The Pocket Oxford Italian Dictionary

Edited by Lexus with

Debora Mazza

Oxford   New York

OXFORD UNIVERSITY PRESS

1997

Oxford University Press, Great Clarendon Street, Oxford OX2 6DP

Oxford New York

Athens Auckland Bangkok Bogota Bombay
Buenos Aires Calcutta Cape Town Dar es Salaam
Delhi Florence Hong Kong Istanbul Karachi
Kuala Lumpur Madras Madrid Melbourne
Mexico City Nairobi Paris Singapore
Taipei Tokyo Toronto

and associated companies in
Berlin Ibadan

Oxford is a trade mark of Oxford University Press

British Library Cataloguing in Publication Data
Data available

Library of Congress Cataloging in Publication Data
Data available
ISBN 0–19–860008–9 (hardback edition)
ISBN 0–19–860007–0 (paperback edition)

Printed in Great Britain by
Mackays plc
Chatham, Kent

Contents/Indice

Editors/Redazione

Debora Mazza   Jane Goldie

Donatella Boi   Francesca Logi   Peter Terrell

Sonia Tinagli-Baxter   Carla Zipoli

Allan Cameron   Michela Masci   Ilaria Panuccio

Copy editors/Segreteria di redazione

Alice Grandison   Mary Rigby   Daphne Trotter

Project management by/A cura di

LEXUS

Preface

This new addition to the Oxford range of Italian dictionaries has been designed to meet the needs of students, tourists and all those who require quick and reliable answers to their translation questions. It provides clear guidance on selecting the most appropriate translation, illustrative examples to help with construction and usage, and precise information on grammar and style.

Focussing on everyday, idiomatic Italian and English, both spoken and written, this easy-to-use dictionary also offers generous treatment of business and computing vocabulary. Its up-to-the-minute coverage and wealth of accurate translations make it an ideal reference tool and study aid.

Prefazione

Questo nuovo dizionario, che viene ad aggiungersi alla serie dei dizionari inglese-italiano della Oxford, è stato creato per soddisfare le esigenze degli studenti, dei turisti e di tutti coloro che hanno bisogno di risposte rapide e sicure ai problemi di traduzione. Il lettore viene guidato con chiarezza nella scelta del termine più appropriato, con esempi di uso della lingua e con indicazioni precise di grammatica e di stile.

Basandosi sull'uso dell'inglese e dell'italiano contemporaneo, sia scritto che parlato, questo dizionario di facile consultazione dedica particolare attenzione al lessico dell'informatica e degli affari. Estremamente attuale e aggiornato, e grazie all'abbondante e precisa terminologia, rappresenta uno strumento di consultazione ideale e un valido sussidio didattico.

Proprietary terms

This dictionary includes some words which are, or are asserted to be, proprietary names or trademarks. Their inclusion does not imply that they have acquired for legal purposes a non-proprietary or general significance, nor is any other judgment implied concerning their legal status. In cases where the editor has some evidence that a word is used as a proprietary name or trademark this is indicated by the symbol ®, but no judgment concerning the legal status of such words is made or implied thereby.

Marche depositate

Questo dizionario include alcune parole che sono o vengono considerate nomi di marche depositate. La loro presenza non implica che abbiano acquisito legalmente un significato generale, né si suggerisce alcun altro giudizio riguardo il loro stato giuridico. Qualora il redattore abbia trovato testimonianza dell'uso di una parola come marca depositata, quest'ultima è stata contrassegnata dal simbolo ®, ma nessun giudizio riguardo lo stato giuridico di tale parola viene espresso o suggerito in tal modo.

Introduction

Here is some basic information on the way the entries in this dictionary are organized.

A swung dash ~ is used to replace the headword within the entry.

Compounds are listed in alphabetical order. Remember this when looking for a word. The entry 'password', for example, is entered alphabetically – at some distance from the entry 'pass'. Likewise 'paintbrush' and 'paintpot' will have 'painter', 'pain threshold' and 'painting' entered in between.

Indicators are provided to guide the user to the best translation for a specific sense of a word. Types of indicator are:

field labels (see the list on pp viii-ix), which indicate a general area of usage (commercial, computing, photography etc);

sense indicators, eg: **bore** *n* (*of gun*) calibro *m*; (*person*) seccatore, -trice *mf*;

typical subjects of verbs, eg: **bond** *vt* ⟨*glue:*⟩ attaccare;

typical objects of verbs, placed after the translation of the verb, eg: **boost** *vt* stimolare ⟨*sales*⟩; sollevare ⟨*morale*⟩;

nouns that typically go together with certain adjectives, eg: **rich** *a* ricco; ⟨*food*⟩ pesante.

A solid black circle means that the same word is being translated as a different part of speech, eg. **partition** *n* ... ● *vt* ...

A solid black square is used to identify phrasal verbs, eg ■ **strip down** *vt* ... Phrasal verbs are listed in alphabetical order directly after the main verb. So 'strip down' comes after 'strip' and before 'strip cartoon'.

English pronunciation is given for the Italian user in the International Phonetic Alphabet (see p vii).

Italian stress is shown by a ' placed in front of the stressed syllable in a word.

Square brackets are used around parts of an expression which can be omitted without altering the sense.

Introduzione

Ecco le informazioni essenziali su come sono organizzate le voci nel dizionario.

Un trattino ondulato ~ è utilizzato al posto del lemma all'interno della voce.

I vocaboli composti sono in ordine alfabetico. È importante ricordarlo quando si cerca la parola che interessa. La voce 'password', ad esempio, essendo in ordine alfabetico, compare a una certa distanza dopo la voce 'pass'. Per la stessa ragione fra 'paintbrush' and 'paintpot' compaiono 'painter', 'pain threshold' e 'painting'.

Degli indicatori vengono forniti per indirizzare l'utente verso la traduzione corrispondente al senso voluto di una parola. I tipi di indicatori sono:

etichette semantiche (vedi la lista a pp viii-ix), indicanti l'ambito specifico in cui la parola viene generalmente usata in quel senso (commercio, informatica, fotografia ecc);

indicatori di significato, es.: **redazione** *nf* (*ufficio*) editorial office; (*di testi*) editing;

soggetti tipici di verbi, es.: **trovarsi** *vr* ⟨*luogo:*⟩ be;

complementi oggetti tipici di verbi, collocati dopo la traduzione dello stesso verbo, es: **superare** *vt* overtake ⟨*veicolo*⟩; pass ⟨*esame*⟩;

sostantivi che ricorrono tipicamente con certi aggettivi, es.: **solare** *a* ⟨*energia, raggi*⟩ solar; ⟨*crema*⟩ sun.

Un pallino nero indica che la stessa parola viene tradotta come una diversa parte del discorso, es. **calcolatore** *a* ... ● *nm* ...

Un quadratino nero viene utilizzato per indicare i phrasal verbs, ad esempio: ■ **strip down** *vt* ... I phrasal verbs si trovano in ordine alfabetico immediatamente dopo il verbo principale. Così 'strip down' viene subito dopo 'strip' e subito prima di 'strip cartoon'.

La pronuncia inglese è data usando l'Alfabetico Fonetico Internazionale (vedi p vii).

L'accento tonico nelle parole italiane è indicato dal segno ' collocato davanti alla sillaba accentata.

Delle parentesi quadre racchiudono parti di espressioni che possono essere omesse senza alterazioni di senso.

Pronunciation of Italian

Vowels:

a	is broad like *a* in *father*: **casa**.
e	has two sounds: closed like *ey* in *they*: **sera**; open like *e* in *egg*: **sette**.
i	is like *ee* in *feet*: **venire**.
o	has two sounds: closed like *o* in *show*: **bocca**; open like *o* in *dog*: **croma**.
u	is like *oo* in *moon*: **luna**.

When two or more vowels come together each vowel is pronounced separately: **buono**; **baia**.

Consonants:

b, d, f, l, m, n, p, t, v are pronounced as in English. When these are double they are sounded distinctly: **bello**.

c	before **a**, **o** or **u** and before consonants is like *k* in *king*: **cane**.
	before **e** or **i** is like *ch* in *church*: **cena**.
ch	is also like *k* in *king*: **chiesa**.
g	before **a**, **o**, or **u** is hard like *g* in *got*: **gufo**.
	before **e** or **i** is like *j* in *jelly*: **gentile**.
gh	is like *g* in *gun*: **ghiaccio**.
gl	when followed by **a, e, o, u** is like *gl* in *glass*: **gloria**.
gli	is like *lli* in *million*: **figlio**.
gn	is like *ni* in *onion*: **bagno**.
h	is silent.
ng	is like *ng* in *finger* (not *singer*): **ringraziare**.
r	is pronounced distinctly.
s	between two vowels is like *s* in *rose*: **riso**.
	at the beginning of a word it is like *s* in *soap*: **sapone**.
sc	before **e** or **i** is like *sh* in *shell*: **scienza**.
z	sounds like *ts* within a word: **fazione**; like *dz* at the beginning: **zoo**.

The stress is shown by the sign ' printed before the stressed syllable.

Pronuncia Inglese

SIMBOLI FONETICI

Vocali e dittonghi

æ bad	ʊ put	aʊ now
ɑ: ah	u: too	aʊə flour
e wet	ə ago	ɔɪ coin
ɪ sit	ɜ: work	ɪə here
i: see	eɪ made	eə hair
ɒ got	əʊ home	ʊə poor
ɔ: door	aɪ five	
ʌ cup	aɪə fire	

Consonanti

b boy	l leg	t ten
d day	m man	tʃ chip
dʒ page	n new	θ three
f foot	ŋ sing	ð this
g go	p pen	v verb
h he	r run	w wet
j yes	s speak	z his
k coat	ʃ ship	ʒ pleasure

Note: ' precede la sillaba accentata.

La vocale nasale in parole quali *nuance* è indicata nella trascrizione fonetica come ɒ̃: njuːɒ̃s.

Abbreviations/Abbreviazioni

adjective	*a*	aggettivo
abbreviation	*abbr*	abbreviazione
administration	*Admin*	amministrazione
adverb	*adv*	avverbio
aeronautics	*Aeron*	aeronautica
American	*Am*	americano
anatomy	*Anat*	anatomia
archaeology	*Archaeol*	archeologia
architecture	*Archit*	architettura
attributive	*attrib*	attributo
astrology, astronomy	*Astr*	astrologia, astronomia
automobiles	*Auto*	automobile
auxiliary	*aux*	ausiliario
biology	*Biol*	biologia
botany	*Bot*	botanica
British English	*Br*	inglese britannico
Chemistry	*Chem*	chimica
commerce	*Comm*	commercio
computers	*Comput*	informatica
conjunction	*conj*	congiunzione
cooking	*Culin*	cucina
definite article	*def art*	articolo determinativo
	ecc	eccetera
economics	*Econ*	economia
electricity	*Electr*	elettricità
et cetera	*etc*	
feminine	*f*	femminile
familiar	*fam*	familiare
figurative	*fig*	figurato
finance	*Fin*	finanza
formal	*fml*	formale
geography	*Geog*	geografia
geology	*Geol*	geologia
grammar	*Gram*	grammatica
humorous	*hum*	umoristico
indefinite article	*indef art*	articolo indeterminativo
interjection	*int*	interiezione
interrogative	*inter*	interrogativo
invariable	*inv*	invariabile
(*no plural form*)		
journalism	*Journ*	giornalismo
law	*Jur*	legge/giuridico
literary	*liter*	letterario
masculine	*m*	maschile
mathematics	*Math*	matematica
mechanics	*Mech*	meccanica

medicine	*Med*	medicina
meteorology	*Metereol*	meteorologia
masculine or feminine	*mf*	maschile o femminile
military	*Mil*	militare
music	*Mus*	musica
noun	*n*	sostantivo
nautical	*Naut*	nautica
old use	*old*	antiquato
pejorative	*pej*	peggiorativo
personal	*pers*	personale
photography	*Phot*	fotografia
physics	*Phys*	fisica
plural	*pl*	plurale
politics	*Pol*	politica
possessive	*poss*	possessivo
past participle	*pp*	participio passato
prefix	*pref*	prefisso
preposition	*prep*	preposizione
present tense	*pres*	presente
pronoun	*pron*	pronome
psychology	*Psych*	psicologia
past tense	*pt*	tempo passato
	qcno	qualcuno
	qcsa	qualcosa
proprietary term	®	marca depositata
rail	*Rail*	ferrovia
reflexive	*refl*	riflessivo
religion	*Relig*	religione
relative pronoun	*rel pron*	pronome relativo
somebody	*sb*	
school	*Sch*	scuola
singular	*sg*	singolare
slang	*sl*	gergo
something	*sth*	
suffix	*suff*	suffisso
technical	*Techn*	tecnico
telephone	*Teleph*	telefono
theatrical	*Theat*	teatrale
television	*TV*	televisione
typography	*Typ*	tipografia
university	*Univ*	università
auxiliary verb	*v aux*	verbo ausiliare
intransitive verb	*vi*	verbo intransitivo
reflexive verb	*vr*	verbo riflessivo
transitive verb	*vt*	verbo transitivo
transitive and intransitive	*vt/i*	verbo transitivo e intransitivo
vulgar	*vulg*	volgare
cultural equivalent	≈	equivalenza culturale

Aa

a (**ad** *before vowel*) *prep* to; (*stato in luogo, tempo, età*) at; (*con mese, città*) in; (*mezzo, modo*) by; **dire qcsa a qcno** tell sb sth; **alle tre** at three o'clock; **a vent'anni** at the age of twenty; **a Natale** at Christmas; **a dicembre** in December; **ero al cinema** I was at the cinema; **vivo a Londra** I live in London; **a due a due** two by two; **a piedi** on *o* by foot; **maglia a maniche lunghe** long-sleeved sweater; **casa a tre piani** house with three floors; **giocare a tennis** play tennis; **50 km all'ora** 50 km an hour; **2 000 lire al chilo** 2,000 lire a kilo; **al mattino/alla sera** in the morning/ evening; **a venti chilometri/due ore da qui** twenty kilometres/two hours away

'abaco *nm* abacus

a'bate *nm* abbot

abbacchia'mento *nm fam* dejection

abbacchi'ato *a fam* dejected, downhearted

ab'bacchio *nm* [young] lamb. **~ alla romana** spring lamb

abbaci'nare *vt* dazzle, blind; *fig* deceive

abbagli'ante *a* dazzling ● *nm* headlight; **mettere gli abbaglianti** put the headlights on full beam

abbagli'are *vt* dazzle

ab'baglio *nm* blunder; **prendere un ~** make a blunder

abbaia'mento *nm* barking

abbai'are *vi* bark

abba'ino *nm* dormer window; (*mansarda*) loft

abbando'nare *vt* abandon; leave ⟨*luogo*⟩; give up ⟨*piani ecc*⟩; **~ il campo** *Mil* desert in the face of the enemy

abbando'narsi *vr* let oneself go; **~ a** give oneself up to ⟨*ricordi ecc*⟩

abbando'nato *a* abandoned

abban'dono *nm* abandoning; *fig* abandon; (*stato*) neglect

abbarbi'carsi *vr* **~ a** cling to

abbassa'mento *nm* (*di temperatura, acqua, prezzi*) drop

abbas'sare *vt* lower; turn down ⟨*radio, TV*⟩; **~ i fari** dip the headlights

abbas'sarsi *vr* stoop; ⟨*sole ecc*⟩ sink; *fig* demean oneself

ab'basso *adv* below ● *int* down with

abba'stanza *adv* enough; (*alquanto*) quite; **~ nuovo** newish; **ne ho ~!** I've had enough!, I'm fed up!

ab'battere *vt* demolish; shoot down ⟨*aereo*⟩; put down ⟨*animale*⟩; topple ⟨*regime*⟩; (*fig: demoralizzare*) dishearten

ab'battersi *vr* (*cadere*) fall; *fig* be discouraged. **~ a terra/al suolo** fall down

abbatti'mento *nm* (*morale*) despondency

abbat'tuto *a* despondent, down-in-the-mouth

abba'zia *nf* abbey

abbelli'mento *nm* embellishment

abbel'lire *vt* embellish

abbel'lirsi *vr* adorn oneself

abbeve'rare *vt* water

abbevera'toio *nm* drinking trough

ab'bicci *nm inv fig* rudiments *pl*; **l'~ di** the ABC of

abbi'ente *a* well-to-do

abbi'etto *a* despicable, abject

abbiglia'mento *nm* clothes *pl*; (*industria*) clothing industry, rag trade. **~ da bambino** children's wear. **~ da donna** ladies' wear. **~ per uomo** menswear

abbigli'are *vt* dress

abbigli'arsi *vr* dress up

abbina'mento *nm* combining

abbi'nare *vt* combine; match ⟨*colori*⟩

abbindo'lare *vt* cheat

abbocca'mento *nm* interview; (*conversazione*) talk

abboc'care *vi* bite; ⟨*tubi:*⟩ join; *fig* swallow the bait

abboc'cato *a* ⟨*vino*⟩ fairly sweet

abbof'farsi = **abbuffarsi**

abbona'mento *nm* subscription; (*ferroviario ecc*) season-ticket; **fare l'~** take out a subscription. **~ all'autobus** bus pass. **~ mensile** monthly ticket. **~ alla televisione** television licence

abbo'nare *vt* make a subscriber

abbo'narsi *vr* subscribe (**a** to); take out a season-ticket (**a** for) ⟨*teatro, stadio*⟩

abbo'nato, -a *nmf* subscriber

abbon'dante *a* abundant; ⟨*quantità*⟩ copious; ⟨*nevicata*⟩ heavy; ⟨*vestiario*⟩ roomy; **~ di** abounding in

abbondante'mente *adv* ⟨*mangiare*⟩ copiously

abbon'danza *nf* abundance

abbon'dare *vi* abound

abbor'dabile *a* ⟨*persona*⟩ approachable; ⟨*prezzo*⟩ reasonable

abbor'daggio *nm Mil* boarding

abbor'dare *vt* board ⟨*nave*⟩; approach ⟨*persona*⟩; (*fam: attaccar bottone a*) chat up; tackle ⟨*compito ecc*⟩

abbotto'nare *vt* button up

abbotto'nato *a fig* tight-lipped

abbottona'tura *nf* [row of] buttons; **con ~**

da donna/uomo ⟨*giacca*⟩ that buttons on the left/right

abboz'zare *vt* sketch [out]; ~ **un sorriso** give a little smile ● *vi fam* ⟨*rassegnarsi*⟩ resign oneself

ab'bozzo *nm* sketch

abbracci'are *vt* embrace; hug, embrace ⟨*persona*⟩; take up ⟨*professione*⟩; *fig* include

ab'braccio *nm* hug

abbrevi'are *vt* shorten; ⟨*ridurre*⟩ curtail; abbreviate ⟨*parola*⟩

abbreviazi'one *nf* abbreviation

abbron'zante *nm* suntan lotion

abbron'zare *vt* bronze; tan ⟨*pelle*⟩

abbron'zarsi *vr* get a tan

abbron'zato *a* tanned

abbronza'tura *nf* [sun]tan

abbrusto'lire *vt* toast; roast ⟨*caffè ecc*⟩

abbruti'mento *nm* brutalization

abbru'tire *vt* brutalize; ⟨*lavoro:*⟩ stultify

abbru'tirsi *vr* become brutalized

abbuf'farsi *vr fam* stuff oneself

abbuf'fata *nf fam* blowout

abbuo'nare *vt* reduce; *fig* overlook ⟨*mancanza, errore*⟩

abbu'ono *nm* allowance; *Sport* handicap

abdi'care *vi* abdicate

abdicazi'one *nf* abdication

aber'rante *a* aberrant

aberrazi'one *nf* aberration

abe'taia *nf* wood of fir trees

a'bete *nm* fir

abi'etto *a* despicable

abiezi'one *nf* degradation

abige'ato *nm Jur* cattle-stealing, rustling

'abile *a* able; ⟨*idoneo*⟩ fit; ⟨*astuto*⟩ clever

abilità *nf inv* ability; ⟨*idoneità*⟩ fitness; ⟨*astuzia*⟩ cleverness

abili'tante *a* **corso** ~ [officially recognized] training course

abili'tare *vt* qualify

abili'tato *a* qualified

abilitazi'one *nf* qualification; ⟨*titolo*⟩ diploma

abil'mente *adv* ably; ⟨*con astuzia*⟩ cleverly

abis'sale *a* abysmal

a'bisso *nm* abyss

abi'tabile *a* inhabitable

abitabilità *nf* fitness for human habitation; **licenza di** ~ *document certifying that a building is fit for human habitation*

abi'tacolo *nm Auto* passenger compartment

abi'tante *nmf* inhabitant

abi'tare *vi* live

abi'tato *a* inhabited ● *nm* built-up area

abitazi'one *nf* house; **crisi delle abitazioni** housing problem

abi'tino *nm Relig* scapular

'abito *nm* ⟨*da donna*⟩ dress; ⟨*da uomo*⟩ suit; **abiti** *pl* clothes. ~ **da ballo** ball dress. ~ **da cerimonia** formal dress. ~ **da cocktail** cocktail dress. ~ **mentale** mentality. '~ **scuro'** ⟨*su inviti*⟩ 'black tie'. ~ **da sera** evening dress. ~ **talare** cassock. ~ **da uomo** suit

abitu'ale *a* usual, habitual

abitual'mente *adv* usually

abitu'are *vt* accustom

abitu'arsi *vr* ~ **a** get used to

abitu'ato *a* ~ **a** used to

abitudi'nario, -a *a* of fixed habits ● *nmf* person of fixed habits

abi'tudine *nf* habit; **d'**~ usually; **per** ~ out of habit; **avere l'**~ **di fare qcsa** be in the habit of doing sth; **abitudini** *pl* customs

abiu'rare *vt* renounce

abla'tivo *nm* ablative

abluzi'oni *nfpl* **fare le** ~ wash

abnegazi'one *nf* self-sacrifice

ab'norme *a* abnormal

abo'lire *vt* abolish; repeal ⟨*legge*⟩

abolizi'one *nf* abolition; ⟨*di legge*⟩ repeal

abolizio'nismo *nm* abolitionism

abolizio'nista *a* & *nmf* abolitionist

abomi'nevole *a* abominable

abo'rigeno, -a *a* & *nmf* aboriginal

abor'rire *vt* abhor

abor'tire *vi* miscarry; ⟨*volontariamente*⟩ have an abortion; *fig* fail

abor'tista *a* pro-choice

abor'tivo *a* abortive

a'borto *nm* miscarriage; ⟨*volontario*⟩ abortion

abrasi'one *nf* abrasion

abra'sivo *a* & *nm* abrasive

abro'gare *vt* repeal

abroga'tivo **a referendum** ~ referendum to repeal a law

abrogazi'one *nf* repeal

abruz'zese *a* Abruzzi *attrib* ● *nmf* person from the Abruzzi ● *nm* Abruzzi dialect

'abside *nf* apse

abu'lia *nf* apathy

a'bulico *a* apathetic

abu'sare *vi* ~ **di** abuse; over-indulge in ⟨*alcol*⟩; ⟨*approfittare di*⟩ take advantage of; ⟨*violentare*⟩ rape

abu'sivo *a* illegal

abusi'vismo *nm* large-scale abuse; ~ **edilizio** building without planning permission

a'buso *nm* abuse; **'ogni** ~ **sarà punito'** 'penalty for misuse'. ~ **di confidenza** breach of confidence

a.C. *abbr* ⟨**avanti Cristo**⟩ BC

a'cacia *nf* acacia

'acaro *nm Zool* mite

'acca *nf fam* **non ho capito un'**~ I understood damn all

acca'demia *nf* academy. **A**~ **di Belle Arti** Academy of Fine Arts. ~ **militare** military academy

acca'demico, -a *a* academic ● *nmf* academician

acca'dere *vi* happen; **accada quel che accada** come what may

acca'duto *nm* event

accalappia'cani *nm inv* dog-catcher

accalappi'are *vt* catch; *fig* allure

accal'care *vt* cram together

accal'carsi *vr* crowd

accal'darsi *vr* get overheated; (*per fatica*) get hot; *fig* get excited

accal'dato *a* overheated; (*per fatica*) hot; *fig* excited

accalo'rarsi *vr* get excited

accampa'mento *nm* camp

accam'pare *vt fig* put forth

accam'parsi *vr* camp

accani'mento *nm* tenacity; (*odio*) rage

acca'nirsi *vr* persist; (*infierire*) rage

accanita'mente *adv* ⟨*odiare*⟩ fiercely; ⟨*insistere*⟩ persistently; ⟨*lavorare*⟩ assiduously

acca'nito *a* persistent; ⟨*odio*⟩ fierce; ⟨*fumatore*⟩ inveterate; ⟨*lavoratore*⟩ assiduous

ac'canto *adv* near; **~ a** *prep* next to; **la ragazza della porta ~** the girl next door

accanto'nare *vt* set aside; *Mil* billet

accaparra'mento *nm* hoarding; *Comm* cornering

accapar'rare *vt* hoard

accapar'rarsi *vr* grab; corner ⟨*mercato*⟩

accaparra'tore, -'trice *nmf* hoarder

accapigli'arsi *vr* scuffle; (*litigare*) squabble

accappa'toio *nm* bathrobe; (*per spiaggia*) beachrobe

accappo'nare *vt* **fare ~ la pelle a qcno** make sb's flesh creep

accarez'zare *vt* caress, stroke; *fig* cherish

accartocci'are *vt* scrunch up

accartocci'arsi *vr* curl up

acca'sarsi *vr* get married

accasci'arsi *vr* flop down; *fig* lose heart

accata'stare *vt* pile up

accatti'vante *a* beguiling

accatti'varsi *vr* **~ le simpatie/la stima/ l'affetto di qcno** gain sb's sympathy/respect/affection

accatto'naggio *nm* begging

accat'tone, -a *nmf* beggar

accaval'lare *vt* cross ⟨*gambe*⟩

accaval'larsi *vr* pile up; *fig* overlap

acce'cante *a* ⟨*luce*⟩ blinding

acce'care *vt* blind ● *vi* go blind

ac'cedere *vi* access; **~ a** enter; (*acconsentire*) comply with; *Comput* access

accele'rare *vi* accelerate ● *vt* speed up, accelerate; **~ il passo** quicken one's pace

accele'rata *nf* sudden acceleration

accele'rato *a* rapid

accelera'tore *nm* accelerator. **~ grafico** *Comput* graphics accelerator

accelerazi'one *nf* acceleration

ac'cendere *vt* light; turn on, switch on ⟨*luce, TV ecc*⟩; *fig* inflame; **ha da ~?** have you got a light?

ac'cendersi *vr* catch fire; (*illuminarsi*) light up; *fig* become inflamed; ⟨*tv, computer:*⟩ turn on, switch on

accendi'gas *nm inv* gas lighter; (*su cucina*) automatic ignition

accen'dino *nm* lighter

accendi'sigari *nm* cigar-lighter

accen'nare *vt* indicate; hum ⟨*melodia*⟩; give a hint of ⟨*sorriso*⟩ ● *vi* **~ a** beckon to; *fig* hint at; (*far l'atto di*) make as if to; **accenna a piovere** it looks like rain

ac'cenno *nm* gesture; (*con il capo*) nod; *fig* hint

accensi'one *nf* lighting; (*di motore*) ignition

accen'tare *vt* accent; (*con accento tonico*) stress

accentazi'one *nf* accentuation

ac'cento *nm* accent; (*tonico*) stress. **~ acuto** acute [accent]. **~ circonflesso** circumflex [accent]. **~ grave** grave [accent]

accentra'mento *nm* centralizing

accen'trare *vt* centralize

accentra'tore *a* ⟨*persona*⟩ who refuses to delegate; ⟨*politica*⟩ of centralization

accentu'are *vt* accentuate

accentu'arsi *vr* become more noticeable

accentu'ato *a* marked

accerchia'mento *nm* surrounding

accerchi'are *vt* surround

accerchi'ato *a* surrounded

accer'tabile *a* ascertainable

accerta'mento *nm* check; **accertamenti** *pl* **[medici]** tests

accer'tare *vt* ascertain; (*controllare*) check; assess ⟨*reddito*⟩

ac'ceso *a* lighted; ⟨*radio, TV ecc*⟩ on; ⟨*colore*⟩ bright

acces'sibile *a* accessible; ⟨*persona*⟩ approachable; ⟨*spesa*⟩ reasonable

ac'cesso *nm* access; (*Med: di rabbia*) fit; **'vietato l'~'** 'no entry'; **'~ riservato a...'** 'access restricted to...'. **~ diretto** *Comput* direct access. **~ multiplo** *Comput* multi-access. **~ di pazzia** fit of madness. **~ remoto** *Comput* remote access

accessori'ato *a* accessorized

acces'sorio *a* accessory; (*secondario*) of secondary importance ● *nm* accessory; **accessori** *pl* (*rifiniture*) fittings. **accessori** *pl* **per il bagno** bathroom fittings. **accessori** *pl* **moda** fashion accessories

ac'cetta *nf* hatchet

accet'tabile *a* acceptable

accet'tare *vt* accept; (*aderire a*) agree to

accettazi'one *nf* acceptance; (*luogo*) reception; **[banco] ~** check-in [desk]. **~ [bagagli]** check-in

ac'cetto *a* agreeable; **essere bene ~** be very welcome

accezi'one *nf* meaning

acchiap'pare *vt* catch

+acchiotto *suff* **lupacchiotto** *nm* wolf cub; (*affettuoso*) baby wolf; **orsacchiotto** *nm* teddy bear; **fessacchiotto** *nm* nitwit

ac'chito *nm* **di primo ~** at first

acciac'care *vt* crush; *fig* prostrate

acciac'cato, -a *a* **essere ~** ache all over

acci'acco *nm* infirmity; **acciacchi** (*pl: afflizioni*) aches and pains

acciaie'ria *nf* steelworks

acci'aio *nm* steel; ~ **inossidabile** stainless steel

acciambel'larsi *vr* curl up

acciden'tale *a* accidental

acciden'talmente *adv* accidentally

acciden'tato *a* ‹*terreno*› uneven

acci'dente *nm* accident; *Med* stroke; **non capisce/non vede un** ~ *fam* he doesn't understand/can't see a damn thing; **mandare un** ~ **a** qcno *fam* tell sb to go to hell

acci'denti *int fam* damn!; ~ **a te!** damn you!, blast you!

ac'cidia *nf* sloth

accigli'arsi *vr* frown

accigli'ato *a* frowning

ac'cingersi *vr* ~ **a** be about to

+accio *suff* **erbaccia** *nf* weed; **donnaccia** *nf* tart; **faticaccia** *nf* hard slog; **lavoraccio** *nm* (*lavoro faticoso*) helluva job *fam*; (*lavoro malfatto*) botched job; **parolaccia** *nf* swear word; **avaraccio** *nm* skinflint

acciotto'lato *nm* cobbled paving, cobblestones *pl*

acci'picchia *int* good Lord!

acciuf'fare *vt* catch

acci'uga *nf* anchovy

accla'mare *vt* applaud; (*eleggere*) acclaim

acclamazi'one *nf* applause

acclima'tare *vt* acclimatize

acclima'tarsi *vr* get acclimatized

acclimatazi'one *nf* acclimatization

ac'cludere *vt* enclose

ac'cluso *a* enclosed

accocco'larsi *vr* squat

acco'darsi *vr* tag along

accogli'ente *a* welcoming; (*confortevole*) cosy

accogli'enza *nf* welcome

ac'cogliere *vt* receive; (*conpiacere*) welcome; (*contenere*) hold

accol'lare *vt* ~ qcsa a qcno *fig* saddle sb with sth

accol'larsi *vr* take on ‹*responsabilità, debiti, doveri*›

accol'lato *a* ‹*maglia*› high-necked

accoltel'lare *vt* knife

accoman'dante *nmf Jur* sleeping partner

accomanda'tario, -a *nmf Jur* general partner

accoman'dita *nf Jur* limited partnership. ~ **per azioni** limited partnership based on shares

accomia'tare *vt* dismiss

accomia'tarsi *vr* take one's leave (**da** of)

accomoda'mento *nm* arrangement

accomo'dante *a* accommodating

accomo'dare *vt* (*riparare*) mend; (*disporre*) arrange

accomo'darsi *vr* make oneself at home; **si accomodi!** come in!; (*si sieda*) take a seat!

accompagna'mento *nm* accompaniment; (*seguito*) retinue

accompa'gnare *vt* accompany; ~ qcno a casa see sb home; ~ qcno alla porta show sb to the door; ~ **qcno con lo sguardo** follow sb with one's eyes

accompa'gnarsi *vr* ‹*cibi, colori ecc:*› go [well] together; ~ **con** *o* **a** qcno accompany sb

accompagna'tore, -'trice *nmf* companion; (*di comitiva*) escort; *Mus* accompanist. ~ **turistico** tour guide

accomu'nare *vt* pool

acconci'are *vt* arrange

acconci'arsi *vr* do one's hair

acconcia'tura *nf* hair-style; (*ornamento*) head-dress; **'acconciature'** 'ladies' hairdresser'

accondiscen'dente *a* too obliging

accondiscen'denza *nf* excessive desire to please

accondi'scendere *vi* ~ **a** condescend; comply with ‹*desiderio*›; (*acconsentire*) consent to

acconsen'tire *vi* consent

acconten'tare *vt* satisfy

acconten'tarsi *vr* be content (**di** with)

ac'conto *nm* deposit; **in** ~ on account; **lasciare un** ~ leave a deposit. ~ **di dividendo** interim dividend

accop'pare *vt fam* bump off

accoppia'mento *nm* coupling; (*di animali*) mating

accoppi'are *vt* couple; mate ‹*animali*›

accoppi'arsi *vr* pair off; ‹*animali:*› mate

accoppi'ata *nf* (*scommessa*) bet placed on two horses for first and second place; **sono una strana** ~ they make strange bedfellows; ~ **vincente** *fig* winning combination

accoppia'tore *nm* ~ **acustico** *Comput* acoustic coupler

acco'rato *a* sorrowful

accorci'are *vt* shorten

accorci'arsi *vr* get shorter

accor'dare *vt* concede; match ‹*colori ecc*›; *Mus* tune

accor'darsi *vr* agree

accorda'tore, -'trice *nmf Mus* tuner

ac'cordo *nm* agreement; *Mus* chord; (*armonia*) harmony; **andare d'**~ get on well; **d'**~! agreed!; **essere d'**~ agree; **in** ~ **con** in collusion with; **prendere accordi con** qcno make arrangements with sb. ~ **collettivo** joint agreement

ac'corgersi *vr* ~ **di** notice; (*capire*) realize

accorgi'mento *nm* shrewdness; (*espediente*) device

accorpa'mento *nm* amalgamation

accor'pare *vt* amalgamate

ac'correre *vi* hasten

accorta'mente *adv* astutely

accor'tezza *nf* (*previdenza*) forethought

ac'corto *a* shrewd; **mal** ~ incautious

accosta'mento *nm* (*di colori*) combination

acco'stare *vt* draw close to; approach ‹*persona*›; put ajar ‹*porta ecc*›

acco'starsi *vr* ~ **a** come near to

accovacci'arsi *vr* crouch, squat down

5

accovacci'ato *a* squatting
accoz'zaglia *nf* jumble; (*di persone*) mob
accoz'zare *vt* ~ **colori** mix colours that clash
accredi'tabile *a* reliable
accredita'mento *nm* credit. ~ **tramite bancogiro** Bank Giro Credit
accredi'tare *vt* confirm ‹*notizia*›; *Comm* credit
accredi'tato *a* accredited; ‹*notizia*› reliable
ac'crescere *vt* increase
ac'crescersi *vr* grow larger
accresci'mento *nm* increase
accresci'tivo *a* augmentative
accucci'arsi *vr* ‹*cane:*› lie down; ‹*persona:*› crouch
accu'dire *vi* ~ **a** attend to
accumu'lare *vt* accumulate
accumu'larsi *vr* pile up, accumulate
accumula'tore *nm* accumulator; *Auto, Comput* battery
accumulazi'one *nf* accumulation
ac'cumulo *nm* (*di merce*) build-up
accurata'mente *adv* carefully
accura'tezza *nf* care
accu'rato *a* careful
ac'cusa *nf* accusation; *Jur* charge; **essere in stato di** ~ *Jur* have been charged; **mettere qcno sotto** ~ *Jur* charge sb; **la Pubblica A~** *Jur* the public prosecutor
accu'sare *vt* accuse; *Jur* charge; complain of ‹*dolore*›; ~ **ricevuta di** *Comm* acknowledge receipt of
accusa'tivo *nm* *Gram* accusative
accu'sato, -a *nmf* accused
accusa'tore *a* accusing ● *nm* *Jur* prosecutor
a'cerbo *a* sharp; (*non maturo*) unripe
'acero *nm* maple
a'cerrimo *a* implacable
ace'tato *nm* acetate
a'ceto *nm* vinegar
ace'tone *nm* nail polish remover
ace'tosa *nf* *Culin* [edible] sorrel
aceto'sella *nf* *Bot* sorrel
A.C.I. *nf* *abbr* (**Automobile Club d'Italia**) Italian Automobile Association
acidità *nf* acidity. ~ **di stomaco** acid stomach
'acido *a* acid; ‹*persona*› sour ● *nm* acid. ~ **cloridrico** hydrochloric acid
a'cidulo *a* slightly sour
'acino *nm* berry; (*chicco*) grape
'acme *nf* acme
'acne *nf* acne
'acqua *nf* water; **fare** ~ *Naut* leak; ~ **in bocca!** *fig* mum's the word!; **avere l'**~ **alla gola**, **essere con l'**~ **alla gola** *fig* be pushed for time; **ho fatto un buco nell'**~ *fig* I had no luck whatsoever; **in cattive acque** in deep water; **navigare in cattive acque** be in financial difficulties. ~ **calda** hot water. ~ **di Colonia** eau de Cologne. ~ **corrente** running water. ~ **dolce** fresh wa-

ter. ~ **minerale** mineral water. ~ **minerale gassata** fizzy mineral water. ~ **naturale** still mineral water. ~ **potabile** drinking water. ~ **del rubinetto** tap water. ~ **salata** salt water. ~ **saponata** suds. ~ **tonica** tonic water
acqua'forte *nf* etching
ac'quaio *nm* sink
acquama'rina *a* aquamarine
acqua'plano *nm* hydroplane
acqua'rello *nm* water-colour
a'cquario *nm* aquarium; *Astr* Aquarius
acquartie'rare *vt* *Mil* billet
acqua'santa *nf* holy water
acquasanti'era *nf* font
acqua'scooter *nm* *inv* water-scooter
a'cquata *nf* *fam* downpour
a'cquatico *a* aquatic; **sport** ~ water sport
acquat'tarsi *vr* crouch
acqua'vite *nf* brandy
acquaz'zone *nm* downpour
acque'dotto *nm* aqueduct
'acqueo *a* **vapore** ~ water vapour
acque'rello *nm* water-colour
acquicol'tura *nf* aquaculture
acquie'scente *a* acquiescent
acquie'tare *vt* appease; calm ‹*dolore*›
acquie'tarsi *vr* calm down
acqui'rente *nmf* purchaser
acqui'sire *vt* acquire
acqui'sito *a* acquired
acquisizi'one *nf* attainment
acqui'stare *vt* purchase; (*ottenere*) acquire; ~ **in** ‹*prestigio, bellezza*› gain in
a'cquisto *nm* purchase; ~ **rateale** hire purchase, HP, installment plan *Am*; **uscire per acquisti** go shopping; **fare acquisti** shop; **ufficio acquisti** purchasing department. ~ **per impulso** impulse buy. ~ **a termine** *Fin* forward buying
acqui'trino *nm* marsh
acquo'lina *nf* **far venire l'**~ **in bocca a qcno** make sb's mouth water; **ho l'**~ **in bocca** my mouth is watering
a'cquoso *a* watery
'acre *a* acrid; (*al gusto*) sour; *fig* harsh
a'credine *nf* acridness; (*al gusto*) sourness; *fig* harshness
acre'mente *adv* acridly
a'crilico *nm* acrylic
a'critico *a* acritical
acro'batica *nmf* acrobat
acro'batico *a* acrobatic
acroba'zia *nf* acrobatics *pl*
acroba'zie *nfpl* acrobatics; **fare** ~ *fig* do acrobatics
a'cronimo *nm* acronym
a'cropoli *nf* acropolis
acu'ire *vt* sharpen
acu'irsi *vr* become more intense
a'culeo *nm* sting; *Bot* prickle
a'cume *nm* acumen
acumi'nato *a* pointed
a'custica *nf* acoustics *pl*
acustica'mente *adv* acoustically
a'custico *a* acoustic

acuta'mente *adv* shrewdly

acu'tezza *nf* acuteness; *fig* shrewdness; (*di suoni*) shrillness

acutiz'zare *vt* aggravate ⟨*dolore*⟩

acutiz'zarsi *vr* become worse

a'cuto *a* sharp; ⟨*suono*⟩ shrill; ⟨*freddo, odore*⟩ intense; *Gram, Math, Med* acute ● *nm Mus* high note

ad (*before vowel*) *prep* = **a**

A.D. *abbr Pol* (**Alleanza Democratica**) Democratic Alliance

adagi'are *vt* lay down

adagi'arsi *vr* lie down

a'dagio *adv* slowly ● *nm Mus* adagio; (*proverbio*) adage

ada'mitico *a* **in costume** ~ in one's birthday suit, stark naked

adat'tabile *a* adaptable

adattabilità *nf* adaptability

adatta'mento *nm* adaptation; **avere spirito di** ~ be adaptable. ~ **cinematografico** film adaptation, adaptation for the cinema

adat'tare *vt* adapt; (*aggiustare*) fit

adat'tarsi *vr* adapt

adatta'tore *nm* adaptor

a'datto *a* suitable (**a** for); (*giusto*) right

addì *adv* ~ **15 settembre 1995** on 15th September 1995

addebita'mento *nm* debit. ~ **diretto** direct debit

addebi'tare *vt* debit; *fig* ascribe ⟨*colpa*⟩

ad'debito *nm* charge

addensa'mento *nm* thickening; (*di persone*) gathering

adden'sare *vt* thicken

adden'sarsi *vr* thicken; (*affollarsi*) gather

adden'tare *vt* bite

adden'trarsi *vr* penetrate

ad'dentro *adv* deeply; **essere** ~ **in** be in on

addestra'mento *nm* training. ~ **iniziale** basic training

adde'strare *vt* train

adde'strarsi *vr* train

addestra|'tore, -'trice *nmf* trainer

ad'detto, -a *a* assigned ● *nmf* employee; (*diplomatico*) attaché. ~ **commerciale** salesman. **adetti** *pl* **ai lavori** persons involved in the work; **'vietato l'ingresso ai non addetti ai lavori'** 'staff only'. ~ **culturale** cultural attaché. ~ **stampa** information officer, press officer. ~ **ai traslochi** removal man

addi'accio *nm* **dormire all'**~ sleep in the open

addi'etro *adv* (*indietro*) back; (*nel passato*) before

ad'dio *nm & int* goodbye. ~ **al celibato** stag night, stag party. **cena d'**~ farewell dinner

addirit'tura *adv* (*perfino*) even; (*assolutamente*) absolutely; ~**!** really!

ad'dirsi *vr* ~ **a** suit

addi'tare *vt* point at; (*per identificare*) point out; *fig* point to

addi'tivo *a & nm* additive

addizio'nale *a* additional ● *nf* (*imposta*) surtax

addizional'mente *adv* additionally

addizio'nare *vt* add [up]

addiziona'trice *nf* adding machine

addizi'one *nf* addition

addob'bare *vt* decorate

ad'dobbo *nm* decoration

addol'cire *vt* sweeten; tone down ⟨*colore*⟩; *fig* soften

addol'cirsi *vr fig* mellow

addolo'rare *vt* grieve

addolo'rarsi *vr* be upset (**per** by)

addolo'rato *a* pained, distressed

ad'dome *nm* abdomen

addomesti'care *vt* tame

addomestica'tore *nm* tamer

addomi'nale *a* abdominal ● *nmpl* **addominali** abdominals

addormen'tare *vt* put to sleep

addormen'tarsi *vr* go to sleep

addormen'tato *a* asleep; *fig* slow

addos'sare *vt* ~ **a** (*appoggiare*) lean against; (*attribuire*) lay on

addos'sarsi *vr* (*ammassarsi*) crowd; shoulder ⟨*responsabilità ecc*⟩

ad'dosso *adv* on; ~ **a** *prep* on; (*molto vicino*) right next to; **andare/venire** ~ **qcno** run into sb; **mettere gli occhi** ~ **a qcno/qcsa** hanker after sb/sth; **non mettermi le mani** ~**!** keep your hands off me!; **stare** ~ **a qcno** *fig* be on sb's back; **farsela** ~ (*fam: bisogni corporali*) dirty oneself; (*pipì*) wet oneself

ad'durre *vt* produce ⟨*prova, documento*⟩; give ⟨*pretesto, esempio*⟩

adegua'mento *nm* adjustment

adegu'are *vt* adjust

adegu'arsi *vr* conform

adeguata'mente *adv* suitably

adegu'atezza *nf* suitability

adegu'ato *a* suitable; ~ **a** suited to, suitable for

a'dempiere *vt* fulfil

adempi'mento *nm* fulfilment

adem'pire *vt* fulfil

ade'noidi *nfpl* adenoids

a'depto, -a *nmf* adherent

ade'rente *a* adhesive; ⟨*vestito*⟩ tight ● *nmf* follower

ade'renza *nf* adhesion; **aderenze** *pl* connections

ade'rire *vi* ~ **a** stick to, adhere to; support ⟨*sciopero, petizione*⟩; agree to ⟨*richiesta*⟩

adesca'mento *nm Jur* soliciting

ade'scare *vt* bait; *fig* entice

adesca'trice *nf* fille de joie

adesi'one *nf* adhesion; *fig* agreement

ade'sivo *a* adhesive ● *nm* sticker; *Auto* bumper sticker

a'desso *adv* now; (*poco fa*) just now; (*tra poco*) any moment now; **da** ~ **in poi** from now on; **per** ~ for the moment; **fino** ~ up till now

adia'cente *a* adjacent; ~ **a** next to

adia'cenze *nfpl* adjacent areas

adi'bire *vt* ~ **a** put to use as

'adipe *nm* adipose tissue
adi'poso *a* adipose
adi'rarsi *vr* get irate
adi'rato *a* irate
a'dire *vt* resort to; **~ le vie legali** take legal proceedings. **~ la successione** *Jur* take possession of an inheritance
'adito *nm* **dare ~ a** give rise to
adocchi'are *vt* eye; (*con desiderio*) covet
adole'scente *a & nmf* adolescent *attrib*
adole'scenza *nf* adolescence
adolescenzi'ale *a* adolescent
adombra'mento *nm* darkening
adom'brare *vt* darken; *fig* veil
adom'brarsi *vr* (*offendersi*) take offence
adope'rare *vt* use
adope'rarsi *vr* take trouble
ado'rabile *a* adorable
ado'rare *vt* adore
adorazi'one *nf* adoration; **in ~** adoring
ador'nare *vt* adorn
a'dorno *a* adorned (**di** with)
adot'tare *vt* adopt
adot'tivo *a* adoptive
adozi'one *nf* adoption
adrena'lina *nf* adrenalin
adri'atico *a* Adriatic ● *nm* **l'A~** the Adriatic
adu'lare *vt* flatter
adula|'tore, -'trice *nmf* flatterer
adula'torio *a* sycophantic
adulazi'one *nf* flattery
a'dultera *nf* adulteress
adulte'rare *vt* adulterate
adulte'rato *a* adulterated
adulte'rino *a* adulterous
adul'terio *nm* adultery
a'dultero *a* adulterous ● *nm* adulterer
a'dulto, -a *a & nmf* adult; (*maturo*) mature
adu'nanza *nf* assembly
adu'nare *vt* gather
adu'nata *nf Mil* parade
a'dunco *a* hooked
adunghi'are *vt* claw
ae'rare *vt* air (*stanza*)
aera'tore *nm* ventilator
aerazi'one *nf* ventilation
a'ereo *a* aerial; (*dell'aviazione*) air ● *nm* aeroplane, plane; **andare in ~** fly. **~ da carico** cargo plane. **~ da guerra** warplane. **~ di linea** airliner. **~ navetta** shuttle. **~ a reazione** jet [plane]
ae'robica *nf* aerobics
ae'robico *a* aerobic
aerodi'namica *nf* aerodynamics *sg*
aerodi'namico *a* aerodynamic
aero'grafo *nm* airbrush
aero'gramma *nm* aerogram[me]
aero'linea *nf* airline
aero'mobile *nm* aircraft
aeromo'dello *nm* model aircraft
aero'nautica *nf* aeronautics; *Mil* Air Force
aero'nautico *a* aeronautical
aerona'vale *a* air and sea *attrib*
aero'plano *nm* aeroplane

aero'porto *nm* airport
aeroportu'ale *a* airport *attrib*
aero'scalo *nm* cargo and servicing area
aero'sol *nm inv* aerosol
aerospazi'ale *a* aerospace *attrib*
aero'statico *a* **pallone ~** aerostat
ae'rostato *nm* aerostat
aerostazi'one *nf* air terminal
aerosti'ere *nm* balloonist
aero'via *nf* air-corridor
A.F. *abbr* (**alta frequenza**) HF
'afa *nf* sultriness
af'fabile *a* affable
affabilità *nf* affability
affaccen'darsi *vr* busy oneself (**a** with)
affacci'arsi *vr* show oneself; **~ alla finestra** appear at the window
affacen'dato *a* busy
affa'mare *vt* starve [out]
affa'mato *a* starving
affan'nare *vt* leave breathless
affan'narsi *vr* busy oneself; (*agitarsi*) get worked up
affan'nato *a* breathless; **dal respiro ~** wheezy
af'fanno *nm* breathlessness; *fig* worry; **essere in ~ per** be anxious about
affannosa'mente *adv* breathlessly
affan'noso *a* exhausting; **respiro ~** heavy breathing
af'fare *nm* matter; (*occasione*) bargain; *Comm* transaction, deal; **pensa agli affari tuoi** mind your own business; **non sono affari tuoi** *fam* it's none of your business; **fare affari d'oro** have a field day; **af'fari** *pl* business; **d'affari** (*uomo, cena, viaggio*) business. **ministro degli affari esteri** Foreign Secretary *Br*, Secretary of State *Am*
affa'rismo *nm pej* wheeling and dealing
affa'rista *nmf* wheeler-dealer
affasci'nante *a* fascinating; (*persona, sorriso*) bewitching
affasci'nare *vt* bewitch; *fig* charm
affastel'lare *vt* tie up in bundles
affatica'mento *nm* fatigue
affati'care *vt* tire; (*sfinire*) exhaust
affati'carsi *vr* tire oneself out; (*affannarsi*) strive
affati'cato *a* fatigued, suffering from fatigue
af'fatto *adv* completely; **non... ~** not... at all; **niente ~!** not at all!
affer'mare *vt* affirm; (*sostenere*) assert
affer'marsi *vr* establish oneself
affermativa'mente *adv* in the affirmative
afferma'tivo *a* affirmative
affer'mato *a* established
affermazi'one *nf* assertion; (*successo*) achievement
affer'rare *vt* seize; catch (*oggetto*); (*capire*) grasp; **~ al volo** *fig* be quick on the uptake
affer'rarsi *vr* **~ a** grasp at, clutch at

affet'tare *vt* slice; *(ostentare)* affect
affet'tato *a* sliced; *(sorriso, maniere)* affected ● *nm* cold meat, sliced meat
affetta'trice *nf* bacon-slicer
affettazi'one *nf* affectation
affet'tivo *a* affective; **rapporto** ~ emotional tie
af'fetto¹ *nm* affection; **con** ~ affectionately; **gli affetti familiari** family ties
af'fetto² *a* ~ **da** suffering from
affettuosa'mente *adv* affectionately
affettuosità *nf inv (gesto)* affectionate gesture
affettu'oso *a* affectionate
affezio'narsi *vr* ~ **a** grow fond of
affezio'nato *a* devoted **(a** to)
affezi'one *nf* affection; *Med* ailment
affian'care *vt* put side by side; *Mil* flank; *fig* support
affian'carsi *vr* come side by side; *fig* stand together, stand shoulder to shoulder; ~ **a qcno** *fig* help sb out
affia'mento *nm* harmony
affia'tarsi *vr* get on well together
affia'tato *a* close-knit; **una coppia affiatata** a very close couple
affibbi'are *vt* ~ **qcsa a qcno** saddle sb with sth; ~ **un pugno a qcno** let fly at sb
affi'dabile *a* reliable, dependable
affidabilità *nf* reliability, dependability
affida'mento *nm (Jur: dei minori)* custody; **fare** ~ **su qcno** rely on sb; **non dare** ~ **(a qcno)** not inspire confidence (in sb)
affi'dare *vt* entrust
affi'darsi *vr* ~ **a** rely on
affievoli'mento *nm* weakening
affievo'lirsi *vr* grow weak
af'figgere *vt* affix
affilacol'telli *nm inv* knife sharpener
affi'lare *vt* sharpen
affili'are *vt* affiliate
affili'arsi *vr* become affiliated
affiliazi'one *nf* affiliation
affi'nare *vt* sharpen; *(perfezionare)* refine
affinché *conj* so that, in order that
af'fine *a* similar
affinità *nf inv* affinity
affiora'mento *nm* emergence; *Naut* surfacing
affio'rare *vi* emerge; *fig* come to light
affissi'one *nf* bill-posting; **'divieto di** ~' 'stick no bills'
af'fisso *nm* bill; *Gram* affix
affitta'camere *nm inv* landlord ● *nf inv* landlady
affit'tare *vt (dare in affitto)* let; *(prendere in affitto)* rent. **af'fittasi** to let, for rent
af'fitto *nm* rent; **contratto d'**~ lease; **dare in** ~ let; **prendere in** ~ rent
affittu'ario, -a *nmf Jur* lessee
af'fliggere *vt* torment
af'fliggersi *vr* distress oneself
af'flitto *a* distressed
afflizi'one *nf* distress; *fig* affliction
afflosci'are *vt* **la pioggia ha afflosciato**
le foglie the rain has made the leaves go all limp; **mi hai afflosciato il morale** you've demoralized me
afflosci'arsi *vr* become floppy; *(accasciarsi)* flop down; *(morale:)* decline
afflu'ente *a & nm* tributary
afflu'enza *nf* flow; *(di gente)* crowd
afflu'ire *vi* flow; *fig* pour in
af'flusso *nm* influx
affoga'mento *nm* drowning
affo'gare *vt/i* drown; *Culin* poach; ~ **in** *fig* be swamped with
affo'garsi *vr (suicidarsi)* drown oneself
affo'gato *a (persona)* drowned; *(uova)* poached ● *nm* ~ **al caffè** ice cream with hot espresso poured over it
affolla'mento *nm* crowd
affol'lare *vt* crowd
affol'larsi *vr* crowd
affol'lato *a* crowded
affonda'mento *nm* sinking
affon'dare *vt/i* sink
affon'darsi *vr* sink
affossa'mento *nm (avvallamento)* pothole; *fig* burial
affran'care *vt* redeem *(bene)*; stamp *(lettera)*; free *(schiavo)*
affran'carsi *vr* free oneself
affran'cato *a (lettera)* stamped; *(schiavo)* freed; **già** *(lettera)* prepaid
affranca'trice *nf* franking machine, franker
affranca'tura *nf* stamping; *(di spedizione)* postage. ~ **per l'estero** postage abroad
af'franto *a* prostrate with grief, grief-stricken; *(esausto)* worn out
affre'scare *vt* paint a fresco on
af'fresco *nm* fresco
affret'tare *vt* speed up
affret'tarsi *vr* hurry
affrettata'mente *adv* hastily
affret'tato *a (passo)* fast; *(decisione)* hasty; *(lavoro)* rushed
affron'tare *vt* face; confront *(nemico)*; meet *(spese)*
affron'tarsi *vr* clash
af'fronto *nm* affront, insult; **fare un** ~ **a qcno** insult sb
affumi'care *vt* fill with smoke; *Culin* smoke
affumi'cato *a (prosciutto, formaggio)* smoked; *(lenti, vetro)* tinted
affuso'lare *vt* taper [off]
affuso'lato *a* tapering
Af'ganistan *nm* Afghanistan
af'gano *a & nmf* Afghani, Afghan
AFI *nm abbr* **(Alfabeto Fonetico Internazionale)** IPA
aficio'nado, -a *nmf* aficionado
'afide *nm* aphid
'afono *a (senza voce)* unvoiced
afo'risma *nm* aphorism
a'foso *a* sultry
'Africa *nf* Africa. ~ **orientale** East Africa. ~ **nera** Black Africa. ~ **del Nord** North Africa

afri'cano, -a *a* & *nmf* African
afri'kaans *nm* Afrikaans
afroameri'cano *a* Afro-American
afroasi'atico *a* Afro-Asian
afroca'ribico *a* Afro-Caribbean
afrocu'bano *a* Afro-Cuban
afrodi'siaco *a* & *nm* aphrodisiac
a'genda *nf* diary. ~ **elettronica** personal organizer. ~ **da tavolo** desk diary
agen'dina *nf* pocket-diary
a'gente *nm* agent; **agenti** *pl* **atmosferici** atmospheric agents. ~ **di cambio** stockbroker. ~ **di custodia** prison warder. ~ **del fisco** assessor. ~ **immobiliare** estate agent, realtor *Am*. ~ **marittimo** shipping agent. ~ **di polizia** police officer. ~ **segreto** secret agent. ~ **teatrale** theatrical agent; (*di compagnia*) impresario. ~ **di viaggio** travel agent
agen'zia *nf* agency; (*filiale*) branch office; (*di banca*) branch. ~ **di collocamento** employment exchange. ~ **immobiliare** estate agency, realtor *Am*. ~ **matrimoniale** dating agency. ~ **pubblicitaria** advertising agency. ~ **di recupero crediti** debt collection agency. ~ **di stampa** news agency, press agency. ~ **di viaggi** travel agency
agevo'lare *vt* facilitate
agevolazi'one *nf* facilitation. **agevolazioni** *pl* **fiscali** tax breaks **a'gevole** *a* easy; (*strada*) smooth
agevol'mente *adv* easily
aggan'ciare *vt* hook up; *Rail* couple
aggan'ciarsi *vr* (*vestito:*) hook up; ~ **a** (*maglia:*) catch on; (*rimorchio:*) hook onto
ag'gancio *nm* Aeron docking
ag'geggio *nm* gadget
agget'tivo *nm* adjective
agghiacci'ante *a* terrifying
agghiacci'are *vt fig* ~ **qcno** make sb's blood run cold
agghiacci'arsi *vr* freeze
agghin'dare *vt fam* dress up
agghin'darsi *vr fam* doll oneself up
agghin'dato *a* dressed up; (*sala*) decorated; (*fig: stile*) stilted
aggiornabilità *nf Comput* upgradability
aggiorna'mento *nm* update; (*azione*) updating; **corso di** ~ refresher course
aggior'nare *vt* (*rinviare*) postpone; (*mettere a giorno*) bring up to date, update
aggior'narsi *vr* get up to date
aggior'nato *a* up-to-date; (*versione*) updated
aggio'taggio *nm Jur* manipulation of the market
aggira'mento *nm Mil* outflanking
aggi'rare *vt* surround; (*fig: ingannare*) trick
aggi'rarsi *vr* hang about; ~ **su** (*discorso ecc:*) be about; (*somma:*) be around
aggiudi'care *vt* award; (*all'asta*) knock down
aggiudi'carsi *vr* win
aggi'ungere *vt* add
aggi'unta *nf* addition; **in** ~ in addition

aggiun'tivo *a* supplementary
aggi'unto *a* added ● **a** & *nm* (*assistente*) assistant
aggiu'stare *vt* mend; (*sistemare*) settle; (*fam: mettere a posto*) fix; **ora l'aggiusto io** *fig* I'll sort him out
aggiu'starsi *vr* adapt; (*mettersi in ordine*) tidy oneself up; (*decidere*) sort things out; (*tempo:*) clear up
aggiusta'tina *nf* **dare un'**~ **a** neaten
agglomera'mento *nm* conglomeration
agglome'rante *nm* binder
agglome'rato *nm* built-up area
aggrap'pare *vt* grasp
aggrap'parsi *vr* ~ **a** cling to
aggrava'mento *nm* worsening; (*di pena*) increase
aggra'vante *Jur nf* aggravation ● **a** aggravating; **circostanza** ~ aggravation
aggra'vare *vt* (*peggiorare*) make worse; increase (*pena*); (*appesantire*) weigh down
aggra'varsi *vr* worsen
ag'gravio *nm* ~ **fiscale** tax burden
aggrazi'ato *a* graceful
aggre'dire *vt* attack
aggre'gare *vt* add; (*associare a un gruppo ecc*) admit
aggre'garsi *vr* ~ **a** join
aggre'gato *a* associated ● *nm* aggregate; (*di case*) block
aggregazi'one *nf* (*di persone*) gathering
aggressi'one *nf* aggression; (*atto*) attack. ~ **a mano armata** armed assault
aggressività *nf* aggressiveness
aggres'sivo *a* aggressive
aggres'sore *nm* aggressor
aggrin'zare, aggrin'zire *vt* wrinkle
aggrin'zirsi *vr* wrinkle
aggrot'tare *vt* ~ **le ciglia/la fronte** frown
aggrovigli'are *vt* tangle
aggrovigli'arsi *vr* get entangled; *fig* get complicated
aggrovigli'ato *a* entangled; *fig* confused
agguan'tare *vt* catch
agguan'tarsi *vr* ~ **a** grasp
aggu'ato *nm* ambush; (*tranello*) trap; **stare in** ~ lie in wait; **tendere un** ~ **a qcno** set an ambush for sb
agguer'rito *a* fierce
agiata'mente *adv* comfortably
agia'tezza *nf* comfort
agi'ato *a* (*persona*) well off; (*vita*) comfortable
a'gibile *a* (*palazzo*) fit for human habitation
agibilità *nf* fitness for human habitation
'agile *a* agile
agilità *nf* agility
agil'mente *adv* agilely
'agio *nm* ease; **mettersi a proprio** ~ make oneself at home
a'gire *vi* act; (*comportarsi*) behave; (*funzionare*) work; ~ **su** affect
agi'tare *vt* shake; wave (*mano*); (*fig: turbare*) trouble; **'**~ **prima dell'uso'** 'shake before using'

agi'tarsi vr toss about; (essere inquieto) be restless; ⟨mare:⟩ get rough
agi'tato a restless; ⟨mare⟩ rough
agita|'tore, -'trice nmf (persona) agitator
agitazi'one nf agitation; **mettere in ~ qcno** send sb into a flat spin
'agli = a + gli
'aglio nm garlic
a'gnello nm lamb
agno'lotti nmpl ravioli sg
a'gnostico, -a a & nmf agnostic
'ago nm needle; **a 9 aghi** ⟨stampante⟩ 9-pin. **~ di pino** pine-needle
ago'gnare vt liter yearn for, thirst for
ago'nia nf agony
ago'nismo nm competitiveness
ago'nistica nf competition
ago'nistico a competitive
agoniz'zante a in one's death throes
agoniz'zare vi be on one's deathbed
agopun|'tore, -'trice nmf acupuncturist
agopun'tura nf acupuncture
agorafo'bia nf agoraphobia
ago'rafobo, -a nmf agoraphobic
agostini'ano, -a a & nmf Augustinian
a'gosto nm August
a'graria nf agriculture
a'grario a agricultural ● nm landowner
a'greste a rustic
a'gricolo a agricultural
agricol'tore nm farmer
agricol'tura nf agriculture. **~ biologica** organic farming
agri'foglio nm holly
agrimen'sore nm land-surveyor
agritu'rismo nm farm holidays, agro-tourism
'agro¹ a sour; **all'~** Culin pickled
'agro² nm countryside around a town
agroalimen'tare a food attrib
agro'dolce a bitter-sweet; Culin sweet-and-sour; **in ~** sweet and sour
agrono'mia nf agronomy
a'gronomo, -a nmf agriculturalist
agropasto'rale a based on farming
a'grume nm citrus fruit; (pianta) citrus tree
agru'meto nm citrus plantation
aguz'zare vt sharpen; **~ le orecchie** prick up one's ears; **~ la vista** look hard
aguz'zino nm slave-driver; (carceriere) jailer
a'guzzo a pointed
ah int ah!; **ah, davvero?** oh really?
ahi int ow!
ahimè int alas!
'ai = a + i
'aia nf threshing-floor
'Aia nf **L'~** The Hague
Aids nm Aids
AIE abbr (**Associazione Italiana degli Editori**) association of Italian publishers
air bag nm inv Auto air bag
ai'rone nm heron
air terminal nm inv air terminal
ai'tante a sturdy
aiu'ola nf flower-bed

aiu'tante nmf assistant ● nm Mil adjutant. **~ di campo** aide-de-camp
aiu'tare vt help
ai'uto nm help, aid; (assistente) assistant; **dare un ~** lend a hand; **venire in ~ a qcno** come to sb's rescue; **~!** help!. **~ chirurgo** assistant surgeon. **~ domestico** mother's help. **~ infermiere** nursing auxiliary. **~ in linea** Comput on-line help
aiz'zare vt incite; **~ contro** set on
al = a + il
'ala nf wing; **fare ~** make way; **avere le ali ai piedi** fig run like the wind; **tarpare le ali a qcno** fig clip sb's wings. **~ destra/sinistra** (in calcio) right/left wing
ala'bastro nm alabaster
'alacre a brisk
alam'bicco nm alembic
a'lano nm Great Dane
a'lare nm firedog; **apertura ~** wingspan
A'laska nf Alaska
'alba nf dawn
alba'nese a & nmf Albanian
Alba'nia nf Albania
'albatro nm albatross
albeggi'are vi dawn
albe'rare vt line with trees ⟨strada⟩
albe'rato a wooded; ⟨viale⟩ tree-lined
albera'tura nf Naut masts pl
albe'rello nm sapling
alber'gare vt ⟨edificio:⟩ accommodate ● vi liter lodge
alberga|'tore, -'trice nmf hotel-keeper
alberghi'ero a hotel attrib
al'bergo nm hotel; **~ diurno** hotel where rooms are rented during the daytime; **~ a 3 stelle** 3-star hotel
'albero nm tree; Naut mast; Mech shaft. **~ a camme** camshaft. **~ a foglie caduche** deciduous tree. **~ da frutto** fruit tree. **~ genealogico** family tree. **~ a gomiti** crankshaft. **~ maestro** Naut mainmast. **~ di Natale** Christmas tree. **~ di trasmissione** Mech transmission shaft, prop shaft
albi'cocca nf apricot
albi'cocco nm apricot-tree
al'bino nm albino
'albo nm register; (libro ecc) album; (per avvisi) notice board **'album** nm inv album. **~ da colorare** colouring book. **~ da disegno** sketch-book
al'bume nm albumen
albu'mina nf albumin
alca'lino a alkaline
'alce nm elk
alchi'mia nf alchemy
alchi'mista nm alchemist
'alcol nm alcohol; Med spirit; (liquori forti) spirits pl; **darsi all'~** take to drink. **~ denaturato** meths. **~ etilico** ethyl alcohol
alcolicità nf alcohol content
al'colico a alcoholic ● nm alcoholic drink
alco'lismo nm alcoholism
alco'lista nmf alcoholic
alcoliz'zato, -a a & nmf alcoholic

alco'test® *nm inv* Breathalyser [R]

al'cova *nf* alcove

al'cun, al'cuno *a & pron* any; **non ha ~ amico** he hasn't any friends, he has no friends. **alcuni** *pl* some, a few; **~i suoi amici** some of his friends

aldilà *nm* next world, hereafter

alea'torio *a* unpredictable; *Jur* aleatory

aleggi'are *vi* ⟨*brezza:*⟩ blow gently; ⟨*profumo:*⟩ waft

a'letta *nf Mech* fin

alet'tone *nm Aeron* aileron; *Auto* stabilizer

'alfa *nf inv* alpha

alfa'betico *a* alphabetical

alfabetizzazi'one *nf* ~ **della popolazione** teaching people to read and write; **tasso di ~** literacy rate

alfa'beto *nm* alphabet. **A~ Fonetico Internazionale** International Phonetic Alphabet. **~ Morse** Morse code

alfanu'merico *a* alphanumeric

alfi'ere *nm (negli scacchi)* bishop

al'fine *adv* eventually, in the end

'alga *nf* weed. **alghe** *pl* **marine** seaweed

'algebra *nf* algebra

Al'geri *nf* Algiers

Alge'ria *nf* Algeria

alge'rino, -a *a & nmf* Algerian

algocol'tura *nf* seaweed farming

algo'ritmo *nm* algorithm

ali'ante *nm* glider

'alibi *nm inv* alibi

a'lice *nf* anchovy

alie'nabile *a Jur* alienable

alie'nare *vt* alienate

alie'narsi *vr* become estranged; **~ le simpatie di qcno** lose sb's good will

ali'enato, -a *a* alienated ● *nmf* lunatic

alienazi'one *nf* alienation

a'lieno, -a *nmf* alien ● *a* **è ~ da invidia** envy is foreign *or* alien to him

alimen'tare *vt* feed; *fig* foment ● *a* food *attrib*; ⟨*abitudine*⟩ dietary ● *nm* **alimentari** *pl* food-stuffs

alimenta'tore *nm* power unit. **~ automatico di documenti** automatic paper feed

alimentazi'one *nf* feeding; *(cibo)* food; *(elettrica, a gas ecc)* supply

ali'mento *nm* food. **alimenti** *pl* food; *Jur* alimony

a'liquota *nf* share; *(di imposta)* rate. **~ minima** basic rate. **ad ~ zero** zero-rated

ali'scafo *nm* hydrofoil

'alito *nm* breath; **~ cattivo** bad breath

ali'tosi *nf inv* halitosis

all. *abbr* **(allegato)** encl

'alla = **a** + **la**

allaccia'mento *nm* connection

allacci'are *vt* fasten ⟨*cintura*⟩; lace up ⟨*scarpe*⟩; do up ⟨*vestito*⟩; *(collegare)* connect; form ⟨*amicizia*⟩

allacci'arsi *vr* do up, fasten ⟨*vestito, cintura*⟩

allaga'mento *nm* flooding

alla'gare *vt* flood

alla'garsi *vr* to become flooded

allampa'nato *a* lanky

allarga'mento *nm (di strada, ricerche)* widening

allar'gare *vt* widen; open ⟨*braccia, gambe*⟩; let out ⟨*vestito ecc*⟩; *fig* extend

allar'garsi *vr* to widen

allar'mante *a* alarming

allar'mare *vt* alarm

allar'mato *a* panicky

al'larme *nm* alarm; **dare l'~** raise the alarm; **mettere in ~ qcno** alarm sb; **far scattare il campanello d'~** set the alarm bells ringing; **falso ~** *fig* false alarm. **~ aereo** air-raid siren; *(suono)* air-raid warning. **~ antincendio** fire alarm

allar'mismo *nm* alarmism

allar'mista *nmf* alarmist

allatta'mento *nm (di animale)* suckling; *(di neonato)* feeding

allat'tare *vt* suckle ⟨*animale*⟩; feed ⟨*neonato*⟩; **~ artificialmente** bottle feed

'alle = **a** + **le**

alle'anza *nf* alliance. **A~ Democratica** *Pol* Democratic Alliance. **A~ Nazionale** *Pol* National Alliance

alle'are *vt* unite

alle'arsi *vr* form an alliance

alle'ato, -a *a* allied ● *nmf* ally

alle'gare¹ *vt Jur* allege

alle'gare² *vt (accludere)* enclose; set on edge ⟨*denti*⟩

alle'gato *a* enclosed ● *nm* enclosure; **in ~** attached, appended

allegazi'one *nf Jur* allegation

alleggeri'mento *nm* alleviation

allegge'rire *vt* lighten; *fig* alleviate

allegge'rirsi *vr* become lighter; *(vestirsi leggero)* put on lighter clothes

allego'ria *nf* allegory

alle'gorico *a* allegorical

allegra'mente *adv* breezily

alle'gria *nf* gaiety

al'legro *a* cheerful; ⟨*colore*⟩ bright; *(brillo)* tipsy ● *nm Mus* allegro

alle'luia *int* hallelujah

allena'mento *nm* training

alle'nare *vt* train

alle'narsi *vr* train

allena'|tore, -'trice *nmf* trainer, coach

allen'tare *vt* loosen; *fig* relax

allen'tarsi *vr* become loose; *Mech* work loose

aller'gia *nf* allergy

al'lergico *a* allergic

aller'gologo, -a *nmf* allergist

al'lerta *nf* **stare ~** be alert, be on the alert; **essere in stato di ~** *Mil* be in a state of alert; **mettere in stato di ~** put on the alert

allesti'mento *nm* preparation; **in ~** in preparation; **~ scenico** *Theat* set

alle'stire *vt* prepare; stage ⟨*spettacolo*⟩; *Naut* fit out

allet'tante *a* alluring; **poco ~** unattractive

allet'tare *vt* entice

alleva'mento *nm* breeding; (*processo*) bringing up; (*luogo*) farm; (*per piante*) nursery; **pollo di ~** battery chicken. **~ in batteria** battery farming

alle'vare *vt* bring up ⟨*bambini*⟩; breed ⟨*animali*⟩; grow ⟨*piante*⟩

alleva|'tore, -'trice *nmf* breeder

allevia'mento *nm* alleviation

allevi'are *vt* alleviate; *fig* lighten

alli'bito *a* astounded; **rimanere ~** be astounded

allibra'tore *nm* bookmaker

allie'tare *vt* gladden

allie'tarsi *vr* rejoice

alli'evo, -a *nmf* pupil ● *nm Mil* cadet

alliga'tore *nm* alligator

allinea'mento *nm* alignment

alline'are *vt* line up; *Typ* align; *Fin* adjust

alline'arsi *vr* line up into line; **~ con qcno** *fig* align oneself with sb

alline'ato *a* lined up; **i paesi non allineati** the non-aligned states

'allo = **a** + **lo**

allo'care *vt* allocate

al'locco *nm* tawny owl

al'locco, -a *nmf fig* idiot

allocuzi'one *nf* speech

al'lodola *nf* [sky]lark

alloggi'are *vt* ⟨*persona:*⟩ put up; ⟨*casa:*⟩ provide accommodation for; *Mil* billet ● *vi* put up, stay; *Mil* be billeted

al'loggio *nm* (*appartamento*) flat, apartment *Am*; *Mil* billet. **~ popolare** council flat

allontana'mento *nm* removal

allonta'nare *vt* move away; (*licenziare*) dismiss; avert ⟨*pericolo*⟩

allonta'narsi *vr* go away

allopa'tia *nf Med* allopathy

al'lora *adv* then; (*in quel tempo*) at that time; (*in tal caso*) in that case; **~ ~** just then; **d'~ in poi** from then on; **e ~?** what now?; (*e con ciò?*) so what?; **fino ~** until then

allorchè *conj* when, as soon as

al'loro *nm* laurel; *Culin* bay; **dormire sugli allori** rest on one's laurels

'alluce *nm* big toe

alluci'nante *a fam* incredible; **sostanza ~** hallucinogen

alluci'nato, -a *nmf person who suffers from hallucinations*; *fam* space cadet

allucina'torio *a* hallucinatory

allucinazi'one *nf* hallucination

allucino'geno *a* ⟨*sostanza*⟩ hallucinogen

al'ludere *vi* **~ a** allude to

allu'minio *nm* aluminium

allu'naggio *nm* moon-landing

allu'nare *vi* land on the moon

allun'gabile *a* ⟨*tavolo*⟩ extending

allun'gare *vt* lengthen; stretch out ⟨*mano*⟩; stretch ⟨*gamba*⟩; extend ⟨*tavolo*⟩; (*diluire*) dilute; **~ il collo** crane one's neck; **~ il muso** pull a long face; **~ il passo** quicken one's step; **~ le mani su qcno** touch sb up; (*picchiare*) start fighting with sb; **~ uno schiaffo a qcno** slap sb

allun'garsi *vr* grow longer; (*crescere*) grow taller; (*sdraiarsi*) lie down, stretch out

al'lungo *nm* (*nel calcio*) pass; (*nella corsa*) spurt; (*nel pugilato*) lunge

allusi'one *nf* allusion

allu'sivo *a* allusive

alluvio'nale *a* alluvial

alluvio'nato *a* ⟨*popolazione*⟩ flooded out; ⟨*territorio*⟩ flooded

alluvi'one *nf* flood

alma'nacco *nm* almanac. **~ nobiliare** peerage

al'meno *adv* at least; [**se**] **~ venisse il sole!** if only the sun would come out!

a'logena *nf* halogen lamp

a'logeno *nm* halogen ● *a* **lampada alogena** halogen lamp

a'lone *nm* halo

alo'pecia *nf Med* alopecia

al'paca *nm inv* alpaca

al'pestre *a* Alpine

'Alpi *nfpl* **le ~** the Alps

alpi'nismo *nm* mountaineering

alpi'nista *nmf* mountaineer

alpi'nistico *a* mountaineering *attrib*

al'pino *a* Alpine ● *nm Mil* **gli alpini** the Alpine troops

al'quanto *a* a certain amount of ● *adv* rather

Al'sazia *nf* Alsace

alt *int* stop; **intimare l'~** give the order to halt

alta'lena *nf* swing; (*tavola in bilico*) see-saw

altale'nare *vi fig* vacillate

alta'mente *adv* highly

al'tare *nm* altar

alta'rino *nm* **scoprire gli altarini di qcno** reveal sb's guilty secrets

alte'rabile *a* which can be changed, alterable

alte'rare *vt* alter; adulterate ⟨*vino*⟩; (*falsificare*) falsify

alte'rarsi *vr* be altered; ⟨*cibo:*⟩ go bad; ⟨*merci:*⟩ deteriorate; (*arrabbiarsi*) get angry

alte'rato *a* ⟨*suono*⟩ distorted; ⟨*viso*⟩ careworn; ⟨*cibo*⟩ spoilt; ⟨*vino*⟩ adulterated; (*arrabbiato*) angry

alterazi'one *nf* alteration; (*di vino*) adulteration

al'terco *nm* altercation

alte'rigia *nf* haughtiness

alter'nanza *nf* alternation; (*in agricoltura*) rotation; *Pol* regular change in government

alter'nare *vt* alternate

alter'narsi *vr* alternate

alterna'tiva *nf* alternative

alterna'tivo *a* alternate; **medicina alternativa** alternative medicine

alter'nato *a* alternating

alterna'tore *nm Electr* alternator

al'terno *a* alternate; **a giorni alterni** every other day

al'tero *a* haughty

al'tezza *nf* height; (*profondità*) depth;

(*suono*) pitch; (*di tessuto*) width; (*titolo*) Highness; **essere all'~ di** be on a level with; *fig* be up to. **~ libera di passaggio** headroom

altezzosa'mente *adv* haughtily

altezzosità *nf* haughtiness

altez'zoso *a* haughty

al'ticcio *a* tipsy, merry

al'timetro *nm* altimeter

altipi'ano *nm* plateau

altiso'nante *a* high-sounding

alti'tudine *nf* altitude

'alto *a* high; (*di statura*) tall; (*profondo*) deep; (*suono*) high-pitched; (*tessuto*) wide; *Geog* northern; **a notte alta** in the middle of the night; **avere degli alti e bassi** have some ups and downs; **di ~ bordo** high-class; **di ~ rango** high-ranking; **ad alta definizione** high-definition; **ad alta fedeltà** high-fidelity; **ad ~ livello** high-level; **a voce alta, ad alta voce** in a loud voice; (*leggere*) aloud; **essere in ~ mare** be on the high seas; *fig* be all at sea. **alta borghesia** *nf* gentry. **~ commissariato** *nm* High Commission. **alta finanza** *nf* high finance. **alta frequenza** *nf* high frequency. **~ medioevo** *nm* Dark Ages. **alta moda** *nf* high fashion. **alta pressione** *nf* (*metereologica*) high pressure. **alta società** *nf* high society. **alta tensione** *nf* high voltage. **~ tradimento** *nm* high treason ● *adv* high; **in ~** (*essere*) at the top; (*guardare*) up; **mani in ~!** hands up!; **dall'~** from above; **guardare qcno dall'~ in basso** look down on sb

altoate'sino *a* South Tirolese

alto'forno *nm* blast-furnace

altolà *int* halt there!

altolo'cato *a* highly placed

altopar'lante *nm* loudspeaker

altopi'ano *nm* plateau

altret'tanto *a & pron* as much; (*pl*) as many ● *adv* likewise; **buona fortuna! – grazie, ~** good luck! – thank you, the same to you

altri'menti *adv* otherwise

'altro *a* other; **un ~, un'altra** another; **l'altr'anno** last year; **l'~ ieri** the day before yesterday; **domani l'~** the day after tomorrow; **l'ho visto l'~ giorno** I saw him the other day ● *pron* other [one]; **un ~, un'altra** another [one]; **ne vuoi dell'~?** would you like some more?; **l'un l'~** one another; **nessun ~** nobody else; **gli altri** (*la gente*) other people ● *nm* something else; **non fa ~ che lavorare** he does nothing but work; **desidera ~?** (*in negozio*) anything else?; **più che ~, sono stanco** I'm tired more than anything; **se non ~** at least; **senz'~** certainly; **tra l'~** what's more; **~ che!** absolutely!

altrochè *adv* absolutely!

altroi'eri *nm* **l'~** the day before yesterday

al'tronde **d'~** *adv* on the other hand

al'trove *adv* elsewhere

al'trui *a* other people's ● *nm* other people's belongings *pl*

altru'ismo *nm* altruism

altru'ista *nmf* altruist

al'tura *nf* high ground; *Naut* deep sea

a'lunno, -a *nmf* pupil

alve'are *nm* hive

'alveo *nm* bed

alzabandi'era *nm inv* flag-raising

alzacri'stallo *nm Auto* window winder

al'zare *vt* lift, raise; (*costruire*) build; *Naut* hoist; **~ le spalle** shrug one's shoulders; **~ i tacchi** *fig* take to one's heels; **~ la voce** raise one's voice; **~ il volume** turn up the volume

al'zarsi *vr* (*in piedi*) stand up; (*da letto*) get up; (*vento, temperatura:*) rise

al'zata *nf* lifting; (*aumento*) rise; (*da letto*) getting up; *Archit* elevation. **~ di spalle** shrug of the shoulders

alza'taccia *nf fam* **fare un'~** get up at the crack of dawn

al'zato *a* up

A.M. *abbr* (**aeronautica militare**) Air Force

a'mabile *a* lovable; (*vino*) sweet

amabilità *nf* kindness

amabil'mente *adv* kindly

a'maca *nf* hammock

a'malgama *nm* amalgam

amalga'mare *vt* amalgamate

amalga'marsi *vr* amalgamate

ama'nita *nf Bot* amanita

a'mante *a* **~ di** fond of ● *nm* lover. **~ degli animali** animal lover ● *nf* mistress. **~ della lettura** book lover

amara'mente *adv* bitterly

ama'ranto *nm Bot* amarant[h]us; (*colore*) rich purple ● *a* rich purple

a'mare *vt* love; be fond of (*musica, sport ecc*)

amareggia'mento *nm* bitterness

amareggi'are *vt* embitter

amareggi'arsi *vr* become embittered

amareggi'ato *a* embittered

ama'rena *nf* sour black cherry

ama'retto *nm* macaroon

ama'rezza *nf* bitterness; (*dolore*) sorrow

a'maro *a* bitter ● *nm* bitterness; (*liquore*) bitters *pl*

ama'rognolo *a* rather bitter

a'mato, -a *a* loved ● *nmf* beloved

ama|'tore, -'trice *nmf* lover

a'mazzone *nf* (*in mitologia*) Amazon; **all'~** side saddle

Amaz'zonia *nf* Amazonia

amaz'zonico *a* Amazonian

ambasce'ria *nf* diplomatic mission

ambasci'ata *nf* embassy; (*messaggio*) message

ambascia|'tore, -'trice *nm* ambassador ● *nf* ambassadress

ambe'due *a & pron* both

ambi'destro *a* ambidextrous

ambien'tale *a* environmental

ambienta'lismo *nm* environmentalism

ambienta'lista *a & nmf* environmentalist

ambienta'mento *nm* acclimatization

ambien'tare *vt* acclimatize; set (*personaggio, film ecc*)

ambien'tarsi *vr* get acclimatized

ambi'ente *nm* environment; (*stanza*) room

ambiguità *nf inv* ambiguity; (*di persona*) shadiness

am'biguo *a* ambiguous; (*persona*) shady

am'bire *vi* ~ **a** aspire to

am'bito *a* (*lavoro, incarico*) much sought-after

'ambito *nm* sphere

ambiva'lente *a* ambivalent

ambiva'lenza *nf* ambivalence

ambizi'one *nf* ambition

ambizi'oso *a* ambitious

amblio'pia *nf* lazy eye

'ambo *a inv* both ● *nm* (*in tombola, lotto*) double

'ambra *nf* amber

am'brato *a* amber

ambu'lante *a* wandering; **venditore** ~ hawker

ambu'lanza *nf* ambulance

ambulatori'ale *a* **essere trattato con intervento** ~ have day surgery

ambula'torio *nm* (*di medico*) surgery; (*di ospedale*) out-patients' [department]. ~ **dentistico** dental clinic

Am'burgo *nf* Hamburg

a'meba *nf* amoeba

a'mebico *a* amoebic

'amen *int* amen; **e allora** ~! well, so be it!

amenità *nf inv* (*facezia*) pleasantry

a'meno *a* pleasant

amenor'rea *nf Med* amenorrhoea

A'merica *nf* America. ~ **centrale** Central America. ~ **Latina** Latin America. ~ **del nord/sud** North/South America

america'nata *nf* (*pej: film*) American rubbish

america'nismo *nm* Americanism; (*patriottismo*) flag-waving

americaniz'zarsi *vr* become Americanized

ameri'cano, -a *a & nmf* American

ame'rindio *a* Native American

ame'tista *nf* amethyst

ami'anto *nm* asbestos

ami'chevole *a* friendly

ami'cizia *nf* friendship; **fare** ~ **con qcno** make friends with sb; **amicizie** *pl* (*amici*) friends

a'mico, -a *a* (*parola, persona*) friendly ● *nmf* friend; ~ **del cuore** bosom friend. ~ **d'infanzia** childhood friend. ~ **intimo** close friend. ~ **di penna** penfriend, penpal

'amido *nm* starch

ammac'care *vt* dent (*metallo*); bruise (*frutto*)

ammac'carsi *vr* (*metallo:*) get dented; (*frutto:*) bruise

ammac'cato *a* (*metallo*) dented; (*frutto*) bruised

ammacca'tura *nf* dent; (*livido*) bruise

ammaestra'mento *nm* training

ammae'strare *vt* (*istruire*) teach; train (*animale*)

ammae'strato *a* trained

ammaestra|'tore, -'trice *nmf* trainer

ammainabandi'era *nm inv* flag-lowering

ammai'nare *vt* lower (*bandiera*); furl (*vele*)

amma'larsi *vr* fall ill

amma'lato, -a *a* ill ● *nmf* sick person; (*paziente*) patient

ammali'are *vt* bewitch

ammali'ato *a* bewitched

ammalia|'tore, -'trice *a* bewitching ● *nm* enchanter ● *nf* enchantress

am'manco *nm* deficit

ammanet'tare *vt* handcuff

ammani'carsi *vr fig* acquire connections

ammani'cato *a* **essere** ~ have connections

ammanigli'arsi *vr fig* = **ammanicarsi**

ammanigli'ato *a fig* = **ammanicato**

amman'sire *vt* tame, domesticate (*animali*); *fig* pacify, placate

amman'sirsi *vr* (*animali:*) become tame; *fig* calm down

amman'tarsi *vr* (*persona:*) wrap oneself up in a cloak; ~ **di** *fig* feign (*virtù*)

amma'raggio *nm* splashdown

amma'rare *vi* put down on the sea; (*nave spaziale:*) splash down

ammassa'mento *nm Mil* build-up

ammas'sare *vt* amass

ammas'sarsi *vr* crowd together

am'masso *nm* mass; (*mucchio*) pile

ammat'tire *vi* go mad

ammazzacaffè *nm inv* liqueur

ammazza'fame *nm inv* stodge

ammaz'zare *vt* kill

ammaz'zarsi *vr* (*suicidarsi, fig*) kill oneself; (*rimanere ucciso*) be killed

am'menda *nf* amends *pl*; (*multa*) fine; **fare** ~ **di qcsa** make amends for sth

am'messo *pp di* **ammettere** ● *conj* ~ **che** supposing that

am'mettere *vt* admit; (*riconoscere*) acknowledge; (*supporre*) suppose; **ammettiamo che...** let's suppose [that]...

ammez'zato *nm* (*piano ammezzato*) mezzanine

ammic'care *vi* wink

ammini'strare *vt* administer; (*gestire*) run

ammini'strarsi *vr fig* manage one's finances

amministra'tivo *a* administrative

amministra|'tore, -'trice *nmf* administrator; (*di azienda*) manager; (*di società*) director; ~ **aggiunto** associate director. ~ **del condominio** property manger. ~ **delegato** managing director. ~ **unico** sole director

amministrazi'one *nf* administration; **fatti di ordinaria** ~ *fig* routine matters. ~ **aziendale** (*studi*) business studies. ~ **comunale** local council. ~ **controllata** receivership. ~ **pubblica** civil service. ~ **regionale** regional council

ammino'acido *nm* amino acid

ammi'rabile *a* admirable

ammi'raglia *nf* flag-ship

ammiragli'ato *nm* admiralty

ammi'raglio *nm* admiral

ammi'rare *vt* admire

ammi'rato *a* **restare/essere ~** be full of admiration

ammira|'tore, -'trice *nmf* admirer

ammirazi'one *nf* admiration

ammi'revole *a* admirable

ammis'sibile *a* admissible

ammissibilità *nf* acceptability

ammissi'one *nf* admission; (*approvazione*) acknowledgement

ammobili'are *vt* furnish

ammobili'ato *a* furnished; **stanza ammo-biliata** furnished room

ammoderna'mento *nm* modernization

ammoder'nare *vt* modernize

ammoder'narsi *vr* move with the times

am'modo *a* proper ● *adv* properly

ammogli'are *vt* marry off

ammogli'arsi *vr* get married

ammogli'ato *a* married ● *nm* married man

am'mollo *nm* **in ~** soaking; **mettere in ~** pre-soak

ammo'niaca *nf* ammonia

ammoni'mento *nm* warning; (*di rim-provero*) admonishment

ammo'nire *vt* warn; (*rimproverare*) admonish

ammoni'tore *a* admonishing

ammonizi'one *nf* Sport warning; (*rim-provero*) admonishment

ammon'tare *vi* **~ a** amount to ● *nm* amount

ammonticchi'are *vt* heap up, pile up

ammonticchi'arsi *vr* pile up

ammor'bare *vt* (*con odore*) pollute; (*con malattie*) infect

ammorbi'dente *nm* (*per panni*) softener

ammorbi'dire *vt* soften

ammorbi'dirsi *vr* soften

ammorta'mento *nm* Comm amortization

ammor'tare *vt* pay off (*spesa*); Comm amor-tize (*debito*)

ammortiz'zare *vt* Comm = **ammortare**; Mech damp

ammortizza'tore *nm* shock-absorber

ammosci'are *vt* make flabby

ammosci'arsi *vi* get flabby

ammucchi'are *vt* pile up

ammucchi'arsi *vr* pile up

ammucchi'ata *nf* (*sl: orgia*) orgy; **un'~ di** (*fam: ammasso*) loads of

ammuf'fire *vi* go mouldy

ammuf'firsi *vr* go mouldy

ammuf'fito *a* mouldy; *fig* stuffy

ammutina'mento *nm* mutiny

ammuti'narsi *vr* mutiny

ammuti'nato *a* mutinous ● *nm* mutineer

ammuto'lire *vi* be struck dumb

ammuto'lirsi *vr* fall silent

amne'sia *nf* amnesia

amni'stia *nf* amnesty

amnisti'are *vt* amnesty

'amo *nm* hook; *fig* bait

amo'rale *a* amoral

amoralità *nf* amorality

a'more *nm* love; **d'~** (*canzone, film*) love; **fare l'~** make love; **per l'amor di Dio/del cielo!** for heaven's sake!; **andare d'~ e d'accordo** get on like a house on fire; **amor proprio** self-respect; **amor cortese** courtly love; **è un ~** (*persona:*) he's/she's a darling; **per ~ di** for the sake of; **amori** *pl* love affairs

amoreggi'are *vi* flirt

amo'revole *a* loving

amorevol'mente *adv* lovingly

a'morfo *a* shapeless; (*persona*) colourless, grey

amo'rino *nm* cherub

amorosa'mente *adv* lovingly

amo'roso *a* loving; (*sguardo ecc*) amorous; (*lettera, relazione*) love *attrib*

am'pere *nm inv* ampere; **da 15 ~** 15-amp

ampe'rometro *nm* ammeter

ampia'mente *adv* widely

ampi'ezza *nf* (*di esperienza*) breadth; (*di stanza*) spaciousness; (*di gonna*) fullness; (*importanza*) scale. **~ di vedute** broad-mindedness

'ampio *a* ample; (*esperienza*) wide; (*stanza*) spacious; (*vestito*) loose; (*gonna, descrizione*) full; (*pantaloni*) baggy; **~ di vedute** broadminded

am'plesso *nm* embrace

amplia'mento *nm* (*di casa, porto*) enlarge-ment; (*di strada, conoscenze*) broadening

ampli'are *vt* broaden, widen (*strada, conoscenze*); enlarge (*casa*)

ampli'arsi *vr* broaden, grow wider

amplifi'care *vt* amplify; *fig* magnify

amplifica'tore *nm* amplifier

amplificazi'one *nf* amplification

am'polla *nf* cruet

ampol'loso *a* pompous

ampu'tare *vt* amputate

amputazi'one *nf* amputation

amu'leto *nm* amulet

A.N. *abbr Pol* (**Alleanza Nazionale**) Na-tional Alliance (*right-wing party*)

anabbagli'ante *a* *Auto* dipped ● *nm* **anabbaglianti** *pl* dipped headlights

anaboliz'zante *nm* anabolic steroid

ana'cardi *nmpl* cashew nuts

ana'cardio *nm* cashew

ana'conda *nf* Zool anaconda

anacro'nismo *nm* anachronism

anacro'nistico *a* anachronistic; **essere ~** be an anachronism

anae'robico *a* anaerobic

anafi'lattico *a* shock **~** Med anaphylactic shock

a'nagrafe *nf* (*ufficio*) registry office; (*registro*) register of births, marriages and deaths

ana'grafico *a* **dati** *pl* **anagrafici** personal data

ana'gramma *nm* anagram

anal'colico *a* non-alcoholic ● *nm* soft drink, non-alcoholic drink

a'nale *a* anal

analfa'beta *a & nmf* illiterate

analfabe'tismo *nm* illiteracy

anal'gesico *nm* painkiller

a'nalisi *nf inv* analysis; *Med* test; **in ultima ~** in the final analysis. **~ grammaticale/del periodo/logica** parsing. **~ di mercato** market research. **~ del percorso critico** critical path analysis. **~ del sangue** blood test

ana'lista *nmf* analyst. **~ economico** economic analyst. **~ finanziario** business analyst

ana'litico *a* analytical

analiz'zabile *a* analysable

analiz'zare *vt* analyse; *Med* test, analyse

anal'lergico *a* hypoallergenic

analoga'mente *adv* analogously

analo'gia *nf* analogy

ana'logico *a* analogue

analo'gismo *nm* reasoning by analogy

a'nalogo *a* analogous

anam'nesi *nf inv* medical history

'ananas *nm inv* pineapple

anar'chia *nf* anarchy

a'narchico, -a *a* anarchic ● *nmf* anarchist

anar'chismo *nm* anarchism

A.N.A.S. *nf abbr* (**Azienda Nazionale Autonoma delle Strade**) *national road maintenance authority*

ana'tema *nm* anathema

anato'mia *nf* anatomy

ana'tomico *a* anatomical; ‹*sedia*› contoured, ergonomic

'anatra *nf* duck. **~ selvatica** mallard

ana'troccolo *nm* duckling

'anca *nf* hip; (*di animale*) flank

ance'strale *a* ancestral

'anche *conj* also, too, as well; (*persino*) even; **parla ~ francese** he also speaks French, he speaks French too, he speaks French as well; **~ se** even if

ancheggi'are *vi* wiggle one's hips

anchilo'sarsi *vr fig* stiffen up

anchilo'sato *a fig* stiff

an'cora *adv* still; (*con negazione*) yet; (*di nuovo*) again; (*di più*) some more; **~ una volta** once more; **non ~** not yet; **~ esistente** extant; **~ più bello** even more beautiful; **~ una birra** another beer, one more beer

'ancora *nf* anchor; **gettare l'~** drop anchor. **~ di salvezza** last hope

anco'raggio *nm* anchorage

anco'rare *vt* anchor

anco'rarsi *vr* anchor, drop anchor; **~ a** *fig* cling to

Andalu'sia *nf* Andalusia

anda'luso, -a *a & nmf* Andalusian

anda'mento *nm* (*del mercato, degli affari*) trend

an'dante *a* (*corrente*) current; (*di poco valore*) cheap ● *nm Mus* andante

an'dare *vi* go; (*funzionare*) work; (*essere di moda*) be in; **~ via** (*partire*) leave; ‹*macchia*:› come out; **~ a piedi** walk; **~ a sciare** go skiing; **~** [**bene**] (*confarsi*) suit; ‹*taglia*:› fit; **ti va bene alle tre?** does three o'clock suit you?; **non mi va di mangiare** I don't feel like eating; **~ di fretta** be in a hurry; **~ fiero di** be proud of; **~ di moda** be in fashion; **va per i 20 anni** he's nearly 20; **ma va'** [**là**]! I come on!; **come va?** how are things?; **~ a male** go off; **~ a fuoco** go up in flames; **~ perduto** be lost; **va spedito** [**entro**] **stamattina** it must be sent this morning; **ne va del mio lavoro** my job is at stake; **come è andata a finire?** how did it turn out?; **cosa vai dicendo?** what are you talking about?; **andarsene** go away; (*morire*) pass away ● *nm* going; **~ e venire** (*andirivieni*) comings and goings *pl*; **a lungo ~** eventually; **a tutto ~** at full speed; **con l'~ del tempo** with the passing of time

an'data *nf* going; (*viaggio*) outward journey; **biglietto di sola ~/di ~ e ritorno** single/return [ticket]

anda'tura *nf* walk; (*portamento*) bearing; *Naut* tack; *Sport* pace

an'dazzo *nm fam* turn of events; **prendere un brutto ~** turn nasty

'Ande *nfpl* **le ~** the Andes

an'dino *a* Andean

andirivi'eni *nm inv* comings and goings *pl*

'andito *nm* passage

An'dorra *nf* Andorra

an'drone *nm* entrance

andro'pausa *nf hum* male menopause

a'neddoto *nm* anecdote

ane'lare *vt* **~ a** long for

a'nelito *nm* longing

a'nello *nm* ring; (*di catena*) link. **~ di fidanzamento** engagement ring. **~ d'oro** gold ring

ane'mia *nf* anaemia

a'nemico *a* anaemic

a'nemone *nm* anemone

aneste'sia *nf* anaesthesia; (*sostanza*) anaesthetic. **~ epidurale** epidural

aneste'sista *nmf* anaesthetist

ane'stetico *a & nm* anaesthetic

anestetiz'zare *vt* anaesthetize

a'neto *nm* dill

anfeta'mina *nf* amphetamine

an'fibi *nmpl* (*stivali*) army boots

an'fibio *nm* amphibian ● *a* amphibious

anfite'atro *nm* amphitheatre

'anfora *nf* amphora

an'fratto *nm* ravine

an'gelico *a* angelic

'angelo *nm* angel. **~ custode** guardian angel

anghe'ria *nf* harassment

an'gina *nf inv* **~** [**pectoris**] angina [pectoris]

angi'ologo, -a *nmf Med* angiologist

anglica'nesimo *nm Relig* Anglicanism

angli'cano, -a *a & nmf Relig* Anglican

angli'cismo *nm* Anglicism

angliciz'zare *vt* anglicize

anglo+ *pref* Anglo+

angloameri'cano, -a *nmf* Anglo-American

an'glofilo, -a *a & nmf* Anglophile

an'glofono, -a *nmf* English-speaker

anglofran'cese *a* Anglo-French

anglo'sassone *a & nmf* Anglo-Saxon

An'gola *nf* Angola

ango'lano, -a *a & nmf* Angolan

ango'lare *a* angular

angolazi'one *nf* angle shot; *fig* point of view

angoli'era *nf* (*mobile*) corner cupboard

'angolo *nm* corner; *Math* angle; **dietro l'~** round the corner; **fare ~ con** ⟨*negozio, casa:*⟩ be on the corner of. **~ acuto** acute angle. **~ [di] cottura** kitchenette. **~ retto** right angle

ango'loso *a* angular; ⟨*carattere*⟩ difficult to get on with

'angora *nf* [**lana d'**]**~** angora

an'goscia *nf* anguish

angosci'are *vt* torment

angosci'arsi *vr* (*preoccuparsi*) worry oneself sick, torment oneself

angosci'ato *a* agonized

angosci'oso *a* (*disperato*) anguished; (*che dà angoscia*) distressing

angu'illa *nf* eel

an'guria *nf* water-melon

an'gustia *nf* (*ansia*) anxiety; (*penuria*) poverty

angusti'are *vt* distress

angusti'arsi *vr* be distressed (**per** about)

angusti'ato *a* distressed

an'gusto *a* narrow

'anice *nm* anise; *Culin* aniseed; (*liquore*) anisette

ani'cino *nm* (*biscotto*) aniseed biscuit

ani'dride *nf* **~ carbonica** carbon dioxide. **~ solforosa** sulphur dioxide

'anima *nf* soul; **non c'era ~ viva** there was not a soul about; **all'~!** good grief!; **mi fa dannare l'~!** he'll be the death of me!; **l'~ della festa** the life and soul of the party; **un'~ in pena** a soul in torment; **volere un bene dell'~ a qcno** love sb to death; **la buon'~ della zia** my late aunt, God rest her soul. **~ gemella** soul mate

ani'male *a & nm* animal. **animali** *pl* **domestici** pets. **animali** *pl* **selvatici** wild animals

anima'lesco *a* animal

anima'lista *nmf* animal activist

ani'mare *vt* give life to; (*ravvivare*) enliven; (*incoraggiare*) encourage

ani'marsi *vr* come to life; (*accalorarsi*) become animated

ani'mato *a* animate; ⟨*discussione*⟩ animated; ⟨*strada, paese*⟩ lively

anima|'tore, -'trice *nmf* leading spirit; *Cinema* animator

animazi'one *nf* animation; **con ~** animatedly

ani'melle *nfpl* (*di agnello, vitello*) sweetbread

'animo *nm* (*mente*) mind; (*indole*) disposition; (*cuore*) heart; **perdersi d'~** lose heart; **farsi ~** take heart

animosa'mente *adv* boldly

animosità *nf* animosity

ani'moso *a* brave; (*ostile*) hostile

ani'setta *nf* anisette

'anitra *nf* duck

annacqua'mento *nm fig* watering down, dilution

annac'quare *vt anche fig* water down

annac'quato *a* watered down; ⟨*colore, resoconto*⟩ insipid

annaffi'are *vt* water

annaffia'toio *nm* watering-can

an'nali *nmpl* annals; **restare negli ~** go down in history

anna'spare *vi* flounder

an'nata *nf* year; (*importo annuale*) annual amount; (*di vino*) vintage; **vino d'~** vintage wine

annebbia'mento *nm* fog build-up; *fig* clouding

annebbi'are *vt* cloud ⟨*vista, mente*⟩

annebbi'arsi *vr* get misty; (*in città, su autostrada*) get foggy; ⟨*vista, mente:*⟩ grow dim

annega'mento *nm* drowning

anne'gare *vt/i* drown

anne'rire *vt/i* blacken

anne'rirsi *vr* become black

an'nessi *nmpl* (*costruzioni*) outbuildings; **tutti gli ~ e i connessi** all the appurtenances

annessi'one *nf* (*di nazione*) annexation

an'nesso *pp di* **annettere ●** *a* attached; ⟨*Stato*⟩ annexed

an'nettere *vt* add; (*accludere*) enclose; annex ⟨*Stato*⟩

annichi'lire *vt* annihilate

anni'darsi *vr* nest

annienta'mento *nm* annihilation

annien'tare *vt* annihilate

annien'tarsi *vr* abase oneself

anniver'sario *a & nm* anniversary. **~ di matrimonio** wedding anniversary

'anno *nm* year; **Buon A~!** Happy New Year!; **quanti anni ha?** how old are you?; **Tommaso ha dieci anni** Thomas is ten [years old]; **gli anni '30** the '30s. **~ accademico** academic year. **~ bisestile** leap year. **~ civile** calendar year. **~ giudiziario** law year. **~ luce** light year. **~ nuovo** New Year. **~ sabbatico** *Univ* sabbatical. **anni** *pl* **verdi** salad days

anno'dare *vt* knot; do up ⟨*cintura*⟩; *fig* form

anno'darsi *vr* become knotted

annoi'are *vt* bore; (*recare fastidio*) annoy

annoi'arsi *vr* get bored; (*condizione*) be bored

annoi'ato *a* bored

an'noso *a* ⟨*questione*⟩ age-old

anno'tare *vt* note down; annotate ⟨*testo*⟩

annotazi'one *nf* note

annove'rare vt number

annu'ale a annual, yearly

annual'mente adv annually

annu'ario nm year-book

annu'ire vi nod; (acconsentire) agree

annulla'mento nm annulment; (di appuntamento) cancellation

annul'lare vt annul; cancel (appuntamento); (togliere efficacia a) undo; disallow (gol); (distruggere) destroy

annul'larsi vr cancel each other out

an'nullo nm (timbro) franking

annunci'are vt announce; (preannunciare) foretell

annuncia|'tore, -'trice nmf announcer

annunciazi'one nf Annunciation

an'nuncio nm announcement; (pubblicitario) advertisement; (notizia) news. **annunci** pl **economici** classified advertisements. **annunci** pl **mortuari** obituaries, death notices. ~ **pubblicitario** advertisement

'annuo a annual, yearly

annu'sare vt sniff

annu'sata nf **dare un'**~ **a** have a sniff at

annuvola'mento nm clouding over

annuvo'lare vt cloud

annuvo'larsi vr cloud over

'ano nm anus

a'nodino a anodyne

'anodo nm anode

anoma'lia nf anomaly

a'nomalo a anomalous

a'nonima nf A~ **Alcolisti** Alcoholics Anonymous. ~ **sequestri** Italian criminal organization specializing in kidnapping

anoni'mato nm **mantenere l'**~ remain anonymous

anonimità nf anonymity

a'nonimo, -a a anonymous ● nmf unknown person; (pittore, scrittore) anonymous painter/writer

anores'sia nf Med anorexia

ano'ressico, -a nmf anorexic

anor'male a abnormal ● nmf deviant, abnormal person

anormalità nf inv abnormality

ANSA nf abbr (**Agenzia Nazionale Stampa Associata**) Italian press agency

'ansa nf handle; (di fiume) bend

an'sante a panting

an'sare vi pant

'ansia, ansietà nf anxiety; **stare/essere in** ~ **per** be anxious about

ansi'mante a breathless

ansi'mare vi gasp for breath

ansio'litico nm tranquillizer

ansi'oso a anxious

'anta nf (di finestra) shutter; (di armadio) door

antago'nismo nm antagonism

antago'nista nmf antagonist

antago'nistico a antagonistic

an'tartico a & nm Antarctic

An'tartide nf Antarctica

ante'bellico a pre-war

antece'dente a preceding ● nm precedent

ante'fatto nm prior event

ante'guerra a pre-war ● nm pre-war period

ante'nato, -a nmf ancestor

an'tenna nf Radio, TV aerial; (di animale) antenna; Naut yard; **rizzare le antenne** fig prick up one's ears. ~ **parabolica** satellite dish. ~ **radar** radar scanner

ante'porre vt put before

ante'prima nf preview; **vedere qcsa in** ~ have a sneak preview of sth

anteri'ore a front attrib; (nel tempo) previous

anterior'mente adv (nel tempo) previously; (nello spazio) in front

antesi'gnano, -a nmf fig forerunner

anti+ pref anti+

antiabor'tista nmf antiabortionist ● a antiabortion attrib

anti'acido nm antacid

antiade'rente a (padella) nonstick

antia'ereo a anti-aircraft attrib

antial'lergico a hypoallergenic

antia'partheid a inv antiapartheid

antia'tomico a anti-nuclear; **rifugio** ~ fall-out shelter

antibat'terico a antibacterial

antibi'otico a & nm antibiotic

antibloc'caggio a inv antilock attrib

anti'caglia nf (oggetto) piece of old junk

anti-cal'care nm softener

antica'mente adv in ancient times, long ago

anti'camera nf ante-room; **fare** ~ be kept waiting

antichità nf inv antiquity; (oggetto) antique

antici'clone nm anticyclone

antici'clonico a (area) anti-cyclonic

antici'pare vt advance; Comm pay in advance; (prevedere) anticipate; (prevenire) forestall ● vi be early

anticipata'mente adv in advance

antici'pato a upfront; **pagamento** ~ advance payment

anticipazi'one nf anticipation; (notizia) advance news

an'ticipo nm advance; (caparra) deposit; **in** ~ early; (nel lavoro) ahead of schedule; **giocare d'**~ Sport, fig anticipate the next move

an'tico a ancient; (mobile ecc) antique; (vecchio) old; **all'antica** old-fashioned ● nm **gli antichi** the ancients

anticomu'nista a & nmf anti-communist

anticoncezio'nale a & nm contraceptive

anticonfor'mismo nm unconventionality

anticonfor'mista nmf nonconformist

anticonfor'mistico a unconventional, nonconformist

anticonge'lante a & nm anti-freeze

anticonsu'mismo nm anti-consumerism

anti'corpo nm antibody

anticostituzio'nale a unconstitutional

anti'crimine a inv (squadra) crime attrib

antidemo'cratico *a* undemocratic

antidepres'sivo *nm* antidepressant

antidiluvi'ano *a fig* antediluvian

antidolo'rifico *nm* painkiller

anti'doping *nm inv Sport* dope test

an'tidoto *nm* antidote

anti'droga *a inv* ⟨campagna⟩ anti-drugs; ⟨squadra⟩ drug *attrib*

antie'stetico *a* ugly

antifa'scismo *nm* anti-fascism

antifa'scista *a & nmf* anti-fascist

an'tifona *nf fig* dull and repetitive speech; **capire l'~** take the hint; **sempre la stessa ~** always the same old story

anti'forfora *a inv* dandruff *attrib*

anti'fumo *a inv* anti-smoking

anti'furto *nm* anti-theft device; ⟨allarme⟩ alarm ● *a inv* ⟨sistema⟩ anti-theft

anti'gelo *a inv* anti-freeze ● *nm* antifreeze; ⟨parabrezza⟩ defroster

anti'gene *nm* antigen

antigi'enico *a* unhygienic

anti-inflazi'one *a inv* anti-inflation

An'tille *nfpl* **le ~** the West Indies

an'tilope *nf* antelope

anti'mafia *a inv* anti-Mafia

antimilita'rista *a inv* anti-militaristic ● *nmf* anti-militarist

antin'cendio *a inv* **allarme ~** fire alarm; **porta ~** fire door

anti'nebbia *a inv* [faro] **~** *Auto* foglamp, foglight

antine'vralgico *a* pain-killing ● *nm* painkiller

antinfiamma'torio *a & nm* anti-inflammatory

antinflazio'nistico *a* anti-inflationary

antinquina'mento *a inv* anti-pollution

antinucle'are *a* anti-nuclear

antio'rario *a* anti-clockwise

antiparassi'tario *nm* insecticide

antiparlamen'tare *a* unparliamentary

antipasti'era *nf* hors d'oeuvre dish

anti'pasto *nm* hors d'oeuvre, starter. **antipasti** *pl* **caldi** hot starters. **antipasti** *pl* **freddi** cold starters. **antipasti** *pl* **misti** variety of starters

antipa'tia *nf* antipathy

anti'patico *a* unpleasant

an'tipodi *nmpl* Antipodes; **essere agli ~** *fig* be poles apart

anti'polio *nf inv* ⟨vaccino⟩ polio vaccine; **fare l'~** have a polio injection ● *a* ⟨siero, vaccino⟩ polio *attrib*

antipopo'lare *a* anti-working-class

antiprobizio'nismo *nm* anti-prohibitionism

antiproibizio'nista *a & nmf* anti-prohibitionist

antiproi'ettile *a inv* bullet-proof

antiquari'ato *nm* antique trade; **pezzo d'~** antique

anti'quario, -a *nmf* antique dealer

anti'quato *a* antiquated

antiraz'zismo *nm* antiracism

antireu'matico *a & nm* anti-rheumatic

antiri'flesso *a inv* antiglare

anti'ruggine *nm inv* rust-inhibitor ● *a* anti-rust

anti'rughe *a inv* anti-wrinkle *attrib*

anti'scasso *a inv* ⟨porta⟩ burglar-proof

antisci'opero *a inv* anti-strike

anti'scippo *a inv* theft-proof

anti'scivolo *a inv* nonskid

antise'mita *a* anti-Semitic

antisemi'tismo *nm* anti-Semitism

anti'settico *a & nm* antiseptic

antisinda'cale *a* ⟨comportamento⟩ anti-trade-union

anti'sismico *a* earthquake-proof

antisoci'ale *a* anti-social

antiso'lare *a & nm* suntan

antisommer'gibile *a inv* anti-submarine ● *nm* submarine hunter

antista'minico *nm* antihistamine

anti'stante *prep* **~ a** in front of

anti'tarlo *nm inv* woodworm treatment

anti'tarmico *a* mothproof

antiterro'rismo *nm* counter-terrorism

antiterro'rista *a* antiterrorist

antiterro'ristico *a* antiterrorist

an'titesi *nf inv* antithesis

antite'tanica *nf* tetanus injection

antite'tanico *a* tetanus *attrib*

anti'tetico *a* antithetical

anti'trust *a* antitrust

antitumo'rale *a* which stops the growth of tumours

anti'urto *a* shockproof

antivaio'losa *nf* smallpox injection

anti'vipera *a* **siero ~** snakebite antidote

antivi'rale *a* anti-viral

antolo'gia *nf* anthology

an'tonimo *nm* antonym

antono'masia: per ~ *a* ⟨poeta⟩ quintessential

antra'cite *nf* anthracite; ⟨colore⟩ charcoal [grey]

'antro *nm* cavern

antro'pofago *a* man-eating, cannibalistic

antropolo'gia *nf* anthropology

antropo'logico *a* anthropological

antro'pologo, -a *nmf* anthropologist

anu'lare *nm* ring-finger

An'versa *nf* Antwerp

'anzi *conj* in fact; ⟨o meglio⟩ or better still; ⟨al contrario⟩ on the contrary

anzianità *nf* old age; ⟨di servizio⟩ seniority

anzi'ano, -a *a* old, elderly; ⟨di grado ecc⟩ senior ● *nmf* elderly person

anziché *conj* rather than

anzi'tempo *adv* prematurely

anzi'tutto *adv* first of all

a'orta *nf* aorta

A'pache *mf inv* Apache

apar'theid *nf* apartheid

apar'titico *a* unaligned

apa'tia *nf* apathy

a'patico *a* apathetic

'ape *nf* bee. **~ regina** queen bee

aperi'tivo *nm* aperitif

aperta'mente *adv* openly

a'perto *a* open; **all'aria aperta** in the open air; **all'~** ⟨*piscina, teatro*⟩ open-air. **~ a tutti** open to all comers. **rimanere a bocca aperta** be dumbfounded

aper'tura *nf* opening; (*inizio*) beginning; (*ampiezza*) spread; (*di arco*) span; *Pol* overtures *pl*; *Phot* aperture. **~ alare** wing span. **~ di credito** loan agreement. **~ mentale** openness

api'ario *nm* apiary

'apice *nm* apex; **l'~ di** the acme of

apicol|'tore, -'trice *nmf* beekeeper

apicol'tura *nf* beekeeping

a'plomb *nm inv* (*di un abito*) hang; *fig* aplomb, self-assuredness

ap'nea *nf* **immersione in ~** free diving

Apoca'lisse *nf* **l'~** the Apocalypse

apoca'littico *a* apocalyptic

a'pocrifo *a* apocryphal

apo'geo *nm* apogee

a'polide *a* stateless ● *nmf* stateless person

apo'litico *a* apolitical

A'pollo *nm* Apollo

apolo'geta *nmf* apologist (**di** for)

apolo'gia *nf* apologia; (*celebrazione*) eulogy. **~ di reato** condoning of a criminal act

apoples'sia *nf* apoplexy

apo'plettico *a* apoplectic

a'postolo *nm* apostle

apostro'fare *vt* (*mettere un apostrofo a*) write with an apostrophe; reprimand ⟨*persona*⟩

a'postrofo *nm* apostrophe

apote'osi *nf* apotheosis

appaga'mento *nm* fulfilment

appa'gare *vt* satisfy

appa'garsi *vr* **~ di** be satisfied with

appa'gato *a* sated

appai'are *vt* pair; mate ⟨*animali*⟩

appallotto'lare *vt* roll into a ball

appallotto'larsi *vr* ⟨*gatto:*⟩ curl up in a ball; ⟨*farina:*⟩ become lumpy

appalta'tore *nm* contractor

ap'palto *nm* contract; **dare in ~** contract out; **gara di ~** call for tenders

appan'naggio *nm* (*in denaro*) annuity; *fig* prerogative

appan'nare *vt* mist ⟨*vetro*⟩; dim ⟨*vista*⟩

appan'narsi *vr* mist over; ⟨*vista:*⟩ grow dim

appa'rato *nm* apparatus; (*apparecchiamento*) array; (*pompa*) display. **~ digerente** digestive system. **~ scenico** set

apparecchi'are *vt* prepare ● *vi* lay the table *Br*, set the table

apparecchia'tura *nf* (*impianti*) equipment

appa'recchio *nm* apparatus; (*congegno*) device; (*radio, tv ecc*) set; (*aeroplano*) aircraft; (*telefono*) phone. **~ acustico** hearing aid

appa'rente *a* apparent

apparente'mente *adv* apparently

appa'renza *nf* appearance; **in ~** apparently

appa'rire *vi* appear; (*sembrare*) look

appari'scente *a* striking; *pej* gaudy

apparizi'one *nf* apparition

apparta'mento *nm* flat, apartment *Am*. **~ ammobiliato** furnished flat. **~ in multiproprietà** timeshare

appar'tarsi *vr* withdraw

appar'tato *a* secluded

apparte'nente *a* **~ a** belonging to

apparte'nenza *nf* membership

apparte'nere *vi* belong

appassio'nante *a* ⟨*storia, argomento*⟩ exciting

appassio'nare *vt* excite; (*commuovere*) move

appassio'narsi *vr* **~ a** become excited by

appassio'nato *a* passionate; **~ di** (*entusiastico*) fond of

appas'sire *vi* wither

appas'sirsi *vr* fade

appas'sito *a* faded

appel'larsi *vr* **~ a** appeal to

ap'pello *nm* appeal; (*chiamata per nome*) rollcall; (*esami*) exam session; **fare l'~** call the roll

ap'pena *adv* just; (*a fatica*) hardly ● *conj* [**non**] **~** as soon as, no sooner... than; **~ prima di** just before

ap'pendere *vt* hang [up]

appendi'abiti *nm inv* hat-stand, hallstand

appen'dice *nf* appendix; **romanzo d'~** novel serialized in a magazine or newspaper

appendi'cite *nf* appendicitis

Appen'nini *nmpl* **gli ~** the Apennines

appen'ninico *a* Apennine

appesan'tire *vt* weigh down

appesan'tirsi *vr* become heavy

ap'peso *pp di* **appendere** ● *a* hanging; (*impiccato*) hanged

appe'tito *nm* appetite; **aver ~** be hungry; **buon ~!** enjoy your meal!

appeti'toso *a* appetizing; *fig* tempting

appezza'mento *nm* plot of land

appia'nare *vt* level; *fig* smooth over

appia'narsi *vr* improve

appiat'tire *vt* flatten

appiat'tirsi *vr* flatten oneself; *fig* level out

appic'care *vt* **~ il fuoco a** set fire to

appicci'care *vt* stick; **~ a** (*fig: appioppare*) palm off on ● *vi* be sticky

appicci'carsi *vr* stick; ⟨*cose:*⟩ stick together; **~ a qcno** *fig* stick to sb like glue

appiccica'ticcio *a* sticky; *fig* clingy

appicci'cato *a* **stare ~ a qcno** be all over sb

appicci'coso *a* sticky; *fig* clingy

appie'dato *a* **sono ~** I don't have the car; **sono rimasto ~** I was stranded

appi'eno *adv* fully

appigli'arsi *vr* **~ a** get hold of; *fig* stick to

ap'piglio *nm* fingerhold; (*per piedi*) foothold; *fig* pretext

appiop'pare *vt* **~ a** palm off on; (*fam: dare*) give; **~ un ceffone a qcno** slap sb

appiso'larsi *vr* doze off

applau'dire *vt/i* applaud

ap'plauso *nm* applause

appli'cabile *a* applicable

appli'care *vt* apply; enforce ‹*legge ecc*›

appli'carsi *vr* apply oneself

appli'cato *nmf (impiegato)* senior clerk ● *a (nel ricamo)* appliqué; **matematica applicata** applied mathematics

applica'tore *nm* applicator

applicazi'one *nf* application; *(di legge)* enforcement. **applicazioni** *pl* **tecniche** handicrafts

appoggi'are *vt* lean (**a** against); *(mettere)* put; *(sostenere)* back

appoggi'arsi *vr* ~ **a** lean against; *fig* rely on

appoggi'ato *a* leaning (**su** on; **contro, a** against)

ap'poggio *nm* support; **appoggi** *pl fig* influential contacts

appollai'arsi *vr fig* perch

ap'porre *vt* affix

appor'tare *vt* bring; *(causare)* cause; **~ delle modifiche a qcsa** modify sth

ap'porto *nm* contribution

apposita'mente *adv (specialmente)* especially; **fatto ~** purpose-made

ap'posito *a* proper

apposizi'one *nf* apposition

ap'posta *adv* on purpose; *(espressamente)* specially; **neanche a farlo ~!** what a coincidence!

apposta'mento *nm* ambush; *(caccia)* lying in wait

appo'stare *vt* post ‹*soldati*›

appo'starsi *vr* lie in wait

ap'prendere *vt* understand; *(imparare)* learn

apprendi'mento *nm* learning

appren'dista *nmf* apprentice

apprendi'stato *nm* apprenticeship

apprensi'one *nf* apprehension; **essere in ~ per** be anxious about

appren'sivo *a* apprehensive

ap'presso *adv & prep (vicino)* near; *(dietro)* behind; **come ~** as follows

appre'stare *vt* prepare

appre'starsi *vr* get ready

apprez'zabile *a* appreciable

apprezza'mento *nm* appreciation; *(giudizio)* opinion

apprez'zare *vt* appreciate

apprez'zato *a* appreciated

ap'proccio *nm* approach

appro'dare *vi* land; **~ a** *fig* come to; **non ~ a nulla** come to nothing

ap'prodo *nm* landing; *(luogo)* landing-stage

approfit'tare *vi* take advantage (**di** of), profit (**di** by)

approfitta'|tore, -'trice *nmf* chancer

approfondi'mento *nm* deepening; **di ~** ‹*corso*› advanced

approfon'dire *vt* broaden, widen ‹*indagine, conoscenze*›

approfon'dirsi *vr* ‹*divario:*› widen

approfon'dito *a* ‹*studio, ricerca*› in-depth

appron'tare *vt* get ready, prepare

appropri'arsi *vr* ~ **a** *(essere adatto a)* suit; **~ di** take possession of; **~ indebitamente di** embezzle, misappropriate

appropri'ato *a* appropriate

appropriazi'one *nf* Jur appropriation. **~ indebita** *Jur* embezzlement

approssi'mare *vt* **~ per eccesso/difetto** round up/down

approssi'marsi *vr* draw near

approssimativa'mente *adv* approximately

approssima'tivo *a* approximate

approssimazi'one *nf* approximation

appro'vare *vt* approve of; approve ‹*legge*›

approvazi'one *nf* approval

approvvigiona'mento *nm* supplying; **approvvigionamenti** *pl* provisions

approvvigio'nare *vt* supply

approvvigio'narsi *vr* stock up

appunta'mento *nm* appointment; *fam* date; **fissare un ~, prendere un ~** make an appointment; **darsi ~** decide to meet

appun'tare *vt (annotare)* take notes; *(fissare)* fix; *(con spillo)* pin; *(appuntire)* sharpen

appun'tarsi *vr* **~ su** ‹*teoria:*› be based on

appun'tato *nm (carabiniere)* lowest rank in the carabinieri

appuntel'larsi *vr (sostenersi)* support oneself

appun'tino *adv* meticulously

appun'tire *vt* sharpen

appun'tito *a* ‹*matita*› sharp; ‹*mento*› pointed

ap'punto¹ *nm* note; *(piccola critica)* niggle

ap'punto² *adv* exactly; **per l'~!** exactly!; **stavo ~ dicendo...** I was just saying...

appura'mento *nm* verification

appu'rare *vt* verify

a'pribile *a* that can be opened; **tettuccio ~** *Auto* sun roof

apribot'tiglie *nm inv* bottle-opener

a'prile *nm* April; **primo d'~** April Fool's Day

aprio'ristico *a* a priori

a'prire *vt* open; turn on ‹*luce, acqua ecc*›; *(con chiave)* unlock; open up ‹*ferita ecc*›; **~ le ostilità** *Mil* commence hostilities; **apriti cielo!** heavens above!

a'prirsi *vr* open; *(spaccarsi)* split; *(confidarsi)* confide (**con** in)

apri'scatole *nf inv* tin opener *Br*, can opener

APT *abbr* (**Azienda di Promozione Turistica**) Tourist Board

aqua'planing *nm* andare in ~ aquaplane

'aquila *nf* eagle; **non è un' ~!** *fig* he's no genius!

aqui'lino *a* aquiline

aqui'lone *nm (giocattolo)* kite

aqui'lotto *nm (piccolo dell'aquila)* eaglet

AR *abbr* (**andata e ritorno**) return [ticket];

abbr (**avviso di ricevimento**) return receipt for registered letters

ara'besco *nm* arabesque; *hum* scribble

A'rabia *nf* Arabia. l'~ **Saudita** Saudi Arabia

'arabo, -a *a* Arab; ⟨*lingua*⟩ Arabic ● *nmf* Arab ● *nm* (*lingua*) Arabic

arabo-israeli'ano *a* Arab-Israeli

a'rachide *nf* peanut

arago'nese *a* Aragonese

ara'gosta *nf* lobster

a'raldica *nf* heraldry

a'raldico *nm* herald ● *a* heraldic

aran'ceto *nm* orange grove

a'rancia *nf* orange; **succo d'~** orange juice

aranci'ata *nf* orangeade

a'rancio *nm* orange-tree; (*colore*) orange

aranci'one *a & nm* orange

a'rare *vt* plough

ara'tore *nm* ploughman

a'ratro *nm* plough

ara'tura *nf* ploughing

a'razzo *nm* tapestry

arbi'traggio *nm* Comm arbitrage; *Sport* refereeing; *Jur* arbitration

arbi'trare *vt* arbitrate in; *Sport* referee

arbitrarietà *nf* arbitrariness

arbi'trario *a* arbitrary

arbi'trato *nm* arbitration

ar'bitrio *nm* will; **è un ~** it's very high-handed

'arbitro *nm* arbiter; *Sport* referee; (*nel baseball*) umpire

arboricol'tura *nf* arboriculture

ar'busto *nm* shrub

'arca *nf* ark; (*cassa*) chest. l'~ **di Noè** Noah's Ark

ar'caico *a* archaic

arca'ismo *nm* archaism

ar'cangelo *nm* archangel

ar'cano *a* mysterious ● *nm* mystery

ar'cata *nf* arch; (*serie di archi*) arcade

archeolo'gia *nf* archaeology

archeo'logico *a* archaeological

arche'ologo, -a *nmf* archaeologist

ar'chetipo *nm* archetype

ar'chetto *nm* Mus bow

architet'tare *vt fig* devise; **cosa state architettando?** *fig* what are you plotting?

archi'tetto *nm* architect. ~ **d'interni** interior designer

architet'tonico *a* architectural

architet'tura *nf anche Comput* architecture

archi'trave *nm* lintel

archivi'abile *a* that can be filed

archivi'are *vt* file; *Jur* close

archiviazi'one *nf* filing; (*Jur: di caso*) closing. ~ **dati** data storage

ar'chivio *nm* archives *pl*; *Comput* file

archi'vista *nmf* filing clerk

archi'vistica *nf rules governing the keeping of archives and records*

ARCI *nf abbr* (**Associazione Ricreativa Culturale Italiana**) *Italian cultural and leisure association*

arci'duca *nm* archduke

arcidu'chessa *nf* archduchess

arci'ere *nm* archer

ar'cigno *a* grim

arci'one *nm* saddle

arci'pelago *nm* archipelago

arci'vescovo *nm* archbishop

'arco *nm* arch; *Math* arc; (*arma, Mus*) bow; **nell'~ di una giornata/due mesi** in the space of a day/two months. ~ **rampante** flying buttress

arcoba'leno *nm* rainbow

arcu'are *vt* bend; ~ **la schiena** ⟨*gatto:*⟩ arch its back

arcu'arsi *vr* bend

arcu'ato *a* bent; ⟨*schiena di gatto*⟩ arched

ar'dente *a* burning; *fig* ardent; **camera ~** chapel of rest

ardente'mente *adv* ardently

'ardere *vt/i* burn; **legna da ~** fire-wood

ar'desia *nf* slate

ardi'mento *nm* boldness

ar'dire *vi* dare ● *nm* (*coraggio*) daring, boldness; (*sfrontatezza*) impudence

ar'dito *a* daring; (*coraggioso*) bold; (*sfacciato*) impudent

ar'dore *nm* (*calore*) heat; *fig* ardour

'arduo *a* arduous; (*ripido*) steep

'area *nf* area; (*superficie*) surface. ~ **fabbricabile** building land. ~ **di rigore** (*in calcio*) penalty area, penalty box. ~ **di servizio** service area

a'rena *nf* arena

are'naria *nf* sandstone

are'narsi *vr* run aground; ⟨*fig: trattative*⟩ reach deadlock; **mi sono arenato** I'm stuck

are'nile *nm* stretch of sand

areo'plano *nm* aeroplane

'argano *nm* winch

argen'tato *a* silver-plated

ar'genteo *a* silvery

argente'ria *nf* silver[ware]

argenti'ere *nm* silversmith

Argen'tina *nf* Argentina

argen'tina *nf* (*maglia*) round-necked pullover

argen'tino *a* silvery

argen'tino, -a *a & nmf* Argentinian

ar'gento *nm* silver; **d'~** silver. ~ **vivo** Chem quicksilver

ar'gilla *nf* clay

argil'loso *a* ⟨*terreno*⟩ clayey; (*simile all'argilla*) clay-like

argi'nare *vt* embank; *fig* hold in check, contain

'argine *nm* embankment; (*diga*) dike; **fare ~ a** *fig* hold in check, contain

argomen'tare *vi* argue

argo'mento *nm* argument; (*motivo*) reason; (*soggetto*) subject

argu'ire *vt* deduce

arguta'mente *adv* (*con astuzia*) shrewdly; (*con facezia*) wittily

ar'guto *a* witty; (*astuto*) shrewd

ar'guzia *nf* wit; (*battuta*) witticism; (*astuzia*) shrewdness

'aria *nf* air; (*aspetto*) appearance; *Mus* tune; **avere l'~...** look...; **corrente d'~** draught; **mandare all'~** qcsa *fig* ruin sth; **andare all'~** *fig* fall through; **a tenuta d'~** draughtproof; **avere la testa per ~** *fig* be absent-minded, have one's head in the clouds; **che ~ tirava?** *fig* what was the atmosphere like?; **cambiare ~** *fig* have a change of scene; **cambia ~!** *hum* get out of here!. **~-~ a** *inv Mil* air-to-air. **~ conditionata** air-condition-ing. **~-terra** *a inv* air-to-ground

ari'ano *a* Aryan

arida'mente *adv* without emotion

aridità *nf* aridity

'arido *a* arid

arieggi'are *vt* air; **~ una stanza** give a room an airing

arieggi'ato *a* airy

ari'ete *nm* ram; (*strumento*) battering-ram; **A~** *Astr* Aries

ari'etta *nf* (*brezza*) breeze

a'ringa *nf* herring

ari'oso *a* (*locale*) light and airy

'arista *nf* chine of pork

aristo'cratico, -a *a* aristocratic ● *nmf* aristocrat

aristocra'zia *nf* aristocracy

arit'metica *nf* arithmetic

arit'metico *a* arithmetical

arlec'chino *nm* Harlequin; *fig* buffoon

'arma *nf* weapon; (*forze armate*) [armed] forces; **armi** *pl* arms; **chiamare alle armi** call up; **sotto le armi** in the army; **alle prime armi** *fig* inexperienced, fledg[e]ling; **prendere/deporre le armi** take up arms/ put down one's arms; **passare qcno per le armi** execute sb; **confrontarsi ad armi pari** compete on an equal footing. **~ bianca** knife. **~ a doppio taglio** *fig* double-edged sword. **~ da fuoco** firearm. **~ impropria** makeshift weapon. **armi** *pl* **nucleari** nuclear weapons

armadi'etto *nm* locker, cupboard; (*in aereo*) overhead locker. **~ del bagno** bathroom cabi-net. **~ dei medicinali** medicine cabinet

arma'dillo *nm* armadillo

ar'madio *nm* cupboard; (*guardaroba*) ward-robe. **~ a muro** fitted cupboard

armamen'tario *nm* tools *pl*; *fig* parapher-nalia

arma'mento *nm* armament; *Naut* fitting out

ar'mare *vt* arm; (*equipaggiare*) fit out; *Archit* reinforce

ar'marsi *vr* arm oneself (**di** with)

ar'mata *nf* army; (*flotta*) fleet

ar'mato *a* armed; **rapina a mano armata** armed robbery

arma'tore *nm* shipowner

arma'tura *nf* framework; (*impalcatura*) scaffolding; (*di guerriero*) armour

armeggi'are *vi fig* manoeuvre

Ar'menia *nf* Armenia

ar'meno, -a *a & nmf* Armenian

arme'ria *nf Mil* armoury

armi'stizio *nm* armistice

armo'nia *nf* harmony

ar'monica *nf* **~ [a bocca]** mouth-organ

ar'monico *a* harmonic

armoniosa'mente *adv* harmoniously

armoni'oso *a* harmonious

armoniz'zare *vt* harmonize ● *vi* match

armoniz'zarsi *vr* (*colori:*) go together, match

ar'nese *nm* tool; (*oggetto*) thing; (*congegno*) gadget; **male in ~** in bad condition

'arnia *nf* beehive

a'roma *nm* aroma; **aromi** *pl* herbs; **aromi** *pl* **naturali/artificiali** natural/artificial fla-vourings

aromatera'pia *nf* aromatherapy

aro'matico *a* aromatic

aromatiz'zare *vt* flavour

'arpa *nf* harp

ar'peggio *nm* arpeggio

ar'pia *nf* harpy

arpi'one *nm* hook; (*pesca*) harpoon

ar'pista *nmf* harpist

arrabat'tarsi *vr* do all one can

arrabbi'arsi *vr* get angry

arrabbi'ato *a* angry

arrabbia'tura *nf* rage; **prendersi un'~** fly into a rage

arraf'fare *vt* grab

arraf'fone *nmf fam* thief

arrampi'carsi *vr* climb [up]; **~ sugli specchi** *fig* clutch at straws

arrampi'cata *nf* climb

arrampica'tore, -'trice *nmf* climber. **~ sociale** social climber

arran'care *vi* limp, hobble; *fig* struggle, limp along

arrangia'mento *nm* arrangement

arrangi'are *vt* arrange

arrangi'arsi *vr* manage; **~ alla meglio** get by; **ar'rangiati!** get on with it!

arrangia'tore, -'trice *nmf Mus* arranger

arra'parsi *vr vulg* get randy

arre'care *vt* bring; (*causare*) cause

arreda'mento *nm* interior decoration; (*l'arredare*) furnishing; (*mobili ecc*) furnish-ings *pl*

arre'dare *vt* furnish

arreda'tore, -'trice *nmf* interior designer

ar'redo *nm* furnishings *pl*

arrem'baggio *nm* **buttarsi all'~** *fig* stam-pede

ar'rendersi *vr* surrender; **~ all'evidenza dei fatti** face facts

arren'devole *a* (*persona*) yielding

arrendevo'lezza *nf* softness

arre'stare *vt* arrest; (*fermare*) stop

arre'starsi *vr* halt

ar'resto *nm* stop; *Jur* arrest; **la dichiaro in [stato d']~** you are under arrest; **mandato di ~** warrant. **~ cardiaco** heart failure, car-diac arrest. **arresti** *pl* **domiciliari** *Jur* house arrest

arretra'mento *nm* withdrawal

arre'trare *vt* withdraw; pull back ⟨*giocatore*⟩ ● *vi* withdraw

arre'trato *a* ⟨*paese ecc*⟩ backward; ⟨*Mil: posizione*⟩ rear; **numero ~** ⟨*di rivista*⟩ back number; **del lavoro ~** a backlog of work ● *nm* ⟨*di stipendio*⟩ back pay; **essere in ~** be behind schedule; **arretrati** *pl* arrears. **arretrati** *pl* **di paga** back pay

arricchi'mento *nm* enrichment

arric'chire *vt* enrich

arric'chirsi *vr* get rich

arric'chito, -a *nmf* nouveau riche

arricciaca'pelli *nm inv* tongs

arricci'are *vt* curl; **~ il naso** turn up one's nose

ar'ridere *vi* **~ a qcno** ⟨*sorte:*⟩ smile on sb

ar'ringa *nf Jur* closing address

arrin'gare *vt* harangue

arrischi'arsi *vr* dare

arrischi'ato *a* risky; ⟨*imprudente*⟩ rash

arri'vare *vi* arrive; **~ a** ⟨*raggiungere*⟩ reach; ⟨*ridursi*⟩ be reduced to

arri'vato, -a *a* successful; **il primo/secondo ~** ⟨*in gare*⟩; **ben ~!** welcome! ● *nmf* successful person

arrive'derci *int* goodbye; **~ a domani** see you tomorrow

arri'vismo *nm* social climbing; ⟨*nel lavoro*⟩ careerism

arri'vista *nmf* social climber; ⟨*nel lavoro*⟩ careerist

ar'rivo *nm* arrival; *Sport* finish; **~ previsto per le ore...** expected time of arrival...

arro'gante *a* arrogant

arro'ganza *nf* arrogance

arro'garsi *vr* **~ il diritto di fare qcsa** take it upon oneself to do sth; **~ il merito** take the credit

arrossa'mento *nm* reddening

arros'sare *vt* make red, redden ⟨*occhi*⟩

arros'sarsi *vr* go red

arros'sire *vi* blush, go red

arro'stire *vt* roast; toast ⟨*pane*⟩; ⟨*ai ferri*⟩ grill

arro'stirsi *vr fig* broil

ar'rosto *a & nm* roast; **molto fumo e niente ~** *fig* all show and no substance. **~ d'agnello** roast lamb

arro'tare *vt* sharpen; ⟨*fam: investire*⟩ run over

arro'tino *nm* knife-sharpener

arroto'lare *vt* roll up

arroton'dare *vt* round; *Math ecc* round off; **~ lo stipendio** supplement one's income

arroton'darsi *vr* become round; ⟨*persona:*⟩ get plump

arrovel'larsi *vr* **~ il cervello** rack one's brains

arroven'tare *vt* make red-hot

arroven'tarsi *vr* become red-hot

arroven'tato *a* red-hot; ⟨*fig: discorso*⟩ fiery

arruf'fare *vt* ruffle; *fig* confuse

arruf'farsi *vr* become ruffled

arruf'fato *a* ⟨*capelli*⟩ dishevelled

arruffia'narsi *vr* **~ [con] qcno** *fig* butter sb up

arruggi'nire *vt* rust

arruggi'nirsi *vr* go rusty; *fig* ⟨*fisicamente*⟩ stiffen up; ⟨*conoscenze:*⟩ go rusty

arruggi'nito *a* rusty

arruola'mento *nm* enlistment

arruo'lare *vt/i* enlist

arruo'larsi *vr* enlist

arse'nale *nm* arsenal; ⟨*cantiere*⟩ [naval] dockyard

ar'senico *nm* arsenic

'arso *pp di* **ardere** ● *a* burnt; ⟨*arido*⟩ dry

ar'sura *nf* burning heat; ⟨*sete*⟩ parching thirst

art déco *nf* art deco

'arte *nf* art; ⟨*abilità*⟩ craftsmanship; **senza ~ né parte** incapable; **nome d'~** professional name. **~ drammatica** dramatics. **le belle arti** *pl* the fine arts. **arti** *pl* **figurative** figurative arts. **arti** *pl* **dello spettacolo** performing arts

arte'fare *vt* adulterate ⟨*vino*⟩; disguise ⟨*voce*⟩

arte'fatto *a* fake; ⟨*vino*⟩ adulterated

ar'tefice *nm* craftsman; *fig* author ● *nf* craftswoman

ar'teria *nf* artery. **~ [stradale]** arterial road

arterio'sclerosi *nf* arteriosclerosis, hardening of the arteries

arteriosle'rotico *a* senile

arteri'oso *a Anat* arterial

'Artico *nm* **l'~** the Arctic

'artico *a* Arctic

artico'lare *a* articular ● *vt* articulate; ⟨*suddividere*⟩ divide

artico'larsi *vr fig* **~ in** consist of

artico'lato *a Auto* articulated; *fig* well-constructed

articolazi'one *nf Anat* articulation

ar'ticolo *nm* article. **articoli** *pl* **per la casa** household goods. **~ civetta** *Comm* loss leader. **articoli** *pl* **per la cucina** kitchenware. **~ determinativo** *Gram* definite article. **~ di fondo** leader, leading article. **~ indeterminativo** *Gram* indefinite article. **articoli** *pl* **di marca** brand name goods. **~ di prima pagina** *Journ* cover story. **articoli** *pl* **da regalo** gifts. **articoli** *pl* **da spiaggia** things for the beach. **articoli** *pl* **sportivi** sports gear; **negozio di ~ ~** sports shop

'Artide *nf* **l'~** the Arctic [region]

artifici'ale *a* artificial

artifici'ere *nm Mil* explosives expert, bomb disposal expert

arti'ficio *nm* artifice; ⟨*affettazione*⟩ affectation

artificiosità *nf* artificiality

artifici'oso *a* artful; ⟨*affettato*⟩ affected

artigi'ana *nf* craftswoman

artigia'nale *a* made by hand; *hum* amateurish

artigianal'mente *adv* with craftsmanship; *hum* amateurishly

artigia'nato *nm* craftsmanship; *(ceto)* craftsmen *pl*

artigi'ano *nm* craftsman

artigli'ato *a* with claws

artigli'ere *nm* artilleryman

artiglie'ria *nf* artillery. **~ antiaerea** flak

ar'tiglio *nm* claw; *fig* clutch; **sfoderare gli artigli** *fig* show one's claws

ar'tista *nmf* artist

artistica'mente *adv* artistically

ar'tistico *a* artistic

arti'stoide *a* arty

art nouveau *nf* art nouveau

'arto *nm* limb

ar'trite *nf* arthritis

ar'tritico, -a *nmf* arthritic

ar'trosi *nf* rheumatism

arzigogo'lato *a* fantastic, bizarre

ar'zillo *a* sprightly

a'scella *nf* armpit

ascen'dente *a* ascending ● *nm (antenato)* ancestor; *(influenza)* ascendancy; *Astr* ascendant

ascen'denza *nf* ancestry

a'scendere *vi* ascend

ascensi'one *nf* ascent; **l'A~** the Ascension

ascen'sore *nm* lift, elevator *Am*

a'scesa *nf* ascent; *(al trono)* accession; *(al potere)* rise

a'scesi *nf* asceticism

a'scesso *nm* abscess

a'sceta *nmf* ascetic

a'scetico *a* ascetic

'ascia *nf* axe

asciugabianche'ria *nm inv (stenditoio)* clothes horse; *(macchina)* tumble dryer

asciugaca'pelli *nm inv* hair dryer, hairdrier

asciuga'mano *nm* towel. **~ di carta** paper towel

asciu'gare *vt* dry; **~ le stoviglie** do the drying-up

asciu'garsi *vr* dry oneself; *(diventare asciutto)* dry up; **~ le mani** dry one's hands

asciuga'trice *nf* tumble dryer

asci'utto *a* dry; *(magro)* wiry; *(risposta)* curt; **essere all'~** *fig* be hard up

ascol'tare *vt* listen to ● *vi* listen

ascolta|'tore, -'trice *nmf* listener

a'scolto *nm* listening; **dare ~ a** listen to; **essere in ~** *Radio* be listening; **mettersi in ~** *Radio* tune in; **prestare ~** listen

a'scrivere *vt (attribuire)* ascribe; **~ a** *(annoverare)* number among

asessu'ato *a* asexual

a'settico *a* aseptic

asfal'tare *vt* asphalt

asfal'tato *a* tarmac

a'sfalto *nm* asphalt

asfis'sia *nf* asphyxia

asfissi'ante *a (caldo)* oppressive; *(fig: persona)* annoying

asfissi'are *vt* asphyxiate; *fig* annoy

'Asia *nf* Asia. **~ Minore** Asia Minor

asi'ago *nm* full-fat white cheese

asi'atico, -a *a & nmf* Asian

a'silo *nm* shelter; *(d'infanzia)* nursery school. **~ infantile** day nursery. **~ nido** day nursery. **~ politico** political asylum

asim'metrico *a* asymmetric[al]

a'sincrono *a* asynchronous

'asino *nm* donkey; *(fig: persona stupida)* ass; *Sch* dunce; **qui casca l'~!** *fig* that's where it falls down!

'asma *nf* asthma

a'smatico *a* asthmatic

asoci'ale *a* asocial

'asola *nf* buttonhole

a'sparagi *nmpl* asparagus *sg*

aspara'gina *nf Bot* asparagus fern

a'sparago *nm* asparagus

a'spergere *vt* **~ con/di** sprinkle with

asperità *nf inv* harshness; *(di terreno)* roughness

asper'sorio *nm* aspergillum, holy-water sprinkler

aspet'tare *vt* wait for; *(prevedere)* expect; **~ un bambino** be expecting [a baby]; **fare ~ qcno** keep sb waiting ● *vi* wait

aspet'tarsi *vr* expect

aspetta'tiva *nf* expectation; *(nel lavoro)* leave of absence; **all'altezza delle aspettative** up to expectations; **inferiore alle aspettative** not up to expectations. **~ per malattia** sick leave. **~ per maternità** maternity leave

a'spetto[1] *nm* look; *(di problema)* aspect; **di bell'~** good-looking

a'spetto[2] *nm* **sala d'~** waiting room

aspi'rante *a* aspiring; *(pompa)* suction *attrib* ● *nmf (a un posto)* applicant; *(al trono)* aspirant; **gli aspiranti al titolo** the contenders for the title

aspira'polvere *nm inv* vacuum cleaner; **passare l'~** vacuum, hoover

aspi'rare *vt* inhale; *Mech* suck in; *(con elettrodomestici)* vacuum, hoover ● *vi* **~ a** aspire to

aspi'rato *a* aspirate

aspira'tore *nm* extractor fan

aspirazi'one *nf* inhalation; *Mech* suction; *(ambizione)* ambition

aspi'rina *nf* aspirin

aspor'tare *vt* take away

aspra'mente *adv (duramente)* severely

a'sprezza *nf (al gusto)* sourness; *(di clima)* severity; *(di carattere, parole, suono)* harshness; *(di odore)* pungency; *(di litigio)* bitterness

a'sprigno *a* slightly sour

'aspro *a (al gusto)* sour; *(clima)* severe; *(suono, parole)* harsh; *(odore)* pungent; *(litigio)* bitter

assaggi'are *vt* taste

assaggia|'tore, -'trice *nmf* taster

assag'gini *nmpl Culin* samples

as'saggio *nm* tasting; *(piccola quantità)* taste; *(fig: campione)* sample

as'sai *adv* very; *(moltissimo)* very much; *(abbastanza)* enough

assa'lire *vt* attack

assali|'tore, -'trice *nmf* assailant

assal'tare *vt Mil* attack, charge; hold up ⟨*banca, treno*⟩

assalta'tore *nm* hold-up man

as'salto *nm* attack; **d'~** ⟨*giornalismo*⟩ aggressive; **prendere d'~** storm ⟨*città*⟩; *fig* mob ⟨*persona*⟩; hold up ⟨*banca*⟩

assapo'rare *vt* savour

assas'sina *nf* murderess

assassi'nare *vt* murder, assassinate; *fig* murder

assas'sinio *nm* murder, assassination

assas'sino *a* murderous ● *nm* murderer

'asse *nf* board ● *nm Techn* axle; *Math* axis. **~ da stiro** ironing board

assecon'dare *vt* satisfy; (*favorire*) support; **~ i capricci di qcno** indulge sb's every whim; **~ i desideri di qcno** comply with sb's wishes

assedi'are *vt* besiege

assedi'ato *a* besieged

as'sedio *nm* siege

assegna'mento *nm* allotment; **fare ~ su** rely on

asse'gnare *vt* allot; award ⟨*premio*⟩

assegna'tario, -a *nmf* recipient

assegnazi'one *nf* (*di alloggio, denaro, borsa di studio*) allocation; (*di premio*) award

as'segno *nm* allowance; (*bancario*) cheque; **contro ~** cash on delivery; **pagare con un ~** pay by cheque. **~ circolare** bank draft. **assegni** *pl* **familiari** family allowance, child benefit. **~ post-datato** post-dated cheque. **~ sbarrato** crossed cheque. **~ non trasferibile** cheque made out to "account payee only". **~ turistico** traveller's cheque. **~ a vuoto** bad cheque, dud cheque

assem'blaggio *nm* assemblage

assem'blare *vt* assemble

assem'blea *nf* assembly; (*adunanza*) gathering. **~ generale annuale** Annual General Meeting, AGM

assembra'mento *nm* gathering

assem'brare *vt* gather

assen'nato *a* sensible

as'senso *nm* assent

assen'tarsi *vr* go away; (*da stanza*) leave the room

as'sente *a* absent; (*distratto*) absent-minded ● *nmf* absentee

assente'ismo *nm* absenteeism

assente'ista *nmf* frequent absentee

assen'tire *vi* acquiesce (**a** in)

as'senza *nf* absence; (*mancanza*) lack. **~ di gravità** zero gravity

asse'rire *vt* assert

asserragli'arsi *vr* barricade oneself

asser'tivo *a* assertive

asser|'tore, -'trice *nmf* supporter

asservi'mento *nm* subservience

asser'vire *vt fig* enslave

asser'virsi *vr fig* be subservient

asserzi'one *nf* assertion

assesso'rato *nm* [council] department

asses'sore *nm* councillor

assesta'mento *nm* settlement

asse'stare *vt* arrange; **~ un colpo** deal a blow

asse'starsi *vr* settle oneself

asse'stato *a* **ben ~** well-judged

asse'tato *a* parched

as'setto *nm* order; *Naut, Aeron* trim; **in ~ di guerra** on a war footing; **cambiare l'~ territoriale dell'Europa** change the map of Europe

assi'cella *nf* lath

assicu'rabile *a* insurable

assicu'rare *vt* assure; *Comm* insure; register ⟨*posta*⟩; (*fissare*) secure; (*accertare*) ensure

assicu'rarsi *vr* (*con contratto*) insure oneself; (*legarsi*) fasten oneself; **~ che** make sure that

assicu'rata *nf* registered letter

assicura'tivo *a* insurance *attrib*

assicu'rato *a* insured; **lettera assicurata** registered letter

assicura|'tore, -'trice *nmf* insurance agent ● *a* insurance; **società assicuratrice** insurance company

assicurazi'one *nf* assurance; (*contratto*) insurance; **fare un'~** take out insurance. **~ multirischi** blanket cover. **~ sanitaria** medical insurance. **~ di viaggio** travel insurance

assidera'mento *nm* exposure

asside'rarsi *vr fam* be frozen; *Med* be suffering from exposure

asside'rato *a Med* suffering from exposure; *fam* frozen

assidua'mente *adv* assiduously

assidu'ità *nf* assiduity

as'siduo *a* assiduous; ⟨*cliente*⟩ regular

assi'eme *a* [together] with

assil'lante *a* ⟨*persona, pensiero*⟩ nagging

assil'lare *vt* pester

assil'larsi *vr* torment oneself

as'sillo *nm* worry

assimi'lare *vt* assimilate

assimilazi'one *nf* assimilation

assi'oma *nm* axiom

assio'matico *a* axiomatic

As'siria *nf* Assyria

as'sise *nfpl* assizes; **Corte d'A~** Court of Assize[s]

assi'stente *nmf* assistant. **~ sociale** social worker. **~ universitario** assistant lecturer. **~ di volo** flight attendant

assi'stenza *nf* assistance; (*presenza*) presence. **~ medica** medical care. **~ ospedaliera** hospital treatment. **~ sanitaria** health care. **~ sociale** social work

assistenzi'ale *a* welfare

assistenzia'lismo *nm* abuse of the welfare state

as'sistere *vt* assist; (*curare*) nurse ● *vi* **~ a** (*essere presente*) be present at; watch ⟨*spettacolo ecc*⟩

assi'stito *a* **~ da computer** computer-aided

'asso nm ace; **piantare in ~** leave in the lurch. **~ nella manica** trump card

associ'are vt join; (collegare) associate

associ'arsi vr join forces; Comm enter into partnership. **~ a** join; subscribe to ⟨giornale ecc⟩

associ'ato, -a a associate ● nmf partner

associazi'one nf association. **~ di categoria** trade-union. **~ per delinquere** criminal organization. **A~ Europea di Libero Scambio** European Free Trade Association. **~ in partecipazione** Comm joint venture

associazio'nismo nm Pol excessive tendency to form associations; Psych associationism

asso'dare vt ascertain ⟨verità⟩

assogget'tare vt subject

assogget'tarsi vr submit

asso'lato a sunny

assol'dare vt recruit

as'solo nm Mus solo

as'solto pp di **assolvere**

assoluta'mente adv absolutely

assolu'tismo nm absolutism

assolu'tista nmf absolutist

assolu'tistico a absolutist

asso'luto a absolute

assolu'torio a **formula assolutoria** acquittal

assoluzi'one nf acquittal; Relig absolution

as'solvere vt perform ⟨compito⟩; Jur acquit; Relig absolve

assolvi'mento nm performance

assomigli'are vi **~ a** be like, resemble

assomigli'arsi vr resemble each other

assom'marsi vr combine; **~ a qcsa** add to sth

asso'nanza nf assonance

asson'nato a drowsy

asso'pirsi vr doze off

assor'bente a & nm absorbent. **~ igienico** sanitary towel

assor'bire vt absorb

assor'dante a deafening

assor'dare vt deafen

assorti'mento nm assortment

assor'tire vt match ⟨colori⟩

assor'tito a assorted; ⟨colori, persone⟩ matched

as'sorto a engrossed

assottiglia'mento nm thinning; (aguzzamento) sharpening

assottigli'are vt make thin; (aguzzare) sharpen; (ridurre) reduce

assottigli'arsi vr grow thin; ⟨finanze:⟩ be whittled away

assue'fare vt accustom

assue'farsi vr **~ a** get used to

assue'fatto a (a caffè, aspirina) immune to the effects; (a droga) addicted

assuefazi'one nf (a caffè, aspirina) immunity to the effects; (a droga) addiction

as'sumere vt assume; take on ⟨impiegato⟩; **~ informazioni** make inquiries

as'sunto pp di **assumere** ● nm task

assunzi'one nf (di impiegato) employment; **l'A~** Assumption

assurdità nf inv absurdity; **dire delle ~** talk nonsense

as'surdo a absurd

'asta nf pole; Mech bar; Comm auction; **a mezz'~** at half-mast. **~ di livello** [dell'olio] Auto dip-stick

a'stemio a abstemious

aste'nersi vr abstain (**da** from)

astensi'one nf abstention

astensio'nismo nm persistent abstention

astensio'nista nmf persistent abstainer

astensio'nistico a **tendenza astensionistica** tendency to abstain

aste'nuto, -a nmf abstainer

aste'risco nm asterisk

aste'roide nm asteroid

'astice nm crayfish

asti'cella nf stick; (in salto in alto) bar

astig'matico a astigmatic

astigma'tismo nm astigmatism

asti'nenza nf abstinence; **crisi di ~** withdrawal symptoms

'astio nm rancour; **avere ~ contro qcno** bear sb a grudge

asti'oso a resentful

a'stragalo nm anklebone

'astrakan nm astrakhan

astrat'tezza nf abstractness

astrat'tismo nm abstractionism

a'stratto a abstract

astrin'gente a & nm astringent

'astro nm star

+astro suff **giovinastro** nm lout; **giallastro** a yellowish; **dolciastro** a sweetish; **fattaccio** nm hum foul deed

astro'fisica nf astrophysics

astro'fisico, -a a astrophysical ● nmf astrophysicist

astrolo'gia nf astrology

astro'logico a astrological

a'strologo, -a nmf astrologer

astro'nauta nmf astronaut

astro'nautica nf astronautics

astro'nave nf spaceship

astrono'mia nf astronomy

astro'nomico a (anche fig) astronomic, astronomical

a'stronomo nm astronomer

astrusità nf abstruseness

a'struso a abstruse

a'stuccio nm case

a'stuto a shrewd; (furbo) cunning

a'stuzia nf shrewdness; (azione) trick

a'tavico a atavistic

ate'ismo nm atheism

ate'lier nm inv (di alta moda) atelier; (di artista) [artist's] studio

A'tene nf Athens

ate'neo nm university

ateni'ese a & nmf Athenian

'ateo, -a a & nmf atheist

a'tipico a atypical

at'lante *nm* atlas; **i monti dell'A~** the Atlas Mountains

at'lantico *a* Atlantic; **l'[Oceano] A~** the Atlantic [Ocean]

at'leta *nmf* athlete

a'tletica *nf* athletics *sg*. **~ leggera** track and field events. **~ pesante** *weight-lifting, boxing, wrestling, etc*

a'tletico *a* athletic

atle'tismo *nm* athleticism

atmo'sfera *nf* atmosphere

atmo'sferico *a* atmospheric

a'tollo *nm* atoll

a'tomica *nf* atom bomb

a'tomico *a* atomic

atomiz'zare *vt* atomize

atomizza'tore *nm* atomizer

'atomo *nm* atom

'atono *a* unstressed

'atrio *nm* entrance hall, lobby

a'troce *a* atrocious; (*terrible*) dreadful

atroce'mente *adv* atrociously

atrocità *nf inv* atrocity

atro'fia *nf* atrophy

atrofiz'zare *vt* atrophy

atrofiz'zarsi *vr Med, fig* atrophy

attac'cabile *a* attachable

attaccabot'toni *nmf inv* [crashing] bore

attacca'brighe *nmf inv* troublemaker

attacca'mento *nm* attachment

attac'cante *a* attacking ● *nm Sport* forward

attacca'panni *nm inv* [coat-]hanger; (*a muro*) [clothes-]hook

attac'care *vt* attach; (*legare*) tie; (*appendere*) hang; (*cucire*) sew on; (*contagiare*) pass on; (*assalire*) attack; (*iniziare*) start ● *vi* stick; (*diffondersi*) catch on

attac'carsi *vr* cling; (*affezionarsi*) become attached; (*litigare*) quarrel

attacca'ticcio *a* sticky; *fig* clinging and tiresome

attac'cato *a* stuck

attacca'tura *nf* junction. **~ dei capelli** hairline

attac'chino *nm* billposter

at'tacco *nm* attack; (*punto d'unione*) junction; (*accesso*) fit. **~ cardiaco** heart attack. **~ epilettico** epileptic fit

attanagli'are *vt* (*fig: tormentare*) haunt

attar'darsi *vr* stay late; (*indugiare*) linger

attec'chire *vi* take; (*moda ecc:*) catch on

atteggia'mento *nm* attitude

atteggi'are *vt* assume

atteggi'arsi *vr* **~ a** pose as

attem'pato *a* elderly

atten'darsi *vr* camp, pitch camp

atten'dente *nm Mil* batman

at'tendere *vt* wait for ● *vi* **~ a** attend to

at'tendersi *vr* expect

atten'dibile *a* reliable

attendibilità *nf* reliability

atte'nersi *vr* **~ a** stick to

attenta'mente *adv* attentively

atten'tare *vi* **~ a** make an attempt on

atten'tato *nm* act of violence; (*contro politico ecc*) assassination attempt; **~ alla vita di** attempted murder of. **~ dinamitardo** bombing

attenta|'tore, -'trice *nmf* attacker; (*a scopo politico*) terrorist

at'tento *a* attentive; (*accurato*) careful; **~!** look out!; **stare ~** pay attention; **'attenti al cane'** 'beware of the dog'

attenu'ante *nf* extenuating circumstance

attenu'are *vt* attenuate; (*minimizzare*) minimize; subdue (*colori ecc*); calm (*dolore*); soften (*colpo*)

attenu'arsi *vr* diminish

attenuazi'one *nf* lessening

attenzi'one *nf* attention; (*cura*) care; **fare ~** be careful; **~!** watch out!; **~, prego** your attention, please; **coprire di attenzioni** lavish attention on

atter'raggio *nm* landing. **~ di fortuna** emergency landing

atter'rare *vt* knock down ● *vi* land

atter'rire *vt* terrorize

atter'rirsi *vr* be terrified

at'tesa *nf* waiting; (*aspettativa*) expectation; **in ~ di** waiting for

at'teso *pp di* **attendere**

atte'stabile *a* certifiable

atte'stare *vt* state; (*certificare*) certify

atte'stato *nm* certificate

attestazi'one *nf* certificate; (*dichiarazione*) declaration

'Attica *nf* Attica

'attico¹ *nm* (*lingua*) Attic

'attico² *nm* (*appartamento*) penthouse

at'tiguo *a* adjacent

attil'lato *a* (*vestito*) close-fitting

'attimo *nm* second; **un ~!** just a sec!; **in un ~** in double-quick time; **non ho avuto un ~ di respiro** I haven't had time to draw breath

atti'nente *a* **~ a** pertaining to

at'tingere *vt* draw; *fig* obtain

atti'rare *vt* attract

atti'rarsi *vr* draw (*attenzione*); incur (*odio*)

attitudi'nale *nm* **test ~** aptitude test

atti'tudine *nf* (*disposizione*) aptitude; (*atteggiamento*) attitude

atti'vare *vt* activate

attivazi'one *nf* setting in motion, turning on; *Phys, Chem* activation

atti'vismo *nm* activism

atti'vista *nmf* activist

attività *nf inv* activity; *Comm* assets *pl*. **~ pl fisse** fixed assets. **~ pl liquide** *Comm* liquid assets

at'tivo *a* active; *Comm* productive ● *nm* assets *pl*

attiz'zare *vt* poke; *fig* stir up

attizza'toio *nm* poker

'atto *nm* act; (*azione*) action; *Comm, Jur* deed; (*certificato*) certificate; **fare ~ di presenza** put in an appearance; **mettere in ~** put into action; **atti** *pl* (*di società ecc*) proceedings. **atti** *pl* **di libidine violenta** indecent assault. **atti** *pl* **osceni** gross indecency. **~ di vendita** bill of sale

+attolo *suff* **vermiciattolo** *nm* slimy individual

at'tonito *a* astonished

attorcigli'are *vt* twist

attorcigli'arsi *vr* get twisted

at'tore *nm* actor

attorni'are *vt* surround

attorni'arsi *vr* ~ **di** surround oneself with

at'torno *adv* around, about ● *prep* ~ **a** around, about

attrac'care *vt/i* dock

attra'ente *a* attractive

at'trarre *vt* attract

at'trarsi *vr* be attracted to each other

attrat'tiva *nf* charm, attraction

attraversa'mento *nm* (*di strada*) crossing. ~ **pedonale** pedestrian crossing, crosswalk *Am*

attraver'sare *vt* cross; (*passare*) go through

attra'verso *prep* through; (*obliquamente*) across

attrazi'one *nf* attraction. **attrazioni** *pl* **turistiche** tourist attractions

attrez'zare *vt* equip; *Naut* rig

attrez'zarsi *vr* kit oneself out

attrezza'tura *nf* equipment; *Naut* rigging. ~ **da campeggio** camping equipment

at'trezzo *nm* tool. **at'trezzi** *pl* equipment; *Sport* appliances *pl*

attribu'ibile *a* attributable

attribu'ire *vt* attribute

attribu'irsi *vr* ascribe to oneself; ~ **il merito di** claim credit for

attri'buto *nm* attribute

attribuzi'one *nf* attribution

at'trice *nf* actress

at'trito *nm* friction

attrup'pare *vt* assemble

attrup'parsi *vr* gather

attu'abile *a* feasible

attuabilità *nf* viability

attu'ale *a* present; (*di attualità*) topical; (*effettivo*) actual

attualità *nf inv* topicality; (*avvenimento*) news; **programma di** ~ current affairs programme

attualiz'zare *vt* update

attual'mente *adv* at present

attu'are *vt* carry out

attu'ario, -a *nmf* actuary

attu'arsi *vr* be realized

attua'tore *nm Techn* actuator

attuazi'one *nf* carrying out

attuti'mento *nm* (*di colpo*) softening; (*di suoni*) muffling

attu'tire *vt* deaden; ~ **il colpo** soften the blow

au'dace *a* daring, bold; (*insolente*) audacious

au'dacia *nf* daring, boldness; (*insolenza*) audacity

audiapprendi'mento *nm* audio-based learning

'audience *nf inv* (*telespettatori*) audience

'audio *nm* audio

audiocas'setta *nf* audio cassette

audio'leso *a* hearing-impaired

audio'libro *nm* audiobook

audio'metrico *a Med* aural

audiovi'sivo *a* audiovisual

'auditing *nm* auditing

audi'torio *nm* auditorium

audizi'one *nf* audition; *Jur* hearing

'auge *nm* height; **essere in** ~ be popular

augu'rare *vt* wish

augu'rarsi *vr* hope

au'gurio *nm* wish; (*presagio*) omen; **auguri!** all the best!; (*a Natale*) Happy Christmas!; **tanti auguri** best wishes

au'gusto *a* august

'aula *nf* classroom; *Univ* lecture-hall; (*sala*) hall; **silenzio in** ~! silence in court!. ~ **bunker** (*in tribunale*) secure courtroom. ~ **magna** *Univ* great hall. ~ **del tribunale** courtroom

aumen'tare *vt/i* increase; ~ **di peso** gain weight

au'mento *nm* increase; (*di stipendio*) [pay] rise. ~ **di prezzo** price increase

'aureo *a* golden

au'reola *nf* halo

au'rora *nf* dawn. ~ **boreale** aurora borealis, Northern Lights

auscul'tare *vt Med* auscultate

ausili'are *a* & *nmf* auxiliary

auspi'cabile *a* **è** ~ **che...** it is to be hoped that...

auspi'care *vt* hope for

au'spicio *nm* omen; **auspici** *pl* (*protezione*) auspices; **è di buon** ~ it is a good omen

austerità *nf* austerity

au'stero *a* austere

Austra'lasia *nf* Australasia

au'strale *a* southern

Au'stralia *nf* Australia

australi'ano, -a *a* & *nmf* Australian

'Austria *nf* Austria

au'striaco, -a *a* & *nmf* Austrian

austroun'garico *a* Austro-Hungarian

autar'chia *nf* autarchy

au'tarchico *a* autarchic

aut aut *nm inv* either-or [choice]

autenti'care *vt* authenticate

autenticità *nf* authenticity

au'tentico *a* authentic; (*vero*) true

au'tismo *nm* autism

au'tista *nm* driver

au'tistico *a* autistic

'auto *nf inv* car; **viaggiare in** ~ travel by car. ~ **blindata** armour-plated car. ~ **a quattro ruote motrici** four-wheel drive car. ~ **sportiva** sports car. ~ **a trazione anteriore** front-wheel drive car. ~ **usata** second-hand car

auto+ *pref* self+

autoabbron'zante *nm* self-tan ● *a* self-tanning

autoaccesso'rista *nmf* car accessory supplier

autoade'sivo *a* self-adhesive ● *nm* sticker

autoaffermazi'one *nf* self-assertion

autoambu'lanza *nf* ambulance

autoa'nalisi *nf* self-analysis

autoartico'lato *nm* articulated lorry

autobiogra'fia *nf* autobiography

autobio'grafico *a* autobiographical

auto'blinda *nf* armoured car

auto'bomba *nf* car-bomb

auto'botte *nf* tanker

'autobus *nm inv* bus

auto'carro *nm* lorry

autocertificazi'one *nf* self-certification

autoci'sterna *nf* tanker

auto'clave *nf* ⟨*contenitore ad alta pressione*⟩ autoclave; ⟨*idraulica*⟩ surge tank

autocombusti'one *nf* spontaneous combustion

autocommiserazi'one *nf* self-pity

autocompiaci'mento *nm* smugness, self-satisfaction

autocompiaci'uto *a* smug, self-satisfied

autoconcessio'nario *nm* car dealer

autocon'trollo *nm* self-control

au'tocrate *nm* autocrat

auto'cratico *a* autocratic

auto'critica *nf* self-criticism

au'toctono *a* native, aboriginal

autodemolizi'one *nf* self-destruction

autode'nuncia *nf* spontaneous confession

autodeterminazi'one *nf* self-determination

autodi'datta *a* self-taught ● *nmf* self-educated person, autodidact

autodi'fesa *nf* self-defence

autodisci'plina *nf* self-discipline

autodi'struggersi *vr* self-destruct

autoferrotranvi'ario *a* public-transport *attrib*

autoferrotranvi'eri *nmpl* public-transport workers

autoffi'cina *nf* garage

autofinanzia'mento *nm* self-financing

autofinanzi'arsi *vr* be self-financing; ⟨*persona:*⟩ use one's own finance

autogesti'one *nf* self-management

autoge'stirsi *vr* ⟨*operai, studenti*⟩ be self-managing; **mio figlio si autogestisce** my son can cope by himself

autoge'stito *a* self-managed

auto'gol *nm inv Sport* own goal

au'tografo *a & nm* autograph

auto'grill *nm inv* motorway café

autogrù *nf inv* breakdown truck

autogui'dato *a* homing *attrib*

autoim'mune *a* autoimmune

autoiro'nia *nf* self-mockery

autola'vaggio *nm* car wash

autolesi'one *nf* self-inflicted wound

autolesio'nismo *nm fig* self-destruction

autolesio'nistico *a* self-destructive

auto'linea *nf* bus line

au'toma *nm* robot

automatica'mente *adv* automatically

auto'matico *a* automatic; **auto con il cambio ~** automatic ● *nm* ⟨*bottone*⟩ press-stud; ⟨*fucile*⟩ automatic

automatiz'zare *vt* automate

automatizzazi'one *nf* automation

automazi'one *nf* automation

auto'mezzo *nm* motor vehicle; **uscita automezzi** motor vehicles exit

auto'mobile *nf* [motor] car. **~ da corsa** racing car

automobi'lina *nf* toy car

automobi'lismo *nm* motoring

automobi'lista *nmf* motorist

automobi'listico *a* ⟨*industria*⟩ automobile *attrib*

automodel'lismo *nm* model car making; ⟨*collezione*⟩ model car collecting

autono'leggio *nm* car rental

autonoma'mente *adv* autonomously

autono'mia *nf* autonomy; *Auto* range; ⟨*di laptop, cellulare*⟩ battery life

au'tonomo *a* autonomous

auto'parco *nm* ⟨*insieme di auto*⟩ fleet of cars

autopat'tuglia *nf* patrol car

auto'pista *nf* [fairground] race track

auto'pompa *nf* fire engine

auto'psia *nf* autopsy

autopunizi'one *nf* self-punishment

auto'radio *nf inv* car radio; ⟨*veicolo*⟩ radio car

au'|tore, -'trice *nmf* author; ⟨*di pitture*⟩ painter; ⟨*di furto ecc*⟩ perpetrator; **quadro d'~** genuine master

autoregolamentazi'one *nf* self-regulation

autore'parto *nm Mil* mechanized unit

auto'revole *a* authoritative; ⟨*che ha influenza*⟩ influential

autorevo'lezza *nf* authority

autoriduzi'one *nf* protest which takes the form of paying less than the requisite amount

autori'messa *nf* garage

autoriparazi'oni *nfpl* '~' 'car repairs', 'auto repairs'

autorità *nf inv* authority

autori'tario *a* autocratic

autorita'rismo *nm* authoritarianism

autori'tratto *nm* self-portrait

autoriz'zare *vt* authorize

autorizzazi'one *nf* authorization

auto'scatto *nm Phot* automatic shutter release

auto'scontro *nm inv* bumper car

autoscu'ola *nf* driving school

autosno'dato *nm* articulated bus

autosoc'corso *nm* breakdown service; ⟨*veicolo*⟩ breakdown van, breakdown truck

auto'starter *nm inv Auto* self-starter

auto'stop *nm* hitch-hiking, hitching; **fare l'~** hitch-hike, hitch

autostop'pista *nmf* hitch-hiker

auto'strada *nf* motorway, highway *Am*. **A~ del Sole** Highway of the Sun (*connecting Milan and Reggio Calabria*)

autostra'dale *a* motorway *attrib*, highway *attrib Am*

autosuffici'ente *a* self-sufficient

autosuffici'enza *nf* self-sufficiency

autosuggesti'one *nf* autosuggestion

autotrasporta'tore, -'trice *nmf* haulier, carrier

autotra'sporto *nm* road haulage

auto'treno *nm* articulated lorry, roadtrain

autove'icolo *nm* motor vehicle

auto'velox *nm inv* speed camera

autovet'tura *nf* motor vehicle

autun'nale *a* autumnal; ⟨giornata, vestiti⟩ autumn *attrib*

au'tunno *nm* autumn

aval'lare *vt* endorse, back ⟨cambiale⟩; *fig* endorse

a'vallo *nm* endorsement

avam'braccio *nm* forearm

avam'posto *nm Mil* forward position

A'vana *nf* Havana

a'vana *nm inv* (*sigaro*) Havana [cigar]; (*colore*) tobacco, dark brown ● *a inv* ⟨colore⟩ tobacco-coloured, dark brown

avangu'ardia *nf* vanguard; *fig* avant-garde; **essere all'~** be in the forefront; *Techn* be at the leading edge; **d'~** avant-garde

avansco'perta *nf* reconnaissance; **andare in ~** reconnoitre

avanspet'tacolo *nm* **da ~** in poor taste

a'vanti *adv* (*in avanti*) forward; (*davanti*) in front; (*prima*) before; **~!** (*entrate*) come in!; (*suvvia*) come on!; **'~'** (*su semaforo*) 'cross now', 'walk' *Am*; **~ diritto** straight ahead; **più ~** further on; **va' ~!** go ahead!; **andare ~** (*precedere*) go ahead; ⟨orologio:⟩ be fast; **~ e indietro** backwards and forwards ● *a* (*precedente*) before ● *prep* **~ a** before; (*in presenza di*) in the presence of

avanti'eri *adv* the day before yesterday

avan'treno *nm* front axle assembly

avanza'mento *nm* progress; (*promozione*) promotion

avan'zare *vi* advance; (*progredire*) progress; (*essere d'avanzo*) be left [over] ● *vt* advance; (*superare*) surpass; (*promuovere*) promote

avan'zarsi *vr* advance; (*avvicinarsi*) approach

avan'zata *nf* advance

avan'zato *a* advanced; (*nella notte*) late; **in età avanzata** elderly

a'vanzo *nm* remainder; *Comm* surplus; **avanzi** *pl* (*rovine*) remains; (*di cibo*) leftovers. **~ di galera** jailbird

ava'raccio *nm* Scrooge

ava'ria *nf* (*di motore*) engine failure

avari'arsi *vr* spoil

avari'ato *a* ⟨frutta, verdura⟩ rotten; ⟨carne⟩ tainted

ava'rizia *nf* avarice

a'varo, -a *a* stingy ● *nmf* miser

a'vena *nf* oats *pl*

a'vere *vt* have; (*ottenere*) get; (*indossare*) wear; (*provare*) feel; **ho trent'anni** I'm thirty; **ha avuto il posto** he got the job; **~ fame/freddo** be hungry/cold; **ho mal di denti** I've got toothache; **cos'ha a che fare con lui?** what has it got to do with him?; **~ da fare** be busy; **~ luogo** take place; **che hai?** what's the matter with you?; **nei hai per molto?** will you be long?; **quanti ne abbiamo oggi?** what date is it today?; **avercela con qcno** have it in for sb ● *v aux* have; **non l'ho visto** I haven't seen him; **lo hai visto?** have you seen him?; **l'ho visto ieri** I saw him yesterday ● *nm* **averi** *pl* wealth *sg*

avia'|tore, -'trice *nmf* aviator

aviazi'one *nf* aviation; *Mil* Air Force

avicol'tura *nf* poultry farming

avida'mente *adv* avidly

avidità *nf* avidness

'avido *a* avid

avi'ere *nm* aircraft[s]man

avio'getto *nm* jet [plane]

avio'linea *nf* airline

aviotraspor'tato *a* airborne

avitami'nosi *nf* vitamin deficiency

a'vito *a* ancestral

'avo, -a *nmf* ancestor

avo'cado *nm inv* avocado

a'vorio *nm* ivory

a'vulso *a* **~ dal contesto** *fig* taken out of context

Avv. *abbr* **avvocato**

avva'lersi *vr* avail oneself (**of** di)

avvalla'mento *nm* depression

avvalo'rare *vt* bear out ⟨tesi⟩; endorse ⟨documento⟩; (*accrescere*) enhance

avvam'pare *vi* flare up; (*arrossire*) blush

avvantaggi'are *vt* favour

avvantaggi'arsi *vr* **~ di** benefit from; (*approfittare*) take advantage of

avve'dersi *vr* (*accorgersi*) notice; (*capire*) realize

avve'duto *a* shrewd

avvelena'mento *nm* poisoning

avvele'nare *vt* poison

avvele'narsi *vr* poison oneself

avvele'nato *a* poisoned

avve'nente *a* attractive

avve'nenza *nf* attraction, charm

avveni'mento *nm* event

avve'nire *vi* happen; (*aver luogo*) take place ● *nm* future

avveni'rismo *nm* excessive confidence in the future

avveni'ristico *a* futuristic

avven'tarsi *vr* fling oneself

avventata'mente *adv* recklessly

avven'tato *a* ⟨decisione⟩ rash

avven'tizio *a* (*personale*) temporary; (*guadagno*) casual

av'vento *nm* advent; *Relig* Advent

avven'tore *nm* regular customer

avven'tura *nf* adventure; (*amorosa*) affair; **d'~** ⟨film⟩ adventure *attrib*

avventu'rarsi *vr* venture

avventuri'ero, -a *nm* adventurer ● *nf* adventuress

avventu'rismo *nm* adventurism

avventu'ristico *a* adventurist

avventu'roso *a* adventurous

avve'rabile *a* ⟨*previsione*⟩ that may come true

avve'rarsi *vr* come true

av'verbio *nm* adverb

avver'sare *vt* oppose

avver'sario, -a *a* opposing ● *nmf* opponent

avversi'one *nf* aversion

avversità *nf inv* adversity

av'verso *a* (*sfavorevole*) adverse; (*contrario*) averse

avver'tenza *nf* (*cura*) care; (*avvertimento*) warning; (*avviso*) notice; (*premessa*) foreword; **avvertenze** *pl* (*istruzioni*) instructions

avver'tibile *a* (*disagio*) perceptible

avverti'mento *nm* warning

avver'tire *vt* warn; (*informare*) inform; (*sentire*) feel

avvertita'mente *adv* deliberately

avvez'zare *vt* accustom

avvez'zarsi *vr* accustom oneself

av'vezzo *a* ~ **a** used to

avvia'mento *nm* starting; *Comm* goodwill

avvi'are *vt* start

avvi'arsi *vr* set out

avvi'ato *a* under way; **bene** ~ thriving

avvicenda'mento *nm* (*in agricoltura*) rotation; (*nel lavoro*) replacement; (*delle stagioni*) change

avvicen'dare *vt* rotate

avvicen'darsi *vr* take turns, alternate

avvicina'mento *nm* approach

avvici'nare *vt* bring near; approach ⟨*persona*⟩

avvici'narsi *vr* come nearer, approach; **avvicinarsi a** come nearer to, approach

avvi'lente *a* demoralizing; (*umiliante*) humiliating

avvili'mento *nm* despondency; (*degradazione*) degradation

avvi'lire *vt* dishearten; (*degradare*) degrade

avvi'lirsi *vr* lose heart; (*degradarsi*) degrade oneself

avvi'lito *a* disheartened; (*degradato*) degraded

avvilup'pare *vt* envelop

avvilup'parsi *vr* wrap oneself up; (*aggrovigliarsi*) get entangled

avvinaz'zato *a* drunk

avvin'cente *a* ⟨*libro ecc*⟩ enthralling

av'vincere *vt* enthral

avvinghi'are *vt* clutch

avvinghi'arsi *vr* cling

av'vio *nm* start-up; **dare l'~ a qcsa** get sth under way; **prendere l'~** get under way

avvi'saglia *nf* (*di malattia*) first sign

avvi'sare *vt* inform; (*mettere in guardia*) warn

av'viso *nm* notice; (*annuncio*) announcement; (*avvertimento*) warning; (*pubblicitario*) advertisement; **a mio** ~ in my opinion. ~ **di garanzia** *Jur* notification that one is to be the subject of a legal enquiry

avvista'mento *nm* sighting

avvi'stare *vt* catch sight of; ~ **terra** make landfall

avvi'tare *vt* screw in; screw down ⟨*coperchio*⟩

avvi'tarsi *vr* ⟨*aereo:*⟩ go into a spin

avvi'tata *nf* (*di aereo*) spin

avviz'zire *vi* wither

avviz'zito *a* withered

avvo'cato *nm* lawyer; *fig* advocate. ~ **del diavolo** devil's advocate

avvoca'tura *nf* legal profession; (*insieme di avvocati*) lawyers

av'volgere *vt* wrap [up]

av'volgersi *vr* wrap oneself up

avvol'gibile *nm* roller blind

avvolgi'mento *nm* winding

av'volto *a* ~ **in** wrapped in

avvol'toio *nm* vulture

aza'lea *nf* azalea

Azerbaigi'an *nm* Azerbaijan

azerbaigi'ano, -a *a & nmf* Azerbaijani

azi'enda *nf* business, firm. ~ **agricola** farm. ~ **elettrica** electricity board. ~ **a partecipazioni statali** enterprise in which the government has a shareholding. ~ **di soggiorno** tourist bureau

azien'dale *a* ⟨*politica, dirigente*⟩ company *attrib*; ⟨*giornale*⟩ in-house

azienda'listico *a* company *attrib*

azio'nabile *a* which can be operated

aziona'mento *nm* operation

azio'nare *vt* operate

azio'nario *a* share *attrib*; **mercato** ~ share market

azi'one *nf* action; *Fin* share; **d'~** ⟨*romanzo, film*⟩ action[-packed]; **ad** ~ **ritardata** delayed action. ~ **sindacale** industrial action

azio'nista *nmf* shareholder

a'zoto *nm* nitrogen

az'teco, -a *a & nmf* Aztec

azzan'nare *vt* seize with its teeth; sink its teeth into ⟨*gamba*⟩

azzar'dare *vt* risk

azzar'darsi *vr* dare

azzar'dato *a* risky; (*precipitoso*) rash

az'zardo *nm* hazard; **gioco d'~** game of chance

azzec'care *vt* hit; (*fig: indovinare*) guess

azzera'mento *nm* setting to zero; *fig* **corso di** ~ remedial classes *pl*

azze'rare *vt* reset

azzi'mato *a* dapper

'azzimo *a* unleavened

azzit'tirsi *vr* go quiet, fall silent

azzit'tire *vt* silence, hush

azzop'pare *vt* lame

Az'zorre *nfpl* **le** ~ the Azores

azzuf'farsi *vr* come to blows

azzur'rato *a* ⟨*lenti*⟩ blue-tinted

az'zurro *a & nm* blue; **principe** ~ Prince Charming; **gli azzurri** the Italian national team

azzur'rognolo *a* bluish

babà *nm inv* ~ **al rum** rum baba
bab'beo *a* foolish ● *nm* idiot
'**babbo** *nm fam* dad, daddy. **B~ Natale** Father Christmas
bab'buccia *nf* slipper
babbu'ino *nm* baboon
ba'bordo *nm Naut* port side
baby boom *nm* baby boom
baby'sitter *nmf inv* baby-sitter; **fare il/la ~** babysit, do baby-sitting
ba'cato *a* wormeaten; **avere il cervello ~** have a slate loose
'**bacca** *nf* berry
baccalà *nm inv* dried salted cod
bac'cano *nm* din
bac'cello *nm* pod
bac'chetta *nf* rod; (*magica*) wand; (*di direttore d'orchestra*) baton; (*di tamburo*) drumstick
ba'checa *nf* showcase; (*in ufficio*) notice board. **~ elettronica** *Comput* bulletin board
bacia'mano *nm* kiss on the hand; **fare il ~ a qcno** kiss sb's hand
baci'are *vt* kiss
baci'arsi *vr* kiss [each other]
ba'cillo *nm* bacillus
baci'nella *nf* basin; (*contenuto*) basinful
ba'cino *nm* basin; *Anat* pelvis; (*di porto*) dock; (*di minerali*) field. **~ d'utenza** catchment area
'**bacio** *nm* kiss; **~ sulla bocca** kiss on the lips
backgammon *nm* backgammon
'**baco** *nm* worm. **~ da seta** silkworm
'**bacon** *nm* bacon
ba'cucco *a* **un vecchio ~** a senile old man
'**bada** *nf* **tenere qcno a ~** keep sb at bay
ba'dare *vi* take care (**a** of); (*fare attenzione*) look out; **bada ai fatti tuoi!** mind your own business!
ba'dia *nf* abbey
ba'dile *nm* shovel
'**badminton** *nm* badminton
'**baffi** *nmpl* moustache *sg*; (*di animale*) whiskers; **mi fa un baffo** I don't give a damn; **ridere sotto i ~** laugh up one's sleeve
baf'futo *a* moustached
ba'gagli *nmpl* luggage, baggage; **ritiro bagagli** baggage claim
bagagli'aio *nm Rail* luggage van, baggage car *Am*; *Auto* boot
ba'gaglio *nm* luggage, baggage; *Mil* kit; **un ~** a piece of luggage. **~ a mano** hand-luggage, hand-baggage. **~ in eccesso, ~ eccedente** excess baggage
baga'rino *nm* ticket tout
baga'tella *nf* trifle; *Mus* bagatelle
baggia'nata *nf* piece of nonsense; **non dire baggianate** don't talk nonsense
Bagh'dad *nf* Baghdad
bagli'ore *nm* glare; (*improvviso*) flash; (*fig: di speranza*) glimmer
bagna'cauda *nf* vegetables (*especially raw*) in an oil, garlic and anchovy sauce
ba'gnante *nmf* bather
ba'gnare *vt* wet; (*inzuppare*) soak; (*immergere*) dip; (*innaffiare*) water; (*mare, lago:*) wash; (*fiume:*) flow through
ba'gnarsi *vr* get wet; (*al mare ecc*) swim, bathe; **'vietato ~'** 'no bathing'
bagnasci'uga *nm inv* edge of the water, waterline
ba'gnato *a* wet; **~ fradicio** soaked
ba'gnino, -a *nmf* life guard
'**bagno** *nm* bath; (*stanza*) bathroom; (*gabinetto*) toilet; (*al mare*) swim, bathe; **bagni** *pl* (*stabilimento*) lido; **fare un ~** have a bath; (*nel mare ecc*) [have a] swim, bathe; **andare in ~** go to the bathroom, go to the toilet; **mettere a ~** soak; **con ~** (*camera*) en suite. **~ oculare** eyebath. **~ rivelatore** *Phot* developing bath. **~ di sangue** bloodbath. **~ di sviluppo** *Phot* developing bath. **~ turco** Turkish bath
bagnoma'ria *nm* **cuocere a ~** cook in a double saucepan
bagnoschi'uma *nm inv* bubble bath
ba'guette *nf inv* French loaf, baguette
Ba'hamas *nfpl* **le ~** the Bahamas
Bah'rain *nm* Bahrain, Bahrein
'**baia** *nf* bay
baio'netta *nf* bayonet
'**baita** *nf* mountain chalet
bala'ustra, balau'strata *nf* balustrade
balbet'tare *vt/i* stammer; (*bambino:*) babble
balbet'tio *nm* stammering; (*di bambino*) babble
bal'buzie *nf* stutter
balbuzi'ente *a* stuttering ● *nmf* stutterer
Bal'cani *nmpl* Balkans
bal'canico *a* Balkan
balco'nata *nf Theat* balcony, dress circle
balcon'cino *nm* **reggiseno a ~** underwired bra
bal'cone *nm* balcony
baldac'chino *nm* canopy; **letto a ~** four-poster bed

bal'danza *nf* boldness
baldan'zoso *a* bold
bal'doria *nf* revelry; **far ~** have a riotous time
Bale'ari *nfpl* **le [isole] ~** the Balearics, the Balearic Islands
ba'lena *nf* whale
bale'nare *vi* lighten; *fig* flash; **mi è balenata un'idea** I've just had an idea
bale'niera *nf* whaler
ba'leno *nm* **in un ~** in a flash
balenot'tera *nf* **~ azzurra** blue whale
ba'lera *nf* dance hall
ba'lestra *nf* crossbow
'balia *nf* wetnurse
ba'lia *nf* **in ~ di** at the mercy of
ba'listico *a* ballistic; **perito ~** ballistics expert
'balla *nf* bale; (*fam: frottola*) tall story
bal'labile *a* **essere ~** be good for dancing to
bal'lare *vi* dance; **andare a ~** go dancing
bal'lata *nf* ballad
balla'toio *nm* (*nelle scale*) landing
balle'rino, -a *nmf* dancer; (*classico*) ballet dancer ● *nf nf* (*classica*) ballet dancer, ballerina
bal'letto *nm* ballet
bal'lista *nmf fam* bull-shitter
'ballo *nm* dance; (*il ballare*) dancing; **sala da ~** ballroom; **essere in ~** ‹*lavoro, vita:*› be at stake; ‹*persona:*› be committed; **tirare qcno in ~** involve sb. **~ liscio** ballroom dancing. **~ in maschera** masked ball
ballonzo'lare *vi* skip about
ballot'taggio *nm* second count [of votes]
balne'are *a* bathing *attrib*; **stagione ~** swimming season; **stazione ~** seaside resort
balneazi'one *nf* **'divieto di ~'** 'no bathing'
ba'lordo *a* foolish; (*stordito*) stunned; **tempo ~** nasty weather
bal'samico *a* ‹*aria*› balmy
'balsamo *nm* balsam; (*per capelli*) conditioner; (*lenimento*) remedy
'baltico *a* Baltic. **il [mar] B~** The Baltic [Sea]
balu'ardo *nm* bulwark
'balza *nf* crag; (*di abito*) flounce
bal'zano *a* (*idea*) weird
bal'zare *vi* bounce; (*saltare*) jump; **~ in piedi** leap to one's feet
'balzo *nm* bounce; (*salto*) jump; **prendere la palla al ~** *fig* seize an opportunity
bam'bagia *nf* cotton wool; **vivere nella ~** *fig* be in clover
bam'bina *nf* little girl; (*piccola*) baby; **ha avuto una ~** she had a [baby] girl
bambi'naia *nf* nursemaid, nanny
bambi'nata *nf* childish thing to do/say
bam'bino *nm* child; (*appena nato*) baby; **avere un ~** have a baby; (*maschio*) have a [baby] boy; **bambini** *pl* children, kids; (*piccoli*) babies. **~ prodigio** child prodigy
bambi'none, -a *nmf pej* big *or* overgrown child

bam'boccio *nm* chubby child; (*sciocco*) simpleton; (*fantoccio*) rag doll
'bambola *nf* doll
bambo'lotto *nm* male doll
bambù *nm* bamboo
ba'nale *a* banal
banalità *nf inv* banality
banaliz'zare *vt* trivialize
ba'nana *nf* banana
ba'nano *nm* banana-tree
'banca *nf* bank. **~ d'affari** merchant bank, investment bank. **~ [di] dati** databank. **B~ Europea per la Ricostruzione e lo Sviluppo** European Bank for Reconstruction and Development. **~ degli occhi** eye bank. **~ del sangue** blood bank. **~ dello sperma** sperm bank
banca'rella *nf* stall
bancarel'lista *nmf* stallholder
ban'cario, -a *a* banking *attrib*; **trasferimento ~** bank transfer ● *nmf* bank employee
banca'rotta *nf* bankruptcy; **fare ~** go bankrupt
banchet'tare *vi* banquet
ban'chetto *nm* banquet
banchi'ere *nm* banker
ban'china *nf Naut* quay; (*in stazione*) platform; (*di strada*) path. **~ spartitraffico** central reservation, median strip *Am*. **~ non transitabile** soft verge
ban'chisa *nf* floe
'banco *nm* (*di scuola*) desk; (*di negozio*) counter; (*di officina*) bench; (*di gioco, banca*) bank; (*di mercato*) stall; (*degli imputati*) dock; **sotto ~** under the counter; **medicinale da ~** over the counter medicines. **~ dei formaggi** (*in supermercato*) cheese counter; (*in mercato*) cheese stall. **~ di ghiaccio** ice floe. **~ informazioni** information desk. **~ di nebbia** fog bank. **~ di sabbia** sandbank
'bancomat® *nm inv* autobank, cashpoint; (*carta*) bank card, cash card
ban'cone *nm* counter; (*in bar*) bar
banco'nota *nf* banknote, bill *Am*; **banco'note** *pl* paper currency
'banda *nf* band; (*di delinquenti*) gang. **~ d'atterraggio** *Aeron* landing strip. **~ passante** bandwidth. **~ rumorosa** rumble strip
banderu'ola *nf* weathercock; *Naut* pennant
bandi'era *nf* flag; **cambiare ~** change sides, switch allegiances
bandie'rina *nf* (*nel calcio*) corner flag
bandie'rine *nfpl* bunting
ban'dire *vt* banish; (*pubblicare*) publish; *fig* dispense with ‹*formalità, complimenti*›
ban'dista *nmf* bandsman
bandi'tismo *nm* banditry
ban'dito *nm* bandit
bandi'tore *nm* (*di aste*) auctioneer
'bando *nm* proclamation; **~ di concorso** job advertisement (*published in an official gazette for a job for which a competitive examination has to be sat*)

bang *nm inv* wham. ~ **sonico** sonic boom
Bangla'desh *nm* Bangladesh
bar *nm inv* bar
'bara *nf* coffin
ba'racca *nf* hut; (*catapecchia*) hovel;
mandare avanti la ~ keep the ship afloat
barac'cato, -a *a* living in a shanty town
● *nmf* shanty town dweller
barac'chino *nm* (*di gelati, giornali*) kiosk;
Radio CB radio
barac'cone *nm* (*roulotte*) circus caravan;
(*in luna park*) booth; (*fig: organizzazione*)
lumbering great dinosaur of an organization
barac'copoli *nf inv* shanty town
bara'onda *nf* chaos; **non fare ~** don't make
a mess
ba'rare *vi* cheat
'baratro *nm* chasm
barat'tare *vt* barter
ba'ratto *nm* barter
ba'rattolo *nm* jar; (*di latta*) tin
'barba *nf* beard; (*fam: noia*) bore; **farsi la ~**
shave; **in ~ a** in spite of; **è una ~** (*noia*) it's
boring
barbabi'etola *nf* beetroot; **barbabietole** *pl*
beetroot. ~ **da zucchero** sugar-beet
Bar'bados *nfpl* **le ~** Barbados
barbagi'anni *nm inv* barn owl
bar'barico *a* barbaric
bar'barie *nf inv* barbarity
barba'rismo *nm* barbarism
'barbaro *a* barbarous ● *nm* barbarian
'barbecue *nm inv* barbecue
bar'betta *nf* *Naut* painter
barbi'ere *nm* barber; (*negozio*) barber's
bar'biglio *nm* barb
barbi'turico *nm* barbiturate
bar'bone, -a *nm* (*vagabondo*) vagrant;
(*cane*) poodle ● *nf* bag lady
bar'boso *a* *fam* boring
barbu'gliare *vi* mumble
bar'buto *a* bearded
'barca *nf* boat; **una ~ di** *fig* a lot of. ~ **a**
motore motorboat. ~ **da pesca** fishing
boat. ~ **a remi** rowing boat, rowboat *Am*. ~
di salvataggio lifeboat. ~ **a vela** sailing
boat, sailboat *Am*
barcai'olo *nm* boatman
barcame'narsi *vr* manage
barca'rola *nf* *Mus* barcarolle
Barcel'lona *nf* Barcelona
barcol'lare *vi* stagger
barcol'loni *adv* **camminare ~** stagger
bar'cone *nm* barge; (*di ponte*) pontoon
bar'dare *vt* harness
bar'darsi *vr* *hum* dress up
barda'tura *nf* (*per cavallo*) harness
ba'rella *nf* stretcher
barelli'ere *nm* stretcher-bearer
'Barents: **mare di ~** Barents Sea
ba'rese *a* from Bari
bari'centro *nm* centre of gravity
ba'rile *nm* barrel
bari'lotto *nm* *fig* tub of lard
ba'rista *nm* barman ● *nf* barmaid

ba'ritono *nm* baritone
bar'lume *nm* glimmer; **un ~ di speranza** a
glimmer of hope
'barman *nm inv* barman
'baro *nm* cardsharper
ba'rocco *a & nm* baroque
ba'rometro *nm* barometer
baro'nale *a* baronial
ba'rone *nm* baron; **i baroni** *fig* the top brass
baro'nessa *nf* baroness
'barra *nf* bar; (*lineetta*) oblique; *Naut* tiller. ~
retroversa backslash. ~ **di rimorchio** tow
bar. ~ **spazio** space bar. ~ **di stato** *Comput*
status bar. ~ **strumenti** *Comput* tool bar
bar'rage *nm inv* *Sport* jump-off
bar'rare *vt* block off (*strada*)
barri'care *vt* barricade
barri'cata *nf* barricade
barri'era *nf* barrier; (*stradale*) road-block;
Geol reef. ~ **corallina** coral reef. ~
linguistica language barrier. ~ **razziale** colour bar. ~ **del suono** sound barrier
bar'rire *vi* trumpet
bar'rito *nm* trumpeting
ba'ruffa *nf* scuffle. **far ~** quarrel
barzel'letta *nf* joke; ~ **sporca** *o* **spinta**
dirty joke
basa'mento *nm* base; *Geol* bedrock
ba'sare *vt* base
ba'sarsi *vr* ~ **su** be based on; **mi baso su**
ciò che ho visto I'm going on [the basis of]
what I saw
'basco, -a *a & nmf* Basque ● *nm* (*copricapo*)
beret
'base *nf* basis; (*fondamento*) foundation; *Mil*
base; *Pol* rank and file; **in ~ a** containing; **in**
~ **a** on the basis of. ~ **di controllo** ground
control. ~ **[di] dati** database. ~ **d'intesa**
common ground. ~ **logica** logical basis. ~
navale naval base
'baseball *nm* baseball
ba'setta *nf* sideburn
basi'lare *a* basic
ba'silica *nf* basilica
Basili'cata *nf* Basilicata
ba'silico *nm* basil
ba'sista *nm* grass roots politician; (*di un*
crimine) mastermind
'basket *nm* basketball
bas'sezza *nf* lowness; (*di statura*) shortness; (*viltà*) vileness
bas'sista *nmf* bassist
'basso *a* low; (*di statura*) short; (*acqua*) shallow; (*televisione*) quiet; (*vile*) despicable;
parlare a bassa voce speak quietly, speak
in a low voice. **la bassa Italia** southern Italy
● *nm* lower part; *Mus* bass; **guardare in ~**
look down
basso'fondo *nm* (*pl* **bassifondi**) shallows;
bassifondi *pl* (*quartieri poveri*) slums
bassorili'evo *nm* bas-relief
bas'sotto *nm* dachshund
ba'stardo, -a *a* bastard; (*di animale*) mongrel ● *nmf* bastard; (*animale*) mongrel
ba'stare *vi* be enough; (*durare*) last; **basta!**

that's enough!, that'll do!; **basta che** (*purchè*) provided that; **basta così** that's enough; **basta così?** is that enough?, will that do?; (*in negozio*) will there be anything else?; **basta andare alla posta** you only have to go to the post office; **basta che tu lo faccia bene** make sure you do it well

Basti'an con'trario *nm* contrary old so-and-so

basti'mento *nm* ship; (*carico*) cargo

basti'one *nm* bastion

basto'nare *vt* beat

basto'nata *nf* **dare una ~ a** beat with a stick

baston'cino *nm* (*da sci*) ski pole. **~ di pesce** fish finger, fish stick *Am*

ba'stone *nm* stick; (*da golf*) club; (*da passeggio*) walking stick. **~ da hockey** hockey stick

ba'tosta *nf* blow

bat'tage *nm inv* **~ pubblicitario** media hype

bat'taglia *nf* battle; (*lotta*) fight

battagli'are *vi* battle; *fig* fight

bat'taglio *nm* (*di campana*) clapper; (*di porta*) knocker

battagli'one *nm* battalion

bat'tello *nm* boat; (*motonave*) steamer

bat'tente *nm* (*di porta*) wing; (*di finestra*) shutter; (*battaglio*) knocker

'battere *vt* beat; hit, knock ‹testa, spalla›; (*percorrere*) scour; thresh ‹grano›; break ‹record› ● *vi* (*bussare, urtare*) knock; ‹cuore:› beat; ‹ali ecc:› flap; *Tennis* serve; **~ a macchina** type; **~ gli occhi** blink; **~ il piede** tap one's foot; **~ le mani** clap [one's hands]; **~ le ore** strike the hours

bat'teri *nmpl* bacteria

batte'ria *nf* battery; *Mus* drums *pl*; (*Sport: eliminatoria*) heat

bat'terico *a* bacterial

bat'terio *nm* bacterium

batteriolo'gia *nf* bacteriology

batterio'logico *a* bacteriological

batte'rista *nmf* drummer

'battersi *vr* fight

bat'tesimo *nm* baptism, christening

battez'zare *vt* baptize, christen

battiba'leno *nm* **in un ~** in a flash

batti'becco *nm* squabble

batticu'ore *nm* palpitation; **mi venne il ~** I was scared

bat'tigia *nf* water's edge

batti'mano *nm* applause

batti'panni *nm inv* carpetbeater

batti'scopa *nm inv* skirting board

batti'stero *nm* baptistery

batti'strada *nm inv* outrider; (*di pneumatico*) tread; *Sport* pacesetter

battitap'peto *nm inv* carpet sweeper

'battito *nm* (*alle tempie*) throbbing; (*di orologio*) ticking; (*della pioggia*) beating. **~ cardiaco** heartbeat

batti'tore, -'trice *nmf Sport* batsman

bat'tuta *nf* beat; (*colpo*) knock; (*spirito-*

saggine) wisecrack; (*osservazione*) remark; *Mus* bar; *Tennis* service; *Theat* cue; (*dattilografia*) stroke. **~ d'arresto** setback

ba'tuffolo *nm* flock

ba'ule *nm* trunk

bau'xite *nf* bauxite

'bava *nf* dribble; (*di cane ecc*) slobber; **aver la ~ alla bocca** foam at the mouth

bava'glino *nm* bib

ba'vaglio *nm* gag

bava'rese *nf* ice-cream cake with milk, eggs and cream

'bavero *nm* collar

ba'zar *nm inv* bazaar

ba'zooka *nm inv* bazooka

baz'zecola *nf* trifle

bazzi'care *vt/i* haunt

baz'zotto *a* softboiled

be'arsi *vr* delight (**di** in)

beata'mente *adv* blissfully

beatifi'care *vt* beatify

beati'tudine *nf* bliss

be'ato *a* blissful; *Relig* blessed; **~ te!** lucky you!

beauty-'case *nm inv* toilet bag

bebè *nm inv* baby

bec'caccia *nf* woodcock

bec'care *vt* peck; *fig* catch

bec'carsi *vr* (*litigare*) quarrel

bec'cata *nf* beakful; (*colpo*) peck

beccheggi'are *vi* pitch

bec'chime *nm* birdseed

bec'chino *nm* grave-digger

'becco *nm* beak; (*di caffettiera ecc*) spout; **chiudi il ~** *fam* shut your trap; **non ha il ~ di un quattrino** *fam* he's skint; **restare a ~ asciutto** *fam* end up with nothing. **~ Bunsen** Bunsen [burner]. **~ a gas** gas burner

bec'cuccio *nm* spout

'beeper *nm inv* beeper

be'fana *nf* legendary old woman who brings presents to children on Twelfth Night; (*giorno*) Twelfth Night; (*donna brutta*) old witch

'beffa *nf* hoax; **farsi beffe di qcno** mock sb

bef'fardo *a* derisory; ‹persona› mocking

bef'fare *vt* mock

bef'farsi *vr* **~ di** make fun of

beffeggi'are *vt* taunt

'bega *nf* quarrel; **è una bella ~** it's really annoying

be'gonia *nf* begonia

beh *int* well

'beige *a & nm* beige

Bei'rut *nf* Beirut

be'lare *vi* bleat

be'lato *nm* bleating

'belga *a & nmf* Belgian

'Belgio *nm* Belgium

Bel'grado *nf* Belgrade

Be'lize *nm* Belize

'bella *nf* (*in carte, Sport*) decider; (*innamorata*) sweetheart. **~ di giorno** *Bot* morning glory. **~ di notte** *fig* lady of the night

bel'lezza *nf* beauty; **che ~!** how lovely!; **per ~** (*per decorazione*) for decoration; **chiudere/finire in ~** end on a high note; **la ~ di tre mesi/200 000 lire** all of three months/200,000 lire

belli'cismo *nm* warmongering

belli'cistico *a* warmongering

'bellico *a* war *attrib*; **periodo ~** wartime

bellicosità *nf* belligerence

belli'coso *a* warlike

bellige'rante *a* & *nmf* belligerent

bellige'ranza *nf* belligerence

bellim'busto *nm* dandy

'bello *a* nice; (*di aspetto*) beautiful; ⟨*uomo*⟩ handsome; (*moralmente*) good; **cosa fai di ~ stasera?** what are you up to tonight?; **oggi fa ~** it's a nice day; **una bella cifra** a lot; **un bel piatto di pasta** a big plate of pasta; **nel bel mezzo** right in the middle; **un bel niente** absolutely nothing; **bell'e fatto** over and done with; **bell'amico!** fine friend he is/you are!; **questa è bella!** that's a good one!; **bel voto** good mark; **il bel mondo** the beautiful people; **le belle arti** the fine arts; **bella lì!** *sl* hi!; (*arrivederci*) bye!, see you! ● *nm* (*bellezza*) beauty; (*innamorato*) sweetheart; **sul più ~** at the crucial moment; **il ~ è che...** the funny thing is that...

beltà *nf liter* beauty

'belva *nf* wild beast

be'molle *nm Mus* flat

ben *vedi* **bene**

benché *conj* though, although

'benda *nf* bandage; (*per occhi*) blindfold

ben'dare *vt* bandage; blindfold ⟨*occhi*⟩

bendi'sposto *a* **essere ~ verso** be well-disposed towards

'bene *adv* well; **ben ~** thoroughly; **~!** good!; **star ~** (*di salute*) be well; ⟨*vestito, stile:*⟩ suit; (*finanziariamente*) be well off; **non sta ~** (*non è educato*) it's not nice; **sta/va ~!** all right!; **ti sta ~!** [it] serves you right!; **ti auguro ~** I wish you well; **voler ~ a** love; **di ~ in meglio** better and better; **fare ~** (*aver ragione*) do the right thing; **fare ~ a** ⟨*cibo:*⟩ be good for; **una persona per ~** a good person; **per ~** ⟨*fare*⟩ properly; **è ben difficile** it's very difficult; **ben cotto** well done; **come tu ben sai** as you well know; **lo credo ~!** I can well believe it! ● *nm* good; **per il tuo ~** for your own good. **beni** *pl* (*averi*) property *sg*; **un ~ di famiglia** a family heirloom. **beni pl ambientali** environment. **beni pl di consumo** consumer products, consumer goods. **beni pl culturali** cultural heritage. **beni pl immobili** real estate, realty *Am*. **beni pl mobili** movables

benedet'tino *a* & *nm* Benedictine

bene'detto *a* blessed

bene'dire *vt* bless; **mandare qcno a farsi ~** *fam* tell sb to get lost

benedizi'one *nf* blessing

benedu'cato *a* well-mannered

benefat|'tore, -'trice *nmf* benefactor; benefactress

benefi'care *vt* help

benefi'cenza *nf* charity

benefici'are *vi* **~ di** profit by

benefici'ario, -a *a* & *nmf* beneficiary

bene'ficio *nm* benefit; **con ~ di inventario** with reservations. **~ accessorio** perquisite

be'nefico *a* beneficial; (*di beneficenza*) charitable

'Benelux *nm* Benelux

beneme'renza *nf* benevolence

bene'merito *a* worthy

bene'placito *nm* consent, approval

be'nessere *nm* well-being

bene'stante *a* well off ● *nmf* well-off person

bene'stare *nm* consent

benevo'lenza *nf* benevolence

be'nevolo *a* benevolent

ben'fatto *a* well-made

Ben'gala *nm* Bengal

ben'godi *nm* **il paese di ~** a land of plenty

'beni *nmpl* property *sg*; *Fin* assets; **~ di consumo** consumer goods

benia'mino *nm* favourite

be'nigno *a* kindly; *Med* benign

Be'nin *nm* Benin

beninfor'mato *a* well-informed ● *npl* **i beninformati** those in the know

benintenzio'nato, -a *a* well-meaning ● *nmf* well-meaning person

benin'teso *adv* needless to say, of course; **~ che...** of course,...

be'nissimo *int* fine

benpen'sante *a* & *nmf* self-righteous

benser'vito *nm* **dare il ~ a qcno** give sb the sack

bensì *conj* but rather

benve'nuto *a* & *nm* welcome; **benvenuta!** welcome!

ben'visto *a* **essere ~** (**da qcno**) go down well (with sb)

benvo'lere *vt* **farsi ~ da qcno** win sb's affection; **prendere qcno in ~** take a liking to sb; **essere benvoluto da tutti** be well-liked by everyone

benvo'luto *a* well-liked

ben'zene *nm* benzene

ben'zina *nf* petrol, gas *Am*; **far ~** get petrol. **~ avio** aviation fuel. **~ senza piombo** leadfree petrol. **~ super** four-star petrol, premium gas *Am*. **~ verde** unleaded petrol

benzi'naio, -a *nm* petrol station attendant, gas station attendant *Am*

be'one, -a *nmf fam* boozer

'berbero, -a *a* & *nmf* Berber

'bere *vt* drink; (*assorbire*) absorb; *fig* swallow; **~ una tazza di tè** have a cup of tea ● *nm* drinking; **da ~ e da mangiare** food and drink

berga'motto *nm* bergamot

'Bering *nm* **il mare di ~** the Bering Sea; **lo stretto di ~** the Bering Straits

ber'lina *nf Auto* saloon; **mettere alla ~ qcno** ridicule sb

berli'nese *nmf* Berliner ● *a* Berlin *attrib*

Ber'lino *nm* Berlin. **~ Est** East Berlin
Ber'muda *nfpl* **le ~** the Bermudas
ber'muda *nfpl* (*pantaloni*) Bermuda shorts
'Berna *nf* Berne
ber'noccolo *nm* bump; (*disposizione*) flair
ber'retto *nm* beret, cap. **~ a pompon** bobble hat
bersagli'are *vt fig* bombard
ber'saglio *nm* target
bescia'mella *nf* béchamel, white sauce
be'stemmia *nf* swear-word; (*maledizione*) oath; (*sproposito*) blasphemy
bestemmi'are *vi* swear
'bestia *nf* animal; (*persona brutale*) beast; (*persona sciocca*) fool; **andare in ~** *fam* blow one's top; **lavorare come una ~** slave away
besti'ale *a* bestial; ⟨*espressione, violenza*⟩ brutal; ⟨*fam: freddo, fame*⟩ terrible; **fa un caldo/freddo ~** it's dreadfully hot/cold
bestialità *nf inv* bestiality; *fig* nonsense
besti'ame *nm* livestock
betabloc'cante *nm* betablocker
Be'tlemme *nf* Bethlehem
betoni'era *nf* concrete mixer
'bettola *nf fig* dive
be'tulla *nf* birch
be'vanda *nf* drink. **~ alcolica** alcoholic drink
bevi'|tore, -'trice *nmf* drinker
be'vuta *nf* drink
be'vuto *pp di* **bere**
Bhu'tan *nm* Bhutan
bi+ *pref* bi+
bi'ada *nf* fodder
bianche'ria *nf* linen. **~ per la casa** white goods, household linen. **~ intima** underwear; (*da donna*) lingerie. **~ da letto** bed linen
bian'chetto *nm* whitener
bi'anco, -a *a* white; ⟨*foglio*⟩ blank; **voce bianca** treble voice ● *nmf* white ● *nm* white; **mangiare in ~** eat bland food; **andare in ~** *fam* not score; **in ~ e nero** ⟨*film, fotografia*⟩ black and white, monochrome; **passare una notte in ~** have a sleepless night. **~ sporco** off white. **~ d'uovo** egg white
biancomangi'are *nm* blancmange
bian'core *nm* (*bianchezza*) whiteness
bianco'segno *nm Jur blank document bearing a signature*
bianco'spino *nm* hawthorn
biasci'care *vt* (*mangiare*) eat noisily; (*parlare*) mumble
biasi'mare *vt* blame
biasi'mevole *a* blameworthy
bi'asimo *nm* blame
'Bibbia *nf* Bible
bibe'ron *nm inv* [baby's] bottle
'bibita *nf* [soft] drink. **~ gasata** fizzy drink
'biblico *a* biblical
bibliogra'fia *nf* bibliography
biblio'grafico *a* bibliographical
biblio'teca *nf* library; (*mobile*) bookcase
bibliote'cario, -a *nmf* librarian

bicame'rale *a* two-chamber *attrib*, bicameral
bicarbo'nato *nm* bicarbonate. **~ di sodio** bicarbonate of soda
bicchie'rata *nf* glassful
bicchi'ere *nm* glass
bicchie'rino *nm fam* tipple
bicente'nario *nm* bicentenary
bici'cletta *nf* bicycle, bike; **andare in ~** cycle, go by bike; (*sapere*) ride a bicycle. **~ da corsa** racer
bi'cipite *nm* biceps
bi'cocca *nf* hovel
bico'lore *a* two-coloured
bidè *nm inv* bidet
bi'dello, -a *nmf* janitor, [school] caretaker
bidirezio'nale *a* bidirectional
bido'nare *vt* con, swindle; **farsi ~** be conned
bido'nata *nf fam* swindle
bi'done *nm* bin; (*fam: truffa*) swindle; **fare un ~ a qcno** *fam* stand sb up. **~ dell'immondizia, ~ della spazzatura** rubbish bin, trash can *Am*
bidon'ville *nf inv* shantytown
bi'eco *a* callous
bi'ella *nf* connecting rod
Bielo'russia *nf* Belarus
bielo'russo, -a *a & nmf* Belorussian
bien'nale *a* biennial
bi'ennio *nm* two-year period
bi'erre *nfpl* (*Brigate Rosse*) Red Brigades
bi'etola *nf* beet
bifo'cale *a* bifocal
bi'folco, -a *nmf fig* boor
bifor'carsi *vr* fork
biforcazi'one *nf* fork
bifor'cuto *a* forked
biga'mia *nf* bigamy
'bigamo, -a *a* bigamous ● *nmf* bigamist
big bang *nm* big bang
bighello'nare *vi* loaf around
bighel'lone *nm* loafer
bigliotte'ria *nf* costume jewellery; (*negozio*) jeweller's
bigliet'taio *nm* booking clerk; (*sui treni*) ticket-collector
bigliette'ria *nf* ticket-office; *Theat* box-office. **~ automatica** ticket vending machine
bigli'etto *nm* ticket; (*lettera breve*) note; (*cartoncino*) card; (*di banca*) banknote. **~ di sola andata** single [ticket]. **~ di andata e ritorno** return [ticket]. **~ di auguri** card. **~ chilometrico** *ticket allowing travel up to a maximum specified distance*. **~ collettivo** group ticket. **~ giornaliero** day pass. **~ d'ingresso** entrance ticket. **~ della lotteria** lottery ticket. **~ da visita** business card
bigliet'tone *nm* (*fam: soldi*) big one
bignè *nm inv* puff. **~ alla crema** cream puff
bigo'dino *nm* roller
bi'gotto *nm* bigot
bi'kini *nm inv* bikini
bi'lancia *nf* scales *pl*; (*di orologio, Comm*) balance; **B~** *Astr* Libra. **~ commerciale** balance of trade. **~ da cucina** kitchen scales.

~ dei pagamenti balance of payments. **~ pesapersone** scales
bilanci'are vt balance; fig weigh
bilancia'tura nf **~ gomme** wheel-balancing
bilanci'ere nm (in sollevamento pesi) barbell; (di orologio) balance wheel
bi'lancio nm budget; Comm balance [sheet]; **fare il ~** balance the books; fig take stock; **chiudere il ~ in attivo/passivo** to end the financial year in profit/with a loss. **~ preventivo** budget
bilate'rale a bilateral
'**bile** nf bile; fig rage
bili'ardo nm billiards sg
'**bilico** nm equilibrium; **in ~** in the balance
bi'lingue a bilingual
bilingu'ismo nm bilingualism
bili'one nm billion
bili'oso a bilious
bilo'cale a two-room ● nm two-room flat
'**bimbo, -a** nmf child. **~ in fasce** babe in arms
bimen'sile a fortnightly Br, twice-monthly
bime'strale a bimonthly
bi'mestre nm two months
bi'nario nm track; (piattaforma) platform
bi'nocolo nm binoculars pl
bi'nomio nm binomial
bio+ pref bio+
bioagricol'tore nm organic farmer
bioagricol'tura nf organic farming
bio'chimica nf biochemistry
bio'chimico, -a nmf biochemist ● a biochemical
biodegra'dabile a biodegradable
biodiversità nf biodiversity
bio'etica nf bioethics
bio'fisica nf biophysics
biogra'fia nf biography
bio'grafico a biographical
bi'ografo, -a nmf biographer
bioingegne'ria nf bioengineering
biolo'gia nf biology
biologica'mente adv biologically
bio'logico a biological
bi'ologo, -a nmf biologist
bi'onda nf blonde. **~ ossigenata** peroxide blonde
bi'ondo a blond ● nm fair colour; (uomo) fair-haired man. **~ cenere** ash blond. **~ platino** platinum blonde
bi'onico a bionic
bio'psia nf biopsy
bio'ritmo nm biorhythm
bio'sfera nf biosphere
bi'ossido nm dioxide. **~ di carbonio** carbon dioxide
biotecnolo'gia nf biotechnology
bip nm inv blip
bipar'titico a bipartisan
biparti'tismo nm two-party system
bipar'tito a bipartite, two-party attrib ● nm two-party coalition
bipartizi'one nf division into two parts

bipo'lare a Electr bipolar; Pol dominated by two large parties
bipola'rismo nm Pol system in which the numerous parties line up behind two main parties
bipolarizazzi'one nf Pol tendency towards 'bipolarismo'
bi'posto a inv & nm inv two-seater
'**birba** nf, **bir'bante** nm rascal, rogue
birbo'nata nf trick
bir'bone a wicked
birdie nm inv (golf) birdie
biri'chino, -a a naughty ● nmf little devil
bi'rillo nm skittle
Bir'mania nf Burma
bir'mano, -a a & nmf Burmese
'**birra** nf beer; **a tutta ~** fig flat out. **~ chiara** lager. **~ grande** ≈ pint. **~ piccola** ≈ half-pint. **~ scura** dark beer, brown ale Br
birre'ria nf beer-house; (fabbrica) brewery
bis nm inv encore
bi'saccia nf haversack
bi'sbetica nf shrew
bi'sbetico a bad-tempered
bisbigli'are vt/i whisper
bi'sbiglio nm whisper
bi'sboccia nf **fare ~** make merry
'**bisca** nf gambling-house
Bi'scaglia nf **il golfo di ~** the Bay of Biscay
'**biscia** nf snake
biscotti'era nf biscuit barrel, biscuit tin
bi'scotto nm biscuit. **~ per cani** dog-biscuit
bisessu'ale a & nmf bisexual
bise'stile a **anno ~** leap year
bisettima'nale a twice-weekly
biset'trice nf bisector
bisezi'one nf bisection
bisil'labico a two-syllable attrib, bisyllabic
bi'slacco a peculiar
bi'slungo a oblong
bi'snonno, -a nm great-grandfather ● nf great-grandmother
biso'gnare vi **bisogna agire subito** we must act at once; **bisogna farlo** it is necessary to do it; **non bisogna venire** you don't have to come
bi'sogno nm need; (povertà) poverty; **aver ~ di** need
biso'gnoso a needy; (povero) poor; **~ di** in need of
bi'sonte nm bison
bi'stecca nf steak. **~ di cavallo** horsemeat steak. **~ ai ferri** grilled steak. **~ alla fiorentina** large grilled beef steak
bi'sticci nmpl bickering
bisticci'are vi quarrel
bi'sticcio nm quarrel; (gioco di parole) pun
bistrat'tare vt mistreat
bistrò nm inv bistro
'**bisturi** nm inv scalpel
bi'sunto a very greasy
bit nm inv bit
bito'nale a two-tone
bi'torzolo nm lump

'bitter *nm inv* bitter aperitif
bi'tume *nm* bitumen
bivac'care *vi* bivouac
bi'vacco *nm* bivouac
'bivio *nm* crossroads; (*di strada*) fork
bizan'tino *a* Byzantine
'bizza *nf* tantrum; **fare le bizze** ⟨*bambini:*⟩ play up
bizzar'ria *nf* eccentricity
biz'zarro *a* bizarre
biz'zeffe *adv* **a ~** galore
'blackjack *nm* blackjack
blan'dire *vt* soothe; (*allettare*) flatter
'blando *a* mild
bla'sfemo *a* blasphemous
bla'sone *nm* coat of arms
blate'rare *vi* blether, blather; **~ di qcsa** burble on about sth
'blatta *nf* cockroach
'bleso *a* lisping
blin'dare *vt* armour-plate
blin'dato *a* armoured
'blinker *nm inv* blinker
'blister *nm inv* blister pack
blitz *nm inv* blitz
bloc'care *vt* block; (*isolare*) cut off; *Mil* blockade; *Comm* freeze; stop ⟨*assegno*⟩; **~ l'accesso a** seal off
bloc'carsi *vr Mech* jam
blocca'sterzo *nm* steering lock
bloc'cato *a* blocked
bloc'chetto *nm* **~ per appunti** memo pad. **~ di biglietti** book of tickets
'blocco *nm* block; *Mil* blockade; (*dei fitti*) restriction; (*di carta*) pad; (*unione*) coalition; **in ~** *Comm* in bulk. **~ per appunti** notepad. **~ psicologico** mental block. **~ stradale** roadblock
block-notes *nm inv* memo pad
blu *a & nm* blue
blu'astro *a* bluish
blue chip *nf inv Fin* blue chip
blue-'jeans *nmpl* jeans
bluff *nm inv* (*carte, fig*) bluff
bluf'fare *vi* (*carte, fig*) bluff
'blusa *nf* blouse
'boa *nm* boa [constrictor]; (*sciarpa*) [feather] boa ● *nf Naut* buoy
bo'ato *nm* rumbling
bo'bina *nf* spool; (*di film*) reel; *Electr* coil
bobi'nare *vt* spool
'bocca *nf* mouth; **a ~ aperta** *fig* dumbfounded; **in ~ al lupo!** *fam* break a leg!; **fare la respirazione ~ a ~ a qcno** give sb mouth to mouth resuscitation, give sb the kiss of life; **essere di ~ buona** eat anything; *fig* be easily satisfied; **essere sulla ~ di tutti** be the talk of the town. **~ del camino** chimneybreast. **~ di leone** snapdragon
boccac'cesco *a* licentious
boc'caccia *nf* grimace; **far boccacce** make faces
boc'caglio *nm* nozzle
boc'cale *nm* jug; (*da birra*) mug
bocca'porto *nm Naut* hatch

bocca'scena *nm inv* proscenium
boc'cata *nf* (*di fumo*) puff; **prendere una ~ d'aria** get a breath of fresh air
boc'cetta *nf* small bottle
boccheggi'are *vi* gasp
boc'chino *nm* cigarette holder; (*di pipa, Mus*) mouthpiece
'boccia *nf* (*palla*) bowl; **bocce** *pl* (*gioco*) bowls *sg*; **giocare a bocce** play bowls
bocci'are *vt* (*agli esami*) fail; (*respingere*) reject; (*alle bocce*) hit; **essere bocciato** fail; (*ripetere*) repeat a year
boccia'tura *nf* failure
bocci'olo *nm* bud
'boccolo *nm* ringlet
boccon'cino *nm* morsel
boc'cone *nm* mouthful; (*piccolo pasto*) snack
boc'coni *adv* face down[wards]
Bo'emia *nf* Bohemia
bo'emo, -a *a & nmf* Bohemian
bo'ero, -a *nmf* Afrikaner
bofonchi'are *vi* grumble
boh *int* dunno
'boia *nm* executioner; **fa un freddo ~** *fam* it's brass-monkey weather; **ho un sonno ~** *fam* I can't keep my eyes open
boi'ata *nf fam* rubbish
boicot'taggio *nm* boycotting
boicot'tare *vt* boycott
bo'lero *nm* bolero
'bolgia *nf* (*caos*) bedlam
'bolide *nm* meteor; **passare come un ~** shoot past [like a rocket]
Bo'livia *nf* Bolivia
bolivi'ano, -a *a & nmf* Bolivian
'bolla *nf* bubble; (*vescica, in tappezzeria*) blister; **finire in una ~ di sapone** go up in smoke. **~ di accompagnamento** packing list. **~ d'aria** (*in acqua*) air bubble. **~ di consegna** packing list
bol'lare *vt* stamp; *fig* brand
bol'lato *a fig* branded; **carta bollata** *paper with stamp showing payment of duty*
bol'lente *a* boiling [hot]
bol'letta *nf* bill; **essere in ~** be hard up
bollet'tino *nm* bulletin; *Comm* list. **~ d'informazione** fact sheet. **~ meteorologico** weather report. **~ ufficiale** gazette
bolli'latte *nm* milk pan
bol'lino *nm* coupon
bol'lire *vt/i* boil
bol'lito *nm* boiled meat
bolli'tore *nm* boiler; (*per l'acqua*) kettle
bolli'tura *nf* boiling
'bollo *nm* stamp; *Auto* tax disc
bol'lore *nm* boil; (*caldo*) intense heat; *fig* ardour
Bo'logna *nf* Bologna
bolo'gnese *nmf* person from Bologna; **spaghetti alla ~** spaghetti bolognese
'bomba *nf* bomb; **a prova di ~** bomb-proof; **tornare a ~** get back to the point. **~ atomica** nuclear bomb. **~ a mano** hand gre-

nade. **~ molotov** petrol bomb. **~ ad orologeria** time bomb

bombarda'mento *nm* shelling; *(con aerei)* bombing; *fig* bombardment. **~ aereo** air raid

bombar'dare *vt* shell; *(con aerei)* bomb; *fig* bombard

bombardi'ere *nm* bomber

bom'bato *a* domed

'bomber *nm inv* bomber jacket

bom'betta *nf* bowler [hat]

'bombo *nm* bumblebee

'bombola *nf* cylinder. **~ di gas** gas bottle, gas cylinder

bombo'lone *nm* doughnut

bomboni'era *nf* wedding keep-sake

bo'naccia *nf Naut* calm

bonacci'one, -a *nmf* good-natured person ● *a* good-natured

bo'nario *a* kindly

bo'nifica *nf* land reclamation

bonifi'care *vt* reclaim

bo'nifico *nm Comm* discount; **~ [bancario]** [credit] transfer

bontà *nf* goodness; *(gentilezza)* kindness

'bonus-'malus *nm inv Auto* car-insurance policy with no claims bonus clause

'boogie *nm* boogie

'bookmaker *nm inv* bookmaker

'boomerang *nm inv* boomerang

boot *nm Comput* boot-up; **eseguire il ~** boot up

'bora *nf* cold north-east wind in the upper Adriatic

borbot'tare *vi* mumble; *⟨stomaco:⟩* rumble

borbot'tio *nm* mumbling; *(di stomaco)* rumbling

'borchia *nf* stud

borchi'ato *a* studded

bor'dare *vt* border

bor'data *nf Naut* broadside

borda'tura *nf* border

bor'deaux *nm inv (vino)* claret, Bordeaux ● *a inv (colore)* claret

bor'dello *nm* brothel; *fig* bedlam; *(disordine)* mess

bor'dino *nm* narrow border

'bordo *nm* border; *(estremità)* edge; **a ~** *Aeron, Naut* on board; **d'alto ~** *⟨prostituta⟩* high-class. **~ d'attacco** *Aeron* leading edge

bor'dura *nf* border

bor'gata *nf* hamlet

bor'ghese *a* bourgeois; *⟨abito⟩* civilian; **in ~** in civilian dress; *⟨poliziotto⟩* in plain clothes

borghe'sia *nf* middle classes *pl*

'borgo *nm* village; *(quartiere)* district

'boria *nf* conceit

bori'oso *a* conceited

bor'lotto *nm* **[fagiolo] ~** borlotto bean

'Borneo *nm* Borneo

boro'talco *nm* talcum powder

bor'raccia *nf* flask

'Borsa *nf* **~ [valori]** Stock Exchange

'borsa *nf* bag; *(borsetta)* handbag. **~ dell'acqua calda** hot-water bottle. **~ frigo**

cool-box. **~ della spesa** shopping bag. **~ di studio** scholarship. **~ termica** cool bag. **~ da viaggio** travel bag

borsai'olo *nm* pickpocket

bor'seggio *nm* pickpocketing

borsel'lino *nm* purse

bor'sello *nm (portamonete)* purse; *(borsetto)* man's handbag

bor'setta *nf* handbag

bor'setto *nm* man's handbag

bor'sino *nm Fin* dealing room

bor'sista *nmf Fin* speculator; *Sch* scholarship holder

bo'scaglia *nf* woodlands *pl*

boscai'olo *nm* woodman; *(guardaboschi)* forester

bo'schetto *nm* grove

'bosco *nm* wood

bo'scoso *a* wooded

'Bosnia *nf* Bosnia

bos'niaco, -a *a & nmf* Bosnian

Bosnia-Erzego'vina *nf* Bosnia-Herzegovina

boss *nm inv* **~ mafioso** Mafia boss

'bosso *nm* boxwood

'bossolo *nm* cartridge case

Bot *nm abbr* (**Buoni Ordinari Del Tesoro**) T-bills

bo'tanica *nf* botany

bo'tanico *a* botanical ● *nm* botanist

'botola *nf* trapdoor

Bot'swana *nm* Botswana

'botta *nf* blow; *(rumore)* bang; **fare a botte** come to blows. **~ e risposta** *fig* thrust and counter-thrust

botta'trice *nf* monkfish

'botte *nf* barrel

bot'tega *nf* shop; *(di artigiano)* workshop

botte'gaio, -a *nmf* shopkeeper

botte'ghino *nm Theatr* box-office; *(del lotto)* lottery-shop

bot'tiglia *nf* bottle; **in ~** bottled

bottiglie'ria *nf* wine shop

bot'tino *nm* loot; *Mil* booty

'botto *nm* bang. **di ~** all of a sudden

bot'tone *nm* button; *Bot* bud. **~ di carica** winder

botu'lismo *nm* botulism

'bourbon *nm inv* bourbon

bo'vini *nmpl* cattle

bo'vino *a* bovine

'bowling *nm* bowling

box *nm inv (per cavalli)* loosebox; *(recinto per bambini)* play-pen

'boxe *nf* boxing

'bozza *nf* draft; *Typ* proof; *(bernoccolo)* bump; **~ in colonna** galley [proof]. **~ definitiva** page proof. **~ impaginata** page proof. **~ di stampa** page proofs

boz'zetto *nm* sketch

'bozzolo *nm* cocoon

BR *nfpl abbr* (**Brigate Rosse**) Red Brigades

brac'care *vt* hunt

brac'cetto *nm* **a ~** arm in arm

bracci'ale *nm* bracelet; *(fascia)* armband

braccia'letto *nm* bracelet; (*di orologio*) watch-strap

bracci'ante *nm* day labourer

bracci'ata *nf* (*nel nuoto*) stroke

'**braccio** *nm* (*pl nf* **braccia**) arm; (*di fiume*, *pl* **bracci**) arm. ~ **di ferro** arm wrestling

bracci'olo *nm* (*di sedia*) arm[rest]; (*da nuoto*) armband

'**bracco** *nm* hound

bracconi'ere *nm* poacher

'**brace** *nf* embers *pl*; **alla** ~ char-grilled

'**brache** *nfpl* (*fam: pantaloni*) britches; **calare le** ~ *fig* chicken out

braci'ere *nm* brazier

braci'ola *nf* chop. ~ **di maiale** pork chop

'**brado** *a* **allo stato** ~ in the wild

braille *nm* Braille

brain-'storming *nm inv* brainstorming

'**brama** *nf* longing

bra'mare *vt* long for

bra'mino *nm* Brahmin

bramo'sia *nf* yearning

'**branca** *nf* branch

'**branchia** *nf* gill

'**branco** *nm* (*di cani*) pack; (*pej: di persone*) gang

branco'lare *vi* grope

'**branda** *nf* camp-bed

bran'dello *nm* scrap; **a brandelli** in tatters

bran'dina *nf* cot

bran'dire *vt* brandish

'**brandy** *nm inv* brandy

'**brano** *nm* piece; (*di libro*) passage

bran'zino *nm* sea bass

bra'sare *vt* braise

bra'sato *nm* braised beef with herbs

Bra'sile *nm* Brazil

brasili'ano, -a *a & nmf* Brazilian

bra'vata *nf* bragging

'**bravo** *a* good; (*abile*) clever; (*coraggioso*) brave; ~! well done!

bra'vura *nf* skill

'**breccia** *nf* breach; **sulla** ~ *fig* very successful, at the top

brecci'ame *nm* loose chippings *pl*

bre'saola *nf* dried, salted beef sliced thinly and eaten cold

Bre'tagna *nf* Brittany

bre'tella *nf* shoulder-strap; *Mech* brace; **bretelle** *pl* (*di calzoni*) braces, suspenders *Am*

'**bretone** *a & nmf* Breton

'**breve** *a* brief, short; **in** ~ briefly; **tra** ~ shortly

brevet'tare *vt* patent

bre'vetto *nm* patent; (*attestato*) licence

brevità *nf* shortness

'**brezza** *nf* breeze

'**bricco** *nm* jug. ~ **del latte** milk jug

bricco'nata *nf* dirty trick

bric'cone *nm* blackguard; *hum* rascal

bri'ciola *nf* crumb; *fig* grain

bri'ciolo *nm* fragment; **non hai un** ~ **di cervello!** you don't have an ounce of common sense!

bridge *nm inv* (*carte*) bridge

'**briga** *nf* (*fastidio*) trouble; (*lite*) quarrel; **attaccar** ~ pick a quarrel; **prendersi la** ~ **di fare qcsa** go to the trouble of doing sth

brigadi'ere *nm* (*dei carabinieri*) sergeant

brigan'taggio *nm* highway robbery

bri'gante *nm* bandit; *hum* rogue

bri'gare *vi* to intrigue

bri'gata *nf* brigade; (*gruppo*) group

briga'tista *nmf Pol* member of the Red Brigades

'**briglia** *nf* rein; **a** ~ **sciolta** at full gallop; *fig* at breakneck speed

bril'lante *a* brilliant; (*scintillante*) sparkling ● *nm* diamond

brillan'tina *nf* brilliantine

bril'lare *vi* shine; (*metallo:*) glitter; (*scintillare*) sparkle

'**brillo** *a* tipsy

'**brina** *nf* hoar-frost

brin'dare *vi* toast; ~ **a qcno** drink a toast to sb

'**brindisi** *nm inv* toast

'**brio** *nm* vivacity

bri'oche *nf inv* croissant

bri'oso *a* vivacious

'**briscola** *nf* (*seme*) trumps

bri'tannico *a* British

'**brivido** *nm* shiver; (*di paura ecc*) shudder; (*di emozione*) thrill; **avere i brividi** have the shivers; **dare i brividi a qcno** give sb the shivers

brizzo'lato *a* (*capelli, barba*) greying

'**brocca** *nf* jug

broc'cato *nm* brocade

'**broccoli** *nmpl* broccoli

bro'daglia *nf pej* dishwater

'**brodo** *nm* broth; (*per cucinare*) stock. ~ **di manzo** beef tea. ~ **di pollo** chicken broth; (*per cucinare*) chicken stock. ~ **ristretto** consommé. ~ **vegetale** clear broth; (*per cucinare*) vegetable stock

'**broglio** *nm* ~ **elettorale** gerrymandering

'**broker** *nmf inv* broker; ~ **d'assicurazioni** insurance broker

'**bromo** *nm Chem* bromine

bro'muro *nm* bromide

bronchi'ale *a* bronchial

bron'chite *nf* bronchitis

bron'chitico *a* chesty

'**broncio** *nm* sulk; **fare il** ~ sulk

bronto'lare *vi* grumble; (*tuono ecc:*) rumble; ~ **contro qcno/qcsa** grumble *or* grouch about sb/sth

bronto'lio *nm* grumbling; (*di tuono*, *stomaco*) rumbling

bronto'lone, -a *nmf* grumbler

'**bronzo** *nm* bronze; **una faccia di** ~ *fam* a brass neck

bros'sura *nf* **edizione in** ~ paperback

bru'care *vt* (*pecora:*) graze

bruciacchi'are *vt* scorch

bruci'ante *a* burning

brucia'pelo *adv* **a** ~ point-blank

bruci'are vt burn; (scottare) scald; (incendiare) set fire to ● vi burn; (scottare) scald
bruci'arsi vr burn oneself
bruci'ato a burnt; fig burnt-out
brucia'tore nm burner
brucia'tura nf burn
bruci'ore nm burning sensation
'bruco nm grub
'brufolo nm spot
brughi'era nf heath
bruli'care vi swarm
bruli'chio nm swarming
'brullo a bare
'bruma nf mist
Bru'nei nm Brunei
'bruno a brown; ⟨occhi, capelli⟩ dark
brusca'mente adv (di colpo) suddenly
bru'schetta nf toasted bread rubbed with garlic and sprinkled with olive oil
'brusco a sharp; ⟨persona⟩ brusque, abrupt; (improvviso) sudden
bru'sio nm buzzing
bru'tale a brutal
brutalità nf brutality
brutaliz'zare vt brutalize
'bruto a & nm brute
brut'tezza nf ugliness
'brutto a ugly; ⟨tempo, tipo, situazione, affare⟩ nasty; (cattivo) bad. **brutta copia** nf rough copy. **~ tiro** nm dirty trick
brut'tura nf ugly thing
bub'bone nm Med swelling
'buca nf hole; (avvallamento) hollow. **~ delle lettere** letter-box
buca'neve nm inv snowdrop
bucani'ere nm buccaneer
bu'care vt make a hole in; (pungere) prick; punch ⟨biglietti⟩ ● vi have a puncture
'Bucarest nf Bucharest
bu'carsi vr prick oneself; (con droga) shoot up
buca'tini nmpl pasta similar to spaghetti but thicker and hollow
bu'cato nm washing; **fare il ~** do the washing
'buccia nf peel, skin; **bucce** pl (di frutta) parings. **~ di banana** banana skin
bucherel'lare vt riddle
bucherel'lato a pitted
'buco nm hole. **~ della serratura** keyhole
bu'colica nf bucolic
bu'colico nm bucolic
'Budda nm Buddha
bud'dista nmf Buddhist
bu'dello nm (pl nf **budella**) bowel
'budget nm inv budget; **~ provvisorio** minibudget
budge'tario a budgetary
bu'dino nm pudding
'bue nm (pl **buoi**) ox; **carne di ~** beef
'bufalo nm buffalo
bu'fera nf storm; (di neve) blizzard
bufferiz'zato a Comput buffered
buf'fet nm inv snack bar; (mobile) sideboard; (pasto) buffet
buf'fetto nm cuff

'buffo a funny; Theat comic ● nm funny thing
buffo'nata nf (scherzo) joke
buf'fone nm buffoon; **fare il ~** play the fool
bu'gia nf lie; **~ pietosa** white lie
bugi'ardo, -a a lying ● nmf liar
bugi'gattolo nm cubby-hole
'buio a dark ● nm darkness; **al ~** in the dark; **~ pesto** pitch dark
'bulbo nm bulb; (dell'occhio) eyeball
Bulga'ria nf Bulgaria
'bulgaro, -a a & nmf Bulgarian
buli'mia nf bulimia
bu'limico nmf bulimic
'bullo nm bully
bul'lone nm bolt
'bunker nm inv bunker
buona'fede nf good faith
buo'nanima nf **quella ~ di mio zio** my late uncle, God rest his soul
buona'notte int good night
buona'sera int good evening
buonco'stume nf Vice Squad
buondì int good day!
buon'giorno int good morning; (di pomeriggio) good afternoon
buon'grado nm **di ~** willingly
buongu'staio, -a nmf gourmet
buon'gusto nm good taste
bu'ono a good; ⟨momento⟩ right; **dar ~** (convalidare) accept; **alla buona** easy-going; ⟨cena⟩ informal; **buona fortuna!** good luck!; **buona notte/sera** good night/evening; **buon compleanno/Natale!** happy birthday/merry Christmas!; **buon viaggio!** have a good trip!; **buon appetito!** enjoy your meal!; **~ senso** common sense; **di buon'ora** early; **a buon mercato** cheap; **una buona volta** once and for all; **buona parte di** the best part of; **tre ore buone** three good hours ● nm good; (in film) goody; (tagliando) voucher; (titolo) bond; **con le buone** gently. **~ acquisto** gift token. **~ sconto** money-off-coupon ● nmf **buono, -a a nulla** dead loss
buontem'pone, -a nmf happy-go-lucky person
buonu'more nm good temper
buonu'scita nf retirement bonus; (di dirigente) golden handshake
buratti'naio nm puppeteer
burat'tino nm puppet
'burbero a surly; (nei modi) rough
bu'rino, -a nmf hick
'burla nf joke; **fare una ~ a** play a trick on; **per ~** for fun
bur'lare vt make a fool of
bur'larsi vr **~ di** make fun of
bu'rocrate nm bureaucrat
burocra'tese nm gobbledygook
buro'cratico a bureaucratic
burocra'zia nf bureaucracy
bu'rotica nf office automation
bur'rasca nf storm
burra'scoso a stormy
'burro nm butter. **~ di arachidi** peanut butter

bur'rone *nm* ravine

Bu'rundi *nm* Burundi

bus *nm inv Comput* bus. **~ locale** local bus

bu'scare *vt* catch; **buscarle** *fam* get a hiding

bu'scarsi *vr* catch

bus'sare *vt* knock

'bussola *nf* compass; **perdere la ~** lose one's bearings

'busta *nf* envelope; (*astuccio*) case. **~ affrancata** business reply envelope. **~ a finestra** window envelope. **~ imbottita** Jiffy bag®, padded envelope. **~ paga** pay packet

busta'rella *nf* bribe

bu'stina *nf* (*di tè*) tea bag; (*per medicine*) sachet

'busto *nm* bust; (*indumento*) girdle; **a mezzo ~** half-length

bu'tano *nm* Calor gas®

buttafu'ori *nm inv* bouncer

but'tare *vt* throw; **~ giù** (*demolire*) knock down; (*inghiottire*) gulp down; scribble down ⟨*scritto*⟩; *fam* put on ⟨*pasta*⟩; (*scoraggiare*) dishearten; **~ via** throw away

but'tarsi *vr* throw oneself; (*saltare*) jump

butte'rato *a* pitted

buz'zurro *nm fam* yokel

byte *nm inv Comput* byte

Cc

ca. *abbr* (**circa**) c.

caba'ret *nm inv* cabaret

cabaret'tisco *a* cabaret *attrib*

ca'bina *nf Naut, Aeron* cabin; (*al mare*) beach hut; (*di funivia*) [cable] car. **~ elettorale** polling booth. **~ di pilotaggio** cockpit; (*di aereo di linea*) flight deck. **~ di prova** fitting room. **~ telefonica** telephone box *Br*, phone booth

cabi'nato *nm* cabin cruiser

ca'blaggio *nm Electr* wiring

ca'blato *a* ⟨*messaggio*⟩ cable *attrib*

cablo'gramma *nm* cablegram

cabo'taggio *nm Naut* coastal navigation

cabrio'let *nm inv Auto* convertible

ca'cao *nm* cocoa

ca'care *vi vulg* have a crap

caca'toa *nm inv* cockatoo

'cacca *nf fam* poo, number two

'cacchio *nm fam* hell; **ma che ~ fai/dici?** *fam* what the hell are you doing/saying?

'caccia *nf* hunt; (*con fucile*) shooting; (*inseguimento*) chase; (*selvaggina*) game ● *nm inv* Aeron fighter; *Naut* destroyer; **andare a ~** go hunting. **~ grossa** big game. **~ all'uomo** man-hunt

cacciabombardi'ere *nm Aeron* fighter-bomber

cacciagi'one *nf* game

cacci'are *vt* hunt; (*mandar via*) chase away; (*scacciare*) drive out; (*ficcare*) shove; **caccia [fuori] i soldi!** *fam* out with the money!; **~ un urlo** *fam* let out a yell ● *vi* go hunting

cacci'arsi *vr* (*nascondersi*) hide; (*andare a finire*) get to; **~ nei guai** get into trouble

caccia'tora: alla ~ *a Culin* chasseur

caccia'tore, -'trice *nmf* hunter. **~ di dote** gold digger. **~ di frodo** poacher. **~ di taglie** bounty hunter. **~ di teste** *Comm* head-hunter

cacciatorpedini'ere *nm inv* destroyer

caccia'vite *nm inv* screwdriver

cacci'ucco *nm* **~ alla livornese** soup of seafood, tomato and wine served with bread

cache-'sexe *nm inv* thong

ca'chet *nm inv Med* capsule; (*colorante*) colour rinse; (*stile*) cachet

'cachi *nm inv* persimmon ● *a inv* (*colore*) khaki

'cacio *nm* (*formaggio*) cheese

caci'otta *nf* creamy, fairly soft cheese

'caco *nm fam* persimmon

cacofo'nia *nf* cacophony

'cactus *nm inv* cactus

cada'uno *a* each

ca'davere *nm* corpse

cada'verico *a fig* deathly pale

ca'dente *a* falling; ⟨*casa*⟩ crumbling

ca'denza *nf* cadence; (*ritmo*) rhythm; *Mus* cadenza

caden'zare *vt* give rhythm to

caden'zato *a* measured

ca'dere *vi* fall; ⟨*capelli ecc.*⟩ fall out; (*capitombolare*) tumble; ⟨*vestito ecc.*⟩ hang; **far ~** (*di mano*) drop; **~ dal sonno** feel very sleepy; **lasciar ~** drop; **~ dalle nuvole** *fig* be taken aback; **~ dalla finestra** fall out of the window

ca'detto *nm* cadet

ca'duta *nf* fall; *fig* downfall. **~ dei capelli** hair loss. **~ libera** freefall. **~ massi** falling rocks

ca'duto *nm* **i caduti** the dead; **monumento ai caduti** war memorial

caffè *nm inv* coffee; (*locale*) café. **~ corretto** espresso with a dash of liqueur. **~ lungo** weak black coffee. **~ macchiato** coffee with a dash of milk. **~ ristretto** extra-strong espresso coffee. **~ solubile** instant coffee

caffe'ina *nf* caffeine

caffel'latte *nm inv* white coffee

caffette'ria *nf* coffee bar

caffetti'era *nf* coffee-pot

cafo'naggine *nf* boorishness

cafo'nata *nf* boorishness

ca'fone, -a *nmf* boor

cafone'ria *nf (comportamento)* boorishness; **è stata una ~** it was boorish

ca'gare *vi vulg* crap; **va' a ~!** go and get stuffed!

cagio'nare *vt* cause

cagio'nevole *a* delicate

cagli'are *vi* curdle

cagli'arsi *vr* curdle

cagli'ata *nf* curd cheese

caglia'tura *nf* curdling

'cagna *nf* bitch

ca'gnara *nf fam* din

ca'gnesco *a* **guardare qcno in ~** scowl at sb

ca'gnetto *nm* lapdog

C.A.I. *nm abbr* **(Club Alpino Italiano)** *Italian mountain sports association*

cai'mano *nm* cayman

'caio *nm* so-and-so

'Cairo *nm* **il ~** Cairo

'cala *nf* creek

cala'brese *a & nmf* Calabrian

Ca'labria *nf* Calabria

cala'brone *nm* hornet

Cala'hari *nm* **il ~** the Kalahari [Desert]

ca'lamaio *nm* inkpot

cala'maretto *nm* small squid

cala'mari *nmpl* squid *sg*

cala'maro *nm* squid

cala'mita *nf* magnet

calamità *nf inv* calamity. **~ pl naturali** natural disasters

calami'tare *vt* draw *⟨attenzione⟩*

ca'lante *a* waning

ca'lare *vi* come down; *⟨vento:⟩* drop; *(diminuire)* fall; *(tramontare)* set; **~ di peso** lose weight; **~ di tono** *fig* drag ● *vt (abbassare)* lower; *(nei lavori a maglia)* decrease ● *nm (di luna)* waning

ca'larsi *vr* lower oneself

ca'lata *nf (invasione)* invasion

'calca *nf* throng

cal'cagno *nm (pl f* **calcagna)** heel; **stare alle calcagna di qcno** *fig* follow sb around

cal'care¹ *nm* limestone

cal'care² *vt* tread; *(premere)* press [down]; **~ la mano** *fig* exaggerate; **~ le orme di qcno** *fig* follow in sb's footsteps; **~ le scene** *fig* tread the boards

'calce¹ *nf* lime. **~ viva** quicklime

'calce² *nm* **in ~** at the foot of the page

calce'struzzo *nm* concrete

cal'cetto *nm Sport* five-a-side [football]; *(da tavolo)* table football

calci'are *vt* kick

calcia'tore *nm* footballer

calcifi'carsi *vr* calcify

calcificazi'one *nf* calcification

cal'cina *nf* mortar

calci'naccio *nm (pezzo di intonaco)* flake of plaster; *(pezzo di muro)* piece of rubble

'calcio¹ *nm* kick; *Sport* football; *(di arma da fuoco)* butt; **dare un ~ a** kick; **giocare a ~** play football. **~ d'angolo** corner [kick]. **~ di punizione** free kick. **~ di rigore** penalty [kick]

'calcio² *nm Chem* calcium

calcio-mer'cato *nm inv* transfer market

'calco *nm (con carta)* tracing; *(arte)* cast

calco'lare *vt* calculate; *(considerare)* consider

calco'lato *a* calculated

calco'latore *a* calculating ● *nm* calculator; *(macchina elettronica)* computer. **~ digitale** *(calcolatrice)* calculator

calcola'trice *nf* calculating machine

'calcolo *nm* calculation; *Med* stone; **per ~** *fig* out of self-interest; **mi sono fatto i calcoli** *fig* I've weighed up the pros and cons. **~ approssimativo** guesstimate. **~ biliare** gallstone. **~ renale** kidney stone

cal'daia *nf* boiler

caldar'rosta *nf* roast chestnut

caldeggi'are *vt* support

'caldo *a* warm; *(molto caldo)* hot; *⟨situazione, zona⟩* dangerous; *⟨notizie⟩* latest; **non gli fa né ~ né freddo** *fig* he doesn't give a damn; **ondata di ~** heatwave; **tavola calda** snack bar ● *nm* heat; **avere ~** be warm, be hot; **fa ~** it's warm, it's hot

caleido'scopio *nm* kaleidoscope

calen'dario *nm* calendar. **~ sportivo** sporting calendar

ca'lesse *nm* gig

cali'brare *vt* calibrate

cali'brato *a* calibrated; *fig* balanced; **taglie pl calibrate** clothes for non-standard sizes

'calibro *nm* calibre; *(strumento)* callipers *pl*; **di grosso ~** *⟨persona⟩* top attrib

'calice *nm* goblet; *Relig* chalice

californi'ano, -a *a & nmf* Californian

ca'ligine *nm* fog; *(industriale)* smog

call-girl *nf inv* call girl

calligra'fia *nf* handwriting; *(cinese)* calligraphy

calli'grafico *a* **perizia calligrafica** handwriting analysis

cal'ligrafo, -a *nmf* calligrapher

cal'lista *nmf* chiropodist

'callo *nm* corn; **fare il ~ a** become hardened to

cal'loso *a* callous

'calma *nf* calm; **mantenere la ~** keep calm; **prendersela con ~** *fig* take it easy; **fare qcsa con ~** take one's time doing sth

cal'mante *a* calming ● *nm* sedative

cal'mare *vt* calm [down]; *(lenire)* soothe

cal'marsi *vr* calm down; *⟨vento:⟩* drop; *⟨dolore:⟩* die down

calmie'rare *vt* control the prices of

calmi'ere *nm* price control

'calmo *a* calm

'calo *nm Comm* fall; (*di volume*) shrinkage; (*di peso*) loss; **in ~** dwindling

ca'lore *nm* heat; (*moderato*) warmth; **in ~** (*di animale*) on heat

calo'ria *nf* calorie

ca'lorico *a* calorific

calo'rifero *nm* radiator

calorosa'mente *adv* warmly

calorosità *nf fig* warmth

calo'roso *a* warm

ca'lotta *nf* **~ cranica** skullcap. **~ glaciale** icecap. **~ polare** polar icecap

calpe'stare *vt* trample [down]; *fig* trample on ⟨*diritti, sentimenti*⟩; **'vietato ~ l'erba'** 'keep off the grass'

calpe'stio *nm* (*passi*) footsteps *pl*; (*rumore*) stamping

ca'lunnia *nf* slander

calunni'are *vt* slander

calunni'oso *a* slanderous

ca'lura *nf* heat

cal'vario *nm* Calvary; *fig* trial

calvi'nismo *nm* Calvinism

calvi'nista *nmf* Calvinist

cal'vizie *nf* baldness

'calvo *a* bald

'calza *nf* (*da reggicalze*) stocking; (*da uomo*) sock. **~ della befana** ≈ Christmas stocking

calza'maglia *nf* tights *pl*; (*per danza*) leotard

cal'zante *a fig* fitting

cal'zare *vt* (*indossare*) wear; (*mettersi*) put on ● *vi* fit; **~ a pennello** ⟨*indumenti:*⟩ fit like a glove

calza'scarpe *nm inv* shoehorn

calza'tura *nf* footwear; **calzature** *pl* footwear *sg*

calzatu'rificio *nm* shoe factory

cal'zetta *nf* ankle sock; **è una mezza ~** *fig* he's no use

calzet'tone *nm* knee-length woollen sock

cal'zino *nm* sock

calzo'laio *nm* shoe mender

calzole'ria *nf* (*negozio*) shoe shop

calzon'cini *nmpl* shorts. **~ da bagno** swimming trunks

cal'zone *nm Culin* folded pizza with tomato, mozzarella etc inside

cal'zoni *nmpl* trousers, pants *Am.* **~ alla cavallerizza** jodhpurs

camale'onte *nm* chameleon

cambi'ale *nf Comm* bill of exchange

cambia'mento *nm* change

cambi'are *vt* change; move ⟨*casa*⟩; (*fare cambio di*) exchange; **~ canale** *TV* switch over; **~ rotta** *Naut* alter course; **~ l'aria in una stanza** air a room ● *vi* change; (*fare cambio*) exchange

cambi'arsi *vr* change

cambiava'lute *nm* bureau de change

'cambio *nm* change; (*Comm, scambio*) exchange; *Mech* gear; **dare il ~ a qcno** relieve sb; **in ~ di** in exchange for. **~ della guardia** changeover. **~ dell'olio** oil change

Cam'bogia *nf* Cambodia

cambogi'ano *a & nmf* Cambodian

cam'busa *nf* pantry

ca'melia *nf* camellia

'camera *nf* room: (*mobili*) [bedroom] suite; *Phot* camera; **C~** *Pol, Comm* Chamber. **~ ammobiliata** bedsit. **~ ardente** chapel of rest. **~ d'aria** inner tube. **~ blindata** strong room. **C~ di Commercio** Chamber of Commerce. **C~ dei Comuni** House of Commons. **C~ dei Deputati** *Pol* ≈ House of Commons. **~ doppia** double room. **~ a gas** gas chamber. **~ da letto** bedroom. **~ a due letti** twin room. **~ matrimoniale** double room. **~ oscura** darkroom. **~ degli ospiti** guest room. **~ singola** single room

came'rata[1] *nf* (*dormitorio*) dormitory; *Mil* barrack room

came'rata[2] *nmf* mate

camera'tesco *a* comradely

camera'tismo *nm* comradeship

cameri'era *nf* maid; (*di ristorante*) waitress; (*in albergo*) chamber-maid

cameri'ere *nm* manservant; (*di ristorante*) waiter

came'rino *nm* dressing-room

came'ristico *a Mus* chamber

'Camerun *nm* **il ~** Cameroon

'camice *nm* overall

camice'ria *nf* shirt shop

cami'cetta *nf* blouse

ca'micia *nf* shirt; **essere nato con la ~** *fig* be born lucky; **uovo in ~** poached egg. **~ di forza** strait-jacket. **~ nera** Blackshirt. **~ da notte** nightdress; (*da uomo*) nightshirt

camici'aio *nm* (*venditore*) shirtseller; (*sarto*) shirtmaker

camici'ola *nf* vest

cami'netto *nm* fireplace

ca'mino *nm* chimney; (*focolare*) fireplace, hearth

'camion *nm inv* lorry *Br*, truck

camion'cino *nm* van

camio'netta *nf* jeep

camio'nista *nmf* lorry driver *Br*, truck driver

'camma *nf* cam; **albero a camme** *Auto* camshaft

cam'mello *nm* camel; (*tessuto*) camel-hair ● *a inv* (*colore*) camel

cam'meo *nm* cameo

cammi'nare *vi* walk; ⟨*auto, orologio:*⟩ go; **~ avanti e indietro** pace up and down

cammi'nata *nf* walk; **fare una ~** go for a walk

cam'mino *nm* way; **essere in ~** be on the way; **mettersi in ~** set out; **cammin facendo** on the way

camo'milla *nf* camomile; (*bevanda*) camomile tea

camo'millarsi *vr sl* **camomillati!** don't get your knickers in a twist!, cool it!

Ca'morra *nf* local mafia

camor'rista *nmf* member of the 'Camorra'

ca'moscio *nm* chamois; (*pelle*) suede

cam'pagna *nf* country; (*paesaggio*) countryside; *Comm, Mil* campaign; **in ~** in the country. **~ elettorale** election campaign. **~ promozionale** promotional campaign, marketing campaign. **~ pubblicitaria** publicity campaign

campa'gnola *nf Auto* cross-country vehicle

campa'gnolo, -a *a* rustic ● *nm* countryman ● *nf* countrywoman

cam'pale *a* field *attrib;* **giornata ~** *fig* strenuous day

cam'pana *nf* bell; (*di vetro*) belljar; **a ~** bell-shaped; **essere sordo come una ~** be as deaf as a doorpost; **sentire anche l'altra ~** *fig* hear the other side of the story; **vivere sotto una ~ di vetro** *fig* be mollycoddled. **campane** *pl* **a morto** death knell

campa'naccio *nm* cowbell

campa'naro *nm* bell-ringer

campa'nella *nf* (*di tenda*) curtain ring

campa'nello *nm* door-bell; (*cicalino*) buzzer

Cam'pania *nf* Campania

campa'nile *nm* bell tower

campani'lismo *nm* parochialism

campani'lista *nmf* person with a parochial outlook

campani'listico *a* parochial

cam'panula *nf Bot* campanula

cam'pare *vi* live; (*a stento*) get by; **tirare a ~** *fig* live from day to day

cam'pato *a* **~ in aria** unfounded

campeggi'are *vi* camp; (*spiccare*) stand out; **'vietato ~'** 'no camping'

campeggia'tore, -'trice *nmf* camper

cam'peggio *nm* camping; (*terreno*) campsite; **andare in ~** go camping; **fare ~ libero** camp in the wild. **~ per roulotte** caravan site

cam'pestre *a* rural

Campi'doglio *nm* Capitol

'camping *nm inv* campsite

campiona'mento *nm* sampling

campio'nario *nm* [set of] samples ● *a* **fiera campionaria** trade fair

campio'nato *nm* championship. **C~ Mondiale di Calcio** World Cup

campiona'tura *nf* (*di merce*) range of samples; (*in statistica*) sampling. **~ casuale** random sample

campi'one *nm* champion; *Comm* sample; (*esemplare*) specimen; **indagine ~** (*in statistica*) sample. **~ gratuito** free sample. **'~ senza valore'** 'sample, no commercial value'

campio'nessa *nf* ladies' champion

'campo *nm* field; (*accampamento*) camp; *Mil* encampment; **abbandonare il ~** *Mil* desert in the face of the enemy; *fig* throw in the towel; **a tutto ~** *fig* wide-ranging; **avere ~ libero** *fig* have a free hand; **giocare a tutto ~** *Sport* cover the entire pitch. **~ base** base camp. **~ di battaglia** battlefield. **~ da calcio** football pitch. **~ di concentramento** concentration camp. **~ da golf** golf course. **~ di grano** cornfield. **~ da hockey** hockey field. **~ di mais** cornfield. **~ sportivo** sports ground. **~ di sterminio** death camp. **~ da tennis** tennis court

campo'santo *nm* cemetery

'campus *nm inv* (*di università*) campus

camuf'fare *vt* disguise

camuf'farsi *vr* disguise oneself

ca'muso *a* **naso ~** snub nose

'Canada *nm* Canada

cana'dese *a* & *nmf* Canadian

ca'naglia *nf* scoundrel; (*plebaglia*) rabble

ca'nale *nm* channel; (*artificiale*) canal. **Canal Grande** Gran Canal. **~ della Manica** English Channel. **~ di scolo** dyke

canaliz'zare *vt* channel (*acque, energie*)

canalizzazi'one *nf* channelling; (*rete*) pipes *pl*

'canapa *nf* hemp. **~ indiana** (*droga*) cannabis

Ca'narie *nfpl* **le ~** the Canaries

cana'rino *nm* canary

ca'nasta *nf* (*gioco*) canasta

cancel'labile *a* erasable; (*impegno, incontro*) which can be cancelled

cancel'lare *vt* cross out; (*con la gomma*) rub out; *fig* wipe out; (*annullare*) cancel; *Comput* delete, erase

cancel'larsi *vr* be erased, be wiped out

cancel'lata *nf* railings *pl*

cancel'lato *a* cancelled

cancella'tura *nf* erasure

cancellazi'one *nf* cancellation; *Comput* deletion

cancelle'ria *nf* chancellery; (*articoli per scrivere*) stationery

cancelli'ere *nm* chancellor; (*di tribunale*) clerk

cancel'lino *nm* duster

can'cello *nm* gate

cance'rogeno *nm* carcinogen ● *a* carcinogenic

cance'roso *a* cancerous

can'crena *nf* gangrene; **andare in ~** become gangrenous

cancre'noso *a* gangrenous

'cancro *nm* cancer. **C~** *Astr* Cancer; **tropico del C~** Tropic of Cancer

candeggi'are *vt* bleach

candeg'gina *nf* bleach

can'deggio *nm* bleaching

can'dela *nf* candle; *Auto* spark plug; **a lume di ~** by candle-light; (*cena*) candlelit; **tenere la ~** *fig* play gooseberry; **il gioco non vale la ~** the game is not worth the candle

cande'labro *nm* candelabra

cande'letta *nf Med* pessary

candeli'ere *nm* candlestick

cande'line *nfpl* candles

cande'lotto *nm* (*di dinamite*) stick. **~ lacrimogeno** tear gas grenade

candida'mente *adv* innocently

candi'dare *vt* put forward as a candidate

candi'darsi *vr* stand as a candidate

candi'dato, -a *nmf* candidate

candida'tura *nf Pol* candidacy; (*per lavoro*) application '**candido** *a* snow-white; (*sincero*) candid; (*puro*) pure

can'dito *a* candied ● *nm* piece of candied fruit

can'dore *nm* whiteness; *fig* innocence

'**cane** *nm* dog; (*di arma da fuoco*) cock; **un tempo da cani** foul weather; **fa un freddo ~** it's bitterly cold; **non c'era un ~** *fig* there wasn't a soul about; **solo come un ~** *fig* all on one's own; **essere come ~ e gatto** *fig* fight like cat and dog; **essere un ~** ‹*attore, cantante*› be appalling, be a dog *sl*; **fatto da cani** *fig* ‹*lavoro*› botched; **mangiare da cani** *fig* eat very badly; **figlio di un ~** *fam* son of a bitch. **~ da caccia** hunting dog. **~ per ciechi** guide-dog. **~ da corsa** greyhound. **~ da guardia** guard-dog. **~ lupo** alsatian. **~ poliziotto** police dog. **~ da salotto** lapdog. **~ sciolto** *fig* maverick

ca'nestro *nm* basket; **fare ~** score a basket

'**canfora** *nf* camphor

cangi'ante *a* iridescent; **seta ~** shot silk

can'guro *nm* kangaroo

ca'nicola *nf* scorching heat

ca'nile *nm* kennel; (*di allevamento*) kennels *pl*. **~ municipale** dog pound

ca'nino *a & nm* canine

ca'nizie *nm* white hair

'**canna** *nf* reed; (*da zucchero*) cane; (*di fucile*) barrel; (*bastone*) stick; (*di bicicletta*) crossbar; (*asta*) rod; (*fam: hascisch*) joint; **povero in ~** destitute. **~ fumaria** flue. **~ da pesca** fishing-rod

'**cannabis** *nm inv* cannabis

can'nella *nf* cinnamon

cannel'loni *nmpl* **~ al forno** *rolls of pasta stuffed with meat and baked in the oven*

can'neto *nm* bed of reeds

can'nibale *nm* cannibal

canniba'lismo *nm* cannibalism

cannocchi'ale *nm* telescope

can'noli *nmpl* **~ alla siciliana** *cylindrical pastries filled with ricotta and candied fruit*

canno'nata *nf* cannon shot; **è una ~** *fig* it's brilliant

cannon'cino *nm* (*dolce*) cream horn

can'none *nm* cannon; *fig* ace

cannoneggia'mento *nm* cannonade

caneggi'era *nf* gunboat

cannoni'ere *nm* (*soldato*) gunner; (*calciatore*) top goal scorer

can'nuccia *nf* [drinking] straw; (*di pipa*) stem

ca'noa *nf* canoe

'**canone** *nm* canon; (*affitto*) rent; **equo ~** rent set by law

ca'nonica *nf* manse

ca'nonico *nm* canon

canoniz'zare *vt* canonize

canonizzazi'one *nf* canonization

ca'noro *a* melodious

ca'notta *nf* (*estiva*) vest top

canot'taggio *nm* canoeing; (*voga*) rowing

canotti'era *nf* vest

canotti'ere *nm* oarsman

ca'notto *nm* [rubber] dinghy

cano'vaccio *nm* (*trama*) plot; (*straccio*) duster; (*per ricamo*) canvas

can'tante *nmf* singer. **~ lirico** opera-singer

can'tare *vt/i* sing; **~ vittoria** *fig* crow; **fare ~ qcno** *sl* make sb talk; **me le ha cantate** *fam* he told me off

canta'storie *nmf inv* story-teller

can'tata *nf Mus* cantata

can'tato *a* sung

cantau'tore, -'trice *nmf* singer-songwriter

canticchi'are *vt* sing softly; (*a bocca chiusa*) hum

'**cantico** *nm* hymn

canti'ere *nm* yard; *Naut* shipyard; (*di edificio*) construction site. **~ navale** naval dockyard; (*per piccole imbarcazioni*) boatyard

cantie'ristica *nf* construction

canti'lena *nf* singsong; (*ninna-nanna*) lullaby

can'tina *nf* cellar; (*osteria*) wine shop

'**canto**[1] *nm* singing; (*canzone*) song; *Relig* chant; (*poesia*) poem. **~ di Natale, ~ natalizio** Christmas carol. **~ degli uccelli** birdsong

'**canto**[2] *nm* (*angolo*) corner; (*lato*) side; **dal ~ mio** for my part; **d'altro ~** on the other hand

canto'nale *a* cantonal

canto'nata *nf* **prendere una ~** *fig* be sadly mistaken

can'tone *nm* canton; (*angolo*) corner

can'tore *nm* chorister

can'tuccio *nm* nook; **stare in un ~** *fig* hold oneself aloof

ca'nuto *a liter* whitehaired

canzo'nare *vt* tease

canzona'torio *a* teasing

canzona'tura *nf* teasing

can'zone *nf* song. **~ d'amore** love song

canzo'netta *nf fam* pop song

canzoni'ere *nm* songbook

'**caos** *nm* chaos

ca'otico *a* chaotic

C.A.P. *nm abbr* (**Codice di Avviamento Postale**) post code, zip code *Am*

cap. *abbr* (**capitolo**) chap

ca'pace *a* able; (*esperto*) skilled; ‹*stadio, contenitore*› big; **~ di** (*disposto a*) capable of; **è ~ a cantare?** can he sing?

capacità *nf inv* ability; (*attitudine*) skill; (*capienza*) capacity. **~ d'assorbimento** absorbency. **~ di credito** creditworthiness. **~ di memorizzazione** retentiveness. **~ produttiva** production capacity. **~ di resistenza** staying power

capaci'tarsi *vr* **~ di** (*rendersi conto*) understand; (*accorgersi*) realize

ca'panna *nf* hut

capan'nello *nm* knot of people; **fare ~ intorno a qcno/qcsa** gather round sb/sth

ca'panno *nm* **~ degli attrezzi** garden shed. **~ da spiaggia** beach hut, cabana

capan'none *nm* shed; *Aeron* hangar

caparbietà *nf* obstinacy

ca'parbio *a* obstinate

ca'parra *nf* deposit

capa'tina *nf* short visit; **fare una ~ in città/da qcno** pop into town/in on sb

ca'pello *nm* hair; **non torcere un ~ a qcno** *fig* not lay a finger on sb; **capelli** *pl* (*capigliatura*) hair *sg*; **asciugarsi/lavarsi i capelli** dry/wash one's hair; **avere i capelli a spazzola** have a crew-cut; **spaccare il ~ in quattro** split hairs; **averne fin sopra i capelli** *fig* be fed up to the back teeth; **mettersi le mani nei capelli** *fig* tear one's hair out. **capelli** *pl* **d'angelo** vermicelli

capel'lone *nm* long-haired type, hippie

capel'luto *a* hairy; **cuoio ~** scalp

ca'pestro *nm* noose; **contratto ~** strait-jacket of a contract

capez'zale *nm* bolster; *fig* bedside

ca'pezzolo *nm* nipple

capi'ente *a* capacious

capi'enza *nf* capacity

capiglia'tura *nf* hair

capil'lare *a* capillary

ca'pire *vt* understand; **non capisco** I don't understand; **~ male** misunderstand; **si capisce!** naturally!; **sì, ho capito** yes, I see

capi'tale *a Jur* capital; (*principale*) main ● *nf* (*città*) capital ● *nm Comm* capital. **~ di avviamento** start-up capital. **~ azionario** *Fin* equity capital, share capital. **~ di investimento** investment capital. **~ di rischio** venture capital. **~ sociale** *Fin* share capital

capita'lismo *nm* capitalism

capita'lista *nmf* capitalist

capita'listico *a* capitalist

capitaliz'zare *vt* capitalize

capitalizzazi'one *nf* capitalization

capita'nare *vt* lead ⟨*rivolta*⟩; *Sport* captain

capitane'ria *nf* **~ di porto** port authorities *pl*

capi'tano *nm* captain. **~ di lungo corso** *Naut* captain

capi'tare *vi* (*giungere per caso*) come; (*accadere*) happen

'capite: pro ~ *adv* per capita

capi'tello *nm Archit* capital

capito'lare *vi* capitulate

capitolazi'one *nf* capitulation

ca'pitolo *nm* chapter

capi'tombolo *nm* headlong fall; **fare un ~** tumble down

'capo *nm* head; (*chi comanda*) boss *fam*; (*di vestiario*) item; *Geog* cape; (*in tribù*) chief; (*parte estrema*) top; **a ~** (*in dettato*) new paragraph; **da ~** over again; **giramento di ~** dizziness; **mal di ~** headache; **in ~ a un mese** within a month; **non ha né ~ né coda** ⟨*discorso, ragionamento*⟩ I can't make head nor tail of it. **~ d'abbigliamento** item of clothing. **~ d'accusa** *Jur* charge, count. **~ di bestiame** head of cattle. **C~ di Buona Speranza** Cape of Good Hope. **~ reparto** head of department. **il C~ Verde** Cape Verde

capo'banda *nm Mus* band-master; (*di delinquenti*) ringleader

capocameri'ere, -a *nm* head waiter ● *nf* head waitress

ca'pocchia *nf* **~ di spillo** pinhead

ca'poccia *nm* (*fam: testa*) nut

capocci'one, -a *nmf fam* brainbox

capo'classe *nmf* ≈ form captain

capocor'data *nmf* (*alpinista*) leader

capocu'oco, -a *nmf* headcook

capo'danno *nm* New Year's Day

capofa'miglia *nm* head of the family

capo'fitto *nm* **a ~** headlong

capo'giro *nm* giddiness

capo'gruppo *nm* group leader

capola'voro *nm* masterpiece

capo'linea *nm* terminus

capo'lino *nm* **fare ~** peep in

capo'lista *nmf Sport* league leaders *pl*; *Pol* candidate whose name appears first on the list

capolu'ogo *nm* main town

capo'mafia *nm* Mafia boss

capo'mastro *nm* master builder

capo'rale *nm* lance-corporal

capore'parto *nmf* department head, head of department

capo'sala *nf inv Med* ward sister

capo'saldo *nm* stronghold

capo'scalo *nm* airline manager

capo'squadra *nm inv* foreman; *Sport* team captain

capostazi'one *nm inv* stationmaster

capo'stipite *nmf* (*di famiglia*) progenitor; (*di esemplare*) archetype

capo'tavola *nmf* (*persona*) head of the table; **sedere a ~** sit at the head of the table

capo'treno *nm* guard

ca'potta *nf* top

capot'tare *vi* somersault

capouf'ficio *nmf* department head

capo'verso *nm* first line; *Jur* paragraph

capo'volgere *vt* overturn; *fig* reverse

capo'volgersi *vr* overturn; ⟨*barca:*⟩ capsize; *fig* be reversed

capovolgi'mento *nm* turnaround

capo'volto *pp di* **capovolgere** ● *a* upside-down

'cappa *nf* cloak; (*di camino*) cowl; (*di cucina*) hood

cappa'santa *nf Culin* scallop

cap'pella *nf* chapel. **la C~ Sistina** the Sistine Chapel

cappel'lano *nm* chaplain

cappel'letti *nmpl* small filled pasta parcels

cappelli'era *nf* hatbox

cappel'lino *nm* **~ di carta** party hat

cap'pello *nm* hat; **tanto di ~!** I take my hat off to you!. **~ a cilindro** top hat. **~ da cow boy** stetson, cowboy hat. **~ di feltro** homburg. **~ di paglia** straw hat. **~ da sole** sun hat

'cappero *nm* caper; **capperi!** *fam* gosh!

'cappio *nm* noose; **avere il ~ al collo** *fig* have a millstone round one's neck; ⟨*marito:*⟩ be henpecked

cap'pone nm capon

cap'potto nm [over]coat

cappuc'cino nm (frate) Capuchin [friar]; (bevanda) white coffee

cap'puccio nm hood; (di penna stilografica) cap

'capra nf goat; salvare ~ e cavoli fig run with the hare and hunt with the hounds

ca'pretto nm kid

ca'priccio nm whim; (bizzarria) freak; fare i capricci have tantrums

capricci'oso a capricious; ⟨bambino⟩ naughty

Capri'corno nm Astr Capricorn

capri'foglio nm honeysuckle

ca'prino nm goat's cheese

capri'ola nf somersault

capri'olo nm roe-deer

'capro nm [billy-]goat. ~ espiatorio scape-goat

ca'prone nm [billy-]goat

'capsula nf capsule; (di proiettile) cap; (di dente) crown

cap'tare vt Radio, TV pick up; catch ⟨attenzione⟩

C.A.R. nm abbr (Centro Addestramento Reclute) basic training camp

cara'bina nf carbine

carabini'ere nm carabiniere; carabini'eri pl Italian police force (which is a branch of the army)

ca'raffa nf carafe

Ca'raibi nmpl (zona) Caribbean sg; (isole) Caribbean Islands; il mar dei ~ the Caribbean [Sea]

cara'ibico a Caribbean

cara'mella nf sweet. ~ alla menta mint

cara'mello nm caramel

ca'rato nm carat

ca'rattere nm character; (caratteristica) characteristic; di buon ~ good-natured; in ~ con (intonato) in keeping with; è una persona di ~ (deciso) he's got character. ~ jolly Comput wild card. ~ tipografico typeface

caratte'rino nm difficult nature

caratte'rista nm character actor ● nf character actress

caratte'ristico, -a a characteristic; (pittoresco) quaint ● nf characteristic

caratteriz'zare vt characterize

caratterizzazi'one nf characterization

cara'tura nf carats; Comm part-ownership

'caravan nm inv caravan

carboi'drato nm carbohydrate

car'bonchio nm anthrax

carbon'cino nm (per disegno) charcoal

car'bone nm coal; stare sui carboni ardenti fig be on tenterhooks. ~ fossile anthracite

carbo'nifero a carboniferous

car'bonio nm carbon. ~ 14 carbon-14

carboniz'zare vt burn to a cinder, burn to a crisp; è morto carbonizzato he was burned to death

carbu'rante nm fuel

carbu'rare vt carburize ● vi fig be firing on all four cylinders; il motore carbura male the mixture is wrong

carbura'tore nm carburettor

carburazi'one nf carburation

car'cassa nf carcass; fig old wreck

carce'rario a prison attrib

carce'rato, -a nmf prisoner

carcerazi'one nf imprisonment. ~ preventiva preventive detention

'carcere nm prison; (punizione) imprisonment. ~ di massima sicurezza maximum-security prison

carceri'ere, -a nmf gaoler

carci'noma nm carcinoma

carcio'fino nm baby artichoke

carci'ofo nm artichoke

cardel'lino nm goldfinch

car'diaco a cardiac; disturbo ~ heart disease

'cardigan nm inv cardigan

cardi'nale a & nm cardinal

'cardine nm hinge

cardiochi'rurgo nm heart surgeon

cardiolo'gia nf cardiology

cardi'ologo nm heart specialist

cardio'patico nmf person suffering from a heart complaint

cardio'tonico nm heart stimulant

cardiovasco'lare a cardiovascular

'cardo nm thistle

ca'rena nf Naut bottom

care'naggio nm bacino di ~ dry dock

ca'rente a ~ di lacking in

ca'renza nf lack; (scarsità) scarcity

care'stia nf famine; (mancanza) dearth

ca'rezza nf stroke; (di madre, amante) caress; fare una ~ a stroke; ⟨madre, amante:⟩ caress

carez'zare vt stroke; ⟨madre, amante:⟩ caress

carez'zevole a fig sweet

'cargo nm inv (nave) cargo boat, freighter; (aereo) cargo plane, freight plane

cari'are vt decay

cari'arsi vi decay

cari'ato a decayed

'carica nf office; Mil, Electr charge; fig drive; dotato di una forte ~ di simpatia really likeable. ~ esplosiva payload

caricabatte'ria nm inv battery charger

cari'care vt load ⟨camion, software⟩; Mil, Electr charge; wind up ⟨orologio⟩

cari'carsi vr Electr charge [up]; ~ di lavoro take on too much work

cari'cato a fig affected

carica'tore nm (per proiettile) magazine; (per diapositive) carousel

carica'tura nf caricature

caricatu'rale a grotesque

caricatu'rista nmf caricaturist

'carico a loaded (di with); ⟨colore⟩ strong; ⟨orologio⟩ wound [up]; ⟨batteria⟩ charged ● nm load; (di nave) cargo; (il caricare) loading; avere un ~ di lavoro have a heavy workload; **testimone a** ~ *Jur* witness for the prosecution; **a** ~ **di** *Comm* to be charged to; ⟨*persona*⟩ dependent on. ~ **utile** payload

'**carie** *nf* [tooth] decay

caril'lon *nm inv* musical box

ca'rino *a* pretty; (*piacevole*) agreeable

ca'risma *nm* charisma

cari'smatico *a* charismatic

carità *nf* charity; **per** ~! (*come rifiuto*) God forbid!

carita'tevole *a* charitable

car'linga *nf* fuselage

car'lino *nm* pug

carnagi'one *nf* complexion

car'naio *nm fig* shambles

car'nale *a* carnal; **cugino** ~ first cousin

'**carne** *nf* flesh; (*alimento*) meat; **di** ~ meaty. ~ **macinata** mince, ground beef *Am*. ~ **di maiale** pork. ~ **di manzo** beef. ~ **di vitello** veal

car'nefice *nm* executioner

carnefi'cina *nf* slaughter

carne'vale *nm* carnival

carneva'lesco *a* carnival

car'nivoro *nm* carnivore ● *a* carnivorous

car'noso *a* fleshy

'**caro, -a** *a* dear; **cari saluti** kind regards ● *nmf fam* darling, dear; **i miei cari** my nearest and dearest

ca'rogna *nf* carcass; *fig* bastard

caro'sello *nm* merry-go-round

ca'rota *nf* carrot

caro'vana *nf* caravan; (*di veicoli*) convoy

caro'vita *nm* high cost of living

'**carpa** *nf* carp

car'paccio *nm finely sliced raw beef with oil, lemon and grated Parmesan*

Car'pazi *nmpl* **i** ~ the Carpathians

carpenti'ere *nm* carpenter

car'pire *vt* seize; (*con difficoltà*) extort

car'pone, car'poni *adv* on all fours; **camminare** ~ crawl

car'rabile *a* suitable for vehicles; **passo** ~ = **passo carraio**

car'raio *a* **passo** ~ *entrance to driveway, garage etc where parking is forbidden*

carreggi'ata *nf* roadway; **doppia** ~ dual carriageway, divided highway *Am*; **rimettersi in** ~ *fig* straighten oneself out

carrel'lata *nf* (*fig: di notizie*) TV pan; round-up

car'rello *nm* trolley; (*di macchina da scrivere*) carriage; *Aeron* undercarriage; *Cinema, TV* dolly. ~ **d'atterraggio** *Aeron* landing gear. ~ **dei dolci** dessert trolley. ~ **portabagagli** luggage trolley, baggage cart *Am*

car'retta *nf* (*veicolo vecchio*) old banger; **tirare la** ~ *fig* plod along

car'retto *nm* cart

carri'era *nf* career; **di gran** ~ at full speed; **fare** ~ get on

carrie'rismo *nm* careerism

carrie'rista *nmf* **è un** ~ his career is all that matters

carri'ola *nf* wheelbarrow

'**carro** *nm* cart. ~ **armato** tank. ~ **attrezzi** breakdown vehicle, wrecker *Am*. ~ **funebre** hearse. ~ **merci** truck

car'rozza *nf* carriage; *Rail* coach, car. ~ **bagagliaio** *Rail* guard's van. ~ **belvedere** *Rail* observation car. ~ **cuccette** sleeping car. ~ **fumatori** *Rail* smoker. ~ **letti** *Rail* sleeping car. ~ **ristorante** *Rail* restaurant car, buffet car

carroz'zella *nf* (*per bambini*) pram; (*per invalidi*) wheelchair

carrozze'ria *nf* bodywork; (*officina*) bodyshop

carrozzi'ere *nm* panel beater

carroz'zina *nf* pram; (*pieghevole*) pushchair, stroller *Am*

carroz'zone *nm* (*di circo*) caravan; (*fig: organizzazione*) slow-moving great monster of an organization

car'ruba *nf* carob

car'rubo *nm* carob

car'rucola *nf* pulley

'**carta** *nf* paper; (*da gioco*) card; (*statuto*) charter; *Geog* map. ~ **di addebito** charge card, debit card. ~ **d'argento** senior citizens' railcard. ~ **assegni** cheque card. ~ **assorbente** blotting-paper. ~ **carbone** carbon paper. ~ **di credito** credit card. ~ **crespata** crepe paper. ~ **geografica** map. ~ **d'identità** identity card. ~ **igienica** toilet-paper. ~ **d'imbarco** boarding pass, boarding card. ~ **intelligente** smart card. ~ **da lettere** writing-paper. ~ **millimetrata** graph paper. ~ **da pacchi** wrapping paper. ~ **da parati** wallpaper. ~ **da regali** giftwrap. ~ **di riso** rice paper. ~ **smerigliata** emery paper. ~ **stagnola** silver paper; *Culin* aluminium foil. ~ **straccia** waste paper. ~ **stradale** road map. ~ **termica** thermal paper. ~ **topografica** ≈ Ordnance Survey Map. ~ **velina** tissue-paper. ~ **verde** *Auto* green card. ~ **vetrata** sandpaper. ~ **dei vini** wine-list

cartacar'bone *nf* carbon paper

car'taccia *nf* waste paper

car'taceo *a* paper

carta'modello *nm* pattern

cartamo'neta *nf* paper money

carta'pecora *nf* vellum

carta'pesta *nf* papier mâché

carta'straccia *nf* waste paper

cartave'trare *vt* sand [down]

car'teggio *nm* correspondence

car'tella *nf* (*per documenti ecc*) briefcase; (*di cartone*) folder; (*di scolaro*) satchel. ~ **clinica** medical record

cartel'lina *nf* document wallet, folder

cartel'lino *nm* (*etichetta*) label; (*dei prezzi*) price-tag; (*di presenza*) time-card; **timbrare il** ~ clock in; (*all'uscita*) clock out

car'tello *nm* sign; (*pubblicitario*) poster; (*stradale*) road sign; (*di protesta*) placard; (*Comm, di droga*) cartel

cartel'lone *nm* poster; *Theat* bill. ~ **pubblicitario** billboard

cartello'nista *nmf* poster designer
cartello'nistica *nf* poster designing
carti'era *nf* paper-mill
carti'lagine *nf* cartilage
car'tina *nf* map. ~ **di tornasole** litmus paper
car'toccio *nm* paper bag; **al ~** *Culin* baked in foil
cartogra'fia *nf* cartography
car'tografo *nm* cartographer
carto'laio, -a *nmf* stationer
cartole'ria *nf* stationer's [shop]
cartolibre'ria *nf* stationer's and book shop
carto'lina *nf* postcard. ~ **postale** postcard. ~ **[precetto]** call-up papers
carto'mante *nmf* fortune-teller
carton'cino *nm* (*materiale*) card; (*biglietto*) card
car'tone *nm* cardboard; (*arte*) cartoon. ~ **animato** [animated] cartoon. ~ **ondulato** corrugated cardboard. ~ **di uova** egg box
car'tuccia *nf* cartridge; **mezza ~** *fig* weakling. ~ **d'inchiostro** ink cartridge
'casa *nf* house; (*abitazione propria*) home; (*ditta*) firm; **amico di ~** family friend; **andare a ~** go home; **uscire di ~** leave the house; **essere di ~** be like one of the family; **fatto in ~** home-made. ~ **di correzione** ≈ reform school. ~ **di cura** nursing home. ~ **del custode** gatehouse. ~ **madre** *Comm* parent company. ~ **di moda** fashion house. ~ **in multiproprietà** timeshare. ~ **popolare** council house. ~ **di riposo** old people's home. ~ **di sartoria** fashion house. ~ **dello studente** hall of residence. ~ **per le vacanze** holiday home
ca'sacca *nf* military coat; (*giacca*) jacket
ca'saccio *adv* **a ~** at random; **sparare a ~ su qcno/qcsa** take a potshot at sb/sth
ca'sale *nm* (*gruppo di case*) hamlet; (*casolare*) farmhouse
casa'linga *nf* housewife
casa'lingo *a* domestic; (*fatto in casa*) home-made; (*amante della casa*) home-loving; (*semplice*) homely ● *nm* **casalinghi** *pl* household goods
casa'nova *nm inv* (*donnaiolo*) Casanova
ca'sata *nf* family
ca'sato *nm* family name
ca'scante *a* falling; (*floscio*) flabby
ca'scare *vi* fall [down]
ca'scata *nf* (*di acqua*) waterfall
casca'tore, -'trice *nm* stuntman ● *nf* stuntwoman
cas'chetto *nm* **[capelli a] ~** bob
ca'scina *nf* farm building
casci'nale *nf* farmhouse
'casco *nm* crash-helmet; (*asciuga-capelli*) [hair-]drier. ~ **di banane** bunch of bananas. **Caschi pl blu** *Mil* Blue Helmets, Blue Berets
caseggi'ato *nm* block of flats *Br*, apartment block
casei'ficio *nm* dairy
ca'sella *nf* pigeon-hole. ~ **postale** post office box, PO box; (*elettronica*) mailbox

casel'lante *nmf* (*per treni*) signalman; (*in autostrada*) toll collector
casel'lario *nm* (*mobile*) filing cabinet; (*di documenti*) file. ~ **giudiziario** record of convictions; **avere il ~ giudiziario vuoto** have no criminal record
ca'sello *nm* (*di autostrada*) [motorway] toll booth
case'reccio *a* home-made
ca'serma *nf* barracks *pl*; (*dei carabinieri*) [police] station; **da ~** (*linguaggio*) barrack room *attrib*. ~ **dei carabinieri** military police station. ~ **dei pompieri, ~ dei vigili del fuoco** fire station
caser'mone *nm pej* barracks *pl*
cash and carry *nm inv* cash-and-carry
casi'nista *nmf fam* muddler
ca'sino *nm fam* (*bordello*) brothel; (*fig sl: confusione*) mess; **da ~** (*disordine*) mess; **un ~ di** loads of; **è un ~** (*complicato*) it's too complicated
casinò *nm inv* casino
ca'sistica *nf* (*classificazione*) record of occurrences
'caso *nm* chance; (*fatto, circostanza, Med, Gram*) case; **a ~** at random; **se mai** if need be; **far ~** a pay attention to; **non far ~ a** take no account of; **per ~** by chance. ~ **[giudiziario]** [legal] case. ~ **urgente** *Med* emergency case
caso'lare *nm* farmhouse
'caspita *int* good gracious
'cassa *nf* till; (*di legno*) crate; *Comm* cash; (*luogo di pagamento*) cash desk; (*mobile*) chest; (*istituto bancario*) bank. ~ **automatica prelievi** cash dispenser, automatic teller. ~ **comune** kitty ~ **continua** autobank. ~ **da morto** coffin. ~ **di risparmio** savings bank. ~ **toracica** ribcage
cassa'forte *nf* safe
cassa'panca *nf* linen chest
cas'sata *nf* ice-cream cake
cas'sero *nm Naut* quarterdeck
casseru'ola *nf* saucepan
cas'setta *nf* case; (*per registratore*) cassette. **far buona ~** *Theatr* be good box-office. ~ **degli attrezzi** toolbox. ~ **delle lettere** post-box, letterbox. ~ **delle offerte** charity box. ~ **portapane** breadbin. ~ **portavalori** cash box. ~ **del pronto soccorso** first-aid kit. ~ **di sicurezza** strong-box
cas'setto *nm* drawer; (*di fotocopiatrice ecc*) tray. ~ **di inserimento [dei] fogli** paper feed tray
casset'tone *nm* chest of drawers
cassi'ere, -a *nmf* cashier; (*di supermercato*) checkout assistant, checkout operator; (*di banca*) teller
cassinte'grato *nmf* person who has been laid off
cas'sone *nm* (*cassa*) chest; (*per acqua*) cofferdam
casso'netto *nm* rubbish bin, trash can *Am*
'casta *nf* caste
ca'stagna *nf* chestnut; **prendere qcno in**

~ *fig* catch sb in the act. ~ **d'India** horse chestnut

casta'gnaccio *nm tart from Tuscany made with chestnut flour*

casta'gneto *nm* chestnut grove

ca'stagno *nm* chestnut[-tree]

casta'gnola *nf (petardo)* firecracker

ca'stano *a* chestnut; ⟨*occhi, capelli*⟩ brown

ca'stello *nm* castle; *(impalcatura)* scaffold. ~ **incantato** enchanted castle. ~ **di sabbia** sandcastle

casti'gare *vt* punish

casti'gato *a (casto)* chaste; ⟨*abito, atteggiamento*⟩ prim and proper

ca'stigo *nm* punishment

castità *nf* chastity

'casto *a* chaste

ca'storo *nm* beaver

ca'strante *a fig* frustrating

ca'strare *vt* castrate

ca'strato *a* castrated; *(inibito)* inhibited; *(cantante)* castrato

castrazi'one *nf* gelding

ca'strone *nm* gelding

castrone'ria *nf fam* rubbish

'casual *nm inv* casual wear

casu'ale *a* chance *attrib*

casual'mente *adv* by chance

ca'supola *nf* little house

cata'clisma *nm fig* upheaval

cata'comba *nf* catacomb

cata'falco *nm* catafalque

cata'fascio *nm* **andare a** ~ go to rack and ruin

cata'litico *a* **marmitta catalitica** *Auto* catalytic converter

cataliz'zare *vt fig* heighten

cataliz'zato *a Auto* fitted with a catalytic converter

catalizza'tore *a Phys* catalysing; **centro** ~ *fig* catalyst ● *nm Auto* catalytic converter; *fig* catalyst

catalo'gabile *a* which can be listed

catalo'gare *vt* catalogue

catalogazi'one *nf* cataloguing

cata'logna *nf type of chicory with large leaves*

ca'talogo *nm* catalogue

catama'rano *nm (da diporto)* catamaran

cata'pecchia *nf* hovel; *fam* dump

cata'pulta *nf* catapult

catapul'tare *vt (scaraventare fuori)* eject

catapul'tarsi *vr (precipitarsi)* dive

catarifran'gente *nm* reflector

ca'tarro *nm* catarrh

catar'roso *a* ⟨*voce*⟩ catarrhal

ca'tarsi *nf inv* catharsis

ca'tartico *a* cathartic

ca'tasta *nf* pile

cata'stale *a* **registro** ~ land registry; **rendita** ~ revenue from landed property

ca'tasto *nm* land register

ca'tastrofe *nf* catastrophe

cata'strofico *a* catastrophic

catastro'fismo *nm* catastrophe theory

catch *nm* all-in wrestling

cate'chismo *nm* catechism

catego'ria *nf* category

cate'gorico *a* categorical

ca'tena *nf* chain. ~ **montuosa** mountain range. **catene** *pl* **da neve** [snow] chains

cate'naccio *nm* bolt

cate'nella *nf (collana)* chain; *(di orologio)* watch chain; **tirare la** ~ *(del gabinetto)* flush, pull the plug

cate'nina *nf* chain

cate'ratta *nf* cataract

ca'terva *nf* **una** ~ **di** heaps of, loads of

ca'tetere *nm* catheter

'catgut *nm inv* catgut

cati'nella *nf* basin; **piovere a catinelle** bucket down

ca'tino *nm* basin

ca'todico *a* cathode; **raggi catodici** cathode rays

ca'torcio *nm fam* old wreck

catra'mare *vt* tar

ca'trame *nm* tar

'cattedra *nf (tavolo di insegnante)* desk; *(di università)* chair

catte'drale *nf* cathedral

catte'dratico, -a *nmf* professor ● *a (pedante)* pedantic; ⟨*insegnamento*⟩ university *attrib*

catti'veria *nf* wickedness; *(azione)* wicked action; **fare una** ~ **a qcno** be nasty to sb

cattività *nf* captivity

cat'tivo *a* bad; ⟨*bambino*⟩ naughty

cattocomu'nista *nmf* Catholic-communist

cattoli'cesimo *nm* Catholicism

cat'tolico, -a *a & nmf* [Roman] Catholic

cat'tura *nf* capture

cattu'rare *vt* capture

cau'casico, -a *nmf* Caucasian

'Caucaso *nm* **il** ~ the Caucasus

caucciù *nm* rubber

'causa *nf* cause; *Jur* lawsuit; **far** ~ **a qcno** sue sb; ~ **di forza maggiore** circumstances beyond one's control; *(in assicurazione)* act of God

cau'sale *a* causal

cau'sare *vt* cause

'caustico *a* caustic

cauta'mente *adv* cautiously

cau'tela *nf* caution

caute'lare *vt* protect

caute'larsi *vr* take precautions

cauteriz'zare *vt* cauterize

cauterizzazi'one *nf* cauterization

'cauto *a* cautious

cauzi'one *nf* security; *(per libertà provvisoria)* bail; *(deposito)* deposit

cav. *abbr* **(cavaliere)** Kt, Knight

'cava *nf* quarry; *fig* mine

caval'care *vt* ride; *(stare a cavalcioni)* sit astride

caval'cata *nf* ride; *(corteo)* cavalcade

cavalca'via *nm* flyover

cavalci'oni: a ~ *adv* astride

cavali'ere *nm* rider; (*titolo*) knight; (*accompagnatore*) escort; (*al ballo*) partner

cavalle'resco *a* chivalrous

cavalle'ria *nf* chivalry; *Mil* cavalry

cavalle'rizzo, -a *nm* horseman ● *nf* horse-woman

caval'letta *nf* grasshopper

caval'letto *nm* trestle; (*di macchina fotografica*) tripod; (*di pittore*) easel

caval'lina *nf* (*ginnastica*) horse; (*gioco*) leap-frog; **correre la ~** *fig* pursue a life of pleasure

caval'lino *a* equine

ca'vallo *nm* horse; (*misura di potenza*) horsepower; (*scacchi*) knight; (*dei pantaloni*) crotch; **a ~** on horseback; **andare a ~** go horse-riding. **~ di battaglia** war horse. **~ a dondolo** rocking-horse. **~ da tiro** carthorse. **~ di Troia** Trojan horse

caval'lona *nf pej* ungainly female

caval'lone *nm* (*ondata*) roller

caval'luccio *nm* **~ marino** sea horse

ca'vare *vt* take out; (*di dosso*) take off; **cavarsela** get away with it; **se la cava bene** he's/she's doing all right

cavasti'vali *nm inv* bootjack

cava'tappi *nm inv* corkscrew

ca'veau *nm inv* (*di banca*) vault

ca'verna *nf* cave

caver'nicolo, -a *nmf* cave dweller

caver'noso *a* (*voce*) deep

ca'vetto *nm Electr* lead

ca'vezza *nf* halter; **mettere la ~ al collo a qcno** put sb on a tight rein

'cavia *nf* guinea-pig

cavi'ale *nm* caviar

ca'viglia *nf* ankle

cavil'lare *vi* quibble

ca'villo *nm* quibble

cavil'loso *a* pettifogging

cavità *nf inv* cavity

'cavo *a* hollow ● *nm* cavity; (*di metallo*) cable; *Naut* rope; **televisione via ~** cable TV. **~ di collegamento** [connecting] cable. **~ seriale** serial cable. **~ di spiegamento** rip-cord

cavo'lata *nf fam* rubbish; **non dire cavolate** *fam* don't talk rubbish; **non fare cavolate** *fam* don't act like an idiot

cavo'letto *nm* **~ di Bruxelles** Brussels sprout

cavolfi'ore *nm* cauliflower

'cavolo *nm* cabbage; **~!** *fam* sugar!; **non ho capito un ~** *fam* I understood bugger-all; **che ~ succede?** what the heck is going on?. **~ cappuccio** spring cabbage

caz'zata *nf vulg* shit; **non dire cazzate** don't talk shit; **non fare cazzate** don't fuck things up

'cazzo *vulg nm* prick ● *int* fuck!; **non capisce un ~** he doesn't understand a fucking thing; **non me ne importa un ~!** I don't give a fuck!; **sono cazzi miei!** it's my fucking business!

caz'zotto *nm* punch; **prendere qcno a cazzotti** beat sb up

cazzu'ola *nf* trowel

CB *nf abbr* (**banda cittadina**) CB

cc *abbr* (**centimetri cubi**) cc

c/c *abbr* (**conto corrente**) c/a

CCT *nm abbr* (**Certificato di Credito del Tesoro**) T-bill

CD *nm inv* CD

CD-ROM *nm inv* CD-Rom

ce *pers pron* (*a noi*) us; **ce lo ha dato** he gave it to us ● *adv* there; **ce ne sono molti** there are many; **ce ne vuole!** it takes some doing!

cec'chino *nm* sniper; *Pol* MP who votes against his own party

'cece *nm* chick-pea

cecità *nf* blindness

ceco, -a *a & nmf* Czech; **la Repubblica Ceca** the Czech Republic

Cecoslo'vacchia *nf* Czechoslovakia

cecoslo'vacco, -a *a & nmf* Czechoslovak

'cedere *vi* (*arrendersi*) surrender; (*concedere*) yield; (*sprofondare*) subside ● *vt* give up; make over (*proprietà ecc*)

ce'devole *a* (*terreno ecc*) soft; *fig* yielding

ce'diglia *nf* cedilla

cedi'mento *nm* (*di terreno*) subsidence

'cedola *nf* coupon

'cedro *nm* (*albero*) cedar; (*frutto*) citron

C.E.E. *nf abbr* (**Comunità Economica Europea**) E[E]C

cefa'lea *nf* headache

ce'falo *nm* mullet

'ceffo *nm* (*muso*) snout; (*pej: persona*) mug

cef'fone *nm* slap

ce'lare *vt* conceal

ce'larsi *vr* conceal oneself

ce'lato *a* concealed

cele'brare *vt* celebrate, observe (*festività*)

celebra'tivo *a* celebratory

celebrazi'one *nf* celebration

'celebre *a* famous

celebrità *nf inv* celebrity

'celere *a* swift; **corso ~** crash course ● *nf* (*polizia*) flying squad

celerità *nf* speed; **con ~** speedily

ce'leste *a* (*divino*) heavenly ● *a & nm* (*colore*) pale blue

celesti'ale *a* celestial

celi'bato *nm* celibacy

'celibe *a* single ● *nm* bachelor

'cella *nf* cell. **~ frigorifera** cold store. **~ di isolamento** solitary confinement

+cello *suff* **monticello** *nm* mound; **praticello** *nm* small meadow

'cellofan *nm inv* cellophane; *Culin* cling film

cellofa'nare *vt* wrap in cling film

'cellula *nf* cell. **~ fotoelettrica** electronic eye

cellu'lare *nm* (*telefono*) cellular [phone] ● *a* **furgone ~** police van; **telefono ~** cellular [phone]

cellu'lite *nf* cellulite

cellu'litico *a* full of cellulite

cellu'loide *a* celluloid; **il mondo della ~** *fig* the celluloid world

cellu'losa *nf* cellulose

'Celsius *a inv* Celsius

'celta *nm* Celt

'celtico *a* Celtic

'cembalo *nm Mus* cembalo, harpsichord

cemen'tare *vt* cement

cementifi'care *vt* turn into a cement jungle

cementificazi'one *nf* turning into a cement jungle

cementi'ficio *nm* cement factory

ce'mento *nm* cement. **~ armato** reinforced concrete

'cena *nf* dinner; (*leggera*) supper; (*festa*) dinner party

ce'nacolo *nm* circle

ce'nare *vi* have dinner; **~ fuori** eat out

'cencio *nm* rag; (*per spolverare*) duster; **bianco come un ~** white as a sheet

cenci'oso *a* in rags

'cenere *nf* ash; (*di carbone ecc*) cinders *pl*; **Ceneri** *pl* Ash Wednesday

Cene'rentola *nf* Cinderella

ce'netta *nf* (*cena semplice*) informal dinner; (*cena intima*) romantic dinner

'cenno *nm* sign; (*col capo*) nod; (*con la mano*) wave; (*allusione*) hint; (*breve resoconto*) mention; **far ~ di sì** nod

ce'none *nm* il **~ di Capodanno/Natale** special New Year's Eve/Christmas Eve dinner

ceno'tafio *nm* cenotaph

censi'mento *nm* census

cen'sire *vt* take a census of

CENSIS *nm abbr* (**Centro Studi Investimenti Sociali**) *national opinion research institute*

cen'sore *nm* censor

cen'sura *nf* censorship

censu'rare *vt* censor

centelli'nare *vt* sip; *fig* measure out carefully

cente'nario, -a *a & nmf* centenarian ● *nm* (*commemorazione*) centenary

centen'nale *a* centennial

cen'tesimo *a* hundredth ● *nm* hundredth; (*di dollaro*) cent; **non avere un ~** be penniless

cen'tigrado *a* centigrade

cen'tilitro *nm* centilitre

cen'timetro *nm* centimetre

centi'naia *nfpl* hundreds

centi'naio *nm* hundred

'cento *a & nm* a *or* one hundred; **per ~** per cent

centodi'eci *nm* a *or* one hundred and ten; **~ e lode** *Univ* ≈ first class honours

centome'trista *nmf Sport* one hundred metres runner

cento'mila *nm* a *or* one hundred thousand

cen'trale *a* central ● *nf* (*di società ecc*) head office. **~ atomica** atomic power station. **~ elettrica** power station. **~ idroelettrica** hydroelectric power station. **~ nucleare** nuclear power station. **~ operativa** (*di polizia*)

operations room. **~ telefonica** [telephone] exchange

centra'lina *nf Teleph* switchboard; (*apparecchiatura*) junction box

centrali'nista *nmf* [switchboard] operator

centra'lino *nm Teleph* exchange; (*di albergo ecc*) switchboard

centra'lismo *nm* centralism

centraliz'zare *vt* centralize

cen'trare *vt* ~ **qcsa** hit sth in the centre; (*fissare nel centro*) centre; *fig* hit on the head (*idea*)

cen'trato *a* (*tiro, colpo*) well-aimed; (*fig: osservazione*) right on target

centrat'tacco *nm Sport* centre forward

centra'vanti *nm Sport* centre forward

cen'trifuga *nf* spin-drier. **~** [**asciugaverdure**] shaker. **~ elettrica** juice extractor

centrifu'gare *vt Techn* centrifuge; (*lavatrice:*) spin

cen'trino *nm* doily

cen'trismo *nm Pol* centrism

cen'trista *a Pol* centrist

'centro *nm* centre; **in ~** (*essere*) in town; (*andare*) into town. **~ di accoglienza** reception centre. **~ di attrazione** focal point. **~ città** city centre. **~ commerciale** shopping centre, mall. **~ di costi** *Comm* cost centre. **~ culturale** arts centre. **~ di gravità** centre of gravity. **~ di informazioni turistiche** tourist information office. **~ operativo** *Mil* operations room. **~ di riabilitazione** halfway house. **~ sociale** community centre. **~ sportivo** leisure centre. **~ storico** old town

centrocam'pista *nm Sport* midfield player, midfielder

centro'campo *nm* midfield

centro'destra *nm inv Pol* centre right

centromedi'ano *nm Sport* centre half

centrosi'nistra *nm inv Pol* centre left

centro'tavola *nm inv* centre-piece

centupli'care *vt fig* multiply

'ceppo *nm* (*di albero*) stump; (*da ardere*) log; (*fig: gruppo*) stock

'cera *nf* wax; (*aspetto*) look. **~ d'api** beeswax. **~ per auto** car wax. **~ per il pavimento** floor-polish

cera'lacca *nf* sealing-wax

ce'ramica *nf* (*arte*) ceramics; (*materia*) pottery; (*oggetto*) piece of pottery

cera'mista *nmf* ceramicist

ce'rato *a* (*tela*) waxed

cerbi'atto *nm* fawn

cerbot'tana *nf* blowpipe

'cerca *nf* **andare in ~ di** look for

cercaper'sone *nm inv* beeper; **chiamare con il ~** beep

cer'care *vt* look for ● *vi* **~ di** try to

cerca|'tore, -'trice *nmf* **~ d'oro** gold seeker

'cerchia *nf* circle. **~ familiare** family circle

cerchi'are *vt* circle, draw a circle around (*parola*)

cerchi'ato *a* (*occhi*) black-ringed

cerchi'etto *nm* (*per capelli*) hairband

'cerchio *nm* circle; (*giocattolo*) hoop

cerchi'one *nm* alloy wheel

cere'ale *nm* cereal

cerea'licolo *a* grain *attrib*, cereal *attrib*

cere'brale *a* cerebral

'cereo *a* waxen

ce'retta *nf* depilatory wax; **fare la ~** wax

cer'foglio *nm* chervil

ceri'monia *nf* ceremony. **~ inaugurale** induction ceremony. **~ nuziale** marriage ceremony. **~ di premiazione** awards ceremony

cerimoni'ale *nm* ceremonial

cerimoni'ere *nm* master of ceremonies

cerimoni'oso *a* ceremonious

ce'rino *nm* [wax] match

cerni'era *nf* hinge; (*di borsa*) clasp. **~ lampo** zip[-fastener], zipper *Am*

'cernita *nf* selection

'cero *nm* candle

ce'rone *nm* greasepaint

ce'rotto *nm* [sticking] plaster. **~ callifugo** corn plaster

certa'mente *adv* certainly

cer'tezza *nf* certainty

certifi'care *vt* certify

certifi'cato *nm* certificate. **~ medico** doctor's note. **~ di morte** death certificate

certificazi'one *nf* certification. **~ di bilancio** *Fin* auditors' report

'certo *a* certain; (*notizia*) definite; (*indeterminativo*) some; **sono ~ di riuscire** I am certain to succeed; **a una certa età** at a certain age; **certi giorni** some days; **un ~ signor Giardini** a Mr Giardini; **una certa Anna** somebody called Anna; **certa gente** *pej* some people; **ho certi dolori!** I'm in such pain!. **certi** *pron pl* some; (*alcune persone*) some people ● *adv* of course; **sapere per ~** know for certain, know for sure; **di ~** surely; **~ che...** surely...

cer'tosa *nf* Carthusian monastery

certo'sino *nm* Carthusian [monk]; **pazienza certosina** exceptional patience

cer'tuni *pron* some

ce'rume *nm* earwax

cer'vello *nm* brain; **avere un ~ da gallina** be a bird-brain

cervel'lone, -a *nmf hum* brainbox

cervel'lotico *a* (*macchinoso*) over-elaborate

cervi'cale *a* cervical

'cervice *nf* cervix

'cervo *nm* deer

ce'sareo *a Med* Caesarean; **parto ~** Caesarean

cesel'lare *vt* chisel

cesel'lato *a* chiselled

cesella'tura *nf* chiselling

ce'sello *nm* chisel

ce'soie *nfpl* shears

'cespite *nm* source of income

ce'spuglio *nm* bush

cespugli'oso *a* (*terreno*) bushy

ces'sare *vi* stop, cease ● *vt* stop

ces'sate *nm* **~ il fuoco** ceasefire

ces'sato *a* **~ allarme/pericolo** all clear

cessazi'one *nf* cessation. **~ d'esercizio** closing down

cessi'one *nf* handover

'cesso *nm sl* (*gabinetto*) bog, john *Am*; (*fig: locale, luogo*) dump

'cesta *nf* [large] basket

ce'stello *nm* (*per lavatrice*) drum

cesti'nare *vt* throw away; bin (*lettera*); turn down (*proposta*)

ce'stino *nm* [small] basket; (*per la carta straccia*) waste-paper basket

'cesto *nm* basket. **~ della biancheria** linen basket

ce'sura *nf* caesura

ce'taceo *nm* cetacean

'ceto *nm* [social] class

'cetra *nf* lyre

cetrio'lino *nm* gherkin

cetri'olo *nm* cucumber

cfr *abbr* (**confronta**) cf

C.G.I.L. *nf abbr* (**Confederazione Generale Italiana del Lavoro**) *trades union* organization

cha'let *nm inv* chalet

cham'pagne *nm inv* champagne

'chance *nf inv* chance

char'lotte *nf* ice-cream cake with fresh cream, biscuits and fruit

'charter *nm inv* charter plane; **volo ~** charter flight

che *rel pron* (*persona: soggetto*) who; (*persona: oggetto*) whom; (*cosa, animale*) which; **questa è la casa ~ ho comprato** this is the house [that] I've bought; **il ~ mi sorprende** which surprises me; **dal ~ deduco che...** from which I gather that...; **avere di ~ vivere** have enough to live on; **grazie! – non c'è di che!** thank you – don't mention it; **il giorno ~ ti ho visto** *fam* the day I saw you ● *inter a* what; (*esclamativo: con aggettivo*) how; (*con nome*) what a; **~ macchina prendiamo, la tua o la mia?** which car are we taking, yours or mine?; **~ bello!** how nice!; **~ idea!** what an idea!; **~ bella giornata!** what a lovely day! ● *inter pron* what; **a ~ pensi?** what are you thinking about? ● *conj* that; (*con comparazioni*) than; **credo ~ abbia ragione** I think [that] he is right; **era così commosso ~ non riusciva a parlare** he was so moved, [that] he couldn't speak; **aspetto ~ telefoni** I'm waiting for him to phone; **è da un po' ~ non lo vedo** it's been a while since I saw him; **mi piace più Roma ~ Milano** I like Rome better than Milan; **~ ti piaccia o no** whether you like it or not; **~ io sappia** as far as I know

'checca *nf fam* queen

checché *pron* whatever

check-'in *nm inv* check-in; **fare il ~** check in

check-'up *nm inv Med* check-up; **fare un ~** have a check-up

cheese'burger *nm inv* cheeseburger

'chef *nm inv* chef

'**chela** *nf* nipper

chemiotera'pia *nf* chemotherapy, chemo *fam*

chemisi'er *nm inv* chemise

chero'sene *nm* paraffin

cheru'bino *nm* cherub

che'tare *vt* quieten

che'tarsi *vr* quieten down

cheti'chella: **alla ~** *adv* silently

'**cheto** *a* quiet

chi *rel pron* whoever; (*coloro che*) people who; **ho trovato ~ ti può aiutare** I found somebody who can help you; **c'è ~ dice che...** some people say that...; **senti ~ parla!** listen to who's talking! ● *inter pron* (*soggetto*) who; (*oggetto, con preposizione*) whom; (*possessivo*) **di ~** whose; **~ sei?** who are you?; **~ hai incontrato?** who did you meet?, whom did you meet? *fml*; **di ~ sono questi libri?** whose books are these?; **con ~ parli?** who are you talking to?, to whom are you talking? *fml*; **a ~ lo dici!** tell me about it!

chi'acchiera *nf* chat; (*pettegolezzo*) gossip; **chiacchiere** *pl* chitchat; **far quattro chiacchiere** have a chat

chiacchie'rare *vi* chat; (*far pettegolezzi*) gossip

chiacchie'rato *a* **essere ~** ⟨*persona:*⟩ be the subject of gossip

chi'acchiere *nfpl* (*dolci*) *sweet pastries fried and sprinkled with fine sugar*

chiacchie'rone, -a *a* talkative ● *nmf* chatterer

chia'mare *vt* call; (*far venire*) send for; **come ti chiami?** what's your name?; **mi chiamo Roberto** my name is Robert; **~ alle armi** call up; **mandare a ~** send for; **~ a rapporto** debrief

chia'marsi *vr* be called

chia'mata *nf* call; *Mil* call-up. **~ a carico del destinatario** reverse charge call. **~ interurbana** long-distance call. **~ in teleselezione** direct dialling. **~ urbana** local call

chi'appa *nf fam* cheek

chiara'mente *adv* clearly

chia'rezza *nf* clarity; (*limpidezza*) clearness

chiarifi'care *vt* clarify

chiarifica'tore *a* clarificatory

chiarificazi'one *nf* clarification

chiari'mento *nm* clarification

chia'rire *vt* make clear; (*spiegare*) clear up

chia'rirsi *vr* become clear

chi'aro *a* clear; (*luminoso*) bright; ⟨*colore*⟩ light

chia'rore *nm* glimmer

chiaro'scuro *nm* (*tecnica*) chiaroscuro

chiaroveg'gente *a* clear-sighted ● *nmf* clairvoyant

chi'asso *nm* din

chiassosa'mente *adv* (*rumorosamente*) rowdily; (*vistosamente*) gaudily

chias'soso *a* (*rumoroso*) rowdy; (*vistoso*) gaudy

chi'atta *nf* canal boat, canal barge

chi'ave *nf* key; **chiudere a ~** lock. **~ dell'accensione** ignition key. **~ di basso** *Mus* bass clef. **~ inglese** monkey-wrench. **~ [inglese] a rullino** adjustable spanner

chia'vetta *nf* (*in tubi*) key

chiavi'stello *nm* latch

chi'azza *nf* stain. **~ di petrolio** oil-slick

chiaz'zare *vt* stain

chiaz'zato *a* dappled

chic *a inv* chic

chicches'sia *pron* anybody

chicchirichi *nm inv* cock-a-doodle-doo

'**chicco** *nm* grain; (*di caffe*) bean; (*d'uva*) grape. **~ di caffè** coffee bean. **~ di grandine** hailstone. **~ d'orzo** barleycorn

chi'edere *vt* ask; (*per avere*) ask for; (*esigere*) demand; **~ notizie di** ask after

chi'edersi *vr* wonder

chieri'chetto *nm* altar boy

chi'erico *nm* cleric

chi'esa *nf* church

chi'esto *pp di* **chiedere**

chif'fon *nm* chiffon

'**chiglia** *nf* keel

chi'gnon *nm inv* bun

'**chilo** *nm* kilo

chilo'grammo *nm* kilogram[me]

chilo'hertz *nm inv* kilohertz

chilome'traggio *nm Auto* ≈ mileage

chilo'metrico *a* in kilometres; *fig* endless

chi'lometro *nm* kilometre

'**chilowatt** *nm inv* kilowatt

chilowat'tora *nm inv* kilowatt hour

chi'mera *nf fig* illusion

'**chimica** *nf* chemistry. **~ organica** organic chemistry

'**chimico, -a** *a* chemical ● *nmf* chemist

chi'mono *nm* kimono

'**china** *nf* (*declivio*) slope; **inchiostro di ~** Indian ink

chi'nare *vt* lower

chi'narsi *vr* stoop

chincaglie'rie *nfpl* knick-knacks

chinesitera'pia *nf* physiotherapy

chi'nino *nm* quinine

'**chino** *a* bent

chi'notto *nm* sparkling soft drink

chintz *nm* chintz

chi'occia *nf* sitting hen

chi'occiola *nf* snail; **scala a ~** spiral staircase

chio'dato *a* **pneumatici chiodati** snow tyres; **scarpe chiodate** shoes with crampons

chi'odo *nm* nail; (*idea fissa*) obsession. **~ di garofano** clove

chi'oma *nf* [head of] hair; (*fogliame*) foliage

chi'osco *nm* kiosk; (*per giornali*) newsstand

chi'ostro *nm* cloister

chip *nm inv* **~ [di silicio]** chip

'**chipset** *nm inv* chipset

chiro'mante *nmf* fortune teller, palmist

chiroman'zia *nf* palmistry

chirur'gia *nf* surgery. ~ **estetica** cosmetic surgery

chirurgica'mente *adv* surgically

chi'rurgico *a* surgical

chi'rurgo *nm* surgeon

chissà *adv* who knows; ~ **quando arriverà** I wonder when he will arrive

chi'tarra *nf* guitar. ~ **acustica** acoustic guitar

chitar'rista *nmf* guitarist

chi'udere *vt* shut, close; (*con chiave*) lock; turn off, switch off (*luce ecc*); turn off (*acqua*); (*per sempre*) close down (*negozio, fabbrica ecc*); (*recingere*) enclose; **chiudi il becco!** shut up! ● *vi* shut, close; (*con chiave*) lock up

chi'udersi *vr* shut; (*tempo:*) cloud over; (*ferita:*) heal over; *fig* withdraw into oneself

chi'unque *pron* anyone, anybody ● *rel pron* whoever

chi'usa *nf* enclosure; (*di canale*) lock; (*conclusione*) close

chi'uso *pp di* **chiudere** ● *a* closed, shut; (*tempo*) overcast; (*persona*) reserved; **'~ per turno'** 'closing day'

chiu'sura *nf* closing; (*sistema*) lock; (*allacciatura*) fastener; **'~ settimanale il lunedì'** 'closed on Mondays'. ~ **centralizzata** *Auto* central locking. ~ **lampo** zip, zipper *Am*

ci *pron* (*personale*) us; (*riflessivo*) ourselves; (*reciproco*) each other; (*a ciò, di ciò ecc*) about it; **non ci disturbare** don't disturb us; **aspettateci** wait for us; **ci ha detto tutto** he told us everything; **ci consideriamo...** we consider ourselves...; **ci laviamo le mani** we wash our hands; **ci odiamo** we hate each other; **non ci penso mai** I never think about it; **pensaci!** think about it! ● *adv* (*qui*) here; (*lì*) there; (*moto per luogo*) through it; **ci siamo** here we are; **ci siete?** are you there?; **ci siamo passati tutti** we all went through it; **c'è** there is; **ci vuole pazienza** it takes patience; **non ci vedo/sento** I can't see/hear

C.ia *abbr* (**compagnia**) Co.

cia'batta *nf* slipper

ciabat'tare *vi* shuffle

ciabat'tino *nm* cobbler

ci'ac *nm inv Cinema* ~ **si gira!** action!

ci'alda *nf* wafer

cial'trone *nm* (*mascalzone*) scoundrel; (*fannullone*) wastrel

ciam'bella *nf Culin* ring-shaped cake; (*salvagente*) lifebelt; (*gonfiabile*) rubber ring

ci'ance *nfpl* yapping

cianci'are *vi* gossip

cianfru'saglie *nfpl* knick-knacks

cia'notico *a* (*viso*) puce

cia'nuro *nm* cyanide

ci'ao *int fam* (*all'arrivo*) hello!, hi!; (*alla partenza*) bye-bye!, cheerio!

ciar'lare *vi* chat

ciarla'tano *nm* charlatan

ciarli'ero *a* (*loquace*) talkative

cia'scuno *a* each ● *pron* everyone, everybody; (*distributivo*) each [one]; **per** ~ each

ci'bare *vt* feed

ci'barie *nfpl* provisions

ci'barsi *vr* eat; ~ **di** live on

ciber'netica *nf* cybernetics

ciber'netico *a* cybernetic

ciber'spazio *nm* cyberspace

'cibo *nm* food; **non toccare** ~ leave one's food untouched; **non ha toccato** ~ **da ieri** he hasn't had a bite to eat since yesterday. **cibi** *pl* **precotti** ready meals

ci'cala *nf* cicada

cica'lino *nm* buzzer

cica'trice *nf* scar

cicatriz'zante *nm* ointment

cicatriz'zare *vi* heal [up]

cicatriz'zarsi *vr* heal [up]

cicatrizzazi'one *nf* healing

'cicca *nf* cigarette end; (*fam: sigaretta*) fag; (*fam: gomma*) [chewing] gum

cic'chetto *nm fam* (*bicchierino*) nip; (*rimprovero*) telling-off

'ciccia *nf fam* fat, flab

cicci'one, -a *nmf fam* fatty, fatso

cice'rone *nm* guide

cicla'mino *nm* cyclamen

ciclica'mente *adv* cyclically

'ciclico *a* cyclical

ci'clismo *nm* cycling

ci'clista *nmf* cyclist

'ciclo *nm* cycle; (*di malattia*) course. ~ **economico** business cycle

ciclo'cross *nm inv* cyclo-cross

ciclomo'tore *nm* moped

ci'clone *nm* cyclone

ci'clonico *a* cyclonic

ciclosti'lare *vt* duplicate

ciclosti'lato *nm* duplicate [copy] ● *a* duplicate

ci'cogna *nf* stork

ci'coria *nf* chicory

ci'cuta *nf* hemlock

ci'eco, -a *a* blind ● *nmf* blind man; blind woman; **i parzialmente ciechi** the partially sighted

ciel'lino *nmf Pol* member of the Comunione e Liberazione movement

ci'elo *nm* sky; *Relig* heaven; **al settimo** ~ in seventh heaven; **santo ~!** good heavens!

'cifra *nf* figure; (*somma*) sum; (*monogramma*) monogram; (*codice*) code; **una** ~ *sl* like crazy

ci'frare *vt* embroider with a monogram; (*codificare*) code

ci'frato *a* monogrammed; (*codificato*) coded

'ciglio *nm* (*bordo*) edge; (*degli occhi*) eyelash; **ciglia** *pl* eyelashes

'cigno *nm* swan

cigo'lante *a* squeaky

cigo'lare *vt* squeak

cigo'lio *nm* squeak

'Cile *nm* Chile

ci'lecca *nf* far ~ miss

ci'leno, -a *a & nmf* Chilean

cili'egia *nf* cherry

cili'egio *nm* cherry[-tree]

cilin'drata *nf* cubic capacity, c.c.; **macchina di alta** ~ highpowered car

ci'lindro *nm* cylinder; (*cappello*) top hat, topper

'**cima** *nf* top; (*fig: persona*) genius; **in** ~ **a** at the top of; **da** ~ **a fondo** from top to bottom. ~ **alla genovese** *baked veal stuffed with chicken and chopped vegetables, served cold*. **cime** *pl* **di rapa** turnip greens

ci'melio *nm* relic; **cimeli** *pl* memorabilia

cimen'tare *vt* put to the test

cimen'tarsi *vr* (*provare*) try one's hand; ~ **in** (*arrischiarsi*) venture into

'**cimice** *nf* bug; (*puntina*) drawing pin, thumbtack *Am*

cimini'era *nf* chimney; *Naut* funnel

cimi'tero *nm* cemetery. ~ **delle macchine** breaker's yard

ci'mosa *nf* selvage, selvedge

ci'murro *nm* distemper

'**Cina** *nf* China

cincial'legra *nf* great tit

cincia'rella *nf* blue tit

cincillà *nm inv* chinchilla

cin cin *int* cheers!

cincischi'are *vi* fiddle

cincischi'arsi *vr* mess around

'**cine** *nm fam* cinema

cine'asta *nmf* film maker

Cinecittà *nf* (*stabilimento*) *film complex in the suburbs of Rome*

cine'club *nm inv* film club

ci'nefilo, -a *nmf* cinemagoer

cinegior'nale *nm* newsreel

'**cinema** *nm inv* cinema. ~ **d'essai** arts cinema

cine'matica *nf* kinematics

cinematogra'fare *vt* film

cinematogra'fia *nf* cinematography

cinemato'grafico *a* film *attrib*

cinema'tografo *nm* cinema

cine'presa *nf* cine-camera

ci'nereo *a* ashen

ci'nese *a* & *nmf* Chinese

cinese'rie *nfpl* chinoiserie

cine'teca *nf* (*raccolta*) film collection

ci'netico *a* kinetic

'**cingere** *vt* (*circondare*) surround

'**cinghia** *nf* strap; (*cintura*) belt. ~ **del ventilatore** fanbelt. ~ **della ventola** fanbelt

cinghi'ale *nm* wild boar; **pelle di** ~ pigskin

cinghi'ata *nf* lash

cingo'lato *a* ⟨*mezzi*⟩ caterpillar *attrib* ● *nm* caterpillar

'**cingolo** *nm Mech* belt

cinguet'tare *vi* twitter

cinguet'tio *nm* twittering

cinica'mente *adv* cynically

'**cinico** *a* cynical

ci'niglia *nf* (*tessuto*) chenille

ci'nismo *nm* cynicism

ci'nofilo *a* ⟨*unità*⟩ dog-loving

cin'quanta *a* & *nm* fifty

cinquanten'nale *nm* fiftieth anniversary

cinquan'tenne *a* & *nmf* fifty-year-old

cinquan'tesimo *a* & *nm* fiftieth

cinquan'tina *nf* **una** ~ **di** about fifty

'**cinque** *a* & *nm* five

cinquecen'tesco *a* sixteenth-century

cinque'cento *a* five hundred ● *nm* **il C**~ the sixteenth century

cinque'mila *a* & *nm* five thousand

cin'quina *nf* (*in tombola*) five in a row

'**cinta** *nf* (*di pantaloni*) belt; **muro di** ~ [boundary] wall

cin'tare *vt* enclose

'**cintola** *nf* (*di pantaloni*) belt

cin'tura *nf* belt. ~ **nera** black belt. ~ **di salvataggio** lifebelt. ~ **di sicurezza** *Aeron, Auto* seat belt

cintu'rato *nm Auto* radial tyre

cintu'rino *nm* ~ [**dell'orologio**] watchstrap; (*di metallo*) bracelet

ciò *pron* this; that; ~ **che** what; ~ **nondimeno** nevertheless

ci'occa *nf* lock

ciocco'lata *nf* chocolate; (*bevanda*) [hot] chocolate. ~ **in polvere** drinking chocolate

cioccola'tino *nm* chocolate

ciocco'lato *nm* chocolate. ~ **fondente** plain chocolate, dark chocolate. ~ **al latte** milk chocolate. ~ **da pasticceria** cooking chocolate

cioè *adv* that is

ciondo'lare *vi* dangle

ciondo'lio *nm* dangling

ci'ondolo *nm* pendant

ciondo'loni *adv fig* hanging about

cionono'stante *adv* nonetheless

ci'otola *nf* bowl

ci'ottolo *nm* pebble; **ciottoli** *pl* (*in spiaggia*) shingle

ci'piglio *nm* frown; **con** ~ with a frown

ci'polla *nf* onion; (*bulbo*) bulb

ci'presso *nm* cypress

'**cipria** *nf* [face] powder

cipri'ota *a* & *nmf* Cypriot

'**Cipro** *nm* Cyprus

'**circa** *adv* & *prep* about

cir'cense *a* circus *attrib*

'**circo** *nm* circus

circo'lare *a* circular ● *nf* circular; (*di metropolitana*) circle line ● *vi* circulate

circola'torio *a Med* circulatory

circolazi'one *nf* circulation; (*traffico*) traffic

'**circolo** *nm* circle; (*società*) club. ~ **del golf** golf-club. **C**~ **polare antartico** Antarctic Circle. **C**~ **polare artico** Arctic Circle

circon'cidere *vt* circumcise

circoncisi'one *nf* circumcision

circon'dare *vt* surround

circon'dario *nm* (*amministrativo*) administrative district; (*vicinato*) neighbourhood

circon'darsi *vr* ~ **di** surround oneself with

circonfe'renza *nf* circumference. ~ **del**

collo collar size. **~ dei fianchi** hip measurement. **~ [della] vita** waist measurement

circon'flesso *a* **e con l'accento ~** circumflex e

circonvallazi'one *nf* ring road

circo'scritto *pp di* **circoscrivere ●** *a* limited

circo'scrivere *vt* circumscribe

circoscrizio'nale *a* area

circoscrizi'one *nf* area. **~ elettorale** constituency

circo'spetto *a* wary

circospezi'one *nf* **con ~** warily

circo'stante *a* surrounding

circo'stanza *nf* circumstance; *(occasione)* occasion

circostanzi'ato *a* circumstantial

circu'ire *vt (ingannare)* trick

circuite'ria *nf* circuitry

cir'cuito *nm* circuit

circumnavi'gare *vt* circumnavigate

circumnavigazi'one *nf* circumnavigation

ci'rillico *a* Cyrillic

cir'ripede *nm* barnacle

cir'rosi *nf* cirrhosis

Cisgior'dania *nf* West Bank

C.I.S.L. *nf abbr* (**Confederazione Italiana Sindacati Lavoratori**) *trades union organization*

C.I.S.N.A.L. *nf abbr* (**Confederazione Italiana Sindacati Nazionali dei Lavoratori**) *trades union organization*

'cispa *nf (nell'occhio)* sleep

ci'sposo *a* bleary-eyed

'ciste *nf inv* cyst

ci'sterna *nf* cistern; *(serbatoio)* tank

'cisti *nf* cyst

cisti'fellea *nf* gall bladder

ci'stite *nf* cystitis

C.I.T. *nm abbr* (**Compagnia Italiana Turismo**) *Italian tourist organization*

ci'tare *vt (riportare brani ecc)* quote; *(come esempio)* cite; *Jur* summons

citazi'one *nf* quotation; *Jur* summons *sg*

citofo'nare *vt* buzz

ci'tofono *nm* entry phone; *(in ufficio, su aereo ecc)* intercom

cito'logico *a* cytological

'citrico *a* citric

ci'trullo *nmf fam* dimwit

città *nf inv* town; *(grande)* city. **C~ del Capo** Cape Town. **~ fantasma** ghost town. **~ giardino** garden city. **C~ del Vaticano** Vatican City

citta'della *nf* citadel

citta'dina *nf* town

cittadi'nanza *nf* citizenship; *(popolazione)* citizens *pl*

citta'dino, -a *nmf* citizen; *(abitante di città)* city dweller

ciucci'are *vt fam* suck

ci'uccio *nm fam* dummy

ci'uco *nm* ass

ci'uffo *nm* tuft

ci'urma *nf Naut* crew

ciur'maglia *nf (gentaglia)* rabble

ci'vetta *nf* owl; *(fig: donna)* flirt; **[auto] ~** unmarked police car

civet'tare *vi* flirt

civette'ria *nf* flirtatiousness, coquettishness

civettu'olo *a* flirtatious, coquettish

'civico *a* civic

ci'vile *a* civil **●** *nm* civilian

civi'lista *nmf (avvocato)* specialist in civil law

civiliz'zare *vt* civilize

civiliz'zarsi *vr* become civilized

civiliz'zato *a* ⟨*paese*⟩ civilized

civilizzazi'one *nf* civilization

civil'mente *adv* civilly

civiltà *nf* civilization; *(cortesia)* civility

ci'vismo *nm* public spirit

CL *nf abbr* (**Comunione e Liberazione**) *young Catholics association*

cl *abbr* (**centilitri**) centilitre(s)

'clacson *nm inv* horn

clacso'nare *vi* beep the horn, hoot

cla'more *nm* clamour; **fare ~** cause a sensation

clamorosa'mente *adv* ⟨*sbagliare*⟩ sensationally

clamo'roso *a* noisy; ⟨*sbaglio*⟩ sensational

clan *nm inv* clan; *fig* clique

clandestina'mente *adv* secretly

clandestinità *nf* secrecy; **vivere nella ~** live underground

clande'stino *a* clandestine; **movimento ~** underground movement; **passeggero ~** stowaway

claque *nf inv* claque

clarinet'tista *nmf* clarinettist

clari'netto *nm* clarinet

'classe *nf* class; *(aula)* classroom; **di prima ~** first-class. **~ economica** economy class. **~ operaia** working class. **~ turistica** tourist class

classicheggi'ante *a* classical

classi'cismo *nm* classicism

classi'cista *nmf* classicist

'classico *a* classical; *(tipico)* classic **●** *nm* classic

clas'sifica *nf* classification; *Sport* results *pl*

classifi'cabile *a* classifiable

classifi'care *vt* classify

classifi'carsi *vr* be placed

classifica'tore *nm (cartella)* folder; *(mobile)* filing cabinet

classificazi'one *nf* classification

clas'sista *a* class-conscious **●** *nmf* class-conscious person

'clausola *nf* clause. **~ penale** *Jur, Comm* penalty clause. **~ di recesso** *Jur, Comm* escape clause

claustrofo'bia *nf* claustrophobia

claustro'fobico *a* claustrophobic

clau'sura nf Relig cloistered life; **di ~** ‹suora› cloistered; **essere in ~** fig shut oneself up; **vivere in ~** fig live like a hermit
'clava nf club
clavicemba'lista nmf harpsichord player
clavi'cembalo nm harpsichord
cla'vicola nf collar-bone
clavi'cordo nm clavichord
cle'mente a merciful; ‹tempo› mild
cle'menza nf mercy, clemency
clep'tomane nmf kleptomaniac
cleptoma'nia nf kleptomania
cleri'cale a clerical
'clero nm clergy
cles'sidra nf hourglass
clic nm inv Comput click; **fare ~ su** click on
clic'care vi Comput click; **~ su** click on
cliché nm inv cliché
click = **clic**
cli'ente nmf client; ‹di negozio› customer
clien'tela nf customers pl, clientèle; ‹di avvocato› clientèle
cliente'lare a Pol nepotistic
cliente'lismo nm nepotism
'clima nm climate
clima'terio nm climacteric
climatica'mente adv climatically
cli'matico a climatic; **stazione climatica** health resort
climatizza'tore nm air conditioner
climatizzazi'one nf air conditioning
'clinica nf clinic. **~ odontoiatrica** dental clinic. **~ ostetrica** maternity hospital. **~ psichiatrica** mental hospital
'clinico a clinical ● nm clinician
clip nf inv paper-clip; ‹di orecchino› clip
cli'stere nm Med enema
clo'aca nf sewer
cloche nf inv cloche hat
clo'nare vt clone
'clone nm clone
clo'rato a chlorate
'cloro nm chlorine
cloro'filla nf chlorophyll
clorofluorocar'buro nm chlorofluorocarbon, CFC
cloro'formio nm chloroform
clou a inv **momenti ~** highlights
club-'sandwich nm inv club sandwich
cm abbr (**centimetro**) cm
CNR nm abbr (**Consiglio Nazionale delle Ricerche**) national research council
Co. abbr (**compagnia**) Co
coabi'tare vi live together
coabitazi'one nf ‹di razze› coexistence
coadiu'tore, -'trice nmf ‹in ufficio› assistant
coadiu'vare vt cooperate with
coagu'lante nm coagulant
coagu'lare vt coagulate
coagu'larsi vr coagulate
coagulazi'one nf coagulation
coalizi'one nf coalition
coaliz'zare vt fig unite
coaliz'zarsi vr unite

co'atto a Jur compulsory
co'balto nm cobalt; ‹colore› cobalt blue
COBAS nmpl abbr (**Comitati di Base**) independent trade unions
'cobra nm inv cobra
'Coca® nf Coke®
Coca 'cola® nf Coca Cola
coca'ina nf cocaine
cocai'nomane nmf cocaine addict
coc'carda nf rosette
cocchi'ere nm coachman
coc'chio nm coach
'coccige nm coccyx
cocci'nella nf ladybird
'coccio nm earthenware; ‹frammento› fragment
cocciu'taggine nf stubbornness
cocciuta'mente adv stubbornly
cocci'uto a stubborn
'cocco nm coconut palm; fam love; **noce di ~** coconut
coccodè nm inv cluck
cocco'drillo nm crocodile
cocco'lare vt cuddle
co'cente a ‹sole› burning; ‹lacrime, delusione› bitter
'cocker nm inv **~ [spaniel]** cocker spaniel
'cocktail nm inv ‹ricevimento› cocktail party
co'comero nm watermelon
co'cuzzolo nm top; ‹di testa, cappello› crown
'coda nf tail; ‹di abito› train; ‹fila› queue; ‹di traffico› tailback; **fare la ~** queue [up], stand in line Am. **~ di cavallo** ‹acconciatura› pony tail. **~ dell'occhio** corner of one's eye. **~ di paglia** guilty conscience
co'dardo, -a a cowardly ● nmf coward
co'dazzo nm train
code'ina nf codeine
co'desto a that
'codice nm code; **in ~** ‹messaggio› coded, in code; **mettere in ~** encode. **~ di avviamento postale** postal code, zip code Am. **~ a barre** bar-code. **~ civile** civil code. **~ fiscale** tax code. **~ penale** penal code. **~ segreto** ‹di carta di credito› PIN. **~ della strada** highway code
codi'cillo nm codicil
co'difica nf coding
codifi'care vt encode; codify ‹legge›
codifica'tore, -'trice nmf Comput encoder
codificazi'one nf encoding; ‹di legge› codification
co'dini nmpl bunches
coeffici'ente nm coefficient
coercizi'one nf coercion
coe'rente a consistent
coe'renza nf consistency
coesi'one nf cohesion
coe'sistere vi coexist
coe'sivo a cohesive
coe'taneo, -a a & nmf contemporary
cofa'netto nm casket

'**cofano** *nm* (*forziere*) chest; *Auto* bonnet, hood *Am*

cofirma'tario, -a *nmf* cosignatory

coge'stire *vt* co-manage

cogi'tare *vi* ponder

'**cogliere** *vt* pick; (*sorprendere*) catch; (*afferrare*) seize; (*colpire*) hit; **~ la palla al balzo** seize the opportunity; **~ di sorpresa** take by surprise

co'glione *nm vulg* ball; (*sciocco*) dickhead; **rompere i coglioni a qcno** get on sb's tits

'**Cognac** *nm* cognac

co'gnato, -a *nm* brother-in-law ● *nf* sister-in-law

cognizi'one *nf* knowledge; **con ~ di causa** on an informed basis

co'gnome *nm* surname. **~ da ragazza/da nubile** maiden name

cogu'aro *nm* cougar

'**coi** = con + i

coi'bente *a* insulating

coinci'denza *nf* coincidence; (*di treno ecc*) connection

coin'cidere *vi* coincide

coinqui'lino *nm* flatmate

coin'volgere *vt* involve

coinvolgi'mento *nm* involvement

coin'volto *a* involved

'**coito** *nm* coitus

col = con + il

colà *adv* there

cola'brodo *nm inv* strainer; **ridotto a un ~** *fam* full of holes

cola'pasta *nm inv* colander

co'lare *vt* strain; (*versare lentamente*) drip ● *vi* (*gocciolare*) drip; (*perdere*) leak; **~ a picco** *Naut* sink

co'lata *nf* (*di metallo*) casting; (*di lava*) flow

colazi'one *nf* (*del mattino*) breakfast; (*di mezzogiorno*) lunch; **prima ~** breakfast; **far ~** have breakfast/lunch. **~ di lavoro** working lunch. **~ al sacco** packed lunch

col'bacco *nm* fur hat

co'lei *pron f* the one

co'lera *nm* cholera

coleste'rolo *nm* cholesterol

colf *nf abbr* (**collaboratrice familiare**) home help

colibrì *nm inv* humming-bird

'**colica** *nf* colic

co'lino *nm* [tea] strainer

'**colla** *nf* glue; (*di farina*) paste. **~ di pesce** gelatine

collabo'rare *vi* collaborate; **~ con** (*polizia*) co-operate with; **~ a** (*rivista*) contribute to

collabora|'tore, -'trice *nmf* collaborator; (*di rivista*) contributor. **~ familiare** domestic help

collaborazi'one *nf* collaboration; (*con polizia*) co-operation

collaborazio'nista *nmf* collaborator

col'lage *nm inv* collage

col'lana *nf* necklace; (*serie*) series. **~ di perle** pearl necklace

col'lant *nmpl* tights. **~ velati** sheer tights

col'lante *a* adhesive

col'lare *nm* collar

colla'rino *nm* dog collar

col'lasso *nm* collapse. **~ cardiaco** syncope. **~ renale** kidney failure

collate'rale *a* collateral

collau'dare *vt* test

collauda|'tore, -'trice *nmf* tester

col'laudo *nm* test

collazio'nare *vt* collate

'**colle** *nm* hill; (*passo*) pass

col'lega *nmf* colleague

collega'gabile *a* compatible (**a** with)

collega'mento *nm* connection; *Mil* liaison; *Radio ecc* link. **~ dati** data link. **~ in rete** networking

colle'gare *vt* connect

colle'garsi *vr* TV, Radio link up (**a** with); (*Comput: a una rete ecc*) go on line (**a** to)

collegi'ale *nmf* boarder ● *a* (*responsabilità, decisione*) collective

col'legio *nm* (*convitto*) boarding-school. **~ elettorale** constituency

'**collera** *nf* anger; **andare in ~** get angry

col'lerico *a* irascible

col'letta *nf* collection

collettività *nf inv* community

collet'tivo *a* collective; (*interesse*) general; **biglietto ~** group ticket ● *nm* (*studentesco, femminista*) collective

col'letto *nm* collar

collet'tore *nm* (*di fognatura*) main sewer. **~ delle imposte** collector of taxes

collezio'nare *vt* collect

collezi'one *nf* collection. **~ invernale** winter collection

collezio'nismo *nm* collecting

collezio'nista *nmf* collector. **~ di francobolli** stamp collector

colli'mare *vi* coincide

col'lina *nf* hill

colli'nare *a* hill *attrib*

colli'netta *nf* knoll

colli'noso *a* (*terreno*) hilly

col'lirio *nm* eyewash

collisi'one *nf* collision

'**collo** *nm* neck; (*pacco*) package; **a ~ alto** high-necked; **a rotta di ~** breakneck. **~ del piede** instep

colloca'mento *nm* placing; (*impiego*) employment

collo'care *vt* place

collo'carsi *vr* take one's place

collocazi'one *nf* placing

colloqui'ale *a* (*termine*) colloquial; (*tono*) informal

col'loquio *nm* conversation; (*udienza ecc*) interview; (*esame*) oral [exam]

col'loso *a* glutinous

col'lottola *nf* nape

collusi'one *nf* collusion

colluttazi'one *nf* scuffle

col'mare *vt* fill; bridge (*divario*); **~ qcno di gentilezze** overwhelm sb with kindness '**colmo** *a* full ● *nm* top; *fig* height; **al ~ della disperazione** in the depths of despair; **questo è il ~!** (*con indignazione*) this is the last straw!; (*con stupore*) I don't believe it!; **per ~ di sfortuna** to crown it all

+**colo** *suff* **poetucolo** second rate poet

co'**lomba** *nf* dove. **~ pasquale** *dove-shaped cake with candied fruit eaten at Easter*

colom'**baccio** *nm* wood pigeon

colom'**baia** *nf* dovecote

Co'**lombia** *nf* Colombia

colombi'**ano** *a & nmf* Colombian

co'**lombo** *nm* pigeon; **colombi** *pl* (*innamorati*) lovebirds

Co'**lonia** *nf* Cologne; [**acqua di**] **c~** [eau de] Cologne

co'**lonia** *nf* colony; (*per bambini*) holiday camp

coloni'**ale** *a* colonial

co'**lonico** *a* ⟨*terreno, casa*⟩ farm *attrib*

coloniz'**zare** *vt* colonize

colonizza'**tore, -trice** *nmf* colonizer

co'**lonna** *nf* column; (*di auto*) tailback. **~ sonora** sound-track. **~ vertebrale** spine

colon'**nato** *nm* colonnade

colon'**nello** *nm* colonel

colon'**nina** *nf* (*distributore*) petrol pump, gas pump *Am*

co'**lono** *nm* tenant farmer

colo'**rante** *nm* colouring. **~ alimentare** food colouring

colo'**rare** *vt* colour; colour in ⟨*disegno*⟩

co'**lore** *nm* colour; (*carte*) suit; **a colori** in colour; **di ~** coloured; **farne di tutti i colori** get up to all sorts of mischief; **passarne di tutti i colori** go through hell. **diventare di tutti i colori** *fig* turn scarlet. **~ a olio** oil paint

colori'**ficio** *nm* paint and dyes shop

colo'**rito** *a* coloured; ⟨*viso*⟩ rosy; ⟨*racconto, linguaggio*⟩ colourful ● *nm* complexion

co'**loro** *pron pl* the ones

colos'**sale** *a* colossal

Colos'**seo** *nm* Coliseum

co'**losso** *nm* colossus

'**colpa** *nf* fault; (*biasimo*) blame; (*colpevolezza*) guilt; (*peccato*) sin; **dare la ~ a** blame; **essere in ~** be at fault; **per ~ di** because of; **è ~ mia** it's my fault

col'**pevole** *a* guilty ● *nmf* culprit

col'**pire** *vt* hit, strike; *fig* strike; **~ nel segno** hit the nail on the head

'**colpo** *nm* blow; (*di arma da fuoco*) shot; (*urto*) knock; (*emozione*) shock; *Med, Sport* stroke; (*furto*) robbery; **di ~** suddenly; **far ~** make a strong impression; **far venire un ~ a qcno** *fig* give sb a fright; **perdere colpi** ⟨*motore:*⟩ keep missing; **a ~ d'occhio** at a glance; **a ~ sicuro** for certain. **~ d'aria** chill. **~ basso** blow below the belt. **~ di frusta** *Med* whiplash injury. **~ di grazia** kiss of death. **~ da maestro** masterstroke. **~ di scena** sensational development. **~ di sole** sunstroke. **colpi** *pl* **di sole** (*su capelli*) highlights. **~ di Stato** coup [d'état]. **~ di**

telefono ring, call; **dare un ~ di telefono a qn** give sb a ring *or* call. **~ di testa** [sudden] impulse. **~ di vento** gust of wind

col'**poso** *a* **omicidio ~** manslaughter

coltel'**lata** *nf* stab

coltelle'**ria** *nf* cutlery shop

col'**tello** *nm* knife; **avere il ~ dalla parte del manico** have the upper hand. **~ per il pane** breadknife. **~ a serramanico** jack-knife

colti'**vare** *vt* cultivate

coltiva'**tore, -trice** *nmf* farmer

coltivazi'**one** *nf* farming; (*di piante*) growing. **~ intensiva** intensive farming

'**colto** *pp di* cogliere ● *a* cultured

'**coltre** *nf* blanket

col'**tura** *nf* cultivation. **~ alternata** crop rotation

co'**lui** *pron m* the one

'**colza** *nf Bot* rape

'**coma** *nm inv* coma; **in ~** in a coma; **in ~ irreversibile** brain dead

comanda'**mento** *nm* commandment

coman'**dante** *nm* commander; *Naut, Aeron* captain

coman'**dare** *vt* command; *Mech* control; **~ a qcno di fare qcsa** order sb to do sth ● *vi* be in charge

co'**mando** *nm* command; (*di macchina*) control

co'**mare** *nf* (*pettegola*) gossip

coma'**toso** *a Med* comatose

combaci'**are** *vi* fit together; ⟨*testimonianze:*⟩ concur

combat'**tente** *a* fighting ● *nm* combatant. **ex ~** ex-serviceman

com'**battere** *vt/i* fight

combatti'**mento** *nm* fight; *Mil* battle; **fuori ~** ⟨*pugilato*⟩ knocked out

combat'**tuto** *a* ⟨*gara*⟩ hard fought; (*tormentato*) torn; ⟨*discussione*⟩ heated

combi'**nare** *vt/i* arrange; (*mettere insieme*) combine; (*fam: fare*) do; **cosa stai combinando?** what are you doing?

combi'**narsi** *vr* combine; (*mettersi d'accordo*) come to an agreement

combinazi'**one** *nf* combination; (*caso*) coincidence; **per ~** by chance

com'**briccola** *nf* gang

combu'**stibile** *a* combustible ● *nm* fuel

combusti'**one** *nf* combustion

com'**butta** *nf* gang; **in ~** in league

'**come** *adv* like; (*in qualità di*) as; (*interrogativo, esclamativo*) how; **questo vestito è ~ il tuo** this dress is like yours; **~? pardon?; ~ stai?** how are you?; **~ va?** how are things?; **~ mai?** how come?; **~?** what?; **non sa ~ fare** he doesn't know what to do; **~ sta bene!** how well he looks!; **~ no!** that will be right!; **~ tu sai** as you know; **fa ~ vuoi** do as you like; **~ se** as if ● *conj* (*non appena*) as soon as

come'**done** *nm* blackhead

co'meta *nf* comet

'comfort *nm inv* comfort; **con tutti i ~** with all mod cons

'comico *a* comical; *(teatro, attore)* comic ● *nm* funny side; *(attore)* comic actor, comedian ● *nf* comedienne; *(attrice)* comic actress, comedienne; *(a torte in faccia)* slapstick sketch

co'mignolo *nm* chimney-pot

cominci'are *vt/i* begin, start; **a ~ da oggi** from today; **per ~** to begin with; **cominciamo bene!** we're off to a fine start!

comi'tato *nm* committee. **~ consultivo** advisory committee. **~ direttivo** steering committee. **~ esecutivo** executive committee. **~ di gestione** management committee

comi'tiva *nf* party, group

co'mizio *nm* meeting. **~ elettorale** election rally

'comma *nm (capoverso)* paragraph

com'mando *nm inv* commando

com'media *nf* comedy; *(opera teatrale)* play; *fig* sham. **~ musicale** musical

commedi'ante *nm* comic actor; *fig pej* phoney ● *nf* comic actress; *fig pej* phoney

commedi'ografo, -a *nmf* playwright

commemo'rare *vt* commemorate

commemorazi'one *nf* commemoration. **~ dei defunti** *2 novembre)* All Souls' Day

commenda'tore *nm* commander

commen'sale *nmf* fellow diner

commen'tare *vt* comment on; *(annotare)* annotate

commen'tario *nm* commentary

commenta|'tore, -'trice *nmf* commentator

com'mento *nm* comment; *TV, Radio* commentary. **~ musicale** music

commerci'ale *a* commercial; *(relazioni, trattative)* trade; *(attività)* business; **centro ~** shopping centre

commercia'lista *nmf* business consultant; *(contabile)* accountant

commercializ'zare *vt* market; *pej* commercialize

commercializzazi'one *nf* marketing; *pej* commercialization

commerci'ante *nmf* trader, merchant; *(negoziante)* shopkeeper. **~ all'ingrosso** wholesaler. **~ di oggetti d'arte** art dealer

commerci'are *vi* **~ in** deal in

com'mercio *nm* commerce; *(internazionale)* trade; *(affari)* business; **in ~** *(prodotto)* on sale. **~ all'ingrosso** wholesale trade. **~ al minuto** retail trade

com'messo, -a *pp di* **commettere** ● *nmf* shop assistant; **commessi** *pl* counter staff. **~ viaggiatore** commercial traveller ● *nf (ordine)* order

comme'stibile *a* edible ● *nm* **commestibili** *pl* groceries

com'mettere *vt* commit; make *(sbaglio)*; **~ un reato** commit an offence

commi'ato *nm* leave; **prendere ~ da** take leave of

commise'rare *vt* commiserate

commise'rarsi *vr* feel sorry for oneself

commissari'ato *nm (di polizia)* police station

commis'sario *nm* ≈ [police] superintendent; *(membro di commissione)* commissioner; *Sport* steward; *Comm* commission agent. **~ di bordo** purser. **~ capo** chief superintendent. **~ d'esame** examiner. **~ di gara** race official, steward. **~ tecnico** *(della nazionale)* national team manager

commissi'one *nf (incarico)* errand; *(comitato, percentuale)* commission; *(Comm: di merce)* order; **commissioni** *pl (acquisti)* **fare commissioni** go shopping. **~ d'esame** board of examiners. **C~ Europea** European Commission. **~ d'inchiesta** court of inquiry

commit'tente *nmf* purchaser

com'mosso *pp di* **commuovere** ● *a* moved

commo'vente *a* moving

commozi'one *nf* emotion. **~ cerebrale** concussion

commu'overe *vt* touch, move

commu'oversi *vr* be touched

commu'tare *vt* change; *Jur* commute

commuta'tore *nm Electr* commutator

commutazi'one *nf (di pena)* commutation

comò *nm inv* chest of drawers

coda'mente *adv* comfortably

como'dino *nm* bedside table

comodità *nf inv* comfort; *(convenienza)* convenience

'comodo *a* comfortable; *(conveniente)* convenient; *(spazioso)* roomy; *(facile)* easy; **stia comodo!** don't get up!; **far ~** be useful ● *nm* comfort; **fare il proprio ~** do as one pleases; **prendila con ~!** take it easy!

'compact disc *nm inv* compact disc

compae'sano, -a *nm* fellow countryman ● *nf* fellow countrywoman

com'pagine *nf (squadra)* team

compa'gnia *nf* company; *(gruppo)* party; **fare ~ a qcno** keep sb company; **essere di ~** be sociable. **~ aerea** airline. **~ di bandiera** *(aerea)* national airline

com'pagno, -a *nmf* companion; *(Comm, Sport, in coppia)* partner; *Pol* comrade. **~ di classe** classmate. **~ di scuola** schoolmate. **~ di squadra** team-mate. **~ di viaggio** fellow traveller

compa'rabile *a* comparable

compa'rare *vt* compare

compara'tivo *a & nm* comparative

comparazi'one *nf* comparison

com'pare *nm* sidekick

compa'rire *vi* appear; *(spiccare)* stand out. **~ in giudizio** appear in court

com'parso, -a *pp di* **comparire** ● *nf* appearance; *Cinema* extra; *Theat* walk-on

compartecipazi'one *nf* sharing; *(quota)* share

comparti'mento *nm* compartment; *(amministrativo)* department

compas'sato *a* calm and collected

compassi'one *nf* compassion; **aver ~ per** feel pity for; **far ~** arouse pity

compassio'nevole *a* compassionate

com'passo *nm* [pair of] compasses *pl*

compa'tibile *a* (*conciliabile*) compatible; (*scusabile*) excusable

compatibilità *nf* compatibility

compatibil'mente *adv* **~ con i miei impegni** if my commitments allow

compati'mento *nm* **un'aria di ~** air of condescension

compa'tire *vt* pity; (*scusare*) make allowances for

compatri'ota *nmf* compatriot

compat'tezza *nf* (*di materia*) compactness; (*fig: di partito*) solidarity

com'patto *a* compact; (*denso*) dense; (*solido*) solid; *fig* united

compendi'are *vt* (*fare un sunto*) summarize

com'pendio *nm* outline; (*sunto*) synopsis; (*libro*) compendium

compene'trare *vt* pervade

compen'sare *vt* compensate; (*supplire*) make up for

compen'sarsi *vr* balance each other out

compen'sato *nm* (*legno*) plywood

compensazi'one *nf* compensation

com'penso *nm* compensation; (*retribuzione*) remuneration; **in compenso** (*in cambio*) in return; (*d'altra parte*) on the other hand; (*invece*) instead

'compera *nf* purchase; **far compere** do some shopping

compe'rare *vt* buy

compe'tente *a* competent; (*ufficio*) appropriate

compe'tenza *nf* competence; (*responsabilità*) responsibility; **competenze** *pl* (*onorari*) fees

com'petere *vi* compete; **~ a** (*compito:*) be the responsibility of

competitività *nf* competitiveness

competi'tivo *a* (*prezzo, carattere*) competitive

competi|'tore, -'trice *nmf* competitor

competizi'one *nf* competition

compia'cente *a* obliging

compia'cenza *nf* obligingness; **avere la ~ di...** be so obliging as to...

compia'cere *vt/i* please

compia'cersi *vr* (*congratularsi*) congratulate; **~ di** (*degnarsi*) condescend to

compiaci'mento *nm* satisfaction; *pej* smugness

compiaci'uto *a* satisfied; (*aria, sorriso*) smug

compi'angere *vt* pity; (*per lutto ecc*) sympathize with

'compiere *vt* (*concludere*) complete; commit (*delitto*); **~ gli anni** have one's birthday

'compiersi *vr* end; (*avverarsi*) come true

compi'lare *vt* compile; fill in (*modulo*)

compila|'tore, -'trice *nmf* compiler

compilazi'one *nf* compilation

compi'mento *nm* completion; **portare a ~ qcsa** conclude sth

com'pire *vt* = **compiere**

compi'tare *vt* spell

'compito¹ *nm* task; (*dovere*) duty; *Sch* homework; **fare i compiti** do one's homework

com'pito² *a* polite

compiu'tezza *nf* completeness

compi'uto *a* **avere 30 anni compiuti** be over 30

comple'anno *nm* birthday

complemen'tare *a* complementary; (*secondario*) subsidiary

comple'mento *nm* complement; *Mil* draft. **~ oggetto** *Gram* direct object

comples'sato *a* hung-up

complessità *nf* complexity

complessiva'mente *adv* on the whole; (*in totale*) altogether

comples'sivo *a* comprehensive; (*totale*) total

com'plesso *a* complex; (*difficile*) complicated ● *nm* complex, hang up *fam*; *Psych* complex; (*di cantanti ecc*) group; (*di circostanze, fattori*) combination; **in ~** on the whole; (*in totale*) altogether. **~ di inferiorità** inferiority complex

completa'mente *adv* completely

completa'mento *nm* completion

comple'tare *vt* complete

comple'tezza *nf* completeness

com'pleto *a* complete; (*pieno*) full [up]; **al ~** (*teatro:*) sold out; (*albergo*) full; **'~'** 'no vacancies'; **la famiglia al ~** the whole family ● *nm* (*vestito*) suit; (*insieme di cose*) set

compli'care *vt* complicate

compli'carsi *vr* become complicated

compli'cato *a* complicated

complicazi'one *nf* complication; **salvo complicazioni** all being well

'complice *nmf* accomplice ● *a* (*sguardo*) knowing

complicità *nf* complicity

complimen'tare *nm* compliment ● *vt* compliment

complimen'tarsi *vr* **~ con** congratulate

compli'mento *nm* compliment. **complimenti** *pl* (*ossequi*) regards; (*congratulazioni*) congratulations; **far complimenti** stand on ceremony

complot'tare *vi* plot

com'plotto *nm* plot

compo'nente *a & nm* component ● *nmf* member

componen'tistica *nf* (*per auto, elettronica*) accessories *pl*

compo'nibile *a* (*cucina*) fitted; (*mobili*) modular

componi'mento *nm* composition; (*letterario*) work

com'porre *vt* compose; (*sistemare*) put in order; *Typ* set; lay out (*salma*); settle (*lite*)

com'porsi *vr* **~ di** be made up of

comportamen'tale *a* behavioural

comporta'mento *nm* behaviour

compor'tare *vt* (*implicare*) involve

compor'tarsi *vr* behave

com'posito *a* Chem, Phot composite

composi|'tore, -'trice *nmf* composer; *Typ* compositor

composizi'one *nf* composition. **~ floreale** flower arrangement

com'posta *nf* stewed fruit; (*concime*) compost

compo'stezza *nf* composure

com'posto *pp di* **comporre** ● *a* (*parola*) compound; **essere ~ da** consist of, comprise; **stai ~!** sit properly! ● *nm* Chem compound; *Culin* mixture

com'prare *vt* buy; (*fig: corrompere*) buy off, bribe

compra|'tore, -'trice *nmf* buyer

compra'vendita *nf* buying and selling; **atto di ~** deed of sale

com'prendere *vt* understand; (*includere*) comprise

compren'donio *nm* **essere duro di ~** be slow on the uptake

compren'sibile *a* understandable

comprensibil'mente *adv* understandably

comprensi'one *nf* understanding

compren'sivo *a* understanding; (*che include*) inclusive

com'preso *pp di* **comprendere** ● *a* included; **tutto ~** (*prezzo*) all-in; **da lunedì a venerdì ~** Monday to Friday inclusive

com'pressa *nf* compress; (*pastiglia*) tablet

compressi'one *nf* compression. **~ dati** *Comput* data compression

com'presso *pp di* **comprimere** ● *a* compressed

compres'sore *nm* (*rullo*) steamroller

compri'mario *nm* Theat supporting actor ● *nf* supporting actress

com'primere *vt* press; (*reprimere*) repress

compro'messo *pp di* **compromettere** ● *nm* compromise; (*contratto*) preliminary but binding agreement

compromet'tente *a* compromising

compro'mettere *vt* compromise

compropri età *nf* multiple ownership

comproprie'tario, -a *nmf* joint owner

compro'vare *vt* prove

com'punto *a* contrite

compunzi'one *nf* compunction

compu'tare *vt* calculate; (*addebitare*) estimate

com'puter *nm inv* computer. **~ da casa** home computer

computeriz'zare *vt* computerize

computeriz'zato *a* computerized

computerizzazi'one *nf* computerization

computiste'ria *nf* book-keeping

'computo *nm* calculation

comu'nale *a* municipal

co'mune *a* common; (*parti*) communal, common; (*amico*) mutual; (*ordinario*) ordinary ● *nm* municipality; **fuori del ~** out of the ordinary; **avere qcsa in ~** have sth in common ● *nf* collective farm

comu'nella *nf* **fare ~** form a clique

comune'mente *adv* commonly

comuni'cante *a* interconnecting

comuni'care *vt* communicate; pass on (*malattia*); Relig administer Communion to

comuni'carsi *vr* receive Communion

comunica'tiva *nf* communicativeness

comunica'tivo *a* communicative

comuni'cato *nm* communiqué. **~ commerciale** Radio commercial. **~ stampa** press release

comunicazi'one *nf* communication; *Teleph* [phone] call; **avere la ~** get through; **dare la ~ a qcno** put sb through. **~ dati** *Comput* data communications

comuni'one *nf* communion; Relig [Holy] Communion

comu'nismo *nm* communism

comu'nista *a & nmf* communist

comunità *nf inv* community. **C~** **[Economica] Europea** European [Economic] Community. **C~ degli Stati Indipendenti** Commonwealth of Independent States. **~ terapeutica** residential therapy group

co'munque *conj* however ● *adv* anyhow

con *prep* with; (*mezzo*) by; **~ facilità** easily; **~ mia grande gioia** to my great delight; **è gentile ~ tutti** he is kind to everyone; **col treno** by train; **~ questo tempo** in this weather

co'nato *nm* **~ di vomito** retching

'conca *nf* basin; (*valle*) dell

concate'nare *vt* link together

concate'narsi *vr* (*idee:*) be connected

concatenazi'one *nf* connection

'concavo *a* concave

con'cedere *vt* grant; award (*premio*); (*ammettere*) admit

con'cedersi *vr* allow oneself (*pausa*); treat oneself to (*lusso, vacanza*)

concentra'mento *nm* concentration

concen'trare *vt* concentrate

concen'trarsi *vr* concentrate

concen'trato *a* concentrated ● *nm* concentrate. **~ di pomodoro** tomato pureé

concentrazi'one *nf* concentration

con'centrico *a* concentric

concepi'mento *nm* conception

conce'pire *vt* conceive (*bambino*); (*capire*) understand; (*figurarsi*) conceive of; devise (*piano ecc*)

con'cernere *vt* concern

concer'tare *vt* Mus harmonize; (*organizzare*) arrange

concer'tarsi *vr* agree

concer'tista *nmf* concert performer

con'certo *nm* concert; (*composizione*) concerto. **~ rock** rock concert

concessio'nario *nm* agent

concessi'one *nf* concession

con'cesso *pp di* **concedere**
con'cetto *nm* concept; (*opinione*) opinion
concet'toso *a* cerebral
concezi'one *nf* conception; (*idea*) concept
con'chiglia *nf* [sea] shell. **~ del pelle-grino, ~ di san Giacomo** scallop shell
'concia *nf* tanning; (*di tabacco*) curing
conci'are *vt* tan; cure ‹*tabacco*›; **~ qcno per le feste** give sb a good hiding
conci'arsi *vr* (*sporcarsi*) get dirty; (*vestirsi male*) dress badly
conci'ato *a* ‹*pelle, cuoio*› tanned; **essere ~ come un barbone** look like something the cat dragged in
concili'abile *a* compatible
concili'abolo *nm* private meeting
concili'ante *a* conciliatory
concili'are *vt* reconcile; pay ‹*contravvenzione*›; (*favorire*) induce
concili'arsi *vr* go together; (*mettersi d'accordo*) become reconciled
conciliazi'one *nf* reconciliation; *Jur* settlement
con'cilio *nm Relig* council; (*riunione*) assembly
conci'maia *nf* dunghill
conci'mare *vt* feed ‹*pianta*›
con'cime *nm* manure; (*chimico*) fertilizer
concisi'one *nf* conciseness
con'ciso *a* concise
conci'tato *a* excited
concitta'dino, -a *nmf* fellow citizen
concla'mato *a Med* full blown
con'clave *nm* conclave
con'cludere *vt* conclude; (*finire con successo*) successfully complete
con'cludersi *vr* come to an end
conclusi'one *nf* conclusion; **in ~** (*insomma*) in short
conclu'sivo *a* conclusive
con'cluso *pp di* **concludere**
concomi'tante *a* contributory
concomi'tanza *nf* (*di circostanze, fatti*) combination; **in ~ con** combined with, in conjunction with
concor'danza *nf* agreement
concor'dare *vt* agree [on]; *Gram* make agree ● *vi* (*sul prezzo*) agree
concor'dato *nm* agreement; *Jur, Comm* composition
con'corde *a* in agreement; (*unanime*) unanimous
con'cordia *nf* concord
concor'rente *a* concurrent; (*rivale*) competing ● *nmf Comm, Sport* competitor; (*candidato*) candidate; (*a quiz, concorso di bellezza*) contestant
concor'renza *nf* competition. **~ sleale** unfair competition
concorrenzi'ale *a* competitive
con'correre *vi* (*contribuire*) combine; (*andare insieme*) go together; (*competere*) compete
con'corso *pp di* **concorrere** ● *nm* competition; **fuori ~** not in the official competition.

~ di bellezza beauty contest. **~ di circostanze** combination of circumstances. **~ di colpa** contributory negligence. **~ ippico** showjumping event. **~ a premi** prize-winning competition. **~ in reato** *Jur* complicity. **~ per titoli** competition in which exam results are not the sole criterion
concreta'mente *adv* concretely
concre'tare, concretiz'zare *vt* put into concrete form
con'creto *a* concrete; **in ~** in concrete terms
concu'bina *nf* concubine
concussi'one *nf* acceptance of a bribe
con'danna *nf* sentence; **pronunziare una ~** hand down a sentence. **~ a morte** death sentence. **~ penale** prison sentence
condan'nare *vt* (*disapprovare*) condemn; *Jur* sentence
condan'nato, -a *a* (*destinato*) forced ● *nmf* prisoner
con'densa *nf* condensation
conden'sare *vt* condense
conden'sarsi *vr* condense
condensa'tore *nm Electr* condenser
condensazi'one *nf* condensation
condi'mento *nm* seasoning; (*salsa*) dressing. **~ per insalata** salad dressing
con'dire *vt* flavour; dress ‹*insalata*›
condiscen'dente *a* indulgent; *pej* condescending; (*arrendevole*) compliant
condiscen'denza *nf* indulgence; *pej* condescension; (*arrendevolezza*) compliance
con'dito *a Culin* seasoned
condi'videre *vt* share
condizio'nale *a & nm* conditional ● *nf Jur* suspended sentence
condiziona'mento *nm Psych* conditioning
condizio'nare *vt* condition
condizionata'mente *adv* conditionally
condizio'nato *a* conditional (**da** on); **aria condizionata** air-conditioning
condiziona'tore *nm* air conditioner
condizi'one *nf* condition; **a ~ che** on condition that. **condizioni** *pl* **di credito** credit terms. **~ imprescindibile** precondition
condogli'anze *nfpl* condolences; **fare le ~ a** offer one's condolences to
'condom *nm inv* condom
condomini'ale *a* ‹*spese*› common; ‹*riunione*› tenants' *attrib*
condo'minio *nm* joint ownership; (*edificio*) condominium
condo'mino, -a *nmf* joint owner
condo'nare *vt* remit
con'dono *nm* remission
con'dotta *nf* conduct, (*circoscrizione di medico*) country practice; (*di gara ecc*) management; (*tubazione*) pipe
con'dotto *pp di* **condurre** ● *a* **medico ~** country doctor ● *nm* pipe; *Anat* duct. **~ dell'aria** air duct. **~ sotterraneo** culvert
condu'cente *nm* driver. **~ di autobus** bus driver

con'durre *vt* lead; drive ⟨*veicoli*⟩; (*accompagnare*) take; conduct ⟨*gas, elettricità ecc*⟩; (*gestire*) run; **~ a termine** complete; **~ delle indagini** carry out an investigation

con'dursi *vr* behave

condut'tore *a* **filo ~** leitmotif

condut'|tore, -'trice *nmf* TV presenter; (*di veicolo*) driver ● *nm Electr* conductor

condut'tura *nf* duct. **~ del gas** gas main

conduzi'one *nf* conduction

confabu'lare *vi* have a confab

confa'cente *a* suitable

con'farsi *vr* **confarsi a** suit

confederazi'one *nf* confederation. **C~ elvetica** Swiss Confederation

confe'renza *nf* (*discorso*) lecture; (*congresso*) conference. **~ stampa** press conference, news conference

conferenzi'ere, -a *nmf* lecturer, speaker

confe'rire *vt* (*donare*) confer ● *vi* (*consultarsi*) confer

con'ferma *nf* confirmation; **dare ~** confirm

confer'mare *vt* confirm

confes'sare *vt* confess

confes'sarsi *vr* confess

confessio'nale *a* ⟨*segreto*⟩ of the confession ● *nm* confessional

confessi'one *nf* confession

confes'sore *nm* confessor

con'fetto *nm* (*di mandorla*) sugared almond

confet'tura *nf* jam

confezio'nare *vt* manufacture; make ⟨*abiti*⟩; package ⟨*merci*⟩

confezio'nato *a* ⟨*vestiti*⟩ off-the-peg; ⟨*gelato*⟩ wrapped

confezi'one *nf* manufacture; (*di abiti*) making; (*di pacchi*) packaging; **di ~** ⟨*abiti*⟩ off-the-peg; **confezioni** *pl* clothes. **~ economica** economy pack, economy size. **~ famiglia** family size. **~ regalo** gift set. **~ da sei** (*di bottiglie, lattine*) six-pack

confic'care *vt* thrust

confic'carsi *vr* lodge

confic'cato *a* **~ in** lodged in, embedded in

confi'dare *vt* confide ● *vi* **~ in** trust

confi'darsi *vr* **~ con** confide in

confi'dente *a* confident ● *nmf* confidant; (*informatore*) informer

confi'denza *nf* confidence; (*familiarità*) familiarity; **prendersi delle confidenze** take liberties

confidenzi'ale *a* confidential; ⟨*tono*⟩ familiar; **in via ~** confidentially

configu'rare *vt Comput* configure

configurazi'one *nf* configuration

confi'nante *a* neighbouring

confi'nare *vt* (*relegare*) confine ● *vi* **~ con** border on

confi'narsi *vr* (*ritirarsi*) withdraw

confi'nato *a* confined ● *nm* prisoner

con'fine *nm* border; (*tra terreni*) boundary

con'fino *nm* political exile

con'fisca *nf* (*di proprietà*) confiscation

confi'scare *vt* confiscate

conflagrazi'one *nf* conflagration

con'flitto *nm* conflict

conflittu'ale *a* adversarial

conflittualità *nf* adversarial nature

conflu'enza *nf* confluence; (*di strade*) junction

conflu'ire *vi* ⟨*fiumi:*⟩ flow together; ⟨*strade:*⟩ meet

con'fondere *vt* confuse; (*imbarazzare*) embarrass

con'fondersi *vr* (*mescolarsi*) mingle; (*sbagliarsi*) be mistaken

confor'mare *vt* standardize (**a** in line with)

confor'marsi *vr* conform

conformazi'one *nf* conformity (**a** with); (*del terreno*) nature

con'forme *a* standard

conforme'mente *adv* accordingly

confor'mismo *nm* conformity

confor'mista *nmf* conformist

conformità *nf* (**a** *norma*) conformity (**a** with); **in ~ a** in accordance with, in conformity with

confor'tante *a* comforting

confor'tare *vt* comfort

confor'tevole *a* (*comodo*) comfortable

con'forto *nm* comfort; **a ~ di** ⟨*una tesi*⟩ in support of; **conforti** *pl* **religiosi** last rites

confra'telli *nmpl* brethren

confra'ternita *nf* brotherhood

confron'tare *vt* compare

con'fronto *nm* comparison; **in ~ a** by comparison with; **nei tuoi confronti** towards you; **senza ~** far and away, by far. **~ diretto** head to head

confusio'nario *a* ⟨*persona*⟩ muddle-headed

confusi'one *nf* confusion; (*baccano*) racket; (*disordine*) mess; (*imbarazzo*) embarrassment

con'fuso *pp di* **confondere** ● *a* confused; (*indistinto*) indistinct; (*imbarazzato*) embarrassed

confu'tare *vt* confute

conge'dare *vt* dismiss; *Mil* discharge

conge'darsi *vr* take one's leave

con'gedo *nm* leave; **essere in ~** be on leave. **~ malattia** sick leave. **~ [di] maternità** maternity leave. **~ [di] paternità** paternity leave

conge'gnare *vt* devise; (*mettere insieme*) assemble

con'gegno *nm* device

congela'mento *nm* freezing; *Med* frostbite

conge'lare *vt* freeze

conge'lato *a* ⟨*cibo*⟩ deep-frozen

congela'tore *nm* freezer

congeni'ale *a* congenial

con'genito *a* congenital

congestio'nare *vt* congest

congestio'nato *a* ⟨*traffico*⟩ congested; ⟨*viso*⟩ flushed

congesti'one *nf* congestion

conget'tura *nf* conjecture

congi'ungere *vt* join, connect; join ‹mani›; combine ‹sforzi›

congi'ungersi *vr* join, connect

congiunti'vite *nf* conjunctivitis

congiun'tivo *nm* subjunctive

congi'unto *pp di* **congiungere** ● *a* joined; ‹azione› joint; ‹forze, sforzo› combined ● *nm* relative

congiun'tura *nf* junction; (*situazione*) situation

congiuntu'rale *a* economic

congiunzi'one *nf Gram* conjunction

congi'ura *nf* conspiracy

congiu'rare *vi* conspire

conglome'rato *nm* conglomerate; *fig* conglomeration; (*da costruzione*) concrete

'Congo *nm* Congo

congo'lese *a & nmf* Congolese

congratu'larsi *vr* ~ **con qcno per** congratulate sb on

congratulazi'oni *nfpl* congratulations

con'grega *nf* band

congre'gare *vt* gather

congre'garsi *vr* congregate

congregazi'one *nf* congregation

congres'sista *nmf* convention participant

con'gresso *nm* congress, convention; (*americano*) Congress. **C~ Nazionale Africano** African National Congress

'congrua *nf* stipend

'congruo *a* proper; (*giusto*) fair

conguagli'are *vt* balance

congu'aglio *nm* balance

coni'are *vt* coin

conia'tura *nf* coinage

coniazi'one *nf* coinage

'conico *a* conical

co'nifera *nf* conifer

co'niglia *nf* female rabbit, doe

conigli'era *nf* rabbit hutch

conigli'etta *nf* bunny girl

conigli'etto *nm* bunny

co'niglio *nm* rabbit

coniu'gale *a* marital; ‹vita› married

coniu'gare *vt* conjugate

coniu'garsi *vr* get married; *Gram* conjugate

coniu'gato *a* (*sposato*) married

coniugazi'one *nf* conjugation

'coniuge *nmf* spouse

connazio'nale *nmf* compatriot

connessi'one *nf* connection

con'nesso *pp di* **connettere**

con'nettere *vt* connect ● *vi* think rationally

con'nettersi *vr* (*Comput: a bacheca elettronica*) log on (**a** to)

connet'tore *nm* connector

conni'vente *a* conniving

conno'tare *vt* connote

conno'tato *nm* distinguishing feature; **connotati** *pl* description; **rispondere ai connotati** fit the description; **cambiare i connotati a qcno** *hum* re-arrange sb's face

con'nubio *nm fig* union

'cono *nm* cone

cono'scente *nmf* acquaintance

cono'scenza *nf* knowledge; (*persona*) acquaintance; (*sensi*) consciousness; **perdere** ~ lose consciousness; **riprendere** ~ regain consciousness, come to. ~ **di lavoro** business contact

co'noscere *vt* know; (*essere a conoscenza di*) be acquainted with; (*fare la conoscenza di*) meet; ~ **qcsa a fondo** know sth inside out

conosci'|tore, -'trice *nmf* connoisseur

conosci'uto *pp di* **conoscere** ● *a* well-known

con'quista *nf* conquest

conqui'stare *vt* conquer; *fig* win

conquista'tore *nm* conqueror; *fig* lady-killer

consa'crare *vt* consecrate; ordain ‹sacerdote›; (*dedicare*) dedicate

consa'crarsi *vr* devote oneself

consa'crato *a* ‹suolo› hallowed

consacrazi'one *nf* consecration

consangu'ineo, -a *nmf* blood-relation

consa'pevole *a* conscious

consapevo'lezza *nf* consciousness

consapevol'mente *adv* consciously

conscia'mente *adv* consciously

'conscio *a* conscious

consecu'tivo *a* consecutive; (*seguente*) next

con'segna *nf* delivery; (*merce*) consignment; (*custodia*) care; (*di prigioniero*) handover; (*Mil: ordine*) orders *pl*; (*Mil: punizione*) confinement to barracks; **pagamento alla** ~ cash on delivery. ~ **della posta** mail delivery

conse'gnare *vt* deliver; *Mil* confine to barracks; hand over ‹prigioniero, chiavi›

consegna'tario *nm* consignee

consegu'ente *a* consequent

consegu'enza *nf* consequence; **di** ~ (*perciò*) consequently; ‹agire, comportarsi› accordingly

consegui'mento *nm* achievement

consegu'ire *vt* achieve ● *vi* follow

con'senso *nm* consent; (*della popolazione*) consensus

consensu'ale *a* consensus-based

consen'tire *vi* consent ● *vt* allow

consenzi'ente *a* consenting

con'serto *a* **a braccia conserte** with one's arms folded

con'serva *nf* preserve; (*di frutta*) jam; (*di agrumi*) marmalade. ~ **di pomodoro** tomato sauce

conser'vare *vt* preserve; (*mantenere*) keep; ~ **in frigo** keep refrigerated; ~ **in luogo asciutto** keep dry

conser'varsi *vr* keep; ~ **in salute** keep well

conserva'|tore, -'trice *a & nmf Pol* conservative; **partito** ~ Conservative Party, Tory Party *Br*

conserva'torio *nm* conservatory, school of music

conservato'rismo *nm* conservatism
conservazi'one *nf* preservation; **a lunga ~** long-life
con'sesso *nm* assembly
conside'rare *vt* consider; *(stimare)* regard
conside'rato *a (stimato)* esteemed
considerazi'one *nf* consideration; *(osservazione, riflessione)* remark; *(stima)* respect
conside'revole *a* considerable
consigli'abile *a* advisable
consigli'are *vt* advise; *(raccomandare)* recommend
consigli'arsi *vr* **~ con qcno** ask sb's advice
consigli'ere, -a *nmf* adviser; *(membro di un consiglio)* councillor. **~ d'amministrazione** board member. **~ delegato** managing director
con'siglio *nm* advice; *(ente)* council; **un ~ a** piece of advice. **~ d'amministrazione** board of directors. **~ di guerra** war cabinet. **~ d'istituto** parent-teacher association. **~ dei ministri** Cabinet. **~ scolastico** education committee. **C~ di Sicurezza** *(dell'ONU)* Security Council. **C~ Superiore della Magistratura** *body responsible for ensuring the independence of the judiciary*
con'simile *a* similar
consi'stente *a* substantial; *(spesso)* thick; *(fig: argomento)* solid
consi'stenza *nf* consistency; *(spessore)* thickness; *(fig: di argomento)* solidity
con'sistere *vi* **~ in** consist of
consoci'arsi *vr* go into partnership
consoci'ata *nf (azienda)* subsidiary
consociati'vismo *nm* excessive tendency to form associations
consoci'ato *nm* associate
con'socio, -a *nmf* fellow-member
conso'lante *a* consoling
conso'lare[1] *a* consular
conso'lare[2] *vt* console
conso'larsi *vr* console oneself
conso'lato *nm* consulate
consolazi'one *nf* consolation
'console *nm* consul
con'sole *nf inv (tastiera)* console
consolida'mento *nm* consolidation
consoli'dare *vt* consolidate
consoli'darsi *vr* consolidate
consommé *nm inv* consommé
conso'nante *nf* consonant
conso'nanza *nf* consonance
'consono *a* appropriate (**a** to), suitable (**a** for)
con'sorte *nmf* consort
con'sorzio *nm* consortium
con'stare *vi* **~ di** consist of; *(risultare)* appear; **a quanto mi consta** as far as I know; **mi consta che...** seemingly,...
consta'tare *vt* ascertain
constatazi'one *nf* statement of fact
consu'eto *a* usual ● *nm* **più del ~** more than usual

consuetudi'nario *a (diritto)* common; *(persona)* set in one's ways
consue'tudine *nf* habit; *(usanza)* custom
consu'lente *nmf* consultant. **~ aziendale** management consultant; *(azienda)* management consultancy. **~ matrimoniale** marriage guidance counsellor
consu'lenza *nf* consultancy
consul'tare *vt* consult
consul'tarsi *vr* **~ con** consult with
consultazi'one *nf* consultation
consul'tivo *a* consultative
con'sulto *nm* consultation
consul'torio *nm* free clinic providing treatment for sexual problems and advice
consu'mare *vt (usare)* consume; wear out *(abito, scarpe)*; consummate *(matrimonio)*; commit *(delitto)*
consu'marsi *vr* consume; *(abito, scarpe:)* wear out; *(struggersi)* pine; **'da ~ preferibilmente entro il...'** 'best before...'
consu'mato *a (politico)* consummate; *(scarpe, tappeto)* worn [out]
consuma|'tore, -'trice *nmf* consumer
consumazi'one *nf* consumption; *(bibita)* drink; *(spuntino)* snack; *(di matrimonio)* consummation; *(di delitto)* commission
consu'mismo *nm* consumerism
consu'mista *nmf* consumerist
con'sumo *nm* consumption; *(uso)* use; **generi di ~** consumer goods. **~ [di carburante]** [fuel] consumption
consun'tivo *nm* **bilancio ~** balance sheet; **fare il ~ di** *fig* take stock of
con'sunto *a* well-worn
conta'balle *nmf fam* storyteller
con'tabile *a* book-keeping ● *nmf* accountant
contabilità *nf inv* accounting; *(ufficio)* accounts department; **tenere la ~** keep the accounts. **~ di gestione** management accounts. **~ in partita doppia** double entry book-keeping
contachi'lometri *nm inv* mileometer, odometer *Am*
conta'dino, -a *nmf* farm-worker, agricultural labourer; *(proprietario)* farmer; *(medievale)* peasant
contagi'are *vt* infect; **la sua allegria contagia tutti** his cheerfulness is very contagious
contagi'ato *a* infected
con'tagio *nm* contagion
contagi'oso *a* contagious
conta'giri *nm inv* rev counter
conta'gocce *nm inv* dropper; **dare qcsa col ~** *fig* dole sth out in dribs and drabs
contami'nare *vt* contaminate
contaminazi'one *nf* contamination
contami'nuti *nm inv* timer
con'tante *nm* cash; **pagare in contanti** pay cash
con'tare *vt* count; *(tenere conto di)* take into

account; **devi ~ un'ora per il viaggio** you have to allow an hour for the journey ● *vi* count; **~ di fare qcsa** plan to do sth

conta'scatti *nm inv Teleph* time-unit counter

con'tato *a* ⟨giorni, ore⟩ numbered

conta'tore *nm* meter. **~ del gas** gas meter

contat'tare *vt* contact

con'tatto *nm* contact; **essere in ~ con** be in touch *or* contact with; **mettersi in ~ con** contact, get in touch with

'conte *nm* count, earl *Br*

con'tea *nf* county

conteggi'are *vt* include ● *vi* calculate

con'teggio *nm* calculation. **~ alla rovescia** countdown

con'tegno *nm* behaviour; (*atteggiamento*) attitude; **darsi un ~** pull oneself together

conte'gnoso *a* dignified

contem'plare *vt* contemplate; (*fissare*) gaze at

contempla'tivo *a* contemplative

contemplazi'one *nf* contemplation

con'tempo *nm* **nel ~** in the meantime

contemporanea'mente *adv* at the same time

contempo'raneo, -a *a* & *nmf* contemporary

conten'dente *nmf* competitor

con'tendere *vi* compete; (*litigare*) quarrel ● *vt* dispute

con'tendersi *vr* **~ qcsa** compete for sth

conte'nere *vt* contain; (*reprimere*) repress

conte'nersi *vr* contain oneself

conteni'tore *nm* container

conten'tabile *a* **facilmente ~** easy to please

conten'tare *vt* please

conten'tarsi *vr* **~ di** be content with

conten'tezza *nf* happiness

conten'tino *nm* placebo

con'tento *a* glad; (*soddisfatto*) happy

conte'nuto *nm* contents *pl*; (*di libro, testo*) content

contenzi'oso *a* contentious ● *nm* dispute; (*ufficio*) legal department

con'tesa *nf* disagreement; *Sport* contest

con'teso *pp di* **contendere** ● *a* contested

con'tessa *nf* countess

conte'stare *vt* contest; *Jur* give notification of ⟨*contravvenzione*⟩; **~ un reato a qcno** charge sb with an offence

contesta|'tore, -'trice *nmf* person who is anti-authority ● *a* anti-authority

contestazi'one *nf* (*disputa*) dispute; (*protesta*) protest; (*di contravvenzione*) notification

con'testo *nm* context

con'tiguo *a* adjacent

continen'tale *a* continental

conti'nente *nm* continent

conti'nenza *nf* continence

contin'gente *nm* contingent; (*quota*) quota

contin'genza *nf* contingency

continua'mente *adv* (*senza interruzione*) continuously; (*frequentemente*) continually

continu'are *vt/i* continue; (*riprendere*) resume; **~ gli studi** stay on at school

continua'tivo *a* on-going, continuous

continuazi'one *nf* continuation

continuità *nf* continuity

con'tinuo *a* continuous; (*molto frequente*) continual; **di ~** continuously; (*frequentemente*) continually; **corrente continua** direct current

con'tinuum *nm inv* continuum

'conto *nm* calculation; (*in banca, negozio*) account; (*di ristorante ecc*) bill; (*stima*) consideration; **a conti fatti** all things considered; **ad ogni buon ~** in any case; **di poco/nessun ~** of little/no importance; **in fin dei conti** when all's said and done; **per ~ di** on behalf of; **per ~ mio** (*a mio parere*) in my opinion; (*da solo*) on my own; **per ~ terzi** for a third party; **sul ~ di** (*voci, informazioni*) about sb; **far ~ di** (*supporre*) suppose; (*proporsi*) intend; **far ~ su** rely on; **fare i propri conti** do one's accounts; **fare i conti con qcno** *fig* sort sb out; **fare i conti in tasca a qcno** estimate how much sb is worth; **fare i conti senza l'oste** forget the most important thing; **render ~ a qcno di qcsa** be accountable to sb for sth; **rendersi ~ di qcsa** realize sth; **starsene per ~ proprio** be on one's own; **tener ~ di qcsa** take sth into account; **tenere da ~ qcsa** look after sth. **~ in banca** bank account. **~ congiunto** joint account. **~ corrente** current account, checking account *Am*. **~ [corrente] comune** joint account. **~ corrente postale** Giro account. **~ profitti e perdite** profit and loss account. **~ alla rovescia** countdown. **~ spese** expense account

con'torcere *vt* twist

con'torcersi *vr* twist about

contor'nare *vt* surround

con'torno *nm* contour; *Culin* vegetables *pl*

contorsi'one *nf* contortion

contorsio'nista *nmf* contortionist

con'torto *pp di* **contorcere** ● *a* twisted

contrabban'dare *vt* smuggle

contrabbandi'ere, -a *nmf* smuggler

contrab'bando *nm* contraband

contrabbas'sista *nmf* double bass player

contrab'basso *nm* double bass

contraccambi'are *vt* return

contrac'cambio *nm* return

contraccet'tivo *nm* contraceptive

contraccezi'one *nf* contraception

contrac'colpo *nm* rebound; (*di arma da fuoco*) recoil; *fig* repercussion

con'trada *nf* (*rione*) district

contrad'detto *pp di* **contraddire**

contrad'dire *vt* contradict

contraddi'stinguere *vt* differentiate, distinguish

contraddi'stinto *pp di* **distinguere** ● *a* ~ **da** distinguished by

contraddit'torio *a* contradictory

contraddizi'one *nf* contradiction

contra'ente *nmf* contracting party

contra'ereo *a* anti-aircraft

contraf'fare *vt* disguise

contraf'fatto *pp di* **contraffare** ● *a* disguised

contraffazi'one *nf* disguising

contraf'forte *nm* buttress

con'tralto *nm* countertenor ● *nf* contralto

contrap'peso *nm* counterbalance

contrap'porre *vt* (*confrontare*) compare; ~ **A a B** counter B with A

contrap'porsi *vr* be in opposition; ~ **a** contrast with; (*opporsi a*) be opposed to

contrap'punto *nm* Mus counterpoint

contraria'mente *adv* ~ **a** contrary to; ~ **a me** unlike me

contrari'are *vt* oppose; (*infastidire*) annoy

contrari'arsi *vr* get annoyed

contrarietà *nf* adversity; (*ostacolo*) setback

con'trario *a* contrary, opposite; ⟨*direzione*⟩ opposite; ⟨*esito, vento*⟩ unfavourable ● *nm* contrary, opposite; **al** ~ on the contrary

con'trarre *vt* contract

contrasse'gnare *vt* mark

contras'segno *nm* mark; [**in**] ~ ⟨*spedizione*⟩ cash on delivery, COD. ~ **IVA** VAT receipt

contra'stante *a* contrasting

contra'stare *vt* oppose; (*contestare*) contest ● *vi* contrast; ⟨*colori:*⟩ clash

con'trasto *nm* contrast; (*di colori*) clash; (*litigio*) dispute

contrattac'care *vt* counter-attack

contrat'tacco *nm* counter-attack

contrat'tare *vt/i* negotiate; (*mercanteggiare*) bargain

contrattazi'one *nf* contravention; (*multa*) fine; (*salariale*) bargaining. ~ **di azioni** share dealing

contrat'tempo *nm* hitch

con'tratto *pp di* **contrarre** ● *nm* contract. ~ **di lavoro** employment contract. ~ **a termine** fixed-term contract. **contratti** *pl* **a termine** Fin futures

contrattu'ale *a* contractual

contravve'nire *vi* contravene a law

contrazi'one *nf* contraction; (*di prezzi*) reduction

contribu'ente *nmf* contributor; (*del fisco*) taxpayer

contribu'ire *vi* contribute

contribu'tivo *a* contributory

contri'buto *nm* contribution. **contributi** *pl* **pensionistici** pension contributions

con'trito *a* contrite

'contro *prep* against; ~ **di me** against me ● *nm* **il pro e il** ~ the pros and cons *pl*

contro'battere *vt* counter

controbilanci'are *vt* counterbalance

controcor'rente *a* ⟨*idee, persona*⟩ non-conformist ● *adv* upriver; *fig* upstream; **andare** ~ *fig* swim against the tide

controcul'tura *nf* counterculture

contro'curva *nf* second bend

contro'esodo *nm* massive return from holiday

controfa'gotto *nm* double bassoon

controffen'siva *nf* counter-offensive

controfi'gura *nf* stand-in

controfi'letto *nm* sirloin

controfir'mare *vt* countersign

controindicazi'one *nf* Med contraindication

controinterroga'torio *nm* cross-examination

control'labile *a* ⟨*emozione*⟩ controllable; Tech which can be monitored

control'lare *vt* control; (*verificare*) check

control'larsi *vr* control oneself

control'lato *a* controlled

con'troller *nm inv* Fin controller

con'trollo *nm* control; (*verifica*) check; Med check-up; **perdere il** ~ **di** lose control of. ~ **degli armamenti** arms control. ~ **automatico della velocità** automatic speed check. ~ **bagagli** baggage control. ~ **biglietti** ticket inspection. ~ **dei cambi** exchange control. ~ **del credito** credit control. ~ **medico** check-up. ~ **delle nascite** birth control. ~ **passaporti** passport control. ~ [**di**] **qualità** quality control. ~ **radar della velocità** radar speed check

control'lore *nm* controller; (*sui treni ecc*) [ticket] inspector. ~ **di volo** air-traffic controller

contro'luce *nf* **in** ~ against the light

contro'mano *adv* in the wrong direction

contromi'sura *nf* countermeasure

contropar'tita *nf* compensation; **in** ~ in return

contropi'ede *nm* Sport breakaway; **prendere in** ~ *fig* catch off guard

controprodu'cente *a* counter-productive

contro'prova *nf* cross-check; **fare la** ~ **di qcsa** cross-check sth

con'trordine *nm* counter order; **salvo contrordini** unless I/you hear to the contrary

contro'senso *nm* contradiction in terms

controspio'naggio *nm* counterespionage

controten'denza *nf* countertrend

controva'lore *nm* equivalent

contro'vento *adv* against the wind

contro'versia *nf* controversy; Jur dispute

contro'verso *a* controversial

contro'voglia *adv* unwillingly

contu'mace *a* Jur in default, absent

contu'macia *nf* default; **in** ~ in one's absence

contun'dente *a* ⟨*corpo, arma*⟩ blunt

contur'bante *a* perturbing

contur'bare *vt* perturb

contusi'one *nf* bruise

con'tuso *nm* person suffering from cuts and bruises

convale'scente *a & nmf* convalescent

convale'scenza *nf* convalescence; **essere in ~** be convalescing

con'valida *nf* ratification; (*di nomina*) confirmation; (*di biglietto*) validation

convali'dare *vt* ratify; confirm ‹*nomina*›; validate ‹*atto, biglietto*›

con'vegno *nm* meeting; (*congresso*) convention, congress

conve'nevole *a* suitable

conve'nevoli *nmpl* pleasantries

conveni'ente *a* convenient; (*vantaggioso*) advantageous; ‹*prezzo*› attractive

conveni'enza *nf* convenience; (*interesse*) advantage; (*di prezzo*) attractiveness

conve'nire *vi* agree; (*riunirsi*) gather; (*essere opportuno*) be convenient; **ci conviene andare** it's better to go; **non mi conviene stancarmi** I'd better not tire myself out ● *vt* agree [on]

conven'ticola *nf* clique

con'vento *nm* (*di suore*) convent; (*di frati*) monastery

conve'nuto *a* agreed

convenzio'nale *a* conventional

convenzio'nato *a* ‹*prezzo*› controlled

convenzi'one *nf* convention

conver'gente *a* converging

conver'genza *nf* convergence

con'vergere *vi* converge

con'versa *nf* lay sister

conver'sare *vi* converse

conversa|'tore, -'trice *nmf* conversationalist

conversazi'one *nf* conversation

conversi'one *nf* conversion

con'verso *pp di* **convergere**

conver'tibile *nf Auto* convertible

conver'tire *vt* convert

conver'tirsi *vr* convert

conver'tito, -a *a* converted ● *nmf* convert

converti'tore *nm* converter

con'vesso *a* convex

convezi'one *nf* convection

convin'cente *a* convincing

con'vincere *vt* convince

con'vinto *a* convinced

convinzi'one *nf* conviction

convi'tato *nm* guest

con'vitto *nm* boarding school

convi'vente *nm* common-law husband ● *nf* common-law wife

convi'venza *nf* cohabitation

con'vivere *vi* live together

convivi'ale *a* convivial

convo'care *vt* summon; *Jur* summons; convene ‹*riunione*›

convocazi'one *nf* summoning; *Jur* summonsing; (*atto*) summons; (*riunione*) meeting

convogli'are *vt* convey; ‹*navi:*› convoy

con'voglio *nm* convoy; (*ferroviario*) train

convo'lare *vi* **~ a giuste nozze** *hum* tie the knot

convulsa'mente *adv* convulsively

convulsi'one *nf* convulsion; *fig* fit

convul'sivo *a Med* convulsive; ‹*riso*› hysterical

coope'rare *vi* co-operate

coopera'tiva *nf* co-operative

cooperazi'one *nf* co-operation

coordina'mento *nm* co-ordination

coordi'nare *vt* co-ordinate

coordi'nata *nf Math* co-ordinate; **coordinate** *pl* (*su mappa*) grid reference. **coordinate** *pl* **bancarie** [bank] sort code

coordi'nato *a* co-ordinated

coordina|'tore, -'trice *nmf* co-ordinator

coordinazi'one *nf* co-ordination

co'perchio *nm* lid; (*copertura*) cover

co'perta *nf* blanket; (*copertura*) cover; *Naut* deck. **~ elettrica** electric blanket

coper'tina *nf* cover; (*di libro*) dust-jacket

co'perto *pp di* **coprire** ● *a* covered; ‹*vestito*› wrapped up; ‹*cielo*› overcast; ‹*piscina*› indoor ● *nm* (*a tavola*) place; (*prezzo del coperto*) cover charge; **al ~** under cover

coper'tone *nm* tarpaulin; (*gomma*) tyre

coper'tura *nf* cover; (*azione*) covering; (*di strada*) surfacing; (*di malefatta*) cover-up. **~ globale** blanket coverage

'copia *nf* copy; **bella/brutta ~** fair/rough copy; **essere la ~ spiccicata di qcno** be the spitting image of sb. **~ su carta** hardcopy. **~ pirata** pirate copy. **~ di riserva** *Comput* backup copy

copi'are *vt* copy

copia'trice *nf* copier

copi'lota *nmf* co-pilot; (*di auto*) co-driver

copi'one *nm Cinema, TV* script

copi'oso *a* copious

'coppa *nf* (*calice*) goblet; (*bicchiere*) glass; (*per gelato ecc*) dish; *Sport* cup. **~ [di] gelato** ice-cream (*served in a dish*). **~ del mondo** World Cup

cop'petta *nf* (*di ceramica, vetro*) bowl; (*di gelato*) small tub

'coppia *nf* couple; (*in carte, voga*) pair

co'prente *a* (*cipria, vernice*) thick; ‹*collant*› opaque

copri'capo *nm* head covering

coprifu'oco *nm* curfew

copri'letto *nm* bedspread

copri'mozzo *nm* hub-cap

copripiu'mino *nm* duvet cover

co'prire *vt* cover; drown [out] ‹*suono*›; hold ‹*carica*›

co'prirsi *vr* (*vestirsi*) cover oneself up; (*vestirsi pesante*) dress warmly; *fig* cover up; (*proteggersi*) cover oneself; ‹*cielo:*› become overcast

copritei'era *nm* tea cosy

co-protago'nista *nmf Cinema* co-star

'coque: alla ~ *a* ‹*uovo*› soft-boiled

co'raggio *nm* bravery, courage; (*sfacciataggine*) nerve; **~!** chin up!

coraggiosa'mente *adv* bravely, courageously

coraggi'oso *a* brave, courageous

co'rale *a* choral

co'rallo nm coral

co'rano nm Koran

co'razza nf armour; (di animali) shell

coraz'zata nf battleship

coraz'zato a ‹nave› armour-plated

corazza'tura nf armour plate, armour plating

corazzi'ere nm cuirassier

corbelle'ria nf piece of nonsense; **dire corbellerie** talk nonsense

'corda nf cord; (spago, Mus) string; (fune) rope; (cavo) cable; **essere giù di ~** be down; **dare ~ a qcno** encourage sb; **tagliare la ~** cut and run; **tenere qcno sulla ~** keep sb on tenterhooks. **corde** pl **vocali** vocal cords

cor'data nf roped party

cordi'ale a cordial ● nm (bevanda) cordial; **cordiali saluti** best wishes

cordialità nf cordiality; **~** pl (saluti) best wishes

cor'doglio nm grief; (lutto) mourning

cor'done nm cord; (schieramento) cordon. **~ ombelicale** umbilical cord. **~ sanitario** cordon sanitaire

Co'rea nf Korea

core'ano, -a a & nmf Korean

coreogra'fia nf choreography; **fare la ~ di** choreograph

core'ografo, -a nmf choreographer

Corfù nf Corfu

cori'aceo a tough

cori'andoli nmpl (di carta) confetti sg

cori'andolo nm (spezia) coriander

cori'care vt put to bed

cori'carsi vr go to bed

Co'rinto nf Corinth

co'rista nmf choir member

'corna vedi **corno**

cor'nacchia nf crow

corna'musa nf bagpipes pl

'cornea nf cornea

'corner nm inv corner; **salvarsi in ~** fig have a lucky escape

cor'netta nf Mus cornet; (del telefono) receiver

cor'netto nm (brioche) croissant. **~ acustico** ear trumpet

cor'nice nf frame

cornici'one nm cornice

cornifi'care vt fam cheat on

'corno nm (pl f **corna**) horn; **fare le corna a qcno** fam cheat on sb; **fare le corna** (per scongiuro) ≈ touch wood; **un ~!** you must be joking!; (per niente) nonsense!. **~ da caccia** French horn

Corno'vaglia nf Cornwall

cornu'copia nf cornucopia

cor'nuto a horned ● nm (fam: marito tradito) cuckold; (insulto) bastard

'coro nm chorus; Relig choir

co'rolla nf corolla

corol'lario nm corollary

co'rona nf crown; (di fiori) wreath; (rosario) rosary

corona'mento nm (di sogno) fulfilment; (di carriera) crowning achievement

coro'nare vt fulfil ‹sogno›

coro'nario a ‹arteria› coronary

cor'petto nm bodice

'corpo nm body; (Mil, diplomatico) corps inv; [a] **~ a ~** Mil hand to hand; **lottare** [a] **~ a ~** have a punch-up, slug it out; **dare ~ a qcsa** give substance to sth; **buttarsi a ~ morto in qcsa** throw oneself desperately into sth; **andare di ~** move one's bowels. **~ di ballo** corps de ballet. **~ insegnante** teaching staff. **~ del reato** incriminating piece of evidence

corpo'rale a corporal

corporati'vismo nm corporatism

corpora'tura nf build

corporazi'one nf corporation

cor'poreo a bodily

cor'poso a full-bodied

corpu'lento a stout

'corpus nm inv corpus

cor'puscolo nm corpuscle

corre'dare vt (di note) supply (di with); **corredato di curriculum** accompanied by a CV

corre'dino nm (per neonato) layette

cor'redo nm (nuziale) trousseau; (di informazioni ecc) set

cor'reggere vt correct; lace ‹bevanda›

corre'lare vt correlate

cor'rente a running; (in vigore) current; (frequente) everyday; ‹inglese ecc› fluent ● nf current; (d'aria) draught; **essere al ~ di qcsa** be aware of sth; **tenersi al ~** keep up to date (**di** with). **~ continua** direct current. **~ trasversale** cross current

corrente'mente adv ‹parlare› fluently; (comunemente) commonly

'correre vi run; (affrettarsi) hurry; Sport race; ‹notizie:› circulate; **lascia ~!** let it go!; **~ dietro a** run after; **tra loro non corre buon sangue** there is bad blood between them ● vt run; **~ un pericolo** run a risk; **corre voce che...** there's a rumour that...

correspon'sabile nmf person jointly responsible

corresponsi'one nf payment

corretta'mente adv correctly; ‹sedersi, mangiare› properly; ‹trattare, fare qcsa› right

corret'tivo nm corrective

cor'retto pp di **correggere** ● a correct; ‹caffè› with a drop of alcohol

corret'|tore, -'trice nmf **~ di bozze** proof-reader ● nm **~ grammaticale** Comput grammar checker. **~ ortografico** Comput spellcheck[er]

correzi'one nf correction. **~ di bozze** proof-reading. **~ errori** Comput error correction

cor'rida nf bullfight

corri'doio nm corridor; Aeron aisle

corri'|dore, -'trice *nmf* (*automobilistico*) driver; (*ciclista*) cyclist; (*a piedi*) runner

corri'era *nf* coach, bus

corri'ere *nm* courier; (*posta*) mail; (*spedizioniere*) carrier

corri'mano *nm* banister

corrispet'tivo *nm* amount due

corrispon'dente *a* corresponding ● *nmf* correspondent

corrispon'denza *nf* correspondence; **tenersi in ~ con** correspond with; **per ~** ⟨*fare un corso*⟩ by correspondence; **corso per ~** correspondence course; **vendite per ~** mail-order [shopping]

corri'spondere *vi* correspond; ⟨*stanza:*⟩ communicate; **~ a** (*contraccambiare*) return

corri'sposto *a* ⟨*amore*⟩ reciprocated

corrobo'rare *vt* strengthen; *fig* corroborate

cor'rodere *vt* corrode

cor'rodersi *vr* corrode

cor'rompere *vt* corrupt; (*con denaro*) bribe

corrosi'one *nf* corrosion

corro'sivo *a* corrosive

cor'roso *pp di* **corrodere**

cor'rotto *pp di* **corrompere** ● *a* corrupt

corrucci'arsi *vr* be vexed

corrucci'ato *a* vexed

corru'gare *vt* wrinkle; **~ la fronte** knit one's brows

corrut'tela *nf* depravity

corruzi'one *nf* corruption; (*con denaro*) bribery

'corsa *nf* running; (*rapida*) dash; *Sport* race; (*di treno ecc*) journey; **di ~** at a run; **di gran ~** in a great hurry; **fare una ~** (*sbrigarsi*) run, hurry. **~ agli armamenti** arms race. **~ ciclistica** cycle race. **~ a ostacoli** obstacle race. **~ piana** flat racing. **~ semplice** one way [ticket]

cor'sia *nf* gangway; (*di ospedale*) ward; *Auto* lane; (*di supermercato*) aisle. **~ autobus** bus lane. **~ d'emergenza** *Auto* hard shoulder. **~ di sorpasso** fast lane, outside lane

'Corsica *nf* Corsica

cor'sivo *nm* italics *pl*; **in ~** in italics

'corso *pp di* **correre** ● *nm* course; (*strada*) main street; *Comm* circulation; (*in borsa*) price, quotation; **essere in ~** be underway; **lavori in ~** work in progress; **nel ~ di** during; **avere ~ legale** be legal tender. **~ d'acqua** waterway. **~ per corrispondenza** correspondence course. **~ di formazione professionale** training course. **~ del giorno** current daily price. **~ di laurea** degree course. **~ serale** evening class

'corso, -a *a & nmf* (*della Corsica*) Corsican

'corte *nf* [court]yard; (*Jur, regale*) court; **fare la ~ a** qcno court sb. **~ d'appello** court of appeal. **~ d'assise** ≈ crown court. **C~ di cassazione** supreme court of appeal. **C~ dei conti** ≈ National Audit Office. **C~ europea per i diritti dell'uomo** European Court of Human Rights. **C~ europea di giustizia** European Court of Justice. **~ di giustizia** court of law

cor'teccia *nf* bark

corteggia'mento *nm* courtship

corteggi'are *vt* court

corteggia'tore *nm* admirer

cor'teo *nm* procession. **~ di auto** motorcade. **~ funebre** funeral cortège. **~ nuziale** bridal party

cor'tese *a* courteous

corte'sia *nf* courtesy; **per ~** please

cortigi'ano, -a *nmf* courtier ● *nf* courtesan

cor'tile *nm* courtyard

cor'tina *nf* curtain; (*schermo*) screen

'corto *a* short; **per farla corta** to cut a long story short; **a ~ di** short of, hard up for. **~ circuito** *nm* short [circuit]

cortome'traggio *nm Cinema* short

cor'vino *a* jet-black

'corvo *nm* raven

'cosa *nf* thing; (*faccenda*) matter; *inter, rel* what; [**che**] **~** what; **nessuna ~** nothing; **ogni ~** everything; **per prima ~** first of all; **tante cose** [so] many things; (*augurio*) all the best; **~?** what?; **~ hai detto?** what did you say?; **le cose le vanno bene** she's doing all right

'cosca *nf* clan

'coscia *nf* thigh; *Culin* leg; **cosce pl di rana** frogs' legs

cosci'ente *a* conscious

cosci'enza *nf* conscience; (*consapevolezza*) consciousness; **mettersi la ~ a posto** salve one's conscience

coscienziosa'mente *adv* conscientiously

coscienzi'oso *a* conscientious

cosci'otto *nm* leg

co'scritto *nm* conscript

coscrizi'one *nf* conscription

così *adv* so; (*in questo modo*) like this, like that; (*perciò*) therefore; **le cose stanno ~** that's how things stand; **fermo ~!** hold it; **proprio ~!** exactly!; **basta ~!** that will do!; **ah, è ~?** it's like that, is it?; **~ ~** so-so; **e ~ via** and so on; **per ~ dire** so to speak; **più di ~** any more; **una ~ cara ragazza!** such a nice girl!; **è stato ~ generoso da aiutarti** he was kind enough to help you ● *conj* (*allora*) so ● *a inv* (*tale*) like that, such; **una ragazza ~** a girl like that, such a girl

cosicché *conj* and so

cosid'detto *a* so-called

co'smesi *nf* beauty treatment

co'smetico *a* cosmetic ● *nm* **cosmetici pl** cosmetics; (*trucchi*) make-up

'cosmico *a* cosmic

'cosmo *nm* cosmos

cosmo'nauta *nmf* cosmonaut

cosmopo'lita *a* cosmopolitan

co'spargere *vt* sprinkle; (*disseminare*) scatter; **~ il pavimento di cera** spread wax on the floor

co'spetto *nm* **al ~ di** in the presence of

co'spicuo *a* conspicuous; ⟨*somma ecc*⟩ considerable

cospi'rare *vi* conspire, plot

cospira|'tore, -'trice *nmf* conspirator, plotter

cospirazi'one *nf* conspiracy, plot

'**costa** *nf* coast, coastline; *Anat* rib; **sotto ~** inshore. **C~ d'Avorio** Ivory Coast. **C~ Azzurra** Côte d'Azur. **C~ Smeralda** Emerald coast (*in Sardinia*)

costà *adv* there

co'stante *a & nf* constant

co'stanza *nf* constancy

co'stare *vi* cost; **quanto costa?** how much is it?; **costi quel che costi** whatever the cost

co'stata *nf* chop. **~ [di manzo]** rib steak

co'stato *nm* ribs *pl*

costeggi'are *vt* (*per mare*) coast; (*per terra*) skirt

co'stei *pers pron* (*soggetto*) she; (*complemento*) her

costellazi'one *nf* constellation

coster'nato *a* dismayed

costernazi'one *nf* consternation

costi'era *nf* stretch of coast

costi'ero *a* coastal

co'stine *nfpl* (*di maiale*) spare ribs

'**costing** *nm inv* costing

costi'pato *a* constipated; **essere ~** (*raffreddato*) have a bad cold

costipazi'one *nf* constipation; (*raffreddore*) bad cold

costitu'ire *vt* constitute; (*essere*) be; (*formare*) form; (*nominare*) appoint

costitu'irsi *vr* (*criminale:*) give oneself up

costituzio'nale *a* constitutional

costituzional'mente *adv Pol* constitutionally

costituzi'one *nf* constitution; (*formazione*) formation

'**costo** *nm* cost; **a nessun ~** on no account; **a ~ di perdere la salute** at the cost of one's health; **sotto ~** at less than cost price. **~ del denaro** *Fin* cost of money. **costi** *pl* **di gestione** administration costs. **costi** *pl* **di spedizione** freight charges. **~ unitario** unit cost. **~ della vita** cost of living

'**costola** *nf* rib; (*di libro*) spine; **stare alle costole di qcno** follow sb around

costo'letta *nf* cutlet

co'storo *pron* (*soggetto*) they; (*complemento*) them

co'stoso *a* costly

co'stretto *pp di* **costringere**

co'stringere *vt* force, compel

costrit'tivo *a* coercive

costrizi'one *nf* compulsion

costru'ire *vt* build, construct

costrut'tivo *a* constructive

costruzi'one *nf* building, construction; (*edificio*) building

co'stui *pers pron* (*soggetto*) he; (*complemento*) him

co'stume *nm* (*usanza*) custom; (*indumento*) costume; **buon ~** vice squad; **costumi** *pl* (*morale*) morals. **~ da bagno** swim-suit; (*da uomo*) swimming trunks. **~ tradizionale** traditional costume

costu'mista *nmf* wardrobe assistant

cote'chino *nm* spiced pork sausage

co'tenna *nf* pigskin; (*della pancetta*) rind. **~ arrostita** crackling

co'togna *nf* quince

coto'letta *nf* cutlet. **~ alla milanese** veal cutlet in breadcrumbs

coto'nato *a* (*capelli*) back-combed

co'tone *nm* cotton. **~ idrofilo** cotton wool, absorbent cotton *Am*

cotoni'ficio *nm* cotton mill

'**cotta** *nf Relig* surplice; (*fam: innamoramento*) crush; **prendere una ~ per qcno** *fam* have a crush on sb

'**cottimo** *nm* piece-work

'**cotto** *pp di* **cuocere** ●*a* done; (*fam: innamorato*) in love; (*sbronzo*) drunk; **ben ~** well cooked; (*carne*) well done; **poco ~** undercooked; (*carne*) underdone; **troppo ~** overcooked; (*carne*) overdone

'**cotton fi'oc®** *nm inv* cotton bud

cot'tura *nf* cooking

'**country** *nm inv* country and western

cou'pon *nm inv* coupon

cou'scous *nm inv* couscous

co'vare *vt* hatch; sicken for (*malattia*); harbour (*rancore*)

co'vata *nf* brood

'**covo** *nm* den

co'vone *nm* sheaf

cow-'boy *nm inv* cowboy

'**cozza** *nf* mussel. **cozze** *pl* **alla marinara** moules marinière

coz'zare *vi* **~ contro** bump into

'**cozzo** *nm fig* clash

C.P. *abbr* (**Casella Postale**) PO Box

crac *nm inv* crack; (*di tessuto*) rip

crack *nm* (*droga*) crack

Cra'covia *nf* Cracow

'**crafen** *nm inv* cream doughnut

'**crampo** *nm* cramp

'**cranio** *nm* skull

cra'tere *nm* crater

cra'vatta *nf* tie; (*a farfalla*) bow-tie

cre'anza *nf* manners; **mala ~** bad manners

cre'are *vt* create; **~ assuefazione** be habit-forming

creatività *nf* creativity

crea'tivo *a* creative

cre'ato *nm* creation

crea|'tore, -'trice *nmf* creator; **andare al ~** go to meet one's maker

crea'tura *nf* creature; (*bambino*) baby; **povera ~!** poor thing!

creazi'one *nf* creation

cre'dente *nmf* believer

cre'denza *nf* belief; *Comm* credit; (*mobile*) sideboard

credenzi'ali *nfpl* credentials

'**credere** *vt* believe; (*pensare*) think ●*vi* **~ in** believe in; **credo di sì** I think so; **non ti credo** I don't believe you; **non posso crederci** I can't believe it!

'**credersi** *vr* think oneself to be; **si crede uno scrittore** he flatters himself he is a writer

cre'dibile *a* credible, believable

credibilità *nf* credibility

credi'tizio *a* credit *attrib*

'**credito** *nm* credit; (*stima*) esteem; **comprare a ~** buy on credit; **dare ~ a qcsa** give credence to sth; **fare ~** give credit. **~ all'esportazione** export credit. **~ inesigibile** bad debt

credi'tore, -'trice *nmf* creditor

'**credo** *nm inv* credo

credulità *nf* credulity

'**credulo** *a* credulous

credu'lone, -a *nmf* simpleton

'**crema** *nf* cream; (*di uova e latte*) custard. **~ base per il trucco** vanishing cream. **~ depilatoria** depilatory [cream]. **~ detergente** cleansing cream. **~ idratante** moisturizer. **~ per le mani** hand cream. **~ pasticciera** confectioner's custard. **~ per la pelle** skin cream. **~ protettiva** barrier cream. **~ solare** suntan lotion. **~ per il viso** face cream

cremagli'era *nf* ratchet

cre'mare *vt* cremate

crema'torio *nm* crematorium

cremazi'one *nf* cremation

crème cara'mel *nf* crème caramel

creme'ria *nf* dairy (*also selling ice cream and cakes*)

Crem'lino *nm* Kremlin

cre'moso *a* creamy

cren *nm* horseradish

'**crepa** *nf* crack

cre'paccio *nm* cleft; (*di ghiacciaio*) crevasse

crepacu'ore *nm* heart-break

crepa'pelle: a ~ *adv* fit to burst

cre'pare *vi* crack; (*fam: morire*) kick the bucket; **~ dal ridere** laugh fit to burst

crepa'tura *nf* crevice

crêpe *nf inv* pancake

crepi'tare *vi* crackle

crepi'tio *nm* crackling

cre'puscolo *nm* twilight

cre'scendo *nm* crescendo

cre'scenza *nf* creamy white cheese

'**crescere** *vi* grow; (*aumentare*) increase, grow ● *vt* (*allevare*) bring up; (*aumentare*) increase

cresci'one *nm* watercress

'**crescita** *nf* growth; (*aumento*) increase, growth

cresci'uto *pp di* **crescere**

'**cresima** *nf* confirmation

cresi'mare *vt* confirm

cre'spato *a* crinkly

cre'spella *nf* pancake

'**crespo** *a* (*capelli*) frizzy ● *nm* crêpe

'**cresta** *nf* crest; (*cima*) peak; **abbassare la ~** become less cocky; **alzare la ~** become cocky; **sulla ~ dell'onda** on the crest of a wave

'**creta** *nf* clay

'**Creta** *nf* Crete

cre'tese *a & nmf* Cretan

creti'nata *nf* something stupid: **dire cretinate** talk nonsense

cre'tino, -a *a* stupid ● *nmf* idiot

C.R.I. *abbr* (**Croce Rossa Italiana**) Italian Red Cross

'**cribbio** *int* gosh!, golly!

cric *nm inv* jack

'**cricca** *nf* gang

'**cricco** *nm* jack

cri'ceto *nm* hamster

'**cricket** *nm* cricket

crimi'nale *a & nmf* criminal

criminalità *nf* crime. **~ organizzata** organized crime

'**crimine** *nm* crime

criminolo'gia *nf* criminology

crimi'nologo, -a *nmf* criminologist

crimi'noso *a* criminal

'**crine** *nm* horsehair

crini'era *nf* mane

crino'lina *nf* crinoline

'**cripta** *nf* crypt

crisan'temo *nm* chrysanthemum

'**crisi** *nf inv* crisis; *Med* fit; **essere in ~ di astinenza** be having withdrawal symptoms, be cold turkey *fam.* **~ di nervi** hysterics. **~ del settimo anno** seven-year itch

cristal'lino *a* crystal clear ● *nm* crystalline lens

cristalliz'zare *vt* crystallize

cristalliz'zarsi *vr* crystallize; ⟨*fig: parola, espressione:*⟩ become part of the language

cri'stallo *nm* crystal

Cristia'nesimo *nm* Christianity

cristianità *nf* Christendom

cristi'ano, -a *a a & nmf* Christian

'**Cristo** *nm* Christ; **avanti ~** BC; **dopo ~** AD; **un povero c~** a poor beggar

cri'terio *nm* criterion; (*buon senso*) [common] sense

'**critica** *nf* criticism; (*recensione*) review; **fare la ~ di** review ⟨*film, libro*⟩

criti'care *vt* criticize

'**critico** *a* critical ● *nm* critic. **~ letterario** literary critic

criti'cone, -a *nmf* fault finder

crittazi'one *nf* **~ [dei] dati** *Comput* data encryption

crivel'lare *vt* riddle (**di** with)

cri'vello *nm* sieve

cro'atc, -a *a & nmf* Croatian, Croat

Cro'azia *nf* Croatia

croc'cante *a* crisp ● *nm* type of crunchy nut biscuit

croc'chetta *nf* croquette

'**crocchia** *nf* bun

'**crocchio** *nm* cluster

'**croce** *nf* cross; **a occhio e ~** roughly; **fare testa e ~** toss a coin; **fare** *o* **mettere una ~ sopra qcsa** *fig* forget about sth; **mettere in ~** (*criticare*) crucify; (*tormentare*) nag nonstop. **C~ Rossa** Red Cross

crocero'sina *nf* Red Cross nurse

croce'via *nm inv* crossroads *sg*

croci'ata *nf* crusade

croci'ato a cruciform ● nm crusader

cro'cicchio nm crossroads sg

croci'era nf cruise; **velocità di ~** cruising speed

croci'figgere vt crucify

crocifissi'one nf crucifixion

croci'fisso pp di **crocifiggere** ● a crucified ● nm crucifix

crogi'olo nm crucible; fig melting pot

crogio'larsi vr bask

crogiu'olo nm = **crogiolo**

crois'sant nm inv croissant

crol'lare vi collapse; ⟨prezzi⟩ slump

'crollo nm collapse; ⟨dei prezzi⟩ slump

'croma nf quaver

cro'mato a chromium-plated

'cromo nm chrome

cromo'soma nm chromosome

'cronaca nf chronicle; (di giornale) news; TV, Radio commentary; **fatto di ~** news item. **~ mondana** gossip column. **~ nera** crime news

'cronico a chronic

cro'nista nmf reporter; (di partita) commentator

croni'storia nf chronicle

cro'nografo nm chronograph

cronolo'gia nf chronology

cronologica'mente adv chronologically

crono'logico a chronological

cronome'traggio nm timing

cronome'trare vt time

cronome'trista nmf Sport timekeeper

cro'nometro nm chronometer; Sport stopwatch

cross nm (corsa campestre) cross-country; (motocross) motocross

cros'sista nmf scrambler; (a piedi) cross-country runner

'crosta nf crust; (di formaggio) rind; (di ferita) scab; (quadro) daub

cro'staceo nm shellfish

cro'stata nf tart. **~ di frutta** fruit tart. **~ di mele** apple pie

cro'stino nm croûton; **crostini** pl pieces of toasted bread served as a starter

croupi'er nmf inv croupier

crucci'are vt torment

crucci'arsi vr torment oneself

'cruccio nm torment

cruci'ale a crucial

cruci'verba nm inv crossword [puzzle]

cru'dele a cruel

crudel'mente adv cruelly

crudeltà nf cruelty

'crudo a raw; ⟨linguaggio⟩ crude

cru'ento a bloody

cru'miro nm blackleg, scab

'crusca nf bran

cru'scotto nm dashboard

C.S.I. nf abbr (**Comunità degli Stati Indipendenti**) CIS

'Cuba nf Cuba

cu'bano, -a a & nmf Cuban

cu'betto nm **~ di ghiaccio** ice cube

'cubico a cubic

cu'bismo nm cubism

cu'bista a & nmf cubist

cubi'tale a **a caratteri cubitali** in enormous letters

'cubo nm cube

cuc'cagna nf abundance; (baldoria) merrymaking; **paese della ~** land of plenty

cuc'cetta nf (su un treno) couchette; Naut berth

cucchiai'ata nf spoonful

cucchia'ino nm teaspoon; (contenuto) teaspoon[ful]

cucchi'aio nm spoon; **un ~** a spoon[ful] (**di** of); **al ~** ⟨dolce⟩ creamy. **~ di legno** wooden spoon. **~ da minestra** soup-spoon. **~ da tavola** tablespoon; (contenuto) tablespoon[ful]

cucchiai'one nm serving spoon

'cuccia nf basket; (in giardino) kennel; [**fa' la**] **~!** down!

cuccio'lata nf litter

'cucciolo nm puppy

cu'cina nf kitchen; (il cucinare) cooking; (cibo) food; (apparecchio) cooker; **far da ~** cook; **libro di ~** cook[ery] book. **~ a gas** gas cooker. **~ componibile** fitted kitchen. **~ economica** cooker

cuci'nare vt cook

cuci'nino nm kitchenette

cu'cire vt sew; **macchina per ~** sewing-machine; **cucilo a macchina** do it on the machine

cu'cito nm sewing

cuci'tura nf seam

cucù nm inv cuckoo; **~!** peekaboo!

'cuculo nm cuckoo

'cuffia nf bonnet; (ricevitore) headphones pl. **~ da bagno** bathing cap

cu'gino, -a nmf cousin

'cui pron rel (persona: con prep) who[m]; (cose, animali: con prep) which; (tra articolo e nome) whose; **la persona con ~ ho parlato** the person I spoke to, the person to whom I spoke fml; **la ditta per ~ lavoro** the company I work for, the company for which I work; **l'amico il ~ libro è stato pubblicato** the friend whose book was published; **in ~** (dove) where; (quando) that; **per ~** (perciò) so; **la città in ~ vivo** the city I live in, the city where I live; **il giorno in ~ l'ho visto** the day [that] I saw him

cu'latta nf breech

culi'naria nf cookery

culi'nario a culinary

'culla nf cradle

cul'lare vt rock; fig cherish ⟨sogno, speranza⟩

cul'larsi vr **~ nella speranza di** liter cherish the fond hope that

culmi'nante a culminating

culmi'nare vi culminate

'culmine nm peak

'culo nm vulg arse; (fortuna) luck; **prendere qcno per il ~** take the piss out of sb

'culto nm cult; Relig religion; (adorazione) worship

cul'tura *nf* culture. ~ **generale** general knowledge. ~ **di massa** mass culture
cultu'rale *a* cultural
cultu'rismo *nm* body-building
cultu'rista *nmf* body-builder
cu'mino *nm* ~ **nero** cumin
cumula'tivo *a* cumulative; ⟨*prezzo*⟩ all-in, all-inclusive; **biglietto** ~ group ticket
'cumulo *nm* pile; (*mucchio*) heap; (*nuvola*) cumulus
'cuneo *nm* wedge
cu'netta *nf* gutter
cu'nicolo *nm* tunnel
cu'ocere *vt* cook; fire ⟨*ceramica*⟩ ● *vi* cook; ⟨*ceramica:*⟩ fire
cu'oco, -a *nmf* cook
cu'oia *nfpl* **tirare le** ~ *fam* kick the bucket
cu'oio *nm* leather. ~ **capelluto** scalp
cu'ore *nm* heart; **cuori** *pl* ⟨*carte*⟩ hearts; **di [buon]** ~ ⟨*persona*⟩ kind-hearted; **di tutto** ~ wholeheartedly; **ti ringrazio di tutto** ~ many thanks; **nel profondo del** ~ in one's heart of hearts; **nel** ~ **della notte** in the middle of the night; **senza** ~ heartless; **mettersi il** ~ **in pace** come to terms with it; **parlare a** ~ **aperto** have a heart-to-heart (**con** with); **stare a** ~ **a qcno** be very important to sb. ~ **tenero** (*persona*) softy
cupa'mente *adv* darkly
cupi'digia *nf* greed
Cu'pido *nm* Cupid
'cupo *a* gloomy; (*voce*) deep
'cupola *nf* dome; **a** ~ domed
'cura *nf* care; (*amministrazione*) management; *Med* treatment; **aver** ~ **di** look after; **a** ~ **di** ⟨*libro*⟩ edited by; **in** ~ under treatment; **fare delle cure termali** take the waters. ~ **dimagrante** diet
cu'rabile *a* curable
cu'rante *a* **medico** ~ GP, doctor
cu'rare *vt* take care of, look after; *Med* treat; (*guarire*) cure; edit ⟨*testo*⟩
cu'rarsi *vr* take care of oneself, look after oneself; ~ **dei fatti propri** mind one's own business

cu'rato *nm* parish priest
cura'tore, -'trice *nmf* trustee; (*di testo*) editor. ~ **fallimentare** official receiver
'curcuma *nf* turmeric
curcu'mina *nf* turmeric
'curdo, -a *nmf* Kurd ● *a* Kurdish
'curia *nf* curia
curio'saggine *nf* nosiness
curio'sare *vi* be curious; (*mettere il naso*) pry (**in** into); (*nei negozi*) look around
curiosità *nf inv* curiosity
curi'oso *a* curious; (*strano*) odd, curious ● *nm* busybody
'curling *nm inv* *Sport* curling
cur'ricolo *nm* curriculum
cur'riculum *nm inv* curriculum
'curry *nm inv* curry. ~ **in polvere** curry powder
cur'sore *nm* *Comput* cursor
'curva *nf* curve; (*stradale*) bend. ~ **a gomito** dogleg. ~ **di apprendimento** learning curve
cur'vare *vt/i* bend, curve
cur'varsi *vr* bend, curve
'curvo *a* curved; (*piegato*) bent
cusci'netto *nm* pad; *Mech* bearing. ~ **puntaspilli** pincushion. ~ **a sfere** ball bearing
cu'scino *nm* cushion; (*guanciale*) pillow. ~ **gonfiabile** air cushion
cu'scus *nm inv* couscous
'cuspide *nf* spire
cu'stode *nm* caretaker; (*di abitazione*) concierge; (*di fabbrica*) guard; (*di museo*) custodian. ~ **giudiziario** official receiver
cu'stodia *nf* care; *Jur* custody; (*astuccio*) case; **ottenere la** ~ **di** get custody of. ~ **cautelare** remand
custo'dire *vt* keep; (*badare*) look after
cu'taneo *a* skin *attrib*
'cute *nf* skin
cu'ticola *nf* cuticle
'cutter *nm inv* cutter
CV *abbr* **(cavallo vapore)** hp
cyber'spazio *nm* cyberspace
cy'clette® *nf inv* exercise bicycle

Dd

da *prep* from; (*con verbo passivo*) by; (*moto a luogo*) to; (*moto per luogo*) through; (*stato in luogo*) at; (*temporale*) since; (*continuativo*) for; (*causale*) with; (*in qualità di*) as; (*con caratteristica*) with; (*come*) like; **da Roma a Milano** from Rome to Milan; **staccare un quadro dalla parete** take a picture off the wall; **i bambini dai 5 ai 10 anni** children between 5 and 10; **vedere qcsa da vicino/lontano** see sth from up close/from a dis-

tance; **amato da tutti** loved by everybody; **scritto da** written by; **andare dal panettiere** go to the baker's; **passo da te più tardi** I'll come over to your place later; **passiamo da qui** let's go this way; **un appuntamento dal dentista** an appointment at the dentist's; **il treno passa da Venezia** the train goes through Venice; **dall'anno scorso** since last year; **vivo qui da due anni** I've been living here for two years; **da domani** from tomorrow; **piangere dal dolore** cry with pain; **ho molto da fare** I have a lot to do; **occhiali da sole** sunglasses; **qualcosa da mangiare** something to eat; **un uomo dai capelli scuri** a man with dark hair; **è un oggetto da poco** it's not worth much; **da solo** alone; **l'ho fatto da solo** I did it by myself; **si è fatto da sé** he is a self-made man; **vive da re** he lives like a king; **non è da lui** it's not like him

dab'bene *a* honest

dac'capo *adv* again; (*dall'inizio*) from the beginning

dacché *conj* since

dada'ismo *nm* (*arte*) Dadaism

dada'ista *a & nmf* Dadaist

'**dado** *nm* dice; *Culin* stock cube; *Techn* nut. **~ ad alette** wing nut

daf'fare *nm* work

'**dagli** = da + gli

'**dai**[1] = da + i

'**dai**[2] *int* come on!; **~, non fare così!** come on, don't be like that!; **~, sbrigati!** come on, get a move on!

'**daino** *nm* deer; (*pelle*) buckskin

dal = da + il

'**dalla** = da + la

'**dalle** = da + le

'**dallo** = da + lo

'**dalia** *nf* dahlia

'**dalmata** *nmf* (*cane*) Dalmatian

Dal'mazia *nf* Dalmatia

dal'tonico *a* colour-blind

'**dama** *nf* lady; (*nei balli*) partner; (*gioco*) draughts. **~ di compagnia** lady's companion. **~ di corte** lady-in-waiting

dama'scato *a* damask

da'masco *nm* (*tessuto*) damask

dame'rino *nm* (*bellimbusto*) dandy

dami'gella *nf* (*di sposa*) bridesmaid

damigi'ana *nf* demijohn

dam'meno *adv* **non essere ~** be no less good (**di** than)

DAMS *nm abbr* (**Discipline delle Arti, della Musica e dello Spettacolo**) (*corso di laurea*) degree in fine art, music and drama

da'naro *nm* = **denaro**

dana'roso *a* (*fam: ricco*) loaded

da'nese *a* Danish ● *nmf* Dane ● *nm* (*lingua*) Danish

Dani'marca *nf* Denmark

dan'nare *vt* damn; **far ~ qcno** drive sb mad

dan'narsi *vr/fig* wear oneself out; **~ l'anima (a fare qcsa)** wear oneself out (doing sth)

dan'nato, -a *a* damned, damn *fam* ● *nmf* damned person; **lavorare/studiare come un ~** *fig* work/study like mad

dannazi'one *nf* damnation

danneggia'mento *nm* damage

danneggi'are *vt* damage; (*nuocere*) harm

danneggi'ato *a* *Jur* injured

'**danno** *nm* damage; (*a persona*) harm; **danni** *pl* damage

dan'noso *a* harmful

dan'tesco *a* Dantean, Dantesque

danubi'ano *a* Danubian

Da'nubio *nm* Danube

'**danza** *nf* dance; (*il danzare*) dancing. **~ folcloristica** country dancing

dan'zante *a* **serata ~** dance

dan'zare *vi* dance

danza|'tore, -'trice *nmf* dancer. **danzatrice del ventre** belly dancer

dapper'tutto *adv* everywhere

dap'poco *a* worthless

dap'prima *adv* at first

Darda'nelli *nmpl* **i ~** the Dardanelles

'**dardo** *nm* dart

'**dare** *vt* give; sit (*esame*); have (*festa*); **~ qcsa a qcno** give sb sth; **~ da mangiare a qcno** give sb something to eat; **~ fuoco a qcsa** set fire to sth; **~ il benvenuto a qcno** welcome sb; **~ la buonanotte a qcno** say good night to sb; **~ del tu/del lei a qcno** address sb as "tu"/"lei"; **~ del cretino a qcno** call sb an idiot; **~ qcsa per scontato** take sth for granted; **~ fastidio a** annoy; **~ cosa danno alla TV stasera?** what's on TV tonight?; **darle a qcno** (*picchiare*) give sb a walloping ● *vi* **~ nell'occhio** be conspicuous; **~ alla testa** go to one's head; **~ su** (*finestra, casa:*) look on to; **~ sui o ai nervi a qcno** get on sb's nerves ● *nm Comm* debit

'darsena *nf* dock

'**darsi** *vr* (*scambiarsi*) give each other; **~ da fare** get down to it; **si è dato tanto da fare!** he went to so much trouble!; **~ a** (*cominciare*) take up; **~ al bere** take to drink; **~ per** (*malato*) pretend to be; **~ per vinto** give up; **può ~** maybe

darvini'ano *a* Darwinian

darvi'nista *nmf* Darwinist

'**data** *nf* date; **di lunga ~** old-established. **~ di emissione** date of issue. **~ di nascita** date of birth. **~ di scadenza** expiry date; (*su cibo*) best before date

data'base *nm inv* database. **~ relazionale** relational database

da'tabile *a* dateable

da'tare *vt* date; **a ~ da** as from

da'tario *nm* (*su orologio*) calendar

da'tato *a* dated

da'tivo *nm* dative

'**dato** *a* given; (*dedito*) addicted; **~ che** seeing that, given that ● *nm* datum; **dati** *pl* data. **~ di fatto** well established fact

da'tore *nm* giver. **~ di lavoro** employer

'dattero *nm* date

dattilogra'fare *vt/i* type; **~ a tastiera cieca** touch-type

dattilogra'fia *nf* typing. **~ a tastiera cieca** touch-typing

datti'lografo, -a *nmf* typist

dattilo'scritto *a* (*copia*) typewritten, typed

dat'torno *adv* **togliersi ~** clear off

da'vanti *adv* before; (*dirimpetto*) opposite; (*di fronte*) in front ● *a inv* front ● *nm* front; **~ di dietro** (*maglia*) back-to-front · **~ a** *prep* before, in front of; **passare ~ a** pass, go past

davan'zale *nm* window sill

da'vanzo *adv* **ce n'è ~** there is more than enough

dav'vero *adv* really; **per ~** in earnest; **dici ~?** honestly?

dazi'ario *a* excise

'dazio *nm* duty; *(ufficio)* customs *pl.* **dazi** *pl* **doganali** customs duties. **~ d'importazione** import duty

D.C. *nf abbr* **(Democrazia Cristiana)** Christian Democratic Party

d.C. *abbr* **(dopo Cristo)** AD

D.D.T. *nm (insetticida)* DDT

'dea *nf* goddess

deambula'torio *a* ambulatory

debel'lare *vt* defeat

debili'tante *a* weakening

debili'tare *vt* weaken

debili'tarsi *vr* become debilitated

debilitazi'one *nf* debilitation

debita'mente *adv* duly

'debito *a* due; **a tempo ~** in due course ● *nm* debt. **~ pubblico** national debt

debi|'tore, -'trice *nmf* debtor

'debole *a* weak; *(luce)* dim; *(suono)* faint ● *nm* weak point; **avere un ~ per qcno** have a soft spot for sb; **avere un ~ per qcsa** have a weakness for sth

debo'lezza *nf* weakness

debor'dare *vi* overflow

debosci'ato *a* debauched

debrai'ata *nf Auto* declutching

debut'tante *a* beginner ● *nmf* beginner; *(attore)* actor/actress making his/her début

debut'tare *vi* make one's début

de'butto *nm* début

'decade *nf* period of ten days

deca'dente *a* decadent

decaden'tismo *nm* decadence

deca'denza *nf* decline; *Jur* loss

deca'dere *vi* lapse

decadi'mento *nm (delle arti)* decline

deca'duto *a* *(persona)* impoverished; *(decreto, norma)* no longer in force

decaffei'nato *a* decaffeinated ● *nm* decaffeinated coffee, decaf *fam*

deca'grammo *nm* decagram

decal'care *vt* trace

decalcifi'carsi *vr* become brittle

decalcificazi'one *nf (condizione)* brittle bones

decalcoma'nia *nf* transfer

de'calitro *nm* decalitre

de'calogo *nm fig* rule book

de'cametro *nm* decametre

de'cano *nm* dean

decan'tare *vt (lodare)* praise

decapi'tare *vt* decapitate; behead *(condannato)*

decapitazi'one *nf* decapitation; beheading

decappot'tabile *a* convertible

decappot'tare *vt* take down the hood of

'decathlon *nm inv* decathlon

de'cedere *vi (morire)* die

dece'duto *a* deceased

decele'rare *vt/i* slow down, decelerate

decelerazi'one *nf* deceleration

decen'nale *a* ten-yearly ● *nm (anniversario)* tenth anniversary

de'cenne *a* *(bambino)* ten-year-old

de'cennio *nm* decade

de'cente *a* decent

decente'mente *adv* decently

decentraliz'zare *vt* decentralize

decentra'mento *nm* decentralization

decen'trare *vt* decentralize

de'cenza *nf* decency

de'cesso *nm* death, decease *fml*; **atto di ~** death certificate

'decibel *nm inv* decibel

de'cidere *vt* decide; settle *(questione)*

de'cidersi *vr* make up one's mind

deci'frabile *a* decipherable

deci'frare *vt* decipher; *(documenti cifrati)* decode

decifrazi'one *nf* deciphering

de'cigrado *nm* tenth of a degree

deci'grammo *nm* decigram[me]

de'cilitro *nm* decilitre

deci'male *a* decimal

deci'mare *vt* decimate

de'cimetro *nm* decimetre

'decimo *a & nm* tenth

de'cina *nf Math* ten; **una ~ di** *(circa dieci)* about ten

decisa'mente *adv* definitely, decidedly

decisio'nale *a* decision-making

decisi'one *nf* decision; **prendere una ~** make or take a decision; **con ~** decisively

decisio'nismo *nm* tendency to make decisions without consulting others

decisio'nista *nmf* person who does not consult others before making decisions

deci'sivo *a* decisive

de'ciso *pp di* **decidere** ● *a* decided

decla'mare *vt/i* declaim

declama'torio *a* *(stile)* declamatory

declas'sare *vt* downgrade

decli'nabile *a Gram* declinable; *(offerta)* that can be refused

decli'nare *vt* decline; turn down, refuse *(invito)*; **~ ogni responsabilità** disclaim all responsibility ● *vi* go down; *(tramontare)* set

declinazi'one *nf Gram* declension

de'clino *nm* decline; **in ~** *(popolarità)* on the decline

de'clivio *nm* downward slope

dé'co *a inv* Art Deco

deco'difica *nf* decoding

decodifi'care *vt* decode

decodifica'tore *nm TV* descrambler

decodificazi'one *nf* decoding

decol'lare *vi* take off

décolle'té *a inv* low cut ● *nm inv* low neckline

de'collo *nm* take-off

decolonizzazi'one *nf* decolonization

decolo'rante *nm* bleach

decolo'rare *vt* bleach

decolorazi'one *nf* bleaching

decom'porre *vt* decompose

decom'porsi *vr* decompose

decomposizi'one *nf* decomposition

decompressi'one *nf* decompression

deconcen'trarsi *vr* become distracted

deconge'lare *vt* defrost

decongestio'nare *vt Med, fig* relieve congestion in

decontami'nare *vt Techn* decontaminate

decontaminazi'one *nf* decontamination

decontrazi'one *nf* relaxation

deco'rare *vt* decorate

decora'tivo *a* decorative

deco'rato *a* (*ornato*) decorated

decora'|tore, -'trice *nmf* decorator

decorazi'one *nf* decoration. **~ floreale** flower arranging

de'coro *nm* decorum

decorosa'mente *adv* decorously

deco'roso *a* dignified

decor'renza *nf* **~ dal...** with effect from..., effective...

de'correre *vi* pass; **a ~ da** with effect from

de'corso *pp di* decorrere ● *nm* passing; *Med* course

decre'mento *nm* decrease

de'crepito *a* decrepit

decre'scente *a* decreasing

de'crescere *vi* decrease; (*prezzi:*) go down; (*acque:*) subside

decre'tare *vt* decree; **~ lo stato d'emergenza** declare a state of emergency

de'creto *nm* decree. **~ ingiuntivo** decree. **~ legge** decree which has the force of law. **~ legislativo** decree requiring the approval of Parliament

decre'tone *nm Pol* portmanteau bill

de'cubito *nm* **piaghe da ~** bedsores

decur'tare *vt* reduce

decurtazi'one *nf* reduction

'dedalo *nm* maze

'dedica *nf* dedication

dedi'care *vt* dedicate

dedi'carsi *vr* dedicate oneself

'dedito *a* **~ a** given to; (*assorto*) engrossed in; addicted to (*vizi*)

dedizi'one *nf* dedication

de'dotto *pp di* dedurre ● *a* deduced

dedu'cibile *a* (*tassa*) allowable

de'durre *vt* deduce; (*sottrarre*) deduct

dedut'tivo *a* deductive

deduzi'one *nf* deduction

défail'lance *nf inv* (*cedimento*) collapse

defal'care *vt* deduct

defalcazi'one *nf* deduction

defe'care *vi* defecate

defecazi'one *nf* defecation

defene'strare *vt fig* remove from office

defe'rente *a* deferential

defe'renza *nf* deference

deferi'mento *nm* referral

defe'rire *vt Jur* remit

defezio'nare *vi* (*abbandonare*) defect

defezi'one *nf* defection

defezio'nista *nmf* defector

defici'ente *a* (*mancante*) deficient; *Med* mentally deficient ● *nmf* mental defective; *pej* half-wit

defici'enza *nf* deficiency; (*lacuna*) gap; *Med* mental deficiency

'deficit *nm inv* deficit, shortfall; **essere in ~** be in deficit

defici'tario *a* (*bilancio*) deficit *attrib*; (*sviluppo*) insufficient

defi'larsi *vr* (*scomparire*) slip away; **~ da qcsa** sneak away from sth

défi'lé *nm inv* fashion show

defi'nibile *a* definable; **~ dall'utente** *Comput* user-definable

defi'nire *vt* define; (*risolvere*) settle

definitiva'mente *adv* for good

defini'tivo *a* definitive

defi'nito *a* definite

definizi'one *nf* definition; (*soluzione*) settlement

defiscaliz'zare *vt* abolish the tax on

defiscalizzazi'one *nf* abolition of tax

defla'grare *vt* (*esplodere*) explode

deflagrazi'one *nf* (*esplosione*) explosion

deflazio'nare *vt* deflate

deflazi'one *nf* deflation

deflazio'nistico *a* deflationary

deflet'tore *nm Auto* quarterlight

deflu'ire *vi* (*liquidi:*) flow away; (*persone:*) stream out

de'flusso *nm* (*di marea*) ebb

defogli'ante *a* defoliating ● *nm* defoliant

deforestazi'one *nf* deforestation

defor'mante *a* **artrite ~** acute arthritis

defor'mare *vt* deform (*arto*); *fig* distort

defor'marsi *vr* lose its shape

defor'mato *a* warped

deformazi'one *nf* (*di fatti*) distortion; **è una ~ professionale** put it down to the job

de'forme *a* deformed

deformità *nf inv* deformity

defrau'dare *vt* defraud

de'funto, -a *a & nmf* deceased

degene'rare *vi* degenerate

degene'rativo *a* (*processo*) degenerative

degene'rato *a* degenerate

degenerazi'one *nf* degeneration

de'genere *a* degenerate

de'gente *a* bedridden ● *nmf* patient

de'genza *nf* confinement. **~ ospedaliera** stay in hospital

'degli = *di* + *gli*

deglu'tire *vt* swallow

deglutizi'one *nf* swallowing

de'gnare *vt* **~ qcno/qcsa di uno sguardo** deign *or* condescend to look at sb/sth

de'gnarsi *vr* deign, condescend

'degno *a* worthy; (*meritevole*) deserving. **~ di lode** praiseworthy. **~ di nota** noteworthy

degrada'mento *nm* degradation

degra'dante *a* demeaning

degra'dare *vt* degrade

degra'darsi *vr* lower oneself; (*città:*) fall into a state of disrepair

degradazi'one *nf* degradation

de'grado *nm* deterioration; **~ ambientale**

environmental damage. **~ urbano** urban blight, urban decay

degu'stare *vt* taste

degustazi'one *nf* tasting. **~ di vini** wine tasting

'**dei** = di + i

deindiciz'zare *vt* deindex

déjà vu *nm inv* déjà vu

del = di + il

dela|'tore, -'trice *nmf* [police] informer

delazi'one *nf* informing

'**delega** *nf* proxy; **legge** *~ law that does not require Parliamentary approval*

dele'gante *nmf Jur* representative

dele'gare *vt* delegate

dele'gato *nm* delegate

delegazi'one *nf* delegation

dele'terio *a* harmful

del'fino *nm* dolphin; (*stile di nuoto*) butterfly [stroke]; **nuotare a ~** do the butterfly

de'libera *nf* bylaw

delibe'rante *a* ⟨*organo*⟩ decision making

delibe'rare *vt/i* deliberate; **~ su/in** rule on/in

deliberata'mente *adv* deliberately

delibe'rato *a* (*intenzionale*) deliberate

delicata'mente *adv* delicately

delica'tezza *nf* delicacy; (*fragilità*) frailty; (*tatto*) tact

deli'cato *a* delicate; ⟨*salute*⟩ frail; ⟨*suono, colore*⟩ soft

deligitti'mare *vt* delegitimize

delimi'tare *vt* define

delimita'tivo *a* defining

delimitazi'one *nf* definition

deline'are *vt* outline

deline'arsi *vr* be outlined; *fig* take shape

deline'ato *a* outlined

delineazi'one *nf* outline

delinqu'ente *nmf* delinquent. **~ minorenne** young offender

delinqu'enza *nf* delinquency. **~ minorile** juvenile crime

delinquenzi'ale *a* criminal

de'linquere *vi* commit a criminal act; **associazione per ~** conspiracy [to commit a crime]; **istigazione a ~** incitement to crime

de'liquio *nm* **cadere in ~** swoon

deli'rante *a Med* delirious; (*assurdo*) insane; (*sfrenato*) frenzied

deli'rare *vi* be delirious

de'lirio *nm* delirium; *fig* frenzy; **mandare/andare in ~** *fig* send/go into a frenzy

de'litto *nm* crime. **~ passionale** crime of passion

delittu'oso *a* criminal

de'lizia *nf* delight

delizi'are *vt* delight

delizi'arsi *vr* **~ di** delight in

delizi'oso *a* delightful; (*cibo*) delicious

'**della** = di + la

'**delle** = di + le

'**dello** = di + lo

'**delta** *nm inv* delta

delta'plano *nm* hang-glider; **fare ~** go hang-gliding

deluci'dare *vt fig* clarify

delucidazi'one *nf* clarification

delu'dente *a* disappointing

de'ludere *vt* disappoint

delusi'one *nf* disappointment

de'luso *a* disappointed; **essere ~ di qcsa/qcno** be disillusioned with sth/sb

dema'gogico *a* popularity-seeking, demagogic

dema'gogo *nm* demagogue

deman'dare *vt* entrust

demani'ale *a* ⟨*proprietà*⟩ government *attrib*

de'manio *nm* government property

demar'care *vt* demarcate

demarcazi'one *nf* demarcation; **linea di ~** demarcation line

de'mente *a* demented

de'menza *nf* dementia. **~ senile** senile dementia

demenzi'ale *a* (*assurdo*) zany

de'merito *nm* **nota di ~** demerit mark

demilitariz'zare *vt* demilitarize

demilitarizzazi'one *nf* demilitarization

demistifi'care *vt* debunk

demistifica|'tore, -'trice *nmf* debunker

demistifica'torio *a* debunking

demistificazi'one *nf* debunking

demitiz'zare *vt* demythologize

demitizzazi'one *nf* demythologization

democratica'mente *adv* democratically

demo'cratico *a* democratic

democratiz'zare *vt* democratize

democra'zia *nf* democracy

democristi'ano, -a *a & nmf* Christian Democrat

'**demodisk** *nm inv Comput* demo disk

demogra'fia *nf* demography

demo'grafico *a* demographic; **incremento ~** increase in population

demo'lire *vt* demolish

demo'lito *a* demolished

demolizi'one *nf* demolition

'**demone** *nm* demon

demo'niaco *a* demonic

de'monio *nm* demon

demoniz'zare *vt* demonize

demonizzazi'one *nf* demonization

demoraliz'zante *a* demoralizing

demoraliz'zare *vt* demoralize

demoraliz'zarsi *vr* become demoralized

demoraliz'zato *a* demoralized

de'mordere *vi* give up

demoti'vare *vt* demotivate

demoti'varsi *vr* become demotivated

demoti'vato *a* demotivated

demotivazi'one *nf* demotivation

de'nari *nmpl* (*nelle carte*) diamonds

de'naro *nm* money

denatu'rato *a* **alcol ~** methylated spirits

denazionaliz'zare *vt* denationalize

deni'grare *vt* denigrate

denigra|'tore, -'trice *a* denigrating ● *nmf* denigrator

denigra'torio *a* denigratory
denigrazi'one *nf* denigration
denomi'nare *vt* name
denomi'narsi *vr* be named
denomina'tivo *a* denominative
denomina'tore *nm* denominator
denominazi'one *nf* denomination. **~ di origine controllata** *mark guaranteeing the quality of a wine*
deno'tare *vt* denote
denotazi'one *nf* denotation
densa'mente *adv* densely
densità *nf* density. **ad alta/bassa ~ di popolazione** densely/sparsely populated
'denso *a* thick, dense
den'tale *a* dental
den'tario *a* dental
den'tata *nf* bite
den'tato *a* ‹*lama*› serrated
denta'tura *nf* teeth *pl*; *Techn* serration
'dente *nm* tooth; (*di forchetta*) prong; (*di montagna*) jagged peak; **al ~** *Culin* just slightly firm; **lavarsi i denti** brush one's teeth. **~ del giudizio** wisdom tooth. **~ di latte** milk tooth. **~ di leone** *Bot* dandelion
'dentice *nm* dentex (*type of sea bream*)
denti'era *nf* dentures *pl*, false teeth *pl*; **mettersi la ~** put one's false teeth in
denti'fricio *nm* toothpaste
den'tista *nmf* dentist
'dentro *adv* in, inside; (*in casa*) indoors; **da ~** from within; **qui ~** in here; **metter ~** (*fam: in prigione*) lock up, put inside ● *prep* in, inside; (*di tempo*) within, by ● *nm* inside
denuclеariz'zare *vt* denuclearize
denucleariz'zato *a* nuclear-free, denuclearized
denuclearizzazi'one *nf* denuclearization
denu'dare *vt* bare
denu'darsi *vr* strip
de'nuncia *nf* denunciation; (*alla polizia*) re-porting; **fare una ~** draw up a report. **~ dei redditi** income tax return
denunci'are *vt* denounce; (*accusare*) report
de'nunzia = **denuncia**
denu'trito *a* underfed
denutrizi'one *nf* malnutrition
deodo'rante *a* & *nm* deodorant. **~ antitraspirante** antiperspirant. **~ a sfera** roll-on
deodo'rare *vt* deodorize
deontolo'gia *nf* (*etica professionale*) code of conduct
depenaliz'zare *vt* decriminalize
depenalizzazi'one *nf* decriminalization
dépen'dance *nf inv* outbuilding
depe'ribile *a* perishable
deperi'mento *nm* wasting away; (*di merci*) deterioration
depe'rire *vi* waste away
depe'rito *a* wasted
depi'lare *vt* depilate
depi'larsi *vr* shave ‹*gambe*›; pluck ‹*sopracciglia*›

depila'tore *a* depilatory ● *nm* (*apparecchio*) hair remover
depila'torio *nm* depilatory
depilazi'one *nf* hair removal. **~ diatermica** electrolysis
depi'staggio *nm fig* diversionary manoeu-vre
depi'stare *vt fig* throw off the track
dépli'ant *nm inv* brochure, leaflet
deplo'rabile *a* deplorable
deplo'rare *vt* deplore; (*dolersi di*) grieve over
deplo'revole *a* deplorable
depoliticiz'zare *vt* depoliticize
de'porre *vt* put down; lay down ‹*armi*›; lay ‹*uova*›; (*togliere da una carica*) depose; (*testimoniare*) testify
depor'tare *vt* deport
depor'tato, -a *nmf* deportee
deportazi'one *nf* deportation
deposi'tante *nmf Fin* depositor
deposi'tare *vt* deposit; (*lasciare in custodia*) leave; (*in magazzino*) store
deposi'tario, -a *nmf* (*di segreto*) repository
deposi'tarsi *vr* settle
de'posito *nm* deposit; (*luogo*) warehouse; *Mil* depot. **~ d'armi** arms dump. **~ bagagli** left-luggage office, baggage checkroom *Am*. **~ bancario** deposit account. **~ bancario vincolato** fixed term deposit account
deposizi'one *nf* deposition; (*da una carica*) removal
de'posto *a* deposed
depotenzi'are *vt* weaken
depra'vare *vt* deprave
depra'vato *a* depraved
depravazi'one *nf* depravity
depre'cabile *a* appalling
depre'care *vt* deprecate
depre'dare *vt* plunder
depressio'nario *a* **area depressionaria** *Meteoreol* area of low pressure
depressi'one *nf* depression; **area di ~** *Meteoreol* area of low pressure; *Econ* depressed area
depres'sivo *a* depressive
de'presso *pp di* **deprimere** ● *a* depressed
depressuriz'zare *vt* depressurize
depressurizzazi'one *nf* depressurization
deprezza'mento *nm* depreciation
deprez'zare *vt* depreciate
deprez'zarsi *vr* depreciate
depri'mente *a* depressing
de'primere *vt* depress
de'primersi *vr* get depressed
deprivazi'one *nf* deprivation
depu'rare *vt* purify
depu'rarsi *vr* be purified
depura'tore *nm* purifier
depurazi'one *nf* purification; (*di detriti*) ef-fluent
depu'tare *vt* delegate
depu'tato, -a *nmf* ≈ Member of Parlia-ment, MP
deputazi'one *nf* deputation

dequalifi'care *vt* disqualify
dequalifi'carsi *vr* disqualify oneself
dequalificazi'one *nf* disqualification
deraglia'mento *nm* derailment
deragli'are *vi* go off the lines; **far ~** derail
deraglia'tore *nm* derailleur gears *pl*
dera'pare *vi Auto* skid; ‹*sciatore:*› sideslip
derattiz'zare *vt* clear of rats
derattizzazi'one *nf* rodent control
'derby *nm inv Sport* local Derby
deregolamen'tare *vt Comm* deregulate
deregolamentazi'one *nf* deregulation
dere'litto *a* derelict
deresponsabiliz'zare *vt* deprive of responsibility
deresponsabiliz'zarsi *vr* abdicate responsibility
deresponsabilizzazi'one *nf* depriving of responsibility
dere'tano *nm* backside, bottom
de'ridere *vt* deride
derisi'one *nf* derision
deri'sorio *a* derisory
de'riva *nf* drift; **andare alla ~** drift
deri'vabile *a* derivable
deri'vare *vi* **~ da** (*provenire*) derive from ● *vt* derive; (*sviare*) divert
deri'vata *nf Math* derivative
deri'vato *a* derived ● *nm* by-product
derivazi'one *nf* derivation; (*di fiume*) diversion
derma'tite *nf* dermatitis
dermatolo'gia *nf* dermatology
dermato'logico *a* dermatological
derma'tologo, -a *nmf* dermatologist
derma'tosi *nf* dermatosis
dermoprotet'tivo *a* ‹*crema*› skin *attrib*; ‹*azione*› protective
'deroga *nf* dispensation
dero'gare *vi* **~ a** depart from
deroga'torio *a* derogatory
der'rata *nf* merchandise. **derrate** *pl* **alimentari** foodstuffs
deru'bare *vt* rob
deru'bato *a* robbed
desaliniz'zare *vt* desalinate
desalinizzazi'one *nf* desalination
desapare'cido *nmf* (*pl* ~**s**) disappeared man/woman, desaparecido
descolarizzazi'one *nf* deschooling
descrit'tivo *a* descriptive
de'scritto *pp di* **descrivere**
de'scrivere *vt* describe
descri'vibile *a* describable
descrizi'one *nf* description
desensibiliz'zare *vt* desensitize
desensibilizzazi'one *nf* desensitization
de'sertico *a* desert
de'serto *a* uninhabited ● *nm* desert
deside'rabile *a* desirable
deside'rare *vt* wish; (*volere*) want; (*intensamente*) long for; (*bramare*) desire; **desidera?** what would you like?, can I help you?; **lasciare a ~** leave a lot to be desired
deside'rato *a* intended

desi'derio *nm* wish; (*brama*) desire; (*intenso*) longing
deside'roso *a* desirous; (*bramoso*) longing
desi'gnare *vt* appoint, designate; (*fissare*) fix
desi'gnato *a* designate *attrib*
designazi'one *nf* appointment
de'signer *nmf inv* designer
desi'nare *vi* dine ● *nm* dinner
desi'nenza *nf* ending
de'sistere *vi* **~ da** desist from
'desktop 'publishing *nm inv* desktop publishing, DTP
deso'lante *a* distressing
deso'lare *vt* distress
deso'lato *a* desolate; (*spiacente*) sorry; **siamo desolati di dovervi comunicare che...** (*in lettere*) we are sorry to have to inform you that...
desolazi'one *nf* desolation
'despota *nm* despot
desqua'marsi *vr* flake off
desquamazi'one *nf* flaking off
destabiliz'zante *a* destabilizing
destabiliz'zare *vt* destabilize
destabilizzazi'one *nf* destabilization
de'stare *vt* waken; *fig* awaken
de'starsi *vr* waken; *fig* awaken
desti'nare *vt* destine; (*nominare*) appoint; (*assegnare*) assign; (*indirizzare*) address
destina'tario *nm* (*di lettera, pacco*) addressee
desti'nato *a* **essere ~ a fare qcsa** be destined *or* fated to do sth
destinazi'one *nf* destination; *fig* purpose; **con ~ Parigi** ‹*aereo, treno*› destined for Paris
de'stino *nm* destiny; (*fato*) fate
destitu'ire *vt* dismiss
destitu'ito *a* **~ di** devoid of
destituzi'one *nf* dismissal
'desto *a liter* awake
'destra *nf* (*parte*) right; (*mano*) right hand; **prendere a ~** turn right; **a ~** ‹*essere*› on the right; ‹*andare*› to the right; **la prima a ~** the first on the right; **di ~** *Pol* right wing; **la ~** *Pol* the Right
destreggi'are *vi* manoeuvre
destreggi'arsi *vr* manoeuvre
de'strezza *nf* dexterity; (*abilità*) skill
'destro *a* right; (*abile*) skilful
de'stroide *a Pol* right-wing
destruttu'rato *a* (*incoerente*) unstructured
desu'eto *a* obsolete
de'sumere *vt* (*congetturare*) infer; (*ricavare*) obtain
desu'mibile *a* inferable
detas'sare *vt* abolish the tax on
detassazi'one *nf* abolition of tax
detei'nato *a* tannin free
dete'nere *vt* hold; ‹*polizia:*› detain
deten'tivo *a* **pena detentiva** custodial sentence
deten|'tore, -'trice *nmf* holder. **~ del titolo** title-holder
dete'nuto, -a *nmf* prisoner

detenzi'one *nf* detention

deter'gente *a* cleaning; ⟨*latte, crema*⟩ cleansing ● *nm* detergent; (*per la pelle*) cleanser

deteriora'mento *nm* deterioration

deterio'rare *vt* cause to deteriorate ⟨*cibo, relazione*⟩

deterio'rarsi *vr* deteriorate

determi'nabile *a* determinable

determinabilità *nf* determinability

determi'nante *a* decisive

determi'nare *vt* determine

determi'narsi *vr* ~ **a** resolve to

determina'tezza *nf* determination

determina'tivo *a* ⟨*articolo*⟩ definite; **pronome** ~ determiner

determi'nato *a* (*risoluto*) determined; (*particolare*) specific; (*stabilito*) certain

determinazi'one *nf* determination; (*decisione*) decision

determi'nismo *nm* determinism

deter'rente *a & nm* deterrent

deter'sivo *nm* detergent. ~ **biologico** biological powder. ~ **per bucato** washing powder. ~ **per i piatti** washing-up liquid, dishwashing liquid *Am*

dete'stare *vt* detest, hate

dete'starsi *vr* hate oneself

deto'nare *vi* detonate

detona'tore *nm* detonator

detonazi'one *nf* detonation

detra'ibile *a* deductible

de'trarre *vt* deduct (**da** from)

de'tratto *pp di* detrarre ● *a* deducted

detrat|'tore, -'trice *nmf* detractor

detrazi'one *nf* deduction; (*da tasse*) tax allowance

detri'mento *nm* detriment; **a** ~ **di** to the detriment of

de'trito *nm* debris; **detriti** *pl* (*di fiume*) detritus. ~ **di falda** scree

detroniz'zare *vt* dethrone

'detta *nf* **a** ~ **di** according to

dettagli'ante *nmf Comm* retailer

dettagli'are *vt* detail

dettagli'ata'mente *adv* in detail

det'taglio *nm* detail; **al** ~ *Comm* retail

det'tame *nm* dictate; **i dettami della moda** the dictates of fashion

det'tare *vt* dictate; ~ **legge** *fig* lay down the law

det'tato *nm Sch* dictation

detta'tura *nf* dictation

'detto *a* said; (*chiamato*) called; (*soprannominato*) nicknamed; ~ **fatto** no sooner said than done ● *nm* ~ **[popolare]** saying

detur'pare *vt* disfigure

deturpazi'one *nf* disfigurement

deumidifi'care *vt* dehumidify

deumidifica'tore *nm* dehumidifier

deumidificazi'one *nf* dehumidification

devalutazi'one *nf* devaluation

deva'stante *a* devastating

deva'stare *vt* devastate

deva'stato *a* devastated

devasta|'tore, -'trice *a* destructive; *fig* devastating ● *nmf* destroyer

devastazi'one *nf* devastation; *fig* ravages *pl*

devi'ante *a* deviant

devi'anza *nf* deviance

devi'are *vi* deviate ● *vt* divert

devi'ato *a* ⟨*mente*⟩ warped

deviazi'one *nf* deviation; (*stradale*) diversion; **fare una** ~ *Auto* make a detour

devitaliz'zare *vt* kill the nerve of, devitalize *fml*

devitalizzazi'one *nf* killing of the nerve, devitalization *fml*

devo'luto *pp di* devolvere ● *a* devolved

devoluzi'one *nf* devolution

de'volvere *vt* devolve; ~ **qcsa in beneficenza** give sth to charity

devota'mente *adv* devoutly

de'voto *a* devout; (*affezionato*) devoted

devozi'one *nf* devotion

dg *abbr* (**decigrammi**) decigrams

di *prep* of; (*partitivo*) some; (*scritto da*) by; ⟨*parlare, pensare ecc*⟩ about; (*con causa, mezzo*) with; (*con provenienza*) from; (*in comparazioni*) than; (*con infinito*) to; **la casa di mio padre/dei miei genitori** my father's house/my parents' house; **compra del pane** buy some bread; **hai del pane?** do you have any bread?; **un film di guerra** a war film; **piangere di dolore** cry with pain; **coperto di neve** covered with snow; **sono di Genova** I'm from Genoa; **uscire di casa** leave one's house; **mi è uscito di mente** it slipped my mind; **più alto di te** taller than you; **è ora di partire** it's time to go; **crede di aver ragione** he thinks he's right; **dire di sì** say yes; **di domenica** on Sundays; **di sera** in the evening; **una pausa di un'ora** an hour's break; **un corso di due mesi** a two-month course

dia'bete *nm* diabetes

dia'betico, -a *a & nmf* diabetic

diabolica'mente *adv* devilishly

dia'bolico *a* diabolic[al]

di'acono *nm* deacon

dia'critico *a* diacritic

dia'dema *nm* diadem; (*di donna*) tiara

di'afano *a* diaphanous

dia'framma *nm* diaphragm; (*divisione*) screen

di'agnosi *nf inv* diagnosis

dia'gnostica *nf Med* diagnostics

diagnosti'care *vt* diagnose

dia'gnostici *nmpl Comput* diagnostics

dia'gnostico *a* diagnostic

diago'nale *a & nf* diagonal

diagonal'mente *adv* diagonally

dia'gramma *nm* diagram. ~ **a barre** bar chart. ~ **di flusso** flowchart

dialet'tale *a* dialect *attrib*; **poesia** ~ poetry in dialect

dialettaleggi'ante *a* dialect *attrib*

dia'lettica *nf* dialectics

dia'lettico *a* dialectic

dia'letto *nm* dialect

di'alisi *nf* dialysis

dialo'gante *a* unità ~ *Comput* interactive terminal

dialo'gare *vt* write the dialogue for ‹scena› ● *vi* ~ **con** converse with

dialo'gato *a* in dialogue

dialo'ghista *nmf* (scrittore) dialogue writer

di'alogo *nm* dialogue

dia'mante *nm* diamond

diaman'tifero *a* diamond bearing

diametral'mente *adv* diametrically

di'ametro *nm* diameter

di'amine *int* **che ~...** what on earth...

di'apason *nm inv* (per accordartura) tuning fork

diaposi'tiva *nf* slide

di'aria *nf* daily allowance

di'ario *nm* diary. ~ **di bordo** logbook. ~ **di classe** class register

dia'rista *nmf* (scrittore) diarist

diar'rea *nf* diarrhoea

di'aspora *nf* Diaspora

dia'triba *nf* diatribe

diavole'ria *nf* (azione) devilment; (marchingegno) weird contraption

diavo'letto *nm* imp; (hum: bambino) little devil

di'avolo *nm* devil; **va' al ~!** *fam* go to hell!; **che ~ fai?** *fam* what the hell are you doing?

di'battere *vt* debate

di'battersi *vr* struggle

dibattimen'tale *a* *Jur* of the hearing

dibatti'mento *nm* (discussione) debate; *Jur* hearing

di'battito *nm* debate; (meno formale) discussion

dica'stero *nm* office

di'cembre *nm* December

dice'ria *nf* rumour

dichia'rare *vt* state; (ufficialmente) declare; ~ **colpevole** *Jur* convict; **niente da ~?** anything to declare?

dichia'rarsi *vr* (in amore) declare one's love; ~ **soddisfatto** declare oneself satisfied; **si dichiara innocente** he says he's innocent; ~ **a favore di qcsa** declare oneself in favour of sth; **si dichiara che...** (in documenti) it is hereby declared that...; ~ **vinto** acknowledge defeat

dichia'rato *a* avowed

dichiarazi'one *nf* statement; (documento, di guerra, d'amore) declaration; **fare una ~** (ufficialmente) make a statement. ~ **dei diritti** *Pol* bill of rights. ~ **doganale** customs declaration. ~ **dei redditi** [income] tax return

dician'nove *a & nm* nineteen

dicianno'venne *a & nmf* nineteen-year-old

dicianno'vesimo *a & nm* nineteenth

dicias'sette *a & nm* seventeen

diciasset'tenne *a & nmf* seventeen-year-old

diciasset'tesimo *a & nm* seventeenth

diciot'tenne *a & nmf* eighteen-year-old

diciot'tesimo *a & nm* eighteenth

dici'otto *a & nm* eighteen

dici'tura *nf* wording

dicoto'mia *nf* dichotomy

didasca'lia *nf* (di film) subtitle; (di illustrazione) caption; *Theat* stage direction

dida'scalico *a* ‹letteratura› didactic

di'dattica *nf* didactics

didattica'mente *adv* didactically

di'dattico *a* didactic; ‹televisione› educational

di'dentro *adv* inside

didi'etro *adv* behind ● *nm hum* hindquarters *pl*

di'eci *a & nm* ten

dieci'mila *a & nm* ten thousand

die'cina = **decina**

di'eresi *nf* diaeresis

'diesel *a & nm inv* diesel

di'esis *nm inv* sharp

di'eta *nf* diet; **a ~** on a diet

die'tetica *nf* dietetics

die'tetico *a* diet

die'tista *nmf* dietician

die'tologo *nmf* dietician

di'etro *adv* behind ● *prep* behind; (dopo) after ● *a* back; (di zampe) hind ● *nm* back; **le stanze di ~** the back rooms; **le zampe di ~** the hind legs

dietro'front *nm inv* about-turn; *fig* U-turn; ~**!** about turn!

dietrolo'gia *nf* investigative journalism

di'fatti *adv* in fact

di'fendere *vt* defend

di'fendersi *vr* defend oneself; (fam: cavarsela) get by

difen'dibile *a* defendable, defensible

difen'siva *nf* **stare sulla ~** be on the defensive

difen'sivo *a* defensive

difen'sore *a* **avvocato ~** defence counsel ● *nm* defender. ~ **civico** ombudsman

di'fesa *nf* defence; **prendere le difese di qcno** come to sb's defence. ~ **civile** Civil Defence

di'feso *pp di* **difendere** ● *a* defended; ‹luogo› sheltered

difet'tare *vi* be defective; ~ **di** lack

difet'tivo *a* defective

di'fetto *nm* defect; (morale) fault, flaw; (mancanza) lack; (in tessuto, abito) flaw; **essere in ~** be at fault; **far ~** be lacking

difet'toso *a* defective; ‹abito› flawed

diffa'mare *vt* (con parole) slander; (per iscritto) libel

diffama|'tore, -'trice *nmf* slanderer; (per iscritto) libeller

diffama'torio *a* slanderous; (per iscritto) libellous

diffamazi'one *nf* slander; (scritta) libel

diffe'rente *a* different

differente'mente *adv* differently

diffe'renza *nf* difference; **a ~ di** unlike; **non fare ~** make no distinction (**fra** between)

differenzi'abile *a* differentiable

differenzi'ale *a & nm* differential

differenzi'are *vt* differentiate

differenzi'arsi *vr ~* **da** differ from

differenzi'ato *a* differentiated

differenziazi'one *nf* differentiation

diffe'ribile *a* postponable

diffe'rire *vt* postpone ● *vi* be different

diffe'rita *nf* **in ~** *TV* prerecorded

dif'ficile *a* difficult; (*duro*) hard; (*improbabile*) unlikely ● *nm* difficulty

difficil'mente *adv* with difficulty

difficoltà *nf* difficulty; **trovarsi in ~** be in trouble; **mettere qcno in ~** put sb on the spot

dif'fida *nf* warning

diffi'dare *vi ~* **di** distrust ● *vt* warn

diffi'dente *a* mistrustful

diffi'denza *nf* mistrust

dif'fondere *vt* spread; diffuse ⟨calore, luce ecc⟩

dif'fondersi *vr* spread

difformità *nf inv* deformation; (*di opinioni*) difference of opinion

diffusa'mente *adv* at length

diffusi'one *nf* diffusion; (*di giornale*) circulation

dif'fuso *pp di* **diffondere** ● *a* common; ⟨malattia⟩ widespread; ⟨luce⟩ diffuse

diffu'sore *nm* (*per asciugacapelli*) diffuser

difi'lato *adv* straight; (*subito*) straightaway

di'fronte *a inv & adv* opposite; **~ all'ingresso** in front of the entrance; (*dall'altro lato della strada*) opposite the entrance

difte'rite *nf* diphtheria

'diga *nf* dam; (*argine*) dike

dige'rente *a* alimentary

dige'ribile *a* digestible

digeribilità *nf* digestibility

dige'rire *vt* digest; *fam* stomach

digesti'one *nf* digestion

dige'stivo *a* digestive ● *nm* digestive; (*dopo cena*) liqueur

Digi'one *nf* Dijon

digi'tale *a* digital; (*delle dita*) finger *attrib* ● *nf* (*fiore*) foxglove

digitalizzazi'one *nf* digitalizing

digi'tare *vt* key in ⟨dati⟩

digiu'nare *vi* fast

digi'uno *a* **essere ~** have an empty stomach ● *nm* fast; **a ~** ⟨bere ecc⟩ on an empty stomach

dignità *nf* dignity

digni'tario *nm* dignitary

dignitosa'mente *adv* with dignity

digni'toso *a* dignified

DIGOS *nf abbr* (**Divisione Investigazioni Generali e Operazioni Speciali**) ≈ riot police

digressi'one *nf* digression

digri'gnare *vi ~* **i denti** grind one's teeth

digros'sare *vt fig* impart basic concepts to

dik'tat *nm inv* (*trattato*) diktat

dila'gare *vi* flood; *fig* spread

dilani'are *vt* tear to pieces

dilapi'dare *vt* squander

dilapidazi'one *nf* squandering

dila'tare *vt* dilate

dila'tarsi *vr* dilate; ⟨legno:⟩ swell; ⟨metallo, gas:⟩ expand

dila'tato *a* dilated; ⟨legno⟩ swollen; ⟨metallo, gas⟩ expanded

dilatazi'one *nf* dilation; (*di legno*) swelling; (*di metallo, gas*) expansion

dilazio'nabile *a* postponable

dilazio'nare *vt* delay

dilazi'one *nf* delay

dileggi'are *vt* mock

dilegu'are *vt* disperse

dilegu'arsi *vr* disappear

di'lemma *nm* dilemma

dilet'tante *nmf* amateur

dilettan'tesco *a* amateurish

dilettan'tismo *nm* amateurism

dilettan'tistico *a* amateurish

dilet'tare *vt* delight

dilet'tarsi *vr ~* **in** delight in

dilet'tevole *a* delightful

di'letto, -a *a* beloved ● *nm* (*piacere*) delight ● *nmf* (*persona*) beloved

dili'gente *a* diligent; ⟨lavoro⟩ accurate

dili'genza *nf* diligence

dilu'ente *nm* diluent

dilu'ire *vt* dilute

diluizi'one *nf* dilution

dilun'gare *vt* prolong

dilun'garsi *vr ~* **su** dwell on ⟨argomento⟩

diluvi'are *vi* pour [down]

di'luvio *nm* downpour; *fig* flood. **il ~ universale** the Flood

dima'grante *a* slimming, diet

dimagri'mento *nm* loss of weight

dima'grire *vi* lose weight

dima'grirsi *vr* lose weight

dime'nare *vt* wave; wag ⟨coda⟩

dime'narsi *vr* be agitated

dimensio'nare *vt fig* get into proportion

dimensi'one *nf* dimension; (*misura*) size

dimenti'canza *nf* forgetfulness; (*svista*) oversight; **per ~** accidentally

dimenti'care *vt* forget; **l'ho dimenticato a casa** I left it at home

dimenti'carsi *vr ~* [**di**] forget

dimentica'toio *nm* **andare/finire nel ~** *hum* fall into oblivion

di'mentico *a ~* **di** (*che non ricorda*) forgetful of; (*non curante*) oblivious of

dimessa'mente *adv* modestly

di'messo *pp di* **dimettere** ● *a* humble; (*trasandato*) shabby; ⟨voce⟩ low

dimesti'chezza *nf* familiarity

di'mettere *vt* dismiss; (*da ospedale ecc*) discharge

di'mettersi *vr* resign

dimez'zare *vt* halve

diminu'ire *vt/i* diminish; (*in maglia*) decrease

diminu'ito *a Mus* diminished

diminu'tivo *a & nm* diminutive

diminuzi'one *nf* decrease; *(riduzione)* reduction; **in ~** dwindling

dimissio'nario *a* outgoing ● *nmf* outgoing chairman/president etc

dimissi'oni *nfpl* resignation *sg*; **dare le ~** resign

di'mora *nf* residence

dimo'rare *vi* reside

dimo'strabile *a* demonstrable

dimostrabilità *nf* demonstrability

dimo'strante *nmf* demonstrator

dimo'strare *vt* demonstrate; *(provare)* prove; *(mostrare)* show

dimo'strarsi *vr* prove [to be]

dimostra'tivo *a* demonstrative

dimostrazi'one *nf* demonstration; *Math* proof

di'namica *nf* dynamics; **~ dei fatti** sequence of events

di'namico *a* dynamic

dina'mismo *nm* dynamism

dinami'tardo *a* **attentato ~** bomb attack ● *nmf* bomber

dina'mite *nf* dynamite

'dinamo *nf inv* dynamo

di'nanzi *adv* in front ● *prep* **~ a** in front of

'dinaro *nm (moneta)* dinar

dina'stia *nf* dynasty

di'nastico *a* dynastic

din'don *nm inv* dingdong

'dingo *nm (cane)* dingo

dini'ego *nm* denial

dinocco'lato *a* lanky

dino'sauro *nm* dinosaur

din'torni *nmpl* outskirts; **nei ~ di** in the vicinity of

din'torno *adv* around

'dio *nm (pl* **'dei)** god; **D~** God; **D~ mio!** my God!

dioce'sano *a* diocesan

di'ocesi *nf inv* diocese

dioni'siaco *a* Dionysian

dios'sina *nf* dioxin

diot'tria *nf* dioptre

dipa'nare *vt* wind into a ball; *fig* unravel

diparti'mento *nm* department

dipen'dente *a* depending ● *nmf* employee

dipen'denza *nf* dependence; *(edificio)* annexe

di'pendere *vi* **~ da** depend on; *(provenire)* derive from; **dipende** it depends

di'pingere *vt* paint; *(descrivere)* describe

di'pinto *pp di* **dipingere** ● *a* painted ● *nm* painting

di'ploma *nm* diploma

diplo'mare *vt* graduate

diplo'marsi *vr* graduate

diplomatica'mente *adv* diplomatically

diplo'matico *a* diplomatic ● *nm* diplomat; *(pasticcino)* millefeuille *(with alcohol)*

diplo'mato *nmf* person with school qualification ● *a* qualified

diploma'zia *nf* diplomacy

di'porto *nm* **imbarcazione da ~** pleasure craft

dirada'mento *nf* thinning out

dira'dare *vt* thin out; make less frequent *(visite)*

dira'darsi *vr* thin out; *(nebbia)* clear

dira'mare *vt* issue

dira'marsi *vr* branch out

diramazi'one *nf (di strada, fiume)* fork; *(di albero, impresa)* branch; *(di ordine)* issuing

'dire *vt* say; *(raccontare, riferire)* tell; **~ quello che si pensa** speak one's mind; **voler ~** mean; **volevo ben ~!** I wondered!; **~ di sì/no** say yes/no; **si dice che...** rumour has it that...; **come si dice "casa" in inglese?** what's the English for "casa"?; **questo nome mi dice qualcosa** the name rings a bell; **che ne dici di...?** how about...?; **non c'è che ~** there's no disputing that; **e ~ che...** to think that...; **a dir poco/tanto** at least/most ● *vi* **~ bene/male di** speak highly/ill of sb; **dica pure** *(in negozio)* how can I help you?; **dici sul serio?** are you serious?; **per modo di ~** as it were

di'retta *nf TV* live broadcast; **in ~** live

diretta'mente *adv* directly

diret'tissima *nf (strada)* main route; **per ~** *Jur (processare)* without going through the normal procedures

diret'tissimo *nm* fast train

diret'tiva *nf* directive; **direttive** *pl (indicazioni)* guidelines

diret'tivo *a (dirigente)* management *attrib*, managerial ● *nm Pol* executive

di'retto *pp di* **dirigere** ● *a* direct; **il mio ~ superiore** my immediate superior; **~ a** *(inteso)* meant for; **essere ~ a** be heading for; **in diretta** *(trasmissione)* live ● *nm (treno)* through train

diret'tore *nm* manager; *(più in alto nella gerarchia)* director; *(di scuola)* headmaster. **~ amministrativo** company secretary. **~ artistico** artistic director. **~ del carcere** prison governor. **~ di filiale** branch manager. **~ di gara** referee. **~ generale** managing director, chief executive officer. **~ di giornale** newspaper editor. **~ d'istituto** *Univ* department head. **~ d'orchestra** conductor. **~ del personale** personnel manager/director. **~ di produzione** production manager/director. **~ spirituale** spiritual advisor. **~ sportivo** team manager. **~ tecnico** *Sport* manager. **~ di zona** area manager; regional director

diret'trice *nf* manageress; *(di scuola)* headmistress; *(indirizzo)* guiding principle

direzio'nale *a* directional

direzio'nare *vt* direct

direzi'one *nf* direction; *(di società)* management; *Sch* headmaster's/headmistress's office *(primary school)*; **in ~ nord** *(traffico)* northbound; **'tutte le direzioni'** *Auto* 'all routes'

diri'gente *a* ruling ● *nmf* executive. **~ di partito** *Pol* party leader

diri'genza nf management; Pol leadership. **~ aziendale** business management

dirigenzi'ale a management attrib, managerial

di'rigere vt direct; conduct ⟨orchestra⟩; run ⟨impresa⟩

di'rigersi vr **~ verso** head for

diri'gibile nm airship

dirim'petto adv opposite ● prep **~ a** facing

di'ritto¹ a straight; ⟨destro⟩ right ● adv straight; **andare ~** go straight on; **sempre ~** straight ahead, straight on ● nm right side; Tennis forehand; **fare un ~** ⟨a maglia⟩ knit one

di'ritto² nm right; Jur law. **diritti** pl **d'autore** royalties. **~ civile** civil law. **diritti** pl **civili** civil rights. **~ commerciale** commercial law. **~ penale** criminal law. **diritti** pl **di prelievo** Fin drawing rights. **diritti** pl **umani** human rights. **~ di voto** right to vote, suffrage

dirit'tura nf straight line; fig honesty. **~ d'arrivo** Sport, fig home straight

diroc'cato a tumbledown

dirom'pente a anche fig explosive

dirotta'mento nm hijacking

dirot'tare vt reroute ⟨treno, aereo⟩; ⟨illegalmente⟩ hijack; divert ⟨traffico⟩ ● vi alter course

dirotta|'tore, -'trice nmf hijacker

di'rotto a ⟨pioggia⟩ pouring; ⟨pianto⟩ uncontrollable; **piovere a ~** rain heavily

di'rupo nm precipice

di'sabile a disabled ● nmf disabled person

disabili'tare vt disable

disabi'tato a uninhabited

disabitu'arsi vr **~ a** get out of the habit of

disac'cordo nm disagreement

disadatta'mento nm maladjustment

disadat'tato, -a a maladjusted ● nmf misfit

disa'dorno a unadorned

disaffezi'one nf disaffection

disa'gevole a ⟨scomodo⟩ uncomfortable; ⟨difficile⟩ inconvenient

disagi'ato a poor; ⟨vita⟩ hard; ⟨scomodo⟩ uncomfortable

di'sagio nm discomfort; ⟨difficoltà⟩ inconvenience; ⟨imbarazzo⟩ embarrassment; **sentirsi a ~** feel uncomfortable; **disagi** pl ⟨privazioni⟩ hardships

di'samina nf close examination

disamora'mento nm estrangement

disanco'rare vt Fin de-link

disappro'vare vt disapprove of

disapprovazi'one nf disapproval

disap'punto nm disappointment; **con suo grande ~** [much] to his chagrin

disarcio'nare vt unseat

disar'mante a fig disarming

disar'mare vt/i disarm

disar'mato a disarmed; fig defenceless

di'sarmo nm disarmament

disartico'lato a fig disjointed

disa'strato, -a a devastated ● nmf victim ⟨of flood, earthquake ecc⟩

di'sastro nm disaster; ⟨fam: grande confusione⟩ mess; ⟨fam: persona⟩ disaster area

disastrosa'mente adv disastrously

disa'stroso a disastrous

disat'tento a inattentive

disatten'zi'one nf inattention; ⟨svista⟩ oversight

disatti'vare vt de-activate

disa'vanzo nm deficit

disavve'duto a thoughtless

disavven'tura nf misadventure

disavver'tenza nf inadvertence

di'sbrigo nm dispatch

di'scapito nm **a ~ di** to the detriment of

di'scarica nf scrap-yard

di'scarico nm ⟨di merce⟩ unloading; **prova a ~** evidence for the defence; **testimone a ~** witness for the defence

discen'dente a descending ● nmf descendant

discen'denza nf descent; ⟨discendenti⟩ descendants pl

di'scendere vi ⟨dal treno⟩ get off; ⟨da cavallo⟩ dismount; ⟨sbarcare⟩ land. **~ da** ⟨trarre origine da⟩ be a descendant of ● vt descend

discen'sore nm ⟨attrezzo⟩ karabiner

di'scepolo, -a nmf disciple

di'scernere vt discern

discerni'mento nm discernment

di'scesa nf descent; ⟨pendio⟩ slope; **~ in picchiata** ⟨di aereo⟩ nosedive; **essere in ~** ⟨strada:⟩ go downhill. **~ libera** ⟨in sci⟩ downhill race

disce'sista nmf ⟨sciatore⟩ downhill skier

di'sceso pp di **discendere**

di'schetto nm Comput diskette

dischi'udere vt open; ⟨svelare⟩ disclose

dischi'udersi vr open up

di'scinto a scantily dressed

disci'ogliere vt dissolve; thaw ⟨neve⟩; ⟨fondere⟩ melt

disci'ogliersi vr dissolve; ⟨neve:⟩ thaw; ⟨fondersi⟩ melt

disci'olto pp di **disciogliere**

disci'plina nf discipline

discipli'nare a disciplinary ● vt discipline

discipli'nato a disciplined

disc-'jockey nm inv disc jockey, DJ

'disco nm disc; Sport discus; Mus record; **ernia del ~** slipped disc. **~ a 33 giri** L.P. **~ a 45 giri** single. **~ fisso** Comput fixed disk, hard disk. **~ dei freni** brake disc. **~ master** Comput master disk. **~ rigido** Comput hard disk. **~ volante** flying saucer

discogra'fia nf ⟨insieme di incisioni⟩ discography; ⟨industria⟩ record industry

disco'grafico a ⟨industria⟩ record attrib, recording; ⟨mercato, raccolta⟩ record attrib; **casa discografica** record company, recording company ● nmf record producer

'discolo nmf rascal ● a unruly

di'scolpa *nf* clearing; **a sua ~ si deve dire che...** in his defence it must be said that...
discol'pare *vt* clear
discol'parsi *vr* clear oneself
disco'noscere *vt* deny; disown ⟨*figlio*⟩
discontinuità *nf inv* (*nel lavoro*) irregularity; (*di stile*) unevenness
discon'tinuo *a* intermittent; ⟨*fig: impegno, rendimento*⟩ uneven
discopa'tia *nf* disc problems *pl*
discor'dante *a* discordant
discor'danza *nf* discordance; **essere in ~** clash
discor'dare *vi* ⟨*opinioni:*⟩ conflict
di'scorde *a* clashing
di'scordia *nf* discord; (*dissenso*) dissension
di'scorrere *vi* talk (**di** about)
discor'sivo *a* colloquial
di'scorso *pp di* **discorrere** ● *nm* speech; (*conversazione*) talk. **~ di ringraziamento** vote of thanks
di'scosto *a* distant ● *adv* far away; **stare ~** stand apart
disco'teca *nf* disco; (*raccolta*) record library
discote'caro *nmf pej* disco freak
di'scount *nm inv* discount store
discredi'tare *vt* discredit
di'scredito *nm* discredit
discre'pante *a* contradictory
discre'panza *nf* discrepancy
di'screto *a* discreet; (*moderato*) moderate; (*abbastanza buono*) fairly good
discrezionalità *nf* discretion
discrezi'one *nf* discretion; (*giudizio*) judgement; **a ~ di** at the discretion of
discrimi'nante *a* extenuating ● *nf Jur* extenuating circumstances *pl*
discrimi'nare *vt* discriminate
discrimina'tivo *a* (*provvedimento*) discriminatory
discrimina'torio *a* ⟨*atteggiamento*⟩ discriminatory
discriminazi'one *nf* discrimination
discussi'one *nf* discussion; (*alterco*) argument; **messa in ~** questioning
di'scusso *pp di* **discutere** ● *a* controversial
di'scutere *vt* discuss; (*formale*) debate; (*litigare*) argue ● *vi* **~ su qcsa** discuss sth
discu'tibile *a* debatable; ⟨*gusto*⟩ questionable
disde'gnare *vt* disdain
di'sdegno *nm* disdain
disde'gnoso *a* disdainful
di'sdetta *nf* retraction; (*sfortuna*) bad luck; *Comm* cancellation
di'sdetto *pp di* **disdire**
disdi'cevole *a* unbecoming
di'sdire *vt* retract; (*annullare*) cancel
disedu'care *vt* have a bad effect on
diseduca'tivo *a* bad for children
dise'gnare *vt* draw; (*progettare*) design
disegna|'tore, -'trice *nmf* designer. **~ di moda** fashion designer

di'segno *nm* drawing; (*progetto, linea*) design. **~ di legge** bill
diser'bante *nm* herbicide, weed-killer ● *a* herbicidal, weed-killing
diser'bare *vt* weed
disere'dare *vt* disinherit
disere'dato *a* dispossessed ● *nmf* **i diseredati** the dispossessed
diser'tare *vt/i* desert; **~ la scuola** stay away from school
diser'tore *nm* deserter
diserzi'one *nf* desertion
disfaci'mento *nm* decay; *fig* decline; **in ~** decaying; *fig* in decline
di'sfare *vt* undo; strip ⟨*letto*⟩; (*smantellare*) take down; (*annientare*) defeat; **~ le valigie** unpack [one's bags]
di'sfarsi *vr* fall to pieces; (*sciogliersi*) melt; **~ di** (*liberarsi di*) get rid of; **~ in lacrime** dissolve into tears
di'sfatta *nf* defeat
disfat'tismo *nm* defeatism
disfat'tista *a & nmf* defeatist
di'sfatto *a fig* worn out
disfunzi'one *nf* disorder
disge'lare *vt/i* thaw
disge'larsi *vr* thaw
di'sgelo *nm* thaw
disgi'ungere *vt* disconnect
disgi'unto *a* ⟨*firme*⟩ separate
di'sgrazia *nf* misfortune; (*incidente*) accident; (*sfavore*) disgrace
disgraziata'mente *adv* unfortunately
disgrazi'ato, -a *a* unfortunate ● *nmf* wretch
disgrega'mento *nm* disintegration
disgre'gare *vt* break up
disgre'garsi *vr* disintegrate
disgrega'tivo *a* disintegrating
disgrega'tore *a* disintegrating
disgregazi'one *nf* (*di società*) break-up
disgu'ido *nm* **~ postale** mistake in delivery
disgu'stare *vt* disgust
disgu'starsi *vr* **~ di** be disgusted by
di'sgusto *nm* disgust
disgustosa'mente *adv* disgustingly; **~ dolce** nauseatingly sweet
disgu'stoso *a* disgusting
disidra'tante *a* dehydrating
disidra'tare *vt* dehydrate
disidra'tarsi *vr* become dehydrated
disidra'tato *a* dehydrated
disidratazi'one *nf* dehydration
disil'ludere *vt* disenchant, disillusion
disil'ludersi *vr* become disenchanted, become disillusioned
disillusi'one *nf* disenchantment, disillusionment
disil'luso *a* disenchanted, disillusioned
disimbal'laggio *nm* unpacking
disimbal'lare *vt* unpack
disimpa'rare *vt* forget
disimpe'gnare *vt* release; (*compiere*) fulfil; redeem ⟨*oggetto dato in pegno*⟩

disimpe'gnarsi vr disengage oneself; (cavarsela) manage

disim'pegno nm (locale) vestibule; (disinteresse) lack of interest

disimpi'ego nm re-allocation; (di truppe) re-assignment

disincagli'are vt Naut refloat

disincagli'arsi vr Naut float off

disincan'tato a (disilluso) disillusioned

disincar'nato a disembodied

disincenti'vante a demotivating

disincenti'vare vt demotivate

disincen'tivo nm disincentive

disincroci'are vt uncross

disinfe'stare vt disinfest

disinfestazi'one nf disinfestation

disinfet'tante a & nm disinfectant

disinfet'tare vt disinfect

disinfezi'one nf disinfection

disinfiam'marsi vr become less inflamed

disinflazio'nare vt disinflate

disinflazi'one nf disinflation

disinflazio'nistico a disinflationary

disinfor'mato a uninformed

disinformazi'one nf lack of information; (informazione erronea) misinformation

disingan'nare vt disabuse

disin'ganno nm disillusion

disini'birsi vr lose one's inhibitions

disini'bito a uninhibited

disinne'scare vt defuse

disin'nesco nm (di bomba) bomb disposal

disinne'stare vt disengage

disinne'starsi vr disengage

disin'nesto nm disengagement

disinquina'mento nm cleaning up

disinqui'nare vt clean up

disinse'rire vt disconnect

disinse'rito a disconnected

disinte'grare vt disintegrate

disinte'grarsi vr disintegrate

disintegrazi'one nf disintegration

disinteressa'mento nm lack of interest

disinteres'sarsi vr ~ **di** take no interest in

disinteressata'mente adv without interest; (senza secondo fine) disinterestedly

disinteres'sato a uninterested; (senza secondo fine) disinterested

disinte'resse nm indifference; (oggettività) disinterestedness

disintossi'care vt detoxify

disintossi'carsi vr come off drugs; ‹alcolizzato:› dry out

disintossicazi'one nf giving up alcohol/drugs; **programma di** ~ detox programme

disinvolta'mente adv in a relaxed way

disin'volto a relaxed

disinvol'tura nf confidence

disi'stima nf lack of respect

disles'sia nf dyslexia

di'slessico a dyslexic

disli'vello nm difference in height; fig inequality

disloca'mento nm Mil posting

dislo'care vt Mil post

dismenor'rea nf dysmenorrhoea

dismi'sura nf excess; **a** ~ excessively

disobbedi'ente a disobedient

disobbe'dire vt disobey

disoccu'pato, -a a unemployed ● nmf unemployed person

disoccupazi'one nf unemployment

disonestà nf dishonesty

diso'nesto a dishonest

disono'rare vt dishonour

disono'rato a dishonoured

diso'nore nm dishonour

di'sopra adv above ● a upper ● nm top

disordi'nare vt disarrange

disordinata'mente adv untidily

disordi'nato a untidy; (sregolato) immoderate

di'sordine nm disorder, untidiness; (sregolatezza) debauchery

disores'sia nf eating disorder

disor'ganico a inconsistent

disorganiz'zare vt disorganize

disorganiz'zato a disorganized

disorganizzazi'one nf disorganization

disorienta'mento nm disorientation

disorien'tare vt disorientate

disorien'tarsi vr lose one's bearings

disorien'tato a fig bewildered

disos'sare vt bone

disos'sato a boned

di'sotto adv below ● a lower ● nm bottom

di'spaccio nm dispatch

dispa'rato a disparate

'dispari a odd, uneven

dispa'rire vi disappear

disparità nf inv disparity

di'sparte adv in ~ apart; **stare in** ~ stand aside

di'spendio nm expenditure; pej waste

dispendiosa'mente adv extravagantly

dispendi'oso a expensive

di'spensa nf pantry; (distribuzione) distribution; (mobile) cupboard; Jur exemption; Relig dispensation; (pubblicazione periodica) number

dispen'sare vt distribute; (esentare) exonerate

dispen'sario nm dispensary

di'spenser nm inv display rack; (confezione) dispenser

dispe'rare vi despair (di of)

dispe'rarsi vr despair

disperata'mente adv ‹piangere› desperately; ‹studiare› like mad

dispe'rato a desperate

disperazi'one nf despair

di'sperdere vt scatter, disperse

di'sperdersi vr scatter, disperse

dispersi'one nf dispersion; (di truppe) dispersal

disper'sivo a disorganized

di'sperso pp di **disperdere** ● a scattered; (smarrito) lost ● nm missing soldier

di'spetto nm spite; **a** ~ **di** in spite of; **fare un** ~ **a qcno** spite sb

dispet'toso *a* spiteful

dispia'cere *nm* upset; (*rammarico*) regret; (*dolore*) sorrow; (*preoccupazione*) worry ● *vi* **mi dispiace** I'm sorry; **non mi dispiace** I don't dislike it; **se non ti dispiace** if you don't mind

dispiaci'uto *a* sorry

dispie'gare *vt* unfold

dispie'garsi *vr* unfurl

dispo'nibile *a* available; (*gentile*) helpful

disponibilità *nf* availability; (*gentilezza*) helpfulness. ~ *pl* **correnti** *Fin* current assets

di'sporre *vt* arrange ● *vi* dispose; (*stabilire*) order; ~ **di** have at one's disposal

di'sporsi *vr* (*in fila*) line up

disposi'tivo *nm* device. ~ **di emergenza** emergency button/handle. ~ **di puntamento** *Comput* pointing device

disposizi'one *nf* disposition; (*ordine*) order; (*libera disponibilità*) disposal

di'sposto *pp di* **disporre** ● *a* ready; (*incline*) disposed; **essere ben disposto verso** be favourably disposed towards

dispotica'mente *adv* despotically

di'spotico *a* despotic

dispo'tismo *nm* despotism

dispregia'tivo *a* disparaging

disprez'zabile *a* despicable

disprez'zare *vt* despise

di'sprezzo *nm* contempt

'**disputa** *nf* dispute

dispu'tare *vi* dispute; (*gareggiare*) compete

dispu'tarsi *vr* ~ **qcsa** contend for sth

disqui'sire *vi* discourse

disquisizi'one *nf* disquisition

dissa'crante *a* debunking

dissa'crare *vt* debunk

dissacra'|tore, -'trice *nmf* debunker

dissacra'torio *a* debunking

dissacrazi'one *nf* debunking

dissangua'mento *nm* loss of blood; *fig* impoverishment

dissangu'are *vt* bleed; *fig* bleed dry

dissangu'arsi *vr* bleed; *fig* become impoverished

dissangu'ato *a* bloodless; *fig* impoverished

dissa'pore *nm* disagreement

dissec'care *vt* dry up

dissec'carsi *vr* dry up

dissemi'nare *vt* disseminate; (*notizie*) spread

dissen'nato *a* (*politica*) senseless

dis'senso *nm* dissent; (*disaccordo*) disagreement

dissente'ria *nf* dysentery

dissen'tire *vi* disagree (**da** with)

dissepelli'mento *nm* exhumation

dissepel'lire *vt* exhume (*cadavere*); disinter (*rovine*); *fig* unearth

dissertazi'one *nf* dissertation

disser'vizio *nm* poor service

disse'stare *vt* upset; *Comm* damage

disse'stato *a* (*strada*) uneven; (*azienda*) shaky

dis'sesto *nm* ruin

disse'tante *a* thirst-quenching

disse'tare *vt* ~ **qcno** quench sb's thirst

disse'tarsi *vr* quench one's thirst

dissezio'nare *vr* dissect

dissezi'one *nf* dissection

dissi'dente *a & nmf* dissident

dissi'denza *nf* dissidence

dis'sidio *nm* disagreement

dis'simile *a* unlike, dissimilar

dissimu'lare *vt* conceal

dissimu'lato *a* concealed

dissimula'|tore, -'trice *nmf* dissembler

dissimulazi'one *nf* concealment

dissi'pare *vt* dissipate; (*sperperare*) squander

dissi'parsi *vr* (*nebbia:*) clear; (*dubbio:*) disappear

dissipa'tezza *nf* dissipation

dissi'pato *a* dissipated

dissipa'tore *nm* ~ **termico** heat sink

dissipazi'one *nf* squandering

dissoci'abile *a* separable

dissoci'are *vt* dissociate

dissoci'arsi *vr* dissociate oneself

dissoci'ato, -a *a Pol* dissenting ● *nmf Pol* dissenter

dissociazi'one *nf Pol* dissociation

dissoda'mento *nm* tillage

disso'dare *vt* till

dis'solto *pp di* **dissolvere**

disso'lubile *a* dissoluble

dissolu'tezza *nf* dissoluteness

dissolu'tivo *a* divisive

disso'luto *a* dissolute

dissol'venza *nf* (*di immagine*) fade-out, dissolve

dis'solvere *vt* dissolve; (*disperdere*) dispel

dis'solversi *vr* dissolve; (*disperdersi*) clear

disso'nante *a* dissonant

disso'nanza *nf* dissonance

dissotterra'mento *nm* disinterment

dissotter'rare *vt* disinter (*bara*); *fig* resurrect (*rancore*)

dissua'dere *vt* dissuade

dissuasi'one *nf* dissuasion

dissua'sivo *a* dissuasive

distacca'mento *nm Mil* detachment

distac'care *vt* detach; *Sport* leave behind

distac'carsi *vr* be detached

distac'cato *a* (*tono, voce*) expressionless

di'stacco *nm* detachment; (*separazione*) separation; *Sport* lead

di'stante *a* far away; (*fig: person*) detached ● *adv* far away

di'stanza *nf* distance

distanzia'mento *nm* spacing [out]; *Sport* outdistancing

distanzi'are *vt* space out; *Sport* outdistance

di'stare *vi* be distant; **quanto dista?** how far is it?; **Roma dista 20 chilometri da qui** Rome is 20 kilometres away, Rome is 20 kilometres from here

di'stendere *vt* stretch out ⟨*parte del corpo*⟩; (*spiegare*) spread; (*deporre*) lay

di'stendersi *vr* stretch; (*sdraiarsi*) lie down; (*rilassarsi*) relax

disten'sione *nf* stretching; (*rilassamento*) relaxation; *Pol* détente

disten'sivo *a* relaxing

di'stesa *nf* expanse

di'steso *pp di* distendere

distil'lare *vt/i* distil

distil'lato *a* distilled ● *nm* distillate

distillazi'one *nf* distillation

distille'ria *nf* distillery

di'stinguere *vt* distinguish

di'stinguersi *vr* (*per bravura ecc*) distinguish oneself; **si distingue dagli altri per...** it is distinguished from the others by...

distin'guibile *a* distinguishable

di'stinguo *nm inv* distinction

di'stinta *nf Comm* list. **~ di pagamento** receipt. **~ di versamento** paying-in slip

distinta'mente *adv* (*separatamente*) individually, separately; (*chiaramente*) clearly; (*in modo elegante*) in a distinguished way; **vi saluto ~** yours truly

distin'tivo *a* distinctive ● *nm* badge

di'stinto *pp di* distinguere ● *a* distinct; (*signorile*) distinguished; **distinti saluti** Yours faithfully

distinzi'one *nf* distinction

di'stogliere *vt* **~ da** (*allontanare*) remove from; (*dissuadere*) dissuade from

di'stolto *pp di* distogliere

di'storcere *vt* twist; distort ⟨*suono*⟩

di'storcersi *vr* sprain ⟨*la caviglia*⟩

distorsi'one *nf Med* sprain; (*alterazione*) distortion

di'storto *a* warped; ⟨*suono*⟩ distorted

di'strarre *vt* distract; (*divertire*) amuse

di'strarsi *vr* (*deconcentrarsi*) be distracted; (*svagarsi*) amuse oneself; **non ti distrarre!** pay attention!

distratta'mente *adv* absently

di'stratto *pp di* distrarre ● *a* absent-minded; (*disattento*) inattentive

distrazi'one *nf* absent-mindedness; (*errore*) inattention; (*svago*) amusement; **errore di ~** absent-minded mistake

di'stretto *nm* district

distrettu'ale *a* district *attrib*

distribu'ire *vt* distribute; (*disporre*) arrange; deal ⟨*carte*⟩

distribu'tore *nm* distributor; (*di benzina*) petrol pump, gas pump *Am*; (*automatico*) slot-machine. **~ automatico di biglietti** ticket machine. **~ di bevande** drinks dispenser. **~ di monete** change machine

distribuzi'one *nf* distribution

distri'care *vt* disentangle

distri'carsi *vr fig* get out of it

distro'fia *nf* **~ muscolare** muscular dystrophy

di'strofico *a* dystrophic

di'struggere *vt* destroy

di'struggersi *vr* **si distrugge col bere** he is destroying himself with drink; **la macchina si è distrutta** the car has been written off

distruttività *nf* destructiveness

distrut'tivo *a* destructive; ⟨*critica*⟩ negative

di'strutto *pp di* distruggere ● *a* destroyed; **un uomo ~** a broken man

distrut'tore *nm* **~ di documenti** paper shredder

distruzi'one *nf* destruction

distur'bare *vt* disturb; (*sconvolgere*) upset

distur'barsi *vr* trouble oneself; **non si disturbi** please don't trouble yourself

distur'bato *a* ⟨*Med: mente*⟩ disordered; ⟨*intestino*⟩ upset

di'sturbo *nm* bother; (*indisposizione*) trouble; *Med* problem; *Radio, TV* interference; **disturbi** *pl Radio, TV* static. **disturbi** *pl di* **stomaco** stomach trouble

disubbidi'ente *a* disobedient

disubbidi'enza *nf* disobedience

disubbi'dire *vi* **~ a** disobey

disuguagli'anza *nf* disparity; (*eterogeneità*) irregularity

disugu'ale *a* unequal; (*eterogeneo*) irregular

disumanità *nf* inhumanity

disu'mano *a* inhuman

disuni'one *nf* disunity

disu'nire *vt* divide

di'suso *nm* **cadere in ~** fall into disuse

di'tale *nm* thimble

di'tata *nf* poke; (*impronta*) finger-mark

'dito *nm* (*pl nf* dita) finger; (*di vino, acqua*) finger. **~ del piede** toe

'ditta *nf* firm. **~ di vendita per corrispondenza** mail order firm

dit'tafono *nm* dictaphone

ditta'tore *nm* dictator

dittatori'ale *a* dictatorial

ditta'tura *nf* dictatorship

dit'tongo *nm* diphthong

diu'retico *a* diuretic

di'urno *a* daytime; **spettacolo ~** matinée

'diva *nf* diva

diva'gare *vi* digress

divagazi'one *nf* digression. **~ sul tema** digression

divam'pare *vi* burst into flames; *fig* spread like wildfire

di'vano *nm* settee, sofa. **~ letto** sofa bed

divari'care *vt* open

divari'carsi *vr* splay

divari'cata *nf* splits *pl*

divari'cato *a* ⟨*gambe, braccia*⟩ splayed

di'vario *nm* discrepancy; **un ~ di opinioni** a difference of opinion

di'vellere *vt* (*sradicare*) uproot

di'velto *pp di* divellere

dive'nire *vi* = diventare

diven'tare *vi* become; (*lentamente*) grow; (*rapidamente*) turn

dive'nuto *pp di* divenire

di'verbio *nm* squabble

diver'gente *a* divergent

diver'genza *nf* divergence; **~ di opinioni** difference of opinion

di'vergere *vi* diverge

diversa'mente *adv* (*altrimenti*) otherwise; (*in modo diverso*) differently

di'versi *a & pron* (*parecchi*) several

diversifi'care *vt* diversify

diversifi'carsi *vr* differ, be different

diversifi'cato *a* broad-based

diversificazi'one *nf* diversification

diversi'one *nf* diversion

diversità *nf inv* diversity; **ci sono molte ~** there are many differences

diver'sivo *a* diversionary ● *nm* diversion

di'verso *a* different ● *nm* (*omosessuale*) deviant

diver'tente *a* amusing

diver'ticolo *nm* digression

diverti'mento *nm* fun, amusement; **buon ~!** enjoy yourself!, have fun!

diver'tire *vt* amuse

diver'tirsi *vr* enjoy oneself, have fun

diver'tito *a* amused

divi'dendo *nm* dividend

di'videre *vt* divide; (*condividere*) share

di'vidersi *vr* (*separarsi*) separate

divi'eto *nm* prohibition; '**~ di pesca**' 'fishing prohibited'; '**~ di sosta**' 'no parking'

divina'mente *adv* divinely

divinco'larsi *vr* wriggle

divinità *nf inv* divinity

di'vino *a* divine

di'visa *nf* uniform; *Comm* currency

divi'sibile *a* divisible

divisi'one *nf* division

divisio'nismo *nm* (*in arte*) pointillism

di'vismo *nm* worship; (*atteggiamento*) superstar mentality

di'viso *pp di* **dividere** ● *a* divided

divi'sore *nm* divisor

divi'sorio *a* dividing; **muro ~** partition wall

'divo, -a *nmf* star

divo'rare *vt* devour

divo'rarsi *vr* **~ da** be consumed with

divorzi'are *vi* divorce

divorzi'ato, -a *nmf* divorcee

di'vorzio *nm* divorce

divul'gare *vt* divulge; (*rendere popolare*) popularize

divul'garsi *vr* spread

divulga'tivo *a* popular

divulgazi'one *nf* spread; (*di cultura, scienza*) popularization

dizio'nario *nm* dictionary. **~ dei sinonimi** thesaurus

dizi'one *nf* diction

DJ *nm inv* DJ

DNA *nm inv* DNA

do *nm Mus* (*chiave, nota*) C

'doccia *nf* shower; (*grondaia*) gutter; **fare la ~** have a shower, shower

doccia'tura *nf Med* douche

D.O.C. *abbr* (**Denominazione di Origine Controllata**) *mark guaranteeing the quality of a wine*

do'cente *a* teaching ● *nmf* teacher; (*di università*) lecturer

do'cenza *nf* university teacher's qualification

D.O.C.G. *abbr* (**Denominazione di Origine Controllata e Garantita**) *mark guaranteeing the high quality of a wine*

'docile *a* docile

docilità *nf* docility

documen'tare *vt* document

documen'tario *a & nm* documentary

documen'tarsi *vr* gather information (**su** about)

documen'tato *a* well-documented; (*persona*) well-informed

documentazi'one *nf* documentation

docu'mento *nm* document; **documenti** *pl* papers. **~ d'identità** ID

dodeca'fonico *a Mus* dodecaphonic

Dodecan'neso *nm* **il ~** the Dodecanese

dodi'cenne *a & nmf* twelve-year-old

dodi'cesimo *a & nm* twelfth

'dodici *a & nm* twelve

do'gana *nf* customs *pl*; (*dazio*) duty. **~ merci** customs for freight. **~ passeggeri** passenger customs

doga'nale *a* customs *attrib*

dogani'ere *nm* customs officer

'doglie *nfpl* labour pains

'dogma *nm* dogma

dog'matico *a* dogmatic

dogma'tismo *nm* dogmatism

'dolce *a* sweet; (*clima*) mild; (*voce, consonante*) soft; (*acqua*) fresh ● *nm* (*portata*) dessert; (*torta*) cake; **non mangio dolci** I don't eat sweet things; **dolci** *pl* **della casa** (*in menu*) home-made cakes

dolce'mente *adv* sweetly

dolce'vita *a inv* (*maglione*) rollneck

dol'cezza *nf* sweetness; (*di clima*) mildness

dolci'ario *a* confectionery

dolci'astro *a* sweetish

dolcifi'cante *nm* sweetener ● *a* sweetening

dolcifica'tore *nm* (*per acqua*) softener

dolci'umi *nmpl* sweets

do'lente *a* painful; (*spiacente*) sorry; **punto ~** sore point

do'lere *vi* ache, hurt; (*dispiacere*) regret

do'lersi *vr* regret; (*protestare*) complain; **~ di** be sorry for

'dollaro *nm* dollar

'dolly *nm inv Cinema, TV* dolly

'dolmen *nm inv* dolmen

'dolo *nm Jur* malice; (*truffa*) fraud

Dolo'miti *nfpl* **le ~** the Dolomites

dolo'mitico *a* Dolomite, of the Dolomites

dolo'rante *a* aching

do'lore *nm* pain; (*morale*) sorrow; **avere dei dolori** be in pain. **dolori** *pl* post-partum after-pains

dolorosa'mente *adv* painfully

dolo'roso *a* painful

do'loso *a* malicious

do'manda *nf* question; (*richiesta*) request; (*scritta*) application; *Comm* demand; ~ **e offerta** supply and demand; **fare una ~ (a qcno)** ask (sb) a question. ~ **di impiego** job application. ~ **riconvenzionale** counterclaim

doman'dare *vt* ask; (*esigere*) demand; ~ **qcsa a qcno** ask sb for sth

doman'darsi *vr* wonder

do'mani *adv* tomorrow; ~ **sera** tomorrow evening; **a ~** see you tomorrow ● *nm* **il ~** the future

do'mare *vt* tame; *fig* control (*emozioni*)

doma|'tore, -'trice *nmf* tamer. ~ **di cavalli** horsebreaker

domat'tina *adv* tomorrow morning

doma'tura *nf* (*di cavallo*) breaking

do'menica *nf* Sunday; **di ~** on Sundays. ~ **delle palme** Palm Sunday

domeni'cale *a* Sunday *attrib*

domeni'cano *a* Dominican

do'mestico, -a *a* domestic; **le pareti domestiche** one's own four walls ● *nm* servant ● *nf* maid

domicili'are *a* **arresti domiciliari** *Jur* house arrest; **perquisizione ~** *Jur* house search

domicili'arsi *vr* settle

domi'cilio *nm* domicile; (*abitazione*) home; **recapitiamo a ~** we do home deliveries

domi'nante *a* (*nazione, colore*) dominant; (*caratteri*) chief; (*opinione*) prevailing; (*motivo*) main

domi'nanza *nf* Biol, Zool dominance

domi'nare *vt* dominate; (*controllare*) control ● *vi* rule over; (*prevalere*) be dominant

domi'narsi *vr* control oneself

domina|'tore, -'trice *a* domineering ● *nmf* ruler

dominazi'one *nf* domination

domini'cano *a* **la Repubblica Dominicana** the Dominican Republic

do'minio *nm* control; *Pol* dominion; (*ambito*) field; **di ~ pubblico** common knowledge

'domino *nm* (*gioco*) dominoes

don *nm inv* (*ecclesiastico*) Father

do'nare *vt* give; donate (*sangue, organo*) ● *vi* ~ **a** (*giovare esteticamente*) suit

do'narsi *vr* dedicate oneself

dona|'tore, -'trice *nmf* donor. ~ **di organi** organ donor

donazi'one *nf* donation

dondo'lare *vt* swing; (*cullare*) rock ● *vi* sway

dondo'larsi *vr* swing

dondo'lio *nm* rocking

'dondolo *nm* swing; **cavallo/sedia a ~** rocking-horse/chair

dongio'vanni *nm inv* Romeo, Don Juan

'donna *nf* woman; **fare la prima ~** act like a prima donna; **'donne'** 'ladies'. ~ **d'affari** businesswoman. ~ **delle pulizie** cleaner. ~ **di servizio** domestic help. ~ **di vita** (*prostituta*) lady of the night

don'naccia *nf pej* hussy

donnai'olo *nm* womanizer

donnicci'ola *nf fig* old woman

'donnola *nf* weasel

'dono *nm* gift

'doping *nm inv* Sport drug-taking; **fa uso di ~** he takes drugs

'dopo *prep* after; (*a partire da*) since ● *adv* after, afterwards; (*più tardi*) later; (*in seguito*) later on; ~ **di me** after me

dopo'barba *nm inv* aftershave

dopo'cena *nm inv* evening

dopodiché *adv* after which

dopodo'mani *adv* the day after tomorrow

dopogu'erra *nm inv* post-war period

dopola'voro *nm inv* working man's club

dopo'pranzo *nm inv* afternoon

dopo'sci *a & nm inv* après-ski

doposcu'ola *nm inv* after-school activities *pl*

dopo-'shampoo *nm inv* conditioner ● *a inv* conditioning

dopo'sole *nm inv* aftersun cream ● *a inv* aftersun

dopo'tutto *adv* after all

doppi'aggio *nm* dubbing

doppia'mente *adv* (*in misura doppia*) doubly

doppi'are *vt* Naut double; Sport lap; Cinema dub

doppia|'tore, -'trice *nmf* dubber

doppi'etta *nf* (*fucile*) double-barrelled shotgun; Auto double-declutch; (*in calcio*) two goals; (*in pugilato*) one-two

doppi'ezza *nf* duplicity

'doppio *a & adv* double. ~ **clic** Comput double click; **fare un ~ su** double-click on. ~ **fallo** *nm* Tennis double fault. ~ **gioco** *nm* double-dealing. ~ **mento** *nm* double chin. ~ **senso** *nm* double entendre. **doppi vetri** *nmpl* double glazing ● *nm* double, twice the quantity; Tennis doubles *pl.* ~ **misto** Tennis mixed doubles

doppio'fondo *nm* Naut double hull; (*in valigia*) false bottom

doppiogio'chista *nmf* double-dealer

doppi'one *nm* duplicate

doppio'petto *a* double-breasted

dop'pista *nmf* Tennis doubles player

do'rare *vt* gild; Culin brown

do'rato *a* gilt; (*color oro*) golden

dora'tura *nf* gilding

'dorico *a* Archit Doric

do'rifora *nf* Colorado beetle

dormicchi'are *vi* doze

dormigli'one, -a *nmf* sleepyhead; *fig* lazybones

dor'mire *vi* sleep; (*essere addormentato*) be asleep; *fig* be asleep; **andare a ~** go to bed; ~ **come un ghiro** sleep like a log; ~ **in piedi** *fig* be half asleep; (*essere stanco*) be dead tired; **dormirci sopra** sleep on it

dor'mita *nf* good sleep; **fare una bella ~** have a good sleep

dormi'tina *nf* nap

dormi'torio *nm* dormitory. **~ pubblico** night shelter

dormi'veglia *nm* **essere nel ~** be half asleep

dor'sale *a* dorsal ● *nf* (*di monte*) ridge

dor'sista *nmf* backstroke swimmer

'dorso *nm* back; (*di libro*) spine; (*di monte*) crest; (*nel nuoto*) backstroke; **a ~ di cavallo** on horseback

do'saggio *nm* dosage; *fig* weighing; **sbagliare il ~** get the amount wrong

do'sare *vt* dose; *fig* measure; **~ le parole** weigh one's words

do'sato *a* measured

dosa'tore *nm* measuring jug

'dose *nf* dose; **~ eccessiva** overdose; **in buona ~** *fig* in good measure

dos'sier *nm inv* (*raccolta di dati, fascicolo*) file

'dosso *nm* (*dorso*) back; **levarsi di ~ gli abiti** take off one's clothes

do'tare *vt* endow; (*di accessori*) equip

do'tato *a* ⟨*persona*⟩ gifted; (*fornito*) equipped

dotazi'one *nf* (*attrezzatura*) equipment; (*mezzi finanziari*) endowment; **avere qcsa in ~** be equipped with sth

'dote *nf* dowry; (*qualità*) gift

dott. *abbr* (**dottore**) Dr.

'dotto *a* learned ● *nm* scholar; *Anat* duct

dotto'rale *a* doctoral; *pej* pedantic

dotto'rando, -a *nmf* postgraduate student

dotto'rato *nm* doctorate

dot'tor|e, ~'essa *nmf* doctor

dot'trina *nf* doctrine

dott.ssa *abbr* (**dottoressa**) Dr.

'dove *adv* where; **di ~ sei?** where do you come from; **fin ~?** how far?; **per ~?** which way?

do'vere *vi* (*obbligo*) have to, must; **devo andare** I have to go, I must go; **devo venire anch'io?** do I have to come too?; **avresti dovuto dirmelo** you should have told me, you ought to have told me; **devo sedermi un attimo** I must sit down for a minute, I need to sit down for a minute; **dev'essere successo qualcosa** something must have happened; **come si deve** properly ● *vt* (*essere debitore di, derivare*) owe; **essere dovuto a** be due to ● *nm* duty; **per ~** out of duty; **rivolgersi a chi di ~** apply to the appropriate authorities

dove'roso *a* right and proper, only right

do'vizia *nf* **con ~ di particolari** in great detail

do'vunque *adv* (*dappertutto*) everywhere; (*in qualsiasi luogo*) anywhere ● *conj* wherever

dovuta'mente *adv* duly

do'vuto *a* due; (*debito*) proper; **essere ~ a** be attributable to; **ha fatto più del ~** he did more than he had to

Down: **sindrome di ~** *Med* Down's syndrome

doz'zina *nf* **una ~ di uova** a dozen eggs; **mezza ~ di uova** half a dozen eggs

dozzi'nale *a* cheap

'draga *nf* (*scavatrice*) dredger

draga'mine *nf* minesweeper

dra'gare *vt* dredge

'drago *nm* dragon

'dramma *nm* drama; **fare un ~ di qcsa** *fig* make a drama out of sth

drammatica'mente *adv* dramatically

drammaticità *nf* dramatic force

dram'matico *a* dramatic

drammatiz'zare *vt* dramatize

drammatizzazi'one *nf* dramatization

drammatur'gia *nf* (*genere*) drama

dramma'turgo *nm* playwright

dram'mone *nm* (*film*) tear-jerker, weepy

drappeggi'are *vt* drape

drap'peggio *nm* drapery

drap'pello *nm* *Mil* squad; (*gruppo*) band

'drappo *nm* (*tessuto*) cloth

drastica'mente *adv* drastically

'drastico *a* drastic

dre'naggio *nm* drainage. **~ di capitali** transfer of capital. **~ fiscale** fiscal drag

dre'nare *vt* drain

'Dresda *nf* Dresden

dres'sage *nm inv* (*gara*) dressage

drib'blare *vt* (*in calcio*) dribble; *fig* dodge

'dribbling *nm inv* (*in calcio*) dribble

'dritta *nf* (*mano destra*) right hand; *Naut* starboard; (*informazione*) pointer, tip; **a ~ e a manca** (*dappertutto*) left, right and centre

dritta'mente *adv* (*furbescamente*) craftily

'dritto *a* = **diritto**[1] ● *nmf fam* crafty so-and-so

drive *nm inv* *Comput* drive

drive-in *nm inv* drive-in

driz'zare *vt* straighten; (*rizzare*) prick up

driz'zarsi *vr* straighten [up]; (*alzarsi*) raise; **mi sono drizzati i capelli** *fig* my hair stood on end

'droga *nf* drug. **~ leggera** soft drug. **~ pesante** hard drug

dro'gare *vt* drug

dro'garsi *vr* take drugs

dro'gato, -a *nmf* drug addict

droghe'ria *nf* grocery

droghi'ere, -a *nmf* grocer

drome'dario *nm* dromedary

'druso *nmf* Druse

dua'lismo *nm* dualism; (*contrasto*) conflict

'dubbio *a* doubtful; (*ambiguo*) dubious ● *nm* doubt; (*sospetto*) suspicion; **mettere in ~** doubt; **essere fuori ~** be beyond doubt; **essere in ~** be doubtful

dubbiosa'mente *adv* doubtfully

dubbi'oso, dubi'tante *a* doubtful

dubi'tare *vi* doubt; **~ di** doubt; (*diffidare*) mistrust; **dubito che venga** I doubt whether he'll come

dubita'tivo *a* (*ambiguo*) ambiguous

duble-'face *a inv* reversible

Du'blino *nf* Dublin

'duca *nm* duke

du'cale *a* ducal

'duce *nm* (*capo del fascismo*) Duce

du'chessa *nf* duchess

'due *a* & *nm* two

duecen'tesco *a* thirteenth-century

duecen'tesimo two hundredth

due'cento *a* & *nm* two hundred

duel'lante *nmf* dueller

duel'lare *vi* duel

du'ello *nm* duel

due'mila *a* & *nm* two thousand

due'pezzi *nm inv* (*bikini*) bikini; (*vestito*) two-piece suit

du'etto *nm* duo; *Mus* duet

'dumping *nm inv Fin* dumping

'duna *nf* dune

dune 'buggy *nm inv* beach buggy

'dunque *conj* therefore; (*allora*) well [then]; **arrivare al ~** get down to the nitty-gritty

'duo *nm inv* duo; *Mus* duet

duodeci'male *a* duodecimal

duode'nale *a* **ulcera ~** duodenal ulcer

duo'deno *nm* duodenum

du'omo *nm* cathedral

'duplex *nm Teleph* party line

dupli'care *vt* duplicate

dupli'cato *nm* duplicate

duplicazi'one *nf* duplication

'duplice *a* double; **in ~** in duplicate

duplicità *nf* duplicity

dura'mente *adv* (*lavorare*) hard; (*rimproverare*) harshly

du'rante *prep* during

du'rare *vi* last; (*cibo:*) keep; (*resistere*) hold out; **così non può ~** this can't go on any longer; **~ in carica** remain in office; **finché dura** as long as it lasts ● *vt* **~ fatica** sweat blood

du'rata *nf* duration. **~ del collegamento** on-line time. **~ di conservazione** shelflife. **~ della vita** life span

dura'turo *a* lasting

du'revole *a* (*pace*) lasting, enduring

du'rezza *nf* hardness; (*di carne*) toughness; (*di voce, padre*) harshness

'duro, -a *a* hard; (*persona, carne*) tough; (*voce*) harsh; (*pane*) stale; **tieni ~!** (*resistere*) hang in there!; **~ d'orecchio** hard of hearing ● *nmf* (*persona*) tough person, toughie *fam*

du'rone *nm* hardened skin

'duttile *a* (*materiale*) ductile; (*carattere, persona*) malleable

duttilità *nf* (*di materiale*) ductility; (*di individuo*) malleability

'duty free *nm inv* duty-free shop

Ee

---

e *conj* and

eba'nista *nmf* cabinet-maker

'ebano *nm* ebony

eb'bene *conj* well [then]

eb'brezza *nf* inebriation; (*euforia*) elation; **guida in stato di ~** drink-driving; **l'~ della velocità** the thrill of speed

'ebbro *a* inebriated; **~ di gioia** delirious with joy

'ebete *a* stupid

ebollizi'one *nf* boiling

e'braico *a* & *nm* Hebrew

ebra'ismo *nm* Judaism

e'breo, -a *a* Jewish ● *nm* Jew ● *nf* Jewess

'Ebridi *nfpl* **le ~** the Hebrides

eca'tombe *nf* **fare un'~** wreak havoc

ecc *abbr* (**eccetera**) etc

ecce'dente *a* (*peso, bagaglio*) excess

ecce'denza *nf* excess; (*d'avanzo*) surplus; **avere qcsa in ~** have an excess of sth; **bagagli in ~** excess baggage. **~ di cassa** surplus. **~ di peso** excess weight

ec'cedere *vt* exceed ● *vi* go too far; **~ nel bere** drink to excess; **~ nel mangiare** overeat

eccel'lente *a* excellent

eccel'lenza *nf* excellence; (*titolo*) Excellency; **per ~** par excellence

ec'cellere *vi* excel (**in** at)

eccentricità *nf* eccentricity

ec'centrico, -a *a* & *nmf* eccentric

ecce'pire *vt* object to

eccessiva'mente *adv* excessively

ecces'sivo *a* excessive

ec'cesso *nm* excess; **andare agli eccessi** go to extremes; **dare in eccessi** fly into a temper; **all'~** to excess. **~ di personale** overmanning. **~ di peso** excess weight. **~ di velocità** speeding

ec'cetera *adv* et cetera

ec'cetto *prep* except; **~ che** (*a meno che*) unless

eccettu'are *vt* except

eccezio'nale *a* exceptional; **in via [del tutto] ~** as an exception

eccezional'mente *adv* exceptionally; (*contrariamente alla regola*) as an exception

eccezi'one *nf* exception; *Jur* objection; **a ~ di** with the exception of; **d'~** exceptional

ec'chimosi *nf inv* bruising

eccì *int* atishoo

ec'cidio *nm* massacre

ecci'tabile *a* (*persona, carattere*) excitable

eccita'mento *nm* excitement

ecci'tante *a* exciting; (*sostanza*) stimulant ● *nm* stimulant

ecci'tare *vt* excite; (*sessualmente*) excite, arouse

ecci'tarsi *vr* get excited; (*sessualmente*) become aroused *or* excited

ecci'tato *a* excited; (*sessulamente*) excited, aroused; **~ da** flushed with

eccitazi'one *nf* excitement; (*sessuale*) arousal, excitement

ecclesi'astico *a* ecclesiastical ● *nm* priest

'ecco *adv* (*qui*) here; (*là*) there; **~!** (*con approvazione*) that's right!; **~ qua!** (*dando qcsa*) here you are!; **~ la tua borsa** here is your bag; **~ mio figlio** there is my son; **eccomi** here I am; **~ fatto** there we are; **~ perché** this is why; **~ tutto** that is all

ec'come *adv & int* and how!

ECG *abbr* (**elettrocardiogramma**) ECG

echeggi'are *vi* echo

e'clettico *a* eclectic

eclet'tismo *nm* eclecticism

eclis'sare *vt fig* eclipse

eclis'sarsi *vr* (*sparire*) disappear

e'clissi *nf inv* eclipse

'eco *nmf* (*pl m* **echi**) echo; **ha suscitato una vasta ~** it caused a great stir

eco+ *pref* eco+

ecogra'fia *nf* scan

ecolo'gia *nf* ecology

eco'logico *a* ecological; (*prodotto*) environmentally friendly, eco-friendly

e'cologo, -a *nmf* ecologist

e commerci'ale *nf* ampersand

econo'mia *nf* economy; (*scienza*) economics; **fare ~** economize (**di** on); [*fatto*] **in ~** [done] on the cheap; **senza ~** unstintingly; **fare qcsa senza ~** spare no expense doing sth. **~ aziendale** business administration. **~ domestica** *Sch* home economics. **~ di mercato** market economy. **~ mista** mixed economy. **~ sommersa** black economy

economicità *nf* economy

eco'nomico *a* economic; (*a buon prezzo*) cheap; (*con pochi costi*) economical; **difficoltà economiche** financial difficulties; **classe economica** economy class; **edizione economica** paperback

econo'mie *nfpl* (*risparmi*) savings

econo'mista *nmf* economist

economiz'zare *vt* save (*tempo, denaro*) ● *vi* economize (**su** on)

economizza'tore *nm Auto* fuel economizer

e'conomo, -a *a* thrifty ● *nmf* (*di collegio*) bursar

ecosi'stema *nm* ecosystem

é'cru *a inv* fawn

'Ecu *nm inv* ECU, ecu

Ecua'dor *nm* Ecuador

ecuadori'ano, -a *a & nmf* Ecuadorian

ecu'menico *a* ecumenical

ec'zema *nm* eczema

ed *conj vedi* **e**

e'dema *nm* oedema

'Eden *nm* Eden

'edera *nf* ivy

e'dicola *nf* [newspaper] kiosk

edifi'cabile *a* ⟨*area, terreno*⟩ classified as suitable for development

edifi'cante *a* edifying

edifi'care *vt* build; (*indurre al bene*) edify

edi'ficio *nm* building; *fig* structure

e'dile *a* building *attrib* ● *nm* **edili** *pl* construction workers

edi'lizia *nf* building trade

edi'lizio *a* building *attrib*

Edim'burgo *nf* Edinburgh

E'dipo *nm* Oedipus; **complesso di ~** Oedipus complex

edi'tare *vt* edit

'editing *nm* editing

'edito *a* published

edi'tore, -'trice *a* publishing ● *nmf* publisher; (*curatore*) editor

edito'ria *nf* publishing. **~ elettronica** desktop publishing. **~ telematica** online publishing

editori'ale *a* publishing ● *nm* (*articolo*) editorial, leader

e'ditto *nm* edict

edizi'one *nf* edition; (*di manifestazione*) performance; **in ~ italiana** ⟨*film*⟩ dubbed into Italian. **~ ridotta** abridgement, abridged version. **~ della sera** (*di telegiornale*) evening news

edo'nismo *nm* hedonism

edo'nistico *a* hedonistic

educagi'oco *nm* edutainment

edu'canda *nf* [convent school] boarder; *fig* prim and proper girl

edu'care *vt* educate; (*allevare*) bring up

educa'tivo *a* educational

edu'cato *a* polite

educa'tore, -'trice *nmf* educator

educazi'one *nf* education; (*di bambini*) upbringing; (*buone maniere*) [good] manners *pl*; **bella ~!** what manners!. **~ fisica** physical education

edulco'rare *vt* **~ la pillola** sweeten the pill

e'felide *nf* freckle

effemi'nato *a* effeminate

effe'rato *a* brutal

efferve'scente *a* effervescent; (*frizzante*) fizzy; (*aspirina*) soluble

effettiva'mente *adv* è **troppo tardi – ~** it's too late – so it is

effet'tivo *a* actual; (*efficace*) effective; ⟨*personale*⟩ permanent; *Mil* regular ● *nm* (*somma totale*) sum total

ef'fetto *nm* effect; (*impressione*) impression; (*cambiale*) bill; **fare ~** ⟨*medicina:*⟩ take effect; **fare ~ su** have an effect on, affect; **in effetti** in fact; **a tutti gli effetti** to all intents and purposes; **ad effetto** ⟨*frase*⟩ catchy; **la vista del sangue mi fa ~** I can't stand the sight of blood; **tiro con ~** spin. **~ boomerang** boomerang effect. **~ di luce** trick of the light. **effetti** *pl* **personali** personal belongings, personal effects *fml*. **~ ritardato** delayed effect. **~ serra** greenhouse effect. **~**

sonoro sound effect. **~ speciale** *Cinema, TV* special effect

effettu'are *vt* effect; carry out ⟨*controllo, sondaggio*⟩

effettu'arsi *vr* take place; **'si effettua dal... al...'** 'this service is available from... till...'

effi'cace *a* effective

effi'cacia *nf* effectiveness

effici'ente *a* efficient

effici'enza *nf* efficiency; **in piena ~** in full swing

ef'figie *nf* effigy

ef'fimero *a* ephemeral

ef'flusso *nm* outflow

ef'fluvio *nm* stink

ef'fondersi *vr* **~ in ringraziamenti** be profuse in one's thanks

effrazi'one *nf* **~ con scasso** *Jur* breaking and entering

effusi'one *nf* effusion

'Egadi *nfpl* **le [isole] ~** the Egadi Islands

egemo'nia *nf* hegemony

E'geo *nm* **l'~** the Aegean [Sea]

e'gida *nf* **sotto l'~ di** under the aegis of

E'gitto *nm* Egypt

egizi'ano, -a *a & nmf* Egyptian

e'gizio, -a *a & nmf* Ancient Egyptian

'egli *pers pron* he; **~ stesso** he himself

ego'centrico, -a *a* egocentric ● *nmf* egocentric person

egocen'trismo *nm* egocentricity

ego'ismo *nm* selfishness

ego'ista *a* selfish ● *nmf* selfish person

egoistica'mente *adv* selfishly

ego'istico *a* selfish

Egr. *abbr* **(egregio) ~ Sig.** (*su busta*) Mr.

e'gregio *a* distinguished; **E~ Signore** Dear Sir

eguali'tario *a & nm* egalitarian

eh *int* huh!

'ehi *int* hey!

ehilà *int* hi!

ehm *int* um

eiacu'lare *vi* ejaculate

eiaculazi'one *nf* ejaculation

eiet'tabile *a* ⟨*sedile*⟩ ejector

eiezi'one *nf Aeron* ejection

'Eire *nf* Eire

elabo'rare *vt* elaborate; process ⟨*dati*⟩

elabo'rato *a* elaborate ● *nm* (*tabulato*) pre-printed form

elabora'tore *nm* **~ [di testi]** word processor

elaborazi'one *nf* elaboration; (*di dati*) processing. **~ [dei] dati** data processing. **~ sequenziale** *Comput* batch processing. **~ [di] testi** word processing

elar'gire *vt* lavish

elasticità *nf* elasticity. **~ mentale** mental agility. **~ di movimento** litheness

elasticiz'zato *a* ⟨*stoffa*⟩ elasticated

e'lastico *a* elastic; ⟨*tessuto*⟩ stretch; ⟨*passo*⟩ springy; ⟨*orario, mente*⟩ flexible; ⟨*persona*⟩ easy-going; ⟨*morale*⟩ lax; **collant** *pl* **elastici** support tights ● *nm* elastic; (*fascia*) rubber band

'Elba *nf* Elba

eldo'rado *nm* eldorado

ele'fante *nm* elephant; **avere una memoria da ~** have a memory like an elephant; **fare passi da ~** thump about. **~ marino** sea-elephant

elefan'tesco *a* elephantine

elefan'tessa *nf* cow[-elephant]

elefan'tiaco *a* (*enorme*) elephantine

ele'gante *a* elegant

elegante'mente *adv* elegantly

ele'ganza *nf* elegance

e'leggere *vt* elect

eleg'gibile *a* eligible

ele'gia *nf* elegy

elemen'tare *a* elementary; **scuola ~** primary school

ele'mento *nm* element; (*componente*) part; **trovarsi nel proprio ~** be in one's element; **elementi** *pl* (*fatti*) data; (*rudimenti*) elements

ele'mosina *nf* charity; **chiedere l'~** beg. **vivere d'~** live on charity; **fare l'~** give money to beggars

elemosi'nare *vt/i* beg

elen'care *vt* list

e'lenco *nm* list. **~ [degli] abbonati** *Teleph* telephone directory. **~ telefonico** telephone directory

elet'tivo *a* ⟨*carica*⟩ elective

e'letto, -a *pp di* **eleggere** ● *a* chosen ● *nmf* (*nominato*) elected member; **per pochi eletti** *fig* for the chosen few

eletto'rale *a* electoral

eletto'ralismo *nm* electioneering

eletto'rato *nm* electorate

elet'|tore, -'trice *nmf/v* voter

elet'trauto *nm* electrics garage

elettri'cista *nm* electrician

elettricità *nf* electricity; **togliere l'~** cut the electricity off; **è mancata l'~** there was a power cut

e'lettrico *a* electric

elettriz'zante *a* ⟨*notizia, gara*⟩ electrifying

elettriz'zare *vt fig* electrify

elettriz'zato *a fig* electrified

elettro+ *pref* electro+

elettrocardio'gramma *nm* electrocardiogram, ECG

elettrocuzi'one *nf* electrocution

e'lettrodo *nm* electrode

elettrodo'mestico *nm* [electrical] household appliance

elettroencefalo'gramma *nm* electroencephalogram

elettroesecuzi'one *nf* electrocution

elet'trogeno *a* **gruppo ~** generator

elet'trolisi *nf* electrolysis

elettromo'tore *nm* electric motor

elettromo'trice *nf* electric train

elet'trone *nm* electron

elet'tronico, -a *a* electronic ● *nf* electronics

elettroshocktera'pia *nf* electroshock therapy, electroshock treatment, EST

elettro'tecnica *nf* electrical engineering

elettro'tecnico *nm* electrical engineer

elettro'treno *nm* electric train

ele'vare *vt* raise; (*promuovere*) promote; (*erigere*) erect; (*fig: migliorare*) better; ~ **al quadrato/cubo** square/cube

ele'varsi *vr* rise; (*edificio:*) stand

ele'vato *a* high; (*fig: sentimento*) lofty; ~ **al cubo/al quadrato** cubed/squared; ~ **a dieci** raised to the power of ten

eleva'tore *nm* fork-lift truck

elevazi'one *nf* elevation

elezi'one *nf* election. **elezioni** *pl* **amministrative** local council elections. **elezioni** *pl* **politiche** general election

eliambu'lanza *nf* air ambulance

'elica *nf Naut* screw, propeller; *Aeron* propeller; (*del ventilatore*) blade

eli'cottero *nm* helicopter

elimi'nabile *a* which can be eliminated

elimi'nare *vt* eliminate

elimina'toria *nf Sport* [preliminary] heat

eliminazi'one *nf* elimination

'elio *nm* (*gas*) helium

eli'porto *nm* heliport

elisabetti'ano *a* & *nmf* Elizabethan

é'lite *nf inv* élite

eli'tista *a* élitist

'ella *pers pron liter* she; ~ **stessa** she herself

el'lenico *a* Hellenic

elle'nistico *a* Hellenistic

ellepì *nm inv* LP

+ellino *suff* **campanellino** *nm* [small] bell; **fiorellino** *nm* [little] flower; **gonnellina** *nf* short skirt

el'lisse *nf* ellipse

el'lissi *nf inv* ellipsis

el'littico *a* elliptical

+ello *suff* **finestrella** *nf* little window; **pecorella** *nf* woolly sheep; **saltello** *nm* skip

el'metto *nm* helmet

elogi'are *vt* praise

elogia'tivo *a* laudatory

e'logio *nm* praise; (*discorso, scritto*) eulogy; **degno di** ~ laudable, praiseworthy; **ti faccio i miei elogi per** congratulations on. ~ **funebre** funeral oration

elo'quente *a* eloquent; *fig* tell-tale

elo'quenza *nf* eloquence

El Salva'dor *nm* El Salvador; **nel Salvador** in El Salvador

e'ludere *vt* elude; evade (*sorveglianza, controllo*)

elusi'one *nf* ~ **fiscale** tax avoidance

elu'sivo *a* elusive

el'vetico *a* Swiss; **Confederazione Elvetica** Swiss Confederation

emaci'ato *a* emaciated

'E-mail *nf* e-mail; **mandare per** ~ e-mail, send by e-mail

ema'nare *vt* give off; pass (*legge*) ● *vi* emanate

emanazi'one *nf* giving off; (*di legge*) enactment

emanci'pare *vt* emancipate

emanci'parsi *vr* become emancipated

emanci'pato *a* emancipated

emancipazi'one *nf* emancipation

emargi'nato *nm* marginalized person

emarginazi'one *nf* marginalization

ema'toma *nm* haematoma

em'bargo *nm* embargo

em'blema *nm* emblem

emble'matico *a* emblematic

embo'lia *nf* embolism

'embolo *nm* embolus

embrio'nale *a Biol, fig* embryonic; **allo stato** ~ (*progetto, idea*) embryonic

embri'one *nm* embryo

emenda'mento *nm* amendment

emen'dare *vt* amend

emen'darsi *vr* reform

emer'gente *a* emergent

emer'genza *nf* emergency; **in caso di** ~ in an emergency; **di** ~ (*di riserva*) stand-by; **uscita d'**~ emergency exit. ~ **sanitaria** ambulance

e'mergere *vi* emerge; (*sottomarino:*) surface; (*distinguersi*) stand out

e'merito *a* (*professore*) emeritus; **un** ~ **imbecille** a prize idiot

e'merso *pp di* **emergere**

e'messo *pp di* **emettere**

e'metico *a* emetic

e'mettere *vt* emit; give out (*luce, suono*); let out (*grido*); (*mettere in circolazione*) issue

emi'crania *nf* migraine

emi'grare *vi* emigrate

emi'grato, -a *nmf* immigrant

emigrazi'one *nf* emigration

emi'nente *a* eminent

emi'nenza *nf* eminence; **Sua E**~ His/Your Eminence. ~ **grigia** éminence grise

emi'rato *nm* emirate; **Emirati** *pl* **Arabi Uniti** United Arab Emirates

e'miro *nm* emir

emi'sfero *nm* hemisphere

emis'sario *nm* emissary; (*fiume*) effluent

emissi'one *nf* emission; (*di denaro, francobolli*) issue; (*trasmissione*) broadcast; **'**~ **del biglietto'** 'take your ticket here'

emit'tente *a* issuing; (*trasmittente*) broadcasting ● *nf Radio* transmitter

'emmenthal *nm* Emmenthal

emofi'lia *nf* haemophilia

emofi'liaco, -a *nmf* haemophiliac

emoglo'bina *nf* haemoglobin

emorra'gia *nf* haemorrhage; **avere un'**~ haemorrhage

emor'roidi *nfpl* haemorrhoids, piles

emo'statico *a* haemostatic

emotività *nf* emotional make-up

emo'tivo *a* emotional

emozio'nante *a* exciting; (*commovente*) moving

emozio'nare *vt* excite; (*commuovere*) move

emozio'narsi *vr* become excited; (*commuoversi*) be moved

emozio'nato *a* excited; (*commosso*) moved

emozi'one *nf* emotion; (*agitazione*) excitement

empietà *nf* impiety

'empio *a* impious; (*spietato*) pitiless; (*malvagio*) wicked

em'pirico *a* empirical

empi'rismo *nm* empiricism

empi'rista *nmf* empiricist

em'porio *nm* emporium; (*negozio*) general store

emù *nm inv* emu

emu'lare *vt* emulate

emulazi'one *nf* emulation. **~ di terminale** terminal emulation

emulsio'nare *vt* emulsify

emulsio'narsi *vr* emulsify

emulsi'one *nf* emulsion

ena'lotto *nm weekly lottery*

encefa'lite *nf* **~ bovina spongiforme** Bovine Spongiform Encephalopathy, BSE

encefalo'gramma *nm* encephalogram

en'ciclica *nf* encyclical

enciclope'dia *nf* encyclopaedia

enciclo'pedico *a* ⟨*mente, cultura, dizionario*⟩ encyclopaedic

encomi'are *vt* commend

en'comio *nm* commendation

ende'mia *nf* (*situazione*) endemic

en'demico *a* endemic

en'divia *nf* Belgian endive

endocrinolo'gia *nf* endocrinology

endo'vena *nf* intravenous injection ● *adv* intravenously

endove'noso *a* intravenous; **per via endovenosa** intravenously

ener'getico *a* ⟨*risorse, crisi*⟩ energy *attrib*; ⟨*alimento*⟩ energy-giving

ener'gia *nf* energy; **pieno di ~** full of energy. **~ atomica** atomic energy. **~ elettrica** electricity. **~ eolica** wind power. **~ nucleare** nuclear energy, nuclear power. **~ solare** solar energy, solar power

energica'mente *adv* energetically

e'nergico *a* energetic; (*efficace*) strong

ener'gumeno *nm* Neanderthal

'enfasi *nf* emphasis

en'fatico *a* emphatic

enfatiz'zare *vt* emphasize

enfi'sema *nm* emphysema

e'nigma *nm* enigma

enig'matico *a* enigmatic

enig'mistica *nf* puzzles *pl*

E.N.I.T. *nm abbr* (**Ente Nazionale Italiano per il Turismo**) Italian State Tourist Office

en'nesimo *a* Math nth; *fam* umpteenth; **all'ennesima potenza** Math, *fig* to the nth power/degree

eno'logico *a* wine *attrib*

e'norme *a* enormous; **è un'ingiustizia ~** it's enormously unfair

enorme'mente *adv* massively

enormità *nf inv* enormity; (*assurdità*) absurdity

eno'teca *nf* wine-tasting shop

eno'tera *nf* evening primrose

en pas'sant *adv* in passing

'ente *nm* board; (*società*) company; (*in filosofia*) being

ente'rite *nf* enteritis

entero'clisma *nm Med* enema

entità *nf inv* (*filosofia*) entity; (*gravità*) seriousness; (*dimensione*) extent

entomolo'gia *nf* entomology

entou'rage *nm inv* entourage

en'trambi *a & pron* both

en'trare *vi* go in, enter; **~ in** go into; (*stare in, trovar posto in*) fit into; (*arruolarsi*) join; **entrarci** (*avere a che fare*) have to do with; **tu che c'entri?** what has it got to do with you?; **da che parte si entra?** how do you get in?; **fallo ~** (*in ufficio, dal medico ecc*) show him in; **'vietato ~'** 'no entry'

en'trata *nf* entry, entrance; **~ libera** admission free; **en'trate** *pl Comm* takings; (*reddito*) income *sg*

entre'côte *nf* beef entrecote

'entro *prep* (*tempo*) within; **~ oggi** by the end of today

entro'bordo *nm* (*motore*) inboard motor; (*motoscafo*) speedboat

entro'terra *nm inv* hinterland

entusia'smante *a* fascinating, exciting

entusia'smare *vt* arouse enthusiasm in

entusia'smarsi *vr* be enthusiastic (**per** about)

entusi'asmo *nm* enthusiasm

entusi'asta *a* enthusiastic ● *nmf* enthusiast

entusi'astico *a* enthusiastic

enucle'are *vt* define

enume'rare *vt* enumerate

enumerazi'one *nf* enumeration

enunci'are *vt* enunciate

enunciazi'one *nf* enunciation

E'olie *nfpl* **le ~** the Aeolian Islands

epa'tite *nf* hepatitis

epi'centro *nm* epicentre

'epico *a* epic

epide'mia *nf* epidemic

epi'dermide *nf* epidermis

epidu'rale *a* (*Med: anestesia*) epidural

Epifa'nia *nf* Epiphany

epi'gramma *nm* epigram

epiles'sia *nf* epilepsy

epi'lettico, -a *a & nmf* epileptic

e'pilogo *nm* epilogue

episco'pato *nm* episcopacy

epi'sodico *a* episodic; **caso ~** one-off case

epi'sodio *nm* episode

e'pistola *nf* epistle

episto'lare *a* epistolary

episto'lario *nm* correspondence, letters *pl*

epi'taffio *nm* epitaph

e'piteto *nm* epithet

'epoca *nf* age; (*periodo*) period; **a quell'~** in those days; **un avvenimento che ha fatto**

~ an epoch-making event; **auto d'**~ vintage car; **mobile d'**~ period furniture

e'ponimo *a* eponymous

epo'pea *nf* epic

ep'pure *conj* [and] yet

E.P.T. *abbr* (**Ente Provinciale per il Turismo**) *Italian local tourist board*

epu'rare *vt* purge; purify ⟨*acqua*⟩

epura'tore *nm* water purifier

epurazi'one *nf* purging; (*di acqua*) purification. ~ **etnica** ethnic cleansing

equalizza'tore *nm* equalizer

e'quanime *a* level-headed; (*imparziale*) impartial

equa'tore *nm* equator

equatori'ale *a* equatorial

equazi'one *nf* equation

e'questre *a* equestrian; **circo** ~ circus

equidi'stante *a* equidistant

equi'latero *a* equilateral

equili'brare *vt* balance

equili'brato *a* ⟨*persona*⟩ well-balanced

equi'librio *nm* balance; (*buon senso*) common sense; (*di bilancia*) equilibrium

equili'brismo *nm* **fare** ~ do a balancing act

equili'brista *nmf* tightrope walker

e'quino *a* horse *attrib*

equi'nozio *nm* equinox

equipaggia'mento *nm* equipment

equipaggi'are *vt* equip; (*di persone*) man

equi'paggio *nm* crew; *Aeron* cabin crew. ~ **di volo** aircrew

equipa'rare *vt* make equal

equipa'rato *a* equal

é'quipe *nf inv* team

equità *nf* equity

equitazi'one *nf* riding

equiva'lente *a* & *nm* equivalent

equiva'lenza *nf* equivalence

equiva'lere *vi* ~ **a** be equivalent to

equivo'care *vi* misunderstand

e'quivoco *a* equivocal; (*sospetto*) suspicious; **un tipo** ~ a shady character ● *nm* misunderstanding; **a scanso di equivoci** to avoid any misunderstandings; **giocare sull'**~ equivocate

'equo *a* fair, just

'era *nf* era. ~ **glaciale** Ice Age

'erba *nf* grass; (*aromatica, medicinale*) herb; **in** ~ ⟨*atleta, attore*⟩ budding. ~ **cipollina** chives

er'baccia *nf* weed

er'baceo *a* herbaceous

erbi'cida *nm* weed-killer

erbi'voro *a* herbivorous ● *nm* herbivore

erbo'rista *nmf* herbalist

erboriste'ria *nf* herbalist's shop

er'boso *a* grassy

Erco'lano *nf* Herculaneum

'Ercole *nm* Hercules

er'culeo *a* ⟨*forza*⟩ herculean

e'rede *nm* heir ● *nf* heiress

eredità *nf inv* inheritance; *Biol* heredity

eredi'tare *vt* inherit

ereditarietà *nf* heredity

eredi'tario *a* hereditary

erediti'era *nf* heiress

+erello *suff* **furterello** *nm* petty theft; **pioggerella** *nf* drizzle

ere'mita *nm* hermit

'eremo *nm* isolated place; *fig* retreat

ere'sia *nf* heresy

e'retico, -a *a* heretical ● *nmf* heretic

e'retto *pp di* **erigere** ● *a* erect

erezi'one *nf* erection; (*costruzione*) building

ergasto'lano, -a *nmf* prisoner serving a life sentence, lifer *fam*

er'gastolo *nm* life sentence; (*luogo*) prison

ergono'mia *nf* ergonomics

ergo'nomico *a* ergonomic

ergotera'pia *nf* occupational therapy

ergotera'pista *nmf* occupational therapist

'erica *nf* heather

e'rigere *vt* erect; (*fig: fondare*) found

eri'tema *nm* (*cutaneo*) inflammation; (*solare*) sunburn; ~ **da pannolini** nappy rash

Eri'trea *nf* Eritrea

eri'treo, -a *a* & *nmf* Eritrean

ermafro'dito *a* & *nm* hermaphrodite

ermel'lino *nm* ermine

ermetica'mente *adv* hermetically

er'metico *a* hermetic; (*a tenuta d'aria*) airtight

'ernia *nf* hernia

e'rodere *vi* erode

e'roe *nm* hero

ero'gare *vt* distribute; (*fornire*) supply

erogazi'one *nf* supply

e'rogeno *a* erogenous

eroica'mente *adv* heroically

e'roico *a* heroic

ero'ina *nf* heroine; (*droga*) heroin

ero'ismo *nm* heroism

'eros *nm* Eros

erosi'one *nf* erosion

e'rotico *a* erotic

ero'tismo *nm* eroticism

'erpice *nm* harrow

er'rante *a* wandering

er'rare *vi* (*vagare*) wander; (*sbagliare*) be mistaken

er'rato *a* (*sbagliato*) mistaken; **se non vado** ~ if I'm not mistaken

'erre *nf* ~ **moscia** burr

erronea'mente *adv* mistakenly

er'rore *nm* error, mistake; (*di stampa*) misprint; **essere in** ~ be wrong. ~ **giudiziario** miscarriage of justice. ~ **di stampa** printing error, typo

'erta *nf* **stare all'**~ be on the alert

eru'dirsi *vr* get educated

eru'dito *a* learned

erut'tare *vt* ⟨*vulcano:*⟩ erupt ● *vi* (*ruttare*) belch

eruzi'one *nf* eruption; *Med* rash

Es *nm Psych* **l'**~ the id

es. *abbr* (**esempio**) eg.

esacer'bare *vt* exacerbate

esage'rare *vt* exaggerate; ~ **le cose** exaggerate things, go over the top ● *vi* exaggerate; (*nel comportamento*) go over the top; **~ nel mangiare** eat too much

esagerata'mente *adv* excessively

esage'rato *a* exaggerated; ⟨*prezzo*⟩ exorbitant ● *nm* **è un ~** he exaggerates

esagerazi'one *nf* exaggeration; **è costato un'~** it cost the earth; **senza ~** with no exaggeration

esago'nale *a* hexagonal

e'sagono *nm* hexagon

esa'lare *vt* give off; **~ l'ultimo respiro** breathe one's last ● *vi* emanate

esalazi'one *nf* emission; **esalazioni** *pl* fumes

esal'tare *vt* exalt; (*entusiasmare*) elate

esal'tarsi *vr* (*entusiasmarsi*) get excited (**per** about)

esal'tato *a* (*fanatico*) fanatical ● *nm* fanatic

esaltazi'one *nf* exaltation; (*in discorso*) fervour

e'same *nm* examination, exam; **dare un ~** take *or* sit an exam; **prendere in ~** examine. **~ di ammissione** *Sch* entrance examination. **~ di coscienza** soul-searching. **~ di guida** driving test. **esami** *pl* **di maturità** ≈ A-levels. **~ orale** *Sch, Univ* viva. **~ del sangue** blood test. **~ della vista** eye test

esami'nando, -a *nmf* examinee

esami'nare *vt* examine

esamina'tore, -'trice *nmf* examiner

e'sangue *a* bloodless

e'sanime *a* lifeless

esaspe'rante *a* exasperating

esaspe'rare *vt* exasperate

esaspe'rarsi *vr* get exasperated

esasperazi'one *nf* exasperation

esatta'mente *adv* exactly

esat'tezza *nf* exactness; (*precisione*) precision; (*di risposta, risultato*) accuracy

e'satto *pp di* **esigere** ● *a* exact; ⟨*risposta, risultato*⟩ correct; ⟨*orologio*⟩ right; **hai l'ora ~?** do you have the right time?; **sono le due esatte** it's two o'clock exactly

esat'tore *nm* collector. **~ dei crediti** *Fin* debt collector. **~ delle imposte** tax collector, tax man

esau'dire *vt* grant; fulfil ⟨*speranze*⟩

esauri'ente *a* exhaustive

esauri'mento *nm* exhaustion; **'fino ad ~ delle scorte'** 'subject to availability'. **~ nervoso** nervous breakdown

esau'rire *vt* exhaust

esau'rirsi *vr* exhaust oneself; ⟨*merci ecc:*⟩ run out

esau'rito *a* exhausted; ⟨*merci*⟩ sold out; ⟨*libro*⟩ out of print; **fare il tutto ~** ⟨*spettacolo:*⟩ play to a full house

esazi'one *nf* collection. **~ crediti** debt collection

'esca *nf* bait

escande'scenza *nf* outburst; **dare in escandescenze** lose one's temper

escava'tore *nm* excavator

escava'trice *nf* excavator

escla'mare *vi* exclaim

esclama'tivo *a* exclamatory

esclamazi'one *nf* exclamation

e'scludere *vt* exclude; rule out ⟨*possibilità, ipotesi*⟩

esclusi'one *nf* exclusion; **senza ~ di colpi** ⟨*attacco*⟩ all-out

esclu'siva *nf* exclusive right, sole right; **in ~** exclusive

esclusiva'mente *adv* exclusively

esclusi'vista *nmf* exclusive agent

esclu'sivo *a* exclusive

e'scluso *pp di* **escludere** ● *a* **non è ~ che ci sia** it's not out of the question that he'll be there; **esclusi i presenti** with the exception of those present; **esclusi sabati e festivi** except Saturdays and Sundays/holidays ● *nm* outcast

escogi'tare *vt* contrive

escoriazi'one *nf* graze

escre'mento *nm* excrement; **escrementi** *pl* excrement

escursi'one *nf* excursion; (*scorreria*) raid; **~ termica** difference between the lowest and the highest temperature in a 24 hours period

ese'crabile *a* abominable

ese'crare *vt* abhor

esecu'tivo *a & nm* executive

esecu'tore, -'trice *nmf* executor; *Mus* performer

esecuzi'one *nf* execution; *Mus* performance. **~ capitale** capital punishment

esegu'ibile *nm* *Comput* executable file

esegu'ire *vt* carry out; *Jur* execute; *Mus* perform

e'sempio *nm* example; **ad** *o* **per ~** for example; **dare l'~ a qcno** set sb an example; **fare un ~** give an example

esem'plare *a* examplary ● *nm* specimen; (*di libro*) copy

esemplifi'care *vt* exemplify

esen'tare *vt* exempt

esen'tarsi *vr* free oneself

esen'tasse *a* tax-free

e'sente *a* exempt. **~ da imposta** duty-free. **~ da IVA** VAT exempt

e'sequie *nfpl* funeral rites

eser'cente *nmf* shopkeeper

eserci'tare *vt* exercise; (*addestrare*) train; (*fare uso di*) exert; (*professione*) practise

eserci'tarsi *vr* practise; **~ nella danza** practise dancing

eserci'tato *a* ⟨*occhio*⟩ practised; **tenere la memoria esercitata** give one's memory some exercise

esercitazi'one *nf* exercise; *Mil* drill; (*di musica, chimica*) practical class

e'sercito *nm* army. **E~ della Salvezza** Salvation Army

eser'cizio *nm* exercise; (*pratica*) practice; *Comm* financial year; (*azienda*) business; **essere fuori ~** be out of practice; **nell'~ delle proprie funzioni** in the line of duty. **~**

finanziario financial year. ~ **fiscale** fiscal year, tax year. **esercizi** *pl* **a terra** floor exercises. ~ **tributario** fiscal year, tax year

esi'bire *vt* show off; produce ‹*documenti*›

esi'birsi *vr Theat* perform; *fig* show off

esibizi'one *nf Theat* performance; *(di documenti)* production

esibizio'nismo *nm* showing off

esibizio'nista *nmf* exhibitionist

esi'gente *a* exacting; *(pignolo)* fastidious

esi'genza *nf* demand; *(bisogno)* need

e'sigere *vt* demand; *(riscuotere)* collect

e'siguo *a* meagre

esila'rante *a* exhilarating

esila'rare *vt* exhilarate

'esile *a* slender; ‹*voce*› thin

esili'are *vt* exile

esili'arsi *vr* go into exile

esili'ato, -a *a* exiled ● *nmf* exile

e'silio *nm* exile

e'simere *vt* release

e'simersi *vr* ~ **da** get out of

e'simio *a* distinguished

esi'stente *a* existing

esi'stenza *nf* existence

esistenzi'ale *a* existential

esistenzia'lismo *nm* existentialism

e'sistere *vi* exist

esi'tante *a* hesitating; ‹*voce*› faltering

esi'tare *vi* hesitate

esitazi'one *nf* hesitation

'esito *nm* result; **avere buon** ~ be a success

'esodo *nm* exodus

e'sofago *nm* oesophagus

esone'rare *vt* exempt

e'sonero *nm* exemption

esorbi'tante *a* exorbitant

esorbi'tare *vi* ~ **da** exceed

esor'cismo *nm* exorcism

esor'cista *nmf* exorcist

esorciz'zare *vt* exorcize

esordi'ente *nmf* person making his/her début

e'sordio *nm* opening; *(di attore)* début

esor'dire *vi* début

esor'tare *vt (pregare)* beg; *(incitare)* urge

eso'terico *a* esoteric

e'sotico *a* exotic

espa'drillas *nfpl* espadrilles

e'spandere *vt* expand

e'spandersi *vr* expand; *(diffondersi)* extend

espan'dibile *a Comput* upgradeable

espandibilità *nf inv Comput* upgradeability

espansi'one *nf* expansion; **in** ~ expanding

espansio'nista *nmf* expansionist

espansio'nistico *a* expansionist

espan'sivo *a* expansive; ‹*persona*› friendly

espatri'are *vi* leave one's country

espatri'ato, -a *nmf* expatriate, expat *fam*

e'spatrio *nm* expatriation

espedi'ente *nm* expedient; **vivere di espedienti** live by one's wits

e'spellere *vt* expel; send off ‹*calciatore*›

esperi'enza *nf* experience; **per** ~ ‹*sapere,*

parlare› from experience; **non ha** ~ he doesn't have any experience

esperi'mento *nm* experiment

e'sperto, -a *a* & *nmf* expert. ~ **di computer** computer expert

espi'are *vt* atone for

espia'torio *a* expiatory

espi'rare *vt/i* breathe out

espirazi'one *nf* exhalation; *(scadenza)* expiry

espli'care *vt* carry on

esplicita'mente *adv* explicitly

e'splicito *a* explicit

e'splodere *vi* explode ● *vt* ‹*arma:*› fire

esplo'rare *vt* explore

esplora|'tore, -'trice *nmf* explorer; **giovane** ~ boy scout; **giovane esploratrice** girl guide

esplorazi'one *nf* exploration

esplosi'one *nf* explosion

esplo'sivo *a* & *nm* explosive

espo'nente *nm* exponent; **2 all'**~ superscript 2

esponenzi'ale *a* exponential

e'sporre *vt* expose; display ‹*merci*›; *(spiegare)* expound; exhibit ‹*quadri ecc*›

e'sporsi *vr (compromettersi)* compromise oneself; *(al sole)* expose oneself; *(alle critiche)* lay oneself open

espor'tare *vt Comm, Comput* export

esporta|'tore, -'trice *nmf* exporter

esportazi'one *nf* export

espo'simetro *nm* light meter

esposi|'tore, -'trice *nmf* exhibitor ● *nm* display rack

esposizi'one *nf (mostra)* exhibition; *(in vetrina)* display; *(spiegazione ecc)* exposition; *(posizione, fotografia)* exposure; **con** ~ **a nord/sud** north-/south-facing

e'sposto *pp di* **esporre** ● *a* exposed; ‹*merce*› on show; ‹*spiegato*› set out; ~ **a nord/sud** north-/south-facing ● *nm* submission

espressa'mente *adv* expressly; **non l'ha detto** ~ he didn't put it in so many words

espressi'one *nf* expression

espressio'nismo *nm* expressionism

espressio'nista *a* & *nmf* expressionist

espressio'nistico *a* expressionistic

espres'sivo *a* expressive

e'spresso *pp di* **esprimere** ● *a* express ● *nm (lettera)* special delivery; *(treno)* express train; *(caffè)* espresso; **per** ~ ‹*spedire*› [by] express [post]; **piatto** ~ meal made to order

e'sprimere *vt* express

e'sprimersi *vr* express oneself

espropri'are *vt* dispossess

espropriazi'one *nf Jur* expropriation

e'sproprio *nm* expropriation

espulsi'one *nf* expulsion

e'spulso *pp di* **espellere**

esqui'mese *a* & *nmf* Eskimo

es'senza *nf* essence

essenzi'ale *a* essential ● *nm* important thing; **l'~** (*di teoria ecc*) the bare bones; **l'~ è...** (*la cosa più importante*) the main thing is...
essenzial'mente *a* essentially
'essere *vi* be; **c'è** there is; **ci sono** there are; **ci sono!** (*ho capito*) I've got it!; **ci siamo!** (*siamo arrivati*) here we are at last!; **non ce n'è più** there's none left; **c'è di che essere contenti** there's a lot to be happy about; **che ora è? – sono le dieci** what time is it? – it's ten o'clock; **chi è? – sono io** who is it? – it's me; **è stato detto che** it has been said that; **siamo in due** there are two of us; **questa camicia è da lavare** this shirt is to be washed; **non è da te** it's not like you; **~ di** belong to; (*provenire da*) be from; **~ per** (*favorevole*) be in favour of; **se fossi in te,...** if I were you,...; **sarà!** if you say so!; **come sarebbe a dire?** what are you getting at? ● *v aux* have; (*in passivi*) be; **siamo arrivati** we have arrived; **ci sono stato ieri** I was there yesterday; **sono nato a Torino** I was born in Turin; **è riconosciuto come...** he is recognized as... ● *nm* being. **~ umano** human being; **~ vivente** living creature
essic'care *vt* dry
essic'cato *a* dried; (*noce di cocco*) desiccated
'esso, -a *pers pron* he, she; (*cosa, animale*) it
est *nm* east; **l'E~ europeo** Eastern Europe
'estasi *nf* ecstasy; **andare in ~ per** go into raptures over
estasi'are *vt* enrapture
estasi'arsi *vr* go into raptures
e'state *nf* summer
e'statico *a* ecstatic
estempo'raneo *a* impromptu
e'stendere *vt* extend
e'stendersi *vr* spread; (*allungarsi*) stretch
estensi'one *nf* extension; (*ampiezza*) expanse; *Mus* range
esten'sivo *a* extensive
estenu'ante *a* exhausting
estenu'are *vt* exhaust
estenu'arsi *vr* exhaust oneself
'estere *nm* ester
esteri'ore *a* & *nm* exterior
esteriorità *nf inv* outward appearance; **badare all'~** judge by appearances
esterioriz'zare *vt* externalize
esterior'mente *adv* externally; (*di persone*) outwardly
esterna'mente *adv* on the outside
ester'nare *vt* express, show
e'sterno, -a *a* external; (*scala*) outside; **per uso ~** for external use only ● *nm Archit* exterior; (*in film*) location shot ● *nmf* day-pupil
'estero *a* foreign ● *nm* foreign countries *pl*; **all'~** abroad; **ministero degli esteri** ≈ Foreign Office *Br*, State Department *Am*
esterofi'lia *nf* xenophilia
este'rofilo *a* xenophile
esterre'fatto *a* horrified
e'steso *pp di* **estendere** ● *a* extensive; (*diffuso*) widespread; **per ~** (*scrivere*) in full
e'steta *nmf* aesthete

e'stetica *nf* aesthetics
estetica'mente *adv* aesthetically
esteticità *nf* aestheticism
e'stetico *a* aesthetic; (*chirurgia, chirurgo*) plastic
este'tismo *nm* (*dottrina, carattere*) aestheticism
este'tista *nmf* beautician
estima'tore, -'trice *nmf* fan
'estimo *nm* estimate
e'stinguere *vt* extinguish; close (*conto*)
e'stinguersi *vr* die out
e'stinto, -a *pp di* **estinguere** ● *nmf* deceased
estin'tore *nm* [fire] extinguisher
estinzi'one *nf* extinction; (*di incendio*) putting out
estir'pare *vt* uproot; extract (*dente*); *fig* eradicate (*crimine, malattia*)
estirpazi'one *nf* eradication; (*di dente*) extraction
e'stivo *a* summer *attrib*
'estone *a* & *nm* Estonian
E'stonia *nf* Estonia
e'storcere *vt* extort
estorsi'one *nf* extortion
e'storto *pp di* **estorcere**
estradizi'one *nf* extradition
estra'gone *nm* tarragon
estra'ibile *a* removable
e'straneo, -a *a* extraneous; (*straniero*) foreign ● *nmf* stranger
estrani'are *vt* estrange
estrani'arsi *vr* become estranged
estrapo'lare *vt* extrapolate
e'strarre *vt* extract; (*sorteggiare*) draw
e'stratto *pp di* **estrarre** ● *nm* extract; (*brano*) excerpt; (*documento*) abstract. **~ conto** statement [of account], bank statement
estrazi'one *nf* extraction; (*a sorte*) draw
estrema'mente *adv* extremely
estre'mismo *nm* extremism
estre'mista *nmf* extremist
estremità *nf inv* extremity; (*di una corda*) end; ● *pl Anat* extremities
e'stremo *a* extreme; (*ultimo*) last; **misure estreme** drastic measures; **fare un ~ tentativo** make one last try; **l'E~ Oriente** the Far East; **~ saluto** *Mil* military funeral; **l'estrema unzione** last rites ● *nm* (*limite*) extreme; **all'~** in the extreme; **passare da un ~ all'altro** go from one extreme to the other; **estremi** *pl* (*di documento*) main points; (*di reato*) essential elements; **essere agli estremi** be at the end of one's tether; **andare agli estremi** go to extremes; **essere all'~ delle forze** have no strength left
'estro *nm* (*disposizione artistica*) talent; (*ispirazione*) inspiration; (*capriccio*) whim
e'strogeno *nm* oestrogen
estro'mettere *vt* expel
estromissi'one *nf* ejection
e'stroso *a* talented; (*capriccioso*) unpredictable

estro'verso *a* extroverted ● *nm* extrovert

estu'ario *nm* estuary

esube'rante *a* exuberant

esube'ranza *nf* exuberance

e'subero *nm* ~ **cassa integrazione** voluntary redundancy

esu'lare *vt* ~ **da** be beyond the scope of

'esule *nmf* exile

esul'tante *a* exultant

esul'tanza *nf* exultation

esul'tare *vi* rejoice

esu'mare *vt* exhume

età *nf* age; **raggiungere la maggiore ~** come of age; **un uomo di mezz'~** a middle-aged man; **avere la stessa ~** be the same age; **che ~ gli daresti?** how old would you say he was?; **fin dalla più tenera ~** from his/her etc earliest years; **in ~ avanzata** of advanced years; **è senza ~** it's hard to tell his age. **~ del Bronzo** Bronze Age. **~ della pensione** retirement age

e'tano *nm* ethane

eta'nolo *nm* ethanol

'etere *nm* ether. **~ etilico** ether

e'tereo *a* ethereal

eterna'mente *adv* eternally

eternità *nf* eternity; **è un'~ che non la vedo** I haven't seen her for ages

e'terno *a* eternal; ⟨*questione, problema*⟩ age-old; ⟨*fig: dicorso, conferenza*⟩ never-ending; **in ~** *fam* for ever; **giurare ~ amore** swear undying love; **un ~ bambino** a child

etero'geneo *a* diverse, heterogeneous

eterosessu'ale *a & nmf* heterosexual

eterosessualità *nf* heterosexuality

'etica *nf* ethics

eti'chetta¹ *nf* label; (*con il prezzo*) price-tag

eti'chetta² *nf* (*cerimoniale*) etiquette

etichet'tare *vt* label

etichetta'trice *nf* labelling machine

etichetta'tura *nf* (*operazione*) labelling

'etico *a* ethical

eti'lometro *nm* Breathalyzer®

etimolo'gia *nf* etymology

e'tiope *a & nmf* Ethiopian

Eti'opia *nf* Ethiopia

eti'opico *a* Ethiopian

'Etna *nm* Etna

et'nia *nf* ethnic group

'etnico *a* ethnic

etnolo'gia *nf* ethnology

e'trusco *a & nmf* Etruscan

'ettaro *nm* hectare

+ettino *suff* **cosettina** *nf* small thing; **è una cosettina da niente** it's nothing

'etto, etto'grammo *nm* hundred grams, quarter pound

+etto *suff* **cameretta** *nf* little bedroom; **scherzetto** *nf* prank; **piccoletto** *nm pej* shorty

et'tolitro *nm* hectolitre

euca'lipto *nm* eucalyptus

eucari'stia *nf* Eucharist

eufe'mismo *nm* euphemism

eufe'mistico *a* euphemistic

eufo'ria *nf* elation; *Med* euphoria

eu'forico *a* elated; *Med* euphoric

euge'netica *nf* eugenics

eu'nuco *nm* eunuch

Eur'asia *nf* Eurasia

eurasi'atico *a* Eurasian

'EURATOM *nf abbr* (**Comunità Europea dell'Energia Atomica**) EURATOM

euro+ *pref* Euro+

eurobbligazi'one *nf* Eurobond

euro'cheque *nm inv* Eurocheque

Euro'city *nm inv Rail* international Intercity

eurodepu'tato *nm* Euro MP, MEP

eurodi'visa *nf* Eurocurrency

euro'dollaro *nm* Eurodollar

Eu'ropa *nf* Europe

europe'ismo *nm* Europeanism

euro'peo, -a *a & nmf* European

euro'scettico *nm* eurosceptic

eutana'sia *nf* euthanasia

evacu'are *vt* evacuate

evacuazi'one *nf* evacuation

e'vadere *vt* evade; (*sbrigare*) deal with ● *vi* **~ da** escape from

evane'scente *a* vanishing

evan'gelico *a* evangelical

evange'lista *nm* evangelist

evan'gelo *nm* = **vangelo**

evapo'rare *vi* evaporate

evaporazi'one *nf* evaporation

evasi'one *nf* escape; (*fiscale*) evasion; *fig* escapism

evasiva'mente *adv* evasively

eva'sivo *a* evasive

e'vaso, -a *pp di* **evadere** ● *nmf* fugitive

eva'sore *nm* ~ **fiscale** tax evader

eveni'enza *nf* eventuality; **in ogni ~** if need be

e'vento *nm* event

eventu'ale *a* possible

eventualità *nf inv* eventuality; **in ogni ~** at all events; **nell'~ che** in the event that

eventual'mente *adv* if necessary

ever'sivo *a* subversive

evi'dente *a* evident

evidente'mente *adv* evidently

evi'denza *nf* evidence; **mettere in ~** emphasize; **mettersi in ~** make oneself conspicuous; **arrendersi all'~** face the facts

evidenzi'are *vt* highlight

evidenzia'tore *nm* (*penna*) highlighter

evi'rare *vt* emasculate

evi'tare *vt* avoid; (*risparmiare*) spare

'evo *nm* age

evo'care *vt* evoke

evolu'tivo *a* evolutionary

evo'luto *pp di* **evolvere** ● *a* evolved; (*progredito*) progressive; ⟨*civiltà, nazione*⟩ advanced; **una donna evoluta** a modern woman

evoluzi'one *nf* evolution; (*di ginnasta, aereo*) circle

e'volvere *vt* develop

e'volversi *vr* evolve

ev'viva *int* hurray; **~ il Papa!** long live the

Pope!; **gridare ~ cheer; ~ la modestia!** what modesty!

ex *prep* ex, former; **ex moglie** ex-wife

ex 'aequo *adv* **arrivare ~ ~** come in joint first

ex-Jugo'slavia *nf* ex-Yugoslavia

ex-jugo'slavo *a & nmf* ex-Yugoslav

ex 'libris *nm inv* bookplate

ex'ploit *nm inv* feat, exploit

'extra *a inv* extra; ⟨*qualità*⟩ first-class ● *nm*
inv extra

extracomuni'tario *a* non-EC, non-EU

extraconiu'gale *a* extramarital

extraeuro'peo *a* non-European

extraparlamen'tare *a* extraparliamentary

extrasco'lastico *a* extra-curricular

extrasensori'ale *a* extrasensory

extrater'restre *nmf* extra-terrestrial

extrauniversi'tario *a* extramural

ex 'voto *nm inv* ex voto

fa¹ *nm inv* Mus ⟨*chiave, nota*⟩ F

fa² *adv* ago; **due mesi ~** two months ago

fabbi'sogno *nm* requirements *pl*, needs *pl*. **~ dello Stato** government spending estimates

'fabbrica *nf* factory

fabbri'cabile *a* ⟨*area, terreno*⟩ that can be built on

fabbri'cante *nm* manufacturer. **~ d'armi** arms manufacturer

fabbri'care *vt* build; ⟨*produrre*⟩ manufacture; ⟨*fig: inventare*⟩ fabricate

fabbri'cato *nm* building

fabbricazi'one *nf* manufacturing; ⟨*costruzione*⟩ building

'fabbro *nm* blacksmith

fac'cenda *nf* matter; **faccende** *pl* **domestiche** housework *sg*

faccendi'ere *nm* wheeler-dealer

fac'chino *nm* porter

'faccia *nf* face; ⟨*di foglio*⟩ side; **~ a ~** face to face; **~ tosta** cheek; **voltar ~** change sides; **di ~** ⟨*palazzo*⟩ opposite; **alla ~ di** ⟨*fam: a dispetto di*⟩ in spite of; **alla ~!** ⟨*stupore*⟩ bloody hell!

facci'ata *nf* façade; ⟨*di foglio*⟩ side; ⟨*fig: esteriorità*⟩ outward appearance

fa'cente *nmf* **~ funzioni** deputy

fa'ceto *a* facetious; **tra il serio e il ~** half joking

fa'cezia *nf* ⟨*battuta*⟩ witticism

fa'chiro *nm* fakir

'facile *a* easy; ⟨*affabile*⟩ easy-going; **essere ~ alle critiche** be quick to criticize; **essere ~ al riso** laugh a lot; **~ a farsi** easy to do; **è ~ che piova** it's likely to rain

facilità *nf inv* ease; ⟨*disposizione*⟩ aptitude; **avere ~ di parola** express oneself well. **~ d'uso** ease of use, user-friendliness

facili'tare *vt* facilitate

facilitazi'one *nf* facility; **facilitazioni** *pl* *Fin* special terms; **facilitazioni** *pl* **di pagamento** *Fin* easy terms

facil'mente *adv* ⟨*con facilità*⟩ easily; ⟨*probabilmente*⟩ probably

faci'lone *a* slapdash

facilone'ria *nf* slapdash attitude

facino'roso *a* violent

facoltà *nf inv* faculty; ⟨*potere*⟩ power; **essere nel pieno possesso delle proprie ~** be compos mentis

facolta'tivo *a* optional; **fermata facoltativa** request stop

facol'toso *a* wealthy

fac'simile *nm* facsimile

fac'totum *nm inv* man Friday ● *nf inv* girl Friday

'faggio *nm* beech

fagi'ano *nm* pheasant

fagio'lino *nm* French bean

fagi'olo *nm* bean; **a ~** ⟨*arrivare, capitare*⟩ at the right time. **~ borlotto** borlotti bean. **~ di Spagna** runner bean, string bean

fagoci'tare *vt* gobble up ⟨*società*⟩

fa'gotto *nm* bundle; *Mus* bassoon

Fahren'heit *a* Fahrenheit

'faida *nf* feud

fai da te *nm* do-it-yourself, DIY

fa'ina *nf* weasel

fa'lange *nf* ⟨*dito, Mil*⟩ phalanx

fal'cata *nf* stride

'falce *nf* scythe; **~ e martello** ⟨*simbolo*⟩ the hammer and sickle

fal'cetto *nm* sickle

falci'are *vt* cut; *fig* mow down

falci'ata *nf* ⟨*quantità d'erba*⟩ swathe

falcia'trice *nf* [lawn-]mower

'falco *nm* hawk

fal'cone *nm* falcon

'falda *nf* stratum; ⟨*di neve*⟩ flake; ⟨*di cappello*⟩ brim; ⟨*di cappotto, frac*⟩ coat-tails; ⟨*pendio*⟩ slope. **~ freatica** water table

fale'gname *nm* carpenter

falegname'ria *nf* carpentry

fa'lena *nf* moth

'Falkland *nfpl* **le [isole] ~** the Falklands

'falla *nf* leak

fal'lace *a* deceptive

'fallico *a* phallic

fallimen'tare *a* disastrous; *Jur* bankruptcy
falli'mento *nm Comm* bankruptcy; *fig* failure
fal'lire *vi Comm* go bankrupt; *fig* fail ● *vt* miss ‹*colpo*›
fal'lito *a* unsuccessful ● *a & nm* bankrupt
'**fallo** *nm* fault; (*errore*) mistake; *Sport* foul; (*imperfezione*) flaw; **senza ~** without fail; **cogliere in ~** catch red-handed; **mettere un piede in ~** slip. **~ di mano** (*in calcio*) handball
falò *nm inv* bonfire
fal'sare *vt* alter; (*falsificare*) falsify
falsa'riga *nf* **sulla ~ di** along the same lines as
fal'sario, -a *nmf* forger; (*di documenti*) counterfeiter
fal'setto *nm* falsetto
falsifi'care *vt* fake; (*contraffare*) forge
falsificazi'one *nf* (*di documento*) falsification
falsità *nf* falseness
'**falso** *a* false; (*sbagliato*) wrong; ‹*opera d'arte ecc*› fake; ‹*gioielli, oro*› imitation; **essere un ~ magro** be fatter than one looks ● *nm* forgery; **giurare il ~** commit perjury. **~ in atto pubblico** forgery of a legal document
'**fama** *nf* fame; (*reputazione*) reputation
'**fame** *nf* hunger; **aver ~** be hungry; **fare la ~** barely scrape a living; **da ~** ‹*stipendio*› miserly; **avere una ~ da lupo** be ravenous
fa'melico *a* ravenous
famige'rato *a* infamous
fa'miglia *nf* family
famili'are *a* family *attrib*; (*ben noto*) familiar; (*senza cerimonie*) informal ● *nm* relative, relation
familiarità *nf* familiarity; (*informalità*) informality
familiariz'zarsi *vr* familiarize oneself
fa'moso *a* famous
fa'nale *nm* lamp; *Auto ecc* light. **fanali** *pl* **posteriori** *Auto* rear lights
fana'lino *nm* **~ di coda** *Auto* tail light; **essere il ~ di coda** *fig* bring up the rear, be the back marker
fa'natico, -a *a* fanatical; **essere ~ di calcio/cinema** be a football/cinema fanatic ● *nmf* fanatic
fana'tismo *nm* fanaticism
fanciul'lezza *nf* childhood
fanci'ullo, -a *nmf* young boy; young girl
fan'donia *nf* lie; **fandonie!** nonsense!
fan'fara *nf* fanfare; (*complesso*) brass band
fanfaro'nata *nf* brag; **fanfaronate** *pl* bragging
fanfa'rone, -a *nmf* braggart
fan'ghiglia *nf* mud
'**fango** *nm* mud
fan'goso *a* muddy
fannul'lone, -a *nmf* idler
fantasci'enza *nf* science fiction
fanta'sia *nf* fantasy; (*immaginazione*) imagination; (*capriccio*) fancy; (*di tessuto*) pattern; **fantasie** *pl* (*sciocchezze*) moonshine

fantasi'oso *a* ‹*stilista, ragazzo*› imaginative; ‹*resoconto*› improbable, fanciful
fan'tasma *nm* ghost; **essere il ~ di se stesso** be a shadow of one's former self; **città ~** ghost town; **governo ~** shadow cabinet
fantasti'care *vi* day-dream, fantasize
fantasti'cheria *nf* day-dream, fantasy
fan'tastico *a* fantastic; ‹*racconto*› fantasy *attrib*
'**fante** *nm* infantryman; (*nelle carte*) jack
fante'ria *nf* infantry
fan'tino *nm* jockey
fan'toccio *nm* puppet
fanto'matico *a* (*inafferrabile*) phantom *attrib*; (*immaginario*) mythical
fara'butto *nm* trickster
fara'ona *nf* (*uccello*) guinea-fowl
'**farcia** *nf* stuffing; ‹*di torta*› filling
far'cire *vt* stuff; fill ‹*torta*›
far'cito *a* stuffed; ‹*dolce*› filled
fard *nm inv* blusher
far'dello *nm* bundle; *fig* burden
'**fare** *vt* do; make ‹*dolce, letto, ecc*›; (*recitare la parte di*) play; (*trascorrere*) spend; **~ una pausa/un sogno** have a break/a dream; **~ colpo su** impress; **~ paura a** frighten; **~ piacere a** please; **farla finita** put an end to it; **~ l'insegnante** be a teacher; **~ lo scemo** play the idiot; **~ una settimana al mare** spend a week at the seaside; **3 più 3 fa 6** 3 and 3 makes 6; **quanto fa?** – **fanno 10 000 lire** how much is it? – it's 10,000 lire; **far ~ qcsa a qcno** get sb to do sth; (*costringere*) make sb do sth; **~ vedere** show; **fammi parlare** let me speak; **niente a che ~ con** nothing to do with; **non c'è niente da ~** (*per problema*) there is nothing we/you etc can do; **fa caldo/buio** it's warm/dark; **non fa niente** it doesn't matter; **strada facendo** on the way. **farcela** (*riuscire*) manage ● *vi* **fai in modo di venire** try and come; **~ da** act as; **~ per** make as if to; **~ presto** be quick; **non fa per me** it's not for me ● *nm* (*comportamento*) manner; **sul far del giorno** at daybreak
fa'retto *nm* spot[light]
far'falla *nf* butterfly
farfal'lino *nm* (*cravatta*) bow tie
farfugli'are *vt* mutter
fa'rina *nf* flour. **~ di ceci** chickpea flour, gram flour. **~ gialla** maize flour. **~ integrale** wholemeal flour. **~ lattea** powdered milk for babies. **~ d'ossa** bonemeal
fari'nacei *nmpl* starchy food *sg*
fa'ringe *nf* pharynx
farin'gite *nf* pharyngitis
fari'noso *a* ‹*neve*› powdery; ‹*mela*› soft; ‹*patata*› floury
farma'ceutico *a* pharmaceutical; **industria farmaceutica** pharmaceuticals industry
farma'cia *nf* pharmacy; (*negozio*) chemist's [shop]. **~ di turno** duty pharmacy
farma'cista *nmf* chemist, pharmacist

'farmaco *nm* drug; **essere sotto farmaci** be on medication

'faro *nm Auto* headlight; *Aeron* beacon; *(costruzione)* lighthouse; **abbassare i fari** dip one's headlights; **accendere i fari** switch on one's lights. **fari** *pl* **antinebbia** fog lamps. **fari** *pl* **posteriori** rear lights

farragi'noso *a* confused

'farsa *nf* farce

far'sesco *a* farcical

'farsi *vr (diventare)* get; *(sl: drogarsi)* shoot up; **~ avanti** come forward; **~ i fatti propri** mind one's own business; **~ la barba** shave; **~ la villa** *fam* buy a villa; **~ il ragazzo** *fam* find a boyfriend; **~ due risate** have a laugh; **~ male** hurt oneself; **~ un nome** make a name for oneself; **farsela sotto** *fam* wet oneself

Far 'west *nm* Wild West

fa'scetta *nf* strip; *(per capelli)* hair band; *(di giornale)* wrapper

'fascia *nf* band; *(zona)* area; *(ufficiale)* sash; *(benda)* bandage; *(di smoking)* cummerbund; *(in statistica)* bracket. **~ per capelli** hair band. **~ elastica** crepe bandage; *(ventriera)* girdle. **~ d'età** age bracket, age group. **~ d'ozono** ozone layer. **~ di reddito** income bracket

fasci'are *vt* bandage; cling to *(fianchi)*

fasci'arsi *vr* bandage; **~ la testa prima di rompersela** worry about something that might never happen

fascia'tura *nf* dressing; *(azione)* bandaging

fascicola'tore, -'trice *nmf* sorter

fa'scicolo *nm* file; *(di rivista)* issue; *(libretto)* booklet

fa'scina *nf* faggot

'fascino *nm* fascination

fasci'noso *a* charming

'fascio *nm* bundle; *(di fiori)* bunch. **~ di luce** beam of light

fa'scismo *nm* fascism

fa'scista *a* & *nmf* fascist

'fase *nf* phase; **il motore è fuori ~** the timing is wrong; **sono fuori ~** I'm not firing on all four cylinders; **essere in ~ di miglioramento** be on the mend, be recovering; **essere in ~ di espansione** be expanding

fast 'food *nm inv* fast food; *(ristorante)* fast food restaurant

fa'stidio *nm* nuisance; *(scomodo)* inconvenience. **~** *pl (preoccupazioni)* worries; *(disturbi)* troubles; **dar ~ a qcno** bother sb

fastidi'oso *a* tiresome

'fasto *nm* pomp

fa'stoso *a* sumptuous

fa'sullo *a* bogus

'fata *nf* fairy

fa'tale *a* fatal; *(inevitabile)* fated; **donna ~** femme fatale

fata'lismo *nm* fatalism

fata'lista *nmf* fatalist ● *a* fatalistic

fatalità *nf inv* fate; *(caso sfortunato)* misfortune

fatal'mente *adv* inevitably

fa'tato *a (anello, bacchetta)* magic

fa'tica *nf* effort; *(lavoro faticoso)* hard work; *(stanchezza, di metalli)* fatigue; **a ~** with great difficulty; **è ~ sprecata** it's a waste of time; **fare ~ a fare qcsa** find it difficult to do sth; **senza [nessuna] ~** without [any] effort; **fare ~ a finire qcsa** struggle to finish sth; **uomo di ~** odd-job man

fati'caccia *nf* pain

fati'care *vi* toil; **~ a** *(stentare)* find it difficult to

fati'cata *nf* effort; *(sfacchinata)* grind

fati'coso *a* tiring; *(difficile)* difficult

fati'scente *a* crumbling

'fato *nm* fate

fat'taccio *nm hum* foul deed

fat'tezze *nfpl* features

fat'tibile *a* feasible

fatti'specie *nf* **nella ~** in this case

'fatto *pp di* **fare**; **ormai è fatta!** what's done is done ● *a* made; **~ a mano/in casa** handmade/home-made; **essere ben ~** *(persona)* have a nice figure; **un uomo ~** a grown man ● *nm* fact; *(azione)* action; *(avvenimento)* event; *(faccenda)* business, matter; **sa il ~ suo** he knows his business; **le ho detto il ~ suo** I told her what I thought of her; **di ~** in fact; **in ~ di** as regards; **~ sta che** the fact remains that; **mettere di fronte al ~ compiuto** present with a fait accompli

fat'tore *nm (causa, Math)* factor; *(di fattoria)* farm manager

fatto'ria *nf* farm; *(casa)* farmhouse

fatto'rino *nm* messenger [boy]. **~ d'albergo** bellboy

fattucchi'era *nf* witch

fat'tura *nf (stile)* cut; *(lavorazione)* workmanship; *Comm* invoice. **~ di acquisto** purchase invoice. **~ pro-forma** pro forma [invoice]. **~ di vendita** sales invoice

fattu'rare *vt* invoice; *(adulterare)* adulterate

fattu'rato *nm* turnover, sales *pl*

fatturazi'one *nf* invoicing, billing

'fatuo *a* fatuous

'fauci *nfpl (di leone)* maw *sg*

'fauna *nf* fauna

'fausto *a* propitious

fau'tore *nm* supporter

'fava *nf* broad bean

fa'vella *nf* speech

fa'villa *nf* spark

'favo *nm* honeycomb

'favola *nf* fable; *(fiaba)* story; *(oggetto di pettegolezzi)* laughing-stock; **è una ~!** *(meraviglia)* it's divine!

favo'loso *a* fabulous

fa'vore *nm* favour; **essere a ~ di** be in favour of; **per ~** please; **di ~** *(condizioni, trattamento)* preferential; **col ~ delle tenebre** under cover of darkness

favoreggia'mento *nm Jur* aiding and abetting

favo'revole *a* favourable

favorevol'mente *adv* favourably

favo'rire vt favour; (promuovere) promote; **vuol ~?** (a cena, pranzo) will you have some?; (entrare) will you come in?; **favorisca alla cassa** please pay at the cash-desk; **favorisca i documenti** your papers please

favo'rito, -a a & nmf favourite

fax nm inv fax; **inviare via ~** fax, send by fax. **~ a carta comune** plain paper fax

fa'xare vt fax

fazi'one nf faction

faziosità nf bias

fazi'oso nm sectarian

fazzolet'tino nm ~ **[di carta]** [paper] tissue

fazzo'letto nm handkerchief; (da testa) headscarf

feb'braio nm February

'febbre nf fever; **avere la ~** have o run a temperature; **~ da fieno** hay fever

febbrici'tante a fevered

feb'brile a feverish

febbril'mente adv feverishly

'feccia nf dregs pl

'fecola nf potato flour

fecon'dare vt fertilize

feconda'tore nm fertilizer

fecondazi'one nf fertilization; **~ artificiale** artificial insemination. **~ in vitro** in vitro fertilization, IVF

fe'condo a fertile

'fede nf faith; (fiducia) trust; (anello) wedding ring; **in buona/mala ~** in good/bad faith; **prestar ~ a** believe; **tener ~ alla parola** keep one's word; **aver ~ in qcno** have faith in sb, believe in sb; **degno di ~** reliable; **in ~** Yours faithfully

fe'dele a faithful ● nmf believer; (seguace) follower; **i fedeli** the faithful

fedel'mente adv faithfully

fedeltà nf faithfulness; **alta ~** high fidelity

'federa nf pillowcase

fede'rale a federal

federa'lismo nm federalism

federa'lista a federalist

fede'rato a federate

federazi'one nf federation

fe'difrago, -a a faithless; (hum) two-timing ● nm faithless wretch; (hum) two-timer

fe'dina nf **avere la ~ penale sporca/pulita** have a/no criminal record

fega'telli nmpl (di maiale) pork liver

fega'tino nm **fegatini** pl **di pollo** chicken livers

'fegato nm liver; fig guts pl; **mangiarsi il ~**, **rodersi il ~** be consumed with rage

'felce nf fern

fe'lice a happy; (fortunato) lucky; **~ come una Pasqua** blissfully happy

felice'mente adv happily; (con successo) successfully

felicità nf happiness

felici'tarsi vr **~ con** congratulate

felicitazi'oni nfpl congratulations

fe'lino a feline

'felpa nf (indumento) sweatshirt; (stoffa) felt

fel'pato a brushed; (passo) stealthy

'feltro nm felt; (cappello) felt hat

'femmina nf female

femmi'nile a feminine; (rivista, abbigliamento) women's; (sesso) female ● nm feminine

femminilità nf femininity

femmi'nismo nm feminism

'femore nm femur

'fendere vt split

fendi'nebbia nm inv fog lamp

fendi'tura nf split; (in roccia) crack

fe'nice nf phoenix

feni'cottero nm flamingo

fenome'nale a phenomenal

fe'nomeno nm phenomenon

'feretro nm coffin

feri'ale a weekday; **giorno ~** weekday

'ferie nfpl holidays; (di università, tribunale ecc) vacation sg; **andare in ~** go on holiday; **prendere le ~** go on holiday; **prendere delle ~** take time off; **prendere un giorno di ~** take a day off

feri'mento nm wounding

fe'rire vt wound; (in incidente) injure; fig hurt

fe'rirsi vr injure oneself

fe'rita nf wound

fe'rito a wounded ● nm wounded person; Mil casualty; **~ grave** seriously injured person

feri'toia nf loophole; **feritoie** pl **per le schede di espansione** Comput expansion slots

'ferma nf Mil period of service

fermacal'zoni nm inv cycle clip

fermaca'pelli nm inv hair slide

ferma'carte nm inv paperweight

fermacra'vatta nm inv tiepin

ferma'fogli nm inv bulldog clip

fer'maglio nm clasp; (spilla) brooch; (per capelli) hair slide

ferma'mente adv firmly

ferma'porta nm inv doorstop

fer'mare vt stop; (fissare) fix; Jur detain ● vi stop

fer'marsi vr stop

fer'mata nf stop; **'~ prenotata'** 'bus stopping'; **senza fermate** (tragitto) non-stop. **~ dell'autobus** bus stop. **~ obbligatoria** compulsory stop. **~ a richiesta** request stop

fermen'tare vi ferment

fermentazi'one nf fermentation

fer'mento nm ferment; (lievito) yeast; **essere in ~** be in/get into a tizzy

fer'mezza nf firmness

'fermo a still; (veicolo) stationary; (stabile) steady; (orologio) not working; **~!** don't move!; **~ restando che...** it being understood that... ; **'~ per manutenzione'** 'closed for repairs' ● nm Jur detention; Mech catch; **in stato di ~** in custody. **~ immagine** TV freeze frame. **~ posta** poste restante, general delivery Am

fer'net® *nm inv bitter digestive liqueur*
fe'roce *a* fierce, ferocious; ⟨*bestia*⟩ wild; ⟨*freddo, dolore*⟩ unbearable
feroce'mente *adv* fiercely, ferociously
fe'rocia *nf* ferocity
fer'raglia *nf* scrap iron
ferra'gosto *nm* 15 August (*bank holiday in Italy*); (*periodo*) August holidays *pl*
ferra'menta *nfpl* ironmongery *sg*; **negozio di ~** ironmonger's
fer'rare *vt* shoe ⟨*cavallo*⟩
fer'rato *a* ~ **in** (*preparato in*) well up in
'ferreo *a* iron
'ferro *nm* iron; (*attrezzo*) tool; (*di chirurgo*) instrument; **di ~** ⟨*memoria*⟩ excellent; ⟨*alibi*⟩ cast-iron; **salute di ~** iron constitution; **ai ferri** ⟨*bistecca*⟩ grilled; **essere ai ferri corti** be at daggers drawn; **mettere il paese a ~ e fuoco** put a country to the sword; **i ferri del mestiere** the tools of the trade. **~ battuto** wrought iron. **~ da calza** knitting needle. **~ di cavallo** horseshoe. **~ da stiro** iron. **~ a vapore** steam iron
fer'roso *a* ferrous
ferro'vecchio *nm* scrap merchant
ferro'via *nf* railway, railroad *Am*; **Ferrovie** *pl* **dello Stato** Italian State Railways
ferrovi'ario *a* railway *attrib*, railroad *Am attrib*
ferrovi'ere *nm* railwayman, railroad worker *Am*
'fertile *a* fertile
fertilità *nf* fertility
fertiliz'zante *nm* fertilizer
fertilizzazi'one *nf* fertilization
fer'vente *a* blazing; *fig* fervent
fervente'mente *adv* fervently
'fervere *vi* ⟨*preparativi:*⟩ be well under way
fervida'mente *adv* fervently
'fervido *a* fervent; **fervidi auguri** best wishes
fer'vore *nm* fervour; (*di discussione*) heat
'fesa *nf* (*carne*) rump
fesse'ria *nf* **dire/fare una ~** *fam* say/do something stupid
'fesso *pp di* **fendere** ● *a* cracked; (*fam: sciocco*) foolish ● *nm* (*fam: idiota*) fool; **far ~ qcno** *fam* con sb
fes'sura *nf* crack; (*per gettone ecc*) slot. **~ [per la scheda] di espansione** *Comput* expansion slot
'festa *nf* feast; (*giorno festivo*) holiday; (*compleanno*) birthday; (*ricevimento*) party; *fig* joy; **fare ~ a qcno** welcome sb; **essere in ~** be on holiday; **far ~** celebrate; **della ~** ⟨*vestito, tovaglia*⟩ best; **conciare qcno per le feste** give sb a sound thrashing; **le feste** (*Natale, Capodanno ecc*) the holidays. **~ di compleanno** birthday party. **~ della mamma** Mother's Day, Mothering Sunday. **~ nazionale** public holiday. **~ del papà** Father's Day
festai'olo *a* festive
festeggia'mento *nm* celebration; (*mani-*

festazione) festivity; **festeggiamenti** *pl* celebrations
festeggi'are *vt* celebrate; (*accogliere festosamente*) give a hearty welcome to
fe'stino *nm* party
festività *nfpl* festivities
fe'stivo *a* holiday; (*lieto*) festive; **festivi** *pl* public holidays
fe'stone *nm* (*nel cucito*) scallop, scollop; (*di carta*) paper chain
fe'stoso *a* merry
fe'tente *a* evil smelling; *fig* revolting ● *nmf fam* bastard
fe'ticcio *nm* fetish
'feto *nm* foetus
fe'tore *nm* stench
'fetta *nf* slice; **a fette** sliced. **~ biscottata** *slices of crispy toast-like bread*
fet'tina *nf* thin slice
fet'tuccia *nf* tape; (*con nome*) name tape
fettuc'cine *nfpl* ribbon-shaped pasta
feu'dale *a* feudal
'feudo *nm* feud
fez *nm inv* fez
FFSS *abbr* (**Ferrovie dello Stato**) Italian State Railways
fi'aba *nf* fairy-tale
fia'besco *a* fairy-tale *attrib*
fi'acca *nf* weariness; (*indolenza*) laziness; **battere la ~** be sluggish
fiac'care *vt* weaken
fi'acco *a* weak; (*indolente*) slack; (*stanco*) weary; ⟨*partita*⟩ dull
fi'accola *nf* torch
fiacco'lata *nf* torchlight procession
fi'ala *nf* phial
fia'letta *nf* phial; **~ puzzolente** stink bomb
fi'amma *nf* flame; *Naut* pennant; **in fiamme** in flames; **andare in fiamme** go up in flames; **dare alle fiamme** commit to the flames; **alla ~** *Culin* flambé. **le Fiamme Gialle** body responsible for border control and investigating fraud. **~ ossidrica** blowtorch
fiam'mante *a* flaming; **nuovo ~** brand new
fiam'mata *nf* blaze
fiammeggi'are *vi* blaze ● *vt* singe ⟨*pollo*⟩
fiam'mifero *nm* match
fiam'mingo, -a *a & nm* Flemish ● *nmf* Fleming
fian'cata *nf* wing
fiancheggi'are *vt* border; *fig* support
fi'anco *nm* side; (*di persona*) hip; (*di animale*) flank; *Mil* wing; **al mio ~** by my side; **~ a** ⟨*lavorare*⟩ side by side
Fi'andre *nfpl* **le ~** Flanders
fia'schetta *nf* hip flask
fiaschet'teria *nf* wine shop
fi'asco *nm* flask; *fig* fiasco; **fare ~** be a fiasco
fia'tare *vi* breathe; (*parlare*) breathe a word
fi'ato *nm* breath; (*vigore*) stamina; **strumenti a ~** wind instruments; **avere il ~ corto** be short of breath; **senza ~** breathlessly; **tutto d'un ~** ⟨*bere, leggere*⟩ all in one go
'fibbia *nf* buckle

'**fibra** nf fibre; **fibre** pl (alimentari) roughage. **fibre** pl **artificiali** man-made fibres. ~ **ottica** optical fibre; **a fibre ottiche** ‹cavo› fibre optic. ~ **sintetica** man-made fibre, synthetic. ~ **di vetro** fibreglass

fi'**broma** nm fibroid

fi'**broso** a fibrous

ficca'**naso** nmf nosey parker

fic'**care** vt thrust; drive ‹chiodo ecc›; (fam: mettere) shove

fic'**carsi** vr thrust oneself; (nascondersi) hide; ~ **nei guai** get oneself into trouble

'**fiche** nf inv (gettone) chip

'**fico** nm (albero) fig-tree; (frutto) fig. ~ **d'India** prickly pear; **non me ne importa un ~** [secco] fam I don't give a damn; **non capisce un ~** [secco] fam he doesn't understand a bloody thing; **non vale un ~** [secco] fam it's totally worthless

'**fico, -a** fam nmf cool sort ● a cool

fidanza'**mento** nm engagement; **rompere il ~** break off one's engagement, break it off

fidan'**zarsi** vr get engaged

fidan'**zata** nf (ufficiale) fiancée; (innamorata) girlfriend

fidan'**zato** nm (ufficiale) fiancé; (innamorato) boyfriend

fi'**darsi** vr ~ **di** trust

fi'**dato** a trustworthy

'**fido** a ‹compagno› loyal ● nm devoted follower; Comm credit

fi'**ducia** nf confidence; **degno di ~** trustworthy; **persona di ~** reliable person; **di ~** ‹fornitore, banca› regular, usual; **avere ~ in se stessi** believe in oneself; **incarico di ~** important job

fiduci'**ario, -a** a ‹rapporto, transazione› based on trust ● nmf trustee

fiduci'**oso** a hopeful

fi'**ele** nm bile; fig bitterness; **amaro come il ~** bitter

fienagi'**one** nf haymaking

fie'**nile** nm barn

fi'**eno** nm hay

fi'**era** nf fair. ~ **commerciale** trade fair. ~ **del libro** book fair

fie'**rezza** nf (dignità) pride

fi'**ero** a proud

fi'**evole** a faint; ‹luce› dim

'**fifa** nf fam jitters; **aver ~** have the jitters

fi'**fone, -a** nmf fam chicken, yellowbelly

FIGC nf abbr (**Federazione Italiana Gioco Calcio**) Italian Football Association

'**figli** nmpl children

'**figlia** nf daughter; ~ **unica** only child

figli'**are** vi ‹animale:› calve

figli'**astra** nf stepdaughter

figli'**astro** nm stepson

'**figlio** nm son; (generico) child; **è ~ d'arte** he was born in a trunk. ~ **adottivo** adopted child. ~ **di papà** spoilt brat. ~ **di puttana** vulg son of a bitch. ~ **unico** only child

figli'**occia** nf goddaughter

figli'**occio** nm godson

figli'**ola** nf girl

figlio'**lanza** nf offspring

figli'**olo** nm boy; **figlioli** pl children

'**figo, -a** a vedi **fico, -a**

fi'**gura** nf figure; (aspetto esteriore) shape; (illustrazione) illustration; **far bella/brutta ~** make a good/bad impression; **mi hai fatto fare una brutta ~** you made me look a fool; **che ~!** how embarrassing!. ~ **paterna** father figure. ~ **retorica** figure of speech

figu'**raccia** nf bad impression

figu'**rare** vt represent; (simboleggiare) symbolize; (immaginare) imagine ● vi (far figura) cut a fine figure; (in lista) appear, figure; ~ **in testa al cartellone** Theat get top billing

figu'**rarsi** vr (immaginarsi) imagine; **figurati!** imagine that!; **posso? – [ma] figurati!** may I? – of course!

figura'**tivo** a figurative

figu'**rina** nf (da raccolta) cigarette card; (statuetta) figurine

figuri'**nista** nmf dress designer

figu'**rino** nm fashion sketch

figu'**rone** nm **fare un ~** make an excellent impression

fi'**guro** nm **un losco ~** a shady character

fil nm ~ **di ferro** wire

'**fila** nf line; (di soldati ecc) file; (di oggetti) row; (coda) queue; **di ~** in succession; **fare la ~** queue [up], stand in line Am; **in ~ indiana** single file

fila'**mento** nm filament

fi'**lanca®** nf type of synthetic stretch fabric

fi'**lante** a ‹formaggio› stringy; **stella ~** (di carta) streamer

filantro'**pia** nf philanthropy

filan'**tropico** a philanthropic

fi'**lantropo, -a** nmf philanthropist

fi'**lare** vt spin; Naut pay out ● vi (andarsene) run away; ‹liquido:› trickle; **fila!** fam scram!; ~ **con** (fam: amoreggiare) go out with; ~ **dritto** toe the line ● vi ‹ragionamento:› hang together ● nm (di viti, di alberi) row

filar'**monica** nf (orchestra) orchestra

filar'**monico** a philharmonic

fila'**strocca** nf rigmarole; (per bambini) nursery rhyme

filate'**lia** nf philately, stamp collecting

fila'**telico, -a** nmf philatelist

fi'**lato** a spun; (ininterrotto) running; (continuato) uninterrupted; **di ~** (subito) immediately; **andare dritto ~ a** go straight to ● nm yarn

fila'**tore, -'trice** nmf spinner

fila'**tura** nf spinning; (filanda) spinning mill

file nm inv Comput file

filetta'**tura** nf (di vite) thread

fi'**letto** nm (bordo) border; (di vite) thread; Culin fillet. ~ **ai ferri** grilled fillet of beef

fili'**ale** a filial ● nf Comm branch

filibusti'**ere** nm rascal

fili'**forme** a stringy

fili'**grana** nf filigree; (su carta) watermark

fi'**lippica** nf invective

Filip'pine nfpl **le ~** the Philippines

filip'pino, -a *a & nmf* Filipino

film *nm inv* film. **~ comico** comedy. **~ drammatico** drama. **~ di fantascienza** science fiction film. **~ giallo** thriller. **~ a lungo metraggio** feature film. **~ dell'orrore** horror film. **~ poliziesco** detective film

fil'mare *vt* film

fil'mato *a* filmed ● *nm* short film

fil'mina *nf* film strip

fil'mino *nm* cine film

'**filo** *nm* thread; (*tessile*) yarn; (*metallico*) wire; (*di lama*) edge; (*venatura*) grain; (*di perle*) string; (*d'erba*) blade; (*di luce*) ray; **un ~ di** (*poco*) a drop of; **con un ~ di voce** in a whisper; **per ~ e per segno** in detail; **fare il ~ a qcno** fancy sb; **perdere il ~** lose the thread; **essere appeso a un ~** be hanging by a thread; **essere sul ~ del rasoio** be on a knife-edge; **un ~ d'aria** a breath of air; **un ~ di speranza** a glimmer of hope. **~ interdentale** dental floss. **~ a piombo** plumb-line. **~ spinato** barbed wire

filo+ *pref* philo+

filoameri'cano *a* pro-American

'**filobus** *nm inv* trolleybus

filocomu'nista *a* pro-communist

filodiffusi'one *nf* rediffusion

filodram'matica *nf* amateur dramatic society

filolo'gia *nf* philology

filo'logico *a* philological

fi'lologo, -a *nmf* philologist

filon'cino *nm* ≈ French stick

fi'lone *nm* vein; (*di pane*) long loaf, Vienna loaf

fi'loso *a* stringy

filoso'fia *nf* philosophy

fi'losofo, -a *nmf* philosopher

fil'traggio *nm* filtering

fil'trare *vt* filter

'**filtro** *nm* filter. **~ dell'olio** oil filter

'**filza** *nf* string

fin *vedi* **fine, fino¹**

fi'nale *a* final ● *nm* end ● *nf Sport* final

fina'lista *nmf* finalist

finalità *nf inv* finality; (*scopo*) aim

final'mente *adv* at last; (*in ultimo*) finally

fi'nanza *nf* finance

finanzia'mento *nm* funding

finanzi'are *vt* fund, finance

finanzi'aria *nf* investment company; (*holding*) holding company; *Jur* finance bill

finanzi'ario *a* financial

finanzia|'tore, -'trice *nmf* backer

finanzi'ere *nm* financier; (*guardia di finanza*) customs officer

finché *conj* until; (*per tutto il tempo che*) as long as

'**fine** *a* fine; (*sottile*) thin; ⟨*udito, vista*⟩ keen; (*raffinato*) refined ● *nf* end; **alla ~** in the end; **alla fin ~** after all; **in fin dei conti** when all's said and done; **andare a buon ~** be successful; **te lo dico a fin di bene** I'm telling you for your own good; **che ~ ha fatto Anna?** what became of Anna?; **che ~**

hanno fatto le chiavi? where have the keys got to?; **senza ~** endless ● *nm* aim. **~ settimana** weekend

fi'nestra *nf* window. **~ a battenti** casement window

fine'strella *nf* **~ di aiuto** *Comput* help window. **~ di dialogo** *Comput* dialog box

fine'strino *nm Rail, Auto* window

fi'nezza *nf* fineness; (*sottigliezza*) thinness; (*raffinatezza*) refinement

'**fingere** *vt* pretend; feign ⟨*affetto ecc*⟩

'**fingersi** *vr* pretend to be

fini'menti *nmpl* finishing touches; (*per cavallo*) harness *sg*

fini'mondo *nm* end of the world; *fig* pandemonium

fi'nire *vt/i* finish, end; (*smettere*) stop; (*diventare, andare a finire*) end up; **finiscila!** stop it!

fi'nito *a* finished; (*abile*) accomplished

fini'tura *nf* finish

finlan'dese *a* Finnish ● *nmf* Finn ● *nm* (*lingua*) Finnish

Fin'landia *nf* Finland

'**fino¹** *prep* **~ a** till, until; (*spazio*) as far as; **~ all'ultimo** to the last; **~ alla nausea** ⟨*ripetere, leggere*⟩ ad nauseam; **fin da** (*tempo*) since; (*spazio*) from; **fin dall'inizio** from the beginning; **fin qui** as far as here; **fin troppo** too much; **~ a che punto** how far

'**fino²** *a* fine; (*acuto*) subtle; (*puro*) pure

fi'nocchio *nm* fennel; (*fam: omosessuale*) poof

fi'nora *adv* so far, up till now

'**finta** *nf* pretence, sham; *Sport* feint; **far ~ di** pretend to; **far ~ di niente** act as if nothing had happened; **per ~** (*per scherzo*) for a laugh

'**finto, -a** *pp di* **fingere** ● *a* false; (*artificiale*) artificial; **finta pelle** fake leather; **fare il ~ tonto** act dumb

finzi'one *nf* pretence

fi'occo *nm* bow; (*di neve*) flake; (*nappa*) tassel; *Naut* jib; **coi fiocchi** *fig* excellent; **fiocchi** *pl* **di avena** oatmeal; (*cotti*) porridge; **fiocchi** *pl* **di granoturco** cornflakes. **fiocchi** *pl* **di latte** cottage cheese. **~ di neve** snowflake

fi'ocina *nf* harpoon

fi'oco *a* weak; ⟨*luce*⟩ dim

fi'onda *nf* catapult

fio'raio, -a *nmf* florist

fiorda'liso *nm* cornflower

fi'ordo *nm* fiord

fi'ore *nm* flower; (*parte scelta*) cream; **a fior d'acqua** on the surface of the water; **a fiori** flowery; **in ~** flowering; **fior di** (*abbondanza*) a lot of; **il fior ~ di** the cream of; **ha i nervi a fior di pelle** his nerves are on edge; **nel ~ degli anni** in one's prime; **è il suo ~ all'occhiello** that's a feather in his cap; **suo figlio è il suo ~ all'occhiello** his son is his pride and joy. **fiori** *pl* **d'arancio** orange blossom. **~ di campo** wild flower. **fior di latte** (*formaggio*) soft cheese. **~ selvatico** wild flower. **fiori** *pl* **di zucca fritti** fried pumpkin flowers

fio'rente *a* ⟨*industria*⟩ booming

fioren'tina *nf* (*bistecca*) T-bone steak

fioren'tino *a* Florentine

fio'retto *nm* (*scherma*) foil; *Relig* act of mortification

fi'ori *nmpl* (*nelle carte*) clubs

fiori'era *nf* container

fio'rino *nm* ~ **olandese** guilder

fio'rire *vi* flower; ⟨*albero:*⟩ blossom; *fig* flourish

fio'rista *nmf* florist; (*negozio*) florist's

fiori'tura *nf* flowering; (*di albero*) blossoming; (*insieme di fiori*) flowers *pl*

fio'rone *nm* (*fico*) early fig

fi'otto *nm* (*di sangue*) spurt; **scorrere a fiotti** pour out; **piove a fiotti** the rain is pouring down

Fi'renze *nf* Florence

'firma *nf* signature; (*nome*) name

firma'mento *nm* firmament

fir'mare *vt* sign

firma'tario, -a *nmf* signatory

fir'mato *a* ⟨*quadro, lettera*⟩ signed; ⟨*abito, borsa*⟩ designer *attrib*

fisar'monica *nf* accordion

fi'scale *a* fiscal

fisca'lista *nmf* tax consultant

fiscaliz'zare *vt* finance with government funds

fischi'are *vi* whistle ● *vt* whistle; (*in segno di disapprovazione*) boo; **mi fischiano le orecchie** I've got a ringing noise in my ears; *fig* my ears are burning

fischi'ata *nf* whistle

fischiet'tare *vt* whistle

fischiet'tio *nm* whistling

fischi'etto *nm* whistle

'fischio *nm* whistle; **fischi** *pl Theat* booing; **prendere fischi per fiaschi** get hold of the wrong end of the stick

'fisco *nm* treasury; (*tasse*) taxation; **il** ~ the taxman

fisica'mente *adv* physically

'fisico, -a *a* physical ● *nmf* physicist. ~ **nucleare** atomic scientist ● *nm* physique ● *nf* physics. ~ **nucleare** nuclear physics

'fisima *nf* whim

fisiolo'gia *nf* physiology

fisio'logico *a* physiological

fisi'ologo, -a *nmf* physiologist

fisiono'mia *nf* features *pl*, face; (*di paesaggio*) appearance

fisiotera'pia *nf* physiotherapy

fisiotera'pista *nmf* physiotherapist, physio *fam*

fissa'mente *adv* fixedly; (*permanentemente*) steadily

fis'sare *vt* fix, fasten; (*guardare fissamente*) stare at; arrange (*appuntamento, ora*)

fis'sarsi *vr* (*stabilirsi*) settle; (*fissare lo sguardo*) stare; ~ **su** (*ostinarsi*) set one's mind on; ~ **di fare qcsa** become obsessed with doing sth

fissa'tivo *nm Phot* fixative

fis'sato, -a *a* (*al muro*) fixed; ⟨*prezzo*⟩ agreed ● *nm* (*persona*) person with an obsession

fissa'tore *nm* hair spray

fissazi'one *nf* fixation; (*osessione*) obsession

'fisso *a* fixed; **un lavoro** ~ a regular job; **senza fissa dimora** of no fixed abode; **avere una ragazza fissa** have a steady girlfriend ● *adv* fixedly; **guardare** ~ **negli occhi qcno** stare at sb; ⟨*innamorato:*⟩ gaze into sb's eyes

fitotera'pia *nf* herbalism; (*per piante*) plant health

'fitta *nf* sharp pain

fit'tavolo *nm* tenant

fit'tizio *a* fictitious

'fitto¹ *a* thick; ~ **di** full of ● *nm* depth

fitto² *nm* (*affitto*) rent; **dare a** ~ let; **prendere a** ~ rent; (*noleggiare*) hire

fiu'mana *nf* swollen river; *fig* stream

fi'ume *nm* river; *fig* stream ● *a inv* ⟨*discussione*⟩ endless, never-ending; **romanzo** ~ roman-fleuve

fiu'tare *vt* smell; ⟨*animale:*⟩ scent; snort ⟨*cocaina*⟩

fi'uto *nm* [sense of] smell; *fig* nose

'flaccido *a* flabby

fla'cone *nm* bottle

flagel'lare *vt* flog

flagellazi'one *nf* flagellation

fla'gello *nm* scourge

fla'grante *a* flagrant; **in** ~ in the act

fla'menco *nm* flamenco

flan *nm inv* baked custard

fla'nella *nf* flannel

'flangia *nf* (*su ruota*) flange

flash *nm inv Journ* newsflash

flau'tista *nmf* flautist

'flauto *nm* flute. ~ **diritto** recorder. ~ **traverso** flute

'flebile *a* feeble

fle'bite *nf* phlebitis

flebo'clisi *nf* drip

'flemma *nf* calm; *Med* phlegm

flem'matico *a* phlegmatic

fles'sibile *a* flexible

flessibilità *nf* flexibility

flessi'one *nf* (*del busto in avanti*) forward bend; (*a terra*) sit-up; (*delle ginocchia*) knee-bend; (*di vendite, produzione*) drop, fall

fles'sivo *a Gram* inflected

'flesso *pp di* **flettere** ● *a Gram* inflected

flessu'oso *a* supple

'flettere *vt* bend

flip-'flop *nm inv* flip flop

flir'tare *vi* flirt

F.lli *abbr* (*fratelli*) Bros.

'floppy disk *nm inv* floppy disk

'flora *nf* flora

'florido *a* flourishing

floroviva'istica *nf* ⟨*attività*⟩ growing under glass

'floscio *a* limp; (*flaccido*) flabby

'**flotta** *nf* fleet
flot'tiglia *nf* flotilla
flu'ente *a* fluent
fluidità *nf* fluidity; (*nel parlare*) fluency
flu'ido *nm* fluid
flu'ire *vi* flow
fluore'scente *a* fluorescent
fluore'scenza *nf* fluorescence
flu'oro *nm* fluorine
fluo'ruro *nm* fluoride
'**flusso** *nm* flow; *Med* flux; (*del mare*) flood-tide; **~ e riflusso** ebb and flow. **~ di cassa** cash flow
'**flutti** *nmpl* billows
fluttu'ante *a* fluctuating
fluttu'are *vi* ⟨*prezzi:*⟩ fluctuate; ⟨*moneta:*⟩ float
fluttuazi'one *nf* fluctuation; (*di moneta*) floating
fluvi'ale *a* river
fo'bia *nf* phobia
'**fobico** *a* phobic
'**foca** *nf* seal
fo'caccia *nf* (*pane*) flat bread; (*dolce*) ≈ raisin bread
fo'cale *a* ⟨*distanza, punto*⟩ focal
focaliz'zare *vt* get into focus ⟨*fotografia*⟩; focus ⟨*attenzione*⟩; define ⟨*problema*⟩
'**foce** *nf* mouth
fo'chista *nm* stoker
foco'laio *nm Med* focus; *fig* centre
foco'lare *nm* hearth; (*caminetto*) fireplace; *Techn* furnace
fo'coso *a* fiery
'**fodera** *nf* lining; (*di libro*) dust-jacket; (*di poltrona ecc*) loose cover
fode'rare *vt* line; cover ⟨*libro*⟩
fode'rato *a* lined; ⟨*libro*⟩ covered
'**foga** *nf* impetuosity
'**foggia** *nf* fashion; (*maniera*) manner; (*forma*) shape
foggi'are *vt* mould
'**foglia** *nf* leaf; (*di metallo*) foil; **mangiare la ~** catch on. **~ di alloro** bay leaf
fogli'ame *nm* foliage
fogliet'tino *nm* **~ igienico** (*per pannolini*) nappy liner
fogli'etto *nm* (*pezzetto di carta*) piece of paper
'**foglio** *nm* sheet; (*pagina*) leaf; (*di domanda, di iscrizione*) form. **~ di carta** sheet of paper. **~ elettronico** *Comput* spreadsheet. **~ illustrativo** instruction leaflet. **~ protocollo** foolscap. **~ rosa** provisional driving licence. **~ di via** expulsion order
'**fogna** *nf* sewer
fogna'tura *nf* sewerage
fohn *nm inv* hair dryer
fo'lata *nf* gust
fol'clore *nm* folklore
folclo'ristico *a* folk; (*bizzarro*) weird
folgo'rante *a* ⟨*idea*⟩ brilliant
folgo'rare *vi* (*splendere*) shine ● *vt* (*con un fulmine*) strike

folgo'rato *a fig* thunderstruck
folgorazi'one *nf* (*da fulmine, elettrica*) electrocution; (*fig: idea*) brainwave
'**folgore** *nf* thunderbolt
'**folio: in ~** *a* folio
'**folla** *nf* crowd
'**folle** *a* mad; ⟨*velocità*⟩ breakneck; **in ~** *Auto* in neutral; **andare in ~** *Auto* coast
folleggi'are *vi* paint the town red
folle'mente *adv* madly
fol'letto *nm* elf
fol'lia *nf* madness; **alla ~** ⟨*amare*⟩ to distraction; **costare una ~** cost the earth; **fare una ~** go mad; **farei follie per lei** I'd do anything for her
'**folto** *a* thick
fomen'tare *vt* stir up
fond'ale *nm Theat* backcloth. **~ marino** sea bed
fonda'menta *nfpl* foundations
fondamen'tale *a* fundamental
fondamenta'lismo *nm* fundamentalism
fondamenta'lista *nmf* fundamentalist
fonda'mento *nm* (*di principio, teoria*) foundation; **privo di ~** groundless, without foundation
fon'dant *nm inv* fondant
fon'dare *vt* establish; base ⟨*ragionamento, accusa*⟩
fon'darsi *vr* be based (**su** on)
fon'dato *a* ⟨*ragionamento*⟩ well-founded; **~ su** based on
fondazi'one *nf* establishment; **fondazioni** *pl* (*di edificio*) foundations
fon'delli *nmpl* **prendere qcno per i ~** *fam* pull sb's leg
fon'dente *a* ⟨*cioccolato*⟩ dark
'**fondere** *vt* melt; fuse ⟨*metallo*⟩ ● *vi* melt; ⟨*metallo:*⟩ fuse; ⟨*colori:*⟩ blend
fonde'ria *nf* foundry
'**fondersi** *vr* melt; *Comm* merge
'**fondo** *a* deep; **è notte fonda** it's the middle of the night ● *nm* bottom; (*fine*) end; (*sfondo*) background; (*indole*) nature; (*somma di denaro*) fund; (*feccia*) dregs *pl;* (*terreno*) land; [**sci di**] **~** cross-country skiing; **andare a ~** ⟨*nave:*⟩ sink; **in ~** after all; **in ~ a** at the end/bottom of; **in ~ in ~** deep down; **fino in ~** right to the end; ⟨*capire*⟩ thoroughly; **andare fino in ~ a qcsa** get to the bottom of sth; **dar ~ a** use up; **a doppio ~** false bottomed; **toccare il ~** touch bottom; *fig* hit rock bottom; **senza ~** bottomless; **articolo di ~** (*in giornale*) editorial; **fondi** *pl* (*denaro*) funds; (*di caffè*) grounds. **~ fiduciario** trust fund. **~** [**comune**] **di investimento** investment trust. **fondi** *pl* **di magazzino** old stock. **F~ Monetario Internazionale** International Monetary Fund. **fondi** *pl* **neri** slush fund. **~ pensione** pension fund. **~ per la ricostruzione** disaster fund. **~ sopravvenienze passive** contingency fund. **~ stradale** road surface
fondo'tinta *nm inv* foundation [cream]
fon'due *nf* (*di formaggio*) fondue

fon'duta *nf* fondue

fo'nema *nm* phoneme

fo'netica *nf* phonetics

fo'netico *a* phonetic

fonolo'gia *nf* phonology

fon'tana *nf* fountain; (*di farina*) well

fonta'nella *nf* drinking fountain; *Anat* fontanelle

'fonte *nf* spring; *fig* source ● *nm* font

fon'tina *nf* soft, mature cheese often used in cooking

'football *nm* ~ **americano** American football

foraggi'are *vt* fodder

fo'raggio *nm* forage

fo'rare *vt* pierce; punch ⟨*biglietto*⟩ ● *vi* puncture

fo'rarsi *vr* ⟨*gomma, pallone:*⟩ go soft

fora'tura *nf* puncture

'forbici *nfpl* scissors; **un paio di** ~ a pair of scissors. ~ **da siepe** garden shears. ~ **a zigzag** pinking shears, pinking scissors

forbi'cina *nf* earwig; **forbicine** *pl* (*per le unghie*) nail scissors

for'bito *a* erudite

'forca *nf* fork; (*patibolo*) gallows *pl*

for'cella *nf* fork; (*per capelli*) hairpin

for'chetta *nf* fork; **essere una buona** ~ enjoy one's food

forchet'tata *nf* (*quantità*) forkful

forchet'tone *nm* carving fork

for'cina *nf* hairpin

'forcipe *nm* forceps *pl*

for'cone *nm* pitchfork

fo'rense *a* forensic

fo'resta *nf* forest. ~ **equatoriale** rain forest. **F~ Nera** Black Forest

fore'stale *a* forest *attrib*; **la F~** *branch of the police with responsibility for national forests*

foreste'ria *nf* guest rooms *pl*

foresti'ero, -a *a* foreign ● *nmf* foreigner.

for'fait *nm inv* fixed price; **dare** ~ (*abbandonare*) give up; **prezzo [a]** ~ all-in price; **contratto [a]** ~ lump-sum contract

forfe'tario *a* flat rate

'forfora *nf* dandruff

'forgia *nf* forge

forgi'are *vt* forge

'forma *nf* form; (*sagoma*) shape; *Culin* mould; (*per scarpe*) shoe tree; (*di calzolaio*) last; **essere in** ~ be in good form; **in (gran)** ~ (very) fit, on (top) form; **a** ~ **di** in the shape of; **sotto** ~ **di** in the form of; **forme** *pl* (*del corpo*) curves; (*convenzioni*) appearances

formag'gera *nf* [covered] cheese board

formag'gino *nm* processed cheese

for'maggio *nm* cheese

for'male *a* formal

forma'lina *nf* formalin

forma'lismo *nm* formalism

forma'lista *nmf* formalist

formalità *nf inv* formality

formaliz'zare *vt* formalize

formaliz'zarsi *vr* stand on ceremony, be formal

formal'mente *adv* formally

'forma 'mentis *nf inv* way of thinking, mindset

for'mare *vt* form; *dial* ⟨*numero di telefono*⟩

for'marsi *vr* form; (*svilupparsi*) develop

for'mato *nm* size; (*di libro, dischetto*) format; ~ **famiglia** economy pack, economy size; ~ **tessera** ⟨*fotografia*⟩ passport-size

format'tare *vt* format

formattazi'one *nf* formatting

formazi'one *nf* formation; *Sport* line-up; **in** ~ in the process of being formed. ~ **professionale** vocational training

for'mella *nf* tile

for'mica *nf* ant

'formica® *nf* Formica

formi'caio *nm* anthill

formichi'ere *nm* anteater

formico'lare *vi* ⟨*braccio ecc:*⟩ tingle; ~ **di** be swarming with; **mi formicola la mano** I have pins and needles in my hand

formico'lio *nm* swarming; (*di braccio ecc*) pins and needles *pl*

formi'dabile *a* (*tremendo*) formidable; (*eccezionale*) tremendous

for'mina *nf* mould

for'moso *a* curvy

'formula *nf* formula; **assolvere con** ~ **piena** acquit. ~ **di cortesia** polite form of address

formu'lare *vt* formulate; (*esprimere*) express

formulazi'one *nf* formulation

for'nace *nf* furnace; (*per laterizi*) kiln

for'naio, -a *nmf* baker; (*negozio*) bakery

fornel'letto *nm* ~ **da campeggio** camping stove. ~ **a gas** gas stove

for'nello *nm* stove; (*di pipa*) bowl. ~ **da campeggio** camping stove

fornicazi'one *nf* fornication

for'nire *vt* supply (**di** with); ~ **qcsa a qcno** supply sb with sth

for'nirsi *vr* ~ **di** provide oneself with

forni'tore *nm* supplier. ~ **di servizi** service provider

forni'tura *nf* supply; **forniture** *pl* **per ufficio** office supplies

'forno *nm* oven; (*panetteria*) bakery; **al** ~ roast; **da** ~ ⟨*stoviglie*⟩ ovenproof. ~ **crematorio** cremator. ~ **elettrico** electric oven. ~ **a gas** gas oven. ~ **a microonde** microwave [oven]

'foro *nm* hole; (*romano*) forum; (*tribunale*) [law] court

'forse *adv* perhaps, maybe; **essere in** ~ be in doubt

forsen'nato, -a *a* mad ● *nmf* madman; madwoman

'forte *a* strong; ⟨*colore*⟩ bright; ⟨*suono*⟩ loud; (*resistente*) tough; ⟨*spesa*⟩ considerable; ⟨*dolore*⟩ severe; ⟨*pioggia*⟩ heavy; (*fam: simpatico*) great; ⟨*taglia*⟩ large; **essere** ~ **in qcsa**

be good at sth ● *adv* strongly; ⟨*parlare*⟩ loudly; ⟨*velocemente*⟩ fast; ⟨*piovere*⟩ heavily ● *nm* (*fortezza*) fort; (*specialità*) strong point

for'tezza *nf* fortress; (*forza morale*) fortitude

fortifi'care *vt* fortify

fortifi'cato *a* ⟨*città*⟩ walled

for'tino *nm* Mil blockhouse

for'tissimo *a* ⟨*caffè, liquore*⟩ extra-strong

for'tuito *a* fortuitous; **incontro ~** chance encounter

for'tuna *nf* fortune; (*successo*) success; (*buona sorte*) luck; **atterraggio di ~** forced landing; **aver ~** be lucky; **buona ~!** good luck!; **di ~** makeshift; **per ~** luckily; **hai una ~ sfacciata!** *fam* you lucky blighter!

fortu'nale *nm* storm

fortunata'mente *adv* fortunately

fortu'nato *a* lucky, fortunate; ⟨*impresa*⟩ successful

fortu'noso *a* ⟨*giornata*⟩ eventful

fo'runcolo *nm* pimple; (*grosso*) boil

forunco'loso *a* spotty

'forza *nf* strength; (*potenza*) power; (*fisica*) force; **di ~** by force; **a ~ di** by dint of; **con ~** hard; **~!** come on!; **in ~ di** under, in accordance with; **~ maggiore** circumstances beyond one's control; **la ~ pubblica** the police; **le forze armate** the armed forces; **per ~** against one's will; (*naturalmente*) of course; **farsi ~** bear up; **mare ~ 8** force 8 gale; **bella ~!** *fam* big deal!; **che ~!** (*che simpatico, divertente*) cool eh?. **~ di gravità** [force of] gravity. **~ lavoro** workforce. **forze** *pl* **di mercato** market forces. **~ di volontà** willpower

for'zare *vt* force; (*scassare*) break open; (*sforzare*) strain

for'zato *a* forced; ⟨*sorriso*⟩ strained ● *nm* convict

forza'tura *nf* (*di cassaforte*) forcing; **sostenere che... è una ~** to maintain that... is forcing things

forzi'ere *nm* coffer

for'zuto *a* strong

fo'schia *nf* haze

'fosco *a* dark

fo'sfato *nm* phosphate

'fosforo *nm* phosphorus

'fossa *nf* pit; (*tomba*) grave. **~ biologica** cesspool. **~ comune** mass grave. **~ dell'orchestra** orchestra pit

fos'sato *nm* (*di fortificazione*) moat

fos'setta *nf* (*di guancia*) dimple

'fossile *nm* fossil

'fosso *nm* ditch; *Mil* trench

'foto *nf inv fam* photo; **fare delle ~** take some photos

foto'cellula *nf* photocell

fotocomposi'tore, -'trice *nmf* filmsetter

fotocomposizi'one *nf* filmsetting, photocomposition

foto'copia *nf* photocopy

fotocopi'are *vt* photocopy

fotocopia'trice *nf* photocopier

foto'finish *nm inv* photo finish

foto'genico *a* photogenic

fotogiorna'lista *nmf* photojournalist

fotogra'fare *vt* photograph

fotogra'fia *nf* (*arte*) photography; (*immagine*) photograph; **fare fotografie** take photographs

foto'grafico *a* photographic; **macchina fotografica** camera

fo'tografo, -a *nmf* photographer; (*negozio*) photographer's

foto'gramma *nm* frame

fotoincisi'one *nf* photoengraving

fotomo'dello, -a *nmf* [photographer's] model

fotomon'taggio *nm* photomontage

foto'ottica *nf* camera shop and optician's

fotorepor'tage *nm inv* photo essay

fotore'porter *nmf inv* newspaper photographer; (*di rivista*) magazine photographer

fotori'tocco *nm* retouching

foto'manzo *nm* photo story

foto'sintesi *nf* photosynthesis

'fottere *vt* (*sl: rubare*) nick; (*sl: imbrogliare*) screw; *vulg* fuck, screw

'fottersene *vr vulg* not give a fuck; **va' a farti ~!** *vulg* fuck off!

fot'tuto *a* (*sl: maledetto*) bloody

fou'lard *nm inv* scarf

'foxhound *nm inv* foxhound

fox-'terrier *nm inv* fox terrier

fo'yer *nm inv* foyer

fra *prep* (*in mezzo a due*) between; (*in un insieme*) among; (*tempo, distanza*) in; **detto ~ noi** between you and me; **~ sé e sé** to oneself; **~ l'altro** what's more; **~ breve** soon; **~ quindici giorni** in two weeks' time; **~ tutti, siamo in venti** there are twenty of us altogether

fracas'sare *vt* smash

fracas'sarsi *vr* shatter

fracas'sato *a* smashed

fra'casso *nm* din; (*di cose che cadono*) crash

fracas'sone, -a *nmf* clumsy person

'fradicio *a* (*bagnato*) soaked; **ubriaco ~** blind drunk

'fragile *a* fragile; *fig* frail

fragilità *nf* fragility; *fig* frailty

'fragola *nf* strawberry

fra'gore *nm* uproar; (*di cose rotte*) clatter; (*di tuono*) rumble

frago'roso *a* uproarious; ⟨*tuono*⟩ rumbling; ⟨*suono*⟩ clanging

fra'grante *a* fragrant

fra'granza *nf* fragrance

frain'tendere *vt* misunderstand

frain'tendersi *vr* be at cross-purposes

frain'teso *pp di* **fraintendere**

frammen'tario *a* fragmentary

fram'mento *nm* fragment

fram'misto *a* **~ di** interspersed with

'frana *nf* landslide; (*fam: persona*) walking disaster area

fra'nare *vi* slide down

franca'mente *adv* frankly

france'scano *a & nm* Franciscan

fran'cese *a* French ● *nm* Frenchman; (*lingua*) French ● *nf* Frenchwoman

france'sina *nf* (*scarpa*) brogue

fran'chezza *nf* frankness; **in tutta ~** in all honesty

fran'chigia *nf* **~ bagaglio** (*per aereo*) baggage allowance

'Francia *nf* France

'franco¹ *a* frank; *Comm* free; **farla franca** get away with sth; **parlare ~** speak frankly. **~ a bordo** free on board. **~ domicilio** delivered free of charge. **~ fabbrica** ex-works; **~ di porto** carriage free, carriage paid

'franco² *nm* (*moneta*) franc

franco'bollo *nm* stamp

franco-cana'dese *a & nmf* French Canadian

fran'cofono *a* Francophone

Franco'forte *nf* Frankfurt

fran'gente *nm* (*onda*) breaker; (*scoglio*) reef; (*fig: momento difficile*) crisis; **in quel ~** in the circumstances

fran'getta *nf* fringe

'frangia *nf* fringe

frangi'flutti *nm inv* bulwark

frangi'vento *nm* windbreak

fra'noso *a* subject to landslides

fran'toio *nm* olive-press

frantu'mare *vt* shatter

frantu'marsi *vr* shatter

fran'tumi *nmpl* splinters; **in ~** smashed; **andare in ~** be smashed to smithereens

frappé *nm inv* milkshake

frap'porre *vt* interpose

frap'porsi *vr* intervene

fra'sario *nm* vocabulary; (*libro*) phrase book

'frasca *nf* [leafy] branch; **saltare di palo in ~** jump from subject to subject

'frase *nf* sentence; (*espressione*) phrase. **~ fatta** cliché

fraseolo'gia *nf* phrases *pl*

'frassino *nm* ash[-tree]

frastagli'are *vt* make jagged

frastagl'iato *a* jagged

frastor'nare *vt* daze

frastor'nato *a* dazed

frastu'ono *nm* racket

'frate *nm* friar; (*monaco*) monk

fratel'lanza *nf* brotherhood

fratel'lastro *nm* half-brother

fratel'lino *nm* little brother

fra'tello *nm* brother; **fratelli** *pl* (*fratello e sorella*) brother and sister; *Relig* brethren. **~ gemello** twin brother. **~ di sangue** blood brother

fraternità *nf* brotherhood

fraterniz'zare *vi* fraternize

fra'terno *a* brotherly

fratri'cida *a* fratricidal ● *nm* fratricide

frat'taglie *nfpl* (*di pollo ecc*) giblets

frat'tanto *adv* in the meantime

frat'tura *nf* fracture

frattu'rare *vt* break

frattu'rarsi *vr* break

fraudo'lento *a* fraudulent

frazi'one *nf* fraction; (*borgata*) hamlet; (*paese*) administrative division of a municipality

'freccia *nf* arrow; *Auto* indicator

frecci'ata *nf* (*osservazione pungente*) cutting remark

fredda'mente *adv* coldly

fred'dare *vt* cool; (*fig: con sguardo, battuta*) cut down; (*uccidere*) kill

fred'dezza *nf* coldness

'freddo *a & nm* cold; **aver ~** be cold; **fa ~** it's cold; **a ~** (*sparare*) in cold blood; (*lavare*) in cold water

freddo'loso *a* sensitive to cold, chilly

fred'dura *nf* pun

fre'gare *vt* rub; (*fam: truffare*) cheat; (*fam: rubare*) swipe; **fregarsene** *fam* not give a damn; **me ne frego!** I don't give a damn!; **chi se ne frega!** what the heck!

fre'garsi *vr* rub (*occhi, mani*)

fre'gata *nf* rub; (*nave*) frigate

frega'tura *nf fam* (*truffa*) swindle; (*delusione*) letdown

'fregio *nm Archit* frieze; (*ornamento*) decoration

'fregola *nf* rutting; **avere la ~ di fare qcsa** *fam* have a craze for doing sth

fre'mente *a* quivering

'fremere *vi* quiver

'fremito *nm* quiver

fre'nare *vt* brake; *fig* restrain; hold back (*lacrime, impazienza*) ● *vi* brake

fre'narsi *vr* check oneself

fre'nata *nf* **fare una ~ brusca** hit the brakes

fre'nesia *nf* frenzy; (*desiderio smodato*) craze

frenetica'mente *adv* frantically

fre'netico *a* frantic

'freno *nm* brake; *fig* check; **togliere il ~** release the brake; **usare il ~** apply the brake; **tenere a ~** restrain; **tenere a ~ la lingua** hold one's tongue; **porre un ~ a** *fig* rein in. **freni** *pl* **a disco** disc brakes. **~ a mano** handbrake. **~ a pedale** footbrake

frequen'tare *vt* frequent; attend (*scuola ecc*); mix with (*persone*); **non ci frequentiamo più** we don't see each other any more

fre'quente *a* frequent; **di ~** frequently

fre'quenza *nf* frequency; (*assiduità*) attendance

'fresa *nf* mill

fre'sare *vt* mill

fre'schezza *nf* freshness; (*di temperatura*) coolness

'fresco *a* fresh; (*temperatura*) cool; **~ di studi** fresh out of school; **stai ~!** *fam* you're for it!; **se ti vede, stai ~** *fam* you're done for if he sees you ● *nm* coolness; **far ~** be cool; **mettere/tenere in ~** put/keep in a cool place; **al ~** (*fam: in prigione*) inside

fre'scura *nf* cool

'fresia *nf* freesia

'fretta *nf* hurry, haste; **aver ~** be in a hurry; **far ~ a qcno** hurry sb; **in ~ e furia** in a

great hurry; **andarsene in** ~ rush away; **senza [nessuna]** ~ at your/his etc leisure
frettolosa'mente *adv* hurriedly
fretto'loso *a* ⟨*persona*⟩ hasty; ⟨*lavoro*⟩ rushed, hurried
fri'abile *a* crumbly
fricas'sea *nf stewed meat served with an egg and lemon sauce*
'**friggere** *vt* fry; **vai a farti** ~**!** get lost! ● *vi* sizzle; ~ **di impazienza** be on tenterhooks
friggi'trice *nf* electric chip pan
frigidità *nf* frigidity
'**frigido** *a* frigid
fri'gnare *vi* whine
fri'gnone, -a *nmf* whiner
'**frigo** *nm inv* fridge
frigo'bar *nm inv* minibar
frigo'rifero *a* refrigerating; ⟨*camion*⟩ refrigerated ● *nm* refrigerator
fringu'ello *nm* chaffinch
'**frisbee**® *nm inv* frisbee
frit'tata *nf* omelette
frit'tella *nf* fritter; (*fam: macchia d'unto*) grease stain
'**fritto** *pp di* **friggere** ● *a* fried; **essere** ~ be done for ● *nm* fried food. ~ **misto** mixed fried fish/vegetables
frit'tura *nf* (*pietanza*) fried dish. ~ **di pesce** variety of fried fish
frivo'lezza *nf* frivolity
'**frivolo** *a* frivolous
frizio'nare *vt* rub
frizi'one *nf* friction; *Mech* clutch; (*di pelle*) rub
friz'zante *a* fizzy; ⟨*vino*⟩ sparkling; ⟨*aria*⟩ bracing
'**frizzo** *nm* gibe
fro'dare *vt* defraud
'**frode** *nf* fraud. ~ **fiscale** tax evasion; **con la** ~ *Jur* under false pretences
frol'lino *nm* (*biscotto*) ≈ shortbread biscuit
'**frollo** *a* tender; ⟨*selvaggina*⟩ high; ⟨*persona*⟩ spineless; **pasta frolla** short[crust] pastry
'**fronda** *nf* [leafy] branch; *fig* rebellion
fron'doso *a* leafy
fron'tale *a* frontal; ⟨*scontro*⟩ head-on
'**fronte** *nf* forehead; (*di edificio*) front ● *nm Mil, Pol* front; **di** ~ opposite; **di** ~ **a** opposite, facing; (*a paragone*) compared with; **far** ~ **a** face
fronteggi'are *vt* face
fronte'spizio *nm* title page
fronti'era *nf* frontier, border
fron'tone *nm* pediment
'**fronzolo** *nm* frill
'**frotta** *nf* swarm; (*di animali*) flock
'**frottola** *nf* fib; **frottole** *pl* nonsense *sg*
fru'gale *a* frugal
fru'gare *vi* rummage ● *vt* search
fru'ire *vi* ~ **di** make use of, take advantage of
frul'lare *vt Culin* whisk ● *vi* ⟨*ali:*⟩ whirr
frul'lato *nm* ~ **di frutta** *fruit drink with milk and crushed ice*
frulla'tore *nm* [electric] mixer
frul'lino *nm* whisk

fru'mento *nm* wheat
frusci'are *vi* rustle
fru'scio *nm* rustle; (*radio, giradischi*) ground noise; (*di acque*) murmur
'**frusta** *nf* whip; (*frullino*) whisk
fru'stare *vt* whip
fru'stata *nf* lash
fru'stino *nm* riding crop
fru'strare *vt* frustrate
fru'strato *a* frustrated
frustrazi'one *nf* frustration
'**frutta** *nf* fruit; **negozio di** ~ **e verdura** greengrocer's. ~ **esotica** exotic fruit, tropical fruit. ~ **fresca di stagione** seasonal fruit. ~ **secca** nuts *pl*
frut'tare *vi* bear fruit; *Comm* give a return ● *vt* yield
frut'teto *nm* orchard
frutticol'tore *nm* fruit farmer
frutticol'tura *nf* fruit farming, fruit growing
frutti'era *nf* fruit bowl
frut'tifero *a* ⟨*albero*⟩ fruit-bearing; ⟨*Fin:* *deposito*⟩ interest-bearing
frutti'vendolo, -a *nmf* greengrocer
'**frutto** *nm anche fig* fruit; *Fin* yield. **frutti** *pl* **di bosco** fruits of the forest. **frutti** *pl* **di mare** seafood *sg*. ~ **della passione** passion fruit
fruttu'oso *a* profitable
FS *abbr* (**Ferrovie dello Stato**) Italian State Railways
f.to *abbr* (**firmato**) signed
fu *a* (*defunto*) late; **il fu signor Rossi** the late Mr Rossi
fuci'lare *vt* shoot, execute by firing squad
fucilazi'one *nf* execution [by firing squad]
fu'cile *nm* rifle. ~ **ad aria compressa** air rifle
fucil'lata *nf* shot
fu'cina *nf* forge
'**fuco** *nm* kelp
'**fucsia** *nf* fuchsia
'**fuga** *nf* escape; (*perdita*) leak; (*di ciclisti*) breakaway; *Mus* fugue; **darsi alla** ~ take to flight; **mettere qcno in** ~ put sb to flight. ~ **di cervelli** brain drain. ~ **di gradini** flight of steps. ~ **di notizie** leak. ~ **romantica** elopement
fu'gace *a* fleeting
fug'gevole *a* short-lived
fuggi'asco, -a *nmf* fugitive
fuggi'fuggi *nm* stampede
fug'gire *vi* flee; ⟨*innamorati:*⟩ elope; *fig* fly
fuggi'tivo, -a *nmf* fugitive
'**fulcro** *nm* fulcrum
ful'gore *nm* splendour
fu'liggine *nf* soot
fuliggi'noso *a* sooty
full *nm inv* (*nel poker*) full house
fulmi'nante *a* (*sguardo*) withering; **è morto di leucemia** ~ he died very soon after contracting leukaemia
fulmi'nare *vt* strike by lightning; (*con sguardo*) look daggers at; (*con scarica elettrica*) electrocute

fulmi'narsi *vr* burn out

fulmi'nato *a* **rimanere ~** electrocute oneself

'fulmine *nm* lightning; **colpo di ~** *fig* love at first sight; **un ~ a ciel sereno** a bolt from the blue

ful'mineo *a* rapid; ‹*sguardo*› withering

'fulvo *a* tawny

fumai'olo *nm* funnel; (*di casa*) chimney

fu'mante *a* ‹*minestra, tazza*› steaming

fu'mare *vt/i* smoke; (*in ebollizione*) steam; **'vietato ~'** 'no smoking'

fu'mario *a* (*canna*) flue

fu'mata *nf* (*segnale*) smoke signal

fuma|'tore, -'trice *nmf* smoker; **non fumatori** ‹*Rail: scompartimento*› non-smoker, non-smoking

fu'metto *nm* comic strip; **fumetti** *pl* comics

'fumo *nm* smoke; (*vapore*) steam; *fig* hot air; **andare in ~** vanish; **vendere ~** put on an act; **cercava di vendere ~** it was all hot air; **fumi** *pl* (*industriali*) fumes; **sotto i fumi dell'alcol** under the influence of alcohol. **~ passivo** passive smoking

fu'mogeno *a* **cortina fumogena** smoke screen

fu'moso *a* ‹*ambiente*› smoky; ‹*discorso*› vague

funambo'lesco *a* acrobatic

fu'nambolo, -a *nmf* tightrope walker

'fune *nf* rope; (*cavo*) cable

'funebre *a* a funeral; (*cupa*) gloomy

fune'rale *nm* funeral

fu'nereo *a* ‹*aria*› funereal

fu'nesto *a* sad

'fungere *vi* **~ da** act as

'fungo *nm* mushroom; *Bot, Med* fungus; **funghi** *pl Bot* fungi. **~ atomico** mushroom cloud. **~ commestibile** edible mushroom

funico'lare *nf* funicular [railway]

funi'via *nf* cableway

funzio'nale *a* functional

funzionalità *nf* functionality

funziona'mento *nm* functioning

funzio'nare *vi* work, function; **~ da** (*fungere da*) act as

funzio'nario *nm* official. **~ statale** civil servant

funzi'one *nf* function; (*carica*) office; *Relig* service; **entrare in ~** take up office; **mettere in ~** ‹*motore*› start up; **vivere in ~ di** live for

fu'oco *nm* fire; (*fisica, fotografia*) focus; **far ~** fire; **dar ~ a** set fire to; **andare a ~** go up in flames; **prendere ~** catch fire; **a ~ vivo** ‹*cuocere*› on a high heat; **a ~ lento** ‹*cuocere*› on a low heat; **'vietato accendere fuochi'** 'no campfires'. **fuochi** *pl* **d'artificio** fireworks. **~ di paglia** nine-days' wonder. **fuochi** *pl* **pirotecnici** pyrotechnics

fuorché *prep* except

fu'ori *adv* out; (*all'esterno*) outside; (*all'aperto*) outdoors; **~!** *fam* get out!; **~ i soldi!** fork up!; **andare di ~** (*traboccare*)

spill over; **essere ~ di sé** be beside oneself; **essere in ~** (*sporgere*) stick out; **far ~** *fam* get rid of; **~ commercio** not for sale; **~ luogo** (*inopportuno*) out of place; **~ mano** out of the way; **~ moda** old-fashioned; **~ pasto** between meals; **~ pericolo** out of danger; **~ programma** unscheduled; **~ questione** out of the question; **~ uso** out of use ● *nm* outside

fuori'bordo *nm* speedboat (*with outboard motor*)

fuori'campo *a inv* ‹*Cinema: voce*› off-screen

fuori'classe *nmf inv* champion

fuoricombatti'mento *nm* knockout

fuorigi'oco *nm & adv* offside

fuori'legge *nmf* outlaw

fuori'pista *nm inv* (*sci*) off-piste skiing

fuori'serie *a* custom-made ● *nf Auto* custom-built model

fuori'strada *nm inv* off-road vehicle

fuoriu'scita *nf* (*perdita*) leak

fuoriu'scito, -a *nmf* exile

fuorvi'are *vt* lead astray ● *vi* go astray

furbacchi'one *nm* crafty old devil

fur'bastro, -a *nmf* crafty devil

furbe'ria *nf* cunning

fur'besco *a* sly, cunning

fur'bizia *nf* cunning

'furbo *a* sly, cunning; (*intelligente*) clever; (*astuto*) shrewd; **bravo ~!** nice one!; **fare il ~** try to be clever

fu'rente *a* furious

fur'fante *nm* scoundrel

furgon'cino *nm* delivery van

fur'gone *nm* van. **~ postale** mail van

'furia *nf* fury; (*fretta*) haste; **a ~ di** by dint of; **andare su tutte le furie** fly into a rage

furi'bondo *a* furious

furi'ere *nm Mil* quartermaster

furiosa'mente *adv* furiously

furi'oso *a* furious; ‹*litigio*› violent

fu'rore *nm* fury; (*veemenza*) frenzy; **far ~** be all the rage

furoreggi'are *vi* be a great success

furtiva'mente *adv* covertly

fur'tivo *a* furtive

'furto *nm* theft; **commettere un ~** steal; **è un ~!** *fig* it's daylight robbery!. **~ con scasso** burglary

'fusa *nfpl* **fare le ~** purr

fu'scello *nm* (*di legno*) twig; (*di paglia*) straw; **sei un ~** you're as light as a feather

fu'seaux *mpl* leggings

fu'sibile *nm* fuse

fu'silli *nmpl* pasta twirls

fusi'one *nf* fusion; *Comm* merger

'fuso *pp di* **fondere** ● *a* melted ● *nm* spindle; **a ~** spindle-shaped. **~ orario** time zone

fusoli'era *nf* fuselage

fu'stagno *nm* corduroy

fu'stella *nf* (*talloncino*) part of packaging on prescribed medicine returned by the pharmacist to claim a refund

fusti'gare *vt* flog; *fig* castigate

fu'stino *nm* (*di detersivo*) box

'fusto *nm* stem; (*tronco*) trunk; (*recipiente di metallo*) drum; (*di legno*) barrel. **~ del letto** bedstead

'futile *a* futile

futilità *nf* futility

futu'rismo *nm* futurism

futu'rista *nmf* futurist

fu'turo *a* & *nm* future; **predire il ~** tell fortunes, foretell. **~ anteriore** *Gram* future perfect

....

Gg

....

gabar'dine *nf* (*tessuto*) gabardine

gab'bare *vt* cheat

gab'barsi *vr* **~ di** make fun of

'gabbia *nf* cage; (*da imballaggio*) crate. **~ dell'ascensore** lift cage. **~ degli imputati** dock. **~ toracica** rib cage

gabbi'ano *nm* [sea]gull. **~ comune** common gull

gabi'netto *nm* (*di medico*) consulting room; *Pol* cabinet; (*toletta*) toilet; (*laboratorio*) laboratory; **andare al ~** go to the toilet. **gabinetti** *pl* **pubblici** public convenience

'Gabon *nm* Gabon

ga'elico *nm* Gaelic

'gaffa *nf* boathook

'gaffe *nf inv* blunder

gagli'ardo *a* vigorous

gai'ezza *nf* gaiety

'gaio *a* cheerful

'gala *nf* gala

ga'lante *a* gallant

galante'ria *nf* gallantry

galantu'omo *nm* (*pl* **galantuomini**) gentleman

ga'lassia *nf* galaxy

gala'teo *nm* [good] manners *pl*; (*trattato*) book of etiquette

gale'otto *nm* (*rematore*) galley-slave; (*condannato*) convict

ga'lera *nf* (*nave*) galley; *fam* slammer

'galla *nf Bot* gall; **a ~** afloat; **venire a ~** surface

galleggi'ante *a* floating ●*nm* craft; (*boa*) float

galleggi'are *vi* float

galle'ria *nf* (*traforo*) tunnel; (*d'arte*) gallery; *Theat* circle; (*arcata*) arcade; **prima ~** dress circle. **~ aerodinamica** wind tunnel. **~ d'arte** art gallery

'Galles *nm* Wales

gal'lese *a* Welsh ●*nm* Welshman; (*lingua*) Welsh ●*nf* Welshwoman

gal'letta *nf* cracker

gal'letto *nm* cockerel; **fare il ~** show off, impress the girls

'gallico *a* Gallic

gal'lina *nf* hen

galli'nella *nf* **~ d'acqua** moorhen

gal'lismo *nm* machismo

'gallo *nm* cock. **~ cedrone** capercaillie

gal'lone *nm* stripe; (*misura*) gallon

galop'pante *a* galloping

galop'pare *vi* gallop

galop'pino *nm* **fare da ~ a qcno** *fam* be sb's gopher

ga'loppo *nm* gallop; **al ~** at a gallop

galvaniz'zare *vt* galvanize

'gamba *nf* leg; (*di lettera*) stem; **a quattro gambe** on all fours; **darsela a gambe** take to one's heels; **essere in ~** (*essere forte*) be strong; (*capace*) be smart

gam'bale *nm* leg; **gambali** *pl* (*calzamaglia*) leggings

gamba'letto *nm* pop sock

gambe'retti *nmpl* shrimps. **~ in salsa rosa** prawn cocktail

'gambero *nm* prawn; (*di fiume*) crayfish

gambe'roni *nmpl* king prawns

'Gambia *nf* the Gambia

gambiz'zare *vt* kneecap

'gambo *nm* stem; (*di pianta*) stalk

ga'mella *nf* billy

game point *nm inv* game point

ga'mete *nm* gamete

'gamma *nf Mus* scale; *fig* range. **~ d'onda** waveband. **~ di prezzi** price range. **~ di prodotti** product range

ga'nascia *nf* jaw; **ganasce** *pl* **del freno** brake shoes

'gancio *nm* hook

'Gange *nm* Ganges

'ganghero *nm* **uscire dai gangheri** *fig* get into a temper

'gangster *nm inv* gangster

'gara *nf* competition; (*di velocità*) race; **fare a ~** compete. **~ d'appalto** call for tenders. **~ a cronometro** time-trial

ga'rage *nm inv* garage

gara'gista *nmf* garage owner

ga'rante *nmf* guarantor

garan'tire *vt* guarantee; (*rendersi garante*) vouch for; (*assicurare*) assure

garan'tirsi *vr* **~ contro, ~ da** guard against, insure against

garan'tismo *nm* protection of civil liberties

garan'tito *a* guaranteed

garan'zia *nf* guarantee; **in ~** under guarantee. **~ collaterale** collateral. **~ di rimborso** money-back guarantee. **~ a vita** lifetime guarantee

gar'bare *vi* like; **non mi garba** I don't like it
gar'bato *a* courteous
'garbo *nm* courtesy; (*grazia*) grace; **con ~** graciously
gar'buglio *nm* muddle
gar'denia *nf* gardenia
gareggi'are *vi* compete
garga'nella *nf* **a ~** from the bottle
garga'rismo *nm* gargle; **fare i gargarismi** gargle
ga'ritta *nf* sentry box
ga'rofano *nm* carnation; **chiodo di ~** clove
gar'retto *nm* shank
gar'rire *vi* chirp
gar'rotta *nf* garrotte
'garrulo *a* garrulous
'garza *nf* gauze
gar'zone *nm* boy. **~ di stalla** stable-boy
gas *nm inv* gas; **dare ~** *Auto* accelerate; **a ~** gas-fired; **a tutto ~** flat out. **~ asfissiante** poisonous gas. **~ esilarante** laughing gas. **~ lacrimogeno** tear gas. **~ nobile** inert gas. **~ propellente** propellant. **~ pl di scarico** exhaust fumes
gas'dotto *nm* natural gas pipeline
ga'solio *nm* diesel oil. **~ invernale** diesel containing anti-freeze
ga'sometro *nm* gasometer
gas'sare *vt* aerate; (*uccidere col gas*) gas
gas'sato *a* gassy
gas'soso, -a *a* gassy; ‹*bevanda*› fizzy ● *nf* lemonade
'gastrico *a* gastric
ga'strite *nf* gastritis
gastroente'rite *nf* gastro-enteritis
gastrono'mia *nf* gastronomy
gastro'nomico *a* gastronomic[al]
ga'stronomo, -a *nmf* gourmet
'gatta *nf* **una ~ da pelare** a headache
gatta'buia *nf hum* clink
gatta'iola *nf* catflap
gat'tino, -a *nmf* kitten
'gatto, -a *nmf* cat; **c'erano solo quattro gatti** there weren't many. **~ delle nevi** snowmobile. **~ a nove code** cat-o'-nine-tails. **~ selvatico** wildcat
gat'toni *adv* on all fours
gat'tuccio *nm* dogfish
gau'dente *a* pleasure-loving
'gaudio *nm* joy
ga'vetta *nf* mess tin; **fare la ~** rise through the ranks
gay *a inv* gay
ga'zebo *nm inv* gazebo
'gazza *nf* magpie
gaz'zarra *nf* racket; **fare ~** make a racket
gaz'zella *nf* gazelle; *Auto* police car
gaz'zetta *nf* gazette. **G~ Ufficiale** official journal
gazzet'tino *nm* (*titolo*) title page; (*rubrica*) page
gaz'zosa *nf* clear lemonade
GB *abbr* (**Gran Bretagna**) GB

'geco *nm* gecko
ge'lare *vt/i* freeze; **far ~ il sangue** make sb's blood run cold
ge'lata *nf* frost
gela'taio, -a *nmf* ice-cream seller ● *nm* (*negozio*) ice-cream shop
gelate'ria *nf* ice-cream parlour
gelati'era *nf* ice-cream maker
gela'tina *nf* gelatine; (*dolce*) jelly. **~ di frutta** fruit jelly
gelati'noso *a* gelatinous
ge'lato *a* frozen ● *nm* ice-cream. **~ alla vaniglia** vanilla ice-cream
'gelido *a* freezing
'gelo *nm* (*freddo intenso*) freezing cold; (*brina*) frost; *fig* chill
ge'lone *nm* chilblain
gelosa'mente *adv* jealously
gelo'sia *nf* jealousy
ge'loso *a* jealous
'gelso *nm* mulberry[-tree]
gelso'mino *nm* jasmine
gemel'laggio *nm* twinning
gemel'lare *vt* twin ● *a* twin
ge'mello, -a *a & nmf* twin; **gemelli** *pl* (*di polsino*) cuff-link; **Gemelli** *pl Astr* Gemini *sg*
'gemere *vi* groan
'gemito *nm* groan
'gemma *nf* gem; *Bot* bud
gemmolo'gia *nf* gemology
gen'darme *nm* gendarme
'gene *nm* gene
genealo'gia *nf* genealogy
genea'logico *a* genealogical
gene'rale[1] *a* general; **in ~** (*tutto sommato*) in general, on the whole; **parlando in ~** generally speaking
gene'rale[2] *nm Mil* general. **~ di divisione** major-general
generalità *nf inv* (*qualità*) generality, general nature; (*maggior parte*) majority; **~ pl** (*dati*) particulars *pl*
generaliz'zare *vt* generalize
generalizzazi'one *nf* generalization
general'mente *adv* generally
gene'rare *vt* give birth to; (*causare*) breed; *Techn* generate
genera'tore *nm Techn* generator
generazio'nale *a* generation
generazi'one *nf* generation; **di ~ in ~** from generation to generation
'genere *nm* kind; *Biol* genus; *Gram* gender; (*letterario, artistico*) genre; (*prodotto*) product; **cose del ~** such things; **il ~ umano** mankind; **in ~** generally. **generi** *pl* **alimentari** provisions. **generi** *pl* **di prima necessità** essentials
generica'mente *adv* generically
ge'nerico *a* generic; **medico ~** general practitioner
'genero *nm* son-in-law
generosa'mente *adv* generously
generosità *nf* generosity
gene'roso *a* generous
'genesi *nf* genesis

genetica'mente *adv* genetically

ge'netico, -a *a* genetic ● *nf* genetics

gene'tista *nmf* geneticist

gen'giva *nf* gum

geni'ale *a* ingenious; *(congeniale)* congenial

geni'ere *nm Mil* sapper

'genio *nm* genius; **andare a ~** be to one's taste. **~ civile** civil engineering. **~ incompreso** misunderstood genius. **~ [militare]** Engineers

geni'tale *a* genital ● *nm* **genitali** *pl* genitals

geni'tore *nm* parent

gen'naio *nm* January

geno'cidio *nm* genocide

'Genova *nf* Genoa

geno'vese *a* Genoese

gen'taglia *nf* rabble

'gente *nf* people *pl*

gen'tile *a* kind; **G~ Signore** *(in lettere)* Dear Sir

genti'lezza *nf* kindness; **per ~** *(per favore)* please

gentil'mente *adv* kindly

gentilu'omo *(pl* **gentilu'omini)** *nm* gentleman

genu'flettersi *vr* kneel down

genuina'mente *adv* genuinely

genu'ino *a* genuine; *⟨cibo, prodotto⟩* natural

genzi'ana *nf* gentian

geo'fisica *nf* geophysics

geo'fisico, -a *nmf* geophysician

geogra'fia *nf* geography

geo'grafico *a* geographical

ge'ografo, -a *nmf* geographer

geolo'gia *nf* geology

geo'logico *a* geological

ge'ologo, -a *nmf* geologist

ge'ometra *nmf* surveyor

geome'tria *nf* geometry

geometrica'mente *adv* geometrically

geo'metrico *a* geometric[al]

geopo'litico *a* geopolitical

geo'termico *a* geothermal, geothermic

ge'ranio *nm* geranium

gerar'chia *nf* hierarchy

gerarchica'mente *adv* hierarchically

ge'rarchico *a* hierarchic[al]

ger'billo *nm* gerbil

ge'rente *nm* manager ● *nf* manageress

'gergo *nm* jargon; *(dei giovani)* slang. **~ burocratico** bureaucratic jargon

geri'atra *nmf* geriatrician

geria'tria *nf* geriatrics

geri'atrico *a* geriatric

'gerla *nf* wicker basket

Ger'mania *nf* Germany. **~ [dell']Est** East Germany. **~ [dell']Ovest** West Germany

ger'manico *a* Germanic

'germe *nm* germ; *(fig: principio)* seed. **~ di grano** seedcorn

germogli'are *vi* sprout

ger'moglio *nm* sprout; **in ~** *Bot* sprouting. **germogli** *pl* **di soia** beansprouts

gero'glifico *nm* hieroglyph

geron'tologo, -a *nmf* gerontologist

ge'rundio *nm* gerund

Gerusa'lemme *nf* Jerusalem

ges'setto *nm* chalk

'gesso *nm* chalk; *(Med, scultura)* plaster

ge'staccio *nm* V-sign

gestazi'one *nf* gestation

gestico'lare *vi* gesticulate

gestio'nale *a* management *attrib*

gesti'one *nf* management. **~ aziendale** business management. **~ dei dati** *Comput* data management. **~ disco** *Comput* disk management. **~ dell'energia** energy resource management. **~ del flusso di cassa** cashflow management. **~ patrimoniale** financial mangement

ge'stire *vi* manage; **~ male** mishandle

ge'stirsi *vr* budget one's time and money

'gesto *nm* gesture; *(azione: pl f* **gesta)** deed

ge'store *nm* manager

Gesù *nm* Jesus. **~ bambino** baby Jesus

gesu'ita *nm* Jesuit

gesu'itico *a* Jesuit *attrib*

get'tare *vt* throw; *(scagliare)* fling; *(emettere)* spout; *Techn, fig* cast; **~ via** throw away

get'tarsi *vr* throw oneself; **~ in** *⟨fiume:⟩* flow into

get'tata *nf* throw; *Techn* casting

'gettito *nm* **~ fiscale** tax revenue

'getto *nm* throw; *(di liquidi, gas)* jet; **a ~ continuo** in a continuous stream; **di ~** straight off

getto'nato *a* *⟨canzone⟩* popular

get'tone *nm* token; *(per giochi)* counter

gettoni'era *nf* coin box

'geyser *nm inv* geyser

'Ghana *nm* Ghana

ghe'pardo *nm* cheetah

'gheppio *nm* kestrel

gher'mire *vt* grasp

'ghette *nfpl* *(per neonato)* leggings

ghettiz'zare *vt* ghettoize

'ghetto *nm* ghetto

ghiacci'aia *nf* glacier

ghiacci'aio *nm* glacier

ghiacci'are *vt/i* freeze

ghiacci'ato *a* frozen; *(freddissimo)* ice-cold

ghi'accio *nm* ice; *Auto* black ice. **~ secco** dry ice

ghiacci'olo *nm* icicle; *(gelato)* ice lolly

ghi'aia *nf* gravel

ghiai'oso *a* gritty

ghi'anda *nf* acorn

ghi'andola *nf* gland. **~ pituitaria** pituitary gland. **~ sudoripara** sweat gland. **~ surrenale** adrenal gland

ghigliot'tina *nf* guillotine

ghi'gnare *vi* sneer

'ghigno *nm* sneer

ghi'otto *a* greedy, gluttonous; *(appetitoso)* appetizing

ghiot'tone, -a *nmf* glutton

ghiottone'ria *nf* *(caratteristica)* gluttony; *(cibo)* tasty morsel

ghiri'goro *nm* flourish

ghir'landa *nf* (*corona*) wreath; (*di fiori*) garland

'ghiro *nm* dormouse; **dormire come un ~** sleep like a log

'ghisa *nf* cast iron

già *adv* already; (*un tempo*) formerly; **~!** indeed!; **~ da ieri** since yesterday

gi'acca *nf* jacket. **~ a vento** wind-cheater

giacché *conj* since

giac'cone *nm* jacket

gia'cenza *nf* **giacenze** *pl* **di magazzino** unsold stock

gia'cere *vi* lie

giaci'mento *nm* deposit. **~ di petrolio** oil deposit

gia'cinto *nm* hyacinth

gi'ada *nf* jade

giaggi'olo *nm* iris

giagu'aro *nm* jaguar

gial'lastro *a* yellowish

gi'allo *a & nm* yellow; [**libro**] **~** crime novel; [**film**] **~** thriller. **~ dell'uovo** egg yolk

Gia'maica *nf* Jamaica

giamai'cano, -a *a & nmf* Jamaican

Giap'pone *nm* Japan

giappo'nese *a & nmf* Japanese

gi'ara *nf* jar

giardi'naggio *nm* gardening

giardini'era *nf* **~ di verdure** *diced, mixed vegetables, cooked and pickled*

giardini'ere, -a *nmf* gardener ● *nf Auto* estate car; (*sottaceti*) pickles *pl*

giar'dino *nm* garden. **~ d'infanzia** kindergarten. **~ pensile** roof-garden. **giardini** *pl* **pubblici** park. **~ zoologico** zoo

giarretti'era *nf* garter

giavel'lotto *nm* javelin

gi'gante *nm* giant

gigan'tesco *a* gigantic

gigantogra'fia *nf* blow-up

'giglio *nm* lily

gilè *nm inv* waistcoat

gin *nm inv* gin

gin'cana *nf* gymkhana

ginecolo'gia *nf* gynaecology

gineco'logico *a* gynaecological

gine'cologo, -a *nmf* gynaecologist

gi'nepro *nm* juniper

gi'nestra *nf* broom

Gi'nevra *nf* Geneva

gingil'larsi *vr* fiddle; (*perder tempo*) potter

gin'gillo *nm* plaything; (*ninnolo*) knick-knack

gin'nasio *nm* (*scuola*) grammar school

gin'nasta *nmf* gymnast

gin'nastica *nf* gymnastics; (*esercizi*) exercises *pl*. **~ ritmica** eurhythmics

ginocchi'ata *nf* **prendere una ~** bang one's knee

ginocchi'era *nf* knee-pad

gi'nocchio *nm* (*pl m* **ginocchi** *o f* **ginocchia**) knee; **in ~** on one's knees, kneeling; **mettersi in ~** kneel down; (*per supplicare*) go down on one's knees; **al ~** ⟨*gonna*⟩ knee-length

ginocchi'oni *adv* kneeling

gio'care *vt/i* play; (*giocherellare*) toy; (*d'azzardo*) gamble; (*puntare*) stake; (*ingannare*) trick; **~ a calcio/a pallavolo** play football/volleyball; **~ d'astuzia** be crafty; **~ d'azzardo** gamble; **~ in Borsa** speculate on the Stock Exchange; **~ in casa** *Sport, fig* play on one's home ground, play at home

gio'carsi *vr* **~ la carriera** throw one's career away

gioca'|tore, -'trice *nmf* player; (*d'azzardo*) gambler

gio'cattolo *nm* toy

giocherel'lare *vi* toy; (*nervosamente*) fiddle

giocherel'lone *a* skittish

gi'oco *nm* game; (*di bambini, Techn*) play; (*d'azzardo*) gambling; (*scherzo*) joke; (*insieme di pezzi ecc*) set; **essere in ~** be at stake; **fare il doppio ~ con qcno** double-cross sb; **è un ~ da ragazzi** *fam* it's a cinch. **~ elettronico** computer game. **giochi** *pl* **della gioventù** nation-wide sports tournament for children. **~ dell'oca** snakes and ladders. **Giochi** *pl* **Olimpici** Olympic Games. **~ di parole** play on words. **~ di pazienza** game of manual skill. **~ di prestigio** conjuring trick. **~ di società** board game

giocoli'ere *nm* juggler

gio'coso *a* playful

gi'ogo *nm* yoke

gi'oia *nf* joy; (*gioiello*) jewel; (*appellativo*) sweetie

gioiel'leria *nf* jeweller's [shop]

gioi'elli *nmpl* jewellery

gioielli'ere, -a *nmf* jeweller; (*negozio*) jeweller's

gioi'ello *nm* jewel

gioiosa'mente *adv* joyfully

gioi'oso *a* joyful

gio'ire *vi* **~ per** rejoice at

Gior'dania *nf* Jordan

gior'dano, -a *a & nmf* Jordanian

giorna'laio, -a *nmf* newsagent, newsdealer

gior'nale *nm* [news]paper; (*diario*) journal. **~ di bordo** logbook. **~ gratuito** freebie. **~ del mattino** morning paper. **~ radio** radio news. **~ della sera** evening paper

giornali'ero *a* daily ● *nm* (*per sciare*) day pass

giorna'lino *nm* comic

giorna'lismo *nm* journalism

giorna'lista *nmf* journalist

giornal'mente *adv* daily

gior'nata *nf* day; **buona ~!** have a good day!; **in ~** today; **a ~** ⟨*essere pagato*⟩ on a day-to-day basis; **vivere alla ~** live from day to day. **~ lavorativa** working day

gi'orno *nm* day; **al ~** per day; **al ~ d'oggi** nowadays; **di ~** by day; **in pieno ~** in broad daylight; **un ~ sì, un ~ no** every other day; **~ per ~** day by day. **~ di chiusura** closing day. **~ fatidico** (*importante*) D-day. **~ feriale** weekday. **~ festivo** public holiday. **~ del giudizio** Judgement Day

gi'ostra nf merry-go-round

gio'strarsi vr manage

giova'mento nm trarre ~ **da** derive benefit from

gi'ovane a young; (giovanile) youthful ● nm youth, young man ● nf girl, young woman; **giovani** pl young people

giova'nile a youthful; (scritto) early

giova'notto nm young man

gio'vare vi ~ **a** be useful to; (far bene a) be good for

gio'varsi vr ~ **di** avail oneself of

giovedì nm inv Thursday; **di** ~ on Thursdays. ~ **grasso** last Thursday before Lent. ~ **santo** Maundy Thursday

Gi'ove nm Jupiter, Jove

gioventù nf youth; (i giovani) young people pl. ~ **bruciata** young drop-outs pl

giovi'ale a jovial

giovi'nezza nf youth

gi'rabile a (assegno) endorsable

gira'dischi nm inv record-player

gi'raffa nf giraffe; Cinema boom

gira'mondo nmf inv globetrotter; **da** ~ globetrotting

gi'randola nf (fuoco d'artificio) Catherine wheel; (giocattolo) windmill; (banderuola) weathercock

gi'rare vt turn; (andare intorno, visitare) go round; Comm endorse; Cinema shoot ● vi turn; (aerei, uccelli:) circle; (andare in giro) wander; ~ **sotto...** Comput run under...; **mi gira la testa** I feel dizzy; **far** ~ **la testa a qcno** make sb's head spin; **far** ~ **le scatole a qcno** fam drive sb round the twist; ~ **al largo** steer clear

girar'rosto nm spit

gi'rarsi vr turn [round]

gira'sole nm sunflower

gi'rata nf turn; Comm endorsement; (in macchina ecc) ride; **fare una** ~ (a piedi) go for a walk; (in macchina) go for a ride

gira'volta nf spin; fig U-turn

gi'rello nm (per bambini) babywalker; Culin topside

gi'revole a revolving; **ponte** ~ swing bridge

gi'rino nm tadpole

'giro nm turn; (circolo) circle; (percorso) round; (viaggio) tour; (passeggiata) short walk; (in macchina) drive; (in bicicletta) ride; (circolazione di denaro) circulation; **andare a fare un** ~ (a piedi) go for a stroll; (in macchina) go for a drive; (in bicicletta) go for a cycle ride; **fare il** ~ **di** go round; **nel** ~ **di un mese/anno** within a month/year; **prendere in** ~ **qcno** pull sb's leg; **sentir dire in** ~ **qcsa** hear sth on the grapevine; **a** ~ **di posta** by return mail. ~ **d'affari** Comm turnover. ~ **in barca** boat trip. ~ **guidato** guided tour. ~ [**della**] **manica** armhole. **giri** pl **al minuto** revs per minute, rpm. ~ **d'onore** lap of honour. **giri** pl **di parole** beating about the bush. ~ **di pista** lap. ~ **di prova** trial lap. ~ **turistico** sightseeing tour. ~ **vita** waist measurement

giro'collo nm choker; **a** ~ roundneck

gi'rone nm round. ~ **di andata** first half of the season. ~ **di ritorno** second half of the season

gironzo'lare vi wander about

giro'tondo nm ring-a-ring-o'-roses

girova'gare vi wander about

gi'rovago nm wanderer

'gita nf trip; **andare in** ~ go on a trip. ~ **organizzata** package tour. ~ **in pullman** coach trip. ~ **scolastica** school trip

gi'tano, -a nmf gipsy

gi'tante nmf tripper

giù adv down; (sotto) below; (dabbasso) downstairs; **a testa in** ~ (a capofitto) headlong; **essere** ~ (di morale) be down, be depressed; (di salute) be run down; ~ **di corda** down; ~ **di lì, su per** ~ more or less; **non andare** ~ **a qcno** stick in sb's craw

gi'ubba nf jacket; Mil tunic

giub'botto nm bomber jacket, jerkin. ~ **antiproiettile** bulletproof vest. ~ **di pelle** leather jacket. ~ **di salvataggio** lifejacket

gi'ubilo nm rejoicing

giudi'care vt judge; (ritenere) consider

gi'udice nm judge. ~ **conciliatore** justice of the peace. ~ **di gara** umpire. ~ **di linea** linesman

giudizi'ario a legal, judicial

giu'dizio nm judg[e]ment; (opinione) opinion; (senno) wisdom; (processo) trial; (sentenza) sentence; **mettere** ~ become wise. ~ **universale** Last Judgement

giudizi'oso a sensible

gi'ugno nm June

giugu'lare nf jugular

giul'lare nm jester

giu'menta nf mare

giun'chiglia nf jonquil

gi'unco nm reed

gi'ungere vi arrive; ~ **a** (riuscire) succeed in; **mi giunge nuovo** it's news to me ● vt (unire) join

gi'ungla nf jungle. ~ **d'asfalto** concrete jungle

gi'unta nf addition; Mil junta; **per** ~ in addition. ~ **comunale** district council. ~ [**militare**] [military] junta

gi'unto pp di **giungere** ● nm Mech joint. ~ **sferico** ball-and-socket joint

giun'tura nf joint

giuo'care, giu'oco = **giocare, gioco**

giura'mento nm oath; **sotto** ~ under oath; **prestare** ~ take the oath. ~ **d'Ippocrate** Hippocratic oath

giu'rare vt/i swear

giu'rato, -a a sworn ● nmf juror

giu'ria nf jury

giu'ridico a legal

giurisdizi'one nf jurisdiction

giurispru'denza nf jurisprudence

giu'rista nmf jurist

giu'stezza nf justness

giustifi'care vt justify

giustifi'carsi *vr* justify oneself; ~ **di** *o* **per qcsa** give an explanation for sth

giustificazi'one *nf* justification

giu'stizia *nf* justice; **farsi** ~ **da sé** take the law into one's own hands

giustizi'are *vt* execute

giustizi'ere *nm* executioner

gi'usto *a* just, fair; *(adatto)* right; *(esatto)* exact ● *nm (uomo retto)* just man; *(cosa giusta)* right ● *adv* exactly; ~ **ora** just now

glaci'ale *a* glacial

gladia'tore *nm* gladiator

gla'diolo *nm* gladiolus

'glassa *nf Culin* icing

glau'coma *nm* glaucoma

gli *def art m pl* the; *vedi* **il** ● *pers pron (a lui)* [to] him; *(a esso)* [to] it; *(a loro)* [to] them; **non** ~ **credo** I don't believe him/them

glice'mia *nf* glycaemia

glice'rina *nf* glycerine

'glicine *nm* wisteria

gli'elo *pron (a lui)* to him; *(a lei)* to her; *(a loro)* to them; *(a Lei, forma di cortesia)* to you; ~ **prestai** I lent it to him/her etc; **gliel'ho chiesto** I've asked him/her etc

glie'ne *pron (di ciò)* of it; ~ **ho dato un po'** I gave him/her/them/you some [of it]; ~ **ho parlato** I've talked to him/her etc about it

glis'sare *vi* avoid the issue; ~ **su qcsa** skate over sth

glo'bale *a* global; *fig* overall

global'mente *adv* globally

'globo *nm* globe. ~ **oculare** eyeball. ~ **terrestre** globe

'globulo *nm* globule; *Med* corpuscle. ~ **bianco** white cell, white corpuscle. ~ **rosso** red cell, red corpuscle

'gloria *nf* glory

glori'arsi *vr* ~ **di** be proud of

glorifi'care *vt* glorify

gloriosa'mente *adv* gloriously

glori'oso *a* glorious

'glossa *nf* gloss

glos'sario *nm* glossary

glottolo'gia *nf* linguistics

glu'cosio *nm* glucose

glutam'mato *nm* ~ **di sodio** monosodium glutamate

'gluteo *nm* buttock

'gnocchi *nmpl small flour and potato dumplings*

'gnomo *nm* gnome

'gnorri *nm* **fare lo** ~ play dumb

goal *nm inv* goal; **fare un** ~ score *or* get a goal

'gobba *nf* hump

'gobbo, -a *a* hunchbacked ● *nmf* hunchback

goc'cetto *nm* pick-me-up

'goccia *nf* drop; *(di sudore)* bead; **è stata l'ultima** ~ it was the last straw. ~ **di pioggia** raindrop. ~ **di rugiada** dewdrop

goccio'lare *vi* drip

goccio'lio *nm* dripping

go'dere *vi (sl: sessualmente)* come; ~ **di qcsa** enjoy sth, make the most of sth

go'dersi *vr* ~ **qcsa** enjoy sth; **godersela** have a good time

godi'mento *nm* enjoyment

gof'faggine *nf* awkwardness

goffa'mente *adv* awkwardly

'goffo *a* awkward

go-'kart *nm inv* go-kart

'gola *nf* throat; *(ingordigia)* gluttony; *Geog* gorge; *(di camino)* flue; **avere mal di** ~ have a sore throat; **far** ~ **a qcno** tempt sb

go'letta *nf* schooner

golf *nm inv* jersey; *Sport* golf

gol'fino *nm* jumper

'golfo *nm* gulf

goli'ardico *a* student *attrib*

golosità *nf inv* greediness; *(cibo)* tasty morsel

go'loso *a* greedy

'golpe *nm inv* coup

go'mena *nf* painter

gomi'tata *nf* nudge; **dare una** ~ **a qcno** elbow sb

'gomito *nm* elbow; **alzare il** ~ *(fam: bere)* raise one's elbow; ~ **a** ~ *‹lavorare›* side by side

go'mitolo *nm* ball

'gomma *nf* rubber; *(colla, da masticare)* gum; *(pneumatico)* tyre; **avere una** ~ **a terra** have a flat. ~ **arabica** gum arabic. ~ **da masticare** chewing gum. ~ **di scorta** spare tyre

gommapi'uma® *nf* foam rubber

gom'mino *nm* rubber tip

gom'mista *nm* tyre specialist

gom'mone *nm* [rubber] dinghy

gom'moso *a* chewy

'gondola *nf* gondola

gondoli'ere *nm* gondolier

gonfa'lone *nm* banner

gonfi'abile *a* inflatable

gonfi'are *vi* swell ● *vt* blow up; pump up *‹pneumatico›*; *(esagerare)* exaggerate

gonfi'arsi *vr* swell; *‹acque:›* rise

'gonfio *a* swollen; *‹pneumatico›* inflated

gonfi'ore *nm* swelling

gongo'lante *a* overjoyed

gongo'lare *vi* be overjoyed

goni'ometro *nm* protractor

'gonna *nf* skirt. ~ **pantalone** culottes *pl*. ~ **a pieghe** pleated skirt. ~ **a portafoglio** wrapover skirt

gonor'rea *nf* gonorrh[o]ea

'gonzo *nm* simpleton

gorgheggi'are *vi* warble

gor'gheggio *nm* warble

'gorgo *nm* whirlpool

gorgogli'ante *a* burbling, gurgling

gorgogli'are *vi* gurgle

gor'goglio *nm* burble

gorgon'zola *nf* strong, soft blue cheese

go'rilla *nm inv* gorilla; *(guardia del corpo)* bodyguard, minder

'gota *nf* cheek

'gotico *a & nm* Gothic

'gotta *nf* gout

gover'nante *nf* housekeeper

gover'nare *vt* govern; (*dominare*) rule; (*dirigere*) manage; (*curare*) look after

governa'tivo *a* government

governa'tore *nm* governor

go'verno *nm* government; (*dominio*) rule; **al ~** in power. **~ ombra** shadow government

'gozzo *nm* (*di animale*) crop; *Med* goitre; *fam* throat

gozzovigli'are *vi* eat, drink and be merry

gracchi'are *vi* caw; (*fig: persona:*) screech

'gracchio *nm* caw

graci'dare *vi* croak

'gracile *a* delicate

gra'dasso *nm* braggart

gradata'mente *adv* gradually

gradazi'one *nf* gradation. **~ alcoolica** alcohol[ic] content

gra'devole *a* agreeable

gradevol'mente *adv* pleasantly, agreeably

gradi'ente *nm* gradient

gradi'mento *nm* liking; **indice di ~** *Radio, TV* popularity rating; **non è di mio ~** it's not to my liking

gradi'nata *nf* flight of steps; (*di stadio, teatro*) tiers *pl*

gra'dino *nm* step

gra'dire *vt* like; (*desiderare*) wish

gra'dito *a* pleasant; (*bene accetto*) welcome

'grado *nm* degree; (*rango*) rank; **di buon ~** willingly; **essere in ~ di fare qcsa** be in a position to do sth; (*essere capace a*) be able to do sth; **per gradi** (*procedere*) by degrees

gradu'ale *a* gradual

gradual'mente *adv* gradually

gradu'are *vt* graduate

gradu'ato *a* graded; (*provvisto di scala graduata*) graduated ● *nm Mil* noncommissioned officer

gradua'toria *nf* list

graduazi'one *nf* graduation

'graffa *nf* clip; (*segno grafico*) brace

graf'fetta *nf* staple

graffi'are *vt* scratch

graffia'tura *nf* scratch

'graffio *nm* scratch

gra'fia *nf* [hand]writing; (*ortografia*) spelling

'grafica *nf* graphics; (*disciplina*) graphics, graphic design. **~ pubblicitaria** commercial art

grafica'mente *adv* in graphics, graphically

'grafico *a* graphic ● *nm* graph; (*persona*) graphic designer. **~ a torta** pie chart

gra'fite *nf* graphite

gra'fologo, -a *nmf* graphologist

gra'migna *nf* weed

gram'matica *nf* grammar

grammati'cale *a* grammatical

grammatical'mente *adv* grammatically

gram'matico *nm* grammarian

'grammo *nm* gram[me]

gram'mofono *nm* gramophone

gran *vedi* **grande**

'grana *nf* grain; (*formaggio*) parmesan; (*fam: seccatura*) trouble; (*fam: soldi*) readies *pl*

gra'naio *nm* barn

gra'nata *nf Mil* grenade; (*frutto*) pomegranate

granati'ere *nm Mil* grenadier

gra'nato *nm* garnet

Gran Bre'tagna *nf* Great Britain

gran'cassa *nf* bass drum

gran'cevola *nf* spiny spider crab

'granchio *nm* crab; (*fig: errore*) blunder; **prendere un ~** make a blunder

grandango'lare *nm* wide-angle lens

gran'dangolo *nm* wide-angle lens

'grande (*a volte* **gran**) *a* (*ampio*) large; (*grosso*) big; (*alto*) tall; (*largo*) wide; (*fig: senso morale*) great; (*grandioso*) grand; (*adulto*) grown-up; **~ e grosso** beefy; **ho una gran fame** I'm very hungry; **fa un gran caldo** it is very hot; **in ~** on a large scale; **in gran parte** to a great extent; **non è un gran che** it is nothing much; **di gran carriera** hotfoot; **un gran ballo** a grand ball; **alla ~** *sl* in a big way ● *nmf* (*persona adulta*) grown-up; (*persona eminente*) great man/woman

grandeggi'are *vi* **~ su** tower over; (*darsi arie*) show off

gran'dezza *nf* greatness; (*ampiezza*) largeness; (*larghezza*) width, breadth; (*dimensione*) size; (*fasto*) grandeur; (*prodigalità*) lavishness; **a ~ naturale** life-size

grandi'nare *vi* hail; **grandina** it's hailing

'grandine *nf* hail

grandiosità *nf* grandeur

grandi'oso *a* grand

gran'duca *nm* grand duke

grandu'cato *nm* grand duchy

grandu'chessa *nf* grand duchess

gra'nello *nm* grain; (*di frutta*) pip

gra'nita *nf* crushed ice drink

gra'nito *nm* granite

'grano *nm* grain; (*frumento*) wheat. **~ di pepe** peppercorn. **~ saraceno** buckwheat

gran[o]'turco *nm* corn

'granulo *nm* granule

'grappa *nf* very strong, clear spirit distilled from grapes; (*morsa*) cramp

'grappolo *nm* bunch. **~ d'uva** bunch of grapes

gras'setto *nm* bold [type]

gras'sezza *nf* fatness; (*untuosità*) greasiness

'grasso *a* fat; (*cibo*) fatty; (*unto*) greasy; (*terreno*) rich; (*grossolano*) coarse ● *nm* fat; (*sostanza*) grease; **a basso contenuto di grassi** low-fat; **senza grassi** nonfat, fat-free

gras'soccio *a* plump

gras'sone, -a *nmf* dumpling

'grata *nf* grating

gra'tella *nf Culin* grill

gra'ticcio *nm* (*per piante*) trellis; (*stuoia*) rush matting

gra'ticola *nf Culin* grill

gra'tifica *nf* bonus

gratificazi'one *nf* satisfaction

gra'tin *nm inv* gratin. ~ **di patate** *potatoes with grated cheese*

grati'nare *vt* cook au gratin

grati'nato *a* au gratin

'gratis *adv* free

grati'tudine *nf* gratitude

'grato *a* grateful; (*gradito*) pleasant

gratta'capo *nm* trouble

grattaci'elo *nm* skyscraper

grat'tare *vt* scratch; (*raschiare*) scrape; (*grattugiare*) grate; (*fam: rubare*) pinch ● *vi* grate

grat'tarsi *vr* scratch oneself

grat'tugia *nf* grater

grattugi'are *vt* grate

gratuita'mente *adv* free [of charge]

gra'tuito *a* free [of charge]; (*ingiustificato*) gratuitous

gra'vare *vt* burden ● *vi* ~ **su** weigh on

'grave *a* (*pesante*) heavy; (*serio*) serious; (*difficile*) hard; ⟨*voce, suono*⟩ low; (*fonetica*) grave; **essere** ~ (*gravemente ammalato*) be seriously ill

grave'mente *adv* seriously, gravely

gravi'danza *nf* pregnancy. ~ **extrauterina** ectopic pregnancy. ~ **indesiderata** unwanted pregnancy

'gravido *a* pregnant

gravità *nf* seriousness; *Phys* gravity

gravi'tare *vi* gravitate

gra'voso *a* onerous

'grazia *nf* grace; (*favore*) favour; *Jur* pardon; **entrare nelle grazie di qcno** get into sb's good books; **ministero di** ~ **e giustizia** Ministry of Justice

grazi'are *vt* pardon

'grazie *int* thank you!, thanks!; ~ **mille!** many thanks!, thanks a lot!; ~ **a Dio/al cielo!** thank God/goodness!; ~ **a** thanks to

grazi'oso *a* charming; (*carino*) pretty

'Grecia *nf* Greece

'greco, -a *a & nmf* Greek; ~ **antico** (*lingua*) classical Greek

gre'gario *a* gregarious ● *nm* (*ciclismo*) supporting rider

'gregge *nm* flock

'greggio *a* raw ● *nm* (*petrolio*) crude [oil]

grembi'ale, grembi'ule *nm* apron

'grembo *nm* lap; (*utero*) womb; *fig* bosom

gre'mire *vt* pack

gre'mirsi *vr* become crowded (**di** with)

gre'mito *a* packed

'gretto *a* stingy; (*di vedute ristrette*) narrow-minded

'greve *a* heavy

'grezzo *a* = **greggio**

gri'dare *vi* shout; (*di dolore*) scream; ⟨*animale:*⟩ cry ● *vt* shout; ~ **qcsa ai quattro venti** shout sth from the rooftops

'grido *nm* (*pl m* **gridi** *o pl f* **grida**) shout, cry; (*di animale*) cry; **all'ultimo** ~ the latest fashion; **scrittore di** ~ celebrated writer. ~ **d'aiuto** cry for help. ~ **di battaglia** battle cry

'grigio *a & nm* grey. ~ **perla** pearl grey

'griglia *nf* grill; **alla** ~ grilled; **cuocere alla** ~ grill

grigli'ata *nf* barbecue. ~ **mista** mixed grill. ~ **di pesce** grilled fish

gril'letto *nm* trigger

'grillo *nm* cricket; (*fig: capriccio*) whim

grimal'dello *nm* picklock

'grinfia *nf fig* clutch

'grinta *nf* grit

grin'toso *a* determined

'grinza *nf* wrinkle; (*di stoffa*) crease; **non fare una** ~ ⟨*fig: ragionamento:*⟩ be flawless

grip'pare *vi Mech* seize up

gri'sou *nm* firedamp

gris'sino *nm* bread-stick

'grizzly *nm inv* grizzly

groenlan'dese *a* of Greenland ● *nmf* Greenlander

Groen'landia *nf* Greenland

'groggy *a inv* punch-drunk

'gronda *nf* eaves *pl*

gron'daia *nf* gutter

gron'dare *vi* pour; (*essere bagnato fradicio*) be dripping wet

'groppa *nf* back

'groppo *nm* knot; **avere un** ~ **alla gola** have a lump in one's throat

gros'sezza *nf* size; (*spessore*) thickness

gros'sista *nmf* wholesaler

'grosso *a* big, large; (*spesso*) thick; (*grossolano*) coarse; (*grave*) serious ● *nm* big part; (*massa*) bulk; **farla grossa** do a stupid thing

grossolanità *nf inv* (*qualità*) coarseness; (*di errore*) grossness; (*gesto*) boorishness

grosso'lano *a* coarse; ⟨*errore*⟩ gross; ⟨*comportamento*⟩ boorish

grosso'modo *adv* roughly

'grotta *nf* cave, grotto

grot'tesco *a & nm* grotesque

grovi'era *nmf* Gruyère

gro'viglio *nm* tangle; *fig* muddle

gru *nf inv* (*uccello, edilizia*) crane

'gruccia *nf* (*stampella*) crutch; (*per vestito*) hanger

gru'gnire *vi* grunt

gru'gnito *nm* grunt

'grugno *nm* snout

'grullo *a* silly

'grumo *nm* clot; (*di farina ecc*) lump

gru'moso *a* lumpy

grunge *nm inv* grunge

'gruppo *nm* group; (*comitiva*) party. ~ **pop** pop group. ~ **sanguigno** blood group

gruvi'era *nmf* = **groviera**

'gruzzolo *nm* nest-egg

guada'gnare *vt* earn; gain ⟨*tempo, forza ecc*⟩

guada'gnarsi *vr* ~ **da vivere** earn a living

gua'dagno *nm* gain; (*profitto*) profit; (*entrate*) earnings *pl*. **guadagni** *pl* **illeciti** ill-gotten gains

gu'ado *nm* ford; **passare a** ~ ford

gua'ina *nf* sheath; (*busto*) girdle

gu'aio *nm* trouble; **che** ~! that's just brilliant!; **essere nei guai** be in a fix; **guai a te se lo tocchi!** don't you dare touch it!

gua'ire *vi* yelp

gua'ito *nm* yelp; **guaiti** *pl* yelping

gu'ancia *nf* cheek

guanci'ale *nm* pillow

gu'anto *nm* glove. ~ **da forno** oven glove. ~ **di spugna** face cloth

guan'tone *nm* mitt. **guantoni** *pl* [da boxe] boxing gloves

guarda'boschi *nm inv* forester

guarda'caccia *nm inv* gamekeeper

guarda'coste *nm inv* coastguard

guarda'linee *nm inv* Sport linesman

guarda'macchine *nmf* car-park attendant

guarda'parco *nm inv* park ranger

guar'dare *vt* look at; (*osservare*) watch; (*badare a*) look after; ⟨*finestra:*⟩ look out on; ~ **la televisione** watch television ● *vi* look; (*essere orientato verso*) face; ~ **in su** look up

guarda'roba *nm inv* wardrobe; (*di locale pubblico*) cloakroom

guardarobi'ere, -a *nmf* cloakroom attendant

guar'darsi *vr* look at oneself; ~ **da** beware of; (*astenersi*) refrain from

gu'ardia *nf* guard; (*poliziotto*) policeman; (*vigilanza*) watch; **essere di** ~ be on guard; ⟨*medico:*⟩ be on duty; **fare la** ~ **a** keep guard over; **mettere in** ~ **qcno** warn sb; **stare in** ~ be on one's guard. ~ **carceraria** prison warder. ~ **del corpo** bodyguard, minder. ~ **di finanza** *body responsible for border control and for investigating fraud*. ~ **forestale** forest ranger. ~ **medica** duty doctor

guardi'ano, -a *nmf* caretaker. ~ **notturno** night watchman

guar'dingo *a* cautious

guardi'ola *nf* gatekeeper's lodge

guarigi'one *nf* recovery

gua'rire *vt* cure ● *vi* recover; ⟨*ferita:*⟩ heal [up]

gua'rito *a* cured

guari|'tore, -'trice *nmf* healer

guarnigi'one *nf* garrison

guar'nire *vt* trim; *Culin* garnish

guarnizi'one *nf* trimming; *Culin* garnish; *Mech* gasket. ~ **del freno** brake lining

guasta'feste *nmf inv* spoilsport

gua'stare *vt* spoil; (*rovinare*) ruin; break ⟨*meccanismo*⟩

gua'starsi *vr* spoil; (*andare a male*) go bad; ⟨*tempo:*⟩ change for the worse; ⟨*meccanismo:*⟩ break down

gu'asto *a* broken; ⟨*ascensore, telefono*⟩ out of order; ⟨*auto*⟩ broken down; ⟨*cibo, dente*⟩ bad ● *nm* breakdown; (*danno*) damage; **ho un** ~ **alla macchina** my car's not working. ~ **al motore** engine failure

guazza'buglio *nm* muddle

guaz'zare *vi* wallow

gu'ercio *a* cross-eyed

gu'erra *nf* war; (*tecnica bellica*) warfare. ~ **batteriologica** germ warfare. ~ **biologica** biological warfare. ~ **civile** civil war. ~ **fredda** Cold War. ~ **del Golfo** Gulf War. ~ **lampo** blitzkrieg. ~ **mondiale** world war. ~ **dei prezzi** price war. ~ **di secessione** American Civil War

guerrafon'daio, -a *nmf* warmonger

guerreggi'are *vi* wage war

guer'resco *a* (*di guerra*) war; (*bellicoso*) warlike

guerri'ero *nm* warrior

guer'riglia *nf* guerrilla warfare

guerrigli'ero, -a *nmf* guerrilla

'gufo *nm* owl

'guglia *nf* spire

gu'ida *nf* guide; (*direzione*) guidance; (*comando*) leadership; (*elenco*) directory; *Auto* driving; (*tappeto*) runner; **chi era alla** ~**?** who was driving?; **essere alla** ~ **di** *fig* be the head of; **fare da** ~ be a guide (**a** to). ~ **commerciale** trade directory. ~ **a destra** right-hand drive. ~ **a sinistra** left-hand drive. ~ **telefonica** phone book, telephone directory. ~ **turistica** tourist guide

gui'dare *vt* guide; *Auto* drive; steer ⟨*nave*⟩; ~ **a passo d'uomo** drive at walking speed

guida|'tore, -'trice *nmf* driver. ~ **della domenica** Sunday driver

guin'zaglio *nm* leash

gu'isa *nf* **a** ~ **di** like

guiz'zare *vi* dart; ⟨*luce:*⟩ flash

gu'izzo *nm* dart; (*di luce*) flash

'gulag *nm inv* Gulag

'gulasch *nm inv* goulash

'guru *nm inv* high priest

'guscio *nm* shell

gu'stare *vt* taste ● *vi* like

'gusto *nm* taste; (*piacere*) liking; **mangiare di** ~ eat heartily; **prenderci** ~ come to enjoy it, develop a taste for it; **al** ~ **di pistacchio** pistachio flavoured. **buon** ~ good taste

gu'stoso *a* tasty; *fig* delightful

guttu'rale *a* guttural

Hh

'habitat nm inv habitat
habitué nmf inv regular [customer]
'hacker nmf inv Comput hacker
Ha'iti nf Haiti
haiti'ano, -a a & nmf Haitian
hall nf inv foyer; (di stazione) concourse
ham'burger nm inv hamburger
'handicap nm inv handicap
handicap'pare vt handicap
handicap'pato, -a a disabled ● nmf disabled person. **~ mentale** mentally handicapped person
'hangar nm inv hangar
hard[-core] a hard core
hard disk nm inv hard disk
hard rock nm hard rock
'hardware nm inv Comput hardware
'harem nm inv harem
'hascish nm hashish
hawai'ano, -a a & nmf Hawaiian

Ha'waii nfpl **le ~** Hawaii
'heavy 'metal nm Mus heavy metal
henné nm henna
'herpes nm inv herpes; (su labbra) cold sore. **~ zoster** shingles
hi-fi nm inv hi-fi
high tech nf high tech
Hima'laia nm Himalayas pl
'hinterland nm inv hinterland
'hippy a & nmf hippy
'hit parade nf hit parade, charts pl
HIV nm HIV
'hockey nm hockey. **~ su ghiaccio** ice hockey. **~ su prato** field hockey
'holding nf inv holding company
hollywoodi'ano a Hollywood
Hong Kong nf Hong Kong
'hostess nf inv stewardess
hot dog nm inv hot dog
ho'tel nm inv hotel
'humus nm humus

Ii

i def art mpl the; vedi **il**
i'ato nm hiatus
i'berico a Iberian
iber'nare vi hibernate
ibernazi'one nf hibernation
i'bisco nm hibiscus
ibri'dare vt interbreed
ibridazi'one nf interbreeding
'ibrido a & nm hybrid
'iceberg nm inv iceberg; **la punta dell'~** fig the tip of the iceberg
i'cona nf icon
icono'clasta a & nmf iconoclast
icono'clastico a iconoclastic
Id'dio nm God
i'dea nf idea; (opinione) opinion; (ideale) ideal; (indizio) inkling; (piccola quantità) hint; (intenzione) intention; **cambiare ~** change one's mind; **neanche per ~!** not on your life!; **chiarirsi le idee** get one's ideas straight; **dare l'~ di...** give the impression that...; **essere dell'~ che...** be of the opinion that...; **non ne ho ~!** I've no idea!. **~ fissa** obsession
ide'ale a & nm ideal

idea'lista nmf idealist
idealiz'zare vt idealize
ide'are vt conceive
idea'|tore, -'trice nmf originator
'idem adv the same
identica'mente adv identically
i'dentico a identical
identifi'cabile a identifiable
identifi'care vt identify
identificazi'one nf identification
identi'kit[R] nm inv identikit
identità nf inv identity
ideo'gramma nm ideogram
ideolo'gia nf ideology
ideologica'mente adv ideologically
ideo'logico a ideological
idillica'mente adv idyllically
i'dillico a idyllic
i'dillio nm idyll
idi'oma nm language
idio'matico a idiomatic; **espressione idiomatica** idiom, idiomatic expression
idiosincra'sia nf fig aversion; Med allergy
idi'ota a idiotic ● nmf idiot
idio'zia nf idiocy; **dire/fare un'~** do/say

something stupid; **dire idiozie** talk nonsense; **non fare idiozie!** don't act daft!
idola'trare *vt* worship
idoleggi'are *vt* idolize
'**idolo** *nm* idol
idoneità *nf* suitability; *Mil* fitness; **esame di ~** qualifying examination
i'**doneo** *a* ~ **a** suitable for; *Mil* fit for
i'**drante** *nm* hydrant; (*tubo*) hose
idra'**tante** *a* ⟨*crema*⟩ moisturizing
idra'**tare** *vt* hydrate; ⟨*cosmetico:*⟩ moisturize
idratazi'**one** *nf* moisturizing
i'**draulico** *a* hydraulic ● *nm* plumber
'**idrico** *a* water *attrib*
idrocar'**buro** *nm* hydrocarbon
idroelettricità *nf* hydroelectricity
idroe'lettrico *a* hydroelectric
i'**drofilo** *a* **cotone** ~ cotton wool, absorbent cotton *Am*
idrofo'**bia** *nf* rabies *sg*
i'**drofobo** *a* rabid; *fig* furious
i'**drofugo** *a* water-repellent
i'**drogeno** *nm* hydrogen
idrogra'**fia** *nf* hydrography
i'**drolisi** *nf* hydrolysis
idromas'**saggio** *nm* (*sistema*) whirlpool bath
idro'**mele** *nm* mead
idrorepel'**lente** *a* & *nm* water-repellent
idroso'**lubile** *a* water-soluble
idrotera'**pia** *nf* hydrotherapy
idrovo'**lante** *nm* seaplane
i'**druro** *nm* hydride
i'**ella** *nf fam* bad luck; **portare** ~ be bad luck
iel'**lato** *a fam* jinxed, plagued by bad luck
i'**ena** *nf* hyena
i'**eri** *adv* yesterday; ~ **l'altro, l'altro** ~ the day before yesterday; **il giornale di** ~ yesterday's paper; ~ **mattina** yesterday morning; ~ **notte** last night; ~ **pomeriggio** yesterday afternoon; ~ **sera** yesterday evening
ietta|'**tore, -trice** *nmf* jinx
ietta'**tura** *nf* (*sfortuna*) bad luck
igi'**ene** *nf* hygiene; **ufficio d'**~ ≈ Public Health Service. ~ **mentale** mental health. ~ **personale** personal hygiene. ~ **pubblica** public health
igienica'**mente** *adv* hygienically
igi'**enico** *a* hygienic
igie'**nista** *nmf* hygienist
ig'**loo** *nm inv* igloo
i'**gname** *nm* yam
i'**gnaro** *a* unaware
i'**gnifugo** *a* flame-retardant
i'**gnobile** *a* despicable
ignobil'**mente** *adv* despicably
igno'**minia** *nf* disgrace
igno'**rante** *a* ignorant ● *nmf* ignoramus
igno'**ranza** *nf* ignorance; ~ **crassa** crass ignorance
igno'**rare** *vt* (*non sapere*) be unaware of; (*trascurare*) ignore; **essere ignorato** go unheeded
i'**gnoto** *a* unknown
i'**guana** *nf* iguana

il *def art m* the; **il latte fa bene** milk is good for you; **il signor Magnetti** Mr Magnetti; **il dottor Piazza** Doctor Piazza; **ha il naso grosso** he's got a big nose; **ha gli occhi azzurri** he's got blue eyes; **mettiti il cappello** put your hat on; **il lunedì** on Mondays; **il 1986** 1986; **5 000 lire il chilo** it costs 5,000 lire a kilo
'**ilare** *a* merry
ilarità *nf* hilarity
i'**leo** *nm* hipbone
illangui'**dire** *vi* grow weak
illazi'**one** *nf* inference
illecita'**mente** *adv* illicitly
il'**lecito** *a* illicit
ille'**gale** *a* illegal
illegalità *nf* illegality
illegal'**mente** *adv* illegally
illeg'**gibile** *a* illegible; ⟨*libro*⟩ unreadable
illegittimità *nf* illegitimacy
ille'**gittimo** *a* illegitimate
il'**leso** *a* unhurt
illette'**rato, -a** *a* & *nmf* illiterate
illi'**bato** *a* chaste
illimitata'**mente** *adv* indefinitely
illimi'**tato** *a* unlimited
illivi'**dire** *vt* bruise ● *vi* (*per rabbia*) turn livid
illogica'**mente** *adv* illogically
il'**logico** *a* illogical
il'**ludere** *vt* deceive
il'**ludersi** *vr* deceive oneself
illumi'**nare** *vt* light up; *fig* enlighten; ~ **a giorno** floodlight
illumi'**narsi** *vr* light up
illuminazi'**one** *nf* lighting; *fig* enlightenment. ~ **a gas** gas lighting
Illumi'**nismo** *nm* Enlightenment
illusi'**one** *nf* illusion; **farsi illusioni** delude oneself. ~ **ottica** optical illusion
illusio'**nismo** *nm* conjuring
illusio'**nista** *nmf* conjurer
il'**luso, -a** *pp di* **illudere** ● *a* deluded ● *nmf* day-dreamer
illu'**sorio** *a* illusory
illu'**strare** *vt* illustrate
illustra'**tivo** *a* illustrative
illustra|'**tore, -trice** *nmf* illustrator
illustrazi'**one** *nf* illustration. ~ **a colori/in bianco e nero** colour/black and white illustration
il'**lustre** *a* distinguished
imbacuc'**care** *vt* wrap up
imbacuc'**carsi** *vr* wrap up
imbacuc'**cato** *a* wrapped up
imbal'**laggio** *nm* packing
imbal'**lare** *vt* pack; *Auto* race
imballa|'**tore, -trice** *nmf* packer
imbalsa'**mare** *vt* embalm; stuff ⟨*animale*⟩
imbalsa'**mato** *a* embalmed; ⟨*animale*⟩ stuffed
imbambo'**lato** *a* vacant
imban'**dito** *a* ⟨*tavolo*⟩ covered with food

imbaraz'zante *a* embarrassing

imbaraz'zare *vt* embarrass; (*ostacolare*) encumber

imbaraz'zato *a* embarrassed

imba'razzo *nm* embarrassment; (*ostacolo*) hindrance; **trarre qcno d'~** help sb out of a difficulty; **avere l'~ della scelta** be spoilt for choice. **~ di stomaco** indigestion.

imbarba'rire *vt* barbarize

imbarba'rirsi *vr* become barbarized

imbarca'dero *nm* landing-stage

imbar'care *vt* embark; (*fam: rimorchiare*) score; **~ acqua** ship water

imbar'carsi *vr* go on board; *fig* embark (**in** on)

imbarcazi'one *nf* boat. **~ da pesca** fishing boat. **~ di salvataggio** lifeboat

im'barco *nm* boarding; (*banchina*) landing-stage. **'~ immediato'** 'now boarding'

imbastar'dire *vt* debase

imbastar'dirsi *vr* become debased

imba'stire *vt* tack, baste; *fig* sketch

imbasti'tura *nf* tacking, basting

im'battersi *vr* **~ in** run into

imbat'tibile *a* unbeatable

imbat'tuto *a* unbeaten

imbavagli'are *vt* gag

imbec'cata *nf Theat* prompt

imbe'cille *a* stupid ● *nmf Med* imbecile

imbellet'tarsi *vr hum* doll oneself up

imbel'lire *vt* embellish

im'berbe *a* beardless; *fig* inexperienced

imbestia'lire *vi* fly into a rage; **far ~ qcno** drive sb crazy

imbestia'lirsi *vr* fly into a rage

imbestia'lito *a* enraged

im'bevere *vt* imbue (**di** with)

im'beversi *vr* absorb

imbe'vibile *a* undrinkable

imbe'vuto *a* **~ di** (*acqua*) soaked in; (*nozioni*) imbued with

imbian'care *vt* whiten ● *vi* turn white

imbian'chino *nm* [house] painter

imbion'dire *vt* bleach ● *vi* become bleached

imbion'dirsi *vr* become bleached

imbizzar'rire *vi* become restless; (*arrabbiarsi*) become angry

imbizzar'rirsi *vr* become restless; (*arrabbiarsi*) become angry

imboc'care *vt* feed; (*entrare*) enter; *fig* prompt

imbocca'tura *nf* opening; (*ingresso*) entrance; (*Mus: di strumento*) mouthpiece

im'bocco *nm* entrance

imboni'mento *nm* spiel

imboni'tore *nm* clever talker

imborghe'sire *vi* become middle class

imborghe'sirsi *vr* become middle class

imbo'scare *vt* hide

imbo'scarsi *vr Mil* shirk military service

imbo'scata *nf* ambush

imbo'scato *nm* draft dodger

imbottiglia'mento *nm* traffic jam

imbottigli'are *vt* bottle

imbottigli'arsi *vr* get snarled up in a traffic jam

imbottigli'ato *a* (*vino, acqua*) bottled; (*auto*) stuck in a traffic jam, snarled up; **nave imbottigliata** ship in a bottle

imbot'tire *vt* stuff; pad (*giacca*); *Culin* fill

imbot'tirsi *vr* **~ di** (*fig: di pasticche*) stuff oneself with

imbot'tita *nf* quilt

imbot'tito *a* (*spalle*) padded; (*cuscino*) stuffed; (*panino*) filled

imbotti'tura *nf* stuffing; (*di giacca*) padding; *Culin* filling

imbraca'tura *nf* harness

imbracci'are *vt* shoulder (*fucile*); grasp (*scudo*)

imbra'nato *a* clumsy

imbrat'tare *vt* mark

imbrat'tarsi *vr* dirty oneself

imbrigli'are *vt* bridle (*cavallo*); dam (*acque*)

imbroc'care *vt* hit; **imbroccarla giusta** hit the nail on the head

imbrogli'are *vt* muddle; (*raggirare*) cheat. **~ le carte** *fig* confuse the issue

imbrogli'arsi *vr* get tangled; (*confondersi*) get confused

im'broglio *nm* tangle; (*pasticcio*) mess; (*inganno*) trick

imbrogli'one, -a *nmf* cheat

imbronci'are *vi* sulk

imbronci'arsi *vr* sulk

imbronci'ato *a* sulky

imbru'nire *vi* get dark; **all'~** at dusk

imbrut'tire *vt* make ugly ● *vi* become ugly

imbu'care *vt* post, mail; (*nel biliardo*) pot

imbu'cato *a fam* **è ~** he only got the job because of who he knows

imbufa'lirsi *vr* hit the roof

imbur'rare *vt* butter

im'buto *nm* funnel

i'mene *nm* hymen

imi'tare *vt* imitate

imita|'tore, -'trice *nmf* imitator, impersonator

imitazi'one *nf* imitation; **'diffidare delle imitazioni'** 'beware of imitations'

immaco'lato *a* spotless, immaculate; **l'Immacolata Concezione** the Immaculate Conception

immagazzi'nare *vt* store

immagi'nare *vt* imagine; (*supporre*) suppose; **s'immagini!** imagine that!

immagi'nario *a* imaginary

immaginazi'one *nf* imagination; **è frutto della tua ~** it's a figment of your imagination

im'magine *nf* image; (*rappresentazione, idea*) picture. **~ aziendale** corporate image. **~ della marca** brand image. **~ speculare** mirror image

immagi'noso *a* full of imagery

immalinco'nire *vt* sadden

immalinco'nirsi *vr* grow melancholy

imman'cabile *a* unfailing

immancabil'mente *adv* without fail

im'mane a huge; (*orribile*) terrible

imma'nente a immanent

immangi'abile a inedible

immatrico'lare vt register

immatrico'larsi vr ‹*studente:*› matriculate

immatricolazi'one nf registration; (*di studente*) matriculation

immaturità nf immaturity

imma'turo a unripe; ‹*persona*› immature; (-*precoce*) premature

immedesi'marsi vr ~ **in** identify oneself with

immedesimazi'one nf identification

immediata'mente adv immediately

immedia'tezza nf immediacy

immedi'ato a immediate; **nell'~ futuro** in the immediate future

immemo'rabile a immemorial

im'memore a oblivious

immensa'mente adv enormously

immensità nf immensity

im'menso a immense

immensu'rabile a immeasurable

im'mergere vt immerse

im'mergersi vr plunge; ‹*sommergibile:*› dive; ~ **in** immerse oneself in

immeritata'mente adv undeservedly

immeri'tato a undeserved

immeri'tevole a undeserving

immersi'one nf immersion; (*di sommergibile, palombaro*) dive. ~ **[subacquea]** skin diving, scuba diving

im'merso pp di **immergere**

im'mettere vt introduce

im'mettersi vr introduce oneself

immi'grante a & nmf immigrant

immi'grare vi immigrate

immi'grato, -a nmf immigrant

immigrazi'one nf immigration. ~ **interna** migration

immi'nente a imminent

immi'nenza nf imminence

immischi'are vt involve

immischi'arsi vr ~ **in** meddle in

immi'scibile a immiscible

immis'sario nm tributary

immissi'one nf insertion; *Techn* intake; (*introduzione*) introduction. ~ **[di] dati** data entry

im'mobile a motionless

im'mobili nmpl real estate

immobili'are a **società** ~ building society, savings and loan *Am*

immobilità nf immobility

immobiliz'zare vt immobilize; *Comm* tie up

immobiliz'zato a immobilized. ~ **a letto** confined to bed

immobilizzazi'one nf immobilization; *Fin* fixed asset; **spese d'~** capital expenditure

immoderata'mente adv immoderately

immode'rato a immoderate

immo'destia nf immodesty

immo'desto a immodest

immo'lare vt sacrifice

immo'larsi vr sacrifice oneself

immondez'zaio nm rubbish tip

immon'dizia nf filth; (*spazzatura*) rubbish

im'mondo a filthy

immo'rale a immoral

immoral'mente adv immorally

immorta'lare vt immortalize

immor'tale a immortal

immortalità nf immortality

immoti'vato a unjustified

im'moto a motionless

im'mune a exempt; *Med* immune

immunità nf immunity. ~ **diplomatica** diplomatic immunity. ~ **parlamentare** parliamentary privilege

immuniz'zare vt immunize

immunizzazi'one nf immunization

immunodefici'enza nf immunodeficiency

immunolo'gia nf immunology

immuno'logico a immunological

immuso'nirsi vr sulk

immuso'nito a sulky

immu'tabile a unchangeable

immu'tato a unchanging

impacchet'tare vt wrap up

impacci'are vt hamper; (*disturbare*) inconvenience; (*imbarazzare*) embarrass

impacciata'mente adv awkwardly

impacci'ato a embarrassed; (*goffo*) awkward

im'paccio nm embarrassment; (*ostacolo*) hindrance; (*situazione difficile*) awkward situation; **trarsi d'~** get out of an awkward situation

im'pacco nm compress

impadro'nirsi vr ~ **di** take possession of; (*fig: imparare*) master

impa'gabile a priceless

impagi'nare vt paginate

impaginazi'one nf pagination

impagli'are vt stuff ‹*animale*›

impa'lare vt impale

impa'lato a fig stiff

impalca'tura nf scaffolding; *fig* structure

impal'lare vt snooker

impalli'dire vi turn pale; (*fig: perdere d'importanza*) pale into insignificance

impalli'nare vt riddle with bullets

impal'pabile a impalpable; ‹*tessuto*› gossamer-like

impa'nare vt *Culin* bread

impa'nato a breaded

impanta'narsi vr get bogged down

impape'rarsi vr falter, stammer

impappi'narsi vr falter, stammer

impa'rare vt learn; ~ **a proprie spese** learn to one's cost

impara'ticcio nm half-baked

impareggi'abile a incomparable

imparen'tarsi vr ~ **con** become related to

imparen'tato a related

'impari a unequal; (*dispari*) odd

impar'tire vt impart

imparzi'ale a impartial

imparzialità *nf* impartiality
im'passe *nf inv* impasse
impas'sibile *a* impassive; **con aria ~** impassively
impa'stare *vt* Culin knead; blend ⟨*colori*⟩
impasta'tura *nf* kneading
impastic'carsi *vr* pop pills
impasticci'are *vt* make a mess of
im'pasto *nm* Culin dough; (*miscuglio*) mixture
im'patto *nm* impact. **~ ambientale** environmental impact
impau'rire *vt* frighten
impau'rirsi *vr* get frightened
im'pavido *a* fearless
impazi'ente *a* impatient; **~ di fare qcsa** eager to do sth
impazien'tirsi *vr* lose patience
impazi'enza *nf* impatience
impaz'zata *nf* **all'~** at breakneck speed
impaz'zire *vi* go mad; ⟨*maionese:*⟩ separate; **far ~ qcno** drive sb mad; **~ per** be crazy about; **da ~** ⟨*mal di testa*⟩ blinding
impaz'zito *a* crazed
impec'cabile *a* impeccable
impeccabil'mente *adv* impeccably
impedi'mento *nm* hindrance; (*ostacolo*) obstacle
impe'dire *vt* (*impacciare*) hinder; (*ostruire*) obstruct; **~ di** prevent from; **~ a qcno di fare qcsa** prevent sb [from] doing sth
impe'gnare *vt* (*dare in pegno*) pawn; (*vincolare*) bind; (*prenotare*) reserve; (*assorbire*) take up
impe'gnarsi *vr* apply oneself; **~ a fare qcsa** commit oneself to doing sth
impegna'tiva *nf* referral
impegna'tivo *a* binding; ⟨*lavoro*⟩ demanding
impe'gnato *a* politically committed
im'pegno *nm* engagement; Comm commitment; (*zelo*) care; **con ~** with dedication; **ho un ~** I'm doing something
impego'larsi *vr* **~ in** become enmeshed in
impel'lente *a* pressing
impene'trabile *a* impenetrable
impen'narsi *vr* ⟨*cavallo:*⟩ rear; *fig* bristle
impen'nata *nf* (*di prezzi*) sharp rise; (*di cavallo*) rearing; (*di moto*) wheelie; (*di aereo*) climb
impen'sabile *a* unthinkable
impen'sato *a* unexpected
impensie'rire *vt* worry
impensie'rirsi *vr* worry
impe'rante *a* prevailing
impe'rare *vi* reign
impera'tivo *a & nm* imperative
impera‖'tore, -'trice *nm* emperor ● *nf* empress
impercet'tibile *a* imperceptible
impercettibil'mente *adv* imperceptibly
imperdo'nabile *a* unforgivable
imperfetta'mente *adv* imperfectly
imper'fetto *a & nm* imperfect
imperfezi'one *nf* imperfection

imperi'ale *a* imperial
imperia'lismo *nm* imperialism
imperia'lista *a & nmf* imperialist
imperia'listico *a* imperialistic
imperi'oso *a* imperious; (*impellente*) urgent
imperi'turo *a* immortal
impe'rizia *nf* lack of skill
imper'lare *vt* bead
imperma'lire *vt* offend
imperma'lirsi *vr* take offence
imperme'abile *a* ⟨*orologio*⟩ waterproof; ⟨*terreno*⟩ impermeable ● *nm* raincoat
imperni'are *vt* pivot; (*fondare*) base
imperni'arsi *vr* **~ su** be based on
im'pero *nm* empire; (*potere*) rule; **stile ~** empire style
imperscru'tabile *a* inscrutable
imperso'nale *a* impersonal
imperso'nare *vt* personify; (*interpretare*) act [the part of]
imper'territo *a* undaunted
imperti'nente *a* impertinent
imperti'nenza *nf* impertinence
impertur'babile *a* imperturbable
impertur'bato *a* unperturbed
imperver'sare *vi* rage
im'pervio *a* inaccessible
'impeto *nm* impetus; (*impulso*) impulse; (*slancio*) transport
impet'tito *a* stiff
impetuosa'mente *adv* impetuously
impetu'oso *a* impetuous; ⟨*vento*⟩ blustering
impiallacci'are *vt* veneer
impiallacci'ato *a* veneered
impian'tare *vt* install; set up ⟨*azienda*⟩
impi'anto *nm* plant; (*sistema*) system; (*operazione*) installation. **~ di amplificazione** public address system, PA system. **~ audio** sound system. **~ elettrico** electrical system. **impianti** *pl* **fissi** fixtures and fittings. **~ radio** Auto car stereo system. **~ di riscaldamento** heating system. **~ stereo** hi-fi
impia'strare *vt* plaster; (*sporcare*) dirty
impia'strarsi *vr* get dirty; **~ le mani** get one's hands dirty
impi'astro *nm* poultice; (*persona noiosa*) bore; (*pasticcione*) cack-handed person
impiccagi'one *nf* hanging
impic'care *vt* hang
impic'carsi *vr* hang oneself
impic'cato, -a *nm* hanged man ● *nf* hanged woman
impicci'arsi *vr* meddle
im'piccio *nm* hindrance; (*seccatura*) bother
impicci'one, -a *nmf* nosey parker
impie'gare *vt* employ; (*usare*) use; spend ⟨*tempo, denaro*⟩; Fin invest; **l'autobus ha impiegato un'ora** it took the bus an hour
impie'garsi *vr* get [oneself] a job
impie'gatizio *a* clerical
impie'gato, -a *nmf* employee; (*di ufficio*) office worker. **~ di banca** bank clerk. **~ di concetto** administrative employee. **~ in prova** probationer. **~ statale** civil servant
impi'ego *nm* employment; (*posto*) job; Fin

investment; **pubblico** ~ public sector. ~ **fisso** permanent job. **impieghi** pl **saltuari** odd jobs, casual employment. ~ **temporaneo** temporary job

impieto'sire vt move to pity

impieto'sirsi vr be moved to pity

impie'toso a pitiless

impie'trito a petrified

impigli'are vt entangle

impigli'arsi vr get entangled

impi'grire vt make lazy

impi'grirsi vr get lazy

impi'lare vt stack

impingu'are vt fig fill

impiom'bare vt seal ⟨cassa, porta⟩

impla'cabile a implacable

implemen'tare vt implement

impli'care vt implicate; (sottintendere) imply

impli'carsi vr become involved

implicazi'one nf implication

implicita'mente adv implicitly

im'plicito a implicit

implo'rante a imploring

implo'rare vt implore

implorazi'one nf entreaty

implosi'one nf implosion

impolli'nare vt pollinate

impollinazi'one nf pollination

impoltro'nire vt make lazy

impoltro'nirsi vr become lazy

impolve'rare vt cover with dust

impolve'rarsi vr get covered with dust

impolve'rato a dusty

impoma'tare vt put brilliantine on

impoma'tarsi vr put brilliantine on ⟨capelli⟩

imponde'rabile a imponderable; ⟨causa, evento⟩ unpredictable

impo'nente a imposing

impo'nenza nf impressiveness

impo'nibile a taxable ● nm taxable income

impopo'lare a unpopular

impopolarità nf unpopularity

imporpo'rarsi vr turn red

im'porre vt impose; (ordinare) order

im'porsi vr assert oneself; (aver successo) be successful; ~ **di** (prefiggersi di) set oneself the task of

impor'tante a important ● nm important thing

impor'tanza nf importance; **di vitale** ~ crucially important

impor'tare vt Comm, Comput import; (comportare) cause ● vi matter; (essere necessario) be necessary. **non importa!** it doesn't matter!; **non me ne importa niente!** I couldn't care less!

importa|'tore, -'trice a importing ● nmf importer

importazi'one nf importation; (merce importata) import

import-'export nm inv import-export

im'porto nm amount

importu'nare vt pester; ~ **qcno per qcsa** pester sb for sth

impor'tuno a troublesome; (inopportuno) untimely

imposizi'one nf imposition; (imposta) tax

imposses'sarsi vr ~ **di** seize

impos'sibile a impossible ● nm **fare l'**~ do absolutely all one can

impossibilità nf impossibility

im'posta[1] nf tax. ~ **fondiaria** land tax. ~ **patrimoniale** property tax. ~ **sul reddito** income tax. ~ **sui redditi di capitale** capital gains tax. ~ **sulle società** corporation tax. ~ **supplementare** surtax. ~ **sul valore aggiunto** value added tax

im'posta[2] nf (di finestra) shutter

impo'stare vt (progettare) plan; (basare) base; Mus pitch; (imbucare) post, mail; set out ⟨domanda, problema⟩

impostazi'one nf planning; (di voce) pitching

im'posto pp di **imporre**

impo'store, -a nmf impostor

impo'stura nf imposture

impo'tente a powerless; Med impotent

impo'tenza nf powerlessness; Med impotence

impoveri'mento nm impoverishment

impove'rire vt impoverish

impove'rirsi vr become poor; ⟨risorse:⟩ become depleted; ⟨linguaggio:⟩ become impoverished

imprati'cabile a impracticable; ⟨strada⟩ impassable

impraticabilità nf per ~ **del terreno/delle strade** because of the state of the pitch/roads

imprati'chire vt train

imprati'chirsi vr ~ **in** o **a** get practice in

impre'care vi curse

imprecazi'one nf curse

impreci'sabile a indeterminable

impreci'sato a indeterminate

imprecisi'one nf inaccuracy

impre'ciso a inaccurate

impre'gnare vt impregnate; (imbevere) soak; fig imbue

impre'gnarsi vr become impregnated with

imprendi|'tore, -'trice nmf entrepreneur

imprenditori'ale a entrepreneurial

imprepa'rato a unprepared

im'presa nf undertaking; (gesta) exploit; (azienda) firm. ~ **edile** property developer. ~ **familiare** family business. ~ **di pompe funebri** undertakers, funeral directors. ~ **pubblica** state-owned company. ~ **di traslochi** furniture remover

impre'sario nm impresario; (appaltatore) contractor. ~ **di pompe funebri** undertaker, funeral director, mortician Am. ~ **teatrale** theatre manager

imprescin'dibile a inescapable

impressio'nabile a impressionable

impressio'nante a impressive; (spaventoso) frightening

impressio'nare vt impress; (spaventare) frighten; expose ⟨foto⟩

impressio'narsi *vr* be affected; (*spaventarsi*) be frightened

impressi'one *nf* impression; (*sensazione*) sensation; (*impronta*) mark; **far ~ a qcno** upset sb; **dare l'~ di essere...** give the impression of being...

impressio'nismo *nm* impressionism

impressio'nista *a & nmf* impressionist

impressio'nistico *a* impressionistic

im'presso *pp di* **imprimere** ● *a* printed

impre'stare *vt* lend

impreve'dibile *a* unforeseeable; ⟨*persona*⟩ unpredictable

imprevedibil'mente *adv* unexpectedly

imprevi'dente *a* improvident

impre'visto *a* unforeseen ● *nm* unforeseen event; **salvo imprevisti** all being well

imprigiona'mento *nm* imprisonment

imprigio'nare *vt* imprison

im'primere *vt* impress; (*stampare*) print; (*comunicare*) impart; **rimanere impresso a qcno** stick in sb's mind

impro'babile *a* unlikely, improbable; **è ~ che ci sia** he is unlikely to be there

improbabilità *nf* improbability

improdut'tivo *a* unproductive

im'pronta *nf* impression; *fig* mark. **~ digitale** fingerprint. **impronte** *pl* **genetiche** genetic fingerprinting. **~ del piede** footprint

impron'tato *a* **~ all'ironia** tinged with irony

impronunci'abile *a* unpronounceable

impro'perio *nm* insult; **improperi** *pl* abuse *sg*

impropo'nibile *a* unrealistic

im'proprio *a* improper

improro'gabile *a* which cannot be extended

improvvisa'mente *adv* suddenly

improvvi'sare *vt/i* improvise

improvvi'sarsi *vr* turn oneself into a

improvvi'sata *nf* surprise

improvvi'sato *a* ⟨*discorso*⟩ unrehearsed

improvvisazi'one *nf* improvisation

improv'viso *a* unexpected, sudden; **all'~** unexpectedly, suddenly

impru'dente *a* imprudent

imprudente'mente *adv* imprudently

impru'denza *nf* imprudence

impu'dente *a* impudent

impudente'mente *adv* impudently

impu'denza *nf* impudence

impu'dico *a* immodest

impu'gnare *vt* grasp; *Jur* contest

impugna'tura *nf* grip; (*manico*) handle. **~ a due mani** two-handed grip

impulsiva'mente *adv* impulsively

impulsività *nf* impulsiveness

impul'sivo *a* impulsive

im'pulso *nm* impulse; **agire d'~** act on impulse

impune'mente *adv* with impunity

impunità *nf* impunity

impu'nito *a* unpunished

impun'tarsi *vr fig* dig one's heels in

impun'tura *nf* stitching

impuntu'rare *vt* backstitch

impurità *nf inv* impurity

im'puro *a* impure

impu'tabile *a* attributable (**a** to); *Jur* indictable

impu'tare *vt* attribute; *Jur* charge

impu'tato, -a *nmf* accused

imputazi'one *nf* charge. **~ di omicidio** murder charge

imputri'dire *vi* putrefy

imputri'dito *a* putrefied

in *prep* in; (*moto a luogo*) to; (*su*) on; (*dentro*) within; (*mezzo*) by; (*con materiale*) made of; **essere in casa/ufficio** be at home/at the office; **in mano/tasca** in one's hand/pocket; **in fondo alla strada/borsa** at the bottom of the street/bag; **andare in Francia/campagna** go to France/the country; **salire in treno** get on the train; **versa la birra nel bicchiere** pour the beer into the glass; **in alto** up there; **in giornata** within the day; **nel 1997** in 1997; **una borsa in pelle** a bag made of leather, a leather bag; **alzarsi in piedi** stand up; **in macchina** ⟨*viaggiare, venire*⟩ by car; **in contanti** [in] cash; **in vacanza** on holiday; **di giorno in giorno** from day to day; **se fossi in te** if I were you; **siamo in sette** there are seven of us

inabbor'dabile *a* unapproachable

i'nabile *a* incapable; (*fisicamente*) unfit

inabilità *nf* incapacity

inabi'tabile *a* uninhabitable

inacces'sibile *a* inaccessible; ⟨*persona*⟩ unapproachable

inaccet'tabile *a* unacceptable

inaccettabilità *nf* unacceptability

inacer'barsi *vr* grow bitter

inacer'bire *vt* embitter; exacerbate ⟨*rapporto*⟩

inaci'dire *vt* turn sour

inaci'dirsi *vr* go sour; ⟨*persona:*⟩ become embittered

ina'datto *a* unsuitable

inadegua'tezza *nf* inadequacy

inadegu'ato *a* inadequate

inadempi'ente *nmf* defaulter

inadempi'enza *nf* nonfulfilment (**a** of). **~ contrattuale** breach of contract

inadempi'mento *nm* nonfulfilment

inaffer'rabile *a* elusive

inaffon'dabile *a* unsinkable

ina'lare *vt* inhale

inala'tore *nm* inhaler

inalazi'one *nf* inhalation

inalbe'rare *vt* hoist

inalbe'rarsi *vr* ⟨*cavallo:*⟩ rear [up]; (*adirarsi*) lose one's temper

inalie'nabile *a* inalienable

inalte'rabile *a* unchanging; ⟨*colore*⟩ fast

inalte'rato *a* unchanged

inami'dare *vt* starch

inami'dato *a* starched

inammis'sibile *a* inadmissible

inamovi'bile *a* ⟨*disco ecc*⟩ non-removable

inanel'lato a bejewelled

inani'mato a inanimate; (senza vita) lifeless

inappa'gabile a unsatisfiable

inappaga'mento nm nonfulfilment

inappa'gato a unfulfilled

inappel'labile a final

inappe'tenza nf lack of appetite

inappli'cabile a inapplicable

inappropri'ato a inapt

inappun'tabile a faultless

inar'care vt arch; raise (sopracciglia)

inar'carsi vr (legno:) warp; (ripiano:) sag; (linea:) curve

inari'dire vt parch; empty of feelings (persona)

inari'dirsi vr dry up; (persona:) become empty of feelings

inarre'stabile a unstoppable

inartico'lato a inarticulate

inascol'tato a unheard

inaspettata'mente adv unexpectedly

inaspet'tato a unexpected

inaspri'mento nm (di carattere) embitterment; (di conflitto) worsening

ina'sprire vt embitter

ina'sprirsi vr become embittered

inattac'cabile a unassailable; (irreprensibile) irreproachable

inatten'dibile a unreliable

inat'teso a unexpected

inattività nf inactivity

inat'tivo a inactive

inattu'abile a impracticable

inau'dito a unheard of

inaugu'rale a inaugural; **cerimonia ~** official opening; **viaggio ~** maiden voyage

inaugu'rare vt inaugurate; open (mostra); unveil (statua); christen (lavastoviglie ecc)

inaugurazi'one nf inauguration; (di mostra) opening; (di statua) unveiling

inavve'duto a inadvertent; (sbadato) careless

inavver'tenza nf inadvertence

inavvertita'mente adv inadvertently

inavvici'nabile a unapproachable

in'breeding nm inv inbreeding

incagli'are vi ground ● vt hinder

incagli'arsi vr run aground

in'caglio nm running aground; fig obstacle

'inca a & nmf (pl **inca** o **incas**) Inca

incalco'labile a incalculable

incal'lirsi vr grow callous; (abituarsi) become hardened

incal'lito a callous; (abituato) hardened

incal'zante a (ritmo) driving; (richiesta) urgent; (crisi) imminent

incal'zare vt pursue; fig press

incame'rare vt appropriate

incammi'nare vt get going; (fig: guidare) set off

incammi'narsi vr set out

incanala'mento nm canalization; fig channelling

incana'lare vt canalize; fig channel

incana'larsi vr converge on

incancel'labile a indelible

incande'scente a incandescent; (discussione) burning

incande'scenza nf incandescence

incan'tare vt enchant

incan'tarsi vr stand spellbound; (incepparsi) jam

incanta|'tore, -'trice nmf enchanter; enchantress. **~ di serpenti** snake charmer

incan'tesimo nm spell

incan'tevole a enchanting

in'canto nm spell; fig delight; (asta) auction; **come per ~** as if by magic

incanu'tire vt turn white

incanu'tito a white

inca'pace a incapable; **~ d'intendere e di volere** Jur unfit to plead

incapacità nf incapability

incapo'nirsi vr be set

incap'pare vi **~ in** run into

incappucci'arsi vr wrap up

incapretta'mento nm method of trussing up a victim by the ankles

incapricci'arsi vr **~ di** take a fancy to

incapsu'lare vt seal; crown (dente)

incarce'rare vt imprison

incarcerazi'one nf imprisonment

incari'care vt charge

incari'carsi vr take upon oneself; **me ne incarico io** I will see to it

incari'cato, -a a in charge ● nmf representative. **~ d'affari** chargé d'affaires

in'carico nm charge; **per ~ di** on behalf of

incar'nare vt embody

incar'narsi vr become incarnate

incarnazi'one nf incarnation

incarta'mento nm documents pl

incartapeco'rito a shrivelled up

incar'tare vt wrap [in paper]

incasel'lare vt pigeonhole

incasi'nato a fam (vita) screwed up; (stanza) messed up

incas'sare vt pack; Mech embed; (incastonare) set; (riscuotere) cash; take (colpo)

incas'sato a set; (fiume) deeply embanked

in'casso nm collection; (introito) takings pl

incasto'nare vt set

incasto'nato a embedded; (anello) inset (**di** with)

incastona'tura nf setting

inca'strare vt fit in; (fam: in situazione) corner

inca'strarsi vr fit

in'castro nm joint; **a ~** (pezzi) interlocking. **~ a coda di rondine** dovetail joint

incate'nare vt chain

incatra'mare vt tar

incatti'vire vt turn nasty

incauta'mente adv imprudently

in'cauto a imprudent

inca'vare vt hollow out

inca'vato a hollow

incava'tura nf hollow

in'cavo nm hollow; (scanalatura) groove

incavo'larsi *vr fam* get shirty

incavo'lato *a fam* shirty

in'cedere *fml vi* advance solemnly ● *nm* solemn gait

incendi'are *vt* set fire to; *fig* inflame

incendi'ario, -a *a* incendiary; ⟨*fig: discorso*⟩ inflammatory; ⟨*fig: bellezza*⟩ sultry ● *nmf* arsonist

incendi'arsi *vr* catch fire

in'cendio *nm* fire. **~ doloso** arson; **incendi** *pl* **dolosi** cases of arson

inceneri'mento *nm* incineration; ⟨*cremazione*⟩ cremation

incene'rire *vt* burn to ashes; ⟨*cremare*⟩ cremate

incene'rirsi *vr* be burnt to ashes

inceneri'tore *nm* incinerator

in'censo *nm* incense

incensu'rabile *a* irreproachable

incensu'rato *a* blameless; **essere ~** *Jur* have a clean record

incenti'vare *vt* motivate

incen'tivo *nm* incentive. **~ fiscale** tax incentive

incen'trarsi *vr* **~ su** centre on

incep'pare *vt* block; *fig* hamper

incep'parsi *vr* jam

ince'rata *nf* oilcloth

incerot'tato *a* with a plaster on

incer'tezza *nf* uncertainty

in'certo *a* uncertain ● *nm* uncertainty; **sono gli incerti del mestiere** that's the way it goes in this business

incespi'care *vi* ⟨*inciampare*⟩ stumble

inces'sante *a* unceasing

incessante'mente *adv* incessantly

in'cesto *nm* incest

incestu'oso *a* incestuous

in'cetta *nf* buying up; **fare ~ di** stockpile

inchi'esta *nf* investigation; **fare un'~** conduct an inquiry. **~ giudiziaria** criminal investigation. **~ parlamentare** parliamentary inquiry

inchi'nare *vt* bow

inchi'narsi *vr* bow

in'chino *nm* bow; ⟨*di donna*⟩ curtsy

inchio'dare *vt* nail; nail down ⟨*coperchio*⟩; **~ a letto** ⟨*malattia:*⟩ confine to bed

inchi'ostro *nm* ink. **~ di china** Indian ink. **~ simpatico** invisible ink. **~ di stampa** newsprint

inciam'pare *vi* stumble; **~ in** trip over; ⟨*imbattersi*⟩ run into

inci'ampo *nm* hindrance

inciden'tale *a* incidental

inci'dente *nm* ⟨*episodio*⟩ incident; ⟨*infortunio*⟩ accident. **~ aereo** plane crash. **~ d'auto** car accident. **~ sul lavoro** industrial accident. **~ stradale** road accident

inci'denza *nf* incidence

in'cidere *vt* cut; ⟨*arte*⟩ engrave; ⟨*registrare*⟩ record ● *vi* **~ su** ⟨*gravare*⟩ weigh upon

in'cinta *a* pregnant

incipi'ente *a* incipient

incipri'are *vt* powder

incipri'arsi *vr* powder one's face

in'circa *adv* **all'~** more or less

incisi'one *nf* incision; ⟨*arte*⟩ engraving; ⟨*acquaforte*⟩ etching; ⟨*registrazione*⟩ recording

inci'sivo *a* incisive ● *nm* ⟨*dente*⟩ incisor

in'ciso *nm* **per ~** incidentally

inci'sore *nm* engraver

incita'mento *nm* incitement

inci'tare *vt* incite

inci'vile *a* uncivilized; ⟨*maleducato*⟩ impolite

inciviltà *nf* barbarism; ⟨*maleducazione*⟩ rudeness

inclassifi'cabile *adv* unclassifiable

incle'mente *a* harsh

incle'menza *nf* harshness

incli'nabile *a* reclining

incli'nare *vt* tilt ● *vi* **~ a** be inclined to

incli'narsi *vr* list

incli'nato *a* tilted; ⟨*terreno*⟩ sloping

inclinazi'one *nf* slope, inclination

in'cline *a* inclined

in'cludere *vt* include; ⟨*allegare*⟩ enclose

inclusi'one *nf* inclusion

inclu'sivo *a* inclusive

in'cluso *pp di* **includere** ● *a* included; ⟨*compreso*⟩ inclusive; ⟨*allegato*⟩ enclosed

incoe'rente *a* ⟨*contraddittorio*⟩ inconsistent

incoerente'mente *adv* inconsistently

incoe'renza *nf* inconsistency

in'cognita *nf* unknown quantity

in'cognito *a* unknown ● *nm* **in ~** incognito

incol'lare *vt* stick; ⟨*con colla liquida*⟩ glue; *Comput* paste

incol'larsi *vr* stick to; **~ a qcno** stick close to sb

incolla'tura *nf* ⟨*nell'ippica*⟩ neck

incolle'rirsi *vr* lose one's temper

incolle'rito *a* enraged

incol'mabile *a* ⟨*differenza*⟩ unbridgeable; ⟨*vuoto*⟩ unfillable

incolon'nare *vt* line up

inco'lore *a* colourless

incol'pare *vt* blame

in'colto *a* uncultivated; ⟨*persona*⟩ uneducated

in'columeità *a* unhurt

in'columeità *a* unhurt

in'colume *a* unhurt

incom'bente *a* impending

incom'benza *nf* task

in'combere *vi* **~ su** hang over; **~ a** ⟨*spettare*⟩ be incumbent on

incombu'stibile *a* noncombustible

incominci'are *vt/i* begin, start

incommensu'rabile *a* immeasurable

incomo'dare *vt* inconvenience

incomo'darsi *vr* trouble

in'comodo *a* uncomfortable; ⟨*inopportuno*⟩ inconvenient ● *nm* inconvenience; **fare il terzo ~** play gooseberry

incompa'rabile *a* incomparable

incompa'tibile *a* incompatible

incompatibilità *nf inv* incompatibility. **~ di carattere** incompatibility

incompe'tente *a* incompetent

incompe'tenza *nf* incompetence

incompi'uto *a* unfinished

incom'pleto *a* incomplete

incompren'sibile *a* incomprehensible

incomprensibil'mente *adv* incomprehensibly

incomprensi'one *nf* lack of understanding; (*malinteso*) misunderstanding

incom'preso *a* misunderstood

inconce'pibile *a* inconceivable

inconcili'abile *a* irreconcilable

inconclu'dente *a* inconclusive; (*persona*) ineffectual

incondizionata'mente *adv* unconditionally

incondizio'nato *a* unconditional

inconfes'sabile *a* unmentionable

inconfon'dibile *a* unmistakable

inconfondibil'mente *adv* unmistakably

inconfu'tabile *a* irrefutable

inconfutabil'mente *adv* irrefutably

incongru'ente *a* inconsistent

incongru'enza *nf* incongruity

in'congruo *a* inadequate

inconsa'pevole *a* unaware; (*inconscio*) unconscious

inconsapevol'mente *adv* unwittingly

inconscia'mente *adv* unconsciously

in'conscio *a & nm Psych* unconscious

inconsegu'ente *a* **essere** ~ be a non sequitur

inconside'rabile *a* negligible

inconside'rato *a* inconsiderate

inconsi'stente *a* insubstantial; (*notizia ecc*) unfounded

inconsi'stenza *nf* (*di ragionamento, prove*) flimsiness

inconso'labile *a* inconsolable

inconsu'eto *a* unusual

incon'sulto *a* rash

incontami'nato *a* uncontaminated

inconte'nibile *a* irrepressible

inconten'tabile *a* insatiable; (*esigente*) hard to please

inconte'stabile *a* indisputable

inconte'stato *a* unchallenged

inconti'nente *a* incontinent

inconti'nenza *nf* incontinence

incon'trare *vt* meet; encounter, meet with (*difficoltà*)

incon'trario: **all'~** *adv* the other way around; (*in modo sbagliato*) the wrong way around

incon'trarsi *vr* meet (**con qcno** sb)

incontra'stabile *a* incontrovertible

incontra'stato *a* undisputed

in'contro *nm* meeting; (*casuale*) encounter; (*di calcio, rugby*) match; (*di tennis*) game; (*di pugilato*) fight. ~ **al vertice** summit meeting ● *prep* ~ **a** towards; **andare** ~ **a qcno** go to meet sb; *fig* meet sb half way

incontrol'labile *a* uncontrollable

incontrollata'mente *adv* uncontrollably

inconveni'ente *nm* drawback

incoraggia'mento *nm* encouragement

incoraggi'ante *a* encouraging

incoraggi'are *vt* encourage

incor'nare *vt* gore

incornici'are *vt* frame

incornicia'tura *nf* framing

incoro'nare *vt* crown

incoronazi'one *nf* coronation

incorpo'rare *vt* incorporate; (*mescolare*) blend

incorpo'rarsi *vr* blend; (*territori*) merge

incorreg'gibile *a* incorrigible

in'correre *vt* ~ **in** incur; ~ **nel pericolo di...** run the risk of...

incorrut'tibile *a* incorruptible

incosci'ente *a* unconscious; (*irresponsabile*) reckless ● *nmf* irresponsible person

incosci'enza *nf* unconsciousness; (*irresponsabilità*) recklessness

inco'stante *a* changeable; (*persona*) fickle

inco'stanza *nf* changeableness; (*di persona*) fickleness

incostituzio'nale *a* unconstitutional

incostituzionalità *nf* unconstitutionality

incre'dibile *a* incredible, unbelievable

incredibil'mente *adv* incredibly, unbelievably

incredulità *nf* incredulity

in'credulo *a* incredulous

incremen'tale *a Comput, Math* incremental

incremen'tare *vt* increase; (*intensificare*) step up

incre'mento *nm* increase. ~ **demografico** population growth. ~ **produttivo** increase in production

incresci'oso *a* regrettable

incre'spare *vt* ruffle; wrinkle (*tessuto*); make frizzy (*capelli*); ~ **la fronte** frown

incre'sparsi *vr* (*acqua*) ripple; (*tessuto*) wrinkle; (*capelli*) go frizzy

incrimi'nabile *a* indictable

incrimi'nare *vt* indict; *fig* incriminate

incriminazi'one *nf* indictment

incri'nare *vt* crack; *fig* affect (*amicizia*)

incri'narsi *vr* crack; (*amicizia*) be affected

incrina'tura *nf* crack

incroci'are *vt* cross ● *vi Naut, Aeron* cruise

incroci'arsi *vr* cross; (*razze*) interbreed

incroci'ato *a* crossover

incrocia'tore *nm* cruiser

in'crocio *nm* crossing; (*di strade*) crossroads *sg*

incrol'labile *a* indestructible

incro'stare *vt* encrust

incrostazi'one *nf* encrustation

incuba'trice *nf* incubator

incubazi'one *nf* incubation

'incubo *nm* nightmare; **da** ~ nightmarish

in'cudine *nf* anvil

incul'care *vt* inculcate

incune'are *vt* wedge

incune'arsi *vr* slot in

incune'ato *a Med* impacted

incu'pirsi *vr fig* darken

incu'rabile *a* incurable
incu'rante *a* careless
in'curia *nf* negligence
incurio'sire *vt* make curious
incurio'sirsi *vr* become curious
incursi'one *nf* raid. **~ aerea** air raid
incurva'mento *nm* bending
incur'vare *vt* bend
incur'varsi *vr* bend
incurva'tura *nf* bending
in'cusso *pp di* **incutere**
incusto'dito *a* unguarded
in'cutere *vt* arouse; **~ spavento a qcno**
strike fear into sb
'indaco *nm* indigo
indaffa'rato *a* busy
inda'gare *vt/i* investigate
in'dagine *nf* research; *(giudiziaria)* investigation. **~ demoscopica** public opinion poll.
~ di mercato market survey
indebi'tare *vt* get into debt
indebi'tarsi *vr* get into debt
in'debito *a* undue
indeboli'mento *nm* weakening
indebo'lire *vt* weaken
indebo'lirsi *vr* weaken
inde'cente *a* indecent
indecente'mente *adv* indecently
inde'cenza *nf* indecency; *(vergogna)* disgrace
indeci'frabile *a* indecipherable
indecisi'one *nf* indecision
inde'ciso *a* undecided
indecli'nabile *a* indeclinable
indeco'roso *a* indecorous
inde'fesso *a* tireless
indefi'nibile *a* indefinable
indefi'nito *a* indefinite
indefor'mabile *a* crushproof
in'degno *a* unworthy
inde'lebile *a* indelible
indelebil'mente *adv* indelibly
indelicata'mente *adv* indiscreetly
indelica'tezza *nf* indelicacy; *(azione)* tactless act
indeli'cato *a* indiscreet; *(grossolano)* indelicate
indemagli'abile *a* ladderproof
indemoni'ato *a* possessed
in'denne *a* uninjured; *(da malattia)* unaffected
inden'nità *nf inv* allowance; *(per danni)*
compensation. **~ di accompagnamento**
mobility allowance. **~ di contingenza** cost-
of-living allowance. **~ di fine rapporto** severance payment. **~ parlamentare** MP's salary. **~ di trasferimento** relocation allowance. **~ di trasferta** travel allowance
indenniz'zare *vt* compensate
inden'nizzo *nm* compensation
indepen'denza *nf* independence
indero'gabile *a* binding
indescri'vibile *a* indescribable
indescrivibil'mente *adv* indescribably
indeside'rabile *a* undesirable

indeside'rato *a* ⟨*figlio, ospite*⟩ unwanted
indetermi'nabile *a* indeterminable
indetermina'tezza *nf* vagueness
indetermina'tivo *a* indefinite
indetermi'nato *a* indeterminate
'India *nf* India
indi'ano, -a *a & nmf* Indian; **in fila indiana**
in single file. **~ d'America** American Indian
indiavo'lato *a* possessed; *(vivace)* wild
indi'care *vt* show, indicate; *(col dito)* point
at; *(far notare)* point out; *(consigliare)* advise
indicativa'mente *adv* as an idea; **può**
dirmi quanto costa ~? can you give me an
idea of the price?
indica'tivo *a* indicative; ⟨*prezzo, cifra*⟩
rough ● *nm Gram* indicative
indica'tore *nm* indicator; *Techn* gauge;
(prontuario) directory. **~ di direzione** indicator light. **~ economico** economic indicator. **~ [del livello] dell'olio** oil gauge. **~ di**
velocità speedometer
indicazi'one *nf* indication; *(istruzione)* direction. **~ stradale** road sign
'indice *nm* *(dito)* forefinger; *(lancetta)*
pointer; *(di libro, statistica)* index; *(fig:*
segno) sign. **~ di ascolto** audience rating. **~**
azionario share index. **~ di gradimento**
popularity rating. **~ di mortalità** death rate.
~ di natalità birth rate
indi'cibile *a* inexpressible
indiciz'zare *vt* index-link
indiciz'zato *a* index-linked
indicizzazi'one *nf* indexing
indietreggi'are *vi* draw back; *Mil* withdraw
indi'etro *adv* back, behind; **all'~** backwards; **essere ~** be behind; *(mentalmente)*
be backward; *(con pagamenti)* be in arrears;
(di orologio) be slow; **fare marcia ~** reverse;
rimandare ~ send back; **rimanere ~** be left
behind; **torna ~!** come back!
indifen'dibile *a* indefensible
indi'feso *a* undefended; *(inerme)* helpless
indiffe'rente *a* indifferent; **mi è ~** it's all
the same to me
indifferente'mente *adv* *(senza fare*
distinzioni) without distinction; *(con*
indifferenza) indifferently; **funziona ~ con i**
due programmi it works equally well with
either program
indiffe'renza *nf* indifference
in'digeno, -a *a* indigenous ● *nmf* native
indi'gente *a* needy
indi'genza *nf* poverty
indigesti'one *nf* indigestion
indi'gesto *a* indigestible
indi'gnare *vt* make indignant
indi'gnarsi *vr* be indignant
indi'gnato *a* indignant
indignazi'one *nf* indignation
indimenti'cabile *a* unforgettable
'indio, -a *a* Indian ● *nmf (mpl* **indii** *o* **indios)**
Indian
indipen'dente *a* independent; *(economica-*
mente) self-supporting

indipendente'mente *adv* independently;
  ~ **da** regardless of
in'dire *vt* announce
indiretta'mente *adv* indirectly
indi'retto *a* indirect
indiriz'zare *vt* address; (*mandare*) send;
  (*dirigere*) direct
indiriz'zario *nm* mailing list
indiriz'zarsi *vr* direct one's steps
indi'rizzo *nm* address; (*direzione*) direction.
  ~ **di consegna** delivery address. '~ **del**
  destinatario' 'addressee'. ~ **di memoria**
  Comput memory address. '~ **del mittente'**
  'sender's address'. ~ **di posta elettronica** e-
  mail address
indisci'plina *nf* lack of discipline
indiscipli'nato *a* undisciplined
indi'screto *a* indiscreet; **in modo** ~ indiscreetly
indiscrezi'one *nf* indiscretion
indiscriminata'mente *adv* indiscriminately
indiscrimi'nato *a* indiscriminate
indi'scusso *a* unquestioned
indiscu'tibile *a* unquestionable
indiscutibil'mente *adv* unquestionably
indispen'sabile *a* essential; ‹*persona*› indispensable
indispet'tire *vt* irritate
indispet'tirsi *vr* get irritated
indi'sporre *vt* anger
indisposizi'one *nf* indisposition
indi'sposto *pp di* **indisporre** ● *a* indisposed
indisso'lubile *a* indissoluble
indissolubil'mente *adv* indissolubly
indistin'guibile *a* indiscernible
indistinta'mente *adv* without exception
indi'stinto *a* indistinct
indistrut'tibile *a* indestructible
indistur'bato *a* undisturbed
in'divia *nf* endive
individu'abile *a* detectable
individu'ale *a* individual
individua'lista *nmf* individualist
individua'listico *a* individualistic
individualità *nf* individuality
individu'are *vt* individualize; (*localizzare*)
  locate; (*riconoscere*) single out
indi'viduo *nm* individual
indivi'sibile *a* indivisible
indivisibilità *nf* indivisibility
indi'viso *a* undivided
indizi'are *vt* throw suspicion on
indizi'ario *a* circumstantial
indizi'ato, -a *a* suspected ● *nmf* suspect
in'dizio *nm* sign; *Jur* circumstantial evidence
Indo'cina *nf* Indochina
indoeuro'peo *a* Indo-European
'**indole** *nf* nature
indo'lente *a* indolent
indo'lenza *nf* indolence
indolenzi'mento *nm* stiffness, ache
indolen'zire *vt* stiffen up

indolen'zirsi *vr* stiffen up, go stiff
indolen'zito *a* stiff
indo'lore *a* painless
indo'mabile *a* untameable
indo'mani *nm* l'~ the following day
in'domito *a* untamed
Indo'nesia *nf* Indonesia
indonesi'ano, -a *a & nmf* Indonesian
indo'rare *vt* gild; ~ **la pillola** sugar the pill
indos'sare *vt* wear; (*mettere addosso*) put on
indossa'|tore, -'trice *nm* [male] model
  ● *nf* model
in'dotto *pp di* **indurre**
indottri'nare *vt* indoctrinate
indovi'nare *vt* guess; (*predire*) foretell
indovi'nato *a* successful; (*scelta*) well-cho-
  sen
indovi'nello *nm* riddle
indo'vino, -a *nmf* fortune-teller
indù *a inv & nmf inv* Hindu
indubbia'mente *adv* undoubtedly
in'dubbio *a* undoubted
indubi'tabile *a* indubitable
indubitabil'mente *adv* indubitably
indugi'are *vi* linger
indugi'arsi *vr* linger
in'dugio *nm* delay
indu'ismo *nm* Hinduism
indul'gente *a* indulgent
indul'genza *nf* indulgence
in'dulgere *vi* ~ **a** indulge in
in'dulto *pp di* **indulgere** ● *nm Jur* pardon
indu'mento *nm* garment; **indumenti** *pl*
  clothes. **indumenti** *pl* **intimi** underwear
induri'mento *nm* hardening
indu'rire *vt* harden
indu'rirsi *vr* harden
in'durre *vt* induce; ~ **qcno a fare** induce sb
  to do; ~ **in tentazione** lead into temptation
in'dustria *nf* industry. ~ **dell'ab-**
  bigliamento clothing industry, rag trade
  fam. ~ **leggera** light industry. ~ **pesante**
  heavy industry. ~ **dello spettacolo** show
  business, showbiz *fam.* ~ **terziaria** service
  industry. ~ **tessile** textile industry, textiles
industri'ale *a* industrial; **zona** ~ industrial
  estate ● *nmf* industrialist
industrializ'zare *vt* industrialize
industrializ'zato *a* industrialized
industrializzazi'one *nf* industrialization
industrial'mente *adv* industrially
industri'arsi *vr* ~ **per guadagnare**
  qualcosa set to and earn some money
industriosa'mente *adv* industriously
industri'oso *a* industrious
indut'tivo *a* inductive
indut'tore *nm* inductor
induzi'one *nf* induction
inebe'tire *vt* daze
inebe'tito *a* stunned
inebri'ante *a* intoxicating, exciting
inebri'are *vt* intoxicate
inebri'arsi *vr* become inebriated
inecce'pibile *a* unexceptionable
i'nedia *nf* starvation

i'nedito a unpublished
inedu'cato a impolite
inef'fabile a inexpressible
ineffi'cace a ineffective
ineffici'ente a inefficient
ineffici'enza nf inefficiency
ineguagli'abile a incomparable
ineguagli'ato a unequalled
inegu'ale a unequal; ⟨superficie⟩ uneven
inelut'tabile a inescapable
inenar'rabile a indescribable
inequivo'cabile a unequivocal
inequivocabil'mente adv unequivocally
ine'rente a ~ **a** inherent in
inerente'mente adv ~ **a** concerning
i'nerme a unarmed; fig defenceless
inerpi'carsi vr ~ **su** clamber up
i'nerte a inactive; Phys inert
i'nerzia nf inactivity; Phys inertia
inesat'tezza nf inaccuracy
ine'satto a inaccurate; ⟨erroneo⟩ incorrect; ⟨non riscosso⟩ uncollected
inesau'ribile a inexhaustible
inesi'stente a non-existent
inesi'stenza nf non-existence
ineso'rabile a inexorable
inesorabil'mente adv inexorably
inesperi'enza nf inexperience
ine'sperto a inexperienced
inespli'cabile a inexplicable
inesplicabil'mente adv inexplicably
inesplo'rato a undiscovered
ine'sploso a unexploded
inespres'sivo a expressionless
inespri'mibile a inexpressible
inespu'gnabile a impregnable
ineste'tismo nm blemish
inesti'mabile a inestimable
inestin'guibile a ⟨sete⟩ insatiable; ⟨odio⟩ undying
inestir'pabile a impossible to eradicate
inestri'cabile a inextricable
inestricabil'mente adv inextricably
inetti'tudine nf ineptitude
i'netto a inept. ~ **a** unsuited to
ine'vaso a ⟨pratiche, corrispondenza⟩ pending
inevi'tabile a inevitable
inevitabil'mente adv inevitably
in ex'tremis adv ⟨segnare un gol⟩ in the nick of time; ⟨prima di morire⟩ in extremis
i'nezia nf trifle
infagot'tare vt wrap up
infagot'tarsi vr wrap [oneself] up
infal'libile a infallible
infa'mante a defamatory
infa'mare vt defame
infama'torio a defamatory
in'fame a infamous; ⟨fam: orrendo⟩ awful, shocking
in'famia nf infamy
infan'gare vt cover with mud; fig sully
infan'garsi vr get muddy
infanti'cida nmf infanticide
infanti'cidio nm infanticide

infan'tile a ⟨letteratura, abbigliamento⟩ children's attrib; ⟨ingenuità⟩ childlike; pej childish
in'fanzia nf childhood; ⟨bambini⟩ children pl; **prima ~** infancy
infar'cire vt stuff (**di** with)
infari'nare vt flour; ~ **di** sprinkle with
infarina'tura nf fig smattering
in'farto nm coronary
infasti'dire vt irritate
infasti'dirsi vr get irritated
infati'cabile a untiring
infaticabil'mente adv tirelessly
in'fatti conj as a matter of fact; ⟨veramente⟩ indeed
infatu'arsi vr ~ **di** become infatuated with
infatu'ato a infatuated
infatuazi'one nf infatuation
in'fausto a ill-omened
infecondità nf infertility
infe'condo a infertile
infe'dele a unfaithful
infedeltà nf unfaithfulness
infe'lice a unhappy; ⟨inappropriato⟩ unfortunate; ⟨cattivo⟩ bad
infelicità nf unhappiness
infel'trire vi matt
infel'trirsi vr matt
infel'trito a matted
inferi'ore a ⟨più basso⟩ lower; ⟨qualità⟩ inferior ● nmf inferior
inferiorità nf inferiority
infe'rire vt infer; strike ⟨colpo⟩
inferme'ria nf infirmary; ⟨di nave⟩ sick-bay
infermi'ere, -a nm [male] nurse ● nf nurse
infermità nf sickness. ~ **mentale** mental illness
in'fermo, -a a sick ● nmf invalid
infer'nale a infernal; ⟨spaventoso⟩ hellish
in'ferno nm hell; **va' all'~!** go to hell!
infero'cirsi vr become fierce
inferri'ata nf grating
infervo'rare vt arouse enthusiasm in
infervo'rarsi vr get excited
infe'stare vt infest
infestazi'one nf infestation
infet'tare vt infect
infet'tarsi vr become infected
infet'tivo a infectious
in'fetto a infected
infezi'one nf infection
infiac'chire vt/i weaken
infiac'chirsi vr weaken
infiam'mabile a [in]flammable
infiam'mare vt set on fire; Med, fig inflame
infiam'marsi vr catch fire; Med become inflamed
infiammazi'one nf Med inflammation
infia'scare vt bottle
infici'are vt Jur invalidate
in'fido a treacherous
infie'rire vi ⟨imperversare⟩ rage; ~ **su** attack furiously
in'figgere vt drive
in'figgersi vr ~ **in** penetrate

infi'lare *vt* thread; (*mettere*) insert; (*indossare*) put on

infi'larsi *vr* slip on ‹*vestito*›; ~ **in** (*introdursi*) slip into

infil'trarsi *vr* infiltrate

infil'trato, -a *nmf* infiltrator

infiltrazi'one *nf* infiltration; (*d'acqua*) seepage; (*Med: iniezione*) injection

infil'zare *vt* pierce; (*infilare*) string; (*conficcare*) stick

'infimo *a* lowest

in'fine *adv* finally; (*insomma*) in short

infin'gardo *a* slothful

infinità *nf* infinity; **un'~ di** masses of

infinita'mente *adv* infinitely

infinitesi'male *a* infinitesimal

infi'nito *a* infinite; *Gram* infinitive ● *nm* infinite; *Gram* infinitive; *Math* infinity; **all'~** endlessly

infinocchi'are *vt fam* hoodwink

infiocchet'tare *vt* tie up with ribbons

infiore'scenza *nf* inflorescence

infischi'arsi *vr* ~ **di** not care about; **me ne infischio** *fam* I couldn't care less

in'fisso *pp di* **infiggere** ● *nm* fixture; (*di porta, finestra*) frame

infit'tire *vt/i* thicken

infit'tirsi *vr* thicken

inflazi'one *nf* inflation. ~ **galoppante** galloping inflation. ~ **strisciante** creeping inflation

inflazio'nistico *a* inflationary

infles'sibile *a* inflexible

inflessibilità *nf* inflexibility

inflessi'one *nf* inflection, inflexion

in'fliggere *vt* inflict

in'flitto *pp di* **infliggere**

influ'ente *a* influential

influ'enza *nf* influence; *Med* influenza; **prendere l'~** catch the flu. ~ **gastro-intestinale** gastric flu

influen'zabile *a* ‹*mente, opinione*› impressionable

influen'zare *vt* influence

influen'zato *a* **essere ~** (*con febbre*) have the flu

influ'ire *vi* ~ **su** influence

in'flusso *nm* influence

info'carsi *vr* catch fire; (*viso:*) go red; ‹*discussione:*› become heated

info'gnarsi *vr fam* get into a mess

infol'tire *vt/i* thicken

infon'dato *a* unfounded

in'fondere *vt* instil

infor'care *vt* fork ‹*fieno*›; get on ‹*bici*›; put on ‹*occhiali*›

inforca'tura *nf* crotch

infor'male *a* informal

infor'mare *vt* inform

infor'marsi *vr* inquire (**di** about)

infor'matica *nf* information technology, IT

infor'matico *a* computer *attrib*

informa'tivo *a* informative

infor'mato *a* informed; **male ~** ill-informed

informa'|tore, -'trice *nmf* (*di polizia*) informer. ~ **medico scientifico** representative of a pharmaceutical company

informazi'one *nf* information; **un'~** a piece of information; **informazioni** *pl* information; **servizio informazioni** enquiries. ~ **genetica** genetic code. ~ **riservata** confidential information. **informazioni** *pl* **sbagliate** misinformation

infor'nare *vt* put into the oven

infortu'narsi *vr* have an accident

infortu'nato, -a *a* injured ● *nmf* injured person; **gli infortunati** the injured

infor'tunio *nm* accident. ~ **sul lavoro** industrial accident

infortu'nistica *nf* study of industrial accidents

infos'sarsi *vr* sink; ‹*guance, occhi:*› become hollow

infos'sato *a* sunken, hollow

infradici'are *vt* drench

infradici'arsi *vr* get drenched; (*diventare marcio*) rot

infra'dito *nmpl* (*scarpe*) flip-flops

in'frangere *vt* break; (*in mille pezzi*) shatter

in'frangersi *vr* break; (*in mille pezzi*) shatter

infran'gibile *a* unbreakable

in'franto *pp di* **infrangere** ● *a* shattered; ‹*fig: cuore*› broken

infra'rosso *a* infra-red

infrasettima'nale *a* midweek

infrastrut'tura *nf* infrastructure

infrazi'one *nf* offence. ~ **al codice della strada** traffic offence

infredda'tura *nf* cold

infreddo'lirsi *vr* feel cold

infreddo'lito *a* cold

infre'quente *a* infrequent

infruttu'oso *a* fruitless

infuo'care *vt* make red-hot

infuo'cato *a* burning

infu'ori *adv* **all'~** outwards; **all'~ di** except; **denti ~** buck teeth

infuri'are *vi* rage

infuri'arsi *vr* fly into a rage

infuri'ato *a* blustering

infusi'one *nf* infusion

in'fuso *pp di* **infondere** ● *nm* infusion

Ing. *abbr* **ingegnere**

ingabbi'are *vt* cage; (*fig: mettere in prigione*) jail

ingaggi'are *vt* engage; sign up ‹*calciatori ecc*›; begin ‹*lotta, battaglia*›

in'gaggio *nm* engagement; (*di calciatore*) signing [up]

ingan'nare *vt* deceive; (*essere infedele a*) be unfaithful to; ~ **l'attesa** kill time

ingan'narsi *vr* deceive oneself; **se non m'inganno** if I am not mistaken

ingan'nevole *a* deceptive

in'ganno *nm* deceit; (*frode*) fraud; **trarre in ~** deceive

ingarbugli'are *vt* entangle; (*confondere*) confuse

ingarbugli'arsi *vr* get entangled; (*confondersi*) become confused

ingarbu'gliato *a* confused

inge'gnarsi *vr* do one's best; ~ **per vivere** try to scrape a living

inge'gnere *nm* engineer. ~ **aeronautico** aeronautical engineer. ~ **civile** civil engineer. ~ **edile** structural engineer. ~ **meccanico** mechanical engineer. ~ **minerario** mining engineer. ~ **navale** marine engineer

ingegne'ria *nf* engineering. ~ **aeronautica** aeronautical engineering. ~ **civile** civil engineering. ~ **edile** structural engineering. ~ **genetica** genetic engineering. ~ **meccanica** mechanical engineering

in'gegno *nm* brains *pl*; (*genio*) genius; (*abilità*) ingenuity

ingegnosa'mente *adv* ingeniously

ingegnosità *nf* ingenuity

inge'gnoso *a* ingenious

ingelo'sire *vt* make jealous

ingelo'sirsi *vr* become jealous

in'gente *a* huge

ingenua'mente *adv* artlessly

ingenuità *nf* ingenuousness

in'genuo *a* ingenuous; (*credulone*) naïve

inge'renza *nf* interference

inge'rire *vt* swallow

inges'sare *vt* put in plaster

ingessa'tura *nf* plaster

Inghil'terra *nf* England

inghiot'tire *vt* swallow

in'ghippo *nm* trick

ingial'lire *vi* turn yellow

ingial'lirsi *vr* turn yellow

ingial'lito *a* yellowed

ingigan'tire *vt* magnify; blow up out of proportion (*problema*) ● *vi* take on gigantic proportions

ingigan'tirsi *vr* take on gigantic proportions

inginocchi'arsi *vr* kneel [down]

inginocchi'ato *a* kneeling

inginocchia'toio *nm* prie-dieu

ingioiel'larsi *vr* put on one's jewels

ingioiel'lato *a* bejewelled

ingiù *adv* down; **all'~** downwards; **a testa ~** head downwards

ingi'ungere *vt* order

ingiunzi'one *nf* injunction, court order. ~ **di pagamento** final demand

ingi'uria *nf* insult; (*torto*) wrong; (*danno*) damage

ingiuri'are *vt* insult; (*fare un torto a*) wrong

ingiuri'oso *a* insulting

ingiusta'mente *adv* unjustly

ingiustifi'cabile *a* unjustifiable; (*comportamento*) indefensible

ingiustifi'cato *a* unjustified

ingiu'stizia *nf* injustice

ingi'usto *a* unjust

in'glese *a* English ● *nm* Englishman; (*lingua*) English; **gli inglesi** the English ● *nf* Englishwoman

inglori'oso *a* inglorious

ingob'bire *vi* become stooped

ingoi'are *vt* swallow

ingol'fare *vt* flood ‹*motore*›

ingol'farsi *vr* *fig* get involved; ‹*motore:*› flood

ingol'lare *vt* gulp down

ingom'brante *a* cumbersome

ingom'brare *vt* clutter up; *fig* cram ‹*mente*›

in'gombro *nm* encumbrance; **essere d'~** be in the way

ingor'digia *nf* greed

in'gordo *a* greedy

ingor'gare *vt* block

ingor'garsi *vr* be blocked [up]

in'gorgo *nm* blockage; (*del traffico*) jam

ingoz'zare *vt* gobble up; (*nutrire eccessivamente*) stuff; fatten ‹*animali*›

ingoz'zarsi *vr* stuff oneself (**di** with)

ingra'naggio *nm* gear; *fig* mechanism

ingra'nare *vt* engage ● *vi* be in gear

ingrandi'mento *nm* enlargement

ingran'dire *vt* enlarge; (*esagerare*) magnify

ingran'dirsi *vr* become larger; (*aumentare*) increase

ingrandi'tore *nm* *Phot* enlarger

ingras'saggio *nm* greasing, lubrication

ingras'sare *vt* fatten [up]; *Mech* lubricate, grease ● *vi* put on weight

ingras'sarsi *vr* put on weight

in'grasso *nm* **mettere all'~** force-feed

ingrati'tudine *nf* ingratitude

in'grato *a* ungrateful; (*sgradevole*) thankless

ingrazi'arsi *vr* ingratiate oneself with

ingredi'ente *nm* ingredient

in'gresso *nm* entrance; (*accesso*) admittance; (*sala*) hall; *Comput* input ~ **gratuito** *o* **libero** admission free; **'vietato l'~'** 'no entry; no admittance'. ~ **degli artisti** stage door. ~ **principale** main entrance. ~ **di servizio** tradesmen's entrance. ~**/uscita** *Comput* input/output. ~ **video** *Techn* video input

ingros'sare *vt* make big; (*gonfiare*) swell ● *vi* grow big; (*gonfiare*) swell

ingros'sarsi *vr* grow big; (*gonfiare*) swell

in'grosso: **all'~** *adv* wholesale; (*pressappoco*) roughly

ingrai'arsi *vr* get into trouble

inguai'nare *vt* sheathe

ingual'cibile *a* crease-resistant

ingua'ribile *a* incurable

inguaribil'mente *adv* incurably

'inguine *nm* groin

ingurgi'tare *vt* gulp down

ini'bire *vt* inhibit; (*vietare*) forbid

ini'bito *a* inhibited

inibi'tore *nm* suppressant

inibizi'one *nf* inhibition; (*divieto*) prohibition

iniet'tare *vt* inject

iniet'tarsi *vr* ~ **di sangue** ‹*occhi:*› become bloodshot

iniezi'one *nf* injection. ~ **endovenosa** intravenous injection. ~ **intramuscolare** intramuscular injection

inimic'arsi vr ~ qcno make an enemy of sb
inimi'cizia nf enmity
inimi'tabile a inimitable
inimmagi'nabile a unimaginable
ininfiam'mabile a nonflammable
intelli'gibile a unintelligible
ininterrotta'mente adv continuously
ininter'rotto a continuous
iniquità nf inv iniquity
i'niquo a iniquitous
inizi'ale a & nf initial
inizial'mente adv initially
inizi'are vt begin; (avviare) open; ~ a fare qcsa begin doing sth; ~ qcno a qcsa initiate sb in sth ● vi begin
inizia'tiva nf initiative; **prendere l'~** take the initiative. ~ **privata** private enterprise
inizi'ato, -a nmf initiated
inizia|'tore, -'trice nmf initiator
iniziazi'one nf initiation
i'nizio nm beginning; **dare ~ a** start; **avere ~** get under way
innaffi'are vt water
innaffia'toio nm watering-can
innal'zare vt raise; (erigere) erect
innal'zarsi vr rise
innamo'rarsi vr fall in love (di with)
innamo'rato a in love ● nm boyfriend
in'nanzi adv (stato in luogo) in front; (di tempo) ahead; (avanti) forward; (prima) before; **d'ora ~** from now on ● prep (prima) before; ~ **a** in front of; ~ **tutto** = **innanzitutto**
innanzi'tutto adv (soprattutto) above all; (per prima cosa) first of all
in'nato a innate
innatu'rale a unnatural
inne'gabile a undeniable
innegabil'mente adv undeniably
inneggi'are vi praise
innervo'sire vt make nervous
innervo'sirsi vr get irritated
inne'scare vt prime
in'nesco nm primer
inne'stare vt graft; Mech engage; (inserire) insert
in'nesto nm graft; Mech clutch; Electr connection
inneva'mento nm snowfall. ~ **artificiale** snow-making
inne'vato a covered in snow
'inno nm hymn. ~ **nazionale** national anthem
inno'cente a innocent; Jur not guilty
innocente'mente adv innocently
inno'cenza nf innocence
in'nocuo a innocuous
inno'vare vt update
innova'tivo a innovative
innova'tore a trail-blazing
innovazi'one nf innovation
innume'revole a innumerable
+ino suff **fratellino** nm little brother; **sorellina** nf little sister; **freddino** (piuttosto freddo) chilly; **bellino** a (abbastanza bello) pretty; **benino** adv (così così) not bad;

pochino a (troppo poco) not enough; **un pochino** a little bit
inocu'lare vt inoculate
ino'doro a odourless
inoffen'sivo a inoffensive, harmless; (animale) harmless
inol'trare vt forward
inol'trarsi vr advance
inol'trato a late
i'noltre adv besides
i'noltro nm forwarding
inon'dare vt flood
inondazi'one nf flood
inope'roso a idle
inopi'nabile a unimaginable
inoppor'tuno a untimely
inor'ganico a inorganic
inorgo'glire vt make proud
inorgo'glirsi vr become proud
inorri'dire vt horrify ● vi be horrified
inospi'tale a inhospitable
inosser'vato a unobserved; (non rispettato) disregarded; **passare ~** go unobserved
inossi'dabile a stainless
'inox a inv (acciaio) stainless; (pentole) stainless steel
'input nm inv ~ **dati** data input
inqua'drare vt frame; fig set
inqua'drarsi vr ~ **in** fit into
inquadra'tura nf framing
inqualifi'cabile a unspeakable
inquie'tante a unnerving
inquie'tare vt worry
inquie'tarsi vr get worried; (impazientirsi) get cross
inqui'eto a restless; (preoccupato) worried
inquie'tudine nf anxiety
inqui'lino, -a nmf tenant
inquina'mento nm pollution. ~ **acustico** noise pollution. ~ **atmosferico** air pollution. ~ **delle prove** Jur tampering with the evidence
inqui'nare vt pollute
inqui'nato a polluted
inqui'rente a Jur (magistrato) examining; (commissione) of investigation
inqui'sire vt/i investigate
inqui'sito a under investigation ● nm person under investigation
inquisi|'tore, -'trice a inquiring ● nmf inquisitor
inquisi'torio a questioning
inquisizi'one nf inquisition
insabbi'are vt bury
insabbi'arsi vr run aground
insa'lata nf salad. ~ **belga** Belgian endive. ~ **di mare** seafood salad. ~ **mista** mixed salad. ~ **di riso** rice salad. ~ **russa** Russian salad
insalati'era nf salad bowl
insa'lubre a unhealthy
insa'nabile a incurable
insangui'nare vt stain with blood
insangui'nato a blood-stained
insapo'nare vt soap

insapo'narsi *vr* soap oneself
insapo'nata *nf* soaping
insa'pore *a* tasteless
insapo'rire *vt* flavour
insa'puta *nf* all'~ **di** unknown to
in'saturo *a* unsaturated
insazi'abile *a* insatiable
inscato'lare *vt* can
inscatola'trice *nf* canning machine
insce'nare *vt* stage
inscin'dibile *a* inseparable
in'scrivere *vt Math* inscribe
insec'chire *vt/i* wither
insedia'mento *nm* installation
insedi'are *vt* install
insedi'arsi *vr* install oneself
in'segna *nf* sign; (*bandiera*) flag; (*decorazione*) decoration; (*emblema*) insignia *pl*; (*stemma*) symbol. ~ **luminosa** neon sign
insegna'mento *nm* teaching
inse'gnante *a* teaching ● *nmf* teacher. ~ **di matematica** maths teacher. ~ **di sostegno** tutor
inse'gnare *vt/i* teach; ~ **qcsa a qcno** teach sb sth
insegui'mento *nmf* pursuit
insegu'ire *vt* pursue
insegui'tore, -'trice *nmf* pursuer
inselvati'chire *vt* make wild ● *vi* grow wild
inselvati'chirsi *vr* grow wild
insemi'nare *vt* inseminate
inseminazi'one *nf* insemination. ~ **artificiale** artificial insemination
insena'tura *nf* inlet
insensata'mente *adv* senselessly
insen'sato *a* senseless; (*folle*) crazy
insen'sibile *a fig* insensitive; **avere le gambe insensibili** have no feeling in one's legs
insensibilità *nf* lack of feeling; *fig* insensitivity
insepa'rabile *a* inseparable
inseri'mento *nm* insertion
inse'rire *vt* insert; place ‹*annuncio*›; *Electr* connect
inse'rirsi *vr* ~ **in** get into
inseri'tore *nm inv* ~ **fogli** (**singoli**) (single) sheetfeed
in'serto *nm* file; (*in un film ecc*) insert
inservi'ente *nmf* attendant
inserzi'one *nf* insertion; (*avviso*) advertisement; **inserzioni** *pl* classified ads
inserzio'nista *nmf* advertiser
insetti'cida *nm* insecticide
insetti'fugo *nm* insect repellent
in'setto *nm* insect
insicu'rezza *nf* insecurity
insi'curo *a* insecure
in'sidia *nf* trick; (*tranello*) snare
insidi'are *vt/i* lay a trap for
insidi'oso *a* insidious
insi'eme *adv* together; (*contemporaneamente*) at the same time ● *prep* ~ **a** [together] with ● *nm* whole; (*completo*) outfit; *Theat* en-

semble; *Math* set; **nell'**~ as a whole; **tutto** ~ (*in una volta*) at one go
insie'mistica *nf* set theory
in'signe *a* renowned
insignifi'cante *a* insignificant
insi'gnire *vt* decorate
insin'cero *a* insincere
insinda'cabile *a* final
insinu'ante *a* insinuating
insinu'are *vt* insinuate
insinu'arsi *vr* penetrate; ~ **in** *fig* creep into
insinuazi'one *nf* insinuation
in'sipido *a* insipid
insi'stente *a* insistent
insistente'mente *adv* repeatedly
insi'stenza *nf* insistence
in'sistere *vi* insist; (*perseverare*) persevere
'insito *a* inherent
insoddisfa'cente *a* unsatisfactory
insoddi'sfatto *a* unsatisfied; (*scontento*) dissatisfied
insoddisfazi'one *nf* dissatisfaction
insoffe'rente *a* intolerant
insoffe'renza *nf* intolerance
insolazi'one *nf* sunstroke
inso'lente *a* rude, insolent
insolente'mente *adv* insolently
inso'lenza *nf* rudeness, insolence; (*commento*) insolent remark
insolita'mente *adv* unusually
in'solito *a* unusual
inso'lubile *a* insoluble
inso'luto *a* unsolved; (*non pagato*) unpaid
insol'vente *a Jur* insolvent
insol'venza *nf* insolvency
insol'vibile *a* insolvent
in'somma *adv* in short; ~**!** well!
inson'dabile *a* unfathomable
in'sonne *a* sleepless
in'sonnia *nf* insomnia
insonno'lito *a* sleepy
insonoriz'zare *vt* soundproof
insonoriz'zato *a* soundproofed
insoppor'tabile *a* unbearable
insoppri'mibile *a* unsuppressible
insor'genza *nf* onset
in'sorgere *vi* revolt, rise up; ‹*problema:*› arise
insormon'tabile *a* ‹*ostacolo, difficoltà*› insurmountable
in'sorto *pp di* **insorgere** ● *a* rebellious ● *nm* rebel
insospet'tabile *a* unsuspected
insospet'tire *vt* make suspicious ● *vi* become suspicious
insospet'tirsi *vr* become suspicious
insoste'nibile *a* untenable; (*insopportabile*) unbearable
insostitu'ibile *a* irreplaceable
insoz'zare *vt* dirty
inspe'rabile *a* hopeless; (*insperato*) unhoped-for
inspe'rato *a* unhoped-for
inspie'gabile *a* inexplicable
inspiegabil'mente *adv* inexplicably

inspi'rare vt breathe in

in'stabile a unstable; (variabile) unsettled

instabilità nf instability; (di tempo) changeability

instal'lare vt install

instal'larsi vr (in casa, lavoro) settle in

installa|'tore, -'trice nmf fitter

installazi'one nf installation. **installazioni** pl **di bordo** on-board equipment

instan'cabile a untiring

instancabil'mente adv tirelessly

instau'rare vt found

instau'rarsi vr become established

instaurazi'one nf foundation

instra'dare vt direct

insù: **all'~** adv upwards; **naso all'~** turned-up nose

insubordi'nato a insubordinate

insubordinazi'one nf insubordination

insuc'cesso nm failure

insudici'are vt dirty

insudici'arsi vr get dirty

insuffici'ente a insufficient; (inadeguato) inadequate ● nf Sch fail

insufficiente'mente adv insufficiently

insuffici'enza nf insufficiency; (inadeguatezza) inadequacy; Sch fail. **~ cardiaca** cardiac insufficiency. **~ di prove** lack of evidence

insu'lare a insular

insu'lina nf insulin

in'sulso a insipid; (sciocco) silly

insul'tare vt insult

in'sulto nm insult; **coprire qcno di insulti** heap abuse on sb

insupe'rabile a insuperable; (eccezionale) incomparable

insurrezi'one nf insurrection

insussi'stente a groundless

intac'cabile a subject to corrosion; fig open to criticism

intac'care vt nick; (corrodere) corrode; draw on (capitale); (danneggiare) damage

intagli'are vt carve

in'taglio nm carving

intan'gibile a untouchable

in'tanto adv meanwhile; (per ora) for the moment; (avversativo) but; **~ che** while

intarsi'are vt inlay

intarsi'ato a **~ di** inset with

in'tarsio nm inlay

intasa'mento nm (ostruzione) blockage; (ingorgo) traffic jam

inta'sare vt block, clog

inta'sarsi vr become blocked

inta'sato a blocked

inta'scare vt pocket

in'tatto a intact

intavo'lare vt start

inte'gerrimo a of integrity

inte'grale a whole; **edizione ~** unabridged edition; **pane ~** wholemeal bread; **versione ~** (di film) uncut version; (di romanzo) unabridged version

integra'lista nmf fundamentalist

integral'mente adv fully

inte'grante a integral

inte'grare vt integrate; (aggiungere) supplement

inte'grarsi vr integrate

integra'tivo a supplementary, additional; **esame ~** test taken by pupil wishing to tranfer from arts to a scientific stream etc

integra'tore nm **~ alimentare** dietary supplement

integrazi'one nf integration

integrità nf integrity

'integro a complete; (retto) upright

intelaia'tura nf framework

intellet'tivo a intellectual

intel'letto nm intellect

intellettu'ale a & nmf intellectual

intellettual'mente adv intellectually

intelli'gente a intelligent

intelligente'mente adv intelligently

intelli'genza nf intelligence. **~ artificiale** artificial intelligence

intelli'ghenzia nf intelligentsia

intelli'gibile a intelligible

intelligibil'mente adv intelligibly

intelligi'oco nm computer game

intempe'rante a intemperate

intempe'ranza nf intemperance; **intemperanze** pl excesses

intem'perie nfpl bad weather

intempe'stivo a untimely

inten'dente nm superintendent

inten'denza nf **~ di finanza** inland revenue office

in'tendere vt (comprendere) understand; (udire) hear; (avere intenzione) intend; (significare) mean; [**siamo**] **intesi?** is that clear?

in'tendersi vr (capirsi) understand each other; **~ di** (essere esperto in) have a good knowledge of; **intendersela con** (fam: avere una relazione con) have it off with

intendi'mento nm understanding; (intenzione) intention

intendi|'tore, -'trice nmf connoisseur; **intenditori** pl cognoscenti

intene'rire vt soften; (commuovere) touch

intene'rirsi vr be touched

intensa'mente adv intensely

intensifi'care vt intensify

intensifi'carsi vr intensify

intensità nf intensity

intensiva'mente adv intensively

inten'sivo a intensive

in'tenso a intense

inten'tare vt start up; **~ causa contro qcno** bring o institute proceedings against sb

inten'tato a **non lasciare nulla di ~** try everything

in'tento a engrossed (**a** in) ● nm purpose

intenzio'nale a intentional

intenzio'nato a **essere ~ a fare qcsa** have the intention of doing sth

intenzi'one *nf* intention; **senza ~** unintentionally; **avere ~ di fare qcsa** intend to do sth, have the intention of doing sth

intera'gire *vi* interact

intera'mente *adv* completely, entirely

interat'tivo *a* interactive

interazi'one *nf* interaction

interca'lare *nm* stock phrase ● *vt* insert ‹*esclamazione*›

intercambi'abile *a* interchangeable

interca'pedine *nf* cavity

inter'cedere *vi* intercede

intercessi'one *nf* intercession

intercet'tare *vt* intercept; tap ‹*telefono*›

intercettazi'one *nf* interception. **~ telefonica** telephone tapping

inter'city *nm inv* inter-city

intercomuni'cante *a* [inter]communicating

interconfessio'nale *a* interdenominational

intercon'nettere *vt* interconnect

intercontinen'tale *a* intercontinental

inter'correre *vi* ‹*tempo:*› elapse; (*esistere*) exist

interco'stale *a* intercostal; **dolori intercostali** *fam* growing pains

interden'tale *a* between the teeth; **filo ~** dental floss

inter'detto *pp di* **interdire** ● *a* astonished; (*proibito*) forbidden; **rimanere ~** be taken aback; **lasciare qcno ~** astonish sb, dumbfound sb ● *nm Relig* interdict

interdipartimen'tale *a* interdepartmental

interdipen'dente *a* interdependent

interdipen'denza *nf* interdependence

inter'dire *vt* ban; (*nel calcio*) intercept; *Jur* deprive of civil rights; *Relig* interdict; **~ a qcno di fare qcsa** forbid sb to do sth

interdiscipli'nare *a* interdisciplinary

interdizi'one *nf* ban; (*nel calcio*) interception; *Relig* interdict. **~ giudiziale** *appointment of a legal guardian to a minor of unsound mind.* **~ legale** *legally imposed ban.* **~ dai pubblici uffici** *ban on taking public office*

interessa'mento *nm* interest

interes'sante *a* interesting; **essere in stato ~** be pregnant

interes'sare *vt* interest; (*riguardare*) concern ● *vi* **~ a** interest; **non mi interessa** I'm not interested; (*non mi importa*) I don't care, it doesn't matter to me

interes'sarsi *vr* **~ a** take an interest in; **~ di** take care of

interes'sato *a* (*attento*) interested; *pej* self-interested; **diretto ~** person concerned

inte'resse *nm* interest; **fare qcsa per ~** do sth out of self-interest; **essere nell'~ di qcno** be in sb's interest; **un ~ del 4%** 4% interest. **~ attivo** interest charge. **~ maturato** accrued interest. **~ privato in atti di ufficio** abuse of public office. **~ a tasso variabile** floating rate interest

interes'senza *nf Econ* profit-sharing

inter'faccia *nf* interface. **~ uomo/macchina** man/machine interface. **~ utente** user interface

interfacci'are *vt* interface

interfacci'arsi *vr* interface

interfe'renza *nf* interference

interfe'rire *vi* interfere

inter'fono *nm* intercom

interga'lattico *a* intergalactic

interiet'tivo *a* interjectory

interiezi'one *nf* interjection

'interim *nm inv* (*incarico*) temporary appointment; (*periodo*) interim; **ad ~** on a temporary basis; ‹*presidente*› acting

interi'ora *nfpl* entrails

interi'ore *a* inner

interioriz'zare *vt* internalize

interior'mente *adv* (*nella parte interiore*) internally; (*emotivamente*) inwardly

inter'linea *nf* line spacing; *Typ* leading. **~ doppia** double spacing

interline'are *vt* space out ● *a* line *attrib*

interlocu'tore, -'trice *nmf* speaker, interlocutor *fml*; **il mio ~** the person I am/was speaking to

inter'ludio *nm* interlude

intermedi'ario, -a *a & nmf* intermediary; *Econ* middleman

intermediazi'one *nf* (*intervento*) mediation

inter'medio *a* in-between

inter'mezzo *nm Theat, Mus* intermezzo

intermi'nabile *a* interminable

interministeri'ale *a* interdepartmental

intermissi'one *nf* intermission

intermit'tente *a* intermittent; ‹*vulcano*› dormant

intermit'tenza *nf* **a ~** intermittent

interna'mente *adv* internally

interna'mento *nm* internment; (*in manicomio*) committal

inter'nare *vt* intern; (*in manicomio*) commit [to a mental institution]

inter'nato, -a *a* interned ● *nmf* internee ● *nm* boarding school

internazio'nale *a* international

internazional'mente *adv* internationally

'Internet *nm* Internet; **in ~** on the Internet; **via ~** through the Internet

inter'nista *nmf* internist

in'terno *a* internal; *Geog* inland; (*interiore*) inner; ‹*politica*› national; **alunno ~** boarder ● *nm* interior; (*di condominio*) flat; *Teleph* extension; *Cinema* interior shot; **all'~** inside; **ministero degli interni** Ministry of the Interior, ≈ Home Office

in'tero *a* whole, entire; *Math* whole; (*intatto*) intact; (*completo*) complete; **per ~** in full ● *nm* (*totalità*) whole

interparlamen'tare *a* interparliamentary

interpel'lanza *nf* parliamentary question

interpel'lare *vt* consult

interpel'lato, -a *nmf* person being questioned

interperso'nale a interpersonal

interplane'tario a interplanetary

interpo'lare vt interpolate

inter'porre vt interpose; use ⟨influenza⟩; ~ **ostacoli a** put obstacles in the way of

inter'porsi vr intervene; ~ **tra** come between

inter'posto a **per interposta persona** through a third party

interpre'tare vt interpret; Mus perform; ~ **male** misinterpret

interpretari'ato nm interpreting

interpretazi'one nf interpretation; Mus performance

in'terprete nmf interpreter; Mus performer

interpunzi'one nf punctuation

inter'rare vt ⟨seppellire⟩ bury; ⟨riempire⟩ fill in; lay underground ⟨cavo, tubo⟩; plant ⟨pianta, seme⟩

inter'rato nm basement

interregio'nale nm long-distance train, stopping at all stations

interro'gante nmf questioner

interro'gare vt question; Sch examine

interrogativa'mente adv ⟨guardare⟩ inquiringly

interroga'tivo a interrogative; ⟨sguardo⟩ questioning ● nm question

interro'gato a ⟨studente⟩ examinee; Jur person questioned

interroga'torio a & nm questioning

interrogazi'one nf question; Sch oral [test]. ~ **ciclica** polling. ~ **parlamentare** parliamentary question

inter'rompere vt interrupt; ⟨sospendere⟩ stop; cut off ⟨collegamento⟩

inter'rompersi vr break off

interrut'tore nm switch. ~ **a reostato** dimmer

interruzi'one nf interruption; **senza** ~ non-stop. ~ **della corrente** power cut. ~ **di gravidanza** termination of pregnancy

interscambi'abile a interchangeable

inter'scambio nm import-export trade

interse'care vt intersect

interse'carsi vr intersect

intersezi'one nf intersection

inter'stizio nm interstice

interur'bana nf long-distance call

interur'bano a inter-city; **telefonata interurbana** long-distance call

interval'lare vt space out

inter'vallo nm interval; ⟨spazio⟩ space; ⟨in ufficio⟩ tea/coffee break; TV, Sch break; **fare un** ~ have a break; **a intervalli regolari** at regular intervals. ~ **del pranzo** lunch hour, lunch break. ~ **pubblicitario** commercial break

interve'nire vi intervene; ⟨Med: operare⟩ operate; ~ **a** take part in

inter'vento nm intervention; ⟨presenza⟩ presence; ⟨chirurgico⟩ operation; **pronto** ~ emergency services. **un** ~ **a cuore aperto** open-heart surgery

inter'vista nf interview. ~ **esclusiva** exclusive interview

intervi'stare vt interview

intervi'stato, -a nmf interviewee

intervista|'tore, -'trice nmf interviewer

in'tesa nf understanding; **d'**~ ⟨cenno⟩ of acknowledgment

in'teso, -a pp di **intendere** ● a **resta** ~ **che...** needless to say,...; ~ **a** meant to; [siamo] **intesi!** agreed! ● nf understanding

in'tessere vt weave together

inte'stare vt head; write one's name and address at the top of ⟨lettera⟩; Comm register

inte'starsi vr ~ **a fare qcsa** take it into one's head to do sth

intesta'tario, -a nmf holder

intestazi'one nf heading; ⟨su carta da lettere⟩ letterhead

intesti'nale a intestinal

inte'stino a ⟨lotte⟩ internal ● nm intestine. ~ **crasso** large intestine. ~ **tenue** small intestine

intiepi'dire vt ⟨scaldare⟩ warm; cool ⟨passione, desiderio⟩

intiepi'dirsi vr cool [down]; ⟨scaldarsi⟩ warm [up]; ⟨fede:⟩ wane

intima'mente adv ⟨conoscere⟩ intimately

inti'mare vt order; ~ **l'alt** give the order to halt; ~ **l'alt a qcno** order sb to stop

intimazi'one nf order. ~ **di sfratto** eviction notice

intimida'torio a threatening

intimidazi'one nf intimidation

intimi'dire vt intimidate

intimi'dirsi vr be overwhelmed with shyness

intimità nf cosiness

'intimo a intimate; ⟨interno⟩ innermost; ⟨amico⟩ close ● nm ⟨amico⟩ close friend; ⟨dell'animo⟩ heart

intimo'rire vt frighten

intimo'rirsi vr get frightened

intimo'rito a frightened

in'tingere vt dip

in'tingolo nm sauce; ⟨pietanza⟩ stew

intiriz'zire vt numb

intiriz'zirsi vr grow numb

intiriz'zito a **essere** ~ ⟨dal freddo⟩ be perished

intito'lare vt entitle; ⟨dedicare⟩ dedicate

intito'larsi vr be called

intolle'rabile a intolerable

intolle'rante a intolerant

intona'care vt plaster

intonaca'tore nm plasterer

in'tonaco nm plaster. ~ **a pinocchino** pebbledash

into'nare vt start to sing; tune ⟨strumento⟩; ⟨accordare⟩ match

into'narsi vr match

into'nato a ⟨persona⟩ able to sing in tune; ⟨voce, strumento⟩ in tune; ⟨colore⟩ matching

intonazi'one nf ⟨inflessione⟩ intonation; ⟨ironica⟩ tone; ⟨cantando⟩ ability to sing in tune

in'tonso a ⟨libro⟩ untouched

inton'tire vt ⟨botta:⟩ stun, daze; ⟨gas:⟩ make dizzy; fig stun ● vi go ga-ga

inton'tito *a* dazed; *fig* stunned; *(con l'età)* ga-ga

intop'pare *vi* ~ **in** run into

in'toppo *nm* **c'è un** ~ something's come up

in'torno *adv* around ● *prep* ~ **a** around; *(circa)* about

intorpi'dire *vt* numb

intorpi'dirsi *vr* become numb

intorpi'dito *a* torpid

intossi'care *vt* poison

intossi'carsi *vr* be poisoned

intossicazi'one *nf* poisoning. ~ **alimentare** food poisoning

intra-azien'dale *a* in-house

intradu'cibile *a* untranslatable

intralci'are *vt* hamper

in'tralcio *nm* hitch; **essere d'~ (a qcno/ qcsa)** be a hindrance (to sb/sth)

intrallaz'zare *vi* intrigue

intral'lazzo *nm* racket

intramon'tabile *a* timeless

intramusco'lare *a* intramuscular

intransi'gente *a* intransigent, uncompromising

intransi'genza *nf* intransigence

intransi'tivo *a* intransitive

intrappolato *a* **rimanere** ~ be trapped

intrapren'dente *a* enterprising

intrapren'denza *nf* initiative

intra'prendere *vt* undertake

intrat'tabile *a* very difficult

intratte'nere *vt* entertain

intratte'nersi *vr* linger

intratteni'mento *nm* entertainment

intrave'dere *vt* catch a glimpse of; *(presagire)* foresee

intrecci'are *vt* interweave; plait *(capelli, corda)*; ~ **le mani** clasp one's hands

intrecci'are *vt* interweave

intrecci'arsi *vr* intertwine; *(aggrovigliarsi)* become tangled

in'treccio *nm* *(trama)* plot; *(di nastri, strade)* tangle

in'trepido *a* intrepid

intri'cato *a* tangled

intri'gante *a* intriguing ● *nmf* schemer

intri'gare *vt* entangle; *(incuriosire)* intrigue ● *vi* be intriguing

intri'garsi *vr* become entangled; *(immischiarsi)* meddle

in'trigo *nm* plot; **intrighi** *pl* plotting; *(di corte)* intrigues

intrinseca'mente *adv* intrinsically

in'trinseco *a* intrinsic

in'triso *a* ~ **di** soaked with; *fig* imbued with

intri'stire *vt* sadden

intri'stirsi *vr* grow sad

intro'durre *vt* introduce; *(inserire)* insert; ~ **a** *(iniziare a)* introduce to

intro'dursi *vr* get in; ~ **in** get into

introdut'tivo *a* *(pagine, discorso)* introductory

introduzi'one *nf* introduction

in'troito *nm* income, revenue; *(incasso)* takings *pl*

intro'mettere *vt* introduce

intro'mettersi *vr* interfere; *(interporsi)* intervene

intromissi'one *nf* intervention

introspet'tivo *a* introspective

intro'vabile *a* unobtainable

intro'verso, -a *a* introverted ● *nmf* introvert

intrufo'larsi *vr* sneak in

in'truglio *nm* concoction

intrusi'one *nf* intrusion

in'truso, -a *nmf* intruder

intu'ibile *a* deducible

intu'ire *vt* perceive

intuitiva'mente *adv* intuitively

intui'tivo *a* intuitive

in'tuito *nm* intuition

intuizi'one *nf* intuition

inguagli'anza *nf* inequality

inu'mano *a* inhuman

inu'mare *vt* inter

inumi'dire *vt* dampen; moisten *(labbra)*

inumi'dirsi *vr* become damp

i'nutile *a* useless; *(superfluo)* unnecessary

inutilità *nf* uselessness

inutiliz'zabile *a* unusable

inutiliz'zato *a* unused

inutil'mente *adv* fruitlessly

inva'dente *a* intrusive

in'vadere *vt* invade; *(affollare)* overrun

inva'ghirsi *vr* ~ **di** take a fancy to

invali'cabile *a* impassable; **'limite ~'** *Mil* 'no access beyond this point'

invali'dare *vt* invalidate

invalidità *nf* disability; *Jur* invalidity

in'valido, -a *a* invalid; *(handicappato)* disabled ● *nmf* disabled person; **gli invalidi** the handicapped. ~ **di guerra** disabled ex-serviceman. ~ **del lavoro** industrial accident victim

in'vano *adv* in vain

invari'abile *a* invariable

invariabil'mente *adv* invariably

invari'ato *a* unchanged

invasi'one *nf* invasion

in'vaso *pp* di **invadere**

inva'sore *a* invading ● *nm* invader

invecchia'mento *nm* *(di vino)* maturation

invecchi'are *vt/i* age

in'vece *adv* instead; *(anzi)* but; ~ **di** instead of

inve'ire *vi* ~ **contro** inveigh against

invele'nito *a* embittered

inven'dibile *a* unsaleable

inven'duto *a* unsold

inven'tare *vt* invent

inventari'are *vt* make an inventory of

inven'tario *nm* inventory

inven'tato *a* made-up

inven'tiva *nf* inventiveness

inven'tivo *a* inventive

inven|'tore, -'trice *nmf* inventor

invenzi'one *nf* invention

inver'nale *a* wintry; **sport** *pl* **invernali** winter sports

in'verno *nm* winter
invero'simile *a* improbable
inverosimil'mente *adv* incredibly
inversa'mente *adv* inversely; ~ **proporzionale** in inverse proportion
inversi'one *nf* inversion; *Mech* reversal; **fare un'~ a U** do a U-turn. ~ **di fondo** *Comput* reverse video. ~ **di tendenza** turnaround
in'verso *a* inverse; (*opposto*) opposite ● *nm* opposite
inverte'brato *a & nm* invertebrate
inver'tire *vt* reverse; (*capovolgere*) turn upside-down
inver'tito, -a *nmf* homosexual
investi'gare *vt* investigate
investiga|'tore, -'trice *nmf* investigator. ~ **privato** private investigator
investigazi'one *nf* investigation
investi'mento *nm* investment; (*incidente*) crash
inve'stire *vt* invest; (*urtare*) collide with; (*travolgere*) run over; ~ **qcno di** invest sb with
investi'tura *nf* investiture
invete'rato *a* inveterate
invet'tiva *nf* invective
invi'are *vt* send
invi'ato, -a *nmf* envoy; (*di giornale*) correspondent. ~ **di pace** peace envoy
in'vidia *nf* envy
invidi'are *vt* envy
invidi'oso *a* envious
invigo'rire *vt* invigorate
invigo'rirsi *vr* become strong
invin'cibile *a* invincible
in'vio *nm* dispatch; *Comput* enter
invio'labile *a* inviolable
invipe'rirsi *vr* get nasty
invipe'rito *a* furious
invischi'arsi *vr* get involved (**in** in)
invi'sibile *a* invisible
invisibilità *nf* invisibility
invi'tante *a* (*piatto, profumo*) enticing
invi'tare *vt* invite
invi'tato, -a *nmf* guest
in'vito *nm* invitation
invo'care *vt* invoke; (*implorare*) beg
invocazi'one *nf* invocation
invogli'are *vt* tempt; (*indurre*) induce
invogli'arsi *vr* ~ **di** take a fancy to
involga'rire *vt* vulgarize
involontaria'mente *adv* involuntarily
involon'tario *a* involuntary
invol'tini *nmpl* stuffed rolls (*of meat, pastry*)
in'volto *nm* parcel; (*fagotto*) bundle
in'volucro *nm* wrapping
invo'luto *a* involved
invulne'rabile *a* invulnerable
inzacche'rare *vt* splash with mud
inzup'pare *vt* soak; (*intingere*) dip
inzup'parsi *vr* get soaked
'io *pers pron* I; **sono io** it's me; **l'ho fatto io** [**stesso**] I did it myself ● *nm* **l'io** the ego
i'odio *nm* iodine

i'one *nm* ion
i'onico *a* Ionic
l'onio *nm* **lo** ~ the Ionian [Sea]
iono'sfera *nf* ionosphere
i'osa: **a iosa** *adv* in abundance
iperattività *nf* hyperactivity
iperat'tivo *a* hyperactive
i'perbole *nf* hyperbole
iper'critico *a* hypercritical
ipermer'cato *nm* hypermarket
iper'metrope *a* long-sighted
ipersen'sibile *a* hypersensitive
ipertensi'one *nf* high blood pressure
iper'testo *nm* *Comput* hypertext
iperventi'lare *vi* hyperventilate
ip'nosi *nf* hypnosis
ipnotera'pia *nf* hypnotherapy
ip'notico *a* hypnotic
ipno'tismo *nm* hypnotism
ipnotiz'zare *vt* hypnotize
ipoaller'genico *a* hypoallergenic
ipoca'lorico *a* low-calorie
ipo'centro *nm* focus
ipocon'dria *nf* hypochondria
ipocon'driaco, -a *a & nmf* hypochondriac
ipocri'sia *nf* hypocrisy
i'pocrita *a* hypocritical ● *nmf* hypocrite
ipocrita'mente *adv* hypocritically
ipo'dermico *a* hypodermic
i'pofisi *nf inv* pituitary gland
ipo'teca *nf* mortgage
ipote'cabile *a* mortgageable
ipote'care *vt* mortgage
ipote'cario *a* mortgage *attrib*
ipote'nusa *nf* hypotenuse
ipo'termia *nf* hypothermia
i'potesi *nf inv* hypothesis; (*caso, eventualità*) eventuality; **nella migliore delle** ~ at best; **nella peggiore delle** ~ if the worst comes to the worst
ipo'tetico *a* hypothetical
ipotiz'zare *vt* hypothesize
'ippico, -a *a* horse *attrib* ● *nf* riding
ippoca'stano *nm* horse-chestnut
ip'podromo *nm* racecourse
ippo'potamo *nm* hippopotamus
'ipsilon *nf inv* [the letter] y
'ira *nf* anger
ira'scibile *a* irascible
i'rato *a* irate
'iride *nf Anat* iris; (*arcobaleno*) rainbow
'iris *nm inv Bot* iris
Ir'landa *nf* Ireland. ~ **del Nord** Northern Ireland
irlan'dese *a* Irish ● *nm* Irishman; (*lingua*) Irish ● *nf* Irishwoman
iro'nia *nf* irony
i'ronico *a* ironic[al]
irradi'are *vt/i* radiate
irradiazi'one *nf* radiation
irraggiun'gibile *a* unattainable
irragio'nevole *a* unreasonable; (*speranza, timore*) irrational; (*assurdo*) absurd
irranci'dire *vi* go rancid
irrazio'nale *a* irrational

irrazionalità *a* irrationality
irrazional'mente *adv* irrationally
irre'ale *a* unreal
irrea'listico *a* unrealistic
irrealiz'zabile *a* unattainable
irrealtà *nf* unreality
irrecupe'rabile *a* irrecoverable
irrecu'sabile *a* incontrovertible
irredi'mibile *a* irredeemable
irrefre'nabile *a* uncontrollable
irrefu'tabile *a* irrefutable
irrego'lare *a* irregular
irregolarità *nf inv* irregularity; (*di terreno*) unevenness; *Sport* foul
irregolar'mente *adv* 〈*frequentare*〉 irregularly; 〈*comportarsi*〉 erratically; 〈*disporre*〉 unevenly
irremo'vibile *a fig* adamant
irrepa'rabile *a* irreparable
irrepe'ribile *a* 〈*persona*〉 not to be found; **sarò irreperibile** I'm not going to be contactable
irrepren'sibile *a* irreproachable
irrepri'mibile *a* irrepressible
irrequi'eto *a* restless
irresi'stibile *a* irresistible
irresistibil'mente *adv* irresistibly
irreso'luto *a* irresolute
irrespon'sabile *a* irresponsible
irresponsabilità *nf* irresponsibility
irrestrin'gibile *a* preshrunk
irre'tire *vt* seduce
irrever'sibile *a* irreversible
irreversibil'mente *adv* irreversibly
irrevo'cabile *a* irrevocable
irrevocabil'mente *adv* irrevocably
irricono'scibile *a* unrecognizable
irridu'cibile *a* irreducible
irri'gare *vt* irrigate; 〈*fiume:*〉 flow through
irrigazi'one *nf* irrigation
irrigidi'mento *nm* (*di muscoli*) stiffening; (*di disciplina*) tightening
irrigi'dire *vt* stiffen up
irrigi'dirsi *vr* stiffen up
irrile'vante *a* unimportant
irrimedi'abile *a* irreparable
irrimediabil'mente *adv* irreparably
irripe'tibile *a* unrepeatable
irri'solto *a* unresolved
irri'sorio *a* derisive; (*insignificante*) derisory
irri'tabile *a* irritable
irri'tante *a* aggravating
irri'tare *vt* irritate
irri'tarsi *vr* get annoyed
irri'tato *a* irritated; 〈*gola*〉 sore
irritazi'one *nf* irritation
irrive'renza *nf* (*qualità*) irreverence; (*azione*) irreverent action
irrobu'stire *vt* fortify
irrobu'stirsi *vr* get stronger
ir'rompere *vi* burst (**in** into)
irro'rare *vt* sprinkle
irrorazi'one *nf* (*di piante*) crop spraying
irru'ente *a* impetuous

irruvi'dire *vt* roughen
irruvi'dirsi *vr* become rough
irruzi'one *nf* raid; *fig* eruption; **fare ~ in** burst into
ir'suto *a* shaggy
'irto *a* bristly
i'scritto, -a *pp di* **iscrivere** ● *a* registered ● *nmf* member; **per ~** in writing
i'scrivere *vt* register
i'scriversi *vr* **~ a** register at, enrol at 〈*scuola*〉; join 〈*circolo ecc*〉
iscrizi'one *nf* registration; (*epigrafe*) inscription
i'slamico *a* Islamic
isla'mismo *nm* Islam
l'slanda *nf* Iceland
islan'dese *a* Icelandic ● *nmf* Icelander
'ismi *nmpl* isms
i'sobara *nf* isobar
'isola *nf* island. **le isole britanniche** the British Isles. **~ deserta** desert island. **~ pedonale** traffic island. **~ spartitraffico** traffic island
iso'lano, -a *a* insular ● *nmf* islander
iso'lante *a* insulating ● *nm* insulator
iso'lare *vt* isolate; *Mech, Electr* insulate; (*acusticamente*) soundproof
iso'lato *a* isolated ● *nm* (*di appartamenti*) block
isolazio'nismo *nm* isolationism
iso'metrico *a* isometric
i'soscele *a* isosceles
is'panico *a* Hispanic
ispessi'mento *nm* thickening
ispes'sire *vt* thicken
ispes'sirsi *vr* thicken
ispet'torato *nm* inspectorate
ispet'tore *nm* inspector. **~ capo** chief inspector. **~ di polizia** police inspector. **~ scolastico** inspector of schools. **~ di zona** *Comm* area manager
ispezio'nare *vt* inspect
ispezi'one *nf* inspection; (*di nave*) boarding
'ispido *a* bristly
ispi'rare *vt* inspire; suggest 〈*idea, soluzione*〉
ispi'rarsi *vr* **~ a** be based on
ispi'rato *a* inspired
ispirazi'one *nf* inspiration; (*idea*) idea
Isra'ele *nm* Israel
israeli'ano, -a *a* & *nmf* Israeli
is'sare *vt* hoist
ist. *abbr* (**istituto**) dept
istan'taneo, -a *a* instantaneous ● *nf* snapshot
i'stante *nm* instant; **all'~** instantly
i'stanza *nf* petition. **~ di divorzio** petition for divorce
isterecto'mia *nf* hysterectomy
i'sterico *a* hysterical; **attacco ~** hysterics *pl*
iste'rismo *nm* hysteria. **~ di massa** mass hysteria
isti'gare *vt* instigate; **~ qcno al male** incite sb to evil
istiga|'tore, -'trice *nmf* instigator

istigazi'one *nf* instigation. **~ a delinquere** incitement to crime
istintiva'mente *adv* instinctively
istin'tivo *a* instinctive
i'stinto *nm* instinct; **d'~** instinctively. **~ di conservazione** instinct of self-preservation. **~ materno** maternal instinct
istitu'ire *vt* institute; (*fondare*) found; initiate (*manifestazione*)
isti'tuto *nm* institute; *Sch* secondary school; *Univ* department. **~ di bellezza** beauty salon. **~ commerciale** business college. **~ di credito** bank. **~ per l'infanzia** children's home
istitu'|tore, -'trice *nmf* (*insegnante*) tutor; (*fondatore*) founder
istituzio'nale *a* institutional
istituzionaliz'zare *vt* institutionalize
istituzionaliz'zarsi *vr* become an institution
istituzionalizzazi'one *nf* institutionalization
istituzi'one *nf* institution; **le istituzioni** state institutions
'istmo *nm* isthmus
isto'gramma *nm* bar chart
istolo'gia *nf* histology
istra'dare *vt* divert; *fig* guide (**a** towards)

'istrice *nm* porcupine
istri'one *nm* clown; *Theat sl* ham
istru'ire *vt* instruct; (*addestrare*) train; (*informare*) inform; *Jur* prepare
istru'ito *a* well-educated
istrut'tivo *a* instructive
istrut'|tore, -'trice *nmf* instructor; **giudice ~** examining magistrate. **~ di guida** driving instructor. **~ di nuoto** swimming instructor
istrut'toria *nf Jur* investigation
istruzi'one *nf* instruction; *Sch* education; **ministero della pubblica ~** Department of Education. **istruzioni** *pl* **per l'uso** instructions for use
istupi'dire *vt* stupefy
l'talia *nf* Italy
itali'ano, -a *a & nmf* Italian
itine'rante *a* wandering
itine'rario *nm* route, itinerary. **~ turistico** tourist route
itte'rizia *nf* jaundice
'ittico *a* fishing *attrib*
i'uta *nf* jute
I.V.A. *nf abbr* (**imposta sul valore aggiunto**) VAT; **~ compresa** inclusive of VAT, VAT inclusive
'ivi *adv* (*linguaggio burocratico*) therein

ja'bot *nm inv* jabot
jack *nm inv* jack
jac'quard *a inv* (*nella maglia*) jacquard
'jais *nm* jet
'jam-session *nf inv* jam-session
jazz *nm* jazz
jaz'zista *nmf* jazz player
jeep *nf inv* jeep
'jersey *nm* jersey
jet *nm inv* jet. **~ privato** private jet
jet-'set *nm* jet set
'jingle *nm inv* jingle
'jodel *nm inv* yodel

'jogging *nm* jogging
joint venture *nf inv Comm* joint venture
'jolly *nm inv* (*carta da gioco*) joker ● *a Comput* **carattere ~** wildcard [character]
'joystick *nm inv* joystick
Jugo'slavia *nf* Yugoslavia
jugo'slavo, -a *a & nmf* Yugoslav[ian]
juke box *nm inv* juke box
jumbo-'jet *nm inv* jumbo jet
junghi'ano, -a *a & nmf* Jungian
'junior *a inv* junior ● *nm* (*pl* **juniores**) junior
'juta *nf* jute

kafki'ano *a* Kafkan, Kafkaesque
ka'jal *nm inv* kohl
'kaki *a inv* khaki ● *nm inv* persimmon
ka'pok *nm* kapok
ka'putt *a inv* kaput
kara'kiri *nm* **fare ~** commit hara-kiri
kara'oke *nm inv* karaoke
kara'te *nm* karate
kart *nm inv* go-kart
kar'tismo *nm* go-karting; **fare del ~** go go-karting
'kasher *a inv* kosher
'Kashmir *nm* Kashmir
ka'yak *nm inv* kayak
KB *Comput abbr* (**kilobyte**) K, KB
Kbyte *Comput abbr* (**kilobyte**) kbyte
ker'messe *nf inv* fair; *fig* rowdy celebration
kero'sene *nm* paraffin
'ketchup *nm* ketchup
kg *abbr* (**chilogrammo**) kg

kib'butz *nm inv* kibbutz
'killer *mf inv* assassin, hit man
'kilo *nm* kilo
kilt *nm inv* kilt
ki'mono *nm inv* kimono
kinesitera'pia *nf* physiotherapy
kit *nm inv* **~ di aggiornamento** upgrade kit. **~ multimediale** multimedia kit
kitsch *a inv* kitschy
'kleenex® *nm inv* Kleenex
km *abbr* (**chilometro**) km
km/h *abbr* (**chilometri all'ora**) kph
kmq *abbr* (**chilometro quadrato**) km²
ko'ala *nm inv* koala
'krapfen *nm inv* doughnut
'kripton *nm* krypton
'Kurdistan *nm* Kurdistan
kuwaiti'ano *nm* Kuwaiti
kW *abbr* (**kilowatt**) kW
K-'way® *nm inv* cagoule
kWh *abbr* (**kilowatt all'ora**) kWh

l' *def art mf* (*before vowel*) the; *vedi* **il**
la *def art f* the; *vedi* **il** ● *pron* (*oggetto, riferito a persona*) her; (*riferito a cosa, animale*) it; (*forma di cortesia*) you ● *nm inv Mus* (*chiave, nota*) A
là *adv* there; **di là** (*in quel luogo*) in there; (*da quella parte*) that way; **eccolo là!** there he is!; **farsi più in là** (*far largo*) make way; **là dentro** in there; **là fuori** out there; [**ma**] **va là!** come off it!; **più in là** (*nel tempo*) later on; (*nello spazio*) further on
'labbro *nm* (*pl nf* **labbra**) lip; **pendere dalle labbra di qcno** hang on sb's every word. **~ leporino** harelip
labi'ale *a & nf* labial
'labile *a* fleeting
labiolet'tura *nf* lip-reading
labi'rinto *nm* labyrinth; (*di sentieri ecc*) maze
labora'torio *nm* laboratory; (*di negozio, officina ecc*) workshop. **~ linguistico** language lab
laboriosa'mente *adv* laboriously
labori'oso *a* (*operoso*) industrious; (*faticoso*) laborious

labra'dor *nm inv* labrador
labu'rista *a* Labour ● *nmf* member of the Labour Party
'lacca *nf* lacquer; (*per capelli*) hairspray
lac'care *vt* lacquer
lacchè *nm inv* lackey
'laccio *nm* noose; (*lazo*) lasso; (*trappola*) snare; (*stringa*) lace. **~ emostatico** tourniquet
lace'rante *a* (*grido*) earsplitting
lace'rare *vt* tear; lacerate (*carne*)
lace'rarsi *vr* tear
lacerazi'one *nf* laceration
'lacero *a* torn; (*cencioso*) ragged
la'conico *a* laconic
'lacrima *nf* tear; (*goccia*) drop
lacri'male *a* (*condotto, ghiandola*) tear *attrib*
lacri'mare *vi* weep
lacri'mevole *a* tear-jerking
lacri'mogeno *a* gas **~** tear gas
lacri'moso *a* tearful
la'cuna *nf* gap
lacu'noso *a* (*preparazione, resoconto*) incomplete

la'custre *a* lake *attrib*

lad'dove *conj* whereas

'ladro, -a *a* thieving ● *nmf* thief; **al ~!** stop thief!

ladro'cinio *nm* theft

la'druncolo *nm* petty thief

'lager *nm inv* concentration camp

laggiù *adv* down there; *(lontano)* over there

'lagna *nf (fam: persona)* moaning Minnie; *(film)* bore

la'gnanza *nf* complaint

la'gnarsi *vr* moan; *(protestare)* complain *(di about)*

la'gnoso *a ⟨persona⟩* moaning; *⟨film⟩* weepy

'lago *nm* lake. **~ di Garda** Lake Garda. **~ di sangue** pool of blood

la'guna *nf* lagoon

lagu'nare *a* lagoon *attrib*

laiciz'zare *vt* laicize

'laico, -a *a* lay; *⟨vita⟩* secular ● *nm* layman ● *nf* laywoman

'lama *nf* blade; **a doppia ~** *⟨rasoio⟩* twin-blade ● *nm inv (animale)* llama

lambic'carsi *vr* **~ il cervello** rack one's brains

lam'bire *vt* lap

lamé *nm inv* lamé

la'mella *nf (di fungo)* lamella; *(di metallo, plastica)* sheet

lamen'tare *vt* lament

lamen'tarsi *vr* moan; **~ di** *(lagnarsi)* complain about

lamen'tela *nf* complaint

lamen'tevole *a* mournful; *(pietoso)* pitiful

la'mento *nm* moan

la'metta *nf* **~ [da barba]** razor blade

lami'era *nf* sheet metal. **~ ondulata** corrugated iron

'lamina *nf* foil. **~ d'oro** gold leaf

lami'nare *vt* laminate

lami'naria *nf* kelp

lami'nato *a* laminated ● *nm* laminate; *(tessuto)* lamé

'lampada *nf* lamp. **~ abbronzante** sunlamp. **~ alogena** halogen lamp. **~ da comodino** bedside lamp. **~ a gas** gas lamp. **~ a olio** oil lamp. **~ a pila** torch. **~ da soffitto** overhead light. **~ da tavolo** table lamp

lampa'dario *nm* chandelier

lampa'dato *nm sl* sun-bed freak

lampa'dina *nf* light bulb

lam'pante *a* clear

lam'para *nf* light used when fishing at night

lampeggi'are *vi* flash

lampeggia'tore *nm* Auto indicator

lampi'one *nm* street lamp

'lampo *nm* flash of lightning; *(luce)* flash; **lampi** *pl* lightning *sg;* **cerniera ~** zip [fastener], zipper *Am.* **~ di genio** stroke of genius. **~ al magnesio** magnesium flash

lam'pone *nm* raspberry

'lana *nf* wool; **di ~** woollen. **~ d'acciaio** steel wool. **~ grossa** double knitting [wool]. **~ merino** botany wool. **~ vergine** new wool. **~ di vetro** glass wool

lan'cetta *nf* pointer; *(di orologio)* hand. **~ dei minuti** minute hand. **~ delle ore** hour hand. **~ dei secondi** second hand

'lancia *nf (arma)* spear, lance; *Naut* launch. **~ di salvataggio** lifeboat

lanciafi'amme *nm inv* flamethrower

lancia'missili *nm inv* missile launcher

lancia'palle *a inv* **macchina ~** ball launcher for tennis practice

lancia'razzi *a inv* **pistola ~** Very pistol ● *nm inv* rocket launcher

lanci'are *vt* throw; *(da un aereo)* drop; launch *⟨missile, prodotto, attacco⟩;* give *⟨grido⟩; Comput* run *⟨file⟩;* **~ uno sguardo a** glance at; **~ in alto** throw up

lanci'arsi *vr* fling oneself; *(intraprendere)* launch out

lanci'nante *a* piercing

'lancio *nm* throwing; *(da aereo)* drop; *(di missile, prodotto)* launch; *(Comput: di file)* running. **~ del disco** discus [throwing]. **~ del giavellotto** javelin [throwing]. **~ con paracadute** airdrop. **~ del peso** putting the shot

'landa *nf* moor

languida'mente *adv* languidly

'languido *a* languid; *(debole)* feeble

langu'ore *nm* languor; *(spossatezza)* listlessness; **~ di stomaco** hunger pangs *pl*

lani'ero *a* wool; **industria laniera** wool industry

lani'ficio *nm* woollen mill

lano'lina *nf* lanolin

la'noso *a* woolly

lan'terna *nf* lantern; *(faro)* lighthouse

la'nugine *nf* down

lapalissi'ano *a* obvious

laparosco'pia *nf* laparoscopy

lapi'dare *vt* stone; *fig* demolish

lapi'dario *a (conciso)* terse; **arte lapidaria** stone carving

'lapide *nf* tombstone; *(commemorativa)* memorial tablet

'lapis *nm inv* pencil

lapi'slazzuli *nm inv* lapis lazuli

'lappa *nf Bot* burr

Lap'ponia *nf* Lapland

'lapsus *nm inv* lapse, error. **~ freudiano** Freudian slip

'laptop *nm inv* laptop

lardel'lare *vt Culin* lard

'lardo *nm* lard

larga'mente *adv (ampiamente)* widely

larcheggi'are *vi* **~ in** be free with

lar'ghezza *nf* width; *(di spalle)* breadth; *fig* liberality. **~ di vedute** broad-mindedness

'largo *a* wide; *(ampio)* broad; *⟨abito⟩* loose; *(liberale)* liberal; *(abbondante)* generous; **stare alla larga** keep away; **~ di manica** *fig* generous; **~ di spalle/vedute** broad-shouldered/-minded; **a gambe larghe** with one's legs wide apart; **di larghe vedute** broadminded ● *nm* width; **andare al ~** *Naut* go out to sea; **fare ~** make room; **farsi ~** make one's way; **al ~ di** off the coast of

'**larice** *nm* larch

la'**ringe** *nf* larynx

larin'**gite** *nf* laryngitis

'**larva** *nf* larva; (*persona emaciata*) shadow. ~ **di pidocchio** a louse

la'**sagne** *nfpl* lasagna

'**lasca** *nf* roach

lasciapas'**sare** *nm inv* pass

lasci'**are** *vt* leave; (*rinunciare*) give up; (*rimetterci*) lose; (*smettere di tenere*) let go [of]; (*concedere*) let; ~ **a desiderare** leave a lot to be desired; ~ **di fare qcsa** (*smettere*) stop doing sth; **lascia perdere!** forget it!; **lascialo venire, lascia che venga** let him come

lasci'**arsi** *vr* (*reciproco*) leave each other, split up; ~ **andare** let oneself go

'**lascito** *nm* legacy

la'**scivo** *a* lascivious

'**laser** *a & nm inv* [**raggio**] ~ laser [beam]

lassa'**tivo** *a & nm* laxative

las'**sismo** *nm* laxity

'**lasso** *nm* ~ **di tempo** period of time

lassù *adv* up there

'**lastra** *nf* slab; (*di ghiaccio*) sheet; (*di metallo, Phot*) plate; (*radiografia*) X-ray [plate]. ~ **di pietra** paving slab, paving stone

lastri'**care** *vt* pave

lastri'**cato** *nm* pavement

'**lastrico** *nm* paving; **sul** ~ on one's beam-ends

la'**tente** *a* latent

late'**rale** *a* side *attrib*; *Med, Techn ecc* lateral; **via** ~ side street

lateral'**mente** *adv* sideways

late'**rizi** *nmpl* bricks

'**latice** *nm* latex

latifon'**dista** *nm* big landowner

lati'**fondo** *nm* large estate

lati'**nismo** *nm* Latinism

la'**tino** *a & nm* Latin

latino-ameri'**cano, -a** *a & nmf* Latin American

lati'**tante** *a* in hiding ● *nmf* fugitive [from justice]

lati'**tanza** *nf* **darsi alla** ~ go into hiding

lati'**tudine** *nf* latitude

'**lato** *a* (*ampio*) broad; **in senso** ~ broadly speaking ● *nm* side; (*aspetto*) aspect; **a** ~ **di** beside; **dal** ~ **mio** (*punto di vista*) for my part; **d'altro** ~ *fig* on the other hand. ~ **B** B side

la'|**tore, -'trice** *nmf Comm* bearer

la'**trare** *vi* bark

la'**trato** *nm* barking

la'**trina** *nf* latrine

'**latta** *nf* tin, can

lat'**taio, -a** *nm* milkman ● *nf* milkwoman

lat'**tante** *a* breast-fed ● *nmf* suckling

'**latte** *nm* milk. ~ **acido** sour milk. ~ **condensato** condensed milk. ~ **detergente** cleansing milk. ~ **di gallina** eggnog. ~ **intero** whole milk. ~ **a lunga conservazione** long-life milk. ~ **materno** mother's milk, breast milk. ~ **parzialmente scremato** semi-skimmed milk. ~ **in pol-**

vere powdered milk. ~ **scremato** skimmed milk. ~ **di soia** soya milk

lat'**teo** *a* milky; **dieta lattea** milk diet. **la Via Lattea** the Milky Way

latte'**ria** *nf* dairy

'**lattice** *nm* latex

latti'**cello** *nm* buttermilk

latti'**cini** *nmpl* dairy products

latti'**era** *nf* milk jug

lattigi'**noso** *a* milky

lat'**tina** *nf* can

lat'**tosio** *nm* lactose

lat'**tuga** *nf* lettuce. ~ **romana** cos lettuce

'**laudano** *nm* laudanum

'**laurea** *nf* degree; **prendere la** ~ graduate. ~ **breve** *degree that takes less than the standard period of time.* ~ **in Lettere** arts degree

laure'**ando, -a** *nmf* final-year student

laure'**are** *vt* confer a degree on

laure'**arsi** *vr* graduate

laure'**ato, -a** *a & nmf* graduate

'**lauro** *nm* laurel

'**lauto** *a* lavish; ~ **guadagno** handsome profit

'**lava** *nf* lava

la'**vabile** *a* washable

la'**vabo** *nm* wash-basin

lavacri'**stallo** *nm* windscreen wiper

la'**vaggio** *nm* washing. ~ **automatico** (*per auto*) carwash. ~ **del cervello** brainwashing. ~ **a secco** dry-cleaning

la'**vagna** *nf* slate; *Sch* blackboard. ~ **a fogli mobili** flipchart. ~ **luminosa** overhead projector

lava'**macchine** *nmf inv* car washer

la'**vanda** *nf* wash; *Bot* lavender; **gli hanno fatto la** ~ **gastrica** he had his stomach pumped

lavan'**daia** *nf* washerwoman

lavande'**ria** *nf* laundry. ~ **automatica** launderette

lavan'**dino** *nm* sink; (*hum: persona*) bottomless pit

lavapi'**atti** *nmf inv* dishwasher

la'**vare** *vt* wash; ~ **i piatti** wash up; ~ **a secco** dry-clean; ~ **a mano** wash by hand; ~ **i panni** do the washing

la'**varsi** *vr* wash, have a wash; ~ **i denti** brush one's teeth; ~ **le mani/il viso** wash one's hands/face; ~ **la testa** *o* **i capelli** wash one's hair

lava'**secco** *nmf inv* dry-cleaner's

lavasto'**viglie** *nf inv* dishwasher

la'**vata** *nf* wash; **darsi una** ~ have a wash; ~ **di capo** *fig* scolding

lava'**tivo, -a** *nmf* idler

lava'**trice** *nf* washing-machine

lava'**vetri** *nm inv* squeegee

la'**vello** *nm* kitchen sink

'**lavico** *a* formed by lava

la'**vina** *nf* snowslide

lavo'**rante** *nmf* worker

lavo'rare *vi* work; ~ **di fantasia** (*sognare*) day-dream ● *vt* work; knead (*pasta ecc*); till (*la terra*); ~ **a maglia** knit; ~ **troppo** overwork

lavora'tivo *a* working; **giorno** ~ workday; **settimana lavorativa** working week

lavo'rato *a* (*pietra, legno*) carved; (*cuoio*) tooled; (*metallo*) wrought; (*golf*) patterned; (*terra*) cultivated

lavora|'tore, -'trice *nmf* worker. ~ **a domicilio** outworker, homeworker ● *a* working

lavorazi'one *nf* manufacture; (*di terra*) working; (*del terreno*) cultivation. ~ [**artigianale**] workmanship. ~ **del metallo** metalwork. ~ **in serie** mass production

lavo'rio *nm* intense activity

la'voro *nm* work; (*faticoso, sociale*) labour; (*impiego*) job; *Theat* play; **andare al** ~ go to work; **essere senza** ~ be out of work; **mettersi al** ~ (**su qcsa**) set to work (on sth); **ministero del** ~ Department of Employment; **ministero dei lavori pubblici** Department of Public Works. **lavori** *pl* **di casa** housework. **lavori** *pl* **in corso** roadworks. **lavori** *pl* **forzati** hard labour *sg*. ~ **di gruppo** *Sch* working in groups, group work. ~ **a maglia** knitting. ~ **nero** moonlighting. ~ **part time** part-time job. **lavori** *pl* **stradali** roadworks. ~ **straordinario** overtime. ~ **teatrale** play. ~ **a tempo pieno** full-time job

lazza'rone *nm* rascal

le *def art fpl* the; *vedi* **il** ● *pers pron* (*oggetto*) them; (*a lei*) her; (*forma di cortesia*) you

'leader *nm inv* leader. ~ **della marca** brand leader ● *a inv* leading; **prodotto** ~ market leader

le'ale *a* loyal

leal'mente *adv* loyally

lealtà *nf* loyalty

'leasing *nm inv* lease-purchase

'lebbra *nf* leprosy

lecca 'lecca *nm inv* lollipop

leccapi'edi *nmf inv pej* bootlicker

lec'care *vt* lick; *fig* suck up to

lec'carsi *vr* lick; (*fig: agghindarsi*) doll oneself up; **da** ~ **i baffi** mouth-watering

lec'cata *nf* lick

lec'cato *a* (*persona*) dressed to kill

'leccio *nm* holm oak

leccor'nia *nf* delicacy

lecita'mente *adv* lawfully

'lecito *a* lawful; (*permesso*) permissible

'ledere *vt* damage; *Med* injure

'lega *nf* league; (*di metalli*) alloy; **far** ~ **con qcno** take up with sb. ~ **doganale** customs union

le'gaccio *nm* string; (*delle scarpe*) shoelace

le'gale *a* legal ● *nm* lawyer

legalità *nf* legality

legaliz'zare *vt* authenticate; (*rendere legale*) legalize

legalizzazi'one *nf* legalization

legal'mente *adv* legally

le'game *nm* tie; (*amoroso*) liaison; (*connes-*

sione). link. ~ **di parentela** family relationship. ~ **di sangue** blood relationship. ~ **sentimentale** emotional relationship

lega'mento *nm Med* ligament

le'gare *vt* tie; tie up (*persona*); tie together (*due cose*); (*unire, rilegare*) bind; alloy (*metalli*); (*connettere*) connect; **legarsela al dito** *fig* bear a grudge ● *vi* (*far lega*) get on well

le'garsi *vr* bind oneself; ~ **a qcno** become attached to sb

lega'tario, -a *nmf* legatee

le'gato *nm* legacy; *Relig* legate

lega'tura *nf* tying; (*di libro*) binding

legazi'one *nf* legation

le'genda *nf* legend

'legge *nf* law; (*parlamentare*) act; **a norma di** ~ by law. ~ **marziale** martial law

leg'genda *nf* legend; (*didascalia*) caption

leggen'dario *a* legendary

'leggere *vt/i* read; ~ **male** (*sbagliato*) misread

legge'rezza *nf* lightness; (*frivolezza*) frivolity; (*incostanza*) fickleness

legger'mente *adv* slightly

leg'gero *a* light; (*bevanda*) weak; (*lieve*) slight; (*frivolo*) frivolous; (*incostante*) fickle; ~ **come una piuma** [as] light as a feather; **alla leggera** lightly

leggi'adro *a* liter graceful

leg'gibile *a* (*scrittura*) legible; (*stile*) readable

leg'gio *nm* lectern; *Mus* music stand

legife'rare *vi* legislate

legio'nario *nm* legionary

legi'one *nf* legion

legisla'tivo *a* legislative

legisla'tore *nm* legislator

legisla'tura *nf* legislature

legislazi'one *nf* legislation

legittima'mente *adv* legitimately

legittimità *nf* legitimacy

le'gittimo *a* legitimate; (*giusto*) proper; **legittima difesa** self-defence

'legna *nf* firewood

le'gnaia *nf* woodshed

le'gname *nm* timber

le'gnata *nf* blow with a stick

'legno *nm* wood; **di** ~ wooden; **legni** *pl Mus* woodwind. ~ **compensato** plywood

le'gnoso *a* woody; (*di legno*) wooden; (*gambe*) stiff; (*movimento*) wooden

le'gume *nm* pod

'lei *pers pron* (*soggetto*) she; (*oggetto, con prep*) her; (*forma di cortesia*) you; **lo ha fatto** ~ **stessa** she did it herself

'lembo *nm* edge; (*di terra*) strip

'lemma *nm* headword

'lemming *nm inv* lemming

'lena *nf* vigour

'lendine *nm* nit

le'nire *vt* soothe

lenta'mente *adv* slowly

'lente *nf* lens. ~ **a contatto** contact lens; **mettersi le lenti a contatto** put in one's contact lenses. **~ a contatto morbida** soft lens. **~ a contatto rigida** hard lens. **~ d'ingrandimento** magnifying glass. **~ semi-rigida** gas-permeable lens

len'tezza nf slowness

len'ticchia nf lentil

len'tiggine nf freckle

'lento a slow; ⟨allentato⟩ slack; ⟨abito⟩ loose

'lenza nf fishing-line

len'zuolo nm sheet; **le lenzuola** the sheets. **~ con gli angoli** fitted sheet. **~ funebre** shroud

leon'cino nm lion cub

le'one nm lion; Astr Leo. **~ marino** sea lion

leo'nessa nf lioness

leo'pardo nm leopard

lepo'rino a **labbro ~** hare-lip

'lepre nf hare

le'protto nm leveret

'lercio a filthy

lerci'ume nm filth

'lesbica nf lesbian

'lesbico a lesbian

lesi'nare vt grudge ● vi be stingy

lesio'nare vt damage

lesi'one nf lesion; ⟨danno⟩ damage. **~ cerebrale** brain damage. **~ interna** internal injury. **lesioni** pl **personali** grievous bodily harm, GBH

'leso pp di **ledere** ● a injured; **lesa maestà** high treason

les'sare vt boil

lessi'cale a lexical

'lessico nm vocabulary

lessicogra'fia nf lexicography

lessi'cografo, -a nmf lexicographer

'lesso a boiled ● nm boiled meat

'lesto a quick; ⟨mente⟩ sharp. **~ di mano** light-fingered

le'tale a lethal

leta'maio nm dunghill; fig pigsty

le'tame nm dung

le'targico a lethargic

le'targo nm lethargy; ⟨di animali⟩ hibernation

le'tizia nf joy

'lettera nf letter; **alla ~** literally; **eseguire qcsa alla ~** carry out sth to the letter; **lettere** pl ⟨letteratura⟩ literature sg; Univ Arts; **dottore in lettere** BA, Bachelor of Arts. **~ d'accompagnamento** covering letter. **~ d'amore** love letter. **~ assicurata** registered letter. **~ di cambio** bill of exchange. **~ di credito** letter of credit. **~ maiuscola** capital [letter]. **~ minuscola** small letter. **~ di presentazione** letter of introduction. **~ raccomandata** recorded delivery letter. **~ di scuse** letter of apology. **~ di trasporto aereo** air waybill

lette'rale a literal

letteral'mente adv literally

lette'rario a literary

lette'rato a well-read ● nm scholar; **letterati** pl literati

lettera'tura nf literature

letti'era nf ⟨per gatto⟩ litter

let'tiga nf stretcher

let'tino nm cot; Med couch. **~ [pieghevole]** camp bed

'letto nm bed; **andare a ~** go to bed; **[ri]fare il ~** make the bed. **~ a castello** bunkbed. **~ di fiume** river bed. **letti** pl **gemelli** twin beds. **~ matrimoniale** double bed. **~ a una piazza** single bed. **~ a due piazze** double bed. **~ singolo** single bed

Let'tonia nf Latvia

letto'rato nm ⟨corso⟩ tutorial

let|**'tore, -'trice** nmf reader; Univ language assistant ● nm Comput disk drive. **~ di CD** CD player, CD system. **~ [di] CD-ROM** CD-Rom drive. **~ di codice a barre** barcode reader, scanner. **~ di compact disc** compact disc player. **~ di disco** disk drive. **~ di floppy** floppy [disk] drive

let'tura nf reading

leuce'mia nf leukaemia

'leva nf lever; Mil call-up; **nuove leve** pl new blood, young blood; **far ~** lever. **~ del cambio** gear lever. **~ di comando** control lever

le'vante nm East; ⟨vento⟩ east wind

leva'punti nm inv staple remover

le'vare vt ⟨alzare⟩ raise; ⟨togliere⟩ take away; ⟨rimuovere⟩ take off; ⟨estrarre⟩ pull out; lift, abolish ⟨divieto, tassa⟩; **~ di mezzo qcsa** get sth out of the way

le'varsi vr move ⟨da away from⟩; ⟨vento:⟩ get up; ⟨sole:⟩ rise; **~ di mezzo** get out of the way

le'vata nf rising; ⟨di posta⟩ collection

leva'taccia nf **fare una ~** get up at the crack of dawn

leva'toio a **ponte ~** drawbridge

leva'trice nf midwife

leva'tura nf intelligence

levi'gare vt smooth; ⟨con carta vetro⟩ rub down

levi'gato a ⟨superficie⟩ polished; ⟨pelle⟩ smooth

leviga'trice nf sander

levi'tare vi levitate

levitazi'one nf levitation

Le'vitico nm Leviticus

levri'ero nm greyhound. **~ afgano** Afghan hound

lezi'one nf lesson; Univ lecture; ⟨rimprovero⟩ rebuke. **~ di guida** driving lesson. **~ di italiano** Italian lesson, Italian class

lezi'oso a ⟨stile, modi⟩ affected

'lezzo nm stench

li pers pron mpl them

lì adv there; **fin lì** as far as there; **giù di lì** thereabouts; **lì per lì** there and then; **la cosa è finita lì** that was the end of it

li'ana nf liana

liba'nese a & nmf Lebanese

Li'bano nm Lebanon

'libbra nf ⟨peso⟩ pound

li'beccio nm south-west wind

li'bello nm libel

li'bellula nf dragon-fly

libe'rale *a* liberal; (*generoso*) generous ● *nmf* liberal

libera'lismo *nm* ~ [**economico**] economic liberalism

liberalità *nf* generosity

liberal'mente *adv* liberally

libe'rare *vt* free; release ⟨*prigioniero*⟩; vacate ⟨*stanza*⟩; (*salvare*) rescue

libe'rarsi *vr* ⟨*stanza:*⟩ become vacant; *Teleph* become free; (*da impegno*) get out of it; ~ **di** get rid of

libera|'tore, -'trice *a* liberating ● *nmf* liberator

libera'torio *a* liberating; **pagamento** ~ full and final payment

liberazi'one *nf* liberation; **la L~** (*ricorrenza*) Liberation Day. ~ **della donna** women's liberation, women's lib

libe'rismo *nm* free trade

'libero *a* free; ⟨*strada*⟩ clear; ~ **come l'aria** free as a bird. ~ **arbitrio** *nm* free will. ~ **docente** *nm* qualified university lecturer. ~ **professionista** *nm* self-employed person

libertà *nf* freedom; (*di prigioniero*) release; ~ *pl* (*confidenze*) liberties; **prendersi la** ~ **di fare qcsa** take the liberty of doing sth. ~ **di espressione** freedom of speech. ~ **di pensiero** freedom of thought. ~ **provvisoria** *Jur* bail. ~ **di stampa** freedom of the press. ~ **vigilata** probation

liber'tino, -a *a* dissolute, libertine ● *nmf* libertine

'liberty *nm & a inv* Art Nouveau

'Libia *nf* Libya

'libico, -a *a a & nmf* Libyan

li'bidine *nf* lust

libidi'noso *a* lustful

li'bido *nf* libido

libra'io *nm* bookseller

libre'ria *nf* (*biblioteca*) library; (*negozio*) bookshop; (*mobile*) bookcase

li'bretto *nm* booklet; *Mus* libretto. ~ **degli assegni** cheque book. ~ **di circolazione** logbook. ~ **d'istruzioni** instruction booklet. ~ **di risparmio** savings account; (*documento*) passbook, savings book. ~ **universitario** *book held by students which records details of their exam performances*

'libro *nm* book. ~ **bianco** White Paper. ~ **dei canti** hymn-book. ~ **contabile** account book. ~ **di esercizi** workbook. ~ **di fumetti** comic book. ~ **giallo** crime novel. ~ **mastro** *Comm* ledger. ~ **paga** payroll. ~ **di ricette** cookbook, recipe book. **libri** *pl* **sociali** company's books. ~ **tascabile** paperback. ~ **di testo** course book

li'cantropo *nm* werewolf

lice'ale *nmf* secondary-school student ● *a* secondary-school *attrib*

li'cenza *nf* licence; (*permesso*) permission; *Mil* leave; *Sch* school-leaving certificate; **essere in** ~ be on leave. ~ **di caccia** hunting licence. ~ **di esportazione** export licence. ~ **matrimoniale** marriage licence. ~

di pesca fishing licence. ~ **poetica** poetic licence. ~ **di porto d'armi** gun licence

licenzia'mento *nm* dismissal

licenzi'are *vt* dismiss, sack *fam*; (*conferire un diploma*) grant a school-leaving certificate to

licenzi'arsi *vr* (*da un impiego*) resign; (*accomiatarsi*) take one's leave

licenzi'oso *a* licentious

li'ceo *nm* secondary school, high school. ~ **classico** *secondary school with an emphasis on humanities*. ~ **scientifico** *secondary school with an emphasis on sciences*

li'chene *nm* lichen

'lido *nm* beach

'Liechtenstein *nm* Liechtenstein

lieta'mente *adv* happily

li'eto *a* glad; ⟨*evento*⟩ happy; **molto** ~! pleased to meet you!

li'eve *a* light; (*debole*) faint; (*trascurabile*) slight

lievi'tare *vi* rise ● *vt* leaven

li'evito *nm* yeast. ~ **in polvere** baking powder

lift *nm inv* liftboy

'lifting *nm inv* face-lift

'ligio *a* **essere** ~ **al dovere** have a sense of duty

li'gnaggio *nm* lineage

'ligneo *a* wooden

'lilla *nf Bot* lilac ● *nm* (*colore*) lilac

'lima *nf* file

limacci'oso *a* slimy

li'manda *nf* dab

li'mare *vt* file

lima'tura *nf* (*atto*) filing; (*residui*) filings *pl*

'limbo *nm* limbo

li'metta *nf* ~ [**da unghie**] nail file; (*di carta*) emery board

limi'tare *nm* threshold ● *vt* limit

limi'tarsi *vr* ~ **a fare qcsa** restrict oneself to doing sth; ~ **in qcsa** cut down on sth

limitata'mente *adv* to a limited extent

limita'tivo *a* limiting

limi'tato *a* limited

limitazi'one *nf* limitation

'limite *a* ⟨*caso*⟩ extreme ● *nm* limit; (*confine*) boundary; **entro certi limiti** within certain limits. ~ **di credito** credit limit, credit ceiling. ~ **di sopportazione** breaking point. ~ **di sosta'** 'restricted parking'. ~ **di tempo** time limit. ~ **di velocità** speed limit; **rispettare il** ~ ~ ~ keep to the speed limit

li'mitrofo *a* neighbouring

'limo *nm* slime

limo'nata *nf* (*bibita*) lemonade; (*succo*) lemon juice. ~ **amara** bitter lemon

li'mone *nm* lemon; (*albero*) lemon tree

'limpido *a* clear; ⟨*occhi*⟩ limpid

'lince *nf* lynx

linci'are *vt* lynch

'lindo *a* neat; (*pulito*) clean

'linea *nf* line; (*di autobus, aereo*) route; (*di metro*) line; (*di abito*) cut; (*di auto, mobile*) design; (*fisico*) figure; **in** ~ **d'aria** as the crow flies; **è caduta la ~** I've been cut off; **in ~ di massima** as a rule; **a grandi linee** in outline; **mantenere la ~** keep one's figure; **in ~** *Comput* on-line; **in prima ~** in the front line; **mettersi in ~** line up; **nave di ~** liner; **volo di ~** scheduled flight. **~ aerea** airline. **~ d'arrivo** *Sport* finishing line. **~ commutata** *Teleph* switched line. **~ di confine** boundary. **~ continua** unbroken line. **~ dedicata** dedicated line. **~ di demarcazione** border line. **~ ferroviaria** railway line. **~ di fondo** baseline. **~ d'immersione** water line. **~ laterale** *Sport* touch line. **linee** *pl* **della mano** lines of the hand. **~ di marea** tidemark. **~ mediana** *Sport* halfway line. **~ di partenza** *Sport* starting line. **~ principale** *Rail* main line. **~ punteggiata** dotted line. **~ secondaria** *Rail* branch line. **~ di tiro** line of fire. **~ tratteggiata** broken line

linea'menti *nmpl* features

line'are *a* linear; ⟨*discorso*⟩ to the point; ⟨*ragionamento*⟩ consistent

line'etta *nf* (*tratto lungo*) dash; (*d'unione*) hyphen

'linfa *nf* *Anat* lymph; *Bot* sap. **~ vitale** *fig* life blood

lin'fatico *a Anat* lymphatic

linfoghi'andola *nf* lymph gland

linfo'nodo *nm* lymph node

linge'rie *nf* lingerie

lin'gotto *nm* ingot

'lingua *nf* tongue; (*linguaggio*) language; **avere la ~ lunga** *fig* have a big mouth. **~ moderna** modern language. **~ morta** dead language. **~ straniera** foreign language

lingu'accia *nf* (*persona*) backbiter; **fare le linguacce** put one's tongue out (**a at**)

lingu'aggio *nm* language. **~ infantile** babytalk. **~ dei segni** sign language

lingu'etta *nf* (*di scarpa*) tongue; (*di strumento*) reed; (*di busta*) flap; *Mus* reed; (*per tirare*) tab

lingu'ista *nmf* linguist

lingu'istica *nf* linguistics

lingu'istico *a* linguistic

'lino *nm* *Bot* flax; (*tessuto*) linen

li'noleum *nm* linoleum

liofiliz'zare *vt* freeze-dry

liofiliz'zato *a* freeze dried

li'pide *nm* lipid

liposuzi'one *nf* liposuction

li'quame *nm* slurry

lique'fare *vt* liquefy; (*sciogliere*) melt

lique'farsi *vr* liquefy; (*sciogliersi*) melt

liqui'dare *vt* liquidate; settle ⟨*conto*⟩; pay off ⟨*debiti*⟩; clear ⟨*merce*⟩; (*fam: uccidere*) get rid of

liquida'tore *nm* liquidator

liquidazi'one *nf* liquidation; (*di conti*) settling; (*di merce*) clearance sale. **~ totale** [**per cessata attività**] closing-down sale

'liquido *a & nm* liquid. **~ dei freni** brake fluid. **~ scongelante** *Auto* de-icer. **~ tergicristallo** screen wash

liqui'gas® *nm inv* Calor gas®

liqui'rizia *nf* liquorice

li'quore *nm* liqueur; **liquori** *pl* (*bevande alcooliche*) liquors

'lira *nf* lira; *Mus* lyre. **~ sterlina** pound sterling

'lirico, -a *a* lyrical; ⟨*poesia*⟩ lyric; ⟨*cantante, musica*⟩ opera *attrib* ● *nf* lyric poetry; *Mus* opera

li'rismo *nm* lyricism

'lisca *nf* fishbone; **avere la ~** (*fam: nel parlare*) have a lisp

lisci'are *vt* smooth; (*accarezzare*) stroke

'liscio *a* smooth; ⟨*capelli*⟩ straight; ⟨*liquore*⟩ neat, straight; ⟨*acqua minerale*⟩ still; **passarla liscia** get away with it

li'seuse *nf inv* bed jacket, liseuse

'liso *a* worn [out]

'lista *nf* list; (*striscia*) strip; **fare una ~** make out a list. **~ di attesa** waiting list; **in ~ ~ ~** on the waiting list; *Aeron* on stand-by. **~ elettorale** list of candidates. **~ degli invitati** guest list. **~ nera** blacklist. **~ di nozze** wedding list. **~ della spesa** shopping list. **~ dei vini** wine list

li'stare *vt* edge; *Comput* list

li'stino *nm* list. **~ di borsa** Stock-Exchange list. **~ dei cambi** exchange rates *pl*. **~ [dei] prezzi** price list

Lit. *abbr* (**lire italiane**) Italian lire

lita'nia *nf* litany

'litchi *nm inv* lychee

'lite *nf* quarrel; (*baruffa*) row; *Jur* lawsuit

liti'gante *nmf* *Jur* litigant

liti'gare *vi* quarrel; *Jur* litigate

li'tigio *nm* quarrel

litigi'oso *a* quarrelsome

'litio *nm* lithium

litogra'fia *nf* (*procedimento*) lithography; (*stampa*) lithograph

li'tografo, -a *nmf* lithographer

lito'rale *a* coastal ● *nm* coast

lito'raneo *a* coastal

'litro *nm* litre

Litu'ania *nf* Lithuania

litu'ano, -a *a & nmf* Lithuanian

litur'gia *nf* liturgy

li'turgico *a* liturgical

li'uto *nm* lute

li'vella *nf* level. **~ a bolla d'aria** spirit level

livella'mento *nm* levelling out, levelling off

livel'lare *vt* level

livel'larsi *vr* level out

livella'tore *a* levelling

livella'trice *nf* bulldozer

li'vello *nm* level; **passaggio a ~** level crossing; **sotto/sul ~ del mare** below/above sea level; **ad alto ~** ⟨*conferenza, trattative*⟩ toplevel, high-level; **a più livelli** multilevel. **~ di guardia** danger level. **~ di magazzino** stock level. **~ occupazionale** level of employment

'livido *a* livid; (*per il freddo*) blue; (*per una botta*) black and blue; **~ di rabbia** livid ● *nm* bruise

li'vore *nm* spite

Li'vorno *nf* Leghorn

li'vrea *nf* livery

'lizza *nf* lists *pl*; **essere in ~ per qcsa** be in the running for sth

lo *def art m* (*before s + consonant, gn, ps, z*) the; *vedi* **il ●** *pron* (*riferito a persona*) him; (*riferito a cosa*) it; **non lo so** I don't know

'lobbia *nf* Homburg [hat]

lob'bista *nmf* lobbyist

'lobby *nf inv* lobby

lo'belia *nf* lobelia

'lobo *nm* lobe

loboto'mia *nf* lobotomy

lo'cale *a* local **●** *nm* (*stanza*) room; (*treno*) local train; **locali** *pl* (*edifici*) premises. **~ notturno** night-club

località *nf* locality. **~ balneare** seaside resort. **~ turistica** tourist resort. **~ di villeggiatura** holiday resort

localiz'zare *vt* localize; (*reperire*) locate

localiz'zarsi *vr* **~ in** be located in

localiz'zato *a* localized

localizzazi'one *nf* localization; (*reperimento*) location

local'mente *adv* locally

lo'canda *nf* inn

locandi'ere, -a *nmf* innkeeper

locan'dina *nf* bill, poster

loca'tario, -a *nmf* tenant. **~ residente** sitting tenant

loca'tivo *a* *Gram* locative; *Jur* rental

loca'|tore, -'trice *nm* landlord **●** *nf* landlady

locazi'one *nf* tenancy

locomo'tiva *nf* locomotive. **~ a vapore** steam engine

locomo'tore *nm* locomotive, engine

locomozi'one *nf* locomotion; **mezzi di ~** means of transport

'loculo *nm* burial niche

lo'custa *nf* locust

locuzi'one *nf* expression

lo'dare *vt* praise

'lode *nf* praise; **degno di ~** praiseworthy; **laurea con ~** first-class degree

'loden *nm inv* (*cappotto*) loden [coat]; (*stoffa*) loden

lo'devole *a* praiseworthy

'lodola *nf* lark

loga'ritmo *nm* logarithm

'loggia *nf* loggia; (*massonica*) lodge

loggi'one *nm* gallery, gods *pl*

'logica *nf* logic

logica'mente *adv* (*in modo logico*) logically; (*ovviamente*) of course

logicità *nf* logic

'logico *a* logical

lo'gistica *nf* logistics

lo'gistico *a* logistic[al]

'logo *nm inv* logo

logope'dia *nf* speech therapy

logope'dista *nmf* speech therapist

logo'rante *a* (*attesa, esperienza*) wearing

logo'rare *vt* wear out; (*sciupare*) waste

logo'rarsi *vr* wear out; (*persona:*) wear oneself out

logo'rio *nm* wear and tear; (*stress*) stress

'logoro *a* worn-out

logor'roico *a* loquacious

lom'baggine *nf* lumbago

Lombar'dia *nf* Lombardy

lom'bardo *a* Lombardy *attrib*

lom'bare *a* lumbar

lom'bata *nf* loin. **~ di manzo** sirloin

'lombo *nm* *Anat* loin

lom'brico *nm* earthworm

londi'nese *a* London *attrib* **●** *nmf* Londoner

'Londra *nf* London

long-'drink *nm inv* long drink

longevità *nf* longevity

lon'gevo *a* long-lived

longhe'rone *nm* strut

longi'lineo *a* rangy

longitudi'nale *a* lengthwise

longitudinal'mente *adv* lengthwise

longi'tudine *nf* longitude

long 'playing *nm inv* LP, long-playing record

lontana'mente *adv* distantly; (*vagamente*) vaguely; **neanche ~** not for a moment

lonta'nanza *nf* distance; (*separazione*) separation; **in ~** in the distance

lon'tano *a* far; (*distante*) distant; (*nel tempo*) far-off, distant; (*parente*) distant; (*vago*) vague; (*assente*) absent; **più ~** further; **è ~ un paio di chilometri** it is a couple of kilometres away **●** *adv* far [away]; **da ~** from a distance; **tenersi ~ da** keep away from; **andare ~** (*allontanarsi*) go away; (*avere successo*) go far

'lontra *nf* otter

'lonza *nf* (*lombata*) loin

lo'quace *a* talkative

'lordo *a* dirty; (*somma, peso*) gross; **al ~ di imposte** pre-tax

'loro[1] *pers pron pl* (*soggetto*) they; (*oggetto*) them; (*forma di cortesia*) you; **sta a ~** it is up to them

'loro[2] (**il ~** *m*, **la ~** *f*, **i ~** *mpl*, **le ~** *fpl*) *poss a* their; (*forma di cortesia*) your; **un ~ amico** a friend of theirs; (*forma di cortesia*) a friend of yours **●** *poss pron* theirs; (*forma di cortesia*) yours; **i ~** (*famiglia*) their folk

lo'sanga *nf* lozenge; **a losanghe** diamond-shaped

losca'mente *adv* suspiciously

'losco *a* suspicious

'loto *nm* lotus

'lotta *nf* fight, struggle; (*contrasto*) conflict; *Sport* wrestling. **~ di classe** class struggle. **~ libera** all-in wrestling

lot'tare *vi* fight, struggle; *Sport, fig* wrestle

lotta'|tore, -'trice *nmf* wrestler

lotte'ria *nf* lottery

lottiz'zare *vt* divide up (*terreno*); *fig* parcel out

lottizzazi'one *nf* (*di terreno*) division into lots; *fig* parcelling out

'lotto *nm* [state] lottery; (*porzione*) lot; (*di terreno*) plot

lozi'one *nf* lotion. **~ idratante** moisturizer. **~ solare** suntan lotion

lubrifi'cante *a* lubricating ● *nm* lubricant
lubrifi'care *vt* lubricate
luc'chetto *nm* padlock
lucci'cante *a* sparkling
lucci'care *vi* sparkle
lucci'chio *nm* sparkle
lucci'cone *nm* **far venire i luccicconi** bring tears to the eyes
'luccio *nm* pike
'lucciola *nf* glow-worm; (*prostituta*) lady of the night
'luce *nf* light; *Auto* highlight; **accendere/ spegnere la** ~ switch the light on/off; **far ~ su** *fig* shed light on; **dare alla** ~ give birth to; **venire alla** ~ come to light. **luci** *pl* **di arresto** *Auto* stop lights. **luci** *pl* **d'atterraggio** landing lights. **luci** *pl* **d'emergenza** *Auto* hazard [warning] lights, hazards. ~ **della luna** moonlight. **luci** *pl* **di posizione** *Auto* sidelights. **luci** *pl* **posteriori** *Auto* rear-lights. **luci** *pl* **di retromarcia** *Auto* reversing lights. ~ **del sole** sunlight. ~ **stroboscopica** strobe
lu'cente *a* shining
lucen'tezza *nf* shine
lucer'nario *nm* skylight
lu'certola *nf* lizard
lucida'labbra *nm inv* lip gloss
luci'dare *vt* polish
lucida'trice *nf* [floor-]polisher
'lucido *a* shiny; (*pavimento, scarpe*) polished; (*chiaro*) clear; (*persona, mente*) lucid; (*occhi*) watery ● *nm* shine. ~ [**da scarpe**] [shoe] polish
lucra'tivo *a* lucrative
'lucro *nm* lucre; **senza fini di** ~ non-profit-making, not-for-profit *Am*
luculli'ano *a* (*pranzo*) lavish
ludo'teca *nf* playroom
'luglio *nm* July
'lugubre *a* gloomy
'lui *pers pron* (*soggetto*) he; (*oggetto, con prep*) him; **lo ha fatto ~ stesso** he did it himself
lu'maca *nf* (*mollusco*) snail; *fig* slowcoach
'lume *nm* lamp; (*luce*) light; **a ~ di candela** by candlelight; **perdere il ~ della ragione** be beside oneself with rage
lumi'nare *nmf* luminary
lumi'narie *nfpl* illuminations
lumine'scente *a* luminescent
lumine'scenza *nf* luminescence
lu'mino *nm* ~ **da notte** nightlight
luminosa'mente *adv* luminously
luminosità *nf* brightness
lumi'noso *a* luminous; (*stanza, cielo ecc*) bright; **idea luminosa** brain wave
'luna *nf* moon; **chiaro di** ~ moonlight; **avere la ~ storta** be in a bad mood. ~ **di miele** honeymoon. ~ **piena** full moon
'luna park *nm inv* fairground
lu'nare *a* lunar
lu'naria *nf* moonstone
lu'nario *nm* almanac; **sbarcare il** ~ make

[both] ends meet
lu'natico *a* moody
lunedì *nm inv* Monday; **di** ~ on Mondays
lu'netta *nf* half-moon [shape]
lun'gaggine *nf* slowness
lunga'mente *adv* at great length
lun'ghezza *nf* length; **di** ~ **media** medium-length. ~ **d'onda** wavelength
'lungi *adv* **ero** [**ben**] ~ **dall'immaginare che...** I never dreamt for a moment that...
lungimi'rante *a* far-seeing
lungimi'ranza *nf* far-sightedness
'lungo *a* long; (*diluito*) weak; (*lento*) slow; **a ~ andare** in the long run; **saperla lunga** be shrewd ● *nm* length; **andare per le lunghe** drag on; **di gran lunga** by far ● *prep* (*durante*) throughout; (*per la lunghezza di*) along
lungofi'ume *nm* riverside
lungo'lago *nm* lakeside
lungo'mare *nm inv* sea front
lungome'traggio *nm* feature film
lu'notto *nm* rear window. ~ **termico** heated rear window
'lunula *nf* half-moon
lu'ogo *nm* place; (*punto preciso*) spot; (*passo d'autore*) passage; **aver** ~ take place; **dar** ~ **a** give rise to; **fuori** ~ out of place; **del** ~ (*usanze*) local. ~ **comune** cliché. ~ **di nascita** birthplace. ~ **natale** birthplace. ~ **pubblico** public place. ~ **di villeggiatura** holiday resort
luogote'nente *nm Mil* lieutenant
'lupa *nf* she-wolf
lu'para *nf* sawn-off shotgun
lu'petto *nm* Cub [Scout]
'lupo *nm* wolf. ~ **mannaro** werewolf
'luppolo *nm* hop
'lurido *a* filthy
luri'dume *nm* filth
lu'singa *nf* flattery
lusin'gare *vt* flatter
lusin'garsi *vr* flatter oneself; (*illudersi*) fool oneself
lusinghi'ero *a* flattering
lus'sare *vt* dislocate
lus'sarsi *vr* dislocate
lussazi'one *nf* dislocation
Lussem'burgo *nm* Luxembourg
'lusso *nm* luxury; **di** ~ luxury *attrib*
lussuosa'mente *adv* luxuriously
lussu'oso *a* luxurious
lussureggi'ante *a* luxuriant
lus'suria *nf* lust
lussuri'oso *a* dissolute
lu'strare *vt* polish
lu'strino *nm* sequin
'lustro *a* shiny ● *nm* sheen; *fig* prestige; (*quinquennio*) five-year period
lute'rano *a & nmf* Lutheran
'lutto *nm* mourning; **parato a** ~ draped in black; ~ **stretto** deep mourning
luttu'oso *a* mournful

Mm

m *abbr* (**metro**) m

ma *conj* but; (*eppure*) yet; **ma!** (*dubbio*) I don't know; (*indignazione*) really!; **ma davvero?** really?; **ma va?** really?; **ma sì!** why not!; (*certo che sì*) of course!

'macabro *a* macabre

macché *int* of course not!

macche'roni *nmpl* macaroni *sg*

macche'ronico *a* ‹*italiano*› broken

'macchia¹ *nf* stain; (*di diverso colore*) spot; (*piccola*) speck; **senza ~** spotless; **spargersi a ~ d'olio** spread rapidly. **~ di colore** splash of colour. **~ d'inchiostro** ink stain. **~ di sangue** bloodstain

'macchia² *nf* (*boscaglia*) scrub; **darsi alla ~** take to the woods

macchi'are *vt* stain

macchi'arsi *vr* stain

macchi'ato *a* ‹*caffè*› with a dash of milk; ‹*pelo*› spotted; **~ di** ‹*sporco*› stained with; **~ d'inchiostro** ink-stained, inky. ● *nm* ‹*caffè*› espresso with a dash of milk

macchi'etta *nf* spot

'macchina *nf* machine; (*motore*) engine; (*automobile*) car; **in ~** by car; **giro in ~** drive; **cimitero delle macchine** scrapyard. **~ del caffè** coffee-maker. **~ da cucire** sewing machine. **~ per l'espresso** coffee machine. **~ fotografica** camera. **~ obliteratrice** ticket-stamping machine. **~ da presa** cine camera. **~ da scrivere** typewriter. **~ sverniciante** paint stripper. **~ utensile** machine tool. **~ della verità** lie detector

macchinal'mente *adv* mechanically

macchi'nare *vt* plot

macchi'nario *nm* machinery

macchinazi'oni *nfpl* machinations, scheming

macchi'netta *nf* (*per i denti*) brace; (*per il caffè*) espresso coffee maker; (*accendino*) lighter

macchi'nista *nm* Rail engine driver; *Naut* engineer; *Theat* stagehand

macchi'noso *a* complicated

Mace'donia *nf* Macedonia

mace'donia *nf* fruit salad

macel'laio *nm* butcher

macel'lare *vt* slaughter

macellazi'one *nf* slaughtering

macelle'ria *nf* butcher's [shop]

ma'cello *nm* (*mattatoio*) slaughterhouse; *fig* shambles *sg*; **andare al ~** *fig* go to the slaughter; **mandare al ~** *fig* send to his/her death

mace'rare *vt* macerate; *fig* distress

mace'rarsi *vr* be consumed

macerazi'one *nf* maceration

ma'cerie *nfpl* rubble *sg*; (*rottami*) debris *sg*

'macero *nm* pulping; (*stabilimento*) pulping mill

Mach *nm inv* Mach

ma'chete *nm inv* machete

machia'vellico *a* Machiavellian

ma'chismo *nm* machismo

'macho *a* macho

ma'cigno *nm* boulder

maci'lento *a* emaciated

'macina *nf* millstone

macinacaffè *nm inv* coffee mill

macina'pepe *nm inv* pepper mill

maci'nare *vt* mill

maci'nato *a* ground ● *nm* (*carne*) mince

maci'nino *nm* mill; (*hum: macchina*) old banger

maciul'lare *vt* (*stritolare*) crush

'macro *nf inv* Comput macro

macrobi'otica *nf* **negozio di ~** health-food shop

macrobi'otico *a* macrobiotic

macro'clima *nm* macroclimate

macro'cosmo *nm* macrocosm

macrofotogra'fia *nf* macrophotography

macro'scopico *a* macroscopic

macu'lato *a* spotted

Madaga'scar *nm* Madagascar

madami'gella *nf* young lady

'madia *nf* cupboard with a covered trough on top for making bread

'madido *a* **~ di** damp with ‹*sudore*›

Ma'donna *nf* Our Lady

mador'nale *a* gross

'madre *nf* mother

madre'lingua *a inv* **inglese ~** English native speaker

madre'patria *nf* native land

madre'perla *nf* mother-of-pearl

ma'drepora *nf* madrepore

madri'gale *nm* madrigal

ma'drina *nf* godmother

maestà *nf* majesty

maestosa'mente *adv* majestically

maestosità *nf* majesty

mae'stoso *a* majestic

ma'estra *nf* teacher; *Sch* primary school teacher. **~ d'asilo** kindergarten teacher. **~ di canto** singing teacher. **~ di piano** piano teacher. **~ di sci** ski instructor

mae'strale *nm* northwest wind

mae'stranza *nf* workers *pl*

mae'stria *nf* mastery

ma'estro *nm* teacher; *Sch* primary school teacher; *Mus* maestro; (*esperto*) master. **colpo da ~** masterstroke. **~ d'asilo** kindergarten teacher. **~ di canto** singing teacher. **~ di cerimonie** master of ceremonies. **~ di piano** piano teacher. **~ di sci** ski instructor ● *a* (*principale*) main; (*di grande abilità*) skilful

'mafia *nf* Mafia

mafi'oso *a* of the Mafia ● *nm* member of the Mafia, Mafioso

'maga *nf* sorceress, magician

ma'gagna *nf* fault

ma'gari *adv* (*forse*) maybe ● *int* I wish! ● *conj* (*per esprimere desiderio*) if only; (*anche se*) even if

magazzini'ere *nm* storeman, warehouseman

magaz'zino *nm* warehouse; (*emporio*) shop; **grande ~** department store. **magazzini** *pl* **portuali** naval stores

Magg. *abbr* (**maggiore**) Maj

mag'gese *nm* field lying fallow

'maggio *nm* May

maggio'lino *nm* May bug

maggio'rana *nf* marjoram

maggio'ranza *nf* majority

maggio'rare *vt* increase

maggior'domo *nm* butler

maggi'ore *a* (*di dimensioni, numero*) bigger, larger; (*superlativo*) biggest, largest; (*di età*) older; (*superlativo*) oldest; (*di importanza, Mus*) major; (*superlativo*) greatest; **la maggior parte di** most; **la maggior parte del tempo** most of the time ● *pron* (*di dimensioni*) the bigger, the larger; (*superlativo*) the biggest, the largest; (*di età*) the older; (*superlativo*) the oldest; (*di importanza*) the major; (*superlativo*) the greatest ● *nm Mil* major; *Aeron* squadron leader

maggio'renne *a* of age ● *nmf* adult

maggiori'tario *a* (*della maggioranza*) majority; (*sistema*) first-past-the-post *attrib*

maggior'mente *adv* [all] the more; (*più di tutto*) most

'Magi *nmpl* **i re ~** the Magi

ma'gia *nf* magic; (*trucco*) magic trick

magica'mente *adv* magically

'magico *a* magic

magi'stero *nm* (*insegnamento*) teaching; (*maestria*) skill; **facoltà di ~** arts faculty

magi'strale *a* masterly; **istituto ~** teacher-training college

magistral'mente *adv* in a masterly fashion

magi'strato *nm* magistrate

magistra'tura *nf* magistrature. **la ~** the Bench

'maglia *nf* stitch; (*lavoro ai ferri*) knitting; (*tessuto*) jersey; (*di rete*) mesh; (*di catena*) link; (*indumento*) vest; **fare la ~** knit. **~ diritta** knit. **~ rosa** (*ciclismo*) ≈ yellow jersey. **~ rovescia** purl

magli'aia *nf* knitter

maglie'ria *nf* knitwear

magli'etta *nf* **~** [**a maniche corte**] tee-shirt

magli'ficio *nm* knitwear factory

ma'glina *nf* (*tessuto*) jersey

'maglio *nm* mallet

magli'one *nm* sweater, jumper. **~ dolcevita** polo neck [jumper]. **~ a girocollo** crew neck [sweater]. **~ a V** V-neck [sweater]

'magma *nm* magma

ma'gnaccia *nm inv fam* pimp

ma'gnanimo *a* magnanimous

ma'gnate *nm* magnate

ma'gnesia *nf* magnesia

ma'gnesio *nm* magnesium

ma'gnete *nm* magnet

magnetica'mente *adv* magnetically

ma'gnetico *a* magnetic

magne'tismo *nm* magnetism

magne'tofono *nm* tape recorder

magnifica'mente *adv* magnificently

magnifi'cenza *nf* magnificence; (*generosità*) munificence

ma'gnifico *a* magnificent; (*generoso*) munificent

magni'tudine *nf Astr* magnitude

'magno *a* **aula magna** main hall

ma'gnolia *nf* magnolia

'magnum *nm inv* (*bottiglia*) magnum ● *nf inv* (*pistola*) magnum

'mago *nm* magician

ma'gone *nm* **avere il ~** be down; **mi è venuto il ~** I've got a lump in my throat

'magra *nf* low water

ma'grezza *nf* thinness

'magro *a* thin; (*carne*) lean; (*scarso*) meagre; **magra consolazione** cold comfort

'mai *adv* never; (*inter, talvolta*) ever; **caso ~** if anything; **caso ~ tornasse** in case he comes back; **come ~?** why?; **cosa ~?** what on earth?; **~ più** never again; **più che ~** more than ever; **quando ~?** whenever?; **quasi ~** hardly ever

mai'ale *nm* pig; (*carne*) pork. **~ arrosto** roast pork

maia'lino *nm* piglet

mai'olica *nf* majolica

maio'nese *nf* mayonnaise

'mais *nm* maize

mai'uscola *nf* capital [letter]

mai'uscolo *a* capital

mai'zena [R] *nf* cornflour

mal *vedi* **male**

'mala *nf sl* **la ~** the underworld

malac'corto *a* unwise

mala'fede *nf* bad faith

malaf'fare *nm* **gente di ~** shady characters *pl*

mala'lingua *nf* backbiter

mala'mente *adv* (*ridotto*) badly; (*rispondere*) rudely

malan'dato *a* in bad shape; (*di salute*) in poor health

ma'lanimo *nm* ill will

ma'lanno *nm* misfortune; (*malattia*) illness; **prendersi un ~** catch something

mala'pena *adv* **a ~** hardly

ma'laria *nf* malaria

mala'ticcio *a* sickly

ma'lato, -a *a* ill, sick; ⟨pianta⟩ diseased ● *nmf* sick person. **~ di mente** mentally ill person

malat'tia *nf* disease, illness; **ho preso due giorni di ~** I had two days off sick; **essere in ~** be on sick leave. **~ nervosa** nervous disease. **~ venerea** venereal disease, VD

malaugurata'mente *adv* unfortunately

malaugu'rato *a* ill-omened

malau'gurio *nm* bad *o* ill omen

mala'vita *nf* underworld

malavi'toso, -a *nmf* gangster

mala'voglia *nf* unwillingness; **di ~** unwillingly

malcapi'tato *a* wretched

malce'lato *a* ill-concealed

mal'concio *a* battered

malcon'tento *nm* discontent

malco'stume *nm* immorality

mal'destro *a* awkward; ⟨inesperto⟩ inexperienced

maldi'cente *a* slanderous

maldi'cenza *nf* slander

maldi'sposto *a* ill-disposed

'**male** *adv* badly; **funzionare ~** not work properly; **star ~** be ill; **star ~ a qcno** ⟨vestito ecc.⟩ not suit sb; **rimanerci ~** be hurt; **ho dormito ~** I didn't sleep well; **non c'è ~!** not bad at all! ● *nm* evil; ⟨dolore⟩ pain, ache; ⟨malattia⟩ illness; ⟨danno⟩ harm. **distinguere il bene dal ~** know right from wrong; **andare a ~** go off; **aver ~ a** have a pain in; **dove hai ~?** where does it hurt?, where is the pain?; **far ~ a qcno** ⟨provocare dolore⟩ hurt sb; ⟨cibo:⟩ be bad for sb; **le cipolle mi fanno ~** onions don't agree with me; **mi fa ~ la schiena** my back is hurting; **farsi ~ alla schiena** hurt one's back. **mal d'aereo** airsickness. **mal d'aria** airsickness; **soffrire il ~ ~** be airsick. **mal d'auto** carsickness. **mal di denti** toothache. **mal di gola** sore throat. **mal di mare** seasickness; **avere il ~ ~ ~** be seasick. **mal d'orecchi** earache. **mal di pancia** stomach-ache. **mal di testa** headache

maledetta'mente *adv* flipping

male'detto *a* cursed; ⟨orribile⟩ awful

male'dire *vt* curse

maledizi'one *nf* curse; **~!** damn!

maleducata'mente *adv* rudely

maledu'cato *a* ill-mannered

maleducazi'one *nf* rudeness

male'fatta *nf* misdeed

male'ficio *nm* witchcraft

ma'lefico *a* ⟨azione⟩ evil; ⟨nocivo⟩ harmful

maleodo'rante *a* foul-smelling

ma'lese *a & nmf* Malaysian

Ma'lesia *nf* Malaysia

ma'lessere *nm* indisposition; *fig* uneasiness

ma'levolo *a* malevolent

malfa'mato *a* of ill repute

mal'fatto *a* badly done; ⟨malformato⟩ ill-shaped

malfat'tore *nm* wrongdoer

mal'fermo *a* unsteady; ⟨salute⟩ poor

malfor'mato *a* misshapen

malformazi'one *nf* malformation

mal'gascio, -a *a & nmf* Malagasy

malgo'verno *nm* misgovernment

mal'grado *prep* in spite of ● *conj* although

'**Mali** *nm* Mali

ma'lia *nf* spell

maligna'mente *adv* maliciously

mali'gnare *vi* malign

malignità *nf* malice; *Med* malignancy

ma'ligno *a* malicious; ⟨perfido⟩ evil; *Med* malignant

malinco'nia *nf* melancholy

malinconica'mente *adv* melancholically

malin'conico *a* melancholy

malincu'ore: a ~ *adv* unwillingly, reluctantly

malinfor'mato *a* misinformed

malintenzio'nato, -a *nmf* miscreant

malin'teso *a* mistaken ● *nm* misunderstanding

ma'lizia *nf* malice; ⟨astuzia⟩ cunning; ⟨espediente⟩ trick

maliziosa'mente *adv* mischievously, naughtily

maliziosità *nf* naughtiness

malizi'oso *a* ⟨birichino⟩ mischievous, naughty

malle'abile *a* malleable

mal'leolo *nm Anat* malleolus

malleva'dore *nm* guarantor

'**mallo** *nm* husk

mal'loppo *nm fam* loot

malme'nare *vt* ill-treat

mal'messo *a* ⟨vestito male⟩ shabbily dressed; ⟨casa⟩ poorly furnished; ⟨fig: senza soldi⟩ hard up

malnu'trito *a* undernourished

malnutrizi'one *nf* malnutrition

'**malo** *a* **in ~ modo** badly

ma'locchio *nm* evil eye

ma'lora *nf* ruin; **della ~** awful; **andare in ~** go to ruin

ma'lore *nm* illness; **essere colto da ~** be suddenly taken ill

malri'dotto *a* ⟨persona⟩ in a sorry state; ⟨auto, casa⟩ dilapidated, in a sorry state

mal'sano *a* unhealthy

malsi'curo *a* unsafe; ⟨incerto⟩ uncertain

'**malta** *nf* mortar

mal'tempo *nm* bad weather

mal'tese *a & nmf* Maltese

'**malto** *nm* malt

mal'tosio *nm* maltose

maltratta'mento *nm* ill-treatment

maltrat'tare *vt* ill-treat

malu'more *nm* bad mood; **di ~** in a bad mood

'**malva** *a inv* mauve

mal'vagio *a* wicked

malvagità *nf* wickedness

malva'sia *nf* type of dessert wine
malversazi'one *nf* embezzlement
mal'visto *a* unpopular (**da** with)
malvi'vente *nm* criminal
malvolenti'eri *adv* unwillingly
malvo'lere *vt* **farsi ~** make oneself unpopular; **prendere qcno a ~** take a dislike to sb
'mamma *nf* mummy, mum; **~ mia!** good gracious!
mam'mario *a* mammary
mam'mella *nf* breast
mam'mifero *nm* mammal
mam'mismo *nm* (*del figlio*) dependency on the mother figure; (*della madre*) excessive motherliness
mammogra'fia *nf* mammograph
'mammola *nf* violet
mammo'letta *nf* shrinking violet
mam'mone *nm* mummy's boy
mam'mut *nm inv* mammoth
ma'nata *nf* handful; (*colpo*) slap
'manca *nf* vedi **manco**
manca'mento *nm* **avere un ~** faint
man'cante *a* missing
man'canza *nf* lack; (*assenza*) absence; (*insufficienza*) shortage; (*fallo*) fault; (*imperfezione*) defect; **in ~ d'altro** failing all else; **sento la sua ~** I miss him. **~ di tatto** lack of tact, indelicacy
man'care *vi* be lacking; (*essere assente*) be missing; (*venir meno*) fail; (*morire*) pass away; **~ di** be lacking in; **~ a** fail to keep 〈*promessa*〉; **mi manca casa** I miss home; **mi manchi** I miss you; **mi è mancato il tempo** I didn't have [the] time; **mi mancano 1000 lire** I'm 1,000 lire short; **quanto manca alla partenza?** how long before we leave?; **è mancata la corrente** there was a power failure; **sentirsi ~** feel faint; **sentirsi ~ il respiro** be unable to breathe [properly] ● *vt* miss 〈*bersaglio*〉; **è mancato poco che cadesse** he nearly fell
man'cato *a* 〈*appuntamento*〉 missed; 〈*tentativo*〉 unsuccessful; 〈*occasione*〉 wasted
'manche *nf inv* heat
man'chevole *a* defective
'mancia *nf* tip. **~ competente** reward
manci'ata *nf* handful
man'cino *a* left-handed
'manco, -a *a* left ● *nf* left hand ● *adv* (*nemmeno*) not even
man'dante *nmf* (*di delitto*) instigator; *Jur* principal
manda'rancio *nm* clementine
man'dare *vt* send; (*emettere*) give off; utter 〈*suono*〉; **~ a chiamare** send for; **~ avanti la casa** run the house; **~ giù** (*ingoiare*) swallow
manda'rino *nm Bot* mandarin
man'data *nf* consignment; (*di serratura*) turn; **chiudere a doppia ~** double lock
manda'tario *nm Jur* agent
man'dato *nm* (*incarico*) mandate; *Jur* warrant; (*di pagamento*) money order. **~ di comparizione** [**in giudizio**] subpoena. **~ di**

pagamento money order. **~ di perquisizione** search warrant
man'dibola *nf* jaw
mando'lino *nm* mandolin
'mandorla *nf* almond; **a ~** 〈*occhi*〉 almond-shaped. **~ amara** bitter almond
mandor'lato *nm* nut brittle (*type of nougat*)
'mandorlo *nm* almond[-tree]
man'dragola *nf* mandrake
'mandria *nf* herd
mandri'ano *nm* cowherd
man'drillo *nm* (*scimmia*) mandrill; (*attrezzo*) mandrel; *fig fam* goat
maneg'gevole *a* easy to handle
maneggi'are *vt* handle
ma'neggio *nm* handling; (*intrigo*) plot; (*scuola di equitazione*) riding school
ma'nesco *a* quick to hit out
ma'netta *nf* lever; **a tutta ~** flat out; **manette** *pl* handcuffs
man'forte *nm* **dare ~ a qcno** support sb
manga'nello *nm* truncheon
manga'nese *nm* manganese
mange'reccio *a* edible
mangiacas'sette *nm inv* cassette player
mangia'dischi[R] *nm inv* portable record player
mangia'fumo *a inv* **candela ~** air-purifying candle
mangia'nastri *nm inv* cassette player
mangi'are *vt/i* eat; (*consumare*) eat up; (*corrodere*) eat away; take 〈*scacchi, carte ecc*〉 ● *nm* eating; (*cibo*) food; (*pasto*) meal; **dar da ~ al gatto/cane** feed the cat/dog
mangi'arsi *vr* **~ le parole** mumble; **~ le unghie** bite one's nails
mangia'soldi *a inv* **macchinetta ~** one-armed bandit
mangi'ata *nf* big meal; **farsi una bella ~ di…** feast on…
mangia'toia *nf* manger
mangia|'tore, -'trice *nmf* eater. **~ di fuoco** fire-eater. **mangiatrice di uomini** man-eater
man'gime *nm* fodder. **~ per i polli** chicken feed
mangi'one, -a *nmf fam* glutton
mangiucchi'are *vt* nibble
'mango *nm* mango
man'grovia *nf* mangrove
man'gusta *nf* mongoose
ma'nia *nf* mania. **~ di grandezza** delusions of grandeur. **~ di persecuzione** persecution complex
mania'cale *a* manic
ma'niaco, -a *a* maniacal ● *nmf* maniac. **~ sessuale** sex maniac
ma'niaco-depres'sivo *a & nmf* manic-depressive
'Manica *nf* **la ~** the [English] Channel
'manica *nf* sleeve; (*fam: gruppo*) band; **a maniche lunghe** long-sleeved; **senza maniche** sleeveless; **essere in maniche di camicia** be in shirt sleeves; **essere di ~ larga** be generous; **essere di ~ stretta** be strict. **~ a vento** wind sock

manica'retto *nm* tasty dish

maniche'ismo *nm* Manicheism

mani'chetta *nf* hose

mani'chino *nm* (*da sarto, vetrina*) dummy

'manico *nm* handle; *Mus* neck. **~ di scopa** broom handle

mani'comio *nm* mental home; (*fam: confusione*) tip

mani'cotto *nm* muff; *Mech* sleeve

mani'cure *nf* manicure ● *nmf inv* (*persona*) manicurist

mani'era *nf* manner; **in ~ che** so that

manie'rato *a* affected; (*stile*) mannered

manie'rismo *nm* mannerism

mani'ero *nm* manor

manifat'tura *nf* manufacture; (*fabbrica*) factory

manifatturi'ero *a* manufacturing

manifesta'mente *adv* demonstrably, manifestly

manife'stante *nmf* demonstrator

manife'stare *vt* show; (*esprimere*) express ● *vi* demonstrate

manifes'tarsi *vr* show oneself

manifestazi'one *nf* show; (*espressione*) expression; (*sintomo*) manifestation; (*dimostrazione pubblica*) demonstration

mani'festo *a* evident ● *nm* poster; (*dichiarazione pubblica*) manifesto

ma'niglia *nf* handle; (*sostegno, in autobus ecc*) strap

manipo'lare *vt* handle; (*massaggiare*) massage; (*alterare*) adulterate; *fig* manipulate

manipola'tore, -'trice *nmf* manipulator

manipolazi'one *nf* handling; (*massaggio*) massage; (*alterazione*) adulteration; *fig* manipulation

mani'scalco *nm* smith

'manna *nf* **~ dal cielo** manna from heaven

man'naia *nf* (*scure*) axe; (*da macellaio*) cleaver

man'naro *a* **lupo ~** werewolf

'mano *nf* hand; (*strato di vernice ecc*) coat; **alla ~** informal; **fuori ~** out of the way; **man ~ little by little; man ~ che** as; **sotto ~** to hand; **di seconda ~** secondhand; **a mani vuote** empty-handed; **a ~** (*scritto, ricamato, fatto*) by hand; (*trapano ecc*) hand[-held]; **dare una ~ a qcno** give *or* lend sb a hand; **ha le mani di pastafrolla** he is a butterfingers

mano'dopera *nf* labour

ma'nometro *nm* manometer, pressure gauge

mano'mettere *vt* tamper with; (*violare*) violate

ma'nopola *nf* (*di apparecchio*) knob; (*guanto*) mitten; (*su pullman*) handle

mano'scritto *a* handwritten ● *nm* manuscript

mano'vale *nm* labourer

mano'vella *nf* handle; *Techn* crank. **~ alzacristalli** winder

ma'novra *nf* manoeuvre; *Rail* shunting;

fare le manovre *Auto* manoeuvre. **manovre** *pl* **di corridoio** lobbying

mano'vrabile *a* manoeuvrable; (*fig: persona*) easy to manipulate

mano'vrare *vt* (*azionare*) operate; *fig* manipulate (*persona*) ● *vi* manoeuvre

manro'vescio *nm* slap

man'sarda *nf* attic

mansio'nario *nm* job description

mansi'one *nf* task; (*dovere*) duty

mansu'eto *a* meek; (*animale*) docile

'manta *nf Zool* manta

mante'cato *nm* soft ice cream ● *a* creamy

man'tella *nf* cape

man'tello *nm* cloak; (*soprabito, di animale*) coat; (*di neve*) mantle

mante'nere *vt* (*conservare*) keep; (*in buono stato, sostentare*) maintain

mante'nersi *vr* **~ in forma** keep fit

manteni'mento *nm* maintenance. **~ della pace** *Mil, Pol* peacekeeping

mante'nuta *nf* kept woman

'mantice *nm* bellows *pl*; (*di automobile*) hood, top

'mantide *nf* mantis

man'tiglia *nf* mantilla

'manto *nm* cloak; (*coltre*) mantle

'Mantova *nf* Mantua

manto'vana *nf* (*di tende*) pelmet

manu'ale *a & nm* manual. **~ di conversazione** phrasebook. **~ d'uso** user manual

manual'mente *adv* manually

ma'nubrio *nm* handle; (*di bicicletta*) handlebars *pl*; (*per ginnastica*) dumb-bell

manu'fatto *a* manufactured

manutenzi'one *nf* maintenance

'manzo *nm* steer; (*carne*) beef

maomet'tano *a & nm* Muslim

ma'ori *a inv & nm* Maori

'mappa *nf* map

mappa'mondo *nm* globe

mar *vedi* **mare**

mara'chella *nf* prank

maragià *nm inv* maharajah

maran'tacea *nf Bot* arrowroot

mara'schino *nm* maraschino, *sweet liqueur*

ma'rasma *nm fig* decline

mara'tona *nf* marathon

marato'neta *nmf* marathon runner

'marca *nf* mark; *Comm* brand; (*fabbricazione*) make; (*scontrino*) ticket. **~ da bollo** *stamp showing that the necessary duties have been paid*

mar'care *vt* mark; *Sport* score

marcata'mente *adv* markedly

mar'cato *a* (*tratto, accento*) strong, marked

marca'tore *nm* (*nel calcio*) scorer; (*chi marca un avversario*) marker; (*pennarello*) marker pen

'Marche *nfpl* Marches

mar'chese, -a *nm* marquis ● *nf* marchioness

mar'chetta *nf* (*assicurativa*) National In-

surance stamp; **fare marchette** *fam* be on
the game
marchi'are *vt* brand
'**marchio** *nm* brand; (*caratteristica*) mark. ~
depositato registered trademark. ~ **di**
fabbrica trademark. ~ **registrato** registered trademark
'**marcia** *nf* march; *Auto* gear; *Sport* walk;
mettere in ~ put into gear; **mettersi in** ~
start off; **cambiare** ~ change gear; ~ **a**
senso unico alternato temporary one way
system in operation. ~ **forzata** forced march.
~ **funebre** funeral march. ~ **indietro** reverse gear; **fare** ~ ~ reverse; *fig* back-pedal.
~ **nuziale** wedding march
marcia'longa *nf* (*di sci*) cross-country skiing race; (*a piedi*) long-distance race
marciapi'ede *nm* pavement, sidewalk *Am*;
(*di stazione*) platform
marci'are *vi* march; (*funzionare*) go, work
marcia'|tore, -'trice *nmf* walker
'**marcio** *a* rotten ● *nm* rotten part; *fig* corruption
mar'cire *vi* go bad, rot
mar'cita *nf* water meadow
'**marco** *nm* (*moneta*) mark
marco'nista *nmf* radio operator
'**mare** *nm* sea; (*luogo di mare*) seaside; **sul** ~
‹*casa*› at the seaside; ‹*città*› on the sea;
andare al ~ go to the sea; **in alto** ~ on the
high seas; **d'alto** ~ ocean-going; **essere in**
alto ~ *fig* not know which way to turn. ~
Adriatico Adriatic Sea. **mar Cinese** China
Sea. **mar Ionio** Ionian Sea. **mar**
Mediterraneo Mediterranean. **mar Morto**
Dead Sea. **mar Nero** Black Sea. ~ **del Nord**
North Sea. **mar Tirreno** Tyrrhenian Sea
ma'rea *nf* tide; **una** ~ **di** hundreds of; **alta/**
bassa ~ high/low tide. ~ **montante** flood
tide
mareggi'ata *nf* [sea] storm
mare'moto *nm* tidal wave, seaquake
maresci'allo *nm* (*ufficiale*) marshal;
(*sottufficiale*) warrant-officer
ma'retta *nf* choppiness; *fig* tension
marga'rina *nf* margarine
marghe'rita *nf* marguerite. ~ **settem-**
brina Michaelmas daisy
margheri'tina *nf* daisy
margi'nale *a* marginal
marginal'mente *adv* marginally
'**margine** *nm* margin; (*orlo*) brink; (*bordo*)
border. ~ **di errore** margin of error. ~ **di**
sicurezza safety margin. ~ **di vendita**
mark-up
mari'ano *a Relig* Marian
ma'rina *nf* navy; (*costa*) seashore; (*quadro*)
seascape. ~ **mercantile** merchant navy. ~
militare navy
mari'naio *nm* sailor. ~ **d'acqua dolce** landlubber
mari'nare *vt* marinate; ~ **la scuola** play
truant
mari'naro *a* seafaring
mari'nata *nf* marinade

mari'nato *a Culin* marinated
ma'rino *a* sea *attrib*, marine
mario'netta *nf* puppet
mari'tare *vt* marry
mari'tarsi *vr* get married
ma'rito *nm* husband
mari'tozzo *nm* currant bun
ma'rittimo *a* maritime
mar'maglia *nf* rabble
marmel'lata *nf* jam; (*di agrumi*) marmalade
mar'mitta *nf* pot; *Auto* silencer. ~ **cata-**
litica catalytic converter
'**marmo** *nm* marble
mar'mocchio *nm fam* brat
mar'moreo *a* marble
marmoriz'zato *a* marbled
mar'motta *nf* marmot
maroc'chino *a & nmf* Moroccan
Ma'rocco *nm* Morocco
ma'roso *nm* breaker
mar'rone *a* brown ● *nm* brown; (*castagna*)
chestnut. **marroni** *pl* **canditi** marrons
glacés
mar'sina *nf* tails *pl*
marsupi'ale *nm* marsupial
mar'supio *nm* (*borsa*) bumbag
martedì *nm* Tuesday; **di** ~ on Tuesdays. ~
grasso Shrove Tuesday
martel'lante *a* ‹*mal di testa*› pounding;
hanno fatto una pubblicità ~ they hyped
the product, they bombarded the market with
publicity
martel'lare *vt* hammer ● *vi* throb
martel'lata *nf* hammer blow
martel'letto *nm* (*di giudice*) gavel; (*di pi-*
anoforte) hammer; (*di medico*) percussion
hammer
martel'lio *nm* hammering
mar'tello *nm* hammer; (*di battente*) knocker.
~ **pneumatico** pneumatic drill
marti'netto *nm Mech* jack
mar'tin pesca'tore *nm inv* kingfisher
'**martire** *nmf* martyr
mar'tirio *nm* martyrdom
'**martora** *nf* marten
martori'are *vt* torment
mar'xismo *nm* Marxism
mar'xista *a & nmf* Marxist
marza'pane *nm* marzipan
marzi'ale *a* martial
marzi'ano, -a *a & nmf* Martian
'**marzo** *nm* March
mascal'zone *nm* rascal
ma'scara *nm inv* mascara
mascar'pone *nm full-fat cream cheese often*
used for desserts
ma'scella *nf* jaw
'**maschera** *nf* mask; (*costume*) fancy dress;
Cinema, Theat usher *m*, usherette *f*; (*nella*
commedia dell'arte) stock character. ~
antigas gas mask. ~ **di bellezza** face pack.
~ **mortuaria** death mask. ~ **ad ossigeno**
oxygen mask

maschera'mento *nm* masking; *Mil* camouflage

masche'rare *vt* mask; *fig* camouflage

masche'rarsi *vr* put on a mask; **~ da** dress up as

masche'rata *nf* masquerade

maschi'accio *nm* (*ragazza*) tomboy

ma'schile *a* masculine; ⟨*sesso*⟩ male ● *nm* masculine [gender]

maschi'lista *a* sexist

'maschio *a* male; (*virile*) manly ● *nm* male; (*figlio*) son

masco'lino *a* masculine

ma'scotte *nf inv* mascot

maso'chismo *nm* masochism

maso'chista *a* & *nmf* masochist

'massa *nf* mass; *Electr* earth, ground *Am*; **comunicazioni di ~** mass media; **una ~** [**di gente**] a crowd [of people]

massa'crante *a* gruelling

massa'crare *vt* massacre

mas'sacro *nm* massacre; *fig* mess

massaggi'are *vt* massage

massaggia'tore, -'trice *nm* masseur ● *nf* masseuse

mas'saggio *nm* massage. **~ cardiaco** heart massage

mas'saia *nf* housewife

mas'sello *nm* (*metallo*) ingot ● *a* ⟨*legno*⟩ solid

masse'rizie *nfpl* household effects

massiccia'mente *adv* on a big scale

massicci'ata *nf* hard core

mas'siccio *a* massive; ⟨*oro ecc*⟩ solid; ⟨*corporatura*⟩ heavy ● *nm* massif

massifi'care *vt* de-individualize ⟨*società*⟩

massificazi'one *nf* de-individualization

'massima *nf* maxim; (*temperatura*) maximum

massi'male *nm* (*assicurazione*) limit of indemnity

massimizzazi'one *nf* maximization

'massimo *a* greatest; ⟨*quantità*⟩ maximum, greatest ● *nm* **il ~** the maximum; **al ~ at** [the] most, as a maximum. **~ storico** all-time high

'masso *nm* rock

mas'sone *nm* [Free]mason

masso'neria *nf* Freemasonry

mastecto'mia *nf* mastectomy

ma'stello *nm* wooden box for the grape or olive harvest

masti'care *vt* chew; (*borbottare*) mumble

'mastice *nm* mastic; (*per vetri*) putty

ma'stino *nm* mastiff

masto'dontico *a* gigantic

ma'stoide *nm* mastoid

'mastro *nm* master; **libro ~** ledger

mastur'barsi *vr* masturbate

masturbazi'one *nf* masturbation

ma'tassa *nf* skein

match 'point *nm inv* Tennis match point

matelassé *nm inv* quilting

mate'matica *nf* mathematics, maths, math *Am*. **~ pura** pure mathematics

mate'matico, -a *a* mathematical ● *nmf* mathematician

materas'sino *nm* small mattress. **~ gonfiabile** air bed, lilo®

mate'rasso *nm* mattress. **~ ad acqua** water bed. **~ di gommapiuma** foam mattress. **~ a molle** spring mattress

ma'teria *nf* matter; (*materiale*) material; (*di studio*) subject. **~ grigia** grey matter. **~ prima** raw material

materi'ale *a* material; (*grossolano*) coarse ● *nm* material. **~ da costruzione** building material. **~ pubblicitario** publicity material. **~ di scarto** waste material

materia'lismo *nm* materialism

materia'lista *a* materialistic; **non ~** unworldly ● *nmf* materialist

materializ'zarsi *vr* materialize

material'mente *adv* physically

materna'mente *adv* maternally

maternità *nf* motherhood; **è alla prima ~** it's her first baby; **ospedale di ~** maternity hospital

ma'terno *a* maternal; **lingua materna** mother tongue

ma'tita *nf* pencil. **matite** *pl* **colorate** colour[ed] pencils. **~ emostatica** styptic pencil. **~ per gli occhi** eyeliner pencil

matriar'cale *a* matriarchal

ma'trice *nf* matrix; (*origini*) roots *pl*; *Comm* counterfoil. **~ attiva** *Comput* active matrix. **~ passiva** *Comput* passive matrix

ma'tricola *nf* (*registro*) register; *Univ* fresher; **numero di ~** (*di studente*) matriculation number

ma'trigna *nf* stepmother

matrimoni'ale *a* matrimonial; **vita ~** married life

matri'monio *nm* marriage; (*cerimonia*) wedding. **~ in bianco** white wedding. **~ civile** civil wedding. **~ di convenienza** marriage of convenience

ma'trona *nf* matron

'matta *nf* (*nelle carte*) joker

mattacchi'one, -a *nmf* rascal

mat'tanza *nf* (*di tonni*) tuna fishing; *fig* killings *pl*

matta'toio *nm* slaughterhouse

matta'tore *nm* (*artista*) star performer

matte'rello *nm* rolling-pin

mat'tina *nf* morning; **la ~, alla ~** in the morning; **domani ~** tomorrow morning; **ieri ~** yesterday morning

matti'nata *nf* morning; *Theat* matinée

mattini'ero *a* **essere ~** be an early riser

mat'tino *nm* morning

'matto, -a *a* mad, crazy; *Med* insane; (*falso*) false; (*opaco*) matt; **~ da legare** barking mad; **avere una voglia matta di...** be dying for... ● *nm* madman ● *nf* madwoman

mat'tone *nm* brick; (*libro*) bore

matto'nella *nf* tile

mattu'tino *a* morning *attrib*

matu'rare *vt* ripen; *Fin* mature

maturazi'one *nf* ripening; *Fin* maturity;

(*fig: di idea ecc*) gestation; **arrivare a ~** ⟨*frutta:*⟩ ripen; ⟨*polizza:*⟩ mature

maturità *nf* maturity; *Sch* school-leaving certificate

ma'turo *a* mature; ⟨*frutto*⟩ ripe

ma'tusa *nm* old fogey

Mau'rizio *nf* **[isola di]** ~ Mauritius

mauso'leo *nm* mausoleum

maxi+ *pref* maxi+

'mayday *nm inv Radio* Mayday

'mazza *nf* club; (*martello*) hammer; (*da baseball, cricket*) bat. ~ **da golf** golf-club

maz'zata *nf* blow

maz'zetta *nf* (*di banconote*) bundle; (*tangente*) bribe

'mazzo *nm* bunch; (*carte da gioco*) pack

Mb *nm abbr* (**megabyte**) *Comput* Mb

me *pers pron* me; **me lo ha dato** he gave it to me; **secondo me** in my opinion; **fai come me** do as I do; **è più veloce di me** he is faster than me *o* faster than I am

me'andro *nm* meander

M.E.C. *nm abbr* (**Mercato Comune Europeo**) EEC

'Mecca *nf* **La ~** Mecca

mec'canica *nf* mechanics. ~ **quantistica** quantum mechanics

meccanica'mente *adv* mechanically

mec'canico *a* mechanical ● *nm* mechanic. ~ **laser** laser engine

mecca'nismo *nm* mechanism

meccanogra'fia *nf* data processing

meccano'grafico *a* data processing *attrib*

mece'nate *nmf* patron

mèche *nfpl* highlights; **[farsi] fare le ~** have highlights put in, have one's hair streaked

me'daglia *nf* medal. ~ **al valore** medal for valour

medagli'ere *nm* medal collection

medagli'one *nm* medallion; (*gioiello*) locket. **medaglioni** *pl* **di vitello** *Culin* medallions of veal

me'desimo *a* same

'media *nf* average; *Sch* average mark; *Math* mean; **essere nella ~** be in the mid-range

medi'ano *a* middle ● *nm* (*calcio*) half-back. ~ **di mischia** scrum half

medi'ante *prep* by

medi'are *vt* act as intermediary in

media'tore, -'trice *nmf* mediator; *Comm* middleman. ~ **d'affari** business agent

mediazi'one *nf* mediation

medica'mento *nm* medicine

medi'care *vt* treat; dress ⟨*ferita*⟩

medi'cato *a* ⟨*shampoo*⟩ medicated

medicazi'one *nf* medication; (*di ferita*) dressing

me'diceo *a* from the period of the Medici, Medicean

medi'cina *nf* medicine. ~ **alternativa** alternative medicine. ~ **del lavoro** occupational health. ~ **legale** forensic medicine. ~ **popolare** folk medicine

medici'nale *a* medicinal ● *nm* medicine

'medico *a* medical ● *nm* doctor. ~ **di base** general practitioner, GP. ~ **di famiglia** family doctor. ~ **generico** general practitioner, GP. ~ **legale** forensic scientist. ~ **di turno** duty doctor

medie'vale *a* medieval

'medio *a* average; ⟨*punto*⟩ middle; ⟨*statura*⟩ medium; **scuola media** secondary school ● *nm* (*dito*) middle finger. **M~ Oriente** Middle East

medi'ocre *a* mediocre; (*scadente*) poor

mediocre'mente *adv* indifferently

medio'evo *nm* Middle Ages *pl*

medi'tare *vt* meditate; (*progettare*) plan; (*considerare attentamente*) think over ● *vi* meditate

medita'tivo *a* meditative

meditazi'one *nf* meditation

mediter'raneo *a* Mediterranean; **il [mar] M~** the Mediterranean [Sea]

me'dusa *nf* jellyfish

'megabyte *nm inv Comput* megabyte

me'gafono *nm* megaphone

megaga'lattico *a* gigantic

mega'lite *nm* megalith

mega'lomane *nmf* megalomaniac

me'gera *nf* hag

'meglio *adv* better; **tanto ~**, ~ **così** so much the better ● *a* better; (*superlativo*) best ● *nmf* best ● *nf* **avere la ~ su** have the better of; **fare qcsa alla [bell'e] ~** do sth as best one can ● *nm* **fare del proprio ~** do one's best; **fare qcsa il ~ possibile** make an excellent job of sth; **al ~ to** the best of one's ability; **per il ~** for the best

'mela *nf* apple; **succo di ~** apple juice. ~ **cotogna** quince

mela'grana *nf* pomegranate

mé'lange *nm inv* flecked wool ● *a inv* ⟨*lana*⟩ flecked

mela'nina *nf* melanin

melan'zana *nf* aubergine, eggplant *Am*. **melanzane** *pl* **alla parmigiana** baked layers of aubergine, tomato and cheese

me'lassa *nf* molasses *sg*

me'lenso *a* ⟨*persona, film*⟩ dull

me'leto *nm* apple orchard

mel'lifluo *a* ⟨*parole*⟩ honeyed; ⟨*voce*⟩ sugary

'melma *nf* slime

mel'moso *a* slimy

'melo *nm* apple[-tree]

melo'dia *nf* melody

me'lodico *a* melodic

melodi'oso *a* melodious

melo'dramma *nm* melodrama

melodrammatica'mente *adv* melodramatically

melodram'matico *a* melodramatic

melo'grano *nm* pomegranate tree

me'lone *nm* melon

mem'brana *nf* membrane

'membro *nm* member; (*pl nf* **membra** *Anat*) limb

memo'rabile *a* memorable

'memore *a* mindful; (*riconoscente*) grateful

me'moria *nf* memory; (*oggetto ricordo*) souvenir; **imparare a ~** learn by heart; **memorie** *pl* (*biografiche*) memoirs. **~ cache** *Comput* cache memory. **~ collettiva** folk memory. **~ dinamica** *Comput* RAM. **~ di massa** *Comput* mass storage. **~ permanente** *Comput* non-volatile memory; **~ di sola lettura** *Comput* read-only memory, ROM. **~ a tampone** *Comput* buffer [memory]. **~ volatile** *Comput* volatile memory

memori'ale *nm* memorial

memoriz'zare *vt* memorize; *Comput* save, store

niena'dito: a ~ *adv* perfectly

me'nare *vt* lead; (*fam: picchiare*) hit; **~ la coda** ‹*cane:*› wag its tail; **~ qcno per il naso** pull sb's leg

mendi'cante *nmf* beggar

mendi'care *vt/i* beg

menefre'ghista *a* devil-may-care

mene'strello *nm* minstrel

me'ningi *nfpl* **spremersi le ~** rack one's brains

menin'gite *nf* meningitis

me'nisco *nm* meniscus

'meno *adv* less; (*superlativo*) least; (*in operazioni, con temperatura*) minus; **~ di** less than; **di ~** less; **~ moderno** less modern; **il ~ moderno di tutti** the least modern of all; **far qcsa alla ~ peggio** do sth as best one can; **fare a ~ di qcsa** do without sth; **non posso fare a ~ di ridere** I can't help laughing; **~ male!** thank goodness!; **sempre ~** less and less; **venir ~** (*svenire*) faint; **venir ~ a qcno** ‹*coraggio:*› fail sb; **sono le tre ~ un quarto** it's a quarter to three; **che tu venga o ~** whether you're coming or not; **quanto ~** at least ● **a** *inv* less; (*con nomi plurali*) fewer ● *nm* least; *Math* minus sign; **il ~ possibile** as little as possible; **per lo ~** at least ● *prep* except [for] ● *conj* **a ~ che** unless

meno'mare *vt* ‹*incidente:*› maim

meno'mato *a* disabled ● *nmf* disabled person

meno'pausa *nf* menopause

'mensa *nf* table; *Mil* mess; *Sch, Univ* refectory

men'sile *a* monthly ● *nm* (*stipendio*) [monthly] salary; (*rivista*) monthly

mensili'tà *nf inv* monthly salary

mensil'mente *adv* monthly

'mensola *nf* bracket; (*scaffale*) shelf

'menta *nf* mint; **al gusto di ~** mint-flavoured. **~ peperita** peppermint. **~ verde** spearmint

men'tale *a* mental

mentali'tà *nf inv* mentality

'mente *nf* mind; **a ~ fredda** in cold blood; **cosa ti è saltato in ~?** what possessed you?; **venire in ~ a qcno** occur to sb

men'tina *nf* mint

men'tire *vi* lie

'mento *nm* chin

men'tolo *nm* menthol; **al ~** mentholated

'mentre *conj* (*temporale*) while; (*invece*) whereas

me'nu *nm inv* menu. **~ a discesa** *Comput* pull-down menu. **~ fisso** set menu. **~ a tendina** *Comput* pull-down menu. **~ turistico** tourist menu

menzio'nare *vt* mention

menzi'one *nf* mention. **~ speciale** special mention

men'zogna *nf* lie

mera'viglia *nf* wonder; **a ~** marvellously; **che ~!** how wonderful!; **con mia grande ~** much to my amazement; **mi fa ~ che...** I am surprised that...

meravigli'are *vt* surprise

meravigli'arsi *vr* **~ di** be surprised at

meravigliosa'mente *adv* marvellously

meravigli'oso *a* marvellous, wonderful

mer'cante *nm* merchant. **~ d'arte** art dealer. **~ di schiavi** slave trader

mercanteggi'are *vi* trade; (*sul prezzo*) bargain

mercan'tile *a* mercantile ● *nm* merchant ship

mercan'zia *nf* merchandise, goods *pl*

merca'tino *nm* (*di quartiere*) local street market; *Fin* unlisted securities market

mer'cato *nm* market; *Fin* market[place]. **a buon ~** ‹*comprare*› cheap[ly]; ‹*articolo*› cheap. **~ aperto** *Econ* open market. **~ azionario** *Fin* equity market, share market. **~ dei cambi** foreign exchange market. **M~ Comune [Europeo]** [European] Common Market. **~ coperto** covered market, indoor market. **~ dell'eurovaluta** eurocurrency market. **~ immobiliare** property market. **~ libero** free market. **~ di massa** mass market. **~ nero** black market. **~ di prova** test market. **~ al rialzo** *Fin* bull market. **~ al ribasso** *Fin* bear market. **~ specializzato** niche market. **~ unico** Single Market

'merce *nf* goods *pl*, merchandise; **la venduta non si cambia senza lo scontrino** goods will not be exchanged without a receipt. **~ in conto vendita** sale or return goods. **~ deperibile** perishable goods

merce' *nf* **alla ~ di** at the mercy of

merce'nario *a & nm* mercenary

merceolo'gia *nf* study of commodities

merce'ria *nf* haberdashery; (*negozio*) haberdasher's

mercifi'care *vt* commercialize

mercificazi'one *nf* commercialization

mercoledì *nm inv* Wednesday; **di ~** on Wednesdays. **~ delle Ceneri** Ash Wednesday

mer'curio *nm* mercury

me'renda *nf* afternoon snack; **far ~** have an afternoon snack

meridi'ana *nf* sundial

meridi'ano *a* midday ● *nm* meridian

meridio'nale *a* southern ● *nmf* southerner

meridi'one *nm* south

me'ringa *nf* meringue

merin'gata *nf* meringue pie

meri'tare *vt* deserve

meri'tato *a* deserved
meri'tevole *a* deserving
'merito *nm* merit; *(valore)* worth; **in ~ a** as to; **per ~ di** thanks to
merito'cratico *a* meritocratic
meri'torio *a* meritorious
merla'tura *nf* battlements *pl*
merlet'taia *nf* lacemaker
mer'letto *nm* lace
'merlo *nm* blackbird; **bravo ~!** you fool!
mer'luzzo *nm* cod
'mero *a* mere
mesca'lina *nf* mescaline
'mescere *vt* pour out
meschine'ria *nf* meanness
me'schino *a* wretched; *(gretto)* mean ● *nm* wretch
'mescita *nf* wine shop
mescola'mento *nm* mixing
mesco'lanza *nf* mixture
mesco'lare *vt* mix; shuffle ‹carte›; *(confondere)* mix up; blend ‹tè, tabacco ecc›
mesco'larsi *vr* mix; *(immischiarsi)* meddle
mesco'lata *nf* (*a carte*) shuffle; *Culin* stir
'mese *nm* month. **~ civile** calendar month
me'setto *nm* **un ~** about a month, a month or so
'messa¹ *nf* Mass. **~ nera** black mass. **~ da requiem** requiem mass. **~ solenne** High Mass
'messa² *nf* *(il mettere)* putting. **~ in moto** *Auto* starting. **~ in piega** *(di capelli)* set; **farsi fare la ~ ~ ~** have one's hair set. **~ a punto** adjustment. **~ in scena** production; *fig* production number. **~ a terra** earthing, grounding *Am*
messag'gero *nm* messenger
mes'saggio *nm* message. **~ di errore** *Comput* error message
mes'sale *nm* missal
'messe *nf* harvest
Mes'sia *nm* Messiah
messi'cano, -a *a & nmf* Mexican
'Messico *nm* Mexico
messin'scena *nf* staging; *fig* act
'messo *pp di* **mettere** ● *nm* messenger
mesti'ere *nm* trade; *(lavoro)* job; **essere del ~** be an expert, know one's trade
'mesto *a* sad
'mestola *nf* *(di cuoco)* ladle; *(di muratore)* trowel
mestru'ale *a* menstrual
mestruazi'one *nf* menstruation; **mestruazioni** *pl* period
'meta *nf* destination; *fig* aim
metà *nf inv* half; *(centro)* middle; **~ prezzo** half price; **a ~ strada** half-way; **a ~ serata** half-way through the evening; **fare a ~ con qcno** go halves with sb, go fifty-fifty with sb; **fare [a] ~ e ~** go fifty-fifty, go halves
metabo'lismo *nm* metabolism
meta'carpo *nm* metacarpus
meta'done *nm* methadone
meta'fisica *n* metaphysics
meta'fisico *a* metaphysical

me'tafora *nf* metaphor
metafora'mente *adv* metaphorically
meta'forico *a* metaphorical
me'tallico *a* metallic
metalliz'zato *a* ‹grigio› metallic
me'tallo *nm* metal. **~ vile** base metal
metal'loide *nm* metalloid
metallur'gia *nf* metallurgy
metal'lurgico *a* metallurgical
metalmec'canico *a* engineering ● *nm* engineering worker
meta'morfosi *nf* metamorphosis
me'tano *nm* methane
metano'dotto *nm* methane pipeline
meta'nolo *nm* methanol
me'tastasi *nf inv* metastasis
meta'tarso *nm* metatarsus
me'teora *nf* meteor
meteo'rite *nm* meteorite
meteorolo'gia *nf* meteorology
meteoro'logico *a* meteorological
meteo'rologo *nm* meteorologist
me'ticcio, -a *nmf* half-caste
meticolosa'mente *adv* meticulously
metico'loso *a* meticulous
me'tile *nm* methyl
me'todico *a* methodical
meto'dista *a & nmf* Methodist
'metodo *nm* method
metodolo'gia *nf* methodology
metodo'logico *a* methodological
me'traggio *nm* length *(in metres)*; **vendere a ~** sell by the metre
'metrico, -a *a* metric; *(in poesia)* metrical ● *nf* metrics
'metro *nm* metre; *(nastro)* tape measure. **~ cubo** cubic metre. **~ quadrato** square metre
'metro *nf inv fam* underground, subway *Am*
me'tronomo *nm* metronome
metro'notte *nmf inv* night security guard
me'tropoli *nf inv* metropolis
metropoli'tana *nf* underground, subway *Am*
metropoli'tano *a* metropolitan
'mettere *vt* put; *(indossare)* put on; *(fam: installare)* put in; **~ al mondo** bring into the world; **~ da parte** set aside; **~ fiducia** inspire trust; **~ qcsa in chiaro** make sth clear; **~ in mostra** display; **~ a posto** tidy up; **~ in vendita** put up for sale; **~ su** set up ‹casa, azienda›; **metter su famiglia** start a family; **ci ho messo un'ora** it took me an hour; **mettiamo che...** let's suppose that...
'mettersi *vr* *(indossare)* put on; *(diventare)* turn out; **~ a** start to; **~ con qcno** *(fam: formare una coppia)* start to go out with sb; **~ a letto** go to bed; **~ a sedere** sit down; **~ in viaggio** set out
metti'foglio *nm* feeder
'mezza *nf* **è la ~** it's half past twelve; **sono le quattro e ~** it's half past four
mez'zadria *nf* sharecropping
mezza'luna *nf* half moon; *(simbolo islamico)* crescent; *(coltello)* two-handled chopping knife; **a ~** half-moon

mezza'manica nf a ~ ⟨maglia⟩ short-sleeved; **mezzemaniche** pl pej lowest grade of clerks, pen-pushers

mezze'nino nm mezzanine

mez'zano, -a a middle

mezza'notte nf midnight; **aspettare la ~** see in the New Year

mezz'asta: a ~ at half mast

mezze'ria nf centre line

'mezzo a half; **di mezza età** middle aged; **~ bicchiere** half a glass; **una mezza idea** a vague idea; **siamo mezzi morti** we're half dead; **sono le quattro e ~** it's half past four. **mezza cartuccia** nf runt. **mezza dozzina** nf half-dozen. **mezza età** nf midlife. **mezza giornata** nf half day. **~ guanto** nm mitt. **~ litro** nm half a litre. **mezz'ora** nf half an hour. **mezza pensione** nf half board. **mezza stagione** nf **una giacca di ~** a spring/autumn jacket. **mezza verità** nf half-truth ● adv (a metà) half; **~ addormentato** half asleep; **~ morto** half-dead; **~ morto di paura** petrified; **~ e ~** ⟨così così⟩ so so ● nm (metà) half; (centro) middle; (per raggiungere un fine) means sg; **uno e ~** one and a half; **tre anni e ~** three and a half years; **in ~ a** in the middle of; **il giusto ~** the happy medium; **levare di ~** clear away; **per ~ di** by means of; **a ~ posta** by mail; **via di ~** fig halfway house; (soluzione) middle way; **mezzi** pl (denaro) means pl. **mezzi** pl **di comunicazione di massa** mass media. **mezzi** pl **pubblici** public transport. **mezzi** pl **di trasporto** [means of] transport

mezzo'busto nm (statua) bust; TV talking head; **a ~** ⟨foto, ritratto⟩ half-length

mezzo'fondo nm middle-distance running

mezzogi'orno nm midday, noon; (sud) South. **il M~** Southern Italy. **~ in punto** high noon

mezzo'sangue nmf crossbreed

mezzo'servizio nm **lavorare a ~** do part-time cleaning work

mi pers pron me; (refl) myself; **mi ha dato un libro** he gave me a book; **mi lavo le mani** I wash my hands; **eccomi** here I am ● nm Mus (chiave, nota) E

mia vedi mio

miago'lare vi miaow

miago'lio nm miaowing

mi'ao nm miaow

'mica[1] nf mica

'mica[2] adv fam (per caso) by any chance; **hai ~ visto Paolo?** have you seen Paul, by any chance?; **non è ~ bello** it is not at all nice; **~ male** not bad

'miccia nf fuse

micidi'ale a deadly

'micio nm pussy-cat

mi'cosi nf athlete's foot

mi'cotico a fungal

microbiolo'gia nf microbiology

'microbo nm microbe

microchirur'gia nf microsurgery

micro'clima nm microclimate

microcom'puter nm inv microcomputer

micro'cosmo nm microcosm

micro'fiche nf inv microfiche

micro'film nm inv microfilm

micro'fisica nf microphysics

mi'crofono nm microphone. **~ con la clip** clip-on microphone. **~ spia** bugging device, bug. **~ a stelo** boom microphone

microfotogra'fia nf Phot micrograph; (tecnica) micrography

microinfor'matica nf microcomputing

micro'onda nf microwave

microorga'nismo nm microorganism

microproces'sore nm microprocessor

micro'scheda nf microfiche

micro'scopico a microscopic

micro'scopio nm microscope; **passare qcsa al ~** fig examine sth in microscopic detail

microse'condo nm microsecond

micro'solco nm (disco) long-playing record

micro'spia nf bug

mi'dollo nm (pl nf midolla, Anat) marrow; **fino al ~** ⟨bagnato⟩ through and through; ⟨corrotto⟩ to the core. **~ osseo** bone marrow. **~ spinale** spinal cord

'mie vedi mio

mi'ei vedi mio

mi'ele nm honey. **~ d'acacia** acacia honey

mi'etere vt reap

mietitrebbia'trice nf combine harvester

mieti'trice nf harvester

mieti'tura nf harvest

migli'aia nfpl thousands

migli'aio nm (pl nf migliaia) thousand. **a migliaia** in thousands

'miglio nm Bot millet; (misura: pl f miglia) mile. **~ nautico** nautical mile. **miglia** pl **all'ora** miles per hour, mph. **~ terrestre** mile

migliora'mento nm improvement

miglio'rare vt/i improve

migli'ore a better; (superlativo) the best; **~ amico** best friend; **i migliori auguri** best wishes ● nmf **il/la ~** the best

miglio'ria nf improvement

mi'gnatta nf leech

'mignolo nm little finger, pinkie fam; (del piede) little toe

mi'gnon a inv (bottiglie) miniature

mi'grare vi migrate

migra'tore a migratory

migra'torio a migratory

migrazi'one nf migration

'mila vedi mille

mila'nese a & nmf Milanese

Mi'lano nf Milan

miliar'dario, -a nm millionaire; (pluri-miliardario) billionaire ● nf millionairess; billionairess

mili'ardo nm billion

mili'are a **pietra ~** milestone

milio'nario, -a nm millionaire ● nf millionairess

mili'one nm million

milio'nesimo *a & nm* millionth

mili'tante *a & nmf* militant

mili'tanza *nf* militancy

mili'tare *vi* ~ **in** be a member of ⟨*un partito ecc*⟩ ● *a* military ● *nm* soldier; **fare il** ~ do one's military service. ~ **di carriera** regular [soldier]. ~ **di leva** National Serviceman

milita'rismo *nm* militarism

milita'rista *a* militaristic

militariz'zare *vt* militarize

militas'solto *a* having done National Service

'milite *nm* soldier

milite'sente *a* exempt from National Service

mil'izia *nf* militia

millanta|'tore, -'trice *nmf* boaster

'mille *a & nm* (*pl* **mila**) *a o* one thousand; **due/tre mila** two/three thousand; ~ **grazie!** thanks a lot!; **millenovecentonovantaquattro** *nm* nineteen ninety-four

mille'foglie *nm inv Culin* vanilla slice

mil'lennio *nm* millennium

millepi'edi *nm inv* centipede

mil'lesimo *a & nm* thousandth

milli'bar *nm inv* millibar

milli'grammo *nm* milligram

mil'lilitro *nm* millilitre

mil'limetro *nm* millimetre

'milza *nf* spleen

mi'mare *vt* mimic ⟨*persona*⟩ ● *vi* mime

mi'metico *a* **tuta** *f* **mimetica** camouflage; **animale** ~ animal which has the ability to camouflage itself; **vernice mimetica** camouflage paint

mime'tismo *nm* ability to camouflage itself; ~ **politico** chameleon-like political traits

mimetiz'zare *vt* camouflage

mimetiz'zarsi *vr* camouflage oneself

'mimica *nf* mime. ~ **facciale** facial expressions *pl*

'mimico *a* mimic

'mimo *nm* mime

mi'mosa *nf* mimosa

'mina *nf* mine; (*di matita*) lead

mi'naccia *nf* threat. **avere una** ~ **di aborto** come close to having a miscarriage. ~ **di morte** death threat

minacci'are *vt* threaten

minacciosa'mente *adv* threateningly, menacingly

minacci'oso *a* threatening; ⟨*onde*⟩ menacing

mi'nare *vt* mine; *fig* undermine

mina'reto *nm* minaret

mina'tore *nm* miner

mina'torio *a* threatening

mine'rale *a & nm* mineral

mineralo'gia *nf* mineralogy

mine'rario *a* mining *attrib*

mi'nestra *nf* soup. ~ **in brodo** noodle soup. ~ **di verdure** vegetable soup

mine'strone *nm* minestrone (*vegetable soup*); (*fam: insieme confuso*) hotchpotch

mingher'lino *a* skinny

'mini *nf inv* (*gonna*) mini ● *a inv* mini

mini+ *pref* mini+

miniapparta'mento *nm* studio flat *Br*, studio apartment

minia'tura *nf* miniature

miniaturiz'zato *a* miniaturized

mini'bus *nm inv* minibus

mini'disco *nm* minidiskette

mini'era *nf* mine; **una** ~ **di notizie** a mine of information; **è una** ~ **di idee** he's full of ideas. ~ **a cielo aperto** opencast mine. ~ **d'oro** gold-mine

mini'golf *nm* minigolf, miniature golf

mini'gonna *nf* miniskirt, mini

'minima *nf* (*atmosferica*) minimum temperature; *Med* minimum blood-pressure level; *Mus* minim

minima'lista *nmf* minimalist

minima'mente *adv* minimally

mini'market *nm inv* minimarket

minimiz'zare *vt* minimize

'minimo *a* least, slightest; (*il più basso*) lowest; ⟨*salario, quantità ecc*⟩ minimum ● *nm* minimum; **girare al** ~ *Auto* idle; **toccare il** ~ **storico** be at an all-time low; **come** ~ at least, as a minimum

'minio *nm* red lead

ministeri'ale *a* (*di ministero*) ministerial; (*di governo*) government

mini'stero *nm* ministry; (*governo*) government. ~ **degli [affari] esteri** Foreign Office, State Department *Am*. ~ **della difesa** Department of Defence. ~ **della pubblica istruzione** Department of Education. ~ **della sanità** Department of Health

mi'nistro *nm* minister. ~ **della difesa** Defence Minister, Defense Secretary *Am*. ~ **degli esteri** Foreign Secretary, Secretary of State *Am*. ~ **di grazia e giustizia** ≈ Attorney General. ~ **dell'interno** Home Secretary, Secretary of the Interior *Am*. ~ **del lavoro** Employment Minister, Employment Secretary. ~ **del tesoro** Chancellor of the Exchequer, Secretary of the Treasury *Am*

mini'tower *nm Comput* minitower

mino'ranza *nf* minority

mino'rato, -a *a* disabled ● *nmf* disabled person

Mi'norca *nf* Menorca

mi'nore *a* ⟨*gruppo, numero*⟩ smaller; (*superlativo*) smallest; ⟨*distanza*⟩ shorter; (*superlativo*) shortest; ⟨*prezzo*⟩ lower; (*superlativo*) lowest; (*di età*) younger; (*superlativo*) youngest; (*di importanza*) minor; (*superlativo*) least important ● *nmf* younger; (*superlativo*) youngest; *Jur* minor; **il** ~ **dei mali** the lesser of two evils; **i minori di 14 anni** children under 14

mino'renne *a* under age ● *nmf* minor

minori'tario *a* minority *attrib*

minu'etto *nm* minuet

mi'nuscolo, -a *a* tiny ● *nf* small letter

mi'nuta *nf* rough copy

minuta'mente *adv* ‹*esaminato*› in minute detail, minutely; ‹*lavorato, tritato*› finely

mi'nuto[1] *a* minute; ‹*persona*› delicate; ‹*ricerca*› detailed; ‹*pioggia, neve*› fine; **al ~** *Comm* retail

mi'nuto[2] *nm* ‹*di tempo*› minute; **spaccare il ~** be dead on time. **minuti** *pl* **di recupero** *Sport* injury time

mi'nuzia *nf* trifle; **minuzie** *pl* minutiae

minuziosa'mente *adv* minutely

minuzi'oso *a* minute, detailed; ‹*persona*› meticulous

'mio (**il mio** *m,* **la mia** *f,* **i miei** *mpl,* **le mie** *fpl*) *poss a* my; **questa macchina è mia** this car is mine; **~ padre** my father; **un ~ amico** a friend of mine ● *poss pron* mine; **i miei** ‹*genitori ecc*› my folks

'miope *a* short-sighted

mio'pia *nf* short-sightedness

'mira *nf* aim; ‹*bersaglio*› target; **prendere la ~** take aim; **prendere di ~ qcno** *fig* have it in for sb

mi'rabile *a* admirable

miraco'lato *a* ‹*malato*› miraculously cured

mi'racolo *nm* miracle

miracolosa'mente *adv* miraculously

miraco'loso *a* miraculous

mi'raggio *nm* mirage

mi'rare *vi* [take] aim; **~ alto** aim high

mi'rarsi *vr* ‹*guardarsi*› look at oneself

mi'riade *nf* myriad

mi'rino *nm* sight; *Phot* view-finder

'mirra *nf* myrrh

mir'tillo *nm* blueberry

'mirto *nm* myrtle

mi'santropo, -a *nmf* misanthropist

mi'scela *nf* mixture; ‹*di caffè, tabacco ecc*› blend

misce'lare *vt* mix

miscela'tore *nm* ‹*apparecchio*› blender; ‹*di acqua*› mixer tap

miscel'lanea *nf* miscellany

'mischia *nf* scuffle; ‹*nel rugby*› scrum

mischi'are *vt* mix; shuffle ‹*carte da gioco*›

mischi'arsi *vr* mix; ‹*immischiarsi*› interfere

misco'noscere *vt* not appreciate

miscre'dente *nmf* heretic

mi'scuglio *nm* mixture; *fig* medley

mise'rabile *a* wretched

misera'mente *adv* ‹*finire*› miserably; ‹*vivere*› in abject poverty; ‹*vestito*› shabbily

mi'seria *nf* poverty; ‹*infelicità*› misery; **guadagnare una ~** earn a pittance; **miserie** *pl* ‹*disgrazie*› misfortunes; **porca ~!** *fam* hell!

miseri'cordia *nf* mercy

misericordi'oso *a* merciful

'misero *a* ‹*miserabile*› wretched; ‹*povero*› poor; ‹*scarso*› paltry

mi'sfatto *nm* misdeed

mi'sogino *nm* misogynist

mis'saggio *nm* vision mixer

'missile *nm* missile. **~ cruise** cruise missile. **~ terra-aria** surface-to-air missile

missi'listico *a* missile *attrib*

missio'nario, -a *nmf* missionary

missi'one *nf* mission. **~ di pace** peace mission

misteriosa'mente *adv* mysteriously

misteri'oso *a* mysterious

mi'stero *nm* mystery

'mistica *nf* mysticism

misti'cismo *nm* mysticism

'mistico *a* mystic[al] ● *nm* mystic

mistifi'care *vt* distort ‹*verità*›

mistificazi'one *nf* ‹*della verità*› distortion

'misto *a* mixed; **scuola mista** mixed *o* co-educational school ● *nm* mixture; ‹*di oggetti*› miscellany. **~ lana** wool mixture; **~ lana/cotone** wool/cotton mix

mi'sura *nf* measure; ‹*dimensione*› measurement; ‹*taglia*› size; ‹*limite*› limit; **su ~** ‹*abiti*› made to measure; ‹*mobile*› custom-made; **a ~** ‹*andare, calzare*› perfectly; **a ~ che** as; **nella ~ in cui** insofar as. **~ di sicurezza** safety measure. **~ di capacità** unit of capacity. **~ di lunghezza** unit of length. **~ profilattica** prophylactic

misu'rare *vt* measure; try on ‹*indumenti*›; ‹*limitare*› limit

misu'rarsi *vr* **~ con** ‹*gareggiare*› compete with

misu'rato *a* measured

misu'rino *nm* measuring spoon

'mite *a* mild; ‹*prezzo*› moderate

'mitico *a* mythical

miti'gare *vt* mitigate

miti'garsi *vr* calm down; ‹*clima:*› become mild

'mitilo *nm* mussel

mitiz'zare *vt* mythicize

'mito *nm* myth

mitolo'gia *nf* mythology

mito'logico *a* mythological

mi'tomane *nmf* compulsive liar

'mitra *nf* *Relig* mitre ● *nm inv* *Mil* machine-gun

mitragli'are *vt* machine-gun; **~ di domande** fire questions at

mitraglia'trice *nf* machine-gun

mitt. *abbr* (**mittente**) sender

mitteleuro'peo *a* Central European

mit'tente *nmf* sender

'mixer *nm inv* mixer

mne'monico *a* mnemonic; **frase mnemonica** mnemonic

mo' *nm* **a mo' di** by way of ‹*esempio, consolazione*›

'mobile[1] *a* mobile; ‹*volubile*› fickle; ‹*che si può muovere*› movable; **beni** *pl* **mobili** moveable personal estate; **squadra ~** flying squad

'mobile[2] *nm* piece of furniture; **mobili** *pl* furniture *sg*. **~ bar** drinks cabinet. **mobili** *pl* **da giardino** garden furniture. **mobili** *pl* **in stile** reproduction furniture

mo'bilia *nf* furniture

mobili'are *a* ‹*capitale*› movable; ‹*credito*› medium-term; ‹*mercato*› share *attrib*; **patrimonio ~** non-property assets

mobili'ere *nm* furniture dealer

mobili'ficio *nm* furniture factory

mo'bilio *nm* furniture

mobilità *nf* mobility

mobili'tare *vt* mobilize

mobilitazi'one *nf* mobilization

'moca *nm inv* mocha

mocas'sino *nm* moccasin

mocci'coso, -a *a* snotty ● *nmf* snotty-nosed kid, brat

'moccolo *nm* (*di candela*) candle-end; (*moccio*) snot

'moda *nf* fashion; **di ~** in fashion; **andare di ~** be in fashion; **alla ~** ⟨*musica, vestiti*⟩ up-to-date; **fuori ~** unfashionable

mo'dale *a* ⟨*verbo*⟩ modal

modalità *nf inv* formality; **~ d'uso** instruction

modana'tura *nf* moulding

mo'della *nf* model

model'lare *vt* model

model'lino *nm* model

model'lismo *nm* model-making; (*collezionismo*) collecting models

model'lista *nmf* model-maker; (*moda*) [fashion] designer

mo'dello *nm* model; (*stampo*) mould; (*di carta*) pattern; (*modulo*) form; (*moda*) male model. **~ in scala** scale model

'modem *nm inv* modem; **mandare per ~** modem, send by modem

'modem-fax *nm* fax-modem

mode'rare *vt* moderate; (*diminuire*) reduce

mode'rarsi *vr* control oneself

moderata'mente *adv* moderately

mode'rato *a* moderate

modera'|tore, -'trice *nmf* (*in tavola rotonda*) moderator ● *a* moderating

moderazi'one *nf* moderation

moderna'mente *adv* (*in modo moderno*) in a modern style

modernari'ato *nm* collecting 20th-century art and products

moder'nismo *nm* modernism

modernità *nf* modernity

moderniz'zare *vt* modernize

modernizzazi'one *nf* modernization

mo'derno *a* modern

mo'destia *nf* modesty

mo'desto *a* modest

'modico *a* reasonable

mo'difica *nf* modification

modifi'care *vt* modify

modifica'tore *nm* modifier

modificazi'one *nf* modification

mo'dista *nf* milliner

'modo *nm* way; (*garbo*) manners *pl*; (*occasione*) chance; *Gram* mood; **ad ogni ~** anyhow; **di ~ che** so that; **fare in ~ di** try to; **in che ~** (*inter*) how; **in qualche ~** somehow; **in questo ~** like this; **~ di dire** idiom; **per ~ di dire** so to speak; **in ~ ottimistico/ pessimistico/anormale** optimistically/pessimistically/abnormally

modu'lare *vt* modulate

modula'tore *nm* modulator. **~ di frequenza** frequency modulator

modulazi'one *nf* modulation. **~ di frequenza** frequency modulation

'modulo *nm* form; (*lunare, di comando*) module. **~ continuo** continuous paper. **~ di domanda** application form. **~ di iscrizione** enrolment form. **~ di ordinazione** order form

'modus ope'randi *nm inv* modus operandi

'modus vi'vendi *nm inv* modus vivendi

mof'fetta *nf* skunk

'mogano *nm* mahogany

'mogio *a* dejected

'moglie *nf* wife

moi'cano *a* **taglio [di capelli] alla moicana** mohican [haircut]

mo'ine *nfpl* **fare le ~** behave in an affected way

'mola *nf* millstone; *Mech* grindstone

mo'lare *nm* molar

mo'lato *a* ⟨*vetro*⟩ cut

mola'trice *nf Mech* grinder

'mole *nf* mass; (*dimensione*) size

mo'lecola *nf* molecule

moleco'lare *a* molecular

mole'stare *vt* bother; (*più forte*) molest

molesta'|tore, -'trice *nmf* molester

mo'lestia *nf* nuisance. **molestie** *pl* **sessuali** sexual harassment *sg*

mo'lesto *a* bothersome

Mo'lise *nm* Molise

'molla *nf* spring; **molle** *pl* tongs; **prendere qcno con le molle** handle sb with kid gloves

mol'lare *vt* let go; (*fam: lasciare*) leave; *fam* give ⟨*ceffone*⟩; *Naut* cast off ● *vi* cease; **mollala!** *fam* stop that!

'molle *a* soft; (*bagnato*) wet

molleggi'are *vi* be springy ● *vt* spring

molleggi'arsi *vr* bend at the knees

molleggi'ato *a* bouncy

mol'leggio *nm* (*di auto*) suspension; (*di letto*) springs *pl*; (*esercizio*) knee-bends *pl*

mol'letta *nf* (*per capelli*) hairgrip, barrette *Am*; (*per bucato*) clothes-peg; **mollette** *pl* (*per ghiaccio ecc*) tongs. **~ da bucato** clothes peg

mollet'tone *nm* (*per tavolo*) padded table cloth

mol'lezza *nf* softness; **mollezze** *pl fig* luxury

'mollica *nf* crumb

mol'liccio *a* squidgy

mol'lusco *nm* mollusc

'molo *nm* pier; (*banchina*) dock

'molotov *a inv* **bottiglia ~** Molotov cocktail

mol'teplice *a* manifold; (*numeroso*) numerous

molteplicità *nf* multiplicity

mol'tiplica *nf* (*di bicicletta*) gear ratio

moltipli'care *vt* multiply

moltipli'carsi *vr* multiply

moltiplica'tore *nm* multiplier

moltiplica'trice *nf* calculating machine

moltiplicazi'one *nf* multiplication

molti'tudine *nf* multitude

'**molto** *a* a lot of; (*con negazione e interrogazione*) much, a lot of; (*con nomi plurali*) many, a lot of; **non ~ tempo** not much time, not a lot of time; **molte grazie** thank you very much ● *adv* very; (*con verbi*) a lot; (*con avverbi*) much; **~ stupido** very stupid; **~ bene, grazie** very well, thank you; **mangiare ~** eat a lot; **~ più veloce** much faster; **non mangiare ~** not eat a lot, not eat much ● *pron* a lot; (*molto tempo*) a lot of time; (*con negazione e interrogazione*) much, a lot; (*plurale*) many; **non ne ho ~** I don't have much, I don't have a lot; **non ne ho molti** I don't have many, I don't have a lot; **non ci metterò ~** I won't be long; **fra non ~** before long; **molti** (*persone*) a lot of people; **eravamo in molti** there were a lot of us

momentanea'mente *adv* momentarily; **è ~ assente** he's not here at the moment

momen'taneo *a* momentary

mo'mento *nm* moment; **a momenti** (*a volte*) sometimes; (*fra un momento*) in a moment; **dal ~ che** since; **per il ~** for the time being; **al ~** at the moment; **da un ~ all'altro** (*cambiare idea ecc*) from one moment to the next; (*aspettare qcno ecc*) at any moment

'**monaca** *nf* nun

'**Monaco** *nm* Monaco ● *nf* (*di Baviera*) Munich

'**monaco** *nm* monk

mo'narca *nm* monarch

monar'chia *nf* monarchy

mo'narchico, -a *a* monarchic ● *nmf* monarchist

mona'stero *nm* (*di monaci*) monastery; (*di monache*) convent

mo'nastico *a* monastic

monche'rino *nm* stump

'**monco** *a* maimed; (*fig: troncato*) truncated; **~ di un braccio** one-armed

mon'dana *nf* lady of the night

mondanità *nf* (*gente*) beau monde; **~** *pl* pleasures of the world

mon'dano *a* worldly; **vita mondana** social life

mon'dare *vt* (*sbucciare*) peel; shell (*piselli*); (*pulire*) clean

mondi'ale *a* world *attrib*; (*scala*) worldwide; (*fam: fantastico*) fantastic; **di fama ~** world-famous

mondi'ali *nmpl* World Cup

mondial'mente *adv* (*operare*) worldwide; **~ noto** world-famous

mon'dina *nf* seasonal worker in the rice fields

'**mondo** *nm* world; **il bel ~** fashionable society; **un ~** (*molto*) a lot. **non è la fine del ~** it's not the end of the world; **è la fine del ~** (*fam: fantastico*) it's out of this world; **~ cane!** *fam* damn!. **~ accademico** academia; **~ del lavoro** world of work. **~ dei sogni** never-never land. **~ dello spettacolo** show biz

mondovisi'one *nf* **in ~** transmitted worldwide

monelle'ria *nf* prank

mo'nello, -a *nmf* urchin

mo'neta *nf* coin; (*denaro*) money; (*denaro spicciolo*) [small] change. **~ estera** foreign currency. **~** [**a corso**] **legale** legal tender. **~ unica** single currency

mone'tario *a* monetary

mongolfi'era *nf* hot air balloon

'**mongolo** *a* Mongol; *Med* mongol

mo'nile *nm* jewel

'**monito** *nm* warning

'**monitor** *nm inv* monitor

monito'raggio *nm* monitoring

moni'tore *nm* monitor

mono'albero *a inv* single-camshaft *attrib*

mono'blocco *nm Auto* cylinder block ● *a inv* (*cucina*) fitted

mo'nocolo *nm* monocle

monoco'lore *a Pol* one-party

monocro'matico *a* monochrome

mono'dose *a inv* individually packaged

monoga'mia *nf* monogamy

mo'nogamo *a* monogamous

monogra'fia *nf* monograph

mono'gramma *nm* monogram

mono'kini *nm inv* monokini

mono'lingue *a* monolingual

mono'lito *nm* monolith

monolo'cale *nm* studio flat *Br*, studio apartment

mo'nologo *nm* monologue

monoma'nia *nf* monomania

mononucle'osi *nf inv* **~ infettiva** glandular fever

mono'pattino *nm* [child's] scooter

mono'petto *a* single-breasted

mono'plano *nm* monoplane

mono'polio *nm* monopoly. **~ di Stato** state monopoly

monopoliz'zare *vt* monopolize

mono'posto *nm* single-seater

mono'reddito *a* single-income *attrib*

monosac'caride *nm* monosaccharide

mono'sci *nm inv* monoski

monosil'labico *a* monosyllabic

mono'sillabo *nm* monosyllable ● *a* monosyllabic

mo'nossido *nm* **~ di carbonio** carbon monoxide

monote'istico *a* monotheistic

monotona'mente *adv* monotonously

monoto'nia *nf* monotony

mo'notono *a* monotonous

mono'uso *a* disposable

monou'tente *a inv* single-user *attrib*

monsi'gnore *nm* monsignor

mon'sone *nm* monsoon

'**monta** *nf Zool* covering; (*modo di cavalcare*) riding style; **stallone da ~** stud horse

monta'carichi *nm inv* hoist

mon'taggio *nm Mech* assembly; *Cinema* editing; **scatola di ~** assembly kit; **catena di ~** production line

mon'tagna *nf* mountain; *(zona)* mountains *pl*; **montagne** *pl* **russe** roller coaster, big dipper

monta'gnoso *a* mountainous

monta'naro, -a *nmf* highlander

mon'tano *a* mountain *attrib*

mon'tante *nm (di finestra, porta)* upright; *Fin* total amount; *(nel pugilato)* upper cut

mon'tare *vt/i* mount; get on *(veicolo)*; *(aumentare)* rise; *Mech* assemble; frame *(quadro)*; *Culin* whip; edit *(film)*; *(a cavallo)* ride; *fig* blow up

mon'tarsi *vr* ~ **la testa** get big-headed

mon'tato, -a *nmf fam* poser

monta'|tore, -'trice *nmf* assembler

monta'tura *nf Mech* assembling; *(di occhiali)* frame; *(di gioiello)* mounting; *fig* exaggeration

'monte *nm anche fig* mountain; **a** ~ upstream; **andare a** ~ be ruined; **mandare a** ~ **qcsa** ruin sth. **M~ Bianco** Mont Blanc. ~ **di pietà** pawnshop

monte'premi *nm inv* jackpot

mont'gomery *nm inv* duffle coat

mon'tone *nm* ram; **carne di** ~ mutton

montu'oso *a* mountainous

monumen'tale *a* monumental

monu'mento *nm* monument. ~ **ai caduti** war memorial. ~ **commemorativo** memorial. ~ **nazionale** national monument

mo'plen® *nm* moulded plastic

mo'quette *nf (tappeto)* fitted carpet

'mora *nf (del gelso)* mulberry; *(del rovo)* blackberry

mo'rale *a* moral ● *nf* morals *pl*; *(di storia)* moral ● *nm* morale

mora'lista *nmf* moralist

mora'listico *a* moralistic

moralità *nf inv* morality; *(condotta)* morals *pl*

moraliz'zare *vt/i* moralize

moral'mente *adv* morally

mora'toria *nf* moratorium

morbida'mente *adv* softly

morbi'dezza *nf* softness

'morbido *a* soft

mor'billo *nm* measles *sg*

'morbo *nm* disease. ~ **della mucca pazza** mad cow disease

morbosa'mente *adv* morbidly

morbosità *nf (qualità)* morbidity

mor'boso *a* morbid

'morchia *nf* sludge

mor'dace *a* cutting

mor'dente *a* biting

'mordere *vt* bite; *(corrodere)* bite into

mordicchi'are *vt* gnaw

mo'rello *nm* black horse ● *a* blackish

mo'rena *nf* moraine

mo'rente *a* dying

mo'resco *a* Moorish

mor'fina *nf* morphine

morfi'nomane *nmf* morphine addict

morfolo'gia *nf* morphology

morfo'logico *a* morphological

mori'bondo *a* dying; *(istituzione)* moribund

morige'rato *a* moderate

mo'rire *vi* die; *fig* die out; **fa un freddo da** ~ it's freezing cold, it's perishing; ~ **di noia** be bored to death; **c'era da** ~ **dal ridere** it was hilariously funny; **morir di fame** starve to death; *fig* starve

mor'mone *nmf* Mormon

mormo'rare *vt/i* murmur; *(brontolare)* mutter

mormo'rio *nm* murmuring; *(lamentela)* grumbling

'moro *a* dark ● *nm* Moor; *(negro)* black

mo'roso *a* in arrears

'morra *nf* game for two players where each shouts a number at the same time as showing a number of fingers

'morsa *nf* vice; *fig* grip

'morse *a* **alfabeto** ~ Morse code

mor'setto *nm* clamp; *(stringinaso)* nose clip. ~ **per batteria** battery lead connection

morsi'care *vt* bite

morsica'tura *nf* [snake] bite

'morso *nm* bite; *(di cibo, briglia)* bit; **i morsi della fame** hunger pangs

morta'della *nf* mortadella *(type of salted pork)*

mor'taio *nm* mortar

mor'tale *a* mortal; *(simile a morte)* deadly; **di una noia** ~ deadly

mortalità *nf* mortality

mortal'mente *adv (ferito)* fatally; *(offeso)* mortally; *(annoiato)* to death. ~ **stanco** *fam* dead tired

morta'retto *nm* firecracker

'morte *nf* death; **non è la** ~ **di nessuno** it's not the end of the world; **lo odia a** ~ *fam* she can't stand the sight of him; **annoiarsi a** ~ *fam* be bored to death. ~ **cerebrale** brain death

mortifi'cante *a* mortifying

mortifi'care *vt* mortify

mortifi'carsi *vr* be mortified

mortifi'cato *a* mortified

mortificazi'one *nf* mortification

'morto, -a *pp di* **morire** ● *a* dead; ~ **di freddo** frozen to death; **stanco** ~ dead tired ● *nm* dead man ● *nf* dead woman

mor'torio *nm* funeral

mo'saico *nm* mosaic

'Mosca *nf* Moscow

'mosca *nf* fly; *(barba)* goatee; **cadere come le mosche** be dropping like flies; **essere una** ~ **bianca** be a rarity; **non si sentiva volare una** ~ you could have heard a pin drop. ~ **cieca** blindman's buff

mo'scato *a* muscat. **noce moscata** nutmeg ● *nm* muscatel

mosce'rino *nm* midge; *(fam: persona)* midget

mo'schea *nf* mosque

moschetti'ere *nm* musketeer

mo'schetto *nm* musket

moschet'tone *nm (in alpinismo)* snaplink; *(gancio)* spring clip

moschi'cida *a inv* **carta ~** flypaper; **liquido ~** fly spray

'**moscio** *a* limp; **avere l'erre moscia** not be able to say one's r's properly

mo'scone *nm* bluebottle; *(barca)* pedalo

Mosè *nm* Moses

'**mossa** *nf* movement; *(passo)* move

'**mosso** *pp di* **muovere** ● *a (mare)* rough; *(capelli)* wavy; *(fotografia)* blurred

mo'starda *nf* mustard. **~ di Cremona** preserve made from candied fruit in grape must or sugar with mustard

'**mostra** *nf* show; *(d'arte)* exhibition; **far ~ di** pretend; **in ~** on show; **mettersi in ~** make oneself conspicuous; **far ~ di sé** show off; **far bella ~ di sé** look impressive

'**mostra-mer'cato** *nf* trade fair

mo'strare *vt* show; *(indicare)* point out; *(spiegare)* explain; **~ di** *(sembrare)* seem; *(fingere)* pretend

mos'trarsi *vr* show oneself; *(apparire)* appear

mo'strina *nf* flash

'**mostro** *nm* monster; *(fig: persona)* genius; **~ sacro** *fig* sacred cow

mostruosa'mente *adv* tremendously

mostru'oso *a* monstrous; *(incredibile)* enormous

mo'tel *nm inv* motel

moti'vare *vt* cause; *Jur* justify

moti'vato *a (persona)* motivated; *(azione)* justified

motivazi'one *nf* motivation; *(giustificazione)* justification

mo'tivo *nm* reason; *(movente)* motive; *(in musica, letteratura)* theme; *(disegno)* pattern, motif; **senza ~** for no reason; *(senza giustificazione)* unjustifiably. **~ a scacchi** chequered pattern

'**moto** *nm* motion; *(esercizio)* exercise; *(gesto)* movement; *(sommossa)* rising. **~ ondoso** swell. **~ perpetuo** perpetual motion ● *nf inv (motocicletta)* motor bike; **mettere in ~** start *(motore)*

moto'carro *nm* three-wheeler

motoci'cletta *nf* motor cycle. **~ da corsa** racing motorbike, racer

motoci'clismo *nm* motorcycling

motoci'clista *nmf* motorcyclist

moto'cross *nm* motocross

motocros'sista *nmf* scrambler

moto'lancia *nf* motor launch

moto'nautica *nf* speedboat racing

moto'nave *nf* motor vessel

mo'tore *a* motor *attrib* ● *nm* motor, engine; **con ~ turbo** turbocharged. . **~ diesel** diesel engine. **~ a iniezione** fuel injection engine. **~ raffreddato ad aria** air-cooled engine. **~ a reazione** jet [engine]. **~ a scoppio** internal combustion engine

moto'retta *nf* motor scooter

moto'rino *nm* moped. **~ d'avviamento** starter motor

mo'torio *a* motor *attrib*

moto'rista *mf* **~ di bordo** flight engineer

motoriz'zare *vt* motorize

motoriz'zato *a Mil* motorized

motorizzazi'one *nf (ufficio)* vehicle licensing office

moto'scafo *nm* motorboat

moto'sega *nf* chain saw

motove'detta *nf* patrol vessel

mo'trice *nf* engine

'**motto** *nm* motto; *(facezia)* witticism; *(massima)* saying

'**mountain bike** *nf inv* mountain bike

mouse *nm inv* Comput mouse

mousse *nf inv* Culin mousse. **~ al cioccolato** chocolate mousse

mo'vente *nm* motive

mo'venze *nfpl* movements

movimen'tare *vt* enliven

movimen'tato *a* lively

movi'mento *nm* movement; **essere sempre in ~** be always on the go. **~ passeggeri e merci** passenger and freight traffic

mozi'one *nf* motion. **~ d'ordine** point of order

mozzafi'ato *a inv* nail-biting

moz'zare *vt* cut off; dock *(coda)*; **~ il fiato a qcno** take sb's breath away

mozza'rella *nf* mozzarella *(mild, white cheese)*

mozzi'cone *nm (di sigaretta)* stub

'**mozzo** *nm* Mech hub; *Naut* ship's boy ● *a (coda)* truncated; *(testa)* severed

ms *abbr* **(manoscritto)** MS

'**mucca** *nf* cow; **morbo della ~ pazza** mad cow disease

'**mucchio** *nm* heap, pile; **un ~ di** *fig* lots of

mucil'lagine *nf Bot* mucilage

'**muco** *nm* mucus

'**muffa** *nf* mould; **fare la ~** go mouldy

muf'fire *vi* go mouldy

muf'fola *nf* mitt

mu'flone *nm* Zool mouflon

mugghi'are *vi (vento, mare:)* roar

mug'gire *vi (mucca:)* moo, low; *(toro:)* bellow

mug'gito *nm* moo; *(di toro)* bellow; *(azione)* mooing; bellowing

mu'ghetto *nm* lily of the valley

mugo'lare *vi* whine; *(persona:)* moan

mugo'lio *nm* whining

mugu'gnare *vt fam* mumble

mulat'tiera *nf* mule track

mu'latto, -a *nmf* mulatto

mu'leta *nf inv* muleta

muli'ebre *a* liter feminine

muli'nare *vi* spin

muli'nello *nm (d'acqua)* whirlpool; *(di vento)* eddy; *(giocattolo)* windmill

mu'lino *nm* mill. **~ a vento** windmill

'**mulo** *nm* mule

'**multa** *nf* fine. **~ per divieto di sosta** parking ticket

mul'tare *vt* fine

multico'lore *a* multicoloured

multicultu'rale *a* multicultural

multifunzio'nale *a* multifunction[al]
multilate'rale *a* multilateral
multi'lingue *a* multilingual
multi'media *mpl* multimedia
multimedi'ale *a* multimedia *attrib*
multimedialità *nf* multimedia
multimiliar'dario, -a *nmf* multi-million-
aire
multinazio'nale *a & nf* multinational
'multiplo *a & nm* multiple
multiproprietà *nf inv* time-share; **una
casa in ~** a time-share
multi'sale *a inv* **cinema ~** multiplex [cin-
ema]
multi'tasking *nm Comput* multitasking
multi'uso *a* ⟨*utensile*⟩ all-purpose
'mummia *nf* mummy; (*fig: persona*) old fogey
mummifi'care *vt* mummify
'mungere *vt* milk
mungi'tura *nf* milking
munici'pale *a* municipal
municipalità *nf inv* town council
muni'cipio *nm* town hall
munifi'cenza *nf* munificence, bounty
mu'nifico *a* munificent
mu'nire *vt* fortify; **~ di** (*provvedere*) supply
with; **munitevi di un carrello/cestino**
please take a trolley/basket
munizi'oni *nfpl* ammunition *sg*
'munto *pp di* **mungere**
mu'overe *vt* move; (*suscitare*) arouse
mu'oversi *vr* move; **muoviti!** hurry up!,
come on!
'mura *nfpl* (*cinta di città*) walls
mu'raglia *nf* wall
mu'rale *a* mural; ⟨*pittura*⟩ wall *attrib*
mur'are *vt* wall up
mu'rario *a* masonry *attrib*; **cinta muraria**
walls *pl*; **opera muraria** masonry
mura'tore *nm* bricklayer; (*con pietre*) mason; (*operaio edile*) builder
mura'tura *nf* (*di pietra*) masonry, stonework; (*di mattoni*) brickwork
mu'rena *nf* moray eel
'muro *nm* wall; (*di nebbia*) bank; **a ~**
⟨*armadio*⟩ built-in. **~ divisorio** partition
wall. **~ di gomma** *fig* wall of indifference. **~
a intercapedine** cavity wall. **M~ del
pianto** Wailing Wall. **~ portante** load-bear-
ing wall. **~ del suono** sound barrier
'musa *nf anche fig* muse
muschi'ato *a* musky
'muschio *nm Bot* moss

musco'lare *a* muscular
muscola'tura *nf* muscles *pl*
'muscolo *nm* muscle
musco'loso *a* muscular
mu'seo *nm* museum
museru'ola *nf* muzzle
'musica *nf* music
musica folk *nf* folk [music]
'musical *nm inv* musical
musi'cale *a* musical
musi'care *vt* set to music
musicas'setta *nf* cassette
musi'cista *nmf* musician
musicolo'gia *nf* musicology
'muso *nm* muzzle; (*pej: di persona*) mug; (*di
aeroplano*) nose; **fare il ~** sulk
mu'sone, -a *nmf* sulker
'mussola *nf* muslin
mussul'mano, -a *a & nmf* Muslim, Moslem
'muta *nf* (*cambio*) change; (*di penne*) moult;
(*di cani*) pack; (*per immersione subacquea*)
wetsuit
muta'mento *nm* change
mu'tande *nfpl* pants
mutan'dine *nfpl* panties; **~ da bagno** bathing trunks; (*da donna*) bikini bottom
mutan'doni *nmpl* (*da uomo*) long johns; (*da
donna*) bloomers
mu'tante *nmf* mutant
mu'tare *vt* change
mutazi'one *nf* mutation
mu'tevole *a* changeable
muti'lare *vt* mutilate
muti'lato, -a *a* crippled ● *nmf* disabled person. **~ di guerra** disabled ex-serviceman. **~
del lavoro** person disabled at work
mutilazi'one *nf* mutilation
mu'tismo *nm* dumbness; *fig* obstinate silence
'muto *a* dumb; (*silenzioso*) silent; (*fonetica*)
mute
'mutua *nf* [**cassa**] **~** sickness benefit fund
mutu'abile *a* ⟨*farmaco*⟩ prescribable on the
NHS
mutu'are *vt* borrow ⟨*teoria, parola*⟩
mutua'tario, -a *nmf Fin* borrower
mutu'ato, -a *nmf* ≈ NHS patient
'mutuo[1] *a* mutual
'mutuo[2] *nm* loan; (*per la casa*) mortgage;
fare un ~ take out a mortgage; **società di ~
soccorso** friendly society. **~ per la casa**
home loan. **~ ipotecario** mortgage

Nn

na'babbo *nm* nabob; **vivere come un ~** live in the lap of luxury

'nacchera *nf* castanet

na'dir *nm* nadir

'nafta *nf* naphtha; (*per motori*) diesel oil; **a ~** ⟨*bruciatore*⟩ oil-burning

'naia *nf* cobra; (*sl: servizio militare*) national service

'nailon *nm* nylon

Na'mibia *nf* Namibia

na'nismo *nm* dwarfism

'nanna *nf* (*sl: infantile*) byebyes; **andare a ~** go byebyes; **fare la ~** sleep

'nano, -a *a* & *nmf* dwarf

'napalm *nm* napalm

napole'tana *nf* (*caffettiera*) Neapolitan coffee maker

napole'tano, -a *a* & *nmf* Neapolitan

'Napoli *nf* Naples

'nappa *nf* tassel; (*pelle*) soft leather

narci'sismo *nm* narcissism

narci'sista *a* & *nmf* narcissist

nar'ciso *nm* narcissus

nar'cosi *nf* general anaesthesia

nar'cotici *nf* Drug Squad

nar'cotico *a* & *nm* narcotic

na'rice *nf* nostril

nar'rare *vt* tell

narra'tivo, -a *a* narrative ● *nf* fiction

narra|'tore, -'trice *nmf* narrator

narrazi'one *nf* narration; (*racconto*) story

na'sale *a* nasal

na'scente *a* budding

'nascere *vi* (*venire al mondo*) be born; (*germogliare*) sprout; (*sorgere*) rise; **~ da** *fig* arise from

'nascita *nf* birth

nasci'turo *nm* unborn child

na'scondere *vt* hide

na'scondersi *vr* hide

nascon'diglio *nm* hiding-place

nascon'dino *nm* hide-and-seek

na'scosto *pp di* **nascondere** ● *a* hidden; **di ~** secretly

na'sello *nm* (*pesce*) hake

'naso *nm* nose

na'sone *nm* big nose, hooter *fam*

'nassa *nf* lobster pot

'nastro *nm* ribbon; (*di registratore ecc*) tape. **~ adesivo** adhesive tape. **~ isolante** insulating tape. **~ magnetico** magnetic tape, mag tape *fam*. **~ trasportatore** conveyor belt

Na'tale *nm* Christmas

na'tale *a* ⟨*giorno, paese*⟩ of one's birth

na'tali *nmpl* parentage

natalità *nf* [number of] births, birthrate

nata'lizio *a* (*del Natale*) Christmas *attrib*; (*di nascita*) of one's birth

na'tante *a* floating ● *nm* craft

'natica *nf* buttock

na'tio *a* native

Nati'vità *nf* Nativity

na'tivo, -a *a* & *nmf* native

NATO *nf* Nato, NATO

'nato *pp di* **nascere** ● *a* born; **uno scrittore ~** a born writer; **nata Rossi** née Rossi

na'tura *nf* nature; **pagare in ~** pay in kind; **di ~ politica** of a political nature. **~ morta** still life

natu'rale *a* natural; **al ~** ⟨*alimento*⟩ plain, natural; **~!** naturally, of course

natura'lezza *nf* naturalness

naturaliz'zare *vt* naturalize

natural'mente *adv* (*ovviamente*) naturally, of course

natu'rista *nmf* naturalist

natu'ristico *a* naturist

naufra'gare *vi* be wrecked; ⟨*persona:*⟩ be shipwrecked

nau'fragio *nm* shipwreck; *fig* wreck

'naufrago, -a *nmf* survivor

'nausea *nf* nausea; **avere la ~** feel sick

nausea'bondo *a* nauseating

nause'ante *a* nauseating

nause'are *vt* nauseate

'nautica *nf* navigation

'nautico *a* nautical

na'vale *a* naval

na'vata *nf* (*centrale*) nave; (*laterale*) aisle

'nave *nf* ship. **~ ammiraglia** flagship. **~ da carico** cargo boat. **~ cisterna** tanker. **~ da crociera** cruise liner. **~ fattoria** factory ship. **~ da guerra** warship. **~ di linea** liner. **~ passeggeri** passenger ship. **~ portacontainer** container ship. **~ spaziale** spaceship. **~ traghetto** ferry

na'vetta *nf* shuttle

navi'cella *nf* **~ spaziale** nose cone

navi'gabile *a* navigable

navi'gare *vi* sail; **~ in Internet** surf the Net

naviga|'tore, -'trice *mf* navigator; (*in Internet*) surfer; **~ solitario** lone yachtsman. **~ spaziale** spaceman

navigazi'one *nf* navigation; **della ~** navigational

na'viglio *nm* fleet; (*canale*) canal

nazifa'scismo *nm* Nazi fascism

nazifa'scista *nmf* Nazi fascist

nazio'nale *a* national ● *nf* *Sport* national team

naziona'lismo *nm* nationalism

naziona'lista *nmf* nationalist

nazionalità *nf inv* nationality

nazionaliz'zare *vt* nationalize

nazi'one *nf* nation. **Nazioni** *pl* **Unite** United Nations

na'zista *a* & *nmf* Nazi

N.B. *abbr* (**nota bene**) NB

n.d.r. *abbr* (**nota del redattore**) editor's note

'n'drangheta *nf* Calabrian Mafia

n.d.t. *abbr* (**nota del traduttore**) translator's note

NE *abbr* (**nord-est**) NE

ne *pron* (*di lui*) about him; (*di lei*) about her; (*di loro*) about them; (*di ciò*) about it; (*da ciò*) from that; (*di un insieme*) of it; (*di un gruppo*) of them; **ne sono contento** I'm happy about it; **non ne conosco nessuno** I don't know any of them; **ne ho** I have some; **non ne ho più** I don't have any left ● *adv* from there; **ne vengo ora** I've just come from there; **me ne vado** I'm off; **ne va della mia reputazione** my reputation is at stake

né *conj* **né... né...** neither... nor...; **non ne ho il tempo né la voglia** I don't have either the time or the inclination; **né tu né io vogliamo andare** neither you nor I want to go; **né l'uno né l'altro** neither [of them/us]

ne'anche *adv* (*neppure*) not even; (*senza neppure*) without even ● *conj* (*e neppure*) neither... nor; **non parlo inglese, e lui ~** I don't speak English, neither does he *o* and he doesn't either

'nebbia *nf* mist; (*in città, autostrada*) fog

nebbi'oso *a* misty; (*in città, autostrada*) foggy

nebuliz'zare *vt* atomize

nebulizza'tore *nm* atomizer; (*per il naso*) nasal spray

nebulizzazi'one *nf* atomizing; **fare delle nebulizzazioni** take nasal sprays

nebulosità *nf* vagueness

nebu'loso *a* hazy; ⟨*teoria*⟩ nebulous; ⟨*discorso*⟩ woolly

necessaria'mente *adv* necessarily

neces'sario *a* necessary ● *nm* **fare il ~** do the necessary, do the needful

necessità *nf inv* necessity; (*bisogno*) need

necessi'tare *vi* **~ di** need; (*essere necessario*) be necessary

necro'logio *nm* obituary

ne'cropoli *nf inv* necropolis

ne'crosi *nf* necrosis

ne'fando *a* wicked

ne'fasto *a* ill-omened

ne'frite *nf* nephritis

nefrolo'gia *nf* nephrology

ne'frologo, -a *nmf* nephrologist

ne'gabile *a* deniable

ne'gare *vt* deny; (*rifiutare*) refuse; **essere negato per qcsa** be no good at sth

nega'tiva *nf* negative

nega'tivo *a* negative

negazi'one *nf* negation; (*diniego*) denial; *Gram* negative; **essere la ~ per** know nothing about

ne'gletto *a* neglected

'negli = **in** + **gli**

negli'gente *a* negligent

negli'genza *nf* negligence

negozi'abile *a* negotiable

negozi'ante *nmf* dealer; (*bottegaio*) shopkeeper

negozi'are *vt* negotiate ● *vi* **~ in** trade in, deal in

negozi'ati *nmpl* negotiations

ne'gozio *nm* shop. **~ di abbigliamento** fashion boutique. **~ di alimentari** grocer's. **~ di antiquariato** antique shop. **~ duty free** duty-free shop. **~ giuridico** legal transaction

'negro, -a *a* Negro, black ● *nmf* Negro, black; (*scrittore*) ghost writer; **come un ~** ⟨*lavorare*⟩ like a slave

negro'mante *nmf* necromancer

'nei = **in** + **i**

nel = **in** + **il**

'nella = **in** + **la**

'nelle = **in** + **le**

'nello = **in** + **lo**

'nembo *nm* nimbus

ne'mesi *nf* nemesis

ne'mico, -a *a* hostile ● *nmf* enemy

nem'meno *conj* not even

'nenia *nf* dirge; (*per bambini*) lullaby; (*piagnucolio*) wail

'neo *nm* mole; (*applicato*) beauty spot

neo+ *pref* neo+

neo'classico *a* neoclassical

neocolonia'lismo *nm* neocolonialism

neofa'scismo *nm* neofascism

neola'tino *a* Romance

neolaure'ato, -a *nmf* recent graduate

neo'litico *a* Neolithic

neolo'gismo *nm* neologism

'neon *nm* neon

neo'nato, -a *a* newborn ● *nmf* newborn baby

neona'zismo *nm* Neonazism

neona'zista *a* & *nmf* Neonazi

neozelan'dese *a* New Zealand *attrib* ● *nmf* New Zealander

nep'pure *conj* not even

ne'rastro *a* blackish

'nerbo *nm* (*forza*) strength; *fig* backbone; **senza ~** effete

nerbo'ruto *a* brawny

ne'retto *nm* *Typ* bold [type]

'nero *a* black; (*fam: arrabbiato*) fuming ● *nm* black; **l'ho visto ~ su bianco** I've seen it in black and white; **mettere ~ su bianco** put in writing. **~ pieno** *Typ* solid. **~ di seppia** sepia

nerva'tura *nf* nerves *pl*; *Bot* veining; (*di libro*) band

ner'vetti *nmpl* chopped beef and veal with onions

ner'vino *a* ⟨*gas*⟩ nerve *attrib*

'**nervo** *nm* nerve; *Bot* vein; **avere i nervi** be bad-tempered; **dare ai nervi a qcno** get on sb's nerves

nervo'sismo *nm* nerviness

ner'voso *a* nervous; (*irritabile*) bad-tempered; **avere il ~** be irritable; **esaurimento ~** nervous breakdown

'**nespola** *nf* medlar

'**nespolo** *nm* medlar[-tree]

'**nesso** *nm* link, connection

nes'suno *a* no, not... any; (*qualche*) any; **non ho nessun problema** I don't have any problems, I have no problems; **non ha nessun valore** it hasn't any value, it has no value; **da nessuna parte** nowhere; **non lo trovo da nessuna parte** I can't find it anywhere; **in nessun modo** on no account; **per nessun motivo** for no reason; **nessuna notizia?** any news? ● *pron* nobody, no one, not ... anybody, not... anyone; (*qualcuno*) anybody, anyone; **hai delle domande? – nessuna** do you have any questions? – none; **~ di voi** none of you; **~ dei due** (*di voi due*) neither of you; **non ho visto ~ dei tuoi amici** I haven't seen any of your friends; **c'è ~?** is anybody there?

'**nesting** *nm inv Comput* nesting

net *nm inv Tennis* net cord

'**nettare** *nm* nectar

net'tare *vt* clean

net'tezza *nf* cleanliness. **~ urbana** cleansing department

'**netto** *a* clean; (*chiaro*) clear; *Comm* net; **di ~** just like that

Net'tuno *nm* Neptune

nettur'bino *nm* dustman

'**neuro** *nf* neurological clinic

neuro+ *pref* neuro+

neurochirur'gia *nf* brain surgery

neurochi'rurgo *nm* brain surgeon

neurolo'gia *nf* neurology

neurologico *a* neurological

neuropsichi'atra *nm* neuropsychiatry

neuropsichia'tria *nf* neuropsychiatrist

neu'trale *a & nm* neutral

neutralità *nf* neutrality

neutraliz'zare *vt* neutralize

'**neutro** *a* neutral; *Gram* neuter ● *nm Gram* neuter

neu'trone *nm* neutron

ne'vaio *nm* snow-field

'**neve** *nf* snow

nevi'care *vi* snow; **nevica** it is snowing

nevi'cata *nf* snowfall

ne'vischio *nm* sleet

ne'voso *a* snowy

nevral'gia *nf* neuralgia

ne'vralgico *a* neuralgic; **punto ~** nerve centre; (*di questione ecc*) crucial point

nevraste'nia *nf* neurasthenia

nevra'stenico *a* neurasthenic; (*irritabile*) hot tempered

ne'vrite *nf* neuritis

ne'vrosi *nf inv* neurosis

ne'vrotico *a* neurotic

'**nibbio** *nm* kite

Nica'ragua *nm* Nicaragua

nicara'guense *a & nmf* Nicaraguan

'**nicchia** *nf* niche

nicchi'are *vi* shilly-shally

'**nichel** *nm* nickel

nichi'lista *nmf* nihilist ● *a* nihilistic

nico'tina *nf* nicotine

nidi'ace *nm* nestling

nidi'ata *nf* brood

nidifi'care *vi* nest

nidifi'cato *a Comput* nested

nidificazi'one *nf Zool* nesting

'**nido** *nm* nest; (*giardino d'infanzia*) crèche; **a ~ d'ape** (*tessuto*) honeycomb. **~ di uccello** bird's nest. **~ di vipere** *fig* nest of vipers

ni'ente *pron* nothing, not... anything; (*qualcosa*) anything; **non ho fatto ~ di male** I didn't do anything wrong, I did nothing wrong; **nient'altro?** anything else?; **grazie! – di ~!** thank you! – don't mention it!; **non serve a ~** it is no use; **vuoi ~?** do you want anything?; **dal ~** (*venire su*) from nothing; **da ~** (*poco importante*) minor; (*di poco valore*) worthless ● *a inv fam* ~ **pesci oggi** no fish today; **non ho ~ fame** I'm not the slightest bit hungry ● *adv* **non fa ~** (*non importa*) it doesn't matter; **per ~** at all; (*litigare*) over nothing; **~ affatto!** no way! ● *nm* **un bel ~** absolutely nothing, damn-all *fam*; **basta un ~ per spaventarlo** it doesn't take much to scare him

nientedi'meno, **niente'meno** *adv* ~ **che** no less than ● *int* fancy that!

night *nm inv* night club

'**Nilo** *nm* Nile

'**ninfa** *nf* nymph

nin'fea *nf* water-lily

nin'fomane *nf* nymphomaniac; **da ~** nymphomaniac

ninna'nanna *nf* lullaby

'**ninnolo** *nm* plaything; (*fronzolo*) knick-knack

ni'pote *nm* (*di zii*) nephew; (*di nonni*) grandson, grandchild; **nipoti** *pl* grandchildren, nephews and nieces ● *nf* (*di zii*) niece; (*di nonni*) granddaughter, grandchild

nip'ponico *a* Japanese

'**nisba** *pron* (*sl: niente*) zilch

'**nitido** *a* neat; (*chiaro*) clear

ni'trato *nm* nitrate

'**nitrico** *a* nitric

ni'trire *vi* neigh

ni'trito *nm* (*di cavallo*) neigh; *Chem* nitrite

nitro+ *pref* nitro+

nitroglice'rina *nf* nitroglycerine

'**niveo** *a* snow-white

N.N. *abbr* (**numeri**) Nos

NO *abbr* (**nord-ovest**) NW

N° *abbr* (**numero**) No.

no *adv* no; **credo di no** I don't think so; **perché no?** why not?; **io no** not me; **sì o no?** yes or no?; **ha detto così, no?** he said so, didn't he?; **fa freddo, no?** it's cold, isn't it?; **se no** otherwise ● *nm* no; (*nelle votazioni*) nay

nobil'donna *nf* noblewoman

'**nobile** *a* noble; **metallo ~** noble metal; **di animo ~** noble-minded ● *nm* noble, nobleman ● *nf* noble, noblewoman

nobili'are *a* noble

nobiltà *nf* nobility

nobilu'omo *nm* nobleman

'**nocca** *nf* knuckle

'**nocci'ola** *nf* hazelnut

noccio'line [americane] *nfpl* peanuts

nocci'olo *nm* (*albero*) hazel

'**nocciolo** *nm* stone; *Phys* core; *fig* heart; **il ~ della questione** the heart of the matter

'**noce** *nf* walnut. **~ moscata** nutmeg. **~ pecan** pecan. **~ di vitello** veal with mushrooms ● *nm* (*legno*) walnut; (*albero*) walnut [tree]

noce'pesca *nf* nectarine

no'cino *nm* walnut liqueur

no'civo *a* harmful

no'dino *nm* veal chop

'**nodo** *nm* knot; *fig* lump; *Comput* node; **fare il ~ della cravatta** do up one's tie. **~ alla gola** lump in the throat; **~ della questione** crux of the matter. **~ ferroviario** railway junction. **~ piano** reef knot. **~ scorsoio** slipknot

no'doso *a* knotty

nodulo *nm* nodule

Noè *nm* Noah

'**noi** *pers pron* (*soggetto*) we; (*oggetto, con prep*) us; **chi è? – siamo ~** who is it? – it's us; **noi due** the two of us

'**noia** *nf* boredom; (*fastidio*) bother; (*persona*) bore; **dar ~** annoy

noi'altri *pers pron* we

noi'oso *a* boring; (*fastidioso*) tiresome

noleggi'are *vt* hire; (*dare a noleggio*) hire out; charter ‹*nave, aereo*›

no'leggio *nm* hire; (*di nave, aereo*) charter. **~ barche/biciclette/sci** boat/cycle/ski hire

'**nolo** *nm* hire; *Naut* freight; **a ~** for hire

'**nomade** *a* nomadic ● *nmf* nomad

'**nome** *nm* name; *Gram* noun; **a ~ di** ‹*da parte di*› on behalf of; **di ~** by name; **farsi un ~** make a name for oneself; **nel ~ di...** in the name of.... **~ d'arte** professional name. **~ di battaglia** nom de guerre. **~ di battesimo** first name, Christian name. **~ depositato** trade-name. **~ di famiglia** surname, family name. **~ proprio** proper name, proper noun. **~ da ragazza** maiden name. **~ da sposata** married name

no'mea *nf* reputation

nomencla'tura *nf* nomenclature

no'mignolo *nm* nickname

'**nomina** *nf* appointment; **di prima ~** newly appointed

nomi'nale *a* nominal; *Gram* noun *attrib*

nomi'nare *vt* name; (*menzionare*) mention; (*eleggere*) appoint

nomina'tivo *a* nominative; *Comm* registered ● *nm* nominative; (*nome*) name; **caso ~** nominative case

non *adv* not; **~ ti amo** I do not *o* don't love you; **~ c'è di che** not at all; **~ più** no longer

nonché *conj* (*tanto meno*) let alone; (*e anche*) as well as

nonconfor'mista *a & nmf inv* nonconformist

nonconformità *nf* noncompliance

noncu'rante *a* nonchalant; (*negligente*) indifferent

noncu'ranza *nf* nonchalance; (*negligenza*) indifference

nondi'meno *conj* nevertheless

'**nonna** *nf* grandmother, grandma *fam*, gran *fam*

'**nonno** *nm* grandfather, grandpa *fam*; **nonni** *pl* grandparents

non'nulla *nm inv* trifle

'**nono** *a & nm* ninth

nono'stante *prep* in spite of ● *conj* although

non stop *a inv & adv* nonstop

nontiscordardimé *nm inv* forget-me-not

nonvio'lento *a* nonviolent

nonvio'lenza *nf* nonviolence

nor'cino *nm* pig butcher

nord *nm* north; **del ~** northern

nord-'est *nm* northeast; **a ~** northeasterly; **del ~** northeastern; **vento di ~** northeasterly [wind]

'**nordico** *a* northern

nor'dista *a & nmf* Yankee

nordocciden'tale *a* northwestern

nordorien'tale *a* northeastern

nord-'ovest *nm* northwest; **a ~** northwesterly; **del ~** northwestern **vento di ~** northwesterly [wind]

'**norma** *nf* norm; (*regola*) rule; (*per l'uso*) instruction; **a ~ di legge** according to law; **è buona ~** it's advisable; **di ~** as a rule, normally

nor'male *a* normal ● *nm* **fuori del ~** out of the ordinary; **superiore al ~** above average

normalità *nf* normality; **rientrare nella ~** be quite normal

normaliz'zare *vt* normalize

normal'mente *adv* normally

Norman'dia *nf* Normandy

nor'manno *a* from Normandy; (*storico*) Norman

norma'tivo *a* normative, prescriptive

nor'mografo *nm* stencil

nor'reno *a* Norse

norve'gese *a & nmf* Norwegian

Nor'vegia *nf* Norway

noso'comio *nm fml* hospital

nossi'gnore *adv* (*assolutamente no*) no way

nostal'gia *nf* (*di casa, patria*) homesickness; (*del passato*) nostalgia; **aver ~** be homesick; **aver ~ di qcno** miss sb

no'stalgico, -a *a* nostalgic ● *nmf* reactionary

nostra *vedi* **nostro**

no'strale *a* local

no'strano *a* local; (*fatto in casa*) home-made

'**nostre** *vedi* **nostro**

'**nostri** *vedi* **nostro**

'**nostro** (**il nostro** *m*, **la nostra** *f*, **i nostri** mpl, **le nostre** fpl) poss a our; **quella macchina è nostra** that car is ours; **~ padre** our father; **un ~ amico** a friend of ours ● poss pron ours

no'stromo nm bo's'n, boatswain

'**nota** nf (segno) sign; (comunicazione, commento, Mus) note; (conto) bill; (lista) list; **degno di ~** noteworthy; **prendere ~** take note; **una ~ di colore** a touch of colour; **mettere in ~ qcsa** add sth to the list. **~ di accredito** Comm credit note. **note** pl **caratteristiche** distinguishing marks. **~ spese** expense account

no'tabile a & nm notable

no'taio nm notary

no'tare vt (segnare) mark; (annotare) note down; (osservare) notice; **far ~ qcsa** point sth out; **farsi ~** get oneself noticed; **nota bene che...** please note that...

notazi'one nf marking; (annotazione) notation

'**notebook** nm inv Comput notebook

'**notes** nm inv notepad

no'tevole a (degno di nota) remarkable; (grande) considerable

no'tifica nf notification

notifi'care vt notify; Comm advise; **~ un ordine di comparizione** [**in giudizio**] subpoena

notificazi'one nf notification

no'tizia nf **una ~** a piece of news, some news; (informazione) a piece of information, some information; **le notizie** the news sg; **per avere ~ di** (telefonare) for news of; **non ha più dato notizie di sé** he hasn't been in touch since. **~ di attualità** news item

notizi'ario nm news sg

'**noto** a [well-]known; **rendere ~** (far sapere) announce

notorietà nf fame; **raggiungere la ~** become famous

no'torio a well-known; pej notorious

not'tambulo nm night-bird

not'tata nf night; **far ~** stay up all night

'**notte** nf night; **di ~** at night; **a ~ fatta** when night had fallen; **la ~** (durante la notte) at night; **buona ~** good night; **fermarsi per la ~** stay overnight; **peggio che andar di ~** worse than ever; **prima ~ di nozze** wedding night. **~ bianca** sleepless night

notte'tempo adv at night[time]

not'turno a nocturnal; (servizio ecc) night attrib; **in notturna** (partita) under floodlights

'**notula** nf (conto) fee note

no'vanta a & nm ninety

novan'tenne a & nmf ninety year old

novan'tesimo a & nm ninetieth

novan'tina nf about ninety

'**nove** a & nm nine; **prova del nove** Math casting out nines

nove'cento a & nm nine hundred. **il N~** the twentieth century; **stile ~** twentieth-century

no'vella nf short story

novelli'ere nm short-story writer

novel'lino, -a a inexperienced ● nmf novice, beginner

no'vello a new

no'vembre nm November

nove'mila a & nm nine thousand

no'vena nf novena

novi'lunio nm new moon

novità nf inv novelty; (notizie) news sg; **l'ultima ~** (moda) the latest fashion

novizi'ato nm Relig novitiate; (tirocinio) apprenticeship

nozi'one nf notion; **perdere la ~ del tempo** lose track of time; **non avere la ~ del tempo** have no sense of time; **nozioni** pl rudiments; **poche nozioni di inglese** very basic English

nozio'nismo nm accumulation of facts

'**nozze** nfpl marriage sg; (cerimonia) wedding sg; **andare a ~** (godersela) have a field day. **~ d'argento** silver wedding [anniversary]. **~ di diamante** diamond wedding [anniversary]. **~ d'oro** golden wedding [anniversary]

'**nube** nf cloud. **~ di mistero** shroud of mystery. **~ tossica** toxic cloud

nubi'fragio nm cloudburst

'**nubile** a unmarried ● nf unmarried woman

'**nuca** nf nape

nucle'are a nuclear

'**nucleo** nm nucleus; (unità) unit

nu'dismo nm nudism

nu'dista nmf nudist

nudità nf nudity, nakedness

'**nudo** a naked; (spoglio, terra) bare; **a occhio ~** to the naked eye; **verità nuda e cruda** naked truth; **a piedi nudi** bare-foot

'**nugolo** nm large number

'**nulla** pron = **niente**; **da ~** worthless; **per ~** for nothing

nulla'osta nm inv permit

nullate'nente nm **i nullatenenti** the have-nots

nullità nf inv (persona) nonentity

'**nullo** a Jur null and void

'**nume** nm numen

nume'rabile a countable

nume'rale a & nm numeral

nume'rare vt number

numera'tore nm Math numerator

numerazi'one nf numbering

nu'merico a numerical

'**numero** nm number; (romano, arabo) numeral; (di scarpe ecc) size; **fare o comporre il ~** dial [the number]; **dare i numeri** fam be off one's head; **avere tutti i numeri per** have what it takes to. **~ arretrato** back issue. **~ cardinale** cardinal [number]. **~ di conto** account number. **~ decimale** decimal. **~ intero** whole number. **~ ordinale** ordinal [number]. **~ d'ordine** Comm order number. **~ di previdenza sociale** ≈ National Insurance number. **~ di protocollo** reference number. **~ di scarpa** shoe size. **~ di telefono** phone number. **~ uno** number one. **~ verde** ≈ Freephone number, toll-free number Am. **~ di volo** flight number

nume'roso *a* numerous
numi'smatico *a* numismatic
'nunzio *nm* nuncio
nu'ocere *vi* ~ **a** harm
nu'ora *nf* daughter-in-law
nuo'tare *vi* swim; *fig* wallow; ~ **come un pesce** swim like a fish; ~ **nell'oro** be stinking rich, be rolling in it
nuo'tata *nf* swim; **fare una** ~ have a swim
nuota|'tore, -'trice *nmf* swimmer
nu'oto *nm* swimming; **stili** *mpl* **del** ~ swimming strokes
nu'ova *nf* piece of news; **buone nuove** good news; **nessuna** ~**, buona** ~ no news is good news
Nu'ova Cale'donia *nf* New Caledonia
Nu'ova Gui'nea *nf* New Guinea
nuova'mente *adv* again
Nu'ova Ze'landa *nf* New Zealand
nu'ovo *a* new; **di** ~ again; **uscire di nuovo** go/come back out, go/come out again; **mi risulta** ~ that's news to me; ~ **di pacca** o

zecca brand new; **rimettere a** ~ give a new lease of life to; ~ **del mestiere** new to the job; **il** ~ **anno** [the] New Year. **nuova linfa** *nf* new blood. ~ **stile** *nm* new look. **N**~ **Testamento** *nm* New Testament
'nursery *nf* nursery
nutri'ente *a* nourishing
nutri'mento *nm* nourishment
nu'trire *vt* feed ⟨*animale, malato, pianta*⟩; harbour ⟨*sentimenti*⟩; cherish ⟨*sogno*⟩ ●*vi* (*essere nutriente*) be nourishing
nu'trirsi *vr* eat; ~ **di** *fig* live on
nutri'tivo *a* nourishing, nutritional
nutrizi'one *nf* nutrition
'nuvola *nf* cloud; **avere la testa fra le nuvole** have one's head in the clouds; **vivere fra le nuvole** live in cloud cuckoo land; **cadere dalle nuvole** be astounded
nuvo'loso *a* cloudy
nuzi'ale *a* nuptial; ⟨*vestito, anello ecc*⟩ wedding *attrib*; **pranzo** ~ wedding breakfast

O *abbr* (**ovest**) W
o *conj* or; ~ **l'uno** ~ **l'altro** one or the other, either; **o... o...** either... or...
'oasi *nf inv* oasis
obbedi'ente = **ubbidiente**
obbedi'enza = **ubbidienza**
obbe'dire = **ubbidire**
obbli'gare *vt* force, oblige
obbli'garsi *vr* ~ **a** undertake to
obbli'gato *a* obliged
obbligatoria'mente *adv* **fare qcsa** ~ be obliged to do sth; **bisogna** ~ **farlo** you absolutely have to do it
obbliga'torio *a* compulsory
obbligazi'one *nf* obligation; *Comm* bond
'obbligo *nm* obligation; (*dovere*) duty; **avere obblighi verso** be under an obligation to; **d'**~ obligatory
ob'brobrio *nm* disgrace
obbrobri'oso *a* disgraceful
obe'lisco *nm* obelisk
obe'rare *vt* overburden
obesità *nf* obesity
o'beso *a* obese
obiet'tare *vt/i* object; ~ **su** object to
obiettiva'mente *adv* objectively
obiettività *nf* objectivity
obiet'tivo *a* objective ● *nm* objective; (*scopo*) object
obiet'tore *nm* objector. ~ **di coscienza** conscientious objector
obiezi'one *nf* objection; **fare** ~ **di coscienza** be a conscientious objector

obi'torio *nm* mortuary
o'blio *nm* oblivion
o'bliquo *a* oblique; *fig* underhand
oblite'rare *vt* obliterate
oblò *nm inv* porthole
ob'lungo *a* oblong
'oboe *nm* oboe
obsole'scenza *nf* obsolescence
obso'leto *a* obsolete
'oca *nf* (*pl* **oche**) goose; (*donna*) silly girl
occasio'nale *a* occasional
occasional'mente *adv* occasionally
occasi'one *nf* occasion; (*buon affare*) bargain; (*motivo*) cause; (*opportunità*) chance; **d'**~ secondhand
occhi'aia *nf* eye socket; **occhiaie** *pl* shadows under the eyes
occhi'ali *nmpl* glasses, spectacles. ~ **scuri** dark glasses. ~ **da sole** sunglasses. ~ **da vista** glasses, spectacles
occhia'luto *a* wearing glasses
occhi'ata *nf* look; **dare un'**~ **a** have a look at
occhieggi'are *vt* ogle ● *vi* (*far capolino*) peep
occhi'ello *nm* buttonhole; (*asola*) eyelet
'occhio *nm* eye; ~**!** watch out!; ~ **ai falsi** beware of imitations; **a quattr'occhi** in private; **abbassare gli occhi** look down, lower one's eyes; **sollevare gli occhi** look up, raise one's eyes; **tenere d'**~ **qcno** keep an eye on sb; **perdere d'**~ lose sight of; **a** ~ **[e croce]** roughly; **chiudere un'**~ **(su qcsa)** turn a

blind eye (to sth); **dare nell'~** attract attention; **pagare** o **spendere un ~** [**della testa**] pay an arm and a leg; **saltare agli occhi** be blindingly obvious. **~ di falco** eagle eye. **~ nero** (*pesto*) black eye. **~ di pernice** (*callo*) corn

occhio'lino *nm* **fare l'~ a qcno** wink at sb, give sb a wink

occiden'tale *a* western ● *nmf* westerner

occi'dente *nm* west; (*paesi capitalisti*) West

oc'cludere *vt* obstruct

occlusi'one *nf* occlusion

occor'rente *a* necessary ● *nm* the necessary

occor'renza *nf* need; **all'~** if need be

oc'correre *vi* be necessary; **non occorre farlo** there is no need to do it

occulta'mento *nm* **~ di prove** concealment of evidence

occul'tare *vt* hide

occul'tismo *nm* occult

oc'culto *a* hidden; (*magico*) occult

occu'pante *nmf* occupier; (*abusivo*) squatter

occu'pare *vt* occupy; spend ⟨*tempo*⟩; take up ⟨*spazio*⟩; (*dar lavoro a*) employ

occu'parsi *vr* occupy oneself; (*trovare lavoro*) find a job; **~ di** (*badare*) look after; **occupati dei fatti tuoi!** mind your own business!

occu'pato *a* engaged; ⟨*persona*⟩ busy; ⟨*posto*⟩ taken; **casa occupata** (*alloggio abusivo*) squat

occupazi'one *nf* occupation; *Comm* employment; (*passatempo*) pastime; **trovarsi un'~** (*interesse*) find oneself something to do

o'ceano *nm* ocean. **~ Atlantico** Atlantic [Ocean]. **~ Indiano** Indian Ocean. **~ Pacifico** Pacific [Ocean]

'ocra *nf* ochre

OCSE *nf abbr* (**Organizzazione per la Cooperazione e lo Sviluppo Economico**) OECD

ocu'lare *a* ocular; ⟨*testimone, bagno*⟩ eye *attrib*

ocula'tezza *nf* care

ocu'lato *a* ⟨*scelta, persona*⟩ prudent

ocu'lista *nmf* optician; (*per malattie*) ophthalmologist

od *conj* (*davanti alla vocale o*) or

'ode *nf* ode

odi'are *vt* hate; **~ a morte** not be able to stand

odi'erno *a* of today; (*attuale*) present

'odio *nm* hatred; **avere in ~** hate

odi'oso *a* hateful

odis'sea *nf* odyssey

o'dometro *nm* *Auto* mileometer, odometer *Am*

odo'rare *vt* smell; (*profumare*) perfume ● *vi* **~ di** smell of

odo'rato *nm* sense of smell

o'dore *nm* smell; (*profumo*) scent; **c'è ~ di...**

there's a smell of...; **avere un buon/cattivo ~** smell nice/awful; **sentire ~ di** smell; **odori** *pl Culin* herbs

odo'roso *a* fragrant

of'fendere *vt* offend; (*ferire*) injure

of'fendersi *vr* take offence

offen'siva *nf Mil, fig* offensive

offen'sivo *a* offensive

offen'sore *nm* offender

offe'rente *nmf* offerer; (*in aste*) bidder; **il miglior ~** the highest bidder

of'ferta *nf* offer; (*donazione*) donation; *Comm* supply; (*nelle aste*) bid; (*di appalto*) tender; **in ~ speciale** on special offer; **"offerte d'impiego"** "situations vacant". **~ pubblica di acquisto** takeover bid

of'ferto *pp di* **offrire**

offer'torio *nm* offertory

of'fesa *nf* offence

of'feso *pp di* **offendere** ● *a* offended

offi'ciare *vt* officiate

offi'cina *nf* workshop; **~** [**meccanica**] garage; **capo** [**di**] **~** foreman

of'frire *vt* offer

of'frirsi *vr* offer oneself; ⟨*occasione:*⟩ present itself; **~ di fare qcsa** offer to do sth

off'set *nm inv* offset printing

off'shore *nm inv* (*motoscafo*) speedboat

offu'scare *vt* darken; *fig* dull ⟨*memoria, bellezza*⟩; blur ⟨*vista*⟩

offu'scarsi *vr* darken; ⟨*fig: memoria, bellezza:*⟩ fade away; ⟨*vista:*⟩ become blurred

of'talmico *a* ophthalmic

ogget'tistica *nf* manufacture and selling of household and gift items; (*oggetti*) household and gift items; **negozio di ~** gift shop

oggettività *nf* objectivity

ogget'tivo *a* objective

og'getto *nm* object; (*argomento*) subject; **oggetti** *pl* **smarriti** lost property, lost and found *Am*

'oggi *adv* & *nm* today; (*al giorno d'oggi*) nowadays; **da ~ in poi** from today on; **~** [**a**] **otto** a week today; **dall'~ al domani** overnight; **il giornale di ~** today's paper; **al giorno d'~** these days, nowadays

oggigi'orno *adv* nowadays

o'giva *nf Mil* warhead

'ogni *a inv* every; (*qualsiasi*) any; **~ tre giorni** every three days; **ad ~ costo** at any cost; **ad ~ modo** anyway; **~ ben di Dio** all sorts of good things; **~ cosa** everything; **~ tanto** now and then; **~ volta che** every time, whenever

o'gnuno *pron* everyone, everybody; **~ di voi** each of you

ohibò *int* oh dear!

ohimè *int* oh dear!

o'kay *nm* **dare l'~ a qcno/qcsa** give sb/sth the OK

'ola *nf inv* Mexican wave

O'landa *nf* Holland

olan'dese *a* Dutch ● *nm* Dutchman; (*lingua*) Dutch; (*formaggio*) Edam ● *nf* Dutchwoman

ole'andro *nm* oleander

ole'ato *a* oiled; **carta oleata** grease-proof paper

oleo'dotto *nm* oil pipeline

ole'oso *a* oily

ol'fatto *nm* sense of smell

oli'are *vt* oil

olia'tore *nm* oilcan

oli'era *nf* cruet

olim'piadi *nfpl* Olympic games, Olympics

o'limpico *a* Olympic

olim'pionico *a* ⟨*primato, squadra*⟩ Olympic; **costume ~** Olympic swimming costume

+olino *suff* **bestiolina** *nf* ⟨*affettuoso*⟩ little creature; **macchiolina** *nf* spot; **pesciolino** *nm* little fish; **risolino** *nm* giggle; **sassolino** *nm* pebble; **strisciolina** *nf* thin strip; **magrolino** *a* skinny

'olio *nm* oil; **sott'~** in oil; **colori a ~** oils; **quadro a ~** oil painting. **~ di fegato di merluzzo** cod-liver oil. **~ di gomito** elbow grease. **~ lubrificante** lubricating oil. **~ di mais** corn oil. **~ minerale** mineral oil. **~ [del] motore** engine oil. **~ d'oliva** olive oil. **~ di semi** vegetable oil. **~ [di semi] di lino** linseed oil. **~ solare** suntan oil

o'liva *nf* olive

oli'vastro *a* olive

oli'veto *nm* olive grove

oli'vetta *nf* toggle

o'livo *nm* olive tree

'olmo *nm* elm

olo'causto *nm* holocaust; **l'O~** the Holocaust

o'lografo *a* holograph

olo'gramma *nm* hologram

oltraggi'are *vt* offend

ol'traggio *nm* offence. **~ al pudore** *Jur* gross indecency

oltraggi'oso *a* offensive

ol'tranza *nf* **ad ~** to the bitter end

'oltre *adv* (*di luogo*) further; (*di tempo*) longer ●*prep* (*nello spazio*) beyond; (*di tempo*) later than; (*più di*) more than; (*in aggiunta*) besides; **~ a** (*eccetto*) except, apart from; **per ~ due settimane** for more than two weeks; **una settimana e ~** a week and more

oltrecon'fine *a* cross-border

oltre'mare *adv* overseas

oltre'modo *adv* extremely

oltrepas'sare *vt* go beyond; (*eccedere*) exceed; **oltrepassi il semaforo** go past the traffic lights; **~ il limite di velocità** break the speed limit; **'non ~'** 'no trespassing'

OM *abbr Radio* (**onde medie**) MW

omacci'one *nm* bruiser

o'maggi *nmpl* (*saluti*) respects

o'maggio *nm* homage; (*dono*) gift; **in ~ con** free with

ombeli'cale *a* umbilical; **cordone ~** umbilical cord

ombe'lico *nm* navel

'ombra *nf* (*zona*) shade; (*immagine oscura*) shadow; **all'~** in the shade

ombreggi'are *vt* shade

ombreggia'ture *nfpl* shading

om'brello *nm* umbrella

ombrel'lone *nm* beach umbrella

om'bretto *nm* eye-shadow

om'broso *a* shady; ⟨*cavallo*⟩ skittish; ⟨*persona*⟩ touchy

ome'lette *nf inv* omelette

ome'lia *nf Relig* sermon

omeopa'tia *nf* homoeopathy

omeo'patico *a* homoeopathic ● *nm* homoeopath

omertà *nf inv* conspiracy of silence

o'messo *pp di* **omettere**

o'mettere *vt* omit

omi'cida *a* murderous ● *nmf* murderer

omi'cidio *nm* murder. **~ colposo** manslaughter. **~ di massa** mass murder. **~ volontario** *Jur* culpable homicide

omissi'one *nf* omission

'omnibus *nm inv* omnibus

omofo'bia *nf* homophobia

omogeneiz'zare *vt* homogenize

omogeneiz'zato *a* homogenized

omo'geneo *a* homogeneous

o'mografo *nm* homograph

omolo'gare *vt* approve; **fare ~ un testamento** prove a will

omologazi'one *nf* probate

o'monimo, -a *nmf* namesake ● *nm* (*parola*) homonym ● *a* of the same name

omosessu'ale *a & nmf* homosexual

omosessualità *nf* homosexuality

On. *abbr* (**onorevole**) MP

'oncia *nf* ounce. **~ fluida** fluid ounce

'onda *nf* wave; **andare in ~** *TV, Radio* go on the air; **seguire l'~** go with the crowd. **onde** *pl* **corte** short wave. **onde** *pl* **lunghe** long wave. **~ di maremoto** tidal wave. **onde** *pl* **medie** medium wave. **onde** *pl* **radio** radio waves. **~ d'urto** shock wave

on'data *nf* wave; **a ondate** in waves. **~ di freddo** cold snap

'onde *conj fml* so that

ondeggi'are *vi* wave; ⟨*barca:*⟩ roll

ondu'lato *a* wavy

ondula'torio *a* undulating

ondulazi'one *nf* undulation; (*di capelli*) wave

+one *suff* **cucchiaione** *nm* big spoon; **gattone** *nm* fat cat; **bacione** *nm* smacker; **bacioni** *pl* (*in lettera*) love and kisses; **omone** *nm* big guy; **nasone** *nm* big nose; **nebbione** *nm* dense fog, peasouper *fam*; **simpaticone** *nm* very friendly person; **lumacone** *nm* slowcoach; **testone** *nm* mule; **facilone** *nm pej* over-casual sort of person; **grassone** *nm pej* fat slob; **pigrone** *nm* lazybones *sg*; **chiacchierone** *nm* chatterbox; **criticone** *nm* nit-picker; **pasticcione** *nm* bungler

'onere *nm* burden

oner'oso *a* onerous

onestà *nf* honesty; (*rettitudine*) integrity, honesty

o'nesto *a* honest; (*giusto*) just

'onice *nf* onyx

o'nirico *a* dream *attrib*

o'nisco *nm* slater

onnipo'tente *a* omnipotent

onnipre'sente *a* ubiquitous; *Rel* omnipresent

onnisci'ente *a* omniscient

ono'mastico *nm* name-day

onomato'pea *nf* onomatopoeia

onomato'peico *a* onomatopoeic

ono'rabile *a* honourable

ono'rare *vt* (*fare onore a*) be a credit to; honour (*promessa*)

ono'rario *a* honorary ● *nm* fee

ono'rarsi *vr* ~ **di** be proud of

ono'rato *a* (*famiglia, professione*) respectable; **considerarsi** ~ **da qcsa** consider oneself honoured by sth. **l'onorata società** *nf* the Mafia

o'nore *nm* honour; **in** ~ **di** (*festa, ricevimento*) in honour of; **fare** ~ **a** do justice to (*pranzo*); **farsi** ~ **in** excel in; **a onor del vero** to tell the truth; **fare gli onori di casa** do the honours

ono'revole *a* honourable ● *nmf* Member of Parliament

onorifi'cenza *nf* honour; (*decorazione*) decoration

ono'rifico *a* honorary

'onta *nf* shame

on'tano *nm* alder

O.N.U. *nf abbr* (**Organizzazione delle Nazioni Unite**) UN

opacità *nf* opaqueness, opacity

o'paco *a* opaque; (*colori ecc*) dull; (*fotografia, rossetto*) matt

o'pale *nf* opal

OPEC *nf inv* Opec, OPEC

'opera *nf* (*lavoro*) work; (*azione*) deed; *Mus* opera; (*teatro*) opera house; (*ente*) institution; **mettere in** ~ put into effect; **mettersi all'**~ get to work. ~ **d'arte** work of art. ~ **lirica** opera. **opere** *pl* **pubbliche** public works

ope'rabile *a* operable

ope'raio, -a *a* working ● *nmf* worker. ~ **edile** building worker. ~ **specializzato** skilled worker

ope'rare *vt Med* operate on; ~ **qcno al cuore** operate on sb's heart; **farsi** ~ have an operation ● *vi* operate; (*agire*) work

opera'tivo, opera'torio *a* operating *attrib*

opera'|tore, -'trice *nmf* operator; *TV* cameraman. ~ **ecologico** refuse collector. ~ **sanitario** health worker. ~ **turistico** tour operator

operazi'one *nf* operation; *Comm* transaction. ~ **antidroga** anti-drug operation. **operazioni** *pl* **di soccorso** rescue operations. ~ **d'urgenza** emergency operation

ope'retta *nf* operetta

ope'roso *a* industrious

opini'one *nf* opinion; **rimanere della propria** ~ still feel the same way. ~ **pubblica** public opinion, vox pop

oplà *int* oops

o'possum *nm inv* possum

'oppio *nm* opium

oppo'nente *a* opposing ● *nmf* opponent

op'porre *vt* oppose; (*obiettare*) object; ~ **resistenza** offer resistance

op'porsi *vr* ~ **a** oppose

opportu'nismo *nm* expediency

opportu'nista *nmf* opportunist

opportunità *nf inv* opportunity; (*l'essere opportuno*) timeliness; **avere il senso dell'**~ have a sense of what is appropriate

oppor'tuno *a* opportune; (*adeguato*) appropriate; **ritenere** ~ **fare qcsa** think it appropriate to do sth; **il momento** ~ the right moment

opposi'tore *nm* opposer

opposizi'one *nf* opposition; **d'**~ (*giornale, partito*) opposition *attrib*; **in** ~ in opposition

op'posto *pp di* **opporre** ● *a* opposite; (*opinioni*) opposing ● *nm* opposite; **all'**~ on the contrary

oppressi'one *nf* oppression

oppres'sivo *a* oppressive

op'presso *pp di* **opprimere** ● *a* oppressed

oppres'sore *nm* oppressor

oppri'mente *a* oppressive

op'primere *vt* oppress; (*gravare*) weigh down

op'pure *conj* otherwise, or [else]; **lunedì** ~ **martedì** Monday or Tuesday

ops *int* oops

op'tare *vi* ~ **per** opt for

'optional *nm inv* optional extra

opu'lento *a* opulent

opu'lenza *nf* opulence

o'puscolo *nm* booklet; (*pubblicitario*) brochure

opzio'nale *a* optional

opzi'one *nf* option

'ora[1] *nf* time; (*unità*) hour; **di buon'**~ early; **che** ~ **è?, che ore sono?** what time is it?; **a che** ~? at what time?; **mezz'**~ half an hour; **a ore** (*lavorare, pagare*) by the hour; **50 km all'**~ 50 km an hour; **è** ~ **di finirla!** that's enough now!; **a un'**~ **di macchina** one hour by car; **non vedo l'**~ **di vederti** I can't wait to see you; **fare le ore piccole** stay up until the small hours. ~ **d'arrivo** arrival time. ~ **di cena** dinnertime. **l'**~ **esatta** *Teleph* speaking clock. ~ **legale** daylight saving time. ~ **locale** local time. ~ **di pranzo** dinnertime. ~ **di punta, ore** *pl* **di punta** peak time; (*per il traffico*) rush hour. ~ **solare** Greenwich Mean Time, GMT. ~ **zero** *Mil, fig* zero hour

'ora[2] *adv* now; (*tra poco*) presently; ~ **come** ~ just now, at the moment; **d'**~ **in poi** from now on; **per** ~ for the time being, for now; ● *conj* (*dunque*) now [then]; ~ **che ci penso,...** now that I [come to] think about it...

o'racolo *nm* oracle

'orafo *nm* goldsmith

o'rale *a & nm* oral; **per via ~** by mouth

ora'mai *adv* = ormai

o'rario *a* ⟨*tariffa*⟩ hourly; ⟨*segnale*⟩ time *attrib*; ⟨*velocità*⟩ per hour; **in senso ~** clockwise ● *nm* time; (*tabella dell'orario*) timetable, schedule *Am*; **essere in ~** be on time; **partire in ~** leave on time; **lavorare fuori ~** work outside normal hours. **~ di apertura** opening hours *pl*. **~ di chiusura** closing time. **~ estivo** summer timetable. **~ ferroviario** railway timetable, railroad schedule *Am*. **~ flessibile** flexitime. **~ invernale** winter timetable. **~ di lavoro** working hours *pl*. **~ degli spettacoli** performance times *pl*. **~ di sportello** banking hours *pl*. **~ d'ufficio** business hours *pl*. **~ di visita** visiting hours *pl*, visiting time; (*del medico*) consulting hours *pl*. **~ di volo** flight time

o'rata *nf* gilthead

ora'|tore, -'trice *nmf* orator; (*conferenziere*) speaker

ora'torio, -a *a* oratorical ● *nm Mus* oratorio ● *nmf* oratory

orazi'one *nf Relig* prayer

'orbita *nf* orbit; *Anat* [eye-]socket

'Orcadi *nfpl* Orkneys

or'chestra *nf* orchestra; (*parte del teatro*) pit. **~ da camera** chamber orchestra

orche'strale *a* orchestral ● *nmf* member of an/the orchestra

orche'strare *vt* orchestrate

orchi'dea *nf* orchid

'orco *nm* ogre

'orda *nf* horde

or'digno *nm* device; (*arnese*) tool. **~ esplosivo** explosive device. **~ incendiario** incendiary device

ordi'nale *a & nm* ordinal

ordina'mento *nm* order; (*leggi*) rules *pl*

ordi'nanza *nf* (*del sindaco*) bylaw; **d'~** ⟨*soldato*⟩ on duty

ordi'nare *vt* (*sistemare*) arrange; (*comandare*) order; (*prescrivere*) prescribe; *Relig* ordain

ordi'nario *a* ordinary; (*grossolano*) common; ⟨*professore*⟩ with a permanent position; **di ordinaria amministrazione** routine ● *nm* ordinary; *Univ* professor; **fuori dell'~** out of the ordinary

ordi'nato *a* (*in ordine*) tidy

ordinazi'one *nf* order; **fare un'~** place an order

'ordine *nm* order; (*di avvocati, medici*) association; **mettere in ~** put in order; tidy up ⟨*appartamento ecc*⟩; **di prim'~** first-class; **di terz'~** ⟨*film, albergo*⟩ third-rate; **di ~ pratico/economico** ⟨*problema*⟩ of a practical/economic nature; **fino a nuovo ~** until further notice; **parola d'~** password. **~ di acquisto** *Comm* purchase order. **~ del giorno** agenda. **~ di pagamento** banker's order. **~ permanente** *Fin* standing order. **ordini** *pl* **sacri** Holy Orders

or'dire *vt* (*tramare*) plot

orecchi'ette *nfpl* small pasta shells

orec'chino *nm* ear-ring. **orecchini** *pl* **con le clip** clip-ons

o'recchio *nm* (*pl nf* **orecchie**) ear; **avere ~** have a good ear; **esser duro d'~** be hard of hearing; **mi è giunto all'~ che...** I've heard that...; **parlare all'~ a qcno** whisper in sb's ear; **suonare a ~** play by ear

orecchi'oni *nmpl Med* mumps *sg*

o'refice *nm* jeweller

orefice'ria *nf* (*arte*) goldsmith's art; (*negozio*) goldsmith's [shop]

'orfano, -a *a* orphan ● *nmf* orphan

orfano'trofio *nm* orphanage

orga'netto *nm* barrel-organ; (*a bocca*) mouth-organ; (*fisarmonica*) accordion

or'ganico *a* organic ● *nm* personnel

orga'nino *nm* hurdy-gurdy

orga'nismo *nm* organism; (*corpo umano*) body

orga'nista *nmf* organist

organiz'zare *vt* organize

organiz'zarsi *vr* get organized

organizza'tivo *a* organizational

organizza'|tore, -'trice *nmf* organizer

organizzazi'one *nf* organization. **~ dei soccorsi** relief organization

'organo *nm* organ

or'gasmo *nm* orgasm; *fig* agitation

'orgia *nf* orgy

or'goglio *nm* pride

orgogli'oso *a* proud

orien'tale *a* eastern; (*cinese ecc*) oriental

orienta'mento *nm* orientation; **perdere l'~** lose one's bearings; **senso dell'~** sense of direction. **~ professionale** careers guidance. **~ scolastico** educational guidance

orien'tare *vt* orientate

orien'tarsi *vr* find one's bearings; (*tendere*) tend

ori'ente *nm* east. **l'Estremo O~** the Far East. **il Medio O~** the Middle East

orien'teering *nm inv* orienteering

o'rigano *nm* oregano

origi'nale *a* original; (*eccentrico*) odd ● *nm* original

originalità *nf* originality

origi'nare *vt/i* originate

origi'nario *a* (*nativo*) native

o'rigine *nf* origin; **in ~** originally; **aver ~ da** originate from; **dare ~ a** give rise to

origli'are *vi* eavesdrop

o'rina *nf* urine

ori'nale *nm* chamber-pot

ori'nare *vi* urinate

ori'undo *a* native

orizzon'tale *a* horizontal

orizzon'tare *vt* = orientare

oriz'zonte *nm* horizon

or'lare *vt* hem

orla'tura *nf* hem

'orlo *nm* edge; (*di vestito ecc*) hem

'orma *nf* track; (*di piede*) footprint; (*impronta*) mark

or'mai *adv* by now; (*passato*) by then; (*quasi*) almost

ormegg'iare *vt* moor

or'meggio *nm* mooring

ormo'nale *a* hormonal

or'mone *nm* hormone

ornamen'tale *a* ornamental

orna'mento *nm* ornament; **d'~** (*oggetto*) ornamental

or'nare *vt* decorate

or'narsi *vr* deck oneself

or'nato *a* (*stile*) ornate

ornitolo'gia *nf* ornithology

orni'tologo, -a *nmf* ornithologist

ornito'rinco *nm* platypus

'oro *nm* gold; **d'~** gold; *fig* golden; **una persona d'~** a wonderful person. **~ nero** black gold

orologe'ria *nf* watchmaker

orologi'aio, -a *nmf* clockmaker, watchmaker

oro'logio *nm* (*portatile*) watch; (*da tavolo, muro ecc*) clock. **~ biologico** biological clock. **~ a carica automatica** self-winding watch. **~ a cucù** cuckoo clock. **~ digitale** digital clock. **~ a pendolo** grandfather clock. **~ da polso** wrist-watch. **~ al quarzo** quartz watch. **~ a sveglia** alarm clock

o'roscopo *nm* horoscope

or'rendo *a* awful, dreadful

or'ribile *a* horrible

orribil'mente *adv* horribly

orripi'lante *a* horrifying

or'rore *nm* horror; **avere qcsa in ~** hate sth; **~!** heck!; **film/romanzo dell'~** horror film/story

orsacchi'otto *nm* teddy bear

or'setto *nm* **~ lavatore** raccoon

'orso *nm* bear; (*persona scontrosa*) hermit. **~ bianco** polar bear. **~ bruno** brown bear

orsù *int* come now!

or'taggio *nm* vegetable

or'tensia *nf* hydrangea

or'tica *nf* nettle; **buttare qcsa alle ortiche** *fig fam* chuck in

orti'caria *nf* nettle-rash

orticol'tura *nf* horticulture

'orto *nm* vegetable plot

orto'dontico *a* orthodontic

ortodon'zia *nf* orthodontics

ortodos'sia *nf* conformity

orto'dosso *a* orthodox

ortofrut'ticolo *a* **mercato ~** fruit and vegetable market

ortofrutticol'tore *nm* market gardener, truck farmer *Am*

ortogo'nale *a* perpendicular

ortogra'fia *nf* spelling

orto'grafico *a* spelling *attrib*

orto'lano *nm* market gardener, truck farmer *Am;* (*negozio*) greengrocer's

ortope'dia *nf* orthopaedics

orto'pedico *a* orthopaedic ● *nm* orthopaedic specialist

orzai'olo *nm* sty

or'zata *nf* barley-water

'orzo *nm* barley. **~ perlato** pearl barley

osan'nato *a* (*esaltato*) praised to the skies

o'sare *vt/i* dare; (*avere audacia*) be daring

oscenità *nf inv* obscenity

o'sceno *a* obscene

oscil'lare *vi* swing; (*prezzi ecc:*) fluctuate; *Tech* oscillate; (*fig: essere indeciso*) vacillate

oscillazi'one *nf* swinging; (*di prezzi*) fluctuation; *Tech* oscillation

oscura'mento *nm* darkening; (*fig: di vista, mente*) dimming; (*totale*) black-out

oscu'rare *vt* darken; *fig* obscure

oscu'rarsi *vr* get dark

oscurità *nf* darkness; (*incomprensibilità*) obscurity; **uscire dall'~** *fig* emerge from obscurity; **morire nell'~** *fig* die in obscurity

o'scuro *a* dark; (*triste*) gloomy; (*incomprensibile*) obscure

o'smosi *nf inv* osmosis

ospe'dale *nm* hospital

ospedali'ero *a* hospital *attrib*

ospi'tale *a* hospitable

ospitalità *nf* hospitality; **non voglio abusare della tua ~** I don't want to outstay my welcome

ospi'tare *vt* give hospitality to

'ospite *nm* (*chi ospita*) host; (*chi viene ospitato*) guest ● *nf* hostess; guest

o'spizio *nm* (*per vecchi*) [old people's] home

ossa'tura *nf* bone structure; (*di romanzo*) structure, framework

'osseo *a* bone *attrib*

osse'quente *a* deferential; **~ alla legge** law-abiding

ossequi'are *vt* pay one's respects to

os'sequio *nm* homage; **ossequi** *pl* respects

ossequi'oso *a* obsequious

osser'vabile *a* observable

osser'vante *a* (*cattolico*) practising

osser'vanza *nf* observance

osser'vare *vt* observe; (*notare*) notice; keep (*ordine, silenzio*)

osserva'tore, -'trice *nmf* observer

osserva'torio *nm* *Astr* observatory; *Mil* observation post

osservazi'one *nf* observation; (*rimprovero*) reproach

ossessio'nante *a* haunting; (*persona*) nagging

ossessio'nare *vt* obsess; (*infastidire*) nag

ossessi'one *nf* obsession; (*assillo*) pain in the neck

osses'sivo *a* obsessive; (*paura*) neurotic

os'sesso *a* obsessed

os'sia *conj* that is

ossi'dabile *a* liable to tarnish

ossi'dante *a* tarnishing

ossi'dare *vt* oxidize

ossi'darsi *vr* oxidize

'ossido *nm* oxide. **~ di carbonio** carbon monoxide. **~ di zinco** zinc oxide

os'sidrico *a* **fiamma ossidrica** blowlamp

ossige'nare *vt* oxygenate; (*decolorare*) bleach

ossige'narsi *vr* put back on its feet ⟨*azienda*⟩; ~ **i capelli** dye one's hair blonde

os'sigeno *nm* oxygen

'osso *nm* (*Anat pl nf* **ossa**) bone; (*di frutto*) stone; **senz'~** boneless. ~ **mascellare** jawbone

osso'buco *nm* marrowbone

os'suto *a* bony

ostaco'lare *vt* hinder, obstruct

ostaco'lista *nmf* hurdler

o'stacolo *nm* obstacle; *Sport* hurdle

o'staggio *nm* hostage; **prendere in ~** take hostage

o'stello *nm* ~ **della gioventù** youth hostel

osten'tare *vt* show off; ~ **indifferenza** pretend to be indifferent

ostentata'mente *adv* ostentatiously

ostentazi'one *nf* ostentation

osteopo'rosi *nf inv* osteoporosis

oste'ria *nf* inn

oste'tricia *nf* obstetrics

o'stetrico, -a *a* obstetric ● *nmf* obstetrician

'ostia *nf* host; (*cialda*) wafer

'ostico *a* tough

o'stile *a* hostile

ostilità *nf inv* hostility

osti'narsi *vr* ~ persist (**a** in)

osti'nato *a* obstinate

ostinazi'one *nf* obstinacy

ostra'cismo *nm* ostracism

'ostrica *nf* oyster

ostro'goto *nm* **parlare ~** talk double Dutch

ostru'ire *vt* obstruct

ostruzi'one *nf* obstruction

ostruzio'nismo *nm* obstructionism; *Sport* obstruction. ~ **sindacale** work-to-rule

oto'rino *nm* ear, nose and throat *attrib*

otorinolaringoi'atra *nmf* ear, nose and throat specialist

'otre *nm* leather bottle

ottago'nale *a* octagonal

ot'tagono *nm* octagon

ot'tanta *a & nm* eighty

ottan'tenne *a & nmf* eighty-year-old

ottant'tesimo *a & nm* eightieth

ottant'tina *nf* about eighty

ot'tava *nf* octave

ot'tavo *a & nm* eighth

otte'nere *vt* obtain; (*più comune*) get; (*conseguire*) achieve

ot'tetto *nm Mus* octet

'ottico, -a *a* optic[al] ● *nmf* optician ● *nf* (*scienza*) optics *sg*; (*di lenti ecc*) optics *pl*

otti'male *a* optimum

ottima'mente *adv* very well

otti'mismo *nm* optimism

otti'mista *nmf* optimist

otti'mistico *a* optimistic

ottimiz'zare *vt* optimize

'ottimo *a* very good ● *nm* optimum; **essere all'~ della forma** be on top form

'otto *a & nm* eight

+otto *suff* **bassotto** (*piuttosto basso*) quite short; **contadinotto** *nm pej* (*semplicotto*) country bumpkin; **paesotto** *nm* hamlet; **leprotto** *nm* leveret; (*affettuoso*) baby hare; **pienotto** *a* ⟨*viso*⟩ chubby

ot'tobre *nm* October

otto'cento *a & nm* eight hundred; **l'O~** the nineteenth century

ot'tone *nm* brass; **gli ottoni** *Mus* the brass

ottuage'nario, -a *a & nmf* octogenarian

ot'tundere *vt* blunt

ottu'rare *vt* block; fill ⟨*dente*⟩

ottu'rarsi *vr* clog

ottura'tore *nm Phot* shutter

otturazi'one *nf* stopping; (*di dente*) filling

ot'tuso *pp di* **ottundere** ● *a* obtuse

ouver'ture *nf inv* overture

o'vaia *nf* ovary

o'vale *a & nm* oval

o'vatta *nf* cotton wool, absorbent cotton *Am*

ovat'tato *a* ⟨*suono, passi*⟩ muffled

ovazi'one *nf* ovation

'ove *adv liter* where

over'dose *nf inv* overdose

'overdrive *nm inv Auto* overdrive

'ovest *nm* west

o'vile *nm* sheep-fold, pen

o'vino *a* sheep *attrib*

ovoi'dale *a* egg-shaped

ovo'via *nf* two-seater cable car

ovulazi'one *nf* ovulation

o'vunque *adv* = **dovunque**

ov'vero *conj* or; (*cioè*) that is

ovvia'mente *adv* obviously

ovvi'are *vi* ~ **a qcsa** counter sth

'ovvio *a* obvious

ozi'are *vi* laze around

'ozio *nm* idleness; **stare in ~** idle about

ozi'oso *a* idle; ⟨*questione*⟩ pointless

o'zono *nm* ozone; **buco nell'~** hole in the ozone layer

Pp

pa'care *vt* calm
paca'tezza *nf* calm[ness]
pa'cato *a* calm
'pacca *nf* slap
pac'chetto *nm* packet; (*postale*) parcel, package; (*di sigarette*) pack, packet. ~ **integrato** *Comput* integrated package; ~ **software** software package
'pacchia *nf* (*fam: situazione*) bed of roses
pacchia'nata *nf* è una ~ it's so garish
pacchi'ano *a* garish
'pacco *nm* parcel; (*involto*) bundle; **disfare un** ~ unwrap a parcel; **fare un** ~ make up a parcel. **pacchi** *pl* **postali** parcels, packages. ~ **regalo** gift-wrapped package; **le faccio un** ~ ~? would you like it gift-wrapped?
paccot'tiglia *nf* (*roba scadente*) junk, rubbish
'pace *nf* peace; **darsi** ~ forget it; **fare** ~ **con qcno** make it up with sb; **lasciare in** ~ **qcno** leave sb in peace; **mettere** ~ **fra** pacify, make [the] peace between; **andate in** ~ *Relig* peace be with you; **in tempo di** ~ in peacetime; **del tempo di** ~ peacetime; **di** ~ ⟨*milizia*⟩ peacekeeping; **firmare la** ~ sign a peace treaty; **per amor di** ~ for a quiet life
pace-'maker *nm* (*apparecchio*) pacemaker
pachi'derma *nm* (*animale*) pachyderm; *fig* thick-skinned person
pachi'stano, -a *nmf & a* Pakistani
paci'ere *nm* peacemaker
pacifi'care *vt* reconcile; (*mettere pace*) pacify
pacificazi'one *nf* reconciliation
pa'cifico *a* pacific; (*calmo*) peaceful; **è** ~ **che...** (*comunemente accettato*) it is clear that... ● *nm* **il P~** the Pacific
paci'fismo *nm* pacifism
paci'fista *a & nmf* pacifist
pacioc'cone, -a *nmf fam* chubby-chops
paci'ugo *nm* (*poltiglia*) mush
pa'dano *a pianura padana* Po Valley
pa'della *nf* frying-pan; (*per malati*) bedpan; **cuocere in** ~ fry; **dalla** ~ **alla brace** out of the frying pan into the fire
padel'lata *nf* **una** ~ **di** a frying-panful of
padigli'one *nm* pavilion. ~ **auricolare** auricle
'Padova *nf* Padua
'padre *nm* father; **padri** *pl* (*antenati*) forefathers; **i padri della chiesa** the Church Fathers; **di** ~ **in figlio** from father to son. ~ **adottivo** (*marito della madre*) stepfather. ~ **di famiglia** father, paterfamilias; **sono** ~ ~ ~ I have a family to look after. ~ **spirituale** spiritual father
padre'nostro *nm* **il** ~ the Lord's Prayer
padre'terno *nm* God Almighty
pa'drino *nm* godfather; ~ **e madrina** godparents
padro'nale *a* principal
padro'nanza *nf* mastery. ~ **di sé** self-control
pa'drone, -a *nmf* master; mistress; (*datore di lavoro*) boss; (*proprietario*) owner. ~ **di casa** (*di inquilini*) landlord; landlady; (*in ricevimento*) master of the house; lady of the house
padroneggi'are *vt* master
padro'nesco *a* domineering
padro'nissimo *a* **essere** ~ **di fare qcsa** be quite at liberty to do sth
pae'saggio *nm* scenery; (*pittura*) landscape. ~ **marino** seascape. ~ **montano** mountain landscape
paesag'gista *nmf* landscape architect
paesag'gistico *a* landscape *attrib*
pae'sano, -a *a* country *attrib* ● *nmf* villager
pa'ese *nm* (*nazione*) country; (*territorio*) land; (*villaggio*) village; **il Bel Paese** Italy; **va' a quel** ~! get lost!; **il mio** ~ **natio** where I was born; **Paesi** *pl* **Bassi** Netherlands. **paesi** *pl* **dell'est** Eastern Bloc countries
paf'futo *a* plump
pag. *abbr* (**pagina**) p.
'paga *nf* pay, wages *pl*
pa'gabile *a* payable
pa'gaia *nf* paddle
paga'mento *nm* payment; **a** ~ ⟨*parcheggio*⟩ which you have to pay to use. ~ **anticipato** *Comm* advance payment. ~ **alla consegna** cash on delivery, COD. ~ **pedaggio** toll
paga'nesimo *nm* paganism
pa'gano, -a *a & nmf* pagan
pa'gante *nmf* payer
pa'gare *vt/i* pay; ~ **da bere a qcno** buy sb a drink; **pagato in anticipo** prepaid, paid in advance; **te la faccio** ~ you'll pay for this; **quanto pagherei per poter venire!** what I wouldn't give to be able to come!
pa'gella *nf* [school] report
pagg. *abbr* (**pagine**) pp.
'pagina *nf* page; **prima** ~ *Journ* front page; ~ **economica** financial news, financial pages; **pagine** *pl* **gialle** Yellow Pages. ~ **mastra** master page. ~ **web** *Comput* web page
pagi'none *nm* centre-fold

'paglia nf straw; ~ **e fieno** Culin mixture of ordinary and green tagliatelle

pagliac'cesco a farcical

pagliac'cetto nm (per bambini) rompers pl; (da donna) camiknickers

pagliac'ciata nf farce

pagli'accio nm clown; **fare il** ~ act or play the clown

pagli'aio nm haystack

paglie'riccio nm straw mattress

pagli'etta nf (cappello) boater; (per pentole) steel wool

pagli'uzza nf wisp of straw; (di metallo) particle

pa'gnotta nf [round] loaf

'pago a satisfied

pa'goda nf pagoda

pa'guro nm hermit crab

pail'lard nf inv slice of grilled veal

pail'lette nf inv sequin

'paio nm (pl nf **paia**) pair; **un** ~ (circa due) a couple; **un** ~ **di** ‹scarpe, forbici› a pair of; **è un altro** ~ **di maniche** fig that's a different kettle of fish

pai'olo nm copper pot

'Pakistan nm Pakistan

paki'stano, -a a & nmf Pakistani

'pala nf shovel; (di remo, elica) blade; (di ruota) paddle; (di mulino) blade, vane. ~ **d'altare** altar piece. ~ **da fornaio** shovel. ~ **meccanica** mechanical digger

pala'dino nm paladin; fig champion

pala'fitta nf pile-dwelling

palan'drana nf (abito largo) big long coat

pala'sport nm inv indoor sports arena

pa'late nfpl **a** ~ ‹fare soldi› hand over fist

pa'lato nm palate

palaz'zetto nm ~ **dello sport** indoor sports arena

palaz'zina nf villa

pa'lazzo nm palace; (edificio) building. ~ **comunale** town hall. **P~ Ducale** Doge's Palace. ~ **delle esposizioni** exhibition centre. ~ **di giustizia** law courts pl, courthouse. ~ **dello sport** indoor sports arena

'palco nm (pedana) platform; Theat box; (palcoscenico) stage

palco'scenico nm stage

paleogra'fia nf palaeography

paleo'grafico a palaeographical

pale'ografo, -a nmf palaeographer

paleo'litico a palaeolithic

pale'sare vt disclose

pale'sarsi vr reveal oneself

pa'lese a evident

Pale'stina nf Palestine

palesti'nese a & nmf Palestinian

pa'lestra nf gymnasium, gym; (ginnastica) gymnastics pl

pa'letta nf spade; (per focolare) shovel. ~ **[della spazzatura]** dustpan

palet'tata nf shovelful

pa'letto nm peg

palin'sesto nm (documento) palimpsest; TV programme schedule

'palio nm (premio) prize. **il P~** horse-race held at Siena

palis'sandro nm rosewood

paliz'zata nf fence

'palla nf ball; (proiettile) bullet; (fam: bugia) porkie; **prendere la** ~ **al balzo** seize an opportunity; **essere una** ~ sl be a drag; **che palle!** vulg this is a pain in the arse!, what a drag!. ~ **da biliardo** billiard ball. ~ **medica** medicine ball. ~ **di neve** snowball. ~ **al piede** fig millstone round one's neck

pallaca'nestro nf basketball

palla'mano nf handball

pallanuo'tista nmf water polo player

pallanu'oto nf water polo

palla-'goal nf **hanno avuto molte palle-goal** they had a lot of goal-scoring opportunities

pallavo'lista nmf volleyball player

palla'volo nf volleyball

palleggi'are vi (calcio) practise ball control; Tennis knock up

pal'leggio nm Sport warm-up

'pallet nm inv pallet

pallet'toni nmpl buckshot

pallia'tivo nm palliative

'pallido a pale; **non ne ho la più pallida idea** I don't have the faintest or foggiest idea

pal'lina nf (di vetro) marble

pal'lino nm **avere il** ~ **del calcio** be crazy about football, be football crazy

pallon'cino nm balloon; (lanterna) Chinese lantern; (fam: etilometro) Breathalyzer ®

pal'lone nm ball; (calcio) football; (aerostato) balloon; **essere/andare nel** ~ be/become confused. ~ **da calcio** football. ~ **gonfiato: è un** ~ ~ he's so puffed-up. ~ **sonda** weather balloon

pallo'netto nm lob

pal'lore nm pallor

pal'loso a sl boring

pal'lottola nf pellet; (proiettile) bullet. ~ **dum-dum** dumdum bullet

pallottoli'ere nm abacus

'palma nf Bot palm. ~ **da cocco** coconut palm. ~ **da datteri** date palm

palmarès nm inv (di festival) award winners pl; (fig: i migliori) top names pl

pal'mato a ‹piede› webbed

pal'mento nm **mangiava a quattro palmenti** he was really tucking in

pal'meto nm palm grove

palmi'pede nm web-footed animal

'palmo nm Anat palm; (misura) hand's-breadth; **restare con un** ~ **di naso** feel disappointed

'palo nm pole; (di sostegno) stake; (in calcio) goalpost; **fare il** ~ ‹ladro:› keep a lookout. ~ **d'arrivo** (in ippica) finishing post ~ **della luce** lamppost. ~ **di partenza** (in ippica) starting post

palom'baro nm diver

pa'lombo *nm* dogfish
pal'pare *vt* feel
pal'pata *nf* **dare una ~ a qcsa** give sth a feel
'**palpebra** *nf* eyelid
palpeggi'are *vt* feel
palpi'tare *vi* throb; (*fremere*) quiver
palpitazi'one *nf* palpitation; **avere le palpitazioni** have palpitations
'**palpito** *nm* throb; (*del cuore*) beat
paltò *nm inv* overcoat
pa'lude *nf* marsh, swamp
palu'doso *a* marshy
pa'lustre *a* marshy; (*piante, uccelli*) marsh *attrib*
'**pampas** *nfpl* pampas
'**pamphlet** *nm inv* pamphlet
pamphlet'tista *nmf* pamphleteer
'**pampino** *nm* vine leaf
pan *nm vedi* **pane**
pana'cea *nf* panacea
pa'nache *nm inv* **far ~** (*in ippica*) fall
'**panca** *nf* bench; (*in chiesa*) pew
pancarré *nm* sliced bread
pan'cetta *nf* Culin bacon; (*di una certa età*) paunch. **~ affumicata** smoked bacon
pan'chetto *nm* [foot]stool
pan'china *nf* garden seat; (*in calcio*) bench
'**pancia** *nf* belly, tummy *fam*; (*di bottiglia, vaso*) body; **mal di ~** stomach-ache; **a ~ piena/vuota** on a full/empty stomach; **metter su ~** develop a paunch; **a ~ in giù** lying face down
panci'ata *nf* **prendere una ~** (*in tuffo*) do a belly flop
panci'era *nf* corset
panci'olle: stare in ~ lounge about
panci'one *nm* (*persona*) pot belly
panci'otto *nm* waistcoat
panci'uto *a* potbellied
'**pancreas** *nm inv* pancreas
pancre'atico *a* pancreatic
'**panda** *a* panda
pande'monio *nm* pandemonium
pan'dolce *nm* Christmas cake similar to *panettone*
pan'doro *nm* kind of sponge cake traditionally eaten at Christmas time
'**pane** *nm* bread; (*pagnotta*) loaf; (*di burro*) block. **~ casereccio** home-made bread. **~ a cassetta** sliced bread. **pan grattato** breadcrumbs *pl*. **~ integrale** wholemeal bread. **~ nero** blackbread. **~ di segale** rye bread. **pan di Spagna** sponge cake. **~ tostato** toast
'**panel** *nm inv* (*gruppo*) panel
panette'ria *nf* bakery; (*negozio*) baker's [shop]
panetti'ere, -a *nmf* baker
panet'tone *nf* dome-shaped cake with sultanas and candied fruit eaten at Christmas
'**panfilo** *nm* yacht
pan'forte *nm* nougat-like spicy delicacy from Siena

'**panico** *nm* panic; **lasciarsi prendere dal ~** panic
pani'ere *nm* basket; (*cesta*) hamper
pani'ficio *nm* bakery; (*negozio*) baker's [shop]
pani'naro *nm sl* preppie
pa'nino *nm* [bread] roll. **~ imbottito** filled roll. **~ al prosciutto** ham roll
panino'teca *nf* sandwich bar
'**panna** *nf* cream. **~ cotta** *kind of creme caramel*. **~ da cucina** [single] cream. **~ montata** whipped cream
'**panne** *nf* Mech **in ~** broken down; **restare in ~** break down
panneggi'ato *a* draped
pan'neggio *nm* drapery
pan'nello *nm* panel. **~ comandi** control panel. **~ solare** solar panel
'**panno** *nm* cloth; (*di tavolo da gioco e da biliardo*) baize; **panni** *pl* (*abiti*) clothes; **mettersi nei panni di qcno** *fig* put oneself in sb's shoes
pan'nocchia *nf* (*di granoturco*) cob
panno'lenci[R] *nm inv* brightly coloured felt
panno'lino *nm* (*per bambini*) nappy; (*da donna*) sanitary towel
pano'rama *nm* panorama; *fig* overview
pano'ramica *nf* (*rassegna*) overview
pano'ramico *a* panoramic
panpe'pato *nm* type of gingerbread
pantacol'lant *nmpl* leggings
pantagru'elico *a* (*pranzo*) gargantuan
pantalon'cini *nmpl* shorts. **~ da ciclista** cycling shorts. **~ corti** shorts
panta'loni *nmpl* trousers, pants *Am*. **~ da sci** ski pants. **~ a tubo** drain-pipe trousers. **~ a zampa d'elefante** bell-bottoms
pan'tano *nm* bog
panta'noso *a* marshy
pan'tera *nf* panther; (*auto della polizia*) high-speed police car. **~ nera** black panther
pan'tofola *nf* slipper
pantofo'laio, -a *nmf/fig* stay-at-home
panto'mima *nf* pantomime; *fig* act
pan'zana *nf* fib
'**panzer** *nm inv* Mil tank
pao'nazzo *a* purple
'**papa** *nm* Pope; **a ogni morte di ~** *fig* once in a blue moon
papà *nm inv* dad[dy]
pa'paia *nf* papaw, papaya
pa'pale *a* papal
papa'lina *nf* skull-cap
papa'razzo *nm* paparazzo
pa'pato *nm* papacy
pa'pavero *nm* poppy
'**papera** *nf* (*errore*) slip of the tongue
'**papero** *nm* gosling
pa'pilla *nf* **~ gustativa** taste bud
papil'lon *nm inv* bow tie
pa'piro *nm* papyrus
'**pappa** *nf* (*per bambini*) baby food; **trovare la ~ pronta** *fig* have everything ready and waiting
pappagal'lino *nm* budgerigar, budgie

pappa'gallo *nm* parrot
pappa'gorgia *nf* double chin
pappa'molle *nmf* wimp
pap'parsi *vr fam* tuck away
pappar'delle *nfpl strips of pasta with a meat sauce*
pap'pone *nm sl* (*mangione*) pig; (*sfruttatore*) pimp
'paprica *nf* paprika
Pap test *nm inv* smear test
'para *nf* **suole di** ~ crêpe soles
parà *nm inv* para
pa'rabola *nf* parable; (*curva*) parabola
para'bolico *a* parabolic
para'brezza *nm inv* windscreen, windshield *Am*
paracadu'tare *vt* parachute
paracadu'tarsi *vr* parachute
paraca'dute *nm inv* parachute
paracadu'tismo *nm* parachuting. ~ **ascensionale** parascending
paracadu'tista *nmf* parachutist
para'carro *nm* roadside post
para'digma *nm Gram* paradigm
paradi'siaco *a* heavenly
para'diso *nm* paradise. ~ **fiscale** tax haven. ~ **terrestre** Eden, earthly paradise
parados'sale *a* paradoxical
para'dosso *nm* paradox
para'fango *nm* mudguard
paraf'fina *nf* paraffin
parafra'sare *vt* paraphrase
pa'rafrasi *nf inv* paraphrase
para'fulmine *nm* lightning-conductor
para'fuoco *nm* fire-screen
pa'raggi *nmpl* neighbourhood *sg*
parago'nabile *a* comparable (**a** to)
parago'nare *vt* compare
parago'narsi *vr* compare oneself
para'gone *nm* comparison; **a** ~ **di** in comparison with; **non c'è** ~! there's no comparison!
paragra'fare *vt* paragraph
pa'ragrafo *nm* paragraph
paraguai'ano, -a *a & nmf* Paraguyan
Paragu'ay *nm* Paraguay
pa'ralisi *nf inv* paralysis
para'litico, -a *a & nmf* paralytic
paraliz'zante *a* crippling
paraliz'zare *vt* paralyse
paraliz'zato *a* (*dalla paura*) transfixed
paral'lela *nf* parallel line; **è una** ~ **di...** ⟨*strada:*⟩ it runs parallel to...; **parallele** *pl* parallel bars
parallela'mente *adv* in parallel
paralle'lismo *nm* parallelism
paral'lelo *a & nm* parallel; **fare un** ~ **tra** draw a parallel between
parallelo'gramma *nm* parallelogram
para'lume *nm* lampshade
para'medico *nm* paramedic
para'mento *nm* hangings *pl*
pa'rametro *nm* parameter
paramili'tare *a* paramilitary
pa'ranco *nm* block and tackle

para'noia *nf* paranoia
para'noico, -a *a & nmf* paranoid
paranor'male *a & nm* paranormal
para'occhi *nmpl* blinkers
parao'recchie *nm* earmuffs
parapen'dio *nm* paragliding
para'petto *nm* parapet
para'piglia *nm* turmoil
para'plegico, -a *a & nmf* paraplegic
pa'rare *vt* (*addobbare*) adorn; (*riparare*) shield; save ⟨*tiro, pallone*⟩; ward off, parry ⟨*schiaffo, pugno*⟩ ● *vi* (*mirare*) lead up to
pa'rarsi *vr* (*abbigliarsi*) dress up; (*da pioggia, pugni*) protect oneself; ~ **dinanzi a qcno** appear in front of sb
parasco'lastico *a* ⟨*attività*⟩ extracurricular
para'sole *nm inv* parasol
paras'sita *a* parasitic ● *nm* parasite
parassi'tario *a anche fig* parasitic
parassi'tismo *nm* parasitism
parasta'tale *a* government-controlled
para'stinchi *nm inv* shin-guard
pa'rata *nf* parade; (*in calcio*) save; (*in scherma, pugilato*) parry. ~ **aerea** flypast
para'tia *nf* bulkhead
parauniversi'tario *a* at university level
para'urti *nm inv Auto* bumper, fender *Am*
para'vento *nm* screen
par'boiled *a* **riso** ~ parboiled rice
par'cella *nf* bill
parcheggi'are *vt anche fig* park; ~ **in doppia fila** double-park
parcheggia'|tore, -'trice *nmf* parking attendant. ~ **abusivo** person who illegally earns money by looking after parked cars
par'cheggio *nm* parking; (*posteggio*) carpark, parking lot *Am*. ~ **carta** *Comput* paper park. ~ **custodito** car park with attendant. ~ **incustodito** unattended car park. ~ **a pagamento** paying car-park. ~ **sotterraneo** underground car park, underground parking garage *Am*
par'chimetro *nm* parking meter
'parco[1] *a* sparing; (*moderato*) moderate; **essere** ~ **nel mangiare** eat sparingly
'parco[2] *nm* park. ~ **di divertimenti** fun-fair. ~ **giochi** playground. ~ **macchine** *Auto* fleet of cars. ~ **naturale** wildlife park. ~ **nazionale** national park. ~ **regionale** [regional] wildlife park
pa'recchio *a* quite a lot of; **parecchi** *pl* several, quite a lot of ● *pron* quite a lot; **parecchi** *pl* several, quite a lot ● *adv* rather; (*parecchio tempo*) quite a time
pareggi'are *vt* level; (*eguagliare*) equal; *Comm* balance; ~ **il bilancio** balance the scales ● *vi* draw
pa'reggio *nm Comm* balance; *Sport* draw
paren'tado *nm* relatives *pl*; (*vincolo di sangue*) relationship
pa'rente *nmf* relative, relation. ~ **acquisito** relation by marriage. ~ **alla lontana** distant relation. ~ **stretto** close relation
paren'tela *nf* relatives *pl*; (*vincolo di*

sangue) relationship; **grado di ~** degree of kinship

pa'rentesi *nf inv* parenthesis; (*segno grafico*) bracket; (*fig: pausa*) break; **aprire una ~** *fig* digress. **~** *pl* **graffe** curly brackets. **~ quadre** square brackets. **~ tonde** round brackets; **fra ~,...** (*tra l'altro*) in parenthesis

pa'reo *nm* (*copricostume*) sarong; **a ~** (*gonna*) wrap-around

pa'rere[1] *nm* opinion; **a mio ~** in my opinion; **essere del ~ che** be of the opinion that

pa'rere[2] *vi* seem; (*pensare*) think; **che te ne pare?** what do you think of it?; **pare di sì** it seems so; **mi pare che...** I think that...; **non mi par vero** I can't believe it; **mi pareva bene!** I thought as much!

pa'rete *nf* wall; (*in alpinismo*) face. **~ divisoria** partition wall

'pargolo *nf liter* child

'pari *a inv* equal; (*numero*) even; **andare di ~ passo** keep pace; **essere ~** be even *o* quits; **arrivare ~** draw; **~ ~** (*copiare, ripetere*) word for word; **fare ~ o dispari** toss a coin ● *nmf inv* equal, peer; **ragazza alla ~** au pair [girl]; **lavorare alla ~** work [as an] au pair; **mettersi in ~ con qcsa** catch up with sth ● *nm* (*titolo nobiliare*) peer

'paria *nm inv* pariah

parifi'cato *a* (*scuola*) state-recognized

Pa'rigi *nf* Paris

pari'gino, -a *a & nmf* Parisian

pa'riglia *nf* pair; **rendere la ~ a qcno** give sb tit for tat

parità *nf* equality; *Tennis* deuce; **a ~ di condizioni/voti** if all circumstances/the votes are equal; **finire in ~** (*partita:*) end in a draw. **~ dei diritti** equal rights. **~ monetaria** monetary parity. **~ dei sessi** sexual equality, equality of the sexes

pari'tario *a* parity *attrib*

'parka *nm inv* parka

parlamen'tare *a* parliamentary ● *nmf* Member of Parliament ● *vi* discuss

parla'mento *nm* Parliament. **Il P~ europeo** the European Parliament

parlan'tina *nf* avere la **~** be a chatterbox

par'lare *vt/i* speak, talk; speak (*inglese, italiano*); (*confessare*) talk; **~ bene/male di qcno** speak well/ill of somebody; **~ da solo** speak to oneself; **chi parla?** *Teleph* who's speaking?; **senti chi parla!** look who's talking!; **non parliamone più** let's forget about it; **non se ne parla nemmeno!** don't even mention it!; **~ a braccio** speak off the top of one's head; **far ~ qcno** make sb talk

par'lato *a* (*lingua*) spoken

parla|'tore, -'trice *nmf* speaker

parla'torio *nm* parlour; (*in prigione*) visiting room

parlot'tare *vi* mutter

parlot'tio *nm* muttering

parlucchi'are *vt* speak a little, have a smattering of (*lingua*)

parmigi'ano *nm* Parmesan

paro'dia *nf* parody; **fare la ~ di** parody

parodi'are *vt* parody

paro'distico *a* (*tono*) parodying; **programma ~** parody

pa'rola *nf* word; (*facoltà*) speech; **è una ~!** it is easier said than done!; **parole** *pl* (*di canzone*) words, lyrics; **rivolgere la ~ a** address; **passare ~** spread the word; **non fare ~ di qcsa con nessuno** not breathe a word of sth to anybody; **ti credo sulla ~** I'll take your word for it; **togliere la ~ di bocca a qcno** take the words [right] out of sb's mouth; **voler sempre l'ultima ~** always want to have the last word; **dire due parole a qcno** have a word *o* chat with sb; **di poche parole** (*persona*) of few words; **dare a qcno la propria ~** give sb one's word; **~ per ~** word-for-word; **in parole povere** crudely speaking. **~ chiave** *inv* keyword. **parole** *pl* **incrociate** crossword [puzzle]. **~ di moda** buzzword. **~ d'onore** word of honour. **~ d'ordine** password

paro'laccia *nf* swear-word

paro'lina *nf* **dire due paroline a qcno** have a word *o* chat with sb

paro'loni *nmpl* mumbo jumbo

paros'sismo *nm* paroxysm

paros'sistico *a Med* paroxysmal

par'quet *nm inv* (*pavimento*) parquet flooring

parri'cida *nmf* parricide

parri'cidio *nm* parricide

par'rocchia *nf* parish

parrocchi'ale *a* parish *attrib*

parrocchi'ano, -a *nmf* parishioner

'parroco *nm* parish priest

par'rucca *nf* wig

parrucchi'ere, -a *nmf* hairdresser

parruc'chino *nm* toupée, hairpiece

parsi'monia *nf* thrift

parsimoni'oso *a* thrifty

'parso *pp di* **parere**

'parte *nf* part; (*lato*) side; (*partito*) party; (*porzione*) share; (*fazione*) group; **a ~** apart from; **in ~** in part; **la maggior ~ di** the majority of; **d'altra ~** on the other hand; **da ~** aside; (*in disparte*) to one side; **farsi da ~** stand aside; **da ~ di** from; (*per conto di*) on behalf of; **è gentile da ~ tua** it is kind of you; **fare una brutta ~ a qcno** behave badly towards sb; **da che ~ è...?** whereabouts is...?; **da una parte..., dall'altra...** on the one hand..., on the other hand...; **dall'altra ~ di** on the other side of; **da nessuna ~** nowhere; **da qualche ~** somewhere; **da qualche altra ~** somewhere else, elsewhere; **da tutte le parti** (*essere*) everywhere; **da questa ~** (*in questa direzione*) this way; **da queste parti** hereabouts; **da un anno a questa ~** for about a year now; **mettere qcsa da ~** put sth aside; **essere dalla ~ di qcno** be on sb's side; **prendere le parti di qcno** take sb's side; **dalla ~ della ragione/del torto** in the right/the wrong; **essere ~ in causa** be involved; **fare ~ di** (*appartenere* *a)* be a member of; **fare la propria ~** do one's share *o* bit; **far ~ di qcsa a qcno** inform sb of sth; **rendere ~ a** take part in; **prendere ~ a qcsa** take part in sth. **~ civile** plaintiff. **~ del discorso** part of speech

parteci'pante *nmf* participant

parteci'pare *vi* **~ a** participate in, take part in; *(condividere)* share in

partecipazi'one *nf* participation; *(annuncio)* announcement; *Fin* shareholding; *(presenza)* presence; **con la ~** [**straordinaria**] **di...** featuring... **~ statale** *(quota)* state interest

par'tecipe *a* participating

parteggi'are *vi* **~ per** side with

par'tenza *nf* departure; *Sport* start; **in ~ per** leaving for; **falsa ~** false start

parti'cella *nf* particle

parti'cina *nf* bit part

parti'cipio *nm* participle. **~ passato** past participle. **~ presente** present participle

partico'lare *a* particular; *(privato)* private; *(speciale)* special, particular ● *nm* detail, particular; **fin nei minimi particolari** down to the smallest detail; **in ~** *(particolarmente)* in particular

particolareggi'ato *a* detailed

particolarità *nf inv* particularity; *(dettaglio)* detail

particolar'mente *adv* particularly

partigi'ano, -a *a & nmf* partisan

par'tire *vi* leave; *(aver inizio)* start; *(fam: rompersi)* break. **a ~ da** [beginning] from; **~ molto bene** get off to a flying start; **~ in quarta** go off at half cock; **è partito** *(fam: ubriaco)* he's away

par'tita *nf* game; *(incontro)* match; *Comm* lot; *(contabilità)* entry; **dare ~ vinta a qcno** *fig* give in to sb. **~ amichevole** friendly [match]. **~ di calcio** football match. **~ a carte** game of cards. **~ doppia** *Comm* double-entry book keeping. **~ di ritorno** *Sport* return match, rematch. **~ semplice** *Comm* single-entry book keeping

parti'tario *nm Comm* ledger. **~ vendite** sales ledger

par'tito *nm* party; *(scelta)* choice; *(occasione di matrimonio)* match; **per ~ preso** out of sheer pig-headedness. **~ di governo** governing party. **~ di maggioranza** majority party. **~ politico** political party

partitocra'zia *nf* concentration of power in the hands of political parties to the detriment of parliamentary democracy

partizi'one *nf (divisione)* division; *(Comput: di disco)* partition

'partner *nmf inv (in affari, coppia)* partner

'parto *nm* childbirth; **un ~ facile** an easy birth *o* labour; **dolori** *pl* **del ~** labour pains; **morire di ~** die in childbirth. **~ cesareo** Caesarian section. **~ indolore** natural childbirth. **~ indotto** induction, induced labour. **~ prematuro** premature birth

partori'ente *nf* woman in labour

parto'rire *vt anche fig* give birth to

part-'time *a* part-time ● *nm* **chiedere il ~** ask to work part-time

pa'rure *nf inv (di gioielli)* set of jewellery; *(di biancheria intima)* set of matching lingerie

par'venza *nf* appearance

parzi'ale *a* partial

parzialità *nf* partiality; **fare ~ per qcno** be biased towards sb

parzial'mente *adv* partially; *(con parzialità)* with bias; **~ cieco** partially sighted; **~ scremato** semi-skimmed

'pascere *vi ⟨mucche:⟩* graze ● *vt* graze on *⟨erba⟩*

pasci'uto *a* **ben ~** plump

pasco'lare *vt* graze

'pascolo *nm* pasture

'Pasqua *nf* Easter

pa'squale *a* Easter *attrib*; **l'isola di P~** Easter Island

pa'squetta *nf (lunedì di Pasqua)* Easter Monday

'passa: e ~ *adv (e oltre)* plus

pas'sabile *a* passable

pas'saggio *nm* passage; *(traversata)* crossing; *Sport* pass; *(su veicolo)* lift, ride; **essere di ~** be passing through; **è stato un ~ obbligato** *fig* it was something essential, it had to be done. **~ a livello** level crossing, grade crossing *Am.* **~ pedonale** pedestrian crossing, crosswalk *Am.* **~ di proprietà** transfer of ownership

passamane'ria *nf* braid

passamon'tagna *nm inv* balaclava

pas'sante *nmf* passer-by ● *nm (di cintura)* loop ● *a Tennis* passing

passa'porto *nm anche fig* passport. **~ europeo** European passport, Europassport

pas'sare *vi* pass; *(attraversare)* pass through; *(far visita)* call; *(andare)* go; *(essere approvato)* be passed; **~ davanti a qcno** go in front of sb; **~ alla storia** go down in history; **~ di moda** go out of fashion; **mi è passato di mente** it slipped my mind; **~ sopra a qcsa** pass over sth; **~ per un genio/idiota** be taken for a genius/an idiot; **farsi ~ per qcno** pass oneself off as sb; **passo!** *(nelle carte)* pass!; *(per radio)* over! ● *vt (far scorrere)* pass over; *(sopportare)* go through; *(al telefono)* put through; *Culin* strain; pass *⟨esame, visita⟩*; **~ in rivista** review; **~ qcsa a qcno** pass sth to sb; **le passo il signor Rossi** *Teleph* I'll put you through to Mr Rossi; **~ qcsa su qcsa** *⟨crema, cera ecc⟩* give sth a coat of sth; **~ il limite** go over the limit; **passarsela bene** be well off; **come te la passi?** how are you doing? ● *nm* **col ~ del tempo** with the passing *or* passage of time

pas'sata *nf (di vernice)* coat; *(spolverata)* dusting; *(occhiata)* look

passa'tempo *nm* pastime

pas'sato *a* past; **l'anno ~** last year; **sono le tre passate** it's past *o* after three o'clock ● *nm* past; *Culin* purée; *Gram* past tense; **in ~** in the past. **~ di moda** old-fashioned. **~**

prossimo *Gram* present perfect. ~ **remoto** *Gram* [simple] past. ~ **di verdure** cream of vegetable soup

passaver'dure *nm inv* food mill

passavi'vande *nm inv* serving hatch

passeg'gero, -a *a* passing ● *nmf* passenger. ~ **in transito** transit passenger

passeggi'are *vi* walk, stroll

passeg'giata *nf* walk, stroll; *(luogo)* public walk; *(in bicicletta)* ride; **fare una ~** go for a walk

passeggia'trice *nf* streetwalker

passeg'gino *nm* pushchair, stroller *Am*

pas'seggio *nm* walk; *(luogo)* promenade; **andare a ~** go for a walk; **scarpe da ~** walking shoes

passe-par'tout *nm inv* master-key

passe'rella *nf* gangway; *Aeron* boarding bridge; *(per sfilate)* catwalk

'passero *nm* sparrow

passe'rotto *nm (passero)* sparrow

pas'sibile *a* ~ **di** liable to

passio'nale *a* passionate; **delitto ~** crime of passion

passi'one *nf* passion; **avere la ~ del gioco** have a passion for gambling

passiva'mente *adv* passively

passività *nf (inerzia)* passiveness, passivity; *Fin* liabilities *pl*. ~ **pl correnti** current liabilities

pas'sivo *a* passive ● *nm* passive; *Fin* liabilities *pl*; **in ~** ⟨*azienda*⟩ in deficit; ⟨*bilancio*⟩ debit, in deficit

'passo *nm* step; *(orma)* footprint; *(andatura)* pace, step; *(di libro)* passage; *(valico)* pass; **a due passi da qui** a stone's throw away; **a ~ d'uomo** at walking pace; **di buon ~** at a spanking pace, at a cracking pace; **a passi felpati** stealthily; **di questo ~** at this rate; **~** step by step; **fare due passi** go for a stroll; **allungare il ~** quicken one's pace, step out; **tornare sui propri passi** retrace one's steps; **fare un ~ avanti** *anche fig* take a step forward; **fare un ~ falso** *fig* make a wrong move; **di pari ~** *fig* hand in hand; **stare al ~ con i tempi** keep up with the times, keep abreast of the times; **tenere il ~** keep up. **~ carrabile**, **~ carraio** driveway. **~ dell'oca** goose-step

'pasta *nf (impasto per pane ecc)* dough; *(per dolci, pasticcino)* pastry; *(pastasciutta)* pasta; *(massa molle)* paste; *fig* nature; **sono fatti della stessa ~** they're birds of a feather. **~ e fagioli** very thick soup with blended borlotti beans and small pasta. **~ al forno** *pasta baked in white sauce with grated cheese*. **~ frolla** shortcrust pastry. **~ al ragù** pasta with Bolognese sauce

pastasci'utta *nf* pasta

pa'stella *nf* batter

pa'stello *nm* pastel

pa'sticca *nf* pastille; *(fam: pastiglia)* pill

pasticce'ria *nf* cake shop, patisserie; *(pasticcini)* pastries *pl*; *(arte)* confectionery

pasticci'are *vi* make a mess ● *vt* make a mess of

pasticci'ere, -a *nmf* confectioner

pastic'cino *nm* little cake

pa'sticcio *nm Culin* pie; *(lavoro disordinato)* mess; **mettersi nei pasticci** get into trouble

pasticci'one, -a *nmf* bungler ● *a* bungling

pasti'ficio *nm* pasta factory

pa'stiglia *nf Med* pill, tablet; *(di menta)* sweet. **~ dei freni** brake pad. **~ per la gola** throat pastille. **~ per la tosse** cough sweet

pa'stina *nf* small pasta shape. **~ in brodo** noodle soup

'pasto *nm* meal; **fuori ~** between meals; **dare qcsa in ~ a** *fig* serve sth up on a platter to ⟨*pubblico, stampa*⟩

pa'stora *nf* shepherdess

pasto'rale *a* pastoral

pa'store *nm* shepherd; *Relig* pastor, vicar. **~ scozzese** collie. **~ tedesco** German shepherd, Alsatian

pasto'rizia *a* sheep farming *attrib*

pastoriz'zare *vt* pasteurize

pastoriz'zato *a* pasteurized

pastorizzazi'one *nf* pasteurization

pa'stoso *a* doughy; *fig* mellow

pa'strocchio *nm* mess

pa'stura *nf* pasture; *(per pesci)* bait

pa'tacca *nf (macchia)* stain; *(fig: oggetto senza valore)* piece of junk

pa'tata *nf* potato. **patate** *pl* **arrosto** roast potatoes. **patate** *pl* **al cartoccio** jacket potatoes. **patate** *pl* **fritte** chips *Br*, French fries. **patate** *pl* **in insalata** potato salad. **patate** *pl* **lesse** boiled potatoes

pata'tine *nfpl* [potato] crisps, chips *Am*

pata'trac *nm inv (crollo)* crash

patch'work *nm inv* patchwork

pâté *nm inv* pâté. **~ di fegato** liver pâté

pa'tella *nf* limpet

pa'tema *nm* anxiety

pa'tente *nf* licence; **prendere la ~** get one's driving licence. **~ di guida** driving licence, driver's license *Am*

pater'nale *nf* scolding

paterna'lismo *nm* paternalism

paterna'lista *nm* paternalist

paterna'listico *a* paternalistic

paternità *nf inv* paternity

pa'terno *a* paternal; ⟨*affetto ecc*⟩ fatherly

pa'tetico *a* pathetic; **cadere nel ~** become over-sentimental

'pathos *nm* pathos

pa'tibolo *nm* gallows *sg*

pati'mento *nm* suffering

'patina *nf* patina; *(sulla lingua)* coating

'patio *nm* patio garden

pa'tire *vt/i* suffer

pa'tito, -a *a* suffering ● *nmf* fanatic. **~ della musica** music lover

patolo'gia *nf* pathology

pato'logico *a* pathological

pa'tologo, -a *nmf* pathologist

'**patria** *nf* native land; **amor di** ~ love of one's country

patri'arca *nm* patriarch

patriar'cale *a* patriarchal

patriar'cato *nm* patriarchy

pa'trigno *nm* stepfather

patrimoni'ale *a* property *attrib*

patri'monio *nm* estate

patri'ota *nmf* patriot

patri'ottico *a* patriotic

patriot'tismo *nm* patriotism

pa'trizio, -a *a & nmf* patrician

patroci'nante *a* sponsoring

patroci'nare *vt* support

patro'cinio *nm* support; **sotto il** ~ **di** under the sponsorship of; *Jur* defended by. ~ **gratuito** legal aid

patro'nato *nm* patronage

pa'trono *nm Relig* patron saint; *Jur* counsel

'**patta¹** *nf* (*di tasca*) flap

'**patta²** *nf* (*pareggio*) draw

patteggia'mento *nm* bargaining

patteggi'are *vt/i* negotiate

patti'naggio *nm* skating. ~ **artistico** figure skating. ~ **su ghiaccio** ice skating. ~ **a rotelle** roller skating

patti'nare *vi* skate; ⟨*auto:*⟩ skid

pattina|'tore, -'trice *nmf* skater

'**pattino** *nm* skate; *Aeron* skid. ~ **da ghiaccio** ice skate. ~ **a rotelle** roller skate

'**patto** *nm* deal; *Pol* pact; **a** ~ **che** on condition that; **scendere a patti, venire a patti** reach a compromise

pat'tuglia *nf* patrol; **essere di** ~ be on patrol. ~ **stradale** highway patrol *Am*, ≈ patrol car; police motorbike

pattu'ire *vt* negotiate

pat'tume *nm* rubbish

pattumi'era *nf* dustbin, trashcan *Am*

pa'ura *nf* fear; (*spavento*) fright; **aver** ~ be afraid; **mettere** ~ **a** frighten; **per** ~ **di** for fear of; **da** ~ ⟨*sl: libro, film*⟩ brilliant

pau'roso *a* (*che fa paura*) frightening; (*che ha paura*) fearful; (*fam: enorme*) awesome

'**pausa** *nf* pause; (*nel lavoro*) break; **fare una** ~ pause; (*nel lavoro*) have a break. ~ **per il caffè** coffee break. ~ **del pranzo** lunch break, lunch hour

pavida'mente *adv* timidly

'**pavido** *a* cowardly ● *nm* coward

pavimen'tare *vt* pave ⟨*strada*⟩

pavimentazi'one *nf* paving

pavi'mento *nm* floor

pa'vone *nm* peacock

pavoneggi'arsi *vr* strut

pay tv *nf inv* pay TV

pazien'tare *vi* be patient

pazi'ente *a & nmf* patient

paziente'mente *adv* patiently

pazi'enza *nf* patience; ~! never mind!; **perdere la** ~ lose one's patience

'**pazza** *nf* madwoman

pazza'mente *adv* madly

pazzerel'lone, -a *nmf* madcap

paz'zesco *a* foolish; (*esagerato*) crazy

paz'zia *nf* madness; (*azione*) [act of] folly

'**pazzo** *a* mad; *fig* crazy; **sei** ~**?** you must be crazy!, are you crazy? ● *nm* madman; **essere** ~ **di/per** be crazy about; ~ **di gioia** mad with joy; **da pazzi** *fam* crackpot; **darsi alla pazza gioia** live it up

paz'zoide *a fam* whacky

P.C.I. *nm abbr* (**Partito Comunista Italiano**) Italian Communist Party

'**pecan** *nm inv* pecan

'**pecca** *nf* fault; **senza** ~ flawless

peccami'noso *a* sinful

pec'care *vi* sin; ~ **di** be guilty of ⟨*ingratitudine*⟩

pec'cato *nm* sin; ~ **che...** it's a pity that...; [**che**] ~! [what a] pity!. ~ **di gioventù** youthful folly

pecca|'tore, -'trice *nmf* sinner

'**pece** *nf* pitch; **nero come la** ~ black as pitch

pechi'nese *nm* Pekin[g]ese

Pe'chino *nf* Peking

'**pecora** *nf* sheep. ~ **nera** black sheep

peco'raio *nm* shepherd

peco'rella *nf* **cielo a pecorelle** sky full of fluffy white clouds. ~ **smarrita** lost sheep

peco'rino *nm* (*formaggio*) sheep's milk cheese

peculi'are *a* ~ **di** peculiar to

peculiarità *nf inv* peculiarity

pecuni'ario *a* money *attrib*

pe'daggio *nm* toll

pedago'gia *nf* pedagogy

peda'gogico *a* pedagogical

peda'gogo, -a *nmf* pedagogue

peda'lare *vi* pedal

peda'lata *nf* push on the pedals

pe'dale *nm* pedal. ~ **del freno** brake pedal

pedalò *nm inv* pedalo

pe'dana *nf* footrest; *Sport* springboard

pe'dante *a* pedantic

pedante'ria *nf* pedantry

pedan'tesco *a* pedantic

pe'data *nf* (*in calcio*) kick; (*impronta*) footprint

pede'rasta *nm* pederast

pe'destre *a* pedestrian

pedi'atra *nmf* paediatrician

pedia'tria *nf* paediatrics

pedi'atrico *a* paediatric

pedi'cure *nmf inv* chiropodist, podiatrist *Am* ● *nm* (*cura dei piedi*) pedicure

pedi'gree *nm inv* pedigree

pedi'luvio *nm* footbath

pe'dina *nf* (*alla dama*) piece; *fig* pawn

pedina'mento *nm* shadowing

pedi'nare *vt* shadow

pedofi'lia *nf* paedophilia

pe'dofilo, -a *nmf* paedophile

pedo'nale *a* pedestrian

pe'done, -a *nmf* pedestrian

pedula *nf* desert boot

peeling *nm inv* exfoliation treatment

'**peggio** *adv* worse; ~ **per te!** too bad!, tough!; ~ **di così** any worse; **la persona** ~

vestita the worst dressed person ● *a* worse; **niente di** ~ nothing worse; **stare** ~ **di** be worse off than ● *nm* **il** ~ **è che...** the worst of it is that...; **pensare al** ~ think the worst ● *nf* **alla** ~ at worst; **avere la** ~ get the worst of it; **alla meno** ~ as best I can

peggiora'mento *nm* worsening

peggio'rare *vt* make worse, worsen ● *vi* get worse, worsen

peggiora'tivo *a* pejorative

peggi'ore *a* worse; (*superlativo*) worst; **nella** ~ **delle ipotesi** if the worst comes to the worst; **tanto** ~ too bad ● *nmf* **il/la** ~ the worst

'**pegno** *nm* pledge; (*nei giochi di società*) forfeit; *fig* token; **dare qcsa in** ~ pawn sth; **in** ~ **d'amicizia** as a token of friendship

pelan'drone *nm* slob

pe'lare *vt* (*spennare*) pluck; (*spellare*) skin; (*sbucciare*) peel; (*fam: spillare denaro*) fleece

pe'larsi *vr fam* lose one's hair

pe'lati *nmpl* (*pomodori*) peeled tomatoes

pe'lato *a* (*calvo*) bald

pel'lame *nm* skins *pl*

'**pelle** *nf* skin; (*cuoio*) leather; (*buccia*) peel; **avere la** ~ **d'oca** have goose-flesh; **non stare più nella** ~ be beside oneself; **salvare la** ~ save one's skin; **lasciarci la** ~ buy it; **essere** ~ **e ossa** be all skin and bones; **avere la** ~ **dura** be tough; **borsa di** ~ leather bag. ~ **scamosciata** suede

pellegri'naggio *nm* pilgrimage

pelle'grino, -a *nmf* pilgrim

pelle'rossa *nmf* Red Indian, Redskin

pellette'ria *nf* leather goods *pl*

pelli'cano *nm* pelican

pellicce'ria *nf* furrier's [shop]

pel'liccia *nf* fur; (*indumento*) fur [coat]

pellicci'aio, -a *nmf* furrier

pel'licola *nf* Phot, Cinema film. ~ **a colori** colour film. ~ **trasparente** Culin cling film

'**pelo** *nm* hair; (*di animale*) coat; (*di lana*) pile; **per un** ~ by the skin of one's teeth; **cavarsela per un** ~ have a narrow escape; **cercare il** ~ **nell'uovo** nitpick

pe'loso *a* hairy

'**peltro** *nm* pewter

pe'luche *nm inv* **giocattolo di** ~ soft toy; **orsetto di** ~ teddy bear

pe'luria *nf* down

'**pelvico** *a* pelvic

'**pena** *nf* (*punizione*) punishment; (*sofferenza*) pain; (*dispiacere*) sorrow; (*disturbo*) trouble; **a mala** ~ hardly; **mi fa** ~ I pity him; **vale la** ~ **andare** it is worth [while] going. **pene** *pl* **dell'inferno** hellfire. ~ **di morte** death sentence

pe'nale *a* criminal; **diritto** ~ criminal law

pena'lista *nmf* criminal lawyer

penalità *nf inv* penalty

penaliz'zare *vt* penalize

penalizzazi'one *nf* (*penalità*) penalty

pe'nare *vi* suffer; (*faticare*) find it difficult

pen'daglio *nm* pendant

pen'dant *nm inv* **fare** ~ [**con**] match

pen'dente *a* hanging; *Comm* outstanding ● *nm* (*ciondolo*) pendant; **pendenti** *pl* drop earrings

pen'denza *nf* slope; *Comm* outstanding account

'**pendere** *vi* hang; (*superficie:*) slope; (*essere inclinato*) lean

pen'dio *nm* slope; **in** ~ sloping

'**pendola** *nf* clock

pendo'lare *a* pendulum ● *nmf* commuter

pendo'lino *nm* (*treno*) special, first class only, fast train

'**pendolo** *nm* pendulum; **orologio a** ~ pendulum clock

'**pene** *nm* penis

pene'trante *a* penetrating; (*freddo*) biting

pene'trare *vt/i* penetrate; (*trafiggere*) pierce ● *vt* (*odore:*) get into ● *vi* (*entrare furtivamente*) steal in

penetrazi'one *nf* penetration

penicil'lina *nf* penicillin

pe'nisola *nf* peninsula

peni'tente *a* & *nmf* penitent

peni'tenza *nf* penitence; (*punizione*) penance; (*in gioco*) forfeit

penitenzi'ario *nm* penitentiary

'**penna** *nf* (*da scrivere*) pen; (*di uccello*) feather. ~ **a feltro** felt-tip[ped pen]. ~ **ottica** light pen. ~ **a sfera** ball-point [pen]. ~ **stilografica** fountain-pen

pen'nacchio *nm* plume

penna'rello *nm* felt-tip[ped pen]

'**penne** *nfpl* pasta quills

pennel'lare *vt* paint

pennel'lata *nf* brushstroke

pen'nello *nm* brush; **a** ~ (*a perfezione*) perfectly. ~ **da barba** shaving brush

pen'nino *nm* nib

pen'none *nm* (*di bandiera*) flagpole

pen'nuto *a* feathered

pe'nombra *nf* half-light

pe'noso *a* (*fam: pessimo*) painful

pen'sabile *a* **non è** ~ it's unthinkable

pen'sare *vi* think; **penso di sì** I think so; ~ **a** think of; remember to (*chiudere il gas ecc*); **pensa ai fatti tuoi!** mind your own business!; **ci penso io** I'll take care of it; ~ **di fare qcsa** think of doing sth; **a pensarci bene** on second thoughts; ~ **tra sé e sé** think to oneself; **pensarci su** think over ● *vt* think

pen'sata *nf* idea

pensa|'tore, -'trice *nmf* thinker

pensi'ero *nm* thought; (*mente*) mind; (*preoccupazione*) worry; **stare in** ~ **per** be anxious about; **levarsi il** ~ to get something out of the way

pensie'roso *a* pensive

'**pensile** *a* hanging; **giardino** ~ roof-garden ● *nm* (*mobile*) wall unit

pensi'lina *nf* (*di fermata d'autobus*) bus shelter

pensio'nante *nmf* boarder; (*ospite pagante*) lodger

pensio'nato, -a *nmf* pensioner ● *nm* (*per*

anziani) [old folks'] home; (*per studenti*) hostel

pensi'one *nf* pension; (*albergo*) boarding-house; (*vitto e alloggio*) board and lodging; **andare in ~** retire; **essere in ~** be retired; **mezza ~** half board. **~ di anzianità** old-age pension. **~ completa** full board. **~ di invalidità** disability pension

pen'soso *a* pensive

pen'tagono *nm* pentagon; **il P~** the Pentagon

pen'tathlon *nm inv* pentathlon

Pente'coste *nf* Whitsun

penti'mento *nm* repentance

pen'tirsi *vr* **~ di** repent of; (*rammaricarsi*) regret

penti'tismo *nm* turning informant

pen'tito *nm* Mafioso turned informant

'pentola *nf* saucepan; (*contenuto*) potful. **~ a pressione** pressure cooker

pento'lino *nf* saucepan

pe'nultimo *a* last but one, penultimate

pe'nuria *nf* shortage

penzo'lare *vi* dangle

penzo'loni *adv* dangling

pe'onia *nf* peony

pepai'ola *nf* pepper pot

pe'pare *vt* pepper

pe'pato *a* peppery

'pepe *nm* pepper; **grano di ~** peppercorn. **~ di Caienna** cayenne pepper. **~ in grani** whole peppercorns. **~ macinato** ground pepper. **~ nero** black pepper

pepero'nata *nf dish of green peppers and tomatoes*

peperon'cino *nm* chilli pepper

pepe'rone *nm* [sweet] pepper; **rosso come un ~** red as a beetroot; **peperoni** *pl* **ripieni** stuffed peppers. **~ verde** green pepper

pepi'era *nf* pepper pot; (*macinino*) pepper mill

pe'pita *nf* nugget

'peptico *a* peptic

'per *prep* for; (*attraverso*) through; (*stato in luogo*) in, on; (*distributivo*) per; (*mezzo, entro*) by; (*causa*) with; (*in qualità di*) as; **mi è passato per la mente** it crossed my mind; **~ strada** on the street; **~ la fine del mese** by the end of the month; **in fila ~ due** in double file; **l'ho sentito ~ telefono** I spoke to him on the phone; **~ iscritto** in writing; **~ caso** by chance; **~ esempio** for example; **ho aspettato ~ ore** I've been waiting for hours; **~ tutta la durata del viaggio** for the entire journey; **~ tempo** in time; **~ sempre** forever; **~ scherzo** as a joke; **gridare ~ il dolore** scream with pain; **vendere ~ 10 milioni** sell for 10 million; **uno ~ volta** one at a time; **uno ~ uno** one by one; **venti ~ cento** twenty per cent; **~ fare qcsa** [in order to] do sth; **stare ~** be about to; **è troppo bello ~ essere vero** it's too good to be true

'pera *nf* pear; **farsi una ~** (*sl: di eroina*) shoot up

perbe'nismo *nm* prissiness

perbe'nista *a inv* prissy

per'calle *nm* gingham

per'cento *adv* per cent

percentu'ale *nf* percentage

perce'pibile *a* perceivable; (*somma*) payable

perce'pire *vt* perceive; (*riscuotere*) cash

percet'tibile *a* perceptible

percettibil'mente *adv* perceptibly

percezi'one *nf* perception

perché *conj* (*in interrogazioni*) why; (*per il fatto che*) because; (*affinché*) so that; **~ non vieni?** why don't you come?; **dimmi ~** tell me why; **~ no/sì!** because!; **la ragione ~ l'ho fatto** the reason [that] I did it, the reason why I did it; **è troppo difficile ~ lo possa capire** it's too difficult for me to understand ● *nm inv* reason [why]; **senza un ~** without any reason

perciò *conj* so

per'correre *vt* cover (*distanza*); (*viaggiare*) travel

percor'ribile *a* (*strada*) driveable, passable

percorribilità *nf* **~ delle strade** road conditions *pl*

per'corso *pp di* **percorrere** ● *nm* (*tragitto*) course, route; (*distanza*) distance; (*viaggio*) journey. **~ ecologico** nature trail. **~ di guerra** assault course. **~ a ostacoli** obstacle course

per'cossa *nf* blow; **percosse** *pl* Jur assault and battery

per'cosso *pp di* **percuotere**

percu'otere *vt* strike

percussi'one *nf* percussion; **strumenti a ~** percussion instruments

percussio'nista *nmf* percussionist

per'dente *nmf* loser

'perdere *vt* lose; (*sprecare*) waste; (*non prendere*) miss; (*fig: vizio:*) ruin; **~ tempo** waste time; **lascia ~!** forget it!; **~ di vista** lose touch [with each other] ● *vi* lose; (*recipiente:*) leak; **a ~** (*vuoto*) nonreturnable; **non avere niente da ~** have nothing to lose

'perdersi *vr* get lost; (*reciproco*) lose touch

perdifi'ato: a ~ *adv* (*gridare*) at the top of one's voice

perdigi'orno *nmf inv* idler

'perdita *nf* loss; (*spreco*) waste; (*falla*) leak; **a ~ d'occhio** as far as the eye can see; **chiudere in ~** (*azienda:*) show a loss. **~ di gas** gas leak. **~ di sangue** loss of blood, bleeding. **~ di tempo** waste of time

perdi'tempo *nm* waste of time

perdizi'one *nf* perdition

perdo'nare *vt* forgive; (*scusare*) excuse; **mi perdoni se interrompo** sorry to interrupt, excuse me for interrupting; **per farsi ~** as an apology ● *vi* **~ a qcno** forgive sb; **un male che non perdona** an incurable disease

per'dono *nm* forgiveness; Jur pardon; **chiedere ~** ask for forgiveness; (*scusarsi*) apologize

perdu'rare *vi* last; (*perseverare*) persist

perduta'mente *adv* hopelessly

per'duto *pp di* **perdere** ● *a* lost; (*rovinato*) ruined

pe'renne *a* everlasting; *Bot* perennial; **nevi perenni** perpetual snow

perenne'mente *adv* perpetually

peren'torio *a* peremptory

per'fetto *a* perfect ● *nm Gram* perfect [tense]

perfezio'nare *vt* perfect; (*migliorare*) improve

perfezio'narsi *vr* improve oneself; (*specializzarsi*) specialize

perfezi'one *nf* perfection; **alla ~** to perfection

perfezio'nismo *nm* perfectionism

perfezio'nista *nmf* perfectionist

per'fidia *nf* wickedness; (*atto*) wicked act

'perfido *a* treacherous; (*malvagio*) perverse

per'fino *adv* even

perfo'rare *vt* pierce; punch (*schede*); *Mech* drill

perfora'tore *nm* (*apparecchio*) punch. **~ di schede** card punch

perfora|'tore, -'trice *nmf* punch-card operator

perforazi'one *nf* perforation; (*di schede*) punching

per'formance *nf inv Theat* performance

perga'mena *nf* parchment

'pergola *nf* pergola

pergo'lato *nm* bower

periar'trite *nf* rheumatoid arthritis

perico'lante *a* precarious; (*azienda*) shaky

pe'ricolo *nm* danger; (*rischio*) risk; **mettere in ~** endanger; **essere fuori ~** be out of danger. **~ pubblico** danger to society. **~ di valanghe** danger of avalanches

pericolosa'mente *adv* dangerously

pericolosità *nf* danger

perico'loso *a* dangerous

peridu'rale *nf* epidural

perife'ria *nf* periphery; (*di città*) outskirts *pl*; *fig* fringes *pl*

peri'ferica *nf* peripheral; (*strada*) ring road. **~ di input** *Comput* input device

peri'ferico *a* peripheral; (*quartiere*) outlying

pe'rifrasi *nf inv* circumlocution

perime'trale *a* (*muro*) perimeter *attrib*

pe'rimetro *nm* perimeter

peri'odico *nm* periodical ● *a* periodical; (*vento, mal di testa, Math*) recurring

pe'riodo *nm* period; *Gram* sentence. **~ nero** bad patch. **~ di prova** trial period. **~ di ripensamento** cooling-off period. **~ di riposo** breathing space. **~ di transizione** transitional period, interim. **~ di validità** period of validity

peripe'zie *nfpl* misadventures

pe'rire *vi* perish

peri'scopio *nm* periscope

pe'rito, -a *a* skilled ● *nmf* expert. **~ agrario** agriculturalist. **~ di assicurazione** *Comm* loss adjuster. **~ edile** chartered surveyor. **~ elettronico** electronics engineer

perito'nite *nf* peritonitis

pe'rizia *nf* skill; (*valutazione*) survey

peri'zoma *nm inv* loincloth

'perla *nf* pearl. **~ coltivata** cultured pearl

per'lina *nf* bead

perli'nato *nm* matchboard

perlo'meno *adv* at least

perlu'strare *vt* patrol

perlustrazi'one *nf* patrol; **andare in ~** go on patrol

perma'loso *a* touchy

perma'nente *a* permanent ● *nf* perm; **farsi [fare] la ~** have a perm

perma'nenza *nf* permanence; (*soggiorno*) stay; **in ~** permanently. **~ in carica** tenure

perma'nere *vi* remain

perme'are *vt* permeate

perme'ato *a* **~ di** *fig* permeated with

per'messo *pp di* **permettere** ● *nm* permission; (*autorizzazione*) permit, licence; *Mil* leave; [**è**] **~?, con ~** (*posso entrare?*) may I come in?; (*posso passare?*) excuse me. **~ di lavoro** work permit. **~ di soggiorno** residence permit

per'mettere *vt* allow, permit; **potersi ~ qcsa** (*finanziariamente*) be able to afford sth

per'mettersi *vr* **~ di fare qcsa** allow oneself to do sth; **come si permette?** how dare you?

permis'sivo *a* permissive

permutazi'one *nf* exchange; *Math* permutation

per'nacchia *nf* (*sl: con la bocca*) raspberry *sl*

per'nice *nf* partridge

perni'cioso *a* pernicious

'perno *nm* pivot

pernot'tare *vi* stay overnight

'pero *nm* pear-tree

però *conj* but; (*tuttavia*) however

pe'rone *nm Anat* fibula

pero'rare *vt* plead

perpendico'lare *a & nf* perpendicular

perpe'trare *vt* perpetrate

per'petua *nf* (*di prete*) priest's housekeeper

perpetu'are *vt* perpetuate

per'petuo *a* perpetual

perplessità *nf inv* perplexity; (*dubbio*) doubt

per'plesso *a* perplexed

perqui'sire *vt* search

perquisizi'one *nf* search. **~ domiciliare** search of the premises

persecu|'tore, -'trice *nmf* persecutor

persecuzi'one *nf* persecution

persegu'ire *vt* pursue

persegui'tare *vt* persecute

persegui'tato, -a *nmf* victim of persecution

perseve'rante *a* persevering

perseve'ranza *nf* perseverance

perseve'rare *vi* persevere

'Persia *nf* Persia

persi'ana *nf* shutter. **~ avvolgibile** roller shutter

persi'ano, -a *a & nmf* Persian

'persico *a* Persian

per'sino *adv* = **perfino**

persi'stente *a* persistent; ⟨*dubbio*⟩ nagging

persi'stenza *nf* persistence

per'sistere *vi* persist; **~ nel fare qcsa** persist in doing sth

'perso *pp di* **perdere ●** *a* lost; **a tempo ~** in one's spare time

per'sona *nf* person; ⟨*un tale*⟩ somebody; **di ~, in ~** in person, personally; **per ~** per person, a head; **per interposta ~** through an intermediary; **curare la propria ~** look after oneself, look after number one; **persone** *pl* people. **~ a carico** dependant. **~ di colore** nonwhite, coloured person. **~ giuridica** legal person. **~ di servizio** domestic

perso'naggio *nm* ⟨*persona di riguardo*⟩ personality; *Theat ecc* character

perso'nale *a* personal **●** *nm* staff; ⟨*aspetto*⟩ build. **~ di terra** ground crew

personalità *nf inv* personality

personaliz'zare *vt* customize ⟨*auto ecc*⟩; personalize ⟨*penna ecc*⟩

personifi'care *vt* personify

personificazi'one *nf* personification

perspi'cace *a* shrewd

perspi'cacia *nf* shrewdness

persua'dere *vt* convince; impress ⟨*critici*⟩; **~ qcno a fare qcsa** persuade sb to do sth

persuasi'one *nf* persuasion; **fare opera di ~ su qcno** try to persuade sb

persuasività *nf* persuasiveness

persua'sivo *a* persuasive

persu'aso *pp di* **persuadere**

persua'sore *nm* persuader

per'tanto *conj* therefore

'pertica *nf* pole

perti'nace *a* pertinacious

perti'nente *a* relevant

per'tosse *nf* whooping cough

per'tugio *nm* opening

pertur'bare *vt* perturb

perturbazi'one *nf* disturbance. **~ atmosferica** atmospheric disturbance

Perù *nm* Peru

peruvi'ano, -a *a & nmf* Peruvian

per'vadere *vt* pervade

perva'sivo *a* pervasive

per'vaso *pp di* **pervadere**

perven'ire *vi* reach; **far ~ qcsa a qcno** send sth to sb

perversa'mente *adv* perversely

perversi'one *nf* perversion

perversità *nf* perversity

per'verso *a* perverse

perver'tire *vt* pervert

perver'tirsi *vr* ⟨*gusti, costumi:*⟩ become debased

perver'tito *a* perverted **●** *nm* pervert

pervi'cace *a* obstinate

pervicace'mente *adv* obstinately

pervi'cacia *nf* obstinacy

per'vinca *nm* ⟨*colore*⟩ blue with a touch of purple

per'vinca *nf Bot* periwinkle

p. es. *abbr* ⟨**per esempio**⟩ e.g.

'pesa *nf* weighing; ⟨*bilancia*⟩ weighing machine; ⟨*per veicoli*⟩ weighbridge

pe'sante *a* heavy; ⟨*stomaco*⟩ overfull; ⟨*accusa, ingiuria*⟩ serious; ⟨*noioso*⟩ boring; **andarci ~ con qcno** be heavy-handed with sb **●** *adv* ⟨*vestirsi*⟩ warmly

pesante'mente *adv* ⟨*cadere*⟩ heavily; ⟨*insultare*⟩ seriously

pesan'tezza *nf* heaviness

pesaper'sone *nm inv* scales

pe'sare *vt* weigh; **~ le parole** weigh one's words **●** *vi* weigh; ⟨*essere pesante*⟩ be heavy; **~ su** *fig* lie heavy on

pe'sarsi *vr* weigh oneself

'pesca[1] *nf* ⟨*frutto*⟩ peach

'pesca[2] *nf* fishing; **andare a ~** go fishing. **~ di beneficenza** lucky dip. **~ con la lenza** angling. **~ subaquea** underwater fishing

pe'scare *vt* ⟨*andare a pesca di*⟩ fish for; ⟨*prendere*⟩ catch; ⟨*fam: trovare*⟩ dig up, find; **guai se ti pesco!** there will be trouble if I catch you!

pesca'tore *nm* fisherman. **~ di frodo** poacher. **~ di perle** pearl diver

'pesce *nm* fish; **non sapere che pesci pigliare** *fig* not know which way to turn; **prendere qcno a pesci in faccia** *fig* treat sb like dirt; **sentirsi un ~ fuor d'acqua** feel like a fish out of water. **~ d'aprile!** April Fool!. **~ in carpione** soused fish. **~ al cartoccio** fish baked in foil. **~ gatto** catfish. **~ grosso** *fig* big fish. **~ persico** perch. **~ piccolo** *fig* small fry. **~ rosso** goldfish. **~ spada** swordfish

pesce'cane *nm* shark

pesche'reccio *nm* fishing boat

pesche'ria *nf* fishmonger's [shop]

peschi'era *nf* fish-pond

'Pesci *nmpl Astr* Pisces

pescio'lino *nm* **~ d'acqua dolce** minnow

pesci'vendolo *nm* fishmonger

'pesco *nm* peach tree

pe'scoso *a* teeming with fish

pe'seta *nf* peseta

pe'sista *nm* ⟨*in sollevamento pesi*⟩ weightlifter; ⟨*in lancio del peso*⟩ shotputter

'peso *nm* weight; **essere di ~ per qcno** be a burden to sb; **alzare di ~** lift up in one go; **avere un ~ sullo stomaco** have a lead weight on one's stomach; **di poco ~** ⟨*senza importanza*⟩ not very important; **non dare ~ a qcsa** not attach any importance to sth. **~ massimo** ⟨*nel pugilato*⟩ heavy weight. **~ medio** ⟨*nel pugilato*⟩ middleweight. **~ morto** dead weight. **~ netto** net weight. **~ piuma** ⟨*nel pugilato*⟩ featherweight **~ specifico** specific gravity

pessi'mismo *nm* pessimism

pessi'mista *nmf* pessimist **●** *a* pessimistic

pessimistica'mente *adv* pessimistically

'pessimo *a* very bad

pe'staggio *nm* beating-up

pe'stare vt tread on; (*picchiare*) beat; crush ⟨*aglio, prezzemolo, uva*⟩; ~ **i piedi** [**per terra**] stamp one's feet [on the ground]; ~ **un piede a qcno** tread on sb's foot

pe'stata nf bash; **dare una ~ a un piede a qcno** tread on sb's foot

'peste nf plague; (*persona*) pest; **dire ~ e corna di qcno** tear sb to bits. ~ **bubbonica** bubonic plague

pe'stello nm pestle

pesti'cida nm pesticide

pe'stifero a (*fastidioso*) pestilential

pesti'lenza nf pestilence; (*fetore*) stench, stink

pestilenzi'ale a ⟨*odore, aria*⟩ noxious

'pesto a ground; **occhio ~** black eye ● nm basil and garlic sauce

'petalo nm petal

pe'tardo nm banger

petizi'one nf petition; **fare una ~** draw up a petition

petrol'chimico a petrochemical

petrol'dollaro nm petrodollar

petroli'era nf [oil] tanker

petroli'ere nm oilman

petro'lifero a oil-bearing

pe'trolio nm oil

pettego'lare vi gossip

pettego'lezzo nm piece of gossip; **pettegolezzi** pl gossip sg; **far pettegolezzi** gossip

pet'tegolo, -a a gossipy ● nmf gossip

petti'nare vt comb

petti'narsi vr comb one's hair

petti'natura nf combing; (*acconciatura*) hairstyle. ~ **a caschetto** bob

'pettine nm comb

'petting nm petting

petti'nino nm (*fermaglio*) comb

petti'rosso nm robin [redbreast]

'petto nm chest; (*seno*) breast; **a doppio ~** double-breasted; **prendere qcsa/qcno di ~** face up to sth/sb. ~ **pl di pollo** chicken breasts

petto'rale nm Sport number ● a pectoral

petto'rina nf (*di salopette*) bib

petto'ruto a ⟨*donna*⟩ full-breasted; ⟨*uomo*⟩ broad-chested

petu'lante a impertinent

petu'lanza nf impertinence

pe'tunia nf petunia

'pezza nf cloth; (*toppa*) patch; (*rotolo di tessuto*) roll; **trattare qcno come una ~ da piedi** walk all over sb. ~ **d'appoggio** voucher. ~ **giustificativa** voucher

pez'zato a ⟨*cavallo, mucca*⟩ piebald

pez'zente nmf tramp; (*avaro*) miser

'pezzo nm piece; (*parte*) part; Mus piece. **un bel ~ d'uomo** a fine figure of a man; **un ~** (*di tempo*) some time; (*di spazio*) a long way; **al ~** ⟨*costare*⟩ each; **essere a pezzi** (*stanco*) be shattered; **fare a pezzi** tear to shreds; **andare in mille pezzi** break into a thousand pieces; **cadere a pezzi** fall to pieces, fall to bits. ~ **forte** centre-piece. **pezzi** pl **grossi**

top brass. ~ **grosso** bigwig, big shot. ~ **di imbecille** stupid idiot. ~ **di ricambio** spare [part]

pezzu'ola nf scrap of material

photo'fitᴿ nm inv Photofit

pia'cente a attractive

pia'cere nm pleasure; (*favore*) favour; **a ~** as much as one likes; **per ~!** please!; ~ **[di conoscerla]**! (*nelle presentazioni*) pleased to meet you!; **con ~** with pleasure; **fare un ~ a qcno** do sb a favour ● vi **la Scozia mi piace** I like Scotland; **mi piacciono i dolci** I like sweets; **mi piacerebbe venire** I'd like to come; **faccio come mi pare e piace** I do as I please; **ti piace?** do you like it?; **lo spettacolo è piaciuto** the show was a success

pia'cevole a pleasant

piacevol'mente adv agreeably

piaci'mento nm **a ~** as much as you like

pia'dina nf unleavened focaccia bread

pi'aga nf sore; fig scourge; (*fig: persona noiosa*) pain; (*fig: ricordo doloroso*) wound

pia'gato a covered with sores

piagni'steo nm whining

piagnuco'lare vi whimper

piagnuco'lio nm whimpering

piagnuco'loso a maudlin

pi'alla nf plane

pial'lare vt plane

pialla'tura nf planing

pi'ana nf (*pianura*) plane

pianeggi'ante a level

piane'rottolo nm landing

pia'neta nm planet

pi'angere vi cry; (*disperatamente*) weep; **mi piange il cuore** my heart bleeds; **mettersi a ~ come una fontana** turn the waterworks on; ~ **sul latte versato** cry over spilt milk ● vt (*lamentare*) lament; (*per un lutto*) mourn; ~ **la morte di qcno** mourn sb's death

pianifi'care vt plan

pianificazi'one nf planning. ~ **aziendale** corporate planning. ~ **familiare** family planning

pia'nista nmf Mus pianist

pi'ano a flat; (*a livello*) flush; (*regolare*) smooth; (*facile*) easy; **i 400 metri piani** the 400 metres flat race ● adv slowly; (*con cautela*) gently; (*sottovoce*) quietly; **andarci ~** go carefully ● nm plain; (*di edificio*) floor, storey; (*livello*) plane; (*progetto*) plan; Mus piano; **di primo ~** first-rate; **primo ~** Phot close-up; **in ~ piano** in the foreground; **essere/mettersi in ~ piano** fig take/occupy centre-stage; **secondo ~** middle distance. ~ **d'emergenza** contingency plan. ~ **di lavoro** work surface; (*programma*) work schedule. ~ **di pensionamento** pension plan, pension scheme. ~ **regolatore** town plan. ~ **di sopra** upstairs. ~ **di sotto** downstairs. ~ **di studi** syllabus. ~ **superiore** upper floor

piano'forte nm piano. ~ **bar** piano bar. ~ **a**

coda grand [piano]. **~ verticale** upright [piano]

pia'nolaᴿ *nf* pianola

piano'terra *nm inv* ground floor, first floor *Am*

pi'anta *nf* plant; (*del piede*) sole; (*disegno*) plan; (*di città*) map; **di sana ~** (*totalmente*) entirely; **in ~ stabile** permanently. **~ da appartamento** house-plant. **~ stradale** road map

piantagi'one *nf* plantation

pianta'grane *nmf fam* **è un/una ~** he's/she's bolshy

pian'tare *vt* plant; (*conficcare*) drive; pitch ‹*tenda*›; (*fam: abbandonare*) dump; **piantala!** *fam* stop it!; **piantato in** ‹*spina, chiodo*› embedded in; **~ baracca e burattini** drop everything; (*per sempre*) chuck everything in

pian'tarsi *vr* plant oneself; (*fam: lasciarsi*) leave each other

pianta|'tore, -'trice *nmf* planter

pianter'reno *nm* ground floor, first floor *Am*

pi'anto *pp di* **piangere** ● *nm* crying; (*disperato*) weeping; (*lacrime*) tears *pl*

pianto'nare *vt* guard

pian'tone *nm* guard; **stare di ~** stand guard; **mettere di ~** put on guard. **~ dello sterzo** *Auto* steering column

pia'nura *nf* plain. **~ padana** Po valley

pi'astra *nf* plate; (*lastra*) slab; *Culin* griddle. **~ elettronica** circuit board. **~ madre** *Comput* motherboard. **~ di registrazione** cassette deck

pia'strella *nf* tile

pia'strina *nf Mil* identity disc; *Med* platelet; *Comput* chip. **~ di riconoscimento** identity tag. **~ di silicio** silicon chip

piatta'forma *nf* platform. **~ di lancio** launch pad. **~ petrolifera** oil platform, offshore rig. **~ rivendicativa** *o* **sindacale** union claims *pl*

piat'tino *nm* saucer

pi'atto *a* flat; (*monotono*) dull ● *nm* plate; (*da portata, vivanda*) dish; (*portata*) course; (*parte piatta*) flat; (*di giradischi*) turntable; (*di bilancia*) pan. **piatti** *pl Mus* cymbals; **lavare i piatti** do the dishes, do the washing-up. **piatti** *pl* **caldi** hot dishes. **piatti** *pl* **carne** meat dishes. **~ fondo** soup plate. **~ del giorno** dish of the day. **~ piano** [ordinary] plate. **~ di portata** serving dish, server. **~ unico** cold sliced meat with pickles

pi'azza *nf* square; *Comm* market; **letto a una ~** single bed; **letto a due piazze** double bed; **far ~ pulita** make a clean sweep; **mettere qcsa in ~** *fig* make sth public; **scendere in ~** *fig* take to the streets. **~ d'armi** parade ground. **~ del mercato** market square. **P~ San Pietro** St Peter's Square

piazza'forte *nf* stronghold

piaz'zale *nm* large square

piazza'mento *nm* (*in classifica*) placing

piaz'zare *vt* place

piaz'zarsi *vr Sport* be placed; **~ secondo** come second, be placed second

piaz'zato *a* ‹*cavallo*› placed; **ben ~** (*robusto*) well-built

piaz'zista *nm* salesman ● *nf* saleswoman

piaz'z[u]ola *nf* **~ di partenza** (*nel golf*) tee. **~ di sosta** pull-in

pic'cante *a* hot; (*pungente*) sharp; (*salace*) spicy

pic'carsi *vr* (*risentirsi*) take offence; **~ di** (*vantarsi di*) claim to

pic'cata *nf* veal in sour lemon sauce

'picche *nfpl* (*in carte*) spades

picchet'taggio *nm* picketing

picchet'tare *vt* stake; ‹*scioperanti:*› picket

pic'chetto *nm* picket

picchi'are *vt* hit; **~ la testa** (**contro qcsa**) bang *o* hit one's head (against sth) ● *vi* (*bussare*) knock; *Aeron* nosedive; **~ in testa** ‹*motore:*› knock

picchi'arsi *vr* **~ il petto** beat one's breast

picchi'ata *nf* beating; *Aeron* nosedive; **scendere in ~** nosedive

picchi'ato *a* (*matto*) touched

picchia'tore *nm* goon

picchiet'tare *vt* tap; (*punteggiare*) spot

picchiet'tato *a* spotted

picchiet'tio *nm* tapping

'picchio *nm* woodpecker

pic'cino *a* tiny; (*gretto*) mean; (*di poca importanza*) petty ● *nm* little one, child

piccion'cini *nmpl fam* lovebirds; **fare i ~** get all lovey-dovey

picci'one *nm* pigeon; **prendere due piccioni con una fava** kill two birds with one stone. **~ viaggiatore** carrier pigeon

'picco *nm* peak; **a ~** vertically; **colare a ~** sink

picco'lezza *nf* (*di persona, ambiente*) smallness; (*grettezza*) meanness; (*inezia*) trifle

'piccolo, -a *a* small, little; ‹*vacanza, pausa*› little, short; (*di statura*) short; (*gretto*) petty ● *nmf* child, little one; **da ~** as a child; **in ~** in miniature; **nel mio ~** in my own small way

pic'cone *nm* pickaxe. **~ da ghiaccio** ice pick

pic'cozza *nf* ice axe

pic'nic *nm inv* picnic

pi'docchio *nm* louse

pidocchi'oso *a* flea-bitten; (*fam: avaro*) stingy ● *nm fam* miser

piè *nm inv* **a ~ di pagina** at the foot of the page; **saltare a ~ pari** skip; **ad ogni ~ sospinto** all the time, endlessly

pi'ede *nm* foot; (*di armadio, letto*) leg; **a piedi** on foot; **andare a piedi** walk; **a piedi nudi** barefoot; **avere i piedi piatti** have flat feet, be flat-footed; **a ~ libero** free; **in piedi** standing; **alzarsi in piedi** stand up; **in punta di piedi** on tiptoe; **ai piedi di** ‹*montagna*› at the foot of; **avere qcno ai propri piedi** have sb at one's feet; **essere sul ~ di guerra** be ready for action; ‹*nazione:*› be on war footing; **prendere ~** *fig* gain ground; ‹*moda:*› catch on; **partire col ~ sbagliato** get off on the wrong foot; **mettere in piedi** (*allestire*) set up; **togliti dai piedi!** get out of the way!. **~ di insalata** head of lettuce. **~ di porco** (*strumento*) jemmy

pie'dino *nm* **fare ~ a qcno** *fam* play footsie with sb

piedi'stallo *nm* pedestal

pi'ega *nf* (*piegatura*) fold; (*di gonna*) pleat; (*di pantaloni*) crease; (*grinza*) wrinkle; (*andamento*) turn; **a pieghe** with pleats, pleated; **non fare una ~** (*ragionamento:*) be flawless; (*persona:*) not bat an eyelid; **prendere una brutta ~** get into bad ways

pie'gare *vt* fold; (*flettere*) bend ● *vi* bend

pie'garsi *vr* bend; **~ a** *fig* yield to

piega'tura *nf* folding; (*piega*) fold

pieghet'tare *vt* pleat

pieghet'tato *a* pleated

pie'ghevole *a* pliable; (*tavolo*) folding ● *nm* leaflet

Pie'monte *nm* Piedmont

piemon'tese *a* & *nmf* Piedmontese

pi'ena *nf* (*di fiume*) flood; (*folla*) crowd

pi'eno *a* full; (*massiccio*) solid; **in piena estate** in the middle of summer; **a pieni voti** (*diplomarsi*) ≈ with A-grades, with first class honours ● *nm* (*colmo*) height; (*carico*) full load; **in ~** (*completamente*) fully; **fare il ~** (*di benzina*) fill up; **nel ~ delle forze** in top physical form

pie'none *nm* **c'era il ~** the place was packed

pietà *nf* pity; (*misericordia*) mercy; **senza ~** (*persona*) pitiless; (*spietatamente*) pitilessly; **avere ~ di qcno** take pity on sb; **far ~** (*far pena*) be pitiful; (*fam: essere orrendo*) be useless

pie'tanza *nf* dish

pie'toso *a* pitiful, merciful; (*fam: pessimo*) terrible

pi'etra *nf* stone. **~ dura** semiprecious stone. **~ preziosa** precious stone. **~ dello scandalo** cause of the scandal

pie'traia *nf* scree

pie'trame *nm* stones *pl*

pietrifi'care *vt* petrify

pie'trina *nf* (*di accendino*) flint

pie'troso *a* stony

'piffero *nm* fife

pigi'ama *nm* pyjamas *pl*, pajamas *Am*

'pigia 'pigia *nm inv* crowd, crush

pigi'are *vt* press

pigia'trice *nf* winepress

pigi'one *nf* rent; **dare a ~** let, rent out; **prendere a ~** rent

pigli'are *vt* (*fam: afferrare*) catch

'piglio *nm* air

pig'mento *nm* pigment

pig'meo, -a *a* & *nmf* pygmy

'pigna *nf* cone. **~ di abete** fir cone

pi'gnolo *a* pedantic

pignora'mento *nm* Jur distraint

pigno'rare *vt* Jur distrain upon

pigo'lare *vi* chirp

pigo'lio *nm* chirping

pigra'mente *adv* lazily

pi'grizia *nf* laziness

'pigro *a* lazy; (*intelletto*) slow

PIL *abbr* (**prodotto interno lordo**) GDP

'pila *nf* pile; *Electr* battery; (*fam: lampadina tascabile*) torch; (*vasca*) basin; **a pile** battery operated, battery powered

pi'lastro *nm* pillar

'pillola *nf* pill; **prendere la ~** be on the pill. **~ del giorno dopo** morning-after pill

pi'lone *nm* pylon; (*di ponte*) pier

pi'lota *nmf* pilot. **~ automatico** automatic pilot. **~ di caccia** fighter pilot ● *nm* Auto driver ● *a inv* **progetto ~** pilot project

pilo'taggio *nm* flying; **cabina di ~** flight deck

pilo'tare *vt* pilot; drive (*auto*)

pinaco'teca *nf* art gallery

'Pinco Pal'lino *nm* so-and-so

pi'neta *nf* pine-wood

ping-'pong *nm* table tennis, ping-pong *fam*

'pingue *a* fat

pingu'edine *nf* fatness

pingu'ino *nm* penguin; (*gelato*) choc ice on a stick

'pinna *nf* fin; (*per nuotare*) flipper

pi'nacolo *nm* pinnacle

'pino *nm* pine[-tree]. **~ marittimo** cluster pine, maritime pine

pi'nolo *nm* pine kernel

'pinta *nf* pint

pin-'up *nf inv* pin-up [girl]

'pinza *nf* pliers *pl*; *Med* forceps *pl*; **prendere qcsa con le pinze** *fig* treat sth cautiously

pin'zare *vt* (*con pinzatrice*) staple

pin'zatrice *nf* stapler

pin'zette *nfpl* tweezers

pinzi'monio *nm* sauce for crudités

'pio *a* pious; (*benefico*) charitable

piogge'rella *nf* drizzle

pi'oggia *nf* rain; (*fig: di pietre, insulti*) hail, shower; **sotto la ~** in the rain. **~ acida** acid rain. **~ radioattiva** radioactive fallout

pi'olo *nm* (*di scala*) rung

piom'bare *vi* fall heavily; **~ su** fall upon; **~ all'improvviso nella stanza** suddenly burst into the room ● *vt* **~ qcno nella disperazione** plunge sb into despair

piom'bino *nm* (*sigillo*) [lead] seal; (*da pesca*) sinker; (*in gonne*) weight

pi'ombo *nm* lead; (*sigillo*) [lead] seal; **a ~** plumb; **senza ~** (*benzina*) lead-free; **avere un sonno di ~** be a very heavy sleeper; **andare con i piedi di ~** tread carefully; **anni di ~** *years when terrorism was at its height*

pioni'ere, -a *nmf* pioneer

pi'oppo *nm* poplar

pior'rea *nf* pyorrhoea

pio'vano *a* **acqua piovana** rainwater

pi'overe *vi* rain; **~ it's raining; **~ addosso a qcno** (*guai, debiti:*) rain down on sb; **non ci piove [sopra]** *fam* that's for sure

pioviggi'nare *vi* drizzle

pio'voso *a* rainy

pi'ovra *nf* octopus

pio'vuto *a* ~ **dal cielo** fallen into one's lap

'**pipa** *nf* pipe

pipe'rito *a* **menta piperita** peppermint

pipi *nf* **fare [la]** ~ pee, piddle; **andare a fare [la]** ~ go for a pee

pipi'strello *nm* bat

piqué *nm inv* piqué

'**pira** *nf* pyre

pi'ramide *nf* pyramid

pi'ranha *nf inv* piranha

pi'rata *nm* pirate. ~ **della strada** hit-and-run driver; (*prepotente*) road-hog ● *a inv* pirate

pirate'ria *nf* piracy. ~ **informatica** hacking

pi'rite *nf* pyrite

piro'etta *nf* pirouette

pi'rofila *nf* (*tegame*) oven-proof dish

pi'rofilo *a* heat-resistant

pi'romane *nmf* pyromaniac

piroma'nia *nf* pyromania

pi'roscafo *nm* steamer. ~ **di linea** liner

'**piscia** *nf* *vulg* piss

pisci'are *vi* *vulg* piss

pisci'ata *nf* *vulg* piss

pi'scina *nf* [swimming] pool. ~ **coperta** indoor [swimming] pool. ~ **gonfiabile** [inflatable] paddling pool. ~ **olimpionica** Olympic [swimming] pool. ~ **scoperta** outdoor [swimming] pool, lido

pi'sello *nm* pea; (*fam: pene*) willie. **piselli** *pl* **odorosi** sweetpeas

piso'lino *nm* nap; **fare un** ~ have a nap

'**pista** *nf* track; *Aeron* runway, tarmac; (*orma*) footprint; (*sci*) slope, piste. ~ **da ballo** dance floor. ~ **ciclabile** cycle track. ~ **da fondo** cross-country ski track. ~ **da pattinaggio** ice rink. ~ **per principianti** nursery slope. ~ **da sci** ski slope, ski run, piste. ~ **per slitte** toboggan run

pi'stacchio *nm* pistachio

pi'stola *nf* pistol; (*per spruzzare*) spray-gun. ~ **a capsule** cap gun. ~ **a spruzzo** paint spray. ~ **a tamburo** revolver

pisto'lero *nm* gunslinger

pi'stone *nm* piston

pi'tone *nm* python

pitto'gramma *nm* pictogram

pit'tore, -'trice *nmf* painter

pitto'resco *a* picturesque

pit'torico *a* pictorial

pit'tura *nf* painting. **pitture** *pl* **di guerra** warpaint. ~ **rupestre** cave painting

pittu'rare *vt* paint

pitui'tario *a* pituitary

più *adv* more; (*superlativo*) most; *Math* plus; ~ **importante** more important; **il** ~ **importante** the most important; ~ **caro/ grande** dearer/bigger; **il** ~ **caro/grande** the dearest/biggest; **di** ~ more; **una coperta in** ~ an extra blanket; **non ho** ~ **soldi** I don't have any more money; **non vive** ~ **a Milano**

he no longer lives in Milan; ~ **o meno** more or less; **il** ~ **lentamente possibile** as slow as possible; **al** ~ **presto** as soon as possible; **per di** ~ what's more; **mai** ~! never again!; ~ **di** more than; **sempre** ~ more and more ● *a* more; (*superlativo*) most; ~ **tempo** more time; **la classe con** ~ **alunni** the class with most pupils; ~ **volte** several times ● *nm* most; *Math* plus sign; **il** ~ **è fatto** the worst is over; **parlare del** ~ **e del meno** make small talk; **i** ~ the majority

piuccheper'fetto *nm* pluperfect

pi'uma *nf* feather

piu'maggio *nm* plumage

piu'mato *a* plumed

piu'mino *nm* (*di cigni*) down; (*copriletto*) eiderdown; (*per cipria*) powder-puff; (*per spolverare*) feather duster; (*giacca*) down jacket

piu'mone[R] *nm* duvet, continental quilt

piut'tosto *adv* rather; (*invece*) instead

'**piva** *nf* **con le pive nel sacco** empty-handed

pi'vello *nm* *fam* greenhorn

'**pivot** *nm inv* (*in pallacanestro*) centre

'**pizza** *nf* pizza; *Cinema* reel; (*fam: noia*) bore. ~ **margherita** tomato and mozzarella pizza. ~ **marinara** pizza with tomato, oregano, garlic and anchovies. ~ **napoletana** pizza with tomato, mozzarella and anchovies. ~ **quattro stagioni** pizza with tomato, mozzarella, ham, mushrooms and baby artichokes

pizzai'ola: alla ~ with tomatoes, garlic and oregano

pizze'ria *nf* pizza restaurant, pizzeria

piz'zetta *nf* small pizza

pizzi'care *vt* pinch; (*pungere*) sting; (*di sapore*) taste sharp; (*fam: sorprendere*) catch; *Mus* pluck ● *vi* scratch; ⟨*cibo:*⟩ be spicy

'**pizzico, pizzi'cotto** *nm* pinch

'**pizzo** *nm* lace; (*di montagna*) peak

pla'care *vt* placate; assuage ⟨*fame, dolore*⟩

pla'carsi *vr* calm down

'**placca** *nf* plate; (*commemorativa, dentale*) plaque; *Med* patch. ~ **batterica** plaque

plac'care *vt* plate

plac'cato *a* ~ **d'argento** silver-plated. ~ **d'oro** gold-plated

placca'tura *nf* plating

pla'cebo *nm inv* placebo; **effetto** ~ placebo effect

pla'centa *nf* placenta, afterbirth

'**placido** *a* placid

pla'fond *nm inv* *Comm* ceiling

plafoni'era *nf* ceiling light

plagi'are *vt* plagiarize; pressure ⟨*persona*⟩

'**plagio** *nm* plagiarism

plaid *nm inv* tartan rug

pla'nare *vi* glide

'**plancia** *nf* *Naut* bridge; (*passerella*) gang-plank

'**plancton** *nm* plankton

plane'tario *a* planetary ● *nm* planetarium

pla'smare *vt* mould

'**plastica** *nf* (*materia*) plastic; *Med* plastic

surgery; (*arte*) plastic art; **sacchetto di ~** plastic bag

'**plastico** *a* plastic; ⟨*rappresentazione*⟩ three-dimensional ● *nm* plastic model

'**platano** *nm* plane tree

pla'**tea** *nf* stalls *pl*; (*pubblico*) audience

'**platino** *nm* platinum

pla'**tonico** *a* platonic

plau'**sibile** *a* plausible; **poco ~** implausible

plausibi'**lità** *nf* plausibility

'**plauso** *nm* (*consenso*) approval

play'**back** *nm* **cantare in ~** mime

play'**boy** *nm inv* playboy

play'**maker** *nm inv Sport* playmaker

p.le *abbr* (**piazzale**) Sq.

ple'**baglia** *nf pej* mob

'**plebe** *nf* common people

ple'**beo, -a** *a & nmf* plebeian

plebi'**scito** *nm* plebiscite

ple'**nario** *a* plenary

pleni'**lunio** *nm* full moon

'**plettro** *nm* plectrum

pleu'**rite** *nf* pleurisy

'**plico** *nm* packet; **in ~ a parte** under separate cover

plissé *a inv* plissé; ⟨*gonna*⟩ accordeon pleated

plop *nm inv* plop; **fare ~** plop

plo'**tone** *nm* platoon; (*di ciclisti*) group. **~ d'esecuzione** firing squad

'**plotter** *nm inv Comput* plotter. **~ da tavolo** flatbed plotter

'**plumbeo** *a* leaden

plum-'**cake** *nm inv* fruit cake

plu'**rale** *a & nm* plural; **al ~** in the plural

plurali'**tà** *nf* (*maggioranza*) majority

pluridiscipli'**nare** *a* multidisciplinary

plurien'**nale** *a* **~ esperienza** many years' experience

plurigemel'**lare** *a* ⟨*parto*⟩ multiple

pluripar'**titico** *a Pol* multi-party

plu'**tonio** *nm* plutonium

pluvi'**ale** *a* rain *attrib*

pluvi'**ometro** *nm* rain gauge

pneu'**matico** *a* pneumatic ● *nm* tyre. **~ radiale** radial [tyre]

pneu'**monia** *nf* pneumonia

PNL *abbr* (**prodotto nazionale lordo**) GNP

Po *nm* Po

po' *vedi* poco

po'**chette** *nf inv* clutch bag

po'**chino** *nm* **un ~** a little bit

'**poco** *a* little; ⟨*tempo*⟩ short; (*con nomi plurali*) few ● *pron* little; (*poco tempo*) a short time; (*plurale*) few ● *nm* little; **un po'** a little [bit]; **un po' di** a little, some; (*con nomi plurali*) a few; **a ~ a ~** a little by little; **fra ~** soon; **per ~** (*a poco prezzo*) cheap; (*quasi*) nearly; **~ fa** a little while ago; **sono arrivato da ~** I have just arrived; **un bel po'** quite a lot; **un bel po' di più/meno** quite a lot more/less; **un ~ di buono** a shady character ● *adv* (*con verbi*) not much; (*con avverbi, aggettivi*) not very; **parla ~** he doesn't speak much; **lo conosco ~** I don't know him very well; **~ spesso** not very often

po'**dere** *nm* farm

pode'**roso** *a* powerful

'**podio** *nm* dais; *Mus* podium

po'**dismo** *nm* walking

po'**dista** *nmf* walker

po'**ema** *nm* poem. **~ epico** epic [poem]. **~ sinfonico** symphonic poem

poe'**sia** *nf* poetry; (*componimento*) poem

po'**eta** *nm* poet

poe'**tessa** *nf* poetess

po'**etico** *a* poetic

poggiapi'**edi** *nm inv* footrest

poggi'**are** *vt* lean; (*posare*) place ● *vi* **~ su** be based on

poggia'**testa** *nm inv* head-rest

'**poggio** *nm* hillock

poggi'**olo** *nm* balcony

'**poi** *adv* (*dopo*) then; (*più tardi*) later [on]; (*finalmente*) finally. **d'ora in ~** from now on; **questa ~!** well! ● *nm* **pensare al ~** think of the future

poi'**ché** *conj* since

pois *nm inv* **a ~** polka-dot

'**poker** *nm* poker

po'**lacco, -a** *a* Polish ● *nmf* Pole ● *nm* (*lingua*) Polish

po'**lare** *a* polar

polari'**tà** *nf inv* polarity

polariz'**zare** *vt* polarize

'**polca** *nf* polka

po'**lemica** *nf* controversy

polemica'**mente** *adv* controversially

polemiciz'**zare** *vi* engage in controversy

po'**lemico** *a* controversial

po'**lenta** *nf* cornmeal porridge

poli'**clinico** *nm* general hospital

policro'**mia** *nf* polychromy

po'**licromo** *a* polychrome

poli'**estere** *nm* polyester

polieti'**lene** *nm* polyethylene

poliga'**mia** *nf* polygamy

poli'**gamico** *a* polygamous

po'**ligamo** *a* polygamous

poli'**glotta** *nmf* polyglot

po'**ligono** *nm* polygon; (*di tiro*) rifle range

po'**limero** *nm* polymer

Poli'**nesia** *nf* Polynesia

polinesi'**ano** *a & nmf* Polynesian

'**polio[mie'lite]** *nf* polio[myelitis]

'**polipo** *nm* polyp

polisti'**rolo** *nm* polystyrene

poli'**tecnico** *nm* polytechnic

po'**litica** *nf* politics *sg*; (*linea di condotta*) policy; **fare ~** be in politics; **darsi alla ~** go into politics. **~ estera** foreign policy. **~ monetaria** monetary policy

politica'**mente** *adv* politically; **~ corretto** politically correct, pc

politi'**chese** *nm* political jargon

politiciz'**zare** *vt* politicize

po'**litico, -a** *a* political ● *nmf* politician

poliva'lente *a* all-purpose

poli'zia *nf* police. ~ **giudiziaria** ≈ Criminal Investigation Department, CID. ~ **stradale** traffic police

polizi'esco *a* police *attrib*; ⟨*romanzo, film*⟩ detective *attrib*

polizi'otto *nm* policeman. ~ **in borghese** plain clothes policeman. ~ **privato** private detective ● *a* police *attrib*

'polizza *nf* policy. ~ **di assicurazione** insurance policy

pol'laio *nm* chicken run; (*fam: luogo chiassoso*) mad house

pol'lame *nm* poultry

polla'strella *nf* spring chicken; *fig fam* bird

polla'strello *nm* spring chicken

pol'lastro *nm* cockerel

polle'ria *nf* poultry butcher, poulterer

'pollice *nm* thumb; (*unità di misura*) inch

'polline *nm* pollen; **allergia al** ~ hay fever

polli'vendolo, -a *nmf* poulterer

'pollo *nm* chicken; (*fam: semplicione*) simpleton; **far ridere i polli** be ridiculous. ~ **arrosto** roast chicken. ~ **alla cacciatora** chicken chasseur

polmo'nare *a* pulmonary

pol'mone *nm* lung. ~ **d'acciaio** iron lung

polmo'nite *nf* pneumonia

'polo *nm* pole; *Sport* polo; (*maglietta*) polo top; *Pol* party; (*conservatori*) Italian Conservatives. ~ **magnetico** magnetic pole. ~ **nord** North Pole. ~ **sud** South Pole

Po'lonia *nf* Poland

'polpa *nf* pulp

pol'paccio *nm* calf

polpa'strello *nm* fingertip

pol'petta *nf* meatball. ~ **di carne** meatball

polpet'tone *nm* meatloaf. ~ **sentimentale** *fam* hokum

'polpo *nm* octopus

pol'poso *a* fleshy

pol'sino *nm* cuff

'polso *nm* pulse; *Anat* wrist; *fig* authority; **avere** ~ be strict; **essere privo di** ~ be soft

pol'tiglia *nf* mush

pol'trire *vi* lie around

pol'trona *nf* armchair; *Theat* seat in the stalls

pol'trone *a* lazy

'polvere *nf* dust; (*sostanza polverizzata*) powder; **in** ~ powdered; **sapone in** ~ soap powder. ~ **da sparo** gun powder

polveri'era *nf* gunpowder magazine; *fig* tinderbox

polve'rina *nf* (*medicina*) powder

polveriz'zare *vt* pulverize; (*nebulizzare*) atomize; smash, shatter ⟨*record*⟩; ~ **qcno** pulverize sb

polve'rone *nm* cloud of dust

polve'roso *a* dusty

po'mata *nf* ointment, cream. ~ **cicatrizzante** healing cream for cuts

pomel'lato *a* dappled

po'mello *nm* knob; (*guancia*) cheek

pomeridi'ano *a* afternoon *attrib*; **alle tre**

pomeridiane at three in the afternoon, at three pm

pome'riggio *nm* afternoon; **buon** ~! have a good afternoon!; **oggi** ~ this afternoon; **questo** ~ this afternoon

'pomice *nf* pumice

pomici'are *vi fam* snog, neck

pomici'ata *nf fam* snogging, necking

'pomo *nm* (*oggetto*) knob. ~ **d'Adamo** Adam's apple

pomo'doro *nm* tomato

'pompa *nf* pump; (*sfarzo*) pomp. ~ **della benzina** petrol pump, gas pump *Am*. **pompe** *pl* **funebri** (*funzione*) funeral

pom'pare *vt* pump; (*gonfiare d'aria*) pump up; (*fig: esagerare*) exaggerate; ~ **fuori** pump out

pompei'ano, -a *a & nmf* Pompeian

pom'pelmo *nm* grapefruit

pompi'ere *nm* fireman; **i pompieri** the fire brigade

pom'pon *nm inv* pompom

pom'poso *a* pompous

'poncho *nm inv* poncho

ponde'rare *vt* ponder

ponde'roso *a* ponderous

po'nente *nm* west

'ponte *nm* bridge; *Naut* deck; (*impalcatura*) scaffolding; **fare il** ~ *fig* make a long weekend of it; **legge** ~ interim *or* bridging law; **governo** ~ interim government. ~ **aereo** airlift. ~ **di coperta** main deck. ~ **levatoio** drawbridge. ~ **radio** radio link. ~ **dei Sospiri** Bridge of Sighs. ~ **di volo** flight deck

pon'tefice *nm* pontiff

pontifi'care *vi* pontificate

pontifi'cato *nm* pontificate

ponti'ficio *a* papal

pon'tile *nm* jetty

'pony *nm inv* pony. ~ **express** express delivery service

pool *nm inv Comm* consortium; (*di giornalisti*) team; (*di esperti*) pool, team. ~ **genico** gene pool

pop'corn *nm inv* popcorn

'popelin *nm* poplin

popò *nm inv fam* bottie, bum

popò *nf inv fam* pooh

popo'lano *a* of the [common] people

popo'lare *a* popular; (*comune*) common ● *vt* populate; **essere popolato da** (*pieno di*) be full by

popolarità *nf* popularity

popo'larsi *vr* get crowded

popolazi'one *nf* population

'popolo *nm* people

popo'loso *a* populous

'poppa *nf Naut* stern; (*mammella*) breast; **a** ~ astern

pop'pare *vt* suck

pop'pata *nf* (*pasto*) feed

poppa'toio *nm* [feeding-]bottle

popu'lista *nmf* populist

por'caio *nf anche fig* pigsty; **fare un** ~ *fam* make a mess

por'cata *nf* load of rubbish; **porcate** *pl* (*fam: cibo*) junk food; **fare una ~ a qcno** play a dirty trick on sb

porcel'lana *nf* porcelain, china. **~ fine** bone china

porcel'lino *nm* piglet. **~ d'India** guinea-pig

porche'ria *nf* dirt; (*fig: cosa orrenda*) piece of filth; (*fam: robaccia*) rubbish

por'chetta *nf* roast sucking pig

por'cile *nm* pigsty

por'cino *a* pig *attrib* ● *nm* (*fungo*) cep (*edible mushroom*)

'porco *nm* pig; (*carne*) pork

porco'spino *nm* porcupine

'porfido *nm* porphyry

'porgere *vt* give; (*offrire*) offer; **~ orecchio** lend an ear; **porgo distinti saluti** (*in lettera*) I remain, yours sincerely

'porno *a inv* porn

pornogra'fia *nf* pornography

porno'grafico *a* pornographic

'poro *nm* pore

po'roso *a* porous

'porpora *nf* purple

'porre *vt* put; (*collocare*) place; (*supporre*) suppose; ask ⟨*domanda*⟩; present ⟨*candidatura*⟩; **~ una domanda a qcno** ask sb a question; **poniamo [il caso] che...** let us suppose that...; **~ fine** *o* **termine a** put an end to

'porro *nm* Bot leek; (*verruca*) wart

'porsi *vr* put oneself; **~ a sedere** sit down; **~ in cammino** set out

'porta *nf* door; *Sport* goal; (*di città*) gate; *Comput* port. **~ a ~** door-to-door; **mettere alla ~** show sb the door; **a porte chiuse** ⟨*riunione, processo*⟩ behind closed doors, in camera; **essere alle porte** (*vicino*) be on the doorstep. **~ a due battenti** double door[s]. **~ d'ingresso** front door. **~ parallela** *Comput* parallel port. **~ seriale** *Comput* serial port. **~ di servizio** tradesman's entrance. **~ di sicurezza** emergency exit. **~ per la stampante** *Comput* printer port. **~ a vento** swing-door

portaba'gagli *nm inv* (*facchino*) porter; (*di treno ecc*) luggage-rack; *Auto* boot, trunk *Am*; (*sul tetto di un'auto*) roof-rack

portabandi'era *nmf inv* standard-bearer

portabici'clette *nm inv* cycle rack

portabot'tiglie *nm inv* bottle rack, wine rack

porta'burro *nm inv* butter dish

porta'cenere *nm inv* ashtray

portachi'avi *nm inv* keyring

porta'cipria *nm inv* compact

portacon'tainers *nm inv* container truck

portadocu'menti *nm inv* document wallet

porta'erei *nf inv* aircraft carrier

portafi'nestra *nf* French window

porta'foglio *nm* wallet; (*per documenti*) portfolio; (*ministero*) ministry

portafor'tuna *nm inv* lucky charm ● *a inv* lucky

portagi'oie *nm inv* jewellery box

por'tale *nm* door

portama'tite *nm inv* pencil case

porta'mento *nm* carriage; (*condotta*) behaviour

porta'mina *nm inv* propelling pencil

portamo'nete *nm inv* purse

por'tante *a* bearing *attrib*

portan'tina *nf* sedan-chair

portaom'brelli *nm inv* umbrella stand

porta'pacchi *nm inv* roof rack; (*su bicicletta*) luggage rack

porta'penne *nm inv* pencil case

por'tare *vt* (*verso chi parla*) bring; (*lontano da chi parla*) take; (*sorreggere, Math*) carry; (*condurre*) lead; (*indossare*) wear; (*avere*) bear; **~ a spasso il cane** take the dog for a walk; **~ a termine** bring to a close; **~ avanti** carry on; **~ ~ bene/male** bring good/bad luck; **~ fortuna** be lucky; **~ rancore** bear a grudge; **~ via** take away

portari'viste *nm inv* magazine rack

por'tarsi *vr* (*trasferirsi*) move; (*comportarsi*) behave; **~ bene/male gli anni** look young/old for one's age

porta'sci *nm inv* ski rack

portasciuga'mano *nm* towel rail

portasiga'rette *nm inv* cigarette-case

porta'spilli *nm inv* pin-cushion

por'tata *nf* (*di pranzo*) course; *Auto* carrying capacity; (*di arma*) range; (*fig: abilità*) capability; **a ~ di mano** within reach; **alla ~ di tutti** accessible to all; (*finanziariamente*) within everybody's reach; **di grande** ⟨*scoperta*⟩ with far-reaching consequences

por'tatile *a & nm* portable

por'tato *a* (*indumento*) worn; (*dotato*) gifted; **essere ~ per qcsa** have a gift for sth; **essere ~ a** (*tendere a*) be inclined to

porta|'tore, -'trice *nmf* bearer; **al ~ to the bearer. **~ di handicap** disabled person

portatovagli'olo *nm* napkin ring

portau'ovo *nm inv* egg-cup

porta'voce *nm inv* spokesman ● *nf inv* spokeswoman

por'tello *nm* hatch. **~ di sicurezza** escape hatch

por'tento *nm* marvel; (*persona dotata*) prodigy

porten'toso *a* wonderful

port'folio *nm inv* (*di fotografie ecc*) portfolio

porti'cato *nm* portico

'portico *nm* portico

porti'era *nf* door; (*tendaggio*) door curtain

porti'ere *nm* porter, doorman; *Sport* goalkeeper. **~ di notte** night porter

porti'naio, -a *nmf* caretaker, concierge

portine'ria *nf* concierge's room; (*di ospedale*) porter's lodge

'porto *pp di* **porgere** ● *nm* harbour; (*complesso*) port; (*vino*) port [wine]; (*spesa di trasporto*) carriage; **andare in ~** succeed. **~ d'armi** gun licence. **~ container** container port. **~ fluviale** river port. **~ franco** free port. **~ marittimo** seaport

Porto'gallo *nm* Portugal

porto'ghese a & nmf Portuguese

por'tone nm main door

portori'cano, -a a & nmf Puerto Rican

Porto'rico nf Puerto Rico

portu'ale nm dockworker, docker

porzi'one nf portion

'posa nf laying; (riposo) rest; Phot exposure; (atteggiamento) pose; **mettersi in ~** pose; **senza ~** without rest

po'sare vt put; (giù) put [down] ● vi (poggiare) rest; (per un ritratto) pose

po'sarsi vr alight; (sostare) rest; Aeron land

po'sata nf piece of cutlery; **posate** pl cutlery sg, flatware sg Am

po'sato a sedate

po'scritto nm postscript

posi'tivo a positive

posizio'nare vt position

posizi'one nf position; **farsi una ~** get ahead; **prendere ~** take a stand

posolo'gia nf dosage

po'sporre vt place after; (posticipare) postpone

po'sposto pp di posporre

posse'dere vt possess, own

possedi'mento nm possession

posses'sivo a possessive

pos'sesso nm possession, ownership; (bene) possession; **entrare in ~ di** come into possession of; **essere in ~ di** be in possession of; **prendere ~ di** take possession of

posses'sore nm owner

pos'sibile a possible; **il più presto ~** as soon as possible ● nm **fare [tutto] il ~** do one's best

possibilità nf inv possibility; (occasione) chance; **avere la ~ di fare qcsa** have the chance o opportunity to do sth ● nfpl (mezzi) means

possi'dente nmf land-owner

'posso vedi potere

'posta nf post, mail; (ufficio postale) post office; (al gioco) stake; **spese di ~** postage; **per ~** by post, by mail; **la ~ in gioco è… ** fig what's at stake is…; **a bella ~** on purpose; **Poste e Telecomunicazioni** [Italian] Post Office. **~ aerea** airmail. **~ centrale** main post office, central post office. **~ del cuore** agony column. **~ elettronica** electronic mail, e-mail; **spedire via ~** e-mail. **~ elettronica vocale** voicemail

posta'giro nm postal giro

po'stale a postal

postazi'one nf position; Mil emplacement

post'bellico a postwar

postda'tare vt postdate (assegno)

posteggi'are vt/i park

posteggia|'tore, -'trice nmf parking attendant

po'steggio nm car-park, parking lot Am; (di taxi) taxi-rank

'posteri nmpl descendants

posteri'ore a back attrib, rear attrib; (nel tempo) later ● nm fam posterior, behind

posterità nf posterity

po'sticcio a artificial; (baffi, barba) false ● nm hair-piece

postici'pare vt postpone

po'stilla nf note; Jur rider

po'stino nm postman, mailman Am

'posto pp di porre ● nm place; (spazio) room; (impiego) job; Mil post; (sedile) seat; **a/fuori ~** in/out of place; **prendere ~** take up room; **sul ~** on-site; **essere a ~** (casa, libri) be tidy; **non grazie, sono a ~** no thanks, I'm all right; **mettere a ~** tidy (stanza); **fare ~** a make room for; **al ~ di** (invece di) in place of, instead of. **~ di blocco** checkpoint. **~ di guardia** guard post. **~ di guida** driving seat. **~ di lavoro** job; Comput workstation. **posti** pl **in piedi** standing room. **~ di polizia** police station. **posti** pl **a sedere** seating, seats

post-'partum a post-natal

'postumo a posthumous ● nm after-effect; **postumi** pl **della sbornia** hangover

po'tabile a drinkable; **acqua ~** drinking water; **non ~** undrinkable

po'tare vt prune

po'tassa nf potash

po'tassio nm potassium

po'tente a powerful; (efficace) potent

po'tenza nf power; (efficacia) potency. **~ nucleare** nuclear power

potenzi'ale a & nm potential

po'tere nm power; **al ~** in power. **~ d'acquisto** purchasing power. **il quarto ~** the fourth estate ● vi can, be able to; **posso entrare?** can I come in?; (formale) may I come in?; **mi spiace, non posso venire alla festa** I'm sorry, I can't come to the party or I won't be able to come to the party; **posso fare qualche cosa?** can I do something?; **che tu possa essere felice!** may you be happy!; **non ne posso più** (sono stanco) I can't go on; (sono stufo) I can't take any more; **può darsi** perhaps; **può darsi che sia vero** perhaps it's true; **potrebbe aver ragione** he could be right, he might be right; **avresti potuto telefonare** you could have phoned, you might have phoned; **spero di poter venire** I hope to be able to come; **senza poter telefonare** without being able to phone; **spero che potremo incontrarci presto** I hope we can meet soon

potestà nf power

pot-pour'ri nm inv medley

'povero, -a a poor; (semplice) plain; **~ di** (paese, terreno) lacking in; **in parole povere** in a few words ● nf poor woman ● nm poor man; **i poveri** the poor

povertà nf poverty

pozi'one nf potion

'pozza nf pool

poz'zanghera nf puddle

'pozzo nm well; (minerario) pit. **~ petrolifero** oil well. **~ di petrolio** oil well. **~ di ventilazione** air shaft

pp. (pagine) abbr pp

PP.TT. abbr (**Poste e Telecomunicazioni**) [Italian] Post Office

PR *nfpl abbr* PR

'Praga *nf* Prague

prag'matico *a* pragmatic

prali'nato *a* ⟨*mandorla, gelato*⟩ praline-coated

pram'matica *nf* **essere di ~** be customary

pranotera'pia *nf* laying on of hands

pran'zare *vi* dine; (*a mezzogiorno*) lunch

'pranzo *nm* dinner; (*a mezzogiorno*) lunch. **~ di lavoro** business lunch, working lunch. **~ di nozze** wedding breakfast

'prassi *nf* standard procedure

prate'ria *nf* grassland

'pratica *nf* practice; (*esperienza*) experience; (*documentazione*) file; **avere ~ di qcsa** be familiar with sth, have experience of sth; **mettere qcsa in ~** put sth into practice; **far ~** gain experience; **fare le pratiche per** gather the necessary papers for

prati'cabile *a* practicable; ⟨*strada*⟩ passable

pratica'mente *adv* practically

prati'cante *nmf* apprentice; *Relig* [regular] church-goer

prati'care *vt* practise; (*frequentare*) associate with; (*fare*) make

praticità *nf* practicality

'pratico *a* practical; (*esperto*) experienced, knowledgeable; ⟨*comodo*⟩ convenient; **essere ~ di qcsa** know about sth; **all'atto ~** in practice

'prato *nm* meadow; (*di giardino*) lawn. **~ all'inglese** lawn

preaccensi'one *nf Auto* pre-ignition

pre'ambolo *nm* preamble

preannunci'are *vt* give advance notice of

prean'nuncio *nm* advance notice

preavvi'sare *vt* forewarn

preav'viso *nm* warning

precari'cato *a* preloaded

precarietà *nf inv* frailty

pre'cario *a* precarious

precauzi'one *nf* precaution; (*cautela*) care

prece'dente *a* previous ● *nm* precedent; **avere dei precedenti penali** have a police record; **senza precedenti** ⟨*successo*⟩ unprecedented

precedente'mente *adv* previously

prece'denza *nf* precedence; (*di veicoli*) right of way; **dare la ~ a** give priority to; *Auto* give way to; **avere la ~** have priority; *Auto* have right of way; **~ assoluta** top priority

pre'cedere *vt* precede

pre'cetto *nm* precept

precet'tore, -'trice *nmf* tutor

precipi'tare *vt* **~ le cose** precipitate events; **~ qcno nella disperazione** cast sb into a state of despair ● *vi* fall headlong; ⟨*situazione, eventi:*⟩ come to a head

precipi'tarsi *vr* (*gettarsi*) throw oneself; (*affrettarsi*) rush; **~ a fare qcsa** rush to do sth

precipitazi'one *nf* (*fretta*) haste; (*atmosferica*) precipitation

precipi'toso *a* hasty; (*avventato*) reckless; ⟨*caduta*⟩ headlong

preci'pizio *nm* precipice; **a ~** headlong

preci'sabile *a* specifiable

precisa'mente *adv* precisely

preci'sare *vt* specify; (*spiegare*) clarify; **ci tengo a ~ che...** I want to make the point that...

precisazi'one *nf* clarification

precisi'one *nf* precision

pre'ciso *a* precise; ⟨*calcolo, risposta*⟩ accurate; ⟨*ore*⟩ sharp; (*identico*) identical

pre'cludere *vt* preclude

pre'cludersi *vr* **~ ogni possibilità** preclude every possibility

pre'cluso *pp di* **precludere**

pre'coce *a* precocious; (*prematuro*) premature

precocità *nf* precociousness

precon'cetto *a* preconceived ● *nm* prejudice

preconfezio'nato *a* pre-packed

preconfigu'rato *a* preconfigured

pre'correre *vt* (*anticipare*) anticipate; **~ i tempi** be ahead of one's time

precorri'|tore, -'trice *nmf* precursor, forerunner

precur'sore *nm* forerunner, precursor

'preda *nf* prey; (*bottino*) booty; **essere in ~ al panico** be panic-stricken; **in ~ alle fiamme** engulfed in flames

pre'dare *vt* plunder

preda'tore *nm* predator

predeces'sore *nmf* predecessor

pre'della *nf* platform

predel'lino *nm* step

predesti'nare *vt* predestine

predesti'nato *a* predestined, preordained

predestinazi'one *nf* predestination

predetermi'nare *vt* predetermine

predetermi'nato *a* predetermined, preordained

pre'detto *pp di* **predire**

'predica *nf* sermon; *fig* lecture

predi'care *vt* preach

predi'cato *nm* predicate

predige'rito *a* predigested

predi'letto, -a *pp di* **prediligere** ● *a* favourite ● *nmf* pet

predilezi'one *nf* predilection; **avere una ~ per** have a predilection for, be partial to

predi'ligere *vt* prefer

prediposizi'one *nf* predisposition; (*al disegno ecc*) bent (**a** for)

pre'dire *vt* foretell

predi'sporre *vt* arrange; **~ qcno a qcsa** *Med* predispose sb to sth; (*preparare*) prepare sb for sth

predi'sporsi *vr* **~ a** prepare oneself for

predi'sposto *pp di* **predisporre**

predizi'one *nf* prediction

predomi'nante *a* predominant

predomi'nare *vi* predominate

predo'minio *nm* predominance

pre'done *nm* robber

prefabbri'cato *a* prefabricated ● *nm* prefabricated building

prefazi'one *nf* preface

prefe'renza *nf* preference; **di ~** preferably

preferenzi'ale *a* preferential; **corsia ~** bus and taxi lane

prefe'ribile *a* preferable

preferibil'mente *adv* preferably

prefe'rire *vt* prefer

prefe'rito, -a *a & nmf* favourite

pre'fetto *nm* prefect

prefet'tura *nf* prefecture

pre'figgere *vt* decide in advance, pre-arrange ⟨*termine*⟩

pre'figgersi *vr* **~ uno scopo** set oneself an objective

prefigu'rare *vt* ⟨*anticipare*⟩ foreshadow

prefinanzia'mento *nm* bridging loan

prefis'sare *vt* pre-arrange ⟨*data, appuntamento*⟩

pre'fisso *pp di* **prefiggere** ● *nm* prefix; *Teleph* [dialling] code

pre'gare *vi Relig* pray ● *vt Relig* pray to; ⟨*supplicare*⟩ beg; **farsi ~** need persuading; **~ qcno di fare qcsa** ask sb to do sth; **si prega di...** please...; **si prega di non...** please do not...; **si prega di non fumare** please refrain from smoking

pre'gevole *a* valuable

preghi'era *nf* prayer; ⟨*richiesta*⟩ request

pregi'arsi *vr* **si pregia di non essere mai in ritardo** he prides himself on never being late

pre'giato *a* esteemed; ⟨*prezioso*⟩ valuable

'pregio *nm* esteem; ⟨*valore*⟩ value; ⟨*di persona*⟩ good point; **di ~** valuable

pregiudi'care *vt* prejudice; ⟨*danneggiare*⟩ harm

pregiudi'cato *a* prejudiced ● *nm Jur* previous offender

pregiu'dizio *nm* prejudice; ⟨*danno*⟩ detriment

pre'gnante *a* ⟨*parola*⟩ pregnant, pregnant with meaning

'pregno *a* ⟨*parola*⟩ pregnant; ⟨*pieno*⟩ full; **~ di** ⟨*umidità*⟩ saturated with; ⟨*significato*⟩ pregnant with

'prego *int* ⟨*non c'è di che*⟩ don't mention it!; ⟨*per favore*⟩ please; **~?** I beg your pardon?; **posso? - ~** may I? - please do

pregu'stare *vt* look forward to

preinstal'lato *a* preinstalled

prei'storia *nf* prehistory

prei'storico *a* prehistoric

pre'lato *nm* prelate

prela'vaggio *nm* prewash

preleva'mento *nm* withdrawal

prele'vare *vt* withdraw ⟨*denaro*⟩; collect ⟨*merci*⟩; *Med* take

preli'evo *nm* ⟨*di soldi*⟩ withdrawal. **~ di sangue** blood sample

prelimi'nare *a* preliminary ● *nm* **preliminari** *pl* preliminaries

pre'ludere *vi* **~ a** herald

pre'ludio *nm* prelude

prema'man *nm inv* maternity dress ● *a* maternity *attrib*

prematrimoni'ale *a* premarital

prematura'mente *adv* prematurely

prema'turo, -a *a* premature ● *nmf* premature baby

premedi'tare *vt* premeditate

premeditazi'one *nf* premeditation; **con ~** ⟨*omicidio*⟩ premeditated

'premere *vt* press; *Comput* hit ⟨*tasto*⟩ ● *vi* **~ a** ⟨*importare*⟩ matter to; **mi preme sapere** I need to know; **~ su** press on; push ⟨*pulsante*⟩; ⟨*fig: fare pressione su*⟩ put pressure on, pressure; **~ per ottenere qcsa** push for sth

pre'messa *nf* introduction; **senza tante premesse** without further ado

pre'messo *pp di* **premettere**; **~ che** bearing in mind that

pre'mettere *vt* ⟨*mettere prima*⟩ put before; **premetto che...** I want to make it clear first that...; **~ un'introduzione a un libro** put an introduction at the beginning of a book

premi'are *vt* give a prize to; ⟨*ricompensare*⟩ reward

premi'ato *a* award-winning

premiazi'one *nf* prize giving

premi'nente *a* pre-eminent

premi'nenza *nf* pre-eminence

'premio *nm* prize; ⟨*ricompensa*⟩ reward; ⟨*di produzione ecc*⟩ bonus; *Fin* premium. **~ di assicurazione** insurance premium. **~ di consolazione** consolation prize; ⟨*ridicolo*⟩ booby prize. **~ di ingaggio** *Sport* signing fee. **~ di produzione** productivity bonus

premoni'tore *a* ⟨*sogno, segno*⟩ premonitory

premonizi'one *nf* premonition

premu'nire *vt* fortify

premu'nirsi *vr* take protective measures; **~ di** provide oneself with; **~ contro** protect oneself against

pre'mura *nf* ⟨*fretta*⟩ hurry; ⟨*cura*⟩ care; **far ~ a qcno** hurry sb up

premu'roso *a* thoughtful

prena'tale *a* antenatal

'prendere *vt* take; ⟨*afferrare*⟩ seize; catch ⟨*treno, malattia, ladro, pesce*⟩; have ⟨*cibo, bevanda*⟩; ⟨*far pagare*⟩ charge; ⟨*assumere*⟩ take on; ⟨*ottenere*⟩ get; ⟨*occupare*⟩ take up; ⟨*guadagnare*⟩ earn; **~ informazioni** make inquiries; **~ qcno in giro** pull sb's leg; **~ a calci/pugni** kick/punch; **che ti prende?** what's got into you?; **quanto prende?** what do you charge?; **~ una persona per un'altra** mistake a person for somebody else; **passare a ~ qcno** collect sb, pick sb up ● *vi* ⟨*voltare*⟩ turn; ⟨*attecchire*⟩ take root; ⟨*rapprendersi*⟩ set; ⟨*fuoco*⟩ catch, take; **~ a destra/sinistra** turn right/left; **~ a fare qcsa** start doing sth; **la colla non ha preso** the glue didn't take

'prendersi *vr* **~ a pugni** come to blows; **~ cura di** take care of ⟨*ammalato*⟩; **prendersela** take it to heart; **si prende troppo sul serio** he takes himself too seriously

prendi'sole *nm* sundress

preno'tare *vt* book, reserve

preno'tarsi *vr* ~ **per** put one's name down for

preno'tato *a* booked, reserved

prenotazi'one *nf* booking, reservation

'prensile *a* prehensile

preoccu'pante *a* alarming

preoccu'pare *vt* worry

preoccu'parsi *vr* ~ worry (**di** about); ~ **di fare qcsa** take the trouble to do sth

preoccu'pato *a* (*ansioso*) worried

preoccupazi'one *nf* worry; (*apprensione*) concern

preopera'torio *a* preoperative

prepa'rare *vt* prepare; study for ‹*esame*›; ~ **da mangiare** prepare a meal

prepa'rarsi *vr* get ready

prepa'rativi *nmpl* preparations

prepa'rato *nm* (*prodotto*) preparation

prepara'torio *a* preparatory

preparazi'one *nf* preparation; (*competenza*) knowledge

prepensiona'mento *nm* early retirement

preponde'rante *a* predominant, preponderant

preponde'ranza *nf* preponderance, prevalence

pre'porre *vt* place before

preposizi'one *nf* preposition

pre'posto *pp di* **preporre** ● *a* ~ **a** (*addetto a*) in charge of

prepo'tente *a* overbearing ● *nmf* bully; **fare il** ~ **con qcno** bully sb

prepo'tenza *nf* high-handedness

preprogram'mato *a* *Comput* preprogrammed

pre'puzio *nm* foreskin, prepuce

preroga'tiva *nf* prerogative

'presa *nf* taking; (*conquista*) capture; (*stretta*) hold; (*di cemento ecc*) setting; *Electr* socket; (*di gas, acqua*) inlet, connection; (*pizzico*) pinch; **essere alle prese con** be struggling *o* grappling with; **macchina da** ~ cine camera; **a** ~ **rapida** ‹*cemento, colla*› quick-setting; **fare** ~ **su qcno** influence sb. ~ **d'aria** air vent. ~ **in giro** leg-pull. ~ **multipla** adaptor

pre'sagio *nm* omen

presa'gire *vt* foretell

presa'lario *nm* maintenance grant

'presbite *a* long-sighted

presbiteri'ano, -a *a & nmf* Presbyterian

presbi'terio *nm* presbytery

pre'scelto *a* selected

pre'scindere *vi* ~ **da** leave aside; **a** ~ **da** apart from

presco'lare *a* pre-school; **in età** ~ pre-school

pre'scritto *pp di* **prescrivere**

pre'scrivere *vt* prescribe

prescrizi'one *nf* prescription; (*norma*) rule; **cadere in** ~ cease to be valid as a result of the statute of limitations

preselezi'one *nf* preliminary selection;

(*per il traffico*) advance lane markings; *Sport* [qualifying] heats *pl*

presen'tare *vt* present; (*far conoscere*) introduce; show ‹*documento*›; (*inoltrare*) submit

presen'tarsi *vr* present oneself; (*farsi conoscere*) introduce oneself; (*a ufficio*) attend; (*alla polizia ecc*) report; (*come candidato*) stand, run (**a** for); ‹*occasione:*› occur; ~ **bene/male** ‹*persona:*› make a good/bad impression; ‹*situazione:*› look good/bad

presenta'tore, -'trice *nmf* presenter; (*di notizie*) announcer

presentazi'one *nf* presentation; (*per conoscersi*) introduction; **fare le presentazioni** do the introductions; **dietro** ~ **di ricetta medica** on doctor's prescription only

pre'sente *a* present; (*attuale*) current; (*questo*) this; **aver** ~ remember ● *nm* present; **i presenti** those present ● *nf* **allegato alla** ~ (*in lettera*) enclosed

presenti'mento *nm* foreboding

pre'senza *nf* presence; (*aspetto*) appearance; **in** ~ **di, alla** ~ **di** in the presence of; **di bella** ~ personable. ~ **di spirito** presence of mind

presenzi'are *vi* ~ **a** attend

pre'sepe *nm*, **pre'sepio** *nm* crib

preser'vare *vt* preserve; (*proteggere*) protect (**da** from)

preserva'tivo *nm* condom

preservazi'one *nf* preservation

'preside *nm* headmaster; *Univ* dean ● *nf* headmistress; *Univ* dean

presi'dente *nm* chairman; *Pol* president ● *nf* chairwoman; *Pol* president. ~ **del consiglio [dei ministri]** Prime Minister. ~ **della repubblica** President of the Republic

presiden'tessa *nf* chairwoman

presi'denza *nf* presidency; (*di assemblea*) chairmanship

presidenzi'ale *a* presidential

presidi'are *vt* garrison

pre'sidio *nm* garrison

presi'edere *vt* preside over

'preso *pp di* **prendere**

'pressa *nf* *Mech* press

press-'agent *mf inv* publicist, press agent

pres'sante *a* urgent

pressap'poco *adv* about

pres'sare *vt* press

pressi'one *nf* pressure; **far** ~ **su** put pressure on; **essere sotto** ~ *fig* be under pressure; **esercitare pressioni su qcno** put pressure on sb; **a/di alta** ~ high pressure. ~ **fiscale** tax burden. ~ **gomme** tyre pressure. ~ **del sangue** blood pressure

'presso *prep* near; (*a casa di*) with; (*negli indirizzi*) care of, c/o; ‹*lavorare*› for; **richiedere qcsa** ~ **una società** request sth from a company ● *nmpl* **pressi: nei pressi di...** in the neighbourhood *or* vicinity of...

pressoché *adv* almost

pressuriz'zare *vt* pressurize

pressuriz'zato *a* pressurized

prestabi'lire *vt* arrange in advance

prestabi'lito *a* agreed, predetermined

prestam'pato *a* printed ● *nm* (*modulo*) form

pre'stante *a* good-looking

pre'stanza *nf* good looks *pl*

pre'stare *vt* lend; **~ attenzione** pay attention; **~ aiuto** lend a hand; **~ ascolto** lend an ear; **~ fede a** give credence to; **~ giuramento** take the oath; **farsi ~** borrow (**da** from)

pre'starsi *vr* (*frase:*) lend itself; (*persona:*) offer

prestazi'one *nf* performance; **prestazioni** *pl* (*servizi*) services

prestigia|'tore, -'trice *nmf* conjurer

pre'stigio *nm* prestige; **gioco di ~** conjuring trick

prestigi'oso *nm* prestigious

'prestito *nm* loan; **dare in ~** lend; **prendere in ~** borrow. **~ bancario** bank loan. **~ con garanzia collaterale** collateral loan

'presto *adv* soon; (*di buon'ora*) early; (*in fretta*) quickly; **a ~** see you soon; **al più ~** as soon as possible; **~ o tardi** sooner or later; **far ~** be quick

pre'sumere *vt* presume; (*credere*) think

presu'mibile *a* è ~ **che...** presumably,...

pre'sunto *a* (*colpevole*) presumed

presuntu'oso *a* presumptuous ● *nmf* presumptuous person

presunzi'one *nf* presumption

presup'porre *vt* suppose; (*richiedere*) presuppose

presupposizi'one *nf* presupposition

presup'posto *nm* essential requirement

prêt-à-por'ter *nm* ready-to-wear clothing

'prete *nm* priest

preten'dente *nmf* pretender ● *nm* (*corteggiatore*) suitor

pre'tendere *vt* (*sostenere*) claim; (*esigere*) demand ● *vi* **~ a** claim to; **~ di** (*esigere*) demand to

pretensi'one *nf* pretension

pretenzi'oso *a* pretentious

preterintenzio'nale *a* **omicidio ~** manslaughter

pre'terito *nm* preterite

pre'tesa *nf* pretension; (*esigenza*) claim; **senza pretese** unpretentious

pre'teso *pp di* **pretendere**

pre'testo *nm* pretext

pre'tore *nm* magistrate

pretta'mente *adv* decidedly

'pretto *a* pure

pre'tura *nf* magistrate's court

preva'lente *a* prevalent

prevalente'mente *adv* primarily

preva'lenza *nf* prevalence

preva'lere *vi* prevail

pre'valso *pp di* **prevalere**

preve'dere *vt* foresee; forecast (*tempo*); (*legge ecc:*) provide for

preve'nire *vt* precede; (*evitare*) prevent; (*avvertire*) forewarn

preventi'vare *vt* estimate; (*aspettarsi*) budget for

preven'tivo *a* preventive; **bilancio ~** budget ● *nm Comm* estimate

preve'nuto *a* forewarned; (*mal disposto*) prejudiced

prevenzi'one *nf* prevention; (*preconcetto*) prejudice

previ'dente *a* provident

previ'denza *nf* foresight. **~ integrativa** supplementary social security, supplementary welfare *Am*. **~ sociale** social security, welfare *Am*

previdenzi'ale *a* provident

'previo *a* **~ pagamento** on payment

previsi'one *nf* forecast; **in ~ di** in anticipation of. **previsioni** *pl* **del tempo** weather forecast

pre'visto *pp di* **prevedere** ● *a* foreseen ● *nm* **più/meno/prima del ~** more/less/earlier than expected

prezi'oso *a* precious

prez'zemolo *nm* parsley

'prezzo *nm* price; [**a**] **metà ~** half price; **a ~ ribassato** at a reduced price; **non aver ~** *fig* be priceless. **~ d'acquisto** purchase price. **~ di costo** cost price. **~ al dettaglio** retail price. **~ di fabbrica** factory price. **~ di favore** special price. **~ all'ingrosso** wholesale price. **~ intero** full price. **~ di mercato** market price. **~ al minuto** retail price. **~ d'offerta** offer price. **~ politico** subsidized price. **~ di riferimento** benchmark price. **~ sorvegliato** controlled price. **~ stracciato** slashed price, drastically reduced price. **~ trattabile** price negotiable. **~ unitario** unit price. **~ di vendita** selling price

prigi'one *nf* prison; (*pena*) imprisonment; **mettere in ~** imprison, put in prison

prigio'nia *nf* imprisonment

prigioni'ero, -a *a* imprisoned ● *nmf* prisoner; **tenere ~** qcno keep sb prisoner. **~ di guerra** prisoner of war, POW

'prima *adv* before; (*più presto*) earlier; (*in anticipo*) beforehand; (*in primo luogo*) first; **~, finiamo questo** let's finish this first; **puoi venire ~?** (*di giorni*) can't you come any sooner?; (*di ore*) can't you come any earlier?; **~ o poi** sooner or later; **quanto ~** as soon as possible ● *prep* **~ di** before; **~ di mangiare** before eating; **~ d'ora** before now ● *conj* **~ che** before; **~ che posso** as soon as I can ● *nf* first class; *Theat* first night; *Auto* first [gear]

pri'mario *a* primary; (*principale*) principal

pri'mate *nm* primate

pri'mato *nm* supremacy; *Sport* record

prima'vera *nf* spring

primave'rile *a* spring *attrib*

primeggi'are *vi* excel

primi'tivo *a* primitive; (*originario*) original

pri'mizie *nfpl* early produce *sg*

'primo *a* first; (*fondamentale*) principal; (*in*

importanza) main; (*precedente di due*) former; (*iniziale*) early; (*migliore*) best ● *nm* first; **il ~ d'aprile** April the first, April Fools' Day; **primi** *pl* (*i primi giorni*) the beginning; **in un ~ tempo** at first. **prima colazione** *nf* breakfast. **prima copia** *nf* master copy. **prima linea** *nf Mil* front line. **prima serata** *nf* prime time; **in ~ ● trasmetteremo…** in the early evening slot we're bringing you…

primo'genito, -a *a & nmf* first-born

primogeni'tura *nf* primogeniture; **vendere la ~** sell one's birthright

primordi'ale *a* primordial

'primula *nf* primrose

princi'pale *a* main ● *nm* head, boss *fam*

princi'pato *nm* principality

'principe *nm* prince; **da ~** princely. **~ ereditario** crown prince. **~ del foro** famous lawyer

princi'pesco *a* princely

princi'pessa *nf* princess

principi'ante *nmf* beginner

principi'are *vt/i* begin, start

prin'cipio *nm* beginning; (*concetto*) principle; (*causa*) cause; **per ~** on principle; **una questione di ~** a matter of principle. **~ attivo** active ingredient

pri'ore *nm* prior

pri'ori: a ~ *adv* ⟨*decidere*⟩ a priori; **farsi ~ ~ un'opinione di** prejudge ● *a* a priori

priorità *nf inv* priority

priori'tario *a* having priority; ⟨*obiettivo*⟩ priority *attrib*; **la nostra scelta prioritaria** our decision, which must take priority

'prisma *nm* prism

'privacy *nf* privacy

pri'vare *vt* deprive

pri'varsi *vr* deprive oneself

privatiz'zare *vt* privatize

privatizzazi'one *nf* privatization

pri'vato, -a *a* private ● *nmf* private citizen; **in ~** in private; **ritirarsi a vita privata** withdraw from public life

privazi'one *nf* deprivation

privilegi'are *vt* privilege; (*considerare più importante*) favour

privi'legio *nm* privilege; **avere il ~ di** have the privilege of; **questo dizionario ha il ~ della chiarezza** this dictionary has the merit of clarity

'privo *a* **~ di** devoid of; (*mancante*) lacking in

pro *prep* for ● *nm* advantage; **a che ~?** what's the point?; **il ~ e il contro** the pros and cons

pro'babile *a* probable

probabilità *nf inv* probability; **avere buone ~** have a fighting chance; **~ di riuscita** chances of success

probabil'mente *adv* probably

pro'bante *a* convincing

probità *nf* probity

pro'blema *nm* problem; **non c'è ~** no problem

proble'matico *a* problematic

pro'boscide *nf* trunk

procacci'are *vt* obtain

procacci'arsi *vr* obtain

pro'cace *a* ⟨*ragazza*⟩ provocative

pro'cedere *vi* (*in percorso, discorso*) go on, proceed *fml*; (*iniziare*) start; **il lavoro procede bene** the work is going well; **~ contro** *Jur* start legal proceedings against

procedi'mento *nm* process; *Jur* proceedings *pl*

proce'dura *nf* procedure. **~ civile** civil proceedings *pl*. **~ fallimentare** bankruptcy proceedings *pl*

procedu'rale *a* procedural

proces'sare *vt Jur* try

processi'one *nf* procession

pro'cesso *nm* process; *Jur* trial; **essere sotto ~** be on trial; **mettere sotto ~** put on trial

proces'sore *nm Comput* processor

processu'ale *a* trial *attrib*

pro'cinto *nm* **essere in ~ di** be about to

proci'one *nm* raccoon

pro'clama *nm* proclamation

procla'mare *vt* proclaim

proclamazi'one *nf* proclamation

procrasti'nare *vt liter* postpone

procre'are *vt* procreate

procreazi'one *nf* procreation

pro'cura *nf* power of attorney; **per ~** by proxy. **P~ [della Repubblica]** Public Prosecutor's office

procu'rare *vt/i* procure; (*causare*) cause; (*cercare*) try

procura'tore *nm* attorney. **P~ Generale** Attorney General. **~ legale** ≈ lawyer. **~ della repubblica** public prosecutor

'prode *a* brave

pro'dezza *nf* bravery

prodi'gare *vt* lavish

prodi'garsi *vr* do one's best

pro'digio *nm* prodigy

prodigi'oso *a* prodigious

pro'digo *a* prodigal

prodi'torio *a* treasonable

pro'dotto *pp di* **produrre** ● *nm* product. **prodotti** *pl* **agricoli** farm produce *sg*. **~ artigianalmente** *a* made by craftsmen. **prodotti** *pl* **di bellezza** cosmetics. **~ derivato** by-product. **~ di fabbrica** *a* factory-made. **~ finito** end product, finished product. **~ interno lordo** gross domestic product. **~ nazionale lordo** gross national product

pro'durre *vt* produce

pro'dursi *vr* ⟨*attore:*⟩ play; (*accadere*) happen, occur

produttività *nf* productivity

produt'tivo *a* productive

produt|'tore, -'trice *a* producing; **~ di petrolio** oil-producing ● *nmf* producer

produzi'one *nf* production. **~ in serie** mass production

Prof. *abbr* (**professore**) Prof.

profa'nare *vt* desecrate

profanazi'one *nf* desecration

pro'fano a profane ● nm **i profani** pl the un-initiated

profe'rire vt utter

Prof.essa abbr (**Professoressa**) Prof.

profes'sare vt profess; practise ⟨professione⟩

professio'nale a professional; **istituto ~** training college

professionalità nf professionalism

professi'one nf profession; **libera ~** profession

professio'nismo nm professionalism

professio'nista nmf professional

professo'rale a professorial

profes'sor|e, -'essa nmf Sch teacher; Univ lecturer; (titolare di cattedra) professor

pro'feta nm prophet

pro'fetico a prophetic

profetiz'zare vt prophesy

profe'zia nf prophecy

pro'ficuo a profitable

profi'lare vt outline; (ornare) border; Aeron streamline

profi'larsi vr stand out

profi'lattico a prophylactic ● nm condom

pro'filo nm profile; (breve studio) outline; **di ~** in profile

profite'roles nmpl profiteroles

profit'tare vi **~ di** (avvantaggiarsi) profit by; (approfittare) take advantage of

pro'fitto nm profit; (vantaggio) advantage; **mettere qcsa a ~** turn sth to one's advantage; **trarre ~ da** (vantaggio) derive benefit from

profonda'mente adv deeply, profoundly

profondità nf inv depth; (del pensiero ecc) depth, profundity; **in ~** in depth; **passaggio in ~** Sport deep pass [down the field]. **~ di campo** Phot depth of field

pro'fondo a deep; ⟨pensiero ecc⟩ profound; ⟨cultura⟩ great

pro 'forma routine; **fattura ~** pro forma [invoice] ● adv as a formality ● nm formality

'profugo, -a nmf refugee

profu'mare vt perfume

profu'marsi vr put on perfume

profumata'mente adv **pagare ~** pay through the nose

profu'mato a ⟨fiore⟩ fragrant; ⟨fazzoletto ecc⟩ scented

profume'ria nf perfumery

pro'fumo nm perfume, scent

profusi'one nf profusion; **a ~** in profusion

pro'fuso pp di **profondere** ● a profuse

pro'genie nf progeny

progeni|'tore, -'trice nmf ancestor

proget'tare vt plan; plan, design ⟨costruzione⟩

progettazione nf planning, design. **~ assistita da computer** computer-aided design, CAD

proget'tista nmf designer

pro'getto nm plan; (di lavoro importante) project. **~ di legge** bill

prog'nosi nf inv prognosis; **in ~ riservata** on the danger list

pro'gramma nm programme; Comput program; **avere qcsa in ~** have sth planned, have sth on. **~ di antivirus** Comput antivirus program. **~ assemblatore** Comput assembler. **~ aziendale** business plan. **~ per la gestione dei file** Comput file manager. **~ di grafico** Comput graphics program. **~ politico** manifesto. **~ scolastico** syllabus. **~ di setup** Comput setup program. **~ di utilità** Comput utility

program'mare vt programme; Comput program

program'mato a ⟨sviluppo⟩ planned

programma|'tore, -'trice nmf [computer] programmer

programmazi'one nf programming

progre'dire vi [make] progress

progres'sione nf progression

progres'sista nmf progressive

progres'sivo a progressive

pro'gresso nm progress; **fare progressi** make progress

proi'bire vt forbid

proibi'tivo a prohibitive

proibito a forbidden; **è ~ fumare qui** it's no smoking here

proibizi'one nf prohibition

proibizio'nismo nm prohibition

proiet'tare vt project; show ⟨film⟩

proi'ettile nm bullet

proiet'tore nm projector; Auto headlight

proiezi'one nf projection

'prole nf offspring

proletari'ato nm proletariat

prole'tario a & nm proletarian

prolife'rare vi proliferate

pro'lifico a prolific

prolissità nf prolixity, diffuseness

pro'lisso a verbose, prolix

pro 'loco nf tourist office (in small places)

'prologo nm prologue

pro'lunga nf Electr extension

prolunga'mento nm extension

prolun'gare vt extend ⟨contratto, scadenza, strada⟩; prolong ⟨vita⟩; lengthen ⟨vita, strada⟩

prolun'garsi vr continue, go on; **~ su** (dilungarsi) dwell upon

prome'moria nm memo; (per se stessi) reminder, note; (formale) memorandum

pro'messa nf promise; **era già una ~ del...** he was already a promising new talent in...

pro'messo pp di **promettere** ● a ⟨terra⟩ promised. **promessa sposa** nf betrothed. **~ sposo** nm betrothed

promet'tente a promising

pro'mettere vt/i promise

promi'nente a prominent

promi'nenza nf prominence

promiscuità nf promiscuity

pro'miscuo a promiscuous

promon'torio nm promontory

pro'mosso *pp di* **promuovere** ● *a Sch* who has gone up a year; *Univ* who has passed an exam

promo'|tore, -'trice *nmf* promoter

promozio'nale *a* promotional; **vendita ~** special offer

promozi'one *nf* promotion

promul'gare *vt* promulgate

promulgazi'one *nf* promulgation

promu'overe *vt* promote; *Sch* move up a class; **essere promosso** *Sch, Univ* pass one's exams

proni'pote *nm* (*di bisnonno*) great-grandson; (*di prozio*) great-nephew; **pronipoti** *pl* great-grandchildren ● *nf* (*di bisnonno*) great-granddaughter; (*di prozio*) great-niece

pro'nome *nm* pronoun

pronomi'nale *a* pronominal

pronosti'care *vt* forecast, predict

pronostica'|tore, -trice *nmf* forecaster

pro'nostico *nm* forecast

pron'tezza *nf* readiness; (*rapidità*) quickness; **~ di riflessi** quick reflexes *pl*; **con ~ di spirito** quick-wittedly

'pronto *a* ready; (*rapido*) quick; **~!** *Teleph* hello!; **tenersi ~ (per qcsa)** be ready (*for* sth); **pronti, via!** (*in gare*) ready! steady! go!; **a pronta cassa** cash on delivery. **~ intervento** *nm* emergency service. **~ soccorso** *nm* first aid; (*in ospedale*) accident and emergency, A&E

prontu'ario *nm* handbook

pro'nuncia *nf* pronunciation

pronunci'are *vt* pronounce; (*dire*) utter; deliver ⟨*discorso*⟩

pronunci'arsi *vr* (*su un argomento*) give one's opinion; **~ a favore/contro qcsa** pronounce oneself in favour of/against sth

pronunci'ato *a* pronounced; (*prominente*) prominent

pro'nunzia = **pronuncia**

pronunzi'are = **pronunciare**

propa'ganda *nf* propaganda. **~ elettorale** electioneering. **~ di partito** party political propaganda

propa'gare *vt* propagate

propa'garsi *vr* spread

propagazi'one *nf* propagation

prope'deutico *a* introductory

propel'lente *nm* propellant

pro'pendere *vi* **~ per** be in favour of

propensi'one *nf* inclination, propensity

pro'penso *pp di* **propendere** ● *a* **essere ~ a fare qcsa** be inclined to do sth

propi'nare *vt* administer

pro'pizio *a* favourable

proponi'mento *nm* resolution

pro'porre *vt* propose; (*suggerire*) suggest

pro'porsi *vr* set oneself ⟨*obiettivo, meta*⟩; **~ di** intend to

proporzio'nale *a* proportional

proporzio'nare *vt* proportion

proporzio'nato *a* proportioned

proporzi'one *nf* proportion

pro'posito *nm* intention; **ho fatto il ~ di...**
I have made the decision to...; **a ~** by the way; **a ~ di** with regard to; **di ~** (*apposta*) on purpose; **capitare a ~, giungere a ~** come at just the right time. **propositi** *pl* **per l'anno nuovo** New Year's resolutions

proposizi'one *nf* clause; (*frase*) sentence

pro'posta *nf* proposal, suggestion. **~ di legge** bill. **~ di matrimonio** [marriage] proposal

pro'posto *pp di* **proporre**

propriamente *adv* **~ detto** in the strict sense of the word

proprietà *nf inv* property; (*diritto*) ownership; (*correttezza*) propriety; **essere di ~ di qcno** be sb's property. **~ collettiva** collective ownership. **~ immobiliare** property. **~ di linguaggio** correct use of language. **~ privata** private property

proprie'taria *nf* owner; (*di casa affittata*) landlady

proprie'tario *nm* owner; (*di casa affittata*) landlord

'proprio *a* one's [own]; (*caratteristico*) typical; (*appropriato*) proper ● *adv* just; (*veramente*) really; **non ~** not really, not exactly; (*affatto*) not... at all ● *pron* one's own ● *nm* one's own; **lavorare in ~** be one's own boss; **mettersi in ~** set up on one's own

propu'gnare *vt* support

propulsi'one *nf* propulsion; **a ~ atomica** atomic[-powered]. **~ a getto** jet propulsion

propul'sore *nm* propeller

'prora *nf Naut* prow

'proroga *nf* extension

proro'gabile *a* extendable

proro'gare *vt* extend

pro'rompere *vi* burst out

'prosa *nf* prose

pro'saico *a* prosaic

pro'sciogliere *vt* release; *Jur* acquit

prosciogli'mento *nm* release

pro'sciolto *pp di* **prosciogliere**

prosciu'gare *vt* dry up; (*bonificare*) reclaim

prosciu'garsi *vr* dry up

prosci'utto *nm* ham. **~ cotto** cooked ham. **~ crudo** type of dry-cured ham, Parma ham

pro'scritto, -a *pp di* **proscrivere** ● *nmf* exile

pro'scrivere *vt* exile, banish

proscrizi'one *nf* exile, banishment

prosecuzi'one *nf* continuation

prosegui'mento *nm* continuation; **buon ~!** (*viaggio*) have a good journey!; (*festa*) enjoy the rest of the party!

prosegu'ire *vt* continue ● *vi* go on, continue

pro'selito *nm* convert

prospe'rare *vi* prosper

prosperità *nf* prosperity

'prospero *a* prosperous; (*favorevole*) favourable

prospe'roso *a* flourishing; ⟨*ragazza*⟩ buxom

prospet'tare *vt* show

prospet'tarsi *vr* seem

prospet'tiva *nf* perspective; (*panorama*) view; *fig* prospect

pro'spetto *nm* (*vista*) view; (*facciata*) façade; (*tabella*) table

prospici'ente *a* facing

prossima'mente *adv* soon

prossimità *nf* proximity; **in ~ di** near

'prossimo, -a *a* near; (*seguente*) next; (*molto vicino*) close; **l'anno ~** next year; **~ venturo** next; **essere ~ a fare qcsa** be about to do sth ● *nmf* neighbour

'prostata *nf* prostate

prostitu'irsi *vr* prostitute oneself

prosti'tuta *nf* prostitute

prostituzi'one *nf* prostitution

pro'strare *vt* prostrate

pro'strarsi *vr* prostrate oneself

pro'strato *a* prostrate

protago'nista *nmf* protagonist

pro'teggere *vt* protect; (*favorire*) favour

pro'teico *a* protein *attrib*; **molto ~** rich in protein

prote'ina *nf* protein

pro'tendere *vt* stretch out

pro'tendersi *vr* (*in avanti*) lean out

pro'teso *pp di* **protendere**

pro'testa *nf* protest; (*dichiarazione*) protestation

prote'stante *a & nmf* Protestant

prote'stare *vt/i* protest

prote'starsi *vr* **~ innocente** protest one's innocence

protet'tivo *a* protective

pro'tetto *pp di* **proteggere**

protetto'rato *nm* protectorate

protet'|tore, -'trice *nmf* protector; (*sostenitore*) patron ● *nm* (*di prostituta*) pimp

protezi'one *nf* protection. **~ civile** civil defence. **~ della natura** nature conservancy

protocol'lare *a* (*visita*) protocol ● *vt* register

proto'collo *nm* protocol; (*registro*) register; **carta ~** official stamped paper

pro'totipo *nm* prototype

pro'trarre *vt* protract; (*differire*) postpone

pro'trarsi *vr* go on, continue

pro'tratto *pp di* **protrarre**

protube'rante *a* protuberant

protube'ranza *nf* protuberance

'prova *nf* test; (*dimostrazione*) proof; (*tentativo*) try, attempt; (*di abito*) fitting; *Sport* heat; *Theat* rehearsal; (*bozza*) proof; **prove** *pl* evidence; **fino a ~ contraria** until I'm told otherwise; **in ~** (*assumere*) for a trial period; **mettere alla ~** put to the test; **a ~ di bomba** bombproof; **a ~ di ladro** burglarproof. **~ del fuoco** acid test. **~ generale** dress rehearsal

pro'vare *vt* test; (*dimostrare*) prove; (*tentare*) try; try on (*abiti ecc*); (*sentire*) feel; *Theat* rehearse; **proval** just try!

pro'varsi *vr* try

proveni'enza *nf* origin

prove'nire *vi* **~ da** come from

pro'vento *nm* proceeds *pl*

prove'nuto *pp di* **provenire**

pro'verbio *nm* proverb

pro'vetta *nf* test-tube; **bambino in ~** test-tube baby

pro'vetto *a* skilled

pro'vincia *nf* province; (*strada*) B road, secondary road

provinci'ale *a* provincial; **strada ~** B road, secondary road

pro'vino *nm* specimen; *Cinema* screen test

provo'cante *a* provocative

provo'care *vt* provoke; (*causare*) cause

provoca'|tore, -'trice *nmf* trouble-maker

provoca'torio *a* provocative

provocazi'one *nf* provocation

provo'lone *nm* type of cheese with a slightly smoked flavour

provve'dere *vi* **~ a** provide for

provvedi'mento *nm* measure; (*previdenza*) precaution. **~ disciplinare** disciplinary measure

provvedito'rato *nm* **~ agli studi** education department

provvedi'tore *nm* **~ agli studi** director of education

provvi'denza *nf* providence

provvidenzi'ale *a* providential

provvigi'one *nf Comm* commission; **lavorare a ~** work on commission

provvi'sorio *a* provisional; **in via provvisoria** provisionally, for the time being

prov'vista *nf* supply

pro'zia *nf* great-aunt

pro'zio *nm* great-uncle

'prua *nf Naut* prow

pru'dente *a* prudent

pru'denza *nf* prudence; **per ~** as a precaution

prudenzi'ale *a* prudential

'prudere *vi* itch

'prugna *nf* plum. **~ secca** prune. **~ selvatica** damson

'prugno *nm* plum[-tree]

'prugnolo *nm* sloe

pruri'gi'noso *a* itchy

pru'rito *nm* itch

P.S. *abbr* (**Pubblica Sicurezza**) police

pseu'donimo *nm* pseudonym

psica'nalisi *nf* psychoanalysis

psicana'lista *nmf* psychoanalyst

psicanaliz'zare *vt* psychoanalyse

'psiche *nf* psyche

psiche'delico *a* psychedelic

psichi'atra *nmf* psychiatrist

psichia'tria *nf* psychiatry

psichi'atrico *a* psychiatric

'psichico *a* mental

psico'farmaco *nm* drug that affects the mind

psicolo'gia *nf* psychology

psico'logico *a* psychological

psi'cologo, -a *nmf* psychologist

psico'patico, -a *a* psychopathic ● *nmf* psychopath

psicopedago'gia *nf* educational psychology

psi'cosi *nf inv* psychosis

psicoso'matico *a* psychosomatic

psicotera'peuta *nmf* psychotherapist

psicotera'pista *nmf* psychotherapist

psi'cotico, -a *a & nmf* psychotic

PT *abbr* (**Posta e Telegrafi**) PO

puàh *int* yuck!

pub *nm* pub

pubbli'care *vt* publish

pubblicazi'one *nf* publication. **pubblicazioni** *pl* (*di matrimonio*) banns. **~ periodica** periodical

pubbli'cista *nmf Journ* correspondent

pubblicità *nf inv* publicity, advertising; (*annuncio*) advertisement, advert; **fare ~ a qcsa** advertise sth; **piccola ~** small advertisements

pubblici'tario *a* advertising

'pubblico *a* public; **scuola pubblica** state school ● *nm* public; (*spettatori*) audience; **in ~** in public; **grande ~** general public. **Pubblica Sicurezza** police. **~ ministero** public prosecutor. **~ ufficiale** civil servant

'pube *nm* pubis

pubertà *nf* puberty

pu'dico *a* modest

pu'dore *nm* modesty

pue'rile *a* children's; *pej* childish

'puerpera *nf* new mother

puerpe'rale *a* of childbirth, puerperal *fml*; (*depressione*) postnatal

puer'perio *nm* postnatal period

pugi'lato *nm* boxing

'pugile *nm* boxer

'Puglia *nf* Apulia

pugli'ese *a & nmf* Apulian

pugna'lare *vt* stab

pugna'lata *nf* stab

pu'gnale *nm* dagger

'pugno *nm* fist; (*colpo*) punch; (*manciata*) fistful; (*fig: numero limitato*) handful; **dare un ~ a** punch; **di proprio ~** (*scrivere*) in one's own hand; **fare a pugni** (*colori:*) clash; **tenere in ~** (*situazione*) have under control; have in the palm of one's hand (*persona*); **un ~ in un occhio** *fig* an eyesore. **~ di ferro** iron fist

'pula *nf sl* **la ~** the fuzz

'pulce *nf* flea; (*microfono*) bug; **mettere la ~ nell'orecchio a qcno** sow a doubt in sb's mind

pul'cino *nm* chick; (*nel calcio*) junior

pu'ledra *nf* filly

pu'ledro *nm* foal, colt

pu'leggia *nf* pulley

pu'lire *vt* clean. **~ a secco** dry-clean; **far ~ qcsa** have sth cleaned

puliscipi'edi *nm inv* boot scraper

pu'lito *a* clean

puli'tura *nf* cleaning

puli'zia *nf* (*il pulire*) cleaning; (*l'essere pulito*) cleanliness; **pulizie** *pl* housework;

fare le pulizie do the cleaning. **~ personale** personal hygiene

'pullman *nm inv* coach, bus; (*urbano*) bus; **gita in ~** coach trip

pull'over *nm* pullover

pul'mino *nm* minibus

'pulpito *nm* pulpit

pul'sante *nm* button; *Electr* [push-]button. **~ di accensione** on/off switch. **~ di alimentazione** power switch

pul'sare *vi* pulsate

pulsazi'one *nf* pulsation

pul'viscolo *nm* dust

'puma *nm inv* puma

pun'gente *a* prickly; (*insetto*) stinging; (*odore ecc*) sharp

'pungere *vt* prick; (*insetto:*) sting; **~ qcno sul vivo** cut sb to the quick

pungersi *vr* prick oneself; **~ un dito** prick one's finger

pungigli'one *nm* sting

pungo'lare *vt* goad

pu'nire *vt* punish

puni'tivo *a* punitive

punizi'one *nf* punishment; *Sport* penalty; (*in calcio*) free kick. **~ corporale** corporal punishment

'punta *nf* point; (*estremità*) tip; (*di monte*) peak, top; (*un po'*) pinch; *Sport* forward; **doppie punte** (*di capelli*) split ends; **di ~** (*ore*) peak; (*personaggio*) leading

pun'tare *vt* point; (*spingere con forza*) push; (*scommettere*) bet; (*fam: appuntare*) fasten ● *vi* **~ su** *fig* rely on; (*scommettere*) bet on; **~ verso** (*dirigersi*) head for; **~ a** aspire to; **punta e clicca** *Comput* point and click

punta'spilli *nm inv* pincushion

pun'tata *nf* (*di una storia*) instalment; (*televisiva*) episode; (*al gioco*) stake, bet; (*breve visita*) flying visit; **a puntate** serialized, in instalments; **fare una ~ a/in** pop over to (*luogo*)

punteggia'tura *nf* punctuation

pun'teggio *nm* score

puntel'lare *vt* prop

pun'tello *nm* prop

punteru'olo *nm* awl

pun'tiglio *nm* spite; (*ostinazione*) obstinacy

puntigli'oso *a* punctilious, pernickety *pej*

pun'tina *nf* (*da disegno*) drawing pin, thumb tack *Am*; (*di giradischi*) stylus. **~ da disegno** drawing pin, thumb tack *Am*

pun'tine *nf pl* points

pun'tino *nm* dot; **a ~** perfectly; (*cotto*) to a T. **puntini** *pl* [**di sospensione**] suspension points

'punto *nm* point; (*in cucito, Med*) stitch; (*in punteggiatura*) full stop; **in che ~?** where, exactly?; **di ~ in bianco** all of a sudden; **essere sul ~ di fare qcsa** be on the point of doing sth, be about to do sth; **in ~** sharp; **mettere a ~** put right; *fig* fine-tune; tune up (*motore*); **messa a ~** fine tuning; **due punti** colon. **punti** *pl* **cardinali** points of the compass. **~ cieco** blind spot. **~ di congela-**

mento freezing point. **~ croce** cross-stitch. **~ debole** blind spot. **~ di domanda** question mark. **~ di ebollizione** boiling point. **~ esclamativo** exclamation mark. **~ di fuga** vanishing point. **~ di fusione** melting point. **~ d'incontro** meeting-point. **~ di infiammabilità** flashpoint. **~ interrogativo** question mark. **~ nero** *Med* blackhead. **~ di pareggio** *Fin* breakeven point. **~ di partenza** starting point. **~ di riferimento** landmark; *(per la qualità)* benchmark. **~ di rottura** breaking point. **~ a smerlo** blanket stitch. **~ di vendita** point of sale, outlet; **pubblicità al ~ ~ ~** point-of-sale publicity. **~ e virgola** semicolon. **~ di vista** point of view

puntu'ale *a* punctual; **essere ~** be punctual, be on time

puntualità *nf* punctuality

puntualiz'zare *vt* make clear, clarify

puntual'mente *adv* punctually, on time; *(come al solito)* as usual

pun'tura *nf (di insetto)* sting; *(di ago ecc)* prick; *Med* puncture; *(iniezione)* injection; *(fitta)* stabbing pain. **~ d'ape** bee sting. **~ d'insetto** insect bite. **~ di spillo** pinprick. **~ di zanzara** mosquito bite

punzecchi'are *vt* prick; *fig* tease

punzo'nare *vt Techn* punch, stamp

pun'zone *nm* punch

può *vedi* **potere**; **~ darsi** maybe, perhaps

'pupa *nf* doll

pu'pazzo *nm* puppet. **~ di neve** snowman

pup'illa *nf Anat* pupil

pu'pillo, -a *nmf Jur* ward; *(di professore)* favourite

purché *conj* provided

'pure *adv* too, also; *(concessivo)* **fate ~!** please do! ● *conj (tuttavia)* yet; *(anche se)* even if; **pur di** just to; **io ~** me too; **è venuto ~ lui** he came too, he also came

purè *nm inv* purée. **~ di patate** mashed potatoes, creamed potatoes

pu'rezza *nf* purity

'purga *nf* purge

pur'gante *nm* laxative

pur'gare *vt* purge

purga'torio *nm* purgatory

purifi'care *vt* purify

purificazi'one *nf* purification

pu'rista *nmf* purist

puri'tano, -a *a & nmf* Puritan

'puro *a* pure; *(vino ecc)* undiluted; **per ~ caso** by sheer chance, purely by chance. **~ cotone** *nm* pure cotton, 100% cotton. **pura lana vergine** *nf* pure new wool. **pura seta** *nf* pure silk

puro'sangue *a & nm* thoroughbred

pur'troppo *adv* unfortunately

'pus *nm* pus

'pustola *nf* pimple

puti'ferio *nm* uproar

putre'fare *vi* putrefy

putre'farsi *vr* putrefy

putre'fatto *a* rotten

putrefazi'one *nf* putrefaction

'putrido *a* putrid

putt *nm inv* putt

put'tana *nf vulg* whore

'puzza *nf* stink; **avere la ~ sotto il naso** be sniffy

puz'zare *vi anche fig* stink; **~ di bruciato** *fig* smell fishy; **~ d'imbroglio** stink; **~ di corruzione** stink of corruption; **questa storia mi puzza** the story stinks

'puzzo *nm* stink

'puzzola *nf* polecat

puzzo'lente *a* stinking

puz'zone *nm fam* bastard

p.zza *abbr* **(piazza)** Sq.

QI *abbr* **(quoziente di intelligenza)** IQ

qua *adv* here; **da un anno in ~** for the last year; **da quando in ~?** since when?; **di ~** this way; **di ~ di** on this side of; **~ dentro** in here; **~ sotto** under here; **~ vicino** near here; **~ e là** here and there

'quacchero, -a *nmf* Quaker

qua'derno *nm* exercise book; *(per appunti)* notebook. **~ a quadretti** maths exercise book. **~ a righe** lined exercise book

quadrango'lare *a (forma)* quadrangular; **incontro ~** *Sport* four-sided tournament

qua'drangolo *nm* quadrangle

qua'drante *nm* quadrant; *(di orologio)* dial

qua'drare *vt* square; *(contabilità)* balance ● *vi* fit in

qua'drato *a* square; *(equilibrato)* level-headed ● *nm* square; *(nel pugilato)* ring; **al ~** squared

quadra'tura *nf Math* squaring; *(di bilancio)* balancing

quadret'tare *vt* divide into small squares

quadret'tato *a* squared; *(carta)* graph *attrib*; *(tessuto)* check, checked

qua'dretto *nm* square; *(piccolo quadro)* small picture; **a quadretti** *(tessuto)* check

quadrico'mia *nf* four-colour printing

quadrien'nale *a (che dura quattro anni)* four-year; *(ogni quattro anni)* four-yearly

quadri'foglio nm four-leaf clover
qua'driglia nf square dance
quadri'latero nm quadrilateral
quadri'mestre nm (periodo) four-month period; Sch term
quadrimo'tore nm four-engined plane
quadri'nomio nm Math quadrinomial
quadripar'tito a four-party ● nm (politica) four-party government
quadri'plegico a quadriplegic
'quadro nm picture, painting; (quadrato) square; (fig: scena) sight; (tabella) table; Theat scene; (dirigente) executive; **fare il ~ della situazione** outline the situation; **fuori ~** Cinema, TV out of shot; **quadri** pl (carte) diamonds; **a quadri** ‹tessuto, giacca, motivo› check, checked. **~ clinico** case history. **~ di comando** control panel. **quadri** pl **direttivi** senior management. **~ di distribuzione** Electr switchboard. **quadri** pl **intermedi** middle management. **~ degli interruttori** switch panel
qua'drupede nm quadruped
quadrupli'care vt quadruple
quadrupli'carsi vr quadruple
qua'druplice a quadruple
'quadruplo a & nm quadruple
quaggiù adv down here
'quaglia nf quail
'qualche a (alcuni) a few, some; (un certo) some; (in interrogazioni) any; **ho ~ problema** I have a few problems, I have some problems; **~ tempo fa** some time ago; **hai ~ libro italiano?** have you any Italian books?; **posso prendere ~ libro?** can I take some books?; **in ~ modo** somehow; **in ~ posto** somewhere; **~ volta** sometimes; **~ cosa = qualcosa**
qualche'duno pron somebody, someone
qual'cosa pron something; (in interrogazioni) anything; **qualcos'altro** something else; **vuoi qualcos'altro?** would you like anything else?; **~ di strano** something strange; **vuoi ~ da mangiare?** would you like something to eat?; **vuoi ~ da bere?** would you like a drink?, would you like something to drink?
qual'cuno pron someone, somebody; (in interrogazioni) anyone, anybody; (alcuni) some; (in interrogazioni) any; **c'è ~?** is anybody in?; **qualcun altro** someone else, somebody else; **c'è qualcun altro che aspetta?** is anybody else waiting?; **ho letto ~ dei suoi libri** I've read some of his books; **conosci ~ dei suoi amici?** do you know any of his friends?
'quale a which; (indeterminato) what; (come) as, like; **~ macchina è la tua?** which car is yours?; **~ motivo avrà di parlare così?** what reason would he have to speak like that?; **~ onore!** what an honour!; **città quali Venezia** towns like Venice; **~ che sia la tua opinione** whatever you may think ● pron inter which [one]; **~ preferisci?** which [one] do you prefer? ● pron rel **il/la ~** (persona)

who; (animale, cosa) that, which; (oggetto: con prep) whom; (oggetto: animale, cosa) which; **ho incontrato tua madre, la ~ mi ha detto...** I met your mother who told me...; **l'ufficio nel ~ lavoro** the office in which I work; **l'uomo con il ~ parlavo** the man to whom I was speaking ● adv (come) as
qua'lifica nf qualification; (titolo) title
qualifi'cabile a qualifiable
qualifi'care vt qualify; (definire) define
qualifi'carsi vr be placed
qualifica'tivo a qualifying
qualifi'cato a ‹operaio› semi-skilled
qualificazi'one nf qualification
qualità nf inv quality; (specie) kind; **in ~ di** in one's capacity as; **di prima ~** high quality; **di ottima/cattiva ~** top/poor quality
qualitativa'mente adv qualitatively
qualita'tivo a qualitative
qua'lora conj in case
qual'siasi, qua'lunque a any; (non importa quale) whatever; (ordinario) ordinary; **dammi una penna ~** give me any pen [whatsoever]; **farei ~ cosa** I would do anything; **~ cosa io faccia** whatever I do; **~ persona** anyone, anybody; **in ~ caso** in any case; **uno ~** any one, whichever; **l'uomo qualunque** the man in the street; **vivo in una casa ~** I live in an ordinary house
qualunqu'ismo nm lack of political views
qualunqu'ista nmf (menefreghista) person with no political views
'quando conj & adv when; **da ~ ti ho visto** since I saw you; **da ~ esci con lui?** how long have you been going out with him?; **da ~ in qua?** since when?; **~... ~...** sometimes..., sometimes...; **continua ad insistere ~ sa di avere torto** he keeps on insisting even when he knows he's wrong
quantifi'cabile a quantifiable
quantifi'care vt quantify
quantità nf inv quantity; **una ~ di** (gran numero) a great deal of
quantitativa'mente adv quantitatively
quantita'tivo nm amount ● a quantitative
'quanto a inter how much; (con nomi plurali) how many; (in esclamazione) what a lot of; ‹tempo› how long; **quanti anni hai?** how old are you? ● a rel as much... as; ‹tempo› as long as; (con nomi plurali) as many... as; **prendi ~ denaro ti serve** take as much money as you need; **prendi quanti libri vuoi** take as many books as you like ● pron inter how much; (quanto tempo) how long; (plurale) how many; **quanti ne abbiamo oggi?** what date is it today? ● pron rel as much as; (quanto tempo) as long as; (plurale) as many as; **prendine ~/quanti ne vuoi** take as much/as many as you like; **stai ~ vuoi** stay as long as you like; **questo è ~** that's it ● adv inter how much; (quanto tempo) how long; **~ sei alto?** how tall are you?; **~ hai aspettato?** how long did you wait for?; **~ costa?** how much is it?; **~ mi dispiace!** I'm so sorry!; **~ è bello!** how nice! ● adv rel as much as; **lavoro ~ posso** I

work as much as I can; **è tanto intelligente ~ bello** he's as intelligent as he's good-looking; **in ~** (*in qualità di*) as; (*poiché*) since; **~ a** as for; **in ~ a me** as far as I'm concerned; **per ~ however; per ~ ne sappia** as far as I know; **per ~ mi riguarda** as far as I'm concerned; **per ~ mi sia simpatico** much as I like him; **~ prima** (*al più presto*) as soon as possible

quan'tunque *conj* although

qua'ranta *a & nm* forty

quaran'tena *nf* quarantine

quaran'tenne *a* forty-year-old; (*sulla quarantina*) in his/her forties ● *nmf* forty-year-old; (*sulla quarantina*) person in his/her forties

quaran'tennio *nm* period of forty years

quaran'tesimo *a & nm* fortieth

quaran'tina *nf* **una ~** about forty

qua'resima *nf* Lent

quar'tetto *nm* quartet

quarti'ere *nm* district, area; *Mil* quarters *pl.* **quartieri** *pl* **alti** smart districts. **quartieri** *pl* **bassi** poor areas. **~ cinese** Chinatown. **~ dormitorio** dormitory town. **~ generale** headquarters. **~ residenziale** residential area

quar'tino *nm* (*strumento musicale*) instrument similar to a clarinet; *Typ* quarto; (*di vino*) quarter litre

'quarto *a* fourth ● *nm* fourth; (*quarta parte*) quarter; **le sette e un ~** [a] quarter past seven, [a] quarter after seven *Am*; **a tre quarti** (*giacca, maniche*) three-quarter length. **quarti** *pl* **di finale** quarter-finals. **~ d'ora** quarter of an hour ● *nf* (*marcia*) fourth [gear]

quarto'genito, -a *nmf* fourth child

quar'tultimo, -a *a a & nmf* fourth last

'quarzo *nm* quartz; **al ~** quartz. **~ rosa** rose quartz

'quasi *adv* almost, nearly; **~ mai** hardly ever ● *conj* (*come se*) as if; **~ ~ sto a casa** I'm tempted to stay home

quas'sù *adv* up here

qua'terna *nf* (*lotto, tombola*) set of four winning numbers

quater'nario *nm* (*era*) Quaternary

'quatto *a* crouching; (*silenzioso*) silent; **starsene ~ ~** keep very quiet

quattordi'cenne *a & nmf* fourteen-year-old

quattordi'cesimo *a & nm* fourteenth

quat'tordici *a & nm* fourteen

quat'trini *nmpl* money *sg*, dosh *sg fam*

'quattro *a & nm* four; **dirne ~ a qcno** give sb a piece of one's mind; **farsi in ~** (**per qcno/per fare qcsa**) go to a lot of trouble (*for sb/to do sth*); **in ~ e quattr'otto** in a flash. **~ per ~** *nm inv Auto* four-wheel drive [vehicle]; **a ~ tempi** *Auto* four-stroke

quat'trocchi *adv* **a ~** in private

quattrocen'tesco *a* fifteenth-century

quattro'cento *a & nm* four hundred; **il Q~** the fifteenth century

quattro'mila *a & nm* four thousand

Qué'bec *nm* Quebec

'quello *a* that (*pl* those); **quell'albero** that tree; **quegli alberi** those trees; **quel cane** that dog; **quei cani** those dogs ● *pron* that [one] (*pl* those [ones]); **~ lì** that one over there; **~ che** the one that; (*ciò che*) what; **quelli che** the ones that, those that; **~ a destra** the one on the right

'quercia *nf* oak; **di ~** oak

que'rela *nf* [legal] action

que'relante *nmf* plaintiff

quere'lare *vt* bring an action against

quere'lato, -a *nmf* defendant

que'sito *nm* question

questio'nare *vi* dispute

questio'nario *nm* questionnaire

quest'ione *nf* question; (*faccenda*) matter; (*litigio*) quarrel; **in ~** in doubt; **è fuori ~** it's out of the question; **è ~ di vita o di morte** it's a matter of life and death; **mettere qcsa in ~** cast doubt on sth; **una ~ personale** a personal matter

'questo *a* this (*pl* these) ● *pron* this [one] (*pl* these [ones]); **~ qui, ~ qua** this one here; **~ è quello che a detto** that's what he said; **per ~** for this *or* that reason; **quest'oggi** today

que'store *nm* chief of police

'questua *nf* collection

que'stura *nf* police headquarters

qui *adv* here; **da ~ in poi, da ~ in avanti** from now on; **di ~ a una settimana** in a week's time; **fin ~** (*di tempo*) up till now, until now; **~ dentro** in here; **~ sotto** under here; **qui vicino** *adv* near here ● *nm* **~ pro quo** misunderstanding

quie'scenza *nf* (*di vulcano*) dormancy; (*pensione*) retirement; **trattamento di ~** retirement package

quie'tanza *nf* receipt

quie'tare *vt* calm

quie'tarsi *vr* calm down

qui'ete *nf* quiet; **disturbo della ~ pubblica** breach of the peace; **stato di ~** *Phys* state of rest

qui'eto *a* quiet

'quindi *adv* then ● *conj* therefore

quindi'cenne *a & nmf* fifteen-year-old

quindi'cesimo *a & nm* fifteenth

'quindici *a & nm* fifteen; **~ giorni** a fortnight *Br*, two weeks *pl*

quindi'cina *nf* **una ~** about fifteen; **una ~ di giorni** a fortnight *Br*, two weeks *pl*

quindici'nale *a* fortnightly *Br*, twice-monthly ● *nm* fortnightly magazine *Br*, twice-monthly magazine

quinquen'nale *a* (*che dura cinque anni*) five-year; (*ogni cinque anni*) five-yearly

quin'quennio *nm* [period of] five years

'quinta *nf Auto* fifth [gear], overdrive

quin'tale *nm* a hundred kilograms

'quinte *nfpl Theat* wings

quintes'senza *nf* quintessence

quin'tetto *nm* quintet

'**quinto** *a & nm* fifth

quintupli'care *vt* quintuple

quin'tuplo *a* quintuple

qui'squiglia *nf* trifle; **perdersi in quisquiglie** get bogged down in details

quiz *nm inv* [**gioco a**] ~ quiz game. ~ **radiofonico** radio quiz

'**quota** *nf* quota; (*rata*) instalment; (*altitudine*) height; *Aeron* altitude, height; (*ippica*) odds *pl*; **perdere/prendere** ~ lose/gain altitude *o* height; **da alta** ~ high-flying. ~ **fissa** fixed amount. ~ **non imponibile** personal allowance. ~ **di iscrizione** entry

fee; (*di club*) membership fee. ~ **di mercato** market share. ~ **zero** sea level

quo'tare *vt Comm* quote

quo'tato *a* quoted; **essere** ~ **in Borsa** be quoted on the Stock Exchange

quotazi'one *nf* quotation. ~ **d'acquisto** buying rate. ~ **ufficiale** (*in Borsa*) official quotation. ~ **di vendita** selling rate

quotidiana'mente *adv* daily

quotidi'ano *a* daily; (*ordinario*) everyday ● *nm* daily [paper]

'**quoto** *nm Math* quotient

quozi'ente *nm* quotient. ~ **d'intelligenza** intelligence quotient, IQ. ~ **di purezza** purity

---

Rr

---

ra'barbaro *nm* rhubarb

'**rabbia** *nf* rage; (*ira*) anger; *Med* rabies *sg*; **che** ~! what a nuisance!; **mi fa** ~ it makes me angry

'**rabbico** *a* ⟨*virus*⟩ rabies *attrib*

rab'bino *nm* rabbi

rabbiosa'mente *adv* furiously

rabbi'oso *a* hot-tempered; *Med* rabid; (*violento*) violent

rabboc'care *vt* top up ⟨*fiasco*⟩

rabbo'nire *vt* pacify

rabbo'nirsi *vr* calm down

rabbri'vidire *vi* shudder; (*di freddo*) shiver

rabbuf'fare *vt* reprimand; ruffle ⟨*capelli*⟩

rab'buffo *nm* reprimand

rabbui'arsi *vr* get dark; ⟨*viso:*⟩ darken

rabdo'mante *nmf* water diviner

rabdoman'zia *nf* water divining

raccapez'zare *vt* put together

raccapez'zarsi *vr* see one's way ahead

raccapricci'ante *a* horrifying

raccatta'palle *nm inv* ball boy ● *nf inv* ball girl

raccat'tare *vt* pick up

rac'chetta *nf* racket. ~ **da neve** snowshoe. ~ **da ping pong** table-tennis bat. ~ **da sci** ski stick, ski pole. ~ **da tennis** tennis racket

'**racchio** *a fam* ugly

racchi'udere *vt* contain

rac'cogliere *vt* pick; (*da terra*) pick up; (*mietere*) harvest; (*collezionare*) collect; (*radunare*) gather; win ⟨*voti ecc*⟩; (*dare asilo a*) take in

rac'cogliersi *vr* gather; (*concentrarsi*) collect one's thoughts

raccogli'mento *nm* concentration

raccogli'tore, -'trice *nmf* collector ● *nm* ~ [**a fogli mobili**] ring-binder

rac'colta *nf* collection; (*di scritti*) compilation; (*del grano ecc*) harvesting; (*adunata*)

gathering; **chiamare a** ~ call *o* gather together. ~ **differenziata** collection of items for recycling. ~ **di fondi** fund-raising

rac'colto, -a *pp di* **raccogliere** ● *a* (*rannicchiato*) hunched; (*intimo*) cosy; (*concentrato*) engrossed ● *nm* (*mietitura*) harvest

raccoman'dabile *a* advisable; **poco** ~ ⟨*persona*⟩ shady

raccoman'dare *vt* recommend; (*affidare*) entrust

raccoman'darsi *vr* (*implorare*) beg

raccoman'data *nf* letter sent by recorded delivery; **per** ~ by recorded delivery. ~ **con ricevuta di ritorno** *letter sent by recorded delivery with acknowledgement of receipt*

raccoman'data-e'spresso *nf express recorded delivery service*

raccomandazi'one *nf* recommendation

raccomo'dare *vt* repair

raccon'tare *vt* tell

rac'conto *nm* story

raccorci'are *vt* shorten

raccorci'arsi *vr* become shorter; ⟨*giorni:*⟩ draw in

raccor'dare *vt* join

rac'cordo *nm* connection; (*stradale*) feeder. ~ **anulare** ring road. ~ **autostradale** motorway junction *Br*, intersection. ~ **ferroviario** siding. ~ **a gomito** elbow

ra'chitico *a* rickety; (*poco sviluppato*) stunted

racimo'lare *vt* scrape together

'**racket** *nm inv* racket

'**rada** *nf Naut* roads *pl*

'**radar** *nm* radar; **uomo** ~ air traffic controller

radden'sare *vt* thicken

radden'sarsi *vr* thicken

raddob'bare *vt* refit

rad'dobbo *nm* refit

raddol'cire vt sweeten; fig soften

raddol'cirsi vr become milder; ‹carattere:› mellow

raddoppia'mento nm doubling

raddoppi'are vt double

rad'doppio nm doubling; (equitazione) gallop; (biliardo) double

raddriz'zabile a which can be straightened

raddriz'zare vt straighten

raddrizza'tore nm (di corrente) rectifier

ra'dente a grazing, shaving; **tiro ~** Mil grazing fire; Sport low shot just skimming the surface; **volo ~** Aeron hedge-hopping

'radere vt shave; graze ‹muro›; **~ al suolo** raze [to the ground]

'radersi vr shave

radi'ale a radial

radi'ante a radiant ● nm Math radian

radi'are vt strike off; **~ dall'albo** strike off ‹medico›; debar ‹avvocato›

radia'tore nm radiator

radiazi'one nf radiation. **~ nucleare** nuclear radiation

'radica nf briar

radi'cale a radical ● nm Gram root; Pol radical

radical'mente adv radically

radi'carsi vr **~ in** be rooted in

radi'cato a deep-seated

ra'dicchio nm chicory

ra'dice nf root; **mettere [le] radici** ‹pianta:› take root; fig put down roots. **~ quadrata** square root

'radio nf inv radio; **via ~** by radio; **contatto ~** radio contact; **ponte ~** radio link. **~ pirata** pirate radio. **~ portatile** portable radio. **~ ricevente** receiver. **~ [a] transistor** transistor radio. **~ trasmittente** transmitter ● nm Chem radium

radioama'tore, -'trice nmf radio ham

radioascolta'tore, -'trice nmf listener

radioassi'stito a radio-assisted

radioattività nf radioactivity

radioat'tivo a radioactive

radiobiolo'gia nf radiobiology

radio'bussola nf radio compass

radiocoman'dare vt operate by remote control

radiocoman'dato a remote-controlled, radio-controlled

radio'cronaca nf radio commentary; **fare la ~ di** commentate on

radiocro'nista nmf radio reporter

radiodiffusi'one nf broadcasting

radio'faro nm radio beacon

radio'fonico a radio attrib

radiofre'quenza nf radio frequency

radiogo'niometro nm direction finder, radiogoniometer

radiogra'fare vt X-ray

radiogra'fia nf X-ray [photograph]; (radiologia) radiography; **fare una ~** ‹paziente:› have an X-ray; ‹dottore:› take an X-ray

radio'lina nf transistor

radiolocaliz'zare vt locate by radar

radi'ologo, -a nmf radiologist

radio'onda nf radio wave

radioregistra'tore nm **~ portatile** portable radio cassette recorder

radiosco'pia nf Med radioscopy

radio'scopico a radioscopic

radi'oso a radiant

radio'spia nf bug

radio'sveglia nf radio alarm, clock radio

radio'taxi nm inv radio taxi

radiote'lefono nm radio-telephone; (privato) cordless [phone]

radiotelevi'sivo a broadcasting attrib

radiotera'pia nf radiotherapy

radiotra'smettere vt radio

radiotrasmetti'tore nm radio

radiotrasmit'tente nf radio station

'rado a sparse; (non frequente) rare; **di ~** seldom

radu'nare vt gather [together]

radu'narsi vr gather [together]

radu'nata nf gathering. **~ sediziosa** seditious assembly

ra'duno nm meeting; Sport rally

ra'dura nf clearing

'rafano nm horseradish

raffazzo'nato a ‹discorso, lavoro› botched

raf'fermo a stale

'raffica nf gust; (di armi da fuoco) burst; (di domande, insulti) barrage

raffigu'rare vt represent

raffigurazi'one nf representation

raffi'nare vt refine

raffinata'mente adv elegantly

raffina'tezza nf refinement

raffi'nato a refined

raffine'ria nf refinery. **~ di petrolio** oil refinery

rafforza'mento nm reinforcement; (di muscolatura, carattere) strengthening

rafforz'are vt reinforce

rafforza'tivo a Gram intensifying ● nm Gram intensifier

raffredda'mento nm (processo) cooling; **di ~** cooling. **~ ad acqua** water-cooling. **~ ad aria** air-cooling

raffred'dare vt cool

raffred'darsi vr get cold; (prendere un raffreddore) catch a cold; (sentimento, passione:) cool [off]

raffred'dato a **essere ~** ‹persona› have a cold

raffred'dore nm cold; **avere il ~** have a cold. **~ da fieno** hay fever

raf'fronto nm comparison

'rafia nf raffia

Rag. abbr **ragioniere**

ra'gazza nf girl; (fidanzata) girlfriend; **nome da ~** maiden name. **~ copertina** cover girl. **~ madre** unmarried mother. **~ alla pari** au pair [girl]. **~ squillo** call girl

ragaz'zata nf prank

ra'gazzo *nm* boy; (*fidanzato*) boyfriend; **da ~** (*da giovane*) as a boy. **~ padre** unmarried father. **~ di strada** guttersnipe. **~ di vita** rent boy

ragge'lare *vt fig* freeze

ragge'larsi *vr fig* turn to ice

raggi'ante *a* radiant; **~ di successo** flushed with success

raggi'era *nf* **a ~** with a pattern like spokes radiating from a centre

raggi'era *nf* (*di ruota*) spokes *pl*

'raggio *nm* ray; *Math* radius; (*di ruota*) spoke; **a raggi infrarossi** infrared. **~ d'azione** range. **~ laser** laser beam. **~ di luna** moonbeam. **~ di sole** ray of sunshine, sunbeam. **~ di speranza** ray of hope. **~ ultravioletto** ultraviolet ray. **raggi** *pl* **X** X-rays

raggi'rare *vt* trick

rag'giro *nm* trick

raggi'ungere *vt* reach; (*conseguire*) achieve

raggiun'gibile *a* (*luogo*) within reach

raggiungi'mento *nm* attainment

raggomito'lare *vt* wind

raggomito'larsi *vr* curl up

raggranel'lare *vt* scrape together

raggrin'zire *vt* wrinkle

raggrin'zirsi *vr* wrinkle

raggru'mare *vt* curdle (*latte*)

raggru'marsi *vr* (*latte:*) curdle

raggruppa'mento *nm* (*gruppo*) group; (*azione*) grouping; *Comm* groupage

raggrup'pare *vt* group together

ragguagli'are *vt* compare; (*informare*) inform

raggu'aglio *nm* comparison; (*informazione*) information

ragguar'devole *a* considerable

'ragia *nf* resin; **acqua ~** turpentine

ragià *nm inv* rajah

ragiona'mento *nm* reasoning; (*discussione*) discussion. **~ per assurdo** reductio ad absurdum

ragio'nare *vi* reason; (*discutere*) discuss

ragio'nato *a* (*argomento*) reasoned; (*cruciverba*) cryptic

ragi'one *nf* reason; (*ciò che è giusto*) right; **a ~ o a torto** rightly or wrongly; **aver ~** be right; **perdere la ~** go out of one's mind; **ragion veduta** after due consideration; **prenderle/darle di santa ~** get/give a good walloping. **ragion d'essere** raison d'être. **~ di scambio** terms of trade. **~ sociale** company name. **ragion di Stato** reasons of State

ragione'ria *nf* accountancy; (*scuola*) secondary school which provides training in accountancy

ragio'nevole *a* reasonable

ragionevol'mente *adv* reasonably

ragioni'ere, -a *nmf* accountant

ra'glan *a inv* (*manica*) raglan

ragli'are *vi* bray

'raglio *nm* bray

ragna'tela *nf* cobweb

'ragno *nm* spider

ragù *nm inv* meat sauce

RAI *nf abbr* (**Radio Audizioni Italiane**) Italian public broadcasting company

'raid *nm inv* raid

'raionᴿ *nm* rayonᴿ

ra'lenti *nm* **al ~** in slow motion

rallegra'menti *nmpl* congratulations

ralle'grare *vt* gladden

ralle'grarsi *vr* rejoice; **~ con qcno** congratulate sb

rallenta'mento *nm* slowing down

rallen'tare *vt/i* slow down; (*allentare*) slacken

rallen'tarsi *vr* slow down

rallenta'tore *nm* (*su strada*) speed bump; **al ~** in slow motion

'rally *nm inv* rally

RAM *nf inv* RAM

ramai'olo *nm* ladle

raman'zina *nf* reprimand

ra'mare *vt* stake (*pianta*)

ra'marro *nm* (*animale*) type of lizard

ra'mato *a* (*capelli*) copper[-coloured], coppery

'rame *nm* copper; **color ~** copper-coloured

ramifi'care *vi* (*pianta:*) put out branches

ramifi'carsi *vr* (*pianta:*) put out branches; (*strada, fiume, matematica ecc:*) branch; (*teoria:*) ramify, branch

ramificazi'one *nf* ramification

ra'mino *nm* rummy

rammari'carsi *vr* **~ di** regret; (*lamentarsi*) complain (**di** about)

ram'marico *nm* regret

rammen'dare *vt* darn

ram'mendo *nm* darning

rammen'tare *vt* remember; **~ qcsa a qcno** (*richiamare alla memoria*) remind sb of sth

rammen'tarsi *vr* remember

rammol'lire *vt* soften

rammol'lirsi *vr* go soft

rammol'lito, -a *nmf* wimp

'ramo *nm* branch

ramo'scello *nm* twig

'rampa *nf* (*di scale*) flight. **~ d'accesso** slip road. **~ di carico** loading ramp. **~ di lancio** launch[ing] pad

ram'pante *a* (*leone, cavallo*) rampant; **giovane ~** yuppie

rampi'cante *a* climbing ● *nm Bot* creeper

ram'pino *nm* hook; *fig* pretext

ram'pollo *nm hum* brat; (*discendente*) descendant

ram'pone *nm* harpoon; (*per scarpe*) crampon

'rana *nf* frog; (*nel nuoto*) breaststroke; **uomo ~** frogman

ranch *nm inv* ranch

'rancido *a* rancid

'rancio *nm* rations *pl*

ran'core *nm* rancour, resentment; **serbare ~ verso qcno** bear sb a grudge

'randa *nf* mainsail

ran'dagio *a* stray

randel'lata *nf* blow with a club

ran'dello *nm* club
'rango *nm* rank
rannicchi'arsi *vr* huddle up
rannuvola'mento *nm* clouding over
rannuvo'larsi *vr* cloud over
ra'nocchio *nm* frog
ranto'lare *vi* wheeze
'rantolo *nm* wheeze; (*di moribondo*) death-rattle
ra'nuncolo *nm* buttercup
'rapa *nf* turnip
ra'pace *a* rapacious; ‹*uccello*› predatory
rapa'nello *nm* radish
ra'pare *vt* crop
ra'parsi *vr fam* have one's head shaved
'rapida *nf* rapids *pl*
rapida'mente *adv* quickly, rapidly
rapidità *nf* speed
'rapido *a* fast, quick; ‹*guarigione, sviluppo*› rapid ● *nm* (*treno*) express [train]
rapi'mento *nm* (*crimine*) kidnapping
ra'pina *nf* robbery, hold-up *fam;* ~ **a mano armata** armed robbery. ~ **in banca** bank robbery
rapi'nare *vt* rob
rapina'tore *nm* robber. ~ **di banca** bank robber
ra'pire *vt* abduct; (*per riscatto*) kidnap; (*fig: estasiare*) ravish
ra'pito, -a *a* abducted; (*per riscatto*) kidnapped; (*estasiato*) rapt ● *nmf* kidnap victim
rapi'tore, -'trice *nmf* kidnapper
rappacifi'care *vt* pacify
rappacifi'carsi *vr* be reconciled, make it up
rappacificazi'one *nf* reconciliation
'rapper *nmf inv Mus* rapper
rappez'zare *vt* patch up
rappor'tare *vt* reproduce ‹*disegno*›; (*confrontare*) compare
rap'porto *nm* report; (*connessione*) relation; (*legame*) relationship; *Math, Techn* ratio; **rapporti** *pl* relations, relationship; **essere in buoni rapporti** be on good terms. **rapporti** *pl* **d'affari** business relations. ~ **di amicizia** friendship; **avere un** ~ ~ ~ **con qcno** be friends with sb. ~ **di lavoro** working relationship. ~ **di parentela** family relationship; **aver un** ~ ~ ~ **con qcno** be related to sb. **rapporti** *pl* **prematrimoniali** premarital sex. ~ **prezzo-prestazioni** price/performance ratio. ~ **prezzo-qualità** value for money. **rapporti** *pl* **sessuali** sexual intercourse. ~ **di trasmissione** *Auto* gear
rap'prendersi *vr* set; ‹*latte:*› curdle
rappre'saglia *nf* reprisal
rappresen'tante *nmf* representative. ~ **di classe** class representative. ~ **di commercio** sales representative, [sales] rep *fam*. ~ **sindacale** trade union representative
rappresen'tanza *nf* delegation; *Comm* agency; **spese di** ~ entertainment expenses; **di** ~ ‹*appartamento, macchina*› company

attrib. ~ **esclusiva** sole agency. ~ **legale** legal representation. ~ **proporzionale** proportional representation, PR
rappresen'tare *vt* represent; *Theat* perform
rappresentativa *nf* representatives *pl*
rappresenta'tivo *a* representative
rappresentazi'one *nf* representation; (*spettacolo*) performance
rap'preso *pp di* **rapprendersi**
rapso'dia *nf* rhapsody
'raptus *nm inv* fit of madness
rara'mente *adv* rarely, seldom
rare'fare *vt* rarefy
rare'farsi *vr* rarefy
rare'fatto *a* rarefied
rarità *nf inv* rarity
'raro *a* rare
ra'sare *vt* shave; trim ‹*siepe ecc*›
ra'sarsi *vr* shave
ra'sato *a* shaved
rasa'tura *nf* shaving
raschia'mento *nm Med* curettage
raschi'are *vt* scrape; (*togliere*) scrape off
raschi'arsi *vr* ~ **la gola** clear one's throat
rasen'tare *vt* go close to
ra'sente *prep* very close to
'raso *pp di* **radere** ● *a* smooth; (*colmo*) full to the brim; ‹*barba*› close-cropped; ~ **terra** close to the ground; **un cucchiaio** ~ a level spoonful ● *nm* satin
ra'soio *nm* razor. ~ **elettrico** electric shaver. ~ **a mano libera** cut-throat razor
'raspa *nf* rasp
'raspo *nm* (*di uva*) small bunch
ras'segna *nf* review; (*mostra*) exhibition; (*musicale, cinematografica*) festival; **passare in** ~ review; *Mil* inspect
rasse'gnare *vt* present
rasse'gnarsi *vr* resign oneself
rassegnata'mente *adv* with resignation
rasse'gnato *a* ‹*persona, aria, tono*› resigned
rassegnazi'one *nf* resignation
rassere'nare *vt* clear; *fig* cheer up
rassere'narsi *vr* become clear; *fig* cheer up
rasset'tare *vt* tidy up; (*riparare*) mend
rassicu'rante *a* ‹*persona, parole, presenza*› reassuring
rassicu'rare *vt* reassure
rassicurazi'one *nf* reassurance
rasso'dare *vt* harden; *fig* strengthen
rassomigli'ante *a* similar
rassomigli'anza *nf* resemblance
rassomigli'are *vi* ~ **a** resemble
rastrella'mento *nm* (*di fieno*) raking; (*perlustrazione*) combing
rastrel'lare *vt* rake; (*perlustrare*) comb
rastrelli'era *nf* rack; (*per biciclette*) bicycle rack; (*scolapiatti*) [plate] rack
ra'strello *nm* rake
'rata *nf* instalment; (*di mutuo*) mortgage repayment; **pagare a rate** pay by instalments; **comprare qcsa a rate** buy sth on hire purchase, buy sth on the installment plan *Am*

rate'ale *a* by instalments; **pagamento ~** payment by instalments; **vendita ~** hire purchase

rate'are, rateiz'zare *vt* divide into instalments

ra'tifica *nf Jur* ratification

ratifi'care *vt Jur* ratify

'ratto¹ *nm* (*rapimento*) abduction

'ratto² *nm* (*roditore*) rat. **~ comune** black rat

rattop'pare *vt* patch

rat'toppo *nm* patch

rattrap'pire *vt* make stiff

rattrap'pirsi *vr* become stiff

rattri'stare *vt* sadden

rattri'starsi *vr* become sad

rau'cedine *nf* hoarseness

'rauco *a* hoarse

rava'nello *nm* radish

ravi'oli *nmpl* ravioli *sg*

ravve'dersi *vr* mend one's ways

ravvi'are *vt* tidy (*capelli, stanza*)

ravvicina'mento *nm* (*tra persone*) reconciliation; *Pol* rapprochement

ravvici'nare *vt* bring closer; (*riconciliare*) reconcile

ravvici'narsi *vr* be reconciled

ravvi'sare *vt* recognize

ravvi'vare *vt* revive; *fig* brighten up

ravvi'varsi *vr* revive

rav'volgere *vt* roll up

rav'volgersi *vr* wrap oneself up

'rayon *nm* rayon

razio'cinio *nm* rational thought; (*buon senso*) common sense

razio'nale *a* rational

razionalità *nf* (*raziocinio*) rationality; (*di ambiente*) functional nature

razionaliz'zare *vt* rationalize (*programmi, metodi, spazio*)

razional'mente *adv* (*con raziocinio*) rationally

raziona'mento *nm* rationing

razio'nare *vt* ration

razi'one *nf* ration

'razza *nf* race; (*di cani ecc*) breed; (*genere*) kind; **che ~ di idiota!** *fam* what an idiot!

raz'zia *nf* raid

razzi'ale *a* racial

raz'zismo *nm* racism

raz'zista *a & nmf* racist

'razzo *nm* rocket. **~ da segnalazione** flare

razzo'lare *vi* (*polli:*) scratch about

re *nm inv* king; (*Mus: chiave, nota*) D. **Re** *pl* **Magi** Wise Men

rea'gente *a & nm* reactant

rea'gire *vi* react

re'ale *a* real; (*di re*) royal

rea'lismo *nm* realism

rea'lista *nmf* realist; (*fautore del re*) royalist

realistica'mente *adv* realistically

rea'listico *a* realistic

realiz'zabile *a* feasible

realiz'zare *vt* (*attuare*) carry out, realize; *Comm* make; score (*gol, canestro*); (*rendersi conto di*) realize

realiz'zarsi *vr* come true; (*nel lavoro ecc*) fulfil oneself

realiz'zato *a* (*persona*) fulfilled

realizzazi'one *nf* realization; (*di sogno, persona*) fulfilment. **~ scenica** production

rea'lizzo *nm* (*vendita*) proceeds *pl*; (*riscossione*) yield

real'mente *adv* really

realtà *nf inv* reality; **in ~** in reality; (*a dire il vero*) actually. **~ virtuale** virtual reality

re'ame *nm* realm

re'ato *nm* crime, criminal offence. **~ minore** minor offence

reattività *nf* reactivity; (*a farmaco*) reaction

reat'tivo *a* reactive

reat'tore *nm* reactor; *Aeron* jet [aircraft]. **~ nucleare** atomic reactor

reazio'nario, -a *a & nmf* reactionary

reazi'one *nf* reaction; **a ~** (*motore, aereo*) jet. **~ a catena** chain reaction. **~ chimica** chemical reaction

'rebus *nm inv* rebus; (*enigma*) puzzle

recapi'tare *vt* deliver

re'capito *nm* address; (*consegna*) delivery; **in caso di mancato ~...** if undelivered.... **~ a domicilio** home delivery. **~ telefonico** contact telephone number

re'care *vt* bear; (*produrre*) cause

re'carsi *vr* go

re'cedere *vi* recede; *fig* give up

recensi'one *nf* review

recen'sire *vt* review

recen'sore *nm* reviewer

re'cente *a* recent; **di ~** recently

recente'mente *adv* recently

re'ception *nf inv* reception [desk]

re'ceptionist *nmf* receptionist

recessi'one *nf* recession

reces'sivo *a* *Biol* recessive; *Econ* recessionary

re'cesso *nm* recess

re'cidere *vt* cut off

reci'diva *nf Jur* recidivism; *Med* relapse; **furto con ~** repeat offence of theft

recidività *nf inv* recidivism

reci'divo, -a *a Med* recurrent ● *nmf* repeat offender, recidivist *fml*; **è ~** *fig* he's lapsed back into his old ways

recin'tare *vt* close off

re'cinto *nm* enclosure; (*per animali*) pen; (*per bambini*) play-pen. **~ delle grida** *Fin* [trading] floor. **~ del peso** (*ippica*) weigh-in room

recinzi'one *nf* (*azione*) enclosure; (*muro*) wall; (*rete*) wire fence; (*cancellata*) railings *pl*

recipi'ente *nm* container

re'ciproco *a* reciprocal

re'ciso *pp di* **recidere** ● *a* (*risoluto*) definite

'recita *nf* performance. **~ scolastica** school play

re'cital *nm inv* recital

reci'tare *vt* recite; *Theat* act; play ⟨*ruolo*⟩ ● *vi* act; ~ **a soggetto** improvise

recitazi'one *nf* recitation; *Theat* acting; **scuola di** ~ drama school

recla'mare *vi* protest ● *vt* claim

ré'clame *nf inv* advertising; (*avviso pubblicitario*) advertisement

reclamiz'zare *vt* advertise

re'clamo *nm* complaint; **ufficio reclami** complaints department

recli'nabile *a* reclining; **sedile** ~ reclining seat

recli'nare *vt* tilt ⟨*sedile*⟩; lean ⟨*capo*⟩

reclusi'one *nf* imprisonment

re'cluso, -a *a* secluded ● *nmf* prisoner

'recluta *nf* recruit

recluta'mento *nm* recruitment

reclu'tare *vt* recruit

re'condito *a* secluded; (*intimo*) secret

'record *nm inv* record; **a tempo di** ~ in record time ● *a inv* ⟨*cifra*⟩ record *attrib*

recrimi'nare *vi* recriminate

recriminazi'one *nf* recrimination

recrude'scenza *nf Med* fresh outbreak; *fig* (*di violenza*) renewed outbreak; (*di criminalità*) upsurge

recupe'rare *vt* recover; rehabilitate ⟨*tossicodipendente*⟩; make up ⟨*ore di assenza*⟩; ~ **il tempo perduto** make up for lost time ● *vi* catch up

re'cupero *nm* recovery; (*di tossicodipendenti*) rehabilitation; (*salvataggio*) rescue; **corso di** ~ additional classes *pl*; **materiali di** ~ recycled material; (*che possono essere recuperati*) recyclable material; [**minuti di**] ~ *Sport* injury time; **partita di** ~ rematch. ~ **crediti** debt collection. ~ [**dei**] **dati** data recovery

redargu'ire *vt* rebuke

re'datto *pp di* **redigere**

redat|'tore, -'trice *nmf* editor; (*di testo*) writer. ~ **capo** editor in chief

redazi'one *nf* (*ufficio*) editorial office; (*di testi*) editing

redditività *nf* earning power

reddi'tizio *a* profitable

'reddito *nm* income; **imposta sul** ~ income tax. ~ **complessivo** gross income. ~ **imponibile** taxable income. ~ **non imponibile** non-taxable income. ~ **da lavoro** earned income. **redditi** *pl* **occasionali** casual earnings. ~ **pubblico** government revenue

re'dento *pp di* **redimere**

reden'tore *nm* redeemer

redenzi'one *nf* redemption

re'digere *vt* write; draw up ⟨*documento*⟩

re'dimere *vt* redeem

re'dimersi *vr* redeem oneself

redi'mibile *a* ⟨*titoli*⟩ redeemable

'redine *nf* rein

redin'gote *nf inv* frock-coat; **abito a** ~ fitted button-through dress

'redini *nfpl* reins

redi'vivo *a* restored to life

'reduce *a* ~ **da** back from ● *nmf* survivor

refe'rendum *nm inv* referendum

refe'renza *nf* reference

referenzi'ato *a* with references

re'ferto *nm* report. ~ **medico** medical report

refet'torio *nm* refectory

reflazio'nare *vt Econ* reflate

reflazi'one *nf Econ* reflation

'reflex *nm inv* reflex camera

'refluo *nm* effluent

refrat'tario *a* refractory; **essere** ~ **a** *fig* be insensitive to ⟨*sentimenti*⟩; **sono** ~ **alla matematica** maths are a closed book to me

refrige'rante *a* cooling *attrib*

refrige'rare *vt* refrigerate

refrigerazi'one *nf* refrigeration

refur'tiva *nf* stolen goods *pl*

re'fuso *nm Typ* literal, typo

rega'lare *vt* give

re'gale *a* regal

re'galo *nm* present, gift; **articoli da** ~ gifts ● *a* **confezione** ~ gift set

re'gata *nf* regatta

'reggae *nm inv Mus* reggae

reg'gente *nmf* regent

reg'genza *nf* regency

'reggere *vt* (*sorreggere*) bear; (*tenere in mano*) hold; (*dirigere*) run; (*governare*) govern; *Gram* take ● *vi* (*resistere*) hold out; (*durare*) last; *fig* stand

'reggersi *vr* stand

'reggia *nf* royal palace

reggi'calze *nm inv* suspender belt

reggi'mento *nm* regiment; (*fig: molte persone*) army

reggi'petto, reggi'seno *nm* bra

re'gia *nf Cinema* direction; *Theat* production

re'gime *nm* regime; (*dieta*) diet; (*di fiume*) rate of flow; **a** ~ **torrenzizio** in spate; **a pieno** ~ (*funzionare*) at full speed. ~ **alimentare** diet. ~ **fiscale** tax system. ~ **di giri** (*di motore*) revs per minute, rpm. ~ **militare** military regime. ~ **monetario aureo** gold standard. ~ **di vita** lifestyle

re'gina *nf* queen; **ape** ~ queen bee. ~ **madre** queen mother

'regio *a* royal

regio'nale *a* regional

regiona'lismo *nm* (*parola*) regionalism

regional'mente *adv* regionally

regi'one *nf* region

re'gista *nmf Cinema, TV* director; *Theat* producer

regi'strare *vt* register; *Comm* enter; (*incidere su nastro*) tape, record; (*su disco*) record

registra'tore *nm* recorder; (*magnetofono*) tape-recorder. ~ **di cassa** cash register. ~ **a cassette** tape recorder, cassette recorder. ~ **di volo** flight recorder

registrazi'one *nf* registration; *Comm* entry; (*di programma*) recording; **sala di** ~ recording studio. ~ [**dei**] **dati** data capture

re'gistro *nm* register; (*ufficio*) registry. ~ **di**

bordo log. ~ **di cassa** ledger. ~ **di classe** class register. ~ **linguistico** register

re'gnare vi reign

'regno nm kingdom; (sovranità) reign. ~ **animale** animal kingdom. **R~ Unito** United Kingdom. ~ **vegetale** plant kingdom

'regola nf rule; **essere in** ~ be in order; ⟨persona:⟩ have one's papers in order; **a** ~ **d'arte** in a workmanlike fashion

rego'labile a ⟨velocità, luminosità⟩ adjustable

regola'mento nm regulation; Comm settlement. ~ **di conti** settling of scores

rego'lare a regular ● vt regulate; (ridurre, moderare) limit; (sistemare) settle

regolarità nf inv regularity

regolariz'zare vt settle ⟨debito⟩; regularize ⟨situazione⟩

rego'larsi vr (agire) act; (moderarsi) control oneself

rego'lata nf **darsi una** ~ pull oneself together

regola'tore, -'trice a **piano** ~ urban development plan ● nmf regulator

'regolo nm ruler. ~ **calcolatore** slide-rule

regre'dire vi Biol, Psych regress

regressi'one nf regression

regres'sivo a regressive

re'gresso nm decline

reincar'narsi vr ~ **in...** be reincarnated as...

reincarnazi'one nf reincarnation

reinseri'mento nm (di persona) reintegration

reinser'irsi vr (in ambiente) reintegrate

reinte'grare vt restore

reinven'tare vt reinvent

reinvesti'mento nm reinvestment

reinve'stire vt reinvest ⟨soldi⟩

reite'rare vt reiterate

reiterazi'one nf reiteration

re'lais nm inv relay

relativa'mente adv relatively; ~ **a** as regards

relatività nf relativity

rela'tivo a relative

rela|'tore, -'trice nmf (in una conferenza) speaker; (di tesi) supervisor

re'lax nm relaxation

relazi'one nf relation; (di lavoro ecc) relationship; (rapporto amoroso) [love] affair; (resoconto) report; **pubbliche relazioni** pl public relations. ~ **extraconiugale** extramarital relationship

rele'gare vt relegate

relegazi'one nf relegation

religi'one nf religion

religi'oso, -a a religious ● nm monk ● nf nun

re'liquia nf relic

reliqui'ario nm reliquary

re'litto nm wreck

re'mainder nm inv (libro) remainder

re'make nm inv remake

re'mare vi row

rema|'tore, -'trice nmf rower

remini'scenza nf reminiscence

remissi'one nf remission; (sottomissione) submissiveness. ~ **del debito** remission of debt. ~ **di querela** withdrawal of an action

remissiva'mente adv submissively

remis'sivo a submissive

re'mix nm inv Mus remix

'remo nm oar

'remora nf **senza remore** without hesitation

re'moto a remote

remo'vibile a removeable

remune'rare vt remunerate

remunera'tivo a remunerative

remunerazi'one nf remuneration

re'nale a renal

'rendere vt (restituire) return; (esprimere) render; (fruttare) yield; (far diventare) make

'rendersi vr become; ~ **conto di qcsa** realize sth; ~ **utile** make oneself useful

rendi'conto nm report

rendi'mento nm rendering; (produzione) yield

'rendita nf income; (dello Stato) revenue; **vivere di** ~ fig rest on one's laurels. ~ **vitalizia** life annuity

'rene nm kidney. ~ **artificiale** kidney machine

'reni nfpl (schiena) back

reni'tente a **essere** ~ **a** ⟨consigli di qcno⟩ be loth to accept; refuse to obey ⟨legge⟩ ● nm ~ **alla leva** person who fails to report for military service after being called up

'renna nf reindeer (pl inv); (pelle) buckskin

'Reno nm Rhine

'reo, -a a guilty ● nmf criminal. ~ **confesso** self-confessed criminal

Rep. abbr (**repubblica**) Rep.

re'parto nm department; Mil unit. **reparti** pl **d'assalto** Mil assault troops. ~ **d'attacco** Sport attack. ~ **difensivo** Sport defence. ~ **grandi ustionati** Med burns unit. ~ **maternità** obstetrics [department]

repel'lente a repulsive

repen'taglio nm **mettere a** ~ risk

repentina'mente adv suddenly

repen'tino a sudden

reper'ibile a available; **non è** ~ (perduto) it's not to be found

reperibilità nf availability

repe'rire vt trace ⟨fondi⟩

re'perto nm ~ **archeologico** find. ~ **giudiziario** exhibit

reper'torio nm repertory; (elenco) index; **immagini** pl **di** ~ archive footage

re'play nm inv [instant] replay

'replica nf reply; (obiezione) objection; (copia) replica; Theat repeat performance

repli'care vt reply; Theat repeat

repor'tage nm inv report

repressi'one nf repression

repres'sivo a repressive

re'presso pp di **reprimere**

re'primere vt repress

re'pubblica *nf* republic. **R~ Ceca** Czech Republic. **R~ Dominicana** Dominican Republic. **R~ Federale Tedesca** Federal Republic of Germany. **R~ d'Irlanda** Republic of Ireland. **~ parlamentare** parliamentary republic. **R~ Popolare cinese** People's Republic of China. **~ presidenziale** presidential-style republic. **R~ Slovacca** Slovakia
repubbli'cano, -a *a & nmf* republican
repu'tare *vt* consider
repu'tarsi *vr* consider oneself
reputazi'one *nf* reputation
'requiem *nm inv* requiem
requi'sire *vt* requisition
requi'sito *nm* requirement
requisi'toria *nf* (*arringa*) closing speech
requisizi'one *nf* requisition
'resa *nf* surrender; *Comm* rendering. **~ dei conti** rendering of accounts. **~ incondizionata** unconditional surrender
re'scindere *vt* cancel
'residence *nm inv* residential hotel
resi'dente *a & nmf* resident
resi'denza *nf* residence; (*soggiorno*) stay
residenzi'ale *a* residential; **zona ~** residential district
re'siduo *a* residual ● *nm* remainder. **residui** *pl* **industriali** industrial waste
'resina *nf* resin
resi'stente *a* resistant; **~ all'acqua** water resistant
resi'stenza *nf* resistance; (*fisica*) stamina; *Electr* resistor; **la ~ the** Resistance. **~ passiva** passive resistance. **~ a pubblico ufficiale** resisting arrest
re'sistere *vi* **~ [a]** resist; (*a colpi, scosse*) stand up to; **~ alla pioggia/al vento** be rain-/wind-resistant
'reso *pp di* **rendere**
reso'conto *nm* report
respin'gente *nm Rail* buffer
re'spingere *vt* repel; (*rifiutare*) reject; (*bocciare*) fail
re'spinto *pp di* **respingere**
respi'rare *vt/i* breathe
respira'tore *nm* respirator; **~ [a tubo]** snorkel
respira'torio *a* respiratory
respirazi'one *nf* breathing; *Med* respiration. **~ artificiale** artificial respiration. **~ bocca a bocca** mouth-to-mouth resuscitation, kiss of life
re'spiro *nm* breath; (*il respirare*) breathing; *fig* respite. **~ di sollievo** sigh of relief
respon'sabile *a* responsible (**di** for); *Jur* liable ● *nmf* person responsible. **~ della produzione** production manager
responsabilità *nf inv* responsibility; *Jur* liability. **~ civile** *Jur* civil liability. **~ limitata** limited liability. **~ penale** criminal liability
responsabiliz'zare *vt* give responsibiity to (*dipendente*); give a sense of responsibility to (*gente*)
responsabil'mente *adv* responsibly

re'sponso *nm* response
'ressa *nf* crowd
re'stante *a* remaining ● *nm* remainder
re'stare *vi* = **rimanere**
restau'rare *vt* restore
restaura|'tore, -'trice *nmf* restorer
restaurazi'one *nf* restoration
re'stauro *nm* (*riparazione*) repair
re'stio *a* restive; **~ a** reluctant to
restitu'ibile *a* returnable
restitu'ire *vt* return; (*reintegrare*) restore
restituzi'one *nf* return; *Jur* restitution
'resto *nm* rest, remainder; (*saldo*) balance; (*denaro*) change; **resti** *pl* (*avanzi*) remains; **del ~** besides
re'stringere *vt* contract; take in (*vestiti*); (*limitare*) restrict; shrink (*stoffa*)
re'stringersi *vr* contract; (*farsi più vicini*) close up; (*stoffa:*) shrink
restringi'mento *nm* (*di tessuto*) shrinkage
restrit'tivo *a* restrictive
restrizi'one *nf* restriction
resurrezi'one *nf* resurrection
resusci'tare *vt* revive; resuscitate (*moribondo*) ● *vi* (*Cristo:*) rise again; *fig* revive
re'taggio *nm* hangover
re'tata *nf* round-up
'rete *nf* net; (*sistema*) network; (*televisiva*) channel; (*in calcio, hockey*) goal; *fig* trap; (*per la spesa*) string bag. **~ commutata pubblica** *Teleph* switched public network. **~ di distribuzione** *Comm* distribution network. **~ locale** *Comput* local [area] network, LAN. **~ di protezione** (*per acrobata*) safety net. **~ stradale** road network. **~ telematica** communications network. **~ televisiva** television channel
reti'cente *a* reticent
reti'cenza *nf* reticence
retico'lato *nm* grid; (*rete metallica*) wire netting
re'ticolo *nm* network. **~ geografico** grid
re'tina *nf* (*per capelli*) hair net
'retina *nf Anat* retina
re'tino *nm* net
retorica'mente *adv* rhetorically
re'torico, -a *a* rhetorical; **domanda retorica** rhetorical question; **figura retorica** figure of speech ● *nf* rhetoric
re'trattile *a* (*punta:*) retractable
retribu'ire *vt* remunerate
retribu'tivo *a* salary *attrib*
retribuzi'one *nf* remuneration
'retro *adv* behind; **vedi ~** see over ● *nm inv* back. **~ di copertina** outside back cover
retroat'tivo *a* retroactive
retrobot'tega *nm inv* back shop
retro'cedere *vi* retreat ● *vt Mil* demote; *Sport* relegate
retrocessi'one *nf Sport* relegation
retroda'tare *vt* backdate
retro'fit *nm inv Auto* retrofitted catalytic converter

re'trogrado *a* retrograde; *fig* old-fashioned; *Pol* reactionary

retrogu'ardia *nf Mil* rearguard

retro'gusto *nm* after-taste

retro'marcia *nf* reverse [gear]

retro'scena *nm inv Theat* backstage; **i ~** *fig* the real story

retrospettiva'mente *adv* retrospectively

retrospet'tivo *a* retrospective

retro'stante *a* **il palazzo ~** the building behind

retro'via *nf Mil* area behind the front lines

retro'virus *nm inv* retrovirus

retrovi'sore *nm* rear-view mirror

'retta¹ *nf Math* straight line; *(di collegio, pensionato)* fee

'retta² *nf* **dar ~ a qcno** take sb's advice

rettango'lare *a* rectangular

ret'tangolo *a* right-angled ● *nm* rectangle

ret'tifica *nf* rectification

rettifi'care *vt* rectify

'rettile *nm* reptile

retti'lineo *a* rectilinear; *(retto)* upright ● *nm Sport* back straight

retti'tudine *nf* rectitude

'retto *pp di* **reggere** ● *a* straight; *fig* upright; *(giusto)* correct; **angolo ~** right angle

'retto *nm* rectum

ret'tore *nm Relig* rector; *Univ* chancellor

reu'matico *a* rheumatic

reuma'tismi *nmpl* rheumatism

reve'rendo *a* reverend

rever'sibile *a* reversible

revisio'nare *vt* revise; *Comm* audit; *Auto* overhaul

revisi'one *nf* revision; *Comm* audit; *Auto* overhaul. **~ di bilancio** audit. **~ di bozze** proof-reading. **~ dello stipendio** salary review

revisio'nismo *nm Pol* revisionism

revisio'nista *a ‹politica›* revisionist

revi'sore *nm (di conti)* auditor; *(di bozze)* proof-reader; *(di traduzioni)* revisor. **~ di bozze** proof-reader. **~ dei conti** auditor

re'vival *nm inv* revival

'revoca *nf* repeal

revo'care *vt* repeal

revolve'rata *nf* revolver shot

rhythm and blues *nm* rhythm and blues, R & B

riabbas'sare *vt* lower again

riabbas'sarsi *vr ‹acque:›* recede; *‹temperatura:›* fall again

riabbotto'nare *vt* button up again

riabbracci'are *vt (abbracciare di nuovo)* embrace again; *(fig: rivedere)* see again

riabili'tare *vt* rehabilitate

riabilitazi'one *nf* rehabilitation; **centro di ~** rehabilitation centre

riabitu'are *vt* **~ qcno a qcsa** reaccustom sb to sth, get sb used to sth again

riabitu'arsi *vr* **~ a qcsa** get used to sth again, reaccustom oneself to sth

riac'cendere *vt* switch on again *‹luce, tv›*; rekindle, revive *‹interesse, passione›*; rekindle *‹fuoco›*

riac'cendersi *vr ‹luce:›* come back on; *‹interesse, passione:›* rekindle, revive

riaccensi'one *nf* **la continua ~** continual switching on and off

riaccer'tare *vt* reassess

riacqui'stare *vt* buy back; regain *‹libertà, prestigio›*; recover *‹vista, udito›*

riacutiz'zarsi *vr* get worse again

riadatta'mento *nm* readjustment

riadat'tare *vt* convert *‹stanza›*; alter *‹indumento›*

riadat'tarsi *vr* readjust

riaddormen'tare *vt* get [back] to sleep again

riaddormen'tarsi *vr* fall asleep again

riadope'rare *vt* reuse

riaffacci'arsi *vr (alla finestra)* appear again; *‹idea:›* surface again

riaffer'mare *vt* reaffirm

riaffon'dare *vi* sink again

riaffron'tare *vt* deal with again *‹situazione›*; take up again *‹argomento›*

riagganci'are *vt* replace *‹ricevitore›*; **~ la cornetta** hang up ● *vi* hang up

riaggre'garsi *vr* regroup

riallac'ciare *vt* refasten; reconnect *‹corrente›*; renew *‹amicizia›*

riallar'gare *vt* widen again *‹tunnel, strada›*

riallinea'mento *nm* realignment

rialline'are *vt* realign

rialloggi'are *vt* rehouse

rial'zare *vt* raise ● *vi* rise

rial'zarsi *vr* get up again

rial'zato *a* piano **~** mezzanine

ri'alzo *nm* rise; **al ~** *Fin* bullish

ria'mare *vt* **~ qcno** reciprocate sb's love, love sb back

riamma'larsi *vr* fall ill again

riam'mettere *vt* readmit *‹socio, studente›*

rian'dare *vi* return

riani'mare *vt Med* resuscitate; *(ridare forza a)* revive; *(ridare coraggio a)* cheer up

riani'marsi *vr* regain consciousness; *(riprendere forza)* revive; *(riprendere coraggio)* cheer up

rianimazi'one *nf* intensive care [unit]; **centro di ~** intensive care unit

rianno'dare *vt* retie *‹filo›*; renew *‹rapporti›*

riaper'tura *nf* reopening

riappa'rire *vi* reappear

riap'pendere *vt* replace *‹cornetta›*; **mi ha riappeso il telefono in faccia** he hung up on me, he slammed the phone down on me

riappiso'larsi *vr* doze off again

riappropri'arsi *vr* **~ di** take back

ria'prire *vt* reopen

ria'prirsi *vr* reopen

ri'armo *nm* rearmament

riascol'tare *vt* listen to again

riasse'gnare *vt* reallocate

riassicu'rare *vt* reinsure

riassicurazi'one *nf* reinsurance

riassorbi'mento *nm* reabsorption

riassor'bire *vt* reabsorb

rias'sumere *vt* re-employ, take on again ⟨*impiegato*⟩; ⟨*ricapitolare*⟩ resume

riassu'mibile *a* ⟨*riepilogabile*⟩ which can be summarized, summarizable

riassun'tivo *a* summarizing

rias'sunto *pp di* **riassumere** ● *nm* summary

riattac'care *vt* ~ **il telefono** hang up ● *vi* ⟨*al telefono*⟩ hang up

riatti'vare *vt* reactivate ⟨*processo*⟩; reintroduce, bring back ⟨*servizio*⟩; start up again, restart ⟨*congegno*⟩; stimulate ⟨*circolazione sanguigna*⟩

ria'vere *vt* get back; regain ⟨*salute, vista*⟩

ria'versi *vr* recover

riavvicina'mento *nm* ⟨*tra persone*⟩ reconciliation; ⟨*tra paesi*⟩ rapprochement

riavvici'nare *vt fig* reconcile ⟨*paesi, persone*⟩

riavvici'narsi *vr* ⟨*riconciliarsi*⟩ be reconciled, make it up *fam*

riav'volgere *vt* rewind

riba'dire *vt* ⟨*confermare*⟩ reaffirm

ri'balta *nf* flap; *Theat* footlights *pl*; *fig* limelight

ribal'tabile *a* tip-up

ribal'tare *vt/i* tip over; *Naut* capsize

ribal'tarsi *vr* tip over; *Naut* capsize

ribas'sare *vt* lower ● *vi* fall

ribas'sato *a* reduced

ri'basso *nm* fall; ⟨*sconto*⟩ discount

ri'battere *vt* ⟨*a macchina*⟩ retype; ⟨*controbattere*⟩ deny ● *vi* answer back

ribattez'zare *vt* rename

ribel'larsi *vr* rebel

ri'belle *a* rebellious ● *nmf* rebel

ribelli'one *nf* rebellion

'**ribes** *nm inv* ⟨*rosso*⟩ redcurrant; ⟨*nero*⟩ blackcurrant

ribol'lire *vi* ⟨*fermentare*⟩ ferment; *fig* seethe

ri'brezzo *nm* disgust; **far ~ a** disgust

ribut'tante *a* repugnant

ribut'tare *vt* ⟨*buttare di nuovo*⟩ throw back

rica'dere *vi* fall back; ⟨*nel peccato ecc*⟩ lapse; ⟨*pendere*⟩ hang [down]; ~ **su** ⟨*riversarsi*⟩ fall on

rica'duta *nf* relapse; **avere una ~** to have a relapse

rical'care *vt* trace

ricalci'trante *a* recalcitrant

ricalco'lare *vt* recalculate

rica'mare *vt* embroider

rica'mato *a* embroidered

ri'cambi *nmpl* spare parts

ricambi'are *vt* return; reciprocate ⟨*sentimento*⟩; ~ **qcsa a qcno** repay sb for sth

ri'cambio *nm* replacement; *Biol* metabolism; **pezzo di ~** spare [part]

ri'camo *nm* embroidery

ricandi'dare *vt* ⟨*a elezioni*⟩ put forward as a candidate again

ricandi'darsi *vr* ⟨*a elezioni*⟩ stand again

ricapito'lare *vt* sum up; **ricapitoliamo** let's recap

ricapitolazi'one *nf* summary, recap *fam*

ri'carica *nf* ⟨*di sveglia*⟩ winder; ⟨*di batteria*⟩ recharging; ⟨*di penna*⟩ refill; ⟨*di fucile*⟩ reloading

ricari'care *vt* reload ⟨*macchina fotografica, fucile, camion*⟩; recharge ⟨*batteria*⟩; *Comput* reboot; rewind ⟨*orologio*⟩

ricat'tare *vt* blackmail

ricatta'|tore, -'trice *nmf* blackmailer

ricatta'torio *a* blackmail *attrib*

ri'catto *nm* blackmail. ~ **morale** moral blackmail, emotional blackmail

rica'vare *vt* get ⟨*ottenere*⟩ obtain; ⟨*dedurre*⟩ draw

rica'vato *nm* proceeds *pl*

ri'cavo *nm* proceeds *pl*

'**ricca** *nf* rich woman

ricca'mente *adv* lavishly

ric'chezza *nf* wealth; *fig* richness; **ricchezze** *pl* riches

'**riccio** *a* curly ● *nm* curl; ⟨*animale*⟩ hedgehog. ~ **di mare** sea-urchin

'**ricciolo** *nm* curl

riccio'luto *a* curly

ricci'uto *a* ⟨*barba*⟩ curly; ⟨*persona*⟩ curlyhaired

'**ricco** *a* rich. ~ **sfondato** *fam* filthy rich ● *nm* rich man

ri'cerca *nf* search; ⟨*indagine*⟩ investigation; ⟨*scientifica*⟩ research; *Sch* project. ~ **sul campo** field work. ~ **di mercato** market research. ~ **operativa** operational research. ~ **scientifica** scientific research

ricer'care *vt* search for; ⟨*fare ricerche su*⟩ research

ricer'cata *nf* wanted woman

ricercata'mente *adv* ⟨*vestire*⟩ with refinement; ⟨*parlare*⟩ in a refined way

ricerca'tezza *nf* refinement

ricer'cato *a* sought-after; ⟨*raffinato*⟩ refined ● *nm* ⟨*dalla polizia*⟩ wanted man

ricerca'|tore, -'trice *nmf* researcher

ricetrasmit'tente *nf* transceiver

ri'cetta *nf* *Culin* recipe; *Med* prescription

ricet'tacolo *nm* receptacle

ricet'tario *nm* ⟨*di cucina*⟩ recipe book; ⟨*di medico*⟩ prescription pad

ricetta'|tore, -'trice *nmf* receiver of stolen goods, fence *fam*

ricettazi'one *nf* receiving [stolen goods]

rice'vente *a* ⟨*apparecchio, stazione*⟩ receiving ● *nmf* receiver

ri'cevere *vt* receive; ⟨*dare il benvenuto*⟩ welcome; ⟨*di albergo*⟩ accommodate

ricevi'mento *nm* receiving; ⟨*accoglienza*⟩ welcome; ⟨*trattenimento*⟩ reception

ricevi'tore *nm* receiver. ~ **delle imposte** tax man. ~ **del lotto** lottery ticket agent

ricevito'ria *nf* ~ **delle imposte** ≈ Inland Revenue. ~ **del lotto** *agency authorized to sell lottery tickets*

rice'vuta *nf* receipt. ~ **doganale** docket. ~ **fiscale** tax receipt. ~ **di ritorno** acknowledgement of receipt. ~ **di versamento** receipt ⟨*given for bills etc paid at the Post Office*⟩

rice'vuto *int* roger

ricezi'one *nf Radio, TV* reception

richia'mare *vt* (*al telefono*) call back; (*far tornare*) recall; (*rimproverare*) rebuke; (*attirare*) draw; **~ alla mente** call to mind

richi'amo *nm* recall; (*attrazione*) call

richie'dente *nmf* applicant

richi'edere *vt* ask for; (*di nuovo*) ask again for; **~ a qcno di fare qcsa** ask *o* request sb to do sth

richi'esta *nf* request; *Comm* demand. **~ di indennizzo** claim for damages

richi'esto *a* sought-after

ri'chiudere *vt* shut again, close again

ri'chiudersi *vr* (*ferita:*) heal; (*porta:*) shut again, close again

rici'clabile *a* recyclable

rici'claggio *nm* recycling; (*di denaro*) laundering

rici'clare *vt* recycle

rici'clarsi *vr* retrain; (*cambiare lavoro*) change one's line of work

'ricino *nm* **olio di ~** castor oil

ricogni'tore *nm* reconnaissance plane

ricognizi'one *nf Mil* reconnaissance

ricolle'gare *vt* (*collegare di nuovo*) reconnect

ricolle'garsi *vr* **~ a** (*evento, fatto:*) relate to, tie up with

ricol'mare *vt* fill to the brim

ri'colmo *a* full

ricominci'are *vt/i* start again; **~ da capo** start all over again

ricompa'rire *vi* reappear

ricom'parsa *nf* reappearance

ricom'pensa *nf* reward

ricompen'sare *vt* reward

ricom'porre *vt* (*riscrivere*) rewrite; (*ricostruire*) reform; *Typ* reset

ricom'porsi *vr* regain one's composure

riconcili'are *vt* reconcile

riconcili'arsi *vr* be reconciled

riconciliazi'one *nf* reconciliation

riconfer'mare *vt* reappoint

ricongi'ungere *vt* reunite

ricongi'ungersi *vr* become reunited

ricono'scente *a* grateful

ricono'scenza *nf* gratitude

rico'noscere *vt* recognize; (*ammettere*) acknowledge

riconosci'mento *nm* recognition; (*ammissione*) acknowledgement; (*per la polizia*) identification

riconosci'uto *a* recognized

ricon'quista *nf* reconquest

riconqui'stare *vt Mil* reconquer

ricon'segna *nf* return

riconse'gnare *vt* return

riconside'rare *vt* rethink

ricontrol'lare *vt* double-check

riconversi'one *nf Econ* restructuring

ricopi'are *vt* copy again

rico'prire *vt* re-cover; (*rivestire*) coat; (*di insulti*) shower (**di** with); hold (*carica*); **~ qcno di attenzioni** lavish attention on sb

ricor'dare *vt* remember; (*richiamare alla memoria*) recall; (*far ricordare*) remind; (*rassomigliare*) look like

ricor'darsi *vr* **~** [**di**] remember; **~ di fare qcsa** remember to do sth

ri'cordo *nm* memory; (*oggetto*) memento; (*di viaggio*) souvenir; **ricordi** *pl* (*memorie*) memoirs. **~ di famiglia** family heirloom

ricor'reggere *vt* correct again

ricor'rente *a* recurrent

ricor'renza *nf* recurrence; (*anniversario*) anniversary

ri'correre *vi* recur; (*accadere*) occur; (*data:*) fall; **~ a** have recourse to; (*rivolgersi a*) turn to

ri'corso *pp di* **ricorrere** ● *nm* recourse; *Jur* appeal

ricostitu'ente *nm* tonic

ricostitu'ire *vt* re-establish

ricostru'ire *vt* reconstruct

ricostruzi'one *nf* reconstruction

ricove'rare *vt* give shelter to; **~ in ospedale** admit to hospital, hospitalize

ricove'rato, -a *nmf* hospital patient

ri'covero *nm* shelter; (*ospizio*) home

ricre'are *vt* re-create; (*ristorare*) restore

ricre'arsi *vr* amuse oneself

ricrea'tivo *a* recreational

ricreazi'one *nf* recreation; *Sch* break

ri'credersi *vr* change one's mind

ri'crescere *vi* grow again

ricu'cire *vt* sew up; stitch up (*ferita*)

ricupe'rare, ri'cupero = **recuperare, recupero**

ri'curvo *a* bent

ricu'sare *vt* refuse

ridacchi'are *vi* giggle

ri'dare *vt* give back, return

rida'rella *nf* giggles *pl*

ridefi'nire *vt* redefine

ri'dente *a* (*piacevole*) pleasant

'ridere *vi* laugh; **~ di** (*deridere*) laugh at

ride'stare *vt* reawaken (*ricordo, sentimento*)

ri'detto *pp di* **ridire**

ridicoliz'zare *vt* ridicule

ri'dicolo *a* ridiculous

ridimensiona'mento *nm* restructuring

ridimensio'nare *vt* restructure (*azienda*); *fig* get into perspective

ridi'pingere *vt* repaint

ri'dire *vt* repeat; **trova sempre da ~** he's always finding fault; **hai qualcosa da ~?** do you have something to say?; **se non hai niente da ~,...** if you've no objection...

ridi'scendere *vi* go back down

ridistribu'ire *vt* redistribute

ridistribuzi'one *nf* redistribution

ridon'dante *a* redundant

ri'dosso: a ~ di *adv* behind

ri'dotto *pp di* **ridurre** ● *a* **essere ~ a uno straccio** be worn out ● *nm Theat* foyer ● *a* reduced

ri'durre *vt* reduce

ri'dursi *vr* diminish; **~ a fare qcsa** be reduced to doing sth; **~ a** ⟨*problema:*⟩ come down to

ridut'tivo *a* reductive

ridut'tore *nm Electr* adaptor

riduzi'one *nf* reduction; (*per cinema, teatro*) adaptation. **~ cinematografica** film adaptation. **~ della pena** reduced sentence. **~ teatrale** adaptation for the theatre

riedifi'care *vt* rebuild

rieducazi'one *nf* (*di malato*) rehabilitation

rie'leggere *vt* re-elect

rielezi'one *nf* re-election

rie'mergere *vi* resurface

riem'pire *vt* fill [up]; fill in ⟨*moduli ecc*⟩

riem'pirsi *vr* fill [up]

riempi'tivo *a* filling ● *nm* filler

rien'tranza *nf* recess

rien'trare *vi* go/come back in; (*tornare*) return; (*piegare indentro*) recede; **~ in** (*far parte*) fall within

ri'entro *nm* return; (*di astronave*) re-entry

riepilo'gare *vt* recapitulate

rie'pilogo *nm* summing-up

rie'same *nm* reassessment

riesami'nare *vt* reappraise

ri'essere *vi* **ci risiamo!** here we go again!

riesu'mare *vt* exhume

rievo'care *vt* (*commemorare*) commemorate; recall ⟨*passato*⟩

rievocazi'one *nf* (*commemorazione*) commemoration; (*ricordo*) recollection

rifaci'mento *nm* remake

ri'fare *vt* do again; (*creare*) make again; (*riparare*) repair; (*imitare*) imitate; make ⟨*letto*⟩

ri'farsi *vr* (*rimettersi*) recover; (*vendicarsi*) get even; **~ una vita/carriera** make a new life/career for oneself; **~ il trucco** touch up one's makeup; **~ di** make up for

ri'fatto *pp di* **rifare**

riferi'mento *nm* reference

rife'rire *vt* report; **~ a** attribute to ● *vi* make a report

rife'rirsi *vr* **~ a** refer to

rifi'lare *vt* (*tagliare a filo*) trim; (*fam: affibbiare*) saddle

rifi'nire *vt* finish off

rifini'tura *nf* finish

rifio'rire *vi* blossom again; *fig* flourish again

rifiu'tare *vt* refuse; **~ di fare qcsa** refuse to do sth

rifi'uto *nm* refusal; **acque** *pl* **di ~** waste water; **rifiuti** *pl* (*immondizie*) rubbish. **rifiuti** *pl* **industriali** industrial waste. **rifiuti** *pl* **urbani** urban waste

riflessi'one *nf* reflection; (*osservazione*) remark

rifles'sivo *a* thoughtful; *Gram* reflexive

ri'flesso *pp di* **riflettere** ● *nm* (*luce*) reflection; *Med* reflex; **per ~** indirectly

ri'flettere *vt* reflect ● *vi* think (**su** about)

ri'flettersi *vr* be reflected

riflet'tore *nm* reflector; (*proiettore*) searchlight

ri'flusso *nm* ebb

rifocil'lare *vt* restore

rifocil'larsi *vr liter, hum* take some refreshment

rifondazi'one *nf* refounding; **R~ Comunista** *diehard Communist party*

ri'fondere *vt* (*rimborsare*) refund

ri'forma *nf* reform; *Relig* reformation; *Mil* exemption on medical grounds

rifor'mare *vt* re-form; (*migliorare*) reform; *Mil* declare unfit for military service

rifor'mato *a* ⟨*chiesa*⟩ Reformed; ⟨*recluta, soldato*⟩ unfit for military service

riforma'tore, -'trice *nmf* reformer

riforma'torio *nm* reformatory

riformat'tare *vt Comput* reformat

rifor'mista *a & nmf* reformist

riformu'lare *vt* recast

riforni'mento *nm* supply; (*scorta*) stock; (*di combustibile*) refuelling; **stazione di ~** petrol station

rifor'nire *vt* restock; **~ di** provide with

rifor'nirsi *vr* restock, stock up (**di** with)

ri'frangere *vt* refract

ri'fratto *pp di* **rifrangere**

rifrazi'one *nf* refraction

rifug'gire *vt* shun ⟨*gloria, celebrità*⟩ ● *vi* escape again; **~ da** *fig* shun

rifugi'arsi *vr* take refuge

rifugi'ato, -a *nmf* refugee

ri'fugio *nm* shelter; (*nascondiglio*) hideaway. **~ antiaereo** bomb shelter. **~ antiatomico** fallout shelter

'riga *nf* line; (*fila*) row; (*striscia*) stripe; (*scriminatura*) parting; (*regolo*) rule; **a righe** ⟨*stoffa*⟩ striped; ⟨*quaderno*⟩ ruled; **mettersi in ~** line up

ri'gaglie *nfpl* (*interiora*) giblets

ri'gagnolo *nm* rivulet

ri'gare *vt* rule ⟨*foglio*⟩ ● *vi* **~ dritto** behave well

riga'toni *nmpl* small ridged pasta tubes

rigatti'ere *nm* junk dealer

rigene'rante *a* regenerative

rigene'rare *vt* regenerate

riget'tare *vt* (*gettare indietro*) throw back; (*respingere*) reject; (*vomitare*) throw up

ri'getto *nm* rejection

ri'ghello *nm* ruler

rigida'mente *adv* rigidly

rigidità *nf* rigidity; (*di clima*) severity; (*severità*) strictness. **~ cadaverica** rigor mortis

'rigido *a* rigid; (*freddo*) severe; (*severo*) strict

rigi'rare *vt* turn again; (*ripercorrere*) go round; *fig* twist ⟨*argomentazione*⟩ ● *vi* walk about

rigi'rarsi *vr* turn round; (*nel letto*) turn over

ri'giro *nm* (*imbroglio*) trick

'rigo *nm* line; *Mus* staff

ri'goglio *nm* bloom

rigogliosa'mente *adv* luxuriantly

rigogli'oso *a* luxuriant

rigonfia'mento *nm* swelling

rigonfi'are *vt* reinflate

ri'gonfio *a* swollen

ri'gore *nm* rigours *pl*; **a rigor di logica** strictly speaking; **calcio di ~** penalty [kick]; **area di ~** penalty area; **essere di ~** be compulsory

rigorosa'mente *adv* ‹giudicare› severely; ‹seguire istruzioni› exactly; **vestito ~ in giacca e cravatta** wearing the obligatory jacket and tie

rigo'roso *a* ‹severo› strict; ‹scrupoloso› rigorous

rigover'nare *vt* wash up

riguada'gnare *vt* regain, win back ‹stima›; win more ‹tempo, punti›

riguar'dare *vt* look at again; ‹considerare› regard; ‹concernere› concern; **per quanto riguarda...** with regard to...

riguar'darsi *vr* take care of oneself

rigu'ardo *nm* care; ‹considerazione› consideration; **nei riguardi di** towards; **~ a** with regard to

rigurgi'tante *a* **~ di** swarming with

rigurgi'tare *vt* regurgitate ● *vi* **~ di** *fig* be swarming with

ri'gurgito *nm* regurgitation; ‹di rabbia› fit; ‹di razzismo› resurgence

rilanci'are *vt* throw back ‹palla›; ‹di nuovo› throw again; increase ‹offerta›; revive ‹moda›; relaunch ‹prodotto› ● *vi* ‹a carte› raise the stakes; **rilancio di dieci** I'll raise you ten

ri'lancio *nm* ‹di offerta› increase; ‹di prodotto› re-launch

rilasci'are *vt* ‹concedere› grant; ‹liberare› release; issue ‹documento›

rilasci'arsi *vr* relax

ri'lascio *nm* release; ‹di documento› issue

rilassa'mento *nm* relaxation. **~ cutaneo** sagging of the skin

rilas'sare *vt* relax

rilas'sarsi *vr* relax

rilas'sato *a* relaxed

rile'gare *vt* bind ‹libro›

rile'gato *a* bound

rilega|'tore, -'trice *nmf* bookbinder

rilega'tura *nf* binding

ri'leggere *vt* reread

ri'lento: **a ~** *adv* slowly

rileva'mento *nm* survey; *Comm* buyout. **~ dirigenti** management buyout, MBO

rile'vante *a* considerable

rile'vanza *nf* significance

rile'vare *vt* ‹trarre› get; ‹mettere in evidenza› point out; ‹notare› notice; ‹topografia› survey; *Comm* take over; *Mil* relieve

rilevazi'one *nf* ‹statistica› survey

rili'evo *nm* relief; *Geog* elevation; ‹topografia› survey; ‹importanza› importance; ‹osservazione› remark; **mettere in ~ qcsa** point sth out

rilut'tante *a* reluctant

rilut'tanza *nf* reluctance

'rima *nf* rhyme; **far ~ con qcsa** rhyme with sth; **rispondere a qcno per le rime** give sb

as good as one gets. **~ alternata** alternate rhyme. **~ baciata** rhyming couplet

riman'dare *vt* ‹posporre› postpone; ‹mandare indietro› send back; ‹mandare di nuovo› send again; ‹far ridare un esame› make resit an examination

ri'mando *nm* return; ‹in un libro› cross-reference

rimaneggia'mento *nm* rejig

rimaneggi'are *vt* rejig, recast

rima'nente *a* remaining ● *nm* remainder

rima'nenza *nf* remainder; **rimanenze** *pl* remnants. **rimanenze** *pl* **di magazzino** unsold stock

rima'nere *vi* stay, remain; ‹essere d'avanzo› be left; ‹venirsi a trovare› be; ‹restare stupito› be astonished; ‹restare d'accordo› agree; **~ senza parole** be speechless

rimangi'are *vt* ‹mangiare di nuovo› have again, eat again

rimangi'arsi *vr* **~ la parola** break one's promise

rimar'care *vt* remark

rimar'chevole *a* remarkable

ri'mare *vt/i* rhyme

rimargi'nare *vt* heal

rimargi'narsi *vr* heal

ri'masto *pp di* rimanere

rima'sugli *nmpl* ‹di cibo› leftovers

rimbal'zare *vi* rebound; ‹proiettile:› ricochet; **far ~** bounce

rim'balzo *nm* rebound; ‹di proiettile› ricochet

rimbam'bire *vi* be in one's dotage ● *vt* stun

rimbam'bito *a* in one's dotage

rimbec'care *vi* retort

rimbecil'lire *vt* make brain-dead

rimbecil'lito *a* ‹stupido› brain-dead; ‹frastornato› stunned

rimboc'care *vt* turn up; roll up ‹maniche›; tuck in ‹coperte›; **~ le coperte a qcno** tuck sb into bed

rimboc'carsi *vr* **~ le maniche** roll up one's sleeves

rimbom'bare *vi* boom, resound

rim'bombo *nm* boom

rimbor'sare *vt* reimburse, repay

rim'borso *nm* reimbursement, repayment. **~ d'imposta** tax rebate. **~ spese** reimbursement of expenses

rimboschi'mento *nm* reafforestation *Br*, reforestation

rim'brotto *nm* reproach

rimedi'abile *a* ‹errore› which can be remedied

rimedi'are *vi* **~ a** remedy; make up for ‹errore›; ‹procurare› scrape up

ri'medio *nm* remedy

rimesco'lare *vt* mix [up]; shuffle ‹carte›; ‹rivangare› rake up; **mi fa ~ il sangue** it makes my blood boil

rimesco'lio *nm* ‹turbamento› shock

ri'messa *nf* ‹locale per veicoli› garage; ‹per aerei› hangar; ‹per autobus› depot; ‹di denaro› remittance; *(di merci)* consignment. **~ laterale** *Sport* throw-in

ri'messo *pp di* **rimettere**

rime'stare *vt* stir well

ri'mettere *vt (a posto)* put back; *(restituire)* return; *(affidare)* entrust; *(perdonare)* remit; *(rimandare)* put off; *(vomitare)* bring up; **~ in gioco** *(nel calcio)* throw in; **rimetterci** *(fam: perdere)* lose [out]

ri'mettersi *vr (ristabilirsi)* recover; *(tempo:)* clear up; **~ a** start again

'rimmel® *nm inv* mascara

rimoder'nare *vt* modernize

ri'monta *nf Sport* recovery

rimon'tare *vt (risalire)* go up; *Mech* reassemble ● *vi* remount; **~ a** *(risalire)* go back to

rimorchi'are *vt* tow; *fam* pick up *(ragazza)*

rimorchia'tore *nm* tug[boat]

ri'morchio *nm* tow; *(veicolo)* trailer

ri'mordere *vt* **mi rimorde la coscienza** *fig* it's preying on my conscience

ri'morso *nm* remorse

rimo'stranza *nf* complaint

rimo'vibile *a* removable

rimozi'one *nf* removal; *(da un incarico)* dismissal. **~ forzata** illegally parked vehicles removed at owner's expense

rimpagi'nare *vt* regret

rim'pallo *nm* bounce

rim'pasto *nm Pol* reshuffle

rimpatri'are *vt* repatriate ● *vi* return home

rimpatri'ata *nf* reunion

rim'patrio *nm* repatriation

rim'piangere *vt* regret

rimpiangi'mento *pp di* **rimpiangere** ● *nm* regret

rimpiat'tino *nm* hide-and-seek

rimpiaz'zare *vt* replace

rimpi'azzo *nm* replacement

rimpiccioli'mento *nm* shrinkage

rimpiccio'lire *vt* make smaller ● *vi* become smaller

rimpin'zare *vt* **~ di** stuff with

rimpin'zarsi *vr* stuff oneself

rimpol'pare *vt (ingrassare)* fatten up; *fig* pad out *(scritto)*

rimprove'rare *vt* reproach; **~ qcsa a qcno** reproach sb for sth

rim'provero *nm* reproach

rimugi'nare *vt* rummage; *fig* **~ su** brood over

rimune'rare *vt* remunerate

rimunera'tivo *a* remunerative

rimunerazi'one *nf* remuneration

ri'muovere *vt* remove

ri'nascere *vi* be reborn, be born again

rinascimen'tale *a* Renaissance

Rinasci'mento *nm* Renaissance

ri'nascita *nf* rebirth

rincal'zare *vt (sostenere)* support; *(rimboccare)* tuck in

rin'calzo *nm* support; **rincalzi** *pl Mil* reserves

rincantucci'arsi *vr* hide oneself away in a corner

rinca'rare *vt* increase the price of ● *vi* become more expensive

rin'caro *nm* price increase

rincar'tare *vt* rewrap

rinca'sare *vi* return home

rinchi'udere *vt* shut up

rinchi'udersi *vr* shut oneself up

rincon'trare *vt* meet again

rincon'trarsi *vr* meet [each other] again

rin'correre *vt* run after

rin'corsa *nf* run-up

rin'corso *pp di* **rincorrere**

rin'crescere *vi* **mi rincresce di non...** I'm sorry *o* I regret that I can't...; **se non ti rincresce** if you don't mind; **rincresce vedere...** it's sad to see...

rincresci'mento *nm* regret

rincresci'uto *pp di* **rincrescere**

rincreti'nire *vt* make brain-dead ● *vi* go brain-dead

rincu'lare *vi (arma:)* recoil; *(cavallo:)* shy

rin'culo *nm* recoil

rincuo'rare *vt* encourage

rincuo'rarsi *vr* take heart

rinfacci'are *vt* **~ qcsa a qcno** throw sth in sb's face

rinfode'rare *vt* sheathe

rinfor'zare *vt* strengthen; *(rendere più saldo)* reinforce

rinfor'zarsi *vr* become stronger

rin'forzo *nm* reinforcement; *fig* support; **rinforzi** *pl Mil* reinforcements

rinfran'care *vt* reassure

rinfre'scante *a* cooling

rinfre'scare *vt* cool; *(rinnovare)* freshen up ● *vi* get cooler

rinfre'scarsi *vr* freshen [oneself] up

rin'fresco *nm* light refreshment; *(ricevimento)* party

rin'fusa *nf* **alla ~** at random

ringalluz'zire *vt* make cocky ● *vi* get cocky

ringhi'are *vi* snarl

ringhi'era *nf* railing; *(di scala)* banisters *pl*

ringhi'oso *a* snarling

ringiova'nire *vt* rejuvenate *(pelle, persona)*; *(vestito:)* make look younger ● *vi* become young again; *(sembrare)* look young again

ringrazia'mento *nm* thanks *pl*

ringrazi'are *vt* thank

rinne'gare *vt* disown

rinne'gato, -a *nmf* renegade

rinno'vabile *a* renewable

rinnova'mento *nm* renewal; *(di edifici)* renovation

rinno'vare *vt* renew; renovate *(edifici)*

rinno'varsi *vr* be renewed; *(ripetersi)* recur, happen again

rin'novo *nm* renewal

rinoce'ronte *nm* rhinoceros

rino'mato *a* renowned

rinsal'dare *vt* consolidate

rinsa'vire *vi* come to one's senses

rinsec'chire *vi* shrivel up

rinsec'chito *a* shrivelled up

rinta'narsi *vr* hide oneself away; ⟨*animale:*⟩ retreat into its den

rintoc'care *vi* ⟨*campana:*⟩ toll; ⟨*orologio:*⟩ strike

rin'tocco *nm* toll; (*di orologio*) stroke

rinton'tire *vt anche fig* stun

rinton'tito *a* (*stordito*) dazed

rintracci'are *vt* trace

rintro'nare *vt* stun ● *vi* boom

rintuz'zare *vt* blunt; (*ribattere*) retort; (*reprimere*) repress

ri'nuncia *nf* renunciation

rinunci'are *vi* ~ **a** renounce, give up

rinuncia'tario *a* defeatist

ri'nunzia, rinunzi'are = **rinuncia, rinunciare**

rinveni'mento *nm* (*di reperti*) discovery; (*di refurtiva*) recovery

rinve'nire *vt* find ● *vi* (*riprendere i sensi*) come round; (*ridiventare fresco*) revive

rinvi'are *vt* put off; (*mandare indietro*) return; (*in libro*) refer; ~ **a giudizio** indict

rinvigo'rire *vt* strengthen

rin'vio *nm Sport* goal kick; (*in libro*) cross-reference; (*di appuntamento*) postponement; (*di merce*) return. ~ **a giudizio** indictment

rioccu'pare *vt* reoccupy

rio'nale *a* local

ri'one *nm* district

riordina'mento *nm* reorganization

riordi'nare *vt* tidy [up]; (*ordinare di nuovo*) reorder

riorganiz'zare *vt* reorganize

riorganizzazi'one *nf* reorganization

R.I.P. *abbr* (**riposi in pace**) RIP

ripa'gare *vt* repay

ripa'rare *vt* (*proteggere*) shelter, protect; (*aggiustare*) repair; (*porre rimedio*) remedy ● *vi* ~ **a** make up for

ripa'rarsi *vr* take shelter

ripa'rato *a* ⟨*luogo*⟩ sheltered

riparazi'one *nf* repair; *fig* reparation

ripar'lare *vi* **ne riparliamo stasera** we'll talk about it again tonight

ri'paro *nm* shelter; (*rimedio*) remedy

ripar'tire *vt* (*dividere*) divide ● *vi* leave again

ripartizi'one *nf* division

ripas'sare *vt* recross; (*rivedere*) revise ● *vi* pass again

ripas'sata *nf* (*spolverata*) quick dust; (*stirata*) quick iron; (*di vernice*) second coat; (*fam: rimprovero*) telling-off; **dar una ~ a** ⟨*lezione*⟩ revise

ri'passo *nm* (*di lezione*) revision

ripensa'mento *nm* second thoughts *pl*

ripen'sare *vi* ~ **a** think back to; **ripensarci** (*cambiare idea*) change one's mind; **ripensaci!** think again!

riper'correre *vt* (*con la memoria*) go back over; trace ⟨*storia*⟩; ~ **la strada fatta** go back the way one came

riper'cosso *pp di* **ripercuotere**

ripercu'otere *vt* strike again

ripercu'otersi *vr* ⟨*suono:*⟩ reverberate; ~ **su qcsa** (*fig: avere conseguenze*) impact on sth

ripercussi'one *nf* repercussion

ripe'scare *vt* (*recuperare*) fish out; (*ritrovare*) find again

ripe'tente *nmf* student who is repeating a year

ri'petere *vt* repeat

ri'petersi *vr* ⟨*evento:*⟩ recur; ⟨*persona:*⟩ repeat oneself

ripeti'tore *nm TV* relay

ripetizi'one *nf* repetition; (*di lezione*) revision; (*lezione privata*) private lesson

ripetuta'mente *adv* repeatedly

ri'piano *nm* (*di scaffale*) shelf; (*terreno pianeggiante*) terrace

ri'picca *nf* spite; **fare qcsa per ~** do sth out of spite

ri'picco = **ripicca**

ripida'mente *adv* steeply

'ripido *a* steep

ripie'gare *vt* refold; (*abbassare*) lower ● *vi* (*indietreggiare*) retreat

ripie'garsi *vr* bend; ⟨*sedile:*⟩ fold

ripi'ego *nm* expedient; (*via d'uscita*) way out

ripi'eno *a* full; *Culin* stuffed ● *nm* filling; *Culin* stuffing

ripiom'bare *vi* (*per terra*) fall down again; (*fig: tornare*) turn up on the doorstep again; (*nello sconforto*) sink back

ripopo'lare *vt* repopulate

ripopo'larsi *vr* be repopulated

ri'porre *vt* put back; (*mettere da parte*) put away; (*collocare*) place; repeat ⟨*domanda*⟩

ripor'tare *vt* (*restituire*) bring/take back; (*riferire*) report; (*subire*) suffer; *Math* carry; win ⟨*vittoria*⟩; transfer ⟨*disegno*⟩

ripor'tarsi *vr* go back; (*riferirsi*) refer

ri'porto *nm* (*su abito, scarpa*) appliqué; ~ **di 4** *Math* carry 4; **cane da ~** gun dog, retriever; **nascondere la calvizie con un ~** comb one's hair over a bald spot

ripo'sante *a* restful

ripo'sare *vi* rest ● *vt* put back

ripo'sarsi *vr* rest

ripo'sato *a* ⟨*mente*⟩ fresh; ⟨*viso*⟩ rested

ri'poso *nm* rest; **andare a ~** retire; **~!** *Mil* at ease!; **giorno di ~** day off

ripo'stiglio *nm* cupboard

ri'posto *pp di* **riporre**

ri'prendere *vt* take again; (*prendere indietro*) take back; (*riconquistare*) recapture; (*ricuperare*) recover; (*ricominciare*) resume; (*rimproverare*) reprimand; take in ⟨*cucitura*⟩; *Cinema* shoot

ri'prendersi *vr* recover; (*correggersi*) correct oneself

ri'presa *nf* resumption; (*ricupero*) recovery; *Theat* revival; *Cinema* shot; *Auto* acceleration; *Mus* repeat; ~ **aerea** bird's-eye view

ripresen'tare *vt* resubmit ⟨*domanda, certificato*⟩; reintroduce ⟨*problema, persona*⟩

ripresen'tarsi *vr* (*a ufficio*) go/come back again; (*come candidato*) stand again, run again; (*occasione:*) arise again; (*problema:*) come up again, reappear; (*a esame*) resit

ri'preso *pp di* **riprendere**

ripristi'nare *vt* restore

ripro'dotto *pp di* **riprodurre**

ripro'durre *vt* reproduce

ripro'dursi *vr Biol* reproduce; (*fenomeno:*) happen again, recur

riprodut'tivo *a* reproductive

riproduzi'one *nf* reproduction. **'~ vietata'** 'copyright'

ripro'mettersi *vr* (*intendere*) intend

ripro'porre *vt* put forward again

ripro'porsi *vr* ~ **di fare qcsa** intend to do sth; (*come candidato*) stand again; (*problema:*) come up again, reappear

ri'prova *nf* confirmation; **a ~ di** as confirmation of

ripro'vare *vt/i Comput* retry

riprovazi'one *nf* ~ **generale** outcry

riprove'vole *a* reprehensible

ripubbli'care *vt* republish

ripudi'are *vt* repudiate

ripu'gnante *a* repugnant

ripu'gnanza *nf* disgust

ripu'gnare *vi* ~ **a** disgust

ripu'lire *vt* clean [up]; *fig* polish

ripu'lita *nf* quick clean; **darsi una ~** have a wash and brushup

ripulsi'one *nf* repulsion

ripul'sivo *a* repulsive

ri'quadro *nm* square; (*pannello*) panel

ri'sacca *nf* undertow

ri'saia *nf* rice field, paddy field

risa'lire *vt* go back up ● *vi* ~ **a** (*nel tempo*) go back to; (*essere datato a*) date back to, go back to

risa'lita *nf* ascent; **impianto di ~** ski lift

risal'tare *vi* (*emergere*) stand out

ri'salto *nm* prominence; (*rilievo*) relief

risana'mento *nm* improvement

risa'nare *vt* heal; (*bonificare*) reclaim

risa'puto *a* well-known

risar'cibile *a* indemnifiable

risarci'mento *nm* compensation

risar'cire *vt* indemnify; **mi hanno risarcito i danni** they compensated me for the damage

ri'sata *nf* laugh

riscalda'mento *nm* heating. **~ autonomo** central heating (*for one flat*). **~ centralizzato** *central heating system for whole block of flats*

riscal'dare *vt* heat; warm (*persona*)

riscal'darsi *vr* warm up

riscat'tabile *a* redeemable

riscat'tare *vt* ransom

riscat'tarsi *vr* redeem oneself

ri'scatto *nm* ransom; (*morale*) redemption

rischia'rare *vt* light up; brighten (*colore*)

rischia'rarsi *vr* light up; (*cielo:*) clear up

rischi'are *vt* risk ● *vi* run the risk; **~ inutilmente** take needless risks

'rischio *nm* risk

rischi'oso *a* risky

risciac'quare *vt* rinse

risci'acquo *nm* rinse

risciò *nm inv* rickshaw

riscon'trare *vt* (*confrontare*) compare; (*verificare*) verify; (*rilevare*) find

ri'scontro *nm* comparison; (*verifica*) verification; (*Comm: risposta*) reply

risco'prire *vt* rediscover

ri'scossa *nf* revolt; (*riconquista*) recovery

riscossi'one *nf* collection

ri'scosso *pp di* **riscuotere**

ri'scrivere *vt* (*scrivere di nuovo*) rewrite; (*rispondere*) write back

riscu'otere *vt* shake; (*percepire*) draw; (*ottenere*) gain; cash (*assegno*)

riscu'otersi *vr* rouse oneself

risen'tire *vt* hear again; (*provare*) feel ● *vi* ~ **di** feel the effect of

risen'tirsi *vr* (*offendersi*) take offence

risenta'mente *adv* resentfully

risen'tito *a* resentful

ri'serbo *nm* reserve; **mantenere il ~** remain tight-lipped

ri'serva *nf* reserve; (*di caccia, pesca*) preserve; *Sport* substitute, reserve; **di ~** spare. **~ di caccia** game reserve. **~ indiana** Indian reservation. **~ naturale** wildlife reserve

riser'vare *vt* reserve; (*prenotare*) book; (*per occasione*) keep

riser'varsi (*ripromettersi*) plan for oneself (*cambiamento*); **mi riservo la sorpresa** I want it to be a surprise

riserva'tezza *nf* reserve

riser'vato *a* reserved; **'~ ai clienti dell'albergo'** 'for hotel guests only'; **'~ carico'** 'loading only'

ri'sguardo *nm* endpaper

ri'siedere *vi* ~ **a** reside in

'risma *nf* ream; *fig* kind

'riso[1] *pp di* **ridere** ● *nm* (*pl nf* **risa**) laughter; (*singolo*) laugh

'riso[2] *nm* (*cereale*) rice. **~ integrale** brown rice

riso'lino *nm* giggle

risolle'vare *vt* raise again; raise (*il morale*); raise again, bring up again (*problema, questione*); increase, improve (*le sorti*)

risolle'varsi *vr* (*da terra*) rise again; *fig* pick up

ri'solto *pp di* **risolvere**

risoluta'mente *adv* energetically

risolu'tezza *nf* determination

risolu'tivo *a* (*determinante*) decisive; **scelta risolutiva** solution

riso'luto *a* resolute, determined

risoluzi'one *nf* resolution

ri'solvere *vt* resolve; *Math* solve

ri'solversi *vr* (*decidersi*) decide; **~ in** turn into

riso'nanza *nf* resonance; **aver ~** *fig* arouse great interest. **~ magnetica** magnetic resonance

riso'nare *vi* resound; (*rimbombare*) echo

ri'sorgere *vi* rise again

risorgi'mento *nm* revival; **il R~** (*storico*) the Risorgimento

ri'sorsa *nf* resource; (*espediente*) resort.
risorse *pl* **energetiche** energy resources.
risorse *pl* **naturali** natural resources.
risorse *pl* **umane** human resources

ri'sorto *pp di* **risorgere**

ri'sotto *nm* risotto. **~ alla marinara** seafood risotto. **~ alla milanese** risotto with saffron

ri'sparmi *nmpl* (*soldi*) savings

risparmi'are *vt* save; (*salvare*) spare

risparmia|'tore, -'trice *nmf* saver

ri'sparmio *nm* saving. **~ energetico** energy saving

rispecchi'are *vt* reflect

rispe'dire *vr* send back, return

rispet'tabile *a* respectable

rispettabilità *nf* respectability

rispet'tare *vt* respect; **farsi ~** command respect

rispet'tivo *a* respective

ri'spetto *nm* respect; **~ a** as regards; (*in paragone a*) compared to

rispettosa'mente *adv* respectfully

rispet'toso *a* respectful

risplen'dente *a* shining

ri'splendere *vi* shine

rispon'dente *a* **~ a** in keeping with

rispon'denza *nf* correspondence

ri'spondere *vi* answer; (*rimbeccare*) answer back; (*obbedire*) respond; **~ a** reply to; **~ di** (*rendersi responsabile*) answer for

rispo'sare *vt* remarry

rispo'sarsi *vr* remarry

ri'sposta *nf* answer, reply; (*reazione*) response

ri'sposto *pp di* **rispondere**

rispun'tare *vi* (*persona, sole:*) reappear

'rissa *nf* brawl

ris'soso *a* pugnacious

ristabi'lire *vt* re-establish

ristabi'lirsi *vr* (*in salute*) recover

rista'gnare *vi* stagnate; (*sangue:*) coagulate

ri'stagno *nm* stagnation

ri'stampa *nf* reprint; (*azione*) reprinting

ristam'pare *vt* reprint

risto'rante *nm* restaurant

risto'rare *vt* refresh

risto'rarsi *vr liter* take some refreshment; (*riposarsi*) take a rest

ristora|'tore, -'trice *nmf* (*proprietario di ristorante*) restaurateur; (*fornitore*) caterer ● *a* refreshing

ri'storo *nm* refreshment; (*sollievo*) relief; **servizio di ~** refreshments *pl*

ristret'tezza *nf* narrowness; (*povertà*) poverty; **vivere in ristrettezze** live in straitened circumstances

ri'stretto *pp di* **restringere** ● *a* narrow; (*condensato*) condensed; (*limitato*) restricted; **di idee ristrette** narrow-minded

ristruttu'rante *a* (*cosmetico*) conditioning

ristruttu'rare *vt Comm* restructure; renovate (*casa*); repair (*capelli*)

ristrutturazi'one *nf Comm* restructuring; (*di casa*) renovation

risucchi'are *vt* suck in

ri'succhio *nm* whirlpool; (*di corrente*) undertow

risul'tare *vi* result; (*riuscire*) turn out

risul'tato *nm* result. **risultati** *pl* **parziali** (*di elezioni*) preliminary results; (*di partite*) half-time results

risuo'nare *vt* play again (*pezzo musicale*); ring again (*campanello*) ● *vi* (*grida, parola:*) echo; *Phys* resonate

risurrezi'one, risusci'tare = **resurrezione, resuscitare**

risvegli'are *vt* reawaken (*interesse*)

risvegli'arsi *vr* wake up; (*natura:*) awake; (*desiderio:*) be aroused

ri'sveglio *nm* waking up; (*dell'interesse*) revival; (*del desiderio*) arousal

ri'svolto *nm* (*di giacca*) lapel; (*di pantaloni*) turn-up, cuff *Am*; (*di manica*) cuff; (*di tasca*) flap; (*di libro*) inside flap

ritagli'are *vt* cut out

ri'taglio *nm* cutting; (*di stoffa*) scrap

ritar'dare *vi* be late; (*orologio:*) be slow ● *vt* delay; slow down (*progresso*); (*differire*) postpone

ritarda'tario, -a *nmf* latecomer

ritar'dato *a Psych* retarded

ri'tardo *nm* delay; **essere in ~** be late; (*volo:*) be delayed

ri'tegno *nm* reserve

ritem'prare *vt* restore

rite'nere *vt* retain; deduct (*somma*); (*credere*) believe

riten'tare *vt* try again

rite'nuta *nf* (*sul salario*) deduction. **~ d'acconto** tax deducted in advance from payments made to self-employed people. **~ diretta** taxation at source. **~ alla fonte** taxation at source, deduction at source

ritenzi'one *nf Med* retention

riti'rare *vt* throw back (*palla*); (*prelevare*) withdraw; (*riscuotere*) draw; collect (*pacco*)

riti'rarsi *vr* withdraw; (*stoffa:*) shrink; (*da attività*) retire; (*marea:*) recede

riti'rata *nf* retreat; (*WC*) toilet

ri'tiro *nm* withdrawal; *Relig* retreat; (*da attività*) retirement; **~ bagagli** baggage reclaim

'ritmica *nf* rhythmic gymnastics

ritmica'mente *adv* rhythmically

'ritmico *a* rhythmic[al]

'ritmo *nm* rhythm; **a ~ serrato** at a cracking pace

'rito *nm* rite; **di ~** customary. **~ funebre** funeral service

ritoc'care *vt* (*correggere*) touch up

ri'tocco *nm* alteration; **ritocchi** *pl Phot* retouching

ri'torcersi *vr* **~ contro qcno** boomerang on sb

ritor'nare *vi* return; (*andare/venire indietro*) go/come back; (*ricorrere*) recur; (*ridiventare*) become again

ritor'nello *nm* refrain

ri'torno *nm* return

ritorsi'one *nf* retaliation

ritra'durre *vt* (*tradurre di nuovo*) re-translate

ri'trarre *vt* (*ritirare*) withdraw; (*distogliere*) turn away; (*rappresentare*) portray

ritra'smettere *vt* TV show again, re-broadcast

ritrat'tabile *a* ⟨*accuso*⟩ which can be withdrawn

ritrat'tare *vt* retract, withdraw ⟨*dichiarazione*⟩

ritrattazi'one *nf* withdrawal, retraction

ritrat'tista *nmf* portrait painter

ri'tratto *pp di* **ritrarre** ● *nm* portrait

ritrazi'one *nf* retraction

ritrosa'mente *adv* shyly

ritro'sia *nf* shyness

ri'troso *a* (*timido*) shy; **a ~** backwards; **~ a** reluctant to

ritrova'mento *nm* (*azione*) finding; (*cosa*) find

ritro'vare *vt* find [again]; regain ⟨*salute*⟩

ritro'varsi *vr* meet; (*di nuovo*) meet again; (*capitare*) find oneself; (*raccapezzarsi*) see one's way

ritro'vato *nm* discovery

ri'trovo *nm* meeting-place. **~ notturno** night club

'ritto *a* upright; (*diritto*) straight

ritu'ale *a & nm* ritual

ritual'mente *adv* ritually

riunifi'care *vt* reunify

riunifi'carsi *vr* be reunited

riunificazi'one *nf* reunification

riuni'one *nf* meeting; (*dopo separazione*) reunion

riu'nire *vt* (*unire*) join together; (*radunare*) gather

riu'nirsi *vr* be reunited; (*adunarsi*) meet

riu'sare *vt* reuse

riusc'ire *vi* (*aver successo*) succeed; (*in matematica ecc*) be good (**in** at; (*aver esito*) turn out; **le è riuscito simpatico** she found him likeable

riu'scita *nf* (*esito*) result; (*successo*) success

ri'uso *nm* reuse

riutiliz'zare *vt* reuse

'riva *nf* (*di mare, lago*) shore; (*di fiume*) bank

rivacci'nare *vt* revaccinate

ri'vale *nmf* rival

rivaleggi'are *vi* compete (**con** with)

rivalità *nf inv* rivalry

ri'valsa *nf* revenge; **prendersi una ~ su qcno** take revenge on sb

rivalu'tare *vt* reappraise

rivalutazi'one *nf* revaluation

rivan'gare *vt* dig up again

rive'dere *vt* see again; revise ⟨*lezione*⟩; review ⟨*accordo*⟩; (*verificare*) check

rive'dibile *a* ⟨*accordo*⟩ reviewable; ⟨*recluta*⟩ temporarily unfit

rive'lare *vt* reveal

rive'larsi *vr* (*dimostrarsi*) turn out

rivela'tore *a* revealing ● *nm* Techn detector. **~ di mine** mine detector

rivelazi'one *nf* revelation

ri'vendere *vt* resell

rivendi'care *vt* claim

rivendicazi'one *nf* claim

ri'vendita *nf* (*negozio*) shop. **~ autorizzata** authorized retailer

rivendi|'tore, -'trice *nmf* retailer. **~ autorizzato** authorized retailer

riverbe'rare *vt* reflect ⟨*luce*⟩

ri'verbero *nm* reverberation; (*bagliore*) glare

rive'renza *nf* reverence; (*inchino*) curtsy; (*di uomo*) bow

rive'rire *vt* respect; (*ossequiare*) pay one's respects to

rivernici'are *vt* repaint; (*con flatting*) revarnish

river'sare *vt* pour

river'sarsi *vr* ⟨*fiume:*⟩ flow

river'sibile *a* reversible

rivesti'mento *nm* covering

rive'stire *vt* (*rifornire di abiti*) clothe; (*ricoprire*) cover; (*internamente*) line; hold ⟨*carica*⟩

rive'stirsi *vr* get dressed again; (*per una festa*) dress up

rive'stito *a* **~ di** covered with

rivi'era *nf* coast; **la ~ ligure** the Italian Riviera

ri'vincita *nf* Sport return match; (*vendetta*) revenge

rivis'suto *pp di* **rivivere**

ri'vista *nf* review; (*pubblicazione*) magazine; *Theat* revue; **passare in ~** review

rivitaliz'zare *vt* revitalize

rivitalizzazi'one *nf* revitalization

ri'vivere *vi* come to life again; (*riprendere le forze*) revive ● *vt* relive

'rivo *nm* stream

rivo'lere *vt* (*volere di nuovo*) want again; (*volere indietro*) want back

ri'volgere *vt* turn; (*indirizzare*) address; **~ da** (*distogliere*) turn away from

ri'volgersi *vr* turn round; **~ a** (*indirizzarsi*) turn to

rivolgi'mento *nm* upheaval

ri'volta *nf* revolt

rivol'tante *a* revolting, disgusting

rivol'tare *vt* turn [over]; (*mettendo l'interno verso l'esterno*) turn inside out; (*sconvolgere*) upset

rivol'tarsi *vr* (*ribellarsi*) revolt

rivol'tella *nf* revolver

ri'volto *pp di* **rivolgere**

rivol'toso, -a *nmf* rebel, insurgent

rivoluzio'nare *vt* revolutionize

rivoluzio'nario, -a *a & nmf* revolutionary

rivoluzi'one *nf* revolution; (*fig: disordine*) chaos. **~ francese** French Revolution. **~ industriale** Industrial Revolution

riz'zare *vt* raise; (*innalzare*) erect; prick up ⟨*orecchie*⟩

riz'zarsi *vr* stand up; ⟨*capelli:*⟩ stand on end; ⟨*orecchie:*⟩ prick up '**roast-beef** *nm inv* thin slices of roast beef served cold with lemon

'**roba** *nf* stuff; (*personale*) belongings *pl*, stuff; (*faccenda*) thing; (*sl: droga*) drugs *pl*; ~ **da matti!** absolute madness!. ~ **da bere** drink. ~ **da lavare** washing. ~ **da mangiare** food, things to eat. ~ **da stirare** ironing

ro'**baccia** *nf* rubbish

robi'**vecchi** *nm inv* second-hand dealer

ro'**bot** *nm inv* robot; (*da cucina*) food processor

ro'**botica** *nf* robotics

ro'**botico** *a* robotic

robotiz'**zato** *a* robotic, robotized

robu'**stezza** *nf* sturdiness, robustness; (*forza*) strength

ro'**busto** *a* sturdy, robust; (*forte*) strong

rocambo'**lesco** *a* incredible

'**rocca** *nf* fortress

rocca'**forte** *nf* stronghold

rocchetti'**era** *nf* winder

roc'**chetto** *nm* reel

'**roccia** *nf* rock; (*sport*) rock-climbing

rock *nm* rock [music]. ~ **acrobatico** rock 'n' roll

'**roco** *a* throaty

ro'**daggio** *nm* running in

'**Rodano** *nm* Rhone

ro'**dare** *vt* run in

ro'**deo** *nm* rodeo

'**rodere** *vt* gnaw; (*corrodere*) corrode

'**rodersi** *vr* ~ **da** (*logorarsi*) be consumed with

rodi'**tore** *nm* rodent

rodo'**dendro** *nm* rhododendron

ro'**gito** *nm Jur* deed

'**rogna** *nf* scabies *sg*; *fig* nuisance

ro'**gnone** *nm Culin* kidney

ro'**gnoso** *a* scabby

'**rogo** *nm* (*supplizio*) stake; (*per cadaveri*) pyre

rol'**lare** *vt* roll ‹sigaretta› ● *vi* ‹aereo, nave:› roll

ROM *nf inv Comput* ROM

'**Roma** *nf* Rome

Roma'**nia** *nf* Romania

ro'**manico** *a* Romanesque

ro'**mano, -a** *a & nmf* Roman

romantica'**mente** *adv* romantically

romanti'**cismo** *nm* romanticism

ro'**mantico** *a* romantic

ro'**manza** *nf* romance

roman'**zato** *a* romanticized

roman'**zesco** *a* fictional; (*stravagante*) wild, unrealistic

roman'**zetto** *nm* ~ **rosa** novelette

romanzi'**ere** *nm* novelist

ro'**manzo** *a* Romance ● *nm* novel; (*storia incredibile romantica*) romance. ~ **d'appendice** serial story. ~ **giallo** thriller. ~ **sceneggiato** novel adapted for television/radio

rom'**bare** *vi* rumble

'**rombo** *nm* rumble; *Math* rhombus; (*pesce*) turbot

romboi'**dale** *a* rhomboid, diamond-shaped

'**rompere** *vt* break; break off ‹relazione›; **non** ~ **[le scatole]!** (*fam: seccare*) don't be a pain [in the neck]!

'**rompersi** *vr* break; ~ **una gamba** break one's leg

rompi'**capo** *nm* nuisance; (*indovinello*) puzzle

rompi'**collo** *nm* daredevil; **a** ~ at breakneck speed

rompighi'**accio** *nm* ice-breaker

rompi'**mento** *nm fam* pain

rompi'**scatole** *nmf inv fam* pain

'**ronda** *nf* rounds *pl*

ron'**della** *nf Mech* washer

'**rondine** *nf* swallow

ron'**done** *nm* swift

ron'**fare** *vi* (*russare*) snore; (*fare le fusa*) purr

ron'**zare** *vi* buzz; ~ **attorno a qcno** *fig* hang about sb

ron'**zino** *nm* jade

ron'**zio** *nm* buzz

'**rosa** *nf* rose. ~ **rampicante** rambler, rambling rose. ~ **selvatica** wild rose. ~ **dei venti** wind rose ● *a & nm* (*colore*) pink

ro'**saio** *nm* rosebush

ro'**sario** *nm* rosary

ro'**sato** *a* rosy ● *nm* (*vino*) rosé

'**rosbif** = **roast-beef**

rosé *nm inv* rosé

'**roseo** *a* pink

ro'**seto** *nm* rose garden

ro'**setta** *nf* (*coccarda*) rosette; *Mech* washer

rosicchi'**are** *vt* nibble; (*rodere*) gnaw

rosma'**rino** *nm* rosemary

'**roso** *pp di* **rodere**

roso'**lare** *vt* brown

roso'**lato** *a* sauté

roso'**lia** *nf* German measles *sg*

ro'**sone** *nm* rosette; (*apertura*) rose window

'**rospo** *nm* toad

ros'**setto** *nm* (*per labbra*) lipstick

'**rosso** *a & nm* red; **diventare** ~ go red; **passare col** ~ go through a red light, jump a red light. ~ **carota** *a* ‹capelli› ginger. ~ **mattone** *a* brick red. ~ **sangue** *a* blood red. ~ **scarlatto** *a* scarlet. ~ **d'uovo** [egg] yolk. ~ **vermiglio** *a* vermilion

ros'**sore** *nm* redness; (*della pelle*) flush

rosticce'**ria** *nf* shop selling cooked meat and other prepared food

'**rostro** *nm* rostrum; (*becco*) bill

ro'**tabile** *a* **strada** ~ carriageway

ro'**taia** *nf* rail; (*solco*) rut

ro'**tante** *a* rotating

ro'**tare** *vt/i* rotate

rota'**tiva** *nf* rotary press

rota'**torio** *a* rotary

rotazi'**one** *nf* rotation; (*di personale*) turnover. ~ **delle colture** crop rotation

rote'**are** *vt/i* roll

ro'**tella** *nf* small wheel; (*di mobile*) castor

roto'calco *nm* (*sistema*) rotogravure; (*rivista*) illustrated magazine

roto'lare *vt/i* roll

roto'larsi *vr* roll [about]

roto'lio *nm* rolling

'rotolo *nm* roll; **andare a rotoli** go to rack and ruin. ~ **di carta igienica** toilet roll

roto'loni *adv* **cadere** ~ tumble

ro'tonda *nf* roundabout, traffic circle *Am*

rotondità *nf* (*qualità*) roundness; ~ *pl* (*curve femminili*) curves *pl*, curvaceousness

ro'tondo, -a *a* round ● *nf* (*spiazzo*) terrace

ro'tore *nm* rotor

'rotta[1] *nf* *Naut, Aeron* course; **far** ~ **per** set a course for; **fuori** ~ off course; **in** ~ **di collisione** on a collision course

'rotta[2] *nf* **a** ~ **di collo** at breakneck speed; **essere in** ~ **con** be on bad terms with

rotta'maio *nm* junkyard

rot'tame *nm* scrap; *fig* wreck

'rotto *pp di* **rompere** ● *a* broken; (*stracciato*) torn

rot'tura *nf* break; **che** ~ **di scatole!** *fam* what a pain!

'rotula *nf* kneecap

rou'lette *nf* *inv* roulette. ~ **russa** Russian roulette

rou'lotte *nf* *inv* caravan, trailer *Am*

rou'tine *nf* *inv* routine; **di** ~ ⟨*operazioni, controlli*⟩ routine

ro'vente *a* scorching

'rovere *nm* (*legno*) oak

rovescia'mento *nm* overthrow

rovesci'are *vt* (*buttare a terra*) knock over; (*sottosopra*) turn upside down; (*rivoltare*) turn upside down; spill ⟨*liquido*⟩; overthrow ⟨*governo*⟩; reverse ⟨*situazione*⟩

rovesci'arsi *vr* (*capovolgersi*) overturn; (*riversarsi*) pour

ro'vescio *a* (*contrario*) reverse; **alla rovescia** (*capovolto*) upside down; (*con l'interno all'esterno*) inside out ● *nm* reverse; (*nella maglia*) purl; (*di pioggia*) downpour; *Tennis* backhand

ro'vina *nf* ruin; (*crollo*) collapse; **in** ~ in ruins

rovi'nare *vt* ruin; (*guastare*) spoil ● *vi* crash

rovi'narsi *vr* be ruined; ⟨*persona:*⟩ ruin oneself

rovi'nato *a* ruined

ro'vine *nfpl* ruins

rovi'noso *a* ruinous

rovi'stare *vt* ransack

'rovo *nm* bramble

rozza'mente *adv* crudely

roz'zezza *nf* indelicacy

'rozzo *a* rough

R.R. *abbr* (**ricevuta di ritorno**) acknowledgment of receipt

R.U. *abbr* (**Regno Unito**) UK

'ruba *nf* **andare a** ~ sell like hot cakes

rubacchi'are *vt* pilfer

rubacu'ori *nm inv* heart-throb

ru'bare *vt* steal

rubi'condo *a* ruddy

rubi'netto *nm* tap, faucet *Am*

ru'bino *nm* ruby

ru'bizzo *a* spry

'rublo *nm* rouble

ru'brica *nf* (*in giornale*) column; (*in programma televisivo*) TV report; (*quaderno con indice*) address book. ~ **sportiva** sports column. ~ **telefonica** telephone and address book

'rucola *nf* rocket

'rude *a* rough

'rudere *nm* ruin

ru'dezza *nf* bluntness

rudimen'tale *a* rudimentary

rudi'menti *nmpl* rudiments

ruffi'ana *nf* procuress

ruffi'ano *nm* pimp; (*adulatore*) bootlicker

'ruga *nf* wrinkle

'ruggine *nf* rust; **fare la** ~ go rusty

ruggi'noso *a* rusty

rug'gire *vi* roar

rug'gito *nm* roar

rugi'ada *nf* dew

ru'goso *a* wrinkled

rul'lare *vi* roll; *Aeron* taxi

rul'lino *nm* film

rul'lio *nm* rolling; *Aeron* taxiing

'rullo *nm* roll; *Techn* roller

rum *nm inv* rum

ru'meno, -a *a & nmf* Romanian

rumi'nante *nm* ruminant

rumi'nare *vt* ruminate

ru'more *nm* noise; *fig* rumour

rumoreggi'are *vi* rumble

rumorosa'mente *adv* noisily

rumo'roso *a* noisy; (*sonoro*) loud

ru'olo *nm* roll; *Theat* role; **di** ~ on the staff. ~ **delle imposte** tax notice. ~ **primario/ secondario** major/minor role

ru'ota *nf* wheel; **andare a** ~ **libera** free-wheel; **fare la** ~ do a cartwheel. ~ **dentata** cogwheel. ~ **di scorta** spare wheel. ~ **di stampa** (*di stampante*) print wheel. ~ **del timone** helm

'rupe *nf* cliff

ru'pestre *a* ⟨*pittura*⟩ rock *attrib*

ru'pia *nf* rupee

ru'rale *a* rural

ru'scello *nm* stream

'ruspa *nf* bulldozer

ru'spante *a* free-range

rus'sare *vi* snore

'Russia *nf* Russia

'russo, -a *a & nmf* Russian ● *nm* (*lingua*) Russian

'rustico *a* rural; ⟨*carattere*⟩ rough

'ruta *nf* *Bot* rue

rut'tare *vi* belch, burp

rut'tino *nm* (*di bambino*) burp

'rutto *nm* belch, burp

'ruvido *a* coarse

ruzzo'lare *vi* tumble down

ruzzo'lone *nm* tumble; **cadere ruzzoloni** tumble down, tumble [helter-skelter]

Ss

S. *abbr* (**santo, santa**) St.; *abbr* (**sud**) south

'sabato *nm* Saturday; **di ~** on Saturdays

sab'batico *a* sabbatical; **anno ~** sabbatical [year]

'sabbia *nf* sand. **sabbie** *pl* **mobili** quick-sand

sabbi'are *vt* sandblast

sabbia'tura *nf* (*di vetro, metallo*) sandblasting; (*terapeutica*) sand-bath

sabbi'oso *a* sandy

sabo'taggio *nm* sabotage

sabo'tare *vt* sabotage

sabota|'tore, -'trice *nmf* saboteur

'sacca *nf* bag. **~ di resistenza** pocket of resistance. **~ da viaggio** travel[ling]-bag

sacca'rina *nf* saccharin

sac'cente *a* conceited ● *nmf* know-all, know-it-all *Am*

saccente'ria *nf* conceit

saccheggi'are *vt* sack; *hum* plunder ‹*frigo*›

saccheggia|'tore, -'trice *nmf* plunderer

sac'cheggio *nm* sack

sac'chetto *nm* bag. **~ di plastica** plastic bag. **~ per la spazzatura** bin liner

'sacco *nm* sack; *Anat* sac; (*sl: biglietto da mille lire*) thousand lire note; (*contenuto*) sack[ful]; **mettere nel ~** *fig* swindle; **un ~** (*moltissimo*) a lot; **un ~ di** (*gran quantità*) lots of. **~ a pelo** sleeping-bag. **~ postale** mail-bag

saccope'lista *nmf* backpacker

sacer'dote *nm* priest

sacer'dozio *nm* priesthood

sacra'mento *nm* sacrament

sacrifi'cale *a* sacrificial

sacrifi'care *vt* sacrifice

sacrifi'carsi *vr* sacrifice oneself

sacrifi'cato *a* sacrificed; (*non valorizzato*) wasted

sacri'ficio *nm* sacrifice

sacri'legio *nm* sacrilege

sa'crilego *a* sacrilegious

'sacro *a* sacred ● *nm* *Anat* sacrum

sacro'santo *a* sacrosanct; ‹*verità*› gospel; ‹*diritto*› sacred

'sadico, -a *a* sadistic ● *nmf* sadist

sa'dismo *nm* sadism

sa'etta *nf* arrow; (*fulmine*) thunderbolt; **correre come una ~** run like the wind

sa'fari *nm inv* safari

'saga *nf* saga

sa'gace *a* shrewd

sa'gacia *nf* sagacity

sag'gezza *nf* wisdom

saggia'mente *adv* sagely

saggi'are *vt* test

'saggio[1] *nm* (*scritto*) essay; (*prova*) proof; (*di metallo*) assay; (*campione*) sample; (*esempio*) example

'saggio[2] *a* wise ● *nm* (*persona*) sage

sag'gista *nmf* essayist

sag'gistica *nf* non-fiction

Sagit'tario *nm* *Astr* Sagittarius

'sago = sagù

'sagoma *nf* shape; (*profilo*) outline; (*in falegnameria*) template; **che ~!** *fam* what a character!

sago'mare *vt* make according to a template

'sagra *nf* festival

sa'grato *nm* churchyard

sagre'stano *nm* sacristan

sagre'stia *nf* sacristy

sagù *nm inv* sago

Sa'hara *nm* Sahara

'sala *nf* hall; (*salotto*) living room; (*per riunioni ecc*) room; (*di cinema*) cinema. **~ arrivi** arrivals lounge. **~ d'aspetto** waiting room. **~ d'attesa** waiting room. **~ da ballo** ballroom. **~ di comando** control room. **~ conferenze** conference hall. **~ giochi** amusement arcade. **~ d'imbarco** departure lounge. **~ di lettura** reading room. **~ macchine** engine room. **~ operatoria** operating theatre *Br*, operating room *Am*. **~ parto** delivery room. **~ da pranzo** dining room. **~ professori** staff room, common room. **~ di regia** *Radio, TV* control room. **~ di ricevimento** function room. **~ riunioni** conference room. **~ da tè** tea shop

sa'lace *a* salacious

sa'lame *nm* salami

salame'lecchi *nmpl* **fare ~** bow and scrape; **prendi quello che vuoi senza tanti ~** don't stand on ceremony, take what you want

sala'moia *nf* brine

sa'lare *vt* salt

salari'ato *nm* wage earner

sa'lario *nm* wages *pl*

salas'sare *vt Med* bleed; *fig* bleed dry

sa'lasso *nm* bleeding; **essere un ~** *fig* cost a fortune

sala'tini *nmpl* savouries (*eaten with aperitifs*)

sa'lato *a* salty; (*costoso*) dear; **acqua salata** salt water

sal'ciccia *nf* = **salsiccia**

sal'dare *vt* weld; set ‹*osso*›; pay off ‹*debito*›; settle ‹*conto*›; **~ a stagno** solder

sal'darsi *vr* ⟨*osso:*⟩ knit; ⟨*ferita:*⟩ heal
saldat'rice *nf* soldering iron
salda'tura *nf* soldering; (*giunzione*) join
'**saldo** *a* firm; (*resistente*) strong; **~ come una roccia** solid as a rock; **essere ~ nei propri principi** stick to one's principles ● *nm* (*pagamento*) settlement; *Comm* balance; (*di conto corrente*) bank balance; **saldi** *pl* sale; **i ~ di fine stagione** the end of season sales; **in ~** ⟨*essere*⟩ on sale; ⟨*comprato*⟩ in a sale. **~ iniziale** opening balance
'**sale** *nm* salt; **non ha ~ in zucca** *fam* he hasn't got an ounce of common sense; **restare di ~** be struck dumb [with astonishment]; **sali** *pl Med* smelling salts. **sali** *pl* **da bagno** bath salts. **~ da cucina** cooking salt. **~ fino** table salt. **~ grosso** cooking salt. **sali** *pl* **e tabacchi** (*negozio*) tobacconist's shop
'**salice** *nm* willow. **~ piangente** weeping willow
sali'ente *a* outstanding; **i punti salienti** the main points, the highlights
sali'era *nf* salt-cellar
sa'lina *nf* salt-works *sg*
salinità *nf* saltiness
sa'lino *a* saline
sa'lire *vi* go/come up; (*levarsi*) rise; (*su treno ecc*) get on; (*in macchina*) get in ● *vt* go/come up ⟨*scale*⟩
sa'lita *nf* climb; (*aumento*) rise; **in ~** uphill
sa'liva *nf* saliva
sali'vare *vt* salivate ● *a* ⟨*ghiandola*⟩ salivary
'**salma** *nf* corpse
sal'mastro *a* brackish ● *nm* salt air
salmì *nm* **in ~** marinated and slowly cooked in the marinade
salmi'strare *vt Culin* cure
'**salmo** *nm* psalm
sal'mone *nm* & *a inv* salmon. **~ affumicato** smoked salmon
salmo'nella *nf* salmonella
sa'lone *nm* (*salotto*) living room; (*di parrucchiere*) salon. **~ dell'automobile** motor show. **~ di bellezza** beauty parlour. **~ del libro** book fair
salo'pette *nf inv* dungarees *pl*
salotti'ero *a pej* mundane; **discorso ~** small talk
salot'tino *nm* bower
sa'lotto *nm* drawing room; (*soggiorno*) sitting room; (*mobili*) [three-piece] suite; **fare ~** chat. **~ letterario** literary salon
sal'pare *vi* sail ● *vt* **~ l'ancora** weigh anchor
'**salsa** *nf* sauce; *Mus* salsa. **~ di pomodoro** tomato sauce. **~ di soia** soy sauce. **~ tartara** tartar sauce
sal'sedine *nf* saltiness
sal'siccia *nf* sausage
salsi'era *nf* sauce-boat
sal'tare *vi* jump; (*venir via*) come off; (*balzare*) leap; (*esplodere*) blow up; **saltar fuori** spring from nowhere; ⟨*oggetto cercato:*⟩ turn up; **è saltato fuori che...** it emerged

that...; **~ fuori con...** come out with...; **salta agli occhi** (*è evidente*) it hits you; **~ in aria** blow up; **~ in mente** spring to mind ● *vt* jump [over]; skip ⟨*pasti, lezioni*⟩; *Culin* sauté
sal'tato *a Culin* sautéed
saltel'lare *vi* hop; (*di gioia*) skip
saltim'banco *nm* acrobat
saltim'bocca *nm inv* slice of veal rolled with ham and sage and fried
'**salto** *nm* jump; (*balzo*) leap; (*dislivello*) drop; (*fig: omissione, lacuna*) gap; **fare un ~ da** (*visitare*) drop in on; **in un ~** *fig* in a jiffy; **fare i salti mortali** *fig* go to great lengths; **fare quattro salti** *fam* go dancing; **fare un ~ nel buio** *fig* take a leap in the dark. **~ in alto** high jump. **~ con l'asta** pole-vault. **~ della corda** skipping. **~ in lungo** long jump. **~ pagina** *Comput* page down. **~ di qualità** quality leap
saltuaria'mente *adv* occasionally, from time to time
saltu'ario *a* desultory; **lavoro ~** casual work
sa'lubre *a* healthy
salume'ria *nf* delicatessen
sa'lumi *nmpl* cold cuts
salumi'ere *nm* person who sells cold meat
salu'tare *vt* greet; (*congedandosi*) say goodbye to; (*portare i saluti a*) give one's regards to; *Mil* salute; **ti saluto!** *fam* cheerio! ● *a* healthy
salu'tarsi *vr* (*all'arrivo*) greet each other; (*in partenza*) say goodbye to each other
sa'lute *nf* health; **godere di ottima ~** be in the best of health, enjoy excellent health; **in ~** in good health; **~!** (*dopo uno starnuto*) bless you!; (*a un brindisi*) cheers!. **~ di ferro** iron constitution
salu'tista *nmf* health fanatic; (*dell'Esercito della Salvezza*) Salvationist
sa'luto *nm* greeting; (*di addio*) goodbye; *Mil* salute; **saluti** *pl* (*ossequi*) regards
'**salva** *nf* salvo; **sparare a salve** shoot blanks; **a salve** ⟨*pistola*⟩ loaded with blank cartridges
salvacon'dotto *nm* safe conduct
salvada'naio *nm* money box
salva'gente *nm* lifebelt; (*a giubbotto*) life-jacket; (*ciambella*) rubber ring; (*spartitraffico*) traffic island
salvaguar'dare *vt* protect, safeguard
salvaguar'darsi *vr* protect oneself
salvagu'ardia *nf* safeguard
sal'vare *vt* save; (*proteggere*) protect; **~ la faccia** save face; **~ la pelle** save one's skin
sal'varsi *vr* save oneself
salva'schermo *nm Comput* screen saver
salva'slip *nm inv* panty-liner
salva'taggio *nm* rescue; *Naut* salvage; *Comput* saving; **battello di ~** lifeboat
salva‖**'tore**, **-'trice** *nmf* saviour
'**salve** *vedi* **salva**
sal'vezza *nf* safety: *Relig* salvation; **ancora di ~** *fig* salvation
'**salvia** *nf* sage

salvi'etta *nf* serviette

'salvo *a* safe ● *nm* **trarre in ~** rescue ● *prep* except [for] ● *conj* **~ che** (*a meno che*) unless; (*eccetto che*) except that

samari'tano, -a *a a & nmf* Samaritan

'samba *nf* samba

sam'buca *nf* sambuca

sam'buco *nm* elder

san *nm* (*before proper names starting with a consonant*) saint; *vedi* **santo**

sa'nabile *a* curable

sa'nare *vt* heal; (*bonificare*) reclaim; **~ il bilancio** balance the books

sana'toria *nf* decree legitimizing a situation which is in principle illegal

sana'torio *nm* sanatorium

san'cire *vt* sanction

'sandalo *nm* sandal; *Bot* sandalwood

sandi'nista *a & nmf* Sandinista

'sandwich *nm inv* sandwich; **uomo ~** sand-wich-man

san'gallo *nm* (*tessuto*) broderie anglaise

san'gria *nf* sangria

'sangue *nm* blood; **a ~ freddo** in cold blood; **al ~** *Culin* rare; **appena al ~** *Culin* medium-rare; **farsi cattivo ~ per** worry about; **iniettato di** ‹*occhio*› bloodshot; **all'ultimo ~** ‹*lotta*› to the death; **di ~ blu** blue-blooded; **sudare ~** sweat blood. **~ freddo** composure. **~ da naso** nose bleed

sangue'misto *nm* half-caste

sangu'igno *a* blood *attrib*

sangui'naccio *nm* *Culin* black pudding

sangui'nante *a* bleeding

sangui'nare *vi* bleed

sangui'nario *a* bloodthirsty

sangui'noso *a* bloody

sangui'suga *nf* leech

sanità *nf* soundness; (*salute*) health; **ministero della ~** Department of Health. **~ di costumi** morality. **~ mentale** sanity, mental health

sani'tario *a* sanitary; **servizio ~** health service ● *nm* doctor

San Ma'rino *nm* San Marino

'sano *a* sound; (*salutare*) healthy; **~ di mente** sane; **~ come un pesce** as fit as a fiddle

'sansa *nf* husk

San Sil'vestro *nm* New Year's Eve

santifi'care *vt* sanctify

santità *nf* sainthood

'santo, -a *a* holy; (*con nome proprio*) saint; **Sant'Antonio** St Anthony; **San Francesco d'Assisi** St Francis of Assisi; **di santa ragione** in no uncertain terms ● *nmf* saint. **~ patrono, -a** patron saint

san'tone *nm* guru

santo'reggia *nf* *Bot* savory

santu'ario *nm* sanctuary

san Valen'tino *nm* St Valentine's Day; **giorno di ~ ~** Valentine's Day

sanzio'nare *vt* sanction

sanzi'one *nf* sanction. **~ amministrativa** administrative sanction. **~ penale** legal sanction

sa'pere *vt* know; (*essere capace di*) be able to; (*venire a sapere*) hear; **saperla lunga** know a thing or two; **non lo so** I don't know; **non so che farci** there's nothing I can do about it; **~ a memoria** know by heart; **~ il fatto proprio** know what one is talking about; **per quanto ne sappia** insofar as I know ● *vi* **~ di** know about; (*aver sapore di*) taste of; (*aver odore di*) smell of; **saperci fare** know how to go about it; **saperci fare con i bambini** be good with children ● *nm* knowledge

sapi'ente *a* wise; (*esperto*) expert ● *nm* sage

sapiente'mente *adv* wisely; (*abilmente*) skilfully

sapien'tone *nm* smart alec[k]

sapi'enza *nf* wisdom

sa'pone *nm* soap; **bolla di ~** soap bubble; **finire in una bolla di ~** *fig* come to nothing. **~ da barba** shaving soap. **~ da bucato** washing soap

sapo'netta *nf* bar of soap

sapo'noso *a* soapy

sa'pore *nm* taste; **sentire ~ di** detect a hint of

saporita'mente *adv* ‹*condire*› skilfully; ‹*mangiare*› appreciatively; ‹*dormire*› soundly

sapo'rito *a* tasty

sapu'tello, -a *a & nm sl* know-all, know-it-all *Am*

sara'banda *nf* *fig* uproar

sara'ceno, -a *a & nmf* Saracen; **grano ~** buckwheat

saraci'nesca *nf* roller shutter; (*di chiusa*) sluice gate

'sarago *nm* white bream

sar'casmo *nm* sarcasm

sarcastica'mente *adv* sarcastically

sar'castico *a* sarcastic

sar'cofago *nm* sarcophagus

Sar'degna *nf* Sardinia

sar'dina *nf* sardine

'sardo, -a *a & nmf* Sardinian

sar'donico *a* sardonic

sarti'ame *nm* rigging

'sarto, -a *nm* tailor ● *nf* dressmaker

sarto'ria *nf* (*da uomo*) tailor's; (*da donna*) dressmaker's; (*arte*) couture

s.a.s. *abbr* **società in accomandita semplice**

sas'saia *nf* stony ground

sassai'ola *nf* hail of stones

sas'sata *nf* blow with a stone; **una ~ ha rotto il vetro** a stone broke the window; **prendere a sassate** throw stones at, stone

'sasso *nm* stone; (*ciottolo*) pebble; **sono rimasto di ~** I was struck dumb [with aston-ishment]

sassofo'nista *nmf* saxophonist

sas'sofono *nm* saxophone

'sassone *nmf* Saxon; **genitivo ~** Saxon genitive

sas'soso *a* stony

'**Satana** *nm* Satan

sa'**tanico** *a* satanic

sa'**tellite** *a inv & nm* satellite; **città ~** satellite town

sati'**nare** *vt* glaze; polish ⟨*metallo*⟩

sati'**nato** *a* glazed; ⟨*metallo*⟩ polished

'**satira** *nf* satire

sa'**tirico** *a* satirical

satol'**lare** *vt hum* stuff

sa'**tollo** *a hum* replete, full

satu'**rare** *vt* saturate

saturazi'**one** *nf* saturation

satur'**nismo** *nm* lead poisoning

Sa'**turno** *nm* Saturn

'**saturo** *a* saturated; (*pieno*) full

S.A.U.B. *nf abbr* (**Struttura Amministrativa Unificata di Base**) *Italian national health service*

'**sauna** *nf* sauna

sa'**vana** *nf* savannah

savoi'**ardo** *nm* (*biscotto*) sponge finger

savoir-'**faire** *nm inv* expertise, know-how

sazi'**are** *vt* satiate

sazi'**arsi** *vr* ~ **di** *fig* weary of, grow tired of

sazi'**età** *nf* **mangiare a** ~ eat one's fill

'**sazio** *a* satiated

sbaciucchi'**are** *vt* smother with kisses

sbaciucchi'**arsi** *vr* kiss and cuddle

sbada'**taggine** *nf* carelessness; **è stata una** ~ it was careless

sbada'**mente** *adv* carelessly

sba'**dato** *a* careless

sbadigli'**are** *vi* yawn

sba'**diglio** *nm* yawn

sba'**fare** *vt* sponge

sba'**fata** *nf fam* nosh; **farsi una** ~ *fam* have a nosh-up

'**sbaffo** *nm* smear

'**sbafo** *nm* sponging; **a** ~ (*gratis*) without paying

sbagli'**are** *vi* make a mistake; (*aver torto*) be wrong ● *vt* make a mistake in; ~ **strada** go the wrong way; ~ **numero** get the number wrong; *Teleph* dial a wrong number; **sbagliando s'impara** practice makes perfect

sbagli'**arsi** *vr* make a mistake; **ti sbagli** you're mistaken, you're wrong; ~ **di grosso** be totally wrong

sbagli'**ato** *a* wrong

'**sbaglio** *nm* mistake; **per** ~ by mistake

sbale'**strare** *vt fig* disconcert

sbale'**strato** *a* disconcerted

sbal'**lare** *vt* unpack; *fam* screw up ⟨*conti*⟩ ● *vi fam* go crazy

sbal'**lato** *a* (*squilibrato*) unbalanced

'**sballo** *nm fam* scream; (*per droga*) trip; **da** ~ *sl* terrific

sballot'**tare** *vt* toss about

sbalordi'**mento** *nm* amazement

sbalor'**dire** *vt* stun ● *vi* be stunned

sbalordi'**tivo** *a* amazing

sbalor'**dito** *a* stunned; **restare** ~ be stunned

sbal'**zare** *vt* throw; (*da una carica*) dismiss ● *vi* bounce; (*saltare*) leap

'**sbalzo** *nm* bounce; (*sussulto*) jolt; (*di temperatura*) sudden change; **a sbalzi** in spurts; **a** ~ (*a rilievo*) embossed

sban'**care** *vt* bankrupt; excavate ⟨*terreno*⟩; ~ **il banco** break the bank

sbanda'**mento** *nm Auto* skid; *Naut* list; *fig* going off the rails

sban'**dare** *vi Auto* skid; *Naut* list

sban'**darsi** *vr* (*disperdersi*) disperse

sban'**data** *nf* skid; *Naut* list; **prendere una** ~ **per** get a crush on

sban'**dato, -a** *a* mixed-up ● *nmf* mixed-up person

sbandie'**rare** *vt* wave; *fig* display

sbarac'**care** *vt/i* clear up

sbaragli'**are** *vt* rout

sba'**raglio** *nm* rout; **mettere allo** ~ rout

sbaraz'**zare** *vt* clear

sbaraz'**zarsi** *vr* ~ **di** get rid of

sbaraz'**zino, -a** *a* mischievous ● *nmf* scamp

sbar'**bare** *vt* shave

sbar'**barsi** *vr* shave

sbarba'**tello, -a** *a & nmf* novice

sbar'**care** *vt/i* disembark; ~ **il lunario** make ends meet

'**sbarco** *nm* landing; (*di merci*) unloading

'**sbarra** *nf* bar; (*di passaggio a livello*) barrier. ~ **spaziatrice** space bar

sbarra'**mento** *nm* barricade

sbar'**rare** *vt* bar; (*ostruire*) block; cross ⟨*assegno*⟩; (*spalancare*) open wide

sbar'**retta** *nf* oblique

sbatacchi'**are** *vt/i sl* bang, slam

'**sbattere** *vt* bang; slam, bang ⟨*porta*⟩; (*urtare*) knock; *Culin* beat; flap ⟨*ali*⟩; shake ⟨*tappeto*⟩; ~ **le palpebre** blink ● *vi* bang; ⟨*porta:*⟩ slam, bang; ~ **contro** knock against; **andare a** ~ **contro** run into

sbat'**tersi** *vr sl* rush around; **sbattersene di qcsa** not give a toss about sth

sbat'**tuto** *a* tossed; *Culin* beaten; *fig* run down

sba'**vare** *vi* dribble; ⟨*colore:*⟩ smear

sbava'**tura** *nf* smear; **senza sbavature** *fig* faultless

sbeccucci'**are** *vt* chip

sbeccucci'**ato** *a* chipped

sbeffeggi'**are** *vt* mock

sbelli'**carsi** *vr* ~ **dalle risa** split one's sides [with laughter]

sben'**dare** *vt* unbandage

'**sberla** *nf* slap

sbevaz'**zare** *vi fam* tipple

sbia'**dire** *vt/i* fade

sbia'**dirsi** *vr* fade

sbia'**dito** *a* faded; *fig* colourless

sbian'**cante** *nm* whitener

sbian'**care** *vt/i* whiten

sbian'**carsi** *vr* whiten

sbi'**eco** *a* slanting; **di** ~ on the slant;

⟨*guardare*⟩ sidelong; **guardare qcno di ~** look askance at sb; **tagliare di ~** cut on the bias

sbigot'tire *vt* dismay ● *vi* be dismayed

sbigot'tirsi *vr* be dismayed

sbigot'tito *a* dismayed

sbilanci'are *vt* unbalance ● *vi* (*perdere l'equilibrio*) overbalance

sbilanci'arsi *vr* lose one's balance

sbi'lancio *nm* lack of balance; *Comm* deficit

sbirci'are *vt* cast sidelong glances at

sbirci'ata *nf* furtive glance

sbircia'tina *nf* **dare una ~ a** sneak a glance at

'sbirro *nm pej* cop

sbizzar'rirsi *vr* satisfy one's whims

sbloc'care *vt* unblock; *Mech* release; decontrol ⟨*prezzi*⟩

'sbobba *nf fam* pigswill

sboc'care *vi* **~ in** ⟨*fiume:*⟩ flow into; ⟨*strada:*⟩ lead to; ⟨*folla:*⟩ pour into

sboc'cato *a* foul-mouthed

sbocci'are *vi* blossom

'sbocco *nm* flowing; (*foce*) mouth; *Comm* outlet

sbolo'gnare *vt fam* get rid of

'sbornia *nf* **prendere una ~** get drunk; **smaltire la ~** sober up

sbor'sare *vt* pay out

sbot'tare *vi* burst out

sbotto'nare *vt* unbutton

sbotto'narsi *vr* (*fam: confidarsi*) open up; **~ la camicia** unbutton one's shirt

sboz'zare *vt* draft; sketch out ⟨*dipinto*⟩

sbra'carsi *vr* put on something more comfortable; **~ dalle risate** *fam* kill oneself laughing

sbracci'arsi *vr* wave one's arms

sbracci'ato *a* bare-armed; ⟨*abito*⟩ sleeveless

sbrai'tare *vi* bawl

sbra'nare *vt* tear to shreds *or* pieces

sbra'narsi *vr* tear each other to shreds

sbrat'tare *vt* clean up

sbrec'cato *a* chipped

sbricio'lare *vt* crumble

sbricio'larsi *vr* crumble

sbri'gare *vt* expedite; (*occuparsi di*) attend to

sbri'garsi *vr* hurry up, be quick

sbriga'tivo *a* hurried, quick

sbrigli'ato *a* ⟨*fantasia*⟩ unbridled

sbri'nare *vt* defrost; *Auto* de-ice

sbrina'tore *nm Auto* de-icer; (*di frigo*) defrost button

sbrindel'lare *vt* tear to shreds

sbrindel'lato *a* in rags

sbrodo'lare *vt* stain

sbrodo'lone, -a *nmf* messy eater

sbrogli'are *vt* disentangle

'sbronza *nf fam* **prendersi una ~** get drunk

sbron'zarsi *vr* get drunk

'sbronzo *a* (*ubriaco*) drunk

sbruffo'nata *nf* boast

sbruf'fone, -a *nmf* boaster

sbu'care *vi* come out

sbucci'are *vt* peel; shell ⟨*piselli*⟩

sbucci'arsi *vr* graze oneself

sbuccia'tore *nm* parer

sbuccia'tura *nf* graze

sbudel'lare *vt* gut ⟨*pesce*⟩; draw ⟨*pollo*⟩; disembowel ⟨*persona*⟩

sbudel'larsi *vr* **~ dal ridere** die laughing

sbuf'fare *vi* snort; (*per impazienza*) fume

'sbuffo *nm* puff; **a ~** ⟨*maniche*⟩ puff *attrib*

sbugiar'dare *vt* show to be a liar

sbuz'zare *vt* gut ⟨*pesce*⟩; draw ⟨*pollo*⟩; disembowel ⟨*persona*⟩

'scabbia *nf* scabies *sg*

'scabro *a* rough; ⟨*terreno*⟩ uneven; ⟨*stile*⟩ bald

sca'broso *a* rough; ⟨*terreno*⟩ uneven; ⟨*fig: questione*⟩ difficult; ⟨*scena*⟩ offensive

scacchi'era *nf* chess-board

scacciapensi'eri *nm inv Mus* Jew's harp

scacci'are *vt* chase away

'scacco *nm* check; **scacchi** *pl* (*gioco*) chess; (*pezzi*) chessmen; **dare ~ matto a** checkmate; **a scacchi** ⟨*tessuto*⟩ checked; **subire uno ~** *fig* suffer a humiliating defeat

sca'dente *a* shoddy

sca'denza *nf* (*di contratto*) expiry; (*di progetto, candidatura*) deadline; *Comm* maturity; **a breve/lunga ~** short-/long-term

scaden'zario *nm* schedule

sca'dere *vi* expire; ⟨*valore:*⟩ decline; ⟨*debito:*⟩ be due

sca'duto *a* ⟨*biglietto*⟩ out-of-date

sca'fandro *nm* diving suit; (*di astronauta*) spacesuit

scaffala'tura *nf* shelves *pl*, shelving

scaf'fale *nm* shelf; (*libreria*) bookshelf

'scafo *nm* hull

scagion'are *vt* exonerate

'scaglia *nf* scale; (*di sapone*) flake; (*scheggia*) chip

scagli'are *vt* fling

scagli'arsi *vr* fling oneself; **~ contro** *fig* rail against

scaglio'nare *vt* space out

scaglio'ne *nm* group; **a scaglioni** in groups. **~ di reddito** tax bracket

sca'gnozzo *nm* henchman

'scala *nf* staircase; (*portatile*) ladder; (*Mus, misura*) scale; **scale** *pl* stairs; **in ~** to scale; **modello in ~** scale model; **su larga ~** large-scale *attrib*. **~ allungabile** extension ladder. **~ antincendio** fire escape. **~ Beaufort** Beaufort scale. **~ a chiocciola** spiral staircase. **~ mobile** escalator; (*dei salari*) cost of living index. **~ Richter** Richter scale. **~ di servizio** backstairs. **~ di sicurezza** fire escape. **~ di valori** scale of values

sca'lare *a* scalar ● *vt* climb; layer ⟨*capelli*⟩; (*detrarre*) deduct

sca'lata *nf* climb; (*dell'Everest ecc*) ascent; **fare delle scalate** go climbing

scala|'tore, -'trice *nmf* climber

scalca'gnato *a* down at heel

scalci'are *vi* kick

scalci'nato *a* shabby

scalda'bagno *nm* water heater

scalda'muscoli *nm inv* legwarmer

scal'dare *vt* heat

scal'darsi *vr* warm up; *(eccitarsi)* get excited

sca'leno *a* scalene

sca'leo *nm* step-ladder

scal'fire *vt* scratch

scalfit'tura *nf* scratch

scali'nata *nf* flight of steps. **~ di piazza di Spagna** Spanish Steps

sca'lino *nm* step; *(di scala a pioli)* rung

scalma'narsi *vr* rush about; *(nel parlare)* get worked up

scalma'nato *a* worked up; **è ~** *(vivace)* he can't sit still

'scalmo *nm* rowlock

'scalo *nm* slipway; *Naut* port of call; **fare ~ a** call at; *Aeron* land at; **senza ~** nonstop. **~ merci** freight depot, goods yard. **~ passeggeri** stopover

sca'logna *nf fam* bad luck

scalo'gnato *a fam* unlucky

sca'logno *nm Bot* scallion

scalop'pina *nf* escalope

scal'pare *vt* scalp

scalpel'lare *vt* chisel

scalpel'lino *nm* stone-cutter

scal'pello *nm* chisel

scalpi'tare *vi* paw the ground; *fig* champ at the bit

scalpi'tio *nm* pawing of the ground

'scalpo *nm* scalp

scal'pore *nm* noise; **far ~** *fig* cause a sensation

scal'trezza *nf* shrewdness

scal'trirsi *vr* get shrewder

'scaltro *a* shrewd

scal'zare *vt* bare the roots of *⟨albero⟩*; *fig* undermine; *(da una carica)* oust

'scalzo *a & adv* barefoot

scambi'are *vt* exchange; **~ qcno per qualcun altro** mistake sb for somebody else

scambi'arsi *vr* exchange; **~ i saluti** exchange greetings

scambi'evole *a* reciprocal

'scambio *nm* exchange; *Comm* trade; **libero ~** free trade. **~ di persona** mistaken identity

scamici'ato *nf* pinafore [dress]

sca'morza *nf* soft cheese

scamosci'ato *a* suede

scampa'gnata *nf* trip to the country

scampa'nato *a ⟨gonna⟩* flared

scampanel'lata *nf* [loud] ring

scampanel'lio *nm* ringing

scampan'io *nm* peal[ing]

scam'pare *vt* save; *(evitare)* escape; **scamparla bella** have a lucky escape

scam'pato *a* **lo ~ pericolo** the escape from danger ● *nmf* survivor

'scampi *nmpl (crostaceo)* scampi

'scampo *nm* escape; **non c'è ~** there's no way out

'scampolo *nm* remnant

scanala'tura *nf* groove

scandagli'are *vt* sound

scanda'lismo *nm* muckraking

scanda'listico *a* sensational; *⟨giornale⟩* sensationalist

scandaliz'zare *vt* scandalize

scandaliz'zarsi *vr* be scandalized

'scandalo *nm* scandal

scanda'loso *a* scandalous; *⟨somma ecc⟩* scandalous; *⟨fortuna⟩* outrageous

Scandi'navia *nf* Scandinavia

scan'dinavo, -a *a & nmf* Scandinavian

scan'dire *vt* scan *⟨verso⟩*; pronounce clearly *⟨parole⟩*; **~ il tempo** beat time

scandi'tore *nm* **~ ottico** *Comput* optical scanner

scan'nare *vt* slaughter

scan'nello *nm* lectern

'scanner *nm inv* scanner. **~ manuale** *Comput* handheld scanner

scanneriz'zare *vt Comput* scan

scansafa'tiche *nmf inv* lazybones *sg*

scan'sare *vt* shift; *(evitare)* avoid

scan'sarsi *vr* get out of the way

scan'sia *nf* shelves *pl*

scansi'one *nf Comput* scanning

'scanso *nm* **a ~ di** in order to avoid; **a ~ di equivoci** to avoid any misunderstanding

scanti'nato *nm* basement

scanto'nare *vi* turn the corner; *(svignarsela)* sneak off

scanzo'nato *a* easy-going

scapacci'one *nm* smack

scape'strato *a* dissolute

scapigli'ato *a* dishevelled

'scapito *nm* loss; **a ~ di** to the detriment of

'scapola *nf* shoulder-blade

'scapolo *nm* bachelor

scappa'mento *nm Auto* exhaust

scap'pare *vi* escape; *(andarsene)* dash [off]; *(sfuggire)* slip; **mi scappa da ridere!** I want to burst out laughing; **mi scappa la pipì** I'm bursting, I need a pee; **mi ha fatto ~ la pazienza** he tried my patience a bit too far; **lasciarsi ~ l'occasione** let the opportunity slip; **scappar via** run off *or* away

scap'pata *nf fam* short visit

scappa'tella *nf* escapade; *(infedeltà)* fling

scappa'toia *nf* way out

scappel'lotto *nm* cuff

scara'beo¹ *nm* scarab beetle

scara'beo²® *nm* Scrabble®

scarabocchi'are *vt* scribble

scara'bocchio *nm* scribble

scara'faggio *nm* cockroach

scara'mantico *a ⟨gesto⟩* to ward off the evil eye

scaraman'zia *nf* superstition

scara'mazzo *a ⟨perla⟩* baroque

scara'muccia *nf* skirmish

scaraven'tare *vt* hurl

scarcas'sato *a* ⟨*fam: macchina*⟩ beat-up

scarce'rare *vt* release [from prison]

scardi'nare *vt* unhinge

'**scarica** *nf* discharge; (*di arma da fuoco*) volley; *fig* shower; **una ~ di botte** a hail of blows

scaricaba'rili *nm* **fare a ~** blame each other

scari'care *vt* discharge; unload ⟨*arma, merci, auto*⟩; *fig* unburden

scari'carsi *vr* ⟨*fiume:*⟩ flow; ⟨*orologio, batteria:*⟩ run down; *fig* unwind

scarica'tore *nm* loader; (*di porto*) docker

'**scarico** *a* unloaded; (*vuoto*) empty; ⟨*orologio*⟩ run-down; ⟨*batteria*⟩ flat; *fig* untroubled ●*nm* unloading; (*di rifiuti*) dumping; (*di acqua*) draining; (*di sostanze inquinanti*) discharge; (*luogo*) [rubbish] dump; *Auto* exhaust; (*idraulico*) drain; (*tubo*) waste pipe; '**divieto di ~**' 'no dumping'; **tubo di ~** waste pipe

scarlat'tina *nf* scarlet fever

scar'latto *a* scarlet

scarmigli'ato *a* ruffled

sca'rnire *vt fig* simplify

'**scarno** *a* thin; ⟨*fig: stile*⟩ bare

sca'rogna, **scaro'gnato** = **scalogna**, **scalognato**

sca'rola *nf* curly endive

'**scarpa** *nf* shoe; (*fam: persona*) dead loss; **fare le scarpe a qcno** *fig* double-cross sb. **scarpe** *pl* **basse** flat shoes, flats. **scarpe** *pl* **da danza** ballet shoes. **scarpe** *pl* **da ginnastica** trainers. **scarpe** *pl* **col tacco** high heels. **scarpe** *pl* **col tacco a spillo** stilettos. **scarpe** *pl* **con la zeppa** platform shoes

scar'pata *nf* slope; (*burrone*) escarpment

scarpi'era *nf* shoe rack

scarpi'nare *vi* hike

scar'pone *nm* boot. **~ da alpinismo** climbing boot. **scarponi** *pl* **da sci** ski boots. **scarponi** *pl* **da trekking** walking boots

scarroz'zare *vt/i* drive around

scarroz'zata *nf fam* trip

scarruf'fato *a* ruffled

scarseggi'are *vi* be scarce; **~ di** (*mancare*) be short of

scar'sezza *nf* scarcity, shortage

scarsità *nf* shortage

'**scarso** *a* scarce; (*manchevole*) short

scartabel'lare *vt* skim through

scarta'mento *nm Rail* gauge. **~ ridotto** narrow gauge

scar'tare *vt* discard; unwrap ⟨*pacco*⟩; (*respingere*) reject ●*vi* (*deviare*) swerve

scartave'trare *vt* sand

'**scarto** *nm* scrap; (*in carte*) discard; (*deviazione*) swerve; (*distacco*) gap

scartocci'are *vt* unwrap

scar'toffie *nfpl* bumf, bumph

scas'sare *vt* break

scas'sato *a fam* clapped out

scassi'nare *vt* force open

scassina|'tore, -'trice *nmf* burglar

'**scasso** *nm* (*furto*) house-breaking

scata'fascio = **catafascio**

scate'nare *vt fig* stir up ⟨*folla*⟩; arouse ⟨*sentimenti*⟩

scate'narsi *vr* break out; ⟨*fig: temporale:*⟩ break; (*fam: darsi alla pazza gioia*) go crazy, go wild; (*fam: infiammarsi*) get excited

scate'nato *a* crazy, wild; **pazzo ~** *fam* off his head

'**scatola** *nf* box; (*di latta*) can, tin *Br*; **in ~** ⟨*cibo*⟩ canned, tinned *Br*; **rompere le scatole a qcno** *fam* get on sb's nerves; **a ~ chiusa** ⟨*comprare*⟩ sight unseen. **~ del cambio** gearbox. **~ nera** *Aeron* black box

scato'lame *nm* (*cibo*) canned food

scato'letta *nf* small box

scato'logico *a* scatological

scat'tante *a* zippy

scat'tare *vi* go off; (*balzare*) spring up; (*adirarsi*) lose one's temper; take ⟨*foto*⟩

'**scatto** *nm* (*balzo*) spring; (*d'ira*) outburst; (*di telefono*) unit; (*dispositivo*) release; **a scatti** jerkily; **di ~** suddenly

scatu'rire *vi* spring

scaval'care *vt* jump over ⟨*muretto*⟩; climb over ⟨*muro*⟩; (*fig: superare*) overtake

sca'vare *vt* dig ⟨*buca*⟩; dig up ⟨*tesoro*⟩; excavate ⟨*città sepolta*⟩

scava'trice *nf* excavator

scavezza'collo *nm* daredevil

'**scavo** *nm* excavation

scazzot'tare *vt fam* beat up

scazzot'tata *nf fam* punch-up; **prendersi una ~** get beaten up

'**scegliere** *vt* choose, select

sce'icco *nm* sheikh

scelle'rato *a* wicked

'**scelta** *nf* choice; (*di articoli*) range; **...a ~** (*in menù*) choice of...; **prendine uno a ~** take your choice *o* pick; **di prima ~** top-grade, choice; ⟨*albergo*⟩ first-rate; **di seconda ~** second grade; *pej* second-rate

'**scelto** *pp di* **scegliere** ●*a* select; ⟨*merce ecc*⟩ choice; **tiratore ~** marksman

sce'mare *vt/i* diminish

sce'menza *nf* silliness; (*azione*) silly thing to do/say; **non diciamo scemenze!** let's not be silly!

'**scemo** *a* idiotic ●*nm* idiot

scempi'aggine *nf* foolish thing to do/say

'**scempio** *nm* havoc; (*fig: di paesaggio*) ruination; **fare ~ di** play havoc with

'**scena** *nf* scene; (*palcoscenico*) stage; **entrare in ~** *Theat* go/come on [stage]; *fig* come on the scene; **fare ~** put on an act; **fare una ~** make a scene; **fare scene** make a fuss; **andare in ~** ⟨*Theat: spettacolo:*⟩ be staged, be put on; **fare ~ muta** not open one's mouth; **scomparire dalla ~** *fig* vanish from the scene; **mettere in ~** produce, stage; **messa in ~** production, staging; *fig* set-up

sce'nario *nm* scenery

sce'nata *nf* row, scene

'**scendere** *vi* go/come down; (*da treno, autobus*) get off; (*da macchina*) get out;

⟨*strada:*⟩ slope; ⟨*notte, prezzi:*⟩ fall ● *vt* go/come down ⟨*scale*⟩

scendi'letto *nm* bedside rug

seneggi'are *vt* dramatize

seneggi'ato *nm* television serial

seneggia'tura *nf* screenplay

'scenico *a* scenic

senogra'fia *nf* set design

sce'nografo, -a *nmf* set designer

sce'riffo *nm* sheriff

scervel'larsi *vr* rack one's brains

scervel'lato *a* brainless

'sceso *pp di* **scendere**

scetti'cismo *nm* scepticism

'scettico, -a *a* sceptical ● *nmf* sceptic

'scettro *nm* sceptre

'scheda *nf* card. **~ audio** *Comput* sound card. **~ elettorale** ballot-paper. **~ di espansione** *Comput* expansion card. **~ grafica** *Comput* graphics card. **~ madre** *Comput* motherboard. **~ magnetica** card key. **~ perforata** punch card. **~ di rete** *Comput* network card. **~ sonora** *Comput* sound card. **~ telefonica** phonecard. **~ video** *Comput* video card

sche'dare *vt* file

sche'dario *nm* file; ⟨*mobile*⟩ filing cabinet

sche'dato, -a *a* with a police record ● *nmf* person with a police record

sche'dina *nf* ≈ pools coupon; **giocare la ~** ≈ do the pools

'scheggia *nf* fragment; ⟨*di legno*⟩ splinter

scheggi'are *vt* splinter

scheggi'arsi *vr* chip; ⟨*legno:*⟩ splinter

sche'letrico *a* skeletal

'scheletro *nm* skeleton; **essere ridotto ad uno ~** be all skin and bones

'schema *nm* diagram; ⟨*abbozzo*⟩ outline; **uscire dagli schemi** break with tradition

schematica'mente *adv* schematically

sche'matico *a* schematic

schematiz'zare *vt* present schematically

'scherma *nf* fencing

scher'maglia *nf* skirmish

scher'mirsi *vr* protect oneself

'schermo *nm* screen; **grande ~** big screen; **farsi ~ con** shield oneself with. **~ panoramico** wide screen. **~ a sfioramento** *Comput* touch-sensitive screen

scher'nire *vt* mock

'scherno *nm* mockery

scher'zare *vi* joke; ⟨*giocare*⟩ play; **c'è poco da ~!** it's nothing to laugh about!

'scherzo *nm* joke; ⟨*trucco*⟩ trick; ⟨*effetto*⟩ play; *Mus* scherzo; **fare uno ~ a qcno** play a joke on sb; **giocare brutti scherzi (a qcno)** ⟨*memoria, vista:*⟩ play tricks (on sb); **per ~** for fun; **scherzi a parte** joking apart, seriously; **stare allo ~** take a joke. **~ di natura** freak of nature

scher'zoso *a* playful

schiaccia'noci *nm inv* nutcrackers *pl*

schiacci'ante *a* damning; ⟨*vittoria*⟩ crushing

schiacci'are *vt* crush; ⟨*in tennis ecc*⟩ smash; press ⟨*pulsante*⟩; crack ⟨*noce*⟩; **~ un pisolino** grab forty winks

schiacci'arsi *vr* get crushed

schiaccia'sassi *nf inv* steamroller

schiaf'fare *vt fam* shove

schiaffeggi'are *vt* slap

schi'affo *nm* slap; **dare uno ~ a** slap. **~ morale** slap in the face; **avere una faccia da schiaffi** have the kind of face you'd love to take a swipe at

schiamaz'zare *vi* make a racket; ⟨*galline:*⟩ cackle

schia'mazzo *nm* din. **schiamazzi** *pl* **notturni** disturbing the peace

schian'tare *vt* break

schian'tarsi *vr* crash ● *vi* **schianto dalla fatica** I'm wiped out

'schianto *nm* crash; *fam* knock-out; ⟨*divertente*⟩ scream

schia'rire *vt* clear; ⟨*sbiadire*⟩ fade ● *vi* brighten up

schia'rirsi *vr* brighten up; **~ la gola** clear one's throat; **~ le idee** get things clear in one's head; ⟨*dopo aver bevuto*⟩ clear one's head

schia'rita *nf* sunny interval

schiat'tare *vi* burst; **~ di invidia** be green with envy

schia'vista *nmf* slave-driver

schiavitù *nf* slavery

schi'avo, -a *nmf* slave

schi'ena *nf* back; **mal di ~** backache

schie'nale *nm* ⟨*di sedia*⟩ back

schi'era *nf* *Mil* rank; ⟨*moltitudine*⟩ crowd

schiera'mento *nm* lining up; *Mil* battle line. **~ di forze** rallying of the troops

schie'rare *vt* draw up; rally ⟨*forze*⟩

schie'rarsi *vr* draw up; ⟨*forze:*⟩ rally; **~ dalla parte di qcno, ~ con qcno** rally [in support] to sb; **~ contro qcno** rally in opposition to sb

schiet'tezza *nf* frankness

schi'etto *a* frank; ⟨*puro*⟩ pure

schi'fezza *nf* **è una ~** it's disgusting; ⟨*film, libro:*⟩ it's rubbish

schifil'toso *a* fussy

'schifo *nm* disgust; **fare ~** be disgusting; **è uno ~!** it's disgusting!

schi'foso *a* disgusting; ⟨*di cattiva qualità*⟩ rubbishy

schioc'care *vt* crack ⟨*frusta*⟩; snap, click ⟨*dita*⟩; click ⟨*lingua*⟩ ● *vi* crack

schi'occo *nm* ⟨*di frusta*⟩ crack; ⟨*di bacio*⟩ smack; ⟨*di dita, lingua*⟩ click

schioppet'tata *nf* shot

schi'oppo *nm fam* rifle; **a un tiro di ~** *fig* a stone's throw away

schiri'bizzo *nm fam* fancy; **se mi salta lo ~...** if it takes my fancy...

schi'udere *vt* open

schi'udersi *vr* open

schi'uma *nf* foam; ⟨*di sapone*⟩ lather; ⟨*di bucato*⟩ suds; ⟨*feccia*⟩ scum. **~ da barba** shaving foam

schiu'mare *vt* skim ● *vi* foam

schiuma'rola nf Culin skimmer

schiu'mogeno a foaming

schiu'moso a ⟨birra, crema⟩ frothy, foamy; ⟨liquido⟩ scummy

schi'uso pp di **schiudere**

schi'vare vt avoid

'schivo a bashful

schizofre'nia nf schizophrenia

schizo'frenico, -a a & nmf schizophrenic

schiz'zare vt squirt; (inzaccherare) splash; (abbozzare) sketch; ~ **qcno/qcsa di qcsa** splatter sb/sth with sth ● vi spurt ~ **via** fig scurry away

schiz'zato, -a a & nmf fam loony

schizzi'noso a squeamish

'schizzo nm squirt; (di fango) splash; (abbozzo) sketch

sci nm inv ski; (sport) skiing. ~ **d'acqua**, ~ **acquatico** water-skiing. ~ **acrobatico** hot dogging. ~ **di fondo** cross-country skiing

'scia nf wake; (di fumo ecc) trail; **sulla ~ di qcno** following in sb's footsteps

sci'abola nf sabre

sciabor'dare vt/i lap

sciabor'dio nm lapping

sciacal'laggio nm profiteering

scia'callo nm jackal; fig profiteer

sciac'quare vt rinse

sciac'quarsi vr rinse oneself

sci'acquo nm mouthwash

scia'gura nf disaster

sciagu'rato a unfortunate; (scellerato) wicked

scialac'quare vt squander

scialacqua|'tore, -'trice nmf squanderer

scia'lare vi spend money like water

sci'albo a pale; fig dull

sci'alle nm shawl

scia'luppa nf dinghy. ~ **di salvataggio** lifeboat

sciaman'nato a good-for-nothing

scia'mano n shaman

scia'mare vi swarm

sci'ame nm swarm; **a sciami** in swarms

sci'ampo nm shampoo

scian'cato a lame

sci'are vi ski; **andare a ~** go skiing

sci'arpa nf scarf

sci'atica nf Med sciatica

scia|'tore, -'trice nmf skier

sciatte'ria nf slovenliness

sci'atto a slovenly; ⟨stile⟩ careless

sciat'tone, -a nmf slovenly person

'scibile nm knowledge; **lo ~ umano** the sum of human knowledge

scic'coso a fam snazzy

scienti'fico a scientific

sci'enza nf science; (sapere) knowledge; **avere la ~ infusa** be naturally talented

scienzi'ato, -a nmf scientist

sci'ita a & nmf Shiite

scilin'guagnolo nm fig **avere lo ~** be a chatterbox

'scimmia nf monkey

scimmiot'tare vt ape

scimpanzé nm inv chimpanzee, chimp

scimu'nito a idiotic

'scindere vt separate; ~ **in** break down into

'scindersi vr divide; ~ **in** divide into

scin'tilla nf spark

scintil'lante a sparkling

scintil'lare vi sparkle

scintil'lio nm sparkle

sciò int shoo!

scioc'cante a shocking

scioc'care vt shock

scioc'chezza nf foolishness; (assurdità) foolish thing; **sciocchezze!** nonsense!

sci'occo a foolish

sci'ogliere vt untie; undo, untie ⟨nodo⟩; (liberare) release; (liquefare) melt; dissolve ⟨contratto, qcsa nell'acqua⟩; loosen up ⟨muscoli⟩

sci'ogliersi vr ⟨nodo:⟩ come undone; (liquefarsi) melt; ⟨contratto:⟩ be dissolved; ⟨pastiglia:⟩ dissolve

sciogli'lingua nm inv tongue-twister

scio'lina nf ski wax

sciol'tezza nf agility; (disinvoltura) ease

sci'olto pp di **sciogliere** ● a loose; (agile) agile; (disinvolto) easy; **versi** pl **sciolti** blank verse

sciope'rante nmf striker

sciope'rare vi go on strike, strike

sci'opero nm strike; **in ~** on strike. ~ **bianco** work-to-rule. ~ **generale** general strike. ~ **a singhiozzo** on-off strike

sciori'nare vt fig show off

sciovi'nismo nm chauvinism

sciovi'nista nmf Pol chauvinist

sciovi'nistico a Pol chauvinistic

sci'pito a insipid

scip'pare vt fam snatch; ~ **qcno** snatch sb's bag/bracelet etc

scippa|'tore, -trice nmf bag-snatcher

'scippo nm bag-snatching

sci'rocco nm sirocco

scirop'pato a ⟨frutta⟩ in syrup

sci'roppo nm syrup

scirop'poso a syrupy

'scisma nm schism

scissi'one nf division

scissio'nista a breakaway attrib

'scisso pp di **scindere**

sciupacchi'are vt spoil

sciupacchi'ato a spoilt

sciu'pare vt spoil; (sperperare) waste

sciu'parsi vr get spoiled; (deperire) wear oneself out

sciu'pio nm waste

scivo'lare vi slide; (involontariamente) slip

'scivolo nm slide; Techn chute

scivo'lone nm fall; (fig: errore) blunder

scivo'loso a slippery

scle'rosi nf sclerosis. ~ **multipla**, ~ **a placche** multiple sclerosis, MS

scoc'care vt fire ⟨freccia⟩; strike ⟨ore⟩ ● vi ⟨scintilla:⟩ shoot out; **sono scoccate le cinque** five o'clock has just struck

scocci'are *vt fam* (*dare noia a*) bother

scocci'arsi *vr fam*; **mi sono scocciato di aspettare** I'm fed up waiting

scocci'ato *a fam* fed up

scoccia|'tore, -'trice *nmf* nuisance

scoccia'tura *nf fam* nuisance

sco'della *nf* bowl

scodel'lare *vt* dish out, dish up

scodinzo'lare *vi* wag its tail

scogli'era *nf* cliff; (*a fior d'acqua*) reef

'scoglio *nm* rock; (*fig: ostacolo*) stumbling block

scoglio'nato *a vulg* pissed off

scoi'attolo *nm* squirrel

scola'pasta *nm inv* colander

scolapi'atti *nm inv* dish drainer

sco'lara *nf* schoolgirl

sco'lare¹ *vt* drain; strain ⟨*pasta, verdura*⟩ ● *vi* drip

sco'lare² *a* school *attrib*; **in età ~** ⟨*bambino*⟩ school-age

scola'resca *nf* pupils *pl*

sco'laro *nm* schoolboy

sco'lastico *a* school *attrib*; **gita scolastica** school trip

scoli'osi *nf* curvature of the spine

scollacci'ato *a* low-cut

scol'lare *vt* cut away the neck of ⟨*abito*⟩; (*staccare*) unstick

scol'lato *a* ⟨*abito*⟩ low-necked

scolla'tura *nf* neckline; **~ profonda** plunging neckline

scolle'gare *vt* disconnect

'scollo *nm* neckline

'scolo *nm* drainage

scolo'rare *vt* fade

scolori'mento *nm* fading

scolo'rire *vt* fade

scolo'rirsi *vr* fade

scolo'rito *a* faded

scol'pire *vt* carve; (*imprimere*) engrave

scombi'nare *vt* upset

scombusso'lare *vt* muddle up

scom'messa *nf* bet

scom'messo *pp di* **scommettere**

scom'mettere *vt* bet; **ci puoi ~!** you bet!

scomo'dare *vt* trouble

scomo'darsi *vr* trouble

scomodità *nf inv* discomfort

'scomodo *a* uncomfortable ● *nm* essere di **~ a qcno** be a trouble to sb

scompagin'are *vt* mess up

scompa'gnare *vt* split

scompa'gnato *a* odd

scompa'rire *vi* disappear; (*morire*) pass away

scom'parsa *nf* disappearance; (*morte*) death, passing

scom'parso, -a *pp di* **scomparire** ● *a* departed ● *nmf* departed

scomparti'mento *nm* compartment

scom'parto *nf* compartment

scompen'sare *vt* throw off balance

scom'penso *nm* imbalance. **~ cardiaco** cardiac insufficiency

scompigli'are *vt* disarrange

scom'piglio *nm* confusion

scompisci'arsi *vr fam* **~** [**dalle risa**] wet oneself, split one's sides laughing

scom'porre *vt* break down; ruffle ⟨*capelli*⟩; (*fig: turbare*) upset

scom'porsi *vr* lose one's composure

scomposizi'one *nf* breaking down

scom'posto *pp di* **scomporre** ● *a* (*sguaiato*) unseemly; (*disordinato*) untidy

sco'munica *nf* excommunication

scomuni'care *vt* excommunicate

sconcer'tante *a* disconcerting; (*che rende perplesso*) bewildering

sconcer'tare *vt* disconcert; (*rendere perplesso*) bewilder

sconcer'tato *a* disconcerted; (*perplesso*) bewildered

scon'cezza *nf* indecency

'sconcio *a* indecent ● *nm* è uno **~ che...** it's a disgrace that...

sconclusio'nato *a* incoherent

scon'dito *a* unseasoned; (*insalata*) with no dressing

sconfes'sare *vt* disown

scon'figgere *vt* defeat

sconfi'nare *vi* cross the border; (*in proprietà privata*) trespass

sconfi'nato *a* unlimited

scon'fitta *nf* defeat; **subire una ~** be defeated, suffer defeat

scon'fitto *pp di* **sconfiggere**

sconfor'tante *a* disheartening, discouraging

scon'forto *nm* discouragement; **farsi prendere dallo ~** get discouraged, get disheartened

sconge'lare *vt* thaw out ⟨*cibo*⟩; defrost ⟨*frigo*⟩

scongiu'rare *vt* beseech; (*evitare*) avert

scongi'uro *nm* **fare gli scongiuri** ≈ touch wood, knock on wood *Am*

scon'nesso *pp di* **sconnettere** ● *a fig* incoherent

scon'nettere *vt* disconnect

sconosci'uto, -a *a* unknown ● *nmf* stranger

sconquas'sare *vt* smash; (*sconvolgere*) upset

sconsa'crare *vt* deconsecrate

sconsiderata'mente *adv* inconsiderately

sconsidera'tezza *nf* lack of consideration, thoughtlessness

sconside'rato *a* inconsiderate, thoughtless

sconsigli'abile *a* not advisable

sconsigli'are *vt* advise against

sconso'lato *a* disconsolate

scon'tare *vt* discount; (*dedurre*) deduct; (*pagare*) pay off; serve ⟨*pena*⟩; **~ la propria colpa** pay for one's sins

scon'tato *a* discounted; (*ovvio*) expected; **~ del 10%** with 10% discount; **era ~** it was to be expected; **dare qcsa per ~** take sth for granted

scon'tento *a* displeased ● *nm* discontent

'sconto *nm* discount; **fare uno ~** give a discount. **~ commerciale** trade discount

scon'trarsi *vr* clash; (*urtare*) collide

scon'trino *nm* ticket; (*di cassa*) receipt; **'munirsi dello ~ alla cassa'** sign reminding customers that payment must be made at the cash desk beforehand

'scontro *nm* clash; (*urto*) collision. **~ frontale** head-on collision. **~ a fuoco** shoot-out

scontrosità *nf* blackness

scon'troso *a* disagreeable

sconveni'ente *a* unprofitable; (*scorretto*) unseemly

sconvol'gente *a* mind-blowing

scon'volgere *vt* upset; (*mettere in disordine*) disarrange

sconvolgi'mento *nm* upheaval

scon'volto *pp di* **sconvolgere** ● *a* distraught

'scooter *nm inv* scooter

'scopa *nf* broom; (*gioco di carte*) type of card game

sco'pare *vt* sweep; *vulg* shag

sco'pata *nf* sweep; *vulg* shag; **dare una ~ per terra** give the floor a sweep

scoperchi'are *vt* take the lid off ⟨*pentola*⟩; take the roof off ⟨*casa*⟩

sco'perta *nf* discovery

sco'perto *pp di* **scoprire** ● *a* uncovered; (*senza riparo*) exposed; (*conto*) overdrawn; (*spoglio*) bare

'scopo *nm* aim; **a ~ di** for the sake of; **allo ~ di** in order to

sco'pone *nm* (*gioco di carte*) type of card game

scoppi'are *vi* burst; *fig* break out

scoppiet'tare *vi* crackle

'scoppio *nm* burst; (*di guerra*) outbreak; (*esplosione*) explosion; **a ~ ritardato** ⟨*bomba*⟩ delayed action; **ha reagito a ~ ritardato** he did a double take

sco'prire *vt* discover; (*togliere la copertura a*) uncover; unveil ⟨*statua*⟩; **~ gli altarini** *fam* reveal his/her etc guilty secrets

scoraggia'mento *nm* discouragement

scoraggi'ante *a* discouraging

scoraggi'are *vt* discourage

scoraggi'arsi *vr* lose heart

scor'butico *a* *Med* suffering from scurvy; (*fig: scontroso*) disagreeable

scor'buto *nm* *Med* scurvy

scorci'are *vt* shorten

scorcia'toia *nf* short cut

'scorcio *nm* (*di cielo*) patch; (*in arte*) foreshortening; **di ~** ⟨*vedere*⟩ from an angle. **~ panoramico** panoramic view. **~ del secolo** end of the century

scor'dare *vt* forget; **~ qcsa a casa** leave sth at home

scor'darsi *vr* forget; **~ di qcsa** forget sth

scor'dato *a* *Mus* out of tune

scorda'tura *nf* *Mus* going out of tune

sco'reggia *nf* *fam* fart

scoreggi'are *vi* *fam* fart

'scorfano *nm* scorpion fish

'scorgere *vt* make out; (*notare*) notice

'scoria *nf* waste; (*di carbone*) slag

scor'nare *vt* *fig* humiliate

scor'narsi *vr* *fig* come a cropper

scor'nato *a* *fig* hangdog

'scorno *nm* humiliation

scorpacci'ata *nf* bellyful; **fare una ~ di** stuff oneself with

scorpi'one *nm* scorpion; *Astr* Scorpio

scorraz'zare *vi* run about

'scorrere *vt* (*dare un'occhiata*) glance through ● *vi* run; (*scivolare*) slide; (*fluire*) flow; *Comput* scroll; (*attorno a un oggetto*) wrap

scorre'ria *nf* raid

scorret'tezza *nf* (*mancanza di educazione*) bad manners *pl*

scor'retto *a* incorrect; (*sconveniente*) improper

scor'revole *a* **porta ~** sliding door

scorri'banda *nf* raid; *fig* excursion

scorri'mento *nm* *Comput* scrolling; (*attorno a un oggetto*) wrapping

'scorsa *nf* glance; **dare una ~ a** glance through

'scorso *pp di* **scorrere** ● *a* last; **l'anno ~** last year

scor'soio *a* **nodo ~** noose

'scorta *nf* escort; (*provvista*) supply

scor'tare *vt* escort

scortecci'are *vt* debark ⟨*albero*⟩; strip ⟨*muro*⟩

scor'tese *a* rude

scorte'sia *nf* rudeness

scorti'care *vt* skin

scortica'tura *nf* graze

'scorto *pp di* **scorgere**

'scorza *nf* peel; (*crosta*) crust; (*corteccia*) bark; *fig* exterior. **~ d'arancia** orange peel

scorzo'nera *nf* salsify

sco'sceso *a* steep

'scossa *nf* shake; *Electr, fig* shock; **prendere la ~** get an electric shock. **~ elettrica** electric shock. **~ sismica** earth tremor

'scosso *pp di* **scuotere** ● *a* shaken; (*sconvolto*) upset

scos'sone *nm* jolt

sco'stante *a* off-putting

sco'stare *vt* push away

sco'starsi *vr* stand aside

scostu'mato *a* dissolute; (*maleducato*) ill-mannered

scoten'nare *vt* skin ⟨*maiale*⟩; scalp ⟨*persona*⟩

scot'tante *a* ⟨*argomento*⟩ burning; (*fig: notizia*⟩ sensational

scot'tare *vt* burn; (*con liquido, vapore*) scald; *Culin* blanch ● *vi* ⟨*bevanda, cibo:*⟩ be too hot; ⟨*sole, pentola:*⟩ be very hot

scot'tarsi *vr* burn oneself; (*con liquido, vapore*) scald oneself; (*al sole*) get sunburnt; *fig* get one's fingers burnt

scot'tato *a* *Culin* blanched

scotta'tura *nf* burn; (*da liquido*) scald; *fig* painful experience; **~ solare** sunburn

'**Scottex**[R] *nm* paper towel

'**scotto**[1] *a* overcooked

'**scotto**[2] *nm* score; **pagare lo ~ di qcsa** pay for sth

scout *a inv* scout *attrib* ● *nmf inv* scout

scou'tismo *nm* scout movement

sco'vare *vt* (*scoprire*) discover

scovo'lino *nm* bottle brush; (*per pipa*) pipe cleaner

'**Scozia** *nf* Scotland

scoz'zese *a* Scottish ● *nmf* Scot

'**scrambler** *nm inv Radio, Teleph* scrambler

screan'zato *a* rude

scredi'tare *vt* discredit

scre'mare *vt* skim

screpo'lare *vt* chap

screpo'larsi *vr* get chapped; (*intonaco:*) crack

screpo'lato *a* chapped; (*intonaco*) cracked

screpola'tura *nf* crack

screzi'ato *a* speckled

'**screzio** *nm* disagreement

scribacchi'are *vt* scribble

scribac'chino, -a *nmf* scribbler; (*impiegato*) penpusher

scricchio'lante *a* creaky

scricchio'lare *vi* creak

scricchio'lio *nm* creaking

'**scricciolo** *nm* wren; *fig* delicate-looking creature

'**scrigno** *nm* casket

scrimina'tura *nf* parting

scriteri'ato *a* empty-headed

'**scritta** *nf* writing; (*su muro*) graffiti

'**scritto** *pp di* **scrivere** ● *a* written; **~ col computer** word-processed; **~ a macchina** typed; **~ a mano** handwritten ● *nm* writing; (*lettera*) letter

scrit'toio *nm* writing-desk

scrit|'tore, -'trice *nmf* writer

scrit'tura *nf* writing; *Relig* scripture; (*calligrafia*) handwriting. **scritture** *pl* **contabili** account books. **~ privata** *Jur* legal document drawn up by an individual

scrittu'rare *vt* engage

scriva'nia *nf* desk

scri'vente *nmf* writer

'**scrivere** *vt* write; (*descrivere*) write about; **~ a macchina** type

scroc'care *vt fam* **~ a sponge** off

scrocchi'are *vi* crack

'**scrocco**[1] *nm fam* **a ~** without paying; **vivere a ~** sponge off other people

'**scrocco**[2] *nm* **coltello a ~** pocket knife; **serratura a ~** spring lock

scroc'cone, -a *nmf fam* sponger

'**scrofa** *nf* sow

scrol'lare *vt* shake; **~ le spalle** shrug one's shoulders; **~ la testa** shake one's head

scrol'larsi *vr* shake oneself; **~ qcsa di dosso** shake sth off

'**scrolling** *nm Comput* scrolling

scrosci'ante *a* pouring; (*applausi*) thunderous

scrosci'are *vi* roar; (*pioggia:*) pelt down

'**scroscio** *nm* roar; (*di pioggia*) pelting; **uno ~ di applausi** thunderous applause; **piovere a ~** lash down

scro'stare *vt* scrape

scro'starsi *vr* flake

scro'stato *a* flaky

'**scroto** *nm* scrotum

'**scrupolo** *nm* scruple; (*diligenza*) care; **senza scrupoli** unscrupulous, without scruples; **farsi scrupoli per qcsa** have scruples about sth

scrupo'loso *a* scrupulous

scru'tare *vt* scan; (*indagare*) search

scruta'tore *nm* (*di voti*) returning officer

scruti'nare *vt* scrutinize

scru'tinio *nm* (*di voti*) poll; *Sch* assessment of progress; **scrutini** *pl Sch* meeting of teachers to discuss pupils' work and assign marks. **~ segreto** secret ballot

scu'cire *vt* unstitch; **scuci i soldi!** *fig fam* cough up [the money]!

scu'cirsi *vr* come unstitched; (*fig: parlare*) talk; **non si scuce** he won't talk

scuci'tura *nf* unstitching

scude'ria *nf* stable; **scuderie** *pl* mews

scu'detto *nm Sport* championship shield; (*campionato*) national championship

scudi'ero *nm* squire

scudisci'ata *nf* whipping

'**scudo** *nm* shield; **farsi ~ con qcsa** shield oneself with sth

scuffi'are *vi* capsize

scu'gnizzo *nm* street urchin

sculacci'are *vt* spank

sculacci'ata *nf* spanking; **prendere a sculacciate** spank

sculacci'one *nm* spanking

sculet'tare *vi* wiggle one's hips

scul|'tore, -'trice *nm* sculptor ● *nf* sculptress

scul'tura *nf* sculpture

scu'ola *nf* school. **~ allievi ufficiali** cadet school. **~ elementare** primary school. **~ guida** driving school. **~ materna** day nursery. **~ media** secondary school. **~ media inferiore** secondary school (*10-13*). **~ media superiore** secondary school (*13-18*). **~ dell'obbligo** compulsory education. **~ privata** private school, public school *Br*. **~ di sci** ski school. **~ serale** evening school. **~ statale** state school. **~ superiore** high school

scu'otere *vt* shake

scu'otersi *vr* (*destarsi*) rouse oneself; **~ qcsa di dosso** *fig* shake sth off

'**scure** *nf* axe

scu'rire *vt/i* darken

'**scuro** *a* dark ● *nm* darkness; (*imposta*) shutter

scur'rile *a* scurrilous

'**scusa** *nf* excuse; (*giustificazione*) apology;

(*pretesto*) pretext; **chiedere** ~ apologize; [**chiedo**] ~! [I'm] sorry!

scu'sare *vt* excuse

scu'sarsi *vr* apologize (**di** for); [**mi**] **scusi!** excuse me!; (*chiedendo perdono*) [I'm] sorry!

'**sdarsi** *vr fam* lose interest

sdebi'tarsi *vr* repay the kindness

sde'gnare *vt* despise; (*fare arrabbiare*) enrage

sde'gnarsi *vr* become angry

sde'gnato *a* indignant

'**sdegno** *nm* disdain; (*ira*) indignation

sde'gnoso *a* disdainful

sden'tato *a* toothless

sdipa'nare *vt* wind

sdogana'mento *nm* customs clearance

sdoga'nare *vt* clear through customs

sdolci'nato *a* sentimental, schmaltzy

sdoppia'mento *nm* splitting. ~ **della personalità** split personality

sdoppi'are *vt* halve

sdrai'arsi *vr* lie down

'**sdraio** *nm* [**sedia a**] ~ deckchair

sdrammatiz'zare *vt* take the heat out of ● *vi* take the heat out of the situation

sdruccio'lare *vi* slither

sdruccio'levole *a* slippery

sdruccio'lone *nm* slip

SE *abbr* (**sud-est**) SE

se *conj* if; (*interrogativo*) whether, if; **se mai** (*caso mai*) if need be; **se mai telefonasse,...** should he call,..., if he calls,...; **se no** otherwise, or else; **se non altro** at least, if nothing else; **se pure** (*sebbene*) even though; (*anche se*) even if; **non so se sia vero** I don't know whether it's true, I don't know if it's true; **come se** as if; **se lo avessi saputo prima!** if only I had known before!; **e se andassimo fuori a cena?** how about going out for dinner? ● *nm inv* if; **non voglio né se né ma** I don't want any ifs or buts

sé *pers pron* oneself; (*lui*) himself; (*lei*) herself; (*esso, essa*) itself; (*loro*) themselves; **l'ha fatto da sé** he did it himself; **ha preso i soldi con sé** he took the money with him; **si sono tenuti le notizie per sé** they kept the news to themselves

se'baceo *a* sebaceous

seb'bene *conj* although

'**sebo** *nm* sebum

sec. *abbr* (**secolo**) c.

'**secca** *nf* shallows *pl*; **in** ~ ‹*nave*› grounded

sec'cante *a* annoying

sec'care *vt* dry; (*importunare*) annoy ● *vi* dry up

sec'carsi *vr* dry up; (*irritarsi*) get annoyed

secca|'**tore, -'trice** *nmf* nuisance

secca'tura *nf* bother; **dare una** ~ **a qcno** trouble sb, bother sb; **non voglio seccature!** I don't want the bother!

secchi'ata *nf* bucketful

secchi'ello *nm* bucket. ~ **del ghiaccio** ice bucket

'**secchio** *nm* bucket. ~ **della spazzatura** rubbish bin, trash can *Am*

'**secco, -a** *a* dry; (*disseccato*) dried; (*magro*) thin; (*brusco*) curt; (*preciso*) sharp; **restare a** ~ be left penniless; **restarci** ~ (*fam: morire di colpo*) be killed on the spot; **frutta secca** nuts *pl* ● *nm* (*siccità*) drought; **lavare a** ~ dry-clean

secessi'one *nf* secession; **guerra di** ~ War of Secession

seco'lare *a* age-old; (*laico*) secular

'**secolo** *nm* century; (*epoca*) age; **è un** ~ **che non lo vedo** *fam* I haven't seen him for ages *o* yonks

se'conda *nf Sch, Rail* second class; *Auto* second [gear] ● *prep* **a** ~ **di** according to

secon'dario *a Jur* collateral; **effetto** ~ side effect

se'condo *a* second ● *nm* second, sec *fam*; (*secondo piatto*) main course; **un** ~! just a sec[ond]! ● *prep* according to; ~ **me** in my opinion

secondo'genito, -a *a & nm* second-born

secrezi'one *nf* secretion

'**sedano** *nm* celery. ~ **rapa** celeriac

se'dare *vt* put down, suppress ‹*rivolta*›; *fig* soothe

seda'tivo *a & nm* sedative; **somministrare sedativi a** sedate

'**sede** *nf* seat; (*centro*) centre; *Relig* see; *Comm* head office; **in** ~ **di esami** during the exams; **in separata** ~ in private. ~ **centrale** head office. ~ **sociale** registered office

seden'tario *a* sedentary

se'dere *vi* sit

se'dersi *vr* sit down ● *nm* (*deretano*) bottom

'**sedia** *nf* chair. ~ **a dondolo** rocking chair. ~ **elettrica** electric chair. ~ **da giardino** garden seat. ~ **a rotelle** wheelchair. ~ **a sdraio** deckchair

sedi'cenne *a & nmf* sixteen-year-old

sedi'cente *a* self-styled

sedi'cesimo, -a *a & nm* sixteenth

'**sedici** *a & nm* sixteen

se'dile *nm* seat

sedimen'tare *vi* leave a sediment

sedi'mento *nm* sediment

sedizi'one *nf* sedition

sedizi'oso *a* seditious

se'dotto *pp di* sedurre

sedu'cente *a* seductive; (*allettante*) enticing

se'durre *vt* seduce

se'duta *nf* session; (*di posa*) sitting. ~ **stante** *adv* here and now

se'duto *a* sitting

sedut|'**tore, -'trice** *nm* charmer ● *nf* temptress

seduzi'one *nf* seduction

seg. *abbr* (**seguente**) foll.

'**sega** *nf* saw; *vulg* wank; **mezza** ~ *vulg* tosser; **non capire una** ~ understand damn all. ~ **circolare** circular saw. ~ **a mano** handsaw. ~ **a nastro** band saw

'**segale** *nf* rye; **pane di** ~ rye bread

sega'ligno *a* wiry

se'gare *vt* saw

sega'trice *nf* saw. **~ a nastro** band saw
sega'tura *nf* sawdust
'seggio *nm* seat. **~ elettorale** polling station
seg'giola *nf* chair
seggio'lino *nm* seat; (*da bambino*) child's seat; **~ regolabile** adjustable seat
seggio'lone *nm* (*per bambini*) high chair
seggio'via *nf* chair lift
seghe'ria *nf* sawmill
se'ghetto *nm* hacksaw
segmen'tare *vt* segment
seg'mento *nm* segment
segna'carte *nm* bookmark
segna'lare *vt* signal; (*annunciare*) announce; (*indicare*) point out
segna'larsi *vr* distinguish oneself
segnalazi'one *nf* signals *pl*; (*di candidato*) recommendation. **~ stradale** road signs *pl*
se'gnale *nm* signal; (*stradale*) sign. **~ acustico** beep. **~ d'allarme** alarm; (*in treno*) communication cord *Br*, emergency brake; *fig* danger signal. **~ digitale** *Comput* digital signal. **~ di libero** *Teleph* dialling tone. **~ orario** time signal
segna'letica *nf* signals *pl*; **'~ in rifacimento'** 'road signs being repainted'. **~ orizzontale** painted road markings *pl*. **~ stradale** road signs *pl*
segna'letico *a* **dati segnaletici** description; **foto segnaletica** *photograph used for identification purposes*
segna'libro *nm* bookmark
segna'punti *nm inv* pegboard
se'gnare *vt* mark; (*prendere nota*) note; (*indicare*) indicate; *Sport* score; **~ la fine di qcsa** sound the death knell for sth; **~ il passo** mark time
se'gnarsi *vr* cross oneself
se'gnato *a* marked
'segno *nm* sign; (*traccia, limite*) mark; (*bersaglio*) target; **far ~** (*col capo*) nod; (*con la mano*) beckon; **fare ~ di no** (*con la testa*) shake one's head; **fare ~ di sì** (*con la testa*) nod [one's head]; **lasciare il ~** leave a mark; **non dare segni di vita** give no sign of life; **oltrepassare il ~** *fig* overstep the mark. **~ della croce** sign of the cross. **~ premonitore** early warning. **~ zodiacale** sign of the Zodiac, birth sign
segre'gare *vt* segregate
segre'garsi *vr* cut oneself off
segre'gato *a* in isolation
segregazi'one *nf* segregation
segretari'ato *nm* secretariat
segre'tario, -a *nmf* secretary; **fare da ~ a qcno** be sb's secretary. **~ bilingue** bilingual secretary. **~ comunale** town clerk. **~ di direzione** executive secretary. **~ personale** personal assistant, PA. **S~ di Stato** Secretary of State. **segretaria tuttofare** girl Friday
segrete'ria *nf* (*ufficio*) administrative office; (*segretariato*) secretariat. **~ telefonica** answering machine, answerphone

segre'tezza *nf* secrecy
se'greto *a & nm* secret; **in ~** in secret
segu'ace *nmf* follower; **avere molti seguaci** have a large following
segu'ente *a* following, next
se'gugio *nm* bloodhound
segu'ire *vt/i* follow; (*continuare*) continue; **~ con lo sguardo** follow with one's eyes; **~ le orme di qcno** follow in sb's footsteps; **~ un corso** take a course
segui'tare *vt/i* continue
'seguito *nm* retinue; (*sequela*) series; (*continuazione*) continuation; **di ~** in succession; **in ~** later on; **in ~ a** following; **al ~** in his/her wake; (*a causa di*) owing to; **fare ~ a** *Comm* follow up; **di ~** one after the other
'sei *a & nm* six
sei'cento *a & nm* six hundred; **il S~** the seventeenth century
sei'mila *a & nm* six thousand
'selce *nf* flint
sel'ciato *nm* paving
se'lenio *nm* selenium
selettività *nf* selectivity
selet'tivo *a* selective; **memoria selettiva** selective memory
selet'tore *nm* selector
selezio'nare *vt* select; **'~ il numero'** 'dial [the number]'
selezi'one *nf* selection. **~ naturale** natural selection
self-con'trol *nm* self-control
self-'service *a & nm inv* self-service
'sella *nf* saddle
sel'lare *vt* saddle
seltz *nm inv* soda water
'selva *nf* forest; (*fig: di errori, capelli*) mass; (*di ammiratori*) horde
selvag'gina *nf* game
sel'vaggio, -a *a* wild; (*primitivo*) savage ● *nmf* savage
sel'vatico *a* wild
selvicol'tura *nf* forestry
se'maforo *nm* traffic lights *pl*
se'mantica *nf* semantics
se'mantico *a* semantic
sembi'anza *nf* semblance; **sembianze** *pl* (*di persona*) appearance
sem'brare *vi* seem; (*assomigliare*) look like; **che te ne sembra?** what do you think?; **mi sembra che...** I think...; **sembra che vada bene** it's fine, seemingly *or* apparently
'seme *nm* seed; (*di mela*) pip; (*di carte*) suit; (*sperma*) semen. **~ della discordia** seeds *pl* of discord
se'mente *nf* seed
seme'strale *a* ⟨*corso*⟩ six-month; ⟨*pagamento*⟩ six-monthly, half-yearly
se'mestre *nm* six months; *Univ* term, semester *Am*
semia'perto *a* half-open
semi'asse *nm* axle
semiauto'matico *a* semiautomatic
semi'breve *nf Mus* semibreve
semi'cerchio *nm* semicircle

semicirco'lare *a* semicircular
semicirconfe'renza *nf* semicircle
semicondut'tore *a & nm* semiconductor
semicon'vitto *nm* **scuola a ~** *school for dayboarders*
semicosci'ente *a* semi-conscious, half-conscious
semi'croma *nf Mus* semiquaver
semifi'nale *nf* semifinal
semi'freddo *nm* cold dessert resembling ice cream
semilavo'rato *a* semi-finished ● *nm* **semilavorati** *pl* semi-finished goods
semi'minima *nf Mus* crotchet
'semina *nf* sowing
semi'nare *vt* sow; *fam* shake off ⟨*inseguitori*⟩; **seminar zizzania** cause trouble
semi'nario *nm* seminar; *Relig* seminary
semina'rista *nm* seminarist
seminfermità *nf* partial disability. **~ mentale** diminished responsibility
seminter'rato *nm* basement
semi'nudo *a* half-naked
semioscurità *nf* semi-darkness
semiprezi'oso *a* semiprecious
semi'secco *a* medium-dry
semi'serio *a* semi-serious
se'mitico *a* Semitic
semi'tono *nm Mus* semitone
sem'mai *conj* in case ● *adv* **è lui, ~, che**... if anyone, it's him who...
'semola *nf* bran
semo'lato *a* ⟨*zucchero*⟩ caster *attrib*
semo'lino *nm* semolina
'semplice *a* simple; **in parole semplici** in plain words
semplice'mente *adv* simply
semplici'otto, -a *nmf* simpleton
sempli'cistico *a* simplistic
semplicità *nf* simplicity
semplifi'care *vt* simplify
'sempre *adv* always; ⟨*ancora*⟩ still; **per ~** for ever; **~ più** more and more; **pur ~** still, nevertheless
sempre'verde *a & nm* evergreen
'senape *nf* mustard
se'nato *nm* senate
sena|'tore, -'trice *nmf* senator
se'nile *a* senile
senilità *nf* senility
'senior *a* senior ● *nmf* (*pl* **seniores**) *Sport* senior
'senno *nm* sense; **giudicare col ~ del poi** use hindsight
sennò *adv* otherwise, or else
sennonché *conj* but, except that; ⟨*fuorché*⟩ but, except
'seno *nm* (*petto*) breast; *Math* sine; **in ~ a** in the bosom of
sen'sale *nm* broker
sen'sato *a* sensible
sensazio'nale *a* sensational
sensazi'one *nf* sensation; **fare ~** ⟨*notizia, scoperta:*⟩ cause a sensation
sen'sibile *a* sensitive; (*percepibile*) percepti-

ble; (*notevole*) considerable; **mondo ~** tangible world
sensibilità *nf* sensitivity
sensibiliz'zare *vt* make more aware (**a** of)
sensibil'mente *adv* appreciably
sensi'tivo *a* sensory ● *nmf* sensitive person; (*medium*) medium
'senso *nm* sense; (*significato*) meaning; (*direzione*) direction; **far ~ a qcno** make sb shudder; **in ~ orario/antiorario** clockwise/anticlockwise; **ai sensi della legge** in accordance with the law; **non ha ~** it doesn't make sense; **avere il ~ degli affari** have good business sense; **di buon ~** ⟨*persona*⟩ sensible; **senza ~** meaningless; **in un certo ~**... in a sense *o* way...; **perdere i sensi** lose consciousness; **a ~** ⟨*ripetere, tradurre*⟩ in general terms; **in ~ opposto** in the opposite direction; **a ~ unico** ⟨*strada*⟩ one-way; **a doppio ~** [**di marcia**] ⟨*strada*⟩ two-way; **a doppio ~** ⟨*parola, espressione*⟩ with a double meaning. **~ dell'umorismo** sense of humour. **'~ vietato'** 'no entry'
sen'sore *nm* sensor
sensu'ale *a* sensual
sensualità *nf* sensuality
sen'tenza *nf* sentence; (*massima*) saying; **pronunciare una ~** hand down a sentence; **pronunciare la ~** pronounce sentence
sentenzi'are *vi* pass judgment
senti'ero *nm* path. **~ luminoso di avvicinamento** *Aeron* approach lights
sentimen'tale *a* sentimental
sentimenta'lista *nmf* sentimentalist
sentimental'mente *adv* sentimentally
senti'mento *nm* feeling; **essere fuori di ~** be out of one's mind
sen'tina *nf Naut* bilge
senti'nella *nf* sentry; **essere di ~** be on guard
sen'tire *vt* feel; (*udire*) hear; (*ascoltare*) listen to; (*gustare*) taste; (*odorare*) smell ● *vi* feel; (*udire*) hear; **~ caldo/freddo** feel hot/cold
sen'tirsi *vr* feel; **~ di fare qcsa** feel like doing sth; **~ bene/male** feel well/ill; **sen'tirsela di fare qcsa** feel up to doing sth
sen'tito *a* (*sincero*) sincere; **per ~ dire** by hearsay
sen'tore *nm* inkling
'senza *prep* without; **~ ombrello** without an umbrella; **~ correre** without running; **senz'altro** certainly; **~ un soldo** penniless; **'~ conservanti'** 'no preservatives'; **fare ~** do without
senza'tetto *nm inv* **i ~** the homeless
'sepalo *nm* sepal
sepa'rare *vt* separate
sepa'rarsi *vr* separate; ⟨*prendere commiato*⟩ part; **~ da** be separated from
separata'mente *adv* separately
separa'tista *nmf* separatist
sepa'rato *a* separate
separazi'one *nf* separation. **~ consensuale** separation by mutual consent. **~ legale** legal separation

sepol'crale *a liter* sepulchral

se'polcro *nm* sepulchre

se'polto *pp di* seppellire ● *a* buried; **morto e ~** *fig* dead and buried

sepol'tura *nf* burial; **dare ~ a** qcno bury sb

seppel'lire *vt* bury

seppel'lirsi *vr fig* cut oneself off

'seppia *nf* cuttle fish ● *a inv* sepia

sep'pure *conj* even if

se'quela *nf* series, succession; *(di insulti)* string

se'quenza *nf* sequence

sequenzi'ale *a* sequential

seque'strare *vt (rapire)* kidnap; *(confiscare)* confiscate; *Jur* impound

sequestra'|tore, -'trice *nmf* kidnapper

se'questro *nm Jur* impounding; *(di persona)* kidnap[ping]

se'quoia *nf* sequoia

'sera *nf* evening, night; **di ~, la ~** in the evening; **da ~** ⟨abito⟩ evening *attrib*; **alle 8 di ~** at 8 o'clock in the evening, at 8 o'clock at night; **buona ~!** good evening!; **dalla mattina alla ~** from morning to night; **ieri ~** yesterday evening, last night; **questa ~** this evening, tonight

se'rale *a* evening *attrib*

seral'mente *adv* every evening, every night

se'rata *nf* evening; *(ricevimento)* party. **~ danzante** dance. **~ di gala** gala night

ser'bare *vt* keep; harbour ⟨odio⟩; cherish ⟨speranza⟩

serba'toio *nm* tank. **~ d'acqua** water tank; *(per una città)* reservoir. **~ della benzina** petrol tank, gas tank *Am*

'Serbia *nf* Serbia

'serbo, -a *a & nmf* Serbian ● *nm (lingua)* Serbian

'serbo *nm* mettere in **~** put aside

serbo-cro'ato *nmf* Serbo-Croat[ian]

sere'nata *nf* serenade

serenità *nf* serenity

se'reno *a* serene; ⟨cielo⟩ clear; **un fulmine a ciel ~** *fam* bolt from the blue

ser'gente *nm* sergeant

'serial *nm* **~ [televisivo]** television serial

seri'ale *a* serial

seria'mente *adv* seriously

'serico *a* silk

'serie *nf inv* series; *(complesso)* set; *Sport* division; **~ A** *(di calcio)* ≈ Premier League; **~ B** *(di calcio)* ≈ First Division; **di ~ B** *fig* second-rate; **fuori ~** custom-built; **produzione in ~** mass production. **~ numerica** numerical series

serietà *nf* seriousness

'serio *a* serious; *(degno di fiducia)* reliable; **sul ~** seriously; *(davvero)* really

ser'mone *nm* sermon

'serpe *nf liter* viper

serpeggi'ante *a* ⟨strada⟩ twisting, winding

serpeggi'are *vi* ⟨strada:⟩ twist, wind; *(fig: diffondersi)* spread

ser'pente *nm* snake. **~ a sonagli** rattlesnake. **~ velenoso** poisonous snake

serpen'tina *nf* **a ~** twisting and turning, winding; **fare una ~** weave

'serra *nf* greenhouse; **effetto ~** greenhouse effect

ser'raglio *nm* harem

ser'randa *nf* shutter

ser'rare *vt* shut; *(stringere)* tighten; *(incalzare)* press on

ser'rata *nf* lockout

serra'tura *nf* lock

ser'vibile *a* usable

ser'vile *a* servile

servi'lismo *nm* servility

ser'vire *vt* serve; *(al ristorante)* wait on ● *vi* serve; *(essere utile)* be of use; **non serve** it's no good; **'~ freddo'** 'serve chilled'

ser'virsi *vr (di cibo)* help oneself; **~ da** buy from; **~ di** use

servi'|tore, -'trice *nmf* retainer ● *nm Comput* server

servitù *nf* servitude; *(personale di servizio)* servants *pl*

servizi'evole *a* obliging

ser'vizio *nm* service; *(da caffè ecc)* set; *(di cronaca, sportivo)* report; *(in tennis)* serve. **servizi** *pl* bathroom; **donna di ~** maid; **essere di ~** be on duty; **fare ~** ⟨autobus ecc:⟩ run; **fuori ~** ⟨bus⟩ not in service; ⟨ascensore⟩ out of order; **~ compreso** service charge included; **~ escluso** not including service charge; **area di ~** service station; **servizi** *pl (terziario)* services. **~ bancario a domicilio** home banking. **~ in camera** room service. **~ civile** civilian duties done instead of national service. **~ filmato** film report. **servizi** *pl* **igienici** toilet block. **~ di linea** passenger service. **~ militare** military service. **servizi** *pl* **di pronto intervento** emergency services. **~ pubblico** utility company. **servizi** *pl* **pubblici** *(bagni)* public toilets. **servizi** *pl* **sociali** welfare services. **~ al tavolo** waiter service. **~ traghetto** passenger ferry

'servo, -a *nmf* servant

servo'freno *nm* servo brake

servo'sterzo *nm* power steering

'sesamo *nm* sesame

ses'santa *a & nm* sixty

sessan'tenne *a & nmf* sixty-year-old

sessan'tesimo *a & nm* sixtieth

sessan'tina *nf* **una ~ di** about sixty

Sessan'totto *nm* protest movement of 1968

sessi'one *nf* session

ses'sista *a* sexist

'sesso *nm* sex; **fare ~** *sl* have sex. **~ forte** stronger sex. **gentil ~** fair sex. **~ sicuro** safe sex

sessu'ale *a* sexual

sessualità *nf* sexuality

'sesto¹ *a & nm* sixth

'sesto² *nm* rimettere in **~** put back on its feet ⟨azienda⟩; restore ⟨vestito⟩; recondition ⟨motore, auto⟩

set *nm inv* set

'**seta** *nf* silk; **di ~** silk *attrib*

setacci'are *vt* sieve

se'taccio *nm* sieve; **passare qcsa al ~** *fig* go through sth with a fine-tooth comb

'**sete** *nf* thirst; **avere ~** be thirsty. **~ di sangue** blood lust

'**setola** *nf* bristle

'**setta** *nf* sect

set'tanta *a & nm* seventy

settan'tenne *a & nmf* seventy-year-old

settan'tesimo *a & nm* seventieth

settan'tina *nf* **una ~ di** about seventy

set'tario *a* sectarian

'**sette** *a & nm* seven

sette'cento *a & nm* seven hundred; **il S~** the eighteenth century

set'tembre *nm* September

settentrio'nale *a* northern ● *nmf* northerner

settentri'one *nm* north

'**setter** *nm inv* setter

'**settico** *a* septic

setti'mana *nf* week; **alla ~** per week; **a metà ~** midweek, half-way through the week. **~ corta** five-day week. **~ lavorativa** working week

settima'nale *a & nm* weekly

setti'mino, -a *a born two months premature* ● *nmf* baby born two months premature

'**settimo** *a & nm* seventh

set'tore *nm* sector

settori'ale *a* sector-based

severità *nf* severity

se'vero *a* severe; (*rigoroso*) strict

se'vizia *nf* torture; **se'vizie** *pl* torture *sg*

sevizi'are *vt* torture

sezio'nare *vt* divide; *Med* dissect

sezi'one *nf* section; (*reparto*) department; *Med* dissection

sfaccen'dare *vi* bustle about

sfaccen'dato *a* idle

sfacet'tare *vt* cut

sfaccet'tato *a* cut; *fig* many-sided, multi-faceted

sfaccetta'tura *nf* cutting; *fig* facet

sfacchi'nare *vi* toil

sfacchi'nata *nf* drudgery

sfaccia'taggine *nf* cheek

sfacciata'mente *adv* cheekily

sfacci'ato *a* cheeky, fresh *Am*

sfa'celo *nm* ruin; **in ~** in ruins

sfagio'lare *vi fam* **non mi sfagiola** it's/ he's/she's not my cup of tea

sfal'darsi *vr* flake off

sfal'sare *vt* stagger; **~ il tiro** shoot wide

sfa'mare *vt* feed

sfa'marsi *vr* satisfy one's hunger, eat one's fill

sfarfal'lio *nm* (*di schermo, luce*) flicker

'**sfarzo** *nm* pomp

sfar'zoso *a* sumptuous

sfa'sato *a fam* confused; (*motore*) which needs tuning; **sentirsi ~** *fam* be out of sync[h]

sfasci'are *vt* unbandage; (*fracassare*) smash

sfasci'arsi *vr* fall to pieces

sfasci'ato *a* beat-up

'**sfascio** *nm* ruin; **andare allo ~** go to rack and ruin

sfa'tare *vt* explode

sfati'cato *a* lazy

'**sfatto** *a* unmade

sfavil'lante *a* sparkling

sfavil'lare *vi* sparkle

sfavo'revole *a* unfavourable

sfavo'rire *vt* disadvantage, put at a disadvantage

sfeb'brare *vi* **comincia a ~** his temperature is starting to come down

'**sfera** *nf* sphere. **~ affettiva** area of feelings and emotions. **~ celeste** celestial sphere. **~ di cristallo** crystal ball. **~ di influenza** sphere of influence

'**sferico** *a* spherical

sfer'rare *vt* unshoe (*cavallo*); give (*calcio, pugno*)

sferruz'zare *vi* knit

sfer'zare *vt* whip

sfer'zata *nf* whip; *fig* telling-off

sfian'cante *a* wearing

sfian'care *vt* wear out

sfian'carsi *vr* wear oneself out

sfiata'toio *nm* blowhole

sfi'brare *vt* exhaust

sfi'brato *a* exhausted

'**sfida** *nf* challenge

sfi'dare *vt* challenge

sfi'ducia *nf* mistrust

sfiduci'ato *a* discouraged

'**sfiga** *nf sl* bloody bad luck; **avere ~** be bloody unlucky

sfi'gato, -a *sl a* bloody unlucky ● *nmf* unlucky beggar

sfigu'rare *vt* disfigure ● *vi* (*far cattiva figura*) look out of place

sfilacci'are *vt* fray

sfilacci'arsi *vr* fray

sfi'lare *vt* unthread; (*togliere di dosso*) take off ● *vi* (*truppe:*) march past; (*in parata*) parade

sfi'larsi *vr* come unthreaded; (*collant:*) ladder; take off (*pantaloni*)

sfi'lata *nf* parade; (*sfilza*) series. **~ di moda** fashion show

sfila'tino *nm* long, thin loaf

'**sfilza** *nf* string

'**sfinge** *nf* sphinx

sfi'nirsi *vr* wear oneself out

sfi'nito *a* worn out

sfio'rare *vt* skim; touch on (*argomento*)

sfio'rire *vi* wither; (*bellezza:*) fade

sfis'sare *vt* cancel

'**sfitto** *a* vacant

'**sfizio** *nm* whim, fancy; **togliersi uno ~** satisfy a whim

sfizi'oso *a* nifty

sfo'cato *a* out of focus

sfoci'are *vi* **~ in** flow into

sfode'rare vt draw ⟨pistola, spada⟩; fig show off ⟨cultura⟩; **~ un sorriso** smile insincerely

sfode'rato a ⟨giacca⟩ unlined

sfo'gare vt vent

sfo'garsi vr give vent to one's feelings

sfoggi'are vt/i show off

'sfoggio nm show, display; **fare ~ di** show off

'sfoglia nf sheet of pastry; **pasta ~** puff pastry

sfogli'are vt leaf through

sfogli'ata¹ nf flaky pastry with filling

sfogli'ata² nf **dare una ~ a** ⟨libro, giornale⟩ flick through

'sfogo nm outlet; fig outburst; Med rash; **dare ~ a** give vent to

sfolgo'rante a blazing

sfolgo'rare vi blaze

sfolla'gente nm truncheon, billy Am

sfol'lare vt clear ● vi Mil be evacuated

sfol'lato, -a nmf evacuee

sfol'tire vt thin [out]; **farsi ~ i capelli** have one's hair thinned

sfon'dare vt break down ● vi (aver successo) make a name for oneself

'sfondo nm background

sfon'done nm fam blunder

sfor'mare vt pull out of shape ⟨tasche⟩

sfor'marsi vi lose its shape; ⟨persona:⟩ lose one's figure

sfor'mato nm Culin flan

sfor'nito a **~ di** ⟨negozio⟩ out of

sfor'tuna nf bad luck

sfortunata'mente adv unfortunately

sfortu'nato a unlucky

sfor'zare vt force

sfor'zarsi vr try hard

sfor'zato a forced

'sforzo nm effort; (tensione) stress

'sfottere vt sl tease

sfracel'larsi vr smash; **~ al suolo** crash to the ground

sfrangi'ato a fringed

sfrat'tare vt evict

'sfratto nm eviction

sfrecci'are vi flash past

sfrega'mento nm crackling

sfre'gare vt rub

sfregi'are vt slash

sfregi'ato, -a a scarred ● nmf scarface

'sfregio nm slash

sfre'narsi vr run wild

sfre'nato a wild

sfrigo'lio nm crackling

sfron'dare vt prune

sfron'tato a shameless

sfrutta'mento nm exploitation

sfrut'tare vt exploit; take advantage of, make the most of ⟨occasione⟩

sfug'gente a elusive; ⟨mento⟩ receding

sfug'gire vi escape; **~ a** escape [from]; **mi sfugge** it escapes me; **mi è sfuggito [di mente]** it [completely] slipped my mind; **mi è sfuggito di mano** I lost hold of it;

lasciarsi **~ un'occasione** let an opportunity slip; **mi è sfuggito un rutto** I just came out with a belch; **gli è sfuggito un colpo dal fucile** the rifle just went off in his hands ● vt avoid

sfug'gita nf **di ~** in passing

sfu'mare vi (svanire) vanish; ⟨colore:⟩ shade off ● vt soften ⟨colore⟩

sfuma'tura nf shade

sfuri'ata nf outburst [of anger]

sga'bello nm stool

sgabuz'zino nm cupboard

sgam'bato a ⟨costume da bagno⟩ high-cut

sgambet'tare vi kick one's legs; (camminare) trot

sgam'betto nm **fare lo ~ a qcno** trip sb up

sganasci'arsi vr **~ dalle risa** roar with laughter

sganci'are vt unhook; Rail uncouple; drop ⟨bombe⟩; fam cough up ⟨denaro⟩

sganci'arsi vr become unhooked; fig get away

sganghe'rato a ramshackle

sgar'bato a rude

'sgarbo nm discourtesy; **fare uno ~ a qcno** be rude to sb; **ricevere uno ~** be treated rudely

sgargi'ante a garish

sgar'rare vi be wrong; (da regola) stray from the straight and narrow

'sgarro nm mistake, slip

sga'sato a flat

sgattaio'lare vi sneak away; **~ via** decamp

sge'lare vt/i thaw

'sghembo a slanting; **a ~** obliquely

sghiacci'are vt defrost; thaw out ⟨carne⟩

sghignaz'zare vi laugh scornfully

sghiri'bizzo nm whim, fancy

sgob'bare vi slog; ⟨fam: studente:⟩ swot

sgob'bone, -a nmf slogger; (fam: studente) swot

sgoccio'lare vi drip

'sgocciolo nm dripping

sgo'larsi vr shout oneself hoarse

sgomb[e]'rare vt clear [out]

'sgombro a clear ● nm (trasloco) removal; (pesce) mackerel

sgomen'tare vt dismay

sgomen'tarsi vr be dismayed

sgo'mento nm dismay

sgomi'nare vt defeat

sgom'mare vi make the tyres screech

sgom'mata nf screech of tyres

sgonfi'are vt deflate

sgonfi'arsi vr go down

'sgonfio a flat

'sgorbio nm scrawl; (fig: vista sgradevole) sight

sgor'gare vi gush [out] ● vt flush out, unblock ⟨lavandino⟩

sgoz'zare vt **~ qcno** cut sb's throat

sgra'devole a disagreeable

sgra'dito a unwelcome

sgraffi'are vt scratch

'sgraffio nm scratch

sgrammaticata'mente *adv* ungrammatically

sgrammati'cato *a* ungrammatical

sgra'nare *vt* shell 〈*piselli*〉; open wide 〈*occhi*〉

sgra'nato *a* grainy; 〈*fagioli*〉 shelled; 〈*occhi*〉 wide-open

sgran'chire *vt* stretch

sgran'chirsi *vr* stretch

sgranocchi'are *vt* munch

sgras'sare *vt* remove the grease from

'sgravio *nm* relief. **~ fiscale** tax relief

sgrazi'ato *a* ungainly

sgreto'lare *vt* crumble

sgreto'larsi *vr* crumble

sgri'dare *vt* scold

sgri'data *nf* scolding

sgron'dare *vt* drain

sgros'sare *vt* rough-hew 〈*marmo*〉; *fig* polish

sguai'ato *a* coarse

sgual'cire *vt* crumple

sgual'drina *nf* slut

sgu'ardo *nm* look; (*breve*) glance; **dare uno ~ a** glance at 〈*giornale, testo*〉. **~ di insieme** overview

sguar'nito *a* unadorned; (*privo di difesa*) undefended

'sguattero, -a *nmf* skivvy

sguaz'zare *vi* splash; (*nel fango*) wallow

'sguincio *nm* sidelong glance

sguinzagli'are *vt* unleash

sgusci'are *vt* shell ● *vi* (*sfuggire*) slip away; **~ fuori** slip out

'shaker *nm inv* shaker

shake'rare *vt* shake

'shampoo *nm inv* shampoo; **~ e messa in piega** shampoo and set

'shopper *nm inv* carrier bag

'shuttle *nm inv* [space] shuttle

si *pers pron* (*riflessivo*) oneself; (*lui*) himself; (*lei*) herself; (*esso, essa*) itself; (*loro*) themselves; (*reciproco*) each other; (*tra più di due*) one another; (*impersonale*) you, one *fml*; **lavarsi** wash [oneself]; **si è lavata** she washed [herself]; **lavarsi le mani** wash one's hands; **si è lavata le mani** she washed her hands; **si è mangiato un pollo intero** he ate an entire chicken by himself; **incontrarsi** meet each other; **la gente si aiuta a vicenda** people help one another; **si potrebbe pensare che...** you might think that..., one might think that... *fml*; **non si sa mai** you never know, one never knows; **queste cose si dimenticano facilmente** these things are easily forgotten

si *nm Mus* (*chiave, nota*) B

sì *adv* yes; **credo di sì** I believe so; **penso di sì** I think so; **ha detto di sì** she said yes; **sì?** really?; **sì che mi piace!** yes I do like it!

'sia¹ *vedi* **essere**

'sia² *conj* **~...~...** (*entrambi*) both...and...; (*o l'uno o l'altro*) either...or...**~ che venga, ~ che non venga** whether he comes or not; **scegli ~ questo ~ quello** choose either

this one or that one; **voglio ~ questo che quello** I want both this one and that one; **verranno ~ Giuseppe ~ Giacomo** both Giuseppe and Giacomo are coming

sia'mese *a* Siamese

sibi'lare *vi* hiss

sibil'lino *a* sibylline

'sibilo *nm* hiss

si'cario *nm* hired killer

sicché *conj* (*perciò*) so [that]; (*allora*) then

siccità *nf* drought

sic'come *conj* as

Si'cilia *nf* Sicily

sicili'ano, -a *a & nmf* Sicilian

sico'moro *nm* sycamore

si'cura *nf* safety catch; (*di portiera*) child-proof lock

sicura'mente *adv* definitely; **~, sarà arrivato** he must have arrived by now

sicu'rezza *nf* (*certezza*) certainty; (*salvezza*) safety; **di ~** 〈*dispositivo*〉 safety *attrib*; **uscita di ~** emergency exit; **di massima ~** top security

si'curo *a* (*non pericoloso*) safe; (*certo*) sure; 〈*saldo*〉 steady; *Comm* sound ● *adv* certainly ● *nm* safety; **al ~** safe; **andare sul ~** play [it] safe; **di ~** definitely; **di ~, sarà arrivato** he must have arrived; **~!** sure!

'sidecar *nm inv* sidecar

siderur'gia *nf* iron and steel industry

side'rurgico *a* iron and steel *attrib*

'sidro *nm* cider

si'epe *nf* hedge

si'ero *nm* serum

sieroposi'tivo, -a *a* HIV positive ● *nmf* person who is HIV positive

Si'erra Le'one *nf* Sierra Leone

si'esta *nf* afternoon nap, siesta; **fare la ~** have an afternoon nap

si'fone *nm* siphon

Sig. *abbr* (**signore**) Mr

Sig.a *abbr* (**signora**) Mrs, Ms

siga'retta *nf* cigarette; **pantaloni** *pl* **a ~** drainpipes

'sigaro *nm* cigar

Sigg. *abbr* (**signori**) Messrs

sigil'lare *vt* seal

si'gillo *nm* seal

'sigla *nf* initials *pl*. **~ musicale** signature tune

si'glare *vt* initial

Sig.na *abbr* (**signorina**) Miss, Ms

signifi'care *vt* mean

significa'tivo *a* significant

signifi'cato *nm* meaning

si'gnora *nf* lady; (*davanti a nome proprio*) Mrs; (*non sposata*) Miss; (*in lettere ufficiali*) Dear Madam; **la ~ Rossi** Mrs Rossi; **il signor Vené e ~** Mr and Mrs Vené

si'gnore *nm* gentleman; *Relig* lord; (*davanti a nome proprio*) Mr; **il signor Rossi** Mr Rossi

signo'rile *a* gentlemanly; (*di lusso*) luxury

signo'rina *nf* young lady; (*seguito da nome proprio*) Miss; **la ~ Rossi** Miss Rossi

silenzia'tore *nm* silencer

si'lenzio *nm* silence. **~ di tomba** deathly hush

silenzi'oso *a* silent

'silfide *nf* sylph

silhou'ette *nf inv* silhouette, outline; **che ~!** you're so slim!

si'licio *nm* **piastrina di ~** silicon chip

sili'cone *nm* silicone

'sillaba *nf* syllable

silla'bario *nm* primer

sillaba'tore *nm Comput* hyphenation program

sillo'gismo *nm* syllogism

silu'rare *vt* torpedo

si'luro *nm* torpedo

simbi'osi *nf* symbiosis; **vivere in ~** need each other, have a symbiotic relationship

simboleggi'are *vt* symbolize

sim'bolico *a* symbolic[al]

simbo'lismo *nm* symbolism

simbo'lista *nmf* symbolist

'simbolo *nm* symbol

similarità *nf inv* similarity

'simile *a* similar; *(tale)* such; **è ~ a...** it's like..., it's similar to...; **qualcosa di ~** something similar ● *nm (il prossimo)* fellow human being, fellow man

simili'tudine *nf Gram* simile

simil'mente *adv* similarly

simil'pelle *nf* Leatherette®

simme'tria *nf* symmetry

sim'metrico *a* symmetric[al]

simpa'tia *nf* liking; *(compenetrazione)* sympathy; **prendere qcno in ~** take a liking to sb; **provare ~ per** like

sim'patico *a* nice; **inchiostro ~** invisible ink

simpatiz'zante *nmf* well-wisher

simpatiz'zare *vt* **~ con** take a liking to; **~ per qcsa/qcno** lean towards sth/sb

sim'posio *nm* symposium

simu'lare *vt* simulate; feign *(amicizia, interesse)*

simula'tore *nm* simulator

simulazi'one *nf* simulation. **~ di reato** *Jur* making of false accusations

simul'tanea *nf* **in ~** simultaneously

simul'taneo *a* simultaneous

sina'goga *nf* synagogue

sincera'mente *adv* sincerely; *(a dire il vero)* honestly

since'rarsi *vr* make sure

sincerità *nf* sincerity

sin'cero *a* sincere

'sincope *nf* syncopation; *Med* fainting fit

sincron'ia *nf* sync[h]

sincro'nismo *nm* synchronism

sincroniz'zare *vt* synchronize

sincroniz'zato *a* synchronized; **essere ben ~ con** be in sync[h] with

sincronizzazi'one *nf* synchronization

'sincrono *a* synchronous

sinda'cabile *a* arguable

sinda'cale *a* [trade] union *attrib*, [labor] union *Am*

sindaca'lista *nmf* trade unionist, labor union member *Am*

sinda'care *vt* inspect

sinda'cato *nm* [trade] union, [labor] union *Am*; *(associazione)* syndicate. **~ di categoria** trade union

'sindaco *nm* mayor

'sindrome *nf* syndrome. **~ di Down** Down's syndrome. **~ premestruale** premenstrual syndrome, PMS

sinfo'nia *nf* symphony

sin'fonico *a* symphonic

singhioz'zare *vi (di pianto)* sob

singhi'ozzo *nm* hiccup; *(di pianto)* sob; **avere il ~** have the hiccups

'single *nmf inv* single

singo'lare *a* singular; *(strano)* peculiar ● *nm Gram* singular

singolar'mente *adv* individually; *(stranamente)* peculiarly

'singolo *a* single ● *nm* individual; *Tennis* singles *pl*

si'nistra *nf* left; **a ~** on the left; **girare a ~** turn to the left; **la seconda a ~** the second on the left; **con la guida a ~** *(auto)* with left-hand drive; **la ~** *Pol* the left; **di ~** *Pol* left wing

sini'strare *vt* injure; damage *(casa)*

sini'strato *a* injured; *(casa)* damaged

si'nistro *a* left[-hand]; *(avverso)* sinister ● *nm* accident

sini'strorso, -a *nmf pej* leftie

'sino *prep* = **fino**

si'nonimo *a* synonymous ● *nm* synonym

sin'tassi *nf* syntax

sin'tattico *a* syntactic[al]

'sintesi *nf* synthesis; *(riassunto)* summary

sin'tetico *a* synthetic; *(conciso)* summary

sintetiz'zare *vt* summarize

sintetizza'tore *nm* synthesizer

sinto'matico *a* symptomatic

'sintomo *nm* symptom

sinto'nia *nf* tuning; **in ~** on the same wavelength; **in ~ con** in harmony with, in tune with

sintonizza'tore *nm* tuner

sinu'oso *a (strada)* winding

sinu'site *nf* sinusitis

sio'nismo *nm* Zionism

sio'nista *a* & *nmf* Zionist

si'pario *nm* curtain

si'rena *nf* siren; *(di nave)* hooter

'Siria *nf* Syria

siri'ano, -a *a* a & *nmf* Syrian

si'ringa *nf* syringe

'sismico *a* seismic

si'smografo *nm* seismograph

sismolo'gia *nf* seismology

si'stema *nm* system; **non è il ~!** that's no way to behave!. **~ di gestione banca dati** database management system, DBMS. **~ immunitario** immune system. **S~ Monetario Europeo** European Monetary System. **~**

nervoso nervous system. **~ operativo** *Comput* operating system. **~ solare** solar system. **~ di vita** way of life

siste'mare *vt* (*mettere*) put; tidy up ⟨*casa, camera*⟩; (*risolvere*) sort out; (*procurare lavoro a*) fix up with a job; (*trovare alloggio a*) find accommodation for; (*sposare*) marry off; (*fam: punire*) sort out

siste'marsi *vr* settle down; (*trovare un lavoro*) find a job; (*trovare alloggio*) find accommodation; (*sposarsi*) marry

sistematica'mente *adv* systematically

siste'matico *a* systematic

sistemazi'one *nf* arrangement; (*di questione*) settlement; (*lavoro*) job; (*alloggio*) accommodation; (*matrimonio*) marriage

siste'mista *nmf Comput* systems engineer

'sistole *nf* systole

'sit-in *nm inv* sit-in

'sito *nm* site. **~ web** *Comput* web site

situ'are *vt* place

situazi'one *nf* situation; **essere all'altezza della ~** be equal to the situation, be up to the situation

'skai *nm* Leatherette®

'skateboard *nm inv* skateboard

sketch *nm inv* sketch

ski-'lift *nm* ski tow

'skipper *nmf inv* skipper

slab'brare *vt* stretch out of shape ⟨*maglia, tasca*⟩

slab'brato *a* ⟨*maglia, tasca*⟩ shapeless

slacci'are *vt* unfasten

'slalom *nm inv* slalom; **a ~** slalom *attrib*

slanci'arsi *vr* hurl oneself

slanci'ato *a* slender

'slancio *nm* impetus; (*impulso*) impulse; **agire di ~** act on impulse

sla'vato *a* ⟨*carnagione, capelli*⟩ fair

'slavo *a* Slav[onic]

sle'ale *a* disloyal; **concorrenza ~** unfair competition

slealtà *nf* disloyalty

sle'gare *vt* untie

sle'garsi *vr* untie oneself

slip *nmpl* underpants

'slitta *nf* sledge; (*trainata*) sleigh

slitta'mento *nm* (*di macchina*) skid; (*fig: di riunione*) postponement

slit'tare *vi Auto* skid; ⟨*riunione:*⟩ be put off

slit'tata *nf* skid

slit'tino *nm* toboggan

'slogan *nm inv* slogan

slo'gare *vt* dislocate

slo'garsi *vr* **~ una caviglia** sprain one's ankle

slo'gato *a* sprained

sloga'tura *nf* sprain

sloggi'are *vt* dislodge ● *vi* move out

slot *nm* **~ di espansione** *Comput* expansion slot

slot-ma'chine *nf inv* slot-machine, one-armed bandit

Slo'vacchia *nf* Slovakia

slo'vacco, -a *a & nmf* Slovak

Slo'venia *nf* Slovenia

smacchi'are *vt* clean

smacchia'tore *nm* stain remover

'smacco *nm* humiliating defeat

smache'rarsi *vr* (*tradirsi*) give oneself away

smagli'ante *a* dazzling

smagli'arsi *vr* ⟨*calza:*⟩ ladder *Br*, run

smaglia'tura *nf* ladder *Br*, run

smagnetiz'zare *vt* demagnetize

smagnetiz'zatore *nm* demagnetizer

sma'grito *a* thinner

smal'tare *vt* enamel; glaze ⟨*ceramica*⟩; varnish ⟨*unghie*⟩

smal'tato *a* enamelled; ⟨*ceramica*⟩ glazed; ⟨*unghie*⟩ varnished

smalta'tura *nf* enamelling; (*di ceramica*) glazing

smalti'mento *nm* disposal; (*di merce*) selling off. **~ rifiuti** waste disposal; (*di grassi*) burning off

smal'tire *vt* burn off; (*merce*) sell off; *fig* get through ⟨*corrispondenza*⟩; **~ la sbornia** sober up

'smalto *nm* enamel; (*di ceramica*) glaze; (*per le unghie*) nail varnish, nail polish

smance'ria *nf* **fare smancerie** be overpolite

smance'roso *a* simpering

'smania *nf* fidgets *pl*; (*desiderio*) longing; **avere la ~ di** have a craving for

smani'are *vi* have the fidgets; **~ per** long for

smani'oso *a* restless

smantella'mento *nm* dismantling

smantel'lare *vt* dismantle

smarri'mento *nm* loss; (*psicologico*) bewilderment

smar'rire *vt* lose; (*temporaneamente*) mislay

smar'rirsi *vr* get lost; (*turbarsi*) be bewildered

smar'rito *a* lost; ⟨*sguardo*⟩ bewildered, lost

smasche'rare *vt* unmask

smasche'rarsi *vr fig* reveal oneself

SME *nm abbr* (**Sistema Monetario Europeo**) EMS

smem'brare *vt* dismember

smemo'rato, -a *a* forgetful ● *nmf* scatter-brain

smen'tire *vt* deny

smen'tita *nf* denial

sme'raldo *nm & a* emerald

smerci'are *vt* sell off

'smercio *nm* sale

smerigli'ato *a* emery; **vetro ~** frosted glass

sme'riglio *nm* emery

smer'lare *vt* scallop

'smerlo *nm* scallop

'smesso *pp di* **smettere** ● *a* ⟨*abiti*⟩ cast-off

'smettere *vt* stop; stop wearing ⟨*abiti*⟩; **smettila!** stop it!

smidol'lato *a* spineless

smilitariz'zare *vt* demilitarize

'smilzo *a* thin

sminu'ire *vt* diminish
sminu'irsi *vr/fig* belittle oneself
sminuz'zare *vt* crumble; (*fig: analizzare*) analyse in detail
smista'mento *nm* clearing; (*postale*) sorting; **stazione di ~** shunting yard, marshalling yard. **~ rifiuti** sorting of waste
smi'stare *vt* sort; *Mil* post; *Rail* marshall
smisu'rato *a* boundless; (*esorbitante*) excessive
smitiz'zare *vt* demythologize
smobili'tare *vt* demobilize
smobilitazi'one *nf* demobilization
smo'dato *a* immoderate
smog *nm* smog
'smoking *nm inv* dinner jacket, tuxedo *Am*
smon'tabile *a* jointed
smon'taggio *nm* disassembly
smon'tare *vt* take to pieces; (*scoraggiare*) dishearten; take down (*tenda*) ● *vi* (*da veicolo*) get off; (*da cavallo*) dismount; (*dal servizio*) go off duty
smon'tarsi *vr* lose heart
'smorfia *nf* grimace; (*moina*) simper; **fare smorfie** make faces
smorfi'oso *a* affected
'smorto *a* pale; (*colore*) dull
smor'zare *vt* dim (*luce*); tone down (*colori*); deaden (*suoni*); quench (*sete*)
smor'zata *nf Sport* drop shot
'smosso *pp di* **smuovere**
smotta'mento *nm* landslide
'smunto *a* emaciated
smu'overe *vt* shift; (*commuovere*) move
smu'oversi *vr* move; (*commuoversi*) be moved
smus'sare *vt* round off; (*fig: attenuare*) tone down
smus'sarsi *vr* go blunt
smussa'tura *nf* bevel
snack bar *nm inv* snack bar
snatu'rato *a* inhuman
snazionaliz'zare *vt* denationalize
S.N.C. *abbr* **società in nome collettivo**
snel'lire *vt* slim down
snel'lirsi *vr* slim [down]
'snello *a* slim
sner'vante *a* enervating
sner'vare *vt* enervate
sner'varsi *vr* get exhausted
sni'dare *vt* drive out
snif'fare *vt* snort
snob'bare *vt* snub
sno'bismo *nm* snobbery
snoccio'lare *vt* stone; *fig* blurt out
snoccio'lato *a* (*olive*) pitted, with the stones removed
sno'dabile *a* jointed
sno'dare *vt* untie; (*sciogliere*) loosen
sno'darsi *vr* come untied; (*strada:*) wind
sno'dato *a* (*persona*) double-jointed; (*dita*) flexible
'snodo *nm* coupling. **~ ferroviario** coupling
SO *abbr* (**sud-ovest**) SW
soap 'opera *nf inv* soap [opera]

so'ave *a* gentle
sobbal'zare *vi* jerk; (*trasalire*) start
sob'balzo *nm* jerk; (*trasalimento*) start
sobbar'carsi *vr* **~ a** undertake
sobbol'lire *vi* simmer
sob'borgo *nm* suburb
sobil'lare *vt* stir up
sobilla'tore, -'trice *nm* instigator
sobrietà *nf inv* sobriety
'sobrio *a* sober
soc'chiudere *vt* half-close
socchi'uso *pp di* **socchiudere** ● *a* (*occhi*) half-closed; (*porta*) ajar
soc'combere *vi* succumb
soc'correre *vt* assist
soc'corso *pp di* **soccorrere** ● *nm* assistance, help; **venire in ~** come to help, come to the rescue; **venire in ~ a qcno** come to sb's rescue; **soccorsi** *pl* help; (*persone*) rescuers; (*dopo disastro*) relief workers. **~ alpino** mountain rescue. **~ stradale** breakdown service, wrecking service *Am*
socialdemo'cratico, -a *a* Social Democratic ● *nmf* Social Democrat
socialdemocra'zia *nf* Social Democracy
soci'ale *a* social
socia'lismo *nm* Socialism
socia'lista *a & nmf* Socialist
socializ'zare *vi* socialize
società *nf inv* society; *Comm* company. **~ in accomandita semplice** limited partnership. **~ per azioni** public limited company, plc. **~ dei consumi** consumer society. **~ in nome collettivo** commercial partnership. **~ a responsabilità limitata** limited liability company
soci'evole *a* sociable
'socio, -a *nmf* member; *Comm* partner
socioeco'nomico *a* socio-economic
soci'ologa *nf* sociologist
sociolo'gia *nf* sociology
socio'logico *a* sociological
soci'ologo *nm* sociologist
'soda *nf* soda. **~ da bucato** washing soda
soda'lizio *nf* association, society
soddisfa'cente *a* satisfactory
soddi'sfare *vt/i* satisfy; meet (*richiesta*); make amends for (*offesa*)
soddi'sfatto *pp di* **soddisfare** ● *a* satisfied
soddisfazi'one *nf* satisfaction
'sodo *a* hard; *fig* firm; (*sodo*) hard-boiled ● *adv* hard; **dormire ~** sleep soundly ● *nm* **venire al ~** get to the point
sofà *nm inv* sofa
soffe'rente *a* (*malato*) ill
soffe'renza *nf* suffering
soffer'marsi *vr* pause; **~ su** dwell on
sof'ferto *pp di* **soffrire**
soffi'are *vt* blow; reveal (*segreto*); (*rubare*) pinch *fam* ● *vi* blow
soffi'ata *nf* **datti una ~ al naso** blow your nose; **fare una ~ a qcno** *fig sl* tip sb off, give sb a tip-off

'**soffice** *a* soft

soffi'etto *nm* bellows; **a ~** ⟨*borsa*⟩ expanding. **~ editoriale** blurb

'**soffio** *nm* puff; *Med* murmur

sof'fitta *nf* attic

sof'fitto *nm* ceiling

soffoca'mento *nm* suffocation

soffo'cante *a* suffocating

soffo'care *vt/i* suffocate; *fig* stifle

sof'friggere *vt* fry lightly

sof'frire *vt/i* suffer; ⟨*sopportare*⟩ bear; **~ di** suffer from; **~ di** [**mal di**] **cuore** suffer from *o* have a heart condition

sof'fritto *pp di* **soffriggere** ● *nm* fried ingredients *pl*

sof'fuso *a* ⟨*luce*⟩ soft, suffused

sofisti'care *vt* ⟨*adulterare*⟩ adulterate ● *vi* ⟨*sottilizzare*⟩ quibble

sofisti'cato *a* sophisticated

soft *a* soft

'**softcopy** *nf Comput* soft copy

'**soft-core** *nm* softcore, soft porn ● *a inv* **pornografia ~** soft porn

'**software** *nm inv* software; **dei ~** software packages. **~ di accesso** access software. **~ applicativo** application software. **~ di autoapprendimento** tutorial package, tutorial software. **~ di comunicazione** communications software, comms software. **~ didattico** educational software. **~ di gestione errori** error correction software. **~ di OCR** OCR software. **~ di sistema** system software

softwa'rista *nm Comput* software engineer

soggettiva'mente *adv* subjectively

sogget'tivo *a* subjective

sog'getto *nm* subject; **cattivo ~** bad sort ● *a* subject; **essere ~ a** be subject to

soggezi'one *nf* subjection; ⟨*rispetto*⟩ awe

sogghi'gnare *vi* sneer

sog'ghigno *nm* sneer

soggio'gare *vt* subdue

soggior'nare *vi* stay

soggi'orno *nm* stay; ⟨*stanza*⟩ living room; **permesso di ~** residence permit

soggi'ungere *vt* add

'**soglia** *nf* threshold; **alle soglie di qcsa** on the threshold of sth. **~ del dolore** pain threshold

'**sogliola** *nf* sole. **~ limanda** lemon sole

so'gnare *vt/i* dream; **~ a occhi aperti** daydream; **non te lo sogni neppure!** forget it!, don't even think of it!

so'gnarsi *vr* dream

sogna|'**tore, -'trice** *nmf* dreamer

'**sogno** *nm* dream; **fare un ~** have a dream; **neanche per ~!** not on your life!; **essere un ~** ⟨*bellissimo*⟩ be a dream; **il mio ~ nel cassetto** my secret dream

'**soia** *nf* soya

sol *nm Mus* ⟨*chiave, nota*⟩ G

so'laio *nm* attic

sola'mente *adv* only

so'lare *a* ⟨*energia, raggi*⟩ solar; ⟨*crema*⟩ sun *attrib*

so'larium *nm inv* solarium

sol'care *vt* plough

'**solco** *nm* furrow; ⟨*di ruota*⟩ track; ⟨*di nave*⟩ wake; ⟨*di disco*⟩ groove

sol'dato *nm* soldier. **~ semplice** private

'**soldo** *nm* **non ha un ~** he hasn't got a penny to his name; **senza un ~** penniless; **al ~ di** in the pay of; **soldi** *pl* ⟨*denaro*⟩ money *sg*; **fare** [**i**] **soldi** make money; **prelevare dei soldi** withdraw money; **da quattro soldi** cheapo, nickel-and-dime *Am*

'**sole** *nm* sun; ⟨*luce del sole*⟩ sun[light]; **al ~** in the sun; **prendere il ~** sunbathe

sole'cismo *nm* solecism

soleggi'ato *a* sunny

so'lenne *a* solemn

solennità *nf* solemnity

so'lere *vi* be in the habit of; **come si suol dire** as they say

so'letta *nf* insole

sol'fato *nm* sulphate

sol'feggio *nm* solfa

'**solfuro** *nm* sulphur

soli'dale *a* in agreement

solidarietà *nf* solidarity

solidifi'care *vt/i* solidify

solidifi'carsi *vr* solidify

solidità *nf* solidity; ⟨*di colori*⟩ fastness

'**solido** *a* solid; ⟨*robusto*⟩ sturdy; ⟨*colore*⟩ fast; **in ~** *Jur* jointly and severally ● *nm* solid

soli'loquio *nm* soliloquy

so'lista *a* solo ● *nmf* soloist

solita'mente *adv* usually

soli'tario *a* solitary; ⟨*isolato*⟩ lonely ● *nm* ⟨*brillante*⟩ solitaire; ⟨*gioco di carte*⟩ patience, solitaire

'**solito** *a* usual; **essere ~ fare qcsa** be in the habit of doing sth ● *nm* the usual; **di ~** usually

soli'tudine *nf* solitude

solleci'tare *vt* speed up; urge ⟨*persona*⟩

sollecitazi'one *nf* ⟨*richiesta*⟩ request; ⟨*preghiera*⟩ entreaty

sol'lecito *a* prompt ● *nm* reminder

solleci'tudine *nf* promptness; ⟨*interessamento*⟩ concern; **con la massima ~** *Comm* as soon as possible

solle'one *nm* noonday sun; ⟨*periodo*⟩ dog days of summer

solleti'care *vt* tickle

sol'letico *nm* tickling; **fare il ~ a qcno** tickle sb; **soffrire il ~** be ticklish

solleva'mento *nm* **~ pesi** weightlifting

solle'vare *vt* lift; ⟨*elevare*⟩ raise; ⟨*confortare*⟩ comfort; **~ una questione** raise a question; **~ qcno da un incarico** relieve sb of a responsibility

solle'varsi *vr* rise; ⟨*riaversi*⟩ recover

solle'vato *a* relieved

solli'evo *nm* relief; **che ~!** what a relief!

'**solo, -a** *a* alone; ⟨*isolato*⟩ lonely; ⟨*unico*⟩ only; *Mus* solo; **da ~** by myself/yourself/himself etc ● *nmf* **il ~, la sola** the only one ● *nm Mus* solo ● *adv* only; **~ il sabato/la**

domenica Saturdays/Sundays only, only on Saturdays/Sundays
sol'stizio *nm* solstice
sol'tanto *adv* only
so'lubile *a* soluble; ⟨*caffè*⟩ instant
soluzi'one *nf* solution; *Comm* payment; **senza ~ di continuità** without interruption; **in unica ~** *Comm* as a lump sum. **~ salina per lenti** soaking solution
sol'vente *nm* solvent. **~ per lo smalto** nail varnish remover. **~ per unghie** nail polish remover ● *a* solvent; **reparto ~** pay ward
solvibilità *nf Fin* solvency
'**soma** *nf* load; **bestia da ~** beast of burden
'**somalo, -a** *a & nmf* Somali
so'maro *nm* ass, donkey; *Sch* dunce
so'matico *a* somatic; **tratti somatici** physical features
somatiz'zare *vt* react psychosomatically to
som'brero *nm* sombrero
somigli'ante *a* similar
somigli'anza *nf* resemblance
somigli'are *vi* ~ **a** look like, resemble; **chi si somiglia si piglia** birds of a feather flock together
somigli'arsi *vr* be alike
'**somma** *nf* sum; *Math* addition
som'mare *vt* add; ⟨*totalizzare*⟩ add up
sommaria'mente *adv* summarily
som'mario *a & nm* summary
som'mato *a* **tutto ~** all things considered
somme'lier *nm inv* wine waiter
som'mergere *vt* submerge
sommer'gibile *nm* submarine
som'merso *pp di* **sommegere** ● *nm Econ* black economy
som'messo *a* soft
sommini'strare *vt* administer
somministrazi'one *nf* administration; **~ per via orale** to be taken orally
sommità *nf inv* summit
'**sommo** *a* highest; *fig* supreme ● *nm* summit
som'mossa *nf* rising
sommozza'tore *nm* frogman
so'naglio *nm* bell
'**sonar** *nm* sonar
so'nata *nf* sonata; *fig fam* beating
'**sonda** *nf Mech* drill; ⟨*spaziale, Med*⟩ probe
son'daggio *nm* drilling; ⟨*spaziale, Med*⟩ probe; ⟨*indagine*⟩ survey. **~ d'opinioni** opinion poll
son'dare *vt* sound; ⟨*investigare*⟩ probe
so'netto *nm* sonnet
sonnambu'lismo *nm* sleepwalking
son'nambulo, -a *nmf* sleepwalker
sonnecchi'are *vi* doze
son'nifero *nm* sleeping-pill
'**sonno** *nm* sleep; **aver ~** be sleepy; **morire di ~** be dead tired, be dead on one's feet; **morto di ~** ⟨*fam: stupido*⟩ zombie; **perdere il ~** *anche fig* lose sleep. **~ eterno** *Relig* eternal rest
sonno'lenza *nf* sleepiness
'**sono** *vedi* **essere**

sonoriz'zare *vt* add a soundtrack to
so'noro *a* resonant; ⟨*rumoroso*⟩ loud; ⟨*onde, scheda*⟩ sound *attrib* ● *nm* (*Tech:* di film) soundtrack
sontu'oso *a* sumptuous
sopo'rifero *a* soporific
sop'palco *nm* platform
soppe'rire *vi* ~ **a qcsa** provide for sth
soppe'sare *vt* weigh up ⟨*situazione*⟩
soppi'atto: **di ~** *adv* furtively
soppor'tare *vt* support; ⟨*tollerare*⟩ stand; bear ⟨*dolore*⟩
sopportazi'one *nf* patience
soppressi'one *nf* removal; ⟨*di legge*⟩ abolition; ⟨*di diritti, pubblicazione*⟩ suppression; ⟨*annullamento*⟩ cancellation
sop'presso *pp di* **sopprimere**
sop'primere *vt* get rid of; abolish ⟨*legge*⟩; suppress ⟨*diritti, pubblicazione*⟩; ⟨*annullare*⟩ cancel
'**sopra** *adv* on top; ⟨*più in alto*⟩ higher [up]; ⟨*al piano superiore*⟩ upstairs; ⟨*in testo*⟩ above; **mettilo lì ~** put it up there; **di ~** upstairs; **dormirci ~** *fig* sleep on it; **pensarci ~** think about it; **vedi ~** see above ● *prep* ~ **[a]** on; ⟨*senza contatto, oltre*⟩ over; ⟨*riguardo a*⟩ about; **è ~ al tavolo, è ~ il tavolo** it's on the table; **il quadro è appeso ~ al camino** the picture is hanging over the fireplace; **il ponte passa ~ all'autostrada** the bridge crosses over the motorway; **è caduto ~ il tetto** it fell on the roof; **l'uno sopra l'altro** one on top of the other; ⟨*senza contatto*⟩ one above the other; **abita ~ di me** he lives upstairs from me; **i bambini ~ i dieci anni** children over ten; **20° ~ lo zero** 20° above zero; **~ il livello del mare** above sea level; **rifletti ~ quello che è successo** think about what happened; **prendere ~ di sé la responsabilità di qcsa** assume responsibility for sth; **scaricare la colpa ~ qcno** put the blame on sb; **non ha nessuno ~ di sé** he has nobody above him; **al di ~ di** over; **al di ~ di ogni sospetto** beyond suspicion ● *nm* **il [di] ~** the top
so'prabito *nm* overcoat
soprac'ciglio *nm* (*pl nf* **sopracciglia**) eyebrow
sopracco'perta *nf* ⟨*di letto*⟩ bedspread; ⟨*di libro*⟩ [dust-]jacket
sopraccoper'tina *nf* book jacket
soprad'detto *a* above-mentioned
sopraele'vare *vt* raise
sopraele'vata *nf* elevated railway
sopraele'vato *a* raised
sopraf'fare *vt* overwhelm
sopraf'fatto *pp di* **sopraffare**
sopraffazi'one *nf* abuse of power
sopraf'fino *a* excellent; ⟨*gusto, udito*⟩ highly refined
sopraggi'ungere *vi* ⟨*persona:*⟩ turn up; ⟨*accadere*⟩ happen; **è sopraggiunta la pioggia** and then it started to rain
soprallu'ogo *nm* inspection
sopram'mobile *nm* ornament

soprannatu'rale *a & nm* supernatural

sopran'nome *nm* nickname

soprannomi'nare *vt* nickname

sopran'numero *adv* **sono in ~** there are too many of them; **ce ne sono 15 in ~** there are 15 too many of them, there are 15 of them too many

so'prano *nmf* soprano

soprappensi'ero *adv* lost in thought

sopras'salto *nm* **di ~** with a start

soprasse'dere *vi* **~ a** postpone

soprat'tassa *nf* surtax. **~ postale** excess postage

soprat'tenda *nm* fly sheet

soprat'tetto *nm* fly sheet

soprat'tutto *adv* above all

sopravvalu'tare *vt* overvalue; overestimate ⟨*forze*⟩

sopravvalutazi'one *nf* overvaluation; (*di forze*) overestimation

sopravve'nire *vi* turn up; (*accadere*) happen

soprav'vento *nm fig* upper hand; **prendere il ~** take the upper hand

sopravvis'suto, -a *pp di* **sopravvivere** ● *nmf* survivor

sopravvi'venza *nf* survival

soprav'vivere *vi* survive; **~ a** outlive ⟨*persona*⟩

soprinten'dente *nmf* supervisor; (*di museo ecc*) keeper

soprinten'denza *nf* supervision; (*ente*) board

so'pruso *nm* abuse of power

soq'quadro *nm* **mettere a ~** turn upside down

sor'betto *nm* sorbet

sor'bire *vt* sip; *fig* put up with

'sorcio *nm* mouse; **far vedere i sorci verdi a qcno** give sb a rough time

'sordido *a* sordid; (*avaro*) stingy

sor'dina *nf* mute; **in ~** *fig* on the quiet

sordità *nf* deafness

'sordo, -a *a* deaf; ⟨*rumore, dolore*⟩ dull ● *nmf* deaf person

sordo'muto, -a *a* deaf-and-dumb ● *nmf* deaf mute

so'rella *nf* sister. **~ gemella** twin sister

sorel'lastra *nf* stepsister

sor'gente *nf* spring; (*fonte*) source; **programma ~** *Comput* source program

'sorgere *vi* rise; *fig* arise

sormon'tare *vt* surmount

sorni'one *a* sly

sorpas'sare *vt* surpass; (*eccedere*) exceed; overtake, pass *Am* ⟨*veicolo*⟩

sorpas'sato *a* old-fashioned

sor'passo *nm* overtaking, passing *Am*

sorpren'dente *a* surprising; (*straordinario*) remarkable

sorprendente'mente *adv* surprisingly

sor'prendere *vt* surprise; (*cogliere in flagrante*) catch

sor'prendersi *vr* be surprised; **~ a fare**

qcsa catch oneself doing sth; **non c'è da ~** it's hardly surprising

sor'presa *nf* surprise; **di ~** by surprise; **provare ~** feel surprised

sor'preso *pp di* **sorprendere**

sor'reggere *vt* support; (*tenere*) hold up

sor'reggersi *vr* support oneself

sor'retto *pp di* **sorreggere**

sorri'dente *a* smiling

sor'ridere *vi* smile; **la fortuna mi ha sorriso** fortune smiled on me

sor'riso *pp di* **sorridere** ● *nm* smile

sorseggi'are *vt* sip

'sorso *nm* sip; (*piccola quantità*) drop

'sorta *nf* sort; **di ~** whatever; **ogni ~ di** all sorts of

'sorte *nf* fate; (*caso imprevisto*) chance; **tirare a ~** draw lots; **per buona ~** *liter* by good fortune

sorteggi'are *vt* draw lots for

sor'teggio *nm* draw

sorti'legio *nm* witchcraft

sor'tire *vi* come out ● *vt* bring about ⟨*effetto*⟩

sor'tita *nf Mil* sortie; (*battuta*) witticism

'sorto *pp di* **sorgere**

sorvegli'ante *nmf* keeper; (*controllore*) overseer

sorvegli'anza *nf* watch; *Mil ecc* surveillance

sorvegli'are *vt* watch over; (*controllare*) oversee; ⟨*polizia:*⟩ watch, keep under surveillance

sorvegli'ato, -a *a* under surveillance ● *nmf* **~ speciale** person kept under special surveillance

sorvo'lare *vt* fly over; *fig* skip

SOS *nm* SOS

'sosia *nm inv* double

so'spendere *vt* hang; (*interrompere*) stop; (*privare di una carica*) suspend

sospensi'one *nf* suspension

sospen'sorio *nm Sport* jockstrap

so'speso *pp di* **sospendere** ● *a* ⟨*impiegato, alunno*⟩ suspended; **~ a** hanging from; **~ a un filo** *fig* hanging by a thread ● *nm* **in ~** pending; (*emozionato*) in suspense

sospet'tare *vt* suspect

so'spetto *a* suspicious ● *nm* suspicion; (*persona*) suspect; **al di sopra di ogni ~** above suspicion

sospet'toso *a* suspicious

so'spingere *vt* drive

so'spinto *pp di* **sospingere**

sospi'rare *vi* sigh ● *vt* long for

so'spiro *nm* sigh

'sosta *nf* stop; (*pausa*) pause; **senza ~** nonstop; **'divieto di ~'** 'no parking'; **'~ autorizzata...'** 'parking permitted for...'

sostan'tivo *nm* noun

so'stanza *nf* substance; **sostanze** *pl* (*patrimonio*) property *sg*; **in ~** to sum up; **la ~ della questione** the nub of the matter

sostanzi'oso *a* substantial; ⟨*cibo*⟩ nourishing; **poco ~** insubstantial

so'stare *vi* stop; (*fare una pausa*) pause

so'stegno *nm* support. **~ morale** moral support

soste'nere *vt* support; (*sopportare*) bear; (*resistere*) withstand; (*affermare*) maintain; (*nutrire*) sustain; sit ‹*esame*›; **~ le spese** meet the costs; **~ delle spese** incur expenditure; **~ una carica** hold a position; **~ una parte** play a role

soste'nersi *vr* support oneself

sosteni'|tore, -'trice *nmf* supporter

sostenta'mento *nm* maintenance

soste'nuto *a* ‹*stile*› formal; ‹*velocità*› high; ‹*mercato, prezzi*› steady ● *nm* **fare il ~** be stand-offish

sostitu'ire *vt* substitute (**a** for), replace (**con** with)

sostitu'irsi *vr* **~ a** replace

sosti'tuto, -a *nmf* replacement, stand-in ● *nm* (*surrogato*) substitute

sostituzi'one *nf* substitution

sotta'ceto *a* pickled; **sottaceti** *pl* pickles

sot'tacqua *adv* underwater

sot'tana *nf* petticoat; (*di prete*) cassock

sotter'fugio *nm* subterfuge; **di ~** secretly

sotter'raneo *a* underground ● *nm* cellar

sotter'rare *vt* bury

sottigli'ezza *nf* slimness; *fig* subtlety

sot'tile *a* thin; ‹*udito, odorato*› keen; ‹*osservazione, distinzione*› subtle

sotti'letta® *nf* cheese slice

sottiliz'zare *vi* split hairs

sottin'tendere *vt* imply

sottin'teso *pp di* **sottintendere** ● *nm* allusion; **senza sottintesi** openly ● *a* implied

'sotto *adv* below; (*più in basso*) lower [down]; (*al di sotto*) underneath; (*al piano di sotto*) downstairs; **è lì ~** it's underneath; **~ ~** deep down; (*di nascosto*) on the quiet; **di ~** downstairs; **mettersi ~** *fig* get down to it; **mettere ~** (*fam: investire*) knock down; **fatti ~!** *fam* get stuck in! ● *prep* **~ [a]** under; (*al di sotto di*) under[neath]; **il fiume passa ~ un ponte** the river passes under[neath] a bridge; **è ~ il tavolo, è ~ al tavolo** it's under[neath] the table; **abita ~ di me** he lives downstairs from me; **i bambini ~ i dieci anni** children under ten; **20°. ~ zero** 20° below zero; **~ il livello del mare** below sea level; **~ la pioggia** in the rain; **~ Elisabetta I** under Elizabeth I; **~ calmante** under sedation; **~ chiave** under lock and key; **~ condizione che...** on condition that...; **~ giuramento** under oath; **~ sorveglianza** under surveillance; **~ Natale/gli esami** around Christmas/exam time; **al di ~ di** under; **andare ~ i 50 all'ora** do less than 50km an hour ● *nm* **il [di] ~** the bottom

sotto'banco *adv* ‹*vendere, comprare*› under the counter

sottobicchi'ere *nm* coaster

sotto'bosco *nm* undergrowth

sotto'braccio *adv* arm in arm

sottoccu'pato *a* underemployed

sottochi'ave *adv* under lock and key

sotto'costo *a* & *adv* at less than cost price

sottodi'rectory *nf* Comput subdirectory

sottoe'sporre *vt* underexpose

sotto'fondo *nm* background

sotto'gamba *adv* **prendere qcsa ~** take sth lightly

sotto'gonna *nf* underskirt

sottoindi'cato *a* undermentioned

sottoinsi'eme *nm* Math subset

sottoline'are *vt* underline; *fig* underline ‹*importanza*›; emphasize ‹*forma degli occhi ecc*›

sot'tolio *adv* in oil

sotto'mano *adv* within reach

sottoma'rino *a* & *nm* submarine

sotto'messo *pp di* **sottomettere** ● *a* (*remissivo*) submissive

sotto'mettere *vt* submit; subdue ‹*popolo*›

sotto'mettersi *vr* submit

sottomissi'one *nf* submission

sottopa'gare *vt* underpay

sottopas'saggio *nm* underpass; (*pedonale*) subway

sottopi'atto *nm* place mat

sotto'porre *vt* submit; (*costringere*) subject

sotto'porsi *vr* submit oneself; **~ a** undergo

sotto'posto *pp di* **sottoporre**

sottoproletari'ato *nm* underclass

sotto'scala *nm* cupboard under the stairs

sotto'scritto *pp di* **sottoscrivere** ● *nm* undersigned

sotto'scrivere *vt* sign; (*approvare*) sanction, subscribe to

sottoscrizi'one *nf* (*petizione*) petition; (*approvazione*) sanction; (*raccolta di denaro*) appeal

sottosegre'tario *nm* undersecretary

sotto'sopra *adv* upside-down

sotto'stante *a* **la strada ~** the road below

sottosu'olo *nm* subsoil

sottosvilup'pato *a* underdeveloped

sottosvi'luppo *nm* underdevelopment

sottote'nente *nm* second lieutenant; Naut sub-lieutenant

sotto'terra *adv* underground

sotto'titolo *nm* subtitle

sottovalu'tare *vt* underestimate

sotto'vento *adv* downwind

sotto'veste *nf* slip

sotto'voce *adv* in a low voice

sottovu'oto *a* vacuum-packed

sotto'zero *a inv* subzero

sot'trarre *vt* remove; embezzle ‹*fondi*›; Math subtract

sot'trarsi *vr* **~ a** escape from; avoid ‹*responsabilità*›

sot'tratto *pp di* **sottrarre**

sottrazi'one *nf* removal; (*di fondi*) embezzlement; Math subtraction

sottuffici'ale *nm* non-commissioned officer; Naut petty officer

sou'brette *nf* showgirl

souf'flé *nm inv* soufflé

souve'nir *nm inv* souvenir; **negozio di ~** souvenir shop

so'vente *adv* liter often

soverchie'ria *nf* bullying; **fare sover-chierie a** bully

so'vietico, -a *a & nmf* Soviet

sovrabbon'danza *nf* overabundance

sovraccari'care *vt* overload

sovrac'carico *a* overloaded (**di** with) ● *nm* overload

sovraffati'carsi *vr* overexert oneself

sovraffolla'mento *nm* overcrowding

sovralimen'tare *vt* overfeed

sovrannatu'rale *a & nm* = **sopran-naturale**

sovrannazio'nale *a* supranational

so'vrano, -a *a* sovereign; *fig* supreme ● *nmf* sovereign

sovrappopo'lato *a* overpopulated

sovrap'porre *vt* superimpose

sovrap'porsi *vr* overlap

sovrapposizi'one *nf* superimposition

sovrapro'fitto *nm* excess profits

sovra'stare *vt* dominate; ⟨*fig: pericolo:*⟩ hang over

sovrastrut'tura *nf* superstructure

sovratensi'one *nf* Electr overload, over-tension

sovrecci'tarsi *vr* get overexcited

sovrecci'tato *a* overexcited

sovresposizi'one *nf Phot* overexposure

sovrimpressi'one *nf Phot* double expo-sure

sovrinten'dente, sovrinten'denza = **soprintendente, soprintendenza**

sovru'mano *a* superhuman

sovvenzio'nare *vt* subsidize

sovvenzi'one *nf* subsidy

sovver'sivo, -a *a & nmf* subversive

sovver'tire *vt* subvert

'sozzo *a* filthy

SP *nf abbr* (**strada provinciale**) secondary road

S.p.A. *abbr* (**società per azioni**) plc

spac'care *vt* split; chop ⟨*legna*⟩; **~ il minuto** keep perfect time; **~ il muso a qcno** *sl* smash sb's face in; **o la va o la spacca** it's all or nothing; **un sole che spacca le pietre** a sun hot enough to fry an egg

spac'carsi *vr* split

spacca'tura *nf* split

spacci'are *vt* deal in, push ⟨*droga*⟩; **~ qcsa per qcsa** pass sth off as sth; **essere spacciato** be done for, be a goner

spacci'arsi *vr* **~ per** pass oneself off as

spaccia'tore, -'trice *nmf* (*di droga*) pusher; (*di denaro falso*) distributor of forged bank notes

'spaccio *nm* (*di droga*) dealer, pusher; (*negozio*) shop

'spacco *nm* split

spacco'nate *nfpl* blustering

spac'cone, -a *nmf* boaster

'spada *nf* sword

spadac'cino *nm* swordsman

spadroneggi'are *vi* act the boss

spae'sato *a* disorientated

spa'ghetti *nmpl* spaghetti *sg.* **~ in bianco**

spaghetti with butter, oil and cheese. **~ alla carbonara** *spaghetti with egg, cheese and diced bacon.* **~ al sugo** *spaghetti with a sauce*

spa'ghetto *nm* (*fam: spavento*) fright

'Spagna *nf* Spain

spagno'letta *nf* spool

spa'gnolo, -a *a* Spanish ● *nmf* Spaniard ● *nm* (*lingua*) Spanish

'spago *nm* string; (*fam: spavento*) fright; **dare ~ a qcno** encourage sb

spai'ato *a* odd

spalan'care *vt* open wide

spalan'carsi *vr* open wide

spalan'cato *a* wide open

spa'lare *vt* shovel

'spalla *nf* shoulder; (*di comico*) straight man; **spalle** *pl* (*schiena*) back; **alzata di spalle** shrug [of the shoulders]; **alle spalle di** be-hind; **alle spalle di qcno** ⟨*ridere*⟩ behind sb's back; **avere qnco/qcsa alle spalle** have sb/sth behind one; **di ~** ⟨*violino ecc*⟩ sec-ond; **vivere alle spalle di qcno** live off sb; **con le spalle al muro** *anche fig* with one's back to the wall; **voltare le spalle** turn one's back

spal'lata *nf* push with the shoulder; (*alzata di spalle*) shrug [of the shoulders]

spalleggi'are *vt* back up

spal'letta *nf* parapet

spalli'era *nf* back; (*di letto*) headboard; (*ginnastica*) wall bars *pl*

spal'lina *nf* strap; (*imbottitura*) shoulder pad; **senza spalline** strapless

spal'mare *vt* spread

spal'marsi *vr* cover oneself

spa'nato *a* ⟨*vite*⟩ threadless

spanci'ata *nf* belly flop

'spandere *vt* spread; (*versare*) spill; **spendere e ~** spend and spend

'spandersi *vr* spread

spandighi'aia *nm inv* gritter

'spaniel *nm inv* spaniel

spappo'lare *vt* crush

spa'rare *vt/i* shoot; **spararle grosse** talk big; **~ fandonie** talk nonsense

spa'rarsi *vr* shoot oneself; **si è sparato un colpo di pistola alla tempia** he shot him-self in the temple

spa'rata *nf fam* tall story

spa'rato *nm* (*della camicia*) dicky

spara'toria *nf* shooting

sparecchi'are *vt* clear

spa'reggio *nm Comm* deficit; *Sport* play-off

'spargere *vt* scatter; (*diffondere*) spread; shed ⟨*lacrime, sangue*⟩

'spargersi *vr* spread

spargi'mento *nm* scattering; (*di lacrime, sangue*) shedding; **~ di sangue** bloodshed

spa'rire *vi* disappear; **sparisci!** get lost!, scram!

sparizi'one *nf* disappearance

spar'lare *vi* **~ di** run down

'sparo *nm* shot

sparpagli'are *vt* scatter

sparpagli'arsi *vr* scatter

sparpagli'ato *a* far-flung

'sparso *pp di* **spargere** ● *a* scattered; ⟨*sciolto*⟩ loose

sparti'neve *nm inv* snowplough

spar'tire *vt* share out; ⟨*separare*⟩ separate

spar'tirsi *vr* share

spar'tito *nm Mus* score

sparti'traffico *nm inv* traffic island; ⟨*di autostrada*⟩ central reservation, median strip *Am*

spartizi'one *nf* division

spa'ruto *a* gaunt; ⟨*gruppo*⟩ small; ⟨*peli, capelli*⟩ sparse

sparvi'ero *nm* sparrow-hawk

spasi'mante *nm hum* admirer

spasi'mare *vi* suffer agonies; **~ per** be madly in love with

'spasimo *nm* spasm

spa'smodico *a* spasmodic

spas'sarsi *vr* amuse oneself; **spas'sarsela** have a good time

spassio'nato *a* ⟨*osservatore*⟩ dispassionate, impartial

'spasso *nm* fun; **essere uno ~** be hilarious; **andare a ~** go for a walk; **essere a ~** be out of work

spas'soso *a* hilarious

'spastico *a* spastic

'spatola *nf* spatula

spau'racchio *nm* scarecrow; *fig* bugbear

spau'rire *vt* frighten

spa'valdo *a* defiant

spaventa'passeri *nm inv* scarecrow

spaven'tare *vt* frighten, scare

spaven'tarsi *vr* be frightened, be scared

spa'vento *nm* fright; **brutto da fare ~** incredibly ugly

spaven'toso *a* frightening; ⟨*fam: enorme*⟩ incredible

spazi'ale *a* spatial; ⟨*cosmico*⟩ space *attrib*

spazi'are *vt* space out ● *vi* range

spazien'tirsi *vr* lose [one's] patience

'spazio *nm* space. **~ aereo** airspace. **~ indietro** *Comput* backspace. **~ di tempo** period of time. **~ vitale** elbowroom

spazi'oso *a* spacious

spazio-tempo'rale *a* spatiotemporal

spazzaca'mino *nm* chimney sweep

spazza'neve *nm inv* ⟨*anche sci*⟩ snowplough

spaz'zare *vt* sweep; **~ via** sweep away; ⟨*fam: mangiare*⟩ devour

spazza'trice *nf* sweeper

spazza'tura *nf* ⟨*immondizia*⟩ rubbish

spaz'zino *nm* road sweeper; ⟨*netturbino*⟩ dustman

'spazzola *nf* brush; ⟨*di tergicristallo*⟩ blade; **capelli a ~** crew cut

spazzo'lare *vt* brush

spazzo'larsi *vr* **~ i capelli** brush one's hair

spazzo'lino *nm* small brush. **~ da denti** toothbrush. **~ per le unghie** nailbrush

spazzo'lone *nm* scrubbing brush

'speaker *nm inv Radio, TV* announcer

specchi'arsi *vr* look at oneself in a/the mirror; ⟨*riflettersi*⟩ be mirrored; **~ in qcno** model oneself on sb

specchi'ato *a di* **specchiata onestà** of spotless integrity

specchi'etto *nm* small mirror. **~ laterale** wing mirror. **~ retrovisore** driving mirror, rear-view mirror

'specchio *nm* mirror

speci'ale *a* special ● *nm TV* special [programme]

specia'lista *nmf* specialist

specialità *nf inv* speciality, specialty

specializ'zare *vt* specialize

specializ'zarsi *vr* specialize

specializ'zato *a* ⟨*operaio*⟩ skilled; **siamo specializzati in...** we specialize in...

special'mente *adv* especially

'specie *nf* ⟨*scientifico*⟩ species; ⟨*tipo*⟩ kind; **fare ~ a** surprise; **in ~** especially

specifi'care *vt* specify

specificata'mente *adv* specifically

spe'cifico *a* specific

speci'oso *a* specious

specu'lare *vi* speculate; **~ su** ⟨*indagare*⟩ speculate on; *Fin* speculate in

specu'lare *a* mirror *attrib*

specula'tivo *a* speculative

specula'tore *nm* speculator

speculazi'one *nf* speculation

spe'dire *vt* send; **~ per posta** mail, post *Br*; **~ qcno all'altro mondo** send sb to meet his/ her maker

spe'dito *pp di* **spedire** ● *a* quick; ⟨*parlata*⟩ fluent

spedizi'one *nf* ⟨*di lettere ecc*⟩ dispatch; *Comm* consignment, shipment; ⟨*scientifica*⟩ expedition

spedizioni'ere *nm Comm* freight forwarder

'spegnere *vt* put out; turn off, switch off ⟨*motore, luce, televisione*⟩; turn off ⟨*gas*⟩; quench, slake ⟨*sete*⟩

'spegnersi *vr* go out; ⟨*morire*⟩ pass away

spegni'mento *nm* standby

spelacchi'ato *a* ⟨*tappeto*⟩ threadbare; ⟨*cane*⟩ mangy

spe'lare *vt* remove the fur of ⟨*coniglio*⟩

spe'larsi *vr* ⟨*cane, tappeto:*⟩ moult; ⟨*persona:*⟩ peel

speleolo'gia *nf* potholing, speleology

spel'lare *vt* skin; *fig* fleece

spel'larsi *vr* ⟨*serpente:*⟩ shed its skin; ⟨*per il sole*⟩ peel; **mi sono spellato un ginocchio** I grazed *or* skinned my knee

spe'lonca *nf* cave; *fig* dingy hole

spendacci'one, -a *nmf* spendthrift

'spendere *vt* spend; **~ fiato** waste one's breath

spen'nare *vt* pluck; *fam* fleece ⟨*cliente*⟩

spennel'lare *vt* brush ● *vi* paint

spensierata'mente *adv* blithely

spensiera'tezza *nf* lightheartedness

spensie'rato *a* lighthearted, carefree

'spento *pp di* **spegnere** ● *a* off; ⟨*gas*⟩ out; ⟨*smorto*⟩ dull; ⟨*vulcano*⟩ extinct

spenzo'lare *vt* dangle

spe'ranza *nf* hope; **pieno di** ~ hopeful; **senza** ~ hopeless

spe'rare *vt* hope for; *(aspettarsi)* expect ● *vi* ~ **in** trust in; **spero di sì** I hope so

'sperdersi *vr* get lost

sper'duto *a* lost; *(isolato)* secluded

spergiu'rare *vi* commit perjury

spergi'uro, -a *nmf* perjurer ● *nm* perjury

sperico'lato *a* swashbuckling

sperimen'tale *a* experimental

sperimen'tare *vt* experiment with; test ⟨*resistenza, capacità, teoria*⟩

sperimen'tato *a* ⟨*metodo*⟩ tried and tested

sperimentazi'one *nf* experimentation; ~ **sugli animali** animal testing

'sperma *nm* sperm

spermi'cida *a* spermicidal ● *nm* spermicide

spero'nare *vt* ram

spe'rone *nm* spur

sperpe'rare *vt* squander

'sperpero *nm* waste, squandering

spersonaliz'zare *vt* depersonalize

spersonaliz'zarsi *vr* become depersonalized

spersonalizzazi'one *nf* depersonalization

'spesa *nf* expense; *(acquisto)* purchase; **andare a far spese** go shopping; **fare la** ~ do the shopping; **fare le spese di** pay for; **a proprie spese** at one's own expense. **spese** *pl* **bancarie** bank charges. **spese** *pl* **di capitale** capital expenditure. **spese** *pl* **a carico del destinatario** carriage forward. **spese** *pl* **di esercizio** business expenses. **spese** *pl* **extra** out-of-pocket expenses. **spese** *pl* **di gestione** operating costs. **spese** *pl* **di spedizione** shipping costs. **spese** *pl* **di viaggio** travel expenses

spe'sare *vt* pay expenses for; **spesato della ditta** paid for by the company, on the company

spe'sato *a* all-expenses-paid

'speso *pp di* **spendere**

'spesso¹ *a* thick

'spesso² *adv* often

spes'sore *nm* thickness; *(fig: consistenza)* substance

spet'tabile *a* (*Comm abbr* **Spett.**) **S~ ditta Rossi** Messrs Rossi

spettaco'lare *a* spectacular

spet'tacolo *nm* spectacle; *(rappresentazione)* show; **dare** ~ **di sé** make a spectacle *o* an exhibition of oneself; **il mondo dello** ~ show business. ~ **di burattini** Punch-and-Judy show

spettaco'loso *a* spectacular

spet'tanza *nf* concern

spet'tare *vi* ~ **a** be up to; ⟨*diritto:*⟩ be due to

spetta'tore, -'trice *nmf* spectator; **spettatori** *pl (di cinema ecc)* audience *sg*

spettego'lare *vi* gossip

spetti'nare *vt* ~ **qcno** ruffle sb's hair

spetti'narsi *vr* ruffle one's hair

spet'trale *a* ghostly

'spettro *nm* ghost; *(fig: della fame)* spectre; *Phys* spectrum; **ad ampio** ~ ⟨*medicina*⟩ broad-spectrum

spezi'are *vt* add spices to, spice

spezi'ato *a* spicy

'spezie *nfpl* spices

spez'zare *vt* break

spez'zarsi *vr* break

spezza'tino *nm* stew

spez'zato *a* broken ● *nm* coordinated jacket and trousers

spezzet'tare *vt* break into small pieces

spez'zone *nm Cinema* clip, footage *no pl*; *(bomba)* cluster bomb

'spia *nf* spy; *(della polizia)* informer; *(di porta)* peep-hole; **fare la** ~ sneak. ~ **di accensione** power-on light. ~ **di attività dell'hard disk** *Comput* hard disk activity light. ~ **della benzina** petrol gauge. ~ **[luminosa]** light. ~ **dell'olio** oil [warning] light

spiacci'care *vt* squash

spia'cente *a* sorry

spia'cevole *a* unpleasant

spi'aggia *nf* beach

spia'nare *vt* level; *(rendere liscio)* smooth; roll out ⟨*pasta*⟩; raze to the ground ⟨*edificio*⟩

spia'nata *nf* flat ground

spi'ano *nm* **a tutto** ~ flat out

spian'tato *a fig* penniless

spi'are *vt* spy on; wait for ⟨*occasione ecc*⟩

spiattel'lare *vt* blurt out; shove ⟨*oggetto*⟩

spiaz'zare *vt* wrong-foot

spi'azzo *nm (radura)* clearing

spic'care *vt* ~ **un salto** jump; ~ **il volo** take flight ● *vi* stand out

spic'cato *a* marked

'spicchio *nm (di agrumi)* segment; *(di aglio)* clove

spicci'arsi *vr* hurry up

spiccia'tivo *a* speedy

'spiccio *a* no-nonsense

'spiccioli *nmpl* change

'spicciolo *a (comune)* banal; ⟨*denaro,* 10 000 *lire*⟩ in change

'spicco *nm* relief; **fare** ~ stand out; **di** ~ high-profile

'spider *nmf inv* open-top sports car

spie'dino *nm* kebab

spi'edo *nm* spit; **allo** ~ on a spit, spit-roasted

spiega'mento *nm* deployment

spie'gare *vt* explain; open out ⟨*cartina*⟩; unfurl ⟨*vele*⟩

spie'garsi *vr* explain oneself; ⟨*vele, bandiere:*⟩ unfurl; **non so se mi spiego** need I say more?; **mi sono spiegato?** *(minaccia)* do I make myself clear?; **non riesco a spiegarmi come...** I can't understand how...

spie'gato *a (ale)* outspread; **a sirene spiegate** with sirens blaring; **a voce spiegata** at the top of one's voice; **a vele spiegate** under full sail, with all sails in the wind

spiegazi'one *nf* explanation; **venire a una ~ con qcno** sort things out with sb

spiegaz'zare *vt* crumple

spiegaz'zato *a* crumpled

spieta'tezza *nf* ruthlessness

spie'tato *a* ruthless

spiffe'rare *vt* blurt out ● *vi* ⟨*vento:*⟩ whistle

'spiffero *nm* (*corrente d'aria*) draught

'spiga *nf* spike; *Bot* ear

spi'gato *a* herringbone

spigli'ato *a* self-possessed

'spigola *nf* sea bass

spigo'lare *vt* glean

'spigolo *nm* edge; (*angolo*) corner

'spilla *nf* (*gioiello*) brooch. **~ da balia** safety pin. **~ di sicurezza** safety pin

spil'lare *vt* tap

'spillo *nm* pin. **~ di sicurezza** safety pin; (*in arma*) safety catch

spil'lone *nm* hatpin

spilluzzi'care *vt* pick at

spi'lorcio, -a *a* stingy ● *nm* miser, skinflint

spilun'gone, -a *nmf* beanpole

'spina *nf* thorn; (*di pesce*) bone; *Electr* plug; **a ~ di pesce** (*tessuto, disegno*) herringbone; ⟨*parcheggio*⟩ in two angled rows; **stare sulle spine** be on tenterhooks. **~ dorsale** spine; **essere una ~ nel fianco** thorn in one's side

spi'naci *nmpl* spinach

spi'nale *a* spinal

spi'nato *a* ⟨*filo*⟩ barbed; ⟨*pianta*⟩ thorny ● *nm* herringbone

spi'nello *nm* (*fam: droga*) joint

'spingere *vt* push; *fig* drive

'spingersi *vr* (*andare*) proceed

spinnaker *nm* spinnaker

spi'noso *a* thorny

spi'notto *nm* *Electr* plug

'spinta *nf* push; (*violenta*) thrust; *fig* spur; **dare una ~ a** qcsa/qcno give sb/sth a push; **farsi largo a spinte** push one's way through

'spinto *pp di* **spingere**

spio'naggio *nm* espionage, spying

spi'one, -a *nmf* tell-tale

spio'vente *a* ⟨*tetto*⟩ sloping ● *nm* slope

spi'overe *vi liter* stop raining; (*ricadere*) fall; (*scorrere*) flow down

'spira *nf* coil

spi'raglio *nm* small opening; (*soffio d'aria*) breath of air; (*raggio di luce*) gleam of light

spi'rale *a* spiral ● *nm* spiral; (*negli orologi*) hairspring; (*anticoncezionale*) coil; **a ~** spiral-shaped

spi'rare *vi* (*soffiare*) blow; (*morire*) pass away

spiri'tato *a* possessed; ⟨*espressione*⟩ wild

spiri'tismo *nm* spiritualism

spiri'tista *nmf* spiritualist

spiri'tistico *a* spiritualist

'spirito *nm* spirit; (*arguzia*) wit; (*intelletto*) mind; **fare dello ~** be witty; **persona di ~** witty person; **sotto ~** in brandy. **~ civico** community spirit. **~ di contraddizione** contrariness. **S~ Santo** Holy Spirit, Holy Ghost

spirito'saggine *nf* witticism

spiri'toso *a* witty

spiritu'ale *a* spiritual

spiritual'mente *adv* spiritually

splen'dente *a* shining

'splendere *vi* shine

'splendido *a* splendid

splen'dore *nm* splendour

spocchia *nf* conceit

spocchi'oso *a* conceited

spode'stare *vt* dispossess; depose ⟨*re*⟩

spoetiz'zare *vt* disenchant

'spoglia *nf* (*di animale*) skin; **spoglie** *pl* (*salma*) mortal remains; (*bottino*) spoils; **sotto false spoglie** under false pretences

spogli'are *vt* strip; (*svestire*) undress; (*fare lo spoglio di*) go through; **~ qcno di un diritto** divest sb of a right

spoglia'rello *nm* strip-tease

spogliarel'lista *nf* strip-tease artist, stripper

spogli'arsi *vr* strip, undress

spoglia'toio *nm* dressing room; *Sport* changing room; (*guardaroba*) cloakroom, checkroom *Am*

'spoglio *a* undressed; ⟨*albero, muro*⟩ bare. **~ di** (*privo*) stripped of ● *nm* (*scrutinio*) perusal

'spoiler *nm inv* *Auto* spoiler

'spola *nf* shuttle; **fare la ~** shuttle

spo'letta *nf* spool

spolmo'narsi *vr* shout oneself hoarse

spol'pare *vt* take the flesh off; *fig* fleece

spolve'rare *vt* dust; *fam* devour ⟨*cibo*⟩

'sponda *nf* (*di mare, lago*) shore; (*di fiume*) bank; (*bordo*) edge

sponsoriz'zare *vt* sponsor

sponsorizzazi'one *nf* sponsorship

spontaneità *nf* spontaneity

spon'taneo *a* spontaneous

'spooling *nm* *Comput* spooling

spopo'lare *vt* depopulate ● *vi* (*avere successo*) draw the crowds

spopo'larsi *vr* become depopulated

'spora *nf* spore

sporadica'mente *adv* sporadically

spo'radico *a* sporadic

sporcacci'one, -a *nmf* dirty pig

spor'care *vt* dirty; (*macchiare*) soil

spor'carsi *vr* get dirty

spor'cizia *nf* dirt

'sporco *a* dirty; **avere la coscienza sporca** have a guilty conscience ● *nm* dirt

spor'gente *a* jutting

spor'genza *nf* projection

'sporgere *vt* stretch out; **~ querela contro** take legal action against ● *vi* jut out

'sporgersi *vr* lean out

sport *nm inv* sport; **fare qcsa per ~** do sth for fun. **~ invernali** *pl* winter sports

'sporta *nf* shopping basket

spor'tello *nm* door; (*di banca ecc*) window. **~ automatico** cash dispenser, cash point. **~ pacchi** parcels counter

spor'tivo, -a *a* sports *attrib*; ⟨*persona*⟩ sporty ● *nm* sportsman ● *nf* sportswoman

'sporto *pp di* **sporgere**

'**sposa** *nf* bride; **dare in** ~ give in marriage, give away; **prendere in** ~ marry

sposa'lizio *nm* wedding

spo'sare *vt* marry; *fig* espouse

spo'sarsi *vr* get married; ⟨*vino:*⟩ go (**con** with)

spo'sato *a* married

spo'sini *nmpl* newly-weds

'**sposo** *nm* bridegroom; **sposi** *pl* [**novelli**] newlyweds

spossa'tezza *nf* exhaustion

spos'sato *a* exhausted, worn out

sposses'sato *a* dispossessed

sposta'mento *nm* displacement. ~ **d'aria** airflow

spo'stare *vt* move; (*differire*) postpone; (*cambiare*) change

spo'starsi *vr* move

spo'stato, -a *a* ill-adjusted ● *nmf* (*disadattato*) misfit

spot *nm inv* ~ [**pubblicitario**] commercial

'**spranga** *nf* bar

spran'gare *vt* bar

'**sprazzo** *nm* (*di colore*) splash; (*di luce*) flash; *fig* glimmer

spre'care *vt* waste

'**spreco** *nm* waste

spre'cone *a* spendthrift

spre'gevole *a* despicable

spregia'tivo *a* pejorative

'**spregio** *nm* contempt; **fare uno** ~ **a qcno** offend sb

spregiudi'cato *a* unprejudiced; *pej* unscrupulous

'**spremere** *vt* squeeze

'**spremersi** *vr* ~ **le meningi** rack one's brains

spremi'aglio *nm inv* garlic press

spremia'grumi *nm inv* lemon squeezer

spremili'moni *nm inv* lemon squeezer

spre'muta *nf* juice. ~ **d'arancia** fresh orange [juice], freshly squeezed orange juice

spre'tato *nm* former priest

sprez'zante *a* contemptuous

sprigio'nare *vt* emit

sprigio'narsi *vr* burst out

sprint *nm* sprint; **fare uno** ~ put on a spurt

spriz'zare *vt/i* spurt; be bursting with ⟨*salute, gioia*⟩

sprofon'dare *vi* sink; (*crollare*) collapse

sprofon'darsi *vr* ~ **in** sink into; *fig* be engrossed in

spron *nm vedi* **sprone**

spro'nare *vt* spur on

'**sprone** *nm* spur; (*sartoria*) yoke; **a spron battuto** instantly; **andare a spron battuto** go hell-for-leather

sproporzio'nato *a* disproportionate

sproporzi'one *nf* disproportion

sproposi'tato *a* full of blunders; (*enorme*) huge

spro'posito *nm* blunder; (*eccesso*) excessive amount; **a** ~ inopportunely

sprovve'duto *a* unprepared; ~ **di** lacking in

sprov'visto *a* ~ **di** out of; lacking in ⟨*fantasia, pazienza*⟩; **alla sprovvista** unexpectedly

spruz'zare *vt* sprinkle; (*vaporizzare*) spray; (*inzaccherare*) spatter

spruzza'tore *nm* spray

'**spruzzo** *nm* spray; (*di fango*) splash

spudorata'mente *adv* shamelessly

spudora'tezza *nf* shamelessness

spudo'rato *a* shameless

'**spugna** *nf* sponge; (*tessuto*) towelling

spu'gnoso *a* spongy

'**spuma** *nf* foam; (*schiuma*) froth; *Culin* mousse

spu'mante *nm* sparkling wine, spumante

spumeggi'ante *a* bubbly; ⟨*mare*⟩ foaming

spumeggi'are *vi* ⟨*champagne:*⟩ bubble; ⟨*birra:*⟩ foam

spun'tare *vt* (*rompere la punta di*) break the point of; trim ⟨*capelli*⟩; **spuntarla** *fig* win ● *vi* ⟨*pianta:*⟩ sprout; ⟨*capelli:*⟩ begin to grow; (*sorgere*) rise; (*apparire*) appear

spun'tarsi *vr* get blunt

spun'tata *nf* trim

spun'tino *nm* snack

'**spunto** *nm* cue; *fig* starting point; **dare** ~ **a** give rise to

spur'gare *vt* purge

spur'garsi *vr Med* expectorate

'**spurio** *a* spurious

spu'tacchio *nm* spittle

spu'tare *vt/i* spit; spit out ⟨*cibo*⟩; ~ **sentenze** pass judgment; ~ **l'osso** *sl* spit it out

'**sputo** *nm* spit

'**squadra** *nf* (*gruppo*) team, squad; (*di polizia ecc*) squad; (*da disegno*) square; **lavoro di** ~ teamwork. ~ **del buoncostume** Vice Squad. ~ **mobile** Flying Squad. ~ **narcotici** Drug Squad. ~ **soccorso** rescue team

squa'drare *vt* square; (*guardare*) look up and down

squa'driglia *nf*, **squadrigli'one** *nm* squadron

squa'drone *nm* squadron

squagli'are *vt* melt

squagli'arsi *vr* melt; **squagliarsela** (*fam: svignarsela*) steal out

squa'lifica *nf* disqualification

squalifi'care *vt* disqualify

'**squallido** *a* squalid

squal'lore *nm* squalor

'**squalo** *nm* shark

'**squama** *nf* scale; (*di pelle*) flake

squa'mare *vt* scale

squa'marsi *vr* ⟨*pelle:*⟩ flake off

squa'moso *a* scaly; ⟨*pelle*⟩ flaky

squarcia'gola: a ~ *adv* at the top of one's voice

squarci'are *vt* rip

'**squarcio** *nm* rip; (*di ferita, in nave*) gash; (*di cielo*) patch

squar'tare *vt* quarter; dismember ⟨*animale*⟩

squarta'tore *nm* **Jack lo** ~ Jack the Ripper

squash *nm inv* squash
squas'sare *vt* shake
squattri'nato *a* penniless
squaw *nf inv* squaw
squilib'rare *vt* unbalance
squili'brato, -a *a* unbalanced ● *nmf* lunatic
squi'librio *nm* imbalance
squil'lante *a* shrill
squil'lare *vi* ⟨*campana:*⟩ peal; ⟨*tromba:*⟩ blare; ⟨*telefono:*⟩ ring
'squillo *nm* blare; *Teleph* ring; ⟨*ragazza*⟩ call girl
squinter'nato *a anche fig* crazy
squisi'tezza *nf* refinement
squi'sito *a* exquisite
squit'tire *vi* ⟨*pappagallo, fig:*⟩ squawk; ⟨*topo:*⟩ squeak
sradi'care *vt* uproot; eradicate ⟨*vizio, male*⟩
sragio'nare *vi* rave
sregola'tezza *nf* dissipation
srego'lato *a* inordinate; ⟨*dissoluto*⟩ dissolute
s.r.l. *abbr* (**società a responsabilità limitata**) Ltd
sroto'lare *vt* uncoil
SS *abbr* (**strada statale**) national road; *abbr* (**Santissimo**) Most Holy
ss *abbr* (**seguenti**) following
sst *int* sh!
'stabile *a* stable; ⟨*permanente*⟩ lasting; ⟨*saldo*⟩ steady; **compagnia ~** *Theat* repertory company ● *nm* ⟨*edificio*⟩ building
stabili'mento *nm* factory; ⟨*industriale*⟩ plant; ⟨*edificio*⟩ establishment. **~ balneare** lido
stabi'lire *vt* establish; ⟨*decidere*⟩ decide
stabi'lirsi *vr* settle
stabilità *nf* stability
stabi'lito *a* established
stabiliz'zare *vt* stabilize
stabiliz'zarsi *vr* stabilize
stabilizza'tore *nm* stabilizer
stacano'vista *nmf* workaholic
stac'care *vt* detach; pronounce clearly ⟨*parole*⟩; ⟨*separare*⟩ separate; turn off ⟨*corrente*⟩; **~ gli occhi da** take one's eyes off ● *vi* ⟨*fam: finire di lavorare*⟩ knock off
stac'carsi *vr* come off; **~ da** break away from ⟨*partito, famiglia*⟩; **si stacca alle cinque** knocking off time is five o'clock
staccata'mente *adv* staccato
stac'cato *a Mus* staccato
staccio'nata *nf* fence
'stacco *nm* gap
'stadio *nm* stadium
'staffa *nf* stirrup; **perdere le staffe** *fig* fly off the handle
staf'fetta *nf* dispatch rider
staffet'tista *nmf Sport* anchorman
stagio'nale *a* seasonal
stagio'nare *vt* season ⟨*legno*⟩; mature ⟨*formaggio*⟩
stagio'nato *a* ⟨*legno*⟩ seasoned; ⟨*formaggio*⟩ matured

stagiona'tura *nf* ⟨*di legno*⟩ seasoning; ⟨*di formaggio*⟩ maturation, maturing
stagi'one *nf* season; **alta/bassa ~** high/low season; **di ~** in season; **fuori ~** out of season. **~ lirica** opera season
stagli'arsi *vr* stand out
sta'gnante *a* stagnant
sta'gnare *vt* ⟨*saldare*⟩ solder; ⟨*chiudere ermeticamente*⟩ seal ● *vi* ⟨*acqua:*⟩ stagnate
'stagno *a* ⟨*a tenuta d'acqua*⟩ watertight ● *nm* ⟨*acqua ferma*⟩ pond; ⟨*metallo*⟩ tin
sta'gnola *nf* tinfoil
stalag'mite *nf* stalagmite
stalat'tite *nf* stalactite
'stalla *nf* stable; ⟨*per buoi*⟩ cowshed
stalli'ere *nm* groom
stal'lone *nm* stallion
sta'mani, stamat'tina *adv* this morning
stam'becco *nm* ibex
stam'berga *nf* hovel
'stampa *nf Typ* printing; ⟨*giornali, giornalisti*⟩ press; ⟨*riproduzione*⟩ print. **stampe** ⟨*postale*⟩ printed matter. **~ fronte retro** two-sided printing, duplex printing. **~ scandalistica** gutter press, tabloid press
stam'pante *nf* printer. **~ ad aghi** dot matrix [printer]. **~ a getto d'inchiostro** inkjet [printer]. **~ laser** laser [printer]. **~ a matrice di punti** dot matrix [printer]. **~ seriale** serial printer. **~ termica** thermal printer
stam'pare *vt* print
stam'patello *nm* block letters *pl*, block capitals *pl*
stam'pato *a* printed ● *nm* leaflet; *Comput* hard copy, printout; ⟨*modulo*⟩ print; **stampati** ⟨*pubblicità*⟩ promotional literature
stam'pella *nf* crutch
stampigli'are *vt* stamp
stampiglia'tura *nf* stamping; ⟨*dicitura*⟩ stamp
stam'pino *nm* stencil
'stampo *nm* mould; **di vecchio ~** ⟨*persona*⟩ of the old school
sta'nare *vt* drive out
stan'care *vt* tire; ⟨*annoiare*⟩ bore
stan'carsi *vr* get tired
stan'chezza *nf* tiredness
'stanco *a* tired; **~ di** ⟨*stufo*⟩ fed up with. **~ morto** dead tired, knackered *fam*
stand *nm inv* stand
'standard *a & nm inv* standard
standardiz'zare *vt* standardize
standardizzazi'one *nf* standardization
'stand-by *a inv* stand-by
'stanga *nf* bar; ⟨*persona*⟩ beanpole
stan'gare *vt fam* fail ⟨*studente*⟩; ⟨*con le tasse ecc*⟩ clobber
stan'gata *nf fig* blow; ⟨*fam: nel calcio*⟩ big kick; **prendere una ~** ⟨*fam: agli esami, economica*⟩ come a cropper
stan'ghetta *nf* ⟨*di occhiali*⟩ leg
sta'notte *nf* tonight; ⟨*la notte scorsa*⟩ last night
'stante *prep* on account of; **a sé ~** separate

stan'tio *a* stale

stan'tuffo *nm* piston

'**stanza** *nf* room; (*metrica*) stanza. ~ **dei giochi** games room. ~ **da pranzo** dining room

stanzia'mento *nm* appropriation

stanzi'are *vt* allocate

stan'zino *nm* walk-in

stap'pare *vt* uncork

star *nf inv Cinema* star

'**stare** *vi* (*rimanere*) stay; (*abitare*) live; (*con gerundio*) be; **sto solo cinque minuti** I'll stay only five minutes; **sto in piazza Peyron** I live in Peyron Square; **sta dormendo** he's sleeping; ~ **a** (*attenersi*) keep to; (*spettare*) be up to; ~ **bene** (*economicamente*) be well off; (*di salute*) be well; (*addirsi*) suit; **sta bene!** that's fine!; ~ **dietro a** (*seguire*) follow; (*sorvegliare*) keep an eye on; (*corteggiare*) run after; ~ **in piedi** stand; ~ **per** be about to; ~ **sempre a fare qcsa** be always doing sth; **ben ti sta!** it serves you right!; **come stai/sta?** how are you?; **lasciar** ~ leave alone; **starci** (*essere contenuto*) go into; (*essere d'accordo*) agree; **il 3 nel 12 ci sta 4 volte** 3 into 12 goes 4; **non sa** ~ **agli scherzi** he can't take a joke; ~ **su** (*con la schiena*) sit up straight; ~ **sulle proprie** keep oneself to oneself

'**starna** *nf* partridge

starnaz'zare *vi* quack; *fig* shriek

starnu'tire *vi* sneeze

star'nuto *nm* sneeze

'**starsene** *vr* (*rimanere*) stay

'**starter** *nm inv* choke

sta'sera *adv* this evening, tonight

'**stasi** *nm* stasis

sta'tale *a* state *attrib* ● *nmf* state employee, civil servant ● *nf* (*strada*) main road, trunk road

'**statico** *a* static

sta'tista *nm* statesman

sta'tistica *nf* statistics *sg*

sta'tistico *a* statistical

'**Stati 'Uniti [d'America]** *nmpl* **gli** ~ ~ the United States [of America]

'**stato** *pp di* **essere, stare** ● *nm* state; (*posizione sociale*) position; *Jur* status; **lo S**~ *Pol* the state. ~ **d'animo** frame of mind. ~ **di attesa** *Comput* wait state. ~ **civile** marital status. ~ **cuscinetto** buffer state. **S**~ **Maggiore** *Mil* General Staff. ~ **di salute** state of health

stato-nazi'one *nm* nation-state

'**statua** *nf* statue

statu'ario *a* statuesque

statuni'tense *a* United States *attrib*, US *attrib* ● *nmf* citizen of the United States, US citizen

sta'tura *nf* height; **di alta** ~ tall; **di bassa** ~ short; **di media** ~ of average height. ~ **morale** moral stature

sta'tuto *nm* statute

stazio'nario *a* stationary

stazi'one *nf* station; (*città*) resort. ~ **degli autobus** bus station. ~ **balneare** seaside resort. ~ **climatica** health resort. ~ **delle corriere** coach station *Br*, bus station. ~ **ferroviaria** railway station *Br*, train station. ~ **marittima** ferry terminal. ~ **master** *Comput* master station. ~ **multimediale** *Comput* multimedia station. ~ **dei pullman** coach station *Br*, bus station. ~ **di servizio** petrol station *Br*, service station. ~ **slave** *Comput* slave station ~ **termale** spa, health resort

'**stecca** *nf* stick; (*di ombrello*) rib; (*da biliardo*) cue; *Med* splint; (*di sigarette*) carton; (*di reggiseno*) stiffener; **fare una** ~ *Mus* fluff a note

stec'cato *nm* fence

stec'chino *nm* cocktail stick

stec'chito *a* skinny; (*rigido*) stiff; (*morto*) stone cold dead

'**stele** *nf* stele

'**stella** *nf* star; **salire alle stelle** (*prezzi:*) rise sky-high, rocket. ~ **alpina** edelweiss. ~ **cadente** shooting star. ~ **del cinema** movie star. ~ **cometa** comet. ~ **filante** streamer. ~ **di mare** starfish. ~ **polare** Pole Star, North Star

stel'lare *a* star *attrib*; (*grandezza*) stellar

stel'lato *a* starry

stel'lina *nf* starlet

'**stelo** *nm* stem; **lampada a** ~ standard lamp *Br*, floor lamp

'**stemma** *nm* coat of arms

stempe'rare *vt* dilute

stempi'ato *a* bald at the temples

sten'dardo *nm* standard

'**stendere** *vt* spread out; (*appendere*) hang out; (*distendere*) stretch [out]; (*scrivere*) write down

'**stendersi** *vr* stretch out

stendibian'cheria *nm inv* clothes horse

stendi'toio *nm* clothes horse

stenodattilogra'fia *nf* shorthand typing

stenodatti'lografo, -a *nmf* shorthand typist

stenogra'fare *vt* take down in shorthand

stenogra'fia *nf* shorthand

sten'tare *vi* ~ **a** find it hard to

sten'tato *a* laboured

'**stento** *nm* (*fatica*) effort; **a** ~ with difficulty; **stenti** *pl* hardships, privations

'**steppa** *nf* steppe

'**sterco** *nm* dung

stereo['fonico] *a* stereo[phonic]

stereo'scopico *a* stereoscopic

stereoti'pato *a* stereotyped; (*sorriso*) insincere

stere'otipo *nm* stereotype

'**sterile** *a* sterile; (*terreno*) barren

sterilità *nf* sterility

steriliz'zare *vt* sterilize

sterilizzazi'one *nf* sterilization

ster'lina *nf* pound; **lira** ~ [pound] sterling

stermi'nare *vt* exterminate

stermi'nato *a* immense

ster'minio *nm* extermination

'**sterno** *nm* breastbone
sternu'tire, ster'nuto = **starnutire, starnuto**
ste'roide *nm* steroid
ster'paglia *nf* brushwood
ster'rare *vt* excavate; dig up ⟨*strada*⟩
ster'rato *a* ⟨*strada*⟩ dug up ● *nm* excavation; (*di strada*) digging up
ster'zare *vi* steer
'**sterzo** *nm* steering; (*volante*) steering wheel
'**steso** *pp di* **stendere**
'**stesso** *a* same; **io ~** myself; **tu ~** yourself; **me ~** myself; **se ~** himself; **in quel momento ~** at that very moment; **è stato ricevuto dalla stessa regina** (*in persona*) he was received by the Queen herself; **tuo fratello ~ dice che hai torto** even your brother says you're wrong; **l'ho visto coi miei stessi occhi** I saw it with my own eyes; **con le mie stesse mani** with my own hands ● *pron* **lo ~** the same one; (*la stessa cosa*) the same; **fa lo ~** it's all the same; **ci vado lo ~** I'll go just the same; **è venuto il giorno ~** he came the same day, he came that very day; **lo farò oggi ~** I'll do it straight away today
ste'sura *nf* drawing up; (*documento*) draft
steto'scopio *nm* stethoscope
'**steward** *nm inv* steward
stick *nm inv* **colla a ~** glue stick; **deodorante a ~** stick deodorant
stiepi'dire *vt* warm
'**stigma** *nm* stigma
'**stigmate** *nfpl* stigmata
sti'lare *vt* draw up
'**stile** *nm* style; **in grande ~** in style; **essere nello ~ di qcno** be typical of sb, be just like sb. **~ libero** (*nel nuoto*) freestyle, crawl. **~ di vita** life style
sti'lista *nmf* [fashion] designer; (*parrucchiere*) stylist
stiliz'zato *a* stylized
'**stilla** *nf* drop
stil'lare *vi* ooze
stilo'grafica *nf* fountain pen
stilo'grafico *a* **penna stilografica** fountain pen
'**stima** *nf* esteem; (*valutazione*) estimate
sti'mare *vt* esteem; (*valutare*) estimate; (*ritenere*) consider
sti'marsi *vr* consider oneself
sti'mato *a* well-thought-of
stimo'lante *a* stimulating ● *nm* stimulant
stimo'lare *vt* stimulate; (*incitare*) incite
'**stimolo** *nm* stimulus; (*fitta*) pang
'**stinco** *nm* shin; **non è uno ~ di santo** *fam* he's no saint
'**stingere** *vt/i* fade
'**stingersi** *vr* fade
'**stinto** *pp di* **stingere**
sti'pare *vt* cram
sti'parsi *vr* crowd together
stipendi'are *vt* pay a salary to
stipendi'ato *a* salaried ● *nm* salaried worker

sti'pendio *nm* salary. **~ base** basic salary. **~ iniziale** starting salary
'**stipite** *nm* doorpost
stipu'lare *vt* stipulate
stipulazi'one *nf* stipulation; (*accordo*) agreement
stira'mento *nm* sprain
sti'rare *vt* iron; (*distendere*) stretch
sti'rarsi *vr* (*distendersi*) stretch; pull ⟨*muscolo*⟩
stira'tura *nf* ironing
'**stiro** *nm* **ferro da ~** iron
'**stirpe** *nf* stock
stiti'chezza *nf* constipation
'**stitico** *a* constipated
'**stiva** *nf Naut* hold
sti'vale *nm* boot; **lo S~** (*Italia*) Italy. **stivali** *pl* **di gomma** Wellington boots, Wellingtons; **poeta dei miei stivali!** *fam* poet my eye!, poet my foot!
stiva'letto *nm* ankle boot
stiva'lone *nm* high boot; **stivaloni** *pl* **da caccia** hunting boots; **stivaloni** *pl* **di gomma** waders
sti'vare *vt* load
'**stizza** *nf* anger
stiz'zire *vt* irritate
stiz'zirsi *vr* become irritated
stiz'zito *a* irritated
stiz'zoso *a* peevish
stocca'fisso *nm* stockfish
stoc'cata *nf* stab; (*battuta pungente*) gibe
stock *nm Comm* stock
'**stock-car** *nm inv* stock car
'**stoffa** *nf* material; *fig* stuff; **avere ~** have what it takes
stoi'cismo *nm* stoicism
'**stoico** *a & nm* stoic
sto'ino *nm* doormat
'**stola** *nf* stole
'**stolido** *a* stolid
'**stolto** *a* foolish
stoma'chevole *a* revolting
'**stomaco** *nm* stomach; **mal di ~** stomach-ache
stoma'tite *nf* stomatitis
sto'nare *vt/i* sing/play out of tune ● *vi* (*non intonarsi*) clash
sto'nato *a* out of tune; (*discordante*) clashing; (*confuso*) bewildered
stona'tura *nf* false note; (*discordanza*) clash
stop *nm inv* (*segnale stradale*) stop sign; (*in telegramma*) stop
stop'pare *vt* stop
'**stopper** *nm Sport* fullback
'**stoppia** *nf* stubble
stop'pino *nm* wick
stop'poso *a* tough
'**storcere** *vt* twist
'**storcersi** *vr* twist
stor'dire *vt* stun; (*intontire*) daze
stor'dirsi *vr* dull one's senses
stor'dito *a* stunned; (*intontito*) dazed; (*sventato*) heedless
'**storia** *nf* history; (*racconto, bugia*) story;

(pretesto) excuse; **senza storie!** no fuss!; **fare [delle] storie** make a fuss. ~ **d'amore** love story

'**storico** *a* historical; *(di importanza storica)* historic ● *nm* historian

stori'ella *nf fam* little story

storiogra'fia *nf* historiography

stori'ografo *nm* historiographer

stori'one *nm* sturgeon

'**stormo** *nm* flock

stor'nare *vt* avert; transfer *(somma)*

'**storno** *nm* starling

storpi'are *vt* cripple; mangle *(parole)*

storpia'tura *nf* deformation

'**storpio, -a** *a* crippled ● *nmf* cripple

'**storta** *nf (distorsione)* sprain; **prendere una ~ alla caviglia** sprain one's ankle

'**storto** *pp di* storcere ● *a* crooked; *(ritorto)* twisted; *(gambe)* bandy; *fig* wrong

stor'tura *nf* deformity; ~ **mentale** twisted way of thinking

sto'viglie *nfpl* crockery *sg*, flatware *Am*

'**strabico** *a* cross-eyed; **essere ~** be cross-eyed, [have a] squint

strabili'ante *a* astonishing

strabili'are *vt* astonish

stra'bismo *nm* squint

straboc'care *vi* overflow

strabuz'zare *vt* ~ **gli occhi** goggle; **ha strabuzzato gli occhi** his eyes popped out of his head

straca'narsi *vr fam* work like a slave, slave away

stra'carico *a* overloaded

strac'chino *nm soft cheese from Lombardy*

stracci'are *vt* tear; *(fam: vincere)* thrash

straccia'tella *nf* vanilla ice cream with chocolate chips

stracci'ato *a* torn; *(persona)* in rags; *(prezzi)* slashed; **a un prezzo ~** at a knock-down price, dirt cheap

'**straccio** *a* torn ● *nm* rag; *(strofinaccio)* cloth; **essere ridotto ad uno ~** feel like a wet rag

stracci'one *nm* tramp

stracci'vendolo *nm* ragman

stracol'larsi *vr* sprain

stra'cotto *a* overdone; *(fam: innamorato)* head over heels ● *nm* stew

'**strada** *nf* road; *(di città)* street; *(fig: cammino)* way; **essere fuori ~** be on the wrong track; **fare ~** lead the way; **tener la macchina in ~** keep the car on the road; *(parcheggiare)* keep the car on the street; **su ~** *(trasportare)* by road; **farsi ~** *(aver successo)* make one's way [in the world]. ~ **d'accesso** approach road. ~ **camionabile** road for heavy vehicles. ~ **maestra** main road. ~ **pedonale** pedestrianized street. ~ **principale** main road. ~ **privata** private road. ~ **secondaria** secondary road. ~ **a senso unico** one-way street. ~ **senza uscita** dead end, cul-de-sac. ~ **di terra battuta** dirt track

stra'dale *a* road *attrib* traffic police ● *nm* **la S~** *fam* traffice police

stra'dina *nf* little street; *(in campagna)* little road

strafalci'one *nm* blunder

stra'fare *vi* overdo it, overdo things

stra'foro: di ~ *adv* on the sly

strafot'tente *a* arrogant

strafot'tenza *nf* arrogance

'**strage** *nf* slaughter

stra'grande *a* vast

stralci'are *vt* remove

'**stralcio** *nm* removal; *(parte)* extract

stralu'nare *vt* ~ **gli occhi** open one's eyes wide

stralu'nato *a (occhi)* staring; *(persona)* distraught

stramaz'zare *vi* fall heavily; ~ **al suolo** crash to the ground

strambe'ria *nf* oddity

'**strambo** *a* strange

strampa'lato *a* odd

stra'nezza *nf* strangeness

strango'lare *vt* strangle

strangugli'one *nm* tonsillitis

strani'ero, -a *a* foreign ● *nmf* foreigner

'**strano** *a* strange; ~ **ma vero** surprisingly enough, funnily enough

straordinaria'mente *adv* extraordinarily

straordi'nario *a* extraordinary; *(notevole)* remarkable; *(edizione)* special; **lavoro ~** overtime; **treno ~** special [train]

strapaz'zare *vt* ill-treat; scramble *(uova)*

strapaz'zarsi *vr* tire oneself out

stra'pazzo *nm* strain; **da ~** *fig* worthless

strapi'eno *a* overflowing

strapi'ombo *nm* projection; **a ~** sheer

strapo'tere *nm* overwhelming power

strappa'lacrime *a inv* weepy

strap'pare *vt* tear; *(per distruggere)* tear up; pull out *(dente, capelli)*; *(sradicare)* pull up; *(estorcere)* wring

strap'parsi *vr* get torn; *(allontanarsi)* tear oneself away; ~ **i capelli** *fig* be tearing one's hair out

'**strappo** *nm* tear; *(strattone)* jerk; *(fam: passaggio)* lift; **fare uno ~ alla regola** make an exception to the rule. ~ **muscolare** muscle strain

strapun'tino *nm* folding seat

strari'pare *vi* flood

strasci'care *vt* trail; shuffle *(piedi)*; drawl *(parole)*

'**strascico** *nm* train; *fig* after-effect

strasci'coni: a ~ *adv* dragging one's feet

straseco'lare *vi* be amazed

strass *nm inv* rhinestone

strata'gemma *nm* stratagem

stra'tega *nmf* strategist

strate'gia *nf* strategy

stra'tegico *a* strategic; **mossa strategica** strategic move

stratifi'care *vt* stratify

stratigra'fia *nf Geol* stratigraphy

'**strato** *nm* layer; *(di vernice ecc)* coat, layer; *(roccioso, sociale)* stratum. ~ **di nuvole** cloud layer

strato'sfera *nf* stratosphere

strato'sferico *a* stratospheric; *fig* sky-high

stravac'carsi *vr fam* slouch

stravac'cato *a fam* slouching

strava'gante *a* extravagant; (*eccentrico*) eccentric

strava'ganza *nf* extravagance; (*eccentricità*) eccentricity

stra'vecchio *a* ancient

strave'dere *vt* ~ **per** worship

stravizi'are *vi* indulge oneself

stra'vizio *nm* excess

stra'volgere *vt* twist; (*turbare*) upset

stravolgi'mento *nm* twisting

stra'volto *a* distraught; (*fam: stanco*) done in

strazi'ante *a* heartrending; ⟨*dolore*⟩ agonizing

strazi'are *vt* grate on ⟨*orecchie*⟩; break ⟨*cuore*⟩

'strazio *nm* agony; **essere uno** ~ be agony; **che** ~! *fam* it's awful!; **fare** ~ **di qcsa** ⟨*fam: attore, cantante:*⟩ murder sth

'streamer *nm inv Comput* streamer

'strega *nf* witch

stre'gare *vt* bewitch

stre'gone *nm* wizard

stregone'ria *nf* witchcraft

'stregua *nf* **alla** ~ **di** in the same way as; **alla stessa** ~ ⟨*giudicare*⟩ by the same yardstick; **a questa** ~ at this rate

stre'mare *vt* exhaust

stre'mato *a* exhausted

'stremo *a* extreme ● *nm* **ridotto allo** ~ at the end of one's tether

'strenna *nf* present

'strenuo *a* strenuous

strepi'tare *vi* make a din

strepi'tio *nm* din, uproar

strepi'toso *a* noisy; *fig* resounding

strepto'cocco *nm Med* streptococcus

streptomi'cina *nf Med* streptomycin

stress *nm* stress

stres'sante *a* ⟨*lavoro, situazione*⟩ stressful

stres'sare *vt* put under stress, be stressful for

stres'sarsi *vr* get stressed

stres'sato *a* stressed [out]

'stretta *nf* grasp; (*dolore*) pang; **essere alle strette** be in dire straits; **mettere alle strette qcno** have sb's back up against the wall; **provare una** ~ **al cuore** feel a pang. ~ **di mano** handshake

stret'tezza *nf* narrowness; **stret'tezze** *pl* (*difficoltà finanziarie*) financial difficulties

'stretto *pp di* **stringere** ● *a* narrow; (*serrato*) tight; (*vicino*) close; (*dialetto*) broad; (*rigoroso*) strict; **lo** ~ **necessario** the bare minimum ● *nm Geog* strait. ~ **di Messina** Straits of Messina

stret'toia *nf* bottleneck; (*fam: difficoltà*) tight spot

stri'ato *a* striped

stria'tura *nf* streak

stri'dente *a* strident

'stridere *vi* squeak; *fig* clash

stri'dore *nm* screech

'stridulo *a* shrill

strigli'are *vt* groom

strigli'ata *nf* grooming; *fig* dressing down

stril'lare *vi/t* scream

'strillo *nm* scream

stril'lone *nm* newspaper seller

strimin'zito *a* skimpy; (*magro*) skinny

strimpel'lare *vt* strum

stri'nare *vt* singe, scorch

'stringa *nf* lace; *Comput* string

strin'gato *a fig* terse

'stringere *vt* press; (*serrare*) squeeze; (*tenere stretto*) hold tight; take in ⟨*abito*⟩; (*comprimere*) be tight; (*restringere*) tighten; ~ **la mano a** shake hands with ● *vi* (*premere*) press

'stringersi *vr* (*accostarsi*) draw close (**a** to); (*avvicinarsi*) squeeze up

strip'pata *nf fam* nosh-up; **farsi una** ~ have a nosh-up

strip-'tease *nm* striptease

'striscia *nf* strip; (*riga*) stripe; **a strisce** striped. **strisce** *pl* **di mezzeria** *Auto* lane markings. **strisce** *pl* [**pedonali**] zebra crossing *sg*, crosswalk *Am*

strisci'are *vi* crawl; (*sfiorare*) graze ● *vt* drag ⟨*piedi*⟩

strisci'arsi *vr* ~ **a** rub against

strisci'ata *nf* scratch

'striscio *nm* graze; *Med* smear; **colpire di** ~ graze

strisci'one *nm* banner

strito'lare *vt* grind

strizzacer'velli *nmf sl* shrink

striz'zare *vt* squeeze; (*torcere*) wring [out]; ~ **l'occhio** wink

'strofa *nf* strophe

strofi'naccio *nm* cloth; (*per spolverare*) duster. ~ **da cucina** tea towel

strofi'nare *vt* rub

strofi'nio *nm* rubbing

strom'bare *vt* splay

strombaz'zare *vt* boast about ● *vi* hoot

strombaz'zata *nf* (*di clacson*) hoot

stron'care *vt* cut off; (*reprimere*) crush; (*criticare*) tear to shreds

stron'zate *nfpl vulg* crap

'stronzo *nm vulg* shit

stropicci'are *vt* rub; crumple ⟨*vestito*⟩

stropicci'ata *nf* rub

stro'piccio *nm* rubbing

stroppi'are *vt* **il troppo stroppia** enough is as good as a feast

stroz'zare *vt* strangle

strozza'tura *nf* strangling; (*di strada*) narrowing

strozzi'naggio *nm* loan-sharking

stroz'zino *nm pej* usurer; (*truffatore*) shark

struc'cante *nm* make-up remover

struc'carsi *vr* remove one's make-up

strug'gente *a* all-consuming

'struggersi *vr liter* pine [away]; ~ **di invidia/desiderio** be consumed with envy/desire

struggi'mento nm yearning
strumen'tale a instrumental
strumentaliz'zare vt make use of
strumen'tario nm instruments pl
strumentazi'one nf instrumentation
strumen'tista nm instrumentalist
stru'mento nm instrument; (arnese) tool. ~ **a corda/fiato** string/wind instrument. ~ **musicale** musical instrument. ~ **a percussione** percussion instrument
strusci'are vt rub
strusci'arsi vr ⟨gatto:⟩ rub itself; ⟨due innamorati:⟩ caress each other; ~ **intorno a qcno** fam suck up to sb
'strutto nm lard
strut'tura nf structure
struttu'rale a structural
struttura'lismo nm structuralism
struttural'mente adv structurally
struttu'rare vt structure
strutturazi'one nf structuring
'struzzo nm ostrich
stuc'care vt plaster; (per decorazione) stucco; put putty in ⟨vetri⟩
stucca'tore nm plasterer; (decorativo) stucco worker
stucca'tura nf plastering; (decorativo) stucco work
stuc'chevole a nauseating
'stucco nm plaster; (decorativo) stucco; (per vetro) putty; **rimanere di** ~ be thunderstruck
stu'dente, studen'tessa nmf student; (di scuola) schoolboy; schoolgirl
studen'tesco a student; (di scolaro) school attrib
studi'are vt study
studi'arsi vr ~ **di** try to
'studio nm studying; (stanza, ricerca) study; (di artista, TV ecc) studio; (di professionista) office. ~ **dentistico** dental surgery
studi'oso, -a a studious ● nmf scholar
'stufa nf stove. ~ **elettrica** electric fire. ~ **a gas** gas fire. ~ **a legna** wood[-burning] stove
stu'fare vt Culin stew; (dare fastidio) bore
stu'farsi vr get bored
stu'fato nm stew
'stufo a bored; **essere** ~ **di** be bored with, be fed up with
stu'oia nf mat
stu'olo nm crowd
stupefa'cente a amazing ● nm drug
stupe'fare vt stun
stu'pendo a stupendous; ~**!** brilliant!
stupi'daggine nf (azione) stupid thing; (cosa da poco) nothing; **non dire stupidaggini!** don't talk stupid!
stupi'data nf stupid thing
stupidità nf stupidity
'stupido a stupid
stu'pire vt astonish ● vi be astonished
stu'pirsi vr be astonished
stu'pore nm amazement
stu'prare vt rape
stupra'tore nm rapist

'stupro nm rape
sturabot'tiglie nm inv corkscrew
sturalavan'dini nm inv plunger
stu'rare vt uncork; unblock ⟨lavandino⟩
stuzzica'denti nm inv toothpick
stuzzi'care vt prod [at]; pick ⟨denti⟩; poke ⟨fuoco⟩; (molestare) tease; whet ⟨appetito⟩
stuzzi'chino nm Culin appetizer
su prep on; (senza contatto) over; (riguardo a) about; (circa, intorno a) about, around; **le chiavi sono sul tavolo** the keys are on the table; **il quadro è appeso sul camino** the picture is hanging over the fireplace; **un libro sull'antico Egitto** a book on o about Ancient Egypt; **sarò lì sulle cinque** I'll be there about five, I'll be there around five; **è durato sulle tre ore** it lasted for about three hours; **costa sulle 50 000 lire** it costs about 50,000 lire; **decidere sul momento** decide at the time; **su commissione** on commission; **su due piedi** on the spot; **su misura** made to measure; **uno su dieci** one out of ten; **stare sulle proprie** keep oneself to oneself; **sul mare** ⟨casa⟩ by the sea ● adv (sopra) up; (al piano di sopra) upstairs; (addosso) on; **andare su** go up; (al piano di sopra) go upstairs; **ho su il cappotto** I've got my coat on; **in su** ⟨guardare⟩ up; **dalla vita in su** from the waist up; **su!** come on!
sua'dente a persuasive
sub nmf inv skin-diver
sub+ pref sub+
su'bacqueo, -a a underwater ● nmf skindiver
subaffit'tare vt sublet
subaf'fitto nm sublet; **in** ~ sublet
suba'gente nm subagent
subal'terno a & nm subordinate
subappal'tare vt subcontract
subappalta|'tore, -'trice nmf subcontractor
subap'palto nm subcontract; **in** ~ subcontracted; **dare in** ~ subcontract; **prendere in** ~ take on a subcontract basis
sub'buglio nm turmoil
sub'conscio a & nm subconscious
subconti'nente nm subcontinent
subcosci'ente a & nm subconscious
subdi'rectory nf Comput subdirectory
subdola'mente adv deviously
'subdolo a devious, underhand
suben'trare vi (circostanze:) come up; ~ **a** take the place of
su'bentro nm changeover
subequatori'ale a subequatorial
su'bire vt undergo; (patire) suffer
subis'sare vt fig ~ **di** overwhelm with
subi'taneo a sudden
'subito adv at once, immediately; ~ **dopo** straight after; **vengo** ~ I'll be right there
subli'mare vt sublimate
su'blime a sublime
sublimi'nale a subliminal
sublingu'ale a sublingual
sublo'care vt sublease

subloca'tario *nm* sublessor
sublocazi'one *nf* sublease
subnor'male *a* subnormal
subodo'rare *vt* suspect
subordi'nare *vt* subordinate
subordi'nato, -a *a & nmf* subordinate
su'bordine *nm* **in ~** second in order of importance
subrou'tine *nf Comput* subroutine
subsi'denza *nf Geol* subsidence
sub'strato *nm* substratum, substrate
subto'tale *nm* subtotal
subtropi'cale *a* subtropical
subu'mano *a* subhuman
subur'bano *a* suburban
suc'cedere *vi (accadere)* happen; **~ a** succeed; *(venire dopo)* follow; **~ al trono** succeed to the throne
suc'cedersi *vr* happen one after the other; **si sono succeduti molti...** there was a series of...
successi'one *nf* succession; **in ~** in succession
successiva'mente *adv* subsequently
succes'sivo *a* successive; *(mese, giorno)* following
suc'cesso *pp di* **succedere ●** *nm* success; *(esito)* outcome; *(disco ecc)* hit
succes'sone *nm* huge success
succes'sore *nm* successor
succhi'are *vt* suck [up]; **~ il sangue a qcno** *fig* bleed sb dry
succhi'ello *nm* gimlet
succinta'mente *adv* succinctly
suc'cinto *a (conciso)* concise; *(abito)* scanty
'succo *nm* juice; *fig* essence. **~ d'arancia** orange juice. **~ di frutta** fruit juice. **~ di limone** lemon juice
suc'coso *a* juicy
'succube *nm* **essere ~ di qcno** be totally dominated by sb
succu'lento *a* succulent
succur'sale *nf* branch [office]
sud *nm* south; **del ~** southern; **a ~ di** [to the] south of
Sud 'Africa *nm* South Africa
sudafri'cano *a & nmf* South African
Suda'merica *nf* South America
sudameri'cano, -a *a & nmf* South American
Su'dan *nm* **il ~** the Sudan
suda'nese *a & nmf* Sudanese
su'dare *vi* sweat, perspire; *(faticare)* sweat blood; **~ freddo** be in a cold sweat; **~ sangue** sweat blood; **mi fa ~ freddo** it brings me out in a cold sweat; **~ sette camicie** sweat blood
su'data *nf anche fig* sweat
suda'ticcio *a* sweaty
su'dato *a* sweaty; *(vittoria)* hard-won; *(pane)* hard-earned
sud'detto *a* above-mentioned
'suddito, -a *nmf* subject
suddi'videre *vt* subdivide
suddivisi'one *nf* subdivision

su'd-est *nm* southeast
'sudicio *a* dirty, filthy
sudici'ume *nm* dirt, filth
sudocciden'tale *a* southwestern
sudorazi'one *nf* perspiring
su'dore *nm* sweat, perspiration; *fig* sweat; **in un bagno di ~** bathed in sweat. **~ freddo** cold sweat; **con il ~ della fronte** *fig* by the sweat of one's brow
sudo'riparo *a* sweat *attrib*
su'd-ovest *nm* southwest
'sue *vedi* **suo**
suffici'ente *a* sufficient; *(presuntuoso)* conceited **●** *nm* bare essentials *pl; Sch* pass mark
suffici'enza *nf* sufficiency; *(presunzione)* conceit; *Sch* pass; **a ~** enough; **prendere la ~** get the pass-mark
suf'fisso *nm* suffix
sufflè *nm Culin* soufflé
suffra'getta *nf* suffragette
suf'fragio *nm (voto)* vote; **in ~ di qcno** in homage to. **~ universale** universal suffrage
suffu'migio *nm* inhalation
suggel'lare *vt* seal
suggeri'mento *nm* suggestion
sugge'rire *vt* suggest; *Theat* prompt
suggeri'|tore, -'trice *nmf Theat* prompter
suggestio'nabile *a* suggestible
suggestio'nare *vt* influence
suggestio'nato *a* influenced
suggesti'one *nf* influence
sugge'stivo *a* suggestive; *(musica ecc)* evocative
'sughero *nm* cork
'sugli = **su + gli**
'sugo *nm (di frutta)* juice; *(di carne)* gravy; *(salsa)* sauce; *(sostanza)* substance
'sui = **su + i**
sui'cida *a* suicidal **●** *nmf* suicide
suici'darsi *vr* commit suicide
sui'cidio *nm anche fig* suicide; **commettere ~** commit suicide; **tentato ~** attempted suicide
su'ino *a* **carne suina** pork **●** *nm* swine
suite *nf* suite
sul = **su + il**
sulfa'midico *nm* sulphonamide/sulpha drug
sul'fureo *a* sulphuric
'sulla = **su + la**
'sulle = **su + le**
'sullo = **su + lo**
sul'tana *nf (persona)* sultana
sulta'nina *a* **uva ~** sultana
sul'tano *nm* sultan
'sunto *nm* summary
'suo, -a *poss a* **il ~, i suoi** his; *(di cosa, animale)* its; *(forma di cortesia)* your; **la sua, le sue** her; *(di cosa, animale)* its; *(forma di cortesia)* your; **questa macchina è sua** this car is his/hers; **~ padre** his/her/your father; **un ~ amico** a friend of his/hers/yours **●** *poss pron* **il ~, i suoi** his; *(di cosa, animale)* its;

(*forma di cortesia*) yours; **la sua, le sue** hers; (*di cosa animale*) its; (*forma di cortesia*) yours; **i suoi** his/her folk[s]

su'ocera *nf* mother-in-law

su'ocero *nm* father-in-law

su'oi *vedi* **suo**

su'ola *nf* sole. **suole** *pl* **di para** crepe soles

su'olo *nm* ground; (*terreno*) soil; ~ **pubblico** public land

suo'nare *vt Mus* play; ring ‹*campanello*›; sound ‹*allarme, clacson*›; ‹*orologio:*› strike; ~ **il clacson** sound the horn, hoot the horn; (*fam: imbrogliare*) do ●*vi* ‹*campanello, telefono, sveglia:*› ring; ‹*clacson:*› hoot; ‹*sirena:*› go [off]; ‹*giradischi:*› play

suo'nato *a fam* bonkers

suona|'tore, -'trice *nmf* player

suone'ria *nf* alarm

su'ono *nm* sound

su'ora *nf* nun; **Suor Maria** Sister Maria

'super *nf* 4-star [petrol], premium [gas] *Am*

super+ *pref* super+

supe'rabile *a* surmountable

superal'colico *nm* spirit ●*a* **bevande superalcoliche** spirits

supera'mento *nm* (*di timidezza*) overcoming; (*di esame*) success (**di** in)

supe'rare *vt* surpass; (*eccedere*) exceed; (*vincere*) overcome; overtake, pass *Am* ‹*veicolo*›; pass ‹*esame*›; ~ **la barriera del suono** break the sound barrier; ~ **se stessi** surpass oneself; **ha superato la trentina** he's over thirty

su'perbia *nf* haughtiness

su'perbo *a* haughty; (*magnifico*) superb

super'donna *nf* superwoman

superdo'tato *a* highly gifted, super-talented

superfici'ale *a* superficial ●*nmf* superficial person

superficialità *nf* superficiality

super'ficie *nf* surface; (*area*) area; **in** ~ on the surface; ‹*fig: esaminare*› superficially

su'perfluo *a* superfluous

superi'ora *nf* superior; *Relig* mother superior

superi'ore *a* superior; (*di grado*) senior; (*più elevato*) higher; (*sovrastante*) upper; (*al di sopra*) above ●*nm* superior

superiorità *nf* superiority

Super-'Io *nm Psych* superego

superla'tivo *a* & *nm* superlative

supermer'cato *nm* supermarket

supermo'della *nf* supermodel

super'nova *nf Astr* supernova

superpetroli'era *nf Naut* supertanker

superpo'tenza *nf* superpower

super'sonico *a* supersonic

su'perstite *a* surviving ●*nmf* survivor

superstizi'one *nf* superstition

superstizi'oso *a* superstitious

super'strada *nf* toll-free motorway. ~ **dell'informatica** information superhighway

superu'omo *nm* superman

supervalu'tare *vt* overvalue

supervalutazi'one *nf* overvaluation

supervisi'one *nf* supervision

supervi'sore *nm* supervisor

su'pino *a* supine

suppel'lettili *nfpl* furnishings

suppergiù *adv* about

supplemen'tare *a* additional, supplementary

supple'mento *nm* supplement. ~ **illustrato** colour supplement. ~ **rapido** express train supplement

sup'plente *a* temporary ●*nmf Sch* supply teacher

sup'plenza *nf* temporary post

'supplica *nf* plea; (*domanda*) petition

suppli'care *vt* beg

suppli'chevole *a* imploring

sup'plire *vt* replace ●*vi* ~ **a** (*compensare*) make up for

sup'plizio *nm* torture

sup'porre *vt* suppose

supportare *vt Comput* support

sup'porto *nm* support. ~ **di sistema** *Comput* system support

supposizi'one *nf* supposition

sup'posta *nf* suppository

sup'posto *pp* di **supporre**

suppu'rare *vi* fester

suppurazi'one *nf* suppuration; **andare in** ~ fester

suprema'zia *nf* supremacy

su'premo *a* supreme

surclas'sare *vt* outclass

surf *nm* surfboard; (*sport*) surfboarding

sur'fare *vi* ~ **in Internet** surf the Net

sur'fista *nmf Sport, Comput* surfer

surge'lare *vt* deep-freeze

surge'lato *a* frozen ●*nm* **surgelati** *pl* frozen food *sg*

'surplus *nm* surplus

surre'ale *a* surreal

surrea'lismo *nm* surrealism

surrea'lista *nmf* surrealist

surrea'listico *a* surrealist

surre'nale *a* adrenal

surriscal'dare *vt* overheat

surriscal'darsi *vr* overheat

surro'gato *nm* substitute

suscet'tibile *a* touchy

suscettibilità *nf* touchiness

susci'tare *vt* stir up; arouse ‹*ammirazione ecc*›

su'sina *nf* plum. ~ **selvatica** damson

su'sino *nm* plumtree

su'spense *nf* suspense

sussegu'ente *a* subsequent

sussegu'irsi *vr* follow one after the other

sussidi'are *vt* subsidize

sussidi'ario *a* subsidiary

sus'sidio *nm* subsidy; (*aiuto*) aid. ~ **di disoccupazione** unemployment benefit. ~ **di malattia** sickness benefit

sussi'ego *nm* haughtiness; **con** ~ haughtily

sussi'stenza *nf* subsistence

sus'sistere vi subsist; (essere valido) hold good

sussul'tare vi start; **far ~ qcno** give sb a start

sus'sulto nm start

sussur'rare vt/i whisper; **si sussurra che...** it is rumoured that...

sussur'rio nm murmur

sus'surro nm whisper

su'tura nf suture

sutu'rare vt suture

suv'via int come on!

sva'gare vt amuse

sva'garsi vr amuse oneself

'svago nm relaxation; (divertimento) amusement; **prendersi un po' di ~** have a break

svaligi'are vt rob; burgle (casa)

svalu'tare vt devalue; fig underestimate

svalu'tarsi vr lose value

svalutazi'one nf devaluation

svam'pito a absent-minded

sva'nire vi vanish

sva'nito, -a a (persona) absent-minded; (sapore, sogno) faded ● nmf absent-minded person

svantaggi'ato a at a disadvantage; (bambino, paese) disadvantaged

svan'taggio nm disadvantage; **essere in ~** Sport be losing; **in ~ di tre punti** three points down; **in ~ rispetto a qcno** at a disadvantage compared with sb

svantaggi'oso a disadvantageous

svapo'rare vi evaporate

svari'ato a varied

svari'one nm blunder

sva'sare vt splay; flare (gonna)

sva'sato a (gonna) flared

svasa'tura nf flare

'svastica nf swastika

sve'dese a & nm (lingua) Swedish ● nmf Swede

'sveglia nf (orologio) alarm [clock]; **~!** get up!; **mettere la ~** set the alarm [clock]. **~ automatica** alarm call. **~ telefonica** wake-up call

svegli'are vt wake up; fig awaken; **~ l'appetito a qcno** whet sb's appetite

svegli'arsi vr wake up

'sveglio a awake; (di mente) alert, sharp

sve'lare vt reveal

svel'tezza nf speed; fig quick-wittedness

svel'tire vt quicken

svel'tirsi vr (persona:) liven up

'svelto a quick; (slanciato) svelte; **alla svelta** quickly; **a passo ~** quickly

sve'narsi vr slash one's wrists; fig reduce oneself to poverty

'svendere vt undersell

'svendita nf [clearance] sale

sve'nevole a sentimental

sveni'mento nm fainting fit

sve'nire vi faint; **da ~** incredibly

sven'tare vt foil

sven'tato a thoughtless ● nmf thoughtless person

'sventola nf slap; **orecchie a ~** protruding ears, jug-handle ears fam

svento'lare vt/i wave

svento'larsi vr fan oneself

svento'lio nm flutter

sventra'mento nm disembowelment; (di pollo) gutting; (fig: di edificio) demolition (edificio)

sven'trare vt disembowel; gut (pollo); fig demolish (edificio)

sven'tura nf misfortune

sventu'rato a unfortunate

sve'nuto pp di svenire

svergi'nare vt deflower

svergo'gnato a shameless

sver'nare vi winter

svernici'ante nm paint stripper

svernici'are vt strip

sve'stire vt undress

sve'stirsi vr undress, get undressed

svet'tare vi (albero, torre:) stand out; **~ verso il cielo** stretch skywards

'Svezia nf Sweden

svezza'mento nm weaning

svez'zare vt wean

svi'are vt divert; (corrompere) lead astray

svi'arsi vr fig go astray

svico'lare vi turn down a side street; (fig: dalla questione ecc) evade the issue; (fig: da una persona) dodge out of the way

svi'gnarsela vr slip away

svigo'rire vt emasculate

svili'mento nm debasement

svi'lire vt debase

svilup'pare vt develop

svilup'parsi vr develop

sviluppa|'tore, -'trice nmf developer

svi'luppo nm development; **paese in via di ~** developing country

svinco'lare vt release; clear (merce); redeem (deposito)

svinco'larsi vr free oneself

'svincolo nm clearance; (di autostrada) exit; **~ di un deposito cauzionale** redemption of a deposit

svioli'nata nf fawning

svisce'rare vt gut; fig dissect

svisce'rato a (amore) passionate; (ossequioso) obsequious

'svista nf oversight

svi'tare vt unscrew

svi'tato a (fam: matto) cracked, nutty

'Svizzera nf Switzerland

'svizzera nf hamburger

'svizzero, -a a & nmf Swiss

svoglia'taggine nf laziness; (riluttanza) unwillingness

svogli'atamente adv half-heartedly; (senza energia) listlessly

svogli'atezza nf half-heartedness; (mancanza di energia) listlessness

svogli'ato a half-hearted; (senza energia) listless

svolaz'zante a (capelli) wind-swept

svolaz'zare vi flutter

svolaz'zio *nm* flutter

'svolgere *vt* unwind; unwrap ⟨*pacco*⟩; (*risolvere*) solve; (*portare a termine*) carry out; (*sviluppare*) develop

'svolgersi *vr* (*accadere*) take place

svolgi'mento *nm* course; (*sviluppo*) development

'svolta *nf* turning; *fig* turning-point

svol'tare *vi* turn

'svolto *pp di* **svolgere**

svuo'tare *vt* empty [out]; (*fig: di significato*) deprive

swing *nm Mus* swing

switch *nm Comput* switch

T *abbr* (**tabaccheria**) tobacconist

tabac'caio, -a *nmf* tobacconist

tabacche'ria *nf* tobacconist's (*which also sells stamps, postcards etc*)

ta'bacco *nm* tobacco; **tabacchi** *pl* cigarettes and tobacco

taba'gismo *nm* nicotine addiction

ta'bella *nf* table; (*lista*) list. **~ di conversione** conversion table. **~ di marcia** *fig* schedule. **~ dei prezzi** price list. **~ retributiva** salary scale

tabel'lina *nf Math* multiplication table

tabel'lone *nm* wall chart. **~ degli arrivi** arrivals board. **~ del canestro** backboard. **~ delle partenze** departures board. **~ segnapunti** scoreboard

taber'nacolo *nm* tabernacle

tabù *a & nm inv* taboo

tabu'lare *vt* tabulate

tabu'lato *nm Comput* [data] printout

tabula'tore *nm* tabulator

tabulazi'one *nf* tabulation

'tacca *nf* notch; **di mezza ~** ⟨*attore, giornalista*⟩ second-rate

taccagne'ria *nf* penny-pinching

tac'cagno *a fam* stingy

taccheggia'|tore, -'trice *nmf* shoplifter

tac'cheggio *nm* shoplifting

tac'chetto *nm Sport* stud

tac'chino *nm* turkey

tacci'are *vt* **~ qcno di qcsa** accuse sb of sth

'tacco *nm* heel; **alzare i tacchi** take to one's heels; **scarpe senza ~** flat shoes, flats; **colpo di ~** backheel; **tacchi** *pl* **a spillo** stiletto heels, stilettos

taccu'ino *nm* notebook

ta'cere *vi* be silent ● *vt* say nothing about; **mettere a ~ qcsa** ⟨*scandalo*⟩ hush sth up; **mettere a ~ qcno** silence sb

tachicar'dia *nf* tachycardia

ta'chigrafo *nm* tachograph

ta'chimetro *nm* speedometer

tacita'mente *adv* tacitly; (*in silenzio*) silently

'tacito *a* tacit; (*silenzioso*) silent

taci'turno *a* taciturn

ta'fano *nm* horsefly

taffe'ruglio *nm* scuffle

taffettà *nm* taffeta

'taglia *nf* (*riscatto*) ransom; (*ricompensa*) reward; (*statura*) height; (*di abiti*) size; **per taglie forti** outsize, OS. **~ unica** one size

taglia'carte *nm inv* paperknife

taglia'erba *nm inv* lawn-mower

tagliafu'oco *a inv* **porta ~** fire door; **striscia ~** fire break ● *nm* (*in bosco*) fire break

tagli'ando *nm* coupon; **fare il ~** ≈ put one's car in for its MOT. **~ di controllo** manufacturer's sticker; (*da raccogliere*) token. **~ controllo bagaglio** baggage claim sticker. **~ di garanzia** warranty

taglia'pasta *a* **a rotella ~** pastry cutter ● *nm inv* pastry cutter

tagliapa'tate *nm inv* potato peeler

tagli'are *vt* cut; (*attraversare*) cut across; cut off ⟨*telefono, elettricità*⟩; carve ⟨*carne*⟩; mow ⟨*erba*⟩; **farsi ~ i capelli** have a haircut, have one's hair cut; **~ i viveri a qcno** stop sb's allowance ● *vi* cut

tagli'arsi *vr* cut oneself; **~ i capelli** have a haircut, have one's hair cut

taglia'sigari *nm inv* cigar cutter

tagli'ata *nf finely-cut beef fillet*; **dare una ~ a qcsa** give sth a cut, cut sth

tagli'ato *a* (*a pezzi*) jointed; **essere ~ per qcsa** *fig* be cut out for sth

taglia'unghie *nm inv* nail clippers *pl*

taglieggi'are *vt* extort money from

tagli'ente *a* sharp ● *nm* cutting edge

tagli'ere *nm* chopping board. **~ per il pane** breadboard

taglie'rina *nf* (*per carta*) guillotine; (*per foto*) trimmer; (*per metallo, vetro*) cutter

'taglio *nm* cut; (*di stoffa*) length; (*di capelli*) [hair-]cut; (*parte tagliente*) cutting edge; **di ~** edgeways; **a doppio ~** *fig* double-edged; **~ e cucito** dressmaking; **dacci un ~!** *fam* put a sock in it!. **~ di carne** cut of meat. **~ cesareo** Caesarean section. **~ di personale** personnel cut. **~ dei prezzi** price cutting

tagli'ola *nf* trap

taglio'lini *nmpl* thin soup noodles

tagli'one *nm* **legge del ~** an eye for an eye and a tooth for a tooth, law of talion

tagliuz'zare *vt* cut into small pieces

tail'leur *nm inv* [lady's] suit

ta'lare *a* **prendere la veste ~** take holy orders

talassotera'pia *nf therapy based on seawater*

'talco *nm* talcum powder, talc

'tale *a* such a; (*con nomi plurali*) such; **c'è un ~ disordine** there is such a mess; **non accetto tali scuse** I won't accept such excuses; **è un ~ bugiardo!** he's such a liar!; **il rumore era ~ che non si sentiva nulla** there was so much noise you couldn't hear yourself think; **il ~ giorno** on such and such a day; **quel tal signore** that gentleman; **~ padre ~ figlio** like father like son; **~ quale** just like ● *pron* **un ~** someone; **quel ~** that man; **il tal dei tali** such and such a person

ta'lea *nf* cutting

ta'lento *nm* talent

'talent scout *nmf inv* talent scout

tali'smano *nm* talisman

tallo'nare *vt* be hot on the heels of

tallon'cino *nm* coupon. **~ del prezzo** price tag

tal'lone *nm* heel. **~ di Achille** *fig* Achilles' heel. **~ aureo** *Econ* gold standard

tal'mente *adv* so

ta'lora *adv* = **talvolta**

'talpa *nf* mole

tal'volta *adv* sometimes

tamburel'lare *vi* (*con le dita*) drum; ⟨*pioggia:*⟩ beat, drum

tambu'rello *nm* tambourine

tambu'rino *nm* drummer

tam'buro *nm* drum. **~ del freno** brake drum

tame'rice *nf* tamarisk

'tamia *nm inv* chipmunk

Ta'migi *nm* Thames

tampona'mento *nm* *Auto* collision; (*di ferita*) dressing; (*di falla*) plugging. **~ a catena** pile-up

tampo'nare *vt* (*urtare*) crash into; plug ⟨*falla*⟩; dress ⟨*ferita*⟩

tam'pone *nm* swab; (*per timbri*) pad; (*per mestruazioni*) tampon; (*per treni, Comput*) buffer

tam'tam *nm inv* bush telegraph

'tana *nf* den

'tandem *nm inv* tandem; **in ~** ⟨*lavorare*⟩ in tandem

'tanfo *nm* stench

'tanga *nm inv* tanga

tan'gente *a* tangent ● *nf* tangent; (*somma*) bribe

tangen'topoli *nf widespread corruption in Italy in the early 90s*

tangenzi'ale *nf* orbital road

tan'gibile *a* tangible

tangibil'mente *adv* tangibly

'tango *nm inv* tango

'tanica *nf* (*contenitore*) jerry can; (*serbatoio di nave*) tank

tan'nino *nm* tannin

tan'tino: un ~ *adv* a little [bit]

'tanto *a* [so] much; (*con nomi plurali*) [so] many, [such] a lot of; **~ tempo** [such] a long time; **non ha tanta pazienza** he doesn't have much patience; **~ tempo quanto ti serve** as much time as you need; **non è ~ intelligente quanto suo padre** he's not as intelligent as his father; **tanti amici quanti parenti** as many friends as relatives ● *pron* much; (*plurale*) many; (*tanto tempo*) much time; **è un uomo come tanti** he's just an ordinary man; **tanti** (*molte persone*) many people; **non ci vuole così ~** it doesn't take that long; **~ quanto** as much as; **tanti quanti** as many as ● *conj* (*comunque*) anyway, in any case ● *adv* (*così*) so; (*con verbi*) so much; **è ~ debole che non sta in piedi** he's so weak that he can't stand; **è ~ ingenuo da crederle** he's naive enough to believe her; **di ~ in ~** every now and then; **~ l'uno come l'altro** both; **~ quanto** as much as; **tre volte ~** three times as much; **una volta ~** once in a while; **~ meglio così!** so much the better!; **tant'è** so much so; **~ vale che andiamo a casa** we might as well go home; **~ per cambiare** for a change

tapi'oca *nf* tapioca

ta'piro *nm* tapir

ta'pis rou'lant *nm inv* conveyor belt

'tappa *nf* (*parte di viaggio*) stage; **fare ~ a** break one's journey in

tappa'buchi *nm inv* stopgap

tap'pare *vt* plug, cork ⟨*bottiglia*⟩; **~ la bocca a qcno** *fam* shut sb up

tappa'rella *nf fam* roller blind; **tirar su la ~** pull the blind up

tap'parsi *vr* **~ gli occhi** cover one's eyes; **~ il naso** hold one's nose; **~ le orecchie** put one's fingers in one's ears

tappe'tino *nm* mat; *Comput* mouse mat. **~ antiscivolo** [anti-slip] safety bathmat. **~ da bagno** bathmat

tap'peto *nm* carpet; (*piccolo*) rug; **andare al ~** ⟨*pugilato:*⟩ hit the canvas; **mandare qcno al ~** knock sb down; **bombardamento a ~** carpet bombing. **~ erboso** lawn. **~ persiano** Persian carpet. **~ stradale** road surface. **~ verde** (*tavolo*) card table. **~ volante** magic carpet

tappez'zare *vt* paper ⟨*pareti*⟩; (*con manifesti*) cover

tappezze'ria *nf* tapestry; (*di carta*) wallpaper; (*arte*) upholstery; **fare da ~** *fig* be a wallflower

tappezzi'ere *nm* upholsterer; (*imbianchino*) decorator

'tappo *nm* plug; (*di sughero*) cork; (*di metallo, per penna*) top; (*fam: persona piccola*) dwarf. **~ di bottiglia** bottle top. **~ a corona** crown cap. **tappi** *pl* **per le orecchie** earplugs. **~ salvagocce** anti-drip top. **~ di scarico** [della coppa] sump drain plug. **~ a strappo** ring-pull. **~ di sughero** cork. **~ a vite** screw top

'**tara** *nf* (*difetto*) flaw; (*ereditaria*) hereditary defect; (*peso*) tare
taran'tella *nf* tarantella
ta'rantola *nf* tarantula
ta'rare *vt Techn* calibrate; *Comm* discount
ta'rato *a Comm* discounted; *Techn* calibrated; *Med* with a hereditary defect; *fam* crazy
tarchi'ato *a* stocky
tar'dare *vi* be late ● *vt* delay
'**tardi** *adv* late; **al più ~** at the latest; **più ~** later [on]; **sul ~** late in the day; **far ~** (*essere in ritardo*) be late; (*con gli amici*) stay up late; **a più ~** see you later; **svegliarsi troppo ~** oversleep
tardiva'mente *adv* late
tar'divo *a* late; ⟨*bambino*⟩ retarded
'**tardo** *a* slow; ⟨*pomeriggio, mattinata*⟩ late
'**targa** *nf* plate; *Auto* numberplate
tar'gato *a* **un'auto targata...** a car with the registration number...
targ'hetta *nf* (*su porta*) nameplate; (*sulla valigia*) name tag. **~ di circolazione** numberplate. **~ commemorativa** memorial plaque. **~ stradale** street sign
ta'riffa *nf* rate, tariff; **a ~ ridotta** *Teleph* off-peak. **~ doganale** customs tariff. **~ ferroviaria** [rail] fares. **~ interna** inland postage. **~ professionale** [professional] fee. **~ telefonica** telephone charges. **~ unica** flat rate
tarif'fario *a* tariff *attrib* ● *nm* price list
tar'larsi *vr* get worm-eaten
tar'lato *a* worm-eaten
'**tarlo** *nm* woodworm
'**tarma** *nf* moth
tar'marsi *vr* get moth-eaten
tarmi'cida *nm* ≈ moth-repellent
ta'rocco *nm* tarot; **tarocchi** *pl* tarot
tar'pare *vt* clip
tartagli'are *vi* stutter
'**tartaro** *a* & *nm* tartar; **salsa tartara** tartar[e] sauce
tarta'ruga *nf* tortoise; (*di mare*) turtle; (*per pettine ecc*) tortoiseshell
tartas'sare *vt* (*angariare*) harass
tar'tina *nf* canapé
tar'tufo *nm* truffle
'**tasca** *nf* pocket; (*in borsa*) compartment; *Culin* icing bag; **da ~** pocket *attrib*; **avere le tasche piene di qcsa** *fam* have had a bellyful of sth; **se ne è stato con le mani in ~** *fig* he didn't lift a finger [to help]. **~ a battente** flap pocket. **~ del nero** (*di polpo, seppia*) ink sac. **~ da pasticciere** icing bag. **~ tagliata** slit pocket. **~ a toppa** patch-pocket
ta'scabile *a* pocket *attrib* ● *nm* paperback
tasca'pane *nm inv* haversack
ta'schino *nm* breast pocket
'**tassa** *nf* tax; (*d'iscrizione ecc*) fee; (*doganale*) duty. **~ di circolazione** road tax. **~ di esportazione** export duty. **~ d'iscrizione** registration fee. **~ di soggiorno** tourist tax, visitors' tax

tas'sabile *a* taxable
tas'sametro *nm* meter
tas'sare *vt* tax
tassativa'mente *adv* without fail
tassa'tivo *a* strict
tassazi'one *nf* taxation
tas'sello *nm* wedge; (*di stoffa*) gusset
tassì *nm inv* taxi
tas'sista *nmf* taxi driver
'**tasso**[1] *nm Bot* yew; (*animale*) badger
'**tasso**[2] *Comm* rate. **~ agevolato** cut rate; **prestito a ~ agevolato** soft loan. **~ base** base rate. **~ base di interesse** base lending rate. **~ di cambio** exchange rate. **~ di crescita** growth rate. **~ inquinamento** pollution level. **~ di interesse** interest rate. **~ di mortalità** death rate. **~ di sconto** discount rate
ta'stare *vt* feel; **~ il terreno** *fig* test the water *or* ground
tasti'era *nf* keyboard. **~ numerica** *Comput* numeric keypad
tasti'rino *nm* **~ numerico** numeric keypad
tasti'rista *nmf* keyboarder
'**tasto** *nm* key; (*tatto*) touch. **~ di controllo** *Comput* control key. **~ cursore** *Comput* cursor key. **~ delicato** *fig* touchy subject. **~ funzione** *Comput* function key. **~ numerico** *Comput* numeric[al] key. **~ di ritorno a margine** return key. **~ tabulatore** tab [key]
ta'stoni: **a ~** *adv* gropingly; **camminare a ~** grope around; **cercare qcsa a ~** grope for sth
'**tattica** *nf* tactics *pl*
'**tattico** *a* tactical
'**tattile** *a* tactile
'**tatto** *nm* (*senso*) touch; (*accortezza*) tact; **aver ~** be tactful
tatu'aggio *nm* tattoo
tatu'are *vt* tattoo
tautolo'gia *nf* tautology
tauto'logico *a* tautological
'**tavola** *nf* table; (*illustrazione*) plate; (*asse*) plank; **saper stare a ~** have good table manners; **calmo come una ~** ⟨*mare*⟩ like a mill pond. **~ calda** snackbar. **~ fredda** salad bar. **~ periodica degli elementi** periodic table. **~ pitagorica** multiplication table. **~ rotonda** *fig* round table. **~ a vela** sailboard; **fare ~ ~ ~** sailboard, windsurf
tavo'lato *nm* (*pavimento*) wooden flooring
tavo'letta *nf* bar; (*medicinale*) tablet; **andare a ~** *Auto* drive flat out. **~ di cioccolata** chocolate bar. **~ grafica** *Comput* digitizer
tavo'lino *nm* [small] table; (*da salotto*) occasional table
'**tavolo** *nm* table. **~ anatomico** mortuary table, slab *fam*. **~ da cucina** kitchen table. **~ da gioco** card table. **~ operatorio** *Med* operating table. **~ da pranzo** dining-table
tavo'lozza *nf* palette
'**tazza** *nf* cup; (*del water*) bowl. **~ da caffè/tè** coffee-cup/teacup

taz'zina *nf* ~ **da caffè** espresso coffee cup

TBC *abbr* (**tubercolosi**) TB

T.C.I. *abbr* (**Touring Club Italiano**) *association promoting tourism nationally and internationally*

te *pers pron* you; **te l'ho dato** I gave it to you

tè *nm inv* tea. **tè al latte** tea with milk. **tè al limone** lemon tea

tea'trale *a* theatre *attrib*; (*affettato*) theatrical

te'atro *nm* theatre. ~ **all'aperto** open-air theatre. ~ **lirico** opera [house]. ~ **neorealista** kitchen sink drama. ~ **di posa** *Cinema* set. ~ **tenda** *marquee for theatre performances*

'tecnico, -a *a* technical ● *nmf* technician. ~ **elettronico** electronics engineer. ~ **informatico** computer engineer. ~ **delle luci** *Cinema, TV* gaffer. ~ **del suono** sound technician ● *nf* technique

tec'nigrafo *nm* drawing board

tec'nocrate *nmf* technocrat

tecnolo'gia *nf* technology

tecno'logico *a* technological

te'desco, -a *a & nmf* German. ~ **dell'est** East German

'tedio *nm* tedium

tedi'oso *a* tedious

TEE *nm abbr* (**treno espresso trans-europeo**) Trans-Europe-Express [train]

te'game *nm* saucepan; **uova al** ~ fried eggs

'teglia *nf* baking tin

'tegola *nf* tile; *fig* blow

tei'era *nf* teapot

te'ina *nf* theine

tek *nm* teak

tel. *abbr* (**telefono**) tel.

'tela *nf* cloth; (*per quadri, vele*) canvas; *Theat* curtain. ~ **cerata** oilcloth. ~ **indiana** cheesecloth. ~ **di iuta** hessian. ~ **di lino** linen. ~ **rigida** buckram

te'laio *nm* (*di bicicletta, finestra*) frame; *Auto* chassis; (*per tessere*) loom

'tele *nf fam* telly, TV

tele'camera *nf* television camera

telecoman'dato *a* remote-controlled, remote control *attrib*

teleco'mando *nm* remote control

'Telecom I'talia *nf* Italian State telephone company

telecomunicazi'oni *nfpl* telecommunications, telecomms

teleconfe'renza *nf* teleconference

tele'cronaca *nf* [television] commentary; **fare la** ~ **di** commentate on. ~ **diretta** live [television] coverage. ~ **registrata** recording

telecro'nista *nmf* television commentator

tele'ferica *nf* cableway

tele'film *nm inv* film [made] for television; ~ **a episodi** series

telefo'nare *vt/i* [tele]phone, ring

telefo'nata *nf* call, [tele]phone call; **fare una** ~ make a phone call. ~ **anonima** nuisance call. ~ **a carico del destinatario** reverse charge [phone] call; **fare una** ~ **a carico [del destinatario]** reverse the charges. ~ **interurbana** long-distance call. ~ **di lavoro** business call. ~ **in teleselezione** ≈ STD call. ~ **urbana** local call

telefonica'mente *adv* by [tele]phone

tele'fonico *a* [tele]phone *attrib*

telefo'nino *nm* mobile [phone]

telefo'nista *nmf* operator

te'lefono *nm* [tele]phone; **numero di** ~ [tele]phone number. ~ **azzurro** children in need help line. ~ **cellulare** cellular [tele]phone, cellular. ~ **senza filo** cordless [phone]. ~ **a gettoni** pay phone. ~ **interno** intercom. ~ **a monete** pay phone. ~ **pubblico** public telephone. ~ **rosso** *Mil, Pol* hotline. ~ **a scatti** *telephone with call charges based on time-units*. ~ **a schede** cardphone. ~ **a tastiera** push-button phone

tele'genico *a* telegenic

telegior'nale *nm* television news

telegra'fare *vt* telegraph

telegra'fia *nf* telegraphy

telegrafica'mente *adv* (*con telegrafo*) by telegram

tele'grafico *a* telegraphic; (*risposta*) monosyllabic; **sii** ~ keep it brief

te'legrafo *nm* telegraph

tele'gramma *nm* telegram

tele'matica *nf* data communications, telematics

teleno'vela *nf* soap opera

teleobiet'tivo *nm* telephoto lens

telepa'tia *nf* telepathy

tele'patico *a* telepathic

tele'quiz *nm inv* TV quiz programme

teleradiotra'smettere *vt* simulcast

telero'manzo *nm* television serial

tele'schermo *nm* television screen

tele'scopio *nm* telescope

telescri'vente *nf* telex [machine]

teleselet'tivo *a* direct dialling

teleselezi'one *nf* subscriber trunk dialling, STD; **chiamare in** ~ call direct, dial direct. ~ **internazionale** international direct dialling

telespetta'|tore, -'trice *nmf* viewer; **i telespettatori** the viewing public

tele'text® *nm* Teletext

'telethon *nm inv* telethon

tele'video *nm* videophone

televisi'one *nf* television; **guardare la** ~ watch television; **alla** ~ on television. ~ **in bianco e nero** black and white television. ~ **via cavo** cable TV. ~ **a circuito chiuso** closed-circuit television, CCT. ~ **a colori** colour television set

televi'sivo *a* television, TV *attrib*; **operatore** ~ television cameraman; **apparecchio** ~ television set

televi'sore *nm* television [set], TV [set]. ~ **portatile** portable [TV], portable [television set]

'telex *nm inv* telex ● *a inv* telex *attrib*

tel'lurico *a* telluric

'telo *nm* [piece of] cloth; ~ **da bagno** beach towel. ~ **di salvataggio** rescue blanket

'tema *nm* theme; *Sch* essay

te'matica *nf* main theme

teme'rario *a* reckless

te'mere *vt* be afraid of ● *vi* be afraid

tem'paccio *nm* filthy weather

'tempera *nf* tempera; (*pittura*) painting in tempera

temperama'tite *nm inv* pencil-sharpener

tempera'mento *nm* temperament

tempe'rare *vt* temper; sharpen ‹*matita*›

tempe'rato *a* temperate

tempera'tura *nf* temperature. ~ **ambiente** room temperature

tempe'rino *nm* penknife

tem'pesta *nf* storm. ~ **magnetica** magnetic storm. ~ **di neve** snowstorm. ~ **di sabbia** sandstorm

tempe'stare *vt* ~ **qcno di colpi** rain blows on sb; ~ **qcno di domande** bombard sb with questions

tempe'stato *a* ‹*anello, diadema*› encrusted (**di** with)

tempestiva'mente *adv* quickly, in a short space of time

tempe'stivo *a* timely

tempe'stoso *a* stormy

'tempia *nf Anat* temple

'tempio *nm Relig* temple

tem'pismo *nm* timing

'tempo *nm* time; (*atmosferico*) weather; *Mus* tempo; *Gram* tense; (*di film*) part; (*di partita*) half; **a suo** ~ in due course; ~ **fa** some time ago; **per molto** ~, **per tanto** ~ for a long time; **tanto** ~ **fa** a long time ago; **un** ~ once; **ha fatto il suo** ~ it's out of date; **a** ~ **indeterminato** ‹*contratto*› permanent; **primo** ~ (*di film, partita*) first half. ~ **di accesso** *Comput* access time. ~ **di cottura** cooking time. ~ **di esposizione** *Phot* exposure time. ~ **libero** free time, leisure time. ~ **limite di accettazione** latest check-in time. ~ **di pace** peacetime. ~ **reale** *Comput* real time; **in** ~ ~ real-time *attrib*. ~ **supplementare** extra time; *Sport* extra time, overtime *Am*; **andare ai tempi supplementari** *Sport* go into extra time

tempo'rale *a* temporal ● *nm* [thunder]storm

temporanea'mente *adv* temporarily

tempo'raneo *a* temporary

temporeggi'are *vi* play for time

tem'prare *vt* form

te'nace *a* tenacious

tenace'mente *adv* tenaciously

te'nacia *nf* tenacity

te'naglia *nf* pincers *pl*

'tenda *nf* curtain; (*per campeggio*) tent; (*tendone*) awning; **tirare le tende** draw the curtains. ~ **della doccia** shower curtain. ~ **a ossigeno** oxygen tent

ten'denza *nf* tendency. ~ **al rialzo/ribasso** *Fin* bull/bear market

tendenzial'mente *adv* by nature

tendenzi'oso *a* tendentious

'tendere *vt* (*allargare*) stretch [out]; (*tirare*) tighten; (*porgere*) hold out; *fig* lay ‹*trappola*› ● *vi* ~ **a** aim at; (*essere portato a*) tend to

'tendersi *vr* tauten

'tendine *nm* tendon. ~ **d'Achille** Achilles tendon. ~ **del garretto** hamstring. ~ **del ginocchio** hamstring

ten'done *nm* awning; (*di circo*) tent. ~ **del circo** big top

ten'dopoli *nf inv* tent city

'tenebre *nfpl* darkness

tene'broso *a* gloomy ● *nm* **bel** ~ dark and handsome man

te'nente *nm* lieutenant. ~ **colonnello** wing commander

tenera'mente *adv* tenderly

te'nere *vt* hold; (*mantenere*) keep; (*gestire*) run; (*prendere*) take; (*seguire*) follow; (*considerare*) consider ● *vi* hold; ~ **stretto** hold tight; ~ **a qcsa** (*oggetto*) be fond of sth; **tengo alla sua presenza** I very much want him to be there; ~ **per** ‹*squadra*› support

tene'rezza *nf* tenderness

'tenero *a* tender

tene'rone, -a *nmf* softie

te'nersi *vr* hold on (**a** to); (*in una condizione*) keep oneself; ~ **indietro** stand back

'tenia *nf* tapeworm

'tennis *nm* tennis. ~ **da tavolo** table tennis

ten'nista *nmf* tennis player

te'nore *nm* standard; *Mus* tenor; **a** ~ **di legge** by law. ~ **di vita** standard of living

tensi'one *nf* tension; *Electr* voltage; **mettere sotto** ~ energize; **in** ~ under stress. **alta** ~ high voltage. ~ **premestruale** premenstrual tension, PMT

ten'tacolo *nm* tentacle

ten'tare *vt* attempt; (*sperimentare*) try; (*indurre in tentazione*) tempt; ~ **la strada di** make a foray or venture into

tenta'tivo *nm* attempt

ten'tato *a* ~ **suicidio** suicide attempt

tentazi'one *nf* temptation

tentenna'mento *nm* wavering; **ha avuto dei tentennamenti** he wavered a bit

tenten'nare *vi* waver

ten'toni *adv* **cercare qcsa a** ~ grope for sth

'tenue *a* fine; (*debole*) weak; (*esiguo*) small; (*leggero*) slight

te'nuta *nf* (*capacità*) capacity; (*Sport: resistenza*) stamina; (*possedimento*) estate; (*divisa*) uniform; (*abbigliamento*) clothes *pl*; **a** ~ **d'aria** airtight. ~ **di strada** road holding

teolo'gia *nf* theology

teo'logico *a* theological

te'ologo *nm* theologian

teo'rema *nm* theorem

teo'ria *nf* theory

teorica'mente *adv* theoretically

te'orico *a* theoretical

te'pore *nm* warmth

'**teppa** *nf* mob
tep'pismo *nm* hooliganism
tep'pista *nm* hooligan
te'quila *nf inv* tequila
tera'peutico *a* therapeutic
tera'pia *nf* therapy; **in ~** in therapy. **~ di gruppo** group therapy. **~ d'urto** shock treatment
tergicri'stallo *nm* windscreen wiper, windshield wiper *Am*
tergilu'notto *nm* rear windscreen wiper
tergiver'sante *a* equivocating, pussyfooting *fam*
tergiver'sare *vi* equivocate, pussyfoot around *fam*
'**tergo** *nm* **a ~** behind; **segue a ~** please turn over, PTO
teri'lene® *nm* Terylene®
'**terital**® *nm* Terylene®
ter'male *a* thermal; **stazione ~** spa
'**terme** *nfpl* thermal baths
'**termico** *a* thermal; **borsa termica** cool bag
'**terminal** *nm inv* air terminal
termi'nale *a & nm* terminal; **malato ~** terminally ill person
termina'lista *nmf* computer operator
termi'nare *vt/i* end, finish
terminazi'one *nf* (*fine*) termination; *Gram* ending. **~ nervosa** nerve ending
'**termine** *nm* (*limite*) limit; (*fine*) end; (*condizione, parola*) term; (*scadenza*) deadline; **ai termini della legge...** under the terms of act...; **contratto a ~** fixed-term contract. **~ di paragone** *Gram* term of comparison. **~ ultimo** final deadline
terminolo'gia *nf* terminology
'**termite** *nf* termite
termoco'perta *nf* electric blanket
ter'mometro *nm* thermometer
'**termos** *nm inv* thermos®
termosi'fone *nm* radiator; (*sistema*) central heating
ter'mostato *nm* thermostat
termotera'pia *nf Med* heat treatment
termoventila'tore *nm* fan heater
'**terra** *nf* earth; (*regione*) land; (*terreno*) ground; (*argilla*) clay; (*cosmetico*) bronzing powder; **a ~** (*sulla costa*) ashore; (*installazioni*) onshore; **essere a ~** (*gomma:*) be flat; *fig* be at rock bottom; **per ~** on the ground; (*su pavimento*) on the floor; **sotto ~** underground; **far ~ bruciata** carry out a scorched earth policy. **~ promessa** Promised Land. **~ di Siena** sienna
terra'cotta *nf* terracotta; **vasellame di ~** earthenware
terra'ferma *nf* dry land
Terra'nova *nf* Newfoundland
terrapi'eno *nm* embankment
ter'razza *nf*, **ter'razzo** *nm* balcony
terremo'tato, -a *a* (*zona*) affected by an earthquake ● *nmf* earthquake victim
terre'moto *nm* earthquake
ter'reno *a* earthly ● *nm* ground; (*suolo*) soil;

(*proprietà terriera*) land; **perdere/guadagnare ~** lose/gain ground. **~ alluvionale** alluvial soil. **~ di bonifica** reclaimed land. **~ edificabile** building land. **~ di gioco** playing field. **~ di scontro** battlefield
ter'restre *a* terrestrial; (*superficie, diametro*) of the earth; **esercito ~** land forces *pl*
ter'ribile *a* terrible
terribil'mente *adv* terribly
ter'riccio *nm* potting compost
'**terrier** *nm inv* terrier
terri'ero *a* (*proprietario*) land *attrib*; (*aristocrazia*) landed; **proprietà** *pl* **terriere** landed property
terrifi'cante *a* terrifying
territori'ale *a* territorial; **acque territoriali** territorial waters
terri'torio *nm* territory
ter'rone, -a *nmf pej* bloody Southerner
ter'rore *nm* terror
terro'rismo *nm* terrorism
terro'rista *nmf* terrorist
terroriz'zare *vt* terrorize
'**terso** *a* clear
'**terza** *nf* (*marcia*) third [gear]
ter'zetto *nm* trio
terzi'ario *a* tertiary ● *nm* service sector, tertiary sector. **~ avanzato** high technology, hi-tech sector
'**terzo** *a* third; **di terz'ordine** (*locale, servizio*) third-rate; **fare il ~ grado a qcno** give sb the third degree; **la terza età** the third age; **il ~ mondo** the Third World ● *nm* third; **terzi** *pl Jur* third party
terzo'genito, -a *nmf* third-born
ter'zultimo, -a *a & n* third from last
'**tesa** *nf* brim
'**teschio** *nm* skull
'**tesi** *nf inv* thesis
'**teso** *pp di* **tendere** ● *a* taut; *fig* tense
tesore'ria *nf* treasury
tesori'ere *nm* treasurer
te'soro *nm* treasure; (*tesoreria*) treasury; **ministro del T~** Finance Minister, ≈ Chancellor of the Exchequer *Br*
'**tessera** *nf* card; (*abbonamento all'autobus*) season ticket; (*di club*) membership card
'**tessere** *vt* weave; hatch (*complotto*); **~ le lodi di qcsa** sing the praises of sth
tesse'rino *nm* travel card
'**tessile** *a* textile ● *nm* **tessili** *pl* textiles; (*operai*) textile workers
tessi'tore, -'trice *nmf* weaver
tessi'tura *nf* weaving
tes'suto *pp di* **tessere** ● *a* woven; **~ a mano** hand-woven ● *nm* fabric, material; *Anat* tissue. **~ sintetico** synthetic material
'**testa** *nf* head; (*cervello*) brain; **essere in ~ a** be ahead of; **in ~** *Sport* in the lead; **~ o croce?** heads or tails?; **fare ~ o croce** spin a coin, toss a coin; **andare a ~ alta** hold one's head up. **~ di rapa** *fam* pinhead. **~ di sbarco** beachhead. **~ di serie** (*squadra*) seeded team. **~ del treno** front of the train

testa-'coda *nm inv* **fare un ~** spin right round

testa'mento *nm* will. **Antico T~** *Relig* Old Testament. **Nuovo T~** *Relig* New Testament

testar'daggine *nf* stubbornness

testarda'mente *adv* stubbornly

te'stardo *a* stubborn

te'stata *nf* head; (*intestazione*) heading; (*colpo*) [head]butt. **~ nucleare** nuclear warhead

'teste *nmf* witness

'tester *nm inv* tester

te'sticolo *nm* testicle

testi'mone *nmf* witness; **essere ~ di qcsa** witness sth. **~ di Geova** Jehovah's Witness. **~ oculare** eye witness

testi'monial *nmf inv* celebrity who promotes a brand of cosmetics

testimoni'anza *nf* testimony; **falsa ~** *Jur* perjury

testimoni'are *vt* testify to ● *vi* testify, give evidence

te'stina *nf* head; (*di stampante*) printhead. **~ di cancellazione** *Comput* erase head. **~ di lettura** *Comput* read head. **~ rotante** (*di macchina da scrivere*) golf-ball. **~ di vitello** *Culin* calf's head

'testo *nm* text; **far ~** be authoritative; **con ~ a fronte** ⟨*traduzione*⟩ with the original text on the opposite page

te'stone, -a *nmf* blockhead

testoste'rone *nm* testosterone

testu'ale *a* textual

'tetano *nm* tetanus

te'traggine *nf* bleakness

tetra'pakᴿ *nm inv* tetrapak

'tetro *a* bleak

tetta'rella *nf* teat

'tetto *nm* roof; **abbandono del ~ coniugale** *Jur* desertion. **~ apribile** (*di auto*) sun[shine] roof. **~ a terrazza** flat roof

tet'toia *nf* roofing

tet'tuccio *nm* **~ apribile** sun-roof

teu'tonico *a* Teutonic

'Tevere *nm* Tiber

ti *pers pron* you; (*riflessivo*) yourself; **ti ha dato un libro** he gave you a book; **lavati le mani** wash your hands; **eccoti!** here you are!; **sbrigati!** hurry up!

ti'ara *nf* tiara

tic *nm inv* tic

ticchet'tare *vi* tick

ticchet'tio *nm* ticking

'ticchio *nm* tic; (*ghiribizzo*) whim

'ticket *nm inv* (*per farmaco, esame*) amount paid by National Health patients

tie-break *nm inv* tie break[er]

tiepida'mente *adv* half-heartedly

ti'epido *a* lukewarm; *fig* half-hearted

ti'fare *vi* **~ per** shout for

'tifo *nm Med* typhus; **far il ~ per** *fig* be a fan of

tifoi'dea *nf* typhoid

ti'fone *nm* typhoon

ti'foso, -a *nmf* fan

tight *nm inv* morning dress

'tiglio *nm* lime

'tigna *nf* ringworm

ti'grato *a* **gatto ~** tabby [cat]

'tigre *nf* tiger

'tilde *nmf* tilde

tim'ballo *nm Culin* pie

tim'brare *vt* stamp; **~ il cartellino** (*all'entrata*) clock in; (*all'uscita*) clock out

'timbro *nm* stamp; (*di voce*) tone. **~ a secco** embossing stamp

time out *nm inv Sport* time-out

'timer *nm inv* timer

timida'mente *adv* timidly, shyly

timi'dezza *nf* timidity, shyness

'timido *a* timid, shy

'timo *nm* thyme

ti'mone *nm* rudder. **~ di direzione** (*di aereo*) rudder. **~ di quota** (*di aereo*) elevator

timoni'ere *nm* helmsman

timo'rato *a* **~ di Dio** God-fearing

ti'more *nm* fear; (*soggezione*) awe

timo'roso *a* timorous

'timpano *nm* eardrum; *Mus* kettledrum; **timpani** *pl Mus* timpani, kettledrums; **rompere i timpani a qcno** *fig* shatter sb's eardrums

ti'nello *nm* dining-room

'tingere *vt* dye; (*macchiare*) stain

'tingersi *vr* ⟨*viso, cielo:*⟩ be tinged (**di** with); **~ i capelli** have one's hair dyed; (*da solo*) dye one's hair

'tino *nm*, **ti'nozza** *nf* tub

'tinta *nf* dye; (*colore*) colour; **in ~ unita** plain, self-coloured

tinta'rella *nf fam* suntan

tintin'nare *vi* tinkle

'tinto *pp di* **tingere**

tinto'ria *nf* (*negozio*) cleaner's

tin'tura *nf* dyeing; (*colorante*) dye. **~ di iodio** iodine

tipica'mente *adv* typically

'tipico *a* typical

'tipo *nm* type; (*fam: individuo*) chap, guy

tipogra'fia *nf* printer's; (*arte*) typography

tipo'grafico *a* typographic[al]

ti'pografo *nm* printer

tip tap *nm* tap dancing

ti'raggio *nm* draught

tiranneggi'are *vt* tyrannize

tiran'nia *nf* tyranny

ti'ranno, -a *a* tyrannical ● *nmf* tyrant

tiranno'sauro *nm* tyrannosaurus

ti'rante *nm* rope

tirapi'edi *nm inv pej* hanger-on

tira'pugni *nm inv* knuckle-duster

ti'rare *vt* pull; (*gettare*) throw; (*nel calcio*) kick; (*tracciare*) draw; (*stampare*) print; *fam* land ⟨*calci, pugni*⟩ ● *vi* pull; ⟨*vento:*⟩ blow; ⟨*abito:*⟩ be tight; (*sparare*) fire; **~ avanti** *fig* get by; **~ su** bring up ⟨*figli*⟩; (*da terra*) pick up; **tirar su** [**col naso**] sniffle

ti'rarsi *vr* **~ indietro** *fig* back out, pull out

tiras'segno *nm* target shooting; (*alla fiera*) rifle range

ti'rata *nf* (*strattone*) pull, tug; **in una ~** in one go; **dare a qcno una ~ d'orecchi** *fig* give sb a telling off

tira'tore *nm* shot. **~ scelto** marksman

tira'tura *nf* printing; (*di giornali*) circulation; (*di libri*) [print]run

tirchie'ria *nf* meanness

'tirchio *a* mean

tiri'tera *nf* spiel

'tiro *nm* (*lancio*) throw; (*azione*) throwing; (*sparo*) shot; (*azione*) shooting; (*scherzo*) trick; **cavallo da ~** draught horse. **~ con l'arco** archery. **~ al bersaglio** target practice. **~ alla fune** tug-of-war. **~ al piattello** clay pigeon shooting. **~ in porta** shot at goal. **~ a segno** rifle-range

tiroci'nante *nmf* trainee

tiro'cinio *nm* training

ti'roide *nf* thyroid

Tir'reno *nm* **il** [**mar**] **~** the Tyrrhenian Sea

ti'sana *nf* herb[al] tea

'tisi *nf* consumption

ti'tanio *nm* titanium

tito'lare *a* permanent ● *nmf* (*proprietario*) owner; (*calcio*) regular player; (*Jur: di diritto*) holder

'titolo *nm* title; (*accademico*) qualification; *Comm security;* **a ~ di** as; **a ~ di favore** as a favour; **titoli** *pl* (*di giornale, telegiornale*) headlines. **titoli** *pl* **di coda** closing credits. **~ di credito** credit instrument. **~ mondiale** world title. **~ obbligazionario** bond. **titoli** *pl* **delle principali notizie** news headlines. **~ in sovrimpressione** superimposed title. **~ di Stato** government security. **titoli** *pl* **di studio** qualifications. **titoli** *pl* **di testa** *Cinema, TV* opening credits. **~ a tutta pagina** banner headline

titu'bante *a* hesitant

titu'banza *nf* hesitation

titu'bare *vi* hesitate

tivù *nf* *inv* *fam* TV, telly

'tizio, -a *nm* so-and-so; **un ~** some man ● *nf* **una tizia** some woman

tiz'zone *nm* brand

toc'cante *a* touching

toc'care *vt* touch; touch on ⟨*argomento*⟩; (*tastare*) feel; (*riguardare*) concern ● *vi* **~ a** (*capitare*) happen to; **mi tocca aspettare** I'll have to wait; **tocca a te** it's your turn; (*da pagare da bere*) it's your round; **'non ~'** 'please do not touch'

tocca'sana *nm* *inv* panacea

toc'cato *a* (*fam: matto*) touched

'tocco *nm* touch; (*di pennello, orologio*) stroke; (*di pane ecc*) chunk; **il ~ finale** the finishing touches ● *a fam* crazy, touched

toc 'toc *nm* *inv* knock, knock

'toga *nf* toga; (*accademica, di magistrato*) gown

'togliere *vt* take off ⟨*coperta*⟩; (*Math, da scuola*) take away; quench ⟨*sete*⟩; take out, remove ⟨*tonsille, dente ecc*⟩; **~ qcsa a qcno** take sth away from sb; **~ qcno dei guai** get sb out of trouble; **ciò non toglie**

che... nevertheless..., the fact remains that...; **farsi ~ le tonsille** have one's tonsils [taken] out

'togliersi *vr* take off ⟨*abito*⟩; **~ la vita** take one's [own] life; **~ di mezzo** get out of the way; **togliti dai piedi!** get out of the way!

toi'lette *nf* *inv* toilet; (*mobile*) dressing table

to'letta *nf* toilet; (*mobile*) dressing table

tolle'rante *a* tolerant

tolle'ranza *nf* tolerance; **casa di ~** brothel

tolle'rare *vt* tolerate

'tolto *pp di* **togliere**

to'maia *nf* upper

'tomba *nf* grave

tom'bino *nm* manhole cover

'tombola *nf* bingo; (*caduta*) tumble

to'mino *nm* goat cheese

'tomo *nm* tome

tomogra'fia *nf* *Med* tomography. **~ assiale computerizzata** computerized axial tomography, CAT

'tonaca *nf* habit

to'nale *a* tonal

tonalità *nf* *inv* *Mus* tonality

to'nante *a* booming

'tondo *a* ⟨*cifra*⟩ round ● *nm* circle

'toner *nm* *inv* toner

'tonfo *nm* thud; (*in acqua*) splash

'tonica *nf* *Mus* keynote

'tonico *a* ⟨*sillaba*⟩ stressed; ⟨*muscoli*⟩ well toned ● *nm* tonic

tonifi'care *vt* tone up ⟨*muscoli*⟩

ton'nara *nf* tuna-fishing net

ton'nato *a* **vitello ~** veal with a tuna and mayonnaise sauce

tonnel'laggio *nm* tonnage

tonnel'lata *nf* ton. **~ corta americana** short ton, net ton

'tonno *nm* tuna [fish]

'tono *nm* tone

ton'sille *nfpl* tonsils

tonsil'lite *nf* tonsillitis

'tonto *a* *fam* thick

to'pazio *nm* topaz

'topless *nm* *inv* **in ~** topless

top 'model *nf* *inv* supermodel, top model

'topo *nm* mouse. **~ di albergo/appartamento** thief *in a hotel/block of flats.* **~ di biblioteca** bookworm. **~ domestico** domestic mouse

topogra'fia *nf* topography

topo'grafico *a* topographic[al]

to'ponimo *nm* place name

topo'ragno *nm* shrew

'toppa *nf* (*rattoppo*) patch; (*serratura*) keyhole

to'race *nm* chest

to'racico *a* thoracic; **gabbia toracica** rib cage

'torba *nf* peat

'torbido *a* cloudy; *fig* troubled

'torcere *vt* twist; wring [out] ⟨*biancheria*⟩

'torcersi *vr* twist

'torchio *nm* press

'torcia *nf* torch. **~ elettrica** torch
torci'collo *nm* stiff neck
'tordo *nm* thrush
to'rero *nm* bullfighter
To'rino *nf* Turin
tor'menta *nf* snowstorm
tormen'tare *vt* torment
tormen'tato *a* tormented
tor'mento *nm* torment
torna'conto *nm* benefit
tor'nado *nm* tornado
tor'nante *nm* hairpin bend
tor'nare *vi* return, go/come back; *(ridiventare)* become again; *‹conto:›* add up; **~ a sorridere** smile again; **~ su** go back up
tor'neo *nm* tournament
'tornio *nm* lathe
'torno *nm* **togliersi di ~** get out of the way
'toro *nm* bull; *Astr* Taurus
tor'pedine *nf* torpedo
torpedini'era *nf* torpedo boat
tor'pore *nm* torpor
'torre *nf* tower; *(scacchi)* castle. **~ d'avorio** ivory tower. **~ di controllo** control tower. **~ di osservazione** observation tower. **~ pendente, ~ di Pisa** Leaning Tower of Pisa
torrefazi'one *nf* roasting; *(negozio)* coffee retailer
tor'rente *nm* torrent, mountain stream; *(fig: di lacrime)* flood; *(fig: di parole)* torrent
torrenzi'ale *a* torrential; **in regime ~** in spate
tor'retta *nf* turret
'torrido *a* torrid
torri'one *nm* keep
tor'rone *nm* nougat
torsi'one *nf* twisting; *(in ginnastica)* twist
'torso *nm* torso; *(di mela, pera)* core; **a ~ nudo** bare-chested
'torsolo *nm* core
'torta *nf* cake; *(crostata)* tart. **~ di compleanno** birthday cake. **~ di mele** apple tart. **~ nuziale** wedding cake. **~ pasqualina** spinach pie
torti'era *nf* cake tin
tor'tino *nm* pie
'torto *pp di* torcere ● *a* twisted ● *nm* wrong; *(colpa)* fault; **aver ~** be wrong; **a ~** wrongly; **far ~ a qcno** wrong sb; *fig* not do sb justice; **non hai tutti i torti** you're not altogether wrong
'tortora *nf* turtle-dove
tortuosa'mente *adv* tortuously
tortu'oso *a* winding; *(ambiguo)* tortuous
tor'tura *nf* torture
tortu'rare *vt* torture
'torvo *a ‹sguardo›* menacing
tosa'erba *nm inv* lawnmower
to'sare *vt* shear
tosasi'epi *nm inv* hedge trimmer
tosa'tura *nf* shearing
To'scana *nf* Tuscany
to'scano, -a *a & nmf* Tuscan
'tosse *nf* cough
'tossico *a* toxic ● *nm* poison

tossicodipen'denza *nf* drug addiction
tossi'comane *nmf* drug addict, drug user
tos'sire *vi* cough
tosta'pane *nm inv* toaster. **~ a espulsione automatica** pop-up toaster
to'stare *vt* toast *‹pane›*; roast *‹caffè›*
'tosto *adv (subito)* soon ● *a fam* cool; **faccia tosta** cheek
tot *a inv* **una cifra ~** such and such a figure ● *nm* **un ~** so much
to'tale *a & nm* total. **~ parziale** subtotal
totalità *nf* entirety; **la ~ dei presenti** all those present
totali'tario *a* totalitarian
totaliz'zare *vt* total; score *‹punti›*
totalizza'tore *nm (per scommesse)* totalizer, tote
total'mente *adv* totally
'totano *nm* squid
'totem *nm inv* totem pole
toto'calcio *nm ≈* [football] pools *pl*
touche *nf inv* touch line
tou'pet *nm inv* toupee
tournée *nf inv* tour
to'vaglia *nf* tablecloth
tovagli'etta *nf* **~ [all'americana]** place mat
tovagli'olo *nm* napkin. **~ di carta** paper napkin
'tozzo *a* squat ● *nm* **~ di pane** stale piece of bread
tra = fra
trabal'lante *a* staggering; *‹sedia›* rickety, wonky
trabal'lare *vi* stagger; *‹veicolo:›* jolt
tra'biccolo *nm fam* contraption; *(auto)* jalopy
traboc'care *vi* overflow
traboc'chetto *nm* trap
traca'gnotto *a* dumpy
tracan'nare *vt* gulp down
'traccia *nf* track; *(orma)* footstep; *(striscia)* trail; *(residuo)* trace; *fig* sign
tracci'are *vt* trace; sketch out *‹schema›*; draw *‹linea›*
tracci'ato *nm (schema)* layout. **~ di gara** circuit
tra'chea *nf* windpipe, trachea
tra'colla *nf* shoulder-strap; **borsa a ~** shoulder-bag
tra'collo *nm* collapse
tradi'mento *nm* betrayal; *Pol* treason; **alto ~** high treason
tra'dire *vt* betray; be unfaithful to *‹moglie, marito›*
tradi'|tore, -'trice *nmf* traitor
tradizio'nale *a* traditional
tradiziona'lista *nmf* traditionalist
tradizional'mente *adv* traditionally
tradizi'one *nf* tradition
tra'dotto *pp di* tradurre
tra'durre *vt* translate
tradut'|tore, -'trice *nmf* translator. **~ elettronico** electronic phrasebook
traduzi'one *nf* translation. **~ consecutiva**

consecutive interpreting. ~ **simultanea** simultaneous interpreting

tra'ente *nmf Comm* drawer

trafe'lato *a* breathless

traffi'cante *nmf* dealer. ~ **d'armi** arms dealer. ~ **di droga** drug dealer

traffi'care *vi* (*affaccendarsi*) busy oneself; ~ **in** *pej* traffic in

'**traffico** *nm* traffic; *Comm* trade. ~ **aereo** air traffic. ~ **della droga** drug trafficking. ~ **ferroviario** rail traffic. ~ **di stupefacenti** drug trafficking

traffi'cone, -a *nmf fam* wheeler dealer

tra'figgere *vt* penetrate, pierce; *fig* pierce

tra'fila *nf fig* rigmarole

trafi'letto *nm* minor news item

trafo'rare *vt* bore, drill

tra'foro *nm* boring, drilling; (*galleria*) tunnel; **lavoro di** ~ fretwork

trafu'gare *vt* steal

tra'gedia *nf* tragedy

traghet'tare *vt* ferry

tra'ghetto *nm* ferrying; (*nave*) ferry

tragica'mente *adv* tragically

'**tragico** *a* tragic ● *nm* (*autore*) tragedian

tra'gitto *nm* journey; (*per mare*) crossing

tragu'ardo *nm* finishing post; (*meta*) goal

traiet'toria *nf* trajectory

trai'nare *vt* drag; (*rimorchiare*) tow

tralasci'are *vt* interrupt; (*omettere*) leave out; ~ **di fare qcsa** fail to do sth, omit to do sth

'**tralcio** *nm Bot* shoot

tra'liccio *nm* (*tela*) ticking; (*graticcio*) trellis

tra'lice: in ~ *adv* (*tagliare*) on the slant; (*guardare*) sideways

tralu'cente *a* shining

tram *nm inv* tram, streetcar *Am*

'**trama** *nf* weft; (*di film ecc*) plot

traman'dare *vt* hand down

tra'mare *vt* weave; (*macchinare*) plot

tram'busto *nm* turmoil

trame'stio *nm* bustle

tramez'zino *nm* sandwich

tra'mezzo *nm* partition

'**tramite** *prep* through ● *nm* link; **con il** ~ **di** by means of; **fare da** ~ act as go-between

tramon'tana *nf* north wind

tramon'tare *vi* set; (*declinare*) decline

tra'monto *nm* sunset; (*declino*) decline

tramor'tire *vt* stun ● *vi* faint

trampoli'ere *nm* wader

trampo'lino *nm* springboard; (*per lo sci*) ski-jump. ~ **di lancio** *fig* launch pad

'**trampolo** *nm* stilt

tramu'tare *vt* transform

trance *nf inv* trance; **essere in** ~ be in a trance

'**trancia** *nf* shears *pl*; (*fetta*) slice

tra'nello *nm* trap

trangugi'are *vt* gulp down

'**tranne** *prep* except

tranquilla'mente *adv* peacefully

tranquil'lante *nm* tranquillizer

tranquillità *nf* calm; (*di spirito*) tranquillity

tranquilliz'zare *vt* reassure

tran'quillo *a* quiet; (*pacifico*) peaceful; (*coscienza*) easy; **stai** ~**!** (*non preoccuparti*) don't worry!

transa'tlantico *a* transatlantic ● *nm* ocean liner

tran'satto *pp di* **transigere**

transazi'one *nf Comm* transaction; *Jur* settlement

tran'senna *nf* (*barriera*) barrier

transessu'ale *nmf* transsexual

tran'setto *nm* transept

'**transfert** *nm inv Psych* transference

tran'sigere *vi Jur* reach a settlement; (*cedere*) compromise

tran'sistor *nm inv fam* transistor [radio]

transi'tabile *a* passable

transi'tare *vi* pass

transi'tivo *a* transitive

'**transito** *nm* transit; '**divieto di** ~' 'no thoroughfare'; **diritto di** ~ right of way; '~ **alterno**' 'temporary one-way system'

transi'torio *a* transitory

transizi'one *nf* transition; **di** ~ transitional

tran'tran *nm fam* routine

tranvi'ere *nm* tram driver, streetcar driver *Am*

'**trapano** *nm* drill. ~ **elettrico** electric drill

trapas'sare *vt* pierce, penetrate ● *vi* (*morire*) pass away

trapas'sato *nm* pluperfect

tra'passo *nm* passage

trape'lare *vi anche fig* leak out

tra'pezio *nm* trapeze; *Math* trapezium

trapian'tare *vt* transplant

trapi'anto *nm* transplant. ~ **di cuore** heart transplant

'**trappola** *nf* trap

tra'punta *nf* quilt

'**trarre** *vt* draw; (*ricavare*) obtain; ~ **in inganno** deceive

trasa'lire *vi* start

trasan'dato *a* shabby

trasbor'dare *vt* transfer; *Naut* tran[s]ship ● *vi* change

tra'sbordo *nm* trans[s]hipment

trascenden'tale *a* transcendental

tra'scendere *vt* transcend ● *vi* (*eccedere*) go too far

trasci'nare *vt* drag; (*fig: entusiasmo:*) carry away

trasci'narsi *vr* drag oneself; (*camminare piano*) dawdle

tra'scorrere *vt* spend ● *vi* pass

tra'scritto *pp di* **trascrivere**

tra'scrivere *vt* transcribe

trascrizi'one *nf* transcription

trascu'rabile *a* negligible

trascu'rare *vt* neglect; (*non tenere conto di*) disregard

trascurata'mente *adv* carelessly

trascura'tezza *nf* negligence

trascu'rato *a* negligent; (*curato male*) neglected; (*nel vestire*) slovenly

traseco'lato *a* amazed

trasferi'mento *nm* transfer; (*trasloco*) move. ~ **automatico** direct debit. ~ **bancario** bank transfer

trasfe'rire *vt* transfer

trasfe'rirsi *vr* move

tra'sferta *nf* transfer; (*indennità*) subsistence allowance; *Sport* away match; **in ~** ⟨*impiegato*⟩ on secondment; **giocare in ~** play away

trasfigu'rare *vt* transfigure

trasfor'mare *vt* transform; (*in rugby*) convert

trasfor'marsi *vr* be transformed; ~ **in** turn into

trasforma'tore *nm* transformer

trasformazi'one *nf* transformation; (*in rugby*) conversion

trasfor'mista *nmf* (*artista*) quick-change artist

trasfusi'one *nf* transfusion

trasgre'dire *vt* disobey; *Jur* infringe

trasgredi'trice *nf* transgressor

trasgressi'one *nf* infringement; (*di ordine*) failure to obey

trasgres'sivo *a* intended to shock

trasgres'sore *nm* transgressor

tra'slato *a* metaphorical

traslitte'rare *vt* transliterate

traslo'care *vt* move ● *vi* move [house]

traslo'carsi *vr* move [house]

tra'sloco *nm* move; **compagnia di ~** removal company

tra'smesso *pp di* **trasmettere**

tra'smettere *vt* pass on; *TV, Radio* broadcast; *Techn, Med* transmit

trasmetti'tore *nm* transmitter

trasmis'sibile *a* transmissible

trasmissi'one *nf* transmission; *TV, Radio* programme. ~ **dati** data transmission. ~ **via fax** fax transmission. ~ **radiofonica** radio programme. ~ **remota** remote transmission. ~ **televisiva** television programme

trasmit'tente *nm* transmitter ● *nf* broadcasting station

traso'gnare *vi* day-dream

traso'gnato *a* dreamy

traspa'rente *a* transparent

traspa'renza *nf* transparency; **in ~** against the light

traspa'rire *vi* show [through]

traspi'rare *vi* perspire; *fig* transpire

traspirazi'one *nf* perspiration

tra'sporre *vt* transpose

traspor'tare *vt* transport; **lasciarsi ~ da** get carried away by; ~ **con ponte aereo** airlift

traspor'tato *a* transported; ~ **dall'aria** airborne

trasporta'tore *nm* conveyor; (*società*) transport company, road haulier

tra'sporto *nm* transport; (*fig: passione*) passion; **ministro dei trasporti** Ministry of Transport. ~ **aereo** air freight. ~ **ferroviario** rail transport. ~ **pesante** heavy goods transport. **trasporti** *pl* **pubblici** public transport. ~ **stradale** road transport, road haulage

trastul'lare *vt* amuse

trastul'larsi *vr* amuse oneself; (*perdere tempo*) fool around

trasu'dare *vt* ooze [with] ● *vi* ooze

trasver'sale *a* transverse; **strada ~** cross street

trasversal'mente *adv* widthways

trasvo'lare *vt* fly over ● *vi* ~ **su** *fig* skim over

trasvo'lata *nf* crossing [by air]

'tratta *nf* (*traffico illegale*) trade; *Comm* draft. ~ **bancaria** *Fin* banker's draft. ~ **delle bianche** white slave trade. ~ **documentaria** documentary bill

trat'tabile *a* or nearest offer, o.n.o.

tratta'mento *nm* treatment. ~ **automatico delle informazioni** electronic data processing, EDP. ~ **di bellezza** beauty treatment. ~ **di fine rapporto** severance pay. ~ **di riguardo** special treatment

trat'tante *a* conditioning

trat'tare *vt* treat; (*commerciare in*) deal in; (*negoziare*) negotiate ● *vi* ~ **di** deal with

trat'tarsi *vr* **di che si tratta?** what's it about?; **si tratta di...** it's about...

tratta'tive *nfpl* negotiations; **il tavolo delle ~** the negotiating table

trat'tato *nm* treaty; (*opera scritta*) treatise. ~ **di pace** peace treaty

tratteggi'are *vt* outline; (*descrivere*) sketch

tratte'nere *vt* (*far restare*) keep; hold ⟨*respiro, in questura*⟩; hold back ⟨*lacrime, riso*⟩; (*frenare*) restrain; (*da paga*) withhold; **sono stato trattenuto** (*ritardato*) I got held up

tratte'nersi *vr* restrain oneself; (*fermarsi*) stay; ~ **su** (*indugiare*) dwell on

tratteni'mento *nm* entertainment; (*ricevimento*) party

tratte'nuta *nf* deduction

trat'tino *nm* dash; (*in parole composte*) hyphen

'tratto *pp di* **trarre** ● *nm* (*di spazio, tempo*) stretch; (*di penna*) stroke; (*linea*) line; (*brano*) passage; **'tratti** *pl* (*lineamenti*) features; **a tratti** at intervals; **ad un ~** suddenly

trat'tore *nm* tractor

tratto'ria *nf* restaurant

'trauma *nm* trauma

trau'matico *a* traumatic

traumatiz'zante *a* traumatic

traumatiz'zare *vt* traumatize

tra'vaglio *nm* labour; (*angoscia*) anguish

trava'sare *vt* decant

tra'vaso *nm* decanting

trava'tura *nf* beams *pl*

'trave *nf* beam. ~ **a sbalzo** cantilever

tra'veggole *nfpl* **avere le ~** be seeing things

'travellers cheque *nm inv* traveller's cheque

tra'versa *nf* (*nel calcio*) crossbar; **è una ~ di via Roma** it's off via Roma, it crosses via Roma

traver'sare *vt* cross

traver'sata *nf* crossing

traver'sie *nfpl* misfortunes

traver'sina *nf* Rail sleeper

tra'verso *a* crosswise ● *adv* **di ~** crossways; **andare di ~** (*cibo:*) go down the wrong way; **camminare di ~** not walk in a straight line; **guardare qcno di ~** look askance at sb; **sapere per vie traverse** *fam* find out indirectly

traver'sone *nm* (*in calcio*) cross

travesti'mento *nm* disguise

trave'stire *vt* disguise

trave'stirsi *vr* disguise oneself

travesti'tismo *nm* transvestism, cross-dressing

trave'stito *a* disguised ● *nm* transvestite

travi'are *vt* lead astray

travisa'mento *nm* distortion

travi'sare *vt* distort

travol'gente *a* overwhelming

tra'volgere *vt* sweep away; (*sopraffare*) overwhelm

tra'volto *pp di* **travolgere**

trazi'one *nf* traction. **~ anteriore/posteriore** front-/rear-wheel drive

tre *a & nm* three

tre'alberi *nm inv* three-masted ship, three-master

trebbi'are *vt* thresh

trebbia'trice *nf* threshing machine

'treccia *nf* plait, braid; (*in maglia*) cable; **a trecce** cable *attrib*

tre'cento *a & nm* three hundred; **il T~** the fourteenth century

tredi'cesima *nf* extra month's salary paid as a Christmas bonus

tredi'cesimo, -a *a & nm* thirteenth

'tredici *a & nm* thirteen

'tregua *nf* truce; *fig* respite

'trekking *nm* trekking

tre'mante *a* trembling, quivering; (*per il freddo*) shivering

tre'mare *vi* tremble, quiver; (*di freddo*) shiver

trema'rella *nf fam* jitters *pl*

tremenda'mente *adv* terribly, tremendously

tre'mendo *a* terrible, tremendous; **ho una fame tremenda** I'm terribly hungry

tremen'tina *nf* turpentine

tre'mila *a & nm* three thousand

'tremito *nm* tremble, quiver; (*per il freddo*) shiver

tremo'lare *vi* shake; (*luce:*) flicker

tre'more *nm* trembling

'tremulo *a* tremulous

tre'nino *nm* miniature railway

'treno *nm* train. **~ merci** freight train, goods train. **~ navetta** shuttle. **~ passeggeri** passenger train. **~ postale** mail train. **~ straordinario** special train

'trenta *a & nm* thirty; **~ e lode** *Univ* ≈ first-class honours

trentatré 'giri *nm inv* LP

tren'tenne *a & nmf* thirty-year-old

tren'tesimo *a & nm* thirtieth

tren'tina *nf* **una ~ di** about thirty

trepi'dare *vi* be anxious

'trepido *a* anxious

treppi'ede *nm* tripod

'tresca *nf* intrigue; (*amorosa*) affair

'trespolo *nm* perch

triango'lare *a* triangular

tri'angolo *nm* triangle. **~ delle Bermude** Bermuda Triangle. **~ equilatero** equilateral triangle. **~ isoscele** isosceles triangle. **~ rettangolo** right-angled triangle

tri'bale *a* tribal

tribo'lare *vi* (*soffrire*) suffer; (*fare fatica*) go to a lot of trouble

tribolazi'one *nf* suffering

tri'bordo *nm* starboard

tribù *nf inv* tribe

tri'buna *nf* podium, dais; (*per uditori*) gallery; *Sport* stand. **~ coperta** stand. **~ riservata al pubblico** public gallery. **~ della stampa** press gallery

tribu'nale *nm* court. **~ fallimentare** bankruptcy court. **~ minorile** juvenile court

tribu'tare *vt* bestow, confer

tribu'tario *a* tax *attrib*

tri'buto *nm* tribute; (*tassa*) tax

'tricheco *nm* walrus

tri'ciclo *nm* tricycle

trico'lore *a* three-coloured ● *nm* (*bandiera*) Italian flag

tri'dente *nm* trident

tridimensio'nale *a* three-dimensional

trien'nale *a* (*ogni tre anni*) three-yearly; (*lungo tre anni*) three-year

tri'ennio *nm* three-year period

tri'fase *a* three-phase

tri'foglio *nm* clover

trifo'lato *a* sliced thinly and cooked with olive oil, parsley and garlic

tri'gemino *a* **parto ~** birth of triplets

'triglia *nf* mullet

trigonome'tria *nf* trigonometry, trig *fam*

tri'lingue *a* trilingual

tril'lare *vi* trill

'trillo *nm* trill

trilo'gia *nf* trilogy

trime'strale *a* quarterly

tri'mestre *nm* quarter

'trina *nf* lace

trin'cea *nf* trench

trince'rare *vt* entrench

trincia'pollo *nm inv* poultry shears *pl*

trinci'are *vt* cut up

trincia'trice *nf* **~ di documenti** document shredder

Trinità *nf* Trinity

'trio *nm* trio

trion'fale *a* triumphal

trionfal'mente *adv* triumphantly

trion'fante *a* triumphant

trion'fare *vi* triumph (**su** over)

tri'onfo *nm* triumph

tri'pletta *nf Sport* hat trick

tripli'care *vt* triple

'**triplice** *a* triple; **in ~** [*copia*] in triplicate

'**triplo** *a* treble, triple; **una somma tripla del previsto** an amount three times as much as forecast ● *nm* **il ~** (**di**) three times as much (as)

'**trippa** *nf* tripe; (*fam: pancia*) belly

tripudi'are *vi* rejoice

tri'pudio *nm* jubilation

tris *nm* (*gioco*) noughts and crosses, tick-tack-toe *Am*

'**triste** *a* sad; ⟨*luogo*⟩ gloomy

tri'stezza *nf* sadness; (*di luogo*) gloominess

'**tristo** *a* nasty

trita'carne *nm inv* mincer

tritaghi'accio *nm inv* ice-crusher

tri'tare *vt* mince

trita'tutto *nm inv* (*elettrico*) [food] processor

'**trito** *a* **~ e ritrito** well-worn, trite

tri'tolo *nm* TNT

tri'tone *nm* (*mitologia*) Triton; *Zool* newt

'**trittico** *nm* triptych

trit'tongo *nm* triphthong

tritu'rare *vt* chop finely

triumvi'rato *nm* triumvirate

tri'vella *nf* drill

trivel'lare *vt* drill

trivi'ale *a* vulgar

tro'feo *nm* trophy

troglo'dita *nmf* (*preistoria*) cave-dweller; *fig* Neanderthal

'**trogolo** *nm* (*per maiali*) trough

'**troia** *nf* sow; *vulg* bitch; (*sessuale*) whore

'**tromba** *nf* trumpet; *Auto* horn; (*delle scale*) well; **partire in ~** dive in head first. **~ d'aria** whirlwind. **~ di Eustachio** Eustachian tube. **~ di Falloppio** Fallopian tube. **~ delle scale** stairwell

trom'bare *vt vulg* bonk; (*fam: in esame*) fail ● *vi vulg* bonk

trom'betta *nm* toy trumpet

trombetti'ere *nm* bugler

trombet'tista *nmf* trumpet-player

trom'bone *nm* trombone

trom'bosi *nf* thrombosis. **~ coronarica** coronary thrombosis

tron'care *vt* sever; truncate ⟨*parola*⟩

tron'chese *nm* wire cutters *pl*

tronche'sino *nm* (*per le unghie*) nail clippers *pl*

tron'chetto *nm* **~ natalizio** Yule log

'**tronco** *a* truncated; **licenziare in ~** fire on the spot ● *nm* trunk; (*di strada*) section. **~ d'albero** tree trunk. **~ di cono** truncated cone

tron'cone *nm* stump

troneggi'are *vi* **~ su** tower over

'**trono** *nm* throne

tropi'cale *a* tropical

'**tropici** *nmpl* Tropics

'**tropico** *nm* tropic. **~ del Cancro** Tropic of Cancer. **~ del Capricorno** Tropic of Capricorn

'**troppo** *a* too much; (*con nomi plurali*) too many ● *pron* too much; (*plurale*) too many; (*troppo tempo*) too long; **troppi** (*troppa gente*) too many people; **me ne hai dato ~** you gave me too much ● *adv* too; (*con verbi*) too much; **~ stanco** too tired; **ho mangiato ~** I ate too much; **hai fame? – non ~** are you hungry? – not very; **sentirsi di ~** feel unwanted

'**trota** *nf* trout. **~ di mare** sea trout. **~ salmonata** salmon trout

trot'tare *vi* trot

trotterel'lare *vi* trot along; ⟨*bambino:*⟩ toddle

'**trotto** *nm* trot; **andare al ~** trot

'**trottola** *nf* [spinning] top; (*movimento*) spin

troupe *nf inv* **~ televisiva** camera crew

trousse *nf inv* (*per trucco*) make-up bag

tro'vare *vt* find; (*scoprire*) find out; (*incontrare*) meet; (*ritenere*) think; **andare a ~** go to see

trova'robe *nmf* (*persona*) props *sg*

tro'varsi *vr* find oneself; ⟨*luogo:*⟩ be; (*sentirsi*) feel

tro'vata *nf* bright idea. **~ pubblicitaria** advertising gimmick

trova'tello, -a *nmf* foundling

truc'care *vt* make up; cook ⟨*libri contabili*⟩; soup up ⟨*motore*⟩; rig ⟨*partita, elezioni*⟩

truc'carsi *vr* put one's make-up on

truc'cato *a* made-up; ⟨*libri contabili*⟩ cooked; ⟨*partita, elezioni*⟩ rigged; ⟨*motore*⟩ souped up

trucca|'tore, -'trice *nmf* make-up artist

'**trucco** *nm* (*cosmetici*) make-up; (*imbroglio*) trick; **trucchi pl del mestiere** tricks of the trade

'**truce** *a* fierce; ⟨*delitto*⟩ savage

truci'dare *vt* slay

trucio'lato *nm* chipboard

'truciolo *nm* shaving

trucu'lento *a* ⟨*delitto*⟩ savage; ⟨*film*⟩ violent

truffa *nf* fraud

truf'fare *vt* defraud

truffa|'tore, -'trice *nmf* fraudster

'trullo *nm* *traditional house with a conical roof found in Apulia*

'**truppa** *nf* troops *pl*; (*gruppo*) group; **truppe pl d'assalto** assault troops

T-shirt *nf inv* tee-shirt, T-shirt

tu *pers pron* you; **sei tu?** is that you?; **l'hai fatto tu?** did you do it yourself?; **a tu per tu** in private; **darsi del tu** use the familiar *tu* to each other

'**tua** *vedi* **tuo**

'**tuba** *nf Mus* tuba; (*cappello*) top hat

tu'bare *vi* coo; ⟨*innamorati:*⟩ bill and coo

tuba'tura *nf* piping

tubazi'one *nf* piping; **tubazioni pl** piping *sg*, pipes

tuberco'lina *nf* tuberculin

tuberco'losi *nf* tuberculosis

'**tubero** *nm* tuber

tube'rosa *nf* tuberose

tu'betto *nm* tube. **~ di colore** tube of paint

tubino | tweed

tu'bino *nm* (*vestito*) shift; (*cappello*) bowler, derby *Am*

'tubo *nm* pipe; *Anat* canal; **non ho capito un ~** *fam* I understood zilch. **~ digerente** alimentary canal. **~ a raggi catodici** cathode-ray tube. **~ di scappamento** exhaust [pipe]. **~ di scarico** waste pipe

tubo'lare *a* tubular

'tue *vedi* **tuo**

tuf'fare *vt* plunge

tuf'farsi *vr* dive; **'vietato ~'** 'no diving'

tuffa|'tore, -'trice *nmf* diver

'tuffo *nm* dive; (*bagno*) dip; **ho avuto un ~ al cuore** my heart leapt into my mouth. **~ di testa** dive

'tufo *nm* tufa

tu'gurio *nm* hovel

tuli'pano *nm* tulip

'tulle *nm* tulle

tume'fatto *a* swollen

tumefazi'one *nf* swelling

'tumido *a* swollen

tu'more *nm* tumour. **~ benigno** benign tumour. **~ maligno** malignant tumour

tumulazi'one *nf* burial

'tumulo *nm* (*di pietre*) cairn

tu'multo *nm* turmoil; (*sommossa*) riot

tumultu'oso *a* tumultuous

tung'steno *nm* tungsten

'tunica *nf* tunic

Tuni'sia *nf* Tunisia

tuni'sino *a & nmf* Tunisian

'tunnel *nm inv* tunnel. **~ sotto la Manica** Channel Tunnel

'tuo (**il ~** *m*, **la tua** *f*, **i tuoi** *mpl*, **le tue** *fpl*) *poss a* your; **è tua questa macchina?** is this car yours?; **un ~ amico** a friend of yours; **~ padre** your father ● *poss pron* yours; **i tuoi** your folk

tu'oi *vedi* **tuo**

tuo'nare *vi* thunder

tu'ono *nm* thunder

tu'orlo *nm* yolk

tu'racciolo *nm* stopper; (*di sughero*) cork

tu'rare *vt* block; cork ⟨*bottiglia*⟩

tu'rarsi *vr* become blocked; **~ le orecchie** stick one's fingers in one's ears; **~ il naso** hold one's nose

'turba *nf* (*folla*) rabble. **~ psichica** mental illness

turba'mento *nm* disturbance; (*sconvolgimento*) upsetting. **~ della quiete pubblica** breach of the peace

tur'bante *nm* turban

tur'bare *vt* upset

tur'barsi *vr* get upset

tur'bato *a* upset

tur'bina *nf* turbine

turbi'nare *vi* whirl

'turbine *nm* whirl. **~ di polvere** dust storm. **~ di vento** whirlwind

'turbo *nm inv* turbo

turbocompres'sore *nm Tech* turbo-charger

turbo'lento *a* turbulent

turbo'lenza *nf* turbulence

turboreat'tore *nm* turbo-jet

tur'chese *a & nmf* turquoise

Tur'chia *nf* Turkey

tur'chino *a & nm* deep blue

'turco, -a *a* Turkish ● *nmf* Turk; **fumare come un ~** smoke like a chimney; **bestemmiare come un ~** swear like a trooper ● *nm* (*lingua*) Turkish; *fig* double Dutch

'turgido *a* turgid

tu'rismo *nm* tourism

tu'rista *nmf* tourist

tu'ristico *a* tourist *attrib*

tur'nista *nmf* shift-worker

'turno *nm* turn; **a ~** in turn; **fare a ~** take turns; **fare i turni** work shifts; **di ~** on duty. **~ eliminatorio** heat. **~ di giorno** day shift. **~ di guardia** guard duty. **~ di lavoro** shift. **~ di notte** night shift; **del ~ ~** night shift *attrib*; **fare il ~ ~** be on night shift

'turpe *a* base

turpi'loquio *nm* foul language

'tuta *nf* overalls *pl*; *Sport* tracksuit. **~ da ginnastica** tracksuit. **~ da lavoro** overalls *pl*. **~ mimetica** camouflage. **~ spaziale** spacesuit. **~ subacquea** wetsuit

tu'tela *nf Jur* guardianship; (*protezione*) protection. **~ dell'ambiente** environmental protection

tute'lare *vt* protect

tu'tina *nf* sleepsuit; (*da danza*) leotard

tu|'tore, -'trice *nmf* guardian

'tutta *nf* **mettercela ~ per fare qcsa** go flat out for sth

tutta'via *conj* nevertheless, still

'tutto *a* whole; (*con nomi plurali*) all; (*ogni*) every; **tutta la classe** the whole class, all the class; **tutti gli alunni** all the pupils; **a tutta velocità** at full speed; **ho aspettato ~ il giorno** I waited all day [long]; **vestito di ~ punto** all kitted out; **in ~ il mondo** all over the world; **noi tutti** all of us; **era tutta contenta** she was delighted; **tutti e due** both; **tutti e tre** all three ● *pron* all; (*tutta la gente*) everybody; (*tutte le cose*) everything; (*qualunque cosa*) anything; **c'è ancora del dolce? - no, l'ho mangiato ~** is there still some cake? - no, I ate it all; **le finestre sono pulite, le ho lavate tutte** the windows are clean, I washed them all; **raccontami ~** tell me everything; **lo sanno tutti** everybody knows; **è capace di ~** he's capable of anything; **~ compreso** all in; **del ~** quite; **in ~** altogether ● *adv* completely; **tutt'a un tratto** all at once; **tutt'altro** not at all; **tutt'altro che** anything but ● *nm* whole; **tentare il ~ per ~** go for broke; **~ compreso** all-inclusive. **~ esaurito** *Theat* full house

tutto'fare *a inv & nmf* **[impiegato] ~** general handyman

tut'tora *adv* still

tutù *nm inv* tutu; (*lungo*) ballet dress

tv *nf inv* TV. **tv interattiva** interactive TV. **tv via cavo** cable TV

tweed *nm inv* tweed

Uu

ubbidi'ente *a* obedient
ubbidiente'mente *adv* obediently
ubbidi'enza *nf* obedience
ubbi'dire *vi* ~ **(a)** obey
ubi'cato *a* located
ubicazi'one *nf* location
ubiquità *nf* **non ho il dono dell'**~ I can't be in two places at once
ubria'care *vt* get drunk
ubria'carsi *vr* get drunk; ~ **di** *fig* become intoxicated with
ubria'chezza *nf* drunkenness; **in stato di** ~ inebriated; **in stato di** ~ **molesta** drunk and disorderly
ubri'aco, -a *a* drunk; ~ **fradicio** dead *o* blind drunk ● *nmf* drunk
ubria'cone *nm* drunkard ● *a* **un marito** ~ a drunkard of a husband
uccelli'era *nf* aviary
uccel'lino *nm* baby bird
uc'cello *nm* bird; (*vulg: pene*) cock. ~ **acquatico** water fowl. ~ **da cacciagione** game bird. ~ **del malaugurio** bird of ill omen. ~ **notturno** night *o* nocturnal bird. ~ **del paradiso** bird of paradise. ~ **di passo** bird of passage. ~ **rapace** bird of prey
uc'cidere *vt* kill
uc'cidersi *vr* kill oneself; (*morire*) be killed
+uccio *suff* **boccuccia** *nf* pretty little mouth; **calduccio** *nm* cosy warmth; **c'è un bel calduccio** it's nice and cosy; **tesoruccio** *nm* sweetie; **avvocatuccio** *nm* *pej* small town lawyer; **cosuccia** *nf* trifle; **è una cosuccia da niente** it's nothing; **doloruccio** *nm* twinge; **vestituccio** *nm pej* skimpy little dress
uccisi'one *nf* killing
uc'ciso *pp di* **uccidere**
ucci'sore *nm* killer
U'craina *nf* **l'**~ the Ukraine
u'craino, -a *a & nmf* Ukrainian
u'dente *a* **i non udenti** the hearing-impaired
u'dibile *a* audible
udi'enza *nf* audience; (*colloquio*) interview; *Jur* hearing. ~ **a porte chiuse** hearing in camera
u'dire *vt* hear
udi'tivo *a* auditory
u'dito *nm* hearing
udi'tore, -'trice *nmf* listener; *Sch* unregistered student (*allowed to sit in on lectures*)
udi'torio *nm* audience
UE *abbr* (**Unione Europea**) EU
'uffa *int* (*con impazienza*) come on!; (*con tono seccato*) damn!

uffici'ale *a* official ● *nm* officer; (*funzionario*) official; **pubblico** ~ public official. ~ **dell'esercito** army officer. ~ **giudiziario** clerk of the court. ~ **sanitario** health officer. ~ **dello Stato civile** registrar
ufficialità *nf* official status
ufficializ'zare *vt* make official, officialize
ufficial'mente *adv* officially
uf'ficio *nm* office; (*dovere*) duty; (*reparto*) department; **andare in** ~ go to the office; **grazie a suoi buoni uffici** thanks to his kind offices. ~ **acquisti** purchasing department. ~ **cambi** bureau de change, exchange bureau. ~ **di collocamento** employment office, jobcentre *Br.* **U**~ **Dazi e Dogana** Customs and Excise. ~ **funebre** *Relig* funeral service. ~ **informazioni** information office. ~ **di informazioni turistiche** tourist information office *o* centre. ~ **oggetti smarriti** lost property office, lost and found *Am.* ~ **del personale** personnel department. ~ **postale** post office. ~ **prenotazioni** advance booking office. ~ **della redazione** newspaper office. ~ **del turismo** tourist office. ~ **turistico** tourist office
ufficiosa'mente *adv* unofficially
uffici'oso *a* unofficial
uff *int* phew!
'ufo¹ *nm inv* ufo
'ufo²: a ~ *adv* without paying
ufolo'gia *nf* ufology
U'ganda *nf* Uganda
ugan'dese *a & nmf* Ugandan
uggiosità *nf* dullness
uggi'oso *a* boring
uguagli'anza *nf* equality
uguagli'are *vt* make equal; (*essere uguale*) equal; (*livellare*) level
uguagli'arsi *vr* ~ **a** compare oneself to
ugu'ale *a* equal; (*lo stesso*) the same; (*simile*) like; **due più due è** ~ **a quattro** two plus two equals four ● *nm Math* equals sign; **che non ha** ~ unequalled
ugual'mente *adv* equally; (*malgrado tutto*) all the same
'ulcera *nf* ulcer. ~ **gastrica** gastric ulcer. ~ **peptica** peptic ulcer
u'liva *nf vedi* **oliva**
uli'veto *nm* olive grove
u'livo *nm* olive[-tree]
'ulna *nf Anat* ulna
ulteri'ore *a* further
ulterior'mente *adv* further
ultima'mente *adv* lately
ulti'mare *vt* complete

ulti'matum *nm inv* ultimatum

ulti'missime *nfpl Journ* stop press, latest news *sg*

'**ultimo** *a* last; (*notizie ecc*) latest; (*più lontano*) farthest; *fig* ultimate; (*prezzo*) rockbottom ● *nm* last; **fino all'** ~ to the last; **per** ~ at the end; **l'~ piano** the top floor

ultimo'genito, -a *nmf* last-born

ultrà *nmf inv Sport* fanatical supporter

ultramo'derno *a* ultra-modern

ultrapi'atto *a* ultra-thin

ultrapo'tente *a* extra-strong

ultra'rapido *a* extra-fast

ultraresi'stente *a* extra-strong

ultrasen'sibile *a* ultrasensitive

ultra'sonico *a* ultrasonic

ultrasu'ono *nm* ultrasound

ultrater'reno *a* (*vita*) after death

ultravio'letto *a* ultraviolet

ulu'lare *vi* howl

ulu'lato *nm* howling; **gli ululati** the howls, the howling

umana'mente *adv* (*trattare*) humanely; ~ **impossibile** not humanly possible

uma'nesimo *nm* humanism

uma'nista *nmf* humanist

umanità *nf* humanity

umani'tario *a* humanitarian

u'mano *a* human; (*benevolo*) humane

'**Umbria** *nf* Umbria

'**umbro, -a** *a & nmf* Umbrian

umet'tare *vt* moisten

umidifica'tore *nm* humidifier

umidità *nf* dampness; (*di clima*) humidity

'**umido** *a* damp; (*clima*) humid; (*mani, occhi*) moist ● *nm* dampness; **in** ~ *Culin* stewed

'**umile** *a* humble

umili'ante *a* humiliating

umili'are *vt* humiliate

umili'arsi *vr* humble oneself

umiliazi'one *nf* humiliation

umil'mente *adv* humbly

umiltà *nf* humility

u'more *nm* humour; (*stato d'animo*) mood; **di cattivo/buon** ~ in a bad/good mood

umo'rismo *nm* humour

umo'rista *nmf* humorist

umoristica'mente *adv* humorously

umo'ristico *a* humorous

un *vedi* **uno**

un' *vedi* **uno**

'**una** *vedi* **uno**

u'nanime *a* unanimous

unanime'mente *adv* unanimously

unanimità *nf* unanimity; **all'**~ unanimously

unci'nare *vt* hook

unci'nato *a* hooked; (*parentesi*) angle *attrib*

unci'netto *nm* crochet hook

un'cino *nm* hook

undi'cenne *a & nmf* eleven-year-old

undi'cesimo *a & nm* eleventh

'**undici** *a & nm* eleven

'**ungere** *vt* grease; (*sporcare*) get greasy; *Relig* anoint; (*blandire*) flatter

'**ungersi** *vr* (*con olio solare*) oil oneself; ~ **le mani** get one's hands greasy

unghe'rese *a & nmf* Hungarian ● *nm* (*lingua*) Hungarian

Unghe'ria *nf* Hungary

'**unghia** *nf* nail; (*di animale*) claw; **cadere sotto le unghie di qcno** fall into sb's clutches. ~ **fessa** cloven hoof

unghi'ata *nf* (*graffio*) scratch

ungu'ento *nm* ointment

unica'mente *adv* only

unicellu'lare *a* single-cell, unicellular

unicità *nf* uniqueness

'**unico** *a* only; (*singolo*) single; (*incomparabile*) unique

uni'corno *nm* unicorn

unidimensio'nale *a* one-dimensional

unidirezio'nale *a* unidirectional

unifami'liare *a* one-family

unifi'care *vt* unify

unificazi'one *nf* unification

unifor'mare *vt* level

unifor'marsi *vr* conform (**a** to)

uni'forme *a* uniform ● *nf* uniform. ~ **di gala** *Mil* mess dress

uniformità *nf* uniformity

unilate'rale *a* unilateral

unilateral'mente *adv* unilaterally

uninomi'nale *a Pol* single-candidate

uni'one *nf* union; (*armonia*) unity. **U**~ **economica e monetaria** Economic and Monetary Union. **U**~ **Europea** European Union. **U**~ **Monetaria Europea** European Monetary Union. ~ **sindacale** trade union, labor union *Am*. **U**~ **Sovietica** Soviet Union

u'nire *vt* unite; (*collegare*) join; blend (*colori ecc*)

u'nirsi *vr* unite; (*collegarsi*) join

'**unisex** *a inv* unisex

u'nisono *nm* **all'**~ in unison

unità *nf inv* unity; (*Math, Mil, reparto ecc*) unit; *Comput* drive. ~ **di backup a nastro** *Comput* tape backup drive. ~ **centrale di elaborazione** *Comput* central processing unit, CPU. ~ **floppy disk** *Comput* floppy disk drive. ~ **di inizializzazione** *Comput* boot drive. ~ **di memoria di massa** *Comput* mass storage device. ~ **di misura** unit of measurement. ~ **a nastro magnetico** *Comput* tapedrive. ~ **periferica** *Comput* peripheral. ~ **di produzione** factory unit. ~ **socio-sanitaria locale** local health centre. ~ **di visualizzazione** *Comput* visual display unit, VDU

uni'tario *a* unitary; **prezzo** ~ unit price

u'nito *a* united; (*tinta*) plain; (*comunità*) tight-knit

univer'sale *a* universal

universaliz'zare *vt* universalize

universal'mente *adv* universally

università *nf inv* university

universi'tario, -a *a* university *attrib* ● *nmf* (*insegnante*) university lecturer; (*studente*) undergraduate

uni'verso *nm* universe

u'nivoco *a* unambiguous

'**unto** *pp di* **ungere** ● *a* greasy ● *nm* grease

untu'oso *a* greasy

uno, -a *art indef* a; (*davanti a vocale o h muta*) an; **un esempio** an example; ● *pron* one; **a ~ a ~** one by one; **~ alla volta** one at a time; **l'~ e l'altro** both [of them]; **né l'~ né l'altro** neither [of them]; **~ di noi** one of us; **~ fa quello che può** you do what you can ● *a* a, one ● *nm* (*numerale*) one; (*un tale*) some man ● *nf* some woman

unzi'one *nf* **l'Estrema U~** Extreme Unction, last rites

u'omo *nm* (*pl* **uomini**) man; '**uomini**' (*bagni*) 'gents', 'men's room'. **~ d'affari** business man. **~ di colore** black man. **~ di fiducia** right-hand man. **~ di mondo** man of the world. **~-oggetto** toy boy. **~ delle pulizie** cleaner. **~ sandwich** sandwich-man. **~ di Stato** statesman. **~ della strada** man on the street

u'ovo *nm* (*pl f* **uova**) egg. **uova** *pl* **al bacon** bacon and eggs. **~ barzotto** *o* **bazzotto** soft-boiled egg. **~ in camicia** poached egg. **~ di Colombo** obvious simple solution. **~ alla coque** boiled egg. **~ all'occhio di bue** fried egg. **~ all'ostrica** raw egg. **~ di Pasqua** Easter egg. **uova** *pl* **al prosciutto** ham and eggs. **~ sodo** hard-boiled egg. **~ strapazzato** scrambled egg. **~ al tegamino** fried egg

upgra'dabile *a* upgradeable

'**upupa** *nf* hoopoe

ura'gano *nm* hurricane

u'ranio *nm* uranium

urba'nesimo *nm* urbanization

urba'nista *nmf* town planner

urba'nistica *nf* town planning

urba'nistico *a* urban

urbaniz'zare *vt* urbanize

urbanizzazi'one *nf* urbanization

ur'bano *a* urban; (*cortese*) urbane

u'rea *nf* urea

u'retra *nf Anat* urethra

ur'gente *a* urgent

urgente'mente *adv* urgently

ur'genza *nf* urgency; **in caso d'~** in an emergency; **d'~** (*misura, chiamata*) emergency *attrib*; **operare d'~** perform an emergency operation on

'**urgere** *vi* be urgent

u'rina *nf* urine

uri'nare *vi* urinate

ur'lare *vi* shout, yell; (*cane, vento:*) howl

'**urlo** *nm* (*pl m* **urli**, *pl f* **urla**) shout; (*di cane, vento*) howling

'**urna** *nf* urn; (*elettorale*) ballot box; **andare alle urne** go to the polls

urrà *int* hurrah!

URSS *nf abbr* (**Unione delle Repubbliche Socialiste Sovietiche**) USSR

ur'tare *vt* knock against; (*scontrarsi*) bump into; *fig* irritate

ur'tarsi *vr* collide; *fig* clash

'**urto** *nm* knock; (*scontro*) crash; (*contrasto*) conflict; *fig* clash; **d'~** (*misure, terapia*) shock

U.S.A. *nmpl* US[A] *sg*

usa e getta *a inv* (*rasoio, siringa*) throw-away, disposable

u'sanza *nf* custom; (*moda*) fashion

u'sare *vt* use; (*impiegare*) employ; (*esercitare*) exercise; **~ fare qcsa** be in the habit of doing sth ● *vi* (*essere di moda*) be fashionable; **non si usa più** it is out of fashion; (*attrezzatura, espressione:*) it's not used any more

u'sato *a* used; (*non nuovo*) second-hand ● *nm* second-hand goods *pl*; **dell'~** second-hand; **fuori dell'~** unusual

u'sbeco, -a *a* & *nmf* Uzbekistani

u'scente *a* (*presidente*) outgoing

usci'ere *nm* usher

'**uscio** *nm* door

u'scire *vi* come out; (*andare fuori*) go out; (*sfuggire*) get out; (*essere sorteggiato*) come up; (*giornale:*) come out; **~ da** *Comput* exit from, quit; **~ di strada** leave the road

u'scita *nf* exit, way out; (*spesa*) outlay; (*di autostrada*) junction; (*battuta*) witty remark; (*in ginnastica artistica*) dismount; **uscite** *pl Fin* outgoings; **essere in libera ~** be off duty. **~ di servizio** back door. **~ di sicurezza** emergency exit

usi'gnolo *nm* nightingale

'**uso** *nm* use; (*abitudine*) custom; (*usanza*) usage; **fuori ~** out of use; **per ~ esterno** (*medicina*) for external use only; **~ e dosi** use and dosage

us'saro *nm* hussar

U.S.S.L. *nf abbr* (**Unità Socio-Sanitaria Locale**) local health centre

ustio'narsi *vr* burn oneself

ustio'nato, -a *nmf* burns case ● *a* burnt

usti'one *nf* burn; **ustioni di primo grado** first-degree burns

usu'ale *a* usual

usual'mente *adv* usually

usucapi'one *nf Jur* usucaption

usufru'ire *vi* **~ di** take advantage of, make use of

usufruttu'ario, -a *nmf* user, usufructuary *fml*

usu'frutto *nm Jur* use, usufruct *fml*

u'sura *nf* usury

usu'raio *nm* usurer

usur'pare *vt* usurp

usurpa|'tore, -'trice *nmf* usurper

u'tensile *nm* tool; *Culin* utensil; **cassetta degli utensili** tool box; **utensili** *pl* **da cucina** kitchen utensils

u'tente *nmf* user. **~ finale** end user. **utenti** *pl* **della strada** road users

u'tenza *nf* use; (*utenti*) users *pl*; **~ finale** end users *pl*

ute'rino *a* uterine

'**utero** *nm* womb

'**utile** *a* useful ● *nm Comm* profit; **unire l'~ al dilettevole** combine business with pleas-

ure. **~ su cambi** foreign exchange gain. **~ sul capitale investito** return on investment
utilità *nf* usefulness, utility; *Comput* utility
utili'tario, -a *a* utilitarian ● *nf Auto* small car
utilita'ristico *a* utilitarian
u'tility *nm* utility
utiliz'zare *vt* utilize
utilizzazi'one *nf* utilization
uti'lizzo *nm* use
util'mente *adv* usefully
Uto'pia *nf* Utopia

uto'pista *nmf* Utopian
uto'pistico *a* Utopian
UVA *nmpl abbr* (**ultravioletto prossimo**) UV
'uva *nf* grapes *pl*; **chicco d'~** grape. **~ bianca** white grapes. **~ nera** black grapes. **~ passa** raisins *pl*. **~ sultanina** currants *pl*. **~ da tavola** [eating] grapes. **~ da vino** wine grapes
u'vetta *nf* raisins *pl*
uxori'cida *nm* wife-killer, uxoricide *fml* ● *nf* husband-killer
Uzbeki'stan *nm* Uzbekistan

va' *vedi* **andare**
va'cante *a* vacant
va'canza *nf* holiday, vacation *Am*; [**giorno di**] **~** holiday; (*posto vacante*) vacancy; **vacanze** *pl* holidays, vacation *Am*; *Univ* vacation, vac *fam*. **essere in ~** be on holiday/vacation; **prendersi una ~** take a holiday/vacation; **andare in ~** go on holiday/vacation; **è ~** it's a holiday. **vacanze** *pl* **estive** summer holidays/vacation. **vacanze** *pl* **di Natale** Christmas holidays/vacation. **vacanze** *pl* **di Pasqua** Easter holidays/vacation. **vacanze** *pl* **scolastiche** school holidays/vacation
'vacca *nf* cow. **~ da latte** dairy cow
vac'caro m, -a *nf* cowherd
vacci'nare *vt* vaccinate; **farsi ~** get vaccinated
vaccinazi'one *nf* vaccination
vac'cino *nm* vaccine
vacil'lante *a* tottering; ⟨oggetto⟩ wobbly; ⟨luce⟩ flickering; *fig* wavering
vacil'lare *vi* totter; ⟨oggetto:⟩ wobble; ⟨luce:⟩ flicker; *fig* waver
'vacuo *a* (*vano*) vain; *fig* empty ● *nm* vacuum
'vado *vedi* **andare**
vaffan'culo *int vulg* fuck off!
vagabon'daggio *nm Jur* vagrancy
vagabon'dare *vi* wander
vaga'bondo *a* ⟨cane⟩ stray; **gente** *pl* **vagabonda** tramps ● *nmf* tramp
vaga'mente *adv* vaguely
va'gante *a* wandering; **mina ~** floating mine; **proiettile ~** stray bullet
va'gare *vi* wander
vagheggi'are *vt* long for
va'ghezza *nf* vagueness
va'gina *nf* vagina
vagi'nale *a* vaginal
va'gire *vi* whimper
va'gito *nm* whimper

'vaglia *nm inv* money order. **~ bancario** bank draft. **~ cambiario** promissory note. **~ internazionale** international money order. **~ postale** postal order
vagli'are *vt* sift; *fig* weigh
'vaglio *nm* sieve
'vago *a* vague
vagon'cino *nm* (*di funivia*) car. **~ a piattaforma** flat[bed] wagon
va'gone *nm* (*per passeggeri*) carriage, car; (*per merci*) truck, wagon. **~ bagagliaio** luggage van, baggage car *Am*. **~ frigorifero** refrigerator van. **~ letto** sleeper. **~ postale** mail coach. **~ ristorante** restaurant car, dining car
vai'olo *nm* smallpox
va'langa *nf* avalanche
val'chiria *nf* Valkyrie
val'dese *a* & *nmf* Waldensian
va'lente *a* skilful
va'lenza *nf Chem* valency; (*fig: valore*) value
va'lere *vi* be worth; (*contare*) count; ⟨regola:⟩ apply (**per** to); (*essere valido*) be valid; **far ~ i propri diritti** assert one's rights; **farsi ~** assert oneself; **non vale!** that's not fair!; **tanto vale che me ne vada** I might as well go ● *vt* **~ qcsa a qcno** (*procurare*) earn sb sth; **valerne la pena** be worth it; **vale la pena di vederlo** it's worth seeing; **valersi di** avail oneself of
valeri'ana *nf* valerian
va'levole *a* valid
'valgo *a* **alluce ~** hallux valgus; **ginocchia** *pl* **valghe** knock knees
vali'care *vt* cross
'valico *nm* pass
valida'mente *adv* validly; (*efficacemente*) efficiently; ⟨contribuire⟩ effectively
validità *nf inv* validity; **con ~ illimitata** valid indefinitely
'valido *a* valid; (*efficace*) efficient; ⟨contributo⟩ valuable

valige'ria nf (*fabbrica*) leather factory; (*negozio*) leather goods shop

vali'getta nf small case; (*per attrezzi*) box. ~ **del pronto soccorso** first aid kit. ~ **ventiquattrore** overnight bag

va'ligia nf suitcase; **fare le valigie** pack; *fig* pack one's bags. ~ **diplomatica** diplomatic bag

val'lata nf valley

'valle nf valley; **a** ~ downstream

val'letta nf *TV* assistant

val'letto nm valet; *TV* assistant

'vallo nm wall; **il** ~ **Adriano** Hadrian's Wall

val'lone nm (*valle*) deep valley

val'lone, -a a & nmf Walloon

va'lore nm value, worth; (*merito*) merit; (*coraggio*) valour; **valori** pl Comm securities; **di** ~ (*oggetto*) valuable; **oggetti di** ~ valuables; **di grande** ~ of great value; (*medico, scienziato*) top attrib; **senza** ~ worthless; **a** ~ **aggiunto** value-added. ~ **bollato** revenue stamp. ~ **contabile** book value. ~ **effettivo** real value. ~ **di mercato** market value. ~ **mobiliare** security. ~ **nominale** nominal value. ~ **di realizzo** break-up value. ~ **di riscatto** surrender value

valoriz'zare vt (*mettere in valore*) use to advantage; (*aumentare di valore*) increase the value of; (*migliorare l'aspetto di*) enhance

valoriz'zarsi vr **il paese ha bisogno di** ~ **migliorando...** the country needs to enhance the value of its assets by improving...

valorosa'mente adv courageously

valo'roso a courageous

'valso pp di **valere**

va'luta nf currency. ~ **a corso legale** legal tender. ~ **estera** foreign currency

valu'tare vt value; weigh up (*situazione*)

valu'tario a (*mercato, norme*) currency attrib

valuta'tivo a for evaluation, evaluative

valutazi'one nf valuation

'valva nf valve

'valvola nf valve; *Electr* fuse. ~ **a farfalla** butterfly valve. ~ **pneumatica** air valve. ~ **di sicurezza** anche fig safety valve

'valzer nm inv waltz

vamp nf inv vamp

vam'pata nf blaze; (*di calore*) blast; (*al viso*) flush

vam'piro nm vampire; *fig* blood-sucker

va'nadio nm vanadium

vanaglori'oso a vainglorious

vana'mente adv (*inutilmente*) in vain; (*con vanità*) vainly

van'dalico a atto ~ act of vandalism

vanda'lismo nm vandalism

vandalizzare vt vandalize

vandalizzazione nf vandalizing

'vandalo, -a nmf vandal

vaneggia'mento nm delirium

vaneggi'are vi rave

va'nesio a conceited

'vanga nf spade

van'gare vt dig

van'gata nf (*quantità*) spadeful; (*azione*) blow with a spade

van'gelo nm Gospel; (*fam: verità*) gospel [truth]

vanifi'care vt nullify

va'niglia nf vanilla

vanigli'ato a (*zucchero*) vanilla

vanil'lina nf vanillin

vanità nf vanity

vanitosa'mente adv vainly

vani'toso a vain

'vano a vain ●nm (*stanza*) room; (*spazio vuoto*) hollow. ~ **doccia** shower room. ~ **portabagagli** Auto boot, trunk Am

van'taggio nm advantage; Sport lead; Tennis advantage; **trarre** ~ **da qcsa** derive benefit from sth

vantaggiosa'mente adv advantageously

vantaggi'oso a advantageous

van'tare vt praise; (*possedere*) boast

van'tarsi vr boast

vante'ria nf boasting; **vanterie** pl boasting

'vanto nm boast

'vanvera nf a ~ at random; **parlare a** ~ talk nonsense

va'pore nm steam; (*di benzina, cascata*) vapour; **a** ~ steam attrib; **al** ~ Culin steamed; **battello a** ~ steamboat. ~ **acqueo** steam, water vapour

vapo'retto nm ferry

vapori'era nf steam engine

vaporiz'zare vt vaporize

vaporizza'tore nm spray

vapo'roso a (*vestito*) filmy; **capelli** pl **vaporosi** big hair

va'rano nm monitor [lizard]

va'rare vt launch

var'care vt cross

'varco nm passage; **aspettare al** ~ lie in wait

vare'china nf bleach

vari'abile a changeable, variable ●nf Math variable

variabilità nf changeableness, variability

varia'mente adv variously

vari'ante nf variant

vari'are vt/i vary; ~ **di umore** change one's mood

vari'ato a varied

variazi'one nf variation

va'rice nf varicose vein

vari'cella nf chickenpox

vari'coso a varicose

varie'gato a variegated

varietà nf inv variety ●nm inv variety show

'vario a varied; (*al pl, parecchi*) various; **varie** pl (*molti*) several; **varie ed eventuali** any other business

vario'pinto a multicoloured

'varo nm launch

Var'savia Warsaw

vas'aio nm potter

'vasca nf tub; (*piscina*) pool; (*lunghezza*)

length. ~ **da bagno** bath. ~ **di sviluppo**
Phot developing tank

va'scello *nm* vessel; **capitano di ~** captain

va'schetta *nf* tub; *Phot* tray. ~ **per il ghiaccio** ice-tray

vasco'lare *a Anat, Bot* vascular

vasecto'mia *nf* vasectomy

vase'lina *nf* Vaseline®

vasel'lame *nm* china. ~ **d'oro/d'argento** gold/silver plate

va'setto *nm* small pot; (*per marmellata*) jam jar

'vaso *nm* pot; (*da fiori*) vase; *Anat* vessel; (*per cibi*) jar. ~ **da notte** chamberpot. ~ **sanguigno** blood vessel

vasocostrit'tore *a* vasoconstrictor

vasodilata'tore *a* vasodilator

vas'sallo *nm* vassal

vas'soio *nm* tray

vastità *nf* vastness

'vasto *a* vast; **di vaste vedute** broad-minded

Vati'cano *nm* Vatican

vati'cinio *nm* prophecy

vattela'pesca *adv fam* God knows

'vattene! go away!; *vedi* **andarsene**

VCR *abbr* (**videoregistratore**) VCR

ve *pers pron* you; **ve l'ho dato** I gave it to you

'vecchia *nf* old woman

vecchi'aia *nf* old age

'vecchio, -a *a* old ● *nmf* old man; old woman; **i vecchi** old people; ~ **mio** old man

'veccia *nf* vetch

'vece *nf* **in ~ di** in place of; **fare le veci di qcno** take sb's place

ve'dente *a* **i non ~** the visually handicapped

ve'dere *vt* see; see, watch (*film, partita*); **far ~** show; **farsi ~** show one's face; **non si vede** (*macchia, imperfezione:*) it doesn't show; **non veder l'ora di fare qcsa** be raring to go; **non poter ~ qcno** not be able to stand the sight of sb; **vederci doppio** have double vision; **ne ho viste di tutti i colori** *fig* I've really seen life!; **da ~** (*film, spettacolo*) not to be missed; **questo è da ~!** that remains to be seen!; **chi si vede!** *fam* look who it is! ● *vi* see

ve'dersi *vr* see oneself; (*reciproco*) see each other; **vedersela brutta** have a narrow escape

ve'detta *nf* (*luogo*) lookout; *Naut* patrol vessel

'vedova *nf* widow. ~ **nera** *Zool* black widow [spider]

'vedovo *nm* widower

ve'duta *nf* view

vee'mente *a* vehement

vege'tale *a & nm* vegetable

vegetali'ano *a & nmf* vegan

vege'tare *vi* vegetate

vegetari'ano, -a *a & nmf* vegetarian

vegeta'tivo *a* vegetative

vegetazi'one *nf* vegetation

'vegeto *a vedi* **vivo**

veg'gente *nmf* clairvoyant

'veglia *nf* watch; **fare la ~** keep watch. ~ **funebre** vigil

vegli'are *vi* be awake; ~ **su** watch over

vegli'one *nm* ~ **di capodanno** New Year's Eve celebration

veico'lare *vt* carry (*malattia*) ● *a* (*traffico*) vehicular

ve'icolo *nm* vehicle. ~ **pesante** heavy goods vehicle, HGV. ~ **spaziale** spacecraft

'vela *nf* sail; *Sport* sailing; **andare a gonfie vele** *fig* go beautifully; (*affari:*) be booming; **far ~** set sail. ~ **di taglio** mainsail

ve'lare *vt* veil; (*fig: nascondere*) hide

ve'larsi *vr* (*vista:*) mist over; (*voce:*) go husky

velata'mente *adv* indirectly

ve'lato *a* veiled; (*occhi*) misty; (*collant*) sheer

vela'tura *nf* sails *pl*

'velcro® *nm* velcro

veleggi'are *vi* sail

ve'leno *nm* poison

velenosa'mente *adv* (*rispondere*) venomously

vele'noso *a* poisonous; (*frase*) venomous

ve'letta *nf* (*di cappello*) veil

'velico *a* (*circolo*) sailing *attrib*; **superficie velica** sail area

veli'ero *nm* sailing ship

ve'lina *nf* (**carta**) ~ tissue paper; (*copia*) carbon copy

ve'lista *nm* yachtsman ● *nf* yachtswoman

ve'livolo *nm* aircraft

velleità *nf inv* foolish ambition

vellei'tario *a* unrealistic

'vello *nm* fleece

vellu'tato *a* velvety

vel'luto *nm* velvet. ~ **a coste** corduroy

'velo *nm* veil; (*di zucchero, cipria*) dusting; (*tessuto*) voile

ve'loce *a* fast

veloce'mente *adv* quickly

velo'cipede *nm* penny-farthing

velo'cista *nmf Sport* sprinter

velocità *nf inv* speed; (*Auto: marcia*) gear. ~ **di clock** *Comput* clock speed. ~ **di crociera** cruising speed. ~ **di stampa** print speed

velociz'zare *vt* speed up

ve'lodromo *nm* cycle track

'vena *nf* vein; **essere in ~ di** be in the mood for. ~ **poetica** poetic mood

ve'nale *a* venal; (*persona*) mercenary, venal

ve'nato *a* grainy

vena'torio *a* hunting *attrib*

vena'tura *nf* (*di legno*) grain; (*di foglia, marmo*) vein

ven'demmia *nf* grape harvest

vendemmi'are *vt* harvest

vendemmia|'tore, -'trice *nmf* grape-picker

'vendere *vt* sell

'vendersi *vr* sell oneself; **vendesi** for sale

ven'detta *nf* revenge. ~ **trasversale** vendetta

vendi'care *vt* avenge

vendi'carsi vr take revenge, get one's revenge; **~ di qcno** take one's vengeance on sb; **~ di qcsa** take revenge for sth

vendicativa'mente adv vindictively

vendica'tivo a vindictive

vendica|'tore, -'trice nmf avenger

'vendita nf sale; **in ~** on sale. **~ all'asta** sale by auction. **~ di beneficenza** bring and buy sale. **~ per corrispondenza** mail-order; **azienda di ~ ~ ~** mail-order company; **catalogo di ~ ~ ~** mail-order catalogue. **~ al dettaglio** retailing. **~ all'ingrosso** wholesaling. **~ al minuto** retailing. **~ porta a porta** door-to-door selling. **~ a rate** hire purchase, installment plan Am

vendi|'tore, -'trice nmf seller. **~ ambulante** hawker, pedlar. **~ al dettaglio** retailer. **~ all'ingrosso** wholesaler. **~ al mercato** market trader. **~ al minuto** retailer

ven'duto a ⟨merce⟩ sold; ⟨fig: arbitro⟩ bent; **arbitro ~!** whose side are you on, ref!

vene'rabile, vene'rando a venerable

vene'rare vt revere

venerazi'one nf reverence

venerdì nm inv Friday; **di ~** on Fridays. **V~ Santo** Good Friday

'Venere nf Venus

ve'nereo a venereal

'Veneto nm Veneto

'veneto a from the Veneto

Ve'nezia nf Venice

venezi'ano, -a a a & nmf Venetian ● nf ⟨persiana⟩ Venetian blind; Culin sweet bun

Vene'zuela nm Venezuela

venezue'lano, -a a & nmf Venezuelan

'vengo vedi venire

veni'ale a venial

ve'nire vi come; ⟨riuscire⟩ turn out; ⟨costare⟩ cost; ⟨in passivi⟩ be; **quanto viene?** how much is it?; **viene prodotto in serie** it's mass-produced; **~ a sapere** learn; **~ in mente** occur; **mi è venuto un dubbio** I've just had a doubt; **gli è venuta la febbre** he's got a temperature; **~ meno** ⟨svenire⟩ faint; **~ meno a un contratto** go back on a contract, renege on a contract; **~ via** come away; ⟨staccarsi⟩ come off; **mi viene da piangere** I feel like crying; **vieni a prendermi** come and pick me up; **vieni a trovarmi** come and see me; **nei giorni a ~** in [the] days to come

ve'noso a venous

ven'taglio nm fan

ven'tata nf gust [of wind]; fig breath

ven'tenne a & nmf twenty-year-old

ven'tesimo a & nm twentieth

'venti a & nm twenty

venti'lare vt ventilate, air; **~ un'idea** give an idea an airing; **poco ventilato** ⟨stanza⟩ airless

ventila'tore nm fan

ventilazi'one nf ventilation

ven'tina nf una **~** ⟨circa venti⟩ about twenty

ventiquat'trore nf inv ⟨valigia⟩ overnight case ● adv **~ su ventiquattro** ⟨lavorare⟩ round-the-clock; ⟨aperto⟩ 24 hours

'vento nm wind; **c'è molto ~** it's very windy; **farsi ~** fan oneself. **~ contrario** headwind. **~ di prua** headwind. **~ di traverso** crosswind

'ventola nf fan

vento'lina nf fan. **~ di raffeddamento** Comput cooling fan

ven'tosa nf sucker

ven'toso a windy

'ventre nm stomach; ⟨fig: di terra⟩ bowels pl; **basso ~** lower abdomen

ventrico'lare a Med ventricular

ven'tricolo nm ventricle

ven'triloquo nm ventriloquist

ventu'nesimo a & nm twenty-first

ven'tuno a & nm twenty-one

ven'tura nf fortune; **andare alla ~** trust to luck

ven'turo a next

ve'nuta nf coming. **~ meno a** breaking

'vera nf ⟨anello⟩ wedding ring

vera'mente adv really

ve'randa nf veranda

ver'bale a verbal ● nm ⟨di riunione⟩ minutes pl. **~ di contravvenzione** fine

verbal'mente adv verbally

ver'bena nf verbena

'verbo nm verb; **il V~** Relig the Word. **~ ausiliare** auxiliary [verb]. **~ modale** modal auxiliary

ver'boso a verbose

ver'dastro a greenish

'verde a green; **~ d'invidia** green with envy ● nm green; ⟨vegetazione⟩ greenery; ⟨semaforo⟩ green light; **essere al ~** be broke. **~ bottiglia** bottle green. **~ oliva** olive green. **~ pisello** pea green. **~ pubblico** public parks pl

verdeggi'ante a liter verdant

verde'mare a & nm inv sea-green

verde'rame nm verdigris

ver'detto nm verdict. **~ di assoluzione** not guilty verdict. **~ di condanna** guilty verdict

ver'done nm greenfinch

ver'dura nf vegetables pl; **una ~** a vegetable; **verdure** pl miste mixed vegetables

'verga nf rod

ver'gato a lined

vergi'nale a virginal

'vergine nf virgin; Astr Virgo ● a virgin; ⟨cassetta⟩ blank

verginità nf virginity

ver'gogna nf shame; ⟨timidezza⟩ shyness

vergo'gnarsi vr feel ashamed; ⟨essere timido⟩ feel shy

vergogna'mente adv shamefully

vergo'gnoso a ashamed; ⟨timido⟩ shy; ⟨disonorevole⟩ shameful

veridicità nf veracity

ve'rifica nf check. **~ dei bilanci** audit. **~ di cassa** cash check

verifi'cabile a verifiable

verifi'care vt check; verify ⟨teoria⟩

verifi'carsi vr come true

verifica|'tore, -'trice nmf checker

ve'rismo *nm* realism
verità *nf inv* truth
veriti'ero *a* truthful
'verme *nm* worm. ~ solitario tapeworm
vermi'celli *nmpl* vermicelli *sg* (*pasta thinner than spaghetti*)
ver'mifugo *a* vermifugal ● *nm* vermifuge
ver'miglio *a & nm* vermilion
'vermut *nm inv* vermouth
ver'nacolo *nm* vernacular
ver'nice *nf* paint; (*trasparente*) varnish; (*pelle*) patent leather; *fig* veneer; '~ fresca' wet paint. ~ a spirito spirit varnish
vernici'are *vt* paint; (*con vernice trasparente*) varnish
vernicia'tura *nf* painting; (*con vernice trasparente*) varnishing; (*strato*) paintwork; *fig* veneer
vernis'sage *nm inv* vernissage
'vero *a* true; (*autentico*) real; (*perfetto*) perfect; è ~? is that so?; ~ e proprio full-blown; sei stanca, ~? you're tired, aren't you; non ti piace, ~? you don't like it, do you? ~ cuoio real leather ● *nm* truth; (*realità*) life
verosimigli'anza *nf* plausibility
vero'simile *a* probable, likely
verosimil'mente *adv* probably
ver'ruca *nf* wart; (*sotto la pianta del piede*) verruca
versa'mento *nm* (*pagamento*) payment; (*in banca*) deposit
ver'sante *nm* slope
ver'sare *vt* pour; (*spargere*) shed; (*rovesciare*) spill; pay (*denaro*); (*in banca*) pay in ● *vi* (*trovarsi*) be
ver'sarsi *vr* spill; (*sfociare*) flow
ver'satile *a* versatile
versatilità *nf* versatility
ver'sato *a* (*pratico*) versed
ver'setto *nm* verse
versifica|'tore, -'trice *nmf* versifier
versi'one *nf* version; (*traduzione*) translation; '~ integrale' 'unabridged version'; ~ originale original version. '~ ridotta' 'abridged version'. ~ teatrale dramatization
'verso[1] *nm* verse; (*grido*) cry; (*gesto*) gesture; (*senso*) direction; (*modo*) manner; fare il ~ a qcno ape sb; non c'è ~ di there is no way of. versi *pl* sciolti blank verse
'verso[2] *prep* towards; (*nei pressi di*) round about; ~ dove? which way?
'vertebra *nf* vertebra
verte'brale *a* vertebral
verte'brato *nm* vertebrate
ver'tenza *nf* dispute. ~ sindacale industrial dispute
'vertere *vi* ~ su focus on
verti'cale *a* vertical; (*in parole crociate*) down ● *nm* vertical ● *nf* handstand; fare la ~ do a handstand
vertical'mente *adv* vertically
'vertice *nm* summit; *Math* vertex; conferenza al ~ summit conference; incontro al ~ summit meeting
ver'tigine *nf* dizziness; *Med* vertigo; ver-

tigini *pl* giddy spells; aver le vertigini feel dizzy
vertiginosa'mente *adv* dizzily
vertigi'noso *a* dizzy; (*velocità*) breakneck; (*prezzi*) sky-high; (*scollatura*) plunging
'vescia *nf* puffball
ve'scica *nf* bladder; (*sulla pelle*) blister
'vescovo *nm* bishop
'vespa *nf* wasp
vespasi'ano *nm* urinal
'vespro *nm* vespers *pl*
ves'sare *vt fml* oppress
ves'sillo *nm* standard
ve'staglia *nf* dressing gown, robe *Am*
'veste *nf* dress; (*rivestimento*) covering; in ~ di in the capacity of; in ~ ufficiale in an official capacity. ~ da camera dressing gown, robe *Am*. ~ editoriale layout. ~ tipografica typographical design
vesti'ario *nm* clothing
ve'stibolo *nm* hall
ve'stigio *nm* (*pl m* vestigi, *pl f* vestigia) trace
ve'stire *vt* dress
ve'stirsi *vr* get dressed; ~ da dress up as a
ve'stito *a* dressed ● *nm* (*da uomo*) suit; (*da donna*) dress; vestiti *pl* clothes. ~ da sposa wedding dress. ~ da uomo suit
vete'rano, -a *a & nmf* veteran
veteri'nario, -a *a* veterinary ● *nm* veterinary surgeon ● *nf* veterinary science
'veto *nm inv* veto
ve'traio *nm* glazier
ve'trato, -a *a* glazed ● *nf* big window; (*in chiesa*) stained-glass window; (*porta*) glass door
vetre'ria *nf* glass works
ve'trina *nf* [shop-]window; (*mobile*) display cabinet
vetri'nista *nmf* window dresser
ve'trino *nm* (*di microscopio*) slide
vetri'olo *nm* vitriol
'vetro *nm* glass; (*di finestra, porta*) pane. ~ di sicurezza safety glass
vetro'resina *nf* fibreglass
ve'troso *a* vitreous
'vetta *nf* peak
vet'tore *nm* vector
vetto'vaglie *nfpl* provisions
vet'tura *nf* coach; (*ferroviaria*) coach, carriage; *Auto* car. ~ d'epoca vintage car
vettu'rino *nm* coachman
vezzeggi'are *vt* fondle
vezzeggia'tivo *nm* pet name
'vezzo *nm* habit; (*attrattiva*) charm; vezzi *pl* (*moine*) affectation
vez'zoso *a* charming; *pej* affected
VF *abbr* (*Vigili del Fuoco*) fire brigade, fire department *Am*
vi *pers pron* you; (*riflessivo*) yourselves; (*reciproco*) each other; (*tra più persone*) one another; vi ho dato un libro I gave you a book; lavatevi le mani wash your hands; eccovi! here you are! ● *adv* = ci
'via[1] *nf* street, road; *fig* way; *Anat* tract; in ~

di in the course of; **per ~ di** on account of; **per ~ aerea** by airmail. **V~ Lattea** *Astr* Milky Way. **~ di mezzo** halfway house. **~ respiratoria** *Anat* airway. **~ d'uscita** let-out
'via² *adv* away; (*fuori*) out; **andar ~** go away; (*macchia:*) come off, come out; **e così ~** and so on; **e ~ dicendo** and whatnot; **~ ~ che** as ● *int* **~!** I go away!; *Sport* go!; (*andiamo*) come on!; **~, non ci credo** come off it *or* come on, I don't believe it ● *nm* starting signal
viabilità *nf* road conditions *pl*; (*rete*) road network; (*norme*) road and traffic laws *pl*
via'card *nf inv* motorway card
vi'ado *nm* (*pl* **viados**) rent boy
via'dotto *nm* viaduct
viaggi'are *vi* travel; **il treno viaggia con 20 minuti di ritardo** the train is 20 minutes late
viaggia|'tore, -'trice *nmf* traveller
vi'aggio *nm* journey; (*breve*) trip; **buon ~!** safe journey!, have a good trip!; **fare un ~** go on a journey; **essere in ~** be underway; **mettersi in ~** get underway. **~ d'affari** business trip. **~ di lavoro** working trip **~ di nozze** honeymoon. **~ organizzato** package tour
vi'ale *nm* avenue; (*privato*) drive
via'letto *nm* path
via'vai *nm* coming and going
vi'brante *a* vibrant
vi'brare *vi* vibrate; (*fremere*) quiver
vibra'tore *nm* vibrator
vibra'torio *a* vibratory
vibrazi'one *nf* vibration
vi'cario *nm* vicar
'vice *nmf* deputy
vice+ *pref* vice+
vicecoman'dante *nm* *Mil* second in command
vicediret|'tore, -'trice *nm* assistant manager ● *nf* assistant manageress
vi'cenda *nf* event; **a ~** (*fra due*) each other; (*a turno*) in turn[s]
vicendevol'mente *adv* each other
vice'preside *nmf* vice-principal
vicepresi'dente *nm* vice-president; *Comm* vice-chairman, vice-president *Am*
vicepresi'denza *nf* vice-presidency; *Sch* deputy head's office
vicerè *nm inv* viceroy
viceret'tore *nm* vice-chancellor
vice'versa *adv* vice versa
vi'chingo, -a *a* & *nmf* Viking
vi'cina *nf* neighbour
vici'nanza *nf* nearness; **vicinanze** (*pl: paraggi*) neighbourhood
vici'nato *nm* neighbourhood; (*vicini*) neighbours *pl*
vi'cino, -a *a* near; (*accanto*) next ● *adv* near, close ● *prep* **~ a** near [to] ● *nmf* neighbour. **~ di casa** nextdoor neighbour
vicissi'tudine *nf* vicissitude
'vicolo *nm* alley. **~ cieco** *anche fig* blind alley
'video *nm* (*musicale*) video; (*schermo*) screen. **~ interattivo** interactive video

video'camera *nf* camcorder
videocas'setta *nf* video, video cassette
videoci'tofono *nm* video entry phone
video'clip *nm inv* video clip
videoconfe'renza *nf* videoconference
videogi'oco *nm* video game
video'leso, -a *a* visually handicapped ● *nmf* visually handicapped person
videoregistra'tore *nm* videorecorder
videoscrit'tura *nf* word processing
videosorvegli'anza *nf* video surveillance
video'teca *nf* video library
video'telᴿ *nm* ≃ Videotex ᴿ
videote'lefono *nm* view phone
videotermi'nale *nm* visual display unit, VDU
vidi'mare *vt* authenticate
vi'eni *vedi* **venire**
Vi'enna *nf* Vienna
vien'nese *a* & *nmf* Viennese
vie'tare *vt* forbid; **~ qcsa a qcno** forbid sb sth
vie'tato *a* forbidden; **sosta vietata** no parking; **~ fumare** no smoking; **~ ai minori di 18 anni** prohibited to children under the age of 18
Vi'etnam *nm* Vietnam
vietna'mita *a* & *nmf* Vietnamese
vi'gente *a* in force
'vigere *vi* be in force
vigi'lante *a* vigilant
vigi'lanza *nf* vigilance; (*sorveglianza*) (*a scuola*) supervision; (*di polizia*) surveillance. **~ notturna** night security guards *pl.* **~ urbana** traffic police (*in towns*)
vigi'lare *vt* keep an eye on ● *vi* keep watch
vigi'lato, -a *a* under surveillance ● *nmf* person under police surveillance. **~ speciale** person under special police surveillance
'vigile *a* watchful ● *nm* **~ [urbano]** traffic policeman. **~ del fuoco** fireman. **vigili** *pl* **del fuoco** firemen, fire brigade. **vigili** *pl* **urbani** traffic police (*in towns*)
vi'gilia *nf* eve; *Relig* fast. **~ di Natale** Christmas Eve
vigliacca'mente *adv* in a cowardly way
vigliacche'ria *nf* cowardice
vigli'acco, -a *a* cowardly ● *nmf* coward
'vigna *nf*, **vi'gneto** *nm* vineyard
vi'gnetta *nf* cartoon
vignet'tista *nm* cartoonist
vi'gogna *nf* (*tessuto*) vicuña
vi'gore *nm* vigour; **entrare in ~** come into force; **essere in ~** be in force
vigorosa'mente *adv* energetically
vigo'roso *a* vigorous
'vile *a* cowardly; (*abietto*) vile
vili'pendio *nm* scorn, contempt
'villa *nf* villa
vil'laggio *nm* village. **~ olimpico** Olympic village. **~ residenziale** commuter town. **~ satellite** satellite village. **~ turistico** holiday village

villa'nia *nf* rudeness

vil'lano *a* rude ● *nm* boor; (*contadino*) peasant

villeggi'ante *nmf* holiday-maker

villeggi'are *vi* spend one's holidays

villeggia'tura *nf* holiday[s] [*pl*], vacation *Am*

vil'letta *nf* small detached house. **~ bifamiliare** semi-detached house. **villette** *pl* **a schiera** terraced houses

vil'lino *nm* detached house

vil'loso *a* hairy

vil'mente *adv* in a cowardly way; (*in modo spreggevole*) contemptibly

viltà *nf* cowardice

'vimine *nm* wicker; **sedia di vimini** wicker chair

vi'naio, -a *nmf* wine merchant

'vincere *vt* win; (*sconfiggere*) beat; (*superare*) overcome

'vincita *nf* win; (*somma vinta*) winnings *pl*

vinci|'tore, -'trice *nmf* winner; (*di battaglia*) victor, winner ● *a* winning, victorious

vinco'lante *a* binding

vinco'lare *vt* bind; *Comm* tie up

vinco'lato *a* *Fin* nonredeemable; **deposito ~** fixed deposit, term deposit

'vincolo *nm* bond

vi'nicolo *a* wine *attrib*

vi'nile *nm* vinyl

vi'nilico *a* vinyl

vinil'pelle[R] *nm* Leatherette[R]

'vino *nm* wine. **~ d'annata** vintage wine. **~ bianco** white wine. **~ brûlé** mulled wine. **~ della casa** house wine. **~ da dessert** dessert wine. **~ nuovo** new wine. **~ rosato** rosé [wine]. **~ rosé** rosé [wine]. **~ rosso** red wine. **~ spumante** sparkling wine. **~ da taglio** blending wine. **~ da tavola** table wine

vin'santo *nm* *dessert wine from Tuscany*

'vinto *pp di* **vincere**

vi'ola *nf* *Bot* violet; *Mus* viola. **~ del pensiero** *Bot* pansy

vio'laceo *a* purplish; (*labbra*) blue

vio'lare *vt* violate

violazi'one *nf* violation. **~ di contratto** breach of contract. **~ di domicilio** breaking and entering

violen'tare *vt* rape

violente'mente *adv* violently

vio'lento *a* violent

vio'lenza *nf* violence. **~ carnale** rape

vio'letto, -a *a & nm* (*colore*) violet ● *nf* violet

violi'nista *nmf* violinist

vio'lino *nm* violin

violon'cello *nm* cello

vi'ottolo *nm* path

'vipera *nf* viper

vi'raggio *nm* *Phot* toning; *Naut, Aeron* turn

vi'rale *a* viral

vi'rare *vi* turn; (*nave:*) put about; **~ di bordo** change course

vi'rata *nf* (*di aereo*) turning; (*di nave*) coming about; (*nel nuoto*) turn; *fig* change of direction

'virgola *nf* comma; *Math* [decimal] point; **punto e ~** semicolon; **quattro ~ due (4,2)** (*decimali*) four point two (4.2)

virgo'lette *nfpl* inverted commas, quotation marks

vi'rile *a* virile; (*da uomo*) manly

virilità *nf* virility; manliness

viril'mente *adv* in a manly way

vi'rologo *nm* virologist

virtù *nf inv* virtue; **in ~ di** (*legge*) under

virtu'ale *a* virtual

virtual'mente *adv* virtually

virtuo'sismo *nm* bravura

virtu'oso *a* virtuous ● *nm* virtuoso

viru'lento *a* virulent

'virus *nm* virus

visa'gista *nmf* beautician

visce'rale *a* visceral; (*odio*) deep-seated; (*reazione*) gut

'viscere *nm* internal organ ● *nfpl* guts

'vischio *nm* mistletoe

vischi'oso *a* viscous; (*appiccicoso*) sticky

'viscido *a* slimy

vi'sconte *nm* viscount

viscon'tessa *nf* viscountess

vi'scoso *a* viscous

vi'sibile *a* visible

visi'bilio *nm* profusion; **andare in ~** go into ecstasies

visibilità *nf* visibility; **scarsa ~** poor visibility

visi'era *nf* (*di elmo*) visor; (*di berretto*) peak

visio'nare *vt* examine; *Cinema* screen

visio'nario, -a *a & nmf* visionary

visi'one *nf* vision; **prima ~** *Cinema* first showing; **seconda ~** re-release, second showing. **~ notturna** night vision

'visita *nf* visit; (*breve*) call; *Med* examination; **fare ~ a** qcno pay sb a visit. **~ di controllo** *Med* checkup. **~ di convenienza** courtesy visit. **~ doganale** customs inspection. **~ a domicilio** home visit, call-out. **~ fiscale** tax inspection. **~ guidata** guided tour. **~ lampo** flying visit. **~ di leva** medical examination

visi'tare *vt* visit; (*brevemente*) call on; *Med* examine

visita|'tore, -'trice *nmf* visitor

visiva'mente *adv* visually

vi'sivo *a* visual

'viso *nm* face. **~ pallido** paleface

vi'sone *nm* mink

'vispo *a* lively

vis'suto *pp di* **vivere** ● *a* experienced

'vista *nf* sight; (*veduta*) view; **a ~ d'occhio** (*crescere*) visibly; (*estendersi*) as far as the eye can see; **in ~ di** in view of; **perdere di ~** qcno lose sight of sb; *fig* lose touch with sb; **a prima ~** at first sight

'visto *pp di* **vedere** ● *nm* visa. **~ di entrata** *o* **di ingresso** entry visa, entry permit. **~ d'uscita** exit visa ● *conj* **~ che...** seeing that...

vistosa'mente *adv* conspicuously

vi'stoso *a* showy; *(notevole)* considerable

visu'ale *a* visual

visualiz'zare *vt* visualize; *Comput* display

visualizza'tore *nm Comput* display, VDU. **~ a cristalli liquidi** *Comput* liquid crystal display

visualizzazi'one *nf Comput* display

'vita *nf* life; *(durata della vita)* lifetime; *Anat* waist; **a ~ for** life; **essere in fin di ~** be at death's door; **essere in ~** be alive; **fare la bella ~** lead the good life; **costo della ~** cost of living. **~ eterna** eternal life. **~ media** *Biol* life expectancy. **~ mondana** high life; **fare ~ ~** lead the high life. **~ notturna** night life. **~ terrena** *Relig* life on earth

vi'taccia *nf* slog

vi'tale *a* vital

vitalità *nf* vitality

vita'lizio *a* life *attrib* ● *nm* [life] annuity

vita'mina *nf* vitamin

vita'minico *a* vitamin-enriched

vitaminiz'zato *a* vitamin-enriched

'vite *nf Mech* screw; *Bot* vine; **giro di ~** *fig* turn of the screw. **~ canadese** Virginia creeper. **~ di coda** *Aeron* tailspin. **~ perpetua** endless screw

vi'tella *nf (animale)* calf; *(carne)* veal

vi'tello *nm* calf; *(carne)* veal; *(pelle)* calfskin. **~ di latte** milk-fed veal. **~ tonnato** *sliced veal with tuna, anchovy, oil and lemon sauce*

vi'ticcio *nm* tendril

viticol'tore *nm* wine grower

viticol'tura *nf* wine growing

vi'tino *nm* narrow waist; **~ di vespa** slender little waist

'vitreo *a* vitreous; *(sguardo)* glassy

'vittima *nf* victim

'vitto *nm* food; *(pasti)* board. **~ e alloggio** board and lodging

vit'toria *nf* victory

vittori'ano *a* Victorian

vittoriosa'mente *adv* victoriously, triumphantly

vittori'oso *a* victorious

vitupe'rare *vt* vituperate

vitu'perio *nm* insult

vi'uzza *nf* narrow lane

'viva *int* hurrah!; **~ la Regina!** long live the Queen!

vi'vace *a* vivacious; *(mente)* lively; *(colore)* bright

vivace'mente *adv* vivaciously

vivacità *nf* vivacity; *(di mente)* liveliness; *(di colore)* brightness

vivaciz'zare *vt* liven up

vi'vaio *nm* nursery; *(per pesci)* pond; *fig* breeding ground

viva'mente *adv (ringraziare)* warmly

vi'vanda *nf* food; *(piatto)* dish

vi'vente *a* living ● *nmpl* **i viventi** the living

'vivere *vi* live; **~ di** live on; **vive** *Typ* stet ● *vt (passare)* go through ● *nm* life; **modo di ~** way of life

'viveri *nmpl* provisions

vivida'mente *adv* vividly

'vivido *a* vivid

vivi'paro *a* viviparous

vivisezio'nare *vt* vivisect

vivisezi'one *nf* vivisection

'vivo *a* alive; *(vivente)* living; *(vivace)* lively; *(colore)* bright; **~ e vegeto** alive and kicking; **farsi ~** keep in touch; *(arrivare)* turn up ● *nm* **colpire qcno sul ~** cut sb to the quick; **dal ~** *(trasmissione)* live; *(disegnare)* from life; **i vivi** the living

vizi'are *vt* spoil *(bambino ecc)*; *(guastare)* vitiate

vizi'ato *a* spoilt; *(aria)* stale

'vizio *nm* vice; *(cattiva abitudine)* bad habit; *(difetto)* flaw. **~ capitale** deadly sin. **~ di forma** legal technicality. **~ procedurale** procedural error

vizi'oso *a* dissolute; *(difettoso)* faulty; **circolo ~** vicious circle

'vizzo *a (pelle)* wrinked; *(pianta)* withered

V.le *abbr* **(viale)** Ave

vocabo'lario *nm* dictionary; *(lessico)* vocabulary

vo'cabolo *nm* word

vo'cale *a* vocal ● *nf* vowel

vo'calico *a (corde)* vocal; *(suono)* vowel *attrib*

vocazi'one *nf* vocation

'voce *nf* voice; *(diceria)* rumour; *(di bilancio, dizionario)* entry. **~ bianca** *Mus* treble voice. **~ fuori campo** voiceover

voci'are *vi (spettegolare)* gossip ● *nm* buzz of conversation

vocife'rare *vi* shout; **si vocifera che...** it is rumoured that...

'vodka *nf inv* vodka

'voga *nf* rowing; *(lena)* enthusiasm; *(moda)* vogue; **essere in ~** be in vogue

vo'gare *vi* row. **~ a bratto** scull. **~ di coppia** scull

voga'tore *nm* oarsman; *(attrezzo)* rowing machine

'voglia *nf* desire; *(volontà)* will; *(della pelle)* birthmark; **aver ~ di fare qcsa** feel like doing sth; **morire dalla ~ di qcsa** be dying for sth; **di buona ~** willingly

'voglio *vedi* **volere**

vogli'oso *a (occhi, persona)* covetous; **essere ~ di qcsa** want sth

'voi *pers pron* you; **siete ~?** is that you?; **l'avete fatto ~?** did you do it yourself?

voia'ltri *pers pron* you

vo'lano *nm* shuttlecock; *Mech* flywheel

vo'lant *nm inv* valance

vo'lante *a* flying; *(foglio)* loose ● *nm* steering-wheel

volanti'nare *vi* hand out leaflets

volan'tino *nm* leaflet

vo'lare *vi* fly

vo'lata *nf Sport* final sprint; **di ~** in a rush

vo'latile *a (liquido)* volatile ● *nm* bird

volatiliz'zarsi *vr* vanish

vol-au-'vent *nm inv* vol-au-vent

vo'lée *nf inv Tennis* volley

vo'lente *a* ~ **o nolente** whether you like it or not

volente'roso *a* willing

volenti'eri *adv* willingly; ~! with pleasure!

vo'lere *vt* want; (*chiedere di*) ask for; (*aver bisogno di*) need; **non voglio** I don't want to; **vuole che lo faccia io** he wants me to do it; **fai come vuoi** do as you like; **se tuo padre vuole, ti porto al cinema** if your father agrees, I'll take you to the cinema; **questa pianta vuole molte cure** this plant needs a lot of care; **vorrei un caffè** I'd like a coffee; **la leggenda vuole che...** legend has it that...; **la vuoi smettere?** will you stop that!; **senza** ~ without meaning to; **voler bene/male a qcno** love/have something against sb; **voler dire** mean; **ci vuole il latte** we need milk; **ci vuole tempo/pazienza** it takes time/patience; **volerne a** have a grudge against; **vuoi... vuoi...** either... or... ● *nm* will; **voleri** *pl* wishes

vol'gare *a* vulgar; (*popolare*) common

volgarità *nf* vulgarity; **dire** ~ use vulgar language, be vulgar

volgariz'zare *vt* popularize

volgarizzazi'one *nf* popularization

volgar'mente *adv* (*grossolanamente*) vulgarly; (*comunemente*) commonly, popularly

'volgere *vt/i* turn

'volgersi *vr* turn [round]; ~ **a** (*dedicarsi*) take up

'volgo *nm* common people

voli'era *nf* aviary

voli'tivo *a* strong-minded

'volo *nm* flight; **al** ~ (*fare qcsa*) quickly; (*prendere qcsa*) in mid-air; **alzarsi in** ~ (*uccello:*) take off; **in** ~ airborne. ~ **di andata** outward flight. ~ **charter** charter flight. ~ **diretto** direct flight. ~ **di linea** scheduled flight. ~ **nazionale** domestic flight. ~ **di ritorno** return flight. ~ **strumentale** flying on instruments. ~ **a vela** gliding

volontà *nf inv* will; (*desiderio*) wish; **a** ~ (*mangiare*) as much as you like

volontaria'mente *adv* voluntarily

volon'tario *a* voluntary ● *nm* volunteer

volonte'roso *a* willing

'volpe *nf* fox

vol'pino *a* (*astuzia*) fox-like ● *nm* (*cane*) Pomeranian

volt *nm inv* volt

'volta *nf* time; (*turno*) turn; (*curva*) bend; *Archit* vault; **4. volte** 4 4 times 4; **a volte, qualche** ~ sometimes; **c'era una** ~... once upon a time, there was...; **una** ~ once; **due volte** twice; **tre/quattro volte** three/four times; **una** ~ **per tutte** once and for all; **una** ~ **ogni tanto** every so often; **uno alla** ~ one at a time; **alla** ~ **di** in the direction of. ~ **a botte** barrel vault. ~ **celeste** vault of heaven. ~ **cranica** cranial vault. ~ **a crociera** groin vault. ~ **a vela** ribbed vault. ~ **a ventaglio** fan vault

volta'faccia *nm inv* volte-face

voltagab'bana *mf inv* turncoat

vol'taggio *nm* voltage

vol'tare *vt/i* turn; (*rigirare*) turn round; (*rivoltare*) turn over; ~ **pagina** *fig* start with a clean sheet

vol'tarsi *vr* turn [round]

volta'stomaco *nm* nausea; *fig* disgust

volteggi'are *vi* circle; (*ginnastica*) vault

'volto *pp di* **volgere** ● *nm* face; **mi ha mostrato il suo vero** ~ he revealed his true colours

vol'tura *nf* (*catastale*) transfer of property. ~ **di contratto** transfer of contract

vo'lubile *a* fickle

volubil'mente *adv* in a fickle way, inconstantly

vo'lume *nm* volume. ~ **di gioco** *Sport* possession

volumi'noso *a* voluminous

vo'luta *nf* (*spirale*) spiral; (*di capitello*) volute

voluta'mente *adv* deliberately

vo'luto *a* deliberate, intended

voluttà *nf* voluptuousness

voluttu'ario *a* non-essential; **beni** *pl* **voluttuari** non-essentials

voluttu'oso *a* voluptuous

vomi'tare *vt* vomit, be sick

vomi'tevole *a* nauseating

'vomito *nm* vomit

'vongola *nf* clam

vo'race *a* voracious

vorace'mente *adv* voraciously

vo'ragine *nf* abyss

vor'rei *vedi* **volere**

'vortice *nm* whirl; (*gorgo*) whirlpool; (*di vento*) whirlwind

vorticosa'mente *adv* in whirls

'vostro (**il** ~ *m*, **la vostra** *f*, **i vostri** *mpl*, **le vostre** *fpl*) *poss a* your; **è vostra questa macchina?** is this car yours?; **un** ~ **amico** a friend of yours; ~ **padre** your father ● *poss pron* yours; **i vostri** your folk

vo'tante *nmf* voter

vo'tare *vi* vote

votazi'one *nf* voting; *Sch* marks *pl*. ~ **di fiducia** *Pol*, *fig* vote of confidence. ~ **a scrutinio segreto** secret ballot

'voto *nm* vote; *Sch* mark; *Relig* vow. ~ **decisivo** casting vote

vs. *abbr Comm* (**vostro**) yours

'vudu *nm inv* voodoo

vul'canico *a* volcanic

vul'cano *nm* volcano. ~ **intermittente** dormant volcano. ~ **spento** extinct volcano

vulne'rabile *a* vulnerable

vulnerabilità *nf* vulnerability

'vulva *nf* vulva

vuo'tare *vt* empty

vuo'tarsi *vr* empty

vu'oto *a* empty; (*non occupato*) vacant; ~ **di** (*sprovvisto*) devoid of ● *nm* empty space; *Phys* vacuum; *fig* void; **assegno a** ~ dud cheque; **sotto** ~ (*prodotto*) vacuum-packed. ~ **d'aria** air pocket. ~ **a perdere** no deposit. ~ **a rendere** (*bottiglia*) returnable

Ww

W *abbr* (**viva**) long live
'wafer *nm inv* (*biscotto*) wafer
wagon-'lit *nm inv* sleeping car
walkie-'talkie *nm inv* walkie-talkie
'water *nm inv* toilet, loo *fam*
watt *nm inv* watt
wat'tora *nm inv* Phys watt-hour

WC *nm* WC
week'end *nm inv* weekend
'welter *a & nm inv* (*in pugilato*) welterweight
'western *a inv* cowboy *attrib* ● *nm inv* Cinema western
'whisky *nm inv* whisky. ~ **di malto** malt [whisky]

Xx

xenofo'bia *nf* xenophobia
xe'nofobo, -a *a* xenophobic ● *nmf* xenophobe
xe'res *nm inv* sherry
xero'copia *nf* xerox

xerocopi'are *vt* photocopy
xerocopia'trice *nf* photocopier
xilofo'nista *nmf* xylophone player
xi'lofono *nm* xylophone

Yy

yacht *nm inv* yacht
yak *nm inv* Zool yak
'yankee *nmf inv* Yank
'Yemen *nm* Yemen
yeme'nita *nmf* Yemeni
yen *nm inv* yen
'yeti *nm* yeti

'yiddish *a inv & nm* Yiddish
'yoga *nm* yoga ● *a inv* yoga *attrib*
'yogurt *nm inv* yoghurt
yogurti'era *nf* yoghurt-maker
'yorkshire *nm inv* (*cane*) Yorkshire terrier
yo-'yo[®] *nm inv* yoyo
yup'pismo *nm* yuppiedom

zaba[gl]i'one *nm* zabaglione (*dessert made from eggs, wine or marsala and sugar*)
'zacchera *nf* (*schizzo*) splash of mud
zaf'fata *nf* whiff; (*di fumo*) cloud
zaffe'rano *nm* saffron
zaf'firo *nm* sapphire
'zagara *nf* orange-blossom
'zaino *nm* rucksack
'zampa *nf* leg; **a quattro zampe** (*animale*) four-legged; (*carponi*) on all fours. **zampe** *pl* **di gallina** *fig* crow's feet
zam'pata *nf* paw; **dare una ~ a** hit with its paw
zampet'tare *vi* scamper
zam'petto *nm Culin* knuckle
zampil'lante *a* spurting
zampil'lare *vi* spurt
zam'pillo *nm* spurt
zam'pino *nm* paw; **mettere lo ~ in** *fig* have a hand in
zam'pogna *nf* bagpipe
zampo'gnaro *nm* piper
zam'pone *nfpl* stuffed pig's trotter with lentils
'zanna *nf* fang; (*di elefante*) tusk
zan'zara *nf* mosquito
zanzari'era *nf* (*velo*) mosquito net; (*su finestra*) insect screen
'zappa *nf* hoe; **darsi la ~ sui piedi** *fig* shoot oneself in the foot
zap'pare *vt* hoe
zap'pata *nf* **dare una ~ a** hit with a hoe
zappet'tare *vt* hoe
zar *nm inv* tzar
za'rina *nf* tzarina
za'rista *a & nmf* tzarist
'zattera *nf* raft
zatte'roni *nmpl* (*scarpe*) wedge shoes
za'vorra *nf* ballast; *fig* dead wood
zavor'rare *vt* load with ballast
'zazzera *nf* mop of hair
'zebra *nf* zebra; **zebre** *pl* (*passaggio pedonale*) zebra crossing, crosswalk *Am*
ze'brato *a* (*tessuto*) with black and white stripes
zecca[1] *nf* mint; **nuovo di ~** brand-new
zecca[2] *nf* (*parassita*) tick
zec'chino *nm* sequin; **oro ~** pure gold
ze'lante *a* zealous
'zelo *nm* zeal
'zenit *nm* zenith
'zenzero *nm* ginger
'zeppa *nf* wedge
'zeppo *a* packed full; **pieno ~ di** crammed o packed with
zer'bino *nm* doormat
'zero *nm* zero, nought; (*in calcio*) nil; *Tennis*

love; **due a ~** (*in partite*) two nil; **ricominciare da ~** *fig* start again from scratch; **sparare a ~ su qcno** *fig* lay into sb; **avere il morale sotto ~** *fig* be down in the dumps
'zeta *nf* zed, zee *Am*
'zia *nf* aunt
zibel'lino *nm* sable
zi'gano, -a *a a & nmf* gypsy
'zigolo *nm Zool* bunting
'zigomo *nm* cheek-bone
zigri'nato *a* (*pelle*) grained; (*metallo*) milled
zig'zag *nm inv* zigzag; **andare a ~** zigzag
Zim'babwe *nm* Zimbabwe
zim'bello *nm* decoy; (*oggetto di scherno*) laughing-stock
'zinco *nm* zinc
zinga'resco *a* gypsy *attrib*
'zingaro, -a *nmf* gypsy
'zio *nm* uncle
'zippo *nm sl* lighter
zi'tella *nf* spinster; *pej* old maid
zitel'lona *nf pej* old maid
zit'tire *vi* fall silent ● *vt* silence
'zitto *a* silent; **sta' ~!** keep quiet!
ziz'zania *nf* (*discordia*) discord; **seminare ~** cause trouble
'zoccola *nf vulg* whore
'zoccolo *nm* clog; (*di cavallo*) hoof; (*di terra*) clump; (*di parete*) skirting board, baseboard *Am*; (*di colonna*) base. **~ duro** *Pol* hard core. **~ fesso** cloven foot, cloven hoof
zodia'cale *a* of the zodiac; **segno ~** sign of the zodiac, birth sign
zo'diaco *nm* zodiac
zolfa'nello *nm* match
'zolfo *nm* sulphur
'zolla *nf* clod; (*di zucchero*) lump
zol'letta *nf* sugar cube, sugar lump
'zombi *nm inv fig* zombi
zom'pare *vi sl* bonk
'zona *nf* zone; (*area*) area. **~ denuclearizzata** nuclear-free zone. **~ di depressione** area of low pressure. **~ disastrata** disaster area. **~ disco** area for parking discs only. **~ erogena** erogenous zone. **~ giorno** living area. **~ industriale** industrial estate. **~ notte** sleeping area. **~ pedonale** pedestrian precinct. **~ a traffico limitato** restricted traffic area. **~ verde** green belt
zonizzazi'one *nf* zoning
'zonzo: andare a ~ stroll about
zoo *nm inv* zoo
zoolo'gia *nf* zoology
zoo'logico *a* zoological
zo'ologo, -a *nmf* zoologist
zoosa'fari *nm inv* safari park

zootec'nia *nf* animal husbandry

zoo'tecnico *a* ⟨*progresso*⟩ in animal husbandry; **patrimonio ~** livestock

zoppi'cante *a* limping; *fig* shaky

zoppi'care *vi* limp; (*essere debole*) be shaky

'zoppo, -a *a* lame ● *nmf* cripple

'zotico *a* uncouth

zoti'cone *nm* boor

zu'ava *nf* **calzoni** *pl* **alla ~** plus-fours

'zucca *nf* marrow; (*fam: testa*) head; (*fam: persona*) thickie; **cos'hai in quella ~?** haven't you got anything between your ears?

zuc'cata *nf* **prendere una ~** *fam* hit one's head

zucche'rare *vt* sugar

zuccherato *a* sugared; **non ~** ⟨*succo d'arancia ecc*⟩ unsweetened

zuccheri'era *nf* sugar bowl

zuccheri'ficio *nm* sugar refinery

zucche'rino *a* sugary ● *nm* sugar cube, sugar lump; *fig* sweetener; **essere uno ~** *fig* ⟨*persona:*⟩ be a softy; ⟨*cosa:*⟩ be a cinch

'zucchero *nm* sugar. **~ di canna** cane sugar. **~ greggio** brown sugar. **~ vanigliato** vanilla sugar. **~ a velo** icing sugar, confectioners' sugar *Am*

zucche'roso *a fig* honeyed

zuc'china *nf* courgette, zucchini *Am*

zuc'chino *nm* courgette, zucchini *Am*

zuc'cone *nm fam* blockhead

zuc'cotto *nm* dessert made with sponge, cream, chocolate and candied fruit

'zuffa *nf* scuffle

zufo'lare *vt/i* whistle

'zufolo *nm* penny whistle

zu'mare *vi* zoom

zu'mata *nf* zoom

'zuppa *nf* soup. **~ inglese** trifle

zup'petta *nf* **fare ~** [**con**] dunk

zuppi'era *nf* soup tureen

'zuppo *a* soaked

Aa

a, A /eɪ/ (*letter*) a, A *f inv*; *Mus* la *m inv*
a /ə/, *accentato* /eɪ/ (*davanti a una vocale* **an**) *indef art* un *m*, una *f*; (*before* s + *consonant, gn, ps, z*) uno; (*before* nf *starting with vowel*) un'; (*each*) a; **I am a lawyer** sono avvocato; **a tiger is a feline** la tigre è un felino; **a knife and fork** un coltello e una forchetta; **a Mr Smith is looking for you** un certo signor Smith ti sta cercando; **£2 a kilo/a head** due sterline al chilo/a testa ● *n Mus* la *m inv*
A4 *a* A4
AA *n Br abbr* (**Automobile Association**) ≈ A.C.I. *f*; *abbr* **Alcoholics Anonymous**
aback /ə'bæk/ *adv* **be taken ~** essere preso in contropiede
abacus /'æbəkəs/ *n* (*pl* **-cuses**) abaco *m*
abandon /ə'bændən/ *vt* abbandonare; (*give up*) rinunciare a ● *n* abbandono *m*
abandoned /ə'bændnd/ *a* abbandonato; ‹*behaviour*› dissoluto
abandonment /ə'bændnmənt/ *n* (*of strike, plan etc*) rinuncia *f*
abashed /ə'bæʃt/ *a* imbarazzato
abate /ə'beɪt/ *vi* calmarsi
abattoir /'æbətwɑ:(r)/ *n* mattatoio *m*
abbess /'æbes/ *n* badessa *f*
abbey /'æbɪ/ *n* abbazia *f*
abbot /'æbət/ *n* abate *m*
abbreviate /ə'bri:vɪeɪt/ *vt* abbreviare
abbreviation /əbri:vɪ'eɪʃn/ *n* abbreviazione *f*
ABC *n* (*alphabet*) alfabeto *m*; **the ~ of** (*basics*) l'ABC *m inv* di ● *n abbr* (**American Broadcasting Company**) rete *f* televisiva americana
abdicate /'æbdɪkeɪt/ *vi* abdicare ● *vt* rinunciare a
abdication /æbdɪ'keɪʃn/ *n* abdicazione *f*
abdomen /'æbdəmən/ *n* addome *m*
abdominal /əb'dɒmɪnl/ *a* addominale
abduct /əb'dʌkt/ *vt* rapire
abduction /əb'dʌkʃn/ *n* rapimento *m*
abductor /əb'dʌktə(r)/ *n* rapitore, -trice *mf*
aberrant /ə'berənt/ *a* ‹*behaviour, nature*› aberrante
aberration /æbə'reɪʃn/ *n* aberrazione *f*
abet /ə'bet/ *vt* (*pt/pp* **abetted**) **aid and ~** *Jur* essere complice di
abeyance /ə'beɪəns/ *n* **in ~** in sospeso; **fall into ~** cadere in disuso
abhor /əb'hɔ:(r)/ *vt* (*pt/pp* **abhorred**) aborrire
abhorrence /əb'hɒrəns/ *n* orrore *m*
abhorrent /əb'hɒrənt/ *a* ripugnante
abide /ə'baɪd/ *vt* (*pt/pp* **abided**) (*tolerate*) sopportare. ● **abide by** *vi* rispettare

abiding /ə'baɪdɪŋ/ *a* perpetuo
ability /ə'bɪlətɪ/ *n* capacità *f inv*
abject /'æbdʒekt/ *a* ‹*poverty*› degradante; ‹*apology*› umile; ‹*coward*› abietto
ablative /'æblətɪv/ *n* ablativo *m*
ablaze /ə'bleɪz/ *a* in fiamme; **be ~ with light** risplendere di luci
able /'eɪbl/ *a* capace, abile; **be ~ to do sth** poter fare qcsa; **were you ~ to...?** sei riuscito a...?
able-bodied /-'bɒdɪd/ *a* robusto; *Mil* abile
able seaman *n* marinaio *m* scelto
ably /'eɪblɪ/ *adv* abilmente
abnegation /æbnɪ'geɪʃn/ *n* (*of rights, privileges*) rinuncia *f*; (*self-abnegation*) abnegazione *f*
abnormal /æb'nɔ:ml/ *a* anormale
abnormality /æbnɔ:'mælətɪ/ *n* anormalità *f inv*
abnormally /æb'nɔ:məlɪ/ *adv* in modo anormale
aboard /ə'bɔ:d/ *adv & prep* a bordo
abode /ə'bəʊd/ *n* dimora *f*
abolish /ə'bɒlɪʃ/ *vt* abolire
abolition /æbə'lɪʃn/ *n* abolizione *f*
abominable /ə'bɒmɪnəbl/ *a* abominevole
abominably /ə'bɒmɪnəblɪ/ *adv* disgustosamente
abominate /ə'bɒmɪneɪt/ *vt* abominare
aboriginal /æbə'rɪdʒɪnl/ *a & n* (*native*) aborigeno, -a *mf*, indigeno, -a *mf*
Aborigine /æbə'rɪdʒəni:/ *n* aborigeno, -a *mf* d'Australia
abort /ə'bɔ:t/ *vt* fare abortire; *fig* annullare
abortion /ə'bɔ:ʃn/ *n* aborto *m*; **have an ~** abortire
abortionist /ə'bɔ:ʃnɪst/ *n* persona *f* che pratica aborti, specialmente clandestini
abortive /ə'bɔ:tɪv/ *a* ‹*attempt*› infruttuoso
abound /ə'baʊnd/ *vi* abbondare (**in** di)
about /ə'baʊt/ *adv* (*here and there*) [di] qua e [di] là; (*approximately*) circa; **be ~** ‹*illness, tourists*:› essere in giro; **be up and ~** essere alzato; **leave sth lying ~** lasciare in giro qcsa ● *prep* (*concerning*) su; (*in the region of*) intorno a; (*here and there in*) per; **what is the book/the film ~?** di cosa parla il libro/il film?; **he wants to see you – what ~?** ti vuole vedere – a che proposito?; **talk/know ~** parlare/sapere di; **I know nothing ~ it** non ne so niente; **~ 5 o'clock** intorno alle 5; **travel ~ the world** viaggiare per il mondo; **be ~ to do sth** stare per fare qcsa; **how ~ going to the cinema?** e se andassimo al cinema?
about-face *n*, **about-turn** *n* dietro front *m inv*

above /ə'bʌv/ *adv & prep* sopra; **~ all** soprattutto

above: above-board *a* onesto. **aboveground** *adv* in superficie. **above-mentioned** /-'menʃnd/ *a* suddetto. **above-named** /-'neɪmd/ *a* suddetto

abrasion /ə'breɪʒn/ *n* (*injury*) abrasione *f*

abrasive /ə'breɪsɪv/ *a* abrasivo; ⟨*remark*⟩ caustico ● *n* abrasivo *m*

abreast /ə'brest/ *adv* fianco a fianco; **come ~ of** allinearsi con; **keep ~ of** tenersi al corrente di

abridged /ə'brɪdʒd/ *a* ridotto

abridg[e]ment /ə'brɪdʒmnt/ *n* (*version*) edizione *f* ridotta

abroad /ə'brɔːd/ *adv* all'estero

abrupt /ə'brʌpt/ *a* brusco

abruptly /ə'brʌptlɪ/ *adv* bruscamente

ABS *n abbr* (**anti-lock braking system**) ABS *m inv*

abscess /'æbsɪs/ *n* ascesso *m*

abscond /əb'skɒnd/ *vi* fuggire

absence /'æbsəns/ *n* assenza *f*; (*lack*) mancanza *f*

absent¹ /'æbsənt/ *a* assente

absent² /æb'sent/ *vt* **~ oneself** essere assente

absentee /æbsən'tiː/ *n* assente *mf*

absenteeism /æbsən'tiːɪzm/ *n* assenteismo *m*

absentee landlord *n* proprietario *m* che affitta una casa in cui non abita

absently /'æbsəntlɪ/ *adv* ⟨*say, look*⟩ distrattamente

absent-minded /-'maɪndɪd/ *a* distratto

absent-mindedly /-'maɪndɪdlɪ/ *adv* distrattamente

absent-mindedness /-'maɪndɪdnɪs/ *n* distrazione *f*

absolute /'æbsəluːt/ *a* assoluto; **an ~ idiot** un perfetto idiota

absolutely /'æbsəluːtlɪ/ *adv* assolutamente; (*fam: indicating agreement*) esattamente; **~ not** assolutamente no

absolution /æbsə'luːʃn/ *n* assoluzione *f*

absolve /əb'zɒlv/ *vt* assolvere

absorb /əb'sɔːb/ *vt* assorbire; **~ed in** assorto in

absorbency /əb'sɔːbənsɪ/ *n* capacità *f* d'assorbimento

absorbent /əb'sɔːbənt/ *a* assorbente

absorbent cotton *n Am* cotone *m* idrofilo, ovatta *f*

absorbing /əb'sɔːbɪŋ/ *a* avvincente

absorption /əb'sɔːpʃn/ *n* assorbimento *m*; (*in activity*) concentrazione *f*

abstain /əb'steɪn/ *vi* astenersi (**from** da)

abstemious /əb'stiːmɪəs/ *a* moderato

abstention /əb'stenʃn/ *n Pol* astensione *f*

abstinence /'æbstɪnəns/ *n* astinenza *f*

abstract /'æbstrækt/ *a* astratto ● *n* astratto *m*; (*summary*) estratto *m*

abstraction /əb'strækʃn/ *n* **an air of ~** un'aria distratta

absurd /əb'sɜːd/ *a* assurdo

absurdity /əb'sɜːdətɪ/ *n* assurdità *f inv*

absurdly /əb'sɜːdlɪ/ *adv* assurdamente

abundance /ə'bʌndəns/ *n* abbondanza *f*

abundant /ə'bʌndənt/ *a* abbondante

abundantly /ə'bʌndəntlɪ/ *adv* **~ clear** più che chiaro

abuse¹ /ə'bjuːz/ *vt* (*misuse*) abusare di; (*insult*) insultare; (*ill-treat*) maltrattare

abuse² /ə'bjuːs/ *n* abuso *m*; (*verbal*) insulti *mpl*; (*ill-treatment*) maltrattamento *m*; **~ of power** sopraffazione *f*

abusive /ə'bjuːsɪv/ *a* offensivo

abut /ə'bʌt/ *vi* (*pt/pp* **abutted**) confinare (**onto** con)

abysmal /ə'bɪzml/ *a fam* pessimo; ⟨*ignorance*⟩ abissale

abyss /ə'bɪs/ *n* abisso *m*

a/c *abbr* (**account**) c/c

academia /ækə'diːmɪə/ *n* mondo *m* accademico

academic /ækə'demɪk/ *a* teorico; ⟨*qualifications, system*⟩ scolastico; **be ~** ⟨*person:*⟩ avere predisposizione allo studio ● *n* docente *mf* universitario, -a

academically /ækə'demɪklɪ/ *adv* ⟨*gifted*⟩ accademicamente

academician /əkædə'mɪʃn/ *n* accademico, -a *mf*

academy /ə'kædəmɪ/ *n* accademia *f*; (*of music*) conservatorio *m*

ACAS /'eɪkæs/ *n Br abbr* (**Advisory Conciliation and Arbitration Service**) organismo *m* pubblico di mediazione tra i lavoratori e i datori di lavoro

accede /ək'siːd/ *vi* **~ to** accedere a ⟨*request*⟩; salire a ⟨*throne*⟩

accelerate /ək'seləreɪt/ *vt/i* accelerare

acceleration /əkselə'reɪʃn/ *n* accelerazione *f*

accelerator /ək'seləreɪtə(r)/ *n* *Auto, Comput* acceleratore *m*

accent¹ /'æksənt/ *n* accento *m*

accent² /æk'sent/ *vt* accentare

accented /'æksəntɪd/ *a* ⟨*speech*⟩ con accento marcato

accentuate /ək'sentjʊeɪt/ *vt* accentuare

accept /ək'sept/ *vt* accettare

acceptability /æksəptə'bɪlɪtɪ/ *n* ammissibilità *f*

acceptable /ək'septəbl/ *a* accettabile

acceptance /ək'septəns/ *n* accettazione *f*

access /'ækses/ *n* accesso *m* ● *vt* Comput accedere a

accessible /ək'sesəbl/ *a* accessibile

accession /ək'seʃn/ *n* (*to throne*) ascesa *f* al trono

accessory /ək'sesərɪ/ *n* accessorio *m*; *Jur* complice *mf*

accident /'æksɪdənt/ *n* incidente *m*; (*chance*) caso *m*; **by ~** per caso; (*unintentionally*) senza volere; **I'm sorry, it was an ~** mi dispiace, non l'ho fatto apposta

accidental /æksɪ'dentl/ *a* ⟨*meeting*⟩ casuale; ⟨*death*⟩ incidentale; (*unintentional*) involontario

accidentally /ˌæksɪˈdentəlɪ/ *adv* per caso; (*unintentionally*) inavvertitamente

acclaim /əˈkleɪm/ *n* acclamazione *f* ● *vt* acclamare (**as** come)

acclimatization /əˌklaɪmətaɪˈzeɪʃn/ *n* acclimatazione *f*

acclimatize /əˈklaɪmətaɪz/ *vt* **become ~d** acclimatarsi

accolade /ˈækəleɪd/ *n* riconoscimento *m*

accommodate /əˈkɒmədeɪt/ *vt* ospitare; (*oblige*) favorire

accommodating /əˈkɒmədeɪtɪŋ/ *a* accomodante

accommodation /əˌkɒməˈdeɪʃn/ *n* (*place to stay*) sistemazione *f*; **look for ~** cercare una sistemazione

accompaniment /əˈkʌmpənɪmənt/ *n* accompagnamento *m*

accompanist /əˈkʌmpənɪst/ *n Mus* accompagnatore, -trice *mf*

accompany /əˈkʌmpənɪ/ *vt* (*pt/pp* **-ied**) accompagnare

accomplice /əˈkʌmplɪs/ *n* complice *mf*

accomplish /əˈkʌmplɪʃ/ *vt* (*achieve*) concludere; realizzare (*aim*)

accomplished /əˈkʌmplɪʃt/ *a* dotato; ⟨*fact*⟩ compiuto

accomplishment /əˈkʌmplɪʃmənt/ *n* realizzazione *f*; (*achievement*) risultato *m*; (*talent*) talento *m*

accord /əˈkɔːd/ *n* (*treaty*) accordo *m*; **with one ~** tutti d'accordo; **of his own ~** di sua spontanea volontà ● *vt* accordare

accordance /əˈkɔːdəns/ *n* **in ~ with** in conformità di o a

according /əˈkɔːdɪŋ/ *adv* **~ to** secondo

accordingly /əˈkɔːdɪŋlɪ/ *adv* di conseguenza

accordion /əˈkɔːdɪən/ *n* fisarmonica *f*

accost /əˈkɒst/ *vt* abbordare

account /əˈkaʊnt/ *n* conto *m*; (*report*) descrizione *f*; (*of eyewitness*) resoconto *m*; **~s** *pl Comm* conti *mpl*; **on ~ of** a causa di; **on no ~** per nessun motivo; **on this ~** per questo motivo; **on my ~** per causa mia; **of no ~** di nessuna importanza; **take into ~** tener conto di ■ **account for** *vt* (*explain*) spiegare; ⟨*person.*⟩ render conto di; (*constitute*) costituire; (*destroy*) distruggere

accountability /əˌkaʊntəˈbɪlətɪ/ *n* responsabilità *f*

accountable /əˈkaʊntəbl/ *a* responsabile (**for** di)

accountant /əˈkaʊntənt/ *n* (*book-keeper*) contabile *mf*; (*consultant*) commercialista *mf*

account: **account book** *n* libro *m* contabile. **account director** *n* account director *mf inv.* **account holder** /əˈkaʊntəʊldə(r)/ *n* (*with bank, credit company*) titolare *mf* del conto

accounting /əˈkaʊntɪŋ/ *n* (*field*) ragioneria *f*; (*auditing*) contabilità *f*

accounting period *n* periodo *m* contabile

account number *n* numero *m* di conto

accounts: **accounts department** *n* [ufficio *m*] contabilità *f.* **accounts payable** *npl* conto *m* creditori diversi. **accounts receivable** *npl* conto *m* debitori diversi

accoutrements /əˈkuːtrəmənts/ *npl* equipaggiamento *msg*

accredited /əˈkredɪtɪd/ *a* accreditato

accretion /əˈkriːʃn/ *n* accrescimento *m*

accrue /əˈkruː/ *vi* ⟨*interest.*⟩ maturare

accumulate /əˈkjuːmjʊleɪt/ *vt* accumulare ● *vi* accumularsi

accumulation /əˌkjuːmjʊˈleɪʃn/ *n* accumulazione *f*

accumulator /əˈkjuːmjʊleɪtə(r)/ *n Electr* accumulatore *m*

accuracy /ˈækjʊrəsɪ/ *n* precisione *f*

accurate /ˈækjʊrət/ *a* preciso

accurately /ˈækjʊrətlɪ/ *adv* con precisione

accusation /ˌækjʊˈzeɪʃn/ *n* accusa *f*

accusative /əˈkjuːzətɪv/ *a* & *n* **~** [**case**] *Gram* accusativo *m*

accuse /əˈkjuːz/ *vt* accusare; **~ sb of doing sth** accusare qcno di fare qcsa

accused /əˈkjuːzd/ *n* **the ~** l'accusato *m*, l'accusata *f*

accuser /əˈkjuːzə(r)/ *n* accusatore, -trice *mf*

accusing /əˈkjuːzɪŋ/ *a* accusatore

accusingly /əˈkjuːzɪŋlɪ/ *adv* ⟨*say, point*⟩ in modo accusatorio

accustom /əˈkʌstəm/ *vt* abituare (**to** a)

accustomed /əˈkʌstəmd/ *a* abituato; **grow** *or* **get ~ to** abituarsi a

ace /eɪs/ *n* (*in cards*) asso *m*; *Tennis* ace *m inv*

acerbic /əˈsɜːbɪk/ *a* acido

acetate /ˈæsɪteɪt/ *n* acetato *m*

ache /eɪk/ *n* dolore *m* ● *vi* dolere, far male; **~ all over** essere tutto indolenzito

achieve /əˈtʃiːv/ *vt* ottenere (*success*); realizzare ⟨*goal, ambition*⟩

achievement /əˈtʃiːvmənt/ *n* (*feat*) successo *m*

achiever /əˈtʃiːvə(r)/ *n* persona *f* di successo

Achilles' heel /əkɪliːzˈhiːl/ *n* tallone *m* di Achille

aching /ˈeɪkɪŋ/ *a* ⟨*body, limbs*⟩ dolorante; **an ~ void** un vuoto incolmabile

acid /ˈæsɪd/ *a* acido ● *n* acido *m*

acid drop *n* caramella *f* agli agrumi

acidic /əˈsɪdɪk/ *a* acido

acidity /əˈsɪdətɪ/ *n* acidità *f*

acid: **acid rain** *n* pioggia *f* acida. **acid stomach** *n Med* acidità *f* di stomaco. **acid test** *n fig* prova *f* del fuoco

acknowledge /əkˈnɒlɪdʒ/ *vt* riconoscere; rispondere a ⟨*greeting*⟩; far cenno di aver notato ⟨*sb's presence*⟩; **~ receipt of** accusare ricevuta di ; **~ defeat** dichiararsi vinto

acknowledgement /əkˈnɒlɪdʒmənt/ *n* riconoscimento *m*; **send an ~ of a letter** confermare il ricevimento di una lettera

acme /ˈækmɪ/ *n* **the ~ of** l'apice *m* di

acne /ˈæknɪ/ *n* acne *f*

acorn /ˈeɪkɔːn/ *n* ghianda *f*

acoustic /əˈkuːstɪk/ *a* acustico

acoustically /əˈkuːstɪklɪ/ *adv* acusticamente

acoustic guitar *n* chitarra *f* acustica

acoustics /ə'ku:stɪks/ *npl* acustica *fsg*

acquaint /ə'kweɪnt/ *vt* ~ **sb with** metter qcno al corrente di; **be ~ed with** conoscere ‹*person*›; essere a conoscenza di ‹*fact*›

acquaintance /ə'kweɪntəns/ *n* (*person*) conoscente *mf*; **make sb's ~** fare la conoscenza di qcno

acquiesce /ækwɪ'es/ *vi* acconsentire (**to, in** a)

acquiescence /ækwɪ'esəns/ *n* acquiescenza *f*

acquiescent /ækwɪ'esənt/ *a* arrendevole

acquire /ə'kwaɪə(r)/ *vt* acquisire

acquired /ə'kwaɪəd/ *a* ‹*characteristic*› acquisito; **it's an ~ taste** è una cosa che si impara ad apprezzare

acquisition /ækwɪ'zɪʃn/ *n* acquisizione *f*

acquisitive /ə'kwɪzətɪv/ *a* avido

acquit /ə'kwɪt/ *vt* (*pt/pp* **acquitted**) assolvere; ~ **oneself well** cavarsela bene

acquittal /ə'kwɪtəl/ *n* assoluzione *f*

acre /'eɪkə(r)/ *n* acro *m* (= 4 047 *m²*)

acreage /'eɪkərɪdʒ/ *n* superficie *f* in acri

acrid /'ækrɪd/ *a* acre

acrimonious /ækrɪ'məʊnɪəs/ *a* aspro

acrimony /'ækrɪmənɪ/ *n* asprezza *f*

acrobat /'ækrəbæt/ *n* acrobata *mf*

acrobatic /ækrə'bætɪk/ *a* acrobatico

acrobatics /ækrə'bætɪks/ *npl* acrobazie *fpl*

acronym /'ækrənɪm/ *n* acronimo *m*

across /ə'krɒs/ *adv* dall'altra parte; (*wide*) in larghezza; (*not lengthwise*) attraverso; (*in crossword*) orizzontale; **come ~ sth** imbattersi in qcsa; **go ~** attraversare ● *prep* (*crosswise*) di traverso su; (*on the other side of*) dall'altra parte di

across-the-board *a* generale ● *adv* in generale

acrylic /ə'krɪlɪk/ *n* acrilico *m* ● *attrib* ‹*garment*› acrilico

act /ækt/ *n* atto *m*; (*in variety show*) numero *m*; **put on an ~** *fam* fare scena ● *vi* agire; (*behave*) comportarsi; *Theat* recitare; (*pretend*) fingere; ~ **as** fare da ● *vt* recitare ‹*role*›

■ **act for** *vi* agire per conto di

■ **act up** *vi* ‹*child, photocopier:*› fare i capricci

acting /'æktɪŋ/ *a* ‹*deputy*› provvisorio ● *n* *Theat* recitazione *f*; (*profession*) teatro *m*; ~ **profession** professione *f* dell'attore

action /'ækʃn/ *n* azione *f*; *Mil* combattimento *m*; *Jur* azione *f* legale; **out of ~** ‹*machine:*› fuori uso; **take ~** agire; ~ **!** *Cinema* ciac si gira!

action: action-packed *a* ‹*film*› d'azione. **action painting** *n* pittura *f* d'azione. **action replay** *n* replay *m inv*

activate /'æktɪveɪt/ *vt* attivare; (*Chem, Phys*) rendere attivo

active /'æktɪv/ *a* attivo

active duty, active service *n Mil* **be on ~ ~** prestare servizio in zona di operazioni

actively /'æktɪvlɪ/ *adv* attivamente

activist /'æktɪvɪst/ *n* attivista *mf*

activity /æk'tɪvətɪ/ *n* attività *f inv*

activity holiday *n Br* vacanza *f* con attività ricreative

act of God *n* causa *f* di forza maggiore

actor /'æktə(r)/ *n* attore *m*

actress /'æktrəs/ *n* attrice *f*

actual /'æktʃʊəl/ *a* ‹*real*› reale

actually /'æktʃʊəlɪ/ *adv* in realtà

actuary /'æktʃʊərɪ/ *n* attuario, -a *mf*

acumen /'ækjʊmən/ *n* acume *m*

acupuncture /'ækjʊpʌŋktʃə(r)/ *n* agopuntura *f*

acupuncturist /ækjʊ'pʌŋktʃərɪst/ *n* agopuntore, -trice *mf*

acute /ə'kju:t/ *a* acuto; ‹*shortage, hardship*› estremo

acute accent *n* accento *m* acuto

acute angle *n* angolo *m* acuto

acutely /ə'kju:tlɪ/ *adv* acutamente; ‹*embarrassed, aware*› estremamente

AD *abbr* (**Anno Domini**) d.C.

ad /æd/ *n* pubblicità *f inv*; (*in paper*) inserzione *f*, annuncio *m*

adage /'ædɪdʒ/ *n* detto *m*, adagio *m*

adamant /'ædəmənt/ *a* categorico (**that** sul fatto che)

Adam's apple /'ædəmz/ *n* pomo *m* di Adamo

adapt /ə'dæpt/ *vt* adattare ‹*play*› ● *vi* adattarsi

adaptability /ədæptə'bɪlətɪ/ *n* adattabilità *f*

adaptable /ə'dæptəbl/ *a* adattabile

adaptation /ædæp'teɪʃn/ *n* *Theat* adattamento *m*

adapter, adaptor /ə'dæptə(r)/ *n* adattatore *m*; (*two-way*) presa *f* multipla

add /æd/ *vt* aggiungere; *Math* addizionare ● *vi* addizionare. ~ **to** *vi* (*fig: increase*) aggravare

■ **add in** *vt* (*include*) includere

■ **add on** *vt* aggiungere

■ **add up** *vt* addizionare ‹*figures*› ● *vi* addizionare; **it doesn't ~ up** *fig* non quadra; ~ **up to** ammontare a

added /'ædɪd/ *a* maggiore

adder /'ædə(r)/ *n* vipera *f*

addict /'ædɪkt/ *n* tossicodipendente *mf*; *fig* fanatico, -a *mf*

addicted /ə'dɪktɪd/ *a* assuefatto (**to** a); ~ **to drugs** tossicodipendente; **he's ~ to television** è videodipendente

addiction /ə'dɪkʃn/ *n* dipendenza *f*; (*to drugs*) tossicodipendenza *f*

addictive /ə'dɪktɪv/ *a* **be ~** dare assuefazione

addition /ə'dɪʃn/ *n* *Math* addizione *f*; (*thing added*) aggiunta *f*; **in ~** in aggiunta

additional /ə'dɪʃnəl/ *a* supplementare

additionally /ə'dɪʃnəlɪ/ *adv* in più

additive /'ædɪtɪv/ *n* additivo *m*

addled /'ædld/ *a* ‹*thinking*› confuso

add-on *a* accessorio

address /ə'dres/ *n* indirizzo *m*; (*speech*) discorso *m*; **form of ~** formula *f* di cortesia

5 address book | advance

● *vt* indirizzare; (*speak to*) rivolgersi a ‹*person*›; tenere un discorso a ‹*meeting*›
address book *n* rubrica *f*
addressee /ædre'si:/ *n* destinatario, -a *mf*
adenoids /'ædənɔɪdz/ *npl* adenoidi *fpl*
adept /'ædept/ *a* esperto, -a *mf* (**at** in)
adequate /'ædɪkwət/ *a* adeguato
adequately /'ædɪkwətlɪ/ *adv* adeguatamente
adhere /əd'hɪə(r)/ *vi* aderire; **~ to** attenersi a ‹*principles, rules*›
adherence /əd'hɪərəns/ *n* fedeltà *f*
adherent /əd'hɪərənt/ *n* (*of doctrine*) adepto, -a *mf*; (*of policy*) sostenitore, -trice *mf*; (*of cult*) seguace *mf*
adhesion /əd'hi:ʒn/ *n* adesione *f*
adhesive /əd'hi:sɪv/ *a* adesivo ● *n* adesivo *m*
ad hoc /æd'hɒk/ *a* ‹*alliance, arrangement*› ad hoc; ‹*committee, legislation*› apposito; **on an ~ ~ basis** secondo le esigenze del momento
adieu /ə'dju:/ *n* **bid sb ~** dire addio a qcno
ad infinitum /ædɪnfɪ'naɪtəm/ *adv* ‹*continue*› all'infinito
adjacent /ə'dʒeɪsənt/ *a* adiacente
adjective /'ædʒɪktɪv/ *n* aggettivo *m*
adjoin /ə'dʒɔɪn/ *vt* essere adiacente a
adjoining /ə'dʒɔɪnɪŋ/ *a* adiacente
adjourn /ə'dʒɜ:n/ *vt/i* aggiornare (**until** a)
adjournment /ə'dʒɜ:nmənt/ *n* aggiornamento *m*
adjudge /ə'dʒʌdʒ/ *vt* Jur (*decree*) giudicare; aggiudicare ‹*costs, damages*›
adjudicate /ə'dʒu:dɪkeɪt/ *vi* decidere; (*in competition*) giudicare
adjudicator /ə'dʒu:dɪkeɪtə(r)/ *n* giudice *m*, arbitro *m*
adjunct /'ædʒʌŋkt/ *n* aggiunta *f*; (*hum: person*) appendice *f*
adjust /ə'dʒʌst/ *vt* modificare; regolare ‹*focus, sound etc*› ● *vi* adattarsi
adjustable /ə'dʒʌstəbl/ *a* regolabile
adjustable spanner *n* chiave *f* [inglese] a rullino
adjustment /ə'dʒʌstmənt/ *n* adattamento *m*; Techn regolamento *m*
adjutant /'ædʒutənt/ *n* Mil aiutante *mf*
ad lib /æd'lɪb/ *a* improvvisato ● *adv* a piacere ● *vi* (*pt/pp* **ad libbed**) *fam* improvvisare
adman /'ædmæn/ *n fam* pubblicitario *m*
admin /'ædmɪn/ *n Br fam* amministrazione *f*
administer /əd'mɪnɪstə(r)/ *vt* amministrare; somministrare ‹*medicine*›
administration /ədmɪnɪ'streɪʃn/ *n* amministrazione *f*; Pol governo *m*
administration costs *n* costi *mpl* di gestione
administrative /əd'mɪnɪstrətɪv/ *a* amministrativo
administrator /əd'mɪnɪstreɪtə(r)/ *n* amministratore, -trice *mf*
admirable /'ædmərəbl/ *a* ammirevole
admiral /'ædmərəl/ *n* ammiraglio *m*
admiralty /'ædmɪrəltɪ/ *n Br* ministero *m* della marina militare britannica

admiration /ædmə'reɪʃn/ *n* ammirazione *f*
admire /əd'maɪə(r)/ *vt* ammirare
admirer /əd'maɪrə(r)/ *n* ammiratore, -trice *mf*
admiring /əd'maɪrɪŋ/ *a* ‹*person*› pieno d'ammirazione; ‹*look*› ammirativo
admiringly /əd'maɪrɪŋlɪ/ *adv* ‹*look, say*› con ammirazione
admissible /əd'mɪsəbl/ *a* ammissibile
admission /əd'mɪʃn/ *n* ammissione *f*; (*to hospital*) ricovero *m*; (*entry*) ingresso *m*
admit /əd'mɪt/ *vt* (*pt/pp* **admitted**) (*let in*) far entrare; (*to hospital*) ricoverare; (*acknowledge*) ammettere ● *vi* **~ to sth** ammettere qcsa
admittance /əd'mɪtəns/ *n* ammissione *f*; **'no ~'** 'vietato l'ingresso'
admittedly /əd'mɪtɪdlɪ/ *adv* bisogna riconoscerlo
admonish /əd'mɒnɪʃ/ *vt* ammonire
admonition /ædmə'nɪʃn/ *n* ammonimento *m*
ad nauseam /æd'nɔ:zɪæm/ *adv* ‹*discuss, repeat*› fino alla nausea
ado /ə'du:/ *n* **without more ~** senza ulteriori indugi
adolescence /ædə'lesns/ *n* adolescenza *f*
adolescent /ædə'lesnt/ *a* & *n* adolescente *mf*
adopt /ə'dɒpt/ *vt* adottare; Pol scegliere ‹*candidate*›
adopted /ə'dɒptɪd/ *a* ‹*son, daughter*› adottivo
adoption /ə'dɒpʃn/ *n* adozione *f*
adoption agency *n* agenzia *f* di adozioni
adoptive /ə'dɒptɪv/ *a* adottivo
adorable /ə'dɔ:rəbl/ *a* adorabile
adoration /ædə'reɪʃn/ *n* adorazione *f*
adore /ə'dɔ:(r)/ *vt* adorare
adoring /ə'dɔ:rɪŋ/ *a* ‹*fan*› in adorazione; **she has an ~ husband** ha un marito che la adora
adoringly /ə'dɔ:rɪŋlɪ/ *adv* con adorazione
adorn /ə'dɔ:n/ *vt* adornare
adornment /ə'dɔ:nmənt/ *n* ornamento *m*
adrenalin /ə'drenəlɪn/ *n* adrenalina *f*
Adriatic /eɪdrɪ'ætɪk/ *a* & *n* **the ~** [Sea] il mare Adriatico, l'Adriatico *m*
adrift /ə'drɪft/ *a* alla deriva; **be ~** andare alla deriva; **come ~** staccarsi
adroit /ə'drɔɪt/ *a* abile
adroitly /ə'drɔɪtlɪ/ *adv* abilmente
adulation /ædjʊ'leɪʃn/ *n* adulazione *f*
adult /'ædʌlt/ *n* adulto, -a *mf*
Adult Education *n Br* ≈ corsi *mpl* serali
adulterate /ə'dʌltəreɪt/ *vt* adulterare ‹*wine*›
adulterated /ə'dʌltəreɪtɪd/ *a* ‹*wine*› adulterato
adulterous /ə'dʌltərəs/ *a* ‹*relationship*› adulterino; ‹*person*› adultero
adultery /ə'dʌltərɪ/ *n* adulterio *m*
adulthood /'ædʌlthʊd/ *n* età *f* adulta
adult literacy classes *n Br* lezioni *fpl* di alfabetizzazione per adulti
advance /əd'vɑ:ns/ *n* avanzamento *m*; Mil

avanzata *f*; (*payment*) anticipo *m*; **in ~** in anticipo ● *vi* avanzare; (*make progress*) fare progressi ● *vt* promuovere ‹*cause*›; avanzare ‹*theory*›; anticipare ‹*money*›

advance booking *n* prenotazione *f* [in anticipo]

advance booking office *n* ufficio *m* prenotazioni

advanced /əd'vɑːnst/ *a* avanzato

Advanced Level *n Br Sch* = **A-Level**

advancement /əd'vɑːnsmənt/ *n* promozione *f*

advance: advance notice *n* preannuncio *m*. **advance party** *n Mil* avanguardia *f*. **advance payment** *n Comm* pagamento *m* anticipato. **advance warning** *n* preavviso *m*

advantage /əd'vɑːntɪdʒ/ *n* vantaggio *m*; **take ~ of** approfittare di

advantageous /ædvən'teɪdʒəs/ *a* vantaggioso

advent /'ædvent/ *n* avvento *m*; **A~** *Relig* Avvento *m*

adventure /əd'ventʃə(r)/ *n* avventura *f*

adventure playground *n Br* parco *m* giochi

adventurer /əd'ventʃərə(r)/ *n* avventuriero, -a *mf*

adventuress /əd'ventʃərɪs/ *n* avventuriera *f*

adventurous /əd'ventʃərəs/ *a* avventuroso

adverb /'ædvɜːb/ *n* avverbio *m*

adversary /'ædvəsərɪ/ *n* avversario, -a *mf*

adverse /'ædvɜːs/ *a* avverso

adversity /əd'vɜːsətɪ/ *n* avversità *f*

advert /'ædvɜːt/ *n fam* = **advertisement**

advertise /'ædvətaɪz/ *vt* reclamizzare; mettere un annuncio per ‹*job, flat*› ● *vi* fare pubblicità; (*for job, flat*) mettere un annuncio

advertisement /əd'vɜːtɪsmənt/ *n* pubblicità *f inv*; (*in paper*) inserzione *f*, annuncio *m*

advertiser /'ædvətaɪzə(r)/ *n* (*in newspaper*) inserzionista *mf*

advertising /'ædvətaɪzɪŋ/ *n* pubblicità *f* ● *attrib* pubblicitario

advertising: advertising agency *n* agenzia *f* di pubblicità. **advertising campaign** *n* campagna *f* pubblicitaria. **advertising executive** *n* dirigente *mf* pubblicitario, -a. **advertising industry** *n* settore *m* pubblicitario. **Advertising Standards Authority** *n Br* organo *m* di controllo sulla pubblicità

advice /əd'vaɪs/ *n* consigli *mpl*; **piece of ~** consiglio *m*

advice note *n* avviso *m*

advisability /ədvaɪzə'bɪlətɪ/ *n* opportunità *f*

advisable /əd'vaɪzəbl/ *a* consigliabile

advise /əd'vaɪz/ *vt* consigliare; (*inform*) avvisare; **~ sb to do sth** consigliare a qcno di fare qcsa; **~ sb against sth** sconsigliare qcsa a qcno

advisedly /əd'vaɪzɪdlɪ/ *adv* ‹*say*› deliberatamente

adviser /əd'vaɪzə(r)/ *n* consulente *mf*

advisory /əd'vaɪzərɪ/ *a* consultivo

advisory committee *n* comitato *m* consultivo

advocacy /'ædvəkəsɪ/ *n* appoggio *m*

advocate¹ /'ædvəkət/ *n* (*supporter*) fautore, -trice *mf*

advocate² /'ædvəkeɪt/ *vt* propugnare

Aegean /ɪ'dʒɪən/ *n* **the ~** l'Egeo *m*

aegis /'iːdʒɪs/ *n* **under the ~ of** sotto l'egida di

aeon /'iːən/ *n* **~s ago** milioni *mpl* e milioni di anni fa

aerate /'eəreɪt/ *vt* aerare; addizionare anidride carbonica a ‹*water*›

aerial /'eərɪəl/ *a* aereo ● *n* antenna *f*

aerial camera *n* macchina *f* fotografica per fotografie aeree

aerial warfare *n* guerra *f* aerea

aerie /'eərɪ/ *n Am* (*eyrie*) nido *m* [d'aquila]

aerobatics /eərə'bætɪks/ *npl* (*manoeuvres*) acrobazie *fpl* aeree

aerobics /eə'rəʊbɪks/ *n* aerobica *fsg*

aerodrome /'eərədrəʊm/ *n* aerodromo *m*

aerodynamic /eərəʊdaɪ'næmɪk/ *a* aerodinamico

aerodynamics /eərəʊdaɪ'næmɪks/ *n* aerodinamica *f*

aerogram[me] /'eərəʊgræm/ *n* aerogramma *m*

aeronautic[al] /eərə'nɔːtɪk[əl]/ *a* aeronautico

aeronautic[al] engineer *n* ingegnere *m* aeronautico

aeronautic[al] engineering *n* ingegneria *f* aeronautica

aeronautics /eərə'nɔːtɪks/ *n* aeronautica *f*

aeroplane /'eərəpleɪn/ *n* aeroplano *m*

aerosol /'eərəsɒl/ *n* bomboletta *f* spray

aerospace /'eərəspeɪs/ *n* (*industry*) industria *f* aerospaziale ● *attrib* ‹*engineer, company*› aerospaziale

aesthete /'iːsθiːt/ *n* esteta *mf*

aesthetic /iːs'θetɪk/ *a* estetico

aesthetically /iːs'θetɪklɪ/ *adv* ‹*restore*› con gusto; ‹*satisfying*› esteticamente

aestheticism /iːs'θetɪsɪzm/ *n* (*taste*) esteticità *f*; (*doctrine, quality*) estetismo *m*

aesthetics /iːs'θetɪks/ *n* estetica *f*

afar /ə'fɑː(r)/ *adv* **from ~** da lontano

affable /'æfəbl/ *a* affabile

affably /'æfəblɪ/ *adv* affabilmente

affair /ə'feə(r)/ *n* affare *m*; (*scandal*) caso *m*; (*sexual*) relazione *f*

affect /ə'fekt/ *vt* influire su; (*emotionally*) colpire; (*concern*) riguardare; (*pretend*) affettare

affectation /æfek'teɪʃn/ *n* affettazione *f*

affected /ə'fektɪd/ *a* affettato

affectedly /ə'fektɪdlɪ/ *adv* ‹*talk*› con affettazione

affection /ə'fekʃn/ *n* affetto *m*

affectionate /ə'fekʃnət/ *a* affettuoso

affectionately /ə'fekʃnətlɪ/ *adv* affettuosamente

affidavit /æfɪ'deɪvɪt/ *n* affidavit *m inv* (*di-*

chiarazione scritta e giurata davanti a un pubblico ufficiale)

affiliated /əˈfɪlɪeɪtɪd/ *a* affiliato

affiliation /əfɪlɪˈeɪʃn/ *n (process, state)* affiliazione *f*; *(link)* legame *m*

affinity /əˈfɪnətɪ/ *n* affinità *f inv*

affirm /əˈfɜːm/ *vt* affermare; *Jur* dichiarare solennemente

affirmative /əˈfɜːmətɪv/ *a* affermativo ● *n* **in the ~** affermativamente

affix /əˈfɪks/ *vt* affiggere; apporre *(signature)*

afflict /əˈflɪkt/ *vt* affliggere

affliction /əˈflɪkʃn/ *n* afflizione *f*

affluence /ˈæfluəns/ *n* agiatezza *f*

affluent /ˈæfluənt/ *a* agiato

afford /əˈfɔːd/ *vt (provide)* fornire; **be able to ~ sth** potersi permettere qcsa

affordable /əˈfɔːdəbl/ *a* abbordabile

affray /əˈfreɪ/ *n* rissa *f*

affront /əˈfrʌnt/ *n* affronto *m* ● *vt* fare un affronto a

Afghan /ˈæfgæn/ *n (person)* afgano, -a *mf*; *(language)* afgano *m*; *(coat)* pellicciotto *m* afgano

Afghan hound *n* levriero *m* afgano

Afghanistan /æfˈgænɪstæn/ *n* Afganistan *m*

aficionado /æfɪsjəˈnɑːdəʊ/ *n* aficionado, -a *mf*

afield /əˈfiːld/ *adv* **further ~** più lontano

aflame /əˈfleɪm/ *a & adv* liter in fiamme, sfolgorante; **be ~** *(cheek:)* essere in fiamme; **be ~ with desire** ardere dal desiderio

afloat /əˈfləʊt/ *a* a galla

afoot /əˈfʊt/ *a* **there's something ~** si sta preparando qualcosa

aforesaid /əˈfɔːsed/ *a Jur* suddetto

afraid /əˈfreɪd/ *a* **be ~** aver paura; **I'm ~ not** purtroppo no; **I'm ~ so** temo di sì; **I'm ~ I can't help you** mi dispiace, ma non posso esserle d'aiuto

afresh /əˈfreʃ/ *adv* da capo

Africa /ˈæfrɪkə/ *n* Africa *f*

African /ˈæfrɪkən/ *a & n* africano, -a *mf*

Afrikaans /æfrɪˈkɑːns/ *n* afrikaans *m*

Afrikaner /æfrɪˈkɑːnə(r)/ *n* boero, -a *mf*

Afro-American /æfrəʊəˈmerɪkən/ *a & n* afroamericano, -a *mf*

Afro-Caribbean /æfrəʊkærəˈbɪən/ *a & n* afrocaraibico, -a *mf*

aft /ɑːft/ *adv Naut* a poppa; *(towards the stern)* verso poppa

after /ˈɑːftə(r)/ *adv* dopo; **the day ~** il giorno dopo; **be ~** cercare ● *prep* dopo; **~ all** dopotutto; **the day ~ tomorrow** dopodomani ● *conj* dopo che

after: after-birth *n* residui *mpl* di placenta. **after-care** *n Med* ospedalizzazione *f* domiciliare. **after-dinner speaker** *n* persona *f* invitata a tenere un discorso dopo una cena o un ricevimento. **after-effect** *n* conseguenza *f*. **after-life** *n* vita *f* nell'aldilà

aftermath /ˈɑːftəmɑːθ/ *n* conseguenze *fpl*; **the ~ of war** il dopoguerra; **in the ~ of** nel periodo successivo a

after: afternoon *n* pomeriggio *m*; **good ~!** buon giorno!. **afternoon tea** *n* merenda *f*.

after-pains *npl* dolori *mpl* post-partum.

after-sales service *n* servizio *m* assistenza clienti. **aftershave** *n* [lozione *f*] dopobarba *m inv*. **after-shock** *n fig* effetti *mpl*. **aftersun** *n & a* doposole *m inv*. **after-taste** *n* retrogusto *m*. **after-tax** *a (profits, earnings)* al netto. **afterthought** *n* added as an **~** aggiunto in un secondo momento; **as an ~, why not...?** ripensandoci bene, perché non...?

afterwards /ˈɑːftəwədz/ *adv* in seguito

again /əˈgeɪn/ *adv* di nuovo; [then] **~** *(besides)* inoltre; *(on the other hand)* d'altra parte; **~ and ~** continuamente

against /əˈgeɪnst/ *prep* contro

age /eɪdʒ/ *n* età *f inv*; *(era)* era *f*; **~ s fam** secoli; **~s ago** *fam* secoli fa; **what ~ are you?** quanti anni hai?; **be under ~** non avere l'età richiesta; **he's two years of ~** ha due anni ● *vt/i (pres p* ageing*)* invecchiare

age bracket, age group *n* fascia *f* d'età

aged¹ /eɪdʒd/ *a* **~ two** di due anni

aged² /ˈeɪdʒɪd/ *a* anziano ● *n* **the ~** *pl* gli anziani

aged debt *n Fin* somma *f* in scadenza

ageing /ˈeɪdʒɪŋ/ *n* invecchiamento *m* ● *a (person, population)* che sta invecchiando

ageism /ˈeɪdʒɪzm/ *n* discriminazione *f* contro chi non è più giovane

ageless /ˈeɪdʒlɪs/ *a* senza età

agency /ˈeɪdʒənsɪ/ *n* agenzia *f*; **have the ~ for** essere un concessionario di

agency-fee *n* commissione *f*

agency-nurse *n* infermiere, -a *mf* privato, -a

agenda /əˈdʒendə/ *n* ordine *m* del giorno; **on the ~** all'ordine del giorno; *fig* in programma

agent /ˈeɪdʒənt/ *n* agente *mf*

age-old *a* secolare

age range *n* fascia *f* d'età

aggravate /ˈægrəveɪt/ *vt* aggravare; *(annoy)* esasperare

aggravating /ˈægrəveɪtɪŋ/ *a Jur* aggravante; *(fam: irritating)* irritante

aggravation /ægrəˈveɪʃn/ *n* aggravamento *m*; *(annoyance)* esasperazione *f*

aggregate /ˈægrɪgət/ *a* totale ● *n* totale *m*; **on ~** nel complesso

aggression /əˈgreʃn/ *n* aggressione *f*

aggressive /əˈgresɪv/ *a* aggressivo

aggressively /əˈgresɪvlɪ/ *adv* aggressivamente

aggressiveness /əˈgresɪvnɪs/ *n* aggressività *f*

aggressor /əˈgresə(r)/ *n* aggressore *m*

aggrieved /əˈgriːvd/ *a* risentito

aggro /ˈægrəʊ/ *n fam* aggressività *f*; *(problems)* grane *fpl*

aghast /əˈgɑːst/ *a* inorridito

agile /ˈædʒaɪl/ *a* agile

agility /əˈdʒɪlətɪ/ *n* agilità *f*

agitate /ˈædʒɪteɪt/ *vt* mettere in agitazione;

(*shake*) agitare ● *vi fig* ~ **for** creare delle agitazioni per

agitated /'adʒɪteɪtɪd/ *a* agitato

agitation /adʒɪ'teɪʃn/ *n* agitazione *f*

agitator /'adʒɪteɪtə(r)/ *n* agitatore, -trice *mf*

AGM *n abbr* (**annual general meeting**) assemblea *f* generale annuale

agnostic /æg'nɒstɪk/ *a & n* agnostico, -a *mf*

ago /ə'gəʊ/ *adv* fa; **a long time/a month** ~ molto tempo/un mese fa; **how long** ~ **was it?** quanto tempo fa è successo?

agog /ə'gɒg/ *a* eccitato

agonize /'ægənaɪz/ *vi* angosciarsi (**over** per)

agonized /'ægənaɪzd/ *a* ⟨*expression, cry*⟩ angosciato

agonizing /'ægənaɪzɪŋ/ *a* angosciante

agony /'ægənɪ/ *n* agonia *f*; (*mental*) angoscia *f*; **be in** ~ avere dei dolori atroci

agony aunt *n persona f* chi tiene la posta del cuore in una rivista

agoraphobia /ægərə'fəʊbɪə/ *n* agorafobia *f*

agoraphobic /ægərə'fəʊbɪk/ *a* agorafobo, -a *mf*

agree /ə'gri:/ *vt* accordarsi su; ~ **to do sth** accettare di fare qcsa; ~ **that** essere d'accordo [sul fatto] che ● *vi* essere d'accordo; ⟨*figures:*⟩ concordare; (*reach agreement*) mettersi d'accordo; (*get on*) andare d'accordo; (*consent*) acconsentire (**to** a); **it doesn't** ~ **with me** mi fa male; ~ **with sth** (*approve of*) approvare qcsa

agreeable /ə'gri:əbl/ *a* gradevole; (*willing*) d'accordo

agreeably /ə'gri:əblɪ/ *adv* (*pleasantly*) piacevolmente; (*amicably*) in modo amichevole

agreed /ə'gri:d/ *a* convenuto

agreement /ə'gri:mənt/ *n* accordo *m*; **in** ~ d'accordo; **reach** ~ arrivare a un accordo

agricultural /ægrɪ'kʌltʃərəl/ *a* agricolo

agriculturalist /ægrɪ'kʌltʃərəlɪst/ *n* agronomo, -a *mf*

agricultural show *n* fiera *f* agricola

agriculture /'ægrɪkʌltʃə(r)/ *n* agricoltura *f*

agronomy /ə'grɒnəmɪ/ *n* agronomia *f*

aground /ə'graʊnd/ *adv* **run** ~ ⟨*ship:*⟩ arenarsi

ah /ɑː/ *int* ~ **well!** (*resignedly*) va be'!

ahead /ə'hed/ *adv* avanti; **be** ~ **of** essere davanti a; *fig* essere avanti rispetto a; **draw** ~ passare davanti (**of** a); **go on** ~ cominciare ad andare; **get** ~ (*in life*) riuscire; **go** ~! fai pure!; **look** ~ pensare all'avvenire; **plan** ~ fare progetti per l'avvenire

AI *n abbr* (**artificial intelligence**) I.A. *f*

aid /eɪd/ *n* aiuto *m*; **in** ~ **of** a favore di ● *vt* aiutare

aide /eɪd/ *n* assistente *mf*

Aids /eɪdz/ *n* AIDS *m*

ailing /'eɪlɪŋ/ *a* malato

ailment /'eɪlmənt/ *n* disturbo *m*

aim /eɪm/ *n* mira *f*; *fig* scopo *m*; **take** ~ prendere la mira ● *vt* puntare ⟨*gun*⟩ (**at** su) ● *vi* mirare; ~ **to do sth** aspirare a fare qcsa

aimless /'eɪmlɪs/ *a* senza scopo

aimlessly /'eɪmlɪslɪ/ *adv* senza scopo

ain't /eɪnt/ *fam* = **am not; is not; are not; have not; has not**

air /eə(r)/ *n* aria *f*; **be on the** ~ ⟨*programme:*⟩ essere in onda; **put on** ~**s** darsi delle arie; **by** ~ in aereo; (*airmail*) per via aerea ● *vt* arieggiare; far conoscere ⟨*views*⟩; *pej* sfoggiare ⟨*knowledge*⟩

air: air ambulance *n* aereo *m* ambulanza; (*helicopter*) eliambulanza *f*. **air bag** *n Auto* air bag *m inv*. **air-bed** *n* materassino *m* [gonfiabile]

airborne /'eəbɔːn/ *a* ⟨*plane*⟩ in volo; ⟨*troops*⟩ aerotrasportato

air: airbrush *n* aerografo *m*. **airbubble** *n* (*in liquid, plastic, wallpaper*) bolla *f* d'aria. **air-conditioned** *a* con aria condizionata. **air conditioner** *n* condizionatore *m*. **air-conditioning** *n* aria *f* condizionata. **air-cooled** *a* ⟨*engine*⟩ raffreddato ad aria. **aircraft** *n* aereo *m*. **aircraft carrier** *n* portaerei *f inv*. **aircraft[s]man** *n Br* aviere *m*. **aircrew** *n* equipaggio *m* di volo. **air cushion** *n* (*inflatable cushion*) cuscino *m* gonfiabile; (*of hovercraft*) cuscino *m* d'aria. **air disaster** *n* disastro *m* aereo. **airdrop** *n* lancio *m* con paracadute. **air duct** *n* condotto *m* dell'aria. **airfare** *n* tariffa *f* aerea. **airfield** *n* campo *m* d'aviazione. **airflow** *n* spostamento *m* d'aria. **air force** *n* aviazione *f*. **airfreight** *n* (*goods*) merce *f* spedita via aerea; (*method of transport*) trasporto *m* aereo; (*charge*) costo *m* per trasporto aereo. **air freshener** *n* deodorante *m* per l'ambiente. **airgun** *n* fucile *m* pneumatico. **airhead** *n pej fam* idiota *mf*. **air hole** *n* sfiatatoio *m*. **air hostess** *n* hostess *f inv*

airing /'eərɪŋ/ *n* **give a room an** ~ arieggiare una stanza; **give an idea an** ~ *fig* ventilare un'idea

airing cupboard *n Br* sgabuzzino *m* del boiler dove viene riposta la biancheria ad asciugare

airless /'eəlɪs/ *a* ⟨*evening*⟩ senza vento; ⟨*room*⟩ poco ventilato

air: air letter *n* aerogramma *m*. **airlift** *vt* trasportare con ponte aereo ● *n* ponte *m* aereo. **airline** *n* compagnia *f* aerea. **airliner** *n* aereo *m* di linea. **airlock** *n* bolla *f* d'aria. **airmail** *n* posta *f* aerea. **air marshal** *n Br* maresciallo *m* d'aviazione. **airplane** *n Am* aereo *m*. **air pocket** *n* vuoto *m* d'aria. **airport** *n* aeroporto *m*. **air power** *n* potenza *f* aerea. **air-raid** *n* incursione *f* aerea. **air-raid shelter** *n* rifugio *m* antiaereo. **air-raid siren** *n* allarme *m* aereo. **air-raid warning** *n* allarme *m* aereo. **air rifle** *n* fucile *m* ad aria compressa. **air-sea rescue** *n* salvataggio *m* dal mare con impiego di mezzi aerei. **air shaft** *n* (*in mine*) pozzo *m* di ventilazione. **airship** *n* dirigibile *m*. **air show** *n* (*trade exhibition*) salone *m* dell'aviazione; (*flying show*) manifestazione *f* aerea. **airsickness** *n* mal *m* d'aereo. **air sock** *n* manica *f* a vento. **airspeed** *n* velocità *f* relativa all'aria. **airspeed indicator** *n* indicatore *m* di velocità (*su un aereo*). **airstream** *n* corrente *f* d'aria. **airstrip** *n* pista *f* d'atterraggio. **air terminal** *n* (*in town, terminus*) [air-]terminal *m inv*. **airtight** *a* ermetico. **airtime** *n Radio, TV* spazio *m* radiofonico/televisivo. **air-to-air** *a* (*missile*) aria-aria; (*refuelling*) in volo. **air traffic** *n* traffico *m* aereo. **air-traffic controller** *n* controllore *m* di volo. **air valve** *n* valvola *f* pneumatica. **air vent** *n* presa *f* d'aria. **air vice-marshal** *n Br* vice-maresciallo *m* dell'aviazione. **airwaves** *npl Radio, TV* onde *fpl* radio. **airway** *n* (*route*) rotta *f* aerea; (*airline*) compagnia *f* aerea; *Anat* via *f* respiratoria; (*ventilating passage*) pozzo *m* di ventilazione. **air waybill** *n* polizza *f* di carico aerea. **airworthiness** *n* idoneità *f* di volo. **airworthy** *a* idoneo al volo

airy /'eərɪ/ *a* (**-ier, -iest**) arieggiato; (*manner*) noncurante

airy-fairy /ˌeərɪ'feərɪ/ *a Br fam* (*plan, person*) fuori dalla realtà

aisle /aɪl/ *n* corridoio *m*; (*in supermarket*) corsia *f*; (*in church*) navata *f*

ajar /ə'dʒɑː(r)/ *a* socchiuso

aka *abbr* (**also known as**) alias

akin /ə'kɪn/ *a* ~ **to** simile a

alabaster /'æləbɑːstə(r)/ *n* alabastro *m*

alacrity /ə'lækrətɪ/ *n* alacrità *f inv*

alarm /ə'lɑːm/ *n* allarme *m*; **set the** ~ (*of alarm clock*) mettere la sveglia; **in** ~ in stato di allarme ● *vt* allarmare; **don't be** ~ **ed!** non si allarmi!

alarm: alarm bell *n* campanello *m* d'allarme; **set the** ~ ~**s ringing** *n Br fig* far scattare il campanello d'allarme. **alarm call** *n Teleph* sveglia *f* automatica. **alarm clock** *n* sveglia *f*

alarming /ə'lɑːmɪŋ/ *a* allarmante, preoccupante

alarmist /ə'lɑːmɪst/ *a & n* allarmista *mf*

alas /ə'læs/ *int* ahimè

Albania /æl'beɪnɪə/ *n* Albania *f*

Albanian /æl'beɪnɪən/ *n* (*person*) albanese *mf*; (*language*) albanese *m* ● *a* albanese

albatross /'ælbətrɒs/ *n* (*also in golf*) albatro *m*

albeit /ɔːl'biːɪt/ *adv & conj* benché

albino /æl'biːnəʊ/ *a & n* albino, -a *mf*

album /'ælbəm/ *n* album *m inv*

albumen /'ælbjʊmɪn/ *n Biol, Bot* albume *m*

alchemist /'ælkɪmɪst/ *n* alchimista *m*

alchemy /'ælkɪmɪ/ *n Chem, fig* alchimia *f*

alcohol /'ælkəhɒl/ *n* alcool *m*

alcoholic /ælkə'hɒlɪk/ *a* alcolico ● *n* alcolizzato, -a *mf*

Alcoholics Anonymous *n* Anonima *f* Alcolisti

alcoholism /'ælkəhɒlɪzm/ *n* alcolismo *m*

alcove /'ælkəʊv/ *n* alcova *f*

alder /ɔːl'də(r)/ *n* (*tree, wood*) ontano *m*

ale /eɪl/ *n* birra *f*

alert /ə'lɜːt/ *a* attento; (*watchful*) vigile ● *n* segnale *m* d'allarme; **be on the** ~ stare allerta ● *vt* allertare

alertness /ə'lɜːtnɪs/ *n* (*attentiveness*) attenzione *f*; (*liveliness*) vivacità *f*

A-level *n Br Sch* ~**s** ≈ esami *mpl* di maturità; **he got an** ~ **in history** ha portato storia alla maturità

Alexandria /ælɪg'zændrɪə/ *n* Alessandria *f* [d'Egitto]

alfalfa /æl'fælfə/ *n* erba *f* medicinale

alfresco /æl'freskəʊ/ *a & adv* all'aperto

algae /'æ̈ldʒiː/ *npl* alghe *fpl*

algebra /'ældʒɪbrə/ *n* algebra *f*

Algeria /æl'dʒɪərɪə/ *n* Algeria *f*

Algerian /æl'dʒɪərɪən/ *a & n* algerino, -a *mf*

Algiers /æl'dʒɪəz/ *n* Algeri *f*

algorithm /'ælgərɪðm/ *n* algoritmo *m*

alias /'eɪlɪəs/ *n* pseudonimo *m* ● *adv* alias

alibi /'ælɪbaɪ/ *n* alibi *m inv*

alien /'eɪlɪən/ *a* straniero; *fig* estraneo ● *n* straniero, -a *mf*; (*from space*) alieno, -a *mf*

alienate /'eɪlɪəneɪt/ *vt* alienare

alienation /eɪlɪə'neɪʃn/ *n* alienazione *f*

alight[1] /ə'laɪt/ *vi* scendere; (*bird:*) posarsi

alight[2] *a* **be** ~ essere in fiamme; **set** ~ dar fuoco a

align /ə'laɪn/ *vt* allineare

alignment /ə'laɪnmənt/ *n* allineamento *m*; **out of** ~ non allineato

alike /ə'laɪk/ *a* simile; **be** ~ rassomigliarsi ● *adv* in modo simile; **look** ~ rassomigliarsi; **summer and winter** ~ sia d'estate che d'inverno

alimentary /ælɪ'mentərɪ/ *a* (*system*) digerente; (*process*) digestivo

alimentary canal *n* tubo *m* digerente

alimony /'ælɪmənɪ/ *n* alimenti *mpl*

alive /ə'laɪv/ *a* vivo; ~ **with** brulicante di; ~ **to** sensibile a; ~ **and kicking** vivo e vegeto

alkali /'ælkəlaɪ/ *n* alcali *m*

alkaline /'ælkəlaɪn/ *a* alcalino

all /ɔːl/ *a* tutto; ~ **the children,** ~ **children** tutti i bambini; ~ **day** tutto il giorno; **he refused** ~ **help** ha rifiutato qualsiasi aiuto; **for** ~ **that** (*nevertheless*) perciò; **in** ~ **sincerity** in tutta sincerità; **be** ~ **for** essere favorevole a ● *pron* tutto; ~ **of you/them** tutti voi/loro; ~ **of it** tutto; ~ **of the town** tutta la città; ~ **but one** tutti tranne uno; **in** ~ in tutto; ~ **in** ~ tutto sommato; **most of** ~ più di ogni altra cosa; **once and for** ~ una volta per tutte; ~ **being well** salvo complicazioni ● *adv* completamente; ~ **but** quasi; ~ **at once** (*at the same time*) tutto in una volta; ~ **at once,** ~ **of a sudden** all'improvviso; ~ **too soon** troppo presto; ~ **the same** (*nevertheless*) ciononostante; ~ **the better** meglio ancora; **she's not** ~ **that good an actress** non è poi così brava come attrice; ~ **in** in tutto; (*fam* esausto); **thirty/three** ~ (*in sport*) trenta/tre pari; ~ **over** (*finished*) tutto finito; (*everywhere*) dappertutto; **it's** ~ **right** (*I don't mind*) non fa niente; **I'm** ~ **right** (*not hurt*) non ho niente; ~ **right!** va bene!

all-American *a* (*record, champion*) americano; (*girl, boy, hero*) tipicamente americano

all-around *a* (*improvement*) generale

allay /ə'leɪ/ *vt* placare (*suspicions, anger*)

all-clear *n Mil* cessato *m* allarme/pericolo;

(*from doctor*) autorizzazione *f*; **give sb the ~ ~** *fig* dare il via libera a qcno

all-consuming *a* ⟨*passion*⟩ sfrenato; ⟨*ambition*⟩ smisurato

all-day *a* ⟨*event*⟩ che dura tutto il giorno

allegation /ælɪˈgeɪʃn/ *n* accusa *f*

allege /əˈledʒ/ *vt* dichiarare

alleged /əˈledʒd/ *a* presunto

allegedly /əˈledʒɪdlɪ/ *adv* a quanto si dice

allegiance /əˈliːdʒəns/ *n* fedeltà *f*

allegorical /ælɪˈgɒrɪkl/ *a* allegorico

allegory /ˈælɪgərɪ/ *n* allegoria *f*

all-embracing /-əmˈbreɪsɪŋ/ *a* globale

allergic /əˈlɜːdʒɪk/ *a* allergico

allergist /ˈælədʒɪst/ *n* allergologo, -a *mf*

allergy /ˈælədʒɪ/ *n* allergia *f*

alleviate /əˈliːvɪeɪt/ *vt* alleviare

alleviation /əliːvɪˈeɪʃn/ *n* alleviamento *m*, alleggerimento *m*

alley /ˈælɪ/ *n* vicolo *m*; (*for bowling*) corsia *f*

alley-way /ˈælɪweɪ/ *n* vicolo *m*

all-found *a* **£200 ~** 200 sterline inclusi vitto e alloggio

alliance /əˈlaɪəns/ *n* alleanza *f*

allied /ˈælaɪd/ *a* alleato; (*fig: related*) connesso (**to** a)

alligator /ˈælɪgeɪtə(r)/ *n* alligatore *m*

all-important *a* essenziale

all in *a* (*Br fam: exhausted*) distrutto; ⟨*fee, price*⟩ tutto compreso

all-inclusive *a* ⟨*fee, price*⟩ tutto compreso

all-in-one *a* ⟨*garment*⟩ in un pezzo solo

all-in wrestling *n* Sport catch *m*

all-night *a* ⟨*party, meeting*⟩ che dura tutta la notte; ⟨*radio station*⟩ che trasmette tutta la notte; ⟨*service*⟩ notturno

allocate /ˈæləkeɪt/ *vt* assegnare; distribuire ⟨*resources*⟩

allocation /æləˈkeɪʃn/ *n* assegnazione *f*; (*of resources*) distribuzione *f*

all-or-nothing *a* ⟨*approach, policy*⟩ senza vie di mezzo

allot /əˈlɒt/ *vt* (*pt/pp* **allotted**) distribuire

allotment /əˈlɒtmənt/ *n* distribuzione *f*; (*share*) parte *f*; (*land*) piccolo lotto *m* di terreno

all-out *a* ⟨*effort*⟩ estremo; ⟨*attack*⟩ senza esclusione di colpi ● *adv* **go all out to do sth/for sth** mettercela tutta per fare qcsa/per qcsa

all-over *a* ⟨*tan*⟩ integrale

all over *prep* **~ ~ China** in/per tutta la Cina; **the news is ~ ~ the village** lo sanno tutti in paese; **be ~ ~ sb** (*fawning over*) stare appiccicato a qcno ● *adv* **be trembling ~ ~** tremare tutto; **that's Mary ~ ~!** è proprio da Mary! ● *a* **when it's ~ ~** (*finished*) quando è tutto finito

allow /əˈlaʊ/ *vt* permettere; (*grant*) accordare; (*reckon on*) contare; (*agree*) ammettere; **~ for** tener conto di; **~ sb to do sth** permettere a qcno di fare qcsa; **you are not ~ed to...** è vietato...; **how much are you ~ed?** qual è il limite?

allowable /əˈlaʊəbl/ *a* permissibile; *Jur* lecito; ⟨*tax*⟩ deducibile

allowance /əˈlaʊəns/ *n* sussidio *m*; (*Am: pocket money*) paghetta *f*; (*for petrol etc*) indennità *f inv*; (*of luggage, duty free*) limite *m*; (*for tax purposes*) deduzione *f*; **make ~s for** essere indulgente verso ⟨*sb*⟩; tener conto di ⟨*sth*⟩

alloy /ˈælɔɪ/ *n* lega *f*

alloy steel *n* lega *f* d'acciaio

alloy wheel *n* cerchione *m* in lega d'acciaio

all points bulletin *n* Am allarme *m* generale

all-powerful *a* onnipotente

all-purpose *a* ⟨*building*⟩ polivalente; ⟨*utensil*⟩ multiuso

all right *a* **is it ~ ~ if...?** va bene se...?; **is that ~ ~ with you?** ti va bene?; **sounds ~ ~ to me** per me va bene; **that's [quite] ~ ~** (*it doesn't matter*) non c'è problema; **is my hair ~ ~?** sono a posto i miei capelli?; **it's ~ ~ for you!** è facile per te!; **she's ~ ~** (*competent*) è abbastanza brava; (*attractive*) non è niente male; (*pleasant*) è piuttosto simpatica; **will you be ~ ~?** (*able to manage*) te la caverai?; **feel ~ ~** (*well*) sentirsi bene ● *adv* ⟨*function, see*⟩ bene; (*not brilliantly*) così così; **can I? – ~ ~** posso? – d'accordo; **she's doing ~ ~** (*in life*) le cose le vanno bene; (*in health*) sta bene; (*in activity*) se la cava bene; **she knows ~ ~!** (*without doubt*) lei lo sa di sicuro!; **~ ~, ~ ~!** va bene, va bene!

all-risk *a* ⟨*policy, cover*⟩ multirischi

all-round *a* ⟨*improvement*⟩ generale; ⟨*athlete*⟩ completo

all-rounder /-ˈraʊndə(r)/ *n* **be a good ~** essere versatile

allspice /ˈɔːlspaɪs/ *n* pepe *m* della Giamaica

all square *a* **be ~ ~** ⟨*people:*⟩ essere pari; ⟨*accounts:*⟩ quadrare

all-time *a* ⟨*record*⟩ assoluto, senza precedenti; **the ~ greats** (*people*) i grandi; **~ high** massimo *m* storico; **be at an ~ low** ⟨*person, morale:*⟩ essere a terra; ⟨*figures, shares:*⟩ toccare il minimo storico

all told *adv* tutto sommato

allude /əˈluːd/ *vi* alludere

allure /æˈljʊə(r)/ *n* attrattiva *f*

alluring /əˈljʊrɪŋ/ *a* allettante, affascinante

allusion /əˈluːʒn/ *n* allusione *f*

ally[1] /ˈælaɪ/ *n* alleato, -a *mf*

ally[2] /əˈlaɪ/ *vt* (*pt/pp* **-ied**) alleare; **~ oneself with** allearsi con

almighty /ɔːlˈmaɪtɪ/ *a* (*fam: big*) mega *inv* ● *n* **the A ~** l'Onnipotente *m*

almond /ˈɑːmənd/ *n* mandorla *f*; (*tree*) mandorlo *m*

almost /ˈɔːlməʊst/ *adv* quasi

alms /ɑːmz/ *npl* (*liter*) elemosina *f sg*

aloft /əˈlɒft/ *adv* in alto; *Naut* sull'alberatura; **from ~** dall'alto

alone /əˈləʊn/ *a* solo; **leave me ~!** lasciami in pace!; **let ~** (*not to mention*) figurarsi ● *adv* da solo

along /ə'lɒŋ/ *prep* lungo ● *adv* ~ **with** assieme a; **all** ~ tutto il tempo; **come** ~! (*hurry up*) vieni qui!; **I'll bring it** ~ lo porto lì; **I'll be** ~ **in a minute** arrivo tra un attimo; **move** ~ spostarsi; **move** ~! circolare!

alongside /əlɒŋ'saɪd/ *adv* lungo bordo ● *prep* lungo; **work** ~ **sb** lavorare fianco a fianco con qcno

aloof /ə'lu:f/ *a* distante

aloud /ə'laʊd/ *adv* ad alta voce

alpaca /æl'pækə/ *n* alpaca *m inv*

alpha /'ælfə/ *n* (*letter*) alfa *f inv*; *Br Univ* ≈ trenta *m inv* e lode

alphabet /'ælfəbet/ *n* alfabeto *m*

alphabetical /ælfə'betɪkl/ *a* alfabetico

alphabetically /ælfə'betɪklɪ/ *adv* in ordine alfabetico

alpine /'ælpaɪn/ *a* alpino

Alps /ælps/ *npl* Alpi *fpl*

already /ɔ:l'redɪ/ *adv* già

alright /ɔ:l'raɪt/ = **all right**

Alsace /æl'zæs/ *n* Alsazia *f*

Alsatian /æl'seɪʃn/ *n* (*dog*) pastore *m* tedesco

also /'ɔ:lsəʊ/ *adv* anche; ~**, I need...** inoltre, ho bisogno di...

altar /'ɔ:ltə(r)/ *n* altare *m*

altar: **altar boy** *n* chierichetto *m*. **altar cloth** *n* tovaglia *f* da altare. **altar piece** *n* pala *f* d'altare

alter /'ɔ:ltə(r)/ *vt* cambiare; aggiustare ‹*clothes*› ● *vi* cambiare

alteration /ɔ:ltə'reɪʃn/ *n* modifica *f*

altercation /ɔ:ltə'keɪʃn/ *n* alterco *m*

alternate¹ /'ɔ:ltəneɪt/ *vi* alternarsi ● *vt* alternare

alternate² /ɔ:l'tɜ:nət/ *a* alterno; **on** ~ **days** a giorni alterni

alternately /ɔ:l'tɜ:nətlɪ/ *adv* in modo alterno; (*Am: alternatively*) alternativamente

alternating current /'ɔ:ltəneɪtɪŋ/ *n* corrente *f* alternata

alternation /ɔ:ltə'reɪʃn/ *n* alternanza *f*

alternative /ɔ:l'tɜ:nətɪv/ *a* alternativo ● *n* alternativa *f*

alternatively /ɔ:l'tɜ:nətɪvlɪ/ *adv* alternativamente

alternative medicine *n* medicina *f* alternativa

alternative technology *n* tecnologia *f* alternativa

alternator /'ɔ:ltəneɪtə(r)/ *n Electr* alternatore *m*

although /ɔ:l'ðəʊ/ *conj* benché, sebbene

altimeter /'æltɪmi:tə(r)/ *n* altimetro *m*

altitude /'æltɪtju:d/ *n* altitudine *f*

alto /'æltəʊ/ *n* contralto *m*

altogether /ɔ:ltə'geðə(r)/ *adv* (*in all*) in tutto; (*completely*) completamente; **I'm not** ~ **sure** non sono del tutto sicuro

altruism /'æltrʊɪzm/ *n* altruismo *m*

altruistic /æltrʊ'ɪstɪk/ *a* altruistico

aluminium /æljʊ'mɪnɪəm/ *n*, *Am* **aluminum** /ə'lu:mɪnəm/ *n* alluminio *m*

aluminium foil *n* carta *f* stagnola

alumna /ə'lʌmnə/ *n Am Sch, Univ* ex allieva *f*

alumnus /ə'lʌmnəs/ *n Am Sch, Univ* ex allievo *m*

always /'ɔ:lweɪz/ *adv* sempre

am /æm/ *see* **be**

a.m. *abbr* (**ante meridiem**) del mattino

amalgam /ə'mælgəm/ *n* amalgama *m*

amalgamate /ə'mælgəmeɪt/ *vt* fondere ● *vi* fondersi

amalgamation /əmælgə'meɪʃn/ *n* fusione *f*; (*of styles*) amalgama *m*

amass /ə'mæs/ *vt* accumulare

amateur /'æmətə(r)/ *n* non professionista *mf*; *pej* dilettante *mf* ● *attrib* dilettante; ~ **dramatics** filodrammatica *f*

amateurish /'æmətərɪʃ/ *a* dilettantesco

amaze /ə'meɪz/ *vt* stupire

amazed /ə'meɪzd/ *a* stupito

amazement /ə'meɪzmənt/ *n* stupore *m*; **to her** ~ con suo grande stupore; **in** ~ stupito

amazing /ə'meɪzɪŋ/ *a* incredibile

amazingly /ə'meɪzɪŋlɪ/ *adv* incredibilmente

Amazon /'æməzən/ *n* (*in myths*) Amazzone *f*; (*fig: strong woman*) amazzone *f*; (*river*) Rio *m* delle Amazzoni ● *attrib* ‹*basin, forest, tribe*› amazzonico

ambassador /æm'bæsədə(r)/ *n* ambasciatore, -trice *mf*

ambassador-at-large *n Am* ambasciatore, -trice *mf* a disposizione

amber /'æmbə(r)/ *n* ambra *f* ● *a* (*colour*) ambra *inv*

ambidextrous /æmbɪ'dekstrəs/ *a* ambidestro

ambience /'æmbɪəns/ *n* atmosfera *f*

ambient /'æmbɪənt/ *a* ‹*temperature*› ambiente *inv*; ‹*noise*› circostante

ambiguity /æmbɪ'gju:ətɪ/ *n* ambiguità *f inv*

ambiguous /æm'bɪgjʊəs/ *a* ambiguo

ambiguously /æm'bɪgjʊəslɪ/ *adv* in modo ambiguo

ambition /æm'bɪʃn/ *n* ambizione *f*; (*aim*) aspirazione *f*

ambitious /æm'bɪʃəs/ *a* ambizioso

ambivalence /æm'bɪvələns/ *n* ambivalenza *f*

ambivalent /æm'bɪvələnt/ *a* ambivalente

amble /'æmb(ə)l/ *vi* camminare senza fretta

ambulance /'æmbjʊləns/ *n* ambulanza *f*

ambulance man *n* guidatore *m* di ambulanze

ambush /'æmbʊʃ/ *n* imboscata *f* ● *vt* tendere un'imboscata a

ameba /ə'mi:bə/ *n Am* ameba *f*

amen /ɑ:'men/ *int* amen

amenability /əmi:nə'bɪlɪtɪ/ *n* arrendevolezza *f*

amenable /ə'mi:nəbl/ *a* conciliante; ~ **to** sensibile a

amend /ə'mend/ *vt* modificare ● *npl* **make** ~**s** fare ammenda (**for** di, per)

amendment /ə'mendmənt/ *n* modifica *f*

amenities /ə'mi:nətɪz/ *npl* comodità *fpl*

America /ə'merıkə/ n America f
American /ə'merıkən/ a & n americano, -a mf
American: American Civil War n guerra f di secessione [americana]. **American English** n inglese m americano. **American Indian** n indiano, -a mf d'America
Americanism /ə'merıkənızm/ n americanismo m
amethyst /'æməθıst/ n (gem) ametista f
Amex /'æmeks/ n abbr (**American Stock Exchange**) Borsa f valori americana; abbr **American Express**
amiable /'eımıəbl/ a amabile
amicable /'æmıkəbl/ a amichevole
amicably /'æmıkəblı/ adv amichevolmente
amid[st] /ə'mıd[st]/ prep in mezzo a
amino acid /ə'mi:nəʊ/ n amminoacido m
amiss /ə'mıs/ a **there's something** ~ c'è qualcosa che non va ● adv **take sth** ~ prendersela [a male]; **it won't come** ~ non sarebbe sgradito
ammo /'æməʊ/ n abbr (**ammunition**) munizioni fpl
ammonia /ə'məʊnıə/ n ammoniaca f
ammunition /æmjʊ'nıʃn/ n munizioni fpl
amnesia /æm'ni:zıə/ n amnesia f
amnesty /'æmnəstı/ n amnistia f
amoeba /ə'mi:bə/ n ameba f
amoebic /ə'mi:bık/ a ⟨dysentry etc⟩ amebico
amok /ə'mɒk/ adv **run** ~ essere in preda a furore; ⟨imagination:⟩ scatenarsi
among[st] /ə'mʌŋ[st]/ prep tra, fra; **talk** ~ **yourselves** parlate tra [di] voi
amoral /eı'mɒrəl/ a amorale
amorality /eımə'rælətı/ n amoralità f
amorous /'æmərəs/ a amoroso
amorphous /ə'mɔːfəs/ a Chem amorfo; ⟨ideas, plans⟩ confuso; ⟨shape, collection⟩ informe
amount /ə'maʊnt/ n quantità f inv; (sum of money) montante m ● vi ~ **to** ammontare a; fig equivalere a
amp /æmp/ n ampère m inv
ampere /'æmpeə(r)/ n ampere m inv
ampersand /'æmpəsænd/ n e f inv commerciale
amphetamine /æm'fetəmi:n/ n anfetamina f
amphibian /æm'fıbıən/ n anfibio m
amphibious /æm'fıbıəs/ a anfibio
amphitheatre /'æmfıθi:ətə(r)/ n anfiteatro m
ample /'æmpl/ a (large) grande; ⟨proportions⟩ ampio; (enough) largamente sufficiente
amplifier /'æmplıfaıə(r)/ n amplificatore m
amplify /'æmplıfaı/ vt (pt/pp -**ied**) amplificare ⟨sound⟩
amply /'æmplı/ adv largamente
amputate /'æmpjuteıt/ vt amputare
amputation /æmpjʊ'teıʃn/ n amputazione f
amputee /æmpjʊ'ti:/ n mutilato, -a mf (in seguito ad amputazione)
amuse /ə'mju:z/ vt divertire

amused /ə'mju:zd/ a divertito
amusement /ə'mju:zmənt/ n divertimento m
amusement arcade n sala f giochi
amusement park n luna park m inv
amusing /ə'mju:zıŋ/ a divertente
an /ən/, accentato /æn/ see **a**
anabolic steroid /ænə'bɒlık/ n anabolizzante m
anachronism /ə'nækrənızm/ n **be an** ~ ⟨object, custom etc:⟩ essere anacronistico
anaemia /ə'ni:mıə/ n anemia f
anaemic /ə'ni:mık/ a anemico
anaerobic /æneə'rəʊbık/ a anaerobico
anaesthesia /ænəs'θi:zıə/ n anestesia f
anaesthetic /ænəs'θetık/ n anestesia f; **give sb an** ~ somministrare a qcno l'anestesia
anaesthetist /ə'ni:sθətıst/ n anestesista mf
anaesthetize /ə'ni:sθətaız/ vt anestetizzare
anagram /'ænəgræm/ n anagramma m
analgesic /ænəl'dʒi:zık/ a & n analgesico m
analogous /ə'næləgəs/ a analogo
analog[ue] /'ænəlɒg/ a analogico
analogy /ə'nælədʒı/ n analogia f
analyse /'ænəlaız/ vt analizzare
analysis /ə'næləsıs/ n analisi f inv
analyst /'ænəlıst/ n analista mf
analytical /ænə'lıtıkl/ a analitico
anarchic[al] /ə'nɑ:kık[l]/ a anarchico
anarchist /'ænəkıst/ n anarchico, -a mf
anarchy /'ænəkı/ n anarchia f
anathema /ə'næθəmə/ n eresia f
anatomical /ænə'tɒmıkl/ a anatomico
anatomically /ænə'tɒmıklı/ adv anatomicamente
anatomy /ə'nætəmı/ n anatomia f
ANC n abbr (**African National Congress**) Congresso m Nazionale Africano
ancestor /'ænsestə(r)/ n antenato, -a mf
ancestral /æn'sestrəl/ a ancestrale; ⟨home⟩ avito
ancestry /'ænsestrı/ n antenati mpl
anchor /'æŋkə(r)/ n ancora f ● vi gettar l'ancora ● vt ancorare
anchorage /'æŋkərıdʒ/ n ancoraggio m
anchorman /'æŋkəmæn/ n Radio, TV anchor man m inv; Sport staffettista m dell'ultima frazione
anchorwoman /'æŋkəwʊmən/ n Radio TV anchor woman f inv
anchovy /'æntʃəvı/ n acciuga f
ancient /'eınʃənt/ a antico; fam vecchio; ~ **Rome** l'antica Roma f
ancillary /æn'sılərı/ a ausiliario
and /ənd/, accentato /ænd/ conj e; ~ **so on** e così via; **two** ~ **two** due più due; **six hundred** ~ **two** seicentodue; **more** ~ **more** sempre più; **nice** ~ **warm** bello caldo; **try** ~ **come** cerca di venire; **go** ~ **get** vai a prendere
Andean /'ændıən/ a andino
Andes /'ændi:z/ npl **the** ~ le Ande
Andorra /æn'dɔ:rə/ n Andorra f
anecdote /'ænıkdəʊt/ n aneddoto m

anemone /ə'nemənɪ/ n Bot anemone m

anew /ə'nju:/ adv di nuovo

angel /'eɪndʒl/ n angelo m

angel cake n dolce m di pan di Spagna

angelfish /'eɪnʒlfɪʃ/ n angelo m di mare

angelic /æn'dʒelɪk/ a angelico

anger /'æŋgə(r)/ n rabbia f ● vt far arrabbiare

angina (pectoris) /æn'dʒaɪnə('pektərɪs)/ n angina f pectoris

angle¹ /'æŋgl/ n angolo m; fig angolazione f; **at an ~** storto

angle² vi pescare con la lenza; **~ for** fig cercare di ottenere

angle bracket n Techn parentesi f inv uncinata

Anglepoise [lamp] /'æŋglpɔɪz/ n lampada f a braccio estensibile

angler /'æŋglə(r)/ n pescatore, -trice mf

Anglican /'æŋglɪkən/ a & n anglicano, -a mf

anglicism /'æŋglɪsɪzm/ n anglicismo m

anglicize /'æŋglɪsaɪz/ vt anglicizzare

angling /'æŋglɪŋ/ n pesca f con la lenza

Anglo+ /'æŋgləʊ/ pref anglo+

Anglo-American a & n angloamericano, -a mf

Anglophone /'æŋgləfəʊn/ a & n anglofono, -a mf

Anglo-Saxon /æŋgləʊ'sæksn/ a & n anglo-sassone mf

Angola /æŋ'gəʊlə/ n Angola f

angora /æn'gɔ:rə/ n lana f d'angora

angrily /'æŋgrɪlɪ/ adv rabbiosamente

angry /'æŋgrɪ/ a (-ier, -iest) arrabbiato; **get ~** arrabbiarsi; **~ with** or **at sb** arrabbiato con qcno; **~ at** or **about sth** arrabbiato per qcsa

anguish /'æŋgwɪʃ/ n angoscia f; **in ~** in preda all'angoscia

anguished /'æŋgwɪʃt/ a (suffering) straziante; (person) angosciato

angular /'æŋgjʊlə(r)/ a angolare

animal /'ænɪm(ə)l/ a & n animale m

animal: animal activist n animalista mf. **animal experiment** n esperimento m sugli animali. **animal husbandry** n allevamento m. **animal kingdom** n regno m animale. **animal lover** n amante mf degli animali. **animal product** n prodotto m di origine animale. **animal sanctuary** n rifugio m per animali. **animal testing** n sperimentazione f sugli animali

animate¹ /'ænɪmət/ a animato

animate² /'ænɪmeɪt/ vt animare

animated /'ænɪmeɪtɪd/ a animato; (person) vivace

animation /ænɪ'meɪʃn/ n animazione f

animator /'ænɪmeɪtə(r)/ n (film cartoonist) animatore, -trice mf; (director) regista mf di film d'animazione

animosity /ænɪ'mɒsətɪ/ n animosità f inv

aniseed /'ænɪsi:d/ n anice f

ankle /'æŋk(ə)l/ n caviglia f

ankle: anklebone n astragalo m. **ankle-deep** a be **~ in mud** a essere nel fan-

go fino alle caviglie. **ankle-length** a (dress) alla caviglia. **ankle sock** n calzino m

annals /'ænəlz/ npl **go down in the ~** [of history] passare agli annali

annex /ə'neks/ vt annettere

annexation /ænek'seɪʃn/ n (action) annessione f; (land annexed) territorio m annesso

annex[e] /'æneks/ n annesso m

annihilate /ə'naɪəleɪt/ vt annientare

annihilation /ənaɪə'leɪʃn/ n annientamento m

anniversary /ænɪ'vɜ:sərɪ/ n anniversario m

Anno Domini /ænəʊ'dɒmɪnaɪ/ adv dopo Cristo

annotate /'ænəteɪt/ vt annotare

announce /ə'naʊns/ vt annunciare

announcement /ə'naʊnsmənt/ n annuncio m

announcer /ə'naʊnsə(r)/ n annunciatore, -trice mf

annoy /ə'nɔɪ/ vt dare fastidio a; **get ~ed** essere infastidito

annoyance /ə'nɔɪəns/ n seccatura f; (anger) irritazione f

annoying /ə'nɔɪɪŋ/ a fastidioso

annual /'ænjʊəl/ a annuale; (income) annuo ● n Bot pianta f annua; (children's book) almanacco m

Annual General Meeting n assemblea f generale annuale

annually /'ænjʊəlɪ/ adv annualmente; **she earns £50,000 ~** guadagna 50 000 sterline all'anno

annuity /ə'nju:ətɪ/ n annualità f inv

annul /ə'nʌl/ vt (pt/pp annulled) annullare

Annunciation /ənʌnsɪ'eɪʃn/ n Annunciazione f

anode /'ænəʊd/ n anodo m

anodyne /'ænədaɪn/ a liter (bland) anodino; (inoffensive) innocuo

anoint /ə'nɔɪnt/ vt ungere

anomalous /ə'nɒmələs/ a anomalo

anomaly /ə'nɒməlɪ/ n anomalia f

anon /ə'nɒn/ abbr (anonymous) anonimo

anonymity /ænə'nɪmətɪ/ n anonimità f

anonymous /ə'nɒnɪməs/ a anonimo; **remain ~** mantenere l'anonimato

anonymously /ə'nɒnɪməslɪ/ adv anonimamente

anorak /'ænəræk/ n giacca f a vento

anorexia /ænə'reksɪə/ n anoressia f

anorexic /ænə'reksɪk/ a & n anoressico, -a mf

another /ə'nʌðə(r)/ a & pron; **~ [one]** un altro, un'altra; **~ day** un altro giorno; **in ~ way** diversamente; **~ time** un'altra volta; **one ~** l'un l'altro

answer /'ɑ:nsə(r)/ n risposta f; (solution) soluzione f ● vt rispondere a (person, question, letter); esaudire (prayer); **~ the door** aprire la porta; **~ the telephone** rispondere al telefono ● vi rispondere

■ **answer back** vi ribattere

■ **answer for** vt rispondere di

answerable /ˈɑːnsərəbl/ *a* responsabile; **be ~ to sb** rispondere a qcno

answering machine *n Teleph* segreteria *f* telefonica

answering service *n* servizio *m* di segreteria telefonica

answerphone /ˈɑːnsəfəʊn/ *n* segreteria *f* telefonica

ant /ænt/ *n* formica *f*

antacid /ænˈtæsɪd/ *a & n* antiacido *m*

antagonism /ænˈtægənɪzm/ *n* antagonismo *m*

antagonistic /æntægəˈnɪstɪk/ *a* antagonistico

antagonize /ænˈtægənaɪz/ *vt* provocare l'ostilità di

Antarctic /ænˈtɑːktɪk/ *n* Antartico *m* ● *a* antartico

Antarctica /ænˈtɑːktɪkə/ *n* Antartide *f*

Antarctic Circle *n* Circolo *m* polare antartico

Antarctic Ocean *n* mare *m* antartico

anteater /ˈæntiːtə(r)/ *n* formichiere *m*

antecedent /æntrˈsiːdənt/ *n* (*precedent*) antecedente *m*; (*ancestor*) antenato, -a *mf*

antedate /æntrˈdeɪt/ *vt* (*put earlier date on*) retrodatare; (*predate*) precedere

antediluvian /æntɪdrˈluːvɪən/ *a* antidiluviano

antelope /ˈæntɪləʊp/ *n* antilope *m*

antenatal /æntrˈneɪtl/ *a* prenatale

antenatal class *n* corso *m* di preparazione al parto

antenatal clinic *n Br* assistenza *f* medica prenatale

antenna /ænˈtenə/ *n* antenna *f*

anterior /ænˈtɪərɪə/ *a* anteriore

ante-room /ˈæntɪ-/ *n* anticamera *f*

antheap /ˈænthiːp/ = **anthill**

anthem /ˈænθəm/ *n* inno *m*

anthill /ˈænthɪl/ *n* formicaio *m*

anthology /ænˈθɒlədʒɪ/ *n* antologia *f*

anthracite /ˈænθrəsaɪt/ *n* antracite *f*

anthrax /ˈænθræks/ *n* (*disease*) carbonchio *m*; (*pustule*) pustola *f* di carbonchio

anthropological /ænθrəpəˈlɒdʒɪkl/ *a* antropologico

anthropologist /ænθrəˈpɒlədʒɪst/ *n* antropologo, -a *mf*

anthropology /ænθrəˈpɒlədʒɪ/ *n* antropologia *f*

anti /ˈæntɪ/ *pref* anti- ● *prep* be ~ essere contro

anti-abortion *a* antiabortista

anti-abortionist *n* antiabortista *mf*

anti-aircraft *a* antiaereo

anti-apartheid *a* antiapartheid *inv*

antibacterial /æntɪbækˈtɪərɪəl/ *a* antibatterico

antiballistic missile /æntɪbəlɪstɪkˈmɪsaɪl/ *n* missile *m* antimissile

antibiotic /æntɪbaɪˈɒtɪk/ *n* antibiotico *m*

antibody /ˈæntɪbɒdɪ/ *n* anticorpo *m*

anticipate /ænˈtɪsɪpeɪt/ *vt* prevedere; (*forestall*) anticipare

anticipation /æntɪsɪˈpeɪʃn/ *n* anticipo *m*; (*excitement*) attesa *f*; **in ~ of** in previsione di

anticlimax /æntrˈklaɪmæks/ *n* delusione *f*

anticlockwise /æntrˈklɒkwaɪz/ *a & adv* in senso antiorario

antics /ˈæntɪks/ *npl* gesti *mpl* buffi

anticyclone /æntrˈsaɪkləʊn/ *n* anticiclone *m*

antidepressant /æntɪdrˈpres(ə)nt/ *a & n* antidepressivo *m*

antidote /ˈæntɪdəʊt/ *n* antidoto *m*

anti-establishment *a* contestatario

antifreeze /ˈæntɪfriːz/ *n* antigelo *m*

antiglare /æntrˈgleə(r)/ *a* (*screen*) antiriflesso *inv*

antihistamine /æntrˈhɪstəmiːn/ *n* antistaminico *m*

anti-inflammatory /-ɪnˈflæmətrɪ/ *a & n* antinfiammatorio *m*

anti-inflation *a* anti-inflazione *inv*

anti-inflationary /-ɪnˈfleɪʃnərɪ/ *a* antinflazionistico

anti-lock *a* antibloccaggio *inv*

antipathy /ænˈtɪpəθɪ/ *n* antipatia *f*

antiperspirant /æntrˈpɜːspɪrənt/ *n* deodorante *m* antitraspirante

antipodean /æntɪpəˈdiːən/ *a & n* australiano, -a e/o neozelandese *mf*

Antipodes /ænˈtɪpədiːz/ *npl Br* the ~ gli antipodi

antiquarian /æntrˈkweərɪən/ *a* antiquario; ~ **bookshop** negozio *m* di libri antichi

antiquated /ˈæntɪkweɪtɪd/ *a* antiquato

antique /ænˈtiːk/ *a* antico ● *n* antichità *f inv*

antique: antiques fair *n* fiera *f* dell'antiquariato. **antique dealer** *n* antiquario, -a *mf*. **antique shop** *n* negozio *m* d'antiquariato. **antiques trade** *n* antiquariato *m*

antiquity /ænˈtɪkwətɪ/ *n* antichità *f*

anti-racism *n* antirazzismo *m*

anti-riot *a* (*police*) antisommossa *inv*

anti-rust *a* antiruggine *inv*

anti-Semitic /æntɪsɪˈmɪtɪk/ *a* antisemita

anti-Semitism /æntrˈsemɪtɪzm/ *n* antisemitismo *m*

antiseptic /æntrˈseptɪk/ *a & n* antisettico *m*

anti-skid *a* antiscivolo *inv*

anti-smoking *a* contro il fumo, antifumo

antisocial /æntrˈsəʊʃəl/ *a* (*behaviour*) antisociale; (*person*) asociale

anti-terrorist *a* antiterrorista

anti-theft *a* (*lock, device*) antifurto *inv*; (*camera*) di sorveglianza; ~ **steering lock** bloccasterzo *m*

antithesis /ænˈtɪθəsɪs/ *n* antitesi *f*

antitrust /æntrˈtrʌst/ *a* antitrust *inv*

antivirus /æntrˈvaɪrəs/ **program** *n Comput* programma *m* antivirus

antivivisectionist /æntɪvɪvɪˈsekʃənɪst/ *n* antivivisezionista *mf* ● *a* antivivisezionistico

antlers /ˈæntləz/ *npl* corna *fpl*

antonym /ˈæntənɪm/ *n* antonimo *m*

Antwerp /ˈæntwɜːp/ *n* Anversa *f*

anus /ˈeɪnəs/ *n* ano *m*

anvil /ˈænvɪl/ *n* incudine *f*

anxiety /ˈæŋˈzaɪətɪ/ *n* ansia *f*

anxious /ˈæŋkʃəs/ *a* ansioso

anxiously /ˈæŋkʃəslɪ/ *adv* con ansia

any /ˈenɪ/ *a* (*no matter which*) qualsiasi, qualunque; **have we ~ wine/biscuits?** abbiamo del vino/dei biscotti?; **have we ~ jam/ apples?** abbiamo della marmellata/delle mele?; **~ colour/number you like** qualsiasi colore/numero ti piaccia; **we don't have ~ wine/biscuits** non abbiamo vino/biscotti; **I don't have ~ reason to lie** non ho nessun motivo per mentire; **for ~ reason** per qualsiasi ragione ● *pron* (*some*) ne; (*no matter which*) uno qualsiasi; **I don't want ~** [of it] non ne voglio [nessuno]; **there aren't ~** non ce ne sono; **have we ~?** ne abbiamo?; **have you read ~ of her books?** hai letto qualcuno dei suoi libri? ● *adv* **I can't go ~ quicker** non posso andare più in fretta; **is it ~ better?** va un po' meglio?; **would you like ~ more?** ne vuoi ancora?; **I can't eat ~ more** non posso mangiare più niente

anybody /ˈenɪbɒdɪ/ *pron* chiunque; (*after negative*) nessuno; **~ can do that** chiunque può farlo; **I haven't seen ~** non ho visto nessuno

anyhow /ˈenɪhaʊ/ *adv* ad ogni modo, comunque; (*badly*) non importa come

anyone /ˈenɪwʌn/ *pron* = **anybody**

anyplace /ˈenɪpleɪs/ *adv Am* = **anywhere**

anything /ˈenɪθɪŋ/ *pron* qualche cosa, qualcosa; (*no matter what*) qualsiasi cosa; (*after negative*) niente; **take/buy ~ you like** prendi/compra quello che vuoi; **I don't remember ~** non mi ricordo niente; **he's ~ but stupid** è tutto, ma non stupido; **I'll do ~ but that** farò qualsiasi cosa, tranne quello

anytime /ˈenɪtaɪm/ *adv* **if at ~ you feel lonely...** se mai ti dovessi sentire solo...; **he could arrive ~ now** potrebbe arrivare da un momento all'altro; **~ after 2 pm** a qualsiasi ora dopo le due; **at ~ of the day or night** a qualsiasi ora del giorno o della notte; **~ you like** quando vuoi

anyway /ˈenɪweɪ/ *adv* ad ogni modo, comunque

anywhere /ˈenɪweə(r)/ *adv* dovunque; (*after negative*) da nessuna parte; **put it ~** mettilo dove vuoi; **I can't find it ~** non lo trovo da nessuna parte; **~ else** da qualch'altra parte; (*after negative*) da nessun'altra parte; **I don't want to go ~ else** non voglio andare da nessun'altra parte

aorta /eɪˈɔːtə/ *n* aorta *f*

Aosta /æˈɒstə/ *n* Aosta *f*

apace /əˈpeɪs/ *adv liter* rapidamente

apart /əˈpɑːt/ *adv* lontano; **live ~** vivere separati; **100 miles ~** lontani 100 miglia; **born 20 minutes ~** nati a distanza di 20 minuti; **~ from** a parte; **you can't tell them ~** non si possono distinguere; **joking ~** scherzi a parte

apartheid /əˈpɑːthaɪt/ *n* apartheid *f*

apartment /əˈpɑːtmənt/ *n* (*Am: flat*) appartamento *m*; **in my ~** a casa mia

apartment block *n* stabile *m*

apartment house *n* stabile *m*

apathetic /æpəˈθetɪk/ *a* (*by nature*) apatico; **~ about sth/towards sb** (*from illness, depression*) indifferente a qcsa/nei confronti di qcno

apathy /ˈæpəθɪ/ *n* apatia *f*

ape /eɪp/ *n* scimmia *f* ● *vt* scimmiottare

Apennines /ˈæpənaɪnz/ *npl* **the ~** gli Appennini

aperitif /əˈperətiːf/ *n* aperitivo *m*

aperture /ˈæpətʃə(r)/ *n* apertura *f*

apex /ˈeɪpeks/ *n* vertice *m*

aphid /ˈeɪfɪd/ *n* afide *m*

aphrodisiac /æfrəˈdɪzɪæk/ *a & n* afrodisiaco *m*

apiary /ˈeɪpɪərɪ/ *n* apiario *m*

apiece /əˈpiːs/ *adv* ciascuno

aplenty /əˈplentɪ/ *adv* **there were goals ~** c'è stata una valanga di gol

apocalypse /əˈpɒkəlɪps/ *n* Apocalisse *f*; (*disaster, destruction*) apocalisse *f*

apocalyptic /əpɒkəˈlɪptɪk/ *a* apocalittico

apocryphal /əˈpɒkrɪfəl/ *a* apocrifo

apogee /ˈæpədʒiː/ *n* apogeo *m*

apolitical /eɪpəˈlɪtɪkl/ *a* apolitico

Apollo /əˈpɒləʊ/ *n also fig* Apollo *m*

apologetic /əpɒləˈdʒetɪk/ *a* ⟨*air, remark*⟩ di scusa; **be ~** essere spiacente

apologetically /əpɒləˈdʒetɪklɪ/ *adv* per scusarsi

apologist /əˈpɒlədʒɪst/ *n* apologeta *mf* (**for** di)

apologize /əˈpɒlədʒaɪz/ *vi* scusarsi (**for** per)

apology /əˈpɒlədʒɪ/ *n* scusa *f*; *fig* **an ~ for a dinner** una sottospecie di cena

apoplectic /æpəˈplektɪk/ *a* (*furious*) furibondo; ⟨*fit, attack*⟩ apoplettico

apoplexy /ˈæpəpleksɪ/ *n Med* apoplessia *f*; (*rage*) rabbia *f*

apostle /əˈpɒsl/ *n* apostolo *m*

apostrophe /əˈpɒstrəfɪ/ *n* apostrofo *m*

apotheosis /əpɒθɪˈəʊsɪs/ *n* apoteosi *f inv*

appal /əˈpɔːl/ *vt* (*pt/pp* **appalled**) sconvolgere

Appalachians /æpəˈleɪtʃnz/ *npl* **the ~** gli Appalachi

appalling /əˈpɔːlɪŋ/ *a* sconvolgente; **he's an ~ teacher** *fig* è un disastro come professore

appallingly /əˈpɔːlɪŋlɪ/ *adv* ⟨*behave, treat*⟩ orribilmente; **unemployment figures are ~ high** il tasso di disoccupazione è spaventosamente alto; **furnished in ~ bad taste** arredato con pessimo gusto

apparatus /æpəˈreɪtəs/ *n* apparato *m*

apparel /əˈpærəl/ *n* abbigliamento *m*

apparent /əˈpærənt/ *a* evidente; (*seeming*) apparente

apparently /əˈpærəntlɪ/ *adv* apparentemente

apparition /æpəˈrɪʃn/ *n* apparizione *f*

appeal /əˈpiːl/ *n* appello *m*; (*attraction*) attrattiva *f* ● *vi* fare appello; **~ to** (*be attractive to*) attrarre

appeal[s] court *n* corte *f* d'appello

appeal fund *n* raccolta *f* di fondi

appealing /ə'piːlɪŋ/ *a* attraente

appealingly /ə'piːlɪŋlɪ/ *adv* (*beseechingly*) in modo supplichevole; (*attractively*) in modo attraente

appear /ə'pɪə(r)/ *vi* apparire; (*seem*) sembrare; (*publication:*) uscire; *Theat* esibirsi; **he finally ~ed at...** *fam* si è fatto finalmente vedere alle...; **~ in court** comparire in giudizio

appearance /ə'pɪərəns/ *n* apparizione *f*; (*look*) aspetto *m*; **to all ~s** a giudicare dalle apparenze; **keep up ~s** salvare le apparenze

appease /ə'piːz/ *vt* placare

appeasement /ə'piːzmənt/ *n* **a policy of ~** una politica troppo conciliante

append /ə'pend/ *vt* apporre (*signature*) (**to** a)

appendage /ə'pendɪdʒ/ *n* appendice *f*

appendicitis /əpendɪ'saɪtɪs/ *n* appendicite *f*

Appenine /'æpənaɪn/ *a* appenninico

Appenines /'æpənaɪnz/ *npl* Appennini *mpl*

appendix /ə'pendɪks/ *n* (*pl* **-ices** /-ɪsiːz/) (*of book*) appendice *f*; (*pl* **-es**) *Anat* appendice *f*

appertain /æpə'teɪn/ *vi* **~ to** essere pertinente a

appetite /'æpɪtaɪt/ *n* appetito *m*

appetite suppressant *n* pillola *f* antifame

appetizer /'æpɪtaɪzə(r)/ *n* (*drink*) aperitivo *m*; (*starter*) antipasto *m*; (*biscuit, olive etc*) stuzzichino *m*

appetizing /'æpɪtaɪzɪŋ/ *a* appetitoso

applaud /ə'plɔːd/ *vt*/*i* applaudire

applause /ə'plɔːz/ *n* applauso *m*

apple /'æpl/ *n* mela *f*; **she's the ~ of his eye** è la luce dei suoi occhi

apple: apple core *n* torsolo *m* di mela. **apple orchard** *n* meleto *m*. **apple tree** *n* melo *m*

appliance /ə'plaɪəns/ *n* attrezzo *m*; [**electrical**] **~** elettrodomestico *m*

applicable /'æplɪkəbl/ *a* **be ~ to** essere valido per; **not ~** (*on form*) non applicabile

applicant /'æplɪkənt/ *n* candidato, -a *mf*

application /æplɪ'keɪʃn/ *n* applicazione *f*; (*request*) domanda *f*; (*for job*) candidatura *f*; **on ~** su richiesta

application form *n* modulo *m* di domanda

applicator /'æplɪkeɪtə(r)/ *n* applicatore *m*

applied /ə'plaɪd/ *a* applicato

appliqué /ə'pliːkeɪ/ *n* applicazione *f* ● *attrib* (*motif, decoration*) applicato

apply /ə'plaɪ/ *vt* (*pt*/*pp* **-ied**) applicare; **~ oneself** applicarsi; **~ the brakes** frenare ● *vi* applicarsi; (*law:*) essere applicabile; **~ to** rivolgersi a; **~ for** fare domanda per (*job etc*)

appoint /ə'pɔɪnt/ *vt* nominare; fissare (*time*); **well ~ed** ben equipaggiato

appointee /əpɔɪn'tiː/ *n* incaricato, -a *mf*

appointment /ə'pɔɪntmənt/ *n* appuntamento *m*; (*to job*) nomina *f*; (*job*) posto *m*

apportion /ə'pɔːʃn/ *vt* ripartire, attribuire

apposite /'æpəzɪt/ *a* appropriato

apposition /æpə'zɪʃn/ *n* apposizione *f*

appraisal /ə'preɪzəl/ *n* valutazione *f*; **make an ~ of sth** valutare qcsa

appraise /ə'preɪz/ *vt* valutare

appreciable /ə'priːʃəbl/ *a* sensibile

appreciably /ə'priːʃəblɪ/ *adv* sensibilmente

appreciate /ə'priːʃɪeɪt/ *vt* apprezzare; (*understand*) comprendere ● *vi* (*increase in value*) aumentare di valore

appreciation /əpriːsɪ'eɪʃn/ *n* (*gratitude*) riconoscenza *f*; (*enjoyment*) apprezzamento *m*; (*understanding*) comprensione *f*; (*in value*) aumento *m*; **in ~** come segno di riconoscenza (**of** per)

appreciative /ə'priːʃətɪv/ *a* riconoscente

apprehend /æprɪ'hend/ *vt* arrestare

apprehension /æprɪ'henʃn/ *n* arresto *m*; (*fear*) apprensione *f*

apprehensive /æprɪ'hensɪv/ *a* apprensivo

apprehensively /æprɪ'hensɪvlɪ/ *adv* con apprensione

apprentice /ə'prentɪs/ *n* apprendista *mf*

apprenticeship /ə'prentɪsʃɪp/ *n* apprendistato *m*

apprise /ə'praɪz/ *vt fml* informare (**of** di)

approach /ə'prəʊtʃ/ *n* avvicinamento *m*; (*to problem*) approccio *m*; (*access*) accesso *m*; **make ~es to** fare degli approcci con ● *vi* avvicinarsi ● *vt* avvicinarsi a; (*with request*) rivolgersi a; affrontare (*problem*)

approachable /ə'prəʊtʃəbl/ *a* accessibile

approach: approach lights *npl Aeron* sentiero *m* luminoso di avvicinamento. **approach path** *n Aeron* rotta *f* di avvicinamento. **approach road** *n* strada *f* d'accesso

approbation /æprə'beɪʃn/ *n* approvazione *f*

appropriate[1] /ə'prəʊprɪət/ *a* appropriato

appropriate[2] /ə'prəʊprɪeɪt/ *vt* appropriarsi di

appropriately /ə'prəʊprɪətlɪ/ *adv* (*suitably*) in modo appropriato; (*sited*) convenientemente; (*designed, chosen, behave*) adeguatamente

appropriation /əprəʊprɪ'eɪʃn/ *n Am Comm* stanziamento *m*; (*Jur: removal*) appropriazione *f*

approval /ə'pruːvl/ *n* approvazione *f*; **on ~** in prova

approve /ə'pruːv/ *vt* approvare ● *vi* **~ of** approvare (*sth*); avere una buona opinione di (*sb*)

approving /ə'pruːvɪŋ/ *a* (*smile, nod*) d'approvazione

approvingly /ə'pruːvɪŋlɪ/ *adv* con approvazione

approximate[1] /ə'prɒksɪmeɪt/ *vi* **~ to** avvicinarsi a

approximate[2] /ə'prɒksɪmət/ *a* approssimativo

approximately /ə'prɒksɪmətlɪ/ *adv* approssimativamente

approximation /əprɒksɪ'meɪʃn/ *n* approssimazione *f*

APR *n abbr* (**annual percentage rate**) tasso *m* percentuale annuo

apricot /'eɪprɪkɒt/ n albicocca f; ~ **tree** albicocco m

April /'eɪprəl/ n aprile m; **make an ~ Fool of sb** fare un pesce d'aprile a qcno; ~ **Fool's Day** il primo d'aprile

apron /'eɪprən/ n grembiule m

apropos /'æprəpəʊ/ adv ~ [**of**] a proposito [di]

apse /æps/ n abside f

apt /æpt/ a appropriato; ‹pupil› dotato; **be ~ to do sth** avere tendenza a fare qcsa

aptitude /'æptɪtjuːd/ n disposizione f

aptitude test n test m inv attitudinale

aptly /'æptlɪ/ adv appropriatamente

Apulia /ə'pjuːlɪə/ n Puglia f

aqualung /'ækwəlʌŋ/ n autorespiratore m

aquamarine /ækwəmə'riːn/ a & n acquamarina f

aquaplane /'ækwəpleɪn/ vi Sport praticare l'acquaplano; Br Auto andare in aquaplaning

aquarium /ə'kweərɪəm/ n acquario m

Aquarius /ə'kweərɪəs/ n Astr Acquario m; **be ~** essere dell'Acquario

aquatic /ə'kwætɪk/ a acquatico

aqueduct /'ækwədʌkt/ n acquedotto m

aquiline /'ækwɪlaɪn/ a ‹nose, features› aquilino

Arab /'ærəb/ a & n arabo, -a mf

Arabia /ə'reɪbɪə/ n Arabia f

Arabian /ə'reɪbɪən/ a arabo

Arabic /'ærəbɪk/ a arabo; ~ **numerals** numeri mpl arabici f; n arabo m

Arab-Israeli a arabo-israeliano

arable /'ærəbl/ a coltivabile

arbiter /'ɑːbɪtə(r)/ n arbitro m

arbitrarily /ɑːbɪ'trerɪlɪ/ adv arbitrariamente

arbitrary /'ɑːbɪtrərɪ/ a arbitrario

arbitrate /'ɑːbɪtreɪt/ vi arbitrare

arbitration /ɑːbɪ'treɪʃn/ n arbitraggio m

arbitrator /'ɑːbɪtreɪtə(r)/ n arbitro m

arbour /'ɑːbə(r)/ n pergolato m

arc /ɑːk/ n arco m

arcade /ɑː'keɪd/ n portico m; (shops) galleria f

arcane /ɑː'keɪn/ a arcano

arch /ɑːtʃ/ n arco m; (of foot) dorso m del piede ● vt **the cat ~ed its back** il gatto ha arcuato la schiena

archaeological /ɑːkɪə'lɒdʒɪkl/ a archeologico

archaeologist /ɑːkɪ'ɒlədʒɪst/ n archeologo, -a mf

archaeology /ɑːkɪ'ɒlədʒɪ/ n archeologia f

archaic /ɑː'keɪɪk/ a arcaico

archbishop /ɑːtʃ'bɪʃəp/ n arcivescovo m

arched /ɑːtʃt/ a ‹eyebrows› arcuato

arch-enemy n acerrimo nemico m

archer /'ɑːtʃə(r)/ n arciere m

archery /'ɑːtʃərɪ/ n tiro m con l'arco

archetypal /ɑːkɪ'taɪpl/ a **the ~ hero** il prototipo dell'eroe

archetype /'ɑːkɪtaɪp/ n archetipo m

archipelago /ɑːkɪ'peləgəʊ/ n arcipelago m

architect /'ɑːkɪtekt/ n architetto m

architectural /ɑːkɪ'tektʃərəl/ a architettonico

architecturally /ɑːkɪ'tektʃərəlɪ/ adv architettonicamente

architecture /'ɑːkɪtektʃə(r)/ n architettura f

archives /'ɑːkaɪvz/ npl archivi mpl

archiving /'ɑːkaɪvɪŋ/ n Comput archiviazione f

archway /'ɑːtʃweɪ/ n arco m

Arctic /'ɑːktɪk/ a artico ● n **the ~** l'Artico

Arctic Circle n Circolo m polare artico

Arctic Ocean n mare m artico

ardent /'ɑːdənt/ a ardente

ardently /'ɑːdəntlɪ/ adv ardentemente

ardour /'ɑːdə(r)/ n ardore m

arduous /'ɑːdjʊəs/ a arduo

arduously /'ɑːdjʊəslɪ/ adv con fatica, con difficoltà

are /ɑː(r)/ see **be**

area /'eərɪə/ n area f; (region) zona f; (fig: field) campo m

area code n prefisso m [telefonico]

area manager n direttore, -trice mf di zona

aren't /ɑːnt/ = **are not** see **be**

arena /ə'riːnə/ n arena f

Argentina /ɑːdʒən'tiːnə/ n Argentina f

Argentine /'ɑːdʒəntaɪn/ a argentino

Argentinian /ɑːdʒən'tɪnɪən/ a & n argentino, -a mf

arguable /'ɑːgjʊəbl/ a **it's ~ that...** si può sostenere che...

arguably /'ɑːgjʊəblɪ/ adv **he is ~...** è probabilmente...

argue /'ɑːgjuː/ vi litigare (**about**); (debate) dibattere; **don't ~!** non discutere! ● vt (debate) dibattere; (reason) ~ **that** sostenere che

argument /'ɑːgjʊmənt/ n argomento m; (reasoning) ragionamento m; **have an ~** litigare

argumentative /ɑːgjʊ'mentətɪv/ a polemico

aria /'ɑːrɪə/ n aria f

arid /'ærɪd/ a arido

aridity /ə'rɪdɪtɪ/ n also fig aridità f

Aries /'eəriːz/ n Astr Ariete m; **be ~** essere dell'Ariete

arise /ə'raɪz/ vi (pt **arose**, pp **arisen**) ‹opportunity, need, problem:› presentarsi; (result) derivare

aristocracy /ærɪ'stɒkrəsɪ/ n aristocrazia f

aristocrat /'ærɪstəkræt/ n aristocratico, -a mf

aristocratic /ærɪstə'krætɪk/ a aristocratico

arithmetic /ə'rɪθmətɪk/ n aritmetica f

arithmetical /ærɪθ'metɪkl/ a aritmetico

ark /ɑːk/ n **Noah's A~** l'Arca f di Noè

arm /ɑːm/ n braccio m; (of chair) bracciolo m; **~s** pl (weapons) armi fpl; ~ **in ~** a braccetto; **up in ~s** fam furioso (**about** per); fig **with open ~s** a braccia aperte ● vt armare

armadillo /ɑːmə'dɪləʊ/ n armadillo m

armaments /'ɑːməmənts/ npl armamenti mpl

armband /'ɑːmbænd/ n (for swimmer) bracciolo *m* (*per nuotare*); (*for mourner*) fascia *f* al braccio

armchair /ˈɑːmtʃeə(r)/ *n* poltrona *f*

armchair traveller *n persona f che si interessa di viaggi senza viaggiare*

armed /ɑːmd/ *a* armato

armed forces /ˈfɔːsɪz/ *npl* forze *fpl* armate

armed robbery *n* rapina *f* a mano armata

Armenia /ɑːˈmiːnɪə/ *n* Armenia *f*

Armenian /ɑːˈmiːnɪən/ *a & n* (*person*) armeno, -a *mf*; (*language*) armeno *m*

armful /ˈɑːmfʊl/ *n* bracciata *f*

armhole /ˈɑːmhəʊl/ *n* giro *m* manica *inv*

armistice /ˈɑːmɪstɪs/ *n* armistizio *m*

Armistice Day *n* l'Anniversario *m* dell'Armistizio (*1 nov. 1918*)

armour /ˈɑːmə(r)/ *n* armatura *f*

armour-clad /-ˈklæd/ *a* ⟨*vehicle*⟩ blindato; ⟨*ship*⟩ corazzato

armoured /ˈɑːməd/ *a* ⟨*vehicle*⟩ blindato

armoured car *n* autoblinda[ta] *f*

armour plate, armour plating /ˈpleɪtɪŋ/ *n* corazzatura *f*

armour-plated /-ˈpleɪtɪd/ *a* corazzato

armoury /ˈɑːmərɪ/ *n* (*factory*) fabbrica *f* d'armi; (*store*) arsenale *m*, armeria *f*

armpit /ˈɑːmpɪt/ *n* ascella *f*

armrest /ˈɑːmrest/ *n* bracciolo *m* (*di sedia*)

arms: arms control *n* controllo *m* degli armamenti. **arms dealer** *n* trafficante *mf* d'armi. **arms dump** *n* deposito *m* d'armi. **arms factory** *n* fabbrica *f* d'armi. **arms limitation** *n* controllo *m* degli armamenti. **arms manufacturer** *n* fabbricante *mf* d'armi. **arms race** *n* corsa *f* agli armamenti. **arms treaty** *n* trattato *m* sul controllo degli armamenti

arm-twisting /ˈɑːmtwɪstɪŋ/ *n* pressioni *fpl*

arm-wrestling *n* braccio *m* di ferro

army /ˈɑːmɪ/ *n* esercito *m*; **join the ~** arruolarsi

A road *n Br* [strada *f*] statale *f*

aroma /əˈrəʊmə/ *n* aroma *f*

aromatherapy /ərəʊməˈθerəpɪ/ *n* aromaterapia *f*

aromatic /ærəˈmætɪk/ *a* aromatico

arose /əˈrəʊz/ *see* **arise**

around /əˈraʊnd/ *adv* intorno; **all ~** tutt'intorno; **I'm not from ~ here** non sono di qui; **he's not ~** non c'è ● *prep* intorno a; in giro per ⟨*room, shops, world*⟩

arousal /əˈraʊzl/ *n* eccitazione *f*

arouse /əˈraʊz/ *vt* svegliare; (*sexually*) eccitare

arpeggio /ɑːˈpedʒɪəʊ/ *n* arpeggio *m*

arrange /əˈreɪndʒ/ *vt* sistemare ⟨*furniture, books*⟩; organizzare ⟨*meeting*⟩; fissare ⟨*date, time*⟩; **~ to do sth** combinare di fare qcsa

arrangement /əˈreɪndʒmənt/ *n* (*of furniture*) sistemazione *f*; *Mus* arrangiamento *m*; (*agreement*) accordo; (*of flowers*) composizione *f*; **make ~s** prendere disposizioni; **I've made other ~s** ho preso altri impegni

array /əˈreɪ/ *n* (*clothes*) abbigliamento *m*; (*of troops, people*) schieramento *m*; (*of numbers*)

tabella *f*; (*of weaponry*) apparato *m*; (*of goods, products*) assortimento *m*; *Comput* matrice *f* ● *vt* **~ed in ceremonial robes** abbigliato da gran cerimonia

arrears /əˈrɪəz/ *npl* arretrati *mpl*; **be in ~** essere in arretrato; **paid in ~** pagato a lavoro eseguito

arrest /əˈrest/ *n* arresto *m*; **under ~** in stato d'arresto ● *vt* arrestare

arresting /əˈrestɪŋ/ *a* (*striking*) che colpisce

arrival /əˈraɪvl/ *n* arrivo *m*; **new ~s** *pl* nuovi arrivati *mpl*

arrival: arrival lounge *n* sala *f* arrivi. **arrivals board** *n* tabellone *m* degli arrivi. **arrival time** *n* ora *f* d'arrivo

arrive /əˈraɪv/ *vi* arrivare; **~ at** *fig* raggiungere

arrogance /ˈærəg(ə)ns/ *n* arroganza *f*

arrogant /ˈærəg(ə)nt/ *a* arrogante

arrogantly /ˈærəg(ə)ntlɪ/ *adv* con arroganza

arrow /ˈærəʊ/ *n* freccia *f*

arrowhead /ˈærəʊhed/ *n* punta *f* di freccia

arse /ɑːs/ *n vulg* culo *m*

■ **arse about, arse around** *vi vulg* coglioneggiare

arsenal /ˈɑːsən(ə)l/ *n* arsenale *m*

arsenic /ˈɑːsənɪk/ *n* arsenico *m*

arson /ˈɑːsən/ *n* incendio *m* doloso

arsonist /ˈɑːsənɪst/ *n* incendiario, -a *mf*

art /ɑːt/ *n* arte *f*; **work of ~** opera *f* d'arte; **~s and crafts** *pl* artigianato *m*; **the A~s** *pl* l'arte *f*; **A~s degree** *Univ* laurea *f* in Lettere

art: art collection *n* collezione *f* d'arte. **art collector** *n* collezionista *mf* d'arte. **art college** *n* ≈ accademia *f* di belle arti. **art dealer** *n* commerciante *mf* di oggetti d'arte. **art deco** *n* art déco *f*

artefact /ˈɑːtɪfækt/ *n* manufatto *m*

arterial /ɑːˈtɪərɪəl/ *a Anat* arterioso

arterial road *n* arteria *f* [stradale]

artery /ˈɑːtərɪ/ *n* arteria *f*

art exhibition *n* mostra *f* d'arte. **art form** *n* forma *f* d'arte

artful /ˈɑːtfʊl/ *a* scaltro

artfully /ˈɑːtfʊlɪ/ *adv* astutamente

art gallery *n* galleria *f* d'arte

arthritic /ɑːˈθrɪtɪk/ *a & n* artritico, -a *mf*

arthritis /ɑːˈθraɪtɪs/ *n* artrite *f*

artichoke /ˈɑːtɪtʃəʊk/ *n* carciofo *m*

article /ˈɑːtɪkl/ *n* articolo *m*; **~ of clothing** capo *m* d'abbigliamento

articulate¹ /ɑːˈtɪkjʊlət/ *a* ⟨*speech*⟩ chiaro; **be ~** esprimersi bene

articulate² /ɑːˈtɪkjʊleɪt/ *vt* scandire ⟨*words*⟩

articulated lorry /ɑːˈtɪkjʊleɪtɪd/ *n* autotreno *m*

articulately /ɑːˈtɪkjʊlətlɪ/ *adv* chiaramente

articulation /ɑːtɪkjʊˈleɪʃn/ *n* (*pronunciation, Anat*) articolazione *f*; (*expression*) espressione *f*

artifice /ˈɑːtɪfɪs/ *n* artificio *m*

artificial /ɑːtɪˈfɪʃl/ *a* artificiale

artificial insemination *n* inseminazione *f* artificiale

artificial intelligence n intelligenza f artificiale

artificiality /ɑːtɪfɪʃɪˈælətɪ/ n artificiosità f

artificial limb n arto m artificiale

artificially /ɑːtɪˈfɪʃəlɪ/ adv artificialmente; ⟨smile⟩ artificiosamente

artificial respiration n respirazione f artificiale

artillery /ɑːˈtɪlərɪ/ n artiglieria f

artisan /ɑːtɪˈzæn/ n artigiano, -a mf

artist /ˈɑːtɪst/ n artista mf

artiste /ɑːˈtiːst/ n Theat artista mf

artistic /ɑːˈtɪstɪk/ a artistico

artistically /ɑːˈtɪstɪklɪ/ adv artisticamente

artistry /ˈɑːtɪstrɪ/ n arte f, talento m

artless /ˈɑːtlɪs/ a spontaneo

artlessly /ˈɑːtlɪslɪ/ adv ⟨smile⟩ ingenuamente

art nouveau /ɑːnuːˈvəʊ/ a & n liberty m

art school n ≈ accademia f di belle arti

arts: arts degree n laurea f in Lettere. **arts funding** n sovvenzioni fpl alle belle arti. **arts student** n studente, -essa mf di Lettere

art student n studente, -essa mf di belle arti

artwork /ˈɑːtwɜːk/ n illustrazioni fpl

arty /ˈɑːtɪ/ a fam ⟨person⟩ intellettualoide; ⟨district⟩ degli intellettuali

Aryan /ˈeərɪən/ a & n ariano, -a mf

as /æz/ conj come; (since) siccome; (while) mentre; **as he grew older** diventando vecchio; **as you get to know her** conoscendola meglio; **young as she is** per quanto sia giovane ● prep come; **as a friend** come amico; **as a child** da bambino; **as a foreigner** in quanto straniero; **disguised as** travestito da ● adv as well (also) anche; **as soon as I get home** [non] appena arrivo a casa; **as quick as you** veloce quanto te; **as quick as you can** più veloce che puoi; **as far as** (distance) fino a; **as far as I'm concerned** per quanto mi riguarda; **as long as** finché; (provided that) purché

asbestos /æzˈbestɒs/ n amianto m

ascend /əˈsend/ vi salire ● vt salire a ⟨throne⟩

ascendancy /əˈsend(ə)nsɪ/ n **gain the ~ over sb** acquisire una posizione dominante su qcno

ascendant /əˈsend(ə)nt/ n **be in the ~** Astr essere in ascendente; ⟨fig: person⟩ essere in auge

Ascension /əˈsenʃn/ n Relig Ascensione f

ascent /əˈsent/ n ascesa f

ascertain /æsəˈteɪn/ vt accertare

ascetic /əˈsetɪk/ a & n ascetico, -a mf

asceticism /əˈsetɪsɪzm/ n ascesi f

ascribable /əˈskraɪbəbl/ a attribuibile

ascribe /əˈskraɪb/ vt attribuire

aseptic /eɪˈseptɪk/ a asettico

asexual /eɪˈseksjʊəl/ a asessuale, asessuato

ash¹ /æʃ/ n (tree) frassino m

ash² n cenere f

ashamed /əˈʃeɪmd/ a **be/feel ~** vergognarsi

ash blond a biondo cenere

ashen /ˈæʃ(ə)n/ a ⟨complexion⟩ cinereo

ashore /əˈʃɔː(r)/ adv a terra; **go ~** sbarcare

ash: ashtray n portacenere m. **ash tree** n frassino m. **Ash Wednesday** n mercoledì m inv delle Ceneri

Asia /ˈeɪʒə/ n Asia f

Asia Minor n Asia f Minore

Asian /ˈeɪʒ(ə)n/ a & n asiatico, -a mf; (Br: Indian, Pakistani) indiano, -a mf

Asiatic /eɪʒɪˈætɪk/ a asiatico

aside /əˈsaɪd/ adv **take sb ~** prendere qcno a parte; **put sth ~** mettere qcsa da parte; **~ from sb** Am a parte te; **~ from his injuries** Am a parte le sue ferite ● n **in an ~** tra parentesi

asinine /ˈæsɪnaɪn/ a sciocco

ask /ɑːsk/ vt fare ⟨question⟩; (invite) invitare; **~ sb sth** domandare or chiedere qcsa a qcno; **~ sb to do sth** domandare or chiedere a qcno di fare qcsa ● vi **~ about sth** informarsi su qcsa; **~ after** chiedere [notizie] di; **~ for** chiedere ⟨sth⟩; chiedere di ⟨sb⟩; **~ for trouble** fam andare in cerca di guai
■ **ask in** vt **~ sb in** invitare qcno ad entrare
■ **ask out** vt **~ sb out** chiedere a qcno di uscire

askance /əˈskɑːns/ adv **look ~ at sb/sth** guardare qcno/qcsa di traverso

askew /əˈskjuː/ a & adv di traverso

asking price /ˈɑːskɪŋ/ n prezzo m trattabile

asleep /əˈsliːp/ a **be ~** dormire; **fall ~** addormentarsi

asparagus /əˈspærəgəs/ n asparagi mpl

aspect /ˈæspekt/ n aspetto m

aspen /ˈæspən/ n pioppo m tremulo

aspersions /əˈspɜːʃnz/ npl **cast ~ on** diffamare

asphalt /ˈæsfælt/ n asfalto m

asphyxia /əsˈfɪksɪə/ n asfissia f

asphyxiate /əsˈfɪksɪeɪt/ vt asfissiare

asphyxiation /əsfɪksɪˈeɪʃn/ n asfissia f

aspirate¹ /ˈæspəreɪt/ vt aspirare

aspirate² /ˈæspɪrət/ a aspirato

aspirations /æspəˈreɪʃnz/ npl aspirazioni fpl

aspire /əˈspaɪə(r)/ vi **~ to** aspirare a

aspiring /əˈspaɪərɪŋ/ a **~ authors/journalists** aspiranti scrittori/giornalisti

ass /æs/ n asino m

assailant /əˈseɪlənt/ n assalitore, -trice mf

assassin /əˈsæsɪn/ n assassino, -a mf

assassinate /əˈsæsɪneɪt/ vt assassinare

assassination /əsæsɪˈneɪʃn/ n assassinio m

assault /əˈsɔːlt/ n Mil assalto m; Jur aggressione f ● vt aggredire

assault and battery n Jur lesioni fpl personali

assault course n Mil percorso m di guerra

assemblage /əˈsemblɪdʒ/ assemblaggio m

assemble /əˈsembl/ vi radunarsi ● vt radunare; Techn montare

assembler /əˈsemblə(r)/ n (in factory)

montatore, -trice *mf*; *Comput* [programma *m*] assemblatore *m*

assembly /əˈsemblɪ/ *n* assemblea *f*; *Sch assemblea f giornaliera di alunni e professori di una scuola*; *Techn* montaggio *m*

assembly line *n* catena *f* di montaggio

assent /əˈsent/ *n* assenso *m* ● *vi* acconsentire

assert /əˈsɜːt/ *vt* asserire; far valere ⟨*one's rights*⟩; ~ **oneself** farsi valere

assertion /əˈsɜːʃn/ *n* asserzione *f*

assertive /əˈsɜːtɪv/ *a* **be** ~ farsi valere

assertiveness /əˈsɜːtɪvnɪs/ *n* capacità *f* di farsi valere; **lack of** ~ scarsa sicurezza *f* di sé

assess /əˈses/ *vt* valutare; (*for tax purposes*) stabilire l'imponibile di

assessment /əˈsesmənt/ *n* valutazione *f*; (*of tax*) accertamento *m*

assessor /əˈsesə(r)/ *n* (*Jur, in insurance*) perito *m*; (*tax*) agente *m* del fisco

asset /ˈæset/ *n* (*advantage*) vantaggio *m*; (*person*) elemento *m* prezioso. **~s** *pl* beni *mpl*; (*on balance sheet*) attivo *msg*

asset stripping /ˈæsetstrɪpɪŋ/ *n* rilevamento *m* di un'azienda per rivenderne le singole attività fisse

assiduity /æsɪˈdjuːətɪ/ *n* assiduità *f*

assiduous /əˈsɪdjʊəs/ *a* assiduo

assign /əˈsaɪn/ *vt* assegnare

assignation /æsɪgˈneɪʃn/ *n* *hum* appuntamento *m* galante

assignment /əˈsaɪnmənt/ *n* (*task*) incarico *m*

assimilate /əˈsɪmɪleɪt/ *vt* assimilare; integrare ⟨*person*⟩

assimilation /əsɪmɪˈleɪʃn/ *n* assimilazione *f*

assist /əˈsɪst/ *vt/i* assistere; ~ **sb to do sth** assistere qcno nel fare qcsa

assistance /əˈsɪstəns/ *n* assistenza *f*

assistant /əˈsɪstənt/ *n* assistente *mf*; (*in shop*) commesso, -a *mf*

assistant manager *n* vicedirettore, -trice *mf*

assistant professor *n* *Am Univ* docente *mf* universitario, -a del grado più basso

associate¹ /əˈsəʊʃɪeɪt/ *vt* associare (**with** a); **be ~d with sth** (*involved in*) essere coinvolto in qcsa ● *vi* ~ **with** frequentare

associate² /əˈsəʊʃɪət/ *a* associato ● *n* collega *mf*; (*member*) socio, -a *mf*

associate: associate company *n* consociata *f*. **associate director** *n* *Comm* amministratore *m* aggiunto. **associate editor** *n* coredattore, -trice *mf*. **associate member** *n* membro *m* associato

association /əsəʊsɪˈeɪʃn/ *n* associazione *f*

Association Football *n* [gioco *m* del] calcio *m*

assorted /əˈsɔːtɪd/ *a* assortito

assortment /əˈsɔːtmənt/ *n* assortimento *m*

assuage /əˈsweɪdʒ/ *vt* *liter* alleviare

assume /əˈsjuːm/ *vt* presumere; assumere ⟨*control*⟩; ~ **office** entrare in carica; **assuming that you're right,...** ammettendo che tu abbia ragione,...

assumption /əˈsʌmpʃn/ *n* supposizione *f*; **on the ~ that** partendo dal presupposto che; **the A~** *Relig* l'Assunzione *f*

assurance /əˈʃʊərəns/ *n* assicurazione *f*; (*confidence*) sicurezza *f*

assure /əˈʃʊə(r)/ *vt* assicurare; **he ~d me of his innocence** mi ha assicurato di essere innocente

assured /əˈʃʊəd/ *a* sicuro

Assyria /əˈsɪrɪə/ *n* Assiria *f*

asterisk /ˈæstərɪsk/ *n* asterisco *m*

astern /əˈstɜːn/ *adv* a poppa

asteroid /ˈæstərɔɪd/ *n* asteroide *m*

asthma /ˈæsmə/ *n* asma *f*

asthmatic /æsˈmætɪk/ *a* asmatico

astigmatism /əˈstɪgmətɪzm/ *n* astigmatismo *m*

astonish /əˈstɒnɪʃ/ *vt* stupire

astonished /əˈstɒnɪʃt/ *a* sorpreso

astonishing /əˈstɒnɪʃɪŋ/ *a* stupefacente

astonishingly /əˈstɒnɪʃɪŋlɪ/ *adv* sorprendentemente

astonishment /əˈstɒnɪʃmənt/ *n* stupore *m*

astound /əˈstaʊnd/ *vt* stupire

astounding /əˈstaʊndɪŋ/ *a* incredibile

astrakhan /æstrəˈkæn/ *n* astrakan *m*

astray /əˈstreɪ/ *adv* **go** ~ smarrirsi; (*morally*) uscire dalla retta via; **lead** ~ traviare

astride /əˈstraɪd/ *adv* [a] cavalcioni ● *prep* a cavalcioni di

astringent /əˈstrɪndʒənt/ *a* astringente; *fig* austero ● *n* astringente *m*

astrologer /əˈstrɒlədʒə(r)/ *n* astrologo, -a *mf*

astrological /æstrəˈlɒdʒɪkl/ *a* astrologico

astrology /əˈstrɒlədʒɪ/ *n* astrologia *f*

astronaut /ˈæstrənɔːt/ *n* astronauta *mf*

astronomer /əˈstrɒnəmə(r)/ *n* astronomo, -a *mf*

astronomic /æstrəˈnɒmɪk/ *a fig* astronomico

astronomical /æstrəˈnɒmɪkl/ *a* *also fig* astronomico

astronomically /æstrəˈnɒmɪklɪ/ *adv* ~ **expensive** dal prezzo astronomico; **prices are** ~ **high** i prezzi sono astronomici

astronomy /əˈstrɒnəmɪ/ *n* astronomia *f*

astrophysicist /æstrəʊˈfɪzɪsɪst/ *n* astrofisico, -a *mf*

astrophysics /æstrəʊˈfɪzɪks/ *n* astrofisica *f*

astute /əˈstjuːt/ *a* astuto

astutely /əˈstjuːtlɪ/ *adv* con astuzia

astuteness /əˈstjuːtnɪs/ *n* astuzia *f*

asylum /əˈsaɪləm/ *n* [**political**] ~ asilo *m* politico; [**lunatic**] ~ manicomio *m*

asylum-seeker /əˈsaɪləmsiːkə(r)/ *n* persona *f* che chiede asilo politico

asymmetric[al] /æsɪˈmetrɪk, æsɪˈmetrɪkl/ *a* asimmetrico

at /ət/, *accentato* /æt/ *prep* a; **at the station/the market** alla stazione/al mercato; **at the office/the bank** in ufficio/banca; **at the beginning** all'inizio; **at John's** da John; **at the hairdresser's** dal parrucchiere; **at home** a casa; **at work** al lavoro; **at**

school a scuola; **at a party/wedding** a una festa/un matrimonio; **at one o'clock** all'una; **at 50 km an hour** ai 50 all'ora; **at Christmas/Easter** a Natale/Pasqua; **at times** talvolta; **two at a time** due alla volta; **good at languages** bravo nelle lingue; **at sb's request** su richiesta di qcno; **are you at all worried?** sei preoccupato?

atavistic /ˌætə'vɪstɪk/ a atavico

ate /et/ see **eat**

atheism /'eɪθɪɪzm/ n ateismo m

atheist /'eɪθɪɪst/ n ateo, -a mf

atheistic /eɪθɪ'ɪstɪk/ a ⟨principle⟩ ateistico; ⟨person⟩ ateo

Athenian /ə'θiːnɪən/ a & n ateniese mf

Athens /'æθənz/ n Atene f

athlete /'æθliːt/ n atleta mf

athlete's foot n micosi f

athletic /æθ'letɪk/ a atletico

athletics /æθ'letɪks/ n atletica fsg

Atlantic /ət'læntɪk/ a & n **the ~** [Ocean] l'[Oceano m] Atlantico m

atlas /'ætləs/ n atlante m

Atlas Mountains npl Monti mpl dell'Atlante

ATM n abbr (**automatic teller machine**) cassa f continua di prelevamento

atmosphere /'ætməsfɪə(r)/ n atmosfera f

atmospheric /ætməs'ferɪk/ a atmosferico

atom /'ætəm/ n atomo m

atom bomb n bomba f atomica

atomic /ə'tɒmɪk/ a atomico

atomic: atomic power station n centrale f atomica. **atomic reactor** n reattore m nucleare. **atomic scientist** n fisico, -a mf nucleare

atomize /'ætəmaɪz/ vt atomizzare

atomizer /'ætəmaɪzə(r)/ n atomizzatore m

atone /ə'təʊn/ vi **~ for** pagare per

atonement /ə'təʊnmənt/ n espiazione f

atrocious /ə'trəʊʃəs/ a atroce; ⟨fam: meal, weather⟩ abominevole

atrociously /ə'trəʊʃəslɪ/ adv atrocemente; ⟨rude etc⟩ terribilmente

atrocity /ə'trɒsətɪ/ n atrocità f inv

atrophy /'ætrəfɪ/ n Med atrofia f ● vi Med, fig atrofizzarsi

attach /ə'tætʃ/ vt attaccare; attribuire ⟨importance⟩; **be ~ed to** fig essere attaccato a

attaché /ə'tæʃeɪ/ n addetto m

attaché case n ventiquattrore f inv

attachment /ə'tætʃmənt/ n (affection) attaccamento m; (accessory) accessorio m

attack /ə'tæk/ n attacco m; (physical) aggressione f ● vt attaccare; (physically) aggredire

attacker /ə'tækə(r)/ n assalitore, -trice mf; (critic) detrattore, -trice mf

attain /ə'teɪn/ vt realizzare ⟨ambition⟩; raggiungere ⟨success, age, goal⟩

attainable /ə'teɪnəbl/ a ⟨ambition⟩ realizzabile; ⟨success⟩ raggiungibile

attainment /ə'teɪnmənt/ n (of knowledge) acquisizione f; (of goal) realizzazione f, raggiungimento m; (success) risultato m

attempt /ə'tempt/ n tentativo m ● vt tentare

attend /ə'tend/ vt essere presente a; (go regularly to) frequentare; (accompany) accompagnare; ⟨doctor:⟩ avere in cura ● vi essere presente; (pay attention) prestare attenzione

■ **attend to** vt occuparsi di; (in shop) servire

attendance /ə'tendəns/ n presenza f

attendance record n (of MP, committee member, schoolchild) tasso m di presenza

attendance register n Sch registro m

attendant /ə'tendənt/ n guardiano, -a mf

attention /ə'tenʃn/ n attenzione f; **~!** Mil attenti!; **pay ~** prestare attenzione; **need ~** aver bisogno di attenzioni; ⟨skin, hair, plant:⟩ dover essere curato; ⟨car, tyres:⟩ dover essere riparato; **for the ~ of** all'attenzione di

attention-seeking /ə'tenʃnsiːkɪŋ/ n bisogno m di attirare l'attenzione ● a ⟨person⟩ che cerca di attirare l'attenzione.

attention span n he has a very short **~ ~** non è capace di mantenere a lungo la concentrazione

attentive /ə'tentɪv/ a ⟨pupil, audience⟩ attento; ⟨son⟩ premuroso

attentively /ə'tentɪvlɪ/ adv attentamente

attentiveness /ə'tentɪvnɪs/ n (concentration) attenzione f; (solicitude) sollecitudine f

attenuate /ə'tenjʊeɪt/ vt attenuare

attest /ə'test/ vt/i attestare

attic /'ætɪk/ n soffitta f

attic room n mansarda f

attic window n lucernario m

attire /ə'taɪə(r)/ n abiti mpl ● vt vestire (**in** con)

attitude /'ætɪtjuːd/ n atteggiamento m

attorney /ə'tɜːnɪ/ n (Am: lawyer) avvocato m; **power of ~** delega f

Attorney General n Br ≈ Procuratore m Generale; Am ≈ Ministro m di Grazia e Giustizia

attract /ə'trækt/ vt attirare

attraction /ə'trækʃn/ n attrazione f; (feature) attrattiva f

attractive /ə'træktɪv/ a ⟨person⟩ attraente; ⟨proposal, price⟩ allettante

attractiveness /ə'træktɪvnɪs/ n (of person, place) fascino m; (of proposal) carattere m allettante; (of investment) convenienza f

attributable /ə'trɪbjʊtəbl/ a ⟨error, fall, loss etc⟩ attribuibile; **be ~ to** ⟨change, profit, success etc:⟩ essere dovuto a

attribute¹ /'ætrɪbjuːt/ n attributo m

attribute² /ə'trɪbjuːt/ vt attribuire

attribution /ætrɪ'bjuːʃn/ n attribuzione f

attributive /ə'trɪbjutɪv/ a attributivo

attrition /ə'trɪʃn/ n **war of ~** guerra f di logoramento

attune /ə'tjuːn/ vt **be ~d to** (in harmony with) essere sintonizzato con; (accustomed to) essere abituato a

aubergine /'əʊbəʒiːn/ n melanzana f

auburn /'ɔːbən/ a castano ramato

auction /'ɔːkʃn/ n asta f ● vt vendere all'asta

auctioneer /ɔːkʃə'nɪə(r)/ n banditore m

auction rooms npl sala f d'aste

auction sale *n* vendita *f* all'asta

audacious /ɔːˈdeɪʃəs/ *a* sfacciato; (*daring*) audace

audaciously /ɔːˈdeɪʃəslɪ/ *adv* sfacciatamente; (*daringly*) con audacia

audacity /ɔːˈdæsətɪ/ *n* sfacciataggine *f*; (*daring*) audacia *f*

audible /ˈɔːdəbl/ *a* udibile

audience /ˈɔːdɪəns/ *n Theat* pubblico *m*; *TV* telespettatori *mpl*; (*Radio*) ascoltatori *mpl*; (*meeting*) udienza *f*

audience: audience participation *n* partecipazione *f* del pubblico. **audience ratings** *npl* indici *mpl* di ascolto. **audience research** *n* sondaggio *m* tra il pubblico

audio /ˈɔːdɪəʊ/: **audiobook** *n* audiolibro *m*. **audio cassette** *n* audiocassetta *f*. **audio system** *n* impianto *m* stereo. **audiotape** *n* audiocassetta *f*. **audiotyping** *n* trascrizione *f* da audiocassetta. **audio typist** *n* dattilografo, -a *mf* (*che trascrive registrazioni*).

audiovisual *a* audiovisivo

audit /ˈɔːdɪt/ *n* verifica *f* del bilancio ● *vt* verificare

auditing /ˈɔːdɪtɪŋ/ *n* auditing *m inv*

audition /ɔːˈdɪʃn/ *n* audizione *f* ● *vi* fare un'audizione

auditor /ˈɔːdɪtə(r)/ *n* revisore *m* di conti

auditorium /ɔːdɪˈtɔːrɪəm/ *n* sala *f*

auditory /ˈɔːdɪt(ə)rɪ/ *a* acustico, uditivo

augment /ɔːgˈment/ *vt* aumentare

augur /ˈɔːgə(r)/ *vi* ~ **well**/**ill** essere di buon/cattivo augurio

August /ˈɔːgəst/ *n* agosto *m*

august /ɔːˈgʌst/ *a* augusto

Augustinian /ɔːgəˈstɪnɪən/ *a* agostiniano

aunt /ɑːnt/ *n* zia *f*

auntie, aunty /ˈɑːntɪ/ *n fam* zietta *f*

au pair /əʊˈpeə(r)/ *n* ~ [**girl**] ragazza *f* alla pari

aura /ˈɔːrə/ *n* aura *f*

aural /ˈɔːrəl/ *a* uditivo; (*Sch: comprehension, test*) orale; (*Med: test*) audiometrico ● *n Sch* esercizio *m* di comprensione ed espressione orale; *Mus* ≈ dettato *m* musicale

aurora australis/borealis /ɔːˈrɔːrəʊˈstrɑːlɪs/bɔːrɪˈɑːlɪs/ *n* aurora *f* australe/boreale

auspices /ˈɔːspɪsɪz/ *npl* **under the** ~ **of** sotto l'egida di

auspicious /ɔːˈspɪʃəs/ *a* di buon augurio

Aussie /ˈɒzɪ/ *a* & *n fam* australiano, -a *mf*

austere /ɒˈstɪə(r)/ *a* austero

austerity /ɒˈsterətɪ/ *n* austerità *f*

Australasia /ɒstrəˈleɪʒə/ *n* Australasia *f*

Australia /ɒˈstreɪlɪə/ *n* Australia *f*

Australian /ɒˈstreɪlɪən/ *a* & *n* australiano, -a *mf*

Austria /ˈɒstrɪə/ *n* Austria *f*

Austrian /ˈɒstrɪən/ *a* & *n* austriaco, -a *mf*

Austro-Hungarian /ɒstrəʊhʌŋˈgeərɪən/ *a* austroungarico

autarchy /ˈɔːtɑːkɪ/ *n* autarchia *f*

authentic /ɔːˈθentɪk/ *a* autentico

authenticate /ɔːˈθentɪkeɪt/ *vt* autenticare

authenticity /ɔːθenˈtɪsətɪ/ *n* autenticità *f*

author /ˈɔːθə(r)/ *n* autore *m*

authoritarian /ɔːθɒrɪˈteərɪən/ *a* autoritario

authoritative /ɔːˈθɒrɪtətɪv/ *a* autorevole; (*manner*) autoritario

authority /ɔːˈθɒrətɪ/ *n* autorità *f*; (*permission*) autorizzazione *f*; **who's in** ~ **here?** chi è il responsabile qui?; **be in** ~ **over** avere autorità su; **be an** ~ **on** essere un'autorità in materia di

authorization /ɔːθəraɪˈzeɪʃn/ *n* autorizzazione *f*

authorize /ˈɔːθəraɪz/ *vt* autorizzare

authorized dealer /ˈɔːθəraɪzd/ rivenditore *m* autorizzato

autism /ˈɔːtɪzm/ *n* autismo *m*

autistic /ɔːˈtɪstɪk/ *a* autistico

auto /ˈɔːtəʊ/ *n Am fam* auto *f* ● *attrib* (*industry*) automobilistico; (*workers*) dell'industria automobilistica

autobiographical /ɔːtəbaɪəˈgræfɪkl/ *a* autobiografico

autobiography /ɔːtəbaɪˈɒɡrəfɪ/ *n* autobiografia *f*

autocrat /ˈɔːtəkræt/ *n* autocrate *m*

autocratic /ɔːtəˈkrætɪk/ *a* autocratico

autocue /ˈɔːtəʊkjuː/ *n TV* gobbo *m*

autograph /ˈɔːtəgrɑːf/ *n* autografo *m* ● *vt* autografare

autoimmune /ɔːtəʊɪˈmjuːn/ *a* (*disease, system*) autoimmune

automate /ˈɔːtəmeɪt/ *vt* automatizzare

automatic /ɔːtəˈmætɪk/ *a* automatico ● *n* (*car*) macchina *f* col cambio automatico; (*washing machine*) lavatrice *f* automatica

automatically /ɔːtəˈmætɪklɪ/ *adv* automaticamente

automatic pilot *n* (*device*) pilota *m* automatico; **be on** ~ ~ *also fig* viaggiare con il pilota automatico inserito

automatic teller machine /ˈtelə/ *n* cassa *f* continua di prelevamento

automation /ɔːtəˈmeɪʃn/ *n* automazione *f*

automaton /ɔːˈtɒmətən/ *n* automa *m*

automobile /ˈɔːtəməbiːl/ *n* automobile *f*

automotive /ɔːtəˈməʊtɪv/ *a* (*self-propelling*) autopropulso; (*design, industry*) automobilistico

autonomous /ɔːˈtɒnəməs/ *a* autonomo

autonomously /ɔːˈtɒnəməslɪ/ *adv* autonomamente

autonomy /ɔːˈtɒnəmɪ/ *n* autonomia *f*

autopilot /ˈɔːtəʊpaɪlət/ *n Aeron, fig* pilota *m* automatico

autopsy /ˈɔːtɒpsɪ/ *n* autopsia *f*

auto-suggestion /ɔːtəʊsəˈdʒestʃən/ *n* autosuggestione *f*

autumn /ˈɔːtəm/ *n* autunno *m*

autumnal /ɔːˈtʌmnl/ *a* autunnale

auxiliary /ɔːgˈzɪlɪərɪ/ *a* ausiliario ● *n* ausiliare *m*

auxiliary nurse *n* infermiere, -a *mf* ausiliario, -a

auxiliary verb *n* ausiliare *m*

avail /ə'veɪl/ *n* **to no ~** invano ● *vi* **~ oneself of** approfittare di

availability /əveɪlə'bɪlətɪ/ *n* (*of option, service*) disponibilità *f*; (*of drugs*) reperibilità *f*, disponibilità *f*; **subject to ~** fino ad esaurimento

available /ə'veɪləbl/ *a* disponibile; ⟨*book, record etc*⟩ in vendita

avalanche /'ævəla:nʃ/ *n* valanga *f*

avant-garde /ævɒ̃'ga:d/ *n* avanguardia *f* ● *a* d'avanguardia

avarice /'ævərɪs/ *n* avidità *f*

avaricious /ævə'rɪʃəs/ *a* avido

Ave *abbr* (**Avenue**) V.le

avenge /ə'vendʒ/ *vt* vendicare

avenger /ə'vendʒə(r)/ *n* vendicatore, -trice *mf*

avenging /ə'vendʒɪŋ/ *a* vendicatore

avenue /'ævənju:/ *n* viale *m*; *fig* strada *f*

average /'ævərɪdʒ/ *a* medio; (*mediocre*) mediocre ● *n* media *f*; **on ~** in media; **above ~** superiore al normale ● *vt* ⟨*sales, attendance etc:*⟩ raggiungere una media di

■ **average out at** *vt* risultare in media

averse /ə'vɜ:s/ *a* **not be ~ to sth** non essere contro qcsa

aversion /ə'vɜ:ʃn/ *n* avversione *f* (**to** per)

avert /ə'vɜ:t/ *vt* evitare ⟨*crisis*⟩; distogliere ⟨*eyes*⟩

aviary /'eɪvɪərɪ/ *n* uccelliera *f*

aviation /eɪvɪ'eɪʃn/ *n* aviazione *f*

aviation fuel *n* benzina *f* avio

aviation industry *n* industria *f* aeronautica

aviator /'eɪvɪeɪtə(r)/ *n* aviatore, -trice *mf*

avid /'ævɪd/ *a* avido (**for** di); ⟨*reader*⟩ appassionato

avidity /ə'vɪdətɪ/ *n* avidità

avidly /'ævɪdlɪ/ *adv* ⟨*read, collect*⟩ avidamente; ⟨*support*⟩ con entusiasmo

avocado /ævə'ka:dəʊ/ *n* avocado *m*

avoid /ə'vɔɪd/ *vt* evitare

avoidable /ə'vɔɪdəbl/ *a* evitabile

avoidance /ə'vɔɪdəns/ *n* **~ of one's duty** astensione *f* dal proprio dovere

avowed /ə'vaʊd/ *a* dichiarato

avuncular /ə'vʌŋkʊlə(r)/ *a* benevolo

await /ə'weɪt/ *vt* attendere

awake /ə'weɪk/ *a* sveglio; **wide ~** completamente sveglio ● *vi* (*pt* **awoke**, *pp* **awoken**) svegliarsi

awaken /ə'weɪkn/ *vt* svegliare ● *vi* svegliarsi

awakening /ə'weɪknɪŋ/ *n* risveglio *m*

award /ə'wɔ:d/ *n* premio *m*; (*medal*) riconoscimento *m*; (*of prize*) assegnazione *f* ● *vt* assegnare; (*hand over*) consegnare

award: award ceremony *n* cerimonia *f* di premiazione. **award winner** *n* vincitore, -trice *mf* di un premio. **award-winning** *a* ⟨*book, film, design*⟩ premiato

aware /ə'weə(r)/ *a* **be ~ of** (*sense*) percepire; (*know*) essere conscio di; **become ~ of** accorgersi di; (*learn*) venire a sapere di; **be ~ that** rendersi conto che

awareness /ə'weənɪs/ *n* percezione *f*; (*knowledge*) consapevolezza *f*

awash /ə'wɒʃ/ *a* inondato (**with** di)

away /ə'weɪ/ *adv* via; **go/stay ~** andare/stare via; **he's ~ from his desk/the office** non è alla sua scrivania/in ufficio; **far ~** lontano; **four kilometres ~** a quattro chilometri; **play ~** *Sport* giocare fuori casa

away game *n* partita *f* fuori casa

awe /ɔ:/ *n* soggezione *f*; **stand in ~ of sb** avere soggezione di qcno

awe-inspiring *a* maestoso

awesome /'ɔ:səm/ *a* imponente

awful /'ɔ:f(ə)l/ *a* terribile; **that's an ~ pity** è un gran peccato ● *adv fam* estremamente

awfully /'ɔ:f(ʊ)lɪ/ *adv* terribilmente; ⟨*pretty*⟩ estremamente; **that's ~ nice of you** è veramente gentile da parte tua; **thanks ~** grazie mille

awhile /ə'waɪl/ *adv* per un po'

awkward /'ɔ:kwəd/ *a* ⟨*movement*⟩ goffo; ⟨*moment, situation*⟩ imbarazzante; ⟨*time*⟩ scomodo

awkwardly /'ɔ:kwədlɪ/ *adv* ⟨*move*⟩ goffamente; ⟨*say*⟩ con imbarazzo; **the meeting is ~ timed** la riunione è ad un orario scomodo

awkwardness /'ɔ:kwədnɪs/ *n* (*clumsiness*) goffaggine *f*; (*inconvenience*) scomodità *f*; (*embarrassment*) imbarazzo *m*; (*delicacy of situation*) delicatezza *f*

awl /ɔ:l/ *n* (*for wood etc*) punteruolo *m*

awning /'ɔ:nɪŋ/ *n* tendone *m*

awoke(n) /ə'wəʊk(ən)/ *see* **awake**

AWOL /'eɪwɒl/ *a & adv abbr* (**absent without leave**) **be/go ~** *Mil* assentarsi senza permesso; *hum* volatilizzarsi

awry /ə'raɪ/ *adv* storto

axe /æks/ *n* scure *f*; **have an ~ to grind** *fig* avere il proprio tornaconto ● *vt* (*pres p* **axing**) fare dei tagli a ⟨*budget*⟩; sopprimere ⟨*jobs*⟩; annullare ⟨*project*⟩

axiom /'æksɪəm/ *n* assioma *m*

axiomatic /æksɪə'mætɪk/ *a* **it is ~ that...** è indiscutibile che...

axis /'æksɪs/ *n* (*pl* **axes** /-si:z/) asse *m*

axle /'æksl/ *n* *Techn* asse *m*

ay[e] /aɪ/ *adv* sì ● *n* sì *m invar*

Azerbaijan /æzəbaɪ'dʒa:n/ *n* Azerbaigian *m*

Azerbaijani /æzəbaɪ'dʒa:nɪ/ *a & n* (*person*) azerbaigiano, -a *mf*; (*language*) azerbaigiano *m*

Azores /ə'zɔ:z/ *npl* **the ~** le Azzorre

Aztec /'æztek/ *a & n* (*person*) azteco, -a *mf*; (*language*) azteco *m*

azure /'eɪʒə(r)/ *a & n* azzurro *m*

b, B /biː/ n (letter) b, B f inv; Mus si m inv
b abbr **born**
BA abbr **Bachelor of Arts**
BAA n abbr (**British Airports Authority**) ente m che gestisce gli aeroporti britannici
baa /bɑː/ vi belare ● int bee
b. & b. abbr **bed and breakfast**
babble /ˈbæbl/ vi farfugliare; ⟨stream:⟩ gorgogliare
babe /beɪb/ n liter bimbo, -a mf; (fam: woman) ragazza f; (fam: form of address) bella f; **a ~ in arms** un bimbo in fasce; fig uno sprovveduto
baboon /bəˈbuːn/ n babbuino m
baby /ˈbeɪbɪ/ n bambino, -a mf; (fam: darling) tesoro m
baby: baby bird n uccellino m. **baby boom** n baby boom m inv. **baby boomer** n persona f nata durante il baby boom. **baby buggy** n Br carrozzina f. **baby carriage** n Am carrozzina f. **baby carrier** n zaino m portabimbo inv. **baby-faced** a ⟨person⟩ con la faccia da bambino
babyish /ˈbeɪbɪʃ/ a bambinesco
baby: baby-sit vi fare da baby-sitter. **baby-sitter** n baby-sitter mf. **baby-sitting** n do ~ fare il/la baby-sitter. **baby talk** n linguaggio m infantile. **baby tooth** n dente m di latte. **baby walker** n girello m. **babywear** n abbigliamento m per bambini
bachelor /ˈbætʃələ(r)/ n scapolo m; **B~ of Arts/Science** laureato, -a mf in lettere/in scienze
bachelor apartment, bachelor flat Br n appartamento m da scapolo
bachelorhood /ˈbætʃələhʊd/ n celibato m
bacillus /bəˈsɪləs/ n (pl -**lli**) bacillo m
back /bæk/ n schiena f; (of horse, hand) dorso m; (of chair) schienale m; (of house, cheque, page) retro m; (in football) difesa f; **at the ~** in fondo; **in the ~** Auto dietro; **stand ~ to ~** stare in piedi schiena contro schiena. **~ to front** ⟨sweater⟩ il davanti di dietro; **you've got it all ~ to front** fig hai capito tutto all'incontrario; **at the ~ of beyond** in un posto sperduto ● a posteriore; ⟨taxes, payments⟩ arretrato ● adv indietro; (returned) di ritorno; **turn/move ~** tornare/spostarsi indietro; **put it ~ here/there** rimettilo qui/là; **~ at home** di ritorno a casa; **I'll be ~ in five minutes** torno fra cinque minuti; **I'm just ~** sono appena tornato; **when do you want the book ~?** quando rivuoi il libro?; **pay ~** ripagare ⟨sb⟩; restituire ⟨money⟩; **~ in power** di nuovo al potere ● vt (support) sostenere; (with money) finanziare; puntare su ⟨horse⟩;

(cover the back of) rivestire il retro di ● vi Auto fare retromarcia
▪ back away vi tirarsi indietro
▪ back down vi battere in ritirata
▪ back in vi Auto entrare in retromarcia; ⟨person:⟩ entrare camminando all'indietro
▪ back out vi Auto uscire in retromarcia; ⟨person:⟩ uscire camminando all'indietro; fig tirarsi indietro (**of** da)
▪ back up vt sostenere; confermare ⟨person's alibi⟩; Comput fare una copia di salvataggio di; **be ~ed up** ⟨traffic:⟩ essere congestionato ● vi Auto fare retromarcia
back: backache n mal m di schiena. **backbench** n Br Pol scanni mpl del Parlamento dove siedono i parlamentari ordinari. **backbencher** n Br Pol parlamentare mf ordinario, -a. **backbiting** n maldicenza f. **backboard** n (in basketball) tabellone m. **back boiler** n caldaia f (posta dietro un caminetto). **backbone** n spina f dorsale. **back-breaking** a massacrante. **back burner** n put sth on the ~ ~ rimandare qcsa. **backchat** n risposta f impertinente. **backcloth** n Theat fondale m; fig sfondo m. **back comb** vt cotonare. **back copy** n numero m arretrato. **back cover** n retro m di copertina. **backdate** vt retrodatare ⟨cheque⟩; **~d to** valido a partire da. **back door** n porta f di servizio. **backdrop** n Theat fondale m; fig sfondo m. **back-end** n (rear) fondo m
backer /ˈbækə(r)/ n sostenitore, -trice mf; (with money) finanziatore, -trice mf
back: backfire vi Auto avere un ritorno di fiamma; ⟨fig: plan⟩ fallire; **the joke ~d on him** lo scherzo si è ritorto contro di lui. **backgammon** n backgammon m. **background** n sfondo m; (environment) ambiente m. **background noise** n rumore m di sottofondo. **background reading** n letture fpl generali. **backhand** n Tennis rovescio m. **backhanded** a ⟨compliment⟩ implicito. **backhander** n (fam: bribe) bustarella f
backing /ˈbækɪŋ/ n (support) supporto m; (material used) fondo m; Mus accompagnamento m
backing group n gruppo m d'accompagnamento
back issue n numero m arretrato
backlash /ˈbæklæʃ/ n fig reazione f opposta
backless /ˈbæklɪs/ a ⟨dress⟩ scollato dietro
back: backlist n opere fpl pubblicate. **backlog** n ~ **of work** lavoro m arretrato. **back marker** n Sport ultimo, -a mf. **back number** n numero m arretrato. **backpack** n zaino m. **backpacker** n saccopelista mf.

backpacking *n* go ~ viaggiare con zaino e sacco a pelo. **back passage** *n Anat* retto *m*. **back pay** *n* arretrato *m* di stipendio. **backpedal** *vi* pedalare all'indietro; *fig* fare marcia indietro. **back pocket** *n* tasca *f* di dietro. **backrest** *n* schienale *m*. **back room** *n* stanza *f* sul retro. **back room boys** *npl esperti mpl che lavorano dietro le quinte*. **backscratcher** *n* manina *f* grattaschiena *inv*. **back seat** *n* sedile *m* posteriore. **back-seat driver** *n persona f che dà consigli non richiesti*. **backside** *n fam* fondoschiena *m inv*. **backslash** *n Typ* barra *f* retroversa. **backspace** *n Comput* spazio *m* indietro. **backstage** *a & adv* dietro le quinte. **backstairs** *npl* scala *f* di servizio. **backstitch** *n* impuntura *f* ● *vi* impunturare. **backstop** *n Sport* ricevitore *m*. **back straight** *n Sport* rettilineo *m*. **backstreet** *n* vicolo *m* ● *attrib* ⟨*abortionist*⟩ clandestino. **backstroke** *n* dorso *m*. **backtalk** *n Am* = **backchat**. **backtrack** *vi* tornare indietro; *fig* fare marcia indietro. **back translation** *n* traduzione *f* di una traduzione. **backup** *n* rinforzi *mpl*; *Comput* riserva *f*, backup *m inv*; **do a ~** realizzare un backup. **backup copy** *n* copia *f* di riserva. **backup light** *n Am* luce *f* della retromarcia

backward /'bækwəd/ *a* ⟨*step*⟩ indietro; ⟨*child*⟩ lento nell'apprendimento; ⟨*country*⟩ arretrato

backward-looking /'bækwədlʊkɪŋ/ *a* retrogrado

backwards /'bækwədz/ *adv* (*also Am:* **backward**) indietro; ⟨*fall, walk*⟩ all'indietro; **~ and forwards** avanti e indietro

backwater /'bækwɔːtə(r)/ *n fig* luogo *m* allo scarto

backyard /bæk'jɑːd/ *n* cortile *m*; **not in my ~ yard** *fam* non a casa propria

bacon /'beɪk(ə)n/ *n* ≈ pancetta *f*

bacon-slicer /'beɪkənslaɪsə(r)/ *n* affettatrice *f*

bacteria /bæk'tɪərɪə/ *npl* batteri *mpl*

bacterial /bæk'tɪərɪəl/ *a* batterico

bacteriology /bæktɪərɪ'ɒlədʒɪ/ *n* batteriologia *f*

bad /bæd/ *a* (**worse, worst**) cattivo; ⟨*weather, habit, news, accident*⟩ brutto; ⟨*apple etc*⟩ marcio; **the light is ~** non c'è una buona luce; **my eyesight is ~** non ho una buona vista; **use ~ language** dire delle parolacce; **she's going through a ~ patch** sta attraversando un brutto periodo; **feel ~** sentirsi male; (*feel guilty*) sentirsi in colpa; **have a ~ back** avere dei problemi alla schiena; **smoking is ~ for you** fumare fa male; **go ~** andare a male; **that's just too ~!** pazienza!; **not ~** niente male; **things have gone from ~ to worse** le cose sono andate di male in peggio

bad: bad blood *n* **there is ~ ~ between them** tra loro non corre buon sangue. **bad boy** *n* ragazzaccio *m*. **bad breath** *n* alito *m* cattivo. **bad cheque** *n* assegno *m* a vuoto

bad debt *n* credito *m* inesigibile

baddie, baddy /'bædɪ/ *n fam* cattivo, -a *mf*

bade /bæd/ *see* **bid**

bad faith *n* malafede *f*

badge /bædʒ/ *n* distintivo *m*

badger /'bædʒə(r)/ *n* tasso *m* ● *vt* tormentare

badly /'bædlɪ/ *adv* male; ⟨*hurt*⟩ gravemente; **~ off** povero; **~ behaved** maleducato; **need ~** aver estremamente bisogno di

bad-mannered /-'mænəd/ *a* maleducato

badminton /'bædmɪntən/ *n* badminton *m*

bad-tempered /-'tempəd/ *a* irascibile

baffle /'bæfl/ *vt* confondere

baffling /'bæflɪŋ/ *a* sconcertante

bag /bæg/ *n* borsa *f*; (*of paper*) sacchetto *m*; **old ~** *sl* megera *f*; **~s under the eyes** occhiaie *fpl*; **~s of** *fam* un sacco di; **it's in the ~** *fig* è fatta ● *vt* (*pt/pp* **bagged**) (*fam: take*) accaparrarsi; **~ sb a seat** tenere un posto a qcno

bagel /'beɪgəl/ *n* panino *m* a forma di ciambella

baggage /'bægɪdʒ/ *n* bagagli *mpl*

baggage: baggage allowance *n* franchigia *f* bagaglio. **baggage car** *n Rail* bagagliaio *m*. **baggage carousel** *n* nastro *m* trasportatore per ritiro bagagli. **baggage check** *n* controllo *m* bagagli. **baggage handler** *n* addetto, -a *mf* ai bagagli. **baggage locker** *n* armadietto *m* per deposito bagagli. **baggage reclaim** *n* ritiro *m* bagagli

baggy /'bægɪ/ *a* ⟨*clothes*⟩ ampio

Baghdad /bæg'dæd/ *n* Baghdad *f*

bag: bag lady *n fam* barbona *f*. **bag person** *n fam* barbone, -a *mf*. **bagpipes** *npl* cornamusa *fsg*. **bag snatcher** *n* scippatore, -trice *mf*

Bahamas /bə'hɑːməz/ *npl* **the ~** le Bahamas

Bahrain, Bahrein /bɑː'reɪn/ *n* Bahrein *m*

bail /beɪl/ *n* cauzione *f*; **on ~** su cauzione

■ **bail out** *vt Naut* aggottare; **~ sb out** *Jur* pagare la cauzione per qcno; *fig* trarre qcno d'impaccio ● *vi Aeron* paracadutarsi

bail bond *n Am Jur* cauzione *f*

bailiff /'beɪlɪf/ *n* ufficiale *m* giudiziario; (*of estate*) fattore *m*

bait /beɪt/ *n* esca *f*; **rise to the ~** abboccare [all'amo] ● *vt* innescare; (*fig: torment*) tormentare

baize /beɪz/ *n* panno *m* (*di tavolo da gioco e da biliardo*)

bake /beɪk/ *vt* cuocere al forno; (*make*) fare ● *vi* cuocersi al forno

baked beans /beɪkt'biːnz/ *n Culin* fagioli *mpl* al pomodoro

baked potato *n* patata *f* cotta al forno (con la buccia)

baker /'beɪkə(r)/ *n* fornaio, -a *mf*, panettiere, -a *mf*

baker's [shop] /'beɪkəz/ *n* panetteria *f*

bakery /'beɪkərɪ/ *n* panificio *m*, forno *m*

baking /'beɪkɪŋ/ *n* cottura *f* al forno

baking: baking powder *n* lievito *m* in polvere. **baking soda** n *Culin* bicarbonato m di sodio. **baking tin** n teglia f

balaclava /bælə'klɑːvə/ n passamontagna m inv

balance /'bæləns/ n (*equilibrium*) equilibrio m; *Comm* bilancio m; (*outstanding sum*) saldo m; [**bank**] ~ saldo m; **be** or **hang in the** ~ *fig* essere in sospeso; **on** ~ tutto sommato ● vt bilanciare; equilibrare 〈budget〉; *Comm* fare il bilancio di 〈books〉 ● vi bilanciarsi; *Comm* essere in pareggio

balanced /'bælənst/ a equilibrato

balance: balance of payments n bilancia f dei pagamenti. **balance of power** n *Pol* equilibrio m delle forze. **balance sheet** n bilancio m [d'esercizio]. **balance of trade** n bilancia f commerciale

balancing act /'bælənsɪŋ/ n *fig* **do a** ~ ~ fare equilibrismo

balcony /'bælkənɪ/ n balcone m

bald /bɔːld/ a 〈person〉 calvo; 〈tyre〉 liscio; 〈statement〉 nudo e crudo; **go** ~ perdere i capelli

balderdash /'bɔːldədæʃ/ n sciocchezze fpl

balding /'bɔːldɪŋ/ a **be** ~ stare perdendo i capelli

baldly /'bɔːldlɪ/ adv 〈state〉 in modo nudo e crudo

baldness /'bɔːldnɪs/ n calvizie f

bale /beɪl/ n balla f

Balearic Islands /bælɪ'ærɪk/ npl isole fpl Baleari

baleful /'beɪlfl/ a malvagio; (*sad*) triste

balefully /'beɪlfʊlɪ/ adv con malvagità

balk /bɔːlk/ vt ostacolare ● vi ~ **at** 〈horse:〉 impennarsi davanti a; *fig* tirarsi indietro davanti a

Balkans /'bɔːlknz/ npl Balcani mpl

ball[1] /bɔːl/ n palla f; (*football*) pallone m; (*of yarn*) gomitolo m; **on the** ~ *fam* sveglio

ball[2] n (*dance*) ballo m

ballad /'bæləd/ n ballata f

ball and chain n palla f al piede

ball-and-socket joint n giunto m sferico

ballast /'bæləst/ n zavorra f

ball: ball-bearing n cuscinetto m a sfera. **ballboy** n *Tennis* raccattapalle m inv. **ballcock** n *Techn* galleggiante m (*in serbatoio*). **ball control** n controllo m della palla. **ball dress** n abito m da sera

ballerina /bælə'riːnə/ n ballerina f [classica]

ballet /'bæleɪ/ n balletto m; (*art form*) danza f

ballet: ballet dancer n ballerino, -a mf [classico, -a]. **ballet dress** n tutù m inv. **ballet shoes** scarpe fpl da danza

ball: ballgame n gioco m con la palla; *Am* partita f di baseball; **that's a whole different** ~ *fig* è tutto un altro paio di maniche. **ballgirl** n *Tennis* raccattapalle f inv. **ball gown** n abito m da sera

ballistic /bə'lɪstɪk/ a balistico

ballistics n balistica fsg

balloon /bə'luːn/ n pallone m; *Aeron* mongolfiera f

balloonist /bə'luːnɪst/ n aeronauta mf

ballot /'bælət/ n votazione f

ballot box n urna f

ballot paper n scheda f di votazione

ball: ballpark n *Am* stadio m di baseball. **ballpark figure** n *fam* cifra f approssimativa. **ball-point [pen]** n penna f a sfera. **ballroom** n sala f da ballo. **ballroom dancing** n ballo m liscio

■ **balls up** vulg vi incasinarsi ● vt incasinare

ballyhoo /bælɪ'huː/ n (*publicity*) battage m inv pubblicitario; (*uproar*) baccano m

balm /bɑːm/ n balsamo m

balmy /'bɑːmɪ/ a (**-ier, -iest**) mite; (*fam: crazy*) strampalato

balsam /'bɒlsəm/ n (*oily*) balsamo m

Baltic /'bɔːltɪk/ a & n **the** ~ [**Sea**] il [mar] Baltico

balustrade /bælə'streɪd/ n balaustra f

bamboo /bæm'buː/ n bambù m

bamboozle /bæm'buːzl/ vt (*fam: mystify*) confondere

ban /bæn/ n proibizione f ● vt (*pt/pp* **banned**) proibire; ~ **from** espellere da 〈club〉; **she was** ~**ned from driving** le hanno ritirato la patente

banal /bə'nɑːl/ a banale

banality /bə'nælətɪ/ n banalità f inv

banana /bə'nɑːnə/ n banana f

banana republic n *pej* repubblica f delle banane

banana skin n buccia f di banana

band /bænd/ n banda f; (*stripe*) nastro m; (*Mus: pop group*) complesso m; (*Mus: brass* ~) banda f; *Mil* fanfara f

■ **band together** vi riunirsi

bandage /'bændɪdʒ/ n benda f ● vt fasciare

■ **bandage up** vt fasciare

Band-Aid n *Med* cerotto m

bandit /'bændɪt/ n bandito m

band: band leader n leader mf di un complesso. **bandmaster** n capobanda m (*di banda musicale*). **band saw** n segatrice f a nastro. **bandsman** n bandista m. **bandstand** n palco m coperto [dell'orchestra]. **bandwagon** n **jump on the** ~ *fig* seguire la corrente

bandy[1] /'bændɪ/ vt (*pt/pp* **-ied**) scambiarsi 〈words〉

■ **bandy about** vt far circolare

bandy[2] a (**-ier, -iest**) **be** ~ avere le gambe storte

bandy-legged /-'legd/ a con le gambe storte

bane /beɪn/ n **she/it is the** ~ **of my life!** è la mia rovina!

bang /bæŋ/ n (*noise*) fragore m; (*of gun, firework*) scoppio m; (*blow*) colpo m; **go with a** ~ *fam* essere una cannonata ● adv **in the middle of** *fam* proprio nel mezzo di; **go** ~ 〈gun:〉 sparare; 〈balloon:〉 esplodere ● int bum! ● vt battere 〈fist〉; battere su 〈table〉; sbattere 〈door, head〉 ● vi scoppiare; 〈door:〉 sbattere

■ **bang about, bang around** *vi* far rumore

■ **bang into** *vt* sbattere contro

banger /'bæŋə(r)/ *n* (*firework*) petardo *m*; (*fam: sausage*) salsiccia *f*; old ~ (*fam: car*) macinino *m*

Bangladesh /bæŋglə'deʃ/ *n* Bangladesh *m*

bangle /'bæŋgl/ *n* braccialetto *m*

banish /'bænɪʃ/ *vt* bandire

banishment /'bænɪʃmənt/ *n* bando *m*

banisters /'bænɪstəz/ *npl* ringhiera *fsg*

banjo /'bændʒəʊ/ *n* banjo *m inv*

bank¹ /bæŋk/ *n* (*of river*) sponda *f*; (*slope*) scarpata *f* ● *vi* Aeron inclinarsi in virata

bank² *n* banca *f* ● *vt* depositare in banca ● *vi* ~ **with** avere un conto [bancario] presso

■ **bank on** *vt* contare su

bank: bank account *n* conto *m* in banca. **bank balance** *n* saldo *m*. **bank-book** *n* libretto *m* di risparmio. **bank borrowings** *npl* prestiti *mpl* bancari. **bank card** *n* carta *f* assegni. **bank charges** *npl* spese *fpl* bancarie, commissioni *fpl*. **bank clerk** *n* bancario, -a *mf*

banker /'bæŋkə(r)/ *n* banchiere *m*

banker's draft *n* tratta *f* bancaria

banker's order *n* ordine *m* di pagamento

Bank Giro Credit *n* Br accreditamento *m* tramite bancogiro

bank holiday *n* giorno *m* festivo

banking /'bæŋkɪŋ/ *n* bancario *m*

banking hours *npl* orario *m* di sportello (*in banca*)

bank: bank manager *n* direttore, -trice *mf* di banca. **banknote** *n* banconota *f*. **bank raid** *n* rapina *f* in banca. **bank robber** *n* rapinatore, -trice *mf* di banca. **bank robbery** *n* rapina *f* in banca. **bankroll** *n* finanziamento *m* ● *vt* finanziare (*person, party*)

bankrupt /'bæŋkrʌpt/ *a* fallito; **go** ~ fallire ● *n* persona *f* che ha fatto fallimento ● *vt* far fallire

bankruptcy /'bæŋkrʌptsɪ/ *n* bancarotta *f*

bankruptcy court *n* tribunale *m* fallimentare

bankruptcy proceedings *npl* procedura *f* fallimentare

bank statement *n* estratto *m* conto

bank transfer *n* bonifico *m* bancario

banner /'bænə(r)/ *n* stendardo *m*; (*of demonstrators*) striscione *m*

banner headline *n* titolo *m* a tutta pagina

banns /bænz/ *npl* Relig pubblicazioni *fpl* [di matrimonio]

banquet /'bæŋkwɪt/ *n* banchetto *m*

bantam /'bæntəm/ *n* gallo *m* bantam

banter /'bæntə(r)/ *n* battute *fpl* di spirito

baptism /'bæptɪzm/ *n* battesimo *m*; ~ **of fire** *fig* battesimo *m* del fuoco

Baptist /'bæptɪst/ *a & n* battista *mf*

baptize /bæp'taɪz/ *vt* battezzare

bar /bɑː(r)/ *n* sbarra *f*; Jur ordine *m* degli avvocati; (*of chocolate*) tavoletta *f*; (*café*) bar *m inv*; (*counter*) banco *m*; Mus battuta *f*; (*fig: obstacle*) ostacolo *m*; ~ **of soap/gold** sapo-

netta *f*/lingotto *m*; **be called to the** ~ Jur entrare a far parte dell'ordine degli avvocati; **behind** ~**s** *fam* dietro le sbarre ● *vt* (*pt/pp* **barred**) sbarrare (*way*); sprangare (*door*); escludere (*person*) ● *prep* tranne; ~ **none** in assoluto

barb /bɑːb/ *n* barbiglio *m*; (*fig: remark*) frecciata *f*

Barbados /bɑː'beɪdɒs/ *n* Barbados *fsg*

barbarian /bɑː'beərɪən/ *n* barbaro, -a *mf*

barbaric /bɑː'bærɪk/ *a* barbarico

barbarism /'bɑːbərɪzm/ *n* (*brutality, primitiveness*) barbarie *f inv*; (*error of style*) barbarismo *m*

barbarity /bɑː'bærətɪ/ *n* barbarie *f inv*

barbarous /'bɑːbərəs/ *a* barbaro

barbecue /'bɑːbɪkjuː/ *n* barbecue *m inv*; (*party*) grigliata *f*, barbecue *m inv* ● *vt* arrostire sul barbecue

barbed /bɑːbd/ *a* ~ **wire** filo *m* spinato

barber /'bɑːbə(r)/ *n* barbiere *m*

barber's shop *n* barbiere *m*

barbiturate /bɑː'bɪtjʊrət/ *n* barbiturico *m*

bar: bar chart *n* istogramma *m*. **bar code** *n* codice *m* a barre. **bar-coded** *a* con codice a barre. **bar code reader** *n* lettore *m* di codice a barre

bard /bɑːd/ *n* liter bardo *m*

bare /beə(r)/ *a* nudo; (*tree, room*) spoglio; (*floor*) senza moquette; **the** ~ **bones** l'essenziale *m* ● *vt* scoprire; mostrare (*teeth*)

bare: bareback *adv* senza sella. **barefaced** *a* sfacciato. **barefoot** *adv* scalzo. **bareheaded** *a* a capo scoperto

barely /'beəlɪ/ *adv* appena

bareness /'beənɪs/ *n* nudità *f*

bargain /'bɑːgɪn/ *n* (*agreement*) patto *m*; (*good buy*) affare *m*; **into the** ~ per di più ● *vi* contrattare; (*haggle*) trattare

■ **bargain for** *vt* (*expect*) aspettarsi

bargain basement *n* reparto *m* occasioni

bargaining /'bɑːgɪnɪŋ/ *n* (*over pay*) contrattazione *f* ● *attrib* (*power, rights*) contrattuale; (*position*) di negoziato

barge /bɑːdʒ/ *n* barcone *m*

■ **barge in** *vi* *fam* (*to room*) piombare dentro; (*into conversation*) interrompere bruscamente; ~ **into** piombare dentro a (*room*); venire addosso a (*person*)

bargepole /'bɑːdʒpəʊl/ *n* **I wouldn't touch him/it with a** ~ non lo toccherei nemmeno con un dito

baritone /'bærɪtəʊn/ *n* baritono *m*

bark¹ /bɑːk/ *n* (*of tree*) corteccia *f*

bark² *n* abbaiamento *m* ● *vi* abbaiare

barking /'bɑːkɪŋ/ *n* abbaiamento *m* ● *a* (*dog*) che abbaia; (*cough, laugh*) convulso ● *adv* **be** ~ **mad** *Br fam* essere matto da legare

barley /'bɑːlɪ/ *n* orzo *m*

barley: barleycorn *n* orzo *m*; (*grain*) chicco *m* d'orzo. **barley sugar** *n* caramella *f* d'orzo. **barley water** *n* *Br* orzata *f*. **barley wine** *n* *Br* birra *f* molto forte

barmaid /'bɑːmeɪd/ *n* barista *f*

barman /'bɑːmən/ *n* barista *m*

barmy /'bɑ:mɪ/ *a fam* strampalato

barn /bɑ:n/ *n* granaio *m*

barnacle /'bɑ:nəkl/ *n* cirripede *m*

barn: barn dance *n* ballo *m* tradizionale statunitense; (*social gathering*) festa *f* negli USA in cui si fanno balli tradizionali. **barn owl** *n* barbagianni *m inv*. **barnstorming** *a* sensazionale. **barnyard** *n* aia *f*

barometer /bə'rɒmɪtə(r)/ *n* barometro *m*

baron /'bærn/ *n* barone *m*

baroness /'bærənɪs/ *n* baronessa *f*

baronial /bə'rəʊnɪəl/ *a* baronale

baroque /bə'rɒk/ *a & n* barocco *m*

barracking /'bærəkɪŋ/ *n* fischi *mpl* e insulti *mpl*

barrack room *n* camerata *f* ● *attrib pej* ⟨*language*⟩ da caserma

barracks /'bærəks/ *npl* caserma *fsg*

barrage /'bærɑ:ʒ/ *n* (*in river*) [opera *f* di] sbarramento *m*; *Mil* sbarramento *m*; (*fig: of criticism, abuse*) sfilza *f*

barrage balloon *n* pallone *m* di sbarramento

barrel /'bærəl/ *n* barile *m*, botte *f*; (*of gun*) canna *f*

barrel organ *n* organetto *m* [a cilindro]

barren /'bærən/ *a* sterile; ⟨*landscape*⟩ brullo

barrette /bæ'ret/ *n Am* (*for hair*) molletta *f*

barricade /bærɪ'keɪd/ *n* barricata *f* ● *vt* barricare

barrier /'bærɪə(r)/ *n* barriera *f*; *Rail* cancello *m*; *fig* ostacolo *m*

barrier: barrier cream *n* crema *f* protettiva. **barrier method** *n Med* metodo *m* anticoncezionale meccanico. **barrier reef** *n* barriera *f* corallina

barring /'bɑ:rɪŋ/ *prep* ~ **accidents** tranne imprevisti

barrister /'bærɪstə(r)/ *n* avvocato *m*

barrow /'bærəʊ/ *n* carretto *m*; (*wheel~*) carriola *f*

bar stool *n* sgabello *m* da bar

bartender /'bɑ:tendə(r)/ *n* barista *mf*

barter /'bɑ:tə(r)/ *vi* barattare (**for** con)

base /beɪs/ *n* base *f* ● *a* vile ● *vt* basare; **be ~d on** basarsi su

baseball /'beɪsbɔ:l/ *n* baseball *m*

baseball cap *n* berretto *m* da baseball

base: base camp *n* campo *m* base *inv*. **base form** *n* (*of verb*) forma *f* non coniugata di un verbo. **base lending rate** *n* tasso *m* base *inv* di interesse

baseless /'beɪslɪs/ *a* infondato

baseline /'beɪslaɪn/ *n Tennis* linea *f* di fondo; *fig* riferimento *m*

basement /'beɪsmənt/ *n* seminterrato *m*

basement flat *n* appartamento *m* nel seminterrato

base metal *n* metallo *m* vile *inv*

base rate *n* tasso *m* base *inv*

bash /bæʃ/ *n* colpo *m* violento; **have a ~!** *fam* provaci! ● *vt* colpire [violentemente]; (*dent*) ammaccare; **~ed in** ammaccato

■ **bash down** *vt* sfondare ⟨*door*⟩

bashful /'bæʃfl/ *a* timido

bashfully /'bæʃflɪ/ *adv* timidamente

bashing /'bæʃɪŋ/ *n fam* (*beating*) pestaggio *m*; (*criticism*) critica *f* feroce; (*defeat*) batosta *f*; **take a ~** prendere una batosta

basic /'beɪsɪk/ *a* di base; ⟨*condition, requirement*⟩ basilare; ⟨*living conditions*⟩ povero; **my Italian is pretty ~** il mio italiano è abbastanza rudimentale; **the ~s** (*of language, science*) i rudimenti; (*essentials*) l'essenziale *m*

basically /'beɪsɪklɪ/ *adv* fondamentalmente

basic rate *n* tariffa *f* minima; (*in tax*) aliquota *f* minima

basil /'bæzɪl/ *n* basilico *m*

basilica /bə'zɪlɪkə/ *n* basilica *f*

basin /'beɪsn/ *n* bacinella *f*; (*wash-hand* ~) lavabo *m*; (*for food*) recipiente *m*; *Geog* bacino *m*

basinful /'beɪsɪnfʊl/ *n* bacinella *f* (*contenuto*)

basis /'beɪsɪs/ *n* (*pl* **-ses** /'beɪsi:z/) base *f*

bask /bɑ:sk/ *vi* crogiolarsi

basket /'bɑ:skɪt/ *n* cestino *m*

basket: basketball *n* pallacanestro *f*. **basket chair** *n* sedia *m* di vimini. **basketwork** *n* (*objects*) oggetti *mpl* in vimini; (*craft*) lavoro *m* artigianale di oggetti in vimini

Basle /bɑ:l/ *n* Basilea *f*

Basque /bæsk/ *a & n* (*person*) basco, -a *mf*; (*language*) basco *m*

bass /beɪs/ *a* basso; ~ **voice** voce *f* di basso ● *n* basso *m*

bass: bass-baritone *n* baritono *m* basso. **bass clef** *n* chiave *f* di basso. **bass drum** *n* grancassa *f*

basset hound /'bæsɪt/ *n* basset hound *m inv*

bassist /'beɪsɪst/ *n* bassista *mf*

bassoon /bə'su:n/ *n* fagotto *m*

bastard /'bɑ:stəd/ *n* (*illegitimate child*) bastardo, -a *mf*; *sl* figlio *m* di puttana

baste¹ /beɪst/ *vt* (*sew*) imbastire

baste² *vt Culin* ungere con grasso

bastion /'bæstɪən/ *n* bastione *m*

bat¹ /bæt/ *n* mazza *f*; (*for table tennis*) racchetta *f*; **off one's own** ~ *fam* tutto da solo ● *vt* (*pt/pp* **batted**) battere; **she didn't ~ an eyelid** *fig* non ha battuto ciglio

bat² *n Zool* pipistrello *m*

batch /bætʃ/ *n* gruppo *m*; (*of goods*) partita *f*; (*of bread*) infornata *f*

batch file *n Comput* batch file *m inv*

batch processing /'prəʊsesɪŋ/ *n Comput* elaborazione *f* a gruppi

bated /'beɪtɪd/ *a* **with ~ breath** col fiato sospeso

bath /bɑ:θ/ *n* (*pl* ~**s** /bɑ:ðz/) bagno *m*; (*tub*) vasca *f* da bagno; ~**s** *pl* piscina *f*; **have a ~** fare un bagno ● *vt* fare il bagno a ● *vi* fare il bagno

bathe /beɪð/ *n* bagno *m* ● *vi* fare il bagno ● *vt* lavare ⟨*wound*⟩

bather /'beɪðə(r)/ *n* bagnante *mf*

bathing /'beɪðɪŋ/ *n* bagni *mpl*

bathing: bathing cap *n* cuffia *f*. **bathing**

costume n costume m da bagno. **bathing hut** n cabina f (al mare). **bathing suit** n costume m da bagno. **bathing trunks** n calzoncini mpl da bagno

bath mat n tappetino m da bagno

bathrobe /'bæθrəʊb/ n accappatoio m

bathroom /'bæθru:m/ n (also: toilet) bagno m

bathroom: bathroom cabinet n armadietto m del bagno. **bathroom fittings** npl accessori mpl per il bagno. **bathroom scales** npl bilancia f pesapersone

bath: bath salts npl sali mpl da bagno. **bath-towel** n asciugamano m da bagno. **bathtub** n vasca f da bagno

baton /'bæt(ə)n/ n Mus bacchetta f

baton charge n Br carica f con lo sfollagente

baton round n Br proiettile m di gomma

batsman /'bætsmən/ n Sport battitore m

battalion /bə'tæliən/ n battaglione m

batten /'bætn/ n assicella f

batter /'bætə(r)/ n Culin pastella f

battered /'bætəd/ a (car) malandato; (wife, baby) maltrattato

battering /'bæt(ə)rɪŋ/ n take a ~ (from bombs, storm, waves) essere colpito; (from other team) prendersi una batosta; (from other boxer) prendersele

battering ram n ariete m

battery /'bætərɪ/ n batteria f; (of torch, radio) pila f

battery: battery charger n caricabatterie m inv. **battery chicken** n pollo m di allevamento in batteria. **battery controlled** a a pile. **battery farming** n allevamento m in batteria. **battery hen** n gallina f d'allevamento in batteria. **battery life** n autonomia f. **battery operated, battery powered** a a pile

battle /'bæt(ə)l/ n battaglia f; fig lotta f ● vi fig lottare

battle: battleaxe n fam virago f inv. **battle cry** n also fig grido m di battaglia. **battle dress** n uniforme f da combattimento. **battlefield** n, **battleground** n campo m di battaglia; fig terreno m di scontro. **battle lines** npl Mil schieramenti mpl

battlements /'bætlmənts/ npl bordo m merlato; (crenellations) merlatura f

battle: battle order n also fig ordine m di battaglia. **battle-scarred** a aguerrito; fig segnato dalla vita. **battleship** n corazzata f

batty /'bætɪ/ a fam strampalato

bauble /'bɔ:b(ə)l/ n (ornament) gingillo m; (jewellery) ninnolo m

bawdiness /'bɔ:dɪnɪs/ n oscenità f

bawdy /'bɔ:dɪ/ a (-ier, -iest) piccante

bawl /bɔ:l/ vt/i urlare

■ **bawl out** vt fam urlare (name, order); fare una sfuriata a (sb)

bay[1] /beɪ/ n Geog baia f

bay[2] n keep at ~ tenere a bada

bay[3] n Bot alloro m

bay[4] n (horse) baio m

bay leaf n foglia f d'alloro

bayonet /'beɪənet/ n baionetta f

bay window n bay window f inv (grande finestra sporgente)

bazaar /bə'zɑ:(r)/ n bazar m inv

bazooka /bə'zu:kə/ n bazooka m inv

BBC n abbr (British Broadcasting Corporation) BBC f

BC abbr (before Christ) a.C.

BE abbr (bill of exchange) cambiale f

be /bi:/ vi (pres am, is, are; pt was, were; pp been) essere; **he is a teacher** è insegnante, fa l'insegnante; **what do you want to be?** cosa vuoi fare?; **be quiet!** sta' zitto!; **I am cold/hot** ho freddo/caldo; **it's cold/hot, isn't it?** fa freddo/caldo, vero?; **how are you?** come stai?; **I am well** sto bene; **there is** c'è; **there are** ci sono; **I have been to Venice** sono stato a Venezia; **has the postman been?** è passato il postino?; **you're coming too, aren't you?** vieni anche tu, no?; **it's yours, is it?** è tuo, vero?; **was John there? – yes, he was** c'era John? – sì; **John wasn't there – yes he was!** John non c'era – sì che c'era!; **three and three are six** tre più tre fanno sei; **he is five** ha cinque anni; **that will be £10, please** fanno 10 sterline, per favore; **how much is it?** quanto costa?; **that's £5 you owe me** mi devi 5 sterline ● v aux **I am coming/reading** sto venendo/leggendo; **I'm staying** (not leaving) resto; **I am being lazy** sono pigro; **I was thinking of you** stavo pensando a te; **you are not to tell him** non devi dirgielo; **you are to do that immediately** devi farlo subito ● passive essere; **I have been robbed** sono stato derubato

beach /bi:tʃ/ n spiaggia f

beach: beach ball n pallone m da spiaggia. **beach buggy** n dune buggy f inv. **beachcomber** n persona f che vive rivendendo gli oggetti trovati sulla spiaggia. **beachhead** n testa f di sbarco. **beach hut** n cabina f [da spiaggia]. **beachrobe** n accappatoio m. **beachwear** n abbigliamento m da spiaggia

beacon /'bi:k(ə)n/ n faro m; Naut, Aeron fanale m

bead /bi:d/ n perlina f

beady-eyed /bi:dɪ'aɪd/ a (sharp-eyed) a cui non sfugge niente

beagle /'bi:g(ə)l/ n beagle m inv, bracchetto m

beak /bi:k/ n becco m

beaker /'bi:kə(r)/ n coppa f; (in laboratory) becher m inv

beam /bi:m/ n trave f; (of light) raggio m ● vi irradiare; (person:) essere raggiante; ~ **at sb** fare un gran sorriso a qcno

beaming /'bi:mɪŋ/ a raggiante

bean /bi:n/ n fagiolo m; (of coffee) chicco m; **spill the ~s** fam spiattellare tutto

bean: bean bag n (seat) poltrona f imbottita di pallini di polistirolo. **beanfeast** n fam festa f. **beanpole** n (fig fam: tall thin person)

spilungone, -a *mf*. **beansprout** *n* germoglio *m* di soia
bear¹ /beə(r)/ *n* orso *m*
bear² *v* (*pt* **bore**, *pp* **borne**) ● *vt* (*endure*) sopportare; mettere al mondo ⟨*child*⟩; (*carry*) portare; **~ in mind** tenere presente; **~ fruit** ⟨*tree:*⟩ produrre; *fig* dare frutto ● *vi* **~ left/right** andare a sinistra/a destra
■ **bear out** *vt* confermare ⟨*story, statement*⟩
■ **bear with** *vt* aver pazienza con
bearable /ˈbeərəbl/ *a* sopportabile
bear cub *n* cucciolo *m* di orso
beard /bɪəd/ *n* barba *f*; **have a ~** avere la barba
bearded /ˈbɪədɪd/ *a* barbuto
bearer /ˈbeərə(r)/ *n* portatore, -trice *mf*; (*of passport*) titolare *mf*
bearing /ˈbeərɪŋ/ *n* portamento *m*; *Techn* cuscinetto *m* [a sfera]; **have a ~ on** avere attinenza con; **get one's ~s** orientarsi; **lose one's ~s** perdere l'orientamento
bear market *n Fin* mercato *m* al ribasso
bearskin *n* (*pelt*) pelle *f* d'orso; (*hat*) colbacco *m* militare
beast /biːst/ *n* bestia *f*; (*fam: person*) animale *m*
beastly /ˈbiːstlɪ/ *a* (**-ier, -iest**) *fam* orribile
beat /biːt/ *n* battito *m*; (*rhythm*) battuta *f*; (*of policeman*) giro *m* d'ispezione ● *v* (*pt* **beat**, *pp* **beaten**) ● *vt* battere; picchiare ⟨*person*⟩; **~ a retreat** *Mil* battere in ritirata; **~ it!** *fam* darsela a gambe!; **it ~s me why...** *fam* non capisco proprio perché...
■ **beat down** *vt* buttare giù ⟨*door*⟩ ● *vi* ⟨*sun:*⟩ battere a picco
■ **beat off** *vt* respingere ⟨*attacker*⟩
■ **beat out** *vt* domare ⟨*flames*⟩
■ **beat up** *vt* picchiare
beaten /ˈbiːtn/ *a* **off the ~ track** fuori mano
beatify /bɪˈætɪfaɪ/ *vt* beatificare
beating /ˈbiːtɪŋ/ *n* bastonata *f*; **get a ~** (*with fists*) essere preso a pugni; ⟨*team, player:*⟩ prendere una batosta
beating-up *n fam* pestaggio *m*
beat-up *a* ⟨*fam: car*⟩ sfasciato
beau /bəʊ/ *n liter, hum* spasimante *m*
Beaufort scale /ˈbəʊfət/ *n* scala *f* Beaufort
beautician /bjuːˈtɪʃn/ *n* estetista *mf*
beautiful /ˈbjuːtɪfl/ *a* bello; **the ~ people** il bel mondo
beautifully /ˈbjuːtɪfʊlɪ/ *adv* splendidamente
beautify /ˈbjuːtɪfaɪ/ *vt* (*pt/pp* **-ied**) abbellire
beauty /ˈbjuːtɪ/ *n* bellezza *f*
beauty: beauty contest *n* concorso *m* di bellezza. **beauty editor** *n* redattore, -trice *mf* di articoli di bellezza. **beauty parlour** *n* istituto *m* di bellezza. **beauty queen** reginetta *f* di bellezza. **beauty salon** *n* istituto *m* di bellezza. **beauty sleep** *n hum* **need one's ~ ~** aver bisogno delle proprie ore di sonno. **beauty spot** *n* neo *m*; (*place*) luogo *m* pittoresco
beaver /ˈbiːvə(r)/ *n* castoro *m*

■ **beaver away** *vi* (*fam: work hard*) sgobbare
becalmed /bɪˈkɑːmd/ *a* in bonaccia
became /bɪˈkeɪm/ *see* **become**
because /bɪˈkɒz/ *conj* perché; (*at start of sentence*) poiché ● *adv* **~ of** a causa di
beck /bek/ *n* **be at sb's ~ and call** dover essere a completa disposizione di qcno
beckon /ˈbekn/ *vt/i* **~ [to]** chiamare con un cenno
become /bɪˈkʌm/ *v* (*pt* **became**, *pp* **become**) ● *vt* diventare ● *vi* diventare; **what has ~ of her?** che ne è di lei?
becoming /bɪˈkʌmɪŋ/ *a* ⟨*clothes*⟩ bello
bed /bed/ *n* letto *m*; (*of sea, lake*) fondo *m*; (*layer*) strato *m*; (*of flowers*) aiuola *f*; **in ~** a letto; **go to ~** andare a letto; **~ and breakfast** pensione *f* familiare in cui il prezzo della camera comprende anche la prima colazione
■ **bed down** *vi* coricarsi
BEd *n abbr* (**Bachelor of Education**) ≈ laurea *f* in magistero
bed: bed and board *n* vitto e alloggio *m*. **bed base** *n* fondo *m* del letto. **bed bath** *n* **give sb a ~ ~** lavare qcno a letto. **bedbug** *n* cimice *f*. **bedchamber** *n* camera *f* da letto. **bedclothes** *npl* lenzuola e coperte *fpl*
bedding /ˈbedɪŋ/ *n* biancheria *f* per il letto, materasso e guanciali
bedeck /bɪˈdek/ *vt* ornare
bedevil /bɪˈdevəl/ *vt* tormentare ⟨*person*⟩; intralciare ⟨*plans*⟩
bed: bedfellow *n* **make strange ~s** *fig* fare una strana coppia. **bedhead** *n* testata *f* del letto. **bed jacket** *n* liseuse *f inv*
bedlam /ˈbedləm/ *n* baraonda *f*
bed linen *n* biancheria *f* per il letto
bedpan /ˈbedpæn/ *n* padella *f*
bedraggled /bɪˈdrægld/ *a* inzaccherato
bedridden /ˈbedrɪdən/ *a* costretto a letto
bedrock /ˈbedrɒk/ *n* basamento *m*; *fig* fondamento *m*
bedroom /ˈbedruːm/ *n* camera *f* da letto
bedroom: bedroom farce *n Theat* pochade *f inv*. **bedroom slipper** *n* pantofola *f*. **bedroom suburb** *n Am* città *f inv* dormitorio
bed-settee *n* divano *m* letto
bedside /ˈbedsaɪd/ *n* **at his ~** al suo capezzale
bedside: bedside lamp *n* abat-jour *m inv*. **bedside manner** *n* modo *m* di trattare i pazienti; **have a good ~ ~** saperci fare con i pazienti. **bedside rug** *n* scendiletto *m*. **bedside table** *n* comodino *m*
bed: bed-sit *n*, **bed-sitter** *n*, **bed-sitting-room** *n* camera *f* ammobiliata [fornita di cucina]. **bedsock** *n* calzino *m* da notte. **bedsore** *n* piaga *f* da decubito. **bedspread** *n* copriletto *m*. **bedstead** *n* fusto *m* del letto. **bedtime** *n* l'ora *f* di andare a letto. **bedwetting** *n* il bagnare il letto
bee /biː/ *n* ape *f*
beech /biːtʃ/ *n* faggio *m*

beef /biːf/ n manzo m

beef: beefburger n hamburger m inv.
beefeater n guardia f della Torre di Londra.
beefsteak n bistecca f. **beefsteak tomato**
n grosso pomodoro m. **beef stew** n stufato m
di manzo. **beef tea** n brodo m di manzo

beefy /'biːfɪ/ a ⟨flavour⟩ di manzo; ⟨fam:
man⟩ grande e grosso

beehive /'biːhaɪv/ n alveare m

bee: bee-keeper n apicoltore, -trice mf.
bee-keeping n apicoltura f. **bee-line** n
make a ~ **for** fam precipitarsi verso

been /biːn/ see **be**

beep /biːp/ n ⟨of car⟩ suono m di clacson; ⟨of
telephone⟩ segnale m acustico; ⟨of electronic
device, radio⟩ bip m inv ● vi ⟨car, driver:⟩
clacsonare; ⟨device:⟩ fare bip ● vt ⟨with
beeper⟩ chiamare con il cercapersone; ~ **the
horn** clacsonare

beeper /'biːpə(r)/ n cercapersone m inv

beer /bɪə(r)/ n birra f

beer: beer belly n pancia f da beone. **beer
bottle** n bottiglia f da birra. **beer garden** n
giardino m di un pub. **beer mat** n sottobicchiere m. **beerswilling** a pej ubriacone

bee sting n puntura f d'ape

beeswax /'biːzwæks/ n cera f d'api

beet /biːt/ n ⟨Am: beetroot⟩ barbabietola f;
[sugar] ~ barbabietola f da zucchero

beetle /'biːtl/ n scarafaggio m

■ **beetle off** vi ⟨fam: hurry away⟩ scappare

beetroot /'biːtruːt/ n barbabietola f

befall /bɪ'fɔːl/ vt liter accadere a

befit /bɪ'fɪt/ vt liter addirsi a

befitting /bɪ'fɪtɪŋ/ a ⟨modesty, honesty⟩ opportuno

before /bɪ'fɔː(r)/ prep prima di; **the day** ~
yesterday ieri l'altro; ~ **long** fra poco ● adv
prima; **never** ~ **have I seen…** non ho mai
visto prima…; ~ **that** prima; ~ **going** prima
di andare ● conj ⟨time⟩ prima che; ~ **you go**
prima che tu vada

beforehand /bɪ'fɔːhænd/ adv in anticipo

before tax a ⟨profit, income⟩ lordo, al lordo
di imposte

befriend /bɪ'frend/ vt trattare da amico

befuddle /bɪ'fʌdl/ vt confondere ⟨mind⟩

beg /beg/ v ⟨pt/pp begged⟩ ● vi mendicare
● vt pregare; chiedere ⟨favour, forgiveness⟩

began /bɪ'gæn/ see **begin**

beggar /'begə(r)/ n mendicante mf; **you
lucky** ~! che fortuna sfacciata!; **poor** ~! povero cristo!; **you little** ~! monellaccio!

beggarly /'begəlɪ/ a ⟨existence, meal⟩ miserabile; ⟨wage⟩ da fame

begging bowl /'begɪŋ/ n ciotola f del mendicante

begging letter n lettera f che sollecita offerte in denaro

begin /bɪ'gɪn/ vt/i ⟨pt began, pp begun, pres
p beginning⟩ cominciare; **well, to** ~ **with**
dunque, per cominciare

beginner /bɪ'gɪnə(r)/ n principiante mf

beginning /bɪ'gɪnɪŋ/ n principio m

begonia /bɪ'gəʊnɪə/ n begonia f

begrudge /bɪ'grʌdʒ/ vt ⟨envy⟩ essere invidioso di; dare malvolentieri ⟨money⟩

beguile /bɪ'gaɪl/ vt ⟨charm⟩ affascinare;
⟨cheat⟩ ingannare

beguiling /bɪ'gaɪlɪŋ/ a accattivante

begun /bɪ'gʌn/ see **begin**

behalf /bɪ'hɑːf/ n **on** ~ **of** a nome di; **on my**
~ a nome mio; **say hello on my** ~ salutalo
da parte mia

behave /bɪ'heɪv/ vi comportarsi; ~
[oneself] comportarsi bene

behaviour /bɪ'heɪvjə(r)/ n comportamento
m; ⟨of prisoner, soldier⟩ condotta f

behavioural /bɪ'heɪvjərəl/ a comportamentale

behaviourist /bɪ'heɪvjərɪst/ a & n compor-
tamentista mf

behaviour pattern n modello m comportamentale

behead /bɪ'hed/ vt decapitare

beheld /bɪ'held/ see **behold**

behind /bɪ'haɪnd/ prep dietro; ⟨with pronoun⟩
dietro di; **be** ~ **sth** fig stare dietro qcsa ● adv
dietro, indietro; ⟨late⟩ in ritardo; **a long way**
~ molto indietro; **in the car** ~ nella macchina dietro ● n fam didietro m

behindhand /bɪ'haɪndhænd/ adv indietro

behold /bɪ'həʊld/ vt ⟨pt/pp beheld⟩ liter vedere

beholden /bɪ'həʊldn/ a obbligato ⟨to verso⟩

beholder /bɪ'həʊldə(r)/ n **beauty is in the
eye of the** ~ è bello ciò che piace

beige /beɪʒ/ a & n beige m inv

Beijing /beɪ'dʒɪŋ/ n Pechino f

being /'biːɪŋ/ n essere m; **come into** ~ nascere

Beirut /beɪ'ruːt/ n Beirut f

bejewelled /bɪ'dʒuːəld/ a ingioiellato

belated /bɪ'leɪtɪd/ a tardivo

belatedly /bɪ'leɪtɪdlɪ/ adv tardi

belch /beltʃ/ vi ruttare ● vt ~ [out] eruttare
⟨smoke⟩

beleaguered /bɪ'liːgəd/ a ⟨city⟩ assediato;
⟨troops⟩ accerchiato; ⟨fig: person⟩ tormentato;
⟨fig: company⟩ in difficoltà

Belfast /bel'fɑːst/ n Belfast f

belfry /'belfrɪ/ n campanile m

Belgian /'beldʒən/ a & n belga mf

Belgium /'beldʒəm/ n Belgio m

Belgrade /bel'greɪd/ n Belgrado f

belie /bɪ'laɪ/ vt ⟨give false impression of⟩ dissimulare; ⟨disprove⟩ smentire

belief /bɪ'liːf/ n fede f; ⟨opinion⟩ convinzione f

believable /bɪ'liːvəbl/ a credibile

believe /bɪ'liːv/ vt/i credere

■ **believe in** vt avere fiducia in ⟨person⟩; credere a ⟨ghosts⟩

believer /bɪ'liːvə(r)/ n Relig credente mf; **be
a great** ~ in credere fermamente in

belittle /bɪ'lɪtl/ vt sminuire ⟨person,
achievements⟩

belittling /bɪ'lɪtlɪŋ/ a ⟨comment⟩ che sminui-
sce

Belize /be'liːz/ n Belize m

bell /bel/ *n* campana *f*; (*on door*) campanello *m*; **that rings a ~** *fig* mi dice qualcosa

bell-bottoms *npl* pantaloni *mpl* a zampa d'elefante

bellboy /'belbɔɪ/ *n Am* fattorino *m* d'albergo

belle /bel/ *n* bella *f*

bellhop /'belhɒp/ *n Am* fattorino *m* d'albergo

belligerence /bɪ'lɪdʒərəns/ *n* bellicosità *f*; *Pol* belligeranza *f*

belligerent /bɪ'lɪdʒərənt/ *a* belligerante; (*aggressive*) bellicoso

bell-jar *n* campana *f* di vetro

bellow /'beləʊ/ *vi* gridare a squarciagola; (*animal:*) muggire

■ **bellow out** *vt* urlare (*name, order*)

bellows /'beləʊz/ *npl* (*for fire*) soffietto *m*

bell: bell-pull *n* (*rope*) cordone *m* di campanello. **bell-push** *n* pulsante *m* di campanello. **bell-ringer** *n* campanaro *m*. **bell-shaped** *a* a campana. **bell tower** *n* campanile *m*

belly /'belɪ/ *n* pancia *f*

belly: bellyache *n fam* mal *m* di pancia ● *vi fam* lamentarsi. **belly button** *n fam* ombelico *m*. **belly dancer** *n* danzatrice *f* del ventre. **belly flop** *n* (*in swimming*) spanciata *f*

bellyful /'belɪfʊl/ *n fam* **have had a ~ of sth** avere le tasche piene di qcsa

belong /bɪ'lɒŋ/ *vi* appartenere (**to** a); (*be member*) essere socio (**to** di)

belongings /bɪ'lɒŋɪŋz/ *npl* cose *fpl*

beloved /bɪ'lʌvɪd/ *a & n* amato, -a *mf*

below /bɪ'ləʊ/ *prep* sotto; (*with numbers*) al di sotto di ● *adv* sotto, di sotto; *Naut* sotto coperta; **see ~** guardare qui di seguito

belt /belt/ *n* cintura *f*; (*area*) zona *f*; *Techn* cinghia *f* ● *vi* (*fam: rush*) **~ along** filare velocemente ● *vt* (*fam: hit*) picchiare

■ **belt up** *vi* (*in car*) mettersi la cintura [di sicurezza]; **~ up!** (*sl: be quiet*) stai zitto!

bemoan /bɪ'məʊn/ *vt* lamentare

bemused /bɪ'mju:zd/ *a* confuso

bench /bentʃ/ *n* panchina *f*; (*work~*) piano *m* da lavoro; **the B~** *Jur* la magistratura

benchmark /'bentʃmɑ:k/ *n* punto *m* di riferimento; *Comput* paragone *m* con un campione; (*fin: price*) prezzo *m* di riferimento

bend /bend/ *n* curva *f*; (*of river*) ansa *f*; **round the ~** *fam* fuori di testa ● *v* (*pt/pp* **bent**) ● *vt* piegare ● *vi* piegarsi; (*road:*) curvare; **~ [down]** chinarsi

■ **bend over** *vi* inchinarsi

beneath /bɪ'ni:θ/ *prep* sotto, al di sotto di; **he thinks it's ~ him** *fig* pensa che sia sotto al suo livello; **~ contempt** indegno ● *adv* giù

Benedictine /benɪ'dɪkti:n/ *a & n Relig* benedettino *m*

benediction /benɪ'dɪkʃn/ *n Relig* benedizione *f*

benefactor /'benɪfæktə(r)/ *n* benefattore, -trice *mf*

beneficial /benɪ'fɪʃl/ *a* benefico

beneficiary /benɪ'fɪʃərɪ/ *n* beneficiario, -a *mf*

benefit /'benɪfɪt/ *n* vantaggio *m*; (*allowance*)

indennità *f inv* ● *v* (*pt/pp* **-fited**, *pres p* **-fiting**) ● *vt* giovare a ● *vi* trarre vantaggio (**from** da)

Benelux /'benɪlʌks/ *n* Benelux *m* ● *attrib* (*countries, organization*) del Benelux

benevolence /bɪ'nevələns/ *n* benevolenza *f*

benevolent /bɪ'nevələnt/ *a* benevolo

benevolently /bɪ'nevələntlɪ/ *adv* con benevolenza

Bengal /beŋ'gɔ:l/ *n* Bengala *m*

benign /bɪ'naɪn/ *a* benevolo; *Med* benigno

benignly /bɪ'naɪnlɪ/ *adv* con benevolenza

Benin /be'ni:n/ *n* Benin *m*

bent /bent/ *see* **bend** ● *a* (*person*) ricurvo; (*distorted*) curvato; (*fam: dishonest*) corrotto; **be ~ on doing sth** essere ben deciso a fare qcsa ● *n* predisposizione *f*

benzene /'benzi:n/ *n* benzene *m*

benzine /'benzi:n/ *n* benzina *f*

bequeath /bɪ'kwi:ð/ *vt* lasciare in eredità

bequest /bɪ'kwest/ *n* lascito *m*

berate /bɪ'reɪt/ *vt fml* redarguire

bereaved /bɪ'ri:vd/ *n* the **~** *pl* i familiari del defunto

bereavement /bɪ'ri:vmənt/ *n* lutto *m*

bereft /bɪ'reft/ *a* **~ of** privo di

beret /'bereɪ/ *n* berretto *m*

Berlin /bɜ:'lɪn/ *n* Berlino *f*

Berliner /bɜ:'lɪnə(r)/ *n* berlinese *mf*

Bermuda /bə'mju:də/ *n* le Bermuda.

Bermuda shorts *npl* bermuda *m inv*

Berne /bɜ:n/ *n* Berna *f*

berry /'berɪ/ *n* bacca *f*

berserk /bə'sɜ:k/ *a* **go ~** diventare una belva

berth /bɜ:θ/ *n* (*bed*) cuccetta *f*; (*anchorage*) ormeggio *m*; **give a wide ~ to** *fam* stare alla larga da ● *vi* ormeggiare

beseech /bɪ'si:tʃ/ *vt* (*pt/pp* **beseeched** or **besought**) supplicare

beseeching /bɪ'si:tʃɪŋ/ *a* implorante

beset /bɪ'set/ *a* **a country ~ by strikes** un paese vessato dagli scioperi

beside /bɪ'saɪd/ *prep* accanto a; **~ oneself** fuori di sé

besides /bɪ'saɪdz/ *prep* oltre a ● *adv* inoltre

besiege /bɪ'si:dʒ/ *vt* assediare

besotted /bɪ'sɒtɪd/ *a* infatuato (**with** di)

besought /bɪ'sɔ:t/ *see* **beseech**

bespatter /bɪ'spætə(r)/ *vt* schizzare

bespectacled /bɪ'spektək(ə)ld/ *a* con gli occhiali

bespoke /bɪ'spəʊk/ *a* (*suit*) su misura; (*tailor*) che lavora su ordinazione

best /best/ *a* migliore; **the ~ part of a year** la maggior parte dell'anno; **~ before** *Comm* preferibilmente prima di; **~ wishes** migliori auguri ● *n* **the ~** il meglio; (*person*) il/la migliore; **at ~** tutt'al più; **all the ~!** tanti auguri!; **do one's ~** fare del proprio meglio; **to the ~ of my knowledge** per quel che ne so; **make the ~ of it** cogliere il lato buono della cosa ● *adv* meglio, nel modo migliore; **as ~ I could** meglio che potevo; **like ~** preferire

best before date *n* data *f* di scadenza

best friend *n* migliore amico, -a *mf*
bestial /'bestɪəl/ *a also fig* bestiale
bestiality /bestɪ'ælətɪ/ *n* bestialità *f*
best man *n* testimone *m*
bestow /bɪ'stəʊ/ *vt* conferire (**on** a)
best-seller /-'selə(r)/ *n* bestseller *m inv*
best-selling /-'selɪŋ/ *a* ‹*novelist*› più venduto
bet /bet/ *n* scommessa *f* ● *vt/i* (*pt/pp* **bet** *or* **betted**) scommettere
beta blocker /'bi:təblɒkə(r)/ *n* betabloccante *m*
Bethlehem /'beθlɪhem/ *n* Betlemme *f*
betray /bɪ'treɪ/ *vt* tradire
betrayal /bɪ'treɪəl/ *n* tradimento *m*
betrothal /bɪ'trəʊðəl/ *n* fidanzamento *m*
betrothed /bɪ'trəʊðd/ *n liter, hum* promesso sposo *m*; promessa sposa *f*; **be ~** essere fidanzato
better /'betə(r)/ *a* migliore, meglio; **get ~** migliorare; (*after illness*) rimettersi; **I waited the ~ part of a week** ho aspettato buona parte della settimana ● *adv* meglio; **~ off** meglio; (*wealthier*) più ricco; **all the ~** tanto meglio; **the sooner the ~** prima è, meglio è; **I've thought ~ of it** ci ho ripensato; **you'd ~ stay** faresti meglio a restare; **I'd ~ not** è meglio che non lo faccia ● *vt* migliorare; **~ oneself** migliorare le proprie condizioni
betting /'betɪŋ/ *n* (*activity*) scommesse *fpl*; **what's the ~ that...?** quanto scommettiamo che...?
betting shop *n* ricevitoria *f* (*dell'allibratore*)
between /bɪ'twi:n/ *prep* fra, tra; **~ you and me** detto fra di noi; **~ us** (*together*) tra me e te ● *adv* [**in**] **~** in mezzo; (*time*) frattempo
betwixt /bɪ'twɪkst/ *adv* **be ~ and between** essere una via di mezzo
bevel /'bevl/ *n* (*edge*) spigolo *m* smussato; (*tool*) squadra *f* falsa ● *vt* smussare ‹*mirror, edge*›
beverage /'bevərɪdʒ/ *n* bevanda *f*
bevy /'bevɪ/ *n* frotta *f*
beware /bɪ'weə(r)/ *vi* guardarsi (**of** da); **~ of the dog!** attenti al cane!
bewilder /bɪ'wɪldə(r)/ *vt* disorientare
bewildered /bɪ'wɪldəd/ *a* ‹*look, person*› perplesso, sconcertato
bewildering /bɪ'wɪldərɪŋ/ *a* sconcertante
bewilderment /bɪ'wɪldəmənt/ *n* perplessità *f*
bewitch /bɪ'wɪtʃ/ *vt* stregare; *fig* affascinare completamente
beyond /bɪ'jɒnd/ *prep* oltre; **~ reach** irraggiungibile; **~ doubt** senza alcun dubbio; **~ belief** da non credere; **it's ~ me** *fam* non riesco proprio a capire ● *adv* più in là
B film *n* film *m inv* di serie B
bias /'baɪəs/ *n* (*preference*) preferenza *f*; *pej* pregiudizio *m* ● *vt* (*pt/pp* **biased**) (*influence*) influenzare
bias binding, bias tape /'baɪndɪŋ/ *n* (*in sewing*) fettuccia *f* in sbieco

biased /'baɪəst/ *a* parziale
bib /bɪb/ *n* bavaglino *m*
Bible /'baɪbl/ *n* Bibbia *f*
Bible Belt *n* zona *f* del sud degli USA, dove predomina il fondamentalismo protestante
biblical /'bɪblɪkl/ *a* biblico
bibliographic[al] /bɪblɪə'græfɪk[l]/ *a* bibliografico
bibliography /bɪblɪ'ɒgrəfɪ/ *n* bibliografia *f*
bicarbonate /baɪ'ka:bəneɪt/ *n* **~ of soda** bicarbonato *m* di sodio
bicentenary /baɪsen'ti:nərɪ/ *n* bicentenario *m* ● *attrib* ‹*celebration, year*› bicentenario
biceps /'baɪseps/ *n* bicipite *m*
bicker /'bɪkə(r)/ *vi* litigare
bickering /'bɪkərɪŋ/ *n* bisticci *mpl*
bicycle /'baɪsɪkl/ *n* bicicletta *f* ● *vi* andare in bicicletta
bicycle: bicycle clip *n* molletta *f* (*per pantaloni*). **bicycle lane** *n* pista *f* ciclabile. **bicycle rack** *n* (*in yard*) rastrelliera *f* per biciclette; (*on car*) portabiciclette *m inv*
bid¹ /bɪd/ *n* offerta *f*; (*attempt*) tentativo *m* ● *vt/i* (*pt/pp* **bid**, *pres p* **bidding**) offrire; (*in cards*) dichiarare
bid² *vt* (*pt* **bade** *or* **bid**, *pp* **bidden** *or* **bid**, *pres p* **bidding**) *liter* (*command*) comandare; **~ sb welcome** dare il benvenuto a qcno
bidder /'bɪdə(r)/ *n* offerente *mf*
bide /baɪd/ *vt* **~ one's time** aspettare il momento buono
bidet /'bi:deɪ/ *n* bidè *m inv*
biennial /baɪ'enɪəl/ *a* biennale
bier /bɪə(r)/ *n* catafalco *m*
bifocals /baɪ'fəʊklz/ *npl* occhiali *mpl* bifocali
big /bɪg/ *a* (**bigger, biggest**) grande; ‹*brother, sister*› più grande; (*fam: generous*) generoso; **make ~ money** fare i soldi ● *adv* **talk ~** *fam* sparare grosse
bigamist /'bɪgəmɪst/ *n* bigamo, -a *mf*
bigamous /'bɪgəməs/ *a* bigamo
bigamy /'bɪgəmɪ/ *n* bigamia *f*
big: big bang *n* (*in astronomy*) big bang *m*. **big business** *n* le grandi imprese; **be ~ ~** essere un grosso affare. **big cat** *n* grosso felino *m*. **big deal** *n fam* **~ ~!** bella forza!. **big dipper** *n* (*Br: at fair*) montagne *fpl* russe. **big game hunting** *n* caccia *f* grossa. **bighead** *n fam* montato, -a *mf*, gasato, -a *mf*. **big-headed** *a fam* montato, gasato. **big-hearted** *a* generoso. **bigmouth** *n fam pej* chiacchierone, -a *mf*; **he's such a ~!** (*indiscreet*) ha una lingua lunga!. **big name** *n* (*in film, art*) grosso nome *m*. **big noise** *n fam* pezzo *m* grosso
bigot /'bɪgət/ *n* fanatico, -a *mf*
bigoted /'bɪgətɪd/ *a* di mentalità ristretta
big: big screen *n* grande schermo *m*. **big shot** *n fam* pezzo *m* grosso. **Big Smoke** *n Br hum* Londra *f*. **big time** *n* **make** *or* **hit the ~ ~** *n fam* raggiungere il successo ● *attrib* **big-time** ‹*crook*› di alto livello. **big toe** *n* alluce *m*. **big top** *n* (*tent*) tendone *m* del circo; (*fig: circus*) circo *m*. **bigwig** *n fam* pezzo *m* grosso

bike /baɪk/ *n fam* bici *f inv*
biker['s] jacket /'baɪkə(z)dʒækɪt/ *n fam* giubbotto *m* di pelle
bikini /bɪ'kiːnɪ/ *n* bikini *m inv*
bilateral /baɪ'lætrəl/ *a* bilaterale
bilberry /'bɪlbərɪ/ *n* mirtillo *m*
bile /baɪl/ *n* bile *f*
bilge /bɪldʒ/ *n Naut* (*place*) carena *f*; (*substance*) sentina *f*; (*fam: nonsense*) idiozie *fpl*
bilingual /baɪ'lɪŋgwəl/ *a* bilingue
bilingual secretary *n* segretario, -a *mf* bilingue
bilious /'bɪljəs/ *a Med* ~ **attack** attacco *m* di bile
bill¹ /bɪl/ *n* fattura *f*; (*in restaurant etc*) conto *m*; (*poster*) manifesto *m*; *Pol* progetto *m* di legge; (*Am: note*) biglietto *m* di banca; *Theat* **be top of the** ~ essere in testa al cartellone ● *vt* fatturare
bill² *n* (*beak*) becco *m*
billboard /'bɪlbɔːd/ *n* cartellone *m* pubblicitario
billet /'bɪlɪt/ *n Mil* alloggio *m* ● *vt* (*pt/pp* **billeted**) alloggiare (**on** presso)
bill: bill of exchange *n* cambiale *f*. **bill of fare** *n* menù *m inv*. **billfold** *n Am* portafoglio *m*. **bill of rights** *n* dichiarazione *f* dei diritti. **bill of sale** *n* atto *m* di vendita
billiard ball *n* palla *f* da biliardo
billiards /'bɪljədz/ *n* biliardo *m*
billiard table /'bɪljəd/ *n* tavolo *m* da biliardo
billing /'bɪlɪŋ/ *n Comm* fatturazione *f*; **get top** ~ *Theat* comparire in testa al cartellone
billion /'bɪljən/ *n* (*thousand million*) miliardo *m*; (*old-fashioned Br: million million*) mille miliardi *mpl*
billionaire /bɪljə'neə(r)/ *n* miliardario, -a *mf*
billow /'bɪləʊ/ *n* (*of smoke*) nube *f* ● *vi* alzarsi in volute
billposter /'bɪlpəʊstə(r)/ *n* attacchino *m*
billy /'bɪlɪ/ *n* (*Am: truncheon*) sfollagente *m inv*
billycan /'bɪlɪkæn/ *n* gamella *f*
billy goat *n* caprone *m*
bimbo /'bɪmbəʊ/ *n pej fam* bambolona *f*; **his latest** ~ la sua ultima amichetta
bin /bɪn/ *n* bidone *m*
binary /'baɪnərɪ/ *a* binario
bind /baɪnd/ *vt* (*pt/pp* **bound**) legare (**to** a); (*bandage*) fasciare; *Jur* obbligare
binder /'baɪndə(r)/ *n* (*for papers*) raccoglitore *m*; (*for cement, paint*) agglomerante *m*
binding /'baɪndɪŋ/ *a* (*promise, contract*) vincolante ● *n* (*of book*) rilegatura *f*; (*on ski*) attacco *m*
binge /bɪndʒ/ *n fam* **have a** ~ fare baldoria; (*eat a lot*) abbuffarsi ● *vi* abbuffarsi (**on** di)
bingo /'bɪŋgəʊ/ *n* ≈ tombola *f*
bin liner *n Br* sacchetto *m* per la spazzatura
binoculars /bɪ'nɒkjʊləz/ *npl* [**pair of**] ~ binocolo *msg*
biochemist /baɪəʊ'kemɪst/ *n* biochimico, -a *mf*

biochemistry /baɪəʊ'kemɪstrɪ/ *n* biochimica *f*
biodegradable /baɪəʊdɪ'greɪdəbl/ *a* biodegradabile
biodiversity /baɪəʊdaɪ'vɜːsətɪ/ *n* biodiversità *f*
bioengineering /baɪəʊendʒɪ'nɪərɪŋ/ *n* bioingegneria *f*
biographer /baɪ'ɒgrəfə(r)/ *n* biografo, -a *mf*
biographical /baɪə'græfɪkl/ *a* biografico
biography /baɪ'ɒgrəfɪ/ *n* biografia *f*
biological /baɪə'lɒdʒɪkl/ *a* biologico
biological clock *n* orologio *m* biologico
biologically /baɪə'lɒdʒɪklɪ/ *adv* biologicamente
biological powder *n* detersivo *m* biologico
biological warfare *n* guerra *f* biologica
biologist /baɪ'ɒlədʒɪst/ *n* biologo, -a *mf*
biology /baɪ'ɒlədʒɪ/ *n* biologia *f*
bionic /baɪ'ɒnɪk/ *a* bionico
biopic /'baɪəʊpɪk/ *n Cin* film *m* basato su una *biografia*
biopsy /'baɪɒpsɪ/ *n* biopsia *f*
biorhythm /'baɪəʊrɪðəm/ *n* bioritmo *m*
biotechnology /baɪəʊtek'nɒlədʒɪ/ *n* biotecnologia *f*
bipartisan /baɪpɑː'tɪzæn/ *a Pol* bipartitico
bipartite /baɪ'pɑːtaɪt/ *a* bipartito
birch /bɜːtʃ/ *n* (*tree*) betulla *f*
bird /bɜːd/ *n* uccello *m*; (*fam: girl*) ragazza *f*; **kill two** ~**s with one stone** prendere due piccioni con una fava
birdbrain /'bɜːdbreɪn/ *n fam* **he's such a** ~ ha un cervello da gallina
bird call *n* cinguettio *m*
birdie /'bɜːdɪ/ *n* (*in golf*) birdie *m*
birdlike /'bɜːdlaɪk/ *a* come un uccello
bird: bird of paradise *n* uccello *m* del paradiso. **bird of prey** *n* [uccello *m*] rapace *m*. **bird sanctuary** *n* riserva *f* per uccelli. **birdseed** *n* becchime *m*. **bird's eye view** *n* veduta *f* panoramica dall'alto. **bird's nest** *n* nido *m* di uccello. **bird's nest soup** *n* zuppa *f* di nidi di rondine. **birdsong** *n* canto *m* degli uccelli. **birdwatcher** *n* persona *f* che pratica il bird-watching. **bird-watching** *n* **go** ~ fare del bird-watching
Biro® /'baɪrəʊ/ *n* biro® *f inv*
birth /bɜːθ/ *n* nascita *f*; **give** ~ partorire; **give** ~ **to** partorire
birth: birth certificate *n* certificato *m* di nascita. **birth-control** *n* controllo *m* delle nascite. **birthday** *n* compleanno *m*. **birthday party** *n* festa *f* di compleanno. **birthmark** *n* voglia *f*. **birthplace** *n* luogo *m* di nascita. **birth-rate** *n* natalità *f*. **birthright** *n* diritto *m* di nascita. **births column** *n* annunci *mpl* delle nascite (*nel giornale*). **birth sign** *n* segno *m* zodiacale. **births, marriages, and deaths** *npl* annunci *mpl* di nascite, di matrimonio, mortuari (*nel giornale*)
biscuit /'bɪskɪt/ *n* biscotto *m*
biscuit barrel, biscuit tin *n* biscottiera *f*

bisect /bar'sekt/ vt dividere in due [parti]
bisexual /bar'seksjʊəl/ a & n bisessuale mf
bishop /'bɪʃəp/ n vescovo m; Chess alfiere m
bistro /'bi:strəʊ/ n bistrò m inv
bit¹ /bɪt/ n pezzo m; (smaller) pezzetto m; (for horse) morso m; Comput bit m inv; **a ~ of** un pezzo di ⟨cheese, paper⟩; un po' di ⟨time, rain, silence⟩; **~ by ~** poco a poco; **do one's ~** fare la propria parte
bit² see bite
bitch /bɪtʃ/ n cagna f; sl arpia f
bitchy /'bɪtʃɪ/ a velenoso
bite /baɪt/ n morso m; (insect ~) puntura f; (mouthful) boccone m ● vt (pt bit, pp bitten) mordere; ⟨insect:⟩ pungere; **~ one's nails** mangiarsi le unghie ● vi mordere; ⟨insect:⟩ pungere
■ **bite off** vt staccare (con un morso)
biting /'baɪtɪŋ/ a ⟨wind, criticism⟩ pungente; ⟨remark⟩ mordace
bit part n Theat particina f
bitter /'bɪtə(r)/ a amaro ● n Br birra f amara
bitter almond n mandorla f amara
bitter lemon n limonata f amara
bitterly /'bɪtəlɪ/ adv amaramente; **it's ~ cold** c'è un freddo pungente
bitterness /'bɪtənɪs/ n amarezza f
bittersweet /bɪtə'swi:t/ a liter agrodolce
bitty /'bɪtɪ/ a Br fam frammentario
bitumen /'bɪtjʊmɪn/ n bitume m
bivouac /'bɪvʊæk/ n bivacco m ● vi bivaccare
bizarre /bɪ'zɑ:(r)/ a bizzarro
blab /blæb/ vi (pt/pp blabbed) cianciare
black /blæk/ a nero; **be ~ and blue** essere coperto di lividi ● n nero m ● vt boicottare ⟨goods⟩
■ **black out** vt cancellare ● vi (lose consciousness) perdere coscienza
black: Black Africa n Africa f nera. **Black American** n negro, -a americano, -a mf. **black and white** n bianco e nero. **blackball** vt dare voto contrario a. **black belt** n cintura f nera. **blackberry** n mora f. **blackberry bush** n rovo m. **blackbird** n merlo m. **blackboard** n Sch lavagna f. **black box** n Aeron scatola f nera. **black bread** n pane m nero. **blackcurrant** n ribes m inv nero
blacken /'blækən/ vt annerire
black: black eye n occhio m nero. **Black Forest gateau** n dolce m a base di cioccolato, panna e ciliegie. **black gold** n fam oro m nero
blackguard /'blægəd/ n hum brigante m
black: blackhead n Med punto m nero. **black-headed gull** n gabbiano m comune. **black humour** umorismo m nero. **black ice** n ghiaccio m (sulla strada)
blacking /'blækɪŋ/ (Br: boycotting) boicottaggio m; (polish) lucido m nero (per scarpe)
blackish /'blækɪʃ/ a nerastro
black: blackjack n blackjack m. **blackleg** n Br crumiro m. **blacklist** vt mettere sulla lista nera. **blackmail** n ricatto m ● vt ricattare. **blackmailer** n ricattatore, -trice mf. **black mark** n fig neo m. **black market** n borsa f

nera. **black marketeer** n borsanerista mf. **black mass** n messa f nera
blackness /'blæknɪs/ n nero m; (evilness) cattiveria f; (of moods) scontrosità f
black: black-out n blackout m inv; **have a ~** Med perdere coscienza. **black pepper** n pepe m nero. **black pudding** n ≈ sanguinaccio m. **Black Sea** n Mar m Nero. **Blackshirt** n camicia f nera. **blacksmith** n fabbro m. **black sheep** n fig pecora f nera. **black spot** n fig luogo m conosciuto per gli incidenti stradali. **black swan** n cigno m nero. **black tie** (on invitation) abito scuro. **black widow** [spider] n vedova f nera
bladder /'blædə(r)/ n Anat vescica f
blade /bleɪd/ n lama f; (of grass) filo m
blame /bleɪm/ n colpa f ● vt dare la colpa a; **~ sb for doing sth** dare la colpa a qcno per aver fatto qcsa; **no one is to ~** non è colpa di nessuno
blameless /'bleɪmlɪs/ a innocente
blameworthy /'bleɪmwɜ:ðɪ/ a biasimevole
blanch /blɑ:ntʃ/ vi sbiancare ● vt Culin sbollentare
blancmange /blə'mɒnʒ/ n biancomangiare m
bland /blænd/ a ⟨food⟩ insipido; ⟨person⟩ insulso
blandly /'blændlɪ/ adv ⟨say⟩ in modo piatto
blank /blæŋk/ a bianco; ⟨look⟩ vuoto ● n spazio m vuoto; (cartridge) cartuccia f a salve
blank cheque n assegno m in bianco
blanket /'blæŋkɪt/ n coperta f; **wet ~** fam guastafeste mf inv
blanket: blanket box, blanket chest n Br cassapanca f. **blanket cover** n (in insurance) assicurazione f che copre tutti i rischi. **blanket stitch** n punto m di rinforzo
blankly /'blæŋklɪ/ adv (uncomprehendingly) con espressione attonita; (without expression) senza espressione
blank verse n versi mpl sciolti
blare /bleə(r)/ vi suonare a tutto volume
■ **blare out** vt strombazzare rumorosamente
blarney /'blɑ:nɪ/ n fam lusinga f
blasé /'blɑ:zeɪ/ a blasé inv
blaspheme /blæs'fi:m/ vi bestemmiare
blasphemous /'blæsfəməs/ a blasfemo
blasphemy /'blæsfəmɪ/ n bestemmia f
blast /blɑ:st/ n (gust) raffica f; (sound) scoppio m ● vt (with explosive) far saltare ● int sl maledizione!
blasted /'blɑ:stɪd/ a sl maledetto
blast furnace n altoforno m
blasting /'blɑ:stɪŋ/ n brillamento m
blast-off n (of missile) lancio m
blatant /'bleɪtənt/ a sfacciato
blatantly /'bleɪtəntlɪ/ adv ⟨copy, disregard⟩ sfacciatamente; **it's ~ obvious** è lampante
blather /'blæðə(r)/ vi fam blaterare
blaze /bleɪz/ n incendio m; **a ~ of colour** un'esplosione f di colori ● vi ardere
■ **blaze down** vi ⟨sun:⟩ essere cocente
blazer /'bleɪzə(r)/ n blazer m inv

bleach /bliːtʃ/ n decolorante m; (for cleaning) candeggina f, varechina f ● vt sbiancare; ossigenare ⟨hair⟩

bleak /bliːk/ a desolato; ⟨fig: prospects, future⟩ tetro

bleakly /ˈbliːklɪ/ adv ⟨stare, say⟩ in modo tetro

bleakness /ˈbliːknɪs/ n (of weather) tetraggine f; (of surroundings, future) desolazione f

bleary-eyed /blɪərɪˈaɪd/ a **be** ~ avere gli occhi gonfi

bleat /bliːt/ vi belare ● n belato m

bleed /bliːd/ v (pt/pp **bled**) ● vi sanguinare ● vt spurgare ⟨brakes, radiator⟩

bleeding /ˈbliːdɪŋ/ n perdita di sangue f; (heavy) emorragia f; (deliberate) salasso m ● a ⟨wound, hand⟩ sanguinante; sl = **bloody**

bleeding heart n fig pej cuore m troppo tenero

bleep /bliːp/ n bip m ● vi suonare ● vt chiamare col cercapersone

bleeper /ˈbliːpə(r)/ n cercapersone m inv

blemish /ˈblemɪʃ/ n macchia f

blend /blend/ n (of tea, coffee, whisky) miscela f; (of colours) insieme m ● vt mescolare ● vi ⟨colours, sounds:⟩ fondersi (**with** con)

blender /ˈblendə(r)/ n Culin frullatore m

blending /ˈblendɪŋ/ n (of coffees, whiskies) miscela f

bless /bles/ vt benedire

blessed /ˈblesɪd/ a also sl benedetto

blessing /ˈblesɪŋ/ n benedizione f

blew /bluː/ see **blow²**

blight /blaɪt/ n Bot ruggine f ● vt far avvizzire ⟨plants⟩

blighter /ˈblaɪtə(r)/ (Br fam: annoying person) idiota mf; **you lucky** ~ hai una fortuna sfacciata!; **poor** ~ povero diavolo m

blimey /ˈblaɪmɪ/ int Br fam accidenti!

blind /blaɪnd/ a cieco; ~ **man/woman** cieco/cieca ● npl **the** ~ i ciechi ● vt accecare ● n [**roller**] ~ avvolgibile m; [**Venetian**] ~ veneziana f

blind: blind alley n vicolo m cieco. **blind date** n appuntamento m galante con una persona sconosciuta. **blind drunk** a ubriaco fradicio. **blindfold** adv con gli occhi bendati ● a **be** ~ avere gli occhi bendati ● n benda f ● vt bendare gli occhi a

blinding /ˈblaɪndɪŋ/ a ⟨light⟩ accecante; ⟨headache⟩ da impazzire, tremendo

blindingly /ˈblaɪndɪŋlɪ/ adv ⟨shine⟩ in modo accecante; **be** ~ **obvious** essere così lampante

blindly /ˈblaɪndlɪ/ adv ciecamente

blind-man's buff n moscacieca f

blindness /ˈblaɪndnɪs/ n cecità f

blind spot n (in car, on hill) punto m privo di visibilità; (in eye) punto m cieco; (fig: point of ignorance) punto m debole

blink /blɪŋk/ vi sbattere le palpebre; ⟨light:⟩ tremolare

blinkered /ˈblɪŋkəd/ a ⟨fig: attitude, approach⟩ ottuso; **be** ~ avere i paraocchi

blinkers /ˈblɪŋkəz/ npl paraocchi mpl

blinking /ˈblɪŋkɪŋ/ n (of light) intermittenza f; (of eye) battere m

blip /blɪp/ n (on screen) segnale m luminoso a intermittenza; (on graph, line) piccola irregolarità f; (sound) ticchettio m; (hitch) intoppo m

bliss /blɪs/ n Rel beatitudine f; (happiness) felicità f

blissful /ˈblɪsfʊl/ a beato; (happy) meraviglioso

blissfully /ˈblɪsfəlɪ/ adv beatamente; ~ **ignorant** beatamente ignaro

blister /ˈblɪstə(r)/ n Med vescica f; (in paint) bolla f ● vi ⟨paint:⟩ formare una bolla/delle bolle

blistering /ˈblɪst(ə)rɪŋ/ n (of skin) vescica f; (of paint) bolle fpl ● a ⟨sun⟩ scottante; ⟨heat⟩ soffocante; ⟨attack, criticism⟩ feroce

blister pack n blister m inv

blithe /blaɪð/ a (cheerful) gioioso; (nonchalant) spensierato

blithely /ˈblaɪðlɪ/ adv (nonchalantly) spensieratamente

blitz /blɪts/ n bombardamento m aereo; **have a** ~ **on sth** fig darci sotto con qcsa

blitzkrieg /ˈblɪtskriːg/ n guerra f lampo

blizzard /ˈblɪzəd/ n tormenta f

bloated /ˈbləʊtɪd/ a gonfio

blob /blɒb/ n goccia f

bloc /blɒk/ n Pol blocco m

block /blɒk/ n blocco m; (building) isolato m; (building ~) cubo m (per giochi di costruzione); ~ **of flats** palazzo m ● vt bloccare

■ **block up** vt bloccare

blockade /blɒˈkeɪd/ n blocco m ● vt bloccare

blockage /ˈblɒkɪdʒ/ n ostruzione f

block: block and tackle n paranco m. **block book** vt prenotare in blocco. **block booking** n prenotazione f in blocco. **blockbuster** n (fam: book, film) successone m; Mil bomba f potente. **block capital** n **in** ~ **~s** in stampatello. **blockhead** n fam testone, -a mf. **blockhouse** n Mil fortino m. **block letters** npl stampatello m. **block vote** n voto m per delega. **block voting** n votazione f per delega

bloke /bləʊk/ n fam tizio m

blonde /blɒnd/ a biondo ● n bionda f

blood /blʌd/ n sangue m

blood: blood-and-thunder a ⟨novel, film⟩ pieno di sangue. **blood bank** n banca f del sangue. **blood bath** n bagno m di sangue. **blood blister** n vescica f di sangue. **blood brother** n fratello m di sangue. **blood cell, blood corpuscle** n globulo m. **blood count** n esame m emocromocitometrico. **blood-curdling** a raccapricciante. **blood donor** n donatore, -trice mf di sangue. **blood group** n gruppo m sanguigno. **bloodhound** n segugio m

bloodless /ˈblʌdlɪs/ a (pale) esangue; ⟨revolution, coup⟩ senza spargimento di sangue

blood: blood-letting n Med salasso m; (killing) spargimento m di sangue. **blood lust** n sete f di sangue. **blood money** n compenso versato ad un killer o delatore. **blood**

orange *n* arancia *f* sanguigna. **blood poisoning** *n* setticemia *f*. **blood pressure** *n* pressione *f* del sangue. **blood-red** *a* rosso sangue *inv*. **blood relative** *n* parente *mf* consanguineo, -a. **bloodshed** *n* spargimento *m* di sangue. **bloodshot** *a* iniettato di sangue. **blood sports** *npl* sport *mpl* cruenti. **bloodstained** *a* macchiato di sangue. **bloodstream** *n* sangue *m*. **bloodsucker** *n* *also fig* sanguisuga *f*. **blood test** *n* analisi *f* del sangue. **bloodthirsty** *a* assetato di sangue. **blood transfusion** *n* trasfusione *f* del sangue. **blood type** *n* gruppo *m* sanguigno. **blood vessel** *n* vaso *m* sanguigno

bloody /'blʌdɪ/ *a* (**-ier, -iest**) insanguinato; *sl* maledetto ● *adv sl* ~ **easy/difficult** facile/difficile da matti; ~ **tired/funny** stanco/divertente da morire; **you** ~ **well will!** e, accidenti, lo farai!

bloody-minded /blʌdɪ'maɪndɪd/ *a* scorbutico

bloom /blu:m/ *n* fiore *m*; **in** ~ (*of flower*) sbocciato; (*of tree*) in fiore ● *vi* fiorire; *fig* essere in forma smagliante

bloomer /'blu:mə(r)/ *n fam* papera *f*

bloomers /'blu:məz/ *npl* mutandoni *mpl* da donna

blooming /'blu:mɪŋ/ *a fam* maledetto

blossom /'blɒsəm/ *n* fiori *mpl* (*d'albero*); (*single one*) fiore *m* ● *vi* sbocciare

■ **blossom out** *vi fig* trasformarsi

blot /blɒt/ *n also fig* macchia *f*

■ **blot out** *vt* (*pt/pp* **blotted**) *fig* cancellare

blotch /blɒtʃ/ *n* macchia *f*

blotchy /'blɒtʃɪ/ *a* chiazzato

blotter /'blɒtə(r)/ *n* tampone *m* di carta assorbente; (*Am: police*) registro *m* di polizia

blotting paper /'blɒtɪŋ/ *n* carta *f* assorbente

blotto /'blɒtəʊ/ *a fam* ubriaco fradicio

blouse /blaʊz/ *n* camicetta *f*

blow¹ /bləʊ/ *n* colpo *m*

blow² *v* (*pt* **blew**, *pp* **blown**) ● *vi* (*wind:*) soffiare; (*fuse:*) saltare ● *vt* (*fam: squander*) sperperare; ~ **one's nose** soffiarsi il naso; ~ **one's top** *fam* andare in bestia

■ **blow away** *vt* far volar via (*papers*) ● *vi* (*papers:*) volare via

■ **blow down** *vt* abbattere ● *vi* abbattersi al suolo

■ **blow off** *vt* (*wind:*) portar via ● *vi* (*hat, roof:*) volare via

■ **blow out** *vt* (*extinguish*) soffiare ● *vi* (*candle:*) spegnersi

■ **blow over** *vt* (*wind:*) buttare giù ● *vi* (*storm:*) passare; (*fig: fuss, trouble:*) dissiparsi

■ **blow up** *vt* (*inflate*) gonfiare; (*enlarge*) ingrandire (*photograph*); (*shatter by explosion*) far esplodere ● *vi* esplodere

blow: blow-by-blow *a* (*account*) particolareggiato. **blow-dry** *vt* asciugare con l'asciugacapelli. **blowfly** *n* moscone *m* (*della carne*). **blowhole** *n* (*of whale*) sfiatatoio *m*. **blowlamp** *n* fiamma *f* ossidrica

blown /bləʊn/ *see* **blow²**

blow: blowout *n Elec* corto circuito *m*; (*in oil or gas well*) fuga *f*; (*of tyre*) scoppio *m*; (*fam: meal*) abbuffata *f*. **blowpipe** *n* cerbottana *f*. **blowtorch** *n* cannello *m* ossidrico. **blow-up** *n Phot* ingrandimento *m* ● *a* (*doll, toy, dinghy*) gonfiabile

blowy /'bləʊɪ/ *a* ventoso

blowzy /'blaʊzɪ/ *a pej* (*woman*) volgarmente appariscente

blubber /'blʌbə(r)/ *n* (*of whale*) grasso *m* di balena; (*fam: of person*) ciccia *f* ● *vi fam* piagnucolare

bludgeon /'blʌdʒən/ *vt* manganellare

blue /blu:/ *a* (*pale*) celeste; (*navy*) blu *inv*; (*royal*) azzurro; **feel** ~ essere giù di corda; ~ **with cold** livido per il freddo; **once in a** ~ **moon** una volta ogni morte di papa ● *n* blu *m inv*; **have the** ~**s** essere giù di corda; **out of the** ~ inaspettatamente; **a bolt from the** ~ un fulmine a ciel sereno

blue: bluebell *n* giacinto *m* di bosco. **Blue Berets** *npl* Mil Caschi blu *mpl*. **blueberry** *n* mirtillo *m*. **blue blood** *n* sangue *m* blu. **blue-blooded** *a* di sangue blu. **bluebottle** *n* moscone *m*. **blue chip** *a* (*company*) di altissimo livello; (*investment*) sicuro. **blue-collar job** *n* lavoro *m* manuale. **blue-collar worker** *n* operaio *m*. **blue-eyed** *a* con gli occhi azzurri. **blue-eyed boy** *n Br fig fam* prediletto *m*. **blue film** *n* film *m* a luci rosse. **blue jeans** *npl* bluejeans *mpl inv*. **blue light** *n* (*on emergency vehicles*) luce *f* della sirena della macchina della polizia

blueness /'blu:nɪs/ *n* azzurro *m*

blue: blue pencil *n* go through with the ~ ~ (*censor*) censurare qcsa; (*edit*) fare una revisione di qcsa. **blueprint** *n fig* progetto *m*. **blue rinse** *n* she's had a ~ ~ si è tinta i capelli color grigio argentato. **bluestocking** *n pej* [donna] intellettualoide *f*. **blue tit** *n* cinciarella *f*. **blue whale** *n* balenottera *f* azzurra

bluff /blʌf/ *n* bluff *m inv* ● *vi* bluffare

bluish /'blu:ɪʃ/ *a* bluastro, azzurrognolo

blunder /'blʌndə(r)/ *n* gaffe *f inv* ● *vi* fare una/delle gaffe

blundering /'blʌnd(ə)rɪŋ/ *a* ~ **idiot** rimbecillito *m*

blunt /blʌnt/ *a* spuntato; (*person*) reciso

bluntly /'blʌntlɪ/ *adv* schiettamente

bluntness /'blʌntnɪs/ *n* (*of manner*) rudezza *f*; (*of person*) brutale schiettezza *f*

blur /blɜ:(r)/ *n* **it's all a** ~ *fig* è tutto confuso ● *vt* (*pt/pp* **blurred**) rendere confuso

blurb /blɜ:b/ *n* soffietto *m* editoriale

blurred /blɜ:d/ *a* (*vision, photo*) sfocato

■ **blurt out** /blɜ:t/ *vt* spifferare

blush /blʌʃ/ *n* rossore *m* ● *vi* arrossire

blusher /'blʌʃə(r)/ *n* fard *m inv*

bluster /'blʌstə(r)/ *n* (*showing off*) sbruffonata *f*

blustering /'blʌst(ə)rɪŋ/ *n* (*rage*) sfuriata *f*; (*boasting*) spacconata *f* ● *a* (*angry*) infuriato; (*boastful*) sbruffone

blustery /'blʌst(ə)rɪ/ *a* ⟨*wind*⟩ furioso; ⟨*day, weather*⟩ molto ventoso

B movie *n* film *m inv* di serie B

BO *n fam* puzza *f* di sudore

boa /'bəʊə/ *n* boa *m inv*

boa constrictor /kən'strɪktə(r)/ boa *m inv*

boar /bɔ:(r)/ *n* cinghiale *m*

board /bɔ:d/ *n* tavola *f*; (*for notices*) tabellone *m*; (*committee*) assemblea *f*; (*of directors*) consiglio *m*; ~ **of directors** consiglio *m* di amministrazione; **full ~** *Br* pensione *f* completa; **half ~** *Br* mezza pensione *f*; ~ **and lodging** vitto e alloggio *m*; **go by the ~** *fam* andare a monte ● *vt Naut, Aeron* salire a bordo di ● *vi* ⟨*passengers:*⟩ salire a bordo; ~ **with** stare a pensione da

■ **board up** *vt* sbarrare con delle assi

boarder /'bɔ:də(r)/ *n* pensionante *mf*; *Sch* convittore, -trice *mf*

board game *n* gioco *m* da tavolo

boarding /'bɔ:dɪŋ/ *n Aeron, Naut* imbarco *m*; (*by customs officer*) ispezione *f*; *Mil* abbordaggio *m*

boarding: boarding card *n* carta *f* di imbarco. **boarding house** *n* pensione *f*. **boarding party** *n* squadra *f* d'ispezione. **boarding school** *n* collegio *m*

board: board meeting *n* riunione *f* del consiglio di amministrazione. **boardroom** *n* sala *f* consiglio, sala *f* riunioni del consiglio di amministrazione. **boardwalk** *n Am* (*by sea*) lungomare *m*

boast /bəʊst/ *vi* vantarsi (**about** di) ● *vt* vantare

boaster /'bəʊstɪə(r)/ *n* sbruffone, -a *mf*

boastful /'bəʊstfʊl/ *a* vanaglorioso

boat /bəʊt/ *n* barca *f*; (*ship*) nave *f*

boater /'bəʊtə(r)/ *n* (*hat*) paglietta *f*

boat-hook *n* gaffa *f*

boathouse /'bəʊthaʊs/ *n* rimessa *f* [per imbarcazioni]

boating /'bəʊtɪŋ/ *n* canottaggio *m* ● *a* ⟨*accident*⟩ di navigazione

boating trip *n* traversata *f* per mare

boat: boatload *n* carico *m*; ~**s of tourists** navi *fpl* cariche di turisti. **boatswain** /'bəʊs(ə)n/ *n* nostromo *m*. **boatyard** *n* cantiere *m* per imbarcazioni

bob /bɒb/ *n* (*hairstyle*) caschetto *m* ● *vi* (*pt/pp* **bobbed**) (*also* ~ **up and down**) andare su e giù

bobbin /'bɒbɪn/ *n* bobina *f*

bobble hat /'bɒblhæt/ *n* berretto *m* a pompon

bobby /'bɒbɪ/ *n Br fam* poliziotto *m*

bobcat /'bɒbkæt/ *n* lince *f*

bobsleigh /'bɒbsleɪ/ *n* bob *m inv* ● *vi* andare sul bob

bode /bəʊd/ *vi* ~ **well/ill** essere di buono/cattivo augurio

bodge /bɒdʒ/ *Br* = **botch**

bodice /'bɒdɪs/ *n* corpetto *m*

bodily /'bɒdɪlɪ/ *a* fisico ● *adv* (*forcibly*) fisicamente

body /'bɒdɪ/ *n* corpo *m*; (*organization*) ente

m; (*amount: of poems etc*) quantità *f*; **over my dead ~!** *fam* devi passare prima sul mio corpo!

body: body blow *n* deal a ~ ~ **to** *fig* assestare un duro colpo a. **bodybuilder** *n* culturista *mf*. **body-building** *n* culturismo *m*. **bodyguard** *n* guardia *f* del corpo. **body heat** *n* calore *m* del corpo. **body language** *n* linguaggio *m* del corpo. **body odour** *n fam* puzza *f* di sudore. **body politic** *n* corpo *m* sociale. **body shop** *n* autocarrozzeria *f*. **body snatching** *n* furto *m* dei cadaveri. **body stocking, body suit** *n* body *m inv*. **body warmer** *n* gilet *m inv* imbottito. **bodywork** *n* *Auto* auto-carrozzeria *f*

boffin /'bɒfɪn/ *n Br fam* scienziato *m*

bog /bɒg/ *n* palude *f*

■ **bog down** *vt* (*pt/pp* **bogged**) **get ~ged down** impantanarsi

bogey /'bəʊgɪ/ *n* (*evil spirit*) spirito *m* malvagio; (*to frighten people*) spauracchio *m*

boggle /'bɒg(ə)l/ *vi* **the mind** ~**s** non posso neanche immaginarlo

boggy /'bɒgɪ/ *a* (*swampy*) paludoso; (*muddy*) fangoso

bogus /'bəʊgəs/ *a* falso

bohemian /bəʊ'hi:mɪən/ *a* ⟨*lifestyle, person*⟩ bohémien

boil[1] /bɔɪl/ *n Med* foruncolo *m*

boil[2] *n* **bring/come to the ~** portare/arrivare ad ebollizione ● *vt* [far] bollire ● *vi* bollire; (*fig: with anger*) ribollire; **the water** or **kettle's ~ing** l'acqua bolle

■ **boil away** *vi* ⟨*water:*⟩ evaporare

■ **boil down to** *vi fig* ridursi a

■ **boil over** *vi* straboccare (*bollendo*)

■ **boil up** *vt* far bollire

boiler /'bɔɪlə(r)/ *n* caldaia *f*

boiler: boiler house *n* caldaia *f*. **boiler room** *n* locale *m* per la caldaia. **boiler suit** *n* tuta *f*

boiling /'bɔɪlɪŋ/ *a* ⟨*water*⟩ bollente; **it's ~ in here!** qui si bolle!

boiling hot *a fam* ⟨*liquid*⟩ bollente; ⟨*day*⟩ torrido

boiling point *n* punto *m* di ebollizione

boisterous /'bɔɪstərəs/ *a* chiassoso

bold /bəʊld/ *a* audace ● *n Typ* neretto *m*

boldly /'bəʊldlɪ/ *adv* audacemente

boldness /'bəʊldnɪs/ *n* audacia *f*

Bolivia /bə'lɪvɪə/ *n* Bolivia *f*

bollard /'bɒlɑ:d/ *n* colonnina *m* di sbarramento al traffico

Bolognese /bɒlə'neɪz/ *n* sugo *m* al ragù

boloney /bə'ləʊnɪ/ *n fam* idiozie *fpl*

bolshy /'bɒlʃɪ/ *a Br fam* (*on one occasion*) brontolone; **he's/she's ~** (*by temperament*) è un/una piantagrane; **get ~** fare [delle] storie

bolster /'bəʊlstə(r)/ *n* cuscino *m* (*lungo e rotondo*) ● *vt* ~ [**up**] sostenere

bolt /bəʊlt/ *n* (*for door*) catenaccio *m*; (*for fixing*) bullone *m* ● *vt* fissare [con bulloni] (**to** a); chiudere col chiavistello ⟨*door*⟩; ingurgitare ⟨*food*⟩ ● *vi* svignarsela; ⟨*horse:*⟩ scappar via ● *adv* ~ **upright** diritto come un fuso

bolt-hole *n Br* rifugio *m*
bomb /bɒm/ *n* bomba *f* ● *vt* bombardare
■ **bomb along** *vi* (*fam: move quickly*) sfrecciare
bombard /bɒm'bɑːd/ *vt also fig* bombardare
bombardment /bɒm'bɑːdmənt/ *n* bombardamento *m*
bombastic /bɒm'bæstɪk/ *a* ampolloso
bomb: bomb attack *n* bombardamento *m*.
bomb blast *n* esplosione *f*. **bomb disposal**
n disinnesco *m*. **bomb disposal expert** *n*
artificiere *m*. **bomb disposal squad** *n* squadra *f* artificieri
bomber /'bɒmə(r)/ *n Aviat* bombardiere *m*;
(*person*) dinamitardo *m*
bomber jacket *n* bomber *m inv*
bombing /'bɒmɪŋ/ *n Mil* bombardamento *m*;
(*by terrorists*) attentato *m* dinamitardo
bomb: bombproof *a* a prova di bomba.
bombscare *n* stato *m* di allarme per la presunta presenza di una bomba. **bombshell** *n*
(*fig: news*) bomba *f*; **blonde ~** bionda *f* esplosiva. **bomb shelter** *n* rifugio *m* antiaereo.
bombsite *n* zona *f* bombardata; (*fig: mess*)
campo *f* di battaglia. **Bomb Squad** *n* squadra
f artificieri
bona fide /bəʊnə'faɪdɪ/ *a* (*member, refugee*)
autentico; (*attempt*) genuino; (*offer*) serio
bonanza /bə'nænzə/ *n* (*windfall*) momento
m di prosperità; (*in mining*) filone *m*
d'oro/d'argento
bond /bɒnd/ *n fig* legame *m*; *Comm* obbligazione *f* ● *vt* (*glue:*) attaccare
bondage /'bɒndɪdʒ/ *n* schiavitù *f*
bonded warehouse /'bɒndɪd/ *n* magazzino *m* doganale
bonding /'bɒndɪŋ/ *n* (*between mother and
baby*) legame *m* madre-figlio; **male ~** solidarietà *f* maschile
bone /bəʊn/ *n* osso *m*; (*of fish*) spina *f* ● *vt*
disossare (*meat*); togliere le spine da (*fish*)
bone china *n* porcellana *f* fine
boned /bəʊnd/ *a* (*joint, leg, chicken*)
disossato; (*fish*) senza lische; (*corset, bodice*)
con le stecche
bone: bone-dry *a* secco. **bonehead** *n fam*
cretino, -a *mf*. **bone idle** *a fam* fannullone
boneless /'bəʊnlɪs/ *a* (*chicken*) disossato;
(*chicken breast*) senz'osso; (*fish*) senza lische
bone: bone marrow *n* midollo *m* osseo.
bone-marrow transplant *n* trapianto *m* di
midollo osseo. **bonemeal** *n* farina *f* d'ossa
bonfire /'bɒnfaɪə(r)/ *n* falò *m inv*
Bonfire Night *n Br* sera *f* del 5 novembre
festeggiata con falò e fuochi d'artificio
bonk /bɒŋk/ *vt sl* zompare
bonkers /'bɒŋkəz/ *a fam* suonato
bonnet /'bɒnɪt/ *n* cuffia *f*; (*of car*) cofano *m*
bonus /'bəʊnəs/ *n* (*individual*) gratifica *f*;
(*production ~*) premio *m*; (*life insurance*) dividendo *m*; **a ~** *fig* qualcosa in più
bonus point *n* **five ~ ~s** un bonus di cinque punti
bony /'bəʊnɪ/ *a* (**-ier, -iest**) ossuto; (*fish*) pieno di spine

boo /buː/ *interj* (*to surprise or frighten*) bu!
● *vt/i* fischiare
boob /buːb/ *n* (*fam: mistake*) gaffe *f inv*;
(*breast*) tetta *f* ● *vi fam* fare una gaffe
booboo /'buːbuː/ *n fam* gaffe *f inv*
booby prize /'buːbɪ/ *n* premio *m* di consolazione per il peggior contendente
booby trap *n Mil* ordigno *m* che esplode al
contatto; (*joke*) trabocchetto *m* ● *vt Mil* mettere un ordigno esplosivo in
boogie /'buːgɪ/ *n fam* boogie *m*
booing /'buːɪŋ/ *n* fischi *mpl*
book /bʊk/ *n* libro *m*; (*of tickets*) blocchetto
m; **keep the ~s** *Comm* tenere la contabilità;
be in sb's bad/good ~s essere nel libro
nero/nelle grazie di qcno; **do sth by the ~**
seguire strettamente le regole ● *vt* (*reserve*)
prenotare; (*for offence*) multare ● *vi* (*reserve*)
prenotare
bookable /'bʊkəbl/ *a* (*event, ticket*) che si
può prenotare; (*offence*) che può essere multato
book: bookbinder *n* rilegatore, -trice *mf*.
bookbinding *n* rilegatura *f*. **bookcase** *n* libreria *f*. **book club** *n* club *m inv* del libro.
book-ends *npl* reggilibri *mpl*. **book fair** *n*
fiera *f* del libro
bookie /'bʊkɪ/ *n fam* bookmaker *m inv*,
allibratore *m*
booking /'bʊkɪŋ/ *n* (*Br: reservation*) prenotazione *f*; **make a ~** fare una prenotazione; **get
a ~** (*Br: from referee*) ricevere un'ammonizione
booking: booking clerk *n Br* impiegato, -a
mf in un ufficio prenotazioni. **booking form**
n Br modulo *m* di prenotazione. **booking
office** *n* biglietteria *f*
bookish /'bʊkɪʃ/ *a* (*person*) secchione
book: book jacket *n* sopraccoperta *f*.
bookkeeper *n* contabile *mf*. **bookkeeping** *n*
contabilità *f*
booklet /'bʊklɪt/ *n* opuscolo *m*
book: book lover *n* amante *mf* della lettura.
bookmaker *n* allibratore *m*. **bookmark** *n*
segnalibro *m*. **bookplate** *n* ex libris *m inv*.
bookrest *n* leggio *m*. **bookseller** *n* libraio,
-a *mf*. **bookshelf** *n* (*single*) scaffale *f*;
(*bookcase*) libreria *f*. **bookshop** *n* libreria *f*.
bookstall *n* edicola *f*. **bookstore** *n Am* libreria *f*. **book token** *n Br* buono *m* acquisto per
libri. **bookworm** *n* topo *m* di biblioteca
boom /buːm/ *n Comm* boom *m inv*; (*upturn*)
impennata *f*; (*of thunder, gun*) rimbombo *m*
● *vi* (*thunder, gun:*) rimbombare; *fig* prosperare
boomerang /'buːməræŋ/ *n* boomerang *m*
inv ● *vi* **~ on sb** (*plan:*) ritorcersi contro
qcno
boomerang effect *n* effetto *m* boomerang
booming /'buːmɪŋ/ *a* (*sound*) sonoro; (*voice*)
tonante; (*economy*) fiorente; (*demand,
exports, sales*) in crescita
boom microphone *n* microfono *m* a stelo
boon /buːn/ *n* benedizione *f*
boor /bʊə(r)/ *n* zoticone *m*

boorish /'bʊərɪʃ/ a maleducato

boost /buːst/ n spinta f ● vt stimolare ⟨sales⟩; sollevare ⟨morale⟩; far crescere ⟨hopes⟩

booster /'buːstə(r)/ n Med dose f supplementare

boot /buːt/ n stivale m; (up to ankle) stivaletto m; (football) scarpetta f; (climbing) scarpone m; Auto portabagagli m inv ● vt Comput mettere in funzione

■ **boot out** vt fam cacciare

■ **boot up** Comput vi caricarsi ● vt caricare

boot black n lustrascarpe mf inv

boot drive n Comput unità f inv di inizializzazione

bootee /buːˈtiː/ n (knitted) babbuccia f di lana; (leather) stivaletto m

booth /buːð/ n (for phoning, voting) cabina f; (at market) bancarella f

boot: **bootlace** n laccio m, stringa f. **bootlegger** n Am contrabbandiere m di alcolici. **bootlicker** n leccapiedi mf inv. **bootmaker** n calzolaio m. **boot polish** n lucido m da scarpe. **boot scraper** n puliscipiedi m inv. **bootstrap** n (on boot) linguetta f calzastivali; Comput lancio m; **pull oneself up by one's ~s** riuscire con le proprie forze. **boot-up** n Comput boot m inv

booty /'buːtɪ/ n bottino m

booze /buːz/ n fam alcolici mpl

boozer /'buːzə(r)/ n fam (person) beone, -a mf; (Br: pub) bar m inv

booze-up n bella bevuta f

boozy /'buːzɪ/ a fam ⟨laughter⟩ da ubriaco; ⟨meal⟩ in cui si beve molto

bop /bɒp/ fam n (blow) colpo m ● vt dare un colpo a ● vi Br (dance) ballare

border /'bɔːdə(r)/ n bordo m; (frontier) frontiera f; (in garden) bordura f ● vi ~ **on** confinare con; fig essere ai confini di

border: **border dispute** n (fight) conflitto m al confine; (disagreement) contesa f sul confine. **border guard** n guardia f di frontiera. **borderline** n linea f di demarcazione; ~ **case** caso m dubbio. **border raid** n incursione f

bore[1] /bɔː(r)/ see bear[2]

bore[2] vt Techn forare

bore[3] n (of gun) calibro m; (person) seccatore, -trice mf; (thing) seccatura f ● vt annoiare

bored /bɔːd/ a annoiato, stufo; **be ~ (to tears** or **to death)** annoiarsi (da morire)

boredom /'bɔːdəm/ n noia f

boring /'bɔːrɪŋ/ a noioso

born /bɔːn/ pp **be ~** nascere; **I was ~ in 1963** sono nato nel 1963 ● a nato; **a ~ liar/actor** un bugiardo/un attore nato

born-again a convertito alla chiesa evangelica

borne /bɔːn/ see bear[2]

Borneo /'bɔːnɪəʊ/ n Borneo m

borough /'bʌrə/ n municipalità f inv

borough council n Br ≈ comune m

borrow /'bɒrəʊ/ vt prendere a prestito (**from** da); **can I ~ your pen?** mi presti la tua penna?

borrower /'bɒrəʊə(r)/ n debitore, -trice mf

borrowing /'bɒrəʊɪŋ/ n prestito m; **increase in** ~ Fin aumento m dell'indebitamento

borrowing costs n Fin costo m del denaro

borstal /'bɔːstəl/ n Br riformatorio m

Bosnia /'bɒznɪə/ n Bosnia f

Bosnia-Herzegovina /-hɜːtsəgəʊ'viːnə/ n Bosnia-Erzegovina f

Bosnian /'bɒznɪən/ a & n bosniaco, -a mf

bosom /'bʊzm/ n seno m

bosom buddy, bosom friend n fam amico, -a mf del cuore

boss /bɒs/ n direttore, -trice mf ● vt (also ~ **about**) comandare a bacchetta

bossy /'bɒsɪ/ a autoritario

bosun /'bəʊsən/ n nostromo m

botanical /bə'tænɪkl/ a botanico

botanist /'bɒtənɪst/ n botanico, -a mf

botany /'bɒtənɪ/ n botanica f

botch /bɒtʃ/ vt fare un pasticcio con

both /bəʊθ/ a & pron tutti e due, entrambi ● adv ~ **men and women** entrambi uomini e donne; ~ [**of**] **the children** tutti e due i bambini; **they are ~ dead** sono morti entrambi; ~ **of them** tutti e due

bother /'bɒðə(r)/ n preoccupazione f; (minor trouble) fastidio m; **it's no ~** non c'è problema ● int fam che seccatura! ● vt (annoy) dare fastidio a; (disturb) disturbare ● vi preoccuparsi (**about** di); **don't ~** lascia perdere

Botswana /bɒt'swaːnə/ n Botswana m

bottle /'bɒt(ə)l/ n bottiglia f; (baby's) biberon m inv ● vt imbottigliare

■ **bottle up** vt fig reprimere

bottle: **bottle bank** n contenitore m per la raccolta del vetro. **bottle-feed** vt allattare col biberon. **bottle-feeding** n allattamento m col biberon. **bottle green** a & n verde m bottiglia inv. **bottleneck** n fig ingorgo m. **bottle-opener** n apribottiglie m inv. **bottle top** n tappo m di bottiglia. **bottle-washer** n hum **chief cook and ~** tuttofare mf inv

bottom /'bɒtm/ a ultimo; **the ~ shelf** l'ultimo scaffale in basso ● n (of container) fondo m; (of river) fondale m; (of hill) piedi mpl; (buttocks) sedere m; **at the ~** in fondo; **at the ~ of the page** in fondo alla pagina; **get to the ~ of** fig vedere cosa c'è sotto

■ **bottom out** vi ⟨inflation, unemployment etc.⟩ assestarsi

bottom drawer n fig corredo m

bottom gear n Br Auto prima f

bottomless /'bɒtəmlɪs/ a senza fondo

bottom line n Fin utile m; **that's the ~ ~** (decisive factor) la questione è tutta qui

botulism /'bɒtjʊlɪzm/ n botulismo m

bouffant /'buːfɒ̃/ a ⟨hair, hairstyle⟩ cotonato; ⟨sleeve⟩ a sbuffo

bough /baʊ/ n ramoscello m

bought /bɔːt/ see buy

boulder /'bəʊldə(r)/ n masso m

bounce /baʊns/ vi rimbalzare; ⟨fam: cheque:⟩ essere respinto ● vt far rimbalzare ⟨ball⟩

■ **bounce back** vi fig riprendersi

bouncer /'baʊnsə(r)/ n fam buttafuori m inv

bouncy /'baʊnsɪ/ a ⟨ball⟩ che rimbalza bene; ⟨mattress, walk⟩ molleggiato; ⟨fig: person⟩ esuberante

bound¹ /baʊnd/ n balzo m ● vi balzare

bound² see bind ● a ~ for ⟨ship⟩ diretto a; **be ~ to do** (likely) dovere fare per forza; (obliged) essere costretto a fare

boundary /'baʊndərɪ/ n limite m

boundless /'baʊndlɪs/ a illimitato

bounds /baʊndz/ npl fig limiti mpl; **out of ~** fuori dai limiti

bounty /'baʊntɪ/ n (gift) dono m; (generosity) munificenza f

bounty hunter n cacciatore m di taglie

bouquet /bʊ'keɪ/ n mazzo m di fiori; (of wine) bouquet m

bourbon /'bʊəbən/ n bourbon m inv

bourgeois /'bʊəʒwɑː/ a pej borghese

bourgeoisie /bʊəʒwɑː'ziː/ n borghesia f

bout /baʊt/ n Med attacco m; Sport incontro m

boutique /buː'tiːk/ n negozio m; **fashion ~** negozio m di abbigliamento

bovine /'bəʊvaɪn/ a bovino

bow¹ /bəʊ/ n (weapon) arco m; Mus archetto m; (knot) nodo m

bow² /baʊ/ n inchino m ● vi inchinarsi ● vt piegare ⟨head⟩

bow³ /baʊ/ n Naut prua f

■ **bow out** vi (withdraw) ritirarsi (of da)

bowel /'baʊəl/ n intestino m; **have a ~ movement** andare di corpo; **~s** pl intestini mpl

bower /'baʊə(r)/ n (in garden) pergolato m; (liter: chamber) salottino m

bowl¹ /bəʊl/ n (for soup, cereal) scodella f; (of pipe) fornello m

bowl² n (ball) boccia f ● vt lanciare ● vi Cricket servire; (in bowls) lanciare

■ **bowl along** vi (in car etc) andare spedito

■ **bowl over** vt buttar giù; (fig: leave speechless) lasciar senza parole

bow-legged /bəʊ'legd/ a dalle gambe storte

bowler¹ /'bəʊlə(r)/ n Cricket lanciatore m; Bowls giocatore m di bocce

bowler² n ~ [**hat**] bombetta f

bowling /'bəʊlɪŋ/ n gioco m delle bocce

bowling alley /'bəʊlɪŋælɪ/ n pista f da bowling

bowling green n prato m da bocce

bowls /bəʊlz/ n gioco m delle bocce

bow /bəʊ/: **bowstring** n corda f d'arco. **bow tie** n cravatta f a farfalla. **bow window** n bow window f inv

box¹ /bɒks/ n scatola f; Theat palco m

box² vi Sport fare il pugile ● vt ~ **sb's ears** dare uno scapaccione a qcno

boxer /'bɒksə(r)/ n pugile m

boxer shorts npl boxer mpl

boxing /'bɒksɪŋ/ n pugilato m

Boxing Day n Br [giorno m di] Santo Stefano m

box: box number n casella f. **box office** n

Theat botteghino m. **boxroom** n Br sgabuzzino m. **boxwood** n bosso m

boy /bɔɪ/ n ragazzo m; (younger) bambino m

boycott /'bɔɪkɒt/ n boicottaggio m ● vt boicottare

boyfriend /'bɔɪfrend/ n ragazzo m

boyhood /'bɔɪhʊd/ n (childhood) infanzia f; (adolescence) adolescenza f

boyish /'bɔɪʃ/ a da ragazzino

boy scout n boy scout m inv

BR abbr (**British Rail**) ente m ferroviario britannico, ≈ FS

bra /brɑː/ n reggiseno m

brace /breɪs/ n sostegno m; (dental) apparecchio m ● vt ~ **oneself** fig farsi forza (**for** per affrontare)

bracelet /'breɪslɪt/ n braccialetto m

braces /'breɪsɪz/ npl bretelle fpl

bracing /'breɪsɪŋ/ a tonificante

bracken /'brækn/ n felce f

bracket /'brækɪt/ n mensola f; (group) categoria f; Typ parentesi f inv ● vt mettere fra parentesi

brackish /'brækɪʃ/ a salmastro

bradawl /'brædɔːl/ n punteruolo m

brag /bræg/ vi (pt/pp **bragged**) vantarsi (**about** di)

bragging /'brægɪŋ/ n vanterie fpl

Brahmin /'brɑːmɪn/ n Relig bramino m

braid /breɪd/ n (edging) passamano m

braille /breɪl/ n braille m

brain /breɪn/ n cervello m; **~s** pl fig testa f sg

brain: brainbox n fam capoccione m. **brainchild** n invenzione f personale. **brain damage** n lesione f cerebrale. **brain-dead** a Med cerebralmente morto; fig senza cervello. **brain death** n morte f cerebrale. **brain drain** n fuga f di cervelli

brainless /'breɪnlɪs/ a senza cervello

brain: brain scan n scan m inv del cervello. **brain scanner** n scanner m inv (per il cervello). **brainstorm** n Med, fig accesso m di pazzia; (Am: brainwave) lampo m di genio. **brainstorming session** n brain-storming m inv. **brains trust** n brains-trust m inv, gruppo m di esperti. **brain surgeon** n neurochirurgo m. **brain surgery** n chirurgia f cerebrale. **brain teaser** n fam rompicapo m. **brainwash** vt fare il lavaggio del cervello a. **brainwashing** n lavaggio m del cervello. **brainwave** n lampo m di genio

brainy /'breɪnɪ/ a (**-ier, -iest**) intelligente

braise /breɪz/ vt brasare

brake /breɪk/ n freno m ● vi frenare

brake: brake block n pastiglia f. **brake disc** n disco m dei freni. **brake drum** n tamburo m del freno. **brake fluid** n liquido m dei freni. **brake-light** n stop m inv. **brake lining** n guarnizione f del freno. **brake pad** n ganascia f del freno. **brake pedal** n pedale m del freno

bramble /'bræmb(ə)l/ n rovo m; (fruit) mora f

bran /bræn/ n crusca f

branch /brɑːntʃ/ n also fig ramo m; Comm

succursale *f*, filiale *f*; *(of bank)* agenzia *f*; **our Oxford St** ~ *(of store)* il negozio di Oxford St ● *vi* ⟨*road*⟩ biforcarsi

■ **branch off** *vi* biforcarsi

■ **branch out** *vi* ~ **out into** allargare le proprie attività nel ramo di

branch: branch line *n* linea *f* secondaria.
branch manager *n* *(of bank)* direttore, -trice *mf* di agenzia; *(of company)* direttore, -trice *mf* di filiale; *(of shop)* direttore, -trice *mf* di succursale. **branch office** *n* filiale *f*; *(of bank)* agenzia *f*

brand /brænd/ *n* marca *f*; *(on animal)* marchio *m* ● *vt* marcare ⟨*animal*⟩; *fig* tacciare (**as** di)

brand image *n* immagine *f* della marca

brandish /'brændɪʃ/ *vt* brandire

brand: brand leader *n* marca *f* leader *inv*.
brand name *n* marca *f*. **brand-new** *a* nuovo fiammante

brandy /'brændɪ/ *n* brandy *m inv*

brash /bræʃ/ *a* sfrontato

brass /brɑːs/ *n* ottone *m*; **the** ~ *Mus* gli ottoni *mpl*; **top** ~ *fam* pezzi *mpl* grossi

brass band *n* banda *f* (*di soli ottoni*)

brassiere /'bræzɪə(r)/ *n fml, Am* reggipetto *m*

brass: brass instrument *n* *Mus* ottone *m*.
brass neck *n* *Br fam* faccia *f* tosta. **brass rubbing** *n* ricalco *m* di iscrizione tombale o commemorativa

brassy /'brɑːsɪ/ *a* (**-ier, -iest**) *fam* volgare

brat /bræt/ *n pej* marmocchio, -a *mf*

bravado /brə'vɑːdəʊ/ *n* bravata *f*

brave /breɪv/ *a* coraggioso ● *vt* affrontare

bravely /'breɪvlɪ/ *adv* con coraggio

bravery /'breɪvərɪ/ *n* coraggio *m*

bravo /brɑː'vəʊ/ *int* bravo!

bravura /brə'vjʊərə/ *n* virtuosismo *m*

brawl /brɔːl/ *n* rissa *f* ● *vi* azzuffarsi

brawn /brɔːn/ *n Culin* ≈ soppressata *f*

brawny /'brɔːnɪ/ *a* muscoloso

brazen /'breɪzn/ *a* sfrontato

brazier /'breɪzɪə(r)/ *n* braciere *m*

Brazil /brə'zɪl/ *n* Brasile *m*

Brazilian /brə'zɪlɪən/ *a & n* brasiliano, -a *mf*

Brazil [**nut**] *n* noce *f* del Brasile

breach /briːtʃ/ *n* *(of law)* violazione *f*; *(gap)* breccia *f*; *(fig: in party)* frattura *f* ● *vt* recedere ⟨*contract*⟩

breach: breach of contract *n Jur* inadempienza *f* contrattuale. **breach of promise** *n Jur* inadempienza *f* a una promessa di matrimonio. **breach of the peace** *n Jur* violazione *f* dell'ordine pubblico. **breach of trust** *n Jur* abuso *m* di fiducia

bread /bred/ *n* pane *m*; **a slice of** ~ **and butter** una fetta di pane imburrato

bread: breadbasket *n* cestino *m* per il pane; *fig* granaio *m*. **breadbin** *n Br* cassetta *f* portapane *inv*. **breadboard** *n* tagliere *m* per il pane. **breadcrumbs** *npl* briciole *fpl*; *Culin* pangrattato *m*. **breadfruit** *n* frutto *m* dell'albero del pane. **breadknife** *n* coltello *m* per il pane. **breadline** *n* **be on the** ~ essere povero

in canna. **bread roll** *n* panino *m*. **breadstick** *n* filoncino *m*

breadth /bredθ/ *n* larghezza *f*

breadwinner /'bredwɪnə(r)/ *n* quello, -a *mf* che porta il soldi a casa

break /breɪk/ *n* rottura *f*; *(interval)* intervallo *m*; *(interruption)* interruzione *f*; *(fam: chance)* opportunità *f inv* ● *v* (*pt* **broke**, *pp* **broken**) ● *vt* rompere; *(interrupt)* interrompere; ~ **one's arm** rompersi un braccio ● *vi* rompersi; ⟨*day*⟩ spuntare; ⟨*storm*⟩ scoppiare; ⟨*news*⟩ diffondersi; ⟨*boy's voice*⟩ cambiare

■ **break away** *vi* scappare; *fig* chiudere (**from** con)

■ **break down** *vi* ⟨*machine, car*⟩ guastarsi; ⟨*negotiations*⟩ interrompersi; *(in tears)* scoppiare in lacrime ● *vt* sfondare ⟨*door*⟩; ripartire ⟨*figures*⟩

■ **break in** *vi* ⟨*burglar*⟩ introdursi

■ **break into** *vt* introdursi con la forza in; forzare ⟨*car*⟩

■ **break off** *vt* rompere ⟨*engagement*⟩ ● *vi* ⟨*part of whole*⟩ rompersi; *(when speaking)* interrompersi

■ **break out** *vi* ⟨*argument, war*⟩ scoppiare

■ **break through** *vi* ⟨*sun*⟩ spuntare

■ **break up** *vt* far cessare ⟨*fight*⟩; disperdere ⟨*crowd*⟩ ● *vi* ⟨*crowd*⟩ disperdersi; ⟨*marriage*⟩ naufragare; ⟨*couple*⟩ separarsi; *Sch* iniziare le vacanze

breakable /'breɪkəbl/ *a* fragile

breakage /'breɪkɪdʒ/ *n* rottura *f*

breakaway /'breɪkəweɪ/ *n* *(from person)* separazione *f*, allontanamento *m*; *(from organization)* scissione *f*; *Sport* contropiede *m* ● *attrib* ⟨*faction, group, state*⟩ separatista

breakdown /'breɪkdaʊn/ *n* *(of car, machine)* guasto *m*; *Med* esaurimento *m* nervoso; *(of figures)* analisi *f inv*

breaker /'breɪkə(r)/ *n* *(wave)* frangente *m*

breaker's yard *n* *Auto* cimitero *m* delle macchine

break-even *n* pareggio *m*

break-even point *n* punto *m* di pareggio, punto *m* di equilibrio

breakfast /'brekfəst/ *n* [prima] colazione *f*

breakfast: breakfast bar *n* tavolo *m* a penisola. **breakfast bowl** *n* scodella *f* per i cereali. **breakfast cereals** *npl* cereali *mpl* per la colazione. **breakfast television** *n* programmi *mpl* televisivi del mattino

break-in *n* irruzione *f*

breaking /'breɪkɪŋ/ *n* *(of glass, seal, contract)* rottura *f*; *(of bone)* frattura *f*; *(of law, treaty)* violazione *f*; *(of voice)* cambiamento *m*; *(of promise)* venuta *f* meno; *(of horse)* domatura *f*; *(of link, sequence, tie)* interruzione *f*

breaking and entering /breɪkɪŋənd'entərɪŋ/ *n Jur* effrazione *f* con scasso

breaking point *n Techn* punto *m* di rottura; *fig* limite *m* di sopportazione

break: breakneck *a* ⟨*pace, speed*⟩ a rotta di collo. **break-out** *n* *(from prison)* evasione *f*.
breakpoint *n Tennis* breakpoint *m inv*.

breakthrough n (*discovery*) scoperta f; (*in negotiations*) passo m avanti. **break-up** n (*of family, company*) disgregazione f; (*of alliance, relationship*) rottura f; (*of marriage*) dissoluzione f. **breakwater** n frangiflutti m inv

breast /brest/ n seno m

breast: breastbone n sterno m. **breastfeed** vt allattare al seno. **breast pocket** n taschino m. **breast-stroke** n nuoto m a rana

breath /breθ/ n respiro m, fiato m; **out of ~** senza fiato; **under one's ~** sottovoce; **a ~ of air** un filo d'aria

breathalyse /'breθəlaɪz/ vt sottoporre alla prova del palloncino

breathalyser® /'breθəlaɪzə(r)/ n Br alcoltest m inv

breathe /bri:ð/ vt/i respirare; **~ a sigh of relief** tirare un sospiro di sollievo

■ **breathe in** vi inspirare ● vt respirare ‹scent, air›

■ **breathe out** vt/i espirare

breather /'bri:ðə(r)/ n pausa f

breathing /'bri:ðɪŋ/ n respirazione f

breathing apparatus n respiratore m

breathing space n (*respite*) tregua f; **give oneself a ~** riprendere fiato

breathless /'breθlɪs/ a senza fiato

breathlessly /'breθlɪslɪ/ adv senza fiato

breathtaking /'breθteɪkɪŋ/ a mozzafiato

breathtakingly /'breθteɪkɪŋlɪ/ adv **~ audacious** di un'audacia stupefacente; **~ beautiful** di una bellezza mozzafiato

breath test n prova f del palloncino

bred /bred/ *see* **breed**

breech /bri:tʃ/ n Med natiche fpl; (*of gun*) culatta f

breed /bri:d/ n razza f ● v (*pt/pp* **bred**) ● vt allevare; (*give rise to*) generare ● vi riprodursi

breeder /'bri:də(r)/ n allevatore, -trice mf

breeding /'bri:dɪŋ/ n allevamento m; fig educazione f

breeding ground n zona f di riproduzione; fig terreno m fertile

breeding period, breeding season n stagione f di riproduzione

breeze /bri:z/ n brezza f

breeze block n Br mattone m fatto con scorie di coke

breezily /'bri:zɪlɪ/ adv (*confidently*) con sicurezza; (*casually*) con disinvoltura; (*cheerfully*) allegramente

breezy /'bri:zɪ/ a ventoso

brevity /'brevətɪ/ n brevità f

brew /bru:/ n infuso m ● vt mettere in infusione ‹tea›; produrre ‹beer› ● vi fig ‹trouble:› essere nell'aria

brewer /'brʊə(r)/ n birraio m

brewery /'brʊərɪ/ n fabbrica f di birra

brew-up n Br fam tè m inv

briar /'braɪə(r)/ n rosa f selvatica; (*heather*) erica f; (*thorns*) rovo m; (*pipe*) n pipa f in radica

bribe /braɪb/ n (*money*) bustarella f; (*large sum of money*) tangente f ● vt corrompere

bribery /'braɪbərɪ/ n corruzione f

brick /brɪk/ n mattone m

■ **brick up** vt murare

brick: brickbat n fig critica f spietata. **brick-built** a di mattoni. **bricklayer** n muratore m. **bricklaying** n muratura f. **brick red** a rosso mattone inv. **brickwork** n muratura f di mattoni. **brickworks** n fabbrica f di mattoni

bridal /'braɪdl/ a nuziale

bridal: bridal party n corteo m nuziale. **bridal suite** n camera f nuziale. **bridal wear** n confezioni fpl da sposa

bride /braɪd/ n sposa f

bridegroom /'braɪdgru:m/ n sposo m

bridesmaid /'braɪdzmeɪd/ n damigella f d'onore

bridge¹ /brɪdʒ/ n ponte m; (*of nose*) setto m nasale; (*of spectacles*) ponticello m ● vt fig colmare ‹gap›

bridge² n Cards bridge m

bridge-building n costruzione f di ponti provvisori; fig mediazione f

bridging loan /'brɪdʒɪŋ/ n Br Fin prefinanziamento m, credito m provvisorio

bridle /'braɪd(ə)l/ n briglia f

bridle track, bridleway /'braɪd(ə)lweɪ/ n sentiero m per cavalli

brief¹ /bri:f/ a breve; **in ~** in breve

brief² n istruzioni fpl; (*Jur: case*) causa f ● vt dare istruzioni a; *Jur* affidare la causa a

briefcase /'bri:fkeɪs/ n cartella f

briefing /'bri:fɪŋ/ n briefing m inv

briefly /'bri:flɪ/ adv brevemente; **briefly,...** in breve,...

briefness /'bri:fnɪs/ n brevità f

briefs /bri:fs/ npl slip m inv

brigade /brɪ'geɪd/ n brigata f

brigadier /brɪgə'dɪə(r)/ n generale m di brigata

bright /braɪt/ a ‹metal, idea› brillante; ‹day, room, future› luminoso; (*clever*) intelligente; **~ red** rosso m acceso

brighten /'braɪt(ə)n/ v **~ [up]** ● vt ravvivare; rallegrare ‹person› ● vi ‹weather:› schiarirsi; ‹face:› illuminarsi; ‹person:› rallegrarsi

brightly /'braɪtlɪ/ adv ‹shine› intensamente; ‹smile› allegramente

brightness /'braɪtnɪs/ n luminosità f; (*intelligence*) intelligenza f

bright spark n Br fam genio m

bright young things npl Br i giovani di belle speranze

brill /brɪl/ n Zool rombo m liscio ● a Br fam fantastico

brilliance /'brɪljəns/ n luminosità f; (*of person*) genialità f

brilliant /'brɪljənt/ a (*very good*) eccezionale; (*very intelligent*) brillante; ‹sunshine› splendente

brilliantly /'brɪljəntlɪ/ adv ‹shine› intensamente; ‹perform› in modo eccezionale

Brillo pad® /'brɪləʊ/ n paglietta f d'acciaio

brim /brɪm/ n bordo m; (*of hat*) tesa f

■ **brim over** vi (*pt/pp* **brimmed**) traboccare

brine /braɪn/ n salamoia f

bring /brɪŋ/ vt (pt/pp **brought**) portare ⟨person, object⟩

■ **bring about** vt causare

■ **bring along** vt portare [con sé]

■ **bring back** vt restituire ⟨sth borrowed⟩; reintrodurre ⟨hanging⟩; fare ritornare in mente ⟨memories⟩

■ **bring down** vt portare giù; fare cadere ⟨government⟩; fare abbassare ⟨price⟩

■ **bring in** vt introdurre ⟨legislation⟩; **his job ~s in £30,000 a year** guadagna 30 000 sterline all'anno

■ **bring off** vt ~ **sth off** riuscire a fare qcsa

■ **bring on** vt ⟨cause⟩ provocare

■ **bring out** vt ⟨emphasize⟩ mettere in evidenza; pubblicare ⟨book⟩

■ **bring round** vt portare; ⟨persuade⟩ convincere; far rinvenire ⟨unconscious person⟩

■ **bring up** vt ⟨vomit⟩ rimettere; allevare ⟨children⟩; tirare fuori ⟨question, subject⟩

bring and buy sale n Br vendita f di beneficenza

brink /brɪŋk/ n orlo m; **on the ~ of disaster** sull'orlo del disastro

brinkmanship /'brɪŋkmənʃɪp/ n strategia f del rischio calcolato

brisk /brɪsk/ a svelto; ⟨person⟩ sbrigativo; ⟨trade, business⟩ redditizio; ⟨walk⟩ a passo spedito

brisket /'brɪskɪt/ n Culin punta f di petto

briskly /'brɪsklɪ/ adv velocemente; ⟨say⟩ frettolosamente; ⟨walk⟩ di buon passo

bristle /'brɪsl/ n setola f ● vi **bristling with** pieno di

bristly /'brɪslɪ/ a ⟨chin⟩ ispido

Britain /'brɪtn/ n Gran Bretagna f

British /'brɪtɪʃ/ a britannico; ⟨ambassador⟩ della Gran Bretagna ● npl **the ~** il popolo britannico

British: British Airports Authority n ente m che gestisce gli aeroporti britannici. **British Broadcasting Corporation** n ente m radiotelevisivo nazionale britannico. **British Columbia** n Columbia f Britannica

Britisher /'brɪtɪʃə(r)/ n Am britannico, -a mf

British: British Gas n Br società f del gas britannica. **British Isles** npl Isole fpl Britanniche. **British Rail** n ente m ferroviario britannico. **British Telecom** n Br società f britannica di telecomunicazioni

Briton /'brɪtən/ n cittadino, -a britannico, -a mf

Brittany /'brɪtənɪ/ n Bretagna f

brittle /'brɪtl/ a fragile

brittle-bone disease n decalcificazione f ossea, osteoporosi f

broach /brəʊtʃ/ vt toccare ⟨subject⟩

B road n Br ≈ strada f provinciale

broad /brɔːd/ a ampio; ⟨hint⟩ chiaro; ⟨accent⟩ marcato. **two metres ~** largo due metri; **in ~ daylight** in pieno giorno

broad-based /-'beɪst/ a ⟨coalition, education⟩ diversificato; ⟨approach, campaign⟩ su larga scala; ⟨consensus⟩ generale

broad bean n fava f

broadcast /'brɔːdkæst/ n trasmissione f ● vt/i (pt/pp **-cast**) trasmettere

broadcaster /'brɔːdkæstə(r)/ n giornalista mf radiotelevisivo, -a

broadcasting /'brɔːdkæstɪŋ/ n diffusione f radiotelevisiva; **be in ~** lavorare per la televisione/radio

broad-chested a con il torace robusto

broaden /'brɔːdn/ vt allargare; **~ one's horizons** allargare i propri orizzonti ● vi allargarsi

broadly /'brɔːdlɪ/ adv largamente; **~ [speaking]** generalmente

broad-minded /-'maɪndɪd/ a di larghe vedute

broadness /'brɔːdnɪs/ n larghezza f

broad: broadsheet n quotidiano m di grande formato. **broad-shouldered** a con le spalle larghe. **broadside** n ⟨Naut: of ship⟩ fiancata f; ⟨enemy fire⟩ bordata f; n ⟨criticism⟩ attacco m; **deliver a ~** lanciare un attacco ● adv di fianco

brocade /brə'keɪd/ n broccato m

broccoli /'brɒkəlɪ/ n inv broccoli mpl

brochure /'brəʊʃə(r)/ n opuscolo m; ⟨travel ~⟩ dépliant m inv

brogue /brəʊg/ n ⟨shoe⟩ scarpa m da passeggio; ⟨accent⟩ cadenza f dialettale

broil /brɔɪl/ vt Culin cuocere alla griglia ⟨meat⟩ ● vi cuocere alla griglia; fig arrostire

broiler /'brɔɪlə(r)/ n ⟨chicken⟩ pollastro m; ⟨Am: grill⟩ griglia f

broke /brəʊk/ see **break** ● a fam al verde

broken /'brəʊk(ə)n/ see **break** ● a rotto; **~ English** inglese m stentato

broken: broken-down a ⟨machine⟩ guasto; ⟨wall⟩ pericolante. **broken heart** n cuore m infranto; **die of a ~ ~** essere distrutto da una delusione amorosa. **broken-hearted** /-'hɑːtɪd/ a affranto. **broken home** n **he comes from a ~ ~** i suoi sono divisi. **broken marriage** n matrimonio m fallito

broker /'brəʊkə(r)/ n broker m inv

brokerage /'brəʊkərɪdʒ/ n ⟨fee, business⟩ intermediazione f

broking /'brəʊkɪŋ/ n attività f di intermediazione

brolly /'brɒlɪ/ n fam ombrello m

bromide /'brəʊmaɪd/ n ⟨in pharmacy, printing⟩ bromuro m; ⟨fig: comment⟩ banalità f inv

bronchial /'brɒŋkɪəl/ a ⟨infection⟩ bronchiale; ⟨wheeze, cough⟩ di petto

bronchitis /brɒŋ'kaɪtɪs/ n bronchite f

bronze /brɒnz/ n bronzo m ● attrib di bronzo

Bronze Age n età f del Bronzo

brooch /brəʊtʃ/ n spilla f

brood /bruːd/ n covata f; ⟨hum: children⟩ prole f ● vi covare; fig rimuginare

brooding /'bruːdɪŋ/ a ⟨person, face⟩ pensieroso; ⟨landscape⟩ sinistro

broody /'bruːdɪ/ a ⟨depressed⟩ pensieroso; **feel ~** ⟨Br fam: woman:⟩ desiderare un figlio

broody hen n chioccia f

brook¹ /brʊk/ n ruscello m
brook² vt sopportare
broom /bruːm/ n scopa f; Bot ginestra f
broom: broom cupboard n ripostiglio m.
  broom handle n Br manico m di scopa.
  broomstick n manico m di scopa
Bros. abbr (**brothers**) F.lli
broth /brɒθ/ n brodo m
brothel /'brɒθ(ə)l/ n bordello m
brother /'brʌðə(r)/ n fratello m
brotherhood /'brʌðəhʊd/ n (bond) fratellanza f; (of monks) confraternita f
brother-in-law n (pl **-s-in-law**) cognato m
brotherly /'brʌðəlɪ/ a fraterno
brought /brɔːt/ see **bring**
brow /braʊ/ n fronte f; (eye~) sopracciglio m;
  (of hill) cima f
browbeat /'braʊbiːt/ vt (pt **-beat,** pp
  -beaten) intimidire
brown /braʊn/ a marrone; castano (hair) ● n
  marrone m ● vt rosolare (meat) ● vi (meat:)
  rosolarsi
brown: brown ale n Br birra f scura. **brown
  bear** n orso m bruno. **brown bread** n pane m
  integrale
browned-off /braʊnd'ɒf/ a Br fam stufo
  (with di)
brown envelope n busta f di carta da pacchi
Brownie /'braʊnɪ/ n coccinella f (negli scout)
brownie point n fam punto m di merito
brownish /'braʊnɪʃ/ a sul marrone
brown: brownout n Am oscuramento m parziale. **brown owl** n allocco m. **brown paper**
  n carta f da pacchi. **brown rice** n riso m integrale. **brown-skinned** /-'skɪnd/ a scuro di
  pelle. **brownstone** n (Am: house) palazzo m
  in arenaria. **brown sugar** n Culin zucchero
  m greggio
browse /braʊz/ vi (read) leggicchiare; (in
  shop) curiosare
bruise /bruːz/ n livido m; (on fruit) ammaccatura f ● vt ammaccare (fruit); **~ one's arm**
  farsi un livido sul braccio
bruised /bruːzd/ a (physically) contuso;
  (eye) pesto; (fruit) ammaccato; (ego, spirit) ferito
bruiser /'bruːzə(r)/ n fam omaccione m
bruising /'bruːzɪŋ/ n livido m, contusione f
  ● a (game) violento; (emotionally) (remark)
  pesante; (campaign, encounter) traumatizzan-
  te; (defeat) cocente
brunch /brʌntʃ/ n brunch m inv
Brunei /bruː'naɪ/ n Brunei m
brunette /bruː'net/ n bruna f
brunt /brʌnt/ n **bear the ~ of sth** subire
  maggiormente qcsa
brush /brʌʃ/ n spazzola f; (with long handle)
  spazzolone m; (for paint) pennello m; (bushes)
  boscaglia f; (fig: conflict) breve scontro m ● vt
  spazzolare (hair); lavarsi (teeth); scopare
  (stairs, floor)
■ brush against vt sfiorare
■ brush aside vt fig ignorare

■ brush off vt spazzolare; (with hands) togliere; ignorare (criticism)
■ brush up vt/i fig **~ up** [on] rinfrescare
brush: brush-off n fam **give sb the ~** mandare qcno a quel paese. **brushstroke** n pen-
  nellata f. **brushup** n Br **have a** [**wash and**]
  brushup darsi una ripulita. **brushwork** n
  tocco m
brusque /brʊsk/ a brusco
brusquely /'brʊsklɪ/ adv bruscamente
Brussels /'brʌsəlz/ n Bruxelles f
Brussels sprouts npl cavoletti mpl di
  Bruxelles
brutal /'bruːt(ə)l/ a brutale
brutality /bruː'tælətɪ/ n brutalità f inv
brutalize /'bruːtəlaɪz/ vt brutalizzare
brutally /'bruːtəlɪ/ adv brutalmente
brute /bruːt/ n bruto m; **~ force** n forza f
  bruta
brutish /'bruːtɪʃ/ a da bruto
BSc abbr **Bachelor of Science**
BSE n abbr (**bovine spongiform encepha-
  litis**) encefalite f bovina spongiforme
B side n (of record) lato m B
BST abbr (**British Summer Time**) ora f legale in Gran Bretagna
bubble /'bʌbl/ n bolla f; (in drink) bollicina f
bubble: bubble bath n bagnoschiuma m
  inv. **bubble car** n Br fam auto f monoposto a
  tre ruote. **bubblegum** n gomma f da masticare. **bubble pack** n Br (for pills) blister m inv;
  (for small item) involucro m di plastica.
  bubble wrap n plastica f a bolle
bubbling /'bʌblɪŋ/ n (sound) gorgoglio m ● a
  che ribolle
bubbly /'bʌblɪ/ n fam champagne m inv,
  spumante m ● a (liquid) effervescente;
  (personality) spumeggiante
bubonic plague /bjʊbɒnɪk'pleɪg/ n peste f
  bubbonica
buccaneer /bʌkə'nɪə(r)/ n bucaniere m
Bucharest /bjuːkə'rest/ n Bucarest f
buck¹ /bʌk/ n maschio m del cervo; (rabbit)
  maschio m del coniglio ● vi (horse:) saltare a
  quattro zampe
buck² n Am fam dollaro m
buck³ n **pass the ~** scaricare la responsabilità
■ buck up vi fam tirarsi su; (hurry) sbrigarsi ● vt **you'll have to ~ your ideas up** fam
  dovresti darti una regolata
bucket /'bʌkɪt/ n secchio m; **kick the ~**
  (fam: die) crepare ● vi **it's ~ing down** fam
  piove a catinelle
bucketful /'bʌkɪtfʊl/ n secchio m
bucket seat n Auto, Aeron sedile m anatomico
bucket shop n Br fam agenzia f di viaggi
  che vende biglietti a prezzi scontati
bucking bronco /bʌkɪŋ'brɒŋkəʊ/ n cavallo m da rodeo
buckle /'bʌkl/ n fibbia f ● vt allacciare ● vi
  (shelf:) piegarsi; (wheel:) storcersi
■ buckle down vi (to work) mettersi sotto
■ buckle in vt legare

buck: buckram *n* tela *f* rigida. **buckshot** *n* pallettoni *mpl*. **buckskin** *n* pelle *f* di daino.

buck teeth *npl* denti *mpl* da coniglio.

buckwheat *n* grano *m* saraceno

bucolic /bju'kɒlɪk/ *a* & *n* bucolico *m*

bud /bʌd/ *n* bocciolo *m*

Buddha /'bʊdə/ *n* Budda *m inv*

Buddhism /'bʊdɪzm/ *n* buddismo *m*

Buddhist /'bʊdɪst/ *a* & *n* buddista *mf*

budding /'bʌdɪŋ/ *a Bot* (*into leaf*) in germoglio; (*into flower*) in boccio; ‹*athlete, champion, artist*› in erba; ‹*talent, romance*› nascente; ‹*career*› promettente

buddy /'bʌdɪ/ *n fam* amico, -a *mf*

budge /bʌdʒ/ *vt* spostare ● *vi* spostarsi

budgerigar /'bʌdʒərɪɡɑː(r)/ *n* cocorita *f*

budget /'bʌdʒɪt/ *n* bilancio *m*; (*allotted to specific activity*) budget *m inv*; **I'm on a ~** cerco di limitare le spese ● *vi* (*pt/pp* **budgeted**) prevedere le spese; **~ for sth** includere qcsa nelle spese previste

budgetary /'bʌdʒɪt(ə)rɪ/ *a* budgetario; **~ year** esercizio *m* finanziario

budget day *n Br Pol* giorno *m* della presentazione del bilancio dello Stato

budgie /'bʌdʒɪ/ *n fam* = **budgerigar**

buff /bʌf/ *a* (*colour*) [color] camoscio ● *n* [color *m*] camoscio *m*; *fam* fanatico, -a *mf* ● *vt* lucidare

buffalo /'bʌfələʊ/ *n* (*inv or pl* **-es**) bufalo *m*

buffer /'bʌfə(r)/ *n Rail* respingente *m*; *Comput* buffer *m inv*; **old ~** *fam* vecchio bacucco *m*

buffer state *n* stato *m* cuscinetto *inv*

buffer zone *n* zona *f* cuscinetto *inv*

buffet[1] /'bʊfeɪ/ *n* (*meal, in station*) buffet *m inv*

buffet[2] /'bʌfɪt/ *vt* (*pt/pp* **buffeted**) sferzare

buffet car *n Br Rail* carrozza *f* ristorante

buffoon /bə'fuːn/ *n* buffone, -a *mf*

bug /bʌɡ/ *n* (*insect*) insetto *m*; *Comput* bug *m inv*; (*fam: device*) cimice *f* ● *vt* (*pt/pp* **bugged**) *fam* installare le microspie in ‹*room*›; mettere sotto controllo ‹*telephone*›; (*fam: annoy*) scocciare

bugbear /'bʌɡbeə(r)/ *n* (*problem, annoyance*) spauracchio *m*

bugger /'bʌɡə(r)/ *fam n* bastardo *m* ● *int* merda!

■ **bugger about, bugger around** *fam vi* (*behave stupidly*) fare il cretino ● *vt* **~ sb about** creare problemi a qcno

■ **bugger off** *vi* (*fam: go away*) andarsene; **~ off!** vai a farti friggere!

bugging device /'bʌɡɪŋ/ *n* microfono *m* spia

buggy /'bʌɡɪ/ *n* [**baby**] **~** passeggino *m*

bugle /'bjuːɡ(ə)l/ *n* tromba *f*

bugler /'bjuːɡlə(r)/ *n* trombettiere *m*

build /bɪld/ *n* (*of person*) corporatura *f* ● *vt/i* (*pt/pp* **built**) costruire

■ **build on** *vt* aggiungere ‹*extra storey*›; sviluppare ‹*previous work*›

■ **build up** *vt* **~ up one's strength** rimettersi in forza ● *vi* ‹*pressure, traffic:*› aumentare; ‹*excitement, tension:*› crescere

builder /'bɪldə(r)/ *n* (*company*) costruttore *m*; (*worker*) muratore *m*

builder's labourer *n* muratore *m*

builder's merchant *n* fornitore *m* di materiale da costruzione

building /'bɪldɪŋ/ *n* edificio *m*

building: building block *n* (*child's toy*) pezzo *m* delle costruzioni; (*basic element*) componente *m*. **building contractor** *n* imprenditore *m* edile. **building land** *n* terreno *m* edificabile. **building materials** *npl* materiali *mpl* da costruzione. **building permit** *n* permesso *m* per edificare. **building plot** *n* terreno *m* edificabile. **building site** *n* cantiere *m* [di costruzione]. **building society** *n* istituto *m* di credito immobiliare. **building trade** *n* edilizia *f*. **building worker** *n Br* muratore *m*

build-up *n* (*increase*) aumento *m*; (*in tension, of gas, in weapons*) accumulo *m*; (*publicity*) battage *m inv* pubblicitario; **give sth a good ~** (*publicity*) fare buona pubblicità a qcsa

built /bɪlt/ *see* **build**

built-in *a* ‹*unit*› a muro; ‹*fig: feature*› incorporato

built-up area *n Auto* centro *m* abitato

bulb /bʌlb/ *n* bulbo *m*; *Electr* lampadina *f*

bulbous /'bʌlbəs/ *a* grassoccio

Bulgaria /bʌl'ɡeərɪə/ *n* Bulgaria *f*

bulge /bʌldʒ/ *n* rigonfiamento *m*; **it shows all my ~s** mette in evidenza tutti i miei cuscinetti [di grasso] ● *vi* esser gonfio (**with** di); ‹*stomach, wall:*› sporgere; ‹*eyes, with surprise:*› uscire dalle orbite

bulging /'bʌldʒɪŋ/ *a* gonfio; ‹*eyes*› sporgente

bulimia (nervosa) /bʊ'lɪmɪə(nɜː'vəʊsə)/ *n* bulimia *f*

bulimic /bʊ'lɪmɪk/ *a* & *n* bulimico, -a *mf*

bulk /bʌlk/ *n* volume *m*; (*greater part*) grosso *m*; **in ~** in grande quantità; (*loose*) sfuso

bulk: bulk-buy *vt/i* comprare in grandi quantità. **bulk-buying** *n* acquisto *m* in grande quantità. **bulk carrier** *n* mezzo *m* per il trasporto di rinfuse. **bulkhead** *n Naut, Aeron* paratia *f*

bulky /'bʌlkɪ/ *a* voluminoso

bull /bʊl/ *n* toro *m*; **take the ~ by the horns** *fig* prendere il toro per le corna

bull: bulldog *n* bulldog *m inv*. **bulldog clip** *n* fermafogli *m inv*. **bulldoze** *vt* (*knock down*) demolire [con bulldozer]; (*clear*) spianare [con bulldozer]; (*fig: force*) costringere. **bulldozer** /'bʊldəʊzə(r)/ *n* bulldozer *m inv*

bullet /'bʊlɪt/ *n* pallottola *f*

bulletin /'bʊlɪtɪn/ *n* bollettino *m*

bulletin board *n Comput* bacheca *f* elettronica

bulletproof /'bʊlɪtpruːf/ *a* antiproiettile *inv*; ‹*vehicle*› blindato

bulletproof vest giubbotto *m* antiproiettile

bullfight /'bʊlfaɪt/ *n* corrida *f*

bullfighter /'bʊlfaɪtə(r)/ *n* torero *m*

bullion /'bʊlɪən/ *n* **gold ~** oro *m* in lingotti

bullish /'bʊlɪʃ/ *a* (*optimistic*) ottimistico; ‹*market, shares, stocks*› al rialzo

bull market n Fin mercato m al rialzo

bullock /'bʊlək/ n manzo m

bullring /'bʊlrɪŋ/ n arena f

bull's-eye /'bʊlzaɪ/ n centro m del bersaglio; **score a ~** fare centro

bully /'bʊlɪ/ n prepotente mf ● vt fare il/la prepotente con

bullying /'bʊlɪŋ/ n prepotenze fpl

bulrush /'bʊlrʌʃ/ n giunco m di palude

bulwark /'bʊlwək/ n Mil, fig baluardo m; Naut parapetto m; (breakwater) frangiflutti m inv

bum¹ /bʌm/ n sl sedere m

bum² n Am fam vagabondo, -a mf

■ **bum around** vi fam vagabondare

bumbag /'bʌmbæg/ n Br fam marsupio m

bumble-bee /'bʌmblbiː/ n calabrone m

bumbling /'bʌmblɪŋ/ a ⟨attempt⟩ maldestro; ⟨person⟩ inconcludente

bumf /bʌmf/ n (Br: toilet paper) carta f igienica; (fam: documents) scartoffie f pl

bump /bʌmp/ n botta f; (swelling) bozzo m, gonfiore m; (in road) protuberanza f ● vt sbattere

■ **bump into** vt sbattere contro; (meet) imbattersi in

■ **bump off** vt fam far fuori

■ **bump up** vt fam [far] aumentare ⟨prices, salaries⟩

bumper /'bʌmpə(r)/ n Auto paraurti m inv ● a abbondante

bumper car n autoscontro m

bumph /bʌmf/ n = **bumf**

bumpkin /'bʌmpkɪn/ n **country ~** zoticone, -a mf

bumptious /'bʌmpʃəs/ a presuntuoso

bumpy /'bʌmpɪ/ a ⟨road⟩ accidentato; ⟨flight⟩ turbolento

bun /bʌn/ n focaccina f (dolce); (hair) chignon m inv

bunch /bʌntʃ/ n (of flowers, keys) mazzo m; (of bananas) casco m; (of people) gruppo m; **~ of grapes** grappolo m d'uva

bundle /'bʌndl/ n fascio m; (of money) mazzetta f; **a ~ of nerves** fam un fascio di nervi ● vt **~ [up]** affastellare

bung /bʌŋ/ vt fam (throw) buttare

■ **bung up** vt (block) otturare

bungalow /'bʌŋgələʊ/ n bungalow m inv

bungee jumping /'bʌndʒɪdʒʌmpɪŋ/ n salto m da ponti, grattacieli, ecc. con un cavo elastico attaccato alla caviglia

bungle /'bʌŋgl/ vt fare un pasticcio di

bunion /'bʌnjən/ n Med callo m all'alluce

bunk /bʌŋk/ n cuccetta f; **do a ~** fam svignarsela ● vi **~ off school** fam marinare la scuola

bunk beds npl letti mpl a castello

bunker /'bʌŋkə(r)/ n (for coal) carbonaia f; (golf) ostacolo m; Mil bunker m inv

bunkum /'bʌŋkəm/ n fandonie fpl

bunny /'bʌnɪ/ n fam coniglietto m

Bunsen [burner] /'bʌnsən[bɜːnə(r)]/ n becco m Bunsen

bunting /'bʌntɪŋ/ n (flags on ship) gran pavese m; Zool zigolo m

buoy /bɔɪ/ n boa f

■ **buoy up** vt fig sostenere ⟨prices⟩; tirare su ⟨person⟩

buoyancy /'bɔɪənsɪ/ n galleggiabilità f

buoyancy aid n salvagente m

buoyant /'bɔɪənt/ a ⟨boat⟩ galleggiante; ⟨water⟩ che aiuta a galleggiare; ⟨fig: person⟩ allegro; ⟨prices⟩ in aumento

burble /'bɜːb(ə)l/ n (of stream) gorgoglio m; (of voices) borbottio m ● vi ⟨stream:⟩ gorgogliare; **~ on about sth** ⟨person:⟩ blaterare di qcsa

burbling /'bɜːblɪŋ/ n (of stream) gorgoglio m; (rambling talk) borbottio m ● a ⟨stream⟩ gorgogliante; ⟨voice⟩ che borbotta

burden /'bɜːdn/ n carico m ● vt caricare

burdensome /'bɜːdnsəm/ a gravoso

bureau /'bjʊərəʊ/ n (pl **-x** /'bjʊərəʊz/ or **~s**) (desk) scrivania f; (office) ufficio m

bureaucracy /bjʊəˈrɒkrəsɪ/ n burocrazia f

bureaucrat /'bjʊərəkræt/ n burocrate mf

bureaucratic /bjʊərəˈkrætɪk/ a burocratico

burgeon /'bɜːdʒən/ vi ⟨plant:⟩ germogliare; ⟨fig: flourish⟩ fiorire; ⟨fig: multiply⟩ moltiplicarsi rapidamente, crescere rapidamente

burger /'bɜːgə(r)/ n hamburger m inv

burger bar n fast-food m inv

burglar /'bɜːglə(r)/ n svaligiatore, -trice mf

burglar alarm n antifurto m inv

burglarize /'bɜːgləraɪz/ vt Am svaligiare

burglar-proof a a prova di ladro

burglary /'bɜːglərɪ/ n furto m con scasso

burgle /'bɜːgl/ vt svaligiare; **they have been ~d** sono stati svaligiati

Burgundy /'bɜːgəndɪ/ n Borgogna f; **b~** (wine) borgogna m inv ● a (colour) rosso scuro

burial /'berɪəl/ n sepoltura f

burial ground n cimitero m

burlesque /bɜːˈlesk/ n parodia f

burly /'bɜːlɪ/ a (-ier, -iest) corpulento

Burma /'bɜːmə/ n Birmania f

Burmese /bɜːˈmiːz/ a & n birmano, -a mf

burn /bɜːn/ n bruciatura f ● v (pt/pp **burnt** or **burned**) ● vt bruciare; **~ one's boats** or **bridges** fig tagliarsi i ponti alle spalle ● vi bruciare

■ **burn down** vt/i bruciare

■ **burn out** vi fig esaurirsi

burned-out a = **burnt-out**

burner /'bɜːnə(r)/ n (on stove) bruciatore m

burning /'bɜːnɪŋ/ n (setting on fire) incendio m; **I can smell ~!** sento odore di bruciato! ● a ⟨ember, coal⟩ acceso; (on fire) in fiamme; ⟨fig: fever, desire⟩ bruciante; **a ~ sensation** una sensazione di bruciore; **a ~ question** una questione scottante

burnish /'bɜːnɪʃ/ vt lucidare

burns unit n Med reparto m grandi ustionati

burnt /bɜːnt/ see **burn**

burnt-out a ⟨building, car⟩ distrutto dalle fiamme; ⟨fig: person⟩ sfinito

burp /bɜːp/ *n fam* rutto *m* ● *vi fam* ruttare
burr /bɜː(r)/ *n Bot* lappa *f*; *(in language)* erre *f* moscia
burrow /'bʌrəʊ/ *n* tana *f* ● *vt* scavare ⟨*hole*⟩
bursar /'bɜːsə(r)/ *n* economo, -a *mf*
bursary /'bɜːsərɪ/ *n* borsa *f* di studio
burst /bɜːst/ *n* (*of gunfire, energy, laughter*) scoppio *m*; (*of speed*) scatto *m* ● *v* (*pt/pp* **burst**) ● *vt* far scoppiare; ~ **its banks** ⟨*river:*⟩ rompere gli argini ● *vi* scoppiare; ~ **into tears** scoppiare in lacrime; ~ **into flames** andare in fiamme; **she** ~ **into the room** ha fatto irruzione nella stanza; **be** ~**ing at the seams** ⟨*room:*⟩ scoppiare
■ burst in *vi* (*enter suddenly*) fare irruzione
■ burst out *vi* ~ **out laughing/crying** scoppiare a ridere/piangere
Burundi /bʊ'rʊndɪ/ *n* Burundi *m*
bury /'berɪ/ *vt* (*pt/pp* **-ied**) seppellire; (*hide*) nascondere
bus /bʌs/ *n* autobus *m inv*, pullman *m inv*; (*long distance*) pullman *m inv*, corriera *f* ● *vt* (*pt/pp* **bussed**) trasportare in autobus
busby /'bʌzbɪ/ *n* colbacco *m* militare
bus: bus conductor *n* ≈ bigliettaio *m*. **bus conductress** *n* ≈ bigliettaia *f*. **bus driver** *n* conducente *mf* di autobus
bush /bʊʃ/ *n* cespuglio *m*; (*land*) boscaglia *f*
bushed /bʊʃt/ *a* (*fam: tired*) distrutto
bushel /'bʊʃ(ə)l/ *n* **hide one's light under a** ~ essere troppo modesto; *Am fam* ~**s of** un sacco di
bush: bushfighting *n Mil* guerriglia *f*. **bushfire** *n* incendio *m* in aperta campagna. **bush telegraph** *n fig hum* tamtam *m inv*
bushy /'bʊʃɪ/ *a* (**-ier, -iest**) folto
busily /'bɪzɪlɪ/ *adv* con grande impegno
business /'bɪznɪs/ *n* affare *m*; *Comm* affari *mpl*; (*establishment*) attività *f* di commercio; **on** ~ per affari; **he has no** ~ **to** non ha alcun diritto di; **mind one's own** ~ farsi gli affari propri; **that's none of your** ~ non sono affari tuoi
business: business activity *n* attività *f inv* economica; (*of single company*) attività *f inv* aziendale. **business analyst** *n* analista *mf* finanziario, -a. **business associate** *n* socio, -a *mf*. **business call** *n* (*phone call*) telefonata *f* di lavoro; (*visit*) appuntamento *m* di lavoro. **business card** *n* biglietto *m* da visita. **business centre** *n* centro *m* affari. **business class** *n Aeron* business class *f inv*. **business college** *n* scuola *f* di amministrazione aziendale. **business contact** *n* contatto *m* di lavoro. **business cycle** *n* ciclo *m* economico. **business deal** *n* operazione *f* commerciale. **business expenses** *npl* spese *fpl* di lavoro. **business failures** *npl* chiusura *f* di aziende. **business hours** *npl* (*in office*) orario *m* di ufficio; (*of shop*) orario *m* d'apertura. **business-like** *a* efficiente. **business lunch** *n* pranzo *m* di lavoro *or* d'affari
businessman /'bɪznɪsmən/ *n* uomo *m* d'affari
business: business management *n* am-

ministrazione *f* aziendale. **business park** *n* centro *m* affari. **business plan** *n* piano *m* economico; (*of single company*) programma *m* aziendale. **business premises** *npl* sede *f* di un'azienda. **business proposition** *n* proposta *f* d'affari. **business reply envelope** *n* busta *f* affrancata. **business school** *n* scuola *f* di amministrazione aziendale. **business software** *n* software *m* per l'ufficio. **business studies** *npl* economia *f* e commercio. **business suit** *n* (*for man*) abito *m* scuro. **business trip** *n* viaggio *m* di lavoro
businesswoman /'bɪznɪswʊmən/ *n* donna *f* d'affari
busk /bʌsk/ *vi Br* ⟨*singer:*⟩ cantare per strada; ⟨*musician:*⟩ suonare per strada
busker /'bʌskə(r)/ *n* suonatore, -trice *mf* ambulante
bus lane *n* corsia *f* autobus
busload /'bʌsləʊd/ *n* **a** ~ **of tourists** una comitiva di turisti; **by the** ~ in massa
busman's holiday /ˌbʌsmənz'hɒlɪdeɪ/ *n Br* vacanze *fpl* passate a fare quello che si fa normalmente
bus: bus pass *n* abbonamento *m* all'autobus. **bus route** *n* percorso *m* dell'autobus. **bus shelter** *n* pensilina *f* alla fermata dell'autobus. **bus station** *n* stazione *f* degli autobus. **bus stop** *n* fermata *f* d'autobus
bust¹ /bʌst/ *n* busto *m*; (*chest*) petto *m*
bust² *a fam* rotto; **go** ~ fallire ● *v* (*pt/pp* **busted** *or* **bust**) *fam* ● *vt* far scoppiare ● *vi* scoppiare
bustle /'bʌsl/ *n* (*activity*) trambusto *m*
■ bustle about *vi* affannarsi
bustling /'bʌslɪŋ/ *a* animato
bust size *n* circonferenza *f* del torace
bust-up *n fam* lite *f*
busy /'bɪzɪ/ *a* (**-ier, -iest**) occupato; ⟨*day, time*⟩ intenso; ⟨*street*⟩ affollato; (*with traffic*) pieno di traffico; **be** ~ **doing** essere occupato a fare ● *vt* ~ **oneself** darsi da fare
busybody /'bɪzɪbɒdɪ/ *n* ficcanaso *mf inv*
but /bʌt/, *atono* /bət/ *conj* ma ● *prep* eccetto, tranne; **nobody** ~ **you** nessuno tranne te; ~ **for** (*without*) se non fosse stato per; **the last** ~ **one** il penultimo; **the next** ~ **one** il secondo ● *adv* soltanto; **there were** ~ **two** ce n'erano soltanto due
butane /'bjuːteɪn/ *n* butano *m*
butch /bʊtʃ/ *a fam* ⟨*man*⟩ macho *inv*; ⟨*woman*⟩ mascolino
butcher /'bʊtʃə(r)/ *n* macellaio *m* ● *vt* macellare; *fig* massacrare
butcher's [shop] /'bʊtʃəz[ʃɒp]/ *n* macelleria *f*
butchery /'bʊtʃərɪ/ *n* (*trade*) macelleria *f*; (*slaughter*) massacro *m*
butler /'bʌtlə(r)/ *n* maggiordomo *m*
butt /bʌt/ *n* (*of gun*) calcio *m*; (*of cigarette*) mozzicone *m*; (*for water*) barile *m*; (*fig: target*) bersaglio *m* ● *vt* dare una testata a; ⟨*goat:*⟩ dare una cornata a
■ butt in *vi* interrompere
butter /'bʌtə(r)/ *n* burro *m* ● *vt* imburrare

■ **butter up** *vt fam* arruffianarsi

butter: butter-bean *n* fagiolo *m* bianco. **buttercup** *n* ranuncolo *m*. **butter dish** *n* portaburro *m inv*. **butter-fingered** *a* con le mani di pasta frolla. **butter-fingers** *n fam* mani *fpl* di pasta frolla

butterfly /'bʌtəflaɪ/ *n* farfalla *f*

butterfly: butterfly net *n* retino *m* per farfalle. **butterfly nut** *n* dado *m* ad alette. **butterfly stroke** *n* nuoto *m* a farfalla

buttermilk /'bʌtəmɪlk/ *n* latticello *m*

butterscotch /'bʌtəskɒtʃ/ *n* caramella *f* dura a base di burro e zucchero

buttocks /'bʌtəks/ *npl* natiche *fpl*

button /'bʌtn/ *n* bottone *m*; (*on mouse, of status bar*) pulsante *m* ● *vt* ~ [**up**] abbottonare ● *vi* ~ [**up**] abbottonarsi

button: button-down *a* ⟨*collar*⟩ button down, coi bottoni; ⟨*shirt*⟩ con il colletto coi bottoni, button down. **buttonhole** *n* occhiello *m*, asola *f*. **buttonhook** *n* asola *f*, occhiello *m*. **button mushroom** *n* piccolo champignon *m inv*

buttress /'bʌtrɪs/ *n* contrafforte *m* ● *vt fig* sostenere

buxom /'bʌksəm/ *a* formosa

buy /baɪ/ *n* **good/bad** ~ buon/cattivo acquisto *m* ● *vt* (*pt/pp* **bought**) comprare; ~ **sb a drink** pagare da bere a qcno; **I'll** ~ **this one** (*drink*) questo, lo offro io

■ **buy off** *vt* (*bribe*) comprare

■ **buy out** *vt* rilevare la quota di ⟨*one's partner*⟩

■ **buy up** *vt* (*buy all of*) accaparrarsi

buyer /'baɪə(r)/ *n* compratore, -trice *mf*

buyout /'baɪaʊt/ *n Comm* rilevamento *m*

buzz /bʌz/ *n* ronzio *m*; **give sb a** ~ *fam* (*on phone*) dare un colpo di telefono a qcno; (*excite*) mettere in fermento qcno ● *vi* ronzare ● *vt* ~ **sb** chiamare qcno col cicalino

■ **buzz off** *vi fam* levarsi di torno

buzzard /'bʌzəd/ *n* poiana *f*

buzzer /'bʌzə(r)/ *n* cicalino *m*

buzzing /'bʌzɪŋ/ *n* (*of buzzer*) trillo *m*; (*of insects*) ronzio *m* ● *a* ⟨*party, atmosphere, town*⟩ molto animato

buzzword /'bʌzwɜːd/ *n fam* parola *f* di moda

by /baɪ/ *prep* (*near, next to*) vicino a; (*at the latest*) per; **by Mozart** di Mozart; **he was run over by a bus** è stato investito da un autobus; **by oneself** da solo; **by the sea** al mare; **by sea** via mare; **by car/bus** in macchina/ autobus; **by day/night** di giorno/notte; **by the hour/metre** a ore/metri; **six metres by four** sei metri per quattro; **he won by six metres** ha vinto di sei metri; **I missed the train by a minute** ho perso il treno per un minuto; **I'll be home by six** sarò a casa per le sei; **by this time next week** a quest'ora tra una settimana; **he rushed by me** mi è passato accanto di corsa ● *adv* **she'll be here by and by** sarà qui fra poco; **by and by the police arrived** poco dopo, la polizia è arrivata; **by and large** in complesso; **put by** mettere da parte; **go/pass by** passare

bye-bye /baɪ'baɪ/ *int fam* ciao, arrivederci; **go** ~**s** *Br* (*baby talk*) andare a fare la nanna

by-election *n* elezione *f* straordinaria indetta per coprire una carica rimasta vacante in Parlamento

Byelorussia /bjeləʊ'rʌʃə/ *n* Bielorussia *f*

Byelorussian /bjeləʊ'rʌʃn/ *a & n* bielorusso

by: bygone *a* passato. **by-law** *n* legge *f* locale. **by-line** *n* (*in newspaper*) nome *m* dell'autore; *Sport* linea *f* laterale. **bypass** *n* circonvallazione *f*; *Med* by-pass *m inv* ● *vt* evitare. **by-product** *n* sottoprodotto *m*. **by-road** *n* strada *f* secondaria. **bystander** *n* spettatore, -trice *mf*

byte /baɪt/ *n Comput* byte *m inv*

by: byway *n* strada *f* secondaria. **byword** *n* **be a** ~ **for** essere sinonimo di. **by-your-leave** *n* **without so much as a** ~ senza neanche chiedere il permesso

Byzantine /bɪ'zæntaɪn/ *a* bizantino

Cc

c, C /siː/ *n* (*letter*) c, C *f inv*; (*Br Sch: grade*) voto *m* scolastico corrispondente alla sufficienza; *Mus* do *m inv*

c, C *abbr* (**Celsius, centigrade**) C; *abbr* (**cent(s)**) c; *abbr* (**circa**) ca

CA *Br abbr* (**Chartered Accountant**) [dottore *m*] commercialista *m*; *Am abbr* (**California**) Cal; *abbr* (**Central America**) America *f* centrale

CAA *n Br abbr* (**Civil Aviation Authority**) *organismo m di controllo dell'aviazione civile*

CAB *n Br abbr* (**Citizens' Advice Bureau**) *ufficio m di consulenza legale gratuita per i cittadini*

cab /kæb/ *n* taxi *m inv*; (*of lorry, train*) cabina *f*

cabana /kə'bɑːnə/ *n* (*Am: hut*) cabina *f* da spiaggia

cabaret /'kæbəreɪ/ *n* cabaret *m inv*

cabbage /'kæbɪdʒ/ *n* cavolo *m*

cabby /'kæbɪ/ *n fam* tassista *mf*

cab driver *n* tassista *mf*

cabin /'kæbɪn/ *n* (*of plane, ship*) cabina *f*; (*hut*) capanna *f*

cabin: cabin boy *n* mozzo *m*. **cabin crew** *n Aeron* equipaggio *m*. **cabin cruiser** *n* cabinato *m*

cabinet /'kæbɪnɪt/ *n* armadietto *m*; [**display**] ~ vetrina *f*; **C~** *Pol* consiglio *m* dei ministri

cabinet: cabinet-maker *n* ebanista *mf*. **cabinet meeting** *n Br* riunione *f* del governo. **cabinet minister** *n Br* ministro *m*. **cabinet reshuffle** *n Br* rimpasto *m* del governo

cable /'keɪb(ə)l/ *n* cavo *m*

cable: cable car *n* cabina *f* (*della funivia*). **cablegram** *n* cablogramma *m*. **cable-knit** *a* ‹*sweater*› a trecce. **cable railway** *n* funicolare *f*. **cable television** *n* televisione *f* via cavo. **cable TV** *n* TV *f inv* via cavo. **cableway** *n* (*for people*) funivia *f*

caboodle /kə'bu:dl/ *n fam* **the whole ~** baracca e burattini

cab rank, cab stand *n* posteggio *m* dei taxi

cache /kæʃ/ *n* nascondiglio *m*; **~ of arms** deposito *m* segreto di armi

cache memory *n Comput* memoria *f* cache

cachet /'kæʃeɪ/ *n* prestigio *m*

cackle /'kækl/ *vi* ridacchiare

cacophony /kə'kɒfənɪ/ *n* cacofonia *f*

cactus /'kæktəs/ *n* (*pl* **-ti** /'kæktaɪ/ or **-tuses**) cactus *m inv*

CAD /kæd/ *n abbr* (**computer-aided design**) CAD *m inv*

cadaver /kə'dɑ:və(r)/ *n* cadavere *m*

cadaverous /kə'dævərəs/ *a* cadaverico

CADCAM /'kædkæm/ *n abbr* (**computer-aided design and computer-aided manufacture**) CADCAM *m inv*

caddie /'kædɪ/ *n* portabastoni *m inv*

caddy /'kædɪ/ *n* [**tea-**]~ barattolo *m* del tè

cadence /'keɪdəns/ *n* cadenza *f*

cadet /kə'det/ *n* cadetto *m*

cadet corps *n Mil* corpo *m* dei cadetti

cadet school *n* scuola *f* allievi ufficiali

cadge /kædʒ/ *vt/i fam* scroccare

cadre /'kɑ:drə/ *n Admin, Pol* quadri *mpl*

CAE *n abbr* (**computer-aided engineering**) CAE *m inv*

Caesarean /sɪ'zeərɪən/ *n* parto *m* cesareo

café /'kæfeɪ/ *n* caffè *m inv*

cafeteria /kæfə'tɪərɪə/ *n* tavola *f* calda

caffeine /'kæfi:n/ *n* caffeina *f*

cage /keɪdʒ/ *n* gabbia *f*

cage bird *n* uccello *m* da gabbia

cagey /'keɪdʒɪ/ *a fam* riservato (**about** su)

cagoule /kə'gu:l/ *n Br* K-way® *m inv*

cahoots /kə'hu:ts/ *npl fam* **be in ~** essere in combutta

cairn /keən/ *n* (*of stones*) tumulo *m* di pietre

Cairo /'kaɪrəʊ/ *n* il Cairo

cajole /kə'dʒəʊl/ *vt* persuadere con le lusinghe

cake /keɪk/ *n* torta *f*; (*small*) pasticcino *m*; ~ **of soap** saponetta *f*; **it was a piece of ~** *fam* è stato un gioco da ragazzi; **you can't have your ~ and eat it** *fig* non si può avere

la botte piena e la moglie ubriaca; **sell like hot ~s** andare a ruba

caked /keɪkt/ *a* incrostato (**with** di)

cake: cake mix *n* miscela *f* per torte. **cake shop** *n* pasticceria *f*. **cake tin** *n* (*for baking*) tortiera *f*; (*for storing*) scatola *f* di latta (*per torte*)

Calabria /kə'læbrɪə/ *n* Calabria *f*

Calabrian /kə'læbrɪən/ *a & n* calabrese

calamine lotion /'kæləmaɪn/ *n* lozione *f* alla calamina

calamitous /kə'læmɪtəs/ *a* disastroso

calamity /kə'læmətɪ/ *n* calamità *f inv*

calcify /'kælsɪfaɪ/ *vi* calcificarsi

calcium /'kælsɪəm/ *n* calcio *m*

calculate /'kælkjʊleɪt/ *vt* calcolare

calculated /'kælkjʊleɪtɪd/ *a* ‹*risk, insult, decision*› calcolato; ‹*crime*› premeditato

calculating /'kælkjʊleɪtɪŋ/ *a fig* calcolatore

calculating machine *n* calcolatrice *f*

calculation /kælkjʊ'leɪʃn/ *n* calcolo *m*

calculator /'kælkjʊleɪtə(r)/ *n* calcolatrice *f*

calculus /'kælkjʊləs/ *n Math, Med* calcolo *m*

calendar /'kælɪndə(r)/ *n* calendario *m*

calendar month *n* mese *m* civile

calendar year *n* anno *m* civile

calf[1] /kɑ:f/ *n* (*pl* **calves**) vitello *m*

calf[2] *n* (*pl* **calves**) *Anat* polpaccio *m*

calfskin /'kɑ:fskɪn/ *n* [pelle *f* di] vitello *m*

calibrate /'kælɪbreɪt/ *vt* calibrare ‹*instrument*›; tarare ‹*scales*›

calibre /'kælɪbə(r)/ *n* calibro *m*

calico /'kælɪkəʊ/ *n* cotone *m* grezzo

California /kælɪ'fɔ:nɪə/ *n* California *f*

Californian /kælɪ'fɔ:nɪən/ *a & n* californiano, -a *mf*

CALL *n abbr* (**computer-assisted language learning**) CALL *m inv*

call /kɔ:l/ *n* grido *m*; *Teleph* telefonata *f*; (*visit*) visita *f*; **be on ~** ‹*doctor:*› essere di guardia ● *vt* chiamare; indire ‹*strike*›; **be ~ed** chiamarsi ● *vi* chiamare; ~ [**in** or **round**] passare

■ **call back** *vt/i* richiamare

■ **call by** *vi* (*make brief visit*) passare

■ **call for** *vt* (*ask for*) chiedere; (*require*) richiedere; (*fetch*) passare a prendere

■ **call off** *vt* richiamare ‹*dog*›; disdire ‹*meeting*›; revocare ‹*strike*›

■ **call on** *vt* chiamare; (*appeal to*) fare un appello a; (*visit*) visitare

■ **call out** *vt* chiamare ad alta voce ‹*names*› ● *vi* chiamare ad alta voce

■ **call together** *vt* riunire

■ **call up** *vt Mil* chiamare alle armi; *Teleph* chiamare

callback facility /'kɔ:lbæk/ *n Teleph* servizio *m* telefonico che permette di individuare il numero che ha chiamato

call box *n* cabina *f* telefonica

caller /'kɔ:lə(r)/ *n* visitatore, -trice *mf*; *Teleph* persona *f* che telefona

call-girl *n* call-girl *f inv*, [ragazza *f*] squillo *f inv*

calligrapher /kəˈlɪɡrəfə(r)/ n calligrafo, -a mf

calligraphy /kəˈlɪɡrəfɪ/ n calligrafia f

calling /ˈkɔːlɪŋ/ n vocazione f

calliper /ˈkælɪpə(r)/ (for measuring) calibro m; (leg support) tutore m

callisthenics /kælɪsˈθenɪks/ n ginnastica f

callous /ˈkæləs/ a insensibile

callousness /ˈkæləsnɪs/ n insensibilità f

call-out n (doctor) visita f a domicilio; (plumber, electrician) chiamata f

call-out charge n costo m della chiamata

callow /ˈkæləʊ/ a immaturo

call: call sign n Radio segnale m di chiamata. **call-up** n Mil chiamata f alle armi.

call-up papers npl cartolina f precetto

calm /kɑːm/ a calmo ● n calma f

■ **calm down** vt calmare ● vi calmarsi

calmly /ˈkɑːmlɪ/ adv con calma

calmness /ˈkɑːmnɪs/ n calma f

Calor gas® /ˈkælə/ n Br liquigas® m inv

calorie /ˈkælərɪ/ n caloria f

calorific /kæləˈrɪfɪk/ a calorico

calve /kɑːv/ vi figliare

calves /kɑːvz/ npl see calf¹ & ²

cam /kæm/ n Techn camma f

camaraderie /kæməˈrædərɪ/ n cameratismo m

camber /ˈkæmbə(r)/ n curvatura f

Cambodia /kæmˈbəʊdɪə/ n Cambogia f

Cambodian /kæmˈbəʊdɪən/ a & n cambogiano, -a mf

camcorder /ˈkæmkɔːdə(r)/ n videocamera f

came /keɪm/ see come

camel /ˈkæml/ n cammello m

camel hair n cammello m

camellia /kəˈmiːlɪə/ n camelia f

cameo /ˈkæmɪəʊ/ n cammeo m

cameo role n Theat, Cinema breve apparizione f

camera /ˈkæmərə/ n macchina f fotografica; TV telecamera f

camera crew n troupe f inv televisiva

cameraman /ˈkæmərəmæn/ n operatore m [televisivo], cameraman m inv

Cameroon /kæməruːn/ n il Camerun

camisole /ˈkæmɪsəʊl/ n canottiera f

camomile /ˈkæməmaɪl/ n camomilla f

camouflage /ˈkæməflɑːʒ/ n mimetizzazione f ● vt mimetizzare

camp¹ /kæmp/ n campeggio f; Mil campo m ● vi campeggiare; Mil accamparsi

camp² a (affected) affettato

campaign /kæmˈpeɪn/ n campagna f ● vi fare una campagna

campaign trail n be on the ~ ~ fare la campagna elettorale

campaign worker n Br Pol membro m dello staff di una campagna elettorale

camp bed n letto m da campo

camper /ˈkæmpə(r)/ n campeggiatore, -trice mf; Auto camper m inv

campfire /ˈkæmpfaɪə(r)/ n fuoco m di bivacco

camphor /ˈkæmfə(r)/ n canfora f

camping /ˈkæmpɪŋ/ n campeggio m

camping: camping equipment n attrezzatura f da campeggio. **camping gas** n gas m inv da campeggio. **camping holiday** n vacanza f in tenda. **camping site** n campeggio m. **camping stool** n Br sgabello m pieghevole. **camping stove** n fornello m da campeggio

campsite /ˈkæmpsaɪt/ n campeggio m

campus /ˈkæmpəs/ n (pl -puses) Univ città f universitaria, campus m inv

camshaft /ˈkæmʃɑːft/ n albero m a camme

can¹ /kæn/ n (for petrol) latta f; (tin) scatola f; ~ of beer lattina f di birra ● vt mettere in scatola

can² /kæn/, atono /kən/ v aux (pres can; pt could) (be able to) potere; (know how to) sapere; **I cannot** or **can't go** non posso andare; **he could not** or **couldn't go** non poteva andare; **she can't swim** non sa nuotare; **I ~ smell something burning** sento odor di bruciato

Canada /ˈkænədə/ n Canada m

Canadian /kəˈneɪdɪən/ a & n canadese mf

canal /kəˈnæl/ n canale m

canal boat, canal barge n chiatta f

canapé /ˈkænəpeɪ/ n canapè m inv

Canaries /kəˈneərɪz/ npl Canarie fpl

canary /kəˈneərɪ/ n canarino m

cancel /ˈkænsl/ v (pt/pp cancelled) ● vt disdire ‹meeting, newspaper›; revocare ‹contract, order›; annullare ‹reservation, appointment, stamp› ● vi ‹guest, host:› annullare

cancellation /kænsəˈleɪʃn/ n (of meeting, contract) revoca f; (in hotel, restaurant, for flight) cancellazione f

cancer /ˈkænsə(r)/ n cancro m; **C~** Astr Cancro m

cancerous /ˈkænsərəs/ a canceroso

cancer research n ricerca f sul cancro

candelabra /kændəˈlɑːbrə/ n candelabro m

candid /ˈkændɪd/ a franco

candidacy /ˈkændɪdəsɪ/ n Pol candidatura f

candidate /ˈkændɪdət/ n candidato, -a mf

candidly /ˈkændɪdlɪ/ adv francamente

candied /ˈkændɪd/ a candito

candle /ˈkænd(ə)l/ n candela f

candlelight /ˈkænd(ə)llaɪt/ n **by ~** a lume di candela

candlelit dinner /ˈkænd(ə)llɪt/ n cena f a lume di candela

candlestick /ˈkænd(ə)lstɪk/ n portacandele m inv

candlewick bedspread /ˈkænd(ə)lwɪk/ n copriletto m inv di ciniglia

candour /ˈkændə(r)/ n franchezza f

candy /ˈkændɪ/ n Am caramella f; **a [piece of] ~** una caramella

candyfloss /ˈkændɪflɒs/ n zucchero m filato

candy-striped /straɪpt/ a (blue) a righe bianche e celesti; (pink) a righe bianche e rosa

cane /keɪn/ n (stick) bastone m; Sch bacchetta f ● vt prendere a bacchettate ‹pupil›

cane sugar n zucchero m di canna

canine /'keɪnaɪn/ a canino

canine tooth n canino m

canister /'kænɪstə(r)/ n barattolo m

cannabis /'kænəbɪs/ n cannabis f

canned /kænd/ a in scatola; ~ **music** fam musica f registrata

cannibal /'kænɪbl/ n cannibale mf

cannibalism /'kænɪbəlɪzm/ n cannibalismo m

cannibalize /'kænɪbəlaɪz/ vt riciclare parti di

cannon /'kænən/ n inv cannone m

cannon ball n palla f di cannone

cannon fodder n carne f da cannone, carne f da macello

cannot /'kænɒt/ see **can²**

canny /'kænɪ/ a astuto

canoe /kə'nu:/ n canoa f ● vi andare in canoa

canon /'kænən/ n (rule) canone m; (person) canonico m

canonization /kænənaɪ'zeɪʃn/ n canonizzazione f

canonize /'kænənaɪz/ vt canonizzare

canoodle /kə'nu:dl/ vi fam sbaciucchiarsi

can-opener n apriscatole m inv

canopy /'kænəpɪ/ n baldacchino f; (of parachute) calotta f

cant /kænt/ n (hypocrisy) ipocrisia f; (jargon) gergo m

can't /kɑ:nt/ = **cannot** see **can²**

cantankerous /kæn'tæŋkərəs/ a stizzoso

cantata /kæn'tɑ:tə/ n Mus cantata f

canteen /kæn'ti:n/ n mensa f; ~ **of cutlery** servizio m di posate

canter /'kæntə(r)/ n piccolo galoppo m ● vi andare a piccolo galoppo

cantilever /'kæntɪli:və(r)/ n cantilever m inv, trave f a sbalzo

cantonal /'kæntənəl/ a cantonale

canvas /'kænvəs/ n tela f; (painting) dipinto m su tela

canvass /'kænvəs/ vi Pol fare propaganda elettorale

canvassing /'kænvəsɪŋ/ n (door to door for votes) propaganda f porta a porta; (door to door for sales) vendita f porta a porta

canyon /'kænjən/ n canyon m inv

cap /kæp/ n berretto m; (nurse's) cuffia f; (top, lid) tappo m ● vt (pt/pp **capped**) (fig: do better than) superare

capability /keɪpə'bɪlətɪ/ n capacità f

capable /'keɪpəbl/ a capace; (skilful) abile; **be ~ of doing sth** essere capace di fare qcsa

capably /'keɪpəblɪ/ adv con abilità

capacious /kə'peɪʃəs/ a (pocket, car boot) capace

capacity /kə'pæsətɪ/ n capacità f; (function) qualità f; **in my ~ as** in qualità di

cape¹ /keɪp/ n (cloak) cappa f

cape² n Geog capo m

Cape of Good Hope n Capo m di Buona Speranza

caper¹ /'keɪpə(r)/ vi saltellare ● n fam birichinata f

caper² n Culin cappero m

Cape Town n Città f del Capo

capful /'kæpfʊl/ n tappo m

cap gun n pistola f a capsule

capillary /kə'pɪlərɪ/ a & n capillare m

capital /'kæpɪtl/ n (town) capitale f; (money) capitale m; (letter) lettera f maiuscola

capital: capital allowances npl detrazioni mpl per ammortamento. **capital city** n capitale f. **capital expenditure** n spese fpl in conto capitale; (personal) spese fpl di capitale. **capital gains tax** n imposta f sui redditi di capitale. **capital goods** npl beni mpl strumentali. **capital-intensive** a ad uso intensivo da capitale. **capital investment** n investimento m di capitale

capitalism /'kæpɪtəlɪzm/ n capitalismo m

capitalist /'kæpɪtəlɪst/ a & n capitalista mf

capitalize /'kæpɪtəlaɪz/ vi ~ **on** fig trarre vantaggio da

capital: capital letter n lettera f maiuscola. **capital punishment** n pena f capitale. **capital spending** n spese fpl in conto capitale. **capital transfer tax** n imposta f sui trasferimenti di capitale

capitulate /kə'pɪtjʊleɪt/ vi capitolare

capitulation /kəpɪtjʊ'leɪʃn/ n capitolazione f

capon /'keɪpɒn/ n cappone m

caprice /kə'pri:s/ n (whim) capriccio m

capricious /kə'prɪʃəs/ a capriccioso

Capricorn /'kæprɪkɔ:n/ n Astr Capricorno m

capsicum /'kæpsɪkəm/ n peperone m

capsize /kæp'saɪz/ vi capovolgersi ● vt capovolgere

caps lock n Comput bloccamaiuscole m inv

capstan /'kæpstən/ n argano m

capsule /'kæpsju:l/ n capsula f

captain /'kæptɪn/ n capitano m ● vt comandare (team)

caption /'kæpʃn/ n intestazione f; (of illustration) didascalia f

captious /'kæpʃəs/ a (remark) ipercritico

captivate /'kæptɪveɪt/ vt incantare

captive /'kæptɪv/ a prigioniero; **hold/take ~** tenere/fare prigioniero ● n prigioniero, -a mf

captivity /kæp'tɪvətɪ/ n prigionia f; (animals) cattività f

captor /'kæptə(r)/ n (of person) persona f che tiene prigioniero qcno; (of person for ransom) rapitore, -trice mf

capture /'kæptʃə(r)/ n cattura f ● vt catturare; attirare (attention)

car /kɑ:(r)/ n macchina f; **by ~** in macchina

carafe /kə'ræf/ n caraffa f

caramel /'kærəməl/ n (sweet) caramella f al mou; Culin caramello m

carat /'kærət/ n carato m

caravan /'kærəvæn/ n roulotte f inv; (horse-drawn) carovana f

caraway /'kærəweɪ/ n (plant) cumino m dei prati

carbohydrate /kɑ:bə'haɪdreɪt/ n carboidrato m

carbolic /kɑ:'bɒlɪk/ a (soap) al fenolo

car bomb *n* autobomba *f*

carbon /'kɑːbən/ *n* carbonio *m*; (*paper*) carta *f* carbone; (*copy*) copia *f* in carta carbone

carbon: carbon copy *n* copia *f* in carta carbone; (*fig: person*) ritratto *m*. **carbon-date** *vt* datare con il carbonio 14. **carbon dating** *n* datazione *f* con il carbonio 14. **carbon diox-ide** *n* anidride *f* carbonica. **carbon filter** *n* filtro *m* al carbone. **carbon monoxide** *n* monossido *m* di carbonio. **carbon paper** *n* carta *f* carbone

car boot sale *n Br mercatino m di oggetti usati, esposti nei bagagliai delle macchine*

carbuncle /'kɑːbʌŋk(ə)l/ *n Med* foruncolo *m*

carburettor /kɑːbjʊ'retə(r)/ *n* carburato-re *m*

carcass /'kɑːkəs/ *n* carcassa *f*

carcinogen /kɑːˈsɪnədʒən/ *n* canceroge-no *m*

carcinogenic /kɑːsɪnəˈdʒenɪk/ *a* cancero-geno

card /kɑːd/ *n* (*for birthday, Christmas etc*) bi-glietto *m* di auguri; (*playing ~*) carta *f* [da gio-co]; (*membership ~*) tessera *f*; (*business ~*) bi-glietto *m* da visita; (*credit ~*) carta *f* di credito; *Comput* scheda *f*

cardboard /'kɑːdbɔːd/ *n* cartone *m*

cardboard box *n* scatola *f* di cartone; (*large*) scatolone *m*

card game *n* gioco *m* di carte

cardiac /'kɑːdɪæk/ *a* cardiaco

cardigan /'kɑːdɪgən/ *n* cardigan *m inv*

cardinal /'kɑːdɪnl/ *a* cardinale; **~ number** numero *m* cardinale ● *n Relig* cardinale *m*

card index *n* schedario *m*

cardiologist /kɑːdɪˈɒlədʒɪst/ *n* cardiologo, -a *mf*

cardiology /kɑːdɪˈɒlədʒɪ/ *n* cardiologia *f*

cardiovascular /kɑːdɪəˈvæskjʊlə(r)/ *a* car-diovascolare

card: card key *n* scheda *f* magnetica. **card table** *n* tappeto *m* verde. **card trick** *n* trucco *m* con le carte

care /keə(r)/ *n* cura *f*; (*caution*) attenzione *f*; (*worry*) preoccupazione *f*; **~ of** (*on letter abbr* **c/o**) presso; **take ~** (*be cautious*) fare atten-zione; **bye, take ~** ciao, stammi bene; **take ~ of** occuparsi di; **be taken into ~** essere preso in custodia da un ente assistenziale; **'[handle] with ~'** 'fragile' ● *vi* **~ about** inte-ressarsi di; **~ for** (*feel affection for*) volere bene a; (*look after*) aver cura di; **I don't ~ for chocolate** non mi piace il cioccolato; **I don't ~** non me ne importa; **who ~s?** chi se ne fre-ga?; **for all I ~** per quello che me ne importa

care assistant *n Br Med* assistente *mf* a domicilio

career /kəˈrɪə(r)/ *n* carriera *f*; (*profession*) professione *f*. **~ woman** *n* donna in carriera ● *vi* andare a tutta velocità

career: career break *n* pausa *f* nella car-riera. **career move** *n* passo *m* utile per un avanzamento di carriera. **careers adviser** *n* consulente *mf* di orientamento professionale. **careers office** *n* centro *m* di orientamento

professionale. **careers service** *n* servizio *m* di orientamento professionale

carefree /'keəfriː/ *a* spensierato

careful /'keəfʊl/ *a* attento; (*driver*) prudente

carefully /'keəfʊlɪ/ *adv* con attenzione

careless /'keəlɪs/ *a* irresponsabile; (*in work*) trascurato; (*work*) fatto con poca cura; (*driver*) distratto

carelessly /'keəlɪslɪ/ *adv* negligentemente

carelessness /'keəlɪsnɪs/ *n* trascuratezza *f*

carer /'keərə(r)/ *n Br* (*relative*) familiare *m* che assiste un anziano o un handicappato; (*professional*) assistente *mf* a domicilio

caress /kəˈres/ *n* carezza *f* ● *vt* accarezzare

caretaker /'keəteɪkə(r)/ *n* custode *mf*; (*in school*) bidello *m*

careworn /'keəwɔːn/ *a* (*face*) segnato dalle preoccupazioni

car ferry *n* traghetto *m* (*per il trasporto di auto*)

cargo /'kɑːgəʊ/ *n* (*pl* -**es**) carico *m*

cargo plane *n* aereo *m* da carico

cargo ship *n* nave *f* da carico

car hire *n* autonoleggio *m*

Caribbean /kærɪˈbiːən/ *n* **the ~** (*sea*) il Mar *m* dei Caraibi ● *a* caraibico

caricature /'kærɪkətjʊə(r)/ *n* caricatura *f* ● *vt* fare una caricatura di

caricaturist /'kærɪkətjʊərɪst/ *n* caricaturi-sta *mf*

caring /'keərɪŋ/ *a* (*parent*) premuroso; (*attitude*) altruista; **the ~ professions** le at-tività assistenziali

carjacking /'kɑːdʒækɪŋ/ *n* furto *m* d'auto con aggressione al conducente

carload /'kɑːləʊd/ *n* **a ~ of people** un'auto-mobile *f* piena di persone

carnage /'kɑːnɪdʒ/ *n* carneficina *f*

carnal /'kɑːn(ə)l/ *a* carnale

carnation /kɑːˈneɪʃn/ *n* garofano *m*

carnival /'kɑːnɪvl/ *n* carnevale *m*

carnivore /'kɑːnɪvɔː(r)/ *n* carnivoro *m*

carnivorous /kɑːˈnɪvərəs/ *a* carnivoro

carob /'kærəb/ *n* (*pod*) carruba *f*; (*tree*) carrubo *m*

carol /'kærəl/ *n* [**Christmas**] **~** canzone *f* na-talizia; **~ concert** concerto *m* natalizio; **go ~ singing** *andare a cantare le canzoni natali-zie per le strade*

carousel /kærʊˈsel/ *n* (*merry-go-round*) gio-stra *f*; (*for luggage*) nastro *m* trasportatore; (*for slides*) caricatore *m* circolare

carp[1] /kɑːp/ *n inv* carpa *f*

carp[2] *vi* lamentarsi; **~ at** trovare da ridire su

car park *n* parcheggio *m*

carpenter /'kɑːpəntə(r)/ *n* falegname *m*

carpentry /'kɑːpəntrɪ/ *n* falegnameria *f*

carpet /'kɑːpɪt/ *n* tappeto *m*; (*wall-to-wall*) moquette *f inv*; **be on the ~** *fig* essere ammo-nito ● *vt* mettere la moquette in (*room*)

carpet: carpet fitter *n* artigiano *m* che mette in opera la moquette. **carpet slipper** *n* pantofola *f*. **carpet sweeper** *n* battitappeto *m inv*. **carpet tile** *n* riquadro *m* di moquette

car phone *n* telefono *m* in macchina

car radio *n* autoradio *f inv*

carriage /'kærɪdʒ/ *n* carrozza *f*; (*of typewriter*) carrello *m*; (*of goods*) trasporto *m*; (*cost*) spese *fpl* di trasporto; (*bearing*) portamento *m*; **~ paid** *Comm* franco di porto

carriage clock *n* orologio *m* da tavolo

carriageway /'kærɪdʒweɪ/ *n* strada *f* carrozzabile; **north-bound ~** carreggiata *f* nord

carrier /'kærɪə(r)/ *n* (*company*) impresa *f* di trasporti; *Aeron* compagnia *f* di trasporto aereo; (*of disease*) portatore *m*

carrier [**bag**] *n* borsa *f* [per la spesa]

carrier pigeon *n* piccione *m* viaggiatore

carrot /'kærət/ *n* carota *f*

carry /'kærɪ/ *v* (*pt/pp* -**ied**) ● *vt* portare; (*transport*) trasportare; *Math* riportare; **get carried away** *fam* lasciarsi prender la mano ● *vi* (*sound:*) trasmettersi

■ **carry off** *vt* portare via; vincere (*prize*)

■ **carry on** *vi* continuare; (*fam: make scene*) fare delle storie; **~ on with sth** continuare qcsa; **~ on with sb** *fam* intendersela con qcno ● *vt* mantenere (*business*); **~ on doing sth** continuare a fare qcsa

■ **carry out** *vt* portare fuori; eseguire (*instructions, task*); mettere in atto (*threat*); effettuare (*experiment, survey*)

carrycot /'kærɪkɒt/ *n* porte-enfant *m inv*

carry-on *n fam* (*complicated procedure*) impresa *f*; (*bad behaviour*) storie *fpl*

carsick /'kɑːsɪk/ *a* **be ~** avere il mal d'auto

cart /kɑːt/ *n* carretto *m*; **put the ~ before the horse** *fig* mettere il carro davanti ai buoi ● *vt* (*fam: carry*) portare

cartel /kɑːˈtel/ *n* cartello *m*

carthorse /'kɑːθɔːs/ *n* cavallo *m* da tiro

cartilage /'kɑːtɪlɪdʒ/ *n Anat* cartilagine *f*

cartographer /kɑːˈtɒɡrəfə(r)/ *n* cartografo, -a *mf*

cartography /kɑːˈtɒɡrəfɪ/ *n* cartografia *f*

carton /'kɑːt(ə)n/ *n* scatola *f* di cartone; (*for drink*) cartone *m*; (*of cream, yoghurt*) vasetto *m*; (*of cigarettes*) stecca *f*

cartoon /kɑːˈtuːn/ *n* vignetta *f*; (*strip*) vignette *fpl*; (*film*) cartone *m* animato; (*in art*) bozzetto *m*

cartoonist /kɑːˈtuːnɪst/ *n* vignettista *mf*; (*for films*) disegnatore, -trice *mf* di cartoni animati

cartridge /'kɑːtrɪdʒ/ *n* cartuccia *f*; (*for film*) bobina *f*; (*of record player*) testina *f*

cartwheel /'kɑːtwiːl/ *n* (*of cart*) ruota *f* di carro; (*in gymnastics*) ruota *f*; **do a ~** (*in gymnastics*) fare la ruota

carve /kɑːv/ *vt* scolpire; tagliare (*meat*)

carving /'kɑːvɪŋ/ *n* scultura *f*

carving knife *n* trinciante *m*

car wash *n* autolavaggio *m inv*

car worker *n* operaio, -a *mf* dell'industria automobilistica

Casanova /'kæsənəʊvə/ *n* casanova *m inv*

cascade /kæsˈkeɪd/ *vi* scendere a cascata ● *n* cascata *f*

case[1] /keɪs/ *n* caso *m*; **in any ~** in ogni caso;

in that ~ in questo caso; **just in ~** per sicurezza; **in ~ he comes** nel caso in cui venisse; **in ~ of emergency** in caso d'emergenza

case[2] *n* (*container*) scatola *f*; (*crate*) cassa *f*; (*for spectacles*) astuccio *m*; (*suitcase*) valigia *f*; (*for display*) vetrina *f*

case history *n Med* cartella *f* clinica

casement window /'keɪsmənt/ *n* finestra *f* a battenti

case: casenotes *npl* pratica *f*. **case study** *n* analisi *f inv*. **casework** *n* **do ~** occuparsi di assistenza sociale

cash /kæʃ/ *n* denaro *m* contante; (*fam: money*) contanti *mpl*; **pay** [**in**] **~** pagare in contanti; **~ on delivery** pagamento alla consegna ● *vt* incassare (*cheque*)

■ **cash in on** *vt fam* approfittarsi di

cash: cash-and-carry *n* cash and carry *m inv*. **cash box** *n* cassetta *f* portavalori. **cash card** *n* bancomat® *m inv*. **cash desk** *n* cassa *f*. **cash dispenser** *n* sportello *m* automatico, cassa *f* automatica

cashew /kəˈʃuː/ *n* anacardio *m*

cash flow *n* flusso *m* di cassa; **~ difficulties** difficoltà *fpl* di flusso di cassa; **~ management** gestione *f* del flusso di cassa

cashier /kæˈʃɪə(r)/ *n* cassiere, -a *mf*

cashmere /'kæʃmɪə(r)/ *n* cachemire *m inv*

cash: cash on delivery *n* pagamento *m* alla consegna. **cashpoint** *n* sportello *m* automatico. **cash register** *n* registratore *m* di cassa

casing /'keɪsɪŋ/ *n* (*of machinery*) rivestimento *m*; (*of gearbox*) scatola *f*; (*of tyre*) copertone *m*

casino /kəˈsiːnəʊ/ *n* casinò *m inv*

cask /kɑːsk/ *n* barile *m*

casket /'kɑːskɪt/ *n* scrigno *m*; (*Am: coffin*) bara *f*

casserole /'kæsərəʊl/ *n* casseruola *f*; (*stew*) stufato *m*

cassette /kəˈset/ *n* cassetta *f*

cassette: cassette deck *n* piastra *f* di registrazione. **cassette player** *n* mangiacassette *m inv*. **cassette recorder** *n* registratore *m* (*a cassette*). **cassette tape** *n* cassetta *f*

cassock /'kæsək/ *n* tonaca *f*

cast /kɑːst/ *n* (*throw*) lancio *m*; (*mould*) forma *f*; *Theat* cast *m inv*; [**plaster**] **~** *Med* ingessatura *f* ● *vt* (*pt/pp* **cast**) dare (*vote*); *Theat* assegnare le parti di (*play*); fondere (*metal*); (*throw*) gettare; (*shed*) sbarazzarsi di; **~ an actor as** dare ad un attore il ruolo di; **~ a glance at** lanciare uno sguardo a

■ **cast off** *vi Naut* sganciare gli ormeggi ● *vt* (*in knitting*) diminuire

■ **cast on** *vt* (*in knitting*) avviare

castanets /kæstəˈnets/ *npl* nacchere *fpl*

castaway /'kɑːstəweɪ/ *n* naufrago, -a *mf*

caste /kɑːst/ *n* casta *f*

caster /'kɑːstə(r)/ *n* (*wheel*) rotella *f*

caster sugar *n* zucchero *m* raffinato

casting director /'kɑːstɪŋ/ *n* direttore *m* del casting

casting vote *n* voto *m* decisivo

cast iron n ghisa f ● a **cast-iron** di ghisa; fig solido

castle /ˈkɑːsl/ n castello m; (in chess) torre f

cast-offs npl abiti mpl smessi

castor /ˈkɑːstə(r)/ n (wheel) rotella f

castor oil n olio m di ricino

castor sugar n zucchero m raffinato

castrate /kæˈstreɪt/ vt castrare

castration /kæˈstreɪʃn/ n castrazione f

castrato /kæsˈtrɑːtəʊ/ n castrato m

casual /ˈkæʒʊəl/ a (chance) casuale; ⟨remark⟩ senza importanza; ⟨glance⟩ di sfuggita; ⟨attitude, approach⟩ disinvolto; ⟨chat⟩ informale; ⟨clothes⟩ casual inv; ⟨work⟩ saltuario; ~ **wear** abbigliamento m casual

casually /ˈkæʒʊəlɪ/ adv ⟨dress⟩ casual; ⟨meet⟩ casualmente

casualty /ˈkæʒʊəltɪ/ n (injured person) ferito m; (killed) vittima f

casualty [department] n pronto soccorso m

cat /kæt/ n gatto m; pej arpia f

catacombs /ˈkætəkuːmz/ npl catacombe fpl

catalogue /ˈkætəlɒg/ n catalogo m ● vt catalogare

catalyst /ˈkætəlɪst/ n Chem & fig catalizzatore m

catalytic converter /kætəˈlɪtɪk/ n Auto marmitta f catalitica

catamaran /kætəməˈræn/ n catamarano m

catapult /ˈkætəpʌlt/ n catapulta f; (child's) fionda f ● vt fig catapultare

cataract /ˈkætərækt/ n Med cataratta f

catarrh /kəˈtɑː(r)/ n catarro m

catastrophe /kəˈtæstrəfɪ/ n catastrofe f

catastrophic /kætəˈstrɒfɪk/ a catastrofico

cat burglar n Br scassinatore, -trice mf acrobata

catch /kætʃ/ n (of fish) pesca f; (fastener) fermaglio m; (on door) fermo m; (on window) gancio m; (fam: snag) tranello m ● v (pt/pp **caught**) ● vt acchiappare ⟨ball⟩; (grab) afferrare; prendere ⟨illness, fugitive, train⟩; ~ **a cold** prendersi un raffreddore; ~ **sight of** scorgere; **I caught him stealing** l'ho sorpreso mentre rubava; ~ **one's finger in the door** chiudersi il dito nella porta; ~ **sb's eye** or **attention** attirare l'attenzione di qcno ● vi ⟨fire:⟩ prendere; (get stuck) impigliarsi

■ **catch on** vi fam (understand) afferrare; (become popular) diventare popolare

■ **catch out** vt (show to be wrong) prendere in castagna

■ **catch up** vt raggiungere ● vi recuperare; ⟨runner:⟩ riguadagnare terreno; ~ **up with** raggiungere ⟨sb⟩; mettersi in pari con ⟨work⟩

catch-22 situation n situazione f senza uscita

catch-all a ⟨term⟩ polivalente; ⟨clause⟩ che comprende tutte le possibilità

catching /ˈkætʃɪŋ/ a contagioso

catchment area /ˈkætʃmənt/ n bacino m d'utenza

catchphrase /ˈkætʃfreɪz/ n tormentone m

catchword /ˈkætʃwɜːd/ n slogan m inv

catchy /ˈkætʃɪ/ a (-ier, -iest) orecchiabile

catechism /ˈkætɪkɪzm/ n catechismo m

categorical /kætɪˈgɒrɪkl/ a categorico

categorically /kætəˈgɒrɪklɪ/ adv categoricamente

category /ˈkætɪgərɪ/ n categoria f

cater /ˈkeɪtə(r)/ vi ~ **for** provvedere a ⟨needs⟩; fig venire incontro alle esigenze di ● vt occuparsi del rinfresco di ⟨party⟩

caterer /ˈkeɪtərə(r)/ n persona f che si occupa di ristorazione

catering /ˈkeɪtərɪŋ/ n (trade) ristorazione f; (food) rinfresco m

caterpillar /ˈkætəpɪlə(r)/ n bruco m

caterwaul /ˈkætəwɔːl/ vi miagolare

cat: catfish n pesce m gatto. **catflap** n gattaiola f. **catgut** n catgut m inv

cathedral /kəˈθiːdrl/ n cattedrale f

Catherine wheel /ˈkæθ(ə)rɪn/ n girandola f

catheter /ˈkæθɪtə(r)/ n catetere m

cathode-ray tube /kæθəʊdˈreɪ/ n tubo m a raggi catodici

Catholic /ˈkæθəlɪk/ a & n cattolico, -a mf

Catholicism /kəˈθɒlɪsɪzm/ n cattolicesimo m

catkin /ˈkætkɪn/ n Bot amento m

cat: cat litter n lettiera f del gatto. **catnap** vi fare un pisolino ● n pisolino m. **cat-o'-nine-tails** n gatto m a nove code. **cat's-eye** n Br catarifrangente m (inserito nell'asfalto). **catsuit** n tuta f

cattery /ˈkætərɪ/ n pensione f per gatti

cattle /ˈkæt(ə)l/ npl bestiame msg

cattle: cattle grid n recinto m metallico che impedisce al bestiame di accedere a una strada. **cattle market** n mercato m del bestiame; (fig fam: for sexual encounters) locale m dove la gente va per rimorchiare. **cattle shed** n stalla f

catty /ˈkætɪ/ a (-ier, -iest) dispettoso

catwalk /ˈkætwɔːk/ n passerella f

Caucasian /kɔːˈkeɪʒ(ə)n/ n (Geog: inhabitant) caucasico, -a mf; (white person) bianco, -a mf ● a Geog caucasico; ⟨race, man⟩ bianco

caught /kɔːt/ see **catch**

cauldron /ˈkɔːldrən/ n calderone m

cauliflower /ˈkɒlɪflaʊə(r)/ n cavolfiore m

cauliflower cheese n cavolfiori mpl gratinati

causal /ˈkɔːzəl/ a causale

cause /kɔːz/ n causa f; (reason) motivo m; **good** ~ buona causa ● vt causare; ~ **sb to do sth** far fare qcsa a qcno

causeway /ˈkɔːzweɪ/ n strada f sopraelevata

caustic /ˈkɔːstɪk/ a caustico

cauterize /ˈkɔːtəraɪz/ vt cauterizzare

caution /ˈkɔːʃn/ n cautela f; (warning) ammonizione f ● vt mettere in guardia; Jur ammonire

cautious /ˈkɔːʃəs/ a cauto

cautiously /ˈkɔːʃəslɪ/ adv cautamente

cavalcade /kævəlˈkeɪd/ n sfilata f

cavalier /kævəˈlɪə(r)/ a noncurante ● n C~

*sostenitore, -trice mf di Carlo I durante la guer-
ra civile inglese*

cavalry /'kævəlrɪ/ *n* cavalleria *f*

cave /keɪv/ *n* caverna *f*

■ **cave in** *vi* ‹roof:› crollare; (*fig: give in*)
capitolare

caveat /'kævɪæt/ *n* avvertimento *m*

cave: cave dweller *n* cavernicolo, -a *mf*.
caveman *n* cavernicolo *m*. **cave painting** *n*
pittura *f* rupestre

caver /'keɪvə(r)/ *n* speleologo, -a *mf*

cavern /'kævən/ *n* caverna *f*

caviare /'kævɪɑ:(r)/ *n* caviale *m*

caving /'keɪvɪŋ/ *n* speleologia *f*

cavity /'kævətɪ/ *n* cavità *f inv*; (*in tooth*) carie
f inv

cavity wall insulation *n* isolamento *m*
per muri a intercapedine

cavort /kə'vɔ:t/ *vi* saltellare

caw /kɔ:/ *n* (*noise*) gracchio *m* ● *vi* gracchiare

cayenne pepper /'kaɪen/ *n* pepe *m* di
Caienna

cayman /'keɪmən/ *n* caimano *m*

CB *n abbr* (**Citizens' Band**) CB *f inv* ● *attrib*
‹equipment, radio, wavelength› CB

cc *n abbr* (**cubic centimetres**) cc *m inv*

CCTV *abbr* (**closed-circuit television**) televisione *f* a circuito chiuso

CD *n abbr* (**Civil Defence**) difesa *f* civile;
abbr (**compact disc**) CD *m inv*; *Am abbr*
(**Congressional District**) circoscrizione *f*
del Congresso; *abbr* (**corps diplomatique**)
CD *m inv*

CD player *n* lettore *m* [di] compact, lettore
m di CD

CD-Rom /si:di:'rɒm/ *n* CD-Rom *m inv*

CD-Rom drive *n* lettore *m* CD-Rom

cease /si:s/ *n* **without** ~ incessantemente
● *vt/i* cessare

ceasefire /'si:sfaɪə(r)/ *n* cessate il fuoco *m*
inv

ceaseless /'si:slɪs/ *a* incessante

ceaselessly /'si:slɪslɪ/ *adv* incessantemente

cedar /'si:də(r)/ *n* cedro *m*

cede /si:d/ *vt* cedere

ceiling /'si:lɪŋ/ *n* soffitto *m*; *fig* tetto *m* [mas-
simo]

celebrate /'selɪbreɪt/ *vt* festeggiare
‹birthday, victory› ● *vi* far festa

celebrated /'selɪbreɪtɪd/ *a* celebre (**for** per)

celebration /selɪ'breɪʃn/ *n* celebrazione *f*

celebrity /sɪ'lebrətɪ/ *n* celebrità *f inv*

celeriac /sɪ'lerɪæk/ *n* sedano *m* rapa

celery /'selərɪ/ *n* sedano *m*

celestial /sɪ'lestɪəl/ *a* celestiale

celibacy /'selɪbəsɪ/ *n* celibato *m*

celibate /'selɪbət/ *a* ‹man› celibe; ‹woman›
nubile

cell /sel/ *n* cella *f*; *Biol* cellula *f*

cellar /'selə(r)/ *n* scantinato *m*; (*for wine*)
cantina *f*

cellist /'tʃelɪst/ *n* violoncellista *mf*

cello /'tʃeləʊ/ *n* violoncello *m*

Cellophane® /'seləfeɪn/ *n* cellofan® *m inv*

cellphone /'selfəʊn/ *n* [telefono *m*] cellulare *m*

cellular phone /seljʊlə'fəʊn/ *n* [telefono *m*]
cellulare *m*

cellulite /'seljʊlaɪt/ *n* cellulite *f*

celluloid /'seljʊlɔɪd/ *n* celluloide *f*

Celsius /'selsɪəs/ *a* Celsius

Celt /kelt/ *n* celta *mf*

Celtic /'keltɪk/ *a* celtico

cement /sɪ'ment/ *n* cemento *m*; (*adhesive*)
mastice *m* ● *vt* cementare; (*stick*) attaccare
col mastice; *fig* consolidare

cement mixer *n* betoniera *f*

cemetery /'semətrɪ/ *n* cimitero *m*

cenotaph /'senətæf/ *n* cenotafio *m*

censor /'sensə(r)/ *n* censore *m* ● *vt* censurare

censorship /'sensəʃɪp/ *n* censura *f*

censure /'senʃə(r)/ *n* biasimo *m* ● *vt* biasimare

census /'sensəs/ *n* censimento *m*

cent /sent/ *n* (*coin*) centesimo *m*

centenary /sen'ti:nərɪ/ *n*, *Am* **centennial**
/sen'tenɪəl/ *n* centenario *m*

center /'sentə(r)/ *n Am* = **centre**

centigrade /'sentɪgreɪd/ *a* centigrado

centilitre /'sentɪli:tə(r)/ *n* centilitro *m*

centimetre /'sentɪmi:tə(r)/ *n* centimetro *m*

centipede /'sentɪpi:d/ *n* centopiedi *m inv*

central /'sentrəl/ *a* centrale

central heating *n* riscaldamento *m* autonomo

centralize /'sentrəlaɪz/ *vt* centralizzare

central locking *n Auto* chiusura *f* centralizzata

centrally /'sentrəlɪ/ *adv* al centro; ~
heated con riscaldamento autonomo

central: central nervous system *n* sistema *m* nervoso centrale. **central processing
unit** *n Comput* unità *f inv* centrale di elaborazione. **central reservation** *n Auto* banchina
f spartitraffico *inv*

centre /'sentə(r)/ *n* centro *m* ● *v* (*pt/pp
centred*) ● *vt* centrare ● *vi* ~ **on** *fig*
incentrarsi su

centre: centrefold *n* (*pin-up picture*)
paginone *m*; (*model*) pin-up *f inv*. **centre
forward** *n* centravanti *m inv*. **centre half** *n*
Sport centromediano *m*. **centre of gravity** *n*
centro *m* di gravità. **centrepiece** *n* (*of table*)
centrotavola *m*; (*fig: of exhibition*) pezzo *m*
forte. **centre spread** *n* paginone *m*. **centre
stage** *n Theat* centro *m* della scena; **stand** ~
~ tenersi al centro della scena; **take/occupy**
~ ~ *fig* essere/mettersi in primo piano

centrifugal /sentrɪ'fjʊgl/ *a* ~ **force** forza *f*
centrifuga

century /'sentʃərɪ/ *n* secolo *m*

CEO *n abbr* (**Chief Executive Officer**) *n* direttore, -trice *mf* generale

ceramic /sɪ'ræmɪk/ *a* ceramico

ceramics /sɪ'ræmɪks/ *n* (*art*) ceramica *fsg*;
(*objects*) ceramiche *fpl*

cereal /'sɪərɪəl/ *n* cereale *m*

cerebral /'serɪbrl/ a cerebrale
cerebral palsy /'pɔ:lzɪ/ n paralisi f cerebrale
ceremonial /serɪ'məʊnɪəl/ a da cerimonia ● n cerimoniale m
ceremonially /serɪ'məʊnɪlɪ/ adv secondo il rituale
ceremonious /serɪ'məʊnɪəs/ a cerimonioso
ceremoniously /serɪ'məʊnɪəslɪ/ adv in modo cerimonioso
ceremony /'serɪmənɪ/ n cerimonia f; **without ~** senza cerimonie
cert /sɜ:t/ n Br fam **it's a [dead] ~!** ci puoi scommettere!
certain /'sɜ:tn/ a certo; **for ~** di sicuro; **make ~** accertarsi; **he is ~ to win** è certo di vincere; **it's not ~ whether he'll come** non è sicuro che venga
certainly /'sɜ:tnlɪ/ adv certamente; **~ not!** no di certo!
certainty /'sɜ:tntɪ/ n certezza f; **it's a ~** è una cosa certa
certifiable /'sɜ:tɪfaɪəbl/ a (verifiable statement, evidence) dimostrabile; (mad) pazzo
certificate /sə'tɪfɪkət/ n certificato m
certify /'sɜ:tɪfaɪ/ vt (pt/pp -ied) certificare; (declare insane) dichiarare malato di mente
certitude /'sɜ:tɪtju:d/ n certezza f
cervical /'sɜ:vɪkl/ a cervicale
cervix /'sɜ:vɪks/ n cervice f uterina, collo m dell'utero
cessation /se'seɪʃn/ n cessazione f
cesspool /'sespu:l/ n pozzo m nero
cf. abbr (**compare**) cf, cfr
CFC n abbr (**chlorofluorocarbon**) CFC m inv
CFE abbr **College of Further Education**
chafe /tʃeɪf/ vt irritare
chaff /tʃɑ:f/ n pula f
chaffinch /'tʃæfɪntʃ/ n fringuello m
chagrin /'ʃægrɪn/ n **much to his ~** con suo grande dispiacere
chain /tʃeɪn/ n catena f ● vt incatenare (prisoner); attaccare con la catena (dog) (**to** a)
■ **chain up** vt legare alla catena (dog)
chain: chain gang n gruppo m di prigionieri incatenati. **chain letter** n lettera f della catena di Sant'Antonio. **chain mail** n cotta f di maglia. **chain reaction** n reazione f a catena. **chain saw** n motosega f. **chain-smoke** vi fumare una sigaretta dopo l'altra. **chain-smoker** n fumatore, -trice mf accanito, -a. **chain store** n negozio m appartenente a una catena
chair /tʃeə(r)/ n sedia f; Univ cattedra f ● vt presiedere
chairlift /'tʃeəlɪft/ n seggiovia f
chairman /'tʃeəmən/ n presidente m; **~ and managing director** presidente m direttore generale
chairperson /'tʃeəpɜ:s(ə)n/ n presidente m, -essa f
chairwoman /'tʃeəwʊmən/ n presidentessa f

chalet /'ʃæleɪ/ n chalet m inv; (in holiday camp) bungalow m inv
chalice /'tʃælɪs/ n Relig calice m
chalk /tʃɔ:k/ n gesso m
chalky /'tʃɔ:kɪ/ a gessoso
challenge /'tʃælɪndʒ/ n sfida f; Mil intimazione f ● vt sfidare; Mil intimare il chi va là a; fig mettere in dubbio (statement)
challenger /'tʃælɪndʒə(r)/ n sfidante mf
challenging /'tʃælɪndʒɪŋ/ a (job) impegnativo
chamber /'tʃeɪmbə(r)/ n **C~ of Commerce** camera f di commercio
chamber: chambermaid n cameriera f [d'albergo]. **chamber music** n musica f da camera. **Chamber of Commerce** n Camera f di Commercio. **chamber orchestra** n orchestra f da camera. **chamber pot** n vaso m da notte
chambers /'tʃeɪmbəz/ n pl Jur studio m [legale]
chameleon /kə'mi:lɪən/ n also fig camaleonte m
chamois[1] /'ʃæmwɑ:/ n inv (animal) camoscio m
chamois[2] /'ʃæmɪ/ n **~[-leather]** [pelle f di] camoscio m
champagne /ʃæm'peɪn/ n champagne m inv
champion /'tʃæmpɪən/ n Sport campione m; (of cause) difensore m, difenditrice f ● vt (defend) difendere; (fight for) lottare per
championship /'tʃæmpɪənʃɪp/ n Sport campionato m
chance /tʃɑ:ns/ n caso m; (possibility) possibilità f inv; (opportunity) occasione f; **by ~** per caso; **take a ~** provarci; **give sb a second ~** dare un'altra possibilità a qcno ● attrib fortuito ● vt **if you ~ to see him** se ti capita di vederlo; **I'll ~ it** fam corro il rischio
chancel /'tʃɑ:nsəl/ n Archit coro m
chancellor /'tʃɑ:nsələ(r)/ n cancelliere m; Univ rettore m; **C~ of the Exchequer** ≈ ministro m del tesoro
chancy /'tʃɑ:nsɪ/ a rischioso
chandelier /ʃændə'lɪə(r)/ n lampadario m
chandler /'tʃɑ:ndlə(r)/ n fornitore m navale
change /tʃeɪndʒ/ n cambiamento m; (money) resto m; (small coins) spiccioli mpl; **for a ~** tanto per cambiare; **have a ~ of heart** cambiare idea; **a ~ of clothes** un cambio di vestiti; **~ of address** cambiamento m d'indirizzo; **a ~ of scene** also fig un cambiamento di scena; **the ~** [of life] la menopausa ● vt cambiare; (substitute) scambiare (**for** con); **~ one's clothes** cambiarsi [i vestiti]; **~ trains** cambiare treno ● vi cambiare; (~ clothes) cambiarsi; **all ~!** stazione terminale!
■ **change down** vi Auto passare alla marcia inferiore
■ **change up** vi Auto passare alla marcia superiore
changeability /tʃeɪndʒə'bɪlɪtɪ/ n (of weather) instabilità f

changeable /ˈtʃeɪndʒəbl/ *a* mutevole; ⟨*weather*⟩ variabile

changeless /ˈtʃeɪndʒlɪs/ *a* ⟨*appearance*⟩ inalterabile; ⟨*character*⟩ costante; ⟨*law, routine*⟩ immutabile

change machine *n* distributore *m* di monete

changeover /ˈtʃeɪndʒəʊvə(r)/ *n* (*time period*) periodo *m* di transizione; (*transition*) passaggio *m*; (*of leaders*) subentro *m*; (*of employees, guards*) cambio *m*; (*Sport: in relay*) passaggio *m* del testimone; (*Sport: of ends*) cambiamento *m*

changing-room *n* camerino *m*; (*for sports*) spogliatoio *m*

channel /ˈtʃænl/ *n* canale *m*; **the [English] C~** la Manica ● *vt* (*pt/pp* **channelled**) **~ one's energies into sth** convogliare le proprie energie in qcsa

channel: channel ferry *n* traghetto *m* attraverso la Manica. **Channel Islands** *npl* Isole *fpl* del Canale. **Channel Tunnel** *n* tunnel *m inv* sotto la Manica

chant /tʃɑ:nt/ *n* cantilena *f*; (*of demonstrators*) slogan *m inv* di protesta ● *vt* cantare; ⟨*demonstrators*⟩ gridare ● *vi* ⟨*demonstrators*⟩ gridare slogan di protesta

chaos /ˈkeɪɒs/ *n* caos *m*

chaotic /keɪˈɒtɪk/ *a* caotico

chap /tʃæp/ *n fam* tipo *m*

chapel /ˈtʃæpl/ *n* cappella *f*

chaperon /ˈʃæpərəʊn/ *n* chaperon *f inv* ● *vt* fare da chaperon a ⟨*sb*⟩

chaplain /ˈtʃæplɪn/ *n* cappellano *m*

chapped /tʃæpt/ *a* ⟨*skin, lips*⟩ screpolato

chapter /ˈtʃæptə(r)/ *n* capitolo *m*

char[1] /tʃɑ:(r)/ *n fam* donna *f* delle pulizie

char[2] *vt* (*pt/pp* **charred**) (*burn*) carbonizzare

character /ˈkærɪktə(r)/ *n* carattere *m*; (*in novel, play*) personaggio *m*; **that's out of ~** non è da te/lui; **quite a ~** *fam* un tipo particolare

character actor *n* caratterista *mf*

character assassination *n* denigrazione *f*

characteristic /kærəktəˈrɪstɪk/ *a* caratteristico ● *n* caratteristica *f*

characteristically /kærəktəˈrɪstɪlkɪ/ *adv* tipicamente

characterization /kærɪktəraɪˈzeɪʃn/ *n* caratterizzazione *f*

characterize /ˈkærɪktəraɪz/ *vt* caratterizzare

character reference *n* referenze *fpl* (*relative al carattere*)

charade /ʃəˈrɑːd/ *n* farsa *f*; **~s** sciarada *fsg*

charcoal /ˈtʃɑ:kəʊl/ *n* carbonella *f*

charge /tʃɑ:dʒ/ *n* (*cost*) prezzo *m*; *Electr, Mil* carica *f*; *Jur* accusa *f*; **free of ~** gratuito; **be in ~** essere responsabile (**of** di); **take ~** assumersi la responsabilità; **take ~ of** occuparsi di ● *vt* far pagare ⟨*fee*⟩; far pagare a ⟨*person*⟩; *Electr, Mil* caricare; *Jur* accusare (**with** di); **~ sb for sth** far pagare qcsa a qcno; **what do you ~?** quanto prende?; **~ it to my account** lo addebiti sul mio conto ● *vi* (*attack*) caricare

charge card *n* (*credit card*) carta *f* di addebito; (*store card*) carta *f* di credito [di un negozio]

charged /tʃɑ:dʒd/ *a Phys* carico; **emotionally ~** ⟨*atmosphere*⟩ carico di emozione

chargé d'affaires /ʃɑ:ʒeɪdæˈfeə(r)/ *n* incaricato *m* d'affari

charge hand *n* caposquadra *mf*

charge nurse *n* caposala *mf*

char-grilled /-ˈɡrɪld/ *a* alla brace

chariot /ˈtʃærɪət/ *n* cocchio *m*

charisma /kəˈrɪzmə/ *n* carisma *m*

charismatic /kærɪzˈmætɪk/ *a* carismatico

charitable /ˈtʃærɪtəbl/ *a* caritatevole; (*kind*) indulgente

charity /ˈtʃærətɪ/ *n* carità *f*; (*organization*) associazione *f* di beneficenza; **concert given for ~** concerto *m* di beneficenza; **live on ~** vivere di elemosina

charity: charity box *n* (*in church*) cassetta *f* delle offerte. **charity shop** *n* negozio *m* dell'usato a scopo di beneficenza. **charity work** *n* lavoro *m* volontario (*per beneficenza*)

charlady /ˈtʃɑ:leɪdɪ/ *n Br* donna *f* delle pulizie

charlatan /ˈʃɑ:lətən/ *n* ciarlatano, -a *mf*

charm /tʃɑ:m/ *n* fascino *m*; (*object*) ciondolo *m* ● *vt* affascinare

charmer /ˈtʃɑ:mə(r)/ *n* **he's a real ~** è un vero seduttore

charming /ˈtʃɑ:mɪŋ/ *a* affascinante

charmingly /ˈtʃɑ:mɪŋlɪ/ *adv* in modo affascinante

chart /tʃɑ:t/ *n* carta *f* nautica; (*table*) tabella *f*

charter /ˈtʃɑ:tə(r)/ *n* **~** [**flight**] [volo *m*] charter *m inv* ● *vt* noleggiare

chartered: chartered accountant *n* commercialista *mf*. **chartered flight** *n Br* volo *m* charter *inv*. **chartered surveyor** *n Br* perito *m* edile

charter plane *n Br* charter *m inv*

charwoman /ˈtʃɑ:wʊmən/ *n* donna *f* delle pulizie

chase /tʃeɪs/ *n* inseguimento *m*; **give ~** mettersi all'inseguimento ● *vt* inseguire

■ **chase away, chase off** *vt* cacciare via

■ **chase up** *vt fam* cercare

chaser /ˈtʃeɪsə(r)/ *n* (*fam: drink*) liquore *m* bevuto dopo la birra

chasm /ˈkæz(ə)m/ *n* abisso *m*

chassis /ˈʃæsɪ/ *n* (*pl* **chassis** /ˈʃæsɪz/) telaio *m*

chaste /tʃeɪst/ *a* casto

chasten /ˈtʃeɪs(ə)n/ *vt* castigare; **they looked suitably ~ed** avevano l'aria mortificata

chastise /tʃæˈstaɪz/ *vt* castigare

chastity /ˈtʃæstətɪ/ *n* castità *f*

chat /tʃæt/ *n* chiacchierata *f*; **have a ~ with** fare quattro chiacchere con ● *vi* (*pt/pp* **chatted**) chiacchierare

■ **chat up** *vt* abbordare

chat show *n* talk show *m inv*

chattel /'tʃæt(ə)l/ *n Jur* **goods and ~s** beni *mpl* mobili

chatter /'tʃætə(r)/ *n* chiacchiere *fpl* ● *vi* chiacchierare; ⟨*teeth:*⟩ battere

chatterbox /'tʃætəbɒks/ *n fam* chiacchierone, -a *mf*

chatty /'tʃætɪ/ *a* (**-ier, -iest**) chiacchierone; ⟨*style*⟩ familiare

chauffeur /'ʃəʊfə(r)/ *n* autista *mf*

chauvinism /'ʃəʊvɪnɪzm/ *n* sciovinismo *m*

chauvinist /'ʃəʊvɪnɪst/ *n* sciovinista *mf*. **male ~** *fam* maschilista *m*

cheap /tʃi:p/ *a* a buon mercato; ⟨*rate*⟩ economico; (*vulgar*) grossolano; (*of poor quality*) scadente ● *adv* a buon mercato

cheapen /'tʃi:p(ə)n/ *vt* **~ oneself** screditarsi

cheaply /'tʃi:plɪ/ *adv* a buon mercato

cheap rate *a* & *adv Teleph* a tariffa ridotta

cheat /tʃi:t/ *n* imbroglione, -a *mf*; (*at cards*) baro *m* ● *vt* imbrogliare; **~ sb out of sth** sottrarre qcsa a qcno con l'inganno ● *vi* imbrogliare; (*at cards*) barare

■ **cheat on** *vt fam* tradire ⟨*wife*⟩

check¹ /tʃek/ *a* ⟨*pattern*⟩ a quadri ● *n* disegno *m* a quadri

check² *n* verifica *f*; (*of tickets*) controllo *m*; (*in chess*) scacco *m*; (*Am: bill*) conto *m*; (*Am: cheque*) assegno *m*; (*Am: tick*) segnetto *m*; **keep a ~ on** controllare; **keep in ~** tenere sotto controllo ● *vt* verificare; controllare ⟨*tickets*⟩; (*restrain*) contenere; (*stop*) bloccare ● *vi* controllare; **~ on sth** controllare qcsa

■ **check in** *vi* registrarsi all'arrivo (*in albergo*); *Aeron* fare il check-in ● *vt* registrare all'arrivo (*in albergo*)

■ **check out** *vi* (*of hotel*) saldare il conto ● *vt* (*fam: investigate*) controllare

■ **check up** *vi* accertarsi

■ **check up on** *vt* prendere informazioni su

checked /tʃekt/ *a* a quadri

checkers /'tʃekəz/ *n Am* dama *f*

check-in *n* accettazione *f*, check-in *m inv*

check-in desk *n* banco *m* dell'accettazione, banco *m* del check-in

check-in time *n* check-in *m inv*

checking account /'tʃekɪŋ/ *n Am* conto *m* corrente

check: checklist *n* lista *f* di controllo. **check mark** *n Am* segnetto *m*. **checkmate** *int* scacco matto!. **checkout** *n* (*in supermarket*) cassa *f*. **checkout assistant, checkout operator** *n Br* cassiere, -a *mf*. **checkpoint** *n* posto *m* di blocco. **checkroom** *n Am* deposito *m* bagagli. **check-up** *n Med* visita *f* di controllo, check-up *m inv*

cheddar /'tʃedə(r)/ *n formaggio m semi-stagionato*

cheek /tʃi:k/ *n* guancia *f*; (*impudence*) sfacciataggine *f*

cheekbone /'tʃi:kbəʊn/ *n* zigomo *m*

cheekily /'tʃi:kɪlɪ/ *adv* sfacciatamente

cheeky /'tʃi:kɪ/ *a* sfacciato

cheep /tʃi:p/ *vi* pigolare

cheer /tʃɪə(r)/ *n* evviva *m inv*; **three ~s** tre urrà; **~s!** salute!; (*goodbye*) arrivederci!; (*thanks*) grazie! ● *vt/i* acclamare

■ **cheer up** *vt* tirare su [di morale] ● *vi* tirarsi su [di morale]; **~ up!** su con la vita!

cheerful /'tʃɪəfʊl/ *a* allegro

cheerfully /'tʃɪəfʊlɪ/ *adv* allegramente; **I could ~ strangle him!** lo strangolerei volentieri!

cheerfulness /'tʃɪəfʊlnɪs/ *n* allegria *f*

cheerily /'tʃɪərɪlɪ/ *adv* allegramente

cheering /'tʃɪərɪŋ/ *n* acclamazione *f*

cheerio /tʃɪərɪ'əʊ/ *int fam* arrivederci

cheerleader /'tʃɪəli:də(r)/ *n* leader *mf* dei tifosi

cheerless /'tʃɪəlɪs/ *a* triste, tetro

cheery /'tʃɪərɪ/ *a* allegro

cheese /tʃi:z/ *n* formaggio *m*

■ **cheese off** *vt fam* **be ~d off with one's job** essere stufo del proprio lavoro; **I'm really ~d off about it** ne ho le scatole piene

cheese: cheeseboard *n* (*object*) vassoio *m* dei formaggi; (*selection*) piatto *m* di formaggi. **cheeseburger** *n* cheeseburger *m inv*. **cheesecake** *n* dolce *m* al formaggio. **cheesecloth** *n* mussola *f*, tela *f* indiana. **cheese counter** *n* banco *m* dei formaggi

cheesy /'tʃi:zɪ/ *a* ⟨*smell*⟩ di formaggio; ⟨*grin*⟩ smagliante

cheetah /'tʃi:tə/ *n* ghepardo *m*

chef /ʃef/ *n* cuoco, -a *mf*, chef *mf inv*

chemical /'kemɪkl/ *a* chimico ● *n* prodotto *m* chimico

chemically /'kemɪklɪ/ *adv* chimicamente

chemise /ʃə'mi:z/ *n* (*undergarment*) sottoveste *f inv*; (*dress*) chemisier *m inv*

chemist /'kemɪst/ *n* (*pharmacist*) farmacista *mf*; (*scientist*) chimico, -a *mf*

chemistry /'kemɪstrɪ/ *n* chimica *f*

chemist's [shop] *n* farmacia *f*

chemotherapy /ki:məʊ'θerəpɪ/ *n* chemioterapia *f*

cheque /tʃek/ *n* assegno *m*

chequebook /'tʃekbʊk/ *n* libretto *m* degli assegni

cheque card *n* carta *f* assegni

chequer /'tʃekə(r)/ *n* (*square*) scacco *m*; (*pattern*) motivo *m* a scacchi; (*in game*) pedina *f*

chequered /'tʃekəd/ *a* (*patterned*) a scacchi; ⟨*fig: career, history*⟩ movimentato

chequers /'tʃekəz/ *n* dama *f*

cherish /'tʃerɪʃ/ *vt* curare teneramente; (*love*) avere caro; nutrire ⟨*hope*⟩

cherry /'tʃerɪ/ *n* ciliegia *f*; (*tree*) ciliegio *m*

cherry brandy *n* cherry-brandy *m inv*

cherry tree *n* ciliegio *m*

cherub /'tʃerəb/ *n* cherubino *m*

chervil /'tʃɜ:vɪl/ *n* cerfoglio *m*

chess /tʃes/ *n* scacchi *mpl*

chess: chessboard *n* scacchiera *f*. **chessman** *n* pezzo *m* degli scacchi. **chessplayer** *n* scacchista *mf*. **chess set** *n* scacchi *mpl*

chest /tʃest/ *n* petto *m*; (*box*) cassapanca *f*; **get sth off one's ~** *fig* levarsi un peso [dallo stomaco]

chest freezer *n* freezer *m inv* orizzontale, congelatore *m* orizzontale

chestnut /ˈtʃesnʌt/ *n* castagna *f*; (*tree*) castagno *m*

chest of drawers *n* cassettone *m*, comò *m inv*

chesty /ˈtʃestɪ/ *a* ⟨person⟩ che soffre di bronchite; ⟨cough⟩ bronchitico

chew /tʃuː/ *vt* masticare

■ **chew over** *vt* (*fam: think about carefully*) rimuginare su

chewing gum /ˈtʃuːɪŋ/ *n* gomma *f* da masticare

chewy /ˈtʃuːɪ/ *a* ⟨meat⟩ legnoso; ⟨toffee⟩ gommoso

chic /ʃiːk/ *a* chic *inv*

chick /tʃɪk/ *n* pulcino *m*; (*fam: girl*) ragazza *f*

chicken /ˈtʃɪkn/ *n* pollo *m* ● *attrib* ⟨soup, casserole⟩ di pollo ● *a fam* fifone

■ **chicken out** *vi fam* he ~ed out gli è venuta fifa

chicken: chicken breast *n* petto *m* di pollo. **chicken curry** *n* pollo *m* al curry. **chicken feed** *n* mangime *m* per i polli; (*fam: paltry sum*) miseria *f*. **chicken livers** *npl* fegatini *mpl* di pollo. **chicken noodle soup** *n* vermicelli *mpl* in brodo di pollo. **chickenpox** *n* varicella *f*. **chicken wire** *n* rete *f* metallica (*a maglia esagonale*)

chickpea /ˈtʃɪkpiː/ *n* cece *m*

chicory /ˈtʃɪkərɪ/ *n* cicoria *f*

chief /tʃiːf/ *a* principale ● *n* capo *m*

chief executive officer *n* direttore, -trice *mf* generale

chief inspector *n* (*Br: of police*) ispettore *m* capo

chiefly /ˈtʃiːflɪ/ *adv* principalmente

chief superintendent *n* (*Br: of police*) commissario *m* capo

chiffon /ˈʃɪfɒn/ *n* chiffon *m* ● *a* ⟨dress, scarf⟩ di chiffon

chilblain /ˈtʃɪlbleɪn/ *n* gelone *m*

child /tʃaɪld/ *n* (*pl* ~**ren**) bambino, -a *mf*; (*son/daughter*) figlio, -a *mf*

child: child abuse *n* violenza *f* sui minori; (*sexual*) violenza *f* sessuale sui minori. **childbearing** *n* gravidanza *f*; **of ~ age** in età feconda. **child benefit** *n* *Br* assegni *mpl* familiari. **childbirth** *n* parto *m*. **childcare** *n* (*bringing up children*) educazione *f* dei bambini; (*nurseries etc*) strutture *fpl* di assistenza ai bambini

childhood /ˈtʃaɪldhʊd/ *n* infanzia *f*

childish /ˈtʃaɪldɪʃ/ *a* infantile

childishness /ˈtʃaɪldɪʃnɪs/ *n* puerilità *f*

childless /ˈtʃaɪldlɪs/ *a* senza figli

childlike /ˈtʃaɪldlaɪk/ *a* ingenuo

child: child-minder *n* baby-sitter *mf inv*. **child molester** *n* molestatore, -trice *mf* di bambini. **child prodigy** *n* bambino prodigio. **child-proof** *a* ⟨container⟩ a prova di bambino; ~ **lock** sicura *f* a prova di bambino

children /ˈtʃɪldrən/ *npl see* **child**

children's home *n* istituto *m* per l'infanzia

Chile /ˈtʃɪlɪ/ *n* Cile *m*

Chilean /ˈtʃɪlɪən/ *a & n* cileno, -a *mf*

chill /tʃɪl/ *n* freddo *m*; (*illness*) infreddatura *f* ● *vt* raffreddare

chilli /ˈtʃɪlɪ/ *n* (*pl* -**es**) ~ [**pepper**] peperoncino *m*

chilly /ˈtʃɪlɪ/ *a* freddo

chime /tʃaɪm/ *vi* suonare

chimera /kɪˈmɪərə/ *n* (*beast, idea*) chimera *f*

chimney /ˈtʃɪmnɪ/ *n* camino *m*

chimney: chimneybreast *n* bocca *f* del camino. **chimney-pot** *n* comignolo *m*. **chimney-sweep** *n* spazzacamino *m*

chimp /tʃɪmp/ *n fam* scimpanzé *m*

chimpanzee /tʃɪmpænˈziː/ *n* scimpanzé *m inv*

chin /tʃɪn/ *n* mento *m*

China /ˈtʃaɪnə/ *n* Cina *f*

china *n* porcellana *f*

China: China Sea *n* Mar *m* Cinese. **China tea** *n* tè *m inv* cinese. **Chinatown** *n* quartiere *m* cinese

Chinese /tʃaɪˈniːz/ *a & n* cinese *mf*; (*language*) cinese *m*; **the ~** *pl* i cinesi

Chinese lantern *n* lanterna *f* cinese

chink[1] /tʃɪŋk/ *n* (*slit*) fessura *f*

chink[2] *n* (*noise*) tintinnio *m* ● *vi* tintinnare

chinos /ˈtʃiːnəʊz/ *npl* pantaloni *mpl* cachi di cotone

chintz /tʃɪnts/ *n* chintz *m inv*

chip /tʃɪp/ *n* (*fragment*) scheggia *f*; (*in china, paintwork*) scheggiatura *f*; *Comput* chip *m inv*; (*in gambling*) fiche *f inv*; ~**s** *pl Br Culin* patatine *fpl* fritte; *Am Culin* patatine *fpl*; **have a ~ on one's shoulder** avere un complesso di inferiorità ● *vt* (*pt/pp* **chipped**) (*damage*) scheggiare

■ **chip in** *fam vi* intromettersi; (*with money*) contribuire

chipboard /ˈtʃɪpbɔːd/ *n* truciolato *m*

chipmunk /ˈtʃɪpmʌŋk/ *n* tamia *m inv*

chip pan *n* friggitrice *f*

chipped /tʃɪpt/ *a* (*damaged*) scheggiato

chippings /ˈtʃɪpɪŋz/ *npl* (*on road*) breccia *f*; '**loose ~**' 'attenzione: breccia'

chippy /ˈtʃɪpɪ/ *n* (*Br fam: chip shop*) negozio *m* di fish and chips

chip shop *n Br* negozio *m* di fish and chips

chiropodist /kɪˈrɒpədɪst/ *n* podiatra *mf inv*

chiropody /kɪˈrɒpədɪ/ *n* podiatria *f*

chirp /tʃɜːp/ *vi* cinguettare; ⟨cricket:⟩ fare cri cri

chirpy /ˈtʃɜːpɪ/ *a fam* pimpante

chisel /ˈtʃɪzl/ *n* scalpello *m* ● *vt* (*pt/pp* **chiselled**) scalpellare

chit /tʃɪt/ *n* bigliettino *m*

chitchat /ˈtʃɪt(t)ʃæt/ *n fam* chiacchiere *fpl*; **spend one's time in idle ~** *fam* perdere tempo in chiacchiere

chivalrous /ˈʃɪvlrəs/ *a* cavalleresco

chivalrously /ˈʃɪvlrəslɪ/ *adv* con cavalleria

chivalry /ˈʃɪvlrɪ/ *n* cavalleria *f*

chives /tʃaɪvz/ *npl* erba *f* cipollina

chlorine /ˈklɔːriːn/ *n* cloro *m*

chlorofluorocarbon /klɔːˈrəʊfluərəʊ'kɑː-b(ə)n/ n clorofluorocarburo m
chloroform /ˈklɔːrəfɔːm/ n cloroformio m
chlorophyll /ˈklɒrəfɪl/ n clorofilla f
choc ice n Br gelato m ricoperto di cioccolato
chock /tʃɒk/ n zeppa f
chock-a-block /tʃɒkəˈblɒk/, **chock-full** /tʃɒkˈfʊl/ a pieno zeppo
chocolate /ˈtʃɒkələt/ n cioccolato m; (drink) cioccolata f; **a ~** un cioccolatino
choice /tʃɔɪs/ n scelta f ● a scelto
choir /ˈkwaɪə(r)/ n coro m
choirboy /ˈkwaɪəbɔɪ/ n corista m
choirgirl /ˈkwaɪəɡɜːl/ n corista f
choke /tʃəʊk/ n Auto aria f ● vt/i soffocare; **I ~d on a fishbone** mi è rimasta in gola una lisca
choker /ˈtʃəʊkə(r)/ n girocollo m
cholera /ˈkɒlərə/ n colera m
cholesterol /kəˈlestərɒl/ n colesterolo m
■ **chomp on** /tʃɒmp/ vi fam masticare rumorosamente
choose /tʃuːz/ vt/i (pt **chose**, pp **chosen**) scegliere; **~ to do sth** scegliere di fare qcsa; **as you ~** come vuoi
choos[e]y /ˈtʃuːzɪ/ a fam difficile
chop /tʃɒp/ n (blow) colpo m (d'ascia); Culin costata f; **get the ~** (fam: employee) essere licenziato; (project:) essere bocciato ● vt (pt/pp **chopped**) tagliare
■ **chop down** vt abbattere (tree)
■ **chop off** vt spaccare
chopper /ˈtʃɒpə(r)/ n accetta f; fam elicottero m
chopping: chopping block n ceppo m; **put one's head on the ~** ~ fig esporsi a rischi. **chopping board** n tagliere m. **chopping knife** n coltello m
choppy /ˈtʃɒpɪ/ a increspato
chopsticks /ˈtʃɒpstɪks/ npl bastoncini mpl cinesi
choral /ˈkɔːrəl/ a corale; **~ society** coro m
chord /kɔːd/ n Mus corda f
chore /tʃɔː(r)/ n corvé f inv; [household] **~s** faccende fpl domestiche
choreographer /kɒrɪˈɒɡrəfə(r)/ n coreografo, -a f
choreography /kɒrɪˈɒɡrəfɪ/ n coreografia f
chorister /ˈkɒrɪstə(r)/ n corista mf
chortle /ˈtʃɔːtl/ vi ridacchiare
chorus /ˈkɔːrəs/ n coro m; (of song) ritornello m
chorus girl n ballerina f di varietà
chose, chosen /tʃəʊz, ˈtʃəʊzn/ see **choose**
chowder /ˈtʃaʊdə(r)/ n zuppa m di pesce
chow mein /tʃaʊˈmeɪn/ n piatto m cinese di spaghetti fritti con gamberetti, ecc. e verdure
Christ /kraɪst/ n Cristo m; **~ Almighty!** fam porca miseria!
christen /ˈkrɪs(ə)n/ vt battezzare
christening /ˈkrɪsnɪŋ/ n battesimo m
Christian /ˈkrɪstʃən/ a & n cristiano, -a mf
Christianity /krɪstɪˈænətɪ/ n cristianesimo m

Christian name n nome m di battesimo
Christmas /ˈkrɪsməs/ n Natale m ● attrib di Natale
Christmas: Christmas box n Br mancia f natalizia. **Christmas card** n biglietto m d'auguri di Natale. **Christmas carol** n canto m natalizio, canto m di Natale. **Christmas cracker** n tubo m di cartone colorato contente una sorpresa. **Christmas Day** n il giorno di Natale. **Christmas Eve** n la vigilia di Natale. **Christmas present** n regalo m di Natale. **Christmas stocking** n calza f (per i doni di Babbo Natale). **Christmas tree** n albero m di Natale
chrome /krəʊm/ n, **chromium** /ˈkrəʊmɪəm/ n cromo m
chromium-plated /-ˈpleɪtɪd/ a cromato
chromosome /ˈkrəʊməsəʊm/ n cromosoma m
chronic /ˈkrɒnɪk/ a cronico
chronicle /ˈkrɒnɪkl/ n cronaca f
chronological /krɒnəˈlɒdʒɪk/ a cronologico
chronologically /krɒnəˈlɒdʒɪkɪ/ adv (ordered) in ordine cronologico
chrysalis /ˈkrɪsəlɪs/ n crisalide f
chrysanthemum /krɪˈsænθəməm/ n crisantemo m
chubby /ˈtʃʌbɪ/ a (-ier, -iest) paffuto
chuck /tʃʌk/ vt fam buttare
■ **chuck in** vt fam mollare (job, boyfriend)
■ **chuck out** vt fam buttare via (object); buttare fuori (person)
■ **chuck up** vt fam = **chuck in**
chuckle /ˈtʃʌk(ə)l/ vi ridacchiare
chuffed /tʃʌft/ a fam felice come una Pasqua
chug /tʃʌɡ/ vi **the train ~ged into/out of the station** il treno è entrato nella/uscito dalla stazione sbuffando
chum /tʃʌm/ n fam amico, -a mf
chummy /ˈtʃʌmɪ/ a fam **be ~ with** essere amico di
chump /tʃʌmp/ n fam zuccone m, -a f; Culin braciola f
chunk /tʃʌŋk/ n grosso pezzo m
chunky /ˈtʃʌŋkɪ/ a (sweater) di lana grossa; (jewellery) massiccio; (fam: person) tarchiato
Chunnel /ˈtʃʌnl/ n Br fam tunnel m inv sotto la Manica
church /tʃɜːtʃ/ n chiesa f
church hall n sala f parrocchiale
churchyard /ˈtʃɜːtʃjɑːd/ n cimitero m
churlish /ˈtʃɜːlɪʃ/ a sgarbato
churn /tʃɜːn/ n zangola f; (for milk) bidone m ● vt churn out sfornare
chute /ʃuːt/ n scivolo m; (for rubbish) canale m di scarico
chutney /ˈtʃʌtnɪ/ n salsa f piccante a base di frutti e spezie
CID abbr **Criminal Investigation Department**
cider /ˈsaɪdə(r)/ n sidro m
cigar /sɪˈɡɑː(r)/ n sigaro m
cigarette /sɪɡəˈret/ n sigaretta f
cigarette: cigarette butt, cigarette end

n cicca *f*, mozzicone *m* di sigaretta. **cigarette lighter** *n* accendino *m*

cinch /sɪntʃ/ *n fam* **it's a ~** è un gioco da ragazzi

cinder /'sɪndə(r)/ *n (glowing)* brace *f*; **burn sth to a ~** carbonizzare qcsa

Cinderella /sɪndə'relə/ *n* cenerentola *f*

cinder track *n* pista *f* di cenere

cine-camera /'sɪnɪ-/ *n* cinepresa *f*

cine-film *n* filmino *m* a passo ridotto

cinema /'sɪnɪmə/ *n* cinema *m inv*

cinema complex *n* cinema *m inv* multisale

cinemagoer /'sɪnɪməgəʊə(r)/ *n (spectator)* spettatore, -trice *mf*; *(regular)* cinefilo, -a *mf*

cinematography /sɪnəmə'tɒɡrəfɪ/ *n* cinematografia *f*

cinnamon /'sɪnəmən/ *n* cannella *f*

cipher /'saɪfə(r)/ *n (code)* cifre *fpl*; *fig* nullità *f inv*

circa /'sɜːkə/ *prep* circa

circle /'sɜːkl/ *n* cerchio *m*; *Theat* galleria *f*; **in a ~** in cerchio ● *vt* girare intorno a; cerchiare *(mistake)* ● *vi* descrivere dei cerchi

circuit /'sɜːkɪt/ *n* circuito *m*; *(lap)* giro *m*

circuit board *n* circuito *m* stampato

circuitous /sə'kjuːɪtəs/ *a* **~ route** percorso *m* lungo e indiretto

circular /'sɜːkjʊlə(r)/ *a & n* circolare *f*

circular letter *n* circolare *f*

circular saw *n* sega *f* circolare

circulate /'sɜːkjʊleɪt/ *vt* far circolare ● *vi* circolare

circulation /sɜːkjʊ'leɪʃn/ *n* circolazione *f*; *(of newspaper)* tiratura *f*

circulatory /sɜːkjʊ'leɪtərɪ/ *a Med* circolatorio

circumcise /'sɜːkəmsaɪz/ *vt* circoncidere

circumcision /sɜːkəm'sɪʒn/ *n* circoncisione *f*

circumference /ʃə'kʌmfərəns/ *n* conconferenza *f*

circumflex /'sɜːkəmfleks/ *n* accento *m* circonflesso

circumnavigate /sɜːkəm'nævɪɡeɪt/ *vt* doppiare *(cape)*; circumnavigare *(world)*

circumnavigation /sɜːkəmnævɪ'ɡeɪʃn/ *n* circumnavigazione *f*

circumspect /'sɜːkəmspekt/ *a* circospetto

circumspectly /'sɜːkəmspektlɪ/ *adv* in modo circospetto

circumstance /'sɜːkəmstəns/ *n* circostanza *f*; **~s** *pl (financial)* condizioni *fpl* finanziarie

circumstantial /sɜːkəm'stænʃl/ *a (Jur: evidence)* indiziario; *(detailed)* circostanziato

circus /'sɜːkəs/ *n* circo *m*

cirrhosis /sɪ'rəʊsɪs/ *n* cirrosi *f inv*

CIS *abbr* (**Commonwealth of Independent States**) CSI *f*

cistern /'sɪstən/ *n (tank)* cisterna *f*; *(of WC)* serbatoio *m*

citadel /'sɪtədel/ *n* cittadella *f*

cite /saɪt/ *vt* citare

citizen /'sɪtɪzn/ *n* cittadino, -a *mf*; *(of town)* abitante *mf*

citizen: Citizens' Advice Bureau *n* ufficio *m* di consulenza legale gratuita per i cittadini. **citizen's arrest** *n* arresto *m* effettuato da un privato cittadino. **citizens' band** *n* Radio banda *f* cittadina

citizenship /'sɪtɪznʃɪp/ *n* cittadinanza *f*

citric acid /sɪtrɪk'æsɪd/ acido *m* citrico

citrus /'sɪtrəs/ *n* **~** [**fruit**] agrume *m*

city /'sɪtɪ/ *n* città *f inv*; **the C~** la City [di Londra]

city centre *n Br* centro *m* [della città]

city slicker *n fam* cittadino *m* sofisticato

civic /'sɪvɪk/ *a* civico ● **~s** *npl* educazione *fsg* civica

civic centre *n* centro *m* municipale

civil /'ʃɪvl/ *a* civile

civil engineer *n* ingeniere *m* civile

civil engineering *n* ingegneria *f* civile

civilian /sɪ'vɪljən/ *a* civile; **in ~ clothes** in borghese ● *n* civile *mf*

civility /sɪ'vɪlətɪ/ *n* cortesia *f*

civilization /sɪvɪlaɪ'zeɪʃn/ *n* civiltà *f inv*

civilize /'sɪvɪlaɪz/ *vt* civilizzare

civilized /'sɪvɪlaɪzd/ *a (country)* civilizzato; *(person, behaviour)* civile; **become ~** civilizzarsi

civil: civil law *n* diritto *m* civile. **civil liability** *n Jur* responsabilità *f inv* civile. **civil liberty** *n* libertà *f inv* civile

civilly /'sɪvɪlɪ/ *adv* civilmente

civil: civil rights *npl* diritti *mpl* civili ● *attrib (march, activist)* per i diritti civili. **civil servant** *n* impiegato, -a *mf* statale. **Civil Service** *n* pubblica amministrazione *f*. **civil war** *n* guerra *f* civile. **civil wedding** *n* matrimonio *m* civile

civvies /'sɪvɪz/ *npl fam* **in ~** in borghese

cl *abbr* (**centilitre(s)**) cl

clad /klæd/ *a* vestito (**in** di)

cladding /'klædɪŋ/ *n* rivestimento *m*

claim /kleɪm/ *n* richiesta *f*; *(right)* diritto *m*; *(assertion)* dichiarazione *f*; **lay ~ to sth** rivendicare qcsa ● *vt* richiedere; reclamare *(lost property)*; rivendicare *(ownership)*; **~ that** sostenere che

■ **claim back** *vt* reclamare *(money)*

claimant /'kleɪmənt/ *n* richiedente *mf*; *(to throne)* pretendente *mf*

clairvoyant /kleə'vɔɪənt/ *n* chiaroveggente *mf*

clam /klæm/ *n Culin* vongola *f*

■ **clam up** *vi* zittirsi

clamber /'klæmbə(r)/ *vi* arrampicarsi

clammy /'klæmɪ/ *a* (**-ier, -iest**) appiccicaticcio

clamour /'klæmə(r)/ *n (noise)* clamore *m*; *(protest)* rimostranza *f* ● *vi* **~ for** chiedere a gran voce

clamp /klæmp/ *n* morsa *f* ● *vt* ammorsare; *Auto* mettere i ceppi bloccaruote a

■ **clamp down** *vi fam* essere duro

■ **clamp down on** *vt* reprimere

clan /klæn/ *n* clan *m inv*

clandestine /klæn'destɪn/ *a* clandestino

clang /klæŋ/ *n* suono *m* metallico

clanger /'klæŋə(r)/ *n fam* gaffe *f inv*

clank /klæŋk/ *n* rumore *m* metallico ● *vi* fare un rumore metallico

clannish /'klænɪʃ/ *a* ⟨*pej: family, profession*⟩ chiuso

clap /klæp/ *n* **give sb a** ~ applaudire qcno; ~ **of thunder** tuono *m* ● *vt/i* (*pt/pp* **clapped**) applaudire; ~ **one's hands** applaudire

clapboard /'klæpbɔːd/ *n Am* rivestimento *m* di legno ● *attrib Am* rivestito di legno

clapped out /klæpt/ *a fam* (*past it*) sfinito; (*exhausted*) stanco morto; ⟨*car, machine*⟩ scassato

clapping /'klæpɪŋ/ *n* applausi *mpl*

claptrap /'klæptræp/ *n fam* sciocchezze *fpl*

claret /'klærət/ *n* claret *m inv*

clarification /klærɪfɪ'keɪʃn/ *n* chiarimento *m*

clarify /'klærɪfaɪ/ *vt/i* (*pt/pp* **-ied**) chiarire

clarinet /klærɪ'net/ *n* clarinetto *m*

clarinettist /klærɪ'netɪst/ *n* clarinettista *mf*

clarity /'klærətɪ/ *n* chiarezza *f*

clash /klæʃ/ *n* scontro *m*; (*noise*) fragore *m* ● *vi* scontrarsi; ⟨*colours:*⟩ stonare; ⟨*events:*⟩ coincidere

clasp /klɑːsp/ *n* chiusura *f* ● *vt* agganciare; (*hold*) stringere

class /klɑːs/ *n* classe *f*; (*lesson*) corso *m* ● *vt* classificare

class-conscious *a* classista

class-consciousness *n* classismo *m*

classic /'klæsɪk/ *a* classico ● *n* classico *m*; ~**s** *pl Univ* lettere *fpl* classiche

classical /'klæsɪk(ə)l/ *a* classico

classification /klæsɪfɪ'keɪʃn/ *n* classificazione *f*

classified ad /klæsɪfaɪd'æd/ *n* annuncio *m*

classified section *n* pagina *f* degli annunci

classify /'klæsɪfaɪ/ *vt* (*pt/pp* **-ied**) classificare

class: classmate *n* compagno, -a *mf* di classe. **classroom** *n* aula *f*. **class system** *n* sistema *m* classista

classy /'klɑːsɪ/ *a* (**-ier, -iest**) *fam* d'alta classe

clatter /'klætə(r)/ *n* fracasso *m* ● *vi* far fracasso

clause /klɔːz/ *n* clausola *f*; *Gram* proposizione *f*

claustrophobia /klɒstrə'fəʊbɪə/ *n* claustrofobia *f*

claustrophobic /klɒstrə'fəʊbɪk/ *a* claustrofobico

clavichord /'klævɪkɔːd/ *n* clavicordo *m*

clavicle /'klævɪkl/ *n* clavicola *f*

claw /klɔː/ *n* artiglio *m*; (*of crab, lobster & Techn*) tenaglia *f* ● *vt* ⟨*cat:*⟩ graffiare

clay /kleɪ/ *n* argilla *f*

clayey /'kleɪɪ/ *a* ⟨*soil*⟩ argilloso

clay pigeon shooting *n* tiro *m* al piattello

clean /kliːn/ *a* pulito, lindo ● *adv* completa-

mente ● *vt* pulire ⟨*shoes, windows*⟩; ~ **one's teeth** lavarsi i denti; **have a coat** ~**ed** portare un cappotto in lavanderia

■ **clean out** *vt* ripulire ⟨*room*⟩; **be** ~**ed out** (*fig: have no money*) essere senza un soldo

■ **clean up** *vt* pulire ● *vi* far pulizia

clean-cut *a* ⟨*image, person*⟩ rispettabile

cleaner /'kliːnə(r)/ *n* uomo *m*/donna *f* delle pulizie; (*substance*) detersivo *m*; [**dry**] ~**'s** lavanderia *f*, tintoria *f*

cleaning /'kliːnɪŋ/ *n* pulizia *f*; **do the** ~ fare le pulizie

cleaning lady *n* donna *f* delle pulizie

cleaning product *n* detergente *m*

cleanliness /'klenlɪnɪs/ *n* pulizia *f*

clean-living /-'lɪvɪŋ/ *n* vita *f* integra ● *a* ⟨*person*⟩ integro

cleanse /klenz/ *vt* pulire

cleanser /'klenzə(r)/ *n* detergente *m*

clean-shaven /-'ʃeɪvən/ *a* sbarbato

clean sheet *n* **start with a** ~ *fig* voltare pagina

cleansing cream /'klenzɪŋ/ *n* latte *m* detergente

clear /klɪə(r)/ *a* chiaro; ⟨*conscience*⟩ pulito; ⟨*road*⟩ libero; ⟨*profit, advantage, majority*⟩ netto; ⟨*sky*⟩ sereno; ⟨*water*⟩ limpido; ⟨*glass*⟩ trasparente; **make sth** ~ mettere qcsa in chiaro; **have I made myself** ~**?** mi sono fatto capire?; **I'm not** ~ **about what I have to do** non mi è ben chiaro quello che devo fare; **five** ~ **days** cinque giorni buoni; **be in the** ~ essere a posto ● *adv* **stand** ~ **of** allontanarsi da; **keep** ~ **of** tenersi alla larga da ● *vt* sgombrare ⟨*room, street*⟩; sparecchiare ⟨*table*⟩; (*acquit*) scagionare; (*authorize*) autorizzare; scavalcare senza toccare ⟨*fence, wall*⟩; guadagnare ⟨*sum of money*⟩; passare ⟨*Customs*⟩; ~ **one's throat** schiarirsi la gola ● *vi* ⟨*face, sky:*⟩ rasserenarsi; ⟨*fog:*⟩ dissiparsi

■ **clear away** *vt* metter via

■ **clear off** *vi fam* filar via

■ **clear out** *vt* sgombrare ● *vi fam* filar via

■ **clear up** *vt* (*tidy*) mettere a posto; chiarire ⟨*mystery*⟩ ● *vi* ⟨*weather:*⟩ schiarirsi

clearance /'klɪərəns/ *n* ⟨*space*⟩ spazio *m* libero; (*authorization*) autorizzazione *f*; (*Customs*) sdoganamento *m*

clearance sale *n* liquidazione *f*

clear-cut *a* ⟨*plan, division*⟩ ben definito; ⟨*problem, rule*⟩ chiaro; ⟨*difference, outline*⟩ netto; **the matter is not so** ~ la faccenda non è così semplice

clear-headed /-'hedɪd/ *a* lucido

clearing /'klɪərɪŋ/ *n* radura *f*

clearly /'klɪəlɪ/ *adv* chiaramente

clear-sighted /-'saɪtɪd/ *a* perspicace

clearway /'klɪəweɪ/ *n Auto* strada *f* con divieto di sosta

cleavage /'kliːvɪdʒ/ *n* (*woman's*) décolleté *m inv*

cleave /kliːv/ *vt* spaccare

cleaver /'kliːvə(r)/ *n* mannaia *f*

clef /klef/ *n Mus* chiave *f*

cleft /kleft/ *n* fenditura *f*

clemency /'klemənsɪ/ n clemenza f

clement /'klemənt/ a clemente

clench /klentʃ/ vt serrare

clergy /'klɜːdʒɪ/ npl clero m

clergyman /'klɜːdʒɪmən/ n ecclesiastico m

cleric /'klerɪk/ n ecclesiastico m

clerical /'klerɪkl/ a impiegatizio; Relig clericale

clerical assistant n impiegato, -a mf

clerk /klɑːk/, Am /klɜːk/ n impiegato, -a mf; (Am: shop assistant) commesso, -a mf

clever /'klevə(r)/ a intelligente; (skilful) abile

cleverly /'klevəlɪ/ adv intelligentemente; (skilfully) abilmente

cliché /'kliːʃeɪ/ n cliché m inv

clichéd /'kliːʃeɪd/ a (idea, technique) convenzionale; (art, music) stereotipato; ~ expression frase f fatta

click /klɪk/ vi scattare; (Comput: with mouse) cliccare ● n (Comput: with mouse) click m inv
■ **click on** vt Comput cliccare su

client /'klaɪənt/ n cliente mf

clientele /kliːɒn'tel/ n clientela f

cliff /klɪf/ n scogliera f

cliffhanger /'klɪfhæŋə(r)/ n it was a real ~ ci ha lasciato in sospeso

climate /'klaɪmət/ n clima f

climatic /klaɪ'mætɪk/ a climatico

climax /'klaɪmæks/ n punto m culminante

climb /klaɪm/ n salita f ● vt scalare (mountain); arrampicarsi su (ladder, tree) ● vi arrampicarsi; (rise) salire; (road:) salire
■ **climb down** vi scendere; (from ladder, tree) scendere; fig tornare sui propri passi
■ **climb over** vt scavalcare (fence, wall)
■ **climb up** vt salire su (hill)

climber /'klaɪmə(r)/ n alpinista mf; (plant) rampicante m

climbing: climbing boot n scarpone m da alpinismo. **climbing expedition** n scalata f. **climbing frame** n struttura f su cui possono arrampicarsi i bambini

clinch /klɪntʃ/ vt fam concludere (deal) ● n (in boxing) clinch m inv

clincher /'klɪntʃə(r)/ n (fam: act, remark) fattore m decisivo; (argument) argomento m decisivo

cling /klɪŋ/ vi (pt/pp clung) aggrapparsi; (stick) aderire

cling film n pellicola f trasparente

clingy /'klɪŋɪ/ a (dress) attillato; (person) appiccicoso

clinic /'klɪnɪk/ n ambulatorio m

clinical /'klɪnɪkl/ a clinico

clinically /'klɪnɪklɪ/ adv clinicamente

clink /klɪŋk/ n tintinnio m; (fam: prison) galera f ● vi tintinnare

clip¹ /klɪp/ n fermaglio m; (jewellery) spilla f ● vt (pt/pp clipped) attaccare

clip² n (extract) taglio m ● vt obliterare (ticket)

clip: clipboard n fermablocco m. **clip-clop** n rumore m fatto dagli zoccoli dei cavalli. **clip-on** a (bow tie) con la clip. **clip-on**

microphone n microfono m con la clip. **clip-ons** npl (earrings) orecchini mpl con le clip

clippers /'klɪpəz/ npl (for hair) rasoio m; (for hedge) tosasiepi m inv; (for nails) tronchesina f

clipping /'klɪpɪŋ/ n (from newspaper) ritaglio m

clique /kliːk/ n cricca f

cliquey, cliquish /'kliːkɪ, 'kliːkɪʃ/ a (atmosphere) esclusivo; (profession, group) chiuso

cloak /kləʊk/ n mantello m

cloak: cloak-and-dagger a (film) d'avventura; (surreptitious) clandestino. **cloakroom** n guardaroba m inv; (toilet) bagno m. **cloakroom attendant** n (Br: at toilets) addetto, -a mf ai bagni; (in hotel) guardarobiere, -a mf. **cloakroom ticket** n scontrino m del guardaroba

clobber /'klɒbə(r)/ n fam armamentario m ● vt (fam: hit) colpire; (defeat) stracciare

cloche /klɒʃ/ n (in garden) campana f di vetro

cloche hat n cloche f inv

clock /klɒk/ n orologio m; (fam: speedometer) tachimetro m
■ **clock in** vi attaccare
■ **clock out** vi staccare

clock: clock face n quadrante m. **clock radio** n orologio, -a mf. **clock radio** n radiosveglia f. **clock speed** n Comput velocità f di clock. **clock tower** n torre f dell'orologio. **clock-watch** vi guardare continuamente l'orologio. **clockwise** a & adv in senso orario. **clockwork** n meccanismo m; **like ~** fam alla perfezione ● attrib a molla

clod /klɒd/ n zolla f

clog /klɒg/ n zoccolo m ● vt (pt/pp clogged) ~ [up] intasare (drain); inceppare (mechanism) ● vi (drain:) intasarsi

cloister /'klɔɪstə(r)/ n chiostro m

clone /kləʊn/ n Biol, Comput, fig clone m ● vt clonare

close¹ /kləʊs/ a vicino; (friend) intimo; (weather) afoso; **have a ~ shave** fam scamparla bella; **be ~ to sb** essere unito a qcno ● adv vicino; **~ by** vicino; **it's ~ on five o'clock** sono quasi le cinque

close² /kləʊz/ n fine f; **draw to a ~** concludere ● vt chiudere ● vi chiudersi; (shop:) chiudere
■ **close down** vt chiudere ● vi (TV station:) interrompere la trasmissione; (factory:) chiudere
■ **close in** vi (mist:) calare; (enemy:) avvicinarsi da ogni lato
■ **close up** vi (come closer together) stringersi; (shop:) chiudere ● vt (bring closer together) avvicinare; chiudere (shop)

close combat n corpo a corpo m inv

close-cropped /-'krɒpt/ a (hair) rasato

closed-circuit television /kləʊzdsɜːkɪttelɪ'vɪʒən/ n televisione f a circuito chiuso

closed shop /kləʊzd'ʃɒp/ n azienda f che as-

sume solo personale aderente ad un dato sindacato

close-fitting /kləʊsˈfɪtɪŋ/ a ‹garment› attillato

close-knit /kləʊsˈnɪt/ a fig ‹family, group› affiatato

closely /ˈkləʊslɪ/ adv da vicino; ‹watch, listen› attentamente

close season /kləʊs/ n stagione f di chiusura della caccia e della pesca

closet /ˈklɒzɪt/ n Am armadio m

close-up /ˈkləʊs-/ n primo piano m

closing: closing date n data f di scadenza. **closing-down sale** n liquidazione f totale [per cessata attività]. **closing time** n orario m di chiusura

closure /ˈkləʊʒə(r)/ n chiusura f

clot /klɒt/ n grumo m; (fam: idiot) tonto, -a mf ● vi (pt/pp **clotted**) ‹blood:› coagularsi

cloth /klɒθ/ n (fabric) tessuto m; (duster etc) straccio m

clothe /kləʊð/ vt vestire

clothes /kləʊðz/ npl vestiti mpl, abiti mpl

clothes: clothes-brush n spazzola f per abiti. **clothes horse** n stendibiancheria m inv. **clothes-line** n corda f stendibiancheria

clothing /ˈkləʊðɪŋ/ n abbigliamento m

clotted cream n Br panna f rappresa (ottenuta scaldando il latte)

cloud /klaʊd/ n nuvola f

■ **cloud over** vi rannuvolarsi

cloudburst /ˈklaʊdbɜːst/ n acquazzone m

cloudy /ˈklaʊdɪ/ a (-ier, -iest) nuvoloso; ‹liquid› torbido

clout /klaʊt/ n fam colpo m; (influence) impatto m (with su) ● vt fam colpire

clove /kləʊv/ n chiodo m di garofano; ~ **of garlic** spicchio m d'aglio

cloven foot, cloven hoof /ˈkləʊvən/ n (of animal) zoccolo m fesso; (of devil) piede m biforcuto

clover /ˈkləʊvə(r)/ n trifoglio m

clover leaf n raccordo m di due autostrade

clown /klaʊn/ n pagliaccio m ● vi ~ [**about**] fare il pagliaccio

club /klʌb/ n club m inv; (weapon) clava f; Sport mazza f; ~**s** pl ‹Cards› fiori mpl ● v (pt/pp **clubbed**) ● vt bastonare

■ **club together** vi unirsi

club: club foot n piede m deformato. **clubhouse** n (for socializing) circolo m; (Am: for changing) spogliatoio m. **club sandwich** n club-sandwich m inv

cluck /klʌk/ vi chiocciare

clue /kluː/ n indizio m; (in crossword) definizione f; **I haven't a** ~ fam non ne ho idea

clued-up /kluːdˈʌp/ a Br fam beninformato

clueless /ˈkluːlɪs/ a Br fam incapace

clump /klʌmp/ n gruppo m

clump about, clump around vi (walk noisily) camminare con passo pesante

clumsily /ˈklʌmzɪlɪ/ adv in modo maldestro; ‹remark› senza tatto

clumsiness /ˈklʌmzɪnɪs/ n goffaggine f

clumsy /ˈklʌmzɪ/ a (-ier, -iest) maldestro; ‹tool› scomodo; ‹remark› senza tatto

clung /klʌŋ/ see **cling**

cluster /ˈklʌstə(r)/ n gruppo m ● vi raggrupparsi (**round** intorno a)

clutch /klʌtʃ/ n stretta f; Auto frizione f; **be in sb's** ~**es** essere in balia di qcno ● vt stringere; (grab) afferrare ● vi ~ **at** afferrare

clutch bag n pochette f inv

clutch cable n cavo m della frizione

clutter /ˈklʌtə(r)/ n caos m ● vt ~ [**up**] ingombrare

cm abbr (**centimetre**) cm

CND n abbr (**Campaign for Nuclear Disarmament**) campagna f per il disarmo nucleare

Co. abbr (**company**) C., C.ia; **and** ~ hum e compagnia; abbr (**county**) contea f

c/o abbr (**care of**) c/o, presso

coach /kəʊtʃ/ n pullman m inv; Rail vagone m; (horse-drawn) carrozza f; Sport allenatore, -trice mf ● vt fare esercitare; Sport allenare

coach: coach party n Br gruppo m di gitanti (in pullman). **coach station** n Br stazione f dei pullman. **coach trip** n viaggio m in pullman. **coachwork** n Br carrozzeria f

coagulate /kəʊˈægjʊleɪt/ vi coagularsi

coagulation /kəʊəgjʊˈleɪʃn/ n coagulazione f

coal /kəʊl/ n carbone m

coalition /kəʊəˈlɪʃn/ n coalizione f

coal: coal-mine n miniera f di carbone. **coal scuttle** n secchio m del carbone. **coal seam** n giacimento m di carbone

coarse /kɔːs/ a grossolano; ‹joke› spinto

coarse-grained /-ˈɡreɪnd/ a ‹texture› a grana grossa

coarsely /ˈkɔːslɪ/ adv ‹ground› grossolanamente; ‹joke› in modo spinto

coast /kəʊst/ n costa f ● vi (freewheel) scendere a ruota libera; Auto scendere in folle

coastal /ˈkəʊstəl/ a costiero

coastguard /ˈkəʊs(t)ɡɑːd/ n guardia f costiera

coaster /ˈkəʊstə(r)/ n (mat) sottobicchiere m inv

coastline /ˈkəʊstlaɪn/ n litorale m

coat /kəʊt/ n cappotto m; (of animal) manto m; (of paint) mano f; ~ **of arms** stemma f ● vt coprire; (with paint) ricoprire

coat-hanger n gruccia f

coat-hook n gancio m [appendiabiti]

coating /ˈkəʊtɪŋ/ n rivestimento m; (of paint) stato m

coat-tails npl falde fpl; **be always hanging on sb's** ~ attaccarsi sempre alle falde di qcno

coax /kəʊks/ vt convincere con le moine

cob /kɒb/ n (of corn) pannocchia f

cobble /ˈkɒbl/ vt ~ **together** raffazzonare

cobbler /ˈkɒblə(r)/ n ciabattino m

cobblestones /ˈkɒbəlstəʊnz/ npl ciottolato msg

cobra /ˈkəʊbrə/ n cobra m inv

cobweb /ˈkɒbweb/ n ragnatela f

cocaine /kə'keɪn/ n cocaina f

coccyx /'kɒksɪks/ n coccige m

cock /kɒk/ n gallo m; (any male bird) maschio m; vulg cazzo m ● vt sollevare il grilletto di ‹gun›; ~ **its ears** ‹animal:› drizzare le orecchie

■ **cock up** fam vt incasinare ● vi incasinarsi

cock-a-doodle-doo /kɒkədu:d(ə)l'du:/ int chicchirichì

cock-a-hoop a fam al settimo cielo

cock-and-bull story n fam panzana f

cockatoo /kɒkə'tu:/ n cacatoa m inv

cockcrow /'kɒkkrəʊ/ n **at** ~ al primo canto del gallo

cocked hat /kɒkt'hæt/ n fam **knock sb/sth into a** ~ ~ schiacciare qcno/qcsa

cockerel /'kɒkərəl/ n galletto m

cocker spaniel /'kɒkə(r)/ n cocker m inv [spaniel]

cock-eyed /-'aɪd/ a fam storto; (absurd) assurdo

cockfighting /'kɒkfaɪtɪŋ/ n combattimenti mpl di galli

cockle /'kɒkl/ n cardio m

cockney /'kɒknɪ/ n (dialect) dialetto m londinese; (person) abitante mf dell'est di Londra

cockpit /'kɒkpɪt/ n Aeron cabina f

cockroach /'kɒkrəʊtʃ/ n scarafaggio m

cocksure /kɒk'ʃʊə(r)/ a ‹person, manner, attitude› presuntuoso

cocktail /'kɒkteɪl/ n cocktail m inv

cocktail: cocktail bar n [cocktail] bar m inv. **cocktail dress** n abito m da cocktail. cocktail-party m inv. **cocktail party** n cocktail m inv. **cocktail shaker** n shaker m inv. **cocktail stick** n stecchino m

cock-up n sl **make a** ~ fare un casino (**of** con)

cocky /'kɒkɪ/ a (-ier, -iest) fam presuntuoso

cocoa /'kəʊkəʊ/ n cacao m

coconut /'kəʊkənʌt/ n noce f di cocco

coconut palm n palma f di cocco

coconut shy n Br tiro m al bersaglio in cui si devono abbattere noci di cocco

cocoon /kə'ku:n/ n bozzolo m

COD abbr (**cash on delivery**) pagamento m alla consegna

cod /kɒd/ n inv merluzzo m

coddle /'kɒd(ə)l/ vt coccolare

code /kəʊd/ n codice m

coded /'kəʊdɪd/ a codificato

codeine /'kəʊdi:n/ n codeina f

coding /'kəʊdɪŋ/ n Comput codifica f

cod-liver oil n olio m di fegato di merluzzo

coeducational /kəʊedjʊ'keɪʃənəl/ a misto

coefficient /kəʊɪ'fɪʃənt/ n coefficiente m

coerce /kəʊ'ɜ:s/ vt costringere

coercion /kəʊ'ɜ:ʃn/ n coercizione f

coexist /kəʊɪg'zɪst/ vi coesistere

coexistence /kəʊɪg'zɪstəns/ n coesistenza f

coffee /'kɒfɪ/ n caffè m inv

coffee: coffee bar n caffè m inv, bar m inv. **coffee bean** n chicco m di caffè. **coffee bre-**

ak n pausa f per il caffè. **coffee grinder** n macinacaffè m inv. **coffee machine** n (in café) macchina f per l'espresso. **coffee-maker** n (on stove) caffettiera f; (electric) macchina f per il caffè (con il filtro). **coffee morning** n Br riunione m mattutina in cui viene servito il caffè. **coffee percolator** n (on stove) caffettiera f; (electric) macchina f per il caffè (con il filtro). **coffee-pot** n caffettiera f. **coffee shop** n torrefazione f; (café) caffè m inv, bar m inv. **coffee table** n tavolino m inv

coffer /'kɒfə(r)/ n forziere m

coffin /'kɒfɪn/ n bara f

cog /kɒg/ n Techn dente m

cogent /'kəʊdʒənt/ a convincente

cogitate /'kɒdʒɪtɪt/ vi cogitare

cognac /'kɒnjæk/ n Cognac m

cognoscenti /kɒnə'ʃentɪ/ npl intenditori mpl

cogwheel /'kɒgwi:l/ n ruota f dentata

cohabit /kəʊ'hæbɪt/ vi Jur convivere

coherent /kəʊ'hɪərənt/ a coerente; (when speaking) logico

cohesion /kəʊ'hi:ʒən/ n coesione f

cohort /'kəʊhɔ:t/ n fig seguito m

coil /kɔɪl/ n rotolo m; Electr bobina f; ~**s** pl spire fpl ● vt ~[**up**] avvolgere

coin /kɔɪn/ n moneta f ● vt coniare ‹word›

coinage /'kɔɪnɪdʒ/ n (of coins, currency) coniatura f; (word, phrase) neologismo m

coin box n (pay phone) telefono m a monete; (on pay phone, in laundromat) gettoniera f

coincide /kəʊɪn'saɪd/ vi coincidere

coincidence /kəʊ'ɪnsɪdəns/ n coincidenza f

coincidental /kəʊɪnsɪ'dentl/ a casuale

coincidentally /kəʊɪnsɪ'dentlɪ/ adv casualmente

Coke® /kəʊk/ n Coca® f

coke n [carbone m] coke m

colander /'kʌləndə(r)/ n Culin colapasta m inv

cold /kəʊld/ a freddo; **I'm** ~ ho freddo; **get** ~ **feet** farsi prendere dalla fifa; **give sb the** ~ **shoulder** trattare qcno freddamente ● n freddo m; Med raffreddore m

cold: cold-blooded /-'blʌdɪd/ a spietato. **cold calling** n Comm visita f senza preavviso. **cold comfort** n magra consolazione f. **cold frame** n telaio m coperto di vetro per proteggere le piante dal gelo. **cold-hearted** /-'ha:tɪd/ a insensibile

coldly /'kəʊldlɪ/ adv fig freddamente

cold meat n salumi mpl

coldness /'kəʊldnɪs/ n freddezza f

cold: cold shoulder n **give sb the** ~ ~ snobbare qcno ● **cold-shoulder** vt trattare freddamente. **cold snap** n ondata f di freddo. **cold sore** n herpes m inv. **cold store** n cella f frigorifera. **cold sweat** n sudore m freddo; **bring sb out in a** ~ ~ far sudare freddo qcno. **cold turkey** n (reaction) crisi f inv di astinenza; **be** ~ ~ avere una crisi di astinenza; **quit** ~ ~ smettere di colpo di drogarsi.

Cold War n guerra f fredda

coleslaw /ˈkəʊlslɔː/ n insalata f di cavolo crudo, cipolle e carote in maionese

colic /ˈkɒlɪk/ n colica f

collaborate /kəˈlæbəreɪt/ vi collaborare; ~ **on sth** collaborare in qcsa

collaboration /kəlæbəˈreɪʃn/ n collaborazione f; (with enemy) collaborazionismo m

collaborator /kəˈlæbəreɪtə(r)/ n collaboratore, -trice mf; (with enemy) collaborazionista mf

collage /kɒˈlɑːʒ/ n collage m inv; (film) montaggio m

collapse /kəˈlæps/ n crollo m ● vi ⟨person:⟩ svenire; ⟨roof, building:⟩ crollare

collapsible /kəˈlæpsəbl/ a pieghevole

collar /ˈkɒlə(r)/ n colletto m; (for animal) collare m

collarbone /ˈkɒləbəʊn/ n clavicola f

collar size n taglia f di camicia

collate /kəˈleɪt/ vt collazionare

collateral /kɒˈlætərəl/ n garanzia f collaterale; **put up** ~ offrire una garanzia collaterale

collateral loan a Fin prestito m con garanzia collaterale

colleague /ˈkɒliːɡ/ n collega mf

collect /kəˈlekt/ vt andare a prendere ⟨person⟩; ritirare ⟨parcel, tickets⟩; riscuotere ⟨taxes⟩; raccogliere ⟨rubbish⟩; (as hobby) collezionare ● vi riunirsi ● adv **call** ~ Am telefonare a carico del destinatario

collected /kəˈlektɪd/ a controllato

collection /kəˈlekʃn/ n collezione f; (in church) questua f; (of rubbish) raccolta f; (of post) levata f

collective /kəˈlektɪv/ a collettivo

collective: collective bargaining n contrattazione f collettiva. **collective farm** n comune f. **collective noun** n nome m collettivo. **collective ownership** n comproprietà f

collector /kəˈlektə(r)/ n (of stamps etc) collezionista mf

collector's item n pezzo m da collezionista

college /ˈkɒlɪdʒ/ n istituto m parauniversitario; **C~ of...** Scuola f di...

college of education n Br ≈ facoltà f inv di magistero

college of further education n Br istituto m parauniversitario

collide /kəˈlaɪd/ vi scontrarsi

collie /ˈkɒlɪ/ n pastore m scozzese, collie m inv

colliery /ˈkɒlɪərɪ/ n miniera f di carbone

collision /kəˈlɪʒn/ n scontro m; **be on a ~ course** essere in rotta di collisione

colloquial /kəˈləʊkwɪəl/ a colloquiale

colloquialism /kəˈləʊkwɪəlɪzm/ n espressione f colloquiale

colloquially /kəˈləʊkwɪəlɪ/ adv colloquialmente

colloquium /kəˈləʊkwɪəm/ n colloquio m

collude /kəˈl(j)uːd/ vi complottare

collusion /kəˈl(j)uːʒn/ n collusione f; **in ~ with** in accordo con

cologne /kəˈləʊn/ n colonia f

Colombia /kəˈlɒmbɪə/ n Colombia f

Colombian /kəˈlɒmbɪən/ a & n colombiano, -a mf

colon /ˈkəʊlən/ n due punti mpl; Anat colon m inv

colonel /ˈkɜːnl/ n colonnello m

colonial /kəˈləʊnɪəl/ a coloniale

colonize /ˈkɒlənaɪz/ vt colonizzare

colonnade /kɒləˈneɪd/ n colonnato m

colony /ˈkɒlənɪ/ n colonia f

Colorado beetle /kɒləˈrɑːdəʊ/ n dorifora f

colossal /kəˈlɒsl/ a colossale

colour /ˈkʌlə(r)/ n colore m; (complexion) colorito m; ~**s** pl (flag) bandiera fsg; **show one's true ~s** fig buttare giù la maschera; **in ~** a colori; **off** ~ fam giù di tono ● vt colorare; ~ **[in]** colorare ● vi (blush) arrossire

colour: colour bar n discriminazione f razziale. **colour-blind** a daltonico. **colour code** vt distinguere per mezzo di colori diversi

coloured /ˈkʌləd/ a colorato; ⟨person⟩ di colore ● n (person) persona f di colore

colour fast a dai colori resistenti

colour film n film m inv a colori

colourful /ˈkʌləfʊl/ a pieno di colore

colouring /ˈkʌlərɪŋ/ n (of plant, animal) colorazione f; (complexion) colorito m; (dye: for hair) tinta f; (for food) colorante m

colouring book n album m inv da colorare

colourless /ˈkʌləlɪs/ a incolore

colour: colour photo[graph] n fotografia f a colori. **colour scheme** n [combinazione f di] colori mpl. **colour sense** n senso m del colore. **colour supplement** n supplemento m illustrato a colori. **colour television** n televisione f a colori

colt /kəʊlt/ n puledro m

column /ˈkɒləm/ n colonna f

columnist /ˈkɒləmnɪst/ n giornalista mf che cura una rubrica

coma /ˈkəʊmə/ n coma m inv

comatose /ˈkəʊmətəʊz/ a Med in stato comatoso

comb /kəʊm/ n pettine m; (for wearing) pettinino m ● vt pettinare; (fig: search) setacciare; ~ **one's hair** pettinarsi i capelli ◼ **comb through** vt setacciare ⟨files, desk⟩

combat /ˈkɒmbæt/ n combattimento m ● vt (pt/pp **combated**) combattere

combat jacket n giubba f da combattimento

combination /kɒmbɪˈneɪʃn/ n combinazione f

combine[1] /kəmˈbaɪn/ vt unire; ~ **a job with being a mother** conciliare il lavoro con il ruolo di madre ● vi ⟨chemical elements:⟩ combinarsi

combine[2] /ˈkɒmbaɪn/ n Comm associazione f

combine [harvester] n mietitrebbia f

combustible /kəmˈbʌstəbl/ a combustibile

combustion /kəmˈbʌstʃn/ n combustione f

come /kʌm/ vi (pt **came**, pp **come**) venire; **after coming all this way** dopo tutta questa strada; **where do you ~ from?** da dove vieni?; **~ to** (*reach*) arrivare a; **that ~s to £10** fanno 10 sterline; **I've ~ to appreciate her** ho finito per apprezzarla; **I don't know what the world is coming to** mi chiedo dove andremo a finire; **~ into money** ricevere dei soldi; **that's what comes of being ...** ecco cosa significa essere ...; **~ true/open** verificarsi/aprirsi; **~ first** arrivare primo; *fig* venire prima di tutto; **~ in two sizes** esistere in due misure; **the years to ~** gli anni a venire; **how ~?** *fam* come mai?

■ **come about** *vi* succedere

■ **come across** *vi* **~ across as being** *fam* dare l'impressione di essere ● *vt* (*find*) imbattersi in

■ **come after** *vt* (*follow*) venire dopo; (*chase, pursue*) inseguire

■ **come along** *vi* venire; ⟨*job, opportunity:*⟩ presentarsi; (*progress*) andare bene

■ **come apart** *vi* smontarsi; (*break*) rompersi

■ **come at** *vt* (*attack*) avventarsi su

■ **come away** *vi* venir via; ⟨*button, fastener:*⟩ staccarsi

■ **come back** *vi* ritornare

■ **come before** *vt* (*precede*) precedere; (*be more important than*) venire prima di

■ **come by** *vi* passare ● *vt* (*obtain*) avere

■ **come down** *vi* scendere; **~ down to** (*reach*) arrivare a; **the situation comes down to...** la situazione si riduce a...; **don't ~ down too hard on her** vacci piano con lei; **~ down with flu** prendersi l'influenza

■ **come forward** *vi* farsi avanti

■ **come in** *vi* entrare; (*in race*) arrivare; ⟨*tide:*⟩ salire; **~ in with sb** (*in an undertaking*) associarsi a qcno

■ **come in for** *vt* **~ in for criticism** essere criticato

■ **come off** *vi* staccarsi; (*take place*) esserci; (*succeed*) riuscire; **~ off it!** non farmi ridere!

■ **come on** *vi* (*make progress*) migliorare; **~ on!** (*hurry*) dai!; (*indicating disbelief*) ma va là!

■ **come out** *vi* venir fuori; ⟨*book, sun:*⟩ uscire; ⟨*stain:*⟩ andar via; ⟨*homosexual:*⟩ rivelare la propria omosessualità; **~ out [on strike]** scioperare

■ **come out with** *vt* venir fuori con ⟨*joke, suggestion*⟩

■ **come over** *vi* venire; **what's ~ over you?** cosa ti prende?

■ **come round** *vi* venire; (*after fainting*) riaversi; (*change one's mind*) farsi convincere

■ **come through** *vi* ⟨*news:*⟩ arrivare ● *vt* attraversare ⟨*operation*⟩

■ **come to** *vi* (*after fainting*) riaversi.

■ **come under** *vi* trovarsi sotto

■ **come up** *vi* salire; ⟨*sun:*⟩ sorgere; ⟨*plant:*⟩ crescere; ⟨*name, subject:*⟩ venir fuori; ⟨*job, opportunity:*⟩ presentarsi; **something came up** (*I was prevented*) ho avuto un imprevisto

■ **come up against** *vt* incontrare

■ **come up to** *vt* (*reach*) arrivare a; essere all'altezza di ⟨*expectations*⟩

■ **come up with** *vt* tirar fuori

come-back *n* ritorno *m*

comedian /kə'mi:dɪən/ *n* [attore *m*] comico *m*

comedienne /kəmi:dɪ'en/ *n* attrice *f* comica

come-down *n* passo *m* indietro

comedy /'kɒmədɪ/ *n* commedia *f*

comer /'kʌmə(r)/ *n* **open to all ~s** aperto a tutti; **take on all ~s** battersi contro tutti gli sfidanti

comet /'kɒmɪt/ *n* cometa *f*

come-uppance /kʌm'ʌpəns/ *n* **get one's ~** *fam* avere quel che si merita

comfort /'kʌmfət/ *n* benessere *m*; (*consolation*) conforto *m*; **all the ~s** tutti i comfort ● *vt* confortare

comfortable /'kʌmfətəbl/ *a* comodo; **be ~** ⟨*person:*⟩ stare comodo; (*fig: in situation*) essere a proprio agio; (*financially*) star bene

comfortably /'kʌmfətəblɪ/ *adv* comodamente

comforting /'kʌmfətɪŋ/ *a* confortante

comfort station *n Am* bagno *m* pubblico

comfy /'kʌmfɪ/ *a fam* comodo

comic /'kɒmɪk/ *a* comico ● *n* comico, -a *mf*; (*periodical*) fumetto *m*

comical /'kɒmɪk(ə)l/ *a* comico

comically /'kɒmɪk(ə)lɪ/ *adv* comicamente

comic: comic book *n* giornalino *m* [a fumetti]. **comic relief** *n Theat* **provide some ~ ~** fare una parentesi comica; *fig* sdrammatizzare. **comic strip** *n* striscia *f* di fumetti

coming /'kʌmɪŋ/ *a* promettente ● *n* venuta *f*; **~s and goings** viavai *m*

comma /'kɒmə/ *n* virgola *f*

command /kə'mɑ:nd/ *n also Comput* comando *m*; (*order*) ordine *m*; (*mastery*) padronanza *f*; **in ~** al comando ● *vt* ordinare; comandare ⟨*army*⟩

commandant /'kɒməndænt/ *n Mil* comandante *m*

commandeer /kɒmən'dɪə(r)/ *vt* requisire

commander /kə'mɑ:ndə(r)/ *n* comandante *m*

commanding /kə'mɑ:ndɪŋ/ *a* ⟨*view*⟩ imponente; ⟨*lead*⟩ dominante

commanding officer *n* comandante *m*

commandment /kə'mɑ:ndmənt/ *n* comandamento *m*

commando /kə'mɑ:ndəʊ/ *n* commando *m inv*

command performance *n Br Theat* serata *f* di gala (su richiesta del capo di stato)

commemorate /kə'meməreɪt/ *vt* commemorare

commemoration /kəmemə'reɪʃn/ *n* commemorazione *f*

commemorative /kə'memərətɪv/ *a* commemorativo

commence /kə'mens/ *vt/i* cominciare

commencement /kə'mensmənt/ n inizio m

commend /kə'mend/ vt complimentarsi con (**on** per); (recommend) raccomandare (**to** a)

commendable /kə'mendəbl/ a lodevole

commendation /kɒmen'deɪʃn/ n elogio m; (for bravery) riconoscimento m

commensurate /kə'menʃərət/ a proporzionato (**with** a)

comment /'kɒment/ n commento m; **no ~!** no comment! ● vi fare commenti (**on** su)

commentary /'kɒməntrɪ/ n commento m; [running] ~ (on radio, TV) cronaca f diretta

commentate /'kɒmənteɪt/ vt ~ **on** TV, Radio fare la cronaca di

■ **commentate on** vt fare la radiocronaca/telecronaca di (sporting event)

commentator /'kɒmənteɪtə(r)/ n cronista mf

commerce /'kɒmɜːs/ n commercio m

commercial /kə'mɜːʃl/ a commerciale ● n TV pubblicità f inv

commercial break n spot m inv [pubblicitario], interruzione f pubblicitaria

commercialism /kə'mɜːʃ(ə)lɪzm/ n pej affarismo m

commercialize /kə'mɜːʃ(ə)laɪz/ vt commercializzare

commercial law n diritto m commerciale

commercially /kə'mɜːʃ(ə)lɪ/ adv commercialmente

commiserate /kə'mɪzəreɪt/ vi esprimere il proprio rincrescimento (**with** a)

commissar /kɒmɪ'sɑː(r)/ n commissario m

commission /kə'mɪʃn/ n commissione f; **receive one's ~** Mil essere promosso ufficiale; **out of ~** fuori uso ● vt commissionare; Mil promuovere ufficiale; ~ **a painting from sb**, ~ **sb to do a painting** commissionare un dipinto a qcno

commissionaire /kəmɪʃə'neə(r)/ n portiere m

commissioner /kə'mɪʃənə(r)/ n commissario m; **C~ for Oaths** ≈ notaio m

commit /kə'mɪt/ vt (pt/pp committed) commettere; (to prison, hospital) affidare (**to** a); impegnare (funds); ~ **oneself** impegnarsi; ~ **sth to memory** imparare qcsa a memoria

commitment /kə'mɪtmənt/ n impegno m; (involvement) compromissione f

committed /kə'mɪtɪd/ a impegnato

committee /kə'mɪtɪ/ n comitato m

commodity /kə'mɒdətɪ/ n prodotto m

commodore /'kɒmədɔː(r)/ n commodoro m

common /'kɒmən/ a comune; (vulgar) volgare ● n prato m pubblico; **have in ~** avere in comune; **House of C~s** Camera f dei Comuni

common cold n raffreddore m

commoner /'kɒmənə(r)/ n persona f non nobile

common: common ground n fig terreno m d'intesa. **common law** n diritto m consuetudinario. **common-law husband** n convivente m (more uxorio). **common-law wife** n convivente f (more uxorio)

commonly /'kɒmənlɪ/ adv comunemente

common: Common Market n Mercato m Comune. **common-or-garden** a ordinario. **commonplace** a banale. **common-room** n sala f dei professori/degli studenti. **common sense** n buon senso m. **Commonwealth** n Br Commonwealth m inv ● attrib (country, Games) del Commonwealth

commotion /kə'məʊʃn/ n confusione f

communal /'kɒmjʊnəl/ a comune

commune /'kɒmjuːn/ n comune f ● /kə'mjuːn/ vi ~ **with** essere in comunione con (nature); comunicare con (person)

communicable /kə'mjuːnɪkəbl/ a (disease) trasmissibile

communicate /kə'mjuːnɪkeɪt/ vt/i comunicare

communication /kəmjuːnɪ'keɪʃn/ n comunicazione f; (of disease) trasmissione f; **be in ~ with sb** essere in contatto con qcno; ~**s** pl (technology) telecomunicazioni f pl

communication cord n fermata f d'emergenza

communications satellite n satellite m per telecomunicazioni

communications software n software m di comunicazione

communication studies /'stʌdɪz/ n studi mpl di comunicazione

communicative /kə'mjuːnɪkətɪv/ a comunicativo

Communion /kə'mjuːnɪən/ n [Holy] ~ comunione f

communiqué /kə'mjuːnɪkeɪ/ n comunicato m stampa

Communism /'kɒmjʊnɪzm/ n comunismo m

Communist /'kɒmjʊnɪst/ a & n comunista mf

Communist Party n partito m communista

community /kə'mjuːnətɪ/ n comunità f

community: community care n cura f fuori dell'ambito ospedaliero. **community centre** n centro m sociale. **community policing** n polizia f di quartiere. **community service** n servizio m civile (in sostituzione di pene per reati minori). **community spirit** n spirito m civico

commute /kə'mjuːt/ vi fare il pendolare ● vt Jur commutare

commuter /kə'mjuːtə(r)/ n pendolare mf

commuter belt n zona f suburbana abitata dai pendolari

commuter train n treno m dei pendolari

compact¹ /kəm'pækt/ a compatto

compact² /'kɒmpækt/ n portacipria m inv

compact disc n compact disc m inv

compact disc player n lettore m di compact disc

companion /kəm'pænjən/ n compagno, -a mf

companionable /kəm'pænjənəbl/ a ⟨person⟩ socievole; ⟨silence⟩ non pesante

companionship /kəm'pænjənʃɪp/ n compagnia f

company /'kʌmpənɪ/ n compagnia f; (guests) ospiti mpl; **I didn't know you had ~** pensavo che fossi solo

company: company brochure n opuscolo m dell'azienda. **company car** n macchina f della ditta. **company letterhead** n carta f intestata dell'azienda. **company pension scheme** n piano m di pensionamento aziendale. **company policy** n politica f aziendale. **company secretary** n direttore, -trice mf amministrativo, -a

comparable /'kɒmpərəbl/ a paragonabile

comparative /kəm'pærətɪv/ a comparativo; (relative) relativo ● n Gram comparativo m

comparatively /kəm'pærətɪvlɪ/ adv relativamente

compare /kəm'peə(r)/ vt paragonare (**with/to** a) ● vi **it can't ~** non ha paragoni

comparison /kəm'pærɪsn/ n paragone m

compartment /kəm'pɑ:tmənt/ n compartimento m; Rail scompartimento m

compass /'kʌmpəs/ n bussola f

compasses /'kʌmpəsɪz/ npl **pair of ~** compasso msg

compassion /kəm'pæʃn/ n compassione f

compassionate /kəm'pæʃənət/ a compassionevole

compatible /kəm'pætəbl/ a compatibile; **be ~** ⟨people:⟩ avere caratteri compatibili

compatriot /kəm'pætrɪət/ n compatriota mf

compel /kəm'pel/ vt (pt/pp **compelled**) costringere

compelling /kəm'pelɪŋ/ a ⟨reason, argument⟩ convincente; ⟨performance, film, speaker⟩ avvincente

compendium /kəm'pendɪəm/ n (handbook) compendio m; (Br: box of games) scatola f di giochi

compensate /'kɒmpənseɪt/ vt risarcire ● vi **~ for** fig compensare di

compensation /kɒmpən'seɪʃn/ n risarcimento m; (fig: comfort) consolazione f

compère /'kɒmpeə(r)/ n presentatore, -trice mf

compete /kəm'pi:t/ vi competere; (take part) gareggiare

competence /'kɒmpɪtəns/ n competenza f

competent /'kɒmpɪtənt/ a competente

competition /kɒmpə'tɪʃn/ n concorrenza f; (contest) gara f

competitive /kəm'petɪtɪv/ a competitivo; **~ prices** prezzi mpl concorrenziali

competitor /kəm'petɪtə(r)/ n concorrente mf

compilation /kɒmpɪ'leɪʃn/ n compilazione f; (collection) raccolta f

compile /kəm'paɪl/ vt compilare

complacency /kəm'pleɪsənsɪ/ n compiacimento m

complacent /kəm'pleɪsənt/ a compiaciuto

complacently /kəm'pleɪsəntlɪ/ adv con compiacimento

complain /kəm'pleɪn/ vi lamentarsi (**about** di); (formally) reclamare; **~ of** Med accusare

complaint /kəm'pleɪnt/ n lamentela f; (formal) reclamo m; Med disturbo m

complement¹ /'kɒmplɪmənt/ n complemento m; **with a full ~ of 25** con un effettivo al completo di 25

complement² /'kɒmplɪment/ vt complementare; **~ each other** complementarsi a vicenda

complementary /kɒmplɪ'mentərɪ/ a complementare

complete /kəm'pli:t/ a completo; (utter) finito ● vt completare; compilare (form)

completely /kəm'pli:tlɪ/ adv completamente

completion /kəm'pli:ʃn/ n fine f

complex /'kɒmpleks/ a & n complesso m

complexion /kəm'plekʃn/ n carnagione f; **that puts a different ~ on the matter** questo mette la questione in una luce nuova

complexity /kəm'pleksətɪ/ n complessità f inv

compliance /kəm'plaɪəns/ n accettazione f; (with rules) osservanza f; **in ~ with** in osservanza a ⟨law⟩; conformemente a ⟨request⟩

complicate /'kɒmplɪkeɪt/ vt complicare

complicated /'kɒmplɪkeɪtɪd/ a complicato

complication /kɒmplɪ'keɪʃn/ n complicazione f

complicity /kəm'plɪsətɪ/ n complicità f

compliment /'kɒmplɪmənt/ n complimento m; **~s** pl omaggi mpl ● vt complimentare

complimentary /kɒmplɪ'mentərɪ/ a complimentoso; (given free) in omaggio

comply /kəm'plaɪ/ vi (pt/pp **-ied**) **~ with** conformarsi a

component /kəm'pəʊnənt/ a & n **~ [part]** componente m

compose /kəm'pəʊz/ vt comporre; **~ oneself** ricomporsi; **be ~d of** essere composto da

composed /kəm'pəʊzd/ a (calm) composto

composer /kəm'pəʊzə(r)/ n compositore, -trice mf

composite /'kɒmpəzɪt/ a composto; (style) composito

composition /kɒmpə'zɪʃn/ n composizione f; (essay) tema m

compos mentis /kɒmpɒs'mentɪs/ a nel pieno possesso delle proprie facoltà

compost /'kɒmpɒst/ n composta f

composure /kəm'pəʊʒə(r)/ n calma f

compound¹ /kəm'paʊnd/ vt (make worse) aggravare

compound² /'kɒmpaʊnd/ a composto ● n Chem composto m; Gram parola f composta; (enclosure) recinto m

compound fracture n frattura f esposta

compound interest n interesse m composto

comprehend /kɒmprɪ'hend/ vt comprendere

comprehensible /kɒmprɪ'hensəbl/ *a* comprensible

comprehensibly /kɒmprɪ'hensəblɪ/ *adv* comprensibilmente

comprehension /kɒmprɪ'henʃn/ *n* comprensione *f*

comprehensive /kɒmprɪ'hensɪv/ *a & n* comprensivo; **~** [**school**] scuola *f* media in cui gli allievi hanno capacità d'apprendimento diverse

comprehensive insurance *n* Auto polizza *f* casco

compress[1] /'kɒmpres/ *n* compressa *f*

compress[2] /kəm'pres/ *vt* comprimere

compressed air /kəm'prest/ *n* aria *f* compressa

compression /kəm'preʃn/ *n* compressione *f*

comprise /kəm'praɪz/ *vt* comprendere; (*form*) costituire

compromise /'kɒmprəmaɪz/ *n* compromesso *m* ● *vt* compromettere ● *vi* fare un compromesso

compulsion /kəm'pʌlʃn/ *n* desiderio *m* irresistibile

compulsive /kəm'pʌlsɪv/ *a* Psych patologico; **~ eating** voglia *f* ossessiva di mangiare

compulsory /kəm'pʌlsərɪ/ *a* obbligatorio; **~ subject** materia *f* obbligatoria

compulsory purchase *n* Br espropriazione *f* (*per pubblica utilità*)

compunction /kəm'pʌŋkʃn/ *n* liter scrupolo *m*

computation /kɒmpjʊ'teɪʃn/ *n* calcolo *m*

computer /kəm'pju:tə(r)/ *n* computer *m inv*

computer: computer-aided *a* assistito da computer. **computer-aided design** *n* progettazione *f* assistita da computer. **computer-assisted language learning** *n* apprendimento *m* della lingua assistito da computer. **computer dating service** *n* agenzia *f* matrimoniale computerizzata. **computer engineer** *n* tecnico *m* informatico. **computer error** *n* errore *m* informatico. **computer game** *n* gioco *m* su computer; **~ ~s** intelligiochi *mpl*. **computer graphics** *n* grafica *f* su computer. **computer hacker** *n* pirata *m* informatico

computerization /kəmpju:tərər'zeɪʃn/ *n* computerizzazione *f*

computerize /kəm'pju:tərraɪz/ *vt* computerizzare

computer: computer-literate *a* che sa usare il computer. **computer operator** *n* terminalista *mf*. **computer program** *n* programma *m* [di computer]. **computer programmer** *n* programmatore, -trice *mf* di computer. **computer virus** *n* virus *m inv* [su computer]

computing /kəm'pju:tɪŋ/ *n* informatica *f*

comrade /'kɒmreɪd/ *n* camerata *m*; Pol compagno, -a *mf*

comradeship /'kɒmreɪdʃɪp/ *n* cameratismo *m*

con[1] /kɒn/ *see* **pro**

con[2] *n fam* fregatura *f* ● *vt* (*pt/pp* **conned**) *fam* fregare

concave /'kɒnkeɪv/ *a* concavo

conceal /kən'si:l/ *vt* nascondere

concealment /kən'si:lmənt/ *n* dissimulazione *f*

concede /kən'si:d/ *vt* (*admit*) ammettere; (*give up*) rinunciare a; lasciar fare ⟨goal⟩

conceit /kən'si:t/ *n* presunzione *f*

conceited /kən'si:tɪd/ *a* presuntuoso

conceivable /kən'si:vəbl/ *a* concepibile

conceive /kən'si:v/ *vt* Biol concepire ● *vi* aver figli; **~ of** *fig* concepire

concentrate /'kɒnsəntreɪt/ *vt* concentrare ● *vi* concentrarsi ● *n* concentrato *m*

concentration /kɒnsən'treɪʃn/ *n* concentrazione *f*

concentration camp *n* campo *m* di concentramento

concentric /kən'sentrɪk/ *a* concentrico

concept /'kɒnsept/ *n* concetto *m*

conception /kən'sepʃn/ *n* concezione *f*; (*idea*) idea *f*

conceptual /kən'septjʊəl/ *a* concettuale

concern /kən's3:n/ *n* preoccupazione *f*; Comm attività *f inv* ● *vt* (*be about, affect*) riguardare; (*worry*) preoccupare; **be ~ed about** essere preoccupato per; **~ oneself with** preoccuparsi di; **as far as I am ~ed** per quanto mi riguarda

concerning /kən's3:nɪŋ/ *prep* riguardo a

concert /'kɒnsət/ *n* concerto *m*

concerted /kən's3:tɪd/ *a* collettivo

concert hall *n* sala *f* da concerti

concertina /kɒnsə'ti:nə/ *n* piccola fisarmonica *f*

concert master *n* Am primo violino *m*

concerto /kən'tʃeətəʊ/ *n* concerto *m*

concession /kən'seʃn/ *n* concessione *f*; (*reduction*) sconto *m*

concessionary /kən'seʃənrɪ/ *a* (*reduced*) scontato

conciliate /kən'sɪlɪeɪt/ *vt* blandire

conciliation /kənsɪlɪ'eɪʃn/ *n* conciliazione *f*

conciliator /kən'sɪlɪeɪtə(r)/ *n* mediatore, -trice *mf*

concise /kən'saɪs/ *a* conciso

concisely /kən'saɪslɪ/ *adv* in modo conciso

conciseness /kən'saɪsnɪs/ *n* concisione *f*

conclude /kən'klu:d/ *vt* concludere ● *vi* concludersi

concluding /kən'klu:dɪŋ/ *a* finale, conclusivo

conclusion /kən'klu:ʒn/ *n* conclusione *f*; **in ~** per concludere

conclusive /kən'klu:sɪv/ *a* definitivo

conclusively /kən'klu:sɪvlɪ/ *adv* in modo definitivo

concoct /kən'kɒkt/ *vt* confezionare; *fig* inventare

concoction /kən'kɒkʃn/ *n* mistura *f*; (*drink*) intruglio *m*

concord /'kɒŋkɔ:d/ *n* concordia *f*

concordance /kən'kɔ:dəns/ *n* accordo *m*;

(*index*) concordanze *fpl*; **be in ~ with** essere in accordo con

concourse /'kɒŋkɔːs/ *n* atrio *m*

concrete /'kɒŋkriːt/ *a* concreto ● *n* calcestruzzo *m* ● *vt* ricoprire di calcestruzzo

concrete jungle *n* giungla *f* d'asfalto

concrete mixer *n* betoniera *f*

concur /kən'kɜː(r)/ *vi* (*pt/pp* **concurred**) essere d'accordo

concurrently /kən'kʌrəntlɪ/ *adv* contemporaneamente

concussion /kən'kʌʃn/ *n* commozione *f* cerebrale

condemn /kən'dem/ *vt* condannare; dichiarare inagibile ⟨*building*⟩

condemnation /kɒndem'neɪʃn/ *n* condanna *f*

condensation /kɒnden'seɪʃn/ *n* condensazione *f*

condense /kən'dens/ *vt* condensare; *Phys* condensare ● *vi* condensarsi

condensed milk /kəndenst'mɪlk/ *n* latte *m* condensato

condescend /kɒndɪ'send/ *vi* degnarsi

condescending /kɒndɪ'sendɪŋ/ *a* condiscendente

condescendingly /kɒndɪ'sendɪŋlɪ/ *adv* in modo condiscendente

condiment /'kɒndɪmənt/ *n* condimento *m*

condition /kən'dɪʃn/ *n* condizione *f*; **on ~ that** a condizione che ● *vt Psych* condizionare

conditional /kən'dɪʃənəl/ *a* ⟨*acceptance*⟩ condizionato; *Gram* condizionale; **be ~ on** essere condizionato da ● *n Gram* condizionale

conditionally /kən'dɪʃənəlɪ/ *adv* condizionatamente

conditioner /kən'dɪʃənə(r)/ *n* balsamo *m*; (*for fabrics*) ammorbidente *m*

conditioning /kən'dɪʃənɪŋ/ *n* (*of hair*) balsamo *m*; *Psych* condizionamento *m* ● *a* ⟨*shampoo, lotion etc*⟩ trattante

condole /kən'dəʊl/ *vi* fare le condoglianze (**with** a)

condolences /kən'dəʊlənsɪz/ *npl* condoglianze *fpl*

condom /'kɒndəm/ *n* preservativo *m*

condo[minium] /'kɒndəʊ, kɒndə'mɪnɪəm/ *n Am* condominio *m*

condone /kən'dəʊn/ *vt* passare sopra a

conducive /kən'djuːsɪv/ *a* **be ~ to** contribuire a

conduct¹ /'kɒndʌkt/ *n* condotta *f*

conduct² /kən'dʌkt/ *vt* condurre; dirigere ⟨*orchestra*⟩

conduction /kən'dʌkʃn/ *n* conduzione *f*

conductor /kən'dʌktə(r)/ *n* direttore *m* d'orchestra; (*of bus*) bigliettaio *m*; *Phys* conduttore *m*

conductress /kən'dʌktrɪs/ *n* bigliettaia *f*

cone /kəʊn/ *n* cono *m*; *Bot* pigna *f*; *Auto* birillo *m*

■ **cone off** *vt* **be ~d off** *Auto* essere chiuso da birilli

confection /kən'fekʃn/ *n* (*cake, dessert*) dolce *m*; **a ~ of** (*combination*) una combinazione di

confectioner /kən'fekʃənə(r)/ *n* pasticciere, -a *mf*

confectionery /kən'fekʃənərɪ/ *n* pasticceria *f*

confederation /kənfedə'reɪʃn/ *n* confederazione *f*

confer /kən'fɜː(r)/ *v* (*pt/pp* **conferred**) ● *vt* conferire (**on** a) ● *vi* (*discuss*) conferire

conference /'kɒnfərəns/ *n* conferenza *f*

conference room *n* sala *f* riunioni

confess /kən'fes/ *vt* confessare ● *vi* confessare; *Relig* confessarsi

confession /kən'feʃn/ *n* confessione *f*

confessional /kən'feʃənəl/ *n* confessionale *m*

confessor /kən'fesə(r)/ *n* confessore *m*

confetti /kən'fetɪ/ *n* coriandoli *mpl*

confide /kən'faɪd/ *vt* confidare

■ **confide in** *vt* **~ in sb** fidarsi di

confidence /'kɒnfɪdəns/ *n* (*trust*) fiducia *f*; (*self-assurance*) sicurezza *f* di sé; (*secret*) confidenza *f*; **in ~** in confidenza

confidence trick *n* truffa *f*

confidence trickster /'kɒnfɪdəns- trɪkstə(r)/ *n* imbroglione, -a *mf*

confident /'kɒnfɪdənt/ *a* fiducioso; (*self-assured*) sicuro di sé

confidential /kɒnfɪ'denʃl/ *a* confidenziale

confidentiality /kɒnfɪdenʃɪ'ælətɪ/ *n* riservatezza *f*

confidentially /kɒnfɪ'denʃəlɪ/ *adv* confidenzialmente

confidently /'kɒnfɪdəntlɪ/ *adv* con aria fiduciosa; **we ~ expect to win** siamo fiduciosi nella vittoria

confine /kən'faɪn/ *vt* rinchiudere; (*limit*) limitare; **be ~d to bed** essere confinato a letto

confined /kən'faɪnd/ *a* ⟨*space*⟩ limitato

confinement /kən'faɪnmənt/ *n* detenzione *f*; *Med* parto *m*

confines /'kɒnfaɪnz/ *npl* confini *mpl*

confirm /kən'fɜːm/ *vt* confermare; *Relig* cresimare

confirmation /kɒnfə'meɪʃn/ *n* conferma *f*; *Relig* cresima *f*

confirmed /kən'fɜːmd/ *a* incallito; **~ bachelor** scapolo *m* impenitente

confiscate /'kɒnfɪskeɪt/ *vt* confiscare

confiscation /kɒnfɪs'keɪʃn/ *n* confisca *f*

conflagration /kɒnflə'greɪʃn/ *n* conflagrazione *f*

conflate /kən'fleɪt/ *vt* fondere

conflict¹ /'kɒnflɪkt/ *n* conflitto *m*

conflict² /kən'flɪkt/ *vi* essere in contraddizione

conflicting /kən'flɪktɪŋ/ *a* contraddittorio

confluence /'kɒnfluəns/ *n* (*of rivers*) confluenza *f*; *fig* convergenza *f*

conform /kən'fɔːm/ *vi* ⟨*person:*⟩ conformarsi; ⟨*thing:*⟩ essere conforme (**to** a)

conformist /kən'fɔːmɪst/ *n* conformista *mf*

conformity /kən'fɔ:mətɪ/ n conformità f; *Relig* ortodossia f; **in ~ with** in conformità a

confound /kən'faʊnd/ vt (*perplex*) confondere; (*show to be wrong*) confutare

confounded /kən'faʊndɪd/ a fam maledetto

confront /kən'frʌnt/ vt affrontare; **the problems ~ing us** i problemi che dobbiamo affrontare

confrontation /kɒnfrʌn'teɪʃn/ n confronto m

confuse /kən'fju:z/ vt confondere

confused /kən'fju:zd/ a (*presentation, idea*) ingarbugliato

confusing /kən'fju:zɪŋ/ a che confonde

confusion /kən'fju:ʒn/ n confusione f

congeal /kən'dʒi:l/ vi (*blood:*) coagularsi

congenial /kən'dʒi:nɪəl/ a congeniale

congenital /kən'dʒenɪtl/ a congenito

congested /kən'dʒestɪd/ a congestionato

congestion /kən'dʒestʃn/ n congestione f

conglomerate /kən'glɒmərət/ n conglomerato m

Congo /'kɒŋgəʊ/ n Congo m

Congolese /kɒŋgəli:z/ a & n congolese mf

congratulate /kən'grætjʊleɪt/ vt congratularsi con (**on** per)

congratulations /kəngrætjʊ'leɪʃnz/ npl congratulazioni fpl

congregate /'kɒŋgrɪgeɪt/ vi radunarsi

congregation /kɒŋgrɪ'geɪʃn/ n Relig assemblea f

congress /'kɒŋgres/ n congresso m

congressman /'kɒŋgresmən/ n Am Pol membro m del congresso

conical /'kɒnɪkl/ a conico

conifer /'kɒnɪfə(r)/ n conifera f

conjecture /kən'dʒektʃə(r)/ n congettura f ● vt congetturare ● vi fare congetture

conjugal /'kɒndʒʊgl/ a coniugale

conjugate /'kɒndʒʊgeɪt/ vt coniugare

conjugation /kɒndʒʊ'geɪʃn/ n coniugazione f

conjunction /kən'dʒʌŋkʃn/ n congiunzione f; **in ~ with** insieme a

conjunctivitis /kəndʒʌŋktɪ'vaɪtɪs/ n congiuntivite f

■ **conjure up** /'kʌndʒə(r)/ vt evocare (*image*); tirar fuori dal nulla (*meal*)

conjuring /'kʌndʒərɪŋ/ n giochi mpl di prestigio

conjuring trick /'kʌndʒərɪŋ/ n gioco m di prestigio

conjuror /'kʌndʒərə(r)/ n prestigiatore, -trice mf

conk /kɒŋk/ vi **~ out** fam (*machine:*) guastarsi; (*person:*) crollare

conker /'kɒŋkə(r)/ n fam castagna f (d'ippocastano)

conman /'kɒnmæn/ n fam truffatore m

connect /kə'nekt/ vt collegare; **be ~ed with** avere legami con; (*be related to*) essere imparentato con; **be well ~ed** aver conoscenze influenti ● vi essere collegato (**with** a); (*train:*) fare coincidenza

connecting /kə'nektɪŋ/ a (*room*) di comunicazione

connecting flight n coincidenza f

connection /kə'nekʃn/ n (*between ideas*) nesso m; (*in travel*) coincidenza f; Electr, Comput collegamento m; **in ~ with** con riferimento a; **~s** pl (*people*) conoscenze fpl

connector /kə'nektə(r)/ n Comput connettore m

connivance /kə'naɪvəns/ n connivenza f

connive /kə'naɪv/ vi **~ at** essere connivente a

connoisseur /kɒnə's3:(r)/ n intenditore, -trice mf

connotation /kɒnə'teɪʃn/ n connotazione f

connote /kə'nəʊt/ vt evocare; (*in linguistics*) connotare

conquer /'kɒŋkə(r)/ vt conquistare; fig superare (*fear*)

conqueror /'kɒŋkərə(r)/ n conquistatore m

conquest /'kɒŋkwest/ n conquista f

conscience /'kɒnʃəns/ n coscienza f

conscientious /kɒnʃɪ'enʃəs/ a coscienzioso

conscientiously /kɒnsɪ'enʃəslɪ/ adv coscienziosamente

conscientious objector /əb'dʒektə(r)/ n obiettore m di coscienza

conscious /'kɒnʃəs/ a conscio; (*decision*) meditato; [**fully**] **~** cosciente; **be/become ~ of sth** rendersi conto di qcsa

consciously /'kɒnʃəslɪ/ adv consapevolmente

consciousness /'kɒnʃəsnɪs/ n consapevolezza f; Med conoscenza f

conscript[1] /'kɒnskrɪpt/ n coscritto m

conscript[2] /kən'skrɪpt/ vt Mil chiamare alle armi; **~ sb to do sth** fig reclutare qcno per fare qcsa

conscription /kən'skrɪpʃn/ n coscrizione f, leva f

consecrate /'kɒnsɪkreɪt/ vt consacrare

consecration /kɒnsɪ'kreɪʃn/ n consacrazione f

consecutive /kən'sekjʊtɪv/ a consecutivo

consecutively /kən'sekjʊtɪvlɪ/ adv consecutivamente

consensus /kən'sensəs/ n consenso m

consent /kən'sent/ n consenso m ● vi acconsentire

consequence /'kɒnsɪkwəns/ n conseguenza f; (*importance*) importanza f

consequent /'kɒnsɪkwənt/ a conseguente

consequently /'kɒnsɪkwəntlɪ/ adv di conseguenza

conservation /kɒnsə'veɪʃn/ n conservazione f

conservationist /kɒnsə'veɪʃənɪst/ n fautore, -trice mf della tutela ambientale

conservatism /kən's3:vətɪzm/ n conservatorismo m

conservative /kən's3:vətɪv/ a conservativo; (*estimate*) ottimistico; **C~** Pol a conservatore ● n conservatore, -trice mf

conservatory /kən'sɜːvətrɪ/ *n* spazio *m* chiuso da vetrate adiacente alla casa

conserve /kən'sɜːv/ *vt* conservare

consider /kən'sɪdə(r)/ *vt* considerare; ~ **doing sth** considerare la possibilità di fare qcsa

considerable /kən'sɪdərəbl/ *a* considerevole

considerably /kən'sɪdərəblɪ/ *adv* considerevolmente

considerate /kən'sɪdərət/ *a* pieno di riguardo

considerately /kən'sɪdərətlɪ/ *adv* con riguardo

consideration /kənsɪdə'reɪʃn/ *n* considerazione *f*; (*thoughtfulness*) attenzione *f*; (*respect*) riguardo *m*; (*payment*) compenso *m*; **take into** ~ prendere in considerazione

considering /kən'sɪdərɪŋ/ *prep* considerando; ~ **that** considerando che

consign /kən'saɪn/ *vt* affidare

consignment /kən'saɪmmənt/ *n* consegna *f*

consist /kən'sɪst/ *vi* ~ **of** consistere di

consistency /kən'sɪstənsɪ/ *n* coerenza *f*; (*density*) consistenza *f*

consistent /kən'sɪstənt/ *a* coerente; (*loyalty*) costante; **be** ~ **with** far pensare a

consistently /kən'sɪstəntlɪ/ *adv* coerentemente; (*late, loyal*) costantemente

consolation /kɒnsə'leɪʃn/ *n* consolazione *f*

consolation prize *n* premio *m* di consolazione

console /kən'səʊl/ *vt* consolare

consolidate /kən'sɒlɪdeɪt/ *vt* consolidare

consolidation /kənsɒlɪ'deɪʃn/ *n* (*of knowledge, position*) consolidamento *m*

consoling /kən'səʊlɪŋ/ *a* consolante

consonant /'kɒnsənənt/ *n* consonante *f*

consort[1] /'kɒnsɔːt/ *n* consorte *mf*

consort[2] /kən'sɔːt/ *vi* ~ **with** frequentare

consortium /kən'sɔːtɪəm/ *n* consorzio *m*

conspicuous /kən'spɪkjʊəs/ *a* facilmente distinguibile; **be** ~ **by one's absence** brillare per la propria assenza

conspicuously /kən'spɪkjʊəslɪ/ *adv* (*dressed*) vistosamente; (*placed*) in evidenza; (*silent, empty*) in modo evidente

conspiracy /kən'spɪrəsɪ/ *n* cospirazione *f*

conspirator /kən'spɪrətə(r)/ *n* cospiratore, -trice *mf*

conspire /kən'spaɪə(r)/ *vi* cospirare

constable /'kʌnstəbl/ *n* agente *m* [di polizia]

constabulary /kən'stæbjʊlərɪ/ *n* Br polizia *f*

constancy /'kɒnstənsɪ/ *n* costanza *f*

constant /'kɒnstənt/ *a* costante

constantly /'kɒnstəntlɪ/ *adv* costantemente

constellation /kɒnstə'leɪʃn/ *n* costellazione *f*

consternation /kɒnstə'neɪʃn/ *n* costernazione *f*

constipated /'kɒnstɪpeɪtɪd/ *a* stitico

constipation /kɒnstɪ'peɪʃn/ *n* stitichezza *f*

constituency /kən'stɪtjʊənsɪ/ *n* area *f* elettorale di un deputato nel Regno Unito

constituent /kən'stɪtjʊənt/ *n* costituente *m*; Pol elettore, -trice *mf*

constitute /'kɒnstɪtjuːt/ *vt* costituire

constitution /kɒnstɪ'tjuːʃn/ *n* costituzione *f*

constitutional /kɒnstɪ'tjuːʃənl/ *a* costituzionale ● *n* passeggiata *f* salutare

constitutionally /kɒnstɪ'tjuːʃənəlɪ/ *adv* Pol costituzionalmente; (*innately*) di costituzione

constrain /kən'streɪn/ *vt* costringere

constraint /kən'streɪnt/ *n* costrizione *f*; (*restriction*) restrizione *f*; (*strained manner*) disagio *m*

constrict /kən'strɪkt/ *vt* (*tight jacket:*) stringere

constriction /kən'strɪkʃn/ *n* (*of chest, throat*) senso *m* di oppressione; (*constraint*) costrizione *f*; (*of blood vessel*) restrizione *f*

construct /kən'strʌkt/ *vt* costruire

construction /kən'strʌkʃn/ *n* costruzione *f*; (*interpretation*) interpretazione *f*; **under** ~ in costruzione

construction: construction engineer *n* ingegnere *m* edile. **construction site** *n* cantiere *m*. **construction worker** *n* [operaio *m*] edile *m*

constructive /kən'strʌktɪv/ *a* costruttivo

constructively /kən'strʌktɪvlɪ/ *adv* in modo costruttivo

construe /kən'struː/ *vt* interpretare

consul /'kɒnsl/ *n* console *m*

consular /'kɒnsjʊlə(r)/ *a* consolare

consulate /'kɒnsjʊlət/ *n* consolato *m*

consult /kən'sʌlt/ *vt* consultare

consultancy /kən'sʌltənsɪ/ *n* (*advice*) consulenza *f*; (*firm*) ufficio *m* di consulenza; Br Med posto *m* di specialista; **do** ~ fare il/la consulente ● *attrib* (*fees, service, work*) di consulenza

consultant /kən'sʌltənt/ *n* consulente *mf*; Med specialista *mf*

consultation /kɒnsl'teɪʃn/ *n* consultazione *f*; Med consulto *m*

consultative /kən'sʌltətɪv/ *a* di consulenza

consulting hours /kən'sʌltɪŋ/ *npl* Med orario *m* di visita

consulting room *n* Med ambulatorio *m*

consumable /kən'sjuːməbl/ *n* bene *m* di consumo

consume /kən'sjuːm/ *vt* consumare

consumer /kən'sjuːmə(r)/ *n* consumatore, -trice *mf*

consumer: consumer advice *n* consigli *mpl* ai consumatori. **consumer confidence** *n* fiducia *f* del consumatore. **consumer goods** *npl* beni *mpl* di consumo

consumerism /kən'sjuːmərɪzm/ *n* consumismo *m*

consumer: consumer organization *n* organizzazione *f* per la tutela dei consumatori. **consumer products** *npl* beni *mpl* di consumo. **consumer protection** *n* tutela *f* dei consumatori. **consumer society** n società f inv consumista, società f inv dei consumi

consuming /kən'sju:mɪŋ/ a ⟨passion⟩ struggente; ⟨urge⟩ pressante; ⟨hatred⟩ insaziabile

consummate /'kɒnsjʊmeɪt/ vt consumare

consummation /kɒnsjʊ'meɪʃn/ n consumazione f

consumption /kən'sʌmpʃn/ n consumo m

contact /'kɒntækt/ n contatto m; (person) conoscenza f ● vt mettersi in contatto con

contactable /'kɒntæktəbl/ a (person) reperibile

contact lenses npl lenti fpl a contatto

contagious /kən'teɪdʒəs/ a contagioso

contain /kən'teɪn/ vt contenere; ~ **oneself** controllarsi

container /kən'teɪnə(r)/ n recipiente m; (for transport) container m inv

container: container port n porto m container. **container ship** n [nave f] portacontainers f inv. **container truck** n [autocarro m] portacontainers m inv

contaminate /kən'tæmɪneɪt/ vt contaminare

contamination /kəntæmɪ'neɪʃn/ n contaminazione f

contd abbr (**continued**) segue

contemplate /'kɒntəmpleɪt/ vt contemplare; (consider) considerare; ~ **doing sth** considerare di fare qcsa

contemplation /kɒntəm'pleɪʃn/ n contemplazione f

contemplative /kən'templətɪv/ a contemplativo

contemporaneous /kəntempə'reɪnɪəs/ a contemporaneo (**with** a)

contemporaneously /kəntempə'reɪnɪəslɪ/ adv contemporaneamente (**with** a)

contemporary /kən'tempərərɪ/ a & n contemporaneo, -a mf

contempt /kən'tempt/ n disprezzo m; **beneath** ~ più che vergognoso; ~ **of court** oltraggio m alla Corte

contemptible /kən'tem(p)təbl/ a spregevole

contemptuous /kən'tem(p)tjʊəs/ a sprezzante

contemptuously /kən'tem(p)tjʊəslɪ/ adv sprezzantemente

contend /kən'tend/ vi ~ **with** occuparsi di ● vt (assert) sostenere

contender /kən'tendə(r)/ n concorrente mf

content[1] /'kɒntent/ n contenuto m

content[2] /kən'tent/ a soddisfatto ● n **to one's heart's** ~ finché se ne ha voglia ● vt ~ **oneself** accontentarsi (**with** di)

contented /kən'tentɪd/ a soddisfatto

contentedly /kən'tentɪdlɪ/ adv con aria soddisfatta

contention /kən'tenʃn/ n (assertion) opinione f

contentious /kən'tenʃəs/ a (subject) controverso; (view) discutibile; (person, group) polemico

contentment /kən'tentmənt/ n soddisfazione f

contents /'kɒntents/ npl contenuto m

contest[1] /'kɒntest/ n gara f

contest[2] /kən'test/ vt contestare (statement); impugnare (will); Pol (candidates:) contendersi; (one candidate:) aspirare a

contestant /kən'testənt/ n concorrente mf

context /'kɒntekst/ n contesto m

continent /'kɒntɪnənt/ n continente m; **the C**~ l'Europa f continentale

continental /kɒntrɪ'nentl/ a continentale

continental breakfast n prima colazione f a base di pane, burro, marmellata, croissant ecc

continental quilt n piumone m

contingency /kən'tɪndʒənsɪ/ n eventualità f inv

contingency fund n fondo m sopravvenienze passive

contingency plan n piano m d'emergenza

contingent /kən'tɪndʒənt/ a **be** ~ **on** dipendere da ● n Mil contingente m

continual /kən'tɪnjʊəl/ a continuo

continually /kən'tɪnjʊəlɪ/ adv continuamente

continuation /kəntɪnjʊ'eɪʃn/ n continuazione f

continue /kən'tɪnju:/ vt continuare; ~ **doing** or **to do sth** continuare a fare qcsa; **to be** ~**d** continua ● vi continuare

continued /kən'tɪnju:d/ a continuo

continuity /kɒntɪ'nju:ətɪ/ n continuità f

continuity announcer n annunciatore, -trice mf

continuity girl n segretaria f di produzione

continuous /kən'tɪnjʊəs/ a continuo

continuously /kən'tɪnjʊəslɪ/ adv continuamente

continuum /kən'tɪnjʊəm/ n continuum m inv

contort /kən'tɔ:t/ vt contorcere

contortion /kən'tɔ:ʃn/ n contorsione f

contortionist /kən'tɔ:ʃənɪst/ n contorsionista mf

contour /'kɒntʊə(r)/ n contorno m; (line) curva f di livello

contraband /'kɒntrəbænd/ n contrabbando m

contraception /kɒntrə'sepʃn/ n contraccezione f; **use** ~ ricorrere alla contraccezione

contraceptive /kɒntrə'septɪv/ a & n contraccettivo m

contract[1] /'kɒntrækt/ n contratto m

contract[2] /kən'trækt/ vi (get smaller) contrarsi ● vt contrarre (illness)

contraction /kən'trækʃn/ n contrazione f

contract killer n sicario m

contractor /kən'træktə(r)/ n imprenditore, -trice mf

contractual /kən'træktjʊəl/ a contrattuale

contract work n lavoro m su commissione

contract worker n lavoratore, -trice mf con contratto a termine

contradict /kɒntrə'dɪkt/ vt contraddire

contradiction /kɒntrə'dɪkʃn/ n contraddizione f

contradictory /kɒntrə'dɪktəri/ a contradditorio

contraflow /'kɒntrəfləʊ/ n utilizzazione f di una corsia nei due sensi di marcia durante lavori stradali

contraindication /kɒntrəmdr'keɪʃn/ n controindicazione f

contralto /kən'træltəʊ/ n contralto m

contraption /kən'træpʃn/ n fam aggeggio m

contrariness /kən'treərɪnɪs/ n spirito m di contraddizione

contrariwise /kən'treərɪwaɪz/ adv (conversely) d'altra parte, d'altro canto; (in the opposite direction) in direzione opposta

contrary[1] /'kɒntrəri/ a contrario ● adv ~ **to** contrariamente a ● n contrario m; **on the ~** al contrario

contrary[2] /kən'treəri/ a disobbediente

contrast[1] /'kɒntrɑːst/ n contrasto m

contrast[2] /kən'trɑːst/ vt confrontare ● vi contrastare

contrasting /kən'trɑːstɪŋ/ a contrastante

contravene /kɒntrə'viːn/ vt trasgredire

contravention /kɒntrə'venʃn/ n trasgressione f

contribute /kən'trɪbjuːt/ vt/i contribuire

contribution /kɒntrɪ'bjuːʃn/ n contribuzione f; (what is contributed) contributo m

contributor /kən'trɪbjʊtə(r)/ n contributore, -trice mf

contributory /kən'trɪbjʊtəri/ a (factor) concomitante; **be ~ to** contribuire a

contrite /kən'traɪt/ a contrito

contrive /kən'traɪv/ vt escogitare; **~ to do sth** riuscire a fare qcsa

contrived /kən'traɪvd/ a (style, effect) artificioso; (plot, ending) forzato; (incident, meeting) non fortuito

control /kən'trəʊl/ n controllo m; **~s** pl (of car, plane) comandi mpl; **get out of ~** sfuggire al controllo ● vt (pt/pp **controlled**) controllare; **~ oneself** controllarsi

control column n Aeron cloche f inv

control key n Comput tasto m di controllo

controlled /kən'trəʊld/ a (explosion, performance, person) controllato; **Labour-~** dominato dai laburisti

controller /kən'trəʊlə(r)/ n controllore m; Fin controllore m [della gestione]; Radio, TV direttore, -trice mf

control: **control panel** n (on machine) quadro m dei comandi; (for plane) quadro m di comando. **control room** n sala f di comando; Radio, TV sala f di regia. **control tower** n torre f di controllo

controversial /kɒntrə'vɜːʃl/ a controverso

controversy /'kɒntrəvɜːsɪ/ n controversia f

conundrum /kə'nʌndrəm/ n enigma m

conurbation /kɒnɜː'beɪʃn/ n conurbazione f

convalesce /kɒnvə'les/ vi essere in convalescenza

convalescence /kɒnvə'lesəns/ n convalescenza f

convalescent /kɒnvə'lesənt/ a convalescente

convalescent home n convalescenziaria m

convection /kən'vekʃn/ n convezione f

convector /kən'vektə(r)/ n ~ [**heater**] convettore m

convene /kən'viːn/ vt convocare ● vi riunirsi

convener /kən'viːnə(r)/ n (organizer) organizzatore, -trice mf; (chair) presidente m

convenience /kən'viːnɪəns/ n convenienza f; [public] ~ gabinetti mpl pubblici; **with all modern ~s** con tutti i comfort

convenience foods npl cibi mpl precotti

convenience store n negozio m aperto fino a tardi

convenient /kən'viːnɪənt/ a comodo; **be ~ for sb** andar bene per qcno; **if it is ~ [for you]** se ti va bene

conveniently /kən'viːnɪəntlɪ/ adv comodamente; **~ located** in una posizione comoda

convent /'kɒnvənt/ n convento m

convention /kən'venʃn/ n convenzione f; (assembly) convegno m

conventional /kən'venʃnəl/ a convenzionale

conventionally /kən'venʃnəlɪ/ adv convenzionalmente

convention centre n palazzo m dei congressi

convent school n scuola f retta da religiose

converge /kən'vɜːdʒ/ vi convergere

conversant /kən'vɜːsənt/ a ~ **with** pratico di

conversation /kɒnvə'seɪʃn/ n conversazione f

conversational /kɒnvə'seɪʃnəl/ a di conversazione

conversationalist /kɒnvə'seɪʃnəlɪst/ n conversatore, -trice mf

converse[1] /kən'vɜːs/ vi conversare

converse[2] /'kɒnvɜːs/ n inverso m

conversely /'kɒnvɜːslɪ/ adv viceversa

conversion /kən'vɜːʃn/ n conversione f

conversion rate n [tasso m di] cambio m

conversion table n tabella f di conversione

convert[1] /'kɒnvɜːt/ n convertito, -a mf

convert[2] /kən'vɜːt/ vt convertire (**into** in); sconsacrare (church)

converter /kən'vɜːtə(r)/ n Electr convertitore m

convertible /kən'vɜːtəbl/ a convertibile ● n Auto macchina f decappottabile

convex /'kɒnveks/ a convesso

convey /kən'veɪ/ vt portare; trasmettere (idea, message)

conveyance /kən'veɪəns/ n trasporto m; (vehicle) mezzo m di trasporto

conveyor /kən'veɪə(r)/ n (of goods, persons) trasportatore m

conveyor belt n nastro m trasportatore

convict[1] /'kɒnvɪkt/ n condannato, -a mf

convict² /kən'vɪkt/ *vt* giudicare colpevole

conviction /kən'vɪkʃn/ *n* condanna *f*; (*belief*) convinzione *f*; **previous ~** precedente *m* penale

convince /kən'vɪns/ *vt* convincere

convincing /kən'vɪnsɪŋ/ *a* convincente

convincingly /kən'vɪnsɪŋlɪ/ *adv* in modo convincente

convivial /kən'vɪvɪəl/ *a* conviviale

convoluted /'kɒnvəlu:tɪd/ *a* contorto

convoy /'kɒnvɔɪ/ *n* convoglio *m*

convulse /kən'vʌls/ *vt* sconvolgere; **be ~d with laughter** contorcersi dalle risa

convulsion /kən'vʌlʃn/ *n* convulsione *f*

convulsive /kən'vʌlsɪv/ *a* convulso; *Med* convulsivo

convulsively /kən'vʌlsɪvlɪ/ *adv* convulsamente

coo /ku:/ *vi* tubare

cooing /'ku:ɪŋ/ *n* (*of bird, lovers*) tubare *m inv*

cook /kʊk/ *n* cuoco, -a *mf* ● *vt* cucinare; **is it ~ed?** è cotto? **~ the books** *fam* truccare i libri contabili ● *vi* ⟨*food:*⟩ cuocere; ⟨*person:*⟩ cucinare

■ **cook up** *vt* (*fam*) inventare ⟨*excuse, story etc*⟩

cookbook /'kʊkbʊk/ *n* libro *m* di cucina

cooked meats /kʊkt'mi:ts/ *npl* salumi *mpl*

cooker /'kʊkə(r)/ *n* cucina *f*; (*apple*) mela *f* da cuocere

cookery /'kʊkərɪ/ *n* cucina *f*

cookery book *n* libro *m* di cucina

cookie /'kʊkɪ/ *n* *Am* biscotto *m*

cooking /'kʊkɪŋ/ *n* cucina *f*; **be good at ~** saper cucinare bene; **do the ~** cucinare

cooking: cooking apple *n* mela *f* da cuocere. **cooking chocolate** *n* cioccolato *m* da pasticceria. **cooking foil** *n* carta *f* stagnola. **cooking salt** *n* sale *m* da cucina. **cooking time** *n* tempo *m* di cottura

cool /ku:l/ *a* fresco; (*calm*) calmo; (*unfriendly*) freddo ● *n* fresco *m*; **keep/lose one's ~** mantenere/perdere la calma ● *vt* rinfrescare ● *vi* rinfrescarsi

■ **cool down** *vi* ⟨*soup, tea etc:*⟩ raffreddarsi; (*fig: become calm*) calmarsi ● *vt* raffreddare ⟨*soup, tea etc*⟩; (*fig*) calmare

cool: cool bag *n Br* borsa *f* frigo. **cool-box** *n* borsa *f* termica. **cool-headed** *a* equilibrato

cooling /'ku:lɪŋ/ *n* raffreddamento *m* ● *a* ⟨*agent*⟩ refrigerante; ⟨*system, tower*⟩ di raffreddamento; ⟨*drink, swim*⟩ rinfrescante

cooling-off period *n* (*in industrial relations*) periodo *m* di tregua [sindacale]; *Comm* fase *f* di riflessione

coolly /'ku:llɪ/ *adv* freddamente

coolness /'ku:lnɪs/ *n* freddezza *f*

coop /ku:p/ *n* stia *f* ● *vt* **~ up** rinchiudere

co-op /'kəʊɒp/ *n abbr* (**cooperative**) cooperativa *f*

cooperate /kəʊ'ɒpəreɪt/ *vi* cooperare

cooperation /kəʊɒpe'reɪʃn/ *n* cooperazione *f*

cooperative /kəʊ'ɒpərətɪv/ *a & n* cooperativa *f*

co-opt /kəʊ'ɒpt/ *vt* eleggere

coordinate /kəʊ'ɔ:dɪneɪt/ *vt* coordinare

coordinated /kəʊ'ɔ:dɪneɪtɪd/ *a* coordinato

coordination /kəʊɒ:dɪ'neɪʃn/ *n* coordinazione *f*

coordinator /kəʊ'ɔ:dɪneɪtə(r)/ *n* coordinatore, -trice *mf*

co-owner /kəʊ'əʊnə(r)/ *n* comproprietario, -a *mf*

cop /kɒp/ *n fam* poliziotto *m*

cope /kəʊp/ *vi fam* farcela; **can she ~ by herself?** ce la fa da sola?; **~ with** farcela con; **I couldn't ~ with five kids** non ce la farei con cinque bambini

Copenhagen /kəʊpən'heɪgən/ *n* Copenhagen *f*

copier /'kɒpɪə(r)/ *n* fotocopiatrice *f*

co-pilot /'kəʊpaɪlət/ *n* copilota *m*

copious /'kəʊpɪəs/ *a* abbondante

copiously /'kəʊpɪəslɪ/ *adv* abbondantemente

cop-out *n fam* (*evasive act*) bidone *m*; (*excuse*) scappatoia *f*

copper¹ /'kɒpə(r)/ *n* rame *m*; **~s** *pl monete fpl* da uno o due pence ● *attrib* di rame

copper² *n fam* poliziotto *m*

copper: copper beech *n* faggio *m* rosso. **copper-coloured** *a* [color] rame *inv*; ⟨*hair*⟩ ramato. **copperplate** *n* calligrafia *f* ornata

coppice /'kɒpɪs/ *n*, **copse** /kɒps/ *n* boschetto *m*

co-property /'kəʊprɒpətɪ/ *n* comproprietà *f inv*

copulate /'kɒpjʊleɪt/ *vi* accoppiarsi

copulation /kɒpjʊ'leɪʃn/ *n* copulazione *f*

copy /'kɒpɪ/ *n* copia *f* ● *vt* (*pt/pp* **-ied**) copiare

■ **copy down** *vt* = **copy**

■ **copy out** *vt* = **copy**

copy: copybook *n* **blot one's ~** rovinarsi la reputazione. **copycat** *n pej fam* copione, -a *mf* ● *a* ⟨*crime, murder*⟩ ispirato da un altro. **copy editor** *n* segretario, -a *mf* di redazione. **copyright** *n* diritti *mpl* d'autore. **copytypist** *n* dattilografo, -a *mf*. **copywriter** *n* copywriter *mf inv*

coquetry /'kɒkɪtrɪ/ *n* civetteria *f*

coquettish /kɒ'ketɪʃ/ *a* civettuolo

coral /'kɒrəl/ *n* corallo *m*

coral: coral island *n* isola *f* di corallo. **coral pink** *a & n* rosa *m inv* corallo. **coral reef** *n* barriera *f* corallina

cord /kɔ:d/ *n* corda *f*; (*thinner*) cordoncino *m*; (*fabric*) velluto *m* a coste; **~s** *pl* pantaloni *mpl* di velluto a coste

cordial /'kɔ:dɪəl/ *a* cordiale ● *n* analcolico *m*

cordially /'kɔ:dɪəlɪ/ *adv* con tutto il cuore

cordless telephone /'kɔ:dlɪs/ *a* telefono *m* senza fili

cordon /'kɔ:dn/ *n* cordone *m* (*di persone*)

■ **cordon off** *vt* bloccare

corduroy /'kɔ:dərɔɪ/ *n* velluto *m* a coste

core /kɔ:(r)/ *n* (*of apple, pear*) torsolo *m*; (*fig:*

of organization) cuore *m*; (*of problem, theory*) nocciolo *m*

co-respondent /ˌkəʊrɪˈspɒndənt/ *n Jur* correo, -a *mf* in adulterio

Corfu /kɔːˈfuː/ *n* Corfù *f*

coriander /ˌkɒrɪˈændə(r)/ *n* coriandolo *m*

cork /kɔːk/ *n* sughero *m*; (*for bottle*) turacciolo *m*

corkage /ˈkɔːkɪdʒ/ *n* somma *f* pagata a un ristorante per servire una bottiglia di vino portata da fuori

corker /ˈkɔːkə(r)/ *n Br fam* (*story*) storia *f* strabiliante; (*stroke, shot*) tiro *m* da maestro

corkscrew /ˈkɔːkskruː/ *n* cavatappi *m inv*

corkscrew curls *npl* boccoli *mpl*

corn[1] /kɔːn/ *n* grano *m*; (*Am: maize*) granturco *m*

corn[2] *n Med* callo *m*

corncob /ˈkɔːnkɒb/ *n* pannocchia *f* [di mais]

cornea /ˈkɔːnɪə/ *n* cornea *f*

corned beef /kɔːndˈbiːf/ *n* manzo *m* sotto sale

corner /ˈkɔːnə(r)/ *n* angolo *m*; (*football*) calcio *m* d'angolo, corner *m inv* ● *vt fig* bloccare; *Comm* accaparrarsi ⟨*market*⟩

corner shop *n* negozio *m* di quartiere

cornerstone /ˈkɔːnəstəʊn/ *n* pietra *f* angolare

cornet /ˈkɔːnɪt/ *n Mus* cornetta *f*; (*for ice-cream*) cono *m*

cornfield /ˈkɔːnfiːld/ *n* campo *m* di grano; (*sweetcorn*) campo *m* di mais

cornflour /ˈkɔːnflaʊə(r)/ *n* farina *f* finissima di mais

cornflower /ˈkɔːnflaʊə(r)/ *n* fiordaliso *m*

cornice /ˈkɔːnɪs/ *n* (*inside*) cornice *f*; (*outside*) cornicione *m*

Cornish pasty /kɔːnɪʃˈpæstɪ/ *n* fagottino *m* di pasta sfoglia ripieno di carne e verdura

corn: **corn oil** *n* olio *m* di mais. **corn on the cob** *n* pannocchia *f* cotta. **corn plaster** *n* [cerotto *m*] callifugo *m*. **cornstarch** *n Am* farina *f* di granturco

cornucopia /kɔːnjʊˈkəʊpɪə/ *n* cornucopia *f*; *fig* abbondanza *f*

Cornwall /ˈkɔːnwɔːl/ *n* Cornovaglia *f*

corny /ˈkɔːnɪ/ *a* (**-ier, -iest**) ⟨*fam: joke, film*⟩ scontato; ⟨*person*⟩ banale; (*sentimental*) sdolcinato

corollary /kəˈrɒlərɪ/ *n* corollario *m*

coronary /ˈkɒrənərɪ/ *a* coronario ● *n ~* [**thrombosis**] trombosi *f* coronarica

coronation /kɒrəˈneɪʃn/ *n* incoronazione *f*

coroner /ˈkɒrənə(r)/ *n* coroner *m inv* (*nel diritto britannico, ufficiale incaricato delle indagini su morti sospette*)

coronet /ˈkɒrənet/ *n* coroncina *f*

corporal[1] /ˈkɔːpərəl/ *n Mil* caporale *m*

corporal[2] *a* corporale; *~* **punishment** punizione *f* corporale

corporate /ˈkɔːpərət/ *a* ⟨*decision, policy, image*⟩ aziendale; *~* **life** la vita in un'azienda

corporate: **corporate image** *n* immagine *f* aziendale. **corporate lawyer** *n* legale *mf* specializzato, -a in diritto aziendale.

corporate planning *n* pianificazione *f* aziendale

corporation /kɔːpəˈreɪʃn/ *n* ente *m*; (*of town*) ≈ consiglio *m* comunale

corporation tax *n Br* imposta *f* sul reddito delle aziende

corps /kɔː(r)/ *n* (*pl* **corps** /kɔːz/) corpo *m*

corps de ballet /kɔːdəˈbæleɪ/ *n* corpo *m* di ballo

corpse /kɔːps/ *n* cadavere *m*

corpulent /ˈkɔːpjʊlənt/ *a* corpulento

corpus /ˈkɔːpəs/ *n* (*of words*) corpus *m inv*

corpuscle /ˈkɔːpʌsl/ *n* globulo *m*

correct /kəˈrekt/ *a* corretto; **be ~** ⟨*person:*⟩ aver ragione; **~!** esatto! ● *vt* correggere

correcting fluid *n* bianchetto *m*

correction /kəˈrekʃn/ *n* correzione *f*

corrective /kəˈrektɪv/ *n* correttivo *m*

correctly /kəˈrektlɪ/ *adv* correttamente

correlate /ˈkɒrəleɪt/ *vt* correlare ● *vi* essere correlato

correlation /kɒrəˈleɪʃn/ *n* correlazione *f*

correspond /kɒrɪˈspɒnd/ *vi* corrispondere; (**to** a); ⟨*two things:*⟩ corrispondere; (*write*) scriversi

correspondence /kɒrɪˈspɒndəns/ *n* corrispondenza *f*

correspondence course *n* corso *m* per corrispondenza

correspondent /kɒrɪˈspɒndənt/ *n* corrispondente *mf*

corresponding /kɒrɪˈspɒndɪŋ/ *a* corrispondente

correspondingly /kɒrɪˈspɒndɪŋlɪ/ *adv* in modo corrispondente

corridor /ˈkɒrɪdɔː(r)/ *n* corridoio *m*

corroborate /kəˈrɒbəreɪt/ *vt* corroborare

corrode /kəˈrəʊd/ *vt* corrodere ● *vi* corrodersi

corrosion /kəˈrəʊʒn/ *n* corrosione *f*

corrugated /ˈkɒrəgeɪtɪd/ *a* ondulato

corrugated iron *n* lamiera *f* ondulata

corrupt /kəˈrʌpt/ *a* corrotto ● *vt* corrompere

corruption /kəˈrʌpʃn/ *n* corruzione *f*

corset /ˈkɔːsɪt/ *n* & **-s** *pl* busto *m*

Corsica /ˈkɔːsɪkə/ *n* Corsica *f*

Corsican /ˈkɔːsɪkən/ *a* & *n* corso, -a *mf*

cortège /kɔːˈteɪʒ/ *n* [**funeral**] *~* corteo *m* funebre

cosh /kɒʃ/ *n* randello *m*

co-signatory /kəʊˈsɪgnətrɪ/ *n* cofirmatario, -a *mf*

cosily /ˈkəʊzɪlɪ/ *adv* ⟨*sit, lie*⟩ in modo confortevole

cosiness /ˈkəʊzɪnɪs/ *n* (*of room*) comodità *f*; (*intimacy*) intimità *f*

cos lettuce /kɒs/ *n* lattuga *f* romana

cosmetic /kɒzˈmetɪk/ *a* cosmetico ● *n ~s pl* cosmetici *mpl*

cosmetic surgery *n* chirurgia *f* estetica

cosmic /ˈkɒzmɪk/ *a* cosmico

cosmonaut /ˈkɒzmənɔːt/ *n* cosmonauta *mf*

cosmopolitan /kɒzməˈpɒlɪtən/ *a* cosmopolita

cosmos /ˈkɒzmɒs/ *n* cosmo *m*

Cossack /'kɒsæk/ *a & n* cosacco, -a *mf*

cosset /'kɒsɪt/ *vt* coccolare

cost /kɒst/ *n* costo *m*; **~s** *pl Jur* spese *fpl* processuali; **at all ~s** a tutti i costi; **I learnt to my ~** ho imparato a mie spese ● *vt (pt/pp* **cost**) costare; **it ~ me £20** mi è costato 20 sterline ● *vt (pt/pp* **costed**) **~** [**out**] stabilire il prezzo di

co-star /'kəʊstɑː/ *n Cinema, Theat* co-protagonista *mf* ● **film ~ring X and Y** un film con X e Y come protagonisti

cost: cost centre *n* centro *m* di costi. **cost-cutting** *n* tagli *mpl* sulle spese; **as a ~ exercise** [come misura] per ridurre le spese. **cost-effective** *a* conveniente. **cost-effectiveness** *n* convenienza *f*

costing /'kɒstɪŋ/ *n (process)* determinazione *f* dei costi; *(discipline)* costing *m inv*

costly /'kɒstlɪ/ *a* (**-ier, -iest**) costoso

cost of living *n* costo *m* della vita

cost-of-living index *n* indice *m* del costo della vita

cost price *n* prezzo *m* di costo

costume /'kɒstjuːm/ *n* costume *m*

costume drama *n* dramma *m* storico

costume jewellery *n* bigiotteria *f*

cosy /'kəʊzɪ/ *a* (**-ier, -iest**) *(pub, chat)* intimo; **it's nice and ~ in here** si sta bene qui ● *n* **tea ~** copriteiera *m inv*

cot /kɒt/ *n* lettino *m*; (*Am: camp bed*) branda *f*

cot death *n Br* morte *f* inspiegabile di un neonato nel sonno

Côte d'Azur /kəʊtdæ'zʊə(r)/ *n* Costa *f* Azzurra

cottage /'kɒtɪdʒ/ *n* casetta *f*

cottage: cottage cheese *n* fiocchi *mpl* di latte. **cottage hospital** *n Br* piccolo ospedale *m (in zona rurale)*. **cottage industry** *n* attività *f inv* artigianale basata sul lavoro *a domicilio*. **cottage loaf** *n* pagnotta *f* casereccia. **cottage pie** *n Br* pasticcio *m* di patate e carne macinata

cotton /'kɒtn/ *n* cotone *m* ● *attrib* di cotone

■ **cotton on** *vi fam* capire

cotton: cotton bud *n* cotton fioc® *m inv*. **cotton mill** *n* cotonificio *m*. **cotton reel** *n* rocchetto *m*, spagnoletta *f*. **cotton wool** *n Br* cotone *m* idrofilo

couch /kaʊtʃ/ *n* divano *m*

couchette /kuː'ʃet/ *n* cuccetta *f*

couch potato *n* pantofolaio, -a *mf*

cougar /'kuːgə(r)/ *n* coguaro *m*

cough /kɒf/ *n* tosse *f* ● *vi* tossire

■ **cough up** *vt/i* sputare; (*fam: pay*) sborsare

cough mixture *n* sciroppo *m* per la tosse

could /kʊd/, *atono* /kəd/ *v aux* (*see also* **can²**) **~ I have a glass of water?** potrei avere un bicchier d'acqua?; **I ~n't do it even if I wanted** non potrei farlo nemmeno se lo volessi; **I ~n't care less** non potrebbe importarmene di meno; **he ~n't have done it without help** non avrebbe potuto farlo senza aiuto; **you ~ have phoned** avresti potuto telefonare

council /'kaʊnsl/ *n* consiglio *m*

council: council estate *n Br* complesso *m* di case popolari. **council house** *n* casa *f* popolare. **council housing** *n Br* case *fpl* popolari

councillor /'kaʊnsələ(r)/ *n* consigliere, -a *mf*

council tax *n* imposta *f* locale sugli immobili

counsel /'kaʊnsl/ *n* consigli *mpl*; *Jur* avvocato *m* ● *vt (pt/pp* **counselled**) consigliare a *(person)*

counselling, *Am* **counseling** /'kaʊnsəlɪŋ/ *n (psychological)* terapia *f* [psichiatrica]; *Sch* orientamento *m* scolastico; **careers ~** orientamento *m* professionale ● *attrib (group, centre, service)* di assistenza

counsellor /'kaʊnsələ(r)/ *n* consigliere, -a *mf*

count¹ /kaʊnt/ *n (nobleman)* conte *m*

count² *n* conto *m*; **keep ~** tenere il conto ● *vt/i* contare

■ **count against** *vt (inexperience, police record:)* deporre a sfavore di

■ **count among** *vt* **~ sb among one's friends** annoverare qcno tra i propri amici

■ **count in** *vt (include)* includere; **~ me in!** io ci sto!

■ **count on** *vt* contare su

■ **count out** *vt* contare *(money)*; **~ me out!** fate senza di me!

■ **count up** *vt* contare ● *vi* **~ to ten** contare fino a dieci

countable /'kaʊntəbl/ *a (noun)* numerabile

countdown /'kaʊntdaʊn/ *n* conto *m* alla rovescia

countenance /'kaʊntənəns/ *n* espressione *f* ● *vt* approvare

counter¹ /'kaʊntə(r)/ *n* banco *m*; (*in games*) gettone *m*

counter² *adv* **~ to** contro, in contrasto a; **go ~ to sth** andare contro qcsa ● *vt/i* opporre *(measure, effect)*; parare *(blow)*

counteract /kaʊntər'ækt/ *vt* neutralizzare

counter-attack *n* contrattacco *m*

counterbalance /'kaʊntəbæləns/ *n* contrappeso *m* ● *vt* controbilanciare

counter-claim *n* replica *f*

counter-culture /'kaʊntəkʌltʃə(r)/ *n* controcultura *f*

counter-espionage *n* controspionaggio *m*

counterfeit /'kaʊntəfɪt/ *a* contraffatto ● *n* contraffazione *f* ● *vt* contraffare

counterfoil /'kaʊntəfɔɪl/ *n* matrice *f*

counter-inflationary /-ɪn'fleɪʃənərɪ/ *a* antinflazionistico

counter-insurgency /-ɪn'sɜːdʒənsɪ/ *attrib* per reprimere un'insurrezione

counter-intelligence *n* controspionaggio *m*

countermeasure /'kaʊntəmeʒə(r)/ *n* contromisura *f*

counter-offensive *n* controffensiva *f*

counterpane /'kaʊntəpeɪn/ *n* copriletto *m*

counterpart /'kaʊntəpɑːt/ *n* equivalente *mf*

counterpoint /ˈkaʊntəpɔɪnt/ n contrappunto mf

counter-productive a controproduttivo

countersign /ˈkaʊntəsaɪn/ vt controfirmare

counter staff n commessi mpl

counter-terrorism n antiterrorismo m

countess /ˈkaʊntɪs/ n contessa f

countless /ˈkaʊntlɪs/ a innumerevole

countrified /ˈkʌntrɪfaɪd/ a ⟨person⟩ campagnolo

country /ˈkʌntrɪ/ n nazione f, paese m; ⟨native land⟩ patria f; ⟨countryside⟩ campagna f; **in the ~** in campagna; **go to the ~** andare in campagna; Pol indire le elezioni politiche

country: country and western n country m inv. **country bumpkin** n pej buzzurro, -a mf. **country club** n club m inv sportivo e ricreativo in campagna. **country cousin** n pej provinciale mf. **country dancing** n danza f folcloristica. **country house** n villa f di campagna. **countryman** n uomo m di campagna; ⟨fellow ~man⟩ compatriota m. **country music** n country m inv. **countryside** n campagna f. **countrywide** a & adv in tutto il paese

county /ˈkaʊntɪ/ n contea f ⟨unità amministrativa britannica⟩

county council n Br Pol consiglio m di contea

county court n Br Jur tribunale m di contea

coup /kuː/ n Pol colpo m di stato

couple /ˈkʌpl/ n coppia f; **a ~ of** un paio di

coupon /ˈkuːpɒn/ n tagliando m; ⟨for discount⟩ buono m sconto

courage /ˈkʌrɪdʒ/ n coraggio m

courageous /kəˈreɪdʒəs/ a coraggioso

courageously /kəˈreɪdʒəslɪ/ adv coraggiosamente

courgette /kʊəˈʒet/ n zucchino m

courier /ˈkʊrɪə(r)/ n corriere m; ⟨for tourists⟩ guida f

course /kɔːs/ n Sch corso m; Naut rotta f; Culin portata f; ⟨for golf⟩ campo m; **~ of treatment** Med serie f inv di cure; **of ~** naturalmente; **in the ~ of** durante; **in due ~ of** a tempo debito; **~ of action** linea f d'azione

course book n libro m di testo

coursework /ˈkɔːswɜːk/ n Sch, Univ esercitazioni fpl scritte che contano per la media

court /kɔːt/ n tribunale m; Sport campo m; **take sb to ~** citare qcno in giudizio ● vt fare la corte a ⟨woman⟩; sfidare ⟨danger⟩; **~ing couples** coppiette fpl

court circular n bollettino quotidiano f di corte

courteous /ˈkɜːtɪəs/ a cortese

courteously /ˈkɜːtɪəslɪ/ adv cortesemente

courtesy /ˈkɜːtəsɪ/ n cortesia f

courthouse /ˈkɔːthaʊs/ n Jur palazzo m di giustizia, tribunale m

courtier /ˈkɔːtɪə(r)/ n cortigiano, -a mf

court: court martial n (pl **~s martial**) corte f marziale ● **court-martial** vt (pt **~-martialled**) portare davanti alla corte marziale. **court of inquiry** n commissione f d'inchiesta. **court of law** n Jur corte f di giustizia. **court order** n Jur ingiunzione f. **courtroom** n Jur aula f [di tribunale]

courtship /ˈkɔːtʃɪp/ n corteggiamento m

courtyard /ˈkɔːtjɑːd/ n cortile m

cousin /ˈkʌzn/ n cugino, -a mf

cove /kəʊv/ n insenatura f

covenant /ˈkʌvənənt/ n ⟨agreement⟩ accordo m; ⟨payment agreement⟩ impegno m scritto a pagare

cover /ˈkʌvə(r)/ n copertura f; ⟨of cushion, to protect sth⟩ fodera f; ⟨of book, magazine⟩ copertina f; **take ~** mettersi al riparo; **under separate ~** a parte ● vt coprire; foderare ⟨cushion⟩; Journ fare un servizio su

■ **cover for** vt ⟨replace⟩ sostituire ⟨sb⟩

■ **cover up** vt coprire; fig soffocare ⟨scandal⟩

■ **cover up for** vt fare da copertura a ⟨sb⟩

coverage /ˈkʌvərɪdʒ/ n Journ **it got a lot of ~** i media gli hanno dedicato molto spazio

cover charge n coperto m

covered market n mercato m coperto

covered wagon n carro m coperto

cover girl n ragazza f copertina

covering /ˈkʌv(ə)rɪŋ/ n copertura f; ⟨for floor⟩ rivestimento m; **~ of snow** strato m di neve

covering fire n fuoco m di copertura

covering letter n lettera f d'accompagnamento

cover note n ⟨from insurance company⟩ polizza f provvisoria

cover story n ⟨in paper⟩ articolo m di prima pagina

covert /ˈkəʊvɜːt/ a ⟨threat⟩ velato; ⟨operation⟩ segreto; ⟨glance⟩ furtivo

covertly /ˈkəʊvɜːtlɪ/ adv furtivamente; ⟨operate⟩ in segreto

cover-up n messa f a tacere

cover version n Mus versione f non originale

covet /ˈkʌvɪt/ vt bramare

covetous /ˈkʌvətəs/ a avido

covetously /ˈkʌvətəslɪ/ adv avidamente

cow /kaʊ/ n vacca f, mucca f

coward /ˈkaʊəd/ n vigliacco, -a mf

cowardice /ˈkaʊədɪs/ n vigliaccheria f

cowardly /ˈkaʊədlɪ/ a da vigliacco

cowbell /ˈkaʊbel/ n campanaccio m

cowboy /ˈkaʊbɔɪ/ n cowboy m inv; fig fam buffone m

cower /ˈkaʊə(r)/ vi acquattarsi

cowherd /ˈkaʊhɜːd/ n vaccaro m

cowhide /ˈkaʊhaɪd/ n ⟨leather⟩ pelle f di mucca

cowl /kaʊl/ n cappuccio m

cowlick /ˈkaʊlɪk/ n fam ciocca f ribelle

cowl neck n collo m ad anello

cowpat /ˈkaʊpæt/ n sterco m di vacca

cowshed /ˈkaʊʃed/ n stalla f

cox /kɒks/ n, **coxswain** /ˈkɒks(ə)n/ n timoniere, -a mf

coy /kɔɪ/ *a* falsamente timido; *(flirtatiously)* civettuolo; **be ~ about sth** essere evasivo su qcsa

coyly /'kɔɪlɪ/ *adv* con falsa modestia; ⟨*flirtatiously*⟩ con civetteria

CPU *n abbr* (**central processing unit**) CPU *f inv*

crab /kræb/ *n* granchio *m*

crab apple *n* mela *f* selvatica

crack /kræk/ *n* (*in wall*) crepa *f*; (*in china, glass, bone*) incrinatura *f*; (*noise*) scoppio *m*; (*fam: joke*) battuta *f*; **have a ~** (*try*) fare un tentativo ● *a* (*fam: best*) di prim'ordine ● *vt* incrinare ⟨*china, glass*⟩; schiacciare ⟨*nut*⟩; decifrare ⟨*code*⟩; *fam* risolvere ⟨*problem*⟩; **~ a joke** *fam* fare una battuta ● *vi* ⟨*china, glass:*⟩ incrinarsi; ⟨*whip:*⟩ schioccare

■ **crack down** *vi fam* prendere seri provvedimenti

■ **crack down on** *vt fam* prendere seri provvedimenti contro

■ **crack up** *vi* crollare

crackdown /'krækdaʊn/ *n* misure *fpl* (**on** contro)

cracked /krækt/ *a* ⟨*plaster*⟩ crepato; ⟨*skin*⟩ screpolato; ⟨*rib*⟩ incrinato; (*fam: crazy*) svitato

cracker /'krækə(r)/ *n* (*biscuit*) cracker *m inv*; (*firework*) petardo *m*; [**Christmas**] **~** cilindro *m* di cartone contenente una sorpresa che produce una piccola esplosione quando viene aperto

crackers /'krækəz/ *a fam* matto

cracking /'krækɪŋ/ *a Br fam* eccellente; **at a ~ pace** a ritmo incalzante

crackle /'krækl/ *vi* crepitare

crackling /'kræklɪŋ/ *n* (*on radio*) disturbo *m*; (*of foil, cellophane*) sfregamento *m*; (*of fire*) crepitio *m*; (*crisp pork*) cotenna *f* arrostita

crackpot /'krækpɒt/ *fam n* pazzo, -a *mf* ● *a* da pazzi

cradle /'kreɪdl/ *n* culla *f*

cradle-snatcher *n fam* **he's/she's a ~** se la intende con i ragazzini/le ragazzine

craft[1] /krɑːft/ *n inv* (*boat*) imbarcazione *f*

craft[2] *n* mestiere *m*; (*technique*) arte *f*

craftily /'krɑːftɪlɪ/ *adv* con astuzia

craftsman /'krɑːftsmən/ *n* artigiano *m*

craftsmanship /'krɑːftsmənʃɪp/ *n* maestria *f*

crafty /'krɑːftɪ/ *a* (**-ier, -iest**) astuto

crag /kræg/ *n* rupe *f*

craggy /'krægɪ/ *a* scosceso; ⟨*face*⟩ dai lineamenti marcati

cram /kræm/ *v* (*pt/pp* **crammed**) ● *vt* stipare (**into** in) ● *vi* (*for exams*) sgobbare

crammer /'kræmə(r)/ *n* (*Br fam: school*) ≈ istituto *m* di recupero

cramp /kræmp/ *n* crampo *m*

cramped /kræmpt/ *a* ⟨*room*⟩ stretto; ⟨*handwriting*⟩ appiccicato; **it's a bit ~ed in here** si sta un po' stretti qui

crampon /'kræmpən/ *n* rampone *m*

cranberry /'krænbərɪ/ *n Culin* mirtillo *m* rosso

crane /kreɪn/ *n* (*at docks, bird*) gru *f inv* ● *vt* **~ one's neck** allungare il collo

cranium /'kreɪnɪəm/ *n* cranio *m*

crank[1] /kræŋk/ *n* tipo, -a *mf* strampalato, -a

crank[2] *n Techn* manovella *f*

crankshaft /'kræŋkʃɑːft/ *n* albero *m* a gomiti

cranky /'kræŋkɪ/ *a* strampalato; (*Am: irritable*) irritabile

cranny /'krænɪ/ *n* fessura *f*

crap /kræp/ *n sl* (*faeces*) merda *f*; (*film, book etc*) schifezza *f*; (*nonsense*) stronzate *fpl*; **have a ~** cacare

crappy /'kræpɪ/ *a sl* di merda

crash /kræʃ/ *n* (*noise*) fragore *m*; *Auto, Aeron* incidente *m*; *Comm* crollo *m;* *Comput* crash *m inv* ● *vi* schiantarsi (**into** contro); ⟨*plane:*⟩ precipitare ● *vt* schiantare ⟨*car*⟩

■ **crash out** *vi* (*sl: go to sleep*) crollare; (*on sofa etc*) dormire

crash: crash barrier *n* guardrail *m inv*. **crash course** *n* corso *m* intensivo. **crash diet** *n* dieta *f* drastica. **crash-helmet** *n* casco *m*. **crash-land** *vi* fare un atterraggio di fortuna. **crash-landing** *n* atterraggio *m* di fortuna

crass /kræs/ *a* ⟨*ignorance*⟩ crasso

crate /kreɪt/ *n* (*for packing*) cassa *f*

crater /'kreɪtə(r)/ *n* cratere *m*

cravat /krə'væt/ *n* foulard *m inv*

crave /kreɪv/ *vt* morire dalla voglia di

craving /'kreɪvɪŋ/ *n* voglia *f* smodata

crawl /krɔːl/ *n* (*swimming*) stile *m* libero; **do the ~** nuotare a stile libero; **at a ~** a passo di lumaca ● *vi* andare carponi; **~ with** brulicare di

crawler lane /'krɔːlə/ *n Auto* corsia *f* riservata al traffico lento

crayfish /'kreɪfɪʃ/ *n* gambero *m* d'acqua dolce

crayon /'kreɪən/ *n* pastello *m* a cera; (*pencil*) matita *f* colorata

craze /kreɪz/ *n* mania *f*

crazed /kreɪzd/ *a* ⟨*china, glaze*⟩ screpolato; ⟨*animal, person*⟩ impazzito; **power-~** ubriaco di potere

crazy /'kreɪzɪ/ *a* (**-ier, -iest**) matto; **be ~ about** andar matto per

crazy golf *n Br* minigolf *m inv*

crazy paving *n Br* pavimentazione *f* a mosaico irregolare

creak /kriːk/ *n* scricchiolio *m* ● *vi* scricchiolare

creaky /'kriːkɪ/ *a* ⟨*leather*⟩ che cigola; ⟨*door, hinge*⟩ cigolante; ⟨*joint, bone, floorboard*⟩ scricchiolante; ⟨*fig fam: alibi, policy*⟩ traballante

cream /kriːm/ *n* crema *f*; (*fresh*) panna *f* ● *a* (*colour*) [bianco] panna *inv* ● *vt* *Culin* sbattere

■ **cream off** *vt* accaparrarsi ⟨*top pupils, scientists etc*⟩

cream: cream cheese *n* formaggio *m* cremoso. **cream cracker** *n Br* cracker *m inv*. **cream puff** *n* sfogliatina *f* alla panna *inv*. **cream soda** *n* soda *f* aromatizzata alla vaniglia. **cream tea** *n Br* tè *m inv* servito con pasticcini da mangiare con marmellata e panna

creamy /'kri:mɪ/ *a* (**-ier, iest**) cremoso

crease /kri:s/ *n* piega *f* ● *vt* stropicciare ● *vi* stropicciarsi

crease-resistant *a* che non si stropiccia

create /kri:'eɪt/ *vt* creare

creation /kri:'eɪʃn/ *n* creazione *f*

creative /kri:'eɪtɪv/ *a* creativo

creative director *n* direttore, -trice *mf* creativo, -a

creative writing *n* (*school subject*) composizione *f*

creativity /kri:eɪ'tɪvətɪ/ *n* creatività *f*

creator /kri:'eɪtə(r)/ *n* creatore, -trice *mf*

creature /'kri:tʃə(r)/ *n* creatura *f*

creature comforts *npl* comodità *fpl*; **like one's ~** amare le proprie comodità

crèche /kreʃ/ *n* asilo *m* nido *inv*

credence /'kri:dəns/ *n* credito *m*; **give ~ to sth** (*believe*) dare credito a qcsa

credentials /krɪ'denʃlz/ *npl* credenziali *fpl*

credibility /kredə'bɪlətɪ/ *n* credibilità *f*

credible /'kredəbl/ *a* credibile

credit /'kredɪt/ *n* credito *m*; (*honour*) merito *m*; **take the ~ for** prendersi il merito di ● *vt* accreditare; **~ sb with sth** *Comm* accreditare qcsa a qcno; *fig* attribuire qcsa a qcno

creditable /'kredɪtəbl/ *a* lodevole

credit: credit balance *n* saldo *m* attivo. **credit card** *n* carta *f* di credito. **credit control** *n* controllo *m* del credito. **credit limit** *n* limite *m* di credito. **credit note** *n* *Comm* nota *f* di accredito

creditor /'kredɪtə(r)/ *n* creditore, -trice *mf*

credit: credit side *n* on the **~ ~** tra i lati positivi. **credit squeeze** *n* stretta *f* creditizia. **credit terms** *npl* condizioni *fpl* di credito. **credit transfer** *n* bonifico *m*

creditworthiness /'kredɪ(t)wɜ:ðɪnɪs/ *n* capacità *f* di credito

creditworthy /'kredɪ(t)wɜ:ðɪ/ *a* meritevole di credito

credulity /krɪ'dju:lətɪ/ *n* credulità *f*; **strain sb's ~** essere ai limiti della credibilità

credulous /'kredjʊləs/ *a* credulo

creed /kri:d/ *n* credo *m inv*

creek /kri:k/ *n* insenatura *f*; (*Am: stream*) torrente *m*; **up the ~** (*fam: in trouble*) nei guai

creep /kri:p/ *vi* (*pt/pp* **crept**) muoversi furtivamente ● *n fam* tipo *m* viscido; **it gives me the ~s** mi fa venire i brividi

creeper /'kri:pə(r)/ *n* pianta *f* rampicante

creepy /'kri:pɪ/ *a* che fa venire i brividi

creepy-crawly /-'krɔ:lɪ/ *n fam* insetto

cremate /krɪ'meɪt/ *vt* cremare

cremation /krɪ'meɪʃn/ *n* cremazione *f*

crematorium /kremə'tɔ:rɪəm/ *n* crematorio *m*

crepe /kreɪp/ *n* (*fabric*) crespo *m*

crepe: crepe bandage *n* fascia *f* elastica. **crepe paper** *n* carta *f* crespata. **crepe soles** *npl* suole *fpl* di para

crept /krept/ *see* **creep**

crescendo /krɪ'ʃendəʊ/ *n Mus* crescendo *m*; **reach a ~** *fig* (*noise, protests:*) raggiungere il picco; (*campaign:*) raggiungere il culmine

crescent /'kresənt/ *n* mezzaluna *f*

crescent moon *n* mezzaluna *f*

cress /kres/ *n* crescione *m*

crest /krest/ *n* cresta *f*; (*coat of arms*) cimiero *m*; **be on the ~ of a wave** essere sulla cresta dell'onda

crestfallen /'krestfɔ:lən/ *a* mogio

Crete /kri:t/ *n* Creta *f*

crevasse /krɪ'væs/ *n* crepaccio *m*

crevice /'krevɪs/ *n* crepa *f*

crew /kru:/ *n* equipaggio *m*; (*gang*) équipe *f inv*

crew cut *n* capelli *mpl* a spazzola

crew neck *n* girocollo *m*

crew neck sweater *n* maglione *m* a girocollo

crib[1] /krɪb/ *n* (*for baby*) culla *f*

crib[2] *vt/i* (*pt/pp* **cribbed**) *fam* copiare

cribbage /'krɪbɪdʒ/ *n* gioco *m* di carte

crick /krɪk/ *n* **~ in the neck** torcicollo *m*

cricket[1] /'krɪkɪt/ *n* (*insect*) grillo *m*

cricket[2] *n* cricket *m*

cricketer /'krɪkɪtə(r)/ *n* giocatore *m* di cricket

crime /kraɪm/ *n* crimine *m*; (*criminality*) criminalità *f*; **it's a ~** *fig* è un delitto

crime of passion *n* delitto *m* passionale

crime prevention *n* prevenzione *f* della criminalità

criminal /'krɪmɪnl/ *a* criminale; (*law, court*) penale ● *n* criminale *mf*

criminal: criminal charges *npl* **face ~ ~** essere imputato. **criminal investigation** *n* inchiesta *f* giudiziaria. **Criminal Investigation Department** *n Br* ≈ polizia *f* giudiziaria. **criminal justice** *n* sistema *m* penale. **criminal law** *n* diritto *m* penale.

criminally insane /'krɪmɪnəlɪ/ *a* pazzo criminale

criminal offence *n* reato *m*

criminal record *n* **have a/no ~ ~** avere la fedina penale sporca/pulita

criminology /krɪmɪ'nɒlədʒɪ/ *n* criminologia *f*

crimp /krɪmp/ *vt* pieghettare (*fabric*); increspare (*pastry*); arricciare (*hair*)

crimson /'krɪmz(ə)n/ *a* cremisi *inv*

cringe /krɪndʒ/ *vi* (*cower*) acquattarsi; (*at bad joke etc*) fare una smorfia

crinkle /'krɪŋk(ə)l/ *vt* spiegazzare ● *vi* spiegazzarsi

crinkly /'krɪŋklɪ/ *a* (*paper, material*) crespato; (*hair*) crespo

cripple /'krɪpl/ *n* storpio, -a *mf* ● *vt* storpiare; *fig* danneggiare

crippled /'krɪpld/ *a* (*person*) storpio; (*ship*) danneggiato

crippling /'krɪplɪŋ/ *a* (*taxes, debts*) esorbitante; (*disease*) devastante; (*strike, effect*) paralizzante

crisis /'kraısıs/ n (pl **-ses** /'kraısi:z/) crisi f inv

crisp /krısp/ a croccante; ‹air› frizzante; ‹style› incisivo

crispbread /'krıs(p)bred/ n crostini mpl di pane

crisps /krısps/ npl patatine fpl

crispy /'krıspı/ a croccante

criss-cross /'krıs-/ a a linee incrociate

criterion /kraı'tıərıən/ n (pl **-ria** /kraı'tıərıə/) criterio m

critic /'krıtık/ n critico, -a mf

critical /'krıtıkl/ a critico

critically /'krıtıklı/ adv in modo critico; ~ **ill** gravemente malato

critical path analysis n analisi f inv del percorso critico

criticism /'krıtısızm/ n critica f; **he doesn't like** ~ non ama le critiche

criticize /'krıtısaız/ vt criticare

croak /krəʊk/ vi gracchiare; ‹frog:› gracidare

Croatia /krəʊ'eıʃə/ n Croazia f

crochet /'krəʊʃeı/ n lavoro m all'uncinetto ● vt fare all'uncinetto

crochet-hook n uncinetto m

crock /krɒk/ n fam **old** ~ (person) rudere m; (car) macinino m

crockery /'krɒkərı/ n terrecotte fpl

crocodile /'krɒkədaıl/ n coccodrillo m

crocodile tears npl lacrime fpl di coccodrillo

crocus /'krəʊkəs/ n (pl **-es**) croco m

croft /krɒft/ n piccola fattoria f

crone /krəʊn/ n pej vecchiaccia f

crony /'krəʊnı/ n compare m

crook /krʊk/ n (fam: criminal) truffatore, -trice mf

crooked /'krʊkıd/ a storto; ‹limb› storpiato; (fam: dishonest) disonesto; ~ **deal** fregatura f

croon /kru:n/ vt/i canticchiare

crop /krɒp/ n raccolto m; fig quantità f inv ● v (pt/pp **cropped**) ● vt coltivare

■ **crop up** vi fam presentarsi

crop rotation n rotazione f delle colture

crop spraying /'krɒpspreııŋ/ n irrorazione f

croquet /'krəʊkeı/ n croquet m

croquette /krəʊ'ket/ n crocchetta f

cross /krɒs/ a (annoyed) arrabbiato; **talk at** ~ **purposes** fraintendersi ● n croce f; Bot, Zool incrocio m ● vt sbarrare ‹cheque›; incrociare ‹road, animals›; ~ **oneself** farsi il segno della croce; ~ **one's arms** incrociare le braccia; ~ **one's legs** accavallare le gambe; **keep one's fingers** ~**ed for sb** tenere le dita incrociate per qcno; **it** ~**ed my mind** mi è venuto in mente ● vi (go across) attraversare; ‹lines:› incrociarsi

■ **cross off** vt (from list) depennare

■ **cross out** vt sbarrare; (from list) depennare

cross: crossbar n (of goal) traversa f; (on bicycle) canna f. **cross-border** a oltreconfine. **crossbow** n balestra f. **crossbred** a ibrido. **crossbreed** vt ibridare, incrociare ‹animals, plants› ● n (animal) incrocio m, ibrido m. **cross-Channel** a attraverso la Manica; ‹ferry› che attraversa la Manica. **cross-check** n controprova f ● vt fare la controprova di. **cross-country** n Sport corsa f campestre. **cross-country skiing** n sci m di fondo. **cross-court** a ‹shot, volley› diagonale. **cross-cultural** a multiculturale. **crosscurrent** n corrente f trasversale. **cross-dressing** n travestitismo m. **cross-examination** n controinterrogatorio m. **cross-examine** vt sottoporre a controinterrogatorio. **cross-eyed** /'krɒsaıd/ a strabico. **crossfire** n fuoco m incrociato

crossing /'krɒsıŋ/ n (for pedestrians) passaggio m pedonale; (sea journey) traversata f

cross-legged /krɒs'legd/ a & adv con le gambe incrociate

crossly /'krɒslı/ adv con rabbia

cross: crossover a ‹straps› incrociato. **cross-purposes** npl **we are at** ~ non ci siamo capiti. **cross-question** vt interrogare ‹person›. **cross-reference** n rimando m. **crossroads** n incrocio m; **reach a** ~ fig arrivare a un bivio. **cross-section** n sezione f; (of community) campione m. **cross-stitch** n punto m croce. **crosswalk** n Am attraversamento m pedonale. **crosswind** n vento m di traverso. **crosswise** adv in diagonale. **crossword** n ~ **[puzzle]** parole fpl crociate

crotch /krɒtʃ/ n Anat inforcatura f; (in trousers) cavallo m

crotchet /'krɒtʃıt/ n Mus semiminima f

crotchety /'krɒtʃıtı/ a irritabile

crouch /kraʊtʃ/ vi accovacciarsi

croupier /'kru:pıə(r)/ n croupier m inv

crouton /'kru:tɒn/ n crostino m

crow /krəʊ/ n corvo m; **as the** ~ **flies** in linea d'aria ● vi cantare

crowbar /'krəʊbɑ:/ n piede m di porco

crowd /kraʊd/ n folla f ● vt affollare ● vi affollarsi

crowd control n controllo m della folla

crowded /'kraʊdıd/ a affollato

crowd-puller /'kraʊdpʊlə(r)/ n (event) grande attrazione f

crowd scene n Cinema, Theat scena f di massa

crown /kraʊn/ n corona f ● vt incoronare; incapsulare ‹tooth›

Crown court n Br Jur ≈ corte f d'assise

crowning glory /'kraʊnıŋ/ n culmine m; **her hair is her** ~ ~ i capelli sono il suo punto forte

crown jewels npl gioielli mpl della corona

crown prince n principe m ereditario

crow's feet /krəʊz'fi:t/ npl (on face) zampe fpl di gallina

crow's nest /krəʊz'nest/ n coffa f

crucial /'kru:ʃl/ a cruciale

crucially /'kru:ʃəlı/ adv ~ **important** di vitale importanza

crucifix /'kru:sıfıks/ n crocifisso m

crucifixion /kruːsɪˈfɪkʃn/ n crocifissione f
crucify /ˈkruːsɪfaɪ/ vt (pt/pp -ied) crocifiggere
crude /kruːd/ a ⟨oil⟩ greggio; ⟨language⟩ crudo; ⟨person⟩ rozzo
crudely /ˈkruːdlɪ/ adv (vulgarly) in modo crudo; (simply) schematicamente; (roughly: assembled) sommariamente; (painted, made) rozzamente; **~ speaking** in parole povere
crudity /ˈkruːdətɪ/ n (vulgarity) volgarità f
cruel /ˈkruːəl/ a (-ler, -lest) crudele (**to** verso)
cruelly /ˈkruːəlɪ/ adv con crudeltà
cruelty /ˈkruːəltɪ/ n crudeltà f
cruise /kruːz/ n crociera f ● vi fare una crociera; ⟨car:⟩ andare a velocità di crociera
cruise liner n nave f da crociera
cruise missile n missile m cruise inv
cruiser /ˈkruːzə(r)/ n Mil incrociatore m; (motor boat) motoscafo m
cruising speed /ˈkruːzɪŋ/ n velocità m inv di crociera
crumb /krʌm/ n briciola f
crumble /ˈkrʌmbl/ vt sbriciolare ● vi sbriciolarsi; ⟨building, society:⟩ sgretolarsi
crumbling /ˈkrʌmblɪŋ/ a fatiscente
crumbly /ˈkrʌmblɪ/ a friabile
crummy /ˈkrʌmɪ/ a fam (substandard) scadente; (Am: unwell) malato
crumpet /ˈkrʌmpɪt/ n Culin focaccina f da tostare e mangiare con burro e marmellata
crumple /ˈkrʌmpl/ vt spiegazzare ● vi spiegazzarsi
crunch /krʌntʃ/ n fam **when it comes to the ~** quando si viene al dunque ● vt sgranocchiare ● vi ⟨snow:⟩ scricchiolare
crunchy /ˈkrʌntʃɪ/ a ⟨vegetables, biscuits⟩ croccante
crusade /kruːˈseɪd/ n crociata f
crusader /kruːˈseɪdə(r)/ n crociato m
crush /krʌʃ/ n (crowd) calca f; **have a ~ on sb** essersi preso una cotta per qcno ● vt schiacciare; sgualcire ⟨clothes⟩
crushed ice /krʌʃt'aɪs/ n ghiaccio m frantumato
crushed velvet n velluto m stazzonato
crust /krʌst/ n crosta f
crustacean /krʌˈsteɪʃn/ n crostaceo m
crusty /ˈkrʌstɪ/ a ⟨bread⟩ croccante; (irritable) scontroso
crutch /krʌtʃ/ n gruccia f; Anat inforcatura f
crux /krʌks/ n fig punto m cruciale; **~ of the matter** nodo m della questione
cry /kraɪ/ n grido m; **~ for help** grido d'aiuto; **have a ~** farsi un pianto; **a far ~ from** fig tutta un'altra cosa rispetto a ● vi (pt/pp cried) (weep) piangere; (call) gridare
■ **cry out** vi (shout) urlare
crypt /krɪpt/ n cripta f
cryptic /ˈkrɪptɪk/ a criptico
cryptically /ˈkrɪptɪklɪ/ adv (say, speak) in modo enigmatico; **~ worded** espresso in maniera sibillina
crystal /ˈkrɪstl/ n cristallo m; (glassware) cristalli mpl

crystal ball n sfera f di cristallo
crystal clear a ⟨water, sound⟩ cristallino; **let me make it ~ ~** lasciatemelo spiegare chiaramente
crystal-gazing /ˈkrɪstlɡeɪzɪŋ/ n predizione f del futuro (con la sfera di cristallo)
crystallize /ˈkrɪstəlaɪz/ vi (become clear) concretizzarsi
CS gas n Br gas m inv lacrimogeno
cub /kʌb/ n (animal) cucciolo m; **C~** [Scout] lupetto m
Cuba /ˈkjuːbə/ n Cuba f
Cuban /ˈkjuːbən/ a & n cubano -a, mf
cubby-hole /ˈkʌbɪ-/ n (compartment) scomparto m; (room) ripostiglio m
cube /kjuːb/ n cubo m
cubic /ˈkjuːbɪk/ a cubico
cubicle /ˈkjuːbɪkl/ n cabina f
cubism /ˈkjuːbɪzm/ n cubismo m
cubist /ˈkjuːbɪst/ a & n cubista mf
cub reporter n cronista mf alle prime armi
cuckoo /ˈkʊkuː/ n cuculo m
cuckoo clock n orologio m a cucù
cucumber /ˈkjuːkʌmbə(r)/ n cetriolo m
cud /kʌd/ n also fig **chew the ~** ruminare
cuddle /ˈkʌd(ə)l/ vt coccolare ● vi **~ up to** starsene accoccolato insieme a ● n **have a ~** ⟨child:⟩ farsi coccolare; ⟨lovers:⟩ abbracciarsi
cuddly /ˈkʌd(ə)lɪ/ a tenerone; (wanting cuddles) coccolone
cuddly toy n peluche m inv
cudgel /ˈkʌdʒl/ n randello m
cue¹ /kjuː/ n segnale m; Theat battuta f d'entrata
cue² n (in billiards) stecca f
cue ball n pallino m
cuff /kʌf/ n polsino m; (Am: turn-up) orlo m; (blow) scapaccione m; **off the ~** improvvisando ● vt dare una pacca a
cuff link n gemello m
cuisine /kwɪˈziːn/ n cucina f; **haute ~** /əʊt/ haute cuisine f
cul-de-sac /ˈkʌldəsæk/ n vicolo m cieco
culinary /ˈkʌlɪnərɪ/ a culinario
cull /kʌl/ vt scegliere ⟨flowers⟩; (kill) selezionare e uccidere
culminate /ˈkʌlmɪneɪt/ vi culminare
culmination /kʌlmɪˈneɪʃn/ n culmine m
culottes /kjuːˈlɒts/ npl gonna f sg pantalone m
culpable /ˈkʌlpəbl/ a colpevole
culpable homicide n Jur omicidio m colposo
culprit /ˈkʌlprɪt/ n colpevole mf
cult /kʌlt/ n culto m
cultivate /ˈkʌltɪveɪt/ vt coltivare; fig coltivarsi ⟨person⟩
cultivated /ˈkʌltɪveɪtɪd/ a ⟨soil⟩ lavorato; ⟨person⟩ colto
cultural /ˈkʌltʃərəl/ a culturale
cultural attaché n addetto m culturale
culture /ˈkʌltʃə(r)/ n cultura f
cultured /ˈkʌltʃəd/ a colto
cultured pearl n perla f coltivata
culture shock n shock m inv culturale

culture vulture n fam fanatico, -a mf di cultura

culvert /'kʌlvət/ n condotto m sotterraneo

cumbersome /'kʌmbəsəm/ a ingombrante

cumin /'kju:mɪn/ n cumino m nero

cummerbund /'kʌməbʌnd/ n fascia f (dello smoking)

cumulative /'kju:mjʊlətɪv/ a cumulativo

cunning /'kʌnɪŋ/ a astuto ● n astuzia f

cup /kʌp/ n tazza f; (prize, of bra) coppa f

cupboard /'kʌbəd/ n armadio m

cupboard love n Br hum amore m interessato

cupboard space n spazio m negli armadi

Cup Final n finale f di coppa

cupful /'kʌpfʊl/ n tazza f (contenuto)

Cupid /'kju:pɪd/ n Cupido m

cupola /'kju:pələ/ n Archit cupola f

cup tie n Br partita f eliminatoria

cur /kɜ:(r)/ n (pej: dog) cagnaccio m

curable /'kjʊərəbl/ a curabile

curate /'kjʊərət/ n curato m

curator /kjʊə'reɪtə(r)/ n direttore, -trice mf (di museo)

curb /kɜ:b/ vt tenere a freno

curd cheese /kɜ:d/ n cagliata f

curdle /'kɜ:dl/ vi coagularsi

cure /kjʊə(r)/ n cura f ● vt curare; (salt) mettere sotto sale; (smoke) affumicare

cure-all n toccasana m inv, panacea f

curfew /'kɜ:fju:/ n coprifuoco m

curio /'kjʊərɪəʊ/ n curiosità f inv

curiosity /kjʊərɪ'ɒsətɪ/ n curiosità f

curious /'kjʊərɪəs/ a curioso

curiously /'kjʊərɪəslɪ/ adv curiosamente

curl /kɜ:l/ n ricciolo m ● vt arricciare ● vi arricciarsi

■ **curl up** vi raggomitolarsi

curler /'kɜ:lə(r)/ n bigodino m

curling /'kɜ:lɪŋ/ n Sport curling m

curly /'kɜ:lɪ/ a (-ier, -iest) riccio

curly-haired, **curly-headed** /-'heəd, -'hedɪd/ a (tight curls) dai capelli crespi; (loose curls) riccio

currant /'kʌrənt/ n (dried) uvetta f

currency /'kʌrənsɪ/ n valuta f; (of word) ricorrenza f; **foreign ~** valuta f estera

current /'kʌrənt/ a corrente ● n corrente f. **~ affairs** or **events** npl attualità f sg

current: current account n Br conto m corrente. **current assets** n Fin disponibilità fpl correnti. **current liabilities** npl Fin passività fpl correnti

currently /'kʌrəntlɪ/ adv attualmente

curriculum /kə'rɪkjʊləm/ n programma m di studi

curriculum vitae /'vi:taɪ/ n curriculum vitae m inv

curry /'kʌrɪ/ n curry m inv; (meal) piatto m cucinato nel curry ● vt (pt/pp -ied) **~ favour with sb** cercare d'ingraziarsi qcno

curry powder n curry m in polvere

curse /kɜ:s/ n maledizione f; (oath) imprecazione f ● vt maledire ● vi imprecare

cursor /'kɜ:sə(r)/ n cursore m

cursor keys npl tasti mpl cursore

cursory /'kɜ:sərɪ/ a sbrigativo

curt /kɜ:t/ a brusco

curtail /kə'teɪl/ vt ridurre

curtailment /kə'teɪlmənt/ n (of rights, freedom) limitazione f; (of expenditure, service) riduzione f; (of holiday) interruzione f

curtain /'kɜ:tn/ n tenda f; Theat sipario m

■ **curtain off** vt separare con una tenda

curtain call n Theat chiamata f alla ribalta

curtly /'kɜ:tlɪ/ adv bruscamente

curtsy /'kɜ:tsɪ/ n inchino m ● vi (pt/pp -ied) fare l'inchino

curvaceous /kɜ:'veɪʃəs/ a formoso

curve /kɜ:v/ n curva f ● vi curvare; **~ to the right/left** curvare a destra/sinistra

curved /kɜ:vd/ a curvo

curvy /'kɜ:vɪ/ a (-ier, iest) (woman) formoso

cushion /'kʊʃn/ n cuscino m ● vt attutire; (protect) proteggere

cushy /'kʊʃɪ/ a (-ier, -iest) fam facile

custard /'kʌstəd/ n (liquid) crema f pasticciera

custard: custard cream n Br biscotto m farcito alla crema. **custard pie** n torta f alla crema (nei film comici). **custard tart** n torta f alla crema

custodial sentence /kʌ'stəʊdɪəl/ n condanna f a una pena detentiva

custodian /kʌ'stəʊdɪən/ n custode mf

custody /'kʌstədɪ/ n (of child) custodia f; (imprisonment) detenzione f preventiva

custom /'kʌstəm/ n usanza f; Jur consuetudine f; Comm clientela f

customary /'kʌstəmərɪ/ a (habitual) abituale; **it's ~ to...** è consuetudine...

custom-built /-'bɪlt/ a (house) ad hoc

custom car n vettura f personalizzata

customer /'kʌstəmə(r)/ n cliente mf

customer: customer feedback n feedback m inv dai clienti. **customer relations** npl rapporto m con i clienti. **customer service** n assistenza f ai clienti

customize /'kʌstəmaɪz/ vt personalizzare

custom-made /-'meɪd/ a su misura

customs /'kʌstəmz/ npl dogana f

customs: Customs and Excise n Br Ufficio m Dazi e Dogana. **customs clearance** n sdoganamento m. **customs declaration** n dichiarazione f doganale. **customs duties** npl dazi mpl doganali. **customs hall** n dogana f. **customs officer** n doganiere m, guardia f di finanza

cut /kʌt/ n (with knife etc, of clothes) taglio m; (reduction) riduzione f; (in public spending) taglio m ● vt/i (pt/pp cut, pres p cutting) tagliare; (reduce) ridurre; **~ one's finger** tagliarsi il dito; **~ sb's hair** tagliare i capelli a qcno ● vi (with cards) alzare

■ **cut away** vt tagliar via

■ **cut back** vt tagliare (hair); potare (hedge); (reduce) ridurre

■ **cut back on** *vt* (*reduce*) ridurre

■ **cut down** *vt* abbattere ⟨*tree*⟩; (*reduce*) ridurre

■ **cut in** *vi* *Auto* tagliare la strada; (*into conversation*) interrompere ● *vt* ~ **sb in on a deal** dare una percentuale a qcno

■ **cut off** *vt* tagliar via; (*disconnect*) interrompere; *fig* isolare; **I was** ~ **off** *Teleph* la linea è caduta

■ **cut out** *vt* ritagliare; (*delete*) eliminare; **be** ~ **out for** *fam* essere tagliato per; ~ **it out!** *fam* dacci un taglio!

■ **cut up** *vt* (*slice*) tagliare a pezzi

cut-and-dried *a* ⟨*answer, solution*⟩ ovvio; **I like everything to be** ~ mi piace che tutto sia ben chiaro e definito

cut and thrust *n* **the** ~ ~ ~ **of debate** gli scambi *mpl* animati del dibattito

cutback /'kʌtbæk/ *n* riduzione *f*; (*in government spending*) taglio *m*

cute /kju:t/ *a fam* (*in appearance*) carino; (*clever*) acuto

cut glass *n* vetro *m* intagliato

cuticle /'kju:tɪkl/ *n* cuticola *f*

cutlery /'kʌtlərɪ/ *n* posate *fpl*

cutlet /'kʌtlɪt/ *n* cotoletta *f*

cut-off *n* (*upper limit*) limite *m* [massimo]

cut-off date *n* data *f* di scadenza

cut-off point *n* limite *m*; *Comm* data *f* di scadenza

cut-offs *npl* (*jeans*) jeans *mpl* tagliati

cut-out *n* (*outline*) ritaglio *m*

cut-price *a* a prezzo ridotto; ⟨*shop*⟩ che fa prezzi ridotti

cutter /'kʌtə(r)/ *n* (*ship*) cutter *m inv*; (*on ship*) lancia *f*; (*for metal, glass*) taglierina *f*

cut-throat *n* assassino, -a *mf* ● *a* ⟨*competition*⟩ spietato

cut-throat razor *n Br* rasoio *m* da barbiere

cutting /'kʌtɪŋ/ *a* ⟨*remark*⟩ tagliente ● *n* (*from newspaper*) ritaglio *m*; (*of plant*) talea *f*

cutting edge *n* (*blade*) filo *m*; **be at the** ~ ~ *fig* essere all'avanguardia

cuttingly /'kʌtɪŋlɪ/ *adv* ⟨*speak*⟩ in maniera tagliente

cutting room *n Cinema* **end up on the** ~ ~ **floor** essere tagliato in fase di montaggio

CV *abbr of* **curriculum vitae**

cwt *abbr* (**hundredweight**) ≈ 50 kg, *Am* ≈ 45 kg

cyanide /'saɪənaɪd/ *n* cianuro *m*

cybernetics /saɪbə'netɪks/ *n* cibernetica *f*

cyberspace /'saɪbəspeɪs/ *n* ciberspazio *m*

cyclamen /'sɪkləmən/ *n* ciclamino *m*

cycle /'saɪk(ə)l/ *n* ciclo *m*; (*bicycle*) bicicletta *f*, *fam* bici *f inv* ● *vi* andare in bicicletta

cycle: cycle clip *n* fermacalzoni *m inv*. **cycle lane** *n* pista *f* ciclabile. **cycle race** *n* corsa *f* ciclistica. **cycle rack** *n* portabiciclette *m inv*. **cycle track** *n* pista *f* ciclabile

cyclical /'saɪklɪkl/ *a* ciclico

cycling /'saɪklɪŋ/ *n* ciclismo *m*

cycling holiday *n Br* vacanza *f* in bicicletta; **go on a** ~ ~ fare una vacanza in bicicletta

cycling shorts *npl* pantaloncini *mpl* da ciclista

cyclist /'saɪklɪst/ *n* ciclista *mf*

cyclo-cross /'saɪkləʊ-/ *n* ciclocross *m inv*

cyclone /'saɪkləʊn/ *n* ciclone *m*

cygnet /'sɪgnɪt/ *n* cigno *m* giovane

cylinder /'sɪlɪndə(r)/ *n* cilindro *m*

cylindrical /sɪl'lɪndrɪkl/ *a* cilindrico

cymbals /'sɪmblz/ *npl Mus* piatti *mpl*

cynic /'sɪnɪk/ *n* cinico, -a *mf*

cynical /'sɪnɪk(ə)l/ *a* cinico

cynically /'sɪnɪklɪ/ *adv* cinicamente

cynicism /'sɪnɪsɪzm/ *n* cinismo *m*

cypress /'saɪprəs/ *n* cipresso *m*

Cypriot /'sɪprɪət/ *a & n* cipriota *mf*

Cyprus /'saɪprəs/ *n* Cipro *m*

Cyrillic /sɪ'rɪlɪk/ *a* cirillico

cyst /sɪst/ *n* ciste *f*

cystitis /sɪ'staɪtɪs/ *n* cistite *f*

Czar, czar /zɑ:(r)/ *n* zar *m inv*

Czech /tʃek/ *a & n* ceco, -a *mf*

Czechoslovak /tʃekə'sləʊvæk/ *a* cecoslovacco

Czechoslovakia /tʃekəslə'vækɪə/ *n* Cecoslovacchia *f*

Czech Republic *n* Repubblica *f* Ceca

Dd

d, D /diː/ *n* (*letter*) d, D *f inv*; *Mus* re *m inv*

d *abbr* (**died**) morto

dab /dæb/ *n* colpetto *m*; **a ~ of** un pochino di ● *vt* (*pt/pp* **dabbed**) toccare leggermente ⟨*eyes*⟩

■ **dab on** *vt* mettere un po' di ⟨*paint etc*⟩

dabble /'dæbl/ *vi* **~ in sth** *fig* occuparsi di qcsa a tempo perso

dachshund /'dækshʊnd/ *n* bassotto *m*

dad[dy] /'dæd[ɪ]/ *n fam* papà *m inv*, babbo *m*

daddy-long-legs *n* zanzarone *m* [dei boschi]; (*Am: spider*) ragno *m*

daffodil /'dæfədɪl/ *n* giunchiglia *f*

daft /dɑːft/ *a* sciocco

dagger /'dægə(r)/ *n* stiletto *m*; *Typ* croce *f*; **be at ~s drawn** *fam* essere ai ferri corti

dahlia /'deɪlɪə/ *n* dalia *f*

daily /'deɪlɪ/ *a* giornaliero ● *adv* giornalmente ● *n* (*newspaper*) quotidiano *m*; (*fam: cleaner*) donna *f* delle pulizie

daintily /'deɪntɪlɪ/ *adv* delicatamente

dainty /'deɪntɪ/ *a* (**-ier**, **-iest**) grazioso; ⟨*movement*⟩ delicato

dairy /'deərɪ/ *n* caseificio *m*; (*shop*) latteria *f*

dairy cow *n* mucca *f* da latte

dairyman /'deərɪmən/ *n* (*on farm*) operaio *m* addetto all'allevamento di mucche [da latte]; (*Am: farmer*) allevatore *m*

dairy products *npl* latticini *mpl*

dais /'deɪɪs/ *n* pedana *f*

daisy /'deɪzɪ/ *n* margheritina *f*; (*larger*) margherita *f*

dale /deɪl/ *n liter* valle *f*

dally /'dælɪ/ *vi* (*pt/pp* **-ied**) stare a gingillarsi

dam /dæm/ *n* diga *f* ● *vt* (*pt/pp* **dammed**) costruire una diga su

damage /'dæmɪdʒ/ *n* danno *m* (**to** a); **~s** *pl Jur* risarcimento *msg* ● *vt* danneggiare; *fig* nuocere a

damaging /'dæmɪdʒɪŋ/ *a* dannoso

damask /'dæməsk/ *n* damasco *m*

dame /deɪm/ *n liter* dama *f*; *Am sl* donna *f*

dammit /'dæmɪt/ *int Br fam* accidenti

damn /dæm/ *c fam* maledetto ● *adv* ⟨*lucky, late*⟩ maledettamente ● *n* **I don't care** *or* **give a ~** *fam* non me ne frega un accidente ● *vt* dannare

damnation /dæm'neɪʃn/ *n* dannazione *f* ● *int fam* accidenti!

damnedest /'dæmdɪst/ *n* **do one's ~** (**to do**) (*fam: hardest*) fare del proprio meglio (per fare) ● *a* **it was the ~ thing** (*surprising*) era la cosa più straordinaria

damning /'dæmɪŋ/ *a* schiacciante

damp /dæmp/ *a* umido ● *n* umidità *f* ● *vt* = **dampen**

dampen /'dæmpən/ *vt* inumidire; *fig* raffreddare ⟨*enthusiasm*⟩

damper /'dæmpə(r)/ *n* **the news put a ~ on the evening** *fam* la notizia ha raggelato l'atmosfera della serata

dampness /'dæmpnɪs/ *n* umidità *f*

damson /'dæmzən/ *n* (*fruit*) susina *f* selvatica, prugna *f* selvatica

dance /dɑːns/ *n* ballo *m* ● *vt/i* ballare

dance hall *n* sala *f* da ballo

dance music *n* musica *f* da ballo

dancer /'dɑːnsə(r)/ *n* ballerino, -a *mf*

dandelion /'dændɪlaɪən/ *n* dente *m* di leone

dandruff /'dændrʌf/ *n* forfora *f*

Dane /deɪn/ *n* danese *mf*; **Great ~** danese *m*

danger /'deɪndʒə(r)/ *n* pericolo *m*; **in/out of ~** in/fuori pericolo

danger level *n* livello *m* di guardia

danger list *n* **on the ~ ~** in prognosi riservata; **off the ~ ~** fuori pericolo

danger money *n* indennità *f* di rischio

dangerous /'deɪndʒərəs/ *a* pericoloso

dangerously /'deɪndʒərəslɪ/ *adv* pericolosamente; **~ ill** in pericolo di vita

danger signal *n also fig* segnale *m* di pericolo

dangle /'dæŋgl/ *vi* penzolare; *fig* **leave sb dangling** lasciare qcno in sospeso ● *vt* far penzolare

Danish /'deɪnɪʃ/ *a* danese ● *n* (*language*) danese *m*

Danish pastry *n* dolce *m* di pasta sfoglia contenente pasta di mandorle, mele ecc.

dank /dæŋk/ *a* umido e freddo

Danube /'dænjuːb/ *n* Danubio *m*

dapper /'dæpə(r)/ *a* azzimato

dappled /'dæp(ə)ld/ *a* ⟨*grey, horse*⟩ pomellato; ⟨*sky*⟩ screziato; ⟨*shade, surface*⟩ chiazzato

dare /deə(r)/ *vt/i* osare; (*challenge*) sfidare (**to** a); **~ [to] do sth** osare fare qcsa; **I ~ say!** molto probabilmente! ● *n* sfida *f*

daredevil /'deədevl/ *n* spericolato, -a *mf*

daring /'deərɪŋ/ *a* audace ● *n* audacia *f*

dark /dɑːk/ *a* buio; **~ blue/brown** blu/marrone scuro; **it's getting ~** sta cominciando a fare buio; **~ horse** *fig* (*in race, contest*) vincitore *m* imprevisto; (*not much known about*) misterioso *m*; **keep sth ~** *fig* tenere qcsa nascosto ● *n* **after ~** col buio; **in the ~** al buio; **keep sb in the ~** *fig* tenere qcno all'oscuro

Dark Ages *n* alto Medioevo *m*

dark chocolate *n* cioccolato *m* fondente

darken /'dɑːkn/ *vt* oscurare ● *vi* oscurarsi

dark-eyed /-'aɪd/ *a* ⟨*person*⟩ dagli occhi scuri

dark glasses *npl* occhiali *mpl* scuri

darkly /'dɑːklɪ/ *adv* ⟨mutter, hint⟩ cupamente

darkness /'dɑːknɪs/ *n* buio *m*

darkroom /'dɑːkruːm/ *n* camera *f* oscura

dark-skinned *a* ⟨person⟩ dalla pelle scura

darling /'dɑːlɪŋ/ *a* adorabile; **my ~ Joan** carissima Joan ● *n* tesoro *m*; **be a ~ and...** sii gentile e...

darn /dɑːn/ *vt* rammendare

darning needle /'dɑːnɪŋ/ *n* ago *m* da rammendo

dart /dɑːt/ *n* dardo *m*; ⟨in sewing⟩ pince *f inv*; ~s *sg* ⟨game⟩ freccette *fpl* ● *vi* lanciarsi

dartboard /'dɑːtbɔːd/ *n* bersaglio *m* [per freccette]

dash /dæʃ/ *n* Typ trattino *m*; ⟨in Morse⟩ linea *f*; **a ~ of milk** un goccio di latte; **make a ~ for** lanciarsi verso ● *vi* **I must ~** devo scappare ● *vt* far svanire ⟨hopes⟩; ⟨hurl⟩ gettare

■ **dash off** *vi* scappar via ● *vt* ⟨write quickly⟩ buttare giù

■ **dash out** *vi* uscire di corsa

dashboard /'dæʃbɔːd/ *n* cruscotto *m*

dashing /'dæʃɪŋ/ *a* ⟨bold⟩ ardito; ⟨in appearance⟩ affascinante

DAT *abbr* (**digital audio tape**) DAT *f inv*

data /'deɪtə/ *npl & sg* dati *mpl*

data: databank *n* banca *f* di dati. **database** *n* banca *f* dati, database *m* inv. **database management system** *n* sistema *m* di gestione di data base

data: data capture *n* registrazione *f* di dati. **data communications** *npl* comunicazione *f* dati, telematica *f*. **data compression** *n* compressione *f* dati. **data disk** *n* dischetto *m* di dati. **data entry** *n* immissione *f* [di] dati. **data file** *n* file *m inv* dati. **data handling** *n* manipolazione *f* [di] dati. **data input** *n* input *m* dati. **data link** *n* collegamento *m* dati. **data processing** *n* elaborazione *f* [di] dati. **data protection** *n* protezione *f* dati. **data protection act** *n* Jur legge *f* britannica per la salvaguardia delle informazioni personali. **data retrieval** *n* recupero *m* dati. **data security** *n* sicurezza *f* dei dati. **data storage** *n* archiviazione *f* dati. **data transmission** *n* trasmissione *f* dati

date¹ /deɪt/ *n* ⟨fruit⟩ dattero *m*

date² *n* data *f*; ⟨meeting⟩ appuntamento *m*; **to ~** fino ad oggi; **out of ~** ⟨not fashionable⟩ fuori moda; ⟨expired⟩ scaduto; ⟨information⟩ non aggiornato; **make a ~ with sb** dare un appuntamento a qcno; **be up to ~** essere aggiornato ● *vt/i* datare; ⟨go out with⟩ uscire con

■ **date back to** *vi* risalire a

dated /'deɪtɪd/ *a* fuori moda; ⟨language⟩ antiquato

date line *n* linea *f* [del cambiamento] di data

date of issue *n* data *f* di emissione

date stamp *n* ⟨mark⟩ timbro *m* con la data

dating agency /'deɪtɪŋ/ *n* agenzia *f* matrimoniale

dative /'deɪtɪv/ *n* dativo *m*

daub /dɔːb/ *vt* imbrattare ⟨walls⟩

daughter /'dɔːtə(r)/ *n* figlia *f*

daughter-in-law *n* (*pl* ~s-in-law) nuora *f*

daunt /dɔːnt/ *vt* scoraggiare; **nothing ~ed** per niente scoraggiato

daunting /'dɔːntɪŋ/ *a* ⟨task, prospect⟩ poco allettante; ⟨person⟩ che intimidisce; **I'm faced with a ~ amount of work** mi aspetta una quantità di lavoro preoccupante; **it can be ⟨quite⟩ ~** può essere ⟨piuttosto⟩ allarmante

dauntless /'dɔːntlɪs/ *a* intrepido

dawdle /'dɔːdl/ *vi* bighellonare; ⟨over work⟩ cincischiarsi

dawn /dɔːn/ *n* alba *f*; **at ~** all'alba ● *vi* albeggiare; **it ~ed on me** *fig* mi è apparso chiaro

dawn raid *n* ⟨police⟩ raid *m* della polizia all'alba; ⟨stock market⟩ dawn raid *m inv*

day /deɪ/ *n* giorno *m*; ⟨whole day⟩ giornata *f*; ⟨period⟩ epoca *f*; **~ by ~** giorno per giorno; **~ after ~** giorno dopo giorno; **these ~s** oggigiorno; **in those ~s** a quei tempi; **it's had its ~** *fam* ha fatto il suo tempo

day: day-boy *n* Br Sch alunno *m* esterno. **daybreak** *n* **at ~** allo spuntar del giorno. **day-care** *n* ⟨for young children⟩ scuola *f* materna. **day centre** *n* centro *m* di accoglienza. **day-dream** *n* sogno *m* ad occhi aperti ● *vi* sognare ad occhi aperti. **day-girl** *n* Sch alunna *f* esterna. **daylight** *n* luce del giorno *f*. **daylight robbery** *n fam* **it's ~ ~** è un furto!. **daylight saving time** *n* ora *f* legale. **day nursery** *n* ⟨0-3 years⟩ asilo *m* nido; ⟨3-6 years⟩ scuola *f* materna. **day off** *n* giorno *m* di riposo

day pass *n* biglietto *m* giornaliero. **day release** *n* giorno *m* di congedo settimanale dal lavoro da dedicare a corsi di formazione. **day return** *n* ⟨ticket⟩ biglietto *m* di andata e ritorno con validità giornaliera. **day school** *n* scuola *f* che non fornisce alloggio. **daytime** *n* giorno *m*; **in the ~** di giorno. **day-to-day** *a* quotidiano; **on a ~ basis** giorno per giorno. **day trip** *n* gita *f* ⟨di un giorno⟩. **day tripper** *n* gitante *mf*

daze /deɪz/ *n* **in a ~** stordito; *fig* sbalordito

dazed /deɪzd/ *a* stordito; *fig* sbalordito

dazzle /'dæzl/ *vt* abbagliare

DBMS *n abbr* (**database management system**) DBMS *m*

D-day *n* Mil D-day *m inv*; ⟨important day⟩ giorno *m* fatidico

deacon /'diːk(ə)n/ *n* diacono *m*

dead /ded/ *a* morto; ⟨numb⟩ intorpidito; **~ and buried** morto e sepolto **~ body** morto *m*; **~ centre** pieno centro *m* ● *adv* **~ tired** stanco morto; **~ slow/easy** lentissimo/facilissimo; **you're ~ right** hai perfettamente ragione; **stop ~** fermarsi di colpo; **be ~ on time** essere in perfetto orario ● *n* **the ~** *pl* i morti; **in the ~ of night** nel cuore della notte

deaden /'ded(ə)n/ *vt* attutire ⟨sound⟩; calmare ⟨pain⟩

dead: dead end *n* vicolo *m* cieco ● *attrib* **dead-end** ⟨job⟩ senza prospettive. **dead heat** *n* **it was a ~ ~** è finita a pari merito.

deadline *n* scadenza *f*. **deadlock** *n* **reach ~** *fig* giungere a un punto morto. **dead loss** *n fam* (*person*) buono, -a *mf* a nulla; (*thing*) oggetto *m* inutile

deadly /'dedlɪ/ *a* (**-ier, -iest**) mortale; (*fam: dreary*) barboso; **~ sins** peccati *mpl* capitali

dead: dead on arrival *a Med* deceduto durante il trasporto. **deadpan** *a* impassibile; ⟨*humour*⟩ all'inglese. **dead ringer** *n fam* **be a ~ ~ for sb** essere la copia spiccicata di qualcuno. **Dead Sea** *n* Mar *m* Morto. **dead weight** *n* (*fig: burden*) peso *m* morto. **dead wood** *n Br fig* zavorra *f*

deaf /def/ *a* sordo; **~ and dumb** sordomuto

deaf aid *n* apparecchio *m* acustico

deafen /'def(ə)n/ *vt* assordare; (*permanently*) render sordo

deafening /'defənɪŋ/ *a* assordante

deaf mute *a & n* sordomuto, -a *mf*

deafness /'defnɪs/ *n* sordità *f*

deal /di:l/ *n* (*agreement*) patto *m*; (*in business*) accordo *m*; **who's ~?** (*Cards*) a chi tocca dare le carte?; **a good** *or* **great ~** molto; **get a raw ~** *fam* ricevere un trattamento ingiusto ● *v* (*pt/pp* **dealt** /delt/) ● *vt* (*in cards*) dare; **~ sb a blow** dare un colpo a qcno

■ **deal in** *vt* trattare in

■ **deal out** *vt* ⟨*hand out*⟩ distribuire

■ **deal with** *vt* ⟨*handle*⟩ occuparsi di; trattare con ⟨*company*⟩; (*be about*) trattare di; **that's been ~t with** è stato risolto

dealer /'di:lə(r)/ *n* commerciante *mf*; (*in drugs*) spacciatore, -trice *mf*

dealership /'di:ləʃɪp/ *n Comm* concessione *f*

dealing room /'di:lɪŋ/ *n Fin* borsino *m*

dealings /'di:lɪŋz/ *npl* **have ~ with** avere a che fare con

dean /di:n/ *n* decano *m*; *Univ* preside *mf* di facoltà

dear /dɪə(r)/ *a* caro; (*in letter*) Caro; (*formal*) Gentile ● *n* caro, -a *mf* ● *int* **oh ~!** Dio mio!

dearly /'dɪəlɪ/ *adv* ⟨*love*⟩ profondamente; ⟨*pay*⟩ profumatamente

dearth /dɜ:θ/ *n* penuria *f*

death /deθ/ *n* morte *f*

death: deathbed *n* letto *m* di morte. **death camp** *n* campo *m* di sterminio. **death certificate** *n* certificato *m* di morte. **death duty** *n* tassa *f* di successione. **death knell** *n* campane *fpl* a morto; *fig* tramonto *m*. **death list** *n* lista *f* dei bersagli (*di un assassino*)

deathly /'deθlɪ/ *a* **~ silence** silenzio *m* di tomba ● *adv* **~ pale** di un pallore cadaverico

death: death mask *n* maschera *f* mortuaria. **death penalty** *n* pena *f* di morte. **death rate** *n* tasso *m* di mortalità. **death ray** *n* raggio *m* mortale. **death row** *n Am* braccio *m* della morte. **death sentence** *n* *also fig* condanna *f* a morte. **death's head** *n* teschio *m*. **death threat** *n* minaccia *f* di morte. **death throes** *npl* *also fig* agonia *f*. **death toll** *n* bilancio *m* delle vittime. **death trap** *n* trappola *f* mortale. **death warrant** *n* ordine *m* di esecuzione di una condanna a morte. **death wish** *n* desiderio *m* di morire

debacle /deɪ'bɑ:k(ə)l/ *n* sfacelo *m*

debar /dɪ'bɑ:(r)/ *vt* (*pt/pp* **debarred**) escludere

debase /dɪ'beɪs/ *vt* degradare

debatable /dɪ'beɪtəbl/ *a* discutibile

debate /dɪ'beɪt/ *n* dibattito *m* ● *vt* discutere; (*in formal debate*) dibattere ● *vi* **~ whether to...** considerare se

debauchery /dɪ'bɔ:tʃərɪ/ *n* dissolutezza *f*

debenture bond /dɪ'bentʃə(r)/ *n* obbligazione *f* non garantita

debilitating /dɪ'bɪlɪteɪtɪŋ/ *a* ⟨*disease*⟩ debilitante

debility /dɪ'bɪlətɪ/ *n* debilitazione *f*

debit /'debɪt/ *n* debito *m* ● *vt* (*pt/pp* **debited**) *Comm* addebitare ⟨*sum, account*⟩

debonair /debə'neə(r)/ *a* ⟨*person*⟩ elegante e cortese

debrief /di:'bri:f/ *vt* chiamare a rapporto; **be ~ed** ⟨*defector, freed hostage:*⟩ essere interrogato; ⟨*diplomat, agent:*⟩ essere chiamato a rapporto

debriefing /di:'bri:fɪŋ/ *n* (*of hostage, defector*) interrogatorio *m*

debris /'debri:/ *n* macerie *fpl*

debt /det/ *n* debito *m*; **be in ~** avere dei debiti

debt collection *n* esazione *f* crediti

debt collection agency *n* agenzia *f* di recupero crediti

debt collector *n* esattore *m* dei crediti

debtor /'detə(r)/ *n* debitore, -trice *mf*

debug /di:'bʌg/ *vt* (*pt/pp* **debugged**) *Comput* correggere gli errori di; togliere i microfoni spia da ⟨*room*⟩

debunk /dɪ'bʌŋk/ *vt* ridicolizzare ⟨*theory, myth*⟩

début /'deɪbu:/ *n* debutto *m*

decade /'dekeɪd/ *n* decennio *m*

decadence /'dekədəns/ *n* decadenza *f*

decadent /'dekədənt/ *a* decadente

decaffeinated /di:'kæfɪneɪtɪd/ *a* decaffeinato

decalitre /'dekəli:tə(r)/ *n* decalitro *m*

decametre /'dekəmi:tə(r)/ *n* decametro *m*

decamp /dɪ'kæmp/ *vi* sgattaiolare via; **~ with sth** (*steal*) squagliarsela con qcsa

decant /dɪ'kænt/ *vt* travasare

decanter /dɪ'kæntə(r)/ *n* caraffa *f* (*di cristallo*)

decapitate /dɪ'kæpɪteɪt/ *vt* decapitare

decathlon /dɪ'kæθlɒn/ *n* decathlon *m inv*

decay /dɪ'keɪ/ *n* (*also fig*) decadenza *f*; (*rot*) decomposizione *f*; (*of tooth*) carie *f inv* ● *vi* imputridire; (*rot*) decomporsi; ⟨*tooth:*⟩ cariarsi

deceased /dɪ'si:st/ *a* defunto ● *n* **the ~** il defunto; la defunta

deceit /dɪ'si:t/ *n* inganno *m*

deceitful /dɪ'si:tful/ *a* falso

deceitfully /dɪ'si:tfulɪ/ *adv* falsamente

deceive /dɪ'si:v/ *vt* ingannare

decelerate /di:'seləreɪt/ *vi* decelerare

deceleration /di:selə'reɪʃn/ *n* decelerazione *f*

December /dɪ'sembə(r)/ *n* dicembre *m*

decency /'di:sənsɪ/ *n* decenza *f*

decent /'di:sənt/ *a* decente; (*respectable*) rispettabile; **very ~ of you** molto gentile da parte tua

decently /'di:səntlɪ/ *adv* decentemente; (*kindly*) gentilmente

decentralization /di:sentrəlar'zeɪʃn/ *n* decentramento *m*

decentralize /di:'sentrəlaɪz/ *vt* decentrare

deception /dɪ'sepʃn/ *n* inganno *m*

deceptive /dɪ'septɪv/ *a* ingannevole

deceptively /dɪ'septɪvlɪ/ *adv* ingannevolmente; **it looks ~ easy** sembra facile, ma non lo è

decibel /'desɪbel/ *n* decibel *m inv*

decide /dɪ'saɪd/ *vt* decidere; **that's ~d then** siamo d'accordo, allora ● *vi* decidere (**on** di)

decided /dɪ'saɪdɪd/ *a* risoluto

decidedly /dɪ'saɪdɪdlɪ/ *adv* risolutamente; (*without doubt*) senza dubbio

decider /dɪ'saɪdə(r)/ *n* (*point*) punto *m* decisivo; (*goal*) goal *m inv* decisivo; (*game*) spareggio *m*

deciduous /dɪ'sɪdjʊəs/ *a* a foglie decidue

decigram[me] /'desɪgræm/ *n* decigrammo *m*

decilitre /'desɪliːtə(r)/ *n* decilitro *m*

decimal /'desɪml/ *a* decimale ● *n* numero *m* decimale

decimal point *n* virgola *f*

decimal system *n* sistema *m* decimale

decimate /'desɪmeɪt/ *vt* decimare

decimetre /'desɪmiːtə(r)/ *n* decimetro *m*

decipher /dɪ'saɪfə(r)/ *vt* decifrare

decision /dɪ'sɪʒn/ *n* decisione *f*

decision-maker /dɪ'sɪʒnmeɪkə(r)/ *n* persona *f* che ama o ha il potere di prendere decisioni

decision-making /dɪ'sɪʒnmeɪkɪŋ/ *n* **be good/bad at ~** saper/non saper prendere decisioni; **~ process** *n* processo *m* decisionale

decisive /dɪ'saɪsɪv/ *a* decisivo

decisively /dɪ'saɪsɪvlɪ/ *adv* con decisione

deck[1] /dek/ *vt* abbigliare

deck[2] *n Naut* ponte *m*; **on ~** in coperta; **top ~** (*of bus*) piano *m* di sopra; **~ of cards** mazzo *m*

deckchair /'dektʃeə(r)/ *n* [sedia *f* a] sdraio *f inv*

declaration /deklə'reɪʃn/ *n* dichiarazione *f*

declare /dɪ'kleə(r)/ *vt* dichiarare; **anything to ~?** niente da dichiarare?; **~ one's love** dichiararsi

declassify /di:'klæsɪfaɪ/ *vt* rimuovere dai vincoli di segretezza (*document, information*)

declension /dɪ'klenʃn/ *n* declinazione *f*

decline /dɪ'klaɪn/ *n* declino *m* ● *vt also Gram* declinare ● *vi* (*decrease*) diminuire; (*health:*) deperire; (*say no*) rifiutare

declutch /di:'klʌtʃ/ *vi Br* lasciare la frizione

decode /di:'kəʊd/ *vt* decifrare; *Comput* decodificare

decoding /di:'kəʊdɪŋ/ *n* decodifica *f*, decodificazione *f*

décolleté /der'kɒlteɪ/ *a* décolleté *inv*, scollato

decompose /di:kəm'pəʊz/ *vi* decomporsi

decomposition /di:kɒmpə'zɪʃn/ *n* scomposizione *f*

decompression /di:kəm'preʃn/ *n* decompressione *f*

decontaminate /di:kən'tæmɪneɪt/ *vt* decontaminare

décor /'deɪkɔ:(r)/ *n* decorazione *f*; (*including furniture*) arredamento *m*

decorate /'dekəreɪt/ *vt* decorare; (*paint*) pitturare; (*wallpaper*) tappezzare

decoration /dekə'reɪʃn/ *n* decorazione *f*

decorative /'dekərətɪv/ *a* decorativo

decorator /'dekəreɪtə(r)/ *n* **painter and ~** imbianchino *m*

decorous /'dekərəs/ *a* decoroso

decorously /'dekərəslɪ/ *adv* decorosamente

decorum /dɪ'kɔ:rəm/ *n* decoro *m*

decoy[1] /'di:kɔɪ/ *n* esca *f*

decoy[2] /dɪ'kɔɪ/ *vt* adescare

decrease[1] /'di:kri:s/ *n* diminuzione *f*; **be on the ~** essere in diminuzione

decrease[2] /dɪ'kri:s/ *vt/i* diminuire

decreasingly /dɪ'kri:sɪŋlɪ/ *adv* sempre meno

decree /dɪ'kri:/ *n* decreto *m* ● *vt* decretare

decrepit /dɪ'krepɪt/ *a* decrepito

decriminalization /di:krɪmɪnəlar'zeɪʃn/ *n* depenalizzazione *f*

decriminalize /di:'krɪmɪnəlaɪz/ *vt* depenalizzare

dedicate /'dedɪkeɪt/ *vt* dedicare

dedicated /'dedɪkeɪtɪd/ *a* (*person*) scrupoloso

dedication /dedɪ'keɪʃn/ *n* dedizione *f*; (*in book*) dedica *f*

deduce /dɪ'dju:s/ *vt* dedurre (**from** da)

deduct /dɪ'dʌkt/ *vt* dedurre

deduction /dɪ'dʌkʃn/ *n* deduzione *f*

deed /di:d/ *n* azione *f*; *Jur* atto *m* di proprietà

deed of covenant *n Jur* accordo *m* accessorio ad un contratto immobiliare

deed poll *n* **change one's name by ~ ~** cambiare nome con un atto unilaterale

deem /di:m/ *vt* ritenere

deep /di:p/ *a* profondo; **go off the ~ end** *fam* arrabbiarsi

deepen /'di:pn/ *vt* approfondire; scavare più profondamente (*trench*) ● *vi* approfondirsi; (*fig: mystery:*) infittirsi

deep: **deep-fat-fryer** *n* friggitrice *f*. **deep-felt** *a* profondo. **deep-freeze** *n* congelatore *m*. **deep-fried** *a* fritto (*in molto olio*). **deep-frozen** *a* surgelato. **deep-fry** *vt* friggere (*in molto olio*)

deeply *adv* profondamente

deep: **deep-rooted** *a* (*habit, prejudice*) radicato. **deep-sea** *a* (*exploration, diving*) in profondità; (*fisherman, fishing*) d'alto mare. **deep-sea diver** *n* palombaro *m*. **deep-seated** *a* radicato. **deep-set** *a* (*eyes*) infossato. **deep South** *n Am* il profondo Sud

deer /dɪə(r)/ *n inv* cervo *m*

deface /dɪˈfeɪs/ *vt* sfigurare ‹*picture*›; deturpare ‹*monument*›

defamation /defəˈmeɪʃn/ *n* diffamazione *f*

defamatory /dɪˈfæmətərɪ/ *a* diffamatorio

default /dɪˈfɔːlt/ *n* (*Jur: non-payment*) morosità *f*; (*failure to appear*) contumacia *f*; **win by ~** *Sport* vincere per abbandono dell'avversario; **in ~ of** per mancanza di ● *a* **~ drive** *Comput* lettore *m* di default ● *vi* (*not pay*) venir meno a un pagamento

defeat /dɪˈfiːt/ *n* sconfitta *f* ● *vt* sconfiggere; (*frustrate*) vanificare ‹*attempts*›; **that ~s the object** questo fa fallire l'obiettivo

defeatist /dɪˈfiːtɪst/ *a & n* disfattista *mf*

defecate /ˈdefəkeɪt/ *vi* defecare

defect¹ /dɪˈfekt/ *vi Pol* fare defezione

defect² /ˈdiːfekt/ *n* difetto *m*

defective /dɪˈfektɪv/ *a* difettoso

defector /dɪˈfektə(r)/ *n* (*from party*) defezionista *mf*; (*from country*) fuor[i]uscito, -a *mf*

defence /dɪˈfens/ *n* difesa *f*

defenceless /dɪˈfenslɪs/ *a* indifeso

Defence Minister *n* ministro *m* della difesa

defend /dɪˈfend/ *vt* difendere; (*justify*) giustificare

defendant /dɪˈfendənt/ *n Jur* imputato, -a *mf*

defender /dɪˈfendə(r)/ *n* difensore *m*, -ditrice *f*

defensive /dɪˈfensɪv/ *a* difensivo ● *n* difensiva *f*; **on the ~** sulla difensiva

defer /dɪˈfɜː(r)/ *vt* (*pt/pp* **deferred**) (*postpone*) rinviare ● *vi* **~ to sb** rimettersi a qcno

deference /ˈdefərəns/ *n* deferenza *f*

deferential /defəˈrenʃl/ *a* deferente

deferentially /defəˈrenʃəlɪ/ *adv* con deferenza

deferment, deferral /dɪˈfɜːmənt, dɪˈfɜːrəl/ *n* (*postponement*) rinvio *m*

defiance /dɪˈfaɪəns/ *n* sfida *f*; **in ~ of** sfidando

defiant /dɪˈfaɪənt/ *a* ‹*person*› ribelle; ‹*gesture, attitude*› di sfida

defiantly /dɪˈfaɪəntlɪ/ *adv* con aria di sfida

deficiency /dɪˈfɪʃənsɪ/ *n* insufficienza *f*

deficient /dɪˈfɪʃənt/ *a* insufficiente; **be ~ in** mancare di

deficit /ˈdefɪsɪt/ *n* deficit *m inv*

defile /dɪˈfaɪl/ *vt fig* contaminare

define /dɪˈfaɪn/ *vt* definire

defined *a* ‹*role*› definito

definite /ˈdefɪnɪt/ *a* definito; (*certain*) ‹*answer, yes*› definitivo; (*improvement, difference*) netto; **he was ~ about it** è stato chiaro in proposito

definite article *n* (*grammatical*) articolo *m* determinativo

definitely /ˈdefɪnɪtlɪ/ *adv* sicuramente

definition /defɪˈnɪʃn/ *n* definizione *f*

definitive /dɪˈfɪnətɪv/ *a* definitivo

deflate /dɪˈfleɪt/ *vt* sgonfiare

deflation /dɪˈfleɪʃn/ *n Comm* deflazione *f*

deflationary /dɪˈfleɪʃənrɪ/ *a* deflazionistico

deflect /dɪˈflekt/ *vt* deflettere

deformed /dɪˈfɔːmd/ *a* deforme

deformity /dɪˈfɔːmətɪ/ *n* deformità *f inv*

defraud /dɪˈfrɔːd/ *vt* defraudare

defray /dɪˈfreɪ/ *vt fml* sostenere

defrost /diːˈfrɒst/ *vt* sbrinare ‹*fridge*›; scongelare ‹*food*›

deft /deft/ *a* abile

deftly /ˈdeftlɪ/ *adv* con destrezza

deftness /ˈdeftnɪs/ *n* destrezza *f*

defunct /dɪˈfʌŋkt/ *a* morto e sepolto; ‹*law*› caduto in disuso

defuse /diːˈfjuːz/ *vt* disinnescare; calmare ‹*situation*›

defy /dɪˈfaɪ/ *vt* (*pt/pp* **-ied**) (*challenge*) sfidare; resistere a ‹*attempt*›; (*not obey*) disobbedire a

degenerate¹ /dɪˈdʒenəreɪt/ *vi* degenerare; **~ into** *fig* degenerare in

degenerate² /dɪˈdʒenərət/ *a* degenerato

degeneration /dɪdʒenəˈreɪʃn/ *n* degenerazione *f*

degenerative /dɪˈdʒenərətɪv/ *a* degenerativo

degradation /degrəˈdeɪʃn/ *n* (*debasement*) degradazione *f*; (*of culture*) deterioramento *m*; (*squalor*) desolazione *f*

degrade /dɪˈgreɪd/ *vt* (*humiliate*) degradare ‹*person*›; (*damage*) deteriorare ‹*environment*›

degrading /dɪˈgreɪdɪŋ/ *a* degradante

degree /dɪˈgriː/ *n* grado *m*; *Univ* laurea *f*; **20 ~s** 20 gradi; **not to the same ~** non allo stesso livello

degree ceremony *n Br Univ* cerimonia *f* di consegna delle lauree

degree course *n Br Univ* corso *m* di laurea

dehydrate /diːhaɪˈdreɪt/ *vt* disidratare

dehydrated /diːhaɪˈdreɪtɪd/ *a* disidratato

dehydration /diːhaɪˈdreɪʃn/ *n* disidratazione *f*

de-ice /diːˈaɪs/ *vt* togliere il ghiaccio da

de-icer /diːˈaɪsə(r)/ *n* (*mechanical*) sbrinatore *m*; (*chemical*) liquido *m* scongelante

deign /deɪn/ *vi* **~ to do sth** degnarsi di fare qcsa

deity /ˈdiːətɪ/ *n* divinità *f inv*

déjà vu /deɪʒɑːˈvuː/ *n* déjà vu *m inv*

dejected /dɪˈdʒektɪd/ *a* demoralizzato

dejectedly /dɪˈdʒektɪdlɪ/ *adv* con aria demoralizzata

dejection /dɪˈdʒekʃn/ *n* abbacchiamento *m*

delay /dɪˈleɪ/ *n* ritardo *m* **without ~** senza indugio ● *vt* ritardare **be ~ed** ‹*person*:› essere trattenuto; ‹*train, aircraft*:› essere in ritardo ● *vi* indugiare

delayed action /dɪˈleɪd/ *a* ad azione ritardata; ‹*bomb*› a scoppio ritardato

delegate¹ /ˈdelɪgət/ *n* delegato, -a *mf*

delegate² /ˈdelɪgeɪt/ *vt* delegare

delegation /delɪˈgeɪʃn/ *n* delegazione *f*

delete /dɪˈliːt/ *vt* cancellare

deletion /dɪˈliːʃn/ *n* cancellatura *f*

deliberate¹ /dɪˈlɪbərət/ *a* deliberato; (*slow*) posato

deliberate² /dɪˈlɪbəreɪt/ *vt/i* deliberare

deliberately /dɪˈlɪbərətlɪ/ *adv* deliberatamente; (*slowly*) in modo posato

deliberation /dɪlɪbəˈreɪʃn/ *n* deliberazione *f*; **with ~** in modo posato

delicacy /ˈdelɪkəsɪ/ *n* delicatezza *f*; (*food*) prelibatezza *f*

delicate /ˈdelɪkət/ *a* delicato

delicately /ˈdelɪkətlɪ/ *adv* ⟨*handle, phrase*⟩ con delicatezza; ⟨*crafted, flavoured*⟩ con raffinatezza

delicatessen /delɪkəˈtesn/ *n* negozio *m* di specialità gastronomiche

delicious /dɪˈlɪʃəs/ *a* delizioso

delight /dɪˈlaɪt/ *n* piacere *m* ● *vt* deliziare ● *vi* **~ in** dilettarsi con

delighted /dɪˈlaɪtɪd/ *a* lieto

delightful /dɪˈlaɪtfʊl/ *a* delizioso

delineate /dɪˈlɪnɪeɪt/ *vt also fig* delineare

delineation /dɪlɪnɪˈeɪʃn/ *n* delineazione *f*

delinquency /dɪˈlɪŋkwənsɪ/ *n* delinquenza *f*

delinquent /dɪˈlɪŋkwənt/ *a* delinquente ● *n* delinquente *mf*

delirious /dɪˈlɪrɪəs/ *a* **be ~** delirare; (*fig: very happy*) essere pazzo di gioia

delirium /dɪˈlɪrɪəm/ *n* delirio *m*

deliver /dɪˈlɪvə(r)/ *vt* consegnare; recapitare ⟨*post, newspaper*⟩; tenere ⟨*speech*⟩; dare ⟨*message*⟩; tirare ⟨*blow*⟩; (*set free*) liberare; **~ a baby** far nascere un bambino

deliverance /dɪˈlɪv(ə)rəns/ *n* liberazione *f*

delivery /dɪˈlɪvərɪ/ *n* consegna *f*; (*of post*) distribuzione *f*; *Med* parto *m*; **cash on ~** pagamento *m* alla consegna

delivery: delivery address *n* indirizzo *m* del destinatario. **delivery man** *n* fattorino *m*. **delivery room** *n* *Med* sala *f* parto

delta /ˈdeltə/ *n* delta *m inv*

delude /dɪˈluːd/ *vt* ingannare; **~ oneself** illudersi

deluge /ˈdeljuːdʒ/ *n* diluvio *m* ● *vt* (*fig: with requests etc*) inondare

delusion /dɪˈluːʒn/ *n* illusione; **~s of grandeur** mania *f* di grandezza

de luxe /dəˈlʌks/ *a* di lusso

delve /delv/ *vi* **~ into** (*into pocket etc*) frugare in; (*into notes, the past*) fare ricerche in

demagnetize /diːˈmægnətaɪz/ *vt* smagnetizzare

demand /dɪˈmɑːnd/ *n* richiesta *f*; *Comm* domanda *f*; **in ~** richiesto; **on ~** a richiesta ● *vt* esigere (**of/from** da)

demanding /dɪˈmɑːndɪŋ/ *a* esigente

demanning /diːˈmænɪŋ/ *n* *Br* taglio *m* di personale

demarcation /diːmɑːˈkeɪʃn/ *n* demarcazione *f*

demean /dɪˈmiːn/ *vt* **~ oneself** abbassarsi (**to** a)

demeaning /dɪˈmiːnɪŋ/ *a* degradante

demeanour /dɪˈmiːnə(r)/ *n* comportamento *m*

demented /dɪˈmentɪd/ *a* demente

dementia /dɪˈmenʃə/ *n* demenza *f*

demerara [**sugar**] /deməˈreərə/ *n* zucchero *m* grezzo di canna

demilitarization /diːmɪlɪtəraɪˈzeɪʃn/ *n* demilitarizzazione *f*

demilitarize /diːˈmɪlɪtəraɪz/ *vt* smilitarizzare

demise /dɪˈmaɪz/ *n* decesso *m*

demister /diːˈmɪstə(r)/ *n* *Auto* sbrinatore *m*

demo /ˈdeməʊ/ *n* (*pl* **~s**) *fam* manifestazione *f*

demobilize /diːˈməʊbəlaɪz/ *vt* *Mil* smobilitare

democracy /dɪˈmɒkrəsɪ/ *n* democrazia *f*

democrat /ˈdeməkræt/ *n* democratico, -a *mf*

democratic /deməˈkrætɪk/ *a* democratico

democratically /deməˈkrætɪklɪ/ *adv* democraticamente

demo disk *n* *Comput* demodisk *m inv*

demographic /deməˈgræfɪk/ *a* demografico

demolish /dɪˈmɒlɪʃ/ *vt* demolire

demolition /deməˈlɪʃn/ *n* demolizione *f*

demon /ˈdiːmən/ *n* demonio *m*

demonic /dɪˈmɒnɪk/ *a* ⟨*aspect, power*⟩ demoniaco

demonize /ˈdiːmənaɪz/ *vt* demonizzare

demonstrable /ˈdemənstrəbl/ *a* dimostrabile

demonstrably /ˈdemənstrəblɪ/ *adv* ⟨*false, untrue*⟩ manifestamente

demonstrate /ˈdemənstreɪt/ *vt* dimostrare; fare una dimostrazione sull'uso di ⟨*appliance*⟩ ● *vi Pol* manifestare

demonstration /demənˈstreɪʃn/ *n* dimostrazione *f*; *Pol* manifestazione *f*

demonstrative /dɪˈmɒnstrətɪv/ *a* *Gram* dimostrativo; **be ~** essere espansivo

demonstrator /ˈdemənstreɪtə(r)/ *n* *Pol* manifestante *mf*; (*for product*) dimostratore, -trice *mf*

demoralize /dɪˈmɒrəlaɪz/ *vt* demoralizzare

demoralizing /dɪˈmɒrəlaɪzɪŋ/ *a* demoralizzante, avvilente

demote /dɪˈməʊt/ *vt* retrocedere di grado; *Mil* degradare

demur /dɪˈmɜː/ *vi* (*pt/pp* **demurred**) (*complain*) protestare; (*disagree*) obiettare ● *n* **without ~** senza obiezioni

demure /dɪˈmjʊə(r)/ *a* schivo

demurely /dɪˈmjʊəlɪ/ *adv* in modo schivo

den /den/ *n* tana *f*; (*room*) rifugio *m*

denationalize /diːˈnæʃ(ə)nəlaɪz/ *vt* denazionalizzare

denial /dɪˈnaɪəl/ *n* smentita *f*

denier /ˈdenɪə(r)/ *n* denaro *m*

denigrate /ˈdenɪɡreɪt/ *vt* denigrare

denigrating /ˈdenɪɡreɪtɪŋ/ *a* denigratore

denim /ˈdenɪm/ *n* [tessuto *m*] jeans *m*; **~s** *pl* [blue]jeans *mpl*

Denmark /ˈdenmɑːk/ *n* Danimarca *f*

denomination /dɪnɒmɪˈneɪʃn/ *n* *Relig* confessione *f*; (*money*) valore *f*

denote /dɪˈnəʊt/ *vt* denotare

denounce /dɪˈnaʊns/ *vt* denunciare

dense /dens/ *a* denso; ⟨*crowd, forest*⟩ fitto; (*stupid*) ottuso

densely /'denslɪ/ *adv* ⟨*populated*⟩ densamente; ~ **wooded** fittamente ricoperto di alberi

density /'densətɪ/ *n* densità *f inv*; (*of forest*) fittezza *f*

dent /dent/ *n* ammaccatura *f* ● *vt* ammaccare

dental /'dentl/ *a* dei denti; ⟨*treatment*⟩ dentistico; ⟨*hygiene*⟩ dentale

dental: dental appointment *n* appuntamento *m* dal dentista. **dental clinic** *n* (*hospital*) clinica *f* odontoiatrica; (*part of hospital*) reparto *m* odontoiatrico. **dental floss** *n* filo *m* interdentale. **dental plate** *n* dentiera *f*. **dental surgeon** *n* odontoiatra *mf*, medico *m* dentista. **dental surgery** *n Br* (*premises*) studio *m* dentistico; (*treatment*) visita *f* dentistica

dented /'dentɪd/ *a* ammaccato; ~ **pride** orgoglio *m* ferito

dentist /'dentɪst/ *n* dentista *mf*

dentistry /'dentɪstrɪ/ *n* odontoiatria *f*

dentures /'dentʃəz/ *npl* dentiera *fsg*

denude /dɪ'njuːd/ *vt* denudare

denunciation /dɪnʌnsɪ'eɪʃn/ *n* denuncia *f*

deny /dɪ'naɪ/ *vt* (*pt/pp* **-ied**) negare; (*officially*) smentire; ~ **sb sth** negare qcsa a qcno; **I can't ~ it** non posso negarlo

deodorant /diː'əʊdərənt/ *n* deodorante *m*

deodorize /diː'əʊdəraɪz/ *vt* deodorare

depart /dɪ'pɑːt/ *vi* ⟨*plane, train:*⟩ partire; ⟨*liter: person*⟩ andare via; (*deviate*) allontanarsi (**from** da)

departed /dɪ'pɑːtɪd/ *a* (*euph: dead*) scomparso

department /dɪ'pɑːtmənt/ *n* reparto *m*; *Pol* ministero *m*; (*of company*) sezione *f*; *Univ* dipartimento *m*

departmental /diːpɑː'tmentl/ *a* ⟨*Pol: colleague, meeting*⟩ di sezione; (*in business*) di reparto

department: Department of Defense *n Am* ministero *m* della difesa. **Department of Energy** *n Am* ≈ Ministero *m* dell'Industria. **Department of the Environment** *n Br* Ministero *m* dell'Ambiente. **department head** *n* caporeparto *mf*; *Univ* direttore, -trice *mf* d'istituto. **Department of Health** *n* ministero *m* della sanità. **department manager** *n* (*of business*) direttore, -trice *mf* di reparto; (*of store*) caporeparto *mf inv*. **Department of Social Security** *n Br* ≈ Istituto *m* Nazionale della Previdenza Sociale. **department store** *n* grande magazzino *m*. **Department of Trade and Industry** *n Br* Ministero *m* del Commercio e dell'Industria

departure /dɪ'pɑːtʃə(r)/ *n* partenza *f*; (*from rule*) allontanamento *m*; **new ~** svolta *f*

departure: departure gate *n* (*at airport*) uscita *f*. **departure lounge** *n* (*at airport*) sala *f* d'attesa. **departure platform** *n Rail* binario *m*. **departures board** *n* tabellone *m* delle partenze

depend /dɪ'pend/ *vi* dipendere (**on** da); (*rely*)

contare (**on** su); **it all ~s** dipende; **~ing on what he says** a seconda di quello che dice

dependability /dɪpendə'bɪlətɪ/ *n* affidabilità *f*

dependable /dɪ'pendəbl/ *a* fidato

dependant /dɪ'pendənt/ *n* persona *f* a carico

dependence /dɪ'pendəns/ *n* dipendenza *f*

dependent /dɪ'pendənt/ *a* dipendente (**on** da)

depict /dɪ'pɪkt/ *vt* (*in writing*) dipingere; (*with picture*) rappresentare

depiction /dɪ'pɪkʃn/ *n* rappresentazione *f*

depilatory /dɪ'pɪlətərɪ/ *n* (*cream*) crema *f* depilatoria

deplete /dɪ'pliːt/ *vt* ridurre; **totally ~d** completamente esaurito

depletion /dɪ'pliːʃn/ *n* (*of resources, funds*) impoverimento *m*

deplorable /dɪ'plɔːrəbl/ *a* deplorevole

deplore /dɪ'plɔː(r)/ *vt* deplorare

deploy /dɪ'plɔɪ/ *vt Mil* spiegare ● *vi* schierarsi

deployment /dɪ'plɔɪmənt/ *n* schieramento *m*

depoliticize /diːpə'lɪtɪsaɪz/ *vt* depoliticizzare

depopulate /diː'pɒpjʊleɪt/ *vt* spopolare

deport /dɪ'pɔːt/ *vt* deportare

deportation /diːpɔː'teɪʃn/ *n* deportazione *f*

deportee /diːpɔː'tiː/ *n* deportato, -a *mf*

deportment /dɪ'pɔːtmənt/ *n* portamento *m*

depose /dɪ'pəʊz/ *vt* deporre

deposit /dɪ'pɒzɪt/ *n* deposito *m*; (*against damage*) cauzione *f*; (*first instalment*) acconto *m* ● *vt* depositare

deposit account *n* libretto *m* di risparmio; (*without instant access*) conto *m* vincolato

depositor /dɪ'pɒzɪtə(r)/ *n Fin* depositante *mf*

deposit slip *n* (*in bank*) distinta *f* di versamento

depot /'depəʊ/ *n* deposito *m*; *Am Rail* stazione *f* ferroviaria

deprave /dɪ'preɪv/ *vt* depravare

depraved /dɪ'preɪvd/ *a* depravato

depravity /dɪ'prævətɪ/ *n* depravazione *f*

deprecate /'deprəkeɪt/ *vt* disapprovare

deprecatory /deprɪ'keɪtərɪ/ *a* (*disapproving*) di disapprovazione; (*apologetic*) di scusa

depreciate /dɪ'priːʃɪeɪt/ *vi* deprezzarsi

depreciation /dɪpriːsɪ'eɪʃn/ *n* deprezzamento *m*

depress /dɪ'pres/ *vt* deprimere; (*press down*) premere

depressed /dɪ'prest/ *a* depresso; ~ **area** zona *f* depressa

depressing /dɪ'presɪŋ/ *a* deprimente

depression /dɪ'preʃn/ *n* depressione *f*

depressive /dɪ'presɪv/ *a* depressivo ● *n* depresso, -a *mf*

depressurize /diː'preʃəraɪz/ *vi* depressurizzare

deprivation /deprɪ'veɪʃn/ *n* privazione *f*

deprive /dɪˈpraɪv/ *vt* ~ **sb of sth** privare qcno di qcsa

deprived /dɪˈpraɪvd/ *a* ‹*area, childhood*› disagiato

dept *abbr* **department**

depth /depθ/ *n* profondità *f inv*; **in ~** ‹*study, analyse*› in modo approfondito; **in the ~s of winter** in pieno inverno; **in the ~s of despair** nella più profonda disperazione; **be out of one's ~** (*in water*) non toccare il fondo; *fig* sentirsi in alto mare

deputation /depjʊˈteɪʃn/ *n* deputazione *f*

deputize /ˈdepjʊtaɪz/ *vi* ~ **for** fare le veci di

deputy /ˈdepjʊti/ *n* vice *mf*; (*temporary*) sostituto, -a *mf* ● *attrib* ~ **leader** ≈ vicesegretario, -a *mf*; ~ **chairman** vicepresidente *mf*

deputy: deputy chairman *n* vicepresidente *m*. **deputy leader** *n Br Pol* sottosegretario *m*. **deputy premier**, **deputy prime minister** *n Pol* vice primo ministro *m*. **deputy president** *n* vicepresidente *mf*

derail /dɪˈreɪl/ *vt* **be ~ed** ‹*train:*› essere deragliato

derailleur gears /dɪˈreɪljə/ *npl* deragliatore *msg*

derailment /dɪˈreɪlmənt/ *n* deragliamento *m*

deranged /dɪˈreɪndʒd/ *a* squilibrato

deregulate /diːˈregjʊleɪt/ *vt* deregolamentare ‹*market*›

deregulation /diːregjʊˈleɪʃn/ *n* deregolamentazione *f*

derelict /ˈderəlɪkt/ *a* abbandonato

deride /dɪˈraɪd/ *vt* deridere

derision /dɪˈrɪʒn/ *n* derisione *f*

derisive /dɪˈraɪsɪv/ *a* ‹*derisory*›

derisory /dɪˈraɪsəri/ *a* ‹*laughter*› derisorio; ‹*offer*› irrisorio

derivation /derɪˈveɪʃn/ *n* derivazione *f*

derivative /dɪˈrɪvətɪv/ *a* derivato ● *n* derivato *m*

derive /dɪˈraɪv/ *vt* (*obtain*) derivare; **be ~d from** ‹*word:*› derivare da ● *vi* ~ **from** derivare da

dermatitis /dɜːməˈtaɪtɪs/ *n* dermatite *f*

dermatologist /dɜːməˈtɒlədʒɪst/ *n* dermatologo, -a *mf*

derogatory /dɪˈrɒgətri/ *a* ‹*comments*› peggiorativo

derrick /ˈderɪk/ *n* derrick *m inv*

derv /dɜːv/ *n Br* gasolio *m*

descaler /diːˈskeɪlə(r)/ *n Br* disincrostante *m*

descend /dɪˈsend/ *vi* scendere; **be ~ed from** discendere da ● *vt* scendere da

■ **descend on** *vt* (*attack*) piombare su; (*visit*) capitare [all'improvviso]

descendant /dɪˈsendənt/ *n* discendente *mf*

descent /dɪˈsent/ *n* discesa *f*; (*lineage*) origine *f*

descrambler /diːˈskræmblə(r)/ *n Teleph, TV* decodificatore *m*

describe /dɪˈskraɪb/ *vt* descrivere

description /dɪˈskrɪpʃn/ *n* descrizione *f*;

they had no help of any ~ non hanno avuto proprio nessun aiuto

descriptive /dɪˈskrɪptɪv/ *a* descrittivo; (*vivid*) vivido

desecrate /ˈdesɪkreɪt/ *vt* profanare

desecration /desɪˈkreɪʃn/ *n* profanazione *f*

desegregate /diːˈsegrɪgeɪt/ *vt* abolire la segregazione razziale in ‹*school*›

deselect /diːsɪˈlekt/ *vt Br* **be ~ed** *non avere riconferma della candidatura alle elezioni da parte del proprio partito*

desensitize /diːˈsensɪtaɪz/ *vt* desensibilizzare

desert[1] /ˈdezət/ *n* deserto *m* ● *a* deserto; ~ **island** isola *f* deserta

desert[2] /dɪˈzɜːt/ *vt* abbandonare ● *vi* disertare

deserted /dɪˈzɜːtɪd/ *a* deserto

deserter /dɪˈzɜːtə(r)/ *n Mil* disertore *m*

desertion /dɪˈzɜːʃn/ *n Mil* diserzione *f*; (*of family*) abbandono *m*

deserts /dɪˈzɜːts/ *npl* **get one's just ~** ottenere ciò che ci si merita

deserve /dɪˈzɜːv/ *vt* meritare

deservedly /dɪˈzɜːvədlɪ/ *adv* meritatamente

deserving /dɪˈzɜːvɪŋ/ *a* meritevole; ~ **cause** opera *f* meritoria

desiccated /ˈdesɪkeɪtɪd/ *a* essiccato; (*pej: dried up*) secco

design /dɪˈzaɪn/ *n* progettazione *f*; (*fashion ~, appearance*) design *m inv*; (*pattern*) modello *m*; (*aim*) proposito *m*; **have ~s on** aver mire su ● *vt* progettare; disegnare ‹*clothes, furniture, model*›; **be ~ed for** essere fatto per

designate /ˈdezɪgneɪt/ *vt* designare

designation /dezɪgˈneɪʃn/ *n* designazione *f*

design consultant *n* progettista *mf*

designer /dɪˈzaɪnə(r)/ *n* progettista *mf*; (*of clothes*) stilista *mf*; (*Theat: of set*) scenografo, -a *mf*

design fault *n* difetto *m* di concezione

design feature *n* prestazione *f*

designing /dɪˈzaɪnɪŋ/ *a pej* calcolatore

desirable /dɪˈzaɪərəbl/ *a* desiderabile

desire /dɪˈzaɪə(r)/ *n* desiderio *m* ● *vt* desiderare

desist /dɪˈzɪst/ *vi* desistere (**from** da)

desk /desk/ *n* scrivania *f*; (*in school*) banco *m*; (*in hotel*) reception *f inv*; (*cash ~*) cassa *f*; (*check-in ~*) check-in *m inv*

desk: deskbound *a* ‹*job*› sedentario. **desk diary** *n* agenda da tavolo. **desk pad** *n* (*blotter*) tampone *m*; (*notebook*) block-notes *m inv*. **desktop** *n* piano *m* della scrivania; (*computer*) [computer *m inv*] desktop *m inv*. **desktop publishing** *n* desktop publishing *m inv*, editoria *f* da tavolo

desolate /ˈdesələt/ *a* desolato

desolation /desəˈleɪʃn/ *n* desolazione *f*

despair /dɪˈspeə(r)/ *n* disperazione *f*; **in ~** disperato; ‹*say*› per disperazione ● *vi* **I ~ of that boy** quel ragazzo mi fa disperare

desperate /ˈdespərət/ *a* disperato; **be ~** ‹*criminal:*› essere un disperato; **be ~ for sth** morire dalla voglia di

desperately /'despərətlɪ/ *adv* disperatamente; **he said ~** ha detto, disperato

desperation /despə'reɪʃn/ *n* disperazione *f*; **in ~** per disperazione

despicable /dɪ'spɪkəbl/ *a* disprezzevole

despise /dɪ'spaɪz/ *vt* disprezzare

despite /dɪ'spaɪt/ *prep* malgrado

despondency /dɪ'spɒndənsɪ/ *n* abbattimento *m*

despondent /dɪ'spɒndənt/ *a* abbattuto

despot /'despɒt/ *n* despota *m*

despotism /'despətɪzm/ *n* dispotismo *m*

des res /dez'rez/ *n abbr fam* (**desirable residence**) abitazione *f* desiderabile

dessert /dɪ'zɜ:t/ *n* dolce *m*

dessert spoon *n* cucchiaio *m* da dolce

dessert wine *n* vino *m* da dessert

destabilize /di:'sterbɪlaɪz/ *vt* destabilizzare

destination /destɪ'neɪʃn/ *n* destinazione *f*

destine /'destɪn/ *vt* destinare; **be ~d for sth** essere destinato a qcsa; **~d for each other** fatti l'uno per l'altra

destined /'destɪnd/ *a* **~ for Paris** ⟨train, package⟩ a destinazione di Parigi; **it was ~ to happen** era destino che succedesse

destiny /'destɪnɪ/ *n* destino *m*

destitute /'destɪtju:t/ *a* bisognoso

destitution /destɪ'tju:ʃn/ *n* indigenza *f*

destroy /dɪ'strɔɪ/ *vt* distruggere

destroyer /dɪ'strɔɪə(r)/ *n Naut* cacciatorpediniere *m*

destruct /dɪ'strʌkt/ *vi* distruggersi

destruction /dɪ'strʌkʃn/ *n* distruzione *f*

destructive /dɪ'strʌktɪv/ *a* distruttivo; ⟨fig: criticism⟩ negativo

destructiveness /dɪ'strʌktɪvnɪs/ *n* distruttività *f*

desultory /'desəltrɪ/ *a* ⟨conversation⟩ sconnesso; ⟨friendship⟩ incostante; ⟨attempt⟩ poco convinto

detach /dɪ'tætʃ/ *vt* staccare

detachable /dɪ'tætʃəbl/ *a* separabile

detached /dɪ'tætʃt/ *a fig* distaccato; **~ house** villetta *f*

detached retina *n Med* retina *f* distaccata

detachment /dɪ'tætʃmənt/ *n* distacco *m*; *Mil* distaccamento *m*

detail /'di:teɪl/ *n* particolare *m*, dettaglio *m*; **in ~** particolareggiatamente ● *vt* esporre con tutti i particolari; *Mil* assegnare

detail drawing *n* disegno *m* dettagliato

detailed /'di:teɪld/ *a* particolareggiato, dettagliato

detain /dɪ'teɪn/ *vt* ⟨police:⟩ trattenere; ⟨delay⟩ far ritardare

detainee /dɪter'ni:/ *n* detenuto, -a *mf*

detect /dɪ'tekt/ *vt* individuare; ⟨perceive⟩ percepire

detectable /dɪ'tektəbl/ *a* individuabile

detection /dɪ'tekʃn/ *n* scoperta *f*

detective /dɪ'tektɪv/ *n* investigatore, -trice *mf*

detective: detective constable *n Br* agente *mf* della polizia giudiziaria. **detective inspector** *n Br* ispettore, -trice *mf* della polizia giudiziaria. **detective story** *n* racconto *m* poliziesco. **detective work** *n* indagini *f* pl

detector /dɪ'tektə(r)/ *n* ⟨for metal⟩ cercametalli *m inv*, metal detector *m inv*

detention /dɪ'tenʃn/ *n* detenzione *f*; *Sch* punizione *f*

deter /dɪ'tɜ:(r)/ *vt* ⟨pt/pp **deterred**⟩ impedire; **~ sb from doing sth** impedire a qcno di fare qcsa

detergent /dɪ'tɜ:dʒənt/ *n* detersivo *m*

deteriorate /dɪ'tɪərɪəreɪt/ *vi* deteriorarsi

deterioration /dɪtɪərɪə'reɪʃn/ *n* deterioramento *m*

determination /dɪtɜ:mɪ'neɪʃn/ *n* determinazione *f*

determine /dɪ'tɜ:mɪn/ *vt* ⟨ascertain⟩ determinare; **~ to** ⟨resolve⟩ decidere di

determined /dɪ'tɜ:mɪnd/ *a* deciso

determining /dɪ'tɜ:mɪnɪŋ/ *a* determinante

deterrent /dɪ'terənt/ *n* deterrente *m*

detest /dɪ'test/ *vt* detestare

detestable /dɪ'testəbl/ *a* detestabile

detonate /'detəneɪt/ *vt* far detonare ● *vi* detonare

detonation /detə'neɪʃn/ *n* detonazione *f*

detonator /'detəneɪtə(r)/ *n* detonatore *m*

detour /'di:tʊə(r)/ *n* deviazione *f*

detoxify /di:'tɒksɪfaɪ/ *vt* disintossicare

detract /dɪ'trækt/ *vi* **~ from** sminuire ⟨merit⟩; rovinare ⟨pleasure, beauty⟩

detractor /dɪ'træktə(r)/ *n* detrattore, -trice *mf*

detriment /'detrɪmənt/ *n* **to the ~ of** a danno di

detrimental /detrɪ'mentl/ *a* dannoso

detritus /dɪ'traɪtəs/ *n* detriti *mpl*

deuce /dju:s/ *n Tennis* deuce *m inv*

devaluation /di:væljʊ'eɪʃn/ *n* svalutazione *f*

devalue /di:'vælju:/ *vt* svalutare ⟨currency⟩

devastate /'devəsteɪt/ *vt* devastare

devastated /'devəsteɪtɪd/ *a fam* sconvolto

devastating /'devəsteɪtɪŋ/ *a* devastante; ⟨news⟩ sconvolgente

devastation /devə'steɪʃn/ *n* devastazione *f*

develop /dɪ'veləp/ *vt* sviluppare; contrarre ⟨illness⟩; ⟨add to value of⟩ valorizzare ⟨area⟩ ● *vi* svilupparsi; **~ into** divenire

developer /dɪ'veləpə(r)/ *n* [**property**] **~** imprenditore, -trice *mf* edile

developing /dɪ'veləpɪŋ/: **developing bath** *n Phot* bagno *m* di sviluppo, bagno *m* rivelatore. **developing country** *n* paese *m* in via di sviluppo. **developing tank** *n Phot* vasca *f* di sviluppo

development /dɪ'veləpmənt/ *n* sviluppo *m*; ⟨of vaccine etc⟩ messa *f* a punto

development company *n* ⟨for property⟩ impresa *f* edile

deviant /'di:vɪənt/ *a* deviato

deviate /'di:vɪeɪt/ *vi* deviare

deviation /di:vɪ'eɪʃn/ *n* deviazione *f*

device /dɪ'vaɪs/ *n* dispositivo *m*; **leave sb to his own ~s** lasciare qcno per conto suo

devil /'devl/ *n* diavolo *m*

devilish /'dev(ə)lɪʃ/ *a* diabolico

devilishly /'dev(ə)lɪʃlɪ/ *adv fig fam* terribilmente

devil-may-care *a* menefreghista

devilment /'dev(ə)lmənt/ *n Br* cattiveria *f*

devil's advocate *n* avvocato *m* del diavolo

devil worship *n* culto *m* demoniaco

devious /'di:vɪəs/ *a* ⟨person⟩ subdolo; ⟨route⟩ tortuoso

deviously /'di:vɪəslɪ/ *adv* subdolamente

devise /dɪ'vaɪz/ *vt* escogitare

devoid /dɪ'vɔɪd/ *a* ~ **of** privo di

devolution /di:və'lu:ʃn/ *n* (*of power*) decentramento *m*

devote /dɪ'vəʊt/ *vt* dedicare

devoted /dɪ'vəʊtɪd/ *a* ⟨daughter etc⟩ affezionato; **be** ~ **to sth** consacrarsi a qcsa

devotedly /dɪ'vəʊtɪdlɪ/ *adv* con dedizione

devotee /devə'ti:/ *n* appassionato, -a *mf*

devotion /dɪ'vəʊʃn/ *n* dedizione *f*; ~**s** *pl Relig* devozione *fsg*

devour /dɪ'vaʊə(r)/ *vt* divorare

devout /dɪ'vaʊt/ *a* devoto

devoutly /dɪ'vaʊtlɪ/ *adv Relig* devotamente; ⟨sincerely⟩ fervidamente

dew /dju:/ *n* rugiada *f*

dewy /'dju:ɪ/ *a* rugiadoso

dewy-eyed /-'aɪd/ *a* ⟨moved⟩ con gli occhi lucidi; ⟨naive⟩ ingenuo

dexterity /dek'sterətɪ/ *n* destrezza *f*

dexterous /'dekstrəs/ *a* ⟨person, movement⟩ agile, destro; ⟨hand⟩ abile; ⟨mind⟩ acuto

dexterously /'dekstrəslɪ/ *adv* ⟨move⟩ agilmente; ⟨manage⟩ abilmente

dg *abbr* (**decigram**) dg *m*

diabetes /daɪə'bi:ti:z/ *n* diabete *m*

diabetic /daɪə'betɪk/ *a* & *n* diabetico, -a *mf*

diabolical /daɪə'bɒlɪkl/ *a* diabolico

diabolically /daɪə'bɒlɪklɪ/ *adv* ⟨wickedly⟩ diabolicamente; ⟨fam: badly⟩ orribilmente

diacritic /daɪə'krɪtrɪk/ *a* ⟨accent, mark⟩ diacritico

diaeresis /daɪ'erɪsɪs/ *n* dieresi *f inv*

diagnose /daɪəg'nəʊz/ *vt* diagnosticare

diagnosis /daɪəg'nəʊsɪs/ *n* (*pl* -**oses** /daɪəg'nəʊsi:z/) diagnosi *f inv*

diagnostic /daɪəg'nɒstɪk/ *a* diagnostico

diagnostics /daɪəg'nɒstɪks/ *n Med* diagnostica *f*

diagonal /daɪ'ægənl/ *a* & *n* diagonale *f*

diagonally /daɪ'ægənlɪ/ *adv* diagonalmente

diagram /'daɪəgræm/ *n* diagramma *m*

dial /'daɪəl/ *n* (*of clock, machine*) quadrante *m*; *Teleph* disco *m* combinatore ● *v* (*pt/pp* **dialled**) ● *vi Teleph* fare il numero; ~ **direct** chiamare in teleselezione ● *vt* fare ⟨number⟩

dialect /'daɪəlekt/ *n* dialetto *m*

dialectic /daɪə'lektɪk/ *n* dialettica *f* ● *a* dialettico

dialectics /daɪə'lektɪks/ *n* dialettica *f*

dialling code /'daɪəlɪŋ/ *n* prefisso *m*

dialling tone *n* segnale *m* di linea libera

dialogue /'daɪəlɒg/ *n* dialogo *m*

dial tone *n Am Teleph* segnale *m* di linea libera

dial-up *a* ⟨network⟩ collegato telefonicamente

dialysis /daɪ'ælɪsɪs/ *n* dialisi *f*

dialysis machine *n* rene *m* artificiale

diameter /daɪ'æmɪtə(r)/ *n* diametro *m*

diametrically /daɪə'metrɪklɪ/ *adv* ~ **opposed** diametralmente opposto

diamond /'daɪəmənd/ *n* diamante *m*, brillante *m*; (*shape*) losanga *f*; ~**s** *pl* (*in cards*) quadri *mpl*

diamond: diamond jubilee *n* sessantesimo anniversario *m*. **diamond-shaped** *a* romboidale. **diamond wedding** [**anniversary**] *n* nozze *fpl* di diamante

diaper /'daɪəpə(r)/ *n Am* pannolino *m*

diaphanous /daɪ'æfənəs/ *a* diafano

diaphragm /'daɪəfræm/ *n* diaframma *m*

diarist /'daɪərɪst/ *n* ⟨author⟩ diarista *mf*; ⟨journalist⟩ giornalista *mf* di piccola cronaca

diarrhoea /daɪə'ri:ə/ *n* diarrea *f*

diary /'daɪərɪ/ *n* (*for appointments*) agenda *f*; (*for writing in*) diario *m*

diatribe /'daɪətraɪb/ *n* diatriba *f*

dice /daɪs/ *n inv* dadi *mpl* ● *vt Culin* tagliare a dadini

dicey /'daɪsɪ/ *a fam* rischioso

dichotomy /daɪ'kɒtəmɪ/ *n* dicotomia *f*

dicky /'dɪkɪ/ *n* (*shirt front*) pettino *m*, sparato *m* ● *a* ⟨Br fam: heart⟩ malandato

dictate /dɪk'teɪt/ *vt*/*i* dettare

dictation /dɪk'teɪʃn/ *n* dettato *m*

dictator /dɪk'teɪtə(r)/ *n* dittatore *m*

dictatorial /dɪktə'tɔ:rɪəl/ *a* dittatoriale

dictatorship /dɪk'teɪtəʃɪp/ *n* dittatura *f*

diction /'dɪkʃn/ *n* dizione *f*

dictionary /'dɪkʃənrɪ/ *n* dizionario *m*

dictum /'dɪktəm/ *n* (*maxim*) massima *f*; (*statement*) affermazione *f*

did /dɪd/ *see* **do**

didactic /dɪ'dæktɪk/ *a* didattico

diddle /'dɪdl/ *vt fam* gabbare

didn't /'dɪdnt/ = **did not**

die[1] /daɪ/ *n Techn* (*metal mould*) stampo *m*; (*for cutting*) matrice *f*

die[2] *vi* (*pres p* **dying**) morire (**of** di); **be dying to do sth** *fam* morire dalla voglia di fare qcsa; **be dying for a drink** *fam* morire dalla voglia di bere qualcosa

■ **die away** *vi* ⟨noise, applause:⟩ smorzarsi

■ **die down** *vi* calmarsi; ⟨fire, flames:⟩ spegnersi

■ **die off** *vi* morire uno dopo l'altro

■ **die out** *vi* estinguersi; ⟨custom:⟩ morire

diehard /'daɪhɑ:d/ *n* (*pol: in party*) fanatico, -a *mf*; (*stubborn person*) ultraconservatore *mf*

diesel /'di:zl/ *n* diesel *m*. ~ **engine** *n* motore *m* diesel

diesel train *n* treno *m* con locomotiva diesel

diet /'daɪət/ *n* regime *m* alimentare; (*restricted*) dieta *f*; **be on a** ~ essere a dieta ● *vi* essere a dieta

dietary /'daɪətrɪ/ *a* ⟨habit⟩ alimentare

dietary fibre *n* fibre *fpl* alimentari

dietary supplement *n* integratore *m* dietetico

dietician /daɪəˈtɪʃn/ *n* dietologo, -a *mf*

differ /ˈdɪfə(r)/ *vi* differire; *(disagree)* non essere d'accordo

difference /ˈdɪfrəns/ *n* differenza *f*; *(disagreement)* divergenza *f*

different /ˈdɪfrənt/ *a* diverso, differente; *(various)* diversi; **be ~ from** essere diverso da

differential /dɪfəˈrenʃl/ *a* differenziale ● *n* differenziale *m*

differentiate /dɪfəˈrenʃieɪt/ *vt* distinguere **(between** fra); *(discriminate)* discriminare **(between** fra); *(make different)* differenziare

differentiation /dɪfərenʃɪˈeɪʃn/ *n* differenziazione *f*

differently /ˈdɪfrəntlɪ/ *adv* in modo diverso; **~ from** diversamente da

difficult /ˈdɪfɪkəlt/ *a* difficile

difficulty /ˈdɪfɪkəltɪ/ *n* difficoltà *f inv*; **with ~** con difficoltà

diffidence /ˈdɪfɪdəns/ *n* mancanza *f* di sicurezza

diffident /ˈdɪfɪdənt/ *a* senza fiducia in se stesso

diffidently /ˈdɪfɪdəntlɪ/ *adv* senza fiducia in se stesso

diffuse¹ /dɪˈfjuːs/ *a* diffuso; *(wordy)* prolisso

diffuse² /dɪˈfjuːz/ *vt* Phys diffondere

diffuseness /dɪˈfjuːsnɪs/ *n (of organization)* estensione *f*; *(of argument)* prolissità *f*

dig /dɪg/ *n (poke)* spinta *f*; *(remark)* frecciata *f*; Archaeol scavo *m*; **~s** *pl fam* camera *fsg* ammobiliata ● *vt/i (pt/pp* dug, *pres p* digging) scavare *(hole)*; vangare *(garden)*; *(thrust)* conficcare; **~ sb in the ribs** dare una gomitata a qcno

■ **dig out** *vt fig* tirar fuori

■ **dig up** *vt* scavare *(garden, street, object)*; sradicare *(tree, plant)*; *(fig: find)* scovare

digest¹ /ˈdaɪdʒest/ *n* compendio *m*

digest² /daɪˈdʒest/ *vt* digerire

digestible /daɪˈdʒestəbl/ *a* digeribile

digestion /daɪˈdʒestʃn/ *n* digestione *f*

digestive /daɪˈdʒestɪv/ *a* digestivo

digestive: digestive [biscuit] *n Br* biscotto *m* di farina integrale. **digestive system** *n* apparato *m* digerente. **digestive tract** *n* apparato *m* digerente.

digger /ˈdɪgə(r)/ *n* Techn scavatrice *f*

diggings /ˈdɪgɪŋz/ *npl (in archaeology)* scavi *mpl*

digit /ˈdɪdʒɪt/ *n* cifra *f*; *(finger)* dito *m*

digital /ˈdɪdʒɪtl/ *a* digitale

digital: digital audio tape *n* audiocassetta *f* digitale. **digital clock** *n* orologio *m* digitale. **digital computer** *n* computer *m* digitale

digitizer /ˈdɪdʒɪtaɪzə(r)/ *n Comput* tavoletta *f* grafica

dignified /ˈdɪgnɪfaɪd/ *a* dignitoso

dignify /ˈdɪgnɪfaɪ/ *vt* nobilitare *(occasion, building)*

dignitary /ˈdɪgnɪtərɪ/ *n* dignitario *m*

dignity /ˈdɪgnətɪ/ *n* dignità *f*

digress /daɪˈgres/ *vi* divagare

digression /daɪˈgreʃn/ *n* digressione *f*

dike /daɪk/ *n* diga *f*

dilapidated /dɪˈlæpɪdeɪtɪd/ *a* cadente

dilapidation /dɪlæpɪˈdeɪʃn/ *n* rovina *f*

dilate /daɪˈleɪt/ *vt* dilatare ● *vi* dilatarsi

dilation /daɪˈleɪʃn/ *n* dilatazione *f*

dilatory /ˈdɪlətərɪ/ *a* dilatorio

dilemma /dɪˈlemə/ *n* dilemma *m*

dilettante /dɪlɪˈtæntɪ/ *n* dilettante *mf*

diligence /ˈdɪlɪdʒəns/ *n* diligenza *f*

diligent /ˈdɪlɪdʒənt/ *a* diligente

dill /dɪl/ *n* aneto *m*

dilly-dally /ˈdɪlɪdælɪ/ *vi (pt/pp* -ied) *fam* tentennare

dilute /daɪˈljuːt/ *vt* diluire

dilution /daɪˈljuːʃn/ *n also fig* diluizione *f*

dim /dɪm/ *a* **(dimmer, dimmest)** debole *(light)*; *(dark)* scuro; *(prospect, chance)* scarso; *(indistinct)* impreciso; *(fam: stupid)* tonto ● *vt/i (pt/pp* dimmed) affievolire

dime /daɪm/ *n Am* moneta *f* da dieci centesimi

dimension /daɪˈmenʃn/ *n* dimensione *f*

dime store *n Am* grande magazzino *m* con prezzi molto bassi

diminish /dɪˈmɪnɪʃ/ *vt/i* diminuire

diminished /dɪˈmɪnɪʃt/ *a* ridotto; *Mus* diminuito; **on grounds of ~ responsibility** *Jur* per seminfermità mentale

diminutive /dɪˈmɪnjutɪv/ *a & n* diminutivo *m*

dimly /ˈdɪmlɪ/ *adv (see, remember)* indistintamente; *(shine)* debolmente

dimmer /ˈdɪmə(r)/ *n* interruttore *m* a reostato

dimple /ˈdɪmpl/ *n* fossetta *f*

dimwit /ˈdɪmwɪt/ *n fam* stupido *m*

dim-witted /-ˈwɪtɪd/ *a fam* stupido

din /dɪn/ *n* baccano *m*

■ **din into** *vt* **~ sth into sb** ficcare qcsa in testa a qcno

dine /daɪn/ *vi* pranzare

diner /ˈdaɪnə(r)/ *n (Am: restaurant)* tavola *f* calda; **the last ~ in the restaurant** l'ultimo cliente nel ristorante

dingdong /ˈdɪŋdɒŋ/ *n* dindon *m*

dingdong battle *n Br* battibecco *m*

dinghy /ˈdɪŋgɪ/ *n* dinghy *m*; *(inflatable)* canotto *m* pneumatico

dingy /ˈdɪndʒɪ/ *a (-ier, -iest)* squallido e tetro

dining /ˈdaɪnɪŋ/: **dining car** *n* carrozza *f* ristorante. **dining hall** *n* refettorio *m*. **dining room** *n* sala *f* da pranzo. **dining table** *n* tavolo *m* da pranzo

dinky /ˈdɪŋkɪ/ *a Br fam* carino

dinner /ˈdɪnə(r)/ *n* cena *f*; *(at midday)* pranzo *m*

dinner: dinner dance *n* cena *f* danzante. **dinner fork** *n* forchetta *f*. **dinner hour** *n Br Sch* pausa *f* del pranzo. **dinner jacket** *n* smoking *m inv*. **dinner knife** *n* coltello *m*. **dinner money** *n Br Sch* soldi *mpl* dati dai genitori agli scolari per il pranzo. **dinner party** *n* cena *f (con invitati)*. **dinner plate** *n* piatto *m* piano. **dinner service, dinner set** *n* servizio *m* da tavola. **dinner time** *n* (*evening*) ora *f* di cena; (*midday*) ora *f* di pranzo

dinnerware /'dɪnəweə(r)/ *n* servizio *m* da tavola

dinosaur /'daɪnəsɔː(r)/ *n* dinosauro *m*

dint /dɪnt/ *n* **by ~ of** a forza di

diocese /'daɪəsɪs/ *n* diocesi *f inv*

diode /'daɪəʊd/ *n* diodo *m*

dioxide /daɪ'ɒksaɪd/ *n* biossido *m*

dip /dɪp/ *n* (*in ground*) inclinazione *f*; *Culin* salsina *f*; **go for a ~** andare a fare una nuotata ● *v* (*pt/pp* **dipped**) ● *vt* (*in liquid*) immergere; abbassare ⟨*head, headlights*⟩ ● *vi* ⟨*land:*⟩ formare un avvallamento

■ **dip into** *vt* scorrere ⟨*book*⟩

diphtheria /dɪf'θɪərɪə/ *n* difterite *f*

diphthong /'dɪfθɒŋ/ *n* dittongo *m*

diploma /dɪ'pləʊmə/ *n* diploma *m*

diplomacy /dɪ'pləʊməsɪ/ *n* diplomazia *f*

diplomat /'dɪpləmæt/ *n* diplomatico, -a *mf*

diplomatic /dɪplə'mætɪk/ *a* diplomatico

diplomatically /dɪplə'mætɪklɪ/ *adv* con diplomazia

diplomatic bag *n* valigia *f* diplomatica

diplomatic immunity *n* immunità *f* diplomatica

dippy /'dɪpɪ/ *a* (*fam: crazy, weird*) pazzo

dipstick /'dɪpstɪk/ *n Auto* astina *f* dell'olio

dire /'daɪə(r)/ *a* ⟨*situation, consequences*⟩ terribile

direct /daɪ'rekt/ *a* diretto ● *adv* direttamente ● *vt* (*aim*) rivolgere ⟨*attention, criticism*⟩; (*control*) dirigere; fare la regia di ⟨*film, play*⟩; **~ sb** (*show the way*) indicare la strada a qcno; **~ sb to do sth** ordinare a qcno di fare qcsa

direct: direct access *n Comput* accesso *m* diretto. **direct current** *n* corrente *m* continua. **direct debit** *n* addebitamento *m* diretto. **direct dialling** *n* teleselezione *f*. **direct hit** *n Mil* colpo *m* diretto

direction /dɪ'rekʃn/ *n* direzione *f*; (*of play, film*) regia *f*; **~s** *pl* indicazioni *fpl*; **~s for use** istruzioni *fpl* per l'uso

directional /daɪ'rekʃənəl/ *a* direzionale

directive /daɪ'rektɪv/ *n* direttiva *f*

directly /daɪ'rektlɪ/ *adv* direttamente; (*at once*) immediatamente ● *conj* [non] appena

directness /daɪ'rektnɪs/ *n* (*of person, attitude*) franchezza *f*; (*of play, work, writing*) chiarezza *f*

direct object *n* complemento *m* oggetto

director /dɪ'rektə(r)/ *n Comm* direttore, -trice *mf*; (*of play, film*) regista *mf*

directorate /daɪ'rektərət/ *n* (*board*) consiglio *m* d'amministrazione

director general *n* presidente *mf*

Director of Public Prosecutions *n Br* ≈ Procuratore *m* della Repubblica

directorship /dɪ'rektəʃɪp/ *n* posto *m* di direttore

directory /dɪ'rektərɪ/ *n* elenco *m*; *Teleph* elenco *m* [telefonico]; (*of streets*) stradario *m*

directory assistance *n Am* servizio *m* informazioni abbonati

directory enquiries *npl Br* servizio *m* informazioni abbonati

direct: direct rule *n Pol* sottomissione *f* al governo centrale. **direct speech** *n* discorso *m* diretto. **direct transfer** *n* trasferimento *m* automatico

dirt /dɜːt/ *n* sporco *m*; **~ cheap** *fam* a [un] prezzo stracciato

dirtiness /'dɜːtɪnɪs/ *n* (*of person etc*) sporcizia *f*

dirt track *n* (*road*) strada *f* sterrata; *Sport* pista *f* sterrata

dirty /'dɜːtɪ/ *a* (**-ier, -iest**) sporco ● *vt* sporcare

dirty: dirty-minded /-'maɪndɪd/ *a* fissato sul sesso. **dirty trick** *n* brutto scherzo *m*. **dirty tricks** *npl Pol* faccende *fpl* sporche. **dirty weekend** *n fam* weekend *m inv* clandestino con l'amante. **dirty word** *n* parolaccia *f*

disability /dɪsə'bɪlətɪ/ *n* infermità *f inv*

disable /dɪ'seɪbl/ *vt* (*make useless*) mettere fuori uso ⟨*machine*⟩; (*in accident*) rendere invalido; *Comput* disabilitare; **be ~d by arthritis** essere menomato dall'artrite

disabled /dɪ'seɪbld/ *a* invalido

disabled: disabled access *n* (*to public building etc*) accesso *m* per gli invalidi. **disabled driver** *n* guidatore, -trice *mf* invalido, -a. **disabled person** *n* invalido, -a *mf*

disabuse /dɪsə'bjuːz/ *vt* disingannare

disadvantage /dɪsəd'vɑːntɪdʒ/ *n* svantaggio *m*; **at a ~** in una posizione di svantaggio

disadvantaged /dɪsəd'vɑːntɪdʒd/ *a* svantaggiato

disadvantageous /dɪsædvən'teɪdʒəs/ *a* svantaggioso

disaffected /dɪsə'fektɪd/ *a* disilluso

disagree /dɪsə'griː/ *vi* non essere d'accordo; **~ with** ⟨*food:*⟩ far male a

disagreeable /dɪsə'griːəbl/ *a* sgradevole

disagreement /dɪsə'griːmənt/ *n* disaccordo *m*; (*quarrel*) dissidio *m*

disallow /dɪsə'laʊ/ *vt* respingere; *Sport* annullare

disappear /dɪsə'pɪə(r)/ *vi* scomparire

disappearance /dɪsə'pɪərəns/ *n* scomparsa *f*

disappoint /dɪsə'pɔɪnt/ *vt* deludere

disappointed /dɪsə'pɔɪntɪd/ *a* deluso; **I am ~ in you** mi hai deluso

disappointing /dɪsə'pɔɪntɪŋ/ *a* deludente

disappointment /dɪsə'pɔɪntmənt/ *n* delusione *f*

disapproval /dɪsə'pruːvəl/ *n* disapprovazione *f*

disapprove /dɪsə'pruːv/ *vi* disapprovare; **~ of sb/sth** disapprovare qcno/qcsa

disapproving /dɪsə'pruːvɪŋ/ *a* ⟨*look, gesture*⟩ di disapprovazione

disarm /dɪs'ɑːm/ *vt* disarmare ● *vi Mil* disarmarsi

disarmament /dɪs'ɑːməmənt/ *n* disarmo *m*

disarming /dɪs'ɑːmɪŋ/ *a* ⟨*frankness etc*⟩ disarmante

disarrange /dɪsə'reɪndʒ/ *vt* scompigliare

disarray /dɪsə'reɪ/ n **in ~** in disordine

disaster /dɪ'zɑːstə(r)/ n disastro m

disaster: disaster area n zona f disastrata; (fig: person) disastro m. **disaster fund** n fondi mpl a favore dei disastrati. **disaster victim** n disastrato, -a mf

disastrous /dɪ'zɑːstrəs/ a disastroso

disastrously /dɪ'zɑːstrəslɪ/ adv ⟨fail⟩ disastrosamente; ⟨end, turn out⟩ in modo catastrofico; **go ~ wrong** essere un disastro

disband /dɪs'bænd/ vt scogliere; smobilitare ⟨troops⟩ ● vi scogliersi; ⟨regiment:⟩ essere smobilitato

disbelief /dɪsbɪ'liːf/ n incredulità f; **in ~** con incredulità

disbelieve /dɪsbɪ'liːv/ vt non credere

disc /dɪsk/ n disco m; (CD) compact disc m inv

discard /dɪ'skɑːd/ vt scartare; (throw away) eliminare; scaricare ⟨boyfriend⟩

disc brakes npl Auto freni mpl a disco

discern /dɪ'sɜːn/ vt discernere

discernible /dɪ'sɜːnəbl/ a discernibile

discerning /dɪ'sɜːnɪŋ/ a perspicace

discharge[1] /'dɪstʃɑːdʒ/ n Electr scarica f; (dismissal) licenziamento m; Mil congedo m; (Med: of blood) emissione f; (of cargo) scarico m

discharge[2] /dɪs'tʃɑːdʒ/ vt scaricare ⟨battery, cargo⟩; (dismiss) licenziare; Mil congedare; Jur assolvere ⟨accused⟩; dimettere ⟨patient⟩; **~ one's duty** esaurire il proprio compito ● vi Electr scaricarsi

disciple /dɪ'saɪpl/ n discepolo m

disciplinarian /dɪsɪplɪ'neərɪən/ n persona f autoritaria

disciplinary /'dɪsɪplɪnərɪ/ a disciplinare

discipline /'dɪsɪplɪn/ n disciplina f ● vt disciplinare; (punish) punire

disciplined /'dɪsɪplɪnd/ a ⟨person, approach⟩ sistematico

disc jockey n disc jockey m inv

disclaim /dɪs'kleɪm/ vt negare

disclaimer /dɪs'kleɪmə(r)/ n rifiuto m

disclose /dɪs'kləʊz/ vt svelare

disclosure /dɪs'kləʊʒə(r)/ n rivelazione f

disco /'dɪskəʊ/ n discoteca f

discoloration /dɪskʌlə'reɪʃn/ n (process) scolorimento m; (spot) macchia f scolorita

discolour /dɪs'kʌlə(r)/ vt scolorire ● vi scolorirsi

discomfort /dɪs'kʌmfət/ n scomodità f, fig disagio m

disconcert /dɪskən'sɜːt/ vt sconcertare

disconcerting /dɪskən'sɜːtɪŋ/ a sconcertante

disconnect /dɪskə'nekt/ vt disconnettere

disconsolate /dɪs'kɒnsələt/ a sconsolato

discontent /dɪskən'tent/ n scontentezza f

discontented /dɪskən'tentɪd/ a scontento

discontinue /dɪskən'tɪnjuː/ vt cessare, smettere; Comm sospendere la produzione di; **~d line** fine f serie

discontinuity /dɪskɒntɪ'njuːɪtɪ/ n discontinuità f

discord /'dɪskɔːd/ n discordia f; Mus dissonanza f

discordant /dɪ'skɔːdənt/ a **~ note** nota f discordante

discothèque /'dɪskətek/ n discoteca f

discount[1] /'dɪskaʊnt/ n sconto m

discount[2] /dɪs'kaʊnt/ vt (not believe) non credere a; (leave out of consideration) non tener conto di

discount flight n volo m a prezzo ridotto

discount store n discount m inv

discourage /dɪs'kʌrɪdʒ/ vt scoraggiare; (dissuade) dissuadere

discouragement /dɪs'kʌrɪdʒmənt/ n (despondency) scoraggiamento m; (disincentive) disincentivo m

discourse /'dɪskɔːs/ n discorso m

discourteous /dɪs'kɜːtɪəs/ a scortese

discourteously /dɪs'kɜːtɪəslɪ/ adv scortesemente

discover /dɪ'skʌvə(r)/ vt scoprire

discovery /dɪs'kʌvərɪ/ n scoperta f

discredit /dɪs'kredɪt/ n discredito m ● vt screditare

discreet /dɪ'skriːt/ a discreto

discreetly /dɪ'skriːtlɪ/ adv discretamente

discrepancy /dɪs'krepənsɪ/ n discrepanza f

discretion /dɪs'kreʃn/ n discrezione f

discriminate /dɪs'krɪmɪneɪt/ vi discriminare (**against** contro); **~ between** distinguere tra

discriminating /dɪs'krɪmɪneɪtɪŋ/ a esigente

discrimination /dɪskrɪmɪ'neɪʃn/ n discriminazione f; (quality) discernimento m

discriminatory /dɪs'krɪmɪnətərɪ/ a discriminatorio, discriminativo

discus /'dɪskəs/ n disco m

discuss /dɪ'skʌs/ vt discutere; (examine critically) esaminare

discussion /dɪs'kʌʃn/ n discussione f

discussion document, discussion paper n documento m in abbozzo

disdain /dɪs'deɪn/ n sdegno f ● vt sdegnare

disdainful /dɪs'deɪnful/ a sdegnoso

disease /dɪ'ziːz/ n malattia f

diseased /dɪ'ziːzd/ a malato

disembark /dɪsem'bɑːk/ vi sbarcare

disembodied /dɪsem'bɒdɪd/ a ⟨voices⟩ evanescente; ⟨head⟩ senza corpo; ⟨soul⟩ disincarnato

disenchant /dɪsen'tʃɑːnt/ vt disincantare

disenchantment /dɪsen'tʃɑːntmənt/ n disincanto m

disenfranchise /dɪsen'fræntʃaɪz/ vt privare del diritto di voto

disengage /dɪsen'geɪdʒ/ vt disimpegnare; disinnestare ⟨clutch⟩

disentangle /dɪsen'tæŋgəl/ vt districare

disfavour /dɪs'feɪvə(r)/ n sfavore m; **fall into ~** perdere il favore

disfigure /dɪs'fɪgə(r)/ vt deformare

disgorge /dɪs'gɔːdʒ/ vt rigettare

disgrace /dɪz'greɪs/ n vergogna f; **fall into ~** cadere in disgrazia; **I am in ~** sono caduto in disgrazia; **it's a ~** è una vergogna ● *vt* disonorare

disgraceful /dɪz'ɡreɪsfʊl/ *a* vergognoso

disgruntled /dɪs'ɡrʌntld/ *a* malcontento

disguise /dɪs'ɡaɪz/ *n* travestimento *m*; **in ~** travestito ● *vt* contraffare ⟨*voice*⟩; dissimulare ⟨*emotions*⟩; **~d as** travestito da

disgust /dɪs'ɡʌst/ *n* disgusto *m*; **in ~** con aria disgustata ● *vt* disgustare

disgusting /dɪs'ɡʌstɪŋ/ *a* disgustoso

dish /dɪʃ/ *n* piatto *m*; **do the ~es** lavare i piatti

■ **dish out** *vt* ⟨*serve*⟩ servire; ⟨*distribute*⟩ distribuire

■ **dish up** *vt* servire

dishcloth /'dɪʃklɒθ/ *n* strofinaccio *m*

dishearten /dɪs'hɑːt(ə)n/ *vt* scoraggiare

disheartening /dɪs'hɑːt(ə)nɪŋ/ *a* scoraggiante

dishevelled /dɪ'ʃevld/ *a* scompigliato

dishonest /dɪs'ɒnɪst/ *a* disonesto

dishonestly /dɪs'ɒnɪstlɪ/ *adv* disonestamente

dishonesty /dɪs'ɒnɪstɪ/ *n* disonestà *f*

dishonour /dɪs'ɒnə(r)/ *n* disonore *m* ● *vt* disonorare ⟨*family*⟩; non onorare ⟨*cheque*⟩

dishonourable /dɪs'ɒnərəbl/ *a* disonorevole

dishonourably /dɪs'ɒnərəblɪ/ *adv* in modo disonorevole

dishwasher /'dɪʃwɒʃə(r)/ *n* lavapiatti *f inv*

dishy /'dɪʃɪ/ *a* (**-ier, est**) ⟨*Br fam: man, woman*⟩ fico, figo

disillusion /dɪsɪ'luːʒn/ *vt* disilludere

disillusioned /dɪsɪ'luːʒnd/ *a* deluso (**with di**)

disillusionment /dɪsɪ'luːʒnmənt/ *n* disillusione *f*

disincentive /dɪsɪn'sentɪv/ *n* disincentivo *m*

disinclined /dɪsɪn'klaɪnd/ *a* riluttante

disinfect /dɪsɪn'fekt/ *vt* disinfettare

disinfectant /dɪsɪn'fektənt/ *n* disinfettante *m*

disingenuous /dɪsɪn'dʒenjʊəs/ *a* ⟨*comment*⟩ insincero; ⟨*smile*⟩ falso

disinherit /dɪsɪn'herɪt/ *vt* diseredare

disintegrate /dɪs'ɪntɪɡreɪt/ *vi* disintegrarsi

disintegration /dɪsɪntɪ'ɡreɪʃn/ *n* disgregazione *f*

disinterested /dɪs'ɪntərestɪd/ *a* disinteressato

disjointed /dɪs'dʒɔɪntɪd/ *a* sconnesso

disk /dɪsk/ *n* Comput disco *m*; ⟨*diskette*⟩ dischetto *m*

disk drive *n* lettore *m* [di disco]

disk operating system /'dɪskɒpəreɪtɪŋ/ *n* sistema *m* operativo su disco

dislike /dɪs'laɪk/ *n* avversione *f*; **your likes and ~s** i tuoi gusti ● *vt* **I ~ him/it** non mi piace; **I don't ~ him/it** non mi dispiace

dislocate /'dɪsləkeɪt/ *vt* slogare; **~ one's shoulder** slogarsi una spalla

dislocation /dɪslə'keɪʃn/ *n* ⟨*of hip, knee*⟩ lussazione *f*

dislodge /dɪs'lɒdʒ/ *vt* sloggiare

disloyal /dɪs'lɔɪəl/ *a* sleale

disloyally /dɪs'lɔɪəlɪ/ *adv* slealmente

disloyalty /dɪs'lɔɪəltɪ/ *n* slealtà *f*

dismal /'dɪzməl/ *a* ⟨*person*⟩ abbacchiato; ⟨*news, weather*⟩ deprimente; ⟨*performance*⟩ mediocre

dismantle /dɪs'mæntl/ *vt* smontare ⟨*tent, machine*⟩; *fig* smantellare

dismay /dɪs'meɪ/ *n* sgomento *m*; **much to my ~** con mio grande sgomento

dismayed /dɪs'meɪd/ *a* sgomento

dismember /dɪs'membə(r)/ *vt* *also fig* smembrare

dismiss /dɪs'mɪs/ *vt* licenziare ⟨*employee*⟩; ⟨*reject*⟩ scartare ⟨*idea, suggestion*⟩

dismissal /dɪs'mɪsəl/ *n* licenziamento *m*

dismissive /dɪs'mɪsɪv/ *a* ⟨*person, attitude*⟩ sprezzante; **be ~ of** essere sprezzante verso

dismount /dɪs'maʊnt/ *vi* smontare

disobedience /dɪsə'biːdɪəns/ *n* disubbidienza *f*

disobedient /dɪsə'biːdɪənt/ *a* disubbidiente

disobey /dɪsə'beɪ/ *vt* disubbidire a ⟨*rule*⟩ ● *vi* disubbidire

disorder /dɪs'ɔːdə(r)/ *n* disordine *m*; Med disturbo *m*

disordered /dɪs'ɔːdəd/ *a* ⟨*life*⟩ disordinato; ⟨*mind*⟩ disturbato

disorderly /dɪs'ɔːdəlɪ/ *a* disordinato; ⟨*crowd*⟩ turbolento; **~ conduct** turbamento *m* della quiete pubblica

disorganization /dɪsɔːɡənaɪ'zeɪʃn/ *n* disorganizzazione *f*

disorganized /dɪs'ɔːɡənaɪzd/ *a* disorganizzato

disorientate /dɪs'ɔːrɪənteɪt/ *vt* disorientare

disorientation /dɪsɔːrɪen'teɪʃn/ *n* disorientamento *m*

disown /dɪs'əʊn/ *vt* disconoscere; **I'll ~ you** *fam* faccio finta di non conoscerti

disparaging /dɪ'spærɪdʒɪŋ/ *a* sprezzante

disparagingly /dɪ'spærɪdʒɪŋlɪ/ *adv* sprezzantemente

disparate /'dɪspərət/ *a* ⟨*different*⟩ eterogeneo; ⟨*incompatible*⟩ disparato

disparity /dɪ'spærətɪ/ *n* disparità *f inv*

dispassionate /dɪ'spæʃənət/ *a* spassionato

dispassionately /dɪs'pæʃənətlɪ/ *adv* spassionatamente

dispatch /dɪ'spætʃ/ *n* Comm spedizione *f*; ⟨*Mil, report*⟩ dispaccio *m*; **with ~** con prontezza ● *vt* spedire; ⟨*kill*⟩ spedire al creatore

dipatch: Dispatch Box *n Br Pol* postazione *f* da cui parlano i ministri nel Parlamento britannico. **dispatch box** *n* valigia *f* diplomatica. **dispatch rider** *n* staffetta *f*

dispel /dɪ'spel/ *vt* ⟨*pt/pp* dispelled⟩ dissipare

dispensable /dɪ'spensəbl/ *a* dispensabile

dispensary /dɪ'spensərɪ/ *n* farmacia *f*

dispense /dɪ'spens/ *vt* distribuire; **~ with** fare a meno di

dispenser /dɪ'spensə(r)/ *n* ⟨*device*⟩ distributore *m*

dispensing chemist /dɪˈspensɪŋ/ n farmacista mf; (shop) farmacia f

dispensing optician n Br ottico m

dispersal /dɪˈspɜːsl/ n disperzione f

disperse /dɪˈspɜːs/ vt disperdere ● vi dispersi

dispersion /dɪˈspɜːʃn/ n dispersione f

dispirited /dɪˈspɪrɪtɪd/ a scoraggiato

displace /dɪsˈpleɪs/ vt spostare

displaced person n profugo, -a mf

displacement /dɪsˈpleɪsmənt/ n spostamento m

display /dɪˈspleɪ/ n mostra f; Comm esposizione f; (of feelings) manifestazione f; pej ostentazione f; Comput display m inv ● vt mostrare; esporre (goods); manifestare (feelings); Comput visualizzare

display: display advertisement n annuncio m pubblicitario di grande formato. **display cabinet, display case** n vetrina f. **display rack** n espositore m. **display window** n vetrina f

displease /dɪsˈpliːz/ vt non piacere a; **be ~d with** essere scontento di

displeasure /dɪsˈpleʒə(r)/ n malcontento m; **incur sb's ~** scontentare qcno

disposable /dɪˈspəʊzəbl/ a (throwaway) usa e getta; (income) disponibile

disposal /dɪˈspəʊzl/ n (getting rid of) eliminazione f; **be at sb's ~** essere a disposizione di qcno

dispose /dɪˈspəʊz/ vi **~ of** (get rid of) disfarsi di; **be well ~d** essere ben disposto (**to** verso)

disposition /dɪspəˈzɪʃn/ n disposizione f; (nature) indole f

dispossessed /dɪspəˈzest/ a (family) spossessato; (son) diseredato

disproportionate /dɪsprəˈpɔːʃənət/ a sproporzionato

disproportionately /dɪsprəˈpɔːʃənətlɪ/ adv in modo sproporzionato

disprove /dɪsˈpruːv/ vt confutare

dispute /dɪˈspjuːt/ n disputa f; (industrial) contestazione f ● vt contestare (statement)

disqualification /dɪskwɒlɪfɪˈkeɪʃn/ n squalifica f; (from driving) ritiro m della patente

disqualify /dɪsˈkwɒlɪfaɪ/ vt escludere; Sport squalificare; **~ sb from driving** ritirare la patente a qcno

disquiet /dɪsˈkwaɪət/ n inquietudine f

disquieting /dɪsˈkwaɪətɪŋ/ a allarmante

disregard /dɪsrɪˈɡɑːd/ n mancanza f di considerazione ● vt ignorare

disrepair /dɪsrɪˈpeə(r)/ n **fall into ~** deteriorarsi; **in a state of ~** in cattivo stato

disreputable /dɪsˈrepjʊtəbl/ a malfamato

disrepute /dɪsrɪˈpjuːt/ n discredito m; **bring sb into ~** rovinare la reputazione a qcno

disrespect /dɪsrɪˈspekt/ n mancanza f di rispetto

disrespectful /dɪsrɪˈspektfʊl/ a irrispettoso

disrespectfully /dɪsrɪˈspektfʊlɪ/ adv irrispettosamente

disrupt /dɪsˈrʌpt/ vt creare scompiglio in; sconvolgere (plans)

disruption /dɪsˈrʌpʃn/ n scompiglio m; (of plans) sconvolgimento m

disruptive /dɪsˈrʌptɪv/ a (person, behaviour) indisciplinato

dissatisfaction /dɪ(s)sætɪsˈfækʃn/ n malcontento m

dissatisfied /dɪ(s)ˈsætɪsfaɪd/ a scontento

dissect /dɪˈsekt/ vt sezionare

dissection /dɪˈsekʃn/ n dissezione f

disseminate /dɪˈsemɪneɪt/ vt divulgare

dissemination /dɪsemɪˈneɪʃn/ n divulgazione f

dissension /dɪˈsenʃn/ n (discord) dissenso m

dissent /dɪˈsent/ n dissenso m ● vi dissentire

dissertation /dɪsəˈteɪʃn/ n tesi f inv

disservice /dɪ(s)ˈsɜːvɪs/ n **do sb/oneself a ~** rendere un cattivo servizio a qcno/se stesso

dissidence /ˈdɪsɪdəns/ n dissidenza f

dissident /ˈdɪsɪdənt/ n dissidente mf

dissimilar /dɪ(s)ˈsɪmɪlə(r)/ a dissimile (**to** da)

dissimilarity /dɪs(s)ɪmɪˈlærətɪ/ n diversità f inv

dissipate /ˈdɪsɪpeɪt/ vt dissipare (hope, enthusiasm)

dissipated /ˈdɪsɪpeɪtɪd/ a dissipato

dissipation n dissipatezza f, sregolatezza f

dissociate /dɪˈsəʊʃɪeɪt/ vt dissociare; **~ oneself from** dissociarsi da

dissolute /ˈdɪsəluːt/ a dissoluto

dissolution /dɪsəˈluːʃn/ n scioglimento m

dissolve /dɪˈzɒlv/ vt dissolvere ● vi dissolversi

dissonance /ˈdɪsənəns/ n dissonanza f

dissonant /ˈdɪsənənt/ a Mus dissonante

dissuade /dɪˈsweɪd/ vt dissuadere

distance /ˈdɪstəns/ n distanza f; **it's a short ~ from here to the station** la stazione non è lontana da qui; **in the ~** in lontananza; **from a ~** da lontano

distant /ˈdɪstənt/ a distante; (relative) lontano

distantly /ˈdɪstəntlɪ/ adv (reply) con distacco

distaste /dɪsˈteɪst/ n avversione f

distasteful /dɪsˈteɪstfʊl/ a spiacevole

distemper /dɪˈstempə(r)/ n (paint) tempera f; (in horses, dogs) cimurro m

distend /dɪˈstend/ vi dilatarsi

distil /dɪˈstɪl/ vt (pt/pp distilled) distillare

distillation /dɪstɪˈleɪʃn/ n distillazione f

distillery /dɪˈstɪlərɪ/ n distilleria f

distinct /dɪˈstɪŋkt/ a chiaro; (different) distinto

distinction /dɪˈstɪŋkʃn/ n distinzione f; Sch massimo m dei voti

distinctive /dɪˈstɪŋktɪv/ a caratteristico

distinctly /dɪˈstɪŋktlɪ/ adv chiaramente

distinguish /dɪˈstɪŋɡwɪʃ/ vt/i distinguere; **~ oneself** distinguersi

distinguishable /dɪ'stɪŋgwɪʃəbl/ *a* distinguibile

distinguished /dɪ'stɪŋgwɪʃt/ *a* rinomato; ⟨*appearance*⟩ distinto; ⟨*career*⟩ brillante

distort /dɪ'stɔːt/ *vt* distorcere

distortion /dɪ'stɔːʃn/ *n* distorsione *f*

distract /dɪ'strækt/ *vt* distrarre

distracted /dɪ'stræktɪd/ *a* assente; (*fam: worried*) preoccupato

distracting /dɪ'stræktɪŋ/ *a* che distrae; **I found the noise too ~** il rumore mi disturbava troppo

distraction /dɪ'strækʃn/ *n* distrazione *f*; (*despair*) disperazione *f*; **drive sb to ~** portare qcno alla disperazione

distraught /dɪ'strɔːt/ *a* sconvolto

distress /dɪ'stres/ *n* angoscia *f*; (*pain*) sofferenza *f*; (*danger*) difficoltà *f* ● *vt* sconvolgere; (*sadden*) affliggere

distressed /dɪ'strest/ *a* (*upset*) turbato; (*stronger*) afflitto

distressing /dɪ'stresɪŋ/ *a* penoso; (*shocking*) sconvolgente

distress signal *n* segnale *m* di richiesta di soccorso

distribute /dɪ'strɪbjuːt/ *vt* distribuire

distribution /dɪstrɪ'bjuːʃn/ *n* distribuzione *f*

distribution network *n* rete *f* di distribuzione

distributor /dɪ'strɪbjʊtə(r)/ *n* distributore *m*

district /'dɪstrɪkt/ *n* regione *f*; *Admin* distretto *m*

district: district council *n* *Br* consiglio *m* distrettuale. **district court** *n* *Am* corte *f* distrettuale federale. **district manager** *n* direttore, -trice *mf* di zona. **district nurse** *n* infermiere, -a *mf* che fa visite a domicilio

distrust /dɪs'trʌst/ *n* sfiducia *f* ● *vt* non fidarsi di

distrustful /dɪs'trʌstfʊl/ *a* diffidente

disturb /dɪ'stɜːb/ *vt* disturbare; (*emotionally*) turbare; spostare ⟨*papers*⟩

disturbance /dɪ'stɜːbəns/ *n* disturbo *m*; **~s** *pl* (*rioting etc*) disordini *mpl*

disturbed /dɪ'stɜːbd/ *a* turbato; **[mentally] ~** malato di mente

disturbing /dɪ'stɜːbɪŋ/ *a* inquietante

disuse /dɪs'juːs/ *n* **fall into ~** cadere in disuso

disused /dɪs'juːzd/ *a* non utilizzato

ditch /dɪtʃ/ *n* fosso *m* ● *vt* (*fam: abandon*) abbandonare ⟨*plan, car*⟩; piantare ⟨*lover*⟩

ditchwater /'dɪtʃwɔːtə(r)/ *n* **as dull as ~** una barba

dither /'dɪðə(r)/ *vi* titubare

ditto /'dɪtəʊ/ *adv* idem; (*in list*) idem come sopra

ditto marks *npl* virgolette *fpl*

divan /dɪ'væn/ *n* divano *m*

dive /daɪv/ *n* tuffo *m*; *Aeron* picchiata *f*; (*fam: place*) bettola *f* ● *vi* tuffarsi; (*when in water*) immergersi; *Aeron* scendere in picchiata; (*fam: rush*) precipitarsi

dive-bomb *vt* *Mil* bombardare in picchiata

diver /'daɪvə(r)/ *n* (*from board*) tuffatore,

-trice *mf*; (*scuba*) sommozzatore, -trice *mf*; (*deep sea*) palombaro *m*

diverge /daɪ'vɜːdʒ/ *vi* divergere

divergent /daɪ'vɜːdʒənt/ *a* divergente

diverse /daɪ'vɜːs/ *a* vario

diversify /daɪ'vɜːsɪfaɪ/ *vt/i* (*pt/pp* **-ied**) diversificare; *Comm* diversificare

diversion /daɪ'vɜːʃn/ *n* deviazione *f*; (*distraction*) diversivo *m*

diversionary /daɪ'vɜːʃənərɪ/ *a* ⟨*tactic, attack*⟩ diversivo

diversity /daɪ'vɜːsətɪ/ *n* varietà *f*

divert /daɪ'vɜːt/ *vt* deviare ⟨*traffic*⟩; distogliere ⟨*attention*⟩

divest /daɪ'vest/ *vt* privare (**of** di)

divide /dɪ'vaɪd/ *vt* dividere (**by** per); **six ~d by two** sei diviso due ● *vi* dividersi

■ **divide out** *vt* = **divide**

■ **divide up** *vt* = **divide**

dividend /'dɪvɪdend/ *n* dividendo *m*; **pay ~s** *fig* ripagare

divider /dɪ'vaɪdə(r)/ *n* (*in room*) divisorio *m*; (*in file*) cartoncino *m* separatore

dividers /dɪ'vaɪdəz/ *npl* compasso *m* a punte fisse

dividing /dɪ'vaɪdɪŋ/ *a* ⟨*wall, fence*⟩ divisorio

dividing line *n* linea *f* di demarcazione

divine /dɪ'vaɪn/ *a* divino

divinely /dɪ'vaɪnlɪ/ *adv* *also fam* divinamente

diving /'daɪvɪŋ/ *n* (*from board*) tuffi *mpl*; (*scuba*) immersione *f*

diving: diving board *n* trampolino *m*. **diving mask** *n* maschera *f* [subacquea]. **diving suit** *n* muta *f*; (*deep sea*) scafandro *m*

divinity /dɪ'vɪnətɪ/ *n* divinità *f* *inv*; (*subject*) teologia *f*; (*at school*) religione *f*

divisible /dɪ'vɪzəbl/ *a* divisibile (**by** per)

division /dɪ'vɪʒn/ *n* divisione *f*; (*in sports league*) serie *f*

divisional /dɪ'vɪʒənəl/ *a* ⟨*commander, officer*⟩ di divisione

divisive /dɪ'vaɪsɪv/ *a* ⟨*policy*⟩ che crea discordia; **be socially ~** creare delle divisioni sociali

divorce /dɪ'vɔːs/ *n* divorzio *m* ● *vt* divorziare da

divorced /dɪ'vɔːst/ *a* divorziato; **get ~** divorziare

divorcee /dɪvɔː'siː/ *n* divorziato, -a *mf*

divulge /daɪ'vʌldʒ/ *vt* rendere pubblico

■ **divvy up** *vt* *fam* = **divide up**

DIY *abbr* **do-it-yourself**

dizziness /'dɪzɪnɪs/ *n* giramenti *mpl* di testa

dizzy /'dɪzɪ/ *a* (**-ier, -iest**) vertiginoso; **I feel ~** mi gira la testa

DJ *n* *abbr* (**disc jockey**) DJ *m* *inv*; *Br abbr* (**dinner jacket**) smoking *m* *inv*

DNA *n* *abbr* (**deoxyribonucleic acid**) DNA *m* *inv* ● *attrib* ⟨*testing*⟩ del DNA

do /duː/ *n* (*pl* **dos** *or* **do's**) *fam* festa *f* ● *v* (*3 sg pres tense* **does**; *pt* **did**; *pp* **done**) ● *vt* fare; (*fam: cheat*) fregare; **do sb out of sth** (*money*) fregare qcsa a qcno; (*opportunity*) defraudare qcno di qcsa; **be done** *Culin* essere cotto; **well done** bravo; *Culin* ben cotto; **do the flowers** sistemare i fiori; **do the washing up** lavare i piatti; **do one's hair** farsi i capelli ● *vi* (*be suitable*) andare; (*be enough*) bastare; **this will do** questo va bene; **that will do!** basta così!; **do well/badly** cavarsela bene/male; **how is he doing?** come sta? ● *v aux* **do you speak Italian?** parli italiano?; **you don't like him, do you?** non ti piace, vero?; (*expressing agreement*) non dirmi che ti piace!; **yes, I do** sì; (*emphatic*) invece sì; **no, I don't** no; **I don't smoke** non fumo; **don't you/doesn't he?** vero?; **so do I** anch'io; **do come in, John** entra, John; **how do you do?** piacere

■ **do away with** *vt* abolire ⟨*rule*⟩
■ **do for** *vt* (*ruin*) rovinare
■ **do in** *vt* (*fam: kill*) uccidere; farsi male a ⟨*back*⟩; **done in** *fam* esausto
■ **do up** *vt* (*fasten*) abbottonare; (*renovate*) rimettere a nuovo; (*wrap*) avvolgere
■ **do with** *vt* **I could do with a spanner** mi ci vorrebbe una chiave inglese
■ **do without** *vt* fare a meno di

d.o.b. *abbr* (**date of birth**) data *f* di nascita
docile /'dəʊsaɪl/ *a* docile
dock¹ /dɒk/ *n Jur* banco *m* degli imputati
dock² *n Naut* bacino *m* ● *vi* entrare in porto; ⟨*spaceship:*⟩ congiungersi
docker /'dɒkə(r)/ *n* portuale *m*
docket /'dɒkɪt/ *n* (*Comm: label*) etichetta *f*; (*customs certificate*) ricevuta *f* doganale ● *vt Comm* etichettare ⟨*parcel, package*⟩
docking /'dɒkɪŋ/ *n Naut* ormeggio *m*; (*of spaceshuttle*) aggancio *m*
docks /dɒks/ *npl* porto *m*
dockworker /'dɒkwɜ:kə(r)/ *n* portuale *m*
dockyard /'dɒkjɑ:d/ *n* cantiere *m* navale
doctor /'dɒktə(r)/ *n* dottore *m*, dottoressa *f* ● *vt* alterare ⟨*drink*⟩; castrare ⟨*cat*⟩
doctorate /'dɒktərət/ *n* dottorato *m*
Doctor of Philosophy *n* titolare *mf* di un dottorato di ricerca
doctor's note /'dɒktəz/ *n* certificato *m* medico
doctrine /'dɒktrɪn/ *n* dottrina *f*
document /'dɒkjʊmənt/ *n* documento *m*
documentary /dɒkjʊ'mentərɪ/ *a* & *n* documentario *m*
documentation /dɒkjʊmen'teɪʃn/ *n* documentazione *f*
document holder *n* (*for keyboarder*) leggio *m*
document wallet *n* (*folder*) cartellina *f*
doddery /'dɒdərɪ/ *a fam* barcollante
doddle /'dɒd(ə)l/ *n Br fam* **it's a ~** è un gioco da ragazzi
dodge /dɒdʒ/ *n fam* trucco *m* ● *vt* schivare ⟨*blow*⟩; evitare ⟨*person*⟩ ● *vi* scansarsi; **~ out of the way** scansarsi
dodgems /'dɒdʒəmz/ *npl* autoscontro *msg*
dodgy /'dɒdʒɪ/ *a* (**-ier, -iest**) (*fam: dubious*) sospetto
DOE *n Br abbr* (**Department of the Environment**) ministero *m* dell'ambiente; *Am*

abbr (**Department of Energy**) ≈ ministero *m* dell'industria
doe /dəʊ/ *n* femmina *f* (*di daino, renna, lepre*); (*rabbit*) coniglia *f*
does /dʌz/ *see* **do**
doesn't /'dʌznt/ = **does not**
dog /dɒg/ *n* cane *m* ● *vt* (*pt/pp* **dogged**) ⟨*illness, bad luck:*⟩ perseguitare
dog: dog biscuit *n* biscotto *m* per cani. **dog breeder** *n* allevatore, -trice *mf* di cani. **dog collar** *n* collare *m* (*per cani*); *Relig fam* collare *m* del prete. **dog-eared** /-ɪəd/ *a* con le orecchie. **dog-end** *n fam* cicca *f*. **dogfight** *n* combattimento *m* di cani; *Aeron* combattimento *m* aereo
dogged /'dɒgɪd/ *a* ostinato
doggedly /'dɒgɪdlɪ/ *adv* ostinatamente
doggy bag /'dɒgɪ/ *n* sacchetto *m* per portarsi a casa gli avanzi di un pasto al ristorante
doggy-paddle *n fam* nuoto *m* a cagnolino
dog handler *n* addestratore, -trice *mf* di cani
doghouse /'dɒghaʊs/ *n Am* canile *m*; **in the ~** *Br & Am fam* in disgrazia
dogma /'dɒgmə/ *n* dogma *m*
dogmatic /dɒg'mætɪk/ *a* dogmatico
do-gooder /du:'gʊdə(r)/ *n pej* pseudo benefattore, -trice *mf*
dog: dog-paddle *n* nuoto *m* a cagnolino. **dogsbody** *n fam* tirapiedi *mf inv*. **dog tag** *n Am Mil fam* piastrina *f* di riconoscimento
doh /dəʊ/ *n Mus* do *m*
doily /'dɔɪlɪ/ *n* centrino *m*
doing /'du:ɪŋ/ *n* **it's none of my ~** non sono stato io; **this is her ~** questa è opera sua; **it takes some ~!** ce ne vuole!
do-it-yourself /du:ɪtjə'self/ *n* fai da te *m*, bricolage *m*
do-it-yourself shop *n* negozio *m* di bricolage
doldrums /'dɒldrəmz/ *npl* **be in the ~** essere giù di corda; ⟨*business:*⟩ essere in fase di stasi
dole /dəʊl/ *n* sussidio *m* di disoccupazione; **be on the ~** essere disoccupato
■ **dole out** *vt* distribuire
doleful /'dəʊlfl/ *a* triste
dolefully /'dəʊlfʊlɪ/ *adv* tristemente
dole queue *n Br* coda *f* per riscuotere il sussidio di disoccupazione; (*fig: number of unemployed*) numero *m* dei disoccupati
doll /dɒl/ *n* bambola *f*
■ **doll up** *vt fam* **~ oneself up** mettersi in ghingheri
dollar /'dɒlə(r)/ *n* dollaro *m*
dollar: dollar bill *n* banconota *f* da un dollaro. **dollar diplomacy** *n* politica *f* di investimenti all'estero. **dollar sign** *n* simbolo *m* del dollaro
dollop /'dɒləp/ *n fam* cucchiaiata *f*
dolly /'dɒlɪ/ *n* (*fam: doll*) bambola *f*; *Cinema, TV* dolly *m inv*
Dolomites /'dɒləmaɪts/ *npl* Dolomiti *mpl*
dolphin /'dɒlfɪn/ *n* delfino *m*
domain /də'meɪn/ *n* dominio *m*

dome /dəʊm/ n cupola f

domed /dəʊmd/ a ‹skyline, city› ricco di cupole; ‹roof, ceiling› a cupola; ‹forehead, helmet› bombato

domestic /də'mestɪk/ a domestico; Pol interno; Comm nazionale.

domestic animal n animale m domestico

domestic appliance n elettrodomestico m

domesticated /də'mestɪkeɪtɪd/ a ‹animal› addomesticato

domestic flight n volo m nazionale

domestic help n collaboratore, -trice mf familiare

domesticity /dɒme'stɪsəti/ n ‹home life› vita f di famiglia; ‹household duties› faccende fpl domestiche

domestic servant n domestico, -a mf

domiciliary /dɒmɪ'sɪlɪəri/ a ‹visit, care› a domicilio

dominance /'dɒmɪnəns/ n Biol, Zool dominanza f; ‹domination› predominio m; ‹numerical strength› preponderanza f

dominant /'dɒmɪnənt/ a dominante

dominate /'dɒmɪneɪt/ vt/i dominare

domination /dɒmɪ'neɪʃn/ n dominio m

domineering /dɒmɪ'nɪərɪŋ/ a autoritario

Dominican Republic /də'mɪnɪkən/ n Repubblica f Dominicana

dominion /də'mɪnjən/ n Br Pol dominion m inv

domino /'dɒmɪnəʊ/ n (pl -es) tessera f del domino; **~es** sg ‹game› domino m

don[1] /dɒn/ vt (pt/pp **donned**) liter indossare

don[2] n docente mf universitario, -a

donate /dəʊ'neɪt/ vt donare

donation /dəʊ'neɪʃn/ n donazione f

done /dʌn/ see **do**

donkey /'dɒŋki/ n asino m

donkey: donkey jacket n giacca f pesante. **donkey's years** fam **not for ~ ~** non da secoli. **donkey-work** n sgobbata f

donor /'dəʊnə(r)/ n donatore, -trice mf

donor card n tessera f del donatore di organi

don't /dəʊnt/ = **do not**

doodle /'du:dl/ vi scarabocchiare

doom /du:m/ n fato m; ‹ruin› rovina f ● vt **be ~ed to failure** essere destinato al fallimento

doomed /du:md/ a ‹vessel› destinato ad affondare

doomsday /'du:mzdeɪ/ n giorno m del giudizio

doomwatch /'du:mwɒtʃ/ n catastrofismo m

door /dɔː(r)/ n porta f; ‹of car› portiera f; **out of ~s** all'aperto

door: door bell n campanello m. **doorman** n portiere m. **doormat** n zerbino m. **door plate** n ‹of doctor etc› targa f. **doorstep** n gradino m della porta. **doorstop** n fermaporta m inv. **door-to-door** a ‹canvassing, selling› porta a porta ● adv ‹sell› porta a porta. **doorway** n vano m della porta

dope /dəʊp/ n fam ‹drug› droga f leggera; ‹information› indiscrezioni fpl; ‹idiot› idiota mf ● vt drogare; Sport dopare

dope test n Sport antidoping m inv

dopey /'dəʊpi/ a fam addormentato

dormant /'dɔːmənt/ a latente; ‹volcano› inattivo

dormer /'dɔːmə(r)/ n ~ [**window**] abbaino m

dormitory /'dɔːmɪtəri/ n dormitorio m

dormouse /'dɔːmaʊs/ n (pl **dormice** /'dɔː-maɪs/) ghiro m

dosage /'dəʊsɪdʒ/ n dosaggio m

dose /dəʊs/ n dose f

doss /dɒs/ vi sl accamparsi

■ **doss down** vi sistemarsi [a dormire]

dosser /'dɒsə(r)/ n barbone, -a mf

doss-house n dormitorio m pubblico

dot /dɒt/ n punto m; **at 8 o'clock on the ~** alle 8 in punto

dotage /'dəʊtɪdʒ/ n **be in one's ~** essere un vecchio rimbambito

dote /dəʊt/ vi **~ on** stravedere per

dot matrix [**printer**] n stampante f a matrice di punti

dotted /'dɒtɪd/ a ~ **line** linea f punteggiata; **sign on the ~ line** firmare nell'apposito spazio; **be ~ with** essere punteggiato di

dotty /'dɒti/ a (-**ier**, -**iest**) fam tocco; ‹idea› folle

double /'dʌbl/ a doppio ● adv cost ~ costare il doppio; **see ~** vedere doppio; **~ the amount** la quantità doppia ● n doppio m; ‹person› sosia m inv; **~s** pl Tennis doppio m; **at the ~** di corsa ● vt raddoppiare; ‹fold› piegare in due ● vi raddoppiare

■ **double back** vi ‹go back› fare dietro front

■ **double up** vi ‹bend over› piegarsi in due ‹with per›; ‹share› dividere una stanza

double: double act n Theat, fig numero m eseguito da due attori. **double-barrelled** /-'bærəld/ a ‹gun› a doppia canna. **double-barrelled surname** n cognome m doppio. **double-bass** n contrabbasso m. **double bed** n letto m matrimoniale. **double bend** n Auto doppia curva f. **double bill** n Theat rappresentazione f di due spettacoli. **double bluff** n atto m del dire la verità facendola sembrare una menzogna. **double-book** vi ‹hotel, airline, company:› fare prenotazioni doppie ● vt ~ **a room/seat etc** riservare la stessa camera/lo stesso posto a due persone. **double-breasted** a a doppio petto. **double-check** vt/i ricontrollare ● n **double check** ulteriore controllo m. **double chin** n doppio mento m. **double cream** n Br ≈ panna f densa. **double-cross** vt ingannare. **double cuff** n polsino m con risvolto. **double-dealing** n doppio gioco m ● a doppio. **double-decker** n autobus m inv a due piani. **double door**[**s**] n[pl] porta f a due battenti. **double Dutch** n fam ostrogoto m. **double-edged** /-'edʒd/ a also fig a doppio taglio. **double entendre** /du:blɒ'tɒdr(ə)/ n doppio senso m. **double entry book-keeping** n contabilità f in partita doppia. **double exposure** n Phot sovrimpressione f. **double fault** n Tennis doppio fallo m. **double feature** n Cinema proiezione f di due film con biglietto unico. **double-fronted** /-'frʌntɪd/ a ⟨house⟩ con due finestre ai lati della porta principale. **double glazing** n doppiovetro m. **double-jointed** a ⟨person, limb⟩ snodato. **double knitting** [**wool**] n lana f grossa. **double lock** vt chiudere a doppia mandata. **double-park** vt/i parcheggiare in doppia fila. **double-quick** adv rapidissimamente ● a **in ~ time** in un baleno. **double room** n camera f doppia. **double saucepan** n Br bagnomaria m inv. **double spacing** n Typ interlinea f doppia. **double spread** n Journ articolo m/pubblicità f su due pagine. **double standard** n **have ~ ~s** usare metri diversi. **double take** n **do a ~ ~** reagire a scoppio ritardato. **double talk** n pej discorso m ambiguo. **double time** n Am Mil marcia f forzata; **be paid ~ ~** ricevere doppia paga per lo straordinario. **double vision** n **have ~ ~** vederci doppio. **double whammy** n (fam: two bits of bad luck) sfortuna f doppia. **double yellow line[s]** n[pl] Br Aut due linee fpl gialle continue indicanti divieto di fermata e di sosta

doubly /'dʌblɪ/ adv doppiamente

doubt /daʊt/ n dubbio m ● vt dubitare di

doubtful /'daʊtful/ a dubbio; (having doubts) in dubbio

doubtfully /'daʊtfʊlɪ/ adv con aria dubbiosa

doubtless /'daʊtlɪs/ adv indubbiamente

douche /duːʃ/ n (Med: vaginal) irrigazione f

dough /dəʊ/ n pasta f; (for bread) impasto m; (fam: money) quattrini mpl

doughnut /'dəʊnʌt/ n bombolone m, krapfen m inv

dour /'dʊə(r)/ a ⟨mood, landscape⟩ cupo; ⟨person, expression⟩ arcigno; ⟨building⟩ austero

douse /daʊs/ vt spegnere

dove /dʌv/ n colomba f

dovecot[e] /'dʌvkɒt/ n colombaia f

dovetail /'dʌvteɪl/ n Techn incastro m a coda di rondine

dowdy /'daʊdɪ/ a (-ier, -iest) trasandato

down[1] /daʊn/ n (feathers) piumino m

down[2] adv giù; **go/come ~** scendere; **~ there** laggiù; **sales are ~** le vendite sono diminuite; **£50 ~** 50 sterline d'acconto; **~ 10%** ridotto del 10%; **~ with...!** abbasso...! ● prep **walk ~ the road** camminare per strada; **~ the stairs** giù per le scale; **fall ~ the stairs** cadere giù dalle scale; **get that ~ you!** fam butta giù!; **be ~ the pub** fam essere al pub ● vt bere tutto d'un fiato ⟨drink⟩; **~ tools** staccare; (in protest) interrompere il lavoro per protestare

down: **down-and-out** n spiantato, -a mf. **downbeat** a (pessimistic) pessimistico; (laidback) distaccato. **downcast** a abbattuto. **downfall** n caduta f; (of person) rovina f. **downgrade** vt (in seniority) degradare. **down-hearted** /-'hɑːtɪd/ a scoraggiato. **downhill** adv in discesa; **go ~** fig essere in declino. **downhill skiing** n sci m di fondo.

down-in-the-mouth a fam abbattuto. **download** vt Comput scaricare. **downmarket** a ⟨newspaper, programme⟩ rivolto al pubblico delle fasce basse; ⟨products⟩ dozzinale; ⟨area⟩ popolare; ⟨hotel, restaurant⟩ economico. **down payment** n deposito m. **downpipe** n Br tubo m di scolo. **downpour** n acquazzone m. **downright** a (absolute) totale; ⟨lie⟩ bell'e buono; ⟨idiot⟩ perfetto ● adv (completely) completamente

downs /daʊnz/ npl Br ⟨hills⟩ colline fpl di gesso nell'Inghilterra meridionale

downside /'daʊnsaɪd/ n svantaggio m

downside up a & adv Am sottosopra

Down's syndrome /'daʊnz/ n sindrome f di Down

down: downstairs adv al piano di sotto ● a del piano di sotto. **downstream** adv a valle. **down-to-earth** a ⟨person⟩ con i piedi per terra. **downtown** adv Am in centro. **downtrodden** /'daʊntrɒd(ə)n/ a oppresso. **downturn** n (in economy) fase f discendente; (in career) svolta f negativa. **down under** adv fam in Australia e/o Nuova Zelanda

downward[s] /'daʊnwəd[z]/ a verso il basso; ⟨slope⟩ in discesa ● adv verso il basso

downwind /daʊn'wɪnd/ adv sottovento

downy /'daʊnɪ/ a (-ier, -iest) coperto di peluria

dowry /'daʊrɪ/ n dote f

doz abbr (**dozen**) dozzina f

doze /dəʊz/ n sonnellino m ● vi sonnecchiare

■ **doze off** vi assopirsi

dozen /'dʌzn/ n dozzina f; **~s of books** libri a dozzine

DPhil n abbr (**Doctor of Philosophy**) titolare mf di un dottorato di ricerca

DPP n Br abbr (**Director of Public Prosecutions**) ≈ Procuratore m della Repubblica

Dr abbr (**doctor**) Dott. m, Dott.essa f; abbr (**drive**) ≈ via f

drab /dræb/ a ⟨colour⟩ spento; ⟨building⟩ tetro; ⟨life⟩ scialbo

draft[1] /drɑːft/ n abbozzo m; Comm cambiale f; Am Mil leva f ● vt abbozzare; Am Mil arruolare

draft[2] n Am = **draught**

drag /dræg/ n fam scocciatura f; **in ~** fam ⟨man⟩ travestito da donna ● vt (pt/pp **dragged**) trascinare; dragare ⟨river⟩

■ **drag on** vi ⟨time, meeting:⟩ trascinarsi

■ **drag out** vt tirare per le lunghe ⟨discussion⟩; **~ sth out of sb** tirar fuori qcsa a qcno con le pinze

■ **drag up** vt (mention unnecessarily) tirare in ballo

dragon /'drægən/ n drago m

dragonfly /'drægənflaɪ/ n libellula f

drag show n spettacolo m di travestiti

drain /dreɪn/ n tubo m di scarico; (grid) tombino m; **the ~s** le fognature; **be a ~ on sb's finances** prosciugare le finanze di qcno ● vt drenare ⟨land, wound⟩; scolare ⟨liquid, vegetables⟩; svuotare ⟨tank, glass, person⟩

● *vi* ~ [**away**] andar via; **leave sth to** ~ lasciare qcsa a scolare

drainage /'dreɪnɪdʒ/ *n* (*system*) drenaggio *m*; (*of land*) scolo *m*

draining board /'dreɪnɪŋ/ *n* scolapiatti *m inv*

drainpipe /'dreɪnpaɪp/ *n* tubo *m* di scarico

drainpipe trousers *npl* pantaloni *mpl* a tubo

drake /dreɪk/ *n* maschio *m* dell'anatra

drama /'drɑːmə/ *n* arte *f* drammatica; (*play*) opera *f* teatrale; (*event*) dramma *m*

dramatic /drə'mætɪk/ *a* drammatico

dramatically /drə'mætɪklɪ/ *adv* in modo drammatico

dramatics /drə'mætɪks/ *npl* arte *f* drammatica; *pej* atteggiamento *m* teatrale

dramatist /'dræmətɪst/ *n* drammaturgo, -a *mf*

dramatization /dræmətaɪ'zeɪʃn/ *n* (*for cinema*) adattamento *m* cinematografico; (*for stage*) adattamento *m* teatrale; (*for TV*) adattamento *m* televisivo; (*exaggeration*) drammatizzazione *f*

dramatize /'dræmətaɪz/ *vt* adattare per il teatro; *fig* drammatizzare

drank /dræŋk/ *see* **drink**

drape /dreɪp/ *n Am* tenda *f* ● *vt* appoggiare (**over** su)

drastic /'dræstɪk/ *a* drastico

drastically /'dræstɪklɪ/ *adv* drasticamente

draught /drɑːft/ *n* corrente *f* [d'aria]

draught beer *n* birra *f* alla spina

draught-proof *a* a tenuta d'aria ● *vt* tappare le fessure di

draughts /drɑːfts/ *n sg* (*game*) [gioco *m* della] dama *fsg*

draughtsman /'drɑːftsmən/ *n* disegnatore, -trice *mf*

draughty /'drɑːftɪ/ *a* pieno di correnti d'aria; **it's** ~ c'è corrente

draw /drɔː/ *n* (*attraction*) attrazione *f*; *Sport* pareggio *m*; (*in lottery*) sorteggio *m* ● *v* (*pt* **drew**, *pp* **drawn**) ● *vt* tirare; (*attract*) attirare; disegnare ⟨*picture*⟩; tracciare ⟨*line*⟩; ritirare ⟨*money*⟩; attingere ⟨*water*⟩; ~ **lots** tirare a sorte ● *vi* ⟨*tea:*⟩ essere in infusione; *Sport* pareggiare; ~ **near** avvicinarsi

■ **draw back** *vt* tirare indietro; ritirare ⟨*hand*⟩; tirare ⟨*curtains*⟩ ● *vi* ⟨*recoil*⟩ tirarsi indietro

■ **draw in** *vt* ritrarre ⟨*claws etc*⟩ ● *vi* ⟨*train:*⟩ arrivare; ⟨*days:*⟩ accorciarsi

■ **draw on** *vt* attingere a ⟨*savings, sb's experience*⟩

■ **draw out** *vt* (*pull out*) tirar fuori; ritirare ⟨*money*⟩ ● *vi* ⟨*train:*⟩ partire; ⟨*days:*⟩ allungarsi

■ **draw up** *vt* redigere ⟨*document*⟩; accostare ⟨*chair*⟩; ~ **oneself up** [**to one's full height**] drizzarsi ● *vi* (*stop*) fermarsi

drawback /'drɔːbæk/ *n* inconveniente *m*

drawbridge /'drɔːbrɪdʒ/ *n* ponte *m* levatoio

drawee *n* trattario *m*

drawer /drɔː(r)/ *n* cassetto *m*; *Fin* traente *mf*

drawing /'drɔːɪŋ/ *n* disegno *m*

drawing: drawing board *n* tavolo *m* da disegno; *fig* **go back to the** ~ ~ ricominciare da capo. **drawing pin** *n* puntina *f*. **drawing rights** *npl Fin* diritti *mf* di prelievo. **drawing room** *n* salotto *m*

drawl /drɔːl/ *n* pronuncia *f* strascicata

drawn /drɔːn/ *see* **draw**

dread /dred/ *n* terrore *m* ● *vt* aver il terrore di

dreadful /'dredfʊl/ *a* terribile

dreadfully /'dredfʊlɪ/ *adv* terribilmente

dream /driːm/ *n* sogno *m* ● *attrib* di sogno ● *vt/i* (*pt/pp* **dreamt** /dremt/ *or* **dreamed**) sognare (**about/of** di)

dreamer /'driːmə(r)/ *n* (*idealist*) sognatore, -trice *mf*; (*inattentive*) persona *f* con la testa fra le nuvole

dream-world *n* **live in a** ~ vivere tra le nuvole

dreamy /'driːmɪ/ *a fam* ⟨*house etc*⟩ di sogno; ⟨*person*⟩ che è un sogno; (*distracted*) distratto; ⟨*sound, music*⟩ dolce

dreary /'drɪərɪ/ *a* (**-ier, -iest**) tetro; (*boring*) monotono

dredge /dredʒ/ *vt/i* dragare

■ **dredge up** *vt* riesumare ⟨*the past*⟩

dredger /'dredʒə(r)/ *n* draga *f*

dregs /dregz/ *npl* feccia *fsg*

drench /drentʃ/ *vt* **get** ~**ed** inzupparsi

drenched /drentʃt/ *a* zuppo

dress /dres/ *n* (*woman's*) vestito *m*; (*clothing*) abbigliamento *m* ● *vt* vestire; (*decorate*) adornare; *Culin* condire; *Med* fasciare; ~ **oneself, get** ~**ed** vestirsi ● *vi* vestirsi

■ **dress up** *vi* mettersi elegante; (*in disguise*) travestirsi (**as** da)

dress: dress circle *n Theat* prima galleria *f*. **dress designer** *n* stilista *mf*

dresser /'dresə(r)/ *n* (*furniture*) credenza *f*; (*Am: dressing table*) toilette *f inv*

dressing /'dresɪŋ/ *n Culin* condimento *m*; *Med* fasciatura *f*

dressing: dressing down *n fam* sgridata *f*. **dressing gown** *n* vestaglia *f*. **dressing room** *n* (*in gym*) spogliatoio *m*; *Theat* camerino *m*. **dressing table** *n* toilette *f inv*

dress: dressmaker *n* sarta *f*. **dressmaking** *n* confezioni *fpl* (*per donna*). **dress rehearsal** *n* prova *f* generale. **dress sense** *n* **have** ~ ~ saper abbinare i capi d'abbigliamento

dressy /'dresɪ/ *a* (**-ier, -iest**) elegante

drew /druː/ *see* **draw**

dribble /'drɪbl/ *vi* gocciolare; ⟨*baby:*⟩ sbavare; *Sport* dribblare

dribs and drabs /'drɪbzən'dræbz/ *npl* **in** ~ alla spicciolata

dried /draɪd/ *a* ⟨*food*⟩ essiccato

drier /'draɪə(r)/ *n* asciugabiancheria *m inv*

drift /drɪft/ *n* movimento *m* lento; (*of snow*) cumulo *m*; (*meaning*) senso *m* ● *vi* (*off course*) andare alla deriva; ⟨*snow:*⟩ accumularsi; ⟨*fig: person:*⟩ procedere senza meta

■ **drift apart** *vi* ⟨*people:*⟩ allontanarsi l'uno dall'altro

drifter /'drɪftə(r)/ *n* persona *f* senza meta

driftwood /'drɪftwʊd/ *n* pezzi *mpl* di legno galleggianti

drill /drɪl/ *n* trapano *m*; *Mil* esercitazione *f* ● *vt* trapanare; *Mil* fare esercitare ● *vi Mil* esercitarsi; **~ for oil** trivellare in cerca di petrolio

drily /'draɪlɪ/ *adv* seccamente

drink /drɪŋk/ *n* bevanda *f*; (*alcoholic*) bicchierino *m*; **have a ~** bere qualcosa; **a ~ of water** un po' d'acqua ● *vt/i* (*pt* **drank**, *pp* **drunk**) bere

■ **drink to** *vt* (*toast*) brindare a

■ **drink up** *vt* finire ● *vi* finire il bicchiere

drinkable /'drɪŋkəbl/ *a* potabile

drink-driving *n Br* guida *f* in stato di ebbrezza

drinker /'drɪŋkə(r)/ *n* bevitore, -trice *mf*

drinking chocolate /'drɪŋkɪŋ/ *n Br* cioccolata *f* in polvere

drinking water *n* acqua *f* potabile

drink: drink problem *n Br* **he has a ~ ~** beve. **drinks cupboard** *n Br* mobile *m* bar. **drinks dispenser** *n Br* distributore *m* di bevande. **drinks machine** *n Br* distributore *m* di bevande. **drinks party** *n Br* cocktail *m inv*

drip /drɪp/ *n* gocciolamento *m*; (*drop*) goccia *f*; *Med* flebo *f inv*; (*fam: person*) mollaccione, -a *mf* ● *vi* (*pt/pp* **dripped**) gocciolare

drip-dry *a* lavare in stira

drip-feed *n* flebo[clisi] *f inv*

dripping /'drɪpɪŋ/ *n* (*from meat*) grasso *m* d'arrosto ● *a* ~ **[wet]** fradicio

drive /draɪv/ *n* (*in car*) giro *m*; (*entrance*) viale *m*; (*energy*) grinta *f*; *Psych* pulsione *f*; (*organized effort*) operazione *f*; *Techn* motore *m*; *Comput* lettore *m*, unità *f inv* ● *vt* (*pt* **drove** *pp* **driven**) ● *vt* portare ⟨*person by car*⟩; guidare ⟨*car*⟩; (*Sport: hit*) mandare; *Techn* far funzionare; **~ sb mad** far diventare matto qcno ● *vi* guidare

■ **drive at** *vt* **what are you driving at?** dove vuoi arrivare?

■ **drive away** *vt* portare via in macchina; (*chase*) cacciare ● *vi* andare via in macchina

■ **drive in** *vt* piantare ⟨*nail*⟩ ● *vi* arrivare [in macchina]

■ **drive off** *vt* portare via in macchina; (*chase*) cacciare ● *vi* andare via in macchina

■ **drive on** *vi* proseguire; **~ on!** avanti!

■ **drive up** *vi* arrivare (*in macchina*)

drive-in *a* ~ **cinema** cinema *m inv* drive-in

drivel /'drɪvl/ *n fam* sciocchezze *fpl*

driven /'drɪvn/ *see* **drive**

driver /'draɪvə(r)/ *n* guidatore, -trice *mf*; (*of train*) conducente *mf*

drive-through *n Am* drive-in *m inv*

driveway /'draɪvweɪ/ *n* strada *f* d'accesso

driving /'draɪvɪŋ/ *a* ⟨*rain*⟩ violento; ⟨*force*⟩ motore ● *n* guida *f*

driving: driving force *n* spinta *f*; (*person behind*) forza *f* trainante. **driving instructor** *n* istruttore, -trice *mf* di guida. **driving**

lesson *n* lezione *f* di guida. **driving licence** *n* patente *f* di guida. **driving mirror** *n* (*rearview*) specchietto *m* retrovisore. **driving school** *n* scuola *f* guida. **driving seat** *n* **be in the ~ ~** essere alla guida. **driving test** *n* esame *m* di guida; **take one's ~ ~** fare l'esame di guida

drizzle /'drɪzl/ *n* pioggerella *f* ● *vi* piovigginare

droll /drəʊl/ *a* divertente

drone /drəʊn/ *n* (*bee*) fuco *m*; (*sound*) ronzio *m*

■ **drone on** *vi* (*talk boringly*) tirarla per le lunghe

drool /druːl/ *vi* sbavare; **~ over sth/sb** *fig fam* sbavare per qcsa/qcno

droop /druːp/ *vi* abbassarsi; ⟨*flowers:*⟩ afflosciarsi

drop /drɒp/ *n* (*of liquid*) goccia *f*; (*fall*) caduta *f*; (*in price, temperature*) calo *m* ● *v* (*pt/pp* **dropped**) ● *vt* far cadere; sganciare ⟨*bomb*⟩; (*omit*) omettere; (*give up*) abbandonare; **~ the subject** cambiare discorso ● *vi* cadere; ⟨*price, temperature, wind:*⟩ calare; ⟨*ground:*⟩ essere in pendenza

■ **drop behind** *vi* rimanere indietro

■ **drop by** *vi* = **drop in**

■ **drop in** *vi* passare

■ **drop off** *vt* depositare ⟨*person*⟩ ● *vi* cadere; (*fall asleep*) assopirsi

■ **drop out** *vi* cadere; (*from race, society*) ritirarsi; **~ out of school** lasciare la scuola

drop handlebars *npl* manubrio *m* ricurvo

drop-out *n* persona *f* contro il sistema sociale

droppings /'drɒpɪŋz/ *npl* sterco *m*

drop shot *n Sport* drop shot *m inv*, smorzata *f*

drop zone *n* (*for supplies etc*) zona *f* di lancio

drought /draʊt/ *n* siccità *f*

drove /drəʊv/ *see* **drive**

droves /drəʊvz/ *npl* **in ~** in massa

drown /draʊn/ *vi* annegare ● *vt* annegare; coprire ⟨*noise*⟩; **he was ~ed** è annegato

drowse /draʊz/ *vi* sonnecchiare; (*be very sleepy*) essere sonnolento

drowsiness /'draʊzɪnɪs/ *n* sonnolenza *f*

drowsy /'draʊzɪ/ *a* sonnolento

drudgery /'drʌdʒərɪ/ *n* lavoro *m* pesante e noioso

drug /drʌg/ *n* droga *f*; *Med* farmaco *m*; **take ~s** drogarsi ● *vt* (*pt/pp* **drugged**) drogare

drug: drug abuse *n* abuso *m* di stupefacenti. **drug addict** *n* tossicomane, -a *mf*. **drug addiction** *n* tossicodipendenza *f*. **drug dealer** *n* spacciatore, -trice *mf* [di droga]

druggist /'drʌgɪst/ *n Am* farmacista *mf*

drug: Drug Squad *n Br* [squadra *f*] narcotici *f*. **drugs raid** *n* operazione *f* antidroga. **drugs ring** *n* rete *f* di narcotrafficanti. **drugstore** /'drʌgstɔː(r)/ *n Am* negozio *m* di generi vari, inclusi medicinali, che funge anche da bar; (*dispensing*) farmacia *f*. **drug-taking** *n* consumo *m* di stupefacenti; *Sport* doping *m inv*.

drug test *n Sport* antidoping *m inv.* **drug user** *n* tossicomane -a *mf*

drum /drʌm/ *n* tamburo *m*; (*for oil*) bidone *m*; **~s** *pl* (*in pop group*) batteria *f* ● *v* (*pt/pp* **drummed**) ● *vi* suonare il tamburo; (*in pop group*) suonare la batteria ● *vt* **~ sth into sb** *fam* ripetere qcsa a qcno cento volte; **~ one's fingers on the table** taburellare con le dita sul tavolo

drum kit *n* batteria *f*

drummer /'drʌmə(r)/ *n* percussionista *mf*; (*in pop group*) batterista *mf*

drumstick /'drʌmstɪk/ *n* bacchetta *f*; (*of chicken, turkey*) coscia *f*

drunk /drʌŋk/ *see* **drink** ● *a* ubriaco; **get ~** urbiacarsi ● *n* ubriaco, -a *mf*

drunkard /'drʌŋkəd/ *n* ubriacone, -a *mf*

drunken /'drʌŋkən/ *a* ubriaco

drunken driving *n* guida *f* in stato di ebbrezza

dry /draɪ/ *a* (**drier, driest**) asciutto; ⟨*climate, country*⟩ secco ● *vt/i* asciugare; **~ one's eyes** asciugarsi le lacrime

■ **dry out** *vi* ⟨*clothes:*⟩ asciugarsi; ⟨*alcoholic:*⟩ disintossicarsi

■ **dry up** *vi* seccarsi; ⟨*fig: source:*⟩ prosciugarsi; (*fam: be quiet*) stare zitto; (*do dishes*) asciugare i piatti

dry: dry cell *n* cella *f* a secco. **dry-clean** *vt* pulire a secco. **dry-cleaner's** *n* (*shop*) tintoria *f*

dryer /'draɪə/ *n* = **drier**

dry ice *n* ghiaccio *m* secco

drying-up /draɪŋ-'/ *n Br* **do the ~** asciugare i piatti

dryness /'draɪnɪs/ *n* secchezza *f*

dry rot *n* carie *f* del legno

DSS *n Br abbr* (**Department of Social Security**) (*local office*) ≈ Ufficio *m* della Previdenza Sociale; (*ministry*) ≈ Istituto *m* Nazionale della Previdenza Sociale

DTI *n Br abbr* (**Department of Trade and Industry**) ≈ Ministero *m* del Commercio e dell'Industria

DTP *n abbr* (**desktop publishing**) desktop publishing *m inv*

dual /'dju:əl/ *a* doppio

dual carriageway *n* strada *f* a due carreggiate

dual-purpose *a* a doppio uso

dub /dʌb/ *vt* (*pt/pp* **dubbed**) doppiare ⟨*film*⟩; (*name*) soprannominare

dubbing /'dʌbɪŋ/ *n* doppiaggio *m*

dubious /'dju:bɪəs/ *a* dubbio; **be ~ about** avere dei dubbi riguardo

dubiously /'dju:bɪəslɪ/ *adv* ⟨*look at*⟩ con aria dubbiosa; ⟨*say*⟩ con esitazione

Dublin /'dʌblɪn/ *n* Dublino *f*

duchess /'dʌtʃɪs/ *n* duchessa *f*

duck /dʌk/ *n* anatra *f* ● *vt* (*in water*) immergere; **~ one's head** abbassare la testa ● *vi* abbassarsi

■ **duck out of** *vt* sottrarsi a ⟨*task*⟩

duckling /'dʌklɪŋ/ *n* anatroccolo *m*

duct /dʌkt/ *n* condotto *m*; *Anat* dotto *m*

dud /dʌd/ *a Mil fam* disattivato; ⟨*coin*⟩ falso; ⟨*cheque*⟩ a vuoto ● *n fam* (*banknote*) banconota *f* falsa; (*Mil: shell*) granata *f* disattivata

due /dju:/ *a* dovuto; **be ~** ⟨*train:*⟩ essere previsto; **the baby is ~ next week** il bambino dovrebbe nascere la settimana prossima; **~ to** (*owing to*) a causa di; **be ~ to** (*causally*) essere dovuto a; **I'm ~ to...** dovrei...; **in ~ course** a tempo debito ● *adv* **~ north** direttamente a nord

duel /'dju:əl/ *n* duello *m*

dues /dju:z/ *npl* quota *f* [di iscrizione]

duet /dju:'et/ *n* duetto *m*

duffle coat /'dʌf(ə)l/ *n* montgomery *m inv*

dug /dʌg/ *see* **dig**

duke /dju:k/ *n* duca *m*

dull /dʌl/ *a* (*overcast, not bright*) cupo; (*not shiny*) opaco; ⟨*sound*⟩ soffocato; (*boring*) monotono; (*stupid*) ottuso ● *vt* interpidire ⟨*mind*⟩; attenuare ⟨*pain*⟩

dullness /'dʌlnɪs/ *n* (*of life*) monotonia *f*; (*of company, conversation*) noia *f*; (*no shine*) opacità *f*

dully /'dʌllɪ/ *adv* ⟨*say, repeat*⟩ monotonamente

duly /'dju:lɪ/ *adv* debitamente

dumb /dʌm/ *a* muto; (*fam: stupid*) ottuso

dumbfounded /dʌm'faʊndɪd/ *a* sbigottito

dummy /'dʌmɪ/ *n* (*tailor's*) manichino *m*; (*for baby*) succhiotto *m*; (*model*) riproduzione *f*

dummy run *n* (*trial*) prova *f*

dump /dʌmp/ *n* (*for refuse*) scarico *m*; (*fam: town*) mortorio *m*; **be down in the ~s** *fam* essere depresso ● *vt* scaricare; (*fam: put down*) lasciare; (*fam: get rid of*) liberarsi di

dumping /'dʌmpɪŋ/ *n Fin* dumping *m inv*, esportazione *f* sottocosto; **no ~** divieto *m* di scarico

dumpling /'dʌmplɪŋ/ *n* gnocco *m*

dumpy /'dʌmpɪ/ *a* (*plump*) tracagnotto

dunce /dʌns/ *n* zuccone, -a *mf*

dune /dju:n/ *n* duna *f*

dung /dʌŋ/ *n* sterco *m*

dungarees /dʌŋgə'ri:z/ *npl* tuta *fsg*

dungeon /'dʌndʒən/ *n* prigione *f* sotterranea

dunk /dʌŋk/ *vt* inzuppare

dunno /də'nəʊ/ *fam* (*I don't know*) boh

duo /'dju:əʊ/ *n* duo *m inv*; *Mus* duetto *m*

dupe /dju:p/ *n* zimbello *m* ● *vt* gabbare

duplicate¹ /'dju:plɪkət/ *a* doppio ● *n* duplicato *m*; (*document*) copia *f*; **in ~** in duplicato

duplicate² /'dju:plɪkeɪt/ *vt* fare un duplicato di; ⟨*research:*⟩ essere una ripetizione di ⟨*work*⟩

duplicator /'dju:plɪkeɪtə(r)/ *n* duplicatore *m*

duplicity /dju'plɪsətɪ/ *n* duplicità *f*, doppiezza *f*

durable /'djʊərəbl/ *a* resistente; durevole ⟨*basis, institution*⟩

duration /djʊə'reɪʃn/ *n* durata *f*

duress /djʊə'res/ *n* costrizione *f*; **under ~** sotto minaccia

during /'djʊərɪŋ/ *prep* durante

dusk /dʌsk/ *n* crepuscolo *m*

dusky /'dʌskɪ/ *a* ⟨complexion⟩ scuro

dust /dʌst/ *n* polvere *f* ● *vt* spolverare; (*sprinkle*) cospargere ⟨cake⟩ (**with** di) ● *vi* spolverare

dust: dustbin *n* pattumiera *f*. **dustbin man** *n Br* netturbino *m*. **dust-cart** *n* camion *m* della nettezza urbana. **dust cover** *n* (*on book*) sopraccoperta *f*; (*on furniture*) telo *m* di protezione

duster /'dʌstə(r)/ *n* strofinaccio *m*

dust: dust-jacket *n* sopraccoperta *f*. **dustman** *n* spazzino *m*. **dustpan** *n* paletta *f* per la spazzatura. **dust sheet** *n* (*on furniture*) telo *m* di protezione

dusty /'dʌstɪ/ *a* (**-ier, -iest**) polveroso

Dutch /dʌtʃ/ *a* olandese; **go ~** *fam* fare alla romana ● *n* (*language*) olandese *m*; **the ~** *pl* gli olandesi

Dutch courage *n* spavalderia *f* ispirata dall'alcool

Dutchman /'dʌtʃmən/ *n* olandese *m*

dutiable /'dju:tɪəbl/ *a* soggetto a imposta

dutiful /'dju:tɪfl/ *a* rispettoso

dutifully /'dju:tɪfʊlɪ/ *adv* a dovere

duty /'dju:tɪ/ *n* dovere *m*; (*task*) compito *m*; (*tax*) dogana *f*; **be on ~** essere di servizio

duty: duty chemist *n* farmacia *f* di turno. **duty-free** *a* esente da dogana ● *n* duty-free *m* inv. **duty-free allowance** *n* limite *m* d'acquisto di merci esenti da dogana. **duty roster, duty rota** *n* tabella *f* dei turni

duvet /'du:veɪ/ *n* piumone *m*

duvet cover *n Br* copripiumone *m*

dwarf /dwɔ:f/ *n* (*pl* **-s** *or* **dwarves**) nano, -a *mf* ● *vt* rimpicciolire

dwell /dwel/ *vi* (*pt/pp* **dwelt**) *liter* dimorare
■ **dwell on** *vt fig* soffermarsi su

dweller /'dwelə(r)/ *n* **city/town ~** cittadino, -a *mf*

dwelling /'dwelɪŋ/ *n* abitazione *f*

dwindle /'dwɪndl/ *vi* diminuire

dwindling /'dwɪndlɪŋ/ *a* ⟨strength, health⟩ in calo; ⟨resources, audience, interest⟩ in diminuzione

dye /daɪ/ *n* tintura *f* ● *vt* (*pres p* **dyeing**) tingere

dyed-in-the-wool /daɪdɪnðə'wʊl/ *a* inveterato

dying /'daɪɪŋ/ *see* **die²**

dyke /daɪk/ *n* (*to prevent flooding*) diga *f*; (*beside ditch*) argine *m*; (*Br: ditch*) canale *m* di scolo

dynamic /daɪ'næmɪk/ *a* dinamico

dynamics /daɪ'næmɪks/ *n* dinamica *fsg*

dynamism /daɪə'mɪzm/ *n* dinamismo *m*

dynamite /'daɪnəmaɪt/ *n* dinamite *f*

dynamo /'daɪnəməʊ/ *n* dinamo *f* inv

dynasty /'dɪnəstɪ/ *n* dinastia *f*

dysentery /'dɪsəntrɪ/ *n* dissenteria *f*

dyslexia /dɪs'leksɪə/ *n* dislessia *f*

dyslexic /dɪs'leksɪk/ *a* dislessico

e, E /i:/ *n* (*letter*) e, E *f* inv; *Mus* mi *m*

E *abbr* (**east**) E

each /i:tʃ/ *a* ogni ● *pron* ognuno; **£1 ~** una sterlina ciascuno; **they love/hate ~ other** si amano/odiano; **we lend ~ other money** ci prestiamo i soldi; **bet on a horse ~ way** puntare su un cavallo piazzato e vincente

eager /'i:gə(r)/ *a* ansioso (**to do** di fare); ⟨pupil⟩ avido di sapere

eager beaver *n fam* **be an ~ ~** essere pieno di zelo

eagerly /'i:gəlɪ/ *adv* ⟨wait⟩ ansiosamente; ⟨offer⟩ premurosamente

eagerness /'i:gənɪs/ *n* premura *f*

eagle /'i:gl/ *n* aquila *f*

eagle-eyed /'-aɪd/ *a* ⟨sharp-eyed⟩ che ha un occhio di falco

ear /ɪə(r)/ *n* orecchio *m*; (*of corn*) spiga *f*

earache /'ɪəreɪk/ *n* mal *m* d'orecchi

eardrum /'ɪədrʌm/ *n* timpano *m*

earl /ɜ:l/ *n* conte *m*

ear lobe *n* lobo *m* dell'orecchio

early /'ɜ:lɪ/ *a* (**-ier, -iest**) (*before expected time*) in anticipo; ⟨spring⟩ prematuro; ⟨reply⟩ pronto; ⟨works, writings⟩ primo; **be here ~!** sii puntuale!; **you're ~!** sei in anticipo!; **~ morning walk** passeggiata *f* mattutina; **in the ~ morning** la mattina presto; **in the ~ spring** all'inizio della primavera; **~ retirement** prepensionamento *m* ● *adv* presto; (*ahead of time*) in anticipo; **~ in the morning** la mattina presto

early warning *n* **come as an ~ ~ of sth** essere il segno premonitore di qcsa

early warning system *n Mil* sistema *m* d'allarme avanzato

earmark /'ɪəmɑ:k/ *vt* riservare (**for** a)

earmuffs /'ɪəmʌfs/ *npl* paraorecchie *m* inv

earn /ɜ:n/ *vt* guadagnare; (*deserve*) meritare

earned income /ɜ:nd/ *n* reddito *m* da lavoro

earner /'ɜ:nə(r)/ *n* (*person*) persona *f* che guadagna; **the main [revenue] ~** la principale fonte di sostentamento; **a nice little ~** *fam* un'ottima fonte di guadagno

earnest /'ɜ:nɪst/ *a* serio ● *n* **in ~** sul serio

earnestly /'ɜːnɪstlɪ/ *adv* con aria seria

earning power /'ɜːnɪŋ/ *n* (*of person*) capacità *f* di guadagno; (*of company*) redditività *f* *inv*

earnings /'ɜːnɪŋz/ *npl* guadagni *mpl*; (*salary*) stipendio *m*

ear nose and throat department *n* reparto *m* otorinolaringoiatrico

ear: earphones *npl* cuffia *fsg*. **earplug** *n* (*for noise*) tappo *m* per le orecchie. **ear-ring** *n* orecchino *m*. **earshot** *n* **within ~** a portata d'orecchio; **he is out of ~** non può sentire. **ear-splitting** /'ɪəsplɪtɪŋ/ *a* 〈*scream, shout*〉 lacerante

earth /ɜːθ/ *n* terra *f*; (*of fox*) tana *f*; **where/what on ~?** dove/che diavolo? ● *vt Electr* mettere a terra

earthenware /'ɜːθnweə/ *n* terraglia *f*

earthly /'ɜːθlɪ/ *a* terrestre; **be no ~ use** *fam* essere perfettamente inutile

earth: earthquake *n* terremoto *m*. **earth sciences** *npl* scienze *fpl* della terra. **earthshaking** *a* *fam* 〈*news*〉 sconvolgente; 〈*experience*〉 travolgente. **earth tremor** *n* scossa *f* sismica. **earthwork** *n* (*embankment*) terrapieno *m*; (*excavation work*) lavori *mpl* di scavo. **earthworm** *n* lombrico *m*

earthy /'ɜːθɪ/ *a* terroso; (*coarse*) grossolano

earwax /'ɪəwæks/ *n* cerume *m*

earwig /'ɪəwɪg/ *n* forbicina *f*

ease /iːz/ *n* **at ~** a proprio agio; **at ~!** *Mil* riposo!; **ill at ~** a disagio; **with ~** con facilità ● *vt* calmare 〈*pain*〉; alleviare 〈*tension, shortage*〉; (*slow down*) rallentare; (*loosen*) allentare ● *vi* 〈*pain, situation, wind:*〉 calmarsi

■ **ease off** *vi* 〈*pain, pressure, tension:*〉 attenuarsi ● *vt* (*remove gently*) togliere con delicatezza

■ **ease up** *vi* = **ease off**

easel /'iːzl/ *n* cavalletto *m*

easily /'iːzɪlɪ/ *adv* con facilità; **~ the best** certamente il meglio

east /iːst/ *n* est *m*; **to the ~ of** a est di ● *a* dell'est ● *adv* verso est

east: East Africa *n* Africa *f* orientale. **East Berlin** *n* Berlino *f* Est. **eastbound** *a* 〈*carriageway, traffic:*〉 diretto a est. **East End** *n* quartiere *m* nella zona est di Londra

Easter /'iːstə(r)/ *n* Pasqua *f*

Easter: Easter egg *n* uovo *m* di Pasqua; **Easter Monday** *n* lunedì *m* dell'Angelo, Pasquetta *f*. **Easter Sunday** *n* [domenica *f* di] Pasqua *f*

easterly /'iːstəlɪ/ *a* da levante

eastern /'iːstən/ *a* orientale

Eastern block *n* paesi *mpl* dell'est

east: East German *n* *Pol* tedesco, -a *mf* dell'est. **East Germany** *n* *Pol* Germania *f* est. **East Indies** *npl* Indie *fpl* orientali

eastward[s] /'iːstwəd[z]/ *adv* verso est

easy /'iːzɪ/ *a* (**-ier, -iest**) facile; **take it** *or* **things ~** prendersela con calma; **take it ~!** (*don't get excited*) calma!; **go ~ with** andarci piano con

easy: easy-care *a* facilmente lavabile. **easy**

chair *n* poltrona *f*. **easy-going** *a* conciliante; **too ~** troppo accomodante. **easy money** *n* facili guadagni *mpl*. **easy terms** *npl* facilitazioni *fpl* di pagamento

eat /iːt/ *vt/i* (*pt* **ate**, *pp* **eaten**) mangiare

■ **eat into** *vt* intaccare

■ **eat out** *vi* mangiar fuori

■ **eat up** *vt* mangiare tutto 〈*food*〉; *fig* inghiottire 〈*profits*〉

eatable /'iːtəbl/ *a* mangiabile

eater /'iːtə(r)/ *n* (*apple*) mela *f* da tavola; **be a big ~** 〈*person:*〉 essere una buona forchetta; **he's a fast ~** mangia sempre in fretta

eatery /'iːtərɪ/ *n* *fam* tavola *f* calda

eating /'iːtɪŋ/: **eating apple** *n* mela *f* non da cuocere. **eating disorder** *n* disoressia *f*. **eating habits** *npl* abitudini *fpl* alimentari

eau-de-Cologne /əʊdəkə'ləʊn/ *n* acqua *f* di Colonia

eaves /iːvz/ *npl* cornicione *msg*

eavesdrop /'iːvzdrɒp/ *vi* (*pt/pp* **~dropped**) origliare; **~ on** ascoltare di nascosto

ebb /eb/ *n* (*tide*) riflusso *m*; **at a low ~** *fig* a terra ● *vi* rifluire; *fig* declinare

ebony /'ebənɪ/ *n* ebano *m*

EBRD *n* *abbr* (**European Bank for Reconstruction and Development**) BERS *f*

ebullient /ɪ'bʌlɪənt/ *a* esuberante

EC *n* *abbr* (**European Community**) CE *f*

eccentric /ek'sentrɪk/ *a* & *n* eccentrico, -a *mf*

eccentricity /eksen'trɪsətɪ/ *n* eccentricità *f* *inv*

ecclesiastical /ɪkliːzɪ'æstɪkl/ *a* ecclesiastico

ECG *n* *abbr* (**electrocardiogram; electrocardiograph**) ECG

echo /'ekəʊ/ *n* (*pl* **-es**) eco *f* or *m* ● *v* (*pt/pp* **echoed**, *pres p* **echoing**) ● *vt* echeggiare; ripetere 〈*words*〉 ● *vi* risuonare (**with** di)

eclectic /ɪ'klektɪk/ *n* eclettico

eclipse /ɪ'klɪps/ *n* *Astr* eclissi *f* *inv* ● *vt* *fig* eclissare

eco+ /'iːkəʊ/ *pref* eco+

eco-friendly *a* che rispetta l'ambiente

ecological /iːkə'lɒdʒɪkl/ *a* ecologico

ecologist /ɪ'kɒlədʒɪst/ *n* ecologo, -a *mf* ● *a* ecologico

ecology /ɪ'kɒlədʒɪ/ *n* ecologia *f*

economic /iːkə'nɒmɪk/ *a* economico

economical /iːkə'nɒmɪkl/ *a* economico

economically /iːkə'nɒmɪklɪ/ *adv* economicamente; (*thriftily*) in economia; **~ priced** a prezzo economico

economic analyst *n* analista *mf* economico,-a

economics /iːkə'nɒmɪks/ *n* economia *f*

economist /ɪ'kɒnəmɪst/ *n* economista *mf*

economize /ɪ'kɒnəmaɪz/ *vi* economizzare (**on** su)

economy /ɪ'kɒnəmɪ/ *n* economia *f*

economy: economy class *n* *Aeron* classe *f* turistica. **economy drive** *n* campagna *f* di risparmio. **economy pack, economy size** *n* confezione *f* economica *inv*

ecosystem /ˈiːkəʊsɪstəm/ n ecosistema m

ecstasy /ˈekstəsɪ/ n estasi f inv; (drug) ecstasy f

ecstatic /ɪkˈstætɪk/ a estatico

ecstatically /ɪkˈstætɪklɪ/ adv estaticamente

ectopic pregnancy /ekˈtɒpɪk/ n gravidanza f extrauterina

ecu /ˈeɪkjuː/ n ecu m inv

Ecuador /ˈekwədɔː(r)/ n Ecuador m

ecumenical /iːkjʊˈmenɪkl/ a ecumenico

eczema /ˈeksɪmə/ n eczema m

eddy /ˈedɪ/ n vortice m

Eden /ˈiːd(ə)n/ n eden m, paradiso m terrestre

edge /edʒ/ n bordo m; (of knife) filo m; (of road) ciglio m; **on ~** con i nervi tesi; **have the ~ on** fam avere un vantaggio su ● vt bordare

■ **edge forward** vi avanzare lentamente

edgeways /ˈedʒweɪz/ adv di fianco; **I couldn't get a word in ~** non ho potuto infilare neanche mezza parola nel discorso

edging /ˈedʒɪŋ/ n bordo m

edgy /ˈedʒɪ/ a nervoso

edible /ˈedəbl/ a commestibile; **this pizza's not ~** questa pizza è immangiabile

edict /ˈiːdɪkt/ n editto m

edifice /ˈedɪfɪs/ n edificio m

edify /ˈedɪfaɪ/ vt (pt/pp -ied) edificare

edifying /ˈedɪfaɪɪŋ/ a edificante

Edinburgh /ˈedɪmb(ə)rə/ n Edimburgo f

edit /ˈedɪt/ vt (pt/pp edited) far la revisione di ⟨text⟩; curare l'edizione di ⟨anthology, dictionary⟩; dirigere ⟨newspaper⟩; montare ⟨film⟩; editare ⟨tape⟩; **~ed by** ⟨book⟩ a cura di

■ **edit out** vt tagliare

edition /ɪˈdɪʃn/ n edizione f

editor /ˈedɪtə(r)/ n (of anthology, dictionary) curatore, -trice mf; (of newspaper) redattore, -trice mf; (of film) responsabile mf del montaggio

editorial /edɪˈtɔːrɪəl/ a redazionale ● n Journ editoriale m

educate /ˈedjʊkeɪt/ vt istruire; educare ⟨public, mind⟩; **be ~d at Eton** essere educato a Eton

educated /ˈedjʊkeɪtɪd/ a istruito

education /edjʊˈkeɪʃn/ n istruzione f; (culture) cultura f, educazione f

educational /edjʊˈkeɪʃnəl/ a istruttivo; ⟨visit⟩ educativo; ⟨publishing⟩ didattico

educationalist /edjʊˈkeɪʃnəlɪst/ n studioso, -a mf di pedagogia

educationally /edjʊˈkeɪʃnəlɪ/ adv ⟨disadvantaged, privileged⟩ dal punto di vista degli studi; ⟨useless, useful⟩ dal punto di vista didattico

educational: educational psychology n psicopedagogia f, psicologia f dell'educazione. **educational television** n televisione f scolastica

education: education authority n Br autorità fpl scolastiche. **education committee** n Br consiglio m scolastico. **education de-**

partment n Br ministero m della pubblica istruzione; (in local government) provveditorato m agli studi; (in university) istituto m di pedagogia

educative /ˈedjʊkətɪv/ a educativo, istruttivo

educator /ˈedjʊkeɪtə(r)/ n educatore, -trice mf

Edwardian /edˈwɔːdɪən/ n del regno di Edoardo VII

EEC n abbr (**European Economic Community**) CEE f ● attrib ⟨policy, directive⟩ della CEE

eel /iːl/ n anguilla f

eerie /ˈɪərɪ/ a (**-ier, -iest**) inquietante

efface /ɪˈfeɪs/ vt cancellare

effect /ɪˈfekt/ n effetto m; **in ~** in effetti; **take ~** ⟨law:⟩ entrare in vigore; ⟨medicine:⟩ fare effetto ● vt effettuare

effective /ɪˈfektɪv/ a efficace; (striking) che colpisce; (actual) di fatto; **~ from** in vigore a partire da

effectively /ɪˈfektɪvlɪ/ adv efficacemente; (actually) di fatto

effectiveness /ɪˈfektɪvnɪs/ n efficacia f

effeminate /ɪˈfemɪnət/ a effeminato

effervescent /efəˈvesnt/ a effervescente

effete /ɪˈfiːt/ a ⟨person⟩ senza nerbo; ⟨civilization⟩ che ha fatto il suo tempo

efficacious /efɪˈkeɪʃəs/ a efficace

efficacy /ˈefɪkəsɪ/ n efficacia f

efficiency /ɪˈfɪʃənsɪ/ n efficienza f; (of machine) rendimento m

efficient /ɪˈfɪʃənt/ a efficiente

efficiently /ɪˈfɪʃəntlɪ/ adv efficientemente

effigy /ˈefɪdʒɪ/ n effigie f

effluent /ˈeflʊənt/ n (waste) refluo m; (river) emissario m ● attrib ⟨treatment, management⟩ dei reflui

effort /ˈefət/ n sforzo m; **make an ~** sforzarsi

effortless /ˈefətlɪs/ a facile

effortlessly /ˈefətlɪslɪ/ adv con facilità

effrontery /ɪˈfrʌntərɪ/ n sfrontatezza f

effusion /ɪˈfjuːʒn/ n (emotional) effusione f

effusive /ɪˈfjuːsɪv/ a espansivo; ⟨speech⟩ caloroso

EFL n abbr (**English as a Foreign Language**) EFL m ● attrib ⟨teacher, course⟩ di inglese come lingua straniera

EFT n abbr **electronic funds transfer**

EFTA /ˈeftə/ n abbr (**European Free Trade Association**) EFTA f

e.g. abbr (**exempli gratia**) per es.

egalitarian /ɪɡælɪˈteərɪən/ a egalitario

egg /eg/ n uovo m

■ **egg on** vt fam incitare

egg: egg box n cartone m di uova. **eggcup** n portauovo m inv. **egg custard** n crema f pasticciera. **egghead** n pej fam intellettuale mf. **eggplant** n Am melanzana f. **egg-shaped** /ˈegʃeɪpt/ a ovale. **eggshell** n guscio m d'uovo. **egg-timer** n clessidra f per misurare il tempo di cottura delle uova. **egg whisk** n frusta *f*. **egg white** *n* albume *m*, bianco *m* d'uovo. **egg yolk** *n* tuorlo *m*, rosso *m* d'uovo

ego /'i:gəʊ/ *n* ego *m*

egocentric /i:gəʊ'sentrɪk/ *a* egocentrico

egoism /'egəʊɪzm/ *n* egoismo *m*

egoist /'egəʊɪst/ *n* egoista *mf*

egotism /'egəʊtɪzm/ *n* egotismo *m*

egotist /'egəʊtɪst/ *n* egotista *mf*

Egypt /'i:dʒɪpt/ *n* Egitto *m*

Egyptian /ɪ'dʒɪpʃn/ *a & n* egiziano, -a *mf*

eiderdown /'aɪdədaʊn/ *n* (*quilt*) piumino *m*

eight /eɪt/ *a & n* otto *m*

eighteen /eɪ'ti:n/ *a & n* diciotto *m*

eighteenth /eɪ'ti:nθ/ *a & n* diciottesimo, -a *mf*

eighth /eɪtθ/ *a & n* ottavo, -a *mf*

eightieth /'eɪtɪɪθ/ *a & n* ottantesimo, -a *mf*

eighty /'eɪtɪ/ *a & n* ottanta *m*

Eire /'eərə/ *n* Repubblica *f* d'Irlanda

either /'aɪðə(r)/ *a & pron* ~ [of them] l'uno o l'altro; **I don't like** ~ [of them] non mi piace né l'uno né l'altro; **on** ~ **side** da tutte e due le parti ● *adv* **I don't** ~ nemmeno io; **I don't like John or his brother** ~ non mi piace John e nemmeno suo fratello ● *conj* ~ **John or his brother will be there** ci saranno o John o suo fratello; **I don't like** ~ **John or his brother** non mi piacciono né John né suo fratello; ~ **you go to bed or** [**else**]... o vai a letto o [altrimenti]...

ejaculate /ɪ'dʒækjʊleɪt/ *vi* eiaculare ● *vt* (*exclaim*) prorompere

ejaculation /ɪdʒækjʊleɪʃn/ *n* eiaculazione *f*; (*exclamation*) esclamazione *f*

eject /ɪ'dʒekt/ *vt* eiettare 〈*pilot*〉; espellere 〈*tape, drunk*〉

ejection /ɪ'dʒekʃn/ *n* (*of gases, waste, troublemaker*) espulsione *f*; (*of lava*) emissione *f*; *Aeron* eiezione *f*

eke /i:k/ *vt* ~ **out** far bastare; (*increase*) arrotondare; ~ **out a living** arrangiarsi

elaborate¹ /ɪ'læbərət/ *a* elaborato

elaborate² /ɪ'læbəreɪt/ *vi* entrare nei particolari (**on** di)

elaborately /ɪ'læbərətlɪ/ *adv* in modo elaborato

elaboration /ɪlæbə'reɪʃn/ *n* (*of plan, theory*) elaborazione *f*

elapse /ɪ'læps/ *vi* trascorrere

elastic /ɪ'læstɪk/ *a* elastico ● *n* elastico *m*

elasticated /ɪ'læstɪkeɪtɪd/ *a* 〈*waistband, bandage*〉 elastico; 〈*material*〉 elasticizzato

elastic band *n* elastico *m*

elasticity /ɪlæs'tɪsətɪ/ *n* elasticità *f*

elated /ɪ'leɪtɪd/ *a* esultante

elation /ɪ'leɪʃn/ *n* euforia *f*

elbow /'elbəʊ/ *n* gomito *m*

elbow grease *n fam* olio *m* di gomito

elbow room *n* (*room to move*) spazio *m* vitale; **there isn't much** ~~ **in this kitchen** si è un po' allo stretto in questa cucina

elder¹ /'eldə(r)/ *n* (*tree*) sambuco *m*

elder² *a* maggiore ● *n* **the** ~ il/la maggiore

elderberry /'eldəbərɪ/ *n* baca *f* di sambuco

elderly /'eldəlɪ/ *a* anziano

elder statesman *n* decano *m* della politica

eldest /'eldɪst/ *a* maggiore ● *n* **the** ~ il/la maggiore

elect /ɪ'lekt/ *a* **the president** ~ il futuro presidente ● *vt* eleggere; ~ **to do sth** decidere di fare qcsa

election /ɪ'lekʃn/ *n* elezione *f*

electioneering /ɪ'lekʃənɪərɪŋ/ *n* (*campaigning*) propaganda *f* elettorale; *pej* elettoralismo *m*

elective /ɪ'lektɪv/ *a* 〈*office, official*〉 elettivo, eletto; (*empowered to elect*) elettorale; *Sch, Univ* facoltativo; ~ **surgery** interventi *mpl* chirurgici facoltativi

elector /ɪ'lektə(r)/ *n* elettore, -trice *mf*

electoral /ɪ'lektərəl/ *a* elettorale

electoral roll *n* liste *fpl* elettorali

electorate /ɪ'lektərət/ *n* elettorato *m*

electric /ɪ'lektrɪk/ *a* elettrico

electrical /ɪ'lektrɪkl/ *a* elettrico

electrical engineer *n* elettrotecnico *m*

electrical engineering *n* elettrotecnica *f*

electrically /ɪ'lektrɪk(ə)lɪ/ *adv* ~ **driven** [a motore] elettrico

electric blanket *n* termocoperta *f*

electric fire *n* stufa *f* elettrica

electrician /ɪlek'trɪʃn/ *n* elettricista *m*

electricity /ɪlek'trɪsətɪ/ *n* elettricità *f*

electricity board *n Br* azienda *f* elettrica

electricity supply *n* alimentazione *f* elettrica

electric shock *n* **get an** ~ ~ prendere la scossa

electric storm *n* temporale *m*

electrify /ɪ'lektrɪfaɪ/ *vt* (*pt/pp* **-ied**) elettrificare; *fig* elettrizzare

electrifying /ɪ'lektrɪfaɪɪŋ/ *a fig* elettrizzante

electrocute /ɪ'lektrəkju:t/ *vt* fulminare; (*execute*) giustiziare sulla sedia elettrica

electrocution /ɪlektrə'kju:ʃn/ *n* elettrocuzione *f*

electrode /ɪ'lektrəʊd/ *n* elettrodo *m*

electrolysis /ɪlek'trɒlɪsɪs/ *n* *Chem* elettrolisi *f*; (*hair removal*) depilazione *f* diatermica

electron /ɪ'lektrɒn/ *n* elettrone *m*

electronic /ɪlek'trɒnɪk/ *a* elettronico

electronic: electronic banking *n* servizi *mpl* bancari telematici. **electronic engineer** *n* tecnico *m* elettronico; (*with diploma*) perito *m* elettronico; (*with degree*) ingegnere *m* elettronico. **electronic engineering** *n* ingegneria *f* elettronica. **electronic eye** *n* cellula *f* fotoelettrica. **electronic funds transfer** *n* sistemi *mpl* telematici di trasferimento fondi. **electronic mail** *n* posta *f* elettronica

electronics /ɪlek'trɒnɪks/ *n* elettronica *f*

electro-shock therapy, electro-shock treatment /ɪ'lektrəʊ-/ *n* terapia *f* elettroshock

elegance /'elɪgəns/ *n* eleganza *f*

elegant /'elɪgənt/ *a* elegante

elegantly /'elɪgəntlɪ/ *adv* elegantemente

elegy /'elɪdʒɪ/ *n* elegia *f*

element /'elɪmənt/ *n* elemento *m*
elementary /elɪ'mentərɪ/ *a* elementare
elephant /'elɪfənt/ *n* elefante *m*
elephantine /elɪ'fæntaɪn/ *a* ⟨person⟩ mastodontico
elevate /'elɪveɪt/ *vt* elevare
elevation /elɪ'veɪʃn/ *n* elevazione *f*; (*height*) altitudine *f*; (*angle*) alzo *m*
elevator /'elɪveɪtə(r)/ *n Am* ascensore *m*
eleven /ɪ'levn/ *a* & *n* undici *m*
eleven plus *n* (*formerly*) esame *m di ammissione alla scuola secondaria inglese*
elevenses /ɪ'levənzɪz/ *n Br fam* pausa *f* per il caffè (*a metà mattina*)
eleventh /ɪ'levənθ/ *a* & *n* undicesimo, -a *mf*; **at the ~ hour** *fam* all'ultimo momento
elf /elf/ *n* (*pl* **elves**) elfo *m*
elicit /ɪ'lɪsɪt/ *vt* ottenere
eligible /'elɪdʒəbl/ *a* eleggibile; **~ young man** buon partito; **be ~ for** aver diritto a
eliminate /ɪ'lɪmɪneɪt/ *vt* eliminare
elimination /ɪlɪmɪ'neɪʃn/ *n* eliminazione *f*; **by a process of ~** procedendo per eliminazione
élite /eɪ'liːt/ *n* fior fiore *m*
élitist /ɪ'liːtɪst/ *a* elitista
ellipse /ɪ'lɪps/ *n* ellisse *f*
elliptical /ɪ'lɪptɪk(ə)l/ *a also fig* ellittico
elm /elm/ *n* olmo *m*
elocution /elə'kjuːʃn/ *n* elocuzione *f*
elongate /'iːlɒŋɡeɪt/ *vt* allungare
elope /ɪ'ləʊp/ *vi* fuggire [per sposarsi]
elopement /ɪ'ləʊpmənt/ *n* fuga *f* romantica
eloquence /'eləkwəns/ *n* eloquenza *f*
eloquent /'eləkwənt/ *a* eloquente
eloquently /'eləkwəntlɪ/ *adv* con eloquenza
El Salvador /el'sælvədɔː(r)/ *n* El Salvador *m*; **in ~ ~** nel Salvador
else /els/ *adv* altro; **who ~?** e chi altro?; **he did of course, who ~?** l'ha fatto lui e chi, se no?; **nothing ~** nient'altro; **or ~** altrimenti; **someone ~** qualcun altro; **somewhere ~** da qualche altra parte; **anyone ~** chiunque altro; (*as question*) nessun'altro?; **anything ~** qualunque altra cosa; (*as question*) altro?
elsewhere /els'weə(r)/ *adv* altrove
elucidate /ɪ'luːsɪdeɪt/ *vt* delucidare
elude /ɪ'luːd/ *vt* eludere; (*avoid*) evitare; **the name ~s me** il nome mi sfugge
elusive /ɪ'luːsɪv/ *a* elusivo
emaciated /ɪ'meɪsɪeɪtɪd/ *a* emaciato
e-mail *n* e-mail *f*, posta *f* elettronica ● *vt* spedire per e-mail
e-mail address *n* indirizzo *m* di posta elettronica
emanate /'eməneɪt/ *vi* emanare
emancipated /ɪ'mænsɪpeɪtɪd/ *a* emancipato
emancipation /ɪmænsɪ'peɪʃn/ *n* emancipazione *f*; (*of slaves*) liberazione *f*
emasculate /ɪ'mæskjʊleɪt/ *vt* evirare; *fig* svigorire
embalm /ɪm'bɑːm/ *vt* imbalsamare
embankment /ɪm'bæŋkmənt/ *n* argine *m*; *Rail* massicciata *f*
embargo /em'bɑːɡəʊ/ *n* (*pl* **-es**) embargo *m*

embark /ɪm'bɑːk/ *vi* imbarcarsi; **~ on** intraprendere
embarkation /embɑː'keɪʃn/ *n* imbarco *m*
embarrass /em'bærəs/ *vt* imbarazzare
embarrassed /em'bærəst/ *a* imbarazzato
embarrassing /em'bærəsɪŋ/ *a* imbarazzante
embarrassment /em'bærəsmənt/ *n* imbarazzo *m*
embassy /'embəsɪ/ *n* ambasciata *f*
embed /ɪm'bedɪd/ *vt Comput* integrare ⟨command⟩; **~ded in** ⟨gem⟩ incastonato in; ⟨plant⟩ piantato in; ⟨sharp object⟩ conficcato in; ⟨rock⟩ incluso in; **~ded** ⟨traditions, feelings⟩ radicato; **be ~ded in** *fig* radicarsi in
embellish /ɪm'belɪʃ/ *vt* abbellire
embers /'embəz/ *npl* braci *fpl*
embezzle /ɪm'bezl/ *vt* appropriarsi indebitamente di
embezzlement /ɪm'bez(ə)lmənt/ *n* appropriazione *f* indebita
embitter /ɪm'bɪtə(r)/ *vt* amareggiare
emblem /'embləm/ *n* emblema *m*
emblematic /emblə'mætɪk/ *a* emblematico
embodiment /ɪm'bɒdɪmənt/ *n* incarnazione *f*
embody /ɪm'bɒdɪ/ *vt* (*pt/pp* **-ied**) incorporare; **~ what is best in...** rappresentare quanto c'è di meglio di...
embolism /'embəlɪzm/ *n Med* embolia *f*
emboss /ɪm'bɒs/ *vt* sbalzare ⟨metal⟩; stampare in rilievo ⟨paper⟩
embossed /ɪm'bɒst/ *a* in rilievo
embrace /ɪm'breɪs/ *n* abbraccio *m* ● *vt* abbracciare ● *vi* abbracciarsi
embroider /ɪm'brɔɪdə(r)/ *vt* ricamare ⟨design⟩; *fig* abbellire
embroidery /ɪm'brɔɪdərɪ/ *n* ricamo *m*
embroil /ɪm'brɔɪl/ *vt* **become ~ed in sth** rimanere invischiato in qcsa
embryo /'embrɪəʊ/ *n* embrione *m*
embryonic /embrɪ'ɒnɪk/ *a Biol*, *fig* embrionale
emend /ɪ'mend/ *vt* emendare
emerald /'emərəld/ *n* smeraldo *m*
emerge /ɪ'mɜːdʒ/ *vi* emergere; (*come into being: nation*) nascere; ⟨sun, flowers⟩ spuntare fuori
emergence /ɪ'mɜːdʒəns/ *n* emergere *m*; (*of new country*) nascita *f*
emergency /ɪ'mɜːdʒənsɪ/ *n* emergenza *f*; **in an ~** in caso di emergenza
emergency: emergency ambulance service *n* pronto soccorso *m* autoambulanze. **emergency case** *n Med* caso *m* di emergenza. **emergency centre** *n* (*for refugees etc*) centro *m* di accoglienza; *Med* centro *m* di soccorso mobile. **emergency exit** *n* uscita *f* di sicurezza. **emergency landing** *n Aeron* atterraggio *m* di fortuna. **emergency laws** *npl Pol* leggi *fpl* straordinarie. **emergency number** *n* numero *m* di emergenza. **emergency powers** *npl Pol* poteri *mpl* straordinari. **emergency rations** *npl* viveri

mpl di sopravvivenza. **emergency service** *n Med* servizio *m* di pronto soccorso. **emergency services** *npl* servizi *mpl* di pronto intervento. **emergency surgery** *n* undergo **~ ~** essere operato d'urgenza. **emergency ward** *n* [reparto *m* di] pronto soccorso *m*. **emergency worker** *n* addetto *m* a operazioni di soccorso

emergent /ɪ'mɜːdʒənt/ *a* ⟨industry, nation⟩ emergente

emery board /'eməri/n limetta *f* per le unghie (*di carta*).

emery paper *n* carta *f* vetrata

emigrant /'emɪgrənt/ *n* emigrante *mf*

emigrate /'emɪgreɪt/ *vi* emigrare

emigration /emɪ'greɪʃn/ *n* emigrazione *f*

eminence /'emməns/ *n* (*fame*) eminenza *f*, gloria *f*; (*honour*) distinzione *f*; (*hill*) altura *f*

eminent /'emmənt/ *a* eminente

eminently /'emməntlɪ/ *adv* eminentemente

emirate /'emɪərət/ *n* emirato *m*

emissary /'emɪsərɪ/ *n* emissario *m* (**to** di)

emission /ɪ'mɪʃn/ *n* emissione *f*; (*of fumes*) esalazione *f*

emit /ɪ'mɪt/ *vt* (*pt/pp* **emitted**) emettere; esalare ⟨fumes⟩

Emmy /'emɪ/ *n* Emmy *m* Oscar *m inv* televisivo americano

emotion /ɪ'məʊʃn/ *n* emozione *f*

emotional /ɪ'məʊʃənəl/ *a* denso di emozione; ⟨person, reaction⟩ emotivo; **become ~** avere una reazione emotiva; **don't get so ~** non lasciarti prendere dalle emozioni

emotionless /ɪ'məʊʃənlɪs/ *a* impassibile

emotive /ɪ'məʊtɪv/ *a* emotivo

empathize /'empəθaɪz/ *vi* **~ with sb** immedesimarsi nei problemi di qcno

empathy /'empəθɪ/ *n* comprensione *f*

emperor /'empərə(r)/ *n* imperatore *m*

emphasis /'emfəsɪs/ *n* enfasi *f*; **put the ~ on sth** accentuare qcsa

emphasize /'emfəsaɪz/ *vt* accentuare ⟨word, syllable⟩; sottolineare ⟨need⟩

emphatic /ɪm'fætɪk/ *a* categorico

emphatically /ɪm'fætɪklɪ/ *adv* categoricamente

empire /'empaɪə(r)/ *n* impero *m*

empirical /em'pɪrɪkl/ *a* empirico

empiricism /em'pɪrɪsɪzm/ *n* empirismo *m*

employ /em'plɔɪ/ *vt* impiegare; *fig* usare ⟨tact⟩

employable /em'plɔɪəbl/ *a* ⟨person⟩ che ha i requisiti per svolgere un lavoro

employee /emplɔɪ'iː/ *n* impiegato, -a *mf*

employee buyout *n* rilevamento *m* dipendenti

employer /em'plɔɪə(r)/ *n* datore *m* di lavoro

employment /em'plɔɪmənt/ *n* occupazione *f*; (*work*) lavoro *m*

employment: employment agency *n* ufficio *m* di collocamento. **employment contract** *n* contratto *m* di lavoro. **employment exchange** *n* agenzia *f* di collocamento. **employment figures** *npl* dati *mpl* su l'occupazione. **Employment Minister, Em-**

ployment Secretary *n* ministro *m* del lavoro

emporium /em'pɔːrɪəm/ *n hum* emporio *m*

empower /ɪm'paʊə(r)/ *vt* autorizzare; (*enable*) mettere in grado

empress /'emprɪs/ *n* imperatrice *f*

empties /'emptɪz/ *npl* vuoti *mpl*

emptiness /'emptɪnɪs/ *n* vuoto *m*

empty /'emptɪ/ *a* vuoto; ⟨promise, threat⟩ vano ● *v* (*pt/pp* **-ied**) ● *vt* vuotare ⟨container⟩ ● *vi* vuotarsi

■ **empty out** *vt/i* = **empty**

empty-handed /-'hændɪd/ *a* ⟨arrive, leave⟩ a mani vuote

empty-headed /-'hedɪd/ *a* scriteriato

EMS *n abbr* (**European Monetary System**) SME *m*

emulate /'emjʊleɪt/ *vt* emulare

emulsify /ɪ'mʌlsɪfaɪ/ *v* (*pt/pp* **-ied**) ● *vt* emulsionare ● *vi* emulsionarsi

emulsion /ɪ'mʌlʃn/ *n* emulsione *f*

enable /ɪ'neɪbl/ *vt* **~ sb to** mettere qcno in grado di

enact /ɪ'nækt/ *vt Theat* rappresentare; decretare ⟨law⟩

enamel /ɪ'næml/ *n* smalto *m* ● *vt* (*pt/pp* **enamelled**) smaltare

enamelling /ɪ'næməlɪŋ/ *n* (*process*) smaltatura *f*; (*art*) decorazione *f* a smalto

enamoured /ɪ'næməd/ *a* **be ~ of** essere innamorato di

enc. *abbr* (**enclosures**) alleg.

encampment /ɪn'kæmpmənt/ *n* accampamento *m*

encapsulate /en'kæpsjʊleɪt/ *vt* (*include*) incapsulare; (*summarize*) sintetizzare

encase /en'keɪs/ *vt* rivestire (**in** di)

encash /en'kæʃ/ *vt Br* incassare

encephalogram /en'kefələgræm/ *n* encefalogramma *m*

enchant /ɪn'tʃɑːnt/ *vt* incantare

enchanting /ɪn'tʃɑːntɪŋ/ *a* incantevole

enchantment /ɪn'tʃɑːntmənt/ *n* incanto *m*

encircle /ɪn'sɜːkl/ *vt* circondare

encl *abbr* (**enclosed; enclosure**) all.

enclave /'enkleɪv/ *n* enclave *f inv*; *fig* territorio *m*

enclose /ɪn'kləʊz/ *vt* circondare ⟨land⟩; (*in letter*) allegare (**with** a)

enclosed /ɪn'kləʊzd/ *a* ⟨space⟩ chiuso; (*in letter*) allegato

enclosure /ɪn'kləʊʒə(r)/ *n* (*at zoo*) recinto *m*; (*in letter*) allegato *m*

encode /ɪn'kəʊd/ *vt* codificare

encoder /ɪn'kəʊdə(r)/ *n* codificatore, -trice *mf*

encompass /ɪn'kʌmpəs/ *vt* (*include*) comprendere

encore /'ɒŋkɔː(r)/ *n & int* bis *m inv*

encounter /ɪn'kaʊntə(r)/ *n* incontro *m*; (*battle*) scontro *m* ● *vt* incontrare

encourage /ɪn'kʌrɪdʒ/ *vt* incoraggiare; promuovere ⟨the arts, independence⟩

encouragement /ɪn'kʌrɪdʒmənt/ *n* incoraggiamento *m*; (*of the arts*) promozione *f*

encouraging /ɪn'kʌrɪdʒɪŋ/ *a* incoraggiante; ⟨*smile*⟩ di incoraggiamento

encroach /ɪn'krəʊtʃ/ *vt* ~ **on** invadere ⟨*land, privacy*⟩; abusare di ⟨*time*⟩; interferire con ⟨*rights*⟩

encrust /en'krʌst/ *vt* **be ~ed with** ⟨*ice*⟩ essere incrostato di; ⟨*jewels*⟩ essere tempestato di

encumber /ɪn'kʌmbə(r)/ *vt* **~ed with** essere carico di ⟨*children, suitcases*⟩; ingombro di ⟨*furniture*⟩

encumbrance /ɪn'kʌmbrəns/ *n* peso *m*

encyclop[a]edia /ɪnsaɪklə'piːdɪə/ *n* enciclopedia *f*

encyclop[a]edic /ɪnsaɪklə'piːdɪk/ *a* enciclopedico

end /end/ *n* fine *f*; ⟨*of box, table, piece of string*⟩ estremità *f*; ⟨*of town, room*⟩ parte *f*; ⟨*purpose*⟩ fine *m*; **in the ~** alla fine; **at the ~ of May** alla fine di maggio; **at the ~ of the street/garden** in fondo alla strada/al giardino; **on ~** ⟨*upright*⟩ in piedi; **for days on ~** per giorni e giorni; **for six days on ~** per sei giorni di fila; **put an ~ to sth** mettere fine a qcsa; **make ~s meet** *fam* sbarcare il lunario; **no ~ of** *fam* un sacco di ● *vt/i* finire

■ **end in** *vt* ⟨*word:*⟩ terminare in; finire in ⟨*failure, argument*⟩

■ **end off** *vt* concludere ⟨*meal, speech*⟩

■ **end up** *vi* finire; **~ up doing sth** finire col fare qcsa

endanger /ɪn'deɪndʒə(r)/ *vt* rischiare ⟨*one's life*⟩; mettere a repentaglio ⟨*sb else, success of sth*⟩

endear /ɪn'dɪə(r)/ *vt* ~ **oneself to sb** conquistarsi la simpatia di qcno; **~ sb to** conquistare a qcno la simpatia di

endearing /ɪn'dɪərɪŋ/ *a* accattivante

endearingly /ɪn'ɪərɪŋlɪ/ *adv* ⟨*smile*⟩ in modo accattivante; **~ honest** di un'onestà disarmante

endearment /ɪn'dɪəmənt/ *n* **term of ~** vezzeggiativo *m*

endeavour /ɪn'devə(r)/ *n* tentativo *m* ● *vi* sforzarsi (**to** di)

endemic /en'demɪk/ *a* endemico ● *n* ⟨*situation*⟩ endemia *f*

ending /'endɪŋ/ *n* fine *f*; *Gram* desinenza *f*

endive /'endaɪv/ *n* indivia *f*

endless /'endlɪs/ *a* interminabile; ⟨*patience*⟩ infinito

endlessly /'endlɪslɪ/ *adv* continuamente; ⟨*patient*⟩ infinitamente

endocrinology /endəʊkrɪ'nɒlədʒɪ/ *n* endocrinologia *f*

endorse /en'dɔːs/ *vt* girare ⟨*cheque*⟩; ⟨*sports personality:*⟩ fare pubblicità a ⟨*product*⟩; approvare ⟨*plan*⟩

endorsement /en'dɔːsmənt/ *n* ⟨*of cheque*⟩ girata *f*; ⟨*of plan*⟩ conferma *f*; ⟨*on driving licence*⟩ registrazione *f* su patente di un'infrazione

endow /ɪn'daʊ/ *vt* dotare

endowment insurance /ɪn'daʊmənt/ *n*

assicurazione *f* sulla vita che fornisce un reddito in caso di sopravvivenza

end: endpaper *n* risguardo *m*. **end product** *n* prodotto *m* finito. **end result** *n* risultato *m* finale

endurable /ɪn'djʊərəbl/ *a* sopportabile

endurance /ɪn'djʊərəns/ *n* resistenza *f*; **it is beyond ~** è insopportabile

endurance test *n* prova *f* di resistenza

endure /ɪn'djʊə(r)/ *vt* sopportare ● *vi* durare

enduring /ɪn'djʊərɪŋ/ *a* duraturo

end user *n* utente *m* finale

enema /'enɪmə/ *n Med* clistere *m*

enemy /'enəmɪ/ *n* nemico, -a *mf* ● *attrib* nemico

energetic /enə'dʒetɪk/ *a* energico

energetically /enə'dʒetɪklɪ/ *adv* ⟨*speak, promote, publicize*⟩ vigorosamente; ⟨*work, exercise*⟩ con energia; ⟨*deny*⟩ risolutamente

energize /'enədʒaɪz/ *vt* stimolare; *Electr* alimentare [elettricamente]

energizing /'enədʒaɪzɪŋ/ *a* ⟨*influence*⟩ stimolante

energy /'enədʒɪ/ *n* energia *f*

energy: energy efficiency *n* razionalizzazione *f* del consumo energetico. **energy resources** *npl* risorse *fpl* energetiche. **energy saving** *n* risparmio *m* energetico ● *a* **energy-saving** ⟨*device*⟩ che fa risparmiare energia; ⟨*measure*⟩ per risparmiare energia

enervate /'enəveɪt/ *vt* snervare

enfold /en'fəʊld/ *vt* avvolgere

enforce /ɪn'fɔːs/ *vt* far rispettare ⟨*law*⟩

enforced /ɪn'fɔːst/ *a* forzato

enforcement /ɪn'fɔːsmənt/ *n* applicazione *f*; ⟨*of discipline*⟩ imposizione *f*

engage /ɪn'geɪdʒ/ *vt* assumere ⟨*staff*⟩; *Theat* ingaggiare; *Auto* ingranare ⟨*gear*⟩; **~ sb in conversation** fare conversazione con qcno ● *vi Techn* ingranare; **~ in** impegnarsi in

engaged /ɪn'geɪdʒd/ *a* ⟨*in use, busy*⟩ occupato; ⟨*person*⟩ impegnato; ⟨*to be married*⟩ fidanzato; **get ~** fidanzarsi (**to** con)

engaged tone *n Br* segnale *m* di occupato

engagement /ɪn'geɪdʒmənt/ *n* fidanzamento *m*; ⟨*appointment*⟩ appuntamento *m*; *Mil* combattimento *m*

engagement ring *n* anello *m* di fidanzamento

engagements book *n* agenda *f*

engaging /ɪn'geɪdʒɪŋ/ *a* attraente

engender /ɪn'dʒendə(r)/ *vt fig* generare

engine /'endʒɪn/ *n* motore *m*; *Rail* locomotrice *f*

engine driver *n* macchinista *m*

engineer /endʒɪ'nɪə(r)/ *n* ingegnere *m*; ⟨*service, installation*⟩ tecnico *m*; *Naut, Am Rail* macchinista *m* ● *vt fig* architettare

engineering /endʒɪ'nɪərɪŋ/ *n* ingegneria *f*

engine: engine failure *n* guasto *m* [al motore]; ⟨*in jet*⟩ avaria *f*. **engine oil** *n* olio *m* [del] motore. **engine room** *n* sala *f* macchine. **engine shed** *n Rail* deposito *m*

England /'ɪŋglənd/ *n* Inghilterra *f*

English /'ɪŋglɪʃ/ *a* inglese; **the ~ Channel**

la Manica ● *n* (*language*) inglese *m*; **the ~** *pl* gli inglesi

English: English as a Foreign Language *n* inglese *m* come lingua straniera. **English as a Second Language** *n* inglese *m* come seconda lingua. **Englishman** *n* inglese *m*. **English rose** *n* donna *f* dalla bellezza tipicamente inglese. **English speaker** *n* anglofono, -a *mf*. **English-speaking** *a* anglofono. **Englishwoman** *n* inglese *f*

engrave /ɪnˈɡreɪv/ *vt* incidere

engraving /ɪnˈɡreɪvɪŋ/ *n* incisione *f*

engross /ɪnˈɡrəʊs/ *vt* **~ed in** assorto in

engrossing /ɪnˈɡrəʊsɪŋ/ *a* avvincente

engulf /ɪnˈɡʌlf/ *vt* (*fire, waves:*) inghiottire

enhance /ɪnˈhɑːns/ *vt* accrescere (*beauty, reputation*); migliorare (*performance*)

enigma /ɪˈnɪɡmə/ *n* enigma *m*

enigmatic /enɪɡˈmætɪk/ *a* enigmatico

enjoy /ɪnˈdʒɔɪ/ *vt* godere di (*good health*); **~ oneself** divertirsi; **I ~ cooking/painting** mi piace cucinare/dipingere; **I ~ed the meal/film** mi è piaciuto il pranzo/il film; **~ your meal** buon appetito

enjoyable /ɪnˈdʒɔɪəbl/ *a* piacevole

enjoyment /ɪnˈdʒɔɪmənt/ *n* piacere *m*

enlarge /ɪnˈlɑːdʒ/ *vt* ingrandire ● *vi* **~ upon** dilungarsi su

enlargement /ɪnˈlɑːdʒmənt/ *n* ingrandimento *m*

enlarger /ɪnˈlɑːdʒə(r)/ *n Phot* ingranditore *m*

enlighten /ɪnˈlaɪtn/ *vt* illuminare

enlightened /ɪnˈlaɪtənd/ *a* progressista

enlightenment /ɪnˈlaɪtənmənt/ *n* **The E~** l'Illuminismo *m*

enlist /ɪnˈlɪst/ *vt Mil* reclutare; **~ sb's help** farsi aiutare da qcno ● *vi Mil* arruolarsi

enliven /ɪnˈlaɪvn/ *vt* animare

enmesh /enˈmeʃ/ *vt* **become ~ed in** *fig* impegolarsi in

enmity /ˈenmətɪ/ *n* inimicizia *f*

ennoble /enˈnəʊbl/ *vt* nobilitare

enormity /ɪˈnɔːmətɪ/ *n* enormità *f*

enormous /ɪˈnɔːməs/ *a* enorme

enormously /ɪˈnɔːməslɪ/ *adv* estremamente; (*grateful*) infinitamente

enough /ɪˈnʌf/ *a & n* abbastanza; **I didn't bring ~ clothes** non ho portato abbastanza vestiti; **have you had ~?** (*to eat/drink*) hai mangiato/bevuto abbastanza?; **I've had ~!** *fam* ne ho abbastanza!; **is that ~?** basta?; **that's ~!** basta così!; **£50 isn't ~** 50 sterline non sono sufficienti ● *adv* abbastanza; **you're not working fast ~** non lavori abbastanza in fretta; **funnily ~** stranamente

enquire /ɪnˈkwaɪə(r)/ *vi* domandare; **~ about** chiedere informazioni su

enquiry /ɪnˈkwaɪərɪ/ *n* domanda *f*; (*investigation*) inchiesta *f*

enrage /ɪnˈreɪdʒ/ *vt* fare arrabbiare

enrich /ɪnˈrɪtʃ/ *vt* arricchire; (*improve*) migliorare (*vocabulary*)

enrol /ɪnˈrəʊl/ *vi* (*pt/pp* **-rolled**) (*for exam, in club*) iscriversi (**for, in** a)

enrolment /ɪnˈrəʊlmənt/ *n* iscrizione *f*

ensconced /ɪnˈskɒnst/ *a* comodamente sistemato (**in** in)

ensemble /ɒnˈsɒmbl/ *n* (*clothing & Mus*) complesso *m*

ensign /ˈensaɪn/ *n* insegna *f*

enslave /ɪnˈsleɪv/ *vt* render schiavo

ensue /ɪnˈsjuː/ *vi* seguire; **~ from** sorgere da; **the ensuing discussion** la discussione che ne è seguita

en suite /ɒ̃ˈswiːt/ *n* (*bathroom*) camera *f* con bagno annesso ● *a* (*bathroom*) annesso; (*room*) con bagno

ensure /ɪnˈʃʊə(r)/ *vt* assicurare; **~ that** (*person:*) assicurarsi che; (*measure:*) garantire che

ENT *n abbr* (**Ear Nose and Throat**) otorino *m*

entail /ɪnˈteɪl/ *vt* comportare; **what does it ~?** in che cosa consiste?

entangle /ɪnˈtæŋɡl/ *vt* **get ~d in** rimanere impigliato in; *fig* rimanere coinvolto in

entanglement /ɪnˈtæŋɡ(ə)lmənt/ *n* (*emotional*) legame *m* sentimentale; (*complicated situation*) pasticcio *m*

enter /ˈentə(r)/ *vt* entrare in; iscrivere (*horse, runner in race*); cominciare (*university*); partecipare a (*competition*); *Comput* immettere (*data*); (*write down*) scrivere ● *vi* entrare; *Theat* entrare in scena; (*register as competitor*) iscriversi; (*take part*) partecipare (**in** a) *n Comput* invio *m*

■ **enter into** *vt* (*begin*) intavolare (*negotiations, an argument*)

enteritis /entəˈraɪtɪs/ *n* enterite *f*

enterprise /ˈentəpraɪz/ *n* impresa *f*; (*quality*) iniziativa *f*

enterprising /ˈentəpraɪzɪŋ/ *a* intraprendente

entertain /entəˈteɪn/ *vt* intrattenere; (*invite*) ricevere; nutrire (*ideas, hopes*); prendere in considerazione (*possibility*) ● *vi* intrattenersi; (*have guests*) ricevere

entertainer /entəˈteɪnə(r)/ *n* artista *mf*

entertaining /entəˈteɪnɪŋ/ *a* (*person*) di gradevole compagnia; (*evening, film, play*) divertente

entertainment /entəˈteɪnmənt/ *n* (*amusement*) intrattenimento *m*

enthral /ɪnˈθrɔːl/ *vt* (*pt/pp* **enthralled**) **be ~led** essere affascinato (**by** da)

enthralling /ɪnˈθrɔːlɪŋ/ *a* (*novel, performance*) affascinante

enthuse /ɪnˈθjuːz/ *vi* **~ over** entusiasmarsi per

enthusiasm /ɪnˈθjuːzɪæzm/ *n* entusiasmo *m*

enthusiast /ɪnˈθjuːzɪæst/ *n* entusiasta *mf*

enthusiastic /ɪnθjuːzɪˈæstɪk/ *a* entusiastico

enthusiastically /ɪnθjuːzɪˈæstɪklɪ/ *adv* entusiasticamente

entice /ɪnˈtaɪs/ *vt* attirare

enticement /ɪnˈtaɪsmənt/ *n* (*incentive*) incentivo *m*

enticing /ɪnˈtaɪsɪŋ/ *a* (*prospect, offer*) allettante; ⟨*person*⟩ seducente; ⟨*food, smell*⟩ invitante

entire /ɪn'taɪə(r)/ *a* intero

entirely /ɪn'taɪəlɪ/ *adv* del tutto; **I'm not ~ satisfied** non sono completamente soddisfatto

entirety /ɪn'taɪərətɪ/ *n* **in its ~** nell'insieme

entitled /ɪn'taɪtld/ *a* ⟨*book*⟩ intitolato; **be ~ to sth** aver diritto a qcsa

entitlement /ɪn'taɪtlmənt/ *n* diritto *m*

entity /'entətɪ/ *n* entità *f*

entomology /entə'mɒlədʒɪ/ *n* entomologia *f*

entourage /'ɒntʊrɑːʒ/ *n* entourage *m inv*

entrails /'entreɪlz/ *npl* intestini *mpl*

entrance[1] /'entrəns/ *n* entrata *f*; *Theat* entrata *f* in scena; ⟨*right to enter*⟩ ammissione *f*; **'no ~'** 'ingresso vietato'

entrance[2] /ɪn'trɑːns/ *vt* estasiare

entrance: entrance examination *n* esame *m* di ammissione. **entrance fee** *n* **how much is the ~ ~?** quanto costa il biglietto di ingresso? **entrance hall** *n* (*in house*) ingresso *m*. **entrance requirements** *npl* requisiti *mpl* di ammissione. **entrance ticket** *n* biglietto *m* d'ingresso

entrancing /ɪn'trɑːnsɪŋ/ *a* incantevole

entrant /'entrənt/ *n* concorrente *mf*

entreat /ɪn'triːt/ *vt* supplicare

entreatingly /ɪn'triːtɪŋlɪ/ *adv* ⟨*beg, ask*⟩ in tono implorante

entreaty /ɪn'triːtɪ/ *n* supplica *f*

entrée /'ɒtreɪ/ *n Br* (*starter*) primo *m*; ⟨*Am: main course*⟩ secondo *m*; **her wealth gave her an ~ into high society** il denaro le ha aperto le porte dell'alta società

entrenched /ɪn'trentʃt/ *a* ⟨*ideas, views*⟩ radicato

entrepreneur /ɒntrəprə'nɜː(r)/ *n* imprenditore, -trice *mf*

entrepreneurial /ɒntrəprə'nɜːrɪəl/ *a* imprenditoriale; **have ~ skills** avere il senso degli affari

entrust /ɪn'trʌst/ *vt* **~ sb with sth, ~ sth to sb** affidare qcsa a qcno

entry /'entrɪ/ *n* ingresso *m*; (*way in*) entrata *f*; (*in directory etc*) voce *f*; (*in appointment diary*) appuntamento *m*; **no ~** ingresso vietato; *Auto* accesso vietato

entry: entry fee *n* quota *f* di iscrizione. **entry form** *n* modulo *m* di ammissione. **entry permit** *n* visto *m* di entrata. **entryphone** *n* citofono *m*. **entry requirements** *npl* requisiti *mpl* di ammissione. **entry visa** *n* visto *m* di ingresso

entwine /ɪn'twaɪn/ *vt also fig* intrecciare

E-number *n Br* sigla *f* degli additivi

enumerate /ɪ'njuːməreɪt/ *vt* enumerare

enumeration /ɪnjuːmə'reɪʃn/ *n* (*list*) enumerazione *f*; (*counting*) conto *m*

enunciate /ɪ'nʌnsɪeɪt/ *vt* enunciare

enunciation /ɪnʌnsɪ'eɪʃn/ *n* (*of principle, facts*) enunciazione *f*; (*of word*) articolazione *f*

envelop /ɪn'veləp/ *vt* (*pt/pp* **enveloped**) avviluppare

envelope /'envələʊp/ *n* busta *f*

enviable /'envɪəbl/ *a* invidiabile

envious /'envɪəs/ *a* invidioso

enviously /'envɪəslɪ/ *adv* con invidia

environment /ɪn'vaɪrənmənt/ *n* ambiente *m*

environmental /ɪnvaɪrən'mentl/ *a* ambientale

environmental health *n* salute *f* pubblica

environmentalist /ɪnvaɪrən'mentəlɪst/ *n* ambientalista *mf*

environmentally /ɪnvaɪrən'mentəlɪ/ *adv* **~ friendly** che rispetta l'ambiente

environmental scientist *n* studioso, -a *mf* di ecologia applicata

Environmental Studies *npl Br Sch* ecogeografia *f* e ecobiologia *f*

envisage /ɪn'vɪzɪdʒ/ *vt* prevedere

envoy /'envɔɪ/ *n* inviato, -a *mf*

envy /'envɪ/ *n* invidia *f* ● *vt* (*pt/pp* **-ied**) **~ sb sth** invidiare qcno per qcsa

enzyme /'enzaɪm/ *n* enzima *m*

ephemeral /ɪ'femərəl/ *a* effimero

epic /'epɪk/ *a* epico ● *n* epopea *f*

epicentre /'epɪsentə(r)/ *n* epicentro *m*

epidemic /epɪ'demɪk/ *n* epidemia *f*

epidermis /epɪ'dɜːmɪs/ *n* epidermide *f*

epidural /epɪ'djʊərəl/ *n Med* anestesia *f* epidurale

epigram /'epɪɡræm/ *n* epigramma *m*

epilepsy /'epɪlepsɪ/ *n* epilessia *f*

epileptic /epɪ'leptɪk/ *a* & *n* epilettico, -a *mf*

epilogue /'epɪlɒɡ/ *n* epilogo *m*

Epiphany /ɪ'pɪfənɪ/ *n* Epifania *f*

episode /'epɪsəʊd/ *n* episodio *m*

episodic /epɪ'sɒdɪk/ *a* episodico

epistle /ɪ'pɪsl/ *n liter* epistola *f*

epitaph /'epɪtɑːf/ *n* epitaffio *m*

epithet /'epɪθet/ *n* epiteto *m*

epitome /ɪ'pɪtəmɪ/ *n* epitome *f*

epitomize /ɪ'pɪtəmaɪz/ *vt* essere il classico esempio di

epoch /'iːpɒk/ *n* epoca *f*

epoch-making *a* che fa epoca

eponymous /ɪ'pɒnɪməs/ *a* eponimo

equable /'ekwəbl/ *a* ⟨*climate*⟩ temperato; ⟨*temperament*⟩ equilibrato

equably /'ekwəblɪ/ *adv* con serenità

equal /'iːkwl/ *a* ⟨*parts, amounts*⟩ uguale; **of ~ height** della stessa altezza; **be ~ to the task** essere a l'altezza del compito ● *n* pari *m inv*; **treat sb as an ~** trattare qcno da pari a pari ● *vt* (*pt/pp* **equalled**) (*be same in quantity as*) essere pari a; (*rival*) uguagliare; **5 plus 5 ~s 10** 5 più 5 [è] uguale a 10

equality /ɪ'kwɒlətɪ/ *n* uguaglianza *f*

equalize /'iːkwəlaɪz/ *vi Sport* pareggiare

equalizer /'iːkwəlaɪzə(r)/ *n Sport* pareggio *m*; **get the ~** pareggiare

equally /'iːkwəlɪ/ *adv* ⟨*divide*⟩ in parti uguali; **~ intelligent** della stessa intelligenza; **~,...** allo stesso tempo...

equal: equal opportunities *npl* uguaglianza *f* dei diritti. **Equal Opportunities Commission** *n Br commissione f per l'ugua-*

glianza dei diritti nei rapporti di lavoro.
equal opportunity *attrib* ⟨*legislation*⟩ per l'uguaglianza dei diritti nei rapporti di lavoro; ⟨*employer*⟩ che applica l'uguaglianza dei diritti. **equal rights** *npl* parità *f* dei diritti.
equals sign *n* segno *m* uguale
equanimity /ekwə'nımətı/ *n* equanimità *f*
equate /ɪ'kweɪt/ *vt* ~ sth with sth equiparare qcsa a qcsa
equation /ɪ'kweɪʒn/ *n Math* equazione *f*
equator /ɪ'kweɪtə(r)/ *n* equatore *m*
equatorial /ekwə'tɔːrɪəl/ *a* equatoriale
equestrian /ɪ'kwestrɪən/ *a* equestre
equidistant /iːkwɪ'dɪstənt/ *a* equidistante
equilateral /iːkwɪ'lætərəl/ *a* equilatero
equilibrium /iːkwɪ'lɪbrɪəm/ *n* equilibrio *m*
equine /'ekwaɪn/ *a* ⟨*disease, species*⟩ equino; ⟨*features*⟩ cavallino
equinox /'iːkwɪnɒks/ *n* equinozio *m*
equip /ɪ'kwɪp/ *vt* (*pt/pp* **equipped**) equipaggiare; attrezzare ⟨*kitchen, office*⟩
equipment /ɪ'kwɪpmənt/ *n* attrezzatura *f*
equitable /'ekwɪtəbl/ *a* giusto
equity /'ekwətɪ/ *n* ⟨*justness*⟩ equità *f*; *Comm* azioni *fpl*
equity: **equity capital** *n Fin* capitale *m* azionario. **equity financing** *n Fin* finanziamento *m* attraverso l'emissione di azioni. **equity market** *n Fin* mercato *m* azionario
equivalent /ɪ'kwɪvələnt/ *a* equivalente; be ~ **to** equivalere a ● *n* equivalente *m*
equivocal /ɪ'kwɪvəkl/ *a* equivoco
equivocate /ɪ'kwɪvəkeɪt/ *vi* parlare in modo equivoco, giocare sull'equivoco
equivocation /ɪkwɪvə'keɪʃn/ *n* affermazione *f* equivoca; **too much** ~ troppi equivoci
era /'ɪərə/ *n* età *f*; (*geological*) era *f*
eradicate /ɪ'rædɪkeɪt/ *vt* eradicare
erase /ɪ'reɪz/ *vt* cancellare
erase head *n Comput* testina *f* di cancellazione
eraser /ɪ'reɪzə(r)/ *n* gomma *f* [da cancellare]; (*for blackboard*) cancellino *m*
erasure /ɪ'reɪʒə(r)/ *n* (*act*) cancellazione *f*; (*on paper*) cancellatura *f*
erect /ɪ'rekt/ *a* eretto ● *vt* erigere
erection /ɪ'rekʃn/ *n* erezione *f*
ergonomic /ɜːgə'nɒmɪk/ *a* ergonomico; ⟨*seat*⟩ anatomico
ergonomics /ɜːgə'nɒmɪks/ *n* ergonomia *f*
Erie /'ɪərɪ/ *n* Lake ~ il lago Erie
ERM *n abbr* **Exchange Rate Mechanism**
ermine /'ɜːmɪn/ *n* ermellino *m*
erode /ɪ'rəʊd/ *vt* ⟨*water:*⟩ erodere; ⟨*acid:*⟩ corrodere
erogenous /ɪ'rɒdʒɪnəs/ *a* erogeno
erosion /ɪ'rəʊʒn/ *n* erosione *f*; (*by acid*) corrosione *f*
erotic /ɪ'rɒtɪk/ *a* erotico
erotica /ɪ'rɒtɪkə/ *npl* (*art*) arte *f* erotica; (*literature*) letteratura *f* erotica; *Cinema* film *mpl* erotici
eroticism /ɪ'rɒtɪsɪzm/ *n* erotismo *m*
err /ɜː(r)/ *vi* errare; (*sin*) peccare
errand /'erənd/ *n* commissione *f*

errant /'erənt/ *a* ⟨*husband, wife*⟩ infedele
erratic /ɪ'rætɪk/ *a* irregolare; ⟨*person, moods*⟩ imprevedibile; ⟨*exchange rate*⟩ incostante
erroneous /ɪ'rəʊnɪəs/ *a* erroneo
erroneously /ɪ'rəʊnɪəslɪ/ *adv* erroneamente
error /'erə(r)/ *n* errore *m*; **in** ~ per errore
error message *n Comput* messaggio *m* di errore
ersatz /'ɜːsæts/ *n* surrogato *m*; ~ **tobacco** surrogato del tabacco
erudite /'erʊdaɪt/ *a* erudito
erudition /erʊ'dɪʃn/ *n* erudizione *f*
erupt /ɪ'rʌpt/ *vi* eruttare; ⟨*spots:*⟩ spuntare; (*fig: in anger*) dare in escandescenze
eruption /ɪ'rʌpʃn/ *n* eruzione *f*; *fig* scoppio *m*
escalate /'eskəleɪt/ *vi* intensificarsi ● *vt* intensificare
escalation /eskə'leɪʃn/ *n* escalation *f inv*
escalator /'eskəleɪtə(r)/ *n* scala *f* mobile
escapade /'eskəpeɪd/ *n* scappatella *f*
escape /ɪ'skeɪp/ *n* fuga *f*; (*from prison*) evasione *f*; **have a narrow** ~ cavarsela per un pelo ● *vi* ⟨*prisoner:*⟩ evadere (**from** da); sfuggire (**from sb** alla sorveglianza di qcno); ⟨*animal:*⟩ scappare; ⟨*gas:*⟩ fuoriuscire ● *vt* ~ **notice** passare inosservato; **the name** ~s **me** mi sfugge il nome
escape chute *n Aeron* scivolo *m*
escape clause *n* clausola *f* di recesso
escapee /ɪskeɪ'piː/ *n* evaso *m*
escape hatch *n Naut* portello *m* di sicurezza
escape route *n* (*for fugitives*) itinerario *m* di fuga; (*in case of fire etc*) percorso *m* di emergenza
escapism /ɪ'skeɪpɪzm/ *n* evasione *f* dalla realtà
escapologist /eskə'pɒlədʒɪst/ *n* illusionista *mf* capace di liberarsi dalle catene
escarpment /es'kɑːpmənt/ *n* scarpata *f*
eschew /ɪs'tʃuː/ *vt* evitare ⟨*discussion*⟩; rifuggire ⟨*temptation*⟩; rifuggire da ⟨*violence ecc*⟩
escort[1] /'eskɔːt/ *n* (*of person*) accompagnatore, -trice *mf*; *Mil etc* scorta *f*
escort[2] /ɪs'kɔːt/ *vt* accompagnare; *Mil etc* scortare
Eskimo /'eskɪməʊ/ *n* esquimese *mf*
esophagus /ɪ'sɒfəgəs/ *n Am* esofago *m*
esoteric /esə'terɪk/ *a* esoterico
ESP *n abbr* (**extrasensory perception**) ESP *f*; *n abbr* **English for Special Purposes**
esp *abbr* **especially**
especial /ɪ'speʃl/ *a* speciale
especially /ɪ'speʃəlɪ/ *adv* specialmente; ⟨*kind*⟩ particolarmente
espionage /'espɪənɑːʒ/ *n* spionaggio *m*
espouse /ɪ'spaʊz/ *vt* abbracciare ⟨*cause*⟩
espresso /e'spresəʊ/ *n* (*coffee*) espresso *m*
Esq *Br abbr* (**esquire**) **James McBride, ~** Egr. Sig. James McBride
essay /'eseɪ/ *n* saggio *m*; *Sch* tema *f*

essence /'esns/ n essenza f; **in ~** in sostanza

essential /ɪ'senʃl/ a essenziale ● n **the ~s** pl l'essenziale m

essentially /ɪ'senʃəlɪ/ adv essenzialmente

est abbr (**established**) fondato nel

establish /ɪ'stæblɪʃ/ vt stabilire ⟨contact, lead⟩; fondare ⟨firm⟩; ⟨prove⟩ accertare; **~ oneself as** affermarsi come

established /ɪ'stæblɪʃt/ a ⟨way of doing sth, view⟩ generalmente accettato; ⟨company⟩ affidabile; ⟨brand⟩ riconosciuto; **a well ~ fact** un dato di fatto; **the ~ church** la religione di Stato

establishment /ɪ'stæblɪʃmənt/ n (firm) azienda f; **the E~** l'establishment m

estate /ɪ'steɪt/ n tenuta f; (possessions) patrimonio m; (housing) quartiere m residenziale **estate: estate agent** n agente m immobiliare. **estate car** n giardiniera f. **estate duty** n Br imposta f di successione

esteem /ɪ'sti:m/ n stima f ● vt stimare; (consider) giudicare

ester /'estə(r)/ n estere m

estimate[1] /'estɪmət/ n valutazione f; Comm preventivo m; **at a rough ~** a occhio e croce

estimate[2] /'estɪmeɪt/ vt stimare

estimated time of arrival /'estɪmeɪtɪd/ n ora f prevista di arrivo

estimation /estɪ'meɪʃn/ n (esteem) stima f; **in my ~** (judgement) a mio giudizio

Estonia /ɪ'stəʊnɪə/ n Estonia f

estrange /ɪ'streɪndʒ/ vt estraniare; **~d from sb** separato da qcno; **her ~d husband** il marito da cui è separata

estrangement /ɪ'streɪndʒmənt/ n disamoramento m

estuary /'estjʊərɪ/ n estuario m

ETA n abbr **estimated time of arrival**

et al /et'æl/ abbr (**et alii**) e altri

etc /et'setərə/ abbr (**et cetera**) ecc

et cetera, etcetera /et'setərə/ adv eccetera

etch /etʃ/ vt incidere all'acquaforte; **~ed on her memory** fig impresso nella sua memoria

etching /'etʃɪŋ/ n acquaforte f

eternal /ɪ'tɜ:nl/ a eterno

eternal life n vita f eterna

eternally /ɪ'tɜ:nəlɪ/ adv eternamente

eternal triangle n eterno triangolo m

eternity /ɪ'tɜ:nətɪ/ n eternità f

ether /'i:θə(r)/ n etere m

ethereal /ɪ'θɪərɪəl/ a etereo

ethic /'eθɪk/ n etica f

ethical /'eθɪkl/ a etico

ethics /'eθɪks/ n etica f

Ethiopia /i:θɪ'əʊpɪə/ n Etiopia f

ethnic /'eθnɪk/ a etnico

ethnically /'eθnɪklɪ/ adv etnicamente

ethnic cleansing n epurazione f etnica

ethnology /eθ'nɒlədʒɪ/ n etnologia f

ethos /'i:θɒs/ n **company ~** filosofia f dell'azienda

etiquette /'etɪket/ n etichetta f

etymology /etɪ'mɒlədʒɪ/ n etimologia f

EU n abbr (**European Union**) UE f

eucalyptus /ju:kə'lɪptəs/ n eucalipto m

eugenics /ju:'dʒenɪks/ n eugenetica f

eulogize /'ju:lədʒaɪz/ vt fare il panegirico di ● vi **~ over sth** tessere le lodi di qcsa

eulogy /'ju:lədʒɪ/ n elogio m

eunuch /'ju:nək/ n eunuco m

euphemism /'ju:fəmɪzm/ n eufemismo m

euphemistic /ju:fə'mɪstɪk/ a eufemistico

euphemistically /ju:fə'mɪstɪklɪ/ adv eufemisticamente

euphoria /ju:'fɔ:rɪə/ n euforia f

euphoric /ju:'fɒrɪk/ a euforico

Eurasian /jʊ'reɪʒ(ə)n/ a ⟨people, region⟩ eurasiatico

EURATOM /jʊr'ætəm/ n abbr (**European Atomic Energy Community**) EURATOM f

eurhythmics /jʊ'rɪðmɪks/ n ginnastica f ritmica

Euro- /'jʊərəʊ-/: **eurobond** n eurobbligazione f. **Eurocheque** n eurochèque m inv. **eurocurrency** n eurovaluta f. **Eurodollar** n eurodollaro m. **euromarket** n euromercato m. **Euro-MP** n eurodeputato, -a mf

Europe /'jʊərəp/ n Europa f

European /jʊərə'pɪən/ a & n europeo, -a mf

European: European Bank for Reconstruction and Development n Banca f Europea per la Ricostruzione e lo Sviluppo. **European Commission** n Commissione f Europea. **European Community** n Comunità f Europea. **European Court of Human Rights** n Corte f europea per i diritti dell'uomo. **European Court of Justice** n Corte f europea di giustizia. **European Economic Community** n Comunità f Economica Europea. **European Free Trade Association** n Associazione f Europea di Libero Scambio. **European Monetary System** n Sistema m Monetario Europeo. **European Monetary Union** n Unione f Monetaria Europea. **European Parliament** n Parlamento m Europeo. **European Union** n Unione f Europea

Euro-sceptic n Br euroscettico, -a mf

euthanasia /ju:θə'neɪzɪə/ n eutanasia f

evacuate /ɪ'vækjʊeɪt/ vt evacuare ⟨building, area⟩

evacuation /ɪvækjʊ'eɪʃn/ n evacuazione f

evacuee /ɪvækjʊ'i:/ n sfollato m

evade /ɪ'veɪd/ vt evadere ⟨taxes⟩; evitare ⟨the enemy, authorities⟩; **~ the issue** evitare l'argomento

evaluate /ɪ'væljʊeɪt/ vt valutare

evaluation /ɪvæljʊ'eɪʃn/ n valutazione f, stima f

evangelical /i:væn'dʒelɪkl/ a evangelico

evangelist /ɪ'vændʒəlɪst/ n evangelista m

evaporate /ɪ'væpəreɪt/ vi evaporare; fig svanire

evaporation /ɪvæpə'reɪʃn/ n evaporazione f

evasion /ɪ'veɪʒn/ n evasione f

evasive /ɪ'veɪsɪv/ a evasivo

evasively /ɪ'veɪsɪvlɪ/ adv in modo evasivo

eve /i:v/ n liter vigilia f

even /'i:vn/ a (level) piatto; (same, equal) uguale; (regular) regolare; ⟨number⟩ pari;

even out | excess profits

get ~ with vendicarsi di; **now we're ~** adesso siamo pari ● *adv* anche, ancora; **~ if** anche se; **~ so** con tutto ciò; **not ~** nemmeno; **~ bigger/hotter** ancora più grande/caldo ● *vt* **~ the score** *Sport* pareggiare

■ **even out** *vi* livellarsi

■ **even up** *vt* livellare

even-handed /-'hændɪd/ *a* imparziale

evening /'i:vnɪŋ/ *n* sera *f*; (*whole evening*) serata *f*; **this ~** stasera; **in the ~** la sera

evening: evening class *n* corso *m* serale. **evening dress** *n* (*man's*) abito *m* scuro; (*woman's*) abito *m* da sera. **evening performance** *n* spettacolo *m* serale. **evening primrose** *n* enotera *f*. **evening star** *n* Venere *f*

evenly /'i:vnlɪ/ *adv* ⟨*distributed*⟩ uniformemente; ⟨*breathe*⟩ regolarmente; ⟨*divided*⟩ in uguali parti

event /ɪ'vent/ *n* avvenimento *m*; (*function*) manifestazione *f*; *Sport* gara *f*; **in the ~ of** nell'eventualità di; **in the ~** alla fine

even-tempered /-'tempəd/ *a* pacato

eventful /ɪ'ventfʊl/ *a* movimentato

eventing /ɪ'ventɪŋ/ *n Br* concorso *m* ippico completo

eventual /ɪ'ventjʊəl/ *a* **the ~ winner was...** alla fine il vincitore è stato...

eventuality /ɪventjʊ'ælətɪ/ *n* eventualità *f*

eventually /ɪ'ventjʊəlɪ/ *adv* alla fine; **~!** finalmente!

ever /'evə(r)/ *adv* mai; **I haven't ~...** non ho mai...; **for ~** per sempre; **hardly ~** quasi mai; **~ since** da quando; (*since that time*) da allora; **~ so** *fam* veramente

evergreen /'evəgri:n/ *n* sempreverde *m*

everlasting /evə'læstɪŋ/ *a* eterno

every /'evrɪ/ *a* ogni; **~ one** ciascuno; **~ other day** un giorno sì un giorno no

everybody /'evrɪbɒdɪ/ *pron* tutti *pl*

everyday /'evrɪdeɪ/ *a* quotidiano, di ogni giorno

everyone /'evrɪwʌn/ *pron* tutti *pl*; **~ else** tutti gli altri

everyplace /'evrɪpleɪs/ *adv Am fam* = **everywhere**

everything /'evrɪθɪŋ/ *pron* tutto; **~ else** tutto il resto

everywhere /'evrɪweə(r)/ *adv* dappertutto; (*wherever*) dovunque

evict /ɪ'vɪkt/ *vt* sfrattare

eviction /ɪ'vɪkʃn/ *n* sfratto *m*

evidence /'evɪdəns/ *n* evidenza *f*; *Jur* testimonianza *f*; **give ~** testimoniare

evident /'evɪdənt/ *a* evidente

evidently /'evɪdəntlɪ/ *adv* evidentemente

evil /'i:vl/ *a* cattivo ● *n* male *m*

evil-smelling /-'smelɪŋ/ *a* puzzolente

evocative /ɪ'vɒkətɪv/ *a* evocativo; **be ~ of** evocare

evoke /ɪ'vəʊk/ *vt* evocare

evolution /i:və'lu:ʃn/ *n* evoluzione *f*

evolutionary /i:və'lu:ʃn(ə)rɪ/ *a* evolutivo

evolve /ɪ'vɒlv/ *vt* evolvere ● *vi* evolversi

ewe /ju:/ *n* pecora *f*

ex /eks/ *n* (*fam: former partner*) ex *mf*

ex+ *pref* ex+

exacerbate /ɪg'sæsəbeɪt/ *vt* esacerbare ⟨*situation*⟩

exact /ɪg'zækt/ *a* esatto ● *vt* esigere

exacting /ɪg'zæktɪŋ/ *a* esigente

exactitude /ɪg'zæktɪtjʊ:d/ *n* esattezza *f*

exactly /ɪg'zæktlɪ/ *adv* esattamente; **not ~** non proprio

exactness /ɪg'zæktnɪs/ *n* precisione *f*

exaggerate /ɪg'zædʒəreɪt/ *vt/i* esagerare

exaggerated /ɪg'zædʒəreɪtɪd/ *a* esagerato; **he has an ~ sense of his own importance** si crede chissà chi

exaggeration /ɪgzædʒə'reɪʃn/ *n* esagerazione *f*

exalt /ɪg'zɔ:lt/ *vt* elevare; (*praise*) vantare

exam /ɪg'zæm/ *n* esame *m*

examination /ɪgzæmɪ'neɪʃn/ *n* esame *m*; (*of patient*) visita *f*; (*of wreckage*) ispezione *f*

examination paper *n* testo *m* d'esame

examine /ɪg'zæmɪn/ *vt* esaminare; visitare ⟨*patient*⟩

examinee /ɪgzæmɪ'ni:/ *n* esaminando *m*

examiner /ɪg'zæmɪnə(r)/ *n Sch* esaminatore, -trice *mf*

example /ɪg'za:mpl/ *n* esempio *m*; **for ~** per esempio; **make an ~ of sb** punire qcno per dare un esempio; **be an ~ to sb** dare il buon esempio a qcno

exasperate /ɪg'zæspəreɪt/ *vt* esasperare

exasperation /ɪgzæspə'reɪʃn/ *n* esasperazione *f*

excavate /'ekskəveɪt/ *vt* scavare; *Archaeol* fare gli scavi di

excavation /ekskə'veɪʃn/ *n* scavo *m*

excavator /'ekskəveɪtə(r)/ *n* (*machine*) escavatrice *f*, escavatore *m*

exceed /ɪk'si:d/ *vt* eccedere

exceedingly /ɪk'si:dɪŋlɪ/ *adv* estremamente

excel /ɪk'sel/ *v* (*pt/pp* **excelled**) ● *vi* eccellere ● *vt* **~ oneself** superare se stessi

excellence /'eksələns/ *n* eccellenza *f*

Excellency /'eksələnsɪ/ *n* (*title*) Eccellenza *f*

excellent /'eksələnt/ *a* eccellente

excellently /'eksələntlɪ/ *adv* in modo eccellente

except /ɪk'sept/ *prep* eccetto, tranne; **~ for** eccetto, tranne; **~ that...** eccetto che... ● *vt* eccettuare

excepting /ɪk'septɪŋ/ *prep* eccetto, tranne

exception /ɪk'sepʃn/ *n* eccezione *f*; **take ~ to** fare obiezioni a

exceptional /ɪk'sepʃənəl/ *a* eccezionale

exceptionally /ɪk'sepʃənəlɪ/ *adv* eccezionalmente

excerpt /'eksɜ:pt/ *n* estratto *m*

excess /ɪk'ses/ *n* eccesso *m*; **in ~ of** oltre

excess baggage *n* bagaglio *m* eccedente

excess fare *n* supplemento *m*

excessive /ɪk'sesɪv/ *a* eccessivo

excessively /ɪk'sesɪvlɪ/ *adv* eccessivamente

excess postage *n* soprattassa *f* postale

excess profits *npl* sovraprofitto *m*

exchange /ɪks'tʃeɪndʒ/ n scambio m; *Teleph* centrale f; *Comm* cambio m; [**stock**] ~ borsa f valori; **in ~** in cambio (**for** di) ● vt scambiare (**for** con); cambiare ⟨money⟩; ~ **views** scambiarsi i punti di vista; ~ **contracts** fare il rogito

exchange: exchange control n controllo m dei cambi. **exchange controls** npl misure fpl di controllo dei cambi. **exchange rate** n tasso m di cambio. **Exchange Rate Mechanism** n meccanismo m di cambio dello Sme.

exchequer /ɪks'tʃekə(r)/ n *Pol* tesoro m

excise¹ /'eksaɪz/ n dazio m

excise² /ek'saɪz/ vt recidere

excise duty n dazio m

excitable /ɪk'saɪtəbl/ a eccitabile

excite /ɪk'saɪt/ vt eccitare

excited /ɪk'saɪtɪd/ a eccitato; **get ~** eccitarsi

excitedly /ɪk'saɪtɪdlɪ/ adv tutto eccitato

excitement /ɪk'saɪtmənt/ n eccitazione f

exciting /ɪk'saɪtɪŋ/ a eccitante; ⟨story, film⟩ appassionante; ⟨holiday⟩ entusiasmante

excl abbr excluding

exclaim /ɪk'skleɪm/ vt/i esclamare

exclamation /eksklə'meɪʃn/ n esclamazione f

exclamation mark n, *Am* **exclamation point** n punto m esclamativo

exclude /ɪk'sklu:d/ vt escludere

excluding /ɪk'sklu:dɪŋ/ prep escluso

exclusion /ɪk'sklu:ʒn/ n esclusione f

exclusion zone n zona f proibita

exclusive /ɪk'sklu:sɪv/ a ⟨rights, club⟩ esclusivo; ⟨interview⟩ in esclusiva; ~ **of...** ...escluso

exclusively /ɪk'sklu:sɪvlɪ/ adv esclusivamente

excommunicate /ekskə'mju:nɪkeɪt/ vt scomunicare

excrement /'ekskrɪmənt/ n escremento m

excreta /ɪk'skri:tə/ npl escrementi mpl

excrete /ɪk'skri:t/ vt espellere; secernere ⟨liquid⟩

excretion /ɪk'skri:ʃn/ n (of animal, human) escremento m

excruciating /ɪk'skru:ʃɪeɪtɪŋ/ a atroce ⟨pain⟩; ⟨fam: very bad⟩ spaventoso

excursion /ɪk'skɜ:ʃn/ n escursione f

excusable /ɪk'skju:zəbl/ a perdonabile

excuse¹ /ɪk'skju:s/ n scusa f

excuse² /ɪk'skju:z/ vt scusare; ~ **from** esonerare da; ~ **me!** (to get attention) scusi!; (to get past) permesso!, scusi!; (indignant) come ha detto?

ex-directory a be ~ non figurare sull'elenco telefonico

exec /ɪg'zek/ n *Am abbr fam* executive

execrable /'eksɪkrəbl/ a esecrabile

executable file /'eksɪkju:təbl/ n *Comput* eseguibile m

execute /'eksɪkju:t/ vt eseguire; (put to death) giustiziare; attuare ⟨plan⟩

execution /eksɪ'kju:ʃn/ n esecuzione f; (of plan) attuazione f

executioner /eksɪ'kju:ʃənə(r)/ n boia m inv

executive /ɪg'zekjʊtɪv/ a esecutivo ● n dirigente mf; *Pol* esecutivo m

executive: executive committee n comitato m esecutivo. **executive director** n direttore, -trice mf [esecutivo, -a]. **executive jet** n jet m inv privato. **executive producer** n *Cinema* direttore, -trice mf di produzione. **executive secretary** n segretario, -a mf di direzione

executor /ɪg'zekjʊtə(r)/ n *Jur* esecutore, -trice mf

exemplary /ɪg'zemplərɪ/ a esemplare

exemplify /ɪg'zemplɪfaɪ/ vt (pt/pp -**ied**) esemplificare

exempt /ɪg'zempt/ a esente ● vt esentare (**from** da)

exemption /ɪg'zempʃn/ n esenzione f

exercise /'eksəsaɪz/ n esercizio m; *Mil* esercitazione f; **physical ~s** ginnastica f; **take ~** fare del moto; **you need more ~** devi muoverti di più ● vt esercitare ⟨muscles, horse⟩; portare a spasso ⟨dog⟩; usare ⟨patience⟩; mettere in pratica ⟨skills⟩ ● vi esercitarsi; ~ **more** fare più moto

exercise bike n cyclette® f inv

exercise book n quaderno m

exert /ɪg'zɜ:t/ vt esercitare; ~ **oneself** sforzarsi

exertion /ɪg'zɜ:ʃn/ n sforzo m

ex gratia /eks'greɪʃə/ a ⟨award, payment⟩ a titolo di favore

exhale /eks'heɪl/ vt/i esalare

exhaust /ɪg'zɔ:st/ n *Auto* scappamento m; (pipe) tubo m di scappamento

exhausted /ɪg'zɔ:stɪd/ a esausto

exhaust fumes npl fumi mpl di scarico m ● vt esaurire

exhausting /ɪg'zɔ:stɪŋ/ a estenuante; ⟨climate, person⟩ sfibrante

exhaustion /ɪg'zɔ:stʃn/ n esaurimento m

exhaustive /ɪg'zɔ:stɪv/ a fig esauriente

exhibit /ɪg'zɪbɪt/ n oggetto m esposto; *Jur* reperto m ● vt esporre; fig dimostrare

exhibition /eksɪ'bɪʃn/ n mostra f; (of strength, skill) dimostrazione f

exhibition centre n palazzo m delle esposizioni

exhibitionist /eksɪ'bɪʃənɪst/ n esibizionista mf

exhibitor /ɪg'zɪbɪtə(r)/ n espositore, -trice mf

exhilarated /ɪg'zɪləreɪtɪd/ a rallegrato

exhilarating /ɪg'zɪləreɪtɪŋ/ a stimolante; ⟨mountain air⟩ tonificante

exhilaration /ɪgzɪlə'reɪʃn/ n allegria f

exhort /ɪg'zɔ:t/ vt esortare

exhume /ɪg'zju:m/ vt esumare

exile /'eksaɪl/ n esilio m; (person) esule mf ● vt esiliare

exist /ɪg'zɪst/ vi esistere

existence /ɪg'zɪstəns/ n esistenza f; **in ~** esistente; **be in ~** esistere

existential /egzɪ'stenʃ(ə)l/ a esistenziale

existentialism /egzɪ'stenʃəlɪzm/ n esistenzialismo m

existing /ɪgˈzɪstɪŋ/ a ⟨policy, management, leadership⟩ attuale; ⟨laws, order⟩ vigente

exit /ˈeksɪt/ n uscita f; Theat uscita f di scena ● vi Theat uscire di scena; Comput uscire (from da)

exit sign n cartello m di uscita

exodus /ˈeksədəs/ n esodo m

ex officio /eksəˈfɪʃɪəʊ/ a ⟨member⟩ di diritto

exonerate /ɪgˈzɒnəreɪt/ vt esonerare

exorbitant /ɪgˈzɔːbɪtənt/ a esorbitante

exorcism /ˈeksɔːsɪzm/ n esorcismo m

exorcist /ˈeksɔːsɪst/ n esorcista mf

exorcize /ˈeksɔːsaɪz/ vt esorcizzare

exotic /ɪgˈzɒtɪk/ a esotico

exotica /ɪgˈzɒtɪkə/ npl oggetti mpl esotici

expand /ɪkˈspænd/ vt espandere; sviluppare ⟨economy⟩ ● vi espandersi; Comm svilupparsi; ⟨metal⟩ dilatarsi

■ **expand on** vt ⟨explain better⟩ approfondire

expandable /ɪkˈspændəbl/ a ⟨Comput: memory⟩ espandibile

expanding /ɪkˈspændɪŋ/ a ⟨file⟩ a soffietto inv; ⟨population, sector⟩ in espansione; ⟨bracelet⟩ allungabile

expanse /ɪkˈspæns/ n estensione f

expansion /ɪkˈspænʃn/ n espansione f; Comm sviluppo m; ⟨of metal⟩ dilatazione f

expansion board, expansion card n Comput scheda f di espansione

expansionist /ɪkˈspænʃənɪst/ n & a espansionista mf

expansion slot n Comput fessura f [per la scheda] di espansione, slot m di espansione

expansive /ɪkˈspænsɪv/ a espansivo

expatriate /eksˈpætrɪət/ n espatriato, -a mf

expect /ɪkˈspekt/ vt aspettare ⟨letter, baby⟩; ⟨suppose⟩ pensare; ⟨demand⟩ esigere; **I ~ so** penso di sì; **we ~ to arrive on Monday** contiamo di arrivare lunedì; **I didn't ~ that** questo non me lo aspettavo; **she ~s too much from him** pretende troppo da lui; **be ~ing** essere in stato interessante

expectancy /ɪkˈspektənsɪ/ n aspettativa f

expectant /ɪkˈspektənt/ a in attesa; **~ mother** donna f incinta

expectantly /ɪkˈspektəntlɪ/ adv con impazienza

expectation /ekspekˈteɪʃn/ n aspettativa f, speranza f

expediency /ɪkˈspiːdɪənsɪ/ n ⟨appropriateness⟩ opportunità f; ⟨self-interest⟩ opportunismo m

expedient /ɪkˈspiːdɪənt/ a conveniente ● n espediente m

expedite /ˈekspɪdaɪt/ vt fml accelerare

expedition /ekspɪˈdɪʃn/ n spedizione f

expeditionary /ekspɪˈdɪʃənərɪ/ a Mil di spedizione

expeditionary force n corpo m di spedizione

expel /ɪkˈspel/ vt ⟨pt/pp **expelled**⟩ espellere

expend /ɪkˈspend/ vt consumare

expendable /ɪkˈspendəbl/ a sacrificabile

expenditure /ɪkˈspendɪtʃə(r)/ n spesa f

expense /ɪkˈspens/ n spesa f; **business ~s** pl spese fpl; **at my ~** a mie spese; **at the ~ of** fig a spese di

expense account n conto m spese

expensive /ɪkˈspensɪv/ a caro, costoso

expensively /ɪkˈspensɪvlɪ/ adv costosamente

experience /ɪkˈspɪərɪəns/ n esperienza f ● vt provare ⟨sensation⟩; avere ⟨problem⟩

experienced /ɪkˈspɪərɪənst/ a esperto

experiment /ɪkˈsperɪmənt/ n esperimento ● /ɪkˈsperɪment/ vi sperimentare

experimental /ɪksperɪˈmentl/ a sperimentale

experimentation /ɪksperɪmenˈteɪʃn/ n sperimentazione f; **~ with drugs** esperienza f della droga

expert /ˈekspɜːt/ a & n esperto, -a mf

expertise /ekspɜːˈtiːz/ n competenza f

expertly /ˈekspɜːtlɪ/ adv abilmente

expiate /ˈekspɪeɪt/ vt espiare ⟨crime, sin⟩; fare ammenda per ⟨guilt⟩

expiration /ekspɪˈreɪʃn/ n ⟨end, exhalation⟩ espirazione f

expire /ɪkˈspaɪə(r)/ vi scadere

expiry /ɪkˈspaɪərɪ/ n scadenza f

expiry date n data f di scadenza

explain /ɪkˈspleɪn/ vt spiegare

■ **explain away** vt ⟨give reasons for⟩ trovare delle giustificazioni per

explanation /ekspləˈneɪʃn/ n spiegazione f

explanatory /ɪkˈsplænətərɪ/ a esplicativo

expletive /ɪkˈspliːtɪv/ n imprecazione f

explicit /ɪkˈsplɪsɪt/ a esplicito

explicitly /ɪkˈsplɪsɪtlɪ/ adv esplicitamente

explode /ɪkˈspləʊd/ vi esplodere ● vt fare esplodere

exploit¹ /ˈeksplɔɪt/ n impresa f

exploit² /ɪkˈsplɔɪt/ vt sfruttare

exploitation /eksplɔɪˈteɪʃn/ n sfruttamento m

exploitative /ɪkˈsplɔɪtətɪv/ a inteso a sfruttare gli individui; ⟨attitude, system⟩ a carattere di sfruttamento

exploration /ekspləˈreɪʃn/ n esplorazione f

exploratory /ɪkˈsplɒrətərɪ/ a esplorativo

explore /ɪkˈsplɔː(r)/ vt esplorare; fig studiare ⟨implications⟩

explorer /ɪkˈsplɔːrə(r)/ n esploratore, -trice mf

explosion /ɪkˈspləʊʒn/ n esplosione f

explosive /ɪkˈspləʊsɪv/ a & n esplosivo m

exponent /ɪkˈspəʊnənt/ n esponente mf

exponential /ekspəˈnenʃəl/ a esponenziale

export¹ /ˈekspɔːt/ n esportazione f

export² /ekˈspɔːt/ vt esportare

export: export agent n esportatore, -trice mf. **export control** n controllo m delle esportazioni. **export credit** n credito m all'esportazione. **export drive** n campagna f di esportazione. **export duty** n tassa f di esportazione. **export earnings** npl ricavato m delle esportazioni

exporter /ek'spɔ:tə(r)/ *n* esportatore, -trice *mf*

export: **export finance** *n* finanziamento *m* delle esportazioni. **export-import company** *n* azienda di import-export. **export licence** *n* licenza *f* di esportazione. **export market** *n* mercato *m* delle esportazioni. **export trade** *n* commercio *m* di esportazione

expose /ɪk'spəʊz/ *vt* esporre; (*reveal*) svelare; smascherare ⟨*traitor etc*⟩

exposée /ɪk'spəʊzeɪ/ *n* (*of scandal*) rivelazioni *fpl*

exposition /ekspə'zɪʃn/ *n* (*of facts*) esposizione *f*

exposure /ɪk'spəʊʒə(r)/ *n* esposizione *f*; *Med* espozione *f* prolungata al freddo/caldo; (*of crimes*) smascheramento *m*; **24 ~s** *Phot* 24 pose

exposure meter *n* *Phot* esposimetro *m*

exposure time *n* *Phot* tempo *m* di esposizione

expound /ɪk'spaʊnd/ *vt* esporre

express /ɪk'spres/ *a* espresso ● *adv* ⟨*send*⟩ per espresso ● *n* (*train*) espresso *m* ● *vt* esprimere; **~ oneself** esprimersi

expression /ɪk'spreʃn/ *n* espressione *f*

expressionless /ɪk'spreʃənlɪs/ *a* ⟨*tone, voice*⟩ distaccato; ⟨*playing*⟩ piatto; ⟨*eyes, face*⟩ inespressivo

expressive /ɪk'spresɪv/ *a* espressivo

expressively /ɪk'spresɪvlɪ/ *adv* espressamente

expulsion /ɪk'spʌlʃn/ *n* espulsione *f*

expurgate /'ekspəgeɪt/ *vt* espurgare

exquisite /ek'skwɪzɪt/ *a* squisito

exquisitely /ek'skwɪzɪtlɪ/ *adv* ⟨*dressed, written*⟩ in modo elegante e raffinato; **~ beautiful** di una bellezza fine

ex-serviceman /'sɜ:vɪsmən/ *n* ex-combattente *m*

ex-servicewoman /'sɜ:vɪswʊmən/ *n* ex-combattente *f*

extant /ɪk'stænt/ *a* ancora esistente

extempore /ɪk'stempərɪ/ *adv* ⟨*speak*⟩ senza preparazione

extend /ɪk'stend/ *vt* prolungare ⟨*visit, road*⟩; prorogare ⟨*visa, contract*⟩; ampliare ⟨*building, knowledge*⟩; (*stretch out*) allungare; tendere ⟨*hand*⟩ ● *vi* ⟨*garden, knowledge:*⟩ estendersi

extendable /ɪk'stendəbl/ *a* ⟨*cable*⟩ allungabile; ⟨*contract*⟩ prorogabile

extension /ɪk'stenʃn/ *n*) prolungamento *m*; (*of visa, contract*) proroga *f*; (*of treaty*) ampliamento *m*; (*part of building*) annesso *m*; (*length of cable*) prolunga *f*; *Teleph* interno *m*; **~ 226** interno 226

extension ladder *n* scala *f* allungabile

extension lead *n* *Electr* prolunga *f*

extensive /ɪk'stensɪv/ *a* ampio, vasto

extensively /ɪk'stensɪvlɪ/ *adv* ampiamente

extent /ɪk'stent/ *n* (*scope*) portata *f*; **to a certain ~** fino a un certo punto; **to such an ~ that...** fino al punto che...

extenuating /ɪk'stenjʊeɪtɪŋ/ *a* **~ circumstances** attenuanti *fpl*

exterior /ɪk'stɪərɪə(r)/ *a* & *n* esterno *m*

exterminate /ɪk'stɜ:mɪneɪt/ *vt* sterminare

extermination /ɪkstɜ:mɪ'neɪʃn/ *n* sterminio *m*

external /ɪk'stɜ:nl/ *a* esterno; **for ~ use only** *Med* per uso esterno

externalize /ɪk'stɜ:nəlaɪz/ *vt* esteriorizzare

externally /ɪk'stɜ:nəlɪ/ *adv* esternamente

externals /ɪk'stɜ:n(ə)lz/ *npl* apparenze *fpl*

extinct /ɪk'stɪŋkt/ *a* estinto

extinction /ɪk'stɪŋkʃn/ *n* estinzione *f*

extinguish /ɪk'stɪŋgwɪʃ/ *vt* estinguere

extinguisher /ɪk'stɪŋgwɪʃə(r)/ *n* estintore *m*

extol /ɪk'stəʊl/ *vt* (*pt/pp* **extolled**) lodare

extort /ɪk'stɔ:t/ *vt* estorcere

extortion /ɪk'stɔ:ʃn/ *n* estorsione *f*

extortionate /ɪk'stɔ:ʃənət/ *a* esorbitante

extra /'ekstrə/ *a* in più; ⟨*train*⟩ straordinario; **an ~ £10** 10 sterline extra, 10 sterline in più ● *adv* in più; (*especially*) più; **pay ~** pagare in più, pagare extra; **~ strong/busy** fortissimo/occupatissimo ● *n* *Theat* comparsa *f*; **~s** *pl* extra *mpl*

extra charge *n* supplemento *m*; **at no ~ ~** senza ulteriori spese

extract[1] /'ekstrækt/ *n* estratto *m*

extract[2] /ɪk'strækt/ *vt* estrarre ⟨*tooth, oil*⟩; strappare ⟨*secret*⟩; ricavare ⟨*truth*⟩

extraction /ɪk'strækʃn/ *n* (*process*) estrazione *f*; **of French ~** di origine francese

extractor [**fan**] /ɪk'stræktə(r)/ *n* aspiratore *m*

extra-curricular /-kə'rɪkjʊlə(r)/ *a* extrascolastico

extradite /'ekstrədaɪt/ *vt* *Jur* estradare

extradition /ekstrə'dɪʃn/ *n* estradizione *f*

extra-dry *a* ⟨*sherry, wine*⟩ extra dry *inv*

extra-fast *a* ultrarapido

extra-large *a* ⟨*pullover, shirt*⟩ extra large *inv*

extramarital /ekstrə'mærɪtəl/ *a* extraconiugale

extramural /ekstrə'mjʊərəl/ *a* *Br Univ* ⟨*course, lecture*⟩ organizzato dall'università e aperto a tutti

extraneous /ɪk'streɪnɪəs/ *a* (*not essential*) inessenziale; ⟨*issue, detail*⟩ superfluo

extraordinarily /ɪk'strɔ:dɪnərɪlɪ/ *adv* straordinariamente

extraordinary /ɪk'strɔ:dɪnərɪ/ *a* straordinario

extrapolate /ɪk'stræpəleɪt/ *vt* arguire; *Math* estrapolare

extrasensory perception /ekstrə'sensərɪ/ *n* percezione *f* extrasensoriale

extra-special *a* eccezionale

extra-strong *a* ⟨*thread*⟩ robustissimo; ⟨*coffee*⟩ fortissimo; ⟨*disinfectant, weed killer*⟩ potentissimo; ⟨*paper*⟩ ultraresistente *inv*

extraterrestrial /ekstrətɪ'restrɪəl/ *n* & *a* extraterrestre *mf*

extra time n tempo m supplementare; **play ~ ~** giocare i tempi supplementari

extravagance /ɪk'strævəgəns/ n (with money) prodigalità f; (of behaviour) stravaganza f

extravagant /ɪk'strævəgənt/ a spendaccione; (bizarre) stravagante; ‹claim› esagerato

extravagantly /ɪk'strævəgəntlɪ/ adv dispendiosamente

extravaganza /ɪkstrævə'gænzə/ n rappresentazione f spettacolare

extreme /ɪk'striːm/ a estremo ● n estremo m; **in the ~** al massimo

extremely /ɪk'striːmlɪ/ adv estremamente

extremism /ɪk'striːmɪzm/ n estremismo m

extremist /ɪk'striːmɪst/ n estremista mf

extremity /ɪk'stremətɪ/ n (end) estremità f inv

extricate /'ekstrɪkeɪt/ vt districare

extrovert /'ekstrəvɜːt/ n estroverso, -a mf

exuberance /ɪg'zjuːbərəns/ n esuberanza f

exuberant /ɪg'zjuːbərənt/ a esuberante

exude /ɪg'zjuːd/ vt also fig trasudare

exult /ɪg'zʌlt/ vi esultare

exultant /ɪg'zʌltənt/ a esultante; ‹cry› di esultanza

exultantly /ɪg'zʌltəntlɪ/ adv con esultanza

ex-works a ‹price, value› franco fabbrica

eye /aɪ/ n occhio m; (of needle) cruna f; **keep an ~ on** tener d'occhio; **see ~ to ~** aver le stesse idee ● vt (pt/pp **eyed**, pres p **ey[e]ing**) guardare

■ **eye up** vt adocchiare ‹sb›

eye: eyeball n bulbo m oculare. **eyebath** n bagno m oculare. **eyebrow** n sopracciglio m (pl sopracciglia f). **eyebrow pencil** n matita f per le sopracciglia. **eye-catching** /'aɪkætʃɪŋ/ a che attira l'attenzione. **eye contact** n **avoid ~ ~ with sb** evitare di incrociare lo sguardo di qcno; **try to make ~ ~ with sb** tentare di incrociare lo sguardo di qcno. **eyedrops** npl collirio m

eyeful /'aɪfʊl/ n **get an ~** (of sth) avere gli occhi pieni (di qcsa); (fam: good look) lustrarsi la vista

eye: eyeglass n (monocle) monocolo m. **eyeglasses** npl Am occhiali mpl [da vista]. **eyelash** n ciglio m (pl ciglia f)

eyelet /'aɪlɪt/ n occhiello m

eye: eye-level a ‹grill, shelf› all'altezza degli occhi. **eyelid** n palpebra f. **eye make-up** n trucco m per gli occhi. **eye-opener** n rivelazione f. **eyepatch** n benda f per gli occhi. **eye-shade** n visiera f. **eyeshadow** n ombretto m. **eyesight** n vista f. **eyesore** n fam pugno m nell'occhio. **eye strain** n affaticamento m degli occhi. **eye test** n esame m della vista. **eyewash** n bagno m oculare; (fig: nonsense) fumo m negli occhi. **eyewitness** n testimone mf oculare

eyrie /'ɪərɪ/ n nido m d'aquila

Ff

f, F /ef/ n (letter) f, F f inv; Mus fa m inv

FA n Br abbr (Football Association) associazione f calcistica britannica, ≈ FIGC f

fable /'feɪbl/ n favola f

fabric /'fæbrɪk/ n also fig tessuto m

fabricate /'fæbrɪkeɪt/ vt fabbricare; inventare ‹story›

fabrication /fæbrɪ'keɪʃn/ n invenzione f; (manufacture) fabbricazione f

fabric softener /sɒfnə(r)/ n ammorbidente m

fabulous /'fæbjʊləs/ a fam favoloso

façade /fə'sɑːd/ n (of building, person) facciata f

face /feɪs/ n faccia f, viso m; (grimace) smorfia f; (surface) faccia f; (of clock) quadrante m; **pull ~s** far boccacce; **in the ~ of** di fronte a; **on the ~ of it** in apparenza ● vt essere di fronta a; (confront) affrontare; **~ north** ‹house:› dare a nord; **~ the fact that** arrendersi al fatto che

■ **face up to** vt accettare ‹facts›; affrontare ‹person›

face flannel n ≈ guanto m di spugna

faceless /'feɪslɪs/ a anonimo

facelift /'feɪslɪft/ n plastica f facciale

face powder n cipria f

facet /'fæsɪt/ n sfaccettatura f; fig aspetto m

facetious /fə'siːʃəs/ a spiritoso. **~ remarks** spiritosaggini mpl

face: face pack n maschera f di bellezza. **face saving** a ‹plan, solution› per salvare la faccia. **face to face** a ‹meeting› a quattr'occhi ● adv ‹be seated› faccia a faccia; **meet sb ~ to ~** avere un incontro a quattr'occhi con qcno; **come ~ to ~ with** trovarsi di fronte a. **face value** n (of money) valore m nominale; **take sb/sth at ~ ~** fermarsi alle apparenze

facial /'feɪʃl/ a facciale ● n trattamento m di bellezza al viso

facile /'fæsaɪl/ a semplicistico

facilitate /fə'sɪlɪteɪt/ vt rendere possibile; (make easier) facilitare

facility /fə'sɪlətɪ/ n facilità f; **facilities** pl (of area, in hotel etc) attrezzature fpl; **credit facilities** pl facilitazioni fpl di pagamento

facing /'feɪsɪŋ/ prep **~ the sea** ‹house› che

dà sul mare; **the person ~ me** la persona di fronte a me

facsimile /fæk'sɪməlɪ/ n facsimile m

fact /fækt/ n fatto m; **in ~** infatti

fact finding a ⟨mission, tour, trip⟩ di inchiesta

faction /'fækʃn/ n fazione f

factional /'fækʃnəl/ a ⟨leader, activity⟩ di una fazione; ⟨fighting, arguments⟩ tra fazioni

factor /'fæktə(r)/ n fattore m

factory /'fæktərɪ/ n fabbrica f

factory: factory farming n allevamento m su scala industriale. **factory floor** n ⟨place⟩ reparto m produzione; ⟨workers⟩ operai mpl. **factory inspector** n verificatore, -trice mf. **factory made** a prodotto in fabbrica. **factory unit** n unità f inv di produzione. **factory worker** n operaio, -a mf

fact sheet n ⟨one issue⟩ prospetto m illustrativo; ⟨periodical⟩ bollettino m d'informazione

factual /'fæktʃʊəl/ a **be ~** attenersi ai fatti

factually /'fæktʃʊəlɪ/ adv ⟨inaccurate⟩ dal punto di vista dei fatti

faculty /'fækəltɪ/ n facoltà f inv

fad /fæd/ n capriccio m

faddish /'fædɪʃ/ a ⟨person⟩ sempre in preda a una nuova mania

fade /feɪd/ vi sbiadire; ⟨sound, light:⟩ affievolirsi; ⟨flower:⟩ appassire

∎ **fade in** vt cominciare in dissolvenza ⟨picture⟩

∎ **fade out** vt finire in dissolvenza ⟨picture⟩

faded /'feɪdɪd/ a ⟨clothing, carpet, colour⟩ sbiadito; ⟨flower, beauty⟩ appassito; ⟨glory⟩ svanito

faeces /'fi:si:z/ npl feci fpl

fag /fæg/ n ⟨chore⟩ fatica f; (fam: cigarette) sigaretta f; (Am sl: homosexual) frocio m

fag end n fam mozzicone m di sigaretta, cicca f; ⟨of day, decade, conversation⟩ fine f; ⟨of material⟩ scampolo m

fagged /fægd/ a **~ out** fam stanco morto

faggot /'fægət/ n ⟨meatball⟩ polpetta f di carne; ⟨firewood⟩ fascina f

Fahrenheit /'færənhaɪt/ a Fahrenheit

fail /feɪl/ n **without ~** senz'altro ● vi ⟨attempt:⟩ fallire; ⟨eyesight, memory:⟩ indebolirsi; ⟨engine, machine:⟩ guastarsi; ⟨marriage:⟩ andare a rotoli; (in exam) essere bocciato; **~ to do sth** non fare qcsa; **I tried but I ~ed** ho provato ma non ci sono riuscito; **a ~ed politician** un politico fallito ● vt non superare ⟨exam⟩; bocciare ⟨candidate⟩; ⟨disappoint⟩ deludere; **words ~ me** mi mancano le parole; **unless my memory ~s me** se la memoria non mi tradisce

failing /'feɪlɪŋ/ n difetto m ● prep **~ that** altrimenti

fail-safe a ⟨device, system⟩ di sicurezza

failure /'feɪljə(r)/ n fallimento m; ⟨mechanical⟩ guasto m; ⟨person⟩ incapace mf

faint /feɪnt/ a leggero; ⟨memory⟩ vago; **feel ~** sentirsi mancare ● n svenimento m ● vi svenire

faint-hearted /-'hɑːtɪd/ a timido

fainting fit /'feɪntɪŋ/ n svenimento m

faintly /'feɪntlɪ/ adv ⟨slightly⟩ leggermente

faintness /'feɪntnɪs/ n ⟨physical⟩ debolezza f

fair¹ /feə(r)/ n fiera f

fair² a ⟨hair, person⟩ biondo; ⟨skin⟩ chiaro; ⟨weather⟩ bello; (just) giusto; (quite good) discreto; Sch abbastanza bene; **a ~ amount** abbastanza ● adv **play ~** fare un gioco pulito

fair copy n bella copia f

fairground /'feəgraʊnd/ n luna park m inv

fairly /'feəlɪ/ adv con giustizia; (rather) discretamente, abbastanza

fair-minded /feə'maɪndɪd/ a equo

fairness /'feənɪs/ n giustizia f

fair: fair play n fair play m inv. **fair skinned** /-'skɪnd/ a di carnagione chiara. **fairway** n Naut via f d'acqua navigabile; (in golf) fairway m inv. **fair weather friend** n pej amico m finché tutto va bene

fairy /'feərɪ/ n fata f; **good ~** fata [buona]; **wicked ~** strega f

fairy: fairy godmother n fata f buona. **fairy lights** npl Br lampadine fpl colorate. **fairy story, fairy-tale** n fiaba f

faith /feɪθ/ n fede f; (trust) fiducia f; **in good/ bad ~** in buona/mala fede

faithful /'feɪθfl/ a fedele

faithfully /'feɪθfʊlɪ/ adv fedelmente; **yours ~** distinti saluti

faithfulness /'feɪθfʊlnɪs/ n fedeltà f

faith-healer /hi:lə(r)/ n guaritore, -trice mf

faithless /'feɪθlɪs/ a ⟨friend, servant⟩ sleale; ⟨husband⟩ infedele

fake /feɪk/ a falso ● n falsificazione f; ⟨person⟩ impostore m ● vt falsificare; ⟨pretend⟩ fingere

falcon /'fɔːlkən/ n falcone m

Falklands /'fɔːlkləndz/ npl le isole Falkland, le isole Malvine

fall /fɔːl/ n caduta f; (in prices) ribasso m; (Am: autumn) autunno m; **have a ~** fare una caduta ● vi (pt fell, pp fallen) cadere; ⟨night:⟩ scendere; **~ in love** innamorarsi

∎ **fall about** vi (with laughter) morire dal ridere

∎ **fall back on** vt ritornare su

∎ **fall down** vi cadere; ⟨building:⟩ crollare

∎ **fall for** vt fam innamorarsi di ⟨person⟩; cascarci ⟨sth, trick⟩

∎ **fall in** vi caderci dentro; ⟨collapse⟩ crollare; Mil mettersi in riga; **~ in with** concordare con ⟨suggestion, plan⟩

∎ **fall off** vi cadere; ⟨diminish⟩ diminuire

∎ **fall out** vi ⟨quarrel⟩ litigare; **his hair is ~ing out** perde i capelli

∎ **fall over** vi cadere

∎ **fall through** vi ⟨plan:⟩ andare a monte

fallacious /fə'leɪʃəs/ a fallace

fallacy /'fæləsɪ/ n errore m

fallible /'fæləbl/ a fallibile

Fallopian tube /fə'ləʊpɪən/ n tromba f di Falloppio

fallout /'fɔːlaʊt/ n pioggia f radioattiva

fallout shelter n rifugio m antiatomico

fallow /'fæləʊ/ a lie ~ essere a maggese

false /fɔːls/ a falso

false bottom n doppio fondo m

falsehood /'fɔːlshʊd/ n menzogna f

falsely /'fɔːlslɪ/ adv falsamente

falseness /'fɔːlsnɪs/ n falsità f

false: false pretences npl **under ~ ~** sotto false spoglie; Jur con la frode. **false start** n Sport falsa partenza f. **false teeth** npl dentiera f

falsetto /fɔːl'setəʊ/ n (voice) falsetto m inv ● a in falsetto

falsification /fɔːlsɪfɪ'keɪʃn/ n (of document, figures) falsificazione f; (of truth, facts) deformazione f

falsify /'fɔːlsɪfaɪ/ vt (pt/pp -ied) falsificare

falsity /'fɔːlsətɪ/ n falsità f

falter /'fɔːltə(r)/ vi vacillare; (making speech) esitare

fame /feɪm/ n fama f

famed /feɪmd/ a rinomato

familiar /fə'mɪljə(r)/ a familiare; **be ~ with** (know) conoscere; **become too ~** prendersi troppe confidenze

familiarity /fəmɪlɪ'ærətɪ/ n familiarità f

familiarize /fə'mɪlɪəraɪz/ vt familiarizzare; **~ oneself with sth** familiarizzarsi con qcsa

family /'fæmɪlɪ/ n famiglia f

family: family allowance n assegni mpl familiari. **family circle** n (group) cerchia f familiare; Am Theat seconda galleria f. **family doctor** n medico m di famiglia. **family life** n vita f familiare. **family name** n cognome m. **family planning** n pianificazione f familiare. **family tree** n albero m genealogico

famine /'fæmɪn/ n carestia f

famished /'fæmɪʃt/ a **be ~** fam avere una fame da lupo

famous /'feɪməs/ a famoso

fan¹ /fæn/ n ventilatore m; (handheld) ventaglio m ● v (pt/pp **fanned**) ● vt far vento a; **~ oneself** sventagliarsi; fig ~ **the flames** soffiare sul fuoco

▪ **fan out** vi spiegarsi a ventaglio

fan² n (admirer) ammiratore, -trice mf, fan mf; Sport tifoso m; (of Verdi etc) appassionato, -a mf

fanatic /fə'nætɪk/ n fanatico, -a mf

fanatical /fə'nætɪkl/ a fanatico

fanatically /fə'æntɪklɪ/ adv con fanatismo

fanaticism /fə'nætɪsɪzm/ n fanatismo m

fan belt n cinghia f per ventilatore

fanciful /'fænsɪfl/ a fantasioso

fancy /'fænsɪ/ n fantasia f; **I've taken a real ~ to him** mi è molto simpatico; **as the ~ takes you** come ti pare ● a fantasia inv ● vt (believe) credere; (fam: want) aver voglia di; **he fancies you** fam gli piaci; **~ that!** ma guarda un po'!

fancy dress n costume m

fanfare /'fænfeə(r)/ n fanfara f

fang /fæŋ/ n zanna f; (of snake) dente m

fan: fan heater n termoventilatore m.

fanlight n lunetta f. **fan mail** n posta f dei fans

fantasize /'fæntəsaɪz/ vi fantasticare

fantastic /fæn'tæstɪk/ a fantastico

fantasy /'fæntəsɪ/ n fantasia f

far /fɑː(r)/ adv lontano; (much) molto; **by ~** di gran lunga; **~ away** lontano; **as ~ as the church** fino alla chiesa; **how ~ is it from here?** quanto dista da qui? **as ~ as I know** per quanto io sappia ● a ⟨end, side⟩ altro; **the F~ East** l'Estremo Oriente m; **in the ~ distance** in lontananza

farce /fɑːs/ n farsa f

farcical /'fɑːsɪkl/ a ridicolo

fare /feə(r)/ n tariffa f; (food) vitto m

fare-dodger /-dɒdʒə(r)/ n passeggero, -a mf senza biglietto

farewell /feə'wel/ int liter addio! ● n addio m; **~ dinner** cena f d'addio

far-fetched /-'fetʃt/ a improbabile

far flung /-'flʌŋ/ a (remote) remoto; (widely distributed) sparpagliato; ⟨network⟩ esteso

farm /fɑːm/ n fattoria f ● vi fare l'agricoltore ● vt coltivare ⟨land⟩

farmer /'fɑːmə(r)/ n agricoltore m

farmhand /'fɑːmhænd/ n bracciante m

farmhouse /'fɑːmhaʊs/ n casa f colonica

farming /'fɑːmɪŋ/ n agricoltura f

farm produce n prodotto m agricolo

farmyard /'fɑːmjɑːd/ n aia f

far-reaching /-'riːtʃɪŋ/ a ⟨programme, plan, proposal⟩ di larga portata; ⟨effect, implication, change⟩ notevole

far-sighted /-'saɪtɪd/ a ⟨policy⟩ lungimirante; (Am: long-sighted) presbite

fart /fɑːt/fam n scoreggia f ● vi scoreggiare

farther /'fɑːðə(r)/ adv più lontano ● a **the ~ end of** all'altra estremità di

fascia /'feɪʃɪə/ n Br (dashboard) cruscotto m

fascinate /'fæsɪneɪt/ vt affascinare

fascinating /'fæsɪneɪtɪŋ/ a affascinante

fascination /fæsɪ'neɪʃn/ n fascino m

fascism /'fæʃɪzm/ n fascismo m

fascist /'fæʃɪst/ a & n fascista mf

fashion /'fæʃn/ n moda f; (manner) maniera f; **in ~** di moda; **out of ~** non più di moda ● vt modellare

fashionable /'fæʃ(ə)nəbl/ a di moda; **be ~** essere alla moda

fashionably /'fæʃ(ə)nəblɪ/ adv alla moda

fashion: fashion designer n stilista mf. **fashion house** n casa f di moda. **fashion model** n indossatore, -trice mf, modello, -a mf

fast¹ /fɑːst/ a veloce; (colour) indelebile; **be ~** ⟨clock:⟩ andare avanti ● adv velocemente; (firmly) saldamente; **~er!** più in fretta!; **be ~ asleep** dormire profondamente

fast² n digiuno m ● vi digiunare

fasten /'fɑːsn/ vt allacciare; chiudere ⟨window⟩; (stop flapping) mettere un fermo a ● vi allacciarsi

fastener /'fɑːsnə(r)/ n, **fastening** /'fɑːsnɪŋ/ n chiusura f

fast: fast food n fast food m inv ● attrib ⟨chain⟩ di fast food; **~ ~ restaurant** n fast food *m inv.* **fast forward** *n* avanzamento *m* veloce ● *vt* far avanzare velocemente ‹*tape*› ● *attrib* ‹*key, button*› di avanzamento veloce. **fast growing** *a* in rapida espansione.

fastidious /fəˈstɪdɪəs/ *a* esigente

fast: fast lane *n Auto* corsia *f* di sorpasso; **life in the ~ ~ ~** *fig* vita *f* frenetica. **fast-talking** *a* ‹*salesperson*› che raggira con la sua parlantina

fat /fæt/ *a* (**fatter, fattest**) ‹*person, cheque*› grasso; *fam* **that's a ~ lot of use** non serve a un accidente ● *n* grasso *m*

fatal /ˈfeɪtl/ *a* mortale; ‹*error*› fatale

fatalism /ˈfeɪtəlɪzm/ *n* fatalismo *m*

fatalist /ˈfeɪtəlɪst/ *n* fatalista *mf*

fatality /fəˈtælətɪ/ *n* morte *f*

fatally /ˈfeɪtəlɪ/ *adv* mortalmente

fate /feɪt/ *n* destino *m*

fated /ˈfeɪtɪd/ *a* destinato; **it was ~** era destino

fateful /ˈfeɪtfʊl/ *a* fatidico

fat free *a* magro

fat-head *n fam* zuccone, -a *mf*

father /ˈfɑːðə(r)/ *n* padre *m* ● *vt* generare ‹*child*›

father: Father Christmas Babbo *m* Natale. **father confessor** *n Relig* confessore *m*. **father figure** *n* figura *f* paterna. **fatherhood** *n* paternità *f*. **father-in-law** *n* (*pl* **~s-in-law**) suocero *m*. **fatherland** *n* patria *f*

fatherly /ˈfɑːðəlɪ/ *a* paterno

Father's Day /ˈfɑːðəz/ *n* la festa del papà

fathom /ˈfæðəm/ *n Naut* braccio *m* ● *vt* **~ [out]** comprendere

fatigue /fəˈtiːɡ/ *n* fatica *f* ● *vt* affaticare

fatness /ˈfætnɪs/ *n* grassezza *f*

fatten /ˈfætn/ *vt* ingrassare ‹*animal*›

fattening /ˈfætnɪŋ/ *a* **cream is ~** la panna fa ingrassare

fatty /ˈfætɪ/ *a* grasso ● *n fam* ciccione, -a *mf*

fatuous /ˈfætjʊəs/ *a* fatuo

faucet /ˈfɔːsɪt/ *n Am* rubinetto *m*

fault /fɔːlt/ *n* difetto *m*; *Geol* faglia *f*; *Tennis* fallo *m*; **be at ~** avere torto; **find ~ with** trovare da ridire su; **it's your ~** è colpa tua ● *vt* criticare

fault-finding /ˈfɔːltfaɪndɪŋ/ *n* (*of person*) atteggiamento *m* ipercritico; *Techn* localizzazione *f* del guasto ● *a* ‹*attitude*› da criticone; ‹*person*› ipercritico

faultless /ˈfɔːltlɪs/ *a* impeccabile

faultlessly /ˈfɔːltlɪslɪ/ *adv* impeccabilmente

faulty /ˈfɔːltɪ/ *a* difettoso

fauna /ˈfɔːnə/ *n* fauna *f*

faux pas /fəʊˈpɑː/ *n* gaffe *f inv*

favour /ˈfeɪvə(r)/ *n* favore *m*; **be in ~ of sth** essere a favore di qcsa; **do sb a ~** fare un piacere a qcno ● *vt* (*prefer*) preferire

favourable /ˈfeɪv(ə)rəbl/ *a* favorevole

favourably /ˈfeɪv(ə)rəblɪ/ *adv* favorevolmente

favourite /ˈfeɪv(ə)rɪt/ *a* preferito ● *n* preferito, -a *mf*; *Sport* favorito, -a *mf*

favouritism /ˈfeɪv(ə)rɪtɪzm/ *n* favoritismo *m*

fawn /fɔːn/ *a* fulvo ● *n* (*animal*) cerbiatto *m*

fax /fæks/ *n* (*document, machine*) fax *m inv*; **by ~** per fax ● *vt* faxare

fax machine *n* fax *m inv*

fax-modem *n* fax-modem *m inv*

faze /feɪz/ *vt fam* scompaginare

fear /fɪə(r)/ *n* paura *f*; **no ~!** *fam* vai tranquillo! ● *vt* temere ● *vi* **~ for sth** temere per qcsa

fearful /ˈfɪəfl/ *a* pauroso; (*awful*) terribile

fearless /ˈfɪəlɪs/ *a* impavido

fearlessly /ˈfɪəlɪslɪ/ *adv* senza paura

fearsome /ˈfɪəsəm/ *a* spaventoso

feasibility /fiːzɪˈbɪlətɪ/ *n* praticabilità *f*

feasible /ˈfiːzəbl/ *a* fattibile; (*possible*) probabile

feast /fiːst/ *n* festa *f*; (*banquet*) banchetto *m* ● *vi* banchettare

■ **feast on** *vt* godersi

feat /fiːt/ *n* impresa *f*

feather /ˈfeðə(r)/ *n* piuma *f*; **you could have knocked me down with a ~** sono rimasto di sasso

feather: feather-brained /-bremd/ *a* che non ha un briciolo di cervello. **feather duster** *n* piumino *m* (*per spolverare*). **featherweight** *n* peso *m* piuma

feature /ˈfiːtʃə(r)/ *n* (*quality*) caratteristica *f*; *Journ* articolo *m*; **~s** *pl* (*of face*) lineamenti *mpl* ● *vt* ‹*film:*› avere come protagonista ● *vi* (*on a list etc*) comparire

feature film *n* lungometraggio *m*

feature length film *n* lungometraggio *m*

February /ˈfebruərɪ/ *n* febbraio *m*

feces /ˈfiːsiːz/ *npl* feci *fpl*

feckless /ˈfeklɪs/ *a* inetto

fecund /ˈfekənd/ *a* fecondo

fed /fed/ *see* **feed** ● *a* **be ~ up** *fam* essere stufo (**with** di)

federal /ˈfed(ə)rəl/ *a* federale

federalist /ˈfed(ə)rəlɪst/ *n & a* federalista *mf*

Federal Republic of Germany *n* Repubblica *f* Federale Tedesca

federate /ˈfed(ə)rət/ *a* federato

federation /fedəˈreɪʃn/ *n* federazione *f*

fee /fiː/ *n* tariffa *f*; (*lawyer's, doctor's*) onorario *m*; (*for membership, school*) quota *f*

feeble /ˈfiːbl/ *a* debole; (*excuse*) fiacco

feeble minded /-ˈmaɪndɪd/ *a* deficiente

feebleness /ˈfiːblnɪs/ *n* debolezza *f*

feed /fiːd/ *n* mangiare *m*; (*for baby*) pappa *f*; **five ~s a day** cinque pasti al giorno ● *v* (*pt/pp* **fed**) ● *vt* dar da mangiare a ‹*animal*›; (*support*) nutrire; **~ sth into sth** inserire qcsa in qcsa; **~ paper into the printer** alimentare la stampante con fogli ● *vi* mangiare

■ **feed up** *vt* ingrassare ‹*sb*›

feedback /ˈfiːdbæk/ *n* controreazione *f*; (*of information*) reazione *f*, feedback *m*

feeder /ˈfiːdə(r)/ *n* (*for printer, photocopier*) mettifoglio *m inv*; (*Br: bib*) bavaglino *m*; (*road*) raccordo *m*

feeding bottle /ˈfiːdɪŋ/ *n Br* biberon *m inv*

feeding time *n* (*in zoo*) l'ora *f* del pasto degli animali

feel /fiːl/ *v* (*pt/pp* **felt**) ● *vt* sentire; (*experience*) provare; (*think*) pensare; (*touch:*

searching) tastare; (*touch: for texture*) toccare
● *vi* ~ **soft/hard** essere duro/morbido al tatto; ~ **hot/hungry** aver caldo/fame; ~ **ill** sentirsi male; **I don't** ~ **like it** non ne ho voglia; **how do you** ~ **about it?** (*opinion*) che te ne pare?; **it doesn't** ~ **right** non mi sembra giusto

■ **feel for** *vt* (*feel sympathy for*) dispiacersi per

■ **feel up to** *vt* ~ **up to doing sth** sentirsi in grado di fare qcsa; **I don't** ~ **up to it** non me la sento

feeler /ˈfiːlə(r)/ *n* (*of animal*) antenna *f*; **put out ~s** *fig* tastare il terreno

feel-good factor *n* sensazione *f* di benessere

feeling /ˈfiːlɪŋ/ *n* sentimento *m*; (*awareness*) sensazione *f*

fee paying *a* ⟨*school*⟩ a pagamento, privato; ⟨*parent, pupil*⟩ che paga l'iscrizione (*a una scuola privata*)

feet /fiːt/ *see* **foot**

feign /feɪn/ *vt* simulare

feint /feɪnt/ *n* finta *f*

feisty /ˈfaɪstɪ/ *a Am* (*quarrelsome*) stizzoso; (*fam: lively*) esuberante

felicitous /fəˈlɪsɪtəs/ *a* felice

feline /ˈfiːlaɪn/ *a* felino

fell[1] /fel/ *vt* (*knock down*) abbattere

fell[2] *see* **fall**

fellow /ˈfeləʊ/ *n* (*of society*) socio *m*; (*fam: man*) tipo *m*

fellow: fellow citizen *n* concittadino, -a *mf*. **fellow countryman** *n* compatriota *m*. **fellow men** *npl* simili *mpl*

fellowship /ˈfeləʊʃɪp/ *n* cameratismo *m*; (*group*) associazione *f*; *Univ* incarico *m* di ricercatore, -trice *mf*

fellow traveller *n* compagno, -a *mf* di viaggio; *Pol, fig* compagno, -a *mf* di strada

felon /ˈfelən/ *n Jur* criminale *mf*

felony /ˈfelənɪ/ *n* delitto *m*

felt[1] /felt/ *see* **feel**

felt[2] *n* feltro *m*. ~[**-tipped**] **pen** /-tɪpt'pen/ *n* pennarello *m*

female /ˈfiːmeɪl/ *a* femminile; **the ~ antelope** l'antilope femmina ● *n* femmina *f*

feminine /ˈfemɪnɪn/ *a* femminile ● *n Gram* femminile *m*

femininity /femɪˈnɪnətɪ/ *n* femminilità *f*

feminist /ˈfemɪnɪst/ *a & n* femminista *mf*

fen /fen/ *n* zona *f* paludosa

fence /fens/ *n* recinto *m*; (*fam: person*) ricettatore *m* ● *vi Sport* tirar di scherma

■ **fence in** *vt* chiudere in un recinto

fencer /ˈfensə(r)/ *n* schermidore *m*

fencing /ˈfensɪŋ/ *n* steccato *m*; *Sport* scherma *f*

fend /fend/ *vi* ~ **for oneself** badare a se stesso

■ **fend off** *vt* parare; difendersi da ⟨*criticisms*⟩

fender /ˈfendə(r)/ *n* parafuoco *m inv*; *Naut* parabordo *m*; (*Am: on car*) parafango *m*

fennel /ˈfenl/ *n* finocchio *m*

ferment[1] /ˈfɜːment/ *n* fermento *m*

ferment[2] /fəˈment/ *vi* fermentare ● *vt* far fermentare

fermentation /fɜːmenˈteɪʃn/ *n* fermentazione *f*

fern /fɜːn/ *n* felce *f*

ferocious /fəˈrəʊʃəs/ *a* feroce

ferocity /fəˈrɒsətɪ/ *n* ferocia *f*

ferret /ˈferɪt/ *n* furetto *m*

■ **ferret out** *vt* scovare

ferrous /ˈferəs/ *a* ferroso

ferry /ˈferɪ/ *n* traghetto *m* ● *vt* (*pt/pp* **-ied**) traghettare

ferryman /ˈferɪmən/ *n* traghettatore *m*

fertile /ˈfɜːtaɪl/ *a* fertile

fertility /fɜːˈtɪlətɪ/ *n* fertilità *f*

fertility drug *n* farmaco *m* contro la sterilità

fertilize /ˈfɜːtɪlaɪz/ *vt* fertilizzare ⟨*land, ovum*⟩

fertilizer /ˈfɜːtɪlaɪzə(r)/ *n* fertilizzante *m*

fervent /ˈfɜːvənt/ *a* fervente

fervour /ˈfɜːvə(r)/ *n* fervore *m*

fester /ˈfestə(r)/ *vi* suppurare

festival /ˈfestɪvl/ *n Mus, Theat* festival *m*; *Relig* festa *f*

festive /ˈfestɪv/ *a* festivo; ~ **season** periodo *m* delle feste natalizie

festivities /feˈstɪvətɪz/ *npl* festeggiamenti *mpl*

festoon /feˈstuːn/ *vt* ~ **with** ornare di

fetch /fetʃ/ *vt* andare/venire a prendere; (*be sold for*) raggiungere [il prezzo di]

fetching /ˈfetʃɪŋ/ *a* attraente

fête /feɪt/ *n* festa *f* ● *vt* festeggiare

fetid /ˈfetɪd/ *a* fetido

fetish /ˈfetɪʃ/ *n* feticcio *m*

fetter /ˈfetə(r)/ *vt* incatenare

fettle /ˈfetl/ *n* **in fine** ~ in buona forma

fetus /ˈfiːtəs/ *n* (*pl* **-tuses**) feto *m*

feud /fjuːd/ *n* faida *f*

feudal /ˈfjuːdl/ *a* feudale

fever /ˈfiːvə(r)/ *n* febbre *f*

fevered /ˈfiːvəd/ *a* ⟨*brow*⟩ febbricitante; ⟨*imagination*⟩ febbrile

feverish /ˈfiːvərɪʃ/ *a* febbricitante; *fig* febbrile

fever pitch *n* **bring a crowd to** ~ ~ esaltare la folla

few /fjuː/ *a* pochi; **every** ~ **days** ogni due o tre giorni; **a** ~ **people** alcuni; ~ **people know that** poche persone lo sanno; ~**er reservations** meno prenotazioni; **the** ~**est number** il numero più basso ● *pron* pochi; ~ **of us** pochi di noi; **a** ~ alcuni; **quite a** ~ parecchi; ~**er than last year** meno dell'anno scorso

fez /fez/ *n* fez *m inv*

fiancé /fɪˈɒnseɪ/ *n* fidanzato *m*

fiancée /fɪˈɒnseɪ/ *n* fidanzata *f*

fiasco /fɪˈæskəʊ/ *n* fiasco *m*

fib /fɪb/ *n* storia *f*; **tell a** ~ raccontare una storia

fibber /ˈfɪbə(r)/ *n fam* contaballe *mf inv*

fibre /ˈfaɪbə(r)/ *n* fibra *f*

fibre: fibreglass n fibra f di vetro ● *attrib* in fibra di vetro. **fibre optic** a ⟨*cable*⟩ a fibre ottiche. **fibre optics** n fibra f ottica

fibroid /'faɪbrɔɪd/ n fibroma m ● a fibroso

fibula /'fɪbjʊlə/ n Anat perone m

fiche /fi:ʃ/ n microscheda f

fickle /'fɪkl/ a incostante

fiction /'fɪkʃn/ n [**works of**] ~ narrativa f; (*fabrication*) finzione f

fictional /'fɪkʃənəl/ a immaginario

fictitious /fɪk'tɪʃəs/ a fittizio

fiddle /'fɪdl/ n fam violino m; (*cheating*) imbroglio m ● vi gingillarsi (**with** con) ● vt fam truccare ⟨*accounts*⟩

fiddly /'fɪdlɪ/ a intricato

fidelity /fɪ'delətɪ/ n fedeltà f

fidget /'fɪdʒɪt/ vi agitarsi

fidgety /'fɪdʒətɪ/ a agitato

field /fi:ld/ n campo m

field day n have a ~ ~ ⟨*press, critics:*⟩ godersela; (*make money*) fare affari d'oro

fielder /'fi:ldə(r)/ n Sport esterno m

field: field events npl atletica fsg leggera. **field glasses** npl binocolo msg. **Field Marshal** n feldmaresciallo m. **field mouse** n topo m campagnolo. **fieldwork** n ricerche fpl sul terreno

fiend /fi:nd/ n demonio m

fiendish /'fi:ndɪʃ/ a diabolico

fierce /fɪəs/ a feroce

fiercely /'fɪəslɪ/ adv ferocemente

fierceness /'fɪəsnɪs/ n ferocia f

fiery /'faɪərɪ/ a (**-ier, -iest**) focoso

fiesta /fɪ'estə/ n sagra f

fife /faɪf/ n piffero m

fifteen /fɪf'ti:n/ a & n quindici m

fifteenth /fɪf'ti:nθ/ a & n quindicesimo, -a mf

fifth /fɪfθ/ a & n quinto, -a mf

fiftieth /'fɪftɪɪθ/ a & n cinquantesimo, -a mf

fifty /'fɪftɪ/ a & n cinquanta m

fifty-fifty a have a ~ **chance** avere una probabilità su due ● adv **go** ~ fare [a] metà e metà; **split sth** ~ dividersi qcsa a metà

fig /fɪg/ n fico m

fight /faɪt/ n lotta f; (*brawl*) zuffa f; (*argument*) litigio m; (*boxing*) incontro m ● v (*pt/pp* **fought**) ● vt also fig combattere ● vi combattere; (*brawl*) azzuffarsi; (*argue*) litigare

■ **fight back** vi reagire ● vt frenare ⟨*tears*⟩

■ **fight for** vt lottare per ⟨*freedom, independence*⟩

■ **fight off** vt combattere ⟨*cold*⟩

fighter /'faɪtə(r)/ n combattente mf; Aeron caccia m inv; **he's a** ~ ha uno spirito combattivo

fighter-bomber n cacciabombardiere m

fighter pilot n pilota m di cacciabombardiere

fighting /'faɪtɪŋ/ n combattimento m

fighting chance n have a ~ ~ avere buone probabilità

fighting fit a in piena forma

figment /'fɪgmənt/ n **it's a** ~ **of your imagination** questo è tutta una tua invenzione

fig tree n fico m

figurative /'fɪgərətɪv/ a ⟨*sense*⟩ figurato; ⟨*art*⟩ figurativo

figuratively /'fɪgərətɪvlɪ/ adv ⟨*use*⟩ in senso figurato

figure /'fɪgə(r)/ n (*digit*) cifra f; (*carving, sculpture, illustration, form*) figura f; (*body shape*) linea f; ~ **of speech** modo m di dire ● vi (*appear*) figurare ● vt (Am: *think*) pensare

■ **figure out** vt dedurre; capire ⟨*person*⟩

figure: figurehead n figura f simbolica. **figure of speech** n modo m di dire; (*literary device*) figura f retorica. **figure skating** n pattinaggio m artistico

figurine /'fɪgəri:n/ n statuetta f

filament /'fɪləmənt/ n filamento m

filch /fɪltʃ/ vt fam rubacchiare

file[1] /faɪl/ n scheda f; (*set of documents*) incartamento m; (*folder*) cartellina f; Comput file m inv ● vt archiviare ⟨*documents*⟩

file[2] n (*line*) fila f; **in single** ~ in fila

file[3] n Techn lima f ● vt limare

file manager n Comput file manager m inv

filial /'fɪlɪəl/ a filiale

filibuster /'fɪlɪbʌstə(r)/ n ostruzionismo m parlamentare

filigree /'fɪlɪgri:/ n filigrana f

filing /'faɪlɪŋ/ n archiviazione f

filing: filing cabinet n schedario m, classificatore m. **filing card** n scheda f. **filing clerk** n archivista mf

filings /'faɪlɪŋz/ npl limatura fsg

filing system n sistema m di classificazione, sistema m di archivio

fill /fɪl/ n **eat one's** ~ mangiare a sazietà ● vt riempire; otturare ⟨*tooth*⟩ ● vi riempirsi

■ **fill in** vt compilare ⟨*form*⟩

■ **fill in for** vt rimpiazzare ⟨*sb*⟩

■ **fill in on** vt ~ **sb in on sth** mettere qcno al corrente di qcsa

■ **fill out** vt compilare ⟨*form*⟩

■ **fill up** vi ⟨*room, tank:*⟩ riempirsi; Auto far il pieno ● vt riempire

fillet /'fɪlɪt/ n filetto m ● vt (*pt/pp* **filleted**) disossare

fillet steak n bistecca f di filetto

fill in n (*fam: replacement*) rimpiazzo m

filling /'fɪlɪŋ/ n Culin ripieno m; (*of tooth*) piombatura f

filling station n stazione f di rifornimento

filly /'fɪlɪ/ n puledra f

film /fɪlm/ n Cinema film m inv; Phot pellicola f; [**cling**] ~ pellicola f per alimenti ● vt/i filmare

film: film-goer /'fɪlmgəʊə(r)/ n frequentatore, -trice mf di cinema. **film industry** n industria f cinematografica. **filmset** n allestimento m scenico. **film star** n star f inv, divo, -a mf

filmy /'fɪlmɪ/ a (*thin: fabric, screen*) trasparente; (*thin*) sottilissimo

filter /'fɪltə(r)/ n filtro m ● vt filtrare

■ **filter through** vi ⟨*news:*⟩ trapelare

filter: filter cigarette n sigaretta f con filtro. **filter coffee** n (ground coffee) caffè m macinato per filtro; (cup of coffee) caffè m inv fatto con il filtro. **filter-paper** n carta f da filtro. **filter tip** n filtro m; (cigarette) sigaretta f col filtro

filth /fɪlθ/ n sudiciume m

filthy /'fɪlθɪ/ a (-ier, -iest) sudicio; (language) sconcio

filthy rich a fam ricco sfondato

fin /fɪn/ n pinna f

final /'faɪnl/ a finale; (conclusive) decisivo ● n Sport finale f; ~s pl Univ esami mpl finali

finale /fɪ'nɑːlɪ/ n finale m

finalist /'faɪnəlɪst/ n finalista mf

finality /faɪ'nælətɪ/ n finalità f

finalize /'faɪnəlaɪz/ vt mettere a punto (text); definire (agreement)

finally /'faɪnəlɪ/ adv (at last) finalmente; (at the end) alla fine; (to conclude) per finire

finance /'faɪnæns/ n finanza f ● vt finanziare

finance director n direttore, -trice mf finanziario, -a

finance company, finance house n società f finanziaria

financial /faɪ'nænʃl/ a finanziario

financially /faɪ'nænʃəlɪ/ adv finanziariamente

financial year n Br esercizio m [finanziario]

finch /fɪntʃ/ n fringuello m

find /faɪnd/ n scoperta f ● vt (pt/pp found) trovare; (establish) scoprire; ~ sb guilty Jur dichiarare qcno colpevole

■ **find out** vt scoprire ● vi (enquire) informarsi

findings /'faɪndɪŋz/ npl conclusioni fpl

fine[1] /faɪn/ n (penalty) multa f ● vt multare

fine[2] a bello; (slender) fine; **he's ~** (in health) sta bene ● adv bene; **that's cutting it ~** non ci lascia molto tempo. ● int [va] bene

fine arts npl belle arti fpl

finely /'faɪnlɪ/ adv (cut) finemente

finery /'faɪnərɪ/ n splendore m

finesse /fɪ'nes/ n finezza f

fine-tooth[ed] comb /-tuːθ[t]/ n **go over sth with a ~** ~ passare qcsa al setaccio

fine-tune vt mettere a punto

fine tuning n messa f a punto

finger /'fɪŋɡə(r)/ n dito m (pl dita f) ● vt tastare

finger: finger bowl n lavadita m inv. **finger hole** n Mus foro m. **fingermark** n ditata f. **fingernail** n unghia f. **finger-paint** vi dipingere con le dita. **fingerprint** n impronta f digitale. **fingertip** n punta f del dito; **have sth at one's ~s** sapere qcsa a menadito; (close at hand) avere qcsa a portata di mano

finicky /'fɪnɪkɪ/ a (person) pignolo; (task) intricato

finish /'fɪnɪʃ/ n fine f; (finishing line) traguardo m; (of product) finitura f; **have a good ~** (runner:) avere un buon finale ● vt finire; ~ **reading** finire di leggere ● vi finire

■ **finish off** vt finire (sth); (fam: exhaust) sfinire

■ **finish with** vt (no longer be using) finire (di adoperare); (end relationship with) lasciare

■ **finish up** vt finire (drink, meal)

finishing line /'fɪnɪʃɪŋlaɪn/ n traguardo m

finishing touches /'tʌtʃɪz/ npl ritocchi mpl

finite /'faɪnaɪt/ a limitato

Finland /'fɪnlənd/ n Finlandia f

Finn /fɪn/ n finlandese mf

Finnish /'fɪnɪʃ/ a finlandese ● n (language) finnico m

fiord /fjɔːd/ n fiordo m

fir /fɜː(r)/ n abete m

fir cone n pigna f (di abete)

fire /'faɪə(r)/ n fuoco m; (forest, house) incendio m; **be on ~** bruciare; **catch ~** prendere fuoco; **set ~ to** dar fuoco a; **under ~** sotto il fuoco ● vt cuocere (pottery); sparare (shot); tirare (gun); (fam: dismiss) buttar fuori ● vi sparare (at a)

fire: fire alarm n allarme m antincendio inv. **firearm** n arma f da fuoco. **fire brigade** n vigili mpl del fuoco. **fire door** n porta f antincendio. **fire drill** n esercitazione f per l'evacuazione in caso di incendio. **fire engine** n autopompa f. **fire escape** n uscita f di sicurezza. **fire extinguisher** n estintore m. **fireman** n pompiere m, vigile m del fuoco. **fireplace** n caminetto m. **fireside** n **by** or **at the ~** accanto al fuoco. **fire station** n caserma f dei pompieri. **firewood** n legna f (da ardere). **firework** n fuoco m d'artificio; **~s** pl (display) fuochi mpl d'artificio

firing squad /'faɪərɪŋ/ n plotone m d'esecuzione

firm[1] /fɜːm/ n ditta f, azienda f

firm[2] a fermo; (soil) compatto; (stable, properly fixed) solido; (resolute) risoluto

firmly /'fɜːmlɪ/ adv (hold) stretto; (say) con fermezza

first /fɜːst/ a & n primo, -a mf; **at ~** all'inizio; **who's ~?** chi è il primo?; **from the ~** [fin] dall'inizio ● adv (arrive, leave) per primo; (beforehand) prima; (in listing) prima di tutto, innanzitutto

first: first aid n pronto soccorso m. **first-aid kit** n cassetta f di pronto soccorso. **first-class** a di prim'ordine; Rail di prima classe ● adv (travel) in prima classe. **first edition** n prima edizione f. **first floor** n primo piano m; (Am: ground floor) pianterreno m

firstly /'fɜːstlɪ/ adv in primo luogo

first: first name n nome m di battesimo. **first night** n Theat prima f. **first-rate** a ottimo. **first time buyer** n acquirente mf della prima casa

firth /fɜːθ/ n foce f

fiscal /'fɪskəl/ a fiscale

fiscal year n Am esercizio m finanziario

fish /fɪʃ/ n pesce m ● vt/i pescare

■ **fish out** vt tirar fuori

fishbone /'fɪʃbəʊn/ n lisca f

fishmonger /ˈfɪʃmʌŋgə(r)/ n pescivendo-lo m

fisherman /ˈfɪʃəmən/ n pescatore m

fish farm n vivaio m

fish finger n bastoncino m di pesce

fishing /ˈfɪʃɪŋ/ n pesca f

fishing boat n peschereccio m

fishing rod n canna f da pesca

fishnet /ˈfɪʃnet/ a ⟨stockings⟩ a rete

fish slice n paletta f per fritti

fishy /ˈfɪʃɪ/ a (fam: suspicious) sospetto

fission /ˈfɪʃn/ n Phys fissione f

fist /fɪst/ n pugno m

fistful /ˈfɪstfʊl/ n manciata f, pugno m

fit¹ /fɪt/ n (attack) attacco m; (of rage) accesso m; (of generosity) slancio m

fit² a (**fitter, fittest**) (suitable) adatto; (healthy) in buona salute; Sport in forma; **be ~ to do sth** essere in grado di fare qcsa; **~ to eat** buono da mangiare; **keep ~** tenersi in forma; **do as you see ~** fai come ritieni meglio

fit³ n (of clothes) taglio m; **it's a good ~** ⟨coat etc.⟩ ti/le sta bene ● v (pt/pp **fitted**) ● vi (be the right size) andare bene; **it won't ~** (no room) non ci sta ● vt (fix) applicare (**to** a); (install) installare; **it doesn't ~ me** ⟨coat etc.⟩ non mi va bene; **~ with** fornire di

■ **fit in** vi ⟨person:⟩ adattarsi; **it won't ~ in** (no room) non ci sta ● vt (in schedule, vehicle) trovare un buco per

fitful /ˈfɪtfl/ a irregolare

fitfully /ˈfɪtfʊlɪ/ adv ⟨sleep⟩ a sprazzi

fitment /ˈfɪtmənt/ n **~s** (in house) impianti mpl fissi

fitness /ˈfɪtnɪs/ n (suitability) capacità f; [**physical**] **~** forma f, fitness m

fitted: fitted carpet n moquette f inv. **fitted cupboard** n armadio m a muro; (smaller) armadietto m a muro. **fitted kitchen** n cucina f componibile. **fitted sheet** n lenzuolo m con angoli

fitter /ˈfɪtə(r)/ n installatore, -trice mf

fitting /ˈfɪtɪŋ/ a appropriato ● n (of clothes) prova f; Techn montaggio m; **~s** pl accessori mpl

fitting room n camerino m

five /faɪv/ a & n cinque m

five-a-side n Br (football) partita f di calcio con cinque giocatori per squadra

fiver /ˈfaɪvə(r)/ n fam biglietto m da cinque sterline

fix /fɪks/ n (sl: drugs) pera f; **be in a ~** fam essere nei guai ● vt fissare; (repair) aggiustare; preparare ⟨meal⟩

■ **fix up** vt fissare ⟨meeting⟩

fixation /fɪkˈseɪʃn/ n fissazione f

fixative /ˈfɪksətɪv/ n fissativo m

fixed /ˈfɪkst/ a fisso

fixed assets npl attività fpl fisse, immobilizzazioni fpl

fixed price n prezzo m a forfait

fixer /ˈfɪksə(r)/ n Phot fissatore m; (fam: person) trafficone, -a mf

fixture /ˈfɪkstʃə(r)/ n Sport incontro m; **~s and fittings** impianti mpl fissi

fizz /fɪz/ vi frizzare

fizzle /ˈfɪzl/ vi **~ out** finire in nulla

fizzy /ˈfɪzɪ/ a gassoso

fizzy drink n bibita f gassata

fjord /fjɔːd/ n fiordo m

flab /flæb/ n fam ciccia f cascante

flabbergasted /ˈflæbəgɑːstɪd/ a **be ~** rimanere a bocca aperta

flabby /ˈflæbɪ/ a floscio

flag¹ /flæg/ n bandiera f

flag² vi (pt/pp **flagged**) cedere

■ **flag down** vt (pt/pp **flagged**) far segno di fermarsi a ⟨taxi⟩

flagellation /flædʒəˈleɪʃn/ n flagellazione f

flagon /ˈflægən/ n bottiglione m

flagpole /ˈflægpəʊl/ n asta f della bandiera

flagrant /ˈfleɪgrənt/ a flagrante

flagship /ˈflægʃɪp/ n Naut nave f ammiraglia; fig fiore m all'occhiello

flagstone /ˈflægstəʊn/ n pietra f da lastricare

flail /fleɪl/ n (for threshing corn etc) correggiato m ● vt battere ⟨corn⟩

■ **flail about, flail around** vi ⟨arms, legs:⟩ agitare

flair /fleə(r)/ n (skill) talento m; (style) stile m

flak /flæk/ n Mil artiglieria f antiaerea; (fig fam: criticism) valanga f di critiche; **take a lot of ~** subire molte critiche

flake /fleɪk/ n fiocco m ● vi **~ off** cadere in fiocchi

flaky /ˈfleɪkɪ/ a a scaglie

flaky pastry n pasta f sfoglia

flamboyant /flæmˈbɔɪənt/ a ⟨personality⟩ brillante; ⟨tie⟩ sgargiante

flame /fleɪm/ n fiamma f

flamenco /fləˈmeŋkəʊ/ n flamenco m

flame retardant /rɪtɑːdənt/ a ⟨substance, chemical⟩ ignifugo; ⟨furniture, fabric⟩ ignifugante

flame-thrower /-θrəʊə(r)/ n Mil lanciafiamme m inv

flamingo /fləˈmɪŋgəʊ/ n fenicottero m

flammable /ˈflæməbl/ a infiammabile

flan /flæn/ n [**fruit**] **~** crostata f

flange /flændʒ/ n (on pipe etc) flangia f

flank /flæŋk/ n fianco m ● vt fiancheggiare

flannel /ˈflæn(ə)l/ n flanella f; (for washing) ≈ guanto m di spugna

flannelette /flænəˈlet/ n flanella f di cotone

flannels /ˈflæn(ə)lz/ npl (trousers) pantaloni mpl di flanella

flap /flæp/ n (of pocket, envelope) risvolto m; (of table) ribalta f; **in a ~** fam in grande agitazione ● v (pt/pp **flapped**) ● vi sbattere; fam agitarsi ● vt **~ its wings** battere le ali

flapjack /ˈflæpdʒæk/ n Br dolcetto m di fiocchi d'avena; Am frittella f

flare /fleə(r)/ n fiammata f; (device) razzo m

■ **flare up** vi ⟨rash:⟩ venire fuori; ⟨fire:⟩ fare una fiammata; ⟨person, situation:⟩ esplodere

flared /fleəd/ a ⟨garment⟩ svasato

flash /flæʃ/ n lampo m; **in a ~** fam in un attimo ● *vi* lampeggiare; **~ past** passare come un bolide ● *vt* lanciare ‹*smile*›; **~ one's headlights** lampeggiare; **~ a torch at** puntare una torcia su

flash: flashback *n* scena *f* retrospettiva.
flashbulb *n* *Phot* flash *m inv*. **flashcard** *n* *Sch* scheda *f* didattica

flasher /'flæʃə(r)/ *n* *Auto* lampeggiatore *m*

flash: flash flood *n* alluvione *f* improvvisa.
flashgun *n* *Phot* flash *m inv*. **flashlight** *n* *Phot* flash *m inv*; (*Am: torch*) torcia *f* [elettrica]. **flashpoint** *n* (*trouble spot*) punto *m* caldo; *Chem* punto *m* di infiammabilità

flashy /'flæʃɪ/ *a* vistoso

flask /flɑ:sk/ *n* fiasco *m*; (*vacuum ~*) termos *m inv*

flat /flæt/ *a* (**flatter, flattest**) piatto; ‹*refusal*› reciso; ‹*beer*› sgassato; ‹*battery*› scarico; ‹*tyre*› a terra; **A ~** *Mus* la bemolle ● *n* appartamento *m*; *Mus* bemolle *m*; (*puncture*) gomma *f* a terra

flat: flat broke *a fam* completamente al verde. **flat feet** *npl* piedi *mpl* piatti. **flatfish** *n* pesce *m* piatto. **flat-footed** /-'fʊtɪd/ *a* **be ~~** avere i piedi piatti. **flat hunting** *n Br* **go ~ ~** andare in cerca di un appartamento

flatly /'flætlɪ/ *adv* ‹*refuse*› categoricamente

flat: flatmate *n Br* persona *f* con cui si divide un appartamento. **flat out** *adv* ‹*drive, work*› a tutto gas; **it only does 120 kph ~ ~** arriva a 120 km all'ora andando a tutta manetta; **go ~ ~ for sth** mettercela tutta per fare qcsa. **flat racing** *n* corse *fpl* piane. **flat rate** *n* forfait *m inv*; (*unitary rate*) tariffa *f* unica ● *attrib* ‹*fee, tax*› forfettario. **flat spin** *n* *Aeron* virata *f* piatta; **be in a ~ ~** *fam* essere in fibrillazione

flatten /'flætn/ *vt* appiattire

flatter /'flætə(r)/ *vt* adulare

flattering /'flætərɪŋ/ *a* ‹*comments*› lusinghiero; ‹*colour, dress*› che fa sembrare più bello

flattery /'flætərɪ/ *n* adulazione *f*

flat tyre *n* gomma *f* a terra

flatulence /'flætjʊləns/ *n* flatulenza *f*

flaunt /flɔ:nt/ *vt* ostentare

flautist /'flɔ:tɪst/ *n* flautista *mf*

flavour /'fleɪvə(r)/ *n* sapore *m* ● *vt* condire; **chocolate ~ed** al sapore di cioccolato

flavour-enhancer /-ɪnhɑ:nsə(r)/ *n* esaltatore *m* dell'aroma

flavouring /'fleɪvərɪŋ/ *n* condimento *m*

flavourless /'fleɪvəlɪs/ *a* insipido

flaw /flɔ:/ *n* difetto *m*

flawless /'flɔ:lɪs/ *a* perfetto

flax /flæks/ *n* lino *m*

flaxen /'flæksən/ *a* ‹*hair*› biondo platino

flea /fli:/ *n* pulce *f*

flea: flea-bitten /'fli:bɪtən/ *a* infestato dalle pulci; *fig* pidocchioso. **flea market** *n* mercato *m* delle pulci. **fleapit** *n Br fam pej* pidocchietto *m*

fleck /flek/ *n* macchiolina *f*

fled /fled/ *see* **flee**

fledg[e]ling /'fledʒlɪŋ/ *n* uccellino *m* (*che ha* *appena messo le ali*) ● *attrib fig* ‹*democracy, enterprise*› giovane; ‹*party, group*› alle prime armi

flee /fli:/ *vt/i* (*pt/pp* **fled**) fuggire (**from** da)

fleece /fli:s/ *n* pelliccia *f* ● *vt fam* spennare

fleecy /'fli:sɪ/ *a* ‹*lining*› felpato

fleet /fli:t/ *n* flotta *f*; (*of cars*) parco *m*

fleeting /'fli:tɪŋ/ *a* **catch a ~ glance of sth** intravedere qcsa; **for a ~ moment** per un attimo

Flemish /'flemɪʃ/ *a* fiammingo

flesh /fleʃ/ *n* carne *f*; **in the ~** in persona; **one's own ~ and blood** il proprio sangue
■ flesh out *vt* dare più consistenza a ‹*essay etc*›

flesh eating /-i:tɪŋ/ *a* carnivoro

flesh wound *n* ferita *f* superficiale

fleshy /'fleʃɪ/ *a* carnoso

flew /flu:/ *see* **fly**[2]

flex[1] /fleks/ *vt* flettere ‹*muscle*›

flex[2] *n* *Electr* filo *m*

flexibility /fleksə'bɪlətɪ/ *n* flessibilità *f*

flexible /'fleksəbl/ *a* flessibile

flexitime /'fleksɪtaɪm/ *n* orario *m* flessibile

flick /flɪk/ *vt* dare un buffetto a; **~ sth off sth** togliere qcsa da qcsa con un colpetto
■ flick through *vt* sfogliare

flicker /'flɪkə(r)/ *vi* tremolare

flick knife *n Br* coltello *m* a scatto

flier /'flaɪə(r)/ *n* = **flyer**

flight[1] /flaɪt/ *n* (*fleeing*) fuga *f*; **take ~** darsi alla fuga

flight[2] *n* (*flying*) volo *m*; **~ of stairs** rampa *f*

flight: flight attendant *n* assistente *mf* di volo. **flight bag** *n* bagaglio *m* a mano. **flight deck** *n Aeron* cabina *f* di pilotaggio; *Naut* ponte *m* di volo. **flight engineer** *n* motorista *mf* di bordo. **flight lieutenant** *n Mil* capitano *m*. **flight path** *n* traiettoria *f* di volo. **flight recorder** *n* registratore *m* di volo

flighty /'flaɪtɪ/ *a* (**-ier, -iest**) frivolo

flimsy /'flɪmzɪ/ *a* (**-ier, -iest**) ‹*material*› leggero; ‹*shelves*› poco robusto; ‹*excuse*› debole

flinch /flɪntʃ/ *vi* (*wince*) sussultare; (*draw back*) ritirarsi; **~ from a task** *fig* sottrarsi a un compito

fling /flɪŋ/ *n* **have a ~** (*fam: affair*) aver un'avventura ● *vt* (*pt/pp* **flung**) gettare

flint /flɪnt/ *n* pietra *f* focaia; (*for lighter*) pietrina *f*

flip /flɪp/ *v* (*pt/pp* **flipped**) *vt* dare un colpetto a; buttare in aria ‹*coin*›. ● *vi fam* uscire dai gangheri; (*go mad*) impazzire
■ flip through *vt* sfogliare

flip chart *n* lavagna *f* a fogli mobili

flip-flop *n* (*sandal*) infradito *m inv*; (*Comput: device*) flip-flop *m inv*, multivibratore *m* bistabile; (*Am: about face*) voltafaccia *m inv*

flippant /'flɪpənt/ *a* irriverente

flipper /'flɪpə(r)/ *n* pinna *f*

flipping /'flɪpɪŋ/ *Br fam a* maledetto ● *adv* ‹*stupid, painful, cold*› maledettamente

flip side *n* (*of record*) retro *m*; (*fig: other side*) rovescio *m*

flirt /flɜ:t/ *n* civetta *f* ● *vi* flirtare

flirtation /flɜːˈteɪʃn/ n flirt m inv

flirtatious /flɜːˈteɪʃəs/ a civettuolo

flit /flɪt/ vi (pt/pp **flitted**) volteggiare

float /fləʊt/ n galleggiante m; (in procession) carro m; (money) riserva f di cassa ● vi galleggiare; Fin fluttuare

floating rate interest /ˈfləʊtɪŋ/ n Fin interesse m a tasso variabile

floating voter n Pol elettore, -trice mf indeciso,-a

flock /flɒk/ n gregge m; (of birds) stormo m ● vi affollarsi

floe /fləʊ/ n banchisa f

flog /flɒg/ vt (pt/pp **flogged**) bastonare; (fam: sell) vendere

flood /flʌd/ n alluvione f; (of river) straripamento m; (fig: of replies, letters, tears) diluvio m; **be in ~** ⟨river:⟩ essere straripato ● vt allagare ● vi ⟨river:⟩ straripare

flood: flood control n prevenzione f delle inondazioni. **flood damage** n danno m provocato da un'inondazione. **floodgate** n chiusa f; **open the ~s** fig spalancare le porte. **floodlight** n riflettore m ● vt (pt/pp **floodlit**) illuminare con riflettori. **floodplain** n pianura f alluvionale. **flood tide** n marea f montante. **flood waters** npl acque fpl alluvionali

floor /flɔː(r)/ n pavimento m; (storey) piano m; (for dancing) pista f ● vt (baffle) confondere; (knock down) stendere ⟨person⟩

floor: floorboard n asse f del pavimento. **floorcloth** n straccio m per lavare il pavimento. **floor exercises** npl esercizi mpl a terra. **floor manager** n TV direttore, -trice mf di studio; Comm gerente mf di un negozio. **floor polish** n cera f per il pavimento. **floor show** n spettacolo m di varietà. **floor space** n superficie f; **we don't have the ~ ~** non abbiamo lo spazio

flop /flɒp/ n fam (failure) tonfo m; Theat fiasco m ● vi (pt/pp **flopped**) (fam: fail) far fiasco

■ **flop down** vi accasciarsi

floppy /ˈflɒpɪ/ a floscio

floppy disk n floppy disk m inv

floppy [disk] drive n lettore m di floppy

flora /ˈflɔːrə/ n flora f

floral /ˈflɔːrəl/ a floreale

Florence /ˈflɒrəns/ n Firenze f

Florentine /ˈflɒrəntaɪn/ a fiorentino

florid /ˈflɒrɪd/ a ⟨complexion⟩ florido; ⟨style⟩ troppo ricercato

florist /ˈflɒrɪst/ n fioriao, -a mf

flotsam /ˈflɒtsəm/ n relitti mpl alla deriva

flounce /flaʊns/ n balza f ● vi **~ out** uscire con aria melodrammatica

flounder[1] /ˈflaʊndə(r)/ vi dibattersi; ⟨speaker:⟩ impappinarsi

flounder[2] n ⟨fish⟩ passera f di mare

flour /ˈflaʊə(r)/ n farina f

flourish /ˈflʌrɪʃ/ n gesto m drammatico; (scroll) ghirigoro m ● vi prosperare ● vt brandire

floury /ˈflaʊərɪ/ a farinoso

flout /flaʊt/ vt fregarsene di ⟨rules⟩

flow /fləʊ/ n flusso m ● vi scorrere; (hang loosely) ricadere

flow chart n diagramma m di flusso

flower /ˈflaʊə(r)/ n fiore m ● vi fiorire

flower arrangement n composizione f floreale

flower bed n aiuola f

flowered /ˈflaʊəd/ a a fiori

flower garden n giardino m fiorito

flowering /ˈflaʊərɪŋ/ n Bot fioritura f; (fig: development) espansione f ● a ⟨shrub, tree⟩ in fiore; **early/late ~** a fioritura precoce/tardiva

flower: flowerpot n vaso m [per i fiori]. **flower shop** n fiorista m. **flower show** n mostra f floreale

flowery /ˈflaʊərɪ/ a fiorito

flown /fləʊn/ see **fly**[2]

fl oz abbr **fluid ounces**

flu /fluː/ n influenza f

fluctuate /ˈflʌktjʊeɪt/ vi fluttuare

fluctuation /flʌktjʊˈeɪʃn/ n fluttuazione f

flue /fluː/ n (of chimney, stove) canna f fumaria

fluent /ˈfluːənt/ a spedito; **speak ~ Italian** parlare correntemente l'italiano

fluently /ˈfluːəntlɪ/ adv speditamente

fluff /flʌf/ n peluria f

fluffy /ˈflʌfɪ/ a (-ier, -iest) vaporoso; ⟨toy⟩ di peluche

fluid /ˈfluːɪd/ a fluido ● n fluido m

fluid ounce n oncia f fluida

fluke /fluːk/ n colpo m di fortuna

flummox /ˈflʌməks/ vt fam sbalestrare

flung /flʌŋ/ see **fling**

flunk /flʌŋk/ vt Am fam essere bocciato in

fluorescent /flʊəˈresnt/ a fluorescente

fluorescent lighting n luce f fluorescente

fluoride /ˈflʊəraɪd/ n fluoruro m

flurry /ˈflʌrɪ/ n (snow) raffica f; fig agitazione f

flush /flʌʃ/ n (blush) [vampata f di] rossore m ● vi arrossire ● vt lavare con un getto d'acqua; **~ the toilet** tirare l'acqua ● a a livello (with di); (fam: affluent) a soldi

flushed /flʌʃt/ a ⟨cheeks⟩ rosso; **~ with** eccitato da ⟨success⟩; raggiante di ⟨pride⟩

flustered /ˈflʌstəd/ a in agitazione; **get ~** mettersi in agitazione

flute /fluːt/ n flauto m

flutter /ˈflʌtə(r)/ n battito m ● vi svolazzare

flux /flʌks/ n **in a state of ~** in uno stato di flusso

fly[1] /flaɪ/ n (pl **flies**) mosca f

fly[2] v (pt **flew**, pp **flown**) ● vi volare; (go by plane) andare in aereo; ⟨flag:⟩ sventolare; (rush) precipitarsi; **~ open** spalancarsi ● vt pilotare ⟨plane⟩; trasportare [in aereo] ⟨troops, supplies⟩; volare con ⟨Alitalia etc⟩

fly[3] n & **flies** pl (on trousers) patta f

flyaway /ˈflaɪəweɪ/ a ⟨hair⟩ che non stanno a posto

fly: fly-by-night a ⟨person⟩ irresponsabile; ⟨company⟩ non affidabile. **flycatcher**

/'flaɪkætʃə(r)/ n pigliamosche m inv. **fly-drive** a con la formula aereo più auto

flyer /'flaɪə(r)/ n aviatore m; (leaflet) volantino m

fly-fishing n pesca f con la mosca

flying /'flaɪɪŋ/ n aviazione f

flying: flying buttress n arco m rampante. **flying colours: with ~ ~** a pieni voti. **flying saucer** n disco m volante. **flying start** n ottima partenza f; **get off to a ~ ~** partire benissimo. **flying visit** n visita f lampo inv

fly: flyleaf n risguardo m. **fly on the wall** a ⟨documentary⟩ con telecamera nascosta. **flyover** n cavalcavia m inv. **fly-past** n Br Aeron parata f aerea. **flysheet** n (handbill) volantino m; (of tent) sopratenda m inv

foal /fəʊl/ n puledro m

foam /fəʊm/ n schiuma f; (synthetic) gommapiuma* f ● vi spumare; **~ at the mouth** far la bava alla bocca

foam rubber n gommapiuma* f

fob /fɒb/ vt (pt/pp **fobbed**) **~ sth off** affibbiare qcsa (on sb a qcno); **~ sb off** liquidare qcno

focal /'fəʊkl/ a focale

focal point n (of village, building) centro m di attrazione; (main concern) punto m centrale; (in optics) fuoco m; **the room lacks a ~ ~** nella stanza manca un punto che focalizzi l'attenzione

focus /'fəʊkəs/ n fuoco m; **in ~** a fuoco; **out of ~** sfocato ● v (pt/pp **focused** or **focussed**) ● vt fig concentrare (on su) ● vi **~ on sth** Phot mettere a fuoco qcsa; fig concentrarsi su qcsa

fodder /'fɒdə(r)/ n foraggio m

foe /fəʊ/ n nemico, -a mf

foetal /'fiːtl/ a fetale

foetid /'fetɪd/ a fetido

foetus /'fiːtəs/ n (pl **-tuses**) feto m

fog /fɒg/ n nebbia f

fog bank n banco m di nebbia

fogey /'fəʊgɪ/ n **old ~** persona f antiquata

foggy /'fɒgɪ/ a (**foggier, foggiest**) nebbioso; **it's ~** c'è nebbia; **I haven't got the foggiest [idea]** fam hon ne ho la più pallida idea

foghorn /'fɒghɔːn/ n sirena f da nebbia

fog lamp, foglight /'fɒglaɪt/ n Auto [faro m] antinebbia m inv

foible /'fɔɪbl/ n punto m debole

foil¹ /fɔɪl/ n lamina f di metallo

foil² vt (thwart) frustrare

foil³ n (sword) fioretto m

foist /fɔɪst/ vt appioppare (on sb a qcno)

fold¹ /fəʊld/ n (for sheep) ovile m

fold² n piega f ● vt piegare; **~ one's arms** incrociare le braccia ● vi piegarsi; (fail) crollare

■ **fold up** vt ripiegare ⟨chair⟩ ● vi essere pieghevole; ⟨fam: business:⟩ collassare

foldaway /'fəʊldəweɪ/ a ⟨bed⟩ pieghevole; ⟨table⟩ estraibile

folder /'fəʊldə(r)/ n cartella f

folding /'fəʊldɪŋ/ a pieghevole

folding seat n strapuntino m, sedile m pieghevole

folding stool n sgabello m pieghevole

fold-out n (in magazine) pieghevole m

foliage /'fəʊlɪdʒ/ n fogliame m

folk /fəʊk/ npl gente f; **my ~s** (family) i miei; **hello there ~s** ciao a tutti

folk: folk dance n danza f popolare. **folklore** n folclore m. **folk medicine** n rimedio m della nonna. **folk memory** n memoria f collettiva. **folk music** n musica f folk. **folk song** n canto m popolare. **folk wisdom** n saggezza f popolare

follow /'fɒləʊ/ vt/i seguire; **it doesn't ~** non è necessariamente così; **~ suit** fig fare lo stesso; **as ~s** come segue

■ **follow up** vt fare seguito a ⟨letter⟩

follower /'fɒləʊə(r)/ n seguace mf

following /'fɒləʊɪŋ/ a seguente ● n seguito m; (supporters) seguaci mpl ● prep in seguito a

follow-on n seguito m

follow-up n (of social work case) controllo m; (of patient, ex inmate) visita f di controllo; (film, record, single, programme) seguito m ● attrib ⟨survey, work, interview⟩ successivo; **~ letter** lettera f che fa seguito

folly /'fɒlɪ/ n follia f

foment /fə'ment/ vt fig fomentare

fond /fɒnd/ a affezionato; ⟨hope⟩ vivo; **be ~ of** essere appassionato di ⟨music⟩; **I'm ~ of...** ⟨food, person⟩ mi piace moltissimo...

fondle /'fɒndl/ vt coccolare

fondly /'fɒndlɪ/ adv ⟨hope⟩ ingenuamente

fondness /'fɒndnɪs/ n affetto m; (for things) amore m

font /fɒnt/ n fonte f battesimale; Typ carattere m di stampa

food /fuːd/ n cibo m; (for animals, groceries) mangiare m; **let's buy some ~** compriamo qualcosa da mangiare

food: food mixer n frullatore m. **food poisoning** n intossicazione f alimentare. **food processor** n tritatutto m inv elettrico. **foodstuffs** npl generi mpl alimentari

fool¹ /fuːl/ n sciocco, -a mf; **she's no ~** non è una stupida; **make a ~ of oneself** rendersi ridicolo ● vt prendere in giro ● vi **~ around** giocare; ⟨husband, wife:⟩ avere l'amante

fool² n Culin crema f

foolhardy /'fuːlhɑːdɪ/ a temerario

foolish /'fuːlɪʃ/ a stolto

foolishly /'fuːlɪʃlɪ/ adv scioccamente

foolishness /'fuːlɪʃnɪs/ n sciocchezza f

foolproof /'fuːlpruːf/ a facilissimo

foolscap /'fuːlskæp/ n (Br: paper) carta f protocollo

foot /fʊt/ n (pl **feet**) piede m; (of animal) zampa f; (measure) piede (=30,48 cm); **on ~** a piedi; **on one's feet** in piedi; **put one's ~ in it** fam fare una gaffe

footage /'fʊtɪdʒ/ n (piece of film) spezzone m; **news ~** servizio m [filmato]

foot: foot-and-mouth disease n afta f

epizootica. **football** *n* calcio *m*; (*ball*) pallone *m*. **footballer** *n* giocatore *m* di calcio. **football pools** *npl* totocalcio *m*. **footbrake** *n* freno *m* a pedale. **footbridge** *n* passerella *f*. **foothills** *npl* colline *fpl* pedemontane. **foothold** *n* punto *m* d'appoggio. **footing** *n* **lose one's ~** perdere l'appiglio; **on an equal ~** in condizioni di parità. **footlights** *npl* luci *npl* della ribalta. **footloose and fancy-free** *a* libero come l'aria. **footman** *n* valletto *m*. **footnote** *n* nota *f* a piè di pagina. **footpath** *n* sentiero *m*. **footprint** *n* orma *f*; (*of machine*) ingombro *m*. **footrest** *n* poggiapiedi *m inv*. **footsore** *a* **be ~** avere male ai piedi. **footstep** *n* passo *m*; **follow in sb's ~s** *fig* seguire l'esempio di qcno. **footstool** *n* sgabellino *m*. **footwear** *n* calzature *fpl*

for /fə(r)/, *accentato* /fɔ:(r)/ *prep* per; **~ this reason** per questa ragione; **I have lived here ~ ten years** vivo qui da dieci anni; **~ supper** per cena; **~ all that** nonostante questo; **what ~?** a che scopo?; **send ~ a doctor** chiamare un dottore; **fight ~ a cause** lottare per una causa; **go ~ a walk** andare a fare una passeggiata; **there's no need ~ you to go** non c'è bisogno che tu vada; **it's not ~ me to say** no sta a me dirlo; **now you're ~ it** ora sei nei pasticci ● *conj* poiché, perché

forage /'fɒrɪdʒ/ *n* foraggio *m* ● *vi* **~ for** cercare

foray /'fɒreɪ/ *n* *Mil* incursione *f*; **make a ~ into** (*politics, acting*) tentare la strada di

forbade /fə'bæd/ *see* **forbid**

forbearance /fɔ:'beərəns/ *n* pazienza *f*

forbearing /fɔ:'beərɪŋ/ *a* tollerante

forbid /fə'bɪd/ *vt* (*pt* **forbade**, *pp* **forbidden**) proibire

forbidding /fə'bɪdɪŋ/ *a* (*prospect*) che spaventa; (*stern*) severo

force /fɔ:s/ *n* forza *f*; **in ~** in vigore; (*in large numbers*) in massa; **come into ~** entrare in vigore; **the** [armed] **~s** *pl* le forze armate ● *vt* forzare; **~ sth on sb** (*decision*) imporre qcsa a qcno; (*drink*) costringere qcno a fare qcsa

■ **force back** *vt* trattenere (*tears*)

■ **force down** *vt* buttar giù (*controvoglia*) (*food, drink*)

forced /fɔ:st/ *a* forzato

forced landing *n* atterraggio *m* forzato

force-feed *vt* (*pt/pp* **-fed**) nutrire a forza

forceful /'fɔ:sful/ *a* energico

forcefully /'fɔ:sfulɪ/ *adv* (*say, argue*) con forza

forceps /'fɔ:seps/ *npl* forcipe *m*

forcible /'fɔ:səbl/ *a* forzato

forcibly /'fɔ:səblɪ/ *adv* forzatamente

ford /fɔ:d/ *n* guado *m* ● *vt* guadare

fore /fɔ:(r)/ *n* **to the ~** in vista; **come to the ~** salire alla ribalta

forearm /'fɔ:rɑ:m/ *n* avambraccio *m*

forebears /'fɔ:beəz/ *npl* antenati *mpl*

foreboding /fɔ:'bəʊdɪŋ/ *n* presentimento *m*

forecast /'fɔ:kɑ:st/ *n* previsione *f* ● *vt* (*pt/pp* **forecast**) prevedere

forecaster /'fɔ:kɑ:stə(r)/ *n* pronosticatore, -trice *mf*; (*economic*) analista *mf* della congiuntura; (*of weather*) meteorologo, -a *mf*

fore: forecourt *n* (*of garage*) spiazzo *m* [antistante]. **forefathers** *npl* antenati *mpl*. **forefinger** *n* [dito *m*] indice *m*. **forefront** *n* **be in the ~** essere all'avanguardia. **foregone** *a* **be a ~ conclusion** essere una cosa scontata. **foreground** *n* primo piano *m*.

forehand *n* *Tennis* diritto *m*

forehead /'fɒhed, 'fɒrɪd/ *n* fronte *f*

foreign /'fɒrən/ *a* straniero; (*trade*) estero; (*not belonging*) estraneo; **he is ~** è uno straniero

foreign currency *n* valuta *f* estera

foreigner /'fɒrənə(r)/ *n* straniero, -a *mf*

foreign: foreign exchange *n* (*currency*) valuta *f* estera. **foreign language** *n* lingua *f* straniera. **Foreign Office** *n* ministero *m* degli [affari] Esteri. **Foreign Secretary** *n* Ministro *m* degli Esteri

foreleg /'fɔ:leg/ *n* zampa *f* anteriore

foreman /'fɔ:mən/ *n* caporeparto *m*

foremost /'fɔ:məʊst/ *a* principale ● *adv* **first and ~** in primo luogo

forename /'fɔ:neɪm/ *n* nome *m* di battesimo

forensic /fə'rensɪk/ *a* **~ medicine** medicina legale

forensic scientist *n* medico *m* legale

forerunner /'fɔ:rʌnə(r)/ *n* precursore *m*

foresee /fɔ:'si:/ *vt* (*pt* **-saw**, *pp* **-seen**) prevedere

foresight /'fɔ:saɪt/ *n* previdenza *f*

foreskin /'fɔ:skɪn/ *n* *Anat* prepuzio *m*

forest /'fɒrɪst/ *n* foresta *f*

forestall /fɔ:'stɔ:l/ *vt* prevenire

forester /'fɒrɪstə(r)/ *n* guardia *f* forestale

forest fire *n* incendio *m* del bosco

forest ranger /'reɪndʒə(r)/ *n* *Am* guardia *f* forestale

forestry /'fɒrɪstrɪ/ *n* silvicoltura *f*

foretaste /'fɔ:teɪst/ *n* pregustazione *f*

foretell /fɔ:'tel/ *vt* (*pt/pp* **-told**) predire

forethought /'fɔ:θɔ:t/ *n* accortezza *f*, previdenza *f*

forever /fə'revə(r)/ *adv* per sempre; **he's ~ complaining** si lamenta sempre

forewarn /fɔ:'wɔ:n/ *vt* avvertire

foreword /'fɔ:wɜ:d/ *n* prefazione *f*

forfeit /'fɔ:fɪt/ *n* (*in game*) pegno *m*; *Jur* penalità *f* ● *vt* perdere

forfeiture /'fɔ:fɪtʃə(r)/ *n* (*of right*) perdita *f*; (*of property*) confisca *f*

forgave /fə'geɪv/ *see* **forgive**

forge¹ /fɔ:dʒ/ *vi* **~ ahead** (*runner:*) lasciarsi indietro gli altri; *fig* farsi strada

forge² *n* fucina *f* ● *vt* fucinare; (*counterfeit*) contraffare

forger /'fɔ:dʒə(r)/ *n* contraffattore *m*

forgery /'fɔ:dʒərɪ/ *n* contraffazione *f*

forget /fə'get/ *vt/i* (*pt* **-got**, *pp* **-gotten**) dimenticare; dimenticarsi di (*language, skill*); **~ oneself** perdere la padronanza di sé

forgetful /fə'getfʊl/ a smemorato
forgetfulness /fə'getfʊlnɪs/ n smemoratez-za f
forget-me-not n non-ti-scordar-di-mé m inv
forgettable /fə'getəbl/ a ⟨day, fact, film⟩ da dimenticare
forgive /fə'gɪv/ vt (pt **-gave**, pp **-given**) ~ **sb for sth** perdonare qcno per qcsa
forgiveness /fə'gɪvnɪs/ n perdono m
forgiving /fə'gɪvɪŋ/ a ⟨person⟩ indulgente
forgo /fɔː'gəʊ/ vt (pt **-went**, pp **-gone**) rinunciare a
forgot(ten) /fə'gɒt(n)/ see **forget**
fork /fɔːk/ n forchetta f; ⟨for digging⟩ forca f; ⟨in road⟩ bivio m ● vi ⟨road:⟩ biforcarsi; ~ **right** prendere a destra
■ **fork out** vt fam sborsare ● vi sborsare soldi
forked lightning /fɔːkt/ n fulmine m ramificato
fork-lift truck n elevatore m
forlorn /fə'lɔːn/ a ⟨look⟩ perduto; ⟨place⟩ derelitto; ~ **hope** speranza f vana
form /fɔːm/ n forma f; ⟨document⟩ modulo m; Sch classe f ● vt formare; formulare ⟨opinion⟩ ● vi formarsi
formal /fɔːml/ a formale
formalin /fɔːməlɪn/ n formalina f
formality /fɔː'mælətɪ/ n formalità f inv
formally /fɔːməlɪ/ adv in modo formale; (officially) ufficialmente
format /fɔːmæt/ n formato m ● vt formattare ⟨disk, page⟩
formation /fɔː'meɪʃn/ n formazione f
formative /fɔːmətɪv/ a ~ **years** anni formativi
former /fɔːmə(r)/ a precedente; ⟨PM, colleague⟩ ex; **the ~, the latter** il primo, l'ultimo
formerly /fɔːməlɪ/ adv precedentemente; (in olden times) in altri tempi
formidable /fɔːmɪdəbl/ a formidabile
formless /fɔːmlɪs/ a ⟨mass⟩ informe; ⟨novel⟩ che manca di struttura
form teacher n Br Sch ≈ coordinatore, -trice mf del consiglio di classe
formula /fɔːmjʊlə/ n (pl **-ae** /fɔːmjʊliː/ or **-s**) formula f
formulate /fɔːmjʊleɪt/ vt formulare
formulation /fɔːmjʊ'leɪʃn/ n formulazione f
fornication /fɔːnɪ'keɪʃn/ n fornicazione f
forsake /fə'seɪk/ vt (pt **-sook** /fə'sʊk/, pp **-saken**) abbandonare
forseeable /fə'siːəbl/ a **in the ~ future** in futuro per quanto si possa prevedere
forswear /fɔː'sweə(r)/ vt ⟨renounce⟩ abiurare
fort /fɔːt/ n Mil forte m
forte /fɔːteɪ/ n [pezzo m] forte m
forth /fɔːθ/ adv **back and ~** avanti e indietro; **and so ~** e così via
forthcoming /fɔːθ'kʌmɪŋ/ a prossimo; (communicative) comunicativo; **no re-**

sponse was ~ non arrivava nessuna risposta
forthright /fɔːθraɪt/ a schietto
forthwith /fɔːθ'wɪð/ adv immediatamente
fortieth /fɔːtɪθ/ a & n quarantesimo, -a mf
fortification /fɔːtɪfɪ'keɪʃn/ n fortificazione f
fortify /fɔːtɪfaɪ/ vt (pt/pp **-ied**) fortificare; fig rendere forte
fortitude /fɔːtɪtjuːd/ n coraggio m
fortnight /fɔːtnaɪt/ n Br quindicina f
fortnightly /fɔːtnaɪtlɪ/ a bimensile ● adv ogni due settimane
fortress /fɔːtrɪs/ n fortezza f
fortuitous /fɔː'tjuːɪtəs/ a fortuito
fortunate /fɔːtʃənət/ a fortunato; **that's ~!** meno male!
fortunately /fɔːtʃənətlɪ/ adv fortunatamente
fortune /fɔːtʃuːn/ n fortuna f
fortune cookie n Am biscottino m che racchiude un foglietto con una predizione
fortune-teller n indovino, -a mf
forty /fɔːtɪ/ a & n quaranta m; **have ~ winks** fam fare un pisolino
forum /fɔːrəm/ n foro m
forward /fɔːwəd/ adv avanti; (towards the front) in avanti; **move ~** andare avanti ● a in avanti; (presumptuous) sfacciato ● n Sport attaccante m ● vt inoltrare ⟨letter⟩; spedire ⟨goods⟩
forward buying n Fin acquisto m a termine
forwarding address n indirizzo m a cui inoltrare la corrispondenza
forward planning n pianificazione f a lungo termine
forwards /fɔːwədz/ adv avanti
fossil /fɒs(ə)l/ n fossile m
fossil fuel n combustibile m fossile
fossilized /fɒsɪlaɪzd/ a fossile; ⟨ideas⟩ fossilizzato
foster /fɒstə(r)/ vt allevare ⟨child⟩
foster child n figlio, -a mf in affidamento
foster mother n madre f affidataria
fought /fɔːt/ see **fight**
foul /faʊl/ a ⟨smell, taste⟩ cattivo; ⟨air⟩ viziato; ⟨language⟩ osceno; ⟨mood, weather⟩ orrendo ● vt inquinare ⟨water⟩; Sport commettere un fallo contro; ⟨nets, rope:⟩ impigliarsi in
■ **foul up** vt (fam: spoil) mandare in malora
foul-mouthed /-'maʊðd/ a sboccato
foul play n Jur delitto m ● n Sport fallo m
foul-smelling /-'smelɪŋ/ a puzzo. **foul up** n fam intoppo m
found¹ /faʊnd/ see **find**
found² vt fondare
foundation /faʊn'deɪʃn/ n (basis) fondamento m; (charitable) fondazione f; ~**s** pl (of building) fondamenta fpl; **lay the ~-stone** porre la prima pietra
foundation course n Br Univ corso m propedeutico
founder¹ /faʊndə(r)/ n fondatore, -trice mf
founder² vi ⟨ship:⟩ affondare

foundry /ˈfaʊndrɪ/ n fonderia f

fount /faʊnt/ n *Typ* carattere m [stampa]

fountain /ˈfaʊntɪn/ n fontana f

fountain pen n penna f stilografica

four /fɔː(r)/ a & n quattro m

four: four four time n *Mus* quattro quarti. **four-letter word** n parolaccia f. **four-poster [bed]** n letto m a baldacchino

foursome /ˈfɔːsəm/ n quartetto m

four-stroke a ⟨engine⟩ a quattro tempi

fourteen /fɔːˈtiːn/ a & n quattordici m

fourteenth /fɔːˈtiːnθ/ a & n quattordicesimo, -a mf

fourth /fɔːθ/ a & n quarto, -a mf

fourthly /ˈfɔːθlɪ/ adv in quarto luogo

fourth rate a ⟨job, hotel, film⟩ di terz'ordine

four-wheel drive [vehicle] n quattro per quattro m inv

fowl /faʊl/ n pollame m

fox /fɒks/ n volpe f ● vt ⟨puzzle⟩ ingannare

fox: fox cub n volpacchiotto m. **fox fur** n pelliccia f di volpe. **foxglove** n digitale f. **foxhound** n foxhound m inv. **fox-hunt** n caccia f alla volpe. **fox terrier** n fox-terrier m inv.

foxtrot n fox-trot m inv

foxy /ˈfɒksɪ/ a (-ier, -iest) ⟨fam: sexy⟩ sexy inv; ⟨crafty⟩ scaltro

foyer /ˈfɔɪeɪ/ n *Theat* ridotto m; ⟨in hotel⟩ salone m d'ingresso

fracas /ˈfrækɑː/ n baruffa f

fraction /ˈfrækʃn/ n frazione f

fractionally /ˈfrækʃənəlɪ/ adv ⟨slightly⟩ leggermente

fracture /ˈfræktʃə(r)/ n frattura f ● vt fratturare ● vi fratturarsi

fragile /ˈfrædʒaɪl/ a fragile

fragment /ˈfrægmənt/ n frammento m

fragmentary /ˈfrægm(ə)ntərɪ/ a frammentario

fragrance /ˈfreɪgrəns/ n fragranza f

fragrant /ˈfreɪgrənt/ a fragrante

frail /freɪl/ a gracile

frailty /ˈfreɪltɪ/ n ⟨imperfection⟩ debolezza f; ⟨of person: moral⟩ fragilità f inv; ⟨of person: physical⟩ gracilità f; ⟨of health, state⟩ precarietà f inv

frame /freɪm/ n ⟨of picture, door, window⟩ cornice f; ⟨of spectacles⟩ montatura f; *Anat* ossatura f; ⟨structure, of bike⟩ telaio m; **~ of mind** stato m d'animo ● vt incorniciare ⟨picture⟩; fig formulare; ⟨sl: incriminate⟩ montare

framework /ˈfreɪmwɜːk/ n struttura f; **within the ~ of the law** nell'ambito della legge

franc /fræŋk/ n franco m

France /frɑːns/ n Francia f

franchise /ˈfræntʃaɪz/ n *Pol* diritto m di voto; *Comm* franchigia f

Franciscan /frænˈsɪskən/ n francescano m

frank[1] /fræŋk/ vt affrancare ⟨letter⟩

frank[2] a franco

Frankfurt /ˈfræŋkfɜːt/ n Francoforte f

frankfurter /ˈfræŋkfɜːtə(r)/ n würstel m inv

frankincense /ˈfræŋkɪnsens/ n incenso m

franking machine /ˈfræŋkɪŋ/ n affrancatrice f

frankly /ˈfræŋklɪ/ adv francamente

frantic /ˈfræntɪk/ a frenetico; **be ~ with worry** essere agitatissimo

frantically /ˈfræntɪklɪ/ adv freneticamente

fraternal /frəˈtɜːnl/ a fraterno

fraternity /frəˈtɜːnətɪ/ n ⟨club⟩ associazione f; ⟨spirit, brotherhood⟩ fratellanza f

fraud /frɔːd/ n frode f; ⟨person⟩ impostore m

fraudulent /ˈfrɔːdjʊlənt/ a fraudolento

fraught /frɔːt/ a **~ with** pieno di

fray[1] /freɪ/ n mischia f

fray[2] vi sfilacciarsi

frayed /freɪd/ a ⟨cuffs⟩ sfilacciato; ⟨nerves⟩ a pezzi

frazzle /ˈfræz(ə)l/ n **be worn to a ~** essere ridotto uno straccio; **burn sth to a ~** carbonizzare qcsa

freak /friːk/ n fenomeno m; ⟨person⟩ scherzo m di natura; ⟨fam: weird person⟩ tipo m strambo ● a anormale

■ **freak out** vi ⟨fam: lose control, go crazy⟩ andar fuori di testa

freakish /ˈfriːkɪʃ/ a strambo

freckle /ˈfrekl/ n lentiggine f

freckled /ˈfrekld/ a lentigginoso

free /friː/ a (**freer, freest**) libero; ⟨ticket, copy⟩ gratuito; ⟨lavish⟩ generoso; **~ of charge** gratuito; **set ~** liberare; **~ with...** *Comm* in ommaggio per... ● vt (pt/pp **freed**) liberare

free agent n persona f libera di agire come vuole

free and easy a disinvolto

freebee, freebie /ˈfriːbiː/ n fam ⟨free gift⟩ omaggio m; ⟨trip⟩ viaggio m gratuito; ⟨newspaper⟩ giornale m gratuito

freedom /ˈfriːdəm/ n libertà f

free: free enterprise n liberalismo m economico. **free fall** n caduta f libera. **free-for-all** n ⟨disorganized situation, fight⟩ baraonda f. **freehand** adv a mano libera. **freehold** n proprietà f [fondiaria] assoluta. **free house** n Br pub m inv che non è legato a nessun produttore di birra. **free-kick** n calcio m di punizione. **freelance** a & adv indipendente. **freeloader** n fam scroccone m

freely /ˈfriːlɪ/ adv liberamente; ⟨generously⟩ generosamente; **I ~ admit that...** devo ammettere che...

free: Freemason n massone m. **Freemasonry** n massoneria f. **freephone number** n numero m verde. **free-range egg** n uovo m di gallina ruspante. **free sample** n campione m gratuito. **free spirit** n persona f che ama la sua indipendenza. **free-standing** a ⟨heater⟩ non incassato; ⟨statue⟩ a tutto tondo; ⟨lamp⟩ a stelo. **freestyle** n stile m libero. **free trade** n libero scambio m. **free trial period** n periodo m di prova gratuito. **freeway** n Am autostrada f. **freewheel** vi ⟨car:⟩ ⟨in neutral⟩ andare in folle; ⟨with engine switched off⟩ andare a motore spento; ⟨bicycle:⟩ andare a ruota libera

freeze /fri:z/ vt (pt **froze**, pp **frozen**) gelare; bloccare ⟨wages⟩ ● vi ⟨water:⟩ gelare; **it's freezing** si gela; **my hands are freezing** ho le mani congelate

freeze-dried a liofilizzato

freeze-frame n ⟨video⟩ fermo m immagine

freezer /'fri:zə(r)/ n freezer m inv, congelatore m

freezing /'fri:zɪŋ/ a gelido ● n **below** ~ sotto zero

freezing fog n nebbia f ghiacciata

freezing point n punto m di congelamento

freight /freɪt/ n carico m

freight charges npl costi mpl di spedizione

freighter /'freɪtə(r)/ n nave f da carico

freight forwarder n spedizioniere m

freight train n Am treno m merci

French /frentʃ/ a francese ● n ⟨language⟩ francese m; **the** ~ pl i francesi

French: French beans npl fagiolini mpl [verdi]. **French bread** n filone m ⟨di pane⟩. **French Canadian** n canadese mf francofono, -a ● a del Canada francofono. **French doors** npl porta-finestra f inv. **French dressing** n Br vinaigrette f inv. **French fries** npl patate fpl fritte. **French horn** n corno m da caccia. **French kiss** n bacio m profondo. **French knickers** npl culottes fpl. **Frenchman** n francese m. **French polish** n vernice f a olio e gommalacca. **French toast** n pane m immerso nell'uovo sbattuto e fritto. **French window** n porta-finestra f. **Frenchwoman** n francese f

frenetic /frə'netɪk/ a ⟨activity⟩ frenetico

frenzied /'frenzɪd/ a frenetico

frenzy /'frenzɪ/ n frenesia f

frequency /'fri:kwənsɪ/ n frequenza f

frequent¹ /'fri:kwənt/ a frequente

frequent² /frɪ'kwent/ vt frequentare

frequently /'fri:kwəntlɪ/ adv frequentemente

fresco /'freskəʊ/ n affresco m

fresh /freʃ/ a fresco; ⟨new⟩ nuovo; (Am: cheeky) sfacciato

freshen /'freʃn/ vi ⟨wind:⟩ rinfrescare

■ **freshen up** vt dare una rinfrescata a ● vi rinfrescarsi

fresh-faced /-'feɪst/ a dalla faccia giovanile

freshly /'freʃlɪ/ adv di recente

freshman /'freʃmən/ n Am matricola f; (fig: in congress, in firm) nuovo arrivato m

freshness /'freʃnɪs/ n freschezza f

freshwater /'freʃwɔ:tə(r)/ a di acqua dolce

fret /fret/ vi (pt/pp **fretted**) inquietarsi

fretful /'fretfʊl/ a irritabile

fretsaw /'fretsɔ:/ n seghetto m da traforo

fretwork /'fretwɜ:k/ n [lavoro m di] traforo m

Freudian slip /'frɔɪdɪən/ n lapsus m inv freudiano

friar /'fraɪə(r)/ n frate m

friction /'frɪkʃn/ n frizione f

Friday /'fraɪdeɪ/ n venerdì m inv

fridge /frɪdʒ/ n frigo m

fried /fraɪd/ see **fry** ● a fritto; ~ **egg** uovo m fritto

friend /frend/ n amico, -a mf

friendly /'frendlɪ/ a (-**ier, -iest**) ⟨relations, meeting, match⟩ amichevole; ⟨neighbourhood, smile⟩ piacevole; ⟨software⟩ di facile uso; **be** ~ **with** essere amico di

friendship /'frendʃɪp/ n amicizia f

frieze /fri:z/ n fregio m

frigate /'frɪgət/ n fregata f

fright /fraɪt/ n paura f; **take** ~ spaventarsi

frighten /'fraɪt(ə)n/ vt spaventare

■ **frighten away** vt far scappare ⟨bird, intruder⟩

frightened /'fraɪtənd/ a spaventato; **be** ~ aver paura (**of** di)

frightening /'fraɪt(ə)nɪŋ/ a spaventoso

frightful /'fraɪtfʊl/ a terribile

frightfully /'fraɪtfʊlɪ/ adv terribilmente

frigid /'frɪdʒɪd/ a frigido

frigidity /frɪ'dʒɪdətɪ/ n freddezza f; Psych frigidità f

frill /frɪl/ n volant m inv

frilly /'frɪlɪ/ a ⟨dress⟩ con tanti volant

fringe /frɪndʒ/ n frangia f; ⟨of hair⟩ frangetta f; ⟨fig: edge⟩ margine m

fringe benefits npl benefici mpl supplementari

frisk /frɪsk/ vt ⟨search⟩ perquisire

frisky /'frɪskɪ/ a (-**ier, -iest**) vispo

fritter /'frɪtə(r)/ n frittella f

■ **fritter away** vt sprecare

frivolity /frɪ'vɒlətɪ/ n frivolezza f

frivolous /'frɪvələs/ a frivolo

frizzy /'frɪzɪ/ a (-**ier, iest**) crespo

fro /frəʊ/ see **to**

frock /frɒk/ n abito m

frog /frɒg/ n rana f

frog: frogman n uomo m rana inv. **frogmarch** vt Br portare via a forza. **frogs' legs** npl cosce fpl di rana. **frogspawn** n uova fpl di rana

frolic /'frɒlɪk/ vi (pt/pp **frolicked**) ⟨lambs:⟩ sgambettare; ⟨fam: people⟩ folleggiare

from /from/ prep da; ~ **Monday** da lunedì; ~ **that day** da quel giorno; **he's** ~ **London** è di Londra; **this is a letter** ~ **my brother** questa è una lettera di mio fratello; **documents** ~ **the 16th century** documenti del XVI secolo; **made** ~ fatto con; **she felt ill** ~ **fatigue** si sentiva male dalla stanchezza; ~ **now on** d'ora in poi

front /frʌnt/ n parte f anteriore; ⟨fig: organization etc⟩ facciata f; ⟨of garment⟩ davanti m; ⟨sea~⟩ lungomare m; Mil, Pol, Meteorol fronte m; **in** ~ **of** davanti a; **in** or **at the** ~ davanti; **to the** ~ avanti ● a davanti; ⟨page, row, wheel⟩ anteriore

frontage /'frʌntɪdʒ/ n ⟨of house⟩ facciata f; **with ocean/river** ~ ⟨access⟩ prospiciente l'oceano/il fiume

frontal /'frʌntl/ a frontale

front: front bench n Br Pol parlamentari mpl di maggiore importanza. **front door** n porta *f* d'entrata. **front garden** *n* giardino *m* d'avanti

frontier /'frʌntɪə(r)/ *n* frontiera *f*

front: front line *n Mil* prima linea *f*; **be in the ~ ~** *fig* essere in prima linea. **front of house** *n Br Theat* foyer *m inv*. **front runner** *n Sport* concorrente *mf* in testa; (*favourite*) favorito, -a *mf*. **front-wheel drive** *n* trazione *f* anteriore

frost /frɒst/ *n* gelo *m*; (*hoar~*) brina *f*

frostbite /'frɒs(t)baɪt/ *n* congelamento *m*

frostbitten /'frɒs(t)bɪtən/ *a* congelato

frosted /'frɒstɪd/ *a* **~ glass** vetro *m* smerigliato

frostily /'frɒstɪlɪ/ *adv* gelidamente

frosting /'frɒstɪŋ/ *n Am Culin* glassa *f*

frosty /'frɒstɪ/ *a* (**-ier, iest**) *also fig* gelido

froth /frɒθ/ *n* schiuma *f* ● *vi* far schiuma

frothy /'frɒθɪ/ *a* (**-ier, iest**) schiumoso

frown /fraʊn/ *n* cipiglio *m* ● *vi* aggrottare le sopraciglia

■ **frown on** *vt* disapprovare

froze /frəʊz/ *see* **freeze**

frozen /'frəʊzn/ *see* **freeze** ● *a* (*corpse, hand*) congelato; (*wastes*) gelido; *Culin* surgelato; **I'm ~** sono gelato

frozen food *n* surgelati *mpl*

frugal /'fru:gl/ *a* frugale

frugally /'fru:gəlɪ/ *adv* frugalmente

fruit /fru:t/ *n* frutto *m*; (*collectively*) frutta *f*; **eat more ~** mangia più frutta

fruit: fruit bowl *n* fruttiera *f*. **fruit cake** *n* dolce *m* con frutta candita. **fruit cocktail** *n* macedonia *f* [di frutta]. **fruit drop** *n* drop *m inv* alla frutta

fruiterer /'fru:tərə(r)/ *n* fruttivendolo, -a *mf*

fruit farmer *n* frutticoltore *m*

fruit fly *n* moscerino *m* della frutta

fruitful /'fru:tfʊl/ *a fig* fruttuoso

fruit gum *n* caramella *f* alla frutta

fruition /fru:'ɪʃn/ *n* **come to ~** dare dei frutti

fruit juice *n* succo *m* di frutta

fruitless /'fru:tlɪs/ *a* infruttuoso

fruitlessly /'fru:tlɪslɪ/ *adv* senza risultato

fruit machine *n* macchinetta *f* mangiasoldi

fruit salad *n* macedonia *f* [di frutta]

fruity /'fru:tɪ/ *a* (*wine*) fruttato

frump /frʌmp/ *n* donna *f* scialba

frumpy /'frʌmpɪ/ *a* scialbo

frustrate /frʌ'streɪt/ *vt* frustrare; rovinare (*plans*)

frustrating /frʌ'streɪtɪŋ/ *a* frustrante

frustration /frʌ'streɪʃn/ *n* frustrazione *f*

fry[1] /fraɪ/ *n inv* **small ~** *fig* pesce *m* piccolo

fry[2] *vt/i* (*pt/pp* **fried**) friggere

frying pan /'fraɪŋ/ *n* padella *f*

fuchsia /'fju:ʃə/ *n* fucsia *f*

fuck /fʌk/ *vulg vt/i* scopare ● *n* **I don't give a ~** me ne sbatto; **what the ~ are you doing?** che cazzo fai? ● *int* cazzo!

■ **fuck off** *vi* (*vulg*) **~ off!** vaffanculo!

■ **fuck up** *vt* (*vulg: ruin*) mandare a puttane

fucking /'fʌkɪŋ/ *a vulg* del cazzo

fuddled /'fʌd(ə)ld/ *a* (*confused*) confuso; (*slightly drunk*) brillo

fuddy-duddy /'fʌdɪdʌdɪ/ *n fam* matusa *mf inv*

fudge /fʌdʒ/ *n caramella f a base di zucchero, burro e latte*

fuel /'fju:əl/ *n* carburante *m*; *fig* nutrimento *m* ● *vt fig* alimentare

fuel: fuel consumption *n* consumo *m* di carburante. **fuel efficient** *a* economico. **fuel injection** *n* iniezione *f*. **fuel injection engine** *n* motore *m* a iniezione. **fuel oil** *n* nafta *f*. **fuel pump** *n* pompa *f* della benzina. **fuel tank** *n* serbatoio *m*

fuggy /'fʌgɪ/ *a* (*Br: smoky*) fumoso

fugitive /'fju:dʒɪtɪv/ *n* fuggiasco, -a *mf*

fugue /fju:g/ *n Mus* fuga *f*

fulcrum /'fʊlkrəm/ *n* fulcro *m*

fulfil /fʊl'fɪl/ *vt* (*pt/pp* **-filled**) soddisfare (*conditions, need*); adempiere a (*promise*); realizzare (*dream, desire*); **~ oneself** realizzarsi

fulfilling /fʊl'fɪlɪŋ/ *a* soddisfacente

fulfilment /fʊl'fɪlmənt/ *n* **sense of ~** senso *m* di appagamento

full /fʊl/ *a* a pieno (**of** di); (*detailed*) esauriente; (*bus, hotel*) completo; (*skirt*) ampio; **at ~ speed** a tutta velocità; **in ~ swing** in pieno fervore ● *adv* in pieno; **you know ~ well that** sai benissimo che ● *n* **in ~** per intero

full: full-back *n* difensore *m*. **full beam** *n Auto* [fari *mpl*] abbaglianti *mpl*. **full-blown** /-'bləʊn/ *a* (*epidemic*) vero a e proprio; (*disease*) conclamato. **full board** *n* pensione *f* completa. **full-bodied** /-'bɒdɪd/ *a* (*wine*) corposo. **full-frontal** *a* (*photograph*) di nudo frontale. **full house** *n Theat* tutto esaurito *m inv*; (*in poker*) full *m inv*. **full-length** *a* (*dress*) lungo; (*curtain*) lungo fino a terra; (*portrait*) intero; **~ ~ film** lungometraggio *m*. **full moon** *n* luna *f* piena. **full-scale** *a* (*model*) in scala reale; (*alert*) di massima gravità. **full stop** *n* punto *m*. **full-time** *a & adv* a tempo pieno

fully /'fʊlɪ/ *adv* completamente; (*in detail*) dettagliatamente; **~ booked** (*hotel, restaurant*) tutto prenotato

fully fledged /-'fledʒd/ *a* (*bird*) che ha messo tutte le penne; (*lawyer*) con tutte le qualifiche; (*member*) a tutti gli effetti

fulsome /'fʊlsəm/ *a* esagerato

fumble /'fʌmbl/ *vi* **~** in rovistare in; **~ with** armeggiare con; **~ for one's keys** rovistare alla ricerca delle chiavi

fume /fju:m/ *vi* (*be angry*) essere furioso

fumes /fju:mz/ *npl* fumi *mpl*; (*from car*) gas *mpl* di scarico

fumigate /'fju:mɪgeɪt/ *vt* suffumicare

fun /fʌn/ *n* divertimento *m*; **for ~** per ridere; **make ~ of** prendere in giro; **have ~** divertirsi

function /'fʌŋkʃn/ *n* funzione *f*; (*event*) cerimonia *f* ● *vi* funzionare; **~ as** (*serve as*) funzionare da

functional /'fʌŋkʃ(ə)nəl/ *a* funzionale

function key n Comput tasto m [di] funzioni

function room n sala f di ricevimento

fund /fʌnd/ n fondo m; fig pozzo m; ~s pl fondi mpl ● vt finanziare

fundamental /fʌndə'mentl/ a fondamentale

fundamentalist /fʌndə'mentəlɪst/ n fondamentalista mf

funding /'fʌndɪŋ/ n (financial aid) finanziamento m; (of debt) consolidamento m

fund-raiser /-reɪzə(r)/ n (person) promotore, -trice mf di raccolte di fondi; (event) manifestazione f per la raccolta di fondi

fund-raising /-reɪzɪŋ/ n raccolta f di fondi

funeral /'fjuːnərəl/ n funerale m

funeral: funeral directors n impresa f di pompe funebri. **funeral home, funeral parlour** Am n camera f ardente. **funeral march** n marcia f funebre. **funeral service** n rito m funebre

funereal /fjuː'nɪərɪəl/ a lugubre

funfair /'fʌnfeə(r)/ n luna park m inv

fungal /'fʌŋgəl/ a (infection) micotico

fungus /'fʌŋgəs/ n (pl -gi /'fʌŋgaɪ/) fungo m

funicular /fjuː'nɪkjʊlə(r)/ n funicolare f

fun loving /fʌnlʌvɪŋ/ a (person) amante del divertimento

funnel /'fʌnl/ n imbuto m; (on ship) ciminiera f

funnily /'fʌnɪlɪ/ adv comicamente; (oddly) stranamente; ~ **enough** strano a dirsi

funny /'fʌnɪ/ a (-ier, -iest) buffo; (odd) strano

funny bone n osso m del gomito

funny business n fam affare m losco

fur /fɜː(r)/ n pelo m; (for clothing) pelliccia f; (in kettle) deposito m

fur coat n pelliccia f

furious /'fjʊərɪəs/ a furioso

furiously /'fjʊərɪəslɪ/ adv furiosamente

furl /fɜːl/ vt serrare (sail)

furnace /'fɜːnɪs/ n fornace f

furnish /'fɜːnɪʃ/ vt ammobiliare (flat); fornire (supplies)

furnished /'fɜːnɪʃt/ a ~ **room** stanza f ammobiliata

furnishings /'fɜːnɪʃɪŋz/ npl mobili mpl

furniture /'fɜːnɪtʃə(r)/ n mobili mpl

furniture remover /rɪmuːvə(r)/ n Br impresa f di traslochi

furniture van n furgone m per i traslochi

furore /fjʊ'rɔːrɪ/ n (outrage, criticism) scalpore m; (acclaim) entusiasmo m

furred /fɜːd/ a (tongue) impastato

furrow /'fʌrəʊ/ n solco m

furry /'fɜːrɪ/ a (animal) peloso; (toy) di peluche

further /'fɜːðə(r)/ a (additional) ulteriore; **at the ~ end** all'altra estremità; **until ~ notice** fino a nuovo avviso ● adv più lontano; ~,**...** inoltre,....; ~ **off** più lontano ● vt promuovere

further education n istruzione f parauniversitaria

furthermore /fɜːðə'mɔː(r)/ adv per di più

furthest /'fɜːðɪst/ a più lontano ● adv più lontano; **the ~ advanced of the students** lo studente più avanti

furtive /'fɜːtɪv/ a furtivo

furtively /'fɜːtɪvlɪ/ adv furtivamente

fury /'fjʊərɪ/ n furore m

fuse¹ /fjuːz/ n (of bomb) detonatore m; (cord) miccia f

fuse² n Electr fusibile m ● vt fondere; Electr far saltare ● vi fondersi; Electr saltare; **the lights have ~d** sono saltate le luci

fuse box n scatola f dei fusibili

fuselage /'fjuːzəlɑːʒ/ n Aeron fusoliera f

fuse wire n [filo m di] fusibile m

fusillade /fjuːzɪl'ɑːd/ n Mil scarica f; fig raffica f

fusion /'fjuːʒn/ n fusione f

fuss /fʌs/ n storie fpl; **make a ~** fare storie; **make a ~ of** colmare di attenzioni ● vi fare storie

fussy /'fʌsɪ/ a (-ier, -iest) (person) difficile da accontentare; (clothes etc) pieno di fronzoli

fusty /'fʌstɪ/ a che odora di stantio; (smell) di stantio

futile /'fjuːtaɪl/ a inutile

futility /fjʊ'tɪlətɪ/ n futilità f

future /'fjuːtʃə(r)/ a & n futuro; **in ~** in futuro

future perfect n futuro m anteriore

futures npl Fin contratti mpl a termine

futuristic /fjuːtʃə'rɪstɪk/ a futuristico

fuzz /fʌz/ n **the ~** (sl: police) la pula

fuzzy /'fʌzɪ/ a (-ier, -iest) (hair) crespo; (photo) sfuocato

g, G /dʒi:/ n (letter) g, G f inv; Mus sol m inv
g abbr (**gram(s**)) g
gab /gæb/ n fam **have the gift of the ~** avere la parlantina
gabardine /gæbə'di:n/ n gabardine f
gabble /'gæb(ə)l/ vi parlare troppo in fretta
gable /'geɪb(ə)l/ n frontone m
gad /gæd/ vi (pt/pp **gadded**) **~ about** andarsene in giro
gadget /'gædʒɪt/ n aggeggio m
Gaelic /'geɪlɪk/ a & n gaelico m
gaff /gæf/ n Br fam **blow the ~** spifferare un segreto; **blow the ~ on sth** svelare la verità su qcsa
gaffe /gæf/ n gaffe f inv
gaffer /'gæfə(r)/ n (Br: foreman) caposquadra m; (Br: boss) capo m; Cinema, TV tecnico m delle luci
gag /gæg/ n bavaglio m; (joke) battuta f ● vt (pt/pp **gagged**) imbavagliare
gaga /'gɑ:gɑ:/ a fam rimbambito
gage /geɪdʒ/ n & vt Am = **gauge**
gaiety /'geɪətɪ/ n allegria f
gaily /'geɪlɪ/ adv allegramente
gain /geɪn/ n guadagno m; (increase) aumento m ● vt acquisire; **~ weight** aumentare di peso; **~ access** accedere ● vi ⟨clock:⟩ andare avanti
gainful /'geɪnful/ a **~ employment** lavoro m remunerativo
gainsay /geɪn'seɪ/ vt contraddire ⟨person⟩; contestare ⟨argument⟩
gait /geɪt/ n andatura f
gala /'gɑ:lə/ n gala f; **swimming ~** manifestazione f di nuoto ● attrib di gala
galaxy /'gæləksɪ/ n galassia f
gale /geɪl/ n bufera f
gale warning n avvertimento m di imminente bufera
gall /gɔ:l/ n (impudence) impudenza f
gallant /'gælənt/ a coraggioso; (chivalrous) galante
gallantly /'gæləntlɪ/ adv galantemente
gallantry /'gæləntrɪ/ n coraggio m
gall bladder n cistifellea f
gallery /'gælərɪ/ n galleria f
galley /'gælɪ/ n (ship's kitchen) cambusa f
galley [**proof**] n bozza f in colonna
Gallic /'gælɪk/ a francese
gallivant /'gælɪvænt/ vi fam andare in giro
gallon /'gælən/ n gallone m (= 4,5 l; Am = 3,7 l)
gallop /'gæləp/ n galoppo m ● vi galoppare
gallows /'gæləʊz/ n forca f
gallstone /'gɔ:lstəʊn/ n calcolo m biliare
galore /gə'lɔ:(r)/ adv a bizzeffe

galvanize /'gælvənaɪz/ vt Techn galvanizzare; fig stimolare (**into** a)
Gambia /'gæmbɪə/ n Gambia f
gambit /'gæmbɪt/ n prima mossa f
gamble /'gæmbl/ n (risk) azzardo m ● vi giocare; (on Stock Exchange) speculare; **~ on** (rely) contare su
gambler /'gæmblə(r)/ n giocatore, -trice mf [d'azzardo]
gambling /'gæmblɪŋ/ n gioco m [d'azzardo]
gambol /'gæmb(ə)l/ vi saltellare
game /geɪm/ n gioco m; (match) partita f; (animals, birds) selvaggina f; **~s** pl Sch ≈ ginnastica f ● a (brave) coraggioso; **are you ~?** ti va?; **be ~ for** essere pronto per
game: game bird n uccello m da cacciagione. **gamekeeper** n guardacaccia m inv.
game park n = **game reserve**. **game point** n Tennis game point m inv. **game reserve** n (for hunting) riserva f di caccia; (for preservation) parco m naturale [faunistico].
game show n ≈ quiz m inv televisivo
gamesmanship /'geɪmzmənʃɪp/ n strategemmi mpl
game warden n guardacaccia m inv
gaming laws /'geɪmɪŋ/ npl leggi fpl che regolano il gioco d'azzardo
gaming machine n slot machine f inv
gammon /'gæmən/ n coscia f di maiale affumicata
gamut /'gæmət/ n fig gamma f
gander /'gændə(r)/ n oca f maschio; **take a ~ at sth** fam dare un'occhiata a qcsa
gang /gæŋ/ n banda f; (of workmen) squadra f ■ **gang up** vi far comunella (**on** contro)
gangland /'gæŋlænd/ n malavita f
gangleader /'gæŋli:də(r)/ n capobanda mf inv
gangling /'gæŋglɪŋ/ a spilungone
gangplank /'gæŋplæŋk/ n passerella f
gang rape n stupro m collettivo
gangrene /'gæŋgri:n/ n cancrena f
gangrenous /'gæŋgrɪnəs/ a cancrenoso
gangster /'gæŋstə(r)/ n gangster m inv
gangway /'gæŋweɪ/ n passaggio m; Naut, Aeron passerella f
gaol /dʒeɪl/ n carcere m ● vt incarcerare
gaoler /'dʒeɪlə(r)/ n carceriere m
gap /gæp/ n spazio m; (in ages, between teeth) scarto m; (in memory) vuoto m; (in story) punto m oscuro
gape /geɪp/ vi stare a bocca aperta; (be wide open) spalancarsi; **~ at** guardare a bocca aperta
gaping /'geɪpɪŋ/ a aperto
garage /'gærɑ:ʒ/ n garage m inv; (for

repairs) meccanico *m*; *(for petrol)* stazione *f* di servizio

garage mechanic *n* meccanico *m*

garage sale *n vendita f di articoli usati a casa propria*

garb /gɑːb/ *n* tenuta *f*

garbage /ˈgɑːbɪdʒ/ *n* immondizia *f*; *(nonsense)* idiozie *fpl*

garbage can *n Am* bidone *m* dell'immondizia

garbled /ˈgɑːbld/ *a* confuso

garden /ˈgɑːdn/ *n* giardino *m*; [**public**] **~s** *pl* giardini *mpl* pubblici ● *vi* fare giardinaggio

garden centre *n Br* vivaio *m (che vende anche articoli da giardinaggio)*

garden city *n* città *f inv* giardino

gardener /ˈgɑːdnə(r)/ *n* giardiniere, -a *mf*

garden flat *n appartamento m al pianterreno o seminterrato che dà sul giardino*

gardening /ˈgɑːdnɪŋ/ *n* giardinaggio *m*

garden: garden shears *npl* cesoie *fpl*. **garden suburb** *n* periferia *f* verde. **garden-variety** *a ⟨Am: writer, book⟩* insignificante

gargle /ˈgɑːgl/ *n* gargarismo *m* ● *vi* fare gargarismi

gargoyle /ˈgɑːgɔɪl/ *n* gargouille *f inv*

garish /ˈgeərɪʃ/ *a* sgargiante

garland /ˈgɑːlənd/ *n* ghirlanda *f*

garlic /ˈgɑːlɪk/ *n* aglio *m*

garlic bread *n* pane *m* condito con aglio

garlic press *n* spremiaglio *m inv*

garment /ˈgɑːmənt/ *n* indumento *m*

garnet /ˈgɑːnɪt/ *n* granato *m*

garnish /ˈgɑːnɪʃ/ *n* guarnizione *f* ● *vt* guarnire

garret /ˈgærɪt/ *n* soffitta *f*

garrison /ˈgærɪsn/ *n* guarnigione *f*

garrotte /gəˈrɒt/ *n Br* garrotta *f* ● *vt (strangle)* strangolare

garrulous /ˈgærʊləs/ *a* chiacchierone

garter /ˈgɑːtə(r)/ *n* giarrettiera *f*; *(Am: for man's socks)* reggicalze *m inv* da uomo

gas /gæs/ *n* gas *m inv*; *(Am fam: petrol)* benzina *f* ● *v (pt/pp* **gassed***)* ● *vt* asfissiare ● *vi fam* blaterare

gas: gas burner *n* becco *m* a gas. **gas chamber** *n* camera *f* a gas. **gas cooker** *n* cucina *f* a gas

gaseous /ˈgæsɪəs/ *a* gassoso

gas fire *n* stufa *f* a gas

gas-fired /-faɪəd/ *a ⟨boiler, water heater⟩* a gas

gash /gæʃ/ *n* taglio *m* ● *vt* tagliare; **~ one's arm** farsi un taglio nel braccio

gasket /ˈgæskɪt/ *n Techn* guarnizione *f*

gas: gas main *n* conduttura *f* del gas. **gas mask** *n* maschera *f* antigas. **gas meter** *n* contatore *m* del gas

gasoline /ˈgæsəliːn/ *n Am* benzina *f*

gasp /gɑːsp/ *vi* avere il fiato mozzato

gas ring *n Br (fixed)* bruciatore *m*; *(portable)* fornelletto *m* [portatile]

gas station *n Am* distributore *m* di benzina

gassy /ˈgæsɪ/ *a ⟨drink⟩* gassato

gastric /ˈgæstrɪk/ *a* gastrico

gastric flu *n* influenza *f* gastro-intestinale

gastric ulcer *n* ulcera *f* gastrica

gastritis /gæˈstraɪtɪs/ *n* gastrite *f*

gastroenteritis /ˌgæstrəʊentəˈraɪtɪs/ *n* gastroenterite *f*

gastronomy /gæˈstrɒnəmɪ/ *n* gastronomia *f*

gate /geɪt/ *n* cancello *m*; *(at airport)* uscita *f*

gâteau /ˈgætəʊ/ *n* torta *f*

gate: gatecrash *vt* entrare senza invito a ● *vi* entrare senza invito. **gatecrasher** *n* intruso, -a *mf*. **gatehouse** *n ⟨to castle⟩* corpo *m* di guardia; *⟨to park⟩* casa *f* del custode. **gatekeeper** *n* custode *mf*. **gatepost** *n* palo *m* del cancello. **gateway** *n* ingresso *m*

gather /ˈgæðə(r)/ *vt* raccogliere; *(conclude)* dedurre; *(in sewing)* arricciare; **~ speed** acquistare velocità; **~ together** radunare *⟨people, belongings⟩*; *(obtain gradually)* acquistare ● *vi ⟨people:⟩* radunarsi; **a storm is ~ing** si sta preparando un acquazzone

gathering /ˈgæðərɪŋ/ *n* **family ~** ritrovo *m* di famiglia

gauche /gəʊʃ/ *a ⟨person, attitude⟩* impacciato; *⟨remark⟩* inopportuno

gaudy /ˈgɔːdɪ/ *a* **(-ier, -iest)** pacchiano

gauge /geɪdʒ/ *n* calibro *m*; *Rail* scartamento *m*; *(device)* indicatore *m* ● *vt* misurare; *fig* stimare

gaunt /gɔːnt/ *a (thin)* smunto

gauntlet /ˈgɔːntlɪt/ *n* **throw down the ~** lanciare il guanto della sfida

gauze /gɔːz/ *n* garza *f*

gave /geɪv/ *see* **give**

gawky /ˈgɔːkɪ/ *a* **(-ier, -iest)** sgraziato

gawp /gɔːp/ *vi* **~ (at)** *fam* guardare con aria da ebete

gay /geɪ/ *a* gaio; *(homosexual)* omosessuale; *⟨bar, club⟩* gay

gaze /geɪz/ *n* sguardo *m* fisso ● *vi* guardare; **~ at** fissare; **~ into space** avere lo sguardo perso nel vuoto

gazelle /gəˈzel/ *n* gazzella *f*

gazette /gəˈzet/ *n (official journal)* bollettino *m* ufficiale; *(newspaper title)* gazzetta *f*

gazetteer /gæzɪˈtɪə(r)/ *n (book)* dizionario *m* geografico; *(part of book)* indice *m* dei nomi geografici

gazump /gəˈzʌmp/ *vt Comm sl* **we've been ~ed** il proprietario della casa ha optato per un'offerta migliore dopo avere accettato la nostra

GB *abbr* **(Great Britain)** GB

GBH *n abbr* **(grievous bodily harm)** lesioni *fpl* personali grave

GCSE *n Br abbr* **(General Certificate of Secondary Education)** *esami mpl conclusivi della scuola dell'obbligo*

GDP *n abbr* **(gross domestic product)** PIL *m*

gear /gɪə(r)/ *n* equipaggiamento *m*; *Techn* ingranaggio *m*; *Auto* marcia *f*; **in ~** con la marcia innestata; **change ~** cambiare marcia ● *vt* finalizzare **(to** a) ● *vi* **~ up for** prepararsi per *⟨election⟩*

gearbox /'gɪəbɒks/ n Auto scatola f del cambio

gear lever, Am **gear shift** n leva f del cambio

geese /giːs/ see **goose**

geezer /'giːzə(r)/ n sl tipo m

gel /dʒel/ n gel m inv

gelatine /'dʒelətɪn/ n gelatina f

gelatinous /dʒɪ'lætɪnəs/ a gelatinoso

gelding /'geldɪŋ/ n (horse) castrone m; (castration) castrazione f

gelignite /'dʒelɪgnaɪt/ n gelatina f esplosiva

gem /dʒem/ n gemma f

Gemini /'dʒemɪnaɪ/ n Astr Gemelli mpl

gen /dʒen/ n Br fam informazioni fpl; **what's the ~ on this?** cosa c'è da sapere su questo?

gender /'dʒendə(r)/ n Gram genere m

gene /dʒiːn/ n gene m

genealogy /dʒiːnɪ'ælədʒɪ/ n genealogia f

gene pool n pool m genetico

general /'dʒenrəl/ a generale ● n generale m; **in ~** in generale

general election n elezioni fpl politiche

generalization /dʒenrəlaɪ'zeɪʃn/ n generalizzazione f

generalize /'dʒenrəlaɪz/ vi generalizzare

general knowledge n cultura f generale

generally /'dʒenrəlɪ/ adv generalmente

general: general practitioner n medico m generico. **general public** n (grande) pubblico m. **general-purpose** a multiuso inv

generate /'dʒenəreɪt/ vt generare

generation /dʒenə'reɪʃn/ n generazione f

generation gap n gap m inv generazionale

generator /'dʒenəreɪtə(r)/ n generatore m

generic /dʒɪ'nerɪk/ a ~ **term** termine m generico

generosity /dʒenə'rɒsətɪ/ n generosità f

generous /'dʒenərəs/ a generoso

generously /'dʒenərəslɪ/ adv generosamente

genesis /'dʒenəsɪs/ n fig genesi f inv

genetic /dʒɪ'netɪk/ a genetico

genetic engineering n ingegneria f genetica

genetic fingerprinting /'fɪŋgəprɪntɪŋ/ n impronte fpl genetiche

geneticist /dʒɪ'netɪsɪst/ n genetista mf

genetics /dʒɪ'netɪks/ n genetica f

Geneva /dʒɪ'niːvə/ n Ginevra f

genial /'dʒiːnɪəl/ a gioviale

genially /'dʒiːnɪəlɪ/ adv con giovialità

genie /'dʒiːnɪ/ n genio m

genitals /'dʒenɪtlz/ npl genitali mpl

genitive /'dʒenɪtɪv/ a & n ~ [**case**] genitivo m

genius /'dʒiːnɪəs/ n (pl -uses) genio m

Genoa /'dʒenəʊə/ n Genova f

genocide /'dʒenəsaɪd/ n genocidio m

genre /'ʒɒrə/ n genere m (letterario)

gent /dʒent/ n fam signore m; **the ~s** sg il bagno per uomini

genteel /dʒen'tiːl/ a raffinato

gentle /'dʒentl/ a delicato; (breeze, tap, slope) leggero

gentleman /'dʒentlmən/ n signore m; (well-mannered) gentiluomo m

gentleness /'dʒentlnɪs/ n delicatezza f

gently /'dʒentlɪ/ adv delicatamente

gentry /'dʒentrɪ/ n alta borghesia f

genuine /'dʒenjʊɪn/ a genuino

genuinely /'dʒenjʊɪnlɪ/ adv ‹sorry› sinceramente

genus /'dʒiːnəs/ n Biol genere m

geographer /dʒɪ'ɒgrəfə(r)/ n geografo m

geographical /dʒɪə'græfɪkl/ a geografico

geographically /dʒɪə'græfɪklɪ/ adv geographicamente

geography /dʒɪ'ɒgrəfɪ/ n geografia f

geological /dʒɪə'lɒdʒɪkl/ a geologico

geologist /dʒɪ'ɒlədʒɪst/ n geologo, -a mf

geology /dʒɪ'ɒlədʒɪ/ n geologia f

geometric[al] /dʒɪə'metrɪk[l]/ a geometrico

geometry /dʒɪ'ɒmətrɪ/ n geometria f

geophysics /dʒɪəʊ'fɪzɪks/ n geofisica f

geopolitical /dʒɪːəʊpə'lɪtɪkl/ a geopolitico

Georgian /'dʒɔːdʒən/ n & a georgiano, -a mf; (language) georgiano m

geranium /dʒə'reɪnɪəm/ n geranio m

gerbil /'dʒɜːbəl/ n gerbillo m

geriatric /dʒerɪ'ætrɪk/ a geriatrico

geriatrics /dʒerɪ'ætrɪks/ n geriatria f

geriatric ward n reparto m geriatria

germ /dʒɜːm/ n germe m; ~**s** pl microbi mpl

German /'dʒɜːmən/ n & a tedesco, -a mf; (language) tedesco m

germane /dʒə'meɪn/ a ‹point, remark› pertinente

Germanic /dʒə'mænɪk/ a germanico

German measles n rosolia f

German shepherd n pastore m tedesco

Germany /'dʒɜːmənɪ/ n Germania f

germinate /'dʒɜːmɪneɪt/ vi germogliare

germ warfare n guerra f batteriologica

gerrymandering /'dʒerɪmænd(ə)rɪŋ/ n manipolazione f dei confini di una circoscrizione elettorale

gerund /'dʒerənd/ n gerundio m

gestate /dʒe'steɪt/ vi Biol essere incinta; fig maturare

gestation /dʒe'steɪʃən/ n gestazione f

gesticulate /dʒe'stɪkjʊleɪt/ vi gesticolare

gesture /'dʒestʃə(r)/ n gesto m

get /get/ v (pt/pp **got**, pp Am also **gotten**, pres p **getting**) ● vt (receive) ricevere; (obtain) ottenere; trovare ‹job›; (buy, catch, fetch) prendere; (transport, deliver to airport etc) portare; (reach on telephone) trovare; (fam: understand) comprendere; preparare ‹meal›; ~ **sb to do sth** far fare qcsa a qcno ● vi (become) ~ **tired/bored/angry** stancarsi/annoiarsi/arrabbiarsi; **I'm ~ting hungry** mi sta venendo fame; ~ **real!** fatti furbo!; ~ **dressed/married** vestirsi/sposarsi; ~ **sth ready** preparare qcsa; ~ **nowhere** non concludere nulla; **this is ~ting us nowhere** questo non ci è di nessun aiuto; ~ **to** (reach) arrivare a

■ **get about** *vi* ⟨*person:*⟩ muoversi; ⟨*rumour:*⟩ circolare

■ **get along** *vi* = **get on**

■ **get along with** *vt* andare d'accordo con ⟨*sb*⟩

■ **get around** *vi* = **get about**

■ **get at** *vi* (*criticize*) criticare; **I see what you're ~ting at** ho capito cosa vuoi dire; **what are you ~ting at?** dove vuoi andare a parare?

■ **get away** *vi* (*leave*) andarsene; (*escape*) scappare

■ **get back** *vi* tornare; **I'll ~ back to you** ci faccio sapere ● *vt* (*recover*) riavere; **~ one's own back** rifarsi

■ **get behind with** *vt* rimanere indietro con

■ **get by** *vi* passare; (*manage*) cavarsela

■ **get down** *vi* scendere; **~ down to work** mettersi al lavoro ● *vt* (*depress*) buttare giù

■ **get in** *vi* entrare ● *vt* mettere dentro ⟨*washing*⟩; far venire ⟨*plumber*⟩

■ **get off** *vi* scendere; (*from work*) andarsene; *Jur* essere assolto; **~ off the bus/one's bike** scendere dal pullman/dalla bici ● *vt* (*remove*) togliere

■ **get on** *vi* salire; (*be on good terms*) andare d'accordo; (*make progress*) andare avanti; (*in life*) riuscire; **~ on the bus/one's bike** salire sul pullman/sulla bici; **how are you ~ting on?** come va?

■ **get out** *vi* uscire; (*of car*) scendere; **~ out!** fuori! ● *vt* togliere ⟨*cork, stain*⟩

■ **get out of** *vt* (*avoid doing*) evitare

■ **get over** *vi* andare al di là ● *vt fig* riprendersi da ⟨*illness*⟩

■ **get round** *vt* aggirare ⟨*rule*⟩; rigirare ⟨*person*⟩ ● *vi* **I never ~ round to it** non mi sono mai deciso a farlo

■ **get through** *vi* (*on telephone*) prendere la linea

■ **get up** *vi* alzarsi; (*climb*) salire; **~ up a hill** salire su una collina

get: getaway *n* fuga *f*. **get-together** *n* incontro *m* fra amici. **get-up** *n* tenuta *f*. **get-up-and-go** *n* dinamismo *m*

geyser /'gi:zə(r)/ *n* scaldabagno *m*; *Geol* geyser *m inv*

G-force *n* forza *f* di gravità

ghastly /'gɑ:stlɪ/ *a* (**-ier, -iest**) terribile; **feel ~** sentirsi da cani

gherkin /'gɜ:kɪn/ *n* cetriolino *m*

ghetto /'getəʊ/ *n* ghetto *m*

ghetto blaster /blɑ:stə(r)/ *n fam* radioregistratore *m* stereo portatile

ghost /gəʊst/ *n* fantasma *m*

ghostly /'gəʊstlɪ/ *a* spettrale

ghost town *n* città *f inv* fantasma

ghost writer *n* negro *m*

ghoulish /'gu:lɪʃ/ *a* macabro

giant /'dʒaɪənt/ *n* gigante *m* ● *a* gigante

gibberish /'dʒɪbərɪʃ/ *n* stupidaggini *fpl*

gibe /dʒaɪb/ *n* malignità *f inv* ● *vi* beffarsi (**at** di)

giblets /'dʒɪblɪts/ *npl* frattaglie *fpl*

giddiness /'gɪdɪnɪs/ *n* vertigini *fpl*

giddy /'gɪdɪ/ *a* (**-ier, -iest**) vertiginoso; **feel ~** avere le vertigini

giddy spell *n* giramento *m* di testa

gift /gɪft/ *n* dono *m*; (*made to charity*) donazione *f*

gifted /'gɪftɪd/ *a* dotato

gift: gift token *n Br* buono *m* acquisto. **gift voucher** *n Br* buono *m* acquisto. **gift-wrap** *vt* impacchettare in carta da regalo

gig /gɪg/ *n Mus fam* concerto *m*

gigantic /dʒaɪ'gæntɪk/ *a* gigantesco

giggle /'gɪg(ə)l/ *n* risatina *f* ● *vi* ridacchiare

giggly /'gɪglɪ/ *a* ⟨*person*⟩ che ha la ridarella

gild /gɪld/ *vt* dorare

gilding /'gɪldɪŋ/ *n* doratura *f*

gill /dʒɪl/ *n* (*measure*) quarto *m* di pinta

gills /gɪlz/ *npl* branchia *fsg*

gilt /gɪlt/ *a* dorato ● *n* doratura *f*

gilt-edged stock /-edʒd/ *n Fin* investimento *m* sicuro

gimlet /'gɪmlɪt/ *n* succhiello *m*

gimmick /'gɪmɪk/ *n* trovata *f*

gimmicky /'gɪmɪkɪ/ *a* ⟨*production*⟩ pieno di trovate a effetto

gin /dʒɪn/ *n* gin *m inv*

ginger /'dʒɪndʒə(r)/ *a* rosso fuoco *inv*; ⟨*cat*⟩ rosso ● *n* zenzero *m*

ginger: ginger ale *n* bibita *f* gassata allo zenzero. **ginger beer** *n* bibita *f* allo zenzero. **gingerbread** *n* panpepato *m*. **ginger-haired** /-'heəd/ *a* con i capelli rossi

gingerly /'dʒɪndʒəlɪ/ *adv* con precauzione

ginger nut, ginger snap *n* biscotto *m* allo zenzero

gingham /'gɪŋəm/ *n* tessuto *m* vichy

gin rummy *n* variante *f* del gioco del ramino

gipsy /'dʒɪpsɪ/ *n* = **gypsy**

giraffe /dʒɪ'rɑ:f/ *n* giraffa *f*

girder /'gɜ:də(r)/ *n Techn* trave *f*

girdle /'gɜ:dl/ *n* cintura *f*; (*corset*) busto *m*

girl /gɜ:l/ *n* ragazza *f*; (*female child*) femmina *f*

girl: girl Friday *n* segretaria *f* tuttofare *inv*. **girlfriend** *n* amica *f*; (*of boy*) ragazza *f*. **girl guide** *n Br* giovane esploratrice *f*

girlish /'gɜ:lɪʃ/ *a* da ragazza

giro /'dʒaɪərəʊ/ *n* bancogiro *m*; (*cheque*) sussidio *m* di disoccupazione

girth /gɜ:θ/ *n* circonferenza *f*

gist /dʒɪst/ *n* **the ~** la sostanza

give /gɪv/ *n* elasticità *f* ● *v* (*pt* **gave**, *pp* **given**) ● *vt* dare; (*as present*) regalare (**to** a); fare ⟨*lecture, present, shriek*⟩; donare ⟨*blood*⟩; **~ birth** partorire ● *vi* (*to charity*) fare delle donazioni; (*yield*) cedere

■ **give away** *vt* dar via; (*betray*) tradire; (*distribute*) assegnare; **~ away the bride** portare la sposa all'altare

■ **give back** *vt* restituire

■ **give in** *vt* consegnare ● *vi* (*yield*) arrendersi

■ **give off** *vt* emanare

■ **give out** *vi* ⟨*supplies, patience:*⟩ esaurirsi;

⟨*engine, heart:*⟩ fermarsi ● *vt* (*distribute*) distribuire; diffondere ⟨*heat*⟩
■ **give over** *vi* ~ **over!** piantala!
■ **give up** *vt* rinunciare a; ~ **oneself up** arrendersi ● *vi* rinunciare
■ **give way** *vi* cedere; *Auto* dare la precedenza; (*collapse*) crollare
give-and-take *n* concessioni *fpl* reciproche
given /'gɪvn/ *see* **give** ● *a* ~ **name** nome *m* di battesimo
glacier /'glæsɪə(r)/ *n* ghiacciaio *m*
glad /glæd/ *a* contento (**of** di)
gladden /'glædn/ *vt* rallegrare
glade /gleɪd/ *n* radura *f*
gladiator /'glædɪeɪtə(r)/ *n* gladiatore *m*
gladiolus /glædɪ'əʊləs/ *n* gladiolo *m*
gladly /'glædlɪ/ *adv* volentieri
glamorize /'glæmərаɪz/ *vt* rendere affascinante
glamorous /'glæmərəs/ *a* affascinante
glamour /'glæmə(r)/ *n* fascino *m*
glance /glɑːns/ *n* sguardo *m* ● *vi* ~ **at** dare un'occhiata a
■ **glance up** *vi* alzare gli occhi
gland /glænd/ *n* glandola *f*
glandular /'glændjʊlə(r)/ *a* ghiandolare
glandular fever *n* mononucleosi *f*
glare /gleə(r)/ *n* bagliore *m*; (*look*) occhiataccia *f* ● *vi* ~ **at** dare un'occhiataccia a
glaring /'gleərɪŋ/ *a* sfolgorante; ⟨*mistake*⟩ madornale
glass /glɑːs/ *n* vetro *m*; (*for drinking*) bicchiere *m*
glasses /'glɑːsɪz/ *npl* (*spectacles*) occhiali *mpl*
glasshouse /'glɑːshaʊs/ *n* serra *f*
glassy /'glɑːsɪ/ *a* vitreo
glassy-eyed /-'aɪd/ *a* (*from drink, illness*) che ha gli occhi vitrei
glaucoma /glɔː'kəʊmə/ *n* glaucoma *m*
glaze /gleɪz/ *n* smalto *m* ● *vt* mettere i vetri a ⟨*door, window*⟩; smaltare ⟨*pottery*⟩; *Culin* spennellare
glazed /gleɪzd/ *a* ⟨*eyes*⟩ vitreo
glazier /'gleɪzɪə(r)/ *n* vetraio *m*
gleam /gliːm/ *n* luccichio *m* ● *vi* luccicare
glean /gliːn/ *vt* racimolare ⟨*information*⟩
glee /gliː/ *n* gioia *f*
gleeful /'gliːfʊl/ *a* gioioso
gleefully /'gliːfʊlɪ/ *adv* giosamente
glen /glen/ *n* vallone *m*
glib /glɪb/ *a pej* insincero
glibly /'glɪblɪ/ *adv pej* senza sincerità
glide /glaɪd/ *vi* scorrere; (*through the air*) planare
glider /'glaɪdə(r)/ *n* aliante *m*
gliding /'glaɪdɪŋ/ *n* volo *m* a vela
glimmer /'glɪmə(r)/ *n* barlume *m* ● *vi* emettere un barlume
glimpse /glɪmps/ *n* occhiata *f*; **catch a** ~ **of** intravedere ● *vt* intravedere
glint /glɪnt/ *n* luccichio *m* ● *vi* luccicare
glisten /'glɪsn/ *vi* luccicare
glitch /glɪtʃ/ *n Comput* problema *m* tecnico

glitter /'glɪtə(r)/ *vi* brillare
gloat /gləʊt/ *vi* gongolare (**over** su)
global /'gləʊbl/ *a* mondiale
global warming *n* riscaldamento *m* dell'atmosfera terrestre
globe /gləʊb/ *n* globo *m*; (*as a map*) mappamondo *m*
globe-trotting /-trɒtɪŋ/ *n* viaggi *mpl* intorno al mondo ● *a* ⟨*life*⟩ da giramondo; ⟨*person*⟩ giramondo
globule /'glɒbjuːl/ *n* globulo *m*
gloom /gluːm/ *n* oscurità *f*; (*sadness*) tristezza *f*
gloomily /'gluːmɪlɪ/ *adv* (*sadly*) con aria cupa
gloomy /'gluːmɪ/ *a* (**-ier, -iest**) cupo
glorify /'glɔːrɪfaɪ/ *vt* (*pt/pp* **-ied**) glorificare; **a glorified waitress** niente più che una cameriera
glorious /'glɔːrɪəs/ *a* splendido; ⟨*deed, hero*⟩ glorioso
glory /'glɔːrɪ/ *n* gloria *f*; (*splendour*) splendore *m*; (*cause for pride*) vanto *m* ● *vi* ~ **in** vantarsi di
glory-hole *n fam* ripostiglio *m*
gloss /glɒs/ *n* lucentezza *f*
■ **gloss over** *vt* sorvolare su
glossary /'glɒsərɪ/ *n* glossario *m*
gloss paint *n* vernice *f* lucida
glossy /'glɒsɪ/ *a* (**-ier, -iest**) lucido; ⟨*paper*⟩ patinato; ~ [**magazine**] rivista *f* femminile
glottal stop /'glɒt(ə)l/ *n* occlusiva *f* glottale
glove /glʌv/ *n* guanto *m*
glove compartment *n Auto* cruscotto *m*
glove puppet *n* burattino *m*
glow /gləʊ/ *n* splendore *m*; (*in cheeks*) rossore *m*; (*of candle*) luce *f* soffusa ● *vi* risplendere; ⟨*candle:*⟩ brillare; ⟨*person:*⟩ avvampare
glower /'glaʊə(r)/ *vi* ~ (**at**) guardare in cagnesco
glowing /'gləʊɪŋ/ *a* ardente; ⟨*account*⟩ entusiastico
glow-worm *n* lucciola *f*
glucose /'gluːkəʊs/ *n* glucosio *m*
glue /gluː/ *n* colla *f* ● *vt* (*pres p* **gluing**) incollare
glue-sniffing /-snɪfɪŋ/ *n* sniffare *m* la colla
glum /glʌm/ *a* (**glummer, glummest**) tetro
glumly /'glʌmlɪ/ *adv* con aria tetra
glut /glʌt/ *n* eccesso *m*
glutinous /'gluːtɪnəs/ *a* colloso
glutton /'glʌtən/ *n* ghiottone, -a *mf*
gluttonous /'glʌtənəs/ *a* ghiotto
gluttony /'glʌtənɪ/ *n* ghiottoneria *f*
glycerine /'glɪsəriːn/ *n* glicerina *f*
gm *abbr* (**gram**) g
gnarled /nɑːld/ *a* nodoso
gnash /næʃ/ *vt* ~ **one's teeth** digrignare i denti
gnat /næt/ *n* moscerino *m*
gnaw /nɔː/ *vt* rosicchiare
gnome /nəʊm/ *n* gnomo *m*
GNP *n abbr* (**gross national product**) PNL *m*
go /gəʊ/ *n* (*pl* **goes**) energia *f*; (*attempt*) tenta-

tivo *m*; **on the go** in movimento; **at one go** in una sola volta; **it's your go** tocca a te; **make a go of it** riuscire ● *vi* (*pt* **went**, *pp* **gone**) andare; (*leave*) andar via; (*vanish*) sparire; (*become*) diventare; (*be sold*) vendersi; **go and see** andare a vedere; **go swimming/ shopping** andare a nuotare/fare spese; **where's the time gone?** come ha fatto il tempo a volare così?; **it's all gone** è finito; **be going to do** stare per fare; **I'm not going to** non ne ho nessuna intenzione; **to go** ‹*Am: hamburgers etc*› da asporto; **a coffee to go** un caffè da portar via

■ **go about** *vi* andare in giro
■ **go about** *vt* affrontare ‹*task*›
■ **go after** *vt* (*chase, pursue*) correr dietro a
■ **go ahead** *vi* (*event*) aver luogo; **go ahead with** mandare avanti ‹*plans, wedding*›
■ **go away** *vi* andarsene
■ **go back** *vi* ritornare
■ **go by** *vi* passare
■ **go down** *vi* scendere; ‹*sun:*› tramontare; ‹*ship:*› affondare; ‹*swelling:*› diminuire
■ **go for** *vt* andare a prendere; andare a cercare ‹*doctor*›; (*choose*) optare per; (*fam: attack*) aggredire; **he's not the kind I go for** non è il genere che mi attira
■ **go in** *vi* entrare
■ **go in for** *vt* partecipare a ‹*competition*›; darsi a ‹*tennis*›
■ **go off** *vi* andarsene; ‹*alarm:*› scattare; ‹*gun, bomb:*› esplodere; ‹*food, milk:*› andare a male; **go off well** riuscire
■ **go on** *vi* andare avanti; **what's going on?** cosa succede?
■ **go on at** *vt fam* scocciare
■ **go on with** *vt* (*continue*) andare avanti con
■ **go out** *vi* uscire; ‹*light, fire:*› spegnersi
■ **go out with** *vt* uscire con ‹*sb*›
■ **go over** *vi* andare ● *vt* (*check*) controllare
■ **go round** *vi* andare in giro; (*visit*) andare; (*turn*) girare; **is there enough to go round?** ce n'è abbastanza per tutti?
■ **go through** *vi* ‹*bill, proposal:*› passare ● *vt* (*suffer*) subire; (*check*) controllare; (*read*) leggere
■ **go under** *vi* passare sotto; ‹*ship, swimmer:*› andare sott'acqua; (*fail*) fallire
■ **go up** *vi* salire; ‹*Theat: curtain:*› aprirsi
■ **go with** *vt* accompagnare
■ **go without** *vt* fare a meno di ‹*supper, sleep*› ● *vi* fare senza

goad /gəʊd/ *vt* spingere (**into** a); (*taunt*) spronare

go-ahead *a* ‹*person, company*› intraprendente ● *n* okay *m*

goal /gəʊl/ *n* porta *f*; (*point scored*) gol *m inv*; (*in life*) obiettivo *m*; **score a ~** segnare

goalie /ˈgəʊlɪ/ *fam*, **goalkeeper** /ˈgəʊl-kiːpə(r)/ *n* portiere *m*

goalpost /ˈgəʊlpəʊst/ *n* palo *m*

goat /gəʊt/ *n* capra *f*

goatee /gəʊˈtiː/ *n* pizzo *m*

■ **gobble up** /ˈgɒbl/ *vt* tranguigiare

gobbledygook /ˈgɒb(ə)ldɪguːk/ *n* ostrogoto *m*

go-between *n* intermediario, -a *mf*

goblet /ˈgɒblɪt/ *n* calice *m*

goblin /ˈgɒblɪn/ *n* folletto *m*

gobsmacked /ˈgɒbsmækt/ *a Br fam* **I was ~** sono rimasto a bocca aperta

God, god /gɒd/ *n* Dio *m*, dio *m*

god: **godchild** *n* figlioccio, -a *mf*. **goddamn** *a* maledetto. **god-daughter** *n* figlioccia *f*

goddess /ˈgɒdes/ *n* dea *f*

god: **godfather** *n* padrino *m*. **god-fearing** /-fɪərɪŋ/ *a* timorato di Dio. **god-forsaken** /-fəseɪkən/ *a* dimenticato da Dio

godless /ˈgɒdlɪs/ *a* empio

godlike /ˈgɒdlaɪk/ *a* divino

godly /ˈgɒdlɪ/ *a* (**-ier, iest**) pio

god: **godmother** *n* madrina *f*. **godparents** *npl* padrino *m* e madrina *f*. **godsend** *n* manna *f*. **godson** *n* figlioccio *m*

goer /ˈgəʊə(r)/ *n Br* **be a ~** ‹*car:*› essere una bomba

go-getter *n* ambizioso, -a *mf*

go-getter /ˈgəʊgetə(r)/ *n* persona *f* intraprendente

go-getting /-getɪŋ/ *a* intraprendente

goggle /ˈgɒgl/ *vi fam* **~ at** fissare con gli occhi sgranati ·

goggles *npl* occhiali *mpl*; (*of swimmer*) occhialini *mpl* [da piscina]; (*of worker*) occhiali *mpl* protettivi

going /ˈgəʊɪŋ/ *a* ‹*price, rate*› corrente; **~ concern** azienda *f* florida ● *n* **it's hard ~** è una faticaccia; **while the ~ is good** finché si può

going-over *n* (*cleaning*) pulizia *f* da cima a fondo; (*examination*) revisione *f*; **the doctor gave me a thorough ~** il dottore mi ha fatto una visita completa; **give sb a ~** (*beat up*) dare una manica di botte a qcno

goings-on *npl* avvenimenti *mpl*

go-kart /-kɑːt/ *n* go-kart *m inv*

go-karting /-kɑːtɪŋ/ *n* kartismo *m*; **go ~** fare del kartismo

gold /gəʊld/ *n* oro *m* ● *a* d'oro

gold-digger *n fig* cacciatore, -trice *mf* di dote

gold dust *n* polvere *f* d'oro; *fig* cosa *f* rara

golden /ˈgəʊldn/ *a* dorato

golden handshake *n Br* buonuscita *f* (*al termine di un rapporto di lavoro*)

golden wedding *n* nozze *fpl* d'oro

gold: **goldfish** *n inv* pesce *m* rosso. **gold mine** *n* miniera *f* d'oro. **gold-plated** /ˈpleɪtɪd/ *a* placcato d'oro. **goldsmith** *n* orefice *m*

golf /gɒlf/ *n* golf *m*

golf club *n* circolo *m* di golf; (*implement*) mazza *f* da golf

golf course *n* campo *m* di golf

golfer /ˈgɒlfə(r)/ *n* giocatore, -trice *mf* di golf

golliwog /ˈgɒlɪwɒg/ *n* bambolotto *m* negro

gondola /ˈgɒndələ/ *n* gondola *f*

gondolier /gɒndəˈlɪə(r)/ *n* gondoliere *m*

gone /gɒn/ *see* **go**

goner /'gɒnə(r)/ *n fam* **be a ~** essere spacciato

gong /gɒŋ/ *n* gong *m inv*

gonorrh[o]ea /gɒnə'rɪə/ *n* gonorrea *f*

good /gʊd/ *a* (**better, best**) buono; (*child, footballer, singer*) bravo; (*holiday, film*) bello; **~ at** bravo in; **a ~ deal of** anger molta rabbia; **as ~ as** (*almost*) quasi; **~ morning, ~ afternoon** buon giorno; **~ evening** buona sera; **~ night** buonanotte; **have a ~ time** divertirsi ● *n* bene *m*; **for ~** per sempre; **do ~** far del bene; **do sb ~** far bene a qcno; **it's no ~** è inutile; **be up to no ~** combinare qualcosa

goodbye /gʊd'baɪ/ *int* arrivederci

good: good-for-nothing *n* buono, -a *mf* a nulla ● *a* **her ~ son** quel buono a nulla di suo figlio. **Good Friday** *n* Venerdì *m* Santo.

good-humoured /-'hjuː məd/ *a* amichevole; (*remark, smile*) bonario

goodies /'gʊdɪz/ *npl* (*fam: to eat*) bontà *fpl*

good-looking /-'lʊkɪŋ/ *a* bello

good-natured /-'neɪtʃəd/ *a* **be ~** avere un buon carattere

goodness /'gʊdnɪs/ *n* bontà *f*; **my ~!** santo cielo!; **thank ~!** grazie al cielo!

goods /gʊdz/ *npl* prodotti *mpl*

goods train *n* treno *m* merci

good-time girl *n* (*fun-loving*) ragazza *f* allegra; (*euph: prostitute*) donnina *f* allegra

goodwill /gʊd'wɪl/ *n* buona *f* volontà; *Comm* avviamento *m*

goody /'gʊdɪ/ *n* (*fam: person*) buono *m*

goody-goody *n* santarellino, -a *mf*

gooey /'guːɪ/ *a fam* appiccicaticcio; *fig* sdolcinato

goof /guːf/ *vi fam* cannare

goofy /'guːfɪ/ *a fam* sciocco

goon /guːn/ *n* (*clown*) svitato *m*; (*thug*) picchiatore *m*

goose /guːs/ *n* (*pl* **geese**) oca *f*

goose: gooseberry /'gʊzbərɪ/ *n* uva *f* spina. **goose-flesh** *n*, **goose-pimples** *npl* pelle *fsg* d'oca. **goose-step** *n* passo *m* dell'oca

gore¹ /gɔː(r)/ *n* sangue *m*

gore² *vt* incornare

gorge /gɔːdʒ/ *n Geog* gola *f* ● *vt* **~ oneself** ingozzarsi

gorgeous /'gɔːdʒəs/ *a* stupendo

gorilla /gə'rɪlə/ *n* gorilla *m inv*

gormless /'gɔːmlɪs/ *a fam* stupido

gorse /gɔːs/ *n* ginestrone *m*

gory /'gɔːrɪ/ *a* (**-ier, -iest**) cruento

gosh /gɒʃ/ *int fam* caspita

gosling /'gɒzlɪŋ/ *n* ochetta *f*

go-slow *n* forma *f* di protesta che consiste in un rallentamento del ritmo di lavoro

gospel /'gɒspl/ *n* vangelo *m*

gospel truth *n* sacrosanta verità *f*

gossamer /'gɒsəmə(r)/ *n* (*fabric*) mussola *f*; (*cobweb*) fili *mpl* di ragnatela

gossip /'gɒsɪp/ *n* pettegolezzi *mpl*; (*person*) pettegolo, -a *mf* ● *vi* pettegolare

gossip column *n* cronaca *f* mondana

gossipy /'gɒsɪpɪ/ *a* pettegolo

got /gɒt/ *see* **get**; **have ~** avere; **have ~ to do sth** dover fare qcsa

Gothic /'gɒθɪk/ *a* gotico

gotten /'gɒtn/ *Am see* **get**

gouge /gaʊdʒ/ *vt* **~ out** cavare

goulash /'guːlæʃ/ *n* gulash *m inv*

gourd /gʊəd/ *n* (*fruit*) zucca *f*

gourmet /'gʊəmeɪ/ *n* buongustaio, -a *mf*

gout /gaʊt/ *n* gotta *f*

govern /'gʌv(ə)n/ *vt/i* governare; (*determine*) determinare

governess /'gʌvənɪs/ *n* istitutrice *f*

government /'gʌvnmənt/ *n* governo *m*

governmental /gʌvn'mentl/ *a* governativo

government stocks *npl* titoli *mpl* di stato

governor /'gʌvənə(r)/ *n* governatore *m*; (*of school*) amministratore, -trice *mf*; (*of prison*) direttore, -trice *mf*; (*fam: boss*) capo *m*

gown /gaʊn/ *n* vestito *m*; *Univ, Jur* toga *f*

GP *abbr* **general practitioner**

grab /græb/ *vt* (*pt/pp* **grabbed**) **~ [hold of]** afferrare

Grace *n* **his/your ~** (*duke*) il signor duca; (*archbishop*) Sua Eccellenza; **her/your ~** (*duchess*) la signora duchessa

grace /greɪs/ *n* grazia *f*; (*before meal*) benedicite *m inv*; **with good ~** volentieri; **say ~** dire il benedicite; **three days' ~** tre giorni di proroga

graceful /'greɪsfʊl/ *a* aggraziato

gracefully /'greɪsfʊlɪ/ *adv* con grazia

gracious /'greɪʃəs/ *a* cortese; (*elegant*) lussuoso

gradation /grə'deɪʃn/ *n* gradazione *f*

grade /greɪd/ *n* livello *m*; *Comm* qualità *f*; *Sch* voto *m*; (*Am Sch: class*) classe *f*; *Am =* **gradient** ● *vt Comm* classificare; *Sch* dare il voto a

grade crossing *n Am* passaggio *m* a livello

gradient /'greɪdɪənt/ *n* pendenza *f*

gradual /'grædʒʊəl/ *a* graduale

gradually /'grædʒʊlɪ/ *adv* gradualmente

graduate¹ /'grædʒʊət/ *n* laureato, -a *mf*

graduate² /'grædʒʊeɪt/ *vi Univ* laurearsi

graduated /'grædʒʊeɪtɪd/ *a* (*container*) graduato

graduation /grædʒʊ'eɪʃn/ *n* laurea *f*; (*calibration*) graduazione *f*

graduation ceremony *n* cerimonia *f* di consegna dei diplomi di laurea

graffiti /grə'fiːtɪ/ *npl* graffiti *mpl*

graffiti artist *n* pittore, -trice *mf* di graffiti

graft /grɑːft/ *n Bot, Med* innesto *m*; (*Med: organ*) trapianto *m*; (*fam: hard work*) duro lavoro *m*; (*fam: corruption*) corruzione *f* ● *vt* innestare; trapiantare (*organ*)

grain /greɪn/ *n* (*of sand, salt*) granello *m*; (*of rice*) chicco *m*; (*cereals*) cereali *mpl*; (*in wood*) venatura *f*; **it goes against the ~** *fig* è contro la mia/sua natura

grainy /'greɪnɪ/ *a* (*photograph*) sgranato; (*paintwork*) granulato

gram /græm/ *n* grammo *m*

grammar /'græmə(r)/ *n* grammatica *f*

grammarian /grə'meərɪən/ n grammatico, -a mf

grammar school n ≈ liceo m

grammatical /grə'mætɪkl/ a grammaticale

grammatically /grə'mætɪklɪ/ adv grammaticalmente

gran /græn/ n fam nonna f

granary /'grænərɪ/ n granaio m

grand /grænd/ a grandioso; fam eccellente

grand: grandad /'grændæd/ n fam nonno m. **grandchild** n nipote mf. **granddaughter** n nipote f

grandeur /'grændʒə(r)/ n grandiosità f

grand: grandfather n nonno m. **grandfather clock** n pendolo m (che poggia a terra)

grandiose /'grændɪəʊs/ a grandioso

grand: grandmother n nonna f. **grandparents** npl nonni mpl. **grand piano** n pianoforte m a coda. **grand slam** n vittoria f di tutte le fasi di una gara. **grandson** n nipote m. **grandstand** n tribuna f

granite /'grænɪt/ n granito m

granny /'grænɪ/ n fam nonna f

granny flat n Br appartamentino m indipendente per genitori anziani annesso all'abitazione principale

grant /grɑːnt/ n (money) sussidio m; Univ borsa f di studio ● vt accordare; (admit) ammettere; **take sth for ~ed** dare per scontato qcsa; **take sb for ~ed** considerare quello che qcno fa come dovuto

granular /'grænjʊlə(r)/ a granulare

granulated /'grænjʊleɪtɪd/ a ~ **sugar** zucchero m semolato

granule /'grænjuːl/ n granello m

grape /greɪp/ n acino m; **~s** pl uva fsg

grapefruit /'greɪpfruːt/ n inv pompelmo m

grapevine /'greɪpvaɪn/ n vite f; **hear sth on the ~** sentir dire in giro qcsa

graph /grɑːf/ n grafico m

graphic /'græfɪk/ a grafico; (vivid) vivido

graphically /'græfɪklɪ/ adv graficamente; (vividly) vividamente

graphic design n grafica f

graphic designer n grafico, -a mf

graphics /'græfɪks/ n grafica f

graphics card n Comput scheda f grafica

graphite /'græfaɪt/ n grafite f

graphologist /græ'fɒlədʒɪst/ n grafologo, -a mf

graph paper n carta f millimetrata

grapple /'græpl/ vi ~ **with** also fig essere alle prese con

grasp /grɑːsp/ n stretta f; (understanding) comprensione f ● vt afferrare

grasping /'grɑːspɪŋ/ a avido

grass /grɑːs/ n erba f;

grass: grasshopper n cavalletta f. **grassland** n prateria f. **grassroots** npl base f; **at the ~** alla base. **grass snake** n biscia f

grassy /'grɑːsɪ/ a erboso

grate¹ /greɪt/ n grata f

grate² vt Culin grattugiare; ~ **one's teeth** far stridere i denti ● vi stridere

grateful /'greɪtfl/ a grato

gratefully /'greɪtfʊlɪ/ adv con gratitudine

grater /'greɪtə(r)/ n Culin grattugia f

gratification /grætɪfɪ'keɪʃn/ n soddisfazione f

gratified /'grætɪfaɪd/ a appagato

gratify /'grætɪfaɪ/ vt (pt/pp -ied) appagare

gratifying /'grætɪfaɪɪŋ/ a appagante

grating /'greɪtɪŋ/ n grata f

gratis /'grɑːtɪs/ adv gratis

gratitude /'grætɪtjuːd/ n gratitudine f

gratuitous /grə'tjuːɪtəs/ a gratuito

gratuity /grə'tjuːətɪ/ n gratifica f

grave¹ /greɪv/ a grave

grave² n tomba f

gravedigger /'greɪvdɪgə(r)/ n becchino m

gravel /'grævl/ n ghiaia f

gravelly /'grævəlɪ/ a (voice) rauco

gravely /'greɪvlɪ/ adv gravemente

graven image /'greɪvən/ n idolo m

gravestone /'greɪvstəʊn/ n lapide f

graveyard /'greɪvjɑːd/ n cimitero m

gravitate /'grævɪteɪt/ vi gravitare

gravity /'grævɒtɪ/ n gravità f

gravy /'greɪvɪ/ n sugo m della carne

gray /greɪ/ a Am = **grey**

graze¹ /greɪz/ vi (animal:) pascolare

graze² n escoriazione f ● vt (touch lightly) sfiorare; (scrape) escoriare; sbucciarsi (knee)

grease /griːs/ n grasso m ● vt ungere

greasepaint /'griːspeɪnt/ n cerone m

greaseproof paper /griːspruːf'peɪpə(r)/ n carta f oleata

greaser /'griːsə(r)/ n (motorcyclist) componente m di una banda giovanile di motociclisti

greasy /'griːsɪ/ a (-ier, -iest) untuoso; (hair, skin) grasso

great /greɪt/ a grande; (fam: marvellous) eccezionale

great: great-aunt n prozia f. **Great Britain** n Gran Bretagna f. **Great Dane** n danese m. **great-grandchildren** npl pronipoti mpl. **great-grandfather** n bisnonno m. **great-grandmother** n bisnonna f

greatly /'greɪtlɪ/ adv enormemente

greatness /'greɪtnɪs/ n grandezza f

great-uncle n prozio m

Grecian /'griːʃ(ə)n/ a greco

Greece /griːs/ n Grecia f

greed /griːd/ n avidità f; (for food) ingordigia f

greedily /'griːdɪlɪ/ adv avidamente; (eat) con ingordigia

greedy /'griːdɪ/ a (-ier, -iest) avido; (for food) ingordo

Greek /griːk/ a & n greco, -a mf; (language) greco m

green /griːn/ a verde; (fig: inexperienced) immaturo ● n verde m; (grass) prato m; (in golf) green m inv; **~s** pl verdura f; **the G~s** pl Pol i verdi

green: green beans n fagiolini mpl. **green belt** n zona f verde intorno a una città. **green card** n carta f verde; Am permesso m di soggiorno

greenery /'gri:nərɪ/ n verde m
green: green-eyed monster /-aɪd-'mɒnstə(r)/ n gelosia f. **greenfinch** n verdone m. **green fingers** npl **have ~ ~** avere il police verde. **greenfly** n afide m. **greengage** n susina f verde. **greengrocer** n fruttivendolo, -a mf. **greenhorn** n (new) novellino m; (gullible) pivello m. **greenhouse** n serra f. **greenhouse effect** n effetto m serra. **Greenland** n Groenlandia f. **green light** n fam verde m. **green salad** n insalata f verde
greet /gri:t/ vt salutare; (welcome) accogliere
greeting /'gri:tɪŋ/ n saluto m; (welcome) accoglienza f
greetings card /'gri:tɪŋz/ n biglietto m d'auguri
gregarious /grɪ'geərɪəs/ a gregario; (person) socievole
gremlin /'gremlɪn/ n hum spirito m maligno
grenade /grɪ'neɪd/ n granata f
grenadier /grenə'dɪə(r)/ n Mil guardia f reale inglese
grew /gru:/ see **grow**
grey /greɪ/ a grigio; (hair) bianco ● n grigio m ● vi diventare bianco
grey: greyhound n levriero m. **grey matter** n (brain) materia f grigia. **grey squirrel** n scoiattolo m grigio
grid /grɪd/ n griglia f; (on map) reticolato m; Electr rete f
griddle /'grɪd(ə)l/ n (for meat) piastra f
grid: gridiron n griglia f; Am campo m di football americano. **gridlock** n (fig: deadlock) situazione f di stallo; (in traffic) imbottigliamento m. **grid reference** n coordinate fpl
grief /gri:f/ n dolore m; **come to ~** (plans:) naufragare
grief-stricken /-strɪkən/ a affranto dal dolore
grievance /'gri:vəns/ n lamentela f
grieve /gri:v/ vt addolorare ● vi essere addolorato
grievous /'gri:vəs/ a doloroso
grievously /'gri:vəslɪ/ adv tristemente
grill /grɪl/ n graticola f; (for grilling) griglia f; **mixed ~** grigliata f mista ● vt/i cuocere alla griglia; (interrogate) sottoporre al terzo grado
grille /grɪl/ n grata f
grim /grɪm/ a (**grimmer, grimmest**) arcigno; (determination) accanito
grimace /'grɪməs/ n smorfia f ● vi fare una smorfia
grime /graɪm/ n sudiciume m
grimly /'grɪmlɪ/ adv accanitamente
Grim Reaper n Morte f
grimy /'graɪmɪ/ a (-**ier, -iest**) sudicio
grin /grɪn/ n sorriso m ● vi (pt/pp **grinned**) fare un gran sorriso
grind /graɪnd/ n (fam: hard work) sfacchinata f ● vt (pt/pp **ground**) macinare; affilare (knife); (Am: mince) tritare; **~ one's teeth** digrignare i denti
grindstone /'graɪndstəʊn/ n mola f; **keep**

one's nose to the **~** lavorare indefessamente
grip /grɪp/ n presa f; fig controllo m; (bag) borsone m; **be in the ~ of** essere in preda a; **get a ~ of oneself** controllarsi ● vt (pt/pp **gripped**) afferrare; (tyres:) far presa su; tenere avvinto (attention)
gripe /graɪp/ vi (fam: grumble) lagnarsi
gripping /'grɪpɪŋ/ a avvincente
grisly /'grɪzlɪ/ a (-**ier, -iest**) raccapricciante
gristle /'grɪsl/ n cartilagine f
grit /grɪt/ n graniglia f; (for roads) sabbia f; (courage) coraggio m ● vt (pt/pp **gritted**) spargere sabbia su (road); **~ one's teeth** serrare i denti
gritter /'grɪtə(r)/ n Br Aut spandighiaia m inv
gritty /'grɪtɪ/ a (sandy) pieno di terra; (gravelly) ghiaioso; (hard, determined) grintoso; (novel, film) crudo
grizzle /'grɪzl/ vi piagnucolare
grizzly /'grɪzlɪ/ n (bear) grizzly m inv
groan /grəʊn/ n gemito m ● vi gemere
grocer /'grəʊsə(r)/ n droghiere, -a mf
groceries /'grəʊsərɪz/ npl generi mpl alimentari
grocer's [shop] n drogheria f
groggy /'grɒgɪ/ a (-**ier, -iest**) stordito; (unsteady) barcollante
groin /grɔɪn/ n Anat inguine m
groom /gru:m/ n sposo m; (for horse) stalliere m ● vt strigliare (horse); fig preparare; **well-~ed** ben curato
groove /gru:v/ n scanalatura f
grope /grəʊp/ vi brancolare; **~ for** cercare a tastoni
gross /grəʊs/ a obeso; (coarse) volgare; (glaring) grossolano; (salary, weight) lordo ● n inv grossa f
gross domestic product n prodotto m interno lordo
gross indecency n Jur oltraggio m al pudore
grossly /'grəʊslɪ/ adv (very) enormemente
gross national product n prodotto m nazionale lordo
grotesque /grəʊ'tesk/ a grottesco
grotesquely /grəʊ'tesklɪ/ adv in modo grottesco
grotto /'grɒtəʊ/ n (pl -**es**) grotta f
grotty /'grɒtɪ/ a (-**ier, -iest**) (fam: flat, street) squallido
grouch /graʊtʃ/ vi brontolare (**about** contro)
grouchy /'graʊtʃɪ/ a brontolone
ground[1] /graʊnd/ see **grind**
ground[2] n terra f; Sport terreno m; (reason) ragione f; **~s** pl (park) giardini mpl; (of coffee) fondi mpl ● vi (ship:) arenarsi ● vt bloccare a terra (aircraft); Am Electr mettere a terra
ground: ground control n base f di controllo. **ground crew** n personale m di terra. **ground floor** n pianterreno m
grounding /'graʊndɪŋ/ n base f

groundless /'graʊndlɪs/ *a* infondato
ground: ground rules *npl* principi *mpl* fondamentali. **groundsheet** *n* telone *m* impermeabile. **groundwork** *n* lavoro *m* di preparazione
group /gruːp/ *n* gruppo *m* ● *vt* raggruppare ● *vi* raggrupparsi
groupage /'gruːpɪdʒ/ *n Comm* raggruppamento *m*
group leader *n* capogruppo *m*
grouse[1] /graʊs/ *n inv* gallo *m* cedrone
grouse[2] *vi fam* brontolare
grove /grəʊv/ *n* boschetto *m*
grovel /'grɒvl/ *vi* (*pt/pp* **grovelled**) strisciare
grovelling /'grɒv(ə)lɪŋ/ *a* leccapiedi *inv*
grow /grəʊ/ *v* (*pt* **grew**, *pp* **grown**) ● *vi* crescere; (*become*) diventare; ⟨*unemployment, fear:*⟩ aumentare; ⟨*town:*⟩ ingrandirsi ● *vt* coltivare; **~ one's hair** farsi crescere i capelli
■ **grow on** *vt* (*fam: become pleasing to*) **it'll ~ on you** finirà a per piacerti
■ **grow out of** *vt* **he's ~n out of his jumper** il golf gli è diventato troppo piccolo
■ **grow up** *vi* crescere; ⟨*town:*⟩ svilupparsi
growbag /'grəʊbæg/ *n* sacco *m* di terriccio entro cui si coltivano piante
grower /'grəʊə(r)/ *n* coltivatore, -trice *mf*
growing pains /'grəʊɪŋ/ *npl* (*of child*) dolori *mpl* della crescita; (*fig: of firm, project*) difficoltà *fpl* iniziali nello sviluppo
growl /graʊl/ *n* grugnito *m* ● *vi* ringhiare
grown /grəʊn/ *see* **grow** ● *a* adulto
grown-up *a & n* adulto, -a *mf*
growth /grəʊθ/ *n* crescita *f*; (*increase*) aumento *m*; *Med* tumore *m*
growth rate *n* tasso *m* di crescita
groyne /grɔɪn/ *n Br* pennello *m* (*per difendere le spiagge dall'erosione*)
grub /grʌb/ *n* larva *f*; (*fam: food*) mangiare *m*
grubby /'grʌbɪ/ *a* (**-ier, -iest**) sporco
grudge /grʌdʒ/ *n* rancore *m*; **bear sb a ~** portare rancore a qcno ● *vt* dare a malincuore
grudging /'grʌdʒɪŋ/ *a* reluttante
grudgingly /'grʌdʒɪŋlɪ/ *adv* a malincuore
gruelling /'gruːəlɪŋ/ *a* estenuante
gruesome /'gruːsəm/ *a* macabro
gruff /grʌf/ *a* burbero
gruffly /'grʌflɪ/ *adv* in modo burbero
grumble /'grʌmbl/ *vi* brontolare (**at** contro)
grumpy /'grʌmpɪ/ *a* (**-ier, -iest**) scorbutico
grunge /grʌndʒ/ *n* (*dirt*) lerciume *m*; (*style*) grunge *m inv*
grunt /grʌnt/ *n* grugnito *m* ● *vi* fare un grugnito
G-string *n* (*garment*) tanga *m inv*
guarantee /gærən'tiː/ *n* garanzia *f* ● *vt* garantire
guarantor /gærən'tɔː(r)/ *n* garante *mf*
guard /gɑːd/ *n* guardia *f*; (*security*) guardiano *m*; (*on train*) capotreno *m*; *Techn* schermo *m* protettivo; **be on ~** essere di guardia; **on one's ~** in guardia ● *vt* sorvegliare; (*protect*) proteggere
■ **guard against** *vt* guardarsi da

guard-dog *n* cane *m* da guardia
guarded /'gɑːdɪd/ *a* guardingo
guardian /'gɑːdɪən/ *n* (*of minor*) tutore, -trice *mf*
guardian angel *n also fig* angelo *m* custode
guard: guard of honour *n* guardia *f* d'onore. **guardroom** *n* corpo *m* di guardia. **guard's van** *n Br Rail* carrozza *f* bagagliaio
guava /'gwɑːvə/ *n* (*fruit*) guava *f*; (*tree*) albero *m* di guava
guerrilla /gə'rɪlə/ *n* guerrigliero, -a *mf*
guerrilla warfare *n* guerriglia *f*
guess /ges/ *n* supposizione *f* ● *vt* indovinare ● *vi* indovinare; (*Am: suppose*) supporre
guesstimate /'gestɪmət/ *n* calcolo *m* approssimativo
guesswork /'geswɜːk/ *n* supposizione *f*
guest /gest/ *n* ospite *mf*; (*in hotel*) cliente *mf*
guest: guest house *n* pensione *f*. **guest room** *n* camera *f* degli ospiti. **guest worker** *n* lavoratore *m* immigrato; lavoratrice *f* immigrata
guff /gʌf/ *n* (*nonsense*) stupidaggini *fpl*
guffaw /gʌ'fɔː/ *n* sghignazzata *f* ● *vi* sghignazzare
guidance /'gaɪdəns/ *n* guida *f*; (*advice*) consigli *mpl*
guide /gaɪd/ *n* guida *f*; [**Girl**] **G~** giovane esploratrice *f* ● *vt* guidare
guidebook /'gaɪdbʊk/ *n* guida *f* turistica
guided missile /'gaɪdɪd/ *n* missile *m* teleguidato
guide dog *n* cane *m* per ciechi
guided tour *n* giro *m* guidato
guidelines /'gaɪdlaɪnz/ *npl* direttive *fpl*
guiding principle /gaɪdɪŋ'prɪnsɪp(ə)l/ *n* direttrice *f*
guild /gɪld/ *n* corporazione *f*
guile /gaɪl/ *n* astuzia *f*
guileless /'gaɪllɪs/ *a* senza malizia
guillotine /'gɪlətiːn/ *n* ghigliottina *f*; (*for paper*) taglierina *f*
guilt /gɪlt/ *n* colpa *f*
guiltily /'gɪltɪlɪ/ *adv* con aria colpevole
guilty /'gɪltɪ/ *a* (**-ier, -iest**) colpevole; **have a ~ conscience** avere la coscienza sporca
guinea /'gɪnɪ/ *n* ghinea *f*
guinea fowl *n* faraona *f*
guinea pig *n* porcellino *m* d'India; (*in experiments*) cavia *f*
guise /gaɪz/ *n* **in the ~ of** sotto le spoglie di
guitar /gɪ'tɑː(r)/ *n* chitarra *f*
guitarist /gɪ'tɑːrɪst/ *n* chitarrista *mf*
Gulag /'guːlæg/ *n* gulag *m inv*
gulf /gʌlf/ *n Geog* golfo *m*; *fig* abisso *m*
gull /gʌl/ *n* gabbiano *m*
gullet /'gʌlɪt/ *n* esofago *m*; (*throat*) gola *f*
gullible /'gʌləbl/ *a* credulone
gully /'gʌlɪ/ *n* burrone *m*; (*drain*) canale *m* di scolo
gulp /gʌlp/ *n* azione *f* di deglutire; (*of food*) boccone *m*; (*of liquid*) sorso *m* ● *vi* deglutire
■ **gulp down** *vt* tranguigiare ⟨*food*⟩; scolarsi ⟨*liquid*⟩

gum¹ /gʌm/ n Anat gengiva f

gum² n gomma f; (chewing-gum) gomma f da masticare, chewing-gum m inv ● vt (pt/pp **gummed**) ingommare (**to** a)

gumboot /'gʌmbu:t/ n stivale m di gomma

gummed /gʌmd/ see **gum²** ● a ⟨label⟩ adesivo

gumption /'gʌmpʃn/ n fam buon senso m

gumshoe /'gʌmʃu:/ n (fam: private investigator) investigatore m privato

gum tree n fam **be up a ~ ~** essere in difficoltà

gun /gʌn/ n pistola f; (rifle) fucile m; (cannon) cannone m; **he had a ~** era armato ■ **gun down** vt (pt/pp **gunned**) freddare **gun: gun barrel** n canna f di fucile. **gunboat** n cannoniera f. **gun dog** n cane m da caccia. **gunfire** n spari mpl; (of cannon) colpi mpl [di cannone]

gunge /gʌndʒ/ n Br poltiglia f [disgustosa]

gung-ho /gʌŋ'həʊ/ a hum (eager for war) guerrafondaio; (overzealous) esaltato

gunman /'gʌnmən/ n uomo m armato

gunner /'gʌnə(r)/ n artigliere m

gun: gunpoint n **hold sb up at ~** assalire qcno a mano armata. **gunpowder** n polvere f da sparo. **gunshot** n colpo m [di pistola]. **gunslinger** n pistolero m

gurgle /'gɜ:gl/ vi gorgogliare; ⟨baby:⟩ fare degli urletti

guru /'gʊru:/ n guru m inv

gush /gʌʃ/ vi sgorgare; (enthuse) parlare con troppo entusiasmo (**over** di) ■ **gush out** vi sgorgare

gushing /'gʌʃɪŋ/ a eccessivamente entusiastico

gusset /'gʌsɪt/ n gherone m

gust /gʌst/ n (of wind) raffica f

gusto /'gʌstəʊ/ n **with ~** con trasporto

gusty /'gʌstɪ/ a ventoso

gut /gʌt/ n intestino m; **~s** pl pancia f; (fam: courage) fegato m ● vt (pt/pp **gutted**) Culin svuotare delle interiora; **~ted by fire** sventrato da un incendio

gutsy /'gʌtsɪ/ a (brave) coraggioso; (spirited) gagliardo

gutter /'gʌtə(r)/ n canale m di scolo; (on roof) grondaia f; fig bassifondi mpl

guttering /'gʌtərɪŋ/ n grondaie fpl

gutter press n stampa f scandalistica

guttersnipe /'gʌtəsnaɪp/ n ragazzo, -a mf di strada

guttural /'gʌtərəl/ a gutturale

guv, guvnor /gʌv, 'gʌvnə(r)/ n (Br fam: boss) capo m

guy /gaɪ/ n fam tipo m, tizio m

Guy Fawkes Day /fɔ:ks/ n Br anniversario m del fallimento della Congiura delle Polveri (5 novembre)

guzzle /'gʌzl/ vt ingozzarsi con ⟨food⟩; **he's ~d the lot** si è sbafato tutto

gym /dʒɪm/ n fam palestra f; (gymnastics) ginnastica f

gymkhana /dʒɪm'kɑ:nə/ n manifestazione f equestre

gymnasium /dʒɪm'neɪzɪəm/ n palestra f

gymnast /'dʒɪmnæst/ n ginnasta mf

gymnastics /dʒɪm'næstɪks/ n ginnastica f

gym shoes npl scarpe fpl da ginnastica

gym-slip n Sch ≈ grembiule m (da bambina)

gynaecologist /gaɪnɪ'kɒlədʒɪst/ n ginecologo, -a mf

gynaecology /gaɪnɪ'kɒlədʒɪ/ n ginecologia f

gyp /dʒɪp/ n Br **my back is giving me ~** ho un terribile mal di schiena

gypsum /'dʒɪpsəm/ n gesso m

gypsy /'dʒɪpsɪ/ n zingaro, -a mf

gyrate /dʒaɪ'reɪt/ vi roteare

Hh

h, H /eɪtʃ/ n h, H f inv

haberdashery /hæbə'dæʃərɪ/ n merceria f; Am negozio m d'abbigliamento da uomo

habit /'hæbɪt/ n abitudine f; (Relig: costume) tonaca f; **be in the ~ of doing sth** avere l'abitudine di fare qcsa

habitable /'hæbɪtəbl/ a abitabile

habitat /'hæbɪtæt/ n habitat m inv

habitation /hæbɪ'teɪʃn/ n **unfit for human ~** inagibile

habit-forming /-fɔ:mɪŋ/ a **be ~** creare assuefazione

habitual /hə'bɪtjʊəl/ a abituale; ⟨smoker, liar⟩ inveterato

habitually /hə'bɪtjʊəlɪ/ adv regolarmente

hack¹ /hæk/ n (writer) scribacchino, -a mf

hack² vt tagliare; **~ to pieces** tagliare a pezzi

hacker /'hækə(r)/ n Comput pirata m informatico

hacking /'hækɪŋ/ n Comput pirateria f informatica

hacking cough n brutta tosse f

hackles /'hæk(ə)lz/ npl (on animal) pelo m del collo; (on bird) piumaggio m del collo; **make sb's ~ rise** fig far imbestialire qcno

hackney cab /'hæknɪ/ n fml taxi m inv

hackneyed /'hæknɪd/ a trito [e ritrito]

hacksaw /'hæksɔ:/ n seghetto m

had /hæd/ see **have**

haddock /'hædək/ *n inv* eglefino *m*

haematoma /hiːməˈtəʊmə/ *n* ematoma *m*

haemoglobin /hiːməˈɡləʊbɪn/ *n* emoglobina *f*

haemophilia /hiːməˈfɪlɪə/ *n* emofilia *f*

haemophiliac /hiːməˈfɪlɪæk/ *n* emofiliaco, -a *mf*

haemorrhage /'hemərɪdʒ/ *n* emorragia *f*

haemorrhoids /'hemərɔɪdz/ *npl* emorroidi *fpl*

hag /hæɡ/ *n* old ~ vecchia befana *f*

haggard /'hæɡəd/ *a* sfatto

haggis /'hæɡɪs/ *n* piatto *m* scozzese a base di frattaglie di pecora e avena

haggle /'hæɡl/ *vi* contrattare (**over** per)

ha! ha! /hɑːˈhɑː/ *int* ah! ah!

hail¹ /heɪl/ *vt* salutare; far segno a ⟨*taxi*⟩ ● *vi* ~ **from** provenire da

hail² *n* grandine *f* ● *vi* grandinare

hailstone /'heɪlstəʊn/ *n* chicco *m* di grandine

hailstorm /'heɪlstɔːm/ *n* grandinata *f*

hair /heə(r)/ *n* capelli *mpl*; (*on body, of animal*) pelo *m*; **wash one's** ~ lavarsi i capelli

hair: hairband *n* ⟨*rigid*⟩ cerchietto *m*; ⟨*elastic*⟩ fascia *f* [per capelli]. **hairbrush** *n* spazzola *f* per capelli. **hair curler** *n* arricciacapelli *m inv.* **haircut** *n* taglio *m* di capelli; **have a** ~ farsi tagliare i capelli. **hairdo** *n fam* pettinatura *f.* **hairdresser** *n* parrucchiere, -a *mf.* **hairdryer** *n* fon *m inv;* ⟨*with hood*⟩ casco *m* [asciugacapelli]. **hair gel** *n* gel *m inv* [per capelli]. **hairgrip** *n* molletta *f*

hairless /'heəlɪs/ *a* ⟨*animal*⟩ senza peli; ⟨*body, chin*⟩ glabro

hair: hairline *n* (*on head*) attaccatura *f* dei capelli. **hairline crack** *n* incrinatura *f* sottilissima. **hairline fracture** *n Med* frattura *f* capillare. **hairnet** *n* retina *f* per capelli. **hairpiece** *n* toupet *m inv.* **hairpin** *n* forcina *f.* **hairpin bend** *n* tornante *m*, curva *f* a gomito. **hair-raising** /'heəreɪzɪŋ/ *a* terrificante. **hair remover** *n* crema *f* depilatoria. **hairslide** *n Br* fermacapelli *m inv.* **hair-splitting** /'heəsplɪtɪŋ/ *n* pedanteria *f.* **hairspray** *n* lacca *f* [per capelli]. **hairstyle** *n* acconciatura *f.* **hairstylist** *n* parrucchiere, -a *mf.* **hair transplant** *n* trapianto *m* di capelli

hairy /'heərɪ/ *a* (**-ier, -iest**) peloso; (*fam: frightening*) spaventoso

Haiti /'heɪtɪ/ *n* Haiti *m*

Haitian /'heɪʃ(ə)n/ *n & a* haitiano, -a *mf*; (*language*) haitiano *m*

hake /heɪk/ *n inv* nasello *m*

halcyon days /'hælsɪən/ *npl* bei tempi *mpl* andati

hale /heɪl/ *a* ~ **and hearty** in piena forma

half /hɑːf/ *n* (*pl* **halves**) metà *f inv*; **cut in** ~ tagliare a metà; **one and a** ~ uno e mezzo; ~ **a dozen** mezza dozzina; ~ **an hour** mezz'ora ● *a* mezzo; [**at**] ~ **price** [a] metà prezzo ● *adv* a metà; ~ **past two** le due e mezza

half: half-and-half *a* mezzo e mezzo ● *adv* a metà; **go** ~ fare a metà. **half-back** *n* mediano

m. **half-baked** *a fam* che non sta in piedi. **half board** *n* mezza pensione *f.* **half-breed** *n & a* mezzosangue *mf inv.* **half-brother** *n* fratellastro *m.* **half-caste** *a* meticcio, -a *mf.* **half-century** *n* mezzo secolo *m.* **half cock** *n* **go off at** ~ ~ partire col piede sbagliato. **half-conscious** *a* semicosciente. **half-crown, half a crown** *n Br* mezza corona *f.* **half-cut** *a* (*fam: drunk*) ciucco. **half day** *n* mezza giornata *f.* **half-dead** *a also fig* mezzo morto. **half-dozen** *n* mezza dozzina *f.* **half fare** *n* metà tariffa *f.* **half-hearted** /-'hɑːtɪd/ *a* esitante. **half hour** *n* mezz'ora *f.* **half-hourly** *a & adv* ogni mezz'ora. **half-length** *a* ⟨*portrait*⟩ a mezzo busto. **half-light** *n* penombra *f.* **half mast** *n* **at** ~ ~ a mezz'asta. **half measures** *npl* mezze misure *fpl.* **half-moon** *n* mezzaluna *f*; (*of fingernail*) lunula *f* ● *attrib* ⟨*spectacles*⟩ a mezzaluna. **half pay** *n* metà stipendio *m.* **halfpenny** /'heɪpnɪ/ *n Br* mezzo penny *m inv.* **half-pint** *n* mezza pinta *f* (*Br* = 0, 28 l, *Am* = 0, 24 l); (*beer*) piccola *f; fig* mezza calzetta *f.* **half price** *a* a metà prezzo ● *adv* [a] metà prezzo. **half size** *n* (*of shoe*) mezzo numero *m* ● *a* ⟨*copy*⟩ ridotto della metà. **half smile** *n* mezzo sorriso *m.* **half-starved** *a* mezzo morto di fame. **half-term** *n* vacanza *f* di metà trimestre. **half-time** *n Sport* intervallo *m.* **half-truth** *n* mezza verità *f inv.* **halfway** *a* **the** ~ **mark/stage** il livello intermedio ● *adv* a metà strada; **get** ~ *fig* arrivare a metà. **halfway house** *n* ⟨*compromise*⟩ via *f* di mezzo; ⟨*rehabilitation centre*⟩ centro *m* di riabilitazione per ex detenuti. **halfway line** *n Sport* linea *f* mediana. **halfwit** *n* idiota *mf.* **half-year** *n Fin, Comm* semestre *m* ● *attrib* ⟨*profit, results*⟩ semestrale. **half-yearly** *a* ⟨*meeting, payment*⟩ semestrale

halibut /'hælɪbət/ *n inv* ippoglosso *m*

halitosis /hælɪˈtəʊsɪs/ *n* alitosi *f inv*

hall /hɔːl/ *n* ⟨*entrance*⟩ ingresso *m*; (*room*) sala *f*; (*mansion*) residenza *f* di campagna; ~ **of residence** *Univ* casa *f* dello studente

hallelujah /(h)ælɪˈluːjə/ *int* alleluia!

hallmark /'hɔːlmɑːk/ *n* marchio *m* di garanzia; *fig* marchio *m*

hallo /həˈləʊ/ *int* ciao!; (*on telephone*) pronto!; **say** ~ **to** salutare

hall of residence *n* residenza *f* universitaria

hallowed /'hæləʊd/ *a* ⟨*ground*⟩ consacrato; ⟨*tradition*⟩ sacro

Halloween /hæləʊˈiːn/ *n* vigilia *f* d'Ognissanti e notte delle streghe, celebrata soprattutto dai bambini

hallucinate /həˈluːsɪneɪt/ *vi* avere le allucinazioni

hallucination /həluːsɪˈneɪʃn/ *n* allucinazione *f*

hallucinatory /həˈluːsɪnət(ə)rɪ/ *a* ⟨*drug*⟩ allucinogeno

hallucinogen /həˈluːsɪnədʒən/ *n* sostanza *f* allucinante

hallucinogenic /həluːsɪnəˈdʒenɪk/ *a* allucinogeno

hallway /'hɔ:lweɪ/ n ingresso m

halo /'heɪləʊ/ n (pl -es) aureola f; Astr alone m

halogen /'hælədʒən/ n alogeno m

halt /hɔ:lt/ n alt m inv; **come to a ~** fermarsi; ⟨traffic:⟩ bloccarsi ● vi fermarsi; **~!** alt!
● vt fermare

halter /'hɔ:ltə(r)/ n (for horse) cavezza f

halter-neck n modello m con allacciatura dietro il collo che lascia la schiena scoperta

halting /'hɔ:ltɪŋ/ a esitante

haltingly /'hɔ:ltɪŋlɪ/ adv con esitazione

halve /hɑ:v/ vt dividere a metà; ⟨reduce⟩ dimezzare

ham /hæm/ n prosciutto m; Theat attore, -trice mf da strapazzo

hamburger /'hæmbɜ:gə(r)/ n hamburger m inv

ham-fisted /-'fɪstɪd/ a Br fam maldestro

hamlet /'hæmlɪt/ n paesino m

hammer /'hæmə(r)/ n martello m ● vt martellare ● vi **~ at/on** picchiare a
■ **hammer in** vt piantare ⟨nail⟩

hammer and sickle n falce f e martello m

hammock /'hæmək/ n amaca f

hamper[1] /'hæmpə(r)/ n cesto m; [gift] ~ cestino m

hamper[2] vt ostacolare

hamster /'hæmstə(r)/ n criceto m

hamstring /'hæmstrɪŋ/ n (of horse) tendine m del garretto; (of human) tendine m del ginocchio ● vt fig rendere impotente

hand /hænd/ n mano f; (of clock) lancetta f; (writing) scrittura f; (worker) manovale m; **all ~s** Naut l'equipaggio al completo; **at ~, to ~** a portata di mano; **by ~** a mano; **on the one ~** da un lato; **on the other ~** d'altra parte; **out of ~** incontrollabile; ⟨summarily⟩ su due piedi; **in ~** in corso; ⟨situation⟩ sotto controllo; ⟨available⟩ disponibile; **give sb a ~** dare una mano a qcno; **~ in ~** ⟨run, walk⟩ mano nella mano; **go ~ in ~** fig andare di pari passo (with con) ● vt porgere
■ **hand back** vt restituire ⟨sth⟩
■ **hand down** vt tramandare
■ **hand in** vt consegnare
■ **hand on** vt passare
■ **hand out** vt distribuire
■ **hand over** vt passare; (to police) consegnare

hand: handbag n borsa f (da signora). **hand baggage** n bagaglio m a mano. **handball** n pallamano f; (fault in football) fallo m di mano; **~!** mano! **handbasin** n lavandino m. **handbook** n manuale m. **handbrake** n freno m a mano. **handcart** n carretto m. **hand cream** n crema f per le mani. **handcuffs** npl manette fpl. **hand-dryer, hand-drier** n asciugamani m inv ad aria

handful /'hændfʊl/ n manciata f; **be [quite] a ~** fam essere difficile da tenere a freno

hand: hand grenade n bomba f a mano. **handgun** n pistola f. **hand-held** a a mano

handicap /'hændɪkæp/ n handicap m inv

handicapped /'hændɪkæpt/ a **mentally/**

physically ~ mentalmente/fisicamente handicappato

handicraft /'hændɪkrɑːft/ n artigianato m

handiwork /'hændɪwɜ:k/ n opera f

handkerchief /'hæŋkətʃɪf/ n (pl ~s & -chieves) fazzoletto m

handle /'hændl/ n manico m; (of door) maniglia f; **fly off the ~** fam perdere le staffe
● vt maneggiare; occuparsi di ⟨problem, customer⟩; prendere ⟨difficult person⟩; trattare ⟨subject⟩; **be good at handling sb** saperci fare con qcno

handlebar moustache /hændlbɑ:mə-'stɑ:ʃ/ n baffi mpl a manubrio

handlebars /'hændlbɑ:z/ npl manubrio m

handler /'hændlə(r)/ n (of dog) addestratore, -trice mf

hand: hand lotion n lozione f per le mani. **hand-luggage** n bagaglio m a mano. **handmade** a fatto a mano. **handout** n (at lecture) foglio m informativo; (fam: money) elemosina f. **handover** n (of prisoner, ransom) consegna f; (of property, territory) cessione f; **~ of power** passaggio m delle consegne. **hand-pick** vt scegliere ⟨produce⟩; selezionare con cura ⟨staff⟩. **handrail** n corrimano m. **hand-reared** /-'rɪəd/ a ⟨animal⟩ allattato con il biberon. **handset** n Teleph ricevitore m. **handshake** n stretta f di mano. **hand signal** n Auto segnalazione f con la mano. **hands-off** a ⟨policy⟩ di non intervento; ⟨manager⟩ che delega le responsabilità

handsome /'hænsəm/ a bello; (fig: generous) generoso; ⟨salary⟩ considerevole

hand: hands-on a ⟨experience⟩ pratico; ⟨approach⟩ pragmatico; ⟨control⟩ diretto; ⟨manager⟩ che segue direttamente le varie attività. **handspring** n salto m sulle mani. **handstand** n verticale f. **hand-to-hand** a & adv ⟨fight⟩ corpo a corpo. **hand-to-mouth** a ⟨existence⟩ precario. **hand towel** n asciugamano m. **hand-woven** /'wəʊvən/ a tessuto a mano. **handwriting** n calligrafia f. **handwritten** a scritto a mano

handy /'hændɪ/ a (-ier, -iest) pratico; ⟨person⟩ abile; **have/keep ~** avere/tenere a portata di mano

handyman /'hændɪmæn/ n tuttofare m inv

hang /hæŋ/ vt (pt/pp hung) appendere ⟨picture⟩; (pt/pp hanged) impiccare ⟨criminal⟩; **~ oneself** impiccarsi; **~ wallpaper** tappezzare ● vi (pt/pp hung) pendere; ⟨hair:⟩ scendere ● n **get the ~ of it** fam afferrare
■ **hang about** vi gironzolare
■ **hang on** vi tenersi stretto; (fam: wait) aspettare; Teleph restare in linea
■ **hang on to** vt tenersi stretto a; (keep) tenere
■ **hang out** vi spuntare; **where does he usually ~ out?** fam dove bazzica di solito?
● vt stendere ⟨washing⟩
■ **hang up** vt appendere; Teleph riattaccare
● vi essere appeso; Teleph riattaccare

hangar /'hæŋə(r)/ n hangar m inv

hanger /'hæŋə(r)/ n gruccia f

hanger-on *n* leccapiedi *mf inv*
hang-glider *n* deltaplano *m*
hang-gliding *n* deltaplano *m*
hang: hangman *n* boia *m*. **hangover** *n* postumi *mpl* della sbornia. **hang-up** *n fam* complesso *m*
hank /hæŋk/ *n* (*of hair*) ciocca *f*; (*of wool etc*) matassa *f*
hanker /'hæŋkə(r)/ *vi* ~ **after sth** smaniare per qcsa
hanky /'hæŋkɪ/ *n fam* fazzoletto *m*
hanky-panky /hæŋkɪ'pæŋkɪ/ *n fam* qualcosa *m* di losco
ha'penny /'heɪpnɪ/ *n Br abbr* (**halfpenny**) mezzo penny *m inv*
haphazard /hæp'hæzəd/ *a* a casaccio; **in a ~ fashion** a casaccio
haphazardly /hæp'hæzədlɪ/ *adv* a casaccio
hapless /'hæplɪs/ *a* sventurato
happen /'hæpn/ *vi* capitare, succedere; **as it ~s** per caso; **I ~ed to meet him** mi è capitato di incontrarlo; **what has ~ed to him?** cosa gli è capitato?; (*become of*) che fine ha fatto?
happening /'hæp(ə)nɪŋ/ *n* avvenimento *m*
happily /'hæpɪlɪ/ *adv* felicemente; (*fortunately*) fortunatamente
happiness /'hæpɪnɪs/ *n* felicità *f*
happy /'hæpɪ/ *a* (**-ier, -iest**) contento, felice
happy: happy-go-lucky *a* spensierato. **happy hour** *n* ora *f* in cui nei pub le bevande vengono vendute a prezzi scontati. **happy medium** *n* giusto mezzo *m*
harangue /hə'ræŋ/ *vt* (*morally*) fare un sermone a; (*politically*) arringare
harass /'hærəs/ *vt* perseguitare
harassed /'hærəst/ *a* stressato
harassment /'hærəsmənt/ *n* persecuzione *f*; **sexual ~** molestie *fpl* sessuali
harbinger /'hɑːbɪndʒə(r)/ *n liter* segnale *m*; (*person*) precursore *m*; precorritrice *f*
harbour /'hɑːbə(r)/ *n* porto *m* ● *vt* dare asilo a; nutrire (*grudge*)
hard /hɑːd/ *a* duro; (*question, problem*) difficile; **~ of hearing** duro d'orecchi; **be ~ on sb** (*person:*) essere duro con qcno ● *adv* (*work*) duramente; (*pull, hit, rain, snow*) forte; **~ hit by unemployment** duramente colpito dalla disoccupazione; **take sth ~** non accettare qcsa; **think ~!** pensaci bene!; **try ~** mettercela tutta; **try ~er** metterci più impegno; **~ done by** *fam* trattato ingiustamente
hard: hard and fast *a* (*rule, distinction*) preciso. **hardback** *n* edizione *f* rilegata. **hardboard** *n* truciolato *m*. **hard-boiled** /-'bɔɪld/ *a* (*egg*) sodo. **hard cash** *n* contante *m*. **hard copy** *n* copia *f* stampata. **hard core** *n* (*in construction*) massicciata *f*; (*of group, demonstrators*) zoccolo *m* duro ● *a* (*pornography, video*) hard-core; (*supporter, opponent*) irriducibile. **hard disk** *n* hard disk *m inv*, disco *m* rigido. **hard drug** *n* droga *f* pesante. **hard-earned** /-'ɜːnd/ *a* (*cash*) sudato
harden /'hɑːdn/ *vi* indurirsi
hard: hard-faced /-'feɪst/ *a* (*person*) dai tratti duri. **hard-fought** *a* (*battle*) accanito. **hard hat** *n* casco *m*. **hard-headed** /-'hedɪd/ *a* pratico; (*businessman*) dal sangue freddo. **hard-hearted** /-'hɑːtɪd/ *a* dal cuore duro. **hard labour** *n Br* lavori *mpl* forzati. **hard lens** *n* lente *f* a contatto rigida. **hardline** *a* (*policy, regime*) duro ● *n* linea *f* dura; ~ **lines!** che sfortuna!. **hardliner** *n Pol* fautore, -trice *mf* della linea dura. **hard luck** *n* sfortuna *f*.
hard-luck story *n* **give sb a ~ ~** raccontare a qcno le proprie disgrazie
hardly /'hɑːdlɪ/ *adv* appena; ~ **ever** quasi mai
hardness /'hɑːdnɪs/ *n* durezza *f*
hard: hard-nosed /-'nəʊzd/ *a* (*attitude, businessman, government*) duro. **hard-on** *n fam* erezione *f*. **hard porn** *n* pornografia *f* hard-core. **hard-pressed** /-'prest/ *a* in difficoltà; (*for time*) a corto di tempo. **hard rock** *n Mus* hard rock *m*. **hard sell** *n* tecnica *f* di vendita aggressiva
hardship /'hɑːdʃɪp/ *n* avversità *f inv*
hard: hard shoulder *n Auto* corsia *f* d'emergenza. **hard up** *a fam* a corto di soldi; ~ **up for sth** a corto di qcsa. **hardware** *n* ferramenta *fpl*; *Comput* hardware *m inv*. **hard-wearing** /-'weərɪŋ/ *a* resistente. **hardwood** *n* legno *m* duro. **hard-working** /-'wɜːkɪŋ/ *a* **be ~** essere un gran lavoratore
hardy /'hɑːdɪ/ *a* (**-ier, -iest**) dal fisico resistente; (*plant*) che sopporta il gelo
hare /heə(r)/ *n* lepre *f*
hare-brained /'heəbreɪnd/ *a* (*scheme*) da scervellati; (*person*) scervellato
harelip /heə'lɪp/ *n* labbro *m* leporino
harem /hɑːriːm/ *n* serraglio *m*
■ **hark back** /hɑːk/ *vt fig* ~ ~ **to** ritornare su
harm /hɑːm/ *n* male *m*; (*damage*) danni *mpl*; **out of ~'s way** in un posto sicuro; **it won't do any ~** non farà certo male ● *vt* far male a; (*damage*) danneggiare
harmful /'hɑːmfʊl/ *a* dannoso
harmless /'hɑːmlɪs/ *a* innocuo
harmonica /hɑː'mɒnɪkə/ *n* armonica *f* [a bocca]
harmonious /hɑː'məʊnɪəs/ *a* armonioso
harmoniously /hɑː'məʊnɪəslɪ/ *adv* in armonia
harmonize /'hɑːmənaɪz/ *vi fig* armonizzare
harmony /'hɑːmənɪ/ *n* armonia *f*
harness /'hɑːnɪs/ *n* finimenti *mpl*; (*of parachute*) imbracatura *f* ● *vt* bardare (*horse*); sfruttare (*resources*)
harp /hɑːp/ *n* arpa *f*
■ **harp on** *vi fam* insistere (**about** su)
harpist /'hɑːpɪst/ *n* arpista *mf*
harpoon /hɑː'puːn/ *n* arpione *m*
harpsichord /'hɑːpsɪkɔːd/ *n* clavicembalo *m*
harrow /'hærəʊ/ *n* erpice *m*
harrowing /'hærəʊɪŋ/ *a* straziante
harry /'hærɪ/ *vt* (*pursue, harass*) assillare
harsh /hɑːʃ/ *a* duro; (*light*) abbagliante
harshly /'hɑːʃlɪ/ *adv* duramente

harshness /'hɑːʃnɪs/ n durezza f

harvest /'hɑːvɪst/ n raccolta f; (of grapes) vendemmia f; (crop) raccolto m ● vt raccogliere

harvester /'hɑːvɪstə(r)/ n (person) mietitore, -trice mf; (machine) mietitrice f

harvest festival n festa f del raccolto

has /hæz/ see **have**

has-been /-biːn/ n fam (person) persona f che ha fatto il suo tempo; (thing) anticaglia f

hash /hæʃ/ n **make a ~ of** fam fare un casino con

hashish /'hæʃɪʃ/ n hascish m

hassle /'hæsl/ n fam rottura f ● vt rompere le scatole a

hassock /'hæsək/ n cuscino m di inginocchiatoio

haste /heɪst/ n fretta f; **make ~** affrettarsi

hasten /'heɪsn/ vi affrettarsi ● vt affrettare

hastily /'heɪstɪlɪ/ adv frettolosamente

hasty /'heɪstɪ/ a (-ier, -iest) frettoloso; (decision) affrettato

hat /hæt/ n cappello m

hatbox /'hætbɒks/ n cappelliera f

hatch¹ /hætʃ/ n (for food) sportello m passavivande inv; Naut boccaporto m

hatch² vi ~ [**out**] rompere il guscio; (egg:) schiudersi ● vt covare; tramare (plot)

■ **hatch up** vt tramare (plot)

hatchback /'hætʃbæk/ n Auto tre/cinque porte m inv; (door) porta f del bagagliaio

hatchet /'hætʃɪt/ n ascia f

hate /heɪt/ n odio m ● vt odiare

hateful /'heɪtfʊl/ a odioso

hate mail n lettere fpl offensive o minatorie

hatpin /'hætpɪn/ n spillone m

hatred /'heɪtrɪd/ n odio m

hat-trick n tripletta f

haughtily /'hɔːtɪlɪ/ adv altezzosamente

haughty /'hɔːtɪ/ a (-ier, -iest) altezzoso

haul /hɔːl/ n (fish) pescata f; (loot) bottino m; (pull) tirata f ● vt tirare; trasportare (goods) ● vi ~ **on** tirare

haulage /'hɔːlɪdʒ/ n trasporto m

haulier /'hɔːlɪə(r)/ n autotrasportatore m

haunch /hɔːntʃ/ n anca f

haunt /hɔːnt/ n ritrovo m ● vt frequentare; (linger in the mind) perseguitare; **this house is ~ed** questa casa è abitata da fantasmi

have /hæv/ vt (3 sg pres tense has; pt/pp had) avere; fare (breakfast, bath, walk etc); **~ a drink** bere qualcosa; **~ lunch/dinner** pranzare/cenare; **~ a rest** riposarsi; **I had my hair cut** mi sono tagliata i capelli; **we had the flat painted** abbiamo fatto tinteggiare la casa; **I had it made** l'ho fatto fare; **~ to do sth** dover fare qcsa; **~ him telephone me tomorrow** digli di telefonarmi domani; **he has** or **he's got two houses** ha due case; **you've got the money, ~n't you?** hai i soldi, no? ● v aux avere; (with verbs of motion & some others) essere; **I ~ seen him** l'ho visto; **he has never been there** non ci è mai stato ● npl **the ~s and the ~-nots** i ricchi e i poveri

■ **have in** vt avere in casa/ufficio etc (builders etc)

■ **have off** vt fam **he's having it off with his secretary** si fa la segretaria

■ **have on** vt (be wearing) portare; (dupe) prendere in giro; **I've got something on tonight** ho un impegno stasera; **you're having me on!** tu mi stai prendendo in giro!

■ **have out** vt ~ **it out with sb** chiarire le cose con qcno; ~ **a tooth out** farsi togliere un dente

haven /'heɪvn/ n fig rifugio m

haver /'heɪvə(r)/ vi (dither) titubare

haversack /'hævəsæk/ n zaino m

havoc /'hævək/ n strage f; **play ~ with** fig scombussolare

haw /hɔː/ see **hum**

Hawaii /hə'waɪɪ/ n le Hawaii

Hawaiian /hə'waɪən/ n & a hawaiano, -a mf; (language) hawaiano m

hawk¹ /hɔːk/ n falco m

hawk² vt vendere in giro

hawker /'hɔːkə(r)/ n venditore, -trice mf ambulante

hawkish /'hɔːkɪʃ/ a Pol intransigente

hawthorn /'hɔːθɔːn/ n biancospino m

hay /heɪ/ n fieno m

hay: hay fever n raffreddore m da fieno. **hayloft** n fienile m. **haymaking** n fienagione f. **haystack** n pagliaio m. **haywire** a fam **go ~** dare i numeri; (plans:) andare all'aria

hazard /'hæzəd/ n (risk) rischio m ● vt rischiare; ~ **a guess** azzardare un'ipotesi

hazardous /'hæzədəs/ a rischioso

hazard [warning] lights npl Auto luci fpl d'emergenza

haze /heɪz/ n foschia f

hazel /'heɪz(ə)l/ n nocciolo m; (colour) [color m] nocciola m

hazelnut /'heɪz(ə)lnʌt/ n nocciola f

hazy /'heɪzɪ/ a (-ier, -iest) nebbioso; (fig: person) confuso; (memories) vago

he /hiː/ pron lui; **he's tired** è stanco; **I'm going but he's not** io vengo, ma lui no

head /hed/ n testa f; (of firm) capo m; (of primary school) direttore, -trice mf; (of secondary school) preside mf; (on beer) schiuma f; **use your ~!** usa la testa!; **be off one's ~** essere fuori di testa; **have a good ~ for business** avere il senso degli affari; **have a good ~ for heights** non soffrire di vertigini; **10 pounds a ~** 10 sterline a testa; **20 ~ of cattle** 20 capi di bestiame; **~ first** a capofitto; **~ over heels in love** innamorato pazzo; **~s or tails?** testa o croce? ● vt essere a capo di; essere in testa a (list); colpire di testa (ball) ● vi ~ **for** dirigersi verso

head: headache n mal m di testa. **headband** n fascia f per capelli. **head boy** n Br Sch alunno m che rappresenta la scuola nelle manifestazioni ufficiali e che ha responsabilità speciali. **head-butt** vt dare una testata a. **head case** n fam **be a ~** essere matto da legare. **head cold** n raffreddore m di testa. **headcount** n **do a ~** contare i presenti.

head of department n capo mf reparto.
headdress n acconciatura f
header /'hedə(r)/ n colpo m di testa; (dive)
tuffo m di testa; (on document) intestazione f
head: headgear n copricapo m. **head girl** n
Br Sch alunna f che rappresenta la scuola nelle manifestazioni ufficiali e che ha responsabilità speciali. **headhunter** n also Comm cacciatore, -trice mf di teste. **headhunting** n
Comm ricerca f ad hoc di personale. **heading**
n (in list etc) titolo m. **headlamp** n Auto fanale m. **headland** n promontorio m. **headlight**
n Auto fanale m. **headline** n titolo m.
headlong a & adv a capofitto. **head louse** n
pidocchio m. **headmaster** n (of primary
school) direttore m; (of secondary school) preside m. **headmistress** n (of primary school)
direttrice f; (of secondary school) preside f.
head office n sede f centrale. **head-on** a
(collision) frontale ● adv frontalmente.
headphones npl cuffie fpl. **headquarters**
npl sede f sg; Mil quartier msg generale.
headrest n poggiatesta m inv. **headroom** n
sottotetto m; (of bridge) altezza f libera di passaggio. **headscarf** n foulard m inv, fazzoletto
m. **headstand** n do a ~ fare la verticale.
head start n have a ~ ~ partire avvantag-
giato. **headstone** n (of grave) lapide f.
headstrong a testardo. **head teacher** n (of
primary school) direttore, -trice mf; (of
secondary school) preside mf. **head-to-head**
n confronto m diretto ● a diretto. **head
waiter** n capocameriere m. **headway** n progresso m. **headwind** n vento m di prua
heady /'hedɪ/ a che dà alla testa
heal /hiːl/ vt/i guarire
healer /'hiːlə(r)/ n guaritore, -trice mf; **time
is a great ~** il tempo guarisce tutti i mali
health /helθ/ n salute f
health: health care n assistenza f sanitaria. **health centre** n Br ambulatorio m.
health check n controllo m medico. **health
club** n club m ginnico. **health farm** n centro
m di rimessa in forma. **health foods** npl alimenti mpl macrobiotici. **health-food shop**
n negozio m di macrobiotica. **health hazard**
n pericolo m per la salute
healthily /'helθɪlɪ/ adv in modo sano
health: health insurance n assicurazione f
contro malattie. **health officer** n ufficiale m
sanitario. **health resort** n (in mountains, by
sea) stazione f climatica; (spa town) stazione f
termale. **health visitor** n Br infermiere, -a mf
che fa visite a domicilio. **health warning** n
avviso m del ministero della sanità
healthy /'helθɪ/ a (-ier, -iest) sano
heap /hiːp/ n mucchio m; **~s of** fam un sacco
di ● vt ~ [up] ammucchiare; **~ed teaspoon**
un cucchiaino abbondante
hear /hɪə(r)/ vt/i (pt/pp heard) sentire; **~,
~!** bravo!
■ **hear about** vt (learn of) sentir parlare di
■ **hear from** vi aver notizie di
■ **hear of** vi sentir parlare di; **he would not
~ of it** non ne ha voluto sentir parlare

hearing /'hɪərɪŋ/ n udito m; Jur udienza f
hearing aid n apparecchio m acustico
hearing-impaired /-ɪm'peəd/ a audioleso
hearsay /'hɪəseɪ/ n **from ~** per sentito dire
hearse /hɜːs/ n carro m funebre
heart /hɑːt/ n cuore m; **~s** pl (Cards) cuori
mpl; **at ~** di natura; **by ~** a memoria
heart: heartache n pena f. **heart attack** n
infarto m. **heartbeat** n battito m cardiaco.
heartbreak n afflizione f. **heartbreaking** a
straziante. **heart-broken** a avere il cuore spezzato. **heartburn** n mal m di stomaco.
heart disease n malattia f cardiaca
hearten /'hɑːt(ə)n/ vt rincuorare
heart failure n arresto m cardiaco
heartfelt /'hɑːtfelt/ a di cuore
hearth /hɑːθ/ n focolare m
hearthrug /'hɑːθrʌg/ n tappeto m davanti al
camino
heartily /'hɑːtɪlɪ/ adv di cuore; (eat) con appetito; **be ~ sick of sth** non poterne più di
qcsa
heartland /'hɑːtlænd/ n (industrial, rural)
cuore m; Pol roccaforte f
heartless /'hɑːtlɪs/ a spietato
heartlessly /'hɑːtlɪslɪ/ adv in modo spietato
heart: heart-lung machine n polmone m
artificiale. **heart rate** n battito m cardiaco.
heart-rending /-rendɪŋ/ a (sigh, story) straziante. **heart-searching** n esame m di coscienza. **heart surgeon** n cardiochirurgo, -a
mf. **heartthrob** n fam rubacuori m inv.
heart-to-heart n conversazione f a cuore
aperto ● a a cuore aperto. **heart transplant**
n trapianto m di cuore. **heart-warming** a
toccante
hearty /'hɑːtɪ/ a caloroso; (meal) copioso;
(person) gioviale
heat /hiːt/ n calore m; Sport prova f eliminatoria ● vt scaldare ● vi scaldarsi
■ **heat up** vt scaldare (food, drink); riscalda-
re (room)
heated /'hiːtɪd/ a (swimming pool) riscalda-
to; (discussion) animato
heater /'hiːtə(r)/ n (for room) stufa f; (for
water) boiler m; Auto riscaldamento m
heath /hiːθ/ n brughiera f
heat haze n foschia f (dovuta all'afa)
heathen /'hiːðn/ a & n pagano, -a mf
heather /'heðə(r)/ n erica f
heating /'hiːtɪŋ/ n riscaldamento m
heat: heat loss n perdita f di calore.
heat-resistant a resistente al calore. **heat
sink** n dissipatore m termico. **heatstroke** n
colpo m di sole. **heat treatment** n Med
termoterapia f. **heatwave** n ondata f di calore
heave /hiːv/ vt tirare; (lift) tirare su; (fam:
throw) gettare; emettere (sigh) ● vi tirare; **my
stomach ~d** avevo la nausea
heaven /'hev(ə)n/ n paradiso m; **~ help you
if...** Dio ti scampi se...; **raise one's eyes to
~** alzare gli occhi al cielo; **H~s!** santo cielo!
heavenly /'hev(ə)nlɪ/ a celeste; fam delizioso

heaven-sent /-'sent/ a ⟨opportunity⟩ provvidenziale

heavily /'hevɪlɪ/ adv pesantemente; ⟨smoke,
drink etc⟩ molto

heaviness /'hevɪnɪs/ n pesantezza f

heavy /'hevɪ/ a (**-ier, -iest**) pesante; ⟨traffic⟩
intenso; ⟨rain, cold⟩ forte; **be a ~ smoker/
drinker** essere un gran fumatore/bevitore

heavy: heavy-duty a ⟨equipment, shoes⟩
molto resistente. **heavy goods vehicle** n veicolo m pesante da trasporto. **heavy-handed**
/-'hændɪd/ a (severe) severo; (clumsy) maldestro. **heavy industry** n industria f pesante.
heavy metal n Mus heavy metal m.
heavyweight n peso m massimo

Hebrew /'hi:bru:/ a & nm ebreo

heck /hek/ fam int cavolo ● n a ~ **of a lot of**
un sacco di; **what the ~ !** chi se ne frega!;
what the ~ is going on? che cavolo succede?

heckle /'hekl/ vt interrompere di continuo

heckler /'heklə(r)/ n disturbatore, -trice mf

hectare /'hektɛə(r)/ n ettaro m

hectic /'hektɪk/ a frenetico

hectoring /'hektərɪŋ/ a prepotente

hedge /hedʒ/ n siepe f ● vi fig essere evasivo

hedge: hedge-clippers npl cesoie fpl.
hedgehog n riccio m. **hedgerow** n siepe f

hedonism /'hi:dənɪzm/ n edonismo m

hedonistic /hi:də'nɪstɪk/ a edonistico

heebie-jeebies /hi:bɪ'dʒi:bɪz/ npl fam **give
sb the ~** far venire i brividi a qcno

heed /hi:d/ n **pay ~ to** prestare ascolto a ● vt
prestare ascolto a

heedless /'hi:dlɪs/ a noncurante

heel[1] /hi:l/ n tallone m; (of shoe) tacco m;
down at ~ fig trasandato; **take to one's ~s**
fam darsela a gambe

heel[2] vi ~ **over** Naut inclinarsi

heel bar n calzolaio m

hefty /'heftɪ/ a (**-ier, -iest**) massiccio

heifer /'hefə(r)/ n giovenca f

height /haɪt/ n altezza f; (of plane) altitudine
f; (of season, fame) culmine m

heighten /'haɪt(ə)n/ vt fig accrescere

heinous /'hi:nəs/ a abominevole

heir /eə(r)/ n erede mf

heiress /eə'res/ n ereditiera f

heirloom /'eəlu:m/ n cimelio m di famiglia

heist /haɪst/ n Am fam furto m; (armed) rapina f

held /held/ see **hold**[2]

helicopter /'helɪkɒptə(r)/ n elicottero m

heliport /'helɪpɔ:t/ n eliporto m

helium /'hi:lɪəm/ n elio m

helix /'hi:lɪks/ n elica f

hell /hel/ n inferno m; **go to ~!** sl va' al diavolo!; **make sb's life ~** rendere la vita infernale a qcno ● int porca miseria!

hell-bent a ~ **on doing sth** deciso a tutti i
costi a fare qcsa

Hellenic /hɪ'lenɪk/ a ellenico

hellfire /'helfaɪə(r)/ n pene fpl dell'inferno

hell-for-leather adv fam **go ~** andare a
spron battuto

hello /hə'ləʊ/ int & n = **hallo**

Hell's angel n Hell's angel m inv

helm /helm/ n timone m; **at the ~** fig al timone

helmet /'helmɪt/ n casco m

help /help/ n aiuto m; (employee) aiuto m domestico; **that's no ~** non è d'aiuto ● vt aiutare; ~ **oneself to sth** servirsi di qcsa; ~
yourself (at table) serviti pure; **I could not
~ laughing** non ho potuto trattenermi dal ridere; **it cannot be ~ed** non c'è niente da
fare; **I can't ~ it** non ci posso far niente ● vi
aiutare

■ **help out** vt dare una mano a ● vi dare una
mano

helper /'helpə(r)/ n aiutante mf

helpful /'helpfʊl/ a ⟨person⟩ di aiuto; ⟨advice⟩
utile

helping /'helpɪŋ/ n porzione f

helping hand n **give sb a ~ ~** dare una
mano a qcno

helpless /'helplɪs/ a (unable to manage) incapace; (powerless) impotente

helplessly /'helplɪslɪ/ adv con impotenza;
⟨laugh⟩ incontrollatamente

help window n Comput finestrella f di aiuto

helter-skelter /heltə'skeltə(r)/ adv in fretta e furia ● n scivolo m a spirale nei luna park

hem /hem/ n orlo m ● vt (pt/pp **hemmed**) or-
lare

■ **hem in** vt intrappolare

hemisphere /'hemɪsfɪə(r)/ n emisfero m

hemline /'hemlaɪn/ n orlo m

hemlock /'hemlɒk/ n cicuta f

hemp /hemp/ n canapa f

hen /hen/ n gallina f; (any female bird) femmina f

hence /hens/ adv (for this reason) quindi;
(from now on) a partire da ora; (from here) da
qui

henceforth /hens'fɔ:θ/ adv fml (from that
time on) da allora in poi; (from now on) d'ora
in poi

henchman /'hentʃmən/ n pej tirapiedi m
inv

hen-coop n stia f

hen house n pollaio m

henna /'henə/ n henné m

hen-party n fam festa f di addio al celibato
per sole donne

henpecked /'henpekt/ a tiranneggiato dalla moglie

hepatitis /hepə'taɪtɪs/ n epatite f

her /hɜ:(r)/ poss a suo m, sua f, suoi mpl, sue
fpl; ~ **job/house** il suo lavoro/la sua casa;
her mother/father sua madre/suo padre
● pers pron (direct object) la; (indirect object)
le; (after prep) lei; **I know ~** la conosco; **give
~ the money** dalle i soldi; **give it to ~** daglielo; **I came with ~** sono venuto con lei;
it's ~ è lei; **I've seen ~** l'ho vista; **I've seen
~, but not him** ho visto lei, ma non lui

herald /'herəld/ vt annunciare

heraldic /he'rældɪk/ a araldico

heraldry /'herəldrı/ n araldica f
herb /hɜːb/ n erba f
herbaceous /hɜː'beɪʃəs/ a erbaceo; ~
 border aiuola f
herbal /'hɜːb(ə)l/ a alle erbe
herbalist /'hɜːbəlɪst/ n erborista mf
herbal tea n tisana f
herb garden n aromatario m
herbs /hɜːbz/ npl (for cooking) aromi mpl [da
 cucina]; (medicinal) erbe fpl
herb tea n tisana f
herculean /hɜːkjʊ'liːən/ a ‹task› erculeo
herd /hɜːd/ n gregge m ● vt (tend) sorvegliare; (drive) far muovere; fig ammassare
■ **herd together** vi raggrupparsi ● vt raggruppare
here /hɪə(r)/ adv qui, qua; **in ~** qui dentro;
 come/bring ~ vieni/porta qui; **~ is...,** ~
 are... ecco...; **~ you are!** ecco qua!
here: hereabouts /hɪərə'baʊts/ adv Br da
 queste parti. **hereafter** adv in futuro. **here
 and now** adv seduta stante ● n **the ~ ~ ~** il
 presente. **hereby** adv con la presente
hereditary /hɪ'redɪtərɪ/ a ereditario
heredity /hɪ'redɪtɪ/ n ereditarietà f
heresy /'herəsɪ/ n eresia f
heretic /'herətɪk/ n eretico, -a mf
herewith /hɪə'wɪð/ adv Comm con la presente
heritage /'herɪtɪdʒ/ n eredità f
hermetic /hɜː'metɪk/ a ermetico
hermetically /hɜː'metɪklɪ/ adv ermeticamente
hermit /'hɜːmɪt/ n eremita mf
hernia /'hɜːnɪə/ n ernia f
hero /'hɪərəʊ/ n (pl -es) eroe m
heroic /hɪ'rəʊɪk/ a eroico
heroically /hɪ'rəʊɪklɪ/ adv eroicamente
heroin /'herəʊɪn/ n eroina f (droga)
heroine /'herəʊɪn/ n eroina f
heroism /'herəʊɪzm/ n eroismo m
heron /'herən/ n airone m
hero-worship n culto m degli eroi ● vt venerare
herpes /'hɜːpiːz/ n herpes m
herring /'herɪŋ/ n aringa f
herringbone /'herɪŋbəʊn/ a ‹pattern› spigato
hers /hɜːz/ poss pron il suo m, la sua f, i suoi
 mpl, le sue fpl; **a friend of ~** un suo amico;
 friends of ~ dei suoi amici; **that is ~** quello
 è suo; (as opposed to mine) quello è il suo
herself /hə'self/ pers pron (reflexive) si;
 (emphatic) lei stessa; (after prep) sé, se stessa;
 she poured ~ a drink si è versata da bere;
 she told me so ~ me lo ha detto lei stessa;
 she's proud of ~ è fiera di sé; **by ~** da sola
hesitant /'hezɪtənt/ a esitante
hesitantly /'hezɪtəntlɪ/ adv con esitazione
hesitate /'hezɪteɪt/ vi esitare
hesitation /hezɪ'teɪʃn/ n esitazione f
hessian /'hesɪən/ n tela f di iuta
heterogeneous /hetərə'dʒiːnɪəs/ a eterogeneo

heterosexual /hetərəʊ'sekʃʊəl/ a etero-
 sessuale
het up /het/ a fam agitato
hew /hjuː/ vt (pt hewed, pp hewed or hewn)
 spaccare
hexagon /'heksəgən/ n esagono m
hexagonal /hek'sægənl/ a esagonale
hey /heɪ/ int ehi!
heyday /'heɪdeɪ/ n tempi mpl d'oro
hey presto /heɪ'prestəʊ/ int (magic) e voilà!
HGV abbr **heavy goods vehicle**
hi /haɪ/ int ciao!
hiatus /haɪ'eɪtəs/ n (pl **-tuses**) iato m
hibernate /'haɪbəneɪt/ vi andare in letargo
hibernation /haɪbə'neɪʃn/ n letargo m
hiccup /'hɪkʌp/ n singhiozzo m; (fam: hitch)
 intoppo m; **have the ~s** avere il singhiozzo
 ● vi fare un singhiozzo
hick /hɪk/ n Am fam buzzurro, -a mf
hick town n Am fam città f inv provinciale
hid /hɪd/, **hidden** /'hɪdn/ see **hide**²
hide¹ /haɪd/ n (leather) pelle f (di animale)
hide² vt (pt **hid**, pp **hidden**) nascondere ● vi
 nascondersi
hide-and-seek n play ~ giocare a nascon-
 dino
hideaway /'haɪdəweɪ/ n (secluded place) rifugio m; (hiding place) nascondiglio m
hidebound /'haɪdbaʊnd/ a (conventional) limitato
hideous /'hɪdɪəs/ a orribile
hideously /'hɪdɪəslɪ/ adv orribilmente
hideout /'haɪdaʊt/ n nascondiglio m
hiding¹ /'haɪdɪŋ/ n (fam: beating) bastonata;
 (defeat) batosta f
hiding² n go into ~ sparire dalla circolazione
hierarchic[al] /haɪə'rɑːkɪk[l]/ a gerarchico
hierarchy /'haɪərɑːkɪ/ n gerarchia f
hieroglyphics /haɪərə'glɪfɪks/ npl gerogli-
 fici mpl
hi-fi /'haɪfaɪ/ n abbr (**high fidelity**) hi-fi m
 inv; (set of equipment) impianto m hi-fi, stereo
 m inv
higgledy-piggledy /hɪgldɪ'pɪgldɪ/ adv alla
 rinfusa
high /haɪ/ a alto; ‹meat› che comincia ad andare a male; ‹wind› forte; (on drugs) fatto; **it's
 ~ time we did something about it** è ora di
 fare qualcosa in proposito ● adv in alto; **~
 and low** in lungo e in largo ● n massimo m;
 (temperature) massima f; **from on ~** dall'alto; **be on a ~** fam essere fatto
high: high and dry a fig **leave sb ~ ~ ~**
 piantare in asso qcno. **high beam** n Am abbagliante m. **high-born** a nobile. **highbrow** a &
 n intellettuale mf. **high chair** n seggiolone m.
 high-class a ‹hotel, shop, car› d'alta classe;
 ‹prostitute› di alto bordo. **high command** n
 stato m maggiore. **High Commission** n alto
 commissariato m. **High Commissioner** n
 alto commissario m. **High Court** n ≈ Corte f
 Suprema. **high-definition** a ad alta definizione. **high diving** n tuffo m

higher education /haɪərˈedjʊˈkeɪʃn/ *n* istruzione *f* universitaria

higher mathematics *n* matematica *f* avanzata

high: highfaluting /haɪfəˈluːtɪŋ/ *a* ⟨*fam* ⟨*ideas*⟩ pretenzioso; ⟨*language*⟩ pomposo. **high fashion** *n* alta moda *f*. **high-fibre** *a* ⟨*diet*⟩ ricco di fibre. **high-fidelity** *n* alta fedeltà *f* ● *a* ad alta fedeltà. **high finance** *n* alta finanza *f*. **high-flier** *n* (*person*) persona *f* che mira alto. **high-flown** *a* ⟨*phrases*⟩ ampolloso. **high-flying** *a* ⟨*aircraft*⟩ da alta quota; ⟨*career*⟩ ambizioso; ⟨*person*⟩ che mira alto. **high-frequency** *a* alta frequenza *f*. **High German** *n* alto tedesco *m*. **high-grade** *a* ⟨*oil, mineral, product*⟩ di prima qualità. **high ground** *n* collina *f*; **take the moral ~** ~ assumere un atteggiamento moralistico. **high-handed** /-ˈhændɪd/ *a* dispotico. **high-handedly** /-ˈhændɪdlɪ/ *adv* dispoticamente. **high-heeled** /-hiːld/ *a* coi tacchi alti. **high heels** *npl* tacchi *mpl* alti. **high jinks** /dʒɪŋks/ *npl* baldoria *f*. **high jump** *n* salto *m* in alto

Highland games /haɪlənd/ *n manifestazione f tradizionale scozzese con gare sportive e musicali*

Highlands /ˈhaɪləndz/ *npl* Highlands *fpl* (*regione della Scozia del nord*)

high-level *a* ⟨*talks*⟩ ad alto livello; ⟨*official*⟩ di alto livello

high life *n* bella vita *f*

highlight /ˈhaɪlaɪt/ *vt* (*emphasize, with pen*) evidenziare ● *n* (*in art*) luce *f*; (*in hair*) riflesso *m*, colpo *m* di sole; (*of exhibition*) parte *f* saliente; (*of week, year*) avvenimento *m* saliente; (*of match, show*) momento *m* clou

highlighter /ˈhaɪlaɪtə(r)/ *n* (*marker*) evidenziatore *m*

highly /ˈhaɪlɪ/ *adv* molto; **speak ~ of** lodare; **think ~ of** avere un'alta opinione di

highly-paid /-ˈpeɪd/ *a* ben pagato

highlystrung /-ˈstrʌŋ/ *a* nervoso

high: High Mass *n* messa *f* solenne. **high-minded** /-ˈmaɪndɪd/ *a* ⟨*person*⟩ di animo nobile. **high-necked** /-ˈnekt/ *a* a collo alto

Highness /ˈhaɪnɪs/ *n* altezza *f*; **Your ~** Sua Altezza

high: high noon *n* mezzogiorno *m* in punto. **high-performance** *a* ad alta prestazione. **high-pitched** /-ˈpɪtʃt/ *a* ⟨*voice, sound*⟩ acuto. **high point** *n* momento *m* culminante. **high-powered** *a* ⟨*car, engine*⟩ molto potente; ⟨*job*⟩ di alta responsabilità; ⟨*person*⟩ dinamico. **high pressure** *n* Meteorol alta pressione *f* ● *attrib* Techn ad alta pressione; ⟨*job*⟩ stressante. **high priest** *n* Relig gran sacerdote *m*; *fig* guru *m* inv. **high priestess** *n* Relig, fig gran sacerdotessa *f*. **high-principled** *a* ⟨*person*⟩ di alti principi. **high-profile** *a* ⟨*politician, group*⟩ di spicco; ⟨*visit*⟩ di grande risonanza. **high-ranking** *a* di alto rango. **high-rise** *a* ⟨*building*⟩ molto alto ● *n* edificio *m* molto alto. **high road** *n* strada *f* principale. **high school** *n* Am ≈ scuola *f* superiore; Br ≈ scuola *f* media e superiore. **high sea** *n* on

the **~** **~s** in alto mare. **high season** *n* alta stagione *f*. **high society** *n* alta società *f*. **high-sounding** /-ˈsaʊndɪŋ/ *a* ⟨*title*⟩ altisonante. **high-speed** *a* ⟨*train, film*⟩ rapido. **high-spirited** *a* pieno di brio. **high spirits** *npl* brio *m*. **high spot** *n* momento *m* culminante. **high street** *n* strada *f* principale. **high-street shop** *n* negozio *m* popolare. **high tea** *n pasto m pomeridiano servito insieme al tè*. **high tech** /ˈtek/ *n* high tech *f*. **high tide** *n* alta marea *f*. **high treason** *n* alto tradimento *m*. **high voltage** *n* alta tensione *f*

highway /ˈhaɪweɪ/ *n* **public ~** strada *f* pubblica

highway: Highway Code *n* Br Codice *m* stradale. **highwayman** *n* brigante *m*. **highway robbery** *n* brigantaggio *m*

high wire *n* filo *m* (*per acrobati*)

hijack /ˈhaɪdʒæk/ *vt* dirottare ● *n* dirottamento *m*

hijacker /ˈhaɪdʒækə(r)/ *n* dirottatore, -trice *mf*

hijacking /ˈhaɪdʒækɪŋ/ *n* dirottamento *m*

hike /haɪk/ *n* escursione *f* a piedi; (*in price*) aumento *m* ● *vi* fare un'escursione a piedi

hiker /ˈhaɪkə(r)/ *n* escursionista *mf*

hilarious /hɪˈleərɪəs/ *a* da morir dal ridere

hilarity /hɪˈlærətɪ/ *n* ilarità *f*

hill /hɪl/ *n* collina *f*; (*mound*) collinetta *f*; (*slope*) altura *f*

hill-billy /-bɪlɪ/ *n* Am montanaro *m* degli Stati Uniti sudorientali

hillock /ˈhɪlək/ *n* poggio *m*

hillside /ˈhɪlsaɪd/ *n* pendio *m*

hilltop /ˈhɪltɒp/ *n* sommità *f* inv di una collina

hilly /ˈhɪlɪ/ *a* collinoso

hilt /hɪlt/ *n* impugnatura *f*; **to the ~** ⟨*fam: support*⟩ fino in fondo; ⟨*mortgaged*⟩ fino al collo

him /hɪm/ *pers pron* (*direct object*) lo; (*indirect object*) gli; (*with prep*) lui; **I know ~** lo conosco; **give ~ the money** dagli i soldi; **give it to ~** daglielo; **I spoke to ~** gli ho parlato; **it's ~** è lui; **she loves ~** lo ama; a **she loves ~, not you** ama lui, non te

Himalayas /hɪməˈleɪəz/ *npl* Himalaia *msg*

himself /hɪmˈself/ *pers pron* (*reflexive*) si; (*emphatic*) lui stesso; (*after prep*) sé, se stesso; **he poured ~ out a drink** si è versato da bere; **he told me so ~** me lo ha detto lui stesso; **he's proud of ~** è fiero di sé; **by ~** da solo

hind /haɪnd/ *a* posteriore

hinder /ˈhɪndə(r)/ *vt* intralciare

hindquarters /ˈhaɪn(d)kwɔːtəz/ *npl* didietro *m*

hindrance /ˈhɪndrəns/ *n* intralcio *m*

hindsight /ˈhaɪndsaɪt/ *n* **with ~** con il senno del poi

Hindu /ˈhɪnduː/ *a & n* indù *mf* inv

Hinduism /ˈhɪnduɪzm/ *n* induismo *m*

hinge /hɪndʒ/ *n* cardine *m* ● *vi* **~ on** *fig* dipendere da

hint /hɪnt/ *n* (*clue*) accenno *m*; (*advice*) suggerimento *m*; *(indirect suggestion)* allusione *f*; *(trace)* tocco *m* ● *vt* ~ **that...** far capire che... ● *vi* ~ **at** alludere a

hinterland /'hɪntəlænd/ *n* entroterra *m inv*, hinterland *m inv*

hip /hɪp/ *n* fianco *m*

hip bone *n* ileo *m*

hip flask *n* fiaschetta *f*

hippie /'hɪpɪ/ *n* hippy *mf inv*

hippo /'hɪpəʊ/ *n fam* ippopotamo *m*

hip pocket *n* tasca *f* posteriore

Hippocratic oath /hɪpə'krætɪk/ *a* giuramento *m* d'Ippocrate

hippopotamus /hɪpə'pɒtəməs/ *n* (*pl* **-muses** *or* **-mi** /hɪpə'pɒtəmaɪ/) ippopotamo *m*

hip replacement *n* protesi *f inv* all'anca

hire /'haɪə(r)/ *vt* affittare; assumere ⟨*person*⟩; ~ **[out]** affittare ● *n* noleggio *m*; '**for ~**' 'affittasi'

hire car *n* macchina *f* a noleggio

hire purchase *n Br* acquisto *m* rateale; **on ~ ~** a rate

his /hɪz/ *poss a* suo *m*, sua *f*, suoi *mpl*, sue *fpl*; ~ **job/house** il suo lavoro/la sua casa; ~ **mother/father** sua madre/suo padre ● *poss pron* il suo *m*, la sua *f*, i suoi *mpl*, le sue *fpl*; **a friend of ~** un suo amico; **friends of ~** dei suoi amici; **that is ~** questo è suo; *(as opposed to mine)* questo è il suo

Hispanic /hɪ'spænɪk/ *a* ispanico

hiss /hɪs/ *n* sibilo *m*; *(of disapproval)* fischio *m* ● *vt* fischiare ● *vi* sibilare; *(in disapproval)* fischiare

historian /hɪ'stɔːrɪən/ *n* storico, -a *mf*

historic /hɪ'stɒrɪk/ *a* storico

historical /hɪ'stɒrɪkl/ *a* storico

historically /hɪ'stɒrɪklɪ/ *adv* storicamente

history /'hɪstərɪ/ *n* storia *f*; **make ~** passare alla storia

histrionic /hɪstrɪ'ɒnɪk/ *a* istrionico

histrionics /hɪstrɪ'ɒnɪks/ *npl* scene *fpl*

hit /hɪt/ *n* *(blow)* colpo *m*; *(fam: success)* successo *m*; **score a direct ~** *⟨missile:⟩* colpire in pieno ● *vt/i* *(pt/pp* **hit**, *pres p* **hitting**) colpire; ~ **one's head on the table** battere la testa contro il tavolo; **the car ~ the wall** la macchina ha sbattuto contro il muro; ~ **the target** colpire il bersaglio; ~ **the nail on the head** fare centro; ~ **the roof** *fam* perdere le staffe

■ **hit back** *vi* *(retaliate)* ribattere

■ **hit off** *vt* ~ **it off** andare d'accordo

■ **hit on** *vt fig* trovare

hit: **hit-and-miss** *a* *⟨affair, undertaking⟩* imprevedibile; *⟨method⟩* a casaccio. **hit-and-run** *a* *⟨raid, attack⟩* lampo *inv*; *⟨accident⟩* causato da un pirata della strada. **hit-and-run driver** *a* pirata *m* della strada

hitch /hɪtʃ/ *n* intoppo *m*; **technical ~** problema *m* tecnico ● *vt* attaccare; ~ **a lift** chiedere un passaggio

■ **hitch up** *vt* tirarsi su *⟨trousers⟩*

hitch: **hitch-hike** *vi* fare l'autostop. **hitchhiker** *n* autostoppista *mf*. **hitch-hiking** *n* autostop *m*

hi-tech *a see* **high tech**

hither /'hɪðə(r)/ *adv* ~ **and thither** di qua e di là

hitherto /hɪðə'tuː/ *adv* finora

hit: **hit list** *n* lista *f* degli obiettivi. **hit man** *n* sicario *m*. **hit-or-miss** *a* **on a very ~ basis** all'improvvisata. **hit parade** *n* hit parade *f inv*, classifica *f*

HIV *n abbr* **(human immunodeficiency virus)** HIV *m*

hive /haɪv/ *n* alveare *m*; ~ **of industry** fucina *f* di lavoro

■ **hive off** *vt Comm* separare

HIV positive *a* sieropositivo

HMS *abbr* **His/Her Majesty's Ship**

hoard /hɔːd/ *n* provvista *f*; *(of money)* gruzzolo *m* ● *vt* accumulare

hoarding /'hɔːdɪŋ/ *n* palizzata *f*; *(with advertisements)* tabellone *m* per manifesti pubblicitari

hoar frost /'hɔː(r)/ *n* brina *f*

hoarse /hɔːs/ *a* rauco

hoarsely /'hɔːslɪ/ *adv* con voce rauca

hoarseness /'hɔːsnɪs/ *n* raucedine *f*

hoary /'hɔːrɪ/ *a* *⟨person⟩* con i capelli bianchi; ~ **old joke** barzelletta *f* vecchia

hoax /həʊks/ *n* scherzo *m*; *(false alarm)* falso allarme *m*

hoaxer /'həʊksə(r)/ *n* burlone, -a *mf*

hob /hɒb/ *n* piano *m* di cottura

hobble /'hɒbl/ *vi* zoppicare

hobby /'hɒbɪ/ *n* hobby *m inv*

hobby horse *n fig* fissazione *f*

hobnailed /'hɒbneɪld/ *a* ~ **boots** *pl* scarponi *mpl* chiodati

■ **hobnob with** /'hɒbnɒb/ *vt* *(pt/pp* **hobnobbed**) frequentare

hobo /'həʊbəʊ/ *n Am* vagabondo, -a *mf*

hock /hɒk/ *n* vino *m* bianco del Reno

hockey /'hɒkɪ/ *n* hockey *m*

hocus-pocus /həʊkəs'pəʊkəs/ *n* *(trickery)* trucco *m*

hod /hɒd/ *n* *(for coal)* secchio *m* del carbone; *(for bricks)* cassetta *f* *(per trasportare mattoni)*

hoe /həʊ/ *n* zappa *f* ● *vt* *(pres p* **hoeing**) zappare

hog /hɒg/ *n* maiale *m* ● *vt* *(pt/pp* **hogged**) *fam* monopolizzare

hog-tie /'hɒgtaɪ/ *vt* legare le quattro zampe di *⟨pig, cow⟩*; *Am fig* ostacolare *⟨person⟩*

hogwash /'hɒgwɒʃ/ *n fam* cretinate *fpl*

hoi polloi /hɔɪpə'lɔɪ/ *npl* plebaglia *fsg*

hoist /hɔɪst/ *n* montacarichi *m inv*; *(fam: push)* spinta *f* in su ● *vt* sollevare; innalzare *⟨flag⟩*; levare *⟨anchor⟩*

hoity-toity /hɔɪtɪ'tɔɪtɪ/ *a fam* altezzoso

hokum /'həʊkəm/ *n Am fam* *(sentimentality)* polpettone *m* sentimentale; *(nonsense)* cretinate *fpl*

hold¹ /həʊld/ *n Naut, Aeron* stiva *f*

hold² *n* presa *f*; *(fig: influence)* ascendente *m*; **get ~ of** trovare; procurarsi *⟨information⟩* ● *v* *(pt/pp* **held**) ● *vt* tenere; *⟨container:⟩* contenere; essere titolare di *⟨licence, passport⟩*;

161

trattenere ‹breath, suspect›; mantenere vivo ‹interest›; ‹civil servant etc.›› occupare ‹position›; (retain) mantenere; ~ **sb's hand** tenere qcno per mano; ~ **one's tongue** tenere la bocca chiusa; ~ **sb responsible** considerare qcno responsabile; ~ **that** (believe) ritenere che ● vi tenere; ‹weather, luck.›› durare; ‹offer.›› essere valido; Teleph restare in linea; **I don't ~ with the idea that...** fam non sono d'accordo sul fatto che...

■ **hold against** vt ~ **sth against sb** avercela con qcno per qcsa

■ **hold back** vt rallentare ● vi esitare

■ **hold down** vt tenere a bada ‹sb›

■ **hold on** vi (wait) attendere; Teleph restare in linea

■ **hold on to** vt aggrapparsi a; (keep) tenersi

■ **hold out** vt porgere ‹hand›; fig offrire ‹possibility› ● vi (resist) resistere

■ **hold up** vt tenere su; (delay) rallentare; (rob) assalire; ~ **one's head up** fig tenere la testa alta

holdall /ˈhəʊldɔːl/ n borsone m

holder /ˈhəʊldə(r)/ n titolare mf; (of record) detentore, -trice mf; (container) astuccio m

holding /ˈhəʊldɪŋ/ n (land) terreno m in affitto; Comm azioni fpl

holding company n società f inv finanziaria

hold-up n ritardo m; (attack) rapina f a mano armata

hole /həʊl/ n buco m

holiday /ˈhɒlɪdeɪ/ n vacanza f; (public) giorno m festivo; (day off) giorno m di ferie; **go on ~** andare in vacanza ● vi andare in vacanza

holiday: holiday home n casa f per le vacanze. **holiday job** n (Br: in summer) lavoretto m estivo. **holiday-maker** n vacanziere mf. **holiday resort** n luogo m di villeggiatura

holier-than-thou /həʊlɪəðənˈðaʊ/ a ‹attitude› da santerellino

holiness /ˈhəʊlɪnɪs/ n santità f; **Your H~** Sua Santità

Holland /ˈhɒlənd/ n Olanda f

holler /ˈhɒlə(r)/ vi urlare (**at** contro)

hollow /ˈhɒləʊ/ a cavo; (promise) a vuoto; ‹voice› assente; ‹cheeks› infossato ● n cavità f inv; (in ground) affossamento m

■ **hollow out** vt scavare

holly /ˈhɒlɪ/ n agrifoglio m

hollyhock /ˈhɒlɪhɒk/ n malvone m

holocaust /ˈhɒləkɔːst/ n olocausto m

hologram /ˈhɒləgræm/ n ologramma m

holograph /ˈhɒləɡrɑːf/ n documento m olografo

hols /hɒlz/ n Br fam abbr (**holidays**) vacanze fpl

holster /ˈhəʊlstə(r)/ n fondina f

holy /ˈhəʊlɪ/ a (-ier, -est) santo; ‹water› benedetto

holy: Holy Ghost or **Spirit** n Spirito m Santo. **Holy Scriptures** sacre scritture fpl. **Holy Week** n settimana f santa

homage /ˈhɒmɪdʒ/ n omaggio m; **pay ~ to** rendere omaggio a

homburg /ˈhɒmbɜːɡ/ n cappello m di feltro

home /həʊm/ n casa f; (for children) istituto m; (for old people) casa f di riposo; (native land) patria f ● adv **at ~** a casa; (football) in casa; **feel at ~** sentirsi a casa propria; **come/go ~** venire/andare a casa; **drive a nail ~** piantare un chiodo a fondo. ● a domestico; ‹movie, video› casalingo; ‹team› ospitante; Pol nazionale

home: home address n indirizzo m di casa. **home brew** n (beer) birra f fatta in casa. **homecoming** n (return home) ritorno m a casa. **home computer** n computer m inv da casa. **Home Counties** npl contee fpl intorno a Londra. **home economics** n Sch economia f domestica. **home front** n (during war) fronte m interno; (in politics) politica f interna. **home game** n gioco m in casa. **home ground** n play on one's ~ ~ giocare in casa. **home-grown** a ‹produce› del proprio orto; fig nostrano. **home help** n aiuto m domestico (per persone non autosufficienti). **homeland** n patria f

homeless /ˈhəʊmlɪs/ a senza tetto

home loan n mutuo m per la casa

homeloving /ˈhəʊmlʌvɪŋ/ a casalingo

homely /ˈhəʊmlɪ/ a (-ier, -iest) a semplice; ‹atmosphere› familiare; (Am: ugly) bruttino

home-made a fatto in casa

home market n mercato m interno

Home Office n Br ministero m degli interni

homeopathic /həʊmɪəˈpæθɪk/ a omeopatico

homeopathy /həʊmɪˈɒpəθɪ/ n omeopatia f

home: Home Secretary n Br ≈ ministro m degli interni. **homesick** a be ~ avere nostalgia (**for** di). **homesickness** n nostalgia f di casa. **homestead** n fattoria f. **home town** n città f inv natia. **home truth** n **tell sb a few ~ ~s** dirne quattro a qcno. **home video** n filmato m di videoamatore

homeward /ˈhəʊmwəd/ a di ritorno ● adv ~[s] verso casa; ~ **bound** sulla strada del ritorno; **travel ~[s]** tornare a casa

homework /ˈhəʊmwɜːk/ n Sch compiti mpl

homey /ˈhəʊmɪ/ a (home-loving) casalingo; (cosy) accogliente

homicide /ˈhɒmɪsaɪd/ n (crime) omicidio m

homily /ˈhɒmɪlɪ/ n omelia f

homing /ˈhəʊmɪŋ/ a ‹missile, device› autoguidato

homing pigeon piccione f homing

homoeopathic /həʊmɪəˈpæθɪk/ a omeopatico

homoeopathy /həʊmɪˈɒpəθɪ/ n omeopatia f

homogeneous /hɒməˈdʒiːnɪəs/ a omogeneo

homogenize /həˈmɒdʒənaɪz/ vt omogeneizzare

homogenous /həˈmɒdʒənəs/ a omogeneo

homograph /ˈhɒməɡrɑːf/ n omografo m

homonym /ˈhɒmənɪm/ n omonimo m

homophobia /həʊmə'fəʊbɪə/ n omofobia f

homosexual /həʊmə'sekʃʊəl/ a & n omosessuale mf

hone /həʊn/ vt (sharpen) affilare; (perfect) affinare

honest /'ɒnɪst/ a onesto; (frank) sincero

honestly /'ɒnɪstlɪ/ adv onestamente; (frankly) sinceramente; ~! ma insomma!

honesty /'ɒnɪstɪ/ n onestà f; (frankness) sincerità f

honey /'hʌnɪ/ n miele m; (fam: darling) tesoro m

honeycomb /'hʌnɪkəʊm/ n favo m

honeydew melon /'hʌnɪdju:/ n melone m (dalla buccia gialla)

honeymoon /'hʌnɪmu:n/ n luna f di miele

honeysuckle /'hʌnɪsʌkl/ n caprifoglio m

Hong Kong /hɒŋ'kɒŋ/ n Hong Kong f

honk /hɒŋk/ vi Aut clacsonare

honky-tonk /'hɒŋkɪtɒŋk/ a (piano) honky-tonky inv

honorary /'ɒnərərɪ/ a onorario

honorific /ɒnə'rɪfɪk/ a onorifico

honour /'ɒnə(r)/ n onore m ● vt onorare

honourable /'ɒnərəbl/ a onorevole

honourably /'ɒnərəblɪ/ adv con onore

honours degree /'ɒnəz/ n ≈ diploma m di laurea

hood /hʊd/ n cappuccio m; (of pram) tettuccio m; (over cooker) cappa f; Am Auto cofano m

hoodlum /'hu:dləm/ n teppista m

hoodwink /'hʊdwɪŋk/ vt fam infinocchiare

hoof /hu:f/ n (pl ~s or **hooves**) zoccolo m

hoo-ha /'hu:hɑ:/ n fam **cause a ~** fare scalpore

hook /hʊk/ n gancio m; (for crochet) uncinetto m; (for fishing) amo m; **off the ~** Teleph staccato; fig fuori pericolo; **by ~ or by crook** in un modo o nell'altro ● vt agganciare ● vi agganciarsi

hookah /'hʊkə/ n narghilè m inv

hook and eye n gancino m

hooked /hʊkt/ a (nose) adunco; ~ **on** (fam: drugs) dedito a; **be ~ on skiing** essere un fanatico dello sci

hooker /'hʊkə(r)/ n Am sl battona f

hookey /'hʊkɪ/ n **play ~** Am fam marinare la scuola

hooligan /'hu:lɪgən/ n teppista f

hooliganism /'hu:lɪgənɪzm/ n teppismo m

hoop /hu:p/ n cerchio m

hoopla /'hu:plɑ:/ n (Br: at fair) lancio m degli anelli (nei luna park); (Am: fuss) trambusto m

hooray /hʊ'reɪ/ int & n = **hurrah**

hoot /hu:t/ n colpo m di clacson; (of siren) ululato m; (of owl) grido m; **~s of laughter** risate fpl ● vi (owl:) gridare; (car:) clacsonare; (siren:) ululare; (jeer) fischiare

hooter /'hu:tə(r)/ n (siren) sirena f; Auto clacson m inv; (Br fam: nose) nasone m

hoover® /'hu:və(r)/ n aspirapolvere m inv ● vt passare l'aspirapolvere su (carpet); pas-

sare l'aspirapolvere in (room) ● vi passare l'aspirapolvere

hop¹ /hɒp/ n luppolo m

hop² n saltello m; **catch sb on the ~** fam prendere qcno alla sprovvista ● vi (pt/pp **hopped**) saltellare; ~ **it!** fam tela!

■ **hop in** vi fam saltar su

■ **hop out** vi fam saltar giù; ~ ~ **to the shops** fare un salto ai negozi

hope /həʊp/ n speranza f; **there's no ~ of that happening** non c'è nessuna speranza che succeda ● vi sperare (for in); **I ~ so/not** spero di sì/no ● vt ~ **that** sperare che

hopeful /'həʊpfʊl/ a pieno di speranza; (promising) promettente; **be ~ that** avere buone speranze che

hopefully /'həʊpfʊlɪ/ adv con speranza; (it is hoped) se tutto va bene

hopeless /'həʊplɪs/ a senza speranze; (useless) impossibile; (incompetent) incapace

hopelessly /'həʊplɪslɪ/ adv disperatamente; (inefficient, lost) completamente

hopelessness /'həʊplɪsnɪs/ n disperazione f

hopscotch /'hɒpskɒtʃ/ n campana f (gioco)

horde /hɔ:d/ n orda f

horizon /hə'raɪzn/ n orizzonte m; **on the ~** all'orizzonte

horizontal /hɒrɪ'zɒntl/ a orizzontale

horizontal bar n sbarra f orizzontale

horizontally /hɒrɪ'zɒntəlɪ/ adv orizzontalmente

hormonal /hɔ:'məʊnəl/ a ormonale

hormone /'hɔ:məʊn/ n ormone m

hormone replacement therapy n terapia f ormonale sostitutiva

horn /hɔ:n/ n corno m; Auto clacson m inv

hornet /'hɔ:nɪt/ n calabrone m

horn-rimmed /-rɪmd/ a (spectacles) con la montatura di tartaruga

horny /'hɔ:nɪ/ a calloso; (fam: sexually) arrapato

horoscope /'hɒrəskəʊp/ n oroscopo m

horrendous /hə'rendəs/ a spaventoso

horrible /'hɒrəbl/ a orribile

horribly /'hɒrəblɪ/ adv orribilmente

horrid /'hɒrɪd/ a orrendo

horrific /hə'rɪfɪk/ a raccapricciante; (fam: accident, prices, story) terrificante

horrify /'hɒrɪfaɪ/ vt (pt/pp **-ied**) far inorridire; **I was horrified** ero inorridito

horrifying /'hɒrɪfaɪɪŋ/ a terrificante

horror /'hɒrə(r)/ n orrore m

horror film n film m inv dell'orrore

hors-d'œuvre /ɔ:'dɜ:vr/ n antipasto m

horse /hɔ:s/ n cavallo m

horse: horseback n **on ~** a cavallo. **horsebox** n furgone m per il trasporto dei cavalli. **horse chestnut** n ippocastano m. **horsefly** n tafano m. **horsehair** n crine m di cavallo. **horseman** n cavaliere m. **horse manure** n concime m. **horseplay** n gioco m pesante. **horsepower** n cavallo m [vapore]. **horse racing** n corse fpl di cavalli.

horseradish n rafano m. **horseshoe** n ferro m di cavallo

hors[e]y /'hɔ:sɪ/ a ‹person› che adora i cavalli; ‹face› cavallino

horticultural /hɔ:tɪ'kʌltʃʊrəl/ a di orticoltura

horticulture /'hɔ:tɪkʌltʃə(r)/ n orticoltura f

hose /həʊz/ n (pipe) manichetta f
■ **hose down** vt lavare con la manichetta

hosepipe /'həʊzpaɪp/ n manichetta f

hosiery /'həʊʒərɪ/ n maglieria f

hospice /'hɒspɪs/ n (for the terminally ill) ospedale m per i malati in fase terminale

hospitable /hɒ'spɪtəbl/ a ospitale

hospitably /hɒ'spɪtəblɪ/ adv con ospitalità

hospital /'hɒspɪtl/ n ospedale m

hospitality /hɒspɪ'tælətɪ/ n ospitalità f

hospitalize /'hɒspɪtəlaɪz/ vt ricoverare [in ospedale]

host¹ /həʊst/ n **a ~ of** una moltitudine di

host² n ospite m

host³ n Relig ostia f

hostage /'hɒstɪdʒ/ n ostaggio m; **hold sb ~** tenere qcno in ostaggio

hostel /'hɒstl/ n ostello m

hostess /'həʊstɪs/ n padrona f di casa; Aeron hostess f inv

hostile /'hɒstaɪl/ a ostile

hostility /hɒ'stɪlətɪ/ n ostilità f; **hostilities** pl ostilità fpl

hot /hɒt/ a (**hotter, hottest**) caldo; (spicy) piccante; **I am** or **feel ~** ho caldo; **it is ~** fa caldo; **in ~ water** fig nei guai

hot: hot-air balloon n mongolfiera f. **hotbed** n fig focolaio m. **hot-blooded** /-'blʌdɪd/ a ‹person› focoso; ‹reaction› passionale. **hot cake** n **sell like ~ ~s** andare a ruba

hotchpotch /'hɒtʃpɒtʃ/ n miscuglio m

hot: hot cross bun n panino m dolce con spezie e uvette, tipicamente pasquale. **hot dog** n hot dog m inv. **hotdogging** n sci m acrobatico

hotel /həʊ'tel/ n hotel m inv, albergo m

hotelier /həʊ'telɪə(r)/ n albergatore, -trice mf

hot: hotfoot adv hum ‹go› di gran carriera. **hothead** n persona f impetuosa. **hot-headed** /-'hedɪd/ a impetuoso. **hothouse** n serra f. **hotline** n linea f diretta; Mil, Pol telefono m rosso

hotly /'hɒtlɪ/ adv fig accanitamente

hot: hotplate n piastra f riscaldante. **hotshot** n fam persona di successo; pej carrierista mf. **hot tap** n rubinetto m dell'acqua calda. **hot-tempered** /-'tempəd/ a irascibile. **hot-water bottle** n borsa f dell'acqua calda

hound /haʊnd/ n cane da caccia m ● vt fig perseguire

hour /'aʊə(r)/ n ora f

hourglass /'aʊəglɑ:s/ n clessidra f

hourly /'aʊəlɪ/ a ad ogni ora; ‹pay, rate› a ora.
● adv ogni ora

house¹ /haʊs/ n casa f; Pol Camera f; Theat sala f; **at my ~** a casa mia, da me

house² /haʊz/ vt alloggiare ‹person›; incastrare ‹machine›

house: houseboat n casa f galleggiante. **housebreaking** n furto m con scasso. **household** n casa f, famiglia f. **householder** n capo m di famiglia. **housekeeper** n governante f di casa. **housekeeping** n governo m della casa; (money) soldi mpl per le spese di casa. **house plant** n pianta f da appartamento. **house-proud** a orgoglioso della propria casa. **house-trained** /-treɪnd/ a che non sporca in casa. **house-warming [party]** n festa f di inaugurazione della nuova casa. **housewife** n casalinga f. **housework** n lavori mpl domestici

housing /'haʊzɪŋ/ n alloggio m; Techn alloggiamento m

housing estate n zona f residenziale

hovel /'hɒvl/ n tugurio m

hover /'hɒvə(r)/ vi librarsi; (linger) indugiare; **~ on the brink of doing sth** essere sul punto di fare qcsa

hovercraft /'hɒvəkrɑ:ft/ n hovercraft m inv

how /haʊ/ adv come; **~ are you?** come stai?; **~ about a coffee/going on holiday?** che ne diresti di un caffè/di andare in vacanza?; **~ do you do?** molto lieto!; **~ old are you?** quanti anni hai?; **~ long** quanto tempo; **~ many** quanti; **~ much** quanto; **~ often** ogni quanto; **and ~!** eccome!; **~ odd!** che strano!

however /haʊ'evə(r)/ adv (nevertheless) comunque; **~ small** per quanto piccolo

howl /haʊl/ n ululato m ● vi ululare; (cry with laughter) singhiozzare

howler /'haʊlə(r)/ n fam strafalcione m

HP abbr **hire purchase**; abbr (**horse power**) C.V.

HQ n Mil abbr (**headquarters**) Q.G.

HRT n abbr (**hormone replacement therapy**) terapia f ormonale sostitutiva

hub /hʌb/ n mozzo m; fig centro m

hubbub /'hʌbʌb/ n baccano m

hubcap /'hʌbkæp/ n coprimozzo m

huckleberry /'hʌklbərɪ/ n Am mirtillo m americano

huddle /'hʌdl/ vi **~ together** rannicchiarsi l'uno contro l'altro

hue¹ /hju:/ n colore m

hue² n **~ and cry** clamore m

huff /hʌf/ n **be in a/go into a ~** fare il broncio

hug /hʌg/ n abbraccio m; **give sb a ~** abbracciare qcno ● vt (pt/pp **hugged**) abbracciare; (keep close to) tenersi vicino a; aggrapparsi a ‹wall›

huge /hju:dʒ/ a enorme

hugely /'hju:dʒlɪ/ adv enormemente

huh /hʌ/ int (inquiry) eh?; (in surprise) oh!

hulk /hʌlk/ n (of ship, tank etc) carcassa f

hulking /'hʌlkɪŋ/ a fam grosso

hull /hʌl/ n Naut scafo m

hullabaloo /hʌləbə'lu:/ n fam (noise) trambusto m; (outcry) fracasso m

hullo /həˈləʊ/ *int* = **hallo**

hum /hʌm/ *n* ronzio *m* ● *vt* (*pt/pp* **hummed**) canticchiare ● *vi* ⟨*motor:*⟩ ronzare; *fig* fervere di attività; ~ **and haw** esitare

human /ˈhjuːmən/ *a* umano ● *n* essere *m* umano

human being *n* essere *m* umano

human resources *npl* risorse *fpl* umane

humane /hjuːˈmeɪn/ *a* umano

humanely /hjuːˈmeɪnlɪ/ *adv* umanamente

humanitarian /hjuːmænɪˈteərɪən/ *a & n* umanitario, -a *mf*

humanities /hjuːˈmænɪtɪz/ *pl Univ* dottrine *fpl* umanistiche

humanity /hjuːˈmænɪtɪ/ *n* umanità *f*

humble /ˈhʌmbl/ *a* umile ● *vt* umiliare

humbly /ˈhʌmblɪ/ *adv* umilmente

humbug /ˈhʌmbʌg/ *n* (*nonsense*) sciocchezze *fpl*; (*dishonesty*) falsità *f*; (*Br: sweet*) caramella *f* alla menta

humdrum /ˈhʌmdrʌm/ *a* noioso

humid /ˈhjuːmɪd/ *a* umido

humidifier /hjuːˈmɪdɪfaɪə(r)/ *n* umidificatore *m*

humidity /hjuːˈmɪdətɪ/ *n* umidità *f*

humiliate /hjuːˈmɪlɪeɪt/ *vt* umiliare

humiliating /hjuːˈmɪlɪeɪtɪŋ/ *a* avvilente

humiliation /hjuːmɪlɪˈeɪʃn/ *n* umiliazione *f*

humility /hjuːˈmɪlətɪ/ *n* umiltà *f*

hummingbird /ˈhʌmɪŋbɜːd/ *n* colibrì *m inv*

hummock /ˈhʌmək/ *n* (*of earth*) poggio *m*

humorist /ˈhjuːmərɪst/ *n* umorista *mf*

humorous /ˈhjuːmərəs/ *a* umoristico

humorously /ˈhjuːmərəslɪ/ *adv* con spirito

humour /ˈhjuːmə(r)/ *n* umorismo *m*; (*mood*) umore *m*; **have a sense of** ~ avere il senso dell'umorismo ● *vt* compiacere

hump /hʌmp/ *n* protuberanza *f*; (*of camel, hunchback*) gobba *f*; **he's got the** ~ *sl* è di malumore

humpback[ed] bridge /ˈhʌm(p)bæk[t]/ *n* ponte *m* a schiena d'asino

humus /ˈhjuːməs/ *n* humus *m*

hunch /hʌntʃ/ *n* (*idea*) intuizione *f*

hunchback /ˈhʌntʃbæk/ *n* gobbo, -a *mf*

hunched /hʌntʃt/ *a* ~ **up** incurvato

hundred /ˈhʌndrəd/ *a* **one/a** ~ cento ● *n* cento *m inv*; ~**s of** centinaia di

hundredfold /ˈhʌndrədfəʊld/ *adv* **increase a** ~ centuplicare

hundredth /ˈhʌndrədθ/ *a & n* centesimo *m*

hundredweight /ˈhʌndrədweɪt/ *n* cinquanta chili *m*

hung /hʌŋ/ *see* **hang**

Hungarian /hʌŋˈɡeərɪən/ *n & a* ungherese *mf*; (*language*) ungherese *m*

Hungary /ˈhʌŋɡərɪ/ *n* Ungheria *f*

hunger /ˈhʌŋɡə(r)/ *n* fame *f*

■ **hunger for** *vt* aver fame di

hunger strike *n* sciopero *m* della fame

hung-over *a* **be** ~ avere i postumi della sbornia

hungrily /ˈhʌŋɡrɪlɪ/ *adv* con appetito

hungry /ˈhʌŋɡrɪ/ *a* (**-ier, -iest**) affamato; **be** ~ aver fame

hung-up *a fam* (*tense*) complessato; **be** ~ **on sb/sth** (*obsessed*) essere fissato per qcsa

hunk /hʌŋk/ *n* grosso pezzo *m*; (*fam: man*) figo *m*

hunky-dory /hʌŋkɪˈdɔːrɪ/ *a fam* perfetto

hunt /hʌnt/ *n* caccia *f* ● *vt* andare a caccia di ⟨*animal*⟩; dare la caccia a ⟨*criminal*⟩ ● *vi* andare a caccia; ~ **for** cercare

hunter /ˈhʌntə(r)/ *n* cacciatore *m*

hunting /ˈhʌntɪŋ/ *n* caccia *f*

hunt saboteur *n Br* sabotatore, -trice *mf* della caccia

huntsman /ˈhʌntsmən/ *n* (*hunter*) cacciatore *m*; (*fox-hunter*) cacciatore *m* di volpe

hurdle /ˈhɜːdl/ *n Sport & fig* ostacolo *m*

hurdler /ˈhɜːdlə(r)/ *n* ostacolista *mf*

hurdy-gurdy /hɜːdɪˈɡɜːdɪ/ *n* organino *m*

hurl /hɜːl/ *vt* scagliare

hurly-burly /hɜːlɪˈbɜːlɪ/ *n* chiasso *m*

hurrah /hʊˈrɑː/, **hurray** /hʊˈreɪ/ *int* urrà! ● *n* urrà *m*

hurricane /ˈhʌrɪkən/ *n* uragano *m*

hurried /ˈhʌrɪd/ *a* affrettato; ⟨*job*⟩ fatto in fretta

hurriedly /ˈhʌrɪdlɪ/ *adv* in fretta

hurry /ˈhʌrɪ/ *n* fretta *f*; **be in a** ~ aver fretta ● *vi* (*pt/pp* **-ied**) affrettarsi

■ **hurry up** *vi* sbrigarsi ● *vt* mettere fretta a ⟨*person*⟩; accelerare ⟨*things*⟩

hurt /hɜːt/ *n* male *m* ● *v* (*pt/pp* **hurt**) ● *vt* far male a; (*offend*) ferire ● *vi* far male; **my leg** ~**s** mi fa male la gamba

hurtful /ˈhɜːtfʊl/ *a fig* offensivo

hurtle /ˈhɜːtl/ *vi* ~ **along** andare a tutta velocità

husband /ˈhʌzbənd/ *n* marito *m*

hush /hʌʃ/ *n* silenzio *m*

■ **hush up** *vt* mettere a tacere

hushed /hʌʃt/ *a* ⟨*voice*⟩ sommesso

hush-hush *a fam* segretissimo

husky /ˈhʌskɪ/ *a* (**-ier, -iest**) ⟨*voice*⟩ rauco

hussar /hʊˈzɑː(r)/ *n* ussaro *m*

hustings /ˈhʌstɪŋz/ *n* **on the** ~ in campagna elettorale

hustle /ˈhʌsl/ *vt* affrettare ● *n* attività *f* incessante; ~ **and bustle** trambusto *m*

hut /hʌt/ *n* capanna *f*

hutch /hʌtʃ/ *n* conigliera *f*

hyacinth /ˈhaɪəsɪnθ/ *n* giacinto *m*

hybrid /ˈhaɪbrɪd/ *a* ibrido ● *n* ibrido *m*

hydrangea /haɪˈdreɪndʒə/ *n* ortensia *f*

hydrant /ˈhaɪdrənt/ *n* [**fire**] ~ idrante *m*

hydraulic /haɪˈdrɔːlɪk/ *a* idraulico

hydrocarbon /haɪdrəʊˈkɑːbən/ *n* idrocarburo *m*

hydrochloric /haɪdrəˈklɒrɪk/ *a* ~ **acid** acido *m* cloridrico

hydroelectric /haɪdrəʊɪˈlektrɪk/ *a* idroelettrico

hydroelectric power station *n* centrale *f* idroelettrica

hydrofoil /ˈhaɪdrəfɔɪl/ *n* aliscafo *m*

hydrogen /ˈhaɪdrədʒən/ *n* idrogeno *m*

hydrolysis /haɪˈdrɒləsɪs/ *n* idrolisi *f*

hydrophobia /haɪdrəˈfəʊbɪə/ *n* idrofobia *f*

hydroplane /'haɪdrəpleɪn/ n (boat) aliscafo m; (Am: seaplane) idrovolante m
hydrotherapy /haɪdrəʊ'θerəpɪ/ n idroterapia f
hyena /haɪ'iːnə/ n iena f
hygiene /'haɪdʒiːn/ n igiene m
hygienic /haɪ'dʒiːnɪk/ a igienico
hygienically /haɪ'dʒiːnɪklɪ/ adv igienicamente
hymn /hɪm/ n inno m
hymn book n libro m dei canti
hype /haɪp/ n fam grande pubblicità f; **media** ~ battage m pubblicitario
■ **hype up** vt fam fare grande pubblicità a ⟨film, star, book⟩; (exaggerate) gonfiare
hyper /'haɪpə(r)/ a fam eccitato
hyperactive /haɪpər'æktɪv/ a iperattivo
hyperactivity /haɪpəræk'tɪvɪtɪ/ n iperattività f
hyperbole /haɪ'pɜːbəlɪ/ n iperbole f
hypercritical /haɪpə'krɪtɪkl/ a ipercritico
hypermarket /'haɪpəmɑːkɪt/ n ipermercato m
hypersensitive /haɪpə'sensɪtɪv/ a pej permaloso; (physically) ipersensibile
hypertension /haɪpə'tenʃn/ n ipertensione f
hypertext /'haɪpətekst/ n Comput ipertesto m
hyperventilate /haɪpə'ventɪleɪt/ vi iperventilare
hyphen /'haɪfn/ n trattino m
hyphenate /'haɪfəneɪt/ vt unire con trattino
hypnosis /hɪp'nəʊsɪs/ n ipnosi f

hypnotherapy /hɪpnəʊ'θerəpɪ/ n ipnoterapia f
hypnotic /hɪp'nɒtɪk/ a ipnotico
hypnotism /'hɪpnətɪzm/ n ipnotismo m
hypnotist /'hɪpnətɪst/ n ipnotizzatore, -trice mf
hypnotize /'hɪpnətaɪz/ vt ipnotizzare
hypoallergenic /haɪpəʊælə'dʒenɪk/ a anallergico
hypochondria /haɪpə'kɒndrɪə/ n ipocondria f
hypochondriac /haɪpə'kɒndrɪæk/ a & n ipocondriaco, -a mf
hypocrisy /hɪ'pɒkrəsɪ/ n ipocrisia f
hypocrite /'hɪpəkrɪt/ n ipocrita mf
hypocritical /hɪpə'krɪtɪkl/ a ipocrita
hypocritically /hɪpə'krɪtɪklɪ/ adv ipocriticamente
hypodermic /haɪpə'dɜːmɪk/ a & n ~ [syringe] siringa f ipodermica
hypotenuse /haɪ'pɒtənjuːz/ n ipotenusa f
hypothermia /haɪpəʊ'θɜːmɪə/ n ipotermia f
hypothesis /haɪ'pɒθəsɪs/ n ipotesi f inv
hypothetical /haɪpə'θetɪkl/ a ipotetico
hypothetically /haɪpə'θetɪklɪ/ adv in teoria; ⟨speak⟩ per ipotesi
hysterectomy /hɪstə'rektəmɪ/ n isterectomia f
hysteria /hɪ'stɪərɪə/ n isterismo m
hysterical /hɪ'sterɪkl/ a isterico
hysterically /hɪ'sterɪklɪ/ adv istericamente; ~ **funny** da morir dal ridere
hysterics /hɪ'sterɪks/ npl attacco m isterico

i, I /aɪ/ n (letter)i, I f inv
I /aɪ/ pron io; **I'm tired** sono stanco; **he's going, but I'm not** lui va, ma io no
ibex /'aɪbeks/ n stambecco m
ice /aɪs/ n ghiaccio m ● vt glassare ⟨cake⟩
■ **ice over, ice up** vi ghiacciarsi
ice: **ice age** n era f glaciale. **ice axe** n piccozza f per il ghiaccio. **iceberg** n iceberg m inv. **icebox** n Am frigorifero m. **ice-breaker** n Naut rompighiaccio m inv. **ice bucket** n secchiello m del ghiaccio. **ice cap** n calotta f glaciale. **ice-cold** a ghiacciato. **ice cream** n gelato m. **ice-cream parlour** n gelateria f. **ice-cream sundae** n coppa f [di] gelato guarnita. **ice cube** n cubetto m di ghiaccio. **ice dancer** n ballerino, -a mf sul ghiaccio. **ice floe** n banco m di ghiaccio. **ice hockey** hockey m su ghiaccio
Iceland /'aɪslənd/ n Islanda f
Icelander /'aɪsləndə(r)/ n islandese mf
Icelandic /aɪs'lændɪk/ a & n islandese m

ice: **ice lolly** n ghiacciolo m. **ice pack** n impacco m di ghiaccio. **ice pick** n piccone m da ghiaccio. **ice rink** n pista f di pattinaggio. **ice-skate** n pattino m da ghiaccio. **ice-skater** pattinatore, -trice mf sul ghiaccio. **ice-skating** pattinaggio m sul ghiaccio. **ice-tray** n vaschetta f per il ghiaccio
icicle /'aɪsɪkl/ n ghiacciolo m
icily /'aɪsɪlɪ/ adv gelidamente
icing /'aɪsɪŋ/ n glassa f
icing sugar n zucchero m a velo
icon /'aɪkɒn/ n icona f
icy /'aɪsɪ/ a (-ier, -iest) ghiacciato; fig gelido
id /ɪd/ n the ~ l'Es m
ID n abbr (identification, identity) documento m d'identità; **ID card** n carta f d'identità
idea /aɪ'dɪə/ n idea f; **I've no** ~! non ne ho idea!
ideal /aɪ'dɪəl/ a ideale ● n ideale m
idealism /aɪ'dɪəlɪzm/ n idealismo m

idealist /aɪˈdɪəlɪst/ n idealista mf
idealistic /aɪdɪəˈlɪstɪk/ a idealistico
idealize /aɪˈdɪəlaɪz/ vt idealizzare
ideally /aɪˈdɪəlɪ/ adv idealmente
identical /aɪˈdentɪkl/ a identico
identifiable /aɪdentɪˈfaɪəbl/ a identificabile
identification /aɪdentɪfɪˈkeɪʃn/ n identificazione f; (proof of identity) documento m di riconoscimento
identify /aɪˈdentɪfaɪ/ vt (pt/pp -ied) identificare ● vi ~ with identificarsi con
identikit® /aɪˈdentɪkɪt/ n identikit m inv
identikit® picture n identikit m inv
identity /aɪˈdentətɪ/ n identità f inv
identity card n carta f d'identità
identity parade n confronto m all'americana
ideological /aɪdɪəˈlɒdʒɪkl/ a ideologico
ideology /aɪdɪˈɒlədʒɪ/ n ideologia f
idiocy /ˈɪdɪəsɪ/ n idiozia f
idiom /ˈɪdɪəm/ n idioma f
idiomatic /ɪdɪəˈmætɪk/ a idiomatico
idiomatically /ɪdɪəˈmætɪklɪ/ adv in modo idiomatico
idiosyncrasy /ɪdɪəˈsɪŋkrəsɪ/ n idiosincrasia f
idiot /ˈɪdɪət/ n idiota mf
idiotic /ɪdɪˈɒtɪk/ a idiota
idle /ˈaɪd(ə)l/ a (lazy) pigro, ozioso; (empty) vano; (machine) fermo ● vi oziare; (engine:) girare a vuoto
idleness /ˈaɪd(ə)lnɪs/ n ozio m
idly /ˈaɪdlɪ/ adv oziosamente
idol /ˈaɪd(ə)l/ n idolo m
idolize /ˈaɪdəlaɪz/ vt idolatrare
idyll /ˈɪdɪl/ n idillio m
idyllic /ɪˈdɪlɪk/ a idillico
i.e. abbr (id est) cioè
if /ɪf/ conj se; **as if** come se
iffy /ˈɪfɪ/ a incerto
igloo /ˈɪɡluː/ n igloo m inv
ignite /ɪɡˈnaɪt/ vt dar fuoco a ● vi prender fuoco
ignition /ɪɡˈnɪʃn/ n Auto accensione f
ignition key n chiave f d'accensione
ignoramus /ɪɡnəˈreɪməs/ n ignorante mf
ignorance /ˈɪɡnərəns/ n ignoranza f
ignorant /ˈɪɡnərənt/ a (lacking knowledge) ignaro; (rude) ignorante
ignore /ɪɡˈnɔː(r)/ vt ignorare
ill /ɪl/ a ammalato; **feel ~ at ease** sentirsi a disagio ● adv male ● n male m
ill: **ill-advised** /-ədˈvaɪzd/ a avventato. **ill-bred** /-ˈbred/ a maleducato. **ill-considered** /-kənˈsɪdəd/ a (measure, remark) avventato. **ill effect** n effetto m negativo
illegal /ɪˈliːɡl/ a illegale
illegality /ɪlɪˈɡælətɪ/ n illegalità f
illegally /ɪˈliːɡəlɪ/ adv illegalmente
illegible /ɪˈledʒəbl/ a illeggibile
illegibly /ɪˈledʒəblɪ/ adv in modo illeggibile
illegitimacy /ɪlɪˈdʒɪtɪməsɪ/ n illegittimità f
illegitimate /ɪlɪˈdʒɪtɪmət/ a illegittimo
ill: **ill-equipped** /-ɪˈkwɪpt/ a non equipaggiato. **ill-fated** /-ˈfeɪtɪd/ a sfortunato. **ill feeling**

n rancore m. **ill-fitting** a (garment, shoe) che non va bene. **ill-founded** /-ˈfaʊndɪd/ a (argument, gossip) infondato. **ill-gotten gains** /ɪlɡɒ(t)nˈɡeɪnz/ a guadagni mpl illeciti. **ill health** n problemi mpl di salute
illicit /ɪˈlɪsɪt/ a illecito
illicitly /ɪˈlɪsɪtlɪ/ adv illecitamente
ill-informed /-ɪnˈfɔːmd/ a (person) male informato
illiteracy /ɪˈlɪtərəsɪ/ n analfabetismo m
illiterate /ɪˈlɪtərət/ a & n analfabeta mf
ill-mannered /-ˈmænəd/ a maleducato
illness /ˈɪlnɪs/ n malattia f
illogical /ɪˈlɒdʒɪkl/ a illogico
illogically /ɪˈlɒdʒɪklɪ/ adv illogicamente
ill: **ill-prepared** /-prɪˈpeəd/ a impreparato. **ill-timed** /-ˈtaɪmd/ a (arrival) inopportuno; (campaign) fatto al momento sbagliato. **ill-treat** vt maltrattare. **ill-treatment** n maltrattamento m
illuminate /ɪˈluːmɪneɪt/ vt illuminare
illuminating /ɪˈluːmɪneɪtɪŋ/ a chiarificatore
illumination /ɪluːmɪˈneɪʃn/ n illuminazione f
illusion /ɪˈluːʒn/ n illusione f; **be under the ~ that** avere l'illusione che
illusory /ɪˈluːsərɪ/ a illusorio
illustrate /ˈɪləstreɪt/ vt illustrare
illustration /ɪləˈstreɪʃn/ n illustrazione f
illustrative /ˈɪləstrətɪv/ a illustrativo
illustrator /ˈɪləstreɪtə(r)/ n illustratore, -trice mf
illustrious /ɪˈlʌstrɪəs/ a illustre
ill will n malanimo m
image /ˈɪmɪdʒ/ n immagine f; (exact likeness) ritratto m
image-conscious a attento all'immagine
imagery /ˈɪmɪdʒərɪ/ n immagini fpl
imaginable /ɪˈmædʒɪnəbl/ a immaginabile
imaginary /ɪˈmædʒɪnərɪ/ a immaginario
imagination /ɪmædʒɪˈneɪʃn/ n immaginazione f, fantasia f; **it's your ~** è solo una tua idea
imaginative /ɪˈmædʒɪnətɪv/ a fantasioso
imaginatively /ɪˈmædʒɪnətɪvlɪ/ adv con fantasia or immaginazione
imagine /ɪˈmædʒɪn/ vt immaginare; (wrongly) inventare
imbalance /ɪmˈbæləns/ n squilibrio m
imbecile /ˈɪmbəsiːl/ n imbecille mf
imbibe /ɪmˈbaɪb/ vt ingerire; fig assorbire ● vi hum bere
imbue /ɪmˈbjuː/ vt ~d with impregnato di
imitate /ˈɪmɪteɪt/ vt imitare
imitation /ɪmɪˈteɪʃn/ n imitazione f
imitative /ˈɪmɪtətɪv/ a imitativo
imitator /ˈɪmɪteɪtə(r)/ n imitatore, -trice mf
immaculate /ɪˈmækjʊlət/ a immacolato
immaculately /ɪˈmækjʊlətlɪ/ adv immacolatamente
immaterial /ɪməˈtɪərɪəl/ a (unimportant) irrilevante
immature /ɪməˈtʃʊə(r)/ a immaturo
immeasurable /ɪˈmeʒərəbl/ a incommensurabile

immediacy /ɪˈmiːdɪəsɪ/ n immediatezza f

immediate /ɪˈmiːdɪət/ a immediato; ⟨relative⟩ stretto; **in the ~ vicinity** nelle immediate vicinanze

immediately /ɪˈmiːdɪətlɪ/ adv immediatamente; **~ next to** subito accanto a ● conj [non] appena

immemorial /ɪmɪˈmɔːrɪəl/ a **from time ~** da tempo immemorabile

immense /ɪˈmens/ a immenso

immensely /ɪˈmenslɪ/ adv immensamente

immensity /ɪˈmensətɪ/ n immensità f

immerse /ɪˈmɜːs/ vt immergere; **be ~d in** fig essere immerso in

immersion /ɪˈmɜːʃn/ n immersione f

immersion heater n scaldabagno m inv elettrico

immigrant /ˈɪmɪgrənt/ n immigrante mf

immigrate /ˈɪmɪgreɪt/ vi immigrare

immigration /ɪmɪˈgreɪʃn/ n immigrazione f

imminence /ˈɪmɪnəns/ n imminenza f

imminent /ˈɪmɪnənt/ a imminente

immobile /ɪˈməʊbaɪl/ a immobile

immobilize /ɪˈməʊbɪlaɪz/ vt immobilizzare

immoderate /ɪˈmɒdərət/ a smodato

immodest /ɪˈmɒdɪst/ a immodesto

immoral /ɪˈmɒrəl/ a immorale

immorality /ɪməˈrælətɪ/ n immoralità f

immortal /ɪˈmɔːtl/ a immortale

immortality /ɪmɔːˈtælətɪ/ n immortalità f

immortalize /ɪˈmɔːtəlaɪz/ vt immortalare

immovable /ɪˈmuːvəbl/ a fig irremovibile

immune /ɪˈmjuːn/ a immune (**to/from** da)

immune system n sistema m immunitario

immunity /ɪˈmjuːnətɪ/ n immunità f

immunization /ɪmjʊnaɪˈzeɪʃn/ n immunizzazione f

immunize /ˈɪmjʊnaɪz/ vt immunizzare

immunodeficiency /ɪmjʊnəʊdɪˈfɪʃənsɪ/ n immunodeficienza f

immunology /ɪmjʊˈnɒlədʒɪ/ n immunologia f

immutable /ɪˈmjuːtəbl/ a immutabile

imp /ɪmp/ n diavoletto m

impact /ˈɪmpækt/ n impatto m

impacted /ɪmˈpæktɪd/ a ⟨tooth⟩ incluso; ⟨fracture⟩ incuneato

impair /ɪmˈpeə(r)/ vt danneggiare

impale /ɪmˈpeɪl/ vt impalare

impalpable /ɪmˈpælpəbl/ a (intangible) impalpabile

impart /ɪmˈpɑːt/ vt impartire

impartial /ɪmˈpɑːʃl/ a imparziale

impartiality /ɪmpɑːʃɪˈælətɪ/ n imparzialità f

impassable /ɪmˈpɑːsəbl/ a impraticabile

impasse /æmˈpɑːs/ n fig impasse f inv

impassioned /ɪmˈpæʃnd/ a appassionato

impassive /ɪmˈpæsɪv/ a impassibile

impassively /ɪmˈpæsɪvlɪ/ adv impassibilmente

impatience /ɪmˈpeɪʃns/ n impazienza f

impatient /ɪmˈpeɪʃnt/ a impaziente

impatiently /ɪmˈpeɪʃntlɪ/ adv impazientemente

impeach /ɪmˈpiːtʃ/ vt accusare

impeccable /ɪmˈpekəbl/ a impeccabile

impeccably /ɪmˈpekəblɪ/ adv in modo impeccabile

impede /ɪmˈpiːd/ vt impedire

impediment /ɪmˈpedɪmənt/ n impedimento m; (in speech) difetto m

impel /ɪmˈpel/ vt (pt/pp **impelled**) costringere; **~led to** sentire l'obbligo di

impending /ɪmˈpendɪŋ/ a imminente

impenetrable /ɪmˈpenɪtrəbl/ a impenetrabile

imperative /ɪmˈperətɪv/ a imperativo; ● n Gram imperativo m

imperceptible /ɪmpəˈseptəbl/ a impercettibile

imperfect /ɪmˈpɜːfɪkt/ a imperfetto; (faulty) difettoso ● n Gram imperfetto m

imperfection /ɪmpəˈfekʃn/ n imperfezione f

imperial /ɪmˈpɪərɪəl/ a imperiale

imperialism /ɪmˈpɪərɪəlɪzm/ n imperialismo m

imperialist /ɪmˈpɪərɪəlɪst/ n imperialista mf

imperil /ɪmˈperəl/ vt (pt/pp **imperilled**) mettere in pericolo

imperious /ɪmˈpɪərɪəs/ a imperioso

imperiously /ɪmˈpɪərɪəslɪ/ adv di modo imperioso

impermeable /ɪmˈpɜːmɪəbl/ a impermeabile

impersonal /ɪmˈpɜːsənəl/ a impersonale

impersonate /ɪmˈpɜːsəneɪt/ vt impersonare

impersonation /ɪmpɜːsəˈneɪʃn/ n imitazione f

impersonator /ɪmˈpɜːsəneɪtə(r)/ n imitatore, -trice mf

impertinence /ɪmˈpɜːtɪnəns/ n impertinenza f

impertinent /ɪmˈpɜːtɪnənt/ a impertinente

imperturbable /ɪmpəˈtɜːbəbl/ a imperturbabile

impervious /ɪmˈpɜːvɪəs/ a **~ to** fig indifferente a

impetuous /ɪmˈpetjʊəs/ a impetuoso

impetuously /ɪmˈpetjʊəslɪ/ adv impetuosamente

impetus /ˈɪmpɪtəs/ n impeto m

impiety /ɪmˈpaɪətɪ/ n Relig empietà f

■ **impinge on** /ɪmˈpɪndʒ/ vt (affect) influire su; (restrict) condizionare

impious /ˈɪmpɪəs/ a Relig empio

impish /ˈɪmpɪʃ/ a birichino

implacable /ɪmˈplækəbl/ a implacabile

implant¹ /ɪmˈplɑːnt/ vt trapiantare; fig inculcare

implant² /ˈɪmplɑːnt/ n trapianto m

implausible /ɪmˈplɔːzəbl/ a poco plausibile

implement¹ /ˈɪmplɪmənt/ n attrezzo m

implement² /ˈɪmplɪmənt/ vt mettere in atto

implicate /ˈɪmplɪkeɪt/ vt implicare

implication /ɪmplɪˈkeɪʃn/ n implicazione f; **by ~** implicitamente

implicit /ɪmˈplɪsɪt/ a implicito; (absolute) assoluto

implicitly /ɪmˈplɪsɪtlɪ/ *adv* implicitamente; (*absolutely*) completamente

implied /ɪmˈplaɪd/ *a* implicito, sottinteso

implore /ɪmˈplɔː(r)/ *vt* implorare

imploring /ɪmˈplɔːrɪŋ/ *a* implorante

implosion /ɪmˈpləʊʒn/ *n* implosione *f*

imply /ɪmˈplaɪ/ *vt* (*pt/pp* **-ied**) implicare; **what are you ~ing?** che cosa vorresti insinuare?

impolite /ɪmpəˈlaɪt/ *a* sgarbato

impolitely /ɪmpəˈlaɪtlɪ/ *adv* sgarbatamente

import[1] /ˈɪmpɔːt/ *n Comm* importazione *f*; (*importance*) importanza *f*; (*meaning*) rilevanza *f*

import[2] /ɪmˈpɔːt/ *vt* importare

importance /ɪmˈpɔːtəns/ *n* importanza *f*

important /ɪmˈpɔːtənt/ *a* importante

importation /ɪmpɔːˈteɪʃn/ *n Comm* importazione *f*

import duty /ˈɪmpɔːt/ *n* dazio *m* d'importazione

importer /ɪmˈpɔːtə(r)/ *n* importatore, -trice *mf*

import-export /ˈɪmpɔːtˈekspɔːt/ *n* import-export *m*

importing country /ɪmˈpɔːtɪŋ/ *n* paese *m* di importazione

impose /ɪmˈpəʊz/ *vt* imporre (**on** a) ● *vi* imporsi; **~ on** abusare di

imposing /ɪmˈpəʊzɪŋ/ *a* imponente

imposition /ɪmpəˈzɪʃn/ *n* imposizione *f*

impossibility /ɪmˈpɒsɪbɪlətɪ/ *n* impossibilità *f*

impossible /ɪmˈpɒsəbl/ *a* impossibile

impossibly /ɪmˈpɒsəblɪ/ *adv* impossibilmente

impostor /ɪmˈpɒstə(r)/ *n* impostore, -trice *mf*

impotence /ˈɪmpətəns/ *n* impotenza *f*

impotent /ˈɪmpətənt/ *a* impotente

impound /ɪmˈpaʊnd/ *vt* confiscare

impoverished /ɪmˈpɒvərɪʃt/ *a* impoverito

impracticable /ɪmˈpræktɪkəbl/ *a* impraticabile

impractical /ɪmˈpræktɪkl/ *a* non pratico

imprecise /ɪmprɪˈsaɪs/ *a* impreciso

impregnable /ɪmˈpregnəbl/ *a* imprendibile

impregnate /ˈɪmpregneɪt/ *vt* impregnare (**with** di); *Biol* fecondare

impresario /ɪmprɪˈsɑːrɪəʊ/ *n* (*pl* **-os**) impresario *m* (*di spettacoli*)

impress /ɪmˈpres/ *vt* imprimere; *fig* colpire (*positivamente*); **~ sth [up]on sb** fare capire qcsa a qcno

impression /ɪmˈpreʃn/ *n* impressione *f*; (*imitation*) imitazione *f*

impressionable /ɪmˈpreʃənəbl/ *a* (*child, mind*) influenzabile

impressionism /ɪmˈpreʃənɪzm/ *n* impressionismo *m*

impressionist /ɪmˈpreʃənɪst/ *n* imitatore, -trice *mf*; (*artist*) impressionista *mf*

impressionistic /ɪmpreʃəˈnɪstɪk/ *a* impressionista; (*account*) approssimativo

impressive /ɪmˈpresɪv/ *a* imponente

imprint[1] /ˈɪmprɪnt/ *n* impressione *f*

imprint[2] /ɪmˈprɪnt/ *vt* imprimere; **~ed on my mind** impresso nella mia memoria

imprison /ɪmˈprɪzən/ *vt* incarcerare

imprisonment /ɪmˈprɪzənmənt/ *n* reclusione *f*

improbable /ɪmˈprɒbəbl/ *a* improbabile

impromptu /ɪmˈprɒmptjuː/ *a* improvvisato ● *adv* in modo improvvisato

improper /ɪmˈprɒpə(r)/ *a* (*use*) improprio; (*behaviour*) scorretto

improperly /ɪmˈprɒpəlɪ/ *adv* scorrettamente

impropriety /ɪmprəˈpraɪətɪ/ *n* scorrettezza *f*

improve /ɪmˈpruːv/ *vt/i* migliorare

■ **improve [up]on** *vt* perfezionare

improvement /ɪmˈpruːvmənt/ *n* miglioramento *m*

improvident /ɪmˈprɒvɪdənt/ *a* (*heedless of the future*) imprevidente

improvisation /ɪmprəvaɪˈzeɪʃn/ *n* improvvisazione *f*

improvise /ˈɪmprəvaɪz/ *vt/i* improvvisare

imprudent /ɪmˈpruːdənt/ *a* imprudente

impudence /ˈɪmpjʊdəns/ *n* sfrontatezza *f*

impudent /ˈɪmpjʊdənt/ *a* sfrontato

impudently /ˈɪmpjʊdəntlɪ/ *adv* sfrontatamente

impulse /ˈɪmpʌls/ *n* impulso *m*; **on [an] ~** impulsivamente

impulse buying *n* acquisti *mpl* fatti d'impulso

impulsive /ɪmˈpʌlsɪv/ *a* impulsivo

impulsively /ɪmˈpʌlsɪvlɪ/ *adv* impulsivamente

impunity /ɪmˈpjuːnətɪ/ *n* **with ~** impunemente

impure /ɪmˈpjʊə(r)/ *a* impuro

impurity /ɪmˈpjʊərətɪ/ *n* impurità *f inv*; **impurities** *pl* impurità *fpl*

impute /ɪmˈpjuːt/ *vt* imputare (**to** a)

in /ɪn/ *prep* in; (*with names of towns*) a; **in the garden** in giardino; **in the street** in or per strada; **in bed/hospital** a letto/all'ospedale; **in the world** nel mondo; **in the rain** sotto la pioggia; **in the sun** al sole; **in this heat** con questo caldo; **in summer/winter** in estate/inverno; **in 1995** nel 1995; **in the evening** la sera; **he's arriving in two hours' time** arriva fra due ore; **deaf in one ear** sordo da un orecchio; **in the army** nell'esercito; **in English/Italian** in inglese/italiano; **in ink/pencil** a penna/matita; **in red** (*dressed, circled*) di rosso; **the man in the raincoat** l'uomo con l'impermeabile; **in a soft/loud voice** a voce bassa/alta; **one in ten people** una persona su dieci; **in doing this, he...** nel far questo,...; **in itself** in sé; **in that** in quanto ● *adv* (*at home*) a casa; (*indoors*) dentro; **he's not in yet** non è ancora arrivato; **in there/here** lì/qui dentro; **ten in all** dieci in tutto; **day in, day out** giorno dopo giorno; **have it in for sb** *fam* avercela con qcno; **send him in** fallo entrare; **come in** entrare; **bring in the washing** portare dentro i panni ● *a* (*fam: in* *fashion*) di moda ● *n* **the ins and outs** i dettagli

inability /mə'bɪlətɪ/ *n* incapacità *f*

inaccessible /mæk'sesəbl/ *a* inaccessibile

inaccuracy /m'ækjʊrəsɪ/ *n* inesattezza *f*

inaccurate /m'ækjʊrət/ *a* inesatto

inaccurately /m'ækjʊrətlɪ/ *adv* in modo inesatto

inaction /m'ækʃn/ *n* (*not being active*) inazione *f*; (*failure to act*) inerzia *f*

inactive /m'æktɪv/ *a* inattivo

inactivity /mæk'tɪvətɪ/ *n* inattività *f*

inadequacy /m'ædɪkwəsɪ/ *n* inadeguatezza *f*

inadequate /m'ædɪkwət/ *a* inadeguato

inadequately /m'ædɪkwətlɪ/ *adv* inadeguatamente

inadmissible /mæd'mɪsəbl/ *a* inammissibile

inadvertent /məd'vɜːtənt/ *a* involontario

inadvertently /məd'vɜːtəntlɪ/ *adv* inavvertitamente

inadvisable /mæd'vaɪzəbl/ *a* sconsigliabile

inalienable /m'eɪliənəbl/ *a* inalienabile

inane /ɪ'neɪn/ *a* futile

inanely /ɪ'neɪnlɪ/ *adv* in modo vacuo

inanimate /m'ænɪmət/ *a* esanime

inanity /ɪ'nænətɪ/ *n* stupidità *f inv*

inapplicable /mə'plɪkəbl/ *a* inapplicabile

inappropriate /mə'prəʊprɪət/ *a* inadatto

inapt /m'æpt/ *a* (*inappropriate*) inappropriato

inarticulate /mɑːtɪkjʊlət/ *a* inarticolato

inasmuch /məz'mʌtʃ/ *conj* ~ **as** (*insofar as*) in quanto; (*seeing that*) poiché

inattention /mə'tenʃn/ *n* disattenzione *f*

inattentive /mə'tentɪv/ *a* disattento

inaudible /m'ɔːdəbl/ *a* impercettibile

inaudibly /m'ɔːdəblɪ/ *adv* in modo impercettibile

inaugural /ɪ'nɔːgjʊrəl/ *a* inaugurale

inaugurate /ɪ'nɔːgjʊreɪt/ *vt* inaugurare

inauguration /mɔːgjʊ'reɪʃn/ *n* inaugurazione *f*

inauspicious /mɔː'spɪʃəs/ *a* infausto

in-between *a* intermedio

inborn /'mbɔːn/ *a* innato

inbred /m'bred/ *a* congenito

inbreeding /m'briːdɪŋ/ *n* (*in animals*) inbreeding *m*; (*in humans*) unioni *mpl* fra consanguinei

inbuilt /m'bɪlt/ *a* (*feeling*) innato

incalculable /m'kælkjʊləbl/ *a* incalcolabile

incandescence /mkæn'desəns/ *n liter* incandescenza *f*

incandescent /mkæn'desənt/ *a liter* incandescente

incapable /m'keɪpəbl/ *a* incapace

incapacitate /mkə'pæsɪteɪt/ *vt* rendere incapace

incapacity /mkə'pæsətɪ/ *n also Jur* incapacità *f*

incarcerate /m'kɑːsəreɪt/ *vt* incarcerare

incarnate /m'kɑːnət/ *a* **the devil** ~ il diavolo in carne e ossa

incarnation /mkɑː'neɪʃn/ *n* incarnazione *f*

incendiary /m'sendɪərɪ/ *a* incendiario ● *n* ~ [**bomb**] bomba *f* incendiaria

incendiary device *n* ordigno *m* incendiario

incense¹ /'msens/ *n* incenso *m*

incense² /m'sens/ *vt* esasperare

incentive /m'sentɪv/ *n* incentivo *m*

inception /m'sepʃn/ *n* inizio *m*

incessant /m'sesənt/ *a* incessante

incessantly /m'sesəntlɪ/ *adv* incessantemente

incest /'msest/ *n* incesto *m*

incestuous /m'sestjʊəs/ *a* incestuoso

inch /mtʃ/ *n* pollice *m* (= *2.54 cm*) ● *vi* ~ **forward** avanzare gradatamente

incidence /'msɪdəns/ *n* incidenza *f*

incident /'msɪdənt/ *n* incidente *m*

incidental /msɪ'dentl/ *a* incidentale; ~ **expenses** spese *fpl* accessorie

incidentally /msɪ'dent(ə)lɪ/ *adv* incidentalmente; (*by the way*) a proposito

incident room *n* (*for criminal investigation*) centrale *f* operativa

incinerate /m'sməreɪt/ *vt* incenerire

incinerator /m'sməreɪtə(r)/ *n* inceneritore *m*

incipient /m'sɪpɪənt/ *a* incipiente

incision /m'sɪʒn/ *n* incisione *f*

incisive /m'saɪsɪv/ *a* incisivo

incisor /m'saɪzə(r)/ *n* incisivo *m*

incite /m'saɪt/ *vt* incitare

incitement /m'saɪtmənt/ *n* incitamento *m*

incivility /msɪ'vɪlətɪ/ *n* scortesia *f*

incl *abbr* **inclusive**; *abbr* **including**

inclement /m'klemənt/ *a* inclemente

inclination /mklɪ'neɪʃn/ *n* inclinazione *f*

incline¹ /m'klaɪn/ *vt* inclinare; **be ~d to do sth** essere propenso a fare qcsa ● *vi* inclinarsi

incline² /'mklaɪn/ *n* pendio *m*

include /m'kluːd/ *vt* includere

including /m'kluːdɪŋ/ *prep* incluso

inclusion /m'kluːʒn/ *n* inclusione *f*

inclusive /m'kluːsɪv/ *a* incluso; ~ **of** comprendente; **be ~ of** comprendere. ● *adv* incluso

incognito /mkɒg'niːtəʊ/ *adv* incognito

incoherent /mkə'hɪərənt/ *a* incoerente; (*because drunk etc*) incomprensibile

incoherently /mkə'hɪərəntlɪ/ *adv* incoerentemente; (*because drunk etc*) incomprensibilmente

income /'mkəm/ *n* reddito *m*

income bracket *n* fascia *f* di reddito

income tax *n* imposta *f* sul reddito

income tax return *n* dichiarazione *f* dei redditi

incoming /'mkʌmɪŋ/ *a* in arrivo; ~ **tide** marea *f* montante

incommunicado /mkəmjuːnɪ'kɑːdəʊ/ *a* (*involuntarily*) segregato; **he's** ~ (*in meeting*) non vuole essere disturbato

incomparable /ɪn'kɒmp(ə)rəbl/ *a* incomparabile

incompatibility /ɪnkəmpætrɪ'bɪlətɪ/ *n* incompatibilità *f*

incompatible /ɪnkəm'pætəbl/ *a* incompatibile

incompetence /ɪn'kɒmpɪtəns/ *n* incompetenza *f*

incompetent /ɪn'kɒmpɪtənt/ *a* incompetente

incomplete /ɪnkəm'pli:t/ *a* incompleto

incomprehensible /ɪnkɒmprɪ'hensəbl/ *a* incomprensibile

inconceivable /ɪnkən'si:vəbl/ *a* inconcepibile

inconclusive /ɪnkən'klu:sɪv/ *a* inconcludente

incongruity /ɪnkɒŋ'gru:ətɪ/ *n* (*of appearance*) contrasto *m*; (*of situation*) assurdità *f* *inv*

incongruous /ɪn'kɒŋgrʊəs/ *a* contrastante

inconsequential /ɪnkɒnsɪ'kwenʃl/ *a* senza importanza

inconsiderate /ɪnkən'sɪdərət/ *a* trascurabile

inconsistency /ɪnkən'sɪstənsɪ/ *n* incoerenza *f*

inconsistent /ɪnkən'sɪstənt/ *a* incoerente; **be ~ with** non essere coerente con

inconsistently /ɪnkən'sɪstəntlɪ/ *adv* in modo incoerente

inconsolable /ɪnkən'səʊləbl/ *a* inconsolabile

inconspicuous /ɪnkən'spɪkjʊəs/ *a* non appariscente

inconspicuously /ɪnkən'spɪkjʊəslɪ/ *adv* modestamente

inconstancy /ɪn'kɒnstənsɪ/ *n* incostanza *f*

inconstant /ɪn'kɒnstənt/ *a* (*conditions*) variabile; (*lover*) volubile

incontestable /ɪnkən'testəbl/ *a* incontestabile

incontinence /ɪn'kɒntɪnəns/ *n* incontinenza *f*

incontinent /ɪn'kɒntɪnənt/ *a* incontinente

inconvenience /ɪnkən'vi:nɪəns/ *n* scomodità *f*; (*drawback*) inconveniente *m*; **put sb to ~** dare disturbo a qcno

inconvenient /ɪnkən'vi:nɪənt/ *a* scomodo; (*time, place*) inopportuno

inconveniently /ɪnkən'vi:nɪəntlɪ/ *adv* in modo inopportuno

incorporate /ɪn'kɔ:pəreɪt/ *vt* incorporare; (*contain*) comprendere

incorrect /ɪnkə'rekt/ *a* incorretto

incorrectly /ɪnkə'rektlɪ/ *adv* scorrettamente

incorrigible /ɪn'kɒrɪdʒəbl/ *a* incorreggibile

incorruptible /ɪnkə'rʌptəbl/ *a* incorruttibile

increase[1] /'ɪnkri:s/ *n* aumento *m*; **on the ~** in aumento

increase[2] /ɪn'kri:s/ *vt/i* aumentare

increasing /ɪn'kri:sɪŋ/ *a* (*impatience etc*) crescente; (*numbers*) in aumento

increasingly /ɪn'kri:sɪŋlɪ/ *adv* sempre più

incredible /ɪn'kredəbl/ *a* incredibile

incredibly /ɪn'kredəblɪ/ *adv* incredibilmente

incredulity /ɪnkrə'dju:lətɪ/ *n* incredulità *f*

incredulous /ɪn'kredjʊləs/ *a* incredulo

increment /'ɪnkrɪmənt/ *n* incremento *m*

incremental /ɪnkrɪ'mentəl/ *a* Comput, Math incrementale; (*effect, measures*) progressivo

incriminate /ɪn'krɪmɪneɪt/ *vt* Jur incriminare

in-crowd *n* **be in with the ~** frequentare gente alla moda

incubate /'ɪŋkjʊbeɪt/ *vt* incubare

incubation /ɪŋkjʊ'beɪʃn/ *n* incubazione *f*

incubation period *n* Med periodo *m* di incubazione

incubator /'ɪnkjʊbeɪtə(r)/ *n* (*for baby*) incubatrice *f*

inculcate /'ɪnkʌlkeɪt/ *vt* inculcare

incumbent /ɪn'kʌmbənt/ *a* **be ~ on sb** incombere a qcno

incur /ɪn'kɜ:(r)/ *vt* (*pt/pp* **incurred**) incorrere; contrarre (*debts*)

incurable /ɪn'kjʊərəbl/ *a* incurabile

incurably /ɪn'kjʊərəblɪ/ *adv* incurabilmente

incursion /ɪn'kɜ:ʃn/ *n* incursione *f*

indebted /ɪn'detɪd/ *a* obbligato (**to** verso)

indecency /ɪn'di:sənsɪ/ *n* oscenità *f*; (*offence*) atti *mpl* osceni; **gross ~** atti *mpl* osceni

indecent /ɪn'di:sənt/ *a* indecente

indecent assault *n* atti *mpl* di libidine violenta

indecent exposure *n* esibizionismo *m* (*dei genitali*)

indecipherable /ɪndɪ'saɪfərəbl/ *a* indecifrabile

indecision /ɪndɪ'sɪʒn/ *n* indecisione *f*

indecisive /ɪndɪ'saɪsɪv/ *a* indeciso

indecisiveness /ɪndɪ'saɪsɪvnɪs/ *n* indecisione *f*

indeed /ɪn'di:d/ *adv* (*in fact*) difatti; **yes ~!** sì, certamente!; **~ I am/do** veramente!; **very much ~** moltissimo; **thank you very much ~** grazie infinite; **~?** davvero?

indefatigable /ɪndɪ'fætɪgəbl/ *a* instancabile

indefensible /ɪndɪ'fensəbl/ *a* Mil indifendibile; (*morally*) ingiustificabile; (*logically*) insostenibile

indefinable /ɪndɪ'faɪnəbl/ *a* indefinibile

indefinite /ɪn'defnɪt/ *a* indefinito

indefinitely /ɪn'defnɪtlɪ/ *adv* indefinitamente; (*postpone*) a tempo indeterminato

indelible /ɪn'deləbl/ *a* indelebile

indelibly /ɪn'deləblɪ/ *adv* in modo indelebile

indelicacy /ɪn'delɪkəsɪ/ *n* (*tactlessness*) mancanza *f* di tatto; (*coarseness*) rozzezza *f*

indelicate /ɪn'delɪkət/ *a* (*tactless*) privo di tatto; (*coarse*) rozzo

indemnity /ɪn'demnətɪ/ *n* indennità *f* *inv*

indent[1] /'ɪndent/ *n* Typ rientranza *f* dal margine

171

indent | indulgent

indent² /ɪn'dent/ vt Typ fare rientrare dal margine

indentation /ɪnden'teɪʃn/ n (notch) intaccatura f

independence /ɪndɪ'pendəns/ n indipendenza f

Independence Day n Am = anniversario m dell'Indipendenza degli USA (4 luglio)

independent /ɪndɪ'pendənt/ a indipendente

independently /ɪndɪ'pendəntlɪ/ adv indipendentemente

in-depth a ⟨analysis, study, knowledge⟩ approfondito

indescribable /ɪndɪ'skraɪbəbl/ a indescrivibile

indescribably /ɪndɪ'skraɪbəblɪ/ adv indescrivibilmente

indestructible /ɪndɪ'strʌktəbl/ a indistruttibile

indeterminate /ɪndɪ'tɜ:mmət/ a indeterminato

index /'ɪndeks/ n indice m

indexation /ɪndek'seɪʃn/ n indicizzazione f

index: index card n scheda f. **index finger** n dito m indice. **index-linked** a ⟨pension⟩ legato al costo della vita

India /'ɪndɪə/ n India f

Indian /'ɪndɪən/ a indiano; (American) indiano [d'America] ● n indiano, -a mf; (American) indiano [d'America], pellerossa mf inv

Indian: Indian elephant n elefante m indiano. **Indian ink** n inchiostro m di China. **Indian Ocean** n oceano m Indiano. **Indian summer** n estate f di San Martino

indicate /'ɪndɪkeɪt/ vt indicare; (register) segnare ● vi Auto mettere la freccia; ~ **left** mettere la freccia a sinistra

indication /ɪndɪ'keɪʃn/ n indicazione f

indicative /ɪn'dɪkətɪv/ a be ~ **of** essere indicativo di ● n Gram indicativo m

indicator /'ɪndɪkeɪtə(r)/ n Auto freccia f

indict /ɪn'daɪt/ vt accusare

indictment /ɪn'daɪtmənt/ n Jur imputazione f

indie /'ɪndɪ/ a fam Cinema, Mus indipendente; ● n (band) complesso m musicale legato a un'etichetta indipendente; (film) film m prodotto da una casa di produzione indipendente

indifference /ɪn'dɪf(ə)rəns/ n indifferenza f

indifferent /ɪn'dɪf(ə)rənt/ a indifferente; (not good) mediocre

indifferently /ɪn'dɪf(ə)rəntlɪ/ adv in modo indifferente; (not well) in modo mediocre

indigenous /ɪn'dɪdʒɪnəs/ a indigeno

indigestible /ɪndɪ'dʒestəbl/ a indigesto

indigestion /ɪndɪ'dʒestʃn/ n indigestione f

indignant /ɪn'dɪgnənt/ a indignato

indignantly /ɪn'dɪgnəntlɪ/ adv con indignazione

indignation /ɪndɪg'neɪʃn/ n indignazione f

indignity /ɪn'dɪgnətɪ/ n umiliazione f

indigo /'ɪndɪgəʊ/ n indaco m

indirect /ɪndaɪ'rekt/ a indiretto

indirectly /ɪndaɪ'rektlɪ/ adv indirettamente

indiscernible /ɪndɪ'sɜ:nəbl/ a indistinguibile

indiscreet /ɪndɪ'skri:t/ a indiscreto

indiscretion /ɪndɪ'skreʃn/ n indiscrezione f

indiscriminate /ɪndɪ'skrɪmmət/ a indiscriminato

indiscriminately /ɪndɪ'skrɪmmətlɪ/ adv senza distinzione

indispensable /ɪndɪ'spensəbl/ a indispensabile

indisposed /ɪndɪ'spəʊzd/ a indisposto

indisputable /ɪndɪ'spju:təbl/ a indisputabile

indisputably /ɪndɪ'spju:təblɪ/ adv indisputabilmente

indistinct /ɪndɪ'stɪnkt/ a indistinto

indistinctly /ɪndɪ'stɪŋktlɪ/ adv indistintamente

indistinguishable /ɪndɪ'stɪŋgwɪʃəbl/ a indistinguibile

individual /ɪndɪ'vɪdjʊəl/ a individuale ● n individuo m

individualist /ɪndɪ'vɪdjʊəlɪst/ n individualista mf

individualistic /ɪndɪvɪdjʊə'lɪstɪk/ a individualistico

individuality /ɪndɪvɪdjʊ'ælətɪ/ n individualità f

individually /ɪndɪ'vɪdjʊəlɪ/ adv individualmente

indivisible /ɪndɪ'vɪzəbl/ a indivisibile

Indochina /ɪndəʊ'tʃaɪnə/ n Indocina f

indoctrinate /ɪn'dɒktrɪneɪt/ vt indottrinare

Indo-European /ɪndəʊ-jʊərə'pɪən/ a indoeuropeo

indolence /'ɪndələns/ n indolenza

indolent /'ɪndələnt/ a indolente

indomitable /ɪn'dɒmɪtəbl/ a indomito

Indonesia /ɪndə'ni:zjə/ n Indonesia f

Indonesian /ɪndə'ni:zjən/ a & n (person) indonesiano, -a mf; (language) indonesiano m

indoor /'ɪndɔ:(r)/ a interno; ⟨shoes⟩ per casa; ⟨plant⟩ da appartamento; ⟨swimming pool etc⟩ coperto

indoors /ɪn'dɔ:z/ adv dentro; **go ~** andare dentro

indubitable /ɪn'dju:bɪtəbl/ a indubitabile

indubitably /ɪn'dju:bɪtəblɪ/ adv indubitabilmente

induce /ɪn'dju:s/ vt indurre (**to** a); (produce) causare

inducement /ɪn'dju:smənt/ n (incentive) incentivo m

induction /ɪn'dʌkʃn/ n (inauguration) introduzione f; (of labour) parto m indotto; Electr induzione f

induction ceremony n cerimonia f inaugurale

induction course n corso m introduttivo

indulge /ɪn'dʌldʒ/ vt soddisfare; viziare ⟨child⟩ ● vi ~ **in** concedersi

indulgence /ɪn'dʌldʒəns/ n lusso m; (leniency) indulgenza f

indulgent /ɪn'dʌldʒənt/ a indulgente

industrial | inflected

industrial /ɪn'dʌstrɪəl/ a industriale; **take ~ action** scioperare

industrial: industrial accident n infortunio m sul lavoro. **industrial dispute** n vertenza f sindacale. **industrial espionage** n spionaggio m industriale. **industrial estate** n zona f industriale. **industrial tribunal** n tribunale m del lavoro

industrialist /ɪn'dʌstrɪəlɪst/ n industriale mf

industrialized /ɪn'dʌstrɪəlaɪzd/ a industrializzato

industrial tribunal n tribunale m competente per i conflitti di lavoro

industrial waste n rifiuti mpl industriali

industrious /ɪn'dʌstrɪəs/ a industrioso

industriously /ɪn'dʌstrɪəslɪ/ adv in modo industrioso

industry /'ɪndəstrɪ/ n industria f; (zeal) operosità f

inebriated /ɪ'ni:brɪeɪtɪd/ a ebbro

inedible /ɪn'edəbl/ a immangiabile

ineffective /ɪnɪ'fektɪv/ a inefficace

ineffectively /ɪnɪ'fektɪvlɪ/ adv inutilmente, invano

ineffectual /ɪnɪ'fektʃʊəl/ a inutile; (person) inconcludente

inefficiency /ɪnɪ'fɪʃənsɪ/ n inefficienza f

inefficient /ɪnɪ'fɪʃnt/ a inefficiente

ineligible /ɪn'elɪdʒəbl/ a inadatto

inept /ɪ'nept/ a inetto

ineptitude /ɪ'neptɪtju:d/ n inettitudine f

inequality /ɪnɪ'kwɒlətɪ/ n ineguaglianza f

inert /ɪ'nɜ:t/ a inerte

inertia /ɪ'nɜ:ʃə/ n inerzia f

inescapable /ɪnɪ'skeɪpəbl/ a inevitabile

inestimable /ɪn'estɪməbl/ a inestimabile

inevitable /ɪn'evɪtəbl/ a inevitabile

inevitably /ɪn'evɪtəblɪ/ adv inevitabilmente

inexact /ɪnɪg'zækt/ a inesatto

inexcusable /ɪnɪk'skju:zəbl/ a imperdonabile

inexhaustible /ɪnɪg'zɔ:stəbl/ a inesauribile

inexorable /ɪn'eksərəbl/ a inesorabile

inexorably /ɪn'egzərəblɪ/ adv inesorabilmente

inexpensive /ɪnɪk'spensɪv/ a poco costoso

inexpensively /ɪnɪk'spensɪvlɪ/ adv a buon mercato

inexperience /ɪnɪk'spɪərɪəns/ n inesperienza f

inexperienced /ɪnɪk'spɪərɪənst/ a inesperto

inexplicable /ɪnɪk'splɪkəbl/ a inesplicabile

inexplicably /ɪnɪk'splɪkəblɪ/ adv inesplicabilmente, inspiegabilmente

inextricable /ɪnɪk'strɪkəbl/ a inestricabile

inextricably /ɪnɪk'strɪkəblɪ/ adv inestricabilmente

infallibility /ɪnfælɪ'bɪlətɪ/ n infallibilità f

infallible /ɪn'fæləbl/ a infallibile

infamous /'ɪnfəməs/ a infame; (person) famigerato

infamy /'ɪnfəmɪ/ n infamia f

infancy /'ɪnfənsɪ/ n infanzia f; **in its ~** fig agli inizi

infant /'ɪnfənt/ n bambino, -a mf piccolo, -a

infanticide /ɪn'fæntɪsaɪd/ n infanticidio m

infantile /'ɪnfəntaɪl/ a infantile

infantry /'ɪnfəntrɪ/ n fanteria f

infant school n scuola f elementare per bambini dai 5 ai 7 anni

infatuated /ɪn'fætʃʊeɪtɪd/ a infatuato (**with** di)

infatuation /ɪnfætʃʊ'eɪʃn/ n infatuazione f

infect /ɪn'fekt/ vt infettare; **become ~ed** (wound:) infettarsi

infection /ɪn'fekʃn/ n infezione f

infectious /ɪn'fekʃəs/ a infettivo

infer /ɪn'fɜ:(r)/ vt (pt/pp **inferred**) dedurre (**from** da); (imply) implicare

inference /'ɪnfərəns/ n deduzione f

inferior /ɪn'fɪərɪə(r)/ a inferiore; (goods) scadente; (in rank) subalterno ● n inferiore mf; (in rank) subalterno, -a mf

inferiority /ɪnfɪərɪ'ɒrətɪ/ n inferiorità f

inferiority complex n complesso m di inferiorità

infernal /ɪn'fɜ:nl/ a infernale

inferno /ɪn'fɜ:nəʊ/ n inferno m

infertile /ɪn'fɜ:taɪl/ a sterile

infertility /ɪnfə'tɪlətɪ/ n sterilità f

infest /ɪn'fest/ vt **be ~ed with** essere infestato di

infestation /ɪnfe'steɪʃn/ n infestazione f

infidelity /ɪnfɪ'delətɪ/ n infedeltà f inv

infighting /'ɪnfaɪtɪŋ/ n fig lotta f per il potere

infiltrate /'ɪnfɪltreɪt/ vt infiltrare; Pol infiltrarsi in

infiltration /ɪnfɪl'treɪʃn/ n infiltrazione f

infinite /'ɪnfɪnɪt/ a infinito

infinitely /'ɪnfɪnɪtlɪ/ adv infinitamente

infinitesimal /ɪnfɪnɪ'tesɪml/ a infinitesimo

infinitive /ɪn'fɪnɪtɪv/ n Gram infinito m

infinity /ɪn'fɪnətɪ/ n infinità f

infirm /ɪn'fɜ:m/ a debole

infirmary /ɪn'fɜ:m(ə)rɪ/ n infermeria f

infirmity /ɪn'fɜ:mətɪ/ n debolezza f

in flagrante delicto /ɪnfləgræntɪdɪ'lɪktəʊ/ adv in flagrante

inflame /ɪn'fleɪm/ vt infiammare

inflamed /ɪn'fleɪmd/ a infiammato; **become ~** infiammarsi

inflammable /ɪn'flæməbl/ a infiammabile

inflammation /ɪnflə'meɪʃn/ n infiammazione f

inflammatory /ɪn'flæmətrɪ/ a incendiario

inflatable /ɪn'fleɪtəbl/ a gonfiabile

inflate /ɪn'fleɪt/ vt gonfiare

inflated /ɪn'fleɪtɪd/ a (price, fee, claim) eccessivo; (style) ampolloso; (tyre) gonfio; **an ~ ego** un'alta opinione di sé

inflation /ɪn'fleɪʃn/ n inflazione f

inflationary /ɪn'fleɪʃənərɪ/ a inflazionario

inflect /ɪn'flekt/ vt flettere (noun, adjective); modulare (voice)

inflected /ɪn'flektɪd/ a (language) flessivo; (form) flesso

inflection /ɪnˈflekʃn/ n (of voice) modulazione f

inflexible /ɪnˈfleksəbl/ a inflessibile

inflexion /ɪnˈflekʃn/ n inflessione f

inflict /ɪnˈflɪkt/ vt infliggere (**on** a)

in-flight a a bordo

influence /ˈɪnfluəns/ n influenza f; **use one's ~** esercitare la propria influenza ● vt influenzare

influential /ɪnfluˈenʃl/ a influente

influenza /ɪnfluˈenzə/ n influenza f

influx /ˈɪnflʌks/ n afflusso f

info /ˈɪnfəu/ n fam informazione f

inform /ɪnˈfɔːm/ vt informare; **keep sb ~ed** tenere qcno al corrente ● vi ~ **against** denunziare

informal /ɪnˈfɔːməl/ a informale; ⟨agreement⟩ ufficioso

informality /ɪnfəˈmælətɪ/ n informalità f inv

informally /ɪnˈfɔːməlɪ/ adv in modo informale

informant /ɪnˈfɔːmənt/ n informatore, -trice mf

information /ɪnfəˈmeɪʃn/ n informazioni fpl; **a piece of ~** un'informazione

information: information desk n banco m informazioni. **information highway** n autostrada f telematica. **information officer** n addetto, -a mf stampa. **information processing** n elaborazione f dati. **information system** n sistema m informativo. **information technology** n informatica f

informative /ɪnˈfɔːmətɪv/ a informativo; ⟨film, book⟩ istruttivo

informer /ɪnˈfɔːmə(r)/ n informatore, -trice mf; Pol delatore, -trice mf

infra-red /ɪnfrəˈred/ a infrarosso

infrastructure /ˈɪnfrəstrʌktʃə(r)/ n infrastruttura f

infrequent /ɪnˈfriːkwənt/ a infrequente

infrequently /ɪnˈfriːkwəntlɪ/ adv raramente

infringe /ɪnˈfrɪndʒ/ vt ~ **on** usurpare

infringement /ɪnˈfrɪndʒmənt/ n violazione f

infuriate /ɪnˈfjʊərɪeɪt/ vt infuriare

infuriating /ɪnˈfjʊərɪeɪtɪŋ/ a esasperante

infuse /ɪnˈfjuːz/ vi ⟨tea:⟩ restare in infusione

infusion /ɪnˈfjuːʒn/ n ⟨drink⟩ infusione f; ⟨of capital, new blood⟩ afflusso m

ingenious /ɪnˈdʒiːnɪəs/ a ingegnoso

ingenuity /ɪndʒɪˈnjuːətɪ/ n ingegnosità f

ingenuous /ɪnˈdʒenjuəs/ a ingenuo

ingest /ɪnˈdʒest/ vt ingerire ⟨food⟩; assimilare ⟨fact⟩

ingot /ˈɪŋgət/ n lingotto m

ingrained /ɪnˈgreɪnd/ a (in person) radicato; ⟨dirt⟩ incrostato

ingratiate /ɪnˈgreɪʃɪeɪt/ vt ~ **oneself with sb** ingraziarsi qcno

ingratitude /ɪnˈgrætɪtjuːd/ n ingratitudine f

ingredient /ɪnˈgriːdɪənt/ n ingrediente m

ingrowing /ˈɪngrəuɪŋ/ a ⟨nail⟩ incarnito

inhabit /ɪnˈhæbɪt/ vt abitare

inhabitable /ɪnˈhæbɪtəbl/ a abitabile

inhabitant /ɪnˈhæbɪtənt/ n abitante mf

inhale /ɪnˈheɪl/ vt aspirare; Med inalare ● vi inspirare; (when smoking) aspirare

inhaler /ɪnˈheɪlə(r)/ n (device) inalatore m

inherent /ɪnˈhɪərənt/ a inerente

inherit /ɪnˈherɪt/ vt ereditare

inheritance /ɪnˈherɪtəns/ n eredità f inv

inhibit /ɪnˈhɪbɪt/ vt inibire

inhibited /ɪnˈhɪbɪtɪd/ a inibito

inhibition /ɪnhɪˈbɪʃn/ n inibizione f

inhospitable /ɪnhɒˈspɪtəbl/ a inospitale

in-house a ⟨training⟩ interno all'azienda; ⟨magazine⟩ aziendale

inhuman /ɪnˈhjuːmən/ a disumano

inimitable /ɪˈnɪmɪtəbl/ a inimitabile

iniquitous /ɪˈnɪkwɪtəs/ a iniquo

initial /ɪˈnɪʃl/ a iniziale ● n iniziale f ● vt (pt/pp **initialled**) siglare

initially /ɪˈnɪʃəlɪ/ adv all'inizio

initiate /ɪˈnɪʃɪeɪt/ vt iniziare

initiation /ɪnɪʃɪˈeɪʃn/ n iniziazione f

initiative /ɪˈnɪʃətɪv/ n iniziativa f; **take the ~** prendere l'iniziativa

inject /ɪnˈdʒekt/ vt iniettare

injection /ɪnˈdʒekʃn/ n iniezione f

in-joke n **it's an ~** è una battuta tra di noi/loro

injunction /ɪnˈdʒʌŋkʃn/ n ingiunzione f

injure /ˈɪndʒə(r)/ vt ferire; (wrong) nuocere; **the ~d party** la parte lesa

injury /ˈɪndʒərɪ/ n ferita f; (wrong) torto m

injury time n Sport recupero m

injustice /ɪnˈdʒʌstɪs/ n ingiustizia f; **do sb an ~** giudicare qcno in modo sbagliato

ink /ɪŋk/ n inchiostro m

ink-jet printer n stampante f a getto d'inchiostro

inkling /ˈɪŋklɪŋ/ n sentore m

inky /ˈɪŋkɪ/ a macchiato d'inchiostro

inlaid /ɪnˈleɪd/ a intarsiato

inland /ˈɪnlənd/ a interno ● adv all'interno

Inland Revenue n fisco m

in-laws /ˈɪnlɔːz/ npl fam parenti mpl acquisiti

inlay /ˈɪnleɪ/ n intarsio m

inlet /ˈɪnlet/ n insenatura f; Techn entrata f

inmate /ˈɪnmeɪt/ n (of hospital) degente mf; (of prison) carcerato, -a mf

inn /ɪn/ n locanda f

innards /ˈɪnədz/ npl fam frattaglie fpl

innate /ɪˈneɪt/ a innato

inner /ˈɪnə(r)/ a interno

inner city n quartieri mpl nel centro di una città caratterizzati da problemi sociali ● attrib ⟨problems⟩ dell'area urbana con problemi sociali

inner ear n orecchio m interno

innermost /ˈɪnəməust/ a il più profondo

inner tube n camera f d'aria

innings /ˈɪnɪŋz/ nsg (in cricket) turno m di battuta; **have had a good ~** (Br fig: when leaving job etc) aver avuto una carriera lunga e gratificante; (when dead) aver avuto una vita lunga e piena di soddisfazioni

innkeeper | instance

innkeeper /ˈɪnkiːpə(r)/ n locandiere, -a mf
innocence /ˈɪnəsəns/ n innocenza f
innocent /ˈɪnəsənt/ a innocente
innocently /ˈɪnəsəntlɪ/ adv innocentemente
innocuous /ɪˈnɒkjuəs/ a innocuo
innovate /ˈɪnəveɪt/ vi innovare
innovation /ɪnəˈveɪʃn/ n innovazione f
innovative /ˈɪnəvətɪv/ a innovativo
innovator /ˈɪnəveɪtə(r)/ n innovatore, -trice mf
innuendo /ɪnjuˈendəʊ/ n (pl -es) insinuazione f
innumerable /ɪˈnjuːmərəbl/ a innumerevole
inoculate /ɪˈnɒkjʊleɪt/ vt vaccinare
inoculation /ɪnɒkjʊˈleɪʃn/ n vaccinazione f
inoffensive /ɪnəˈfensɪv/ a inoffensivo
inoperable /ɪnˈɒpərəbl/ a inoperabile
inopportune /ɪnˈɒpətjuːn/ a inopportuno
inordinate /ɪˈnɔːdɪnət/ a smodato
inordinately /ɪˈnɔːdɪnətlɪ/ adv smodatamente
inorganic /ɪnɔːˈgænɪk/ a inorganico
in-patient n degente mf
input /ˈɪnpʊt/ n input m inv, ingresso m
inquest /ˈɪnkwest/ n inchiesta f
inquire /ɪnˈkwaɪə(r)/ vi informarsi (**about** su); ~ **into** far indagini su ● vt domandare
inquiring /ɪnˈkwaɪərɪŋ/ a ⟨mind⟩ curioso; ⟨look, voice⟩ interrogativo
inquiry /ɪnˈkwaɪərɪ/ n domanda f; (investigation) inchiesta f
inquisitive /ɪnˈkwɪzətɪv/ a curioso
inquisitively /ɪnˈkwɪzɪtɪvlɪ/ adv con molta curiosità
inroad /ˈɪnrəʊd/ n make ~s into intaccare ⟨savings⟩; cominciare a risolvere ⟨problem⟩
insalubrious /ɪnsəˈluːbrɪəs/ a ⟨dirty⟩ insalubre; ⟨sleazy⟩ sordido
insane /ɪnˈseɪn/ a pazzo; fig insensato
insanitary /ɪnˈsænɪt(ə)rɪ/ a malsano
insanity /ɪnˈsænətɪ/ n pazzia f
insatiable /ɪnˈseɪʃəbl/ a insaziabile
inscribe /ɪnˈskraɪb/ vt iscrivere
inscription /ɪnˈskrɪpʃn/ n iscrizione f
inscrutable /ɪnˈskruːtəbl/ a impenetrabile
insect /ˈɪnsekt/ n insetto m
insecticide /ɪnˈsektɪsaɪd/ n insetticida m
insect repellent n insettifugo m
insecure /ɪnsɪˈkjʊə(r)/ a malsicuro; ⟨fig: person⟩ insicuro
insecurity /ɪnsɪˈkjʊərətɪ/ n mancanza f di sicurezza
insemination /ɪnsemɪˈneɪʃn/ n inseminazione f
insensitive /ɪnˈsensɪtɪv/ a insensibile
inseparable /ɪnˈsep(ə)rəbl/ a inseparabile
insert¹ /ˈɪnsɜːt/ n inserto m
insert² /ɪnˈsɜːt/ vt inserire
insertion /ɪnˈsɜːʃn/ n inserzione f
inset /ˈɪnset/ n (map, photo) dettaglio m ● a ~ **with** ⟨necklace⟩ incastonato di; ⟨table⟩ intarsiato di
inshore /ɪnˈʃɔː(r)/ a ⟨current⟩ diretta a riva;

⟨fishing, waters, current⟩ costiero; ⟨wind⟩ dal mare ● adv ⟨fish⟩ sotto costa
inside /ɪnˈsaɪd/ n interno m; ~**s** pl fam pancia f ● adv dentro; ~ **out** a rovescio; (thoroughly) a fondo ● prep dentro; (of time) entro
inside lane n Auto corsia f interna
inside leg n interno m della gamba
insider /ɪnˈsaɪdə(r)/ n persona f all'interno
insider dealer, insider trader n Fin persona f che pratica l'insider trading
insider dealing, insider trading /ˈdiːlɪŋ, ˈtreɪdɪŋ/ n Fin insider trading m
insidious /ɪnˈsɪdɪəs/ a insidioso
insidiously /ɪnˈsɪdɪəslɪ/ adv insidiosamente
insight /ˈɪnsaɪt/ n intuito m (**into** per); **an ~ into** un quadro di
insignia /ɪnˈsɪgnɪə/ npl insegne fpl
insignificant /ɪnsɪgˈnɪfɪkənt/ a insignificante
insincere /ɪnsɪnˈsɪə(r)/ a poco sincero
insincerity /ɪnsɪnˈserətɪ/ n mancanza f di sincerità
insinuate /ɪnˈsɪnjʊeɪt/ vt insinuare
insinuation /ɪnsɪnjʊˈeɪʃn/ n insinuazione f
insipid /ɪnˈsɪpɪd/ a insipido
insist /ɪnˈsɪst/ vi insistere (**on** per) ● vt ~ **that** insistere che
insistence /ɪnˈsɪstəns/ n insistenza f
insistent /ɪnˈsɪstənt/ a insistente
insistently /ɪnˈsɪstəntlɪ/ adv insistentemente
insofar /ɪnsəˈfɑː(r)/ conj ~ **as** (to the extent that) nella misura in cui; (seeing that) in quanto; ~ **as I know** per quanto ne sappia
insole /ˈɪnsəʊl/ n soletta f
insolence /ˈɪnsələns/ n insolenza f
insolent /ˈɪnsələnt/ a insolente
insolently /ˈɪnsələntlɪ/ adv con insolenza
insoluble /ɪnˈsɒljʊbl/ a insolubile
insolvency /ɪnˈsɒlvənsɪ/ n insolvenza f
insolvent /ɪnˈsɒlvənt/ a insolvente
insomnia /ɪnˈsɒmnɪə/ n insonnia f
insomniac /ɪnˈsɒmɪæk/ n persona f che soffre di insonnia
insomuch /ɪnsəˈmʌtʃ/ conj ~ **as** (to the extent that) nella misura in cui; (seeing that) in quanto
inspect /ɪnˈspekt/ vt ispezionare; controllare ⟨ticket⟩
inspection /ɪnˈspekʃn/ n ispezione f; (of ticket) controllo m
inspector /ɪnˈspektə(r)/ n ispettore, -trice mf; (of tickets) controllore m
inspiration /ɪnspəˈreɪʃn/ n ispirazione f
inspire /ɪnˈspaɪə(r)/ vt ispirare
inspired /ɪnˈspaɪəd/ a ⟨person, performance⟩ ispirato; ⟨idea⟩ luminosa
instability /ɪnstəˈbɪlətɪ/ n instabilità f
install /ɪnˈstɔːl/ vt installare; insediare ⟨person⟩
installation /ɪnstəˈleɪʃn/ n installazione f
instalment /ɪnˈstɔːlmənt/ n Comm rata f; (of serial) puntata f; (of publication) fascicolo m
instance /ˈɪnstəns/ n (case) caso m;

(*example*) esempio *m*; **in the first** ~ in primo luogo; **for** ~ per esempio

instant /'ɪnstənt/ *a* immediato; *Culin* espresso ● *n* istante *m*

instantaneous /ɪnstən'teɪnɪəs/ *a* istantaneo

instant coffee *n* caffè *m* *inv* solubile

instantly /'ɪnstəntlɪ/ *adv* immediatamente

instant replay *n* *Sport* replay *m* *inv*

instead /ɪn'sted/ *adv* invece; ~ **of doing** anziché fare; ~ **of me** al mio posto; ~ **of going** invece di andare

instep /'ɪnstep/ *n* collo *m* del piede

instigate /'ɪnstɪɡeɪt/ *vt* istigare

instigation /ɪnstrɪ'ɡeɪʃn/ *n* istigazione *f*; **at his** ~ dietro suo suggerimento

instigator /'ɪnstɪɡeɪtə(r)/ *n* istigatore, -trice *mf*

instil /ɪn'stɪl/ *vt* (*pt/pp* **instilled**) inculcare (**into** in)

instinct /'ɪnstɪŋkt/ *n* istinto *m*

instinctive /ɪn'stɪŋktɪv/ *a* istintivo

instinctively /ɪn'stɪŋktɪvlɪ/ *adv* istintivamente

institute /'ɪnstɪtjuːt/ *n* istituto *m* ● *vt* istituire ‹*scheme*›; iniziare ‹*search*›; intentare ‹*legal action*›

institution /ɪnstɪ'tjuːʃn/ *n* istituzione *f*; (*home for elderly*) istituto *m* per anziani; (*for mentally ill*) istituto *m* per malati di mente

institutionalize /ɪnstɪ'tjuːʃənəlaɪz/ *vt* istituzionalizzare

institutionalized /ɪnstɪ'tjuːʃənəlaɪzd/ *a* ‹*racism, violence*› istituzionalizzato; **become** ~ (*officially established*) essere istituzionalizzato; **be** ~**d** ‹*person:*› non essere autonomo a causa di un lungo soggiorno in ospedale psichiatrico

instruct /ɪn'strʌkt/ *vt* istruire; (*order*) ordinare

instruction /ɪn'strʌkʃn/ *n* istruzione *f*; ~**s** *pl* (*orders*) ordini *mpl*

instructive /ɪn'strʌktɪv/ *a* istruttivo

instructor /ɪn'strʌktə(r)/ *n* istruttore, -trice *mf*

instrument /'ɪnstrʊmənt/ *n* strumento *m*

instrumental /ɪnstrʊ'ment(ə)l/ *a* strumentale; **be** ~ **in** contribuire a

instrumentalist /ɪnstrʊ'mentəlɪst/ *n* strumentista *mf*

insubordinate /ɪnsə'bɔːdɪnət/ *a* insubordinato

insubordination /ɪnsəbɔːdɪ'neɪʃn/ *n* insubordinazione *f*

insubstantial /ɪnsəb'stænʃəl/ *a* (*unreal*) irreale; ‹*evidence*› inconsistente; ‹*flimsy, building*› poco solido; ‹*meal*› poco sostanzioso

insufferable /ɪn'sʌf(ə)rəbl/ *a* insopportabile

insufficient /ɪnsə'fɪʃənt/ *a* insufficiente

insufficiently /ɪnsə'fɪʃəntlɪ/ *adv* insufficientemente

insular /'ɪnsjʊlə(r)/ *a fig* gretto

insulate /'ɪnsjʊleɪt/ *vt* isolare

insulating tape /'ɪnsjʊleɪtɪŋ/ *n* nastro *m* isolante

insulation /ɪnsjʊ'leɪʃn/ *n* isolamento *m*

insulator /'ɪnsjʊleɪtə(r)/ *n* isolante *m*

insulin /'ɪnsjʊlɪn/ *n* insulina *f*

insult[1] /'ɪnsʌlt/ *n* insulto *m*

insult[2] /ɪn'sʌlt/ *vt* insultare

insuperable /ɪn'suːpərəbl/ *a* insuperabile

insurable value /ɪn'ʃʊərəbl/ *n* valore *m* assicurabile

insurance /ɪn'ʃʊərəns/ *n* assicurazione *f*

insurance: insurance broker *n* broker *mf inv* d'assicurazioni. **insurance claim** *n* richiesta *f* di indennizzo (*ad assicurazione*). **insurance policy** *n* polizza *f* d'assicurazione. **insurance premium** *n* premio *m* assicurativo

insure /ɪn'ʃʊə(r)/ *vt* assicurare

insurgent /ɪn'sɜːdʒənt/ *n* rivoltoso, -a *mf*

insurmountable /ɪnsə'maʊntəbl/ *a* insormontabile

insurrection /ɪnsə'rekʃn/ *n* insurrezione *f*

intact /ɪn'tækt/ *a* intatto

intake /'ɪnteɪk/ *n* immissione *f*; (*of food*) consumo *m*

intangible /ɪn'tændʒəbl/ *a* intangibile

integral /'ɪntɪɡrəl/ *a* integrale

integrate /'ɪntɪɡreɪt/ *vt* integrare ● *vi* integrarsi

integration /ɪntɪ'ɡreɪʃn/ *n* integrazione *f*

integrity /ɪn'teɡrətɪ/ *n* integrità *f*

intellect /'ɪntəlekt/ *n* intelletto *m*

intellectual /ɪntə'lektjʊəl/ *a & n* intellettuale *mf*

intelligence /ɪn'telɪdʒəns/ *n* intelligenza *f*; *Mil* informazioni *fpl*

intelligent /ɪn'telɪdʒənt/ *a* intelligente

intelligently /ɪn'telɪdʒəntlɪ/ *adv* intelligentemente

intelligentsia /ɪntelɪ'dʒentsɪə/ *n* intellighenzia *f*

intelligible /ɪn'telɪdʒəbl/ *a* intelligibile

intemperate /ɪn'temp(ə)rət/ *a* ‹*language, person*› intemperante; ‹*weather*› rigido; ‹*attack*› violento

intend /ɪn'tend/ *vt* destinare; (*have in mind*) aver intenzione di; **be** ~**ed for** essere destinato a

intended /ɪn'tendɪd/ *a* ‹*visit, purchase*› programmato; ‹*result*› voluto, desiderato ● *n her* ~ *hum* il suo fidanzato; **his** ~ *hum* la sua fidanzata

intense /ɪn'tens/ *a* intenso; ‹*person*› dai sentimenti intensi

intensely /ɪn'tenslɪ/ *adv* intensamente; (*very*) estremamente

intensification /ɪntensɪfɪ'keɪʃn/ *n* intensificazione *f*

intensify /ɪn'tensɪfaɪ/ *v* (*pt/pp* **-ied**) ● *vt* intensificare ● *vi* intensificarsi

intensity /ɪn'tensətɪ/ *n* intensità *f*

intensive /ɪn'tensɪv/ *a* intensivo; ~ **care** [**unit**] terapia *f* intensiva; (*for people in coma*) rianimazione *f*

intensive care [unit] *n* [reparto *m*] rianimazione *f*

intensively /ɪn'tensɪvlɪ/ *adv* intensivamente

intent /ɪn'tent/ *a* intento; **~ on** (*absorbed in*) preso da; **be ~ on doing sth** essere intento a fare qcsa ● *n* intenzione *f*; **to all ~s and purposes** a tutti gli effetti

intention /ɪn'tenʃn/ *n* intenzione *f*

intentional /ɪn'tenʃənəl/ *a* intenzionale

intentionally /ɪn'tenʃənəlɪ/ *adv* intenzionalmente

intently /ɪn'tentlɪ/ *adv* attentamente

inter /ɪn'tɜ:(r)/ *vt* (*pt/pp* **interred**) *fml* interrare

interaction /ɪntər'ækʃn/ *n* cooperazione *f*

interactive /ɪntər'æktɪv/ *a* interattivo

interactive video *n* video *m* interattivo

interbreed /ɪntə'bri:d/ *vt* ibridare ● *vi* incrociarsi

interbreeding /ɪntə'bri:dɪŋ/ *n* ibridazione *f*

intercede /ɪntə'si:d/ *vi* intercedere (**on behalf of** a favore di)

intercept /ɪntə'sept/ *vt* intercettare

interchange /'ɪntətʃeɪndʒ/ *n* scambio *m*; *Auto* raccordo *m* [autostradale]

interchangeable /ɪntə'tʃeɪndʒəbl/ *a* interscambiabile

intercity /ɪntə'sɪtɪ/ *n* (*Br: train*) intercity *m inv* ● *a* intercity

intercom /'ɪntəkɒm/ *n* citofono *m*

interconnecting /ɪntəkə'nektɪŋ/ *a* ⟨*rooms*⟩ comunicante

intercontinental /ɪntəkɒntɪ'nentəl/ *a* intercontinentale

intercourse /'ɪntəkɔ:s/ *n* (*sexual*) rapporti *mpl* [sessuali]

interdepartmental /ɪntədi:pɑ:t'ment(ə)l/ *a Univ, Comm* interdipartimentale; *Pol* interministeriale

interdependent /ɪntədɪ'pendənt/ *a* interdipendente

interdisciplinary /ɪntədɪsɪ'plɪnərɪ/ *a* interdisciplinare

interest /'ɪntrəst/ *n* interesse *m*; **have an ~ in** *Comm* essere cointeressato in; **be of ~** essere interessante ● *vt* interessare ● *a* interessato

interest-bearing *a* fruttifero

interest-free loan *n* prestito *m* senza interessi

interesting /'ɪnt(ə)rəstɪŋ/ *a* interessante

interest rate *n* tasso *m* di interesse

interface /'ɪntəfeɪs/ *n Comput, fig* interfaccia *f* ● *vi* interfacciarsi ● *vt* interfacciare

interfere /ɪntə'fɪə(r)/ *vi* interferire; **~ with** interferire con

interference /ɪntə'fɪərəns/ *n* interferenza *f*

interim /'ɪntərɪm/ *a* temporaneo; **~ payment** acconto *m* ● *n* **in the ~** nel frattempo

interior /ɪn'tɪərɪə(r)/ *a* interiore ● *n* interno *m*

interior decorator *n* arredatore, -trice *mf*

interior designer *n* (*of colours, fabrics etc*) arredatore, -trice *mf*; (*of walls, space*) architetto *m* d'interni

interject /ɪntə'dʒekt/ *vt* intervenire

interjection /ɪntə'dʒekʃn/ *n Gram* interiezione *f*; (*remark*) intervento *m*

interlink /ɪntə'lɪŋk/ *vt* connettere; **be ~ed with** essere connesso con

interlocking /ɪntə'lɒkɪŋ/ *a* a incastro

interloper /'ɪntələʊpə(r)/ *n* intruso, -a *mf*

interlude /'ɪntəlu:d/ *n* intervallo *m*

intermarry /ɪntə'mærɪ/ *vi* sposarsi tra parenti; ⟨*different groups:*⟩ contrarre matrimoni misti

intermediary /ɪntə'mi:dɪərɪ/ *n* intermediario, -a *mf*

intermediate /ɪntə'mi:dɪət/ *a* intermedio

interminable /ɪn'tɜ:mɪnəbl/ *a* interminabile

intermission /ɪntə'mɪʃn/ *n* intervallo *m*

intermittent /ɪntə'mɪtənt/ *a* intermittente

intermittently /ɪntə'mɪtəntlɪ/ *adv* a intermittenza

intern /ɪn'tɜ:n/ *vt* internare

internal /ɪn'tɜ:nl/ *a* interno

internal combustion engine *n* motore *m* a scoppio

internally /ɪn'tɜ:nəlɪ/ *adv* internamente; ⟨*deal with*⟩ all'interno

international /ɪntə'næʃ(ə)nəl/ *a* internazionale ● *n* (*game*) incontro *m* internazionale; (*player*) competitore, -trice *mf* in gare internazionali

internationally /ɪntə'næʃ(ə)nəlɪ/ *adv* internazionalmente; **it applies ~** ha validità internazionale

international: international money order *n* vaglia *m inv* postale internazionale. **International Phonetic Alphabet** *n* Alfabeto *m* Fonetico Internazionale. **international reply coupon** *n* tagliando *m* di risposta internazionale

Internet /'ɪntənet/ *n* Internet *m*

internist /ɪn'tɜ:nɪst/ *n Am* internista *mf*

internment /ɪn'tɜ:nmənt/ *n* internamento *m*

interplay /'ɪntəpleɪ/ *n* azione *f* reciproca

interpolate /ɪn'tɜ:pəleɪt/ *vt* interpolare

interpose /ɪntə'pəʊz/ *vt* (*insert*) frapporre; interrompere con ⟨*comment, remark*⟩

interpret /ɪn'tɜ:prɪt/ *vt* interpretare ● *vi* fare l'interprete.

interpretation /ɪntɜ:prɪ'teɪʃn/ *n* interpretazione *f*

interpreter /ɪn'tɜ:prɪtə(r)/ *n* interprete *mf*

interpreting /ɪn'tɜ:prɪtɪŋ/ *n* interpretariato *m*

interrelated /ɪntərɪ'leɪtɪd/ *a* ⟨*facts*⟩ in correlazione

interrogate /ɪn'terəgeɪt/ *vt* interrogare

interrogation /ɪntərə'geɪʃn/ *n* interrogazione *f*; (*by police*) interrogatorio *m*

interrogative /ɪntə'rɒgətɪv/ *a & n* **~ [pronoun]** interrogativo *m*

interrupt /ɪntə'rʌpt/ *vt/i* interrompere

interruption /ɪntə'rʌpʃn/ *n* interruzione *f*

intersect /ɪntə'sekt/ *vi* intersecarsi ● *vt* intersecare

intersection /ɪntə'sekʃn/ *n* intersezione *f*; *(of street)* incrocio *m*

interspersed /ɪntə'spɜːst/ *a* ~ **with** inframmezzato di

interstate /'ɪntəsteɪt/ *Am n* superstrada *f* fra stati ● *a* ‹*commerce, links*› fra stati

intertwine /ɪntə'twaɪn/ *vi* attorcigliarsi

interval /'ɪntəvl/ *n* intervallo *m*; **bright** ~**s** *pl* schiarite *fpl*

intervene /ɪntə'viːn/ *vi* intervenire

intervention /ɪntə'venʃn/ *n* intervento *m*

interview /'ɪntəvjuː/ *n Journ* intervista *f*; *(for job)* colloquio *m* [di lavoro] ● *vt* intervistare

interviewee /ɪntəvjuː'iː/ *n* *(on TV, radio, in survey)* intervistato, -a *mf*; *(for job)* persona *f* sottoposta a un colloquio di lavoro

interviewer /'ɪntəvjuːə(r)/ *n* intervistatore, -trice *mf*

interweave /ɪntə'wiːv/ *vt* intrecciare ‹*themes, threads*›; mischiare ‹*rhythms*›

intestinal /ɪnte'staɪnəl/ *a* intestinale

intestine /ɪn'testɪn/ *n* intestino *m*

intimacy /'ɪntɪməsɪ/ *n* intimità *f*

intimate[1] /'ɪntɪmət/ *a* intimo; **be** ~ **with** *(sexually)* avere relazioni intime con

intimate[2] /'ɪntɪmeɪt/ *vt* far capire; *(imply)* suggerire

intimately /'ɪntɪmətlɪ/ *adv* intimamente

intimidate /ɪn'tɪmɪdeɪt/ *vt* intimidire

intimidation /ɪntɪmɪ'deɪʃn/ *n* intimidazione *f*

into /'ɪntə/, *di fronte a una vocale* /'ɪntʊ/ *prep* dentro, in; **go** ~ **the house** andare dentro [casa] *o* in casa; **be** ~ *(fam: like)* essere appassionato di; **I'm not** ~ **that** questo non mi piace; **7** ~ **21 goes 3** il 7 nel 21 ci sta 3 volte; **translate** ~ **French** tradurre in francese; **get** ~ **trouble** mettersi nei guai

intolerable /ɪn'tɒlərəbl/ *a* intollerabile

intolerance /ɪn'tɒlərəns/ *n* intolleranza *f*

intolerant /ɪn'tɒlərənt/ *a* intollerante

intonation /ɪntə'neɪʃn/ *n* intonazione *f*

intone /ɪn'təʊn/ *vt* recitare ‹*prayer*›

intoxicated /ɪn'tɒksɪkeɪtɪd/ *a* inebriato

intoxication /ɪntʊksɪ'keɪʃn/ *n* ebbrezza *f*

intractable /ɪn'træktəbl/ *a* intrattabile; ‹*problem*› insolubile

intramural /ɪntrə'mjʊərəl/ *a* ‹*studies*› tenuto in sede

intransigence /ɪn'trænzɪdʒəns/ *n* intransigenza *f*

intransigent /ɪn'trænzɪdʒənt/ *a* intransigente

intransitive /ɪn'trænzɪtɪv/ *a* intransitivo

intransitively /ɪn'trænzɪtɪvlɪ/ *adv* intransitivamente

intrauterine device /ɪntrəjuː'tərəmdɪ'vaɪs/ *n Med* spirale *f*, dispositivo *m* anticoncezionale intrauterino

intravenous /ɪntrə'viːnəs/ *a* endovenoso

intravenous drip *n* flebo[clisi] *f inv*

intravenously /ɪntrə'viːnəslɪ/ *adv* per via endovenosa

in-tray *n* vassoio *m* per pratiche e corrispondenza da evadere

intrepid /ɪn'trepɪd/ *a* intrepido

intricacy /'ɪntrɪkəsɪ/ *n* complessità *f*

intricate /'ɪntrɪkət/ *a* complesso

intrigue /ɪn'triːg/ *n* intrigo *m* ● *vt* intrigare ● *vi* tramare

intriguing /ɪn'triːgɪŋ/ *a* intrigante

intrinsic /ɪn'trɪnsɪk/ *a* intrinseco

introduce /ɪntrə'djuːs/ *vt* presentare; *(bring in, insert)* introdurre

introduction /ɪntrə'dʌkʃn/ *n* introduzione *f*; *(to person)* presentazione *f*; *(to book)* prefazione *f*

introductory /ɪntrə'dʌktərɪ/ *a* introduttivo

introspective /ɪntrə'spektɪv/ *a* introspettivo

introvert /'ɪntrəvɜːt/ *n* introverso, -a *mf*

introverted /'ɪntrəvɜːtɪd/ *a* introverso

intrude /ɪn'truːd/ *vi* intromettersi

intruder /ɪn'truːdə(r)/ *n* intruso, -a *mf*

intrusion /ɪn'truːʒn/ *n* intrusione *f*

intuition /ɪntjʊ'ɪʃn/ *n* intuito *m*

intuitive /ɪn'tjuːɪtɪv/ *a* intuitivo

intuitively /ɪn'tjuːɪtɪvlɪ/ *adv* intuitivamente

inundate /'ɪnəndeɪt/ *vt fig* inondare (**with** di)

inure /ɪn'jʊə(r)/ *vt* **become** ~**d to sth** assuefarsi a qcsa

invade /ɪn'veɪd/ *vt* invadere

invader /ɪn'veɪdə(r)/ *n* invasore *m*

invalid[1] /'ɪnvəlɪd/ *n* invalido, -a *mf*

invalid[2] /ɪn'vælɪd/ *a* non valido

invalidate /ɪn'vælɪdeɪt/ *vt* invalidare

invaluable /ɪn'væljʊ(ə)bl/ *a* prezioso; *(priceless)* inestimabile

invariable /ɪn'veərɪəbl/ *a* invariabile

invariably /ɪn'veərɪəblɪ/ *adv* invariabilmente

invasion /ɪn'veɪʒn/ *n* invasione *f*

invective /ɪn'vektɪv/ *n* invettiva *f*

invent /ɪn'vent/ *vt* inventare

invention /ɪn'venʃn/ *n* invenzione *f*

inventive /ɪn'ventɪv/ *a* inventivo

inventor /ɪn'ventə(r)/ *n* inventore, -trice *mf*

inventory /'ɪnvəntrɪ/ *n* inventario *m*

inverse /ɪn'vɜːs/ *a* inverso ● *n* inverso *m*

inversely /ɪn'vɜːslɪ/ *adv* inversamente

invert /ɪn'vɜːt/ *vt* invertire; **in** ~**ed commas** tra virgolette

invertebrate /ɪn'vɜːtɪbrət/ *a* & *n* invertebrato *m*

invest /ɪn'vest/ *vt* investire ● *vi* fare investimenti; ~ **in** *(fam: buy)* comprarsi

investigate /ɪn'vestɪgeɪt/ *vt* investigare

investigation /ɪnvestɪ'geɪʃn/ *n* investigazione *f*

investigative journalism /ɪn'vestɪgətɪv/ *n* dietrologia *f*

investiture /ɪn'vestɪtjə(r)/ *n* investitura *f*

investment /ɪn'vestmənt/ *n* investimento *m*

investment: investment capital *n* capitale *m* di investimento. **investment income** *n* reddito *m* da investimenti. **investment trust** *n* fondo *m* comune di investimento

investor /ɪn'vestə(r)/ *n* investitore, -trice *mf*

inveterate /ɪn'vetərət/ *a* inveterato

invidious /ɪn'vɪdɪəs/ *a* ingiusto; ⟨*position*⟩ antipatico

invigilate /ɪn'vɪdʒɪleɪt/ *vi Sch* sorvegliare lo svolgimento di un esame

invigilator /ɪn'vɪdʒɪleɪtə(r)/ *n persona f che sorveglia lo svolgimento di un esame*

invigorate /ɪn'vɪɡəreɪt/ *vt* rinvigorire

invigorating /ɪn'vɪɡəreɪtɪŋ/ *a* tonificante

invincible /ɪn'vɪnsəbl/ *a* invincibile

inviolable /ɪn'vaɪələbl/ *a* inviolabile

invisible /ɪn'vɪzəbl/ *a* invisibile

invisible ink *n* inchiostro *m* simpatico

invitation /ɪnvɪ'teɪʃn/ *n* invito *m*

invite /ɪn'vaɪt/ *vt* invitare; ⟨*attract*⟩ attirare

■ **invite in** *vt* invitare a entrare

■ **invite round** *vt* invitare a casa

inviting /ɪn'vaɪtɪŋ/ *a* invitante

in vitro fertilization /ˌmviː'trəʊfɜːtɪlaɪ'zeɪʃn/ *n* fecondazione *f* in vitro

invoice /'ɪnvɔɪs/ *n* fattura *f* ● *vt* ~ **sb** emettere una fattura a qcno

invoke /ɪn'vəʊk/ *vt* invocare

involuntarily /ɪn'vɒlʌntərɪlɪ/ *adv* involontariamente

involuntary /ɪn'vɒləntrɪ/ *a* involontario

involve /ɪn'vɒlv/ *vt* comportare; ⟨*affect, include*⟩ coinvolgere; ⟨*entail*⟩ implicare; **get ~d with sb** legarsi a qcno; ⟨*romantically*⟩ legarsi sentimentalmente a qcno

involved /ɪn'vɒlvd/ *a* complesso

involvement /ɪn'vɒlvmənt/ *n* coinvolgimento *m*

invulnerable /ɪn'vʌln(ə)rəbl/ *a* invulnerabile; ⟨*position*⟩ inattaccabile

inward /'ɪnwəd/ *a* interno; ⟨*thoughts etc*⟩ interiore

inward investment *n Comm* investimento *m* di capitali stranieri

inward-looking /'ɪnwədlʊkɪŋ/ *a* ⟨*person*⟩ egocentrico; ⟨*society, policy*⟩ chiuso

inwardly /'ɪnwədlɪ/ *adv* interiormente

inward[s] /'ɪnwəd[z]/ *adv* verso l'interno

iodine /'aɪədiːn/ *n* iodio *m*

Ionian Sea /aɪəʊnɪən/ *n* mar *m* Ionio

iota /aɪ'əʊtə/ *n* briciolo *m*

IOU *abbr* (**I owe you**) pagherò *m inv*

IPA *n abbr* (**International Phonetic Alphabet**) AFI *m*

IQ *abbr* (**intelligence quotient**) Q.I. *m*

IRA *abbr* (**Irish Republican Army**) I.R.A. *f*

Iran /ɪ'rɑːn/ *n* Iran *m*

Iranian /ɪ'reɪnɪən/ *a & n* iraniano, -a *mf*

Iraq /ɪ'rɑːk/ *n* Iraq *m*

Iraqi /ɪ'rɑːkɪ/ *a & n* iracheno, -a *mf*

irascible /ɪ'ræsəbl/ *a* irascibile

irate /aɪ'reɪt/ *a* adirato

Ireland /'aɪələnd/ *n* Irlanda *f*

iris /'aɪrɪs/ *n Anat* iride *f*; *Bot* iris *f inv*

Irish /'aɪrɪʃ/ *a* irlandese ● **n the ~** *pl* gli irlandesi

Irishman /'aɪrɪʃmən/ *n* irlandese *m*

Irishwoman /'aɪrɪʃwʊmən/ *n* irlandese *f*

irk /ɜːk/ *vt* infastidire

irksome /'ɜːksəm/ *a* fastidioso

iron /'aɪən/ *a* di ferro ● *n* ferro *m*; ⟨*appliance*⟩ ferro *m* [da stiro] ● *vt/i* stirare

■ **iron out** *vt* eliminare stirando; *fig* appianare

Iron Curtain *n* cortina *f* di ferro

iron fist *n fig* pugno *m* di ferro

ironic[al] /aɪ'rɒnɪk[l]/ *a* ironico

ironing /'aɪənɪŋ/ *n* stirare *m*; ⟨*articles*⟩ roba *f* da stirare; **do the ~** stirare

ironing board *n* asse *f* da stiro

iron lung *n* polmone *m* d'acciaio

ironmonger /'aɪənmʌŋɡə(r)/ *n* ~**'s** [**shop**] negozio *m* di ferramenta

irony /'aɪərənɪ/ *n* ironia *f*

irradiate /ɪ'reɪdɪeɪt/ *vt* irradiare

irrational /ɪ'ræʃənl/ *a* irrazionale

irreconcilable /ɪ'rekənsaɪləbl/ *a* irreconciliabile

irrecoverable /ɪrɪ'kʌv(ə)rəbl/ *a* ⟨*debt, object*⟩ irrecuperabile; ⟨*loss*⟩ irreparabile

irredeemable /ɪrɪ'diːməbl/ *a* ⟨*Fin: shares, loan*⟩ irredimibile; ⟨*loss*⟩ irreparabile; ⟨*Relig: sinner*⟩ che non è redimibile

irrefutable /ɪrɪ'fjuːtəbl/ *a* irrefutabile

irregular /ɪ'reɡjʊlə(r)/ *a* irregolare

irregularity /ɪreɡjʊ'lærətɪ/ *n* irregolarità *f inv*

irregularly /ɪ'reɡjʊləlɪ/ *adv* in modo irregolare

irrelevant /ɪ'reləvənt/ *a* non pertinente

irreparable /ɪ'repərəbl/ *a* irreparabile

irreparably /ɪ'rep(ə)rəblɪ/ *adv* irreparabilmente

irreplaceable /ɪrɪ'pleɪsəbl/ *a* insostituibile

irrepressible /ɪrɪ'presəbl/ *a* irrefrenabile; ⟨*person*⟩ incontenibile

irreproachable /ɪrɪ'prəʊtʃəbl/ *a* irreprensibile

irresistible /ɪrɪ'zɪstəbl/ *a* irresistibile

irresolute /ɪ'rezəluːt/ *a* irresoluto

irrespective /ɪrɪ'spektɪv/ *a* ~ **of** senza riguardo per

irresponsible /ɪrɪ'spɒnsəbl/ *a* irresponsabile

irresponsibly /ɪrɪ'spɒnsəblɪ/ *adv* irresponsabilmente

irretrievable /ɪrɪ'triːvəbl/ *a* ⟨*loss, harm*⟩ irreparabile

irreverence /ɪ'revərəns/ *n* irriverenza *f*

irreverent /ɪ'revərənt/ *a* irreverente

irreverently /ɪ'revərəntlɪ/ *adv* in modo irreverente

irreversible /ɪrɪ'vɜːsəbl/ *a* irreversibile

irreversibly /ɪrɪ'vɜːsɪblɪ/ *adv* irreversibilmente

irrevocable /ɪ'revəkəbl/ *a* irrevocabile

irrevocably /ɪ'revəkəblɪ/ *adv* irrevocabilmente

irrigate /'ɪrɪɡeɪt/ *vt* irrigare

irrigation /ɪrɪ'ɡeɪʃn/ *n* irrigazione *f*

irritability /ɪrɪtə'bɪlətɪ/ *n* irritabilità *f*

irritable /'ɪrɪtəbl/ *a* irritabile

irritant /'ɪrɪtənt/ n sostanza f irritante; (fig: person) persona f irritante

irritate /'ɪrɪteɪt/ vt irritare

irritated /'ɪrɪteɪtɪd/ a irritato, stizzito

irritating /'ɪrɪteɪtɪŋ/ a irritante

irritation /ɪrɪ'teɪʃn/ n irritazione f

is /ɪz/ see **be**

Islam /'ɪzlɑːm/ n Islam m

Islamic /ɪz'læmɪk/ a islamico

island /'aɪlənd/ n isola f; (in road) isola f spartitraffico

islander /'aɪləndə(r)/ n isolano, -a mf

island hopping /'aɪləndhɒpɪŋ/ n go ~ ~ andare di isola in isola

isle /aɪl/ n liter isola f

isms /'ɪz(ə)mz/ npl pej ismi mpl

isobar /'aɪsəbɑː(r)/ n isobara f

isolate /'aɪsəleɪt/ vt isolare

isolated /'aɪsəleɪtɪd/ a isolato

isolation /aɪsə'leɪʃn/ n isolamento m

isosceles /aɪ'sɒsəliːz/ a isoscele

Israel /'ɪzreɪl/ n Israele m

Israeli /ɪz'reɪlɪ/ a & n israeliano, -a mf

issue /'ɪʃuː/ n (outcome) risultato m; (of magazine) numero m; (of stamps etc) emissione f; (offspring) figli mpl; (matter, question) questione f; **at ~** in questione; **take ~ with sb** prendere posizione contro qcno ● vt distribuire ⟨supplies⟩; rilasciare ⟨passport⟩; emettere ⟨stamps, order⟩; pubblicare ⟨book⟩; **be ~d with sth** ricevere qcsa ● vi ~ **from** uscire da

isthmus /'ɪsməs/ n (pl **-muses**) istmo m

it /ɪt/ pron (direct object) lo m, la f; (indirect object) gli m, le f; **it's broken** è rotto/rotta; **will it be enough?** basterà?; **it's hot** fa caldo; **it's raining** piove; **it's me** sono io; **who is it?** chi è?; **it's two o'clock** sono le due; **I doubt it** ne dubito; **take it with you** prendilo con te; **give it a wipe** dagli una pulita

IT n abbr (**information technology**) informatica f

Italian /ɪ'tæljən/ a & n italiano, -a mf; (language) italiano m

italic /ɪ'tælɪk/ a in corsivo

italics /ɪ'tælɪks/ npl corsivo msg; **in ~** in corsivo

Italy /'ɪtəlɪ/ n Italia f

itch /ɪtʃ/ n prurito m ● vi avere prurito, prudere; **be ~ing to** fam avere una voglia matta di

itching powder /'ɪtʃɪŋ/ n polverina f che dà prurito

itchy /'ɪtʃɪ/ a che prude; **my foot is ~** ho prurito al piede; **have ~ feet** fig avere la terra che scotta sotto i piedi

item /'aɪtəm/ n articolo m; (on agenda, programme) punto m; (on invoice) voce f; ~ [**of news**] notizia f

itemize /'aɪtəmaɪz/ vt dettagliare ⟨bill⟩

itinerant /aɪ'tɪnərənt/ a itinerante

itinerary /aɪ'tɪnərərɪ/ n itinerario m

its /ɪts/ poss pron suo m, sua f, suoi mpl, sue fpl; ~ **mother/cage** sua madre/la sua gabbia

it's = **it is**, **it has**

itself /ɪt'self/ pron (reflexive) si; (emphatic) essa stessa; **the baby looked at ~ in the mirror** il bambino si è guardato nello specchio; **by ~** da solo; **the machine in ~ is simple** la macchina di per sé è semplice

ITV abbr (**Independent Television**) stazione f televisiva privata

IUD n abbr (**intrauterine device**) spirale f

IVF n abbr **in vitro fertilization**

ivory /'aɪvərɪ/ n avorio m ● attrib d'avorio

Ivory Coast n Costa f d'Avorio

ivory tower n fig torre f d'avorio

ivy /'aɪvɪ/ n edera f

Jj

j, J /dʒeɪ/ n (letter) j, J f inv

jab /dʒæb/ n colpo m secco; (fam: injection) puntura f ● vt (pt/pp **jabbed**) punzecchiare

jabber /'dʒæbə(r)/ vi borbottare

jack /dʒæk/ n Auto cric m inv; Teleph jack m inv; (in cards) fante m, jack m inv

■ **jack in** vt sl piantare ⟨job⟩

■ **jack up** vt Auto sollevare [con il cric]; fam aumentare di molto ⟨salary etc⟩

jackal /'dʒæk(ə)l/ n sciacallo m

jackboot /'dʒækbuːt/ n stivale m militare

jackdaw /'dʒækdɔː/ n taccola f

jacket /'dʒækɪt/ n giacca f; (of book) sopraccoperta f

jacket potato n patata f cotta al forno con la buccia

jack-in-the-box n scatola f a sorpresa contenente un pupazzo a molla

jackknife /'dʒæknaɪf/ n coltello m a serramanico ● vi sbandare finendo di traverso rispetto al rimorchio

jackpot /'dʒækpɒt/ n premio m (di una lotteria); **win the ~** vincere alla lotteria; **hit the ~** fig fare un colpo grosso

jackrabbit /'dʒækræbɪt/ n lepre f americana

jade /dʒeɪd/ n giada f ● attrib di giada

jaded /'dʒeɪdɪd/ a spossato

jagged /'dʒægɪd/ a dentellato

jail /dʒeɪl/ = **gaol**
jail: jailbird n avanzo m di galera. **jailbreak** n evasione f. **jail sentence** n condanna f al carcere
jalopy /dʒə'lɒpɪ/ n fam vecchia carretta f
jam¹ /dʒæm/ n marmellata f
jam² n Auto ingorgo m; (fam: difficulty) guaio m ● v (pt/pp **jammed**) ● vt (cram) pigiare; disturbare ⟨broadcast⟩; inceppare ⟨mechanism, drawer etc⟩; **be ~med** ⟨roads:⟩ essere congestionato ● vi ⟨mechanism:⟩ incepparsi; ⟨window, drawer:⟩ incastrarsi
■ **jam on** vt **~ on the brakes** inchiodare
Jamaica /dʒə'meɪkə/ n Giamaica f
Jamaican /dʒə'meɪkən/ a & n giamaicano, -a mf
jam: jam jar n barattolo m per la marmellata. **jam-packed** a fam pieno zeppo. **jampot** n vasetto m per la marmellata
jangle /'dʒæŋgl/ vt far squillare ● vi squillare
janitor /'dʒænɪtə(r)/ n (caretaker) custode m; (in school) bidello, -a mf
January /'dʒænjʊərɪ/ n gennaio m
Japan /dʒə'pæn/ n Giappone m
Japanese /dʒæpə'niːz/ a & n giapponese mf; (language) giapponese m
jar¹ /dʒɑː(r)/ n (glass) barattolo m
jar² vi (pt/pp **jarred**) ⟨sound:⟩ stridere
jargon /'dʒɑːgən/ n gergo m
jarring /'dʒɑːrɪŋ/ a stridente
jasmine /'dʒæsmɪn/ n gelsomino m
jaundice /'dʒɔːndɪs/ n itterizia f
jaundiced /'dʒɔːndɪst/ a fig inacidito
jaunt /dʒɔːnt/ n gita f
jaunty /'dʒɔːntɪ/ a (-ier, -iest) sbarazzino
javelin /'dʒævlɪn/ n giavellotto m
jaw /dʒɔː/ n mascella f; (bone) mandibola f ● vi fam ciarlare
jawbone /'dʒɔːbəʊn/ n Anat osso m mascellare
jaywalker /'dʒeɪwɔːkə(r)/ n pedone m indisciplinato
jazz /dʒæz/ n jazz m
■ **jazz up** vt ravvivare
jazz band n complesso m di jazz
jazzy /'dʒæzɪ/ a vistoso
jealous /'dʒeləs/ a geloso
jealously /'dʒeləslɪ/ adv gelosamente
jealousy /'dʒeləsɪ/ n gelosia f
jeans /dʒiːnz/ npl [blue] jeans mpl
jeep /dʒiːp/ n jeep f inv
jeer /dʒɪə(r)/ n scherno m ● vi schernire; **~ at** prendersi gioco di ● vt (boo) fischiare
jell /dʒel/ vi concretarsi
jellied /'dʒelɪd/ a ⟨eels⟩ in gelatina
jelly /'dʒelɪ/ n gelatina f
jelly: jelly baby n caramella f gommosa a forma di pupazzetto. **jelly bean** n caramella f di gelatina di frutta. **jellyfish** n medusa f
jemmy /'dʒemɪ/ n piede m di porco
jeopardize /'dʒepədaɪz/ vt mettere in pericolo
jeopardy /'dʒepədɪ/ n **in ~** in pericolo
jerk /dʒɜːk/ n scatto m, scossa f ● vt scattare

● vi sobbalzare; ⟨limb, muscle:⟩ muoversi a scatti
jerkily /'dʒɜːkɪlɪ/ adv a scatti
jerkin /'dʒɜːkɪn/ n gilè m inv
jerky /'dʒɜːkɪ/ a traballante
jerry-built /'dʒerɪbɪlt/ a pej costruito alla bell'e meglio
jersey /'dʒɜːzɪ/ n maglia f; Sport maglietta f; (fabric) jersey m
Jerusalem /dʒə'ruːsələm/ n Gerusalemme f
jest /dʒest/ n scherzo m; **in ~** per scherzo ● vi scherzare
jester /'dʒestə(r)/ n buffone m
Jesuit /'dʒezjʊɪt/ n gesuita m ● a gesuitico
Jesus /'dʒiːzəs/ n Gesù m
jet¹ /dʒet/ n (stone) giaietto m
jet² n (of water) getto m; (nozzle) becco m; (plane) aviogetto m, jet m inv
jet: jet-black a nero ebano. **jet engine** n motore m a reazione. **jet fighter** n caccia m inv a reazione. **jetfoil** n aliscafo m. **jet lag** n scombussolamento m da fuso orario. **jet-propelled** /-prə'peld/ a a reazione. **jet propulsion** n propulsione f a getto
jettison /'dʒetɪsn/ vt gettare a mare; fig abbandonare
jetty /'dʒetɪ/ n molo m
Jew /dʒuː/ n ebreo m
jewel /'dʒuːəl/ n gioiello m
jewelled /'dʒuːəld/ a ornato di pietre preziose
jeweller /'dʒuːələ(r)/ n gioielliere m; **~'s [shop]** gioielleria f
jewellery /'dʒuːəlrɪ/ n gioielli mpl
Jewess /'dʒuːɪs/ n ebrea f
Jewish /'dʒuːɪʃ/ a ebreo
Jew's harp n Mus scacciapensieri m inv
jib /dʒɪb/ vi (pt/pp **jibbed**) fig mostrarsi riluttante (**at** a)
jibe /dʒaɪb/ n see **gibe**
jiffy /'dʒɪfɪ/ n fam **in a ~** in un batter d'occhio
Jiffy bag® n busta f imbottita
jig /dʒɪg/ n Mus giga f (danza popolare)
jiggle /'dʒɪg(ə)l/ vt scuotere
jigsaw /'dʒɪgsɔː/ n **~ [puzzle]** puzzle m inv
jilt /dʒɪlt/ vt piantare
jingle /'dʒɪŋgl/ n (rhyme) canzoncina f pubblicitaria ● vi tintinnare ● vt far tintinnare
jingoist /'dʒɪŋgəʊɪst/ n Pol sciovinista mf
jingoistic /dʒɪŋgəʊ'ɪstɪk/ a Pol sciovinistico
jinx /dʒɪŋks/ n fam (person) iettatore, -trice mf; **it's got a ~ on it** è iellato
jinxed /dʒɪŋkst/ a **be ~** essere iellato
jitters /'dʒɪtəz/ npl fam **have the ~** aver una gran fifa
jittery /'dʒɪtərɪ/ a fam in preda alla fifa
jive /dʒaɪv/ n (Am fam: talk) storie fpl
Jnr abbr **junior**
job /dʒɒb/ n lavoro m; **this is going to be quite a ~** fam [questa] non sarà un'impresa facile; **it's a good ~ that ...** meno male che...
job: jobcentre n ufficio m statale di collocamento. **job description** n mansionario m. **job-hunting** n ricerca f impiego
jobless /'dʒɒblɪs/ a senza lavoro

job: job lot *n* *(at auction)* insieme *m* di oggetti disparati. **job satisfaction** *n* soddisfazione *f* nel lavoro. **job security** *n* sicurezza *f* di impiego. **job-share** *n* *(position)* posto *m* condiviso ● *attrib* ⟨scheme⟩ di condivisione del posto di lavoro. **job-sharing** /-'ʃeərɪŋ/ *n* job sharing *m inv*

jockey /'dʒɒkɪ/ *n* fantino *m*

jocular /'dʒɒkjʊlə(r)/ *a* scherzoso

jocularly /'dʒɒkjʊləlɪ/ *adv* scherzosamente

jodhpurs /'dʒɒdpəz/ *npl* calzoni *mpl* alla cavallerizza

Joe Bloggs /dʒəʊ'blɒgz/ *n* l'uomo qualunque

jog /'dʒɒg/ *n* colpetto *m*; **at a ~** in un balzo; *Sport* **go for a ~** andare a fare jogging ● *v* (*pt/pp* **jogged**) ● *vt* (*hit*) urtare; **~ sb's memory** farlo ritornare in mente a qcno ● *vi* *Sport* fare jogging

■ **jog along** *vi fig* tirare avanti

jogging /'dʒɒgɪŋ/ *n* jogging *m*

john /dʒɒn/ *n* (*Am fam: toilet*) gabinetto *m*

John Bull *n* il tipico inglese

John Doe *n Am* uomo *m* non identificato

join /dʒɔɪn/ *n* giuntura *f* ● *vt* raggiungere, unire; raggiungere ⟨person⟩; (*become member of*) iscriversi a; entrare in ⟨firm⟩ ● *vi* ⟨roads:⟩ congiungersi

■ **join in** *vi* partecipare

■ **join up** *vi Mil* arruolarsi ● *vt* unire

■ **join up with** *vt* (*meet*) raggiungere ⟨friends⟩; congiungersi a ⟨road, river⟩

joiner /'dʒɔɪnə(r)/ *n* falegname *m*

joint /dʒɔɪnt/ *a* comune ● *n* articolazione *f*; (*in wood, brickwork*) giuntura *f*; *Culin* arrosto *m*; (*fam: bar*) bettola *f*; (*sl: drug*) spinello *m*

joint account *n* conto *m* [corrente] comune

joint agreement *n* accordo *m* collettivo

jointed /'dʒɔɪntɪd/ *a* ⟨Culin, chicken⟩ tagliato a pezzi; ⟨doll, puppet⟩ snodabile; ⟨rod, pole⟩ smontabile

joint effort *n* collaborazione *f*

joint honours *npl Br Univ* laurea *f* in due discipline

jointly /'dʒɔɪntlɪ/ *adv* unitamente

joint owner *n* comproprietario, -a *mf*

joint venture *n* joint venture *f inv*

joist /dʒɔɪst/ *n* travetto *m*

joke /dʒəʊk/ *n* (*trick*) scherzo *m*; (*funny story*) barzelletta *f* ● *vi* scherzare

joker /'dʒəʊkə(r)/ *n* burlone, -a *mf*; (*in cards*) jolly *m inv*

joking /'dʒəʊkɪŋ/ *n* **~ apart** scherzi a parte

jokingly /'dʒəʊkɪŋlɪ/ *adv* per scherzo

jollity /'dʒɒlətɪ/ *n* allegria *f*

jolly /'dʒɒlɪ/ *a* (**-ier, -iest**) allegro ● *adv fam* molto

Jolly Roger /'rɒdʒə(r)/ *n* bandiera *f* dei pirati

jolt /dʒəʊlt/ *n* scossa *f*, sobbalzo *m* ● *vt* far sobbalzare ● *vi* sobbalzare

Jordan /'dʒɔ:dn/ *n* Giordania *f*; (*river*) Giordano *m*

Jordanian /dʒɔ:'deɪnɪən/ *a* & *n* giordano, -a *mf*

joss stick /'dʒɒs/ *n* bastoncino *m* d'incenso

jostle /'dʒɒsl/ *vt* spingere

jot /dʒɒt/ *n* nulla *f*

■ **jot down** *vt* (*pt/pp* **jotted**) annotare

jotter /'dʒɒtə(r)/ *n* taccuino *m*; (*with a spine*) quaderno *m*

jottings /'dʒɒtɪŋz/ *npl* annotazioni *fpl*

journal /'dʒɜ:nl/ *n* giornale *m*; (*diary*) diario *m*

journalese /dʒɜ:nə'li:z/ *n* gergo *m* giornalistico

journalism /'dʒɜ:nəlɪzm/ *n* giornalismo *m*

journalist /'dʒɜ:nəlɪst/ *n* giornalista *mf*

journey /'dʒɜ:nɪ/ *n* viaggio *m* ● *vi* viaggiare

jovial /'dʒəʊvɪəl/ *a* gioviale

jowl /dʒaʊl/ *n* (*jaw*) mascella *f*; (*fleshy fold*) guancia *f*; **cheek by ~ with sb** fianco a fianco con qcno

joy /dʒɔɪ/ *n* gioia *f*

joyful /'dʒɔɪfʊl/ *a* gioioso

joyfully /'dʒɔɪfʊlɪ/ *adv* con gioia

joyless /'dʒɔɪlɪs/ *a* ⟨occasion⟩ triste; ⟨marriage⟩ infelice

joy: joyride *n fam* giro *m* con una macchina rubata. **joyrider** *n fam* persona *f* che ruba una macchina per andare a fare un giro. **joystick** *n Comput* joystick *m inv*

Jr *abbr* **junior**

jubilant /'dʒu:bɪlənt/ *a* giubilante

jubilation /dʒu:bɪ'leɪʃn/ *n* giubilo *m*

jubilee /'dʒu:bɪlɪ/ *n* giubileo *m*

Judaism /'dʒu:deɪɪzm/ *n* giudaismo *m*

judder /'dʒʌdə(r)/ *vi* vibrare violentemente

judge /dʒʌdʒ/ *n* giudice *m* ● *vt* giudicare; (*estimate*) valutare; (*consider*) ritenere ● *vi* giudicare (**by** da)

judgement /'dʒʌdʒmənt/ *n* giudizio *m*; *Jur* sentenza *f*

judicial /dʒu:'dɪʃl/ *a* giudiziario

judiciary /dʒu:'dɪʃərɪ/ *n* magistratura *f*

judicious /dʒu:'dɪʃəs/ *a* giudizioso

judo /'dʒu:dəʊ/ *n* judo *m*

jug /dʒʌg/ *n* brocca *f*; (*small*) bricco *m*

juggernaut /'dʒʌgənɔ:t/ *n fam* grosso autotreno *m*

juggle /'dʒʌgl/ *vi* fare giochi di destrezza

juggler /'dʒʌglə(r)/ *n* giocoliere, -a *mf*

jugular /'dʒʌgjʊlə(r)/ *n* giugulare *f*; **go straight for the ~** *fig* colpire nel punto debole

juice /dʒu:s/ *n* succo *m*; **~ extractor** *n* spremiagrumi *m inv* elettrico

juicy /'dʒu:sɪ/ *a* (**-ier, -iest**) succoso; (*fam: story*) piccante

jukebox /'dʒu:kbɒks/ *n* juke-box *m inv*

July /dʒʊ'laɪ/ *n* luglio *m*

jumble /'dʒʌmbl/ *n* accozzaglia *f* ● *vt* **~** [**up**] mischiare

jumble sale *n* vendita *f* di beneficenza

jumbo /'dʒʌmbəʊ/ *n* **~** [**jet**] jumbo jet *m inv*

jump /dʒʌmp/ *n* salto *m*; (*in prices*) balzo *m*; (*in horse racing*) ostacolo *m* ● *vi* saltare; (*with fright*) sussultare; ⟨prices:⟩ salire rapidamente; **~ to conclusions** saltare alle conclusioni ● *vt* saltare; **~ the gun** *fig* precipitarsi; **~ the queue** non rispettare la fila

■ **jump at** *vt fig* accettare con entusiasmo ⟨*offer*⟩

■ **jump down** *vt* **~ down sb's throat** saltare addosso a qcno

■ **jump in** *vi* (*to vehicle*) saltar su

■ **jump up** *vi* rizzarsi in piedi

jumped-up /dʒʌmpt'ʌp/ *a* montato

jumper /'dʒʌmpə(r)/ *n* (*sweater*) golf *m inv*

jump: jump jet *n* aeroplano *m* a decollo e atterraggio verticali. **jump leads** *npl* cavi *mpl* per batteria. **jump-start** *vt far partire con i cavi da batteria.* **jumpsuit** *n* tuta *f*

jumpy /'dʒʌmpɪ/ *a* nervoso

junction /'dʒʌŋkʃn/ *n* (*of roads*) incrocio *m*; *Rail* nodo *m* ferroviario

juncture /'dʒʌŋktʃə(r)/ *n* **at this ~** a questo punto

June /dʒuːn/ *n* giugno *m*

Jungian /'jʊŋɪən/ *a* junghiano

jungle /'dʒʌŋgl/ *n* giungla *f*

junior /'dʒuːnɪə(r)/ *a* giovane; (*in rank*) subalterno; *Sport* junior *inv* ● *n* **the ~s** *pl Sch* i più giovani

junior doctor *n* assistente *mf* ospedaliero, -a

junior school *n* scuola *f* elementare

juniper /'dʒuːnɪpə(r)/ *n* ginepro *m*

junk /dʒʌŋk/ *n* cianfrusaglie *fpl*

junk food *n fam* cibo *m* poco sano, porcherie *fpl*

junkie /'dʒʌŋkɪ/ *n sl* tossico, -a *mf*

junk: junk mail *n* posta *f* spazzatura. **junk shop** *n* negozio *m* di rigattiere. **junkyard** *n* (*for scrap*) rottamaio *m*; (*for old cars*) cimitero *m* delle macchine

junta /'dʒʌntə/ *n* giunta *f* militare

jurisdiction /dʒʊərɪs'dɪkʃn/ *n* giurisdizione *f*

jurisprudence /dʒʊrɪs'pruːdəns/ *n* giurisprudenza *f*

jurist /'dʒʊərɪst/ *n* giurista *mf*

juror /'dʒʊərə(r)/ *n* giurato, -a *mf*

jury /'dʒʊərɪ/ *n* giuria *f*

jury box *n* banco *m* dei giurati

jury service *n* do **~ ~** far parte di una giuria popolare

just /dʒʌst/ *a* giusto ● *adv* (*barely*) appena; (*simply*) solo; (*exactly*) esattamente; **~ as tall** altrettanto alto; **~ as I was leaving** proprio quando stavo andando via; **I've ~ seen her** l'ho appena vista; **it's ~ as well** meno male; **~ at that moment** proprio in quel momento; **~ listen!** almeno ascolta!; **I'm ~ going** sto andando proprio ora

justice /'dʒʌstɪs/ *n* giustizia *f*; **do ~ to** rendere giustizia a; **J~ of the Peace** giudice *m* conciliatore

justifiable /dʒʌstɪ'faɪəbl/ *a* giustificabile

justifiably /dʒʌstɪ'faɪəblɪ/ *adv* in modo giustificato

justification /dʒʌstɪfɪ'keɪʃn/ *n* giustificazione *f*

justified /'dʒʌstɪfaɪd/ *a* ⟨*action*⟩ motivato

justify /'dʒʌstɪfaɪ/ *vt* (*pt/pp* **-ied**) giustificare

justly /'dʒʌstlɪ/ *adv* giustamente

justness /'dʒʌstnɪs/ *n* (*of decision*) giustezza *f*; (*of claim, request*) legittimità *f*

jut /dʒʌt/ *vi* (*pt/pp* **jutted**) **~ out** sporgere

jute /dʒuːt/ *n* iuta *f*

juvenile /'dʒuːvənaɪl/ *a* giovanile; (*childish*) infantile; (*for the young*) per i giovani ● *n* giovane *mf*

juvenile: juvenile crime *n* criminalità *f* presso i giovani . **juvenile delinquency** *n* delinquenza *f* giovanile. **juvenile delinquent** *n* delinquente *mf* minorile. **juvenile offender** *n Jur* imputato, -a *mf* minorenne

juxtapose /dʒʌkstə'pəʊz/ *vt* giustapporre

Kk

k, K /keɪ/ *n* (*letter*) k, K *f inv*

K *abbr* (**kilo**) k; *abbr* (**kilobyte**) KB, Kbyte *m inv*; *abbr* **thousand pounds**; **he earns £50 K** guadagna 50 mila sterline

kaleidoscope /kə'laɪdəskəʊp/ *n* caleidoscopio *m*

kangaroo /kæŋgə'ruː/ *n* canguro *m*

kaput /kə'pʊt/ *a fam* kaputt *inv*

karaoke /kærɪ'əʊkɪ/ *n* karaoke *m inv*

karate /kə'rɑːtɪ/ *n* karatè *m*

kart /kɑːt/ *n* kart *m inv*

Kashmir /kæʃ'mɪə(r)/ *n* Kashmir *m*

Kashmiri /kæʃ'mɪərɪ/ *a* del Kashmir ● *n* nativo, -a *mf* del Kashmir

kayak /'kaɪæk/ *n* kayak *m inv*

KB *n abbr* (**kilobyte**) KB, Kbyte *m inv*

kebab /kɪ'bæb/ *n Culin* spiedino *m* di carne

kedgeree /'kedʒərɪ/ *n Br piatto m indiano a base di pesce, riso e uova*

keel /kiːl/ *n* chiglia *f*

■ **keel over** *vi* capovolgersi

keen /kiːn/ *a* (*intense*) acuto; ⟨*interest*⟩ vivo; (*eager*) entusiastico; ⟨*competition*⟩ feroce; ⟨*wind, knife*⟩ tagliente; **~ on** entusiasta di; **she's ~ on him** le piace molto; **be ~ to do sth** avere voglia di fare qcsa

keenly /'kiːnlɪ/ *adv* intensamente

keenness /'kiːnnɪs/ *n* entusiasmo *m*

keep /ki:p/ *n* (*maintenance*) mantenimento *m*; (*of castle*) maschio *m*; **for ~s** per sempre ● *v* (*pt/pp* **kept**) ● *vt* tenere; (*not throw away*) conservare; (*detain*) trattenere; mantenere (*family, promise*); tenere (*shop*); allevare (*animals*); rispettare (*law, rules*); **~ sth hot** tenere qcsa in caldo; **~ sb waiting** far aspettare qcno; **~ sth to oneself** tenere qcsa per sé; **~ vi** (*remain*) rimanere; (*food:*) conservarsi; **~ calm** rimanere calmo; **~ left/right** tenere la sinistra/la destra; **~ [on] doing sth** continuare a fare qcsa

■ **keep at** *vt* (*persevere with*) **~ at it!** non mollare!

■ **keep away** *vi* non avvicinarsi, stare alla larga ● *vt* tenere lontano

■ **keep away from** *vt* non avvicinarsi a (*fire*); stare alla larga da (*sb*); **~ sb away from sth** tener qcno lontano da qcsa

■ **keep back** *vt* trattenere (*person*); **~ sth back from sb** tenere nascosto qcsa a qcno ● *vi* tenersi indietro

■ **keep down** *vi* star giù ● *vt* mandar giù (*food*); mantenere basso (*prices, inflation etc*); **~ one's voice down** non alzare la voce

■ **keep from** *vt* **~ sb from doing sth** prevenire qcno dal fare qcsa; **~ sb from** impedire a qcno di (*falling*); **~ sb from their work** distogliere qcno dal lavoro; **~ sth from sb** tenere nascosto qcsa a qcno; **~ the truth from sb** nascondere la verità a qcno

■ **keep in** *vt* (*in school*) trattenere oltre l'orario per punizione; reprimere (*indignation, anger etc*)

■ **keep in with** *vt* mantenersi in buoni rapporti con

■ **keep off** *vt* (*avoid*) astenersi da (*cigarettes, chocolate etc*); evitare (*delicate subject*)

■ **keep on** *vi* (*continue one's journey*) proseguire; *fam* assillare (**at sb** qcno) ● *vt* non togliersi (*coat, hat*); tenere (*employee*)

■ **keep out of** *vt* (*person:*) non entrare in (*place*); tenersi fuori da (*argument*); **~ sb out of** tenere qcno alla larga da (*place*); **~ me out of this!** lasciamene fuori!

■ **keep to** *vt* non deviare da (*path, subject*); **~ sth to oneself** tenere qcsa per sé

■ **keep up** *vi* (*remain level*) stare al passo; (*rain, good weather:*) mantenersi ● *vt* (*continue*) continuare; (*prevent from going to bed*) tenere alzato; mantenere alto (*prices*); tener su (*trousers*)

keeper /'ki:pə(r)/ *n* custode *mf*

keep-fit *n* ginnastica *f*

keeping /'ki:pɪŋ/ *n* custodia *f*; **be in ~ with** essere in armonia con

keepsake /'ki:pseɪk/ *n* ricordo *m*

keg /keg/ *n* barilotto *m*

kelp /kelp/ *n* laminaria *f*, fuco *m*

kennel /'kenl/ *n* canile *m*; **~s** *pl* (*boarding*) canile *m*; (*breeding*) allevamento *m* di cani

Kenya /'kenjə/ *n* Kenia *m*

Kenyan /'kenjən/ *a* & *n* keniota *mf*

kept /kept/ *see* **keep**

kerb /kɜːb/ *n* bordo *m* del marciapiede

kernel /'kɜːnl/ *n* nocciolo *m*

kerosene /'kerəsi:n/ *n Am* cherosene *m*

kestrel /'kestrəl/ *n* gheppio *m*

ketchup /'ketʃʌp/ *n* ketchup *m*

kettle /'ket(ə)l/ *n* bollitore *m*; **put the ~ on** mettere l'acqua a bollire

kettledrum /'ket(ə)ldrʌm/ *n* timpano *m*

key /ki:/ *n also Mus* chiave *f*; (*of piano, typewriter*) tasto *m* ● *vt* **~ [in]** digitare (*character*); **could you ~ this?** puoi battere questo?

key: keyboard *n Comput, Mus* tastiera *f*. **keyboarder** *n* tastierista *mf*. **keyboard player** *n* tastierista *mf*

keyed-up /ki:d'ʌp/ *a* (*excited*) teso; (*anxious*) estremamente agitato; (*ready to act*) psicologicamente preparato

key: keyhole *n* buco *m* della serratura. **key money** *n* (*for apartment*) somma *f* richiesta ad un affittuario quando si trasferisce nell'abitazione. **keynote** *n Mus* tonica *f*; (*main theme*) tema *m* principale. **keynote speech** *n* discorso *m* programmatico. **keypad** *n Comput* tastiera *f* numerica. **keyring** *n* portachiavi *m inv*. **key signature** *n Mus* armatura *f* di chiave. **keystroke** *n Comput* keystroke *m inv*. **keyword** *n* parola *f* chiave

kg *abbr* (**kilogram**) kg

khaki /'kɑːkɪ/ *a* cachi *inv* ● *n* cachi *m*

kibbutz /kɪ'bʊts/ *n* (*pl* **-es** *or* **-im**) kibbutz *m inv*

kibosh /'kaɪbɒʃ/ *n fam* **put the ~ on sth** mandare all'aria qcsa

kick /kɪk/ *n* calcio *m*; (*fam: thrill*) piacere *m*; **for ~s** *fam* per spasso; **get a ~ out of sth** trovare un piacere incredibile in qcsa ● *vt* dar calci a; **~ the bucket** *fam* crepare ● *vi* (*animal:*) scalciare; (*person:*) dare calci

■ **kick around** *vi fam* essere in giro ● *vt* buttar giù (*idea*)

■ **kick in** *vt* sfondare a calci (*door*)

■ **kick off** *vi Sport* dare il calcio d'inizio; *fam* iniziare

■ **kick out** *vt* (*fam: of school, club etc*) sbatter fuori

■ **kick up** *vt* **~ up a row** fare una scenata

kickback /'kɪkbæk/ *n fam* tangente *f*

kick-off *n Sport* calcio *m* d'inizio; **for a ~** *fam* tanto per cominciare

kid /kɪd/ *n* capretto *m*; (*fam: child*) ragazzino, -a *mf* ● *v* (*pt/pp* **kidded**)● *vt fam* prendere in giro. ● *vi fam* scherzare

kid gloves *npl* guanti *mpl* di capretto; **handle sb with ~ ~** trattare qcno con i guanti

kidnap /'kɪdnæp/ *vt* (*pt/pp* **-napped**) rapire, sequestrare

kidnapper /'kɪdnæpə(r)/ *n* sequestratore, -trice *mf*, rapitore, -trice *mf*

kidnapping /'kɪdnæpɪŋ/ *n* rapimento *m*, sequestro *m* [di persona]

kidney /'kɪdnɪ/ *n* rene *m*; *Culin* rognone *m*

kidney: kidney bean *n* fagiolo *m* comune. **kidney dialysis** *n* dialisi *f*. **kidney failure** *n* collasso *m* renale. **kidney machine** *n* rene *m* artificiale. **kidney-shaped** /'kɪdnɪʃeɪpt/ a a forma di fagiolo. **kidney stone** n calcolo m renale

kill /kɪl/ vt uccidere; fig metter fine a; ammazzare ⟨time⟩

■ **kill off** vt eliminare ⟨people⟩; distruggere ⟨plants, insects⟩

killer /'kɪlə(r)/ n assassino, -a mf; **it was a real ~** fig è stato micidiale

killer instinct n istinto m di uccidere; fig spietatezza f

killer whale n orca f

killing /'kɪlɪŋ/ n uccisione f; ⟨murder⟩ omicidio m

killjoy /'kɪldʒɔɪ/ n guastafeste mf inv

kiln /kɪln/ n fornace f

kilo /'kiːləʊ/ n chilo m

kilo /'kɪlə/: **~byte** kilobyte m inv. **kilogram** n chilogrammo m. **kilohertz** /'kɪləhɜːts/ n chilohertz m inv. **kilometre** n chilometro m. **kilowatt** n chilowatt m inv

kilt /kɪlt/ n kilt m inv ⟨gonnellino degli scozzesi⟩

kimono /kɪ'məʊnəʊ/ n kimono m inv, chimono m inv

kin /kɪn/ n congiunti mpl; **next of ~** parente m stretto

kind¹ /kaɪnd/ n genere m, specie f; ⟨brand, type⟩ tipo m; **what ~ of car?** che tipo di macchina?; **~ of** fam alquanto; **two of a ~** due della stessa specie

kind² a gentile, buono; **~ to animals** amante degli animali; **~ regards** cordiali saluti

kindergarten /'kɪndəgɑːtn/ n asilo m infantile

kind-hearted /-'hɑːtɪd/ a ⟨person⟩ di [buon] cuore

kindle /'kɪndl/ vt accendere

kindly /'kaɪndlɪ/ a (**-ier**, **-iest**) benevolo ● adv gentilmente; ⟨if you please⟩ per favore

kindness /'kaɪndnɪs/ n gentilezza f

kindred /'kɪndrɪd/ a **she's a ~ spirit** è la mia/sua/tua anima gemella

kinetic /kɪ'netɪk/ a cinetico

king /kɪŋ/ n re m inv

kingdom /'kɪŋdəm/ n regno m

kingfisher /'kɪŋfɪʃə(r)/ n martin m inv pescatore

kingly /'kɪŋlɪ/ a also fig regale

king-sized /'kɪŋsaɪzd/ a ⟨cigarette⟩ king-size inv, lungo; ⟨bed⟩ matrimoniale grande

kink /kɪŋk/ n attorcigliamento m

kinky /'kɪŋkɪ/ a fam bizzarro

kinship /'kɪnʃɪp/ n ⟨blood relationship⟩ parentela f; ⟨empathy⟩ affinità f

kiosk /'kiːɒsk/ n chiosco m; Teleph cabina f telefonica

kip /kɪp/ n fam pisolino m; **have a ~** schiacciare un pisolino ● vi (pt/pp **kipped**) fam dormire

kipper /'kɪpə(r)/ n aringa f affumicata

kirk /kɜːk/ n ⟨Scottish⟩ chiesa f

kiss /kɪs/ n bacio m ● vt baciare ● vi baciarsi

kiss of death n colpo m di grazia

kiss of life n respirazione f bocca a bocca;

give sb the ~ ~ ~ fare la respirazione bocca a bocca a qcno

kissogram /'kɪsəgræm/ n servizio m commerciale in cui un messaggio di auguri viene scherzosamente recapitato con un bacio da una ragazza in abiti succinti

kit /kɪt/ n equipaggiamento m, kit m inv; ⟨tools⟩ attrezzi mpl; ⟨construction ~⟩ pezzi mpl da montare, kit m inv ● vt (pt/pp **kitted**) **~ out** equipaggiare

kitbag /'kɪtbæg/ n sacco m a spalla

kitchen /'kɪtʃɪn/ n cucina f ● attrib di cucina

kitchenette /kɪtʃɪ'net/ n cucinino m

kitchen: kitchen foil n carta f di alluminio. **kitchen garden** n orto m. **kitchen paper** n carta f da cucina. **kitchen roll** n Scottex® m inv. **kitchen scales** npl bilancia f da cucina. **kitchensink** n lavello m; **everything bar the ~** fig proprio tutto quanto. **kitchen-sink drama** n teatro m neorealista. **kitchen towel** n Scottex® m inv. **kitchen unit** n elemento m componibile da cucina. **kitchenware** n ⟨crockery⟩ stoviglie fpl; ⟨implements⟩ utensili mpl da cucina

kite /kaɪt/ n aquilone m

kitemark /'kaɪtmɑːk/ n Br marchio m di conformità alle norme britanniche

kith /kɪθ/ n **~ and kin** amici e parenti mpl

kitsch /kɪtʃ/ n kitsch m inv

kitten /'kɪtn/ n gattino m

kitty /'kɪtɪ/ n ⟨money⟩ cassa f comune

kiwi /'kiːwiː/ n Zool kiwi m inv

kiwi fruit n kiwi m inv

kleptomania /kleptə'meɪnɪə/ n cleptomania f

kleptomaniac /kleptə'meɪnɪæk/ n cleptomane mf

km abbr (**kilometre**) km

kmh abbr (**kilometres per hour**) km/h

knack /næk/ n tecnica f; **have the ~ for doing sth** avere la capacità di fare qcsa

knapsack /'næpsæk/ n sacco m da montagna

knave /neɪv/ m ⟨in cards⟩ fante m; ⟨rogue⟩ furfante m

knead /niːd/ vt impastare

knee /niː/ n ginocchio m; **go down on one's ~s to sb** inginocchiarsi davanti qcno

kneecap /'niːkæp/ n rotula f

kneel /niːl/ vi (pt/pp **knelt**) **~** [**down**] inginocchiarsi; **be ~ing** essere inginocchiato

knee-length a ⟨boots⟩ alto; ⟨skirt⟩ al ginocchio; ⟨socks⟩ lungo

knee-pad n ginocchiera f

knees-up /'niːzʌp/ n Br fam festa f

knell /nel/ n campana f a morto; **sound the death ~ for sth** segnare la fine di qcsa

knelt /nelt/ see **kneel**

knew /njuː/ see **know**

knickerbocker glory /nɪkəbɒkə'glɔːrɪ/ n coppa f [gelato] gigante

knickers /'nɪkəz/ npl mutandine fpl

knick-knacks /'nɪknæks/ npl ninnoli mpl

knife /naɪf/ n (pl **knives**) coltello m ● vt fam accoltellare

knife: knife-edge *n* **be on a ~** ⟨*person*:⟩ trovarsi sul filo del rasoio; ⟨*negotiations*:⟩ essere appeso a un filo. **knifepoint** *n* **at ~** sotto la minaccia di un coltello. **knife sharpener** *n* affilacoltelli *m inv*

knight /naɪt/ *n* cavaliere *m*; (*in chess*) cavallo *m* ● *vt* nominare cavaliere

knighthood /'naɪthʊd/ *n* **receive a ~** ricevere il titolo di cavaliere

knit /nɪt/ *vt/i* (*pt/pp* **knitted**) lavorare a maglia; **~ one, purl one** un diritto, un rovescio; **~ one's brow** aggrottare le sopracciglia

knitted /'nɪtɪd/ *a* lavorato a maglia

knitting /'nɪtɪŋ/ *n* lavorare *m* a maglia; (*product*) lavoro *m* a maglia

knitting needle *n* ferro *m* da calza

knitwear /'nɪtweə(r)/ *n* maglieria *f*

knives /naɪvz/ *npl see* **knife**

knob /nɒb/ *n* pomello *m*; (*of stick*) pomo *m*; (*of butter*) noce *f*

knobbly /'nɒblɪ/ *a* nodoso; (*bony*) spigoloso

knock /nɒk/ *n* colpo *m;* **there was a ~ at the door** hanno bussato alla porta ● *vt* bussare a ⟨*door*⟩; (*fam: criticize*) denigrare; **~ a hole in sth** fare un buco in qcsa; **~ one's head** battere la testa (**on** contro) ● *vi* (*at door*) bussare

■ **knock about** *vt* malmenare ● *vi fam* girovagare

■ **knock back** *vt* (*fam: drink quickly*) buttar giù tutto d'un fiato

■ **knock down** *vt* far cadere; (*with fist*) stendere con un pugno; (*in car*) investire; (*demolish*) abbattere; (*fam: reduce*) ribassare ⟨*price*⟩

■ **knock off** *vt* (*fam: steal*) fregare; (*fam: complete quickly*) fare alla bell'e meglio ● *vi* (*fam: cease work*) staccare

■ **knock out** *vt* eliminare; (*make unconscious*) mettere K.O.; (*fam: anaesthetize*) addormentare

■ **knock over** *vt* rovesciare; (*in car*) investire

■ **knock up** *vt fam* (*prepare quickly*) buttare giù; (*sl: make pregnant*) mettere incinta

knock: knockabout *n Sport* **have a ~** palleggiare. **knock-down furniture** *n* mobili *mpl* scomponibili. **knock-down price** *n* prezzo *m* stracciato

knocker /'nɒkə(r)/ *n* battente *m*; (*critic*) denigratore, -trice *mf*

knocking-off time /nɒkɪŋ'ɒf/ *n* ~ **~ is five o'clock** si stacca alle cinque

knock: knock-kneed /-'niːd/ *a* con gambe storte. **knock-on effect** *n* implicazioni *fpl*. **knock-out** *n* knock-out *m inv*; **be a ~** *fig* essere uno schianto

knoll /nəʊl/ *n* collinetta *f*

knot /nɒt/ *n* nodo *m*; **to tie the ~** *fam* convolare a giuste nozze ● *vt* (*pt/pp* **knotted**) annodare; *Br fam* **get ~ted!** vai a farti friggere!

knotty /'nɒtɪ/ *a* (**-ier, -iest**) *fam* spinoso

know /nəʊ/ *v* (*pt* **knew**, *pp* **known**) ● *vt* sapere; conoscere ⟨*person, place*⟩; (*recognize*) riconoscere; **get to ~ sb** conoscere qcno; **~ how to swim** sapere nuotare; **~ right from wrong** saper distinguere il bene dal male ● *vi* sapere; **did you ~ about this?** lo sapevi? ● *n* **in the ~** *fam* al corrente

■ **know of** *vt* conoscere; **not that I ~ of** non che io sappia

know-all *n fam* sapientone, -a *mf*

know-how *n* abilità *f*

knowing /'nəʊɪŋ/ *a* d'intesa

knowingly /'nəʊɪŋlɪ/ *adv* (*intentionally*) consapevolmente; ⟨*smile etc*⟩ con un aria d'intesa

knowledgable /'nɒlɪdʒəbl/ *a* ben informato

knowledge /'nɒlɪdʒ/ *n* conoscenza *f*

known /nəʊn/ *see* **know** ● *a* noto

knuckle /'nʌkl/ *n* nocca *f*

■ **knuckle down** *vi* darci sotto (**to** con)

■ **knuckle under** *vi* sottomettersi

koala [**bear**] /kəʊ'ɑːlə/ *n* koala *m inv*

Koran /kə'rɑːn/ *n* Corano *m*

Korea /kə'rɪə/ *n* Corea *f*

Korean /kə'rɪən/ *a & n* coreano, -a *mf*; (*language*) coreano *m*

Korean // *a & n* coreano, -a *mf*

kosher /'kəʊʃə(r)/ *a* kasher *inv*

kowtow /kaʊ'taʊ/ *vi* piegarsi

kph *abbr* (**kilometres per hour**) km/h

kudos /'kjuːdɒs/ *n fam* gloria *f*

Kurd /'kɜːd/ *n* curdo,-a *mf* ● *a* curdo

Kurdish /'kɜːdɪʃ/ *a & n* (*language*) curdo *m*

Kurdistan /kɜːdɪ'stɑːn/ *n* Kurdistan *m*

Kuwait /kʊ'weɪt/ *n* Kuwait *m*

Kuwaiti /kʊ'weɪtɪ/ *a & n* kuwaitiano, -a *mf*

kW *abbr* (**kilowatt**) kW

kWh *abbr* (**kilowatt-hour**) kWh

Ll

I, L /el/ *n* (*letter*) l, L *f inv*
L *abbr* (**lake**) L; *abbr* (**large**) L; *abbr*
(**learner**) P; *abbr* (**left**) sinistra *f*; *abbr* (**line**)
v; *abbr* (**litre(s)**) l
lab /læb/ *n fam* laboratorio *m*
lab assistant *n* assistente *mf* di laboratorio
lab coat *n* camice *m*
label /'leɪbl/ *n* etichetta *f* ● *vt* (*pt/pp*
labelled) mettere un'etichetta a; *fig* etichettare ⟨*person*⟩
labelling /'leɪbəlɪŋ/ *n* (*act*) etichettatura *f*
laboratory /lə'bɒrətrɪ/ *n* laboratorio *m*
laborious /lə'bɔːrɪəs/ *a* laborioso
laboriously /lə'bɔːrɪəslɪ/ *adv* in modo laborioso
labor union /'leɪbə/ *n Am* sindacato *m*
labour /'leɪbə(r)/ *n* lavoro *m*; (*workers*) manodopera *f*; *Med* doglie *fpl*; **be in** ~ avere le doglie; **L~** *Pol* partito *m* laburista ● *attrib Pol*
laburista ● *vi* lavorare ● *vt* ~ **the point** *fig*
ribadire il concetto
labour camp *n* campo *m* di lavoro
laboured /'leɪbəd/ *a* ⟨*breathing*⟩ affannato
labourer /'leɪbərə(r)/ *n* manovale *m*
labour exchange *n old* ufficio *m* di collocamento
labour force *n* manodopera *f*
labouring /'leɪbərɪŋ/ *n* lavoro *m* manuale
labour: labour-intensive *a* ad uso intensivo
di lavoro; **be** ~ richiedere molta manodopera. **labour market** *n* mercato *m* del lavoro.
Labour Party *n* Partito *m* laburista. **labour**
relations *npl* relazioni *fpl* industriali.
labour-saving /'leɪbəseɪvɪŋ/ *a* che fa risparmiare lavoro e fatica. **labour ward** *n* reparto
m maternità
labrador /'læbrədɔː(r)/ *n* (*dog*) labrador *m*
inv
lab technician *n* technico, -a *mf* di laboratorio
laburnum /lə'bɜːnəm/ *n* maggiociondolo *m*
labyrinth /'læbərɪnθ/ *n* labirinto *m*
lace /leɪs/ *n* pizzo *m*; (*of shoe*) laccio *m*
● *attrib* di pizzo ● *vt* allacciare ⟨*shoes*⟩; correggere ⟨*drink*⟩
lacerate /'læsəreɪt/ *vt* lacerare
laceration /læsə'reɪʃn/ *n* lacerazione *f*
lace-up [**shoe**] *n* scarpa *f* stringata
lack /læk/ *n* mancanza *f*; ~ **of interest**
disinteressamento *m*; ~ **of evidence** insufficienza *f* di prove ● *vt* **the programme ~s**
originality il programma manca di originalità; **I** ~ **the time** mi manca il tempo ● *vi* be
~**ing** mancare; **be** ~**ing in sth** mancare di
qcsa
lackadaisical /lækə'deɪzɪkl/ *a* senza entu-

siasmo
lackey /'lækɪ/ *n* lacchè *m inv*
lacklustre /'læklʌstə(r)/ *a* scialbo
laconic /lə'kɒnɪk/ *a* laconico
laconically /lə'kɒnɪklɪ/ *adv* laconicamente
lacquer /'lækə(r)/ *n* lacca *f*
lactate /læk'teɪt/ *vi* produrre latte
lactation /læk'teɪʃn/ *n* lattazione *f*
lacy /'leɪsɪ/ *a* di pizzo
lad /læd/ *n* ragazzo *m*
ladder /'lædə(r)/ *n* scala *f*; (*in tights*) sfila-
tura *f* ● *vi* sfilarsi
ladderproof /'lædəpruːf/ *a* ⟨*stockings*⟩
indemagliabile
laddish /'lædɪʃ/ *a fam* da ragazzacci
laden /'leɪdn/ *a* carico (**with** di)
la-di-da /lɑːdɪ'dɑː/ *a* affettato
ladle /'leɪdl/ *n* mestolo *m* ● *vt* ~ [**out**] versare
(*col mestolo*)
lady /'leɪdɪ/ *n* signora *f*; (*title*) Lady *f*; **ladies**
[**room**] *n* bagno *m* per donne
lady: ladybird *n*, *Am* **ladybug** *n* coccinella *f*.
lady-in-waiting /-'weɪtɪŋ/ *n* dama *f* di corte.
ladykiller *n fam* dongiovanni *m inv*
ladylike /'leɪdɪlaɪk/ *a* signorile
lady: lady mayoress *n* moglie *f* del Lord
Mayor. **Ladyship** *n* her/your ~ (*to aristocrat*)
≈ Signora Contessa. **lady's maid** *n* cameriera *f* personale
lag¹ /læg/ *vi* (*pt/pp* **lagged**) ~ **behind** restare indietro
lag² *vt* (*pt/pp* **lagged**) isolare ⟨*pipes*⟩
lager /'lɑːgə(r)/ *n* birra *f* chiara
lager lout *n Br pej* giovinastro *m* ubriaco
lagging /'lægɪŋ/ *n* (*for pipes*) materiale *m*
isolante
lagoon /lə'guːn/ *n* laguna *f*
laid /leɪd/ *see* **lay³**; *sl* **get** ~ scopare
laid-back *a fam* rilassato
lain /leɪn/ *see* **lie²**
lair /leə(r)/ *n* tana *f*
laird /leəd/ *n* (*in Scotland*) proprietario *m*
terriero
laity /'leɪətɪ/ *n* laicato *m*
lake /leɪk/ *n* lago *m*. ~ **Garda** lago di Garda
lakeside /'leɪksaɪd/ *n* riva *f* del lago ● *attrib*
⟨*café, scenery*⟩ della/sulla riva del lago
lama /'lɑːmə/ *n* lama *m inv*
lamb /læm/ *n* agnello *m*
lambast[e] /læm'beɪst/ *vt* biasimare ⟨*person, organization*⟩
lamb: lamb chop *n* cotoletta *f* d'agnello.
lambskin *n* pelle *f* d'agnello. **lambswool** *n*
lana *f* d'agnello, lambswool *m inv*
lame /leɪm/ *a* zoppo; *fig* ⟨*argument*⟩ zoppicante; ⟨*excuse*⟩ traballante

lamé /'lɑːmeɪ/ n lamé m

lame duck n (person) inetto, -a mf; (firm) azienda f in cattive acque

lament /lə'ment/ n lamento m ● vt lamentare ● vi lamentarsi

lamentable /'læməntəbl/ a deplorevole

laminated /'læmɪneɪtɪd/ a laminato

lamp /læmp/ n lampada f; (in street) lampione m

lampoon /læm'puːn/ n satira f ● vt fare oggetto di satira

lamp-post n lampione m

lampshade /'læmpʃeɪd/ n paralume m

lance /lɑːns/ n lancia f ● vt Med incidere

lance corporal n appuntato m

lancet /'lɑːnsɪt/ n Med bisturi m inv

land /lænd/ n terreno m; (country) paese m; (as opposed to sea) terra f; **plot of ~** pezzo m di terreno ● vt Naut sbarcare; ⟨fam: obtain⟩ assicurarsi; **be ~ed with sth** fam ritrovarsi fra capo e collo qcsa ● vi Aeron atterrare; ⟨fall⟩ cadere; **~ on one's feet** fig cadere in piedi

■ **land up** vi fam finire

land: land agent n (on estate) fattore m. **land army** n gruppo m di lavoratrici agricole durante la seconda guerra mondiale. **landfall** n Naut approdo m; **make ~** (reach) approdare; (sight) avvistare terra. **landfill site** n discarica f in cui i rifiuti vengono interrati

landing /'lændɪŋ/ n Naut sbarco m; Aeron atterraggio m; (top of stairs) pianerottolo m

landing: landing card n Aeron, Naut carta f di sbarco. **landing craft** n mezzo m da sbarco. **landing gear** n Aeron carrello m d'atterraggio. **landing lights** npl luci fpl d'atterraggio. **landing party** n Mil reparto m da sbarco. **landing-stage** n pontile m da sbarco. **landing strip** n pista f d'atterraggio

land: landlady n proprietaria f; (of flat) padrona f di casa. **landlocked** a privo di sbocco sul mare. **landlord** n proprietario m; (of flat) padrone m di casa. **landlubber** n marinaio m d'acqua dolce. **landmark** n punto m di riferimento; fig pietra f miliare. **land mass** n continente m. **landmine** n Mil mina f terrestre. **landowner** n proprietario, -a mf terriero, -a. **landscape** n paesaggio m. **landscape architect** n paesaggista mf. **landscape gardener** n paesaggista mf. **landslide** n frana f; Pol valanga f di voti. **landslip** n smottamento m

lane /leɪn/ n sentiero m; Auto, Sport corsia f

lane closure n (on motorway) chiusura f di corsia

lane markings n (on road) [strisce fpl di] mezzeria f

langoustine /'lɒŋɡustiːn/ n scampo m

language /'læŋɡwɪdʒ/ n lingua f; (speech, style, Comput) linguaggio m

language barrier n barriera f linguistica

language laboratory n laboratorio m linguistico

languid /'læŋɡwɪd/ a languido

languidly /'læŋɡwɪdlɪ/ adv languidamente

languish /'læŋɡwɪʃ/ vi languire

languor /'læŋɡə(r)/ n languore m

lank /læŋk/ a ⟨hair⟩ liscio

lanky /'læŋkɪ/ a (-ier, -iest) allampanato

lanolin /'lænəlɪn/ n lanolina f

lantern /'læntən/ n lanterna f

lanyard /'lænjəd/ n (Naut: rope) cima f

lap[1] /læp/ n grembo m

lap[2] n (Sport, of journey) tappa f; **~ of honour** giro m d'onore ● v (pt/pp **lapped**) ● vi ⟨water:⟩ **~ against** lambire ● vt Sport doppiare

lap[3] vt (pt/pp **lapped**) **~ up** bere avidamente; bersi completamente ⟨lies⟩; credere ciecamente a ⟨praise⟩

lap and shoulder belt n Auto, Aeron cintura f di sicurezza

laparoscope /'læpərəʃkəʊp/ n laparoscopio m

laparoscopy /læpə'rɒskəpɪ/ n laparoscopia f

lap belt n Auto, Aeron cintura f di sicurezza addominale

lapdog /'læpdɒg/ n cane m da salotto; **he's her ~** è il suo cagnolino

lapel /lə'pel/ n bavero m

Lapland /'læplænd/ n Lapponia f

lapse /læps/ n sbaglio m; (moral) sbandamento m [morale]; (of time) intervallo m ● vi (expire) scadere; (morally) scivolare; **~ into** cadere in

laptop /'læptɒp/ n ~ [**computer**] computer m inv portabile, laptop m inv

larceny /'lɑːsənɪ/ n furto m

larch /lɑːtʃ/ n larice m

lard /lɑːd/ n strutto m

larder /'lɑːdə(r)/ n dispensa f

large /lɑːdʒ/ a & adv grande; ⟨number, amount⟩ grande, grosso; **by and ~** in complesso; **at ~** in libertà; (in general) ampiamente

large intestine n intestino m crasso

largely /'lɑːdʒlɪ/ adv **~ because of** in gran parte a causa di

largeness /'lɑːdʒnɪs/ n grandezza f

large-scale a ⟨map⟩ a grande scala; ⟨operation⟩ su larga scala

largesse /lɑː'ʒes/ n generosità f

lark[1] /lɑːk/ n (bird) allodola f

lark[2] n (joke) burla f

■ **lark about** vi giocherellare

larva /'lɑːvə/ n (pl **-vae** /'lɑːviː/) larva f

laryngitis /lærɪn'dʒaɪtɪs/ n laringite f

larynx /'lærɪŋks/ n laringe f

lasagne /lə'zænjə/ n lasagne fpl

lascivious /lə'sɪvɪəs/ a lascivo

laser /'leɪzə(r)/ n laser m inv

laser disc n disco m laser

laser printer n stampante f laser

lash /læʃ/ n frustata f; (eyelash) ciglio m ● vt (whip) frustare; (tie) legare fermamente

■ **lash out** vi attaccare; (spend) sperperare (**on** in)

lashings /'læʃɪŋz/ npl **~ of** fam una marea di

lass /læs/ n ragazzina f

lasso /ləˈsuː/ n lazo m

last /lɑːst/ a (final) ultimo; (recent) scorso; ~ **year** l'anno scorso; ~ **night** ieri sera; **at** ~ alla fine; **at** ~**!** finalmente!; **that's the** ~ **straw** fam questa è l'ultima goccia ● n ultimo, -a mf; **the** ~ **but one** il penultimo ● adv per ultimo; (last time) l'ultima volta; ~ **but not least** per ultimo ma non il meno importante ● vi durare

lasting /ˈlɑːstɪŋ/ a durevole

lastly /ˈlɑːstlɪ/ adv infine

last: last name n (surname) cognome m. **last rites** npl Relig estrema unzione f. **Last Supper** n Ultima Cena f

latch /lætʃ/ n chiavistello m; (on gate) saliscendi m inv; **leave the door on the** ~ chiudere la porta senza far scattare la serratura

■ **latch on to** vt fissarsi con ⟨person, idea⟩

latchkey /ˈlætʃkiː/ n chiave f di casa

latchkey child n bambino m che ha le chiavi di casa in quanto i genitori lavorano

late /leɪt/ a (delayed) in ritardo; (at a late hour) tardo; (deceased) defunto; **it's** ~ (at night) è tardi; **in** ~ **November** alla fine di Novembre; **of** ~ recentemente; **be a** ~ **developer** ⟨child:⟩ essere lento nell'apprendimento ● adv tardi; **stay up** ~ stare alzati fino a tardi

latecomer /ˈleɪtkʌmə(r)/ n ritardatario, -a mf; (to political party etc) nuovo, -a arrivato, -a mf

lately /ˈleɪtlɪ/ adv recentemente

lateness /ˈleɪtnɪs/ n ora f tarda; (delay) ritardo m

latent /ˈleɪtnt/ a latente

later /ˈleɪtə(r)/ a ⟨train⟩ che parte più tardi; ⟨edition⟩ più recente ● adv più tardi; ~ **on** più tardi, dopo

lateral /ˈlætərəl/ a laterale

late riser /ˈraɪzə(r)/ n dormiglione, -a mf

latest /ˈleɪtɪst/ a ultimo; (most recent) più recente; **the** ~ **[news]** le ultime notizie ● **n six o'clock at the** ~ alle sei al più tardi

latex /ˈleɪteks/ n la[t]tice m

lath /læθ/ n assicella f

lathe /leɪð/ n tornio m

lather /ˈlɑːðə(r)/ n schiuma f ● vt insaponare ● vi far schiuma

Latin /ˈlætɪn/ a latino ● n latino m

Latin America n America f Latina

Latin American n & a latino-americano mf

Latino /ləˈtiːnəʊ/ n Am latino-americano, -a mf

latitude /ˈlætɪtjuːd/ n Geog latitudine f; fig libertà f d'azione

latrine /ləˈtriːn/ n latrina f

latter /ˈlætə(r)/ a ultimo ● n the ~ quest'ultimo

latter-day a moderno

latterly /ˈlætəlɪ/ adv ultimamente

lattice /ˈlætɪs/ n traliccio m

lattice window n finestra f con vetri a losanghe

lattice-work n intelaiatura f a traliccio

Latvia /ˈlætvɪə/ n Lettonia f

Latvian /ˈlætvɪən/ a & n lettone mf; (language) lettone m

laudable /ˈlɔːdəbl/ a lodevole

laudatory /ˈlɔːdətrɪ/ a elogiativo

laugh /lɑːf/ n risata f ● vi ridere (**at/about** di); ~ **at sb** (mock) prendere in giro qcno

laughable /ˈlɑːfəbl/ a ridicolo

laughing gas /ˈlɑːfɪŋ/ n gas m inv esilarante

laughing stock n zimbello m

laughter /ˈlɑːftə(r)/ n risata f

launch[1] /lɔːntʃ/ n (boat) lancia f

launch[2] n lancio m; (of ship) varo m ● vt lanciare ⟨rocket, product⟩; varare ⟨ship⟩; sferrare ⟨attack⟩

■ **launch into** vt intraprendere ⟨career⟩; imbarcarsi in ⟨speech⟩

launcher /ˈlɔːntʃə(r)/ n lanciamissili m inv

launch[ing] pad /ˈlɔːntʃ[ɪŋ]/ n piattaforma f di lancio; fig trampolino m di lancio

launder /ˈlɔːndə(r)/ vt lavare e stirare; ~ **money** fig riciclare denaro sporco

launderette /lɔːndəˈret/ n lavanderia f automatica

laundry /ˈlɔːndrɪ/ n lavanderia f; (clothes) bucato m

laureate /ˈlɒrɪət/ a **poet** ~ poeta m di corte; **Nobel** ~ vincitore, -trice mf del Nobel

laurel /ˈlɒrəl/ n lauro m; **rest on one's** ~**s** fig dormire sugli allori

lav /læv/ n Br fam gabinetto m

lava /ˈlɑːvə/ n lava f

lavatorial /lævəˈtɔːrɪəl/ a ⟨humour⟩ scatologico

lavatory /ˈlævətrɪ/ n gabinetto m

lavender /ˈlævəndə(r)/ n lavanda f

lavender blue a color lavanda

lavish /ˈlævɪʃ/ a copioso; (wasteful) prodigo; **on a** ~ **scale** su vasta scala ● vt ~ **sth on sb** ricoprire qcno di qcsa

lavishly /ˈlævɪʃlɪ/ adv copiosamente

law /lɔː/ n legge f; **study** ~ studiare giurisprudenza, studiare legge; ~ **and order** ordine m pubblico; **take the** ~ **into one's own hands** farsi giustizia da sé; ~ **of the jungle** legge della giungla

law-abiding /ˈlɔːəbaɪdɪŋ/ a che rispetta la legge

lawbreaker /ˈlɔːbreɪkə(r)/ n persona f che infrange la legge

law court n tribunale m

lawful /ˈlɔːfʊl/ a legittimo

lawfully /ˈlɔːfʊlɪ/ adv legittimamente

lawfulness /ˈlɔːfʊlnɪs/ n legalità f

lawless /ˈlɔːlɪs/ a senza legge

lawmaker /ˈlɔːmeɪkə(r)/ n legislatore m

lawn /lɔːn/ n prato m [all'inglese]

lawnmower /ˈlɔːnməʊə(r)/ n tosaerba m inv

law school n facoltà f di giurisprudenza

lawsuit /ˈlɔːsuːt/ n causa f

lawyer /ˈlɔːjə(r)/ n avvocato m

lax /læks/ a negligente; ⟨morals etc⟩ lassista

laxative /ˈlæksətɪv/ n lassativo m

laxity /'læksətɪ/ n lassismo m

lay¹ /leɪ/ a laico; fig profano

lay² see **lie²**

lay³ vt (pt/pp **laid**) porre, mettere; apparecchiare ‹table› ● vi ‹hen:› fare le uova

■ **lay aside** vt mettere da parte

■ **lay down** vt posare; stabilire ‹rules, conditions›

■ **lay in** vt farsi una scorta di ‹coal, supplies etc›

■ **lay into** vt sl picchiare

■ **lay off** vt licenziare ‹workers› ● vi (fam: stop) ~ **off!** smettila!

■ **lay on** vt (organize) organizzare

■ **lay out** vt (display, set forth) esporre; (plan) pianificare ‹garden›; (spend) sborsare; Typ impaginare

■ **lay up** vt **I was laid up in bed for a week** sono stato costretto a letto per una settimana

layabout /'leɪəbaʊt/ n fannullone, -a mf

lay-by n piazzola f di sosta

layer /'leɪə(r)/ n strato m

layette /leɪ'et/ n corredino m

layman /'leɪmən/ n profano m

layout /'leɪaʊt/ n disposizione f; Typ impaginazione f, layout m inv

lay preacher n predicatore m laico

laze /leɪz/ vi ~ [**about**] oziare

lazily /'leɪzɪlɪ/ adv ‹move, wander etc› pigramente

laziness /'leɪzɪnɪs/ n pigrizia f

lazy /'leɪzɪ/ a (-**ier**, -**iest**) pigro

lazybones /'leɪzɪbəʊnz/ n poltrone, -a mf

lazy eye n ambliopia f

lb abbr (**pound**) libbra

LCD n abbr (**liquid crystal display**) LCD m

lead¹ /led/ n piombo m; (of pencil) mina f

lead² /liːd/ n guida f; (leash) guinzaglio m; (flex) filo m; (clue) indizio m; Theat parte f principale; (distance ahead) distanza f (over su); **in the** ~ in testa; **follow sb's** ~ seguire l'esempio di qcno ● vt (pt/pp **led**) condurre; dirigere ‹expedition, party etc›; (induce) indurre; ~ **the way** mettersi in testa; ~ **into temptation** indurre in tentazione ● vi (be in front) condurre; (in race, competition) essere in testa

■ **lead astray** vt sviare

■ **lead away** vt portar via

■ **lead on** vt ingannare

■ **lead off** vi (begin) cominciare ● vt (take away) portare via

■ **lead to** vt portare a

■ **lead up to** vt preludere; **the period ~ing up to the election** il periodo precedente le elezioni; **what's this ~ing up to?** dove porta questo?

leaded /'ledɪd/ a con piombo

leaden /'ledən/ a di piombo

leader /'liːdə(r)/ n capo m; (of orchestra) primo violino m; (in newspaper) articolo m di fondo

leadership /'liːdəʃɪp/ n direzione f, leadership f inv; **show** ~ mostrare capacità di comando

lead-free /'ledfriː/ a senza piombo

lead-in /'liːdɪn/ n presentazione f

leading¹ /'liːdɪŋ/ a principale

leading² /'ledɪŋ/ n Typ interlinea m

leading /'liːdɪŋ/: **leading article** n articolo m di fondo. **leading edge** n Aeron bordo m d'attacco; **at the** ~ ~ **of** (technology) all'avanguardia in. **leading lady** attrice f principale. **leading light** n personaggio m di spicco. **leading man** attore m principale. **leading question** n domanda f che influenza la risposta

lead poisoning n saturnismo m

leaf /liːf/ n (pl **leaves**) foglia f; (of table) asse f; fig **take a** ~ **out of sb's book** imparare la lezione di qcno; **turn over a new** ~ voltare pagina

■ **leaf through** vt sfogliare

leaflet /'liːflɪt/ n dépliant m inv; (advertising) dépliant m inv pubblicitario; (political) manifestino m

leafy /'liːfɪ/ a ‹tree› ricco di foglie; ‹wood› molto verde; ‹suburb, area› ricco di verde

league /liːg/ n lega f; Sport campionato m; **be in** ~ **with** essere in combutta con

league table n classifica f del campionato

leak /liːk/ n (hole) fessura f; Naut falla f; (of gas & fig) fuga f ● vi colare; ‹ship:› fare acqua; ‹liquid, gas:› fuoriuscire ● vt ~ **sth to sb** fig far trapelare qcsa a qcno

leakage /'liːkɪdʒ/ n perdita f; (of gas & fig) fuga f

leaky /'liːkɪ/ a che perde; Naut che fa acqua

lean¹ /liːn/ a magro

lean² v (pt/pp **leaned** or **leant** /lent/) ● vt appoggiare (**against/on** contro/su); ~ **one's elbows on the table** appoggiare i gomiti sul tavolo ● vi appoggiarsi (**against/on** contro/ su); (not be straight) pendere; **be** ~**ing against** essere appoggiato contro; ~ **on sb** (depend on) appoggiarsi a qcno; (fam: exert pressure on) stare col calcagne di qcno

■ **lean back** vi sporgersi indietro

■ **lean forward** vi piegarsi in avanti

■ **lean out** vi sporgersi

■ **lean over** vi piegarsi

■ **lean towards** vt (favour) propendere per

leaning /'liːnɪŋ/ a pendente; **the L~ Tower of Pisa** la torre di Pisa, la torre pendente ● n tendenza f

leanness /'liːnnɪs/ n magrezza f

lean-to n garage m inv adiacente alla casa

leap /liːp/ n salto m ● vi (pt/pp **leapt** /lept/ or **leaped**) saltare; **he leapt at it** fam l'ha preso al volo

leapfrog /'liːpfrɒg/ n cavallina f

leap year n anno m bisestile

learn /lɜːn/ v (pt/pp **learnt** or **learned**) ● vt imparare; ~ **to swim** imparare a nuotare; **I have ~ed that...** (heard) sono venuto a sapere che...; fig **he's ~t his lesson** ha imparato la lezione ● vi imparare; **as I've ~t to my cost** come ho imparato a mie spese

learned /'lɜːnɪd/ a colto

learner /'lɜːnə(r)/ n also Auto principiante mf

learning /'lɜːnɪŋ/ n cultura f

learning: learning curve n curva f di apprendimento. **learning difficulties** npl (of schoolchildren) difficoltà fpl d'apprendimento. **learning disability** n difficoltà fpl d'apprendimento

lease /liːs/ n contratto m d'affitto; (rental) affitto m; **the job has given him a new ~ of life** grazie al lavoro ha ripreso gusto alla vita ● vt affittare

leasehold /'liːshəʊld/ n proprietà f in affitto

leaseholder /'liːshəʊldə(r)/ n titolare mf di un contratto d'affitto

leash /liːʃ/ n guinzaglio m

least /liːst/ a più piccolo; (smallest amount) meno; **you've got ~ luggage** hai meno bagagli di tutti ● n the ~ il meno; **that's the ~ of my worries** questa è la cosa che mi preoccupa di meno; **at ~** almeno; **not in the ~** niente affatto ● adv meno; **the ~ expensive wine** il vino meno caro

leather /'leðə(r)/ n pelle f; (of soles) cuoio m ● attrib di pelle/cuoio; **~ jacket** giubbotto m di pelle

leathery /'leðərɪ/ a (meat, skin) duro

leave /liːv/ n (holiday) congedo m; Mil licenza f; **on ~** in congedo/licenza; **take one's ~** accomiatarsi; **~ of absence** aspettativa f ● v (pt/pp **left**) ● vt lasciare; uscire da (house, office); (forget) dimenticare; **there is nothing left** non è rimasto niente; **~ sb in peace** lasciare in pace qcno ● vi andare via; (train, bus:) partire

■ **leave aside** vt (disregard) lasciare da parte

■ **leave behind** vt lasciare; (forget) dimenticare

■ **leave out** vt omettere; (not put away) lasciare fuori

leaves /liːvz/ see **leaf**

Lebanese /lebə'niːz/ a & n libanese mf

Lebanon /'lebənən/ n Libano m

lecher /'letʃə(r)/ n libertino m

lecherous /'letʃərəs/ a lascivo

lechery /'letʃərɪ/ n lascivia f

lectern /'lektɜːn/ n leggio m, scannello m

lecture /'lektʃə(r)/ n conferenza f; Univ lezione f; (reproof) ramanzina f ● vi fare una conferenza (on su); Univ insegnare (on sth qcsa) ● vt ~ sb rimproverare qcno

lecturer /'lektʃərə(r)/ n conferenziere, -a mf; Univ docente mf universitario, -a

lecture room n Br Univ aula f magna

lectureship /'lektʃəʃɪp/ n Br Univ docenza f universitaria

lecture theatre n Br Univ aula f magna

LED n abbr (**light-emitting diode**) LED m inv

led /led/ see **lead²**

ledge /ledʒ/ n cornice f; (of window) davanzale m

ledger /'ledʒə(r)/ n libro m mastro

leech /liːtʃ/ n sanguisuga f

leek /liːk/ n porro m

leer /lɪə(r)/ n sguardo m libidinoso ● vi ~ (at) guardare in modo libidinoso

lees /liːz/ npl (wine sediment) fondi mpl

leeway /'liːweɪ/ n fig libertà f di azione

left¹ /left/ see **leave**

left² a sinistro ● adv a sinistra ● n also Pol sinistra f; **on the ~** a sinistra

left-hand drive a (car) con la guida a sinistra

left-handed /-'hændɪd/ a mancino; (scissors etc) per mancini

leftie /'leftɪ/ n sinistrorso, -a mf

leftist /'leftɪst/ a & n sinistrorso, -a mf

left: left luggage [office] n deposito m bagagli. **leftovers** npl rimasugli mpl. **left wing** n Pol sinistra f; Sport ala f sinistra. **left-wing** a Pol di sinistra. **left-winger** n Pol persona f di sinistra; Sport ala f sinistra

leg /leg/ n gamba f; (of animal) zampa f; (of journey) tappa f; Culin (of chicken) coscia f; (of lamb) cosciotto m; **be on one's last ~s** (machine:) funzionare per miracolo; **not have a ~ to stand on** non avere una ragione che regga ● vi ~ **it** fam darsela a gambe

legacy /'legəsɪ/ n lascito m

legal /'liːgl/ a legale; **take ~ action** intentare un'azione legale

legal: legal adviser n consulente mf legale. **legal aid** n gratuito patrocinio m. **legal eagle** n hum principe m del foro

legality /lɪ'gælətɪ/ n legalità f

legalization /liːgəlar'zeɪʃn/ n legalizzazione f

legalize /'liːgəlaɪz/ vt legalizzare

legally /'liːgəlɪ/ adv legalmente

legal tender n valuta f a corso legale

legend /'ledʒənd/ n leggenda f

legendary /'ledʒəndərɪ/ a leggendario

leggings /'legɪŋz/ npl (for baby) ghette fpl; (for woman) pantacollant mpl; (for man) gambali mpl

leggy /'legɪ/ a (person) con le gambe lunghe

Leghorn /'leghɔːn/ n Livorno f

legibility /ledʒə'bɪlətɪ/ n leggibilità f

legible /'ledʒəbl/ a leggibile

legibly /'ledʒəblɪ/ adv in modo leggibile

legion /'liːdʒn/ n legione f

legionnaire /liːdʒə'neə(r)/ n Mil legionario m

legionnaire's disease n legionellosi f

legislate /'ledʒɪsleɪt/ vi legiferare

legislation /ledʒɪs'leɪʃn/ n legislazione f

legislative /'ledʒɪslətɪv/ a legislativo

legislator /'ledʒɪsleɪtə(r)/ n legislatore m

legislature /'ledʒɪsleɪtʃə(r)/ n legislatura f

legitimacy /lɪ'dʒɪtɪməsɪ/ n (lawfulness) legittimità f; (of argument) validità f

legitimate /lɪ'dʒɪtɪmət/ a legittimo; (excuse) valido

legitimately /lɪ'dʒɪtɪmətlɪ/ adv legittimamente

legitimize /lɪdʒɪtɪ'maɪz/ vt rendere legittimo

legless /'leglɪs/ a senza gambe; (Br: drunk) ubriaco fradicio

leg: leg-pulling n presa f in giro. **legroom** n spazio m per le gambe. **leg warmer** n scaldamuscoli m inv. **legwork** n fatica f; **do the ~** fare da galoppino

leisure /'leʒə(r)/ n tempo m libero; **at your ~** con comodo

leisure centre n centro m sportivo e ricreativo

leisurely /'leʒəlɪ/ a senza fretta

leisure time n tempo m libero

leisurewear /'leʒəweə(r)/ n abbigliamento m per il tempo libero

lemming /'lemɪŋ/ n lemming m inv

lemon /'lemən/ n limone m

lemonade /lemə'neɪd/ n limonata f

lemon: lemon curd n crema f al limone. **lemon juice** n (drink) succo m di limone. **lemon sole** n sogliola f limanda. **lemon squash** n sciroppo m di limone. **lemon tea** n tè m inv al limone. **lemon yellow** n giallo m limone ● a giallo limone

lend /lend/ vt (pt/pp **lent**) prestare; **~ a hand** fig dare una mano; **~ an ear** prestare ascolto; **~ itself to** prestarsi a

lender /'lendə(r)/ n prestatore, -trice mf

lending library /'lendɪŋ/ n biblioteca f per il prestito

length /leŋθ/ n lunghezza f; (piece) pezzo m; (of wallpaper) parte f; (of visit) durata f; **at ~** a lungo; (at last) alla fine

lengthen /'leŋθən/ vt allungare ● vi allungarsi

lengthways /'leŋθweɪz/ adv per lungo

lengthwise /'leŋθwaɪz/ adv longitudinale

lengthy /'leŋθɪ/ a (**-ier, -iest**) lungo

lenience /'liːnɪəns/ n indulgenza f

lenient /'liːnɪənt/ a indulgente

leniently /'liːnɪəntlɪ/ adv con indulgenza

lens /lenz/ n lente f; Phot obiettivo m; (of eye) cristallino m

Lent /lent/ n Quaresima f

lent see **lend**

lentil /'lentl/ n Bot lenticchia f

Leo /'liːəʊ/ n Astr Leone m

leopard /'lepəd/ n leopardo m

leopardskin /'lepədskɪn/ n pelle f di leopardo ● attrib di [pelle di] leopardo

leotard /'liːətɑːd/ n body m inv

leper /'lepə(r)/ n lebbroso, -a mf; fig appestato, -a mf

leprosy /'leprəsɪ/ n lebbra f

lesbian /'lezbɪən/ a lesbico ● n lesbica f

lesbianism /'lezbɪənɪzm/ n lesbismo m

lesion /'liːʒn/ n lesione f

less /les/ a meno di; **~ and ~** sempre meno; ● adv & prep meno ● n meno m

lessee /le'siː/ n Jur affittuario, -a mf

lessen /'lesn/ vt/i diminuire

lesser /'lesə(r)/ a minore; **the ~ of two evils** il minore fra i due mali

lesson /'lesn/ n lezione f; **teach sb a ~** fig dare una lezione a qcno

lessor /le'sɔː/ n Jur locatore, -trice mf

lest /lest/ conj liter per timore che

let /let/ vt (pt/pp **let**, pres p **letting**) lasciare,

permettere; (rent) affittare; **~ alone** (not to mention) tanto meno; '**to ~**' 'affittasi'; **~ us go** andiamo; **~ sb do sth** lasciare fare qcsa a qcno, permettere a qcno di fare qcsa; **~ me know** fammi sapere; **just ~ him try!** che ci provi solamente!; **~ oneself go** lasciarsi andare; **~ oneself in for sth** fam impelagarsi in qcsa ● n Tennis colpo m nullo; (Br: lease) contratto m d'affitto ● vi **~ fly at sb** aggredire qcno

■ **let down** vt sciogliersi ⟨hair⟩; abbassare ⟨blinds⟩; (lengthen) allungare; (disappoint) deludere; **don't ~ me down** conto su di te

■ **let in** vt far entrare

■ **let off** vt far partire; (not punish) perdonare; **~ sb off doing sth** abbonare qcsa a qcno; **~ off steam** fig scaricarsi

■ **let on** vi sl **don't ~ on** non spifferare niente

■ **let out** vt far uscire; (make larger) allargare; emettere ⟨scream, groan⟩

■ **let through** vt far passare

■ **let up** vi fam diminuire

let-down n delusione f

lethal /'liːθl/ a letale; **~ dose** n dose f letale

lethargic /lɪ'θɑːdʒɪk/ a apatico

lethargy /'leθədʒɪ/ n apatia f

let-out n fam via f d'uscita

letter /'letə(r)/ n lettera f

letter: letter of apology n lettera f di scuse. **letter bomb** n lettera f esplosiva. **letter box** n buca f per le lettere. **letter of credit** n Comm lettera f di credito. **letterhead** n (heading) intestazione f; (paper) carta f intestata

lettering /'letərɪŋ/ n caratteri mpl

letter of introduction n lettera f di presentazione

lettuce /'letɪs/ n lattuga f

let-up n fam pausa f

leukaemia /luː'kiːmɪə/ n leucemia f

level /'levl/ a piano; (in height, competition) allo stesso livello; (spoonful) raso; **draw ~ with sb** affiancare qcno; **do one's ~ best** fare del proprio meglio ● n livello m; **on the ~** fam giusto ● vt (pt/pp **levelled**) livellare; (aim) puntare (at su)

■ **level off** vi ⟨inflation, unemployment:⟩ stabilizzarsi

■ **level out** vi ⟨surface:⟩ diventare pianeggiante; ⟨aircraft:⟩ mettersi in orizzontale

■ **level with** vt (fam: be honest with) essere franco con

level: level crossing n passaggio m a livello. **level-headed** /-'hedɪd/ a posato. **level pegging** n **it's ~ ~ so far** finora sono alla pari

lever /'liːvə(r)/ n leva f

■ **lever off, lever up** vt sollevare (con una leva)

leverage /'liːvərɪdʒ/ n azione f di una leva; fig influenza f

leveret /'levərət/ n leprotto m

levitate /'levɪteɪt/ vi levitare

levity /'levətɪ/ n leggerezza f

levy /'levɪ/ vt (pt/pp **levied**) imporre ‹tax›

lewd /lju:d/ a osceno

lexical /'leksɪkəl/ a lessicale

lexicographer /leksɪ'kɒɡrəfə(r)/ n lessicografo, -a mf

lexicographic /leksɪkə'ɡræfɪk/ a lessicografico

lexicography /leksɪ'kɒɡrəfɪ/ n lessicografia f

lexicon /'leksɪkən/ n lessico m

liability /laɪə'bɪlətɪ/ n responsabilità f; ‹fam: burden› peso m; **liabilities** pl passività fpl

liable /'laɪəbl/ a responsabile (**for** di); **be ~ to** ‹rain, break etc› rischiare di; ‹tend to› tendere a

liaise /lɪ'eɪz/ vi fam essere in contatto

liaison /lɪ'eɪzɒn/ n contatti mpl; Mil collegamento m; ‹affair› relazione f

liar /'laɪə(r)/ n bugiardo, -a mf

Lib Dem /lɪb'dem/ Br Pol abbr **Liberal Democrat**

libel /'laɪbl/ n diffamazione f ● vt (pt/pp **libelled**) diffamare

libellous /'laɪbələs/ a diffamatorio

liberal /'lɪb(ə)rəl/ a ‹tolerant› di larghe vedute; ‹generous› generoso. **L~** a Pol liberale ● n liberale mf

Liberal Democrat n Br Pol liberaldemocratico, -a mf

liberalization /lɪbərəlaɪ'zeɪʃn/ n ‹of trade› liberalizzazione f

liberalize /'lɪbərəlaɪz/ vt liberalizzare

liberally /'lɪbrəlɪ/ adv liberalmente

liberate /'lɪbəreɪt/ vt liberare

liberated /'lɪbəreɪtɪd/ a ‹woman› emancipata

liberating /'lɪbəreɪtɪŋ/ a liberatorio

liberation /lɪbə'reɪʃn/ n liberazione f; ‹of women› emancipazione f

liberator /'lɪbəreɪtə(r)/ n liberatore, -trice mf

libertarian /lɪbə'teərɪən/ a & n liberale nmf

libertarianism /lɪbə'teərɪənɪzm/ n liberalismo m

liberty /'lɪbətɪ/ n libertà f; **take the ~ of doing sth** prendersi la libertà di fare qcsa; **take liberties** prendersi delle libertà; **be at ~ to do sth** essere libero di fare qcsa

libido /lɪ'bi:dəʊ/ n libido f inv

Libra /'li:brə/ n Astr Bilancia f

librarian /laɪ'breərɪən/ n bibliotecario, -a mf

library /'laɪbrərɪ/ n biblioteca f

libretto /lɪ'bretəʊ/ n (pl **-tti** or **-ttos**) libretto m di opera

Libya /'lɪbɪə/ n Libia f

Libyan /'lɪbɪən/ a & n libico, -a mf

lice /laɪs/ see **louse**

licence /'laɪsns/ n licenza f; ‹for TV› canone m televisivo; ‹for driving› patente f; ‹freedom› sregolatezza f

licence number n numero m di targa

licence plate n targa f

license /'laɪsns/ vt autorizzare; **be ~d** ‹car:› avere il bollo; ‹restaurant:› essere autorizzato alla vendita di alcolici

licensee /laɪsən'si:/ n titolare mf di licenza ‹per la vendita di alcolici›

licensing hours /'laɪsənsɪŋ/ npl Br orario m in cui è permessa la vendita di alcolici

licentious /laɪ'senʃəs/ a licenzioso

licentiousness /laɪ'senʃəsnɪs/ n licenziosità f

lichen /'laɪkən/ n Bot lichene m

lick /lɪk/ n leccata f; **a ~ of paint** una passata leggera di pittura ● vt leccare; ‹fam: defeat› battere; leccarsi ‹lips›; fam **~ sb into shape** rendere qcno efficiente

lid /lɪd/ n coperchio m; ‹of eye› palpebra f; **keep the ~ on sth** fam non lasciare trapelare qcsa

lido /'li:dəʊ/ n ‹beach› lido m; ‹Br: pool› piscina f scoperta

lie¹ /laɪ/ n bugia f; **tell a ~** mentire ● vi (pt/pp **lied**, pres p **lying**) mentire

lie² vi (pt **lay**, pp **lain**, pres p **lying**) ‹person:› sdraiarsi; ‹object:› stare; ‹remain› rimanere; **leave sth lying about** or **around** lasciare qcsa in giro; **here ~s...** qui giace...; **~ low** tenersi nascosto

■ **lie back** vi ‹relax› rilassarsi

■ **lie down** vi sdraiarsi

■ **lie in** vi ‹stay in bed› rimanere a letto

Liechtenstein /'lɪktənstaɪn/ n Liechtenstein m

lie detector n macchina f della verità

lie-down n have a **~** fare un riposino

lie-in n fam have a **~** restare a letto fino a tardi

lieu /lju:/ n **in ~ of** in luogo di

lieutenant /lef'tenənt/ n tenente m

life /laɪf/ n (pl **lives**) vita f; **give one's ~ for sb/one's country** dare la vita per qcno/la patria; **give one's ~ to** ‹devote oneself to› dedicare la propria vita a; **lose one's ~** perdere la vita; **for dear ~** per salvare la pelle; **not on your ~!** fam neanche morto!

life: life-and-death a ‹struggle› disperato. **lifebelt** n salvagente m. **lifeblood** n fig linfa f vitale. **lifeboat** n lancia f di salvataggio; ‹on ship› scialuppa f di salvataggio. **lifebuoy** n salvagente m. **life expectancy** n vita f media. **life form** n forma f di vita. **lifeguard** n ‹on beach etc› bagnino, -a mf. **life-imprisonment** n ergastolo m. **life insurance** n assicurazione f sulla vita. **life jacket** n giubbotto m di salvataggio

lifeless /'laɪflɪs/ a inanimato

life: lifelike a realistico. **lifeline** n sagola f di salvataggio. **lifelong** a di tutta la vita

lifer /'laɪfə(r)/ n fam ergastolano, -a mf

life: life sentence n condanna f all'ergastolo. **life-size[d]** /'laɪfsaɪz[d]/ a in grandezza naturale. **lifespan** n durata f della vita. **life story** n biografia f. **lifestyle** n stile m di vita. **lifetime** n vita f; **the chance of a ~** un'occasione unica; **~ guarantee** garanzia f a vita

lift /lɪft/ n ascensore m; Auto passaggio m; **give sb a ~** dare un passaggio a qcno; **I got a ~** mi hanno dato un passaggio ● vt sollevare;

revocare ‹*restrictions*›; (*fam: steal*) rubare
● *vi* ‹*fog:*› alzarsi
■ **lift off** *vi* ‹*rocket:*› partire
■ **lift up** *vt* sollevare
liftboy *n* Br lift *m inv*
lift-off *n* decollo *m* (*di razzo*)
ligament /'lɪgəmənt/ *n* Anat legamento *m*
light[1] /laɪt/ *a* (*not dark*) luminoso; **~ green**
verde chiaro ● *n* luce *f*; (*lamp*) lampada *f*; **in
the ~ of** *fig* alla luce di; **have you got a ~?**
ha da accendere?; **come to ~** essere rivelato
● *vt* (*pt/pp* **lit** *or* **lighted**) accendere; (*illuminate*) illuminare
■ **light up** *vt* accendere ‹*pipe, cigarette*›; illuminare ‹*face*›; rischiarare ‹*sky*› ● *vi* ‹*face:*›
illuminarsi
light[2] *a* (*not heavy*) leggero; **make ~ of** non
dare peso a ● *adv* **travel ~** viaggiare con
poco bagaglio
light bulb *n* lampadina *f*
lighten[1] /'laɪtn/ *vt* illuminare
lighten[2] *vt* alleggerire ‹*load*›
light entertainment *n* varietà *m inv*
lighter /'laɪtə(r)/ *n* accendino *m*
lighter fuel *n* (*liquid*) gas *m inv* da accendino
light: light-fingered /-'fɪŋgəd/ *a* svelto di
mano. **light-headed** /-'hedɪd/ *a* sventato.
light-hearted /-'hɑːtɪd/ *a* spensierato.
lighthouse *n* faro *m*. **light industry** *n* industria *f* leggera
lighting /'laɪtɪŋ/ *n* illuminazione *f*
lightly /'laɪtlɪ/ *adv* leggermente; ‹*accuse*› con
leggerezza; ‹*take sth*› alla leggera; (*without
concern*) senza dare importanza alla cosa; **get
off ~** cavarsela a buon mercato
lightness /'laɪtnɪs/ *n* leggerezza *f*
lightning /'laɪtnɪŋ/ *n* lampo *m*, fulmine *m*
lightning conductor *n* parafulmine *m*
lightning strike *n* sciopero *m* a sorpresa
light: light-pen *n* (*for computer screen*) penna *f* ottica. **lightweight** *a* leggero ● *n* (*in
boxing*) peso *m* leggero. **light year** *n* anno *m*
luce; **it was ~ ~s ago** è stato secoli fa
like[1] /laɪk/ *a* simile ● *prep* come; **~ this/that**
così; **what's he ~?** com'è? ● *conj* (*fam: as*)
come; (*Am: as if*) come se
like[2] *vt* piacere, gradire; **I should** *or* **would
~** vorrei, gradirei; **I ~ him** mi piace; **I ~ this
car** mi piace questa macchina; **I ~ dancing**
mi piace ballare; **I ~ that!** *fam* questa mi è
piaciuta!; **~ it or lump it!** abbozzala! ● *n* **~s
and dislikes** *pl* gusti *mpl*
likeable /'laɪkəbl/ *a* simpatico
likelihood /'laɪklɪhʊd/ *n* probabilità *f*
likely /'laɪklɪ/ *a* (**-ier, -iest**) probabile ● *adv*
probabilmente; **not ~!** *fam* neanche per sogno!
like-minded /laɪk'maɪndɪd/ *a* con gusti affini
liken /'laɪkən/ *vt* paragonare (**to** a)
likeness /'laɪknɪs/ *n* somiglianza *f*
likewise /'laɪkwaɪz/ *adv* lo stesso
liking /'laɪkɪŋ/ *n* gusto *m*; **is it to your ~?** è
di suo gusto?; **take a ~ to sb** prendere qcno
in simpatia

lilac /'laɪlək/ *n* lillà *m* ● *a* color lillà
Lilo® /'laɪləʊ/ *n* materassino *m* gonfiabile
lilting /'lɪltɪŋ/ *a* cadenzato
lily /'lɪlɪ/ *n* giglio *m*
lily of the valley *n* mughetto *m*
lily pond *n* stagno *m* con ninfee
limb /lɪm/ *n* arto *m*
limber /'lɪmbə(r)/ *vi* **~ up** sciogliersi i muscoli
limbo /'lɪmbəʊ/ *n* (*Relig, fig, dance*) limbo *m*;
be in ~ ‹*person:*› essere nel limbo del dubbio;
‹*future of sth.*› essere in sospeso
lime[1] /laɪm/ *n* (*fruit*) cedro *m*; (*tree*) tiglio *m*
lime[2] *n* calce *f*
lime: lime-green *a* & *n* verde *m* limone.
limelight /'laɪmlaɪt/ *n* **be in the ~** essere
molto in vista. **limestone** /'laɪmstəʊn/ *n* cal-
care *m*
limit /'lɪmɪt/ *n* limite *m*; **be the ~** essere il
colmo; **that's the ~!** *fam* questo è troppo!
● *vt* limitare (**to** a)
limitation /lɪmɪ'teɪʃn/ *n* limite *m*
limited /'lɪmɪtɪd/ *a* ristretto
limited: limited company *n* società *f inv* a
responsabilità limitata. **limited edition** *n*
(*book, lithograph*) edizione *f* limitata.
limited liability *n* responsabilità *f* limitata
limitless /'lɪmɪtlɪs/ *a* infinito
limousine /'lɪməziːn/ *n* limousine *f inv*
limp[1] /lɪmp/ *n* andatura *f* zoppicante; **have a
~** zoppicare ● *vi* zoppicare
limp[2] *a* floscio
limpet /'lɪmpɪt/ *n* **be like a ~** *fig* essere at-
taccaticcio
limpid /'lɪmpɪd/ *a* limpido
limp-wristed /-'rɪstɪd/ *a pej* effeminato
linchpin /'lɪntʃpɪn/ *n* ‹*fig: essential element*›
perno *m*
line[1] /laɪn/ *n* linea *f*; (*length of rope, cord*) filo
m; (*of writing*) riga *f*; (*of poem*) verso *m*; (*row*)
fila *f*; (*wrinkle*) ruga *f*; (*of business*) settore *m*;
(*Am: queue*) coda *f*; **in ~ with** in conformità
con; **bring into ~** mettere al passo ‹*structure,
law*›; **in the ~ of duty** (*of policeman*) nel-
l'esercizio delle proprie funzioni; **~ of fire** linea *f* di tiro; **stand in ~** (*Am: queue*) fare la
coda; **in ~ for** ‹*promotion etc*› in lista per; **on
the ~** ‹*job, career*› in serio pericolo; **read
between the ~s** *fig* leggere tra le righe ● *vt*
segnare; fiancheggiare ‹*street*›; foderare
‹*garment*›
■ **line up** *vi* allinearsi ● *vt* allineare
lineage /'lɪnɪɪdʒ/ *n* lignaggio *m*
linear /'lɪnɪə(r)/ *a* lineare
lined[1] /laɪnd/ *a* ‹*face*› rugoso; ‹*paper*› a righe
lined[2] *a* ‹*garment*› foderato
line manager *n* line manager *m inv*
linen /'lɪnɪn/ *n* lino *m*; (*articles*) biancheria *f*
● *attrib* di lino
linen basket *n* cesto *m* della biancheria
liner /'laɪnə(r)/ *n* nave *f* di linea
linesman /'laɪnzmən/ *n* Sport guardalinee *m
inv*
line-up *n* (*personnel, Sport*) formazione *f*;
(*identification*) confronto *m* all'americana

linger /'lɪŋgə(r)/ vi indugiare
lingerie /'lɒʒərɪ/ n biancheria f intima (da donna)
lingering /'lɪŋgərɪŋ/ a ‹illness› lento; ‹look› prolungato; ‹doubt› persistente
linguist /'lɪŋgwɪst/ n linguista mf
linguistic /lɪŋ'gwɪstɪk/ a linguistico
linguistically /lɪŋ'gwɪstɪklɪ/ adv linguisticamente
linguistics /lɪŋ'gwɪstɪks/ n linguistica fsg
lining /'laɪnɪŋ/ n (of garment) fodera f; (of brakes) guarnizione f
link /lɪŋk/ n (of chain) anello m; fig legame m ● vt collegare; ~ **arms** prendersi sotto braccio
■ **link up** vi unirsi (**with** a); TV collegarsi
linkage /'lɪŋkɪdʒ/ n (connection) connessione f; (in genetics) associazione f
links /lɪŋks/ n or npl campo msg da golf
link-up n collegamento m
lino /'laɪnəʊ/ n, **linoleum** /lɪ'nəʊlɪəm/ n linoleum m
linseed oil /'lɪnsiːdɔɪl/ n olio m [di semi] di lino
lint /lɪnt/ n garza f
lintel /'lɪntəl/ n architrave m
lion /'laɪən/ n leone m; **get the ~'s share** fig prendersi la fetta più grossa
lion cub n leoncino m
lioness /'laɪənɪs/ n leonessa f
lip /lɪp/ n labbro m (pl labbra f); (edge) bordo m
lip gloss n lucidalabbra m inv
liposuction /'laɪpəʊsʌkʃn/ n liposuzione f
lip: **lip-read** vi leggere le labbra. **lip-reading** n lettura f delle labbra. **lipsalve** n burro m [di] cacao. **lip-service** n **pay** ~ **to** approvare soltanto a parole. **lipstick** n rossetto m
liquefy /'lɪkwɪfaɪ/ v (pt/pp -**ied**) ● vt liquefare ● vi liquefarsi
liqueur /lɪ'kjʊə(r)/ n liquore m
liquid /'lɪkwɪd/ n liquido m ● a liquido
liquidate /'lɪkwɪdeɪt/ vt liquidare
liquidation /lɪkwɪ'deɪʃn/ n liquidazione f; **go into** ~ Comm andare in liquidazione
liquidator /'lɪkwɪdeɪtə(r)/ n liquidatore, -trice mf
liquid crystal display n visualizzatore m a cristalli liquidi
liquidize /'lɪkwɪdaɪz/ vt rendere liquido
liquidizer /'lɪkwɪdaɪzə(r)/ n Culin frullatore m
liquor /'lɪkə(r)/ n bevanda f alcoolica
liquorice /'lɪkərɪs/ n liquirizia f
liquor store n Am negozio m di alcolici
lira /'lɪərə/ n lira f; **50,000 lire** 50.000 lire
lisp /lɪsp/ n pronuncia f con la lisca; **have a** ~ parlare con la lisca ● vi parlare con la lisca
list[1] /lɪst/ n lista f ● vt elencare
list[2] vi ‹ship:› inclinarsi
listen /'lɪsn/ vi ascoltare; ~ **to** ascoltare
listener /'lɪs(ə)nə(r)/ n ascoltatore, -trice mf
listeria /lɪ'stɪərɪə/ n (illness) listeriosi f; (bacteria) listeria f
listings /'lɪstɪŋz/ npl TV programma m tv
listless /'lɪstlɪs/ a svogliato
listlessly /'lɪstlɪslɪ/ adv in modo svogliato

lit /lɪt/ see **light**[1]
litany /'lɪtənɪ/ n litania f
literacy /'lɪtərəsɪ/ n alfabetizzazione f
literal /'lɪtərəl/ a letterale
literally /'lɪt(ə)rəlɪ/ adv letteralmente
literary /'lɪtərərɪ/ a letterario
literary critic n critico, -a mf letterario, -a
literate /'lɪtərət/ a **be** ~ saper leggere e scrivere
literati /lɪtə'rɑːtiː/ npl letterati mpl
literature /'lɪtrətʃə(r)/ n letteratura f
lithe /laɪð/ a flessuoso
lithographer /lɪ'θɒgrəfə(r)/ n litografo, -a mf
lithography /lɪ'θɒgrəfɪ/ n litografia f
Lithuania /lɪθjʊ'eɪnɪə/ n Lituania f
Lithuanian /lɪθjʊ'eɪnɪən/ a & n lituano, -a mf; (language) lituano m
litigation /lɪtɪ'geɪʃn/ n causa f [giudiziaria]
litmus paper /'lɪtməs/ n cartina f di tornasole
litmus test n Chem test m inv con cartina di tornasole; fig prova f del nove
litre /'liːtə(r)/ n litro m
litter /'lɪtə(r)/ n immondizie fpl; Zool figliata f ● vt **be** ~**ed with sth** essere ingombrato di qcsa
litter-bin n bidone m della spazzatura
litterbug /'lɪtəbʌg/ n persona f che butta per terra cartacce e rifiuti
little /'lɪtl/ a piccolo; (not much) poco ● adv & n poco m; **a** ~ un po'; **a** ~ **water** un po' d'acqua; **a** ~ **better** un po' meglio; ~ **by** ~ a poco a poco
little finger n mignolo m (della mano)
little-known a poco noto
liturgical /lɪ'tɜːdʒɪkl/ a liturgico
liturgy /'lɪtədʒɪ/ n liturgia f
live[1] /laɪv/ a vivo; ‹ammunition› carico; ~ **broadcast** trasmissione f in diretta; **be** ~ Electr essere sotto tensione; ~ **wire** n fig persona f dinamica ● adv ‹broadcast› in diretta
live[2] /lɪv/ vi vivere; (reside) abitare; ~ **with** convivere con
■ **live down** vt far dimenticare
■ **live for** vt vivere solo per ‹one's work, family›
■ **live off** vt vivere alle spalle di
■ **live on** vt vivere di ● vi sopravvivere
■ **live through** vt vivere
■ **live together** vi ‹friends:› vivere insieme; ‹lovers:› convivere
■ **live up** vt ~ **it up** far la bella vita
■ **live up to** vt essere all'altezza di
■ **live with** vt convivere con ‹lover, situation›; vivere con ‹mother etc›
lived-in /'lɪvdɪn/ a **have that** ~ **look** ‹room, flat:› avere un'aria vissuta
live-in a ‹maid, nanny› che vive in casa
livelihood /'laɪvlɪhʊd/ n mezzi mpl di sostentamento
liveliness /'laɪvlɪnɪs/ n vivacità f
lively /'laɪvlɪ/ a (-**ier**, -**iest**) vivace
■ **liven up** /'laɪvn/ vt vivacizzare ● vi vivacizzarsi

liver /'lɪvə(r)/ *n* fegato *m*

liver pâté *n* pâté *m inv* di fegato

Liverpudlian /lɪvə'pʌdlɪən/ *n* (*born there*) originario, -a *mf* di Liverpool; (*living there*) abitante *mf* di Liverpool

lives /laɪvz/ *see* **life**

livestock /'laɪvstɒk/ *n* bestiame *m*

livid /'lɪvɪd/ *a fam* livido

living /'lɪvɪŋ/ *a* vivo ● *n* **earn one's ~** guadagnarsi da vivere; **the ~** *pl* i vivi

living room *n* soggiorno *m*

lizard /'lɪzəd/ *n* lucertola *f*

load /ləʊd/ *n* carico *m*; **~s of** *fam* un sacco di; **that's a ~ off my mind** mi sono tolto un peso [dallo stomaco] ● *vt* ~ **[up]** caricare

loaded /'ləʊdɪd/ *a* carico; (*fam: rich*) ricchissimo; **~ question** domanda *f* esplosiva *f*

loading bay /'ləʊdɪŋ/ *n* piazzola *f* di carico e scarico

loaf¹ /ləʊf/ *n* (*pl* **loaves**) pane *m*; (*round*) pagnotta *f*; **use one's ~** (*fam*) pensare con il proprio cervello

loaf² *vi* oziare

loafer /'ləʊfə(r)/ *n* (*idler*) scansafatiche *mf inv*; (*shoe*) mocassino *m*

loan /ləʊn/ *n* prestito *m*; **on ~** in prestito ● *vt* prestare

loan shark *n fam* strozzino, -a *mf*

loath /ləʊθ/ *a* **be ~ to do sth** essere restio a fare qcsa

loathe /ləʊð/ *vt* detestare

loathing /'ləʊðɪŋ/ *n* disgusto *m*

loathsome /'ləʊðsəm/ *a* disgustoso

loaves /ləʊvz/ *see* **loaf**

lob /lɒb/ *vt* (*pres p etc* **-bb-**) lanciare in alto; *Sport* respingere a pallonetto ● *n Sport* pallonetto *m*

lobby /'lɒbɪ/ *n* atrio *m*; *Pol* gruppo *m* di pressione, lobby *m inv*

lobbyist /'lɒbɪɪst/ *n* lobbista *mf*

lobe /ləʊb/ *n* (*of ear*) lobo *m*

lobelia /lə'bi:lɪə/ *n* lobelia *f*

lobster /'lɒbstə(r)/ *n* aragosta *f*

lobster pot *n* nassa *f* per aragoste

local /'ləʊkl/ *a* locale; **under ~ anaesthetic** sotto anestesia locale; **I'm not ~** non sono del posto ● *n* abitante *mf* del luogo; (*fam: public house*) pub *m inv* locale

local: local authority *n* autorità *f* locale. **local bus** *n* bus *m* locale. **local call** *n* Teleph telefonata *f* urbana. **local government** *n* autorità *f inv* locale. **local network** *n* Comput rete *f* locale

locality /ləʊ'kælətɪ/ *n* zona *f*

localized /'ləʊkəlaɪzd/ *a* localizzato

locally /'ləʊkəlɪ/ *adv* localmente; ⟨*live, work*⟩ nei paraggi

locate /ləʊ'keɪt/ *vt* situare; trovare ⟨*person*⟩; **be ~d** essere situato

location /ləʊ'keɪʃn/ *n* posizione *f*; **filmed on ~** girato in esterni

loch /lɒx/ *n* lago *m*

lock¹ /lɒk/ *n* (*of hair*) ciocca *f*

lock² *n* (*on door*) serratura *f*; (*on canal*) chiu-

sa *f* ● *vt* chiudere a chiave; bloccare ⟨*wheels*⟩ ● *vi* chiudersi

■ **lock in** *vt* chiudere dentro

■ **lock out** *vt* chiudere fuori

■ **lock up** *vt* (*in prison*) mettere dentro ● *vi* chiudere

locker /'lɒkə(r)/ *n* armadietto *m*

locket /'lɒkɪt/ *n* medaglione *m*

lock: lockout *n* serrata *f*. **locksmith** *n* fabbro *m*. **lock-up** *n* (*prison*) guardina *f*

loco /'ləʊkəʊ/ *a* (*Br: crazy*) toccato

locomotion /ləʊkə'məʊʃn/ *n* locomozione *f*

locomotive /ləʊkə'məʊtɪv/ *n* locomotiva *f*

locum /'ləʊkəm/ *n* sostituto, -a *mf*

locust /'ləʊkəst/ *n* locusta *f*

lodge /lɒdʒ/ *n* (*porter's*) portineria *f*; (*masonic*) loggia *f* ● *vt* presentare ⟨*claim, complaint*⟩; (*with bank, solicitor*) depositare; **be ~d** essersi conficcato ● *vi* essere a pensione (**with** da); (*become fixed*) conficcarsi

lodger /'lɒdʒə(r)/ *n* inquilino, -a *mf*

lodgings /'lɒdʒɪŋz/ *npl* camere *fpl* in affitto

loft /lɒft/ *n* soffitta *f*

lofty /'lɒftɪ/ *a* (**-ier, -iest**) alto; (*haughty*) altezzoso

log /lɒg/ *n* ceppo *m*; *Auto* libretto *m* di circolazione; *Naut* giornale *m* di bordo; **sleep like a ~** *fam* dormire come un ghiro ● *vt* (*pt/pp* **logged**) registrare

■ **log in** *vi* aprire una sessione

■ **log off** *vi* disconnettersi

■ **log on** *vi* connettersi (**to** a)

■ **log out** *vi* chiudere una sessione

logarithm /'lɒgərɪðm/ *n* logaritmo *m*

logbook /'lɒgbʊk/ *n Naut* giornale *m* di bordo; *Auto* libretto *m* di circolazione

logger /'lɒgə(r)/ *n* boscaiolo *m*

loggerheads /'lɒgəhedz/ *npl* **be at ~** *fam* essere in totale disaccordo

logic /'lɒdʒɪk/ *n* logica *f*

logical /'lɒdʒɪkl/ *a* logico

logically /'lɒdʒɪklɪ/ *adv* logicamente

logistics /lə'dʒɪstɪks/ *npl* logistica *f*

logo /'ləʊgəʊ/ *n* logo *m inv*

loin /lɔɪn/ *n Culin* lombata *f*

loin chop *n* lombatina *f*

loincloth /'lɔɪnklɒθ/ *n* perizoma *m*

loiter /'lɔɪtə(r)/ *vi* gironzolare

loll /lɒl/ *vi* **~ about** (*posture*) stravaccarsi; (*do nothing*) starsene in panciolle

lollipop /'lɒlɪpɒp/ *n* lecca-lecca *m inv*

lollop /'lɒləp/ *vi* ⟨*rabbit, person*⟩ avanzare a balzi

lolly /'lɒlɪ/ *n* lecca-lecca *m inv*; (*fam: money*) quattrini *mpl*

Lombardy /'lɒmbədɪ/ *n* Lombardia *f*

London /'lʌndən/ *n* Londra *f* ● *attrib* londinese, di Londra

Londoner /'lʌndənə(r)/ *n* londinese *mf*

lone /ləʊn/ *a* solitario

loneliness /'ləʊnlɪnɪs/ *n* solitudine *f*

lonely /'ləʊnlɪ/ *a* (**-ier, -iest**) solitario; ⟨*person*⟩ solo

loner /'ləʊnə(r)/ *n* persona *f* solitaria

lonesome /'ləʊnsəm/ *a* solo

long[1] /lɒŋ/ a (**-er** /'lɒŋɡə(r)/, **-est** /'lɒŋɡɪst/) lungo; **a ~ time** molto tempo; **a ~ way** distante; **in the ~ run** a lungo andare; (*in the end*) alla fin fine ● *adv* a lungo, lungamente; **how ~ is it?** quanto è lungo?; (*in time*) quanto dura?; **all day ~** tutto il giorno; **not ~ ago** non molto tempo fa; **before ~** fra breve; **he's no ~er here** non è più qui; **as** *or* **so ~ as** finché; (*provided that*) purché; **so ~!** *fam* ciao!; **will you be ~?** ti ci vuole molto?

long[2] *vi* **~ for** desiderare ardentemente

long: long-awaited a tanto atteso. **long-distance** a a grande distanza; *Sport* di fondo; ⟨*call*⟩ interurbano. **long division** n divisione f

longevity /lɒn'dʒevətɪ/ n longevità f

long: long face n muso m lungo. **longhand** /'lɒŋhænd/ n **in ~** in scrittura ordinaria. **long-haul** *attrib* su lunga distanza; ⟨*plane*⟩ per lunghi tragitti

longing /'lɒŋɪŋ/ a desideroso ● n brama f

longingly /'lɒŋɪŋlɪ/ adv con desiderio

longitude /'lɒŋɡɪtjuːd/ n *Geog* longitudine f

long: long-life milk n latte m a lunga conservazione. **long-lived** /-'lɪvd/ a longevo. **long jump** n salto m in lungo. **long-playing record** n 33 giri m inv. **long-range** a Mil, Aeron a lunga portata; ⟨*forecast*⟩ a lungo termine. **long-sighted** /-'saɪtɪd/ a presbite. **long-sleeved** /-'sliːvd/ a a maniche lunghe. **longstanding** a di vecchia data. **long-suffering** a infinitamente paziente. **long-term** a a lunga scadenza. **long wave** n onde fpl lunghe. **long-winded** /-'wɪndɪd/ a prolisso

loo /luː/ n *fam* gabinetto m

look /lʊk/ n occhiata f; (*appearance*) aspetto m; [**good**] **~s** pl bellezza f; **have a ~ at** dare un'occhiata a ● *vi* guardare; (*seem*) sembrare; **~ here!** mi ascolti bene!; **~ at** guardare; **~ for** cercare; **~ sb in the eye** guardare negli occhi qcno; **~ sb up and down** guardare qcno dall'alto in basso; **~ a fool** fare la figura del cretino; **~ young/old for one's age** portarsi bene/male gli anni; **~ like** (*resemble*) assomigliare a; **it ~s as if it's going to rain** sembra che stia per piovere; **~ sharp** (*fam: hurry up*) darsi una mossa

■ **look after** *vt* badare a

■ **look ahead** *vi* (*think of the future*) guardare al futuro

■ **look back** *vi* girarsi; (*think of the past*) guardare indietro

■ **look down** *vi* guardare in basso; **~ down on sb** *fig* guardare dall'alto in basso qcno

■ **look forward to** *vt* essere impaziente di

■ **look in on** *vt* passare da

■ **look into** *vt* (*examine*) esaminare

■ **look on** *vi* (*watch*) guardare ● *vt* **~ sb/sth as** (*consider to be*) considerare qcno/qcsa come

■ **look on to** *vt* ⟨*room:*⟩ dare su

■ **look out** *vi* guardare fuori; (*take care*) fare attenzione; **~ out!** attento! ● *vt* cercare ⟨*sth for sb*⟩

■ **look out for** *vt* cercare

■ **look over** *vt* riguardare ⟨*notes*⟩; ispezionare ⟨*house*⟩

■ **look round** *vi* girarsi; (*in shop, town etc*) dare un'occhiata

■ **look through** *vt* dare un'occhiata a ⟨*script, notes*⟩

■ **look to** *vt* (*rely on*) contare su

■ **look up** *vi* guardare in alto ● *vt* cercare [nel dizionario] ⟨*word*⟩; (*visit*) andare a trovare

■ **look up to** *vt fig* rispettare

look-alike n sosia mf inv

looker-on /lʊkər'ɒn/ n (pl **lookers-on**) spettatore, -trice mf

look-in n Br fam **give sb a ~** dare una chance a qcno; **get a ~** avere una chance

lookout /'lʊkaʊt/ n guardia f; (*prospect*) prospettiva f; **be on the ~ for** tenere gli occhi aperti per

loom[1] /luːm/ n telaio m

loom[2] *vi* apparire; *fig* profilarsi

loony /'luːnɪ/ a & n fam matto, -a mf; **~ bin** manicomio m

loop /luːp/ n cappio m; (*on garment*) passante m

loophole /'luːphəʊl/ n (*in the law*) scappatoia f

loopy /'luːpɪ/ a fam matto

loose /luːs/ a libero; ⟨*knot*⟩ allentato; ⟨*page*⟩ staccato; ⟨*clothes*⟩ largo; ⟨*morals*⟩ dissoluto; (*inexact*) vago; **be at a ~ end** non sapere cosa fare; **come ~** ⟨*knot:*⟩ sciogliersi; **set ~** liberare

loose: loose change n spiccioli mpl. **loose chippings** npl ghiaino m. **loose-leaf notebook** n raccoglitore m di fogli

loosely /'luːslɪ/ adv scorrevolmente; ⟨*defined*⟩ vagamente

loosen /'luːsn/ vt sciogliere

■ **loosen up** *vt* sciogliere ⟨*muscles*⟩ ● *vi* (*fam: relax*) rilassarsi

loot /luːt/ n bottino m ● *vt/i* depredare

looter /'luːtə(r)/ n predatore, -trice mf

looting /'luːtɪŋ/ n saccheggio m

lop off /lɒp/ *vt* (*pt/pp* **lopped**) potare

lop-eared /'lɒpɪəd/ a con le orecchie [a] penzoloni

lope off /ləʊp'ɒf/ *vi* andarsene a passi lunghi

lopsided /lɒp'saɪdɪd/ a sbilenco

loquacious /lə'kweɪʃəs/ a loquace

lord /lɔːd/ n signore m; (*title*) Lord m; **House of L~s** Camera f dei Lords; **the L~'s Prayer** il Padrenostro; **good L~!** Dio mio!

Lordship /'lɔːdʃɪp/ n **your/his ~** (*of noble*) Sua Signoria; **your ~** (*to judge*) Signor Giudice

lore /lɔː(r)/ n tradizioni fpl

lorry /'lɒrɪ/ n camion m inv

lorry driver n camionista mf

lose /luːz/ v (*pt/pp* **lost**) ● *vt* perdere; **~ heart** perdersi d'animo; **~ one's inhibitions** disinibirsi; **~ one's nerve** farsi prendere dalla paura; **~ sight of** perdere di vista, perdere d'occhio; **~ touch with** perdere di vista; **~ track of time** perdere la nozione del tempo; **~ weight** calare di peso ● *vi* perdere; ‹*clock:*› essere indietro

■ **lose out** *vi* rimetterci

loser /'luːzə(r)/ *n* perdente *mf*

losing battle /'luːzɪŋ/ *n* battaglia *f* persa

loss /lɒs/ *n* perdita *f*; **~es** *pl Comm* perdite *fpl*; **be at a ~** essere perplesso; **be at a ~ for words** non trovare le parole; **make a ~** *Comm* subire una perdita

loss: loss adjuster /'lɒsədʒʌstə(r)/ *n Comm* perito *m* di assicurazione. **loss-leader** *n* articolo *m* civetta. **loss-making** /'lɒsmeɪkɪŋ/ *a* ‹*company*› in passivo; ‹*product*› che non vende

lost /lɒst/ *see* **lose** ● *a* perduto; **get ~** perdersi; **get ~!** *fam* va a quel paese!

lost and found *n Am* oggetti *mpl* smarriti

lost property office *n* ufficio *m* oggetti smarriti

lot[1] /lɒt/ *(at auction)* lotto *m*; *(piece of land)* lotto *m*; **draw ~s** tirare a sorte

lot[2] *n* **the ~** il tutto; **a ~ of, ~s of** molti; **the ~ of you** tutti voi; **it has changed a ~** è cambiato molto

lotion /'ləʊʃn/ *n* lozione *f*

lottery /'lɒtərɪ/ *n* lotteria *f*

lottery ticket *n* biglietto *m* della lotteria

loud /laʊd/ *a* sonoro, alto; ‹*colours*› sgargiante ● *adv* forte; **out ~** ad alta voce

loud hailer /'heɪlə(r)/ *n* megafono *m*

loudly /'laʊdlɪ/ *adv* forte

loudspeaker /laʊd'spiːkə(r)/ *n* altoparlante *m*

lounge /laʊndʒ/ *n* salotto *m*; *(in hotel)* salone *m* ● *vi* poltrire

■ **lounge about** *vi* stare in panciolle

lounge suit *n* vestito *m* da uomo *(formale)*

louse /laʊs/ *n* *(pl* **lice)** pidocchio *m*

■ **louse up** *vt* *(fam: ruin)* guastare

lousy /'laʊzɪ/ *a* **(-ier, -iest)** *fam* schifoso

lout /laʊt/ *n* zoticone *m*

loutish /'laʊtɪʃ/ *a* rozzo

louvred /'luːvəd/ *a* ‹*door, blinds*› con le gelosie

lovable /'lʌvəbl/ *a* adorabile

love /lʌv/ *n* amore *m*; *(Tennis)* zero *m*; **in ~** innamorato **(with** di) ● *vt* amare ‹*person, country*›; **I ~ watching tennis** mi piace molto guardare il tennis

love: love affair *n* relazione *f* [sentimentale]. **lovebite** *n* succhiotto *m*. **love letter** *n* lettera *f* d'amore. **love life** *n* vita *f* sentimentale. **lovemaking** *n* il fare l'amore

lovely /'lʌvlɪ/ *a* **(-ier, -iest)** bello; *(in looks)* bello, attraente; *(in character)* piacevole; ‹*meal*› delizioso; **have a ~ time** divertirsi molto

lover /'lʌvə(r)/ *n* amante *mf*

love song *n* canzone *f* d'amore

love story *n* storia *f* d'amore

lovey-dovey /lʌvɪ'dʌvɪ/ *a Br fam* **get all ~** fare i piccioncini

loving /'lʌvɪŋ/ *a* affettuoso

lovingly /'lʌvɪŋlɪ/ *adv* affettuosamente

low /ləʊ/ *a* basso; *(depressed)* giù *inv* ● *adv* basso; **feel ~** sentirsi giù ● *n* minimo *m*; *Meteorol* depressione *f*; **at an all-time ~** ‹*prices etc*› al livello minimo

low: lowbrow /'ləʊbraʊ/ *a* di scarsa cultura. **low-calorie** *a* ipocalorico. **low-cut** *a* ‹*dress*› scollato. **low gear** *n Auto* marcia *f* bassa

lower /'ləʊə(r)/ *a & adv see* **low** ● *vt* abbassare; **~ oneself** abbassarsi

lowest common denominator /'ləʊɪst ...dɪ'nɒmɪneɪtə(r)/ *n* minimo denominatore *m* comune

low: low-fat *a* ‹*diet*› a basso contenuto di grassi; ‹*cheese, milk*› magro. **low-grade** *a* di qualità inferiore. **low-key** *a fig* moderato.

lowlands *npl* pianure *fpl*

lowly /'ləʊlɪ/ *a* **(-ier, -iest)** umile

low tide *n* bassa marea *f*

loyal /'lɔɪəl/ *a* leale

loyally /'lɔɪəlɪ/ *adv* lealmente

loyalty /'lɔɪəltɪ/ *n* lealtà *f*

lozenge /'lɒzɪndʒ/ *n* losanga *f*; *(tablet)* pastiglia

LP *n abbr* **(long-playing record)** LP *m inv*

L-plate *n Br Auto* cartello *m* che indica che il conducente non ha ancora preso la patente

LSD *n* LSD *m*

Ltd *abbr* **(Limited)** s.r.l.

lubricant /'luːbrɪkənt/ *n* lubrificante *m*

lubricate /'luːbrɪkeɪt/ *vt* lubrificare

lubrication /luːbrɪ'keɪʃn/ *n* lubrificazione *f*

lucid /'luːsɪd/ *a* ‹*explanation*› chiaro; *(sane)* lucido

lucidity /luː'sɪdətɪ/ *n* lucidità *f*; *(of explanation)* chiarezza *f*

luck /lʌk/ *n* fortuna *f*; **bad ~** sfortuna *f*; **good ~!** buona fortuna!

luckily /'lʌkɪlɪ/ *adv* fortunatamente

lucky /'lʌkɪ/ *a* **(-ier, -iest)** fortunato; **be ~** essere fortunato; ‹*thing:*› portare fortuna

lucky charm *n* portafortuna *m inv*

lucky dip *n* pesca *f* di beneficenza

lucrative /'luːkrətɪv/ *a* lucrativo

lucre /'luːkə(r)/ *n* *(fam: money)* soldi *mpl*

ludicrous /'luːdɪkrəs/ *a* ridicolo

ludicrously /'luːdɪkrəslɪ/ *adv* ‹*expensive, complex*› eccessivamente

ludo /'luːdəʊ/ *n Br* gioco *m* da tavola

lug /lʌg/ *vt* *(pt/pp* **lugged)** *fam* trascinare

luggage /'lʌgɪdʒ/ *n* bagaglio *m*

luggage: luggage-rack *n* portabagagli *m inv*. **luggage trolley** *n* carrello *m* portabagagli. **luggage van** *n* bagagliaio *m*

lughole /'lʌghəʊl/ *n* *(Br fam: ear)* orecchio *m*

lugubrious /lʊ'guːbrɪəs/ *a* lugubre

lukewarm /'luːkwɔːm/ *a* tiepido; *fig* poco entusiasta

lull /lʌl/ *n* pausa *f* ● *vt* **~ to sleep** cullare

lullaby /'lʌləbaɪ/ *n* ninnananna *f*

lumbago /lʌm'beɪgəʊ/ *n* lombaggine *f*

lumbar /'lʌmbə(r)/ *a* lombare

lumber /'lʌmbə(r)/ *n* cianfrusaglie *fpl*; *(Am: timber)* legname *m* ● *vt fam* **~ sb with sth** affibbiare qcsa a qcno

lumberjack /'lʌmbədʒæk/ *n* tagliaboschi *m inv*

luminary /'lu:mɪnərɪ/ n (fig: person) lumina-re mf

luminous /'lu:mɪnəs/ a luminoso

lump¹ /lʌmp/ n (of sugar) zolletta f; (swelling) gonfiore m; (in breast) nodulo m; (in sauce) grumo m; **a ~ in one's throat** un groppo alla gola ● vt **~ together** ammucchiare

lump² vt **~ it** fam **you'll just have to ~ it** che ti piaccia o no è così

lump sugar n zucchero m in zollette

lump sum n somma f globale

lumpy /'lʌmpɪ/ a (-ier, -iest) grumoso

lunacy /'lu:nəsɪ/ n follia f

lunar /'lu:nə(r)/ a lunare

lunatic /'lu:nətɪk/ n pazzo, -a mf

lunch /lʌntʃ/ n pranzo m; **she's gone to ~** è andata a pranzo; **let's have ~ together sometime** pranziamo qualche volta insieme ● vi pranzare

lunch box n cestino m del pranzo

luncheon /'lʌntʃn/ n (formal) pranzo m

luncheon meat n carne f in scatola

luncheon voucher n buono m pasto

lunch hour n intervallo m per il pranzo

lunchtime /'lʌntʃtaɪm/ n ora f di pranzo

lung /lʌŋ/ n polmone m

lung cancer n cancro m al polmone

lunge /lʌndʒ/ vi lanciarsi (**at** su)

lurch¹ /lɜ:tʃ/ n **leave in the ~** fam lasciare nei guai

lurch² vi barcollare

lure /lʊə(r)/ n esca f; fig lusinga f ● vt adescare

lurid /'lʊərɪd/ a (gaudy) sgargiante; (sensational) sensazionalistico

lurk /lɜ:k/ vi appostarsi

luscious /'lʌʃəs/ a saporito; fig sexy inv

lush /lʌʃ/ a lussureggiante

lust /lʌst/ n lussuria f ● vi **~ after** desiderare [fortemente]

lustful /'lʌstfʊl/ a lussurioso

lustre /'lʌstə(r)/ n lustro m

lusty /'lʌstɪ/ a (-ier, -iest) vigoroso

lute /lu:t/ n liuto m

Luxembourg /'lʌksəmbɜ:g/ n (city) Lus-semburgo f; (state) Lussemburgo m

luxuriant /lʌg'ʒʊərɪənt/ a lussureggiante, rigoglioso

luxuriantly /lʌg'ʒʊərɪəntlɪ/ adv rigogliosamente

luxurious /lʌg'ʒʊərɪəs/ a lussuoso

luxuriously /lʌg'ʒʊərɪəslɪ/ adv lussuosamente

luxury /'lʌkʃərɪ/ n lusso m; **live in ~** vivere nel lusso ● attrib di lusso

LV abbr **luncheon voucher**

LW abbr (**long wave**) OL

lychee /'laɪtʃi:/ n litchi m inv

lych-gate /'lɪtʃ-/ n entrata f coperta di un cimitero

lycra® /'laɪkrə/ n lycra f

lying /'laɪɪŋ/ see **lie¹**, **lie²** ● n mentire m

lymph gland /'lɪmf/ n linfoghiandola f

lymph node n linfonodo m

lynch /lɪntʃ/ vt linciare

lynchpin /'lɪntʃpɪn/ n fig pilastro m

lynx /lɪŋks/ n lince f

lyric /'lɪrɪk/ a lirico

lyrical /'lɪrɪkl/ a lirico; (fam: enthusiastic) entusiasta. **~ poetry** n poesia f lirica

lyricism /'lɪrɪsɪzm/ n lirismo m

lyrics /'lɪrɪks/ npl parole fpl

Mm

m, M /em/ n (letter) m, M f inv

m abbr (**metre(s)**) m; abbr (**million**) milione m; abbr (**mile(s)**) miglio

MA n abbr (**Master of Arts**) (diploma) laurea f in lettere; (person) laureato, -a mf in lettere; Am abbr **Massachusetts**

ma'am /mɑ:m/ int signora; (to queen) Sua Altezza

mac /mæk/ n fam impermeabile m

macabre /mə'kɑ:br/ a macabro

macaroni /mækə'rəʊnɪ/ n maccheroni mpl

macaroni cheese n maccheroni mpl gratinati al formaggio

macaroon /mækə'ru:n/ n ≈ amaretto m

mace¹ /meɪs/ n (staff) mazza f

mace² n (spice) macis mf

Macedonia /mæsə'dəʊnɪə/ n Macedonia f

machete /mə'ʃetɪ/ n machete m inv

Machiavellian /mækɪə'velɪən/ a machiavellico

machinations /mækɪ'neɪʃnz/ macchinazioni fpl

machine /mə'ʃi:n/ n macchina f ● vt (sew) cucire a macchina; Techn lavorare a macchina

machine: machine-gun n mitragliatrice f. **machine operator** n addetto, -a mf alle macchine. **machine-readable** a ⟨data, text⟩ leggibile dalla macchina

machinery /mə'ʃi:nərɪ/ n macchinario m; fig meccanismo m

machine: machine-stitch vt cucire a macchina. **machine tool** n macchina f utensile. **machine translation** n traduzione f elettronica

machinist /mə'ʃi:nɪst/ n macchinista mf;

(*on sewing machine*) lavorante *mf* adetto, -a alla macchina da cucire

machismo /mə'kızməʊ/ *n* machismo *m*

macho /'mætʃəʊ/ *a* macho *inv*

mackerel /'mækr(ə)l/ *n inv* sgombro *m*

mackintosh /'mækɪntɒʃ/ *n* impermeabile *m*

macro /'mækrəʊ/ *n Comput* macro *f inv*

macrocosm /'mækrəʊkɒzm/ *n* macrocosmo *m*

mad /mæd/ *a* (**madder, maddest**) pazzo, matto; (*fam: angry*) furioso (**at** con); **like ~** *fam* come un pazzo; **be ~ about sb/sth** (*fam: keen on*) andare matto per qcno/qcsa

Madagascar /mædə'gæskə(r)/ *n* Madagascar *m*

madam /'mædəm/ *n* signora *f*

mad cow disease *n* morbo *m* della mucca pazza

madden /'mædən/ *vt* (*make angry*) far diventare matto

maddening /'mæd(ə)nɪŋ/ *a* ‹*delay, person*› esasperante

made /meɪd/ *see* **make**

Madeira cake /mə'dɪərə/ *n* pan *m* di Spagna

made to measure *a* [fatto] su misura

made-up *a* (*wearing make-up*) truccato; ‹*road*› asfaltata; ‹*story*› inventato

madhouse /'mædhaʊs/ *n fam* manicomio *m*; **it's like a ~ in here!** sembra di essere in un manicomio

madly /'mædlɪ/ *adv fam* follemente; **~ in love** innamorato follemente

madman /'mædmən/ *n* pazzo *m*

madness /'mædnɪs/ *n* pazzia *f*

madonna /mə'dɒnə/ *n* madonna *f*

madwoman /'mædwʊmən/ *n* pazza *f*

mafia /'mæfɪə/ *n also fig* mafia *f*

mag /mæg/ *n abbr* **magazine**

magazine /mægə'zi:n/ *n* rivista *f*; *Mil*, *Phot* magazzino *m*

maggot /'mægət/ *n* verme *m*

maggoty /'mægətɪ/ *a* coi vermi

Magi /'meɪdʒaɪ/ *npl* **the ~** i Re Magi

magic /'mædʒɪk/ *n* magia *f*; (*tricks*) giochi *mpl* di prestigio ● *a* magico; ‹*trick*› di prestigio

magical /'mædʒɪkl/ *a* magico

magic carpet *n* tappeto *m* volante

magician /mə'dʒɪʃn/ *n* mago, -a *mf*; (*entertainer*) prestigiatore, -trice *mf*

magistrate /'mædʒɪstreɪt/ *n* magistrato *m*

magistrate's court /n ≈ pretura *f*

magnanimity /mægnə'nɪmətɪ/ *n* magnanimità *f*

magnanimous /mæg'nænɪməs/ *a* magnanimo

magnesia /mæg'ni:ʃə/ *n* magnesia *f*

magnet /'mægnɪt/ *n* magnete *m*, calamita *f*

magnetic /mæg'netɪk/ *a* magnetico

magnetic tape *n* nastro *m* magnetico

magnetism /'mægnətɪzm/ *n* magnetismo *m*

magnetize /'mægnətaɪz/ *vt* magnetizzare

magnification /mægnɪfɪ'keɪʃn/ *n* ingrandimento *m*

magnificence /mæg'nɪfɪsəns/ *n* magnificenza *f*

magnificent /mæg'nɪfɪsənt/ *a* magnifico

magnificently /mæg'nɪfɪsəntlɪ/ *adv* magnificamente

magnify /'mægnɪfaɪ/ *vt* (*pt/pp* **-ied**) ingrandire; (*exaggerate*) ingigantire

magnifying glass /'mægnɪfaɪɪŋ/ *n* lente *f* d'ingrandimento

magnitude /'mægnɪtju:d/ *n* grandezza *f*; (*importance*) importanza *f*; **a project of this ~** un progetto di tale portata

magnum opus /mægnəm'ɒpəs/ *n* opera *f* principale

magpie /'mægpaɪ/ *n* gazza *f*

mahogany /mə'hɒgənɪ/ *n* mogano *m* ● *attrib* di mogano

maid /meɪd/ *n* cameriera *f*; **old ~** *pej* zitella *f*

maiden /'meɪdn/ *n liter* fanciulla *f* ● *a* ‹*speech, voyage*› inaugurale

maiden aunt *n* zia *f* zitella

maiden name *n* nome *m* da ragazza

mail /meɪl/ *n* posta *f* ● *vt* impostare

mail: mailbag *n* sacco *m* postale. **mail bomb** *n* pacco *m* esplosivo (*arrivato per posta*). **mailbox** *n Am* cassetta *f* delle lettere; (*e-mail*) casella *f* postale. **mail coach** *n Rail* vagone *m* postale. **mail delivery** *n* consegna *f* della posta

mailing address /'meɪlɪŋ/ *n* recapito *m* postale

mailing list *n* elenco *m* d'indirizzi per un *mailing*

mail: mailman /'meɪlmən/ *n Am* postino *m*. **mail order** *n* vendita *f* per corrispondenza ● *attrib* ‹*business*› di vendita per corrispondenza; ‹*goods*› comprati per corrispondenza. **mail-order catalogue** catalogo *m* di vendita per corrispondenza. **mail-order firm** *n* ditta *f* di vendita per corrispondenza. **mail room** *n* reparto *m* spedizioni. **mailshot** *n* mailing *m inv*. **mail train** *n* treno *m* postale. **mail van** *n* (*delivery vehicle*) furgone *m* postale; (*in train*) vagone *m* postale

maim /meɪm/ *vt* menomare

main[1] /meɪn/ *n* (*water, gas, electricity*) conduttura *f* principale

main[2] *a* principale; **the ~ thing is to...** la cosa essenziale è di... ● *n* **in the ~** in complesso

main: main course *n* secondo *m*. **main deck** *n* ponte *m* di coperta. **mainframe** *n Comput* mainframe *m inv*. **mainland** *n* continente *m*. **main line** *n Rail* linea *f* principale ● *attrib* ‹*station, terminus, train*› della linea principale

mainly /'meɪnlɪ/ *adv* principalmente

main: main memory *n Comput* memoria *f* principale. **main office** *n* (*of company*) sede *f* centrale. **main road** *n* strada *f* principale. **mainsail** *n* randa *f*, vela *f* di taglio. **mainstay** *n fig* pilastro *m*. **main street** *n* via *f* principale

maintain /meɪn'teɪn/ *vt* mantenere; (*keep in repair*) curare la manutenzione di; (*claim*) sostenere

maintenance /'meɪntənəns/ n mantenimento m; (care) manutenzione f; (allowance) alimenti mpl

maintenance grant n (for student) presalario m

maintenance order n Br obbligo m degli alimenti

maisonette /meɪzə'net/ n appartamento m a due piani

maize /meɪz/ n granoturco m

Maj abbr (**Major**) Mag

majestic /mə'dʒestɪk/ a maestoso

majestically /mə'dʒestɪklɪ/ adv maestosamente

majesty /'mædʒəstɪ/ n maestà f inv; **His/Her M~** Sua Maestà

major /'meɪdʒə(r)/ a maggiore; ~ **road** strada f con diritto di precedenza ● n Mil, Mus maggiore m ● vi Am ~ **in** specializzarsi in

Majorca /mə'jɔːkə/ n Maiorca f

major general n generale m di divisione

majority /mə'dʒɒrətɪ/ n maggioranza f; **be in the ~** avere la maggioranza

make /meɪk/ n (brand) marca f ● v (pt/pp made) ● vt fare; (earn) guadagnare; rendere ⟨happy, clear⟩; prendere ⟨decision⟩; ~ **sb laugh** far ridere qcno; ~ **sb do sth** far fare qcsa a qcno; ~ **it** (to party, top of hill etc) farcela; **what time do you ~ it?** che ore fai? ● vi ~ **as if to** fare per

■ **make after** vt (chase) inseguire

■ **make do** vi arrangiarsi

■ **make for** vt dirigersi verso

■ **make good** vi riuscire ● vt compensare ⟨loss⟩; risarcire ⟨damage⟩

■ **make off** vi fuggire

■ **make off with** vt (steal) sgraffignare

■ **make out** vt (distinguish) distinguere; (write out) rilasciare ⟨cheque⟩; compilare ⟨list⟩; (claim) far credere

■ **make over** vt cedere

■ **make up** vt (constitute) comporre; (complete) completare; (invent) inventare; (apply cosmetics to) truccare; fare ⟨parcel⟩; ~ **up one's mind** decidersi; ~ **it up** (after quarrel) riconciliarsi ● vi (after quarrel) fare la pace

■ **make up for** vt compensare; ~ **up for lost time** recuperare il tempo perso

■ **make up to** vt arruffianarsi

make: make-believe a finto ● n finzione f. **make-do-and-mend** vi arrangiarsi col poco che si ha. **make-over** n trasformazione f

maker /'meɪkə(r)/ n fabbricante mf; **M~** Relig Creatore m; **send sb to meet his/her ~** spedire qcno all'altro mondo

make: makeshift a di fortuna ● n espediente m. **make-up** n trucco m; (character) natura f. **make-up artist** n truccatore, -trice mf. **make-up bag** n astuccio m per il trucco. **make-up remover** n struccante m

making /'meɪkɪŋ/ n (manufacture) fabbricazione f; **be the ~ of** essere la causa del successo di; **have the ~s of** aver la stoffa di; **in the ~** in formazione

maladjusted /mælə'dʒʌstɪd/ a disadattato

maladjustment /mælə'dʒʌstmənt/ n disadattamento m

Malagasy /mælə'gæzɪ/ n (native of Madagascar) malgascio, -a mf; (language) malgascio m

malaise /mə'leɪz/ n fig malessere m

malaria /mə'leərɪə/ n malaria f

Malaysia /mə'leɪʒə/ n Malesia f

Malaysian /mə'leɪʒən/ n & a malese mf

male /meɪl/ a maschile ● n maschio m

male: male chauvinist [pig] n [sporco m] maschilista m. **male menopause** n andropausa f. **male model** n indossatore m. **male nurse** n infermiere m. **male voice choir** n coro m maschile

malevolence /mə'levələns/ n malevolenza f

malevolent /mə'levələnt/ a malevolo

malformation /mælfɔː'meɪʃn/ n malformazione f

malformed /mæl'fɔːmd/ a malformato

malfunction /mæl'fʌŋkʃn/ n funzionamento m imperfetto ● vi funzionare male

Mali /'mɑːlɪ/ n Mali m

malice /'mælɪs/ n malignità f; **bear sb** ~ voler del male a qcno

malicious /mə'lɪʃəs/ a maligno

maliciously /mə'lɪʃəslɪ/ adv con malignità

malign /mə'laɪn/ vt malignare su

malignancy /mə'lɪgnənsɪ/ n malignità f

malignant /mə'lɪgnənt/ a maligno

malinger /mə'lɪŋgə(r)/ vi fingersi malato

malingerer /mə'lɪŋgərə(r)/ n scansafatiche mf inv

mall /mæl/ n (shopping arcade, in suburb) centro m commerciale; (Am: street) strada f pedonale

mallard /'mælɑːd/ n germano m reale

malleable /'mælɪəbl/ a malleabile

mallet /'mælɪt/ n martello m di legno

malnourished /mæl'nʌrɪʃt/ a malnutrito

malnutrition /mælnjʊ'trɪʃn/ n malnutrizione f

malpractice /mæl'præktɪs/ n negligenza f

malt /mɔːlt/ n malto m

Malta /'mɔːltə/ n Malta f

Maltese /mɔːl'tiːz/ a & n maltese mf

maltreat /mæl'triːt/ vt maltrattare

maltreatment /mæl'triːtmənt/ n maltrattamento m

malt whisky n whisky m inv di malto

mammal /'mæml/ n mammifero m

mammary /'mæmərɪ/ a mammario

mammograph /'mæməgrɑːf/ n mammografia f

mammoth /'mæməθ/ a mastodontico ● n mammut m inv

man /mæn/ n (pl **men**) uomo m; (chess, draughts) pedina f; **the ~ in the street** l'uomo della strada; ~ **to** ~ da uomo a uomo ● vt (pt/pp **manned**) equipaggiare; far funzionare ⟨pump⟩; essere di servizio a ⟨counter, telephones⟩

manacle /'mænəkl/ vt ammanettare

manage /'mænɪdʒ/ vt dirigere; gestire ⟨shop, affairs⟩; (cope with) farcela; ~ **to do sth** riuscire a fare qcsa ● *vi* riuscire; (*cope*) farcela (**on** con)

manageable /'mænɪdʒəbl/ *a* ⟨*hair*⟩ docile; ⟨*size*⟩ maneggevole

management /'mænɪdʒmənt/ *n* gestione *f*; **the ~** la direzione

management: management accounting *n* contabilità *f* di gestione. **management buyout** *n* buyout *m inv* da parte dei manager, rilevamento *m* dirigenti. **management consultancy** *n* (*firm*) consulente *m* aziendale; (*activity*) consulenza *f* aziendale. **management consultant** *n* consulente *mf* aziendale

manager /'mænɪdʒə(r)/ *n* direttore *m*; (*of shop, bar*) gestore *m*; *Sport* manager *m inv*

manageress /mænɪdʒə'res/ *n* direttrice *f*

managerial /mænɪ'dʒɪərɪəl/ *a* **~ staff** personale *m* direttivo

managing /'mænɪdʒɪŋ/ *a* **~ director** direttore, -trice *mf* generale

mandarin /'mændərɪn/ *n* **~ [orange]** mandarino *m*

mandate /'mændeɪt/ *n* mandato *m*

mandatory /'mændətrɪ/ *a* obbligatorio

mandolin /'mændəlɪn/ *n* mandolino *m*

mandrake /'mændreɪk/ *n* mandragola *f*

mane /meɪn/ *n* criniera *f*

manful /'mænfl/ *a* coraggioso

manfully /'mænfʊlɪ/ *adv* coraggiosamente

mangle /'mæŋgl/ *vt* (*damage*) maciullare

mango /'mæŋgəʊ/ *n* (*pl* **-es**) mango *m*

mangrove /'mæŋgrəʊv/ *n* mangrovia *f*

mangy /'meɪndʒɪ/ *a* ⟨*dog*⟩ rognoso

manhandle /'mænhændl/ *vt* malmenare

manhole /'mænhəʊl/ *n* botola *f*

manhole cover *n* tombino *m*

manhood /'mænhʊd/ *n* età *f* adulta; (*quality*) virilità *f*

man-hour *n* ora *f* lavorativa

manhunt /'mænhʌnt/ *n* caccia *f* all'uomo

mania /'meɪnɪə/ *n* mania *f*

maniac /'meɪnɪæk/ *n* maniaco, -a *mf*

manic /'mænɪk/ *a* (*obsessive*) maniacale; (*frenetic*) frenetico

manic depression *n* psicosi *f inv* maniaco-depressiva

manic-depressive *a* maniaco-depressivo

manicure /'mænɪkjʊə(r)/ *n* manicure *f inv* ● *vt* fare la manicure a

manicurist /'mænɪkjʊərɪst/ *n* manicure *f inv*

manifest /'mænɪfest/ *a* manifesto ● *n Comm* manifesto *m* ● *vt* manifestare; **~ itself** manifestarsi

manifestation /mænɪfe'steɪʃn/ *n* manifestazione *f*

manifestly /'mænɪfestlɪ/ *adv* palesemente

manifesto /mænɪ'festəʊ/ *n* manifesto *m*

manifold /'mænɪfəʊld/ *a* molteplice

manipulate /mə'nɪpjuleɪt/ *vt* manipolare

manipulation /mənɪpjʊ'leɪʃn/ *n* manipolazione *f*

mankind /mæn'kaɪnd/ *n* genere *m* umano

manly /'mænlɪ/ *a* virile

man-made *a* artificiale; **~ fibre** *n* fibra *f* sintetica

manna /'mænə/ *n* manna *f*; **~ from heaven** *fig* manna *f* dal cielo

mannequin /'mænɪkɪn/ *n* manichino *m*

manner /'mænə(r)/ *n* maniera *f*; **in this ~** in questo modo; **have no ~s** avere dei pessimi modi; **good/bad ~s** buone/cattive maniere

mannered /'mænəd/ *pej* manierato

mannerism /'mænərɪzm/ *n* affettazione *f*

mannish /'mænɪʃ/ *a* mascolino

manoeuvrable /mə'nu:vrəbl/ *a* manovrabile

manoeuvre /mə'nu:və(r)/ *n* manovra *f* ● *vt* fare manovra con ⟨*vehicle*⟩; manovrare ⟨*person*⟩

manor /'mænə(r)/ *n* maniero *m*

manpower /'mænpaʊə(r)/ *n* manodopera *f*

manse /mæns/ *n* canonica *f*

mansion /'mænʃn/ *n* palazzo *m*

manslaughter /'mænslɔːtə(r)/ *n* omicidio *m* colposo

mantelpiece /'mæntlpiːs/ *n* mensola *f* di caminetto

mantis /'mæntɪs/ *n* mantide *f*

Mantua /'mæntjʊə/ *n* Mantova *f*

manual /'mænjʊəl/ *a* manuale ● *n* manuale *m*

manufacture /mænjʊ'fæktʃə(r)/ *vt* fabbricare ● *n* manifattura *f*

manufacturer /mænjʊ'fæktʃərə(r)/ *n* fabbricante *m*

manure /mə'njʊə(r)/ *n* concime *m*

manuscript /'mænjʊskrɪpt/ *n* manoscritto *m*

Manx /mæŋks/ *n* (*language*) lingua *f* parlata nell'isola di Man; **the ~** *pl* (*people*) gli abitanti dell'isola di Man

many /'menɪ/ *a* & *pron* molti; **there are as ~ boys as girls** ci sono tanti ragazzi quante ragazze; **as ~ as 500** ben 500; **as ~ as that** così tanti; **as ~** altrettanti; **very ~, a good/ great ~** moltissimi; **~ a time** molte volte

many-sided /-'saɪdɪd/ *a* ⟨*personality, phenomenon*⟩ sfaccettato

map /mæp/ *n* carta *f* geografica; (*of town*) mappa *f*

■ **map out** *vt* (*pt/pp* **mapped**) *fig* programmare

maple /'meɪpl/ *n* acero *m*

mar /mɑː(r)/ *vt* (*pt/pp* **marred**) rovinare

marathon /'mærəθən/ *n* maratona *f*

marauder /mə'rɔːdə(r)/ *n* predone *m*

marble /'mɑːbl/ *n* marmo *m*; (*for game*) pallina *f* ● *attrib* di marmo

March /mɑːtʃ/ *n* marzo *m*

march *n* marcia *f*; (*protest*) dimostrazione *f* ● *vi* marciare ● *vt* far marciare; **~ sb off** scortare qcno fuori

marcher /'mɑːtʃə(r)/ *n* (*in procession, band*) persona *f* che marcia in una processione, in un corteo ecc; (*in demonstration*) dimostrante *mf*

marchioness /mɑːʃə'nes/ *n* marchesa *f*

march past *n* sfilata *f*

mare /'meə(r)/ *n* giumenta *f*

margarine /mɑ:dʒə'ri:n/ n margarina f

marge /mɑ:dʒ/ n (Br fam: margarine) margarina f

margin /'mɑ:dʒɪn/ n margine m

marginal /'mɑ:dʒɪnəl/ a marginale

marginally /'mɑ:dʒɪnəlɪ/ adv marginalmen-
te

marigold /'mærɪɡəʊld/ n calendula f

marijuana /mærʊ'wɑ:nə/ n marijuana f

marina /mə'ri:nə/ n porticciolo m

marinade /mærɪ'neɪd/ n marinata f ● vt marinare

marine /mə'ri:n/ a marino ● n (sailor) soldato m di fanteria marina

Marine Corps n i Marine

marine engineer n ingegnere m navale;
(works in engine room) macchinista m

marionette /mærɪə'net/ n marionetta f

marital /'mærɪtl/ a coniugale; ~ **status** stato m civile

maritime /'mærɪtaɪm/ a marittimo

marjoram /'mɑ:dʒərəm/ n maggiorana f

mark[1] /mɑ:k/ n (currency) marco m

mark[2] n (stain) macchia f; (sign, indication)
segno m; Sch voto m; **be the ~** of designare
● vt segnare; (stain) macchiare; Sch correggere; Sport marcare; ~ **time** Mil segnare il passo; fig non far progressi; ~ **my words** ricor-
dati quello che dico

■ **mark down** vt (reduce the price of) ribassare

■ **mark out** vt delimitare; fig designare

■ **mark up** vt (increase the price of) aumentare

marked /mɑ:kt/ a marcato

markedly /'mɑ:kɪdlɪ/ adv notevolmente

marker /'mɑ:kə(r)/ n (for highlighting)
evidenziatore m; Sport marcatore m; (of
exam) esaminatore, -trice mf

marker pen n evidenziatore m

market /'mɑ:kɪt/ n mercato m ● vt vendere al
mercato; (launch) commercializzare; **on the
~** sul mercato

market: market analyst n analista mf di
mercato. **market day** n giorno m di mercato.
market economy n economia f di mercato.
market forces npl forze fpl di mercato.
market garden n orto m. **market gardener**
n ortofrutticoltore, -trice mf

marketing /'mɑ:kɪtɪŋ/ n marketing m

marketing: marketing campaign n campagna f promozionale or pubblicitaria.
marketing department n ufficio m
marketing. **marketing man** n addetto, -a mf
al marketing. **marketing mix** n mix m inv
del marketing. **marketing strategy** n strategia f di marketing

market: market leader n (company,
product) leader m inv del mercato. **market
place** n (square, Fin) mercato m. **market
price** n prezzo m di mercato. **market
research** n ricerca f di mercato. **market
square** n piazza f del mercato. **market stall**
n banco m del mercato. **market survey** n indagine f di mercato. **market town** n cittadi-

na f dove si tiene il mercato. **market trader** n
venditore, -trice mf al mercato. **market
value** n valore m di mercato

markings /'mɑ:kɪŋz/ npl (on animal) colori
mpl

marksman /'mɑ:ksmən/ n tiratore m scelto

marksmanship /'mɑ:ksmənʃɪp/ n abilità f
nel tiro

mark-up n (margin) margine m di vendita;
(price increase) aumento m

marmalade /'mɑ:məleɪd/ n marmellata f
d'arance

maroon /mə'ru:n/ a marrone rossastro

marooned /mə'ru:nd/ a abbandonato

marquee /mɑ:'ki:/ n tendone m; (Am:
awning) pensilina f con pubblicità

marquess /'mɑ:kwɪs/ n marchese m

marquetry /'mɑ:kɪtrɪ/ n intarsio m

marquis /'mɑ:kwɪs/ n marchese m

marriage /'mærɪdʒ/ n matrimonio m

marriage: marriage ceremony n cerimonia f nuziale. **marriage certificate** n certificato m di matrimonio. **marriage guidance
counsellor** n consulente mf matrimoniale.
marriage of convenience n matrimonio m
di convenienza

married /'mærɪd/ a sposato; ⟨life⟩ coniugale

marrow /'mærəʊ/ n Anat midollo m;
(vegetable) zucca f

marrowbone /'mærəʊbəʊn/ n midollo m
osseo

marry /'mærɪ/ vt (pt/pp -ied) sposare; **get
married** sposarsi ● vi sposarsi

marsh /mɑ:ʃ/ n palude f

marshal /'mɑ:ʃl/ n (steward) cerimoniere m
● vt (pt/pp **marshalled**) fig organizzare
⟨arguments⟩

marshmallow /mɑ:ʃ'mæləʊ/ n caramella f
gommosa e pastosa

marshy /'mɑ:ʃɪ/ a paludoso

marsupial /mɑ:'su:pɪəl/ n marsupiale m

marten /'mɑ:tɪn/ n martora f

martial /'mɑ:ʃl/ a marziale

Martian /'mɑ:ʃn/ a & n marziano, -a mf

martinet /mɑ:tɪ'net/ n fanatico, -a mf della
disciplina

martyr /'mɑ:tə(r)/ n martire mf ● vt marti-
rizzare

martyrdom /'mɑ:tədəm/ n martirio m

martyred /'mɑ:təd/ a fam da martire

marvel /'mɑ:vl/ n meraviglia f ● vi (pt/pp
marvelled) meravigliarsi (**at** di)

marvellous /'mɑ:vələs/ a meraviglioso

marvellously /'mɑ:vələslɪ/ adv meravigliosamente

Marxism /'mɑ:ksɪzm/ n marxismo m

Marxist /'mɑ:ksɪst/ a & n marxista mf

marzipan /'mɑ:zɪpæn/ n marzapane m

mascara /mæ'skɑ:rə/ n mascara m inv

mascot /'mæskət/ n mascotte f inv

masculine /'mæskjʊlɪn/ a maschile ● n
Gram maschile m

masculinity /mæskjʊ'lɪnətɪ/ n mascolinità f

mash /mæʃ/ n Culin fam purè m inv ● vt impastare

mashed potatoes /mæʃt/ npl purè m inv di patate

mask /mɑːsk/ n maschera f ● vt mascherare

masked ball /mɑːskt'bɔːl/ n ballo m in maschera

masking tape /ˈmɑːskɪŋ/ n nastro m di carta adesiva

masochism /ˈmæsəkɪzm/ n masochismo m

masochist /ˈmæsəkɪst/ n masochista mf

Mason /ˈmeɪsn/ n massone m

mason n muratore m

Masonic /məˈsɒnɪk/ a massonico

masonry /ˈmeɪsnrɪ/ n muratura f; **two tons of** ~ due tonnellate di pietre

masquerade /mæskəˈreɪd/ n fig mascherata f ● vi ~ **as** (pose) farsi passare per

mass[1] /mæs/ n Relig messa f

mass[2] n massa f; ~**es of** fam un sacco di ● vi ammassarsi

massacre /ˈmæsəkə(r)/ n massacro m ● vt massacrare

massage /ˈmæsɑːʒ/ n massaggio m ● vt massaggiare; fig manipolare (statistics)

masseur /mæˈsɜː(r)/ n massaggiatore m

masseuse /mæˈsɜːz/ n massaggiatrice f

mass grave n fossa f comune

mass hysteria n isterismo m di massa

massive /ˈmæsɪv/ a enorme

massively /ˈmæsɪvlɪ/ adv estremamente

mass: mass market n mercato m di massa ● attrib del mercato di massa. **mass media** npl mezzi mpl di comunicazione di massa, mass media mpl. **mass murder** n omicidio m di massa. **mass murderer** n omicida mf di massa. **mass-produce** vt produrre in serie. **mass production** n produzione f in serie. **mass screening** n Med controllo m su larga scala

mast /mɑːst/ n Naut albero m; (for radio) antenna f

master /ˈmɑːstə(r)/ n maestro m, padrone m; (teacher) professore m; (of ship) capitano m; **M**~ (boy) signorino m ● vt imparare perfettamente; avere padronanza di (language)

master: master bedroom n camera f da letto principale. **master builder** n capomastro m. **master copy** n originale m. **master disk** n Comput disco m master. **master key** n passe-partout m inv

masterly /ˈmɑːstəlɪ/ a magistrale

master: mastermind n cervello m ● vt ideare e dirigere. **Master of Arts** n (diploma) laurea f in lettere; (person) laureato, -a mf in lettere. **master of ceremonies** n (presenting entertainment) presentatore m; (of formal occasion) maestro m delle cerimonie. **Master of Science** n (diploma) laurea f in discipline scientifiche; (person) laureato, -a mf in discipline scientifiche. **masterpiece** n capolavoro m. **master plan** n piano m generale. **master race** n razza f superiore. **master stroke** n colpo m da maestro. **master tape** n nastro m matrice

mastery /ˈmæstərɪ/ n (of subject) padronanza f

masticate /ˈmæstɪkeɪt/ vi masticare

masturbate /ˈmæstəbeɪt/ vi masturbarsi

masturbation /mæstəˈbeɪʃn/ n masturbazione f

mat /mæt/ n stuoia f; (on table) sottopiatto m

match[1] /mætʃ/ n Sport partita f; (equal) uguale mf; (marriage) matrimonio m; (person to marry) partito m; **be a good** ~ (colours:) intonarsi bene; **be no** ~ **for** non essere dello stesso livello di ● vt (equal) uguagliare; (be like) andare bene con ● vi intonarsi

match[2] n fiammifero m

matchbox /ˈmætʃbɒks/ n scatola f di fiammiferi

matching /ˈmætʃɪŋ/ a intonato

match: matchmaker n **he's a successful** ~ (for couples) è stato l'artefice di molti matrimoni. **match point** n Tennis match point m inv. **matchstick** n fiammifero m

mate[1] /meɪt/ n compagno, -a mf; (assistant) aiuto m; Naut secondo m; (fam: friend) amico, -a mf ● vi accoppiarsi ● vt accoppiare

mate[2] n (in chess) scacco m matto

material /məˈtɪərɪəl/ n materiale m; (fabric) stoffa f; **raw** ~**s** pl materie fpl prime ● a materiale

materialism /məˈtɪərɪəlɪzm/ n materialismo m

materialistic /mətɪərɪəˈlɪstɪk/ a materialistico

materialize /məˈtɪərɪəlaɪz/ vi materializzarsi

maternal /məˈtɜːnl/ a materno

maternity /məˈtɜːnətɪ/ n maternità f

maternity: maternity clothes npl abiti mpl pre-maman. **maternity department** n (in store) reparto m pre-maman. **maternity hospital** n maternità f inv. **maternity leave** n congedo m per maternità. **maternity unit** n reparto m maternità. **maternity ward** n maternità f inv

matey /ˈmeɪtɪ/ a fam amichevole

math /mæθ/ n Am matematica f

mathematical /mæθəˈmætɪkl/ a matematico

mathematically /mæθəˈmætɪklɪ/ adv matematicamente

mathematician /mæθəməˈtɪʃn/ n matematico, -a mf

mathematics /mæθəˈmætɪks/ n matematica fsg

maths /mæθs/ n fam matematica fsg

matinée /ˈmætɪneɪ/ n Theat matinée f inv

mating /ˈmeɪtɪŋ/ n accoppiamento m

mating call n richiamo m [per l'accoppiamento]

mating season n stagione f degli amori

matriarchal /meɪtrɪˈɑːkl/ a matriarcale

matriarchy /ˈmeɪtrɪɑːkɪ/ n matriarchia f

matrices /ˈmeɪtrɪsiːz/ see **matrix**

matriculate /məˈtrɪkjʊleɪt/ vi immatricolarsi

matriculation /mətrɪkjʊˈleɪʃn/ n immatricolazione f

matrimonial /mætrɪˈməʊnɪəl/ a matrimoniale

matrimony /'mætrɪmənɪ/ *n* matrimonio *m*

matrix /'meɪtrɪks/ *n* (*pl* **matrices** /'meɪtrɪsiːz/) matrice *f*

matron /'meɪtrən/ *n* (*of hospital*) capoinfermiera *f*; (*of school*) governante *f*

matronly /'meɪtrənlɪ/ *a* matronale

matron of honour *n Br* damigella *f* d'onore (*sposata*)

matt /mæt/ *a* opaco

matted /'mætɪd/ *a* ~ **hair** capelli *mpl* tutti appiccicati tra loro

matter /'mætə(r)/ *n* (*affair*) faccenda *f*; (*question*) questione *f*; (*pus*) pus *m*; (*Phys: substance*) materia *f*; **money ~s** questioni *fpl* di soldi; **as a ~ of fact** a dire la verità; **what is the ~?** che cosa c'è? ● *vi* importare; **~ to sb** essere importante per qcno; **it doesn't ~** non importa

matter-of-fact *a* pratico

matting /'mætɪŋ/ *n* materiale *m* per stuoie

mattress /'mætrɪs/ *n* materasso *m*

maturation /mætʃʊ'reɪʃn/ *n* (*of tree, body*) sviluppo *m*; (*of whisky, wine*) invecchiamento *m*; (*of cheese*) stagionatura *f*

mature /mə'tʃʊə(r)/ *a* maturo; *Comm* in scadenza ● *vi* maturare ● *vt* far maturare

mature student *n Br* persona *f* che riprende gli studi universitari dopo i 25 anni

maturity /mə'tʃʊərətɪ/ *n* maturità *f*; *Comm* maturazione *f*

maudlin /'mɔːdlɪn/ *a* ‹*song*› sdolcinato; ‹*person*› piagnucoloso

maul /mɔːl/ *vt* malmenare

Maundy /'mɔːndɪ/ *n* ~ **Thursday** giovedì *m* santo

Mauritius /mə'rɪʃəs/ *n* [isola *f* di] Maurizio *f*

mausoleum /mɔːsə'lɪəm/ *n* mausoleo *m*

mauve /məʊv/ *a* malva

maverick /'mævərɪk/ *n, a* anticonformista *mf*

mawkish /'mɔːkɪʃ/ *a* sdolcinato

maxi /'mæksɪ/ *n* (*dress*) vestito *m* alla caviglia; (*skirt*) gonna *f* alla caviglia

maxim /'mæksɪm/ *n* massima *f*

maximization /mæksɪmaɪ'zeɪʃn/ *n* massimizzazione *f*

maximum /'mæksɪməm/ *a* massimo; **ten minutes ~** dieci minuti al massimo ● *n* (*pl* -**ima**) massimo *m*

maximum security prison *n* carcere *m* di massima sicurezza

May /meɪ/ *n* maggio *m*

may *v aux* (*solo al presente*) potere; **~ I come in?** posso entrare?; **if I ~ say so** se mi posso permettere; **~ you both be very happy** siate felici; **I ~ as well stay** potrei anche rimanere; **it ~ be true** potrebbe esser vero; **she ~ be old, but...** sarà anche vecchia, ma...

maybe /'meɪbɪ/ *adv* forse, può darsi

may: May-bug *n* maggiolino *m*. **Mayday** *n Radio* mayday *m inv*. **May Day** *n* il primo maggio

mayhem /'meɪhem/ *n* **create ~** creare scompiglio

mayonnaise /meɪə'neɪz/ *n* maionese *f*

mayor /'meə(r)/ *n* sindaco *m*

mayoress /'meə'res/ *n* sindaco *m*; (*wife of mayor*) moglie *f* del sindaco

maypole /'meɪpəʊl/ *n* palo *m* intorno al quale si balla durante la celebrazione del primo maggio

May queen *n* reginetta *f* di calendimaggio

maze /meɪz/ *n* labirinto *m*

Mb *abbr* (**megabyte**) Mb *m inv*

MBA *n abbr* (**Master of Business Administration**) laurea *f inv* in economia e commercio

MBE *n Br abbr* (**Member of the Order of the British Empire**) onorificenza *f* britannica

MBO *n abbr* **management buyout**

MC *n abbr* (**Master of Ceremonies**) (*in cabaret*) presentatore *m*; (*at banquet*) maestro *m* delle cerimonie; *Am abbr* (**Member of Congress**) membro *m* del Congresso

McCoy /mə'kɔɪ/ *n* **this whisky is the real ~** questo è un vero whisky

MD *abbr* (**Managing Director**) direttore, -trice *mf* generale; *abbr* (**Doctor of Medicine**) dottore *m* in medicina; *Am abbr* **Maryland**

ME *n abbr* (**myalgic encephalomyelitis**) encefalomielite *f* mialgica; *Am abbr* **Maine**

me /miː/ *pers pron* (*object*) mi; (*with preposition*) me; **he knows me** mi conosce; **she called me, not you** ha chiamato me, non te; **give me the money** dammi i soldi; **give it to me** dammelo; **he explained it to me** me lo ha spiegato; **it's me** sono io

mead /miːd/ *n* idromele *m*

meadow /'medəʊ/ *n* prato *m*

meagre /'miːgə(r)/ *a* scarso

meal[1] /miːl/ *n* pasto *m*; **did you enjoy your ~?** ha mangiato bene?

meal[2] *n* (*grain*) farina *f*

meal ticket *n* (*fig: quality, qualification*) fonte *f* di guadagno; **he's only a ~ ~ to her** le interessano solo i suoi soldi

mealy-mouthed /miːlɪ'maʊðd/ *a* ambiguo

mean[1] /miːn/ *a* avaro; (*unkind*) meschino; (*low in rank*) basso; (*accommodation*) misero

mean[2] *a* medio ● *n* (*average*) media *f*; **Greenwich ~ time** ora *f* media di Greenwich

mean[3] *vt* (*pt/pp* **meant**) voler dire; (*signify*) significare; (*intend*) intendere; **I ~ it** lo dico seriamente; **~ well** avere buone intenzioni; **be ~t for** ‹*present:*› essere destinato a; ‹*remark:*› essere riferito a

meander /mɪ'ændə(r)/ *vi* vagare

meaning /'miːnɪŋ/ *n* significato *m*

meaningful /'miːnɪŋfʊl/ *a* significativo

meaningless /'miːnɪŋlɪs/ *a* senza senso

meanness /'miːnnɪs/ *n* (*with money*) avarizia *f*; (*unkindness*) meschinità *f*

means /miːnz/ *n* mezzo *m*; ~ **of transport** mezzo *m* di trasporto; **by ~ of** per mezzo di; **by all ~!** certamente!; **by no ~** niente affatto ● *npl* (*resources*) mezzi *mpl*; ~ **test** *n* accertamento *m* patrimoniale

meant /ment/ *see* **mean³**

meantime /'mi:ntaɪm/ *n* **in the ~** nel frattempo ● *adv* intanto

meanwhile /'mi:nwaɪl/ *adv* intanto

measles /'mi:zlz/ *nsg* morbillo *m*

measly /'mi:zlɪ/ *a fam* misero

measurable /'meʒərəbl/ *a* misurabile

measure /'meʒə(r)/ *n* misura *f* ● *vt/i* misurare

■ **measure out** *vt* dosare ‹amount›

■ **measure up to** *vt fig* essere all'altezza di

measured /'meʒed/ *a* misurato

measurement /'meʒəmənt/ *n* misura *f*

measuring jug /'meʒərɪŋ/ *n* dosatore *m*

measuring spoon *n* misurino *m*

meat /mi:t/ *n* carne *f*

meat: meatball *n Culin* polpetta *f* di carne. **meat-eater** *n* ‹animal› carnivoro *m*; **I'm not a ~** non mangio carne. **meat hook** *n* gancio *m* da macellaio. **meat loaf** *n* polpettone *m*. **meat pie** *n* tortino *m* di carne

meaty /'mi:tɪ/ *a* (**-ier, -iest**) di carne; *fig* sostanzioso

Mecca /'mekə/ *n* La Mecca

mechanic /mɪ'kænɪk/ *n* meccanico *m*

mechanical /mɪ'kænɪkl/ *a* meccanico

mechanical engineering *n* ingegneria *f* meccanica

mechanically /mɪ'kænɪklɪ/ *adv* meccanicamente

mechanics /mɪ'kænɪks/ *n* meccanica *f* ● *npl* meccanismo *msg*

mechanism /'mekənɪzm/ *n* meccanismo *m*

mechanize /'mekənaɪz/ *vt* meccanizzare

medal /'medl/ *n* medaglia *f*

medallion /mɪ'dælɪən/ *n* medaglione *m*

medallist /'medəlɪst/ *n* vincitore, -trice *mf* di una medaglia

meddle /'medl/ *vi* immischiarsi (**in** di); ‹tinker› armeggiare (**with** con)

media /'mi:dɪə/ *n see* **medium** ● *npl* **the ~** i mass media

median /'mi:dɪən/ *a* **~ strip** *Am* banchina *f* spartitraffico

media studies *npl* scienze *fpl* delle comunicazioni

mediate /'mi:dɪeɪt/ *vi* fare da mediatore

mediation /mi:dɪ'eɪʃn/ *n* mediazione *f*

mediator /'mi:dɪeɪtə(r)/ *n* mediatore, -trice *mf*

medic /'medɪk/ *n* (*fam:* doctor) medico *m*; (*fam:* student) studente, -essa *mf* di medicina; *Mil fam* infermiere, -a *mf* militare

medical /'medɪkl/ *a* medico ● *n* visita *f* medica

medical: medical care *n* assistenza *f* medica. **medical check-up** *n* controllo *m* medico. **medical history** *n* anamnesi *f* inv. **medical insurance** *n* assicurazione *f* sanitaria

medically /'medɪklɪ/ *adv* **~ qualified** con qualifiche di medico; **~ fit** in buona salute

medical: medical officer *n Mil* ufficiale *m* medico. **medical profession** *n* (occupation) professione *f* del medico; (doctors collectively)

categoria *f* medica. **medical student** *n* studente, -essa *mf* di medicina

medicated /'medɪkeɪtɪd/ *a* medicato

medication /medɪ'keɪʃn/ *n* (drugs) medicinali *mpl*; **are you on any ~?** sta prendendo delle medicine?

medicinal /mɪ'dɪsɪnl/ *a* medicinale

medicine /'medsən/ *n* medicina *f*

medicine: medicine ball *n* palla *f* medica. **medicine bottle** *n* flacone *m*. **medicine cabinet** *n* armadietto *m* dei medicinali. **medicine man** *n* stregone *m*

medieval /medɪ'i:vl/ *a* medievale

mediocre /mi:dɪ'əʊkə(r)/ *a* mediocre

mediocrity /mi:dɪ'ɒkrətɪ/ *n* mediocrità *f*

meditate /'medɪteɪt/ *vi* meditare (**on** su)

meditative /'medɪtətɪv/ *a* ‹music, person› meditativo; ‹mood, expression› meditabondo

Mediterranean /medɪtə'reɪnɪən/ *n* **the ~** [Sea] il [mare] Mediterraneo ● *a* mediterraneo

medium /'mi:dɪəm/ *a* medio; *Culin* di media cottura ● *n* (*pl* **media**) mezzo *m*; (*pl* **-s**) (person) medium *mf inv*

medium: medium dry *a* ‹drink› semisecco. **medium-length** *a* ‹book, film, hair› di media lunghezza. **medium-range** *a* ‹missile› di media portata. **medium-rare** *a* ‹meat› appena al sangue. **medium-sized** /'mi:dɪəmsaɪzd/ *a* di taglia media. **medium wave** *n* onde *fpl* medie

medley /'medlɪ/ *n* miscuglio *m*; *Mus* miscellanea *f*

meek /mi:k/ *a* mite, mansueto

meekly /'mi:klɪ/ *adv* docilmente

meet /mi:t/ *v* (*pt/pp* **met**) ● *vt* incontrare; (*at station, airport*) andare incontro a; (*for first time*) far la conoscenza di; pagare ‹bill›; soddisfare ‹requirements› ● *vi* incontrarsi; ‹committee:› riunirsi; **~ with** incontrare ‹problem›; incontrarsi con ‹person› ● *n* raduno *m* [sportivo]

■ **meet up** *vi* ‹people:› incontrarsi; **~ up with sb** incontrare qcno

meeting /'mi:tɪŋ/ *n* riunione *f*, meeting *m inv*; (large) assemblea *f*; (by chance) incontro *m*; **be in a ~** essere in riunione

meeting-place *n* luogo *m* d'incontro

meeting-point *n* punto *m* d'incontro

mega+ /'megə/ *pref* mega+

megabyte /'megəbaɪt/ *n Comput* megabyte *m inv*

megalith /'megəlɪθ/ *n* megalite *m*

megalomania /megələ'meɪnɪə/ *n* megalomania *f*

megaphone /'megəfəʊn/ *n* megafono *m*

melancholy /'melənkəlɪ/ *a* malinconico ● *n* malinconia *f*

mellow /'meləʊ/ *a* ‹wine› generoso; ‹sound, colour› caldo; ‹person› dolce ● *vi* ‹person:› addolcirsi

melodic /mɪ'lɒdɪk/ *a* melodico

melodious /mɪ'ləʊdɪəs/ *a* melodioso

melodrama /'melədrɑːmə/ *n* melodramma *m*

melodramatic /melədrə'mætɪk/ *a* melodrammatico

melodramatically /melədrə'mætɪklɪ/ *adv* in modo melodrammatico

melody /'melədɪ/ *n* melodia *f*

melon /'melən/ *n* melone *m*

melt /melt/ *vt* sciogliere ● *vi* sciogliersi

■ **melt away** *vi* ‹*snow:*› sciogliersi; ‹*crowd:*› disperdersi; ‹*support:*› venir meno

■ **melt down** *vt* fondere

meltdown /'meltdaʊn/ *n* (*in nuclear reactor*) fusione *f* del nocciolo

melting point /'meltɪŋ/ *n* punto *m* di fusione

melting pot *n fig* crogiuolo *m*

member /'membə(r)/ *n* membro *m*; **be a ~ of the family** far parte della famiglia

member: member countries paesi *mpl* membri. **Member of Parliament** deputato, -a *mf*. **Member of the European Parliament** *n* eurodeputato, -a *mf*

membership /'membəʃɪp/ *n* iscrizione *f*; (*members*) soci *mpl*

membrane /'membreɪn/ *n* membrana *f*

memento /mɪ'mentəʊ/ *n* ricordo *m*

memo /'meməʊ/ *n* promemoria *m inv*

memoirs /'memwɑ:z/ *npl* ricordi *mpl*

memo pad *n* blocchetto *m*

memorabilia /memərə'bɪlɪə/ *npl* cimeli *mpl*

memorable /'memərəbl/ *a* memorabile

memorandum /memə'rændəm/ *n* promemoria *m inv*

memorial /mɪ'mɔ:rɪəl/ *n* monumento *m*

memorial service *n* funzione *f* commemorativa

memorize /'meməraɪz/ *vt* memorizzare

memory /'memərɪ/ *n also Comput* memoria *f*; (*thing remembered*) ricordo *m*; **from ~ a** memoria; **in ~ of** in ricordo di

men /men/ *see* **man**

menace /'menəs/ *n* minaccia *f*; (*nuisance*) piaga *f* ● *vt* minacciare

menacing /'menəsɪŋ/ *a* minaccioso

menacingly /'menəsɪŋlɪ/ *adv* minacciosamente

mend /mend/ *vt* riparare; (*darn*) rammendare ● *n* **on the ~** in via di guarigione

menfolk /'menfəʊk/ *n* uomini *mpl*

menial /'mi:nɪəl/ *a* umile

meningitis /menɪn'dʒaɪtɪs/ *n* meningite *f*

menopause /'menəpɔ:z/ *n* menopausa *f*

Menorca /mɪ'nɔ:kə/ *n* Minorca *f*

men's room *n* toilette *f inv* degli uomini

menstruate /'menstrʊeɪt/ *vi* mestruare

menstruation /menstrʊ'eɪʃn/ *n* mestruazione *f*

menswear /'menzweə(r)/ *n* abbigliamento *m* per uomo

mental /'mentl/ *a* mentale; (*fam: mad*) pazzo

mental: mental arithmetic *n* calcolo *m* mentale. **mental block** *n* blocco *m* psicologico. **mental health** *n* (*of person*) salute *f* mentale. **mental health care** *n* assistenza *f* psi-

chiatrica. **mental home** *n* clinica *f* psichiatrica. **mental illness** *n* malattia *f* mentale

mentality /men'tælətɪ/ *n* mentalità *f inv*

mentally /'mentəlɪ/ *adv* mentalmente; **~ ill** malato di mente

mentholated /'menθəleɪtɪd/ *a* al mentolo

mention /'menʃn/ *n* menzione *f* ● *vt* menzionare; **don't ~ it** non c'è di che

mentor /'mentɔ:(r)/ *n* mentore *m*

menu /'menju:/ *n* menu *m inv*

MEP *n abbr* (**Member of the European Parliament**) eurodeputato, -a *mf*

mercantile /'mɜ:kəntaɪl/ *a* mercantile

mercenary /'mɜ:sɪnərɪ/ *a* mercenario ● *n* mercenario *m*

merchandise /'mɜ:tʃəndaɪz/ *n* merce *f*

merchant /'mɜ:tʃənt/ *n* commerciante *mf*

merchant: merchant bank *n Br* banca *f* d'affari. **merchant banker** *n* (*owner*) proprietario, -a *mf* di una banca d'affari; (*executive*) dirigente *mf* di banca d'affari.

merchant navy *n* marina *f* mercantile

merciful /'mɜ:sɪfl/ *a* misericordioso

mercifully /'mɜ:sɪfʊlɪ/ *adv fam* grazie a Dio

merciless /'mɜ:sɪlɪs/ *a* spietato

mercilessly /'mɜ:sɪlɪslɪ/ *adv* senza pietà

mercurial /mɜ:'kjʊərɪəl/ *a fig* volubile

mercury /'mɜ:kjʊrɪ/ *n* mercurio *m*

mercy /'mɜ:sɪ/ *n* misericordia *f*; **be at sb's ~** essere alla mercé *o* in balia di qcno

mercy killing *n* eutanasia *f*

mere /mɪə(r)/ *a* solo

merely /'mɪəlɪ/ *adv* solamente

merest /'mɪərɪst/ *a* minimo

merge /mɜ:dʒ/ *vi* fondersi ● *vt Comm* fondere

merger /'mɜ:dʒə(r)/ *n* fusione *f*

meridian /mə'rɪdɪən/ *n* meridiano *m*

meringue /mə'ræŋ/ *n* meringa *f*

merit /'merɪt/ *n* merito *m*; (*advantage*) qualità *f inv* ● *vt* meritare

mermaid /'mɜ:meɪd/ *n* sirena *f*

merrily /'merɪlɪ/ *adv* allegramente

merriment /'merɪmənt/ *n* baldoria *f*

merry /'merɪ/ *a* (**-ier, -iest**) allegro; **~ Christmas!** Buon Natale!; **make ~** far festa

merry-go-round *n* giostra *f*

merry-making /'merɪmeɪkɪŋ/ *n* festa *f*

mesh /meʃ/ *n* maglia *f*

mesmerize /'mezməraɪz/ *vt* ipnotizzare

mesmerized /'mezməraɪzd/ *a fig* ipnotizzato

mess /mes/ *n* disordine *m*, casino *m fam*; (*trouble*) guaio *m*; (*something spilt*) sporco *m*; *Mil* mensa *f*; **make a ~ of** (*botch*) fare un pasticcio *m*

■ **mess about** *vi* perder tempo; **~ about with** armeggiare con ● *vt* prendere in giro ‹*person*›

■ **mess up** *vt* mettere in disordine, incasinare *fam*; (*botch*) mandare all'aria

■ **mess with** *vt* (*fam: interfere with*) trafficare con ‹*computer, radio etc*›; contrariare ‹*person*›

message /'mesɪdʒ/ *n* messaggio *m*

mess dress *n Mil* uniforme *f* di gala
messenger /'mesɪndʒə(r)/ *n* messaggero *m*
messenger boy *n* fattorino *m*
Messiah /mɪ'saɪə/ *n* Messia *m*
Messrs /'mesəz/ *npl* (*on letter*) ~ **Smith** Spett. ditta Smith
messy /'mesɪ/ *a* (**-ier, -iest**) disordinato; (*in dress*) sciatto
met /met/ *see* **meet**
metabolism /mɪ'tæbəlɪzm/ *n* metabolismo *m*
metal /'metl/ *n* metallo *m* ● *a* di metallo
metal detector *n* metal detector *m inv*
metal fatigue *n* fatica *f* del metallo
metallic /mɪ'tælɪk/ *a* metallico
metallurgy /mɪ'tælədʒɪ/ *n* metallurgia *f*
metal polish *n* lucido *m* per metalli
metalwork /'metlwɜːk/ *n* lavorazione *f* del metallo
metamorphose /metə'mɔːfəʊz/ *vt* trasformare ● *vi* trasformarsi (**into** in)
metamorphosis /metə'mɔːfəsɪs/ *n* (*pl* **-phoses** /metə'mɔːfəsiːz/) metamorfosi *f inv*
metaphor /'metəfə(r)/ *n* metafora *f*
metaphorical /metə'fɒrɪkl/ *a* metaforico
metaphorically /metə'fɒrɪklɪ/ *adv* metaforicamente
metaphysical /metə'fɪzɪkl/ *a* metafisico; (*abstract*) astruso
meteor /'miːtɪə(r)/ *n* meteora *f*
meteoric /miːtɪ'ɒrɪk/ *a fig* fulmineo
meteorite /'miːtɪəraɪt/ *n* meteorite *m*
meteorological /miːtɪərə'lɒdʒɪkl/ *a* meteorologico
Meteorological Office *n* Ufficio *m* meteorologico
meteorologist /miːtɪə'rɒlədʒɪst/ *n* meteorologo, -a *mf*
meteorology /miːtɪə'rɒlədʒɪ/ *n* meteorologia *f*
meter[1] /'miːtə(r)/ *n* contatore *m*
meter[2] *n Am* = **metre**
meter reader *n* persona *f* incaricata di leggere il contatore (*di gas, elettricità*)
methane /'miːθeɪn/ *n* metano *m*
method /'meθəd/ *n* metodo *m*
method acting *n* metodo *m* dell'Actors' Studio
method actor *n* attore *m* che segue il metodo dell'Actors' Studio
methodical /mɪ'θɒdɪkl/ *a* metodico
methodically /mɪ'θɒdɪklɪ/ *adv* metodicamente
Methodist /'meθədɪst/ *n* metodista *mf*
methodology /meθə'dɒlədʒɪ/ *n* metodologia *f*
meths /meθs/ *n fam* alcol *m* denaturato
methyl /'miːθaɪl/ *n* metile *m*
methylated /'meθɪleɪtɪd/ *a* ~ **spirit[s]** alcol *m* denaturato
meticulous /mɪ'tɪkjʊləs/ *a* meticoloso
meticulously /mɪ'tɪkjʊləslɪ/ *adv* meticolosamente
metre /'miːtə(r)/ *n* metro *m*
metric /'metrɪk/ *a* metrico

metrication /metrɪ'keɪʃn/ *n* conversione *f* al sistema metrico
metronome /'metrənəʊm/ *n* metronomo *m*
metropolis /mɪ'trɒpəlɪs/ *n* metropoli *f inv*
metropolitan /metrə'pɒlɪtən/ *a* metropolitano
metropolitan district *n Br* circoscrizione *f* amministrativa urbana
Metropolitan police *n Br* polizia *f* di Londra
mew /mjuː/ *n* miao *m* ● *vi* miagolare
mews /mjuːz/ *n Br* (*stables*) scuderie *fpl*; (*street*) stradina *f*; (*yard*) cortile *m*
mews flat *n Br* piccolo appartamento *m* ricavato da vecchie scuderie
Mexican /'meksɪkən/ *a & n* messicano, -a *mf*
Mexican wave *n* ola *f inv*
Mexico /'meksɪkəʊ/ *n* Messico *m*
mezzanine /'metsəniːn/ *n* mezzanino *m*
miaow /mɪ'aʊ/ *n* miao *m* ● *vi* miagolare
mice /maɪs/ *see* **mouse**
Michaelmas /'mɪkəlməs/ *n* festa *f* di San Michele (*29 settembre*)
Michaelmas daisy *n Br* margherita *f* settembrina
Michaelmas Term *n Br Univ* primo trimestre *m*
mickey /'mɪkɪ/ *n* **take the** ~ **out of** prendere in giro
Mickey Mouse *n* Topolino *m*
microbe /'maɪkrəʊb/ *n* microbo *m*
microchip /'maɪkrəʊtʃɪp/ *n* microchip *m inv*
microcomputer /'maɪkrəʊkəmpjuːtə(r)/ *n* microcomputer *m inv*
microcosm /'maɪkrəkɒzm/ *n* microcosmo *m*
micro: microfilm *n* microfilm *m inv.* **micromesh tights** *npl* collant *mpl* velati. **microphone** *n* microfono *m.* **microphysics** *n* microfisica *f.* **microprocessor** *n* microprocessore *m.* **microscope** *n* microscopio *m.* **microscopic** *a* microscopico. **microsurgery** *n* microchirurgia *f.* **microwave** *n* microonda *f*; (*oven*) forno *m* a microonde
mid /mɪd/ *a* ~ **May** metà maggio; **in** ~ **air** a mezz'aria
midday /mɪd'deɪ/ *n* mezzogiorno *m*
middle /'mɪdl/ *a* di centro; **the M~ Ages** il medioevo; **the** ~ **class[es]** la classe media; **the M~ East** il Medio Oriente ● *n* mezzo *m*; **in the** ~ **of** ‹*room, floor etc*› in mezzo a; **in the** ~ **of the night** nel pieno della notte, a notte piena
middle: middle-aged /-'eɪdʒd/ *a* di mezza età. **middle-age spread** *n* pancetta *f* di mezza età. **Middle America** *n* (*social group*) ceto *m* medio americano a tendenza conservatrice. **middlebrow** *a* ‹*book*› per il lettore medio; ‹*person*› con interessi culturali convenzionali. **middle-class** *a* borghese. **middle distance** *n Phot, Cinema* secondo piano *m*; **gaze into the** ~ ~ avere lo sguardo perso nel vuoto. **Middle English** *n* medio inglese *m.* **middle finger** *n* dito *m* medio. **middle ground** *m Pol* centro *m*; **occupy the** ~ ~

adottare una posizione intermedia. **middle-income** *a* ⟨*person, family, country*⟩ dal reddito medio

middleman /'mɪdlmæn/ *n Comm* intermediario *m*

middle: middle manager *n* quadro *m* intermedio. **middle-of-the-road** *a* ⟨*ordinary*⟩ ordinario; ⟨*policy*⟩ moderato. **middle-size[d]** /-saɪz[d]/ *a* di misura media. **middleweight** *n* peso *m* medio

middling /'mɪdlɪŋ/ *a* discreto

midfield /mɪd'fiːld/ *n* centrocampo *m*

midfield player *n* centrocampista *m*

midge /mɪdʒ/ *n* moscerino *m*

midget /'mɪdʒɪt/ *n* nano, -a *mf*

Midlands /'mɪdləndz/ *npl* **the ~** l'Inghilterra *fsg* centrale

mid-life *n* mezza età *f*

mid-life crisis *n* crisi *f inv* di mezza età

midnight /'mɪdnaɪt/ *n* mezzanotte *f*

mid-range *attrib* ⟨*car*⟩ (*in price*) di prezzo medio; (*in power*) di media cilindrata; ⟨*hotel*⟩ intermedio; **be in the ~** ⟨*product, hotel:*⟩ essere nella media

midriff /'mɪdrɪf/ *n* diaframma *m*

mid-season *a* di metà stagione

midshipman /'mɪdʃɪpmən/ *n Br* cadetto *m* di marina; *Am* allievo *m* dell'Accademia Navale

midst /mɪdst/ *n* **in the ~ of** in mezzo a; **in our ~** fra di noi, in mezzo a noi

midstream /mɪd'striːm/ *adv* **in ~** (*in river*) nel mezzo della corrente; (*fig: in speech*) nel mezzo del discorso

midsummer /'mɪdsʌmə(r)/ *n* mezza estate *f*

Midsummer's Day *n* festa *f* di San Giovanni (*24 giugno*)

mid-term *attrib Sch* di metà trimestre; *Pol* a metà del mandato del governo

midway /'mɪdweɪ/ *adv* a metà strada

midweek /mɪd'wiːk/ *a* di metà settimana ● *adv* a metà settimana

midwife /'mɪdwaɪf/ *n* ostetrica *f*

midwifery /'mɪdwɪfrɪ/ *n* ostetricia *f*

midwinter /mɪd'wɪntə(r)/ *n* pieno inverno *m*

miffed /mɪft/ *a fam* seccato

might[1] /maɪt/ *v aux* **I ~** potrei; **will you come?** – **I ~** vieni? – può darsi; **it ~ be true** potrebbe essere vero; **I ~ as well stay** potrei anche restare; **he asked if he ~ go** ha chiesto se poteva andare; **you ~ have drowned** avresti potuto affogare; **you ~ have said so!** avresti potuto dirlo!

might[2] *n* potere *m*

mighty /'maɪtɪ/ *a* (**-ier, -iest**) potente ● *adv fam* molto

migraine /'miːgreɪn/ *n* emicrania *f*

migrant /'maɪgrənt/ *a* migratore ● *n* (*bird*) migratore, -trice *mf*; (*person: for work*) emigrante *mf*

migrate /maɪ'greɪt/ *vi* migrare

migration /maɪ'greɪʃn/ *n* migrazione *f*

migratory /maɪ'greɪtərɪ/ *a* ⟨*animal*⟩ migratore

mike /maɪk/ *n fam* microfono *f*

Milan /mɪ'læn/ *n* Milano *f*

Milanese /mɪlə'niːz/ *a* milanese

mild /maɪld/ *a* ⟨*weather*⟩ mite; ⟨*person*⟩ dolce; ⟨*flavour*⟩ delicato; ⟨*illness*⟩ leggero

mildew /'mɪldjuː/ *n* muffa *f*

mildly /'maɪldlɪ/ *adv* moderatamente; ⟨*say*⟩ dolcemente; **to put it ~** a dir poco, senza esagerazione

mildness /'maɪldnɪs/ *n* (*of person, words*) dolcezza *f*; (*of weather*) mitezza *f*

mile /maɪl/ *n* miglio *m* (= *1,6 km*); **~s nicer** *fam* molto più bello; **~s too big** *fam* eccessivamente grande

mileage /'maɪlɪdʒ/ *n* chilometraggio *m*

mileage allowance *n* indennità *f inv* di trasferta per chilometro

milestone /'maɪlstəʊn/ *n* pietra *f* miliare

milieu /'miːljɜ:/ *n* ambiente *m*

militant /'mɪlɪtənt/ *a* & *n* militante *mf*

militarism /'mɪlɪtərɪzm/ *n* militarismo *m*

militarize /'mɪlɪtəraɪz/ *vt* militarizzare

military /'mɪlɪtrɪ/ *a* militare

military: military academy *n* accademia *f* militare. **military policeman** *n* agente *m* di polizia militare. **military service** *n* servizio *m* militare

militate /'mɪlɪteɪt/ *vi* **~ against** opporsi a

militia /mɪ'lɪʃə/ *n* milizia *f*

milk /mɪlk/ *n* latte *m* ● *vt* mungere

milk: milk chocolate *n* cioccolato *m* al latte. **milk float** *n Br* furgone *m* del lattaio. **milk jug** *n* bricco *m* del latte. **milkman** *n* lattaio *m*. **milk pudding** *n* budino *m* a base di latte. **milk shake** *n* frappé *m inv*. **milk train** *n* primo treno *m* del mattino

milky /'mɪlkɪ/ *a* (**-ier, -iest**) latteo; ⟨*tea etc*⟩ con molto latte. **Milky Way** *n Astr* Via *f* Lattea

mill /mɪl/ *n* mulino *m*; (*factory*) fabbrica *f*; (*for coffee etc*) macinino *m* ● *vt* macinare ⟨*grain*⟩

■ **mill about, mill around** *vi* brulicare

millennium /mɪ'lenɪəm/ *n* millennio *m*

miller /'mɪlə(r)/ *n* mugnaio *m*

millet /'mɪlɪt/ *n* miglio *m*

milligram /'mɪlɪgræm/ *n* milligrammo *m*

millimetre /'mɪlɪmiːtə(r)/ *n* millimetro *m*

million /'mɪljən/ *a* & *n* milione *m*; **a ~ pounds** un milione di sterline

millionaire /mɪljə'neə(r)/ *n* miliardario, -a *mf*

millipede /'mɪlɪpiːd/ *n* millepiedi *m inv*

mill: millpond *n* **like a ~** calmo come una tavola. **millstone** *n* **a ~ round one's neck** *fig* un peso; **mill-wheel** *n* ruota *f* di mulino

milometer /maɪ'lɒmɪtə(r)/ *n Br* ≈ contachilometri *m inv*

mime /maɪm/ *n* mimo *m* ● *vt* mimare

mime artist *n* mimo, -a *mf*

mimic /'mɪmɪk/ *n* imitatore, -trice *mf* ● *vt* (*pt/pp* **mimicked**) imitare

mimicry /'mɪmɪkrɪ/ *n* mimetismo *m*

mimosa /mɪ'məʊzə/ *n* mimosa *f*

minaret /mɪnə'ret/ *n* minareto *m*

mince /mɪns/ *n* carne *f* tritata ● *vt Culin* tritare; **not ~ words** parlare senza mezzi termini

mincemeat /'mɪnsmiːt/ n miscuglio m di frutta secca; **make ~ of** fig demolire

mince pie n pasticcino m a base di frutta secca

mincer /'mɪnsə(r)/ n tritacarne m inv

mind /maɪnd/ n mente f; (sanity) ragione f; **to my ~** a mio parere; **give sb a piece of one's ~** dire chiaro e tondo a qcno quello che si pensa; **make up one's ~** decidersi; **have sth in ~** avere qcsa in mente; **bear sth in ~** tenere presente qcsa; **have something on one's ~** essere preoccupato; **have a good ~ to** avere una grande voglia di; **I have changed my ~** ho cambiato idea; **be out of one's ~** essere fuori di sé ● vt (look after) occuparsi di; **I don't ~ the noise** il rumore non mi dà fastidio; **I don't ~ what we do** non mi importa quello che facciamo; **~ the step!** attenzione al gradino! ● vi **I don't ~** non mi importa; **never ~!** non importa!; **do you ~ if...?** ti dispiace se...?
■ **mind out** vi ~ **out!** [fai] attenzione!

mind: mind-bending /-bendɪŋ/ a ⟨problem⟩ complicatissimo; **~ drugs** psicofarmaci mpl. **mind-blowing** /-bləʊɪŋ/ a fam sconvolgente. **mind-boggling** /-bɒglɪŋ/ a fam incredibile

minded /'maɪndɪd/ a **if you're so ~** se vuole

minder /'maɪndə(r)/ n (Br: bodyguard) gorilla m inv; (for child) baby-sitter mf inv

mindful /'maɪndfʊl/ a ~ **of** attento a

mindless /'maɪndlɪs/ a noncurante

mind-reader n persona f che legge nel pensiero; **I'm not a ~** non leggo nel pensiero

mine¹ /maɪn/ poss pron il mio m, la mia f, i miei mpl, le mie fpl; **a friend of ~** un mio amico; **friends of ~** dei miei amici; **that is ~** questo è mio; (as opposed to yours) questo è il mio

mine² n miniera f; (explosive) mina f ● vt estrarre; Mil minare

mine-detector n rivelatore m di mine

minefield /'maɪnfiːld/ n also fig campo m minato

miner /'maɪnə(r)/ n minatore m

mineral /'mɪnərəl/ n minerale m ● a minerale

mineral: mineral oil n (Am: paraffin) olio m minerale. **mineral rights** npl concessioni fpl minerarie. **mineral water** n acqua f minerale

minesweeper /'maɪnswiːpə(r)/ n dragamine m inv

mingle /'mɪŋgl/ vi ~ **with** mescolarsi a

mini /'mɪni/ n see **miniskirt**

mini+ pref mini+

miniature /'mɪnɪtʃə(r)/ a in miniatura ● n miniatura f

miniature golf n minigolf m inv

miniature railway n trenino m

mini: mini-budget n Br Pol budget m inv provvisorio. **minibus** n minibus m inv, pulmino m. **minicab** n taxi m inv

minim /'mɪnɪm/ n Mus minima f

minimal /'mɪnɪməl/ a minimo

minimally /'mɪnɪməlɪ/ adv (very slightly) minimamente

minimarket /'mɪnɪmɑːkɪt/ n minimarket m inv

minimize /'mɪnɪmaɪz/ vt minimizzare

minimum /'mɪnɪməm/ n (pl -ima) minimo m ● a minimo; **ten minutes ~** minimo dieci minuti

mining /'maɪnɪŋ/ n estrazione f ● attrib estrattivo

mining engineer n ingegnere m minerario

miniskirt /'mɪnɪskɜːt/ n minigonna f

minister /'mɪnɪstə(r)/ n ministro m; Relig pastore m

ministerial /mɪnɪ'stɪərɪəl/ a ministeriale

minister of state n Br Pol titolo m di un parlamentare con competenze specifiche in seno a un ministero

ministry /'mɪnɪstrɪ/ n Pol ministero m; **the ~** Relig il ministero sacerdotale

mink /mɪŋk/ n visone m

minnow /'mɪnəʊ/ n (fish) pesciolino m d'acqua dolce

minor /'maɪnə(r)/ a minore ● n minorenne mf

Minorca /mɪ'nɔːkə/ n Minorca f

minority /maɪ'nɒrətɪ/ n minoranza f; (age) minore età f

minority leader n Am Pol leader mf inv dell'opposizione

minority rule n governo m di minoranza

minor offence n Br reato m minore

minor road n strada f secondaria

minster /'mɪnstə(r)/ n (cathedral) cattedrale f

mint¹ /mɪnt/ n zecca f; fam patrimonio m ● a **in ~ condition** in condizione perfetta ● vt coniare

mint² n (herb) menta f

mint-flavoured /-fleɪvəd/ a al gusto di menta

minuet /mɪnjʊ'et/ n minuetto m

minus /'maɪnəs/ prep meno; (fam: without) senza ● n ~ **[sign]** meno m

minute¹ /'mɪnɪt/ n minuto m; **in a ~** (shortly) in un minuto; **~s** pl (of meeting) verbale msg

minute² /maɪ'njuːt/ a minuto; (precise) minuzioso

minute hand /'mɪnɪt/ n lancetta f dei minuti

minutely /maɪ'njuːtlɪ/ adv ⟨vary, differ⟩ di poco; ⟨describe, examine⟩ minuziosamente

minutiae /maɪ'njuːʃɪaɪ/ npl minuzie fpl

miracle /'mɪrəkl/ n miracolo m

miraculous /mɪ'rækjʊləs/ a miracoloso

mirage /'mɪrɑːʒ/ n miraggio m

mire /'maɪə(r)/ n pantano m

mirror /'mɪrə(r)/ n specchio m ● vt rispecchiare

mirror image n (exact replica) copia f esatta; (inverse) immagine f speculare

mirth /mɜːθ/ n ilarità f

misadventure /mɪsæd'ventʃə(r)/ n disavventura f

misanthropist /mɪ'zænθrəpɪst/ n misantropo, -a mf

misapprehension /mɪsæprɪ'henʃn/ n malinteso m; **be under a ~** avere frainteso

misappropriate /mɪsə'prəʊprɪeɪt/ vt appropriarsi indebitamente di ⟨funds⟩

misbehave /mɪsbɪ'heɪv/ vi comportarsi male

misbehaviour /mɪsbɪ'heɪvjə(r)/ n comportamento m scorretto

miscalculate /mɪs'kælkjʊleɪt/ vt/i calcolare male

miscalculation /mɪskælkjʊ'leɪʃn/ n calcolo m sbagliato

miscarriage /'mɪskærɪdʒ/ n aborto m spontaneo; **~ of justice** errore m giudiziario

miscarry /mɪs'kærɪ/ vi abortire

miscellaneous /mɪsə'leɪnɪəs/ a assortito

miscellany /mɪ'selənɪ/ n ⟨of people, things⟩ misto m; ⟨anthology⟩ miscellanea f

mischief /'mɪstʃɪf/ n malefatta f; ⟨harm⟩ danno m

mischievous /'mɪstʃɪvəs/ a ⟨naughty⟩ birichino; ⟨malicious⟩ dannoso

mischievously /'mɪstʃɪvəslɪ/ adv in modo birichino

misconceived /mɪskən'siːvd/ a ⟨argument, project⟩ sbagliato

misconception /mɪskən'sepʃn/ n concetto m erroneo

misconduct /mɪs'kɒndʌkt/ n cattiva condotta f

misconstrue /mɪskən'struː/ vt fraintendere

miscount /mɪs'kaʊnt/ vt/i contare male

misdeed /mɪs'diːd/ n misfatto m

misdemeanour /mɪsdɪ'miːnə(r)/ n reato m

misdirect /mɪsdaɪ'rekt/ vt mettere l'indirizzo sbagliato su ⟨letter, parcel⟩; dare istruzioni sbagliate a ⟨jury⟩; **the letter was ~ed to our old address** la lettera ci è stata erroneamente spedita al vecchio indirizzo

miser /'maɪzə(r)/ n avaro m

miserable /'mɪzrəbl/ a ⟨unhappy⟩ infelice; ⟨wretched⟩ miserabile; ⟨fig: weather⟩ deprimente

miserably /'mɪzrəblɪ/ adv ⟨live, fail⟩ miseramente; ⟨say⟩ tristemente

miserly /'maɪzəlɪ/ a avaro; ⟨amount⟩ ridicolo

misery /'mɪzərɪ/ n miseria f; ⟨fam: person⟩ piagnone, -a mf

misfire /mɪs'faɪə(r)/ vi ⟨gun:⟩ far cilecca; ⟨plan etc:⟩ non riuscire

misfit /'mɪsfɪt/ n disadattato, -a mf

misfortune /mɪs'fɔːtʃuːn/ n sfortuna f

misgivings /mɪs'gɪvɪŋz/ npl dubbi mpl

misguided /mɪs'gaɪdɪd/ a fuorviato

mishandle /mɪs'hændl/ vt gestire male ⟨operation, meeting⟩; non prendere per il verso giusto ⟨person⟩; ⟨roughly⟩ maneggiare senza precauzioni ⟨object⟩; maltrattare ⟨person, animal⟩

mishap /'mɪshæp/ n disavventura f

mishear /mɪs'hɪə(r)/ vt sentire male

mishmash /'mɪʃmæʃ/ n fam guazzabuglio m

misinform /mɪsɪn'fɔːm/ vt informar male

misinformation /mɪsɪnfə'meɪʃn/ n informazioni fpl sbagliate

misinterpret /mɪsɪn'tɜːprɪt/ vt fraintendere

misinterpretation /mɪsɪntɜːprɪ'teɪʃn/ n interpretazione f sbagliata

misjudge /mɪs'dʒʌdʒ/ vt giudicar male; ⟨estimate wrongly⟩ valutare male

mislay /mɪs'leɪ/ vt ⟨pt/pp -laid⟩ smarrire

mislead /mɪs'liːd/ vt ⟨pt/pp -led⟩ fuorviare

misleading /mɪs'liːdɪŋ/ a fuorviante

mismanage /mɪs'mænɪdʒ/ vt amministrare male

mismanagement /mɪs'mænɪdʒmənt/ n cattiva amministrazione f

mismatch /'mɪsmætʃ/ n discordanza f

misname /mɪs'neɪm/ vt dare il nome sbagliato a

misnomer /mɪs'nəʊmə(r)/ n termine m improprio

misogynist /mɪs'ɒdʒənɪst/ n misogino m

misplace /mɪs'pleɪs/ vt mettere in un posto sbagliato; **~ one's trust** riporre male la propria fiducia

misprint /'mɪsprɪnt/ n errore m di stampa

mispronounce /mɪsprə'naʊns/ vt pronunciare male

mispronunciation /mɪsprənʌnsɪ'eɪʃn/ n ⟨act⟩ pronuncia f sbagliata; ⟨instance⟩ errore m di pronuncia

misquote /mɪs'kwəʊt/ vt citare erroneamente

misread /mɪs'riːd/ vt leggere male ⟨sentence, meter⟩; ⟨misinterpret⟩ fraintendere ⟨actions⟩

misrepresent /mɪsreprɪ'zent/ vt rappresentare male

misrepresentation /mɪsreprɪzen'teɪʃn/ n ⟨of facts, opinions⟩ travisamento m

Miss /mɪs/ n ⟨pl -es⟩ signorina f

miss n colpo m mancato ● vt ⟨fail to hit or find⟩ mancare; perdere ⟨train, bus, class⟩; ⟨feel the loss of⟩ sentire la mancanza di; **I ~ed that part** ⟨failed to notice⟩ mi è sfuggita quella parte; **~ the point** non afferrare il punto ● vi **but he ~ed** ⟨failed to hit⟩ ma l'ha mancato

■ **miss out** vt saltare, omettere

misshapen /mɪs'ʃeɪpən/ a malformato

missile /'mɪsaɪl/ n missile m

missing /'mɪsɪŋ/ a mancante; ⟨person⟩ scomparso; Mil disperso; **be ~** essere introvabile; **~ in action** Mil disperso

mission /'mɪʃn/ n missione f

missionary /'mɪʃənrɪ/ n missionario, -a mf

missive /'mɪsɪv/ n missiva f

misspell /mɪs'spel/ vt ⟨pt/pp -spelt, -spelled⟩ sbagliare l'ortografia di

misspent /mɪs'spent/ a **a ~ youth** una gioventù sprecata

mist /mɪst/ n ⟨fog⟩ foschia f; **because of the ~ on the windows** a causa dei vetri appannati

■ **mist up** vi appannarsi, annebbiarsi

mistake /mɪ'steɪk/ n sbaglio m; **by ~** per sbaglio ● vt ⟨pt **mistook**, pp **mistaken**⟩ sbagliare ⟨*road, house*⟩; fraintendere ⟨*meaning, words*⟩; ~ **for** prendere per

mistaken /mɪ'steɪkən/ *a* sbagliato; **be ~** sbagliarsi; ~ **identity** errore *m* di persona

mistakenly /mɪ'steɪkənlɪ/ *adv* erroneamente

mister /'mɪstə(r)/ *n* signore *m*

mistletoe /'mɪsltəʊ/ *n* vischio *m*

mistranslate /mɪstrænz'leɪt/ *vt* tradurre in modo sbagliato

mistranslation /mɪstrænz'leɪʃn/ *n* traduzione *f* sbagliata

mistreat /mɪs'tri:t/ maltrattare

mistreatment /mɪs'tri:tmənt/ *n* maltrattamento *m*

mistress /'mɪstrɪs/ *n* padrona *f*; (*teacher*) maestra *f*; (*lover*) amante *f*

mistrust /mɪs'trʌst/ *n* sfiducia *f* ● *vt* non aver fiducia in

misty /'mɪstɪ/ *a* (**-ier, -iest**) nebbioso; *fig* indistinto

misty-eyed /-'aɪd/ *a* ⟨*look*⟩ commosso; **he goes all ~ about it** a parlarne si commuove

misunderstand /mɪsʌndə'stænd/ *vt* (*pt/pp* **-stood**) fraintendere

misunderstanding /mɪsʌndə'stændɪŋ/ *n* malinteso *m*

misuse[1] /mɪs'ju:z/ *vt* usare male

misuse[2] /mɪs'ju:s/ *n* cattivo uso *m*

mite /maɪt/ *n* Zool acaro *m*; (*child*) piccino, -a *mf*

mitigate /'mɪtɪgeɪt/ *vt* attenuare

mitigating /'mɪtɪgeɪtɪŋ/ *a* attenuante

mitt /mɪt/ *n* (*no separate fingers*) muffola *f*; (*cut-off fingers*) mezzo guanto *m*; (*in baseball*) guantone *m*; (*fam: hand*) mano *f*

mitten /'mɪtn/ *n* manopola *f*, muffola *f*

mix /mɪks/ *n* (*combination*) mescolanza *f*; Culin miscuglio *m*; (*ready-made*) preparato *m* ● *vt* mischiare ● *vi* mischiarsi; ⟨*person:*⟩ inserirsi; ~ **with** (*associate with*) frequentare

■ **mix in** *vt* incorporare ⟨*eggs, flour etc*⟩

■ **mix up** *vt* mescolare ⟨*papers*⟩; (*confuse, mistake for*) confondere

mixed /mɪkst/ *a* misto; ~ **up** ⟨*person*⟩ confuso

mixed: mixed ability *a* ⟨*class, teaching*⟩ per alunni di capacità differenti. **mixed bag: it was a very ~ ~** *n fig* c'era un po' di tutto. **mixed blessing: be a ~ ~** *n* avere vantaggi e svantaggi. **mixed doubles** *npl Tennis* doppio *m* misto. **mixed economy** *n* economia *f* mista. **mixed grill** *n* grigliata *f* di carne mista. **mixed marriage** *n* matrimonio *m* misto. **mixed-media** *a* multimediale. **mixed metaphor** *n* abbinamento *m* di parte di due o più metafore diverse con effetto comico

mixed-up *a* ⟨*person, emotions*⟩ confuso

mixed vegetables *npl* verdure *fpl* miste

mixer /'mɪksə(r)/ *n* Culin frullatore *m*, mixer *m inv*; **he's a good ~** è un tipo socievole

mixing /'mɪksɪŋ/ *n* (*of people, objects, ingredients*) mescolamento *m*; Mus mixaggio *m*

mixture /'mɪkstʃə(r)/ *n* mescolanza *f*; (*medicine*) sciroppo *m*; Culin miscela *f*

mix-up *n* (*confusion*) confusione *f*; (*mistake*) pasticcio *m*

mm *abbr* (**millimetre(s)**) mm

MO *abbr* (**medical officer**) ufficiale *m* medico; *abbr* (**money order**) vaglia *m inv* postale; *Am abbr* **Missouri**

moan /məʊn/ *n* lamento *m* ● *vi* lamentarsi; (*complain*) lagnarsi

moat /məʊt/ *n* fossato *m*

mob /mɒb/ *n* folla *f*; (*rabble*) gentaglia *f*; (*fam: gang*) banda *f* ● *vt* (*pt/pp* **mobbed**) assalire

mobile /'məʊbaɪl/ *a* mobile ● *n* composizione *f* mobile; (*phone*) [telefono *m*] cellulare *m*

mobile: mobile home *n* casa *f* roulotte. **mobile library** *n Br* biblioteca *f* itinerante. **mobile phone** *n* [telefono *m*] cellulare *m*. **mobile shop** *n* furgone *m* attrezzato per la vendita

mobility /mə'bɪlətɪ/ *n* mobilità *f*

mobility allowance *n Br* indennità *f inv* di accompagnamento

mobilization /məʊbɪlaɪ'zeɪʃn/ *n* mobilitazione *f*

mobilize /'məʊbɪlaɪz/ *vt* mobilitare

mocha /'mɒkə/ *n* moca *m inv*

mock /mɒk/ *a* finto ● *vt* canzonare

mockery /'mɒkərɪ/ *n* derisione *f*; **a ~ of** una parodia di

mock-up *n* modello *m* in scala

MoD *n Br abbr* (**Ministry of Defence**) Ministero *m* della Difesa

modal /'məʊdl/ *a* ~ **auxiliary** verbo *m* modale

mod con /mɒd'kɒn/ *Br abbr* (**modern convenience**) **all ~ ~s** tutti i confort

mode /məʊd/ *n* modo *m*; Comput modalità *f*

model /'mɒdl/ *n* modello *m*; (**fashion**) ~ indossatore, -trice *mf*, modello, -a *mf* ● *a* ⟨*yacht, plane*⟩ in miniatura; ⟨*pupil, husband*⟩ esemplare, modello ● *v* (*pt/pp* **modelled**) ● *vt* indossare ⟨*clothes*⟩ ● *vi* fare l'indossatore, -trice *mf*; (*for artist*) posare

modelling /'mɒd(ə)lɪŋ/ *n* (*with clay etc*) modellare *m* con la creta; (*of clothes*) professione *f* di indossatore; **do some ~** (*for artist*) fare il modello

modelling clay *n* creta *f* per modellare

modem /'məʊdem/ *n* modem *m inv* ● *vt* mandare per modem

moderate[1] /'mɒdəreɪt/ *vt* moderare ● *vi* moderarsi

moderate[2] /'mɒdərət/ *a* moderato ● *n Pol* moderato, -a *mf*

moderately /'mɒdərətlɪ/ *adv* ⟨*drink, speak etc*⟩ moderatamente; ⟨*good, bad etc*⟩ relativamente

moderation /mɒdə'reɪʃn/ *n* moderazione *f*; **in ~** con moderazione

modern /'mɒdn/ *a* moderno

modern-day *a* attuale

modernism /'mɒdənɪzm/ *n* modernismo *m*

modernity /mə'dɜ:nətɪ/ *n* modernità *f*

modernization /mɒdənaɪ'zeɪʃn/ *n* modernizzazione *f*

modernize /'mɒdənaɪz/ *vt* modernizzare

modern languages npl lingue fpl moderne

modest /'mɒdɪst/ a modesto

modesty /'mɒdɪstɪ/ n modestia f

modicum /'mɒdɪkəm/ n **a ~ of** un po' di

modification /mɒdɪfɪ'keɪʃn/ n modificazione f

modifier /'mɒdɪfaɪə(r)/ n (in linguistics) modificatore m

modify /'mɒdɪfaɪ/ vt (pt/pp -**fied**) modificare

modular /'mɒdjʊlə(r)/ a ‹course› a moduli; ‹construction, furniture› modulare

modulate /'mɒdjʊleɪt/ vt/i modulare

module /'mɒdjuːl/ n modulo m

modus operandi /məʊdəsɒpə'rændiː/ n modus operandi m inv

mohican /məʊ'hiːkən/ n (hairstyle) taglio m [di capelli] alla moicana

moist /mɔɪst/ a umido

moisten /'mɔɪsn/ vt inumidire

moisture /'mɔɪstʃə(r)/ n umidità f

moisturizer /'mɔɪstʃəraɪzə(r)/ n [crema f] idratante m

molar /'məʊlə(r)/ n molare m

molasses /mə'læsɪz/ n Am melassa f

mole¹ /məʊl/ n (on face etc) neo m

mole² n Zool talpa f

mole³ n (breakwater) molo m

molecular /mə'lekjʊlə(r)/ a molecolare

molecule /'mɒlɪkjuːl/ n molecola f

molehill /'məʊlhɪl/ n monticello m

moleskin /'məʊlskɪn/ n (fur) pelliccia f di talpa

molest /mə'lest/ vt molestare

mollify /'mɒlɪfaɪ/ vt (pt/pp -**ied**) placare

mollusc /'mɒləsk/ n mollusco m

mollycoddle /'mɒlɪkɒdl/ vt tenere nella bambagia

molten /'məʊltən/ a fuso

mom /mɒm/ n Am fam mamma f

moment /'məʊmənt/ n momento m; **at the ~** in questo momento

momentarily /məʊmən'terɪlɪ/ adv (for an instant) per un momento; (Am: at any moment) da un momento all'altro; (Am: very soon) tra un momento

momentary /'məʊməntrɪ/ a momentaneo

momentous /mə'mentəs/ a molto importante

momentum /mə'mentəm/ n impeto m

monarch /'mɒnək/ n monarca m

monarchist /'mɒnəkɪst/ n monarchico, -a mf

monarchy /'mɒnəkɪ/ n monarchia f

monastery /'mɒnəstrɪ/ n monastero m

monastic /mə'næstɪk/ a monastico

Monday /'mʌndeɪ/ n lunedì m inv

monetary /'mʌnɪtrɪ/ a monetario

money /'mʌnɪ/ n denaro m

money: money box n salvadanaio m. **moneylender** n usuraio m. **money order** n vaglia m inv postale

mongrel /'mʌŋgrəl/ n bastardo m

monitor /'mɒnɪtə(r)/ n Techn monitor m inv ● vt controllare

monk /mʌŋk/ n monaco m

monkey /'mʌŋkɪ/ n scimmia f

■ **monkey about with** vt (fam: interfere with) armeggiare con

monkey: monkey business n fam (fooling) scherzi mpl; (cheating) imbrogli mpl. **monkey-nut** n nocciolina f americana. **monkey wrench** n chiave f inglese a rullino

monkfish /'mʌŋkfɪʃ/ n bottatrice f

mono /'mɒnəʊ/ n mono m

monochrome /'mɒnəkrəʊm/ a monocromatico; Cinema, TV in bianco e nero

monocle /'mɒnəkl/ n monocolo m

monogamy /mə'nɒgəmɪ/ n monogamia f

monogram /'mɒnəgræm/ n monogramma m

monograph /'mɒnəgrɑːf/ n monografia f

monolith /'mɒnəlɪθ/ n monolito m

monologue /'mɒnəlɒg/ n monologo m

monomania /mɒnə'meɪnɪə/ n monomania f

monoplane /'mɒnəpleɪn/ n monoplano m

monopolize /mə'nɒpəlaɪz/ vt monopolizzare

monopoly /mə'nɒpəlɪ/ n monopolio m

monoski /'mɒnəʊskiː/ n monosci m inv ● vi praticare il monosci

monosodium glutamate /mɒnəsəʊdɪəm'gluːtəmeɪt/ n glutammato m di sodio

monosyllabic /mɒnəsɪ'læbɪk/ a monosillabico

monosyllable /'mɒnəsɪləbl/ n monosillabo m

monotone /'mɒnətəʊn/ n **speak in a ~** parlare con tono monotono

monotonous /mə'nɒtənəs/ a monotono

monotonously /mə'nɒtənəslɪ/ adv di modo monotono

monotony /mə'nɒtənɪ/ n monotonia f

monsoon /mɒn'suːn/ n monsone m

monster /'mɒnstə(r)/ n mostro m

monstrosity /mɒn'strɒsətɪ/ n mostruosità f

monstrous /'mɒnstrəs/ a mostruoso

montage /mɒn'tɑːʒ/ n montaggio m

Mont Blanc /mɒn'blɒ̃/ n Monte m Bianco

month /mʌnθ/ n mese m

monthly /'mʌnθlɪ/ a mensile ● adv mensilmente ● n (periodical) mensile m

monument /'mɒnjʊmənt/ n monumento m

monumental /mɒnjʊ'mentl/ a fig monumentale

monumentally /mɒnjʊ'mentəlɪ/ adv ‹boring, ignorant› enormemente

moo /muː/ n muggito m ● vi (pt/pp mooed) muggire

mooch /muːtʃ/ vi **~ about** fam gironzolare; **~ about the house** gironzolare per casa

mood /muːd/ n umore m; **be in a good/bad ~** essere di buon/cattivo umore; **be in the ~ for** essere in vena di

moody /'muːdɪ/ a (-ier, -iest) (variable) lunatico; (bad-tempered) di malumore

moon /muːn/ n luna f; **over the ~** fam al settimo cielo

■ **moon about, moon around** vi (fam: wander aimlessly) gironzolare

■ **moon over** *vt fam* sospirare d'amore per ⟨*sb*⟩

moon: moonbeam *n* raggio *m* di luna. **moon buggy** *n* veicolo *m* lunare. **moonlight** *n* chiaro *m* di luna ● *vi fam* lavorare in nero. **moonlighting** *n fam* lavoro *m* nero. **moonlit** *a* illuminato dalla luna. **moonshine** *n* (*nonsense*) fantasie *fpl*; (*Am: liquor*) liquore *m* di contrabbando

moor[1] /'mʊə(r)/ *n* brughiera *f*

moor[2] *vt Naut* ormeggiare

moorhen /'mʊəhen/ *n* gallinella *f* d'acqua

mooring /'mʊərɪŋ/ *n* (*place*) ormeggio *m*; ~**s** *pl* (*chains*) ormeggi *mpl*

Moorish /'mʊərɪʃ/ *a* moresco

moorland /'mʊələnd/ *n* brughiera *f*

moose /mu:s/ *n* (*pl* **moose**) alce *m*

moot /mu:t/ *a* **it's a ~ point** è un punto controverso

mop /mɒp/ *n* mocio[ʀ] *m inv*; ~ **of hair** zazzera *f* ● *vt* (*pt/pp* **mopped**) lavare con il mocio

■ **mop up** *vt* (*dry*) asciugare con il mocio[ʀ]; (*clean*) pulire con il mocio

mope /məʊp/ *vi* essere depresso

■ **mope about, mope around** *vi* trascinarsi

moped /'məʊped/ *n* ciclomotore *m*

moral /'mɒrəl/ *a* morale ● *n* morale *f*

morale /məˈrɑːl/ *n* morale *m*; **be a ~-booster** tirare su di morale

moral fibre *n* forza *f* morale

moralistic /mɒrəˈlɪstɪk/ *a* moralistico

morality /məˈrælətɪ/ *n* moralità *f*

moralize /'mɒrəlaɪz/ *vi* moraleggiare

morally /'mɒrəlɪ/ *adv* moralmente

morals /'mɒrəlz/ *npl* moralità *f*

moratorium /mɒrəˈtɔːrɪəm/ *n* moratoria *f*

morbid /'mɔːbɪd/ *a* morboso

more /mɔː(r)/ *a* più; **a few ~ books** un po' più di libri; **some ~ tea?** ancora un po' di tè?; **there's no ~ bread** non c'è più pane; **there are no ~ apples** non ci sono più mele; **one ~ word and...** ancora una parola e... ● *pron* di più; **would you like some ~?** ne vuoi ancora?; **no ~, thank you** non ne voglio più, grazie ● *adv* più; ~ **interesting** più interessante; ~ (**and ~**) **quickly** (sempre) più veloce; ~ **than** più di; **I don't love him any ~** no lo amo più; **once ~** ancora una volta; ~ **or less** più o meno; **the ~ I see him, the ~ I like him** più lo vedo, più mi piace

moreish /'mɔːrɪʃ/ *a fam* **be ~** tirare per la gola

moreover /mɔːr'əʊvə(r)/ *adv* inoltre

morgue /mɔːɡ/ *n* obitorio *m*

MORI /'mɔːrɪ/ *n abbr* (**Market Opinion Research Institute**) *istituto m di sondaggio e ricerche di mercato*

moribund /'mɒrɪbʌnd/ *a* moribondo

morning /'mɔːnɪŋ/ *n* mattino *m*, mattina *f*; **spend the ~ doing sth** passare la mattinata facendo qcsa; **in the ~** del mattino; (*tomorrow*) domani mattina

morning: morning-after pill *n* pillola *f* del giorno dopo. **morning coffee** *n* caffè *m inv* del mattino. **morning dress** *n* tight *m inv*. **morning sickness** *n* nausea *f* mattutina

Moroccan /məˈrɒk(ə)n/ *a & n* marocchino, -a *mf*

Morocco /məˈrɒkəʊ/ *n* Marocco *m*

morocco leather *n* marocchino *m*

moron /'mɔːrɒn/ *n fam* deficiente *mf*

morose /məˈrəʊs/ *a* scontroso

morosely /məˈrəʊslɪ/ *adv* in modo scontroso

morphine /'mɔːfiːn/ *n* morfina *f*

morris dance /'mɒrɪs/ *n* danza *f* tradizionale inglese

Morse /mɔːs/ *n* ~ [**code**] [codice *m*] Morse *m*

morsel /'mɔːsl/ *n* (*food*) boccone *m*

mortal /'mɔːtl/ *a & n* mortale *mf*

mortal combat *n* duello *m* mortale

mortality /mɔːˈtælətɪ/ *n* mortalità *f*

mortally /'mɔːtəlɪ/ *adv* ⟨*wounded, offended*⟩ a morte; ⟨*afraid*⟩ da morire

mortar /'mɔːtə(r)/ *n* mortaio *m*

mortgage /'mɔːɡɪdʒ/ *n* mutuo *m*; (*money raised on collateral of property*) ipoteca *f* ● *vt* ipotecare

mortgage: mortgage rate *n* tasso *m* d'interesse sui mutui. **mortgage relief** *n* sgravio *m* fiscale sul mutuo. **mortgage repayment** *n* rata *f* del mutuo

mortician /mɔːˈtɪʃn/ *n Am* impresario, -a *mf* di pompe funebri

mortification /mɔːtɪfɪˈkeɪʃn/ *n* (*of the flesh, embarrassment*) mortificazione *f*

mortify /'mɔːtɪfaɪ/ *vt* (*pt/pp* **-ied**) mortificare

mortuary /'mɔːtjʊərɪ/ *n* camera *f* mortuaria

mosaic /məʊˈzeɪɪk/ *n* mosaico *m*

Moscow /'mɒskəʊ/ *n* Mosca *f*

Moselle /məʊˈzel/ *n* (*wine*) vino *m* della Mosella

Moses /'məʊzɪz/ *n* Mosè

Moslem /'mʊzlɪm/ *a & n* musulmano, -a *mf*

mosque /mɒsk/ *n* moschea *f*

mosquito /mɒsˈkiːtəʊ/ *n* (*pl* **-es**) zanzara *f*

mosquito: mosquito bite *n* puntura *m* di zanzara. **mosquito net** *n* zanzariera *f*. **mosquito repellent** *n* antizanzare *m inv*

moss /mɒs/ *n* muschio *m*

mossy /'mɒsɪ/ *a* muschioso

most /məʊst/ *a* (*majority*) la maggior parte di; **for the ~ part** per lo più ● *adv* più, maggiormente; (*very*) estremamente, molto; **the ~ interesting day** la giornata più interessante; **a ~ interesting day** una giornata estremamente interessante; **the ~ beautiful woman in the world** la donna più bella del mondo; ~ **unlikely** veramente improbabile ● *pron* ~ **of them** la maggior parte di loro; **at** [**the**] ~ al massimo; **make the ~ of** sfruttare al massimo; ~ **of the time** la maggior parte del tempo

mostly /'məʊs(t)lɪ/ *adv* per lo più

MOT *n Br* revisione *f* obbligatoria di autoveicoli

motel /məʊˈtel/ *n* motel *m inv*

moth /mɒθ/ *n* falena *f*; [**clothes-**]~ tarma *f*

mothball /'mɒθbɔːl/ *n* pallina *f* di naftalina

moth-eaten /-iːtən/ *a* tarmato
mother /'mʌðə(r)/ *n* madre *f*; **Mother's Day** la festa della mamma ● *vt* fare da madre a
motherboard /'mʌðəbɔːd/ *n* scheda *f* madre
motherhood /'mʌðəhʊd/ *n* maternità *f*
Mothering Sunday /mʌðərɪŋ'sʌndeɪ/ *n* la festa della mamma
mother-in-law *n* (*pl* **mothers-in-law**) suocera *f*
motherland /'mʌðəlænd/ *n* patria *f*
motherless /'mʌðəlɪs/ *a* orfano, -a *mf* di madre
motherly /'mʌðəlɪ/ *a* materno
mother: mother-of-pearl *n* madreperla *f*. **mother's boy** *n* mammone *m*. **Mother's Day** *n* la festa della mamma. **mother's help** *n Br* aiuto *m* domestico. **mother-to-be** *n* futura mamma *f*. **mother tongue** *n* madrelingua *f*
mothproof /'mɒθpruːf/ *a* antitarmico
motif /məʊ'tiːf/ *n* motivo *m*
motion /'məʊʃn/ *n* moto *m*; (*proposal*) mozione *f*; (*gesture*) gesto *m* ● *vt/i* ~ [**to**] **sb to come in** fare segno a qcno di entrare
motionless /'məʊʃ(ə)nlɪs/ *a* immobile
motionlessly /'məʊʃənlɪslɪ/ *adv* senza alcun movimento
motion picture *n* film *m inv* [per il cinema] ● *attrib* (*industry*) cinematografico
motivate /'məʊtɪveɪt/ *vt* motivare
motivation /məʊtɪ'veɪʃn/ *n* motivazione *f*
motive /'məʊtɪv/ *n* motivo *m*
motley /'mɒtlɪ/ *a* disparato
motor /'məʊtə(r)/ *n* motore *m*; (*car*) macchina *f* ● *a* a motore; *Anat* motore ● *vi* andare in macchina
Motorail /'məʊtəreɪl/ *n* treno *m* per trasporto auto
motorbike /'məʊtəbaɪk/ *n fam* moto *f inv*
motor boat *n* motoscafo *m*
motorcade /'məʊtəkeɪd/ *n Am* corteo *m* di auto
motor: motor car *n* automobile *f*. **motorcycle** *n* motocicletta *f*. **motorcycle escort** *n* scorta *f* di motociclette. **motorcycle messenger** *n* corriere *m* in moto. **motorcyclist** *n* motociclista *mf*. **motorhome** *n* camper *m inv*; (*towed*) roulotte *f inv*
motoring /'məʊtərɪŋ/ *n* automobilismo *m*
motorist /'məʊtərɪst/ *n* automobilista *mf*
motor: motor launch *n* motolancia *f*. **motor mechanic** *n* meccanico *m*. **motormouth** *n fam* chiacchierone, -a *mf*. **motor oil** *n* olio *m* lubrificante. **motor racing** *n* corse *fpl* automobilistiche. **motor scooter** *n* vespa *f*. **motor vehicle** *n* autoveicolo *m*. **motorway** *n* autostrada *f*
mottled /'mɒtld/ *a* chiazzato
motto /'mɒtəʊ/ *n* (*pl* **-es**) motto *m*
mould¹ /məʊld/ *n* (*fungus*) muffa *f*
mould² *n* stampo *m* ● *vt* foggiare; *fig* formare
moulder /'məʊldə(r)/ *vi* (*corpse, refuse:*) andare in decomposizione
moulding /'məʊldɪŋ/ *n Archit* cornice *f*
mouldy /'məʊldɪ/ *a* ammuffito; (*fam: worthless*) ridicolo

moult /məʊlt/ *vi* (*bird:*) fare la muta; (*animal:*) perdere il pelo
mound /maʊnd/ *n* mucchio *m*; (*hill*) collinetta *f*
mount /maʊnt/ *n* (*horse*) cavalcatura *f*; (*of jewel, photo, picture*) montatura *f* ● *vt* montare a (*horse*); salire su (*bicycle*); incastonare (*jewel*); incorniciare (*photo, picture*) ● *vi* aumentare
■ **mount up** *vi* aumentare
mountain /'maʊntɪn/ *n* montagna *f*; **make a ~ out of a molehill** fare di una mosca un elefante
mountain bike *n* mountain bike *f inv*
mountain climbing *n* alpinismo *m*
mountaineer /maʊntɪ'nɪə(r)/ *n* alpinista *mf*
mountaineering /maʊntɪ'nɪərɪŋ/ *n* alpinismo *m*
mountainous /'maʊntɪnəs/ *a* montagnoso
mountain range *n* catena *f* montuosa
mountain top *n* cima *f* di montagna
mounted police /maʊntɪdpə'liːs/ *n* polizia *f* a cavallo
mourn /mɔːn/ *vt* lamentare ● *vi* ~ **for** piangere la morte di
mourner /'mɔːnə(r)/ *n* persona *f* che participa a un funerale
mournful /'mɔːnfʊl/ *a* triste
mournfully /'mɔːnfʊlɪ/ *adv* tristemente
mourning /'mɔːnɪŋ/ *n* **in ~** in lutto
mouse /maʊs/ *n* (*pl* **mice**) topo *m*; *Comput* mouse *m inv*
mouse: mousehole *n* tana *f* di topi/di un topo. **mouse mat** *n Comput* tappetino *m*. **mousetrap** *n* trappola *f* [per topi]
mousse /muːs/ *n Culin* mousse *f inv*
moustache /mə'stɑː.ʃ/ *n* baffi *mpl*
mousy /'maʊsɪ/ *a* (*colour*) grigio topo
mouth¹ /maʊð/ *vt* ~ **sth** dire qcsa silenziosamente muovendo solamente le labbra
mouth² /maʊθ/ *n* bocca *f*; (*of river*) foce *f*
mouthful /'maʊθfʊl/ *n* boccone *m*
mouth: mouth organ *n* armonica *f* [a bocca]. **mouthpiece** *n* imboccatura *f*; (*fig: person*) portavoce *m inv*. **mouth-to-mouth resuscitation** *n* respirazione *f* bocca-bocca. **mouthwash** *n* acqua *f* dentifricia. **mouthwatering** /-wɔːtərɪŋ/ *a* che fa venire l'acquolina in bocca
movable /'muːvəbl/ *a* movibile
move /muːv/ *n* mossa *f*; (*moving house*) trasloco *m*; **on the ~** in movimento; **get a ~ on** *fam* darsi una mossa ● *vt* muovere; (*emotionally*) commuovere; spostare (*car, furniture*); (*transfer*) trasferire; (*propose*) proporre; ~ **house** traslocare ● *vi* muoversi; (*move house*) traslocare; **don't ~!** non muoverti!
■ **move about, move around** *vi* (*in house*) muoversi; (*in country*) spostarsi
■ **move along** *vi* andare avanti ● *vt* muovere in avanti
■ **move away** *vi* allontanarsi; (*move house*) trasferirsi ● *vt* allontanare

■ **move forward** *vi* avanzare ● *vt* spostare avanti

■ **move in** *vi* (*to a house*) trasferirsi

■ **move off** *vi* ⟨*vehicle:*⟩ muoversi

■ **move on** *vi* (*move to another place*) muoversi ● *vt* ⟨*police:*⟩ far circolare

■ **move on to** *vt* passare a ⟨*new topic, next question*⟩

■ **move out** *vi* (*of house*) andare via

■ **move over** *vi* spostarsi ● *vt* spostare

■ **move up** *vi* muoversi; (*advance, increase*) avanzare

movement /'mu:vmənt/ *n* movimento *m*; (*of clock*) meccanismo *m*

movie /'mu:vɪ/ *n* film *m inv*; **go to the ~s** andare al cinema

movie: movie camera *n* cinepresa *f*. **movie director** *n* regista *mf* cinematografico, -a. **movie-goer** *n* persona *f* che va al cinema. **movie star** *n* stella *f* del cinema, star *f inv* del cinema

moving /'mu:vɪŋ/ *a* mobile; (*touching*) commovente

mow /məʊ/ *vt* (*pt* **mowed**, *pp* **mown** *or* **mowed**) tagliare ⟨*lawn*⟩

■ **mow down** *vt* (*destroy*) sterminare

mower /'məʊə(r)/ *n* tosaerba *m inv*

MP *abbr* (**Member of Parliament**) deputato, -a *mf*

mpg *abbr* (**miles per gallon**) miglia al gallone

mph *abbr* (**miles per hour**) miglia all'ora

Mr /'mɪstə(r)/ *n* (*pl* **Messrs**) Signor *m*

Mrs /'mɪsɪz/ *n* Signora *f*

Ms /mɪz/ *n* Signora *f* (*modo m formale di rivolgersi ad una donna quando non si vuole connotarla come sposata o nubile*)

MS *n abbr* (**multiple sclerosis**) sclerosi *f* a placche *or* multipla; *abbr* (**manuscript**) ms; *Am abbr* **Mississippi**

MSc *n abbr* (**Master of Science**) (*diploma*) laurea *f* in discipline scientifiche; (*person*) laureato, -a *mf* in discipline scientifiche

much /mʌtʃ/ *a, adv & pron* molto; **~ as** per quanto; **I love you just as ~ as before/him** ti amo quanto prima/lui; **as ~ as £5 million** ben cinque milioni di sterline; **as ~ as that** così tanto; **very ~** tantissimo, moltissimo; **~ the same** quasi uguale

muck /mʌk/ *n* (*dirt*) sporcizia *f*; (*farming*) letame *m*; (*fam: filth*) porcheria *f*

■ **muck about** *vi fam* perder tempo; **~ about with** trafficare con

■ **muck in** *vi fam* dare una mano

■ **muck up** *vt fam* rovinare; (*make dirty*) sporcare

muckraking /'mʌkreɪkɪŋ/ *n* scandalismo *m*

mucky /'mʌkɪ/ *a* (**-ier, -iest**) sudicio

mucus /'mju:kəs/ *n* muco *m*

mud /mʌd/ *n* fango *m*

muddle /'mʌdl/ *n* disordine *m*; (*mix-up*) confusione *f* ● *vt* ~ [**up**] confondere ⟨*dates*⟩

■ **muddle through** *vi* farcela alla bell'e meglio

muddle-headed /-'hedɪd/ *a* ⟨*plan*⟩ confuso; ⟨*person*⟩ confusionario

muddy /'mʌdɪ/ *a* (**-ier, -iest**) ⟨*path*⟩ fangoso; ⟨*shoes*⟩ infangato

mud: mudflat *n* distesa *f* di fango. **mudguard** *n* parafango *m*. **mud hut** *n* capanna *f* di fango. **mudpack** *n* (*for beauty treatment*) maschera *f* di fango. **mud pie** *n* formina *f* di fango. **mudslide** *n* colata *f* di fango. **mud-slinging** /-slɪŋɪŋ/ *n* diffamazione *f*

muesli /'mju:zlɪ/ *n* muesli *m inv*

muffle /'mʌfl/ *vt* smorzare ⟨*sound*⟩

■ **muffle** *vi* (*for warmth*) imbacuccarsi

muffler /'mʌflə(r)/ *n* sciarpa *f*; *Am Auto* marmitta *f*

mug¹ /mʌg/ *n* tazza *f*; (*for beer*) boccale *m*; (*fam: face*) muso *m*; (*fam: simpleton*) pollo *m*

mug² *vt* (*pt/pp* **mugged**) aggredire e derubare

■ **mug up** *vt* (*fam: learn*) imparare alla bell'e meglio

mugger /'mʌgə(r)/ *n* assalitore, -trice *mf*

mugging /'mʌgɪŋ/ *n* aggressione *f* per furto

muggy /'mʌgɪ/ *a* (**-ier, -iest**) afoso

mulatto /mju:'lætəʊ/ *a & n Am* mulatto, -a *mf*

mulberry /'mʌlb(ə)rɪ/ *n Am* (*fruit*) mora *f* di gelso; (*tree*) gelso *m*

mule¹ /mju:l/ *n* mulo *m*

mule² *n* (*slipper*) ciabatta *f*

mulish /'mju:lɪʃ/ *a* testardo

mull /mʌl/ *vt* ~ **over** rimuginare su

mulled /mʌld/ *a* ~ **wine** vin brûlé *m inv*

multi- /mʌltɪ/ *pref* multi+

multi-access *n Comput* accesso *m* multiplo

multichannel /mʌltɪ'tʃænəl/ *a* ⟨*television*⟩ con molti canali

multicoloured /'mʌltɪkʌləd/ *a* variopinto

multicultural /mʌltɪ'kʌltʃərəl/ *a* multiculturale

multidisciplinary /mʌltɪdɪsɪ'plɪnərɪ/ *a* *Sch, Univ* pluridisciplinare

multifaceted /mʌltɪ'fæsɪtɪd/ *a* ⟨*gemstone*⟩ sfaccettato; ⟨*career*⟩ variegato; ⟨*personality*⟩ sfaccettato

multifunction /mʌltɪ'fʌŋkʃn/ *a* multifunzionale

multigym /'mʌltɪdʒɪm/ *n* attrezzo *m* multiuso

multilateral /mʌltɪ'læt(ə)rəl/ *a Pol* multilaterale

multilevel /'mʌltɪlevəl/ *a* ⟨*parking, access*⟩ a più piani; ⟨*analysis*⟩ a più livelli

multilingual /mʌltɪ'lɪŋgwəl/ *a* multilingue *inv*

multimedia /mʌltɪ'mi:dɪə/ *n* multimedia *mpl* ● *a* multimediale

multinational /mʌltɪ'næʃnəl/ *a* multinazionale ● *n* multinazionale *f*

multi-party /'mʌltɪpɑ:tɪ/ *a* ⟨*government, system*⟩ pluripartitico

multiple /'mʌltɪpl/ *a & n* multiplo *m*

multiple: multiple choice question *n Sch* test *m inv* a scelta multipla. **multiple**

ownership n comproprietà f. **multiple pile-up** n tamponamento m a catena. **multiple sclerosis** n sclerosi f a placche or multipla.

multiple store n Br negozio m appartenente a una catena

multiplex /'mʌltɪpleks/ n Teleph multiplex m inv; Cinema cinema m inv multisale ● a Teleph in multiplex

multiplication /mʌltɪplɪ'keɪʃn/ n moltiplicazione f

multiply /'mʌltɪplaɪ/ v (pt/pp -ied) ● vt moltiplicare (**by** per) ● vi moltiplicarsi

multi-purpose a ⟨tool, gadget⟩ multiuso inv; ⟨organization⟩ con più scopi

multi-storey a ~ **car park** parcheggio m a più piani

multi-track a ⟨sound system⟩ a più piste

multitude /'mʌltɪtjuːd/ n moltitudine f; **hide a ~ of sins** ⟨rug etc:⟩ nascondere un sacco di magagne

multi-user a ⟨system, installation⟩ multiutente

mum[1] /mʌm/ a **keep ~** fam non aprire bocca

mum[2] n fam mamma f

mumble /'mʌmbl/ vt/i borbottare

mumbo-jumbo /mʌmbəʊ'dʒʌmbəʊ/ n ⟨fam: speech, writing⟩ paroloni mpl

mummy[1] /'mʌmi/ n fam mamma f

mummy[2] n Archaeol mummia f

mummy's boy n Br pej mammone m

mumps /mʌmps/ n orecchioni mpl

munch /mʌntʃ/ vt/i sgranocchiare

mundane /mʌn'deɪn/ a ⟨everyday⟩ banale

municipal /mjʊ'nɪsɪpl/ a municipale

munitions /mjʊ'nɪʃnz/ npl munizioni fpl

mural /'mjʊərəl/ n dipinto m murale

murder /'mɜːdə(r)/ n assassinio m ● vt assassinare; ⟨fam: ruin⟩ massacrare

murder case n caso m di omicidio

murder charge n imputazione f di omicidio

murderer /'mɜːdərə(r)/ n assassino, -a mf

murderous /'mɜːdərəs/ a omicida

murky /'mɜːkɪ/ a (-ier, -iest) oscuro

murmur /'mɜːmə(r)/ n mormorio m ● vt/i mormorare

murmuring /'mɜːmərɪŋ/ n mormorio m; **~s** pl ⟨of discontent⟩ segnali mpl di malcontento

muscle /'mʌsl/ n muscolo m

■ **muscle in** vi sl intromettersi (**to** in)

muscle strain n strappo m musculare

muscular /'mʌskjʊlə(r)/ a muscolare; ⟨strong⟩ muscoloso

muscular dystrophy /'dɪstrəfɪ/ n distrofia f muscolare

muse /mjuːz/ vi meditare (**on** su)

museum /mjuː'zɪəm/ n museo m

mushroom /'mʌʃrʊm/ n fungo m ● vi fig spuntare come funghi

mushroom cloud n fungo m atomico

mushy /'mʌʃi/ a fig sdolcinato

music /'mjuːzɪk/ n musica f; ⟨written⟩ spartito m; **set to ~** musicare

musical /'mjuːzɪkl/ a musicale; ⟨person⟩ dotato di senso musicale ● n commedia f musicale

musical box n carillon m inv

musical instrument n strumento m musicale

music: music box n carillon m inv. **music centre** n impianto m stereo. **music hall** n teatro m di varietà

musician /mjuː'zɪʃn/ n musicista mf

music lover n amante mf della musica

musicology /mjuːzɪ'kɒlədʒɪ/ n musicologia f

music: music stand n leggio m. **music stool** n sgabello m per pianoforte. **music video** n video clip m inv

musings /'mjuːzɪŋz/ npl riflessioni fpl

musket /'mʌskɪt/ n moschetto m

musketeer /mʌskə'tɪə(r)/ n moschettiere m

musky /'mʌskɪ/ a muschiato

Muslim /'mʊzlɪm/ a & n musulmano, -a mf

mussel /'mʌsl/ n cozza f

must /mʌst/ v aux (solo al presente) dovere; **you ~ not be late** non devi essere in ritardo; **she ~ have finished by now** (probability) deve aver finito ormai ● n **a ~** fam una cosa da non perdere

mustard /'mʌstəd/ n senape f

muster /'mʌstə(r)/ vt radunare ⟨troops⟩; fare appello a ⟨strength⟩

musty /'mʌstɪ/ a (-ier, -iest) stantio

mutant /'mjuːtənt/ n & a mutante mf

mutate /mjuː'teɪt/ vi ⟨cell, organism:⟩ subire una mutazione; **~ into** ⟨alien, monster:⟩ trasformarsi in ● vt far subire una mutazione

mutation /mjuː'teɪʃn/ n Biol mutazione f

mute /mjuːt/ a muto

muted /'mjuːtɪd/ a smorzato

mutilate /'mjuːtɪleɪt/ vt mutilare

mutilation /mjuːtɪ'leɪʃn/ n mutilazione f

mutinous /'mjuːtɪnəs/ a ammutinato

mutiny /'mjuːtɪnɪ/ n ammutinamento m ● vi (pt/pp -ied) ammutinarsi

mutter /'mʌtə(r)/ n borbottio m ● vt/i borbottare

mutton /'mʌtn/ n carne f di montone

mutual /'mjuːtjʊəl/ a reciproco; ⟨fam: common⟩ comune

mutually /'mjuːtjʊəlɪ/ adv reciprocamente

Muzak® /'mjuːzæk/ n musica f di sottofondo

muzzle /'mʌzl/ n ⟨of animal⟩ muso m; ⟨of firearm⟩ bocca f; ⟨for dog⟩ museruola f ● vt fig mettere il bavaglio a

MW abbr (**medium wave**) OM

my /maɪ/ poss a mio m, mia f, miei mpl, mie fpl; **my job/house** il mio lavoro/la mia casa; **my mother/father** mia madre/mio padre

myalgic encephalomyelitis /maɪ-ældʒɪkensefələʊmaɪ'laɪtɪs/ n encefalomielite f mialgica

myopic /maɪ'ɒpɪk/ a miope

myself /maɪ'self/ pers pron ⟨reflexive⟩ mi; (emphatic) me stesso; (after prep) me; **I've seen it ~** l'ho visto io stesso; **by ~** da solo; **I thought to ~** ho pensato tra me e me; **I'm proud of ~** sono fiero di me

mysterious /mɪ'stɪərɪəs/ a misterioso

mysteriously /mɪˈstɪərɪəslɪ/ *adv* misteriosamente

mystery /ˈmɪstərɪ/ *n* mistero *m*; ~ [**story**] racconto *m* del mistero

mystery play *n* mistero *m* (*teatrale*)

mystery tour *n* viaggio *m* con destinazione a sorpresa

mystic[al] /ˈmɪstɪk[l]/ *a* mistico

mysticism /ˈmɪstɪsɪzm/ *n* misticismo *m*

mystification /mɪstɪfɪˈkeɪʃn/ *n* disorientamento *m*

mystified /ˈmɪstɪfaɪd/ *a* disorientato

mystify /ˈmɪstɪfaɪ/ *vt* disorientare

mystique /mɪˈstiːk/ *n* mistica *f*

myth /mɪθ/ *n* mito *m*

mythical /ˈmɪθɪkl/ *a* mitico

mythological /mɪθəˈlɒdʒɪkl/ *a* mitologico

mythology /mɪˈθɒlədʒɪ/ *n* mitologia *f*

Nn

n, N /en/ *n* (*letter*) n, N *f inv*

N *abbr* (**north**) N

n/a, N/A *abbr* (**not applicable**) non pertinente

nab /næb/ *vt* (*pt/pp* **nabbed**) *fam* beccare

nadir /ˈneɪdɪə/ *n* nadir *m*; *fig* punto *m* più basso, fondo *m*

naff /næf/ *a Br fam* banale

nag¹ /næg/ *n* (*horse*) ronzino *m*

nag² *v* (*pt/pp* **nagged**) ● *vt* assillare ● *vi* essere insistente ● *n* (*person*) brontolone, -a *mf*

nagging /ˈnægɪŋ/ *a* ⟨*pain*⟩ persistente

nail /neɪl/ *n* chiodo *m*; (*of finger, toe*) unghia *f*; **on the ~** *fam* sull'unghia

■ **nail down** *vt* inchiodare; **~ sb down to a time/price** far fissare a qcno un'ora/un prezzo

nail: nail-biting /-baɪtɪŋ/ *n* abitudine *f* di mangiarsi le unghie ● *a* ⟨*match, finish*⟩ mozzafiato *inv*; ⟨*wait*⟩ esasperante. **nail brush** *n* spazzolino *m* da unghie. **nail clippers** *npl* tronchesina *m*. **nail file** *n* limetta *f* da unghie. **nail polish** *n* smalto *m* [per unghie]. **nail polish remover** *n* acetone *m*, solvente *m* per unghie. **nail scissors** *npl* forbicine *fpl* da unghie. **nail varnish** *n* smalto *m* [per unghie]

naïve /naɪˈiːv/ *a* ingenuo

naïvely /naɪˈiːvlɪ/ *adv* ingenuamente

naïvety /naɪˈiːvətɪ/ *n* ingenuità *f*

naked /ˈneɪkɪd/ *a* nudo; **with the ~ eye** a occhio nudo

nakedness /ˈneɪkɪdnɪs/ *n* nudità *f*

name /neɪm/ *n* nome *m*; **what's your ~?** come ti chiami?; **my ~ is Matthew** mi chiamo Matthew; **I know her by ~** la conosco di nome; **by the ~ of Bates** di nome Bates; **make a ~ for oneself** farsi un nome; **call sb ~s** *fam* insultare qcno ● *vt* (*to position*) nominare; chiamare ⟨*baby*⟩; (*identify*) citare; **be ~d after** essere chiamato col nome di

name day *n Relig* onomastico *m*

name-drop *vi* **he's always ~ping** si vanta sempre di conoscere persone famose

nameless /ˈneɪmlɪs/ *a* senza nome

namely /ˈneɪmlɪ/ *adv* cioè

name: nameplate *n* targhetta *f*. **namesake** *n* omonimo, -a *mf*. **name tag** *n* targhetta *f* attaccata a un oggetto con il nome del proprietario. **name tape** *n* fettuccia *f* attaccata a un oggetto con il nome del proprietario

Namibia /nəˈmɪbɪə/ *n* Namibia *f*

nanny /ˈnænɪ/ *n* bambinaia *f*

nanny goat *n* capra *f*

nap /næp/ *n* pisolino *m*; **have a ~** fare un pisolino ● *vi* **catch sb ~ping** cogliere qcno alla sprovvista

napalm /ˈneɪpɑːm/ *n* napalm *m*

nape /neɪp/ *n* **~** [**of the neck**] nuca *f*

napkin /ˈnæpkɪn/ *n* tovagliolo *m*

Naples /ˈneɪp(ə)lz/ *n* Napoli *f*

nappy /ˈnæpɪ/ *n* pannolino *m*

nappy liner *n* filtrante *m*

nappy rash *n Br* eritema *m* da pannolini

narcotic /nɑːˈkɒtɪk/ *a & n* narcotico *m*

narcotics agent *n Am* agente *m* della squadra antidroga

narked /nɑːkt/ *a fam* scocciato

narrate /nəˈreɪt/ *vt* narrare

narration /nəˈreɪʃn/ *n* narrazione *f*

narrative /ˈnærətɪv/ *a* narrativo ● *n* narrazione *f*

narrator /nəˈreɪtə(r)/ *n* narratore, -trice *mf*

narrow /ˈnærəʊ/ *a* stretto; ⟨*fig: views*⟩ ristretto; ⟨*margin, majority*⟩ scarso; **have a ~ escape** scamparla per un pelo ● *vi* restringersi

■ **narrow down** *vt* (*reduce*) restringere

narrowly /ˈnærəʊlɪ/ *adv* **~ escape death** evitare la morte per un pelo

narrow-minded /-ˈmaɪndɪd/ *a* di idee ristrette

nasal /ˈneɪzl/ *a* nasale

nasal spray *n* spray *m inv* nasale

nastily /ˈnɑːstɪlɪ/ *adv* (*spitefully*) con cattiveria

nasty /ˈnɑːstɪ/ *a* (**-ier, -iest**) ⟨*smell, person, remark*⟩ cattivo; ⟨*injury, situation, weather*⟩ brutto; **turn ~** ⟨*person:*⟩ diventare cattivo; ⟨*situation:*⟩ mettersi male; ⟨*weather:*⟩ volgere al brutto

nation /ˈneɪʃn/ *n* nazione *f*

national /'næʃən(ə)l/ a nazionale ● n cittadino, -a mf
national: national anthem n inno m nazionale. **National Curriculum** n Br programma m scolastico ministeriale per il Galles e l'Inghilterra. **national debt** n debito m pubblico. **National Front** n Br partito m britannico di estrema destra. **national grid** n Electr rete f elettrica nazionale. **National Health** n Br servizio m nazionale di assistenza sanitaria. **National Health Service** n servizio m sanitario britannico. **National Insurance** n ≈ Previdenza f sociale. **National Insurance number** n numero m di Previdenza sociale
nationalism /'næʃənəlɪzm/ n nazionalismo m
nationality /næʃə'nælətɪ/ n nazionalità f inv
nationalization /næʃənəlaɪ'zeɪʃn/ n nazionalizzazione
nationalize /'næʃənəlaɪz/ vt nazionalizzare
nationally /'næʃənəlɪ/ adv a livello nazionale
national: national monument n monumento m nazionale. **National Savings Bank** n Br Cassa f di risparmio. **national service** n Br servizio m militare. **National Trust** n Br associazione f per la tutela del patrimonio culturale e ambientale in Gran Bretagna
nation state n stato-nazione m
nationwide /'neɪʃnwaɪd/ a su scala nazionale
native /'neɪtɪv/ a nativo; (innate) innato ● n nativo, -a mf; (local inhabitant) abitante mf del posto; (outside Europe) indigeno, -a mf; **she's a ~ of Venice** è originaria di Venezia
native: Native American a & n amerindio, -a mf. **native land** n paese m natio. **native language** n lingua f madre. **native speaker** n persona f di madrelingua; **Italian ~ ~s** Italiani madrelingua
Nativity /nə'tɪvətɪ/ n **the ~** la Natività
Nativity play n rappresentazione f sulla nascita di Gesù
Nato, NATO /'neɪtəʊ/ n abbr (**North Atlantic Treaty Organization**) NATO f
natter /'nætə(r)/ n **have a ~** fam fare quattro chiacchiere ● vi fam chiacchierare
natty /'nætɪ/ a fam (smart) chic inv; (clever) geniale
natural /'nætʃ(ə)rəl/ a naturale
natural: natural childbirth n parto m indolore. **natural gas** n metano m. **natural history** n storia f naturale
naturalist /'nætʃ(ə)rəlɪst/ n naturalista mf
naturalization /nætʃ(ə)rəlaɪ'zeɪʃn/ n naturalizzazione f
naturalize /'nætʃ(ə)rəlaɪz/ vt naturalizzare
naturally /'nætʃ(ə)rəlɪ/ adv (of course) naturalmente; (by nature) per natura
nature /'neɪtʃə(r)/ n natura f; **by ~** per natura
nature: nature conservancy n protezione f della natura. **nature reserve** n riserva f naturale. **nature trail** n percorso m ecologico
naturism /'neɪtʃərɪzm/ n nudismo m

naturist /'neɪtʃərɪst/ n naturista mf ● a naturistico
naught /nɔːt/ n = **nought**
naughtily /'nɔːtɪlɪ/ adv male
naughtiness /'nɔːtɪnɪs/ n (of child, pet) birbanteria f; (of joke, suggestion) maliziosità f inv
naughty /'nɔːtɪ/ a (-ier, -iest) monello; (slightly indecent) spinto
nausea /'nɔːzɪə/ n nausea f
nauseate /'nɔːzɪeɪt/ vt nauseare
nauseating /'nɔːzɪeɪtɪŋ/ a nauseante
nauseatingly /'nɔːzɪeɪtɪŋlɪ/ adv (rich, sweet) disgustosamente
nauseous /'nɔːzɪəs/ a **I feel ~** ho la nausea
nautical /'nɔːtɪkl/ a nautico
nautical mile n miglio m marino
naval /'neɪvl/ a navale
naval: naval base n base f navale. **naval dockyard** n cantiere m navale militare. **naval officer** n ufficiale m di marina. **naval station** n base f navale. **naval stores** npl (depot) magazzini mpl della marina militare
nave /neɪv/ n navata f centrale
navel /'neɪvl/ n ombelico m
navigable /'nævɪgəbl/ a navigabile
navigate /'nævɪgeɪt/ vi navigare; Auto fare da navigatore ● vt navigare su (river)
navigation /nævɪ'geɪʃn/ n navigazione f
navigational /nævɪ'geɪʃənəl/ a (instruments) di navigazione; (science) della navigazione
navigator /'nævɪgeɪtə(r)/ n navigatore m
navvy /'nævɪ/ n manovale m
navy /'neɪvɪ/ n marina f ● **~ [blue]** a blu scuro inv ● n blu m inv scuro
nay /neɪ/ adv anzi ● n (negative vote) no m
Nazi /'nɑːtsɪ/ n & a nazista mf
NBC n abbr (**National Broadcasting Company**) NBC f (rete nazionale televisiva statunitense)
NC Am abbr **North Carolina**
NCO n abbr (**non-commissioned officer**) sottufficiale m
ND Am abbr **North Dakota**
NE abbr (**north-east**) NE
Ne Am abbr **Nebraska**
Neapolitan /nɪə'pɒlɪtən/ a & n napoletano, -a mf
near /nɪə(r)/ a vicino; (future) prossimo; **the ~est bank** la banca più vicina ● adv vicino; **draw ~** avvicinarsi; **~ at hand** a portata di mano ● prep vicino a; **he was ~ to tears** aveva le lacrime agli occhi ● vt avvicinarsi a
nearby /nɪə'baɪ/ a & adv vicino
Near East n Medio Oriente m
nearly /'nɪəlɪ/ adv quasi; **it's not ~ enough** non è per niente sufficiente
near miss n **have a ~ ~** (planes, cars:) evitare per poco uno scontro
nearness /'nɪənɪs/ n vicinanza f
near: nearside n Auto (in Britain) lato m sinistro; (in America, rest of Europe) lato m de-

stro. **near-sighted** /-'saɪtɪd/ a Am miope.
near-sightedness n miopia f
neat /niːt/ a (tidy) ordinato; (clever) efficace; (undiluted) liscio
neaten /'niːtən/ vt riordinare ⟨pile of paper⟩; dare un'aggiustatina a ⟨tie, skirt⟩
neatly /'niːtlɪ/ adv ordinatamente; (cleverly) efficacemente
neatness /'niːtnɪs/ n (tidiness) ordine m
necessarily /nesə'serɪlɪ/ adv necessariamente
necessary /'nesəsərɪ/ a necessario
necessitate /nɪ'sesɪteɪt/ vt rendere necessario
necessity /nɪ'sesətɪ/ n necessità f inv
neck /nek/ n collo m; (of dress) colletto m; ~ **and** ~ testa a testa
necking /'nekɪŋ/ n fam pomiciate fpl
neck: necklace /'neklɪs/ n collana f. **neckline** n scollatura f. **necktie** n cravatta f
nectar /'nektə(r)/ n nettare m
neé /neɪ/ a ~ **Brett** nata Brett
need /niːd/ n bisogno m; **be in** ~ essere bisognoso; **be in** ~ **of** avere bisogno di; **if** ~ **be** se ce ne fosse bisogno; **there is a** ~ **for** c'è bisogno di; **there is no** ~ **for that** non ce n'è bisogno; **there is no** ~ **for you to go** non c'è bisogno che tu vada ● vt aver bisogno di; **I** ~ **to know** devo saperlo; **it** ~**s to be done** bisogna farlo ● v aux **you** ~ **not go** non c'è bisogno che tu vada; ~ **I come?** devo venire?
needful /'niːdfʊl/ a necessario ● n **do the** ~ fare il necessario
needle /'niːdl/ n ago m; (for knitting) uncinetto m; (of record player) puntina f ● vt (fam: annoy) punzecchiare
needless /'niːdlɪs/ a inutile
needlessly /'niːdlɪslɪ/ adv inutilmente
needlework /'niːdlwɜːk/ n cucito m
needs /niːdz/ adv ~ **must** la dovere chiama
need-to-know a **we have a** ~ **policy** la nostra politica consiste nel tenere informati solo i diretti interessati
needy /'niːdɪ/ a (-ier, -iest) bisognoso
negate /nɪ'geɪt/ vt (cancel out) annullare; mettere in forma negativa ⟨sentence⟩; (contradict) contraddire; (deny) negare
negation /nɪ'geɪʃn/ n negazione f
negative /'negətɪv/ a negativo ● n negazione f; Phot negativo m; **in the** ~ Gram alla forma negativa
neglect /nɪ'glekt/ n trascuratezza f; **state of** ~ stato di abbandono ● vt trascurare; **he** ~**ed to write** non si è curato di scrivere
neglected /nɪ'glektɪd/ a trascurato
neglectful /nɪ'glektfʊl/ a negligente; **be** ~ **of** trascurare
negligée /'neglɪʒeɪ/ n négligé m inv
negligence /'neglɪdʒəns/ n negligenza f
negligent /'neglɪdʒənt/ a negligente
negligently /'neglɪdʒəntlɪ/ adv con negligenza
negligible /'neglɪdʒəbl/ a trascurabile
negotiable /nɪ'gəʊʃəbl/ a ⟨road⟩ transitabile; Comm negoziabile; **not** ~ ⟨cheque⟩ non trasferibile
negotiate /nɪ'gəʊʃɪeɪt/ vt negoziare; Auto prendere ⟨bend⟩ ● vi negoziare
negotiating /nɪ'gəʊʃɪeɪtɪŋ/ a ⟨rights⟩ al negoziato; ⟨team, committee⟩ che conduce le trattative; ⟨ploy, position⟩ di negoziato; **the** ~ **table** il tavolo delle trattative
negotiation /nɪgəʊʃɪ'eɪʃn/ n negoziato m
negotiator /nɪ'gəʊʃɪeɪtə(r)/ n negoziatore, -trice mf
Negro /'niːgrəʊ/ a & n (pl **-es**) negro, -a mf
neigh /neɪ/ vi nitrire
neighbour /'neɪbə(r)/ n vicino, -a mf
neighbourhood /'neɪbəhʊd/ n vicinato m; **in the** ~ **of** nei dintorni di; fig circa
neighbourhood watch scheme n vigilanza f da parte della gente del quartiere
neighbouring /'neɪbərɪŋ/ a vicino
neighbourly /'neɪbəlɪ/ a amichevole
neither /'naɪðə(r)/ a & pron nessuno dei due, né l'uno né l'altro ● adv ~... **nor** né... né ● conj nemmeno, neanche; ~ **do/did I** nemmeno io
neo+ /'niːəʊ/ pref neo+
neologism /nɪ'ɒlədʒɪzm/ n neologismo m
neon /'niːɒn/ n neon m
neon light n luce f al neon
nephew /'nevjuː/ n nipote m
nephritis /nɪ'fraɪtəs/ n nefrite f
nepotism /'nepətɪzm/ n nepotismo m
nerve /nɜːv/ n nervo m; (fam: courage) coraggio m; (fam: impudence) faccia f tosta!; **lose one's** ~ perdersi d'animo; **you've got a** ~! hai una bella faccia tosta!; **live on one's** ~**s** vivere con i nervi a fior di pelle; **be a bag of** ~**s** avere i nervi a fior di pelle
nerve-racking /'nɜːvrækɪŋ/ a logorante
nerviness /'nɜːvɪnɪs/ n Br nervosismo m; Am grinta f
nervous /'nɜːvəs/ a nervoso; **he makes me** ~ mi mette in agitazione
nervous breakdown n esaurimento m nervoso
nervous energy n energia f in eccesso
nervously /'nɜːvəslɪ/ adv nervosamente
nervousness /'nɜːvəsnɪs/ n nervosismo m; (before important event) tensione f
nervous system n sistema m nervoso
nervous wreck n fascio m di nervi
nervy /'nɜːvɪ/ a (-ier, -iest) nervoso; (Am: impudent) sfacciato
nest /nest/ n nido m ● vi fare il nido
nested /'nestɪd/ a Comput nidificato
nest egg n gruzzolo m
nesting /'nestɪŋ/ n Zool nidificazione f; Comput nesting m inv, nidificazione f ● attrib ⟨habit⟩ di nidificare; ⟨place⟩ per nidificare; ⟨season⟩ della nidificazione
nestle /'nesl/ vi accoccolarsi
■ **nestle up to** vt accoccolarsi accanto a ⟨sb⟩
nestling /'neslɪŋ/ n nidiace m
net¹ /net/ n rete f ● vt (pt/pp **netted**) (catch) prendere (con la rete)

net² *a* netto; ~ **of VAT** al netto dell'IVA ● *vt* (*pt/pp* **netted**) incassare un utile netto di

netball /'netbɔ:l/ *n sport m inv femminile, simile a pallacanestro*

net cord *n* corda *f* di rete; *Tennis* (*shot*) net *m inv*

Netherlands /'neðələndz/ *npl* **the** ~ i Paesi Bassi

netting /'netɪŋ/ *n* [**wire**] ~ reticolato *m*

nettle /'netl/ *n* ortica *f*

net ton *n Am* tonnellata *f* corta americana

network /'netwɜ:k/ *n* rete *f*

network card *n Comput* scheda *f* di rete

networked /'netwɜ:kt/ *a Comput* collegato in rete

networking /'netwɜ:kɪŋ/ *n* (*establishing contacts*) stabilmento *m* di una rete di contatti; *Comput* collegamento *m* in rete

neuralgia /njʊə'rældʒə/ *n* nevralgia *f*

neuritis /njʊə'raɪtɪs/ *n* nevrite *f*

neurologist /njʊə'rɒlədʒɪst/ *n* neurologo, -a *mf*

neurology /njʊə'rɒlədʒɪ/ *n* neurologia *f*

neurosis /njʊə'rəʊsɪs/ *n* (*pl* **-oses** /njʊə'rəʊsi:z/) nevrosi *f inv*

neurosurgeon /'njʊərəsɜ:dʒən/ *n* neurochirurgo *m*

neurotic /njʊə'rɒtɪk/ *a* nevrotico

neurotically /njʊə'rɒtɪklɪ/ *adv* in modo ossessivo

neuter /'nju:tə(r)/ *a Gram* neutro ● *n Gram* neutro *m* ● *vt* sterilizzare

neutral /'nju:trəl/ *a* neutro; (*country, person*) neutrale ● *n* **in** ~ *Auto* in folle

neutrality /nju:'trælətɪ/ *n* neutralità *f*

neutralize /'nju:trəlaɪz/ *vt* neutralizzare

never /'nevə(r)/ *adv* [non...] mai; (*fam: expressing disbelief*) ma va; ~ **again** mai più; **well I** ~! chi l'avrebbe detto!

never-ending *a* interminabile

nevermore /nevə'mɔ:(r)/ *adv* mai più

never-never *n fam* **buy sth on the** ~ comprare qcsa a rate

never-never land *n* mondo *m* dei sogni

nevertheless /nevəðə'les/ *adv* tuttavia

new /nju:/ *a* nuovo

new: New Age *n* New Age *f inv* ● *attrib* 〈*music, ideas, sect*〉 New Age *inv.* **new blood** *n* nuove leve *fpl.* **newborn** *a* neonato. **New Caledonia** *n* Nuova Caledonia *f.* **newcomer** *n* nuovo, -a arrivato, -a *mf.* **newfangled** *a pej* modernizzante. **newfound** *a* nuovo

Newfoundland /'nju:fən(d)lənd/ *n* Terranova *f*

New Guinea *n* Nuova Guinea *f*

newish /'nju:ɪʃ/ *a* abbastanza nuovo

new: new-laid /'nju:leɪd/ *a* fresco. **new look** *a* 〈*car, team*〉 nuovo; 〈*edition, show*〉 rinnovato; 〈*product*〉 dall'aspetto nuovo ● *n* **they have given the shop a completely** ~ ~ hanno completamente rinnovato il negozio

newly /'nju:lɪ/ *adv* (*recently*) di recente

newly-built *a* costruito di recente

newly-weds /'nju:lɪwedz/ *npl* sposini *mpl*

new moon *n* luna *f* nuova

newness /'nju:nɪs/ *n* novità *f*

news /nju:z/ *n* notizie *fpl; TV* telegiornale *m; Radio* giornale *m* radio; **piece of** ~ notizia *f*

news: news agency *n* agenzia *f* di stampa. **newsagent's** *n Br* giornalaio *m* (*che vende anche tabacchi, caramelle ecc*). **news bulletin** *n* notiziario *m.* **newscast** *n Am* notiziario *m.* **newscaster** *n* giornalista *mf* televisivo, -a/radiofonico, -a. **news conference** *n* conferenza *f* stampa *inv.* **newsdealer** *n Am* giornalaio, -a *mf.* **news desk** *n* (*at newspaper*) redazione *f.* **news editor** *n* caporedattore, -trice *mf* di servizi di cronaca. **newsflash** *n* notizia *f* flash. **news headlines** *npl TV* titoli *mpl* delle principali notizie. **news item** *n* notizia *f* di attualità. **newsletter** *n* bollettino *m* d'informazione

newspaper /'nju:zpeɪpə(r)/ *n* giornale *m;* (*material*) carta *f* di giornale

newspaper: newspaperman *n* giornalista *m.* **newspaper office** *n* ufficio *m* della redazione. **newspaperwoman** *n* giornalista *f*

newspeak /'nju:spi:k/ *n Am* politichese *m*

news: newsprint *n* (*paper*) carta *f* da giornale; (*ink*) inchiostro *m* di stampa. **newsreader** *n* giornalista *mf* televisivo, -a/radiofonico, -a. **newsroom** *n* redazione *f.* **news sheet** *n* bollettino *m.* **newsstand** *n* edicola *f.* **news value** *n* interesse *m* mediatico. **newsworthy** *a* che merita di essere pubblicato

newsy /'nju:zɪ/ *a* 〈*letter*〉 pieno di notizie

newt /nju:t/ *n* tritone *m*

new: new technology *n* nuova technologia *f.* **New Testament** *n* Nuovo Testamento *m.* **new wave** *n & a* new wave *f inv.* **New Year** *n* (*January 1st*) capodanno *m;* (*next year*) l'anno *m* nuovo; **Happy** ~ ~ ! buon anno!; **closed for** ~ ~ chiuso per le feste di capodanno; **see in the** ~ ~ festeggiare il capodanno. **New Year Honours list** *n Br* lista *f* delle persone che ricevono decorazioni il 1 gennaio. **New Year's Day** *n* Capodanno *m.* **New Year's Eve** *n* vigilia *f* di Capodanno. **New Year's resolution** *n* proposito *m* per l'anno nuovo. **New Zealand** *n* Nuova Zelanda *f.* **New Zealander** *n* neozelandese *mf*

next /nekst/ *a* prossimo; (*adjoining*) vicino; **who's** ~? a chi tocca?; **the** ~ **best thing would be to** alternativamente la cosa migliore sarebbe di; ~ **door** accanto; ~ **to nothing** quasi niente; **the** ~ **day** il giorno dopo; ~ **week** la settimana prossima; **the week after** ~ fra due settimane; **the** ~ **thing I knew** la sola cosa che ho saputo dopo ● *adv* dopo; **when will you see him** ~? quando lo rivedi la prossima volta?; ~ **to** accanto a ● *n* seguente *mf;* ~ **of kin** parente *m* prossimo

next door *a* 〈*dog, bell*〉 dei vicini; 〈*office*〉 accanto *inv;* **the girl** ~ *also fig* la ragazza della porta accanto ● *adv* 〈*live, move in*〉 nella casa accanto

next-door neighbour *n* vicino *m* di casa

nexus /'neksəs/ *n* (*network*) rete *f*

NF *n Br Pol abbr* **National Front**

NH *Am abbr* **New Hampshire**
NHS *n abbr* **National Health Service**
NI *n Br abbr* (**National Insurance**) previdenza *f* sociale; *abbr* (**Northern Ireland**) Irlanda *f* del Nord
nib /nɪb/ *n* pennino *m*
nibble /'nɪbl/ *vt/i* mordicchiare
∎ **nibble at, nibble on** *vt* = **nibble**
Nicaragua /nɪkə'ræɡjʊə/ *n* Nicaragua *m*
nice /naɪs/ *a* ⟨day, weather, holiday⟩ bello; ⟨person⟩ gentile, simpatico; ⟨food⟩ buono; **it was ~ meeting you** è stato un piacere conoscerla
nicely /'naɪslɪ/ *adv* gentilmente; (*well*) bene
niceties /'naɪsətɪz/ *npl* finezze *fpl*
niche /niːʃ/ *n* nicchia *f*
niche market *n* mercato *m* specializzato
nick /nɪk/ *n* tacca *f*; (on chin etc) taglietto *m*; (*fam: prison*) galera *f*; (*fam: police station*) centrale *f* [di polizia]; **in the ~ of time** *fam* appena in tempo; **in good ~** *fam* in buono stato ● *vt* intaccare; (*fam: steal*) fregare; (*fam: arrest*) beccare; **~ one's chin** farsi un taglietto nel mento
nickel /'nɪkl/ *n* nichel *m*; *Am* moneta *f* da cinque centesimi
nickel-and-dime *a Am fam* da quattro soldi
nickelodeon /nɪkəl'əʊdɪən/ *n* (*Am: juke box*) juke box *m inv*
nickname /'nɪkneɪm/ *n* soprannome *m* ● *vt* soprannominare
nicotine /'nɪkəti:n/ *n* nicotina *f*
niece /ni:s/ *n* nipote *f*
nifty /'nɪftɪ/ *a fam* (*skilful*) geniale; (*attractive*) sfizioso
Nigeria /naɪ'dʒɪərɪə/ *n* Nigeria *f*
Nigerian /naɪ'dʒɪərɪən/ *a & n* nigeriano, -a *mf*
niggardly /'nɪɡədlɪ/ *a* ⟨person⟩ tirchio; ⟨salary⟩ misero
niggle /'nɪɡl/ *fam n* (*complaint*) cosetta *f* da ridire ● *vi* (*complain*) lamentarsi in continuazione ● *vt* (*irritate*) dar fastidio a
niggling /'nɪɡlɪŋ/ *a* ⟨detail⟩ insignificante; ⟨pain⟩ fastidioso; ⟨doubt⟩ persistente
night /naɪt/ *n* notte *f*; (*evening*) sera *f*; **at ~** la notte, di notte; (*in the evening*) la sera, di sera; **Monday ~** lunedì notte/sera; **work ~s** lavorare la notte ● *a* di notte
night: **nightcap** *n* papalina *f*; (*drink*) bicchierino *m* bevuto prima di andare a letto. **nightclub** *n* locale *m* notturno, night[-club] *m inv.* **nightclubbing** *n* **go ~** andare nei night [club]. **nightdress** *n* camicia *f* da notte. **nightfall** *n* crepuscolo *m*. **nightgown,** *fam* **nightie** *n* camicia *f* da notte. **nightlife** *n* vita *f* notturna. **night light** *n* lumino *m* da notte
nightly /'naɪtlɪ/ *a* di notte, di sera ● *adv* ogni notte, ogni sera
nightmare /'naɪtmeə(r)/ *n also fig* incubo *m*
nightmarish /'naɪtmeərɪʃ/ *a* da incubo
night: **night owl** nottambulo, -a *mf*. **night porter** *n* portiere *m* di notte. **night school** scuola *f* serale. **nightshade** *n Bot* **deadly ~**

belladonna *f*. **night shelter** *n* dormitorio *m* pubblico. **nightshift** *n* (*workers*) turno *m* di notte; **be on the ~** fare il turno di notte.
nightshirt *n* camicia *f* da notte (*da uomo*).
nightspot *n* night club *m inv.* **nightstand** *n Am* comodino *m.* **nightstick** *n* (*Am: truncheon*) manganello *m.* **night-time** *n* **at ~** di notte, la notte. **night vision** *n* visione *f* notturna. **nightwatchman** *n* guardiano *m* notturno. **nightwear** *n* indumenti *mpl* da notte
nil /nɪl/ *n* nulla *m*; *Sport* zero *m*
Nile /naɪl/ *n* Nilo *m*
nimble /'nɪmbl/ *a* agile
nimbly /'nɪmblɪ/ *adv* agilmente
nincompoop /'nɪŋkəmpu:p/ *n fam* scemo *m*
nine /naɪn/ *a & n* nove *m*
ninepin /'naɪnpɪn/ *n* birillo *m*; **be falling like ~s** ⟨troops, guards, candidates:⟩ cadere come le mosche
nineteen /naɪn'ti:n/ *a & n* diciannove *m*
nineteenth /naɪn'ti:nθ/ *a & n* diciannovesimo, -a *mf*
ninetieth /'naɪntɪɪθ/ *a & n* novantesimo, -a *mf*
nine-to-five *a* ⟨job⟩ in un ufficio; ⟨routine⟩ dell'ufficio ● *adv* ⟨work⟩ dalle nove alle cinque
ninety /'naɪntɪ/ *a & n* novanta *m*
ninth /naɪnθ/ *a & n* nono, -a *mf*
nip /nɪp/ *n* pizzicotto *m*; (*bite*) morso *m* ● *vt* pizzicare; (*bite*) mordere; **~ in the bud** *fig* stroncare sul nascere ● *vi* (*fam: run*) fare un salto
nipper /'nɪpə(r)/ *n fam* ragazzino, -a *mf*
nipple /'nɪpl/ *n* capezzolo *m*; (*Am: on bottle*) tettarella *f*
nippy /'nɪpɪ/ *a* (**-ier, -iest**) *fam* (*cold*) pungente; (*quick*) svelto
nit /nɪt/ *n* (*egg*) lendine *m*; (*larva*) larva *f* di pidocchio
nit-pick *vi* cercare il pelo nell'uovo
nitrate /'naɪtreɪt/ *n* nitrato *m*
nitric /'naɪtrɪk/ *a* nitrico
nitrogen /'naɪtrədʒn/ *n* azoto *m*
nitty-gritty /nɪtɪ'ɡrɪtɪ/ *n fam* **the ~** il nocciolo [della questione]; **get down to the ~** arrivare al dunque
nitwit /'nɪtwɪt/ *n fam* imbecille *mf*
NJ *Am abbr* **New Jersey**
NM *Am abbr* **New Mexico**
no /nəʊ/ *adv* no ● *n* (*pl* **noes**) no *m invar* ● *a* nessuno; **I have no time** non ho tempo; **in no time** in un baleno; **'no parking'** 'sosta vietata'; **'no smoking'** 'vietato fumare'; **it's no go** è inutile; **no one** = **nobody**
no., No. *abbr* (**number**) No.
Noah /'nəʊə/ *n* Noè *m*; **~'s Ark** l'arca *f* di Noè
nobility /nəʊ'bɪlətɪ/ *n* nobiltà *f*
noble /'nəʊbl/ *a* nobile
nobleman /'nəʊblmən/ *n* nobile *m*
noble-minded /-'maɪndɪd/ *a* di animo nobile
noble savage *n* buon selvaggio *m*
nobly /'nəʊblɪ/ *adv* (*selflessly*) generosamente; **~ born** di nobili natali

nobody /'nəʊbədɪ/ *pron* nessuno; **he knows ~** non conosce nessuno; **he's ~ important** non è nessuno d'importante ● *n* **he's a ~** non è nessuno

no claims bonus *n* abbuono *m* in assenza di sinistri

nocturnal /nɒk'tɜ:nl/ *a* notturno

nod /nɒd/ *n* cenno *m* del capo; **give a ~** fare un cenno col capo ● *v* (*pt/pp* **nodded**) ● *vi* fare un cenno col capo; (*in agreement*) fare di sì col capo ● *vt* **~ one's head** fare di sì col capo

■ **nod off** *vi* assopirsi

node /nəʊd/ *n* nodo *m*

nodule /'nɒdju:l/ *n* nodulo *m*

no-go *a fam* **it's ~** non è possibile

no-go area *n* quartiere *m* caldo in cui la polizia può accedere solo con la forza

no-hoper /nəʊ'həʊpə(r)/ *n* persona *f* senza prospettive

noise /nɔɪz/ *n* rumore *m*; (*loud*) rumore *m*, chiasso *m*

noiseless /'nɔɪzlɪs/ *a* silenzioso

noiselessly /'nɔɪzlɪslɪ/ *adv* silenziosamente

noise level *n* intensità *f inv* del rumore

noise pollution *n* inquinamento *m* da rumore

noisily /'nɔɪzɪlɪ/ *adv* rumorosamente

noisy /'nɔɪzɪ/ *a* (**-ier, -iest**) rumoroso

nomad /'nəʊmæd/ *n* nomade *mf*

nomadic /nəʊ'mædɪk/ *a* nomade

nominal /'nɒmɪnl/ *a* nominale

nominally /'nɒmɪnəlɪ/ *adv* nominalmente

nominate /'nɒmɪneɪt/ *vt* proporre come candidato; (*appoint*) designare

nomination /nɒmɪ'neɪʃn/ *n* nomina *f*; (*person nominated*) candidato, -a *mf*

nominative /'nɒmɪnətɪv/ *a & n Gram* **~** [**case**] nominativo *m*

nominee /nɒmɪ'ni:/ *n* persona *f* nominata

non+ /nɒn/ *pref* non+, in+

non-academic *a* (*course*) pratico; (*staff*) non insegnante

non-addictive *a* che non dà assuefazione

non-alcoholic *a* analcolico

non-attendance *n* mancata presenza *f*

non-believer *n* non credente *mf*

nonchalant /'nɒnʃələnt/ *a* disinvolto

nonchalantly /'nɒnʃələntlɪ/ *adv* in modo disinvolto

non-classified *a* (*information*) non confidenziale

non-combustible *a* incombustibile

non-commercial *a* (*event, activity*) senza fini di lucro

non-commissioned /-kə'mɪʃnd/ *a* **~ officer** sottufficiale *m*

non-committal /-kə'mɪtəl/ *a* che non si sbilancia

non-compliance *n* (*with standards*) non conformità *f* (**with** a); (*with orders*) inadempienza *f* (**with** a)

nonconformist /nɒnkən'fɔ:mɪst/ *a & n* anticonformista *mf*

non-cooperation *n* non cooperazione *f*

non-denominational /-dɪnɒmɪ'neɪʃənəl/ *a* (*church*) ecumenico; (*school*) laico

nondescript /'nɒndɪskrɪpt/ *a* qualunque

none /nʌn/ *pron* (*person*) nessuno; (*thing*) niente; **~ of us** nessuno di noi; **~ of this** niente di questo; **there's ~ left** non ce n'è più ● *adv* **she's ~ too pleased** non è per niente soddisfatta; **I'm ~ the wiser** non ne so più di prima

non-EC *a* (*national*) extracomunitario; (*country*) che non appartiene alla Comunità Europea

nonentity /nɒ'nentətɪ/ *n* nullità *f inv*

non-essentials /-ɪ'senʃlz/ *npl* (*details*) dettagli *mpl*; (*objects*) cose *fpl* accessorie

nonetheless /nʌnðə'les/ *adv* = **nevertheless**

non-event *n* delusione *f*

non-existent *a* inesistente

non-family *a* al di fuori della famiglia

non-fat *a* magro; (*diet*) senza grassi

non-fiction *n* saggistica *f*

non-flammable *a* non infiammabile

non-fulfilment *n* (*of contract, obligation*) inadempienza *f* (**of** a); (*of desire*) inappagamento *m*

non-infectious *a* non infettivo

non-iron *a* che non si stira

non-judgmental *a* imparziale

non-league *a Sport* fuori campionato

no-no *n fam* cosa *f* proibita; **that's a ~** è un argomento tabù

no-nonsense *a* (*manner, attitude*) diretto; (*tone*) spiccio; (*look, policy*) pratico; (*person*) franco

non-partisan *a* imparziale

non-party *a* (*issue, decision*) apartitico; (*person*) indipendente

non-person *n* (*insignificant person*) nullità *f inv*; **officially, he is a ~** *Pol* ufficialmente non è mai esistito

nonplussed /nɒn'plʌst/ *a* perplesso

non-professional *a* dilettante

non-profit-making /-'prɒfɪtmeɪkɪŋ/ *a* (*organization*) senza fini di lucro

non-redeemable *a Fin* vincolato

non-refillable *a* (*lighter, pen*) non ricaricabile; (*can, bottle*) non riutilizzabile

non-religious *a* laico

non-resident *a* (*job, course*) non residenziale; *Comput* che non risiede in permanenza nella memoria centrale ● *n* non residente *mf*

non-residential *a* (*guest*) di passaggio; (*student, visitor*) non residente; (*caretaker*) che non alloggia sul posto; (*area*) non residenziale

non-returnable *a* (*bottle*) a perdere

non-segregated *a* (*area*) non segregato; (*society*) non segregazionista

nonsense /'nɒnsəns/ *n* sciocchezze *fpl*

nonsensical /nɒn'sensɪkl/ *a* assurdo

non sequitur /nɒn'sekwɪtə(r)/ *n* affermazione *f* senza legame con quanto detto prima

non-skid *a* antiscivolo *inv*

non-smoker *n* non fumatore, -trice *mf*;

(*compartment*) scompartimento *m* non fumatori

non-specialized *a* non specializzato

non-starter *n* be a ~ ⟨*person*:⟩ non avere nessuna probabilità di riuscita; ⟨*plan, idea*:⟩ essere destinato al fallimento

non-stick *a* antiaderente

non-stop *a* ⟨*talk, work, pressure, noise*⟩ continuo; ⟨*train*⟩ diretto; ⟨*journey*⟩ senza fermate; ⟨*flight*⟩ senza scalo ● *adv* ⟨*work, talk*⟩ senza sosta; ⟨*travel, fly*⟩ senza scalo

non-swimmer *n* persona *f* che non sa nuotare

non-taxable *a* non imponibile

non-union *a* ⟨*person*⟩ non iscritto a un sindacato; ⟨*company*⟩ non sindacalizzato

non-violent *a* non violento

non-white, non-White *n* persona *f* di colore

noodles /'nu:dlz/ *npl* taglierini *mpl*

nook /nʊk/ *n* cantuccio *m*

noon /nu:n/ *n* mezzogiorno *m*; **at** ~ a mezzogiorno

no one *pron* nessuno

noose /nu:s/ *n* nodo *m* scorsoio

nor /nɔ:(r)/ *adv & conj* né; ~ **do I** neppure io

Nordic /'nɔ:dɪk/ *a* nordico

norm /nɔ:m/ *n* norma *f*

normal /'nɔ:ml/ *a* normale

normality /nɔ:'mælətɪ/ *n* normalità *f*

normally /'nɔ:məlɪ/ *adv* (*usually*) normalmente

Norman /'nɔ:mən/ *a* normanno; ⟨*landscape, village*⟩ della Normandia ● *n* normanno *m*

Norse /nɔ:s/ *a* ⟨*mythology, saga*⟩ norreno

north /nɔ:θ/ *n* nord *m*; **to the** ~ **of** a nord di ● *a* del nord, settentrionale ● *adv* a nord

North Africa *n* Africa *f* del Nord

North African *a & n* nordafricano, -a *mf*

North America *n* America *f* del Nord

North American *a & n* nordamericano, -a *mf*

Northants /nɔ:'θænts/ *Br abbr* **Northamptonshire**

northbound /'nɔ:θbaʊnd/ *a* ⟨*traffic, carriageway*⟩ in direzione nord

Northd *Br abbr* **Northumberland**

north: north-east *a* di nord-est, nord-orientale ● *n* nord-est *m* ● *adv* a nord-est; ⟨*travel*⟩ verso nord-est. **north-easterly** *a* ⟨*point*⟩ a nord-est; ⟨*wind*⟩ di nord-est ● *n* vento *m* di nord-est. **northeastern** /nɔ:θ'i:stən/ *a* nordorientale

northerly /'nɔ:ðəlɪ/ *a* ⟨*direction*⟩ nord; ⟨*wind*⟩ del nord

northern /'nɔ:ðən/ *a* del nord, settentrionale

Northern Ireland *n* Irlanda *f* del Nord

Northern Lights *npl* aurora *f* boreale

north: North Pole *n* polo *m* nord. **North Sea** *n* Mare *m* del Nord. **North Star** *n* stella *f* polare

northward[s] /'nɔ:θwəd(z)/ *adv* verso nord

north: north-west *a* di nord-ovest, nordoccidentale ● *n* nord-ovest *m* ● *adv* a nord-ovest; ⟨*travel*⟩ verso nord-ovest. **north-**

westerly *a* ⟨*point*⟩ a nord-ovest; ⟨*wind*⟩ di nord-ovest ● *n* vento *m* di nord-ovest. **north-western** *a* nordoccidentale

Norway /'nɔ:weɪ/ *n* Norvegia *f*

Norwegian /nɔ:'wi:dʒn/ *a & n* norvegese *mf*

nose /nəʊz/ *n* naso *m*

■ **nose about** *vi* curiosare

nosebleed /'nəʊzbli:d/ *n* emorragia *f* nasale

nosedive /'nəʊzdaɪv/ *n* *Aeron* picchiata *f*; **take a** ~ ⟨*fig: prices*:⟩ scendere vertiginosamente

nosey /'nəʊzɪ/ *a* = **nosy**

no-show *n* persona *f* che non si è presentata

nosily /'nəʊzɪlɪ/ *adv* in modo indiscreto

nostalgia /nɒ'stældʒɪə/ *n* nostalgia *f*

nostalgic /nɒ'stældʒɪk/ *a* nostalgico

nostril /'nɒstrəl/ *n* narice *f*

nosy /'nəʊzɪ/ *a* (**-ier, -iest**) *fam* ficcanaso *inv*

not /nɒt/ *adv* non; **he is** ~ **Italian** non è italiano; **I hope** ~ spero di no; ~ **all of us have been invited** non siamo stati tutti invitati; **if** ~ se no; ~ **at all** niente affatto; ~ **a bit** per niente; ~ **even** neanche; ~ **yet** non ancora; **in the** ~ **too distant future** in un futuro non troppo lontano; ~ **only... but also...** non solo... ma anche...

notable /'nəʊtəbl/ *a* (*remarkable*) notevole

notably /'nəʊtəblɪ/ *adv* (*in particular*) in particolare

notary /'nəʊtərɪ/ *n* notaio *m*; ~ **public** notaio *m*

notation /nəʊ'teɪʃn/ *n* notazione *f*

notch /nɒtʃ/ *n* tacca *f*

■ **notch up** *vt* (*score*) segnare

note /nəʊt/ *n* nota *f*; (*short letter, banknote*) biglietto *m*; (*memo, written comment etc*) appunto *m*; **of** ~ ⟨*person*⟩ di spicco; ⟨*comments, event*⟩ degno di nota; **make a** ~ **of** prendere nota di; **take** ~ **of** (*notice*) prendere nota di ● *vt* (*notice*) notare; (*write*) annotare

■ **note down** *vt* annotare

notebook /'nəʊtbʊk/ *n* taccuino *m*; *Comput* notebook *m inv*

noted /'nəʊtɪd/ *a* noto, celebre (**for** per)

note: notepad *n* blocco *m* per appunti. **notepaper** *n* carta *f* da lettere. **noteworthy** *a* degno di nota

nothing /'nʌθɪŋ/ *pron* niente, nulla ● *adv* niente affatto; **for** ~ (*free, in vain*) per niente; (*with no reason*) senza motivo; ~ **but** nient'altro che; ~ **much** poco o nulla; ~ **interesting** niente di interessante; **it's** ~ **to do with you** non ti riguarda

notice /'nəʊtɪs/ *n* (*on board*) avviso *m*; (*review*) recensione *f*; (*termination of employment*) licenziamento *m*; [**advance**] ~ preavviso *m*; **two months'** ~ due mesi di preavviso; **at short** ~ con breve preavviso; **until further** ~ fino nuovo avviso; **give** [**in one's**] ~ ⟨*employee*:⟩ dare le dimissioni; **give an employee** ~ dare il preavviso a un impiegato; **take no** ~ **of** non fare caso a; **take no** ~! non farci caso! ● *vt* notare

noticeable /'nəʊtɪsəbl/ *a* evidente

noticeably /'nəʊtɪsəblɪ/ *adv* sensibilmente

noticeboard /'nəʊtɪsbɔːd/ n bacheca f
notification /nəʊtɪfɪ'keɪʃn/ n notifica f
notify /'nəʊtɪfaɪ/ vt (pt/pp -ied) notificare
notion /'nəʊʃn/ n idea f, nozione f; **he hasn't the slightest ~ of time** gli manca completamente la nozione del tempo; **~s** pl (Am: haberdashery) merceria f
notoriety /nəʊtə'raɪətɪ/ n notorietà f
notorious /nəʊ'tɔːrɪəs/ a famigerato; **be ~ for** essere tristemente famoso per
notoriously /nəʊ'tɔːrɪəslɪ/ adv **they're ~ unreliable** tutti sanno che su di loro non si può mai fare affidamento
Notts /nɒts/ Br abbr **Nottinghamshire**
notwithstanding /nɒtwɪð'stændɪŋ/ prep malgrado ● adv ciononostante
nougat /'nʌɡət/ n torrone m
nought /nɔːt/ n zero m
noughts and crosses n tris m
noun /naʊn/ n nome m, sostantivo m
nourish /'nʌrɪʃ/ vt nutrire
nourishing /'nʌrɪʃɪŋ/ a nutriente
nourishment /'nʌrɪʃmənt/ n nutrimento m
novel /'nɒvl/ a insolito ● n romanzo m
novelette /nɒvə'let/ n (oversentimental) romanzetto m rosa
novelist /'nɒvəlɪst/ n romanziere, -a mf
novelty /'nɒvltɪ/ n novità f; **novelties** pl (objects) oggettini mpl
November /nəʊ'vembə(r)/ n novembre m
novice /'nɒvɪs/ n novizio, -a mf
now /naʊ/ adv ora, adesso; **by ~** ormai; **just ~** proprio ora; **right ~** subito; **~ and again, ~ and then** ogni tanto; **~, ~!** su! ● conj **~ [that]** ora che, adesso che
nowadays /'naʊədeɪz/ adv oggigiorno
nowhere /'nəʊweə(r)/ adv in nessun posto, da nessuna parte
noxious /'nɒkʃəs/ a nocivo
nozzle /'nɒzl/ n bocchetta f
nr abbr near
NSPCC n Br abbr (**National Society for the Prevention of Cruelty to Children**) Società f nazionale per la protezione dell'infanzia
NT abbr **New Testament**
nth /enθ/ a Math, fig **to the ~ power/degree** all'ennesima potenza; **for the ~ time** per l'ennesima volta
nuance /'njuːɒs/ n sfumatura f
nub /nʌb/ n **the ~ of the matter** il nocciolo della questione
nubile /'njuːbaɪl/ a ⟨attractive⟩ desiderabile
nuclear /'njuːklɪə(r)/ a nucleare
nuclear: nuclear bomb n bomba f atomica. **nuclear deterrent** n deterrente m nucleare. **nuclear energy** n energia f nucleare. **nuclear-free zone** n Br zona f denuclearizzata. **nuclear physics** n fisica f nucleare. **nuclear power** n (energy) energia f nucleare; (country) potenza f nucleare. **nuclear power station** n centrale f nucleare. **nuclear shelter** n rifugio m antiatomico
nucleus /'njuːklɪəs/ n (pl -lei /'njuːklɪaɪ/) nucleo m

nude /njuːd/ a nudo ● n nudo m; **in the ~** nudo
nudge /nʌdʒ/ n colpetto m di gomito ● vt dare un colpetto col gomito a
nudism /'njuːdɪzm/ n nudismo m
nudist /'njuːdɪst/ n nudista mf
nudity /'njuːdətɪ/ n nudità f
nugget /'nʌɡɪt/ n pepita f
nuisance /'njuːsəns/ n seccatura f; (person) piaga f; **what a ~!** che seccatura!
nuisance call n Teleph telefonata f anonima
null /nʌl/ a **~ and void** nullo
nullify /'nʌlɪfaɪ/ vt (pt/pp -ied) annullare
numb /nʌm/ a intorpidito; **~ with cold** intirizzito dal freddo ● vt intorpidire
number /'nʌmbə(r)/ n numero m; **a ~ of people** un certo numero di persone ● vt numerare; (include) annoverare
numbering /'nʌmbərɪŋ/ n numerazione f
number one n (most important) numero uno m; **look after ~** (oneself) pensare prima di tutto a se stessi
number plate n targa f
numeracy /'njuːmərəsɪ/ n **improve standards of ~** migliorare il livello nel calcolo
numeral /'njuːmərəl/ n numero m, cifra f
numerate /'njuːmərət/ a **be ~** saper fare i calcoli
numerical /njuː'merɪkl/ a numerico; **in ~ order** in ordine numerico
numerically /njuː'merɪklɪ/ adv numericamente
numeric keypad /njuː'merɪk/ n Comput tastierino m numerico
numerous /'njuːmərəs/ a numeroso
nun /nʌn/ n suora f
nuptial /'nʌpʃl/ a nuziale ● **~s** npl nozze fpl
nurse /nɜːs/ n infermiere, -a mf; **children's ~** bambinaia f ● vt curare
nursery /'nɜːsərɪ/ n stanza f dei bambini; (for plants) vivaio m; **[day] ~** asilo m
nursery: nursery rhyme n filastrocca f. **nursery school** n scuola f materna. **nursery slope** n Br pista f per principianti
nurse's aid n Am aiuto infermiere, -a mf
nursing /'nɜːsɪŋ/ n professione f d'infermiere
nursing auxiliary n Br aiuto infermiere, -a mf
nursing home n casa f di cura per anziani
nurture /'nɜːtʃə(r)/ vt allevare; fig coltivare
nut /nʌt/ n noce f; Techn dado m; (fam: head) zucca f
nutcrackers /'nʌtkrækəz/ npl schiaccianoci m inv
nutmeg /'nʌtmeg/ n noce f moscata
nutrient /'njuːtrɪənt/ n sostanza f nutritiva
nutrition /njuː'trɪʃn/ n nutrizione f
nutritionist /njuː'trɪʃənɪst/ n nutrizionista mf
nutritious /njuː'trɪʃəs/ a nutriente
nuts /nʌts/ npl frutta f secca; **be ~** fam essere svitato

nutshell /'nʌtʃel/ n guscio m di noce; **in a ~** *fig* in parole povere

nuzzle /'nʌzl/ vt ⟨horse, dog:⟩ strofinare il muso contro

NV Am abbr **Nevada**

NW abbr (**north-west**) NO

NY Am abbr **New York**

NYC Am abbr **New York City**

nylon /'naɪlɒn/ n nailon m; **~s** pl calze fpl di nailon ● attrib di nailon

nymph /nɪmf/ n ninfa f

nymphomaniac /nɪmfə'meɪnɪæk/ n ninfomane f ● a da ninfomane

NZ abbr **New Zealand**

o, O /əʊ/ n (letter) o, O f inv

O /əʊ/ n Teleph zero m

oaf /əʊf/ n (pl **oafs**) zoticone, -a mf

oak /əʊk/ n quercia f ● attrib di quercia

OAP abbr (**old-age pensioner**) pensionato, -a mf

oar /ɔ:(r)/ n remo m

oarsman /'ɔ:zmən/ n vogatore m

oasis /əʊ'eɪsɪs/ n (pl **oases** /əʊ'eɪsi:z/) oasi f inv

oatcake /'əʊtkeɪk/ n galletta f di avena

oath /əʊθ/ n giuramento m; (swear-word) bestemmia f

oatmeal /'əʊtmi:l/ n farina f d'avena

oats /əʊts/ npl avena fsg; Culin [**rolled**] **~** fiocchi mpl di avena

obdurate /'ɒbdjʊrət/ a (stubborn) irremovibile; (hardhearted) insensibile

OBE n Br abbr (**Officer of the (Order of the) British Empire**) onorificenza f britannica

obedience /ə'bi:dɪəns/ n ubbidienza f

obedient /ə'bi:dɪənt/ a ubbidiente

obediently /ə'bi:dɪəntlɪ/ adv ubbidientemente

obelisk /'ɒbəlɪsk/ n obelisco m

obese /ə'bi:s/ a obeso

obesity /ə'bi:sətɪ/ n obesità f

obey /ə'beɪ/ vt ubbidire a; osservare ⟨instructions, rules⟩ ● vi ubbidire

obituary /ə'bɪtjʊərɪ/ n necrologio m

object[1] /'ɒbdʒɪkt/ n oggetto m; Gram complemento m oggetto; **money is no ~** i soldi non sono un problema

object[2] /əb'dʒekt/ vi (be against) opporsi (**to** a); **~ that...** obiettare che...

objection /əb'dʒekʃn/ n obiezione f; **have no ~** non avere niente in contrario

objectionable /əb'dʒekʃ(ə)nəbl/ a discutibile; ⟨person⟩ sgradevole

objective /əb'dʒektɪv/ a oggettivo ● n obiettivo m

objectively /əb'dʒektɪvlɪ/ adv obiettivamente

objectivity /ɒbdʒek'tɪvətɪ/ n oggettività f

objector /əb'dʒektə(r)/ n oppositore, -trice mf

obligation /ɒblɪ'geɪʃn/ n obbligo m; **be**

under an ~ avere un obbligo; **without ~** senza impegno

obligatory /ə'blɪgətrɪ/ a obbligatorio

oblige /ə'blaɪdʒ/ vt (compel) obbligare; (do a small service for) fare una cortesia a; **much ~d** grazie mille

obliging /ə'blaɪdʒɪŋ/ a disponibile

oblique /ə'bli:k/ a obliquo; fig indiretto. **~ [stroke]** n barra f

obliterate /ə'blɪtəreɪt/ vt obliterare

obliteration /əblɪtə'reɪʃn/ n (of mark, memory) rimozione f; (of city) annientamento m

oblivion /ə'blɪvɪən/ n oblio m

oblivious /ə'blɪvɪəs/ a **be ~** essere dimentico (**of, to** di)

oblong /'ɒblɒŋ/ a oblungo ● n rettangolo m

obnoxious /əb'nɒkʃəs/ a detestabile

oboe /'əʊbəʊ/ n oboe m inv

obscene /əb'si:n/ a osceno; ⟨profits, wealth⟩ vergognoso

obscenity /əb'senətɪ/ n oscenità f inv

obscure /əb'skjʊə(r)/ a oscuro ● vt oscurare; (confuse) mettere in ombra

obscurity /əb'skjʊərətɪ/ n oscurità f

obsequious /əb'si:kwɪəs/ a ossequioso

observable /əb'zɜ:vəbl/ a (discernible) percettibile

observance /əb'zɜ:vəns/ n (of custom) osservanza f

observant /əb'zɜ:vənt/ a attento

observation /ɒbzə'veɪʃn/ n osservazione f

observation car n carrozza f belvedere

observation tower n torre f di osservazione

observatory /əb'zɜ:vətrɪ/ n osservatorio m

observe /əb'zɜ:v/ vt osservare; (notice) notare; (keep, celebrate) celebrare

observer /əb'zɜ:və(r)/ n osservatore, -trice mf

obsess /əb'ses/ vt **be ~ed by** essere fissato con

obsession /əb'seʃn/ n fissazione f

obsessive /əb'sesɪv/ a ossessivo

obsessively /əb'sesɪvlɪ/ adv ossessivamente

obsolescence /ɒbsə'lesəns/ n obsolescenza f; **built-in ~** obsolescenza f programmata

obsolete /'ɒbsəli:t/ a obsoleto; ⟨word⟩ desueto; ⟨idea⟩ sorpassato

obstacle /ˈɒbstəkl/ n ostacolo m
obstacle course n Mil, fig percorso m a ostacoli
obstacle race n corsa f a ostacoli
obstetrician /ɒbstəˈtrɪʃn/ n ostetrico, -a mf
obstetrics /əbˈstetrɪks/ n ostetricia f
obstinacy /ˈɒbstɪnəsɪ/ n ostinazione f
obstinate /ˈɒbstɪnət/ a ostinato
obstinately /ˈɒbstɪnətlɪ/ adv ostinatamente
obstreperous /əbˈstrepərəs/ a turbolento
obstruct /əbˈstrʌkt/ vt ostruire; (hinder) ostacolare
obstruction /əbˈstrʌkʃn/ n ostruzione f; (obstacle) ostacolo m
obstructive /əbˈstrʌktɪv/ a be ~ ⟨person:⟩ creare dei problemi
obtain /əbˈteɪn/ vt ottenere ● vi prevalere
obtainable /əbˈteɪnəbl/ a ottenibile
obtrusive /əbˈtruːsɪv/ a ⟨object⟩ stonato
obtuse /əbˈtjuːs/ a ottuso
obverse /ˈɒbvɜːs/ a the ~ side/face (of coin) l'altra faccia f
obviate /ˈɒbvɪeɪt/ vt fml ovviare a
obvious /ˈɒbvɪəs/ a ovvio
obviously /ˈɒbvɪəslɪ/ adv ovviamente
occasion /əˈkeɪʒn/ n occasione f; (event) evento m; **on** ~ talvolta; **on the** ~ **of** in occasione di ● vt cagionare
occasional /əˈkeɪʒənl/ a saltuario; **he has the** ~ **glass of wine** ogni tanto beve un bicchiere di vino
occasionally /əˈkeɪʒənəlɪ/ adv ogni tanto
occult /ɒˈkʌlt/ a occulto
occupancy /ˈɒkjʊpənsɪ/ n **available for immediate** ~ libero immediatamente; **change of** ~ cambio m di inquilino
occupant /ˈɒkjʊpənt/ n occupante mf; (of vehicle) persona f a bordo
occupation /ɒkjʊˈpeɪʃn/ n occupazione f; (job) professione f
occupational /ɒkjʊˈpeɪʃənl/ a professionale
occupational: occupational hazard n rischio m professionale. **occupational health** n medicina f del lavoro. **occupational pension** n Br pensione f di lavoro. **occupational psychologist** n psicologo, -a mf del lavoro. **occupational therapist** n ergoterapista mf. **occupational therapy** n ergoterapia f
occupier /ˈɒkjʊpaɪə(r)/ n residente mf
occupy /ˈɒkjʊpaɪ/ vt (pt/pp occupied) occupare; (keep busy) tenere occupato
occur /əˈkɜː(r)/ vi (pt/pp occurred) accadere; (exist) trovarsi; **it** ~**red to me that** mi è venuto in mente che
occurrence /əˈkʌrəns/ n (event) fatto m
ocean /ˈəʊʃn/ n oceano m
ocean-going /ˈəʊʃənɡəʊɪŋ/ a ⟨ship⟩ d'alto mare
ochre /ˈəʊkə(r)/ n & a (colour) ocra f
o'clock /əˈklɒk/ adv **it's 7** ~ sono le sette; **at 7** ~ alle sette
octagon /ˈɒktəɡən/ n ottagono m
octagonal /ɒkˈtæɡənl/ a ottagonale

octave /ˈɒktɪv/ n Mus ottava f
octet /ɒkˈtet/ n Mus ottetto m
October /ɒkˈtəʊbə(r)/ n ottobre m
octogenarian /ɒktədʒɪˈneərɪən/ n & a ottantenne mf
octopus /ˈɒktəpəs/ n (pl -puses) polpo m
oculist /ˈɒkjʊlɪst/ oculista mf
OD n abbr (overdose) overdose f inv
odd /ɒd/ a ⟨number⟩ dispari; (not of set) scompagnato; (strange) strano; **forty** ~ quaranta e rotti; ~ **jobs** lavoretti mpl; **the** ~ **one out** l'eccezione f; **at** ~ **moments** a tempo perso; **have the** ~ **glass of wine** avere un bicchiere di vino ogni tanto
oddball /ˈɒdbɔːl/ n fam eccentrico, -a mf
odd bod /ˈɒdbɒd/ n Br fam tipo, -a mf strano, -a
oddity /ˈɒdətɪ/ n stranezza f
odd-job man n tuttofare m inv
oddly /ˈɒdlɪ/ adv stranamente; ~ **enough** stranamente
oddment /ˈɒdmənt/ n (of fabric) scampolo m
odds /ɒdz/ npl (chances) probabilità fpl; **at** ~ in disaccordo; ~ **and ends** cianfrusaglie fpl; **it makes no** ~ non fa alcuna differenza
odds-on a be the ~ **favourite** (in betting) essere il gran favorito; **she has an** ~ **chance of...** ha molte probabilità di...; **it is** ~ **that** è molto probabile che
ode /əʊd/ n ode f
odious /ˈəʊdɪəs/ a odioso
odium /ˈəʊdɪəm/ n odio m
odometer /əʊˈdɒmɪtə(r)/ n Am contachilometri m inv, odometro m
odour /ˈəʊdə(r)/ n odore m
odourless /ˈəʊdəlɪs/ a inodore
odyssey /ˈɒdɪsɪ/ n odissea f
OECD n abbr (Organization for Economic Cooperation and Development) OCSE f
oedema /ɪˈdiːmə/ n edema m
oesophagus /ɪˈsɒfəgəs/ n esofago m
oestrogen /ˈiːstrədʒən/ n estrogeno m
of /ɒv/ prep di; **a cup of tea/coffee** una tazza di tè/caffè; **the hem of my skirt** l'orlo della mia gonna; **the summer of 1989** l'estate del 1989; **the two of us** noi due; **made of** di; **that's very kind of you** è molto gentile da parte tua; **a friend of mine** un mio amico; **a child of three** un bambino di tre anni; **the fourth of January** il quattro gennaio; **within a year of their divorce** a circa un anno dal loro divorzio; **half of it** la metà; **the whole of the room** tutta la stanza
off /ɒf/ prep da; (distant from) lontano da; **take £10** ~ **the price** ridurre il prezzo di 10 sterline; ~ **the coast** presso la costa; **a street** ~ **the main road** una traversa della via principale; (near) una strada vicina alla via principale; **get** ~ **the ladder** scendere dalla scala; **get** ~ **the bus** uscire dall'autobus; **leave the lid** ~ **the saucepan** lasciare la pentola senza il coperchio ● adv ⟨button, handle⟩ staccato; ⟨light, machine⟩ spento; ⟨brake⟩ tolto; ⟨tap⟩ chiuso; **'off'** (on appliance) 'off'; **2 kilometres** ~ a due chilo-

metri di distanza; **a long way** ~ molto distante; (*time*) lontano; ~ **and on** di tanto in tanto; **with his hat/coat** ~ senza il cappotto/ cappello; **with the light** ~ a luce spenta; **20%** ~ 20% di sconto; **be** ~ (*leave*) andar via; *Sport* essere partito; (*food:*) essere andato a male; (*all gone*) essere finito; (*wedding, engagement:*) essere cancellato; **I'm** ~ **drugs/ alcohol** ho smesso di drogarmi/bere; **be** ~ **one's food** non avere appetito; **she's** ~ **today** (*on holiday*) è in ferie oggi; (*ill*) è malata oggi; **I'm** ~ **home** vado a casa; **you'd be better** ~ **doing...** faresti meglio a fare...; **have a day** ~ avere un giorno di vacanza; **drive/sail** ~ andare via

offal /ˈɒfl/ *n Culin* frattaglie *fpl*

offbeat /ˈɒfbiːt/ *a* insolito

off-centre *a Br* fuori centro

off chance *n* **there's an** ~ ~ **that** c'è una remota possibilità che; **just on the** ~ ~ **that** nella remota possibilità che

off colour *a* (*not well*) giù di forma; (*joke, story*) sporco

offence /əˈfens/ *n* (*illegal act*) reato *m*; **give** ~ offendere; **take** ~ offendersi (**at** per)

offend /əˈfend/ *vt* offendere

offender /əˈfendə(r)/ *n Jur* colpevole *mf*

offensive /əˈfensɪv/ *a* offensivo ● *n* offensiva *f*; **go on the** ~ passare all'offensiva

offer /ˈɒfə(r)/ *n* offerta *f*; **on special** ~ in offerta speciale ● *vt* offrire; opporre (*resistance*); ~ **sb sth** offrire qcsa a qcno; ~ **to do sth** offrirsi di fare qcsa

offering /ˈɒfərɪŋ/ *n* offerta *f*

offer price *n Comm* prezzo *m* d'offerta

offertory /ˈɒfətrɪ/ *n Relig* offertorio *m*

offhand /ɒfˈhænd/ *a* (*casual*) spiccio ● *adv* su due piedi

office /ˈɒfɪs/ *n* ufficio *m*; (*post, job*) carica *f*

office: office automation *n* burotica *f*. **office block** *n Br* complesso *m* di uffici. **office building** *n Br* complesso *m* di uffici. **office hours** *npl* orario *m* di ufficio. **office junior** *n* fattorino, -a *mf*. **office politics** *n* intrighi *mpl* di ufficio

officer /ˈɒfɪsə(r)/ *n* ufficiale *m*; (*police*) agente *m* [di polizia]

office worker *n* impiegato, -a *mf*

official /əˈfɪʃl/ *a* ufficiale ● *n* funzionario, -a *mf*; *Sport* dirigente *m*

officialdom /əˈfɪʃəldəm/ *n* burocrazia *f*

officially /əˈfɪʃəlɪ/ *adv* ufficialmente

officiate /əˈfɪʃɪeɪt/ *vi* officiare

officious /əˈfɪʃəs/ *a* autoritario

officiously /əˈfɪʃəslɪ/ *adv* in modo autoritario

offing /ˈɒfɪŋ/ *n* **in the** ~ in vista

off-key *a Mus* stonato

off-licence *n* negozio *m* per la vendita di alcolici

off-limits *a* off-limits *inv*

off-line *a Comput* fuori linea *inv*, off-line *inv*

offload /ɒfˈləʊd/ *vt* scaricare

off-peak *a* (*travel*) fuori dagli orari di punta; (*electricity*) a tariffa notturna ridotta; ~ **call** *Teleph* telefonata *f* a tariffa ridotta

offprint /ˈɒfprɪnt/ *n* estratto *m*

off-putting /-ˈpʊtɪŋ/ *a fam* scoraggiante

off-screen *a* (*voice, action*) fuoricampo *inv*; (*relationship*) nella vita privata ● *adv* nella vita privata

off-season *a* (*losses*) di bassa stagione; (*cruise*) in bassa stagione

offset /ˈɒfset/ *vt* (*pt/pp* -**set**, *pres p* -**setting**) controbilanciare

offset printing *n* offset *m inv*

offshoot /ˈɒfʃuːt/ *n* ramo *m*; *fig* diramazione *f*

offshore /ˈɒfʃɔː(r)/ *a* (*wind*) di terra; (*company, investment*) offshore *inv*

offside /ɒfˈsaɪd/ *a Sport* [in] fuori gioco; (*wheel etc*) (*left*) sinistro; (*right*) destro

offspring /ˈɒfsprɪŋ/ *n* prole *m*

off-stage *adv* dietro le quinte

off-the-cuff *a* (*remark*) spontaneo; (*speech*) improvvisato

off-the-peg *a* (*garment*) prêt-à-porter *inv*, confezionato

off-the-shelf *a Comm* standard *inv*

off-the-shoulder *a* (*dress*) senza bretelle

off-the-wall *a* (*fam: sense of humour*) strano

off-white *a* bianco sporco

often /ˈɒfn/ *adv* spesso; **how** ~ ogni quanto; **every so** ~ una volta ogni tanto

ogle /ˈəʊgl/ *vt* mangiarsi con gli occhi

ogre /ˈəʊgə(r)/ *n* orco *m*

oh /əʊ/ *int* oh!; **oh dear** oh Dio!

OHMS *Br abbr* (**On Her/His Majesty's Service**) *abbreviazione f apposta su corrispondenza ufficiale del governo*

oil /ɔɪl/ *n* olio *m*; (*petroleum*) petrolio *m*; (*for heating*) nafta *f* ● *vt* oliare

oil: oil-burning *a* (*stove, boiler*) a nafta. **oil can** *n* (*applicator*) oliatore *m*. **oil change** *n* cambio *m* dell'olio. **oilcloth** *n* tela *f* cerata. **oilfield** *n* giacimento *m* di petrolio. **oil filter** *n* filtro *m* dell'olio. **oil-fired** /-faɪəd/ *a* (*furnace, heating*) a nafta. **oil gauge** *n* indicatore *m* [del livello] dell'olio. **oil heater** *n* stufa *f* a nafta. **oil lamp** *n* lampada *f* a olio. **oil paint** *n* colore *m* a olio. **oil painting** *n* pittura *f* a olio. **oil pipeline** *n* oleodotto *m*. **oil pressure** *n* pressione *f* dell'olio. **oil-producing** /-prədjuːsɪŋ/ *a* (*country*) produttore di petrolio. **oil refinery** *n* raffineria *f* di petrolio. **oil rig** *n* piattaforma *f* petrolifera, offshore *m inv*. **oilskins** *npl* vestiti *mpl* di tela cerata. **oil slick** *n* chiazza *f* di petrolio. **oil spill** *n* fuoriuscita *f* di petrolio. **oil stove** *n* stufa *f* a nafta. **oil tank** *n* (*domestic*) serbatoio *m* della nafta; (*industrial*) cisterna *f* della nafta. **oil tanker** *n* petroliera *f*. **oil well** *n* pozzo *m* petrolifero

oily /ˈɔɪlɪ/ *a* (-**ier**, -**iest**) unto; *fig* untuoso

ointment /ˈɔɪntmənt/ *n* pomata *f*

OK /əʊˈkeɪ/ *int* va bene, o.k. ● *a* **if that's OK with you** se ti va bene; **she's OK** (*well*) sta bene; **is the milk still OK?** il latte è ancora buono? ● *adv* (*well*) bene ● *vt* (*anche* **okay**) (*pt/pp* **OK'd, okayed**) dare l'o.k. a

old /əʊld/ *a* vecchio; (*girlfriend*) ex; **how ~ is she?** quanti anni ha?; **she is ten years ~** ha dieci anni

old: old age *n* vecchiaia *f*. **old-age pension** *n Br* pensione *f* di vecchiaia. **old-age pensioner** *n* pensionato, -a *mf*. **old boy** *n Sch* ex-allievo *m*. **old country** *n* paese *m* d'origine

olden /'əʊldən/ *a* **the ~ days** i tempi andati

old-established /-ɪ'stæblɪʃt/ *a* di lunga data

olde-worlde /əʊldɪ'wɜːldɪ/ *a hum* dall'aria falsamente antica

old: old-fashioned /-'fæʃ(ə)nd/ *a* antiquato. **old favourite** *n* (*book, play*) classico *m*; (*song, film*) vecchio successo *m*. **old flame** *n fam* vecchia fiamma *f*. **old girl** *n* ex-allieva *f*. **Old Glory** *n* bandiera *f* statunitense. **old hand** *n* **be an ~ ~ at sth/at doing sth** saperci fare con qcsa/a fare qcsa. **old hat** *a fam* **be ~ ~** essere roba vecchia

oldie /'əʊldɪ/ *n* (*person*) vecchio, -a *mf*; (*film, song*) vecchio successo *m*

old: old lady *n* (*elderly woman*) signora *f* anziana; **my ~ ~** (*mother*) la mia vecchia; (*wife*) la mia signora. **old maid** *n* zitella *f*. **old man** *n* (*elderly man*) uomo *m* anziano; (*old: dear chap*) vecchio *m* mio; **my ~ ~** (*father*) il mio vecchio; (*husband*) mio marito *m*; **the ~ ~** (*boss*) il capo. **old master** *n* (*work*) dipinto *m* antico (*specialmente di un pittore europeo del XIII-XVII secolo*). **old people's home** *n* casa *f* di riposo. **old soldier** *n* (*former soldier*) veterano *m*. **Old Testament** *n* Antico Testamento *m*. **old-time** *a* di un tempo; **~ dancing** ballo *m* liscio. **old-timer** *n* veterano, -a *mf*. **old wives' tale** *n* superstizione *f*. **old woman** *n* (*elderly lady*) donna *f* anziana; **my ~ ~** (*mother*) mia madre *f*; (*wife*) la mia signora; **be an ~ ~** (*pej: man:*) essere una donnicciola

olive /'ɒlɪv/ *n* (*fruit, colour*) oliva *f*; (*tree*) olivo *m* ● *a* d'oliva; (*colour*) olivastro

olive: olive branch *n fig* ramoscello *m* d'olivo. **olive grove** *n* oliveto *m*. **olive oil** *n* olio *m* di oliva. **olive-skinned** /-'skɪnd/ *a* olivastro

Olympic /ə'lɪmpɪk/ *a* olimpico

Olympic Games, Olympics *npl* Olimpiadi *fpl*

ombudsman /'ɒmbʊdzmən/ *n* difensore *m* civico

omelette /'ɒmlɪt/ *n* omelette *f inv*

omen /'əʊmən/ *n* presagio *m*

ominous /'ɒmməs/ *a* sinistro

omission /ə'mɪʃn/ *n* omissione *f*

omit /ə'mɪt/ *vt* (*pt/pp* **omitted**) omettere; **~ to do sth** tralasciare di fare qcsa

omnibus /'ɒmnɪbəs/ *n* (*bus*) omnibus *m inv*

omnibus edition *n Br TV* replica *f* delle puntate precedenti

omnipotent /ɒm'nɪpətənt/ *a* onnipotente

on /ɒn/ *prep* su; (*on horizontal surface*) su, sopra; **on Monday** lunedì; **on Mondays** di lu-

nedì; **on the first of May** il primo di maggio; **on arriving** all'arrivo; **on one's finger** nel dito; **on foot** a piedi; **on the right/left** a destra/sinistra; **on the Rhine/Thames** sul Reno/Tamigi; **on the radio/television** alla radio/televisione; **on the bus/train** in autobus/treno; **go on the bus/train** andare in autobus/treno; **get on the bus/train** salire sull'autobus/sul treno; **on me** (*with me*) con me; **it's on me** *fam* tocca a me ● *adv* (*further on*) dopo; (*switched on*) acceso; (*brake*) inserito; (*in operation*) in funzione; **'on'** (*on machine*) 'on'; **he had his hat/coat on** portava il cappello/cappotto; **without his hat/coat on** senza cappello/capotto; **with/without the lid on** con/senza coperchio; **be on** (*film, programme, event:*) esserci; **it's not on** *fam* non è giusto; **be on at** *fam* tormentare (**to** per); **on and on** senza sosta; **on and off** a intervalli; **and so on** e così via; **go on** continuare; **stick on** attaccare; **sew on** cucire

once /wʌns/ *adv* una volta; (*formerly*) un tempo; **~ upon a time there was** c'era una volta; **at ~** subito; (*at the same time*) contemporaneamente; **~ and for all** una volta per tutte ● *conj* [non] appena

once-over *n fam* **give sb/sth the ~** (*look, check*) dare un'occhiata veloce a qcno/qcsa

oncoming /'ɒnkʌmɪŋ/ *a* che si avvicina dalla direzione opposta

one /wʌn/ *a* uno, una; **not ~ person** nemmeno una persona ● *n* uno *m* ● *pron* uno; (*impersonal*) si; **~ another** l'un l'altro; **~ by ~** [a] uno a uno; **~ never knows** non si sa mai

one-armed bandit /wʌnɑːmd'bændɪt/ *n* slot-machine *f inv*

one-dimensional /-daɪ'menʃənəl/ *a* unidimensionale; **be ~** (*fig: character:*) mancare di spessore

one-eyed /-'aɪd/ *a* con un occhio solo

one-for-one *a* = **one-to-one**

one-handed /-'hændɪd/ *adv* (*catch, hold*) con una sola mano

one-horse town *n fam* cittadina *f* di provincia

one-legged /-'legɪd/ *a* con una sola gamba

one-liner *n* battuta *f* d'effetto

one-man *a* (*bobsled*) monoposto *inv*; (*for one person*) per una sola persona; **she's a ~ woman** è una donna fedele; **it's a ~ outfit/operation** manda avanti tutto da solo

one-man band *n* musicista *m* che suona più strumenti contemporaneamente; **be a ~** *fig* mandare avanti tutto da solo

one-off *a Br* (*experiment, order, deal*) unico e irripetibile; (*event, decision, offer, payment*) eccezionale; (*example, design*) unico; (*issue, magazine*) speciale

one-parent family *n* famiglia *f* con un solo genitore

one-room flat, one-room apartment *n* monolocale *m*

one's /wʌnz/ *poss a* **one has to look after**

~ health ci si deve preoccupare della propria salute

oneself /wʌn'self/ *pron* (*reflexive*) si; (*emphatic*) sé, se stesso; **by ~** da solo; **be proud of ~** essere fieri di sé

one-shot *a Am* = **one-off**

one-sided /-'saɪdɪd/ *a* unilaterale

one-time *a* ex *inv*

one-to-one *a* ⟨*personal relationship*⟩ tra due persone; ⟨*private lesson*⟩ individuale; ⟨*correspondence*⟩ di uno a uno

one-upmanship /-'ʌpmənʃɪp/ *n* arte *f* di primeggiare

one-way *a* ⟨*street*⟩ a senso unico; ⟨*ticket*⟩ di sola andata

one-woman *a* **it's a ~ outfit** manda avanti tutto da sola; **he's a ~ man** è un uomo fedele

ongoing /'ɒngəʊɪŋ/ *a* ⟨*process*⟩ continuo; ⟨*battle, saga*⟩ in corso

onion /'ʌnjən/ *n* cipolla *f*

on-line *a* Comput in linea, on-line *inv*; **go ~ to...** connettersi a...; **~ time** durata *f* del collegamento

onlooker /'ɒnlʊkə(r)/ *n* spettatore, -trice *mf*

only /'əʊnlɪ/ *a* solo; **~ child** figlio, -a *mf* unico, -a ● *adv & conj* solo, solamente; **~ just** appena

o.n.o. *Br abbr* (**or nearest offer**) trattabile

on-off *a* ⟨*button, control*⟩ di accensione

onrush /'ɒnrʌʃ/ *n* (*of people, water*) ondata *f*

on-screen *a* sullo schermo

onset /'ɒnset/ *n* (*beginning*) inizio *m*

onshore /'ɒnʃɔ:(r)/ *a* ⟨*wind*⟩ di mare; ⟨*work*⟩ a terra

onside /ɒn'saɪd/ *a & adv* Sport non in fuorigioco

on-site *a* sul posto

onslaught /'ɒnslɔ:t/ *n* attacco *m*

on-stage *a & adv* in scena

on-the-job *a* ⟨*training*⟩ in sede

on-the-spot *a* ⟨*advice, quotation*⟩ immediato

onto /'ɒntu:/ *prep* (*also* **on to**) su

onus /'əʊnəs/ *n* **the ~ is on me** spetta a me la responsabilità (**to** di)

onward[s] /'ɒnwəd[z]/ *adv* in avanti; **from then ~** da allora [in poi]

oodles /'u:dlz/ *n fam* un sacco

ooh /u:/ *int* oh!

oomph /u:mf/ *n fam* verve *f inv*

oops /u:ps/ *int* ops!

ooze /u:z/ *vi* fluire

op /ɒp/ *n* = **operation**

opal /'əʊpl/ *n* opale *f*

opaque /əʊ'peɪk/ *a* opaco

Opec, OPEC /'əʊpek/ *n abbr* (**Organization of Petroleum Exporting Countries**) OPEC *f*

open /'əʊpən/ *a* aperto; (*free to all*) pubblico; ⟨*job*⟩ vacante; **in the ~ air** all'aperto ● *n* **in the ~** all'aperto; *fig* alla luce del sole ● *vt* aprire ● *vi* aprirsi; ⟨*shop:*⟩ aprire; ⟨*flower:*⟩ sbocciare

■ **open onto** *vt* ⟨*door, window;*⟩ dare su

■ **open out** *vi* ⟨*road:*⟩ allargarsi; ⟨*flower:*⟩ aprirsi ● *vt* aprire ⟨*map, newspaper*⟩

■ **open up** *vt* aprire ● *vi* aprirsi

■ **open with** *vi* (*start with*) iniziare con

open: open-air *a* ⟨*pool, market, stage*⟩ all'aperto. **opencast mining** *n Br* miniera *f* a cielo aperto. **open competition** *n* concorso *m*. **open day** *n* giorno *m* di apertura al pubblico. **open-ended** /-'endɪd/ *a* ⟨*relationship, question, contract*⟩ aperto; ⟨*stay*⟩ a tempo indeterminato; ⟨*period*⟩ indeterminato; ⟨*strategy*⟩ flessibile

opener /'əʊpənə(r)/ *n* (*for tins*) apriscatole *m inv*; (*for bottles*) apribottiglie *m inv*

open: open government *n* politica *f* di trasparenza. **open-handed** /-'hændɪd/ *a* generoso. **open-heart surgery** *n* intervento *m* a cuore aperto. **open house** *n* (*Am: open day*) giornata *f* di apertura al pubblico; **it's always ~ ~ at the Batemans'** i Bateman sono sempre molto ospitali

opening /'əʊpənɪŋ/ *n* apertura *f*; (*beginning*) inizio *m*; (*job*) posto *m* libero

opening: opening balance *n Fin* saldo *m* iniziale. **opening ceremony** *n* cerimonia *f* inaugurale. **opening hours** *npl* orario *m* d'apertura

openly /'əʊpənlɪ/ *adv* apertamente

open: open market *n Econ* mercato *m* aperto. **open-minded** /-'maɪndɪd/ *a* aperto; (*broad-minded*) di vedute larghe. **open-mouthed** /-'maʊðd/ *a* a bocca aperta. **open-necked** /-'nekt/ *a* ⟨*shirt*⟩ col colletto sbottonato

openness /'əʊpənnɪs/ *n* (*of government, atmosphere*) trasparenza *f*; (*candour*) franchezza *f*; (*receptiveness*) apertura *f* mentale

open: open-plan *a* a pianta aperta. **open sandwich** *n* tartina *f*. **open scholarship** *n* Univ borsa *f* di studio assegnata per concorso. **open season** *n* (*in hunting*) stagione *f* della caccia. **open secret** *n* segreto *m* di Pulcinella. **open ticket** *n* biglietto *m* aperto. **Open University** *n Br* Univ corsi *mpl* universitari per corrispondenza. **open verdict** *n Jur* verdetto *m* che dichiara non accertabili le cause della morte

opera /'ɒpərə/ *n* opera *f*

operable /'ɒpərəbl/ *a* operabile

opera: opera glasses *npl* binocolo *msg* da teatro. **opera house** *n* teatro *m* lirico. **opera-singer** *n* cantante *mf* lirico, -a

operate /'ɒpəreɪt/ *vt* far funzionare ⟨*machine, lift*⟩; azionare ⟨*lever, brake*⟩; mandare avanti ⟨*business*⟩ ● *vi* Techn funzionare; (*be in action*) essere in funzione; *Mil, fig* operare

■ **operate on** *vt Med* operare

operatic /ɒpə'rætɪk/ *a* lirico, operistico

operating /'ɒpəreɪtɪŋ/: **operating costs** *npl* spese *fpl* di esercizio. **operating instructions** *npl* istruzioni *fpl* per l'uso. **operating room** *n Am* sala *f* operatoria. **operating system** *n Comput* sistema *m* operativo. **operating table** *n Med* tavolo *m* operatorio. **operating theatre** *n Br* sala *f* operatoria

operation /ɒpəˈreɪʃn/ n operazione f; Tech funzionamento m; **in ~** Techn in funzione; **come into ~** fig entrare in funzione; ⟨law:⟩ entrare in vigore; **have an ~** Med subire un'operazione

operational /ɒpəˈreɪʃənəl/ a operativo; ⟨law etc⟩ in vigore

operations room n Mil centro m operativo; (police) centrale f operativa

operative /ˈɒpərətɪv/ a operativo

operator /ˈɒpəreɪtə(r)/ n (user) operatore, -trice mf; Teleph centralinista mf

operetta /ɒpəˈretə/ n operetta f

ophthalmic /ɒfˈθælmɪk/ a oftalmico

opinion /əˈpɪnjən/ n opinione f; **in my ~** secondo me

opinionated /əˈpɪnɪəneɪtɪd/ a dogmatico

opinion poll n sondaggio m di opinione

opium /ˈəʊpɪəm/ n oppio m

opponent /əˈpəʊnənt/ n avversario, -a mf

opportune /ˈɒpətjuːn/ a opportuno

opportunist /ɒpəˈtjuːnɪst/ n opportunista mf

opportunistic /ɒpətjʊˈnɪstɪk/ a opportunistico

opportunity /ɒpəˈtjuːnətɪ/ n opportunità f inv

oppose /əˈpəʊz/ vt opporsi a; **be ~d to sth** esssere contrario a qcsa; **as ~d to** al contrario di

opposing /əˈpəʊzɪŋ/ a avversario; (opposite) opposto

opposite /ˈɒpəzɪt/ a opposto; ⟨house⟩ di fronte; **~ number** fig controparte f; **the ~ sex** l'altro sesso ● n contrario m ● adv di fronte ● prep di fronte a

opposition /ɒpəˈzɪʃn/ n opposizione f

oppress /əˈpres/ vt opprimere

oppression /əˈpreʃn/ n oppressione f

oppressive /əˈpresɪv/ a oppressivo; ⟨heat⟩ opprimente

oppressor /əˈpresə(r)/ n oppressore m

■ **opt for** /ɒpt/ vt optare per

■ **opt out** vi dissociarsi (**of** da)

optic /ˈɒptɪk/ a ⟨nerve, disc, fibre⟩ ottico

optical /ˈɒptɪkl/ a ottico; **~ illusion** illusione f ottica

optician /ɒpˈtɪʃn/ n ottico, -a mf

optics /ˈɒptɪks/ n ottica f

optimism /ˈɒptɪmɪzm/ n ottimismo m

optimist /ˈɒptɪmɪst/ n ottimista mf

optimistic /ɒptɪˈmɪstɪk/ a ottimistico

optimistically /ɒptɪˈmɪstɪklɪ/ adv ottimisticamente

optimize /ˈɒptɪmaɪz/ vt ottimizzare

optimum /ˈɒptɪməm/ a ottimale ● n (pl -ima) optimum m

option /ˈɒpʃn/ n scelta f; Comm opzione f

optional /ˈɒpʃənəl/ a facoltativo; **~ extras** optional m inv

opulence /ˈɒpjʊləns/ n opulenza f

opulent /ˈɒpjʊlənt/ a opulento

opus /ˈəʊpəs/ n (pl **opuses** or **opera**) opera f

or /ɔː(r)/ conj o, oppure; (after negative) né; **or**

[else] se no; **in a year or two** fra un anno o due

oracle /ˈɒrəkl/ n oracolo m

oral /ˈɔːrəl/ a orale ● n fam esame m orale

orally /ˈɔːrəlɪ/ adv oralmente

orange /ˈɒrɪndʒ/ n arancia f; (colour) arancione m ● a arancione

orangeade /ɒrɪndʒˈeɪd/ n aranciata f

orange: orange blossom n fiori mpl d'arancio. **orange juice** n succo m d'arancia. **orange peel** n scorza f d'arancia. **orange squash** n Br succo m d'arancia (diluito in acqua). **orange tree** n arancio m

oration /əˈreɪʃn/ n orazione f

orator /ˈɒrətə(r)/ n oratore, -trice mf

oratorio /ɒrəˈtɔːrɪəʊ/ n oratorio m

oratory /ˈɒrətrɪ/ n oratorio m

orbit /ˈɔːbɪt/ n orbita f ● vt orbitare

orbital /ˈɔːbɪtl/ a **~ road** tangenziale f

orchard /ˈɔːtʃəd/ n frutteto m

orchestra /ˈɔːkɪstrə/ n orchestra f

orchestral /ɔːˈkestrəl/ a orchestrale

orchestra pit n [fossa f dell']orchestra f

orchestrate /ˈɔːkɪstreɪt/ vt orchestrare

orchid /ˈɔːkɪd/ n orchidea f

ordain /ɔːˈdeɪn/ vt decretare; Relig ordinare

ordeal /ɔːˈdiːl/ n fig terribile esperienza f

order /ˈɔːdə(r)/ n ordine m; Comm ordinazione f; **out of ~** ⟨machine⟩ fuori servizio; **in ~ that** affinché; **in ~ to** per; **take holy ~s** prendere i voti ● vt ordinare

■ **order about, order around** vt (give orders to) impartire ordini a

order book n registro m degli ordini

order form n modulo m di ordinazione

orderly /ˈɔːdəlɪ/ a ordinato ● n Mil attendente m; Med inserviente m

orderly officer n Mil attendente m

order number n numero m d'ordine

ordinal /ˈɔːdɪnl/ n & a ordinale m

ordinarily /ɔːdɪˈnerɪlɪ/ adv (normally) normalmente

ordinary /ˈɔːdɪnərɪ/ a ordinario

ordination /ɔːdɪˈneɪʃn/ n Relig ordinazione f

ordnance /ˈɔːdnəns/ n Mil materiale m militare

Ordnance Survey n Br istituto m cartografico; **Ordnance Survey Map** carta f topografica dell'istituto cartografico

ore /ɔː(r)/ n minerale m grezzo

oregano /ɒrɪˈɡɑːnəʊ/ n origano m

organ /ˈɔːɡən/ n Anat, Mus organo m

organ donor n Med donatore, -trice mf di organi

organic /ɔːˈɡænɪk/ a organico; (without chemicals) biologico

organically /ɔːˈɡænɪklɪ/ adv organicamente; **~ grown** coltivato biologicamente

organic: organic chemistry n chimica f organica. **organic farm** n azienda f agricola specializzata in prodotti biologici. **organic farming** n agricoltura f biologica

organism /ˈɔːɡənɪzm/ n organismo m

organist /ˈɔːɡənɪst/ n organista mf

organization /ɔ:gənaɪ'zeɪʃn/ n organizzazione f

organizational /ɔ:gənaɪ'zeɪʃənəl/ a ‹ability, role› organizzativo

organize /'ɔ:gənaɪz/ vt organizzare

organized crime /ɔ:gənaɪzd'kraɪm/ n criminalità f organizzata

organized labour n manodopera f organizzata

organizer /'ɔ:gənaɪzə(r)/ n organizzatore, -trice mf

organ transplant n Med trapianto m di organi

orgasm /'ɔ:gæzm/ n orgasmo m

orgy /'ɔ:dʒɪ/ n orgia f

Orient /'ɔ:rɪənt/ n Oriente m

oriental /ɔ:rɪ'entl/ a orientale; **~ carpet** tappeto m persiano ● n orientale mf

orientate /'ɔ:rɪenteɪt/ vt **~ oneself** orientarsi

orientation /ɔ:rɪən'teɪʃn/ n orientamento m

orienteering /ɔ:rɪen'tɪərɪŋ/ n orientamento m

orifice /'ɒrɪfɪs/ n orifizio m

origin /'ɒrɪdʒɪn/ n origine f

original /ə'rɪdʒɪnl/ a originario; (not copied, new) originale; ● n originale m; **in the ~** in versione originale

originality /ərɪdʒɪ'næləti/ n originalità f

originally /ə'rɪdʒɪnəlɪ/ adv originariamente

originate /ə'rɪdʒɪneɪt/ vi **~ in** avere origine in

originator /ə'rɪdʒɪneɪtə(r)/ n ideatore, -trice mf

Orkney /'ɔ:knɪ/ n (also **Orkney Islands**) Orcadi fpl

ornament /'ɔ:nəmənt/ n ornamento m; (on mantelpiece etc) soprammobile m

ornamental /ɔ:nə'mentl/ a ornamentale

ornamentation /ɔ:nəmen'teɪʃn/ n decorazione f

ornate /ɔ:'neɪt/ a ornato

ornithologist /ɔ:nɪ'θɒlədʒɪst/ n ornitologo, -a mf

ornithology /ɔ:nɪ'θɒlədʒɪ/ n ornitologia f

orphan /'ɔ:fn/ n orfano, -a mf ● vt rendere orfano; **be ~ed** rimanere orfano; **be ~ed by...** essere reso orfano da...

orphanage /'ɔ:fənɪdʒ/ n orfanotrofio m

orphaned /'ɔ:fənd/ a reso orfano

orthodox /'ɔ:θədɒks/ a ortodosso

orthopaedic /ɔ:θə'pi:dɪk/ a ortopedico

orthopaedics /ɔ:θə'pi:dɪks/ n ortopedia f

OS abbr (**outsize**) per taglie forti

oscillate /'ɒsɪleɪt/ vi oscillare

osmosis /ɒz'məʊsɪs/ n osmosi f inv; **by ~** per osmosi

ostensible /ɒ'stensəbl/ a apparente

ostensibly /ɒ'stensəblɪ/ adv apparentemente

ostentation /ɒsten'teɪʃn/ n ostentazione f

ostentatious /ɒsten'teɪʃəs/ a ostentato

ostentatiously /ɒsten'teɪʃəslɪ/ adv ostentatamente

osteopath /'ɒstɪəpæθ/ n osteopata mf

osteoporosis /ɒstɪəʊpə'rəʊsɪs/ n osteoporosi f

ostracism /'ɒstrəsɪzm/ n ostracismo m

ostracize /'ɒstrəsaɪz/ vt ostracizzare

ostrich /'ɒstrɪtʃ/ n struzzo m

other /'ʌðə(r)/ a, pron & n altro, -a mf; **the ~** [one] l'altro, -a mf; **the ~ two** gli altri due; **two ~s** altri due; **~ people** gli altri; **any ~ questions?** altre domande?; **every ~ day** (alternate days) a giorni alterni; **the ~ day** l'altro giorno; **the ~ evening** l'altra sera; **someone/something or ~** qualcuno/qualcosa ● adv **~ than him** tranne lui; **somehow or ~** in qualche modo; **somewhere or ~** da qualche parte

otherwise /'ʌðəwaɪz/ adv altrimenti; (differently) diversamente

other-worldly /ʌðə'wɜ:ldlɪ/ a disinteressato alle cose materiali

OTT abbr fam (**over-the-top**) esagerato

otter /'ɒtə(r)/ n lontra f

OU n Br abbr (**Open University**) corsi mpl universitari per corrispondenza

ouch /aʊtʃ/ int ahi!

ought /ɔ:t/ v aux I/we **~ to stay** dovrei/dovremmo rimanere; **he ~ not to have done it** non avrebbe dovuto farlo; **that ~ to be enough** questo dovrebbe bastare

ounce /aʊns/ n oncia f (= 28,35 g)

our /'aʊə(r)/ poss a il nostro m, la nostra f, i nostri mpl, le nostre fpl; **~ mother/father** nostra madre/nostro padre

ours /'aʊəz/ poss pron il nostro m, la nostra f, i nostri mpl, le nostre fpl; **a friend of ~** un nostro amico; **friends of ~** dei nostri amici; **that is ~** quello è nostro; (as opposed to yours) quello è il nostro

ourselves /aʊə'selvz/ pers pron (reflexive) ci; (emphatic) noi, noi stessi; **we poured ~ a drink** ci siamo versati da bere; **we heard it ~** l'abbiamo sentito noi stessi; **we are proud of ~** siamo fieri di noi; **by ~** da soli

oust /aʊst/ vt rimuovere

out /aʊt/ adv fuori; (not alight) spento; **be ~** ‹flower:› essere sbocciato; ‹workers:› essere in sciopero; ‹calculation:› essere sbagliato; Sport essere fuori; (unconscious) aver perso i sensi; (fig: not feasible) fuori questione; **the sun is ~** è uscito il sole; **~ and about** in piedi; **get ~!** fam fuori!; **you should get ~ more** dovresti uscire più spesso; **~ with it!** fam sputa il rospo!; **be ~ to** avere l'intenzione di; ● prep **~ of** fuori da; **~ of date** non aggiornato; ‹passaporto› scaduto; **~ of order** guasto; **~ of print/stock** esaurito; **~ of sorts** indisposto; **~ of tune** (singer) stonato; (instrument) scordato; **be ~ of bed/ the room** fuori dal letto/dalla stanza; **~ of breath** senza fiato; **~ of danger** fuori pericolo; **~ of work** disoccupato; **nine ~ of ten** nove su dieci; **be ~ of sugar/bread** rimanere senza zucchero/pane; **go ~ of the room** uscire dalla stanza

out-and-out a ‹success, failure› totale; ‹villain, liar› vero e proprio

outback /'aʊtbæk/ n entroterra m inv australiano

outbid /aʊt'bɪd/ vt (pt/pp -bid, pres p -bidding) ~ sb rilanciare l'offerta di qcno

outboard /'aʊtbɔːd/ a ~ motor fuoribordo m inv

outbreak /'aʊtbreɪk/ n (of war) scoppio m; (of disease) insorgenza f

outbuilding /'aʊtbɪldɪŋ/ n costruzione f annessa

outburst /'aʊtbɜːst/ n esplosione f

outcast /'aʊtkɑːst/ n esule mf; (social) escluso m

outclass /aʊt'klɑːs/ vt surclassare

outcome /'aʊtkʌm/ n risultato m

outcrop /'aʊtkrɒp/ n affioramento m

outcry /'aʊtkraɪ/ n protesta f

outdated /aʊt'deɪtɪd/ a sorpassato

outdo /aʊt'duː/ vt (pt -did, pp -done) superare

outdoor /'aʊtdɔː(r)/ a (life, sports) all'aperto; ~ swimming pool piscina f scoperta

outdoors /aʊt'dɔːz/ adv all'aria aperta; go ~ uscire all'aria aperta

outer /'aʊtə(r)/ a esterno

outer space n spazio m cosmico

outfit /'aʊtfɪt/ n equipaggiamento m; (clothes) completo m; (fam: organization) organizzazione f

outfitter /'aʊtfɪtə(r)/ n men's ~'s negozio m di abbigliamento maschile

outflow /'aʊtfləʊ/ n (of money) uscite fpl

outgoing /'aʊtgəʊɪŋ/ a (president) uscente; (mail) in partenza; (sociable) estroverso ● npl ~s uscite fpl

outgrow /aʊt'grəʊ/ vi (pt -grew, pp -grown) diventare troppo grande per

outhouse /'aʊthaʊs/ n costruzione f annessa

outing /'aʊtɪŋ/ n gita f

outlandish /aʊt'lændɪʃ/ a stravagante

outlast /aʊt'lɑːst/ vt durare più a lungo di

outlaw /'aʊtlɔː/ n fuorilegge mf inv ● vt dichiarare illegale

outlay /'aʊtleɪ/ n spesa f

outlet /'aʊtlet/ n sbocco m; fig sfogo m; Comm punto m [di] vendita

outline /'aʊtlaɪn/ n contorno m; (summary) sommario m ● vt tracciare il contorno di; (describe) descrivere

outline agreement n abbozzo m di accordo

outlive /aʊt'lɪv/ vt sopravvivere a

outlook /'aʊtlʊk/ n vista f; (future prospect) prospettiva f; (attitude) visione f

outlying /'aʊtlaɪɪŋ/ a ~ areas zone fpl periferiche

outmanoeuvre /aʊtmə'nuːvə(r)/ vt ~ sb passare in vantaggio su qcno con un'abile manovra

outmoded /aʊt'məʊdɪd/ a fuori moda

outnumber /aʊt'nʌmbə(r)/ vt superare in numero

out of bounds a & adv (area) vietato all'accesso

out-of-date a (theory, concept) sorpassato; (ticket, passport) scaduto

out-of-pocket a be out of pocket essere in perdita; ~ expenses spese fpl extra

out-of-the-way a (places) fuori mano

outpatient /'aʊtpeɪʃnt/ n paziente mf esterno, -a; ~s' department ambulatorio m

outpost /'aʊtpəʊst/ n avamposto m

output /'aʊtpʊt/ n produzione f

outrage /'aʊtreɪdʒ/ n oltraggio m ● vt oltraggiare

outrageous /aʊt'reɪdʒəs/ a oltraggioso; (price) scandaloso

outrider /'aʊtraɪdə(r)/ n battistrada m inv

outright¹ /'aʊtraɪt/ a completo; (refusal) netto

outright² /aʊt'raɪt/ adv completamente; (at once) immediatamente; (frankly) francamente

outrun /aʊt'rʌn/ vt superare

outsell /aʊt'sel/ vt vendere meglio di (product)

outset /'aʊtset/ n inizio m; from the ~ fin dall'inizio

outside¹ /'aʊtsaɪd/ a esterno ● n esterno m; from the ~ dall'esterno; at the ~ al massimo

outside² /aʊt'saɪd/ adv all'esterno, fuori; (out of doors) fuori; go ~ andare fuori ● prep fuori da; (in front of) davanti a

outsider /aʊt'saɪdə(r)/ n estraneo, -a mf

outsize /'aʊtsaɪz/ a smisurato; (clothes) per taglie forti

outskirts /'aʊtskɜːts/ npl sobborghi mpl

outsmart /aʊt'smɑːt/ vt essere più furbo di

outspoken /aʊt'spəʊkn/ a schietto

outspread /'aʊtspred/ a (wings) spiegato; (arms, fingers) disteso

outstanding /aʊt'stændɪŋ/ a eccezionale; (landmark) prominente; (not settled) in sospeso

outstandingly /aʊt'stændɪŋlɪ/ adv eccezionalmente; ~ good eccezionale

outstay /aʊt'steɪ/ vt ~ one's welcome abusare dell'ospitalità di qcno

outstretched /'aʊtstretʃt/ a allungato

outstrip /aʊt'strɪp/ vt (pt/pp -stripped) superare

out-tray n vassoio m per corrispondenza e pratiche evase

outvote /aʊt'vəʊt/ vt mettere in minoranza

outward /'aʊtwəd/ a esterno; (journey) di andata ● adv verso l'esterno

outwardly /'aʊtwədlɪ/ adv esternamente

outwards /'aʊtwədz/ adv verso l'esterno

outweigh /aʊt'weɪ/ vt aver maggior peso di

outwit /aʊt'wɪt/ vt (pt/pp -witted) battere in astuzia

outworker /'aʊtwɜːkə(r)/ n Br lavoratore, -trice mf a domicilio

outworn /aʊt'wɔːn/ a (outmoded) sorpassato

oval /'əʊvl/ a ovale ● n ovale m

ovary /'əʊvərɪ/ n Anat ovaia f

ovation /əʊ'veɪʃn/ n ovazione f

oven /'ʌvn/ n forno m

oven: oven cleaner *n* detergente *m* per il forno. **oven glove** *n* guanto *m* da forno. **ovenproof** *a* da forno. **oven-ready** *a* pronto da mettere in forno

over /'əʊvə(r)/ *prep* sopra; ⟨*across*⟩ al di là di; ⟨*during*⟩ durante; ⟨*more than*⟩ più di; **~ the phone** al telefono; **~ the page** alla pagina seguente; **all ~ Italy** in tutta [l']Italia; ⟨*travel*⟩ per l'Italia ● *adv* sopra; ⟨*ended*⟩ finito; **~ again** un'altra volta; **~ and ~** più volte; **~ and above** oltre a; **~ here/there** qui/là; **all ~** ⟨*everywhere*⟩ dappertutto; **it's all ~** è tutto finito; **I ache all ~** ho male dappertutto; **come/bring ~** venire/portare; **turn ~** girare

over+ *pref* ⟨*too*⟩ troppo

overact /əʊvər'ækt/ *vi* strafare

overactive /əʊvər'æktɪv/ *a* ⟨*imagination*⟩ sbrigliato

overall[1] /'əʊvərɔːl/ *n* grembiule *m*

overall[2] /əʊvər'ɔːl/ *a* complessivo; ⟨*general*⟩ generale ● *adv* complessivamente

overalls /'əʊvərɔːlz/ *npl* tuta *fsg* [da lavoro]

overarm /'əʊvərɑːm/ *a* & *adv* ⟨*throw*⟩ col braccio al di sopra della spalla

overawe /əʊvər'ɔː/ *vt fig* intimidire

overbalance /əʊvə'bæləns/ *vi* perdere l'equilibrio

overbearing /əʊvə'beərɪŋ/ *a* prepotente

overblown /əʊvə'bləʊn/ *a* ⟨*style*⟩ ampolloso

overboard /'əʊvəbɔːd/ *adv Naut* in mare

overbook /əʊvə'bʊk/ *vt accettare un numero di prenotazioni superiore ai posti disponibili*

overburden /əʊvə'bɜːdən/ *vt* sovraccaricare **(with** di)

overcapacity /əʊvəkə'pæsətɪ/ *n* eccesso *m* di capacità produttiva

overcast /'əʊvəkɑːst/ *a* coperto

overcharge /əʊvə'tʃɑːdʒ/ *vt* **~ sb** far pagare più del dovuto a ● *vi* far pagare più del dovuto

overcoat /'əʊvəkəʊt/ *n* cappotto *m*

overcome /əʊvə'kʌm/ *vt* (*pt* **-came**, *pp* **-come**) vincere; **be ~ by** essere sopraffatto da

overcompensate /əʊvə'kɒmpənseɪt/ *vi* compensare eccessivamente

overconfident /əʊvə'kɒnfɪdənt/ *a* troppo sicuro di sé

overcook /əʊvə'kʊk/ *vt* cuocere troppo

overcrowded /əʊvə'kraʊdɪd/ *a* sovraffollato

overcrowding /əʊvə'kraʊdɪŋ/ *n* ⟨*in transport*⟩ calca *f*; ⟨*in city, institution*⟩ sovraffollamento *m*

overdo /əʊvə'duː/ *vt* (*pt* **-did**, *pp* **-done**) esagerare; ⟨*cook too long*⟩ stracuocere; **~ it** ⟨*fam: do too much*⟩ strafare

overdose /'əʊvədəʊs/ *n* overdose *f inv*

overdraft /'əʊvədrɑːft/ *n* scoperto *m*; **have an ~** avere il conto scoperto

overdraw /əʊvə'drɔː/ *vt* (*pt* **-drew**, *pp* **-drawn**) **~ one's account** andare allo scoperto; **be ~n by...** ⟨*account:*⟩ essere scoperto di...

overdressed /əʊvə'drest/ *a* troppo elegante

overdrive /'əʊvədraɪv/ *n Auto* overdrive *m inv*

overdue /əʊvə'djuː/ *a* in ritardo

overeat /əʊvər'iːt/ *vi* mangiare troppo

overemphasize /əʊvər'emfəsaɪz/ *vt* esagerare ⟨*importance*⟩; dare troppo rilievo a ⟨*aspect, fact*⟩

overenthusiastic /əʊvərɪnθjuːzɪ'æstɪk/ *a* troppo entusiasta

overestimate /əʊvər'estɪmeɪt/ *vt* sopravvalutare

overexcited /əʊvərɪk'saɪtɪd/ *a* sovreccitato; **get ~** sovreccitarsi

overexert /əʊvərɪg'zɜːt/ *vt* **~ oneself** sovraffaticarsi

overexposure /əʊvərek'spəʊʒə(r)/ *n Phot* sovresposizione *f*; ⟨*in the media*⟩ attenzione *f* eccessiva da parte dei media

overfeed /əʊvə'fiːd/ *vt* sovralimentare ⟨*child, pet*⟩; concimare troppo ⟨*plant*⟩

overflow[1] /'əʊvəfləʊ/ *n* ⟨*water*⟩ acqua *f* che deborda; ⟨*people*⟩ pubblico *m* in eccesso; ⟨*outlet*⟩ scarico *m*

overflow[2] /əʊvə'fləʊ/ *vi* debordare

overgenerous /əʊvə'dʒenərəs/ *a* ⟨*amount*⟩ troppo generoso

overgrown /əʊvə'grəʊn/ *a* ⟨*garden*⟩ coperto di erbacce

overhang[1] /'əʊvəhæŋ/ *n* sporgenza *f*

overhang[2] /əʊvə'hæŋ/ *v* (*pt/pp* **-hung**) ● *vi* sporgere ● *vt* sovrastare

overhanging /əʊvə'hæŋɪŋ/ *a* ⟨*ledge, cliff*⟩ sporgente

overhaul[1] /'əʊvəhɔːl/ *n* revisione *f*

overhaul[2] /əʊvə'hɔːl/ *vt Techn* revisionare

overhead[1] /əʊvə'hed/ *adv* in alto

overhead[2] /'əʊvəhed/ *a* aereo; ⟨*railway*⟩ sopraelevato; ⟨*lights*⟩ da soffitto ● *npl* **~s** spese *fpl* generali

overhead: overhead light *n* lampada *f* da soffitto. **overhead locker** *n Aeron* armadietto *m* [per il bagaglio a mano]. **overhead projector** *n* lavagna *f* luminosa

overhear /əʊvə'hɪə(r)/ *vt* (*pt/pp* **-heard**) sentire per caso ⟨*conversation*⟩; **I ~d him saying it** l'ho sentito per caso mentre lo diceva

overheat /əʊvə'hiːt/ *vi Auto* surriscaldarsi ● *vt* surriscaldare

over-indulge *vi* eccedere ● *vt* viziare ⟨*child*⟩

over-indulgence *n* ⟨*excess*⟩ eccesso *m*; ⟨*laxity towards*⟩ indulgenza *f* eccessiva

overjoyed /əʊvə'dʒɔɪd/ *a* felicissimo

overkill /'əʊvəkɪl/ *n* ⟨*exaggerated treatment*⟩ esagerazione *f*

overland /'əʊvəlænd/ *a* & *adv* via terra; **~ route** via *f* terrestre

overlap /əʊvə'læp/ *v* (*pt/pp* **-lapped**) ● *vi* sovrapporsi ● *vt* sovrapporre

overlay /əʊvə'leɪ/ *vt* ricoprire

overleaf /əʊvə'liːf/ *adv* sul retro

overload[1] /əʊvə'ləʊd/ *vt* sovraccaricare

overload[2] /'əʊvələʊd/ *n Electr* sovratensioni *pl*

overlook /əʊvə'lʊk/ *vt* dominare; (*fail to see, ignore*) lasciarsi sfuggire

overly /'əʊvəlɪ/ *adv* eccessivamente

overmanned /əʊvə'mænd/ *a* con un'eccedenza di personale

overmanning /əʊvə'mænɪŋ/ *n* eccesso *m* di personale

overmuch /əʊvə'mʌtʃ/ *adv* troppo

overnight¹ /əʊvə'naɪt/ *adv* per la notte; **stay ~** fermarsi a dormire

overnight² /'əʊvənaɪt/ *a* notturno

overnight bag *n* piccola borsa *f* da viaggio

overnight stay *n* sosta *f* per la notte

overpass /'əʊvəpɑːs/ *n* cavalcavia *m inv*

overpay /əʊvə'peɪ/ *vt* (*pt/pp* **-paid**) strapagare

overplay /əʊvə'pleɪ/ *vt* (*exaggerate*) esagerare

overpopulated /əʊvə'pɒpjʊleɪtɪd/ *a* sovrappopolato

overpower /əʊvə'paʊə(r)/ *vt* sopraffare

overpowering /əʊvə'paʊərɪŋ/ *a* insostenibile

overpriced /əʊvə'praɪst/ *a* troppo caro

overproduce /əʊvəprə'djuːs/ *vt* produrre in eccesso

overqualified /əʊvə'kwɒlɪfaɪd/ *a* troppo qualificato

overrate /əʊvə'reɪt/ *vt* sopravvalutare

overrated /əʊvə'reɪtɪd/ *a* sopravvalutato

overreach /əʊvə'riːtʃ/ *vt* **~ oneself** puntare troppo in alto

overreact /əʊvərɪ'ækt/ *vi* avere una reazione eccessiva

overreaction /əʊvərɪ'ækʃn/ *n* reazione *f* eccessiva

override /əʊvə'raɪd/ *vt* (*pt* **-rode**, *pp* **-ridden**) passare sopra a

overriding /əʊvə'raɪdɪŋ/ *a* prevalente

overrule /əʊvə'ruːl/ *vt* annullare (*decision*); **we were ~d by the chairman** il direttore ha prevalso su di noi

overrun /əʊvə'rʌn/ *vt* (*pt* **-ran**, *pp* **-run**, *pres p* **-running**) invadere; oltrepassare (*time*); **be ~ with** essere invaso da

overseas¹ /əʊvə'siːz/ *adv* oltremare

overseas² /'əʊvəsiːz/ *a* d'oltremare

oversee /əʊvə'siː/ *vt* (*pt* **-saw**, *pp* **-seen**) sorvegliare

oversell /əʊvə'sel/ *vt* lodare esageratamente (*idea, plan*)

oversensitive /əʊvə'sensɪtɪv/ *a* (*person*) ipersensibile

oversexed /əʊvə'sekst/ *a fam* **be ~** essere un maniaco/una maniaca del sesso

overshadow /əʊvə'ʃædəʊ/ *vt* adombrare

overshoot /əʊvə'ʃuːt/ *vt* (*pt/pp* **-shot**) oltrepassare

oversight /'əʊvəsaɪt/ *n* disattenzione *f*; **an ~** una svista

oversimplification /əʊvəsɪmplɪfɪ'keɪʃn/ *n* semplificazione *f* eccessiva

oversimplified /əʊvə'sɪmplɪfaɪd/ *a* semplicistico

oversimplify /əʊvə'sɪmplɪfaɪ/ *vt* semplificare eccessivamente

oversize[d] /əʊvə'saɪz[d]/ *a* più grande del normale

oversleep /əʊvə'sliːp/ *vi* (*pt/pp* **-slept**) svegliarsi troppo tardi

overspend /əʊvə'spend/ *vi* spendere troppo

overspending /əʊvə'spendɪŋ/ *n* spese *fpl* eccessive; *Fin* spese *fpl* superiori al bilancio di previsione

overspill /'əʊvəspɪl/ *n* (*excess amount*) eccedenza *f* ● *attrib* **~ housing development** ≈ città *f inv* satellite; **~ population** popolazione *f* in eccesso

overstaffed /əʊvə'stɑːft/ *a* **be ~** avere personale in eccedenza

overstaffing /əʊvə'stɑːfɪŋ/ *n* eccedenza *f* di personale

overstate /əʊvə'steɪt/ *vt* esagerare; **its importance cannot be ~d** la sua importanza non sarà mai sottolineata a sufficienza; **~ the case** esagerare le cose

overstatement /əʊvə'steɪtmənt/ *n* esagerazione *f*

overstay /əʊvə'steɪ/ *vt* **~ one's time** trattenersi troppo a lungo; **~ one's visa** trattenersi oltre la scadenza del visto

overstep /əʊvə'step/ *vt* (*pt/pp* **-stepped**) **~ the mark** oltrepassare ogni limite

overstretched /əʊvə'stretʃt/ *a* (*person*) sovraccarico [di lavoro]; (*budget, resources*) sfruttato fino al limite

oversubscribed /əʊvəsəb'skraɪbd/ *a* (*share issue*) sottoscritto in eccesso; (*offer, tickets*) richiesto oltre la disponibilità

overt /əʊ'vɜːt/ *a* palese

overtake /əʊvə'teɪk/ *vt/i* (*pt* **-took**, *pp* **-taken**) sorpassare

overtaking /əʊvə'teɪkɪŋ/ *n* sorpasso *m*; **no ~** divieto di sorpasso

overtax /əʊvə'tæks/ *vt fig* abusare di

over-the-counter *a* (*medicines*) venduto senza ricetta

over-the-top *a fam* esagerato; **go over the top** esagerare

overthrow¹ /'əʊvəθrəʊ/ *n Pol* rovesciamento *m*

overthrow² /əʊvə'θrəʊ/ *vt* (*pt* **-threw**, *pp* **-thrown**) *Pol* rovesciare

overtime /'əʊvətaɪm/ *n* lavoro straordinario *m* ● *adv* **work ~** fare lo straordinario

overtired /əʊvə'taɪəd/ *a* sovraffaticato

overtly /əʊ'vɜːtlɪ/ *adv* apertamente

overtone /'əʊvətəʊn/ *n fig* sfumatura *f*

overture /'əʊvətjʊə(r)/ *n Mus* preludio *m*; **~s** *pl fig* approccio *msg*; **make ~s to** mostrare un atteggiamento di apertura verso

overturn /əʊvə'tɜːn/ *vt* ribaltare ● *vi* ribaltarsi

overvalue /əʊvə'væljuː/ *vt* sopravvalutare (*currency, property*)

overview /'əʊvəvjuː/ *n* visione *f* d'insieme

overweight /əʊvə'weɪt/ *a* sovrappeso

overwhelm /əʊvə'welm/ *vt* sommergere (**with** di); (*with emotion*) confondere

overwhelming /əʊvə'welmɪŋ/ a travolgente; ⟨victory, majority⟩ schiacciante

overwhelmingly /əʊvə'welmɪŋlɪ/ adv ⟨vote, accept, reject⟩ con una maggioranza schiacciante; ⟨generous⟩ straordinariamente

overwork /əʊvə'wɜːk/ n lavoro m eccessivo ● vt far lavorare eccessivamente ● vi lavorare eccessivamente

overwrite /əʊvə'raɪt/ vt Comput registrare sopra a

overwrought /əʊvə'rɔːt/ a in stato di agitazione

ovulation /ɒvjʊ'leɪʃn/ n ovulazione f

ow /aʊ/ int ahi!

owe /əʊ/ vt also fig dovere ([to] sb a qcno); ~ **sb sth** dovere qcsa a qcno

owing /'əʊɪŋ/ a **be** ~ ⟨money:⟩ essere da pagare ● prep ~ **to** a causa di

owl /aʊl/ n gufo m

own[1] /əʊn/ a proprio ● pron **a car of my** ~ una macchina per conto mio; **on one's** ~ da solo; **hold one's** ~ **with** tener testa a; **get one's** ~ **back** fam prendersi una rivincita

own[2] vt possedere; ⟨confess⟩ ammettere; **I**

don't ~ **it** non mi appartiene

■ **own up** vi confessare (**to sth** qcsa)

owner /'əʊnə(r)/ n proprietario, -a mf

owner: owner-driver n persona f che guida un'auto di sua proprietà. **owner-occupied** /-'ɒkjʊpaɪd/ a abitato dal proprietario. **owner-occupier** n persona f chi abita in una casa di sua proprietà

ownership /'əʊnəʃɪp/ n proprietà f

ox /ɒks/ n (pl **oxen**) bue m (pl buoi)

Oxbridge /'ɒksbrɪdʒ/ n le università di Oxford e Cambridge

oxide /'ɒksaɪd/ n ossido m

oxidize /'ɒksɪdaɪz/ vt ossidare ● vi ossidarsi

oxygen /'ɒksɪdʒən/ n ossigeno m

oxygen mask n maschera f a ossigeno

oyster /'ɔɪstə(r)/ n ostrica f

oz abbr (**ounce(s)**) oncia f

ozone /'əʊzəʊn/ n ozono m

ozone: ozone depletion n distruzione f dell'ozonosfera. **ozone-friendly** a che non danneggia l'ozono. **ozone layer** n fascia f d'ozono

Pp

p, P /piː/ n (letter) p, P f inv; Br abbr **penny, pence**

PA abbr (**personal assistant**) segretario, -a mf personale; Am abbr (**Pennsylvania**) Pennsylvania f

p.a. abbr (**per annum**) all'anno

pace /peɪs/ n passo m; (speed) ritmo m; **keep** ~ **with** camminare di pari passo con ● vi ~ **up and down** camminare avanti e indietro

pacemaker /'peɪsmeɪkə(r)/ n Med pacemaker m inv; (runner) battistrada m inv

pace-setter n (athlete) battistrada m inv

Pacific /pə'sɪfɪk/ a & n **the** ~ [**Ocean**] l'oceano m Pacifico, il Pacifico

pacifier /'pæsɪfaɪə(r)/ n Am ciuccio m, succhiotto m

pacifism /'pæsɪfɪzm/ n pacifismo m

pacifist /'pæsɪfɪst/ n pacifista mf

pacify /'pæsɪfaɪ/ vt (pt/pp **-ied**) placare ⟨person⟩; pacificare ⟨country⟩

pack /pæk/ n (of cards) mazzo m; (of hounds) muta f; (of wolves, thieves) branco m; (of cigarettes etc) pacchetto m; **a** ~ **of lies** un mucchio di bugie ● vt impacchettare ⟨article⟩; fare ⟨suitcase⟩; mettere in valigia ⟨swimsuit etc⟩; (press down) comprimere; ~**ed** (crowded) strapieno, pieno zeppo ● vi fare i bagagli; **send sb** ~**ing** fam mandare qcno a quel paese

■ **pack in** vt fam mollare ⟨job⟩; ~ **it in!** (stop it) piantala!

■ **pack off** vt (send) spedire

■ **pack out** vt **be** ~**ed out** ⟨cinema, shops:⟩ essere strapieno, essere pieno zeppo

■ **pack up** vt impacchettare ● vi fam ⟨machine:⟩ guastarsi

package /'pækɪdʒ/ n pacco m ● vt impacchettare

package: package deal n offerta f tutto compreso. **package holiday** n vacanza f organizzata. **package tour** n viaggio m organizzato

packaging /'pækɪdʒɪŋ/ n (materials) confezione f; (promotion: of product) presentazione f pubblicitaria

packed lunch /pækt/ n pranzo m al sacco

packer /'pækə(r)/ n (in factory) imballatore, -trice mf

packet /'pækɪt/ n pacchetto m; **cost a** ~ fam costare un sacco

pack ice n banchisa f

packing /'pækɪŋ/ n imballaggio m

pact /pækt/ n patto m

pad[1] /pæd/ n imbottitura f; (for writing) bloc-notes m inv, taccuino m; (fam: home) casa f ● vt (pt/pp **padded**) imbottire

pad[2] vi (pt/pp **padded**) camminare con passo felpato

■ **pad out** vt gonfiare

padded /'pædɪd/: **padded bra** n reggiseno m imbottito. **padded cell** n cella f con le pareti imbottite. **padded envelope** n busta f imbottita. **padded shoulders** npl spalline fpl imbottite

padding /'pædɪŋ/ n imbottitura f; (in written work) fronzoli mpl

paddle /'pædl/ n pagaia f; **go for a ~** sguazzare ● vt (row) spingere remando ● vi (wade) sguazzare

paddling pool n (public) piscina f per bambini; (inflatable) piscina f gonfiabile

paddock /'pædək/ n recinto m

padlock /'pædlɒk/ n lucchetto m ● vt chiudere con lucchetto

padre /'pɑ:dreɪ/ n padre m

Padua /'pædjuə/ n Padova f

paediatric /pi:dr'ætrɪk/ a pediatrico

paediatrician /pi:dɪə'trɪʃn/ n pediatra mf

paediatrics /pi:dr'ætrɪks/ n pediatria f

paedophile /'pi:dəʊfaɪl/ n pedofilo, -a mf

paedophilia /pi:dəʊ'fɪlɪə/ n pedofilia f

pagan /'peɪgən/ a & n pagano, -a mf

paganism /'peɪgənɪzm/ n paganesimo m

page[1] /peɪdʒ/ n pagina f

page[2] n (boy) paggetto m; (in hotel) fattorino m ● vt far chiamare ⟨person⟩

pageant /'pædʒənt/ n parata f

pageantry /'pædʒəntrɪ/ n cerimoniale m

page proof n bozza f definitiva

pager /'peɪdʒə(r)/ n cercapersone m inv

page three n Br terza pagina f di quotidiano scandalistico inglese con una pin-up

page three girl n Br pin-up f inv

paid /peɪd/ see pay ● a ~ **employment** lavoro m remunerato; **put ~ to** mettere fine a

paid-up a Br ⟨member⟩ che ha pagato la sua quota; ⟨instalment⟩ versato

pail /peɪl/ n secchio m

pain /peɪn/ n dolore m; **be in ~** soffrire; **take ~s to do sth** fare il possibile per fare qcsa; **~ in the neck** fam rottura f di scatole; ⟨person⟩ rompiscatole mf inv ● vt fig addolorare

pained /peɪnd/ a addolorato

painful /'peɪnfʊl/ a doloroso; (laborious) penoso

painfully /'peɪnfʊlɪ/ adv ~ **shy** incredibilmente timido

painkiller /'peɪnkɪlə(r)/ n calmante m

painkilling /'peɪnkɪlɪŋ/ a antinevralgico

painless /'peɪnlɪs/ a indolore

painlessly /'peɪnlɪslɪ/ adv in modo indolore

painstaking /'peɪnzteɪkɪŋ/ a minuzioso

paint /peɪnt/ n pittura f; **~s** pl colori mpl ● vt/i pitturare; ⟨artist:⟩ dipingere; **~ the town red** folleggiare

■ **paint over** vt (cover with paint) coprire di vernice

paintbox /'peɪntbɒks/ n scatola f di colori

paintbrush /'peɪntbrʌʃ/ n pennello m

painter /'peɪntə(r)/ n pittore, -trice mf; (decorator) imbianchino m

pain threshold n soglia f del dolore

painting /'peɪntɪŋ/ n pittura f; (picture) dipinto m

paint: paintpot n latta f di pittura. **paint remover** n sverniciante m. **paint roller** n rullo m. **paint spray** n pistola f a spruzzo.

paint stripper n (tool) macchina f sverniciante; (chemical) sverniciante m. **paintwork** n pittura f

pair /peə(r)/ n paio m; (of people) coppia f; **a ~ of trousers/scissors** un paio di pantaloni/forbici

■ **pair off** vi mettersi in coppia

pajamas /pə'dʒɑ:məz/ npl Am pigiama msg

Pakistan /pɑ:kɪ'stɑ:n/ n Pakistan m

Pakistani /pɑ:kɪ'stɑ:nɪ/ a & n pakistano, -a mf

pal /pæl/ n fam amico, -a mf

■ **pal up** vi (fam: become friends) fare amicizia (**with** con)

palace /'pælɪs/ n palazzo m

palaeontologist /pælɪɒn'tɒlədʒɪst/ n paleontologo, -a mf

palaeontology /pælɪən'tɒlədʒɪ/ n paleontologia f

palatable /'pælətəbl/ a gradevole al gusto

palate /'pælət/ n palato m

palatial /pə'leɪʃl/ a sontuoso

palaver /pə'lɑ:və(r)/ n (fam: fuss) storie fpl

pale[1] /peɪl/ n (stake) palo m; **beyond the ~** fig inaccettabile

pale[2] a pallido ● vi impallidire; **~ into insignificance** diventare insignificante

paleness /'peɪlnɪs/ n pallore m

Palestine /'pælɪstaɪn/ n Palestina f

Palestinian /pælə'stɪnɪən/ a & n palestinese mf

palette /'pælɪt/ n tavolozza f

palette knife n spatola f

paling /'peɪlɪŋ/ n (stake) palo m; (fence) palizzata f

palisade /pælɪ'seɪd/ n (fence) palizzata f

pall /pɔ:l/ n drappo m funebre; fig velo m di tristezza; (of smoke) cappa f ● vi stufare

pallet /'pælɪt/ n pallet m inv

palliative /'pælɪətɪv/ n palliativo m

pallid /'pælɪd/ a pallido

pallor /'pælə(r)/ n pallore m

palm /pɑ:m/ n palmo m; (tree) palma f

■ **palm off** vt ~ **sth off on sb** rifilare qcsa a qcno

palmist /'pɑ:mɪst/ n chiromante mf

palmistry /'pɑ:mɪstrɪ/ n chiromanzia f

Palm Sunday n domenica f delle palme

palpable /'pælpəbl/ a palpabile; (perceptible) tangibile

palpate /pæl'peɪt/ vi palpare

palpitate /'pælpɪteɪt/ vi palpitare

palpitations /pælpɪ'teɪʃnz/ npl palpitazioni fpl

paltry /'pɔ:ltrɪ/ a (-ier, -iest) insignificante

pampas /'pæmpəs/ n pampas fpl

pamper /'pæmpə(r)/ vt viziare

pamphlet /'pæmflɪt/ n opuscolo m

pan /pæn/ n tegame m, pentola f; (for frying) padella f; (of scales) piatto m ● vt (pt/pp **panned**) (fam: criticize) stroncare

■ **pan out** vi (fam: develop) mettersi

panacea /pænə'si:ə/ n panacea f

panache /pə'næʃ/ n stile m

pancake /'pænkeɪk/ n crêpe f inv, frittella f

Pancake Day *n* martedì *m inv* grasso

pancreas /'pæŋkrɪəs/ *n* pancreas *m inv*

panda /'pændə/ *n* panda *m inv*

panda car *n* macchina *f* della polizia

pandemonium /pændɪ'məʊnɪəm/ *n* pandemonio *m*

pander /'pændə(r)/ *vi* ~ **to sb** compiacere qcno

p & p *n abbr* (**postage and packing**) spese *fpl* di spedizione

pane /peɪn/ *n* ~ **[of glass]** vetro *m*

panel /'pænl/ *n* pannello *m*; (*group of people*) giuria *f*; ~ **of experts** gruppo *m* di esperti; ~ **of judges** giuria *f*

panelling /'pænəlɪŋ/ *n* pannelli *mpl*

panellist /'pænəlɪst/ *n Radio, TV* partecipante *mf*

pan-fry *vt* friggere

pang /pæŋ/ *n* ~**s of hunger** morsi *mpl* della fame; ~**s of conscience** rimorsi *mpl* di coscienza

panic /'pænɪk/ *n* panico *m* ● *vi* (*pt/pp* **panicked**) lasciarsi prendere dal panico

panic: panic button *n fam* **hit the** ~ ~ farsi prendere dal panico. **panic buying** *n* accaparramento *m*. **panic-stricken** /'pænɪk-strɪkən/ *a* in preda al panico

panicky /'pænɪkɪ/ *a* che si lascia prendere dal panico facilmente

pannier /'pænɪə(r)/ *n* (*on bike*) borsa *f*; (*on mule*) bisaccia *f*

panorama /pænə'rɑːmə/ *n* panorama *m*

panoramic /pænə'ræmɪk/ *a* panoramico

pan scourer *n* paglietta *f*

pansy /'pænzɪ/ *n* viola *f* del pensiero; (*fam: effeminate man*) finocchio *m*

pant /pænt/ *vi* ansimare

pantechnicon /pæn'teknɪkən/ *n* furgone *m* per traslochi

panther /'pænθə(r)/ *n* pantera *f*

panties /'pæntɪz/ *npl* mutandine *fpl*

panting /'pæntɪŋ/ *a* ansante

pantomime /'pæntəmaɪm/ *n* pantomima *f*

pantry /'pæntrɪ/ *n* dispensa *f*

pants /pænts/ *npl* (*underwear*) mutande *fpl*; (*woman's*) mutandine *fpl*; (*trousers*) pantaloni *mpl*

panty /'pæntɪ/: **panty girdle** *n* guaina *f*. **pantyhose** *n Am* collant *m inv*. **panty-liner** *n* salvaslip *m inv*

paparazzi /pæpə'rætzɪ/ *npl* paparazzi *mpl*

papal /'peɪpl/ *a* papale

paper /'peɪpə(r)/ *n* carta *f*; (*wallpaper*) carta *f* da parati; (*newspaper*) giornale *m*; (*exam*) esame *m* scritto; (*treatise*) saggio *m*; ~**s** *pl* (*documents*) documenti *mpl*; (*for identification*) documento *msg* [d'identità]; **on** ~ in teoria; **put down on** ~ mettere per iscritto ● *attrib* di carta; (*version*) su carta ● *vt* tappezzare

∎ **paper over** *vt* ~ **over the cracks** dissimulare le divergenze

paper: paperback *n* edizione *f* economica. **paper bank** *n* cassonetto *m* per la raccolta della carta. **paper boy** *n* ragazzo *m* che reca-pita i giornali a domicilio. **paper chain** *n* festone *m* di carta. **paper chase** *n corsa f* campestre in cui i partecipanti seguono una scia di pezzetti di carta. **paper clip** *n* graffetta *f*. **paper currency** *n* banconote *fpl*. **paper feed tray** *n Comput* vassoio *m* della carta. **paperknife** *n* tagliacarte *m inv*. **paper mill** *n* cartiera *f*. **paper money** *n* cartamoneta *f*. **paper napkin** *n* tovagliolo *m* di carta. **paper round** *n* **he does a** ~ ~ recapita i giornali a domicilio. **paper shredder** *n* distruttore *m* di documenti. **paper-thin** *a* sottilissimo. **paper towel** *n* (*toilet*) asciugamano *m* di carta; (*kitchen*) carta *f* asciugatutto. **paperweight** *n* fermacarte *m inv*. **paperwork** *n* lavoro *m* d'ufficio

papery /'peɪpərɪ/ *a* (*texture, leaves*) cartaceo

paprika /pə'priːkə/ *n* paprica *f*

par /pɑː(r)/ *n* (*in golf*) par *m inv*; **on a** ~ **with** alla pari con; **feel below** ~ essere una po' giù di tono

para[1] /'pærə/ *n* (*paragraph*) paragrafo *m*

para[2] *n Br Mil* parà *m inv*

parable /'pærəbl/ *n* parabola *f*

parachute /'pærəʃuːt/ *n* paracadute *m inv* ● *vi* lanciarsi col paracadute

parachutist /'pærəʃuːtɪst/ *n* paracadutista *mf*

parade /pə'reɪd/ *n* (*military*) parata *f* militare; (*display*) sfoggio *m* ● *vi* sfilare ● *vt* (*show off*) far sfoggio di

parade ground *n* piazza *f* d'armi

paradigm /'pærədaɪm/ *n* paradigma *m*

paradise /'pærədaɪs/ *n* paradiso *m*

paradox /'pærədɒks/ *n* paradosso *m*

paradoxical /pærə'dɒksɪkl/ *a* paradossale

paradoxically /pærə'dɒksɪklɪ/ *adv* paradossalmente

paraffin /'pærəfɪn/ *n* paraffina *f*; (*oil*) cherosene *m*

paragliding /'pærəglaɪdɪŋ/ *n* parapendio *m*

paragon /'pærəgən/ *n* ~ **of virtue** modello *m* di virtù

paragraph /'pærəgrɑːf/ *n* paragrafo *m*

parallel /'pærəlel/ *a & adv* parallelo ● *n Geog, fig* parallelo *m*; (*line*) parallela *f* ● *vt* essere paragonabile a

parallel bars *npl* parallele *fpl*

parallelogram /pærə'leləʊgræm/ *n Math* parallelogramma *m*

parallel port *n Comput* porta *f* parallela

paralyse /'pærəlaɪz/ *vt* paralizzare

paralysis /pə'rælɪsɪs/ *n* (*pl* **-ses**) /pə-'rælɪsiːz/ paralisi *f inv*

paralytic /pærə'lɪtɪk/ *a* (*person*) paralitico; (*arm, leg*) paralizzato; (*Br fam: drunk*) ubriaco fradicio

paramedic /pærə'medɪk/ *n* paramedico *m*

parameter /pə'ræmɪtə(r)/ *n* parametro *m*

paramilitary /pærə'mɪlɪtrɪ/ *n* appartenente *mf* a un gruppo paramilitare ● *a* paramilitare

paramount /'pærəmaʊnt/ *a* supremo; **be** ~ essere essenziale

paranoia /pærə'nɔɪə/ *n* paranoia *f*

paranoid /'pærənɔɪd/ *a* paranoico

paranormal /pærə'nɔ:məl/ a & n paranormale m

parapet /'pærəpɪt/ n parapetto m

paraphernalia /pærəfə'neɪlɪə/ n armamentario m

paraphrase /'pærəfreɪz/ n parafrasi f inv ● vt parafrasare

paraplegic /pærə'pli:dʒɪk/ a & n paraplegico, -a mf

parascending /'pærəsendɪŋ/ n Br paracadutismo m ascensionale

parasite /'pærəsaɪt/ n parassita mf

parasitic /pærə'sɪtɪk/ a parassitario

parasol /'pærəsɒl/ n parasole m

paratrooper /'pærətru:pə(r)/ n paracadutista m

parboil /'pɑ:bɔɪl/ vt scottare

parcel /'pɑ:sl/ n pacco m

■ **parcel up** vt impacchettare ⟨clothes etc⟩

parch /pɑ:tʃ/ vt disseccare; **be ~ed** ⟨person:⟩ morire dalla sete

parchment /'pɑ:tʃmənt/ n pergamena f

pardon /'pɑ:dn/ n perdono m; Jur grazia f; **~?** prego?; **I beg your ~?** fml chiedo scusa?; **I do beg your ~** (sorry) chiedo scusa! ● vt perdonare; Jur graziare

pare /peə(r)/ vt (peel) pelare

parent /'peərənt/ n genitore m

parentage /'peərəntɪdʒ/ n natali mpl

parental /pə'rentl/ a dei genitori

parent company n casa f madre

parenthesis /pə'renθəsɪs/ n (pl -ses /pə-'renθəsi:z/) parentesi f inv

parer /'peərə(r)/ n sbucciatore m

pariah /pə'raɪə/ n paria m

parings /'peərɪŋz/ npl (of fruit) bucce fpl; (of nails) ritagli mpl di unghie

Paris /'pærɪs/ n Parigi f

parish /'pærɪʃ/ n parrocchia f

parishioner /pə'rɪʃənə(r)/ n parrocchiano, -a mf

parish priest n (Catholic) parroco m; (Protestant) pastore m

Parisian /pə'rɪzɪən/ a & n parigino, -a mf

parity /'pærətɪ/ n parità f

park /pɑ:k/ n parco m ● vt Auto posteggiare, parcheggiare; **~ oneself** fam installarsi ● vi posteggiare, parcheggiare

parka /'pɑ:kə/ n parka m inv

park-and-ride n parcheggio m collegato al centro di una città da mezzi pubblici

parking /'pɑ:kɪŋ/ n parcheggio m, posteggio m; **'no ~'** 'divieto di sosta'

parking: parking attendant n parcheggiatore, -trice mf, posteggiatore, -trice mf. **parking lot** n Am posteggio m, parcheggio m. **parking meter** n parchimetro m. **parking space** n posteggio m, parcheggio m

park: parkland n parco m. **park ranger, park warden** n guardaparco m inv

parliament /'pɑ:ləmənt/ n parlamento m

parliamentary /pɑ:lə'mentərɪ/ a parlamentare

parlour /'pɑ:lə(r)/ n salotto m

parochial /pə'rəʊkɪəl/ a parrocchiale; fig ristretto

parochialism /pə'rəʊkɪəlɪzm/ n campanilismo m

parody /'pærədɪ/ n parodia f ● vt (pt/pp -ied) parodiare

parole /pə'rəʊl/ n **on ~** sulla parola; **eligible for ~** suscettibile di essere liberato sulla parola ● vt mettere in libertà sulla parola

paroxysm /'pærəksɪzm/ n accesso m

parquet floor /'pɑ:keɪ/ n parquet m

parquet flooring /'flɔ:rɪŋ/ n parquet m inv

parrot /'pærət/ n pappagallo m

parry /'pærɪ/ vt (pt/pp -ied) parare ⟨blow⟩; (in fencing) eludere

parse /pɑ:z/ vt fare l'analisi grammaticale di ⟨sentence⟩; Comput analizzare la sintassi di

parsimonious /pɑ:sɪ'məʊnɪəs/ a parsimonioso

parsing /'pɑ:zɪŋ/ n analisi f grammaticale; Comput analisi f sintattica

parsley /'pɑ:slɪ/ n prezzemolo m

parsnip /'pɑ:snɪp/ n pastinaca f

parson /'pɑ:sn/ n pastore m

part /pɑ:t/ n parte f; (of machine) pezzo m; **for my ~** per quanto mi riguarda; **on the ~ of** da parte di; **take sb's ~** prendere le parti di qcno; **take ~ in** prendere parte a ● adv in parte ● vt **~ one's hair** farsi la riga ● vi ⟨people:⟩ separarsi; **~ with** separarsi da

part exchange n **take in ~** prendere indietro come pagamento parziale

partial /'pɑ:ʃl/ a parziale; **be ~ to** aver un debole per

partiality /pɑ:ʃɪ'ælətɪ/ n (liking) predilezione f

partially /'pɑ:ʃəlɪ/ adv parzialmente; **~ sighted** parzialmente cieco

participant /pɑ:'tɪsɪpənt/ n partecipante mf

participate /pɑ:'tɪsɪpeɪt/ vi partecipare (in a)

participation /pɑ:tɪsɪ'peɪʃn/ n partecipazione f

participatory /pɑ:tɪsɪ'peɪtərɪ/ a partecipativo

participle /'pɑ:tɪsɪpl/ n participio m; **present/past ~** participio presente/passato

particle /'pɑ:tɪkl/ n Phys, Gram particella f

particular /pə'tɪkjʊlə(r)/ a particolare; (precise) meticoloso; pej difficile; **in ~** in particolare

particularly /pə'tɪkjʊləlɪ/ adv particolarmente

particulars /pə'tɪkjʊləz/ npl particolari mpl

parting /'pɑ:tɪŋ/ n separazione f; (in hair) scriminatura f ● attrib di commiato

partisan /pɑ:tɪ'zæn/ n partigiano, -a mf

partition /pɑ:'tɪʃn/ n (wall) parete f divisoria; Pol divisione f ● vt dividere

■ **partition off** vt separare

partly /'pɑ:tlɪ/ adv in parte

partner /'pɑ:tnə(r)/ n Comm socio, -a mf; (sport, in relationship) compagno, -a mf

partnership /'pɑ:tnəʃɪp/ *n Comm* società *f inv*

part: part of speech *n* categoria *f* grammaticale. **part owner** *n* comproprietario, -a *mf*. **part payment** *n* acconto *m*

partridge /'pɑ:trɪdʒ/ *n* pernice *f*

part-time *a & adv* part time; **be** *or* **work ~** lavorare part time

part-way *adv* **~ through the evening** a metà serata

party /'pɑ:tɪ/ *n* ricevimento *m*, festa *f*; (*group*) gruppo *m*; *Pol* partito *m*; *Jur* parte *f*; **be ~ to** essere parte attiva in

party: party dress *n* abito *m* da sera. **party-goer** *n* festaiolo, -a *mf*. **party hat** *n* cappellino *m* di carta. **party leader** *n* dirigente *m* di partito. **party line** *n Teleph* duplex *m inv*; *Pol* linea *f* del partito. **party piece** *n* pezzo *m* forte; **do one's ~ ~** esibirsi nel proprio pezzo forte. **party political broadcast** *n* comunicato *m* di partito (*trasmesso per radio o per televisione*). **party politics** *n* politica *f* di partito. **party wall** *n* muro *m* divisorio

pass /pɑ:s/ *n* lasciapassare *m inv*; (*in mountains*) passo *m*; *Sport* passaggio *m*; (*Sch: mark*) [voto *m*] sufficiente *m*; **get a ~** *Sch* ottenere la sufficienza; **make a ~ at** *fam* fare delle avances a ● *vt* passare; (*overtake*) sorpassare; (*approve*) far passare; (*exceed*) oltrepassare; fare ⟨*remark*⟩; esprimere ⟨*judgement*⟩; *Jur* pronunciare ⟨*sentence*⟩; **~ water** orinare; **~ the time** passare il tempo ● *vi* passare; (*in exam*) essere promosso; **let sth ~** *fig* lasciar correre qcsa; **~!** (*in game*) passo!

■ **pass as** *vt* = **pass for**
■ **pass away** *vi* mancare
■ **pass by** *vi* (*go past*) passare
■ **pass down** *vt* passare; *fig* trasmettere
■ **pass for** *vt* (*be accepted as*) passare per
■ **pass off** *vi* (*disappear*) passare; (*take place*) svolgersi ● *vt* **~ sb/sth off as** far passare qcno/qcsa per
■ **pass on** *vt* passare ⟨*message, information*⟩
■ **pass on to** *vt* passare a ⟨*new subject, next question*⟩
■ **pass out** *vi fam* svenire
■ **pass over** *vt* (*not mention*) passare sopra a; **~ sb over for promotion** non prendere in considerazione qcno per una promozione ● *vi* (*die*) spirare
■ **pass round** *vt* far passare
■ **pass through** *vt* attraversare
■ **pass up** *vt* passare; (*fam: miss*) lasciarsi scappare

passable /'pɑ:səbl/ *a* ⟨*road*⟩ praticabile; (*satisfactory*) passabile

passage /'pæsɪdʒ/ *n* passaggio *m*; (*corridor*) corridoio *m*; (*voyage*) traversata *f*

pass book *n Fin* libretto *m* di risparmio

passé /pæ'seɪ/ *a pej* sorpassato

passenger /'pæsɪndʒə(r)/ *n* passeggero, -a *mf*

passenger: passenger compartment *n Br Auto* abitacolo *m*. **passenger ferry** *n* tra-

ghetto *m*. **passenger plane** *n* aereo *m* passeggeri. **passenger seat** *n* posto *m* accanto al guidatore. **passenger train** *n* treno *m* passeggeri

passepartout /ˌpæspɑ:'tu:/ *n* (*key, frame*) passe-partout *m inv*

passer-by /pɑ:sə'baɪ/ *n* (*pl* **-s-by**) passante *mf*

passing place /'pɑ:sɪŋ/ *n* piazzola *f* di sosta per consentire il transito dei veicoli nei due sensi

passing shot *n Tennis* passante *m*

passion /'pæʃn/ *n* passione *f*

passionate /'pæʃənət/ *a* appassionato

passionately /'pæʃənətlɪ/ *adv* appassionatamente

passion fruit *n* frutto *m* della passione

passive /'pæsɪv/ *a & n* passivo *m*

passively /'pæsɪvlɪ/ *adv* passivamente

passiveness /'pæsɪvnɪs/ *n* passività *f*

passive resistance *n* resistenza *f* passiva

passive smoking *n* fumo *m* passivo

pass: pass-key *n* (*master-key*) passe-partout *m inv*; (*for access*) chiave *f*. **pass-mark** *n Sch* [voto *m*] sufficiente *m*. **Passover** *n* Pasqua *f* ebraica. **passport** *n* passaporto *m*. **password** *n* parola *f* d'ordine

past /pɑ:st/ *a* passato; (*former*) ex; **that's all ~** tutto questo è passato; **in the ~ few days** nei giorni scorsi; **the ~ week** la settimana scorsa ● *n* passato *m* ● *prep* oltre; **at ten ~ two** alle due e dieci ● *adv* oltre; **go/come ~** passare

pasta /'pæstə/ *n* pasta[sciutta] *f*

paste /peɪst/ *n* pasta *f*; (*dough*) impasto *m*; (*adhesive*) colla *f* ● *vt* incollare
■ **paste down** *vt* incollare
■ **paste in** *vt* incollare
■ **paste up** *vt* affiggere ⟨*notice, poster*⟩

paste jewellery *n* bigiotteria *f*

pastel /'pæstl/ *n* pastello *m* ● *attrib* pastello

pasteurization /ˌpɑ:stʃəraɪ'zeɪʃn/ *n* pastorizzazione *f*

pasteurize /'pɑ:stʃəraɪz/ *vt* pastorizzare

pasteurized /'pɑ:stʃəraɪzd/ *a* pastorizzato

pastille /'pæstɪl/ *n* pastiglia *f*

pastime /'pɑ:staɪm/ *n* passatempo *m*

pasting /'peɪstɪŋ/ *n* (*fam: defeat, criticism*) batosta *f*

past master *n* esperto, -a *mf*

pastor /'pɑ:stə(r)/ *n* pastore *m*

pastoral /'pɑ:stərəl/ *a* pastorale

past participle *n* participio *m* passato

pastrami /pæ'strɑ:mɪ/ *n* carne *f* di manzo affumicata

pastry /'peɪstrɪ/ *n* pasta *f*; **pastries** *pl* pasticcini *mpl*

past tense *n* passato *m*

pasture /'pɑ:stʃə(r)/ *n* pascolo *m*

pasty¹ /'pæstɪ/ *n* ≈ pasticcio *m*

pasty² /'peɪstɪ/ *a* smorto

pat /pæt/ *n* buffetto *m*; (*of butter*) pezzetto *m* ● *adv* **have sth off ~** conoscere qcsa a menadito ● *vt* (*pt/pp* **patted**) dare un buffetto a; **~ sb on the back** *fig* congratularsi con qcno

patch /pætʃ/ n toppa f; (spot) chiazza f; (period) periodo m; **not a ~ on** fam molto inferiore a ● vt mettere una toppa su
■ **patch up** vt riparare alla bell'e meglio; appianare ⟨quarrel⟩
patchwork /'pætʃwɜːk/ n patchwork m inv; fig mosaico m
patchy /'pætʃɪ/ a incostante
pâté /'pæteɪ/ n pâté m inv
patent /'peɪtnt/ a palese ● n brevetto m ● vt brevettare
patent leather n vernice m
patently /'peɪtntlɪ/ adv in modo palese
paternal /pə'tɜːnl/ a paterno
paternalism /pə'tɜːnəlɪzm/ n paternalismo m
paternalistic /pətɜːnə'lɪstɪk/ a paternalistico
paternity /pə'tɜːnətɪ/ n paternità f
paternity leave n congedo m di paternità
paternity suit n causa f per il riconoscimento di paternità
path /pɑːθ/ n (pl ~s /pɑːðz/) sentiero m; (orbit) traiettoria f; fig strada f
pathetic /pə'θetɪk/ a patetico; (fam: very bad) penoso
pathological /pæθə'lɒdʒɪkl/ a patologico
pathologist /pə'θɒlədʒɪst/ n patologo, -a mf
pathology /pə'θɒlədʒɪ/ n patologia f
pathos /'peɪθɒs/ n pathos m
patience /'peɪʃns/ n pazienza f; (game) solitario m
patient /'peɪʃnt/ a & n paziente mf
patiently /'peɪʃntlɪ/ adv pazientemente
patio /'pætɪəʊ/ n terrazza f
patio doors npl portafinestra f
patio garden n cortile m
patriarch /'peɪtrɪɑːk/ n patriarca m
patriarchal /peɪtrɪ'ɑːkəl/ a patriarcale
patriarchy /'peɪtrɪɑːkɪ/ n patriarcato m
patriot /'pætrɪət/ n patriota m
patriotic /pætrɪ'ɒtɪk/ a patriottico
patriotism /'pætrɪətɪzm/ n patriottismo m
patrol /pə'trəʊl/ n pattuglia f ● vt/i pattugliare
patrol car n autopattuglia f
patron /'peɪtrən/ n patrono m; (of charity) benefattore, -trice mf; (of the arts) mecenate mf; (customer) cliente mf
patronage /'pætrənɪdʒ/ n patrocinio m; (of shop etc) frequentazione f
patronize /'pætrənaɪz/ vt frequentare abitualmente; fig trattare con condiscendenza
patronizing /'pætrənaɪzɪŋ/ a condiscendente
patronizingly /'pætrənaɪzɪŋlɪ/ adv con condiscendenza
patron saint n [santo, -a mf] patrono, -a mf
patter¹ /'pætə(r)/ n picchiettio m ● vi picchiettare
patter² n (of salesman) chiacchiere fpl
pattern /'pætn/ n motivo m; (for knitting, sewing, in behaviour) modello m
patterned /'pætənd/ a ⟨material⟩ fantasia
paunch /pɔːntʃ/ n pancia f

pauper /'pɔːpə(r)/ n povero, -a mf
pause /pɔːz/ n pausa f ● vi fare una pausa
pave /peɪv/ vt pavimentare; **~ the way** preparare la strada (for a)
pavement /'peɪvmənt/ n marciapiede m
pavilion /pə'vɪljən/ n padiglione m; (Cricket) costruzione f annessa al campo da gioco con gli spogliatoi
paving /'peɪvɪŋ/ n lastricato m
paving slab, paving stone n lastra f di pietra
paw /pɔː/ n zampa f ● vt fam mettere le zampe addosso a
pawn¹ /pɔːn/ n (in chess) pedone m; fig pedina f
pawn² vt impegnare ● n **in ~** in pegno
pawnbroker /'pɔːnbrəʊkə(r)/ n prestatore, -trice mf su pegno
pawnshop /'pɔːnʃɒp/ n monte m di pietà
pawpaw /'pɔːpɔː/ n papaia f
pay /peɪ/ n paga f; **in the ~ of** al soldo di ● v (pt/pp paid) ● vt pagare; prestare ⟨attention⟩; fare ⟨compliment, visit⟩; **~ cash** pagare in contanti ● vi pagare; (be profitable) rendere; **it doesn't ~ to...** fig è fatica sprecata...; **~ in instalments** pagare a rate; **~ through the nose** fam pagare profumatamente
■ **pay back** vt ripagare
■ **pay for** vt pagare per
■ **pay in** vt versare
■ **pay off** vt saldare ⟨debt⟩ ● vi fig dare dei frutti
■ **pay out** vt (spend) pagare
■ **pay up** vi pagare
payable /'peɪəbl/ a pagabile; **make ~ to** intestare a
PAYE Br abbr (**pay-as-you-earn**) trattenute fpl fiscali alla fonte
payee /peɪ'iː/ n beneficiario m
payer /'peɪə(r)/ n pagante mf
paying-in slip /peɪɪŋ'ɪn/ n distinta f di versamento
payload /'peɪləʊd/ n (of bomb) carica f esplosiva; (of aircraft, ship) carico m utile
payment /'peɪmənt/ n pagamento m; **~ by instalments** pagamento rateale
pay: pay packet n busta f paga. **payphone** n telefono m pubblico. **payroll** n (list) libro m paga; (sum of money) paga f del personale; (employees collectively) personale m. **payslip** n busta f paga inv
PC abbr (**personal computer**) PC m inv; abbr (**police constable**) agente m di polizia
pc abbr (**per cent**) per cento; abbr (**politically correct**) politicamente corretto; abbr (**postcard**) cartolina f postale
pd Am abbr (**police department**) reparto m di polizia
PE n abbr (**physical education**) educazione f fisica
pea /piː/ n pisello m
peace /piːs/ n pace f; **~ of mind** tranquillità f
peaceable /'piːsəbl/ a pacifico
peace envoy n mediatore, -trice mf
peaceful /'piːsfʊl/ a calmo, sereno

peacefully /'pi:sfʊlɪ/ adv in pace

peace: peacekeeping n Mil, Pol mantenimento m della pace ● attrib ⟨force, troops⟩ di mantenimento della pace. **peacemaker** n mediatore, -trice mf. **peacetime** n tempo m di pace ● attrib ⟨planning, government⟩ del tempo di pace; ⟨army, alliance, training⟩ in tempo di pace. **peace treaty** n trattato m di pace

peach /pi:tʃ/ n pesca f; (tree) pesco m

peacock /'pi:kɒk/ n pavone m

pea green a verde pisello

peak /pi:k/ n picco m; fig culmine m

peaked cap /pi:kt/ n berretto m a punta

peak hours npl ore fpl di punta

peak season n alta stagione f

peaky /'pi:kɪ/ a malaticcio

peal /pi:l/ n (of bells) scampanio m; **~s of laughter** fragore msg di risate

peanut /'pi:nʌt/ n nocciolina f [americana]; **~s** pl fam miseria fsg

peanut butter n burro m di arachidi

pear /peə(r)/ n pera f; (tree) pero m

pearl /pɜ:l/ n perla f

pearl: pearl barley n orzo m perlato. **pearldiver** n pescatore, -trice mf di perle. **pearl grey** n grigio m perla inv ● a grigio perla inv

Pearly Gates /'pɜ:lɪ/ npl hum porte fpl del paradiso

peasant /'peznt/ n contadino, -a mf

peat /pi:t/ n torba f

pebble /'pebl/ n ciottolo m

pebble-dash n intonaco m a pinocchino

pecan /'pi:kən/ n (tree) pecan m inv; (nut) noce f pecan inv

peck /pek/ n beccata f; (kiss) bacetto m ● vt beccare; (kiss) dare un bacetto a

■ **peck at** vi beccare

pecking order /'pekɪŋ/ n gerarchia f

peckish /'pekɪʃ/ a **be ~** fam avere un languorino allo stomaco

pectoral /'pektərəl/ a & n pettorale m

peculiar /pɪ'kju:lɪə(r)/ a strano; (special) particolare; **~ to** tipico di

peculiarity /pɪkju:lɪ'ærətɪ/ n stranezza f; (feature) particolarità f inv

peculiarly /pɪ'kju:lɪəlɪ/ adv singolarmente

pecuniary /pə'kju:nɪərɪ/ a pecuniario

pedagogical /pedə'gɒdʒɪkl/ a pedagogico

pedagogy /'pedəgɒdʒɪ/ n pedagogia f

pedal /'pedl/ n pedale m ● vi pedalare

pedal bin n pattumiera f a pedale

pedant /'pedənt/ n pedante m

pedantic /pɪ'dæntɪk/ a pedante

pedantically /pɪ'dæntɪklɪ/ adv in modo pedante

pedantry /'pedəntrɪ/ n pedanteria f

peddle /'pedl/ vt vendere porta a porta

pedestal /'pedɪstl/ n piedistallo m

pedestrian /pɪ'destrɪən/ n pedone m ● a fig scadente

pedestrian crossing n passaggio m pedonale

pedestrian precinct n zona f pedonale

pedicure /'pedɪkjʊə(r)/ n pedicure f inv

pedigree /'pedɪgri:/ n pedigree m inv; (of person) lignaggio m ● attrib ⟨animal⟩ di razza, con pedigree

pedlar /'pedlə(r)/ n venditore, -trice mf ambulante

pee /pi:/ fam vi (pt/pp peed) fare la pipì ● n **go for a ~** andare a fare la pipì

peek /pi:k/ fam vi sbirciare ● n **take a ~ at sth** dare una sbirciata a qcsa

peekaboo /pi:kə'bu:/ int cucù

peel /pi:l/ n buccia f ● vt sbucciare ● vi ⟨nose etc.⟩ spellarsi; ⟨paint:⟩ staccarsi

■ **peel off** vt togliersi ⟨item of clothing⟩ ● vi ⟨wallpaper:⟩ staccarsi; ⟨skin:⟩ squamarsi

peeler /'pi:lə(r)/ n sbucciatore m

peelings /'pi:lɪŋz/ npl bucce fpl

peep /pi:p/ n sbirciata f ● vi sbirciare

peephole /'pi:phəʊl/ n spioncino m

Peeping Tom /'pi:pɪŋ/ n fam guardone m

peer[1] /pɪə(r)/ vi **~ at** scrutare

peer[2] n nobile m; **his ~s** pl (in rank) i suoi pari; (in age) i suoi coetanei

peerage /'pɪərɪdʒ/ n Br Pol nobiltà f; (book) almanacco m nobiliare; **be given a ~** essere elevato al rango di pari

peer group n (of same status) pari mpl; (of same age) coetanei mpl; **~ ~ pressure** pressione f esercitata dal gruppo cui si appartiene

peerless /'pɪəlɪs/ a impareggiabile

peeved /pi:vd/ a fam irritato

peevish /'pi:vɪʃ/ a fam irritabile

peg /peg/ n (hook) piolo m; (for tent) picchetto m; (for clothes) molletta f; **off the ~** fam prêt-à-porter ● vt (pt/pp pegged) fissare ⟨prices⟩; stendere con le mollette ⟨washing⟩

pegboard /'pegbɔ:d/ n segnapunti m inv

pejorative /pɪ'dʒɒrətɪv/ a peggiorativo

pejoratively /pɪ'dʒɒrətɪvlɪ/ adv in modo peggiorativo

Peke /pi:k/ n fam (dog) pechinese m

Peking /'pi:kɪŋ/ n Pechino f

Pekin[g]ese /pi:kɪ'ni:z/ n pechinese m

pelican /'pelɪkən/ n pellicano m

pelican crossing n passaggio m pedonale con semaforo

pellet /'pelɪt/ n pallottola f

pell-mell /pel'mel/ adv alla rinfusa

pelmet /'pelmɪt/ n mantovana f

pelt[1] /pelt/ n (skin) pelliccia f

pelt[2] vt bombardare ● vi (fam: run fast) catapultarsi; (rain heavily) venir giù a fiotti

■ **pelt along** vi (move quickly) precipitarsi lungo

■ **pelt down** vi ⟨rain:⟩ venir giù a fiotti

pelvis /'pelvɪs/ n Anat bacino m

pen[1] /pen/ n (for animals) recinto m

pen[2] n penna f; (ball-point) penna f a sfera

penal /'pi:nl/ a penale

penal code n codice m penale

penalize /'pi:nəlaɪz/ vt penalizzare

penalty /'penltɪ/ n sanzione f; (fine) multa f; (in football) [calcio m di] rigore m

penalty: penalty area, penalty box n area f di rigore. **penalty clause** n Comm, Jur clausola *f* penale. **penalty kick** *n* [calcio *m* di] rigore *m*. **penalty shootout** *n* rigori *mpl*

penance /'penəns/ *n* penitenza *f*

pence /pens/ *see* **penny**

penchant /'pɔ̃ʃɒ̃/ *n* debole *m*

pencil /'pensl/ *n* matita *f* ● *vt* (*pt/pp* **pencilled**) segnare a matita

■ **pencil in** *vt* annotare provvisoriamente 〈*date*〉

pencil case *n* [astuccio *m*] portamatite *m inv*

pencil sharpener *n* temperamatite *m inv*

pendant /'pendənt/ *n* ciondolo *m*

pending /'pendɪŋ/ *a* in sospeso ● *prep* in attesa di

pendulum /'pendjʊləm/ *n* pendolo *m*

penetrate /'penɪtreɪt/ *vt/i* penetrare

penetrating /'penɪtreɪtɪŋ/ *a* 〈*sound, stare*〉 penetrante; 〈*remark*〉 acuto

penetration /penɪ'treɪʃn/ *n* penetrazione *f*

penfriend /'penfrend/ *n* amico, -a *mf* di penna

penguin /'peŋgwɪn/ *n* pinguino *m*

penicillin /penɪ'sɪlɪn/ *n* penicillina *f*

peninsula /pɪ'nɪnsjʊlə/ *n* penisola *f*

penis /'piːnɪs/ *n* pene *m*

penitence /'penɪtəns/ *n* penitenza *f*

penitent /'penɪtənt/ *a* & *n* penitente *mf*

penitentiary /penɪ'tenʃərɪ/ *n* Am penitenziario *m*

penknife /'pennaɪf/ *n* temperino *m*

pen-name *n* pseudonimo *m*

pennant /'penənt/ *n* bandiera *f*

penniless /'penɪlɪs/ *a* senza un soldo

penny /'penɪ/ *n* (*pl* **pence**; *single coins* **pennies**) penny *m*; Am centesimo *m*; **spend a ~** *fam* andare in bagno; **the ~'s dropped!** *fam* ci è arrivato!

penny: penny-farthing *n* velocipede *m*. **penny-pinching** /'penɪpɪntʃɪŋ/ *a* taccagno ● *n* taccagneria *f*. **penny whistle** *n* zufolo *m*

pen-pusher *n fam* scribacchino, -a *mf*

pension /'penʃn/ *n* pensione *f*

■ **pension off** *vt* (*force to retire*) mandare in pensione

pensioner /'penʃənə(r)/ *n* pensionato, -a *mf*

pension fund *n* fondo *m* pensioni; (*of an individual*) fondo *m* pensione

pension scheme *n* piano *m* di pensionamento

pensive /'pensɪv/ *a* pensoso

pentagon /'pentəgən/ *n* pentagono *m*; Am Pol **the P~** il Pentagono

pentagonal /pen'tægənəl/ *a* pentagonale

pentathlete /pen'tæθliːt/ *n* pentatleta *mf*

pentathlon /pen'tæθlɒn/ *n* pentathlon *m inv*

Pentecost /'pentɪkɒst/ *n* Pentecoste *f*

pent-up /'pentʌp/ *a* represso

penultimate /pɪ'nʌltɪmət/ *a* penultimo

penury /'penjʊrɪ/ *n* miseria *f*

peony /'pɪənɪ/ *n* peonia *f*

people /'piːpl/ *npl* persone *fpl*, gente *fsg*; (*citizens*) popolo *msg*; **a lot of ~** una marea di gente; **the ~** la gente; **English ~** gli inglesi;

~ say si dice; **for four ~** per quattro ● *vt* popolare

PEP /pep/ Br *abbr* (**personal equity plan**) piano *m* di investimento azionario personale

■ **pep up** *vt* vivacizzare 〈*party, conversation*〉; tirare su 〈*person*〉

pepper /'pepə(r)/ *n* pepe *m*; (*vegetable*) peperone *m* ● *vt* (*season*) pepare

pepper: peppercorn *n* grano *m* di pepe. **peppercorn rent** affitto *m* nominale. **pepper mill** *n* macinapepe *m inv*. **peppermint** *n* menta *f* peperita; (*sweet*) caramella *f* alla menta. **pepper pot** *n* pepiera *f*

pep pill /'peppɪl/ *n fam* stimolante *m*

pep talk *n* discorso *m* d'incoraggiamento

peptic /'peptɪk/ *a* peptico

peptic ulcer *n* ulcera *f* peptica

per /pɜː(r)/ *prep* per

per annum /pər'ænəm/ *adv* all'anno

per capita /pə'kæpɪtə/ *a* & *adv* pro capite

perceive /pə'siːv/ *vt* percepire; (*interpret*) interpretare

per cent *adv* percento

percentage /pə'sentɪdʒ/ *n* percentuale *f*

perceptible /pə'septəbl/ *a* percettibile; *fig* sensibile

perceptibly /pə'septɪblɪ/ *adv* percettibilmente; *fig* sensibilmente

perception /pə'sepʃn/ *n* percezione *f*

perceptive /pə'septɪv/ *a* perspicace

perch[1] /pɜːtʃ/ *n* pertica *f* ● *vi* 〈*bird:*〉 appollaiarsi

perch[2] *n inv* (*fish*) pesce *m* persico

percolate /'pɜːkəleɪt/ *vi* infiltrarsi; 〈*coffee:*〉 passare

percolator /'pɜːkəleɪtə(r)/ *n* caffettiera *f* a filtro

percussion /pə'kʌʃn/ *n* percussione *f*

percussion instrument *n* strumento *m* a percussione

percussionist /pə'kʌʃ(ə)nɪst/ *n* percussionista *mf*

peremptory /pə'remptərɪ/ *a* perentorio

perennial /pə'renɪəl/ *a* perenne ● *n* pianta *f* perenne

perfect[1] /'pɜːfɪkt/ *a* perfetto ● *n* Gram passato *m* prossimo

perfect[2] /pə'fekt/ *vt* perfezionare

perfection /pə'fekʃn/ *n* perfezione *f*; **to ~** alla perfezione

perfectionism /pə'fekʃənɪzm/ *n* perfezionismo *m*

perfectionist /pə'fekʃ(ə)nɪst/ *a* & *n* perfezionista *mf*

perfectly /'pɜːfɪktlɪ/ *adv* perfettamente

perfidious /pə'fɪdɪəs/ *a* perfido

perforate /'pɜːfəreɪt/ *vt* perforare

perforated /'pɜːfəreɪtɪd/ *a* perforato; 〈*ulcer*〉 perforante

perforation /pɜːfə'reɪʃn/ *n* perforazione *f*

perform /pə'fɔːm/ *vt* compiere, fare; eseguire 〈*operation, sonata*〉; recitare 〈*role*〉; mettere in scena 〈*play*〉 ● *vi* Theat recitare; Techn funzionare

performance /pə'fɔːməns/ *n* esecuzione *f*;

(*at theatre, cinema*) rappresentazione *f*; *Techn* rendimento *m*

performance bonus *n* premio *m* di produttività

performance-related *a* commensurato alla produttività

performer /pə'fɔːmə(r)/ *n* artista *mf*

performing arts /pə'fɔːmɪŋ/ *npl* arti *fpl* dello spettacolo

perfume /'pɜːfjuːm/ *n* profumo *m*

perfumed /'pɜːfjuːmd/ *a* profumato

perfunctory /pə'fʌŋktərɪ/ *a* superficiale

perhaps /pə'hæps/ *adv* forse

peril /'perɪl/ *n* pericolo *m*

perilous /'perɪləs/ *a* pericoloso

perilously /'perɪləslɪ/ *adv* pericolosamente

perimeter /pə'rɪmɪtə(r)/ *n* perimetro *m*

period /'pɪərɪəd/ *n* periodo *m*; (*menstruation*) mestruazioni *fpl*; *Sch* ora *f* di lezione; (*full stop*) punto *m* fermo ● *attrib* ‹costume› d'epoca; ‹furniture› in stile

periodic /pɪərɪ'ɒdɪk/ *a* periodico

periodical /pɪərɪ'ɒdɪkl/ *n* periodico *m*, rivista *f*

periodically /pɪərɪ'ɒdɪklɪ/ *adv* periodicamente

period of notice *n* periodo *m* di preavviso

peripheral /pə'rɪfərəl/ *a* periferico ● *n* *Comput* periferica *f*

periphery /pə'rɪfərɪ/ *n* periferia *f*

periscope /'perɪskəʊp/ *n* periscopio *m*

perish /'perɪʃ/ *vi* (*rot*) deteriorarsi; (*die*) perire

perishable /'perɪʃəbl/ *a* deteriorabile ● **~s** *npl* merce *f* deperibile

perished /'perɪʃt/ *a* (*fam: freezing cold*) **be ~** essere intirizzito

perishing /'perɪʃɪŋ/ *a fam* **it's ~** fa freddo da morire

peritonitis /perɪtə'naɪtɪs/ *n* peritonite *f*

perjure /'pɜːdʒə(r)/ *vt* **~ oneself** spergiurare

perjury /'pɜːdʒərɪ/ *n* spergiuro *m*

perk[1] /pɜːk/ *n fam* vantaggio *m*

perk[2] *vi Am* ‹coffee:› passare

■ **perk up** *vt* tirare su ● *vi* tirarsi su

perky /'pɜːkɪ/ *a* allegro

perm /pɜːm/ *n* permanente *f* ● *vt* **~ sb's hair** fare la permanente a qno

permanent /'pɜːmənənt/ *a* permanente; ‹job, address› stabile

permanently /'pɜːmənəntlɪ/ *adv* stabilmente

permeable /'pɜːmɪəbl/ *a* permeabile

permeate /'pɜːmɪeɪt/ *vt* impregnare

permissible /pə'mɪsəbl/ *a* ammissibile

permission /pə'mɪʃn/ *n* permesso *m*

permissive /pə'mɪsɪv/ *a* permissivo

permit[1] /pə'mɪt/ *vt* (*pt/pp* -**mitted**) permettere; **~ sb to do sth** permettere a qcno di fare qcsa

permit[2] /'pɜːmɪt/ *n* autorizzazione *f*

pernicious /pə'nɪʃəs/ *a* pernicioso

pernickety /pə'nɪkətɪ/ *a Br fam* puntiglioso, pignolo; (*about food*) difficile

peroxide blonde /pə'rɒksaɪd/ *n* bionda *f* ossigenata

perpendicular /pɜːpən'dɪkjʊlə(r)/ *a* & *n* perpendicolare *f*

perpetrate /'pɜːpɪtreɪt/ *vt* perpetrare

perpetrator /'pɜːpɪtreɪtə(r)/ *n* autore, -trice *mf*

perpetual /pə'petjʊəl/ *a* perenne

perpetually /pə'petjʊəlɪ/ *adv* perennemente

perpetuate /pə'petjʊeɪt/ *vt* perpetuare

perplex /pə'pleks/ *vt* lasciare perplesso

perplexed /pə'plekst/ *a* perplesso

perplexity /pə'pleksətɪ/ *n* perplessità *f inv*

perquisite /'pɜːkwɪzɪt/ *n* fringe benefit *m inv*, beneficio *m* accessorio

per se /pɜː'seɪ/ *adv* in sé

persecute /'pɜːsɪkjuːt/ *vt* perseguitare

persecution /pɜːsɪ'kjuːʃn/ *n* persecuzione *f*

persecutor /'pɜːsɪkjuːtə(r)/ *n* persecutore, -trice *mf*

perseverance /pɜːsɪ'vɪərəns/ *n* perseveranza *f*

persevere /pɜːsɪ'vɪə(r)/ *vi* perseverare

persevering /pɜːsɪ'vɪərɪŋ/ *a* assiduo

Persian /'pɜːʃn/ *a* persiano

persist /pə'sɪst/ *vi* persistere; **~ in doing sth** persistere nel fare qcsa

persistence /pə'sɪstəns/ *n* persistenza *f*

persistent /pə'sɪstənt/ *a* persistente

persistently /pə'sɪstəntlɪ/ *adv* persistentemente

person /'pɜːsn/ *n* persona *f*; **in ~** di persona

persona /pə'səʊnə/ *n Psych* individuo *m*; *Theat* personaggio *m*

personable /'pɜːsənəbl/ *a* di bella presenza

personage /'pɜːsənɪdʒ/ *n* personaggio *m*

personal /'pɜːsənl/ *a* personale

personal: personal allowance *n* (*in taxation*) quota *f* non imponibile. **personal assistant** *n* segretario, -a *mf* personale. **personal belongings** *npl* effetti *mpl* personali. **personal computer** *n* personal computer *m inv*. **personal hygiene** *n* igiene *f* personale

personality /pɜːsə'nælətɪ/ *n* personalità *f inv*; (*on TV*) personaggio *m*

personalize /'pɜːsənəlaɪz/ *vt* personalizzare ‹stationery, clothing›; mettere sul piano personale ‹issue, dispute›

personal loan *n* prestito *m* a privato

personally /'pɜːsənəlɪ/ *adv* personalmente

personal organizer *n* *Comput* agenda *f* elettronica

personal stereo *n* walkman® *m inv*

personification /pəsɒnɪfɪ'keɪʃn/ *n* **the ~ of** la personificazione di

personify /pə'sɒnɪfaɪ/ *vt* (*pt/pp* -**ied**) personificare

personnel /pɜːsə'nel/ *n* personale *m*

personnel director *n* direttore, -trice *mf* del personale

personnel management *n* gestione *f* del personale

perspective /pə'spektɪv/ *n* prospettiva *f*

perspex® /'pɜːspeks/ *n* plexiglas® *m*

perspicacious /pɜːspɪˈkeɪʃəs/ a perspicace
perspiration /pɜːspɪˈreɪʃn/ n sudore m
perspire /pəˈspaɪə(r)/ vi sudare
persuade /pəˈsweɪd/ vt persuadere
persuasion /pəˈsweɪʒn/ n persuasione f;
  (belief) convinzione f
persuasive /pəˈsweɪsɪv/ a persuasivo
persuasively /pəˈsweɪsɪvlɪ/ adv in modo
  persuasivo
pert /pɜːt/ a (lively) esuberante
pertinent /ˈpɜːtɪnənt/ a pertinente (**to** a)
perturb /pəˈtɜːb/ vt perturbare
perturbing /pəˈtɜːbɪŋ/ a conturbante
Peru /pəˈruː/ n Perù m
peruse /pəˈruːz/ vt leggere
Peruvian /pəˈruːvɪən/ a & n peruviano, -a mf
pervade /pəˈveɪd/ vt pervadere
pervasive /pəˈveɪsɪv/ a pervasivo
perverse /pəˈvɜːs/ a perverso; (illogical) irragionevole
perversely /pəˈvɜːslɪ/ adv in modo perverso
perversion /pəˈvɜːʃn/ n perversione f
perversity /pəˈvɜːsɪtɪ/ n perversità f
pervert[1] /pəˈvɜːt/ vt deviare (course of
  justice)
pervert[2] /ˈpɜːvɜːt/ n pervertito, -a mf
perverted /pəˈvɜːtɪd/ a perverso
pessary /ˈpesərɪ/ n candeletta f
pessimism /ˈpesɪmɪzm/ n pessimismo m
pessimist /ˈpesɪmɪst/ n pessimista mf
pessimistic /pesɪˈmɪstɪk/ a pessimistico
pessimistically /pesɪˈmɪstɪklɪ/ adv in
  modo pessimistico
pest /pest/ n piaga f; (fam: person) peste f
pester /ˈpestə(r)/ vt molestare
pesticide /ˈpestɪsaɪd/ n pesticida m
pestilential /pestɪˈlenʃəl/ a (hum:
  annoying) fastidiosissimo
pestle /ˈpesl/ n pestello m
pet /pet/ n animale m domestico; (favourite)
  cocco, -a mf ● a (favourite) prediletto ● v (pt/
  pp **petted**) ● vt coccolare ● vi (couple:) praticare il petting
petal /ˈpetl/ n petalo m
peter /ˈpiːtə(r)/ vi ~ **out** finire
petite /pəˈtiːt/ a minuto
petition /pəˈtɪʃn/ n petizione f
pet name n vezzeggiativo m
petrified /ˈpetrɪfaɪd/ a (frightened) pietrifi-
  cato
petrify /ˈpetrɪfaɪ/ vt (pt/pp **-ied**) pietrificare
petrochemical /petrəʊˈkemɪkl/ n petrol-
  chimico m
petrodollar /ˈpetrəʊdɒlə(r)/ n petroldolla-
  ro m
petrol /ˈpetrəl/ n Br benzina f
petrol bomb n Br [bomba f] molotov f inv
petroleum /pɪˈtrəʊlɪəm/ n petrolio m
petroleum jelly n vaselina f
petrol: **petrol-pump** n Br pompa f di benzina. **petrol station** n Br stazione f di servizio.
  petrol tank n Br serbatoio m della benzina
pet shop n negozio m di animali
petticoat /ˈpetɪkəʊt/ n sottoveste f
pettifogging /ˈpetɪfɒgɪŋ/ a pej cavilloso

petty /ˈpetɪ/ a (**-ier**, **-iest**) insignificante;
  (mean) meschino
petty cash n cassa f per piccole spese
petty-minded /-ˈmaɪndɪd/ a meschino
petulance /ˈpetjʊləns/ n petulanza f
petulant /ˈpetjʊlənt/ a petulante
pew /pjuː/ n banco m (di chiesa)
pewter /ˈpjuːtə(r)/ n peltro m
phallic /ˈfælɪk/ a fallico
phallic symbol n simbolo m fallico
phallus /ˈfæləs/ n fallo m
phantom /ˈfæntəm/ n fantasma m
Pharaoh /ˈfeərəʊ/ n faraone m
pharmaceutical /fɑːməˈsjuːtɪkl/ a farma-
  ceutico
pharmacist /ˈfɑːməsɪst/ n farmacista mf
pharmacy /ˈfɑːməsɪ/ n farmacia f
phase /feɪz/ n fase f ● vt **phase in/out** intro-
  durre/eliminare gradualmente
Ph.D. abbr (**Doctor of Philosophy**) ≈ dottorato m di ricerca
pheasant /ˈfeznt/ n fagiano m
phenomenal /fɪˈnɒmɪnl/ a fenomenale;
  (incredible) incredibile
phenomenally /fɪˈnɒmɪnəlɪ/ adv incredibilmente
phenomenon /fɪˈnɒmɪnən/ n (pl **-na**) fenomeno m
phew /fjuː/ int (when too hot, in relief) uff!;
  (in surprise) oh!
philanderer /fɪˈlændərə(r)/ n donnaiolo m
philanthropic /fɪlənˈθrɒpɪk/ a filantropico
philanthropist /fɪˈlænθrəpɪst/ n filantropo,
  -a mf
philatelist /fɪˈlætəlɪst/ n filatelico, -a mf
philately /fɪˈlætəlɪ/ n filatelia f
philharmonic /fɪlhɑːˈmɒnɪk/ n (orchestra)
  orchestra f filarmonica ● a filarmonico
Philippines /ˈfɪlɪpiːnz/ npl Filippine fpl
philistine /ˈfɪlɪstaɪn/ a & n filisteo, -a mf
philology /fɪˈlɒlədʒɪ/ n filologia f
philosopher /fɪˈlɒsəfə(r)/ n filosofo, -a mf
philosophical /fɪləˈsɒfɪkl/ a filosofico
philosophically /fɪləˈsɒfɪklɪ/ adv con filosofia
philosophy /fɪˈlɒsəfɪ/ n filosofia f
phlebitis /flɪˈbaɪtɪs/ n flebite f
phlegm /flem/ n Med flemma f
phlegmatic /flegˈmætɪk/ a flemmatico
phobia /ˈfəʊbɪə/ n fobia f
phobic /ˈfəʊbɪk/ a fobico
phoenix /ˈfiːnɪks/ n fenice f
phone /fəʊn/ n telefono m; **be on the** ~ avere il telefono; (be phoning) essere al telefono
  ● vt telefonare a ● vi telefonare
■ **phone back** vt/i richiamare
■ **phone in** vi telefonare al lavoro; **he** ~**d in
  sick** ha telefonato [al lavoro] per dire che è
  ammalato
■ **phone up** vi telefonare ● vt dare un colpo
  di telefono a
phone: **phone book** n guida f del telefono.
  phone box n cabina f telefonica. **phone call**
  telefonata f. **phonecard** n scheda f telefonica.

phone-in *n* trasmissione *f* con chiamate in diretta

phoneme /'fəʊni:m/ *n* fonema *m*

phone number *n* numero *m* telefonico

phonetic /fə'netɪk/ *a* fonetico

phonetics /fə'netɪks/ *n* fonetica *f*

phoney /'fəʊnɪ/ *a* (**-ier, -iest**) fasullo ● *n* ciarlatano, -a *mf*

phonology /fə'nɒlədʒɪ/ *n* fonologia *f*

phosphate /'fɒsfeɪt/ *n* fosfato *m*

phosphorus /'fɒsfərəs/ *n* fosforo *m*

photo /'fəʊtəʊ/ *n* foto *f*

photo: photo album *n* album *m* *inv* di fotografie. **photocell** *n* fotocellula *f*. **photocopier** *n* fotocopiatrice *f*. **photocopy** *n* fotocopia *f* ● *vt* fotocopiare. **photoengraving** *n* fotoincisione *f*. **photo finish** *n* fotofinish *m*. **Photofit®** *n* *Br* photofit *m* *inv*

photogenic /fəʊtəʊ'dʒenɪk/ *a* fotogenico

photograph /'fəʊtəgrɑ:f/ *n* fotografia *f* ● *vt* fotografare

photographer /fə'tɒgrəfə(r)/ *n* fotografo, -a *mf*

photographic /fəʊtə'græfɪk/ *a* fotografico

photography /fə'tɒgrəfɪ/ *n* fotografia *f*

photo: photojournalism *n* fotoreportage *m*. **photojournalist** *n* fotogiornalista *mf*. **photomontage** /fəʊtəʊmɒn'tɑ:ʒ/ *n* fotomontaggio *m*. **photosynthesis** *n* fotosintesi *f*

phrase /freɪz/ *n* espressione *f* ● *vt* esprimere

phrase book *n* libro *m* di fraseologia

phut /fʌt/ *adv* *fam* **go ~** ⟨car, washing machine etc:⟩ scassarsi; ⟨plan:⟩ andare in fumo

physical /'fɪzɪkl/ *a* fisico

physical education *n* educazione *f* fisica

physically /'fɪzɪklɪ/ *adv* fisicamente

physician /fɪ'zɪʃn/ *n* medico *m*

physicist /'fɪzɪsɪst/ *n* fisico, -a *mf*

physics /'fɪzɪks/ *n* fisica *f*

physio /'fɪzɪəʊ/ *n* *Br* *fam* (**physiotherapist**) fisioterapista *mf*; (**physiotherapy**) fisioterapia *f*

physiology /fɪzɪ'ɒlədʒɪ/ *n* fisiologia *f*

physiotherapist /fɪzɪəʊ'θerəpɪst/ *n* fisioterapista *mf*

physiotherapy /fɪzɪəʊ'θerəpɪ/ *n* fisioterapia *f*

physique /fɪ'zi:k/ *n* fisico *m*

pianist /'pɪənɪst/ *n* pianista *mf*

piano /pɪ'ænəʊ/ *n* piano *m*

pianola® /pɪə'nəʊlə/ *n* pianola* *f*

piazza /pɪ'ætsə/ *n* (*public square*) piazza *f*; (*Am: veranda*) veranda *f*

pick¹ /pɪk/ *n* (*tool*) piccone *m*

pick² *n* scelta *f*; **take your ~** prendi quello che vuoi ● *vt* (*select*) scegliere; cogliere ⟨flowers⟩; scassinare ⟨lock⟩; borseggiare ⟨pockets⟩; **~ one's nose** mettersi le dita nel naso; **~ a quarrel** attaccar briga; **~ holes in sth** (*fam: criticize*) criticare qcsa ● *vi* **~ and choose** fare il difficile; **~ at one's food** spilluzzicare

■ **pick off** *vt* (*remove*) togliere

■ **pick on** *vt* (*fam: nag*) assillare; **he always ~s on me** ce l'ha con me

■ **pick out** *vt* (*identify*) individuare

■ **pick up** *vt* sollevare; raccogliere ⟨fallen object, information⟩; prendere in braccio ⟨baby⟩; prendere ⟨passengers, habit⟩; ⟨police:⟩ arrestare ⟨criminal⟩; *fam* rimorchiare ⟨girl⟩; prendersi ⟨illness⟩; captare ⟨signal⟩; (*buy*) comprare; (*learn*) imparare; (*collect*) andare/venire a prendere; **~ oneself up** riprendersi ● *vi* (*improve*) recuperare; ⟨weather:⟩ rimettersi

pickaxe /'pɪkæks/ *n* piccone *m*

picker /'pɪkə(r)/ *n* raccoglitore, -trice *mf*

picket /'pɪkɪt/ *n* picchettista *mf* ● *vt* picchettare

picket line *n* picchetto *m*

pickle /'pɪkl/ *n* **~s** *pl* sottaceti *mpl*; **in a ~** *fig* nei pasticci ● *vt* mettere sottaceto

pick-me-up *n* (*alcohol*) cicchetto *m*; (*medicine*) tonico *m*

pickpocket /'pɪkpɒkɪt/ *n* borsaiolo *m*

pick-up *n* (*truck*) furgone *m*; (*on record-player*) pickup *m* *inv*

picky /'pɪkɪ/ *a* (*fam: choosy, fussy*) difficile

picnic /'pɪknɪk/ *n* picnic *m* ● *vi* (*pt/pp* **-nicked**) fare un picnic

pictogram /'pɪktəgræm/ *n* (*symbol*) pittogramma *m*; (*chart*) tabella *f*

pictorial /pɪk'tɔːrɪəl/ *a* illustrato

picture /'pɪktʃə(r)/ *n* (*painting*) quadro *m*; (*photo*) fotografia *f*; (*drawing*) disegno *m*; (*film*) film *m* *inv*; **as pretty as a ~** ⟨girl⟩ bella come una Madonna; **put sb in the ~** *fig* mettere qcno al corrente; **the ~s** *Br* *fam* il cinema ● *vt* (*imagine*) immaginare

picturesque /pɪktʃə'resk/ *a* pittoresco

piddle /'pɪdl/ *vi* *fam* fare pipì

pie /paɪ/ *n* torta *f*

piece /pi:s/ *n* pezzo *m*; (*in game*) pedina *f*; **a ~ of bread /paper** un pezzo di pane /carta; **a ~ of news /advice/junk** una notizia /un consiglio/una patacca; **take to ~s** smontare

■ **piece together** *vt* montare; *fig* ricostruire

piecemeal /'pi:smi:l/ *adv* un po' alla volta

piecework /'pi:sw3:k/ *n* lavoro *m* a cottimo

pie chart *n* grafico *f* a torta

Piedmont /'pi:dmɒnt/ *n* Piemonte *m*

pier /pɪə(r)/ *n* molo *m*; (*pillar*) pilastro *m*

pierce /pɪəs/ *vt* perforare; **~ a hole in sth** fare un buco in qcsa

piercing /'pɪəsɪŋ/ *a* penetrante

pig /pɪg/ *n* maiale *m*

pigeon /'pɪdʒɪn/ *n* piccione *m*

pigeon-hole *n* casella *f* ● *vt* incasellare

pigeon-toed /-təʊd/ *a* **be ~** camminare con i piedi in dentro

piggery /'pɪgərɪ/ *n* (*pigsty*) porcile *m*; (*fam: overeating*) ingordigia *f*

piggyback /'pɪgɪbæk/ *n* **give sb a ~** portare qcno sulle spalle

piggy bank /'pɪgɪ/ *n* salvadanaio *m*

pig-headed /-'hedɪd/ *a* *fam* cocciuto

piglet /'pɪglət/ n maialino m, porcellino m

pigment /'pɪgmənt/ n pigmento m

pigmentation /pɪgmən'teɪʃn/ n pigmentazione f

pigskin /'pɪgskɪn/ n pelle f di cinghiale

pigtail /'pɪgteɪl/ n (plait) treccina f

pike /paɪk/ n inv (fish) luccio m

pilchard /'pɪltʃəd/ n sardina f

pile /paɪl/ n (heap) pila f ● vt ~ sth on to sth appilare qcsa su qcsa

■ **pile in** vi (enter, get on) entrare disordinatamente

■ **pile up** vt accatastare ● vi ammucchiarsi

piles /paɪlz/ npl emorroidi fpl

pile-up n tamponamento m a catena

pilfering /'pɪlfərɪŋ/ n piccoli furti mpl

pilgrim /'pɪlgrɪm/ n pellegrino, -a mf

pilgrimage /'pɪlgrɪmɪdʒ/ n pellegrinaggio m

pill /pɪl/ n pillola f

pillage /'pɪlɪdʒ/ vt saccheggiare

pillar /'pɪlə(r)/ n pilastro m

pillar box n buca f delle lettere

pillion /'pɪljən/ n sellino m posteriore; **ride ~** viaggiare dietro

pillory /'pɪlərɪ/ vt (pt/pp -ied) fig mettere alla berlina

pillow /'pɪləʊ/ n guanciale m

pillowcase /'pɪləʊkeɪs/ n federa f

pilot /'paɪlət/ n pilota mf ● vt pilotare

pilot light n fiamma f di sicurezza

pimp /pɪmp/ n protettore m

pimple /'pɪmpl/ n foruncolo m

PIN /pɪn/ n abbr (**personal identification number**) [numero m di] codice m segreto

pin /pɪn/ n spillo m; Electr spinotto m; Med chiodo m; **I have ~s and needles in my leg** fam mi formicola una gamba ● vt (pt/pp **pinned**) appuntare (**to/on** su); (sewing) fissare con gli spilli; (hold down) immobilizzare; **~ sb down to a date** ottenere un appuntamento da qcno; **~ sth on sb** fam addossare a qcno la colpa di qcsa

■ **pin up** vt appuntare; (on wall) affiggere

pinafore /'pɪnəfɔː(r)/ n grembiule m

pinafore dress n scamiciato m

pinball /'pɪnbɔːl/ n flipper m inv

pinball machine n flipper m inv

pincers /'pɪnsəz/ npl tenaglie fpl

pinch /pɪntʃ/ n pizzicotto m; (of salt) presa f; **at a ~** fam in caso di bisogno ● vt pizzicare; (fam: steal) fregare ● vi (shoe:) stringere

pincushion /'pɪnkʊʃən/ n puntaspilli m inv

pine[1] /paɪn/ n (tree) pino m

pine[2] vi **she is pining for you** le manchi molto

■ **pine away** vi deperire

pine: pineapple n ananas m inv. **pine cone** n pigna f. **pine-needle** n ago m di pino. **pine nut** n pinolo m

ping /pɪŋ/ n rumore m metallico

ping-pong n ping-pong m

pinhead /'pɪnhed/ n capocchia f di spillo; fam, pej testa f di rapa

pink /pɪŋk/ a rosa inv

pinking shears, pinking scissors /'pɪŋkɪŋ/ npl forbici fpl a zigzag

pinnacle /'pɪnəkl/ n guglia f

PIN number n codice m segreto

pinpoint /'pɪnpɔɪnt/ vt definire con precisione

pinprick /'pɪnprɪk/ n puntura f di spillo; (fig: of jealousy, remorse) punta f

pinstripe /'pɪnstraɪp/ a gessato

pint /paɪnt/ n pinta f (= 0,571, Am: 0,47 l); **a ~** fam una birra media

pin-up n ragazza f da copertina, pin-up f inv

pioneer /paɪə'nɪə(r)/ n pioniere, -a mf ● vt essere un pioniere di

pious /'paɪəs/ a pio

pip[1] /pɪp/ n (seed) seme m

pip[2] n **the ~s** il segnale orario; (telephone) il segnale telefonico

pip[3] vt (pt/pp **pipped**) **be ~ped at the post** essere battuto all'ultimo minuto

pipe /paɪp/ n tubo m; (for smoking) pipa f; **the ~s** pl Mus la cornamusa ● vt far arrivare con tubature (water, gas etc); Culin mettere

■ **pipe down** vi fam abbassare la voce; (shut up) stare zitto

■ **pipe up** vi ~ **with a suggestion** venir fuori con una proposta

pipe-cleaner n scovolino m

piped music /paɪpt/ n musichetta f di sottofondo

pipe dream n illusione f

pipeline /'paɪplaɪn/ n conduttura f; **in the ~** fam in cantiere

piper /'paɪpə(r)/ n suonatore m di cornamusa

piping /'paɪpɪŋ/ a ~ **hot** bollente

pique /pi:k/ n **in a fit of ~** risentito

piracy /'paɪrəsɪ/ n pirateria f

piranha /pɪ'rɑːnə/ n piranha m

pirate /'paɪrət/ n pirata m ● vt pirateggiare

pirate copy n copia f pirata

pirated a /'paɪrətɪd/ pirateggiato

pirate radio n radio f pirata

pirouette /pɪru:'et/ n piroetta f ● vi piroettare

Pisces /'paɪsiːz/ n Astr Pesci mpl

piss /pɪs/ sl n piscia f ● vi pisciare

■ **piss about, piss around** sl vi (waste time, play the fool) cazzeggiare ● vt ~ **sb about** rompere le palle a qcno

■ **piss down** vi sl **it's ~ing down** (raining heavily) piove a dirotto

■ **piss off** sl vt fare incacchiare; **that type of behaviour ~es me off** questi comportamenti mi stanno sulle palle ● vi (leave) filarsela; ~ **off!** levati dalle palle!, va' a cagare!

pissed /pɪst/ a sl sbronzo; ~ **as a newt** sbronzo come una cucuzza

pissed off a sl scoglionato

pistachio [nut] /pɪ'stæʃɪəʊ/ n pistachio m

pistol /'pɪstl/ n pistola f

piston /'pɪstn/ n Techn pistone m

pit /pɪt/ n fossa f; (mine) miniera f; (for orchestra) orchestra f; (of stomach) bocca f ● vt (pt/pp **pitted**) fig opporre (**against** a)

pit-a-pat /'pɪtəpæt/ n **go ~** (heart:) palpitare

pitch¹ /pɪtʃ/ n (tone) tono m; (level) altezza f; (in sport) campo m; (fig: degree) grado m ● vt montare ⟨tent⟩

pitch² n (substance) pece f

■ **pitch in** vi fam mettersi sotto

pitch-black a nero come la pece; ⟨night⟩ buio pesto

pitch-dark a buio pesto

pitcher /'pɪtʃə(r)/ n brocca f

pitchfork /'pɪtʃfɔːk/ n forca f

piteous /'pɪtɪəs/ a pietoso

pitfall /'pɪtfɔːl/ n fig trabocchetto m

pith /pɪθ/ n (of lemon, orange) interno m della buccia; fig essenza f

pithy /'pɪθɪ/ a (-ier, -iest) fig conciso

pitiable /'pɪtɪəbl/ a pietoso

pitiful /'pɪtɪfl/ a pietoso

pitifully /'pɪtɪfʊlɪ/ adv da far pietà

pitiless /'pɪtɪlɪs/ a spietato

pitilessly /'pɪtɪlɪslɪ/ adv senza pietà

pittance /'pɪtns/ n miseria f

pitted /'pɪtɪd/ a ⟨surface⟩ bucherellato; ⟨face, skin⟩ butterato; ⟨olive⟩ snocciolato

pituitary /pɪ'tjuːɪt(ə)rɪ/ a pituitario

pituitary gland n ghiandola f pituitaria, ipofisi f

pity /'pɪtɪ/ n pietà f; [what a] ~! che peccato!; **take ~ on** avere compassione di ● vt aver pietà di

pivot /'pɪvət/ n perno m; fig fulcro m ● vi imperniarsi (**on** su)

pivotal /'pɪvətl/ a ⟨role⟩ centrale; ⟨decision⟩ cruciale

pixel /'pɪksəl/ n pixel m inv

pixie /'pɪksɪ/ n folletto m

pizza /'piːtsə/ n pizza f

placard /'plækɑːd/ n cartellone m

placate /plə'keɪt/ vt placare

place /pleɪs/ n posto m (fam: house) casa f; (in book) segno m; **feel out of ~** sentirsi fuori posto; **take ~** aver luogo; **all over the ~** dappertutto ● vt collocare; (remember) identificare; **~ an order** fare un'ordinazione; **be ~d** (in race) piazzarsi

placebo /plə'siːbəʊ/ n Med placebo m inv; fig contentino m

place mat n sottopiatto m

placement /'pleɪsmənt/ n (act: in accommodation) collocamento m; (Br: job) stage m inv

place name n toponimo m

placenta /plə'sentə/ n placenta f

placid /'plæsɪd/ a placido

plagiarist /'pleɪdʒərɪst/ n plagiario, -a mf

plagiarism /'pleɪdʒərɪzm/ n plagio m

plagiarize /'pleɪdʒəraɪz/ vt plagiare

plague /pleɪg/ n peste f

plaice /pleɪs/ n inv platessa f

plaid /plæd/ n (fabric) plaid m inv; (pattern) motivo m scozzese ● attrib ⟨scarf, shirt⟩ scozzese

plain /pleɪn/ a chiaro; (simple) semplice; (not pretty) scialbo; (not patterned) normale; ⟨chocolate⟩ fondente; **in ~ clothes** in borghese ● adv (simply) semplicemente ● n pianura f

plain-clothes a ⟨policeman etc⟩ in borghese

plainly /'pleɪnlɪ/ adv francamente; (simply) semplicemente; (obviously) chiaramente

plain paper fax n fax m inv a carta comune

plain-spoken a franco

plaintiff /'pleɪntɪf/ n Jur parte f lesa

plaintive /'pleɪntɪv/ a lamentoso

plaintively /'pleɪntɪvlɪ/ adv con aria lamentosa

plait /plæt/ n treccia f ● vt intrecciare

plan /plæn/ n progetto m, piano m ● vt (pt/pp **planned**) progettare; (intend) prevedere

plane¹ /pleɪn/ n (tree) platano m

plane² n aeroplano m; (in geometry) piano m

plane³ n (tool) pialla f ● vt piallare

plane crash n incidente m aereo

planet /'plænɪt/ n pianeta m

plank /plæŋk/ n asse f

■ **plank down** vt (fam: put down) mollare

plankton /'plæŋktən/ n plancton m

planning /'plænɪŋ/ n pianificazione f

planning permission n licenza f edilizia

plant /plɑːnt/ n pianta f; (machinery) impianto m; (factory) stabilimento m ● vt piantare; **~ oneself in front of sb** piantarsi davanti a qcno

plantation /plæn'teɪʃn/ n piantagione f

planter /'plɑːntə(r)/ n (person) piantatore, -trice mf; (machine) piantatrice f

plant life n flora f

plaque /plɑːk/ n placca f

plasma /'plæzmə/ n plasma m

plaster /'plɑːstə(r)/ n intonaco m; Med gesso m; (sticking ~) cerotto m; **in ~** ingessato ● vt intonacare ⟨wall⟩; (cover) ricoprire

plastered /'plɑːstəd/ a (sl: drunk) sbronzo

plasterer /'plɑːstərə(r)/ n intonacatore m

plaster of Paris n gesso m

plastic /'plæstɪk/ n plastica f ● a plastico

Plasticine® /'plæstɪsiːn/ n Plastilina* f

plastic surgeon n chirurgo m plastico

plastic surgery n chirurgia f plastica

plate /pleɪt/ n piatto m; (flat sheet) placca f; (gold and silverware) argenteria f; (in book) tavola f fuori testo ● vt (cover with metal) placcare

plateau /'plætəʊ/ n (pl **~x** /'plætəʊz/) altopiano m ● vi fig livellarsi

platform /'plætfɔːm/ n (stage) palco m; Rail marciapiede m; Pol piattaforma f; **~ 5** binario 5

platform shoes npl scarpe fpl con la zeppa

platinum /'plætɪnəm/ n platino m ● attrib di platino

platitude /'plætɪtjuːd/ n luogo m comune

platonic /plə'tɒnɪk/ a platonico

platoon /plə'tuːn/ n Mil plotone m

platter /'plætə(r)/ n piatto m da portata

platypus /'plætɪpəs/ n ornitorinco m

plausibility /plɔːzɪ'bɪlɪtɪ/ n plausibilità f

plausible /'plɔːzəbl/ a plausibile

play /pleɪ/ n gioco m; Theat, TV dramma m, opera f teatrale; (performance) rappresentazione f; Radio sceneggiato m radiofonico; ~

on words gioco *m* di parole ● *vt* giocare a; (*act*) recitare; suonare ⟨*instrument*⟩; giocare ⟨*card*⟩ ● *vi* giocare; *Mus* suonare; ~ **by the rules** stare alle regole; ~ **with fire** scherzare con il fuoco; ~ **dumb** fare lo gnorri; ~ **safe** non prendere rischi

▪ **play along** *vi* ~ **along with sb** (*fam: cooperate*) fare il gioco di qcno

▪ **play around with** *vt* (*meddle with*) cincischiarsi con

▪ **play back** *vt* riascoltare ⟨*recording*⟩

▪ **play down** *vt* minimizzare

▪ **play on** *vi* (*continue to play*) continuare a giocare ● *vt* (*exploit*) giocare su

▪ **play up** *vi fam* fare i capricci

play-acting *n* commedia *f*

playboy /'pleɪbɔɪ/ *n* playboy *m inv*

player /'pleɪə(r)/ *n* giocatore, -trice *mf*

playful /'pleɪfʊl/ *a* scherzoso

playfully /'pleɪfʊlɪ/ *adv* in modo scherzoso

playground /'pleɪgraʊnd/ *n* Sch cortile *m* (*per la ricreazione*)

playgroup /'pleɪgru:p/ *n* asilo *m*

playing card /'pleɪɪŋ/ *n* carta *f* da gioco

playing field *n* campo *m* da gioco

play: playmate *n* compagno, -a *mf* di gioco. **playpen** *n* box *m inv*. **playroom** /'pleɪru:m/ *n* ludoteca *f*. **plaything** *n* giocattolo *m*. **playwright** /'pleɪraɪt/ *n* drammaturgo, -a *mf*

plaza /'plɑ:zə/ *n* (*public square*) piazza *f*; (*shopping* ~) centro *m* commerciale; (*Am: services point*) area *f* di servizio; (*Am: toll point*) casello *m*

plc *abbr* (**public limited company**) s.r.l.

plea /pli:/ *n* richiesta *f*; **enter a** ~ **of not guilty** *Jur* dichiararsi non colpevole; **make a** ~ **for** fare un appello a

plead /pli:d/ *vi* fare appello (**for** a); ~ **guilty** dichiararsi colpevole; ~ **with sb** implorare qcno ● *vt Jur* perorare ⟨*case*⟩

pleasant /'pleznt/ *a* piacevole

pleasantly /'plezntlɪ/ *adv* piacevolmente; ⟨*say, smile*⟩ cordialmente

pleasantry /'plezntrɪ/ *n* (*joke*) battuta *f*; **pleasantries** (*pl: polite remarks*) convenevoli *mpl*

please /pli:z/ *adv* per favore; ~ **do** prego ● *vt* far contento; ~ **oneself** fare il proprio comodo; ~ **yourself!** come vuoi!; *pej* fai come ti pare!

pleased /pli:zd/ *a* lieto; ~ **with/about** contento di

pleasing /'pli:zɪŋ/ *a* gradevole

pleasurable /'pleʒərəbl/ *a* gradevole

pleasure /'pleʒə(r)/ *n* piacere *m*; **with** ~ con piacere, volentieri

pleat /pli:t/ *n* piega *f* ● *vt* pieghettare

pleated /'pli:tɪd/ *a* a pieghe

pleb /pleb/ *n fam* plebeo, -a *mf*

plebby /'plebɪ/ *a fam* plebeo

plebeian /plɪ'bi:ən/ *pej* *a* plebeo, -a *mf* ● *a* plebeo

plebiscite /'plebɪsɪt/ *n* plebiscito *m*

pledge /pledʒ/ *n* pegno *m*; (*promise*) promes-

sa *f* ● *vt* (*pawn*) impegnare; ~ **to do sth** impegnarsi a fare qcsa

plenary /'pli:nərɪ/ *a* ⟨*session*⟩ plenario; ⟨*powers*⟩ pieno; ⟨*authority*⟩ assoluto

plentiful /'plentɪfl/ *a* abbondante

plenty /'plentɪ/ *n* abbondanza *f*; ~ **of money** molti soldi; ~ **of people** molta gente; **I've got** ~ ne ho in abbondanza

pleurisy /'plʊərəsɪ/ *n* pleurite *f*

pliability /plaɪə'bɪlɪtɪ/ *n* flessibilità *f*

pliable /'plaɪəbl/ *a* flessibile

pliers /'plaɪəz/ *npl* pinze *fpl*

plight /plaɪt/ *n* triste condizione *f*

plimsolls /'plɪmsəlz/ *npl* scarpe *fpl* da ginnastica

plinth /plɪnθ/ *n* plinto *m*

plod /plɒd/ *vi* (*pt/pp* **plodded**) trascinarsi; (*work hard*) sgobbare

plodder /'plɒdə(r)/ *n* sgobbone, -a *mf*

plonk[1] /plɒŋk/ *n fam* vino *m*; (*poor wine*) vinaccio *m*

plonk[2] *vt* (*fam: put*) sbattere

plop /plɒp/ *n* plop *m inv* ● *vi* (*pt/pp* **plopped**) fare plop

plot /plɒt/ *n* complotto *m*; (*of novel*) trama *f*; ~ **of land** appezzamento *m* [di terreno] ● *vt/i* (*pt/pp* **plotted**) complottare

plotter /'plɒtə(r)/ *n* (*schemer*) cospiratore, -trice *mf*; *Comput* plotter *m inv*, tracciatore *m*

plough /plaʊ/ *n* aratro *m* ● *vt/i* arare

▪ **plough back** *vt Comm* reinvestire

▪ **plough into** *vt* (*crash into*) schiantarsi contro

▪ **plough through** *vt* procedere a fatica in

ploughman /'plaʊmən/ *n* aratore *m*

ploughman's lunch *n Br* piatto *m* freddo *a* base di pane formaggio e sottaceti

plow /plaʊ/ *Am n* aratro *m* ● *vt/i* arare

ploy /plɔɪ/ *n fam* manovra *f*

pluck /plʌk/ *n* fegato *m* ● *vt* strappare; depilare ⟨*eyebrows*⟩; spennare ⟨*bird*⟩; cogliere ⟨*flower*⟩

▪ **pluck up** *vt* ~ **up courage** farsi coraggio

plucky /'plʌkɪ/ *a* (**-ier, -iest**) coraggioso

plug /plʌg/ *n* tappo *m*; *Electr* spina *f*; *Auto* candela *f*; (*fam: advertisement*) pubblicità *f inv* ● *vt* (*pt/pp* **plugged**) tappare; (*fam: advertise*) pubblicizzare

▪ **plug away** *vi* (*work hard*) lavorare sodo

▪ **plug in** *vt Electr* inserire la spina di

plughole /'plʌghəʊl/ *n Br* scarico *m*

plug-in *a* con la spina

plum /plʌm/ *n* prugna *f*; (*tree*) prugno *m*

plumage /'plu:mɪdʒ/ *n* piumaggio *m*

plumb /plʌm/ *a* verticale ● *adv* esattamente

▪ **plumb in** *vt* collegare

plumber /'plʌmə(r)/ *n* idraulico *m*

plumbing /'plʌmɪŋ/ *n* impianto *m* idraulico

plumb line *n* filo *m* a piombo

plume /plu:m/ *n* piuma *f*

plummet /'plʌmɪt/ *vi* precipitare; ⟨*prices:*⟩ crollare

plump /plʌmp/ *a* paffuto

▪ **plump down** *vt* (*put down*) lasciare cadere

■ **plump for** *vt* scegliere

plumpness /'plʌmpnɪs/ *n* rotondità *f*

plunder /'plʌndə(r)/ *n* (*booty*) bottino *m* ● *vt* saccheggiare

plunge /plʌndʒ/ *n* tuffo *m*; **take the ~** *fam* buttarsi ● *vt* tuffare; *fig* sprofondare; **~ sb into despair** piombare qcno nella disperazione ● *vi* tuffarsi

plunger /'plʌndʒə(r)/ *n* (*tool*) sturalavandini *m inv*; (*handle*) stantuffo *m*

plunging /'plʌndʒɪŋ/ *a* **~ neckline** scollatura *f* profonda

pluperfect /plu:'pɜ:fɪkt/ *n* trapassato *m* prossimo

plural /'plʊərəl/ *a & n* plurale *m*

plus /plʌs/ *prep* più ● *a* in più; **500 ~** più di 500 ● *n* in più *m*; (*advantage*) extra *m inv*

plush /plʌʃ/ *a* (*hotel etc*) lussuoso

plutonium /plu:'təʊnɪəm/ *n* plutonio *m*

ply /plaɪ/ *vt* (*pt/pp* **plied**) esercitare (*trade*); **~ sb with drink** continuare a offrire da bere a qcno

plywood /'plaɪwʊd/ *n* compensato *m*

PM *abbr* **Prime Minister**

p.m. *abbr* (**post meridiem**) del pomeriggio

PMS *n abbr* (**premenstrual syndrome**) sindrome *f* premestruale

PMT *n abbr* (**premenstrual tension**) tensione *f* premestruale

pneumatic /nju:'mætɪk/ *a* pneumatico

pneumatic drill *n* martello *m* pneumatico

pneumonia /nju:'məʊnɪə/ *n* polmonite *f*

PO *abbr* (**Post Office**) ≈ P.T.; *abbr* (**postal order**) vaglia *m inv* postale

poach /pəʊtʃ/ *vt* Culin bollire; cacciare di frodo (*deer*); pescare di frodo (*salmon*); **~ed egg** uovo *m* in camicia

poacher /'pəʊtʃə(r)/ *n* bracconiere *m*

PO Box *n abbr* (**Post Office Box**) C.P. *f*

pocket /'pɒkɪt/ *n* tasca *f*; **~ of resistance** sacca *f* di resistenza; **be out of ~** rimetterci ● *vt* intascare

pocket-book *n* taccuino *m*; (*wallet*) portafoglio *m*

pocket-money *n* denaro *m* per le piccole spese

pock-marked /'pɒkmɑ:kt/ *a* butterato

pod /pɒd/ *n* baccello *m*

podgy /'pɒdʒɪ/ *a* (**-ier, -iest**) grassoccio

podiatrist /pə'daɪətrɪst/ *n Am* pedicure *mf inv*

podium /'pəʊdɪəm/ *n* podio *m*

poem /'pəʊɪm/ *n* poesia *f*

poet /'pəʊɪt/ *n* poeta *m*

poetic /pəʊ'etɪk/ *a* poetico

poetic licence *n* licenza *f* poetica

Poet Laureate /'lɔ:rɪət/ *n* poeta *m* laureato

poetry /'pəʊɪtrɪ/ *n* poesia *f*

po-faced /pəʊ'feɪst/ *a Br fam* **look/be ~** avere un'aria di disapprovazione

poignancy /'pɔɪnjənsɪ/ *n* pregnanza *f*

poignant /'pɔɪnjənt/ *a* pregnante

point /pɔɪnt/ *n* punto *m*; (*sharp end*) punta *f*; (*meaning, purpose*) senso *m*; *Electr* presa *f*; **what is the ~?** a che scopo?; **the ~ is** il fatto

è; **I don't see the ~** non vedo il senso; **up to a ~** fino a un certo punto; **be on the ~ of doing sth** essere sul punto di fare qcsa; **~s** *pl Rail* scambio *m*; **good/bad ~s** aspetti *mpl* positivi/negativi ● *vt* puntare (**at** verso) ● *vi* (*with finger*) puntare il dito; **~ at/to** (*person:*) mostrare col dito; (*indicator:*) indicare; **~ and click** *Comput* punta e clicca

■ **point out** *vt* far notare (*fact*); **~ sth out to sb** far notare qcsa a qcno

point-blank *a* a bruciapelo

pointed /'pɔɪntɪd/ *a* appuntito; (*question*) diretto

pointer /'pɔɪntə(r)/ *n* (*piece of advice*) consiglio *m*

pointillism /'pwæntɪlɪzm/ *n* divisionismo *m*

pointillist /'pwæntɪlɪst/ *n* divisionista *mf*

pointing /'pɔɪntɪŋ/ *n Constr* rifinitura *f* con la malta

pointing device *n Comput* dispositivo *m* di puntamento

pointless /'pɔɪntlɪs/ *a* inutile

point: point of order *n* mozione *f* d'ordine. **point of sale** *n* (*place*) punto *m* di vendita; (*promotional material*) materiale *m* pubblicitario. **point-of-sale promotion** *n* promozione *f* punto vendita. **point of view** *n* punto *m* di vista

poise /pɔɪz/ *n* padronanza *f*

poised /pɔɪzd/ *a* in equilibrio; (*composed*) padrone di sé; **~ to** sul punto di

poison /'pɔɪzn/ *n* veleno *m* ● *vt* avvelenare

poisoned /'pɔɪz(ə)nd/ *a* avvelenato

poisoner /'pɔɪzənə(r)/ *n* avvelenatore, -trice *mf*

poisonous /'pɔɪzənəs/ *a* velenoso

poison-pen letter *n* lettera *f* anonima diffamatoria

poke /pəʊk/ *n* spintarella *f* ● *vt* spingere; (*fire*) attizzare; (*put*) ficcare; **~ fun at** prendere in giro

■ **poke about** *vi* frugare

■ **poke out** *vi* (*protrude*) spuntare

poker¹ /'pəʊkə(r)/ *n* attizzatoio *m*

poker² *n* (*Cards*) poker *m*

poker-faced /-'feɪst/ *a* (*person*) impassibile

poky /'pəʊkɪ/ *a* (**-ier, -iest**) angusto

Poland /'pəʊlənd/ *n* Polonia *f*

polar /'pəʊlə(r)/ *a* polare

polar bear *n* orso *m* bianco

polarity /pə'lærətɪ/ *n Electr, Phys, fig* polarità *f inv*

polarize /'pəʊləraɪz/ *vt* polarizzare

polarized *a* polarizzato

Pole /pəʊl/ *n* polacco, -a *mf*

pole¹ *n* palo *m*

pole² *n Geog, Electr* polo *m*

polemic /pə'lemɪk/ *n* polemica *f*

polemical /pə'lemɪkl/ *a* polemico

pole star *n* stella *f* polare

pole vault *n* salto *m* con l'asta

police /pə'li:s/ *npl* polizia *f* ● *vt* pattugliare (*area*); sorvegliare (*behaviour*)

police: police car *n* gazzella *f*. **policeman** *n* poliziotto *m*. **police state** *n* stato *m* militarista. **police station** *n* commissariato *m*. **policewoman** *n* donna *f* poliziotto

policy¹ /'pɒlɪsɪ/ *n* politica *f*

policy² *n* (*insurance*) polizza *f*

polio /'pəʊlɪəʊ/ *n* polio *f*

Polish /'pəʊlɪʃ/ *a & n* polacco *m*

polish /'pɒlɪʃ/ *n* (*shine*) lucentezza *f*; (*substance*) lucido *m*; (*for nails*) smalto *m*; *fig* raffinatezza *f* ● *vt* lucidare; *fig* smussare

■ **polish off** *vt fam* finire; far fuori (*food*)

■ **polish up** *vt* rispolverare (*Italian*)

polished /'pɒlɪʃt/ *a* (*manner*) raffinato; (*performance*) senza sbavature

polisher /'pɒlɪʃə(r)/ *n* (*machine*) lucidatrice *f*

polite /pə'laɪt/ *a* cortese

politely /pə'laɪtlɪ/ *adv* cortesemente

politeness /pə'laɪtnɪs/ *n* cortesia *f*

politic /'pɒlɪtɪk/ *a* prudente

political /pə'lɪtɪkl/ *a* politico

politically /pə'lɪtɪklɪ/ *adv* dal punto di vista politico; ~ **correct** politicamente corretto

politician /pɒlɪ'tɪʃn/ *n* politico *m*

politicize /pə'lɪtɪsaɪz/ *vt* politicizzare

politics /'pɒlɪtɪks/ *n* politica *f*

polka /'pɒlkə/ *n* polka *f*

polka dot *n* pois *nm inv*, pallino *m* ● *attrib a* pois

poll /pəʊl/ *n* votazione *f*; (*election*) elezioni *fpl*; [**opinion**] ~ sondaggio *m* d'opinione; **go to the ~s** andare alle urne ● *vt* ottenere (*votes*)

pollen /'pɒlən/ *n* polline *m*

polling booth /'pəʊlɪŋ/ *n* cabina *f* elettorale

polling station *n* seggio *m* elettorale

pollster /'pəʊlstə(r)/ *n* (*person*) persona *f* che esegue un sondaggio d'opinione

poll tax *n* imposta *f* locale sulle persone fisiche

pollutant /pə'lu:tənt/ *n* sostanza *f* inquinante

pollute /pə'lu:t/ *vt* inquinare

polluted /pə'lu:tɪd/ *a* inquinato

polluter /pə'lu:tə(r)/ *n* inquinatore, -trice *mf*

pollution /pə'lu:ʃn/ *n* inquinamento *m*

polo /'pəʊləʊ/ *n* polo *m*

polo neck *n* collo *m* alto

polo shirt *n* dolcevita *f*

poly /'pɒlɪ/ *n* (*Br fam: polytechnic*) politecnico *m*

poly bag *n* sacchetto *m* di plastica

polyester /pɒlɪ'estə(r)/ *n* poliestere *m*

polygamous /pə'lɪgəməs/ *a* poligamico

polygamy /pə'lɪgəmɪ/ *n* poligamia *f*

polymath /'pɒlɪmæθ/ *n* erudito, -a *mf*

polymer /'pɒlɪmə(r)/ *n* polimero *m*

polystyrene® /pɒlɪ'staɪri:n/ *n* polistirolo *m*

polytechnic /pɒlɪ'teknɪk/ *n* politecnico *m*

polythene /'pɒlɪθi:n/ *n* politene *m*

polythene bag *n* sacchetto *m* di plastica

polyunsaturates /pɒlɪʌn'sætjʊreɪts/ *npl* grassi *mpl* polinsaturi

pomade /pə'meɪd/ *n* pomata *f*

pomegranate /'pɒmɪgrænɪt/ *n* melagrana *f*

pomp /pɒmp/ *n* pompa *f*

pompon /'pɒmpɒn/ *n* pompon *m*

pomposity /pɒm'pɒsətɪ/ *n* pomposità *f*

pompous /'pɒmpəs/ *a* pomposo

pompously /'pɒmpəslɪ/ *adv* pomposamente

poncy /'pɒnsɪ/ *a fam* da finocchio; (*person*) finocchio

pond /pɒnd/ *n* stagno *m*

ponder /'pɒndə(r)/ *vt/i* ponderare

ponderous /'pɒndərəs/ *a* ponderoso; *fig* pesante

pong /pɒŋ/ *n fam* puzza *f* ● *vi* puzzare

pontiff /'pɒntɪf/ *n* pontefice *m*

pontificate /pɒn'tɪfɪkeɪt/ *vi* pontificare

pontoon /pɒn'tu:n/ *n* (*float*) galleggiante *m*; (*pier*) pontile *m*; (*Br: game*) ventuno *m*

pony /'pəʊnɪ/ *n* pony *m inv*

ponytail /'pəʊnɪteɪl/ *n* coda *f* di cavallo

pony-trekking /'pəʊnɪtrekɪŋ/ *n* escursioni *fpl* col pony

pooch /pu:tʃ/ *n* (*fam: dog*) cagnetto *m*

poodle /'pu:dl/ *n* barboncino *m*

poof /pʊf/, **poofter** /'pʊftə(r)/ *n* (*Br fam: homosexual*) finocchio *m*

pooh /pu:/ *int* (*scorn, disgust*) puah! ● *n* (*Br: baby talk*) popò *f inv*

pooh-pooh /pu:'pu:/ *vt fam* ridere di (*suggestion*)

pool¹ /pu:l/ *n* (*of water, blood*) pozza *f*; [**swimming**] ~ piscina *f*

pool² *n* (*common fund*) cassa *f* comune; (*in cards*) piatto *m*; (*game*) biliardo *m* a buca; **~s** *pl* ≈ totocalcio *msg* ● *vt* mettere insieme

pooped /pu:pt/ *a fam* **be ~** [**out**] essere stanco morto

poor /pʊə(r)/ *a* povero; (*not good*) scadente; **in ~ health** in cattiva salute ● *npl* **the ~** i poveri

poorly /'pʊəlɪ/ *a* **be ~** non stare bene ● *adv* male

pop¹ /pɒp/ *n* botto *m*; (*drink*) bibita *f* gasata ● *v* (*pt/pp* **popped**) ● *vt* (*fam: put*) mettere; (*burst*) far scoppiare ● *vi* (*burst*) scoppiare

■ **pop in** *vi fam* fare un salto

■ **pop out** *vi fam* fare un salto fuori; ~ **out to the shop** fare un salto al negozio

■ **pop up** *vi* (*fam: appear unexpectedly*) saltare fuori

pop² *n fam* musica *f* pop ● *attrib* pop *inv*

popcorn /'pɒpkɔ:n/ *n* popcorn *m inv*

pope /pəʊp/ *n* papa *m*

poplar /'pɒplə(r)/ *n* pioppo *m*

poppy /'pɒpɪ/ *n* papavero *m*

pop sock *n* gambaletto *m*

populace /'pɒpjʊləs/ *n* popolo *m*

popular /'pɒpjʊlə(r)/ *a* popolare; (*belief*) diffuso

popularity /pɒpjʊ'lærətɪ/ *n* popolarità *f*

popularize /'pɒpjʊləraɪz/ *vt* divulgare

populate /'pɒpjʊleɪt/ *vt* popolare

population /pɒpjʊ'leɪʃn/ *n* popolazione *f*

populist /'pɒpjʊlɪst/ *a & n* populista *mf*

populous /'pɒpjʊləs/ *a* popoloso

pop-up book *n* libro *m* con immagini tridimensionali

pop-up toaster *n* tostapane *m inv* a espulsione automatica

porcelain /'pɔːsəlɪn/ n porcellana f
porch /pɔːtʃ/ n portico m; Am veranda f
porcupine /'pɔːkjʊpaɪn/ n porcospino m
pore[1] /pɔː(r)/ n poro m
pore[2] vi ~ **over** immergersi in
pork /pɔːk/ n carne f di maiale
porn /pɔːn/ n fam porno m
porno /'pɔːnəʊ/ a fam porno inv
pornographic /pɔːnə'græfɪk/ a pornografico
pornography /pɔː'nɒgrəfɪ/ n pornografia f
porous /'pɔːrəs/ a poroso
porpoise /'pɔːpəs/ n focena f
porridge /'pɒrɪdʒ/ n farinata f di fiocchi d'avena
port[1] /pɔːt/ n porto m
port[2] n (Naut: side) babordo m
port[3] n (wine) porto m
portable /'pɔːtəbl/ a & n portatile m
Portakabin® /'pɔːtəkæbɪn/ n baracca f prefabbricata
portcullis /pɔːt'kʌlɪs/ n saracinesca f
portentous /pɔː'tentəs/ a (significant) solenne; (ominous) infausto
porter /'pɔːtə(r)/ n portiere m; (for luggage) facchino m
portfolio /pɔːt'fəʊlɪəʊ/ n cartella f; Comm portafoglio m
porthole /'pɔːthəʊl/ n oblò m inv
portion /'pɔːʃn/ n parte f; (of food) porzione f
portly /'pɔːtlɪ/ a (-ier, -iest) corpulento
portrait /'pɔːtrɪt/ n ritratto m
portrait painter n ritrattista mf
portray /pɔː'treɪ/ vt ritrarre; (represent) descrivere; ⟨actor:⟩ impersonare
portrayal /pɔː'treɪəl/ n ritratto m; (by actor) impersonazione f
Portugal /'pɔːtjʊgl/ n Portogallo m
Portuguese /pɔːtjʊ'giːz/ a & n portoghese mf; (language) portoghese m
pose /pəʊz/ n posa f ● vt porre ⟨problem, question⟩ ● vi (for painter) posare; ~ **as** atteggiarsi a
poser /'pəʊzə(r)/ n fam (puzzle) rompicapo m inv; (person) montato, -a mf
posh /pɒʃ/ a fam lussuoso; (people) danaroso
position /pə'zɪʃn/ n posizione f; (job) posto m; (status) ceto m [sociale] ● vt posizionare
positive /'pɒzɪtɪv/ a positivo; (certain) sicuro; (progress) concreto ● n positivo m
positively /'pɒzɪtɪvlɪ/ adv positivamente; (decidedly) decisamente
posse /'pɒsɪ/ n gruppo m di volontari armati
possess /pə'zes/ vt possedere
possession /pə'zeʃn/ n possesso m; ~s pl beni mpl
possessive /pə'zesɪv/ a possessivo
possessiveness /pə'zesɪvnɪs/ n carattere m possessivo
possessor /pə'zesə(r)/ n possessore, -ditrice mf
possibility /pɒsə'bɪlətɪ/ n possibilità f inv
possible /'pɒsəbl/ a possibile
possibly /'pɒsəblɪ/ adv possibilmente; **I couldn't ~ accept** non mi è possibile accet-

tare; **he can't ~ be right** non è possibile che abbia ragione; **could you ~...?** potrebbe per favore...?

possum /'pɒsəm/ n fam opossum m inv; **play ~** far finta di dormire; (pretend to be dead) fare il morto
post[1] /pəʊst/ n (pole) palo m ● vt affiggere ⟨notice⟩
post[2] n (place of duty) posto m ● vt appostare; (transfer) assegnare
post[3] n (mail) posta f; **by ~** per posta ● vt spedire; (put in letter box) imbucare; (as opposed to fax) mandare per posta; **keep sb ~ed** tenere qcno al corrente
post+ pref post+
postage /'pəʊstɪdʒ/ n affrancatura f; **~ and packaging** spese fpl di posta
postage stamp n francobollo m
postal /'pəʊstl/ a postale
postal order n vaglia m inv postale
post: **postbox** n cassetta f delle lettere. **postcard** n cartolina f. **postcode** n codice m postale. **post-date** vt postdatare
poster /'pəʊstə(r)/ n poster m inv; (advertising, election) cartellone m
posterior /pɒ'stɪərɪə(r)/ n fam posteriore m
posterity /pɒ'sterətɪ/ n posterità f
postgraduate /pəʊs(t)'grædjʊət/ n laureato, -a mf che continua gli studi ● a successivo alla laurea
posthumous /'pɒstjʊməs/ a postumo
posthumously /'pɒstjʊməslɪ/ adv dopo la morte
posting /'pəʊstɪŋ/ n (job) incarico m; (Br: in mail) spedizione f
postman /'pəʊstmən/ n postino m
postmark /'pəʊstmɑːk/ n timbro m postale
post-mortem /-'mɔːtəm/ n autopsia f
post-natal /-'neɪtl/ a post-partum
post office n ufficio m postale
post office box n casella f postale
postpone /pəʊs(t)'pəʊn/ vt rimandare
postponement /pəʊs(t)'pəʊnmənt/ n rinvio m
postscript /'pəʊs(t)skrɪpt/ n poscritto m
posture /'pɒstʃə(r)/ n posizione f
post-war a del dopoguerra
pot /pɒt/ n vaso m; (for tea) teiera f; (for coffee) caffettiera f; (for cooking) pentola f; (sl: marijuana) erba f; **~s of money** fam un sacco di soldi; **go to ~** fam andare in malora
potash /'pɒtæʃ/ n potassa f
potassium /pə'tæsɪəm/ n potassio m
potato /pə'teɪtəʊ/ n (pl -es) patata f
potato-peeler /-'piːlə(r)/ n tagliapatate m inv
pot-bellied /'pɒtbelɪd/ a panciuto
pot-belly /'pɒtbelɪ/ n fam pancione m
potent /'pəʊtənt/ a potente
potentate /'pəʊtənteɪt/ n potentato m
potential /pə'tenʃl/ a potenziale ● n potenziale m
potentially /pə'tenʃəlɪ/ adv potenzialmente
pot: **pothole** n cavità f inv; (in road) buca f. **potholer** n speleologo, -a mf. **pot-luck** n take

~ affidarsi alla sorte. **pot plant** n pianta f da appartamento. **pot-shot** n **take a ~ at** sparare a casaccio a

potted /'pɒtɪd/ a conservato; (*shortened*) condensato

potted plant n pianta f da appartamento

potter¹ /'pɒtə(r)/ vi ~ [**about**] gingillarsi

potter² n vasaio, -a mf

pottery /'pɒtərɪ/ n lavorazione f della ceramica; (*articles*) ceramiche fpl; (*workshop*) laboratorio m di ceramiche

potting compost /'pɒtɪŋ/ n terriccio m

potty /'pɒtɪ/ a (**-ier, -iest**) fam matto ● n vasino m

pouch /paʊtʃ/ n marsupio m

pouffe /puːf/ n pouf m inv

poultry /'pəʊltrɪ/ n pollame m

pounce /paʊns/ vi balzare; ~ **on** saltare su

pound¹ /paʊnd/ n libbra f (= 0,454 kg); (*money*) sterlina f

pound² vt battere ● vi ⟨*heart*:⟩ battere forte; (*run heavily*) correre pesantemente

pound³ n (*for cars*) deposito m auto

pounding /'paʊndɪŋ/ n martellio m ● a martellante

pour /pɔː(r)/ vt versare ● vi riversarsi; (*with rain*) piovere a dirotto

■ **pour out** vi riversarsi fuori ● vt versare ⟨*drink*⟩; sfogare ⟨*troubles*⟩

pout /paʊt/ vi fare il broncio ● n broncio

poverty /'pɒvətɪ/ n povertà f

POW n abbr (**prisoner of war**) prigioniero, -a mf di guerra

powder /'paʊdə(r)/ n polvere f; (*cosmetic*) cipria f ● vt polverizzare; (*face*) incipriare

powder room n euph toilette f inv per signore

powdery /'paʊdərɪ/ a polveroso

power /'paʊə(r)/ n potere m; Electr corrente f [elettrica]; Math potenza f

power cut n interruzione f di corrente

powered /'paʊəd/ a ~ **by electricity** alimentato da corrente elettrica

powerful /'paʊəfʊl/ a potente

powerhouse /'paʊəhaʊs/ n (*fig: person*) persona f dinamica e energica; **a ~ of ideas** un vulcano di idee

powerless /'paʊəlɪs/ a impotente

power: **power-on light** n spia f di accensione. **power station** n centrale f elettrica. **power steering** n Auto servosterzo m. **power switch** n pulsante m di alimentazione. **power unit** n (*of computer etc*) alimentatore m

pow-wow /'paʊwaʊ/ n (*of American Indians*) raduno m tribale; (*fam: discussion*) discussione f

pp abbr (**pages**) pp.; abbr (**per procurationem**) pp.

PR n abbr (**proportional representation**) proporzionale f; abbr (**public relations**) pubbliche relazioni fpl

practicable /'præktɪkəbl/ a praticabile

practical /'præktɪkl/ a pratico

practicality /præktɪ'kælɪtɪ/ n praticità f

practical joke n scherzo m pratico

practically /'præktɪklɪ/ adv praticamente

practice /'præktɪs/ n pratica f; (*custom*) usanza f; (*habit*) abitudine f; (*exercise*) esercizio m; Sport allenamento m; **in ~** (*in reality*) in pratica; **out of ~** fuori esercizio; **put into ~** mettere in pratica

practise /'præktɪs/ vt fare pratica in; (*carry out*) mettere in pratica; esercitare ⟨*profession*⟩ ● vi esercitarsi; ⟨*doctor*:⟩ praticare

practised /'præktɪst/ a esperto

pragmatic /præg'mætɪk/ a pragmatico

pragmatism /'prægmətɪzm/ n pragmatismo m

pragmatist /'prægmətɪst/ n pragmatico, -a mf

praise /preɪz/ n lode f ● vt lodare

praiseworthy /'preɪzwɜːðɪ/ a lodevole

pram /præm/ n carrozzella f

prance /prɑːns/ vi saltellare

prank /præŋk/ n tiro m

prattle /'prætl/ vi parlottare

prawn /prɔːn/ n gambero m

prawn cocktail n cocktail m inv di gamberetti

pray /preɪ/ vi pregare

prayer /preə(r)/ n preghiera f

preach /priːtʃ/ vt/i predicare

preacher /'priːtʃə(r)/ n predicatore, -trice mf

preamble /priː'æmbl/ n preambolo m

pre-arrange /priː-/ vt predisporre

precarious /prɪ'keərɪəs/ a precario

precariously /prɪ'keərɪəslɪ/ adv in modo precario

precast /'priːkɑːst/ a ⟨*concrete*⟩ prefabbricato

precaution /prɪ'kɔːʃn/ n precauzione f; **as a ~** per precauzione

precautionary /prɪ'kɔːʃnərɪ/ a preventivo

precede /prɪ'siːd/ vt precedere

precedence /'presɪdəns/ n precedenza f

precedent /'presɪdənt/ n precedente m

preceding /prɪ'siːdɪŋ/ a precedente

preceptor /prɪ'septə(r)/ n Am Univ precettore m

precinct /'priːsɪŋkt/ n (*traffic-free*) zona f pedonale; (*Am: district*) circoscrizione f

precious /'preʃəs/ a prezioso; ⟨*style*⟩ ricercato ● adv fam ~ **little** ben poco

precipice /'presɪpɪs/ n precipizio m

precipitate¹ /prɪ'sɪpɪtət/ a precipitoso

precipitate² /prɪ'sɪpɪteɪt/ vt precipitare

precipitation /prɪsɪpɪ'teɪʃn/ n precipitazione f

précis /'preɪsiː/ n (*pl* **précis** /'preɪsiːz/) sunto m

precise /prɪ'saɪs/ a preciso

precisely /prɪ'saɪslɪ/ adv precisamente

precision /prɪ'sɪʒn/ n precisione f

preclude /prɪ'kluːd/ vt precludere

precocious /prɪ'kəʊʃəs/ a precoce

precociousness /prɪ'kəʊʃəsnɪs/ n precocità f

preconceived /priːkənˈsiːvd/ a preconcetto

preconception /priːkənˈsepʃn/ n preconcetto m

precondition /priːkənˈdɪʃn/ n presupposto m ● vt Psych condizionare

precook /priːˈkʊk/ vt cuocere in anticipo

precursor /priːˈkɜːsə(r)/ n precursore m

predator /ˈpredətə(r)/ n predatore, -trice mf

predatory /ˈpredət(ə)rɪ/ a rapace

predecessor /ˈpriːdɪsesə(r)/ n predecessore, -a mf

predetermine /priːdɪˈtɜːmɪn/ vt predeterminare

predicament /prɪˈdɪkəmənt/ n situazione f difficile

predicate /ˈpredɪkət/ n Gram predicato m

predicative /prɪˈdɪkətɪv/ a predicativo

predict /prɪˈdɪkt/ vt predire

predictable /prɪˈdɪktəbl/ a prevedibile

prediction /prɪˈdɪkʃn/ n previsione f

predigested /priːdaɪˈdʒestɪd/ a predigerito

predisposition /priːdɪspəˈzɪʃn/ n predisposizione f

predominant /prɪˈdɒmɪnənt/ a predominante

predominate /prɪˈdɒmɪneɪt/ vi predominare

pre-eminent /priːˈemɪnənt/ a preminente

pre-empt /priːˈempt/ vt (prevent) prevenire

pre-emptive /priːˈemptɪv/ a preventivo

preen /priːn/ vt lisciarsi; ~ **oneself** fig farsi bello

prefab /ˈpriːfæb/ n fam casa f prefabbricata

prefabricated /priːˈfæbrɪkeɪtɪd/ a prefabbricato

preface /ˈprefɪs/ n prefazione f

prefatory /ˈprefət(ə)rɪ/ a ⟨comments⟩ preliminare; ⟨pages, notes⟩ introduttivo

prefect /ˈpriːfekt/ n Sch studente, -tessa mf della scuola superiore con responsabilità disciplinari ecc

prefer /prɪˈfɜː(r)/ vt (pt/pp **preferred**) preferire; **I** ~ **to walk** preferisco camminare

preferable /ˈprefərəbl/ a preferibile (to a)

preferably /ˈprefərəblɪ/ adv preferibilmente

preference /ˈprefərəns/ n preferenza f

preferential /prefəˈrenʃl/ a preferenziale

prefix /ˈpriːfɪks/ n prefisso m

pregnancy /ˈpregnənsɪ/ n gravidanza f

pregnant /ˈpregnənt/ a incinta

preheat /priːˈhiːt/ vt preriscaldare ⟨oven⟩

prehensile /priːˈhensaɪl/ a prensile

prehistoric /priːhɪsˈtɒrɪk/ a preistorico

pre-ignition /priːɪgˈnɪʃn/ n preaccensione f

pre-installed /priːɪnˈstɔːld/ a preinstallato

prejudge /priːˈdʒʌdʒ/ vt giudicare prematuramente ⟨issue⟩

prejudice /ˈpredʒʊdɪs/ n pregiudizio m ● vt influenzare (**against** contro); (harm) danneggiare

prejudiced /ˈpredʒʊdɪst/ a prevenuto

preliminary /prɪˈlɪmɪnərɪ/ a preliminare

preloaded /priːˈləʊdɪd/ a precaricato

prelude /ˈpreljuːd/ n preludio m

premarital /priːˈmærɪtl/ a prematrimoniale

premarital sex n rapporti mpl prematrimoniali

premature /ˈpremətjʊə(r)/ a prematuro

premature birth n parto m prematuro

prematurely /ˈpremətjʊəlɪ/ adv prematuramente

premeditated /priːˈmedɪteɪtɪd/ a premeditato

premenstrual syndrome /priːˈmenstrʊəl/ n sindrome f premestruale

premenstrual tension n tensione f premestruale

premier /ˈpremɪə(r)/ a primario ● n Pol primo ministro m, premier m inv

première /ˈpremɪeə(r)/ n prima f

premiership /ˈpremɪəʃɪp/ n Pol carica f di primo ministro nel Regno Unito; ≈ presidenza f del consiglio

premises /ˈpremɪsɪz/ npl locali mpl; **on the** ~ sul posto

premium /ˈpriːmɪəm/ n premio m; **be at a** ~ essere una cosa rara

premonition /preməˈnɪʃn/ n presentimento m

prenatal /priːˈneɪtl/ a esp Am prenatale

preoccupied /priːˈɒkjʊpaɪd/ a preoccupato

preoperative /priːˈɒp(ə)rətɪv/ a preoperatorio

preordained /priːɔːˈdeɪnd/ a prestabilito; ⟨outcome⟩ predestinato

prep /prep/ n Sch compiti mpl

pre-packed /priːˈpækt/ a preconfezionato

prepaid /priːˈpeɪd/ a pagato in anticipo; ⟨envelope⟩ già affrancato

preparation /prepəˈreɪʃn/ n preparazione f; ~**s** pl preparativi mpl

preparatory /prɪˈpærətrɪ/ a preparatorio; ~ **to** come preparazione per

prepare /prɪˈpeə(r)/ vt preparare ● vi prepararsi (**for** per); ~**d to** disposto a

prepay /priːˈpeɪ/ vt (pt/pp -**paid**) pagare in anticipo

preponderance /prɪˈpɒndərəns/ n preponderanza f

preponderantly /prɪˈpɒndərəntlɪ/ adv in modo preponderante

preponderate /prɪˈpɒndəreɪt/ vi predominare

preposition /prepəˈzɪʃn/ n preposizione f

prepossessing /priːpəˈzesɪŋ/ a attraente

preposterous /prɪˈpɒstərəs/ a assurdo

pre-programmed /priːˈprəʊɡræmd/ a programmato; Comput preprogrammato

prep school n scuola f elementare privata

pre-recorded /-rɪˈkɔːdɪd/ a in differita

prerequisite /priːˈrekwɪzɪt/ n condizione f sine qua non

prerogative /prɪˈrɒɡətɪv/ n prerogativa f

Presbyterian /prezbɪˈtɪərɪən/ a & n presbiteriano, -a mf

pre-school /ˈpriːskuːl/ n Am scuola f materna, asilo m ● a ⟨child⟩ in età prescolastica; ⟨years⟩ prescolastico

prescribe /prɪˈskraɪb/ *vt* prescrivere

prescription /prɪˈskrɪpʃn/ *n Med* ricetta *f*

prescriptive /prɪˈskrɪptɪv/ *a* normativo

presence /ˈprezns/ *n* presenza *f*; ~ **of mind** presenza *f* di spirito

present¹ /ˈpreznt/ *a* presente ● *n* presente *m*; **at** ~ attualmente

present² *n* (*gift*) regalo *m*; **give sb sth as a** ~ regalare qcsa a qcno

present³ /prɪˈzent/ *vt* presentare; ~ **sb with an award** consegnare un premio a qcno

presentable /prɪˈzentəbl/ *a* **be** ~ essere presentabile

presentation /prezn'teɪʃn/ *n* presentazione *f*

present-day *a* attuale

presenter /prɪˈzentə(r)/ *n TV, Radio* presentatore, -trice *mf*

presently /ˈprezntlɪ/ *adv* fra poco; (*Am: now*) attualmente

preservation /prezə'veɪʃn/ *n* conservazione *f*

preservative /prɪˈzɜːvətɪv/ *n* conservante *m*

preserve /prɪˈzɜːv/ *vt* preservare; (*maintain, Culin*) conservare ● *n* (*in hunting & fig*) riserva *f*; (*jam*) marmellata *f*

pre-set /priːˈset/ *vt* programmare

pre-shrunk /priːˈʃrʌŋk/ *a* (*fabric*) irrestringibile

preside /prɪˈzaɪd/ *vi* presiedere (**over** a)

presidency /ˈprezɪdənsɪ/ *n* presidenza *f*

president /ˈprezɪdənt/ *n* presidente *m*

presidential /prezɪˈdenʃl/ *a* presidenziale

pre-soak /priːˈsəʊk/ *vt* mettere in ammollo

press /pres/ *n* (*machine*) pressa *f*; (*newspapers*) stampa *f* ● *vt* premere; pressare (*flower*); (*iron*) stirare; (*squeeze*) stringere ● *vi* (*urge*) incalzare

■ **press ahead** *vi* (*continue*) proseguire

■ **press for** *vi* fare pressione per; **be** ~**ed for** (*short of*) essere a corto di

■ **press on** *vi* andare avanti

press: **press conference** *n* conferenza *f* stampa. **press cutting** *n* ritaglio *m* di giornale. **press-gang** *vt* forzare

pressing /ˈpresɪŋ/ *a* urgente

press: **press release** *n* comunicato *m* stampa. **press stud** *n* [bottone *m*] automatico *m*. **press-up** *n* flessione *f*

pressure /ˈpreʃə(r)/ *n* pressione *f* ● *vt* = **pressurize**

pressure-cooker *n* pentola *f* a pressione

pressure group *n* gruppo *m* di pressione

pressurize /ˈpreʃəraɪz/ *vt* far pressione su

pressurized /ˈpreʃəraɪzd/ *a* (*cabin*) pressurizzato

prestige /preˈstiːʒ/ *n* prestigio *m*

prestigious /preˈstɪdʒəs/ *a* prestigioso

presumably /prɪˈzjuːməblɪ/ *adv* presumibilmente

presume /prɪˈzjuːm/ *vt* presumere; ~ **to do sth** permettersi di fare qcsa ● *vi* ~ **on** approfittare di

presumption /prɪˈzʌmpʃn/ *n* presunzione *f*; (*boldness*) impertinenza *f*

presumptuous /prɪˈzʌmptjʊəs/ *a* impertinente

presuppose /priːsəˈpəʊz/ *vt* presupporre

presupposition /priːsʌpəˈzɪʃn/ *n* presupposizione *f*

pre-tax /ˈpriːtæks/ *a* al lordo d'imposta

pretence /prɪˈtens/ *n* finzione *f*; (*pretext*) pretesto *m*; **it's all** ~ è tutta una scena

pretend /prɪˈtend/ *vt* fingere; (*claim*) pretendere ● *vi* fare finta

pretender /prɪˈtendə(r)/ *n* pretendente *mf*

pretentious /prɪˈtenʃəs/ *a* pretenzioso

preterite /ˈpretərɪt/ *n* preterito *m*

pretext /ˈpriːtekst/ *n* pretesto *m*

pretty /ˈprɪtɪ/ *a* (-**ier**, -**iest**) carino ● *adv* (*fam: fairly*) abbastanza

prevail /prɪˈveɪl/ *vi* prevalere; ~ **on sb to do sth** convincere qcno a fare qc

prevailing /prɪˈveɪlɪŋ/ *a* prevalente

prevalence /ˈprevələns/ *n* diffusione *f*

prevalent /ˈprevələnt/ *a* diffuso

prevaricate /prɪˈværɪkeɪt/ *vi* tergiversare

prevent /prɪˈvent/ *vt* impedire; ~ **sb [from] doing sth** impedire a qcno di fare qcsa

preventable /prɪˈventəbl/ *a* evitabile

prevention /prɪˈvenʃn/ *n* prevenzione *f*

preventive /prɪˈventɪv/ *a* preventivo

preview /ˈpriːvjuː/ *n* anteprima *f*

previous /ˈpriːvɪəs/ *a* precedente

previously /ˈpriːvɪəslɪ/ *adv* precedentemente

pre-war /priːˈwɔː/ *a* anteguerra

pre-wash /ˈpriːwɒʃ/ *n* prelavaggio *m*

prey /preɪ/ *n* preda *f*; **bird of** ~ uccello *m* rapace ● *vi* ~ **on** far preda di; ~ **on sb's mind** attanagliare qcno

price /praɪs/ *n* prezzo *m* ● *vt Comm* fissare il prezzo di

price: **price-conscious** *adj* consapevole dell'andamento dei prezzi. **price cutting** *n* taglio *m* dei prezzi. **price increase** *n* aumento *m* di prezzo

priceless /ˈpraɪslɪs/ *a* inestimabile; (*fam: amusing*) spassosissimo

price: **price list** *n* listino *m* prezzi. **price/performance ratio** *n* rapporto *m* prezzo/prestazioni. **price range** *n* gamma *f* di prezzi. **price tag** *n* talloncino *m* del prezzo. **price war** *n* guerra *f* dei prezzi

pricey /ˈpraɪsɪ/ *a fam* caro

pricing policy /ˈpraɪsɪŋ/ *n* politica *f* di determinazione dei prezzi

prick /prɪk/ *n* puntura *f*; *vulg* (*penis*) cazzo *m*; (*person*) stronzo *m* ● *vt* pungere

■ **prick up** *vt* ~ **up one's ears** rizzare le orecchie

prickle /ˈprɪkl/ *n* spina *f*; (*sensation*) formicolio *m*

prickly /ˈprɪklɪ/ *a* pungente; (*person*) irritabile

pride /praɪd/ *n* orgoglio *m*; (*of lions*) branco *m*; ~ **of place** posizione *f* d'onore ● *vt* ~ **oneself on** vantarsi di

priest /priːst/ *n* prete *m*

priesthood /ˈpriːsthʊd/ *n* (*clergy*) clero *m*;

(calling) sacerdozio *m*; **enter the ~** farsi prete

prig /prɪg/ *n* presuntuoso *m*

priggish /'prɪgɪʃ/ *a* presuntuoso

prim /prɪm/ *a* (**primmer**, **primmest**) perbenino

primacy /'praɪməsɪ/ *n* primato *m*; *(of party, power)* supremazia *f*; *Relig* carica *f* di primate

prima facie /praɪmə'feɪʃiː/ *adv* *(at first)* a prima vista ● *a* a prima vista legittimo

primal /'praɪməl/ *a* *(quality, myth, feeling)* primitivo

primarily /'praɪmərɪlɪ/ *adv* in primo luogo

primary /'praɪmərɪ/ *a* primario; *(chief)* principale

primary school *n* scuola *f* elementare

primate /'praɪmeɪt/ *n* Zool, Relig primate *m*

prime¹ /praɪm/ *a* principale, primo; *(first-rate)* eccellente ● *n* **be in one's ~** essere nel fiore degli anni

prime² *vt* preparare *(surface, person)*

Prime Minister *n* Primo Ministro *m*

primer /'praɪmə(r)/ *n* *(paint)* base *f*; *(for detonating)* innesco *m*

prime time *n* prime time *m inv*, fascia *f* di massimo ascolto ● *attrib* *(advertising, programme)* nella fascia di massimo ascolto

primeval /praɪ'miːvl/ *a* primitivo

primitive /'prɪmɪtɪv/ *a* primitivo

primordial /praɪ'mɔːdɪəl/ *a* primordiale

primrose /'prɪmrəʊz/ *n* primula *f*

prince /prɪns/ *n* principe *m*

princely /'prɪnslɪ/ *a* *(life, rôle)* da principe; *(amount, style)* principesco

princess /prɪn'ses/ *n* principessa *f*

principal /'prɪnsəpl/ *a* principale ● *n* Sch preside *m*

principality /prɪnsɪ'pælətɪ/ *n* principato *m*

principally /'prɪnsəplɪ/ *adv* principalmente

principle /'prɪnsəpl/ *n* principio *m*; **in ~** in teoria; **on ~** per principio; **~s** *pl* *(fundamentals)* fondamenti *mpl*

print /prɪnt/ *n* *(mark, trace)* impronta *f*; *Phot* copia *f*; *(letters)* stampatello *m*; *(picture)* stampa *f*; **in ~** *(printed out)* stampato; *(book)* in commercio; **out of ~** esaurito ● *vt/i* stampare; *(write in capitals)* scrivere in stampatello

■ **print out** *vt/i* Comput stampare

printed matter /'prɪntɪd/ *n* stampe *fpl*

printer /'prɪntə(r)/ *n* stampante *f*; *(person)* tipografo, -a *mf*

printer port *n* porta *f* per la stampante

printing /'prɪntɪŋ/ *n* tipografia *f*

printout /'prɪntaʊt/ *n* Comput stampa *f*

print speed *n* velocità *f* di stampa

prior /'praɪə(r)/ *a* precedente ● *prep* **~ to** prima di

priority /praɪ'ɒrətɪ/ *n* precedenza *f*; *(matter)* priorità *f inv*

prise /praɪz/ *vt* **~ open/up** forzare

prism /'prɪzm/ *n* prisma *m*

prison /'prɪzn/ *n* prigione *f*

prisoner /'prɪz(ə)nə(r)/ *n* prigioniero, -a *mf*

prison sentence *n* pena *f* detentiva

prissy /'prɪsɪ/ *a* *(person)* perbenista

pristine /'prɪstiːn/ *a* originario; *(unspoilt)* intatto

privacy /'prɪvəsɪ/ *n* privacy *f*

private /'praɪvət/ *a* privato; *(car, secretary, letter)* personale ● *n* Mil soldato *m* semplice; **in ~** in privato

private enterprise *n* iniziativa *f* privata

private property *n* proprietà *f* privata

privately /'praɪvətlɪ/ *adv* *(funded, educated etc)* privatamente; *(in secret)* in segreto; *(confidentially)* in privato; *(inwardly)* interiormente

privation /praɪ'veɪʃn/ *n* privazione *f*; **~s** *pl* stenti *mpl*

privatization /praɪvətaɪ'zeɪʃn/ *n* privatizzazione *f*

privatize /'praɪvətaɪz/ *vt* privatizzare

privilege /'prɪvəlɪdʒ/ *n* privilegio *m*

privileged /'prɪvəlɪdʒd/ *a* privilegiato

privy /'prɪvɪ/ *a* **be ~ to** essere al corrente di

prize /praɪz/ *n* premio *m* ● *a* *(idiot etc)* perfetto ● *vt* apprezzare

prize: prize-giving /'praɪzgɪvɪŋ/ *n* premiazione *f*. **prizewinner** *n* vincitore, -trice *mf*. **prize-winning** *a* vincente

pro /prəʊ/ *n* *(fam: professional)* professionista *mf*; **the ~s and cons** il pro e il contro

probability /prɒbə'bɪlətɪ/ *n* probabilità *f inv*

probable /'prɒbəbl/ *a* probabile

probably /'prɒbəblɪ/ *adv* probabilmente

probate /'prəʊbeɪt/ *n* Jur omologazione *f*

probation /prə'beɪʃn/ *n* prova *f*; *Jur* libertà *f* vigilata

probationary /prə'beɪʃnərɪ/ *a* in prova; **~ period** periodo *m* di prova

probationer /prə'beɪʃnə(r)/ *n* *(employee on trial)* impiegato, -a *mf* in prova; *(trainee)* apprendista *mf*

probe /prəʊb/ *n* sonda *f*; *(fig: investigation)* indagine *f* ● *vt* sondare; *(investigate)* esaminare a fondo

probing /'prəʊbɪŋ/ *a* *(question)* penetrante

problem /'prɒbləm/ *n* problema *m* ● *attrib* difficile

problematic /prɒblə'mætɪk/ *a* problematico

problem page *n* posta *f* del cuore

procedural /prə'siːdʒərəl/ *a* *(detail, error)* procedurale

procedure /prə'siːdʒə(r)/ *n* procedimento *m*

proceed /prə'siːd/ *vi* procedere ● *vt* **~ to do sth** proseguire facendo qcsa

proceedings /prə'siːdɪŋz/ *npl* *(report)* atti *mpl*; *Jur* azione *fsg* legale

proceeds /'prəʊsiːdz/ *npl* ricavato *msg*

process /'prəʊses/ *n* processo *m*; *(procedure)* procedimento *m*; **in the ~** nel far ciò ● *vt* trattare; *Admin* occuparsi di; *Phot* sviluppare

procession /prə'seʃn/ *n* processione *f*

processor /'prəʊsesə(r)/ *n* Comput processore *m*; *(for food)* tritatutto *m inv*

pro-choice /prəʊ'tʃɔɪs/ *a* abortista

proclaim /prə'kleɪm/ *vt* proclamare

proclamation /prɒklə'meɪʃn/ *n* proclamazione *f*

proclivity /prə'klɪvətɪ/ n tendenza f
procrastinate /prə'kræstɪneɪt/ vi procrastinare
procrastination /prəkræstɪ'neɪʃn/ n procrastinazione f
procreate /'prəʊkrɪeɪt/ vi procreare
procreation /prəʊkrɪ'eɪʃn/ n procreazione f
procure /prə'kjʊə(r)/ vt ottenere
prod /prɒd/ n colpetto m ● vt (pt/pp **prodded**) punzecchiare; fig incitare
prodigal /'prɒdɪgl/ a prodigo
prodigal son n figliol m prodigo
prodigious /prə'dɪdʒəs/ a prodigioso
prodigy /'prɒdɪdʒɪ/ n [infant] ~ bambino m prodigio
produce¹ /'prɒdjuːs/ n prodotti mpl; ~ **of Italy** prodotto in Italia
produce² /prə'djuːs/ vt produrre; (bring out) tirar fuori; (cause) causare; (fam: give birth to) fare
producer /prə'djuːsə(r)/ n produttore m
product /'prɒdʌkt/ n prodotto m
product range n gamma f di prodotti
production /prə'dʌkʃn/ n produzione f; Theat spettacolo m
production: production control n controllo m della produzione. **production director** n direttore, -trice mf della produzione. **production line** n catena f di montaggio. **production management** n gestione f della produzione. **production manager** n direttore, -trice mf della produzione
productive /prə'dʌktɪv/ a produttivo
productivity /prɒdʌk'tɪvətɪ/ n produttività f
product range n gamma f di prodotti
profane /prə'feɪn/ a profano; (blasphemous) blasfemo
profanity /prə'fænətɪ/ n (oath) bestemmia f
profess /prə'fes/ vt (claim) dichiarare
professed /prə'fest/ a (claiming to be) sedicente
profession /prə'feʃn/ n professione f
professional /prə'feʃnəl/ a professionale; (not amateur) professionista; (piece of work) da professionista; (man) di professione ● n professionista mf
professionalism /prə'feʃnəlɪzm/ n (of person, organization, work) professionalità f; Sport professionismo m
professionally /prə'feʃnəlɪ/ adv professionalmente
professor /prə'fesə(r)/ n professore m [universitario]
professorial /prɒfə'sɔːrɪəl/ a (duties, post, salary) professorale
proffer /'prɒfə(r)/ vt (hold out) porgere; (fig: offer) offrire
proficiency /prə'fɪʃnsɪ/ n competenza f
proficient /prə'fɪʃnt/ a competente (in in)
profile /'prəʊfaɪl/ n profilo m
profit /'prɒfɪt/ n profitto m ● vi ~ **from** trarre profitto da
profitable /'prɒfɪtəbl/ a proficuo
profitably /'prɒfɪtəblɪ/ adv in modo proficuo

profit and loss account n conto m profitti e perdite
profiteer /prɒfɪ'tɪə(r)/ n profittatore, -trice mf
profiterole /prə'fɪtərəʊl/ n profiterole m inv
profit margin n margine m di profitto
profit-sharing n partecipazione f agli utili
profligate /'prɒflɪgət/ a (extravagant) spendaccione; (dissolute) dissoluto; (spending) eccessivo
pro forma invoice /fɔːmə/ n fattura f proforma
profound /prə'faʊnd/ a profondo
profoundly /prə'faʊndlɪ/ adv profondamente
profuse /prə'fjuːs/ a ~ **apologies** una profusione di scuse
profusely /prə'fjuːslɪ/ adv profusamente
profusion /prə'fjuːʒn/ n profusione f; **in ~** in abbondanza
progeny /'prɒdʒənɪ/ n progenie f inv
prognosis /prɒg'nəʊsɪs/ n (pl -oses) (prediction) previsione f; Med prognosi f inv
prognosticate /prɒg'nɒstɪkeɪt/ vt pronosticare
program /'prəʊgræm/ n Comput programma m ● vt (pt/pp **programmed**) programmare
programme /'prəʊgræm/ n Br programma m
programmer /'prəʊgræmə(r)/ n Comput programmatore, -trice mf
programming /'prəʊgræmɪŋ/ n programmazione f
progress¹ /'prəʊgres/ n progresso m; **in ~** in corso; **make ~** fig fare progressi
progress² /prə'gres/ vi progredire; fig fare progressi
progressive /prə'gresɪv/ a progressivo; (reforming) progressista
progressively /prə'gresɪvlɪ/ adv progressivamente
prohibit /prə'hɪbɪt/ vt proibire
prohibition /prəʊhɪ'bɪʃn/ n proibizione f; **P~** Am proibizionismo m
prohibitive /prə'hɪbɪtɪv/ a proibitivo
prohibitively /prə'hɪbɪtɪvlɪ/ adv (expensive) in modo proibitivo
project¹ /'prɒdʒekt/ n progetto m; Sch ricerca f
project² /prə'dʒekt/ vt proiettare (film, image) ● vi (jut out) sporgere
projectile /prə'dʒektaɪl/ n proiettile m
projection /prə'dʒekʃn/ n (of figures) proiezione f
projector /prə'dʒektə(r)/ n proiettore m
proletarian /prəʊlə'teərɪən/ a & n proletario, -a mf
proletariat /prəʊlɪ'teərɪət/ n proletariato m
pro-life /prəʊ'laɪf/ a antiabortista
proliferate /prə'lɪfəreɪt/ vi proliferare
proliferation /prəlɪfə'reɪʃn/ n proliferazione f
prolific /prə'lɪfɪk/ a prolifico
prologue /'prəʊlɒg/ n prologo m
prolong /prə'lɒŋ/ vt prolungare

prom /prɒm/ n (*Br fam: at seaside*) lungomare m inv; (*Am fam: at high school*) ballo m studentesco

promenade /prɒmə'nɑːd/ n lungomare m inv

prominence /'prɒmɪnəns/ n (*of person, issue*) importanza f; (*of object*) sporgenza f; (*hill*) rilievo m

prominent /'prɒmɪnənt/ a prominente; (*conspicuous*) di rilievo

promiscuity /prɒmɪ'skjuːəti/ n promiscuità f

promiscuous /prə'mɪskjʊəs/ a promiscuo

promise /'prɒmɪs/ n promessa f ● vt promettere; ~ **sb that** promettere a qcno che; **I ~d to** l'ho promesso

Promised Land /prɒmɪst'lænd/ n Terra f Promessa

promising /'prɒmɪsɪŋ/ a promettente

promo /'prəʊməʊ/ n (*fam: of product*) campagna f promozionale; (*video*) video m inv promozionale

promontory /'prɒmənt(ə)rɪ/ n promontorio m

promote /prə'məʊt/ vt promuovere; **be ~d** essere promosso

promoter /prə'məʊtə(r)/ n promotore, -trice mf

promotion /prə'məʊʃn/ n promozione f

promotional /prə'məʊʃnəl/ a Comm promozionale

prompt /prɒmpt/ a immediato; (*punctual*) puntuale ● adv in punto ● vt incitare (**to** a); Theat suggerire a ● vi suggerire ● n Comput prompt m inv

prompter /'prɒmptə(r)/ n suggeritore, -trice mf

promptly /'prɒmptlɪ/ adv puntualmente

Proms /prɒmz/ npl rassegna f di concerti estivi di musica classica presso l'Albert Hall a Londra

prone /prəʊn/ a prono; **be ~ to do sth** essere incline a fare qcsa

prong /prɒŋ/ n dente m

pronoun /'prəʊnaʊn/ n pronome m

pronounce /prə'naʊns/ vt pronunciare; (*declare*) dichiarare

pronounced /prə'naʊnst/ a (*noticeable*) pronunciato

pronouncement /prə'naʊnsmənt/ n dichiarazione f

pronunciation /prənʌnsɪ'eɪʃn/ n pronuncia f

proof /pruːf/ n prova f; Typ bozza f, prova f; **12% ~** 12° ● a ~ **against** a prova di

proof-reader n correttore, -trice mf di bozze

proof-reading n revisione f di bozze

prop¹ /prɒp/ n puntello m ● vt (pt/pp **propped**) ~ **open** tenere aperto; ~ **against** (*lean*) appoggiare a
 ■ **prop up** vt sostenere

prop² n Theat, fam accessorio m di scena

propaganda /prɒpə'gændə/ n propaganda f

propagate /'prɒpəgeɪt/ vt propagare

propagator /'prɒpəgeɪtə(r)/ n propagatore m

propane /'prəʊpeɪn/ n propano m

propel /prə'pel/ vt (pt/pp **propelled**) spingere

propellant /prə'pelənt/ n (*in aerosol*) gas m inv propellente; (*in rocket*) propellente m

propeller /prə'pelə(r)/ n elica f

propelling pencil /prə'pelɪŋ/ n portamina m inv

propensity /prə'pensəti/ n tendenza f

proper /'prɒpə(r)/ a corretto; (*suitable*) adatto; (*fam: real*) vero [e proprio]

properly /'prɒpəli/ adv correttamente

proper name, proper noun n nome m proprio

property /'prɒpəti/ n proprietà f inv

property developer n impresa f edile; (*person*) impresario m edile

property market n mercato m immobiliare

prophecy /'prɒfəsi/ n profezia f

prophesy /'prɒfɪsaɪ/ vt (pt/pp **-ied**) profetizzare

prophet /'prɒfɪt/ n profeta m

prophetic /prə'fetɪk/ a profetico

prophylactic /prɒfɪ'læktɪk/ n (*condom*) profilattico m, preservativo m; (*Med: treatment*) misura f profilattica ● a profilattico

proponent /prə'pəʊnənt/ n fautore, -trice mf

proportion /prə'pɔːʃn/ n proporzione f; (*share*) parte f; **be in ~** essere proporzionato (**to** a); **be out of ~** essere sproporzionato; ~**s** pl (*dimensions*) proporzioni fpl

proportional /prə'pɔːʃnəl/ a proporzionale

proportionally /prə'pɔːʃnəli/ adv in proporzione

proportional representation n rappresentanza f proporzionale

proposal /prə'pəʊzl/ n proposta f; (*of marriage*) proposta f di matrimonio

propose /prə'pəʊz/ vt proporre; (*intend*) proporsi ● vi fare una proposta di matrimonio

proposition /prɒpə'zɪʃn/ n proposta f; (*fam: task*) impresa f

proprietor /prə'praɪətə(r)/ n proprietario, -a mf

propriety /prə'praɪəti/ n correttezza f; **the proprieties** pl l'etichetta f

propulsion /prə'pʌlʃn/ n propulsione f

pro rata /'rɑːtə/ a **on a ~ basis** in proporzione

prosaic /prə'zeɪɪk/ a prosaico

proscribe vt (*exile*) esiliare; (*ban*) bandire

prose /prəʊz/ n prosa f

prosecute /'prɒsɪkjuːt/ vt intentare azione contro

prosecution /prɒsɪ'kjuːʃn/ n azione f giudiziaria; **the ~** l'accusa f

prosecutor /'prɒsɪkjuːtə(r)/ n [Public] P~ Pubblico Ministero m

prospect¹ /'prɒspekt/ n (*expectation*) prospettiva f; (*view*) vista f

prospect² /prə'spekt/ vi ~ **for** cercare

prospective /prə'spektɪv/ a (*future*) futuro; (*possible*) potenziale

prospector /prə'spektə(r)/ n cercatore m

prospectus /prə'spektəs/ n prospetto m

prosper /'prɒspə(r)/ vi prosperare; ⟨person:⟩ stare bene finanziariamente

prosperity /prɒ'sperətɪ/ n prosperità f

prosperous /'prɒspərəs/ a prospero

prostate /'prɒsteɪt/ n prostata f

prosthesis /prɒs'θiːsɪs/ n protesi f

prostitute /'prɒstɪtjuːt/ n prostituta f ● vt fig prostituire

prostitution /prɒstɪ'tjuːʃn/ n prostituzione f

prostrate /'prɒstreɪt/ a prostrato; ~ **with grief** fig prostrato dal dolore

protagonist /prə'tægənɪst/ n protagonista mf

protect /prə'tekt/ vt proteggere (**from** da)

protection /prə'tekʃn/ n protezione f

protective /prə'tektɪv/ a protettivo

protector /prə'tektə(r)/ n protettore, -trice mf

protégé /'prɒtɪʒeɪ/ n protetto m

protein /'prəʊtiːn/ n proteina f

protest[1] /'prəʊtest/ n protesta f

protest[2] /prə'test/ vt/i protestare

Protestant /'prɒtɪstənt/ a & n protestante mf

Protestantism /'prɒtɪstəntɪzm/ n protestantesimo m

protestation /prɒtɪ'steɪʃn/ n protesta f

protester /prə'testə(r)/ n contestatore, -trice mf; (at demonstration) dimostrante mf

protocol /'prəʊtəkɒl/ n protocollo m

prototype /'prəʊtətaɪp/ n prototipo m

protract /prə'trækt/ vt protrarre

protracted /prə'træktɪd/ a prolungato

protractor /prə'træktə(r)/ n goniometro m

protrude /prə'truːd/ vi sporgere

protuberance /prə'tuːbərəns/ n protuberanza f

proud /praʊd/ a fiero (**of** di)

proudly /'praʊdlɪ/ adv fieramente

prove /pruːv/ vt provare ● vi ~ **to be a lie** rivelarsi una bugia

proven /'pruːvən/ a dimostrato

proverb /'prɒvɜːb/ n proverbio m

proverbial /prə'vɜːbɪəl/ a proverbiale

provide /prə'vaɪd/ vt fornire; ~ **sb with sth** fornire qcsa a qcno ● vi ~ **for** (allow for) tenere conto di; ⟨law:⟩ prevedere

provided /prə'vaɪdɪd/ conj ~ [**that**] purché

providence /'prɒvɪdəns/ n provvidenza f

provident /'prɒvɪdənt/ a previdenziale

providential /prɒvɪ'denʃl/ a provvidenziale

provider /prə'vaɪdə(r)/ n (in family) persona f che mantiene la famiglia

providing /prə'vaɪdɪŋ/ conj = **provided**

province /'prɒvɪns/ n provincia f; fig campo m

provincial /prə'vɪnʃl/ a provinciale

provincialism /prə'vɪnʃəlɪzm/ n provincialismo m

provision /prə'vɪʒn/ n (of food, water) approvvigionamento m (**of** di); (of law) disposizione f; **make** ~ **for** ⟨law:⟩ prevedere; ~**s** pl provviste fpl

provisional /prə'vɪʒ(ə)nəl/ a provvisorio

provisionally /prə'vɪʒ(ə)nəlɪ/ adv provvisoriamente

proviso /prə'vaɪzəʊ/ n condizione f

provocation /prɒvə'keɪʃn/ n provocazione f

provocative /prə'vɒkətɪv/ a provocatorio; (sexually) provocante

provocatively /prə'vɒkətɪvlɪ/ adv in modo provocatorio; ⟨smile, be dressed⟩ in modo provocante

provoke /prə'vəʊk/ vt provocare

provost /'prɒvəst/ n Am Univ decano m; Br Univ, Sch rettore m; (in Scotland) sindaco m

prow /praʊ/ n prua f

prowess /'praʊɪs/ n abilità f inv

prowl /praʊl/ vi aggirarsi ● n **on the** ~ in cerca di preda

prowler /'praʊlə(r)/ n tipo m sospetto

proximity /prɒk'sɪmətɪ/ n prossimità f

proxy /'prɒksɪ/ n procura f; (person) persona che agisce per procura

prude /pruːd/ n **be a** ~ essere eccessivamente pudico

prudence /'pruːdəns/ n prudenza f

prudent /'pruːdənt/ a prudente; (wise) oculatezza f

prudently /'pruːdəntlɪ/ adv con prudenza

prudish /'pruːdɪʃ/ a eccessivamente pudico

prudishness /'pruːdɪʃnɪs/ n eccessivo pudore m

prune[1] /pruːn/ n prugna f secca

prune[2] vt potare

pry /praɪ/ vi (pt/pp pried) ficcare il naso

prying /'praɪɪŋ/ a curioso

PS n abbr (**postscriptum**) PS m inv

psalm /sɑːm/ n salmo m

pseud /sjuːd/ n fam intellettualoide mf

pseudonym /'sjuːdənɪm/ n pseudonimo m

■ **psych out** /saɪk/ vt (fam: unnerve) snervare

■ **psych up** vt (fam: prepare mentally) preparare psicologicamente

psychedelic /saɪkə'delɪk/ a psichedelico

psychiatric /saɪkɪ'ætrɪk/ a psichiatrico

psychiatrist /saɪ'kaɪətrɪst/ n psichiatra mf

psychic /'saɪkɪk/ n sensitivo, -a mf ● a psichico; **I'm not** ~ non sono un indovino

psychoanalyse /saɪkəʊ'ænəlaɪz/ vt psicanalizzare

psychoanalysis /saɪkəʊə'næləsɪs/ n psicanalisi f

psychoanalyst /saɪkəʊ'ænəlɪst/ n psicanalista mf

psychological /saɪkə'lɒdʒɪkl/ a psicologico

psychologically /saɪkə'lɒdʒɪklɪ/ adv psicologicamente

psychologist /saɪ'kɒlədʒɪst/ n psicologo, -a mf

psychology /saɪ'kɒlədʒɪ/ n psicologia f

psychopath /'saɪkəpæθ/ n psicopatico, -a mf

psychopathic /saɪkə'pæθɪk/ a psicopatico

psychosis /saɪ'kəʊsɪs/ n psicosi f inv

psychosomatic /saɪkəʊsə'mætɪk/ a psicosomatico

psychotherapist /saɪkəʊ'θerəpɪst/ n psicoterapista mf, psicoterapeuta mf

psychotic /saɪ'kɒtɪk/ a & n psicotico, -a mf

PT n abbr (**physical training**) educazione f fisica

PTA n abbr (**Parent-Teacher Association**) ≈ consiglio m d'istituto

PTO abbr (**please turn over**) vedi retro

pub /pʌb/ n fam pub m inv

puberty /'pju:bətɪ/ n pubertà f

pubic hair /'pju:bɪk/ n peli mpl del pube

public /'pʌblɪk/ a pubblico; **make ~** rendere pubblico ● n **the ~** il pubblico; **in ~** in pubblico

public address system n impianto m di amplificazione

publican /'pʌblɪkən/ n gestore, -trice mf/proprietario, -a mf di un pub

publication /pʌblɪ'keɪʃn/ n pubblicazione f

public: public convenience n gabinetti mpl pubblici. **public holiday** n festa f nazionale. **public house** n pub m inv

publicist /'pʌblɪsɪst/ n (press agent) pressagent mf inv, addetto, -a mf stampa

publicity /pʌb'lɪsətɪ/ n pubblicità f

publicity department n settore m pubblicità

publicity director n direttore, -trice mf della pubblicità

publicize /'pʌblɪsaɪz/ vt pubblicizzare

public library n biblioteca f pubblica

public limited company /'lɪmɪtɪd/ n società f inv per azioni

publicly /'pʌblɪklɪ/ adv pubblicamente

public: public opinion n opinione f pubblica. **public relations** npl pubbliche relazioni fpl. **public relations department** n ufficio m pubbliche relazioni. **public relations officer** n addetto, -a mf alle pubbliche relazioni. **public school** n scuola f privata; Am scuola f pubblica. **public sector** n settore m pubblico. **public-spirited** a be **~** essere dotato di senso civico. **public transport** n mezzi mpl pubblici

publish /'pʌblɪʃ/ vt pubblicare

publisher /'pʌblɪʃə(r)/ n editore m; (firm) editore m, casa f editrice

publishing /'pʌblɪʃɪŋ/ n editoria f

puce /pju:s/ a color bruno rossastro

puck /pʌk/ n (in ice-hockey) disco m; (sprite) folletto m

pucker /'pʌkə(r)/ vi (material:) arricciarsi

pudding /'pʊdɪŋ/ n dolce m cotto al vapore; (course) dolce m

puddle /'pʌdl/ n pozzanghera f

pudgy /'pʌdʒɪ/ a (-ier, -iest) grassoccio

puerile /'pjʊəraɪl/ a puerile

puff /pʌf/ n (of wind) soffio m; (of smoke) tirata f; (for powder) piumino m ● vt sbuffare

■ **puff at** vt tirare boccate da (pipe)

■ **puff out** vt lasciare senza fiato (person); spegnere (candle)

puffed /pʌft/ a (out of breath) senza fiato

puff pastry n pasta f sfoglia

puff sleeve n manica f a palloncino

puffy /'pʌfɪ/ a gonfio

pug /pʌg/ n (dog) carlino m

pugnacious /pʌg'neɪʃəs/ a aggressivo

pull /pʊl/ n trazione f; (fig: attraction) attrazione f; (fam: influence) influenza f ● vt tirare; estrarre (tooth); stirarsi (muscle); **~ a fast one** fam giocare un brutto tiro; **~ faces** far boccacce; **~ oneself together** ricomporsi; **~ one's weight** mettercela tutta; **~ sb's leg** fam prendere in giro qcno

■ **pull ahead** vi (move in front) passare davanti

■ **pull away** vi (increase one's lead) distanziarsi

■ **pull down** vt (demolish) demolire

■ **pull in** vi Auto accostare

■ **pull off** vt togliere; fam azzeccare

■ **pull out** vt tirar fuori ● vi Auto spostarsi; (of competition) ritirarsi

■ **pull over** vi Aut accostare

■ **pull through** vi (recover) farcela

■ **pull together** vi (co-operate) sommare le forze

■ **pull up** vt sradicare (plant); (reprimand) rimproverare ● vi Auto fermarsi

pull-down menu n Comput menu m inv a discesa

pulley /'pʊlɪ/ n Techn puleggia f

pull-in n Br (lay-by) piazzuola f di sosta; (café) bar m inv sul bordo della strada

pullover /'pʊləʊvə(r)/ n pullover m inv

pulmonary /'pʌlmənərɪ/ a polmonare

pulp /pʌlp/ n poltiglia f; (of fruit) polpa f; (for paper) pasta f

pulpit /'pʊlpɪt/ n pulpito m

pulsar /'pʌlsɑ:(r)/ n pulsar m inv

pulsate /pʌl'seɪt/ vi pulsare

pulse /pʌls/ n polso m

pulses /'pʌlsɪz/ npl legumi mpl secchi

pulverize /'pʌlvəraɪz/ vt polverizzare

puma /'pju:mə/ n puma m inv

pumice /'pʌmɪs/ n pomice f

pummel /'pʌml/ vt (pt/pp **pummelled**) prendere a pugni

pump /pʌmp/ n pompa f ● vt pompare; fam cercare di estorcere informazioni da

■ **pump up** vt (inflate) gonfiare

pumpkin /'pʌmpkɪn/ n zucca f

pun /pʌn/ n gioco m di parole

punch¹ /pʌntʃ/ n pugno m; (device) pinza f per forare ● vt dare un pugno a; forare (ticket); perforare (hole)

punch² n (drink) punch m inv

punch: Punch-and-Judy show n spettacolo m di burattini. **punch-drunk** a (in boxing) groggy inv; fig stordito. **punchline** n battuta f finale. **punch-up** n rissa f

punctual /'pʌŋktjʊəl/ a puntuale

punctuality /pʌŋktjʊ'ælətɪ/ n puntualità f

punctually /'pʌŋktjʊəlɪ/ adv puntualmente

punctuate /'pʌŋktjʊeɪt/ vt punteggiare

punctuation /pʌŋktjʊ'eɪʃn/ n punteggiatura f

punctuation mark n segno m di interpunzione

puncture /'pʌŋktʃə(r)/ *n* foro *m*; (*tyre*) foratura *f* ● *vt* forare
pundit /'pʌndɪt/ *n* esperto *m*
pungency /'pʌndʒənsɪ/ *n* asprezza *f*
pungent /'pʌndʒənt/ *a* acre
punish /'pʌnɪʃ/ *vt* punire
punishable /'pʌnɪʃəbl/ *a* punibile
punishment /'pʌnɪʃmənt/ *n* punizione *f*
punitive /'pju:nɪtɪv/ *a* punitivo
punk /pʌŋk/ *n* punk *m inv*
punk rock *n* punk rock *m inv*
punk rocker /'rɒkə(r)/ *n* punk *mf inv*
punnet /'pʌnɪt/ *n* cestello *m*
punt /pʌnt/ *n* (*boat*) barchino *m*
punter /'pʌntə(r)/ *n* (*gambler*) scommettitore, -trice *mf*; (*fam: client*) consumatore, -trice *mf*
puny /'pju:nɪ/ *a* (**-ier, -iest**) striminzito
pup /pʌp/ *n* = **puppy**
pupil /'pju:pl/ *n* alluno, -a *mf*; (*of eye*) pupilla *f*
puppet /'pʌpɪt/ *n* marionetta *f*; (*glove ~, fig*) burattino *m*
puppy /'pʌpɪ/ *n* cucciolo *m*
purchase /'pɜ:tʃəs/ *n* acquisto *m*; (*leverage*) presa *f* ● *vt* acquistare
purchase: purchase invoice *n* fattura *f* di acquisto. **purchase ledger** *n* libro *m* mastro degli acquisti. **purchase order** *n* ordine *m* di acquisto. **purchase price** *n* prezzo *m* di acquisto
purchaser /'pɜ:tʃəsə(r)/ *n* acquirente *mf*
purchasing [department] /'pɜ:tʃəsɪŋ/ *n* ufficio *m* acquisti
purdah /'pɜ:də/ *n* *reclusione f delle donne in alcune società musulmane e indù*
pure /pjʊə(r)/ *a* puro
pure-bred /-bred/ *n* (*horse*) purosangue *m inv* ● *a* purosangue *inv*
purée /'pjʊəreɪ/ *n* purè *m inv* ● *vt* passare
purely /'pjʊəlɪ/ *adv* puramente
purgatory /'pɜ:gətrɪ/ *n* purgatorio *m*
purge /pɜ:dʒ/ *Pol n* epurazione *f* ● *vt* epurare
purification /pjʊərɪfɪ'keɪʃn/ *n* purificazione *f*
purify /'pjʊərɪfaɪ/ *vt* (*pt/pp* **-ied**) purificare
purist /'pjʊərɪst/ *a* & *n* purista *mf*
puritan /'pjʊərɪtən/ *n* puritano, -a *mf* ● *a fig* puritano
puritanical /pjʊərɪ'tænɪkl/ *a* puritano
purity /'pjʊərɪtɪ/ *n* purità *f*
purl /pɜ:l/ *n* (*Knitting*) maglia *f* rovescia ● *vt/i* lavorare a rovescio
purple /'pɜ:pl/ *a* viola *inv*
purport /pə'pɔ:t/ *vt* ~ **to be** farsi passare per
purpose /'pɜ:pəs/ *n* scopo *m*; (*determination*) fermezza *f*; **on** ~ apposta
purpose-built /-'bɪlt/ *a* costruito ad hoc
purposeful /'pɜ:pəsfʊl/ *a* deciso
purposefully /'pɜ:pəsfʊlɪ/ *adv* con decisione
purposely /'pɜ:pəslɪ/ *adv* apposta
purpose-made *a Br* fatto appositamente
purr /pɜ:(r)/ *vi* (*cat:*) fare le fusa
purse /pɜ:s/ *n* borsellino *m*; (*Am: handbag*) borsa *f* ● *vt* increspare (*lips*)

purser /'pɜ:sə(r)/ *n* commissario *m* di bordo
pursue /pə'sju:/ *vt* inseguire; *fig* proseguire
pursuer /pə'sju:ə(r)/ *n* inseguitore, -trice *mf*
pursuit /pə'sju:t/ *n* inseguimento *m*; (*fig: of happiness*) ricerca *f*; (*pastime*) attività *f inv*; **in** ~ all'inseguimento
pus /pʌs/ *n* pus *m*
push /pʊʃ/ *n* spinta *f*; (*fig: effort*) sforzo *m*; (*drive*) iniziativa *f*; **at a** ~ in caso di bisogno; **get the** ~ *fam* essere licenziato ● *vt* spingere; premere (*button*); (*pressurize*) far pressione su; **be ~ed for time** *fam* non avere tempo ● *vi* spingere
■ **push around** *vt* (*bully*) fare il prepotente con
■ **push aside** *vt* scostare
■ **push back** *vt* respingere
■ **push for** *vt* fare pressione per ottenere (*reform*)
■ **push off** *vt* togliere ● *vi* (*fam: leave*) levarsi dai piedi
■ **push on** *vi* (*continue*) continuare
■ **push over** *vt* (*cause to fall*) far cadere
■ **push through** *vt* (*have accepted quickly*) fare accettare
■ **push up** *vt* alzare (*price*)
push-button *n* pulsante *m*
pushchair /'pʊʃtʃeə(r)/ *n* passeggino *m*
pusher /'pʊʃə(r)/ *n* (*fam: of drugs*) spacciatore, -trice *mf* [di droga]
push: pushover *n fam* bazzecola *f*. **pushstart** *vt* spingere (*per far partire*) (*vehicle*) ● *n* give sth a ~ dare una spinta a qcsa. **push-up** *n* flessione *f*
pushy /'pʊʃɪ/ *a fam* troppo intraprendente
puss /pʊs/ *n*, **pussy** /'pʊsɪ/ *n* micio *m*
■ **pussyfoot around** /'pʊsɪfʊt/ *vi fam* tergiversare
pussyfooting /'pʊsɪfʊtɪŋ/ *n fam* tentennamento *m* ● *a* (*fam: attitude, behaviour*) tergiversante
put /pʊt/ *vt* (*pt/pp* **put**, *pres p* **putting**) mettere; ~ **the cost of sth at £50** valutare il costo di qcsa 50 sterline; ~ **an end to** porre fine o termine a; ~ **in writing** mettere per iscritto; ~ **into effect** mettere in opera ● *vi* ~ **to sea** salpare ● *a* stay ~! rimani lì!
■ **put about** *vt* mettere in giro (*rumour*)
■ **put across** *vt* raccontare (*joke*); esprimere (*message*)
■ **put aside** *vt* mettere da parte
■ **put away** *vt* mettere via
■ **put back** *vt* rimettere; mettere indietro (*clock*)
■ **put by** *vt* mettere da parte
■ **put down** *vt* mettere giù; (*suppress*) reprimere; (*kill*) sopprimere; (*write*) annotare; (*criticize unfairly*) sminuire; ~ **one's foot down** *fam* essere fermo; *Auto* dare un'accelerata; ~ **down to** (*attribute*) attribuire
■ **put forward** *vt* avanzare; mettere avanti (*clock*)
■ **put in** *vt* (*insert*) introdurre; (*submit*) presentare ● *vi* ~ **in for** far domanda di
■ **put off** *vt* spegnere (*light*); (*postpone*) ri-

mandare; **~ sb off** tenere a bada qcno; (*deter*) smontare qcno; (*disconcert*) distrarre qcno; **~ sb off sth** (*disgust*) disgustare qcno di qcsa

■ **put on** *vt* mettersi ⟨*clothes*⟩; mettere ⟨*brake*⟩; *Culin* mettere su; accendere ⟨*light*⟩; mettere in scena ⟨*play*⟩; prendere ⟨*accent*⟩; **~ on weight** mettere su qualche chilo; **he's just ~ting it on** è solo una messa in scena

■ **put on to** *vt* (*help find*) indicare ⟨*doctor, restaurant etc*⟩

■ **put out** *vt* spegnere ⟨*fire, light*⟩; tendere ⟨*hand*⟩; (*inconvenience*) creare degli inconvenienti a

■ **put through** *vt* far passare; *Teleph* **I'll ~ you through to him** glielo passo

■ **put to** *vt* **~ sb to trouble** scomodare qcno; **I ~ it to you that...** ritengo che...

■ **put together** *vt* montare ⟨*machine*⟩; fare ⟨*model, jigsaw*⟩

■ **put up** *vt* alzare; erigere ⟨*building*⟩; montare ⟨*tent*⟩; aprire ⟨*umbrella*⟩; affiggere ⟨*notice*⟩; aumentare ⟨*price*⟩; ospitare ⟨*guest*⟩; **~ sb up to sth** mettere qcsa in testa a qcno ● *vi* (*at hotel*) stare; **~ up with** sopportare

putrefaction /pju:trɪ'fækʃn/ *n* putrefazione *f*
putrefy /'pju:trɪfaɪ/ *vi* (*pt/pp* **-ied**) putrefarsi
putrid /'pju:trɪd/ *a* putrido
putt /pʌt/ *n* putt *m inv* ● *vi* colpire leggermente
putty /'pʌtɪ/ *n* mastice *m*
put-up job *n fam* truffa *f*
puzzle /'pʌzl/ *n* enigma *m*; (*jigsaw*) puzzle *m inv* ● *vt* lasciare perplesso ● *vi* **~ over** scervellarsi su

■ **puzzle out** *vt* trovare ⟨*solution*⟩
puzzling /'pʌzlɪŋ/ *a* inspiegabile
pvc *n* PVC *m* ● *attrib* di PVC
pygmy /'pɪgmɪ/ *n* pigmeo, -a *mf*
pyjamas /pə'dʒɑːməz/ *npl* pigiama *msg*
pylon /'paɪlən/ *n* pilone *m*
pyramid /'pɪrəmɪd/ *n* piramide *f*
pyre /paɪə(r)/ *n* pira *f*
pyrex® /'paɪreks/ *n* Pyrex *m*
pyromaniac /paɪrə'meɪnɪæk/ *n* piromane *mf*
pyrotechnics /paɪrə'teknɪks/ *n* (*display*) fuochi *mpl* pirotecnici
python /'paɪθn/ *n* pitone *m*

Qq

q, Q /kju:/ *n* (*letter*) q, Q *f inv*
QC *n Br Jur* avvocato *m* di rango superiore
QED *abbr* (**quod erat demonstrandum**) qed
quack¹ /kwæk/ *n* qua qua *m inv* ● *vi* fare qua qua
quack² *n* (*doctor*) ciarlatano *m*
quad /kwɒd/ *n* (*fam: court*) = **quadrangle**; **~s** *pl fam* = **quadruplets**
quadrangle /'kwɒdræŋgl/ *n* quadrangolo *m*; (*court*) cortile *m* quadrangolare
quadratic equation /kwɒ'drætɪk/ *n* equazione *f* di secondo grado
quadriplegic /kwɒdrɪ'pli:dʒɪk/ *a* quadriplegico
quadruped /'kwɒdrʊped/ *n* quadrupede *m*
quadruple /'kwɒdrʊpl/ *a* quadruplo ● *vt* quadruplicare ● *vi* quadruplicarsi
quadruplets /kwɒd'ru:plɪts/ *npl* quattro gemelli *mpl*
quadruplicate /kwɒd'ru:plɪkət/ *n* **in ~** in quattro copie
quagmire /'kwɒgmaɪə(r)/ *n* pantano *m*
quail /kweɪl/ *vi* farsi prendere dalla paura
quaint /kweɪnt/ *a* pittoresco; (*odd*) bizzarro
quake /kweɪk/ *n fam* terremoto *m* ● *vi* tremare
Quaker /'kweɪkə(r)/ *n* quacchero, -a *mf*
qualification /kwɒlɪfɪ'keɪʃn/ *n* qualifica *f*; (*reservation*) riserva *f*

qualified /'kwɒlɪfaɪd/ *a* qualificato; (*limited*) con riserva
qualifier /'kwɒlɪfaɪə(r)/ *n Sport* concorrente *mf* qualificato, -a
qualify /'kwɒlɪfaɪ/ *v* (*pt/pp* **-ied**) ● *vt* ⟨*course:*⟩ dare la qualifica a (**as** di); (*entitle*) dare diritto a; (*limit*) precisare ● *vi* ottenere la qualifica; *Sport* qualificarsi
qualitative /'kwɒlɪtətɪv/ *a* qualitativo
quality /'kwɒlətɪ/ *n* qualità *f inv*
quality: quality assurance *n* verifica *f* qualità. **quality control** *n* controllo *m* [di] qualità. **quality controller** *n* addetto, -a *mf* al controllo di qualità
qualm /kwɑːm/ *n* scrupolo *m*
quandary /'kwɒndərɪ/ *n* dilemma *m*
quango /'kwæŋgəʊ/ *n Br* organismo *m* autonomo, ma finanziato dal governo
quantifiable /'kwɒntɪfaɪəbl/ *a* quantificabile
quantitative /'kwɒntɪtətɪv/ *a* quantitativo
quantity /'kwɒntətɪ/ *n* quantità *f inv*; **in ~** in grande quantità
quantity surveyor *n* geometra *mf* che calcola quantità e costo di materiali da costruzione
quantum leap /kwɒntəm'li:p/ *n fig* balzo *m* in avanti
quantum mechanics *n* meccanica *f* quantistica
quarantine /'kwɒrənti:n/ *n* quarantena *f*

quarrel /'kwɒrəl/ n lite f ● vi (pt/pp **quarrelled**) litigare

quarrelsome /'kwɒrəlsəm/ a litigioso

quarry¹ /'kwɒrɪ/ n (prey) preda f

quarry² n cava f

quart /kwɔ:t/ n = 1.14 litro

quarter /'kwɔ:tə(r)/ n quarto m; (of year) trimestre m; Am 25 centesimi mpl; ~s pl Mil quartiere msg; **at [a] ~ to six** alle sei meno un quarto; **from all ~s** da tutti i lati ● vt dividere in quattro

quarterdeck /'kwɔ:tədek/ n Naut cassero m

quarter-final n quarto m di finale

quarterly /'kwɔ:təlɪ/ a trimestrale ● adv trimestralmente

quartermaster /'kwɔ:təmɑ:stə(r)/ n (in navy) timoniere m; (in army) furiere m

quartet /kwɔ:'tet/ n quartetto m

quartz /kwɔ:ts/ n quarzo m; ~ **watch** orologio m al quarzo

quash /kwɒʃ/ vt annullare; soffocare ⟨rebellion⟩

quasi+ /'kweɪzaɪ/ pref semi+

quaver /'kweɪvə(r)/ n Mus croma f ● vi tremolare

quay /ki:/ n banchina f

queasiness /'kwi:zɪnɪs/ n nausea f

queasy /'kwi:zɪ/ a **I feel ~** ho la nausea

Quebec /kwɪ'bek/ n (province) Quebec m; (town) Quebec f

queen /kwi:n/ n regina f

queen bee n ape f regina; **she thinks she's the ~ ~** fig si crede chissà chi

queenly /'kwi:nlɪ/ a da regina

queen mother n regina f madre

Queen: Queen's Counsel n Br Jur avvocato m di rango superiore. **Queen's English** n Br **speak the ~ ~** parlare un inglese corretto e senza accento. **Queen's evidence** n Br Jur **turn ~ ~** deporre contro i propri complici. **Queen's Regulations** npl Br Mil codice m militare

queer /kwɪə(r)/ a strano; (dubious) sospetto; (fam: homosexual) finocchio ● n fam finocchio m

quell /kwel/ vt reprimere

quench /kwentʃ/ vt ~ **one's thirst** dissetarsi

query /'kwɪərɪ/ n domanda f; (question mark) punto m interrogativo ● vt (pt/pp -**ied**) interrogare; (doubt) mettere in dubbio

quest /kwest/ n ricerca f (**for** di)

question /'kwestʃən/ n domanda f; (for discussion) questione f; **out of the ~** fuori discussione; **without ~** senza dubbio; **in ~** in questione ● vt interrogare; (doubt) mettere in dubbio

questionable /'kwestʃ(ə)nəbl/ a discutibile

questioner /'kwestʃ(ə)nə(r)/ n interrogante mf

questioning /'kwestʃ(ə)nɪŋ/ n (of person) interrogatorio m; (of criteria) messa f in discussione ● a ⟨look, tone⟩ inquisitorio

question mark n punto m interrogativo

question master n presentatore, -trice mf di quiz

questionnaire /kwestʃə'neə(r)/ n questionario m

question tag n domanda f di conferma

queue /kju:/ n coda f, fila f ● vi ~ [**up**] mettersi in coda (**for** per)

queue-jump vi Br passare davanti alle altre persone in coda

quibble /'kwɪbl/ vi cavillare

quick /kwɪk/ a veloce; **be ~!** sbrigati!; **have a ~ meal** fare uno spuntino ● adv in fretta ● n **be cut to the ~** fig essere punto sul vivo

quick: quick-assembly a facile da montare. **quick-fire** a ⟨questions⟩ a mitraglia. **quick-freeze** vt surgelare

quickie /'kwɪkɪ/ n fam (question) domanda f rapida; (drink) bicchierino m rapido; (film) cortometraggio m

quicklime /'kwɪklaɪm/ n calce f viva

quickly /'kwɪklɪ/ adv in fretta

quick: quicksand n sabbie fpl mobili. **quick-setting** a ⟨setin⟩ a a presa rapida. **quicksilver** n Chem argento m vivo, mercurio m. **quick-tempered** /-'tempəd/ a collerico. **quick-witted** /-'wɪtɪd/ a ⟨reaction⟩ pronto; ⟨person⟩ sveglio

quid /kwɪd/ n inv fam sterlina f

quid pro quo /kwɪdprəʊ'kwəʊ/ n contraccambio m

quiet /'kwaɪət/ a (calm) tranquillo; (silent) silenzioso; (voice, music) basso; **keep ~ about** fam non raccontare a nessuno ● n quiete f; **on the ~** di nascosto

quieten /'kwaɪətn/ vt calmare

■ **quieten down** vt calmare ● vi calmarsi

quietly /'kwaɪətlɪ/ adv (peacefully) tranquillamente; ⟨say⟩ a bassa voce

quietness /'kwaɪətnɪs/ n quiete f

quiff /kwɪf/ n (Br: hair) ciocca f

quill /kwɪl/ n penna f d'uccello; (spine) spina f

quilt /kwɪlt/ n piumino m

quilted /'kwɪltɪd/ a trapuntato

quilting /'kwɪltɪŋ/ n (fabric) matelassé m inv

quince /kwɪns/ n cotogna f; (tree) melo m cotogno

quinine /'kwɪni:n/ n chinino m

quins /kwɪnz/ npl fam = **quintuplets**

quintessential /kwɪntɪ'senʃl/ a ⟨quality⟩ fondamentale

quintet /kwɪn'tet/ n quintetto m

quintuple /'kwɪntjʊpl/ vt quintuplicare ● a quintuplo

quintuplets /'kwɪntjʊplɪts/ npl cinque gemelli mpl

quip /kwɪp/ n battuta f ● vt (pt/pp **quipped**) dire scherzando

quirk /kwɜ:k/ n stranezza f

quisling /'kwɪzlɪŋ/ n pej collaborazionista mf

quit /kwɪt/ v (pt/pp **quitted** or **quit**) ● vt lasciare; (give up) smettere (**doing** di fare); Comput uscire da ● vi (fam: resign) andarsene; *Comput* uscire; **give sb notice to** ~ dare a qcno preavviso di sfratto

quite /kwaɪt/ *adv* (*fairly*) abbastanza; (*completely*) completamente; (*really*) veramente; ~ [**so**]! proprio così!; ~ **a few** parecchi

quits /kwɪts/ *a* pari

quiver /'kwɪvə(r)/ *vi* tremare

quiz /kwɪz/ *n* (*game*) quiz *m inv* ● *vt* (*pt/pp* **quizzed**) interrogare

quiz game, quiz show *n* quiz *m inv*

quizzical /'kwɪzɪkl/ *a* sardonico

quoit /kwɔɪt/ *n* anello *m* (*del gioco*)

quoits *n* (*game*) gioco *m* degli anelli

quorum /'kwɔːrəm/ *n* quorum *m inv*; **have a** ~ avere il quorum

quota /'kwəʊtə/ *n* quota *f*

quotation /kwəʊ'teɪʃn/ *n* citazione *f*; (*price*) preventivo *m*; (*of shares*) quota *f*

quotation marks *npl* virgolette *fpl*

quote /kwəʊt/ *n fam* = **quotation;** **in** ~**s** tra virgolette ● *vt* citare; quotare ⟨*price*⟩; ~**d on the Stock Exchange** quotato in Borsa

---

Rr

---

r, R /ɑː(r)/ *n a* (*letter*) r, R *f inv*; **the three Rs** leggere, scrivere e contare

R *n Br abbr* (**regina**) regina *f*

rabbi /'ræbaɪ/ *n* rabbino *m*; (*title*) rabbi

rabbit /'ræbɪt/ *n* coniglio *m*

■ **rabbit on** *vi fam* **what's he** ~**ting on about now?** cosa sta blaterando?

rabbit hutch *n* conigliera *f*

rabble /'ræbl/ *n* **the** ~ la plebaglia

rabble rouser /raʊzə(r)/ *n* agitatore, -trice *nmf*

rabble rousing *n* incitazione *f* alla violenza

rabid /'ræbɪd/ *a fig* rabbioso

rabies /'reɪbiːz/ *n* rabbia *f*

raccoon /rə'kuːn/ *n* procione *m*, orsetto *m* lavatore

race¹ /reɪs/ *n* (*people*) razza *f*

race² *n* corsa *f* ● *vi* correre ● *vt* gareggiare con; fare correre ⟨*horse*⟩

racecourse /'reɪskɔːs/ *n* ippodromo *m*

racehorse /'reɪshɔːs/ *n* cavallo *m* da corsa

racer /'reɪsə(r)/ *n* (*bike*) bicicletta *f* da corsa; (*motorbike*) motocicletta *f* da corsa; (*car*) automobile *f* da corsa; (*runner, cyclist etc*) corridore, -trice *mf*

race relations *npl* rapporti *mpl* tra le razze

race riots *npl* scontri *mpl* razziali

racetrack /'reɪstræk/ *n* pista *f*

racial /'reɪʃl/ *a* razziale

racialism /'reɪʃəlɪzm/ *n* razzismo *m*

racially /'reɪʃ(ə)lɪ/ *adv* razzialmente

racing /'reɪsɪŋ/ *n* corse *fpl*; (*horse-*~) corse *fpl* dei cavalli

racing car *n* macchina *f* da corsa

racing driver *n* corridore *m* automobilistico

racism /'reɪsɪzm/ *n* razzismo *m*

racist /'reɪsɪst/ *a & n* razzista *mf*

rack¹ /ræk/ *n* (*for bikes*) rastrelliera *f*; (*for luggage*) portabagagli *m inv*; (*for plates*) scolapiatti *m inv* ● *vt* ~ **one's brains** scervellarsi

rack² *n* **go to** ~ **and ruin** andare in rovina

racket¹ /'rækɪt/ *n Sport* racchetta *f*

racket² *n* (*din*) chiasso *m*; (*swindle*) truffa *f*; (*crime*) racket *m inv*, giro *m*

racketeer /rækɪ'tɪə(r)/ *n* trafficante *m*

racketeering /rækɪ'tɪərɪŋ/ *n* traffici *mpl* illeciti

racking /'rækɪŋ/ *a* ⟨*pain*⟩ atroce

raconteur /'rækɪt/ *n* bravo narratore *m*, brava narratrice *f*

racy /'reɪsɪ/ *a* (**-ier, -iest**) vivace; (*risqué*) osé *inv*, spinto

radar /'reɪdɑː(r)/ *n* radar *m*

radar trap *n Auto* tratto *m* di strada sul quale la polizia controlla la velocità dei veicoli

radial /'reɪdɪəl/ *n* (*tyre*) [pneumatico *m*] radiale *m* ● *a* ⟨*lines, roads*⟩ radiale

radiance /'reɪdɪəns/ *n* radiosità *f*

radiant /'reɪdɪənt/ *a* raggiante

radiate /'reɪdɪeɪt/ *vt* irradiare ● *vi* ⟨*heat:*⟩ irradiarsi; ⟨*roads:*⟩ partire

radiation /reɪdɪ'eɪʃn/ *n* radiazione *f*

radiator /'reɪdɪeɪtə(r)/ *n* radiatore *m*

radical /'rædɪkl/ *a & n* radicale *mf*

radicalism /'rædɪkəlɪzm/ *n* radicalismo *m*

radically /'rædɪklɪ/ *adv* radicalmente

radio /'reɪdɪəʊ/ *n* radio *f inv* ● *vt* mandare via radio ⟨*message*⟩

radioactive /reɪdɪəʊ'æktɪv/ *a* radioattivo

radioactive waste *n* scorie *fpl* radioattive

radioactivity /reɪdɪəʊæk'tɪvətɪ/ *n* radioattività *f*

radio cassette player *n* radioregistratore *m*

radio-controlled *a* radiocomandato

radiographer /reɪdɪ'ɒɡrəfə(r)/ *n* radiologo, -a *mf*

radiography /reɪdɪ'ɒɡrəfɪ/ *n* radiografia *f*

radio ham *n* radioamatore, -trice *mf*

radiologist /ˌreɪdɪˈɒlədʒɪst/ n radiologo, -a mf

radiotherapy /ˌreɪdɪəʊˈθerəpɪ/ n radioterapia f

radish /ˈrædɪʃ/ n ravanello m

radius /ˈreɪdɪəs/ n (pl -dii /ˈreɪdɪaɪ/) raggio m

raffle /ˈræfl/ n lotteria f ● vt mettere in palio

raft /rɑːft/ n zattera f

rafter /ˈrɑːftə(r)/ n trave f

rag[1] /ræg/ n straccio m; (pej: newspaper) giornalaccio m; **in ~s** stracciato

rag[2] vt (pt/pp ragged) fam fare scherzi a ● n Univ festa f di beneficenza organizzata da studenti universitari

ragamuffin /ˈrægəmʌfɪn/ n monellaccio m

rag-and-bone man n Br rigattiere m, straccivendolo m

ragbag /ˈrægbæg/ n fig accozzaglia f

rage /reɪdʒ/ n rabbia f; **all the ~** fam all'ultima moda ● vi infuriarsi; ⟨storm:⟩ infuriare; ⟨epidemic:⟩ imperversare

ragged /ˈrægɪd/ a logoro; ⟨edge⟩ frastagliato

raging /ˈreɪdʒɪŋ/ a ⟨blizzard, sea⟩ furioso; ⟨thirst, pain⟩ atroce; ⟨passion, argument⟩ acceso

raglan /ˈræglən/ a raglan inv ● n manica f raglan

rag trade n fam settore m dell'abbigliamento

rag week n Br Univ settimana f di manifestazioni a scopo benefico organizzate dagli studenti

raid /reɪd/ n (by thieves) rapina f; Mil incursione f, raid m inv; (by police) irruzione f ● vt Mil fare un'incursione in; ⟨police, thieves:⟩ fare irruzione in

raider /ˈreɪdə(r)/ n (of bank) rapinatore, -trice mf

rail[1] /reɪl/ n ringhiera f; Rail rotaia f; Naut parapetto m; **by ~** per ferrovia

rail[2] vi **~ against** or **at** inveire contro

railcard /ˈreɪlkɑːd/ n tessera f di riduzione ferroviaria

railings /ˈreɪlɪŋz/ npl ringhiera f

railroad /ˈreɪlrəʊd/ n Am = **railway** ● vt **~ sb into doing sth** spingere qcno a fare qcsa

railroad schedule n Am orario m ferroviario

rail traffic n traffico m ferroviario

railway /ˈreɪlweɪ/ n ferrovia f

railwayman /ˈreɪlweɪmən/ n ferroviere m

railway station n stazione f ferroviaria

rain /reɪn/ n pioggia f ● vi piovere; **~ down on sb** fig piovere addosso a qcno ● vt **~ blows on sb** tempestare qcno di colpi

■ **rain off** vt be **~ed off** essere annullato a causa della pioggia

rain: rainbow n arcobaleno m. **raincheck** n Am **can I take a ~?** facciamo un'altra volta. **raincoat** n impermeabile m. **raindrop** n goccia f di pioggia. **rainfall** n precipitazione f [atmosferica]. **rainforest** n foresta f pluviale, foresta f equatoriale. **rainstorm** n temporale m. **rain water** n acqua f piovana

rainy /ˈreɪnɪ/ a (-ier, -iest) piovoso

rainy day n **save sth for a ~** ~ fig mettere qcsa in serbo per i tempi di magra

raise /reɪz/ n Am aumento m ● vt alzare; levarsi ⟨hat⟩; allevare ⟨children, animals⟩; sollevare ⟨question⟩; ottenere ⟨money⟩; **~ hell** indiavolarsi; **~ a laugh** ⟨joke, remark:⟩ far ridere; **~ the stakes** rilanciare; **~ one's voice** alzare la voce

raisin /ˈreɪzn/ n uvetta f; **~s** pl uvetta f, uva f passa

Raj /rɑːʒ/ n governo m britannico in India

rake /reɪk/ n rastrello m ● vt rastrellare

■ **rake in** vt fam farsi ⟨profits, money⟩; **he's raking it in** sta facendo un sacco di soldi

■ **rake together** vt fig racimolare ⟨money⟩

■ **rake up** vt raccogliere col rastrello; fam rivangare

rake-off n fam parte f

rakish /ˈreɪkɪʃ/ a (dissolute) dissoluto; (jaunty) disinvolto

rally /ˈrælɪ/ n raduno m; Auto rally m inv; (Tennis) scambio m; (recovery) ripresa f ● v (pt/pp -ied) ● vt radunare ● vi radunarsi; (recover strength) riprendersi

RAM /ræm/ n memoria f RAM

ram /ræm/ n montone m; Astr Ariete m ● vt (pt/pp rammed) cozzare contro

ramble /ˈræmbl/ n escursione f ● vi gironzolare; (in speech) divagare

■ **ramble on** vi fam parlare/scrivere a ruota libera

rambler /ˈræmblə(r)/ n escursionista mf; (rose) rosa f rampicante

rambling /ˈræmblɪŋ/ a (in speech) sconnesso; ⟨club⟩ escursionistico

ramification /ˌræmɪfɪˈkeɪʃən/ n ramificazione f

ramify /ˈræmɪfaɪ/ vi (pt/pp -ied) ramificarsi

ramp /ræmp/ n rampa f; Auto dosso m

rampage /ˈræmpeɪdʒ/ n **be/go on the ~** scatenarsi ● vi **~ through the streets** scatenarsi per le strade

rampant /ˈræmpənt/ a dilagante; (in heraldry) rampante

rampart /ˈræmpɑːt/ n bastione f

ramshackle /ˈræmʃækl/ a sgangherato

ran /ræn/ see **run**

ranch /rɑːntʃ/ n ranch m inv

rancher /ˈrɑːntʃə(r)/ n (worker) cow-boy m inv; (owner) proprietario m di ranch

rancid /ˈrænsɪd/ a rancido

rancour /ˈræŋkə(r)/ n rancore m

R&B n rhythm and blues m

R&D n ricerca f e sviluppo m

random /ˈrændəm/ a casuale; **~ sample** campione m a caso ● n **at ~** a casaccio

random-access a ad accesso casuale

random-access memory n memoria f viva

randy /ˈrændɪ/ a (-ier, -iest) fam eccitato

rang /ræŋ/ see **ring**[2]

range /reɪndʒ/ n serie f; Comm, Mus gamma f; (of mountains) catena f; (distance) raggio m;

(for shooting) portata *f*; *(stove)* cucina *f* economica; **at a ~ of** a una distanza di ● *vi* estendersi; **~ from... to...** andare da... a...

ranger /'reɪndʒə(r)/ *n* guardia *f* forestale

rank¹ /ræŋk/ *n (row)* riga *f*; *Mil* grado *m*; *(social position)* rango *m*; **the ~ and file** la base; **the ~s** *pl Mil* i soldati *mpl* semplici ● *vt (place)* annoverare **(among** tra) ● *vi (be placed)* collocarsi

rank² *a (smell)* puzzolente; ⟨*plants*⟩ rigoglioso; *fig* vero e proprio

rankle /'ræŋkl/ *vi fig* bruciare; **it still ~s with him** gli brucia ancora

ransack /'rænsæk/ *vt* rovistare; *(pillage)* saccheggiare

ransom /'rænsəm/ *n* riscatto *m*; **hold sb to ~** tenere qcno in ostaggio per il riscatto

rant /rænt/ *vi* **~ [and rave]** inveire; **what's he ~ing on about?** cosa sta blaterando?

rap /ræp/ *n* colpo *m* secco; *Mus* rap *m* ● *v (pt/ pp* **rapped)** ● *vt* dare colpetti a; **~ sb over the knuckles** *fig* dare una tirata d'orecchie a qcno ● *vi* **~ at** bussare a

rape¹ /reɪp/ *n Bot* colza *f*

rape² *n (sexual)* stupro *m* ● *vt* violentare, stuprare

rape[seed] oil /'reɪp[si:d]/ *n* olio *m* [di semi] di colza

rapid /'ræpɪd/ *a* rapido

rapidity /rə'pɪdətɪ/ *n* rapidità *f*

rapidly /'ræpɪdlɪ/ *adv* rapidamente

rapids /'ræpɪdz/ *npl* rapida *fsg*

rapist /'reɪpɪst/ *n* violentatore *m*

rapper /'ræpə(r)/ *n (Br: door-knocker)* battiporta *m inv*; *Mus* rapper *mf inv*

rapport /ræ'pɔ:(r)/ *n* rapporto *m* di intesa

rapt /ræpt/ *a ⟨look⟩* rapito; **~ in** assorto in

rapturous /'ræptʃərəs/ *a* entusiastico

rapturously /'ræptʃərəslɪ/ *adv* entusiasticamente

rapture /'ræptʃə(r)/ *n* estasi *f*

rare¹ /reə(r)/ *a* raro

rare² *a Culin* al sangue

rarefied /'reərɪfaɪd/ *a* rarefatto

rarely /'reəlɪ/ *adv* raramente

raring /'reərɪŋ/ *a fam* **be ~ to** non vedere l'ora di

rarity /'reərətɪ/ *n* rarità *f inv*

rascal /'rɑ:skl/ *n* mascalzone *m*

rash¹ /ræʃ/ *n Med* eruzione *f*

rash² *a* avventato

rasher /'ræʃə(r)/ *n* fetta *f* di pancetta

rashly /'ræʃlɪ/ *adv* avventatamente

rashness /'ræʃnɪs/ *n* avventatezza *f*

rasp /rɑ:sp/ *n (noise)* stridio *m*

raspberry /'rɑ:zbərɪ/ *n* lampone *m*

rasping /'rɑ:spɪŋ/ *a* stridente

rat /ræt/ *n* topo *m*; *(fam: person)* carogna *f*; **smell a ~** *fam* sentire puzzo di bruciato ● *vi (pt/pp* **ratted)** *fam* **~ on** far la spia a

rat-a-tat-tat /rætətæ(t)'tæt/ *n* toc toc *m inv*

rat-catcher *n* addetto, -a *mf* alla derattizzazione

ratchet /'rætʃɪt/ *n (toothed rack)* cremagliera *f*

rate /reɪt/ *n (speed)* velocità *f inv*; *(of payment)* tariffa *f*; *(of exchange)* tasso *m*; **~s** *pl (taxes)* imposte *fpl* comunali sui beni immobili; **at any ~** in ogni caso; **at this ~** di questo passo ● *vt* stimare; **~ among** annoverare tra ● *vi* **~ as** essere considerato

ratepayer /'reɪtpeɪə(r)/ *n* contribuente *mf*

rather /'rɑ:ðə(r)/ *adv* piuttosto; **~!** eccome!; **~ too...** un po' troppo...

ratification /rætɪfɪ'keɪʃn/ *n* ratifica *f*

ratify /'rætɪfaɪ/ *vt (pt/pp* **-ied)** ratificare

rating /'reɪtɪŋ/ *n* valutazione *f*; *(class)* livello *m*; *(sailor)* marinaio *m* semplice; **~s** *pl Radio, TV* indice *m* d'ascolto, audience *f inv*

ratio /'reɪʃɪəʊ/ *n* rapporto *m*; **in a ~ of two to one** in [un] rapporto di due a uno

ration /'ræʃn/ *n* razione *f* ● *vt* razionare

rational /'ræʃənl/ *a* razionale

rationale /ræʃə'nɑ:l/ *n (logic)* base *f* logica; *(reasons)* ragioni *fpl*

rationalize /'ræʃ(ə)nəlaɪz/ *vt/i* razionalizzare

rationally /'ræʃ(ə)nəlɪ/ *adv* razionalmente

rationing /'ræʃ(ə)nɪŋ/ *n* razionamento *m*

rat race *n fam* corsa *f* al successo

rattan /rə'tæn/ *n (tree, material)* malacca *f*

rattle /'rætl/ *n* tintinnio *m*; *(toy)* sonaglio *m* ● *vi* tintinnare ● *vt (shake)* scuotere; *fam* innervosire

■ **rattle off** *vt fam* sciorinare

■ **rattle on** *vi (talk at length)* parlare ininterrottamente

■ **rattle through** *vt (say quickly)* dire velocemente; *(do quickly)* fare velocemente

rattlesnake /'rætlsneɪk/ *n* serpente *m* a sonagli

ratty /'rætɪ/ *a (Br fam: grumpy)* irascibile; *⟨Am: hair⟩* sudicio

raucous /'rɔ:kəs/ *a* rauco

raunchy /'rɔ:ntʃɪ/ *a fam ⟨performer, voice, song⟩* sexy *inv*; *(bawdy)* spinto

ravage /'rævɪdʒ/ *vt* devastare

ravages /'rævɪdʒɪz/ *npl* danni *mpl*

rave /reɪv/ *vi* vaneggiare; **~ about** andare in estasi per

raven /'reɪvn/ *n* corvo *m* imperiale

ravenous /'rævənəs/ *a ⟨person⟩* affamato

rave-up *n Br fam* festa *f* animata

ravine /rə'vi:n/ *n* gola *f*

raving /'reɪvɪŋ/ *a* **~ mad** *fam* matto da legare

ravings /'reɪvɪŋz/ *npl* vaneggiamenti *mpl*

ravioli /rævɪ'əʊlɪ/ *n* ravioli *mpl*

ravishing /'rævɪʃɪŋ/ *a* incantevole

raw /rɔ:/ *a* crudo; *(not processed)* grezzo; *⟨weather⟩* gelido; *(inexperienced)* inesperto

raw deal *n* **get a ~** *fam* farsi fregare

rawhide *n (leather)* cuoio *m* grezzo

Rawlplug® /'rɔ:lplʌg/ *n* tassello *m*

raw materials *npl* materie *fpl* prime

ray /reɪ/ *n* raggio *m*; **~ of hope** barlume *m* di speranza

rayon® /'reɪɒn/ *n* raion® *m*

raze /reɪz/ *vt* **~ to the ground** radere al suolo

razor /'reɪzə(r)/ *n* rasoio *m*

razor blade *n* lametta *f* da barba

razor-sharp *a* affilatissimo

razzle /'ræzl/ *n Br fam* **go on the ~** andare a fare baldoria

razzle-dazzle *n fam* baldoria *f*

razzmatazz /ræzmə'tæz/ *n fam* clamore *m*

RC *n* (**Roman Catholic**) cattolico, -a *mf* ● *a* cattolico

re /ri:/ *prep* con riferimento a

reach /ri:tʃ/ *n* portata *f*; (*of river*) tratto *m*; **within ~** a portata di mano; **out of ~ of** fuori dalla portata di; **within easy ~** facilmente raggiungibile ● *vt* arrivare a ⟨*place, decision*⟩; (*contact*) contattare; (*pass*) passare; **I can't ~ it** non ci arrivo ● *vi* arrivare (**to** a); **I can't ~** non ci arrivo; **~ for** allungare la mano per prendere

react /ri'ækt/ *vi* reagire

reaction /ri'ækʃn/ *n* reazione *f*

reactionary /ri'ækʃ(ə)nəri/ *a & n* reazionario, -a *mf*

reactor /ri'æktə(r)/ *n* reattore *m*

read /ri:d/ *vt* (*pt/pp* **read** /red/) leggere; *Univ* studiare ● *vi* leggere; ⟨*instrument:*⟩ indicare

■ **read back** *vt* (*say aloud*) rileggere

■ **read on** *vi* (*continue reading*) continuare a leggere

■ **read out** *vt* leggere ad alta voce

■ **read up on** *vt* studiare a fondo

readable /'ri:dəbl/ *a* piacevole a leggersi; (*legible*) leggibile

reader /'ri:də(r)/ *n* lettore, -trice *mf*; (*book*) antologia *f*

readership /'ri:dəʃɪp/ *n* numero *m* di lettori

read head *n Comput* testina *f* di lettura

readily /'redɪlɪ/ *adv* volentieri; (*easily*) facilmente

readiness /'redɪnɪs/ *n* disponibilità *f*; **in ~** pronto

reading /'ri:dɪŋ/ *n* lettura *f*

readjust /ri:ə'dʒʌst/ *vt* regolare di nuovo ● *vi* riabituarsi (**to** a)

readjustment /ri:ə'dʒʌstmənt/ *n* riadattamento *m*

read-only memory *n Comput* memoria *f* di sola lettura

ready /'redɪ/ *a* (**-ier, -iest**) pronto; (*quick*) veloce; **get ~** prepararsi

ready: ready-made *a* confezionato. **ready-mixed** *a* già miscelato. **ready money** *n* contanti *mpl*. **ready-to-wear** *a* prêt-à-porter

reaffirm /ri:ə'fɜ:m/ *vt* riaffermare

reafforestation /ri:əfɒrɪ'steɪʃn/ *n* rimboschimento *m*

real /ri:l/ *a* vero; ⟨*increase*⟩ reale ● *adv Am fam* veramente

real estate *n* beni *mpl* immobili

realign /ri:ə'laɪn/ *vt* riallineare ● *vi fig* formare nuove alleanze

realignment /ri:ə'laɪnmənt/ *n Pol* formazione *f* di nuove alleanze; *Fin* riallineamento *m*

realism /'rɪəlɪzm/ *n* realismo *m*

realist /'rɪəlɪst/ *n* realista *mf*

realistic /rɪə'lɪstɪk/ *a* realistico

realistically /rɪə'lɪstɪklɪ/ *adv* realisticamente

reality /rɪ'ælətɪ/ *n* realtà *f inv*

realization /rɪəlaɪ'zeɪʃn/ *n* realizzazione *f*

realize /'rɪəlaɪz/ *vt* realizzare

real life *n* realtà *f*; **in ~ life** nella realtà

real-life *attrib* autentico

reallocate /ri:'æləkeɪt/ *vt* riassegnare

reallocation /ri:ælə'keɪʃn/ *n* riassegnazione *f*

really /'rɪəlɪ/ *adv* davvero

realm /relm/ *n* regno *m*

real time *n* tempo *m* reale; **in ~ ~** in tempo reale ● *a* in tempo reale

realtor /'rɪəltə(r)/ *n Am* agente *mf* immobiliare

realty /'rɪəltɪ/ *n Am* beni *mpl* immobili

reanimate /ri:'ænɪmeɪt/ *vt* rianimare

reap /ri:p/ *vt* mietere

reappear /ri:ə'pɪə(r)/ *vi* riapparire

reappearance /ri:ə'pɪərəns/ *n* ricomparsa *f*

reapply /ri:ə'plaɪ/ *vi* (*pt/pp* **-ied**) ripresentare domanda

reappoint /ri:ə'pɔɪnt/ *vt* riconfermare

reappraisal /ri:ə'preɪzl/ *n* riconsiderazione *f*

reappraise /ri:ə'preɪz/ *vt* riesaminare ⟨*question, policy*⟩; rivalutare ⟨*writer, work*⟩

rear[1] /rɪə(r)/ *a* posteriore; *Auto* di dietro

rear[2] *vt* allevare ● *vi* **~ [up]** ⟨*horse:*⟩ impennarsi ● *n* the **~** (*of building*) il retro; (*of bus, plane*) la parte posteriore; **from the ~** da dietro

rear end *n fam* didietro *m*

rearguard /'rɪəgɑ:d/ *n Mil, fig* retroguardia *f*

rear light *n* luce *f* posteriore

rearm /ri:'ɑ:m/ *vt* riarmare ● *vi* riarmarsi

rearmament /ri:'ɑ:məmənt/ *n* riarmo *m*

rearmost /'rɪəməʊst/ *a* ultimo; ⟨*carriage*⟩ di coda

rearrange /ri:ə'reɪndʒ/ *vt* cambiare la disposizione di

rear-view mirror *n Auto* specchietto *m* retrovisore

reason /'ri:zn/ *n* ragione *f*; **within ~** nei limiti del ragionevole; **listen to ~** ascoltare la ragione ● *vi* ragionare; **~ with** cercare di far ragionare

reasonable /'ri:znəbl/ *a* ragionevole

reasonably /'ri:znəblɪ/ *adv* (*in reasonable way, fairly*) ragionevolmente

reasoning /'ri:znɪŋ/ *n* ragionamento *m*

reassemble /ri:ə'semb(ə)l/ *vt* riassemblare

reassembly /ri:ə'semblɪ/ *n* riassemblaggio *m*

reassess /ri:ə'ses/ *vt* riesaminare ⟨*problem, situation*⟩; riaccertare ⟨*tax liability*⟩

reassessment /ri:ə'sesmənt/ *n* (*of situation*) riesame *m*; (*of tax*) nuovo accertamento *m*

reassurance /ri:ə'ʃʊərəns/ *n* rassicurazione *f*

reassure /riːəˈʃʊə(r)/ vt rassicurare; **~ sb of sth** rassicurare qcno su qcsa

reassuring /riːəˈʃʊərɪŋ/ a rassicurante

reawaken /riːəˈweɪkn/ vt fig risvegliare ⟨interest⟩

rebate /ˈriːbeɪt/ n rimborso m; (discount) deduzione f

rebel¹ /ˈrebl/ n ribelle mf

rebel² /rɪˈbel/ vi (pt/pp **rebelled**) ribellarsi

rebellion /rɪˈbeljən/ n ribellione f

rebellious /rɪˈbeljəs/ a ribelle

rebelliousness /rɪˈbeliːəsnɪs/ n spirito m di ribellione

rebirth /riːˈbɜːθ/ n rinascita f

reboot /riːˈbuːt/ vt Comput reinizializzare

reborn /riːˈbɔːn/ a Relig **be ~** rinascere; **be ~ as sth** rinascere come qcsa

rebound¹ /rɪˈbaʊnd/ vi rimbalzare; fig ricadere

rebound² /ˈriːbaʊnd/ n rimbalzo m

rebuff /rɪˈbʌf/ n rifiuto m • vt respingere

rebuild /riːˈbɪld/ vt (pt/pp **-built**) ricostruire

rebuke /rɪˈbjuːk/ n rimprovero m • vt rimproverare

rebut /rɪˈbʌt/ vt confutare

rebuttal /rɪˈbʌtl/ n rifiuto m

recalcitrant /rɪˈkælsɪtrənt/ a fml ricalcitrante

recalculate /riːˈkælkjʊleɪt/ vt ricalcolare

recall /rɪˈkɔːl/ n richiamo m; **beyond ~** irrevocabile • vt richiamare; riconvocare ⟨diplomat, parliament⟩; (remember) rievocare

recant /rɪˈkænt/ vi abiurare

recap /ˈriːkæp/ vt/i fam = **recapitulate** • n ricapitolazione f

recapitulate /riːkəˈpɪtjʊleɪt/ vt/i ricapitolare

recapture /riːˈkæptʃə(r)/ vt riconquistare; ricatturare ⟨person, animal⟩

recast /riːˈkɑːst/ vt rimaneggiare ⟨text, plan⟩; riformulare ⟨sentence⟩

recede /rɪˈsiːd/ vi allontanarsi

receding /rɪˈsiːdɪŋ/ a ⟨forehead, chin⟩ sfuggente; **have ~ hair** essere stempiato

receipt /rɪˈsiːt/ n ricevuta f; (receiving) ricezione f; **~s** pl Comm entrate fpl

receive /rɪˈsiːv/ vt ricevere

receiver /rɪˈsiːvə(r)/ n Teleph ricevitore m; Radio, TV apparecchio m ricevente; (of stolen goods) ricettatore, -trice mf

receivership /rɪˈsiːvəʃɪp/ n Br **go into ~** essere sottomesso all'amministrazione controllata

receiving end /rɪˈsiːvɪŋ/ n **be on the ~** essere dall'altro lato della barricata

recent /ˈriːsnt/ a recente

recently /ˈriːsntlɪ/ adv recentemente

receptacle /rɪˈseptəkl/ n recipiente m

reception /rɪˈsepʃn/ n ricevimento m; (welcome) accoglienza f; Radio ricezione f; **~ [desk]** (in hotel) reception f inv

receptionist /rɪˈsepʃənɪst/ n persona f alla reception

receptive /rɪˈseptɪv/ a ricettivo

recess /rɪˈses/ n rientranza f; (holiday) vacanza f; Am Sch intervallo m

recession /rɪˈseʃn/ n recessione f

recharge /riːˈtʃɑːdʒ/ vt ricaricare

recidivism /rɪˈsɪdɪvɪzm/ n recidività f

recidivist /rɪˈsɪdɪvɪst/ n recidivo, -a mf

recipe /ˈresəpɪ/ n ricetta f

recipe book n libro m di ricette

recipient /rɪˈsɪpɪənt/ n (of letter, parcel) destinatario, -a mf; (of money) beneficiario, -a mf

reciprocal /rɪˈsɪprəkl/ a reciproco

reciprocate /rɪˈsɪprəkeɪt/ vt ricambiare

recital /rɪˈsaɪtl/ n recital m inv

recitation /resɪˈteɪʃn/ n recitazione f

recite /rɪˈsaɪt/ vt recitare; (list) elencare

reckless /ˈreklɪs/ a ⟨action, decision⟩ sconsiderato; **be a ~ driver** guidare in modo spericolato

recklessly /ˈreklɪslɪ/ adv in modo sconsiderato

recklessness /ˈreklɪsnɪs/ n sconsideratezza f

reckon /ˈrekən/ vt calcolare; (consider) pensare; **be ~ed** essere considerato

■ **reckon on, reckon with** vt fare i conti con

■ **reckon without** vt fare i conti senza

reclaim /rɪˈkleɪm/ vt reclamare; bonificare ⟨land⟩

recline /rɪˈklaɪn/ vi sdraiarsi

reclining /rɪˈklaɪnɪŋ/ a ⟨seat⟩ reclinabile

recluse /rɪˈkluːs/ n recluso, -a mf

reclusive /rɪˈkluːsɪv/ a solitario

recognition /rekəgˈnɪʃn/ n riconoscimento m; **in ~** come riconoscimento (**of** per); **beyond ~** irriconoscibile

recognize /ˈrekəgnaɪz/ vt riconoscere

recoil¹ /ˈriːkɔɪl/ n (of gun) rinculo m

recoil² /rɪˈkɔɪl/ vi (in fear) indietreggiare

recollect /rekəˈlekt/ vt ricordare

recollection /rekəˈlekʃn/ n ricordo m

recommence /riːkəˈmens/ vt/i ricominciare

recommend /rekəˈmend/ vt raccomandare

recommendation /rekəmenˈdeɪʃn/ n raccomandazione f

recommended retail price /rekəˈmendɪd/ n Comm prezzo m di vendita raccomandato

recompense /ˈrekəmpens/ n ricompensa f • vt ricompensare

reconcile /ˈrekənsaɪl/ vt riconciliare; conciliare ⟨facts⟩; far quadrare ⟨bank statement⟩; **~ oneself to** rassegnarsi a

reconciliation /rekənsɪlɪˈeɪʃn/ n riconciliazione f

recondition /riːkənˈdɪʃn/ vt ripristinare; **~ed engine** motore m che ha subito riparazioni

reconnaissance /rɪˈkɒnɪsns/ n Mil ricognizione f; **on ~** in ricognizione

reconnoitre /rekəˈnɔɪtə(r)/ vi (pres p **-tring**) fare una recognizione • vt fare una recognizione di

reconsider /ri:kən'sɪdə(r)/ vt riconsiderare

reconstruct /ri:kən'strʌkt/ vt ricostruire

reconstruction /ri:kən'strʌkʃn/ n ricostruzione f

reconvene /ri:kən'vi:n/ vi riunirsi nuovamente

record[1] /rɪ'kɔ:d/ vt registrare; (make a note of) annotare

record[2] /'rekɔ:d/ n (file) documentazione f; Mus disco m; Sport record m inv; ~s pl (files) schedario msg; **keep a ~ of** tener nota di; **off the ~** in via ufficiosa; **have a [criminal] ~** avere la fedina penale sporca

record-breaker /'rekɔ:dbreɪkə(r)/ n **be a ~** battere un record

recorded delivery /rɪ'kɔ:dɪd/ n raccomandata f

recorder /rɪ'kɔ:də(r)/ n Mus flauto m dolce

recording /rɪ'kɔ:dɪŋ/ n registrazione f

recording studio n sala f di registrazione

record player n giradischi m inv

recount /rɪ'kaʊnt/ vt raccontare

re-count[1] /ri:'kaʊnt/ vt ricontare

re-count[2] /'ri:kaʊnt/ n Pol nuovo conteggio m

recoup /rɪ'ku:p/ vt rifarsi di (losses)

recourse /rɪ'kɔ:s/ n **have ~ to** ricorrere a

recover /rɪ'kʌvə(r)/ vt/i recuperare

re-cover /ri:'kʌvə(r)/ vt rifoderare

recovery /rɪ'kʌvərɪ/ n recupero m; (of health) guarigione f

recreation /rekrɪ'eɪʃn/ n ricreazione f

recreational /rekrɪ'eɪʃənəl/ a ricreativo

recrimination /rɪkrɪmɪ'neɪʃn/ n recriminazione f

recruit /rɪ'kru:t/ n Mil recluta f; **new ~** (member) nuovo, -a adepto, -a mf; (worker) neoassunto, -a mf ● vt assumere (staff)

recruitment /rɪ'kru:tmənt/ n assunzione f

rectangle /'rektæŋgl/ n rettangolo m

rectangular /rek'tæŋgjʊlə(r)/ a rettangolare

rectify /'rektɪfaɪ/ vt (pt/pp -ied) rettificare

rector /'rektə(r)/ n Univ rettore m

rectory /'rektərɪ/ n presbiterio m

rectum /'rektəm/ n retto m

recuperate /rɪ'kju:pəreɪt/ vi ristabilirsi

recur /rɪ'kɜ:(r)/ vi (pt/pp recurred) ricorrere; (illness:) ripresentarsi

recurrence /rɪ'kʌrəns/ n ricorrenza f; (of illness) ricomparsa f

recurrent /rɪ'kʌrənt/ a ricorrente

recyclable /ri:'saɪkləbl/ a riciclabile

recycle /ri:'saɪkl/ vt riciclare; **~d paper** carta f riciclata

recycling /ri:'saɪklɪŋ/ n riciclaggio m

red /red/ a (**redder, reddest**) rosso ● n rosso m; **be in the ~** (account:) essere scoperto; (person:) avere il conto scoperto

red: redbrick a Univ di recente fondazione. **Red Cross** n Croce f rossa. **redcurrant** n ribes m rosso

redden /'redn/ vt arrossare ● vi arrossire

reddish /'redɪʃ/ a rossastro

redecorate /ri:'dekəreɪt/ vt (paint) ridipingere; (wallpaper) ritappezzare

redeem /rɪ'di:m/ vt (Relig, from pawnshop) riscattare; **~ing quality** unico aspetto m positivo

redefine /ri:dɪ'faɪn/ vt ridefinire

redemption /rɪ'dempʃn/ n riscatto m

redeploy /ri:dɪ'plɔɪ/ vt ridistribuire

red: red-faced a also fig paonazzo. **redhaired** /-'heəd/ a con i capelli rossi. **redhanded** /-'hændɪd/ a **catch sb ~** cogliere qcno con le mani nel sacco. **red herring** n diversione f. **red-hot** a rovente

redial /ri:'daɪəl/ Teleph vt ricomporre ● vi ricomporre il numero

redirect /ri:dar'rekt/ vt mandare al nuovo indirizzo (letter)

rediscover /ri:dɪ'skʌvə(r)/ vt riscoprire

redistribute /ri:dɪs'trɪbju:t/ vt ridistribuire

redistribution /ri:dɪstrɪ'bju:ʃn/ n ridistribuzione f

red: red-letter day n giorno m memorabile. **red light** n Auto semaforo m rosso; **go through a ~ ~** passare col rosso. **red light district** n quartiere m a luci rosse. **red meat** n carne f rossa

redness /'rednɪs/ n rossore m

redo /ri:'du:/ vt (pt -**did**, pp -**done**) rifare

redolent /'redələnt/ a profumato (**of** di)

redouble /ri:'dʌbl/ vt raddoppiare

redraft /ri:'drɑ:ft/ vt stendere nuovamente

redress /rɪ'dres/ n riparazione f ● vt ristabilire (balance)

red tape n fam burocrazia f

reduce /rɪ'dju:s/ vt ridurre; Culin far consumare

reductio ad absurdum /rɪdʌktɪəʊædæb-'sɜ:dəm/ n ragionamento m per assurdo

reduction /rɪ'dʌkʃn/ n riduzione f

redundancy /rɪ'dʌndənsɪ/ n licenziamento m; (payment) cassa f integrazione

redundant /rɪ'dʌndənt/ a superfluo; **make ~** licenziare; **be made ~** essere licenziato

reed /ri:d/ n Bot canna f

reedy /'ri:dɪ/ a (voice, tone) acuto

reef /ri:f/ n scogliera f

reefer /'ri:fə(r)/ n (jacket) giubbotto m a doppio petto; (fam: dope) spinello m

reef knot n nodo m piano

reek /ri:k/ vi puzzare (**of** di)

reel /ri:l/ n bobina f ● vi (stagger) vacillare

■ **reel off** vt fig snocciolare

re-elect vt rieleggere

re-election n rielezione f

re-emerge vi riemergere

re-emergence n ricomparsa f

re-enact /ri:ɪ'nækt/ vt ricostruire (crime); Jur rimettere in vigore; recitare nuovamente (role)

re-enter /ri:'entə(r)/ vt rientrare in

re-entry n (of spacecraft) rientro m

re-establish vt ristabilire, ripristinare

re-establishment n ripristino m

re-examination n riesame m

re-examine vt riesaminare

refectory /rɪ'fektərɪ/ n refettorio m; Univ mensa f universitaria

refer /rɪ'fɜ:(r)/ v (pt/pp **referred**) ● vt rinviare ‹matter›; indirizzare ‹person› ● vi ~ **to** fare allusione a; (consult) rivolgersi a ‹book›; **are you ~ring to me?** alludi a me?

referee /refə'ri:/ n arbitro m; (for job) garante mf ● vt/i (pt/pp **refereed**) arbitrare

reference /'ref(ə)rəns/ n riferimento m; (in book) nota f bibliografica; (for job) referenza f; Comm **'your ~'** 'riferimento'; **with ~ to** con riferimento a; **make [a] ~ to** fare riferimento a

reference: reference book n libro m di consultazione. **reference library** n biblioteca f per la consultazione. **reference number** n numero m di riferimento

referendum /refə'rendəm/ n referendum m inv

referral /rɪ'fɜ:rəl/ n (of matter, problem) deferimento m; Med (act) invio m di un paziente a un altro medico; (person) paziente mf mandato da un medico a un altro

refill¹ /ri:'fɪl/ vt riempire di nuovo; ricaricare ‹pen, lighter›

refill² /'ri:fɪl/ n (for pen) ricambio m

refine /rɪ'faɪn/ vt raffinare

refined /rɪ'faɪnd/ a raffinato

refinement /rɪ'faɪnmənt/ n raffinatezza f

refinery /rɪ'faɪnərɪ/ n raffineria f

refining /rɪ'faɪnɪŋ/ n Techn raffinazione f

refit¹ /'ri:fɪt/ n Naut raddobbo m; (of shop, factory etc) rinnovo m

refit² /ri:'fɪt/ vt raddobbare ‹ship›; rinnovare ‹shop, factory etc›

reflate /ri:'fleɪt/ vt reflazionare ‹economy›

reflect /rɪ'flekt/ vt riflettere; **be ~ed in** essere riflesso in ● vi (think) riflettere (**on** su); ~ **badly on sb** fig mettere in cattiva luce qcno

reflection /rɪ'flekʃn/ n riflessione f; (image) riflesso m; **on ~** dopo riflessione

reflective /rɪ'flektɪv/ a riflessivo

reflectively /rɪ'flektɪvlɪ/ adv in modo riflessivo

reflector /rɪ'flektə(r)/ n riflettore m

reflex /'ri:fleks/ n riflesso m ● attrib di riflesso

reflexive /rɪ'fleksɪv/ a riflessivo

refloat /ri:'fləʊt/ vt Naut, Comm rimettere a galla

reforestation /ri:fɒrɪ'steɪʃn/ n rimboschimento m

reform /rɪ'fɔ:m/ n riforma f ● vt riformare ● vi correggersi.

reformat /ri:'fɔ:mæt/ vt riformattare

Reformation /refə'meɪʃn/ n Relig Riforma f

reformer /rɪ'fɔ:mə(r)/ n riformatore, -trice mf

refrain¹ /rɪ'freɪn/ n ritornello m

refrain² vi astenersi (**from** da)

refresh /rɪ'freʃ/ vt rinfrescare

refresher course /rɪ'freʃə(r)/ n corso m d'aggiornamento

refreshing /rɪ'freʃɪŋ/ a rinfrescante

refreshments /rɪ'freʃmənts/ npl rinfreschi mpl

refrigerate /rɪ'frɪdʒəreɪt/ vt conservare in frigo; Ind refrigerare

refrigerated lorry /rɪ'frɪdʒəreɪtɪd/ n camion m inv frigorifero

refrigeration /rɪfrɪdʒə'reɪʃn/ n Ind refrigerazione f

refrigerator /rɪ'frɪdʒəreɪtə(r)/ n frigorifero m

refuel /ri:'fjʊəl/ v (pt/pp **-fuelled**) ● vt rifornire di carburante ● vi fare rifornimento

refuge /'refju:dʒ/ n rifugio m; **take ~** rifugiarsi

refugee /refju'dʒi:/ n rifugiato, -a mf

refund¹ /'ri:fʌnd/ n rimborso m

refund² /rɪ'fʌnd/ vt rimborsare

refurbish /ri:'fɜ:bɪʃ/ vt rimettere a nuovo

refurbishment /ri:'fɜ:bɪʃmənt/ n rinnovo m

refusal /rɪ'fju:zl/ n rifiuto m

refuse¹ /rɪ'fju:z/ vt/i rifiutare; ~ **to do sth** rifiutare di fare qcsa

refuse² /'refju:s/ n rifiuti mpl

refuse collection n raccolta f dei rifiuti

refute /rɪ'fju:t/ vt confutare

regain /rɪ'geɪn/ vt riconquistare

regal /'ri:gl/ a regale

regalia /rɪ'geɪlɪə/ npl insegne fpl reali

regard /rɪ'gɑ:d/ n (heed) riguardo m; (respect) considerazione f; ~**s** pl saluti mpl; **send/give my ~s to your brother** salutami tuo fratello; **with ~ to** riguardo a ● vt (consider) considerare (**as** come); **as ~s** riguardo a

regarding /rɪ'gɑ:dɪŋ/ prep riguardo a

regardless /rɪ'gɑ:dlɪs/ adv lo stesso; ~ **of** senza badare a

regatta /rɪ'gætə/ n regata f

regency /'ri:dʒənsɪ/ n reggenza f

regenerate /rɪ'dʒenəreɪt/ vt rigenerare ● vi rigenerarsi

regent /'ri:dʒənt/ n reggente mf

reggae /'regeɪ/ n reggae m

regime /reɪ'ʒi:m/ n regime m

regiment¹ /'redʒɪmənt/ n reggimento m

regiment² /'redʒɪment/ vt irreggimentare

regimental /redʒɪ'mentl/ a reggimentale

regimentation /redʒɪmən'teɪʃn/ n irreggimentazione f

regimented /'redʒɪmentɪd/ a irreggimentato

region /'ri:dʒən/ n regione f; **in the ~ of** fig approssimativamente

regional /'ri:dʒənl/ a regionale

register /'redʒɪstə(r)/ n registro m ● vt registrare; mandare tramite assicurata ‹letter, package›; assicurare ‹luggage›; immatricolare ‹motor vehicle›; mostrare ‹feeling› ● vi ‹instrument:› funzionare; ‹student:› iscriversi (**for** a); **it didn't ~ with me** fig non ci ho fatto attenzione; ~ **with** iscriversi nella lista di ‹doctor›

registered letter /'redʒɪstəd/ n lettera f assicurata

registered trademark n marchio m depositato

registrar /redʒɪ'strɑ:(r)/ n ufficiale m di stato civile

registration /redʒɪ'streɪʃn/ n (of vehicle) immatricolazione f; (of letter, luggage) assicurazione f; (for course) iscrizione f

registration fee n tassa f d'iscrizione

registration number n Auto [numero m di] targa f

registry office /'redʒɪstrɪ/ n anagrafe f

regress /rɪ'gres/ vi Biol, Psych, fig regredire

regression /rɪ'greʃən/ n regressione f

regressive /rɪ'gresɪv/ a Biol, Psych regressivo

regret /rɪ'gret/ n rammarico m ● vt (pt/pp regretted) rimpiangere; **I ~ that** mi rincresce che

regretfully /rɪ'gretfʊlɪ/ adv con rammarico

regrettable /rɪ'gretəbl/ a spiacevole

regrettably /rɪ'gretəblɪ/ adv spiacevolmente; (before adjective) deplorevolmente

regroup /ri:'gru:p/ vi riorganizzarsi

regular /'regjʊlə(r)/ a regolare; (usual) abituale ● n cliente mf abituale

regularity /regjʊ'lærətɪ/ n regolarità f

regularly /'regjʊləlɪ/ adv regolarmente

regulate /'regʊleɪt/ vt regolare

regulation /regjʊ'leɪʃn/ n (rule) regolamento m

regulator /'regjʊleɪtə(r)/ n (person) regolatore, -trice mf; (device) regolatore m

regurgitate /rɪ'gɜ:dʒɪteɪt/ vt rigurgitare; fig pej ripetere meccanicamente

rehabilitate /ri:hə'bɪlɪteɪt/ vt riabilitare

rehabilitation /ri:həbɪlɪ'teɪʃn/ n riabilitazione f

rehash¹ /ri:'hæʃ/ vt rimaneggiare

rehash² /'ri:hæʃ/ n rimaneggiamento m

rehearsal /rɪ'hɜ:sl/ n Theat prova f

rehearse /rɪ'hɜ:s/ vt/i provare

reheat /ri:'hi:t/ vt scaldare di nuovo

rehouse /ri:'haʊz/ vt rialloggiare

reign /reɪn/ n regno m ● vi regnare

reimburse /ri:ɪm'bɜ:s/ vt ~ **sb for sth** rimborsare qcsa a qcno

reimbursement /ri:ɪm'bɜ:smənt/ n rimborso m

rein /reɪn/ n redine f

reincarnate /ri:ɪn'kɑ:neɪt/ vt **be ~d** reincarnarsi

reincarnation /ri:ɪnkɑ:'neɪʃn/ n reincarnazione f

reindeer /'reɪndɪə(r)/ n inv renna f

reinforce /ri:ɪn'fɔ:s/ vt rinforzare

reinforced concrete n cemento m armato

reinforcement /ri:ɪn'fɔ:smənt/ n rinforzo m; ~**s** pl Mil rinforzi mpl

reinstate /ri:ɪn'steɪt/ vt reintegrare

reinstatement /ri:ɪn'steɪtmənt/ n reintegrazione f

reinterpret /ri:ɪn'tɜ:prɪt/ vt reinterpretare

reinterpretation /ri:ɪntɜ:prɪ'teɪʃn/ n reinterpretazione f

reintroduce /ri:ɪntrə'dju:s/ vt reintrodurre

reintroduction /ri:ɪntrə'dʌkʃn/ n reintroduzione f

reiterate /ri:'ɪtəreɪt/ vt reiterare

reiteration /ri:ɪtə'reɪʃn/ n reiterazione f

reject /rɪ'dʒekt/ vt rifiutare

rejection /rɪ'dʒekʃn/ n rifiuto m; Med rigetto m

rejects /'ri:dʒekts/ npl Comm scarti mpl

rejig /ri:'dʒɪg/ vt (pt/pp rejigged) Br riorganizzare

rejoice /rɪ'dʒɔɪs/ vi liter rallegrarsi

rejoicing /rɪ'dʒɔɪsɪŋ/ n gioia f

rejoin /rɪ'dʒɔɪn/ vt riassociarsi a (club, party); Mil reintegrarsi in (regiment); (answer) replicare

rejuvenate /rɪ'dʒu:vəneɪt/ vt rinnovare; ringiovanire (person)

rejuvenation /rɪdʒu:və'neɪʃn/ n rinnovamento m; (of person) ringiovanimento m

rekindle /ri:'kɪndl/ vt riattizzare

relapse /rɪ'læps/ n ricaduta f ● vi ricadere

relate /rɪ'leɪt/ vt (tell) riportare; (connect) collegare

■ **relate to** vt riferirsi a; identificarsi con (person)

related /rɪ'leɪtɪd/ a imparentato (**to** a); (ideas etc) affine

relation /rɪ'leɪʃn/ n rapporto m; (person) parente mf

relationship /rɪ'leɪʃnʃɪp/ n rapporto m; (blood tie) parentela f; (affair) relazione f

relative /'relətɪv/ n parente mf ● a relativo

relatively /'relətɪvlɪ/ adv relativamente

relativity /relə'tɪvətɪ/ n relatività f

relativity theory n Phys teoria f della relatività

relaunch¹ /'ri:lɔ:ntʃ/ n rilancio m

relaunch² /ri:'lɔ:ntʃ/ vt rilanciare

relax /rɪ'læks/ vt rilassare; allentare (pace, grip) ● vi rilassarsi

relaxation /ri:læk'seɪʃn/ n rilassamento m, relax m; (recreation) svago m

relaxed /rɪ'lækst/ a rilassato

relaxing /rɪ'læksɪŋ/ a rilassante

relay¹ /ri:'leɪ/ vt (pt/pp -layed) trasmettere

relay² /'ri:leɪ/ n Electr relais m inv; **work in ~s** fare i turni

relay [race] /'ri:leɪ/ n (corsa f a] staffetta f

release /rɪ'li:s/ n rilascio m; (of film) distribuzione f ● vt liberare; lasciare (hand); togliere (brake); distribuire (film); rilasciare (information etc)

relegate /'relɪgeɪt/ vt relegare; **be ~d** Br Sport essere retrocesso

relegation /relɪ'geɪʃn/ n relegazione f; Br Sport retrocessione f

relent /rɪ'lent/ vi cedere

relentless /rɪ'lentlɪs/ a inflessibile; (unceasing) incessante

relentlessly /rɪ'lentlɪslɪ/ adv incessantemente

relevance /'reləvəns/ n pertinenza f

relevant /'reləvənt/ a pertinente (**to** a)

reliability /rɪlaɪə'bɪlətɪ/ n affidabilità f

reliable /rɪ'laɪəbl/ a affidabile

reliably /rɪ'laɪəblɪ/ adv in modo affidabile; **be ~ informed** sapere da fonte certa

reliance /rɪ'laɪəns/ n fiducia f (**on** in)

reliant /rɪ'laɪənt/ *a* fiducioso (**on** in)

relic /'relɪk/ *n Relig* reliquia *f*; **~s** *pl* resti *mpl*

relief /rɪ'li:f/ *n* sollievo *m*; (*assistance*) soccorso *m*; (*distraction*) diversivo *m*; (*replacement*) cambio *m*; (*in art*) rilievo *m*; **in ~** in rilievo

relief map *n* carta *f* in rilievo

relief train *n* treno *m* supplementare

relieve /rɪ'li:v/ *vt* alleviare; (*take over from*) dare il cambio a; **~ of** liberare da ⟨*burden*⟩

religion /rɪ'lɪdʒən/ *n* religione *f*

religious /rɪ'lɪdʒəs/ *a* religioso

religiously /rɪ'lɪdʒəslɪ/ *adv* (*conscientiously*) scrupolosamente

relinquish /rɪ'lɪŋkwɪʃ/ *vt* abbandonare; **~ sth to sb** rinunciare a qcsa in favore di qcno

relish /'relɪʃ/ *n* gusto *m*; *Culin* salsa *f* ● *vt fig* apprezzare

relive /ri:'lɪv/ *vt* rivivere

reload /ri:'ləʊd/ *vt* ricaricare

relocate /ri:lə'keɪt/ *vt* trasferire ● *vi* trasferirsi

relocation /ri:lə'keɪʃn/ *n* (*of employee, company*) trasferimento *m*

relocation allowance *n* indennità *f inv* di trasferimento

reluctance /rɪ'lʌktəns/ *n* riluttanza *f*

reluctant /rɪ'lʌktənt/ *a* riluttante

reluctantly /rɪ'lʌktəntlɪ/ *adv* con riluttanza, a malincuore

rely /rɪ'laɪ/ *vi* (*pt/pp* **-ied**) **~ on** dipendere da; (*trust*) contare su

remain /rɪ'meɪn/ *vi* restare

remainder /rɪ'meɪndə(r)/ *n* resto *m*; *Comm* rimanenza *f* ● *vt Comm* svendere

remaining /rɪ'meɪnɪŋ/ *a* restante

remains /rɪ'meɪnz/ *npl* resti *mpl*; (*dead body*) spoglie *fpl*

remake /'ri:meɪk/ *n* (*of film, recording*) remake *m inv*

remand /rɪ'mɑ:nd/ *n* **on ~** in custodia cautelare ● *vt* **~ in custody** rinviare con detenzione provvisoria

remark /rɪ'mɑ:k/ *n* osservazione *f* ● *vt* osservare

remarkable /rɪ'mɑ:kəbl/ *a* notevole

remarkably /rɪ'mɑ:kəblɪ/ *adv* notevolmente

remarry /ri:'mærɪ/ *vi* (*pt/pp* **-ied**) risposarsi

remaster /ri:'mɑ:stə(r)/ *vt* incidere di nuovo ⟨*recording*⟩

rematch /'ri:mætʃ/ *n Sport* partita *f* di ritorno; (*in boxing*) secondo incontro *m*

remedial /rɪ'mi:dɪəl/ *a* correttivo; *Med* curativo

remedy /'remədɪ/ *n* rimedio *m* (**for** contro)● *vt* (*pt/pp* **-ied**) rimediare a

remember /rɪ'membə(r)/ *vt* ricordare, ricordarsi; **~ to do sth** ricordarsi di fare qcsa; **~ me to him** salutamelo ● *vi* ricordarsi

Remembrance Day /rɪ'membrəns/ *n* commemorazione *f* dei caduti (*11 novembre*)

remind /rɪ'maɪnd/ *vt* **~ sb of sth** ricordare qcsa a qcno

reminder /rɪ'maɪndə(r)/ *n* ricordo *m*; (*memo*) promemoria *m inv*; (*letter*) lettera *f* di sollecito; (*to pay*) sollecitazione *f* di pagamento

reminisce /remɪ'nɪs/ *vi* rievocare il passato

reminiscences /remɪ'nɪsənsɪz/ *npl* reminiscenze *fpl*

reminiscent /remɪ'nɪsənt/ *a* **be ~ of** richiamare alla memoria

remiss /rɪ'mɪs/ *a* negligente

remission /rɪ'mɪʃn/ *n* remissione *f*; (*of sentence*) condono *m*

remit /rɪ'mɪt/ *vt* (*pt/pp* **remitted**) rimettere ⟨*money*⟩

remittance /rɪ'mɪtəns/ *n* rimessa *f*

remix[1] /ri:'mɪks/ *vt Mus* rimixare

remix[2] /'ri:mɪks/ *n Mus* rimixaggio *m*

remnant /'remnənt/ *n* resto *m*; (*of material*) scampolo *m*; (*trace*) traccia *f*

remonstrate /'remənstreɪt/ *vi* fare rimostranze (**with sb** a qcno)

remorse /rɪ'mɔ:s/ *n* rimorso *m*

remorseful /rɪ'mɔ:sfʊl/ *a* pieno di rimorso

remorsefully /rɪ'mɔ:sfʊlɪ/ *adv* con rimorso

remorseless /rɪ'mɔ:slɪs/ *a* spietato

remorselessly /rɪ'mɔ:slɪslɪ/ *adv* senza pietà

remote /rɪ'məʊt/ *a* remoto; (*slight*) minimo

remote: remote access *n Comput* accesso *m* remoto. **remote control** *n* telecomando *m*. **remote-controlled** *a* telecomandato

remotely /rɪ'məʊtlɪ/ *adv* lontanamente; **be not ~...** non essere lontanamente...

remoteness /rɪ'məʊtnɪs/ *n* lontananza *f*

remould /'ri:məʊld/ *n* pneumatico *m* ricostruito

remount /ri:'maʊnt/ *vt* rimontare in sella a ⟨*bike, horse*⟩

remov[e]able /rɪ'mu:vəbl/ *a* rimovibile

removal /rɪ'mu:vl/ *n* rimozione *f*; (*from house*) trasloco *m*

removal man *n* addetto *m* ai traslochi

removal van *n* camion *m inv* da trasloco

remove /rɪ'mu:v/ *vt* togliere; togliersi ⟨*clothes*⟩; eliminare ⟨*stain, doubts*⟩

remuneration /rɪmju:nə'reɪʃn/ *n* rimunerazione *f*

remunerative /rɪ'mju:nərətɪv/ *a* rimunerativo

renaissance /rə'neɪsəns/ *n* rinascita *f*; **R~** Rinascimento *m*

renal /'ri:nəl/ *a* renale

render /'rendə(r)/ *vt* rendere ⟨*service*⟩

rendering /'rend(ə)rɪŋ/ *n Mus* interpretazione *f*

rendezvous /'rɒndeɪvu:/ *vi esp Mil* incontrarsi

rendition /ren'dɪʃn/ *n* interpretazione *f*

renegade /'renɪgeɪd/ *n* rinnegato, -a *mf*

renege /rɪ'neɪg/ *vi* venire meno (**on** a)

renegotiate /ri:nɪ'gəʊʃɪeɪt/ *vt* rinegoziare

renegotiation /ri:nɪgəʊʃɪ'eɪʃn/ *n* rinegoziato *m*

renew /rɪ'nju:/ *vt* rinnovare ⟨*contract*⟩

renewable /rɪ'nju:əbl/ *a* rinnovabile

renewal /rɪ'nju:əl/ *n* rinnovo *m*

renounce /rɪ'naʊns/ *vt* rinunciare a

renovate /'renəveɪt/ *vt* rinnovare
renovation /renə'veɪʃn/ *n* rinnovo *m*
renown /rɪ'naʊn/ *n* fama *f*
renowned /rɪ'naʊnd/ *a* rinomato
rent /rent/ *n* affitto *m* ● *vt* affittare; ~ [out] dare in affitto
rental /'rentl/ *n* affitto *m*
rent boy *n* ragazzo *m* di vita
rent-free *a* ⟨*accommodation*⟩ gratuito ● *adv* ⟨*live, use*⟩ senza pagare l'affitto
renunciation /rɪnʌnsɪ'eɪʃn/ *n* rinuncia *f*
reopen /ri:'əʊpən/ *vt/i* riaprire
reorganization /ri:ɔːgənaɪ'zeɪʃn/ *n* riorganizzazione *f*
reorganize /ri:'ɔːgənaɪz/ *vt* riorganizzare
rep /rep/ *n* *Comm fam* rappresentante *mf*; *Theat* ≈ teatro *m* stabile
repackage /ri:'pækɪdʒ/ *vt* *Comm* cambiare la confezione di; (*fig: change public image of*) cambiare l'immagine pubblica di; cambiare i termini di ⟨*proposal*⟩
repaint /ri:'peɪnt/ *vt* ridipingere
repair /rɪ'peə(r)/ *n* riparazione *f*; **in good/bad ~** in buone/cattive condizioni ● *vt* riparare
reparation /repə'reɪʃn/ *n* **make ~s for sth** risarcire qcsa
repartee /repɑː'tiː/ *n* botta e risposta *m inv*; **piece of ~** risposta *f* pronta
repatriate /ri:'pætrɪeɪt/ *vt* rimpatriare
repatriation /ri:pætrɪ'eɪʃn/ *n* rimpatrio *m*
repay /ri:'peɪ/ *vt* (*pt/pp* **-paid**) ripagare
repayment /ri:'peɪmənt/ *n* rimborso *m*
repeal /rɪ'pi:l/ *n* abrogazione *f* ● *vt* abrogare
repeat /rɪ'pi:t/ *n* *TV* replica *f* ● *vt/i* ripetere; ~ **oneself** ripetersi
repeated /rɪ'pi:tɪd/ *a* ripetuto
repeatedly /rɪ'pi:tɪdlɪ/ *adv* ripetutamente
repel /rɪ'pel/ *vt* (*pt/pp* **repelled**) respingere; *fig* ripugnare
repellent /rɪ'pelənt/ *a* ripulsivo
repent /rɪ'pent/ *vi* pentirsi
repentance /rɪ'pentəns/ *n* pentimento *m*
repentant /rɪ'pentənt/ *a* pentito
repercussions /ri:pə'kʌʃnz/ *npl* ripercussioni *fpl*
repertoire /'repətwɑː(r)/ *n* repertorio *m*
repertory /'repətrɪ/ *n* ≈ teatro *m* stabile
repertory company *n* compagnia *f* di un teatro stabile
repetition /repɪ'tɪʃn/ *n* ripetizione *f*
repetitious /repɪ'tɪʃəs/, **repetitive** /rɪ'petɪtɪv/ *a* ripetitivo
replace /rɪ'pleɪs/ *vt* (*put back*) rimettere a posto; (*take the place of*) sostituire; ~ **sth with sth** sostituire qcsa con qcsa
replacement /rɪ'pleɪsmənt/ *n* sostituzione *f*; (*person*) sostituto, -a *mf*
replacement part *n* pezzo *m* di ricambio
replant /ri:'plɑːnt/ *vt* ripiantare
replay /'ri:pleɪ/ *n* *Sport* partita *f* ripetuta; [**action**] ~ replay *m inv*
replenish /rɪ'plenɪʃ/ *vt* rifornire ⟨*stocks*⟩; (*refill*) riempire di nuovo
replete /rɪ'pli:t/ *a* ~ **with** riempito di

replica /'replɪkə/ *n* copia *f*
replicate /'replɪkeɪt/ *vt* ripetere ⟨*experiment*⟩
reply /rɪ'plaɪ/ *n* risposta *f* (**to** a) ● *vt/i* (*pt/pp* **replied**) rispondere
reply-paid envelope *n* busta *f* affrancata per rispondere
report /rɪ'pɔːt/ *n* rapporto *m*; *TV, Radio* servizio *m*; *Journ* cronaca *f*; *Sch* pagella *f*; (*rumour*) diceria *f* ● *vt* riportare; ~ **sb to the police** denunciare qcno alla polizia ● *vi* riportare; (*present oneself*) presentarsi (**to** a)
reportedly /rɪ'pɔːtɪdlɪ/ *adv* secondo quanto si dice
reporter /rɪ'pɔːtə(r)/ *n* cronista *mf*, reporter *mf inv*
repose /rɪ'pəʊz/ *n* riposo *m*
repository /rɪ'pɒzɪt(ə)rɪ/ *n* (*place*) deposito *m*; (*of secret, authority*) depositario, -a *mf*
repossess /ri:pə'zes/ *vt* riprendere possesso di
repossession /ri:pə'zeʃn/ *n* esproprio *m*
repot /ri:'pɒt/ *vt* rinvasare ⟨*plant*⟩
reprehensible /reprɪ'hensəbl/ *a* riprovevole
represent /reprɪ'zent/ *vt* rappresentare
representation /reprɪzen'teɪʃn/ *n* rappresentazione *f*; **make ~s to** fare delle rimostranze a
representative /reprɪ'zentətɪv/ *a* rappresentativo ● *n* rappresentante *mf*
repress /rɪ'pres/ *vt* reprimere
repression /rɪ'preʃn/ *n* repressione *f*
repressive /rɪ'presɪv/ *a* repressivo
reprieve /rɪ'priːv/ *n* commutazione *f* della pena capitale; (*postponement*) sospensione *f* della pena capitale; *fig* tregua *f* ● *vt* sospendere la sentenza a; *fig* risparmiare
reprimand /'reprɪmɑːnd/ *n* rimprovero *m* ● *vt* rimproverare
reprint[1] /'riːprɪnt/ *n* ristampa *f*
reprint[2] /riː'prɪnt/ *vt* ristampare
reprisal /rɪ'praɪzl/ *n* rappresaglia *f*; **in ~ for** per rappresaglia contro
reproach /rɪ'prəʊtʃ/ *n* rimprovero *m* ● *vt* rimproverare a (**for doing sth** di fare qcsa)
reproachful /rɪ'prəʊtʃfʊl/ *a* riprovevole
reproachfully /rɪ'prəʊtʃfʊlɪ/ *adv* con aria di rimprovero
reprocess /riː'prəʊses/ *vt* trattare di nuovo
reproduce /riːprə'djuːs/ *vt* riprodurre ● *vi* riprodursi
reproduction /riːprə'dʌkʃn/ *n* riproduzione *f*
reproduction furniture *n* riproduzioni *fpl* di mobili antichi
reproductive /riːprə'dʌktɪv/ *a* riproduttivo
reproof /rɪ'pruːf/ *n* rimprovero *m*
reprove /rɪ'pruːv/ *vt* rimproverare
reptile /'reptaɪl/ *n* rettile *m*
republic /rɪ'pʌblɪk/ *n* repubblica *f*
republican /rɪ'pʌblɪkn/ *a & n* repubblicano, -a *mf*
republish /riː'pʌblɪʃ/ *vt* ripubblicare

repudiate /rɪ'pju:dɪeɪt/ vt ripudiare; respingere ⟨view, suggestion⟩

repugnance /rɪ'pʌgnəns/ n ripugnanza f

repugnant /rɪ'pʌgnənt/ a ripugnante

repulse /rɪ'pʌls/ vt fml respingere ⟨attack⟩; rifiutare ⟨assistance⟩

repulsion /rɪ'pʌlʃn/ n repulsione f

repulsive /rɪ'pʌlsɪv/ a ripugnante

reputable /'repjʊtəbl/ a affidabile

reputation /repjʊ'teɪʃn/ n reputazione f

repute /rɪ'pju:t/ n reputazione f

reputed /rɪ'pju:tɪd/ a presunto; **he is ~ to be** si presume che sia

reputedly /rɪ'pju:tɪdlɪ/ adv presumibilmente

request /rɪ'kwest/ n richiesta f ● vt richiedere

request stop n fermata f a richiesta

requiem /'rekwɪəm/ n requiem m inv

require /rɪ'kwaɪə(r)/ vt (need) necessitare di; (demand) esigere

required /rɪ'kwaɪəd/ a richiesto

requirement /rɪ'kwaɪəmənt/ n esigenza f; (condition) requisito m

requisite /'rekwɪzɪt/ a necessario ● n **toilet/travel ~s** pl articoli mpl da toilette/viaggio

requisition /rekwɪ'zɪʃn/ n ~ **[order]** [domanda f di] requisizione f ● vt requisire

reread /ri:'ri:d/ vt rileggere

re-release /ri:rɪ'li:s/ n (of film) nuova distribuzione f ● vt ridistribuire ⟨film⟩

reroof /ri:'ru:f/ vt rifare il tetto di ⟨building⟩

reroute /ri:'ru:t/ vt dirottare ⟨flight, traffic⟩

rerun /'ri:rʌn/ n (of film, play) replica f; (fig: repeat) ripetizione f

resale /ri:'seɪl/ n rivendita f

reschedule /ri:'ʃedju:l/ vt (change date of) cambiare la data di; (change time of) cambiare l'orario di; rinegoziare ⟨debt⟩

rescind /rɪ'sɪnd/ vt rescindere

rescue /'reskju:/ n salvataggio m ● vt salvare

rescuer /'reskjʊə(r)/ n salvatore, -trice mf

research /rɪ's3:tʃ/ n ricerca f ● vt fare ricerche su; Journ fare un'inchiesta su ● vi ~ **into** fare ricerche su

research and development n ricerca f e sviluppo m

researcher /rɪ's3:tʃə(r)/ n ricercatore, -trice mf

research fellow n Br Univ ricercatore, -trice mf

resell /ri:'sel/ vt (pt/pp resold) rivendere

resemblance /rɪ'zembləns/ n rassomiglianza f

resemble /rɪ'zembl/ vt rassomigliare a

resent /rɪ'zent/ vt risentirsi per

resentful /rɪ'zentfʊl/ a pieno di risentimento

resentfully /rɪ'zentfʊlɪ/ adv con risentimento

resentment /rɪ'zentmənt/ n risentimento m

reservation /rezə'veɪʃn/ n (booking) prenotazione f; (doubt, enclosure) riserva f

reserve /rɪ'z3:v/ n riserva f; (shyness) riserbo m ● vt riservare; riservarsi ⟨right⟩

reserved /rɪ'z3:vd/ a riservato

reservoir /'rezəvwɑ:(r)/ n bacino m idrico

reset /ri:'set/ vt riprogrammare ⟨clock⟩; (zero) azzerare

reshape /ri:'ʃeɪp/ vt ristrutturare

reshuffle /ri:'ʃʌfl/ Pol n rimpasto m ● vt rimpastare

reside /rɪ'zaɪd/ vi risiedere

residence /'rezɪdəns/ n residenza f; (stay) soggiorno m

residence permit n permesso m di soggiorno

resident /'rezɪdənt/ a & n residente mf

residential /rezɪ'denʃl/ a residenziale

residential area n quartiere m residenziale

residual /rɪ'zɪdjʊəl/ a residuo

residue /'rezɪdju:/ n residuo m

resign /rɪ'zaɪn/ vt dimettersi da; ~ **oneself to** rassegnarsi a ● vi dare le dimissioni

resignation /rezɪg'neɪʃn/ n rassegnazione f; (from job) dimissioni fpl

resigned /rɪ'zaɪnd/ a rassegnato

resignedly /rɪ'zaɪnɪdlɪ/ adv con rassegnazione

resilient /rɪ'zɪlɪənt/ a elastico; fig con buone capacità di ripresa

resin /'rezɪn/ n resina f

resist /rɪ'zɪst/ vt resistere a ● vi resistere

resistance /rɪ'zɪstəns/ n resistenza f

resistant /rɪ'zɪstənt/ a resistente

resit /ri:'sɪt/ Br vt (pt/pp resat) ridare ⟨exam⟩ ● n esame m di recupero

resize /ri:'saɪz/ vt ridimensionare

resolute /'rezəlu:t/ a risoluto

resolutely /'rezəlu:tlɪ/ adv con risolutezza

resolution /rezə'lu:ʃn/ n risolutezza f

resolve /rɪ'zɒlv/ n risolutezza f; (decision) risoluzione f ● vt (solve) risolvere; ~ **to do** decidere di fare

resolved /rɪ'zɒlvd/ a risoluto

resonance /'rezənəns/ n risonanza f

resonant /'rezənənt/ a risonante

resonate /'rezəneɪt/ vi risuonare

resort /rɪ'zɔ:t/ n (place) luogo m di villeggiatura; **as a last ~** come ultima risorsa ● vi ~ **to** ricorrere a

resound /rɪ'zaʊnd/ vi risonare (**with** di)

resounding /rɪ'zaʊndɪŋ/ a ⟨success⟩ risonante

resoundingly /rɪ'zaʊndɪŋlɪ/ adv in modo risonante

resource /rɪ'sɔ:s/ n ~**s** pl risorse fpl

resourceful /rɪ'sɔ:sfʊl/ a pieno di risorse; ⟨solution⟩ ingegnoso

resourcefulness /rɪ'sɔ:sfʊlnɪs/ n ingegnosità f

respect /rɪ'spekt/ n rispetto m; (aspect) aspetto m; **with ~ to** per quanto riguarda ● vt rispettare

respectability /rɪspektə'bɪlətɪ/ n rispettabilità f

respectable /rɪ'spektəbl/ a rispettabile

respectably /rɪ'spektəblɪ/ adv rispettabilmente

respectful /rɪ'spektfʊl/ a rispettoso

respectfully /rɪ'spektfʊlɪ/ adv rispettosamente

respective /rɪ'spektɪv/ a rispettivo

respectively /rɪ'spektɪvlɪ/ adv rispettivamente

respiration /respɪ'reɪʃn/ n respirazione f

respirator /'respɪreɪtə(r)/ n (apparatus) respiratore m

respite /'respaɪt/ n respiro m

resplendent /rɪ'splendənt/ a risplendente

respond /rɪ'spɒnd/ vi rispondere; (react) reagire (to a); (patient:) rispondere (to a)

respondent /rɪ'spɒndənt/ n Jur convenuto, -a mf; (to questionnaire) interrogato, -a mf

response /rɪ'spɒns/ n risposta f; (reaction) reazione f

responsibility /rɪspɒnsɪ'bɪlətɪ/ n responsabilità f inv

responsible /rɪ'spɒnsəbl/ a responsabile; (trustworthy) responsabile; (job) impegnativo

responsibly /rɪ'spɒnsəblɪ/ adv in modo responsabile

responsive /rɪ'spɒnsɪv/ a be ~ (audience etc:) reagire; (brakes:) essere sensibile; **she wasn't very ~** non era molto cooperativa

respray[1] /ri:'spreɪ/ vt riverniciare (vehicle)

respray[2] /'ri:spreɪ/ n riverniciatura f; **it's had a ~** è stato riverniciato

rest[1] /rest/ n riposo m; Mus pausa f; **have a ~** riposarsi ● vt riposare; (lean, place) appoggiare (on su) ● vi riposarsi; (elbows:) appoggiarsi; (hopes:) riposare; **it ~s with you** sta a te

∎ **rest up** vi riposars

rest[2] n the ~ il resto; (people) gli altri

restart /ri:'stɑːt/ vt rimettere in moto (engine); riprendere (talks)

restate /ri:'steɪt/ vt (say differently) riformulare; (say again) ribadire

restaurant /'restərɒnt/ n ristorante m

restaurant car n vagone m ristorante

restful /'restfl/ a riposante

rest home n casa f di riposo

restitution /restɪ'tjuːʃn/ n restituzione f

restive /'restɪv/ a irrequieto

restless /'restlɪs/ a nervoso

restlessly /'restlɪslɪ/ adv nervosamente

restlessness /'restlɪsnɪs/ n agitazione f

restock /ri:'stɒk/ vt rifornire (shelf, shop) ● vi rifornirsi

restoration /restə'reɪʃn/ n ristabilimento m; (of building) restauro m; (of stolen property etc) restituzione f

restore /rɪ'stɔː(r)/ vt ristabilire; restaurare (building); (give back) restituire

restorer /rɪ'stɔːrə(r)/ n (person) restauratore, -trice mf

restrain /rɪ'streɪn/ vt trattenere; **~ oneself** controllarsi

restrained /rɪ'streɪnd/ a controllato

restraint /rɪ'streɪnt/ n restrizione f; (moderation) ritegno m

restrict /rɪ'strɪkt/ vt limitare (**to** a)

restriction /rɪ'strɪkʃn/ n limite m; (restraint) restrizione f

restrictive /rɪ'strɪktɪv/ a limitativo

restring /ri:'strɪŋ/ vt rinfilare (necklace, beads); sostituire le corde di (instrument, racket)

restroom /'restruːm/ n Am toilette f inv

restructure /ri:'strʌktʃə(r)/ vt ristrutturare

restructuring /ri:'strʌktʃərɪŋ/ n ristrutturazione f

resubmit /ri:sʌb'mɪt/ vt ripresentare

restyle /ri:'staɪl/ vt cambiare il taglio di (hair); cambiare la linea di (car); rimodernare (shop)

result /rɪ'zʌlt/ n risultato m; **as a ~** di conseguenza; **as a ~ of** a causa di ● vi **~ from** risultare da; **~ in** portare a

resume /rɪ'zjuːm/ vt/i riprendere

résumé /'rezjʊmeɪ/ n riassunto m; Am curriculum m inv vitae

resumption /rɪ'zʌmpʃn/ n ripresa f

resurface /ri:'sɜːfɪs/ vi (sub, person, rumour:) riemergere ● vt rifare la copertura di (road)

resurgence /rɪ'sɜːdʒəns/ n rinascita f

resurrect /rezə'rekt/ vt fig risuscitare

resurrection /rezə'rekʃn/ n the R~ Relig la Risurrezione

resuscitate /rɪ'sʌsɪteɪt/ vt rianimare

resuscitation /rɪsʌsɪ'teɪʃn/ n rianimazione f

retail /'ri:teɪl/ n vendita f al minuto o al dettaglio ● a & adv al minuto ● vt vendere al minuto ● vi ~ **at** essere venduto al pubblico al prezzo di

retailer /'ri:teɪlə(r)/ n dettagliante mf

retail price n prezzo m al minuto

retain /rɪ'teɪn/ vt conservare; (hold back) trattenere

retainer /rɪ'teɪnə(r)/ n (fee) anticipo m; (old: servant) servitore, -trice mf

retake[1] /ri:'teɪk/ vt Cinema girare di nuovo; Sch, Univ ridare; Mil riconquistare

retake[2] /'ri:teɪk/ n Cinema ulteriore ripresa f

retaliate /rɪ'tælɪeɪt/ vi vendicarsi

retaliation /rɪtælɪ'eɪʃn/ n rappresaglia f; **in ~ for** per rappresaglia contro

retarded /rɪ'tɑːdɪd/ a ritardato

retch /retʃ/ vi avere conati di vomito

retention /rɪ'tenʃn/ n conservazione f; (of information) memorizzazione f; (of fluid) ritenzione f

retentive /rɪ'tentɪv/ a (memory) buono

retentiveness /rɪ'tentɪvnɪs/ n capacità f di memorizzazione

rethink /ri:'θɪŋk/ vt (pt/pp rethought) riconsiderare ● n have a ~ riconsiderare la cosa

reticence /'retɪsəns/ n reticenza f

reticent /'retɪsənt/ a reticente

retina /'retɪnə/ n retina f

retinue /'retɪnjuː/ n seguito m

retire /rɪ'taɪə(r)/ vi andare in pensione;

(withdraw) ritirarsi ● *vt* mandare in pensione *(employee)*

retired /rɪˈtaɪəd/ *a* in pensione

retirement /rɪˈtaɪəmənt/ *n* pensione *f*; **since my ~** da quando sono andato in pensione

retirement age *n* età *f* della pensione

retiring /rɪˈtaɪərɪŋ/ *a* riservato

retort /rɪˈtɔːt/ *n* replica *f*; *Chem* storta *f* ● *vt* ribattere

retouch /riːˈtʌtʃ/ *vt Phot* ritoccare

retouching /riːˈtʌtʃɪŋ/ *n Phot* ritocco *m*

retrace /rɪˈtreɪs/ *vt* ripercorrere; **~ one's steps** ritornare sui propri passi

retract /rɪˈtrækt/ *vt* ritirare; ritrattare *(statement, accusation)* ● *vi* ritrarsi

retractable /rɪˈtræktəbl/ *a (landing gear)* retrattile; *(pen)* con la punta retrattile

retraction /rɪˈtrækʃn/ *n* ritiro *m*; *(of statement, accusation)* ritrattazione *f*

retrain /riːˈtreɪn/ *vt* riqualificare ● *vi* riqualificarsi

retread /ˈriːtred/ *n* pneumatico *m* ricostruito

retreat /rɪˈtriːt/ *n* ritirata *f*; *(place)* ritiro *m* ● *vi* ritirarsi; *Mil* battere in ritirata

retrench /rɪˈtrentʃ/ *vi* ridurre le spese

retrenchment /rɪˈtrentʃmənt/ *n* riduzione *f* delle spese

retrial /riːˈtraɪəl/ *n* nuovo processo *m*

retribution /retrɪˈbjuːʃn/ *n* castigo *m*

retrievable /rɪˈtriːvəbl/ *a* recuperabile

retrieval /rɪˈtriːvəl/ *n* recupero *m*

retrieve /rɪˈtriːv/ *vt* recuperare

retroactive /retrəʊˈæktɪv/ *a* retroattivo

retroactively /retrəʊˈæktɪvlɪ/ *adv* retroattivamente

retrograde /ˈretrəɡreɪd/ *a* retrogrado

retrospect /ˈretrəspekt/ *n* **in ~** guardando indietro

retrospective /retrəˈspektɪv/ *a (exhibit)* retrospettivo; *(legislation)* retroattivo ● *n* retrospettiva *f*

retrospectively /retrəˈspektɪvlɪ/ *adv* retrospettivamente

retrovirus /ˈretrəʊvaɪrəs/ *n* retrovirus *m inv*

retry /riːˈtraɪ/ *vt Jur* riprocessare; *Comput* riprovare

return /rɪˈtɜːn/ *n* ritorno *m*; *(giving back)* restituzione *f*; *Comm* profitto *m*; *(ticket)* biglietto *m* di andata e ritorno; **by ~ [of post]** a stretto giro di posta; **in ~** in cambio **(for** di); **many happy ~s!** cento di questi giorni!; **~ on investment** utile *m* sul capitale investito ● *vi* ritornare ● *vt* ridare *(give back)* restituire; ricambiare *(affection, invitation)*; *(put back)* rimettere; *(send back)* mandare indietro; *(elect)* eleggere

returnable /rɪˈtɜːnəbl/ *a* restituibile

return: return flight *n* volo *m* di andata e ritorno. **return match** *n* rivincita *f*. **return ticket** *n* biglietto *m* di andata e ritorno

reunification /riːjuːnɪfɪˈkeɪʃn/ *n* riunificazione *f*

reunify /riːˈjuːnɪfaɪ/ *vt* riunificare

reunion /riːˈjuːnjən/ *n* riunione *f*

reunite /riːjʊˈnaɪt/ *vt* riunire

reusable /riːˈjuːzəbl/ *a* riutilizzabile

reuse /riːˈjuːz/ *vt* riutilizzare

rev /rev/ *n Auto* giro; **~s per minute** regime *m* di giri ● *vt* **~ [up]** far andare su di giri ● *vi* andare su di giri

revaluation /riːvæljuˈeɪʃn/ *n* rivalutazione *f*

revalue /riːˈvæljuː/ *vt Comm* rivalutare

revamp /riːˈvæmp/ *vt* riorganizzare *(company)*; rimodernare *(building, clothing)*

rev counter *n* contagiri *m*

Rev[d] *abbr* **(Reverend)** Reverendo

reveal /rɪˈviːl/ *vt* rivelare; *(dress:)* scoprire

revealing /rɪˈviːlɪŋ/ *a* rivelatore; *(dress)* osé *inv*

revel /ˈrevl/ *vi (pt/pp* **revelled)** **~ in sth** godere di qcsa

revelation /revəˈleɪʃn/ *n* rivelazione *f*

reveller /ˈrevələ(r)/ *n* festaiolo, -a *mf*

revelry /ˈrevəlrɪ/ *n* baldoria *f*

revenge /rɪˈvendʒ/ *n* vendetta *f*; *Sport* rivincita *f*; **take ~** vendicarsi **(on sb for sth** di qcno per qcsa) ● *vt* vendicare

revenue /ˈrevənjuː/ *n* reddito *m*

reverberate /rɪˈvɜːbəreɪt/ *vi* riverberare

reverberations /rɪvɜːbəˈreɪʃnz/ *npl fig* ripercussione *f*

revere /rɪˈvɪə(r)/ *vt* riverire

reverence /ˈrevərəns/ *n* riverenza *f*

Reverend /ˈrevərənd/ *a* reverendo

reverent /ˈrevərənt/ *a* riverente

reverential /revəˈrenʃ(ə)l/ *a* riverente

reverently /ˈrevərəntlɪ/ *adv* rispettosamente

reverie /ˈrevərɪ/ *n* sogno *m* ad occhi aperti

reversal /rɪˈvɜːsl/ *n* inversione *f*

reverse /rɪˈvɜːs/ *a* opposto; **in ~ order** in ordine inverso ● *n* contrario *m*; *(back)* rovescio *m*; *Auto* marcia *m* indietro ● *vt* invertire; **~ the car into the garage** entrare in garage a marcia indietro; **~ the charges** *Teleph* fare una telefonata a carico del destinatario ● *vi Auto* fare marcia indietro

reverse charge [phone-]call *n* telefonata *f* a carico del destinatario

reversing lights /rɪˈvɜːsɪŋ/ *npl* luci *fpl* di retromarcia

revert /rɪˈvɜːt/ *vi* **~ to** tornare a

review /rɪˈvjuː/ *n (survey)* rassegna *f*; *(re-examination)* riconsiderazione *f*; *Mil* rivista *f*; *(of book, play)* recensione *f* ● *vt* riesaminare *(situation)*; *Mil* passare in rivista; recensire *(book, play)*

reviewer /rɪˈvjuːə(r)/ *n* critico, -a *mf*

revile /rɪˈvaɪl/ *vt* ingiuriare

revise /rɪˈvaɪz/ *vt* rivedere; *(for exam)* ripassare

revision /rɪˈvɪʒn/ *n* revisione *f*; *(for exam)* ripasso *m*

revisionism /rɪˈvɪʒənɪzm/ *n* revisionismo *m*

revisionist /rɪˈvɪʒənɪst/ *a & n* revisionista *mf*

revisit /riːˈvɪzɪt/ *vt* rivisitare ⟨*person, museum etc*⟩

revitalization /riːvaɪtəlaɪˈzeɪʃn/ *n* rivitalizzazione *f*

revitalize /riːˈvaɪtəlaɪz/ *vt* rivitalizzare

revival /rɪˈvaɪvl/ *n* ritorno *m*; (*of patient*) recupero *m*; (*from coma*) risveglio *m*

revivalist /rɪˈvaɪvəlɪst/ *a Relig* revivalista

revive /rɪˈvaɪv/ *vt* resuscitare; rianimare ⟨*person*⟩ ● *vi* riprendersi; ⟨*person:*⟩ rianimarsi

revocation /revəˈkeɪʃn/ *n* (*of decision, order*) revoca *f*; (*of law*) abrogazione *f*; (*of will*) annullamento *m*

revoke /rɪˈvəʊk/ *vt* revocare ⟨*decision, order*⟩; abrogare ⟨*law*⟩; annullare ⟨*will*⟩

revolt /rɪˈvəʊlt/ *n* rivolta *f* ● *vi* ribellarsi ● *vt* rivoltare

revolting /rɪˈvəʊltɪŋ/ *a* rivoltante

revolution /revəˈluːʃn/ *n* rivoluzione *f*; ~**s per minute** *Auto* giri *mpl* al minuto

revolutionary /revəˈluːʃənərɪ/ *a & n* rivoluzionario, -a *mf*

revolutionize /revəˈluːʃənaɪz/ *vt* rivoluzionare

revolve /rɪˈvɒlv/ *vi* ruotare; ~ **around** girare intorno a

revolver /rɪˈvɒlvə(r)/ *n* rivoltella *f*, revolver *m inv*

revolving /rɪˈvɒlvɪŋ/ *a* ruotante

revolving doors *npl* porta *f* girevole

revue /rɪˈvjuː/ *n* rivista *f*

revulsion /rɪˈvʌlʃn/ *n* ripulsione *f*

reward /rɪˈwɔːd/ *n* ricompensa *f* ● *vt* ricompensare

rewarding /rɪˈwɔːdɪŋ/ *a* gratificante

rewind /riːˈwaɪnd/ *vt* riavvolgere ⟨*tape, film*⟩

rewind button /ˈriːwaɪnd/ *n* tasto *m* di riavvolgimento

rewire /riːˈwaɪə(r)/ *vt* rifare l'impianto elettrico di

reword /riːˈwɜːd/ *vt* esprimere con parole diverse

rework /riːˈwɜːk/ *vt* modificare

rewrite /riːˈraɪt/ *vt* (*pt* **rewrote**, *pp* **rewritten**) riscrivere

rhapsody /ˈræpsədɪ/ *n* rapsodia *f*

rhesus /ˈriːsəs/ *n* reso *m*

rhesus-negative *a* Rh-negativo

rhesus-positive *a* Rh-positivo

rhetoric /ˈretərɪk/ *n* retorica *f*

rhetorical /rɪˈtɒrɪkl/ *a* retorico

rhetorically /rɪˈtɒrɪklɪ/ *adv* retoricamente

rhetorical question *n* domanda *f* retorica

rheumatic /rʊˈmætɪk/ *a* reumatico

rheumatism /ˈruːmətɪzm/ *n* reumatismo *m*

rheumatoid arthritis /ˈruːmətɔɪd/ *n* periartrite *f*

Rhine /raɪn/ *n* Reno *m*

rhino /ˈraɪnəʊ/ *n fam* rinoceronte *m*

rhinoceros /raɪˈnɒsərəs/ *n* rinoceronte *m*

rhombus /ˈrɒmbəs/ *n* rombo *m*

rhubarb /ˈruːbɑːb/ *n* rabarbaro *m*

rhyme /raɪm/ *n* rima *f*; (*poem*) filastrocca *f* ● *vi* rimare; ~ **with sth** far rima con qcsa

rhythm /ˈrɪðm/ *n* ritmo *m*

rhythmic[al] /ˈrɪðmɪk[l]/ *a* ritmico

rhythmically /ˈrɪðmɪklɪ/ *adv* con ritmo

rhythm method *n* (*of contraception*) metodo *m* Ogino-Knauss

rib /rɪb/ *n* costola *f*; ~**s** *pl Culin* costata *f* ● *vt* (*pt/pp* **ribbed**) *fam* punzecchiare

ribald /ˈrɪbld/ *a* spinto

ribbon /ˈrɪbən/ *n* nastro *m*; **in** ~**s** a brandelli

ribcage /ˈrɪbkeɪdʒ/ *n* gabbia *f* toracica, cassa *f* toracica

rice /raɪs/ *n* riso *m*

ricefield /ˈraɪsfiːld/ *n* risaia *f*

rice-paper *n Culin* carta *f* di riso

rich /rɪtʃ/ *a* ricco; ⟨*food*⟩ pesante ● *n* **the** ~ *pl* i ricchi; ~**es** *pl* ricchezze *fpl*

richly /ˈrɪtʃlɪ/ *adv* riccamente; ⟨*deserve*⟩ largamente

Richter scale /ˈrɪktə(r)/ *n* scala *f* Richter

rick /rɪk/ *vt Br* ~ **one's ankle** prendere una storta alla caviglia

rickets /ˈrɪkɪts/ *n* rachitismo *m*

rickety /ˈrɪkətɪ/ *a* malfermo

rickshaw /ˈrɪkʃɔː/ *n* risciò *m inv*

ricochet /ˈrɪkəʃeɪ/ *vi* rimbalzare ● *n* rimbalzo *m*

rid /rɪd/ *vt* (*pt/pp* **rid**, *pres p* **ridding**) sbarazzare (**of** di); **get** ~ **of** sbarazzarsi di

riddance /ˈrɪdns/ *n* **good** ~! che liberazione!

ridden /ˈrɪdn/ *see* **ride**

riddle /ˈrɪdl/ *n* enigma *m*

riddled /ˈrɪdld/ *a* ~ **with** crivellato di

ride /raɪd/ *n* (*on horse*) cavalcata *f*; (*in vehicle*) giro *m*; (*journey*) viaggio *m*; **take sb for a** ~ *fam* prendere qcno in giro ● *v* (*pt* **rode**, *pp* **ridden**) ● *vt* montare ⟨*horse*⟩; andare su ⟨*bicycle*⟩ ● *vi* andare a cavallo; ⟨*jockey, showjumper:*⟩ cavalcare; ⟨*cyclist:*⟩ andare in bicicletta; (*in vehicle*) viaggiare

rider /ˈraɪdə(r)/ *n* cavallerizzo, -a *mf*; (*in race*) fantino *m*; (*on bicycle*) ciclista *mf*; (*in document*) postilla *f*

ridge /rɪdʒ/ *n* spigolo *m*; (*on roof*) punta *f*; (*of mountain*) cresta *f*; (*of high pressure*) zona *f* a alta pressione [atmosferica]

ridicule /ˈrɪdɪkjuːl/ *n* ridicolo *m* ● *vt* mettere in ridicolo

ridiculous /rɪˈdɪkjʊləs/ *a* ridicolo

ridiculously /rɪˈdɪkjʊləslɪ/ *adv* in modo ridicolo; ~ **expensive/easy** carissimo/facilissimo

riding /ˈraɪdɪŋ/ *n* equitazione *f* ● *attrib* d'equitazione

rife /raɪf/ *a* **be** ~ essere diffuso; ~ **with** pieno di

riff-raff /ˈrɪfræf/ *n* marmaglia *f*

rifle /ˈraɪfl/ *n* fucile *m* ● *vt* ~ [**through**] mettere a soqquadro

rifle-range *n* tiro *m* al bersaglio

rift /rɪft/ *n* fessura *f*; *fig* frattura *f*

rig[1] /rɪg/ *n* equipaggiamento *m*; (*at sea*) piattaforma *f* per trivellazioni subacquee

rig[2] *vt* (*pt/pp* **rigged**) manovrare ⟨*election*⟩

■ **rig out** *vt* equipaggiare; (*with clothes*) parare

■ **rig up** vt allestire

rigging /'rɪgɪŋ/ n Naut sartiame m; (of election, competition) broglio m

right /raɪt/ a giusto; (not left) destro; **be ~** ‹person:› aver ragione; ‹clock:› essere giusto; **put ~** mettere all'ora ‹clock›; correggere ‹person›; rimediare a ‹situation›; **that's ~!** proprio così!; **do you have the ~ time?** ha l'ora esatta? ● adv (correctly) bene; (not left) a destra; (directly) proprio; (completely) completamente; **~ away** immediatamente; **too ~!** altroché! ● n giusto m; (not left) destra f; (what is due) diritto m; **the R~** Pol la destra; **on/to the ~** a destra; **be in the ~** essere nel giusto; **by ~s** secondo giustizia; **be within one's ~s** avere tutti i diritti (**in doing sth** di fare qcsa) ● vt raddrizzare; **~ a wrong** fig riparare a un torto

right angle n angolo m retto

righteous /'raɪtʃəs/ a virtuoso; (cause) giusto

rightful /'raɪtfl/ a legittimo

rightfully /'raɪtfʊlɪ/ adv legittimamente

right-handed /-'hændɪd/ a che usa la mano destra

right-hand man n fig braccio m destro

rightly /'raɪtlɪ/ adv giustamente

right-minded /-'maɪndɪd/ a sensato

right of way n diritto m di transito; (path) passaggio m; Auto precedenza f

right-on int fam bene! ● a fam **they're very ~** sono molto impegnati

rights issue n emissione f riservata agli azionisti

right: right-thinking a sensato. **right turn** n svolta f a destra. **right wing** n Pol destra; Sport ala f destra. **right-wing** a Pol di destra. **right-winger** n Pol persona f di destra; Sport ala f destra

rigid /'rɪdʒɪd/ a rigido

rigidity /rɪ'dʒɪdətɪ/ n rigidità f

rigmarole /'rɪgmərəʊl/ n trafila f; (story) tiritera f

rigor mortis /rɪgə'mɔːtɪs/ n rigidità f cadaverica

rigorous /'rɪgərəs/ a rigoroso

rigorously /'rɪgərəslɪ/ adv rigorosamente

rigour /'rɪgə(r)/ n rigore m

rig-out n (fam: clothes) tenuta f

rile /raɪl/ vt fam irritare

rim /rɪm/ n bordo m; (of wheel) cerchione m

rind /raɪnd/ n (on cheese) crosta f; (on bacon) cotenna f

ring¹ /rɪŋ/ n (circle) cerchio m; (on finger) anello m; (boxing) ring m inv; (for circus) pista f; **stand in a ~** essere in cerchio ● vt accerchiare; **~ in red** fare un cerchio rosso intorno a

ring² n suono m; **give sb a ~** Teleph dare un colpo di telefono a qcno ● v (pt **rang**, pp **rung**) ● vt suonare; Teleph telefonare a; **it ~s a bell** fig mi dice qualcosa; **~ the changes** fig cambiare ● vi suonare; Teleph telefonare; **~ true** aver l'aria di essere vero

■ **ring back** vt/i Teleph richiamare

■ **ring off** vi Teleph riattaccare

■ **ring out** vi ‹voice, shot etc:› risuonare chiaramente

■ **ring round** vi Teleph fare un giro di telefonate

■ **ring up** Teleph vt telefonare a ● vi telefonare

ring-binder /'rɪŋbaɪndə(r)/ n raccoglitore m ad anelli

ring finger n anulare m

ringing /'rɪŋɪŋ/ n (noise of bell, alarm) suono m; (in ears) fischio m

ringleader /'rɪŋliːdə(r)/ n capobanda m

ringlet /'rɪŋlɪt/ n boccolo m

ring: ringmaster n direttore m di circo. **ringpull** n linguetta f. **ring-pull can** n lattina f con linguetta. **ring road** n circonvallazione f. **ringside** n **at the ~** in prima fila; **have a ~ seat** fig essere in prima fila

rink /rɪŋk/ n pista f di pattinaggio

rinse /rɪns/ n risciacquo m; (hair colour) cachet m inv ● vt sciacquare

■ **rinse off** vt sciacquare via

■ **rinse out** vt sciacquare ‹cup, glass›; sciacquare via ‹shampoo, soap›

riot /'raɪət/ n rissa f; (of colour) accozzaglia f; **~s** pl disordini mpl; **run ~** impazzare ● vi creare disordini

riot act n **read the ~ ~ to sb** fig dare una lavata di capo a qcno

rioter /'raɪətə(r)/ n dimostrante mf

riot gear n tenuta f antisommossa

riotous /'raɪətəs/ a sfrenato

riotously /'raɪətəslɪ/ adv **~ funny** divertente da morire

riot police n DIGOS f, Divisione f Investigazioni Generali e Operazioni Speciali

RIP abbr (**rest in peace**) R.I.P.

rip /rɪp/ n strappo m ● v (pt/pp **ripped**) ● vt strappare; **~ open** aprire con uno strappo ● vi strapparsi; **let ~** scatenarsi

■ **rip off** vt (remove) togliere; (fam: cheat) fregare

■ **rip up** vt stracciare ‹letter›

ripcord /'rɪpkɔːd/ n cavo m di spiegamento

ripe /raɪp/ a maturo; ‹cheese› stagionato

ripen /'raɪpn/ vi maturare; ‹cheese:› stagionarsi ● vt far maturare; stagionare ‹cheese›

ripeness /'raɪpnɪs/ n maturazione f

rip-off n fam frode f; **these prices are a ~!** questi prezzi sono un furto!

riposte /rɪ'pɒst/ n replica f

ripple /'rɪpl/ n increspatura f; (sound) mormorio m ● vt increspare ● vi incresparsi

rip-roaring /'rɪprɔːrɪŋ/ a ‹fam: success› travolgente

rise /raɪz/ n (of sun) levata f; (fig: to fame, power) ascesa f; (increase) aumento m; **give ~ to** dare adito a ● vi (pt **rose**, pp **risen**) alzarsi; ‹sun:› sorgere; ‹dough:› lievitare; ‹prices, water level:› aumentare; (to power, position) arrivare (**to** a); (rebel) sollevarsi; ‹Parliament, court:› aggiornare la seduta; (for holidays) sospendere i lavori

■ **rise above** vt superare ‹difficulty›

riser /'raɪzə(r)/ n early ~ persona f mattiniera

rising /'raɪzɪŋ/ a ⟨sun⟩ levante; ~ **generation** nuova generazione f ● n (revolt) sollevazione f

risk /rɪsk/ n rischio m; **run the ~ of** correre il rischio di; **at ~** in pericolo; **at one's own ~** a proprio rischio e pericolo; **at the ~ of doing sth** a costo di fare qcsa ● vt rischiare

risky /'rɪskɪ/ a (-ier, -iest) rischioso

risotto /rɪ'zɒtəʊ/ n risotto m

risqué /'rɪskeɪ/ a spinto

rissole /'rɪsəʊl/ n crocchetta f

rite /raɪt/ n rito m; **last ~s** pl estrema unzione fsg

ritual /'rɪtjʊəl/ a & n rituale m

ritzy /'rɪtsɪ/ a ⟨fam: hotel, style, decoration⟩ lussuoso

rival /'raɪvl/ a rivale ● n rivale mf; ~**s** pl Comm concorrenti mpl ● vt (pt/pp rivalled) rivaleggiare con

rivalry /'raɪv(ə)lrɪ/ n rivalità f inv; Comm concorrenza f

river /'rɪvə(r)/ n fiume m

river: riverbank n riva f di fiume. **river-bed** n letto m del fiume. **riverside** n lungofiume m ● attrib sul fiume

rivet /'rɪvɪt/ n rivetto m ● vt rivettare; **be ~ed by** fig essere avvinto da

riveting /'rɪvɪtɪŋ/ a fig avvincente

Riviera /rɪvɪ'eərə/ n **the French ~** la Costa Azzurra; **the Italian ~** la riviera ligure

roach /rəʊtʃ/ n ⟨fish⟩ lasca f; (Am fam: insect) scarafaggio m

road /rəʊd/ n strada f, via f; **be on the ~** viaggiare

road: roadblock n blocco m stradale. **road haulage** n trasporto m su strada. **road hog** n fam pirata m della strada

roadie /'rəʊdɪ/ n roadie m inv

road: road map n carta f stradale. **road safety** n sicurezza f sulle strade. **road sense** n prudenza f (per strada). **roadshow** n (play, show) spettacolo m di tournée; (publicity tour) giro m promozionale. **roadside** n bordo m della strada. **road sign** cartello m stradale. **road surface** n fondo m stradale. **road sweeper** n (person) spazzino, -a nmf; (machine) autospazzatrice f. **road tax** n tassa f di circolazione. **roadway** n carreggiata f, corsia f. **roadworks** npl lavori mpl stradali. **roadworthy** a sicuro

roam /rəʊm/ vi girovagare

roar /rɔ:(r)/ n ruggito m; ~**s of laughter** scroscio msg di risa ● vi ruggire; ⟨lorry, thunder:⟩ rombare; ~ **with laughter** ridere fragorosamente

■ **roar out** vt gridare

■ **roar past** vi (move noisily) passare rombando

roaring /'rɔ:rɪŋ/ a **do a ~ trade** fam fare affari d'oro ● adv ~ **drunk** fam ubriaco fradicio

roast /rəʊst/ a arrosto; ~ **pork** arrosto m di maiale ● n arrosto m ● vt arrostire ⟨meat⟩ ● vi arrostirsi

roasting [**hot**] /'rəʊstɪŋ/ a fam caldissimo

roasting pan n teglia f per arrosti

rob /rɒb/ vt (pt/pp robbed) derubare (of di); svaligiare ⟨bank⟩

robber /'rɒbə(r)/ n rapinatore m

robbery /'rɒbərɪ/ n rapina f

robe /rəʊb/ n tunica f; (Am: bathrobe) accappatoio m

robin /'rɒbɪn/ n pettirosso m

robot /'rəʊbɒt/ n robot m inv

robotic /rəʊ'bɒtɪk/ a ⟨movement, voice⟩ robotico; ⟨tool, device, machine⟩ robotizzato

robotics n robotica f

robust /rəʊ'bʌst/ a robusto

rock[1] /rɒk/ n roccia f; (in sea) scoglio m; (sweet) zucchero m candito; **on the ~s** ⟨ship⟩ incagliato; ⟨marriage⟩ finito; ⟨drink⟩ con ghiaccio

rock[2] vt cullare ⟨baby⟩; (shake) far traballare; (shock) scuotere ● vi dondolarsi

rock[3] n Mus rock m

rock: rock and roll n rock and roll m. **rock-bottom** a bassissimo ● n livello m più basso; **hit ~** toccare il fondo. **rock-climber** n scalatore, -trice nmf. **rock-climbing** n roccia f

rockery /'rɒkərɪ/ n giardino m roccioso

rocket /'rɒkɪt/ n razzo m; **give sb a ~** fam fare un cicchetto a qcno ● vi salire alle stelle

rocket launcher /'lɔ:ntʃə(r)/ n lanciarazzi m inv

rock face n parete f rocciosa

rocking chair /'rɒkɪŋ/ n sedia f a dondolo

rocking horse n cavallo m a dondolo

rocky /'rɒkɪ/ a (-ier, -iest) roccioso; fig traballante

rod /rɒd/ n bacchetta f; (for fishing) canna f

rode /rəʊd/ see **ride**

rodent /'rəʊdnt/ n roditore m

roe[1] /rəʊ/ n uova fpl di pesce; (soft) latte m di pesce

roe[2] n (pl roe or roes) ~[-deer] capriolo m

roebuck /'rəʊbʌk/ n capriolo m maschio

roger /'rɒdʒə(r)/ int Teleph ricevuto

rogue /rəʊg/ n farabutto m

role /rəʊl/ n ruolo m

role model n Psych modello m comportamentale

role-play, role-playing /'rəʊlpleɪŋ/ n Psych role playing m inv

roll /rəʊl/ n rotolo m; (bread) panino m; (list) lista f; (of ship, drum) rullio m ● vi rotolare; **be ~ing in money** fam nuotare nell'oro ● vt spianare ⟨lawn, pastry⟩; ~**ed into one** allo stesso tempo

■ **roll back** vt ridurre ⟨prices⟩

■ **roll by** vi ⟨time:⟩ passare

■ **roll in** vi (fam: arrive in large quantities) arrivare a valanghe; (arrive) arrivare

■ **roll on** vi ~ **on Friday!** non vedo l'ora che sia venerdì!

■ **roll over** vi rigirarsi; (fam: capitulate) arrendersi

■ **roll up** vt arrotolare; rimboccarsi ⟨sleeves⟩ ● vi fam arrivare

roll-call n appello m

roller /'rəʊlə(r)/ n rullo m; (for hair) bigodino m

roller: rollerblade n pattino m a rotelle in linea ● vi pattinare (con pattini in linea).
roller blind n tapparella f. **roller coaster** n montagne fpl russe. **roller skate** n pattino m a rotelle

rollicking /'rɒlɪkɪŋ/ a **have a ~ time** divertirsi da pazzi

rolling /'rəʊlɪŋ/: **rolling pin** n mattarello m. **rolling stock** n materiale m rotabile. **rolling stone** n fig vagabondo, -a mf

roll: rollneck n collo m alto; (whole sweater) dolcevita f. **roll-on** n (deodorant) deodorante m a sfera. **roll-on roll-off ferry** n traghetto m roll-on roll-off

ROM /rɒm/ n Comput ROM f inv

Roman /'rəʊmən/ a (also print) romano ● n romano, -a mf

Roman Catholic a & n cattolico, -a mf

romance /rəʊ'mæns/ n (love-affair) storia f d'amore; (book) romanzo m rosa

Romania /rəʊ'meɪnɪə/ n Romania f

Romanian /rəʊ'meɪnɪən/ a & n rumeno, -a mf; (language) rumeno m

roman numeral n numero m romano

romantic /rəʊ'mæntɪk/ a romantico

romantically /rəʊ'mæntɪklɪ/ adv romanticamente

romanticism /rəʊ'mæntɪsɪzm/ n romanticismo m

romanticize /rəʊ'mæntɪsaɪz/ vt romanticizzare

romanticized /rəʊ'mæntɪsaɪzd/ a romanzato

Rome /rəʊm/ n Roma f

Romeo /'rəʊmɪəʊ/ n (fam: ladykiller) dongiovanni m inv

romp /rɒmp/ n gioco m rumoroso ● vi giocare rumorosamente

■ **romp home** vi (win easily) vincere senza difficoltà

■ **romp through** vt fam passare senza difficoltà (exam) ● vi riuscire senza difficoltà

rompers /'rɒmpəz/ npl pagliaccetto msg

roof /ru:f/ n tetto m; (of mouth) palato m; **live under one ~** vivere sotto lo stesso tetto; **go through the ~** (fam: increase) andare alle stelle; (be very angry) andare su tutte le furie ● vt mettere un tetto su

roof-rack n portabagagli m inv

rooftop /'ru:ftɒp/ n tetto m; **shout it from the ~s** fig gridarlo ai quattro venti

rook /rʊk/ n corvo m; (in chess) torre f ● vt (fam: swindle) fregare

rookie /'rʊkɪ/ n Am fam novellino, -a mf

room /ru:m/ n stanza f; (bedroom) camera f; (for functions) sala f; (space) spazio m

room: room-mate n (Am: flatmate) compagno, -a mf di appartamento; (in same room) compagno, -a mf di stanza. **room service** n servizio m in camera. **room temperature** n temperatura f ambiente

roomy /'ru:mɪ/ a spazioso; (clothes) ampio

roost /ru:st/ n posatoio m ● vi appollaiarsi

rooster /'ru:stə(r)/ n gallo m

root¹ /ru:t/ n radice f; **take ~** metter radici; **put down ~s** fig metter radici ● vi metter radici

root² vi **~ about** grufolare; **~ for sb** Am fam fare il tifo per qcno

■ **root out** vt fig scovare

rope /rəʊp/ n corda f; **know the ~s** fam conoscere i trucchi del mestiere

■ **rope in** vt fam coinvolgere

rope ladder n scala f di corda

ropey /'rəʊpɪ/ a Br fam scadente; **feel ~** sentirsi poco bene

rosary /'rəʊzərɪ/ n rosario m

rose¹ /rəʊz/ n rosa f; (of watering-can) bocchetta f

rose² see **rise**

rosé /'rəʊzeɪ/ n [vino m] rosé m inv

rosebud /'rəʊzbʌd/ n bocciolo m di rosa

rosehip /'rəʊzhɪp/ n frutto m della rosa canina

rosemary /'rəʊzmərɪ/ n rosmarino m

rose-tinted spectacles /'rəʊztɪntɪd/ npl **wear ~** vedere tutto rosa

rosette /rəʊ'zet/ n coccarda f

roster /'rɒstə(r)/ n tabella f dei turni

rostrum /'rɒstrəm/ n podio m

rosy /'rəʊzɪ/ a (-ier, -iest) roseo

rot /rɒt/ n marciume m; (fam: nonsense) sciocchezze fpl ● vi (pt/pp **rotted**) marcire

rota /'rəʊtə/ n tabella f dei turni

rotary /'rəʊtərɪ/ a rotante

rotate /rəʊ'teɪt/ vt far ruotare; avvicendare (crops) ● vi ruotare

rotation /rəʊ'teɪʃn/ n rotazione f; **in ~** a turno

rote /rəʊt/ n **by ~** meccanicamente

rotten /'rɒtn/ a marcio; fam schifoso; (person) penoso

rotund /rəʊ'tʌnd/ a paffuto

rotunda /rəʊ'tʌndə/ n rotonda f

rouble /'ru:bl/ n rublo m

rough /rʌf/ a (not smooth) ruvido; (ground) accidentato; (behaviour) rozzo; (sport) violento; (area) malfamato; (crossing, time) brutto; (estimate) approssimativo ● adv (play) grossolanamente; **sleep ~** dormire sotto i ponti ● n **do sth in ~** far qcsa alla bell'e meglio ● vt **~ it** vivere senza comfort

■ **rough out** vt abbozzare

■ **rough up** vt fam malmenare (person)

roughage /'rʌfɪdʒ/ n fibre fpl

rough: rough-and-ready a (person, manner) sbrigativo; (conditions, method) rudimentale. **rough-and-tumble** n (rough play) zuffa f. **rough copy** n brutta copia f. **rough draft** n abbozzo m

roughen /'rʌfən/ vt rendere ruvido (surface)

roughly /'rʌflɪ/ adv rozzamente; (more or less) pressappoco

roughness /'rʌfnɪs/ n ruvidità f; (of behaviour) rozzezza f

rough paper n carta f da brutta

roughshod /'rʌfʃɒd/ adv **ride ~ over** infischiarsi di ⟨person, objection⟩; calpestare ⟨feelings⟩

roulette /ruːˈlet/ n roulette f

round /raʊnd/ a rotondo ● n tondo m; (slice) fetta f; (of visits, drinks) giro m; (of competition) partita f; (boxing) ripresa f, round m inv; **do one's ~s** ⟨doctor:⟩ fare il giro delle visite ● prep intorno a; **open ~ the clock** aperto ventiquattr'ore ● adv **all ~** tutt'intorno; **ask sb ~** invitare qcno; **go/come ~ to** (a friend etc) andare da; **turn/look ~** girarsi; **~ about** (approximately) intorno a ● vt arrotondare; girare ⟨corner⟩

■ **round down** vt arrotondare (per difetto)

■ **round off** vt (end) terminare

■ **round on** vt aggredire

■ **round up** vt radunare; arrotondare ⟨prices⟩

roundabout /ˈraʊndəbaʊt/ a indiretto ● n giostra f; (for traffic) rotonda f

round: round bracket n parentesi f tonda. **round figure** n cifra f tonda. **round robin** n petizione f

rounders /ˈraʊndəz/ n Br Sport gioco m simile al baseball

round: round-shouldered /-ˈʃəʊldəd/ a con le spalle curve. **round table** n tavola f rotonda. **round the clock** adv 24 ore su 24. **round-the-clock** a ⟨Br: care, surveillance⟩ ventiquattr'ore su ventiquattro. **round trip** n viaggio m di andata e ritorno. **round-up** n (of suspects) retata f; (of cattle) raduno m; (summary) riepilogo m

rouse /raʊz/ vt svegliare; risvegliare ⟨suspicion, interest⟩

rousing /ˈraʊzɪŋ/ a ⟨speech⟩ che solleva il morale; ⟨music⟩ trionfale

rout /raʊt/ vt Mil, fig sbaragliare ● n disfatta f

route /ruːt/ n itinerario m; Naut, Aeron rotta f; (of bus) percorso m

routine /ruːˈtiːn/ a di routine ● n routine f inv; Theat numero m

routinely /ruːˈtiːnlɪ/ adv d'ufficio

rove /rəʊv/ vi girovagare

roving /ˈrəʊvɪŋ/ a ⟨reporter, ambassador⟩ itinerante

roving eye n **have a ~** essere sempre in cerca di avventure amorose

row[1] /rəʊ/ n (line) fila f; **three years in a ~** tre anni di fila

row[2] vi (in boat) remare ● vt **~ a boat** remare

row[3] /raʊ/ n fam (quarrel) litigata f; (noise) baccano m; **we've had a ~** abbiamo litigato ● vi fam litigare

rowboat /ˈrəʊbəʊt/ n Am barca f a remi

rowdy /ˈraʊdɪ/ a (-ier, -iest) chiassoso ● n attaccabrighe m inv

rower /ˈrəʊə(r)/ n rematore, -trice mf

rowing boat /ˈrəʊɪŋ/ n barca f a remi

rowing machine n vogatore m

rowlock /ˈrɒlək/ n Br scalmo m

royal /ˈrɔɪəl/ a reale ● n membro m della famiglia reale

royally /ˈrɔɪəlɪ/ adv regalmente

royalties /ˈrɔɪəltɪz/ npl (payments) diritti mpl d'autore

royalty /ˈrɔɪəltɪ/ n appartenenza f alla famiglia reale; (persons) i membri della famiglia reale

rpm abbr (**revolutions per minute**) giri mpl al minuto

rub /rʌb/ n sfregata f ● vt (pt/pp **rubbed**) sfregare; **~ one's hands** fregarsi le mani

■ **rub along** vi sopportarsi [a vicenda]

■ **rub down** vt frizionare ⟨person, body⟩; levigare ⟨wood⟩

■ **rub in** vt far assorbire (massaggiando) ⟨cream⟩; **don't ~ it in** fam non rigirare il coltello nella piaga

■ **rub off** vt mandar via sfregando ⟨stain⟩; (from blackboard) cancellare ● vi andar via; **~ off on** essere trasmesso a

■ **rub out** vt cancellare

■ **rub up** vt **~ sb up the wrong way** prendere qcno per il verso sbagliato

rubber /ˈrʌbə(r)/ n gomma f; (eraser) gomma f [da cancellare]

rubber: rubber band n elastico m. **rubber bullet** n proiettile m di gomma. **rubberneck** n fam (onlooker) curioso, -a mf; (tourist) turista mf. **rubber plant** n ficus m inv. **rubber-stamp** vt fig approvare senza discutere

rubbery /ˈrʌbərɪ/ a gommoso

rubbish /ˈrʌbɪʃ/ n immondizie fpl; (fam: nonsense) idiozie fpl; (fam: junk) robaccia f ● vt fam fare a pezzi

rubbish bin n pattumiera f

rubbish dump n discarica f; (official) discarica f comunale

rubbishy /ˈrʌbɪʃɪ/ a fam schifoso

rubble /ˈrʌbl/ n macerie fpl

rub-down n strofinata f

rubella /ruˈbelə/ n rosolia f

rubric /ˈruːbrɪk/ n rubrica f

ruby /ˈruːbɪ/ n rubino m ● attrib di rubini; ⟨lips⟩ scarlatta

rucksack /ˈrʌksæk/ n zaino m

ructions /ˈrʌkʃ(ə)nz/ npl fam finimondo msg; **there'll be ~ if he finds out** se lo scopre, succede il finimondo

rudder /ˈrʌdə(r)/ n timone m

ruddy /ˈrʌdɪ/ a (-ier, -iest) rubicondo; fam maledetto

rude /ruːd/ a scortese; (improper) spinto

rudely /ˈruːdlɪ/ adv scortesemente

rudeness /ˈruːdnɪs/ n scortesia f

rudimentary /ruːdɪˈmentərɪ/ a rudimentale

rudiments /ˈruːdɪmənts/ npl rudimenti mpl

rue[1] /ruː/ vt pentirsi di ⟨decision⟩; **~ the day** maledire il giorno

rue[2] n Bot ruta f

rueful /ˈruːfl/ a rassegnato

ruefully /ˈruːfʊlɪ/ adv con rassegnazione

ruffian /ˈrʌfɪən/ n farabutto m

ruffle /ˈrʌfl/ n gala f ● vt scompigliare ⟨hair⟩

rug /rʌg/ n tappeto m; (blanket) coperta f

rugby /ˈrʌgbɪ/ n ~ [**football**] rugby m

rugby league n rugby m a tredici

rugby union n rugby m a quindici

rugged /ˈrʌgɪd/ a ⟨coastline⟩ roccioso; ⟨face, personality⟩ duro

ruin /'ruːɪn/ *n* rovina *f*; **in ~s** in rovina ● *vt* rovinare

ruined /'ruːɪnd/ *a* ⟨*building, clothes*⟩ rovinato

ruinous /'ruːɪnəs/ *a* estremamente costoso

rule /ruːl/ *n* regola *f*; ⟨*control*⟩ ordinamento *m*; ⟨*for measuring*⟩ metro *m*; **~s** *pl* regolamento *msg*; **as a ~** generalmente; **make it a ~ to do sth** fare qcsa sistematicamente ● *vt* governare; dominare ⟨*colony, behaviour*⟩; **~ that** stabilire che ● *vi* governare

■ **rule out** *vt* escludere

ruled /ruːld/ *a* ⟨*paper*⟩ a righe

rule of thumb *n* principio *m* empirico

ruler /'ruːlə(r)/ *n* capo *m* di Stato; ⟨*sovereign*⟩ sovrano, -a *mf*; ⟨*measure*⟩ righello *m*, regolo *m*

ruling /'ruːlɪŋ/ *a* ⟨*class*⟩ dirigente; ⟨*party*⟩ di governo ● *n* decisione *f*

rum[1] /rʌm/ *n* rum *m inv*

rum[2] *a* ⟨*fam: peculiar*⟩ curioso

rumble /'rʌmbl/ *n* rombo *m*; ⟨*of stomach*⟩ brontolio *m* ● *vi* rombare; ⟨*stomach:*⟩ brontolare

rumble strip *n* banda *f* rumorosa

rumbustious /rʌm'bʌstʃəs/ *a* ⟨*noisy, very lively*⟩ chiassoso

ruminant /'ruːmɪnənt/ *n* ruminante *m*

ruminate /'ruːmɪneɪt/ *vi* ⟨*animals:*⟩ ruminare; ⟨*think*⟩ rimuginare

rummage /'rʌmɪdʒ/ *vi* rovistare (**in/ through** in)

rummy /'rʌmɪ/ *n* ramino *m*

rumour /'ruːmə(r)/ *n* diceria *f* ● *vt* **it is ~ed that** si dice che

rumour-monger /'ruːməmʌŋgə(r)/ *n* persona *f* che sparge pettegolezzi

rump /rʌmp/ *n* natiche *fpl*

rumple /'rʌmpl/ *vt* sgualcire ⟨*clothes, sheets, papers*⟩; scompigliare ⟨*hair*⟩

rump steak *n* bistecca *f* di girello

rumpus /'rʌmpəs/ *n fam* baccano *m*

run /rʌn/ *n* ⟨*on foot*⟩ corsa *f*; ⟨*distance to be covered*⟩ tragitto *m*; ⟨*outing*⟩ giro *m*; *Theat* rappresentazioni *fpl*; ⟨*in skiing*⟩ pista *f*; ⟨*Am: ladder*⟩ smagliatura *f* ⟨*in calze*⟩; **at a ~** di corsa; **~ of bad luck** periodo *m* sfortunato; **on the ~** in fuga; **have the ~ of** avere a disposizione; **in the long ~** a lungo termine ● *v* (*pt* **ran**, *pp* **run**, *pres p* **running**) ● *vi* correre; ⟨*river:*⟩ scorrere; ⟨*nose, makeup:*⟩ colare; ⟨*bus:*⟩ fare servizio; ⟨*play:*⟩ essere in cartellone; ⟨*colours:*⟩ sbiadire; ⟨*in election*⟩ presentarsi [come candidato]; ⟨*software:*⟩ girare; **~ aground** insabbiarsi; **~ low on, ~ short of** essere a corto di ● *vt* ⟨*manage*⟩ dirigere; tenere ⟨*house*⟩; ⟨*drive*⟩ dare un passaggio a; correre ⟨*risk*⟩; *Comput* lanciare; *Journ* pubblicare ⟨*article*⟩; ⟨*pass*⟩ far scorrere ⟨*eyes, hand*⟩; **~ a temperature** avere la febbre; **~ a bath** far scorrere l'acqua per il bagno

■ **run about** *vi* ⟨*children:*⟩ correre di qua e di là; ⟨*be busy*⟩ correre

■ **run across** *vt* imbattersi in

■ **run after** *vt* ⟨*chase*⟩ rincorrere; ⟨*romantically*⟩ andare dietro a

■ **run along** *vi* ⟨*go away*⟩ andare via

■ **run away** *vi* scappare [via], andare via di corsa; ⟨*from home*⟩ scappare di casa

■ **run away with** *vt* scappare con ⟨*lover, money*⟩; **she let her enthusiasm ~ away with her** si è lasciata trasportare dall'entusiasmo

■ **run back** *vi* correre indietro ● *vt* ⟨*transport by car*⟩ riaccompagnare

■ **run back over** *vt* ⟨*review*⟩ rivedere

■ **run down** *vi* ⟨*clock:*⟩ scaricarsi; ⟨*stocks:*⟩ esaurirsi ● *vt Auto* investire; ⟨*reduce*⟩ esaurire; ⟨*fam: criticize*⟩ denigrare

■ **run in** *vi* entrare di corsa

■ **run into** *vi* ⟨*meet*⟩ imbattersi in; ⟨*knock against*⟩ urtare

■ **run off** *vi* scappare [via], andare via di corsa; ⟨*from home*⟩ scappare di casa ● *vt* stampare ⟨*copies*⟩

■ **run off with** *vt* = **run away with**

■ **run on** *vi* ⟨*meeting:*⟩ protrarsi; ⟨*person:*⟩ chiacchierare senza sosta

■ **run out** *vi* uscire di corsa; ⟨*supplies, money:*⟩ esaurirsi; **~ out of** rimanere senza

■ **run over** *vi* correre; ⟨*overflow*⟩ traboccare ● *vt* ⟨*review*⟩ dare una scorsa a; *Auto* investire

■ **run through** *vt* ⟨*use up*⟩ fare fuori; ⟨*be present in*⟩ pervadere; ⟨*review*⟩ dare una scorsa a

■ **run to** *vt* ⟨*be enough for*⟩ essere sufficiente per; ⟨*have enough money for*⟩ potersi permettere

■ **run up** *vi* salire di corsa; ⟨*towards*⟩ arrivare di corsa ● *vt* accumulare ⟨*debts, bill*⟩; ⟨*sew*⟩ cucire

■ **run up against** *vt* incontrare ⟨*difficulties*⟩

run: **runabout** *n* ⟨*vehicle*⟩ utilitaria *f*. **runaround** *n* **he's giving me/her the ~** mi/la sta menando per il naso. **runaway** *n* fuggitivo, -a *mf*, fuggiasco, -a *mf*; ⟨*child*⟩ ragazzo, -a *mf* scappato, -a di casa ● *a* ⟨*person*⟩ in fuga; ⟨*child*⟩ scappato di casa; ⟨*inflation*⟩ galoppante; ⟨*success*⟩ eclatante. **run-down** *a* ⟨*area*⟩ in abbandono; ⟨*person*⟩ esaurito ● *n* analisi *f*

rung[1] /rʌŋ/ *n* ⟨*of ladder*⟩ piolo *m*

rung[2] *see* **ring**[2]

run-in *n* ⟨*fam: argument*⟩ lite *f*

runner /'rʌnə(r)/ *n* podista *mf*; ⟨*in race*⟩ corridore, -trice *mf*; ⟨*on sledge*⟩ pattino *f*; ⟨*carpet*⟩ guida *f*

runner bean *n* fagiolino *m*

runner-up *n* secondo, -a classificato, -a *mf*

running /'rʌnɪŋ/ *a* in corsa; ⟨*water*⟩ corrente; **four times ~** quattro volte di seguito ● *n* corsa *f*; ⟨*management*⟩ direzione *f*; **be in the ~** essere in lizza

running commentary *n* cronaca *f*

runny /'rʌnɪ/ *a* semiliquido; **~ nose** naso *m* che cola

run-of-the-mill *a* ordinario

runs /rʌnz/ *npl* **the ~** ⟨*fam: diarrhoea*⟩ la sciolta

runt /rʌnt/ *n* ⟨*of litter*⟩ animale *m* più piccolo

e debole di una figliata; (*pej: weakling*) mezza cartuccia *f*

run-through *n* prova *f* generale

run-up *n Sport* rincorsa *f*; **the ~ to** il periodo precedente

runway /'rʌnweɪ/ *n* pista *f*

rupee /ru:'pi:/ *n* rupia *f*

rupture /'rʌptʃə(r)/ *n* rottura *f*; *Med* ernia *f* ● *vt* rompere; **~ oneself** farsi venire l'ernia ● *vi* rompersi

rural /'rʊərəl/ *a* rurale

ruse /ru:z/ *n* astuzia *f*

rush¹ /rʌʃ/ *n Bot* giunco *m*

rush² *n* fretta *f*; **in a ~** di fretta ● *vi* precipitarsi ● *vt* far premura a; **~ sb to hospital** trasportare qcno di corsa all'ospedale

■ **rush away, rush off** *vi* andar via in fretta

rush hour *n* ora *f* di punta ● *attrib* delle ore di punta

rusk /rʌsk/ *n* biscotto *m*

Russia /'rʌʃə/ *n* Russia *f*

Russian /'rʌʃən/ *a* & *n* russo, -a *mf*; (*language*) russo *m*

Russian roulette *n* roulette *f* russa

rust /rʌst/ *n* ruggine *f* ● *vi* arrugginirsi ● *vt* arruginire

rustic /'rʌstɪk/ *a* rustico

rustle /'rʌsl/ *vi* frusciare ● *vt* far frusciare; *Am* rubare ⟨*cattle*⟩

■ **rustle up** *vt fam* fare ⟨*meal, cup of coffee*⟩

rustler /'rʌslə(r)/ *n* ladro *m* di bestiame

rustproof /'rʌstpru:f/ *a* a prova di ruggine

rusty /'rʌstɪ/ *a* (**-ier, -iest**) arrugginito

rut /rʌt/ *n* solco *m*; **in a ~** *fam* nella routine

ruthless /'ru:θlɪs/ *a* spietato

ruthlessly /'ru:θlɪslɪ/ *adv* spietatamente

ruthlessness /'ru:θlɪsnɪs/ *n* spietatezza *f*

rutting /'rʌtɪŋ/ *n* accoppiamento *m*

rutting season *n* stagione *f* degli amori

rye /raɪ/ *n* segale *f*

Ss

s, S /es/ *n* (*letter*) s, S *f inv*

S *abbr* **small**; *abbr* (**south**) S

sabbath /'sæbəθ/ *n* domenica *f*; (*Jewish*) sabato *m*

sabbatical /sə'bætɪkl/ *n Univ* anno *m* sabbatico

sable /'seɪbl/ *n* (*animal, fur*) zibellino *m*

sabotage /'sæbətɑ:ʒ/ *n* sabotaggio *m* ● *vt* sabotare

saboteur /sæbə'tɜ:(r)/ *n* sabotatore, -trice *mf*

sabre /'seɪbə(r)/ *n* sciabola *f*

sac /sæk/ *n Anat, Zool* sacco *m*; *Bot* sacca *f*; **honey ~** cestella *f*

saccharin /'sækərɪn/ *n* saccarina *f*

sachet /'sæʃeɪ/ *n* bustina *f*; (*scented*) sacchetto *m* profumato

sack¹ /sæk/ *vt* (*plunder*) saccheggiare

sack² *n* sacco *m*; **get the ~** *fam* essere licenziato; **give sb the ~** licenziare qcno ● *vt fam* licenziare

sackcloth /'sækklɒθ/ *n* tela *f* di sacco; **wear ~ and ashes** cospargersi il capo di cenere

sackful /'sækfʊl/ *n* sacco *m* (*contenuto*)

sacking /'sækɪŋ/ *n* tela *f* per sacchi; (*fam: dismissal*) licenziamento *m*

sackload /'sækləʊd/ *n* sacco *m* (*contenuto*)

sacrament /'sækrəmənt/ *n* sacramento *m*

sacred /'seɪkrɪd/ *a* sacro

sacred cow /kaʊ/ *n* (*institution*) istituzione *f* intoccabile; (*principle*) principio *m* inderogabile; (*person*) mostro *m* sacro

sacrifice /'sækrɪfaɪs/ *n* sacrificio *m* ● *vt* sacrificare; **~ oneself** immolarsi

sacrificial /sækrɪ'fɪʃl/ *a* ⟨*victim*⟩ sacrificale

sacrilege /'sækrɪlɪdʒ/ *n* sacrilegio *m*

sacrilegious /sækrɪ'lɪdʒəs/ *a* sacrilego

sacristy /'sækrɪstɪ/ *n* sagrestia *f*

sacrosanct /'sækrəʊsæŋkt/ *a* sacrosanto

sacrum /'sækrʌm/ *n Anat* osso *m* sacro

sad /sæd/ *a* (**sadder, saddest**) triste

sadden /'sædn/ *vt* rattristare

saddle /'sædl/ *n* sella *f*; **be in the ~** *fig* tenere le redini ● *vt* sellare; **I've been ~d with...** *fig* mi hanno affibbiato...

sadism /'seɪdɪzm/ *n* sadismo *m*

sadist /'seɪdɪst/ *n* sadico, -a *mf*

sadistic /sə'dɪstɪk/ *a* sadico

sadistically /sə'dɪstɪklɪ/ *adv* sadicamente

sadly /'sædlɪ/ *adv* tristemente; (*unfortunately*) sfortunatamente

sadness /'sædnɪs/ *n* tristezza *f*

sadomasochism /seɪdəʊ'mæsəkɪzm/ *n* sadomasochismo *m*

sadomasochist /seɪdəʊ'mæsəkɪst/ *n* sadomasochismo *m*

sadomasochistic /seɪdəʊ'mæsəkɪstɪk/ *a* sadomasochistico

sae *abbr* **stamped addressed envelope**

safari /sə'fɑ:rɪ/ *n* safari *m inv*

safari park *n* zoosafari *m inv*

safe /seɪf/ *a* sicuro; (*out of danger*) salvo; ⟨*object*⟩ al sicuro; **~ and sound** sano e salvo ● *n* cassaforte *f*

safe-breaker *n* scassinatore, -trice *mf*.

safeguard *n* protezione *f* ● *vt* proteggere. **safe keeping** *n* custodia *f*; **for ~ ~** in custodia

safely /'seɪflɪ/ *adv* in modo sicuro; ⟨*arrive*⟩ senza incidenti; ⟨*assume*⟩ con certezza

safe sex n sesso m sicuro
safety /'seɪftɪ/ n sicurezza f
safety: safety belt n cintura f di sicurezza.
safety catch n sicura f. **safety curtain** n
tagliafuoco m. **safety-deposit box** n cassetta f di sicurezza. **safety glass** n vetro m di
sicurezza. **safety net** n (for acrobat) rete f di
protezione; fig protezione. **safety pin** n spilla
f di sicurezza o da balia. **safety razor** n rasoio m di sicurezza. **safety valve** n valvola f di
sicurezza; fig valvola f di sfogo
saffron /'sæfrən/ n zafferano m
sag /sæg/ vi (pt/pp **sagged**) abbassarsi
saga /'sɑːgə/ n saga f
sagacity /sə'gæsətɪ/ n sagacia f
sage¹ /seɪdʒ/ n (herb) salvia f
sage² a & n saggio, -a mf
sagely /'seɪdʒlɪ/ adv (reply, nod) saggiamente
Sagittarius /sædʒɪ'teərɪəs/ n Sagittario m
sago /'seɪgəʊ/ n sagù m
Sahara /sə'hɑːrə/ n Sahara m
said /sed/ see **say**
sail /seɪl/ n vela f; (trip) giro m in barca a vela
● vi navigare; Sport praticare la vela; (leave)
salpare ● vt pilotare
■ **sail through** vt superare senza problemi
(exam)
sailboard /'seɪlbɔːd/ n tavola f del windsurf
sailboarding /'seɪlbɔːdɪŋ/ n windsurf m inv
sailboat /'seɪlbəʊt/ n Am barca f a vela
sailing /'seɪlɪŋ/ n vela f
sailing boat n barca f a vela
sailing ship n veliero m
sailor /'seɪlə(r)/ n marinaio m
saint /seɪnt/ n santo, -a mf
sainthood /'seɪnthʊd/ n santità f
saintly /'seɪntlɪ/ a da santo
sake /seɪk/ n **for the ~ of** (person) per il
bene di; (peace) per amor di; **for the ~ of it**
per il gusto di farlo
salacious /sə'leɪʃəs/ a (joke) salace; (book)
licenzioso; (look) lascivo
salad /'sæləd/ n insalata f
salad: salad bar n tavola f fredda. **salad
bowl** n insalatiera f. **salad cream** n salsa f
per condire l'insalata. **salad days** npl anni
mpl verdi. **salad dressing** n condimento m
per insalata
salami /sə'lɑːmɪ/ n salame m
salaried /'sælərɪd/ a stipendiato
salary /'sælərɪ/ n stipendio m
salary review n revisione f dello stipendio
salary scale n tabella f retributiva
sale /seɪl/ n vendita f; (at reduced prices)
svendita f; **for/on ~** in vendita; **'for ~'**
'vendesi'
sales: sales and marketing n vendite fpl e
marketing. **sales and marketing department** n ufficio m vendite e marketing. **sales
assistant** n commesso, -a mf. **sales director** n capo mf dell'ufficio vendite. **sales engineer** n tecnico m commerciale. **sales figures** npl volumi mpl d'affari. **sales force** n
rappresentanti mpl. **sales invoice** n fattura f
di vendita. **sales ledger** n partitario m

vendite. **salesman** n venditore m; (traveller)
rappresentante m. **salesroom** n (for auc-
tions) sala f d'aste. **sales team** n team m inv
vendite. **saleswoman** n venditrice f
salient /'seɪlɪənt/ a saliente
saline /'seɪlaɪn/ a salino
saliva /sə'laɪvə/ n saliva f
salivary glands /sə'laɪvərɪ/ npl ghiandole
fpl salivari
salivate /'sælɪveɪt/ vi salivare; **the smell of
chicken roasting makes me ~** l'odore di
pollo arrosto mi fa venire l'acquolina in bocca
sallow /'sæləʊ/ a giallastro
sally /'sælɪ/ n (witty remark) battuta f; Mil
sortita f ● vi saltar fuori
salmon /'sæmən/ n salmone m
salmonella /sælmə'nelə/ n salmonella f
salmon-pink a [rosa inv] salmone inv
salmon trout n trota f salmonata
salon /'sælɒn/ n salone m
saloon /sə'luːn/ n Auto berlina f; (Am: bar)
bar m
salsa /'sælsə/ n salsa f
salt /sɔːlt/ n sale m ● a salato; (fish, meat)
sotto sale ● vt salare; (cure) mettere sotto
sale
salt cellar n saliera f
saltiness /'sɔːltɪnɪs/ n salinità f
salt water n acqua f di mare
salt-water fish n pesce m d'acqua salata
salty /'sɔːltɪ/ a salato
salubrious /sə'luːbrɪəs/ a (neighbourhood)
raccomandabile; **it's not a very ~ area** è
una zona poco raccomandabile
salutary /'sæljʊtərɪ/ a salutare
salute /sə'luːt/ Mil n saluto m ● vt salutare
● vi fare il saluto
salvage /'sælvɪdʒ/ n Naut recupero m ● vt
recuperare
salvation /sæl'veɪʃn/ n salvezza f
Salvation Army n Esercito m della Salvezza
salve /sælv/ vt **~ one's conscience** mettersi la coscienza a posto
salver /'sælvə(r)/ n vassoio m (di metallo)
salvo /'sælvəʊ/ n salva f
samba /'sæmbə/ n samba f
same /seɪm/ a stesso (as di) ● pron **the ~** lo
stesso; **be all the ~** essere tutti uguali ● adv
the ~ nello stesso modo; **all the ~** (however)
lo stesso; **the ~ to you** altrettanto
same-day delivery n consegna f in giornata
sample /'sɑːmpl/ n campione m ● vt testare
sanatorium /sænə'tɔːrɪəm/ n casa f di cura
sanctify /'sæŋktɪfaɪ/ vt (pt/pp **-fied**) santifi-
care
sanctimonious /sæŋktɪ'məʊnɪəs/ a mora-
leggiante
sanction /'sæŋkʃn/ n (approval) autorizzazione f; (penalty) sanzione f ● vt autorizzare
sanctity /'sæŋktətɪ/ n santità f
sanctuary /'sæŋktjʊərɪ/ n Relig santuario
m; (refuge) asilo m; (for wildlife) riserva f
sanctum /'sæŋktəm/ n (holy place) santua-

rio *m*; (*private place*) rifugio *m*; **the inner ~** *Relig* il Sancta Sanctorum

sand /sænd/ *n* sabbia *f* ● *vt* ~ [**down**] carteggiare

sandal /'sændl/ *n* sandalo *m*

sand: sandbag *n* sacchetto *m* di sabbia. **sandbank** *n* banco *m* di sabbia. **sand dune** *n* duna *f*. **sandblast** *vt* sabbiare. **sandblasting** *n* sabbiatura *f*. **sandcastle** *n* castello *m* di sabbia

sander /'sændə(r)/ *n* (*machine*) levigatrice *f*

Sandinista /sændr'ni:stə/ *a* & *n* sandinista

sand: sandpaper *n* carta *f* vetrata ● *vt* cartavetrare. **sandpit** *n* recinto *m* contenente sabbia dove giocano i bambini. **sandstone** *n* arenaria *f*. **sandstorm** *n* tempesta *f* di sabbia

sandwich /'sænwidʒ/ *n* tramezzino *m* ● *vt* ~**ed between** schiacciato tra

sandwich course *n* corso *m* che comprende dei periodi di tirocinio

sandwich-man *n* uomo *m* sandwich

sandy /'sændi/ *a* (**-ier, -iest**) (*beach, soil*) sabbioso; (*hair*) biondiccio

sane /sein/ *a* (*not mad*) sano di mente; (*sensible*) sensato

sang /sæŋ/ *see* **sing**

sangria /sæŋ'griə/ *n* sangria *f*

sanguine /'sæŋgwin/ *a* ottimistico

sanitary /'sænitəri/ *a* igienico; (*system*) sanitario

sanitary napkin *n Am*, **sanitary towel** *n* assorbente *m* igienico

sanitation /sænr'teiʃn/ *n* impianti *mpl* igienici

sanity /'sænəti/ *n* sanità *f* di mente; (*sensibleness*) buon senso *m*

sank /sæŋk/ *see* **sink**

Santa [Claus] /'sæntə[klɔːz]/ *n* Babbo *m* Natale

sap /sæp/ *n Bot* linfa *f* ● *vt* (*pt/pp* **sapped**) indebolire

sapling /'sæpliŋ/ *n* alberello *m*

sapper /'sæpə(r)/ *n Br Mil* geniere *m*

sapphire /'sæfaiə(r)/ *n* zaffiro *m* ● *attrib* blu zaffiro *inv*

sarcasm /'sɑːkæzm/ *n* sarcasmo *m*

sarcastic /sɑː'kæstik/ *a* sarcastico

sarcastically /sɑː'kæstikli/ *adv* sarcasticamente

sarcophagus /sɑː'kɒfəgəs/ *n* sarcofago *m*

sardine /sɑː'diːn/ *n* sardina *f*

Sardinia /sɑː'diniə/ *n* Sardegna *f*

Sardinian /sɑː'diniən/ *a* & *n* sardo, -a *mf*

sardonic /sɑː'dɒnik/ *a* sardonico

sardonically /sɑː'dɒnikli/ *adv* sardonicamente

sari /'sɑːri/ *n* sari *m inv*

sarong /sə'rɒŋ/ *n* pareo *m*

SAS *n Br abbr* (**Special Air Service**) commando *mpl* britannici per operazioni speciali

sash /sæʃ/ *n* fascia *f*; (*for dress*) fusciacca *f*

sashay /'sæʃei/ *vi fam* (*casually*) camminare in modo disinvolto; (*seductively*) camminare in modo provocante

sassy /'sæsi/ *a Am fam* (*cheeky*) sfacciato; (*smart*) chic *inv*

sat /sæt/ *see* **sit**

Satan /'seitən/ *n* Satana *m*

satanic /sə'tænik/ *a* satanico

satchel /'sætʃl/ *n* cartella *f*

sated /'seitid/ *a* (*person*) sazio; (*desire*) appagato; (*appetite*) soddisfatto

satellite /'sætəlait/ *n* satellite *m*

satellite dish *n* antenna *f* parabolica

satellite television *n* televisione *f* via satellite

satiate /'seiʃieit/ *vt* saziare (*person*); appagare (*desire*); soddisfare (*appetite*)

satin /'sætin/ *n* raso *m* ● *attrib* di raso

satire /'sætaiə(r)/ *n* satira *f*

satirical /sə'tirikl/ *a* satirico

satirically /sə'tirikli/ *adv* satiricamente

satirist /'sætərist/ *n* scrittore, -trice *mf* satirico, -a; (*comedian*) comico, -a *mf* satirico, -a

satirize /'sætiraiz/ *vt* satireggiare

satisfaction /sætis'fækʃn/ *n* soddisfazione *f*; **be to sb's ~** soddisfare qcno

satisfactorily /sætis'fækt(ə)rili/ *adv* in modo soddisfacente

satisfactory /sætis'fæktəri/ *a* soddisfacente

satisfy /'sætisfai/ *vt* (*pt/pp* -**ied**) soddisfare; (*convince*) convincere; **be satisfied** essere soddisfatto

satisfying /'sætisfaiiŋ/ *a* soddisfacente

saturate /'sætʃəreit/ *vt* inzuppare (**with** di); *Chem, fig* saturare (**with** di)

saturated /'sætʃəreitid/ *a* saturo

saturation /sætʃə'reiʃn/ *n* **reach ~ point** raggiungere il punto di saturazione

Saturday /'sætədei/ *n* sabato *m*

Saturn /'sætən/ *n* Saturno *m*

sauce /sɔːs/ *n* salsa *f*; (*cheek*) impertinenza *f*

saucepan /'sɔːspən/ *n* pentola *f*

saucer /'sɔːsə(r)/ *n* piattino *m*

saucy /'sɔːsi/ *a* (-**ier, -iest**) impertinente

Saudi /'saudi/ *a* saudita ● *n* (*person*) saudita *mf*; (*country*) Arabia *f* Saudita

Saudi Arabia /ə'reibiə/ *n* Arabia *f* Saudita

Saudi Arabian *a* & *n* saudita *mf*

sauerkraut /'sauəkraut/ *n* crauti *mpl*

sauna /'sɔːnə/ *n* sauna *f*

saunter /'sɔːntə(r)/ *vi* andare a spasso

sausage /'sɒsidʒ/ *n* salsiccia *f*; (*dried*) salame *m*

sausage dog /'sɒsidʒdɒg/ *n fam* bassotto *m*

sausage roll *n* involtino *m* di pasta sfoglia con salsiccia

sauté /'səutei/ *vt* rosolare ● *a* rosolato

savage /'sævidʒ/ *a* feroce; (*tribe, custom*) selvaggio ● *n* selvaggio, -a *mf* ● *vt* fare a pezzi

savagely /'sævidʒli/ *adv* (*attack*) selvaggiamente; (*criticize*) ferocemente

savagery /'sævidʒri/ *n* ferocia *f*

save /seiv/ *n Sport* parata *f* ● *vt* salvare (**from** da); (*keep, collect*) tenere; risparmiare (*time, money*); (*avoid*) evitare; *Sport* parare (*goal*); *Comput* salvare, memorizzare; ~ **face** salvar la faccia ● *vi* ~ [**up**] risparmiare ● *prep* salvo

saver /'seɪvə(r)/ n risparmiatore, -trice mf
saving grace /seɪvɪŋ'greɪs/ n that's his one ~ ~ si salva grazie a questo
savings /'seɪvɪŋz/ npl (money) risparmi mpl
savings: savings account n libretto m di risparmio. **savings and loan association** n Am associazione f mutua di risparmi e presti-ti. **savings bank** n cassa f di risparmio
saviour /'seɪvjə(r)/ n salvatore m
savoir faire /sævwɑ:'feə(r)/ n (social) savoir-faire m
savory /'seɪvərɪ/ n Bot santoreggia f
savour /'seɪvə(r)/ n sapore m ● vt assaporare
savoury /'seɪvərɪ/ a salato; fig rispettabile
saw¹ /sɔː/ see **see¹**
saw² n sega f ● vt (pt sawed, pp sawn or sawed) segare
sawdust /'sɔːdʌst/ n segatura f
sawmill /'sɔːmɪl/ n segheria f
Saxon /'sæksən/ a & n sassone mf; (language) sassone m
saxophone /'sæksəfəʊn/ n sassofono m
saxophonist /sæk'sʊfənɪst/ n sassofonista mf
say /seɪ/ n have one's ~ dire la propria; **have a** ~ avere voce in capitolo ● vt/i (pt/pp said) dire; **that is to** ~ cioè; **that goes without** ~ing suono è ovvio; **when all is said and done** alla fine dei conti; ~ **yes/no** dire di si/no; **just** ~ **the word and I'll come** tu chiama e io vengo. **what more can I** ~? che altro dire?; **some time next week** ~? la prossima settimana, diciamo?; **the clock** ~**s ten to six** la sveglia fa le sei meno dieci; **you can** ~ **that again!** puoi dirlo forte!; **the tree is said to be very old** a quanto pare l'albero è vecchissimo; **he said you were to bring the car** ha detto che dovevi portare la mac-china; **it** ~**s a lot for him that...** il fatto che...la dice lunga sul suo conto; **what have you got to** ~ **for yourself?** che scusa hai?; **to** ~ **nothing of...** per non parlare di...; **what would you** ~ **to a new car?** cosa ne diresti di una macchina nuova?
saying /'seɪɪŋ/ n proverbio m
scab /skæb/ n crosta f; pej crumiro m
scabby /'skæbɪ/ a (plant) coperto di galle; (skin) coperto di croste; (animal) rognoso; (fam: nasty) schifoso
scaffold /'skæfəld/ n patibolo m
scaffolding /'skæfəldɪŋ/ n impalcatura f
scalar /'skeɪlə(r)/ a scalare
scald /skɔːld/ vt scottare; (milk) scaldare ● n scottatura f
scalding /'skɔːldɪŋ/ a bollente
scale¹ /skeɪl/ n (of fish) scaglia f
scale² n scala f; on a grand ~ su vasta sca-le; to ~ in scala; ~ of values scala f di valori ● vt (climb) scalare
■ **scale down** vt diminuire
scale model n modello m in scala
scales /skeɪlz/ npl (for weighing) bilancia fsg
scallop /'skɒləp/ n (in sewing) smerlo m, fe-stone m; Zool pettine m; Culin cappasanta f

● vt (in sewing) smerlare; ~**ed potatoes** pa-tate fpl gratinate
scalp /skælp/ n cuoio m capelluto ● vt scalpare
scalpel /'skælpl/ n bisturi m inv
scaly /'skeɪlɪ/ a (wing, fish) squamoso; (plaster, wall) scrostato
scam /skæm/ n fam fregatura f
scamper /'skæmpə(r)/ vi ~ **away** sgattaio-lare via
scampi /'skæmpɪ/ npl scampi mpl
scan /skæn/ n Med scanning m inv, scansioscintigrafia f ● v (pt/pp scanned) ● vt scrutare; (quickly) dare una scorsa a; Med fare uno scanning di; Comput scannerizzare ● vi (poetry:) scandire
scandal /'skændl/ n scandalo m; (gossip) pettegolezzi mpl
scandalize /'skændəlaɪz/ vt scandalizzare
scandalmonger /'skænd(ə)lmʌŋgə(r)/ n malalingua f
scandalous /'skændələs/ a scandaloso
Scandinavia /skændɪ'neɪvɪə/ n Scandina-via f
Scandinavian /skændɪ'neɪvɪən/ a & n scan-dinavo, -a mf
scanner /'skænə(r)/ n Med, Comput scanner m inv; (radar) antenna f radar; (for bar codes) lettore m di codice a barre
scanning /'skænɪŋ/ n Comput scan-nerizzazione f
scant /skænt/ a a scarso
scantily /'skæntɪlɪ/ adv scarsamente; (clothed) succintamente
scanty /'skæntɪ/ a (-ier, -iest) scarso; (clothing) succinto
scapegoat /'skeɪpgəʊt/ n capro m espia-torio
scar /skɑː(r)/ n cicatrice f ● vt (pt/pp scarred) lasciare una cicatrice a
scar tissue n tessuto m di cicatrizzazione
scarce /skeəs/ a scarso; fig raro; **make oneself** ~ fam svignarsela
scarcely /'skeəslɪ/ adv appena; ~ **anything** quasi niente
scarcity /'skeəsɪtɪ/ n scarsezza f
scare /skeə(r)/ n spavento m; (panic) pani-co m ● vt spaventare; **be** ~**d** aver paura (**of** di)
■ **scare away** vt far scappare
scarecrow /'skeəkrəʊ/ n spaventapasseri m inv
scaremonger /'skeəmʌŋgə(r)/ n allarmis-ta mf
scaremongering /'skeəmʌŋgərɪŋ/ n allar-mismo m
scarf /skɑːf/ n (pl scarves) sciarpa f; (square) foulard m inv
scarlet /'skɑːlət/ a scarlatto
scarlet fever n scarlattina f
scarper /'skɑːpə(r)/ vi Br fam squagliarsela
scary /'skeərɪ/ a be ~ far paura
scathing /'skeɪðɪŋ/ a mordace
scatter /'skætə(r)/ vt spargere; (disperse) di-sperdere ● vi disperdersi

scatterbrained /'skætəbreɪnd/ a fam scervellato

scattered /'skætəd/ a sparso

scatty /'skætɪ/ a (**-ier, -iest**) fam svitato

scavenge /'skævɪndʒ/ vi frugare nella spazzatura

scavenger /'skævɪndʒə(r)/ n persona f che fruga nella spazzatura

scenario /sɪ'nɑ:rɪəʊ/ n scenario m

scene /si:n/ n scena f; (quarrel) scenata f; **behind the ~s** dietro le quinte

scenery /'si:nərɪ/ n scenario m

scenic /'si:nɪk/ a panoramico

scent /sent/ n odore m; (trail) scia f; (perfume) profumo m

scented /'sentɪd/ a profumato (**with** di)

sceptic /'skeptɪk/ n scettico, -a mf

sceptical /'skeptɪkl/ a scettico

sceptically /'skeptɪklɪ/ adv in modo scettico

scepticism /'skeptɪsɪzm/ n scetticismo m

schedule /'ʃedju:l/ n piano m, programma m; (of work) programma m; (Am: timetable) orario m; **behind ~** indietro; **on ~** nei tempi previsti; **according to ~** secondo i tempi previsti ● vt prevedere

scheduled flight /ʃedju:ld'flaɪt/ n volo m di linea

schematic /skɪ'mætɪk/ a schematico

scheme /ski:m/ n (plan) piano m; (plot) macchinazione f ● vi pej macchinare

scheming /'ski:mɪŋ/ n pej macchinazioni fpl, intrighi mpl ● a ⟨person⟩ intrigante

schism /'skɪzm/ n scisma m

schizophrenia /skɪtsə'fri:nɪə/ n schizofrenia f

schizoprenic /skɪtsə'frenɪk/ a schizofrenico

schmaltzy /'ʃmɒltsɪ/ a sdolcinato

scholar /'skɒlə(r)/ n studioso, -a mf

scholarly /'skɒləlɪ/ a erudito

scholarship /'skɒləʃɪp/ n erudizione f; (grant) borsa f di studio

scholastic /skə'læstɪk/ a scolastico

school /sku:l/ n scuola f; (in university) facoltà f; (of fish) branco m ● vt addestrare ⟨animal⟩

school: school age n **of ~ ~** in età scolare. **schoolboy** n scolaro m. **schoolchild** n scolaro, -a mf. **schooldays** npl tempi mpl della scuola. **schoolgirl** n scolara f. **school leaver** n ≈ neo-diplomato, -a mf. **school-leaving age** n età f della scuola dell'obbligo

schooling /'sku:lɪŋ/ n istruzione f

school: schoolmaster n maestro m; (secondary) insegnante m. **schoolmistress** n maestra f; (secondary) insegnante f. **schoolteacher** n insegnante mf

schooner /'sku:nə(r)/ n (Am: glass) boccale m da birra; (Br: glass) grande bicchiere m da sherry; (boat) goletta f

sciatica /saɪ'ætɪkə/ n sciatica f

science /'saɪəns/ n scienza f

science fiction n fantascienza f

scientific /saɪən'tɪfɪk/ a scientifico

scientifically /saɪən'tɪfɪklɪ/ adv scientificamente

scientist /'saɪəntɪst/ n scienziato, -a mf

sci-fi /'saɪfaɪ/ n fam fantascienza f

scintillate /'sɪntɪleɪt/ vi fig brillare

scintillating /'sɪntɪleɪtɪŋ/ a brillante

scissors /'sɪzəz/ npl forbici fpl

scoff¹ /skɒf/ vi **~ at** schernire

scoff² vt fam divorare

scold /skəʊld/ vt sgridare

scolding /'skəʊldɪŋ/ n sgridata f

scollop /'skɒləp/ = **scallop**

scone /skɒn/ n pasticcino m da tè

scoop /sku:p/ n paletta f; Journ scoop m inv ■ **scoop out** vt svuotare ■ **scoop up** vt tirar su

scoot /sku:t/ vi fam filare

scooter /'sku:tə(r)/ n motoretta f

scope /skəʊp/ n portata f; (opportunity) opportunità f inv

scorch /skɔ:tʃ/ vt bruciare

scorcher /'skɔ:tʃə(r)/ n fam giornata f torrida

scorching /'skɔ:tʃɪŋ/ a caldissimo

score /skɔ:(r)/ n punteggio m; Mus partitura f; (for film, play) musica f; **a ~** [**of**] (twenty) una ventina [di]; **keep [the] ~** tenere il punteggio; **on that ~** a questo proposito ● vt segnare ⟨goal⟩; (cut) incidere ● vi far punti; (in football etc) segnare; (keep score) tenere il punteggio ■ **score out** vt cancellare

scoreboard n /'skɔ:bɔ:d/ tabellone m segnapunti

scorer /'skɔ:rə(r)/ n segnapunti m inv; (of goals) giocatore, -trice mf che segna; **top ~** cannoniere m

scorn /skɔ:n/ n disprezzo m ● vt disprezzare

scornful /'skɔ:nfʊl/ a sprezzante

scornfully /'skɔ:nfʊlɪ/ adv sdegnosamente

Scorpio /'skɔ:pɪəʊ/ n Astr Scorpione m

scorpion /'skɔ:pɪən/ n scorpione m

Scot /skɒt/ n scozzese mf

Scotch a scozzese ● n (whisky) whisky m [scozzese]

scotch /skɒtʃ/ vt far cessare

Scotch egg n Br polpetta f di salsiccia che racchiude un uovo sodo

scot-free a **get off ~** cavarsela impunemente

Scotland /'skɒtlənd/ n Scozia f

Scots, Scottish /skɒts, 'skɒtɪʃ/ a scozzese

scoundrel /'skaʊndrəl/ n mascalzone m

scour¹ /'skaʊə(r)/ vt (search) perlustrare

scour² vt (clean) strofinare

scourer /'skaʊərə(r)/ n (pad) paglietta f

scouring pad /'skaʊərɪŋ/ n paglietta f in lana d'acciaio

scourge /skɜ:dʒ/ n flagello m

Scout n [**Boy**] **~** [boy]scout m inv

scout /skaʊt/ n Mil esploratore m ● vi **~ for** andare in cerca di

scowl /skaʊl/ n sguardo m torvo ● vi guardare [di] storto

Scrabble® /'skræbl/ n Scarabeo® m

■ **scrabble around** *vi* (*search*) cercare a tastoni

scraggy /'skrægɪ/ *a* (**-ier, -iest**) *pej* scarno

scram /skræm/ *vi fam* levarsi dai piedi

scramble /'skræmbl/ *n* (*climb*) arrampicata *f* ● *vi* (*clamber*) arrampicarsi; **~ for** azzuffarsi per ● *vt Teleph* creare delle interferenze in; (*eggs*) strapazzare

scrambled eggs /'skræmbəld/ *npl* uova *fpl* strapazzate

scrambler /'skræmblə(r)/ *n* (*Br: motorcyclist*) [moto]crossista *mf*

scrap¹ /skræp/ *n* (*fam: fight*) litigio *m*

scrap² *n* pezzetto *m*; (*metal*) ferraglia *f*; **~s** *pl* (*of food*) avanzi *mpl* ● *vt* (*pt/pp* **scrapped**) buttare via

scrapbook /'skræpbʊk/ *n* album *m inv*

scrape /skreɪp/ *vt* raschiare; (*damage*) graffiare

■ **scrape through** *vi* passare per un pelo

■ **scrape together** *vt* racimolare

scraper /'skreɪpə(r)/ *n* raschietto *m*

scrap: scrap heap *n* **be on the ~** *~ fig* essere inutile. **scrap iron** *n* ferraglia *f*. **scrap merchant** *n* ferrovecchio *m*. **scrap paper** *n* carta *f* qualsiasi

scrappy /'skræpɪ/ *a* frammentario

scrapyard /'skræpjɑ:d/ *n* deposito *m* di ferraglia; (*for cars*) cimitero *m* delle macchine

scratch /skrætʃ/ *n* graffio *m*; (*to relieve itch*) grattata *f*; **start from ~** partire da zero; **up to ~** (*work*) all'altezza ● *vt* graffiare; (*to relieve itch*) grattare ● *vi* grattarsi

scratchy /'skrætʃɪ/ *a* (*recording*) pieno di fruscii

scrawl /skrɔ:l/ *n* scarabocchio *m* ● *vt/i* scarabocchiare

scrawny /'skrɔ:nɪ/ *a* (**-ier, -iest**) *pej* magro

scream /skri:m/ *n* strillo *m*; **be a ~** (*fam: situation, film, person:*) essere uno spasso ● *vt/i* strillare

scree /skri:/ *n* ghiaione *m*

screech /skri:tʃ/ *n* stridore *m*; **~ of tyres** sgommata *f* ● *vi* stridere ● *vt* strillare

screen /skri:n/ *n* paravento *m*; *Cinema, TV, Comput* schermo *m* ● *vt* proteggere; (*conceal*) riparare; proiettare (*film*); (*candidates*) passare al setaccio; *Med* sottoporre a visita medica

screening /'skri:nɪŋ/ *n Med* visita *f* medica; (*of film*) proiezione *f*

screen: screenplay *n* sceneggiatura *f*. **screen saver** *n Comput* salvaschermo *m*. **screen test** *n Cinema* provino *m*. **screenwriter** *n Cinema* sceneggiatore, -trice *mf*

screw /skru:/ *n* vite *f* ● *vt* avvitare; *vulg* trombare; **~ sth to sth** avvitare qcsa a qcsa

■ **screw up** *vt* (*crumple*) accartocciare; strizzare (*eyes*); storcere (*face*); (*sl: bungle*) mandare all'aria; **~ up one's courage** prendere il coraggio a due mani

screwdriver /'skru:draɪvə(r)/ *n* cacciavite *m inv*

screwed up /skru:d/ *a fam* incasinato

screw top *n* tappo *m* a vite

screwy /'skru:ɪ/ *a* (**-ier, -iest**) *fam* svitato

scribble /'skrɪbl/ *n* scarabocchio *m* ● *vt/i* scarabocchiare

scrimmage /'skrɪmɪdʒ/ *n* (*struggle*) zuffa *f*; (*Am: in football*) mischia *f*

scrimp /skrɪmp/ *vi* risparmiare; **~ and save** risparmiare fino all'osso; **~ on sth** risparmiare su qcsa

script /skrɪpt/ *n* scrittura *f*; (*of film etc*) sceneggiatura *f*

Scriptures /'skrɪptʃəz/ *npl* Sacre Scritture *fpl*

scriptwriter /'skrɪptraɪtə(r)/ *n* sceneggiatore, -trice *mf*

scroll /skrəʊl/ *n* rotolo *m* (*di pergamena*); (*decoration*) voluta *f* ● *vi Comput* far scorrere

Scrooge /skru:dʒ/ *n fam* tirchio, -a *mf*

scrotum /'skrəʊtəm/ *n* scroto *m*

scrounge /skraʊndʒ/ *vt/i* scroccare

scrounger /'skraʊndʒə(r)/ *n* scroccone, -a *mf*

scrub¹ /skrʌb/ *n* (*land*) boscaglia *f*

scrub² *vt/i* (*pt/pp* **scrubbed**) strofinare; (*fam: cancel*) cancellare (*plan*)

scrubbing brush /'skrʌbɪŋ/ *n* spazzolone *m*

scruff /skrʌf/ *n* **by the ~ of the neck** per la collottola

scruffy /'skrʌfɪ/ *a* (**-ier, -iest**) trasandato

scrum /skrʌm/ *n* (*in rugby*) mischia *f*

scrum half *n* mediano *m* di mischia

scrunch /skrʌntʃ/ *vi* (*footsteps in snow, tyres:*) scricchiolare ● *n* scricchiolio *m*

■ **scrunch up** *vt* accartocciare

scruple /'skru:pl/ *n* scrupolo *m*; **have no ~s** essere senza scrupoli

scrupulous /'skru:pjʊləs/ *a* scrupoloso

scrupulously /'skru:pjʊləslɪ/ *adv* scrupolosamente

scrutinize /'skru:tɪnaɪz/ *vt* scrutinare

scrutiny /'skru:tɪnɪ/ *n* (*look*) esame *m* minuzioso

scuba diver /'sku:bə/ *n* sommozzatore, -trice *mf*

scuba diving *n* immersione *f* subacquea

scud /skʌd/ *vi* (*pt/pp* **scudded**) (*clouds:*) muoversi velocemente

scuff /skʌf/ *vt* strascicare (*one's feet*)

scuffle /'skʌfl/ *n* tafferuglio *m*

scull /skʌl/ *vi* (*with two oars*) vogare di coppia; (*with one oar*) vogare a bratto ● *n* (*boat*) imbarcazione *f* da regata con un vogatore

scullery /'skʌlərɪ/ *n* retrocucina *f*

sculpt /skʌlpt/ *vt/i* scolpire

sculptor /'skʌlptə(r)/ *n* scultore *m*

sculpture /'skʌlptʃə(r)/ *n* scultura *f*

scum /skʌm/ *n* schiuma *f*; (*people*) feccia *f*

scurrilous /'skʌrɪləs/ *a* scurrile

scurry /'skʌrɪ/ *vi* (*pt/pp* **-ied**) affrettare il passo

scuttle¹ /'skʌtl/ *n* secchio *m* per il carbone

scuttle² *vt* affondare (*ship*)

scuttle³ *vi* (*hurry*) **~ away** correre via

scythe /saɪð/ *n* falce *f*

SE *abbr* (**south-east**) SE

sea /si:/ *n* mare *m*; **at** ~ in mare; *fig* confuso; **by** ~ via mare; **by the** ~ sul mare

sea: seabed *n* fondale *m* marino. **seabird** *n* uccello *m* marino. **seaboard** *n* costiera *f*. **seafaring** *a* ⟨nation⟩ marinaro. **seafood** *n* frutti *mpl* di mare. **seagull** *n* gabbiano *m*.

sea horse *n* cavalluccio *m* marino

seal[1] /si:l/ *n* Zool foca *f*

seal[2] *n* sigillo *m*; Techn chiusura *f* ermetica ● *vt* sigillare; Techn chiudere ermeticamente ■ **seal off** *vt* bloccare ⟨area⟩

sea level *n* livello *m* del mare; **above** ~ ~ sopra il livello del mare

sealing wax /'si:lɪŋ/ *n* ceralacca *f*

sea lion *n* leone *m* marino

seam /si:m/ *n* cucitura *f*; (of coal) strato *m*

seaman /'si:mən/ *n* marinaio *m*

seamless /'si:mlɪs/ *a* senza cucitura

seamy /'si:mɪ/ *a* ⟨scandal⟩ sordido; ⟨area⟩ malfamato

seance /'seɪɑ:ns/ *n* seduta *f* spiritica

seaplane /'si:pleɪn/ *n* idrovolante *m*

seaport /'si:pɔ:t/ *n* porto *m* di mare

sear /sɪə(r)/ *vt* cauterizzare ⟨wound⟩; rosolare [a fuoco vivo] ⟨meat⟩; ⟨scorch⟩ disseccare

search /sɜ:tʃ/ *n* ricerca *f*; (official) perquisizione *f*; **in** ~ **of** alla ricerca di ● *vt* frugare (**for** alla ricerca di); perlustrare ⟨area⟩; (officially) perquisire ● *vi* ~ **for** cercare

search and replace *n* Comput ricerca *f* e sostituzione

searching /'sɜ:tʃɪŋ/ *a* penetrante

search: searchlight *n* riflettore *m*. **search party** *n* squadra *f* di ricerca. **search warrant** *n* mandato *m* di perquisizione

searing /'sɪərɪŋ/ *a* bruciante; ⟨pace⟩ travolgente; ⟨pain⟩ lancinante

sea: seascape *n* paesaggio *m* marino. **seasick** *a* **be/get** ~ avere il mal di mare. **seaside** *n* **at/to the** ~ al mare. **seaside resort** *n* stazione *f* balneare. **seaside town** *n* città *f* di mare

season /'si:zn/ *n* stagione *f* ● *vt* (flavour) condire; **in** ~ ⟨fruit⟩ di stagione; ⟨animal⟩ in calore

seasonal /'si:zənəl/ *a* stagionale

seasoned /'si:znd/ *a* ⟨Culin: dish⟩ condito; ⟨timber⟩ stagionato; ⟨actor, politician⟩ consumato; ⟨leader⟩ di provata capacità; ~ **traveller** persona *f* che ha viaggiato molto; ~ **soldier** veterano *m*

seasoning /'si:z(ə)nɪŋ/ *n* condimento *m*

season ticket *n* abbonamento *m*

seat /si:t/ *n* (chair) sedia *f*; (in car) sedile *m*; (place to sit) posto *m* [a sedere]; (bottom) didietro *m*; (of government) sede *f*; **take a** ~ sedersi ● *vt* mettere a sedere; (have seats for) aver posti [a sedere] per; **remain** ~**ed** mantenere il proprio posto

seat belt *n* cintura *f* di sicurezza; **fasten one's** ~ ~ allacciare la cintura di sicurezza

seating /'si:tɪŋ/ *n* (places) posti *mpl* a sedere; (arrangement) disposizione *f* dei posti a sedere

seating capacity *n* numero *m* dei posti a sedere

sea: sea urchin *n* riccio *m* di mare. **seaweed** *n* alga *f* marina. **seaworthy** *a* in stato di navigare

sec /sek/ *n* (fam: short instant) attimo *m*, secondo *m*; *abbr* (**second**) s

secateurs /sekə'tɜ:z/ *npl* cesoie *fpl*

secede /sɪ'si:d/ *vi* staccarsi

secession /sɪ'seʃn/ *n* secessione *f*

secluded /sɪ'klu:dɪd/ *a* appartato

seclusion /sɪ'klu:ʒn/ *n* isolamento *m*

second[1] /sɪ'kɒnd/ *vt* (transfer) distaccare

second[2] /'sekənd/ *a* secondo; **in** ~ **gear** Auto in seconda; **on** ~ **thoughts** ripensandoci meglio; **be having** ~ **thoughts** ripensarci; ● *n* secondo *m*; ~**s** *pl* (goods) merce *fsg* di seconda scelta; **have** ~**s** (at meal) fare il bis; **John the S**~ Giovanni Secondo ● *adv* (in race) al secondo posto ● *vt* assistere; appoggiare ⟨proposal⟩

secondary /'sekəndrɪ/ *a* secondario

secondary school *n* ≈ scuola *f* media (inferiore e superiore)

second: second-best *a* secondo dopo il migliore; **be** ~ *pej* essere un ripiego. **second-class** *a* di seconda classe. **second class** *adv* ⟨travel, send⟩ in seconda classe

seconder /'sekəndə(r)/ *n* (of motion) persona *f* che appoggia una mozione

second-guess *vt* anticipare

second hand *n* (on watch, clock) lancetta *f* dei secondi

second-hand *a* ⟨car, goods, news, information⟩ di seconda mano; ⟨clothes⟩ usato; ⟨market⟩ dell'usato; ⟨opinion⟩ preso a prestito ● *adv* ⟨sell⟩ di seconda mano

second in command *n* vice *mf inv*; Mil vicecomandante *m*

secondly /'sekəndlɪ/ *adv* in secondo luogo

secondment /sɪ'kɒndmənt/ *n* **on** ~ in trasferta

second-rate *a* di second'ordine

secrecy /'si:krəsɪ/ *n* segretezza *f*; **in** ~ in segreto

secret /'si:krɪt/ *a* segreto ● *n* segreto *m*; **make no** ~ **of sth** non fare mistero di qcsa

secret agent *n* agente *m* segreto

secretarial /sekrə'teərɪəl/ *a* ⟨work, staff⟩ di segreteria

secretariat /sekrə'teərɪət/ *n* segretariato *m*

secretary /'sekrətərɪ/ *n* segretario, -a *mf*

Secretary of State *n* Segretario *m* di Stato; *Am Pol* ministro *m* degli Esteri

secret ballot *n* scrutinio *m* segreto, votazione *f* a scrutinio segreto

secrete /sɪ'kri:t/ *vt* secernere ⟨poison⟩

secretion /sɪ'kri:ʃn/ *n* secrezione *f*

secretive /'si:krətɪv/ *a* riservato

secretly /'si:krɪtlɪ/ *adv* segretamente

secretness /'si:krɪtnɪs/ *n* riserbo *m*

secret: secret police *n* polizia *f* segreta. **secret service** *n* servizi *mpl* segreti. **secret society** *n* società *f* segreta

sect /sekt/ *n* setta *f*

sectarian /sek'teəriən/ n & a settario, -a mf
section /'sekʃn/ n sezione f
sector /'sektə(r)/ n settore m
secular /'sekjʊlə(r)/ a secolare; ⟨education⟩ laico
secure /sɪ'kjʊə(r)/ a sicuro ● vt proteggere; chiudere bene ⟨door⟩; rendere stabile ⟨ladder⟩; (obtain) assicurarsi
securely /sɪ'kjʊəlɪ/ adv saldamente
security /sɪ'kjʊərətɪ/ n sicurezza f; (for loan) garanzia f; **securities** pl titoli mpl
security: Security Council n (of the UN) Consiglio m di Sicurezza. **security guard** n guardia f giurata. **security risk** n be a ~ ~ costituire un pericolo per la sicurezza
sedan /sɪ'dæn/ n Am berlina f
sedate¹ /sɪ'deɪt/ a posato
sedate² vt somministrare sedativi a
sedately /sɪ'deɪtlɪ/ adv in modo posato
sedation /sɪ'deɪʃn/ n somministrazione f di sedativi; **be under** ~ essere sotto l'effetto di sedativi
sedative /'sedətɪv/ a sedativo ● n sedativo m
sedentary /'sedəntərɪ/ a sedentario
sediment /'sedɪmənt/ n sedimento m
seduce /sɪ'dju:s/ vt sedurre
seduction /sɪ'dʌkʃn/ n seduzione f
seductive /sɪ'dʌktɪv/ a seducente
seductively /sɪ'dʌktɪvlɪ/ adv con aria seducente
see¹ /si:/ v (pt **saw**, pp **seen**) ● vt vedere; (understand) capire; (escort) accompagnare; **go and** ~ andare a vedere; (visit) andare a trovare; ~ **you!** ci vediamo!; ~ **you later!** a più tardi!; ~**ing that** visto che; ~ **sb out**, ~ **sb to the door** accompagnare qcno alla porta; **I can't** ~ **myself doing this forever** non mi ci vedo a farlo per sempre; **I can't think what she** ~**s in him** non capisco cosa trovi in lui; ~ **reason** ragionare; **you're** ~**ing things** hai le traveggole ● vi vedere; (understand) capire; ~ **that** (make sure) assicurarsi che; **let me** ~ (think) fammi pensare; **I** ~ (understand) ho capito
■ **see about** vt occuparsi di
■ **see off** vt veder partire; (chase away) mandar via
■ **see through** vi vedere attraverso; fig non farsi ingannare da ● vt portare a buon fine
■ **see to** vi occuparsi di
see² n Relig diocesi f inv
seed /si:d/ n seme m; Tennis testa f di serie; **go to** ~ fare seme; fig lasciarsi andare
seeded player /'si:dɪd/ n Tennis testa f di serie
seedless /'si:dlɪs/ a senza semi
seedling /'si:dlɪŋ/ n pianticella f
seedy /'si:dɪ/ a (-ier, -iest) squallido; **feel** ~ fam sentirsi poco bene
seek /si:k/ vt (pt/pp **sought**) cercare
■ **seek out** vt scovare
seeker /'si:kə(r)/ n ~ **after** or **for sth** persona f che è alla ricerca di qcsa; **gold** ~ cercatore, -trice mf d'oro
seem /si:m/ vi sembrare

seeming /'si:mɪŋ/ a apparente
seemingly /'si:mɪŋlɪ/ adv apparentemente
seemly /'si:mlɪ/ a decoroso
seen /si:n/ see **see¹**
seep /si:p/ vi filtrare
seepage /'si:pɪdʒ/ n (leak: from container) perdita f; Geol trasudamento m superficiale; (trickle) lenta fuoriuscita f; (into structure, soil) infiltrazione f
see-saw /'si:sɔ:/ n altalena f
seethe /si:ð/ vi ~ **with anger** ribollire di rabbia
see-through a trasparente
segment /'segmənt/ n segmento m; (of orange) spicchio m
segregate /'segrɪgeɪt/ vt segregare
segregation /segrɪ'geɪʃn/ n segregazione f
seismic /'saɪzmɪk/ a sismico
seismograph /'saɪzməgrɑ:f/ n sismografo m
seismology /saɪz'mɒlədʒɪ/ n sismologia f
seize /si:z/ vt afferrare; Jur confiscare; ~ **the opportunity** prendere la palla al balzo
■ **seize up** vi Techn bloccarsi
seizure /'si:ʒə(r)/ n Jur confisca f; Med colpo m [apoplettico]
seldom /'seldəm/ adv raramente
select /sɪ'lekt/ a scelto; (exclusive) esclusivo ● vt scegliere; selezionare ⟨team⟩
selection /sɪ'lekʃn/ n selezione f
selective /sɪ'lektɪv/ a selettivo
selectively /sɪ'lektɪvlɪ/ adv con criterio
selector /sɪ'lektə(r)/ n Sport selezionatore, -trice mf
self /self/ n io m
self: self-addressed a con il proprio indirizzo. **self-addressed envelope** n busta f affrancata con il proprio indirizzo. **self-adhesive** a autoadesivo. **self-analysis** n autoanalisi f. **self-assembly** a da montare. **self-assurance** n sicurezza f di sé. **self-assured** a sicuro di sé. **self-catering** a in appartamento attrezzato di cucina. **self-centred** a egocentrico. **self-cleaning** a ⟨oven⟩ autopulente. **self-confessed** a dichiarato. **self-confidence** n fiducia f in se stesso. **self-confident** a sicuro di sé. **self-conscious** a impacciato. **self-contained** a ⟨flat⟩ con ingresso indipendente. **self-control** n autocontrollo m. **self-defence** n autodifesa f; Jur legittima difesa f. **self-denial** n abnegazione f. **self-destruct** vi ⟨missile, spacecraft⟩ autodistruggersi. **self-destruction** n autodistruzione f; fig autolesionismo m. **self-determination** n autodeterminazione f. **self-discipline** n autodisciplina f. **self-employed** a che lavora in proprio; **the** ~ i lavoratori autonomi. **self-esteem** n stima f di sé. **self-evident** a ovvio. **self-explanatory** a be ~ parlare da sé. **self-financing** /-faɪ'nænsɪŋ/ n autofinanziamento m. **self-governing** /-'gʌvənɪŋ/ a autonomo. **self-government** n autogoverno m. **self-help** n iniziativa f personale. **self-important** a borioso. **self-imposed** /-ɪm'pəʊzd/ a autoimposto. **self-improvement** n crescita f

personale. **self-indulgent** *a* indulgente con se stesso. **self-inflicted** *a* **Anna's problems are** ~ sono problemi che Anna si è creata da sé; ~ **wound** autolesione *f*. **self-interest** *n* interesse *m* personale

selfish /'selfɪʃ/ *a* egoista

selfishly /'selfɪʃlɪ/ *adv* egoisticamente

selfishness /'selfɪʃnɪs/ *n* egoismo *m*

selfless /'selflɪs/ *a* disinteressato

selflessly /'selflɪslɪ/ *adv* disinteressatamente

selflessness /'selflɪsnɪs/ *n* disinteresse *m*

self: self-locking /-'lɒkɪŋ/ *a* ⟨*door*⟩ a chiusura automatica. **self-made** *a* che si è fatto da sé. **self-pity** *n* autocommiserazione *f*. **self-portrait** *n* autoritratto *m*. **self-possessed** /-pə'zest/ *a* padrone di sé. **self-preservation** *n* istinto *m* di conservazione. **self-raising flour** *Br*, **self-rising flour** *Am* /-'reɪzɪŋ, -'raɪzɪŋ/ *n* farina *f* contenente lievito. **self-respect** *n* amor *m* proprio. **self-righteous** *a* presuntuoso. **self-sacrifice** *n* abnegazione *f*. **selfsame** *a* stesso. **self-satisfied** *a* compiaciuto di sé. **self-service** *n* self-service *m inv* ● *attrib* self-service. **self-styled** *a* sedicente. **self-sufficiency** *n* autosufficienza *f*. **self-sufficient** *a* autosufficiente. **self-supporting** *a* ⟨*person*⟩ indipendente ⟨*economicamente*⟩. **self-tan** *n* autoabbronzante *m*. **self-tanning** /-'tænɪŋ/ *a* autoabbronzante. **self-taught** /-'tɔːt/ *a* ⟨*person*⟩ autodidatta. **self-willed** /-'wɪld/ *a* ostinato

sell /sel/ *v* (*pt/pp* **sold**) ● *vt* vendere; **be sold out** essere esaurito; ~ **sb on the idea of...** *fam* convincere qcno di... ● *vi* vendersi

■ **sell off** *vt* liquidare

■ **sell up** *vi* liquidare i propri beni

sell-by date *n* data *f* di scadenza per la vendita

seller /'selə(r)/ *n* venditore, -trice *mf*

sellers' market /'seləzmɑːkɪt/ *n* mercato *m* al rialzo

selling price /'selɪŋ/ *n* prezzo *m* di vendita

Sellotape® /'seləʊteɪp/ *n* nastro *m* adesivo, scotch® *m*

sell-out *n* (*fam: betrayal*) tradimento *m*; **be a** ~ ⟨*concert:*⟩ fare il tutto esaurito

selvage, selvedge /'selvɪdʒ/ *n* cimosa *f*

selves /selvz/ *pl of* **self**

semantic /sɪ'mæntɪk/ *a* semantico

semantics /sɪ'mæntɪks/ *n* (*subject*) semantica *f*; **that's just** ~ sono solo sfumature di significato

semblance /'sembləns/ *n* parvenza *f*

semen /'siːmən/ *n Anat* liquido *m* seminale

semester /sɪ'mestə(r)/ *n Am* semestre *m*

semi /'semɪ/ *n* (*Br: house*) villetta *f* bifamiliare; *Am Auto* autoarticolato *m*

semi+ *pref* semi+

semi: semi-automatic *a* semiautomatico. **semibreve** *n Mus* semibreve *f*. **semicircle** *n* semicerchio *m*. **semicircular** *a* semicircolare. **semicolon** *n* punto e virgola *m*. **semi-darkness** *n* semioscurità *f*. **semi-**

detached *a* gemella ● *n* casa *f* gemella. **semi-final** *n* semifinale *f*

seminal /'semɪnəl/ *a* (*major*) determinante

seminar /'semɪnɑː(r)/ *n* seminario *m*

seminary /'semɪnərɪ/ *n* seminario *m*

semi: semi-precious *a* semiprezioso; ~ **stone** pietra *f* dura. **semi-skilled** /-'skɪld/ *a* qualificato. **semi-skimmed** /-'skɪmd/ *a* parzialmente scremato. **semitone** *n Mus* semitono *m*

semolina /semə'liːnə/ *n* semolino *m*

senate /'senət/ *n* senato *m*

senator /'senətə(r)/ *n* senatore *m*

send /send/ *vt/i* (*pt/pp* **sent**) mandare; (*by mail*) spedire

■ **send away for** *vt* farsi spedire ⟨*information etc*⟩

■ **send down** *vt* (*send to prison*) mandare in galera

■ **send for** *vt* mandare a chiamare ⟨*person*⟩; far venire ⟨*thing*⟩

■ **send in** *vt* presentare ⟨*application*⟩; far entrare ⟨*person*⟩

■ **send off** *vt* spedire ⟨*letter, parcel*⟩; espellere ⟨*footballer*⟩

■ **send up** *vt fam* parodiare

sender /'sendə(r)/ *n* mittente *mf*; **return to** ~ (*on letter*) rispedire al mittente

send-off *n* commiato *m*

senile /'siːnaɪl/ *a* arteriosclerotico

senile dementia /dɪ'menʃə/ *n* demenza *f* senile

senility /sɪ'nɪlətɪ/ *n* senilismo *m*

senior /'siːnɪə(r)/ *a* più vecchio; (*in rank*) superiore ● *n* (*in rank*) superiore *mf*; (*in sport*) senior *mf*; **she's two years my** ~ è più vecchia di me di due anni

senior citizen *n* anziano, -a *mf*

seniority /siːnɪ'ɒrətɪ/ *n* anzianità *f* di servizio

senior management *n* alta dirigenza *f*

sensation /sen'seɪʃn/ *n* sensazione *f*; **cause a** ~ fare scalpore

sensational /sen'seɪʃənəl/ *a* sensazionale

sensationalize /sen'seɪʃənəlaɪz/ *vt pej* dare un tono scandalistico a

sensationally /sen'seɪʃənəlɪ/ *adv* in modo sensazionale

sense /sens/ *n* senso *m*; (*common* ~) buon senso *m*; **in a** ~ in un certo senso; **make** ~ aver senso ● *vt* sentire

senseless /'senslɪs/ *a* insensato; (*unconscious*) privo di sensi

senselessly /'senslɪslɪ/ *adv* insensatamente

sensible /'sensəbl/ *a* sensato; (*suitable*) appropriato

sensibly /'sensəblɪ/ *adv* in modo appropriato

sensitive /'sensətɪv/ *a* sensibile; (*touchy*) suscettibile

sensitively /'sensətɪvlɪ/ *adv* con sensibilità

sensitivity /sensə'tɪvətɪ/ *n* sensibilità *f inv*

sensitize /'sensɪtaɪz/ *vt* **become** ~**d to** (*allergic to*) diventare ipersensibile a

sensor /'sensə(r)/ n sensore m
sensory /'sensərɪ/ a sensoriale
sensual /'sensjʊəl/ a sensuale
sensuality /sensjʊ'ælətɪ/ n sensualità f inv
sensuous /'sensjʊəs/ a voluttuoso
sent /sent/ see **send**
sentence /'sentəns/ n frase f; Jur sentenza f; (punishment) condanna f ● vt ~ **to** condannare a
sentiment /'sentɪmənt/ n sentimento m; (opinion) opinione f; (sentimentality) sentimentalismo m
sentimental /sentɪ'mentl/ a sentimentale; pej sentimentalista
sentimentality /sentɪmen'tælətɪ/ n sentimentalità f inv
sentinel /'sentɪnəl/ n sentinella f
sentry /'sentrɪ/ n sentinella f
separable /'sepərəbl/ a separabile
separate[1] /'sepərət/ a separato
separate[2] /'sepəreɪt/ vt separare ● vi separarsi
separately /'sepərətlɪ/ adv separatamente
separates /'sepərəts/ npl [indumenti npl] coordinati npl
separation /sepə'reɪʃn/ n separazione f
separatist /'sepərətɪst/ n & a separatista mf
sepia /'si:pɪə/ n (colour) seppia m
September /sep'tembə(r)/ n settembre m
septic /'septɪk/ a settico; **go** ~ infettarsi
septicaemia /septɪ'si:mɪə/ n setticemia f
septic tank n fossa f biologica
sequel /'si:kwəl/ n seguito m
sequence /'si:kwəns/ n sequenza f; **in** ~ nell'ordine giusto
sequential /sɪ'kwenʃəl/ a sequenziale
sequin /'si:kwɪn/ n lustrino m, paillette f inv
Serb /sɜ:b/ a & n serbo, -a mf
Serbia /'sɜ:bɪə/ n Serbia f
Serbian /'sɜ:bɪən/ n serba, -a mf; (language) serbo m ● a serbo
Serbo-Croat[ian] /sɜ:bəʊ'krəʊæt, sɜ:bəʊkrəʊ'eɪʃən/ n (language) serbo-croato m ● a serbo-croato
serenade /serə'neɪd/ n serenata f ● vt fare una serenata a
serene /sɪ'ri:n/ a sereno
serenely /sɪ'ri:nlɪ/ adv serenamente
serenity /sɪ'renətɪ/ n serenità f inv
sergeant /'sɑ:dʒənt/ n sergente m
sergeant major n sergente m maggiore
serial /'sɪərɪəl/ n racconto m a puntate; TV sceneggiato m a puntate; Radio commedia f radiofonica a puntate ● a Comput seriale
serialize /'sɪərɪəlaɪz/ vt pubblicare a puntate; Radio, TV trasmettere a puntate
serial killer n serial killer mf inv
serial number n numero m di serie
serial port n Comput porta f seriale
series /'sɪərɪz/ n serie f inv
serious /'sɪərɪəs/ a serio; (illness, error) grave
seriously /'sɪərɪəslɪ/ adv seriamente; (ill) gravemente; **take** ~ prendere sul serio

seriousness /'sɪərɪəsnɪs/ n serietà f; (of situation) gravità f
sermon /'sɜ:mən/ n predica f
seropositive /sɪərəʊ'pɒzɪtɪv/ a sieropositivo
serpent /'sɜ:pənt/ n serpente m
serrated /se'reɪtɪd/ a dentellato
serum /'sɪərəm/ n siero m
servant /'sɜ:vənt/ n domestico, -a mf
serve /sɜ:v/ n Tennis servizio m ● vt servire; Jur notificare (writ) (**on sb** a qcno); scontare (sentence); ~ **its purpose** servire al proprio scopo; **it** ~**s you right!** ben ti sta!; ~**s two** per due persone ● vi prestare servizio; Tennis servire; ~ **as** servire da
server /'sɜ:və(r)/ n (piece of cutlery) posata f di portata; (plate) piatto m di portata; (tray) vassoio m di portata; Sport giocatore, -trice mf che effettua il servizio; Comput server m inv, servitore m
service /'sɜ:vɪs/ n servizio m; Relig funzione f; (maintenance) revisione f; ~**s** pl forze fpl armate; (on motorway) area f di servizio; **in the** ~**s** sotto le armi; **of** ~ **to** utile a; **out of** ~ (machine:) guasto ● vt Techn revisionare
serviceable /'sɜ:vɪsəbl/ a utilizzabile; (hard-wearing) resistente; (practical) pratico
service: service area n area f di servizio. **service charge** n servizio m. **service company** n compagnia f del settore terziario. **service industry** n industria f terziaria. **serviceman** n militare m. **service provider** n fornitore m di servizi. **service road** n strada f d'accesso. **service station** n stazione f di servizio
serviette /sɜ:vɪ'et/ n tovagliolo m
servile /'sɜ:vaɪl/ a servile
servility /sə'vɪlɪtɪ/ n servilismo m
serving /'sɜ:vɪŋ/ a (officer) di carriera ● n (helping) porzione f
session /'seʃn/ n seduta f; Jur sessione f; Univ anno m accademico
set /set/ n serie f inv, set m inv; (of crockery, cutlery) servizio m; TV, Radio apparecchio m; Math insieme m; Theat scenario m; Cinema, Tennis set m inv; (of people) circolo m; (of hair) messa f in piega ● a (ready) pronto; (rigid) fisso; (book) in programma; **be** ~ **on doing sth** essere risoluto a fare qcsa; **be** ~ **in one's ways** essere abitudinario ● v (pt/pp **set**, pres p **setting**) ● vt mettere, porre; mettere (alarm clock); assegnare (task, homework); fissare (date, limit); chiedere (questions); montare (gem); assestare (bone); apparecchiare (table); Typ comporre; ~ **fire to** dare fuoco a; ~ **free** liberare; ~ **a good example** dare il buon esempio; ~ **sail for** far vela per; ~ **in motion** dare inizio a; ~ **to music** musicare; **the film is** ~ **in Rome/the 18th century** il film è ambientato a Roma/nel XVIII secolo; ~ **to music** musicare; ~ **about doing sth** mettersi a fare qcsa ● vi (sun:) tramontare; (jelly, concrete:) solidificarsi; ~ **to work (on sth)** mettersi al lavoro (su qcsa)

■ **set back** vt mettere indietro; (hold up) ritardare; (fam: cost) costare a

■ **set off** vi partire ● vt avviare; mettere ‹alarm›; fare esplodere ‹bomb›

■ **set out** vi partire; ~ **out to do sth** proporsi di fare qcsa ● vt disporre; (state) esporre

■ **set to** vi mettersi all'opera

■ **set up** vt fondare ‹company›; istituire ‹committee›

setback /'setbæk/ n (hitch) contrattempo m; Mil sconfitta f, scacco m; Fin tracollo m; (in health) ricaduta f

set design n scenografia f

set designer n scenografo, -a mf

set meal n menù m inv fisso

settee /se'ti:/ n divano m

setter /'setə(r)/ n (dog) setter m inv

setting /'setɪŋ/ n scenario m; (position) posizione f; (of sun) tramonto m; (of jewel) montatura f

settle /'setl/ vt (decide) definire; risolvere ‹argument›; fissare ‹date›; calmare ‹nerves›; saldare ‹bill›; **that's ~d then** allora è deciso ● vi (live) stabilirsi; ‹snow, dust, bird:› posarsi; (subside) assestarsi; ‹sediment:› depositarsi

■ **settle down** vi sistemarsi; (stop making noise) calmarsi

■ **settle for** vt accontentarsi di

■ **settle up** vi regolare i conti

settlement /'setlmənt/ n (agreement) accordo m; (of bill) saldo m; Comm liquidazione f; (colony) insediamento m

settler /'setlə(r)/ n colonizzatore, -trice mf

set-to n fam zuffa f; (verbal) battibecco m

set-up n situazione f

seven /'sevn/ a & n sette m

seventeen /sevən'ti:n/ a & n diciassette m

seventeenth /sevən'ti:nθ/ a & n diciassettesimo, -a mf

seventh /'sevnθ/ a & n settimo, -a mf

seventieth /'sevntɪɪθ/ a & n settantesimo, -a mf

seventy /'sevntɪ/ a & n settanta m

seven-year itch n fam crisi f inv del settimo anno

sever /'sevə(r)/ vt troncare ‹relations›

several /'sevrəl/ a & pron parecchi

severance /'sev(ə)rəns/ n ~ **pay** trattamento m di fine rapporto

severe /sɪ'vɪə(r)/ a severo; ‹pain› violento; ‹illness› grave; ‹winter› rigido

severely /sɪ'vɪəlɪ/ adv severamente; ‹ill› gravemente

severity /sɪ'verətɪ/ n severità f; (of pain) violenza f; (of illness) gravità f; (of winter) rigore m

sew /səʊ/ vt/i (pt **sewed**, pp **sewn** or **sewed**) cucire

■ **sew up** vt ricucire

sewage /'su:ɪdʒ/ n acque fpl di scolo

sewer /'su:ə(r)/ n fogna f

sewing /'səʊɪŋ/ n cucito m; (work) lavoro m di cucito

sewing machine n macchina f da cucire

sewn /səʊn/ see **sew**

sex /seks/ n sesso m; **have ~** avere rapporti sessuali, fare l'amore

sex appeal n sex appeal m

sex change operation n intervento m per il cambiamento di sesso

sexism /'seksɪzm/ n sessismo m

sexist /'seksɪst/ a sessista mf

sex: sex life n vita f sessuale. **sex maniac** n maniaco m sessuale. **sex offender** n colpevole mf di delitti a sfondo sessuale

sextet /seks'tet/ n sestetto m

sex tourism n turismo m a scopo sessuale

sexual /'seksjʊəl/ a sessuale

sexual: sexual assault n atti mpl di libidine violenta. **sexual equality** n parità f dei sessi. **sexual harassment** n molestie fpl sessuali. **sexual intercourse** n rapporti mpl sessuali

sexuality /seksjʊ'ælətɪ/ n sessualità f

sexually /'seksjʊəlɪ/ adv sessualmente; **be ~ assaulted** subire atti di libidine violenta

sexually transmitted disease /trænz'mɪtɪd/ n malattia f trasmissibile per via sessuale

sexy /'seksɪ/ a (-ier, -iest) sexy inv

sh /ʃ/ int silenzio!, sst!

shabbily /'ʃæbɪlɪ/ adv in modo scialbo; ‹treat› in modo meschino

shabbiness /'ʃæbɪnɪs/ n trasandatezza f; (of treatment) meschinità f

shabby /'ʃæbɪ/ a (-ier, -iest) scialbo; ‹treatment› meschino

shack /ʃæk/ n catapecchia f

shackles /'ʃæklz/ npl catene fpl

shade /ʃeɪd/ n ombra f; (of colour) sfumatura f; (for lamp) paralume m; (Am: for window) tapparella f; **a ~ better** un tantino meglio ● vt riparare dalla luce; (draw lines on) ombreggiare

shades /ʃeɪdz/ npl fam occhiali mpl da sole

shading /'ʃeɪdɪŋ/ n (slight variation in colour) tonalità f inv; (to give effect of darkness) ombreggiature fpl

shadow /'ʃædəʊ/ n ombra f ● vt (follow) pedinare

shadow boxing n allenamento m di boxe con l'ombra

Shadow Cabinet n governo m ombra

shadowy /'ʃædəʊɪ/ a (indistinct) confuso

shady /'ʃeɪdɪ/ a (-ier, -iest) ombroso; (fam: disreputable) losco

shaft /ʃɑ:ft/ n Techn albero m; (of light) raggio m; (of lift, mine) pozzo m; ~**s** pl (of cart) stanghe fpl

shaggy /'ʃægɪ/ a (-ier, -iest) irsuto; ‹animal› dal pelo arruffato

shaggy dog story n fam barzelletta f interminabile dal finale deludente

shake /ʃeɪk/ n scrollata f ● v (pt **shook**, pp **shaken**) ● vt scuotere; agitare ‹bottle›; far tremare ‹building›; ~ **hands with** stringere la mano a; ~ **one's head** scuotere la testa ● vi tremare

■ **shake off** vt scrollarsi di dosso

shaken [up] /'ʃeɪkən/ *a* (*after accident etc*) scosso

shaker /'ʃeɪkə(r)/ *n* (*for salad*) centrifuga *f* [asciugaverdure]; (*for dice*) bicchiere *m*; (*for cocktails*) shaker *m inv*; (*for pepper*) pepaiola *f*; (*for salt*) saliera *f*

shake-up *n Pol* rimpasto *m*; *Comm* ristrutturazione *f*

shakily /'ʃeɪkɪlɪ/ *adv* ⟨*say sth*⟩ con voce tremante; ⟨*walk*⟩ con passo esitante

shaky /'ʃeɪkɪ/ *a* (**-ier, -iest**) tremante; ⟨*table etc*⟩ traballante; (*unreliable*) vacillante

shall /ʃæl/ *v aux* **I ~ go** andrò; **we ~ see** vedremo; **what ~ I do?** cosa faccio?; **I'll come too, ~ I?** vengo anch'io, no?; **thou shalt not kill** *liter* non uccidere; **passengers ~ remain seated** i passeggeri devono rimanere seduti

shallot /ʃə'lɒt/ *n* scalogno *m*

shallow /'ʃæləʊ/ *a* basso, poco profondo; ⟨*dish*⟩ poco profondo; *fig* superficiale

sham /ʃæm/ *a* falso ● *n* finzione *f*; (*person*) spaccone, -a *mf* ● *vt* (*pt/pp* **shammed**) simulare

shambles /'ʃæmblz/ *n* baraonda *fsg*

shame /ʃeɪm/ *n* vergogna *f*; **it's a ~ that** è un peccato che; **what a ~!** che peccato!; **~ on you!** vergognati!; **put sb/sth to ~** far sfigurare qcno/qcsa

shamefaced /ʃeɪm'feɪst/ *a* vergognoso

shameful /'ʃeɪmfl/ *a* vergognoso

shamefully /'ʃeɪmfʊlɪ/ *adv* vergognosamente

shameless /'ʃeɪmlɪs/ *a* spudorato

shamelessly /'ʃeɪmlɪslɪ/ *adv* spudoratamente

shampoo /ʃæm'puː/ *n* shampoo *m inv*; **~ and set** shampoo *m inv* e messa in piega ● *vt* fare uno shampoo a ⟨*carpet, person's hair etc*⟩

shamrock /'ʃæmrɒk/ *n* trifoglio *m* (*simbolo dell'Irlanda*)

shandy /'ʃændɪ/ *n* bevanda *f* a base di birra e gassosa

shank /ʃæŋk/ *n* garretto *m*; (*of knife*) manico *m*; (*of golf club*) impugnatura *f*; (*of screw*) gambo *m*; (*of anchor*) fuso *m*; (*of person*) gamba *f* (*dal ginocchio in giù*)

shan't /ʃɑːnt/ = **shall not**

shanty /'ʃæntɪ/ *n* (*hut*) baracca *f*; (*song*) marinaro

shanty town /'ʃæntɪtaʊn/ *n* bidonville *f inv*, baraccopoli *f inv*

shape /ʃeɪp/ *n* forma *f*; (*figure*) ombra *f*; **take ~** prendere forma; **get back in ~** ritornare in forma; **be out of ~** non essere in forma ● *vt* dare forma a (**into** di) ● *vi* **~ [up]** mettere la testa a posto; **~ up nicely** mettersi bene

shapeless /'ʃeɪplɪs/ *a* informe

shapely /'ʃeɪplɪ/ *a* (**-ier, -iest**) ben fatto

shard /ʃɑːd/ *n* frammento *m*; (*of clay*) coccio *m*

share /ʃeə(r)/ *n* porzione *f*; *Comm* azione *f* ● *vt* dividere; condividere ⟨*views*⟩ ● *vi* dividere; **~ in** partecipare a

■ **share out** *vt* spartire; (*including oneself*) spartirsi

share: **share capital** *n* capitale *m* azionario. **share dealing** *n* contrattazione *f* di azioni. **shareholder** *n* azionista *mf*. **shareholding** *n* titoli *mpl* azionari. **share index** *n* indice *m* azionario

shark /ʃɑːk/ *n* squalo *m*, pescecane *m*; *fig* truffatore, -trice *mf*

sharp /ʃɑːp/ *a* ⟨*knife etc*⟩ tagliente; ⟨*pencil*⟩ appuntito; ⟨*drop*⟩ a picco; ⟨*reprimand*⟩ severo; ⟨*outline*⟩ marcato; (*alert*) acuto; (*unscrupulous*) senza scrupoli; **~ pain** fitta *f* ● *adv* **at three o'clock ~** alle tre in punto; **look ~!** sbrigati! ● *n Mus* diesis *m inv*

sharpen /'ʃɑːpn/ *vt* affilare ⟨*knife*⟩; appuntire ⟨*pencil*⟩

sharpener /'ʃɑːpnə(r)/ *n* (*for pencils*) temperamatite *m inv*; (*for knife*) affilacoltelli *m inv*

shatter /'ʃætə(r)/ *vt* frantumare; *fig* mandare in frantumi

shattered /'ʃætəd/ *a* (*fam: exhausted*) a pezzi ● *vi* frantumarsi

shave /ʃeɪv/ *n* rasatura *f*; **have a ~** farsi la barba ● *vt* radere ● *vi* radersi

shaver /'ʃeɪvə(r)/ *n* rasoio *m* elettrico

shaving /'ʃeɪvɪŋ/: **shaving-brush** *n* pennello *m* da barba. **shaving foam** *n* schiuma *f* da barba. **shaving soap** *n* sapone *m* da barba

shawl /ʃɔːl/ *n* scialle *m*

she /ʃiː/ *pers pron* lei; **~ is tired** è stanca; **I'm going, but ~ is not** io vado, ma lei no

sheaf /ʃiːf/ *n* (*pl* **sheaves**) fascio *m*

shear /ʃɪə(r)/ *vt* (*pt* **sheared**, *pp* **shorn** or **sheared**) tosare

shears /ʃɪəz/ *npl* (*for hedge*) cesoie *fpl*

sheath /ʃiːθ/ *n* (*pl* **~s** /ʃiːðz/) guaina *f*

sheathe /ʃiːð/ *vt* rinfoderare; rivestire ⟨*cable*⟩

sheaves /ʃiːvz/ *see* **sheaf**

shed¹ /ʃed/ *n* baracca *f*; (*for cattle*) stalla *f*

shed² *vt* (*pt/pp* **shed**, *pres p* **shedding**) perdere; versare ⟨*blood, tears*⟩; **~ light on** far luce su

sheen /ʃiːn/ *n* lucentezza *f*

sheep /ʃiːp/ *n inv* pecora *f*

sheepdog /'ʃiːpdɒg/ *n* cane *m* da pastore

sheepish /'ʃiːpɪʃ/ *a* imbarazzato

sheepishly /'ʃiːpɪʃlɪ/ *adv* con aria imbarazzata

sheepskin /'ʃiːpskɪn/ *n* [pelle *f* di] montone *m*

sheer /ʃɪə(r)/ *a* puro; (*steep*) a picco; (*transparent*) trasparente ● *adv* a picco

sheet /ʃiːt/ *n* lenzuolo *m*; (*of paper*) foglio *m*; (*of glass, metal*) lastra *f*

sheet lightning *n* bagliore *m* diffuso dei lampi; (*without a storm*) lampi *mpl* di calore

sheet music *n* spartiti *mpl*

sheikh /ʃeɪk/ *n* sceicco *m*

shelf /ʃelf/ *n* (*pl* **shelves**) ripiano *m*; (*set of shelves*) scaffale *m*

shelf-life *n* (*of product*) durata *f* di conservazione; (*fig: of technology, pop music*) durata *f* di vita; ⟨*fig: of politician, star*⟩ periodo *m* di gloria

shell /ʃel/ *n* conchiglia *f*; ⟨*of egg, snail, tortoise*⟩ guscio *m*; ⟨*of crab*⟩ corazza *f*; ⟨*of unfinished building*⟩ ossatura *f*; *Mil* granata *f* ● *vt* sgusciare ⟨*peas*⟩; *Mil* bombardare

■ **shell out** *vi fam* sborsare

shell: shellfish *n inv* mollusco *m*; *Culin* frutti *mpl* di mare. **shell-shocked** /ʃelʃɒkt/ *a* ⟨*soldier*⟩ traumatizzato da un bombardamento; *fig* in stato di shock. **shell suit** *n* tuta *f* di acetato

shelter /ʃeltə(r)/ *n* rifugio *m*; ⟨*air raid ~*⟩ rifugio *m* antiaereo; **take ~** rifugiarsi ● *vt* riparare ⟨**from** da⟩; *fig* mettere al riparo; ⟨*give lodging to*⟩ dare asilo a ● *vi* rifugiarsi

sheltered /ʃeltəd/ *a* ⟨*spot*⟩ riparato; ⟨*life*⟩ ritirato

shelve /ʃelv/ *vt* accantonare ⟨*project*⟩ ● *vi* ⟨*slope:*⟩ scendere

shelves /ʃelvz/ *see* **shelf**

shelving /ʃelvɪŋ/ *n* ⟨*shelves*⟩ ripiani *mpl*

shepherd /ʃepəd/ *n* pastore *m* ● *vt* guidare

shepherdess /ʃepədes/ *n* pastora *f*

shepherd's pie /ʃepədzˈpaɪ/ *n* pasticcio *m* di carne tritata e patate

sherbet /sɜːbət/ *n* ⟨*Br: powder*⟩ polverina *f* effervescente al gusto di frutta; ⟨*Am: sorbet*⟩ sorbetto *m*

sheriff /ʃerɪf/ *n* sceriffo *m*

Sherpa /sɜːpə/ *n* scerpa *m*

sherry /ʃerɪ/ *n* sherry *m inv*

shield /ʃiːld/ *n* scudo *m*; ⟨*for eyes*⟩ maschera *f*; *Techn* schermo *m* ● *vt* proteggere ⟨**from** da⟩

shift /ʃɪft/ *n* cambiamento *m*; ⟨*in position*⟩ spostamento *m*; ⟨*at work*⟩ turno *m* ● *vt* spostare; ⟨*take away*⟩ togliere; riversare ⟨*blame*⟩ ● *vi* spostarsi; ⟨*wind:*⟩ cambiare; ⟨*fam: move quickly*⟩ darsi una mossa

shift key *n* tasto *m* delle maiuscole

shiftless /ʃɪftlɪs/ *a* privo di risorse

shift work *n* turni *mpl*

shift worker *n* turnista *mf*

shifty /ʃɪftɪ/ *a* (**-ier, -iest**) *pej* losco; ⟨*eyes*⟩ sfuggente

Shiite /ʃiːaɪt/ *a & n* sciita *mf*

shilling /ʃɪlɪŋ/ *n* scellino *m*

shilly-shally /ʃɪlɪʃelɪ/ *vi* titubare

shimmer /ʃɪmə(r)/ *n* luccichio *m* ● *vi* luccicare

shin /ʃɪn/ *n* stinco *m* ● *vi* **~ up/down sth** ⟨*climb*⟩ arrampicarsi su/scendere giù da qcsa

shin-guard *n* parastinchi *m inv*

shindig /ʃɪndɪg/ *n fam* ⟨*party*⟩ baldoria *f*; ⟨*disturbance*⟩ pandemonio *m*

shindy /ʃɪndɪ/ *n fam* ⟨*disturbance*⟩ pandemonio *m*; ⟨*party*⟩ baldoria *f*

shine /ʃaɪn/ *n* lucentezza *f*; **give sth a ~** dare una lucidata a qcsa ● *v* (*pt/pp* **shone**) ● *vi* splendere; ⟨*reflect light*⟩ brillare; ⟨*hair, shoes:*⟩ essere lucido ● *vt* **~ a light on** puntare una luce su

shingle /ʃɪŋgl/ *n* ⟨*pebbles*⟩ ghiaia *f*

shingles /ʃɪŋglz/ *n Med* fuochi *mpl* di Sant'Antonio

shiny /ʃaɪnɪ/ *a* (**-ier, -iest**) lucido

ship /ʃɪp/ *n* nave *f* ● *vt* (*pt/pp* **shipped**) spedire; ⟨*by sea*⟩ spedire via mare

shipbuilder /ʃɪpbɪldə(r)/ *n* costruttore *m* navale

shipbuilding /ʃɪpbɪldɪŋ/ *n* costruzione *f* di navi

shipment /ʃɪpmənt/ *n* spedizione *f*; ⟨*consignment*⟩ carico *m*

shipowner /ʃɪpəʊnə(r)/ *n* armatore *m*

shipper /ʃɪpə(r)/ *n* spedizioniere *m*

shipping /ʃɪpɪŋ/ *n* trasporto *m*; ⟨*traffic*⟩ imbarcazioni *fpl*

shipping agent *n* spedizioniere *m*

shipping company *n* compagnia *f* di spedizione

ship: shipshape *a & adv* in perfetto ordine. **shipwreck** *n* naufragio *m*. **shipwrecked** *a* naufragato. **shipyard** *n* cantiere *m* navale

shire /ʃaɪə(r)/ *n Br* contea *f*

shire-horse *n* cavallo *m* da tiro

shirk /ʃɜːk/ *vt* scansare

shirker /ʃɜːkə(r)/ *n* scansafatiche *mf inv*

shirt /ʃɜːt/ *n* camicia *f*; **in ~-sleeves** in maniche di camicia

shirty /ʃɜːtɪ/ *a Br fam* incavolato; **get ~ with sb** incavolarsi con qcno

shish kebab /ʃɪʃkɪbæb/ *n* spiedino *m* di carne e verdure

shit /ʃɪt/ *vulg n & int* merda *f* ● *vi* (*pt/pp* **shit**) cagare

shit-scared *a vulg* **be ~** farsela sotto

shiver /ʃɪvə(r)/ *n* brivido *m* ● *vi* rabbrividire

shoal /ʃəʊl/ *n* ⟨*of fish*⟩ banco *m*

shock /ʃɒk/ *n* ⟨*impact*⟩ urto *m*; *Electr* scossa *f* [elettrica]; *fig* colpo *m*, shock *m inv*; *Med* shock *m inv*; **get a ~** *Electr* prendere la scossa; **in ~** *Med* in stato di shock ● *vt* scioccare

shock absorber *n Auto* ammortizzatore *m*

shocking /ʃɒkɪŋ/ *a* scioccante; ⟨*fam: weather, handwriting etc*⟩ tremendo

shockingly /ʃɒkɪŋlɪ/ *adv* ⟨*behave*⟩ in modo pessimo; ⟨*expensive*⟩ eccessivamente

shocking pink *n* rosa *m* shocking

shock: shockproof *a* antiurto. **shock treatment** *n* terapia *f* d'urto. **shock wave** *n* onda *f* d'urto

shod /ʃɒd/ *see* **shoe**

shoddily /ʃɒdɪlɪ/ *adv* in modo scadente

shoddy /ʃɒdɪ/ *a* (**-ier, -iest**) scadente

shoe /ʃuː/ *n* scarpa *f*; ⟨*of horse*⟩ ferro *m* ● *vt* (*pt/pp* **shod**, *pres p* **shoeing**) ferrare ⟨*horse*⟩

shoe: shoehorn *n* calzante *m*. **shoelace** *n* laccio *m* da scarpa. **shoemaker** *n* calzolaio *m*. **shoe rack** *n* scarpiera *f*. **shoe-shop** *n* calzoleria *f*. **shoestring** *n* **on a ~** *fam* con una miseria. **shoe-tree** *n* forma *f* da scarpa

shone /ʃɒn/ *see* **shine**

shoo /ʃuː/ *vt* **~ away** cacciar via ● *int* sciò!

shook /ʃʊk/ *see* **shake**

shoot /ʃuːt/ *n Bot* germoglio *m*; ⟨*hunt*⟩ battuta *f* di caccia ● *v* (*pt/pp* **shot**) ● *vt* sparare; girare ⟨*film*⟩; **~ oneself in the foot** *fig* darsi la zappa sui piedi ● *vi* ⟨*hunt*⟩ andare a caccia

■ **shoot down** *vt* abbattere

■ **shoot out** *vi* (*rush*) precipitarsi fuori
■ **shoot up** *vi* (*grow*) crescere in fretta; ⟨*prices:*⟩ salire di colpo
shooting /'ʃuːtɪŋ/ *n* (*pastime*) caccia *f*; (*killing*) uccisione *f*
shooting range *n* poligono *m* di tiro
shoot-out *n fam* sparatoria *f*
shop /ʃɒp/ *n* negozio *m*; (*workshop*) officina *f*; **talk ~** *fam* parlare di lavoro ● *vi* (*pt*/*pp* **shopped**, *pres p* **shopping**) far compere; **go ~ping** andare a fare compere
■ **shop around** *vi* confrontare i prezzi
■ **shop:** **shop assistant** *n* commesso, -a *mf*. **shop floor** *n* **problems on the ~ ~** problemi tra gli operai. **shopkeeper** *n* negoziante *mf*. **shoplifter** *n* taccheggiatore, -trice *mf*. **shoplifting** *n* taccheggio *m*
shopper /'ʃɒpə(r)/ *n* compratore, -trice *mf*
shopping /'ʃɒpɪŋ/ *n* compere *fpl*; (*articles*) acquisti *mpl*; **do the ~** fare la spesa
shopping: **shopping bag** *n* borsa *f* per la spesa. **shopping centre** *n* centro *m* commerciale. **shopping list** *n* lista *f* della spesa. **shopping mall** *n* centro *m* commerciale. **shopping trolley** *n* carrello *m*
shop steward *n* rappresentante *mf* sindacale
shop window *n* vetrina *f*
shore /ʃɔː(r)/ *n* riva *f*
■ **shore up** *vt* puntellare ⟨*building, wall*⟩
shorn /ʃɔːn/ *see* **shear**
short /ʃɔːt/ *a* corto; (*not lasting*) breve; ⟨*person*⟩ basso; (*curt*) brusco; **a ~ time ago** poco tempo fa; **be ~ of** essere a corto di; **be in ~ supply** essere scarso; *fig* essere raro; **Mick is ~ for Michael** Mick è il diminutivo di Michael; **cut ~** interrompere ⟨*holiday*⟩; **to cut a long story ~...** per farla breve...; **in the ~ term** nell'immediato futuro, a breve termine ● *adv* bruscamente; **in ~** in breve; **~ of doing** a meno di fare; **go ~** essere privato (**of** di); **stop ~ of doing sth** non arrivare fino a fare qcsa; **you're 10p ~** mancano 10 pence ● *n* (*Cinema*) cortometraggio *m*
shortage /'ʃɔːtɪdʒ/ *n* scarsità *f inv*
short: **shortbread** *n* biscotto *m* di pasta frolla. **short-change** *vt* dare meno resto del dovuto a; (*deliberately*) imbrogliare sul resto; *fig* imbrogliare. **short circuit** *n* corto *m* circuito ● *vt* mandare in cortocircuito ● *vi* causare un cortocircuito. **shortcoming** *n* difetto *m*. **shortcrust pastry** *n* pasta *f* frolla. **short cut** *n* scorciatoia *f*
shorten /'ʃɔːtn/ *vt* abbreviare; accorciare ⟨*garment*⟩
short: **shortfall** *n* (*in budget, accounts*) deficit *m inv*. **shorthand** *n* stenografia *f*. **shorthanded** /-'hændɪd/ *a* a corto di personale. **shorthand typist** *n* stenodattilografo, -a *mf*. **short list** *n* lista *f* dei candidati selezionati per un lavoro. **short-lived** /-'lɪvd/ *a* di breve durata
shortly /'ʃɔːtlɪ/ *adv* presto; **~ before/after** poco prima/dopo

shortness /'ʃɔːtnɪs/ *n* brevità *f inv*; (*of person*) bassa statura *f*
short notice *n* **at ~ ~** con poco preavviso
short-range *a* di breve portata
shorts /ʃɔːts/ *npl* calzoncini *mpl* corti
short: **short-sighted** /-'saɪtɪd/ *a* miope. **short-sleeved** /-'sliːvd/ *a* a maniche corte. **short-staffed** /-'stɑːft/ *a* a corto di personale. **short story** *n* racconto *m*, novella *f*. **short-tempered** /-'tempəd/ *a* irascibile. **short time** *n* **be on ~ ~** ⟨*worker:*⟩ fare orario ridotto. **short wave** *n* onde *fpl* corte. **short wave radio** *n* radio *f inv* a onde corte
shot /ʃɒt/ *see* **shoot** ● *n* colpo *m*; (*pellets*) piombini *mpl*; (*person*) tiratore *m*; *Phot* foto *f inv*; (*injection*) puntura *f*; (*fam: attempt*) prova *f*; **like a ~** *fam* come un razzo
shot: **shotgun** *n* fucile *m* da caccia. **shotputter** *n* pesista *mf*. **shot-putting** *n* *Sport* lancio *m* del peso
should /ʃʊd/ *v aux* **I ~ go** dovrei andare; **I ~ have seen him** avrei dovuto vederlo; **you ~n't have said that** non avresti dovuto dire questo; **I ~ like** mi piacerebbe; **this ~ be enough** questo dovrebbe bastare; **if he ~ come** se dovesse venire, se venisse
shoulder /'ʃəʊldə(r)/ *n* spalla *f*; **~ to ~** gomito a gomito ● *vt* mettersi in spalla; *fig* accollarsi
shoulder: **shoulder bag** *n* borsa *f* a tracolla. **shoulder blade** *n* scapola *f*. **shoulder pad** *n* spallina *f*. **shoulder strap** *n* spallina *f*; (*of bag*) tracolla *f*
shout /ʃaʊt/ *n* grido *m* ● *vt/i* gridare
■ **shout at** *vi* alzar la voce con
■ **shout down** *vt* azzittire gridando
shouting /'ʃaʊtɪŋ/ *n* grida *fpl*
shove /ʃʌv/ *n* spintone *m* ● *vt* spingere; (*fam: put*) ficcare ● *vi* spingere
■ **shove off** *vi fam* togliersi di torno
shovel /'ʃʌvl/ *n* pala *f* ● *vt* (*pt*/*pp* **shovelled**) spalare
show /ʃəʊ/ *n* (*display*) manifestazione *f*; (*exhibition*) mostra *f*; (*ostentation*) ostentazione *f*; *Theat, TV* spettacolo *m*; (*programme*) programma *m*; **on ~** esposto ● *v* (*pt* **showed**, *pp* **shown**) ● *vt* mostrare; (*put on display*) esporre; proiettare ⟨*film*⟩; **~ sb to the door** accompagnare qcno alla porta; **~ sb the door** mettere alla porta qcno ● *vi* ⟨*film:*⟩ essere proiettato; **your slip is ~ing** ti si vede la sottoveste
■ **show in** *vt* fare accomodare
■ **show off** *vi fam* mettersi in mostra ● *vt* mettere in mostra
■ **show out** *vt* **~ sb out** fare uscire qcno
■ **show up** *vi* risaltare; (*fam: arrive*) farsi vedere ● *vt* (*fam: embarrass*) far fare una brutta figura a
show: **showbiz** /'ʃəʊbɪz/ *n fam* mondo *m* dello spettacolo. **show business** *n* mondo *m* dello spettacolo. **showcase** *n* *also fig* vetrina *f* ● *attrib* ⟨*village, prison*⟩ modello. **showdown** *n* regolamento *m* dei conti

shower /ˈʃaʊə(r)/ n doccia f; (of rain) acquazzone m; **have a ~** fare la doccia ● vt **~ with** coprire di ● vi fare la doccia

shower: shower-cap n cuffia f da doccia. **shower-curtain** tenda f della doccia. **shower-head** n bocchetta f. **showerproof** a impermeabile

showery /ˈʃaʊərɪ/ a **it was ~** ci sono stati diversi acquazzoni

showjumper /ˈʃəʊdʒʌmpə(r)/ n cavaliere m/cavallerizza f di salto ad ostacoli

showjumping /ˈʃəʊdʒʌmpɪŋ/ n concorso m ippico

shown /ʃəʊn/ see **show**

show: show-off n esibizionista mf. **showpiece** n pezzo m forte. **showplace** n attrazione f. **showroom** n salone m [per] esposizioni

showy /ˈʃəʊɪ/ a appariscente

shrank /ʃræŋk/ see **shrink**

shrapnel /ˈʃræpnl/ n schegge fpl di granata, shrapnel m

shred /ʃred/ n brandello m; fig briciolo m ● vt (pt/pp **shredded**) fare a brandelli; Culin tagliuzzare

shredder /ˈʃredə(r)/ n distruttore m di documenti

shrew /ʃru:/ n Zool toporagno m; (pej: woman) bisbetica f

shrewd /ʃru:d/ a accorto

shrewdly /ˈʃru:dlɪ/ adv con accortezza

shrewdness /ˈʃru:dnɪs/ n accortezza f

shriek /ʃri:k/ n strillo m ● vt/i strillare

shrift /ʃrɪft/ n **give sb short ~** liquidare qcno rapidamente

shrill /ʃrɪl/ a penetrante

shrillness /ˈʃrɪlnɪs/ n acutezza f

shrilly /ˈʃrɪlɪ/ adv in modo penetrante

shrimp /ʃrɪmp/ n gamberetto m

shrine /ʃraɪn/ n (place) santuario m

shrink /ʃrɪŋk/ vi (pt **shrank**, pp **shrunk**) restringersi; (draw back) ritrarsi (**from** da) ● n fam strizzacervelli mf inv

shrinkage /ˈʃrɪŋkɪdʒ/ n (of fabric) restringimento m; (of area, company) rimpicciolimento m; (in a shop) perdite fpl; (of resources) diminuzione f

shrinking violet /ʃrɪŋkɪŋˈvaɪələt/ n hum mammoletta f

shrink: shrink-proof a irrestringibile. **shrink-resistant** a irrestringibile. **shrink-wrap** vt avvolgere nella pellicola trasparente ● n pellicola f trasparente

shrivel /ˈʃrɪvl/ vi (pt/pp **shrivelled**) raggrinzare

shroud /ʃraʊd/ n sudario m; fig manto m; **~ed** in fig avvolto in

Shrove /ʃrəʊv/ n **~ Tuesday** martedì m grasso

shrub /ʃrʌb/ n arbusto m

shrubbery /ˈʃrʌbərɪ/ n (in garden) zona f piantata ad arbusti

shrug /ʃrʌg/ n scrollata f di spalle ● vt/i (pt/ pp **shrugged**) **~ [one's shoulders]** scrollare le spalle

■ **shrug off** vt ignorare

shrunk /ʃrʌŋk/ see **shrink**. **~en** a rimpicciolito

shudder /ˈʃʌdə(r)/ n fremito m ● vi fremere

shuffle /ˈʃʌfl/ vi strascicare i piedi ● vt mescolare (cards) ● n strascicamento m; (at cards) mescolata f

shufty /ˈʃʊftɪ/ n Br fam **have a ~ at sth** dare un'occhiata a qcsa

shun /ʃʌn/ vt (pt/pp **shunned**) rifuggire

shunt /ʃʌnt/ vt smistare

shush /ʃʊʃ/ int zitto!

shut /ʃʌt/ v (pt/pp **shut**, pres p **shutting**) ● vt chiudere ● vi chiudersi; (shop:) chiudere

■ **shut down** vt/i chiudere

■ **shut off** vt chiudere (water, gas)

■ **shut out** vt bloccare (light); impedire (view); scacciare (memory)

■ **shut up** vt chiudere; fam far tacere ● vi fam stare zitto; **~ up!** stai zitto!

shutdown /ˈʃʌtdaʊn/ n chiusura f

shut-eye n (fam: short sleep) **get some ~** fare un pisolino

shutter /ˈʃʌtə(r)/ n serranda f; Phot otturatore m

shuttle /ˈʃʌtl/ n navetta f ● vi far la spola

shuttlecock /ˈʃʌtlkɒk/ n volano m

shuttle service n servizio m pendolare

shy /ʃaɪ/ a (timid) timido ● vi (pt/pp **shied**) (horse:) fare uno scarto

■ **shy away from** vt rifuggire da

shyly /ˈʃaɪlɪ/ adv timidamente

shyness /ˈʃaɪnɪs/ n timidezza f

sibylline /ˈsɪbɪlaɪn/ a sibillino

Siamese /saɪəˈmi:z/ a siamese

Siamese twins npl fratelli mpl/sorelle fpl siamesi

sibling /ˈsɪblɪŋ/ n (brother) fratello m; (sister) sorella f; **~s** pl fratelli mpl

sibling rivalry n rivalità f tra fratelli

Sicilian /sɪˈsɪlɪən/ a & n siciliano, -a mf

Sicily /ˈsɪsɪlɪ/ n Sicilia f

sick /sɪk/ a ammalato; (humour) macabro; **be ~** (vomit) vomitare; **be ~ of sth** fam essere stufo di qcsa; **feel ~** aver la nausea

sicken /ˈsɪkn/ vt disgustare ● vi **be ~ing for something** covare qualche malanno

sickening /ˈsɪkənɪŋ/ a disgustoso

sick leave n congedo m per malattia

sickly /ˈsɪklɪ/ a (**-ier, -iest**) malaticcio

sickness /ˈsɪknɪs/ n malattia f; (vomiting) nausea f

sickness benefit n sussidio m di malattia

sickroom /ˈsɪkru:m/ n camera f dell'ammalato

side /saɪd/ n lato m; (of person, mountain) fianco m; (of road) bordo m; **on the ~** (as sideline) come attività secondaria; **~ by ~** fianco a fianco; **take ~s** immischiarsi; **take sb's ~** prendere le parti di qcno; **be on the safe ~** andare sul sicuro ● attrib laterale ● vi **~ with** parteggiare per

side: sideboard n credenza f. **sideburns** npl

basette *fpl*. **side effect** *n* effetto *m* collaterale. **sidekick** *n fam* (*companion*) compare *mf*; (*assistant*) braccio *m* destro. **sidelights** *npl* luci *fpl* di posizione. **sideline** *n* attività *f inv* complementare. **sidelong** *a* ~ **glance** sguincio *m*. **side road** *n* strada *f* secondaria. **side-saddle** *adv* all'amazzone. **sideshow** *n* attrazione *f*. **sidestep** *vt* schivare. **side street** *n* strada *f* laterale. **sidetrack** *vt* sviare. **sidewalk** *n Am* marciapiede *m*. **sideways** *adv* obliquamente

siding /'saɪdɪŋ/ *n* binario *m* di raccordo

sidle /'saɪdl/ *vi* camminare furtivamente (**up to** verso)

siege /si:dʒ/ *n* assedio *m*

Sierra Leone /sɪeərəlɪ'əʊn/ *n* Sierra Leone *f*

siesta /sɪ'estə/ *n* siesta *f*; **take a** ~ fare una siesta

sieve /sɪv/ *n* setaccio *m* ● *vt* setacciare

sift /sɪft/ *vt* setacciare; ~ [**through**] *fig* passare al setaccio

sigh /saɪ/ *n* sospiro *m*; **give a** ~ sospirare ● *vi* sospirare

sight /saɪt/ *n* vista *f*; (*on gun*) mirino *m*; **the ~s** *pl* le cose da vedere; **at first** ~ a prima vista; **be within/out of** ~ essere/non essere in vista; **within** ~ **of** vicino a; **lose** ~ **of** perdere di vista; **know by** ~ conoscere di vista; **have bad** ~ vederci male ● *vt* avvistare

sightseeing /'saɪtsi:ɪŋ/ *n* **go** ~ andare a visitare posti

sightseer /'saɪtsi:ə(r)/ *n* turista *mf*

sign /saɪn/ *n* segno *m*; (*notice*) insegna *f* ● *vt/i* firmare

■ **sign for** *vt* firmare la ricevuta di (*letter, parcel*); firmare un contratto con (*football club*)

■ **sign in** *vi* (*hotel guest:*) firmare il registro

■ **sign on** *vi* (*as unemployed*) presentarsi all'ufficio di collocamento; *Mil* arruolarsi

■ **sign up** *vi Mil* arruolarsi; ~ **up for a course** iscriversi a un corso

signal /'sɪgnl/ *n* segnale *m* ● *v* (*pt/pp* **signalled**) ● *vt* segnalare ● *vi* fare segnali; ~ **to sb** far segno a qcno (**to** di)

signal box *n* cabina *f* di segnalazione

signalman /'sɪgnəlmən/ *n* casellante *m*

signatory /'sɪgnət(ə)rɪ/ *n* firmatario, -a *mf*

signature /'sɪgnətʃə(r)/ *n* firma *f*

signature tune *n* sigla *f* [musicale]

signet ring /'sɪgnɪt/ *n* anello *m* con sigillo

significance /sɪg'nɪfɪkəns/ *n* significato *m*

significant /sɪg'nɪfɪkənt/ *a* significativo

significantly /sɪg'nɪfɪkəntlɪ/ *adv* in modo significativo

signify /'sɪgnɪfaɪ/ *vt* (*pt/pp* **-ied**) indicare

signing /'saɪnɪŋ/ *n* (*of treaty*) firma *f*; (*of footballer*) ingaggio *m*; (*footballer*) nuovo acquisto *m*; (*sign language*) linguaggio *m* dei segni

sign language *n* linguaggio *m* dei segni

signpost /'saɪnpəʊst/ *n* segnalazione *f* stradale

Sikh /si:k/ *n* sikh *mf inv* ● *a* sikh *inv*

silage /'saɪlɪdʒ/ *n* foraggio *m* conservato in silo

silence /'saɪləns/ *n* silenzio *m*; **in** ~ in silenzio ● *vt* far tacere

silencer /'saɪlənsə(r)/ *n* (*on gun*) silenziatore *m*; *Auto* marmitta *f*

silent /'saɪlənt/ *a* silenzioso; (*film*) muto; **remain** ~ rimanere in silenzio; **the** ~ **majority** la maggioranza silenziosa

silently /'saɪləntlɪ/ *adv* silenziosamente

silhouette /sɪlʊ'et/ *n* sagoma *f*, silhouette *f inv* ● *vt* **be** ~**d** profilarsi

silica gel /'sɪlɪkə/ *n* gel *m inv* di silice

silicon /'sɪlɪkən/ *n* silicio *m*

silicon chip *n Comput* chip *m inv* di silicio, piastrina *f* di silicio

silicone /'sɪlɪkəʊn/ *n Chem* silicone *m*

silicone varnish *n* vernice *f* siliconica

silk /sɪlk/ *n* seta *f* ● *attrib* di seta

silkworm /'sɪlkwɜ:m/ *n* baco *m* da seta

silky /'sɪlkɪ/ *a* (**-ier, -iest**) come la seta

sill /ʃɪl/ *n* davanzale *m*

silly /'ʃɪlɪ/ *a* (**-ier, -iest**) sciocco

silo /'saɪləʊ/ *n* silo *m*

silt /sɪlt/ *n* melma *f*

silver /'sɪlvə(r)/ *a* d'argento; (*paper*) argentato ● *n* argento *m*; (*silverware*) argenteria *f*

silver: silver-plated *a* placcato d'argento. **silver service** *n* servizio *m* a tavola in cui il cameriere fa il giro dei commensali. **silversmith** *n* argentiere *m*. **silverware** *n* argenteria *f*. **silver wedding** *n* nozze *fpl* d'argento

silvery /'sɪlvərɪ/ *a* argentino

similar /'sɪmɪlə(r)/ *a* simile

similarity /sɪmɪ'lærətɪ/ *n* somiglianza *f*

similarly /'sɪmɪləlɪ/ *adv* in modo simile

simile /'sɪmɪlɪ/ *n* similitudine *f*

simmer /'sɪmə(r)/ *vi* bollire lentamente ● *vt* far bollire lentamente

■ **simmer down** *vi* calmarsi

simper /'sɪmpə(r)/ *vi* ostentare un sorriso

simpering /'sɪmp(ə)rɪŋ/ *a* (*smile*) affettato; (*person*) smanceroso

simple /'sɪmpl/ *a* semplice; (*person*) sempliciotto

simple-minded /-'maɪndɪd/ *a* sempliciotto

simpleton /'sɪmpltən/ *n* sempliciotto, -a *mf*

simplicity /sɪm'plɪsətɪ/ *n* semplicità *f*

simplification /sɪmplɪfɪ'keɪʃn/ *n* semplificazione *f*

simplify /'sɪmplɪfaɪ/ *vt* (*pt/pp* **-ied**) semplificare

simplistic /sɪm'plɪstɪk/ *a* semplicistico

simply /'sɪmplɪ/ *adv* semplicemente

simulate /'sɪmjʊleɪt/ *vt* simulare

simulation /sɪmjʊ'leɪʃn/ *n* simulazione *f*

simulcast /'sɪməlkɑ:st/ *vt* teleradiotrasmettere

simultaneous /sɪml'teɪnɪəs/ *a* simultaneo

simultaneously /sɪməl'teɪnɪəslɪ/ *adv* simultaneamente

sin /sɪn/ *n* peccato *m* ● *vi* (*pt/pp* **sinned**) peccare

since /sɪns/ *prep* da; ~ **when?** da quando in qua? ●*adv* da allora ●*conj* da quando; (*because*) siccome

sincere /sɪnˈsɪə(r)/ *a* sincero

sincerely /sɪnˈsɪəlɪ/ *adv* sinceramente; **Yours** ~ Distinti saluti

sincerity /sɪnˈserətɪ/ *n* sincerità *f*

sine /saɪn/ *n* Math seno *m*

sinew /ˈsɪnjuː/ *n* tendine *m*

sinful /ˈsɪnfl/ *a* peccaminoso

sing /sɪŋ/ *vt/i* (*pt* **sang**, *pp* **sung**) cantare

singalong /ˈsɪŋəlɒŋ/ *n* **have a** ~ cantare [tutti] insieme

singe /sɪndʒ/ *vt* (*pres p* **singeing**) bruciacchiare

singer /ˈsɪŋə(r)/ *n* cantante *mf*

singer-songwriter /-ˈsɒŋraɪtə(r)/ *n* cantautore, -trice *mf*

singing /ˈsɪŋɪŋ/ *n* canto *m*

single /ˈsɪŋgl/ *a* solo; (*not double*) semplice; (*unmarried*) celibe; ⟨*woman*⟩ nubile; ⟨*room*⟩ singolo; ⟨*bed*⟩ a una piazza; **I haven't spoken to a ~ person** non ho parlato con nessuno ●*n* (*ticket*) biglietto *m* di sola andata; (*record*) singolo *m*

■ **single out** *vt* scegliere; (*distinguish*) distinguere

single: single-breasted /-ˈbrestɪd/ *a* a un petto. **single cream** *n* panna *f* da cucina fluida. **single currency** *n* (*in Europe*) moneta *f* unica. **single-decker** /-ˈdekə(r)/ *n* autobus *m inv* (*a un piano solo*). **single file** *adv* in fila indiana. **single-handed** /-ˈhændɪd/ *a* & *adv* da solo. **single-handedly** /-ˈhændɪdlɪ/ *adv* da solo. **single market** *n* mercato *m* unico. **single-minded** /-ˈmaɪndɪd/ *a* risoluto. **single parent** *n* genitore *m* che alleva il figlio da solo

singles /ˈsɪŋglz/ *npl* Tennis singolo *m*; (*people*) single *mpl*; **the women's** ~ il singolo femminile

singles bar *n* bar ritrovo *m inv* per single

single-sex *a* (*for boys*) maschile; (*for girls*) femminile

single-storey *a* ⟨*house*⟩ a un piano

singly /ˈsɪŋglɪ/ *adv* singolarmente

sing-song Br *a* ⟨*voice, dialect*⟩ che ha una sua particolare cadenza ●*n* **have a** ~ cantare [tutti] insieme

singular /ˈsɪŋgjʊlə(r)/ *a* Gram singolare; (*uncommon*) eccezionale ●*n* singolare *m*

singularly /ˈsɪŋgjʊləlɪ/ *adv* singolarmente

sinister /ˈsɪnɪstə(r)/ *a* sinistro

sink /sɪŋk/ *n* lavandino *m* ●*v* (*pt* **sank**, *pp* **sunk**) ●*vi* affondare ●*vt* affondare ⟨*ship*⟩; scavare ⟨*shaft*⟩; investire ⟨*money*⟩

■ **sink in** *vi* penetrare; **it took a while to ~ in** (*fam: be understood*) c'è voluto un po' a capirlo

sinker /ˈsɪŋkə(r)/ *n* (*in fishing*) piombo *m*; *Am Culin* ≈ bombolone *m*

sinking /ˈsɪŋkɪŋ/ *n* affondamento *m*

sink unit *n* mobile *m* di cucina comprendente il lavandino

sinner /ˈsɪnə(r)/ *n* peccatore, -trice *mf*

sinuous /ˈsɪnjʊəs/ *a* sinuoso

sinus /ˈsaɪnəs/ *n* seno *m* paranasale

sinusitis /saɪnəˈsaɪtɪs/ *n* sinusite *f*

sip /sɪp/ *n* sorso *m* ●*vt* (*pt/pp* **sipped**) sorseggiare

siphon /ˈsaɪfn/ *n* (*bottle*) sifone *m*

■ **siphon off** *vt* travasare (con sifone)

sir /sɜː(r)/ *n* signore *m*; **S~** (*title*) Sir *m*; **Dear S~** Egregio Signore; **Dear S~s** Spettabile ditta

sire /saɪə(r)/ *vt* generare

siren /ˈsaɪrən/ *n* sirena *f*

sirloin /ˈsɜːlɔɪn/ *n* (*of beef*) controfiletto *m*

sirloin steak *n* bistecca *f* di controfiletto

sissy /ˈsɪsɪ/ *n* feminuccia *f*

sister /ˈsɪstə(r)/ *n* sorella *f*; (*nurse*) [infermiera *f*] caposala *f*

sisterhood /ˈsɪstəhʊd/ *n* Relig congregazione *f* religiosa femminile; (*in feminism*) solidarietà *f inv* femminile

sister-in-law *n* (*pl* ~**s-in-law**) cognata *f*

sisterly /ˈsɪstəlɪ/ *a* da sorella

Sistine Chapel /ˈsɪstiːn/ *n* Cappella *f* Sistina

sit /sɪt/ *v* (*pt/pp* **sat**, *pres p* **sitting**) ●*vi* essere seduto; (*sit down*) sedersi; ⟨*committee:*⟩ riunirsi ●*vt* sostenere ⟨*exam*⟩

■ **sit back** *vi fig* starsene con le mani in mano

■ **sit by** *vi* starsene a guardare

■ **sit down** *vi* mettersi a sedere; **please ~ down** si accomodi; ~ **down!** siediti!

■ **sit for** *vi* posare per ⟨*portrait*⟩

■ **sit on** *vt* far parte di ⟨*committee*⟩

■ **sit up** *vi* mettersi seduto; (*not slouch*) star seduto diritto; (*stay up*) stare alzato

sitcom /ˈsɪtkɒm/ *n fam* situation comedy *f inv*

sit-down *n Br* **have a** ~ sedersi un momento

site /saɪt/ *n* posto *m*; *Archaeol* sito *m*; (*building* ~) cantiere *m* ●*vt* collocare

sit-in /ˈsɪtɪn/ *n* occupazione *f* (*di fabbrica ecc*); sit-in *m inv*

sitter /ˈsɪtə(r)/ *n* (*babysitter*) baby-sitter *mf inv*; (*for artist*) modello *m*

sitting /ˈsɪtɪŋ/ *n* seduta *f*; (*for meals*) turno *m*

sitting: sitting duck *n fam* facile bersaglio *m*. **sitting room** *n* salotto *m*. **sitting tenant** *n* locatario *m* residente

situate /ˈsɪtjʊeɪt/ *vt* situare

situated /ˈsɪtjʊeɪtɪd/ *a* situato

situation /sɪtjʊˈeɪʃn/ *n* situazione *f*; (*location*) posizione *f*; (*job*) posto *m*; '~**s vacant**' 'offerte di lavoro'

situation report *n* quadro *m* della situazione

sit-ups *npl* addominali *mpl*

six /sɪks/ *a* & *n* sei *m*

six-pack *n* confezione *f* da sei (*di bottiglie o lattine*)

sixteen /sɪksˈtiːn/ *a* & *n* sedici *m*

sixteenth /sɪksˈtiːnθ/ *a* & *n* sedicesimo, -a *mf*

sixteenth-century *a* cinquecentesco

sixth /sɪksθ/ *a* & *n* sesto, -a *mf*

sixth form n Sch ultimo biennio m facoltativo della scuola superiore

sixth sense n sesto senso m

sixtieth /'sɪkstɪɪθ/ a & n sessantesimo, -a mf

sixty /'sɪkstɪ/ a & n sessanta m

size /saɪz/ n dimensioni fpl; (of clothes) taglia f, misura f; (of shoes) numero m; **what ~ is the room?** che dimensioni ha la stanza?

■ **size up** vt fam valutare

sizeable /'saɪzəbl/ a piuttosto grande

sizzle /'sɪzl/ vi sfrigolare

skate[1] /skeɪt/ n inv (fish) razza f

skate[2] n pattino m ● vi pattinare

■ **skate over** vt fig glissare su

skateboard /'skeɪtbɔːd/ n skate-board m inv

skateboarder /'skeɪtbɔːdə(r)/ n persona f che va in skate-board

skateboarding /'skeɪtbɔːdɪŋ/ n skate-board m

skater /skeɪt/ n pattinatore, -trice mf

skating /'skeɪtɪŋ/ n pattinaggio m

skating rink n pista f di pattinaggio

skeletal /'skelɪtl/ a also fig scheletrico; ⟨disease⟩ dello scheletro

skeleton /'skelɪtn/ n scheletro m

skeleton key n passe-partout m inv

skeleton staff n personale m ridotto

sketch /sketʃ/ n schizzo m; Theat sketch m inv ● vt fare uno schizzo di

■ **sketch out** vt delineare

sketchbook /'sketʃbʊk/ n (for sketching) album m inv per schizzi; (book of sketches) album m inv di schizzi

sketchily /'sketʃɪlɪ/ adv in modo abbozzato

sketchpad /'sketʃpæd/ n blocco m per schizzi

sketchy /'sketʃɪ/ a (-ier, -iest) abbozzato

skew /skju:/ vt alterare ⟨figures⟩

skewer /'skjuə(r)/ n spiedo m

ski /ski:/ n sci m inv ● vi (pt/pp **skied**, pres p **skiing**) sciare; **go ~ing** andare a sciare

skid /skɪd/ n slittata f; **go into a ~** slittare ● vi (pt/pp **skidded**) slittare

skid mark n segno m di frenata

skier /'ski:ə(r)/ n sciatore, -trice mf

skiing /'ski:ɪŋ/ n sci m

ski instructor n maestro, -a mf di sci

ski jump n (competition) salto m con gli sci; (slope) trampolino m

skilful /'skɪlfl/ a abile

skilfully /'skɪlfʊlɪ/ adv abilmente

ski lift n impianto m di risalita

skill /skɪl/ n abilità f inv

skilled /skɪld/ a dotato; ⟨worker⟩ specializzato

skillet /'skɪlət/ n Am padella f

skim /skɪm/ vt (pt/pp **skimmed**) schiumare; scremare ⟨milk⟩

■ **skim off** vt togliere

■ **skim over** vt sfiorare ⟨surface, subject⟩

■ **skim through** vt scorrere

skimmed milk /skɪmd/ n latte m scremato

skimp /skɪmp/ vi ~ **on** lesinare su

skimpy /'skɪmpɪ/ a (-ier, -iest) succinto

skin /skɪn/ n pelle f; (on fruit) buccia f;

soaked to the ~ fradicio fino all'osso ● vt (pt/pp **skinned**) spellare

skin: skin cancer n cancro m alla pelle. **skincare** n cura f della pelle. **skin cream** n crema f per la pelle. **skin-deep** a superficiale.

skin diver n sub mf inv. **skin diving** n nuoto m subacqueo

skinflint /'skɪnflɪnt/ n miserabile mf

skin graft n innesto m epidermico

skinhead /'skɪnhed/ n skinhead m

skinny /'skɪnɪ/ a (-ier, -iest) molto magro

skint /skɪnt/ a fam al verde

skintight /skɪn'taɪt/ a aderente

skip[1] /skɪp/ n (container) benna f

skip[2] n salto m ● v (pt/pp **skipped**) ● vi saltellare; (with rope) saltare la corda ● vt omettere

ski: ski pants npl pantaloni mpl da sci. **ski pass** n ski-pass m inv. **ski pole** n racchetta f da sci

skipper /'skɪpə(r)/ n skipper m inv

skipping /'skɪpɪŋ/ n salto m della corda

skipping rope n corda f per saltare

ski rack n portasci m inv

ski resort n stazione f sciistica

skirmish /'skɜ:mɪʃ/ n scaramuccia f

skirt /skɜ:t/ n gonna f ● vt costeggiare

skirting board /'skɜ:tɪŋ/ n battiscopa m inv, zoccolo m

ski: ski run n pista f da sci. **ski slope** n pista f da sci. **ski stick** n racchetta f da sci

skit /skɪt/ n bozzetto m comico

skittish /'skɪtɪʃ/ a (difficult to handle) ombroso; (playful) giocherellone

skittle /'skɪtl/ n birillo m

skive /skaɪv/ vi fam fare lo scansafatiche

skivvy /'skɪvɪ/ n Br fam sguattera f

ski wax n sciolina f

skulduggery /skʌl'dʌgərɪ/ n fam imbrogli mpl

skulk /skʌlk/ vi aggirarsi furtivamente

skull /skʌl/ n cranio m

skunk /skʌŋk/ n moffetta f; (person) farabutto m

sky /skaɪ/ n cielo m

sky: skydiving n paracadutismo m in caduta libera. **sky-high** a ⟨prices⟩ alle stelle; ⟨rates⟩ esorbitante ● adv **rise ~** salire alle stelle. **skylight** n lucernario m. **skyline** n (of city) profilo m. **skyrocket** vi ⟨prices:⟩ andare alle stelle. **skyscraper** n grattacielo m

slab /slæb/ n lastra f; (slice) fetta f; (of chocolate) tavoletta f

slack /slæk/ a lento; ⟨person⟩ fiacco ● vi fare lo scansafatiche

■ **slack off** vi rilassarsi

slacken /'slækn/ vi allentare; ~ **[off]** ⟨trade:⟩ rallentare; ⟨speed, rain:⟩ diminuire ● vt allentare; diminuire ⟨speed⟩

slacker /'slækə(r)/ n lazzarone m

slacks /slæks/ npl pantaloni mpl sportivi

slag /slæg/ n scorie fpl

■ **slag off** vt (pt/pp **slagged**) Br fam sparlare di

slain /sleɪn/ see **slay**

slalom /'slɑːləm/ n slalom m inv

slam /slæm/ v (pt/pp **slammed**) ● vt sbattere; (fam: criticize) stroncare ● vi sbattere

slammer /'slæmə(r)/ n (fam: prison) galera f

slander /'slɑːndə(r)/ n diffamazione f ● vt diffamare

slanderer /'slɑːndərə(r)/ n diffamatore, -trice mf

slanderous /'slɑːnd(ə)rəs/ a diffamatorio

slang /slæŋ/ n gergo m

slangy /'slæŋɪ/ a gergale

slant /slɑːnt/ n pendenza f; (point of view) angolazione f; **on the ~** in pendenza ● vt pendere; fig distorcere ‹report›

slanted /'slæntɪd/ a ‹fig: report› tendenzioso

slap /slæp/ n schiaffo m ● vt (pt/pp **slapped**) schiaffeggiare; (put) schiaffare ● adv in pieno

slap: slap bang adv fam **he went ~ ~ into the wall** è andato a sbattere in pieno contro il muro. **slapdash** a fam frettoloso. **slapstick** n farsa f da torte in faccia. **slap-up** a fam di prim'ordine

slash /slæʃ/ n taglio m; Typ barra f obliqua ● vt tagliare; ridurre drasticamente ‹prices›; **~ one's wrists** svenarsi

slat /slæt/ n stecca f

slate /sleɪt/ n ardesia f ● vt fam fare a pezzi

slater /'sleɪtə(r)/ n (roofer) addetto m alla ricopertura dei tetti con tegole di ardesia; Zool onisco m

slatted /'slætɪd/ a ‹shutter› a stecche

slaughter /'slɔːtə(r)/ n macello m; (of people) massacro m ● vt macellare; massacrare ‹people›

slaughterhouse /'slɔːtəhaʊs/ n macello m

Slav /slɑːv/ a slavo ● n slavo, -a mf

slave /sleɪv/ n schiavo, -a mf ● vi **~ [away]** lavorare come un negro

slave-driver n schiavista mf

slavery /'sleɪvərɪ/ n schiavitù f

Slavic /'slɑːvɪk/ a slavo

slavish /'sleɪvɪʃ/ a servile

slavishly /'sleɪvɪʃlɪ/ adv in modo servile

Slavonic /slə'vɒnɪk/ a slavo

slay /sleɪ/ vt (pt **slew**, pp **slain**) ammazzare

sleaze /sliːz/ n fam (pornography) pornografia f; (corruption) corruzione f

sleazy /'sliːzɪ/ a (-ier, -iest) sordido

sled /sled/ n slitta f ● vi andare in slitta

sledge /sledʒ/ n slitta f

sledgehammer /'sledʒhæmə(r)/ n martello m

sleek /sliːk/ a liscio, lucente; (well-fed) pasciuto

sleep /sliːp/ n sonno m; **go to ~** addormentarsi; **put to ~** far addormentare; **in my ~** nel sonno; **a good night's ~** una bella dormita ● v (pt/pp **slept**) ● vi dormire; **~ like a log** dormire come un ghiro; **~ on it** dormirci sopra; **~ with sb** andare a letto con qcno ● vt **~s six** ha sei posti letto

■ **sleep around** vi andare a letto con tutti

■ **sleep in** vi dormire più a lungo

sleeper /'sliːpə(r)/ n Rail treno m con vagoni

letto; (compartment) vagone m letto; (on track) traversina f; **be a light/heavy ~** avere il sonno leggero/pesante

sleepily /'sliːpɪlɪ/ adv con aria assonnata

sleeping /'sliːpɪŋ/: **sleeping bag** n sacco m a pelo. **sleeping car** n vagone m letto. **sleeping partner** n Br Comm socio m accomodante. **sleeping pill** n sonnifero m. **sleeping policeman** n dosso m di rallentamento

sleepless /'sliːplɪs/ a insonne; **have a ~ night** passare una notte insonne

sleeplessness /'sliːplɪsnɪs/ n insonnia f

sleep: sleepsuit n tutina f. **sleepwalk** vi essere sonnambulo. **sleepwalker** n sonnambulo, -a mf. **sleepwalking** n sonnambulismo m

sleepy /'sliːpɪ/ a (-ier, -iest) assonnato; **be ~** aver sonno

sleet /sliːt/ n nevischio m ● vi **it is ~ing** nevischia

sleeve /sliːv/ n manica f; (for record) copertina f

sleeveless /'sliːvlɪs/ a senza maniche

sleigh /sleɪ/ n slitta f

sleight /slaɪt/ n **~ of hand** gioco m di prestigio

slender /'slendə(r)/ a snello; ‹fingers, stem› affusolato; fig scarso; ‹chance› magro

slept /slept/ see **sleep**

sleuth /sluːθ/ n investigatore m, detective m inv

slew¹ /sluː/ vi girare

slew² see **slay**

slice /slaɪs/ n fetta f ● vt affettare; **~d bread** pane m a cassetta

slick /slɪk/ a liscio; (cunning) astuto ● n (of oil) chiazza f di petrolio

slide /slaɪd/ n scivolata f; (in playground) scivolo m; (for hair) fermaglio m [per capelli]; Phot diapositiva f ● v (pt/pp **slid**) ● vi scivolare ● vt far scivolare

slide rule n regolo m calcolatore

sliding /'slaɪdɪŋ/ a ‹door, seat› scorrevole

sliding scale n scala f mobile

slight /slaɪt/ a leggero; ‹importance› poco; (slender) esile; **~est** minimo; **not in the ~est** niente affatto ● vt offendere ● n offesa f

slightly /'slaɪtlɪ/ adv leggermente

slim /slɪm/ a (**slimmer, slimmest**) snello; fig scarso; ‹chance› magro ● vi dimagrire

slime /slaɪm/ n melma f

slimy /'slaɪmɪ/ a melmoso; fig viscido

sling /slɪŋ/ n Med benda f al collo ● vt (pt/pp **slung**) fam lanciare

sling-back n sandalo m (chiuso davanti)

slingshot /'slɪŋʃɒt/ n fionda f

■ **slink in** /slɪŋk/ vi (pt/pp **slunk**) entrare furtivamente

slinky /'slɪŋkɪ/ a ‹fam: dress› sexy inv, attillato

slip /slɪp/ n scivolata f; (mistake) lieve errore m; (petticoat) sottoveste f; (for pillow) federa f; (paper) scontrino m; **give sb the ~** fam sbarazzarsi di qcno; **~ of the tongue** lapsus *m inv* ● *v* (*pt/pp* **slipped**) ● *vi* scivolare; (*go quickly*) sgattaiolare; (*decline*) retrocedere; **let sth ~** (*reveal*) lasciarsi sfuggire qcsa ● *vt* **he ~ped it into his pocket** se l'è infilato in tasca; **~ sb's mind** sfuggire di mente a qcno

■ **slip away** *vi* sgusciar via; ⟨*time:*⟩ sfuggire

■ **slip into** *vi* infilarsi ⟨*clothes*⟩

■ **slip on** *vt* infilarsi ⟨*jacket etc*⟩

■ **slip up** *vi fam* sbagliare

slip-knot *n* nodo *m* scorsoio

slip-on [**shoe**] *n* mocassino *m*

slipped disc /slɪpt'dɪsk/ *n Med* ernia *f* del disco

slipper /'slɪpə(r)/ *n* pantofola *f*

slippery /'slɪpərɪ/ *a* scivoloso

slip road *n* bretella *f*

slipshod /'slɪpʃɒd/ *a* trascurato

slip-up *n fam* sbaglio *m*

slit /slɪt/ *n* spacco *m*; (*tear*) strappo *m*; (*hole*) fessura *f* ● *vt* (*pt/pp* **slit**) tagliare

slither /'slɪðə(r)/ *vi* scivolare

sliver /'slɪvə(r)/ *n* scheggia *f*

slob /slɒb/ *n fam* (*messy*) maiale *m*; (*lazy*) pelandrone *m*

slobber /'slɒbə(r)/ *vi* sbavare

sloe /sləʊ/ *n* (*fruit*) prugnola *f*; (*bush*) prugnolo *m*

slog /slɒg/ *n* [**hard**] **~** sgobbata *f* ● *vi* (*pt/pp* **slogged**) (*work*) sgobbare

slogan /'sləʊgən/ *n* slogan *m inv*

slop /slɒp/ *vt* (*pt/pp* **slopped**) versare

■ **slop over** *vi* versarsi

slope /sləʊp/ *n* pendenza *f*; (*ski ~*) pista *f* ● *vi* essere inclinato, inclinarsi

■ **slope off** *vi* scantonare

sloping /'sləʊpɪŋ/ *a* in pendenza

sloppiness /'slɒpɪnɪs/ *n* (*of work*) sciatteria *f*

sloppy /'slɒpɪ/ *a* (**-ier, -iest**) ⟨*work*⟩ trascurato; ⟨*worker*⟩ negligente; (*in dress*) sciatto; (*sentimental*) sdolcinato

slosh /slɒʃ/ *vi fam* ⟨*person, feet:*⟩ sguazzare; ⟨*water:*⟩ scrosciare ● *vt* (*fam: hit*) colpire

sloshed /slɒʃt/ *a fam* sbronzo

slot /slɒt/ *n* fessura *f*; (*time-~*) spazio *m* ● *vt* (*pt/pp* **slotted**) infilare

■ **slot in** *vi* incastrarsi

sloth /sləʊθ/ *n* accidia *f*

slot machine *n* distributore *m* automatico; (*for gambling*) slot-machine *f inv*

slouch /slaʊtʃ/ *vi* (*in chair*) stare scomposto

Slovak /'sləʊvæk/ *a & n* slovacco, -a *mf*

Slovakia /sləʊ'vækɪə/ *n* Slovacchia *f*

Slovene /'sləʊviːn/ *a & n* sloveno, -a *mf*

Slovenia /sləʊə'viːnɪə/ *n* Slovenia *f*

slovenliness /'slʌvənlɪnɪs/ *n* sciatteria *f*

slovenly /'slʌvnlɪ/ *a* sciatto

slow /sləʊ/ *a* lento; **be ~** ⟨*clock:*⟩ essere indietro; **in ~ motion** al rallentatore ● *adv* lentamente

■ **slow down** *vt/i* rallentare

■ **slow up** *vt/i* rallentare

slowcoach /'sləʊkəʊtʃ/ *n fam* tartaruga *f*

slowly /'sləʊlɪ/ *adv* lentamente

slowness /'sləʊnɪs/ *n* lentezza *f*

slow puncture *n* foratura *f*

sludge /slʌdʒ/ *n* fanghiglia *f*

slug /slʌg/ *n* lumacone *m*; (*bullet*) pallottola *f*

sluggish /'slʌgɪʃ/ *a* lento

sluggishly /'slʌgɪʃnɪs/ *adv* lentamente

sluice /sluːs/ *n* chiusa *f*

sluice gate *n* saracinesca *f* (*di chiusa*)

slum /slʌm/ *n* (*house*) tugurio *m*; **~s** *pl* bassifondi *mpl*

slumber /'slʌmbə(r)/ *n* sonno *m* ● *vi* dormire

slump /slʌmp/ *n* crollo *m*; (*economic*) depressione *f* ● *vi* crollare

slung /slʌŋ/ *see* **sling**

slunk /slʌŋk/ *see* **slink**

slur /slɜː(r)/ *n* (*discredit*) calunnia *f* ● *vt* (*pt/ pp* **slurred**) biascicare

slurp /slɜːp/ *vt/i* bere rumorosamente

slurry /'slʌrɪ/ *n* (*waste from animals*) liquame *m*; (*waste from factory*) fanghiglia *f* semiliquida; (*of cement*) impasto *m* semiliquido

slush /slʌʃ/ *n* pantano *m* nevoso; *fig* sdolcinatezza *f*

slush fund *n* fondi *mpl* neri

slushy /'slʌʃɪ/ *a* fangoso; (*sentimental*) sdolcinato

slut /slʌt/ *n* sgualdrina *f*

sly /slaɪ/ *a* (**-er, -est**) scaltro ● *n* **on the ~** di nascosto

slyly /'slaɪlɪ/ *adv* scaltramente

SM *n abbr* **sadomasochism**

smacker /'smækə(r)/ *n* (*fam: kiss*) bacio *m*; **500 ~s** (*£500*) 500 sterline

smack¹ /smæk/ *n* (*on face*) schiaffo *m*; (*on bottom*) sculaccione *m* ● *vt* (*on face*) schiaffeggiare; (*on bottom*) sculacciare; **~ one's lips** far schioccare le labbra ● *adv fam* in pieno

smack² *vi* **~ of** *fig* sapere di

small /smɔːl/ *a* piccolo; **be out/work until the ~ hours** fare le ore piccole ● *adv* **chop up ~** fare a pezzettini ● *n* **the ~ of the back** le reni

small: small ads *npl* annunci *mpl* [commerciali]. **small business** *n* piccola impresa *f*. **small change** *n* spiccioli *mpl*. **smallholding** *n* piccola tenuta *f*. **small hours** *npl* ore *fpl* piccole. **small letter** *n* lettera *f* minuscola. **small-minded** /-'maɪndɪd/ *a* meschino. **smallpox** *n* vaiolo *m*. **small print** *n* caratteri *mpl* piccoli; **read the ~ ~** *fig* leggere tutto fin nei minimi particolari. **small talk** *n* chiacchiere *fpl*; **make ~** fare conversazione

smarmy /'smɑːmɪ/ *a* (**-ier, -iest**) *fam* untuoso

smart /smɑːt/ *a* elegante; (*clever*) intelligente; (*brisk*) svelto; **be ~** (*fam: cheeky*) fare il furbo ● *vi* (*hurt*) bruciare

smart alec[k] /'smɑːtælɪk/ *n fam* sapientone *m*

smart card *n* carta *f* intelligente

smarten /'smɑːt(ə)n/ *vt* **~ oneself up** farsi bello

smartly /'smɑːtlɪ/ *adv* elegantemente;

(*cleverly*) intelligentemente; (*briskly*) veloce-mente; (*cheekily*) sfacciatamente

smart money *n fam* **the ~ ~ was on Desert Orchid** gli esperti hanno puntato su Desert Orchid

smash /smæʃ/ *n* fragore *m*; (*collision*) scontro *m*; *Tennis* schiacciata *f* ● *vt* spaccare; *Tennis* schiacciare ● *vi* spaccarsi; (*crash*) schiantarsi (**into** contro)

■ **smash up** *vt* distruggere ⟨*car, bar*⟩

smash-and-grab *n Br* rapina *f* a un negozio (*con sfascio di vetrina*)

smashed /smæʃt/ *a* ⟨*window*⟩ in frantumi; ⟨*vehicle*⟩ sfasciato; ⟨*limb*⟩ fracassato; (*fam: on drugs*) fatto; (*fam: on alcohol*) ubriaco fradicio

smash [hit] *n* successo *m*

smashing /'smæʃɪŋ/ *a fam* fantastico

smattering /'smætərɪŋ/ *n* infarinatura *f*

smear /smɪə(r)/ *n* macchia *f*; *Med* striscio *m* ● *vt* imbrattare; (*coat*) spalmare (**with** di); *fig* calunniare ● *vi* sbavare

smear campaign *n* campagna *f* diffamatoria

smear test *n Med* striscio *m*, Pap test *m inv*

smell /smel/ *n* odore *m*; (*sense*) odorato *m* ● *v* (*pt/pp* **smelt** *or* **smelled**) ● *vt* odorare; (*sniff*) annusare ● *vi* odorare (**of** di); **that ~s good** ha un buon odore

smelling salts /'smelɪŋ/ *npl Med* sali *mpl*

smelly /'smelɪ/ *a* (**-ier, -iest**) puzzolente

smelt¹ /smelt/ *see* **smell**

smelt² *vt* fondere

smidgeon /'smɪdʒɪn/ *n* (*of something to eat*) pizzico *m*; (*of something to drink*) goccio *m*

smile /smaɪl/ *n* sorriso *m* ● *vi* sorridere; **~ at** sorridere a ⟨*sb*⟩; sorridere di ⟨*sth*⟩

smirk /smɜːk/ *n* sorriso *m* compiaciuto ● *vi* sorridere con aria compiaciuta

smithereens /smɪðə'riːnz/ *npl* **to/in ~** in mille pezzi

smithy /'smɪðɪ/ *n* fucina *f*

smitten /'smɪtn/ *a* **~ with** tutto preso da

smock /smɒk/ *n* grembiule *m*

smog /smɒg/ *n* smog *m inv*

smoke /sməʊk/ *n* fumo *m* ● *vt/i* fumare

smoked /sməʊkt/ *a* affumicato

smoke-free zone *n* zona *f* non-fumatori; '**~**' 'vietato fumare'

smokeless /'sməʊklɪs/ *a* senza fumo; ⟨*fuel*⟩ che non fa fumo

smoker /'sməʊkə(r)/ *n* fumatore, -trice *mf*; *Rail* vagone *m* fumatori

smokescreen /'sməʊkskriːn/ *n* *also fig* cortina *f* di fumo

smoking /'sməʊkɪŋ/ *n* fumo *m*; '**no ~**' 'vietato fumare'; '**~ or non-~?**' 'fumatori o non fumatori?'

smoky /'sməʊkɪ/ *a* (**-ier, -iest**) fumoso; ⟨*taste*⟩ di fumo

smooch /smuːtʃ/ *vi fam* pomiciare

smooth /smuːð/ *a* liscio; ⟨*movement*⟩ scorrevole; ⟨*sea*⟩ calmo; ⟨*manners*⟩ mellifluo ● *vt* lisciare; **~ things over** sistemare le cose

■ **smooth out** *vt* lisciare

smoothly /'smuːðlɪ/ *adv* in modo scorrevole; **go ~** andare liscio

smooth-tongued /-'tʌŋd/ *a pej* mellifluo

smother /'smʌðə(r)/ *vt* soffocare

smoulder /'sməʊldə(r)/ *vi* fumare; (*with rage*) consumarsi

smudge /smʌdʒ/ *n* macchia *f* ● *vt/i* imbrattare

smug /smʌg/ *a* (**smugger, smuggest**) compiaciuto

smuggle /'smʌgl/ *vt* contrabbandare

smuggler /'smʌglə(r)/ *n* contrabbandiere, -a *mf*

smuggling /'smʌglɪŋ/ *n* contrabbando *m*

smugly /'smʌglɪ/ *adv* con aria compiaciuta

smugness /'smʌgnɪs/ *n* compiacimento *m*

smut /smʌt/ *n* macchia *f* di fuliggine; *fig* sconcezza *f*

smutty /'smʌtɪ/ *a* (**-ier, -iest**) fuligginoso; *fig* sconcio

snack /snæk/ *n* spuntino *m*

snack-bar *n* snack bar *m inv*

snag¹ /snæg/ *n* (*problem*) intoppo *m*

snag² *vt* smagliarsi ⟨*tights*⟩ (**on** con)

snail /sneɪl/ *n* lumaca *f*; **at a ~'s pace** a passo di lumaca

snake /sneɪk/ *n* serpente *m*

snake: **snakebite** *n* morso *m* di serpente. **snake charmer** *n* incantatore, -trice *mf* di serpenti. **snakes and ladders** *n Br* gioco *m* dell'oca

snap /snæp/ *n* colpo *m* secco; (*photo*) istantanea *f* ● *attrib* ⟨*decision*⟩ istantaneo ● *v* (*pt/pp* **snapped**) ● *vi* (*break*) spezzarsi ● *vt* (*break*) spezzare; (*say*) dire seccamente; *Phot* fare un'istantanea di; schioccare ⟨*fingers*⟩

■ **snap at** ⟨*dog:*⟩ cercare di azzannare; ⟨*person:*⟩ parlare seccamente a

■ **snap off** *vt* **~ sb's head off** *fam* aggredire qcno

■ **snap out** *vi* **~ out of it** venirne fuori

■ **snap up** *vt* afferrare

snappy /'snæpɪ/ *a* (**-ier, -iest**) scorbutico; (*smart*) elegante; **make it ~!** sbrigati!

snapshot /'snæpʃɒt/ *n* istantanea *f*

snare /sneə(r)/ *n* trappola *f*

snarl /snɑːl/ *n* ringhio *m* ● *vi* ringhiare

snarled-up /snɑːld'ʌp/ *a* ⟨*traffic*⟩ bloccato

snarl-up *n* (*in traffic, network*) ingorgo *m*

snatch /snætʃ/ *n* strappo *m*; (*fragment*) brano *m*; (*theft*) scippo *m*; **make a ~ at sth** cercare di afferrare qcsa ● *vt* strappare [di mano] (**from** a); (*steal*) scippare; rapire ⟨*child*⟩

snazzy /'snæzɪ/ *a fam* sciccoso

sneak /sniːk/ *n* (*fam: devious person*) tipo, -a *mf* subdolo, -a; (*Br fam: telltale*) spia *f* ● *vt* (*fam: steal*) fregare; rubare ⟨*kiss*⟩; **~ a glance at** dare una sbirciatina a ● *vi* (*Br fam: tell tales*) fare la spia ● *attrib* ⟨*visit*⟩ furtivo; **have a ~ preview of sth** vedere qcsa in anteprima

■ **sneak away** *vi* sgattaiolare via

■ **sneak in** *vi* sgattaiolare dentro

■ **sneak out** *vi* sgattaiolare fuori

sneakers /'sniːkəz/ *npl Am* scarpe *fpl* da ginnastica

sneaking /'sniːkɪŋ/ *a* furtivo; ‹suspicion› vago

sneaky /'sniːkɪ/ *a* sornione

sneer /snɪə(r)/ *n* ghigno *m* ● *vi* sogghignare; **~ at** ‹mock› ridere di

sneeze /sniːz/ *n* starnuto *m* ● *vi* starnutire; **it's not to be ~d at** non ci sputerei sopra

snide /snaɪd/ *a fam* insinuante

sniff /snɪf/ *n* ‹of dog› annusata *f*; **give a ~** ‹person:› tirare su col naso ● *vi* tirare su col naso ● *vt* odorare ‹flower›; sniffare ‹glue›; ‹dog:› annusare

sniffer dog /'snɪfə/ *n* cane *m* poliziotto (antidroga, antiterrorismo)

sniffle /'snɪfl/ *n* **have a ~** or **the ~s** (slight cold) avere un po' di raffreddore; **give a ~** tirar su col naso ● *vi* tirar su col naso

sniffy /'snɪfɪ/ *a* (fam: haughty) con la puzza sotto il naso

snigger /'snɪgə(r)/ *n* risatina *f* soffocata ● *vi* ridacchiare

snip /snɪp/ *n* taglio *m*; (fam: bargain) affare *m* ● *vt/i* **~ [at]** tagliare

snipe /snaɪp/ *vi* **~ at** tirare su; *fig* sparare a zero su

sniper /'snaɪpə(r)/ *n* cecchino *m*

snippet /'snɪpɪt/ *n* **a ~ of information/ news** una breve notizia/informazione

snivel /'snɪvl/ *vi* (*pt/pp* **snivelled**) piagnucolare

snivelling /'snɪv(ə)lɪŋ/ *a* piagnucoloso

snob /snɒb/ *n* snob *mf inv*

snobbery /'snɒbərɪ/ *n* snobismo *m*

snobbish /'snɒbɪʃ/ *a* da snob; **be ~** ‹person:› essere uno/una snob; ‹club etc:› essere molto snob

snobbishness /'snɒbɪʃnɪs/ *n* snobismo *m*

snog /snɒg/ *vi Br sl* pomiciare

snooker /'snuːkə(r)/ *n* (game) snooker *m*; (shot) impallatura *f* ● *vt Sport* impallare; *fig* mettere in difficoltà

snoop /snuːp/ *n* spia *f* ● *vi fam* curiosare

snooper /'snuːpə(r)/ *n* ficcanaso *mf*

snooty /'snuːtɪ/ *a fam* sdegnoso

snooze /snuːz/ *n* sonnellino *m* ● *vi* fare un sonnellino

snore /snɔː(r)/ *vi* russare

snoring /'snɔːrɪŋ/ *n* il russare

snorkel /'snɔːkl/ *n* respiratore *m*

snort /snɔːt/ *n* sbuffo *n* ● *vi* sbuffare ● *vt* fiutare ‹cocaine›

snot /snɒt/ *n* (fam: mucus) moccolo *m*

snotty /'snɒtɪ/ *a fam* ‹nose› moccicoso; (disagreeable) sgradevole

snotty-nosed kid /-nəʊzd/ *n* moccioso, -a *mf*

snout /snaʊt/ *n* grugno *m*

snow /snəʊ/ *n* neve *f* ● *vi* nevicare; **~ed under with** *fig* sommerso di

snow: snowball *n* palla *f* di neve ● *vi fig* fare a palle di neve. **snowdrift** *n* cumulo *m* di neve. **snowdrop** *n* bucaneve *m inv*. **snowfall**

n nevicata *f*. **snowflake** *n* fiocco *m* di neve.

snowman *n* pupazzo *m* di neve.

snowmobile /'snəʊməbiːl/ *n* gatto *m* delle nevi. **snowplough** *n* spazzaneve *m inv*.

snowstorm *n* tormenta *f*. **snow tyres** *npl* pneumatici *mpl* chiodati

snowy /'snəʊɪ/ *a* nevoso

Snr *abbr* **Senior**

snub /snʌb/ *n* sgarbo *m* ● *vt* (*pt/pp* **snubbed**) snobbare

snub-nosed /'snʌbnəʊzd/ *a* dal naso all'insù

snuff[1] /snʌf/ *n* tabacco *m* da fiuto

snuff[2] *vt* **~ [out]** spegnere ‹candle›; **~ it** *fam* tirare le cuoia

snug /snʌg/ *a* (**snugger**, **snuggest**) comodo; (tight) aderente

snuggle /'snʌgl/ *vi* rannicchiarsi (**up to** accanto a)

so /səʊ/ *adv* così; **so far** finora; **so am I** anch'io; **so I see** così pare; **you've left the door open – so I have!** l'ho fatto!; **that is so** è così; **so much** così tanto; **so much the better** tanto meglio; **so it is** proprio così; **if so** se è così; **so as to** in modo da; **so long!** *fam* a presto!; **I hope/think/am afraid so** spero/penso/temo di sì; **I told you so** te l'ho detto; **because I say so** perché lo dico io; **I did so!** l'ho fatto!; **so saying/doing,...** così dicendo/facendo,...; **or so** circa; **very much so** sì, molto; **and so forth** *or* **on** e così via ● *conj* (therefore) perciò; (in order that) così; **so that** affinché; **so there!** ecco!; **so what?** e allora?; **so where have you been?** allora, dove sei stato?

soak /səʊk/ *vt* mettere a bagno ● *vi* stare a bagno

■ **soak in** *vi* penetrare

■ **soak into** *vt* ‹liquid:› penetrare

■ **soak up** *vt* assorbire

soaked /səʊkt/ *a* fradicio; **~ in sth** impregnato di qcsa

soaking /'səʊkɪŋ/ *n* ammollo *m* ● *a & adv* **~ [wet]** *fam* inzuppato

so-and-so *n* Tal dei Tali *mf*; (euphemism) specie *f* di imbecille

soap /səʊp/ *n* sapone *m*

soap opera *n* telenovella *f*, soap opera *f inv*

soap powder *n* detersivo *m* in polvere

soapy /'səʊpɪ/ *a* (**-ier, -iest**) insaponato

soar /sɔː(r)/ *vi* elevarsi; ‹prices:› salire alle stelle

S.O.B. *n Am abbr* **son of a bitch**

sob /sɒb/ *n* singhiozzo *m* ● *vi* (*pt/pp* **sobbed**) singhiozzare

sobbing /'sɒbɪŋ/ *n* singhiozzi *mpl*

sober /'səʊbə(r)/ *a* sobrio; (serious) serio

■ **sober up** *vi* ritornare sobrio

soberly /'səʊbəlɪ/ *adv* sobriamente; (seriously) con aria seria

sobriety /sə'braɪətɪ/ *n* (not drinking) sobrietà *f*; (seriousness) serietà *f*

sob story *n* storia *f* lacrimevole

so-called /'səʊkɔːld/ *a* cosiddetto

soccer /'sɒkə(r)/ *n* calcio *m*

soccer pitch n campo m di calcio
soccer player n giocatore m di calcio
sociable /'səʊʃəbl/ a socievole
social /'səʊʃl/ a sociale; (sociable) socievole
social climber n arrampicatore, -trice mf sociale
social climbing n arrivismo m sociale
socialism /'səʊʃəlɪzm/ n socialismo m
socialist /'səʊʃəlɪst/ a socialista ● n socialista mf
socialite /'səʊʃəlaɪt/ n persona f che fa vita mondana
socialize /'səʊʃəlaɪz/ vi socializzare
socially /'səʊʃəlɪ/ adv socialmente; **know sb ~** frequentare qcno
social: social security n previdenza f sociale. **social services** npl servizi mpl sociali. **social work** n assistenza f sociale. **social worker** n assistente mf sociale
society /sə'saɪətɪ/ n società f inv
socio-economic /səʊsɪəʊi:kə'nɒmɪk/ a socioeconomico
sociological /səʊsɪə'lɒdʒɪkl/ a sociologico
sociologist /səʊsɪ'ɒlədʒɪst/ n sociologo, -a mf
sociology /səʊsɪ'ɒlədʒɪ/ n sociologia f
sock[1] /sɒk/ n calzino m; (kneelength) calza f
sock[2] fam n pugno m ● vt dare un pugno a
socket /'sɒkɪt/ n (of eye) orbita f; (wall plug) presa f [di corrente]; (for bulb) portalampada m inv
sod /sɒd/ n fam stronzo m; **you lucky ~!** che fortuna sfacciata!
■ **sod off** vi fam togliersi dai piedi
soda /'səʊdə/ n soda f; Am gazzosa f
soda water n seltz m inv
sodden /'sɒdn/ a inzuppato
sodium /'səʊdɪəm/ n sodio m
sodium bicarbonate n bicarbonato m di sodio
Sod's Law /sɒdz/ n fam hum regola f per cui, se qualcosa può andare storto, va storto
sofa /'səʊfə/ n divano m
sofa bed n divano m letto
soft /sɒft/ a morbido, soffice; (voice) sommesso; (light, colour) tenue; (not strict) indulgente; (fam: silly) stupido
soft: soft-boiled /-'bɔɪld/ a (egg) bazzotto. **soft contact lenses** npl lenti fpl a contatto morbide. **soft drink** n bibita f analcolica. **soft drug** n droga f leggera
soften /'sɒfn/ vt ammorbidire; fig attenuare ● vi ammorbidirsi
softener /'sɒf(ə)nə(r)/ n (for water) dolcificatore m; (substance) anti-calcare m inv; (for fabrics) ammorbidente m
soft: soft furnishings npl tappeti mpl e tessuti mpl da arredamento. **soft-hearted** a dal cuore tenero. **soft ice-cream** n mantecato m
softie /'sɒftɪ/ n fam = **softy**
softly /'sɒftlɪ/ adv (say) sottovoce; (treat) con indulgenza; (play music) in sottofondo
soft: soft-pedal vt fig minimizzare. **soft porn** n fam pornografia f soft[-core]. **soft sell** n metodo m di vendita basato sulla persuasione. **soft soap** n fig lusinghe fpl. **soft-soap** vt fig lusingare. **soft-spoken** a dalla voce dolce. **soft spot** n have a ~ ~ for sb avere un debole per qcno. **soft-top** n Auto decappottabile f. **soft touch** n be a ~ ~ lasciarsi spremere. **soft toy** n pupazzo m di peluche
software /'sɒftweə(r)/ n software m
software: software engineer n softwarista mf. **software house** n software house f. **software package** n pacchetto m software. **software writer** n scrittore, -trice mf di programmi
softy /'sɒftɪ/ n fam (weak person) pappamolle mf inv; (indulgent person) bonaccione, -a mf
soggy /'sɒgɪ/ a (-ier, -iest) zuppo
soil[1] /sɔɪl/ n suolo m
soil[2] vt sporcare
solace /'sɒləs/ n sollievo m
solar /'səʊlə(r)/ a solare
solar: solar energy n energia f solare. **solar panel** n pannello m solare. **solar power** n energia f solare. **solar system** n sistema m solare
sold /səʊld/ see **sell**
solder /'səʊldə(r)/ n lega f da saldatura ● vt saldare
soldier /'səʊldʒə(r)/ n soldato m
■ **soldier on** vi perseverare
sole[1] /səʊl/ n (of foot) pianta f; (of shoe) suola f
sole[2] n (fish) sogliola f
sole[3] a unico, solo
sole agency n rappresentanza f esclusiva
solecism /'sɒlɪsɪzm/ n (social) scorrettezza f; (linguistic) solecismo m
solely /'səʊllɪ/ adv unicamente
solemn /'sɒləm/ a solenne
solemnity /sə'lemnətɪ/ n solennità f inv
solemnly /'sɒləmlɪ/ adv solennemente
sol-fa /'sɒlfɑ:/ n solfeggio m
solicit /sə'lɪsɪt/ vt sollecitare ● vi (prostitute:) adescare
soliciting /sə'lɪsɪtɪŋ/ n Jur adescamento m
solicitor /sə'lɪsɪtə(r)/ n avvocato m
solicitous /sə'lɪsɪtəs/ a premuroso
solicitously /sə'lɪsɪtəslɪ/ adv premurosamente
solid /'sɒlɪd/ a solido; (oak, gold) massiccio; **it took a ~ hour** ci è voluta ben un'ora ● n (figure) solido m; **~s** pl (food) cibi mpl solidi
solidarity /sɒlɪ'dærətɪ/ n solidarietà f inv
solidify /sə'lɪdɪfaɪ/ vi (pt/pp -ied) solidificarsi
soliloquy /sə'lɪləkwɪ/ n soliloquio m
solitaire /sɒlɪ'teə(r)/ n solitario m
solitary /'sɒlɪtərɪ/ a solitario; (sole) solo
solitary confinement n cella f di isolamento
solitude /'sɒlɪtju:d/ n solitudine f
solo /'səʊləʊ/ n Mus assolo m ● a (flight) in solitario ● adv in solitario
soloist /'səʊləʊɪst/ n solista mf
solstice /'sɒlstɪs/ n solstizio m
soluble /'sɒljʊbl/ a solubile

solution /sə'lu:ʃn/ n soluzione f
solvable /'sɒlvəbl/ a risolvibile
solve /sɒlv/ vt risolvere
solvency /'sɒlvənsɪ/ n Fin solvibilità f
solvent /'sɒlvənt/ a & n solvente m
solvent abuse n uso m di solventi come stupefacenti
Somali /səʊ'mɑ:lɪ/ a & n somalo, -a mf
Somalia /səʊ'mɑ:lɪə/ n Somalia f
sombre /'sɒmbə(r)/ a tetro; ⟨clothes⟩ scuro
some /sʌm/ a (a certain amount of) del; (a certain number of) alcuni, dei; ~ **bread/ water** del pane/dell'acqua; ~ **books/ oranges** dei libri/delle arance; **I need** ~ **money/books** ho bisogno di soldi/libri; **do** ~ **shopping** fare qualche acquisto; ~ **day** un giorno o l'altro ● pron (a certain amount) un po'; (a certain number) alcuni; **I want** ~ ne voglio; **would you like** ~? ne vuoi?; ~ **of the butter** una parte del burro; ~ **of the apples/women** alcune delle mele/donne
somebody /'sʌmbədɪ/ pron qualcuno m; ~ **else will bring it** la porterà un altro ● n **he thinks he's** ~ si crede chissà chi
somehow /'sʌmhaʊ/ adv in qualche modo; ~ **or other** in un modo o nell'altro
someone /'sʌmwʌn/ pron & n = **somebody**
somersault /'sʌməsɔ:lt/ n capriola f; **turn a** ~ fare una capriola ● vi fare una capriola
something /'sʌmθɪŋ/ pron qualche cosa, qualcosa; ~ **different** qualcosa di diverso; ~ **like** un po' come; (approximately) qualcosa come; **see** ~ **of sb** vedere qcno ogni tanto; **she is** ~ **of an expert** è un'esperta
sometime /'sʌmtaɪm/ adv un giorno o l'altro; ~ **last summer** durante l'estate scorsa ● a ex
sometimes /'sʌmtaɪmz/ adv qualche volta
somewhat /'sʌmwɒt/ adv piuttosto
somewhere /'sʌmweə(r)/ adv da qualche parte ● pron ~ **to eat** un posto in cui mangiare
son /sʌn/ n figlio m
sonar /'səʊnɑ:(r)/ n sonar m
sonata /sə'nɑ:tə/ n sonata f
song /sɒŋ/ n canzone f
song: song and dance n **make a** ~ ~ ~ **about sth** (fuss) far tante storie per qcsa.
songbird n uccello m canoro. **songwriter** n compositore, -trice mf di canzoni
sonic /'sɒnɪk/ a sonico
sonic boom n bang m inv sonico
son-in-law n (pl ~s-in-law) genero m
sonnet /'sɒnɪt/ n sonetto m
son of a bitch n fam figlio m di un cane
sonorous /'sɒnərəs/ a sonoro; ⟨name⟩ altisonante
soon /su:n/ adv presto; (in a short time) tra poco; **as** ~ **as** [non] appena; **as** ~ **as possible** il più presto possibile; ~**er or later** prima o poi; **the** ~**er the better** prima è, meglio è; **no** ~**er had I arrived than...** ero appena arrivato quando...; **I would** ~**er go** preferirei andare; ~ **after** subito dopo
soot /sʊt/ n fuliggine f

soothe /su:ð/ vt calmare
soothing /'su:ðɪŋ/ a calmante
sooty /'sʊtɪ/ a fuligginoso
sop /sɒp/ n **throw a** ~ **to** dare un contentino a
sophisticated /sə'fɪstɪkeɪtɪd/ a sofisticato; (complex) complesso
sophistication /səfɪstɪ'keɪʃn/ n (elegance) sofisticatezza f, raffinatezza f; (complexity) complessità f
soporific /sɒpə'rɪfɪk/ a soporifero
soppiness /'sɒpɪnɪs/ n fam svenevolezza f
sopping /'sɒpɪŋ/ a & adv **be** ~ [**wet**] essere bagnato fradicio
soppy /'sɒpɪ/ a (-ier, -iest) fam svenevole
soprano /sə'prɑ:nəʊ/ n soprano m
sorcerer /'sɔ:sərə(r)/ n stregone m
sorceress /'sɔ:sərɪs/ n strega f, maga f
sorcery /'sɔ:sərɪ/ n (witchcraft) stregoneria f
sordid /'sɔ:dɪd/ a sordido
sordidness /'sɔ:dɪdnɪs/ n sordidezza f
sore /sɔ:(r)/ a dolorante; (Am: vexed) arrabbiato; **it's** ~ fa male; **have a** ~ **throat** avere mal di gola; **it's a** ~ **point with her** è un punto delicato per lei ● n piaga f
sorely /'sɔ:lɪ/ adv ⟨tempted⟩ seriamente
soreness /'sɔ:nɪs/ n dolore m
sorrel /'sɒrəl/ n Bot acetosa f
sorrow /'sɒrəʊ/ n tristezza f
sorrowful /'sɒrəʊfʊl/ a triste
sorrowfully /'sɒrəʊfʊlɪ/ adv tristemente
sorry /'sɒrɪ/ a (-ier, -iest) (sad) spiacente; (wretched) pietoso; **you'll be** ~! te ne pentirai!; **I am** ~ mi dispiace; **be** or **feel** ~ **for** provare compassione per; ~! scusa!; (more polite) scusi!
sort /sɔ:t/ n tipo m; **it's a** ~ **of fish** è un tipo di pesce; **be out of** ~**s** (fam: unwell) stare poco bene ● vt classificare; fam sistemare ⟨problem, person⟩
■ **sort out** vt selezionare ⟨papers⟩; fig risolvere ⟨problem⟩; occuparsi di ⟨person⟩
sort code n Fin coordinate fpl bancarie
sorter /'sɔ:tə(r)/ n (on photocopier) fascicolatrice f, fascicolatore m
SOS n SOS m; fig segnale m di soccorso
so-so a & adv così così
sotto voce /sɒtəʊ'vəʊtʃeɪ/ adv ⟨say, add⟩ sottovoce
soufflé /'su:fleɪ/ n sufflè m
sought /sɔ:t/ see **seek**
sought-after a ⟨job, brand, person⟩ richiesto
soul /səʊl/ n anima f; **poor** ~ poveretto; **there was not a** ~ **in sight** non c'era anima viva
soul-destroying /-dɪstrɔɪɪŋ/ a ⟨job⟩ che abbrutisce
soulful /'səʊlfʊl/ a sentimentale
soul: soulmate n anima f gemella. **soul-searching** /-sɜ:tʃɪŋ/ n esame m di coscienza. **soul-stirring** /-stɜ:rɪŋ/ a molto commovente
sound¹ /saʊnd/ a sano; (sensible) saggio;

(secure) solido; *⟨thrashing⟩* clamoroso ● *adv*
~ asleep profondamente addormentato
sound² *n* suono *m*; *(noise)* rumore *m*; **I don't
like the ~ of it** *fam* non mi suona bene ● *vi*
suonare; *(seem)* aver l'aria; **it ~s to me as
if...** mi sa che... ● *vt (pronounce)* pronunciare;
Med auscoltare *⟨chest⟩*
■ **sound off** *vi* fare grandi discorsi
■ **sound out** *vt fig* sondare
sound: sound barrier *n* muro *m* del suono.
sound bite *n breve frase f dal forte impatto
mediatico*. **sound card** *n Comput* scheda *f* sonora. **sound effect** *n* effetto *m* sonoro.
sound engineer *n* tecnico *m* del suono
soundless /'saʊndlɪs/ *a* silenzioso
soundlessly /'saʊndlɪslɪ/ *adv* silenziosamente
soundly /'saʊndlɪ/ *adv ⟨sleep⟩* profondamente; *⟨defeat⟩* clamorosamente
sound: soundproof *a* impenetrabile al suono ● *vt* insonorizzare. **sound system** *n (hifī)*
stereo *m*; *(for disco etc)* impianto *m* audio.
soundtrack *n* colonna *f* sonora
soup /su:p/ *n* minestra *f*; **in the ~** *fam* nei
pasticci
souped-up /su:pt'ʌp/ *a fam ⟨engine⟩* truccato
soup: soup kitchen *n* mensa *f* dei poveri.
soup plate *n* piatto *m* fondo. **soup spoon** *n*
cucchiaio *m* da minestra
sour /'saʊə(r)/ *a* agro; *(not fresh & fig)* acido
source /sɔ:s/ *n* fonte *f*; **at ~** *⟨deducted⟩* alla
fonte
sour: sour cream *n* panna *f* acida. **sour-
faced** /saʊə'feɪst/ *a ⟨person⟩* dall'espressione
dura. **sour grapes** *npl fam* **it's just ~ ~** *[on
his part]* fa come la volpe con l'uva
south /saʊθ/ *n* sud *m*; **to the ~ of** a sud di
● *a* del sud, meridionale ● *adv* a sud
south: South Africa *n* Sudafrica *f*. **South
African** *a & n* sudafricano, -a *mf*. **South
America** *n* America *f* del Sud. **South
American** *a & n* sud-americano, -a *mf*.
southbound *a ⟨traffic⟩* diretto a sud;
⟨carriageway⟩ sud. **south-east** *n* sud-est *m*
southerly /'sʌðəlɪ/ *a* del sud
southern /'sʌðən/ *a* del sud, meridionale; **~
Italy** il Mezzogiorno
southerner /'sʌðənə(r)/ *n* meridionale *mf*
southpaw /'saʊθpɔ:/ *n (in boxing)* pugile *m*
mancino
South Pole *n* polo *m* Sud
southward[s] /'saʊθwəd[z]/ *adv* verso sud
south-west /saʊθ'west/ *n* sud-ovest *m*
south-western /saʊθ'westən/ *a* sudocci-
dentale
souvenir /su:və'nɪə(r)/ *n* ricordo *m*,
souvenir *m inv*
sovereign /'sɒvrɪn/ *a & n* sovrano, -a *mf*
sovereignty /'sɒvrɪntɪ/ *n* sovranità *f inv*
Soviet /'saʊvɪət/ *a* sovietico
Soviet Union *n* Unione *f* Sovietica
sow¹ /saʊ/ *n* scrofa *f*
sow² /səʊ/ *vt (pt sowed, pp sown or sowed)*
seminare

soya bean /'sɔɪə/ *n* soia *f*
soy sauce /sɔɪ/ *n* salsa *f* di soia
sozzled /'sɒzld/ *a fam* sbronzo
spa /spa:/ *n* stazione *f* termale
space /speɪs/ *n* spazio *m* ● *a ⟨research etc⟩*
spaziale ● *vt* ~ **[out]** distanziare
space: space age *n* era *f* spaziale ● *attrib*
dell'era spaziale. **space bar** *n* barra *f* spazio.
spacecraft *n* navetta *f* spaziale. **space
cadet** *n fig fam* allucinato, -a *mf*. **space capsule** *n* capsula *f* spaziale. **spaced out**
/speɪst'aʊt/ *a fam* **he's completely ~ ~** è
completamente fuori di testa. **space-saving**
a poco ingombrante. **spaceship** *n* astronave
f. **space shuttle** *n* shuttle *m*. **space travel** *n*
viaggi *mpl* nello spazio. **space walk** *n* passeggiata *f* nello spazio
spacing /'speɪsɪŋ/ *n* distanziamento *m*;
single/double ~ interlinea *m* semplice/dop-
pio
spacious /'speɪʃəs/ *a* spazioso
spade /speɪd/ *n* vanga *f*; *(for child)* paletta *f*;
~s *pl (Cards)* picche *fpl*; **call a ~ a ~** dire
pane al pane e vino al vino
spadework /'speɪdwɜ:k/ *n fig* lavoro *m* preparatorio
spaghetti /spə'getɪ/ *n* spaghetti *mpl*
spaghetti bolognese /bʊlə'neɪz/ *n* spaghetti *mpl* al ragù
spaghetti junction *n fam* intricato raccordo *m* autostradale
Spain /speɪn/ *n* Spagna *f*
span¹ /spæn/ *n* spanna *f*; *(of arch)* luce *f*; *(of
time)* arco *m*; *(of wings)* apertura *f* ● *vt (pt/pp
spanned)* estendersi su
span² *see* **spick**
Spaniard /'spænjəd/ *n* Spagnolo, -a *mf*
spaniel /'spænjəl/ *n* spaniel *m inv*
Spanish /'spænɪʃ/ *a* spagnolo ● *n (language)*
spagnolo *m*; **the ~** *pl* gli Spagnoli
spank /spæŋk/ *vt* sculacciare
spanking /'spæŋkɪŋ/ *n* sculacciata *f* ● *a fam*
at a ~ pace con passo spedito ● *adv fam* **a ~
new car** una macchina nuova di zecca
spanner /'spænə(r)/ *n* chiave *f* inglese
spar /spa:(r)/ *vi (pt/pp sparred) (boxing)* allenarsi; *(argue)* litigare
spare /speə(r)/ *a (surplus)* in più;
(additional) di riserva; **go ~** *(fam: be very
angry)* andare su tutte le furie ● *n (part)* ricambio *m* ● *vt* risparmiare; *(do without)*
fare a meno di; **can you ~ five minutes?**
avresti cinque minuti?; **no expense was
~d** non si è badato a spese; **to ~** *(surplus)*
in eccedenza
spare: spare part *n* pezzo *m* di ricambio.
spare ribs *npl* costine *fpl*. **spare room** *n*
stanza *f* degli ospiti. **spare time** *n* tempo *m*
libero. **spare tyre** *n Br Auto* gomma *f* di scorta; *(fam: fat)* trippa *f*. **spare wheel** *n* ruota *f*
di scorta
sparing /'speərɪŋ/ *a* parco *(with* di)
sparingly /'speərɪŋlɪ/ *adv* con parsimonia
spark /spa:k/ *n* scintilla *f*
■ **spark off** *vt* far scoppiare

sparkle /'spɑːkl/ *n* scintillio *m* ● *vi* scintillare

sparkling /'spɑːklɪŋ/ *a* frizzante; ⟨*wine*⟩ spumante

spark-plug *n Auto* candela *f*

sparrow /'spærəʊ/ *n* passero *m*

sparse /spɑːs/ *a* rado

sparsely /'spɑːslɪ/ *adv* scarsamente; ~ **populated** ⟨*area*⟩ a bassa densità di popolazione

sparseness /'spɑːsnɪs/ *n* (*of vegetation*) radezza *f*

spartan /'spɑːtn/ *a* spartano

spasm /'spæzm/ *n* spasmo *m*

spasmodic /spæz'mɒdɪk/ *a* spasmodico

spasmodically /spæz'mɒdɪklɪ/ *adv* spasmodicamente

spastic /'spæstɪk/ *a* spastico ● *n* spastico, -a *mf*

spat /spæt/ *see* **spit**[1]

spate /speɪt/ *n* (*series*) successione *f*; **be in full** ~ essere in piena

spatial /'speɪʃl/ *a* spaziale

spatio-temporal /speɪʃɪəʊ'tempərəl/ *a* spazio-temporale

spatter /'spætə(r)/ *vt/i* schizzare

spatula /'spætjʊlə/ *n* spatola *f*

spawn /spɔːn/ *n* uova *fpl* (*di pesci, rane ecc*) ● *vi* deporre le uova ● *vt fig* generare

spay /speɪ/ *vt* sterilizzare

speak /spiːk/ *v* (*pt* **spoke**, *pp* **spoken**) ● *vi* parlare (**to** a); ~**ing!** *Teleph* sono io! ● *vt* dire; ~ **one's mind** dire quello che si pensa

▪ **speak for** *vt* parlare a nome di; ~ **for yourself!** parla per te!

▪ **speak of** *vt* ~ **well/ill of sb** parlare bene/male di qcno; **nothing to** ~ **of** niente di speciale; (*quantity*) non un granché; ~**ing of holidays...** a proposito di vacanze...

▪ **speak out** *vi* (*protest*) parlare

▪ **speak up** *vi* parlare più forte; ~ **up for oneself** farsi valere

speaker /'spiːkə(r)/ *n* parlante *mf*; (*in public*) oratore, -trice *mf*; (*of stereo*) cassa *f*

speaking terms /'spiːkɪŋ/ *npl* **we are not on** ~ ~ non ci parliamo

spear /'spɪə(r)/ *n* lancia *f* ● *vt* trafiggere

spearhead /'spɪəhed/ *vt fig* essere l'iniziatore di

spearmint /'spɪəmɪnt/ *n* menta *f* verde

spec /spek/ *n* **on** ~ *fam* ⟨*take, use*⟩ in prova; ⟨*go somewhere*⟩ per ispezione

special /'speʃl/ *a* speciale

special: special correspondent *n* inviato, -a *mf* speciale. **special delivery** *n* espresso *m*. **special effect** *n Cinema, TV* effetto *m* speciale ● *attrib* ~ ~**s** ⟨*specialist, team*⟩ degli effetti speciali. **special envoy** *n* inviato, -a *mf* speciale

specialist /'speʃəlɪst/ *n* specialista *mf*

speciality /speʃɪ'ælətɪ/ *n* specialità *f inv*

specialize /'speʃəlaɪz/ *vi* specializzarsi

specially /'speʃəlɪ/ *adv* specialmente; (*particularly*) particolarmente

special offer *n* vendita *f* promozionale

special treatment *n* trattamento *m* di riguardo

species /'spiːʃiːz/ *n* specie *f inv*

specific /spə'sɪfɪk/ *a* specifico

specifically /spə'sɪfɪklɪ/ *adv* in modo specifico

specifications /spesɪfɪ'keɪ∫nz/ *npl* descrizione *f*

specify /'spesɪfaɪ/ *vt* (*pt/pp* **-ied**) specificare

specimen /'spesɪmən/ *n* campione *m*

specious /'spiːʃəs/ *a* ⟨*argument, reasoning*⟩ specioso

speck /spek/ *n* macchiolina *f*; (*particle*) granello *m*

speckled /'spekld/ *a* picchiettato

specs /speks/ *npl fam* occhiali *mpl*

spectacle /'spektəkl/ *n* (*show*) spettacolo *m*

spectacles /'spektəklz/ *npl* occhiali *mpl*

spectacular /spek'tækjʊlə(r)/ *a* spettacolare

spectacularly /spek'tækjʊləlɪ/ *adv* in modo spettacolare

spectator /spek'teɪtə(r)/ *n* spettatore, -trice *mf*

spectator sport *n* sport *m inv* di intrattenimento

spectre /'spektə(r)/ *n* spettro *m*

spectrum /'spektrəm/ *n* (*pl* **-tra**) spettro *m*; *fig* gamma *f*

speculate /'spekjʊleɪt/ *vi* speculare

speculation /spekjʊ'leɪ∫n/ *n* speculazione *f*

speculative /'spekjʊlətɪv/ *a* speculativo

speculator /'spekjʊleɪtə(r)/ *n* speculatore, -trice *mf*

sped /sped/ *see* **speed**

speech /spiːt∫/ *n* linguaggio *m*; (*address*) discorso *m*; **make a** ~, **give a** ~ fare un discorso

speech day *n Sch* giorno *m* della premiazione

speechless /'spiːt∫lɪs/ *a* senza parole

speech: speech therapist *n* logoterapista *mf*. **speech therapy** *n* logoterapia *f*. **speech-writer** *n* persona *f* che scrive i discorsi di personaggi pubblici

speed /spiːd/ *n* velocità *f inv*; (*gear*) marcia *f*; **at** ~ a tutta velocità ● *vi* (*pt/pp* **sped**) andare veloce ● (*pt/pp* **speeded**) (*go too fast*) andare a velocità eccessiva

▪ **speed up** (*pt/pp* **speeded up**) *vt/i* accelerare

speed: speedboat *n* motoscafo *m*. **speed bump** *n* rallentatore *m*. **speed camera** *n* autovelox® *m inv*

speedily /'spiːdɪlɪ/ *adv* rapidamente

speeding /'spiːdɪŋ/ *n* eccesso *m* di velocità

speeding fine *n* multa *f* per eccesso di velocità

speed limit *n* limite *m* di velocità

speed merchant *n fam* fanatico, -a *mf* della velocità

speedometer /spiː'dɒmɪtə(r)/ *n* tachimetro *m*

speed skating *n* pattinaggio *m* di velocità

speed trap *n Auto* tratto *m* di strada sul

quale la polizia controlla la velocità dei veicoli

speedy /'spi:dɪ/ *a* (**-ier, -iest**) rapido

speleologist /spi:lɪ'ɒlədʒɪst/ *n* speleologo, -a *mf*

speleology /spi:lɪ'ɒlədʒɪ/ *n* speleologia *f*

spell¹ /spel/ *n* (*turn*) turno *m*; (*of weather*) periodo *m*

spell² *v* (*pt/pp* **spelled** *or* **spelt**) ● *vt* **how do you ~...?** come si scrive...?; **could you ~ that for me?** me lo può compitare?; **~ disaster** *fig* essere disastroso ● *vi* **he can't ~** fa molti errori d'ortografia

spell³ *n* (*magic*) incantesimo *m*

■ **spell out** *vt* compitare; *fig* spiegare

spellbound /'spelbaʊnd/ *a* affascinato

spellchecker /'speltʃekə(r)/ *n Comput* correttore *m* ortografico

spelling /'spelɪŋ/ *n* ortografia *f*

spelt /spelt/ *see* **spell²**

spend /spend/ *vt/i* (*pt/pp* **spent**) spendere; passare ⟨*time*⟩

spending money /'spendɪŋ/ *n* soldi *mpl* per le piccole spese

spendthrift /'spendθrɪft/ *a* spendaccione; ⟨*habit, policy*⟩ dispendioso ● *n* spendaccione, -a *mf*

spent /spent/ *see* **spend**

sperm /spɜ:m/ *n* spermatozoo *m*; (*semen*) sperma *m*

sperm bank *n* banca *f* dello sperma

sperm count *n* conteggio *m* di spermatozoi

spermicidal /spɜ:mɪ'saɪdl/ *a* spermicida *inv*

spermicide /'spɜ:mɪsaɪd/ *n* spermicida *m*

spew /spju:/ *vt/i* vomitare

sphere /sfɪə(r)/ *n* sfera *f*

sphere of influence *n* sfera *f* di influenza

spherical /'sferɪkl/ *a* sferico

spice /spaɪs/ *n* spezia *f*; *fig* pepe *m*

spick /spɪk/ *a* **~ and span** lindo

spicy /'spaɪsɪ/ *a* piccante

spider /'spaɪdə(r)/ *n* ragno *m*

spiel /ʃpiːl/ *n fam* (*sales pitch*) imbonimento *m*; (*long repetitive speech*) tiritera *f*; **he gave me some ~ about...** mi ha raccontato un sacco di storie su...

spike /spaɪk/ *n* punta *f*; *Bot, Zool* spina *f*; (*on shoe*) chiodo *m*

spikes *npl* (*shoes*) scarpe *fpl* chiodate

spiky /'spaɪkɪ/ *a* ⟨*plant*⟩ spinoso

spill /spɪl/ *v* (*pt/pp* **spilt** *or* **spilled**) ● *vt* versare ⟨*blood*⟩; **~ the beans** *fam* vuotare il sacco ● *vi* rovesciarsi

spillage /'spɪlɪdʒ/ *n* (*of oil, chemical*) perdita *f*

spin /spɪn/ *v* (*pt/pp* **spun**, *pres p* **spinning**) ● *vt* far girare; filare ⟨*wool*⟩; centrifugare ⟨*washing*⟩ ● *vi* girare; ⟨*washing machine:*⟩ centrifugare ● *n* rotazione *f*; (*short drive*) giretto *m*

■ **spin out** *vt* far durare

spinach /'spɪnɪdʒ/ *n* spinaci *mpl*

spinal /'spaɪnl/ *a* spinale

spinal column *n* colonna *f* vertebrale

spinal cord *n* midollo *m* spinale

spindle /'spɪndl/ *n* fuso *m*

spindly /'spɪndlɪ/ *a* affusolato

spin doctor *n* persona *f* incaricata di presentare le scelte di un partito politico sotto una luce favorevole

spin-drier *n* centrifuga *f*

spine /spaɪn/ *n* spina *f* dorsale; (*of book*) dorso *m*; *Bot, Zool* spina *f*

spineless /'spaɪnlɪs/ *a fig* smidollato

spinning /'spɪnɪŋ/ *n* filatura *f*

spinning wheel *n* filatoio *m*

spin-off *n* ricaduta *f*

spinster /'spɪnstə(r)/ *n* donna *f* nubile; (*old maid, fam*) zitella *f*

spiny /'spaɪnɪ/ *a* ⟨*plant, animal*⟩ spinoso

spiral /'spaɪrəl/ *a* a spirale ● *n* spirale *f* ● *vi* (*pt/pp* **spiralled**) formare una spirale

spiral staircase *n* scala *f* a chiocciola

spire /'spaɪə(r)/ *n* guglia *f*

spirit /'spɪrɪt/ *n* spirito *m*; (*courage*) ardore *m*; **~s** *pl* (*alcohol*) liquori *mpl*; **in good ~s** di buon umore; **in low ~s** abbattuto

■ **spirit away** *vt* far sparire

spirited /'spɪrɪtɪd/ *a* vivace; (*courageous*) pieno d'ardore

spirit level *n* livella *f* a bolla d'aria

spirit stove *n* fornellino *m* [da campeggio]

spiritual /'spɪrɪtjʊəl/ *a* spirituale ● *n* spiritual *m*

spiritualism /'spɪrɪtjʊəlɪzm/ *n* spiritismo *m*

spiritualist /'spɪrɪtjʊəlɪst/ *n* spiritista *mf*

spit¹ /spɪt/ *n* (*for roasting*) spiedo *m*

spit² *n* sputo *m* ● *vt/i* (*pt/pp* **spat**, *pres p* **spitting**) sputare; ⟨*cat:*⟩ soffiare; ⟨*fat:*⟩ sfrigolare; **it's ~ting [with rain]** piovviggina; **the ~ting image of** il ritratto spiccicato di

spit out *vt* sputare ⟨*food*⟩; **~ it out!** *fam* sputa l'osso!

spite /spaɪt/ *n* dispetto *m*; **in ~ of** malgrado ● *vt* far dispetto a

spiteful /'spaɪtfʊl/ *a* indispettito

spitefully /'spaɪtfʊlɪ/ *adv* con aria indispettita

spittle /'spɪtl/ *n* saliva *f*

splash /splæʃ/ *n* schizzo *m*; (*of colour*) macchia *f*; (*fam: drop*) goccio *m* ● *vt* schizzare; **~ sb with sth** schizzare qcno di qcsa ● *vi* schizzare

■ **splash about** *vi* schizzarsi

■ **splash down** *vi* ⟨*spacecraft:*⟩ ammarare

■ **splash out** *vi* (*spend freely*) darsi alle spese folli

splashdown /'splæʃdaʊn/ *n* ammaraggio *m*

splatter /'splætə(r)/ *vt* schizzare; **~ sb/sth with sth** schizzare qcno/qcsa di qcsa ● *vi* **~ onto/over sth** ⟨*ink, paint:*⟩ schizzare su qcsa

splay /spleɪ/ *vt* divaricare ⟨*legs, feet, fingers*⟩; svasare ⟨*end of pipe etc*⟩; strombare ⟨*side of window, door*⟩; **~ed** ⟨*feet, fingers, legs*⟩ scartato

spleen /spli:n/ *n Anat* milza *f*

splendid /'splendɪd/ *a* splendido

splendidly /'splendɪdlɪ/ *adv* splendidamente

splendour /'splendə(r)/ *n* splendore *m*

splint /splɪnt/ *n Med* stecca *f*

splinter /'splɪntə(r)/ *n* scheggia *f* ● *vi* scheggiarsi

splinter group *n* gruppo *m* scissionista

split /splɪt/ *n* fessura *f*; (*quarrel*) rottura *f*; (*division*) scissione *f*; (*tear*) strappo *m* ● *v* (*pt/pp* **split**, *pres p* **splitting**) ● *vt* spaccare; (*share*, *divide*) dividere; (*tear*) strappare; ~ **hairs** spaccare il capello in quattro; ~ **one's sides** sbellicarsi dalle risa ● *vi* spaccarsi; (*tear*) strapparsi; (*divide*) dividersi; ~ **on sb** *fam* denunciare qcno ● *a* **a** ~ **second** una frazione di secondo

■ **split up** *vt* dividersi ● *vi* ⟨*couple:*⟩ separarsi

split: split ends *npl* (*in hair*) doppie punte *fpl*. **split personality** *n* sdoppiamento *m* della personalità. **split screen** *n* schermo *m* diviso

splitting /'splɪtɪŋ/ *a* **have a** ~ **headache** avere un tremendo mal di testa

splutter /'splʌtə(r)/ *vi* farfugliare

spoil /spɔɪl/ *n* ~**s** *pl* bottino *msg* ● *v* (*pt/pp* **spoilt** *or* **spoiled**) ● *vt* rovinare; viziare ⟨*person*⟩ ● *vi* andare a male

spoiler /'spɔɪlə(r)/ *n Auto*, *Aeron* spoiler *m inv*

spoilsport /'spɔɪlspɔːt/ *n* guastafeste *mf inv*

spoilt /spɔɪlt/ *a* ⟨*child*⟩ viziato; **be** ~ **for choice** non avere che l'imbarazzo della scelta

spoke¹ /spəʊk/ *n* raggio *m*

spoke² *see* **speak**

spoken /'spəʊkən/ *see* **speak** ● *a* ⟨*language*⟩ parlato; **be** ~ **for** essere messo da parte per qualcuno

spokesman /'spəʊksmən/ *n* portavoce *m inv*

spokesperson /'spəʊkspɜːsn/ *n* portavoce *mf*

spokeswoman /'spəʊkswʊmən/ *n* portavoce *f*

sponge /spʌndʒ/ *n* spugna *f* ● *vt* pulire con la spugna ● *vi* ~ **on** *fam* scroccare da

sponge bag *n* nécessaire *m inv*

sponge cake *n* pan *m* di Spagna

sponger /'spʌndʒə(r)/ *n* scroccone, -a *mf*

spongy /'spʌndʒɪ/ *a* spugnoso

sponsor /'spɒnsə(r)/ *n* garante *mf*; *Radio*, *TV* sponsor *m inv*; (*god-parent*) padrino *m*, madrina *f*; (*for membership*) socio, -a *mf* garante ● *vt* sponsorizzare

sponsorship /'spɒnsəʃɪp/ *n* sponsorizzazione *f*

sponsorship deal *n* accordo *m* con uno sponsor

spontaneity /spɒntə'neɪətɪ/ *n* spontaneità *f*

spontaneous /spɒn'teɪnɪəs/ *a* spontaneo

spontaneously /spɒn'teɪnɪəslɪ/ *adv* spontaneamente

spoof /spuːf/ *n fam* parodia *f*

spook /spuːk/ *fam vt* (*haunt*) perseguitare; (*frighten*) spaventare ● *n* (*ghost*) fantasma *m*; (*Am: spy*) spia *f*

spooky /'spuːkɪ/ *a* (**-ier**, **-iest**) *fam* sinistro

spool /spuːl/ *n* bobina *f*

spooling /'spuːlɪŋ/ *n Comput* spooling *m*

spoon /spuːn/ *n* cucchiaio *m* ● *vt* mettere col cucchiaio

spoonerism /'spuːnərɪzm/ *n scambio m delle iniziali di due parole con effetto umoristico*

spoon-feed *vt* (*pt/pp* **-fed**) *fig* imboccare

spoonful /'spuːnfʊl/ *n* cucchiaiata *f*

sporadic /spə'rædɪk/ *a* sporadico

sporadically /spə'rædɪklɪ/ *adv* sporadicamente

spore /spɔː(r)/ *n* spora *f*

sporran /'spɒrən/ *n* borsa *f* di cuoio o pelo *portata alla cintura dagli scozzesi insieme al kilt*

sport /spɔːt/ *n* sport *m inv*; **be a [good]** ~**!** sii sportivo! ● *vt* sfoggiare

sporting /'spɔːtɪŋ/ *a* sportivo

sporting calendar *n* calendario *m* sportivo

sporting chance *n* possibilità *f inv*

sports: sports car *n* automobile *f* sportiva. **sports coat** *n*, **sports jacket** *n* giacca *f* sportiva. **sportsman** *n* sportivo *m*. **sportswoman** *n* sportiva *f*. **sports writer** *n* giornalista *mf* sportivo, -a

sporty /'spɔːtɪ/ *a* (**-ier**, **-iest**) sportivo

spot /spɒt/ *n* macchia *f*; (*pimple*) brufolo *m*; (*place*) posto *m*; (*in pattern*) pois *m inv*; (*of rain*) goccia *f*; (*of water*) goccio *m*; ~**s** *pl* (*rash*) sfogo *msg*; **a** ~ **of** *fam* un po' di; **a** ~ **of bother** qualche problema; **on the** ~ sul luogo; (*immediately*) immediatamente; **in a [tight]** ~ *fam* in difficoltà ● *vt* (*pt/pp* **spotted**) macchiare; (*fam: notice*) individuare

spot check *n* (*without warning*) controllo *m* a sorpresa; **do a** ~ ~ **on sth** dare una controllata a qcsa

spotless /'spɒtlɪs/ *a* immacolato

spot: spotlight *n* riflettore *m*; *fig* riflettori *mpl*. **spot-on** *a Br* esatto. **spot rate** *n Fin* tasso *m* di cambio a vista

spotted /'spɒtɪd/ *a* ⟨*material*⟩ a pois

spotty /'spɒtɪ/ *a* (**-ier**, **-iest**) (*pimply*) brufoloso

spot-weld *vt* saldare a punti

spouse /spaʊz/ *n* consorte *mf*

spout /spaʊt/ *n* becco *m*; **up the** ~ (*fam: ruined*) all'aria ● *vi* zampillare (**from** da)

sprain /spreɪn/ *n* slogatura *f* ● *vt* slogare; ~ **one's ankle** slogarsi la caviglia

sprang /spræŋ/ *see* **spring**²

sprat /spræt/ *n* spratto *m*

sprawl /sprɔːl/ *vi* (*in chair*) stravaccarsi; ⟨*city etc:*⟩ estendersi; **go** ~**ing** (*fall*) cadere disteso

sprawling /'sprɔːlɪŋ/ *a* ⟨*suburb*, *city*⟩ che si propaga disordinatamente; ⟨*handwriting*⟩ che occupa tutta la pagina

spray¹ /spreɪ/ *n* (*of flowers*) rametto *m*; (*bouquet*) mazzolino *m*

spray² *n* spruzzo *m*; (*from sea*) spruzzo *m*; (*preparation*) spray *m inv*; (*container*) spruzzatore *m* ● *vt* spruzzare

spray-gun n pistola f a spruzzo

spray-on a ⟨conditioner, glitter⟩ spray inv

spread /spred/ n estensione f; ⟨of disease⟩ diffusione f; ⟨paste⟩ crema f; ⟨fam: feast⟩ banchetto m ● v ⟨pt/pp **spread**⟩ ● vt spargere; spalmare ⟨butter, jam⟩; stendere ⟨cloth, arms⟩; diffondere ⟨news, disease⟩; dilazionare ⟨payments⟩; **~ sth with** spalmare qcsa di ● vi spargersi; ⟨butter:⟩ spalmarsi; ⟨disease:⟩ diffondersi

■ **spread out** vt sparpagliare ● vi sparpagliarsi

spread-eagled /-'i:gld/ a a gambe e braccia aperte

spreadsheet /'spredʃi:t/ n Comput foglio m elettronico

spree /spri:/ n fam **go on a ~** far baldoria; **go on a shopping ~** fare spese folli

sprig /sprɪg/ n rametto m

sprightly /'spraɪtlɪ/ a (-ier, -iest) vivace

spring¹ /sprɪŋ/ n primavera f; **in ~, in the ~** in primavera ● attrib primaverile

spring² n ⟨jump⟩ balzo m; ⟨water⟩ sorgente f; ⟨device⟩ molla f; ⟨elasticity⟩ elasticità f ● v ⟨pt **sprang**, pp **sprung**⟩ ● vi balzare; ⟨arise⟩ provenire ⟨from da⟩; **~ to mind** saltare in mente ● vt **he just sprang it on me** me l'ha detto a cose fatte compiuto

■ **spring up** vi balzare; fig spuntare

spring: **springboard** n trampolino m. **spring chicken** n Culin pollastrello m, pollastrella f; **she's no ~ ~** fam non è una giovincella. **spring-clean** vt pulire a fondo. **spring-cleaning** n pulizie fpl di Pasqua. **spring onion** n cipollina f. **springtime** n primavera f

sprinkle /'sprɪŋkl/ vt ⟨scatter⟩ spruzzare ⟨liquid⟩; spargere ⟨flour, cocoa⟩; **~ sth with** spruzzare qcsa di ⟨liquid⟩; cospargere qcsa di ⟨flour, cocoa⟩

sprinkler /'sprɪŋklɪə(r)/ n sprinkler m inv; ⟨for garden⟩ irrigatore m

sprinkling /'sprɪŋklɪŋ/ n ⟨of liquid⟩ spruzzatina f; ⟨of pepper, salt⟩ pizzico m; ⟨of flour, sugar⟩ spolveratina f; ⟨of knowledge⟩ infarinatura f; ⟨of people⟩ pugno m

sprint /sprɪnt/ n sprint m inv ● vi fare uno sprint; Sport sprintare

sprinter /'sprɪntə(r)/ n sprinter mf inv

sprite /spraɪt/ n folletto m

spritzer /'sprɪtsə(r)/ n spriz m inv, spritzer m inv

sprout /spraʊt/ n germoglio m; **[Brussels] ~s** pl cavolini mpl di Bruxelles ● vi germogliare

spruce /spru:s/ a elegante ● n abete m

■ **spruce up** vt dare una ripulita a

sprung /sprʌŋ/ see **spring²** ● a molleggiato

spry /spraɪ/ a (-er, -est) arzillo

spud /spʌd/ n fam patata f

spun /spʌn/ see **spin**

spur /spɜ:(r)/ n sperone m; ⟨stimulus⟩ stimolo m; ⟨road⟩ svincolo m; **on the ~ of the moment** su due piedi ● vt ⟨pt/pp **spurred**⟩ **~ [on]** fig spronare

spurious /'spjʊərɪəs/ a falso

spuriously /'spjʊərɪəslɪ/ adv falsamente

spurn /spɜ:n/ vt sdegnare

spurt /spɜ:t/ n getto m; Sport scatto m; **put on a ~** fare uno scatto ● vi sprizzare; ⟨increase speed⟩ scattare

sputter /'spʌtə(r)/ vi ⟨engine:⟩ scoppiettare ● n colpi mpl irregolari del motore

spy /spaɪ/ n spia f ● vi spiare ● vt ⟨fam: see⟩ spiare

■ **spy on** vt spiare

■ **spy out** vt esplorare

spying /'spaɪɪŋ/ n spionaggio m

squabble /'skwɒbl/ n bisticcio m ● vi bisticciare

squabbling /'skwɒblɪŋ/ n bisticci mpl

squad /skwɒd/ n squadra f

squaddie /'skwɒdɪ/ n Br fam soldato m semplice

squadron /'skwɒdrən/ n Mil squadrone m; Aeron, Naut squadriglia f

squalid /'skwɒlɪd/ a squallido

squalidly /'skwɒlɪdlɪ/ adv squallidamente

squall /skwɔ:l/ n ⟨howl⟩ strillo m; ⟨storm⟩ bufera f ● vi strillare

squally /'skwɔ:lɪ/ a burrascoso

squalor /'skwɒlə(r)/ n squallore m

squander /'skwɒndə(r)/ vt sprecare

square /skweə(r)/ a quadrato; ⟨meal⟩ sostanzioso; ⟨fam: old-fashioned⟩ vecchio stampo; **all ~** fam pari ● n quadrato m; ⟨in city⟩ piazza f; ⟨on chessboard⟩ riquadro m; **be back to ~ one** riessere al punto di partenza ● vt ⟨settle⟩ far quadrare; Math elevare al quadrato ● vi ⟨agree⟩ armonizzare

■ **square up** vi ⟨settle accounts⟩ saldare

■ **square up to** vt affrontare

square dance n quadriglia f

squarely /'skweəlɪ/ adv direttamente

square root n radice f quadrata

squash /skwɒʃ/ n calca f; ⟨drink⟩ spremuta f; ⟨sport⟩ squash m; ⟨vegetable⟩ zucca f ● vt schiacciare; soffocare ⟨rebellion⟩

squashy /'skwɒʃɪ/ a floscio

squat /skwɒt/ a tarchiato ● n fam edificio m occupato abusivamente ● vi ⟨pt/pp **squatted**⟩ accovacciarsi; **~ in** occupare abusivamente

squatter /'skwɒtə(r)/ n occupante mf abusivo, -a

squaw /skwɔ:/ n squaw f inv

squawk /skwɔ:k/ n gracchio m ● vi gracchiare

squeak /skwi:k/ n squittio m; ⟨of hinge, brakes⟩ cigolio m ● vi squittire; ⟨hinge, brakes:⟩ cigolare

squeaking /'skwi:kɪŋ/ n ⟨of door, hinge⟩ cigolio m

squeaky /'skwi:kɪ/ a ⟨door, hinge⟩ cigolante

squeaky-clean a fam ⟨glass, hair⟩ lucente; ⟨floor⟩ tirato a specchio; fig ⟨person⟩ senza vizi; ⟨company⟩ al di sopra di ogni sospetto

squeal /skwi:l/ n strillo m; ⟨of brakes⟩ cigolio m ● vi strillare; sl spifferare

squeamish /'skwiːmɪʃ/ a dallo stomaco delicato; (*scrupulous*) troppo scrupoloso

squeegee /'skwiːdʒiː/ n Phot rullo m asciugatore; (*for glasses*) lavavetri m inv

squeeze /skwiːz/ n stretta f; (*crush*) pigia pigia m inv; **give sb's hand a ~** dare a qcno una stretta di mano ● vt premere; (*to get juice*) spremere; stringere ⟨hand⟩; (*force*) spingere a forza; (*fam: extort*) estorcere (**out of** da)

■ **squeeze in/out** vi sgusciare dentro/fuori

■ **squeeze up** vi stringersi

squelch /skweltʃ/ vi sguazzare

squib /skwɪb/ n petardo m

squid /skwɪd/ n calamaro m

squidgy /'skwɪdʒɪ/ a (Br fam: squashy) molliccio

squiggle /'skwɪgl/ n scarabocchio m

squint /skwɪnt/ n strabismo m ● vi essere strabico

squire /'skwaɪə(r)/ n signorotto m di campagna

squirm /skwɜːm/ vi contorcersi; (*feel embarrassed*) sentirsi imbarazzato

squirrel /'skwɪrəl/ n scoiattolo m

squirt /skwɜːt/ n spruzzo m; (*fam: person*) presuntuoso m ● vt/i spruzzare

St abbr (**Saint**) S; abbr **Street**

stab /stæb/ n pugnalata f, coltellata f; (*sensation*) fitta f; (*fam: attempt*) tentativo m ● vt (*pt/pp* stabbed) pugnalare, accoltellare

stability /stə'bɪlətɪ/ n stabilità f inv

stabilization /steɪbɪlaɪ'zeɪʃn/ n stabilizzazione f

stabilize /'steɪbɪlaɪz/ vt stabilizzare ● vi stabilizzarsi

stabilizer /'steɪbɪlaɪzə(r)/ n stabilizzatore m; (*on bike*) rotella f; (*in food*) stabilizzante m

stable¹ /'steɪbl/ a stabile

stable² n stalla f; (*establishment*) scuderia f

staccato /stə'kɑːtəʊ/ a Mus staccato; ⟨gasps, shots⟩ intermittente ● adv ⟨play⟩ staccatamente

stack /stæk/ n catasta f; (*of chimney*) comignolo m; (*chimney*) ciminiera f; (*fam: large quantity*) montagna f; **~s of** ⟨money, time, work⟩ un sacco di ● vt accatastare

stadium /'steɪdɪəm/ n stadio m

staff /stɑːf/ n (*stick*) bastone m; (*employees*) personale m; (*teachers*) corpo m insegnante; Mil Stato m Maggiore ● vt fornire di personale

staffroom /'stɑːfruːm/ n Sch sala f insegnanti

stag /stæg/ n cervo m

stage /steɪdʒ/ n palcoscenico m; (*profession*) teatro m; (*in journey*) tappa f; (*in process*) stadio m; **go on the ~** darsi al teatro; **in ~s** a tappe ● vt mettere in scena; (*arrange*) organizzare

stage: stagecoach n diligenza f. **stage door** n ingresso m degli artisti. **stage fright** n panico m da palcoscenico. **stage-manage** vt fig orchestrare. **stage manager** n direttore, -trice mf di scena. **stage-struck** /-strʌk/ a appassionatissimo di teatro

stagger /'stægə(r)/ vi barcollare ● vt sbalordire; scaglionare ⟨holidays, payments etc⟩; **I was ~ed** sono rimasto sbalordito ● n vacillamento m

staggering /'stægərɪŋ/ a sbalorditivo

stagnant /'stægnənt/ a stagnante

stagnate /stæg'neɪt/ vi fig [ri]stagnare

stagnation /stæg'neɪʃn/ n fig inattività f

stag night, stag party n addio m al celibato

staid /steɪd/ a posato

stain /steɪn/ n macchia f; (*for wood*) mordente m ● vt macchiare; ⟨wood⟩ dare il mordente a

stained glass /steɪnd'glɑːs/ n vetro m colorato

stained-glass window n vetrata f colorata

stainless /'steɪnlɪs/ a senza macchia

stainless steel n acciaio m inossidabile

stain remover n smacchiatore m

stair /steə(r)/ n gradino m; **~s** pl scale fpl

staircase /'steəkeɪs/ n scale fpl

stake /steɪk/ n palo m; (*wager*) posta f; Comm partecipazione f; **at ~** in gioco ● vt puntellare; (*wager*) scommettere; **~ a claim to sth** rivendicare qcsa

stake-out n fam sorveglianza f

stalactite /'stæləktaɪt/ n stalattite f

stalagmite /'stæləgmaɪt/ n stalagmite f

stale /steɪl/ a stantio; ⟨air⟩ viziato; (*uninteresting*) trito [e ritrito]

stalemate /'steɪlmeɪt/ n (*in chess*) stallo m; (*deadlock*) situazione f di stallo

stalk¹ /stɔːk/ n gambo m

stalk² vt inseguire ● vi camminare impettito

stalker /'stɔːkə(r)/ n (*of person*) persona f che perseguita qcno per cui ha una fissazione maniacale

stalking /'stɔːkɪŋ/ n (*of person*) persecuzione f di una persona per cui si ha una fissazione maniacale

stall /stɔːl/ n box m inv; (*in market*) bancarella f; **~s** pl Theat platea f ● vi ⟨engine:⟩ spegnersi; fig temporeggiare ● vt far spegnere ⟨engine⟩; tenere a bada ⟨person⟩

stallholder /'stɔːlhəʊldə(r)/ n bancarellista mf

stallion /'stæljən/ n stallone m

stalwart /'stɔːlwət/ a fedele ● n sostenitore m fedele

stamina /'stæmɪnə/ n [capacità f di] resistenza f

stammer /'stæmə(r)/ n balbettio m ● vt/i balbettare

stamp /stæmp/ n (*postage ~*) francobollo m; (*instrument*) timbro m; fig impronta f ● vt affrancare ⟨letter⟩; timbrare ⟨bill⟩; battere ⟨feet⟩

■ **stamp out** vt spegnere; fig soffocare

stamp collecting n filatelia f

stamp collector n collezionista mf di francobolli

stamped addressed envelope busta *f* affrancata per la risposta

stampede /stæm'piːd/ *n* fuga *f* precipitosa; *fam* fuggifuggi *m inv* ● *vi* fuggire precipitosamente

stance /staːns/ *n* posizione *f*

stand /stænd/ *n* (*for bikes*) rastrelliera *f*; (*at exhibition*) stand *m inv*; (*in market*) bancarella *f*; (*in stadium*) gradinata *f*; *fig* posizione *f* ● *v* (*pt/pp* **stood**) ● *vi* stare in piedi; (*rise*) alzarsi [in piedi]; (*be*) trovarsi; (*be candidate*) essere candidato (**for** a); (*stay valid*) rimanere valido; **I don't know where I ~** non so qual'è la mia posizione; **~ still** non muoversi; **~ firm** *fig* tener duro; **~ on ceremony** formalizzarsi; **~ together** essere solidali; **~ to lose/gain** rischiare di perdere/vincere; **~ to reason** essere logico ● *vt* (*withstand*) resistere a; (*endure*) sopportare; (*place*) mettere; **~ a chance** avere una possiblilità; **~ one's ground** tener duro; **~ the test of time** superare la prova del tempo; **~ sb a beer** offrire una birra a qcno

■ **stand back** *vi* (*withdraw*) farsi da parte

■ **stand by** *vi* stare a guardare; (*be ready*) essere pronto ● *vt* (*support*) appoggiare

■ **stand down** *vi* (*retire*) ritirarsi

■ **stand for** *vt* (*mean*) significare; (*tolerate*) tollerare

■ **stand in for** *vt* sostituire

■ **stand out** *vi* spiccare

■ **stand up** *vi* alzarsi [in piedi]

■ **stand up for** *vt* prendere le difese di; **~ up for oneself** farsi valere

■ **stand up to** *vt* affrontare

stand-alone *a Comput* indipendente

standard /'stændəd/ *a* standard; **be ~ practice** essere pratica corrente ● *n* standard *m inv*; *Techn* norma *f*; (*level*) livello *m*; (*quality*) qualità *f inv*; (*flag*) stendardo *m*; **~s** *pl* (*morals*) valori *mpl*

standardization /stændədaɪ'zeɪʃn/ *n* standardizzazione *f*

standardize /'stændədaɪz/ *vt* standardizzare

standard lamp *n* lampada *f* a stelo

standard of living *n* tenore *m* di vita

standby /'stændbaɪ/ *n* (*person*) riserva *f* ● *attrib* (*circuit, battery*) di emergenza; (*passenger*) in lista di attesa; (*ticket*) stand-by *inv* ● *adv* (*fly*) con biglietto stand-by

stand-in *n* controfigura *f*

standing /'stændɪŋ/ *a* (*erect*) in piedi; (*permanent*) permanente ● *n* posizione *f*; (*duration*) durata *f*

standing: standing order *n* ordine *m* permanente. **standing ovation** *n* **give sb a ~ ~** alzarsi per applaudire qcno. **standing room** *n* posti *mpl* in piedi

stand-offish /stænd'ɒfɪʃ/ *a* scostante

stand: standpoint *n* punto *m* di vista. **standstill** *n* **come to a ~** fermarsi; **at a ~** in un periodo di stasi. **stand-up** *a* (*buffet*) in piedi; (*argument*) accanito ● *n* (*comedy*) recital *m inv* di un comico. **stand-up comedian**

comico *m* che intrattiene il pubblico con barzellette

stank /stæŋk/ *see* **stink**

stanza /'stænzə/ *n* strofa *f*

staple¹ /'steɪpl/ *n* (*product*) prodotto *m* principale

staple² *n* graffa *f*, pinzatrice *f* ● *vt* pinzare

staple diet *n* **a ~ ~ of** una dieta basata principalmente su

staple gun *n* pistola *f* sparachiodi

stapler /'steɪplə(r)/ *n* pinzatrice *f*, cucitrice *f*

staple remover *n* levapunti *m inv*

star /staː(r)/ *n* stella *f*; (*asterisk*) asterisco *m*; *Theat, Cinema, Sport* divo, -a *mf*, stella *f* ● *vi* (*pt/pp* **starred**) essere l'interprete principale (**in** di)

starboard /'staːbəd/ *n* tribordo *m*

starch /staːtʃ/ *n* amido *m* ● *vt* inamidare

starchy /'staːtʃɪ/ *a* ricco di amido; *fig* compito

stardom /'staːdəm/ *n* celebrità *f*

stare /steə(r)/ *n* sguardo *m* fisso ● *vi* **it's rude to ~** è da maleducati fissare la gente; **~ at** fissare; **~ into space** guardare nel vuoto

starfish /'staːfɪʃ/ *n* stella *f* di mare

stark /staːk/ *a* austero; (*contrast*) forte ● *adv* completamente; **~ naked** completamente nudo

starlet /'staːlɪt/ *n* stellina *f*

starling /'staːlɪŋ/ *n* storno *m*

starlit /'staːlɪt/ *a* stellato

starry /'staːrɪ/ *a* stellato

starry-eyed /-'aɪd/ *a fam* ingenuo

star-struck /-strʌk/ *a* ossessionato dalle celebrità

star-studded /-stʌdɪd/ *a* (*cast, line-up*) con molti interpreti famosi; (*sky*) stellato

start /staːt/ *n* inizio *m*; (*departure*) partenza *f*; (*jump*) sobbalzo *m*; **from the ~** [fin] dall'inizio; **for a ~** tanto per cominciare; **give sb a ~** *Sport* dare un vantaggio a qcno ● *vi* [in]cominciare; (*set out*) avviarsi; (*engine, car:*) partire; (*jump*) trasalire; **to ~ with,...** tanto per cominciare,... ● *vt* [in]cominciare; (*cause*) dare inizio a; (*found*) mettere su; mettere in moto (*car*); mettere in giro (*rumour*)

■ **start off** *vi* (*begin*) cominciare

■ **start on** *vt fam* (*attack*) criticare; (*nag*) punzecchiare

■ **start out** *vi* (*on journey*) partire

■ **start up** *vt* mettere in funzione (*engine*); intentare (*business*)

starter /'staːtə(r)/ *n Culin* primo *m* [piatto *m*]; (*in race: giving signal*) starter *m inv*; (*participant*) concorrente *mf*; *Auto* motorino *m* d'avviamento

starting point /'staːtɪŋ/ *n* punto *m* di partenza

starting salary *n* stipendio *m* iniziale

startle /'staːtl/ *vt* far trasalire; (*news:*) sconvolgere

startling /'staːtlɪŋ/ *a* sconvolgente

start-up capital *n* capitale *m* di avviamento

starvation /staː'veɪʃn/ *n* fame *f*

starve /stɑːv/ *vi* morire di fame ● *vt* far morire di fame

stash /stæʃ/ *vt fam* ~ [**away**] nascondere

state /steɪt/ *n* stato *m*; *Pol* Stato *m*; ⟨*grand style*⟩ pompa *f*; ; **be in a** ~ ⟨*person:*⟩ essere agitato; **lie in** ~ essere esposto ● *attrib* di Stato; *Sch* pubblico; ⟨*with ceremony*⟩ di gala ● *vt* dichiarare; ⟨*specify*⟩ precisare

state-aided /-ˈeɪdɪd/ *a* sovvenzionato dallo Stato

State Department *n Am Pol* ministero *m* degli [affari] esteri

stateless /ˈsteɪtlɪs/ *a* apolide

stately /ˈsteɪtlɪ/ *a* (**-ier, -iest**) maestoso

stately home *n* dimora *f* signorile

statement /ˈsteɪtmənt/ *n* dichiarazione *f*; *Jur* deposizione *f*; ⟨*from bank*⟩ estratto *m* conto; ⟨*account*⟩ rapporto *m*

state: state of the art *a* ⟨*technology*⟩ il più avanzato. **state of emergency** *n* stato *m* di emergenza. **state of play** punteggio *m*

stateside /ˈsteɪtsaɪd/ *a* degli Stati Uniti ● *adv* negli Stati Uniti

statesman /ˈsteɪtsmən/ *n* statista *m*

static /ˈstætɪk/ *a* statico

static electricity *n* elettricità *f* statica

station /ˈsteɪʃn/ *n* stazione *f*; ⟨*police*⟩ commissariato *m* ● *vt* appostare ⟨*guard*⟩; **be ~ed in Germany** essere di stanza in Germania

stationary /ˈsteɪʃənərɪ/ *a* immobile

stationer /ˈsteɪʃənə(r)/ *n* ~**'s** [**shop**] cartoleria *f*

stationery /ˈsteɪʃənərɪ/ *n* cartoleria *f*

station wagon *n Am* familiare *f*

statistical /stəˈtɪstɪkl/ *a* statistico

statistically /stəˈtɪstɪklɪ/ *adv* statisticamente

statistician /stætɪsˈtɪʃn/ *n* esperto *m* di statistica

statistics /stəˈtɪstɪks/ *n* ⟨*subject*⟩ statistica *f*; ⟨*pl: figures*⟩ statistiche *fpl*

statue /ˈstætjuː/ *n* statua *f*

statuesque /stætjʊˈesk/ *a* statuario

stature /ˈstætʃə(r)/ *n* statura *f*

status /ˈsteɪtəs/ *n* condizione *f*; ⟨*high rank*⟩ alto rango *m*

status bar *n Comput* barra *f* di stato

status symbol *n* status symbol *m inv*

statute /ˈstætjuːt/ *n* statuto *m*

statutory /ˈstætjʊtərɪ/ *a* statutario

staunch /stɔːntʃ/ *a* fedele

staunchly /ˈstɔːntʃlɪ/ *adv* fedelmente

stave /steɪv/ *vt* ~ **off** tenere lontano

stay /steɪ/ *n* soggiorno *m* ● *vi* restare, rimanere; ⟨*reside*⟩ alloggiare; ~ **the night** passare la notte; ~ **put** non muoversi ● *vt* ~ **the course** resistere fino alla fine

■ **stay away** *vi* stare lontano

■ **stay behind** *vi* non andare con gli altri

■ **stay in** *vi* ⟨*at home*⟩ stare in casa; *Sch* restare a scuola dopo le lezioni

■ **stay on** *vi* ⟨*remain*⟩ rimanere; ~ **on at school** continuare gli studi

■ **stay up** *vi* stare su; ⟨*person:*⟩ stare alzato

staying power /ˈsteɪɪŋ/ *n* capacità *f* di resistenza

STD *abbr* **sexually transmitted disease**

STD [area] code *n Br* prefisso *m* [di teleselezione]

stead /sted/ *n* **in his** ~ in sua vece; **stand sb in good** ~ tornare utile a qcno

steadfast /ˈstedfɑːst/ *a* fedele; ⟨*refusal*⟩ fermo

steadily /ˈstedɪlɪ/ *adv* ⟨*continually*⟩ continuamente

steady /ˈstedɪ/ *a* (**-ier, -iest**) saldo, fermo; ⟨*breathing*⟩ regolare; ⟨*job, boyfriend*⟩ fisso; ⟨*dependable*⟩ serio ● *adv* **be going** ~ ⟨*couple:*⟩ fare coppia fissa

steak /steɪk/ *n* ⟨*for stew*⟩ spezzatino *m*; ⟨*for grilling, frying*⟩ bistecca *f*

steal /stiːl/ *vt* (*pt* **stole**, *pp* **stolen**) rubare (**from** da); ~ **the show** essere al centro d'attenzione

■ **steal in/out** *vi* entrare/uscire furtivamente

stealth /stelθ/ *n* **by** ~ di nascosto

stealthily /ˈstelθɪlɪ/ *adv* furtivamente

stealthy /ˈstelθɪ/ *a* furtivo

steam /stiːm/ *n* vapore *m*; **under one's own** ~ *fam* da solo; **let off** ~ *fig* sfogarsi ● *vt Culin* cucinare a vapore ● *vi* fumare

■ **steam up** *vi* ⟨*window:*⟩ appannarsi

steamed up /stiːmdˈʌp/ *a* **get** ~ **up** ⟨*angry*⟩ andare su tutte le furie

steam engine *n* locomotiva *f*

steam iron *n* ferro *m* [da stiro] a vapore

steamer /ˈstiːmə(r)/ *n* piroscafo *m*; ⟨*saucepan*⟩ pentola *f* a vapore

steamroller /ˈstiːmrəʊlə(r)/ *n* rullo *m* compressore

steamy /ˈstiːmɪ/ *a* appannato; ⟨*fig: scene*⟩ spinto

steel /stiːl/ *n* acciaio *m* ● *vt* ~ **oneself** temprarsi

steel wool *n* lana *f* d'acciaio

steely /ˈstiːlɪ/ *a* d'acciaio

steep[1] /stiːp/ *vt* ⟨*soak*⟩ lasciare a bagno; ~**ed in** *fig* immerso in

steep[2] *a* ripido; ⟨*fam: price*⟩ esorbitante

steeple /ˈstiːpl/ *n* campanile *m*

steeplechase /ˈstiːpltʃeɪs/ *n* corsa *f* ippica a ostacoli

steeplejack /ˈstiːpldʒæk/ *n* persona *f* che ripara campanili e ciminiere

steeply /ˈstiːplɪ/ *adv* ripidamente

steer /stɪə(r)/ *vt/i* guidare; ~ **clear of** stare alla larga da

steering /ˈstɪərɪŋ/ *n Auto* sterzo *m*

steering: steering column *n Auto* piantone *m* dello sterzo. **steering committee** *n* comitato *m* direttivo. **steering lock** *n Auto* bloccasterzo *m*; ⟨*turning circle*⟩ angolo *m* di massima sterzata. **steering wheel** *n* volante *m*

stem[1] /stem/ *n* stelo *m*; ⟨*of glass*⟩ gambo *m*; ⟨*of word*⟩ radice *f* ● *vi* (*pt/pp* **stemmed**) ~ **from** derivare da

stem[2] *vt* (*pt/pp* **stemmed**) contenere

stem ginger *n* zenzero *m* sciroppato

stench /stentʃ/ *n* fetore *m*

stencil /'stensl/ *n* stampino *m*; (*decoration*) stampo *m* ● *vt* (*pt/pp* **stencilled**) stampinare

stenographer /stɪ'nɒgrəfə(r)/ *n* stenografo, -a *mf*

stenography /stɪ'nɒgrəfɪ/ *n* stenografia *f*

step /step/ *n* passo *m*; (*stair*) gradino *m*; **~s** *pl* (*ladder*) scaleo *m*; **in ~** al passo; **be out of ~** non stare al passo; **~ by ~** un passo alla volta ● *vi* (*pt/pp* **stepped**) **~ into** entrare in; **~ into sb's shoes** succedere a qcno; **~ out of** uscire da; **~ out of line** sgarrare

■ **step down** *vi fig* dimettersi

■ **step forward** *vi* farsi avanti

■ **step in** *vi fig* intervenire

■ **step up** *vt* (*increase*) aumentare

step: **stepbrother** *n* fratellastro *m*. **stepchild** *n* figliastro, -a *mf*. **stepdaughter** *n* figliastra *f*. **stepfather** *n* patrigno *m*. **stepladder** *n* scaleo *m*. **stepmother** *n* matrigna *f*

stepping stone /'stepɪŋ/ *n* pietra *f* per guadare; *fig* trampolino *m*

stepsister /'stepsɪstə(r)/ *n* sorellastra *f*

stepson /'stepsʌn/ *n* figliastro *m*

stereo /'sterɪəʊ/ *n* stereo *m*; **in ~** in stereofonia

stereophonic /sterɪəʊ'fɒnɪk/ *a* stereofonico

stereoscopic /sterɪəʊ'skɒpɪk/ *a* stereoscopico

stereotype /'sterɪətaɪp/ *n* stereotipo *m*

stereotyped /'sterɪətaɪpt/ *a* stereotipato

sterile /'steraɪl/ *a* sterile

sterility /stə'rɪlətɪ/ *n* sterilità *f*

sterilization /sterəlaɪ'zeɪʃn/ *n* sterilizzazione *f*

sterilize /'sterɪlaɪz/ *vt* sterilizzare

sterling /'stɜːlɪŋ/ *a fig* apprezzabile ● *n* sterlina *f*

sterling silver *n* argento *m* pregiato

stern[1] /stɜːn/ *a* severo

stern[2] *n* (*of boat*) poppa *f*

sternly /'stɜːnlɪ/ *adv* severamente

steroid /'sterɔɪd/ *n* steroide *m*

stet /stet/ (*in proofreading*) vive

stethoscope /'steθəskəʊp/ *n* stetoscopio *m*

stetson /'stetsən/ *n* cappello *m* da cow boy

stew /stjuː/ *n* stufato *m*; **in a ~** *fam* agitato ● *vt/i* cuocere in umido; **~ed fruit** frutta *f* cotta

steward /'stjuːəd/ *n* (*at meeting*) organizzatore, -trice *mf*; (*on ship, aircaft*) steward *m inv*

stewardess /stjuː'ə'des/ *n* hostess *f inv*

stick[1] /stɪk/ *n* bastone *m*; (*of celery, rhubarb*) gambo *m*; *Sport* mazza *f*

stick[2] *v* (*pt/pp* **stuck**) ● *vt* (*stab*) conficcare; (*glue*) attaccare; (*fam: put*) mettere; (*fam: endure*) sopportare; **be stuck** ⟨*vehicle, person:*⟩ essere bloccato; ⟨*drawer:*⟩ essere incastrato; **stuck in a traffic jam** bloccato nel traffico; **be stuck for an answer** non saper cosa rispondere; **stuck on** *fam* attratto da; **be stuck with sth** *fam* farsi incastrare con qcsa ● *vi* (*adhere*) attaccarsi (**to** a); (*jam*) bloccarsi

■ **stick around** *vi* (*fam: stay*) rimanere

■ **stick at** *vt* **~ at it** *fam* tener duro; **~ at nothing** *fam* non fermarsi di fronte a niente

■ **stick by** *vt* (*be faithful to*) rimanere al fianco di ⟨*sb*⟩

■ **stick down** *vt* incollare ⟨*flap*⟩; (*fam: write down, put down*) mettere

■ **stick out** *vi* (*project*) sporgere; (*fam: catch the eye*) risaltare ● *vt fam* fare ⟨*tongue*⟩; **~ it out** (*endure*) tener duro; **~ one's neck out** sbilanciarsi

■ **stick to** *vt* (*keep to*) attenersi a ⟨*rules, facts*⟩; mantenere ⟨*story*⟩; perseverare in ⟨*task*⟩; **I'll ~ to beer** continuo con la birra

■ **stick up** *vi* (*project*) sporgere

■ **stick up for** *vt fam* difendere

■ **stick with** *vt* (*remain with*) rimanere con ⟨*sb*⟩

sticker /'stɪkə(r)/ *n* autoadesivo *m*

sticking plaster /'stɪkɪŋ/ *n* cerotto *m*

stick insect *n* stecco *m*

stick-in-the-mud *n* retrogrado *m*

stickler /'stɪklə(r)/ *n* **be a ~ for** tenere molto a

stick-up *n fam* rapina *f* a mano armata

sticky /'stɪkɪ/ *a* (**-ier, -iest**) appiccicoso; (*adhesive*) adesivo; (*fig: difficult*) difficile

stiff /stɪf/ *a* rigido; ⟨*brush, task*⟩ duro; ⟨*person*⟩ controllato; ⟨*drink*⟩ forte; ⟨*penalty*⟩ severo; ⟨*price*⟩ alto; **bored ~** *fam* annoiato a morte; **~ neck** torcicollo *m*

stiffen /'stɪfn/ *vt* irrigidire ● *vi* irrigidirsi

stiffly /'stɪflɪ/ *adv* rigidamente; ⟨*smile, answer*⟩ in modo controllato

stiffness /'stɪfnɪs/ *n* rigidità *f*

stifle /'staɪfl/ *vt* soffocare

stifling /'staɪflɪŋ/ *a* soffocante

stigma /'stɪgmə/ *n* marchio *m*

stile /staɪl/ *n* scaletta *f*

stiletto /stɪ'letəʊ/ *n* stiletto *m*; **~ heels** tacchi *mpl* a spillo; **~s** (*pl: shoes*) scarpe *fpl* coi tacchi a spillo

still[1] /stɪl/ *n* distilleria *f*

still[2] *a* fermo; ⟨*drink*⟩ non gasato; **keep/ stand ~** stare fermo ● *n* quiete *f*; (*photo*) posa *f* ● *adv* ancora; (*nevertheless*) nondimeno, comunque; **I'm ~ not sure** non sono ancora sicuro

stillborn /'stɪlbɔːn/ *a* nato morto

still life *n* natura *f* morta

stilted /'stɪltɪd/ *a* artificioso

stilts /stɪlts/ *npl* trampoli *mpl*

stimulant /'stɪmjʊlənt/ *n* eccitante *m*

stimulate /'stɪmjʊleɪt/ *vt* stimolare

stimulating /'stɪmjʊleɪtɪŋ/ *a* stimolante

stimulation /stɪmjʊ'leɪʃn/ *n* stimolo *m*

stimulus /'stɪmjʊləs/ *n* (*pl* **-li** /'stɪmjʊlaɪ/) stimolo *m*

sting /stɪŋ/ *n* puntura *f*; (*organ*) pungiglione *m* ● *v* (*pt/pp* **stung**) ● *vt* pungere; ⟨*jellyfish:*⟩ pizzicare ● *vi* (*insect:*) pungere

stinging nettle /'stɪŋɪŋ/ *n* ortica *f*

stingy /'stɪndʒɪ/ *a* (**-ier, -iest**) tirchio

stink /stɪŋk/ n puzza f ● vi (pt **stank**, pp **stunk**) puzzare

stink bomb n fialetta f puzzolente

stinker /'stɪŋkə(r)/ n (fam: difficult problem etc) rompicapo m

stinking /'stɪŋkɪŋ/ adv be ~ **rich** fam essere ricco sfondato

stint /stɪnt/ n lavoro m; **do one's** ~ fare la propria parte ● vt ~ **on** lesinare su

stipend /'staɪpend/ n congrua f

stipulate /'stɪpjʊleɪt/ vt porre come condizione

stipulation /stɪpjʊ'leɪʃn/ n condizione f

stir /stɜː(r)/ n mescolata f; (commotion) trambusto m ● v (pt/pp **stirred**) ● vt muovere; (mix) mescolare ● vi muoversi

■ **stir up** vt fomentare ‹hatred›

stir-fry vt saltare in padella ● n pietanza f saltata in padella

stirrup /'stɪrəp/ n staffa f

stitch /stɪtʃ/ n punto m; (Knitting) maglia f; (pain) fitta f; **have sb in** ~**es** fam far ridere qcno a crepapelle ● vt cucire

■ **stitch up** vt ricucire ‹wound›; **the deal's** ~**ed up** l'affare è concluso

stoat /stəʊt/ n ermellino m

stock /stɒk/ n (for use or selling) scorta f, stock m inv; (livestock) bestiame m; (lineage) stirpe f; Fin titoli mpl; Culin brodo m; **in** ~ disponibile; **out of** ~ esaurito; **take** ~ fig fare il punto ● a solito ● vt ‹shop:› vendere; approvvigionare ‹shelves›

■ **stock up** vi far scorta (**with** di)

stock: stockbroker n agente m di cambio. **stock car** n (for racing) stock-car m inv. **stock-car racing** n corsa f di stock-car. **stock cube** n dado m [da brodo]. **Stock Exchange** n Borsa f Valori

stocking /'stɒkɪŋ/ n calza f

stockist /'stɒkɪst/ n rivenditore m

stock: stockmarket n mercato m azionario. **stockpile** vt fare scorta di ● n riserva f. **stock-still** a immobile. **stocktaking** n Comm inventario m

stocky /'stɒkɪ/ a (-**ier**, -**iest**) tarchiato

stodge /stɒdʒ/ n (Br fam: food) ammazzafame m inv

stodgy /'stɒdʒɪ/ a indigesto

stoic /'stəʊɪk/ n stoico, -a mf

stoical /'stəʊɪkl/ a stoico

stoically /'stəʊɪklɪ/ adv stoicamente

stoicism /'stəʊɪsɪzm/ n stoicismo m

stoke /stəʊk/ vt alimentare

stole[1] /stəʊl/ n stola f

stole[2], **stolen** /'stəʊln/ see **steal**

stolid /'stɒlɪd/ a apatico

stolidly /'stɒlɪdlɪ/ adv apaticamente

stomach /'stʌmək/ n pancia f; Anat stomaco m ● vt fam reggere

stomach-ache n mal m di pancia

stomp /stɒmp/ vi (walk heavily) camminare con passo pesante

stone /stəʊn/ n pietra f; (in fruit) nocciolo m; Med calcolo m; (weight) 6,348 kg; **within a**

~**'s throw of** a un tiro di schioppo da ● a di pietra ● vt snocciolare ‹fruit›

Stone Age n età f della pietra

stone-cold a gelido

stone-cold sober a perfettamente sobrio

stoned /stəʊnd/ a (fam: on drugs, drink) fatto

stone: stone-deaf a fam sordo come una campana. **stonemason** n scalpellino m. **stonework** n lavoro m in muratura

stony /'stəʊnɪ/ a pietroso; ‹glare› glaciale

stony-broke a Br fam al verde

stood /stʊd/ see **stand**

stooge /stuːdʒ/ n Theat spalla f; (underling) tirapiedi mf inv

stool /stuːl/ n sgabello m

stool-pigeon n fam informatore, -trice mf

stoop /stuːp/ n curvatura f; **walk with a** ~ camminare con la schiena curva ● vi stare curvo; (bend down) chinarsi; fig abbassarsi

stop /stɒp/ n (break) sosta f; (for bus, train) fermata f; Gram punto m; **come to a** ~ fermarsi; **put a** ~ **to sth** mettere fine a qcsa ● v (pt/pp **stopped**) ● vt fermare; arrestare ‹machine›; (prevent) impedire; ~ **sb doing sth** impedire a qcno di fare qcsa; ~ **doing sth** smettere di fare qcsa; ~ **that!** smettila!; ~ **a cheque** bloccare un assegno ● vi fermarsi; ‹rain:› smettere ● int fermo!

■ **stop by** vi (make a brief visit) passare

■ **stop off** vi fare una sosta

■ **stop up** vt otturare ‹sink›; tappare ‹hole›

■ **stop with** vi (fam: stay with) fermarsi da

stop: stopcock n rubinetto m di arresto. **stopgap** n palliativo m; (person) tappabuchi m inv. **stop lights** npl luci fpl di arresto.

stopover n sosta f; Aeron scalo m

stoppage /'stɒpɪdʒ/ n ostruzione f; (strike) interruzione f; (deduction) trattenute fpl

stopper /'stɒpə(r)/ n tappo m

stop press n ultimissime fpl

stopwatch /'stɒpwɒtʃ/ n cronometro m

storage /'stɔːrɪdʒ/ n deposito m; (in warehouse) immagazzinaggio m; Comput memoria f

store /stɔː(r)/ n (stock) riserva f; (shop) grande magazzino m; (depot) deposito m; **in** ~ in deposito; **there's trouble in** ~ **for him** ci sono guai in vista per lui; **what the future has in** ~ **for me** cosa mi riserva il futuro; **set great** ~ **by** tenere in gran conto ● vt tenere; (in warehouse, Comput) immagazzinare

■ **store up** vt (accumulate) far scorte di

store card n carta f di credito di grandi magazzini

storeroom /'stɔːruːm/ n magazzino m

storey /'stɔːrɪ/ n piano m

stork /stɔːk/ n cicogna f

storm /stɔːm/ n temporale m; (with thunder) tempesta f ● vt prendere d'assalto

stormy /'stɔːmɪ/ a tempestoso

story /'stɔːrɪ/ n storia f; (in newspaper) articolo m

storybook /'stɔːrɪbʊk/ n libro m di racconti

storyteller /'stɔːrɪtelə(r)/ n (writer) narratore, -trice mf; (liar) contaballe mf inv

stout /staʊt/ a ⟨shoes⟩ resistente; (fat) robusto; ⟨defence⟩ strenuo ● n birra f scura

stoutly /'staʊtlɪ/ adv strenuamente

stove /stəʊv/ n cucina f [economica]; (for heating) stufa f

stow /stəʊ/ vt metter via

■ **stow away** vi Naut imbarcarsi clandestinamente

stowaway /'stəʊəweɪ/ n passeggero, -a mf clandestino, -a

straddle /'strædl/ vt stare a cavalcioni su; (standing) essere a cavallo su

strafe /streɪf/ vt mitragliare da bassa quota

straggle /'strægl/ vi crescere disordinatamente; (dawdle) rimanere indietro

straggler /'stræglə(r)/ n persona f che rimane indietro

straggly /'strælɪ/ a have ~ hair avere pochi capelli sottili

straight /streɪt/ a diritto, dritto; ⟨answer, question, person⟩ diretto; (tidy) in ordine; ⟨drink, hair⟩ liscio; **three ~ wins** tre vittorie di seguito ● adv diritto, dritto; (directly) direttamente; **~ away** immediatamente; **~ on** or **ahead** diritto; **~ out** fig apertamente; **go ~** fam rigare diritto; **put sth ~** mettere qcsa in ordine; **sit/stand up ~** stare diritto; **let's get something ~** mettiamo una cosa in chiaro

straighten /'streɪtn/ vt raddrizzare ● vi raddrizzarsi; **~ [up]** ⟨person:⟩ mettersi diritto

■ **straighten out** vt fig chiarire ⟨situation⟩

straight: straight face n keep a **~ ~** restare serio. **straight-faced** /-'feɪst/ a con l'aria seria. **straightforward** a franco; (simple) semplice. **straight man** n Theat spalla f

strain[1] /streɪn/ n (streak) vena f; Bot varietà f inv; (of virus) forma f

strain[2] n tensione f; (injury) stiramento m; **~s** pl (of music) note fpl; **put a ~ on** fig introdurre delle tensioni in; **under a lot of ~** estremamente sotto pressione ● vt tirare; sforzare ⟨eyes, voice⟩; stirarsi ⟨muscle⟩; Culin scolare ● vi sforzarsi

strained /streɪnd/ a ⟨relations⟩ teso

strainer /'streɪnə(r)/ n colino m

strait /streɪt/ n stretto m; **in dire ~s** in serie difficoltà

straitjacket /'streɪtdʒækɪt/ n camicia f di forza

strait-laced /-'leɪst/ a puritano

strand[1] /strænd/ n (of thread) gugliata f; (of beads) filo m; (of hair) capello m

strand[2] vt be **~ed** rimanere bloccato

strange /streɪndʒ/ a strano; (not known) sconosciuto; (unaccustomed) estraneo

strangely /'streɪndʒlɪ/ adv stranamente; **~ enough** curiosamente

strangeness /'streɪndʒnɪs/ n stranezza f

stranger /'streɪndʒə(r)/ n estraneo, -a mf

strangle /'stræŋgl/ vt strangolare; fig reprimere

stranglehold /'stræŋglhəʊld/ n (physical grip) presa f alla gola; (fig: powerful control) stretta f mortale; **have a ~ on sth** fig avere in pugno qcsa

strangulation /stræŋgjʊ'leɪʃn/ n strangolamento m

strap /stræp/ n cinghia f; (to grasp in vehicle) maniglia f; (of watch) cinturino m; (shoulder ~) bretella f, spallina f ● vt (pt/pp strapped) legare; **~ in/down** assicurare

strapless /'stræplɪs/ a ⟨bra, dress⟩ senza spalline

strapped /stræpt/ a fam be **~ for** essere a corto di

strapping /'stræpɪŋ/ a robusto

strata /'strɑːtə/ see stratum

stratagem /'strætədʒəm/ n stratagemma m

strategic /strə'tiːdʒɪk/ a strategico

strategically /strə'tiːdʒɪklɪ/ adv strategicamente

strategist /'strætədʒɪst/ n stratega mf

strategy /'strætədʒɪ/ n strategia f

stratosphere /'strɑːtəsfɪə(r)/ n stratosfera f

stratum /'strɑːtəm/ n (pl strata) strato m

straw /strɔː/ n paglia f; (single piece) fuscello m; (for drinking) cannuccia f; **the last ~** l'ultima goccia

strawberry /'strɔːbərɪ/ n fragola f

straw poll n Pol sondaggio m d'opinione non ufficiale

stray /streɪ/ a (animal) randagio ● n randagio m ● vi andarsene per conto proprio; (deviate) deviare (from da)

streak /striːk/ n striatura f; (fig: trait) vena f; **~s** (pl: in hair) mèches fpl ● vi (move fast) sfrecciare

streaky /'striːkɪ/ a striato; ⟨bacon⟩ grasso

stream /striːm/ n ruscello m; (current) corrente f; (of blood, people) flusso m; Sch classe f; **come on ~** (start operating) entrare in attività; ⟨oil:⟩ cominciare a scorrere ● vi scorrere

■ **stream in** vi entrare a fiotti

■ **stream out** vi uscire a fiotti

streamer /'striːmə(r)/ n (paper) stella f filante; (flag) pennone m

streamline /'striːmlaɪn/ vt rendere aerodinamico; (simplify) snellire

streamlined /'striːmlaɪnd/ a aerodinamico; (simplified) snellito

street /striːt/ n strada f

street: streetcar n Am tram m inv. **street cred** n fam immagine f pubblica. **street lamp** n lampione m. **streetwalker** n passeggiatrice f. **streetwise** a ⟨fam: person⟩ che conosce tutti i trucchi per sopravvivere in una metropoli

strength /streŋθ/ n forza f; (of wall, bridge etc) solidità f; **~s** pl punti mpl forti; **on the ~ of** grazie a

strengthen /'streŋθən/ vt rinforzare

strenuous /'strenjʊəs/ a faticoso; ⟨attempt, denial⟩ energico

strenuously /'strenjʊəslɪ/ *adv* energicamente

stress /stres/ *n* (*emphasis*) insistenza *f*; *Gram* accento *m* tonico; (*mental*) stress *m inv*; *Mech* spinta *f* ● *vt* (*emphasise*) insistere su; *Gram* mettere l'accento [tonico] su

stressed /strest/ *a* (*mentally*) ~ [**out**] stressato

stressful /'stresfʊl/ *a* stressante

stretch /stretʃ/ *n* stiramento *m*; (*period*) periodo *m* di tempo; (*of road*) tratto *m*; (*elasticity*) elasticità *f*; **at a ~** di fila; **have a ~** stirarsi ● *vt* tirare; allargare (*shoes, sweater, etc*); ~ **one's legs** stendere le gambe; ~ **a point** fare uno strappo alla regola ● *vi* (*become wider*) allargarsi; (*extend*) estendersi; (*person:*) stirarsi

■ **stretch out** *vt* allungare (*one's hand, legs*); allargare (*arms*) ● *vi* (*person:*) sdraiarsi; (*land:*) estendersi

stretcher /'stretʃə(r)/ *n* barella *f*

stretchy /'stretʃɪ/ *a* elastico

strew /stru:/ *vt* (*pt/pp* **strewn** *or* **strewed**) sparpagliare; ~**n with** coperto di

stricken /'strɪkn/ *a* prostrato; ~ **with** affetto da (*illness*)

strict /strɪkt/ *a* severo; (*precise*) preciso

strictly /'strɪktlɪ/ *adv* severamente; ~ **speaking** in senso stretto

strictness /'strɪktnɪs/ *n* severità *f*

stricture /'strɪktʃə(r)/ *n* critica *f*; (*constriction*) restringimento *m*

stride /straɪd/ *n* [lungo] passo *m*; **make great ~s** *fig* fare passi da gigante; **take sth in one's ~** accettare qcsa con facilità ● *vi* (*pt* **strode**, *pp* **stridden**) andare a gran passi

strident /'straɪdənt/ *a* stridente; (*colour*) vistoso

stridently /'straɪdəntlɪ/ *adv* con voce stridente

strife /straɪf/ *n* conflitto *m*

strike /straɪk/ *n* sciopero *m*; *Mil* attacco *m*; **on ~** in sciopero ● *v* (*pt/pp* **struck**) ● *vt* colpire; accendere (*match*); trovare (*oil, gold*); (*delete*) depennare; (*occur to*) venire in mente a; *Mil* attaccare; ~ **sb a blow** colpire qcno ● *vi* (*lightning:*) cadere; (*clock:*) suonare; *Mil* attaccare; (*workers:*) scioperare; ~ **lucky** azzeccarla

■ **strike back** *vi* fare rappresaglia; (*at critics*) reagire

■ **strike off** *vt* eliminare; **be struck off [the register]** (*doctor:*) essere radiato [dall'albo]

■ **strike out** *vt* eliminare

■ **strike up** *vt* fare (*friendship*); attaccare (*conversation*)

strike-breaker *n persona f* che non aderisce a uno sciopero

striker /'straɪkə(r)/ *n* scioperante *mf*

striking /'straɪkɪŋ/ *a* impressionante; (*attractive*) affascinante

string /strɪŋ/ *n* spago *m*; (*of musical instrument, racket*) corda *f*; (*of pearls*) filo *m*; (*of lies*) serie *f*; **the ~s** *pl Mus* gli archi; **pull ~s** *fam* usare le proprie conoscenze ● *vt* (*pt/pp* **strung**) (*thread*) infilare (*beads*)

■ **string along** *vt* (*fam: deceive*) prendere in giro ● *vi* **I'll ~ along** (*come too*) vengo anch'io; ~ **along with sb** andare/venire con qcno

■ **string out** *vi* (*spread out*) allinearsi ● *vt* disporre in fila; **be strung out** (*sl: on drugs*) essere fatto

■ **string together** *vt* mettere insieme (*words, remarks*)

string bean *n* fagiolino *m*

stringed /strɪŋd/ *a* (*instrument*) a corda

stringent /'strɪndʒnt/ *a* rigido

stringy /'strɪŋɪ/ *a* (*person, build*) asciutto; (*hair*) come spaghetti; *Culin* filaccioso

strip /strɪp/ *n* striscia *f* ● *v* (*pt/pp* **stripped**) ● *vt* spogliare; togliere le lenzuola da (*bed*); scrostare (*wood, furniture*); smontare (*machine*); (*deprive*) privare (**of** di) ● *vi* (*undress*) spogliarsi

■ **strip down** *vt* smontare (*engine*)

strip cartoon *n* striscia *f*

strip club *n* locale *m* di strip-tease

stripe /straɪp/ *n* striscia *f*; *Mil* gallone *m*

striped /straɪpt/ *a* a strisce

stripey /'straɪpɪ/ *a* a strisce, a righe

strip light *n* tubo *m* al neon

stripper /'strɪpə(r)/ *n* spogliarellista *mf*; (*solvent*) sverniciatore *m*

strip-search *n* perquisizione *f* (*facendo spogliare qcno*) ● *vt* perquisire (*facendo spogliare*)

striptease /'strɪptiːz/ *n* spogliarello *m*, strip-tease *m inv*

strive /straɪv/ *vi* (*pt* **strove**, *pp* **striven**) sforzarsi (**to** di); ~ **for** sforzarsi di ottenere

strobe /strəʊb/ *n* luce *f* stroboscopica

strode /strəʊd/ *see* **stride**

stroke[1] /strəʊk/ *n* colpo *m*; (*of pen*) tratto *m*; (*in swimming*) bracciata *f*; *Med* ictus *m inv*; ~ **of luck** colpo *m* di fortuna; **put sb off his ~** far perdere il filo a qcno

stroke[2] ● *vt* accarezzare ● *n* carezza *f*

stroll /strəʊl/ *n* passeggiata *f*; **go for a ~** andare a far due passi ● *vi* passeggiare

stroller /'strəʊlə(r)/ *n* (*Am*: *push-chair*) passeggino *m*

strong /strɒŋ/ *a* (**-er** /'strɒŋgə(r)/, **-est** /'strɒŋgɪst/) forte; (*argument*) valido

strong: **strongbox** /'strɒŋbɒks/ *n* cassaforte *f*. **stronghold** /'strɒŋhəʊld/ *n* roccaforte *f*. **strong language** *n* (*forceful terms*) linguaggio *m* incisivo; (*swearing*) linguaggio *m* offensivo

strongly /'strɒŋlɪ/ *adv* fortemente; **feel ~ about sth** avere molto a cuore qcsa

strong: **strong-minded** /-'maɪndɪd/ *a* risoluto. **strong point** *n* punto *m* di forza. **strongroom** *n* camera *f* blindata. **strong stomach** *n* stomaco *m* di ferro

stroppiness /'strɒpɪnɪs/ *n* scontrosità *f*

stroppy /'strɒpɪ/ *a fam* scorbutico, scontroso

strove /strəʊv/ *see* **strive**

struck /strʌk/ *see* **strike**; ~ **on** *a fam* entusiasta di

structural /'strʌktʃərəl/ *a* strutturale

structurally /'strʌktʃərəlɪ/ *adv* strutturalmente

structure /'strʌktʃə(r)/ *n* struttura *f* ● *vt* strutturare

struggle /'strʌgl/ *n* lotta *f*; **with a** ~ con difficoltà ● *vi* lottare; ~ **for breath** respirare con fatica; ~ **to do sth** fare fatica a fare qcsa; ~ **to one's feet** alzarsi con fatica

strum /strʌm/ *vt/i* (*pt/pp* **strummed**) strimpellare

strung /strʌŋ/ *see* **string**

strut¹ /strʌt/ *n* (*component*) puntello *m*

strut² *vi* (*pt/pp* **strutted**) camminare impettito

stub /stʌb/ *n* mozzicone *m*; (*counterfoil*) matrice *f* ● *vt* (*pt/pp* **stubbed**) ~ **one's toe** sbattere il dito del piede (**on** contro)

■ **stub out** *vt* spegnere ⟨*cigarette*⟩

stubble /'stʌbl/ *n* (*on face*) barba *f* ispida

stubbly /'stʌblɪ/ *a* ispido

stubborn /'stʌbən/ *a* testardo; ⟨*refusal*⟩ ostinato

stubbornly /'stʌbənlɪ/ *adv* testardamente; ⟨*refuse*⟩ ostinatamente

stubbornness /'stʌbənnɪs/ *n* (*of person*) testardaggine *f*

stubby /'stʌbɪ/ *a* (**-ier**, **-iest**) tozzo

stucco /'stʌkəʊ/ *n* stucco *m*

stuck /stʌk/ *see* **stick²**

stuck-up *a fam* snob *inv*

stud¹ /stʌd/ *n* (*on boot*) tacchetto *m*; (*on jacket*) borchia *f*; (*for ear*) orecchino *m* [a bottone]

stud² *n* (*of horses*) scuderia *f*

studded with /'stʌdɪd/ *a fig* tempestato di

student /'stju:dənt/ *n* studente *m*, studentessa *f*; (*school child*) scolaro, -a *mf*

student nurse *n* studente, -tessa *mf* infermiere, -a

stud-horse *n* stallone *m* [da monta]

studied /'stʌdɪd/ *a* intenzionale; ⟨*politeness*⟩ studiato

studio /'stju:dɪəʊ/ *n* studio *m*

studio apartment *n Am* monolocale *m*

studio flat *n* monolocale *m*

studious /'stju:dɪəs/ *a* studioso; ⟨*attention*⟩ studiato

studiously /'stju:dɪəslɪ/ *adv* studiosamente; (*carefully*) attentamente

stud mare *n* giumenta *f* fattrice

study /'stʌdɪ/ *n* studio *m* ● *vt/i* (*pt/pp* **-ied**) studiare; ~ **for an exam** preparare un esame

stuff /stʌf/ *n* materiale *m*; (*fam: things*) roba *f* ● *vt* riempire; (*with padding*) imbottire; *Culin* farcire; ~ **sth into a drawer/one's pocket** ficcare qcsa alla rinfusa in un cassetto/in tasca; ~ **oneself** ingozzarsi (**with** di); **get ~ed!** *fam* va' a quel paese!

stuffing /'stʌfɪŋ/ *n* (*padding*) imbottitura *f*; *Culin* ripieno *m*

stuffy /'stʌfɪ/ *a* (**-ier**, **-iest**) che sa di chiuso; (*old-fashioned*) antiquato

stultifying /'stʌltɪfaɪɪŋ/ *a* che abbrutisce

stumble /'stʌmbl/ *vi* inciampare; ~ **across** *or* **on** imbattersi in

stumbling block /'stʌmblɪŋ/ *n* ostacolo *m*

stump /stʌmp/ *n* ceppo *m*; (*of limb*) moncone *m*

■ **stump up** *vt/i fam* sganciare

stumped /stʌmpt/ *a fam* perplesso

stumpy /'stʌmpɪ/ *a* (**-ier**, **-iest**) ⟨*person, legs*⟩ tozzo

stun /stʌn/ *vt* (*pt/pp* **stunned**) stordire; (*astonish*) sbalordire

stung /stʌŋ/ *see* **sting**

stunk /stʌŋk/ *see* **stink**

stunned /stʌnd/ *a* (⟨*expression*⟩) sbalordito

stunning /'stʌnɪŋ/ *a fam* favoloso; ⟨*blow, victory*⟩ sbalorditivo

stunt¹ /stʌnt/ *n fam* trovata *f* pubblicitaria

stunt² *vt* arrestare lo sviluppo di

stunted /'stʌntɪd/ *a* stentato

stuntman /'stʌntmən/ *n* stuntman *m inv*, cascatore *m*

stuntwoman /'stʌntwʊmən/ *n* stuntwoman *f inv*

stupefaction /stju:pɪ'fækʃn/ *n* stupore *m*

stupefy /'stju:pɪfaɪ/ *vt* (*pt/pp* **-ied**) (*astonish*) stupire

stupefying /'stju:pɪfaɪɪŋ/ *a* stupefacente

stupendous /stju:'pendəs/ *a* stupendo

stupendously /stju:'pendəslɪ/ *adv* stupendamente

stupid /'stju:pɪd/ *a* stupido

stupidity /stju:'pɪdətɪ/ *n* stupidità *f*

stupidly /'stju:pɪdlɪ/ *adv* stupidamente

stupor /'stju:pə(r)/ *n* torpore *m*

sturdy /'stɜ:dɪ/ *a* (**-ier**, **-iest**) robusto; ⟨*furniture*⟩ solido

stutter /'stʌtə(r)/ *n* balbuzie *f*; **have a** ~ balbettare ● *vt/i* balbettare

sty¹ /staɪ/ *n* (*pl* **sties**) porcile *m*

sty², **stye** /staɪ/ *n* (*pl* **styes**) *Med* orzaiolo *m*

style /staɪl/ *n* stile *m*; (*fashion*) moda *f*; (*sort*) tipo *m*; (*hair-*~) pettinatura *f*; **in** ~ in grande stile

stylish /'staɪlɪʃ/ *a* elegante

stylishly /'staɪlɪʃlɪ/ *adv* con eleganza

stylist /'staɪlɪst/ *n* stilista *mf*; (*hair-*~) *n* parrucchiere, -a *mf*

stylistic /staɪ'lɪstɪk/ *a* stilistico

stylistically /staɪ'lɪstɪklɪ/ *adv* stilisticamente

stylized /'staɪlaɪzd/ *a* stilizzato

stylus /'staɪləs/ *n* (*on record player*) puntina *f*

styptic pencil /'stɪptɪk/ *n* matita *f* emostatica

suave /swɑ:v/ *a* dai modi garbati

sub-aqua /sʌb'ækwə/ *a* ⟨*club*⟩ di sport subacquei

subcommittee /'sʌbkəmɪtɪ/ *n* sottocommissione *f*

subconscious /sʌb'kɒnʃəs/ *a* subcosciente ● *n* subcosciente *m*

subconsciously /sʌb'kɒnʃəslɪ/ *adv* in modo inconscio

subcontinent /sʌb'kɒntɪnənt/ n subcontinente m

subcontract /sʌbkən'trækt/ vt subappaltare (**to** a)

subcontractor /'sʌbkəntræktə(r)/ n subappaltatore, -trice mf

subdirectory /'sʌbdaɪrektərɪ/ n Comput sottodirectory f inv

subdivide /sʌbdɪ'vaɪd/ vt suddividere

subdivision /'sʌbdɪvɪʒn/ n suddivisione f

subdue /səb'dju:/ vt sottomettere; (make quieter) attenuare

subdued /səb'dju:d/ a ⟨light⟩ attenuato; ⟨person, voice⟩ pacato

subhuman /sʌb'hju:mən/ a (cruel, not fit for humans) disumano; ⟨fam: appearance⟩ da paleolitico

subject¹ /'sʌbdʒɪkt/ a ~ **to** soggetto a; (depending on) subordinato a; ~ **to availability** nei limiti della disponibilità ● n soggetto m; (of ruler) suddito, -a mf; Sch materia f; **change the** ~ parlare di qualcos'altro

subject² /səb'dʒekt/ vt (to attack, abuse) sottoporre; assoggettare ⟨country⟩

subjective /səb'dʒektɪv/ a soggettivo

subjectively /səb'dʒektɪvlɪ/ adv soggettivamente

subjectiveness /səb'dʒektɪvnɪs/ n soggetività f

subjugate /'sʌbdʒʊgeɪt/ vt soggiogare, sottomettere

subjugation /sʌbdʒə'geɪʃn/ n sottomissione f

subjunctive /səb'dʒʌŋktɪv/ a & n congiuntivo m

sub-let /sʌb'let/ vt (pt/pp **-let**, pres p **-letting**) subaffittare

sublime /sə'blaɪm/ a sublime

sublimely /sə'blaɪmlɪ/ adv sublimamente

subliminal /sə'blɪmɪnl/ a subliminale

sub-machine gun n mitraglietta f

submarine /'sʌbməri:n/ n sommergibile m

submerge /səb'mɜ:dʒ/ vt immergere; **be ~d** essere sommerso ● vi immergersi

submission /səb'mɪʃn/ n sottomissione f

submissive /səb'mɪsɪv/ a sottomesso

submissively /səb'mɪsɪvlɪ/ adv remissivamente

submissiveness /səb'mɪsɪvnɪs/ n remissività f

submit /səb'mɪt/ v (pt/pp **-mitted**, pres p **-mitting**) ● vt sottoporre ● vi sottomettersi

subnormal /sʌb'nɔ:ml/ a ⟨temperature⟩ al di sotto della norma; ⟨person⟩ subnormale

subordinate¹ /sə'bɔ:dɪnət/ a & n subordinato, -a mf

subordinate² /sə'bɔ:dɪneɪt/ vt subordinare (**to** a)

subpoena /səb'pi:nə/ n mandato m di comparizione ● vt citare

subroutine /'sʌbru:ti:n/ n Comput subroutine f

subscribe /səb'skraɪb/ vi contribuire; ~ **to** abbonarsi a ⟨newspaper⟩; sottoscrivere ⟨fund⟩; fig aderire a ⟨theory⟩

subscriber /səb'skraɪbə(r)/ n abbonato, -a mf

subscription /səb'skrɪpʃn/ n (to club) sottoscrizione f; (to newspaper) abbonamento m

subsequent /'sʌbsɪkwənt/ a susseguente

subsequently /'sʌbsɪkwəntlɪ/ adv in seguito

subservience /səb'sɜ:vɪəns/ n asservimento m

subservient /səb'sɜ:vɪənt/ a subordinato; (servile) servile

subserviently /səb'sɜ:vɪəntlɪ/ adv servilmente

subset /'sʌbset/ n Math sottoinsieme m

subside /səb'saɪd/ vi sprofondare; ⟨ground:⟩ avvallarsi; ⟨storm:⟩ placarsi

subsidence /'sʌbsɪdəns/ n (of land) cedimento m

subsidiary /səb'sɪdɪərɪ/ a secondario ● n ~ [**company**] filiale f

subsidize /'sʌbsɪdaɪz/ vt sovvenzionare

subsidy /'sʌbsɪdɪ/ n sovvenzione f

subsist /səb'sɪst/ vi vivere (**on** di)

subsistence /səb'sɪstəns/ n sussistenza f

substance /'sʌbstəns/ n sostanza f

sub-standard /sʌb'stændəd/ a di qualità inferiore

substantial /səb'stænʃl/ a sostanziale; ⟨meal⟩ sostanzioso; (strong) solido

substantially /səb'stænʃəlɪ/ adv sostanzialmente; ⟨built⟩ solidamente

substantiate /səb'stænʃɪeɪt/ vt comprovare

substitute /'sʌbstɪtju:t/ n sostituto m ● vt ~ **A for B** sostituire B con A ● vi ~ **for sb** sostituire qcno

substitution /sʌbstɪ'tju:ʃn/ n sostituzione f

subterfuge /'sʌbtəfju:dʒ/ n sotterfugio m

subterranean /sʌbtə'reɪnɪən/ a sotterraneo

subtext /'sʌbtekst/ n storia f secondaria; fig messaggio m implicito

subtitle /'sʌbtaɪtl/ n sottotitolo m ● vt sottotitolare

subtle /'sʌtl/ a sottile; ⟨taste, perfume⟩ delicato

subtlety /'sʌtltɪ/ n sottigliezza f

subtly /'sʌtlɪ/ adv sottilmente

subtotal /'sʌbtəʊtl/ n totale m parziale

subtract /səb'trækt/ vt sottrare

subtraction /səb'trækʃn/ n sottrazione f

suburb /'sʌbɜ:b/ n sobborgo m; **in the ~s** in periferia

suburban /sə'bɜ:bən/ a suburbano

suburbia /sə'bɜ:bɪə/ n sobborghi mpl

subversive /səb'vɜ:sɪv/ a sovversivo

subway /'sʌbweɪ/ n sottopassaggio m; (Am: railway) metropolitana f, metrò m inv

sub-zero /sʌb'zɪərəʊ/ a sottozero inv

succeed /sək'si:d/ vi riuscire (**in doing sth** a fare qcsa); (follow) succedere (**to** a) ● vt succedere a ⟨king⟩

succeeding /sək'si:dɪŋ/ a successivo

success /sək'ses/ n successo m; **be a** ~ (in life) aver successo

successful /sək'sesfʊl/ a riuscito; ⟨businessman, artist etc⟩ di successo

successfully /sək'sesfʊlɪ/ adv con successo

succession /sək'seʃn/ n successione f; **in ~** di seguito

successive /sək'sesɪv/ a successivo

successively /sə'sesɪvlɪ/ adv successivamente

successor /sək'sesə(r)/ n successore m

succinct /sək'sɪŋkt/ a succinto

succinctly /sək'sɪŋktlɪ/ adv succintamente

succour /'sʌkə(r)/ vt soccorrere ● n soccorso m

succulence /'sʌkjʊləns/ n succuluenza f

succulent /'ʃʌkjʊlənt/ a succulento

succumb /sə'kʌm/ vi soccombere (**to** a)

such /sʌtʃ/ a tale; **~ a book** un libro così; **~ a thing** una cosa del genere; **~ a long time ago** talmente tanto tempo fa; **there is no ~ thing/person** non c'è una cosa/persona così ● pron **as ~** in quanto tale; **~ as** come; **and ~ e simili; ~ as it is** per quel che vale; **if ~ is the case** se questo è il caso

suchlike /'sʌtʃlaɪk/ pron fam di tal genere

suck /ʃʌk/ vt succhiare

■ **suck up** vt assorbire

■ **suck up to** vt fam fare il lecchino con

sucker /'ʃʌkə(r)/ n Bot pollone m; ⟨fam: person⟩ credulone, -a mf

suckle /'ʃʌl/ vt allattare

suction /'sʌkʃn/ n aspirazione f

Sudan /sʊ'dæn/ n Sudan m

Sudanese /sʊdən'iːz/ a & n sudanese mf

sudden /'sʌdn/ a improvviso ● n **all of a ~** all'improvviso

suddenly /'sʌdənlɪ/ adv improvvisamente

suds /sʌdz/ npl ⟨foam⟩ schiuma f; ⟨soapy water⟩ acqua f saponata

sue /su:/ v (pres p **suing**) ● vt fare causa a (**for** per) ● vi fare causa

suede /sweɪd/ n pelle f scamosciata

suet /'su:ɪt/ n grasso m di rognone

suffer /'sʌfə(r)/ vi soffrire (**from** per) ● vt soffrire di ⟨pain⟩; subire ⟨loss etc⟩

sufferance /'sʌf(ə)rəns/ n **you're here on ~** qui tu sei appena tollerato

suffering /'sʌf(ə)rɪŋ/ n sofferenza f

suffice /sə'faɪs/ vi bastare

sufficient /sə'fɪʃənt/ a sufficiente

sufficiently /sə'fɪʃəntlɪ/ adv sufficientemente

suffix /'sʌfɪks/ n suffisso m

suffocate /'sʌfəkeɪt/ vt/i soffocare

suffocation /sʌfə'keɪʃn/ n soffocamento m

suffrage /'sʌfrɪdʒ/ n ⟨right⟩ diritto m di voto; ⟨system⟩ suffragio m

suffragette /sʌfrə'dʒet/ n suffragetta f

sugar /'ʃʊgə(r)/ n zucchero m ● vt zuccherare; **~ the pill** fig addolcire la pillola

sugar: sugar basin, sugar bowl n zuccheriera f. **sugar-coated** /-'kəʊtɪd/ a ricoperto di zucchero. **sugar cube** n zolletta f. **sugar daddy** n fam vecchio amante m danaroso. **sugar lump** n zolletta f

sugary /'ʃʊgərɪ/ a zuccheroso; fig sdolcinato

suggest /sə'dʒest/ vt suggerire; ⟨indicate, insinuate⟩ fare pensare a

suggestible /sə'dʒestəbl/ a suggestionabile

suggestion /sə'dʒestʃən/ n suggerimento m; ⟨trace⟩ traccia f

suggestive /sə'dʒestɪv/ a allusivo; **be ~ of** fare pensare a

suggestively /sə'dʒestɪvlɪ/ adv in modo allusivo

suicidal /su:ɪ'saɪdl/ a suicida

suicide /'su:ɪsaɪd/ n suicidio m; ⟨person⟩ suicida mf; **commit ~** suicidarsi

suicide attempt n tentato suicidio m

suicide pact n patto m suicida

suit /su:t/ n vestito m; ⟨woman's⟩ tailleur m inv; ⟨Cards⟩ seme m; Jur causa f; **follow ~** fig fare lo stesso ● vt andar bene a; ⟨adapt⟩ adattare (**to** a); ⟨be convenient for⟩ andare bene per; **be ~ed to** or **for** essere adatto a; **~ yourself!** fa' come vuoi!

suitability /su:tə'bɪlɪtɪ/ n adeguatezza f

suitable /'su:təbl/ a adatto

suitably /'su:təblɪ/ adv convenientemente

suitcase /'su:tkeɪs/ n valigia f

suite /swi:t/ n suite f inv; ⟨of furniture⟩ divano m e poltrone fpl assortiti

sulk /sʌlk/ vi fare il broncio

sulkily /'sʌlkɪlɪ/ adv con aria imbronciata

sulky /'sʌlkɪ/ a imbronciato

sullen /'sʌlən/ a svogliato

sullenly /'sʌlənlɪ/ adv svogliatamente

sulphur /'sʌlfə(r)/ n zolfo m

sulphur dioxide /daɪ'ɒksaɪd/ n anidride f solforosa

sulphuric acid /sʌl'fjʊərɪk/ n acido m solforico

sultana /sʌl'tɑːnə/ n uva f sultanina

sultry /'sʌltrɪ/ a (**-ier, -iest**) ⟨weather⟩ afoso; fig sensuale

sum /sʌm/ n somma f; Sch addizione f

■ **sum up** v (pt/pp **summed**) ● vi riassumere ● vt valutare

summarily /sʌ'merɪlɪ/ adv sommariamente; ⟨dismissed⟩ sbrigativamente

summarize /'sʌməraɪz/ vt riassumere

summary /'sʌmərɪ/ n sommario m ● a sommario; ⟨dismissal⟩ sbrigativo

summer /'sʌmə(r)/ n estate f; **in ~, in the ~** in estate

summer: summer house n padiglione m. **summertime** n ⟨season⟩ estate f. **summer time** n ⟨clock change⟩ ora f legale

summery /'sʌmərɪ/ a estivo

summing-up /sʌmɪŋ'ʌp/ n riepilogo m; Jur ricapitolazione f del processo

summit /'sʌmɪt/ n cima f

summit conference n vertice m

summon /'sʌmən/ vt convocare; Jur citare

■ **summon up** vt raccogliere ⟨strength⟩; rievocare ⟨memory⟩

summons /'sʌmənz/ n Jur citazione f ● vt citare in giudizio

sump /sʌmp/ n Auto coppa f dell'olio

sumptuous /'sʌmptjʊəs/ a sontuoso

sumptuously /'sʌmptjʊəslɪ/ *adv* sontuosamente

sum total *n* totale *m*

sun /sʌn/ *n* sole *m* ● *vt* (*pt/pp* **sunned**) ~ **oneself** prendere il sole

sun: sunbathe *vi* prendere il sole. **sunbed** *n* lettino *m* solare. **sunblock** *n* prodotto *m* solare a protezione totale. **sunburn** *n* scottatura *f* (*solare*). **sunburnt** *a* scottato (*dal sole*). **sun cream** *n* crema *f* solare

sundae /'sʌndeɪ/ *n* gelato *m* guarnito

Sunday /'sʌndeɪ/ *n* domenica *f*

sundial /'sʌndaɪəl/ *n* meridiana *f*

sun-dried tomatoes /'sʌndraɪd/ *npl* pomodori *mpl* secchi

sundry /'sʌndrɪ/ *a* svariati; **all and ~** tutti quanti

sunflower /'sʌnflaʊə(r)/ *n* girasole *m*

sung /sʌŋ/ *see* **sing**

sunglasses /'sʌnglɑːsɪz/ *npl* occhiali *mpl* da sole

sunk /sʌŋk/ *see* **sink**

sunken /'sʌŋkn/ *a* incavato

sunlamp /'sʌnlæmp/ *n* lampada *f* abbronzante

sunlight /'sʌnlaɪt/ *n* [luce *f* del] sole *m*

sunny /'sʌnɪ/ *a* (**-ier, -iest**) assolato

sun: sunrise *n* alba *f*. **sunroof** *n* *Auto* tettuccio *m* apribile. **sunscreen** *n* (*to prevent sunburn*) crema *f* solare protettiva. **sunset** *n* tramonto *m*. **sunshade** *n* parasole *m*. **sunshine** *n* [luce *f* del] sole *m*. **sunshine roof** *n* tettuccio *m* apribile. **sunstroke** *n* insolazione *f*. **suntan** *n* abbronzatura *f*. **suntan lotion** *n* antisolare *m*. **sun-tanned** *a* abbronzato. **suntan oil** *n* olio *m* solare

super /'suːpə(r)/ *a fam* fantastico

superannuated /suː'pər'ænjʊeɪtɪd/ *a fig* che ha fatto il suo tempo

superannuation /suː'pərænjʊ'eɪʃn/ *n* (*contributions*) contributi *mpl* pensionistici; (*pension*) pensione *f*

superannuation fund *n* fondo *m* pensione

superb /sʊ'pɜːb/ *a* splendido

superbly /sʊ'pɜːblɪ/ *adv* splendidamente

supercilious /suːpə'sɪlɪəs/ *a* altezzoso

superciliously /suːpə'sɪlɪəslɪ/ *adv* in modo altezzoso

superficial /suːpə'fɪʃl/ *a* superficiale

superficiality /suːpəfɪʃɪ'ælɪtɪ/ *n* superficialità *f*

superficially /suːpə'fɪʃəlɪ/ *adv* superficialmente

superfluous /sʊ'pɜːflʊəs/ *a* superfluo

superhighway /'suːpəhaɪweɪ/ *n* [**information**] ~ *Comput* autostrada *f* telematica

superhuman /suːpə'hjuːmən/ *a* sovrumano

superimpose /suːpərɪm'pəʊz/ *vt* sovrapporre (*picture, soundtrack*) (**on** a); **~d title** titolo *m* in sovrimpressione

superintendent /suːpərɪn'tendənt/ *n* (*of police*) commissario *m* di polizia

superior /suː'pɪərɪə(r)/ *a & n* superiore, -a *mf*

superiority /suː'pɪərɪ'ɒrətɪ/ *n* superiorità *f*

superlative /suː'pɜːlətɪv/ *a* eccellente ● *n* superlativo *m*

superlatively /suː'pɜːlətɪvlɪ/ *adv* ‹*perform*› in modo eccezionale; ‹*good*› estremamente

superman /'suːpəmæn/ *n* superuomo *m*

supermarket /'suːpəmɑːkɪt/ *n* supermercato *m*

supermodel /'suːpəmɒdl/ *n* top model *f*, supermodella *f*

supernatural /suːpə'nætʃrəl/ *a* soprannaturale

superpower /'suːpəpaʊə(r)/ *n* superpotenza *f*

superscript /'suːpəskrɪpt/ *a* ‹*number, letter*› all'esponente

supersede /suːpə'siːd/ *vt* rimpiazzare

supersonic /suːpə'sɒnɪk/ *a* supersonico

superstition /suːpə'stɪʃn/ *n* superstizione *f*

superstitious /suːpə'stɪʃəs/ *a* superstizioso

superstitiously /suːpə'stɪʃəslɪ/ *adv* in modo superstizioso

superstore /'suːpəstɔː(r)/ *n* ipermercato *m*

superstructure /'suːpəstrʌktʃə(r)/ *n* sovrastruttura *f*

supertax /'suːpətæks/ *n Fin* soprattassa *f*

supervise /'suːpəvaɪz/ *vt* supervisionare

supervision /suːpə'vɪʒn/ *n* supervisione *f*

supervisor /'suːpəvaɪzə(r)/ *n* supervisore *m*

supervisory /suːpə'vaɪzərɪ/ *a* di supervisione

superwoman /'suːpəwʊmən/ *n* superdonna *f*

supper /'sʌpə(r)/ *n* cena *f*; **have ~** cenare

supple /'sʌpl/ *a* slogato

supplement /'sʌplɪmənt/ *n* supplemento *m* ● *vt* integrare

supplementary /sʌplɪ'mentərɪ/ *a* supplementare

supplier /sə'plaɪə(r)/ *n* fornitore, -trice *mf*

supply /sə'plaɪ/ *n* fornitura *f*; *Econ* offerta *f*; **be in short ~** scarseggiare; **~ and demand** domanda *f* e offerta *f*; **supplies** *pl Mil* approvvigionamenti *mpl* ● *vt* (*pt/pp* **-ied**) fornire; **~ sb with sth** fornire qcsa a qcno

supply teacher *n* supplente *mf*

support /sə'pɔːt/ *n* sostegno *m*; (*base*) supporto *m*; (*keep*) sostentamento *m* ● *vt* sostenere; mantenere ‹*family*›; (*give money to*) mantenere finanziariamente; *Sport* fare il tifo per; *Comput* supportare

supporter /sə'pɔːtə(r)/ *n* sostenitore, -trice *mf*; *Sport* tifoso, -a *mf*

supporting actor /sə'pɔːtɪŋ/ *n* attore *m* non protagonista

supporting actress *n* attrice *f* non protagonista

supportive /sə'pɔːtɪv/ *a* incoraggiante; **be ~ of sb** dare tutto il proprio appoggio a qcno

support stockings *npl* calze *fpl* elastiche

suppose /sə'pəʊz/ *vt* (*presume*) supporre; (*imagine*) pensare; **be ~d to do** dover fare; **not be ~d to** non avere il permesso di; **I ~ so** suppongo di sì

supposedly /sə'pəʊzɪdlɪ/ *adv* presumibilmente

supposition /ˌsʌpəˈzɪʃn/ n supposizione f

suppository /sʌˈpɒzɪtrɪ/ n supposta f

suppress /səˈpres/ vt sopprimere

suppressant /səˈpresənt/ n Med inibitore m

suppression /səˈpreʃn/ n soppressione f

suppurate /ˈsʌpjʊreɪt/ vi suppurare

supremacy /suːˈpreməsɪ/ n supremazia f

supreme /suːˈpriːm/ a supremo

supremo /suːˈpriːməʊ/ n massima autorità f inv

surcharge /ˈsɜːtʃɑːdʒ/ n supplemento m

sure /ʃʊə(r)/ a sicuro, certo; **make ~** accertarsi; **be ~ to do it** accertati di farlo ● adv Am fam certamente; **~ enough** infatti

sure-fire a fam garantito

sure-footed /-ˈfʊtɪd/ a agile

surely /ˈʃʊəlɪ/ adv certamente; (Am: gladly) volentieri

surety /ˈʃʊərətɪ/ n garanzia f; **stand ~ for sb/sth** fare da garante a qcno/per qcsa

surf /sɜːf/ n schiuma f ● vt **~ the Net** surfare in Internet

surface /ˈsɜːfɪs/ n superficie f; **on the ~** fig in apparenza ● vi (emerge) emergere

surface mail n **by ~** per posta ordinaria

surface-to-air missile n missile m terra-aria

surfboard /ˈsɜːfbɔːd/ n tavola f da surf

surfeit /ˈsɜːfɪt/ n eccesso m

surfer /ˈsɜːfə(r)/ n surfista mf

surfing /ˈsɜːfɪŋ/ n surf m

surge /sɜːdʒ/ n (of sea) ondata f; (of interest) aumento m; (in demand) impennata f; (of anger, pity) impeto m ● vi riversarsi; **~ forward** buttarsi in avanti

surgeon /ˈsɜːdʒən/ n chirurgo m

surgery /ˈsɜːdʒərɪ/ n chirurgia f; (place, consulting room) ambulatorio m; (hours) ore fpl di visita; **have ~** subire un'intervento [chirurgico]

surgical /ˈsɜːdʒɪkl/ a chirurgico

surgically /ˈsɜːdʒɪklɪ/ adv chirurgicamente

surliness /ˈsɜːlɪnɪs/ n scontrosità f

surly /ˈsɜːlɪ/ a (-ier, -iest) scontroso

surmise /səˈmaɪz/ vt supporre

surmount /səˈmaʊnt/ vt sormontare

surname /ˈsɜːneɪm/ n cognome m

surpass /səˈpɑːs/ vt superare

surplus /ˈsɜːpləs/ a d'avanzo; **be ~ to requirements** essere in eccedenza rispetto alle necessità ● n sovrappiù m

surprise /səˈpraɪz/ n sorpresa f ● vt sorprendere; **be ~d** essere sorpreso (**at** da)

surprising /səˈpraɪzɪŋ/ a sorprendente

surprisingly /səˈpraɪzɪŋlɪ/ adv sorprendentemente; **~ enough** stranamente

surreal /səˈrɪəl/ a surreale

surrealism /səˈrɪəlɪzm/ n surrealismo m

surrealist /səˈrɪəlɪst/ n surrealista mf ● a surrealistico

surrender /səˈrendə(r)/ n resa f ● vi arrendersi ● vt cedere

surreptitious /ˌsʌrəpˈtɪʃəs/ a furtivo

surreptitiously /ˌsʌrəpˈtɪʃəslɪ/ adv furtivamente

surrogate /ˈsʌrəgət/ n surrogato m

surrogate mother n madre f surrogata o in prestito

surround /səˈraʊnd/ vt circondare; **~ed by** circondato da

surrounding /səˈraʊndɪŋ/ a circostante

surroundings /səˈraʊndɪŋz/ npl dintorni mpl

surtax /ˈsɜːtæks/ n soprattassa f; (on income) imposta f supplementare

surveillance /səˈveɪləns/ n sorveglianza f; **under ~** sotto sorveglianza

survey[1] /ˈsɜːveɪ/ n sguardo m; (poll) sondaggio m; (investigation) indagine f; (of land) rilevamento m; (of house) perizia f

survey[2] /səˈveɪ/ vt esaminare; fare un rilevamento di ‹land›; fare una perizia di ‹building›

surveyor /səˈveɪə(r)/ n perito m; (of land) topografo, -a mf

survival /səˈvaɪvl/ n sopravvivenza f; (relic) resto m

survive /səˈvaɪv/ vt sopravvivere a ● vi sopravvivere

survivor /səˈvaɪvə(r)/ n superstite mf; **be a ~** fam riuscire sempre a cavarsela

susceptible /səˈseptəbl/ a influenzabile; **~ to** sensibile a

suspect[1] /səˈspekt/ vt sospettare; (assume) supporre

suspect[2] /ˈsʌspekt/ a & n sospetto, -a mf

suspend /səˈspend/ vt appendere; (stop, from duty) sospendere

suspender belt /səˈspendə/ n reggicalze m inv

suspenders /səˈspendəz/ npl giarrettiere fpl; (Am: braces) bretelle fpl

suspense /səˈspens/ n tensione f; (in book etc) suspense f

suspension /səˈspenʃn/ n Auto sospensione f

suspension bridge n ponte m sospeso

suspicion /səˈspɪʃn/ n sospetto m; (trace) pizzico m; **under ~** sospettato

suspicious /səˈspɪʃəs/ a sospettoso; (arousing suspicion) sospetto

suspiciously /səˈspɪʃəslɪ/ adv sospettosamente; (arousing suspicion) in modo sospetto

■ **suss out** /sʌs/ vt Br fam intuire ‹person›; capire ‹software, technique›; **I've got you ~ed [out]** ho scoperto il tuo piano

sustain /səˈsteɪn/ vt sostenere; mantenere ‹life›; subire ‹injury›

sustained /səˈsteɪnd/ a ‹effort› prolungato

sustenance /ˈsʌstɪnəns/ n nutrimento m

suture n /ˈsuːtʃə(r)/ sutura f

SW abbr (**south-west**) SO

swab /swɒb/ n Med tampone m

swagger /ˈswægə(r)/ vi pavoneggiarsi

swallow[1] /ˈswɒləʊ/ vt/i inghiottire

■ **swallow up** vt divorare; ‹earth, crowd:› inghiottire

swallow[2] n (bird) rondine f

swam /swæm/ see **swim**

swamp /swɒmp/ n palude f ● vt fig sommergere

swampy /'swɒmpɪ/ a paludoso

swan /swɒn/ n cigno m

swank /swæŋk/ vi fam darsi delle arie

swanky /'swæŋkɪ/ a ⟨fam: posh⟩ snob inv

swap /swɒp/ n fam scambio m ● vt (pt/pp **swapped**) fam scambiare (**for** con) ● vi fare cambio

swarm /swɔ:m/ n sciame m ● vi sciamare; **be ~ing with** fig brulicare di

swarthy /'swɔ:ðɪ/ a (**-ier, -iest**) di carnagione scura

swashbuckling /'swɒʃbʌklɪŋ/ a ⟨hero, appearance⟩ spericolato; ⟨adventure, tale⟩ di cappa e spada

swastika /'swɒstɪkə/ n svastica f

swat /swɒt/ vt (pt/pp **swatted**) schiacciare

swathe /sweɪð/ n (of grass, corn) falciata f; (land) larga striscia f ● vt (in bandages, silk) avvolgere

sway /sweɪ/ n fig influenza f ● vi oscillare; ⟨person:⟩ ondeggiare ● vt (influence) influenzare

swear /sweə(r)/ v (pt **swore**, pp **sworn**) ● vt giurare; **I could have sworn that ...** avrei giurato che ... ● vi giurare; (curse) dire parolacce; **I'd ~ to it!** ci potrei giurare!; **~ at sb** imprecare contro qcno; **~ by** (believe in) credere ciecamente in

■ **swear off** vt (fam: give up) smettere di

swear word n parolaccia f

sweat /swet/ n sudore m ● vi sudare ● vt ~ **blood** sudare sangue

■ **sweat out** vt ~ **it out** (endure to the end) tener duro fino alla fine

sweatband /'swetbænd/ n fascia f per il sudore; (for wrist) polsino m

sweater /'swetə(r)/ n golf m inv

sweatshirt /'swetʃ3:t/ n felpa f

sweaty /'swetɪ/ a sudato

Swede /swi:d/ n svedese mf

swede n rapa f svedese

Sweden /'swi:dn/ n Svezia f

Swedish /'swi:dɪʃ/ a & n svedese m

sweep /swi:p/ n scopata f, spazzata f; (curve) curva f; (movement) movimento m ampio; **make a clean ~** fig fare piazza pulita ● v (pt/pp **swept**) ● vt scopare, spazzare; ⟨wind:⟩ spazzare; **~ the board** fare piazza pulita ● vi (go swiftly) andare rapidamente; ⟨wind:⟩ soffiare

■ **sweep away** vt fig spazzare via

■ **sweep up** vt spazzare

sweeper /'swi:pə(r)/ n (machine) spazzatrice f; (person) spazzino m; (in football) libero m

sweeping /'swi:pɪŋ/ a ⟨gesture⟩ ampio; ⟨statement⟩ generico; ⟨changes⟩ radicale

sweet /swi:t/ a dolce; **have a ~ tooth** essere goloso ● n caramella f; (dessert) dolce m

sweet: **sweet and sour** a agrodolce. **sweetbread** n (veal) animella f di vitello; (lamb) animella f di agnello. **sweetcorn** n mais m, granturco m

sweeten /'swi:tn/ vt addolcire

sweetener /'swi:tnə(r)/ n dolcificante m; (fam: incentive) incentivo m; (fam: bribe) bustarella f

sweetheart /'swi:thɑ:t/ n innamorato, -a mf; **hi, ~** ciao, tesoro

sweetly /'swi:tlɪ/ adv dolcemente

sweetness /'swi:tnɪs/ n dolcezza f

sweet: **sweet pea** n pisello m odoroso. **sweetshop** n negozio m di dolciumi. **sweet-talk** vt ~ **sb into doing sth** convincere qcno a fare qcsa con tante belle parole

swell /swel/ n (of sea) mare m lungo ● v (pt **swelled**, pp **swollen** or **swelled**) ● vi gonfiarsi; (increase) aumentare ● vt gonfiare; (increase) far salire ● a fam eccellente

swelling /'swelɪŋ/ n gonfiore m

swelter /'sweltə(r)/ vi soffocare [dal caldo]

sweltering [**hot**] /'sweltərɪŋ/ a ⟨day⟩ afoso

swept /swept/ see **sweep**

swerve /sw3:v/ vi deviare bruscamente

swift /swift/ a rapido

swiftly /'swiftlɪ/ adv rapidamente

swiftness /'swiftnɪs/ n rapidità f

swig /swɪg/ fam n sorso m ● vt (pt/pp **swigged**) scolarsi

swill /swɪl/ n (for pigs) brodaglia f ● vt ~ [**out**] risciacquare

swim /swɪm/ n **have a ~** fare una nuotata ● vi (pt **swam**, pp **swum**) nuotare; ⟨room:⟩ girare; **go ~ming** andare a nuotare; **my head is ~ming** mi gira la testa ● vt percorrere a nuoto ⟨distance⟩

swimmer /'swɪmə(r)/ n nuotatore, -trice mf

swimming /'swɪmɪŋ/ n nuoto m

swimming baths npl piscina fsg

swimming costume n costume m da bagno

swimmingly /'swɪmɪŋlɪ/ adv **go ~** andar liscio

swimming pool n piscina f

swimming trunks npl calzoncini mpl da bagno

swimsuit /'swɪmsu:t/ n costume m da bagno

swindle /'swɪndl/ n truffa f ● vt truffare

swindler /'swɪndlə(r)/ n truffatore, -trice mf

swine /swaɪn/ n fam porco m

swing /swɪŋ/ n oscillazione f; (shift) cambiamento m; (seat) altalena f; Mus swing m; **in full ~** in piena attività ● (pt/pp **swung**) ● vi oscillare; (on swing, sway) dondolare; (dangle) penzolare; (turn) girare ● vt oscillare; far deviare ⟨vote⟩

swing-door n porta f a vento

swingeing /'swɪndʒɪŋ/ a ⟨increase⟩ drastico

swingometer /swɪŋ'ɒmɪtə(r)/ n strumento m che permette di seguire l'andamento delle votazioni

swipe /swaɪp/ n fam botta f ● vt fam colpire; (fam: steal) rubare; far passare nella macchinetta ⟨credit card⟩

swirl /sw3:l/ n (of smoke, dust) turbine m ● vt far girare ● vi ⟨water:⟩ fare mulinello

swish[1] /swɪʃ/ a fam chic

swish[2] vi schioccare

Swiss /swɪs/ *a & n* svizzero, -a *mf*; **the ~** *pl* gli svizzeri

Swiss roll *n* rotolo *m* di pan di Spagna ripieno di marmellata

switch /swɪtʃ/ *n* interruttore *m*; (*change*) mutamento *m* ●*vt* cambiare; (*exchange*) scambiare ● *vi* cambiare; **~ to** passare a
■ **switch off** *vt* spegnere
■ **switch on** *vt* accendere
■ **switch over** *vi* *TV* cambiare [canale]; **~ over to** passare a
■ **switch round** *vt* (*change one for the other*) scambiare

switch: switchback *n* montagne *fpl* russe. **switchblade** *n* coltello *m* a scatto. **switchboard** *n* centralino *m*

switched line /swɪtʃt/ *n* *Teleph* linea *f* commutata

swither /ˈswɪðə(r)/ *vi* (*fam: hesitate*) tentennare

Switzerland /ˈswɪtsələnd/ *n* Svizzera *f*

swivel /ˈswɪvl/ *v* (*pt/pp* **swivelled**) ● *vt* girare ● *vi* girarsi

swizz /swɪz/ *n* (*fam: swindle*) fregatura *f*

swollen /ˈswəʊlən/ *see* **swell** ● *a* gonfio

swollen-headed /-ˈhedɪd/ *a* presuntuoso

swoon /swuːn/ *vi* svenire

swoop /swuːp/ *n* (*by police*) incursione *f* ● *vi* **~ [down]** ⟨*bird:*⟩ piombare; *fig* fare un'incursione

sword /sɔːd/ *n* spada *f*

swordfish /ˈsɔːdfɪʃ/ *n* pesce *m* spada *inv*

swore /swɔː(r)/ *see* **swear**

sworn /swɔːn/ *see* **swear**

sworn enemy *n* nemico *m* giurato

swot /swɒt/ *n* *fam* sgobbone, -a *mf* ● *vt* (*pt/pp* **swotted**) *fam* sgobbare (**for an exam** per un esame

swum /swʌm/ *see* **swim**

swung /swʌŋ/ *see* **swing**

sycamore /ˈsɪkəmɔː(r)/ *n* sicomoro *m*

sycophant /ˈsɪkəfænt/ *n* adulatore, -trice *mf*

sycophantic /ˌsɪkəˈfæntɪk/ *a* adulatorio

syllable /ˈsɪləbl/ *n* sillaba *f*

syllabus /ˈsɪləbəs/ *n* programma *m* [dei corsi]

syllogism /ˈsɪlədʒɪzm/ *n* sillogismo *m*

sylph /sɪlf/ *n* silfide *f*

symbiosis /sɪmbaɪˈəʊsɪs/ *n* simbiosi *f* *inv*

symbiotic /sɪmbaɪˈɒtɪk/ *a* simbiotico

symbol /ˈsɪmbl/ *n* simbolo *m* (**of** di)

symbolic /sɪmˈbɒlɪk/ *a* simbolico

symbolically /sɪmˈbɒlɪklɪ/ *adv* simbolicamente

symbolism /ˈsɪmbəlɪzm/ *n* simbolismo *m*

symbolist /ˈsɪmbəlɪst/ *n* simbolista *mf*

symbolize /ˈsɪmbəlaɪz/ *vt* simboleggiare

symmetrical /sɪˈmetrɪkl/ *a* simmetrico

symmetrically /sɪˈmetrɪklɪ/ *adv* simmetricamente

symmetry /ˈsɪmɪtrɪ/ *n* simmetria *f*

sympathetic /sɪmpəˈθetɪk/ *a* (*understanding*) comprensivo; (*showing pity*) compassionevole

sympathetically /sɪmpəˈθetɪklɪ/ *adv* con comprensione/compassione

sympathize /ˈsɪmpəθaɪz/ *vi* capire; (*in grief*) solidarizzare; **~ with sb** capire qcno/solidarizzare con qcno

sympathizer /ˈsɪmpəθaɪzə(r)/ *n* *Pol* simpatizzante *mf*

sympathy /ˈsɪmpəθɪ/ *n* comprensione *f*; (*pity*) compassione *f*; (*condolences*) condoglianze *fpl*; **in ~ with** ⟨*strike*⟩ per solidarietà con

symphonic /sɪmˈfɒnɪk/ *a* sinfonico

symphony /ˈsɪmfənɪ/ *n* sinfonia *f*

symptom /ˈsɪmptəm/ *n* sintomo *m*

symptomatic /sɪmptəˈmætɪk/ *a* sintomatico (**of** di)

synagogue /ˈsɪnəgɒg/ *n* sinagoga *f*

sync[h] /sɪŋk/ *n* sincronia *f*; **be out of ~** essere sfasato; **be in ~** essere in sincronia; **be in ~ with/out of ~ with** essere sincronizzato/sfasato rispetto a

synchronize /ˈsɪŋkrənaɪz/ *vt* sincronizzare

synchronous /ˈsɪŋkrənəs/ *a* sincrono

syndicate /ˈsɪndɪkət/ *n* gruppo *m*

syndrome /ˈsɪndrəʊm/ *n* sindrome *f*

synonym /ˈsɪnənɪm/ *n* sinonimo *m*

synonymous /sɪˈnɒnɪməs/ *a* sinonimo

synopsis /sɪˈnɒpsɪs/ *n* (*pl* **-opses** /sɪnˈɒpsiːz/) (*of opera, ballet*) trama *f*; (*of book*) riassunto *m*

syntactic[al] /sɪnˈtæktɪk[l]/ *a* sintattico

syntax /ˈsɪntæks/ *n* sintassi *f* *inv*

synthesis /ˈsɪnθəsɪs/ *n* (*pl* **-theses** /ˈsɪnθəsiːz/) sintesi *f* *inv*

synthesize /ˈsɪnθəsaɪz/ *vt* sintetizzare

synthesizer /ˈsɪnθəsaɪzə(r)/ *n* *Mus* sintetizzatore *m*

synthetic /sɪnˈθetɪk/ *a* sintetico ● *n* fibra *f* sintetica

syphilis /ˈsɪfɪlɪs/ *n* sifilide *f*

Syria /ˈsɪrɪə/ *n* Siria *f*

Syrian /ˈsɪrɪən/ *a & n* siriano, -a *mf*

syringe /sɪˈrɪndʒ/ *n* siringa *f* ● *vt* siringare

syrup /ˈsɪrəp/ *n* sciroppo *m*; *Br* tipo *m* di melassa

syrupy /ˈsɪrəpɪ/ *a* sciropposo

system /ˈsɪstəm/ *n* sistema *m*

systematic /sɪstəˈmætɪk/ *a* sistematico

systematically /sɪstəˈmætɪklɪ/ *adv* sistematicamente

systems: /sɪstəmz/ **systems analysis** *n* analisi *f* dei sistemi. **systems analyst** *n* analista *mf* programmatore, -trice *mf*. **systems design** *n* progettazione *f* di sistemi. **systems engineer** *n* sistemista *mf*

t, T /ti:/ *n* (*letter*) t, T *f inv*
tab /tæb/ *n* linguetta *f*; (*with name*) etichetta *f*; **keep ~s on** *fam* sorvegliare; **pick up the ~** *fam* pagare il conto
tabby /'tæbɪ/ *n* gatto *m* tigrato
tab key *n* tasto *m* tabulatore
table /'teɪbl/ *n* tavolo *m*; (*list*) tavola *f*; **at** [**the**] **~** a tavola
table: ~ of contents tavola *f* delle materie ● *vt* proporre. **table-cloth** *n* tovaglia *f*. **table lamp** *n* lampada *f* da tavolo. **table salt** *n* sale *m* fine. **tablespoon** *n* cucchiaio *m* da tavola. **tablespoonful** *n* cucchiaiata *f*
tablet /'tæblɪt/ *n* pastiglia *f*; (*slab*) lastra *f*; **~ of soap** saponetta *f*
table tennis *n* tennis *m* da tavolo; (*everyday level*) ping pong *m*
tabloid /'tæblɔɪd/ *n* tabloid *m inv*; *pej* giornale *m* scandalistico
taboo /tə'bu:/ *a* tabù *inv* ● *n* tabù *m inv*
tabulate /'tæbjʊleɪt/ *vt* tabulare
tabulation /tæbjʊ'leɪʃn/ *n* (*of data, results*) tabulazione *f*
tabulator /'tæbjʊleɪtə(r)/ *n* tabulatore *m*
tachometer /tæ'kɒmɪtə(r)/ *n* tachimetro *m*
tachograph /'tækəgrɑ:f/ *n* tachigrafo *m*
tacit /'tæsɪt/ *a* tacito
tacitly /'tæsɪtlɪ/ *adv* tacitamente
taciturn /'tæsɪtɜ:n/ *a* taciturno
tack /tæk/ *n* (*nail*) chiodino *m*; (*stitch*) imbastitura *f*; *Naut* virata *f*; *fig* linea *f* di condotta ● *vt* inchiodare; (*sew*) imbastire ● *vi Naut* virare
tackle /'tækl/ *n* (*equipment*) attrezzatura *f*; (*football etc*) contrasto *m*, tackle *m inv* ● *vt* affrontare
tacky /'tækɪ/ *a* (*paint*) non ancora asciutto; (*glue*) appiccicoso; *fig* pacchiano
tact /tækt/ *n* tatto *m*
tactful /'tæktfʊl/ *a* pieno di tatto; (*remark*) delicato
tactfully /'tæktfʊlɪ/ *adv* con tatto
tactical /'tæktɪkl/ *a* tattico
tactically /'tæktɪklɪ/ *adv* tatticamente
tactician /tæk'tɪʃn/ *n* stratega *mf*
tactics /'tæktɪks/ *npl* tattica *fsg*
tactile /'tæktaɪl/ *a* tattile
tactless /'tæktlɪs/ *a* privo di tatto
tactlessly /'tæktlɪslɪ/ *adv* senza tatto
tactlessness /'tæktlɪsnɪs/ *n* mancanza *f* di tatto; (*of remark*) indelicatezza *f*
tadpole /'tædpəʊl/ *n* girino *m*
taffeta /'tæfɪtə/ *n* taffettà *m*
tag¹ /tæg/ *n* (*label*) etichetta *f* ● *vt* (*pt/pp* **tagged**) attaccare l'etichetta a

tag² *n* (*game*) acchiapparello *m*
■ **tag along** *vi* seguire passo passo
■ **tag on** *vt* (*attach*) aggiungere
tail /teɪl/ *n* coda *f*; **~s** *pl* (*tailcoat*) frac *m inv* ● *vt* (*fam: follow*) pedinare
■ **tail off** *vi* diminuire
tail: tailback *n* coda *f*. **tail-end** *n* parte *f* finale; (*of train*) coda *f*. **tail light** *n* fanalino *m* di coda
tailor /'teɪlə(r)/ *n* sarto *m* ● *vt* **~ sth to sb's needs** adattare qcsa alle esigenze di qcno
tailor-made *a* fatto su misura
tailspin /'teɪlspɪn/ *n Aeron* vite *f* di coda
tailwind /'teɪlwɪnd/ *n* vento *m* di coda
taint /teɪnt/ *vt* contaminare
take /teɪk/ *n* (*Cinema*) ripresa *f* ● *v* (*pt* **took**, *pp* **taken**) ● *vt* prendere; (*to a place*) portare ⟨*person, object*⟩; (*contain*) contenere ⟨*passengers etc*⟩; (*endure*) sopportare; (*require*) occorrere; (*teach*) insegnare; (*study*) studiare ⟨*subject*⟩; (*teach*) insegnare; (*study*) studiare ⟨*subject*⟩; fare ⟨*exam, holiday, photograph, walk, bath*⟩; sentire ⟨*pulse*⟩; misurare ⟨*sb's temperature*⟩; **~ sth to the cleaner's** portare qcsa in lavanderia; **~ sb home** (*by car*) portare qcno a casa; **~ sb prisoner** fare prigioniero qcno; **be ~n ill** ammalarsi; **~ sth calmly** prendere con calma qcsa; **~ the dog for a walk** portare a spasso il cane; **~ one's time doing sth** fare qcsa con calma; **this will only ~ a minute** ci vuole solo un minuto; **I ~ it that...** (*assume*) presumo che...; **~ it from me!** (*believe me*) dai retta a me! ● *vi* (*plant:*) attecchire
■ **take aback** *vt* (*surprise*) cogliere di sorpresa
■ **take after** *vt* assomigliare a
■ **take against** *vt* (*turn against*) prendere in antipatia
■ **take apart** *vt* (*dismantle*) smontare
■ **take away** *vt* (*with one*) portare via; (*remove*) togliere; (*subtract*) sottrarre; **'to ~ away'** 'da asporto'
■ **take back** *vt* riprendere; ritirare ⟨*statement*⟩; (*return*) riportare [indietro]; **she took him back** (*as husband, boyfriend*) lo ha perdonato
■ **take down** *vt* portare giù; (*remove*) tirare giù; (*write down*) prendere nota di
■ **take in** *vt* (*bring indoors*) portare dentro; (*to one's home*) ospitare; (*understand*) capire; (*deceive*) ingannare; riprendere ⟨*garment*⟩; (*include*) includere; vedere ⟨*film etc*⟩
■ **take off** *vt* togliersi ⟨*clothes*⟩; (*deduct*) togliere; (*mimic*) imitare; **~ time off** prendere delle vacanze; **~ oneself off** andarsene ● *vi*

Aeron decollare; (*fam: leave*) andarsene; (*become successful*) decollare

■ **take on** *vt* farsi carico di; assumere ⟨*employee*⟩; (*as opponent*) prendersela con; **~ it on oneself to do sth** arrogarsi il diritto di fare qcsa

■ **take out** *vt* portare fuori; togliere ⟨*word, stain*⟩; (*withdraw*) ritirare ⟨*money, books*⟩; **~ out a subscription to sth** abbonarsi a qcsa; **she took a pen out of her pocket** ha preso una penna dalla tasca; **I'm taking my wife out tonight** esco con mia moglie stasera; **~ sb out to dinner** portare a cena fuori qcno; **it'll ~ you out of yourself** (*take your mind off things*) servirà a distrarti; **~ it out on sb** *fam* prendersela con qcno

■ **take over** *vt* assumere il controllo di ⟨*firm*⟩ ● *vi* **~ over from sb** sostituire qcno; (*permanently*) succedere a qcno

■ **take to** *vt* (*as a habit*) darsi a; **I took to her** (*liked*) mi è piaciuta

■ **take up** *vt* portare su; accettare ⟨*offer*⟩; intraprendere ⟨*profession*⟩; dedicarsi a ⟨*hobby*⟩; prendere ⟨*time*⟩; occupare ⟨*space*⟩; tirare su ⟨*floor-boards*⟩; accorciare ⟨*dress*⟩; **~ sth up with sb** discutere qcsa con qcno; **~ sb up on sth** (*question further*) chiedere ulteriori chiarimenti a qcno su qcsa; **I'll ~ you up on your offer** (*accept*) accetto la tua offerta ● *vi* **~ up with sb** legarsi a qcno

takeaway /'teɪkəweɪ/ *n* (*meal*) piatto *m* da asporto; (*restaurant*) *ristorante m che prepara piatti da asporto*

take-home pay *n* stipendio *m* netto

taken /'teɪkən/ *a* ⟨*room etc*⟩ occupato; **be very ~ with sb/sth** essere conquistato da qcno/qcsa

take: take-off *n Aeron* decollo *m.* **takeover** *n* rilevamento *m.* **takeover bid** *n* offerta *f* pubblica di acquisto

takings /'teɪkɪŋz/ *npl* incassi *mpl*

talcum /'tælkəm/ *n* **~ [powder]** talco *m*

tale /teɪl/ *n* storia *f, pej* fandonia *f;* **tell ~s** fare la spia

talent /'tælənt/ *n* talento *m*

talent scout *n* talent scout *mf inv*

talented /'tæləntɪd/ *a* [ricco] di talento

talisman /'tælɪzmən/ *n* talismano *m*

talk /tɔːk/ *n* conversazione *f;* (*lecture*) conferenza *f;* (*gossip*) chiacchere *fpl;* **make small ~** parlare del più e del meno ● *vi* parlare ● *vt* parlare di ⟨*politics etc*⟩; **~ sb into sth** convincere qcno di qcsa

■ **talk about** *vt* parlare di; **~ about bad luck!** e quando si dice la sfortuna!

■ **talk back** *vi* (*reply defiantly*) rispondere

■ **talk down to** *vt* (*patronize*) parlare con condiscendenza a

■ **talk of** *vt* parlare di; **~ing of food...** a proposito di mangiare...

■ **talk over** *vt* discutere

■ **talk to** *vt* parlare con; (*reprimand*) fare un discorsetto a; **~ to oneself** parlare da solo

talkative /'tɔːkətɪv/ *a* loquace

talking head /'tɔːkɪŋ/ *n* mezzobusto *m*

talking-to *n* sgridata *f*

talk show *n* talk show *m inv*

tall /tɔːl/ *a* alto; **how ~ are you?** quanto sei alto?

tall: tallboy *n* cassettone *m.* **~ order** *n* impresa *f* difficile. **tall story** *n* frottola *f*

tally /'tælɪ/ *n* conteggio *m;* **keep a ~ of** tenere il conto di ● *vi* coincidere

talon /'tælən/ *n* artiglio *m*

tambourine /tæmbə'riːn/ *n* tamburello *m*

tame /teɪm/ *a* ⟨*animal*⟩ domestico; (*dull*) insulso ● *vt* domare

tamely /'teɪmlɪ/ *adv* docilmente

tamer /'teɪmə(r)/ *n* domatore, -trice *mf*

tamper /'tæmpə(r)/ *vi* **~ with** manomettere

tampon /'tæmpɒn/ *n* tampone *m*

tan /tæn/ *a* marrone rossiccio *inv* ● *n* marrone *m* rossiccio; (*from sun*) abbronzatura *f* ● *v* (*pt/pp* **tanned**) ● *vt* conciare ⟨*hide*⟩ ● *vi* abbronzarsi

tandem /'tændəm/ *n* tandem *m inv;* **in ~** in tandem

tang /tæŋ/ *n* sapore *m* forte; (*smell*) odore *m* penetrante

tanga /'tæŋgə/ *n* tanga *m inv*

tangent /'tændʒənt/ *n* tangente *f;* **go off at a ~** *fam* partire per la tangente

tangerine /tændʒə'riːn/ *n* (*fruit*) tipo *m* di mandarino; (*colour*) arancione *m* ● *a* arancione

tangible /'tændʒəbl/ *a* tangibile

tangibly /'tændʒəblɪ/ *adv* tangibilmente

tangle /'tæŋgl/ *n* groviglio *m;* (*in hair*) nodo *m* ● *vt* **~ [up]** aggrovigliare ● *vi* aggrovigliarsi

tango /'tæŋgəʊ/ *n* tango *m*

tangy /'tæŋɪ/ *a* forte; (*smell*) penetrante

tank /tæŋk/ *n* contenitore *m;* (*for petrol*) serbatoio *m;* (*fish ~*) acquario *m; Mil* carro *m* armato

tankard /'tæŋkəd/ *n* boccale *m*

tanker /'tæŋkə(r)/ *n* nave *f* cisterna; (*lorry*) autobotte *f*

tank top *n* canottiera *f*

tanned /tænd/ *a* abbronzato

tannin /'tænɪn/ *n* tannino *m*

Tannoy® /'tænɔɪ/ *n Br* sistema *m* di altoparlanti

tantalize /'tæntəlaɪz/ *vt* tormentare

tantalizing /'tæntəlaɪzɪŋ/ *a* allettante; ⟨*smell*⟩ stuzzicante

tantamount /'tæntəmaʊnt/ *a* **~ to** equivalente a

tantrum /'tæntrəm/ *n* scoppio *m* d'ira; **throw a ~** fare i capricci

tap /tæp/ *n* rubinetto *m;* (*knock*) colpo *m;* **on ~** a disposizione ● *v* (*pt/pp* **tapped**) ● *vt* dare un colpetto a; sfruttare ⟨*resources*⟩; mettere sotto controllo ⟨*telephone*⟩ ● *vi* picchiettare

tap-dance *n* tip tap *m* ● *vi* ballare il tip tap

tap-dancer *n* ballerino, -a *mf* di tip tap

tape /teɪp/ *n* nastro *m;* (*recording*) cassetta *f* ● *vt* legare con nastro; (*record*) registrare

tape: tape backup drive *n Comput* unità *f*

di backup a nastro. **tape deck** n piastra f.
tape-measure n metro m [a nastro]
taper /'teɪpə(r)/ n candela f sottile ● vi assottigliarsi
■ **taper off** vi assottigliarsi
tapered /'teɪpəd/ a ‹trousers› affusolato
tape: tape-record vt registrare su nastro.
tape recorder n registratore m. **tape
recording** n registrazione f. **tape streamer**
n Comput unità f a nastro magnetico
tapestry /'tæpɪstrɪ/ n arazzo m
tapeworm /'teɪpwɜːm/ n verme m solitario,
tenia f
tapping /'tæpɪŋ/ n ‹noise› picchiettio m
tap water n acqua f del rubinetto
tar /tɑː(r)/ n catrame m ● vt ‹pt/pp **tarred**) in-
catramare
tardy /'tɑːdɪ/ a (**-ier, -iest**) tardivo
target /'tɑːgɪt/ n bersaglio m; fig obiettivo m
● vt stabilire come obiettivo ‹market›
target market n mercato m obiettivo
target practice n tiro m al bersaglio
tariff /'tærɪf/ n ‹price) tariffa f; ‹duty› dazio m
● a tariffario
Tarmac® /'tɑːmæk/ n macadam m al catrame
tarmac n asfalto m; ‹Br: of airfield› pista f
● attrib ‹road, footpath› asfaltato ● vt
asfaltare
tarnish /'tɑːnɪʃ/ vi ossidarsi ● vt ossidare;
fig macchiare
tarpaulin /tɑːˈpɔːlɪn/ n telone m impermeabile
tarragon /'tærəgən/ n dragoncello m
tart¹ /tɑːt/ a aspro; fig acido
tart² n crostata f; ‹individual› crostatina f;
‹sl: prostitute› donnaccia f
■ **tart up** vt fam ~ **oneself up** agghindarsi
tartan /'tɑːtn/ n tessuto m scozzese, tartan m
inv ● attrib di tessuto scozzese
tartar /'tɑːtə(r)/ n ‹on teeth› tartaro m
tartar sauce n salsa f tartara
task /tɑːsk/ n compito m; **take sb to** ~ riprendere qcno
task force n Pol commissione f; Mil task-
force f inv
tassel /'tæsl/ n nappa f
taste /teɪst/ n gusto m; ‹sample› assaggio m;
get a ~ **of sth** fig assaporare il gusto di qcsa;
in good/bad ~ di buongusto/di cattivo gusto
● vt sentire il sapore di; ‹sample› assaggiare
● vi sapere (**of** di); **it** ~**s lovely** è ottimo; ~
like sth sapere di qcsa
taste buds npl papille fpl gustative
tasteful /'teɪs(t)fʊl/ a di [buon] gusto
tastefully /'teɪs(t)fʊlɪ/ adv con gusto
tasteless /'teɪs(t)lɪs/ a senza gusto
tastelessly /'teɪs(t)lɪslɪ/ adv con cattivo gusto
taster /'teɪstə(r)/ n ‹foretaste› assaggio m;
‹person› assaggiatore, -trice mf
tasty /'teɪstɪ/ a (**-ier, -iest**) saporito
tat /tæt/ see **tit²**
tattered /'tætəd/ a cencioso; ‹pages› stracciato

tatters /'tætəz/ npl **in** ~ a brandelli
tattle /'tætl/ vi spettegolare ● n pettegolezzo m
tattoo¹ /tæˈtuː/ n tatuaggio m ● vt tatuare
tattoo² n Mil parata f militare
tatty /'tætɪ/ a (**-ier, -iest**) ‹clothes, person›
trasandato; ‹book› malandato
taught /tɔːt/ see **teach**
taunt /tɔːnt/ n scherno m ● vt schernire
Taurus /'tɔːrəs/ n Astr Toro m
taut /tɔːt/ a teso
tauten /'tɔːtən/ vt tendere ● vi tendersi
tautology /tɔːˈtɒlədʒɪ/ n tautologia f
tavern /'tævən/ n liter taverna f
tawdry /'tɔːdrɪ/ a (**-ier, -iest**) pacchiano
tawny /'tɔːnɪ/ a fulvo
tax /tæks/ n tassa f; ‹on income› imposte fpl;
before ~ ‹price› tasse escluse; ‹salary› lordo
● vt tassare; fig mettere alla prova; ~ **with**
accusare di
taxable /'tæksəbl/ a tassabile; ~ **income**
reddito m imponibile
taxation /tækˈseɪʃn/ n tasse fpl; ~ **at
source** ritenuta f alla fonte
tax: tax allowance n detrazione f di imposta. **tax avoidance** n elusione f fiscale. **tax
bracket** n scaglione m d'imposta. **tax break**
n agevolazione f fiscale. **tax burden** n
aggravio m fiscale. **tax code** n codice m fiscale. **tax consultant** n fiscalista m. **tax-
deductible** a detraibile. **tax disc** n Auto bollo m. **tax evader** n evasore m fiscale. **tax
evasion** n evasione f fiscale. **tax-free** a esen-
tasse. **tax haven** n paradiso m fiscale. **tax
incentive** n incentivo m fiscale
taxi /'tæksɪ/ n taxi m inv ● vi ‹pt/pp **taxied**,
pres p **taxiing**) ‹aircraft:› rullare
taxi driver n tassista mf
taxing /'tæksɪŋ/ a ‹exhausting› sfiancante
taxi rank n posteggio m per taxi
taxman /'tæksmæn/ n **the** ~ il fisco
tax: taxpayer n contribuente mf. **tax
rebate** n rimborso m d'imposta. **tax return**
n dichiarazione f dei redditi. **tax shelter** n
paradiso m fiscale. **tax system** n regime m
fiscale
TB n abbr (**tuberculosis**) TBC f
tbsp abbr (**tablespoon**)
tea /tiː/ n tè m inv
tea-bag n bustina f di tè
tea-break n intervallo m per il tè
teach /tiːtʃ/ vt/i ‹pt/pp **taught**) insegnare; ~
sb sth insegnare qcsa a qcno; ~ **sb a lesson**
fig dare una lezione a qcno
teacher /'tiːtʃə(r)/ n insegnante mf;
‹primary› maestro, -a mf
teaching /'tiːtʃɪŋ/ n insegnamento m
tea: teacloth n ‹for drying› asciugapiatti m
inv. **tea cosy** n copriteiera f. **teacup** n tazza f
da tè
teak /tiːk/ n tek m
tea leaves npl tè m inv sfuso; ‹when
infused› fondi mpl di tè
team /tiːm/ n squadra f; fig équipe f inv
■ **team up** vi unirsi

team: team captain n caposquadra mf. **team manager** n direttore m sportivo. **team-mate** n compagno m di squadra. **team spirit** n spirito m di squadra. **teamwork** n lavoro m di squadra; fig lavoro m d'équipe

teapot /'ti:pɒt/ n teiera f

tear¹ /teə(r)/ n strappo m ● v (pt **tore**, pp **torn**) ● vt strappare; ~ **to pieces** or **shreds** fare a pezzi; stroncare ⟨book, film⟩ ● vi strappare; ⟨material:⟩ strapparsi; ⟨run⟩ precipitarsi

■ **tear apart** vt (fig: criticize) fare a pezzi; (separate) dividere

■ **tear away** vt ~ **oneself away from** staccarsi da ⟨television⟩; abbandonare a malincuore ⟨party⟩

■ **tear into** vt fam (reprimand) attaccare duramente; (make a vigorous start on) dare dentro a

■ **tear open** vt aprire strappando

■ **tear out** vt staccare; ~ **one's hair out** mettersi le mani nei capelli

■ **tear up** vt strappare; rompere ⟨agreement⟩

tear² /tɪə(r)/ n lacrima f

tearaway /'teərəweɪ/ n giovane teppista mf

tearful /'tɪəful/ a ⟨person⟩ in lacrime; ⟨farewell⟩ lacrimevole

tearfully /'tɪəfulɪ/ adv in lacrime

tear gas /'tɪə/ n gas m lacrimogeno

tearing /'teərɪŋ/ a **be in a ~ hurry** avere una gran fretta

tear-jerker /'tɪədʒɜ:kə(r)/ n fam **this film is a real ~** è davvero un film strappalacrime

tease /ti:z/ vt prendere in giro ⟨person⟩; tormentare ⟨animal⟩

teasel /'ti:zl/ n Bot cardo m

teaset /'ti:set/ n servizio m da tè

tea shop n sala f da tè

teasing /'ti:zɪŋ/ a canzonatorio

tea: teaspoon n cucchiaino m [da tè]. **teaspoon[ful]** n cucchiaino m. **tea-strainer** n colino m per il tè

teat /ti:t/ n capezzolo m; (on bottle) tettarella f

tea towel n strofinaccio m [per i piatti]

technical /'teknɪkl/ a tecnico

technicality /teknɪ'kælətɪ/ n tecnicismo m; Jur cavillo m giuridico

technically /'teknɪklɪ/ adv tecnicamente; (strictly) strettamente

technician /tek'nɪʃn/ n tecnico, -a mf

technique /tek'ni:k/ n tecnica f

technocrat /'teknəkræt/ n tecnocrate m

technological /teknə'lɒdʒɪkl/ a tecnologico

technologically /teknə'lɒdʒɪklɪ/ adv tecnologicamente

technology /tek'nɒlədʒɪ/ n tecnologia f

teddy /'tedɪ/ n ~ [**bear**] orsacchiotto m

tedious /'ti:dɪəs/ a noioso

tedium /'ti:dɪəm/ n tedio m

tee /ti:/ n (Golf) tee m inv

teem /ti:m/ vi (rain) piovere a dirotto; **be ~ing with** (full of) pullulare di

teen /ti:n/ a ⟨fashion, idol⟩ degli adolescenti

teenage /'ti:neɪdʒ/ a per ragazzi; ~ **boy/girl** adolescente mf

teenager /'ti:neɪdʒə(r)/ n adolescente mf

teens /ti:nz/ npl **the ~** l'adolescenza fsg; **be in one's ~** essere adolescente

teeny /'ti:nɪ/ a fam (**-ier, -iest**) piccolissimo

teeny-weeny /'ti:nɪ'wi:nɪ/ a fam minuscolo

tee-shirt n T-shirt f inv, maglietta f [a maniche corte]

teeter /'ti:tə(r)/ vi barcollare

teeth /ti:θ/ see **tooth**

teethe /ti:ð/ vi mettere i primi dent

teething troubles /'ti:ðɪŋ/ npl fig difficoltà fpl iniziali

teetotal /ti:'təutl/ a astemio

teetotaller /ti:'təut(ə)lə(r)/ n astemio, -a mf

TEFL /'tefl/ n insegnamento m dell'inglese come lingua straniera

telebanking /'telɪbæŋkɪŋ/ n servizi mpl bancari telematici

telecast /'telɪkɑ:st/ n trasmissione f televisiva ● vt far vedere in televisione

telecomms /'telɪkɒmz/ npl telecomunicazioni fpl

telecommunications /telɪkəmju:nɪ'keɪʃnz/ npl telecomunicazioni fpl

telecommuter /telɪkə'mju:tə(r)/ n persona f che lavora da casa su computer

telecommuting /telɪkə'mju:tɪŋ/ n lavoro m su computer da casa

teleconference /'telɪkɒnf(ə)r(ə)ns/ n videoconferenza f

telegenic /telɪ'dʒenɪk/ a telegenico

telegram /'telɪgræm/ n telegramma m

telegraph /'telɪgrɑ:f/ n telegrafo m

telegraphic /telɪ'græfɪk/ a telegrafico

telegraph pole n palo m del telegrafo

telematics /telɪ'mætɪks/ n telematica f

telemessage /'telɪmesɪdʒ/ n Br telegramma m

telepathic /telɪ'pæθɪk/ a telepatico

telepathy /tɪ'lepəθɪ/ n telepatia f; **by ~** per telepatia

telephone /'telɪfəun/ n telefono m; **be on the ~** avere il telefono; (be telephoning) essere al telefono ● vt telefonare a ● vi telefonare

telephone: telephone answering service n segreteria f telefonica. **telephone book** n elenco m telefonico. **telephone booking** n prenotazione f telefonica. **telephone booth** n, **telephone box** n cabina f telefonica. **telephone call** n telefonata f. **telephone conversation** n conversazione f telefonica. **telephone directory** n elenco m telefonico. **telephone helpline** n servizio m telefonico. **telephone message** n messaggio m telefonico. **telephone number** n numero m di telefono. **telephone tapping** n intercettazione f telefonica

telephonist /tɪ'lefənɪst/ n telefonista mf

telephoto /telɪ'fəutəu/ a ~ **lens** teleobiettivo m

teleprinter /'telɪprɪntə(r)/ n telescrivente f

telerecording /'telɪkrɪkɔːdɪŋ/ n programma m [televisivo] registrato

telesales /'telɪseɪlz/ n vendita f per telefono

telescope /'telɪskəʊp/ n telescopio m

telescopic /telɪ'skɒpɪk/ a telescopico

teleshopping /'telɪʃɒpɪŋ/ n acquisti mpl per telefono

teletext /'telɪtekst/ n televideo m

telethon /'telɪθɒn/ n telethon m inv

televise /'telɪvaɪz/ vt trasmettere per televisione

television /'telɪvɪʒn/ n televisione f; **watch ~** guardare la televisione; **on ~** alla televisione

television: television channel n rete f televisiva. **television licence** n abbonamento m alla televisione. **television licence fee** n costo m dell'abbonamento alla televisione. **television programme** n programma m televisivo. **television screen** n teleschermo m. **television serial** n sceneggiato m. **television set** n televisore m

televisual /telɪ'vɪʒʊəl/ a televisivo

telex /'teleks/ n telex m inv ● vt mandare via telex ⟨message⟩; mandare un telex a ⟨person⟩

tell /tel/ vt (pt/pp told) dire; raccontare ⟨story⟩; ⟨distinguish⟩ distinguere (**from** da); **~ sb sth** dire qcsa a qcno; **~ sb to do sth** dire a qcno di fare qcsa; **~ the time** dire l'ora; **I couldn't ~ why...** non sapevo perché...; **you're ~ing me!** a chi lo dici! ● vi ⟨produce an effect⟩ avere effetto; **time will ~** il tempo ce lo dirà; **his age is beginning to ~** l'età comincia a farsi sentire [per lui]; **don't ~ me** non dirmelo; **you mustn't ~** non devi dire niente

■ **tell apart** vt distinguere

■ **tell off** vt sgridare

■ **tell on** vt (Sch: inform against) fare la spia a

teller /'telə(r)/ n (in bank) cassiere, -a mf

telling /'telɪŋ/ a significativo; ⟨argument⟩ efficace

telling-off n cicchetto m

tell-tale n spione, -a mf ● a rivelatore

telly /'telɪ/ n fam tv f inv, tele f inv

temerity /tɪ'merətɪ/ n audacia f

temp /temp/ fam n impiegato, -a mf temporaneo, -a ● vi lavorare come impiegato, -a temporaneo, -a

temper /'tempə(r)/ n ⟨disposition⟩ carattere m; ⟨mood⟩ umore m; ⟨anger⟩ collera f; **lose one's ~** arrabbiarsi; **be in a ~** essere arrabbiato; **keep one's ~** mantenere la calma ● vt fig temperare

temperament /'temprəmənt/ n temperamento m

temperamental /temprə'mentl/ a ⟨moody⟩ capriccioso

temperamentally /temprə'mentəlɪ/ adv **they are ~ unsuited** tra loro c'è incompatibilità di carattere

temperance /'tempərəns/ n ⟨abstinence⟩ astinenza f dal bere

temperate /'tempərət/ a ⟨climate⟩ temperato

temperature /'temprətʃə(r)/ n temperatura f; **have** or **run a ~** avere la febbre

tempest /'tempɪst/ n tempesta f

tempestuous /tem'pestjʊəs/ a tempestoso

template /'templɪt/ n sagoma f

temple¹ /'templ/ n tempio m

temple² n Anat tempia f

tempo /'tempəʊ/ n ritmo m; Mus tempo m

temporal /'tempər(ə)l/ a temporale

temporarily /tempə'rerɪlɪ/ adv temporaneamente; ⟨introduced, erected⟩ provvisoriamente

temporary /'tempərərɪ/ a temporaneo; ⟨measure, building⟩ provvisorio

tempt /tempt/ vt tentare; sfidare ⟨fate⟩; **~ sb to** indurre qcno a; **be ~ed** essere tentato (**to** di); **I am ~ed by the offer** l'offerta mi tenta

temptation /temp'teɪʃn/ n tentazione f

tempting /'temptɪŋ/ a allettante; ⟨food, drink⟩ invitante

temptress /'temptrɪs/ n seduttrice f

ten /ten/ a & n dieci m; **the T~ Commandments** i Dieci Comandamenti

tenable /'tenəbl/ a fig sostenibile

tenacious /tɪ'neɪʃəs/ a tenace

tenacity /tɪ'næsətɪ/ n tenacia f

tenant /'tenənt/ n inquilino, -a mf; Comm locatario, -a mf

tend¹ /tend/ vt ⟨look after⟩ prendersi cura di

tend² vi **~ to do sth** tendere a far qcsa

tendency /'tendənsɪ/ n tendenza f

tendentious /ten'denʃəs/ a tendenzioso

tender¹ /'tendə(r)/ n Comm offerta f; **put out to ~** dare in appalto; **be legal ~** avere corso legale ● vt offrire; presentare ⟨resignation⟩

tender² a tenero; ⟨painful⟩ dolorante

tender-hearted /-hɑːtɪd/ a dal cuore tenero

tenderize /'tendəraɪz/ vt rendere tenero ⟨meat⟩

tenderly /'tendəlɪ/ adv teneramente

tenderness /'tendənɪs/ n tenerezza f; ⟨painfulness⟩ dolore m

tendon /'tendən/ n tendine m

tendril /'tendrɪl/ n ⟨of plant⟩ viticcio m

tenement /'tenəmənt/ n casamento m

tenet /'tenɪt/ n principio m

tenner /'tenə(r)/ n fam biglietto m da dieci sterline

tennis /'tenɪs/ n tennis m

tennis: tennis ball n palla f da tennis. **tennis-court** n campo m da tennis. **tennis match** n partita f di tennis. **tennis player** n tennista mf. **tennis racket** n racchetta f da tennis. **tennis shoes** npl scarpe fpl da tennis

tenor /'tenə(r)/ n tenore m

tense¹ /tens/ n Gram tempo m

tense² a teso ● vt tendere ⟨muscle⟩

■ **tense up** vi tendersi

tension /'tenʃn/ n tensione f

tent /tent/ n tenda f

tentacle /'tentəkl/ n tentacolo m

tentative /ˈtentətɪv/ a provvisorio; ⟨smile, gesture⟩ esitante

tentatively /ˈtentətɪvlɪ/ adv timidamente; ⟨accept⟩ provvisoriamente

tent city n tendopoli f inv

tenterhooks /ˈtentəhʊks/ npl **be on ~** essere sulle spine

tenth /tenθ/ a & n decimo, -a mf

tenuous /ˈtenjʊəs/ a fig debole

tenure /ˈtenjə/ n (period of office) permanenza f in carica; (Univ: job security) ruolo m; (of land, property) possesso m; **security of ~** (of land, property) diritto m di possesso

tepid /ˈtepɪd/ a tiepido

tercentenary /tɜːsenˈtiːnərɪ/ n terzo centenario m

term /tɜːm/ n periodo m; Sch Univ trimestre m; (in Italy) Sch quadrimestre m; Univ semestre m; (expression) termine m; **~s** pl (conditions) condizioni fpl; **~ of office** carica f; **in the short/long ~** a breve/lungo termine; **be on good/bad ~s** essere in buoni/cattivi rapporti; **come to ~s with** accettare ⟨past, fact⟩; **easy ~s** facilità fpl di pagamento; **~s of reference** pl (of committee) competenze fpl

terminal /ˈtɜːmɪnl/ a finale; Med terminale ● n Aeron terminal m inv; Rail stazione f di testa; (of bus) capolinea m; (on battery) morsetto m; Comput terminale m

terminally /ˈtɜːmɪnəlɪ/ adv **be ~ ill** essere in fase terminale

terminate /ˈtɜːmɪneɪt/ vt terminare; rescindere ⟨contract⟩; interrompere ⟨pregnancy⟩ ● vi terminare; **~ in** finire in

termination /tɜːmɪˈneɪʃn/ n termine m; Med interruzione f di gravidanza

terminologist /tɜːmɪˈnɒlədʒɪst/ n linguista mf specializzato, -a in terminologia

terminology /tɜːmɪˈnɒlədʒɪ/ n terminologia f

terminus /ˈtɜːmɪnəs/ n (pl **-ni** /ˈtɜːmɪnaɪ/) (for bus) capolinea m; (for train) stazione f di testa

term-time n **during ~** durante il trimestre

terrace /ˈterəs/ n terrazza f; (houses) fila f di case a schiera; **the ~s** pl Sport le gradinate

terraced house /ˈterəsd/ n casa f a schiera

terracotta /terəˈkɒtə/ n (earthenware) terracotta f; (colour) color m terracotta

terrain /teˈreɪn/ n terreno m

terrestrial /tɪˈrestrɪəl/ n terrestre mf ● a terrestre; **~ television** televisione f terrestre

terrible /ˈterəbl/ a terribile

terribly /ˈterəblɪ/ adv terribilmente; **I'm ~ sorry** sono infinitamente spiacente

terrier /ˈterɪə(r)/ n terrier m inv

terrific /təˈrɪfɪk/ a fam (excellent) fantastico; (huge) enorme

terrifically /təˈrɪfɪklɪ/ adv fam terribilmente

terrify /ˈterɪfaɪ/ vt (pt/pp **-ied**) atterrire; **be terrified** essere terrorizzato

terrifying /ˈterɪfaɪɪŋ/ a terrificante

territorial /terɪˈtɔːrɪəl/ a territoriale

territorial waters /ˈwɔːtəz/ npl acque fpl territoriali

territory /ˈterɪtərɪ/ n territorio m

terror /ˈterə(r)/ n terrore m

terrorism /ˈterərɪzm/ n terrorismo m

terrorist /ˈterərɪst/ n terrorista mf

terrorize /ˈterəraɪz/ vt terrorizzare

terror-stricken a terrorizzato

terry towelling /terɪˈtaʊəlɪŋ/ n tessuto m di spugna

terse /tɜːs/ a conciso

tersely /ˈtɜːslɪ/ adv concisamente

tertiary /ˈtɜːʃ(ə)rɪ/ a ⟨era, industry, sector⟩ terziario; ⟨education, college⟩ superiore

Terylene® /ˈterɪliːn/ n terilene® m

test /test/ n esame m; (in laboratory) esperimento m; (of friendship, machine) prova f; (of intelligence, aptitude) test m inv; **put to the ~** mettere alla prova; **pass one's ~** Auto passare l'esame di guida ● vt esaminare; provare ⟨machine⟩

testament /ˈtestəmənt/ n testamento m; **Old/New T~** Antico/Nuovo Testamento m

test-drive vt ⟨manufacturer:⟩ collaudare; ⟨buyer:⟩ provare ● n collaudo m; prova f

tester /ˈtestə(r)/ n (person) collaudatore, -trice mf; (device) tester m inv; (sample: of make-up, perfume) campione m

testicle /ˈtestɪkl/ n testicolo m

testify /ˈtestɪfaɪ/ vt/i (pt/pp **-ied**) testimoniare

testily /ˈtestɪlɪ/ adv ⟨say, reply⟩ in modo scontroso

testimonial /testɪˈməʊnɪəl/ n lettera f di referenze

testimony /ˈtestɪmənɪ/ n testimonianza f

test market n mercato m di prova

test match n partita f internazionale

testosterone /tesˈtɒstərəʊn/ n testosterone m

test: test pilot n pilota mf collaudatore, -trice. **test tube** n provetta f. **test tube baby** n fam bambino, -a mf in provetta

testy /ˈtestɪ/ a irascibile

tetanus /ˈtetənəs/ n tetano m

tetanus injection n antitetanica f

tetchy /ˈtetʃɪ/ a facilmente irritabile

tether /ˈteðə(r)/ n **be at the end of one's ~** non poterne più ● vt legare

Teutonic /tjuːˈtɒnɪk/ a teutonico

text /tekst/ n testo m

textbook /ˈtekstbʊk/ n manuale m

textile /ˈtekstaɪl/ a tessile ● n stoffa f

textual /ˈtekstjʊəl/ a testuale

texture /ˈtekstʃə(r)/ n (of skin) grana f; (of food) consistenza f; **of a smooth ~** (to the touch) soffice al tatto

Thai /taɪ/ a & n tailandese mf; (language) tailandese m

Thailand /ˈtaɪlænd/ n Tailandia f

Thames /temz/ n Tamigi m

than /ðən/ accentato /ðæn/ conj che; (with numbers, names) di; **older ~ me** più vecchio di me

thank /θæŋk/ vt ringraziare; **~ you [very much]** grazie [mille]

thankful /'θæŋkfʊl/ a grato

thankfully /'θæŋkfʊlɪ/ adv con gratitudine; (happily) fortunatamente

thankless /'θæŋklɪs/ a ingrato

thanks /θæŋks/ npl ringraziamenti mpl; **~!** fam grazie!; **~ to** grazie a; **no ~ to you!** non certo grazie a te!

thank-you letter n lettera f di ringraziamento

that /ðæt/ a & pron (pl **those**) quel, quei pl; (before s + consonant, gn, ps, z) quello, quegli pl; (before vowel) quell' mf, quegli mpl, quelle fpl; **~ shop** quel negozio; **those shops** quei negozi; **~ mirror** quello specchio; **~ man/woman** quell'uomo/quella donna; **those men/women** quegli uomini/quelle donne; **~ one** quello; **I don't like those** quelli non mi piacciono; **~ is** cioè; **is ~ you?** sei tu?; **who is ~?** chi è?; **what did you do after ~?** cosa hai fatto dopo?; **like ~** in questo modo, così; **a man like ~** un uomo così; **~ is why** ecco perché; **~ is the reason she gave me** questa è la ragione che mi ha dato; **~ is the easiest thing to do** è la cosa più facile da fare; **~'s it!** (you've understood) ecco!; (I've finished) ecco fatto!; (I've had enough) basta così!; (there's nothing more) tutto qui!; **~'s ~!** (with job) ecco fatto!; (with relationship) è tutto finito!; **and ~'s ~!** punto e basta! ● adv così; **it wasn't ~ good** non era poi così buono ● rel pron che; **the man ~ I spoke to** l'uomo con cui ho parlato; **the day ~ I saw him** il giorno in cui l'ho visto; **all ~ I know** tutto quello che so ● conj che; **I think ~...** penso che...

thatch /θætʃ/ n tetto m di paglia

thatched /θætʃt/ a coperto di paglia

thaw /θɔː/ n disgelo m ● vt fare scongelare ⟨food⟩ ● vi ⟨food:⟩ scongelarsi; **it's ~ing** sta sgelando

the /ðə/ di fronte a una vocale /ðiː/ def art il m, la f; i mpl, le fpl; (before s + consonant, gn, ps, z) lo m, gli mpl; (before vowel) l'mf, gli mpl, le fpl; **at ~ cinema/station** al cinema/alla stazione; **from ~ cinema/station** dal cinema/dalla stazione ● adv **~ more ~ better** più ce n'è meglio è; (with reference to pl) più ce ne sono, meglio è; **all ~ better** tanto meglio

theatre /'θɪətə(r)/ n teatro m; Med sala f operatoria

theatregoer /'θiːətəɡəʊə(r)/ n persona f che va a teatro

theatregoing /'θiːətəɡəʊɪŋ/ n l'andare m a teatro

theatrical /θɪ'ætrɪkl/ a teatrale; (showy) melodrammatico

theft /θeft/ n furto m

theft-proof a antiscippo

their /ðeə(r)/ poss a il loro m, la loro f, i loro mpl, le loro fpl; **~ mother/father** la loro madre/il loro padre

theirs /ðeəz/ poss pron il loro m, la loro f, i loro mpl, le loro fpl; **a friend of ~** un loro amico; **friends of ~** dei loro amici; **those are ~** quelli sono loro; (as opposed to ours) quelli sono i loro

them /ðem/ pers pron (direct object) li m, le f; (indirect object) gli, loro fml; (after prep: with people) loro; (after preposition: with things) essi; **we haven't seen ~** non li/le abbiamo visti/viste; **give ~ the money** dai loro or dagli i soldi; **give it to ~** daglielo; **I've spoken to ~** ho parlato con loro; **it's ~** sono loro

theme /θiːm/ n tema m

theme: theme park n parco m a tema.

theme song n motivo m conduttore

themselves /ðem'selvz/ pron (reflexive) si; (emphatic) se stessi; **they poured ~ a drink** si sono versati da bere; **they said so ~** lo hanno detto loro stessi; **they kept it to ~** se lo sono tenuti per sé; **by ~** da soli

then /ðen/ adv allora; (next) poi; **by ~** (in the past) ormai; (in the future) per allora; **since ~** sin da allora; **before ~** prima di allora; **from ~ on** da allora in poi; **now and ~** ogni tanto; **there and ~** all'istante ● a di allora

thence /ðens/ adv (from there) di là; (therefore) perciò

theologian /θɪə'ləʊdʒɪən/ n teologo, -a mf

theological /θɪə'lɒdʒɪkl/ a teologico

theology /θɪ'ɒlədʒɪ/ n teologia f

theorem /'θɪərəm/ n teorema m

theoretical /θɪə'retɪkl/ a teorico

theoretically /θɪə'retɪklɪ/ adv teoricamente

theorist /'θɪərɪst/ n teorico m

theorize /'θɪəraɪz/ vi teorizzare

theory /'θɪərɪ/ n teoria f; **in ~** in teoria

therapeutic /θerə'pjuːtɪk/ a terapeutico

therapist /'θerəpɪst/ n terapista mf

therapy /'θerəpɪ/ n terapia f

there /ðeə(r)/ adv là, lì; **down/up ~** laggiù/lassù; **~ is/are** c'è/ci sono; **~ he/she is** eccolo/eccola ● int **~**, **~!** dai, su!

there: thereabouts adv [or] **~abouts** (roughly) all'incirca. **thereafter** adv dopo di che. **thereby** adv in tal modo. **therefore** / 'ðeəfɔː(r)/ adv perciò. **therein** adv **~ lies...** in ciò risiede...; **contained ~** (Jur: in contract) contenuto nello stesso

thermal /'θɜːml/ a termico; ⟨treatment⟩ termale

thermal: thermal paper n carta f termica. **thermal printer** n stampante f termica. **thermal underwear** n biancheria f che mantiene la temperatura corporea

thermometer /θə'mɒmɪtə(r)/ n termometro m

Thermos® /'θɜːməs/ n **~ [flask]** termos m inv

thermostat /'θɜːməstæt/ n termostato m

thesaurus /θɪ'sɔːrəs/ n (of particular field) dizionario m specialistico; (of synonyms) dizionario m dei sinonimi

these /ðiːz/ see **this**

thesis /'θiːsɪs/ n (pl **-ses** /-siːz/) tesi f inv

they /ðeɪ/ pers pron loro; **~ are tired** sono stanchi; **we're going, but ~ are not** noi andiamo, ma loro no; **~ say** (generalizing) si dice; **~ are building a new road** stanno costruendo una nuova strada

thick /θɪk/ a spesso; ⟨forest⟩ fitto; ⟨liquid⟩

denso; ⟨*hair*⟩ folto; (*fam: stupid*) ottuso; (*fam: close*) molto unito; **be 5 mm ~** essere 5 mm di spessore; **give sb a ~ ear** *fam* dare uno schiaffone a qcno ● *adv* densamente ● *n* **in the ~ of** nel mezzo di

thicken /ˈθɪkn/ *vt* ispessire ⟨*sauce*⟩ ● *vi* ispessirsi; ⟨*fog:*⟩ infittirsi

thicket /ˈθɪkɪt/ *n* boscaglia *f*

thickhead /ˈθɪkhed/ *n fam* zuccone *mf*

thickie /ˈθɪkɪ/ *n fam* zucca *f* vuota

thickly /ˈθɪklɪ/ *adv* densamente; ⟨*cut*⟩ a fette spesse

thickness /ˈθɪknɪs/ *n* spessore *m*

thicko /ˈθɪkəʊ/ *n fam* zucca *f* vuota

thickset /ˈθɪkset/ *a* tozzo

thick-skinned /-ˈskɪnd/ *a fam* insensibile

thief /θiːf/ *n* (*pl* **thieves**) ladro, -a *mf*

thieving /ˈθiːvɪŋ/ *a* ladro ● *n* furti *mpl*

thigh /θaɪ/ *n* coscia *f*

thimble /ˈθɪmbl/ *n* ditale *m*

thimbleful /ˈθɪmbəlfʊl/ *n* (*of wine etc*) goccino *m*

thin /θɪn/ *a* (**thinner**, **thinnest**) sottile; ⟨*shoes, sweater*⟩ leggero; ⟨*liquid*⟩ liquido; ⟨*person*⟩ magro; ⟨*fig: excuse, plot*⟩ inconsistente; **be [going] ~ on top** (*be going bald*) perdere i capelli; **vanish into ~ air** volatilizzarsi ● *adv* = **thinly** ● *v* (*pt/pp* **thinned**) ● *vt* diluire ⟨*liquid*⟩ ● *vi* diradarsi

■ **thin down** *vt* diluire ⟨*paint etc*⟩ ● *vi* (*become slimmer*) dimagrire

■ **thin out** *vi* diradarsi

thing /θɪŋ/ *n* cosa *f*; **~s** *pl* (*belongings*) roba *fsg*; **for one** ~ in primo luogo; **the right ~** la cosa giusta; **just the ~!** proprio quel che ci vuole!; **how are ~s?** come vanno le cose?; **the latest ~** *fam* l'ultima cosa; **the best ~ would be** la cosa migliore sarebbe; **poor ~!** poveretto!; **have a ~ about** (*be frightened of*) aver la fobia di; (*be attracted to*) avere un debole per

thingumabob /ˈθɪŋəməbɒb/ *n fam* coso *m*

thingumajig /ˈθɪŋəmədʒɪg/ *n fam* coso *m*

think /θɪŋk/ *vt/i* (*pt/pp* **thought**) pensare; (*believe*) credere; **I ~ so** credo di sì; **what do you ~?** (*what is your opinion?*) cosa ne pensi?; **~ of/about** pensare a; **what do you ~ of it?** cosa ne pensi di questo?; **~ of doing sth** pensare di fare qcsa; **~ better of it** ripensarci; **~ for oneself** pensare con la propria testa

■ **think again** *vi* pensarci su; **you can ~ again!** sei matto!

■ **think ahead** *vi* pensare al futuro; **~ ahead to sth** pensare in anticipo a qcsa

■ **think back** *vi* **~ back to sth** ripensare a qcsa

■ **think out** *vt* mettere a punto ⟨*strategy*⟩

■ **think over** *vt* riflettere su

■ **think through** *vt* riflettere bene su ⟨*problem*⟩

■ **think up** *vt* escogitare; trovare ⟨*name*⟩

thinker /ˈθɪŋkə(r)/ *n* pensatore, -trice *mf*

thinking /ˈθɪŋkɪŋ/ *n* (*opinion*) opinione *f*

think-tank *n* gruppo *m* d'esperti

thinly /ˈθɪnlɪ/ *adv* ⟨*populated*⟩ scarsamente; ⟨*disguised*⟩ leggermente; ⟨*cut*⟩ a fette sottili

thinness /ˈθɪnnɪs/ *n* (*of person*) magrezza *f*; (*of material*) finezza *f*

thin-skinned /-ˈskɪnd/ *a* (*sensitive*) permaloso

third /θɜːd/ *a & n* terzo, -a *mf*

third degree *n* **give sb the ~ ~** fare il terzo grado a qcno

third-degree burns *npl* ustioni *fpl* di terzo grado

thirdly /ˈθɜːdlɪ/ *adv* terzo

third: third party *n* (*in insurance, law*) terzi *mpl*. **third-party insurance** *n* assicurazione *f* contro terzi. **third person** *n* terzo *m*. **third-rate** *a* scadente. **Third World** *n* Terzo Mondo *m*

thirst /θɜːst/ *n* sete *f*

thirstily /ˈθɜːstɪlɪ/ *adv* con sete

thirsty /ˈθɜːstɪ/ *a* assetato; **be ~** aver sete

thirteen /θɜːˈtiːn/ *a & n* tredici *m*

thirteenth /θɜːˈtiːnθ/ *a & n* tredicesimo, -a *mf*

thirtieth /ˈθɜːtɪɪθ/ *a & n* trentesimo, -a *mf*

thirty /ˈθɜːtɪ/ *a & n* trenta *m*

this /ðɪs/ *a* (*pl* **these**) questo; **~ man/ woman** quest'uomo/questa donna; **these men/women** questi uomini/queste donne; **~ one** questo; **~ evening/morning** stamattina/stasera ● *pron* (*pl* **these**) questo; **we talked about ~ and that** abbiamo parlato del più e del meno; **like ~** così; **~ is Peter** questo è Peter; *Teleph* sono Peter; **who is ~?** chi è?; *Teleph* chi parla?; **~ is the happiest day of my life** è il giorno più felice della mia vita ● *adv* così; **~ big** così grande

thistle /ˈθɪsl/ *n* cardo *m*

thong /θɒŋ/ *n* (*on whip*) cinghia *f*; (*on shoe, garment*) laccetto *m*; (*underwear*) cache-sexe *m inv*; **~s** (*pl: sandals*) infradito *mpl or fpl*

thorn /θɔːn/ *n* spina *f*

thorny /ˈθɔːnɪ/ *a* spinoso

thorough /ˈθʌrə/ *a* completo; ⟨*knowledge*⟩ profondo; ⟨*clean, search, training*⟩ a fondo; ⟨*person*⟩ scrupoloso

thorough: thoroughbred *n* purosangue *m inv*. **thoroughfare** *n* via *f* principale; **'no ~'** 'strada non transitabile '

thoroughly /ˈθʌrəlɪ/ *adv* ⟨*clean, search, know sth*⟩ a fondo; (*extremely*) estremamente

thoroughness /ˈθʌrənɪs/ *n* completezza *f*

those /ðəʊz/ *see* **that**

though /ðəʊ/ *conj* sebbene; **as ~** come se ● *adv fam* tuttavia

thought /θɔːt/ *see* **think** ● *n* pensiero *m*; (*idea*) idea *f*; **I've given this some ~** ci ho pensato su

thoughtful /ˈθɔːtfʊl/ *a* pensieroso; (*considerate*) premuroso

thoughtfully /ˈθɔːtfʊlɪ/ *adv* pensierosamente; (*considerately*) premurosamente

thoughtfulness /ˈθɔːtfʊlnɪs/ *n* (*kindness*) considerazione *f*

thoughtless /ˈθɔːtlɪs/ *a* (*inconsiderate*) sconsiderato

thoughtlessness /ˈθɔːtlɪsnɪs/ n sconsideratezza f

thoughtlessly /ˈθɔːtlɪslɪ/ adv con noncuranza

thought-provoking a ⟨book, film etc⟩ che fa riflettere

thousand /ˈθaʊznd/ a one/a ~ mille m inv ● n mille m inv; ~s of migliaia fpl di

thousandth /ˈθaʊzndθ/ a & n millesimo

thrash /θræʃ/ vt picchiare; (defeat) sconfiggere

■ **thrash about** vi dibattersi

■ **thrash out** vt mettere a punto

thrashing /ˈθræʃɪŋ/ n (defeat) sconfitta f; **give sb a** ~ (beating) picchiare qcno

thread /θred/ n filo m; (of screw) filetto m ● vt infilare ⟨beads⟩; ~ **one's way through** farsi strada fra

threadbare /ˈθredbeə/ a logoro

threat /θret/ n minaccia f

threaten /ˈθretn/ vt minacciare (**to do** di fare)● vi fig incalzare

threatening /ˈθretnɪŋ/ a minaccioso; ⟨sky, atmosphere⟩ sinistro

threateningly /ˈθretnɪŋlɪ/ adv minacciosamente

three /θriː/ a & n tre m

three-dimensional /-daɪˈmenʃ(ə)nəl/ a tridimensionale

threefold /ˈθriːfəʊld/ a & adv triplo

three: **three-legged** /-ˈleɡɪd/ a con tre gambe. **three-piece suit** n vestito m da uomo con panciotto. **three-piece suite** n insieme m di divano e due poltrone coordinati. **three-quarter length** a ⟨portrait⟩ di tre quarti; ⟨sleeve⟩ a tre quarti. **three-quarters** adv ⟨empty, full, done⟩ per tre quarti

threesome /ˈθriːsəm/ n trio m

three-wheeler /-ˈwiːlə(r)/ n (car) auto f inv a tre ruote

thresh /θreʃ/ vt trebbiare

threshold /ˈθreʃəʊld/ n soglia f

threw /θruː/ see **throw**

thrift /θrɪft/ n economia f

thrifty /ˈθrɪftɪ/ a parsimonioso

thrill /θrɪl/ n emozione f; (of fear) brivido m ● vt entusiasmare; **be ~ed with** essere entusiasta di

thriller /ˈθrɪlə(r)/ n (book) [romanzo m] giallo m; (film) [film m inv] giallo m

thrilling /ˈθrɪlɪŋ/ a eccitante

thrive /θraɪv/ vi (pt thrived or throve, pp thrived) ⟨business:⟩ prosperare; ⟨child, plant:⟩ crescere bene; **I** ~ **on pressure** mi piace essere sotto tensione

thriving /ˈθraɪvɪŋ/ a fiorente

throat /θrəʊt/ n gola f; **sore** ~ mal m di gola

throaty /ˈθrəʊtɪ/ a (husky) roco; (fam: with sore throat) rauco

throb /θrɒb/ n pulsazione f; (of heart) battito m ● vi (pt/pp throbbed) (vibrate) pulsare; ⟨heart:⟩ battere

throes /θrəʊz/ npl **in the** ~ **of** fig alle prese con

thrombosis /θrɒmˈbəʊsɪs/ n trombosi f

throne /θrəʊn/ n trono m

throng /θrɒŋ/ n calca f

throttle /ˈθrɒtl/ n (on motorbike) manopola f di accelerazione ● vt strozzare

through /θruː/ prep attraverso; (during) durante; (by means of) tramite; (thanks to) grazie a; **Saturday** ~ **Tuesday** Am da sabato a martedì incluso ● adv attraverso; ~ **and** ~ fino in fondo; **wet** ~ completamente bagnato; **read sth** ~ dare una lettura a qcsa; **let** ~ lasciar passare ⟨sb⟩ ● a ⟨train⟩ diretto; **be** ~ (finished) aver finito; Teleph avere la comunicazione

throughout /θruːˈaʊt/ prep per tutto ● adv completamente; (time) per tutto il tempo

throve /θrəʊv/ see **thrive**

throw /θrəʊ/ n tiro m ● vt (pt **threw**, pp **thrown**) lanciare; (throw away) gettare; azionare ⟨switch⟩; disarcionare ⟨rider⟩; (fam: disconcert) disorientare; fam dare ⟨party⟩

■ **throw about** vt spargere; ~ **one's money about** sbandierare i propri soldi

■ **throw away** vt gettare via

■ **throw in** vt (include at no extra cost) aggiungere [gratuitamente]; (in football) rimettere in gioco; ~ **the towel** or **the sponge** fig abbandonare il campo

■ **throw off** vt seminare ⟨pursuers⟩; liberarsi di ⟨cold, infection etc⟩

■ **throw together** vt (assemble hastily) mettere insieme; improvvisare ⟨meal⟩; (bring into contact) fare incontrare

■ **throw out** vt gettare via; rigettare ⟨plan⟩; buttare fuori ⟨person⟩

■ **throw up** vt alzare ● vi (vomit) vomitare

throw: throwaway a ⟨remark⟩ buttato lì; ⟨paper cup⟩ usa e getta inv. **throwback** n Biol atavismo m; fig regressione f. **throw-in** n Sport rimessa f laterale

thrush /θrʌʃ/ n tordo m; Med mughetto m; (in woman) candida f

thrust /θrʌst/ n spinta f ● vt (pt/pp **thrust**) (push) spingere; (insert) conficcare; ~ **[up]on** imporre a

thud /θʌd/ n tonfo m

thug /θʌɡ/ n deliquente m

thuggish /ˈθʌɡɪʃ/ a violento

thumb /θʌm/ n pollice m; **as a rule of** ~ come regola generale; **under sb's** ~ succube di qcno ● vt ~ **a lift** fare l'autostop

■ **thumb through** vt sfogliare

thumb: thumb-index n indice m a rubrica. **thumbnail sketch** n breve descrizione f. **thumbs down** n fam **get the** ~ ~ non ottenere l'okay; **give sb/sth the** ~ ~ non dare l'okay a qcno/qcsa. **thumbs up** n fam **get the** ~ ~ ricevere l'okay; **give sb/sth the** ~ ~ dare l'okay a qcno/qcsa. **thumbtack** n Am cimice f, puntina f (da disegno)

thump /θʌmp/ n colpo m; (noise) tonfo m ● vt battere su ⟨table, door⟩; battere ⟨fist⟩; colpire ⟨person⟩ ● vi battere (**on** su); ⟨heart:⟩ battere forte

■ **thump about** vi camminare pesantemente

thumping /'θʌmpɪŋ/ a (fam: very large) enorme; **a ~ headache** un mal di testa martellante

thunder /'θʌndə(r)/ n tuono m; (loud noise) rimbombo m ● vi tuonare; (make loud noise) rimbombare

thunderbolt /'θʌndəbəʊlt/ n folgore f

thunderclap /'θʌndəklæp/ n rombo m di tuono

thundering /'θʌndərɪŋ/ a (fam: very big or great) tremendo

thunderous /'θʌndərəs/ a ‹applause› scrosciante

thunderstorm /'θʌndəstɔːm/ n temporale m

thunderstruck /'θʌndəstrʌk/ a sbigottito

thundery /'θʌndərɪ/ a temporalesco

Thursday /'θɜːzdeɪ/ n giovedì m inv

thus /ðʌs/ adv così

thwack /θwæk/ vt colpire ● n colpo m

thwart /θwɔːt/ vt ostacolare

thyme /taɪm/ n timo m

thyroid /'θaɪrɔɪd/ n tiroide f

tiara /tɪ'ɑːrə/ n diadema m

Tiber /'taɪbə(r)/ n Tevere m

tick[1] /tɪk/ n **on ~** fam a credito

tick[2] n (sound) ticchettio m; (mark) segno m; (fam: instant) attimo m ● vi ticchettare

■ **tick off** vt spuntare; fam sgridare

■ **tick over** vi ‹engine:› andare al minimo

ticket /'tɪkɪt/ n biglietto m; (for item deposited, library) tagliando m; (label) cartellino m; (fine) multa f

ticket: ticket-collector n controllore m. **ticket-holder** n persona f munita di biglietto. **ticket-office** n biglietteria f. **ticket tout** n Br bagarino m

tickle /'tɪkl/ n solletico m ● vt fare il solletico a; (amuse) divertire ● vi fare prurito

ticklish /'tɪklɪʃ/ a che soffre il solletico; ‹problem› delicato

tidal /'taɪdl/ a ‹river, harbour› di marea

tidal wave n onda f di marea

tiddly /'tɪdlɪ/ a (Br fam: drunk) brillo

tiddlywinks /'tɪdlɪwɪŋks/ n gioco m delle pulci

tide /taɪd/ n marea f; (of events) corso m; **the ~ is in/out** c'è alta/bassa marea

■ **tide over** vt **~ sb over** aiutare qcno a andare avanti

tidemark /'taɪdmɑːk/ n linea f di marea; (Br fig: line of dirt) tracce fpl di sporco (nella vasca da bagno)

tidily /'taɪdɪlɪ/ adv in modo ordinato

tidiness /'taɪdɪnɪs/ n ordine m

tidy /'taɪdɪ/ a (-ier, -iest) ordinato; (fam: amount) bello ● vt ordinare

■ **tidy away** vt mettere a posto ‹toys, books›

■ **tidy out** vt mettere in ordine ‹drawer, cupboard›

■ **tidy up** vt ordinare; **~ oneself up** mettersi in ordine

tie /taɪ/ n cravatta f; (cord) legaccio m; (fig: bond) legame m; (restriction) impedimento m;

Sport pareggio m ● v (pres p **tying**) ● vt legare; fare ‹knot›; **be ~d** (in competition) essere in parità ● vi pareggiare

■ **tie down** vt anche fig legare

■ **tie in with** vi corrispondere a

■ **tie on** vt attaccare

■ **tie up** vt legare; vincolare ‹capital›; **be ~d up** (busy) essere occupato

tie: tie-break[er] n Tennis tie-break m inv; (in quiz) spareggio m. **tie-dye** vt tingere annodando. **tie-on** a ‹label› volante. **tiepin** n fermacravatta m

tier /tɪə(r)/ n fila f; (of cake) piano m; (in stadium) gradinata f

tiff /tɪf/ n battibecco m

tiger /'taɪgə(r)/ n tigre f

tiger's-eye /'taɪgəz/ n occhio m di tigre

tight /taɪt/ a stretto; (taut) teso; (fam: drunk) sbronzo; (fam: mean) spilorcio; **~ corner** fam brutta situazione f ● adv strettamente; ‹hold› forte; ‹closed› bene

tighten /'taɪtn/ vt stringere; avvitare ‹screw›; intensificare ‹control›; **~ one's belt** fig tirare la cinghia ● vi stringersi

■ **tighten up** vt stringere ‹screw›; rendere più severo ‹security› ● vi (become stricter) diventare più severo

tight: tight-fisted /-'fɪstɪd/ a tirchio. **tight-fitting** /-'fɪtɪŋ/ a attillato. **tight-knit** a ‹fig: community, group› unito. **tight-lipped** /-'lɪpt/ a **they are remaining ~ about events** mantengono il riserbo riguardo all'accaduto

tightly /'taɪtlɪ/ adv strettamente; ‹hold› forte; ‹closed› bene

tightrope /'taɪtrəʊp/ n fune f (da funamboli)

tights /taɪts/ npl collant m inv

tigress /'taɪgrɪs/ n tigre f femmina

tile /taɪl/ n mattonella f; (on roof) tegola f ● vt rivestire di mattonelle ‹wall›; coprire con tegole ‹roof›

till[1] /tɪl/ prep & conj = **until**

till[2] n cassa f

tiller /'tɪlə(r)/ n barra f del timone

tilt /tɪlt/ n inclinazione f; **at full ~** a tutta velocità ● vt inclinare ● vi inclinarsi

timber /'tɪmbə(r)/ n legname m

time /taɪm/ n tempo m; (occasion) volta f; (by clock) ora f; **two ~s four** due volte quattro; **at any ~** in qualsiasi momento; **this ~** questa volta; **at ~s, from ~ to ~** ogni tanto; **~ and again** cento volte; **two at a ~** due alla volta; **on ~** in orario; **in ~** in tempo; (eventually) col tempo; **in no ~ at all** velocemente; **in a year's ~** fra un anno; **behind ~** in ritardo; **behind the ~s** antiquato; **for the ~ being** per il momento; **what is the ~?** che ora è?; **by the ~ we arrive** quando arriviamo; **do you have the ~?** (what ~ is it?) hai l'ora?; **did you have a nice ~?** ti sei divertito?; **have a good ~!** divertiti! ● vt scegliere il momento per; cronometrare ‹race›; **be well ~d** essere ben calcolato

time: time bomb n bomba f a orologeria. **time-consuming** a che porta via molto tempo. **time-honoured** /-ɒnəd/ a venerando.

timekeeper n Sport cronometrista mf; **be a good ~** (be punctual) essere sempre puntuale. **time lag** n intervallo m [di tempo]

timeless /'taɪmlɪs/ a eterno

time limit n limite m di tempo

timely /'taɪmlɪ/ a opportuno

time off n (leave) permesso m; **take some ~ ~** prendere delle ferie

time-out n (break) pausa f; Sport time out m inv

timer /'taɪmə(r)/ n timer m inv

time: timescale n periodo m. **timeshare** n (apartment) appartamento m in multiproprietà; (house) casa f in multiproprietà. **time sheet** n foglio m di presenza. **time signal** n segnale m orario. **time span** n arco m di tempo. **time switch** n interruttore m a tempo. **timetable** n orario m. **time zone** n fuso m orario

timid /'tɪmɪd/ a (shy) timido; (fearful) timoroso

timidly /'tɪmɪdlɪ/ adv timidamente

timidness /'tɪmɪdnɪs/ n (shyness) timidezza f; (fear) paura f

timing /'taɪmɪŋ/ n Sport, Techn cronometraggio m; **the ~ of the election** il momento scelto per le elezioni; **have no sense of ~** non saper scegliere il momento opportuno

timorous /'tɪm(ə)rəs/ a timoroso

timpani /'tɪmpənɪ/ npl timpani mpl

tin /tɪn/ n stagno m; (container) barattolo m ● vt (pt/pp **tinned**) inscatolare

tin foil n [carta f] stagnola f

tinge /tɪndʒ/ n sfumatura f ● vt **~d with** fig misto a

tingle /'tɪŋgl/ vi pizzicare

tinker /'tɪŋkə(r)/ vi armeggiare

tinkle /'tɪŋkl/ n tintinnio m; (fam: phone call) colpo m di telefono ● vi tintinnare

tinned /tɪnd/ a in scatola

tinnitus /'tɪnɪtəs/ n Med ronzio m auricolare

tinny /'tɪnɪ/ a (sound, music) metallico; (badly made) di latta

tin-opener /-əʊpnə(r)/ n apriscatole m inv

tinpot /'tɪnpɒt/ a pej (firm) da due soldi

tinsel /'tɪnsl/ n filo m d'argento

tint /tɪnt/ n tinta f ● vt tingersi (hair); **~ed glasses** occhiali mpl colorati

tiny /'taɪnɪ/ a (**-ier, -iest**) minuscolo

tip¹ /tɪp/ n (point, top) punta f

tip² n (money) mancia f; (advice) consiglio m; (for rubbish) discarica f ● v (pt/pp **tipped**) ● vt (tilt) inclinare; (overturn) capovolgere; (pour) versare; (reward) dare una mancia a ● vi inclinarsi; (overturn) capovolgersi

■ **tip off** vt **~** sb off (inform) fare una soffiata a qcno

■ **tip out** vt rovesciare

■ **tip over** vt capovolgere ● vi capovolgersi

■ **tip up** vt sollevare (seat); (overturn) rovesciare

tip-off n soffiata f

tipped /tɪpt/ a (cigarette) col filtro

tipple /'tɪpl/ vi bere [alcool] ● n have a ~ prendere un bicchierino; **my favourite ~** il mio liquore preferito

tipster /'tɪpstə(r)/ n esperto m che dà suggerimenti su cavalli da corsa, azioni ecc

tipsy /'tɪpsɪ/ a fam brillo

tiptoe /'tɪptəʊ/ n **on ~** in punta di piedi

tip-top a fam in condizioni perfette

tirade /tar'reɪd/ n filippica f

tire /'taɪə(r)/ vt stancare ● vi stancarsi

tired /'taɪəd/ a stanco; **~ of** stanco di; **~ out** stanco morto

tiredness /'taɪədnɪs/ n stanchezza f

tireless /'taɪəlɪs/ a instancabile

tirelessly /'taɪəlɪslɪ/ adv instancabilmente

tiresome /'taɪəsəm/ a fastidioso

tiring /'taɪərɪŋ/ a stancante

tissue /'tɪʃuː/ n tessuto m; (handkerchief) fazzolettino m di carta

tissue-paper n carta f velina

tit¹ /tɪt/ n (bird) cincia f

tit² n **~ for tat** pan per focaccia

tit³ n fam (breast) tetta f; (fool) stupido m

titbit /'tɪtbɪt/ n ghiottoneria f; (fig: of news) notizia f appetitosa

titillate /'tɪtɪleɪt/ vt titillare

titivate /'tɪtɪveɪt/ vt agghindare; **~ oneself** agghindarsi

title /'taɪtl/ n titolo m

title: title deed n atto m di proprietà. **title-holder** n detentore, -trice mf del titolo. **title-page** n frontespizio m. **title role** n ruolo m principale

titter /'tɪtə(r)/ vi ridere nervosamente ● n risatina f nervosa

tittle-tattle /'tɪtltætl/ n pettegolezzi mpl

titular /'tɪtjʊlə(r)/ a nominale

tizzy /'tɪzɪ/ n fam **in a ~** in grande agitazione

to /tuː/, atono /tə/ prep a; (to countries) in; (towards) verso; (up to, until) fino a; **I'm going to John's/the butcher's** vado da John/dal macellaio; **come/go to sb** venire/andare da qcno; **to Italy/Switzerland** in Italia/Svizzera; **I've never been to Rome** non sono mai stato a Roma; **go to the market** andare al mercato; **to the toilet/my room** in bagno/camera mia; **to an exhibition** a una mostra; **to university** all'università; **twenty/quarter to eight** le otto meno venti/un quarto; **5 to 6 kilos** da 5 a 6 chili; **to the end** alla fine; **to this day** fino a oggi; **to the best of my recollection** per quanto mi possa ricordare; **give/say sth to sb** dare/dire qcsa a qcno; **give it to me** dammelo; **there's nothing to it** è una cosa da niente ● verbal constructions **to go** andare; **learn to swim** imparare a nuotare; **I want to/have to go** voglio/devo andare; **it's easy to forget** è facile da dimenticare; **too ill/tired to go** troppo malato/stanco per andare; **you have to** devi; **I don't want to** non voglio; **he wants to be a teacher** vuole diventare un insegnante; **live to be 90** vivere fino a 90 anni; **he was the last to arrive** è stato l'ultimo ad arrivare; **to be honest,...** per essere sincero,... ● adv **pull to** chiudere; **to and fro** avanti e indietro

toad /təʊd/ n rospo m

toadstool /'təʊdstu:l/ n fungo m velenoso

■ **toady to** /'təʊdɪ/ vi fare da leccapiedi a

toast /təʊst/ n pane m tostato; (drink) brindisi m inv ● vt tostare ⟨bread⟩; (drink a ~ to) brindare a

toaster /'təʊstə(r)/ n tostapane m inv

toastrack /'təʊstræk/ n portatoast m inv

tobacco /tə'bækəʊ/ n tabacco m

tobacconist's [shop] /tə'bækənɪsts [ʃɒp]/ n tabaccheria f

toboggan /tə'bɒgən/ n toboga m inv ● vi andare in toboga

today /tə'deɪ/ a & adv oggi m; **a week ~** una settimana a oggi; **~'s paper** il giornale di oggi

toddle /'tɒdl/ vi ⟨child:⟩ cominciare a camminare; **~ into town** fam fare una passeggiata in centro; **I must be toddling** fam devo scappare

toddler /'tɒdlə(r)/ n bambino, -a mf piccolo, -a

toddy /'tɒdɪ/ n grog m inv

to-do /tə'du:/ n fam baccano m

toe /təʊ/ n dito m del piede; (of footwear) punta f; **on one's ~s** fig pronto ad agire; **big ~** alluce m; **little ~** mignolo m [del piede] ● vt **~ the line** rigar diritto

toe-hold n punto m d'appoggio

toenail n unghia f del piede

toff /tɒf/ n fam elegantone, -a mf

toffee /'tɒfɪ/ n caramella f al mou

toffee apple n mela f caramellata

toffee-nosed a Br fam con la puzza sotto il naso

together /tə'geðə(r)/ adv insieme; (at the same time) allo stesso tempo; **~ with** insieme a

toggle /'tɒgl/ n (fastening) olivetta f

toil /tɔɪl/ n duro lavoro m ● vi lavorare duramente

toilet /'tɔɪlɪt/ n (lavatory) gabinetto m

toilet bag n nécessaire m inv

toilet paper n carta f igienica

toiletries /'tɔɪlɪtrɪz/ npl articoli mpl da toilette

toilet: toilet roll n rotolo m di carta igienica. **toilet soap** n sapone m. **toilet tissue** n carta f igienica. **toilet-train** vt **~ a child** insegnare a un bambino a usare il vasino. **toilet water** n acqua f di colonia

token /'təʊkən/ n segno m; (counter) gettone m; (voucher) buono m ● attrib simbolico

told /təʊld/ see **tell** ● a **all ~** in tutto

tolerable /'tɒl(ə)rəbl/ a tollerabile; (not bad) discreto

tolerably /'tɒl(ə)rəblɪ/ adv discretamente

tolerance /'tɒl(ə)r(ə)ns/ n tolleranza f

tolerant /'tɒl(ə)r(ə)nt/ a tollerante

tolerantly /'tɒl(ə)r(ə)ntlɪ/ adv con tolleranza

tolerate /'tɒləreɪt/ vt tollerare

toll¹ /təʊl/ n pedaggio m; **death ~** numero m di morti; **take a heavy ~** costare gravi perdite

toll² vi suonare a morto

toll-booth n casello m

toll-free number n Am Teleph numero m verde

tom /tɒm/ n (cat) gatto m maschio

tomato /tə'mɑːtəʊ/ n (pl -es) pomodoro m

tomato: tomato ketchup n ketchup m. **tomato purée** n concentrato m di pomodoro. **tomato sauce** n salsa f di pomodoro

tomb /tuːm/ n tomba f

tomboy /'tɒmbɔɪ/ n maschiaccio m

tombstone /'tuːmstəʊn/ n pietra f tombale

tom-cat n gatto m maschio

tome /təʊm/ n tomo m

tomfoolery /tɒm'fuːlərɪ/ n stupidaggini fpl

tomorrow /tə'mɒrəʊ/ a & adv domani; **~ morning** domani mattina; **the day after ~** dopodomani; **see you ~!** a domani!

tom-tom n tamtam m inv

ton /tʌn/ n tonnellata f (= 1,016 kg); **~s of** fam un sacco di

tonal /'təʊnl/ a tonale

tonality /təʊ'nælətɪ/ n tonalità f inv

tone /təʊn/ n tono m; (colour) tonalità f inv

■ **tone down** vt attenuare

■ **tone in** vi intonarsi

■ **tone up** vt tonificare ⟨muscles⟩

tone-deaf a **be ~** non avere orecchio

toneless /'təʊnlɪs/ a (unmusical) piatto

toner /'təʊnə(r)/ n toner m

tongs /tɒŋz/ npl pinze fpl

tongue /tʌŋ/ n lingua f; **~ in cheek** ⟨fam: say⟩ ironicamente

tongue: tongue-lashing n (severe reprimand) strigliata f. **tongue-tied** a senza parole. **tongue-twister** n scioglilingua m inv

tonic /'tɒnɪk/ n tonico m; (for hair) lozione f per i capelli; fig toccasana m inv; **~ [water]** acqua f tonica

tonight /tə'naɪt/ adv stanotte; (evening) stasera ● n questa notte f; (evening) questa sera f

tonnage /'tʌnɪdʒ/ n stazza f

tonne /tʌn/ n tonnellata f metrica

tonsil /'tɒnsl/ n Anat tonsilla f; **have one's ~s out** operarsi di tonsille

tonsillitis /tɒnsə'laɪtɪs/ n tonsillite f; **have ~** avere la tonsillite

too /tuː/ adv troppo; (also) anche; **~ many** troppi; **~ much** troppo; **~ little** troppo poco

took /tʊk/ see **take**

tool /tuːl/ n attrezzo m

tool: tool-bag n borsa f degli attrezzi. **tool bar** n Comput barra f strumenti. **toolbox** n cassetta f degli attrezzi. **tool kit** n astuccio m di attrezzi

toot /tuːt/ n suono m di clacson ● vi Auto clacsonare

tooth /tuːθ/ n (pl teeth) dente m

tooth ache /'tuːθeɪk/ n mal m di denti; **have ~** avere mal di denti

toothbrush /'tuːθbrʌʃ/ n spazzolino m da denti

toothless /'tuːθlɪs/ a sdentato

toothpaste /'tuːθpeɪst/ n dentifricio m

toothpick /'tuːθpɪk/ n stuzzicadenti m inv

toothy /'tu:θɪ/ *a* **give a ~ grin** fare un sorriso a trentadue denti

top[1] /tɒp/ *n* (*toy*) trottola *f*

top[2] *n* cima *f*; *Sch* primo, -a *mf*; (*upper part or half*) parte *f* superiore; (*of page, list, street*) inizio *m*; (*upper surface*) superficie *f*; (*lid*) coperchio *m*; (*of bottle*) tappo *m*; (*garment*) maglia *f*; (*blouse*) camicia *f*; *Auto* marcia *f* più alta; **at the ~** *fig* al vertice; **at the ~ of one's voice** a squarciagola; **on ~/on ~ of** sopra; **on ~ of that** (*besides*) per di più; **from ~ to bottom** da cima a fondo; **blow one's ~** *fam* perdere le staffe; **over the ~** (*fam: exaggerated, too much*) eccessivo ● *a* in alto; (*official, floor of building*) superiore; (*pupil, musician etc*) migliore; (*speed*) massimo ● *vt* (*pt/pp* **topped**) essere in testa a (*list*); (*exceed*) sorpassare; **~ped with ice-cream** ricoperto di gelato; **~ oneself** *sl* suicidarsi
■ **top up** *vt* riempire

topaz /'təʊpæz/ *n* topazio *m*

top: top brass *n fam* pezzi *mpl* grossi. **topcoat** *n* (*of paint*) strato *m* finale. **top floor** *n* ultimo piano *m*. **top gear** *n Auto* marcia *f* più alta. **top hat** *n* cilindro *m*. **top-heavy** *a* con la parte superiore sovraccarica

topic /'tɒpɪk/ *n* soggetto *m*; (*of conversation*) argomento *m*

topical /'tɒpɪkl/ *a* d'attualità; **very ~** di grande attualità

topless /'tɒplɪs/ *a & adv* topless

top-level *a* ad alto livello

topmost /'tɒpməʊst/ *a* più alto

top: top-notch *a fam* eccellente. **top-of-the-range** *a* (*model*) della fascia più alta

topping /'tɒpɪŋ/ *n* **with a chocolate ~** ricoperto di cioccolato; **pizza with a ham and mushroom ~** pizza al prosciutto e funghi

topple /'tɒpl/ *vt* rovesciare ● *vi* rovesciarsi
■ **topple off** *vi* cadere

top: top-ranking *a* (*official*) di massimo grado. **top secret** *a* segretissimo, top secret *inv*. **top security** *a* di massima sicurezza. **topsoil** *n* strato *m* superficiale del terreno. **topspin** *n* topspin *m inv*

topsy-turvy /tɒpsɪ'tɜ:vɪ/ *a & adv* sottosopra

top ten *npl* primi dieci *mpl* in classifica

top-up *n* **would you like a ~?** ti riempio il bicchiere/la tazza?

torch /tɔ:tʃ/ *n* torcia *f* [elettrica]; (*flaming*) fiaccola *f*

torchlight procession /'tɔ:tʃlaɪt/ *n* fiaccolata *f*

tore /tɔ:(r)/ *see* **tear**[1]

torment[1] /'tɔ:ment/ *n* tormento *m*

torment[2] /tɔ:'ment/ *vt* tormentare

tormentor /tɔ:'mentə(r)/ *n* tormentatore, -trice *mf*

torn /tɔ:n/ *see* **tear**[1] ● *a* bucato

tornado /tɔ:'neɪdəʊ/ *n* (*pl* **-es**) tornado *m inv*

torpedo /tɔ:'pi:dəʊ/ *n* (*pl* **-es**) siluro *m* ● *vt* silurare

torpid /'tɔ:pɪd/ *a* intorpidito

torrent /'tɒrənt/ *n* torrente *m*

torrential /tə'renʃl/ *a* (*rain*) torrenziale

torrid /'tɒrɪd/ *a* torrido

torso /'tɔ:səʊ/ *n* torso *m*; (*in art*) busto *m*

tortoise /'tɔ:təs/ *n* tartaruga *f*

tortoiseshell /'tɔ:təsʃel/ *n* tartaruga *f*

tortuous /'tɔ:tʃʊəs/ *a* tortuoso

tortuously /'tɔ:tʃʊəslɪ/ *adv* tortuosamente

torture /'tɔ:tʃə(r)/ *n* tortura *f* ● *vt* torturare

Tory /'tɔ:rɪ/ *Br n* conservatore, -trice *mf* (*appartenente al partito britannico dei conservatori*) ● *a* del partito conservatore

toss /tɒs/ *vt* gettare; (*into the air*) lanciare in aria; (*shake*) scrollare; (*horse:*) disarcionare; mescolare (*salad*); rivoltare facendo saltare in aria (*pancake*); **~ a coin** fare testa o croce ● *vi* **~ and turn** (*in bed*) rigirarsi; **let's ~ for it** facciamo testa o croce

toss-up *n fam* **let's have a ~ to decide** facciamo testa o croce

tot[1] /tɒt/ *n* bimbetto, -a *mf*; (*fam: of liquor*) goccio *m*

tot[2] *vt* (*pt/pp* **totted**) **~ up** *fam* fare la somma di

total /'təʊtl/ *a* totale ● *n* totale *m* ● *vt* (*pt/pp* **totalled**) ammontare a; (*add up*) sommare

totalitarian /təʊtælɪ'teərɪən/ *a* totalitario

totally /'təʊtəlɪ/ *adv* totalmente

tote bag /təʊt/ *n* sporta *f*

totem pole /'təʊtəm/ *n* totem *m inv*

totter /'tɒtə(r)/ *vi* barcollare; (*government:*) vacillare

touch /tʌtʃ/ *n* tocco *m*; (*sense*) tatto *m*; (*contact*) contatto *m*; (*trace*) traccia *f*; (*of irony, humour*) tocco *m*; **get/be in ~** mettersi/essere in contatto ● *vt* toccare; (*lightly*) sfiorare; (*equal*) eguagliare; (*fig: move*) commuovere ● *vi* toccarsi
■ **touch down** *vi Aeron* atterrare
■ **touch off** *vi fig* scatenare
■ **touch on** *vt fig* accennare a
■ **touch up** *vt* ritoccare (*painting*); **~ sb up** (*sexually*) allungare le mani su qcno

touch-and-go *a* incerto

touchdown /'tʌtʃdaʊn/ *n Aeron* atterraggio *m*; *Sport* meta *f*

touché /tu:'ʃeɪ/ *int fig* touché!

touched /tʌtʃt/ *a* (*crazy*) toccato

touching /'tʌtʃɪŋ/ *a* commovente

touchingly /'tʌtʃɪŋlɪ/ *adv* in modo commovente

touch: touchline *n* (*in football*) linea *f* laterale; (*in rugby*) touche *nf inv*. **touch[-sensitive] screen** *n Comput* schermo *m* a sfioramento. **touch-type** *vi* dattilografare a tastiera cieca. **touch-typing** *n* dattilografia *f* a tastiera cieca. **touch-up** *n* (*of paintwork*) ritocco *m*

touchy /'tʌtʃɪ/ *a* permaloso; (*subject*) delicato

tough /tʌf/ *a* duro; (*severe, harsh*) severo; (*durable*) resistente; (*resilient*) forte; **~!** (*fam: too bad*) peggio per te/lui!

toughen /'tʌfn/ *vt* rinforzare
■ **toughen up** *vt* rendere più forte (*person*)

toupee /'tu:peɪ/ *n* toupet *m inv*

tour /tʊə(r)/ *n* giro *m*; (*of building, town*) visita *f*; *Theat, Sport* tournée *f inv*; (*of duty*) servizio *m* ● *vt* visitare ● *vi* fare un giro turistico; *Theat* essere in tournée

tour guide *n* guida *f* turistica

tourism /'tʊərɪzm/ *n* turismo *m*

tourist /'tʊərɪst/ *n* turista *mf* ● *attrib* turistico

tourist: tourist class *n* classe *f* turistica. **tourist office** *n* ufficio *m* turistico. **tourist resort** *n* località *f* turistica. **tourist route** *n* itinerario *m* turistico. **tourist trap** *n locale o località per turisti dove i prezzi sono molto alti*

touristy /'tʊərɪstɪ/ *a fam pej* da turisti; **it's too ~ here** è troppo turistico qui

tournament /'tʊənəmənt/ *n* torneo *m*

tourniquet /'tʊənɪkeɪ/ *n* laccio *m* emostatico

tour operator *n* tour operator *mf inv*, operatore, -trice *mf* turistico, -a

tousle /'taʊzl/ *vt* spettinare

tout /taʊt/ *n* (*ticket* ~) bagarino *m*; (*horse-racing*) informatore *m* ● *vi* ~ **for** sollecitare

tow /təʊ/ *n* rimorchio *m*; **'on ~'** 'a rimorchio'; **in** ~ *fam* al seguito ● *vt* rimorchiare

■ **tow away** *vt* portare via col carro attrezzi

toward[s] /tə'wɔːd(z)/ *prep* verso (*with respect to*) nei riguardi di

tow bar *n* barra *f* di rimorchio

towel /'taʊəl/ *n* asciugamano *m*

■ **towel down** *vt* asciugare

towelling /'taʊəlɪŋ/ *n* spugna *f*

towelling robe *n* accappatoio *m*

towel rail *n* portasciugamano *m*

tower /'taʊə(r)/ *n* torre *f*; **be a ~ of strength to sb** essere di grande conforto per qcno ● *vi* ~ **above** dominare

tower block *n* palazzone *m*

towering /'taʊərɪŋ/ *a* torreggiante; ⟨*rage*⟩ violento

tow line *n* cavo *m* da rimorchio

town /taʊn/ *n* città *f inv*; **in** ~ nel centro

town: town centre *n* centro *m* della città. **town council** *n* municipalità *f inv*. **town hall** *n* municipio *m*. **town planner** *n* urbanista *mf*. **town planning** *n* urbanistica *f*

towpath /'təʊpɑːθ/ *n* strada *f* alzaia

tow rope *n* cavo *m* da rimorchio

toxic /'tɒksɪk/ *a* tossico

toxicity /tɒk'sɪsɪtɪ/ *n* tossicità *f*

toxic waste *n* rifiuti *mpl* tossici

toxicologist /tɒksɪ'kɒlədʒɪst/ *n* tossicologo, -a *mf*

toxicology /tɒksɪ'kɒlədʒɪ/ *n* tossicologia *f*

toxin /'tɒksɪn/ *n* tossina *f*

toy /tɔɪ/ *n* giocattolo *m*

■ **toy with** *vt* giocherellare con

toyboy /'tɔɪbɔɪ/ *n Br fam* uomo-oggetto *m*

toyshop /'tɔɪʃɒp/ *n* negozio *m* di giocattoli

trace /treɪs/ *n* traccia *f* ● *vt* seguire le tracce di; (*find*) rintracciare; (*draw*) tracciare; (*with tracing-paper*) ricalcare

■ **trace back** *vt* trovare tracce di ⟨*family*⟩

■ **trace out** *vt* tracciare

tracer /'treɪsə(r)/ *n Mil* proiettile *m* tracciante

tracing /'treɪsɪŋ/ *n* ricalco *m*

tracing-paper *n* carta *f* da ricalco

track /træk/ *n* traccia *f*; (*path, Sport*) pista *f*; *Rail* binario *m*; **keep ~ of** tenere d'occhio ● *vt* seguire le tracce di

■ **track down** *vt* scovare

trackball /'trækbɔːl/ *n Comput* trackball *inv*

tracker /'trækə(r)/ *n* (*dog*) segugio *m*

track record *n fig* background *m inv*

tracksuit /'træksuːt/ *n* tuta *f* da ginnastica

tract /trækt/ *n* (*pamphlet*) opuscolo *m*

tractable /'træktəbl/ *a* trattabile; (*docile*) maneggevole

traction /'trækʃn/ *n* (*of wheel*) trazione *f*

traction engine *n* trattore *m*

tractor /'træktə(r)/ *n* trattore *m*

trade /treɪd/ *n* commercio *m*; (*line of business*) settore *m*; (*craft*) mestiere *m*; **by ~** di mestiere ● *vt* commerciare; ~ **sth for sth** scambiare qcsa per qcsa ● *vi* commerciare

■ **trade in** *vt* (*give in part exchange*) dare in pagamento parziale

■ **trade off** *vt* scambiare

■ **trade on** *vt* approfittarsi di

trade: trade deficit *n* bilancio *m* commerciale in deficit. **trade discount** *n* sconto *m* commerciale. **trade fair** *n* fiera *f* commerciale. **trade-in** *n* permuta *f* come pagamento parziale. **trade mark** *n* marchio *m* di fabbrica. **trade-name** *n* nome *m* depositato. **trade-off** *n* compromesso *m*. **trade price** *n* prezzo *m* all'ingrosso

trader /'treɪdə(r)/ *n* commerciante *mf*

trade secret *n* segreto *m* commerciale

tradesman /'treɪdzmən/ *n* (*joiner etc*) operaio *m*

trade: trade union *n* sindacato *m*. **trade unionist** *n* sindacalista *mf*. **trade union representative** *n* rappresentante *mf* sindacale

trading /'treɪdɪŋ/ *n* commercio *m*

trading: trading estate *n* zona *f* industriale. **trading floor** *n Fin* sala *f* delle contrattazioni. **trading stamp** *n* bollino *m* premio

tradition /trə'dɪʃn/ *n* tradizione *f*

traditional /trə'dɪʃnl/ *a* tradizionale

traditionalist /trə'dɪʃn(ə)lɪst/ *n* tradizionalista *mf*

traditionally /trə'dɪʃn(ə)lɪ/ *adv* tradizionalmente

traffic /'træfɪk/ *n* traffico *m* ● *vi* trafficare

traffic: traffic calming measures *npl* misure *fpl* per rallentare il traffico in città. **traffic circle** *n Am* isola *f* rotatoria. **traffic island** *n* isola *f* spartitraffico. **traffic jam** *n* ingorgo *m*. **traffic lights** *npl* semaforo *msg*. **traffic offence** *n* infrazione *f* al codice della strada. **traffic warden** *n* vigile *m* [urbano]; (*woman*) vigilessa *f*

tragedy /'trædʒədɪ/ *n* tragedia *f*

tragic /'trædʒɪk/ *a* tragico

tragically /'trædʒɪklɪ/ *adv* tragicamente

trail /treɪl/ n traccia f; (path) sentiero m ● vi strisciare; ⟨plant:⟩ arrampicarsi; ~ **[behind]** rimanere indietro; (in competition) essere in svantaggio ● vt trascinare

trail bike n moto f fuoristrada

trailblazer /ˈtreɪlbleɪzə(r)/ n pioniere, -a mf

trailblazing /ˈtreɪlbleɪzɪŋ/ a innovatore

trailer /ˈtreɪlə(r)/ n Auto rimorchio m; (Am: caravan) roulotte f inv; (film) presentazione f (di un film)

train /treɪn/ n treno m; (of dress) strascico m; **by ~** in treno; **~ of thought** filo m dei pensieri ● vt formare professionalmente; Sport allenare; (aim) puntare; educare ⟨child⟩; addestrare ⟨animal, soldier⟩; far crescere ⟨plant⟩ ● vi fare il tirocinio; Sport allenarsi

trained /treɪnd/ a ⟨animal⟩ addestrato (**to do** a fare)

trainee /treɪˈniː/ n apprendista mf

trainer /ˈtreɪnə(r)/ n Sport allenatore, -trice mf; (in circus) domatore, -trice mf; (of dog, race-horse) addestratore, -trice mf; **~s** (pl: shoes) scarpe fpl da ginnastica

training /ˈtreɪnɪŋ/ n tirocinio m; Sport allenamento m; (of animal, soldier) addestramento m

training college n istituto m professionale

train set n trenino m

traipse /treɪps/ vi **~ around** fam andare in giro

trait /treɪt/ n caratteristica f

traitor /ˈtreɪtə(r)/ n traditore, -trice mf

trajectory /trəˈdʒekt(ə)rɪ/ n traiettoria f

tram /træm/ n tram m inv

tram-lines npl rotaie fpl del tram

tramp /træmp/ n (hike) camminata f; (vagrant) barbone, -a mf; (of feet) calpestio m ● vi camminare con passo pesante; (hike) percorrere a piedi

■ **trample on** /ˈtræmpl/ vt calpestare

trampoline /ˈtræmpəliːn/ n trampolino m

trance /trɑːns/ n trance f inv

tranquil /ˈtræŋkwɪl/ a tranquillo

tranquillity /træŋˈkwɪlətɪ/ n tranquillità f

tranquillizer /ˈtræŋkwɪlaɪzə(r)/ n tranquillante m

transact /trænˈzækt/ vt trattare

transaction /trænˈzækʃn/ n transazione f

transatlantic /trænzətˈlæntɪk/ a ⟨crossing, flight⟩ transatlantico; ⟨attitude, accent⟩ americano

transceiver /trænˈsiːvə(r)/ n ricetrasmittente f

transcend /trænˈsend/ vt trascendere

transcontinental /trænzkɒntɪˈnent(ə)l/ a transcontinentale

transcribe /trænˈskraɪb/ vt trascrivere

transcript /ˈtrænskrɪpt/ n trascrizione f

transcription /trænˈskrɪpʃn/ n trascrizione f

transept /ˈtrænsept/ n transetto m

transfer¹ /ˈtrænsfə(r)/ n trasferimento m; Sport cessione f; (design) decalcomania f

transfer² /trænsˈfɜː(r)/ v (pt/pp trans-

ferred) ● vt trasferire; Sport cedere ● vi trasferirsi; (when travelling) cambiare

transfer fee n (for footballer) prezzo m d'acquisto

transfer list n (in football) lista f di giocatori da cedere

transferable /trænsˈfɜːrəbl/ a trasferibile

transfigure /trænsˈfɪɡə/ vt trasfigurare

transfix /trænsˈfɪks/ vt trafiggere; fig immobilizzare

transfixed /trænsˈfɪkst/ a (with fascination) folgorato; (with horror) paralizzato

transform /trænsˈfɔːm/ vt trasformare

transformation /trænsfəˈmeɪʃn/ n trasformazione f

transformer /trænsˈfɔːmə(r)/ n trasformatore m

transfusion /trænsˈfjuːʒn/ n trasfusione f

transgression /trænsˈɡreʃn/ n Jur trasgressione f; Relig peccato m

transient /ˈtrænzɪənt/ a passeggero

transistor /trænˈzɪstə(r)/ n transistor m inv; (radio) radiolina f a transistor

transit /ˈtrænzɪt/ n transito m; **in ~** ⟨goods⟩ in transito

transition /trænˈzɪʃn/ n transizione f

transitional /trænˈzɪʃənl/ a di transizione

transitive /ˈtrænzɪtɪv/ a transitivo

transitively /ˈtrænzɪtɪvlɪ/ adv transitivamente

transit lounge n sala f d'attesa transiti

transitory /ˈtrænzɪtərɪ/ a transitorio

transit passenger n passeggero m in transito

translate /trænzˈleɪt/ vt tradurre

translation /trænzˈleɪʃn/ n traduzione f

translation agency n agenzia f di traduzioni

translator /trænzˈleɪtə(r)/ n traduttore, -trice mf

translucent /trænzˈluːsnt/ a liter traslucido

transmissible /trænzˈmɪsəbl/ a trasmissibile

transmission /trænzˈmɪʃn/ n trasmissione f

transmit /trænzˈmɪt/ vt (pt/pp **transmitted**) trasmettere

transmitter /trænzˈmɪtə(r)/ n trasmettitore m

transparency /trænˈspærənsɪ/ n Phot diapositiva f

transparent /trænˈspærənt/ a trasparente

transpire /trænˈspaɪə(r)/ vi emergere; (fam: happen) accadere

transplant¹ /ˈtrænsplɑːnt/ n trapianto m

transplant² /trænsˈplɑːnt/ vt trapiantare

transport¹ /ˈtrænspɔːt/ n trasporto m; **do you have ~?** hai un mezzo di trasporto?

transport² /trænˈspɔːt/ vt trasportare

transportation /trænspɔːˈteɪʃn/ n trasporto m

transpose /trænsˈpəʊz/ vt trasporre

transsexual /trænzˈseksʊəl/ n transessuale mf ● a transessuale

trans-shipment /trænz'ʃɪpmənt/ n trasbordo m

transverse /trænz'vɜ:s/ a trasversale

transvestite /trænz'vestaɪt/ n travestito, -a mf

trap /træp/ n trappola f; (fam: mouth) boccaccia f; (carriage) calesse m ● vt (pt/pp **trapped**) intrappolare; schiacciare ⟨finger in door⟩; **be ~ped** essere intrappolato

trapdoor /'træpdɔ:(r)/ n botola f

trapeze /trə'pi:z/ n trapezio m

trappings /'træpɪŋz/ npl (dress) ornamenti mpl; **the ~ of wealth/success** i segni esteriori della ricchezza/del successo

trash /træʃ/ n robaccia f; (rubbish) spazzatura f; (nonsense) schiocchezze fpl

trashcan /'træʃkæn/ n Am pattumiera f, secchio m della spazzatura

trashy /'træʃɪ/ a scadente

trauma /'trɔ:mə/ n trauma m

traumatic /trɔ:'mætɪk/ a traumatico

traumatize /'trɔ:mətaɪz/ vt traumatizzare

travel /'trævl/ n viaggi mpl ● v (pt/pp **travelled**) ● vi viaggiare; (to work) andare ● vt percorrere ⟨distance⟩

travel: travel agency n agenzia f di viaggi. **travel agent** n agente mf di viaggio. **travel expenses** npl spese fpl di viaggio

traveller /'trævələ(r)/ n viaggiatore, -trice mf; Comm commesso m viaggiatore; **~s** pl (gypsies) zingari mpl

traveller's cheque n traveller's cheque m inv

travelling salesman /'trævəlɪŋ/ n commesso m viaggiatore

travelogue /'trævəlɒg/ n (film) documentario m di viaggio; (talk) conferenza f su un viaggio

travel-sick a **be/get ~** (on plane) soffrire il mal d'aria; (in car) soffrire il mal d'auto; (on boat) soffrire il mal di mare

travel-sickness n (on plane) mal m d'aria; (in car) mal m d'auto; (on boat) mal m di mare ● attrib ⟨pills⟩ per il mal d'aria/d'auto/di mare

traverse /trə'vɜ:s/ vt traversare

travesty /'trævɪstɪ/ n (fig: farce) farsa f; **a ~ of justice** una presa in giro della giustizia

trawler /'trɔ:lə(r)/ n peschereccio m

tray /treɪ/ n vassoio m; (for baking) teglia f; (for documents) vaschetta f; (of printer, photocopier) vassoio m, cassetto m

treacherous /'tretʃərəs/ a traditore; ⟨weather, currents⟩ pericoloso

treachery /'tretʃ(ə)rɪ/ n tradimento m

treacle /'tri:kl/ n melassa f

tread /tred/ n andatura f; (step) gradino m; (of tyre) battistrada m inv ● vi (pt **trod**, pp **trodden**) (walk) camminare

■ **tread on** vt calpestare ⟨grass⟩; pestare ⟨foot⟩

treadmill /'tredmɪl/ n fig solito tran tran m

treason /'tri:zn/ n tradimento m

treasonable /'tri:z(ə)nəbl/ a proditorio

treasure /'treʒə(r)/ n tesoro m ● vt tenere in gran conto

treasurer /'treʒərə(r)/ n tesoriere, -a mf

treasury /'treʒərɪ/ n **the T~** il Ministero del Tesoro

treat /tri:t/ n piacere m; (present) regalo m; **give sb a ~** fare una sorpresa a qcno ● vt trattare; Med curare; **~ sb to sth** offrire qcsa a qcno; **~ sb for sth** Med sottoporre qcno ad una cura per qcsa

treatise /'tri:tɪz/ n trattato m

treatment /'tri:tmənt/ n trattamento m; Med cura f

treaty /'tri:tɪ/ n trattato m

treble /'trebl/ a triplo; **~ the amount** il triplo ● n Mus (voice) voce f bianca ● vt triplicare ● vi triplicarsi

treble clef n chiave f di violino

tree /tri:/ n albero m

tree: tree house n capanna f su un albero. **treetop** n cima f di un albero. **tree trunk** n tronco m d'albero

trek /trek/ n scarpinata f; (as holiday) trekking m inv ● vi (pt/pp **trekked**) farsi una scarpinata; (on holiday) fare trekking

trekking /'trekɪŋ/ n trekking m

trellis /'trelɪs/ n graticolato m

tremble /'trembl/ vi tremare (**with** di)

trembling /'tremblɪŋ/ a tremante

tremendous /trɪ'mendəs/ a (huge) enorme; (fam: excellent) formidabile

tremendously /trɪ'mendəslɪ/ adv (very) straordinariamente; (a lot) enormemente

tremor /'tremə(r)/ n tremito m; [**earth**] **~** scossa f [sismica]

tremulous /'tremjʊləs/ a tremulo

trench /trentʃ/ n fosso m; Mil trincea f

trenchant /'trentʃənt/ a ⟨comment, criticism⟩ mordace

trench coat n trench m inv

trend /trend/ n tendenza f; (fashion) moda f

trend-setter n persona f che detta la moda

trend-setting a che detta la moda

trendy /'trendɪ/ a (**-ier**, **-iest**) fam di or alla moda

trepidation /trepɪ'deɪʃn/ n trepidazione f

trespass /'trespəs/ vi **~ on** introdursi abusivamente in; fig abusare di

trespasser /'trespəsə(r)/ n intruso, -a mf

trestle /'tresl/ n cavalletto m

trestle table n tavolo m a cavalletto

trial /'traɪəl/ n Jur processo m; (test, ordeal) prova f; **on ~** in prova; Jur in giudizio; **by ~ and error** per tentativi

trial period n periodo m di prova

trial run n (preliminary test) prova f

triangle /'traɪæŋgl/ n triangolo m

triangular /traɪ'æŋgjʊlə(r)/ a triangolare

tribal /'traɪbl/ a tribale

tribe /traɪb/ n tribù f inv

tribulation /trɪbjʊ'leɪʃn/ n tribolazione f

tribunal /traɪ'bju:nl/ n tribunale m

tributary /'trɪbjʊtərɪ/ n affluente m

tribute /'trɪbju:t/ n tributo m; **pay ~** rendere omaggio

trice /traɪs/ *n* **in a ~** in un attimo

tricentenary /traɪsen'tiːnərɪ/ *n* terzo centenario *m* ● *a* del terzo centenario

trick /trɪk/ *n* trucco *m*; (*joke*) scherzo *m*; (*Cards*) presa *f*; **do the ~** *fam* funzionare; **play a ~ on** fare uno scherzo a ● *vt* imbrogliare; **~ of the trade** trucco *m* del mestiere
■ **trick into** *vt* **~ sb into doing sth** convincere qcno a fare qcsa con l'inganno
■ **trick out** *vt* **~ sb out of sth** fregare qcno a qcsa

trick cyclist *n* (*sl: psychiatrist*) psichiatra *mf*

trickle /'trɪkl/ *vi* colare
■ **trickle in** *vi fig* entrare poco per volta
■ **trickle out** *vi fig* uscire poco per volta

trickster /'trɪkstə(r)/ *n* imbroglione, -a *mf*

tricky /'trɪkɪ/ *a* (**-ier, -iest**) *a* (*operation*) complesso; (*situation*) delicato

tricolour /'trɪkələ(r)/ *n* tricolore *m*

tricycle /'traɪsɪkl/ *n* triciclo *m*

tried /traɪd/ *see* **try**

tried and tested *a* (*method*) sperimentato

trifle /'traɪfl/ *n* inezia *f*; *Culin* zuppa *f* inglese

trifling /'traɪflɪŋ/ *a* insignificante

trig /trɪg/ *n* (*fam: trigonometry*) trigonometria *f*

trigger /'trɪgə(r)/ *n* grilletto *m*; *fig* causa *f* ● *vt* **~ [off]** scatenare

trigger-happy *a fam* dalla pistola facile; *fig* impulsivo

trigonometry /trɪgə'nɒmɪtrɪ/ *n* trigonometria *f*

trilateral /traɪ'lætərəl/ *a* trilaterale

trilby /'trɪlbɪ/ *n* cappello *m* di feltro

trill /trɪl/ *n* *Mus* trillo *m*

trilogy /'trɪlədʒɪ/ *n* trilogia *f*

trim /trɪm/ *a* (**trimmer, trimmest**) curato; (*figure*) snello ● *n* (*of hair, hedge*) spuntata *f*; (*decoration*) rifinitura *f*; **in good ~** in buono stato; (*person*) in forma ● *vt* (*pt/pp* **trimmed**) spuntare (*hair etc*); (*decorate*) ornare; *Naut* orientare
■ **trim off** *vt* tagliare via

trimming /'trɪmɪŋ/ *n* bordo *m*; **~s** *pl* (*of pastry*) ritagli *mpl*; (*decorations*) guarnizioni *fpl*; **with all the ~s** *Culin* guarnito

Trinity /'trɪnətɪ/ *n* **the [Holy] ~** la [Santissima] Trinità

trinket /'trɪŋkɪt/ *n* ninnolo *m*

trio /'triːəʊ/ *n* trio *m*

trip /trɪp/ *n* (*excursion*) gita *f*; (*journey*) viaggio *m*; (*stumble*) passo *m* falso ● *v* (*pt/pp* **tripped**) ● *vt* far inciampare ● *vi* inciampare (**on/over** in)
■ **trip up** *vt* far inciampare

tripartite /traɪ'pɑːtaɪt/ *a* tripartito

tripe /traɪp/ *n* trippa *f*; (*sl: nonsense*) fesserie *fpl*

triple /'trɪpl/ *a* triplo ● *vt* triplicare ● *vi* triplicarsi

triplets /'trɪplɪts/ *npl* tre gemelli *mpl*

triplicate /'trɪplɪkət/ *n* **in ~** in triplice copia

tripod /'traɪpɒd/ *n* treppiede *m inv*

tripper /'trɪpə(r)/ *n* gitante *mf*

trite /traɪt/ *a* banale

triteness /'traɪtnɪs/ *n* banalità *f*

triumph /'traɪʌmf/ *n* trionfo *m* ● *vi* trionfare (**over** su)

triumphant /traɪ'ʌmf(ə)nt/ *a* trionfante

triumphantly /traɪ'ʌmf(ə)ntlɪ/ *adv* (*exclaim*) con tono trionfante

triumvirate /traɪ'ʌmvɪrət/ *n* triumvirato *m*

trivia /'trɪvɪə/ *npl* cose *fpl* secondarie

trivial /'trɪvɪəl/ *a* insignificante

triviality /trɪvɪ'ælətɪ/ *n* banalità *f inv*

trivialize /'trɪvɪəlaɪz/ *vt* sminuire

trod, trodden /trɒd, 'trɒdn/ *see* **tread**

trolley /'trɒlɪ/ *n* carrello *m*; (*Am: tram*) tram *m inv*

trolley bus *n* filobus *m inv*

trombone /trɒm'bəʊn/ *n* trombone *m*

trombonist /trɒm'bəʊnɪst/ *n* trombonista *mf*

troop /truːp/ *n* gruppo *m*; **~s** *pl* truppe *fpl* ● *vi* **~ in/out** entrare/uscire in gruppo

trooper /'truːpə(r)/ *n* *Mil* soldato *m* di cavalleria; (*Am: policeman*) poliziotto *m*

trophy /'trəʊfɪ/ *n* trofeo *m*

tropic /'trɒpɪk/ *n* tropico *m*; **~s** *pl* tropici *mpl*

tropical /'trɒpɪkl/ *a* tropicale

tropical fruit *n* frutta *f inv* esotica

trot /trɒt/ *n* trotto *m* ● *vi* (*pt/pp* **trotted**) trottare
■ **trot out** *vt* (*fam: produce*) tirar fuori

trotter /'trɒtə(r)/ *n* *Culin* piedino *m* di maiale

trouble /'trʌbl/ *n* guaio *m*; (*difficulties*) problemi *mpl*; (*inconvenience, Med*) disturbo *m*; (*conflict*) conflitto *m*; **be in ~** essere nei guai; (*swimmer, climber:*) essere in difficoltà; **get into ~** finire nei guai; **get sb into ~** mettere qcno nei guai; **take the ~ to do sth** darsi la pena di far qcsa; **it's no ~** nessun disturbo; **the ~ with you is...** il tuo problema è... ● *vt* (*worry*) preoccupare; (*inconvenience*) disturbare; (*conscience, old wound:*) tormentare ● *vi* **don't ~!** non ti disturbare!

troubled /'trʌbld/ *a* (*mind*) inquieto; (*person, expression*) preoccupato; (*times, area*) difficile; (*waters, sleep*) agitato

troublemaker /'trʌblmeɪkə(r)/ *n* **be a ~** seminare zizzania

troublesome /'trʌblsəm/ *a* fastidioso

trouble spot *n* zona *f* calda

trough /trɒf/ *n* trogolo *m*; (*atmospheric*) depressione *f*

trounce /traʊns/ *vt* (*in competition*) schiacciare

troupe /truːp/ *n* troupe *f inv*

trouser press *n* stiracalzoni *m inv*

trousers /'traʊzəz/ *npl* pantaloni *mpl*

trouser suit *n* tailleur *m inv* pantalone

trousseau /'truːsəʊ/ *n* corredo *m*

trout /traʊt/ *n inv* trota *f*

trowel /'traʊəl/ *n* (*for gardening*) paletta *f*; (*for builder*) cazzuola *f*

truant /'truːənt/ *n* **play ~** marinare la scuola

truce /truːs/ *n* tregua *f*

truck /trʌk/ n (*lorry*) camion m inv

trucker /'trʌkə(r)/ n (*fam: lorry driver*) camionista mf

truck farmer n Am ortofrutticoltore m, ortolano m

truculent /'trʌkjʊlənt/ a aggressivo

truculently /'trʌkjʊləntlɪ/ adv aggressivamente

trudge /trʌdʒ/ n camminata f faticosa ● vi arrancare

true /tru:/ a vero; **come ~** avverarsi

true-life a ⟨adventure, story⟩ vero

truffle /'trʌfl/ n tartufo m

truism /'tru:ɪzm/ n truismo m

truly /'tru:lɪ/ adv veramente; **Yours ~** Distinti saluti

trump /trʌmp/ n (*Cards*) atout m inv ● vt prendere con l'atout

■ **trump up** vt fam inventare

trump card n fig asso m nella manica

trumpet /'trʌmpɪt/ n tromba f

trumpeter /'trʌmpɪtə(r)/ n trombettista mf

truncate /'trʌŋkeɪt/ vt tagliare ⟨text⟩; interrompere ⟨process, journey, event⟩

truncheon /'trʌntʃn/ n manganello m

trundle /'trʌndl/ vt far rotolare ● vi rotolare

trunk /trʌŋk/ n (*of tree, body*) tronco m; (*of elephant*) proboscide f; (*for travelling, storage*) baule m; (*Am: of car*) bagagliaio m, portabagagli m inv

trunk road n statale f

trunks /trʌŋks/ npl calzoncini mpl da bagno

truss /trʌs/ n Med cinto m erniario

■ **truss up** vt legare

trust /trʌst/ n fiducia f; (*group of companies*) trust m inv; (*organization*) associazione f; **on ~** sulla parola ● vt fidarsi di; (*hope*) augurarsi ● vi **~ in** credere in; **~ to** affidarsi a

trusted /'trʌstɪd/ a fidato

trustee /trʌs'ti:/ n amministratore, -trice mf fiduciario, -a

trustful /'trʌstfʊl/ a fiducioso

trustfully /'trʌstfʊlɪ/ adv fiduciosamente

trust fund n fondo m fiduciario

trusting /'trʌstɪŋ/ a fiducioso

trustworthiness /'trʌstwɜ:ðɪnɪs/ n (*of person*) affidabilità f; (*of source*) attendibilità f

trustworthy /'trʌstwɜ:ðɪ/ a fidato

trusty /'trʌstɪ/ a fam fidato

truth /tru:θ/ n (pl **-s** /tru:ðz/) verità f inv

truthful /'tru:θfʊl/ a ⟨person⟩ sincero; ⟨statement⟩ veritiero

truthfully /'tru:θfʊlɪ/ adv sinceramente

truthfulness /'tru:θfʊlnɪs/ n (*of person*) sincerità f; (*of account*) veridicità f

try /traɪ/ n tentativo m, prova f; (*in rugby*) meta f; **I'll give it a ~** faccio un tentativo ● v (pt/pp **tried**) ● vt provare; (*be a strain on*) mettere a dura prova; Jur processare ⟨person⟩; discutere ⟨case⟩; **~ to do sth** provare a fare qcsa ● vi provare

■ **try for** vi cercare di ottenere

■ **try on** vt provarsi ⟨garment⟩

■ **try out** vt provare

trying /'traɪɪŋ/ a duro; ⟨person⟩ irritante

try-out n **give sb a ~** mettere alla prova qcno

tsar /zɑː/ n zar m inv

tsarina /tsɑːˈriːnə/ n zarina f

tsarist /'tsɑːrɪst/ a zarista

T-shirt n maglietta f

tsp abbr **teaspoonful**

tub /tʌb/ n tinozza f; (*carton*) vaschetta f; (*bath*) vasca f da bagno

tuba /'tju:bə/ n Mus tuba f

tubby /'tʌbɪ/ a (**-ier, -iest**) tozzo

tube /tju:b/ n tubo m; (*of toothpaste*) tubetto m; Br Rail metro f

tuber /'tju:bə(r)/ n tubero m

tuberculosis /tju:bɜ:kjʊˈləʊsɪs/ n tubercolosi f

tubing /'tju:bɪŋ/ n tubi mpl

tubular /'tju:bjʊlə(r)/ a tubolare

tuck /tʌk/ n piega f ● vt (*put*) infilare

■ **tuck away** vt (*put in a safe place*) mettere al sicuro; (*eat*) spolverare

■ **tuck in** vt rimboccare; **~ sb in** rimboccare le coperte a qcno ● vi (*fam: eat*) mangiare con appetito

■ **tuck into** vt mangiare di gusto ⟨meal⟩; **~ sth into one's pocket** infilarsi in tasca qcsa; **~ sb into bed** rimboccare le coperte a qcno

■ **tuck up** vt rimboccarsi ⟨sleeves⟩; (*in bed*) rimboccare le coperte a

Tuesday /'tju:zdeɪ/ n martedì m inv

tuft /tʌft/ n ciuffo m

tug /tʌg/ n strattone m; Naut rimorchiatore m ● v (pt/pp **tugged**) ● vt tirare ● vi dare uno strattone

tug of war n tiro m alla fune

tuition /tju:ˈɪʃn/ n lezioni fpl

tulip /'tju:lɪp/ n tulipano m

tumble /'tʌmbl/ n ruzzolone m ● vi ruzzolare; **~ to sth** (*fam: realize*) afferrare qcsa

tumbledown /'tʌmbəldaʊn/ a cadente

tumble-drier n asciugabiancheria f

tumbler /'tʌmblə(r)/ n bicchiere m (*senza stelo*)

tummy /'tʌmɪ/ n fam pancia f

tummy button n fam ombelico m

tumour /'tju:mə(r)/ n tumore m

tumult /'tju:mʌlt/ n tumulto m

tumultuous /tju:ˈmʌltjʊəs/ a tumultuoso

tuna /'tju:nə/ n tonno m

tune /tju:n/ n motivo m; **out of/in ~** ⟨instrument⟩ scordato/accordato; ⟨person⟩ stonato/intonato; **to the ~ of** fam per la modesta somma di ● vt accordare ⟨instrument⟩; sintonizzare ⟨radio, TV⟩; mettere a punto ⟨engine⟩

■ **tune in** vt sintonizzare ● vi sintonizzarsi (**to** su)

■ **tune up** vi ⟨orchestra:⟩ accordare gli strumenti

tuneful /'tju:nfl/ a melodioso

tuner /'tju:nə(r)/ n accordatore, -trice mf; Radio, TV sintonizzatore m

tune-up n (*of engine*) messa f a punto

tungsten /'tʌŋstən/ n tungsteno m
tunic /'tju:nɪk/ n tunica f; Mil giacca f; Sch ≈ grembiule m
tuning-fork /'tu:nɪŋ/ n diapason m inv
Tunisia /tju:'nɪzɪə/ n Tunisia f
Tunisian /tju:'nɪzɪən/ a & n tunisino, -a mf
tunnel /'tʌnl/ n tunnel m inv ● vi (pt/pp **tunnelled**) scavare un tunnel
tuppence /'tʌpəns/ n due penny
turban /'tɜ:bən/ n turbante m
turbine /'tɜ:baɪn/ n turbina f
turbo /'tɜ:bəʊ/ n turbo m inv
turbocharged /'tɜ:bəʊtʃɑ:dʒd/ a con motore turbo
turbocharger /'tɜ:bəʊtʃɑ:dʒə(r)/ n turbocompressore m
turbot /'tɜ:bət/ n rombo m gigante
turbulence /'tɜ:bjʊləns/ n turbolenza f
turbulent /'tɜ:bjʊlənt/ a turbolento
turd /tɜ:d/ n sl (excrement) stronzo m; (pej: person) stronzo, -a mf
tureen /tjʊ'ri:n/ n zuppiera f
turf /tɜ:f/ n erba f; (segment) zolla f erbosa
■ **turf out** vt fam buttar fuori
turf accountant n allibratore m
turgid /'tɜ:dʒɪd/ a (style, water) turgido
Turin /tjʊ'rɪn/ n Torino m
Turk /tɜ:k/ n turco, -a mf
Turkey /'tɜ:kɪ/ n Turchia f
turkey n tacchino m
Turkish /'tɜ:kɪʃ/ a turco
Turkish bath n bagno m turco
Turkish delight n cubetti mpl di gelatina ricoperti di zucchero a velo
turmeric /'tɜ:mərɪk/ n (spice) curcumina f; (plant) curcuma f
turmoil /'tɜ:mɔɪl/ n tumulto m
turn /tɜ:n/ n (rotation, short walk) giro m; (in road) svolta f, curva f; (development) svolta f; Theat numero m; (fam: attack) crisi f inv; **a ~ for the better/worse** un miglioramento/peggioramento m; **do sb a good ~** rendere un servizio a qcno; **take ~s** fare a turno; **in ~** a turno; **out of ~** (speak) a sproposito; **it's your ~** tocca a te ● vt girare voltare (back, eyes); dirigere (gun, attention) ● vi girare; (person:) girarsi; (leaves:) ingiallire; (become) diventare; **~ right/left** girare a destra/sinistra; **~ sour** inacidirsi; **~ to sb** girarsi verso qcno; fig rivolgersi a qcno
■ **turn against** vi diventare ostile a ● vt mettere contro
■ **turn around** vi (person:) girarsi; (car:) girare ● vt girare (object); risollevare (company)
■ **turn away** vt mandare via (people); girare dall'altra parte (head) ● vi girarsi dall'altra parte
■ **turn back** vi tornare indietro ● vt mandare indietro (people); ripiegare (covers, sheet etc)
■ **turn down** vt piegare (collar); abbassare (heat, gas, sound); respingere (person, proposal)
■ **turn in** vt ripiegare in dentro (edges); con-

segnare (lost object) ● vi (fam: go to bed) andare a letto; **~ in to the drive** entrare nel viale
■ **turn into** vt (become) diventare
■ **turn off** vt spegnere; chiudere (tap, water); **~ sb off** (fam: disgust) fare schifo a qcno ● vi (car:) girare
■ **turn on** vt accendere; aprire (tap, water); (fam: attract) eccitare ● vi (attack) attaccare
■ **turn out** vt (expel) mandar via; spegnere (light, gas); (produce) produrre; (empty) svuotare (room, cupboard) ● vi (transpire) risultare; (to see, do sth) venire; **~ out well/badly** (cake, dress:) riuscire bene/male; (situation:) andare bene/male
■ **turn over** vt girare; **~ sb over to the police** consegnare qcno alla polizia; **he ~ed the business over to her** le ha ceduto l'azienda ● vi girarsi; **please ~ over** vedi retro
■ **turn round** vi girarsi; (car:) girare
■ **turn up** vt tirare su (collar); alzare (heat, gas, sound, radio) ● vi farsi vedere
turn: turn-about n (fig: change of direction) cambiamento m. **turnaround** n (in attitude) dietrofront m inv; (of fortune) capovolgimento m; (for the better) ripresa f. **turncoat** n voltagabbana mf inv
turning /'tɜ:nɪŋ/ n svolta f
turning-point n svolta f decisiva
turnip /'tɜ:nɪp/ n rapa f
turn: turn-off n strada f laterale; **it's a real ~** fam ti fa davvero passar la voglia. **turn-on** n fam **be a real ~** essere veramente eccitante. **turnout** n (of people) affluenza f. **turnover** n Comm giro m d'affari, fatturato m; (of staff) ricambio m. **turnpike** n Am autostrada f. **turnround** n (in policy etc) cambiamento m. **turnstile** n cancelletto m girevole. **turntable** n piattaforma f girevole; (on record-player) piatto m. **turn-up** n (of trousers) risvolto m
turpentine /'tɜ:pəntaɪn/ n trementina f
turquoise /'tɜ:kwɔɪz/ a (colour) turchese ● n turchese m
turret /'tʌrɪt/ n torretta f
turtle /'tɜ:tl/ n tartaruga f acquatica
turtle-dove n tortora f
turtleneck /'tɜ:tlnek/ n collo m a lupetto; (sweater) maglia f a lupetto
Tuscan /'tʌskən/ a toscano
Tuscany /'tʌskənɪ/ n Toscana f
tusk /tʌsk/ n zanna f
tussle /'tʌsl/ n zuffa f ● vi azzuffarsi
tussock /'tʌsək/ n ciuffo m d'erba
tut /tʌt/ vi fare un'esclamazione di disapprovazione ● int ts!
tutor /'tju:tə(r)/ n insegnante mf privato, -a; Univ insegnante mf universitario, -a che segue individualmente un ristretto numero di studenti
tutorial /tju:'tɔ:rɪəl/ n discussione f col tutor
tutorial package n Comput software m di autoapprendimento
tuxedo /tʌk'si:dəʊ/ n Am smoking m inv
TV abbr (**television**) tv f inv, tivù f inv

twaddle /'twɒdl/ *n* scemenze *fpl*

twain /tweɪn/ *npl* **the ~** i due; **and never the ~ shall meet** e mai i due si incontreranno

twang /twæŋ/ *n* (*in voice*) suono *m* nasale ● *vt* far vibrare

tweak /twi:k/ *vt* tirare ⟨*ear, nose*⟩; (*adjust*) apportare delle modifiche a ● *n* (*adjustment*) modifica *f*; **give sb's ears a ~** dare una tirata d'orecchie a qcno

twee /twi:/ *a Br fam* ⟨*manner*⟩ affettato

tweed /twi:d/ *n* tweed *m inv*

tweezers /'twi:zəz/ *npl* pinzette *f*

twelfth /twelfθ/ *a & n* dodicesimo, -a *mf*

twelve /twelv/ *a & n* dodici *m*

twentieth /'twentɪɪθ/ *a & n* ventesimo, -a *mf*

twenty /'twentɪ/ *a & n* venti *m*

twerp /tws:p/ *n fam* stupido, -a *mf*

twice /twaɪs/ *adv* due volte; **she's done ~ as much as you** ha fatto il doppio di quanto hai fatto tu

twiddle /'twɪdl/ *vt* giocherellare con; **~ one's thumbs** *fig* girarsi i pollici

twig[1] /twɪg/ *n* ramoscello *m*

twig[2] *vt/i* (*pt/pp* **twigged**) *fam* intuire

twilight /'twaɪlaɪt/ *n* crepuscolo *m*

twill /twɪl/ *n* spigato *m*

twin /twɪn/ *n* gemello, -a *mf* ● *attrib* gemello

twin beds *npl* letti *mpl* gemelli

twine /twaɪn/ *n* spago *m* ● *vi* intrecciarsi; ⟨*plant:*⟩ attorcigliarsi ● *vt* intrecciare

twinge /twɪndʒ/ *n* fitta *f*; **~ of conscience** rimorso *m* di coscienza

twinkle /'twɪŋkl/ *n* scintillio *m* ● *vi* scintillare

twinning /'twɪnɪŋ/ *n* (*of companies*) gemellaggio *m*

twin town *n* città *f inv* gemellata

twirl /tws:l/ *vt* far roteare ● *vi* volteggiare ● *n* piroetta *f*

twist /twɪst/ *n* torsione *f*; (*curve*) curva *f*; (*in rope*) attorcigliata *f*; (*in book, plot*) colpo *m* di scena; **round the ~** (*fam: crazy*) ammattito ● *vt* attorcigliare ⟨*rope*⟩; torcere ⟨*metal*⟩; girare ⟨*knob, cap*⟩; (*distort*) distorcere; **~ one's ankle** storcersi la caviglia ● *vi* attorcigliarsi; ⟨*road:*⟩ essere pieno di curve

twister /'twɪstə(r)/ *n fam* imbroglione, -a *mf*; (*tornado*) tornado *m inv*

twit /twɪt/ *n fam* cretino, -a *mf*

twitch /twɪtʃ/ *n* tic *m inv*; (*jerk*) strattone *m* ● *vi* contrarsi

twitchy /'twɪtʃɪ/ *a* (*fam: nervous*) nervosetto

twitter /'twɪtə(r)/ *n* cinguettio *m*; **in a ~** *fam* agitato ● *vi* cinguettare; ⟨*person:*⟩ cianciare

■ **twitter on about** *vt* parlare incessantemente di

two /tu:/ *a & n* due *m*; **put ~ and ~ together** fare due più due

two: two-faced /-'feɪst/ *a* falso. **two-piece** *a* (*swimsuit*) due pezzi *m inv*; (*suit*) completo *m*. **two-seater** /-si:tə(r)/ *n* biposto *m* inv. **twosome** /'tu:səm/ *n* coppia *f*. **two-time** *vt fam* fare le corna a. **two-tone** *a* (*in colour*) bicolore; (*in sound*) bitonale. **two-way** *a* ⟨*traffic*⟩ a doppio senso di marcia

tycoon /taɪ'ku:n/ *n* magnate *m*

tying /'taɪɪŋ/ *see* **tie**

type /taɪp/ *n* tipo *m*; (*printing*) carattere *m* [tipografico] ● *vt/i* scrivere a macchina

type: typecast *vt Theat, fig* far fare sempre la stessa parte a ⟨*person*⟩ ● *a* a ruolo fisso. **typeface** *n* carattere *m* tipografico. **typeset** *vt* comporre. **typesetter** *n* compositore *m*. **typewriter** *n* macchina *f* da scrivere. **typewritten** *a* dattiloscritto

typhoid /'taɪfɔɪd/ *n* febbre *f* tifoidea

typhoon /taɪ'fu:n/ *n* tifone *m*

typical /'tɪpɪkl/ *a* tipico

typically /'tɪpɪklɪ/ *adv* tipicamente; (*as usual*) come al solito

typify /'tɪpɪfaɪ/ *vt* (*pt/pp* **-ied**) essere tipico di

typing /'taɪpɪŋ/ *n* dattilografia *f*

typist /'taɪpɪst/ *n* dattilografo, -a *mf*

typo /'taɪpəʊ/ *n* errore *m* di stampa; (*keying error*) errore *m* di battitura

typography /taɪ'pɒgrəfɪ/ *n* tipografia *f*

tyrannical /tɪ'rænɪkl/ *a* tirannico

tyrannize /'tɪrənaɪz/ *vt* tiranneggiare

tyranny /'tɪrənɪ/ *n* tirannia *f*

tyrant /'taɪrənt/ *n* tiranno, -a *mf*

tyre /'taɪə(r)/ *n* gomma *f*, pneumatico *m*

tyre pressure *n* pressione *f* delle gomme

Tyrrhenian Sea /tɪ'ri:nɪən/ *n* mar *m* Tirreno

tzar /zɑ:/ *n* zar *m*

tzarina /tsɑ:'ri:nə/ *n* zarina *f*

Uu

u, U /juː/ *n* (*letter*) u, U *f inv*
u *abbr Cinema* (**universal**) per tutti
U-bend *n* (*in pipe*) gomito *m*; (*in road*) curva *f* a gomito
ubiquitous /juːˈbɪkwɪtəs/ *a* onnipresente
udder /ˈʌdə(r)/ *n* mammella *f* (*di vacca, capra etc*)
UFO *abbr* (**unidentified flying object**) ufo *m inv*
Uganda /juːˈgændə/ *n* Uganda *f*
Ugandan /juːˈgændən/ *a* & *n* ugandese *mf*
ugliness /ˈʌglɪnɪs/ *n* bruttezza *f*
ugly /ˈʌglɪ/ *a* (**-ier, -iest**) brutto
UK *abbr* **United Kingdom**
Ukraine /juːˈkreɪn/ *n* Ucraina *f*
Ukrainian /juːˈkreɪnɪən/ *a* & *n* ucraino, -a *mf*; (*language*) ucraino *m*
ulcer /ˈʌlsə(r)/ *n* ulcera *f*
ulterior /ʌlˈtɪərɪə(r)/ *a* ~ **motive** secondo fine *m*
ultimate /ˈʌltɪmət/ *a* definitivo; (*final*) finale; (*fundamental*) fondamentale
ultimately /ˈʌltɪmətlɪ/ *adv* alla fine
ultimatum /ʌltɪˈmeɪtəm/ *n* ultimatum *m inv*
ultramarine /ʌltrəməˈriːn/ *a* oltremarino ● *n* azzurro *m* oltremarino
ultrasound /ˈʌltrəsaʊnd/ *n Med* ecografia *f*
ultrasound scan *n* ecografia *m*
ultrasound scanner *n* scanner *m inv* per ecografia
ultraviolet /ʌltrəˈvaɪələt/ *a* ultravioletto
umbilical /ʌmˈbɪlɪkl/ *a* ~ **cord** cordone *m* ombelicale
umbrage /ˈʌmbrɪdʒ/ *n* **take** ~ offendersi
umbrella /ʌmˈbrelə/ *n* ombrello *m*
umbrella stand *n* portaombrelli *m inv*
umpire /ˈʌmpaɪə(r)/ *n* arbitro *m* ● *vt/i* arbitrare
umpteen /ʌmpˈtiːn/ *a fam* innumerevole
umpteenth /ʌmpˈtiːnθ/ *a fam* ennesimo; **for the** ~ **time** per l'ennesima volta
UN *abbr* (**United Nations**) ONU *f*
unabashed /ʌnəˈbæʃt/ *a* spudorato
unabated /ʌnəˈbeɪtɪd/ *a* (*enthusiasm*) inalterato; **continue** ~ (*gales:*) continuare con la stessa intensità
unable /ʌnˈeɪbl/ *a* **be** ~ **to do sth** non potere fare qcsa; (*not know how*) non sapere fare qcsa
unabridged /ʌnəˈbrɪdʒd/ *a* integrale
unacceptable /ʌnəkˈseptəbl/ *a* (*proposal, suggestion*) inaccettabile
unaccompanied /ʌnəˈkʌmpnɪd/ *a* non accompagnato; (*luggage*) incustodito

unaccountable /ʌnəˈkaʊntəbl/ *a* inspiegabile
unaccountably /ʌnəˈkaʊntəblɪ/ *adv* inspiegabilmente
unaccounted /ʌnəˈkaʊntɪd/ *a* **be** ~ **for** (*not explained*) non avere spiegazione; (*not found*) mancare
unaccustomed /ʌnəˈkʌstəmd/ *a* insolito; **be** ~ **to** non essere abituato a
unadorned /ʌnəˈdɔːnd/ *a* (*walls*) disadorno
unadulterated /ʌnəˈdʌltəreɪtɪd/ *a* (*water*) puro; (*wine*) non sofisticato; *fig* assoluto
unadventurous /ʌnədˈventʃ(ə)rəs/ *a* (*person, production*) poco avventuroso; (*meal*) poco fantasioso
unaided /ʌnˈeɪdɪd/ *a* senza aiuto
unalloyed /ʌnəˈlɔɪd/ *a fig* puro
unanimity /juːnəˈnɪmətɪ/ *n* unanimità *f*
unanimous /juːˈnænɪməs/ *a* unanime
unanimously /juːˈnænɪməslɪ/ *adv* all'unanimità
unannounced /ʌnəˈnaʊnst/ *a* inaspettato
unanswerable /ʌnˈɑːns(ə)rəbl/ *a* (*remark, case*) irrefutabile; (*question*) senza risposta
unappealing /ʌnəˈpiːlɪŋ/ *a* poco attraente
unappetizing /ʌnˈæpetaɪzɪŋ/ *a* poco appetitoso
unappreciated /ʌnəˈpriːʃɪeɪtɪd/ *a* (*work of art*) incompreso
unappreciative /ʌnəˈpriːʃ(ɪ)ətɪv/ *a* (*audience*) indifferente; (*person*) ingrato
unapproachable /ʌnəˈprəʊtʃəbl/ *a* (*person*) inavvicinabile
unarmed /ʌnˈɑːmd/ *a* disarmato
unarmed combat *n* lotta *f* senza armi
unashamedly /ʌnəˈʃeɪmd/ *adv* sfacciatamente
unasked /ʌnˈɑːskt/ *adv* **he came** ~ è venuto senza che nessuno glielo chiedesse
unassuming /ʌnəˈsjuːmɪŋ/ *a* senza pretese
unattached /ʌnəˈtætʃd/ *a* staccato; (*person*) senza legami
unattainable /ʌnəˈteɪnəbl/ *a* irraggiungibile
unattended /ʌnəˈtendɪd/ *a* incustodito
unattractive /ʌnəˈtræktɪv/ *a* (*person*) poco attraente; (*proposition*) poco allettante; (*characteristic*) sgradevole; (*building, furniture*) brutto
unauthorized /ʌnˈɔːθəraɪzd/ *a* non autorizzato
unavailable /ʌnəˈveɪləbl/ *a* non disponibile
unavoidable /ʌnəˈvɔɪdəbl/ *a* inevitabile
unavoidably /ʌnəˈvɔɪdəblɪ/ *adv* inevitabil-

mente; **I was ~ detained** sono stato trattenuto da cause di forza maggiore

unaware /ʌnə'weə/ a **be ~ of sth** non rendersi conto di qcsa

unawares /ʌnə'weəz/ adv **catch sb ~** prendere qcno alla sprovvista

unbalanced /ʌn'bælənst/ a non equilibrato; (mentally) squilibrato

unbearable /ʌn'beərəbl/ a insopportabile

unbearably /ʌn'beərəblɪ/ adv insopportabilmente

unbeatable /ʌn'biːtəbl/ a imbattibile

unbeaten /ʌn'biːtən/ a imbattuto

unbecoming /ʌnbɪ'kʌmɪŋ/ a (garment) che non dona

unbeknown /ʌnbɪ'nəʊn/ a fam **~ to me** a mia insaputa

unbelievable /ʌnbɪ'liːvəbl/ a incredibile

unbend /ʌn'bend/ vi (pt/pp **-bent**) (relax) distendersi

unbiased /ʌn'baɪəst/ a obiettivo

unblock /ʌn'blɒk/ vt sbloccare

unbolt /ʌn'bəʊlt/ vt togliere il chiavistello di

unborn /ʌn'bɔːn/ a non ancora nato

unbreakable /ʌn'breɪkəbl/ a infrangibile

unbridled /ʌn'braɪdld/ a sfrenato

unbuckle /ʌn'bʌkl/ vt slacciare (belt)

unburden /ʌn'bɜːdən/ vt **~ oneself** fig sfogarsi (**to** con)

unbutton /ʌn'bʌtən/ vt sbottonare

uncalled-for /ʌn'kɔːldfɔː(r)/ a fuori luogo

uncannily /ʌn'kænɪlɪ/ adv incredibilmente

uncanny /ʌn'kænɪ/ a sorprendente; (silence, feeling) inquietante

uncared-for /ʌn'keədfɔː(r)/ a (house, pet) trascurato

uncaring /ʌn'keərɪŋ/ a (world) indifferente

unceasing /ʌn'siːsɪŋ/ a incessante

uncensored /ʌn'sensəd/ a (film, book) non censurato

unceremonious /ʌnserɪ'məʊnɪəs/ a (abrupt) brusco

unceremoniously /ʌnserɪ'məʊnɪəslɪ/ adv senza tante cerimonie

uncertain /ʌn'sɜːtən/ a incerto; (weather) instabile; **in no ~ terms** senza mezzi termini

uncertainty /ʌn'sɜːtəntɪ/ n incertezza f

unchallenged /ʌn'tʃælɪndʒd/ a (statement, decision) incontestato; **I can't let that go ~** non posso non contestarlo

unchanged /ʌn'tʃeɪndʒd/ a invariato

uncharacteristic /ʌnkærəktə'rɪstɪk/ a (generosity) insolito

uncharitable /ʌn'tʃærɪtəbl/ a duro

uncivilized /ʌn'sɪvɪlaɪzd/ a (people, nation) non civilizzato; (treatment, conditions) incivile

unclassified /ʌn'klæsɪfaɪd/ a (document, information) non riservato; (road) non classificato

uncle /'ʌŋkl/ n zio m

unclear /ʌn'klɪːr/ a (instructions, reason, voice, writing) non chiaro; (future) incerto;

be ~ about sth (person:) non aver ben chiaro qcsa

unclog /ʌn'klɒg/ vt sturare (pipe)

uncoil /ʌn'kɔɪl/ vt srotolare

uncomfortable /ʌn'kʌmftəbl/ a scomodo; imbarazzante (silence, situation): **feel ~** fig sentirsi a disagio

uncomfortably /ʌn'kʌmftəblɪ/ adv (sit) scomodamente; (causing alarm etc) spaventosamente

uncommon /ʌn'kɒmən/ a insolito

uncommunicative /ʌnkə'mjuːnɪkətɪv/ a poco comunicativo

uncompromising /ʌn'kɒmprəmaɪzɪŋ/ a intransigente

unconditional /ʌnkən'dɪʃənl/ a incondizionato

unconditionally /ʌnkən'dɪʃnəlɪ/ adv incondizionatamente

unconscious /ʌn'kɒnʃəs/ a privo di sensi; (unaware) inconsapevole; **be ~ of sth** non rendersi conto di qcsa

unconsciously /ʌn'kɒnʃəslɪ/ adv inconsapevolmente

uncontested /ʌnkən'testɪd/ a (Pol: seat) non disputato

uncontrollable /ʌnkən'trəʊləbl/ a incontrollabile; (sobbing) irrefrenabile

uncontrollably /ʌnkən'trəʊləblɪ/ adv (increase) incontrollatamente; (laugh, sob) senza potersi controllare

unconventional /ʌnkən'venʃnəl/ a poco convenzionale

unconvincing /ʌnkən'vɪnsɪŋ/ a poco convincente

uncooked /ʌn'kʊkt/ a crudo

uncooperative /ʌnkəʊ'ɒpr(ə)tɪv/ a poco cooperativo

uncork /ʌn'kɔːk/ vt sturare

uncorroborated /ʌnkə'rɒbəreɪtɪd/ a non convalidato

uncouth /ʌn'kuːθ/ a zotico

uncover /ʌn'kʌvə(r)/ vt scoprire; portare alla luce (buried object)

uncross /ʌn'krɒs/ vt disincrociare (legs, arms)

unctuous /'ʌŋktjʊəs/ a untuoso

uncultivated /ʌn'kʌltɪveɪtɪd/ a incolto

undamaged /ʌn'dæmɪdʒd/ a intatto

undaunted /ʌn'dɔːntɪd/ a imperterrito; **~ by sth** per nulla intimidito da qcsa

undecided /ʌndɪ'saɪdɪd/ a indeciso; (not settled) incerto

undefined /ʌndɪ'faɪnd/ a (objective, nature) indeterminato

undelivered /ʌndɪ'lɪvəd/ a (mail) non recapitato

undeniable /ʌndɪ'naɪəbl/ a innegabile

undeniably /ʌndɪ'naɪəblɪ/ adv innegabilmente

under /'ʌndə(r)/ prep sotto; (less than) al di sotto di; **~ there** lì sotto; **~ repair/ construction** in riparazione/costruzione; **~ way** fig in corso; ● adv (~ water) sott'acqua; (unconscious) sotto anestesia

underachieve /ˌʌndərəˈtʃiːv/ *vi Sch* restare al di sotto delle proprie possibilità

underarm /ˈʌndərɑːm/ *a* ⟨*deodorant*⟩ per le ascelle; ⟨*hair*⟩ sotto le ascelle; ⟨*service, throw*⟩ dal basso verso l'alto

undercarriage /ˈʌndəkærɪdʒ/ *n Aeron* carrello *m*

undercharge /ʌndəˈtʃɑːdʒ/ *vt* far pagare meno del dovuto a

underclothes /ˈʌndəkləʊðz/ *npl* biancheria *fsg* intima

undercoat /ˈʌndəkəʊt/ *n* prima mano *f*

undercook /ʌndəˈkʊk/ *vt* non cuocere abbastanza

undercover /ʌndəˈkʌvə(r)/ *a* clandestino

undercurrent /ˈʌndəkʌrənt/ *n* corrente *f* sottomarina; *fig* sottofondo *m*

undercut /ʌndəˈkʌt/ *vt* (*pt/pp* -**cut**) *Comm* vendere a minor prezzo di

underdeveloped /ˌʌndərɪˈveləpt/ *a* ⟨*country*⟩ sottosviluppato; *Phot* non completamente sviluppato

underdog /ˈʌndədɒg/ *n* perdente *m*

underdone /ʌndəˈdʌn/ *a* ⟨*meat*⟩ al sangue

underemployed /ˌʌndərɪmˈplɔɪd/ *a* ⟨*person*⟩ sottoccupato; ⟨*resources, equipment etc*⟩ non sfruttato completamente

underequipped /ˌʌndərɪˈkwɪpt/ *a* ⟨*army, person*⟩ insufficientemente equipaggiato; ⟨*schools, gym*⟩ insufficientemente attrezzato

underestimate /ʌndərˈestɪmeɪt/ *vt* sottovalutare

underexpose /ˌʌndərɪksˈpəʊz/ *vt Phot* sottoesporre

underfed /ʌndəˈfed/ *a* denutrito

underfloor /ˈʌndəflɔː(r)/ *a* ⟨*pipes, wiring*⟩ sotto il pavimento

underfoot /ʌndəˈfʊt/ *adv* sotto i piedi; **trample ~** calpestare

underfunded /ʌndəˈfʌndɪd/ *a* insufficientemente finanziato

underfunding /ʌndəˈfʌndɪŋ/ *n* finanziamento *m* insufficiente

undergo /ʌndəˈgəʊ/ *vt* (*pt* -**went**, *pp* -**gone**) subire ⟨*operation, treatment*⟩; **~ repair** essere in riparazione

undergraduate /ʌndəˈgrædʒʊət/ *n* studente, -tessa *mf* universitario, -a

underground¹ /ʌndəˈgraʊnd/ *adv* sottoterra

underground² /ˈʌndəgraʊnd/ *a* sotterraneo; ⟨*secret*⟩ clandestino ● *n* ⟨*railway*⟩ metropolitana *f*

underground car park *n* parcheggio *m* sotterraneo

undergrowth /ˈʌndəgrəʊθ/ *n* sottobosco *m*

underhand /ˈʌndəhænd/ *a* subdolo

underlay /ˈʌndəleɪ/ *n* strato *m* di gomma o feltro posto sotto la moquette

underlie /ʌndəˈlaɪ/ *vt* (*pt* -**lay**, *pp* -**lain**, *pres p* -**lying**) *fig* essere alla base di

underline /ʌndəˈlaɪn/ *vt* sottolineare

underling /ˈʌndəlɪŋ/ *n pej* subalterno, -a *mf*

underlying /ʌndəˈlaɪɪŋ/ *a fig* fondamentale

undermanned /ʌndəˈmænd/ *a* ⟨*factory*⟩ a corto di mano d'opera

undermentioned /ʌndəˈmenʃnd/ *a* sottoindicato

undermine /ʌndəˈmaɪn/ *vt fig* minare

underneath /ʌndəˈniːθ/ *prep* sotto; **~ it** sotto ● *adv* sotto

undernourished /ʌndəˈnʌrɪʃt/ *a* denutrito

underpaid /ʌndəˈpeɪd/ *a* mal pagato

underpants /ˈʌndəpænts/ *npl* mutande *fpl*

underpass /ˈʌndəpɑːs/ *n* sottopassaggio *m*

underpay /ʌndəˈpeɪ/ *vt* sottopagare ⟨*employee*⟩

underpin /ʌndəˈpɪn/ *vt* puntellare ⟨*wall*⟩; rafforzare ⟨*currency, power, theory*⟩; essere alla base di ⟨*religion, society*⟩

underpopulated /ʌndəˈpɒpjʊleɪtɪd/ *a* sottopopolato

underprivileged /ʌndəˈprɪvɪlɪdʒd/ *a* non abbiente

underrate /ʌndəˈreɪt/ *vt* sottovalutare

underseal /ˈʌndəsiːl/ *n Auto* antiruggine *m inv*

under-secretary /ʌndəˈsekrət(ə)rɪ/ *n Br Pol* sottosegretario *m*

undersell /ʌndəˈsel/ *vt* vendere a prezzo inferiore rispetto a ⟨*competitor*⟩; pubblicizzare poco ⟨*product*⟩

undersexed /ʌndəˈsekst/ *a* con scarsa libido

undershirt /ˈʌndəʃɜːt/ *n Am* maglia *f* della pelle

undersigned /ʌndəˈsaɪnd/ *a* sottoscritto

undersized /ʌndəˈsaɪzd/ *a* ⟨*portion*⟩ scarso; ⟨*animal*⟩ troppo piccolo; ⟨*person*⟩ di statura inferiore alla media

understaffed /ʌndəˈstɑːft/ *a* a corto di personale

understand /ʌndəˈstænd/ *vt* (*pt/pp* -**stood**) capire; **I ~ that...** (*have heard*) mi risulta che... ● *vi* capire

understandable /ʌndəˈstændəbl/ *a* comprensibile

understandably /ʌndəˈstændəblɪ/ *adv* comprensibilmente

understanding /ʌndəˈstændɪŋ/ *a* comprensivo ● *n* comprensione *f*; (*agreement*) accordo *m*; **reach an ~** trovare un accordo; **on the ~ that** a condizione che

understatement /ˈʌndəsteɪtmənt/ *n* **that's an ~** non è dire abbastanza

understudy /ˈʌndəstʌdɪ/ *n Theat* sostituto, -a *mf*

undertake /ʌndəˈteɪk/ *vt* (*pt* -**took**, *pp* -**taken**) intraprendere; **~ to do sth** impegnarsi a fare qcsa

undertaker /ˈʌndəteɪkə(r)/ *n* impresario *m* di pompe funebri; [**firm of**] **~s** *n* impresa *f* di pompe funebri

undertaking /ʌndəˈteɪkɪŋ/ *n* impresa *f*; (*promise*) promessa *f*

under-the-counter *a* ⟨*goods, supply, trade*⟩ comprato/venduto sottobanco

undertone /ˈʌndətəʊn/ *n fig* sottofondo *m*; **in an ~** sottovoce

undervalue /ʌndə'vælju:/ vt sottovalutare; **the shares are ~d** le azioni si sono svalutate

underwater¹ /'ʌndə'wɔ:tə(r)/ a subacqueo

underwater² /ʌndə'wɔ:tə(r)/ adv sott'acqua

under way a **be ~** ~ ⟨vehicle:⟩ essere in corsa; ⟨filming, talks:⟩ essere in corso; **get ~ ~** ⟨vehicle:⟩ mettersi in viaggio; ⟨preparations, season:⟩ avere inizio

underwear /'ʌndəweə(r)/ n biancheria f intima

underweight /ʌndə'weɪt/ a sotto peso

underworld /'ʌndəwɜ:ld/ n ⟨criminals⟩ malavita f

underwriter /'ʌndəraɪtə(r)/ n assicuratore m

undeserved /ʌndɪ'zɜ:vd/ a ⟨praise, reward, win⟩ immeritato; ⟨blame, punish⟩ ingiusto

undeservedly /ʌndɪ'zɜ:vɪdlɪ/ adv ⟨praise, reward, win⟩ immeritatamente; ⟨blame, punish⟩ ingiustamente

undesirable /ʌndɪ'zaɪərəbl/ a indesiderato; ⟨person⟩ poco raccomandabile

undetected /ʌndɪ'tektɪd/ a ⟨crime, cancer⟩ non scoperto; ⟨flaw, movement, intruder⟩ non visto; **go ~** ⟨cancer, crime:⟩ non essere scoperto; ⟨person:⟩ passare inosservato ● adv ⟨break in, listen⟩ senza essere scoperto

undeveloped /ʌndɪ'veləpt/ a non sviluppato; ⟨land⟩ non sfruttato

undies /'ʌndɪz/ npl fam biancheria f intima (da donna)

undignified /ʌn'dɪgnɪfaɪd/ a poco dignitoso

undisciplined /ʌn'dɪsɪplɪnd/ a indisciplinato

undiscovered /ʌndɪs'kʌvəd/ a ⟨secret⟩ non svelato; ⟨crime, document⟩ non scoperto; ⟨land⟩ inesplorato; ⟨species⟩ sconosciuto; ⟨talent⟩ non ancora scoperto

undiscriminating /ʌndɪs'krɪmɪneɪtɪŋ/ a che non sa fare distinzioni

undisputed /ʌndɪ'spju:tɪd/ a indiscusso

undisturbed /ʌndɪ'stɜ:bd/ a ⟨sleep, night⟩ indisturbato

undivided /ʌndɪ'vaɪdɪd/ a ⟨loyalty, attention⟩ assoluto

undo /ʌn'du:/ vt (pt -did, pp -done) disfare; slacciare ⟨dress, shoes⟩; sbottonare ⟨shirt⟩; fig, Comput annullare

undone /ʌn'dʌn/ a ⟨shirt, button⟩ sbottonato; ⟨shoes, dress⟩ slacciato; ⟨not accomplished⟩ non fatto; **leave ~** ⟨job⟩ tralasciare

undoubted /ʌn'daʊtɪd/ a indubbio

undoubtedly /ʌn'daʊtɪdlɪ/ adv senza dubbio

undress /ʌn'dres/ vt spogliare; **get ~ed** spogliarsi ● vi spogliarsi

undrinkable /ʌn'drɪŋkəbl/ a ⟨unpleasant⟩ imbevibile; ⟨dangerous⟩ non potabile

undue /ʌn'dju:/ a eccessivo

undulating /'ʌndjʊleɪtɪŋ/ a ondulato; ⟨country⟩ collinoso

unduly /ʌn'dju:lɪ/ adv eccessivamente

undying /ʌn'daɪɪŋ/ a eterno

unearned /ʌn'ɜ:nd/ a immeritato; **~ income** rendita f

unearth /ʌn'ɜ:θ/ vt dissotterrare; fig scovare; scoprire ⟨secret⟩

unearthly /ʌn'ɜ:θlɪ/ a soprannaturale; **at an ~ hour** fam a un'ora impossibile

unease /ʌn'i:z/ n disagio m

uneasy /ʌn'i:zɪ/ a a disagio; ⟨person⟩ inquieto; ⟨feeling⟩ inquietante; ⟨truce⟩ precario

uneatable /ʌn'i:təbl/ a immangiabile

uneconomic /ʌni:kə'nɒmɪk/ a poco remunerativo

uneconomical /ʌni:kə'nɒmɪkl/ a poco economico

uneducated /ʌn'edjʊkeɪtɪd/ a ⟨person⟩ non istruito; ⟨tastes⟩ non raffinato; ⟨accent, speech⟩ da persona non istruita

unemployed /ʌnem'plɔɪd/ a disoccupato ● npl **the ~** i disoccupati

unemployment /ʌnem'plɔɪmənt/ n disoccupazione f

unemployment benefit n sussidio m di disoccupazione

unending /ʌn'endɪŋ/ a senza fine

unenthusiastic /ʌnɪmθju:zɪ'æstɪk/ a poco entusiasta

unequal /ʌn'i:kwəl/ a disuguale; ⟨struggle⟩ impari; **be ~ to a task** non essere all'altezza di un compito

unequalled /ʌn'i:kwəld/ a ⟨achievement, quality, record⟩ ineguagliato

unequally /ʌn'i:kwəlɪ/ adv in modo disuguale

unequivocal /ʌnɪ'kwɪvəkl/ a inequivocabile; ⟨person⟩ esplicito

unequivocally /ʌnɪ'kwɪvəklɪ/ adv inequivocabilmente

unerring /ʌn'ɜ:rɪŋ/ a infallibile

unethical /ʌn'eθɪkl/ a immorale

uneven /ʌn'i:vən/ a irregolare; ⟨distribution⟩ ineguale; ⟨number⟩ dispari

unevenly /ʌn'i:vənlɪ/ adv irregolarmente; ⟨distributed⟩ inegualmente

uneventful /ʌnɪ'ventfʊl/ a senza avvenimenti di rilievo

unexciting /ʌnɪk'saɪtɪŋ/ a poco entusiasmante

unexpected /ʌnɪk'spektɪd/ a inaspettato

unexpectedly /ʌnɪk'spektɪdlɪ/ adv inaspettatamente

unexplored /ʌnɪk'splɔ:d/ a inesplorato

unfailing /ʌn'feɪlɪŋ/ a infallibile

unfair /ʌn'feə/ a ingiusto

unfair dismissal n licenziamento m ingiustificato

unfairly /ʌn'feəlɪ/ adv ingiustamente

unfairness /ʌn'feənɪs/ n ingiustizia f

unfaithful /ʌn'feɪθfʊl/ a infedele

unfamiliar /ʌnfə'mɪljə(r)/ a sconosciuto; **be ~ with** non conoscere

unfashionable /ʌn'fæʃnəbl/ a fuori moda

unfasten /ʌn'fɑ:sn/ vt slacciare; ⟨detach⟩ staccare

unfathomable /ʌnˈfæð(ə)məbl/ *a* imperscrutabile

unfavourable /ʌnˈfeɪv(ə)rəbl/ *a* sfavorevole; ⟨*impression*⟩ negativo

unfeeling /ʌnˈfiːlɪŋ/ *a* insensibile

unfinished /ʌnˈfɪnɪʃt/ *a* da finire; ⟨*business*⟩ in sospeso

unfit /ʌnˈfɪt/ *a* inadatto; (*morally*) indegno; *Sport* fuori forma; **~ for work** non in grado di lavorare; **~ for human consumption** non commestibile

unflappable /ʌnˈflæpəbl/ *a fam* calmo

unflattering /ʌnˈflæt(ə)rɪŋ/ *a* ⟨*clothes, hairstyle*⟩ che non dona; ⟨*portrait, description*⟩ poco lusinghiero

unflinching /ʌnˈflɪntʃɪŋ/ *a* risoluto

unfold /ʌnˈfəʊld/ *vt* spiegare; (*spread out*) aprire; *fig* rivelare ● *vi* ⟨*view:*⟩ spiegarsi

unforeseeable /ʌnfɔːˈsiːəbl/ *a* imprevedibile

unforeseen /ʌnfɔːˈsiːn/ *a* imprevisto

unforgettable /ʌnfəˈgetəbl/ *a* indimenticabile

unforgivable /ʌnfəˈgɪvəbl/ *a* imperdonabile

unforgiving /ʌnfəˈgɪvɪŋ/ *a* che non perdona

unfortunate /ʌnˈfɔːtʃənət/ *a* sfortunato; (*regrettable*) spiacevole; ⟨*remark, choice*⟩ infelice

unfortunately /ʌnˈfɔːtʃənətlɪ/ *adv* purtroppo

unfounded /ʌnˈfaʊndɪd/ *a* infondato

unfriendly /ʌnˈfrendlɪ/ *a* ⟨*person, remark*⟩ scortese, poco amichevole; ⟨*place, climate, reception*⟩ ostile; ⟨*software*⟩ difficile da usare

unfulfilled /ʌnfʊlˈfɪld/ *a* ⟨*prophecy*⟩ non avverato; ⟨*promise*⟩ non mantenuto; ⟨*ambition*⟩ non realizzato; ⟨*desire, need*⟩ non soddisfatto; ⟨*condition*⟩ non rispettato; **feel ~** essere insoddisfatto

unfurl /ʌnˈfɜːl/ *vt* spiegare ● *vi* spiegarsi

unfurnished /ʌnˈfɜːnɪʃt/ *a* non ammobiliato

ungainly /ʌnˈgeɪnlɪ/ *a* sgraziato

ungentlemanly /ʌnˈdʒentlmənlɪ/ *a* non da gentiluomo

ungodly /ʌnˈgɒdlɪ/ *a* empio; **~ hour** *fam* ora *f* impossibile

ungracious /ʌnˈgreɪʃəs/ *a* sgarbato

ungrateful /ʌnˈgreɪtfʊl/ *a* ingrato

ungratefully /ʌnˈgreɪtfʊlɪ/ *adv* senza riconoscenza

unhappily /ʌnˈhæpɪlɪ/ *adv* infelicemente; (*unfortunately*) purtroppo

unhappiness /ʌnˈhæpɪnɪs/ *n* infelicità *f*

unhappy /ʌnˈhæpɪ/ *a* infelice; (*not content*) insoddisfatto (**with** di)

unharmed /ʌnˈhɑːmd/ *a* incolume

unhealthy /ʌnˈhelθɪ/ *a* poco sano; (*insanitary*) malsano

unheard-of /ʌnˈhɜːdɒv/ *a* ⟨*actor, brand*⟩ mai sentito; ⟨*levels, price*⟩ incredibile

unheated /ʌnˈhiːtɪd/ *a* senza riscaldamento

unheeded /ʌnˈhiːdɪd/ *a* ignorato; **go ~** ⟨*warning, plea:*⟩ venir ignorato

unhelpful /ʌnˈhelpfʊl/ *a* ⟨*person, attitude*⟩

poco disponibile; ⟨*witness*⟩ che non collabora; ⟨*remark*⟩ di poco aiuto

unholy /ʌnˈhəʊlɪ/ *a* ⟨*alliance, pact*⟩ paradossale; ⟨*fam: mess, hour*⟩ indecente

unhook /ʌnˈhʊk/ *vt* sganciare; staccare ⟨*picture*⟩

unhurt /ʌnˈhɜːt/ *a* illeso

unhygienic /ʌnhaɪˈdʒiːnɪk/ *a* non igienico

unicorn /ˈjuːnɪkɔːn/ *n* unicorno *m*

unidentified /ʌnaɪˈdentɪfaɪd/ *a* non identificato

unification /juːnɪfɪˈkeɪʃn/ *n* unificazione *f*

uniform /ˈjuːnɪfɔːm/ *a* uniforme ● *n* uniforme *f*

uniformly /ˈjuːnɪfɔːmlɪ/ *adv* uniformemente

unify /ˈjuːnɪfaɪ/ *vt* (*pt/pp* **-ied**) unificare

unilateral /juːnɪˈlæt(ə)rəl/ *a* unilaterale

unilaterally /juːnɪˈlæt(ə)rəlɪ/ *adv* unilateralmente

unimaginable /ʌnɪˈmædʒɪnəbl/ *a* inimmaginabile

unimaginative /ʌnɪˈmædʒɪnətɪv/ *a* privo di fantasia

unimportant /ʌnɪmˈpɔːtənt/ *a* irrilevante

uninformed /ʌnɪnˈfɔːmd/ *a* ⟨*person*⟩ disinformato

uninhabited /ʌnɪnˈhæbɪtɪd/ *a* disabitato

uninhibited /ʌnɪnˈhɪbɪtɪd/ *a* ⟨*person, attitude*⟩ disinibito; ⟨*performance, remarks*⟩ disinvolto; **be ~ about doing sth** non avere problemi a fare qcsa

uninitiated /ʌnɪˈnɪʃɪeɪtɪd/ *a* ⟨*person*⟩ non iniziato ● *npl* **the ~** i profani

uninspired /ʌnɪnˈspaɪəd/ *a* privo di immaginazione; ⟨*performance*⟩ piatto; ⟨*times*⟩ banale

unintentional /ʌnɪnˈtenʃənl/ *a* involontario

unintentionally /ʌnɪnˈtenʃənəlɪ/ *adv* involontariamente

uninvited /ʌnɪnˈvaɪtɪd/ *a* ⟨*attentions*⟩ non richiesto; **~ guest** ospite *mf* senza invito

union /ˈjuːnɪən/ *n* unione *f*; (*trade ~*) sindacato *m*

Union Jack *n* bandiera *f* del Regno Unito

unique /juːˈniːk/ *a* unico

uniquely /juːˈniːklɪ/ *adv* unicamente

unisex /ˈjuːnɪseks/ *a* unisex *inv*

unison /ˈjuːnɪsn/ *n* **in ~** all'unisono

unit /ˈjuːnɪt/ *n* unità *f inv*; (*department*) reparto *m*; (*of furniture*) elemento *m*

unit cost *n* costo *m* unitario

unite /juːˈnaɪt/ *vt* unire ● *vi* unirsi

united /juːˈnaɪtɪd/ *a* unito

united: United Kingdom *n* Regno *m* Unito. **United Nations** *n* [Organizzazione *f* delle] Nazioni Unite *fpl*. **United States [of America]** *n* Stati *mpl* Uniti [d'America]

unit trust *n* *Fin* fondo *m* comune di investimento aperto

unity /ˈjuːnətɪ/ *n* unità *f*; (*agreement*) accordo *m*

universal /juːnɪˈvɜːsl/ *a* universale

universally /juːnɪˈvɜːsəlɪ/ *adv* universalmente

universe /ˈjuːnɪvɜːs/ *n* universo *m*

university /juːnɪˈvɜːsətɪ/ *n* università *f inv* ● *attrib* universitario

unjust /ʌnˈdʒʌst/ *a* ingiusto

unjustifiable /ʌnˈdʒʌstɪfaɪəbl/ *a* ingiustificato

unjustifiably /ʌnˈdʒʌstɪfaɪəblɪ/ *adv* ⟨*act*⟩ senza giustificazione

unjustified /ʌnˈdʒʌstɪfaɪd/ *a* ⟨*suspicion*⟩ ingiustificato

unjustly /ʌnˈdʒʌstlɪ/ *adv* ingiustamente

unkempt /ʌnˈkempt/ *a* trasandato; ⟨*hair*⟩ arruffato

unkind /ʌnˈkaɪnd/ *a* scortese

unkindly /ʌnˈkaɪndlɪ/ *adv* in modo scortese

unkindness /ʌnˈkaɪndnɪs/ *n* mancanza *f* di gentilezza

unknown /ʌnˈnəʊn/ *a* sconosciuto

unlawful /ʌnˈlɔːfʊl/ *a* illecito, illegale

unlawfully /ʌnˈlɔːfʊlɪ/ *adv* illegalmente

unleaded /ʌnˈledɪd/ *a* senza piombo

unleash /ʌnˈliːʃ/ *vt fig* scatenare

unless /ənˈles/ *conj* a meno che; **~ I am mistaken** se non mi sbaglio

unlicensed /ʌnˈlaɪsnst/ *a* ⟨*transmitter, activity*⟩ abusivo; ⟨*vehicle*⟩ senza bollo; ⟨*restaurant*⟩ non autorizzato a vendere alcolici

unlike /ʌnˈlaɪk/ *a* (*not the same*) diversi ● *prep* diverso da; **that's ~ him** non è da lui; **~ me, he...** diversamente da me, lui...

unlikely /ʌnˈlaɪklɪ/ *a* improbabile

unlimited /ʌnˈlɪmɪtɪd/ *a* illimitato

unlined /ʌnˈlaɪnd/ *a* ⟨*face*⟩ senza rughe; ⟨*paper*⟩ senza righe; ⟨*garment, curtain*⟩ senza fodera

unlit /ʌnˈlɪt/ *a* ⟨*cigarette, fire*⟩ spento; ⟨*room, street*⟩ non illuminato

unload /ʌnˈləʊd/ *vt* scaricare

unlock /ʌnˈlɒk/ *vt* aprire (*con chiave*)

unloved /ʌnˈlʌvd/ *a* **feel ~** ⟨*person:*⟩ non sentirsi amato

unlucky /ʌnˈlʌkɪ/ *a* sfortunato; **it's ~ to...** porta sfortuna...

unmade /ʌnˈmeɪd/ *a* ⟨*bed*⟩ sfatto

unmade-up *a* ⟨*road*⟩ non asfaltato

unmanageable /ʌnˈmænɪdʒəbl/ *a* ⟨*number, company*⟩ difficile da gestire; ⟨*hair, child, animal*⟩ ribelle; ⟨*size*⟩ ingombrante

unmanly /ʌnˈmænlɪ/ *a* poco virile

unmanned /ʌnˈmænd/ *a* senza equipaggio

unmarked /ʌnˈmɑːkt/ *a* *Sport* smarcato; ⟨*skin*⟩ senza segni; ⟨*container*⟩ non contrassegnato; **~ police car** [auto *f inv*] civetta *f*

unmarried /ʌnˈmærɪd/ *a* non sposato

unmarried mother *n* ragazza *f* madre

unmask /ʌnˈmɑːsk/ *vt fig* smascherare

unmentionable /ʌnˈmenʃnəbl/ *a* innominabile

unmistakable /ʌnmɪˈsteɪkəbl/ *a* inconfondibile

unmistakably /ʌnmɪˈsteɪkəblɪ/ *adv* chiaramente

unmitigated /ʌnˈmɪtɪgeɪtɪd/ *a* assoluto

unmoved /ʌnˈmuːvd/ *a fig* impassibile

unnamed /ʌnˈneɪmd/ *a* (*not having a name*) senza nome; (*name not divulged*) di cui non si conosce il nome; **the as yet ~ winner...** il vincitore di cui ancora non si conosce il nome...

unnatural /ʌnˈnætʃər(ə)l/ *a* innaturale; *pej* anormale

unnaturally /ʌnˈnætʃər(ə)lɪ/ *adv* in modo innaturale; *pej* in modo anormale

unnecessarily /ʌnˈnesəs(ə)rɪlɪ/ *adv* inutilmente

unnecessary /ʌnˈnesəs(ə)rɪ/ *a* inutile

unnerving /ʌnˈnɜːvɪŋ/ *a* inquietante

unnoticed /ʌnˈnəʊtɪst/ *a* inosservato

unobservant /ʌnəbˈzɜːvənt/ *a* senza spirito d'osservazione

unobserved /ʌnəbˈzɜːvd/ *a* inosservato; **go ~** passare inosservato

unobtainable /ʌnəbˈteɪnəbl/ *a* ⟨*product*⟩ introvabile; ⟨*phone number*⟩ non ottenibile

unobtrusive /ʌnəbˈtruːsɪf/ *a* discreto

unobtrusively /ʌnəbˈtruːsɪvlɪ/ *adv* in modo discreto

unoccupied /ʌnˈɒkjuːpaɪd/ *a* ⟨*house, block, shop*⟩ vuoto; ⟨*table, seat*⟩ libero

unofficial /ʌnəˈfɪʃl/ *a* non ufficiale

unofficially /ʌnəˈfɪʃ(ə)lɪ/ *adv* ufficiosamente

unopened /ʌnˈəʊpənd/ *a* ⟨*bottle, packet*⟩ chiuso; ⟨*package*⟩ ancora incartato

unorthodox /ʌnˈɔːθədɒks/ *a* poco ortodosso

unpack /ʌnˈpæk/ *vi* disfare le valigie ● *vt* svuotare ⟨*parcel*⟩; spacchettare ⟨*books*⟩; **~ one's case** disfare la valigia

unpaid /ʌnˈpeɪd/ *a* da pagare; (*work*) non retribuito

unpalatable /ʌnˈpælətəbl/ *a* sgradevole

unparalleled /ʌnˈpærəleld/ *a* senza pari

unpasteurized /ʌnˈpɑːstʃəraɪzd/ *a* non pastorizzato

unperturbed /ʌnpəˈtɜːbd/ *a* imperturbato

unpick /ʌnˈpɪk/ *vt* disfare

unplanned /ʌnˈplænd/ *a* ⟨*stoppage, increase*⟩ imprevisto

unpleasant /ʌnˈplezənt/ *a* sgradevole; ⟨*person*⟩ maleducato

unpleasantly /ʌnˈplezəntlɪ/ *adv* sgradevolmente; ⟨*behave*⟩ maleducatamente

unpleasantness /ʌnˈplezəntnɪs/ *n* (*bad feeling*) tensioni *fpl*

unplug /ʌnˈplʌg/ *vt* (*pt/pp* **-plugged**) staccare

unpolluted /ʌnpəˈluːtɪd/ *a* ⟨*water*⟩ non inquinato; ⟨*mind*⟩ incontaminato

unpopular /ʌnˈpɒpjʊlə(r)/ *a* impopolare

unprecedented /ʌnˈpresɪdentɪd/ *a* senza precedenti

unpredictable /ʌnprɪˈdɪktəbl/ *a* imprevedibile

unprejudiced /ʌnˈpredʒʊdɪst/ *a* ⟨*person*⟩ senza pregiudizi; ⟨*opinion, judgement*⟩ imparziale

unpremeditated /ʌnpriːˈmedɪteɪtɪd/ *a* involontario

unprepared /ʌnprɪ'peəd/ *a* impreparato

unprepossessing /ʌnpri:pə'zesɪŋ/ *a* poco attraente

unpretentious /ʌnprɪ'tenʃəs/ *a* senza pretese

unprincipled /ʌn'prɪnsɪpəld/ *a* senza principi; ⟨*behaviour*⟩ scorretto

unprofessional /ʌnprə'feʃnl/ *a* non professionale; **it's ~** è una mancanza di professionalità

unprofitable /ʌn'prɒfɪtəbl/ *a* non redditizio

unprompted /ʌn'prɒm(p)tɪd/ *a* ⟨*offer*⟩ spontaneo; ⟨*answer*⟩ non suggerito

unpronounceable /ʌnprə'naʊnsəbl/ *a* impronunciabile

unprovoked /ʌnprə'vəʊkt/ *a* ⟨*attack, aggression*⟩ non provocato; **the attack was ~** l'attacco è avvenuto senza provocazione

unqualified /ʌn'kwɒlɪfaɪd/ *a* non qualificato; (*fig: absolute*) assoluto

unquestionable /ʌn'kwestʃənəbl/ *a* incontestabile

unquote /ʌn'kwəʊt/ *vi* chiudere le virgolette

unravel /ʌn'rævl/ *vt* (*pt/pp* -**ravelled**) districare; (*in knitting*) disfare

unreal /ʌn'rɪəl/ *a* irreale; *fam* inverosimile

unrealistic /ʌnrɪə'lɪstɪk/ *a* ⟨*character, presentation*⟩ poco realistico; ⟨*expectation, aim*⟩ irrealistico; ⟨*person*⟩ poco realista

unreasonable /ʌn'ri:z(ə)nəbl/ *a* irragionevole

unrecognizable /ʌn'rekəgnaɪzəbl/ *a* irriconoscibile

unrecorded /ʌnrɪ'kɔ:dɪd/ *a* non documentato; **go ~** non essere documentato

unrefined /ʌnrɪ'faɪnd/ *a* ⟨*person, manners, style*⟩ rozzo; ⟨*oil*⟩ greggio; ⟨*flour, sugar*⟩ non raffinato

unrehearsed /ʌnrɪ'hɜ:st/ *a* ⟨*response, action*⟩ improvvisto; ⟨*speech*⟩ improvvisato

unrelated /ʌnrɪ'leɪtɪd/ *a* ⟨*facts*⟩ senza rapporto (**to** con); ⟨*person*⟩ non imparentato (**to** con)

unrelenting /ʌnrɪ'lentɪŋ/ *a* ⟨*person*⟩ ostinato; ⟨*stare*⟩ insistente; ⟨*pursuit*⟩ continuo; ⟨*heat, zeal*⟩ costante

unreliable /ʌnrɪ'laɪəbl/ *a* inattendibile; ⟨*person*⟩ inaffidabile, che non dà affidamento

unremitting /ʌnrɪ'mɪtɪŋ/ *a* costante; ⟨*struggle*⟩ continuo

unrepeatable /ʌnrɪ'pi:təbl/ *a* ⟨*offer, bargain*⟩ unico; **his comment was ~** il commento che ha fatto è irripetibile

unrepentant /ʌnrɪ'pentənt/ *a* irriducibile; ⟨*sinner*⟩ impenitente

unrequited /ʌnrɪ'kwaɪtɪd/ *a* non corrisposto

unreservedly /ʌnrɪ'zɜ:vɪdlɪ/ *adv* senza riserve; (*frankly*) francamente

unresolved /ʌnrɪ'zɒlvd/ *a* irrisolto

unrest /ʌn'rest/ *n* fermenti *mpl*

unripe /ʌn'raɪp/ *a* ⟨*fruit*⟩ acerbo; ⟨*wheat*⟩ non maturo

unrivalled /ʌn'raɪvəld/ *a* ineguagliato

unroll /ʌn'rəʊl/ *vt* srotolare ● *vi* srotolarsi

unruffled /ʌn'rʌfld/ *a* ⟨*person*⟩ imperturbato; ⟨*hair*⟩ a posto; ⟨*water*⟩ non mosso; **be ~** ⟨*person:*⟩ rimanere imperturbato; ⟨*person, hair:*⟩ essere a posto

unruly /ʌn'ru:lɪ/ *a* indisciplinato

unsafe /ʌn'seɪf/ *a* pericoloso

unsaid /ʌn'sed/ *a* inespresso

unsalaried /ʌn'sælərɪd/ *a* ⟨*post*⟩ non stipendiato

unsalted /ʌn'sɔ:ltɪd/ *a* non salato

unsatisfactory /ʌnsætɪs'fækt(ə)rɪ/ *a* poco soddisfacente

unsavoury /ʌn'seɪvərɪ/ *a* equivoco

unscathed /ʌn'skeɪðd/ *a* illeso

unscheduled /ʌn'ʃedju:ld/ *a* ⟨*flight*⟩ supplementare; ⟨*appearance, speech*⟩ fuori programma; ⟨*stop*⟩ non programmato

unscramble /ʌn'skræmbl/ *vt* decifrare ⟨*code, words*⟩; sbrogliare ⟨*ideas, thoughts*⟩

unscrew /ʌn'skru:/ *vt* svitare

unscrupulous /ʌn'skru:pjʊləs/ *a* senza scrupoli

unseasoned /ʌn'si:znd/ *a* ⟨*wood*⟩ non stagionato; ⟨*food*⟩ scondito

unseemly /ʌn'si:mlɪ/ *a* indecoroso

unselfish /ʌn'selfɪʃ/ *a* disinteressato

unsettled /ʌn'setld/ *a* in agitazione; ⟨*weather*⟩ variabile; ⟨*bill*⟩ non saldato

unshakeable /ʌn'ʃeɪkəbl/ *a* categorico

unshaven /ʌn'ʃeɪvn/ *a* non rasato

unsightly /ʌn'saɪtlɪ/ *a* brutto

unsinkable /ʌn'sɪŋkəbl/ *a* ⟨*ship, object*⟩ inaffondabile; ⟨*hum: personality*⟩ che non si deprime

unskilled /ʌn'skɪld/ *a* non specializzato

unskilled worker *n* manovale *m*

unsmiling /ʌn'smaɪlɪŋ/ *a* ⟨*person*⟩ serioso

unsociable /ʌn'səʊʃəbl/ *a* scontroso

unsolicited /ʌnsə'lɪsɪtɪd/ *a* ⟨*help, advice*⟩ non richiesto; ⟨*job application*⟩ spontaneo

unsophisticated /ʌnsə'fɪstɪkeɪtɪd/ *a* semplice

unsound /ʌn'saʊnd/ *a* ⟨*building, reasoning*⟩ poco solido; ⟨*advice*⟩ poco sensato; **of ~ mind** malato di mente

unspeakable /ʌn'spi:kəbl/ *a* indicibile

unspoiled /ʌn'spɔɪld/ *a* ⟨*town*⟩ non deturpato; ⟨*landscape*⟩ intatto; **she was ~ by fame** la fama non l'ha cambiata

unstable /ʌn'steɪbl/ *a* instabile; (*mentally*) squilibrato

unsteadily /ʌn'stedɪlɪ/ *adv* ⟨*walk, speak*⟩ in modo malsicuro

unsteady /ʌn'stedɪ/ *a* malsicuro

unstoppable /ʌn'stɒpəbl/ *a* ⟨*force, momentum*⟩ inarrestabile

unstressed /ʌn'strest/ *a* ⟨*vowel, word*⟩ atono

unstuck /ʌn'stʌk/ *a* **come ~** staccarsi; (*fam: project*) andare a monte

unsuccessful /ʌnsək'sesfʊl/ *a* fallimentare; **be ~** (*in attempt*) non aver successo

unsuccessfully /ʌnsək'sesfʊlɪ/ *adv* senza successo

unsuitable /ʌn'su:təbl/ *a* (*inappropriate*) inadatto; (*inconvenient*) inopportuno

unsupervised /ʌn'su:pəvaɪzd/ *a* (*activity*) non controllato

unsuspecting /ʌnsə'spektɪŋ/ *a* fiducioso

unsweetened /ʌn'swi:tənd/ *a* senza zucchero

unsympathetic /ʌnsɪmpə'θetɪk/ *a* (*person, attitude, manner, tone*) poco comprensivo; (*person, character*) antipatico; **she is ~ to the cause** non appoggia la causa

untamed /ʌn'teɪmd/ *a* (*lion*) non addomesticato; (*passion, person*) indomito

untangle /ʌn'tæŋgl/ *vt* sbrogliare (*threads*); risolvere (*difficulties, mystery*)

unthinkable /ʌn'θɪŋkəbl/ *a* impensabile

unthought-of /ʌn'θɔ:təv/ *a* impensato; **hitherto ~** finora impensato

untidily /ʌn'taɪdɪlɪ/ *adv* disordinatamente

untidiness /ʌn'taɪdɪnɪs/ *n* disordine *m*

untidy /ʌn'taɪdɪ/ *a* disordinato

untie /ʌn'taɪ/ *vt* slegare

until /ʌn'tɪl/ *prep* fino a; **not ~** non prima di; **~ the evening** fino alla sera; **~ his arrival** fino al suo arrivo ● *conj* finché, fino a quando; **not ~ you've seen it** non prima che tu l'abbia visto

untimely /ʌn'taɪmlɪ/ *a* inopportuno; (*premature*) prematuro

untiring /ʌn'taɪərɪŋ/ *a* instancabile

untold /ʌn'təʊld/ *a* (*wealth*) incalcolabile; (*suffering*) indescrivibile; (*story*) inedito

untouched /ʌn'tʌtʃt/ *a* (*unchanged, undisturbed*) intatto; (*unscathed*) incolume; (*unaffected*) non toccato; **leave one's dinner/a meal** non toccare cibo

untoward /ʌntə'wɔ:d/ *a* **if nothing ~ happens** se non capita un imprevisto

untrained /ʌn'treɪnd/ *a* (*voice*) non impostato; (*eye, artist, actor*) inesperto; **be ~** (*worker:*) non avere una formazione professionale

untranslatable /ʌntrænz'leɪtəbl/ *a* intraducibile

untreated /ʌn'tri:tɪd/ *a* (*sewage, water*) non depurato; (*illness*) non curato

untrue /ʌn'tru:/ *a* falso; **that's ~** non è vero

unused[1] /ʌn'ju:zd/ *a* non usato

unused[2] /ʌn'ju:st/ *a* **be ~ to** non essere abituato a

unusual /ʌn'ju:ʒəl/ *a* insolito

unusually /ʌn'ju:ʒəlɪ/ *adv* insolitamente

unveil /ʌn'veɪl/ *vt* scoprire

unversed /ʌn'vɜ:st/ *a* inesperto (**in** di)

unwanted /ʌn'wɒntɪd/ *a* (*child, pet, visitor*) indesiderato; (*goods, produce*) che non serve; **feel ~** sentirsi respinto

unwarranted /ʌn'wɒrəntɪd/ *a* ingiustificato

unwelcome /ʌn'welkəm/ *a* sgradito

unwell /ʌn'wel/ *a* indisposto

unwieldy /ʌn'wi:ldɪ/ *a* ingombrante

unwilling /ʌn'wɪlɪŋ/ *a* riluttante

unwillingly /ʌn'wɪlɪŋlɪ/ *adv* malvolentieri

unwind /ʌn'waɪnd/ *v* (*pt/pp* **unwound**) ● *vt* svolgere, srotolare ● *vi* svolgersi, srotolarsi; (*fam: relax*) rilassarsi

unwise /ʌn'waɪz/ *a* imprudente

unwisely /ʌn'waɪzlɪ/ *adv* imprudentemente

unwitting /ʌn'wɪtɪŋ/ *a* involontario; (*victim*) inconsapevole

unwittingly /ʌn'wɪtɪŋlɪ/ *adv* involontariamente

unworldly /ʌn'wɜ:ldlɪ/ *a* (*not materialistic*) poco materialista; (*naive*) ingenuo; (*spiritual*) non materialista

unworthy /ʌn'wɜ:ðɪ/ *a* non degno

unwrap /ʌn'ræp/ *vt* (*pt/pp* **-wrapped**) scartare (*present, parcel*)

unwritten /ʌn'rɪtn/ *a* tacito

unyielding /ʌn'ji:ldɪŋ/ *a* rigido

unzip /ʌn'zɪp/ *vt* aprire [la cerniera di] (*garment, bag*)

up /ʌp/ *adv* su; (*not in bed*) alzato; (*road*) smantellato; (*theatre curtain, blinds*) alzato; (*shelves, tent*) montato; (*notice*) affisso; (*building*) costruito; **prices are up** i prezzi sono aumentati; **be up for sale** essere in vendita; **up here/there** quassù/lassù; **time's up** tempo scaduto; **what's up?** *fam* cosa è successo?; **up to** (*as far as*) fino a; **be up to** essere all'altezza di (*task*); **what's he up to?** *fam* cosa sta facendo?; (*plotting*) cosa sta combinando?; **I'm up to page 100** sono arrivato a pagina 100; **feel up to it** sentirsela; **be one up on sb** *fam* essere in vantaggio su qcno; **go up** salire; **lift up** alzare; **up against** *fig* alle prese con ● *prep* su; **the cat ran/is up the tree** il gatto è salito di corsa/è sull'albero; **further up this road** più avanti su questa strada; **row up the river** risalire il fiume; **go up the stairs** salire su per le scale; **be up the pub** *fam* essere al pub; **be up on** *or* **in sth** essere bene informato su qcsa ● *npl* **ups and downs** alti *mpl* e bassi

up-and-coming *a* promettente

upbeat /'ʌpbi:t/ *a* ottimistico

upbringing /'ʌpbrɪŋɪŋ/ *n* educazione *f*

update /ʌp'deɪt/ *vt* aggiornare

upfront /ʌp'frʌnt/ *a* *fam* (*frank*) aperto; (*money*) anticipato ● *adv* (*pay*) in anticipo

upgrade /ʌp'greɪd/ *vt* promuovere (*person*); modernizzare (*equipment*) ● *n* aggiornamento *m*

upheaval /ʌp'hi:vl/ *n* scompiglio *m*

uphill /ʌp'hɪl/ *a* in salita; *fig* arduo ● *adv* in salita

uphold /ʌp'həʊld/ *vt* (*pt/pp* **upheld**) sostenere (*principle*); confermare (*verdict*)

upholster /ʌp'həʊlstə(r)/ *vt* tappezzare

upholsterer /ʌp'həʊlstərə(r)/ *n* tappezziere, -a *mf*

upholstery /ʌp'həʊlstərɪ/ *n* tappezzeria *f*

upkeep /'ʌpki:p/ *n* mantenimento *m*

uplifting /ʌp'lɪftɪŋ/ *a* (*morally*) edificante

up-market *a* di qualità

upon /ə'pɒn/ *prep* su; **~ arriving home** una volta arrivato a casa

upper /'ʌpə(r)/ a superiore ● n (of shoe) tomaia f

upper: upper-case a maiuscolo. **upper circle** n seconda galleria f. **upper class** n alta borghesia f. **upper crust** a hum aristocratico. **upper hand** n **have the ~** ~ avere il sopravvento. **upper middle class** n ceto m medio-alto

uppermost /'ʌpəməʊst/ a più alto; **that's ~ in my mind** è la mia preoccupazione principale

upright /'ʌpraɪt/ a dritto; ⟨piano⟩ verticale; ⟨honest⟩ retto ● n montante m

upright freezer n freezer m inv verticale

uprising /'ʌpraɪzɪŋ/ n rivolta f

upriver /ʌp'rɪvə/ adv ⟨lie⟩ a monte; ⟨sail⟩ controcorrente

uproar /'ʌprɔː(r)/ n tumulto m; **be in an ~** essere in trambusto

uproot /ʌp'ruːt/ vt sradicare

upset¹ /ʌp'set/ vt (pt/pp upset, pres p upsetting) rovesciare; sconvolgere ⟨plan⟩; ⟨distress⟩ turbare; **get ~ about sth** prendersela per qcsa; **be very ~** essere sconvolto; **have an ~ stomach** avere l'intestino disturbato

upset² /'ʌpset/ n scombussolamento m

upshot /'ʌpʃɒt/ n risultato m

upside down adv sottosopra; **turn ~ ~** capovolgere

upstage /ʌp'steɪdʒ/ vt Theat, fig distogliere l'attenzione del pubblico da ● adv Theat ⟨stand⟩ al fondo del palcoscenico; ⟨move⟩ verso il fondo del palcoscenico

upstairs¹ /ʌp'steəz/ adv [al piano] di sopra

upstairs² /'ʌpsteəz/ a del piano superiore

upstart /'ʌpstɑːt/ n arrivato, -a mf

upstream /ʌp'striːm/ adv controcorrente

upsurge /'ʌpsɜːdʒ/ n (in sales) aumento m improvviso; ⟨of enthusiasm, crime⟩ ondata f

uptake /'ʌpteɪk/ n **be slow on the ~** essere lento nel capire; **be quick on the ~** capire le cose al volo

uptight /ʌp'taɪt/ a teso

up-to-date a moderno; ⟨news⟩ ultimo; ⟨person, information, records⟩ aggiornato

up-to-the-minute a ⟨information⟩ dell'ultimo minuto

uptown /'ʌptaʊn/ a (Am: smart) dei quartieri alti

upturn /'ʌptɜːn/ n ripresa f

upward /'ʌpwəd/ a verso l'alto, in su; **~ slope** salita f ● adv **~[s]** verso l'alto; **~s of** oltre

upwardly mobile /ʌpwədlɪ'məʊbaɪl/ a che sale nella scala sociale

uranium /jʊ'reɪnɪəm/ n uranio m

urban /'ɜːbən/ a urbano

urban blight, urban decay n degrado m urbano

urbane /ɜː'beɪn/ a cortese

urban planning n urbanistica f

urge /ɜːdʒ/ n forte desiderio m ● vt esortare (to a)

■ **urge on** vt spronare

urgency /'ɜːdʒənsɪ/ n urgenza f

urgent /'ɜːdʒənt/ a urgente

urgently /'ɜːdʒəntlɪ/ adv urgentemente

urinal /jʊ'raɪnl/ n (fixture) orinale m; (place) vespasiano m

urinate /'jʊərɪneɪt/ vi urinare

urine /'jʊərɪn/ n urina f

urn /ɜːn/ n urna f; (for tea) contenitore m munito di cannella che si trova nei self-service, mense ecc

US n abbr (United States) U.S.A. mpl

us /ʌs/ pers pron ci; (after prep) noi; **they know us** ci conoscono; **give us the money** dateci i soldi; **give it to us** datecelo; **they showed it to us** ce l'hanno fatto vedere; **they meant us, not you** intendevano noi, non voi; **it's us** siamo noi; **she hates us** ci odia

USA n abbr (United States of America) U.S.A. mpl

usable /'juːzəbl/ a usabile

usage /'juːsɪdʒ/ n uso m

use¹ /juːs/ n uso m; **be of ~** essere utile; **be of no ~** essere inutile; **make ~ of** usare; ⟨exploit⟩ sfruttare; **it is no ~** è inutile; **what's the ~?** a che scopo?

use² /juːz/ vt usare

■ **use up** vt consumare

used¹ /juːzd/ a usato

used² /juːst/ pt **be ~ to sth** essere abituato a qcsa; **get ~ to** abituarsi a; **he ~ to say** diceva; **he ~ to live here** viveva qui

useful /'juːsfl/ a utile

usefulness /'juːsflnɪs/ n utilità f

useless /'juːslɪs/ a inutile; ⟨fam: person⟩ incapace; **you're ~!** sei un idiota!

user /'juːzə(r)/ n utente mf

user: user-friendliness n facilità f d'uso. **user-friendly** a facile da usare. **user manual** n manuale m d'uso

usher /'ʌʃə(r)/ n Theat maschera f; Jur usciere m; (at wedding) persona f che accompagna gli invitati a un matrimonio ai loro posti in chiesa

■ **usher in** vt fare entrare ⟨person⟩; inaugurare ⟨new age⟩

usherette /ʌʃə'ret/ n maschera f

USSR n URSS f

usual /'juːʒʊəl/ a usuale; **as ~** come al solito

usually /'juːʒʊəlɪ/ adv di solito

usurp /jʊ'zɜːp/ vt usurpare

usurper /jʊ'zɜːpə(r)/ n usurpatore, -trice mf

utensil /jʊ'tensl/ n utensile m

uterus /'juːtərəs/ n utero m

utilitarian /jʊtɪlɪ'teərɪən/ a funzionale

utility /jʊ'tɪlətɪ/ n utilità f; (public) servizio m

utility: utility company n servizio m pubblico. **utility program** n Comput [programma m di] utilità f. **utility room** n stanza f in casa privata per il lavaggio, la stiratura dei panni ecc

utilize /'juːtɪlaɪz/ vt utilizzare

utmost /'ʌtməʊst/ a estremo ● n **one's ~** tutto il possibile

Utopia /juː'təʊpɪə/ n utopia f
Utopian /juː'təʊpɪən/ n utopista mf ● a uto-
pistico
utter[1] /'ʌtə(r)/ a totale
utter[2] vt emettere ⟨sigh, sound⟩; proferire
⟨word⟩

utterance /'ʌtərəns/ n dichiarazione f
utterly /'ʌtəlɪ/ adv completamente
U-turn n Auto inversione f a U; fig marcia f in
dietro
UV abbr (**ultraviolet**) UVA mpl
Uzbekistan /ʌzbekɪ'stɑːn/ n Uzbekistan m

Vv

---

v, V /viː/ n (letter) v, V f inv
v abbr (**versus**) contro; abbr (**volt**) V m
vac /væk/ n Br abbr (**vacation**) vacanze fpl
vacancy /'veɪk(ə)nsɪ/ n (job) posto m vacante; (room) stanza f disponibile
vacant /'veɪknt/ a libero; ⟨position⟩ vacante;
⟨look⟩ assente
vacant possession n Br Jur bene m immobile libero
vacate /və'keɪt/ vt lasciare libero
vacation /və'keɪʃn/ n Univ & Am vacanza f
vaccinate /'væksmeɪt/ vt vaccinare
vaccination /væksɪ'neɪʃn/ n vaccinazione f
vaccine /'væksiːn/ n vaccino m
vacillate /'væsɪleɪt/ vi tentennare
vacuous /'vækjʊəs/ a ⟨person, look,
expression⟩ vacuo; ⟨person⟩ superficiale
vacuum /'vækjʊəm/ n vuoto m ● vt passare
l'aspirapolvere in/su
vacuum: vacuum cleaner n aspirapolvere
m inv. **vacuum flask** n thermos® m inv.
vacuum-packed a confezionato sottovuoto
vagabond /'vægəbɒnd/ n vagabondo, -a mf
vagaries /'veɪgərɪz/ npl capricci mpl
vagina /və'dʒaɪnə/ n Anat vagina f
vagrancy /'veɪgrənsɪ/ n Jur vagabondaggio m
vagrant /'veɪgrənt/ n vagabondo, -a mf
vague /veɪg/ a vago; ⟨outline⟩ impreciso;
(absent-minded) distratto; **I'm still ~ about
it** non ho ancora le idee chiare in proposito
vaguely /'veɪglɪ/ adv vagamente
vagueness /'veɪgnɪs/ n (imprecision) va-
ghezza f; (of wording, proposals) indetermina-
tezza f; (of image) nebulosità f; (of thinking)
imprecisione f
vain /veɪn/ a vanitoso; ⟨hope, attempt⟩ vano;
in ~ invano
vainly /'veɪnlɪ/ adv vanamente
valance /'væləns/ n (above curtains)
mantovana f; (on bed base) balza f
vale /veɪl/ n liter valle f
valentine /'væləntaɪn/ n (card) biglietto m
di San Valentino
Valentine's Day n giorno m di San
Valentino
valet /'væleɪ/ n servitore m personale
valiant /'vælɪənt/ a valoroso
valiantly /'vælɪəntlɪ/ adv coraggiosamente
valid /'vælɪd/ a valido

validate /'vælɪdeɪt/ vt (confirm) convalidare
validity /və'lɪdətɪ/ n validità f
valley /'vælɪ/ n valle f
valour /'vælə(r)/ n valore m
valuable /'væljʊəbl/ a di valore; fig prezioso
valuables /'væljʊəblz/ npl oggetti mpl di valore
valuation /væljʊ'eɪʃn/ n valutazione f
value /'væljuː/ n valore m; (usefulness) utilità
f ● vt valutare; (cherish) apprezzare
value added tax /'ædɪd/ n imposta f sul
valore aggiunto
valued /'væljuːd/ a (appreciated) apprezzato
valuer /'væljʊə(r)/ n stimatore, -trice mf
valve /vælv/ n valvola f
vamp /væmp/ n vamp f inv
vampire /'væmpaɪə(r)/ n vampiro m
van /væn/ n furgone m
vandal /'vændl/ n vandalo, -a mf
vandalism /'vænd(ə)lɪzm/ n vandalismo m
vandalize /'vænd(ə)laɪz/ vt vandalizzare
vane /veɪn/ n banduerola f
vanguard /'vængɑːd/ n avanguardia f; **in
the ~** all'avanguardia
vanilla /və'nɪlə/ n vaniglia f
vanish /'vænɪʃ/ vi svanire
vanishing: vanishing cream n crema f
base per il trucco. **vanishing point** n punto
m di fuga. **vanishing trick** n trucco m da
illusionista per far sparire un oggetto; **he's
done his ~ ~ again** fam è sparito come al
solito
vanity /'vænətɪ/ n vanità f inv
vanity bag, vanity case n beauty-case m
inv
vanity mirror n Auto specchietto m di cortesia
vanquish /'væŋkwɪʃ/ vt sconfiggere ⟨enemy⟩
vantage point /'vɑːntɪdʒ/ n punto m d'osservazione; fig punto m di vista
vaporize /'veɪpəraɪz/ vt vaporizzare ⟨liquid⟩
vapour /'veɪpə(r)/ n vapore m
vapour trail n scia f
variable /'veərɪəbl/ a variabile; (adjustable)
regolabile
variance /'veərɪəns/ n **be at ~** essere in disaccordo
variant /'veərɪənt/ n variante f
variation /veərɪ'eɪʃn/ n variazione f

varicose /'værɪkəʊs/ *a* ~ **veins** vene *fpl* varicose

varied /'veərɪd/ *a* vario; ⟨*diet*⟩ diversificato; ⟨*life*⟩ movimentato

variegated /'veərɪəgeɪtɪd/ *a* variegato

variety /və'raɪətɪ/ *n* varietà *f inv*

various /'veərɪəs/ *a* vario

variously /'veərɪəslɪ/ *adv* variamente

varnish /'vɑːnɪʃ/ *n* vernice *f*; (*for nails*) smalto *m* ● *vt* verniciare; ~ **one's nails** mettersi lo smalto

vary /'veərɪ/ *vt/i* (*pt/pp* **-ied**) variare

varying /'veərɪɪŋ/ *a* variabile; (*different*) diverso

vascular /'væskjʊlə/ *a* *Anat*, *Bot* vascolare

vase /vɑːz/ *n* vaso *m*

vasectomy /və'sektəmɪ/ *n* vasectomia *f*

vast /vɑːst/ *a* vasto; ⟨*difference, amusement*⟩ enorme

vastly /'vɑːstlɪ/ *adv* ⟨*superior*⟩ di gran lunga; ⟨*different, amused*⟩ enormemente

VAT /viːeɪˈtiː, væt/ *abbr* (**value added tax**) I.V.A. *f*

vat /væt/ *n* tino *m*

vaudeville /'vɔːdəvɪl/ *n Theat* varietà *m*

vault[1] /vɔːlt/ *n* (*roof*) volta *f*; (*in bank*) caveau *m inv*; (*tomb*) cripta *f*

vault[2] *n* salto *m* ● *vt/i* ~ **[over]** saltare

VCR *n abbr* (**video cassette recorder**) VCR *m*

VD *abbr* (**venereal disease**) malattia *f* venerea

VDU *abbr* (**visual display unit**) VDU *m*

veal /viːl/ *n* carne *f* di vitello ● *attrib* di vitello

vector /'vektə(r)/ *n Biol, Math* vettore *m*; *Aeron* rotta *f*

veer /vɪə(r)/ *vi* cambiare direzione; *Naut*, *Auto* virare

vegan /'viːgn/ *n* vegetaliano, -a *mf* ● *a* vegetaliano

vegetable /'vedʒtəbl/ *n* (*food*) verdura *f*; (*when growing*) ortaggio *m* ● *attrib* ⟨*oil, fat*⟩ vegetale

vegetarian /vedʒɪ'teərɪən/ *a* & *n* vegetariano, -a *mf*

vegetate /'vedʒɪteɪt/ *vi* vegetare

vegetation /vedʒɪ'teɪʃn/ *n* vegetazione *f*

vehemence /'viːəməns/ *n* veemenza *f*

vehement /'viːəmənt/ *a* veemente

vehemently /'viːəməntlɪ/ *adv* con veemenza

vehicle /'viːɪkl/ *n* veicolo *m*; (*fig: medium*) mezzo *m*

vehicular /vɪ'hɪkjʊlə/ *a* **no** ~ **access**, **no** ~ **traffic** circolazione vietata

veil /veɪl/ *n* velo *m* ● *vt* velare

vein /veɪn/ *n* vena *f*; (*mood*) umore *m*; (*manner*) tenore *m*

veined /veɪnd/ *a* venato

Velcro® /'velkrəʊ/ *n* ~ **fastening** chiusura *f* con velcro

vellum /'veləm/ *n* pergamena *f*

velocity /vɪ'lɒsətɪ/ *n* velocità *f inv*

velvet /'velvɪt/ *n* velluto *m*

velvety /'velvətɪ/ *a* vellutato

venal /'viːnl/ *a* venale

vendetta /ven'detə/ *n* vendetta *f*

vending machine /'vendɪŋ/ *n* distributore *m* automatico

vendor /'vendə(r)/ *n* venditore, -trice *mf*

veneer /və'nɪə(r)/ *n* impiallacciatura *f*; *fig* vernice *f*

veneered /və'nɪəd/ *a* impiallacciato

venerable /'venərəbl/ *a* venerabile

veneration /venə'reɪʃn/ *n* venerazione *f*

venereal /vɪ'nɪərɪəl/ *a* ~ **disease** malattia *f* venerea

Venetian /və'niːʃn/ *a* & *n* veneziano, -a *mf*

Venetian blind *n* persiana *f* alla veneziana

Venezuela /venɪz'weɪlə/ *n* Venezuela *m*

Venezuelan /venɪz'weɪlən/ *a* & *n* venezuelano, -a *mf*

vengeance /'vendʒəns/ *n* vendetta *f*; **with a** ~ *fam* a più non posso

Venice /'venɪs/ *n* Venezia *f*

venison /'venɪsn/ *n Culin* carne *f* di cervo

venom /'venəm/ *n* veleno *m*

venomous /'venəməs/ *a* velenoso

vent[1] /vent/ *n* presa *f* d'aria; **give** ~ **to** *fig* dar libero sfogo a ● *vt fig* sfogare ⟨*anger*⟩

vent[2] *n* (*in jacket*) spacco *m*

ventilate /'ventɪleɪt/ *vt* ventilare

ventilation /ventɪ'leɪʃn/ *n* ventilazione *f*; (*installation*) sistema *m* di ventilazione

ventilator /'ventɪleɪtə(r)/ *n* ventilatore *m*

ventriloquist /ven'trɪləkwɪst/ *n* ventriloquo, -a *mf*

venture /'ventʃə(r)/ *n* impresa *f* ● *vt* azzardare ● *vi* avventurarsi

venture capital *n* capitale *m* a rischio

venue /'venjuː/ *n* luogo *m* (*di convegno, concerto ecc*)

veracity /və'ræsətɪ/ *n* veridicità *f*

veranda /və'rændə/ *n* veranda *f*

verb /vɜːb/ *n* verbo *m*

verbal /'vɜːbl/ *a* verbale

verbally /'vɜːb(ə)lɪ/ *adv* verbalmente

verbatim /vɜː'beɪtɪm/ *a* letterale ● *adv* parola per parola

verbose /vɜː'bəʊs/ *a* prolisso

verdict /'vɜːdɪkt/ *n* verdetto *m*; (*opinion*) parere *m*

verdigris /'vɜːdɪgriː/ *n* verderame *m*

verge /vɜːdʒ/ *n* orlo *m*; **be on the** ~ **of doing sth** essere sul punto di fare qcsa

■ **verge on** *vt fig* rasentare

verger /'vɜːdʒə(r)/ *n* sagrestano *m*

verification /verɪfɪ'keɪʃn/ *n* verifica *f*

verify /'verɪfaɪ/ *vt* (*pt/pp* **-ied**) verificare; (*confirm*) confermare

veritable /'verɪtəbl/ *a* vero

vermicelli /vɜːmɪ'tʃelɪ/ *n* (*pasta*) capelli *mpl* d'angelo; (*chocolate*) pezzettini *mpl* di cioccolato per decorazione

vermilion /və'mɪljən/ *n* rosso *m* vermiglio ● *a* vermiglio

vermin /'vɜːmɪn/ *n* animali *mpl* nocivi

vermouth /'vɜːməθ/ *n* vermut *m inv*

vernacular /və'nækjʊlə(r)/ *n* vernacolo *m*

verruca /vəˈruːkə/ n verruca f
versatile /ˈvɜːsətaɪl/ a versatile
versatility /vɜːsəˈtɪlətɪ/ n versatilità f
verse /vɜːs/ n verso m; (of Bible) versetto m; (poetry) versi mpl
versed /vɜːst/ a ~ **in** versato in
versifier /ˈvɜːsɪfaɪə(r)/ n pej versificatore, -trice mf
version /ˈvɜːʃn/ n versione f; (translation) traduzione f
versus /ˈvɜːsəs/ prep contro
vertebra /ˈvɜːtɪbrə/ n (pl -**brae** /-briː/) Anat vertebra f
vertebrate /ˈvɜːtɪbrət/ n vertebrato m ● a vertebrato
vertex /ˈvɜːteks/ n Anat sommità f inv del capo; Math vertice m
vertical /ˈvɜːtɪkl/ a & n verticale m
vertically /ˈvɜːtɪklɪ/ adv verticalmente
vertigo /ˈvɜːtɪɡəʊ/ n Med vertigine f
verve /vɜːv/ n verve f
very /ˈverɪ/ adv molto; ~ **much** molto; ~ **little** pochissimo; ~ **many** moltissimi; ~ **few** pochissimi; ~ **probably** molto probabilmente; ~ **well** benissimo; **at the** ~ **most** tut't'al più; **at the** ~ **latest** al più tardi ● a **the** ~ **first** il primissimo; **the** ~ **thing** proprio ciò che ci vuole; **at the** ~ **end/beginning** proprio alla fine/all'inizio; **that** ~ **day** proprio quel giorno; **the** ~ **thought** la sola idea; **only a** ~ **little** solo un pochino
vespers /ˈvespəz/ npl vespri mpl
vessel /ˈvesl/ n nave f; (receptacle) recipiente m; Anat vaso m
vest /vest/ n maglia f della pelle; (Am: waistcoat) gilè m inv ● vt ~ **sth in sb** investire qcno di qcsa
vested interest /vestɪdˈɪntrəst/ n interesse m personale
vestige /ˈvestɪdʒ/ n (of past) vestigio m
vestment /ˈvestmənt/ n Relig paramento m
vestry /ˈvestrɪ/ n sagrestia f
vet /vet/ n veterinario, -a mf ● vt (pt/pp **vetted**) controllare minuziosamente
veteran /ˈvetərən/ n veterano, -a mf
veteran car n auto f inv d'epoca (costruita prima del 1916)
veterinary /ˈvetərɪnərɪ/ a veterinario
veterinary surgeon n medico m veterinario
veto /ˈviːtəʊ/ n (pl -**es**) veto m ● vt proibire
vetting /ˈvetɪŋ/ n verifica f del passato di un individuo
vex /veks/ vt irritare
vexation /vekˈseɪʃn/ n irritazione f
vexatious /vekˈseɪʃəs/ a (person) fastidioso; (situation) spiacevole
vexed /vekst/ a irritato; ~ **question** questione f controversa
vexing /ˈveksɪŋ/ a irritante
VHF abbr (**very high frequency**) VHF
via /ˈvaɪə/ prep via; (by means of) attraverso
viability /vaɪəˈbɪlətɪ/ n probabilità f di sopravvivenza; (of proposition) attuabilità f
viable /ˈvaɪəbl/ a (life form, relationship,

company) in grado di sopravvivere; (proposition) attuabile
viaduct /ˈvaɪədʌkt/ n viadotto m
vibes /vaɪbz/ npl fam **I'm getting good/bad** ~ provo una sensazione gradevole/sgradevole
vibrant /ˈvaɪbrənt/ a fig che sprizza vitalità
vibrate /vaɪˈbreɪt/ vi vibrare
vibration /vaɪˈbreɪʃn/ n vibrazione f
vicar /ˈvɪkə(r)/ n parroco m (protestante)
vicarage /ˈvɪkərɪdʒ/ n casa f parrocchiale
vicarious /vɪˈkeərɪəs/ a indiretto
vice[1] /vaɪs/ n vizio m
vice[2] n Techn morsa f
vice: vice-captain n Sport vicecapitano m.
vice-chairman n vicepresidente mf. **vice-chancellor** n Br Univ vicerettore m; Am Jur vicecancelliere m. **vice-president** n vicepresidente mf. **vice-principal** n (of senior school) vicepreside mf; (of junior school, college) vicedirettore, -trice mf
vice squad n buoncostume f
vice versa /vaɪsəˈvɜːsə/ adv viceversa
vicinity /vɪˈsɪnətɪ/ n vicinanza f; **in the** ~ **of** nelle vicinanze di
vicious /ˈvɪʃəs/ a cattivo; (attack) brutale; (animal) pericoloso
vicious circle n circolo m vizioso
viciously /ˈvɪʃəslɪ/ adv (attack) brutalmente
victim /ˈvɪktɪm/ n vittima f
victimization /vɪktɪmaɪˈzeɪʃn/ n vittimizzazione f
victimize /ˈvɪktɪmaɪz/ vt vittimizzare
victor /ˈvɪktə(r)/ n vincitore m
Victorian /vɪkˈtɔːrɪən/ n persona f vissuta in epoca vittoriana ● a (writer, poverty, age) vittoriano
victorious /vɪkˈtɔːrɪəs/ a vittorioso
victory /ˈvɪktərɪ/ n vittoria f
video /ˈvɪdɪəʊ/ n video m inv; (cassette) videocassetta f; (recorder) videoregistratore m ● attrib video ● vt registrare
video: video camera n videocamera f, telecamera f. **video card** n scheda f video. **video cassette** n videocassetta f. **video clip** n videoclip m inv. **videoconference** n videoconferenza f. **video game** n videogioco m. **video library** n videoteca f. **video nasty** n film m inv con scene violente o pornografiche. **video recorder** n videoregistratore m. **video shop** n negozio m che affitta o vende videocassette. **video surveillance** n videosorveglianza f. **videotape** n videocassetta f
vie /vaɪ/ vi (pres p **vying**) rivaleggiare
Vienna /vɪˈenə/ n Vienna f
Viennese /vɪəˈniːz/ a viennese
Vietnam /vɪetˈnæm/ n Vietnam m
Vietnamese /vɪetnəˈmiːz/ a & n vietnamita mf; (language) vietnamita m
view /vjuː/ n vista f; (photographed, painted) veduta f; (opinion) visione f; **look at the** ~ guardare il panorama; **in my** ~ secondo me; **in** ~ **of** in considerazione di; **on** ~ esposto; **with a** ~ **to** con l'intenzione di ● vt visitare

⟨*house*⟩; (*consider*) considerare ● *vi TV* guardare

viewer /'vju:ə(r)/ *n TV* telespettatore, -trice *mf*; *Phot* visore *m*

viewfinder /'vju:faɪndə(r)/ *n Phot* mirino *m*

viewing /'vju:ɪŋ/ *n TV* programmi *mpl* della televisione; (*of film*) proiezione *f*; (*of new range*) presentazione *f*; (*of exhibition, house*) visita *f*; **it makes good ~** *TV* vale la pena di vederlo; **what's tonight's ~?** cosa danno alla tv stasera? ● *attrib* ⟨*habits, preferences*⟩ dei telespettatori; **the ~ public** i telespettatori

view phone *n* videotelefono *m*

viewpoint /'vju:pɔɪnt/ *n* punto *m* di vista

vigil /'vɪdʒɪl/ *n* veglia *f*

vigilance /'vɪdʒɪləns/ *n* vigilanza *f*

vigilant /'vɪdʒɪlənt/ *a* vigile

vigilante /vɪdʒɪ'læntɪ/ *n* membro *m* di un'organizzazione privata per la prevenzione della criminalità

vigorous /'vɪg(ə)rəs/ *a* vigoroso

vigorously /'vɪg(ə)rəslɪ/ *adv* vigorosamente

vigour /'vɪgə(r)/ *n* vigore *m*

vile /vaɪl/ *a* disgustoso; ⟨*weather*⟩ orribile; ⟨*temper, mood*⟩ pessimo

vilification /vɪlɪfɪ'keɪʃn/ *n* denigrazione *f*

villa /'vɪlə/ *n* (*for holidays*) casa *f* di villeggiatura

village /'vɪlɪdʒ/ *n* paese *m*

village green *n* giardino *m* pubblico nel centro di un paese

village hall *n* sala *f* utilizzata per feste e altre attività

villager /'vɪlɪdʒə(r)/ *n* paesano, -a *mf*

villain /'vɪlən/ *n* furfante *m*; (*in story*) cattivo *m*

villainous /'vɪlənəs/ *a* infame

vim /vɪm/ *n fam* energia *f*

vindicate /'vɪndɪkeɪt/ *vt* (*from guilt*) discolpare; **you are ~d** ti sei dimostrato nel giusto

vindictive /vɪn'dɪktɪv/ *a* vendicativo

vine /vaɪn/ *n* vite *f*

vinegar /'vɪnɪgə(r)/ *n* aceto *m*

vinegary /'vɪnɪg(ə)rɪ/ *a* agro

vineyard /'vɪnjɑːd/ *n* vigneto *m*

vintage /'vɪntɪdʒ/ *a* ⟨*wine*⟩ d'annata ● *n* (*year*) annata *f*

vintage car *n* auto *f inv* d'epoca (*costruita tra il 1917 e il 1930*)

vintage year *n also fig* anno *m* memorabile

vinyl /'vaɪnɪl/ *n* vinile *m* ● *attrib* ⟨*paint*⟩ vinilico

viola /vɪ'əʊlə/ *n Mus* viola *f*

violate /'vaɪəleɪt/ *vt* violare

violation /vaɪə'leɪʃn/ *n* violazione *f*

violence /'vaɪələns/ *n* violenza *f*

violent /'vaɪələnt/ *a* violento

violently /'vaɪələntlɪ/ *adv* violentemente

violet /'vaɪələt/ *a* violetto ● *n* (*flower*) violetta *f*; (*colour*) violetto *m*

violin /vaɪə'lɪn/ *n* violino *m*

violinist /vaɪə'lɪnɪst/ *n* violinista *mf*

VIP *n abbr* (**very important person**) vip *mf*

viper /'vaɪpə(r)/ *n* vipera *f*

virgin /'vɜːdʒɪn/ *a* vergine ● *n* vergine *f*

virginal /'vɜːdʒɪn(ə)l/ *a* verginale

virginals /'vɜːdʒɪn(ə)lz/ *npl Mus* spinetta *f*

Virginia creeper /vədʒɪnɪə'kriːpə(r)/ *n* vite *f* del Canada

virginity /və'dʒɪnətɪ/ *n* verginità *f*

Virgo /'vɜːgəʊ/ *n Astr* Vergine *f*

virile /'vɪraɪl/ *a* virile

virility /vɪ'rɪlətɪ/ *n* virilità *f*

virologist /vaɪ'rɒlədʒɪst/ *n* virologo *m*

virtual /'vɜːtjʊəl/ *a* effettivo

virtually /'vɜːtjʊəlɪ/ *adv* praticamente

virtual reality *n* realtà *f* virtuale

virtue /'vɜːtjuː/ *n* virtù *f inv*; (*advantage*) vantaggio *m*; **by** *or* **in ~ of** a causa di

virtuoso /vɜːtʊ'əʊzəʊ/ *n* (*pl* **-si** /-zi:/) virtuoso *m*

virtuous /'vɜːtjʊəs/ *a* virtuoso

virulent /'vɪrʊlənt/ *a* virulento

virus /'vaɪərəs/ *n* virus *m inv*

visa /'viːzə/ *n* visto *m*

vis-à-vis /viːzɑː'viː/ *prep* rispetto a

visceral /'vɪs(ə)rəl/ *a* ⟨*power, performance*⟩ viscerale

viscount /'vaɪkaʊnt/ *n* visconte *m*

viscous /'vɪskəs/ *a* vischioso

visibility /vɪzə'bɪlətɪ/ *n* visibilità *f*

visible /'vɪzəbl/ *a* visibile

visibly /'vɪzəblɪ/ *adv* visibilmente

vision /'vɪʒn/ *n* visione *f*; (*sight*) vista *f*

visionary /'vɪʒn(ə)rɪ/ *a & n* visionario, -a *mf*

vision mixer *n* (*person*) tecnico *m* del mixaggio video; (*equipment*) mixaggio *m* video

visit /'vɪzɪt/ *n* visita *f* ● *vt* andare a trovare ⟨*person*⟩; andare da ⟨*doctor etc*⟩; visitare ⟨*town, building*⟩

visiting /'vɪzɪtɪŋ/: **visiting card** *n* biglietto *m* da visita. **visiting hours** *npl* orario *m* delle visite. **visiting lecturer** *n* conferenziere, -a *mf*. **visiting team** *n* squadra *f* ospite. **visiting time** *n* orario *m* delle visite

visitor /'vɪzɪtə(r)/ *n* ospite *mf*; (*of town, museum*) visitatore, -trice *mf*; (*in hotel*) cliente *mf*

visitor centre *n* centro *m* di accoglienza e di informazione per i visitatori

visitors' book *n* (*in exhibition*) albo *m* dei visitatori; (*in hotel*) registro *m* dei clienti

visor /'vaɪzə(r)/ *n* visiera *f*; *Auto* parasole *m*

vista /'vɪstə/ *n* (*view*) panorama *m*

visual /'vɪzjʊəl/ *a* visivo

visual: visual aids *npl* supporto *m* visivo. **visual arts** *npl* arti *fpl* visive. **visual display unit** *n* visualizzatore *m*

visualize /'vɪzjʊəlaɪz/ *vt* visualizzare

visually /'vɪzjʊəlɪ/ *adv* visualmente; **~ handicapped** non vedente

vital /'vaɪtl/ *a* vitale

vitality /vaɪ'tælətɪ/ *n* vitalità *f*

vitally /'vaɪtəlɪ/ *adv* estremamente

vital statistics *npl fam* misure *fpl*

vitamin /'vɪtəmɪn/ *n* vitamina *f*

vitreous /'vɪtrɪəs/ *a* vetroso; ⟨*enamel*⟩ vetrificato

vitriolic /vɪtrɪ'ɒlɪk/ a Chem di vetriolo; fig al vetriolo
vituperative /vɪ'tju:p(ə)rətɪv/ a ingiurioso
viva /'vaɪvə/ n Br Univ [esame m] orale m
vivacious /vɪ'veɪʃəs/ a vivace
vivaciously /vɪ'veɪʃəslɪ/ adv vivacemente
vivacity /vɪ'væsətɪ/ n vivacità f
vivid /'vɪvɪd/ a vivido
vividly /'vɪvɪdlɪ/ adv in modo vivido
vivisect /'vɪvɪsekt/ vt vivisezionare
vivisection /vɪvɪ'sekʃn/ n vivisezione f
vixen /'vɪksn/ n volpe f femmina
viz /vɪz/ adv cioè
vocabulary /və'kæbjʊlərɪ/ n vocabolario m; (list) glossario m
vocal /'vəʊkl/ a vocale; (vociferous) eloquente
vocal cords npl corde fpl vocali
vocalist /'vəʊkəlɪst/ n vocalista mf
vocalize /'vəʊkəlaɪz/ vt (fig: express) esprimere a parole; articolare ⟨sound⟩
vocation /və'keɪʃn/ n vocazione f
vocational /və'keɪʃ(ə)nl/ a di orientamento professionale
vociferous /və'sɪfərəs/ a vociante
vodka /'vɒdkə/ n vodka f inv
vogue /vəʊg/ n moda f; **in ~** in voga
voice /vɔɪs/ n voce f ● vt esprimere
voice box n Anat laringe f
voiceless /'vɔɪslɪs/ a ⟨minority⟩ silenzioso; ⟨group⟩ privo del diritto di parola
voicemail /'vɔɪsmeɪl/ n posta f elettronica vocale
voice-over n voce f fuori campo
void /vɔɪd/ a (not valid) nullo; **~ of** privo di ● n vuoto m
vol /vɒl/ abbr (**volume**) vol.
volatile /'vɒlətaɪl/ a volatile; ⟨person⟩ volubile
volcanic /vɒl'kænɪk/ a vulcanico
volcano /vɒl'keɪnəʊ/ n vulcano m
volition /və'lɪʃn/ n **of his own ~** di sua spontanea volontà
volley /'vɒlɪ/ n (of gunfire) raffica f; (Tennis) volée f inv
volleyball /'vɒlɪbɔ:l/ n pallavolo f
volt /vəʊlt/ n volt m inv
voltage /'vəʊltɪdʒ/ n Electr voltaggio m
voluble /'vɒljʊbl/ a loquace
volume /'vɒlju:m/ n volume m; (of work, traffic) quantità f inv
volume control n volume m

voluntarily /'vɒləntərɪlɪ/ adv volontariamente
voluntary /'vɒləntərɪ/ a volontario
voluntary redundancy n Br dimissioni fpl volontarie
voluntary work n volontariato m
volunteer /vɒlən'tɪə(r)/ n volontario, -a mf ● vt offrire volontariamente ⟨information⟩ ● vi offrirsi volontario; Mil arruolarsi come volontario
voluptuous /və'lʌptjʊəs/ a voluttuoso
vomit /'vɒmɪt/ n vomito m ● vt/i vomitare
voodoo /'vu:du:/ n vudu m inv
voracious /və'reɪʃəs/ a vorace
vortex /'vɔ:teks/ n vortice m; fig turbine m
vote /vəʊt/ n voto m; (ballot) votazione f; (right) diritto m di voto; **take a ~ on** votare su ● vi votare ● vt **~ sb president** eleggere qcno presidente
■ **vote down** vt (reject by vote) bocciare ai voti
■ **vote in** vt (elect) eleggere
vote of confidence n Pol, fig voto m di fiducia
vote of thanks n discorso m di ringraziamento
voter /'vəʊtə(r)/ n elettore, -trice mf
voting /'vəʊtɪŋ/ n votazione f
voting age n età f inv per votare
voting booth n cabina f elettorale
vouch /vaʊtʃ/ vi **~ for** garantire per
voucher /'vaʊtʃə(r)/ n buono m
vow /vaʊ/ n voto m ● vt giurare
vowel /'vaʊəl/ n vocale f
vox pop /vɒks'pɒp/ n TV, Radio opinione f pubblica
voyage /'vɔɪɪdʒ/ n viaggio m [marittimo]; (in space) viaggio m [nello spazio]
V-sign n (offensive gesture) gestaccio m; (victory sign) segno m di vittoria
VSO abbr (**Voluntary Service Overseas**) servizio m civile volontario nei paesi in via di sviluppo
vulgar /'vʌlgə(r)/ a volgare
vulgar fraction n Math frazione f ordinaria
vulgarity /vʌl'gærətɪ/ n volgarità f inv
vulnerable /'vʌlnərəbl/ a vulnerabile
vulture /'vʌltʃə(r)/ n avvoltoio m
vying /'vaɪɪŋ/ see **vie**

w, W /'dʌblju:/ *n* (*letter*) w, W *f inv*
W *abbr* (**West**) O; *abbr Electr* (**watt**) w
wad /wɒd/ *n* batuffolo *m*; (*bundle*) rotolo *m*
wadding /'wɒdɪŋ/ *n* ovatta *f*
waddle /'wɒdl/ *vi* camminare ondeggiando
wade /weɪd/ *vi* guadare
▪ **wade in** *vi* (*fam: start working*) mettersi al lavoro; (*take part*) prendere parte
▪ **wade into** *vt* (*attack*) scagliarsi contro
▪ **wade through** *vt fam* procedere faticosamente in ⟨*book*⟩
wader /'weɪdə(r)/ *n Zool* trampoliere *m*; **~s** (*pl: boots*) stivaloni *mpl* di gomma
wafer /'weɪfə(r)/ *n* cialda *f*, wafer *m inv*; *Relig* ostia *f*
wafer-thin *a* sottilissimo
waffle¹ /'wɒfl/ *vi fam* blaterare
waffle² *n Culin* cialda *f*
waft /wɒft/ *vt* trasportare ● *vi* diffondersi
wag /wæg/ *v* (*pt/pp* **wagged**) ● *vt* agitare ● *vi* agitarsi
wage¹ /weɪdʒ/ *vt* dichiarare ⟨*war*⟩; lanciare ⟨*campaign*⟩
wage² *n* & **~s** *pl* salario *msg*
wage earner *n* salariato, -a *mf*
wage packet *n* busta *f* paga
wager /'weɪdʒə(r)/ *n* scommessa *f*
waggle /'wægl/ *vt* dimenare ● *vi* dimenarsi
wagon /'wægən/ *n* carro *m*; *Rail* vagone *m* merci; **be on the ~** *fam* astenersi dall'alcol
waif /weɪf/ *n* trovatello, -a *mf*
wail /weɪl/ *n* piagnucolio *m*; (*of wind*) lamento *m*; (*of baby*) vagito *m* ● *vi* piagnucolare; ⟨*wind:*⟩ lamentarsi; ⟨*baby:*⟩ vagire
Wailing Wall /'weɪlɪŋ/ *n* Muro *m* del pianto
waist /weɪst/ *n* vita *f*
waist: waistband *n* cintura *f*. **waistcoat** *n* gilè *m inv*; (*of man's suit*) panciotto *m*. **waistline** *n* vita *f*. **waist measurement** *n* giro *m* vita
wait /weɪt/ *n* attesa *f*; **lie in ~ for** appostarsi per sorprendere ● *vi* aspettare; **~ at table** servire i tavoli; **~ for** aspettare ● *vt* **~ one's turn** aspettare il proprio turno
▪ **wait about, wait around** *vi* aspettare
▪ **wait behind** *vi* trattenersi
▪ **wait in** *vi* rimanere a casa ad aspettare
▪ **wait on** *vt* servire
▪ **wait up** *vi* rimanere alzato ad aspettare; **don't ~ up for me** non mi aspettare alzato
waiter /'weɪtə(r)/ *n* cameriere *m*
waiter service *n* servizio *m* al tavolo
waiting /'weɪtɪŋ/: **waiting game** *n* **play a ~ ~** *n* temporeggiare. **waiting list** *n* lista *f* d'attesa. **waiting room** *n* sala *f* d'aspetto
waitress /'weɪtrɪs/ *n* cameriera *f*

waive /weɪv/ *vt* rinunciare a ⟨*claim*⟩; non tener conto di ⟨*rule*⟩
waiver /'weɪvə(r)/ *n Jur* rinuncia *f*
wake¹ /weɪk/ *n* veglia *f* funebre ● *v* (*pt* **woke**, *pp* **woken**) **~** [**up**] ● *vt* svegliare ● *vi* svegliarsi
▪ **wake up to** *vt* **~ up to the fact that...** (*realize*) aprire gli occhi di fronte al fatto che...
wake² *n Naut* scia *f*; **in the ~ of** *fig* nella scia di
wakeful /'weɪkfʊl/ *a* ⟨*night*⟩ insonne
waken /'weɪkn/ *vt* svegliare ● *vi* svegliarsi
wake-up call *n* sveglia *f* telefonica
Wales /weɪlz/ *n* Galles *m*
walk /wɔːk/ *n* passeggiata *f*; (*gait*) andatura *f*; (*path*) sentiero *m*; **go for a ~** andare a fare una passeggiata; **~ of life** livello *m* sociale ● *vi* camminare; (*as opposed to drive etc*) andare a piedi; (*ramble*) passeggiare; '**~**' *Am* (*at crossing*) 'avanti' ● *vt* portare a spasso ⟨*dog*⟩; percorrere ⟨*streets*⟩
▪ **walk into** *vt* entrare in ⟨*room*⟩; andare a sbattere contro ⟨*door, lamp post*⟩; cadere in ⟨*trap*⟩; trovare facilmente ⟨*job*⟩
▪ **walk off** *vi* (*leave*) andarsene
▪ **walk off with** *vt* (*win easily*) riportare senza difficoltà; (*take, steal*) portarsi via
▪ **walk out** *vi* ⟨*husband, employee:*⟩ andarsene; ⟨*workers:*⟩ scioperare
▪ **walk out of** *vt* uscire da ⟨*room*⟩; abbandonare ⟨*meeting*⟩
▪ **walk out on** *vt* lasciare
▪ **walk over** *vt* **~ all over sb** (*defeat*) stracciare qcno; (*treat badly*) trattare qcno come una pezza da piedi
▪ **walk through** *vt* superare senza difficoltà ⟨*exam, interview*⟩
▪ **walk up** *vi* (*as opposed to taking the lift*) salire a piedi; (*approach*) avvicinarsi
walkabout /'wɔːkəbaʊt/ *n* escursione *f* periodica degli aborigeni australiani nell'entroterra; (*by royalty*) incontro *m* con la folla; **go ~** ⟨*queen, politician:*⟩ camminare tra la folla
walker /'wɔːkə(r)/ *n* camminatore, -trice *mf*; (*rambler*) escursionista *mf*
walkie-talkie /wɔːkɪ'tɔːkɪ/ *n* walkie-talkie *m inv*
walk-in *a* **~ closet** stanzino *m*
walking /'wɔːkɪŋ/ *n* camminare *m*; (*rambling*) fare *m* delle escursioni
walking: walking boots *npl* scarponi *mpl* [da trekking]. **walking distance** *n* **it's within ~** ci si arriva a piedi. **walking**

frame n Med deambulatore m. **walking pace** n passo m. **walking shoes** npl scarpe fpl da passeggio. **walking-stick** n bastone m da passeggio. **walking wounded** npl feriti mpl in grado di camminare

walk: Walkman® n Walkman m inv. **walk-on** n Theat comparsa f ● a ‹role› piccolo. **walkout** n sciopero m. **walkover** n fig vittoria f facile. **walkway** n passaggio m pedonale

wall /wɔːl/ n muro m; **go to the ~** fam andare a rotoli; **drive sb up the ~** fam far diventare matto qcno

■ **wall up** vt murare

wallchart /'wɔːltʃɑːt/ n tabellone m

walled /wɔːld/ a ‹city› fortificato

wallet /'wɒlɪt/ n portafoglio m

wallflower /'wɔːlflaʊə(r)/ n violaciocca f

wall hanging n decorazione f murale

wallop /'wɒləp/ n fam colpo m ● vt (pt/pp walloped) fam colpire

walloping /'wɒləpɪŋ/ fam a enorme ● adv ~ **great** (very big) enorme ● n **give sb a ~** suonarle a qcno

wallow /'wɒləʊ/ vi sguazzare; (in self-pity, grief) crogiolarsi

wallpaper /'wɔːlpeɪpə(r)/ n tappezzeria f ● vt tappezzare

wall-to-wall a che copre tutto il pavimento

walnut /'wɔːlnʌt/ n noce f

waltz /wɔːlts/ n valzer m inv ● vi ballare il valzer; **he came ~ing up and said** fam è arrivato e ha detto con nonchalance

■ **waltz off with** vt (fam: take, win) portarsi via

■ **waltz through** vt superare facilmente ‹exam›

wan /wɒn/ a esangue

wand /wɒnd/ n (magic ~) bacchetta f [magica]

wander /'wɒndə(r)/ vi girovagare; (fig: digress) divagare

■ **wander about** vi andare a spasso

■ **wander away** vi allontanarsi

■ **wander off** vi allontanarsi; **I'd better be ~ing off** fam è meglio che vada

wanderer /'wɒndərə(r)/ n vagabondo, -a mf

wanderlust /'wɒndəlʌst/ n smania f dei viaggi

wane /weɪn/ n **be on the ~** essere in fase calante ● vi calare

wangle /'wæŋgl/ vt fam rimediare ‹invitation, holiday›

waning /'weɪnɪŋ/ n (of moon) calare m; (weakening) declino m ● a ‹moon› calante; ‹popularity› in declino

wannabee /'wɒnəbiː/ n fam persona f che sogna di diventare famosa

want /wɒnt/ n (hardship) bisogno m; (lack) mancanza f ● vt volere; (need) aver bisogno di; ~ **[to have]** sth volere qcsa; ~ **to do** sth voler fare qcsa; **we ~ to stay** vogliamo rimanere; **I ~ you to go** voglio che tu vada; **it ~s painting** ha bisogno d'essere dipinto; **you ~ to learn to swim** bisogna che impari a nuotare ● vi ~ **for** mancare di

wanted /'wɒntɪd/ a ricercato

wanted list n lista f dei ricercati

wanting /'wɒntɪŋ/ a **be ~** mancare; **be ~ in** mancare di

wanton /'wɒntən/ a ‹cruelty, neglect› gratuito; (morally) debosciato

war /wɔː(r)/ n guerra f; fig lotta f (**on** contro); **at ~** in guerra

warble /'wɔːbl/ vt/i trillare; ‹singer:› gorgheggiare

war cabinet n consiglio m di guerra

war cry n grido m di guerra

ward /wɔːd/ n (in hospital) reparto m; (child) minore m sotto tutela

■ **ward off** vt evitare; parare ‹blow›

warden /'wɔːdn/ n guardiano, -a mf

warder /'wɔːdə(r)/ n guardia f carceraria

wardrobe /'wɔːdrəʊb/ n guardaroba m

wardrobe assistant n costumista mf

ward round n Med giro m delle corsie

ward sister n Br Med caposala f inv

warehouse /'weəhaʊs/ n magazzino m

wares /weəz/ npl merci mpl

warfare /'wɔːfeə/ n guerra f

war: war game n Mil simulazione f di scontro militare. **warhead** n testata f. **warhorse** n cavallo m da battaglia; (fig: campaigner) veterano m

warily /'weərɪlɪ/ adv cautamente

warlike /'wɔːlaɪk/ a bellicoso

warm /wɔːm/ a caldo; ‹welcome› caloroso; **be ~** ‹person:› aver caldo; **it is ~** ‹weather› fa caldo ● vt scaldare

■ **warm up** vt scaldare ● vi scaldarsi; fig animarsi

warm-blooded /-'blʌdɪd/ a Zool con temperatura corporea costante

war memorial n monumento m ai caduti

warm-hearted /-'hɑːtɪd/ a espansivo

warmly /'wɔːmlɪ/ adv ‹greet› calorosamente; ‹dress› in modo pesante

warmongering /'wɔːmʌŋgərɪŋ/ n bellicismo m ● a ‹article› bellicistico; ‹person› guerrafondaio

warmth /wɔːmθ/ n calore m

warm-up n Sport riscaldamento m; (of musicians) prove fpl

warn /wɔːn/ vt avvertire

■ **warn off** vt dare un avvertimento a

warning /'wɔːnɪŋ/ n avvertimento m; (advance notice) preavviso m

warp /wɔːp/ vt deformare; fig distorcere ● vi deformarsi

warpaint /'wɔːpeɪnt/ n Mil pitture fpl di guerra

warpath /'wɔːpɑːθ/ n **on the ~** sul sentiero di guerra

warped /wɔːpt/ a deformato; ‹personality› contorto; ‹sexuality› deviato; ‹view› distorto

warplane /'wɔːpleɪn/ n aereo m da guerra

warrant /'wɒrənt/ n (for arrest, search) mandato m ● vt (justify) giustificare; (guarantee) garantire

warranty /'wɒrəntɪ/ n garanzia f

warren /'wɒr(ə)n/ n (of rabbits) area f piena

di tane di conigli; (*building, maze of streets*) labirinto *m*

warring /ˈwɔːrɪŋ/ *a* in guerra

warrior /ˈwɒrɪə(r)/ *n* guerriero, -a *mf*

Warsaw /ˈwɔːsɔː/ *n* Varsavia *f*

warship /ˈwɔːʃɪp/ *n* nave *f* da guerra

wart /wɔːt/ *n* porro *m*

wartime /ˈwɔːtaɪm/ *n* tempo *m* di guerra

war-torn /ˈwɔːtɔːn/ *a* logorato dalla guerra

wary /ˈweərɪ/ *a* (**-ier, -iest**) (*careful*) cauto; (*suspicious*) diffidente

was /wɒz/ *see* **be**

wash /wɒʃ/ *n* lavata *f*; (*clothes*) bucato *m*; (*in washing machine*) lavaggio *m*; **have a ~** darsi una lavata ● *vt* lavare; (*sea:*) bagnare; **~ one's hands** lavarsi le mani ● *vi* lavarsi

■ **wash away** *vt* (*rain:*) portare via; (*sea, floodwaters:*) spazzare via

■ **wash off** *vt* lavar via (*stain, mud*) ● *vi* andar via

■ **wash out** *vt* sciacquare (*soap*); sciacquarsi (*mouth*)

■ **wash up** *vt* lavare ● *vi* lavare i piatti; *Am* lavarsi

wash: wash-and-wear *a* che non si stira. **washbasin** *n* lavandino *m*. **wash cloth** *n* *Am* ≈ guanto *m* da bagno

washed out /wɒʃt'aʊt/ *a* (*faded*) scolorito; (*tired*) spossato

washed up *a* *fam* (*finished*) finito; (*tired*) distrutto

washer /ˈwɒʃə(r)/ *n* *Techn* guarnizione *f*; (*machine*) lavatrice *f*

washer-dryer /-ˈdraɪə(r)/ *n* asciugabiancheria *m* *inv*

washing /ˈwɒʃɪŋ/ *n* bucato *m*

washing: washing machine *n* lavatrice *f*. **washing powder** *n* detersivo *m*. **washing soda** *n* soda *f* da bucato. **washing-up** *n* **do the ~** lavare i piatti. **washing-up bowl** *n* bacinella *f* (*per i piatti*). **washing-up liquid** *n* detersivo *m* per i piatti. **washing-up water** *n* rigovernatura *f*

wash: wash load *n* carico *m* di lavatrice. **wash-out** *n* disastro *m*. **washroom** *n* bagno *m*

wasp /wɒsp/ *n* vespa *f*

waspish /ˈwɒspɪʃ/ *a* pungente

wastage /ˈweɪstɪdʒ/ *n* perdita *f*

waste /weɪst/ *n* spreco *m*; (*rubbish*) rifiuto *m*; **~s** *pl* distesa *fsg* desolata; **~ of time** perdita *f* di tempo ● *a* (*product*) di scarto; (*land*) desolato; **lay ~** devastare ● *vt* sprecare

■ **waste away** *vi* deperire

waste: wastebasket *n* cestino *m* della carta straccia. **waste bin** *n* (*for paper*) cestino *m* della carta straccia; (*for rubbish*) secchio *m* della spazzatura. **waste disposal unit** *n* eliminatore *m* di rifiuti

wasteful /ˈweɪstfʊl/ *a* dispendioso

waste: waste paper *n* carta *f* straccia. **waste-paper basket** *n* cestino *m* per la carta [straccia]. **waste pipe** *n* tubo *m* di scarico

watch /wɒtʃ/ *n* guardia *f*; (*period of duty*) tur-

no *m* di guardia; (*timepiece*) orologio *m*; **be on the ~** stare all'erta ● *vt* guardare (*film, match, television*); (*be careful of, look after*) stare attento a ● *vi* guardare

■ **watch out** *vi* (*be careful*) stare attento (**for** a)

■ **watch out for** *vt* (*look for*) fare attenzione all'arrivo di (*person*)

watchdog /ˈwɒtʃdɒg/ *n* cane *m* da guardia

watchful /ˈwɒtʃfʊl/ *a* attento

watchfully /ˈwɒtʃfʊlɪ/ *adv* attentamente

watch: watchmaker *n* orologiaio, -a *mf*. **watchman** *n* guardiano *m*. **watch strap** *n* cinturino *m* dell'orologio. **watchtower** *n* torre *f* di guardia. **watchword** *n* motto *m*

water /ˈwɔːtə(r)/ *n* acqua *f*; **~s** *pl* acque *fpl* ● *vt* annaffiare (*garden, plant*); (*dilute*) annacquare; dare da bere a (*horse etc*) ● *vi* (*eyes:*) lacrimare; **my mouth was ~ing** avevo l'acquolina in bocca

■ **water down** *vt* diluire; *fig* attenuare

water: water authority *n* ente *m* dell'acqua. **waterbird** *n* uccello *m* acquatico. **water bottle** *n* borraccia *f*. **watercolour** *n* acquerello *m*. **water company** *n* società *f* *inv* dell'acqua. **watercress** *n* crescione *m*. **water-divining** *n* rabdomanzia *f*. **waterfall** *n* cascata *f*. **waterfront** *n* (*by lakeside, riverside*) riva *f*; (*on harbour*) zona *f* portuale. **waterhole** *n* pozza *f* d'acqua

watering can /ˈwɔːtərɪŋ/ *n* annaffiatoio *m*

water: water lily *n* ninfea *f*. **waterline** *n* linea *f* di galleggiamento. **waterlogged** *a* inzuppato. **water main** *n* conduttura *f* dell'acqua. **watermark** *n* filigrana *f*. **water-meadow** *n* marcita *f*. **watermelon** *n* cocomero *m*. **watermill** *n* mulino *m* ad acqua. **water polo** *n* pallanuoto *f*. **water-power** *n* energia *f* idraulica. **waterproof** *a* (*coat*) impermeabile; (*make-up*) water-proof *inv* ● *n* impermeabile *m*. **waterproofs** *npl* sovrapantaloni *mpl* e giacca impermeabili. **water rates** *mpl* *Br* tariffe *fpl* dell'acqua. **water-resistant** *a* (*sun cream*) resistente all'acqua; (*garment, watch*) impermeabile. **watershed** *n* spartiacque *m* *inv*; *fig* svolta *f*. **waterside** *n* riva *f* ● *attrib* (*cafe, hotel*) sulla riva. **water-skiing** *n* sci *m* nautico. **water softener** *n* (*equipment*) addolcitore *m*; (*substance*) anticalcare *m* *inv*. **water-soluble** *a* idrosolubile. **water sport** *n* sport *m* *inv* acquatico. **water-table** *n* *Geog* superficie *f* freatica. **watertight** *a* stagno; *fig* irrefutabile. **water tower** *n* serbatoio *m* idrico a torre. **waterway** *n* canale *m* navigabile. **water-wheel** *n* ruota *f* idraulica. **water wings** *npl* braccioli *mpl*. **waterworks** *n* impianto *m* idrico; **turn on the ~** *fam* mettersi a piangere come una fontana

watery /ˈwɔːtərɪ/ *a* acquoso; (*eyes*) lacrimoso

watt /wɒt/ *n* watt *m* *inv*

wattage /ˈwɒtɪdʒ/ *n* wattaggio *m*

wave /weɪv/ *n* onda *f*; (*gesture*) cenno *m*; *fig* ondata *f* ● *vt* agitare; **~ one's hand** agitare la mano ● *vi* far segno; (*flag:*) sventolare

■ **wave aside** *vt* respingere ⟨*criticism*⟩

■ **wave down** *vt* far segno di fermarsi a ⟨*vehicle*⟩

waveband /'weɪvbænd/ *n* gamma *f* d'onda

wavelength /'weɪvleŋθ/ *n* lunghezza *f* d'onda; **be on the same ~** *fig* essere sulla stessa lunghezza d'onda

waver /'weɪvə(r)/ *vi* vacillare; (*hesitate*) esitare

wavy /'weɪvɪ/ *a* ondulato

wax[1] /wæks/ *vi* ⟨*moon:*⟩ crescere; (*fig: become*) diventare

wax[2] *n* cera *f*; (*in ear*) cerume *m* ● *vt* dare la cera a

waxworks /'wæksw3:ks/ *n* museo *m* delle cere

waxy /'wæksɪ/ *a* ⟨*skin, texture*⟩ cereo

way /weɪ/ *n* percorso *m*; (*direction*) direzione *f*; (*manner, method*) modo *m*; **~s** *pl* (*customs*) abitudini *fpl*; **be in the ~** essere in mezzo; **on the ~ to Rome** andando a Roma; **I'll do it on the ~** lo faccio mentre vado; **it's on my ~** è sul mio percorso; **a long ~ off** lontano; **this ~** da questa parte; (*like this*) così; **by the ~** a proposito; **by ~ of** come; (*via*) via; **either ~** (*whatever we do*) in un modo o nell'altro; **in some ~s** sotto certi aspetti; **in a ~** in un certo senso; **in a bad ~** ⟨*person*⟩ molto grave; **out of the ~** fuori mano; **under ~** in corso; **lead the ~** far strada; *fig* aprire la strada; **make ~** far posto (**for** a); **give ~** *Auto* dare la precedenza; **go out of one's ~** *fig* scomodarsi (**to** per); **get one's [own] ~** averla vinta ● *adv* **~ behind** molto indietro

way in *n* entrata *f*

waylay /weɪ'leɪ/ *vt* (*pt/pp* **-laid**) aspettare al varco ⟨*person*⟩; intercettare ⟨*letter*⟩

way-out *a fam* eccentrico

way out *n* uscita *f*; *fig* via *f* d'uscita

wayside /'weɪsaɪd/ *n* bordo *m*; **fall by the ~** (*morally*) smarrire la retta via; (*fail*) fallire

wayward /'weɪwəd/ *a* capriccioso

WC *abbr* WC; **the WC** il gabinetto

we /wi:/ *pers pron* noi; **we're the last** siamo gli ultimi; **they're going, but we're not** loro vanno, ma noi no

weak /wi:k/ *a* debole; ⟨*liquid*⟩ leggero; **go ~ at the knees** *fam* sentirsi piegare le ginocchia

weaken /'wi:kn/ *vt* indebolire ● *vi* indebolirsi

weakling /'wi:klɪŋ/ *n* smidollato, -a *mf*

weakly /'wi:klɪ/ *adv* debolmente

weak-minded /-'maɪndɪd/ *a* (*indecisive*) debole; (*simple*) poco intelligente

weakness /'wi:knɪs/ *n* debolezza *f*; (*liking*) debole *m*

weak-willed /-'wɪld/ *a* debole

weal /wi:l/ *n* piaga *f*

wealth /welθ/ *n* ricchezza *f*; *fig* gran quantità *f*

wealthy /'welθɪ/ *a* (**-ier, -iest**) ricco

wean /wi:n/ *vt* svezzare

weapon /'wepən/ *n* arma *f*

wear /weə(r)/ *n* (*clothing*) abbigliamento *m*; **for everyday ~** da portare tutti i giorni; **~ [and tear]** usura *f* ● *v* (*pt* **wore**, *pp* **worn**) ● *vt* portare; (*damage*) consumare; **~ a hole in sth** logorare qcsa fino a fare un buco; **what shall I ~?** cosa mi metto? ● *vi* consumarsi; (*last*) durare

■ **wear away** *vt* consumare ● *vi* consumarsi

■ **wear down** *vt* estenuare ⟨*opposition etc*⟩

■ **wear off** *vi* scomparire; ⟨*effect:*⟩ finire

■ **wear out** *vt* consumare [fino in fondo]; (*exhaust*) estenuare ● *vi* estenuarsi

wearable /'weərəbl/ *a* portabile

wearily /'wɪərɪlɪ/ *adv* stancamente

weariness /'wɪərmɪs/ *n* stanchezza *f*

weary /'wɪərɪ/ *a* (**-ier, -iest**) sfinito ● *v* (*pt/pp* **wearied**) ● *vt* sfinire ● *vi* **~ of** stancarsi di

weasel /'wi:zl/ *n* donnola *f*

weather /'weðə(r)/ *n* tempo *m*; **in this ~** con questo tempo; **under the ~** *fam* giù di corda ● *vt* sopravvivere a ⟨*storm*⟩

weather: **weather balloon** *n* pallone *m* sonda. **weather-beaten** /-bi:tn/ *a* ⟨*face*⟩ segnato dalle intemperie. **weathercock** *n* gallo *m* segnavento. **weather forecast** *n* previsioni *fpl* del tempo. **weatherman** *n* *TV* meteorologo *m*. **weatherproof** *a* ⟨*garment, shoe*⟩ impermeabile; ⟨*shelter, door*⟩ resistente alle intemperie. **weather-vane** *n* banderuola *f*

weave[1] /wi:v/ *vi* (*pt/pp* **weaved**) (*move*) zigzagare

weave[2] *n* (*Tex*) tessuto *m* ● *vt* (*pt* **wove**, *pp* **woven**) tessere; intrecciare ⟨*flowers etc*⟩; intrecciare le fila di ⟨*story etc*⟩

weaver /'wi:və(r)/ *n* tessitore, -trice *mf*

web /web/ *n* rete *f*; (*of spider*) ragnatela *f*

webbed feet /webd'fi:t/ *npl* piedi *mpl* palmati

web page *n* *Comput* pagina *f* web

web site *n* *Comput* sito *m* web

wed /wed/ *vt* (*pt/pp* **wedded**) sposare ● *vi* sposarsi

wedding /'wedɪŋ/ *n* matrimonio *m*

wedding: **wedding bells** *npl* *fig* marcia *f* nuziale. **wedding breakfast** *n* rinfresco *m* di nozze. **wedding cake** *n* torta *f* nuziale. **wedding day** *n* giorno *m* del matrimonio. **wedding dress** *n* vestito *m* da sposa. **wedding march** *n* marcia *f* nuziale. **wedding night** *n* prima notte *f* di nozze. **wedding reception** *n* ricevimento *m* di nozze. **wedding ring** *n* fede *f*. **wedding vows** *npl* voti *mpl* nuziali

wedge /wedʒ/ *n* zeppa *f*; (*for splitting wood*) cuneo *m*; (*of cheese*) fetta *f* ● *vt* (*fix*) fissare

wedlock /'wedlɒk/ *n* **born out of ~** nato fuori dal matrimonio

Wednesday /'wenzdeɪ/ *n* mercoledì *m inv*

wee[1] /wi:/ *a fam* piccolo

wee[2] *n fam* **do a ~** fare la pipì ● *vi fam* fare la pipì

weed /wi:d/ *n* erbaccia *f*; (*fam: person*) mollusco *m* ● *vt* estirpare le erbacce da ● *vi* estirpare le erbacce

■ **weed out** *vt fig* eliminare

weedkiller /'wi:dkɪlə(r)/ *n* erbicida *m*

weedy /'wi:dɪ/ *a fam* mingherlino

week /wi:k/ *n* settimana *f*

weekday /'wi:kdeɪ/ *n* giorno *m* feriale

weekend /'wi:kend/ *n* fine *m* settimana

weekly /'wi:klɪ/ *a* settimanale ● *n* settimanale *m* ● *adv* settimanalmente

weep /wi:p/ *vi* (*pt/pp* **wept**) piangere

weeping willow /wi:pɪŋ'wɪləʊ/ *n* salice *m* piangente

weepy /'wi:pɪ/ ⟨*film*⟩ strappalacrime *inv*

weigh /weɪ/ *vt/i* pesare; **~ anchor** levare l'ancora

■ **weigh down** *vt fig* piegare

■ **weigh in** *vi* (*fam: join in discussion*) intromettersi

■ **weigh out** *vt* pesare ⟨*amount of flour etc*⟩

■ **weigh up** *vt fig* soppesare; valutare ⟨*person*⟩

weighing machine /'weɪŋ/ *n* bilancia *f*

weight /weɪt/ *n* peso *m*; **put on/lose ~** ingrassare/dimagrire

weighting /'weɪtɪŋ/ *n* ⟨*allowance*⟩ indennità *f inv*

weightlessness /'weɪtlɪsnɪs/ *n* assenza *f* di gravità

weight: weightlifter *n* sollevatore *m* di pesi. **weightlifting** *n* sollevamento *m* pesi. **weight training** *n* **do ~ ~** allenarsi con i pesi. **weight-watcher** *n* (*in group*) persona *f* che segue una dieta dimagrante

weighty /'weɪtɪ/ *a* (**-ier, -iest**) pesante; (*important*) di un certo peso

weir /wɪə(r)/ *n* chiusa *f*

weird /wɪəd/ *a* misterioso; (*bizarre*) bizzarro

welcome /'welkəm/ *a* benvenuto; **you're ~!** prego!; **you're ~ to have it/to come** prendilo/vieni pure ● *n* accoglienza *f* ● *vt* accogliere; (*appreciate*) gradire

welcoming /'welkəmɪŋ/ *a* ⟨*ceremony*⟩ di benvenuto; ⟨*committee, smile*⟩ di accoglienza; ⟨*house*⟩ accogliente

weld /weld/ *vt* saldare

welder /'weldə(r)/ *n* saldatore *m*

welfare /'welfeə(r)/ *n* benessere *m*; (*aid*) assistenza *f*; *Am* previdenza *f* sociale

welfare: welfare services *n* servizi *mpl* sociali. **Welfare State** *n* Stato *m* assistenziale. **welfare work** *n* assistenza *m* sociale

well¹ /wel/ *n* pozzo *m*; (*oil ~*) pozzo *m*; (*of staircase*) tromba *f*

well² *adv* (**better, best**) bene; **as ~** anche; **as ~ as** (*in addition*) oltre a; **~ done!** bravo!; **very ~** benissimo ● *a* **he is not ~** non sta bene; **get ~ soon!** guarisci presto! ● *int* beh!; **~ I never!** ma va!

well: well-attended /-ə'tendɪd/ *a* ben frequentato. **well-behaved** /-bɪ'heɪvd/ *a* educato. **well-being** /'welbi:ɪŋ/ *n* benessere *m*. **well-bred** /wel'bred/ *a* beneducato. **well-defined** /-dɪ'faɪnd/ *a* ⟨*role, boundary*⟩ ben definito; ⟨*outline, image*⟩ netto. **well-disposed** /-dɪ'spəʊzd/ *a* benevolo; **be ~ towards** essere bendisposto verso ⟨*person*⟩; essere favorevole

a ⟨*idea*⟩. **well done** /dʌn/ *a* ⟨*task*⟩ ben fatto; *Culin* ben cotto. **well-educated** *a* istruito; (*cultured*) colto. **well-founded** /-'faʊndɪd/ *a* fondato. **well-heeled** /-'hi:ld/ *a fam* danaroso. **well-informed** /-ɪn'fɔ:md/ *a* beninformato

wellingtons /'welɪŋtənz/ *npl* stivali *mpl* di gomma

well: well-judged /-'dʒʌdʒd/ *a* ⟨*performance*⟩ molto intelligente; ⟨*shot*⟩ ben assestato; ⟨*statement, phrase*⟩ ben ponderato. **well-kept** /-'kept/ *a* ⟨*garden*⟩ curato; ⟨*secret*⟩ ben custodito. **well-known** /-'nəʊn/ *a* famoso. **well-liked** /-'laɪkt/ *a* popolare. **well-made** /-'meɪd/ *a* benfatto. **well-mannered** /-'mænəd/ *a* educato. **well-meaning** *a* con buone intenzioni. **well-meant** /-'ment/ *a* con le migliori intenzioni. **well-nigh** /'welnaɪ/ *adv* quasi. **well-off** *a* benestante. **well-read** /-'red/ *a* colto. **well-spoken** /-'spəʊkən/ *a* ⟨*person*⟩ che parla bene. **well-thought-of** *a* stimato. **well-to-do** *a* ricco. **well-trodden** /-'trɒdn/ *a also fig* battuto. **well-wisher** /'welwɪʃə(r)/ *n* simpatizzante *mf*. **well-worn** /-'wɔ:n/ *a* ⟨*steps, floorboards*⟩ consunto; ⟨*carpet, garment*⟩ logoro; ⟨*fig: argument*⟩ trito e ritrito

Welsh /welʃ/ *a & n* gallese *mf*; (*language*) gallese *m*; **the ~** *pl* i gallesi

Welshman /'welʃmən/ *n* gallese *m*

Welsh rabbit *n* toast *m inv* al formaggio

welt /welt/ *n* (*on shoe*) rinforzo *m*; (*on skin*) segno *m* di frustata

went /went/ *see* **go**

wept /wept/ *see* **weep**

were /wɜ:(r)/ *see* **be**

west /west/ *n* ovest *m*; **to the ~ of** a ovest di; **the W~** l'Occidente *m* ● *a* occidentale ● *adv* verso occidente; **go ~** *fam* andare in malora

west: West Bank *n* Cisgiordania *f*. **West Country** *n* sud-ovest *m* dell'Inghilterra. **West End** *n* zona *f* di Londra con un'alta concentrazione di teatri e negozi di lusso

westerly /'westəlɪ/ *a* verso ovest; occidentale ⟨*wind*⟩

western /'westən/ *a* occidentale ● *n* western *m inv*

Westerner /'westənə(r)/ *n* occidentale *mf*

West Germany *n* Germania *f* Occidentale

West Indian *a & n* antillese *mf*

West Indies /'ɪndɪz/ *npl* Antille *fpl*

westward[s] /'westwəd[z]/ *adv* verso ovest

wet /wet/ *a* (**wetter, wettest**) bagnato; fresco ⟨*paint*⟩; (*rainy*) piovoso; ⟨*fam: person*⟩ smidollato; **get ~** bagnarsi ● *vt* (*pt/pp* **wet, wetted**) bagnare

wet: wet blanket *n* guastafeste *mf inv*. **wet fish** *n Br* pesce *m* fresco. **wet-look** *a* ⟨*plastic, leather*⟩ lucido. **wet-nurse** *n* balia *f*. **wetsuit** *n* muta *f*

whack /wæk/ *n fam* colpo *m* ● *vt fam* dare un colpo a

whacked /wækt/ *a fam* stanco morto

whacking /'wækɪŋ/ *a* (*Br fam: enormous*) enorme ● *n fam* sculacciata *f*

whacky /'wækɪ/ a ⟨fam: joke, person etc⟩ demenziale

whale /weɪl/ n balena f; **have a ~ of a time** fam divertirsi un sacco

wham /wæm/ int bum!

wharf /wɔːf/ n banchina f

what /wɒt/ pron che, [che] cosa; **~ for?** perché?; **~ is that for?** a che cosa serve?; **~ is it?** ⟨what do you want⟩ cosa c'è?; **is it like?** com'è?; **~ is your name?** come ti chiami?; **~ is the weather like?** com'è il tempo?; **~ is the film about?** di cosa parla il film?; **~ is he talking about?** di cosa sta parlando?; **he asked me ~ she had said** mi ha chiesto cosa ha detto; **~ about going to the cinema?** e se andassimo al cinema?; **~ about the children?** ⟨what will they do⟩ e i bambini?; **~ if it rains?** e se piove? ● a quale, che; **take ~ books you want** prendi tutti i libri che vuoi; **~ kind of** a che tipo di; **at ~ time?** a che ora? ● adv che; **~ a lovely day!** che bella giornata! ● int ~! [che] cosa!; **~?** [che] cosa?

whatever /wɒt'evə(r)/ a qualunque ● pron qualsiasi cosa; **~ is it?** cos'è?; **~ he does** qualsiasi cosa faccia; **~ happens** qualunque cosa succeda; **nothing ~** proprio niente

whatnot /'wɒtnɒt/ n coso m; ⟨stand⟩ scaffaletto m; **and ~** ⟨and so on⟩ e così via

what's-his-name /'wɒtsɪzneɪm/ n fam coso m

whatsit /'wɒtsɪt/ n fam aggeggio m, coso m

what's-its-name n fam coso, -a mf

whatsoever /wɒtsəʊ'evə(r)/ a & pron = **whatever**

wheat /wiːt/ n grano m, frumento m

wheatgerm /'wiːtdʒɜːm/ n germoglio m di grano

wheatmeal /'wiːtmiːl/ n farina f di frumento

wheedle /'wiːdl/ vt **~ sth out of sb** ottenere qcsa da qualcuno con le lusinghe

wheel /wiːl/ n ruota f; ⟨steering ~⟩ volante m; **at the ~** al volante ● vt ⟨push⟩ spingere ● vi ⟨circle⟩ ruotare; **~ round** ruotare

wheel: wheelbarrow n carriola f. **wheelchair** n sedia f a rotelle. **wheel clamp** n ceppo m bloccaruote

wheeler-dealer /'wiːlə'diːlə(r)/ n trafficone, -a mf

wheeze /wiːz/ vi ansimare

wheezy /'wiːzɪ/ a ⟨voice, cough⟩ dal respiro affannato

when /wen/ adv & conj quando; **the day ~** il giorno in cui; **~ swimming/reading** nuotando/leggendo

whence /wens/ adv liter donde

whenever /wen'evə(r)/ adv & conj in qualsiasi momento; ⟨every time that⟩ ogni volta che; **~ did it happen?** quando è successo?

where /weə(r)/ adv & conj dove; **the street ~ I live** la via in cui abito; **~ do you come from?** da dove vieni?

whereabouts[1] /'weərə'baʊts/ adv dove

whereabouts[2] /'weərəbaʊts/ n **nobody knows his ~** nessuno sa dove si trova

whereas /weər'æz/ conj dal momento che; ⟨in contrast⟩ mentre

whereby /weə'baɪ/ adv attraverso il quale

whereupon /weərə'pɒn/ adv dopo di che

wherever /weər'evə(r)/ adv & conj dovunque; **~ is he?** dov'è mai?; **~ possible** dovunque sia possibile

wherewithal /'weəwɪðɔːl/ n mezzi mpl

whet /wet/ vt (pt/pp **whetted**) aguzzare ⟨appetite⟩

whether /'weðə(r)/ conj se; **~ you like it or not** che ti piaccia o no

which /wɪtʃ/ a & pron quale; **~ one?** quale?; **~ one of you?** chi di voi?; **~ way?** ⟨direction⟩ in che direzione? ● rel pron ⟨object⟩ che; **~ he does frequently** cosa che fa spesso; **after ~** dopo di che; **on/in ~** su/in cui

whichever /wɪtʃ'evə(r)/ a & pron qualunque; **~ it is** qualunque sia; **~ one of you** chiunque tra voi

whiff /wɪf/ n zaffata f; **have a ~ of sth** odorare qcsa

while /waɪl/ n **a long ~** un bel po'; **a little ~** un po' ● conj mentre; ⟨as long as⟩ finché; ⟨although⟩ sebbene; **he met her ~ in exile** l'ha incontrata mentre era in esilio

■ **while away** vt passare ⟨time⟩

whilst /waɪlst/ conj = **while**

whim /wɪm/ n capriccio m

whimper /'wɪmpə(r)/ vi piagnucolare; ⟨dog:⟩ mugolare

whimsical /'wɪmzɪkl/ a capriccioso; ⟨story⟩ fantasioso

whine /waɪn/ n lamento m; ⟨of dog⟩ guaito m ● vi lamentarsi; ⟨dog:⟩ guaire

whinny /'wɪnɪ/ n nitrito m ● vi ⟨horse:⟩ nitrire

whip /wɪp/ n frusta f; ⟨Pol: person⟩ parlamentare mf incaricato, -a di assicurarsi della presenza dei membri del suo partito alle votazioni ● vt (pt/pp **whipped**) frustare; Culin sbattere; ⟨snatch⟩ afferrare; ⟨fam: steal⟩ fregare

■ **whip up** vt ⟨incite⟩ stimolare; fam improvvisare ⟨meal⟩

whiplash injury /'wɪplæʃ/ n Med colpo m di frusta

whipped cream /wɪpt'kriːm/ n panna f montata

whipping boy /'wɪpɪŋ/ n capro m espiatorio

whip-round n fam colletta f; **have a ~** fare una colletta

whirl /wɜːl/ n ⟨movement⟩ rotazione f; **my mind's in a ~** ho le idee confuse ● vi girare rapidamente ● vt far girare rapidamente

whirlpool /'wɜːlpuːl/ n vortice m

whirlwind /'wɜːlwɪnd/ n turbine m

whirr /wɜː(r)/ vi ronzare

whisk /wɪsk/ n Culin frullino m ● vt Culin frullare

■ **whisk away** vt portare via

whisker /'wɪskə(r)/ n **~s** pl ⟨of cat⟩ baffi mpl; ⟨on man's cheek⟩ basette fpl; **by a ~** per un pelo

whisky /'wɪskɪ/ n whisky m inv

whisper /'wɪspə(r)/ n sussurro m; (*rumour*) diceria f ● vt/i sussurrare

whispering gallery /'wɪspərɪŋ/ n galleria f acustica

whistle /'wɪsl/ n fischio m; (*instrument*) fischietto m ● vt fischiettare ● vi fischiettare; ⟨*referee*⟩ fischiare

whistle-stop tour n Pol giro m elettorale

white /waɪt/ a bianco; **go ~** (*pale*) sbiancare ● n bianco m; (*of egg*) albume m; (*person*) bianco, -a mf

white: whitebait n bianchetti npl. **whiteboard** n lavagna f bianca. **white coffee** n caffè m inv macchiato. **white-collar worker** n colletto m bianco. **white elephant** n (*public project*) progetto m dispendioso e di scarsa efficacia; (*building*) cattedrale f nel deserto; (*item, knicknack*) oggetto m inutile. **white goods** n (*linen*) biancheria f per la casa; (*appliances*) elettrodomestici mpl. **Whitehall** n strada f di Londra, sede degli uffici del governo britannico; fig amministrazione f britannica. **white horses** npl cavalloni mpl. **white-hot** a ⟨*metal*⟩ arroventato. **white knight** n Fin white knight m inv. **white lie** n bugia f pietosa

whiten /'waɪtn/ vt imbiancare ● vi sbiancare

whitener /'waɪt(ə)nə(r)/ n (*for shoes*) bianchetto m; (*for clothes*) sbiancante m; (*for coffee, tea*) surrogato m del latte

whiteness /'waɪtnɪs/ n bianchezza f

white: white tie n (*tie*) cravattino m bianco; (*formal dress*) frac m inv. **whitewash** n intonaco m; fig copertura f ● vt dare una mano d'intonaco a; fig coprire. **white water** n rapide fpl. **white wedding** n matrimonio m in bianco

whither /'wɪðə(r)/ adv liter dove

whiting /'waɪtɪŋ/ n (*fish*) merlano m

Whitsun /'wɪtsn/ n Pentecoste f

■ **whittle away** /'wɪtl/ vt intaccare ⟨*savings*⟩; ridurre ⟨*lead in race*⟩

■ **whittle down** vt ridurre

whiz[z] /wɪz/ vi (*pt/pp* whizzed) sibilare

whiz[z]-kid n fam giovane m prodigio

who /hu:/ inter pron chi ● rel pron che; **the children, ~ were all tired, ...** i bambini, che erano tutti stanchi,...

whodunnit /hu:'dʌnɪt/ n fam [romanzo m] giallo m

whoever /hu:'evə(r)/ pron chiunque; **~ he is** chiunque sia; **~ can that be?** chi può mai essere?

whole /həʊl/ a tutto; (*not broken*) intatto; **the ~ truth** tutta la verità; **the ~ world** il mondo intero; **the ~ lot** (*everything*) tutto; (*pl*) tutti; **the ~ lot of you** tutti voi ● n tutto m; **as a ~** nell'insieme; **on the ~** tutto considerato; **the ~ of Italy** tutta l'Italia

whole: wholefood n cibo m macrobiotico. **wholehearted** /'həʊlhɑ:tɪd/ a di tutto cuore. **wholemeal** a integrale. **whole milk** n latte m intero. **whole number** n numero m intero

wholesale /'həʊlseɪl/ a & adv all'ingrosso; fig in massa

wholesaler /'həʊlseɪlə(r)/ n grossista mf

wholesome /'həʊlsəm/ a sano

wholly /'həʊlɪ/ adv completamente

wholly-owned subsidiary n consociata f interamente controllata

whom /hu:m/ rel pron che; **the man ~ I saw** l'uomo che ho visto; **to/with ~** a/con cui ● inter pron chi; **to ~ did you speak?** con chi hai parlato?

whoop /wu:p/ n (*shout*) grido m ● vi gridare

whoopee /'wʊpɪ/ int evviva! ● n hum **make ~** (*have fun*) fare baldoria; (*make love*) fare l'amore

whooping cough /'hu:pɪŋ/ n pertosse f

whoosh /wʊʃ/ int vuum!

whopper /'wɒpə(r)/ n fam (*lie*) balla f; **what a ~!** è veramente gigantesco!

whopping /'wɒpɪŋ/ a fam enorme

whore /hɔ:(r)/ n puttana f vulg

whorl /wɔ:l/ n (*of cream, chocolate etc*) ghirigoro m; (*of fingerprint*) spirale f

whose /hu:z/ rel pron il cui; **people ~ name begins with D** le persone i cui nomi cominciano con la D ● inter pron di chi; **~ is that?** di chi è quello? ● a **~ car did you use?** di chi è la macchina che hai usato?

Who's Who n pubblicazione f annuale con l'elenco delle personalità di spicco

why /waɪ/ adv (*inter*) perché; **the reason ~** la ragione per cui; **that's ~** per questo ● int diamine!

WI abbr (**Women's Institute**); Am abbr **Wisconsin**

wick /wɪk/ n stoppino m

wicked /'wɪkɪd/ a cattivo; (*mischievous*) malizioso

wicker /'wɪkə(r)/ n vimini mpl ● attrib di vimini

wicket /'wɪkɪt/ n (*field gate*) cancelletto m; Sport porta f; (Am: *of ticket office etc*) sportello m; **be a sticky ~** fam essere in una situazione difficile

wide /waɪd/ a (*experience, knowledge*) vasto; (*difference*) profondo; (*far from target*) lontano; **10 cm ~** largo 10 cm; **how ~ is it?** quanto è largo? ● adv (*off target*) lontano dal bersaglio; **~ awake** del tutto sveglio; **~ open** spalancato; **open ~!** apri bene!; **far and ~** in lungo e in largo

wide-angle lens n grandangolo m

wide-eyed /-'aɪd/ a ⟨*person, innocence*⟩ ingenuo; (*with fear, surprise*) con gli occhi sbarrati

widely /'waɪdlɪ/ adv largamente; ⟨*known, accepted*⟩ generalmente; ⟨*different*⟩ profondamente

widen /'waɪdn/ vt allargare; **~ the gap** fig accentuare il contrasto ● vi allargarsi

wide open a ⟨*door, window, eyes*⟩ spalancato

wide screen n Cinema schermo m panoramico

widespread /'waɪdspred/ a diffuso

widow /'wɪdəʊ/ n vedova f

widowed /'wɪdəʊd/ a vedovo

widower /'wɪdəʊə(r)/ n vedovo m

width /wɪdθ/ *n* larghezza *f*; (*of material*) altezza *f*

widthways /ˈwɪdθweɪz/ *adv* trasversalmente

wield /wiːld/ *vt* maneggiare; esercitare ⟨*power*⟩

wife /waɪf/ *n* (*pl* **wives**) moglie *f*

wife battering /ˈwaɪfbæt(ə)rɪŋ/ *n* maltrattamento *m* della coniuge

wig /wɪg/ *n* parrucca *f*

wiggle /ˈwɪgl/ *vi* dimenarsi ● *vt* dimenare

wild /waɪld/ *a* selvaggio; ⟨*animal, flower*⟩ selvatico; (*furious*) furibondo; ⟨*applause*⟩ fragoroso; ⟨*idea*⟩ folle; (*with joy*) pazzo; ⟨*guess*⟩ azzardato; **be ~ about** (*keen on*) andare pazzo per ● *adv* **run ~** crescere senza controllo ● *n* **in the ~** allo stato naturale; **the ~s** *pl* le zone sperdute

wild: wild card *n* jolly *m inv*; *Comput* carattere *m* jolly. **wildcat strike** *n* sciopero *m* selvaggio. **wild dog** *n* cane *m* randagio

wilderness /ˈwɪldənɪs/ *n* deserto *m*; ⟨*fig: garden*⟩ giungla *f*

wild: wild-eyed /-ˈaɪd/ *a* (*distressed*) dall'aria angosciata; (*angry*) dallo sguardo minaccioso. **wildfire** *n* **spread like ~** allargarsi a macchia d'olio. **wild flower** *n* fiore *m* di campo. **wildfowl** *n* (*bird*) uccello *m* selvatico; (*birds collectively*) uccelli *mpl* selvatici; (*game*) selvaggina *f* di penna. **wild-goose chase** *n* ricerca *f* inutile. **wildlife** *n* animali *mpl* selvatici. **wildlife park** *n* parco *m* naturale. **wildlife reserve** *n* riserva *f* naturale. **wildlife sanctuary** *n* riserva *f* naturale

wildly /ˈwaɪldlɪ/ *adv fig* ⟨*exaggerated*⟩ estremamente; ⟨*speak*⟩ senza riflettere; ⟨*applaud*⟩ fragorosamente; ⟨*hit out*⟩ all'impazzata

Wild West *n* far west *m*

wiles /waɪlz/ *npl* astuzie *fpl*

wilful /ˈwɪlful/ *a* intenzionale; ⟨*person, refusal*⟩ ostinato

wilfully /ˈwɪlfulɪ/ *adv* intenzionalmente; ⟨*refuse*⟩ ostinatamente

will¹ /wɪl/ *v aux* **he ~ arrive tomorrow** arriverà domani; **I won't tell him** non glielo dirò; **you ~ be back soon, won't you?** tornerai presto, no?; **he ~ be there, won't he?** sarà là, no?; **she ~ be there by now** sarà là ormai; **~ you go?** (*do you intend to go*) pensi di andare?; **~ you go to the baker's and buy...?** puoi andare dal panettiere a comprare...?; **~ you be quiet!** vuoi stare calmo!; **~ you have some wine?** vuoi del vino?; **the engine won't start** la macchina non parte

will² *n* volontà *f inv*; (*document*) testamento *m*

willing /ˈwɪlɪŋ/ *a* disposto; (*eager*) volonteroso

willingly /ˈwɪlɪŋlɪ/ *adv* volentieri

willingness /ˈwɪlɪŋnɪs/ *n* buona volontà *f*

willow /ˈwɪləʊ/ *n* salice *m*

willowy /ˈwɪləʊɪ/ *a* ⟨*person, figure*⟩ slanciato

will-power *n* forza *f* di volontà

willy-nilly /wɪlɪˈnɪlɪ/ *adv* (*at random*) a casaccio; (*wanting to or not*) volente o nolente

wilt /wɪlt/ *vi* appassire

wily /ˈwaɪlɪ/ *a* (**-ier, -iest**) astuto

wimp /wɪmp/ *n* rammollito, -a *mf*

wimpish /ˈwɪmpɪʃ/ *a* ⟨*fam: behaviour*⟩ da rammollito

wimpy /ˈwɪmpɪ/ *a* ⟨*fam: person*⟩ rammollito

win /wɪn/ *n* vittoria *f*; **have a ~** riportare una vittoria ● *v* (*pt/pp* **won**; *pres p* **winning**) ● *vt* vincere; conquistare ⟨*fame*⟩ ● *vi* vincere

■ win back *vt* recuperare

■ win over *vt* convincere

■ win through *vi* (*fam: be successful*) uscire vittorioso

wince /wɪns/ *vi* contrarre il viso

winch /wɪntʃ/ *n* argano m

■ winch up *vt* tirare con l'argano

wind¹ /wɪnd/ *n* vento *m*; (*breath*) fiato *m*; (*fam: flatulence*) aria *f*; **get/have the ~ up** *fam* aver fifa; **get ~ of** aver sentore di; **in the ~** nell'aria ● *vt* **~ sb** lasciare qcno senza fiato; **~ a baby** far fare il ruttino a un neonato

wind² /waɪnd/ *v* (*pt/pp* **wound**) ● *vt* (*wrap*) avvolgere; (*move by turning*) far girare; ⟨*clock*⟩ caricare ● *vi* (*road:*) serpeggiare

■ wind down *vi* (*relax*) rilassarsi; (*gradually come to an end*) diminuire ● *vt* (*gradually bring to an end*) metter fine in modo graduale a

■ wind up /waɪnd/ *vt* caricare ⟨*clock*⟩; concludere ⟨*proceedings*⟩; *fam* sfottere ⟨*sb*⟩ ● *vi* (*end up*) **~ up doing sth** finire per fare qcsa

wind /wɪnd/: **windbreak** *n* frangivento *m*. **windcheater** *n Br* giacca *f* a vento. **windchill factor** *n* fattore *m* di raffreddamento da vento. **wind energy** *n* forza *f* del vento. **windfall** *n fig* fortuna *f* inaspettata; **~s** *pl* (*fruit*) frutta *f* abbattuta dal vento

winder /ˈwaɪndə(r)/ *n* (*for car window*) manovella *f* alzacristalli; (*for watch*) bottone *m* di carica

winding /ˈwaɪndɪŋ/ *a* tortuoso

wind instrument /ˈwɪnd/ *n* strumento *m* a fiato

windmill /ˈwɪn(d)mɪl/ *n* mulino *m* a vento

window /ˈwɪndəʊ/ *n* finestra *f*; (*of car*) finestrino *m*; (*of shop*) vetrina *f*

window: window box *n* cassetta *f* per i fiori. **window cleaner** *n* (*person*) lavavetri *mf inv*. **window display** *n Comm* esposizione *f* in vetrina. **window dresser** *n* vetrinista *mf*. **window dressing** *n* vetrinistica *f*; *fig* fumo *m* negli occhi. **window envelope** *n* busta *f* a finestra. **window frame** *n* telaio *m* di finestra. **window ledge** *n* davanzale *m*. **window pane** *n* vetro *m*. **window-shopping** *n* **go ~** andare in giro a vedere le vetrine. **window sill** *n* davanzale *m*

wind /wɪnd/: **windpipe** *n* trachea *f*. **windscreen** *n, Am* **windshield** *n* parabrezza *m inv*. **windscreen washer** *n* getto *m* d'acqua. **windscreen-wiper** *n* tergicristallo *m*. **wind-sleeve** *n* manica *f* a vento. **wind-sock** *n* manica *f* a vento. **wind surfing** *n* windsurf *m inv*. **windswept** *a* esposto al vento; ⟨*person*⟩ scompigliato

windy /ˈwɪndɪ/ *a* (**-ier, -iest**) ventoso

wine /waɪn/ n vino m

wine: wine bar n ≈ enoteca f. **wine box** n contenitore m di vino con rubinetto. **wine cooler** n (ice bucket) secchiello m del ghiaccio; (Am: drink) bibita f leggermente alcolica. **wineglass** n bicchiere m da vino. **wine list** n carta f dei vini. **wine merchant** n commerciante mf di vini. **wine producer** n produttore, -trice mf di vini. **wine rack** n portabottiglie m inv

winery /'waɪnərɪ/ n Am vigneto m

wine tasting /'waɪnteɪstɪŋ/ n degustazione f di vini

wing /wɪŋ/ n ala f; Auto parafango m; ~s pl Theat quinte fpl; **under sb's** ~ sotto l'ala [protettiva] di qcno

wing: wing chair n poltrona f con ampio schienale. **wing collar** n colletto m rigido. **wing commander** n tenente m colonnello delle forze aeree

winger /'wɪŋə(r)/ n Sport ala f

wing: wing-half n (in soccer) mediano m. **wing mirror** n Br specchietto m laterale. **wing nut** n dado m ad alette. **wingspan** n apertura f alare

wink /wɪŋk/ n strizzata f d'occhio; **not sleep a** ~ non chiudere occhio ● vi strizzare l'occhio; (light:) lampeggiare

winner /'wɪnə(r)/ n vincitore, -trice mf

winning /'wɪnɪŋ/ a vincente; (smile) accattivante

winning post n linea f d'arrivo

winnings /'wɪnɪŋz/ npl vincite fpl

winning streak n periodo m fortunato; **be on a** ~ essere in un periodo fortunato

winsome /'wɪnsəm/ a accattivante

winter /'wɪntə(r)/ n inverno m

winter sports npl sport mpl invernali

wintertime /'wɪntətaɪm/ n inverno m

wintry /'wɪntrɪ/ a invernale

wipe /waɪp/ n passata f; (to dry) asciugata f ● vt strofinare; (dry) asciugare

■ **wipe off** vt asciugare; (erase) cancellare

■ **wipe out** vt annientare; eliminare (village); estinguere (debt)

■ **wipe up** vt asciugare (dishes)

wiper blade /'waɪpə/ n Auto bordo f gommato del tergicristallo

wire /'waɪə(r)/ n fil m di ferro; (electrical) filo m elettrico

wire: wire brush n spazzola f metallica. **wire-cutters** n tronchese msg. **wire-haired** /-'heəd/ a dal pelo ispido

wireless /'waɪəlɪs/ n radio f inv

wire: wire mesh n rete f metallica. **wire netting** n rete f metallica. **wire wool** n lana f d'acciaio

wiring /'waɪərɪŋ/ n impianto m elettrico

wiry /'waɪərɪ/ a (-ier, -iest) (person) dal fisico asciutto; (hair) ispido

wisdom /'wɪzdəm/ n saggezza f; (of action) sensatezza f

wisdom tooth n dente m del giudizio

wise /waɪz/ a saggio; (prudent) sensato

■ **wise up** fam vi (become more aware) aprire gli occhi ● vt aprire gli occhi a (**to** su)

wisecrack /'waɪzkræk/ fam n battuta f salace ● vi far battute salaci

wise guy n fam sapientone m

wisely /'waɪzlɪ/ adv saggiamente; (act) sensatamente

Wise Men npl Re Magi mpl

wish /wɪʃ/ n desiderio m; **make a** ~ esprimere un desiderio; **with best** ~es con i migliori auguri ● vt desiderare; ~ **sb well** fare tanti auguri a qcno; **I** ~ **you every success** ti auguro buona fortuna; **I** ~ **you could stay** vorrei che tu potessi rimanere; ~ **sth on sb** fam sbolognare qcsa a qcno ● vi ~ **for sth** desiderare qcsa

wishbone /'wɪʃbəʊn/ n forcella f (di pollo o tacchino)

wishful /'wɪʃfʊl/ a ~ **thinking** illusione f

wishy-washy /'wɪʃɪwɒʃɪ/ a (colour) spento; (personality) insignificante

wisp /wɪsp/ n (of hair) ciocca f; (of smoke) filo m; (of grass) ciuffo m

wisteria /wɪs'tɪərɪə/ n glicine m

wistful /'wɪstfʊl/ a malinconico

wistfully /'wɪstfʊlɪ/ adv malinconicamente

wit /wɪt/ n spirito m; (person) persona f di spirito; **be at one's** ~**s' end** non saper che pesci pigliare; **scared out of one's** ~**s** spaventato a morte

witch /wɪtʃ/ n strega f

witch: witchcraft n magia f. **witch doctor** n stregone m. **witch-hunt** n caccia f alle streghe

with /wɪð/ prep con; (fear, cold, jealousy etc) di; **I'm not** ~ **you** fam non ti seguo; **can I leave it** ~ **you?** (task) puoi occupartene tu?; ~ **no regrets/money** senza rimpianti/soldi; **be** ~ **it** fam essere al passo coi tempi; (alert) essere concentrato

withdraw /wɪð'drɔː/ v (pt -drew, pp -drawn) ● vt ritirare; prelevare (money) ● vi ritirarsi

withdrawal /wɪð'drɔː(ə)l/ n ritiro m; (of money) prelevamento m; (from drugs) crisi f inv di astinenza; Psych chiusura f in se stessi

withdrawal symptoms npl sintomi mpl da crisi di astinenza

withdrawn /wɪð'drɔːn/ see **withdraw** ● a (person) chiuso in se stesso

wither /'wɪðə(r)/ vi (flower:) appassire

withering /'wɪðərɪŋ/ a (look) fulminante

withhold /wɪð'həʊld/ vt (pt/pp -held) rifiutare (consent) (from a); nascondere (information) (from a); trattenere (smile)

within /wɪð'ɪn/ prep in; (before the end of) entro; ~ **the law** legale ● adv all'interno

without /wɪð'aʊt/ prep senza; ~ **stopping** senza fermarsi; **how could it have happened** ~ **you noticing it?** come è potuto succedere senza che tu lo notassi?

withstand /wɪð'stænd/ vt (pt/pp -stood) resistere a

witness /'wɪtnɪs/ n testimone mf; **bear** ~ portare testimonianza ● vt ≈ autenticare (signature); essere testimone di (accident)

witness box, *Am* **witness-stand** *n* banco *m* dei testimoni

witticism /'wɪtɪsɪzm/ *n* spiritosaggine *f*

wittingly /'wɪtɪŋlɪ/ *adv* consapevolmente

witty /'wɪtɪ/ *a* (-ier, -iest) spiritoso

wives /waɪvz/ *see* **wife**

wizard /'wɪzəd/ *n* mago *m*

wizardry /'wɪzədrɪ/ *n* stregoneria *f*

wizened /'wɪznd/ *a* raggrinzito

wk *abbr* **week**

wobble /'wɒbl/ *vi* traballare

wobbly /'wɒblɪ/ *a* traballante

wodge /wɒdʒ/ *n fam* mucchio *m*

woe /wəʊ/ *n* afflizione *f*; ~ **is me!** me meschino!

woeful /'wəʊfʊl/ *a* ⟨story, sight⟩ triste; ⟨lack⟩ vergognoso

woke, woken /wəʊk, 'wəʊkn/ *see* **wake**[1]

wolf /wʊlf/ *n* (*pl* **wolves** /wʊlvz/) lupo *m*; (*fam: womanizer*) donnaiolo *m* ● *vt* ~ **[down]** divorare

wolf: **wolf cub** *n* cucciolo *m* di lupo. **wolfhound** *n Br* cane *m* lupo. **wolf whistle** *n* fischio *m* ● *vi* ~**-whistle at sb** fischiare dietro a qcno

woman /'wʊmən/ *n* (*pl* **women**) donna *f*

womanizer /'wʊmənaɪz(r)/ *n* donnaiolo *m*

womanly /'wʊmənlɪ/ *a* femmineo

womb /wuːm/ *n* utero *m*

women /'wɪmɪn/ *see* **woman**

women's: **Women's Institute** *n* associazione *f* che si occupa dei problemi delle donne. **Women's Libber** /wɪmɪnz'lɪbə(r)/ *n* femminista *f*. **Women's Liberation** *n* movimento *m* femminista. **women's movement** *n* movimento *m* per l'emancipazione della donna. **women's studies** *npl* storia *f* dell'emancipazione femminile

won /wʌn/ *see* **win**

wonder /'wʌndə(r)/ *n* meraviglia *f*; (*surprise*) stupore *m*; **no** ~**!** non c'è da stupirsi!; **it's a** ~ **that...** è incredibile che... ● *vi* restare in ammirazione; (*be surprised*) essere sorpreso; **I** ~ è quello che mi chiedo; **I** ~ **whether she is ill** mi chiedo se è malata?

wonderful /'wʌndəfʊl/ *a* meraviglioso

wonderfully /'wʌndəfʊlɪ/ *adv* meravigliosamente

wonderland /'wʌndəlænd/ *n* paese *m* delle meraviglie

wonky /'wɒŋkɪ/ *a Br fam* (*faulty*) difettoso; ⟨furniture⟩ traballante; (*crooked*) storto

wont /wəʊnt/ *n* **as was his** ~ come suo solito ● *a* **he was** ~ **to fall asleep** era solito addormentarsi

won't /wəʊnt/ = **will not**

woo /wuː/ *vt* corteggiare; *fig* cercare di accattivarsi ⟨voters⟩; cercare di ottenere ⟨fame, fortune⟩

wood /wʊd/ *n* legno *m*; (*for burning*) legna *f*; ⟨forest⟩ bosco *m*; **out of the** ~ *fig* fuori pericolo; **touch** ~**!** tocca ferro!

woodcarving /'wʊdkɑːvɪŋ/ *n* scultura *f* di legno

wooded /'wʊdɪd/ *a* boscoso

wooden /'wʊdn/ *a* di legno; *fig* legnoso

wooden horse *n* cavallo *m* di Troia

wooden spoon *n* mestolo *m* di legno; *fig* premio *m* di consolazione

wood: **woodlouse** *n* onisco *m*. **woodpecker** *n* picchio *m*. **wood pigeon** *n* colombaccio *m*. **wood shavings** *npl* trucioli *mpl*. **woodshed** *n* legnaia *f*. **wood stove** *n* stufa *f* a legna. **woodwind** *n* strumenti *mpl* a fiato. **woodwork** *n* (*wooden parts*) parti *fpl* in legno; (*craft*) falegnameria *f*. **woodworm** *n* tarlo *m*

woody /'wʊdɪ/ *a* legnoso; ⟨hill⟩ boscoso

wool /wʊl/ *n* lana *f*; **pull the** ~ **over sb's eyes** gettar fumo negli occhi a qcno ● *attrib* di lana

woollen /'wʊlən/ *a* di lana

woollens /'wʊlənz/ *npl* capi *mpl* di lana

woolly /'wʊlɪ/ *a* (-ier, -iest) ⟨sweater⟩ di lana; *fig* confuso

woozy /'wuːzɪ/ *a* intontito

word /wɜːd/ *n* parola *f*; (*news*) notizia *f*; **by** ~ **of mouth** a viva voce; **have a** ~ **with** dire due parole a; **have** ~**s** bisticciare; **in other** ~**s** in altre parole; **go back on one's** ~ rimangiarsi la parola

word-for-word *a* ⟨translation⟩ letterale ● *adv* parola per parola

wording /'wɜːdɪŋ/ *n* parole *fpl*

word: **word-perfect** *a* che sa a memoria. **word processing** *n Comput* word processing *m*, elaborazione *f* testi. **word processor** *n* sistema *m* di videoscrittura, word processor *m inv*

wordy /'wɜːdɪ/ *a* prolisso

wore /wɔː(r)/ *see* **wear**

work /wɜːk/ *n* lavoro *m*; (*of art*) opera *f*; ~**s** *pl* (*factory*) fabbrica *fsg*; (*mechanism*) meccanismo *msg*; **at** ~ al lavoro; **out of** ~ disoccupato ● *vi* lavorare; ⟨machine, ruse:⟩ funzionare; (*study*) studiare ● *vt* far funzionare ⟨machine⟩; far lavorare ⟨employee⟩; far studiare ⟨student⟩; ~ **one's way through sth** (*read*) leggere attentamente

■ **work off** *vt* sfogare ⟨anger⟩; lavorare per estinguere ⟨debt⟩; fare sport per smaltire ⟨weight⟩

■ **work out** *vt* elaborare ⟨plan⟩; risolvere ⟨problem⟩; calcolare ⟨bill⟩; **I** ~**ed out how he did it** ho capito come l'ha fatto ● *vi* evolvere

■ **work up** *vt* **I've** ~**ed up an appetite** mi è venuto appetito; **don't get** ~**ed up** (*anxious*) non farti prendere dal panico; (*angry*) non arrabbiarti

workable /'wɜːkəbl/ *a* (*feasible*) fattibile

workaday /'wɜːkədeɪ/ *a* ⟨clothes, life⟩ ordinario

workaholic /wɜːkə'hɒlɪk/ *n* staccanovista *mf*

work: **workbench** *n* banco *m* da lavoro. **workbook** *n* (*blank*) quaderno *m*; (*with exercises*) libro *m* di esercizi. **workday** *n* giorno *m* lavorativo

worker /'wɜːkə(r)/ *n* lavoratore, -trice *mf*; (*manual*) operaio, -a *mf*

work: work experience *n* esperienza *f* professionale; (*part of training programme*) stage *m inv.* **workforce** *n* forza *f* lavoro. **workhorse** *n fig* lavoratore, -trice *mf* indefesso, -a

working /'wɜːkɪŋ/ *a* ‹*clothes etc*› da lavoro; ‹*day*› feriale; **in ~ order** funzionante

working: working capital *n* capitale *m* netto di esercizio. **working-class** *a* operaio; **be ~** appartenere alla classe operaia ● **working class** *n* classe *f* operaia. **working week** *n* settimana *f* lavorativa

work: workload *n* carico *m* di lavoro. **workman** *n* operaio *m.* **workmanlike** *a* fatto con competenza. **workmanship** *n* lavorazione *f.* **workmate** *n* collega *mf.* **work of art** *n* opera *f* d'arte. **workout** *n* allenamento *m.* **work permit** *n* permesso *m* di lavoro. **workplace** *n* posto *m* di lavoro. **work-sharing** *n divisione f di un posto di lavoro tra più persone.* **workshop** *n* officina *f*; (*discussion*) dibattito *m.* **work-shy** *a* pigro. **workstation** *n* stazione *f* di lavoro. **work surface** *n* piano *m* di lavoro. **worktop** *n* piano *m* di lavoro. **work-to-rule** *n* sciopero *m* bianco

world /wɜːld/ *n* mondo *m*; **a ~ of difference** una differenza abissale; **out of this ~** favoloso; **think the ~ of sb** andare matto per qcno

world: world-class *a* di livello internazionale. **World Cup** *n* (*in football*) Coppa *f* del Mondo. **world-famous** *a* di fama mondiale

worldly /'wɜːldlɪ/ *a* materiale; ‹*person*› materialista

worldly-wise *a* vissuto

world war *n* guerra *f* mondiale

worldwide /'wɜːldwaɪd/ *a* mondiale ● *adv* mondialmente

worm /wɜːm/ *n* verme *m* ● *vt* **~ one's way into sb's confidence** conquistarsi la fiducia di qcno in modo subdolo

■ **worm out** *vt* **~ sth out of sb** carpire qcsa a qcno

worm-eaten /'wɜːmiːtən/ *a* ‹*wood*› tarlato; ‹*fruit*› bacato

wormhole /'wɜːmhəʊl/ *n* (*in wood*) buco *m* di tarlo; (*in fruit, plant*) buco *m* del verme

worn /wɔːn/ *see* **wear** ● *a* sciupato

worn-out *a* consumato; ‹*person*› sfinito

worried /'wʌrɪd/ *a* preoccupato

worrier /'wʌrɪə(r)/ *n* ansioso, -a *mf*; **he's a terrible ~** è ansioso da morire

worry /'wʌrɪ/ *n* preoccupazione *f* ● *v* (*pt/pp* **worried**) ● *vt* preoccupare; (*bother*) disturbare ● *vi* preoccuparsi

worrying /'wʌrɪɪŋ/ *a* preoccupante

worse /wɜːs/ *a* peggiore ● *adv* peggio ● *n* peggio *m*

worsen /'wɜːsn/ *vt/i* peggiorare

worse off *a* **be ~ ~ than** stare peggio di; **be £100 ~ ~** avere 100 sterline in meno

worship /'wɜːʃɪp/ *n* culto *m*; (*service*) funzione *f*; **Your/His W~** (*to judge*) signor giudice/il

giudice ● *v* (*pt/pp* **-shipped**) ● *vt* venerare ● *vi* andare a messa

worst /wɜːst/ *a* peggiore ● *adv* peggio ● *n* **the ~** il peggio; **get the ~ of it** avere la peggio; **if the ~ comes to the ~** nella peggiore delle ipotesi

worsted /'wʊstɪd/ *n* lana *f* pettinata

worth /wɜːθ/ *n* valore *m*; **£10 ~ of petrol** 10 sterline di benzina ● *a* **be ~** valere; **be ~ it** *fig* valerne la pena; **it is ~ trying** vale la pena di provare; **it's ~ my while** mi conviene; **I'll make it ~ your while** te ne ricompenserò

worthless /'wɜːθlɪs/ *a* senza valore

worthwhile /wɜːθ'waɪl/ *a* che vale la pena; ‹*cause*› lodevole

worthy /'wɜːðɪ/ *a* degno; ‹*cause, motive*› lodevole

would /wʊd/ *v aux* **I ~ do it** lo farei; **~ you go?** andresti?; **~ you mind if I opened the window?** ti dispiace se apro la finestra?; **he ~ come if he could** verrebbe se potesse; **he said he ~n't** ha detto di no; **he said he ~n't have** ha detto che non lo avrebbe fatto; **~ you like a drink?** vuoi qualcosa da bere?; **what ~ you like to drink?** cosa prendi da bere?; **you ~n't, ~ you?** non lo faresti, vero?

would-be *a* ‹*pej: actor, singer etc*› sedicente; ‹*investor, buyer*› aspirante

wound¹ /wuːnd/ *n* ferita *f* ● *vt* ferire

wound² /waʊnd/ *see* **wind²**

wove, woven /wəʊv, 'wəʊvn/ *see* **weave²**

wow /waʊ/ *n* (*fam: success*) successone *m*; (*in sound system*) wow *m* ● *vt fam* entusiasmare ‹*person*› ● *int* caspita!

WP *abbr* (**word processing**) elaborazione *f* testi

wpm *abbr* (**words per minute**) parole *fpl* al minuto

wrangle /'ræŋgl/ *n* litigio *m* ● *vi* litigare

wrap /ræp/ *n* (*shawl*) scialle *m* ● *vt* (*pt/pp* **wrapped**) **~** [**up**] avvolgere; ‹*present*› incartare; **be ~ped up in** *fig* essere completamente preso da ● *vi* **~ up warmly** coprirsi bene

wraparound /'ræpəraʊnd/ *a* ‹*skirt*› a pareo; ‹*window, windscreen*› panoramico

wrapper /'ræpə(r)/ *n* (*for sweet*) carta *f* [di caramella]

wrapping /'ræpɪŋ/ *n* materiale *m* da imballaggio

wrapping paper *n* carta *f* da pacchi; (*for gift*) carta *f* da regalo

wrath /rɒθ/ *n* ira *f*

wreak /riːk/ *vt* **~ havoc with sth** scombussolare qcsa

wreath /riːθ/ *n* (*pl* **~s** /riːðz/) corona *f*

wreathed /riːðd/ *a* **~ in** avvolto in ‹*mists*›; **her face was ~ in smiles** era raggiante

wreck /rek/ *n* (*of ship*) relitto *m*; (*of car*) carcassa *f*; (*person*) rottame *m* ● *vt* far naufragare; demolire ‹*car*›

wreckage /'rekɪdʒ/ *n* rottami *mpl*; *fig* brandelli *mpl*

wrecked /rekt/ *a* ‹*ship, car*› distrutto;

⟨*building*⟩ demolito; (*fig: exhausted*) distrutto

wren /ren/ n scricciolo m

wrench /rentʃ/ n (*injury*) slogatura f; (*tool*) chiave f inglese; (*pull*) strattone m; **it was a ~ leaving home** *fig* è stato un passo difficile andarsene da casa ● vt (*pull*) strappare; slogarsi ⟨*wrist, ankle etc*⟩

wrest /rest/ vt strappare

wrestle /ˈresl/ vi lottare corpo a corpo; *fig* lottare

wrestler /ˈreslə(r)/ n lottatore, -trice mf

wrestling /ˈreslɪŋ/ n lotta f libera; (*all-in*) catch m

wretch /retʃ/ n disgraziato, -a mf

wretched /ˈretʃɪd/ a odioso; ⟨*weather*⟩ orribile; **feel ~** (*unhappy*) essere triste; (*ill*) sentirsi malissimo

wriggle /ˈrɪgl/ n contorsione f ● vi contorcersi; (*move forward*) strisciare; **~ out of sth** *fam* sottrarsi a qcsa

wriggly /ˈrɪglɪ/ a ⟨*person*⟩ che si dimena; ⟨*snake, worm*⟩ che si contorce

wring /rɪŋ/ vt (*pt/pp* wrung) torcere ⟨*sb's neck*⟩; strizzare ⟨*clothes*⟩; **~ one's hands** torcersi le mani; **~ sth out of sb** *fig* estorcere qcsa a qcno; **~ing wet** inzuppato

wrinkle /ˈrɪŋkl/ n grinza f; (*on skin*) ruga f ● vt/i raggrinzire

wrinkled /ˈrɪŋkld/ a ⟨*skin, face*⟩ rugoso; ⟨*clothes*⟩ raggrinzito

wrist /rɪst/ n polso m

wristband /ˈrɪs(t)bænd/ n polsino m; (*on watch*) cinturino m

wristwatch /ˈrɪstwɒtʃ/ n orologio m da polso

writ /rɪt/ n *Jur* mandato m

write /raɪt/ vt/i (*pt* wrote, *pp* written, *pres p* writing) scrivere

■ **write away for** vt richiedere per posta ⟨*information*⟩

■ **write back** vi rispondere

■ **write down** vt annotare

■ **write in** vi scrivere

■ **write off** vt cancellare ⟨*debt*⟩; distruggere ⟨*car*⟩

■ **write out** vt fare ⟨*cheque, prescription*⟩; (*copy*) ricopiare

■ **write up** vt redigere; aggiornare ⟨*diary*⟩; elaborare ⟨*notes*⟩

write-off n (*car*) rottame m

writer /ˈraɪtə(r)/ n autore, -trice mf; **she's a ~** è una scrittrice

writer's block n blocco m dello scrittore

write-up n (*review*) recensione f

writhe /raɪð/ vi contorcersi; **~ with embarrassment** vergognarsi a morte

writing /ˈraɪtɪŋ/ n (*occupation*) scrivere m; (*words*) scritte fpl; (*handwriting*) scrittura f; **~s** pl scritti mpl; **in ~** per iscritto

writing: writing desk n scrivania f. **writing pad** n (*for notes*) bloc-notes m inv; (*for letters*) blocco m di carta da lettere. **writing paper** n carta f da lettera

written /ˈrɪtn/ *see* **write**

wrong /rɒŋ/ a sbagliato; **be ~** ⟨*person:*⟩ sbagliare; **what's ~?** cosa c'è che non va? ● adv ⟨*spelt*⟩ in modo sbagliato; **go ~** ⟨*person:*⟩ sbagliare; ⟨*machine:*⟩ funzionare male; ⟨*plan:*⟩ andar male; **don't get me ~** non fraintendermi ● n ingiustizia f; **in the ~** dalla parte del torto; **know right from ~** distinguere il bene dal male ● vt fare torto a

wrong-foot vt *Sport, fig* prendere in contropiede

wrongful /ˈrɒŋful/ a ingiusto

wrongfully /ˈrɒŋfulɪ/ adv ⟨*accuse*⟩ ingiustamente

wrongly /ˈrɒŋlɪ/ adv in modo sbagliato; ⟨*accuse, imagine*⟩ a torto; ⟨*informed*⟩ male

wrote /rəʊt/ *see* **write**

wrought iron /rɔːˈtaɪən/ n ferro m battuto ● attrib di ferro battuto

wrung /rʌŋ/ *see* **wring**

wry /raɪ/ a (**-er, -est**) ⟨*humour, smile*⟩ beffardo

WYSIWYG /ˈwɪzɪwɪg/ abbr *Comput* (**what you see is what you get**) ciò che vedi è ciò che ottieni

x, X /eks/ n (letter) x, X f inv; (anonymous person, place etc) X
x n Math x f inv
X certificate a Br vietato ai minori di 18 anni
xenophobia /zenə'fəʊbɪə/ n xenofobia f
xerox® /'zɪərɒks/ vt xerocopiare ● n (machine) xerocopiatrice f; (document) xerocopia f

Xmas /'krɪsməs/ n fam Natale m
X-ray n (picture) radiografia f; **have an ~** farsi fare una radiografia ● vt passare ai raggi X
X-ray machine n apparecchio m radiografico
xxx n (at end of letter) baci mpl

y, Y /waɪ/ n (letter) y, Y f inv
yacht /jɒt/ n yacht m inv; (for racing) barca f a vela
yachting /'jɒtɪŋ/ n vela f
yak /jæk/ n Zool yak m inv
Yale® /jeɪl/ n (lock) serratura f di sicurezza
yam /jæm/ n (tropical) igname m; (Am: sweet potato) patata f dolce
Yank /jæŋk/ n fam americano, -a mf
yank vt fam tirare
Yankee /'jæŋkɪ/ n (pej: American) yankee m inv; (soldier) nordista m; (Am: of Northern USA) abitante mf degli USA settentrionali; (Am: inhabitant of New England) abitante mf della Nuova Inghilterra
yap /jæp/ vi (pt/pp yapped) (dog:) guaire
yapping /'jæpɪŋ/ n (of dogs) guaiti mpl; (fam: of people) ciance fpl
yard¹ /jɑːd/ n cortile m; (for storage) deposito m; **the Y~** fam Scotland Yard f (polizia londinese)
yard² n iarda f (= 91,44 cm)
yardstick /'jɑːdstɪk/ n fig pietra f di paragone
yarn /jɑːn/ n filo m; (fam: tale) storia f
yashmak /'jæʃmæk/ n velo m (delle donne musulmane)
yawn /jɔːn/ n sbadiglio m ● vi sbadigliare
yawning /'jɔːnɪŋ/ a ~ gap sbadiglio m
yd abbr **yard**
yeah /je/ adv fam sì; **oh ~ ?** ma davvero?
year /jɪə(r)/ n anno m; (of wine) annata f; **for ~s** fam da secoli
yearbook /'jɪəbʊk/ n annuario m
yearly /'jɪəlɪ/ a annuale ● adv annualmente
yearn /jɜːn/ vi struggersi
yearning /'jɜːnɪŋ/ n desiderio m struggente
year-round a (supply, source) permanente

yeast /jiːst/ n lievito m
yell /jel/ n urlo m ● vi urlare
yelling /'jelɪŋ/ n urla fpl
yellow /'jeləʊ/ a & n giallo m
yellow-belly n fam fifone m
yellow card n Sport cartellino m giallo
yellowish /'jeləʊɪʃ/ a giallastro
yellow pages npl pagine fpl gialle
yellowy /'jeləʊɪ/ a giallastro
yelp /jelp/ n (of dog) guaito m ● vi (dog:) guaire
Yemen /'jemən/ n Yemen m
Yemeni /'jemənɪ/ a & n yemenita mf
yen /jen/ n forte desiderio m (for di)
yeoman /'jəʊmən/ n Br piccolo proprietario m terriero; **Y~ of the Guard** guardiano m della Torre di Londra
yep /jep/ adv fam sì
yes /jes/ adv sì ● n sì m inv
yes-man n fam tirapiedi m inv
yesterday /'jestədeɪ/ n & adv ieri m inv; **~'s paper** il giornale di ieri; **the day before ~** l'altroieri; **~ afternoon** ieri pomeriggio; **~ evening** ieri sera; **~ morning** ieri mattina
yet /jet/ adv ancora; **as ~** fino ad ora; **not ~** non ancora; **the best ~** il migliore finora ● conj eppure
yew /juː/ n tasso m (albero)
Y-fronts npl Br slip m inv da uomo con apertura
YHA Br abbr (Youth Hostels Association) associazione f degli ostelli della gioventù
Yiddish /'jɪdɪʃ/ n yiddish m
yield /jiːld/ n produzione f; (profit) reddito m ● vt produrre; fruttare (profit) ● vi cedere; Am Auto dare la precedenza
yielding /'jiːldɪŋ/ a (submissive) arrendevole; (ground) cedevole; (person) flessibile

YMCA *abbr* (**Young Men's Christian Association**) Associazione *f* Cristiana dei Giovani

yodel /'jəʊdl/ *vi* (*pt/pp* **yodelled**) cantare jodel

yoga /'jəʊgə/ *n* yoga *m*

yoghurt /'jɒgət/ *n* yogurt *m inv*

yoke /jəʊk/ *n* giogo *m*; (*of garment*) carré *m inv*

yokel /'jəʊkl/ *n* zotico, -a *mf*

yolk /jəʊk/ *n* tuorlo *m*

yonder /'jɒndə(r)/ *adv liter* laggiù

yonks /jɒŋks/ *npl fam* **I haven't seen him for ~** è un secolo che non lo vedo

yore /jɔ:(r)/ *n* **in days of ~** un tempo

you /ju:/ *pers pron* (*subject*) tu, voi *pl*; (*formal*) lei, voi *pl*; (*direct/indirect object*) ti, vi *pl*; (*formal: direct object*) la; (*formal: indirect object*) le; (*after prep*) te, voi *pl*; (*formal: after prep*) lei; **~ are very kind** (*sg*) sei molto gentile; (*formal*) è molto gentile; (*pl & formal pl*) siete molto gentili; **~ can stay, but he has to go** (*sg*) tu puoi rimanere, ma lui deve andarsene; (*pl*) voi potete rimanere, ma lui deve andarsene; **all of ~** tutti voi; **I'll give ~ the money** (*sg*) ti darò i soldi; (*pl*) vi darò i soldi; **I'll give it to ~** (*sg*) te/(*pl*) ve lo darò; **it does ~ good** (*sg*) ti/(*pl*) vi fa bene; **it was ~!** (*sg*) eri tu!; (*pl*) eravate voi!; **~ has to be careful these days** si deve fare attenzione di questi tempi; **~ can't tell the difference** non puoi vedere la differenza

you'd /ju:d/ *abbr* **you would**; **you had**

you-know-what *pron fam* sai cosa

you-know-who *pron fam* sai chi

you'll /ju:l/ *abbr* **you will**

you're /jʊə(r)/ *abbr* **you are**

you've /ju:v/ *abbr* **you have**

young /jʌŋ/ *a* giovane; **~ lady** signorina *f*; **~ man** giovanotto *m*; **her ~ man** (*boyfriend*) il suo ragazzo ● *npl* (*animals*) piccoli *mpl*; **the ~** (*people*) i giovani

young blood *n* nuove leve *fpl*

youngish /'jʌŋɪʃ/ *a* abbastanza giovane

young-looking *a* dall'aria giovanile

young offender *n* delinquente *mf* minorenne

youngster /'jʌŋstə(r)/ *n* ragazzo, -a *mf*; (*child*) bambino, -a *mf*

your /jɔ:(r)/ *poss a* tuo *m*, tua *f*, tuoi *mpl*, tue

fpl; (*formal*) suo *m*, sua *f*, suoi *mpl*, sue *fpl*; (*pl & formal pl*) vostro *m*, vostra *f*, vostri *mpl*, vostre *fpl*; **~ task/house** il tuo compito/la tua casa; (*formal*) il suo compito/la sua casa; (*pl & formal pl*) il vostro compito/la vostra casa; **~ mother/father** tua madre/tuo padre; (*formal*) sua madre/suo padre; (*pl & formal pl*) vostra madre/vostro padre

yours /jɔ:z/ *poss pron* il tuo *m*, la tua *f*, i tuoi *mpl*, le tue *fpl*; (*formal*) il suo *m*, la sua *f*, i suoi *mpl*, le sue *fpl*; (*pl & formal pl*) il vostro *m*, la vostra *f*, i vostri *mpl*, le vostre *fpl*; **a friend of ~** un tuo/suo/vostro amico; **friends of ~** dei tuoi/vostri/suoi amici; **that is ~** quello è tuo/vostro/suo; (*as opposed to mine*) quello è il tuo/il vostro/il suo

yourself /jɔ:'self/ *pers pron* (*reflexive*) ti; (*formal*) si; (*emphatic*) te stesso; (*formal*) sé, se stesso; **do pour ~ a drink** versati da bere; (*formal*) si versi da bere; **you said so ~** lo hai detto tu stesso; (*formal*) lo ha detto lei stesso; **you can be proud of ~** puoi essere fiero di te/di sé; **by ~** da solo

yourselves /jɔ:'selvz/ *pers pron* (*reflexive*) vi; (*emphatic*) voi stessi; **do pour ~ a drink** versatevi da bere; **you said so ~** lo avete detto voi stessi; **you can be proud of ~** potete essere fieri di voi; **by ~** da soli

youth /ju:θ/ *n* (*pl* **youths** /ju:ð:z/) gioventù *f inv*; (*boy*) giovanetto *m*; **the ~** (*young people*) i giovani

youthful /'ju:θful/ *a* giovanile

youth: **youth hostel** *n* ostello *m* [della gioventù]; **youth hostelling** *n* viaggiare *m* pernottando in ostelli della gioventù. **youth work** *n* lavoro *m* di educatore. **youth worker** *n* educatore, -trice *mf*

yo-yo® /'jəʊjəʊ/ *n* yo-yo *m inv* ● *vi* ⟨*prices, inflation:*⟩ andare su e giù

yr *abbr* **year**

Yugoslav /'ju:gəslɑ:v/ *a & n* jugoslavo, -a *mf*

Yugoslavia /ju:gə'slɑ:vɪə/ *n* Jugoslavia *f*

Yule log /ju:l/ *n* tronchetto *m* natalizio

yup /jʌp/ *adv fam* sì

yuppie /'jʌpɪ/ *n* yuppie *mf inv*

yuppie flu *n* sindrome *f* da affaticamento cronico

YWCA *abbr* (**Young Women's Christian Association**) Associazione *f* Cristiana delle Giovani

z, Z /zed/ n (letter) z, Z f inv
zany /'zeɪnɪ/ a (-ier, -iest) demenziale
zap /zæp/ n (fam: energy) energia f ● vt (pt/pp
zapped) fam (destroy) distruggere ‹town›; far
fuori ‹person, animal›; (fire at) fulminare;
(Comput: delete) cancellare
zapper /'zæpə(r)/ n (fam: for TV) telecomando m
zeal /ziːl/ n zelo m
zealot /'zelət/ n fig fanatico m
zealous /'zeləs/ a zelante
zealously /'zeləslɪ/ adv con zelo
zebra /'zebrə/ n zebra f
zebra crossing n passaggio m pedonale,
zebre fpl
zenith /'zenɪθ/ n zenit m inv; fig apogeo m
zero /'zɪərəʊ/ n zero m
zero: zero gravity n assenza f di gravità.
zero hour n Mil, fig ora f zero. **zero-rated**
/-'reɪtɪd/ a Br esente [da] IVA
zest /zest/ n gusto m; (peel) scorza f (di agrumi)
zigzag /'zɪgzæg/ n zigzag m inv ● vi (pt/pp
-zagged) zigzagare
zilch /zɪltʃ/ n fam un tubo; **I understood ~**
non ho capito un tubo
Zimbabwe /zɪm'bæbweɪ/ n Zimbabwe m
Zimmer® /'zɪmə(r)/ n Br deambulatore m

zinc /zɪŋk/ n zinco m
zinc oxide n ossido m di zinco
zing /zɪŋ/ n fam (energy) brio m; (sound) sibilo m ● vt (Am: criticize) stroncare
Zionism /'zaɪənɪzm/ n sionismo m
zip /zɪp/ n ~ [**fastener**] cerniera f [lampo]
● vt (pt/pp **zipped**) ~ [**up**] chiudere con la
cerniera [lampo]
■ **zip along** vi (move quickly) procedere velocemente
zip code n Am codice m [di avviamento] postale, C.A.P.
zipper /'zɪpə(r)/ n Am cerniera f [lampo]
zippy /'zɪpɪ/ a ‹fam: vehicle› scattante
zither /'zɪðə(r)/ n cetra f
zodiac /'zəʊdɪæk/ n zodiaco m
zombie /'zɒmbɪ/ n fam zombi mf inv
zone /zəʊn/ n zona f
zoning /'zəʊnɪŋ/ n zonazione f
zonked /zɒŋkt/ a ‹fam: on drugs, drunk,
tired› fatto
zoo /zuː/ n zoo m inv
zoological /zəʊə'lɒdʒɪkl/ a zoologico
zoologist /zəʊ'ɒlədʒɪst/ n zoologo, -a mf
zoology /zəʊ'ɒlədʒɪ/ n zoologia f
zoom /zuːm/ vi sfrecciare
zoom lens n zoom m inv
zucchini /zʊ'kiːnɪ/ n zucchino m, zucchina f

ITALIAN VERB TABLES

REGULAR VERBS:

1. in **-are** (*eg* **compr|are**)

    Present ~o, ~i, ~a, ~iamo, ~ate, ~ano
    Imperfect ~avo, ~avi, ~ava, ~avamo, ~avate, ~avano
    Past historic ~ai, ~asti, ~ò, ~ammo, ~aste, ~arono
    Future ~erò, ~erai, ~erà, ~eremo, ~erete, ~eranno
    Present subjunctive ~i, ~i, ~i, ~iamo, ~iate, ~ino
    Past subjunctive ~assi, ~assi, ~asse, ~assimo, ~aste, ~assero
    Present participle ~ando
    Past participle ~ato
    Imperative ~a (*fml* ~i), ~iamo, ~ate
    Conditional ~erei, ~eresti, ~erebbe, ~eremmo, ~ereste, ~erebbero

2. in **-ere** (*eg* **vend|ere**)

    Pres ~o, ~i, ~e, ~iamo, ~ete, ~ono
    Impf ~evo, ~evi, ~eva, ~evamo, ~evate, ~evano
    Past hist ~ei *or* ~etti, ~esti, ~è *or* ~ette, ~emmo, ~este, ~erono *or* ~ettero
    Fut ~erò, ~erai, ~erà, ~eremo, ~erete, ~eranno
    Pres sub ~a, ~a, ~a, ~iamo, ~iate, ~ano
    Past sub ~essi, ~essi, ~esse, ~essimo, ~este, ~essero
    Pres part ~endo
    Past part ~uto
    Imp ~i (*fml* ~a), ~iamo, ~ete
    Cond ~erei, ~eresti, ~erebbe, ~eremmo, ~ereste, ~erebbero

3. in **-ire** (*eg* **dorm|ire**)

    Pres ~o, ~i, ~e, ~iamo, ~ite, ~ono
    Impf ~ivo, ~ivi, ~iva, ~ivamo, ~ivate, ~ivano
    Past hist ~ii, ~isti, ~ì, ~immo, ~iste, ~irono
    Fut ~irò, ~irai, ~irà, ~iremo, ~irete, ~iranno
    Pres sub ~a, ~a, ~a, ~iamo, ~iate, ~ano
    Past sub ~issi, ~issi, ~isse, ~issimo, ~iste, ~issero
    Pres part ~endo
    Past part ~ito
    Imp ~i (*fml* ~a), ~iamo, ~ite
    Cond ~irei, ~iresti, ~irebbe, ~iremmo, ~ireste, ~irebbero

Notes

- Many verbs in the third conjugation take *isc* between the stem and the ending in the first, second, and third person singular and in the third person plural of the present, the present subjunctive, and the imperative: fin|ire **Pres** ~isco, ~isci, ~isce, ~iscono. **Pres sub** ~isca, ~iscano **Imp** ~isci.

- The three forms of the imperative are the same as the corresponding forms of the present for the second and third conjugation. In the first conjugation the forms are also the same except for the second person singular: present *compri*, imperative *compra*. The negative form of the second person singular is formed by putting *non* before the infinitive for all conjugations: *non comprare*. In polite forms the third person of the present subjunctive is used instead for all conjugations: *compri*.

IRREGULAR VERBS:

Certain forms of all irregular verbs are regular (except for *essere*). These are: the second person plural of the present, the past subjunctive, and the present participle. All forms not listed below are regular and can be derived from the parts given. Only those irregular verbs considered to be the most useful are shown in the tables.

accadere   *as* **cadere**

accendere   • **Past hist** accesi, accendesti • **Past part** acceso

affliggere   • **Past hist** afflissi, affliggesti • **Past part** afflitto

ammettere   *as* **mettere**

andare   • **Pres** vado, vai, va, andiamo, andate, vanno • **Fut** andrò *etc* • **Pres sub** vada, vadano • **Imp** va', vada, vadano

apparire   • **Pres** appaio *or* apparisco, appari *or* apparisci, appare *or* apparisce, appaiono *or* appariscono • **Past hist** apparvi *or* apparsi, apparisti, apparve *or* apparì *or* apparse, apparvero *or* apparirono *or* apparsero • **Pres sub** appaia *or* apparisca

aprire   • **Pres** apro • **Past hist** aprii, apristi • **Pres sub** apra • **Past part** aperto

avere   • **Pres** ho, hai, ha, abbiamo, hanno • **Past hist** ebbi, avesti, ebbe, avemmo, aveste, ebbero • **Fut** avrò *etc* • **Pres sub** abbia *etc* • **Imp** abbi, abbia, abbiate, abbiano

bere   • **Pres** bevo *etc* • **Impf** bevevo *etc* • **Past hist** bevvi *or* bevetti, bevesti • **Fut** berrò *etc* • **Pres sub** beva *etc* • **Past sub** bevessi *etc* • **Pres part** bevendo • **Cond** berrei *etc*

cadere   • **Past hist** caddi, cadesti • **Fut** cadrò *etc*

chiedere   • **Past hist** chiesi, chiedesti • **Pres sub** chieda *etc* • **Past part** chiesto *etc*

chiudere   • **Past hist** chiusi, chiudesti • **Past part** chiuso

cogliere   • **Pres** colgo, colgono • **Past hist** colsi, cogliesti • **Pres sub** colga • **Past part** colto

correre   • **Past hist** corsi, corresti • **Past part** corso

crescere   • **Past hist** crebbi • **Past part** cresciuto

cuocere   • **Pres** cuocio, cuociamo, cuociono • **Past hist** cossi, cocesti • **Past part** cotto

dare   • **Pres** do, dai, da, diamo, danno • **Past hist** diedi *or* detti, desti • **Fut** darò *etc* • **Pres sub** dia *etc* • **Past sub** dessi *etc* • **Imp** da' (*fml* dia)

dire
• **Pres** dico, dici, dice, diciamo, dicono • **Impf** dicevo *etc* • **Past hist** dissi, dicesti • **Fut** dirò *etc* • **Pres sub** dica, diciamo, diciate, dicano • **Past sub** dicessi *etc* • *Pres part* dicendo • **Past part** detto • **Imp** di' (*fml* dica)

dovere
• **Pres** devo *or* debbo, devi, deve, dobbiamo, devono *or* debbono • **Fut** dovrò *etc* • **Pres sub** deva *or* debba, dobbiamo, dobbiate, devano *or* debbano • **Cond** dovrei *etc*

essere
• **Pres** sono, sei, è, siamo, siete, sono • **Impf** ero, eri, era, eravamo, eravate, erano • **Past hist** fui, fosti, fu, fummo, foste, furono • **Fut** sarò *etc* • **Pres sub** sia *etc* • **Past sub** fossi, fossi, fosse, fossimo, foste, fossero • **Past part** stato • **Imp** sii (*fml* sia), siate • **Cond** sarei *etc*

fare
• **Pres** faccio, fai, fa, facciamo, fanno • **Impf** facevo *etc* • **Past hist** feci, facesti • **Fut** farò *etc* • **Pres sub** faccia *etc* • **Past sub** facessi *etc* • **Pres part** facendo • **Past part** fatto • **Imp** fa' (*fml* faccia) • **Cond** farei *etc*

fingere
• **Past hist** finsi, fingesti, finsero • **Past part** finto

giungere
• **Past hist** giunsi, giungesti, giunsero • **Past part** giunto

leggere
• **Past hist** lessi, leggesti • **Past part** letto

mettere
• **Past hist** misi, mettesti • **Past part** messo

morire
• **Pres** muoio, muori, muore, muoiono • **Fut** morirò *or* morrò *etc* • **Pres sub** muoia • **Past part** morto

muovere
• **Past hist** mossi, movesti • **Past part** mosso

nascere
• **Past hist** nacqui, nascesti • **Past part** nato

offrire
• **Past hist** offersi *or* offrii, offristi • **Pres sub** offra • **Past part** offerto

parere
• **Pres** paio, pari, pare, pariamo, paiono • **Past hist** parvi *or* parsi, paresti • **Fut** parrò *etc* • **Pres sub** paia, paiamo *or* pariamo, pariate, paiano • **Past part** parso

piacere
• **Pres** piaccio, piaci, piace, piacciamo, piacciono • **Past hist** piacqui, piacesti, piacque, piacemmo, piaceste, piacquero • **Pres sub** piaccia *etc* • **Past part** piaciuto

porre
• **Pres** pongo, poni, pone, poniamo, ponete, pongono • **Impf** ponevo *etc* • **Past hist** posi, ponesti • **Fut** porrò *etc* • **Pres sub** ponga, poniamo, poniate, pongano • **Past sub** ponessi *etc*

potere
• **Pres** posso, puoi, può, possiamo, possono • **Fut** potrò *etc* • **Pres sub** possa, possiamo, possiate, possano • **Cond** potrei *etc*

prendere
• **Past hist** presi, prendesti • **Past part** preso

ridere
• **Past hist** risi, ridesti • **Past part** riso

rimanere • **Pres** rimango, rimani, rimane, rimaniamo, rimangono • **Past hist** rimasi, rimanesti • **Fut** rimarrò *etc* • **Pres sub** rimanga • **Past part** rimasto • **Cond** rimarrei

salire • **Pres** salgo, sali, sale, saliamo, salgono • **Pres sub** salga, saliate, salgano

sapere • **Pres** so, sai, sa, sappiamo, sanno • **Past hist** seppi, sapesti • **Fut** saprò *etc* • **Pres sub** sappia *etc* • **Imp** sappi (*fml* sappia), sappiate • **Cond** saprei *etc*

scegliere • **Pres** scelgo, scegli, sceglie, scegliamo, scelgono • **Past hist** scelsi, scegliesti *etc* • **Past part** scelto

scrivere • **Past hist** scrissi, scrivesti *etc* • **Past part** scritto

sedere • **Pres** siedo *or* seggo, siedi, siede, siedono • **Pres sub** sieda *or* segga

spegnere • **Pres** spengo, spengono • **Past hist** spensi, spegnesti • **Past part** spento

stare • **Pres** sto, stai, sta, stiamo, stanno • **Past hist** stetti, stesti • **Fut** starò *etc* • **Pres sub** stia *etc* • **Past sub** stessi *etc* • **Past part** stato • **Imp** sta' (*fml* stia)

tacere • **Pres** taccio, tacciono • **Past hist** tacqui, tacque, tacquero • **Pres sub** taccia

tendere • **Past hist** tesi • **Past part** teso

tenere • **Pres** tengo, tieni, tiene, tengono • **Past hist** tenni, tenesti • **Fut** terrò *etc* • **Pres sub** tenga

togliere • **Pres** tolgo, tolgono • **Past hist** tolsi, tolse, tolsero • **Pres sub** tolga, tolgano • **Past part** tolto • *Imp fml* tolga

trarre • **Pres** traggo, trai, trae, traiamo, traete, traggono • **Past hist** trassi, traesti • **Fut** trarrò *etc* • **Pres sub** tragga • **Past sub** traessi *etc* • **Past part** tratto

uscire • **Pres** esco, esci, esce, escono • **Pres sub** esca • **Imp** esci (*fml* esca)

valere • **Pres** valgo, valgono • **Past hist** valsi, valesti • **Fut** varrò *etc* • **Pres sub** valga, valgano • **Past part** valso • **Cond** varrei *etc*

vedere • **Past hist** vidi, vedesti • **Fut** vedrò *etc* • **Past part** visto *or* veduto • **Cond** vedrei *etc*

venire • **Pres** vengo, vieni, viene, vengono • **Past hist** venni, venisti • **Fut** verrò *etc*

vivere • **Past hist** vissi, vivesti • **Fut** vivrò *etc* • **Past part** vissuto • **Cond** vivrei *etc*

volere • **Pres** voglio, vuoi, vuole, vogliamo, volete, vogliono • **Past hist** volli, volesti • **Fut** vorrò *etc* • **Pres sub** voglia *etc* • **Imp** vogliate • **Cond** vorrei *etc*

379

English irregular verbs

Infinitive	Past Tense	Past Participle	Infinitive	Past Tense	Past Participle
Infinito	*Passato*	*Participio passato*	*Infinito*	*Passato*	*Participio passato*
arise	arose	arisen	**feed**	fed	fed
awake	awoke	awoken	**feel**	felt	felt
be	was	been	**fight**	fought	fought
bear	bore	borne	**find**	found	found
beat	beat	beaten	**flee**	fled	fled
become	became	become	**fling**	flung	flung
begin	began	begun	**fly**	flew	flown
behold	beheld	beheld	**forbid**	forbade	forbidden
bend	bent	bent	**forget**	forgot	forgotten
beseech	beseeched besought	beseeched besought	**forgive**	forgave	forgiven
			forsake	forsook	forsaken
bet	bet, betted	bet, betted	**freeze**	froze	frozen
bid	bade, bid	bidden, bid	**get**	got	got, gotten *Am*
bind	bound	bound	**give**	gave	given
bite	bit	bitten	**go**	went	gone
bleed	bled	bled	**grind**	ground	ground
blow	blew	blown	**grow**	grew	grown
break	broke	broken	**hang**	hung, hanged (*vt*)	hung, hanged
breed	bred	bred			
bring	brought	brought	**have**	had	had
build	built	built	**hear**	heard	heard
burn	burnt, burned	burnt, burned	**hew**	hewed	hewed, hewn
burst	burst	burst	**hide**	hid	hidden
bust	busted, bust	busted, bust	**hit**	hit	hit
			hold	held	held
buy	bought	bought	**hurt**	hurt	hurt
cast	cast	cast	**keep**	kept	kept
catch	caught	caught	**kneel**	knelt	knelt
choose	chose	chosen	**know**	knew	known
cling	clung	clung	**lay**	laid	laid
come	came	come	**lead**	led	led
cost	cost, costed (*vt*)	cost, costed	**lean**	leaned, leant	leaned, leant
creep	crept	crept	**leap**	leapt, leaped	leapt, leaped
cut	cut	cut			
deal	dealt	dealt	**learn**	learnt, learned	learnt, learned
dig	dug	dug			
do	did	done	**leave**	left	left
draw	drew	drawn	**lend**	lent	lent
dream	dreamt, dreamed	dreamt, dreamed	**let**	let	let
			lie	lay	lain
drink	drank	drunk	**light**	lit, lighted	lit, lighted
drive	drove	driven			
dwell	dwelt	dwelt	**lose**	lost	lost
eat	ate	eaten	**make**	made	made
fall	fell	fallen	**mean**	meant	meant
			meet	met	met

Infinitive	Past Tense	Past Participle	Infinitive	Past Tense	Past Participle
Infinito	*Passato*	*Participio passato*	*Infinito*	*Passato*	*Participio passato*
mow	mowed	mown, mowed	**spend**	spent	spent
			spill	spilt, spilled	spilt, spilled
overhang	overhung	overhung			
pay	paid	paid	**spin**	spun	spun
put	put	put	**spit**	spat	spat
quit	quitted, quit	quitted, quit	**split**	split	split
			spoil	spoilt, spoiled	spoilt, spoiled
read	read /red/	read /red/			
rid	rid	rid	**spread**	spread	spread
ride	rode	ridden	**spring**	sprang	sprung
ring	rang	rung	**stand**	stood	stood
rise	rose	risen	**steal**	stole	stolen
run	ran	run	**stick**	stuck	stuck
saw	sawed	sawn, sawed	**sting**	stung	stung
			stink	stank	stunk
say	said	said	**strew**	strewed	strewn, strewed
see	saw	seen			
seek	sought	sought	**stride**	strode	stridden
sell	sold	sold	**strike**	struck	struck
send	sent	sent	**string**	strung	strung
set	set	set	**strive**	strove	striven
sew	sewed	sewn, sewed	**swear**	swore	sworn
			sweep	swept	swept
shake	shook	shaken	**swell**	swelled	swollen, swelled
shear	sheared	shorn, sheared			
			swim	swam	swum
shed	shed	shed	**swing**	swung	swung
shine	shone	shone	**take**	took	taken
shit	shit	shit	**teach**	taught	taught
shoe	shod	shod	**tear**	tore	torn
shoot	shot	shot	**tell**	told	told
show	showed	shown	**think**	thought	thought
shrink	shrank	shrunk	**thrive**	thrived, throve	thrived, thriven
shut	shut	shut			
sing	sang	sung	**throw**	threw	thrown
sink	sank	sunk	**thrust**	thrust	thrust
sit	sat	sat	**tread**	trod	trodden
slay	slew	slain	**understand**	understood	understood
sleep	slept	slept	**undo**	undid	undone
slide	slid	slid	**wake**	woke	woken
sling	slung	slung	**wear**	wore	worn
slit	slit	slit	**weave**	wove	woven
smell	smelt, smelled	smelt, smelled	**weep**	wept	wept
			wet	wet, wetted	wet, wetted
sow	sowed	sown, sowed			
			win	won	won
speak	spoke	spoken	**wind**	wound	wound
speed	sped, speeded	sped, speeded	**wring**	wrung	wrung
			write	wrote	written
spell	spelled, spelt	spelled, spelt			